The Continuum Encyclopedia of

YOUNG ADULT
LITERATURE

The Continuum Encyclopedia of

YOUNG ADULT LITERATURE

BERNICE E. CULLINAN,
BONNIE L. KUNZEL,
DEBORAH A. WOOTEN
Editors

A Giniger Book

continuum

NEW YORK • LONDON

2005

The Continuum International Publishing Group Inc
15 East 26 Street, New York, NY 10010

The Continuum International Publishing Group Ltd
The Tower Building, 11 York Road, London SE1 7NX

The K. S. Giniger Company, Inc., Publishers
250 West 57 Street, New York, NY 10107

Printed in the United States of America

Library of Congress Cataloging-in-Publication Data

The continuum encyclopedia of young adult literature / Bernice E. Cullinan,
Bonnie L. Kunzel, Deborah A. Wooten, editors.
    p. cm.
  Includes bibliographical references and index.
  ISBN 0-8264-1710-8 (hardcover : alk. paper)
  1. Young adult literature—Encyclopedias.   2. Young adult
literature—Bio-bibliography—Dictionaries.   3. Young adults—Books and
reading—Encyclopedias.   I. Cullinan, Bernice E.   II. Kunzel, Bonnie, 1944–
III. Wooten, Deborah A.
PN1008.5C67 2005
809′.89283′03—dc22   2005018693

In memory of
Ted Hipple,
who was a leader in young adult literature;
Bruce Cassiday,
who turned ordinary prose into art; and
Will Eisner,
a true pioneer

Contents

Board of Advisers

Guide to Topical Articles

List of Author and Illustrator Photographs

Doublas Adams
David Almond
Laurie Halse Anderson
Brent (Kenneth) Ashabranner
Avi
T. A Barron
Joan Bauer
Marion Dane Bauer
Judy Blume
Sue Ellen Bridgers
Martha Brooks
Michael Cadnum
Michael Cart
Aidan Chambers
Alice Childress
John Christopher
Brock Cole
Carolyn Coman
Caroline B. Cooney
Sharon Creech
Chris Crutcher
Roald Dahl
Sarah Dessen
Carl Deuker
Peter Dickinson
Lois Duncan
Will Eisner
Nancy Farmer
Jean Ferris
Paul Fleischman
E. R. Frank
Russell Freedman
Neil Gaiman

Donald R. Gallo
Nancy Garden
James Cross Giblin
Rosa Guy
Virginia Hamilton
James Haskins
Nat Hentoff
Karen Hesse
Will Hobbs
Kimberley Willis Holt
B. Jacques
Sherryl Jordan
Bel Kaufman
M. E. Kerr
David Klass
Annette Curtis Klaus
Ron Koertge
E. L. Konigsburg
Kathryn Lasky
Madeleine L'Engle
Julius Lester
Gail Carson Levine
Sonia Levitin
C. S. Lewis
Robert Lipsyte
Lois Lowry
Joyce McDonald
Patricia and Fred McKissack
Margaret Mahy
Carol Matas
Harry Mazer
Norma Fox Mazer
Milton Meltzer

Carolyn Meyer
Beverly Naidoo
Phyllis Reynolds Naylor
Garth Nix
Joan Lowry Nixon
Han Nolan
Naomi Shihab Nye
Katherine Paterson
Richard Peck
Tamora Pierce
Daniel Pinkwater
Randy Powell
Philip Pullman
Louise Rennison
Hazel Rochman

J. K. Rowling
Graham Salisbury
William Sleator
Art Spiegelman
Suzanne Fisher Staples
Theodore Taylor
Chris van Allsburg
Vivian Vande
Ruth White
Rita Williams-Garcia
Ellen Wittlinger
Jacqueline Woodson
Tim Wynne-Jones
Jane Yolen

Author and Illustrator Photo Credits

Brent (Kenneth) Ashabranner by Jennifer
    Ashabranner
Avi courtesy HarperCollins
Marion Dane Bauer courtesy Holiday House
Judy Blume courtesy Penguin Putnam
Sue Ellen Bridgers by Ann States
Martha Brooks © Jeff Debooy
Michael Cart by Marilyn Sanders
Aidan Chambers courtesy Penguin Putnam
Alice Childress courtesy Penguin Putnam
John Christopher courtesy Simon and Schuster
Brock Cole © Tobiah Cole
Carolyn Coman © 2000 Steven Holt
Sharon Creech by Karin Leuthy
Chris Crutcher by Kelly Milner Halls
Roald Dahl courtesy Penguin Putnam
Carl Deuker by Marian Mitchell Deuker
Peter Dickinson by Robin McKinley
Lois Duncan courtesy Random House Children's
    Books
Will Eisner courtesy the late Will Eisner
Jean Ferris © Jon Lyons
Paul Fleischmann courtesy HarperCollins
Russell Freedman by Carlo Ontal
Neil Gaiman by Sigrid Estrada
Donald R. Gallo by Chris Perrett
Nancy Garden © Midge Eliassen
James Cross Giblin by Sarah Hoe Sterling
Rosa Guy © Carmen L. deJesus
Virginia Hamilton by Carlo Ontal
James Haskins by George Gray
Nat Hentoff courtesy Random House Children's
    Books

Will Hobbs courtesy HarperCollins
Kimberley Willis Holt by Fuqua Photography, Inc.
Bel Kaufmann by Stanley Gluck
B. Jacques courtesy Penguin Putnam
Sherryl Jordan by Jenny Scown Photography
M. E. Kerr by Allan Einhorn
David Klass © Giselle Benatar
Annette Curtis Klaus courtesy Random House
    Children's Books
Ron Koertge courtesy Candlewick
Kathryn Lasky courtesy HarperCollins
Madeleine L'Engle © Kenneth S. Lewis
Julius Lester by Milan Sabatini
Gail Carson Levine courtesy HarperCollins
C. S. Lewis courtesy HarperCollins
Robert Lipsyte by Gerard Murell
Lois Lowry by Bachrach
Joyce McDonald courtesy Random House Children's
    Books
Margaret Mahy courtesy Simon and Schuster
    Children's Publishing
Carol Mates courtesy Simon and Schuster
Harry Mazer courtesy HarperCollins
Carolyn Meyer by Diane J. Schmidt
Beverly Naidoo courtesy HarperCollins
Phyllis Reynolds Naylor by Katherine Lambert
    Photography
Garth Nix by Robert McFarlane
Joan Lowry Nixon by Gittings
Han Nolan by Brian Nolan
Naomi Shihab Nye by Amy Arbus
Katherine Paterson by Samantha Loomis Paterson
Richard Peck by Sonya Sones

Daniel Pinkwater courtesy HarperCollins

Randy Powell © Judy Powell

Philp Pullman by Jerry Bauer and Random House Children's Books

Louise Rennison by Jason Bell

Hazel Rochman courtesy HarperCollins

J. K. Rowling by Richard Young and Scholastic

Graham Salisbury by Ray Warren

William Sleator by Andrew Bi

Art Spiegelman by Anne Hall

Suzanne Fisher Staples © Virginia Morgan

Theodore Taylor courtesy HarperCollins

Chris Van Allsburg © Constance Brown

Vivian Vande Velde courtesy Simon and Schuster

Ruth White © Beth Agresta

Rita Williams-Garcia courtesy HarperCollins

Ellen Wittlinger by Patsy Kelley

Jacqueline Woodson courtesy Penguin Putnam

Diana Wynne Jones courtesy HarperCollins

Jane Yolen by Julie Offutt

Introduction

Although children's literature blossomed in the late Victorian period in England, young adult or YA literature came of age in the 20th century. YA literature is separate from that written for children, just as its readership is drawn from a separate segment of society, defined and named with the advent of teen culture in the 1930s. Prior to this time, society was divided into children and adults, a development based on the family and the American lifestyle.

Two early writers to gain national attention in what would become the YA genre were Louisa May Alcott and Horatio Alger. Alcott's ever-popular *Little Women* (1868) single-handedly created the rags-to-riches, coming-of-age format repeated in a number of books that were extremely popular, including Alger's *Ragged Dick* (1868). Alger also went on to write one hundred articles for magazines and newspapers.

The growth of public libraries brought both new opportunities for literary education and a new debate focused on fiction. Many librarians and teachers opposed offering novels in libraries or spending time with them in classrooms, describing the reading of fiction as at best wasteful and at worst wicked. Nevertheless, the publishing of YA novels soared as the Boston publishing firm of Lee and Shepard found a format that defined the industry for years to come: the SERIES book. Lee and Shepard published 900 series books in 1887 alone. Edward Stratemeyer is credited with turning series books into the most financially successful industry ever built around adolescent reading: the Lakeport series (1904–12), the Dave Porter series (1905–19), and the highly successful Rover Boys series (30 books published between 1899 and 1926), culminating in the still-popular Nancy Drew and Hardy Boys series.

In the 20th century, the Great Depression eliminated jobs for young people. As a result, children stayed in school for longer periods of time and high-school enrollment rose. Later, teens with discretionary-spending money entered the marketplace and rapidly became a force in the American economy. The category to be known as YA literature finally emerged and it was recognized as such. Advertisements were tailored to the teen market, companies developed teen products, and more publishers produced books with appeal to this age group. For a comprehensive discussion of YA literature and its first golden age, see Michael Cart's entry "YA Literature."

According to YALSA (Young Adult Library Services Association), a division of the American Library Association, a teen is an individual between the ages of twelve and eighteen. This broad age range covers middle-school students (grades 6–8), junior high (grades 7–9), and high school (grades 9–12). Although there is quite a gap between the interests of a twelve-year-old and an eighteen-year-old, some of the genre fiction, especially fantasy and science fiction, bridges this gap successfully since some works appeal more to younger teens, and others to older ones. Today, publishers meet the demand for quality books for teens of all ages with CROSSOVERS in both directions—books issued that appeal to teens and younger children on the one hand, and to teens and adults on the other. John Grisham, Michael Crichton, Robin Cook, Stephen King, Dean Koontz, Barbara Kingsolver, Toni Morrison, and Elizabeth Berg are a few of the adult authors regularly read by young people. This is a growing phenomenon now recognized by the American Library Association (ALA) with its ALEX (Adult Books for Young Adults) award list. Every year ten titles, both fiction and nonfiction, are selected by a committee of YA librarians as the adult books with the greatest degree of teen appeal and potential staying power.

The teenage years are a time of struggle to become an adult, to establish an identity, to belong, to fit into peer groups, and to assume a measure of personal independence. Teens want to read about teens, usually a few years older, coping with and overcoming problems similar to ones that they face. With the new millennium, this body of literature has come of age. Teens have access to works that are increasingly mature and that deal with situations and issues like sexuality with a level of candor practically unheard of in the past. There is a growing demand for GRAPHIC NOVELS, comic compilations, or original works in graphic format. Works of diversity are on the rise, including immigrant experiences as well as settings in various countries around the world.

This encyclopedia celebrates the diversity and complexity of YA literature with an emphasis on contemporary authors and topical articles that cover a spectrum of current teen interests. Our goal is to provide a work that is as reliable, insofar as information is available, informative, and thought provoking, with occasional serendipitous discoveries for those who approach it with specific questions or a general interest in the field. We hope it will be of use to the browser as well as those seeking to increase their knowledge of YA literature in all of its richness.

The Continuum Encyclopedia of Young Adult Literature is intended as a comprehensive single-volume reference describing the development, significant authors, and current trends in YA literature. We emphasize English-speaking authors and works appearing in English translation. To our knowledge, no other reference book in any language compares to it.

The work contains some 95 signed topical entries and approximately 900 (mostly) signed biographical-critical entries by 180 contributors on authors of YA books or books that are embraced by teen readers. In a time of increasingly strained budgets, CROSSOVERS, books written for one age group but also read by another, are increasingly relied upon by librarians.

Aside from this introduction, biographical and topical articles mentioned in an entry are cross-referenced to their main entry in SMALL CAPS. Lists of award-winning books are included, and a more comprehensive awards list appears as an appendix.

THE EDITORS

The Continuum Encyclopedia of

YOUNG ADULT
LITERATURE

ABELOVE, Joan

Author, n.d., n.p.

A. earned her B.A. from Barnard College in 1966 and completed her doctorate in cultural anthropology from The City University of New York in 1978. She married Steve Hoffman (1987) and has one child. A. has taught emotionally disturbed boys at a state hospital, been a part-time teacher of anthropology at colleges in New York City, and currently is a technical writer during the day and a YA fiction writer in her spare time.

Following doctoral work in Peru, A. tried many times to write a book that would share her experiences there. A. first wanted to write the book from an outsider's point of view; then she tried writing it in the third person. Nothing seemed to work. In 1991, A. enrolled in Margaret Gabel's writing workshop at the New School in New York City, where the pieces finally came into place. She wrote two pages of *Go and Come Back*, which she read to her workshop members and got the encouragement she needed to write the remainder of the book. This final version was written from a narrator's point of view. The narrator begins by talking about "Two old white ladies come to my village." These two old white ladies are, of course, A. and a colleague, both in their late twenties when they were in Peru. To members of the village, this was old. A. compares and contrasts two very different cultures, yet shows how similar these cultures can be.

This is A.'s most notable work to date; it grew from her experience of spending two years in the Amazon jungle of Peru in the 1970s. *Go and Come Back* (1998) is the critically acclaimed novel that allows A. to share her experience in another culture.

In her next book, *Saying It out Loud* (1999), A. also writes from her own personal experiences. This time, the story is written as journal entries by Mindy, a girl who is losing her mother to a brain tumor. Although much different from *Go and Come Back,* A. continues to write about people and their experiences with humor, tenderness, and clarity.

AWARDS: For *Go and Come Back*: Notable Children's Book, ALA Best Book for Young Adults, Booklist Editor's Choice, Bulletin of the Center for Children's Book Blue Ribbon, Publishers Weekly Best Book of the Year, SLJ Best Book of the Year.

FURTHER WORKS: Short story in the anthology: *Lost and Found: Award-Winning Authors Sharing Real-Life Experience through Fiction,* ed. Jerry M. Weiss and Helen S. Weiss, 2000.

BIBLIOGRAPHY: Brown, Jennifer. "Flying Starts: Joan Abelove," *Publishers Weekly,* June 29, 1998; Doyle, Miranda. "Review of 'Lost and Found: Award–Winning Authors Sharing Real-Life Experience through Fiction,'" *School Library Journal,* November 2000. *Contemporary Authors* vol. 172; *Best Books for Young Adults,* 2000.

TINA HERTEL

ADAMS, Douglas Noel

Author, b. 11 March 1952, Cambridge, England; d. 11 May 2001, Santa Barbara, California

A. achieved cult-author status with *The Hitchhiker's Guide to the Galaxy.* Not only a book, but a radio program, television show, and movie, the quirky adventures of Arthur Dent and Ford Prefect have captivated readers in all formats. Their fascination remained intact through four sequels—*The Restaurant at the End of the Universe; Life, the Universe, and Everything; So Long and Thanks for All the Fish;* and *Mostly Harmless.* Hilarious, wild, and zany, the books have captured a cadre of dedicated readers since the 1970s.

Although A. is best known for the antic *Hitchhiker's Guide,* he produced many other works. Among them are *Dirk Gently's Holistic Detective Agency* and *The Long Dark Teatime of the Soul.* The *Last Chance to See* (co-authored by Mark Carwardine), *The Meaning of Liff,* and *The Deeper Meaning of Liff: A Dictionary of Things There Aren't Words for Yet—But There Ought to Be* are the other pieces of A.'s work that appeared while he was living. *The Salmon of Doubt: Hitchhiking the Galaxy One Last Time* was published posthumously, and included a short-story fragment, as well as essays and other works in progress.

In addition to being an author, A. also helped to start a business, The Digital Village. Dealing primarily with media, the company produced a computer game, *Starship Titanic.* Other efforts include an online Hitchhiker's Guide to the Galaxy (h2g2.com)—a website. This website still exists as http://www.bbc.co.uk/h2g2. A. appreciated and enjoyed computers, although they occasionally served as a distraction to his writing.

Other career highlights include being a script editor for *Doctor Who*—although that only lasted a year. He also authored three scripts for the show: *Shada, City of Death* (written under the pseudonym David Agnew), and *The Pirate Planet.* A. had also done work for the Cambridge Footlights group. In his youth, A. studied at the Brentwood School, located in Essex, and went on to study (but not graduate) from Cambridge. One of A.'s less glamorous jobs included cleaning chicken sheds, but he more than made up for that in his work guarding an Arab royal and playing guitar in Pink Floyd. Yet it was the radio show *The Hitchhiker's Guide to the Galaxy* that was to lead A. to fame. When he turned the radio series into a book—and subsequently a SERIES of books—he made history. Fans of the books were legion, and they developed their own catchphrases from the book that were as good as a secret language to the uninitiated.

One can only wonder at what else A. might have produced. Although his proclivity for procrastination was well documented, with more time A.'s imagination may have led readers on more fabulous trips. Unfortunately, many of his projects remain unfinished. *The Hitchhiker's Guide to the Galaxy* appeared on the big screen in 2005. Cast members include Mos Def, Martin Freeman, and John Malkovich. When A. was alive, Jim Carrey's name was mentioned as a possible star. Fans eagerly awaited this media event and were not disappointed.

When all is taken into account, what is there really to say except "So long and thanks for all the fish." A. was only forty-nine years old when he died, stricken by a heart attack. His wife, Jane, and daughter, Polly, survive him. His many fans include Neil Gaiman who penned *Don't Panic: The Official Hitchhiker's Guide to the Galaxy Companion* in 1988 and revised it after A.'s death and produced *Don't Panic: Douglas Adams and the Hitchhiker's Guide to the Galaxy,* and M. J. Simpson who wrote *Pocket Essentials: The Hitchhiker's Guide,* as well as the biographical *Hitchhiker: A Biography of Douglas Adams.*

BIBLIOGRAPHY: http://www.amazon.com; http://www.douglasadams.com; http://www.zootle.net/afda/mfaq.shtml; http://www.zootle.net/afda/faq/main.shtml; www.imdb.com; Nick Webb, *Wish You Were Here: The Official Biography of Douglas Adams,* 2005.

JEANNE MARIE RYAN

ADAMS, Richard
Author, b. 9 May 1920, Newbury, Berkshire, England

A. was working as Assistant Secretary for the Department of Environment in London when he began writing a story to entertain his two young daughters, Juliet and Rosamond. The resulting novel, *Watership Down,* was published in 1972 after being rejected seven times. Not a writer by profession, A. lacked knowledge of literary conventions such as book length, age range, level of difficulty, and acceptable subject matter in the genre of juvenile publishing. Yet after spending more than twenty-five years in government service, A. achieved fame unexpectedly at age 52 with the publication of his first novel. *Watership Down,* a FANTASY considered by many critics to be a modern classic, depicts the adventures of a group of rabbits who are forced to find a new home when their old one is destroyed. The rabbits, led by Hazel, Fiver, and Blackberry, finally set up a new home at Watership Down. With American marketing, the novel became an adult and worldwide bestseller, selling over a million copies in record time. In addition, *Watership Down* was released as a full-length animated film by Avco–Embassy in 1978.

Since 1974, A. has been a full-time writer. He is praised for his unique view of nature and for his characterization of animal protagonists. A. used animal protagonists in several of his subsequent novels, including *The Plague Dogs* (1977), *Shardik* (1974), and *Traveller* (1988). These novels as well as *The Girls in a Swing* (1980), a ghost story, and *Maia* (1984), a tale of a slave girl, became bestsellers, despite less favorable reactions from critics. A. produced several major novels, several collections of SHORT STORIES, travel writing, POETRY, and works on natural history. He has been president of the Royal Society for the Prevention of Cruelty to Animals (R.S.P.C.A.) and an animal rights campaigner. A. resides in Hampshire, close to the actual territory in which he set his famed *Watership Down.*

AWARDS: *Watership Down:* 1972 Carnegie Medal and 1973 *Guardian* Award; California Young Readers' Award; Fellow of the Royal Society of Literature.

FURTHER WORKS: *The Tyger Voyage,* 1976; *The Adventures and Brave Deeds of the Ship's Cat on the Spanish Maine: Together with the Most Lamentable Losse of the Alcestis and Triumphant Firing of the Port of Chagres,* 1977; *The Legend of Te Tuna,* 1982; *The Bureaucats,* 1985; *Tales from Watership Down,* 1999; *The Outlandish Knight,* 2000.

BIBLIOGRAPHY: Olendorff, Donna (ed.) *Something about the Author,* vol. 69, 1992; www.findarticles .com

JODI PILGRIM

ADAMSON, Joy

Author, illustrator, b. 20 January 1910 Troppau, Austria; d. 3 January 1980, Shaba Game Reserve, Kenya

A. and her husband, George, gained worldwide fame with *Born Free: A Lioness of Two Worlds,* published in 1960, followed by the film and a television series in 1964. Born Friederike Victoria Gessner, A. grew up a child of privilege in Austria, studying music, art, and psychoanalysis; this led to medical studies in university, though she did not take the qualifying exam. A. sailed for Africa in 1937 at the urging of her first husband, Victor von Klarwill, a Jew, to escape the growing Nazi presence in Austria. She met her second husband, Peter Bally, on the ship to Africa, and they were married in 1938. Bally gave her the name "Joy." As a botanist for the Nairobi Museum, he traveled through Kenya studying plant life. A. painted their findings, eventually illustrating seven books of East African flora. In 1943 A. married George A., a game warden for the Kenyan park service, who in addition to other duties, oversaw the care of orphaned wild animals. In 1956, George brought home three orphaned lion cubs, one of which remained with them, whom they called *Elsa.* Determined that Elsa would not be a pet, and with the offer of a permanent home for her in Meru in northern Tanzania, the A.s kept written records of the 27-month project to turn Elsa from a tame cub to a wild animal capable of surviving in the African bush. Their efforts were successful, and they ultimately released Elsa at age two. To chronicle their experience and raise awareness of wild animals, A. wrote *Born Free.* The book was an international success. "Wild lions had been described, and tame lions had been described," wrote Faith McNulty of the *Washington Post.* "It was Elsa's transition from one to the other that was so enormously revealing." The book "reads like a letter from Eden to homesick humanity" according to a *New York Herald-Tribune* review. A.'s intellect, subtle dry humor, and eye for scientific study keep her prose from being too sentimental, but still evoke emotion in the reader. Although she must have been tempted to anthropomorphize, her early training as a scientist is evident, as is her artist's eye for observation. *Born Free* was followed by *Living Free* in 1961 and *Forever Free* in 1963, which chronicle the story of Elsa's cubs and their relocation to the Serengeti game preserve.

A. continued her work in wild-animal preservation after Elsa's death at age five. In 1964 she took on an 8-month-old cheetah, Pippa, that had been a pet of a British army officer. Pippa's rehabilitation to independence took over four years; her adventures in returning Pippa to the wild are chronicled in *The Spotted Sphinx* (1969) and *Pippa's Challenge* (1972).

AWARDS: Grenfell Gold Medal, Royal Horticultural Society (England), 1947; Award of Merit (Czechoslovakia), 1970; Joseph Wood Krutch Medal, Humane Society (United States), 1971; Cross of Honor for Science and Art (Austria), 1976.

FURTHER WORKS: *The Story of Elsa,* 1966; *The Peoples of Kenya,* 1967; *Joy Adamson's Africa,* 1972; *The Searching Spirit: An Autobiography,* 1978; *Such Agreeable Friends: Adventures with Animals* (contributor), 1978; *Queen of Sheba: The Story of an African Leopard,* 1980; *Friends from the Forest,* 1981.

BIBLIOGRAPHY: Durrell, Gerald. "Living with a Lioness." *New York Times Book Review,* May 22, 1960; Durrell, Gerald. "Out of the Jungle to the Stepmother's House." *New York Times Book Review,* October 15, 1961; Hayes, Harold. "Grown Free." *New York Times Book Review,* April 22, 1979; "Joy Adamson." *Contemporary Authors Online,* Gale 2003. Reproduced in *Biography Resource Center,* 2003. http://0-www.galenet.com.kimbel.coastal.edu:80/servlet/bioRC; Joy Adamson. *Contemporary Heroes and Heroines, Book I.* Edited by Ray B. Brown, 1990. Reproduced in *Center Biography Resource,* 2003. http://0-www.galenet.com.kimbel.coastal.edu:80/servlet/bioRC; "Joy Adamson." *Notable Twentieth-Century Scientists,* Gale, 1995. Reproduced in *Biography Resource Center,* 2003. http://www.galenet.com/servlet/BioRC; "Joy Adamson." *Encyclopedia of World Biography Supplement,* Vol. 18, 1998. Reproduced in *Biography Resource Center,* 2003. http://www.galenet.com/servlet/BioRC; "Life with a Lioness." *Times Literary Supplement,* April 22, 1960; "Life with Lions." *Times Literary Supplement,* December 22, 1961.

C. GOODWIN

ADOFF, Arnold
Author, b. 16 July 1935, New York City

A. grew up in the South Bronx, the son of a Polish–Russian immigrant. His family emphasized the importance of being an American as well as having a strong commitment to social justice. He went to The City College of New York and attended graduate school at Columbia University, with a concentration in American history, and began work on his doctorate. He taught social studies in New York City, and met his future wife, Virginia HAMILTON, an AFRICAN AMERICAN children's writer.

A. realized that there was a lack of good literature in the classroom appropriate for use by black students. He decided to do something about it, publishing his first anthology, *I Am the Darker Brother* in 1968, which led to subsequent anthologies of black poetry and prose. His anthologies have been constantly updated. He has been recognized as one of the first people to champion multiculturalism in Ameri-

can literature. In addition to his poetry anthologies, A. has compiled several collections of fiction and commentary by black authors. In 1973 he edited *Poetry of Black America: Anthology of the 20th Century,* which included works by James Weldon Johnson, Paul Laurence Dunbar, Langston Hughes, Gwendolyn Brooks, and Nikki Giovanni.

During this time, A. also wrote poetry himself, using both form and physical shape in his creations. He often uses the word *music* to describe his poetry, and he uses both sight and sound for his poems. The individual letters and words are specifically placed upon the page to help contribute to its totality. His first book of poetry *MA nDA LA* is a story poem using only words containing the "ah" that relates the cycle of life in a small African village.

His book, *Black Is Brown Is Tan,* is based on his own family and is one of the first to depict interracial families. He continued to depict interracial families in *All the Colors of the Race.* Other books of poetry include *Chocolate Dreams,* a collection of poems about food, as well as *Street Music,* poems about city life.

AWARDS: Children's Books of the Year citation, Child Study Association of American, 1968, for *I Am the Darker Brother;* 1969, for *City in All Directions;* and 1986, for *Sports Pages;* Best Children's Books, *School Library Journal,* 1971, for *It Is the Poem Singing into Your Eyes,* and 1973, for *Black Is Brown Is Tan;* Notable Children's Trade Book citation, National Council for the Social Studies Children's Book Council (NCSS/CBC), both 1974, and Children's Choice citation, INTERNATIONAL READING ASSOCIATION/Children's Book Council (IRA/CBC), 1985, both for *My Black Me: A Beginning Book of Black Poetry;* Art Books for Children Award for *MA nDA LA,* 1975, Books for the Teen Age citation, New York Public Library, 1980, 1981, and 1982, for *It Is the Poem Singing into Your Eyes;* Jane Addams Children's Book Award special recognition, 1983, for *All the Colors of the Race;* Parents Choice Award (picture book), 1988, for *Flamboyan;* National Council of Teachers of English Award for Excellence in Poetry for Children, 1988; American Library Association (ALA) notable book citation, for *Street Music;* ALA Best Book for Young Adults citation, 1996, for *Slow Dance Heartbreak Blues;* Blue Ribbon Award, Bulletin of the Center for Children's Books, for *Love Letters,* Children's Book of Distinction Award, Riverbank Review, for *Love Letters.*

BIBLIOGRAPHY: *Contemporary Authors,* online, 2001; http://dept.kent.edu/virginiahailtoneconf/adoff04.htm; www.arnoldadoff.com

JOAN PEARLMAN

ADULT BOOKS FOR YA

Long before designated literature for children and young adults existed, teens were reading books that were written to, and intended for, an adult audience. Most public and school librarians can testify to the fact that many adult-marketed best-selling authors like Stephen KING, Dean KOONTZ, John GRISHAM, and Mary Higgins Clark are popular with teen readers. There are any number of reasons teenagers seek out these books. Many teens are drawn to trendy best-sellers for the same reasons adults are; they hear them being discussed by others, in the media or within their own social networks. Teens may also be looking to adult books as a way to connect with their parents. One study conducted in Maine during the 1997–98 school year indicated that among the twelve Stephen King–reading teens that took part in the study, several had been introduced to King's HORROR fiction by their parents. The researcher concluded that King's work served as a supportive rather than oppositional force between the teens and their parents.

Teens seem especially drawn to adult genre fiction, including MYSTERIES, horror, and SCIENCE FICTION. In 1994, a study of the reading choices of British eighth graders revealed that the avid attraction teens have for these stories is most likely developmental. Researchers found that, by examining the emotions of characters vicariously, teens can come to terms with their own feelings of disillusionment, fear, and doubt. The study also observed that the violence of a modern supernatural thriller is akin to traditional folk tales and ballads that feature brave champions, intense emotions, and often violent or tragic endings. Teens are responding to the archetypes that are employed in adult genre fiction, where moral clarity is sharply drawn. There are heroes and villains, and good almost always triumphs over evil.

Another reason teens may be reading adult books is because they are curious about adult lifestyles. Most librarians who work with children and teens soon recognize their desire to read about the next stage in their development. Middle-school students want to read books that are about high-school trials and tribulations, and high-school students often are most interested in books that star college students, people looking for their first jobs, or married couples rearing a family. Teens are often drawn to adult characters in a myriad of situations as a means of modeling their behavior and anticipating the rigors of adulthood. Books about adult choices can serve as reliable signposts to teens who are often apprehensive about the uncertain future. Of course, teens also turn to adult nonfiction titles, often as a supplement to the less sophisticated treatment of favorite topics they find in juvenile literature. In addition, there are not nearly as many authors writing nonfiction for young people, so there is often no alternative to adult nonfiction for the young researcher.

Teenagers come to adult literature for an infinite number of reasons. To acknowledge the validity of these reasons, and encourage all types of reading among teenagers, the Young Adult Library Services Association of the American Library Association (ALA) established the Alex Awards, given annually to the best adult books for young adults. In 1998, YALSA initiated a five-year project in which the use of adult books with teenagers would be examined more closely. The project included not only a series of lectures that would be presented at each annual conference during the grant period, but a task force that would create an annual top-ten list of the best adult books published for young adults. When the grant ended in 2002, the Alex Awards were adopted as an official ALA award, and the task force was turned into the Alex Award Committee.

The Alex Award was named for pioneering young adult librarian Margaret Alexander Edwards (known to friends as *Alex*) and the initial project was funded by the trust that was established shortly before her death in 1988. The trust, which was "to be used to experiment with ways of effectively promoting the reading of young adults and inspiring young adult librarians to realize the importance of reading and to perfect themselves as readers' advisors," was both a legacy and testimony to the impressive dedication Edwards showed through her devotion to library service for teenagers. Edwards is widely known in library circles for bringing attention to specialized service for teenagers and setting the standard high for future generations of YA librarians.

At the Enoch Pratt Free Library in Baltimore, from 1933 to 1962, Edwards established outreach programs to local schools, sponsored teen book fairs, and encouraged young book reviewers to voice their opinions in the monthly teen newsletter "You're the Critic." But what Edwards was perhaps best known for was her love and promotion of books. Her famous training regimen for new teen librarians included the daunting task of reading at least three hundred books, and being able to discuss them at length. At the time, there were few books written expressly for teens that were little more than didactic place-holders for readers seen as not ready for adult books. So, Edwards championed the use of adult books with teens since she not only respected teenagers' ability to understand and enjoy them, but since she also hoped that by including adult titles on ALA's Booklist (an early form of today's Best Books for Young Adults list) librarians would feel more comfortable purchasing and promoting adult books for their young adult collections.

The official Alex Awards are still sponsored by the Margaret Alexander Edwards Trust, with *Booklist* magazine as a co-sponsor. The nine-member Alex Awards committee is charged with selecting "ten books written for adults that have special appeal to young adults, ages 12–18." The books may be fiction or nonfiction, meet standard criteria that include origination in a publisher's adult list and have potential teen appeal, besides being "well written and very readable." The top-ten booklist is published annually in *Booklist* in the spring, during or near National Library Week.

BIBLIOGRAPHY: "Alex Awards," YALSA webpage, www.ala.org/Content/NavigationMe.../Alex_Award_ Policies_and_Procedures.htm; Benton, Peter. "Recipe Fictions . . . Literary Fast Food? Reading Interests in Year 8," *Oxford Review of Education,* Mar. 1995, pp. 99–111; Carter, Betty. "Alex: The Why and the How," *Booklist,* 1, Apr. 2003, p. 1389; Carter, Betty. "Margaret Alexander Edwards: Still Reaching out to Young Adult Librarians," *ALAN Review,* Fall 1997; Chandler, Kelly. "Reading Relationships: Parents, Adolescents, and Popular Fiction by Stephen King," *Journal of Adolescent and Adult Literacy,* Nov. 1999, pp. 228–39; Furi-Perry, Ursula. "Dude, that Book was Cool: The Reading Habits of Young Adults," *Reading Today,* April–May 2003, p. 24; Gallik, Jude D. "Do They Read for Pleasure? Recreational Reading Habits of College Students," *Journal of Adolescent and Adult Literacy,* Mar. 1999, pp. 480–89; Kloberdanz, Kristin. "What You Didn't Know About Teenage Readers," *Book,* July–August 1999, pp. 34–38.

JENNIFER HUBERT

ADVENTURE FICTION FOR TEENS

Readers have long been drawn to tales of survival. Travelers since the time of Odysseus have had interesting stories to tell. Modern readers continue to flock to both fiction and nonfiction accounts of remarkable and perilous journeys. For this reason, realistic fiction that focuses on an adventure is ever popular with teens. These stories pit humans against the elements. Many teens enjoy reading passages that produce surges of adrenaline. Adventure fiction is fast-paced and hard to put down. Teen protagonists struggle against seemingly insurmountable odds—and survive. Adventure fiction gives teens a sense of what humans are capable of while providing them with a reminder of their own mortality.

One of the most widely read adventure novels is *The Call of the Wild,* written by Jack London, first published in serial form in the *New York Post* in 1903. In the novel, a mixed-breed dog named Buck, who begins his days as a pet in California, is kidnapped and ends up in the Klondike leading a wolf pack. The tale is filled with challenges for the canine protagonist, but Buck ultimately perseveres. London went on to write *White Fang* (1906), another book with a dog as the central character. Both *White Fang* and *The Call of the Wild* are allegorical works that have been read and enjoyed on many levels by children, teens, and adults.

Gary PAULSEN is one of the best-known contemporary writers of adventure fiction for teens. He draws on experiences from his life to create stories that appeal to readers, especially boys in middle school. *Hatchet* (1987) is one of Paulsen's most popular titles. In this novel, a teen named Brian embarks on a plane trip to visit his father. The pilot suffers a heart attack and Brian miraculously survives a terrifying plane crash, only to find himself stranded in the wilds of Canada. Armed with only a hatchet and the clothes he was wearing at the time of the crash, Brian survives for more than fifty days in the wilderness before he is rescued. Brian's story continues in *The River* (1991), in which he takes part in a psychological study of survival. Paulsen offers fans a parallel-universe approach to Brian's story in *Brian's Winter* (1996), in which Brian was *not* rescued but instead was forced to endure the harsh Canadian winter. Brian feels out of place in the city, returns to the wilderness, and is befriended by the Cree people in *Bri-*

an's Return (1999). Paulsen had originally declared the Brian Robeson SERIES complete but, urged by his adoring fans, revisited Brian's story in *Brian's Hunt* (2003), in which he befriends an injured dog, learns of a bear that has gravely injured his Cree friends, and sets out to hunt the bear. All of Paulsen's stories are filled with detailed descriptions of hunting-and-gathering provisions, creating shelters, narrowly escaping death at the hands of wild animals, and surviving the elements that come from his firsthand experiences with the wilderness. Paulsen has also written numerous nonfiction and biographic titles, some of which focus on his experiences running the *Iditarod.*

Another seminal writer of adventure fiction for teens is Will HOBBS. Cloyd Atcitty, a young Ute boy from Utah, holds center stage in *Bearstone* (1989) and *Beardance* (1993). Cloyd is sent by his tribe to a group home, and from the group home he is sent to live with an elderly rancher named Walter Landis. Clyde and Walter grow closer since their pursuits (Walter wishes to reopen an old mine and Clyde wants to walk in the same places as his ancestors) throw them together. When Clyde witnesses the killing of a protected grizzly bear by a friend of Walter's, he is faced with a moral dilemma. In *Beardance,* Clyde and Walter learn of a mother grizzly and two cubs that may be the last grizzlies left in the region. Clyde must face a cold Colorado winter alone in order to save the lives of the cubs. He must also call upon his ancestors to give him strength during the challenge.

Hobbs has also written numerous stand-alone adventure titles for teens. In *Jason's Gold* (1999), a young man travels from California to the Klondike in order to participate in the Gold Rush. In *The Maze* (1998), a teen in dire straits finds a sense of purpose protecting condors in the Canyonlands National Park in Utah. In *Wild Man Island* (2002), a young man seeking closure after his father's death sneaks away from his kayaking group, is caught in a fierce storm, and ends up stranded on an island with only a reclusive hermit to aid him.

Tom Bodett's *Williwaw!* (1999) is another story about a ferocious storm on Alaskan waters. Left alone for a brief period by their father, September and Ivan Crane make a series of poor choices and find themselves caught on the water during a williwaw, the same type of storm that took their mother's life years

earlier. Teen-adventure fans especially enjoy listening to the audio version of this novel, read by the author.

Joan BAUER, author of many humorous stories geared to a female audience, also succeeds in the adventure arena with her snowy survival tale *Backwater* (1999). Ivy Breedlove, the protagonist, does not wish to follow in the footsteps of so many of her relatives and become an attorney. Ivy's true love is history, and while she is compiling a family genealogy, she learns of another nonlawyer in her family, Josephine, a reclusive aunt who has become a hermit. Ivy sets out to find and interview her family's black sheep, who can only be reached by climbing a mountain in New York's Adirondacks. Led by a woman known as "Mountain Mama," Ivy sets off for her aunt's home in a snowstorm.

Many writers have written adventure stories with nautical themes. *The Wanderer* (2000) by Sharon CREECH is an excellent sailing story, noteworthy because a group must pull together in order to survive the elements, and each other, while at sea. This intricate tale with complex characters is told through the voices of Sophie and Cody, two of three cousins traveling with their fathers and uncles on a sailing vessel headed for their grandfather's home in England. The sailing is not smooth and neither are the dynamics of the group. Creech skillfully reveals hints about Sophie's past and unfolds a beautiful tale of adoption and acceptance of one's past.

Rodman PHILBRICK's *The Young Man and the Sea* (2004) is the tale of Skiff Beaman, a teen from a coastal village in Maine. Skiff's mother has passed away and his father has fallen into a depressed state, refusing to budge off the couch. Their boat, the *Mary Rose,* has sunk while tied up outside their shacklike home, and Skiff is convinced that if he can mend the boat, his father's attitude will turn around. Skiff undertakes the raising and repair of the *Mary Rose,* only to find that the motor has been wrecked by the salt water. After his attempts at earning money to fix the motor through lobstering, Skiff sets his eyes on tuna fishing. The adventures begin as Skiff sets out alone for the deep waters to spear a bluefin tuna.

Life of Pi (2003) by Yann Martel is an unusual story of a teen's survival against the odds after he and several zoo animals survive the sinking of a cargo ship. Pi suffers the precarious fate of being saved by jumping into a lifeboat, but at the same time is endangered, since the lifeboat also contains some hideaway animals. This novel, written for an adult audience but with great teen appeal, presents the particular challenges of being stranded at sea with a hyena, an orangutan, a zebra, and a 450-pound Bengal tiger named Richard Parker.

CATHY DELNEO

AFRICAN AMERICAN LITERATURE

The rise of A. A. literature for YA came with the advent of the civil rights movement in the 1960s. Prior to this time, African Americans were rarely featured in young adult literature, or, if they were, the portrayal was often controversial. 19th century literature for teenagers included, for example, Mark Twain's (pseud. Samuel Clemens) *Adventures of Huckleberry Finn* (1888) and its characterization of the kind but often addle-brained slave, Jim. Early 20th-century literature for teenagers generally featured white characters written by white authors, although southern American authors such as Carson McCullers occasionally included an African American as a noncentral character.

In 1960 Harper LEE, another southern white American writer, published *To Kill a Mockingbird,* a novel at least partly about a white lawyer, Atticus Finch, who defends an African American named Tom Robinson against the charge of raping a white woman. Because this novel is told from the point of view of a young girl, it quickly became part of assigned reading in many American high schools. The novel details the sympathetic position of white liberalism toward African Americans during this time, but ultimately accepts the inevitable tragedy of racism. Although *To Kill a Mockingbird* was written neither for an African American nor for an exclusively YA audience, the novel and film had an effect on the African American writers for young adults who would appear on the scene in the late 1960s and early 1970s.

One of the most important of these early authors is Mildred TAYLOR, who in 1976 published her Newbery medal-winning *Roll of Thunder, Hear My Cry.* This novel was the first of a SERIES of novels about the African American Logan family, living in southern Mississippi during the Great Depression. Like *To Kill a Mockingbird,* the Logan Family series examines ways that racism affects and harms the lives of all people, no matter what their race. However, Taylor's work concentrates on the viewpoint of African Americans, particularly young Cassie Logan, and her struggles to make sense out of a racist world.

Author Virginia HAMILTON, whose first YA novel, *Zeely,* appeared in 1968, also focused on the African American experience, but her novels often included an aspect of fantasy. *Zeely* and *The House of Dies Drear* (1968) both involve mysteries of identity. *The Planet of Junior Brown* (1971) includes a city run by children. Hamilton published a full FANTASY trilogy, beginning with the novel *Justice and Her Brothers* in 1978. She will be most remembered, however, for being the first African American author to win the Newbery Medal for *M. C. Higgins the Great* in 1975.

YA literature about African Americans written in the 1960s and 1970s has not been without controversy, however. White author Theodore TAYLOR has been both criticized and praised for his 1969 novel *The Cay,* about a young boy who has to deal with prejudice when he is shipwrecked alone on an island with a West Indian man. Books such as Taylor's have renewed questions over the legitimacy of white authors writing about black characters, a debate with strong proponents on both sides.

Although the majority of novels about African American young adults have female protagonists, a few authors have focused primarily on the struggles of African American males, including Walter Dean MYERS and Christopher Paul CURTIS. Myers, in books such as *Scorpions* (1988) and *Monster* (1999), showcases the difficulties for African American males of growing up in urban settings where gangs and racism produce a culture of violence. Curtis, whose work spans a readership from older children to YAs and reluctant readers, produced historical fiction set in key moments of 20th-century African American history: *Bud, Not Buddy* (1999) is about the Depression, and *The Watsons Go to Birmingham—1963* (1995) is set during the CIVIL RIGHTS era.

While few novels about African American characters avoid the issue of racism completely, many also deal with other topics typically covered by YA literature. Connie PORTER's *Imani All Mine* (2000) discusses teen pregnancy; Sharon DRAPER's *Tears of a Tiger* (1994) is about the results of drunken driving. African American characters in these novels, however, are typically economically challenged; few YA novels suggest that the African American young adult might live an affluent lifestyle.

Not all YA novels written about blacks by Americans have had characters with slave ancestors in the American South. Rosa GUY, a West Indian writer, often writes about the conflict between those African Americans born in the U.S. and black people born elsewhere, as she does in *The Friends* (1973). In this novel and its sequels, Guy tells the story of West Indian Phyllisia and her struggles to understand American culture. Jamaica KINCAID'S CROSSOVER novel, *Annie John* (1986) is set entirely in the West Indies, although her follow-up novel, *Lucy* (1988), is set in New York City, where Kincaid herself is based. Sonia LEVITIN's *The Return* (1987) and *Dream Freedom* (2000) are about Ethiopia and the Sudan, respectively. C. KESSLER's *No Condition Is Permanent* (2001) concerns Sierra Leone and an American girl's understanding of tribal practices (including female circumcision) there. Even though these novels are not always set in the U.S., they still discuss issues that resonate with African American readers, such as racism, culture, migration, and identity.

Like novels set in or concerning the African diaspora, authors who write about mixed-race relations are expanding the definition of African American YA literature. Carolyn MEYER's *Jubilee Journey* (1997) and Canadian author William BELL's *Zach* (2000) both involve the journey of a biracial teenager to discover her or his African American heritage. Jacqueline WOODSON's *From the Notebooks of Melanin Sun* (1995) gives the viewpoint of an African American teenager on his mother's lesbian relationship with a white woman, tackling issues of race and sexuality.

African American literature for young adults has its base in historical events, primarily the experiences of American slaves and their descendents. However, other historical eras, such as the civil rights movement and the American Depression, have also proved popular with authors writing about African Americans. In addition, realistic fiction in contemporary settings has been an important focus of YA fiction; but it, too, has undergone change. Whereas works of the 1970s and 1980s focused on racism in its many forms, later African American YA literature includes a broader view, both within the African American experience and as a part of the African diaspora. FANTASY and SCIENCE FICTION are still underdeveloped aspects of African American YA literature. Overall, however, African Americans are powerfully represented.

BIBLIOGRAPHY: Harris, Violet J. (ed). *Teaching Multicultural Literature in Grades K–8.* Norwood, Massachusetts: Christopher-Gordon, 1993; Johnson, Dianne. "The International Context of African-American Children's Literature." *The All-White World of Children's Books,* ed. Osayimwense Osa. Trenton, New Jersey: Africa World Press, 1995, 139–46; Kutenplon, Deborah and Ellen Olmstead. *Young Adult Fiction by African-American Authors, 1968–1993: A Critical and Annotated Bibliography,* New York: Garland, 1995; MacCann, Donnarae and Gloria Woodard, eds., *The Black American in Books for Children,* second ed., New York: Rowan and Littlefield, 1993; Mikkelsen, Nina. "Insiders, Outsiders, and the Question of Authenticity: Who Shall Write for African-American Children?," *African American Review* 32.1, Spring 1998, 33–49; Smith, Karen Patricia. *African-American Voices in Young Adult Literature: Tradition, Transition, Transformation,* New York: Rowan and Littlefield, 2001; White, Paul. "Geography, Literature and Migration." *Writing across Worlds: Literature and Migration,* R. King, J. Cornell and Paul White, eds. London: Routledge, 1995.

KAREN SANDS-O'CONNOR

AIKEN, Joan (Delano)
Author, b. 4 September 1924, Rye, Sussex, London

A.'s literary work has been classified as adult FANTASY, crime/MYSTERY, ROMANCE/gothic, and children's FANTASY. The suspenseful, intricate plots and complex characters she invents capture the minds of children and young adults alike.

A. was born into a literary FAMILY. Her father, American poet/writer Conrad Aiken, won the 1930 Pulitzer Prize for his *Selected Poems.* Her mother, Canadian Jessie McDonald Aiken, was also an author. A. was raised in a rural area and home-schooled by her mother until age 12, during which time she was exposed to such authors as Charles Dickens, Mark Twain, Edgar Allan Poe, and Rudyard Kipling. Alone much of the time, she occupied herself by reading and creating stories. When her mother remarried, A. found that her blended family also enjoyed her knack for story development.

A. began writing when she was five years old, having already decided upon a literary career. Her first two poems were published while she was still in school, appearing in the *Abinger Chronicle.* Even though A. was paid, she began to realize that POETRY was not a profitable occupation. Her writing career began in earnest in 1955, following the death of her husband. She started with SHORT STORIES, but soon realized that they did not reap the benefits that a longer piece of literature would. She uncovered a manuscript that she had written at age seventeen, and after careful revisions, the manuscript became her first published novel, *The Kingdom and the Cave* (1959).

A. draws on her personal experiences for creative inspiration. For example, in *Beware of the Bouquet* (1960), the main character is a young female advertising executive who gets caught up in a deadly twist while on a photo shoot for a new product. A. herself worked for an advertising company for five years. She also continues the ADVENTURES of characters that she developed during childhood, such as Dido Twite of *Dido and Pa* (1986).

One of A.'s best-received YA novels is *The Wolves of Willoughby Chase* (1962). Readers are transported back to the beginning of an alternative 19th century where they find young Bonnie and her cousin Sylvia in dire straits. Left alone with their cruel governess while Bonnie's parents are abroad, the two girls find all of their possessions sold off and themselves relocated to a prisonlike orphan school. *Black Hearts in Battersea* (1964) continues this gothic saga. Simon, the boy who aided Bonnie and Sylvia in their escape in *Willoughby Chase,* arrives in London to meet an old friend and pursue the study of painting. Instead he finds himself inadvertently involved in a plot to overthrow King James III and the Duke and Duchess of Battersea. In *Night Fall* (1969), another award-winning novel, a young English girl travels to Cornwall to trace the source of a recurring nightmare.

In addition to being an author, A. has been a librarian, editor, and copywriter. Her various careers have contributed to her creativity and natural ability, supplying the author with knowledge and insight that is later brought into her works. As to why she writes, A. once stated, "Why do we want to have alternate worlds? It's a way of making progress . . . if you write about something, hopefully you write about something that's better or more interesting than circumstances as they are now, and that way you hope to make a step towards it."

AWARDS: 1965 Lewis Carroll Shelf Award, *The Wolves of Willoughby Chase;* 1969 *Guardian* Award, *The Whispering Mountain;* 1968 Carnegie Medal Honor Book, *The Whispering Mountain;* 1972 Edgar Allan Poe Award, *Night Fall;* 1974 *New York Times* outstanding book, *Midnight Is a Place; The Skin*

Spinners was included in the 1975 American Institute of Graphic Arts Book Show.

SELECT FURTHER WORKS: *The Skin Spinners,* 1960; *Nightbirds on Nantucket,* 1966; *The Crystal Crow,* 1968; *The Whispering Mountain,* 1969; *Smoke from Cromwell's Time,* 1970; *The Cuckoo Tree,* 1971; *Died on a Rainy Sunday,* 1972; *Arabel's Raven,* 1974; *Midnight is a Place,* 1974; *Castle Barebane,* 1976; *The Faithless Lollybird,* 1978; *The Shadow Guests,* 1980; *The Stolen Lake,* 1981; *Up the Chimney Down and Other Stories,* 1985; *Mansfield Revisited,* 1985; *The Teeth of the Gale,* 1988; *Morningquest,* 1994; *The Cockatrice Boys,* 1996; *Dangerous Games,* 1999; *Midwinter Nightingale,* 2003; *The Witch of Clatteringshaws,* 2005.

BIBLIOGRAPHY: *Contemporary Authors Online,* 2000; Hipple, Ted. *Writers for Young Adults,* vol. 1, 1993; "Joan Aiken: Wolves and Alternate Worlds," *Locus Magazine,* May, 1998; Kantar, Andrew, "Joan Aiken," *The Continuum Encyclopedia of Children's Literature,* 2001; http://webpages.marshall.edu/~pbostic/bio.html

RACHEL WITMER

ALAN

The Assembly for Adolescent Literature (ALAN) is a subsidiary organization of the National Council of Teachers of English. NCTE established assemblies to serve as special-interest groups for people committed to a particular area of study, but which differed from other subgroups. One can be a member of an assembly without concurrently being a member of NCTE itself.

A. was formed in 1973 at the NCTE Annual Convention in Philadelphia. Paying initial dues of $1.00, the charter members of ALAN included such important names in YA literature as G. Robert Carlsen, Ken Donelson, Aileen Pace Nilsen, and Jerry WEISS. A. was established as an organization open not only to NCTE members, but also to others with an interest in YA literature who would promote the genre through publications and activities that could be held in conjunction with the NCTE Annual Convention. Membership in A. includes authors, librarians, and publishing professionals who share with academics and classroom teachers a professional interest in YA literature.

The A. Constitution calls for an Executive Board composed of nine officers: a president, president-elect, a past president, and nine directors, all of them elected directly by the membership. The presidency is a three-year commitment, first as president-elect, then as president, then as past-president. Directors also serve for three years. The Executive Board meets formally each year at the NCTE Annual Convention in November and, for those able to attend, informally at the NCTE Spring Conference. Additionally, the Executive Board communicates throughout the year via e-mails, mailings, and teleconferences. Presidential duties include chairing board meetings, assigning committee members, and planning and choosing speakers for two major annual events—the Annual Breakfast and the A. Workshop. Marguerite Archer served as the first A. president. Other notable names in YA literature who have served as president include Michael CART, Betty Carter, Don GALLO, Ted Hipple, Virginia Monseau, and Connie Zitlow. To handle the business affairs of the organization, A. created the position of Executive Secretary in 1982.

A major benefit of membership in ALAN is a subscription to *The A. Review,* a journal first published in 1974, then titled *News from A.* What began as a newsletter announcing convention information evolved into an important scholarly journal devoted entirely to the critical study and teaching of YA literature. Published three times during the academic year, *The A. Review* is a peer-reviewed journal devoted solely to the field of literature for adolescents. The journal publishes research studies, papers presented at professional meetings, literary critiques and surveys, articles about and interviews with authors, comparative genre studies, and articles on effective teaching practices for teaching YA literature to adolescents. Contributors to the journal include authors, classroom teachers, college and university professors, librarians, and scholars. Manuscripts submitted to the journal receive a blind review by the editor and at least two members of the editorial review board. Other journal content includes "clip and file" reviews of recently published YA books and regular columns focusing on such topics as nonprint media for adolescents, research in progress, and issues of concern to middle- and high-school classroom teachers.

Two major annual events organized by A. are the A. Breakfast and ALAN Workshop. Since 1975, the A. Breakfast has been held each November on the Saturday of the NCTE Annual Convention. Regularly attracting an audience of three to four hundred, the breakfast program includes the installation of new officers, the presentation of the A. Award, and the

Breakfast Speaker. The speaker is always a high profile YA author. Since 1974, the A. Award has been presented to individuals who have made significant contributions to YA literature. Honorees have included authors, librarians, publishers, scholars, and teachers.

The two-day A. Workshop immediately follows the NCTE Annual Convention. The program usually opens with a keynote speaker, who is often an academic speaking on issues and trends in adolescent literature. Authors, teachers, and librarians participate in debates, individual talks, and panel discussions. Interspersed between the large-group sessions are small-group breakout sessions addressing a variety of adolescent literature topics.

Another important activity of A. is the administration of the A. Foundation. Established in 1983 with the goal of expanding scholarship in adolescent literature, the A. Foundation awards grants of up to $1,000 annually to support research projects in YA literature. Members and nonmembers submit funding requests to the Executive Secretary who sends them on to a standing Foundation Committee made up of the five most recent past presidents. Since its creation, the A. Foundation has funded over fifty proposals representing such topics as using recorded YA literature with reluctant readers, studying the university-level YA literature course, and reader-response to adolescent novels in middle school.

BIBLIOGRAPHY: Hipple, Ted. "A Brief History of ALAN." *Two Decades of The ALAN Review,* Urbana, IL: National Council of Teachers of English, 1999; Nilsen, Alleen Pace. "The Beginnings of *The ALAN Review.*" *Two Decades of The A. Review,* Urbana, IL: National Council of Teachers of English, 1999.

EDWARD T. SULLIVAN

ALCOCK, Vivien Dolores

Author, b. 23 June 1924; d. 2003, Worthing, England

A., author of FANTASY novels for children, began writing professionally after noticing her daughter's enjoyment of her storytelling at home. A. always enjoyed writing and used it to face difficult situations in her life. She was encouraged by a mentor in these efforts. Her works include fantasy and the use of supernatural elements that promote the growth of the characters.

AWARDS: ALA Notable Book of the Year citation: 1982 for *Travelers by Night,* 1985 for *The Cuckoo*

Sister, 1988 for *The Monster Garden;* 1983 Horn Book Honor List, *Travelers by Night;* Voice of Youth Advocate Best Science Fiction/Fantasy Book, *Monster Garden.*

FURTHER WORKS: The *Haunting of Cassie Palmer,* 1980; *The Stonewalkers,* 1981; *The Sylvia Game: A Novel of the Supernatural,* 1982; *Ghostly Companions: A Feast of Chilling Tales,* 1984; *Wait and See,* 1985; *The Mysterious Dr. Ross,* 1987; *The Thing in the Woods,* 1989; *The Trial of Anna Cotman,* 1990; *The Dancing Bush,* 1991; *A Kind of Thief,* 1992; *Singer to the Sea God,* 1992; *Othergran,* 1993; *The Wrecker,* 1994; *The Face at the Window,* 1994 (published *Stranger at the Window,* 1999); *Time Wreck,* 1996; *The Silver Egg,* 1997; *The Red-Eared Ghosts,* 1998; Contributor to *Help Wanted: and Short Stories about Young People Working,* 1997 and *Working Days: Short Stories about Teenagers at Work,* 1997.

BIBLIOGRAPHY: *Contemporary Authors Online,* 2002.

PATRICIA KEANE

ALCOTT, Bronson (Amos Bronson Alcott)

Educator, b. 29 November 1799, nr Wolcott Ct.; d. 4 March 1888, Concord, Massachusetts

A. ended his formal schooling at thirteen, and was largely self-educated from such books as he could borrow in his small farming community, crediting John Bunyan's classic *The Pilgrim's Progress* as his "most efficient teacher." Although he earned his living as a peddler in the South, his ambition was to become a teacher and he finally found work in various New England schools and began to develop an educational philosophy based on the ideas of the Swiss educator, Johann Pestalozzi. Putting his ideas into practice brought him wide attention in Connecticut, and he was invited to manage small, private Quaker schools in Boston and Philadelphia. In 1834, he started his Temple School in Boston to put his theories to the test. Although his school was initially successful, his ideas about the teaching of religion and his admitting a black girl as a student led ultimately to its closing. However, a school based on his ideas, Temple House, was founded in England and became a success.

A. was particularly interested in children's reading and deplored the fact that books did not deal with the real lives of children. His daughter, Louisa May ALCOTT, remedied that with *Little Women* and other books, the success of which enabled A. and his family

to live more comfortably. Louisa May shared a birthday with her father and died only two days after his death. A. is best remembered as a member of the Transcendentalist School of philosophers, which included Ralph Waldo Emerson and Henry David Thoreau.

SELECT FURTHER WORKS: *Principles and Methods of Infant Instruction,* 1830; *Record of a School,* 1835.

BIBLIOGRAPHY: "Orpheus at the Plough," *The New Yorker,* 10 January 2005; *Pedlar's Progress,* Odell Shepard, 1937.

KENNETH SEEMAN GINIGER

ALCOTT, Louisa May (pseud. A. M. Barnard)

Author, b. 29 November 1832, Germantown, Pennsylvania; d. 6 March 1888, Boston, Massachusetts

A. is best known for her classic YA novel, *Little Women* (1868). Her writing talents, however, span more than books for young readers. Born in Germantown, Pennsylvania, she grew up in Concord, Massachusetts. Her father was a brilliant philosopher and educator, but had a difficult time providing for his wife and four daughters. A string of failed enterprises that almost left the family penniless instilled a sense of responsibility in young A. Her father made up for his lack of ability to provide financial stability with his excellent teaching skills. He educated all four daughters at home, and introduced them to great thinkers of the time such as Emerson and Thoreau. A. herself served as a tutor to Emerson's daughter. It was at this time that she began writing fairy stories for fun. Her mother was also a strong individual who loved literature. A.'s parents fostered the skills of observing and writing in their daughters by requiring them to keep journals of their thoughts, experiences, and observations.

As a result, A. grew up well-read, well-educated, and a passionate supporter of many reform movements, including the abolition of slavery and women's right to vote. With such strong literary influences around her, it is not surprising that A.'s writing career began early in life. When she was eighteen and living in Boston with her family, she began writing stories for magazines and newspapers. She wrote suspense and ROMANCE and some stories under the pseudonym A. M. Barnard. Being ambitious and determined to support herself financially, she aspired to do more than write for magazines. At age twenty-three, A.'s first novel, *Flower Fables,* was published. It consisted of the collection of fairy stories she had written earlier while she was a tutor.

Passionate about helping others, A. devoted much of her life to volunteering for charitable causes, caring for others, and promoting the social causes she believed in. She nursed her sister before the sister's death in 1858. Shortly after, she signed up to work as a nurse in a Union hospital during the Civil War. She enjoyed being a nurse, but nothing could keep her from writing. In 1863, *Hospital Sketches* was published, letters A. wrote to her FAMILY, graphically describing her time in the Union hospital and the difficulties of war. It was this book that brought A. recognition and her first success as an author. However, her next novel, *Moods* (1865), was not as well received. In order to support herself in the wake of the book's lackluster success, she went back to writing for magazines. In 1867, A. became editor of the children's MAGAZINE *Merry's Museum.* When she was approached by her publisher to write a book specifically for children, she was reluctant. She did not think of herself as a children's author, and had not set out to become one. But agree she did. She did not enjoy writing the book and did not think it would be of much interest to anyone. Ironically, the result was the classic novel, *Little Women* (1968). She based the story on her own experiences growing up with her three sisters.

Little Women proved to be a huge and instant success, both critically and commercially. A.'s popularity soared. The great success of *Little Women* prompted A. to write seven more novels, including *An Old-Fashioned Girl* (1870), *Little Men* (1871), and *Jo's Boys* (1886), which comprised a SERIES tracking the "little women" throughout their lives. A. achieved a rather large following among young readers, not to mention the financial security she sought. She lived comfortably and used her wealth to take care of her family. A. did not forget her deeply held beliefs. She wrote in support of the suffrage movement for various women's journals and urged women to register to vote. In 1879 she was the first woman to register to vote in the local school election in Concord. A. also wrote numerous SHORT STORIES for young readers.

A. never married or had children of her own, but she did raise her niece and nephew after her two sisters passed away. A. died in 1888 in Boston due to complications from typhoid fever she contracted during the Civil War. *Little Women* is her lasting legacy, through which she has touched the lives of countless young readers. The book has never been out of print. She influenced the entire genre of children's fiction because she was the first author to write realistic fiction specifically for children.

A Long Fatal Love Chase (1866), initially rejected by A.'s publisher, was rediscovered and published in 1995. Several heretofore uncharacteristic novels by A., under the pseudonym A. M. Barnard, were identified in 1942 by the antiquerian-book dealers Leona Rostenberg and Madeleine B. Stern. In 1996, A.'s first novel was unearthed; never published, *The Inheritance* (1849) was written for young people when the author was eighteen. Some of A.'s works have also been made into films including *Little Women, An Old-Fashioned Girl,* and *Little Men.* Today, the Orchard House, a residence of the Alcott family in Concord is a landmark and museum.

SELECT FURTHER WORKS: *Good Wives* (or *Little Women, or Meg, Jo, Beth and Amy, Part Second*), 1869; *Life at Plumfied with Jo's Boys,* 1871; *Eight Cousins,* 1875; *Rose in Bloom,* 1876; *Under the Lilacs,* 1878; *Jack and Jill: A Village Story,* 1880; *Jo's Boys and How They Turned Out,* 1886.

BIBLIOGRAPHY: *Something About the Author,* vol. 100, 1999; "Louisa May Alcott" on Encyclopedia .com: http://www.encyclopedia.com/html/A/Alcott -L1.asp

NANCY A. BUGGÉ

ALDER, Elizabeth
Author, educator, n.d., n.p.

A.'s first book, the award-winning *The King's Shadow,* was published in 1995. The novel is set in England in the tumultuous three years leading up to the Battle of Hastings (1066) and has been designated by many as useful for exposing students to the medieval era (Barnhouse 2000; Manczuk 2002). Although, as Rebecca Barnhouse notes in her book, *Recasting the Past: The Middle Ages in Young Adult Literature* (2000), much of the historical record of the time directly preceding the Battle of Hastings is "not well documented . . . [and] difficult to interpret" (pp. 44–45), Barnhouse acknowledges that "Alder's portrayal of Anglo-Saxon society is remarkably accurate" (p. 48). "I have tried to remain as close as possible to historical fact," states Alder in the "Author's Note" (1995, p. vii).

Barnhouse sees academic value and artistic quality in A.'s *The King's Shadow.* This is especially evident, as Barnhouse notes, in Alder's allusions to many historical texts—*Beowulf, The Song of Roland, The Anglo-Saxon Chronicles.* Barnhouse compliments Alder's use of the texts: "Alder does not give the reader the entire plot of *The Song of Roland* or 'The Battle of Brunanburh' or *Beowulf.* Instead, she presents snatches of poetry. . . . [twisting] poetic lines sinuously . . . through the texture of her tale . . . [and, in so doing,] celebrates poetry and invites the readers to join in the dance" (p. 35).

Chris Sherman (*Booklist*) also sees entertainment value in the book. He notes, "Alder's vivid descriptions of the harsh conditions and customs of medieval life make the story come alive" (1995). In the book a self-taught, resilient Welsh serf, Evyn, himself a storyteller, overcomes brutality, sorrow, and adversity and becomes a personal companion to the King of England. It is from such a vantage point, on the front lines, that the historical events of this significant period are seen.

Crossing the Panther's Path (2002) shares aspects of its structure with *The King's Shadow.* Another young hero, gifted in languages, sees at close range the action that leads to a major battle; this time the Battle of 1812. *Crossing the Panther's Path* follows the son of a British Army Captain, Billy Calder (based on a historical figure), as he serves as interpreter for Tecumseh, the Shawnee warrior. As he matures, Billy learns of the predicament of Native Americans.

Alder lives in Willoughby, Ohio; she is married and is the mother of five children. She teaches English at the junior-high level.

AWARDS: *Crossing the Panther's Path:* Teachers' Choice Book, 2003, and nominated for the American Library Association's Best Books for Young Adults, 2002; The Best Children's Book of the Year, 2003 (Bank Street College of Education); Notable Social Studies Trade Book for Young People, 2003 (the National Council for the Social Studies NCSS); Teacher's Choices, 2003 (International Reading Association). *The King's Shadow:* ALA Best Book for Young Adults, 1996; ALA Popular Paperbacks for Young Adults, 1998; Best Books for Young Adults, 1995 (*School Library Journal*); Popular Paperback for Young Adults, 1998 (Teens from Other Times: historical fiction category); 1996 Friends of American

Writers Award, juvenile category; Best Book of the Year, 1995 (*School Library Journal*); IRA Children's Book Award, older reader category, 1995.

BIBLIOGRAPHY: Alder, E. *The King's Shadow,* 1995; Barnhouse, R. *Recasting the Past: The Middle Ages in Young Adult Literature,* 2000; Manczuk, S. "Medieval Days and Ways: Books for Middle School Readers," *Book Report, 21* (3), 2002, 10, 12–14; Sherman, C. Review of *The King's Shadow, Booklist, 91,* 1995, 1873; Teachers' choices for 2003, *The Reading Teacher, 57,* 271–278.

MARY MCMILLAN TERRY

ALEXANDER, Lloyd (Chudley)
Author, translator, cartoonist, layout artist, advertising copywriter, editor, b. 30 January 1924, Philadelphia, Pennsylvania

A. was born to Alan Audley (a stockbroker and importer) and Edna (Chudley) Alexander. He learned to read by age three or four, and has read avidly ever since. As a boy, he loved classic literature and ancient folktales, often pretending to be his hero, King Arthur. Although A. decided that he wanted to be a writer and poet, his parents said that he needed a more practical job, so he became a bank messenger to save money for college. A. didn't enjoy working at the bank and referred to it as, "feeling like Robin Hood chained in the Sheriff of Nottingham's dungeon." A. attended West Chester State Teachers College for a year before he quit. He then joined the U.S. Army seeking adventures to write about. The Army sent A. from Texas to Maryland, to England and Wales. A. ended up in Paris, where he met his future wife, Janine. There, after marrying her in January 1946, A. applied for a discharge from the Army in order to attend the University of Paris.

No matter where he was, A. was continually writing. After Paris, he took his wife and her daughter, Madeleine, back to the city of his origins. For many years A. was an unpublished writer, initially aiming for an adult audience. He held a series of odd jobs to support his family. Finally, after seven years of writing, A.'s first book, *And Let the Credit Go,* was published. Ten years later A. started writing children's books in the FANTASY genre. The popular five-novel Prydain Chronicles focused on the mystical adventures of Taran, an assistant pig-keeper. For A., the fantasy world is a mirror to the real world. "At heart, the issues raised in a work of fantasy are those we face in real life," he stated in his 1969 Newbery Award acceptance speech. Reprinted in *The Horn Book.* "In whatever guise—our own daily nightmares of war, intolerance, inhumanity; or the struggles of an Assistant Pig-Keeper against the Lord of Death—the problems are agonizingly familiar. And openness to compassion, love, and mercy is as essential to us here and now as it is to any inhabitant of an imaginary kingdom."

In a later book, *The Gawgon and the Boy* (2003), A. writes a story that seems AUTOBIOGRAPHICAL. The book's narrator is an eleven-year-old boy named David, who becomes so ill that he cannot attend school. The book takes place during the Great Depression, and as David's father, an importer, struggles to provide for his family, David explores his imaginary world. Amid a family of interesting and odd characters, Great Aunt Annie (aka the Gawgon, or Gorgon, like Medusa) becomes David's tutor. Once she discovers David's nickname for her, Aunt Annie takes on the name the Gawgon, and David becomes, simply, the Boy.

The Gawgon is no ordinary teacher, giving the Boy his first homework—unraveling a knotted ball of yarn. She teaches all the conventional subjects, but in a way that interests the Boy, who never cared for school. The Boy could be any young boy or girl, and the wonderful imaginary world and stories that the Boy creates could be done by any child. This book paints a wonderful image of childhood. While it takes place in a fictional place, it shows that fantasy worlds exist in the imagination.

While all of A.'s books develop entertaining stories that are accessible and exciting for young readers, he doesn't stop there. The reader can always relate to the characters, even the fantastical ones. These books create stories to be enacted in a child's mind. These books let children know that they are not the only ones who have problems. No matter how difficult and complex a problem may seem, there is most often a solution.

A. continues to produce novels. In addition to young adult and children's literature, A. has written a number of adult novels and translated works by Jean-Paul Sartre, Paul Eluard, and Paul Vialar. Besides writing, A. enjoys his cats, his music (he plays violin, piano, and guitar) and painting. He currently resides with his wife and cats in Drexel Hill, Pennsylvania.

AWARDS: 1959 Isaac Siegel Memorial Juvenile Award, *Border Hawk: August Bondi;* 1966 Newbery Honor Book, *The Black Cauldron;* 1969 Newbery Medal, *The High King;* 1971 National Book Award, *The Marvelous Misadventures of Sebastian;* 1973 Boston Globe–Horn Book Honor Book in Fiction, *The Cat Who Wished to Be a Man; The First Two Lives of Lukas-Kusha:* 1981 Silver Pencil Award and 1984 Austrian Children's Book Award; 1982 American Book Award, *Westmark;* Parents' Choice Awards: *The Kestrel* (1982), *The Beggar Queen* (1984), *The Illyrian Adventure* (1986), *The Fortune-Tellers* (1992); *The Fortune-Tellers: Boston Globe–Horn Book Award and Otter Award (1993).*

FURTHER WORKS: *The Black Cauldron,* 1965; *Taran Wanderer,* 1967; *The High King,* 1968; *The Castle of Llyr,* 1969; *The Book of Three,* 1978; *Westmark,* 1981; *The Beggar Queen,* 1985; *Drackenberg Adventure,* 1988; *The Jedera Adventure,* 1989; *The Remarkable Journey of Prince Jen,* 1991; *The House of Gobbaleen,* 1995; *The Illyrian Adventure,* 1995; *Time Cat: The Remarkable Journeys of Jason & Gareth,* 1996; *The Foundling: And Other Tales of Prydain,* 1996; *The Cat Who Wished to Be a Man,* 1997; *The Fortune-Tellers,* 1997; *The Iron Ring,* 1997; *The Arkadians,* 1998; *The First Two Lives of Lukas-Kasha,* 1998; *The Wizard in the Tree,* 1998; *The Town Cats and Other Tales,* 1998; *Gypsy Rizka,* 2000; *El Dorado Adventure,* 2000; *How the Cat Swallowed Thunder,* 2000; *The Marvelous Misadventures of Sebastian,* 2000; *Kestrel,* 2002; *The Philadelphia Adventure,* 2002; *The Rope Trick,* 2002; *The Xanadu Adventure,* 2005.

BIBLIOGRAPHY: *Children's Books in Print,* 2003; *Something About the Author,* Vol. 81, 1995; *Writers for Young Adults,* Vol. 1, 1993; *Contemporary Authors, New Revision Series,* Vol. 38, 1993; *Something About the Author,* Vol. 49, 1987; Something About the Author, Vol. 3, 1972; http://www.geocities.com/EnchantedForest/4802/#bio; http://www.carr.lib.md.us/authco/alex.htm; http://www.friend.ly.net/scoop/biographies/alexanderlloyd/; http://www.cas.usf.edu/lis/alis/lis5937/prior/eliza.htm

SARAH KATZ

ALMOND, David
Author, b. 15 May 1951, Newcastle-upon-Tyne, England

A. grew up in Felling-on-Tyne, England; his childhood playground eventually became the setting for his YA adult novels. As a child, A. disliked school but loved the library. He always knew he wanted to be a writer, and he dreamed of seeing his books on library shelves.

A. attended the University of East Anglia, where he studied to be a teacher. A. chose a career he thought would provide time for writing. The demands of teaching, however, soon led A. to quit his full-time job in order to concentrate on his writing. A. initially experienced minimal success. He wrote SHORT STORIES for magazines, edited a fiction magazine, *Panurge,* (1987 to 1993), and published *Sleepless Nights* (1985), a collection of stories for adults. A. worked five years on a novel that was rejected by 33 publishers. He eventually found his niche in writing young adult fiction.

A. achieved overnight success with the publication of the YA novel *Skellig* (1998). The book took A. just seven months to write; he claims the story flew into his head. *Skellig* is about a young boy's discovery of a mysterious, possibly supernatural creature in his garage. The creature, named Skellig, has winglike appendages and is dying. The title of the book came from the name of an island off the southwest coast of Ireland. *Skellig* sold out the first printing in four days and received unanimous praise from reviewers.

A. had already finished his second YA novel, *Kit's Wilderness* (1999), before *Skellig* had been nominated for any British awards. The tale of children playing a game of pretend death earned positive reviews and was published in several translations. In *Heaven's Eyes* (2000), A.'s third novel for young adults, escapees of a juvenile home flee on a raft to an old printing press on the River Tyne. In this story and others, A. uses landscapes and memories of his childhood.

A. lives with his family in Northumberland and enjoys writing for teens. He has published over five novels, a collection of short stories, and a play called *Wild Girl, Wild Boy* (2002), all for young adults. A. has been praised for his ability to blend everyday adventures with an element of mystery, while maintaining a story's credibility.

AWARDS: *Skellig:* 1998 Whitbread Children's Book of the Year Award, 1998, Carnegie Medal, 2000, Michael L. Printz Honor Book, *School Library Journal* Best Book, Junior Literary Guild Selection, ALA Notable Children's Book, Lancashire Children's Book of the Year, Stockton Children's Book of the Year, and Sheffield Children's Book of the Year; *Kit's Wilderness:* 1998 Arts Council Award for outstanding literature for young people, 1999 Silver Award of London's *Nestle Smarties Prize,* 2001 Michael L. Printz Award, *School Library Journal* Best Book, ALA Notable Children's Book; ALA Best Books for Young Adults list, 2001.

AWARDS: *Fire-Eaters:* Kirkus Reviews Editor's Choice, 2004; Horn Book Fanfare, 2004; ALA Best Books for Young Adults, 2005; ALA Notable Children's Books, 2005; Bulletin Blue Ribbons, 2004.

FURTHER WORKS: *Counting Stars,* 2001; *Secret Heart,* 2002; *The Fire-Eaters,* 2004.

BIBLIOGRAPHY: *Something about the Author,* vol. 114, 2000; davidalmond.com; jubileebooks.com

JODI PILGRIM

ALPHIN, Elaine Marie

Author, b. 30 October 1955, San Francisco, California

Inspired to write by her father, A. has been making up stories since she was a young girl. Her childhood was full of imagination and a love of words. A.'s novels for young adults reflect the importance of imagination. She says, "My novels deal with serious realities that young people face and overcome by the power of their imagination. There is often danger, and my heroes must find the courage and conviction to put themselves on the line for what they believe." She started writing while working as a journalist in Houston, but found she preferred YA literature. On her website, A. says, "I wanted to write to challenge readers to question their assumptions. . . . Kids are still finding out who they are, like I am, I guess. They're the perfect audience for me, because they want to consider new ideas in order to decide for themselves which ideas they agree with and which they don't, and how they want to live their lives."

A. is interested in the study of history, and she tries to make people real through her stories. Her novel *Ghost Soldier* (2001) combines history and the supernatural, telling the story of a teen helping a ghost from the Civil War. A. also writes suspense and MYSTERY. *Counterfeit Son* (2000) is a "psychological thriller" about the son of a serial killer who finds a place for himself by assuming the identity of one of his father's victims. *Counterfeit Son* won the Edgar Allan Poe Mystery Award. Another novel, *Simon Says* (2002), tells the story of a talented teen artist who goes to a boarding school for the arts, determined to stay true to his nonconformist nature. Instead, he finds himself mirroring the behavior of those around him, with disastrous results. *Picture Perfect* (2003) is a suspenseful story about two boys trying to understand their fathers.

AWARDS: YALSA 2003 Popular Paperbacks for Young Adults for *Counterfeit Son;* Edgar Allan Poe Award for the Best Young Adult Mystery of 2001 for *Counterfeit Son;* 2001 American Library Association Quick Pick for Reluctant Young Adult Readers for *Counterfeit Son;* 1993 American Library Association Quick Pick for Reluctant Young Adult Readers for *The Proving Ground; Counterfeit Son* and *Simon Says* were both nominated for the American Library Association Best Books for Young Adults list.

FURTHER WORKS: *The Ghost Cadet,* 1991; *The Proving Ground,* 1992; *101 Bible Puzzles,* 1993; *Tournament of Time,* 1994; *Rainy Day/Sunny Day/Any Day Activities,* 1994; *A Bear for Miguel,* 1996; *Creating Characters Kids will Love,* 2000; *Around the World in 1500,* 2001; *Germ Hunter: A Story about Louis Pasteur,* 2003; *Davy Crockett,* 2003; *Dinosaur Hunter,* 2003; *Picture Perfect,* 2003. From the "Household History" SERIES: *Vacuum Cleaners,* 1997; *Irons,* 1998; *Toasters,* 1998; *Telephones,* 2000. (Note: these Further Works include A.'s novels for children and nonfiction for adults.)

BIBLIOGRAPHY: *Contemporary Authors Online* (2002); Books in Print Online (2003); A.'s website, http://www.elainemariealphin.com

JENNA OBEE

ALTERNATIVE FORMATS TO THE PRINTED WORD

Audio books offer an alternative to conventional reading. Available currently in both abridged and unabridged editions as well as on tape and compact disc format, they offer the ability to absorb works of literature while at the same time complete other tasks. Useful during family trips or other shared-listening experiences, everyone can listen to a story together. Although not quite as intimate as an oral reading, they do offer a chance for a small group to listen to a tale simultaneously and then discuss it.

Abridged audio books excerpt parts of the complete work, much as an abridged book does. Unabridged audio books offer the work in its totality (with a narrator who reads the book in its entirety). The narrator may influence one's perception of the book by his or her interpretation of the material, not unlike the way actors portray a character from a book in a film or television show and imprint their interpretation. Sometimes authors narrate their own works, which leads to a different type of listening experience, providing a more personal flavor. Noted actors are becoming more prevalent as narrators. Among them is Jim Dale, who has given voice to the Harry Potter series in the U.S. Audio book listeners often have favorite narrators whose work they seek out.

Audio books also may be helpful to those who have learning disabilities because they offer readers a chance to read and listen simultaneously. They also increase the listener's capability to cultivate the skill of paying attention and processing spoken information. Another advantage of listening to audio books is that of learning how to pronounce different words correctly.

A newer alternative to the printed word is an electronic book, although technically this format still requires readers to physically read the text. However, an electronic book is loaded with technical assists—the result is a mixture of book and personal computer. Most electronic book readers offer the option of highlighting a word and instantaneously looking up its definition. It is also possible to electronically bookmark where a reader has left off in the text. There are various other conveniences, including a built-in light to make for easier reading in darker environments. Perhaps the greatest advantage that electronic books and e-books offer to readers is the ability to fit a great deal of text in a small device that is approximately the size of a thick paperback. The practical advantages that these conveniences offer cannot be overlooked, despite the current technological difficulties, and the relative scarcity of YA selections other than the classics found on so many high-school reading lists.

Alternative formats to the printed word will continue to emerge as technology advances. Some consider film and television adaptations of novels and stories as alternatives to the printed word. These formats bring a varied perspective to an author's work, as well as interpretations of each character that are wrought by both the director's and actors' insights. However, the substitution of the film or television version for the original work is often not as fulfilling for the viewer. Sometimes it can enhance one's appreciation of the original work as in Francis Ford Coppola's interpretations of S. E. HINTON's *The Outsiders* and *Rumble Fish.* This is not only true in cinema, but in the medium of television as well—such as *Roswell*

ANDERSON, L. H. ANDERSON, L. H.

based on the novels by Melinda Metz. Conversely, a poor interpretation of a previously enjoyed work can leave a viewer with a feeling of great disappointment—or even, in some cases, the thought that those involved may have read a totally different work. An excellent example of that is the *Nancy Drew* movies of the 1930s that portray a heroine who is more dependent on luck than on logic.

As technology continues to expand, it is difficult to anticipate the next developments. It is necessary to judge each on its own merits, as each one will no doubt offer both advantages and disadvantages. In the meantime, there is always a book.

JEANNE MARIE RYAN

ANDERSON, Laurie Halse
Author, b. 23 October 1961, Potsdam, New York

A. was born in Potsdam in northern New York State. She moved to Syracuse at age five, where her father was a Methodist clergyman involved with campus ministries. An avid reader, her favorite book as a child was *Heidi* by Johanna Spyri. A. enjoyed school and received a scholarship to a private school in the eighth grade. When her father changed positions, necessitating a move, A. attended a large public high school and despite her involvement with the school newspaper, the swim team, and the track team, she was unhappy. A. went to Denmark for her senior year as a foreign exchange student, living on a Danish farm. While in Denmark, she completed high school and took classes at a junior college. Returning to the United States, A. received her Associate of Arts degree in 1981 from Onandaga County Community College and her B.S.L.L. from Georgetown University in 1984. She married Gregory Anderson in 1983; they have two daughters, Stephanie and Meredith.

In 1989 A. began writing for a local newspaper; she later took a position as a reporter for the *Philadelphia Inquirer*. When her work hours began to interfere with her family life, she left the newspaper and started writing PICTURE BOOKS and also mysteries for adults. When the picture books sold and the mysteries did not, A. became a children's book writer. Devoting what time she could find in her busy life, she wrote a few books for middle-grade students, with little success. When she moved and caught mononucleosis, she was forced to slow down her busy schedule, as reflected in her words, ". . . had time to listen to my

soul" (Gallo, 2001). She was awakened one night from a nightmare by the sound of a girl sobbing; from this Melinda, the main character and voice of *Speak*, began to develop. Melinda's story unfolds as a young girl in her first year of high school is ostracized by her classmates and former friends because she called the police to a party during the summer. What no one realizes is that she called the police because she was raped. As a result, she withdraws into a world of silence until she is forced to deal with her attack. A. has created in Melinda a character with the ability to make the reader laugh at her observations and insights of high-school life and cry at her pain and vulnerability. As A. explained in an interview for Gallo's *authors4teens.com*, she didn't set out to write a YOUNG ADULT NOVEL; however, once completed, it was clearly a book for teens. Nominated for a National Book Award and receiving a Printz Honor Book Award, *Speak* catapulted the author into celebrity status among YA readers, teachers, and librarians. Her second book for young adults is a work of historical fiction, set in Philadelphia during a yellow-fever breakout. While working at the *Philadelphia Inquirer*, A. was intrigued after reading a story on the 200-year anniversary of the epidemic. Seven years later, *Fever 1793* (2000) was completed, and A.'s versatility as a YA author was further demonstrated by the many awards and honors she received for it. In her third YA book, *Catalyst* (2002), A. introduces Kate, a high-school senior, whose existence for several years has been focused on her acceptance to MIT. When Kate is not admitted, she is forced to reevaluate her self-worth, goals, and values.

A. is kept busy writing a SERIES for middle-grade readers, as well as other books for young children, yet her enthusiasm and genuine admiration for teens keep her listening for the characters like Melinda, Matilda, and Kate to share their stories through her writing.

AWARDS: National Book Award Finalist, 1999; *School Library Journal* Best Book of the Year, 1999; *Publishers Weekly* Best Book of the Year, 1999; YALSA Quick Pick for Young Adults, 2000. YALSA Best Book for Young Adults, 2000; Printz Award Honor Book, 2000; YALSA Top Ten Best Books for Young Adults, 2000; Golden Kite Award, 2000; IRA Young Adult Choice, 2001; all for *Speak* (1999) American Bookseller Pick of the Lists, 2000; IRA Teacher's Choice Book, 2001; YALSA Best Book for Young Adults, 2001 all for *Fever 1793*, (2000); YALSA Top Ten Best Books for Young Adults (2003) for *Catalyst*.

FURTHER WORKS: *Turkey Pox,* 1996; *Ndito Runs,* 1996; Wild at Heart Series: *Fight for Life,* 2000; *Homeless,* 2000, *Trickster,* 2000; *Manatee Blues,* 2000; *Say Good-bye,* 2001; *Storm Rescue,* 2001; *Teacher's Pet,* 2001; *Fear of Falling,* 2001; *Trapped,* 2002; *Time to Fly,* 2002; *Masks,* 2002. "Passport" in *Dirty Laundry: Stories about Family,* ed. Lisa Rowe Fraustino, 1998; "Snake" in *Love and Sex: Ten Stories of Truth,* edited by Michael CART, 2001; "Speaking Out" in *The* ALAN *Review,* 2000; "The Writing of Fever 1793: A Historical Detective Searches for the Truth" in *School Library Journal,* May 2001; "Dear Friends" in *Voices from the Middle,* Dec. 2001; *The Shy Child: Helping Children Triumph over Shyness,* with Ward K. Swallow, 2000; *Prom,* 2005.

BIBLIOGRAPHY: *Contemporary Authors:* New Revision Series, vol. 103, 2001. www.authors4teens.com; *Something About the Author,* vol. 132, 2002.

CATHY DENMAN

ANDERSON, M. T(obin)

Author, b. 4 November 1968, Cambridge, Massachusetts

Why publish under the initials M. T.? The author says, "I liked the ring of 'Thirsty by M.T.'" Get it? Seriously, Tobin Anderson is a very smart, very funny guy.

A Boston native, A. received his B.A. from Cambridge University and his M.F.A. in writing from Syracuse University. Shedding what he says was a distinctly middle-class background, he admits a fondness for all things British; this includes a penchant for tweed, eccentricities, and sophisticated intellectual pursuits. In addition to his writing and teaching about writing at Vermont College, he is the fiction editor of the online and print journal of surrealist and absurdist literature, "3rd bed" (see http://www.3rdbed.com/).

A. cites Roald DAHL and Tove Jansson as his favorite authors from adolescence, and Mark Twain, Evelyn Waugh, Lawrence Sterne, Denis Diderot, Richard Brautigan, Ralph Ellison, Vladimir Nabokov, Ronald Firbank, Donald Barthelme, John Marston, and Charles Brockden Brown as examples of "great stylists and satirists" whom he now admires.

A.'s first published novel, *Thirsty* (1997), is a realistic FANTASY which describes the tribulations of Chris, a teenage boy who grows to understand that he is becoming a vampire. *Thirsty* is not only a fine mood piece but is also perfect in its portrayal of male adolescent angst. Chris's irresistible urge, or more appropriately his inescapable transformation toward ly-canthropy, serves as a powerful metaphor for every boy's emergent sexuality. The matter-of-fact prose is deliciously jarring in the way it juxtaposes mundane details of contemporary life with extraordinary, even otherworldly, events. For example, rituals that have long held evil powers at bay must now be performed in the parking lot of the White Hen Pantry, as a strip mall has overtaken the sacred site. This wickedly wry commentary on contemporary complacence about things that should raise righteous indignation is a common thread that can be seen throughout the author's work.

A.'s second published novel is *Burger Wuss* (2003). Satiric from start to finish, it describes Anthony who works at a burger joint in an attempt to exact revenge over a love gone wrong. Sadly, he learns that being a nice guy in a world of nasty people only brings him greater pain.

Feed (2004), arguably Anderson's most accomplished work to date, is a highly ironic look at a future in which most people have a permanent electronic stream of information; it is as if the Internet and countless channels of cable TV were fed directly into their brains. Teenaged Titus and his pals are bored; they are consumerist pawns of the powers that be. Unable to communicate on any deep level, unable to love or connect with anyone, in the end there is little hope for their future. A. extrapolates a "culture [that] is becoming palpably more insular and contentedly moronic" but also believes that "there are a huge number of kids that see that this very thing is happening, and get angry about it. These are the kids who are the hope of the future—the ones who feel offended by what they're being fed, and who want to produce their own content that reflects the complications of their own lives."

A fourth novel was written earlier and is aimed at younger readers. Anderson describes *The Game of Sunken Places* (2004) as a "fantasy adventure story—mysterious, spooky, and reasonably fast-paced—a tribute to all those YA and middle-grade novels in which kids on vacation battle evil in knee-socks. It's about this great friendship—very characteristic for that age—and these two kids forced to wear Victorian clothes and face the powers of darkness in the Vermont woods."

In addition to his novels for young adults, A. has written four PICTURE BOOKS for younger readers and several SHORT STORIES for young adults.

AWARDS: *Feed,* ALA Best Books for Young Adults: 2003 *Boston Globe–Horn Book* Honor, Fiction; *Handel, Who Knew What He Liked, Boston Globe–Horn Book* Honor; ALA Notable Children's Books, 2002.

SELECT FURTHER WORKS: *Handel, Who Knew What He Liked,* 2001; "Barcarole for Paper and Bones," in *Shelf Life* (by Gary Paulsen), 2003; "A Brief Guide to the Ghosts of Great Britain" in *Open Your Eyes* (by Jill Davis), 2003; "The Mud and Fever Dialogues" in *Sixteen: Stories About That Sweet and Bitter Birthday* (Megan McCaffrey), 2004; *Whales on Stilts,* 2005.

BIBLIOGRAPHY: Shoemaker, Joel, "Hungry . . . For M. T., A.," *Voice of Youth Advocates,* vol. 27, no. 2, June, 2004, pp. 98–102.

JOEL SHOEMAKER

ANDERSON, Rachel
Author, b. 18 March 1943, Hampton Court, Surrey, England

The daughter of a military historian and a writer, A. writes books for children and YOUNG ADULTS in which she often addresses alienation, disability, and loss. A. has written more than thirty books for readers of all ages. She has worked in the news department of the British Broadcasting Corp. (BBC) and as a broadcaster for the BBC's *Woman's Hour.* In 1975, A. starred in *Fateful Eclipse,* a television drama written by Loalu Oguniyi and later broadcast on Western Nigerian Television. Her SHORT STORIES appear in *The Oxford Christmas Story Book, The Oxford Merry Christmas Book,* and *Stories for Four Year Olds.* She has contributed articles to the *Observer, Good Housekeeping, Home & Gardens, Times,* and other magazines and newspapers in England. A. published her AUTOBIOGRAPHICAL book, *For the Love of Sang,* in 1990. One of her latest works, *Warlands* (2000), is a powerful novel that deals with the psychological scars left behind after the Vietnam War.

AWARDS: *Guardian* Children's Fictional Award, for *Paper Faces.*

FURTHER WORKS: *Happy Christmas Little Angel,* 1991; *Black Water,* 1994; *The Dolls' House,* 1995; *Letters from Heaven,* 1995; *Julie and the Queen of Tonga,* 1996; *Carly's Luck,* 1997; *Ollie and the Trainers,* 1997; *Big Ben,* 1998; *The Scavenger's Tale,* 1998; *Bloom of Youth,* 1999; *Grandmother's Footsteps,* 1999; *Warlands,* 2000; *Joe's Story,* 2001; *Stronger than Mountains,* 2001.

BIBLIOGRAPHY: *Contemporary Authors,* online, 2002; *Writers for Young Adults,* 1993.

HECTOR L. MOREY

ANGELL, Judie (Fran Arrick and Maggie Twohill)
Author, b. 10 July 1937, New York City

A. earned her B.S. from Syracuse University (1959), after working as an elementary-school teacher, associate editor, switchboard operator, waitress, and continuity writer. A. began writing full time in 1968. She has always felt a connection between music and writing; for her, music provides the background and inspiration for her writings, beginning in the mid-1940s when she created a picture while listening to her favorite music.

A. believes her most crucial job as a writer is to relate her personal memories of powerful emotions that adolescents experience. By exploring both common and unique issues that young people face in familial and social circles, A. writes novels that combine serious emotions with humorous circumstances. "Most of A.'s protagonists are experiencing transitions, and they tend to be clever and creative in meeting the challenges involved in moving to adulthood." A.'s novel, *Dear Lola; or, How to Build Your Own Family: A Tale* (1980), focuses on a group of orphaned children who are related only through circumstances and hardships, and follows them as they try to survive in a world of unfriendly adults; the novel was adopted for the video *The Beniker Gang* in 1984.

Although A. has published novels in three different categories, her works for pre-teens and younger teens were written under her real name for the longest period of time. Under the pseudonym Fran Arrick, A. has explored darker subjects for older teens since the late 1970s. By depicting realistic family and community scenarios, she brought prominent social issues such as suicide, prostitution, and AIDS into a personal context. However, A. published *Yours Truly* (1993) under her own name, despite the fact that it contains discussions of AIDS, safe sex, substance abuse, and gangs.

A.'s most recent pseudonym, Maggie Twohill, is used for books directed at a younger audience. As Maggie Twohill, A. continually depicts protagonists who encounter difficult obstacles, but who function on a level of pure entertainment as they become involved in unusual adventures.

Despite the fact that A.'s novels vary as far as subject matter and level of difficulty, they all show A.'s respect for young readers. A. often tells her stories "through her young characters' eyes and insightful perceptions," using first-person narration.

SELECT FURTHER WORKS: Angell: *In Summertime It's Tuffy*, 1977; *Tina Gogo*, 1978; *Secret Selves*, 1979; *A Word from Our Sponsor, or, My Friend Alfred*, 1979; *What's Best for You*, 1981; *The Buffalo Nickel Blues Band*, 1982, 1991; *First, the Good News*, 1983; *Suds, a New Daytime Drama / Brought to You by Judie Angell*, 1983; *A Home Is to Share—and Share—and Share*, 1984; *One-Way to Ansonia*, 1985; *Ronnie and Rosie*, 1985; *The Weird Disappearance of Jordan Hall*, 1987; *What's Best for You*, 1990; *Don't Rent My Room!*, 1990; *Leave the Cooking to Me*, 1990; *Your's Truly: A Novel*, 1993; Fran Arrick: *Steffie Can't Come Out to Play*, 1978; *Tunnel Vision*, 1980; *Chernowitz!*, 1981; *G-d's Radar*, 1983; *Nice Girl from Good Home*, 1984; *Where'd You Get the Gun, Billy?*, 1991; *What You Don't Know Can Kill You*, 1992; Maggie Twohill: *Who Has the Lucky Duck in Class 4-B?*, 1984; *Jeeter, Mason and the Magic Headset*, 1985; *Bigmouth*, 1986; *Vanetine Frankenstein*, 1991; *Superbowl Upset*, 1991; *Hallelujah! The Welcome Table: A Lifetime of Memories with Recipes*, 2004.

BIBLIOGRAPHY: "Judie Angell." U*X*L Junior DISCovering Authors, 1998, reproduced in Discovering Collection, 2001. http://galenet.galegroup.com/servlet/DC/

SARA MARCUS

ANGELOU, Maya

Author, poet, screenwriter, director, educator, b. 4 April 1928, St. Louis, Missouri

Born Marguerite Annie Johnson in St. Louis, and reared in Stamps, Arkansas as well as St. Louis, A. experienced numerous challenges, changes, and transformations in her life that are described in her autobiographical writings. First, her divorcing parents sent her and her brother Bailey to live with their paternal grandmother in Stamps, a small, racially segregated town in Arkansas. For a while the children returned to live with their mother in St. Louis but were returned to their grandmother's custody in the aftermath of A.'s rape by the man who was her mother's boyfriend. A. credits a woman from the Stamps community, Mrs. Flowers, with reviving her sense of pride and providing her with an interest in literature.

San Francisco was the next of several places where A. lived; it was there that she gave birth, at age sixteen, to her son Guy, became the first AFRICAN AMERICAN streetcar conductor in the city, graduated from high school, and took dance and theatre classes. The years that followed drew on both her intellect and her education, as well as on her survival instincts honed through disparate and sometimes despairing circumstances. From a life that included working as a prostitute and a cook, as well as failed marriages, A. emerged as a singer, actress, and dancer; a writer and editor; a civil rights activist; a faculty member and an administrator.

Her first book, *I Know Why the Caged Bird Sings* (1970), won critical praise and a lasting legacy as a significant literary work. Nominated for a National Book Award and listed by the ALA as one of its Outstanding Books for the College Bound, this book tells the story of A.'s turbulent childhood and emergence into young adulthood. Some critics find it to be the most outstanding of her many works. At the same time, the book consistently appears on ALA's list of 100 Most Frequently Challenged Books, ranked as the third most frequently challenged book between the years of 1990–2000.

I Know Why the Caged Bird Sings was followed by other AUTOBIOGRAPHICAL volumes including *A Song Flung up to Heaven* (2002), published more than thirty years after the book that described the first seventeen years of A.'s life. Critical interpretations of these works refer to the way the books tell the story of a 20th-century African American woman while at the same time capturing themes and ideas reminiscent of those voiced by Frederick Douglass in the 19th century. The quest for self-identity and the role of motherhood are also identified as recurring themes in her work. *Just Give Me a Cool Drink of Water 'fore I Die* (1971) was nominated for a Pulitzer Prize.

In addition to her best-selling and acclaimed books, A. is recognized as a poet. Although critical reviews of her POETRY call her verse less powerful than her prose works, A. was distinguished by being asked to write and to read a poem at President Clinton's Inauguration in 1993. On this occasion, A. recited her poem "On the Pulse of Morning." Since then, A. has continued to write poetry, essays, and narrative works; she teaches literature and is in demand as a speaker. She also published several volumes of poetry including *And I Still Rise* (1987).

AWARDS: National Book Award nomination (1970); Pulitzer Prize Nomination (1972); Grammy, Best Spoken Word Album (1994); Presidential Medal of Arts (2000).

FURTHER WORKS: *Gather Together in My Name,* 1974; *Singin' and Swingin' and Gettin' Merry like Christmas,* 1985; *The Complete Collected Poems of Maya Angelou,* 1994; *Life Doesn't Frighten Me,* 1996; *The Heart of a Woman,* 1999.

BIBLIOGRAPHY: M. Angelou, *I Know Why the Caged Bird Sings,* 1970; www.mayaangelou.com; *Something About the Author,* 2003; *Dictionary of Literary Biography,* 1985; www.ala.org,online

JENNIFER B. PIERCE

ANONYMOUS (Sparks, Beatrice Mathews)

Author, editor, psychologist, b. 15 Jan. 1918, Goldberg, Idaho

A. holds a Ph.D. in Human Behavior and specializes in working with young people who have problems. She has been counseling YOUNG ADULTS in seminars, youth conferences, runaway houses, and school assemblies since 1955. A. uses her knowledge of young adults to produce nonfiction works with social messages. Her books, often taken from case histories, focus on youth in trouble. She skillfully edits diaries and journals to provide an inside look at social and health issues such as drugs, suicide, and body image.

A. published her first book for young adults, *Go Ask Alice,* in 1971. *Go Ask Alice* is the story of fifteen-year-old nameless girl whose life takes a downward spiral due to her involvement with drugs. *Go Ask Alice* has sold millions of copies, has been translated into sixteen languages, and has been made into a television movie. The book is also named in the list of the top twenty all-time best-selling PAPERBACK books for young adults. *Go Ask Alice* is widely used as required reading material for schools; with its sexual content and depiction of drug use, its inclusion on school lists has made it among the most frequently challenged books in the country. While the story, published in diary format, has been praised for presenting a positive message, it has also been criticized for containing unrealistic material. When it became known that A. added material from other case studies to the original DIARY, the publisher changed the book's genre from fiction to nonfiction. The book re-mains listed as nonfiction in many bookstores and is often taught as nonfiction in schools.

All of A.'s subsequent works have been nonfiction. They are authored by "Anonymous" in order to protect the youths who wrote the journal entries. *Go Ask Alice* was the only novel that did not contain the name "Beatrice Sparks" as editor. *Jay's Journal* (1979), another huge success, was adapted from the journal of a 16-year-old boy who committed suicide. With *Jay's Journal,* A. captured a large TEEN audience. Although there has been some debate about whether or not any fictionalized material was added, *Jay's Journal* has been translated into at least five languages and was also adapted into a movie. A. experiences great success with her nonfiction, diary-style novels, and has edited eight books in this format.

A. lives in California with her husband. After many years of working to help young people, she continues to write for them, putting real-life situations into book form. A. also speaks on topics related to healing young adults.

AWARDS: ALA Young Adult Notable Award, Christopher Medal, *School Library Journal* Best Books, ALA Quick Pick for Recommended Reading; Iowa's Teen Award: 1996–1997 for *It Happened to Nancy,* 2000–2001 for *Annie's Baby.*

FURTHER WORKS: *Key to Happiness,* 1967; *Voices,* 1978; *It Happened to Nancy: By an Anonymous Teenager,* 1994; *Almost Lost: The True Story of an Anonymous Teenager's Life on the Streets,* 1996; *It's My Candle: By an Anonymous Teenager—A True Story from His Diary,* 1996; *Annie's Baby: The Diary of Anonymous, a Pregnant Teenager,* 1998; *Treacherous Love: The Diary of an Anonymous Teenager,* 2000; *Kim—Empty Inside: The Diary of an Anonymous Teenager,* 2002.

BIBLIOGRAPHY: *Something about the Author,* vol. 44, 1986; www.rickwalton.com

JODI PILGRIM

ANTHONY, Piers

Author, b. 6 August 1934, Oxford, England
Pseud.: Piers Xanthony, Piers A. Jacob

One of America's most popular FANTASY writers, A. was born Piers Anthony Dillingham Jacob. His earliest childhood memories are of Spain, where his Quaker parents, both Oxford graduates, worked with refugee children during the Spanish Civil War.

His U.S.–born father was imprisoned by Franco. Upon his release in 1940, when A. was six, the family left Spain for the United States. After overcoming emotional difficulties and learning disabilities, A. earned a B.A. in Writing at Goddard College, Vermont in 1956, the year of his marriage to Carol Ann Marble ("Cam"). Service in the U.S. Army followed and A. became a U.S. citizen in 1958. After working as a hospital aide, technical writer, and teacher, A. sold his first SCIENCE FICTION stories in 1962. His first novel, *Chthon,* about a quest for freedom on a sentient prison planet, originally written as his B.A. thesis, was published in 1967. Like its sequel *Pthor* (1975), *Chthon* mixes Greek and Scandinavian myths, a feature typical of A.'s eclectic approach.

In 1968 his version of the Arthurian legend of Lancelot, set on a devastated Earth dominated by a duelling code, won the $5,000 Pyramid competition for a new SF novel and was serialized in *The Magazine of Fantasy and Science Fiction*. Published in book form as *Sos the Rope* (1968), it became the first of the Battle Circle trilogy. Endlessly inventive and a self-confessed workaholic, A. often develops his novels into linked SERIES.

With his wife's support, A. became a full-time writer and in 1977 produced his first best-seller, *A Spell for Chameleon*. Set in Xanth, a Florida-shaped enchanted kingdom, populated by intelligent animals, mythical creatures, and humans with magic powers, it set the pattern for the Xanth series. Bink is smart and handsome, but also naive and baffled, features he has in common with most of A's Xanth heroes. Bink undertakes a hazardous quest, saves the kingdom, and rescues a young woman from a spell that changes her intelligence and appearance. Appearance is often the only distinguishing characteristic of A's rather passive female characters. A's sometimes juvenile humor, with wet T-shirts and panty traps, may suit Xanth, where babies are literally delivered by the stork, but it offers little scope for heroines. The picaresque series also draws widely on conventional fantasy and MYTHOLOGY, so that flying carpets, unicorns, basilisks, werewolves, zombies, dragons, and centaurs all make appearances in the infinitely flexible Xanth universe. Comparisons are often made to L. Frank Baum's Oz series.

The Xanth series has grown to over twenty-five volumes since 1977. 1977 was a key year for epic fantasy; Terry BROOKS began his Shannara series and Stephen Donaldson launched the Thomas Covenant saga. Xanth's growing popularity with younger teenage readers encouraged A. to expand humorous content and wordplay. Readers meet the Pet Peeve, a bird that is rude to all, bedbugs that snore, and the colorfruit tree that bears blues, yellows, and oranges. Irritating insects include the cri-tic and depress-ant. Titles like *Isle of View* (1991) also carry loaded puns. *Up In A Heaval* (2002) includes two pages acknowledging puns sent by fans. The enthusiasm of A.'s two daughters for horses helped inspire the animals in *Split Infinity* (1980) and *Night Mare* (1983).

Because of A.'s skillful plot construction, highly professional writing, and logical development of the consequences of magic, the Xanth series is often recommended for beginners crossing the bridge between science fiction and fantasy.

The fifth Xanth novel, *Ogre Ogre* (1982), the story of Smash, a half-human ogre who gained intelligence and acceptance, marked an important stage in A.'s writing. The parallels between A.'s own life and Smash's were noted in A.'s significantly titled autobiography, *Biography of an Ogre* (1988).

A. is generous with his time in responding to fans' e-mail, and has collaborated with some on their novels, a process illustrated by (and described in) *Dream a Little Dream* (1999) by A. and Julie Brady.

Some of A.'s stories for older readers, such as the Incarnations of Immortality series, develop much darker themes in greater depth, examining the human response to catastrophe and death.

An amazingly prolific writer, capable of anything from martial arts action stories to space opera, A. has produced over 100 novels, twenty-one of them listed in the *New York Times* bestseller list. In 1983 three of his novels appeared simultaneously in the annual Locus Poll for the best fantasy novel: *Ogre Ogre* (1982) at sixth place, *Centaur Aisle* (1981) eighth and *Juxtaposition* (1982) ninth.

A. lives with his wife on a tree farm in Inverness Forest, Citrus County, Florida, near a railway cutting resembling The Chasm.

AWARDS: 1967 Pyramid-Fantasy and Science Fiction Novel Contest: Winner: *Sos the Rope;* 1978 August Derleth Fantasy Award: *A Spell for Chameleon;* 1978 Gandalf Award, *A Spell for Chameleon.*

FURTHER WORKS: *Chthon,* 1967; *Prostho Plus,* 1967; *Macroscope,* 1969; *Omnivore,* 1968; *Volk,* 1998; AP-

PRENTICE ADEPT SERIES: *Blue Adept,* 1981; *Out of Phaze,* 1987; *Robot Adept,* 1988; *Unicorn Point,* 1989; *Phaze Doubt,* 1990; BATTLE CIRCLE SERIES: *Var the Stick,* 1972; *Neq the Sword,* 1975; XANTH SERIES: *The Source of Magic,* 1979; *Castle Roogna,* 1979; *Night Mare,* 1983; *Dragon on a Pedestal,* 1983; *Crewel Lye: A Caustic Yarn,* 1984; *Golem in the Gears,* 1986; *Vale of the Vole,* 1987; *Heaven Cent,* 1988; *Man from Mundania,* 1989; *Question Quest,* 1991; *The Colour of her Panties,* 1992; *Demons Don't Dream,* 1992; *Harpy Thyme,* 1994; *Geis of the Gargoyle,* 1994; *Roc and a Hard Place,* 1995; *Yon Ill Wind,* 1996; *Faun and Games,* 1997; *Zombie Lover,* 1998; *Xone of Contention,* 1999; *The Dastard,* 2000; *Swell Foop,* 2001; *Cube Root,* 2003; *Current Events,* 2004.

BIBLIOGRAPHY: Anthony, Piers & Nye, Jody Lynn, *Piers Anthony's Visual Guide to Xanth,* 2000; Anthony, Piers, *Bio of an Ogre: The Autobiography of Piers Anthony to Age Fifty,* New York, NY, Ace Books, 1988; Anthony, Piers, *How Precious Was that While: An Autobiography,* 2001; Collings, Michael R., *Piers Anthony,* 1983; Marowski, Daniel G. Ed. *Contemporary Literary Criticism,* Vol 35, 1985: 34; Piers Anthony's website: www.hipiers.com; The Compleat Piers Anthony: www.piers-anthony.com

TREVOR AGNEW

THE ANTIHERO

An A. is a central character that is not brave, noble, or morally good in the style of a typical hero. The classic A. of 20th century YA literature is Holden Caulfield from J. D. Salinger's *The Catcher in the Rye* (1951). Totally lacking in much of what had constituted a hero up to that point in the 20th century, the foul-mouthed Holden turns out to be heroic in an offbeat way. However, to look at the roots of the A., one could go back to Shakespeare or perhaps the Bible. Either Hamlet or Jacob would fit nicely the description of an A., a protagonist who does not act in the classically defined way. Yet it is in the second half of the 20th and in the beginning of the 21st century that the a. has truly thrived in literature. The place of the A. in modern literature, especially in modern YA literature, is front and center. It is usually easier to find an A. in current literature than a hero.

J. R. R. TOLKIEN's Bilbo Baggins is also something of an A. If not for his cowardice and panic, Bilbo would not have slipped Gollum's ring onto his finger and endangered himself; by doing so, he falls under the supremacy of the ring (*The Hobbit,* 1938).

It causes him to act in ways that are without honor, such as attacking his nephew Frodo in a desperate attempt to regain possession of the ring (*Fellowship of the Ring,* 1954–1955). However, on many other occasions, he demonstrates bravery and adventurousness that is almost unheard of in the Hobbit community. When he finally does manage to turn the stewardship of the ring over to Frodo, Bilbo reveals his true nature and achieves heroic status despite past weakness.

Steve York, protagonist of the acclaimed *Rats Saw God* (1996) by Rob THOMAS, spends a good part of his high-school life trying not to be a hero. According to Steve, heroism is usurped in his family by his father, the astronaut. After nearly hitting bottom through overuse of drugs and alcohol, he jeopardizes his future by barely graduating from high school. Steve not only cleans up his own act but reassesses his relationships; in his self-assessment, this character shows a great deal of heroism. Self-assessment and eventual self-acceptance are keynotes for Paula DANZINGER's antihero, Marcy Lewis. Overweight and miserable, Marcy fumbles in her life until Ms. Finney, a new teacher, helps her find herself. Marcy, in turn, finds the courage to defend Ms. Finney against the anger of the community. Marcy's reluctant evolution is chronicled in *The Cat Ate My Gymsuit* (1974) and *There's a Bat in Bunk Five* (1980).

Eoin Colfer's "Artemis Fowl" series provides another example of an A. in current YA literature. Artemis Fowl is a pre-teen capable of demonstrating an amazing amount of amorality, not to mention that he is a thief. When his back is against a wall, however, Artemis can surprise everyone with his sense of loyalty.

Perhaps, in the current crop of YA literature, the most famous A. is J. K. ROWLING's character Harry Potter. Harry is not conventionally heroic—he breaks rules on an almost constant basis, defies authority on any number of occasions, and generally is in the midst of trouble. However, this does not take away from the fact that his battles with the malevolent wizard Voldemort are classic replays of many other conflicts where good fights evil.

The A. seems particularly suited to these modern cynical times. This is a world that, in the past five decades, saw the Vietnam War, Watergate, the Iran–Contra scandal, the Clinton impeachment hearings, and conflicts with Iraq and North Korea; like Ernest

Hemingway's nihilistic response to World War I, modern and contemporary authors create characters who have experienced their own disillusioning events and cannot fulfill the roles of the classic protagonists. Antiheroes are the new heroes of the 21st century; though they may ultimately prove heroic, their decency is always accompanied with a dose of human nature.

BIBLIOGRAPHY: www.amazon.com; www.novelst4 .epnet.com; *Encarta World English Dictionary,* Bloomsbury Publishing Plc, p. 75, 1999.

JEANNE MARIE RYAN

APPELT, Kathi

Author, b. 6 July 1954, Fayetteville, North Carolina

A. is the creator of delightful PICTURE BOOKS on bats, children, and pets that use language play to sensitively celebrate life's daily events, but her versatility is evident in her POETRY, SHORT STORIES, and INFORMATIONAL books for adolescents. A. did her first writing on the garage walls, with the permission of her parents, although she attributes her beginnings in writing for children to her two sons and the experiences they shared. Her personal focus as a writer is on the people and objects that are part of everyday life, and her commitment to children is evident in her presentation of these everyday events.

As a writer for adolescents, A. speaks through various genres and uses language that is clear and appealing as it speaks to and from the perspective of these younger adults. *Down Cut Shin Creek: The Pack Horse Librarians of Kentucky* (2001), co-authored with Jeanne Cannela Schmitzer, tells the story of the women who delivered reading materials to families living in the Kentucky Mountains in the early 1900s. The Pack Horse Library Project of Eastern Kentucky was part of the Works Progress Administration in the 1933 New Deal initiative. This well-researched historical account shares the often unknown story of these early librarians and their effort to bring hope to rural mountain folk. The book *Kissing Tennessee: And Other Stories from the Stardust Dance* (2000) consists of short stories about young people who are attending a spring dance in the school cafeteria. Each scenario describes a young person grappling with adolescent hopes of love and acceptance. A. captures the simple but encompassing feelings, strategies, and ultimate actions of various teens

at the Stardust Dance and appeals to even reluctant readers through this collection. Adolescents are also the focus of *Poems from Homeroom, A Writer's Place to Start* (2002), in which she shares through her own poetic images the yearnings of adolescents "at the cusp of taking charge of their lives" framed within a homeroom class. Poetry-writing insights and lesson suggestions given in the second half of the book make it so interesting that readers of all ages will want to put pen to paper. A. lives in Texas where she writes, is an instructor of writing at Texas A & M University, and gives presentations at schools as well as state and national conferences.

AWARDS: *The Bat Jamboree,* 1996, Pick of the Lists, American Booksellers Association; *Just People and Paper/Pen/Poem: A Young Writer's Way to Begin,* 1997, Best Book for Young Adults, ALA; *Kissing Tennessee: And Other Stories from the Stardust Dance,* 2000, Best Book for Young Adults, ALA; Quick Pick for Reluctant Readers, ALA; *Down Cut Shin Creek: The Pack Horse Librarians of Kentucky,* 2001, Pick of the Lists, ABA.

FURTHER WORKS: *The Bat Jamboree,* 1996; *The Thunderherd,* 1996; *Just People/Paper/Pen/Poem: A Young Writer's Way to Begin,* 1997; *Cowboy Dreams,* 1999; *Rain Dance,* 2001; *The Alley Cat's Meow,* 2001. *The Best Kind of Gift,* 2003; *My Father's Summers: A Daughter's Memoir,* 2004.

BIBLIOGRAPHY: Appelt, Kathi, *Poems from Homeroom,* 2002; Carton Debbie, review of *Kissing Tennessee, Booklist,* June 1, 2000; Contemporary Authors Online, Gale, 2002; Kathi Appelt website, http://www.kathiappelt.com (April 22, 2003); Meyer, Randy, review of *Down Cut Shin Creek, Booklist,* October 1, 2001.

JANELLE MATHIS

ARCHETYPAL ANALYSES OF YOUNG ADULT LITERATURE

Teenagers can understand and appreciate literary discussions based on archetypal analyses probably because all their lives they have seen media "typecasting" of Destroyers and Heroes, Friends and Lovers, and Innocents and Sages. Identifying and talking about some of the roles which they have observed gives young adults a way to go beyond their typical responses of *I-liked-it* or *I-didn't-like-it* and *It-was-believable* or *It-was-unlikely.* In many ways, basic archetypes (what Carl Jung called the "Collective Unconscious") chart the journeys of people's lives and so at one time or another people fill different archetypal roles. However, it is easier to talk about archetypal roles in books than in real life because authors are usually telling stories about only a small part of a character's life and focus on only one or two archetypes, perhaps tracing the changes that occur as a character moves from filling one role to filling another.

To keep students from overgeneralizing when they assign archetypes to characters, teachers need to talk about variations in the archetypes and in the kinds of transitions that "naturally" occur between one archetype and another. To demonstrate the correlation of particular archetypes with ages or stages of life, some teachers list and study them in the order that they are most likely to occur in people's lives. For example, they start with talking about and illustrating such roles as The Innocent, The Orphan, The Seeker, and The Friend, all roles filled by children. They then move on to young adult years where they talk about characters embarking on The Journey and either being, or coming in contact with, The Fool, The Trickster, The Magician, The Creator, and The Lover. It is usually later in full adulthood or in their senior years that people become The Caregiver, The Hero, The Warrior, The Destroyer, The Ruler, and The Sage.

There is no definitive list of archetypes. The above list is adapted from one that Carol Pearson outlines in her book *Awakening the Heroes Within: Twelve Archetypes to Help Us Find Ourselves and Transform Our World* (1991). Based on discussions in YA literature classes, we divided what Pearson listed as The Lover into two categories: The Lover and The Friend (because books about friendship are an important category in books for young readers). Because teenagers have entered a new phase in their lives when they make their own friends instead of relying on who their parents arrange for them to play with, they are curious about the intricacies and challenges of friendship, quite apart from romantic or sexual interests. Some of the most popular books for middle-school girls have been about all-girl friendships, as in stories by Judy BLUME, Ellen CONFORD, and Paula DANZIGER. Ann Brashares's *Sisterhood of the Traveling Pants* (2001) showed that if such stories were well written, they could also attract older readers. Another addition that we made to Pearson's list was that of the

Junex/Senex Conflict because so many books focus on struggles not just between adults and TEENAGERS, but also between older and younger teens as when older students or siblings bully or take advantage of younger or weaker ones, as in such books as Kathe Kojha's *Buddha Boy* (Farrar, 2003), Rodman PHILBRICK's *The Young Man and the Sea* (2004), and Jan CHERIPKO's *Rat* (Boyds Mills Press, 2002).

The point of talking about archetypes is not to encourage overgeneralizations or to force characters into non-negotiable boxes. Instead it is to give students an entrée into literary criticism that uses what they already know. When Beth Ricks, a doctoral student who did an archetypal analysis for her dissertation, used the approach with her high-school students in Monroe, Louisiana, she wrote to say that for the first time her students "understood that they could criticize texts while being positive."

An important concept that inspires class discussion is that of the Shadow Archetype. A Shadow is a character who has the qualities and characteristics of one of the archetypes to such an extent that they become self-destructive or damaging. Shadow lovers, for example, might be Samson and Delilah, Jay Gatsby and Daisy, Humbert Humbert and Lolita, and perhaps even the gangsters Bonnie and Clyde. The nurse, played by Kathy Bates in the film version of Stephen KING's *Misery,* was a Shadow Caregiver in that she kept her patient from getting well so that she could force him to write the kind of book she wanted. The city counselors who refused to pay the Pied Piper the money they had promised if he would rid their town of rats were Shadow Rulers, while the Pied Piper is a Destroyer, or some would argue, a Trickster.

The archetype that inspires the most discussion from my students is the one about an Innocent Embarking on a Journey. As Joseph Campbell describes it, the journey begins with a worthy young person setting out either willingly or through some kind of coercion on a quest and meeting frightening and terrible challenges. After proving his or her worth, the young person receives help from divine or unexpected sources. The biblical story of Joseph is a prototypical example of a worthy young hero forced to go on a journey. Early in life, Joseph was chosen and marked as a special person. When he was sold to the Egyptian traders, he embarked on a quest for wisdom and knowledge. When all seemed lost, Joseph was released from prison because of being blessed with the ability to interpret dreams. When during the famine, Joseph's brothers came to Egypt to beg for food, Joseph's forgiveness and generosity were final proof of his worthiness.

A distinguishing feature of such ROMANCES is the happy ending, which comes only after the hero's worth is proven through a crisis or an ordeal. If the young traveler has chosen to go searching, as opposed to being forced, then he or she might be referred to as a Seeker. Most such books include an actual journey as in *Whirligig* (Holt, 1998), Christopher Paul CURTIS's *The Watsons Go to Birmingham: 1963* (1995), Sharon CREECH's *Walk Two Moons* (HarperCollins, 1994), Gary PAULSEN's *The Beet Fields: Memories of a Sixteenth Summer* (Delacorte, 2000), and Joan BAUER's *Hope Was Here* (Putnam's Sons, 2000). The literal journey is a concrete representation for something more abstract such as acquiring knowledge or gaining wisdom, but as shown by Virginia Euwer WOLFF's *Make Lemonade* (Holt, 1993) and Paul FLEISHMAN's *Seek* (Marcato/Cricket, 2001), seekers do not always have to travel. One of the reasons that Journey and Seeker stories appeal to teenagers is that they know that sooner or later they will leave their parents' homes and make a life for themselves.

Perhaps the best thing about an archetypal approach to literary criticism is that young people can easily apply what they learn to literary experiences outside of school and books. Video games, recorded songs, advertisements, television programs, movies, and music videos are filled with archetypal images and figures. TEENAGERS who have participated in thoughtful discussions of such archetypes will be in a better position to understand and appreciate all kinds of literature—not just what they meet in school.

These ideas are more fully developed in chapter 3 of the seventh edition of *Literature for Today's Young Adults* by Kenneth L. Donelson and Alleen Pace Nilsen (Allyn and Bacon, 2005).

ALLEEN PACE NILSEN

ARMSTRONG, Jennifer (Julia Winfield)

Author, b. 12 May 1961, Waltham, Massachusetts

A. grew up in South Salem, New York and decided to become a writer when she was in first grade. After attending Smith College she worked as an editor at Cloverdale Press in New York. There she wrote anonymously more than fifty chapter books for children in

the "Sweet Valley High" SERIES and its sister series "Sweet Valley Kids." Following this apprenticeship she wrote books on her own under the pseudonym Julia Winfield.

In 1992 A. published her first and highly acclaimed novel *Steal Away* about a runaway slave and the white girl she accompanies. The novel is partly ADVENTURE story, memoir, and coming-of-age tale, moving back and forth across time by employing three fictional voices. *Steal Away* established A. as a writer of historical fiction. In her six-book series "Wild Rose Inn" she documents the lives of several generations of girls whose families inhabit the same Massachusetts tavern. In writing series books A. welcomed the possibility of tracing narrative life spans across centuries. Although the books stand on their own, the whole series can be greater than the sum of its parts.

A.'s 1996 ambitious Civil War novel *The Dreams of Mairhe Mehan,* and its sequel *Mary Mehan Awake,* tell the story of a young Irish barmaid in a Washington D.C. slum. After her brother decides to fight for the Union and dies, she moves north and accepts a position as a domestic in the house of a naturalist. The love and kindness of her employers and her own interaction with a war veteran help Mary discover her senses, her dreams, and a future. The author has also published picture books.

A.'s 1998 nonfiction account of the Antarctic journey of the explorer Shackleton in *Shipwreck at the Bottom of the World* has been praised for its colorful anecdotes and lively writing style. A. also received exceptional praise for her contributions to Irene Gut Opdyke's *In My Hands: Memories of a Holocaust Survivor* (1999). Both authors succeed in evoking Irene's memories, showing her simultaneously strong and vulnerable throughout her ordeal; the story is inspiring to young readers.

AWARDS: *Steal Away,* 1992, BBYA, 2000; Best Books for Young Adults 1993; The Golden Kite Award; *That Terrible Baby,* 1995, IRA and CBC Children's Choices; *Shipwreck at the Bottom of the World,* 1999, Orbis Pictus Award from NCTE—Outstanding Nonfiction, *Boston Globe–Horn Book* honor in nonfiction; *Shattered,* ALA BBYA, 2003; *The Kindling,* ALA Popular Paperback, 2004.

FURTHER WORKS: *Black-Eyed Susan* (illustrated by Emily Martindale), 1995; *The Snowball* (illustrated by Jean Pidgin), 1996; *Patrick Doyle is Full of Blar-*

ney (illustrated by Krista Brauckmann-Towns), 1996; *Sunshine, Moonshine,* 1997; *Foolish Gretel* (illustrated by Bill Dodge), 1997; *Lili the Brave* (illustrated by Uldis Klavins), 1997; *The Century for Young People* (w/Peter Jennings and Todd Brewster), 1999; (with Nancy Butler) *The Kindling: Fire-Us Trilogy Book One* (2002), *Keepers of the Flame: Fire-Us Book Two* (2002), *The Kiln: Fire-Us Book Three* (2003).

BIBLIOGRAPHY: *The Horn Book Magazine,* March–April, 1996, p. 193; July–August, 1999, pp. 478–79. *Something about the Author,* 1971, Vol. 111, 2000, pp. 1–5; Jennifer Armstrong website http://www.jennifer-armstrong.com

CHRISTINA MARIA WELTER

ARMSTRONG, William H.

b. 14 September 1914, Lexington, Virginia; d. 11 April 1999

A. was born in Lexington, Virginia, during the most violent hailstorm and tornado that people in the region had ever seen. A.'s father, Howard Gratton Armstrong, was a farmer, and his mother, Ida Morris Armstrong, was a homemaker. His mother wept with joy at having a healthy son after having two girls; she cried with fear as she watched all their crops destroyed.

A. developed a love of history as he grew up, partially because he lived in the middle of a historic region. He could walk to Lexington and Concord where Revolutionary War battles were fought. He saw the place George Washington carved his initials on Natural Bridge. He learned that Texas Freedom Fighter Sam Houston was born nearby. His grandfather had ridden with the renowned Confederate General Stonewall Jackson. History surrounded his home.

School, however, was not easy for A. He suffered from chronic asthma, was the smallest boy in his class, and the only one who wore glasses. He was never chosen to play when classmates were picking teams. When he found his favorite pony kicked to death by horses, he developed a stutter and became even more of an outcast. Finally, in the sixth grade his teacher, Mrs. Parker, changed his life. She held up his homework paper and announced that it was the neatest paper in the class. This was the first time he had received any praise for school work. The praise had the effect of a tonic. He accepted his lot and decided to do his best. Praise had a cyclical effect; each

time he received praise, he worked harder. The harder he worked the better his papers became, which led to more praise.

A.'s father taught him how to do hard work while growing up on a farm. He learned how to help with farm chores and how to be responsible for the care of animals. His mother taught him to read the Bible. A. said that years later he finally understood why he liked the Bible stories so much; everything that could be left out of the Bible stories had been left out including descriptions of characters. He could assume the role of David or Jacob because there were no descriptions of David or Jacob; he imagined that he looked exactly like them.

A. excelled in high school and college. He attended Hampden-Sydney College in Prince Edward Island County, Virginia. He wrote for the college newspaper and literary MAGAZINE as well as serving as the magazine's editor. When he graduated in 1936, he considered a career in journalism; however, another teacher, Dr. David C. Wilson, inspired him to teach. A. considers the decision to become a teacher one of the wisest he ever made.

After his wife died in 1952, A. raised his three children without the help of a housekeeper. He cleared a rocky hillside and built a house with his own hands. He taught ancient history and general studies at Kent School in Kent, Connecticut, for fifty-two years. The headmaster at Kent said that A. had the best-disciplined and best-prepared students in the school; he asked A. to write a book to help other teachers. The request resulted in *Study Is Hard Work* (1956).

Sounder (1969) is the best known and probably the most important book that A. wrote. It is based on stories told by an elderly black man who sat around the family kitchen table when A. was a child. The storyteller worked on the farm for A.'s father after school and in the summer, he was a teacher in a one-room school for black children. The stories that came from this man's lips were from Aesop, the Old Testament, Homer, and history. One night he told a story about Argus, Odysseus's faithful dog, who recognized his master when he returned home after twenty years. Then the man told the story of his own faithful coon dog, Sounder. The story was so powerful that A. remembered it fifty years later as he walked along the Housatonic River in Connecticut. He thought about the man who told the story and wondered what had kept the desire to learn alive in him while he faced neglect, oppression, and loneliness. A. knew that he must use the memory, create the man's boyhood revealing his desire to learn, show how he was supported by love and self-respect, which produced the remarkable man. A. wrote the book that winter; it was such a long manuscript that it was broken into three parts to become a trilogy.

AWARDS: 1970 Newbery Award for *Sounder.*

FURTHER WORKS: *Through Troubled Waters,* 1957; *Tools of Thinking: A Self-Help Workbook for Students in Grades 5–9,* 1968; *Barefoot in the Grass: The Story of Grandma Moses,* 1970; *Sour Land,* 1971; *The MacLeod Place,* 1972; *Hadassah: Esther the Orphan Queen,* 1972; *The Mills of God,* 1973; *The Education of Abraham Lincoln,* 1974; *My Animals,* 1974; *Joanna's Miracle,* 1977; *The Tale of Tawny and Dingo,* 1979.

BIBLIOGRAPHY: Sanderson, Jeannette, *A Reading Guide to Sounder by William H. Armstrong,* 2003; *Children's Literature Review,* Volume 1, 1976; *Something About the Author,* Volume 4, 1973; *Something About the Author,* Volume 111, 2000; *Something About the Author,* Volume 7, 1988; *Third Book of Junior Authors,* 1972; *Horn Book Magazine,* August 1970, pp. 352–358; *The New York Times,* April 25, 1999, p. 47; *The New York Times Book Review,* October 26, 1969. p. 42; *Contemporary Authors Online,* 2002; www.galenet.com/servlet/BioRC. Educational Paperback Association: www.edupaperback.org/author bios/Armstrong.William.html

BERNICE E. CULLINAN

ARNOLDI, Katherine
Author, illustrator, n.d., n.p.

A. has worked as a teacher and an advocate for single mothers, and is best known as the author and illustrator of the AUTOBIOGRAPHICAL GRAPHIC NOVEL *The Amazing True Story of a Teenage Single Mom* (1998). The seeds of her book were planted when A. worked with single mothers in high-school equivalency degree programs and ran a program in lower Manhattan called "The Single Mom College Program." A. was often frustrated with the uphill battle that young single mothers faced, as well as with the fact that they were reluctant to apply to college. She gave out copies of what would later become her book to help inspire young mothers and to show them that they were worthy of a bright future.

The Amazing True Story of a Teenage Single Mom is at once poignant and uplifting. The story covers traumatic instances of A.'s life, such as her rape by one man and abuse by several others, yet offers a beacon of hope in the form of her dreams of a good future for her daughter and a chance to attend college. The black-and-white illustrations are vibrant, expressive, and deceptively simple. The writing and style of illustration are appealing to TEENAGE readers. This book was picked by *Entertainment Weekly* as one of the top ten books of 1998. A. is a graduate of The City College Masters Program in Creating Writing and continues to be an advocate for single mothers. She refers to her book as "a support group you can hold in your hand."

BIBLIOGRAPHY: Gonzalez, David. "A Mother: Young, Single and Heroic." *The New York Times,* February 17, 1999: B1; *How I Became a Cartoonist: The Making of The Amazing True Story of a Teenage Single Mom.* Katherine Arnoldi. 14 November 2003. www .girlmom.com/arnoldi.html

ANDREA LIPINSKI

ARONSON, Marc
Author, b. 1950, n.p.

A. is best known for two award-winning, YOUNG ADULT nonfiction titles: *Art Attack: A Short Cultural History of the Avante Garde* (1998) and *Sir Walter Ralegh and the Quest for El Dorado* (2000).

In *Art Attack,* A. summarizes each of the artistic movements of the 20th century, pairing the various movements with relevant (if often anachronistic) musical selections. His writing style and cross-cultural focus make modern art into something accessible and significant outside the community of art scholars. *Art Attack* has been praised as "an exciting invitation to a brisk but rigorous survey that connects . . . Mondrian to . . . the Sex Pistols."

The carefully researched *Sir Walter Ralegh* (as Ralegh spelled it) offers a deep and varied history of the 15th-century explorer, considering both Ralegh's life and the broader significance of the era's events. The *Los Angeles Times* praised it as "both provocative and tantalizing" while *Booklist* called it "sweeping, multilayered nonfiction."

A. combines several of his speeches and articles on YA literature into *Exploding the Myths: The Truth about Teens and Reading* (2001). Critics note that this "thought provoking collection" shows that "teenagers today are more open to . . . diversity in narrative and format than their adult guardians are."

In addition to writing nonfiction, A. has edited literature for children and young adults with several publishers and has taught publishing courses at NYU.

AWARDS: *Art Attack: Publishers Weekly* Best Book of Year and the *New York Times* Notable Book citation, both 1998; *Sir Walter Ralegh:* Robert F. Sibert Award (American Library Association), Most Distinguished Information Book for Children, *Boston Globe–Horn Book* Award for nonfiction, Blue Ribbon Award *(Bulletin of the Center for Children's Books),* all 2000; *Witch-Hunt:* SLJ Best Books for Children, 2003.

FURTHER WORKS: *Day by Day: The Eighties* (1994); *Beyond the Pole: New Essays for a New Era*; *Witch-Hunt: Mysteries of the Salem Witch Trials* (2003); *John Winthrop, Oliver-Cromwell, and the Land of Promise* (2004); *The Real Revolution: The Global Study of American Independence* (2005).

BIBLIOGRAPHY: *Contemporary Authors,* vol. 196.

MYRON A. MYKYTA

ARRICK, Fran. See ANGELL, Judie.

ASHABRANNER, Brent (Kenneth)
Author, b. 3 November 1921, Shawnee, Oklahoma

Although A. grew up in a small Oklahoma town, he was fascinated by books about foreign countries. Books ultimately influenced the direction of A.'s life. At the age of eleven, A. read *Bomba the Jungle Boy,* which inspired him to write a book of his own that was set in Africa, *Barbara the Jungle Girl.* He never completed the book but he continued to pursue writing. In high school, A. won fourth prize in a *Scholastic Magazine* short-story writing contest, and at age twenty, he sold the first of many MAGAZINE stories. A.'s interest in writing still persists.

A. married Martha White in 1941. He served in the Navy during World War II, from 1942 to 1945, and returned to Oklahoma to finish his education. A. graduated from Oklahoma State University with a Bachelor's Degree in 1948 and a Master of Arts Degree in 1951. A. taught English at Oklahoma State University from 1952 to 1955 and published many magazine stories about the American West.

A. is best known for his nonfiction books for children and YOUNG ADULTS; he began writing nonfiction while working overseas in the 1950s. A. accepted an assignment in Africa working with the U.S. Foreign Assistance Program and, accompanied by his wife and daughters, spent two years in Ethiopia, and another two years in Libya. A. then joined the Peace Corps staff, starting the Peace Corps program in Nigeria and directing the Peace Corps in India. After the Peace Corps, A. worked for the Ford Foundation in the Philippines and Indonesia.

A., who has been praised for his knowledge of customs and lifestyles, felt a need to share with young people this knowledge as well as the importance of understanding people from different cultures. A. collaborated with co-worker and writer Russell Davis on his first seven books, including *The Lion's Whiskers* (1959), *Ten Thousand Desert Swords* (1960), *The Choctaw Code* (1961), and *Strangers in Africa* (1963). Most of their books are about the countries they visited, and include people and legends they encountered.

Since returning to the U.S., A. devotes the majority of his time to writing and is an award-winning author. In a span of twenty years, A. published more than thirty informative books for children that largely deal with social issues. He has written several books focusing on Native Americans, referencing his boyhood in Oklahoma, while others spotlight immigrants and refugees and their efforts to find their place in America. For example, *To Live in Two Worlds: American Indian Youth Today* (1984) presents the concerns of Indian youth in the 1980s. In *Dark Harvest* (1985), A. illustrates the plight of America's migrant workers while inspiring hope for social reform. A.'s *Still a Nation of Immigrants* (1993) paints a human face on contemporary immigrant groups.

A.'s success in revealing the individuals behind the stereotypes lies in his comprehensive field research. He interviews subjects whose stories provide interesting insight into individuals struggling in harsh environments. In *Gavriel and Jemal: Two Boys of Jerusalem* (1984), A. documents the experiences of a Jewish boy and an Arab boy, both living in Jerusalem. A. presents an unbiased view of the serious situation which exists in this volatile area of the world. In addition to field research, A. demonstrates the importance of library research. His books are laced with history, consideration of public policy issues, statistics, as well as personal stories.

A. currently resides in Williamsburg, Virginia. A.'s family participates in his life as a writer. A. has collaborated with his photographer daughter, Jennifer, on several books including a series of books about memorials. Books in the series, including *Their Names to Live: What the Vietnam Veterans Memorial Means to America* (1998), *The New African Americans* (1999), *Badge of Valor: The National Law Enforcement Officers Memorial* (2000), *A Date with Destiny: The Women in Military Service for America Memorial* (2000), *No Better Hope: What the Lincoln Memorial Means to America* (2001), *Remembering Korea: The Korean War Veterans Memorial* (2001), *On the Mall in Washington, DC: A Visit to America's Front Yard* (2002), and *The Washington Monument: A Beacon for America* (2002) contain photographs, personal stories, and BIOGRAPHICAL sketches of heroes. These nonfiction books have received praise for their quality as well as for their informative and inspiring tributes. A.'s daughter Martha helps research his books. In addition, his daughter Melissa has twice collaborated with A.—*Into a Strange Land: Unaccompanied Refugee Youth in America* (1987) and *Counting America: The Story of the United States Census* (1989).

A. continues to find ways to make complex social issues interesting and understandable to young readers because he feels that our most important reading takes place when we are young. He proposes that his topics can be made interesting to young readers because they are about real people dealing with serious problems.

AWARDS: *Morning Star, Black Sun: The Northern Cheyenne Indians and America's Energy Crisis* (1982): Notable Children's Trade Book in the Field of Social Studies and the Carter G. Woodson Book Award; *The New Americans: Changing Patterns in U.S. Immigration* (1983): Notable Children's Trade Book in the Field of Social Studies and ALA's Notable Book; *To Live in Two Worlds: American Indian Youth Today* (1984): Notable Children's Trade Book in the Field of Social Studies, ALA Best Book for Young Adults, and the Carter G. Woodson Book Award; *Gavriel and Jemal: Two Boys of Jerusalem* (1984): Notable Children's Book in the Field of Social Studies and ALA Notable Book; *Dark Harvest: Migrant Farmworkers in America* (1985): ALA Notable Book, a *Boston Globe–Horn Book* Honor Book, and a Carter G. Woodson Book Award; *Children of the Maya: A Guatemalan Indian Odyssey* (1986): ALA Notable Book and *School Library Journal's* Best Book of the Year; *Into a Strange Land: Unaccompanied Refugee Youth in America* (1987): Notable

Children's Trade Book in the Field of Social Studies, *SLJ*'s Best Book of the Year, ALA's Notable Book, and the Christopher Award; *The Vanishing Border: A Photographic Journey along Our Frontier with Mexico* (1987): Notable Children's Trade Book in the Field of Social Studies; *Always to Remember: The Story of the Vietnam Veterans Memorial* (1988): ALA Notable Book and Best Book. Six of A.'s novels were named Books for the Teen Age by the New York Public Library, and eleven were named Junior Literary Guild selections.

FURTHER WORKS: *Strangers in Africa* (1963); *Born to the Land: An American Portrait* (1989); *Counting America: The Story of the United States Census* (1989); *I'm in the Zoo, Too!* (1989); *People Who Make a Difference* (1989); *The Times of My Life: A Memoir* (1990); *Crazy about German Shepherds* (1990); *An Ancient Heritage: The Arab-American Minority* (1991); *To Seek a Better World: The Haitian Minority in America* (1997); *No Better Hope: What the Lincoln Memorial Means to America* (2001).

BIBLIOGRAPHY: Peacock, Scott (Ed.), *Contemporary Authors,* Vol. 110, 2002; Peacock, Scott (Ed.), *Something about the Author,* vol. 130, 2002; www.childrens bookguild.org

JODI PILGRIM

ASIAN AMERICAN LITERATURE

A.s have had a unique history. Unlike slaves from Africa, most Asian immigrants came to the U.S. voluntarily, starting in the mid-1800s. Driven from their homelands by natural disasters and political turmoil, they came to seek a better life. Many died on the difficult journey across the Pacific. Their arrival in the U.S. threatened the European American labor class, which quickly led to discriminatory laws limiting their ability to naturalize, marry, own land, and work in most occupations, forcing many Asian Americans to start their own businesses.

According to the 2000 census, Chinese Americans are the largest group of Asian Americans. Recruited to work on plantations in Hawai'i, farms in California, and the transcontinental railroad, they also worked in factories on both the East and West Coasts until they were barred from such work. Laurence YEP recounts the history of the Chinese railroad workers in *Dragon's Gate* (1993), in which fourteen-year-old Otter arrives in America during the California gold rush and finds thousands of fellow Chinese working on the Central Pacific Railroad under brutal—and often deadly—conditions. Urban Chinatowns developed at this time, a setting found in both Yep's *Child of the Owl* (1977) and Frank Chin's *Donald Duk* (1991). Later, second-wave immigrants settled in the suburbs, as in Yep's *Thief of Hearts* (2001), Maxine Hong Kingston's *The Woman Warrior* (1989), and Gish Jen's *Mona in the Promised Land* (1997). Other contemporary books often explore the cultural and generational gaps between the first and second or subsequent generations. These include Mel GLENN's *Split Image: A Story in Poems* (2000), Jen's *Typical American* (1992), and Amy TAN's *The Joy Luck Club* (1989), *Kitchen God's Wife* (1992), *The Hundred Secret Senses* (1996), and *The Bonesetter's Daughter* (2002). Chinese American characters are also starting to appear in popular series such as Randall and Cynthia Farley's *Tournament Crisis (Chip Hilton Sports Series,* Vol 14, 2000).

The Japanese are the sixth most numerous Asian American group. Originally recruited to keep Chinese workers in check, they faced slightly better treatment. Many were allowed to become citizens and to bring wives from Japan, as recounted in Yoshiko Uchida's *Picture Bride* (1997). However, when Pearl Harbor was bombed on December 7, 1941, Japanese Americans were immediately looked upon with suspicion, while other Asian Americans began to experience more tolerance. On December 22, *Time* MAGAZINE printed an article on differentiating the Chinese "friend" from the Japanese "enemy," and on May 7, 1942, over 100,000 Japanese Americans from the western U.S. were stripped of their property and imprisoned in ten internment camps in Utah, Arizona, Colorado, Arkansas, Idaho, Wyoming, and California. Their experiences are recounted in numerous fiction and nonfiction narratives, such as Jeanne Wakatsuki Houston's *Farewell to Manzanar* (1974), Jerry Stanley's *I am an American* (1994), Monica Itoi Sone's *Nisei Daughter* (1979), John Okada's *No-No Boy* (1980), Lawson Fusao Inada's *Only What We Could Carry* (2000), and Yoshiko Uchida's *Journey to Topaz* (1971). Canadians of Japanese descent were also interned, and their ordeals are recounted in Joy Kogawa's *Obasan* (1982) and *Itsuka* (1994). On August 6, 1945, the U.S. ended World War II by dropping an atomic bomb on Hiroshima, Japan. The first nuclear weapon used in a war, it caused massive devastation and suffering for years to come. Toshi Maruki's *Hiroshima No Pika* (1982) and Takayuki Ishii's

One Thousand Paper Cranes (2001) describe the bomb's aftereffects as experienced by young civilians. Other books about the Japanese American experience include Nancy Werlin's *Black Mirror* (2001), Maureen Wartski's *Candle in the Wind* (1995), and Uchida's *A Jar of Dreams* (1981), *The Happiest Ending* (1985), *The Best Bad Thing* (1986), and *The Invisible Thread* (1995).

The fourth largest group of Asian Americans, Koreans began arriving in the U.S. soon after the Chinese and Japanese. Like many first-generation immigrants, first-generation Korean Americans still felt strong attachments to their homeland, even more fiercely due to the war of independence Korea was waging against Japan. Many contributed to the WAR, sometimes an entire month's salary. They also worked hard to differentiate themselves from Japanese Americans, but they had their share of problems fitting in. This and other themes are reflected in stories about young Korean Americans such as Lauren Lee's *Stella: On the Edge of Popularity* (1994), Haemi Balgassi's *Tae's Sonata* (1997), Frances Park's *When My Sister Was Cleopatra Moon* (2001), and prolific writer Marie LEE's *F is for Fabuloso* (1999), *Finding My Own Voice* (2001), *If It Hadn't Been for Yoon Jun* (1995), *Necessary Roughness* (1998), and *Saying Goodbye* (1994).

A little-known fact is that the Asians from India, the third largest group of Asian Americans, are actually Caucasian, and in *U.S. vs. Balsara* (1910) and *Ajkoy Kumar Mazumdar* (1913), the courts held that Asians from India were considered "white persons" and therefore eligible for citizenship under a 1790 law granting naturalization to "free white persons." However, in *U.S. vs. Bhagat Singh Thind* (1923), the Supreme Court ruled that based on the "understanding of the common man," the term "white person" meant an immigrant from northern or western Europe. A year later, Congress passed the 1924 Immigration Act, denying immigration to people ineligible for naturalization, and the numbers of Asians from India in the U.S. dwindled. It wasn't until after World War II, when the laws were lifted, that Asian Indians began immigrating to the U.S. along with other formerly excluded Asians in large numbers. The Asian Indian's experiences in the West are explored in Rachna Gillmore's *A Group of One* (2001), and for mature readers, Bharati Mukherjee's *Tiger's Daughter* (1996) and *Desirable Daughters* (2003). For contemporary stories about India and Pakistan, try Suzanne Fisher STAPLES' *Shiva's Fire* (2000), *Shabanu: Daughter of the Wind* (1989), and *Haveli* (1995).

Filipino Americans, the second largest group of Asian Americans, didn't start arriving in the U.S. in large numbers until the early 1900s. Considered American nationals after the U.S. acquired the Philipines from Spain as a result of the Spanish-American War, they were allowed entry into the U.S. and worked mainly in Alaskan fisheries, agriculture, and the service industry. Their early experiences are recounted in Carlos Bulosan's AUTOBIOGRAPHICAL *America is in the Heart* (1946), Bienvenido N. Santos's *Scent of Apples* (1979), and Peter Bacho's *Dark Blue Suit and Other Stories* (1997). The Phillipines went through further political turmoil during World War II under Japanese occupation, as described in Tess Uriza Holthe's *When the Elephants Dance* (2002) and later during the reign of Ferdinand and Imelda Marcos, as described in Jessica Tarahata Hagedorn's *Dogeaters* (1991). Contemporary stories about Filipinos and Filipino Americans include Cecilia Manguerra Brainard's *Growing Up Filipino* (2003) and Brian Ascalon Roley's *American Son* (2001).

In 1964, there were only 603 South East Asians in the U.S. Today they outnumber Japanese Americans as the fifth most numerous group of Asian Americans. A week before and immediately after the fall of the U.S.-backed South Vietnamese government on April 29, 1975, over 100,000 fled the country from North Vietnamese troops, and in subsequent years several hundred thousand more escaped on crowded leaky boats. Altogether, about 130,000 South East Asians settled in the U.S. Many did not plan on a permanent move, but they had no choice. While some U.S. communities welcomed the refugees, others found them unwelcome reminders of an unpopular war. These and other experiences are recounted in Sara Gogol's *Vatasana's Lucky New Year* (1992), Sherry GARLAND's *Shadow of the Dragon* (1993), Qui Duc Nguyen's *Where the Ashes Are* (1994), Lucy Nguyen-Hong-Nhiem and Joel Halpern's *The Far East Comes Near: Autobiographical Accounts of Southeast Asian Students in America* (1989), Gloria WHELAN's *Good Bye Vietnam* (1993), Duong Van Mai Elliott's *The Sacred Willow* (2000), and for mature readers, Le Ly Hayslip and Jay Wurts' *When Heaven and Earth Changed Places* (1989).

Although most literature about Asians is still set "long ago and far away," books such as these that include images of contemporary Asians and Asian Americans are slowly becoming more numerous. Since many Asian Americans feel more connection to the U.S. than to the country of their cultural origin, it is important for teachers and librarians to balance their collections of Asian folklore and historical fiction with modern Asian American literature.

BIBLIOGRAPHY: Kim, Elaine H. 1982. *Asian American Literature: An Introduction to the Writings and Their Social Context*. Temple University Press, 1994 reprint; Takaki, Ronald. 1989. *Strangers from a Different Shore: A History of Asian Americans*. Back Bay Books 1998 revision.

JULIE SHEN

ASIMOV, Isaac

Author, b. 2 January 1920, Petrovichi, Soviet Union; d. 6 April 1992, New York City

A., one of the best-known SCIENCE FICTION and popular-science writers of his time, produced almost five hundred books during his lifetime, in addition to numerous articles and columns. His Jewish family immigrated to the U.S. when he was three. As a boy, he arose early to deliver papers and hurried home after school to help his father run his Brooklyn candy stores. This work ethic was carried into adulthood, as he wrote at a staggering pace, almost ten books per year, until his life was taken by AIDS, acquired through a blood transfusion.

The science fiction magazines on the candy store newsstands drew A. at an early age to science fiction. In 1941, after three years of submission attempts while continuing to improve his writing skills, the MAGAZINE *Astounding Science Fiction* bought his story "Nightfall." This story was voted as the best science-fiction short story almost thirty years later by the Science Fiction Writers of America. A. earned a B.S. (1939), an M.A. (1941), and a Ph.D. (1948) from Columbia University. He worked as a Navy civilian chemist from 1942–1945 and served in the U.S. Army from 1945–1946. In 1949, he became an Assistant Professor of Biochemistry at Boston University's School of Medicine. "By 1951 I was writing a textbook on biochemistry, and I finally realized the only thing I really wanted to be was a writer," A. said in an interview. He became famous for his *Three Laws* of Robotics, included in *I, Robot* (1950), that govern relations between robots and humans. Soon after came his famous *Foundation Trilogy,* a "future history" that was inspired by Edward Gibbon's *Decline and Fall of the Roman Empire.* The trilogy consists of *Foundation* (1951), *Foundation and Empire* (1952), and *Second Foundation* (1953), and was given a Hugo Award in 1966 as Best All-Time Science-Fiction Series. During this time, he also wrote the *Lucky Starr* SERIES for YOUNG ADULTS. Forty years later, A. added a sequel to the Foundation trilogy, *Foundation's Edge.* This novel was his first book to make the *New York Times* best-seller list. His final novel, *Forward the Foundation,* was published posthumously. In 1978 he wrote his favorite book, *Murder at the A.B.A.,* a MYSTERY in which he appeared as a character.

A. is also famous for his ability to explain the basic framework of many disciplines to his readers. He wrote about physical and biological sciences, humor, satire, and history. *Asimov's New Guide to Science* is revered as one of the greatest science books for laypersons. He also explored human culture and literary classics such as the Bible and Shakespeare through his writings.

In 1942 A. married Gertrude Blugerman; they had two children, David and Robyn. They divorced in 1973, and A. later married Janet Jeppson. His life is well chronicled in three autobiographies: *In Memory Yet Green* (1979), *In Joy Still Felt* (1980), and *I. Asimov* (1994). Select awards for his contributions to writing, science and science fiction are listed here.

AWARDS: Honored guest Thirteenth World Science Fiction Convention, 1955; Edison Foundation National Mass Media Award, 1958; Blakeslee Award for Nonfiction, 1960; Hugo Award, 1963, for science articles, Hugo Award, 1966, for *Foundation, Foundation and Empire, Second Foundation,* Hugo Award, 1973 for *The Gods Themselves,* 1983 for *Foundation's Edge,* James T. Grady Award, American Chemical Society, 1965; American Association for the Advancement of Science-Westinghouse Award for science writing, 1967; Nebula Award, 1973 and 1977 for "The Bicentennial Man." In 1979, "Nightfall" was chosen the best science fiction story of all time in a Science Fiction Writers of America poll.

FURTHER WORKS (SELECT): *How Did We Find out about the Universe?,* 1983; *How Did We Find out about Superconductivity?,* 1988; *How Did We Find out about Microwaves?,* 1989; *How Did We Find out*

about Photosynthesis?, 1989; *Complete Science Fair Handbook,* 1990; *Christopher Columbus: Navigator to the New World,* 1991; *Henry Hudson: Arctic Explorer and North American Adventurer,* 1991.

BIBLIOGRAPHY: Asimov, Janet Jeppson (ed.). *It's Been a Good Life,* 2002; Hutcheon, Pat Duffy. "The Legacy of Isaac Asimov." *Humanist,* 53(2), March/April 1993; "Isaac Asimov," *Contemporary Authors Online,* Gale, 2003; Rothstein, Mervyn. "Isaac Asimov, Whose Thoughts and Books Traveled the Universe, Is Dead at 72." *The New York Times,* 7 April 1992.

RUTH HITCHCOCK

ATKIN, S. Beth
Author, photographer, n.d., n.p.

A. dedicates most of her work to describing the lives of young people at risk who have had to grow up too soon through a combination of words and revealing photographic portraits. After graduating from Barnard College, A. moved to the Salinas Valley in California, and soon became interested in the lives of Mexican American migrant farm workers and their children, whose hard labor in difficult working conditions supplies much of the country's fruits and vegetables. Her first book, *Voices from the Fields: Children of Migrant Farmworkers Tell Their Stories* (1993), an ALA Best Book for Young Adults (BBYA), incorporates photographs, poems, and interviews to honestly and respectfully reveal the stark realities and hopeful yearnings of these children and their families. Each of the nine profiles is accompanied by a poem written in both Spanish and English, which mirror the children themselves who must act as a bridge balanced between their families and the world of the Anglos.

After interviewing a LATINO gang member during her research for *Voices from the Fields,* A. was inspired to write her second book, *Voices from the Streets: Young Former Gang Members Tell Their Stories* (1996), which was also selected as a Best Book for Young Adults. Like its predecessor, *Voices from the Streets* uses interviews, verse, and A.'s trademark black-and-white portraits as it tells the stories of former gang members from across the United States. The book reveals a startling diversity in its profiles, as you are introduced to girls and boys, representing various ethnicities, ranging in age from twelve to twenty-two. A. provides the reader with a view of their young lives, but without a hint of condescension or judgment. In both books, A. portrays her subjects as simultaneously tough and vulnerable, mature and optimistic. This contrast is revealed not only through photography, but also through the uncensored words of the young people themselves, creating an authenticity that makes their commitment to improving their lives so much more poignant.

Educating young people comprises a large part of A.'s work. In order to encourage young people to learn more about the broader issues involved in the lives of her subjects, A. includes glossaries and lists of resources in her books. Her interest in educating young people also extends beyond the printed page into her work as an Internet curriculum specialist. A nationally published photojournalist, A. also lectures on migrant worker issues and speaks to at-risk youth through community outreach programs in and around her home in Santa Monica, CA.

AWARDS: *Voices from the Streets: Young Former Gang Members Tell Their Stories* (1997), ALA Best Books for Young Adults; *Voices from the Fields,* ALA Popular Paperbacks, 2003.

BIBLIOGRAPHY: "S. Beth Atkin," http://www.twbook mark.com/authors/44/836/

MICHELLE CROSWELL FOSSUM

ATKINS, Catherine
Teacher, author, n.d., n.p.

A.'s current career as a teacher in alternative education programs has, without question, informed her work. Over the past decade she has taught people from elementary-school age to adults, but her main focus has been on TEENAGERS. A.'s experience as a teacher has given her an excellent understanding of teens, as well as a clear memory of her own teen years.

When Jeff Comes Home (1999) is a gritty look at how a teen reacts when he is returned to his home after being kidnapped and held for over two years in an abusive environment. His struggles to move beyond his past while holding his abuser responsible are extremely realistic; he continues to face threats from his former captor that place his family in imminent danger. Even after that threat passes, Jeff must live the rest of his life with the events that took place during his kidnapping.

A.'s second novel, *Alt Ed* (2003), is also about teens on the edge. Susan, an overweight tenth-grader, participates in a special after-school counseling class with other troubled students in order to develop a better self-image. Although this is primarily Susan's story, she shares it with the five other members of her Alt Ed group, and their counselor, Mr. Duffy. As the group assesses why they are in the program to begin with, each one must face personal demons. A. reworked a short story that she wrote in high school to create *Alt Ed,* adding enrichment from her teaching experiences. *Alt Ed* was a 2004 American Library Association Best Books for Young Adults nominee.

A.'s advice to aspiring writers: "Write with passion. Believe in yourself. Work to improve. Find a process that works for you and stick to it." A. lives and teaches in Northern California.

AWARDS: ALA Quick Picks for Reluctant Young Adult Readers, 2001; *When Jeff Comes Home,* 2000 American Library Association Best Book for Young Adults; Alt Ed: ALA Popular Paperbacks: 2005.

BIBLIOGRAPHY: www.amazon.com; www.catherine atkins.com; www.cathyatkins.smartwriters.com

JEANNE MARIE RYAN

ATWATER-RHODES, Amelia
Author, b. 16 April 1984, n.p.

On her fourteenth birthday A. learned that *In the Forests of the Night* was accepted for publication. A. writes about vampires, witches, and shapeshifters and has been compared to Anne Rice, S. E. HINTON and Christopher PIKE. A. lives in Concord, MA and attends the University of Massachusetts at Amherst. Amelia, known as Amy, enjoys reading, writing, singing, acting, fencing, playing the piano, and Wicca. She is also interested in helping the environment and endangered animals.

A. has been creating stories from an early age. At three, she was making up elaborate stories about a stuffed animal named Meow Stripe, who ruled the upside-down world of Catland. At age nine, she discovered Christopher Pike's *The Last Vampire,* which served as an inspiration for her own efforts. A. began writing in earnest after completing fifth grade. When she was twelve, she found a book on Wicca during a family trip to Salem. She embraced the book's teachings and with several middle-school friends began practicing Wiccan rites and spell-casting rituals.

Her novels have been described as dark, twisting, suspenseful, and compelling. Elaborate plotlines, complex character lineages, and creative solutions that advance the story are trademarks of A.'s writing. Her books are popular with teen readers because, as she says, "As a teen I bring a different perspective to writing. I can offer immediate emotions, experiences and insight that adult writers often have to reach back and find in order to write about them."

AWARDS: Quick Picks for Reluctant Young Readers citation, ALA, 2001 for *Demon in My View;* "20 Teens Who Will Change the World," *Teen People Magazine*; *Shattered Mirror:* ALA Quick Picks for Reluctant Young Adult Readers, 2002, ALA Popular Paperbacks, 2005; *Midnight Predator:* ALA Quick Picks for Reluctant Young Adult Readers, 2003; *Hawksong:* SLJ Best Books for Children, 2003.

FURTHER WORKS: *Demon In My View,* Delacorte, 2000; *Hawksong,* Delacorte, 2003; *In the Forests of the Night,* Laurel Leaf, 2000; *Midnight Predator,* Delacorte, 2002; *Shattered Mirror,* Delacorte, 2001; The Kiesha'ra vols. 1–3, *Hawksong,* 2003; *Snakecharm,* 2004, *Falcondance,* 2005.

BIBLIOGRAPHY: Alessio, Amy. "Teen Author Creates a New World: An Interview with Amelia Atwater-Rhodes," *Public Libraries,* v. 40, no. 3, May/June 2001; *Authors and Artists for Young People,* Gale Group, 2001; *Contemporary Authors Online,* Gale 2002; http://teenreads.com; http://www.kidzworld .com

MOLLY S. KINNEY, PH.D.

ATWOOD, Margaret
Author, b. 18 November 1939, Ottawa, Ontario, Canada

Survival, nature, alienation: these are the themes of CANADIAN author A., and, she would argue, of Canadian literature altogether. A. is best known for her novels, though she had released six volumes of poetry before her first novel was published.

A. spent significant periods of her childhood in the northern forests of Canada, where her father worked as an entomologist for the Canadian government. The family lived rudimentarily, often without running water or electricity. The natural world was a strong influence; the woods "were both playground and laboratory," and she learned from her father about the destructive organisms invisible to the naked eye that lurked in the trees and soil. Her fiction and POETRY

often pit human beings against nature, and the natural landscapes in her work are richly symbolic. Her mother was trained as a teacher and home economist, and taught the children at home. She had little interest in traditional homemaking skills; instead their house was filled "with books and people reading," notably MYTHOLOGY and the unabridged Grimms' FAIRY TALES. The moralistic violence of these tales and the survivalist nature of the Canadian wilderness permeate A.'s poetry and early fiction.

A. was an early reader and wrote poetry as a child. She decided at age sixteen to become a writer, and in high school wrote poetry largely influenced by Edgar Allan Poe. She enrolled as an English honors student at University of Toronto's Victoria College and published her first poem at age nineteen. Upon graduation in 1961 she published her first volume of poetry, *Double Persephone,* which won the E. J. Pratt Medal. A year later she received a Master of Arts degree from Radcliffe College where she studied Victorian literature. She enrolled in Harvard for a year, and it was here that A. began "thinking seriously about Canada as having a shape and culture of its own." She left school to work odd jobs, during which she wrote book reviews and poetry. She returned to Harvard from 1965 to 1967 and published four more volumes of poetry.

Despite her early and immediate success with poetry, A. is best known for her novels. Her early fiction deals with strong, well-educated, self-conscious women seeking the source of their suffering. In *Cat's Eye* (1988) middle-aged artist Elaine Risely recalls the first subtle, then not so subtle, torture by her childhood "friends" as she returns to the city of her upbringing for a retrospective of her work. *Lady Oracle* (1976) tells of Joan Foster, a former fat child often belittled by her mother. Joan finds success as a clandestine writer of cheap Gothic romances. However, it is *The Handmaid's Tale* (1985) that made A. a popular success. Unlike her early work set in contemporary Canada, *Handmaid* takes place in a dystopian future America, in which religious fundamentalists have taken over the county and reduced women to property as breeders (handmaids) and servants. A.'s recent works include *The Blind Assassin* (2000), a book within a book within a book; *Alias Grace* (1996), historical fiction speculating on the motives of an infamous murderess, and *Oryx and Crake* (2003), a frightening futuristic novel about the last human left in a society of bioengineered life forms.

Regardless of her reputation as a FEMINIST, A. insists she is a humanist, and that the suffering of her characters is not exclusive to gender.

AWARDS: 1961 E. J. Pratt Medal, *Double Persephone;* Governor General's Award: 1966, for *The Circle Game* and 1986 for *The Handmaid's Tale;* 1977 Canadian Booksellers' Association Award, *Dancing Girls and Other Stories;* Molson Award, 1981; 1983 Book of the Year Award, *Bluebeard's Egg and Other Stories;* 1987 Arthur C. Clarke Award for Best Science Fiction, *The Handmaid's Tale;* Humanist of the Year award, 1987; *Cat's Eye:* Coles Book of the Year Award, Canadian Booksellers' Association Author of the Year Award, and Torgi Talking Book Award, all 1989; Order of Ontario, 1990; *Wilderness Tips and Other Stories:* Book of the Year Award, Periodical Marketers of Canada, both 1992; Commemorative Medal, 125th Anniversary of Canadian Confederation; *The Robber Bride:* Trillium Award, Canadian Authors' Association Novel of the Year Award, Commonwealth Writers' Prize for Canadian and Caribbean Region; 1994 Government of France's Chevalier dans l'Ordre des Arts et des Lettres, *The Robber Bride;* 1995 Trillium Award, *Morning in the Burned House;* Norwegian Order of Literary Merit, 1996; 1996 Giller Prize, *Alias Grace; The Blind Assassin:* 2000 Booker Prize, 2001 Dashiell Hammett Award; and many others.

FURTHER WORKS: *The Circle Game,* 1964; *Kaleidoscopes Baroque: A Poem,* 1965; *Talismans for Children,* 1965; *Speeches for Doctor Frankenstein,* 1966; *Expeditions,* 1966; *The Animals in That Country,* 1968; *What Was in the Garden,* 1969; *The Edible Woman,* 1969; *The Journals of Susanna Moodie,* 1970; *Procedures for Underground,* 1970; *Power Politics,* 1971; *Surfacing,* 1972; *You Are Happy,* 1974; *Selected Poems, 1965–1975,* 1976; *Marsh Hawk,* 1977; *Dancing Girls and Other Stories,* 1977; *Two-headed Poems,* 1978; *Life before Man,* 1979; *Bodily Harm,* 1981; *Notes toward a Poem That Can Never Be Written,* 1981; *True Stories,* 1981; *Encounters with the Element Man,* 1982; *Snake Poems,* 1983; *Unearthing Suite,* 1983; *Murder in the Dark: Short Fictions and Prose Poems,* 1983; *Bluebeard's Egg and Other Stories,* 1983; *Interlunar,* 1984; *Selected Poems II: Poems Selected and New, 1976–1986,* 1986; *Wilderness Tips and Other Stories,* 1991; *Good Bones,* 1992; *The Robber Bride,* 1993; *Morning in the Burned House,* 1995; *A Quiet Game: And Other Early Works,* 1997; *Eating Fire: Story Selected Poetry, 1965–1995,* 1998; *Writing with Intent: Essays, Reviews, Personal Prose: 1983–2005,* 2005.

BIBLIOGRAPHY: "Margaret Atwood." *Authors and Artists for Young Adults,* 2003. Reproduced in *Biography Resource Center,* 2003. http://0www.galenet.com .kimbel.coastal.edu:80/servlet/BioRC; "Margaret Atwood." *Newsmakers,* Issue 2, 2001. Reproduced in *Biography Resource Center,* 2003. http://0-www .galenet.com.kimbel.coastal.edu:80/servlet/BioRC; "Margaret Atwood." *Contemporary Authors Online,* 2003. Reproduced in *Biography Resource Center,* 2003. http://0www.galenet.com.kimbel.coastal.edu :80/servlet/BioRC; Simon, Linda. "Words and Their Glories—Margaret Atwood's journey from a childhood in the Canadian forests to the challenge of a prolific author." *World and I* 8.1 (2003): 236. *Info Trac OneFile.* InfoTrac.13 May 2003 <http://infotrac .galegroup.com/itweb/coastcui_kimbel>; Lacayo, Richard. "Science Project: In a grim tale of the future, Atwood gets the gene blues." *Time International.* 28 April 2003: 55. *InfoTrac OneFile.* Info-Trac.13 May 2003 <http://infotrac.galegroup.com/ itweb/coastalcui_kimbel; Hubbard, Kim. "Reflected in Margaret Atwood's Cat's Eye, girlhood home as a time of cruelty and terror." *People Weekly.* 6 March 1989: 205–206. Infotrac OneFile. http://infotrac.gale group.com/itweb/coastalcui_kimbel

CATHY GOODWIN

AUDIO BOOKS: ALTERNATIVE FORMATS TO THE PRINTED WORD

A. offer an alternative to conventional reading. Available currently in both abridged and unabridged formats, as well as being available both as tapes and compact discs, they offer the ability to both absorb works of literature and complete other tasks simultaneously. Also useful for family trips or shared listening experiences, they offer a chance for everyone to listen to a story together. Although not quite as intimate as a family read-aloud, they do offer a chance for a small group to listen to a tale simultaneously and then discuss it.

Abridged audio books excerpt parts of the complete work, much as an abridged book does. Unabridged audio books offer the work in its totality, with a narrator who reads the book in its entirety. However, the narrator may influence one's perception of the book by his or her interpretation of the material, not unlike the way an actor portrays a character from a book in a film or television show and imprints their interpretation over your perceptions of the character forever after. Sometimes authors narrate their own works, which lends to a different type of experience and gives the listening experience a much more personal flavor, almost as if the author is sharing their work directly. Noted actors are also becoming more prevalent as narrators, among them Jim Dale, who has given voice to the HARRY POTTER series. Audiobook listeners often have favorite narrators whose work they seek out for the pleasure of hearing them at work.

A. also may be helpful to those who have learning disabilities, in that they offer readers a chance to read and listen simultaneously. They are also useful in that by listening, it is possible for hearers to cultivate their skill at paying attention and processing spoken information. Another advantage of listening to audiobooks is that it will enhance the listener's ability to pronounce difficult words correctly, although it may then provide them with a spelling challenge.

A newer alternative to the printed word is an electronic book (E-book)—although technically it really does require readers to read the written word. However, it is also loaded with technical assists that make it a cross between a book and a personal computer. Most electronic book readers offer the option of highlighting a word and instantaneously looking up its definition. It is also possible to bookmark electronically where a reader has left off in the text, as well as having various other bells and whistles, including a built-in light to make it easy to read in darker environments. Perhaps the greatest advantage that electronic books and E-book readers offer is the ability to fit a great deal of text in a small device that is approximately the size of a thick PAPERBACK. The practical advantages cannot be overlooked, despite current technological difficulties, and the relative scarcity of YA selections.

Alternative formats to the printed word will continue to emerge as technology advances. Each can be judged on its own merits, and will no doubt offer both advantages and disadvantages.

JEANNE MARIE RYAN

AUEL, Jean
Author, b. 18 February 1936, Chicago, Illinois

A. (pronounced "owl") has created her own literary niche—the pre-historical novel—bringing Paleolithic archaeology and anthropology to life. Born Jean Marie Untinen in Chicago, daughter of a Finnish-descended housepainter, A. married her high-school sweetheart, Ray Auel, in 1954, when she was eighteen. They had five children before she was twenty-five, after which A. worked at a Portland electronics plant at jobs varying from circuit-board designer to technical writer. She earned her MBA from the University of Portland at age forty.

A. had written POETRY and stories but was inspired to write a short story about a young woman becoming aware that she is surrounded by people with a different way of thinking. A. found her starting point in *Shanidar: The Humanity of Neanderthal Man* by Ralph Solecki (1971). At Shanidar in Iraq, Solecki had excavated a fossil Neanderthal, physically deformed from birth. His survival into middle age proved that Neanderthal people cared for each other.

A. made him into Creb the magician (or shaman) of the Clan, a group of Neanderthals who adopt Ayla, a Cro-Magnon child orphaned in an earthquake near the Black Sea. A. found her short-story scenario growing into a novel of nearly half a million words. Restructured into a planned six-book saga set some 30,000 years ago, and signed from a treatment by Crown Publishers for a then-almost unprecedented advance, this became the foundation for her Earth's Children SERIES. Begun with only the hope of success, *The Clan of the Cave Bear* (1980) rapidly became a bestseller.

It is an Ugly Duckling tale of golden-haired Ayla, who grows up surrounded by kindly people who see her as deformed: tall with a high forehead. Ayla is intelligent and swiftly learns the use of plants for healing, but her openess to new ways of thinking, exemplified by her use of a sling for hunting, brings conflict with the rest of the Clan. Cast out, Ayla lives alone in *The Valley of Horses* (1982) with her domesticated wolf and horse, until she saves the life of a wandering hunter, mauled by a cave-lion. He is Jondalar, one of the Other People (Cro-Magnon), and when he teaches her his language, Ayla realizes her origins. Their passionate love affair dominates the subsequent novels.

In *The Mammoth Hunters* (1985), Ayla and Jondalar meet another Cro-Magnon tribe, the Mamutoi, and Ayla learns to interact with larger groups of people. Ayla agrees to travel with Jondalar to his home to begin a new cave. In *The Plains of Passage* (1990), the pair ride horses from the Ukraine to southwest France. Ayla again saves Jondalar and demonstrates her leadership and diplomacy among the groups they encounter. After a glacier-crossing worthy of Indiana Jones, the pair reach the Ninth Cave of the Zelandonii (actually Laugerie Haute in the Dordogne).

There was a thirteen-year hiatus before *The Shelter of Stones* (2003) appeared, during which A. revised the ending of the series. One result was that very little seems to happen in *The Shelter of Stones,* even though Ayla marries and gives birth to a daughter. There are moments of excitement, but much of the narrative concerns ceremonies and Ayla's quest for acceptance by her new in-laws. This novel draws together strands before the surge of action in the final novel.

A member of Mensa, A. regards Ayla's intelligence as the key to her personality. A. also notes her childhood enthusiasm for active heroines, as in the Scandinavian folktale "East of the Sun and West of the Moon," in which a young girl rescues an imprisoned prince. She freely admits to compressing time to give Ayla credit for many of the achievements of the Pleistocene period. Thus Ayla domesticates the wolf and horse, uses flint to create fire, invents a calendar, and even deduces how babies are conceived.

A.'s fascination with the daily detail of prehistoric existence is conveyed to her readers, who learn of the early use of sleeping bags, haversacks, tents, and waterproof baskets, along with the excitement of mammoth hunts. Even Jondalar's six-foot-six-inch physique is based on actual Cro-Magnon remains.

A key feature of the Earth's Children series is the attitude of the various Cro-Magnon groups to the Neanderthals, depicted by A. as 'an ancient dying race.' Ayla is aware of the Neanderthals' talents, language, and accumulated wisdom, but others see them as 'flatheads,' little better than animals. The endless debates on this issue in the series seem to be more about the rights of Native Americans than life in the Paleolithic world. Scientists hold conflicting theories, for example, on whether Cro-Magnon and Neanderthal could interbreed, but a novelist must be specific, so Ayla gives birth to Durc, after being raped by Broud, the resentful son of the Clan's chief. Although archaeologists may quibble at some of A.'s interpretations, they value her ability to bring research findings into public awareness—known jocularly as the Paleolithic Park effect. Her strongest critics are those who cling to the outdated idea of cave-dwellers as primitive and intelligent.

A's wide-ranging research includes practical experience of arctic survival, plant identification, and cooking wild food. With sales of thirty-five million copies, translations into twenty-eight languages, and calendars and posters, the Earth's Children series is sometimes criticized for its popular status, but as A. points out, if she had planned to write a bestseller, she would never have chosen a cavewoman as her main character.

A. has demonstrated that a way of life pruned to the essentials can be spiritually and intellectually fulfilling. The author and her husband live in Portland near many of their fifteen grandchildren.

AWARDS: 1981 Friends of Literature award, *The Clan of the Cave Bear;* 1986 Silver Trowel award, Sacramento Archaeology Society; 1990, Waldo Award (Waldenbrooks), *The Plains of Passage;* 1990 Persie Award (W.I.N.), *The Plains of Passage.*

BIBLIOGRAPHY: Locker, Frances C. ed., *Contemporary Authors,* Vol 103, 1982: 21–22; Stine, Jean C. & Marowski, Daniel G. ed., *Contemporary Literary Criticism,* Vol 31, 1985: 22–24; Note: Articles on Jean Auel also appear in these reference volumes: *Authors and Artists for Young Adults,* Vol. 7; *Bestsellers,* 90:4; *Contemporary Authors,* New Revision Series, Vol 21; website: www.randomhouse.com/features/auel/; http://ecfans.com

                                    TREVOR AGNEW

AUSTRALIAN YOUNG ADULT LITERATURE

In a 1986 speech before the Third Pacific Rim Conference on Children's Literature entitled "Writing for Children in A. Today," author Victor Kelleher commented upon the unique challenges of being a "children's" writer in A. He discussed the difficulty of juggling notions of what Australian literature should look like (according to Australians and those outside Australia) and the reality of what the Australian nation has become, in terms of a more open, multicultural society. Though Kelleher used the term "children's literature," his statement encompasses YA literature as well. Kelleher is a British–born writer who makes A. his permanent home. He is also author of many award-winning works, including the 1983 Children's Book of the Year Award Winner, *Master of the Grove.*

From the 1980s to the present, there has been an extraordinary growth of unique works of young YA literature. This includes nonfiction informational literature, recognized by the CBC Eve Pownall Award for excellence in writing for children and TEENS. It is within the realm of fiction primarily, as well as the more selective area of AUTOBIOGRAPHICAL writing by the Australian Aboriginal people concerning their heritage, that we note the most interesting and varied A. writing achievements for young adults.

Saxby (1969, 1971, 1993), Niall (1984), Alderman (1987), Hazell (1989), McCallum (1996), and Scutter (1999) have noted interesting developments in A. writing for young people over time, as well as the uniqueness of the literary output. Saxby credits Ethel Turner (*Seven Little A.s,* 1894) and Louise Mack (*Teens: A Story of A. Schoolgirls,* 1897) with having addressed aspects of the teenage experience early on. Lees and Macintyre (1993) remind us that the teenage experience of the 19th and early 20th centuries included an awareness of the adult expectation that the young person would quickly assume adult responsibilities. Adolescence as a stage of life, however, was not yet fully acknowledged. Turner and Mack wrote narratives which assumed, by 21st century standards, the relative innocence of life experience. Such narratives did not attempt to address inner adolescent turmoil or the psychological and physiological angst that we now acknowledge to be part of the adolescent experience.

G. Stanley Hall's research recognized adolescence as a stage of life and influenced the thinking in countries outside America including Australia. Authors were inspired to create stories addressing unique adolescent needs using a more authentic voice and viewpoint of the adolescent. Niall points out that the character of J. D. Salinger's Holden Caulfield in *The Catcher in the Rye* (1951), whose voice communicated the persona of the alienated youth, stimulated debate among those concerned with the education of youth. Eventually, strident echoes of the voice of Holden Caulfield resonated in the literary works of Australian authors like Mavis Thorpe Clarke in *The Min-Min* (1966, CBC Winner 1967), Ivan Southall in *Bread and Honey* (1970, CBC Winner 1971) and *Josh* (1971), and in J. M. Couper's *The Thundering Good Today* (1971).

Stories were becoming more introspective, allowing the audience to penetrate the mind of the protagonists. Southall's story *Josh* is revealed from the point of view of Josh, the protagonist. This is also the case

in Southall's *Let the Balloon Go* (1968, CBC Commended 1969) in which John Summer, a disabled young man, attempts to establish his independence from an over-protective mother. In Simon French's *All We Know* (1986, CBC Winner 1987), twelve-year-old Arkie Gerhardt, soon to enter high school, must cope with the pressures and responsibilities of home, look after her young brother, juggle the "difficulties" of school, and develop her own interests in photography.

Author Libby Gleeson also explores inner workings of adolescent minds. Her 1987 work, *I Am Susannah* (CBC Honour 1988), is the story of a girl growing up in Sydney who must cope with a close friend's moving away and the loneliness that ensues. However, through loss and the subsequent bond she develops with a mysterious woman she meets in a graveyard, she becomes a stronger person, ultimately better equipped to deal with the challenges of growing up. Gleeson also writes of a male protagonist's coming of age. Mick Jamieson in *Dodger* (1990) is offered a role in a school play, that of the artful Dodger in "Oliver." He must cope with his fears and insecurities, believing that he may not be able to live up to the task. Gleeson realistically portrays the uncertainties that exist when a young person is caught in the throes of adolescent turmoil and an unstable home environment. Ultimately however, Mick makes decisions which at first appear overwhelming and scary. As his teacher Penny tells Mick: "Just don't decide on the basis of what the others think. You work out what you want." This sentiment is the hallmark of thinking in many contemporary YA literary works.

John Marsden is one of A.'s most popular authors of realistic and "speculative fiction" writing today for primarily a YA audience. His *Checkers* (1999) is a hard-hitting novel whose disclosures resonate with highly publicized corporate finance scandals. A young girl's confinement in a psychiatric hospital is masterfully related in the first person and shows the tragic effects of corporate scandal on the family of a corporate executive. Marsden skillfully leads us to the conclusion that the young daughter becomes stronger as a result of her trauma and will, in fact, most likely recover. This possible ending is strongly hinted at rather than positively assured, since the daughter is still in the psychiatric hospital at the close of the story. In *Tomorrow When the War Began* (1995) a group of teens fight back after their country has been invaded and their families held hostages in the fairgrounds. The resistance continues through subsequent novels that are spine-tingling suspenseful and extremely popular.

Popular author Nick Earls develops an authentic voice in the portrayal of his adolescent protagonists in *48 Shades of Brown* (1999, CBC Winner 2000). Sixteen-year-old Dan shares his story of awakening sexual awareness through a first person point of view and through the use of present tense. Dan's crush on his lesbian aunt's housemate, Naomi, raises blunt issues of adjustment not only to his own budding sexuality, but also to the dilemma of coping with his aunt's revelation of her sexual orientation.

Addressing sexuality has not been avoided by authors considered more "traditional" in their approaches. In 1977, Eleanor Spence ventures into this territory with *A Candle for Saint Antony* (CBC Highly Commended 1978), in which a deep friendship between two fifteen-year-old male students is misconstrued as a homosexual relationship. The same year Ivan Southall in *What About Tomorrow* explores the issue of a young man's coming to terms with his sexual urges through his relationship with three women, Rose, Sally, and Mary who challenge his growing sexual awareness.

The Australian continent has a unique geographical environment which has historically proven to be a challenge to the European Australian people. Australia's major cities and much of its European populace of approximately twenty million persons are situated primarily along the periphery of the continent.

Mavis Thorpe Clarke shares the intrigues of the gold rush in *Gully of Gold* (1958), the story of a 19th-century British family lured to Australia by the possibility of striking it rich. David Martin tells the story of the gold rush from the point of view of a fourteen-year-old Chinese protagonist, Ho, in *The Chinese Boy* (1973), while Frank Kellaway in *The Quest for Golden Dan* (1962, CBC Commended 1963) focuses upon the adventurous life of a young boy who, kidnapped in 1855, is disguised and made to work for a musician in Victoria, Australia.

The gold rush setting serves as a focus for Maureen Pople's *Pelican Creek* (1988), a story bearing supernatural overtones. Here, sixteen-year-old Sally Matthews discovers "a nugget of gold" bearing a mysterious connection to another girl, Ann Bird who lived in Pelican Creek during the 19th century. This nugget functions as the spark for unravelling the mystery of the girl and the meaning of her connection to Sally Matthews.

The threat of wildfires, an ever-present concern particularly in the states of South A. and Victoria, is dramatically explored in Ivan Southall's *Ash Road* (1965, CBC Winner 1966), which tells the story of the lives affected by a group of teenage students who accidentally set a devastating fire. The consequences of fire are also explored in Colin Thiele's *February Dragon* (1965, CBC Commended 1966), Mavis Thorpe Clarke's *Wildfire* (1973), and Roger Vaughn Carr's *Firestorm!* (1985; CBC shortlist 1986), a story about the Ash Wednesday fire that devastated sections of South Australia and Victoria in 1983.

Saxby attributes the strong activity in the area of FANTASY writing for young people to "complexities and uncertainties of life in the 1970s and 1980s." In the 1970s Patricia Wrightson opened the door to new possibilities with her stories involving traditional Aboriginal spiritual beliefs at work in modern times. She was particularly successful with the YA SERIES "The Book of Wirrun" comprising *The Ice Is Coming* (1977, CBC Winner 1978), *The Dark Bright Water* (1979), and *Behind the Wind* (1981, CBC Highly Commended 1982). These dramatic stories feature Aboriginal protagonists and highlight classic themes of good vs. evil, invigorated by Aboriginal creatures who penetrate the modern context.

For many years Wrightson was one of the best-known A. authors in the U.S. and one of the few whose works were widely available there. In approaching her subject matter as a European A., she exhibits the courage and determination of a highly creative literary artist. Not being of Aboriginal heritage, she is clearly working outside her own cultural heritage. But early on, in the Author's Note for *The Ice Is Coming,* she states her focus upon the creatures of Aboriginal belief: "I might have written a story about more familiar spirits, the elves and fairies and dragons and monsters of Europe. Then everyone would have known that the story was mine and the spirits borrowed from an older convention. But for that story I would have to invent a foreign setting, an Earthsea or a Middle Earth; and powerfully magical as those countries are I know one as powerful and as magic. It is the only one I know and the one I want to write about . . . And I claim a writer's leave to employ them in my own stories in my own way." Her *Balyet*

(1989, CBC Shortlist 1990), a YA story features a fourteen-year-old protagonist; it draws upon traditional beliefs as the basis for inventive narrative.

A. writers are fascinated with the theme of displacement, an issue which reflects universal adolescent concerns and the implications of "uneasy" settlement by European A.s. In Ruth Park's fantasy *Playing Beatie Bow* (1980, CBC Winner 1981), rebellious fourteen-year-old Abigail Kirk travels back to the 19th-century Sydney through the vehicle of a children's game. She is mysteriously drawn into the lives of the Bow family and must cope with the dangers of a familiar—yet not familiar—Sydney environment. Lee Harding's *Displaced Person* (1979, CBC Winner 1980) explores the gradual and frightening removal of Graeme Drury from the world he knows as Melbourne by manipulative, extra-terrestrial forces. This stark story with a disquieting ending poses the possibility that we may not be alone in the universe, and that our earthly presence may be subject to manipulation by outside forces.

SCIENCE FICTION and technological narratives are also well represented in Australian writing for young adults. In her first novel, published in 1986, Gillian RUBENSTEIN successfully blends these themes in *Space Demons* (1986, CBC Honour 1987), in which four young people become involved in a dangerous life-threatening computer game. *Skymaze* (1989, CBC Shortlist 1990 continues the adventures of Andrew Hayford, Ben Challis, Mario Ferrone and Elaine Taylor who first meet in *Space Demons,* and other works including *Terra-Farma* (2001). Most of Rubenstein's stories for young adults explore aspects of science fiction, supernatural and/or paranormal phenomena.

Caroline MacDonald explores the relationship of humanity to environment in a futuristic postnuclear holocaust setting in *The Lake at the End of the World* (1988, CBC Honour 1989). Sonya Hartnett writes works of breathtaking prose and striking originality. Her mystical *Forest: A Journey from the Wild* (2001, CBC Winner 2002) is a gripping story of the journey of three domestic cats in a forest inhabited by among other creatures, feral cats, the descendants of domestic creatures cast out from their owners' households. The story challenges the sensibilities—from the brutal treatment of three cats cruelly removed from the security of their home, to their frightening transportation in a box to the midst of a forest. In this story,

Hartnett removes any sense of hope the reader may have that the story will turn out well. The protagonist, Kian, expires at the end of the story. Cats as protagonists with abilities to communicate within a supernatural framework appear in stories by Joan Phipson (*The Cats,* 1976, CBC Highly Commended 1977), Gordon Aalborg's *Cat Tracks* (1981) and Gillian Rubinstein's *Under the Cat's Eye* (1997).

The European A. relationship with the A. Aboriginal people serves as a focus for publication within the YA market. The A. Aboriginal people have begun to publish in this area. One of the earliest works published by an A. Aboriginal author was *Moon and Rainbow: The Autobiography of an Aboriginal,* an account of the early life of Dick Roughsey, a member of the Lardil tribe of Mornington Island. Published in 1971, this book can be read and appreciated by a YA audience. Following the civil-rights demands of the Aboriginal populace during the 1970s and land rights claims from various tribes, there have been a growing number of publications written by A. Aboriginal authors who want to make an impact upon the perceptions of and concerns of their people. They feel, the story needs to be told from a personal point of view. Such narratives provide a different point of view from that seen in YA works by A. European writers like Nan Chauncy, author of *Tangara* (1960, CBC Winner 1961) and David Martin, author of *Hughie* (1971, CBC Commended 1972). Many of the works written by A. Aboriginal people focus upon the efforts of the people to gain acceptance within a white society, and the pain of coping with the legacy of difficulties encountered. There is also a strong focus in Aboriginal writing upon the need to maintain racial identity and the challenges of doing so within a society whose values are often alien to the concerns of Aboriginal people. Authors like Sally Morgan in *My Place: An Aborigine's Stubborn Quest for Her Truth, Heritage, and Origins* (1987) and Glenyse Ward in *Wandering Girl* (1987) focus upon this crucial aspect of Australian social history. *My Place* was published in the United States in 1989. Reviewing for the *New York Times* on February 19, 1989, Janette Turner Hospital wrote: "*My Place* is an historical document which should be (and doubtless will be) on every black studies and women's studies course in Australia and round the world. It is also a book for everyone; a book with the form and texture of a novel and the complexity and pace of a mystery not solved until the final pages.

It is wonderfully entertaining and a luminous prose poem." Magabala Books, the first-ever established Aboriginal Publishing house, and publisher of *Wandering Girl* contributes to the efforts of bringing YA literature to the Australian consciousness.

In summary, Australian YA authors continue to make striking contributions to YA literature. They show a great capacity to confront many coming-of-age issues of concern to young adults, as well as the desire to confront and come to terms with cultural issues emanating from their unique historical context. This is a literature that deserves to be better known and distributed throughout the English-speaking world in particular, and the world at large.

BIBLIOGRAPHY: Arnold, Josie and Tesha Piccinin. *A Practical Guide to Young A. Fiction,* 1985. Bradford, Clare, ed. *Writing the A. Child: Texts and Contexts in Fictions for Children,* 1996. See Robyn McCallum, "Other Selves: Subjectivity and the *Doppelgänger* in A. Adolescent Fiction," pp. 17–36. Hazell, Anne M. *Reflections of Reality?: Female Roles in A. Adolescent Fiction since World War II,* 1989. Lees, Stella and Pam Macintyre. *The Oxford Companion to A. Children's Literature,* 1993. See "Adolescence," pp. 10–12. Niall, Brenda. *A. Through the Looking-Glass: Children's Fiction, 1830–1980.* Ragsdale, Winifred, ed. *A Sea of Upturned Faces: Proceedings of the Third Pacific Rim Conference on Children's Literature,* 1989. See Victor Kelleher, "Writing for Children in A. Today," pp. 213–235. Saxby, Maurice and Gordon Winch, ed. *Give Them Wings: The Experience of Children's Literature,* 1987. See Belle Alderman, "Rites of Passage: Adolescent Literature," pp. 290–307. Saxby, H. M. *A History of A. Children's Literature, 1841–1941,* 1969. Saxby, H. M. *A History of A. Children's Literature, 1941–1970,* 1971. Saxby, Maurice. *The Proof of the Puddin': A. Children's Literature, 1970–1990,* 1993. Scutter, Heather. *Displaced Fictions: Contemporary A. Fiction for Teenagers and Young Adults,* 1999.

KAREN PATRICIA SMITH

AVI
Author, b. 23 December 1937, New York City

Named Avi Wortis at birth, this prolific writer was destined to be a storyteller. Dubbed "Avi" by his sister, the boy grew up in Brooklyn surrounded by family artisans of almost every creative sort. He was an avid reader, but as a student, A. faced a world of struggle. He was afflicted with dysgraphia, a learning disorder that jumbles letters on the page and makes written communication intensely difficult. However, A.'s passion for reading and his personal determination carried him through. An intuitive high-school teacher eventually enlisted private tutors to help lift him out of this disability and the despair that went with it.

Even in the midst of this turmoil, A. insists that he knew he could be a writer, even though some reports suggest that his family discouraged him. "I think you become a writer when you stop writing for yourself or your teacher and start thinking about readers," A. says on his website BIOGRAPHICAL profile. "I made up my mind to do that when a high school senior."

Higher education was A.'s next challenge to conquer, and conquer it he did. After graduating from the University of Wisconsin, A. studied library science at Columbia University, where he got his Master's degree in 1964. For years, he was a librarian at the New York Public Library as well as other facilities.

A. shared an early and accurate high-school prediction about his bibliographic future during his Newbery Medal acceptance speech at the American Library Association convention in Toronto, Canada, on June 22, 2003.

"When assembling our senior yearbook (my school was so small we only needed a year-pamphlet), classmates used Shakespeare to define me by placing right next to my graduation picture Prospero's words: '[I was a] poor man, [but] my library was Dukedom large enough.' Indeed, I worked in libraries some twenty-five years." A. became a respected playwright and taught popular courses on children's literature. He did not tackle literature for young adults until the 1980s and 1990s.

Inspired by fatherhood and children of his own, A. practiced telling impromptu stories at first. A PICTURE BOOK launched his lengthy and evolving career. He has mastered virtually every group within the expansive reach of literature for young people, including the realm of the YA.

Considering his rocky educational beginnings, it is perhaps no surprise that A. sees reading as the golden key to skillful writing. "The more you read, the better your writing can be," he says in his publisher's biography.

In an interview (1999) with Kids Reads, A. admits some parents seem to fear the intensely private relationship young readers experience with their favorite authors and books. What ideas stories inspire, he says, inner thoughts are completely out of parental reach. "They fear it because it's a process they can't control."

A. says "Bully for such a safe harbor. When asked how to advise young writers, A. reflects the same brave determination. A. advises prospective writers: "Listen, and watch the world around you. Don't be satisfied with answers others give you. Don't assume that because everyone believes a thing, that it is right *or* wrong. Reason things out for yourself. Work to get answers on your own. Understand why you believe things. Finally, write what you honestly feel, then learn from the criticism that will always come your way."

The Breakfast Serial, his newspaper serialization of dozens of stories by exceptional authors helped bring good reading material to reluctant readers subscribing to newspapers across the continent.

After A. had published fifty books and received two Newbery honor book awards, he received the Newbery Medal in 2003 for *Crispin: The Cross of Lead* in 2003. And according to his acceptance speech, the announcement made him cry. Tears of joy? Not exactly, he admits. They were more like tears of relief. "My world was telling me an extraordinary simple but powerful thing," he said in the speech. "I had been recognized as a good writer."

Had some crystal ball foretold this award fifty years earlier to teachers wondering about A.'s future, they might have shattered the defective orb. But the little boy would have known better. "I wanted to prove that I could write," he says reflectively on his website biography. He is loved by young readers around the world and honored by educators across the board. By all reasonable accounts he has proved that his early critics were wrong.

AWARDS: 1981 Christopher Award, *Encounter at Easton;* 1985 Scott O'Dell Award, *The Fighting Ground;* Horn Book Award: 1991 for *True Confessions of Charlotte Doyle,* and 1996 for *Poppy;* Newbery Honor Medal: 1991 for *The True Confessions of Charlotte Doyle,* and 1992 for *Nothing but the Truth;* 1992 Horn Book Award Honor, *Nothing but the Truth;* 2003 Newbery Medal, *Crispin: The Cross of Lead.*

SELECT FURTHER WORKS: *Emily Upham's Revenge,* 1979; *A Place Called Ugly,* 1983; *Sometimes I Think I Hear My Name,* 1983; *The Fighting Ground,* 1984; *Wolf Rider: A Tale of Terror,* 1988; *Nothing but the Truth,* 1991; *The Man Who Was Poe,* 1991; *The True Confessions of Charlotte Doyle,* 1991; *Windcatcher,* 1991; *Blue Heron,* 1992; *Who Was That Masked Man, Anyway?,* 1992; *Captain Grey,* 1993; *Encounter at Easton,* 1994; *Beyond the Western Sea 1 and 2,* 1996; *Poppy,* 1997; *Punch with Judy,* 1997; *Perloo the Bold,* 1998; *Poppy and Rye,* 1998; *Ereth's Birthday,* 2000; *Midnight Magic,* 1999; *Never-Mind: A Twin Novel* (with Rachel Vail), 2004; *The Book Without Words: A Fable of Medieval Magic,* 2005; *Poppy's Return,* 2005.

BIBLIOGRAPHY: The Essential Guide to Children's Books and Their Creators, 2002; Avi's website: http://www.avi-writer.com; interview with Avi for Kids Reads, 1996; interview with Avi for Writer's Digest 2001; educational Paperback Association bio; ALA 2003 Acceptance Speech.

KELLY MILNER HALLS

BACHRACH, Susan D.

Author, historian, b. 11 March 1948, Lawrence, Massachusetts

Noted for nonfiction on THE HOLOCAUST for older-elementary and junior-high YA readers, B.'s books are directly tied to her work as a special exhibits curator at the United States Holocaust Memorial Museum. The titles for young adults are related to exhibits there. B. has curated exhibits on the history of the Kovno ghetto, the liberation of the camps in 1945, and the Nazi Olympics in Berlin in 1936. Since 1994, she has received several awards in literature. A major characteristic of her nonfiction is its storytelling quality and the way she demands that the reader pay attention to the lives of individuals in the midst of historic turmoil. B.'s educational background is focused on modern European history. She holds a B.A. from Wellesley, and an M.A. and a Ph.D. from the University of Wisconsin.

AWARDS: *Tell Them We Remember: The Story of the Holocaust:* 1994 Best Nonfiction for Young Adults, 1996 International Reading Association's Young Adult Choices; *The Nazi Olympics: Berlin 1936:* 2001 Wisconsin Library Association's Outstanding Books for Children, ALA Best Books for Young Adults: 2001.

FURTHER WORKS: *The Nazi Olympics: Berlin 1936,* 2000; *Tell Them We Remember: The Story of the Holocaust,* 1994.

BIBLIOGRAPHY: United States Holocaust Memorial website online, 2003; interview via e-mail with author, 2003.

ANDREA L. WILLIAMS

BAGDASARIAN, Adam

Author, n.d., n.p.

B. spent ten years writing his first novel, the widely acclaimed *Forgotten Fire* (2000). This book chronicles in harrowing and vivid first-person detail the experiences of its fourteen-year-old narrator as he and his family are swept away in the violence and suffering of the Armenian genocide. B. was moved to write this book after hearing a tape made by his great uncle, who as a young man survived the genocide. B. has said that he hopes the honest portrayal of violence in the book will help counterbalance the more glamorous images of violence that pervade most young people's worlds. *Forgotten Fire* was a short-list honoree for both the National Book Award and the *Los Angeles Times* Book Prize. It was also named a Top Ten Best Book for Young Adults for 2000 by the Young Adult Library Services Association (YALSA). His second book, *First French Kiss and Other Traumas* (2000), is a more lighthearted and tender take on adolescence, told through a series of vignettes.

AWARDS: *Forgotten Fire:* ALA Popular Paperbacks, 2003; ALA Quick Picks for Reluctant Young Adult Readers, 2001.

CAROL L. TILLEY

BAGLEY, Desmond

Author, b. 29 October 1923, Kendal, England; d. 12 April 1983, Southampton, England

B., author of action novels, began work at age fourteen as a printer's devil and worked at a number of jobs before transferring to an aircraft factory at the start of World War II. After the war B. traveled to South Africa.

B. started freelance writing in South Africa in the 1950s and subsequently turned to writing novels, debuting with the thriller *The Golden Keel* (1963).

B.'s novels are noted for their vivid detail of place and expert technological knowledge. *Running Blind* (1970) takes place in Iceland; B. describes the Icelandic landscape in detail, providing vivid narrative about spouting geysers, hot springs, and bubbling pools, all amidst an exciting spy thriller story.

The Freedom Trap (1971) was made into the movie *The Macintosh Man* (1973) and is one of B.'s most exciting and popular novels.

B.'s sense of moral outrage is depicted through his mild-mannered heroes. *The Enemy* (1978) follows the story of government agencies pressuring geneticists to experiment in genetic mutation without proper controls. The protagonist, Jaggard, an Intelligence Officer, caught up in espionage, finds himself morally outraged by his superiors' inhumane conspiracy and begins to unearth their plot.

B.'s last book, *Juggernaut* (1985), published posthumously, was completed by his wife, Joan Margaret Brown.

At the time of his death, B. was one of the most highly paid thriller writers in the world, with twenty million copies of his sixteen novels in print in twenty-three languages.

FURTHER WORKS: *High Citadel.* 1964; *Wyatt's Hurricane.* 1966; *Landslide,* 1967; *The Vivero Letter,* 1968; *The Spoilers,* 1970; *The Tightrope Men,* 1973; *The Snow Tiger,* 1974; *Flyaway,* 1978; *Bahama Crisis,* 1980; *Windfall,* 1982; *Night of Error.* 1986.

BIBLIOGRAPHY: *Contemporary Authors,* vol. 19–20, vol. 29, vol. 109; *Dictionary of Literary Biography,* vol. 87.

SUSAN E. MORTON

BALDWIN, James Arthur

Author, playwright, b. 2 August 1924, New York City; d. 1 December 1987, St. Paul-de-Vence, France

During the civil-rights movement of the 1950s and 60s, B. was a vital literary voice. In the powerful essay collections *Nobody Knows My Name* (1961) and *The Fire Next Time* (1963), he expressed AFRICAN AMERICAN reaction to racial discrimination. The publication of *The Fire Next Time* coincided with the 1963 March on Washington and secured his reputation as a prophet and fervent social critic. His optimism about a reconciliation in American race relations led to a rift with the more militant Black writers and black nationalists like Eldridge CLEAVER.

B. was the eldest of nine children, and his stepfather was a minister. At the age of fourteen, B. was preaching at the Fireside Pentecostal Church in Harlem. At Frederick Douglass Junior High School he edited the school newspaper and belonged to the literary club. After his high-school graduation in 1942 he took a series of odd jobs in New Jersey. After Harlem riots and the death of his stepfather occurred on the same day in the summer of 1943, he settled in Greenwich Village and decided to focus on his writing. B. met Richard Wright who became his mentor and recommended him for the Eugene Saxon Fellowship that he received in 1945. Although publishers continued to reject B.'s early attempts at a novel, he won a Rosenwald Fellowship in 1948 for his book reviews and essays in *The New Leader, The Nation, Commentary,* and *Partisan Review.* He bought a one-way ticket to Paris with his prize money and left the United States at the age of twenty-four for a stay in Europe that lasted nearly ten years. In Paris he published his first novel *Go Tell It on the Mountain* (1953), a partially AUTOBIOGRAPHICAL account revealing the psychological problems of members of an African American family. His essay collection *Notes of a Native Son* (1955) brought him recognition as a critic of social injustice. Critics note that the cadences of Black churches resonate in his writings. His friends in Paris included Jean-Paul Sartre and fellow American expatriates at that time Saul Bellow, Truman Capote, and Beauford Delaney.

During the height of the civil-rights movement B. began spending half of each year in New York City where he lectured and taught. He became involved in the Southern school desegregation struggle. However, after the assassination of his friends Medgar Evers, the Reverend Dr. Martin Luther King Jr., and Malcolm X, he spent more time in France and settled there again in 1974 and worked on a book about the disillusionment of the times, *If Beale Street Could Talk* (1974). Even if B. expressed much of the anger of the recent struggles, he always remained an advocate for brotherhood and universal love. His novels *Giovanni's Room* (1956) and *Another Country* (1962) deal with homosexuality. His treatment of gay themes met with harsh criticism from the black community, especially from Eldridge Cleaver of the Black Panthers. As an openly gay man, B. condemned discrimination against lesbians and gays. He also wrote several plays and the novel *Harlem Quartet* (1987) which were set in jazz clubs of the 1950s. During the last ten years of his life B. turned to teaching as another way of connecting to the young; he became Five College Professor in Afro-American Studies at the University of Massachusetts in Amherst. By the time he died in 1987, he had become one of the most important and eloquent advocates for equality and a spokesman for his generation of black writers.

AWARDS: The French American Friendship Prize for *Harlem Quartet,* 1987.

FURTHER WORKS: *Four Great Americans: Washington, Franklin, Webster, Lincoln: A Book for Young Americans,* 2000; *Collected Essays,* 1998 (ed. Toni Morrison).

BIBLIOGRAPHY: Africana: Gateway to the Black World, encarta africana http://www.africana.com/research/encarta/tt_099.asp; American Masters James Baldwin, PBS, http://www.pbs.org/wnet/americanmasters/database/baldwin_j.html; Campbell, James, *Talking at the Gates: A Life of James Baldwin,* 1991; Leeming, David, *James Baldwin: A Biography,* 1995; *Something About the Author,* Vol. 9, 1976, p. 15; *Something About the Author,* Vol. 54, 1989, p. 4; Troupe, Quincy, ed., *James Baldwin: The Legacy,* 1989.

CHRISTINE MARIA WELTER

BALLARD, James Graham

Author, b. 8 November 1930, Shanghai, China

B. is well known, particularly in Europe, for his novels and SCIENCE FICTION short stories. His most notable works include *Empire of the Sun* (1984) and *Crash* (1973), both of which were adapted as films.

Born in Shanghai and forced to endure a Japanese internment camp after the World War II invasion, B. began writing science fiction in the 1950s. He avoided traditional spaceship and alien themes and preferred to focus on, as Lanz states, "the convoluted psyche." Symbols that reverberate throughout B.'s fiction include derelict cars, empty swimming pools, and abandoned buildings. His signature touches are heavily symbolic themes and a psychological focus.

B's early novels, such as *The Drowned World* (1962) and *The Crystal World* (1966), depict major catastrophes in which primary characters achieve psychological fulfillment despite material difficulties. His SHORT STORY collections include *The Four-Dimensional Nightmare* (1963) and *The Atrocity Exhibition* (1970), which collect related short stories of violent, sexually charged DEATH. These stories led to *Crash,* which focuses on the eroticism of automobiles and horrific crashes. Other important novels include *Concrete Island* (1974) and *High-Rise* (1975).

After his science fiction career was established, B. wrote the pseudo-AUTOBIOGRAPHICAL *Empire of the Sun,* which maintains a science fiction tone through a surreal world of abandoned mansions and internment camps. In 1987, Steven Spielberg directed the film adaptation. B.'s sequel, *The Kindness of Women,* followed in 1991. *A User's Guide to the Millennium* (1996) collects essays and reviews from throughout B.'s career.

AWARDS: *Empire of the Sun:* 1984 *Guardian* Fiction prize, 1985.

FURTHER WORKS: *The Wind from Nowhere,* 1962; *The Unlimited Dream Company,* 1979; *The Voices of Time and Other Stories,* 1962.

BIBLIOGRAPHY: *Contemporary Authors New Revision Series,* vol. 65; *Contemporary Literary Criticism,* vol. 36; Pringle, David, *Earth Is the Alien Planet,* 1979.

MYRON A. MYKYTA

BANKS, Lynne Reid

Author, b. 31 July 1929, London, England

A teenager during World War II, B. was sent from London to Saskatchewan, Canada, to escape the bombing raids on England. When England was deemed safe, B. returned to her home, attended three drama schools, and eventually became a 1949 graduate of the Royal Academy of Dramatic Arts in London. Although being an actress was B.'s first choice of career, ultimately she became a television journalist and then shifted to scriptwriting. She moved to a kibbutz in Israel where she became successful in teaching English rather than farming; this move also led to her marriage to a sculptor. The couple produced three boys—Adiel, Gillon, and Omri. B. started to write children's books upon her return to Britain. She travels frequently to places such as Africa, AUSTRA-LIA, and India.

B. is best known for her "Indian in the Cupboard Series," that includes *The Indian in the Cupboard* (1980), *The Return of the Indian* (1986), *The Secret of the Indian* (1989), *The Mystery of the Cupboard* (1993), and *The Key to the Indian* (1999). *The Return of the Indian* was a Junior Literary Guild Selection. B. also writes books geared toward YA readers. Among the YA books are the final two books in the Indian in the Cupboard series—the problems Omri and his companions must deal with grow more complex in *The Mystery of the Cupboard* and *The Key to the Indian*. "The Indian in the Cupboard" books begin when Omri accidentally brings his plastic Indian to life with the help of an unexpectedly magical cupboard. The adventures continue through five books and have also been featured in a motion picture.

B.'s BIOGRAPHICAL portrait of the Brontë family, *Dark Quartet: The Story of the Brontës,* was named a Best Book for Young Adults by the American Library Association in 1977. In 1978, B. published a sequel: *Path to the Silent Country: Charlotte Brontë's Years of Fame.* B. returned to fiction with the publication of *Melusine: A Mystery* (1989) in which Roger encounters Mesuline at a chateau in France on a vacation that turns out to be much more than his family expected.

B.'s other books for older readers include *Letters to My Israeli Sons: The Story of Jewish Survival* (1980), a chronicle of Jewish history. Contemporary Jewish history plays a part in *One More River* and its sequel, *Broken Bridge* (1994). B. reworked *One More River,* originally published in 1973, for new release in 1993. In the novel, Lesley is forced by her father to relocate from Canada to Israel, and if that were not enough, he decides that the family will live on a kibbutz on the River Jordan. Much of the story takes place during the 1967 Six-Day War, as Lesley grapples with her new life and new relationships. The book includes a map and a glossary of Hebrew and Yiddish words that are used throughout the book. *Broken Bridge* explores the decisions Lesley's daughter faces when her cousin is murdered, and she is safeguarded, by the terrorists who took his life. *Moses in Egypt* (1998) is a retelling of the story of Moses, done in conjunction with the movie, *The Prince of Egypt.*

B. is an author whose works span fiction and nonfiction. She also has written for adult audiences, as well as children and young adults. She is quite prolific and continues to publish on a regular basis.

AWARDS: New York Times Notable Book: 1981 *Indian in the Cupboard* and 1986 *Return of the Indian.*

FURTHER WORKS: *The L-Shaped Room,* 1960; *The Backward Shadow,* 1970; *Two Is Lonely: A Sequel to the L-Shaped Room and the Backward Shadow,* 1974; *Sarah and After: Five Women Who Founded a Nation,* 1977; *My Darling Villain,* 1977; *Defy the Wilderness,* 1981; *Torn Country: An Oral History of the Israeli War Of Independence,* 1982; *The Writing on the Wall,* 1982, (also published as *Cat and Alex and the Magic Flying Carpet, Maura's Angel,* 1986; *The Warning Bell,* 1987; *Fair Exchange,* 1998; *Angela and Diabola,* 1997; *The Dungeon,* 2002; *Tiger, Tiger,* 2005.

BIBLIOGRAPHY: Sixth Book of Junior Authors, 1989; www.lynnereidbanks.com; http://falcon.jum.edu/~ramseyil/banks.htm; www.edupaperback.org/show auth.cfm?authid=47

JEANNE MARIE RYAN

BANKS, Russell
Author, b. 28 March 1940, Newton, Massachusetts

B. is the author of a novel that was chosen for the 1996 Best Books for Young Adults list, *Rule of the Bone* (1995). He is also the author of a number of essays, small-press volumes of verse, and adult novels. His working-class roots and his parents' divorce when he was twelve years old are key formative elements of his fiction, reflecting the turmoil and discomfort of his childhood years.

The son of a plumber and a bookkeeper, B. grew up in the midst of difficult economic conditions in rural New England. Attending Colgate University on a scholarship, he dropped out and set off for Cuba to join the revolution. Instead, stopping in Islamorada Key, he began to write stories while holding odd jobs. Eventually, he graduated Phi Beta Kappa from the University of North Carolina at Chapel Hill in 1967. Having co-founded the literary magazine, *Lillabulero Press, Inc.* at Chapel Hill, he later continued it as an editor while teaching at Emerson College, Boston and the University of New Hampshire, Durham. He received a Woodrow Wilson Fellowship in 1968, a Guggenheim Fellowship in 1976, and NEA Fellowships in 1977 and 1983.

His novel, *The Book of Jamaica* (1980), won the American Book Award of the Before Columbus Foundation, in 1982. In 1986, he was awarded the

American Academy and Institute of Arts and Letters Award and the John Dos Passos Award. His novels, *The Sweet Hereafter* (1991) and *Affliction* (1989), were produced as major Hollywood movies in 1997 and 1998.

AWARDS: St. Lawrence Award for Fiction from St. Lawrence University and Fiction International, 1975; Fels Award, O'Henry Memorial Award, and other short story awards.

FURTHER WORKS: *Collected Short Stories—Searching for Survivors,* 1975; *Trailerpark,* 1981; *The Relation of My Imprisonment,* 1983; *Continental Drift,* 1985; *Success Stories,* 1986. *Cloudsplitter,* 1997; *The Angel on the Roof: The Stories of Russell Banks,* 2001.

BIBLIOGRAPHY: *Literature Resource Center,* online, 2003; *Wilson Biographies,* online.

CATHERINE GIVEN

BARRETT, Tracy
Author, educator, b. 1 March 1955, Cleveland, Ohio

B. grew up in New York and completed a bachelor's degree with honors in classics–archaeology at Brown University in 1976 and received an M.A. (1979) and a Ph.D. (1987) in medieval Italian literature from the University of California, Berkeley.

Her academic research launched her on the path of serious writing. Her early nonfiction works for young readers (*Nat Turner and the Slave Revolt* in 1993; *Harper's Ferry,* 1994; *Growing up in Colonial America,* 1995) illustrate her capacity for writing enlightening and enlivened historical accounts. Describing *Growing up in Colonial America,* Susan D. Lempke, for *Booklist,* says, "Barrett sprinkles her text with many interesting details," and notes that the book "makes a good choice for reports or pleasure reading" (1995, p. 700).

Later works, *The Ancient Greek World* (2004) and *Anna of Byzantium* (1999) are examples of further (and deeper) coalescence of B.'s academic interest (the ancient world) and her ability to write intriguing works of nonfiction and fiction for YOUNG ADULTS. "I learned about Princess Anna Comnena while doing research on medieval women writers," B. notes on her homepage (2004). Anna Comnena (1083–1153), the daughter of Alexium I, successor to the Byzantine throne and, later, historian of her era, is the eponymous main character in *Anna of Byzantium.* Through her eyes readers see the Byzantine Empire and the

events surrounding the usurpation, as Anna sees it, of the throne by her younger brother. For its historical details, emotional intrigue, and, as Suzanne Manczuk notes in *Book Report* the fact that it is "beautifully written," has garnered the novel scores of accolades.

Commenting on *Anna of Byzantium,* a writer for the *Bulletin of the Center for Children's Books* notes: "[This is] a gripping saga of alliances, intrigues, deceits, and treacheries worthy of a place among the tragic myths" (1999, p. 377). The American Library Association placed it on the Best Books for Young Adults list (2000). *Booklist* named the work Editor's Choice and placed it on the Top Ten Historical Fiction List.

From the realm of history (actual and fictionalized), B. moved into FANTASY with *Cold in Summer* (2003), in which a young girl, recently moved with her family to a new town, befriends another girl who turns out to be a ghost. *Cold in Summer* became another award-winning book for Barrett.

B. has also written books in the "Celebrate the States" SERIES: Kentucky in 1998, Virginia in 1997, and Tennessee in 1995. B.'s next work was a sequel to *Cold in Summer* called *On Etruscan Time* (2005), followed by *The Ancient Chinese World* (with Terry Kleeman), and a middle-grade novel with the working title *The Other Side of the Story.*

Barrett resides with her husband and two children in Nashville, Tennessee, where she is a Senior Lecturer of Italian, women's studies, and humanities at Vanderbilt University. Since 1999 she has been Regional Advisor (mid-south) for the Society of Children's Book Writers and Illustrators.

AWARDS: *Cold in Summer:* VOYA 2003 Science Fiction/Fantasy/Horror List; *Anna of Byzantium:* Best Books for Young Adults 2002; Quick Picks for Reluctant Readers, 2002, 1999 Blue Ribbon Book, *Bulletin of the Center for Children's Books;* Top Ten Historical Fiction, *Booklist.*

FURTHER WORKS: *Celebrate the States: Virginia,* 1997, 2004; *Cover-to-Cover Informational Books: Moments History: Trail of Tears: An American Tragedy,* 2000; *Celebrate the States: Kentucky,* 1999; *Kidding Around Nashville,* 1998; *Celebrate the States: Tennessee,* 1997; *Spotlight on American History: Harper's Ferry: The Story of John Brown's Raid,* 1994; *Gateway to Civil Rights: Nat Turner and the Slave Revolt,* 1993; *Kentucky,* 1999; *On Etruscan Time,* 2005.

BIBLIOGRAPHY: Web Home of Author Barrett http://www.tracybarrett.com; Contemporary Authors online. 2003. http://www.galenet.com/servlet/LitRC?final Auth = true; Lempke, S. D. 1995. Review of *Growing Up in Colonial America. Booklist, 92,* 700; Manczuk, S. (2002). Medieval days and ways: Books for middle school readers. *Book Report, 21* (3), 10, 12–14; Review of *Anna of Byzantium,* 1999. *Bulletin of the Center for Children's Books, 52,* 377.

MARY MCMILLAN TERRY

BARRON, T. A.

Author, b. 26 March 1952, New England

B. spent his boyhood exploring the pristine natural resources of Black Forest, Colorado, near Colorado Springs. He thrived in the embrace of the majesty of the Rocky Mountains; he learned to respect the great outdoors and witnessed the fragility of his homeland. Eventually, he traveled widely and saw lands far removed. He crafted his first work of fiction, *Autobiography of a Big Tree,* (*Booklist* April 25, 2001) as a seven-year-old and later for *Idiot's Odyssey,* a middle-school magazine.

Nature's expansive realm of possibility and a sense of family nurtured B.'s writer's voice and personal ideology. "There is something about the immensity of the Colorado sky," he said in the *Denver Post* (October 28, 1998), "that, when I was a boy gave me the sense that I was bigger than the world thought I was."

That passion for a bigger voice influenced B.'s life and his writing. As a student at Princeton, he gobbled up information, from geology to history, searching for focus. The winner of a Rhodes scholarship to Oxford University, he continued his scholarly quest. Between semesters, he traveled to Siberia, Africa, and Asia—anywhere his heart might lead him.

At Oxford, B. wrote his first novel. More than forty rejection letters later, he set fiction aside to enroll in Harvard Law School with an eye for environmental advocacy. He soon abandoned that ambition to work as a venture capitalist in New York. B. was quite successful in business, but his writer's yearning continued. With the blessing of his wife Currie—whom he met skiing in New York State—and his five children, B. finally made a leap of faith. In 1989, he traded the fast pace of Manhattan for an attic office in Boulder, Colorado, where he set out to write full time. "When I made my decision to leave my business and try to write full time, "B. said in the *Alan Review,* "I knew nothing about the future except that my passion for writing was strong enough that I simply had to give it a try." *Heartlight,* the story of young Kate's determined quest to rescue her grandfather and her universe, was published a year later in 1990.

Magic has been a central theme in many of B.'s novels of outdoor adventure; his Merlin books lead the FANTASY pack. But why Merlin? "Merlin has incredible depth," B. said in a computer-recorded interview. "The reason he endures is that he speaks to so many of our basic problems and struggles. Three of Merlin's greatest qualities continue to draw this continuing interest." Learning from nature was the first of Merlin's traits that B. described. His ability to bridge universal gaps of understanding was the second. Third: the ability to balance darkness with light—to see the importance of both highs and lows in harmony. In *Book Links* (January 1998), B. points to Merlin's whimsy. "Wizards are full of surprises," he explains. "They change faces, personalities, and forms at will. They grow younger, older, or stay forever the same age. They appear when least expected, and often vanish when most needed." Those qualities of magic circle back to B.'s commitment to the natural world and his family. "The world around us is full of wonder, mystery, and surprise, "he says on his personal website http://www.tabarron.com. "It is ours to protect—and also to explore."

B. backs his writing with volunteer work, lending his skills to organizations including the Natural Resources Defense Council and other non-profit organizations. His commitment to planetary stewardship has influenced almost everything B. has done—both before and after writing for young readers captured his imagination.

AWARDS: 1995 Colorado Book Award; 1996 Kansas State Reading Circle Award; 1998 Utah Book Award; 2000 Oppenheim Portfolio Gold Award; 2000 Virginia Young Readers Best Book Award; 2001 Nautilus Award; ALA Popular Paperbacks 2003.

FURTHER WORKS: *The Ancient One,* 1992; *To Walk in Wilderness,* 1993; *The Merlin Effect,* 1994; *Rocky Mountain National Park,* 1995; *The Seven Songs of Merlin,* 1997; *The Lost Years of Merlin,* 1998; *The Mirror of Merlin,* 1999; *The Fires of Merlin,* 2000; *The Wings of Merlin,* 2000; *Where is Grandpa?,* 2000; *Tree Girl,* 2001; *The Hero's Trail: A Hiking Guide for a Heroic Life,* 2002; *High as a Hawk: A Brave Girl's Historic Climb,* 2004.

BIBLIOGRAPHY: T.A. Barron's website: http://www
.tabarron.com/ T.A. Barron e-mail correspondence
Nov. 2003; ALAN Review Interview; *Booklist,* April
2001; *Book Links,* Jan. 1998; *Denver Post,* 1998;
Amazon.com Interview; Natural Resources Defense
Council interview.

KELLY MILNER HALLS

BARRY, Lynda (Jean)

Artist, author, playwright, comics/graphic novel creator; b. 2 January 1956, Richland Center, Wisconsin

B. and her family moved from Wisconsin to a diverse working-class neighborhood in Seattle, Washington. There, her half–Filipino mother felt at home and her Irish-Norwegian father felt outnumbered. It was a chaotic environment, where B.—with her pale complexion and red hair—didn't fit in as white or ASIAN. Occasionally she found a refuge: an elementary teacher gave her space to work on art projects before school; later the junior-high library was a haven where she read art books and POETRY. Still out of place in high school, B. moved to a more affluent school as an Asian transfer student; she made sure school officials didn't see her until the transfer was completed. Her painfully accurate memories of childhood and adolescence became ideas to use in her books.

The first person in her family to go to college, B. attended Evergreen State College and studied painting. She began creating comics to relieve the stress of fine-arts classes and the pain of being dumped by a boyfriend. The school newspaper editor liked and published some of her comics; this friend, Matt Groening, later created *The Simpsons* and the *Life in Hell* comic series. An article Groening wrote about local Seattle artists got the attention of the *Chicago Reader* and an offer to create a weekly cartoon for $80 per strip. B's comic became *Ernie Pook's Comeek* and was eventually syndicated in alternative newspapers around the country. Further work followed for *Esquire, Mother Jones,* and other publications. As her popularity increased, B. became a frequent visitor on David Letterman's *Late Show* and a commentator for National Public Radio.

Awarded a year-long residency by the Ragdale Foundation, B. retreated from public life to concentrate on writing. There she met her husband, Kevin; the two settled in Evanston, IL, where they live with their dogs.

B.'s career, like her artistic process, was not planned. For her, being "in the groove" of creation is more important than knowing what the final product will look like. An example of her creative serendipity is a collection of mixed-media portrayals of American musicians she created for a gallery exhibition in Seattle. She transformed the prose introduction she meant to write for the exhibition catalog into a narrative about an adolescent girl's response to music and racism. It became the novel *The Good Times Are Killing Me* (1988), later adapted into a play produced in Chicago and Off-Broadway. Her next novel, *Cruddy,* received critical acclaim for its depiction of the dark and violent world of its TEENAGE protagonist.

B. is known for her unpretentious painting and drawing style and the ability to pinpoint the pain and humor of growing up. Some critics find her artwork "childlike" or "awkward," but most would agree that her realistic depictions and dialogue magnify the details of childhood with piercing accuracy. *Kirkus Review* calls B. "a visual archaeologist of American childhood."

In her most recent book, *One Hundred Demons* (2002), B. paints with an Asian–style brush technique to incarnate seventeen personal "demons," including lost toys, cooties, broken friendships, and self-conscious dancing. More than previous works, this one is based on her own life—she calls it autobifictionalography. The book's final message is to try making art; B. inspires her readers to express their own creativity as a way to explore being human and to survive their own demons.

AWARDS: *One Hundred Demons,* 2003 Alex Award (YALSA); *My Perfect Life,* ALA Pick for Reluctant Readers; *It's So Magic,* 1994, Best Books for Young Adults list nomination.

FURTHER WORKS: *The Lynda Barry Experience,* (audio) 1996; *Cruddy: An Illustrated Novel,* 1999; *The Freddie Stories,* 1999; *The Greatest of Marlys,* 2000.

BIBLIOGRAPHY: *Time,* September 2, 2002; *Kirkus Reviews,* October 1, 2000; *Contemporary Authors Online,* 2004; *CNN Booknews from Salon.com* May 2, 1999; *Chicago magazine* March 1997; Independent Publisher <www.independentpublisher.com>; <www.marlysmagazine.com>; NPR's *Talk of the Nation,* October 1, 2002.

JENNIFER STILL

BARTOLETTI, Susan
Author, b. 25 June 1958, Harrisburg, Pennsylvania

Admitting quickly to her passion for reading and drawing as a child, B. remembers loving the space, time, and solitude she had growing up in the countryside of Pennsylvania—ingredients necessary, she feels, to develop a sense of FANTASY. Beginning college at age sixteen as an art major, she switched to English. After finishing college, B. began teaching at age twenty—a career she continued for eighteen years. Her early endeavors at writing were as the author of textbooks that developed her own teaching strategies. This led to writing for MAGAZINES and her first PICTURE BOOK publication.

Drawing from the history of her home state, B. is acknowledged for her stories and historical perspectives on coal mines. "Hers are not the usual tales of the coal miner himself, or of the rapacious coal owners; rather B. focuses on what she terms the 'gaps' in history—untold stories of the women and children of the coal mining era" (*Something about the Author*, 2003, p. 11). *Growing up in Coal Country* (1996), *Kids on Strike!* (1999), and *A Coal Miner's Bride* (2000) represent excellence in research as well as a perspective in sharing information as she attempts to fill these gaps. Likewise, *Silver at Night* (1994) reflects her own family's history as it tells the story of the immigration of her husband's grandfather from Italy to the mines in the U.S. First-hand accounts from oral history interviews are interwoven with the information received from period artifacts—newspapers, diaries, photographs, etc.—and provide exceptional resources for cross-curricular use. *Growing up in Coal Country* vividly portrays accounts of children working under harsh conditions and for long hours. Using pictures taken by the well-known photographer Lewis Hine to support her narrative, B. shares the personal stories of these strong children who lived around the turn of the century in Pennsylvania coal towns and places a somewhat tragic but inspiring perspective on both child labor and the coal industry. Similarly, in *Kids On Strike!* B. employs nonfiction to enter the life stories of individual children and confront the struggles they faced as they engaged in strikes—the bootblack action of 1988, the Pennsylvania coal strikes of 1900 and 1902, and the mill-workers' strike in Lawrence, Massachusetts, of 1913. Children making a dif-

ference in the midst of hardship and struggles is a theme in *Kids On Strike!* as well as in other of B.'s titles, such as *No Man's Land: A Young Soldier's Story* (1999), historical fiction about two young boys who join the troops during the Civil War, one fighting for the North and one for the South. The relationship that evolves between the two adolescents in the midst of their developing understanding of war speaks to historical accuracy as well as the creative development of their characters. One reviewer of this novel comments that B. "spins a history as fresh as the day it happened."

A Coal Miner's Bride: The Diary of Anetka Kaminska (2000) continues B.'s exploration into the coal mines but this time through historical fiction. In this title from the Dear America SERIES (Scholastic), Anetka immigrates to America in 1896 from Poland to marry a miner whom she has never met. He later dies and she falls in love with a labor organizer who ultimately leads miners during the Lattimer Massacre, a historical event. Told through the DIARY of Anetka, B.'s research is supported by historical notes. It has been praised for its vivid depiction of the life of immigrants, laborers, and strong women as well as Anetka's spirited use of lively metaphors and the Polish language throughout the story. B. continues to bring historical events to a lively forefront in her book, *Black Potatoes: The Story of the Great Irish Famine, 1845–1850* (2001). She weaves together personal stories, historical records, and photographs to portray this event from the perspective of individuals who were there.

B. hopes to empower young readers through her presentations of the challenges faced by children of the past. Her outstanding sense of the stories that undergird historical events and her desire to share these stories with readers is a perfect complement to her disciplined and well-developed craftsmanship. B. has received numerous awards and citations for her books. *Growing up in Coal Country* alone has been awarded over fifteen citations and awards, including Notable Children's Trade Book in the field of social studies, National Council for the Social Studies/Children's Book Council, Orbis Pictus recommended title. Other titles have also been recognized.

AWARDS: *Growing up in Coal Country:* 1998 BBYA, Jane Addams Children's Book Award, ALA Notable

Book, Orbis Pictus Recommended Title; 2001 BBYA, *Kids on Strike; Black Potatoes:* 2003 ALA Best Books for Young Adults; 2002 ALA Notable Children's Books; 2002 Robert F. Sibert Informational Book Award.

FURTHER WORKS: *Silver at Night,* 1994; *Dancing with Dziadziu,* 1997; *The Christmas Promise,* 2001; *The Journal of Finn Reardon, A Newsie,* 2003; *Hitler Youth: Growing Up in Hitler's Shadow,* 2005.

BIBLIOGRAPHY: Bartoletti, Susan Campbell, interview with J. Sydney Jones, *Authors and Artists for Young Adults,* 44, 2002; Bartoletti, Susan C., "Exploring the Gaps in History," *Book Links,* 2000, pp. 16–21; *Contemporary Authors Online,* 2002; *Publishers Weekly,* 1999, p. 94; *Something About the Author,* 135, 2003, pp. 10–15.

JANELLE MATHIS

BAT-AMI, Miriam
Author, professor, b. 1950, n.p.

B. is the author of several books that appeal to YA, and is a Professor of English at Western Michigan University. Her first children's book was *Sea, Salt, and Air* (1993), in which the oldest of three children tells about her family's trips to visit her grandparents by the shore. With the publication of *When the Frost Is Gone* (1994), B. reached out to an older audience. Natalie's summer is filled with various upheavals as she deals with her addict mother and the loss of her best friend in a fire. Set mostly on a city block that is a virtual melting pot, Natalie grows up a little with the help of a kindly neighbor. In *Dear Elijah* (1997), Rebecca Samuelson deals with her father being in the Cardiac Care Unit by writing letters to the prophet Elijah. Set against the Orthodox Jewish observance of Passover, the novel offers strong religious conviction, a conviction that ultimately helps Rebecca deal with her situation.

B.'s recent and highly successful book, *Two Suns in the Sky* (2001), relies on research done at a refugee camp in Oswego, New York, the only sanctuary for refugees that existed in the U.S. during World War II. *Two Suns in the Sky* is the story of Adam and Christine, the story is of the controversial romance between an all–American Catholic girl and a teenage Jewish refugee from Yugoslavia. B. captures the cultural conflict in both the teenagers' relationship and the townspeople who have mixed feelings toward the

strangers seeking refuge in their town. There is also the frustration felt by the refugees who are supposedly free yet are separated from the townspeople by barbed wire and suspicion.

B. emphasizes research in the beginning stages of a book. There are historical accuracies and accounts from real life that are indispensable when writing about another's experience. B. lives in Mattawan, Michigan.

AWARDS: *Two Suns in the Sky:* 2000 Scott O'Dell Historical Fiction Award, 2000 YALSA Best Books for Young Adults.

BIBLIOGRAPHY: www.amazon.com; www.calvin.edu/academic/engl/conf/program/speakers/bat-ami.htm; http://homepages.wmich.edu/%7Ellhall/interview.htm; www.novelst4.epnet.com

JEANNE MARIE RYAN

BAUER, Cat
Author, n.d., South Carolina

B. is the author of the YA novel *Harley, like a Person* (2000), in which the title character faces a question that many TEENS consider—whether or not the people she lives with are really her parents. Her curiosity about how she is so different from the rest of her family is justified when she finds a note in the attic that says "Papa loves you forever and a day," a note that is not in her father's handwriting. Her rebellion against her restrictive family includes a descent into drug use and failing grades, and only her artistic talent and the faith of the few people who still believe in her keep her life together.

Harley, like a Person, evolved from a SHORT STORY that B. wrote for *Sassy* MAGAZINE. B. was initially inspired by J. D. Salinger's *The Catcher in the Rye* and wanted to write a novel with a similar spirit that would generate interest from both teenagers and adults. The story, called "Run Away," generated fan mail demanding to know what happened to the character next. The short story became the first chapter of the novel that told the rest of Harley's story. *Harley* was a book-club selection for both *Teen People* and *CosmoGirl.*

B. lives in Venice, Italy, and is a regular contributor to the "Italy Daily" section of the *International Herald Tribune.*

AWARDS: *Harley, Like a Person: Booklist* Top Ten Youth First Novel, ALA Best Books For Young Adults (2001) and Quick Picks for Young Adults (2001), New York Public Library's Books for the Teen Age (2001), SCBWI Sue Alexander Most Promising New Work Award.

BIBLIOGRAPHY: *Teensreads.com,* online, 2000.

ANDREA LIPINSKI AND MEGAN PEARLMAN

BAUER, Joan
Author, b. 12 July 1951, Oak Park, Illinois

In her novels, B. has one overarching theme: adversity makes one a stronger person. Strong female characters (and two unforgettable young men), each facing tough times in their young lives, come through their trials thanks in large part to their ability to laugh at themselves. A sense of humor is key to reading and to understanding B.'s writing. Another important component of a B. novel is a caring, understanding adult who assists the protagonist on her or his journey from childhood to adulthood.

B.'s first novel, *Squashed* (1992), received the Delacorte Press Prize for a First Young Novel. This grand entrance onto the YA scene might have intimidated a lesser talent. However, B. followed the success of her first novel with *Thwonk* (1995). Next, B. changed direction and offered *Sticks* (1996), a novel for younger readers. Unlike her two earlier works, *Sticks* focused on a young man and his struggle to prove himself as a pool player.

Following *Sticks,* B. wrote *Rules of the Road.* Jenna Boller, the female protagonist, is a young shoe salesperson who learns a great deal as the traveling companion of the owner of the chain of shoe stores for which she works. As she travels across the country with Mrs. Gladstone, Jenna comes to understand more about the business world. More importantly, Jenna discovers how what she is learning at work applies to her personal life as well.

Hope Was Here (2000), B.'s next story, won many awards including a Newbery Honor Medal in 2001. Hope is a young woman who moves, along with her Aunt Addie, from New York to the "Land of the Lactose." There, Hope helps Addie work in a diner. Hope finds friends and, ultimately, the family Hope has longed for most of her life. *Hope Was Here* is exemplary of B.'s work: a young woman, with the assistance of some wiser adults, discovers the inner

strength she will need to face some terrible obstacles and events.

B.'s writing for YA readers resonates with several truths. First, readers will see that it is possible to get through the tough times, to be what B. terms an "overcomer." Readers will also catch a glimpse of strong characters who are hovering on the verge of independence, characters who use humor to see them through the harsher realities of life. They will come face to face with protagonists who discover their purpose in the world.

AWARDS: *Squashed* (1992): Delacorte Prize for a First Young Adult Novel, YALSA's QuickPicks and Popular Paperback Lists. YALSA Top Ten Best Books for Young Adults for *Thwonk* (1995). *Rules of the Road:* Golden Kite Award; the first LA Times Award in Young Adult Literature, ALA Notable Book, Quick Picks, Popular Paperbacks, and BBYA. *Hope Was Here* (2001): Newbery Honor Book, Top Ten BBYA list, ALA Notable Books, New York Public Library Books for the Teen Age Reader List, IRA Young Adult Choices list, the Christopher Medal. New York Public Library Books for the Teen Age Reader for *Backwater* (1999) and *Stand Tall* (2002).

FURTHER WORKS: *In the Streets,* 1987; *Backwater,* 1999; *Stand Tall,* 2002; *Best Foot Forward,* 2005.

BIBLIOGRAPHY: www.joanbauer.com; www.authors4teens.com

TERI S. LESESNE

BAUER, Marion Dane
Author, b. 30 November 1938, Oglesby, Illinois

B. grew up in a small prairie town where she spent a great deal of her "ideal" childhood creating stories. Her first piece was a poem honoring her teddy bear. B.'s interest in writing led her to a career as an English teacher. After B. graduated from the University of Oklahoma, she devoted her time to teaching and raising children. B. did not write professionally until her daughter Elisabeth entered first grade. At that time B. started her career as a children's author, by researching trends in children's literature. B. eventually published *Foster Child* (1977), loosely based on her experiences as a foster parent. This publication encouraged B. to continue to write professionally. *Shelter from the Wind* (1976) established B.'s ability to handle sensitive subjects with care. Later adapted for television, *Shelter from the Wind* tells the story of a TEENAGER so overwhelmed by troubles at home that she runs away to the Oklahoma prairie, where she is taken in by Old Ella.

B. continued to write novels that focus on young people who face traumatic events in everyday life. *Rain of Fire* (1983) depicts a young boy's relationship with his older brother, a soldier recovering from the effects of World War II. B.'s characters prevail by confronting their problems and teaching children the importance of their own choices. B.'s fiction often evolves from her personal experiences, and are set in places she has lived or visited.

Not only do teens relate to B.'s themes, but also the power of her novels is affirmed by many awards, including a Newbery Honor Book citation for *On My Honor* in 1987. In this powerful story, a teenage boy named Joel witnesses the death of his best friend, Tony, while they are swimming in the river. The reader shares Joel's pain as he learns to cope with his own sense of overwhelming guilt. *Face to Face* (1991), a book about an enraged teen on the brink of committing suicide, and *A Question of Trust* (1994) were also recipients of several literary awards.

B. gained recognition as editor for a collection of SHORT STORIES on gay and lesbian themes. *Am I Blue?: Coming out from the Silence* (1994) won, among other awards, the Gay-Lesbian-Bisexual Book Award for Literature.

In the early 1990s, B. expanded her writing repertoire to include nonfiction, PICTURE BOOKS, and chapter books for a younger audience. B.'s *What's Your Story?: A Young Person's Guide to Writing Fiction* (1992) provides suggestions on determining story ideas, plot, character development, and revision. This informational book, used by both adults and adolescents, was awarded a Notable Children's Book citation by the American Library Association. B. has written two other nonfiction books about writing: *A Writer's Story: From Life to Fiction* (1995) and *Our Stories: A Fiction Workshop for Young Authors* (1996).

Most of B.'s recent work includes chapter books and picture books that appeal to a younger audience as well as several books for YOUNG ADULTS. B. publishes a series of chapter books for beginning readers that focus on Alison, a strong and endearing character. B. has written over thirty books for children and young adults and received the Kerlan Award from the University of Minnesota for the body of her work, which continues to grow.

AWARDS: Golden Kite Honor Book Award from the Society of Children's Book Writers, *Foster Child; Shelter from the Wind:* Notable Book Award and the Japanese Library Association Award; 1984 Jane Addams Peace Association award, *Rain of Fire; On My Honor:* 1987 Newbery Honor Book, ALA Notable Children's Book Award, *School Library Journal's* Best Books list, *Booklist* Editors' Choice, Golden Archer Award, Flicker Tale Children's Book Award, and William Allen White Award; 1991 *Hungry Mind Review* Children's Book of Distinction, *Face to Face;* 1994 ALA Best Book for Young Adults, *Am I Blue?: Coming Out from the Silence; School Library Journal's* Best Books of 1995, *A Question of Trust.*

FURTHER WORKS: *Tangled Butterfly,* 1980; *Like Mother, like Daughter,* 1985; *Touch the Moon,* 1987; *A Dream of Queens and Castles,* 1990; *Ghost Eye,* 1992; *A Taste of Smoke,* 1993; *When I Go Camping with Grandma,* 1995; *Alison's Wings,* 1996; *Alison's Fierce and Ugly Halloween,* 1997; *Alison's Puppy,* 1997; *If You Were Born a Kitten,* 1997; *Turtle Dreams,* 1997; *Bear's Hiccups,* 1998; *An Early Winter,* 1999; *Sleep, Little One, Sleep,* 1999; *Jason's Bears,* 2000; *Grandmother's Song,* 2000; *Runt,* 2002; *Land of the Buffalo Bones: The Diary of Mary Ann Elizabeth Rogers, An English Girl in Minnesota,* 2003.

BIBLIOGRAPHY: *Something about the Author,* vol. 113.

JODI PILGRIM

BEAGLE, Peter S.
Author, b. 20 April 1939, New York City

B., who writes FANTASY books for young people and adults, had early success with writing; he won a scholarship to the University of Pittsburgh with a poem that won first prize in a Scholastic Writing Awards contest. B.'s first book, *A Fine and Private Place* (1960), a story set in a Bronx cemetery, was published when he was just twenty-one. B.'s second novel, *The Last Unicorn* (1968), is his most famous book. It is recognized as a fantasy classic that combines adventure, fairy tale, humor, and tragedy, written in poetic, evocative language. In this book, a unicorn overhears hunters saying that she is the last of her kind, so she leaves her enchanted forest and begins a quest to find the rest of her species. Along the way, she meets many colorful characters such as Molly Grue, Captain Cully, and Schmendrick the Magician. *The Last Unicorn* has been adapted into a play and an animated film. Many of B.'s other novels and stories, also have fantastic elements. In *The Innkeep-*

er's Song (1993), a sorceress, a wizard, and other characters play pivotal roles in a story about magic, fate, and death. In *Tamsin* (1999), a spoiled teenager discovers her connection to a 300-year-old ghost that haunts the farm being restored by her stepfather.

B. has worked as an editor of and contributor to many fantasy anthologies; he has also written articles, screenplays, and nonfiction. B. continues to be compared by critics to other great fantasy writers such as C. S. LEWIS and J. R. R. TOLKIEN.

AWARDS: Mythopoeic Fantasy Award (1987) for *The Folk of the Air;* World Fantasy Award (1998) for *Giant Bones;* World Fantasy Award and Mythopoeic Fantasy Award (both 2000) for *Tamsin.*

FURTHER WORKS: *The Fantasy Worlds of Peter S. Beagle,* 1974; *The Unicorn Sonata,* 1996; *Giant Bones,* 1997; *A Dance For Emilia,* 2000.

BIBLIOGRAPHY: *Authors and Artists For Young Adults,* vol. 47, 2003; *Contemporary Authors,* online, 2002; *Something About The Author,* vol. 130, 2002; *St. James Guide to Young Adult Writers* (second edition), 1999.

ANDREA LIPINSKI

BEALE, Fleur

Author, b. 22 February 1945, Inglewood, Taranaki, New Zealand

Raised on the family dairy farm and educated at Inglewood School and Victoria University of Wellington, B. has taught English in high schools in Hamilton and Wellington since 1985. She began writing stories for *Grampa's Place,* a Radio New Zealand children's program, then developed a three-page draft into her first novel *Slide the Corner* (1993). This exciting story of Greg's finding friendship, job satisfaction, and a purpose in life, as a result of car rallying, established B. as a popular writer for YOUNG ADULTS. It also displays many features typical of her novels.

Although B. and husband Tim have two daughters, many of B.'s stories feature male characters involved in activities mainly of interest to boys. Careful research and inspection of details give her accounts of skateboarding, camping, motor-cycling and car maintenance a ring of authenticity. B's skillful storytelling and characterization have brought her popularity with female readers, but one of her aims is to make her novels accessible to males in the twelve-to-fourteen-age range who are not keen readers.

In *Driving a Bargain* (1994), two friends, Thomas and Jimmy, spend a golden summer holiday learning to drive a decrepit antique Morris 1000 in a paddock. Thomas learns the value of true friendship and both boys develop their personalities through their achievements. *Ambush* (2001) is a reminder of the wit in many of B.'s stories, as a group of students work together to break up a bullying racket. The tense plot of *Against the Tide* (1993) forces David and Chrissie, two teenagers who dislike each other, to co-operate to save David's family from a crazed gunman. The real strength of the novel, however, lies in Chrissie's idiosyncratic personality and the way David's concern later forces her to re-examine her life as a runaway. *Fifteen and Screaming* (1995) introduces Lily who has to organize the family when her mother becomes depressed. In this entertaining examination of responsibility issues, Lily's adventures with housework, chicken pox and budgeting range from serious to hilarious.

B.'s most remarkable achievement is *I Am Not Esther* (1998), an award-winning novel. It describes Kirby's successful struggle to resist her Uncle Caleb's religious cult, which tries to dominate her thinking and personality. As a female, she must defer to males, marry at sixteen, and give up any idea of a career. At the same time, B. shows Caleb's sincerity in opposing the secular world and trying to save Kirby's immortal soul from damnation. Major issues such as these are not commonly discussed in YA novels. Writers of B.'s quality ensure that they are discussed well.

B.'s stories move swiftly, and her plots have impact. She displays an acute ear for dialogue, making her settings and people recognizably from New Zealand (*Slide the Corner* was rejected by an American publisher for this reason). Her characters are convincing. Above all, B. identifies with teenagers' interests and concerns. Almost painlessly, B.'s readers are drawn to examine deeper issues. She shows a good understanding of the issues facing young people and the difficulties they meet in coping with them. Thus *Further Back than Zero* (1998) explores teenage attitudes to alcohol. At the same time, B. has a good sense of humor and, while their themes may be grim, her books are never depressing.

AWARDS: 2002 NZ Post Children's Book Awards, *I Am Not Esther; Ambushed:* 2002 NZ Post Children's Book Awards (Shortlist), Esther Glen Award (Shortlist); ALA Quick Picks for Reluctant Young Adult Readers 2003.

FURTHER WORKS: *The Great Pumpkin Battle*, 1988; *A Surprise for Anna*, 1990; *Over the Edge*, 1994; *Dear Pop*, 1995; *The Rich and Famous Body and the Empty; Chequebook*, 1995; *The Fortune Teller*, 1995; *Rockman*, 1996; *Keep Out*, 1999; *Destination Disorder*, 1999; *Playing to Win*, 1999; *Deadly Prospect*, 2000; *Trucker*, 2000; *Lucky For Some*, 2002.

BIBLIOGRAPHY: Harper, Julie. "Know the Author: Fleur Beale." *Magpies NZ Supplement* 13:4 (Sep 1998): 4–6; Hebley, Diane. "Beale, Fleur." *The Oxford Companion to New Zealand Literature*. Ed. Roger Robinson and Nelson Wattie, 1998; McKenzie, John. "Fleur Beale: A Writer for 1990s Teenagers." *Reading Time* 43 (1) 39–40; New Zealand Book Council website: http://www.bookcouncil.org.nz/writers/bealefleur.htm; Christchurch City Libraries website: http://library.christchurch.org.nz/Childrens/ChildrensAuthors/FleurBeale.asp/.

TREVOR AGNEW

BEAR, Greg
Author, b. 20 August 1951, San Diego, California

B., also known as Gregory Dale Bear, is considered an important writer of SCIENCE FICTION today. The son of a U.S. Navy officer, B. traveled with his family throughout the continental United States, Alaska, the Philippines, and Japan. He wrote his first SHORT STORY at the age of nine and sold his first one at fifteen to Robert Lowndes' *Famous Science Fiction*. B. published his first novel, *Hegira*, in 1979. The short story *Dead Run* was adapted by Alan Brennert for the second *Twilight Zone* television show. B. has served frequently as an advisor to the government on scientific matters including the National Citizens Advisory Council on Space Policy. As a freelance journalist, his articles have appeared in the *Los Angeles Times*, *Newsday*, and the *San Diego Union*.

AWARDS: Nebula Award and Hugo Award (1984) for *Blood Music*; Prix Apollo (1986) for *Blood Music*; Nebula Award and Hugo Award (1987) for the short story *Tangents*; Nebula Award (1994) for best novel, *Moving Mars*; Nebula Award (2001) for *Darwin's Radio*.

FURTHER WORKS: *Queen of Angels*, 1990; *Heads*, 1991; *Anvil of Stars*, 1992; *Sisters*, 1992; *Bear's Fantasies: Six Stories in Old Paradigms*, 1992; *The Venging*, 1992; *Songs of Earth and Power*, 1994; *Legacy*, 1995; *Dinosaur Summer*, 1998; *Foundation and Chaos*, 1998; *Darwin's Radio*, 1999; *Rogue Planet*, 2000; *Vitals*, 2002; *The Collected Stories of Greg Bear*, 2003; *Darwin's Children*, 2003; *Dead Lines: A Novel of Life . . . after Death*, 2004; *Quantico*, 2006.

BIBLIOGRAPHY: *Authors and Artists for Young Adults*, vol. 24, 1998; *Contemporary Authors*, online, 2002.

HECTOR L. MOREY

BECKETT, Bernard
Author, b. 13 October 1967, Featherstone, New Zealand

B. may be the only writer for TEENAGERS ever to admit to having been a bully at school. His youthful misdemeanors may lack political correctness but they certainly bring a sharp reality to his novels about troubled young adults. B.'s characters are often out of step with their family and the world about them.

In B.'s first novel, *Lester* (1999), Michael not only spars with the school authorities but also resists a spiritual revival movement which has been diverted into promoting prejudice in a small town similar to his hometown. Michael's fresh and convincing personality helped make *Lester* a success and established B. as an important writer. Written while B. was teaching in Japan, *Lester* was rewritten under the editorial guidance of Paula BOOCK, who calls it "assured with a clear voice."

As a high-school teacher of economics, math and drama, B. is well aware of teenagers' ideas and emotions; his characters often question authority and are never far from trouble. Samuel in *Red Cliff* (2000) has a record of school arson; the diary of his first year in "a new sub-division with its own brochures" shows the emotional cost of resisting peer pressure from the "back-seaters" on the school bus. Sharon in *No Alarms* (2002) is in trouble at home and school. Desperate to escape her dead-end situation, she becomes involved in bullying and burglary. Her story is convincing, sad, and often witty. *Jolt* (2001) is an exciting thriller about survival when an earthquake triggers a crisis for a party of hikers. The main character, Marko, is a superbly recognizable portrait of a defiantly sullen teenager, who captures our sympathy even as he irritates all around him.

Two interesting recent developments for B. are the publication of *Three Plays* (2003), large-cast dramas written for teenage performers, and his first historical novel, *Home Boys* (2003). Until World War II, many

Pakeha (European-descended) New Zealanders referred to Britain as "Home." After the war some British orphans were sent to New Zealand. The scheme was poorly supervised and the experiences of the runaway boys Colin and Dougal in this novel are grimly realistic.

B.'s work receives high acclaim from critics and is widely read by teenagers.

BIBLIOGRAPHY: Packer, Ann. "Know the Author: Bernard Beckett," *Magpies NZ Supplement,* 17:1 (Mar. 2002): 3–4; http://library.christchurch.org.nz/Chil drens/ChildrensAuthors/BernardBeckett.asp/ http:// www.bookcouncil.org.nz/writers/beckettbernard.htm/.

TREVOR AGNEW

BEDARD, Michael
Author, b. 26 June 1949, Toronto, Ontario, Canada

The oldest of five children, B. currently resides in the town of his birth with his wife and four children. Best known for his YA suspense novels which use "vivid, sometimes disturbing prose," B.'s writing career was inspired by authors such as Emily Dickinson, William Blake, Dylan Thomas, and T. S. Eliot. His own writing did not start until the age of seventeen when he fell under the spell of poetry. Dickinson's influence is recognized in his works through the use of extremes and the suggestion of what lies beneath the surface. By the end of high school, B. had realized his own passion for writing.

After graduating from the University of Toronto with a B.A. in English and philosophy, B. first worked as a library assistant and a pressman. While there, B. published two anthologies of original FAIRY TALES. This was a critical beginning for an author who would carry fairy tales with him throughout his writing career.

B.'s first novel, *A Darker Magic* (1987), tells the story of an elderly woman seeking to destroy an evil magician whom she encountered fifty years earlier. While the content of the book was labeled as horrifying, critics agreed that the story completely captivates its audiences. B. established a chilling and highly imaginative writing style which he retained throughout his further works. One of the main characters, Emily Endicott, reappears as an eccentric aunt in B.'s later book *Painted Devil* (1994), making the evil which emerged in *A Darker Magic* all the more persistent and omnipresent.

Redwork (1990), B.'s second book, received much attention and numerous awards. The story focuses on the relationship between two teenagers and a survivor of World War I, as the three search for a philosopher's stone that would enable them to cure the world of evil and grant immortality.

B. has also written several PICTURE BOOKS including *The Lightening Bolt* (1989), *The Tinderbox* (1990), and *The Nightingale* (1991) which reinterpret stories by Hans Christian Andersen and the Brothers Grimm.

Despite the supernatural nature of B.'s works, they do not fit neatly into one category, as he also "investigates themes of freedom, self-determination, and imagination." He credits his own children as the motivation and inspiration to create works for young readers. He says without the presence of children, one runs the risk of "forget[ting] how fragile a thing childhood is and children are, something a writer of children's books can't afford to be without."

AWARDS: Book of the Year, Canadian Library Association, Governor General's Literary Award for Text, 1990, National Chapter of Canada IODE Violet Downey Book Award, and Young Adult Canadian Book Award runner-up, both 1991, International Board on Books for Young People (IBBY) Honor List, 1992, all for *Redwork;* National Chapter of Canada IODE Violet Downey Book Award, 1991, for *The Nightingale;* nominee, Young Adult Canadian Book Award, Canadian Library Association, 2002, for *Stained Glass.*

SELECT FURTHER WORKS: *Woodsedge and Other Tales,* 1979; *Pipe and Pearls: A Gathering of Tales,* 1980; *Emily,* 1992; *The Divide,* 1997; *Glass Town,* 1997; *The Painted Wall and Other Strange Tales,* 2003.

BIBLIOGRAPHY: *Contemporary Authors Online,* 2002; Jenkinson, Dave, "Michael Bedard," *Emergency Librarian,* vol. 19, 1991; "Michael Bedard," *Authors and Artists for Young Adults,* vol. 22, 1997, reproduced in *Biography Resource Center,* 2003; http:// www.galenet.com/servlet/BioRC.

RACHEL WITMER
AND SARA MARCUS

BELL, Clare Louise
Author, b. 19 June 1952, Hitchin, Hertfordshire, England

B. immigrated with her parents to the U.S. in 1957 at the age of five. She earned a B.A. at the University of California in 1975 and a Masters of Mechanical Engineering at Stanford University in 1983. Her diverse interests include electric cars, music, hiking, cycling, and swimming. She has had a multifaceted career that includes work as a writer and editor, Geological Field Assistant, and Test Engineer for International Business Machines (IBM).

While B. was working for IBM she began writing FANTASY novels for juveniles and YAS. By 1989, her books were successful enough for her to leave her work in engineering. Her novels appeal to a diverse audience and range of age groups. B.'s stories are fantastical for the younger audience and riveting page-turners for adults. Her debut novel, *Rathas Creature* (1983), is the first novel in an award-winning series about prehistoric "sentient" cats. In addition to the Ratha series, B. has written fantasy novels intended for older audiences, including *People of the Sky* (1989) and *Jaguar Princess* (1993). B. co-authored three novels under the joint pseudonym Clare Coleman with M. Coleman Easton. All her works have wide audience appeal for readers of SCIENCE FICTION and fantasy.

The Ratha series is about a society of anthropomorphic cats that is both a prehistoric and futuristic commentary on human social development and interaction. The clans have human social and cultural elements: organized systems of government, family structure, religion, technology, and social hierarchies. Although the elements of society are human, the cats retain a distinct feline quality which is part of the appeal in the stories. There are two competing clans in the books; civilized and domesticated herders (The Named) and the wild hunters (The Unnamed). Ratha, the central character through whom the stories are told, resides among both clans alternately as leader and a banished member from both societies. Leadership and challenge are recurring themes creating conflict and the atmosphere for resolution resulting in the character's growth.

B.'s writings are sociological parables for the meeting between human nature and technology. The exploration of evolution is a common theme in the stories. The future and past meet and resulting social change is examined.

AWARDS: *Ratha's Creature:* 1983 PEN Los Angeles Award, 1983 ALA Best Book for Young People, 1984 International Reading Association's Children's Book Award; ALA Best Book for Young People: 1984 for *Clan Ground,* 1990 for *Ratha and Thistle-Chaser.*

FURTHER WORKS: *Ratha's Creature,* 1983; *Clan Ground,* 1984; *Tomorrow's Sphinx,* 1986; *Ratha and Thistle-Chaser,* 1990; *Ratha's Challenge,* 1995; As Clare Coleman with M. Coleman Easton: *Daughter of the Reef,* 1992; *Sister of the Sun,* 1993; *Child of the Dawn,* 1994.

BIBLIOGRAPHY: Beetz, Kirk H., *Beacham's Guide to Literature for Young Adults,* Volume 6, 1994; *Contemporary Authors Online,* Gale, 2003; Hedblad, Alan, ed., *Something About the Author: Facts and Pictures about Authors and Illustrators of Books for Young People,* Volume 99, 1999; Pringle, David, ed., *St. James Guide to Fantasy Writers,* 1996, pp. 55–6 Bell, Clare and pp. 174–5 Easton, Malcom Coleman.

CLARA HUDSON

BELL, Hilari
Author, b. 1958, Denver, Colorado

B. read her first chapter book, Lloyd Alexander's *The Book of Three,* when she was in the first grade, and she says "I spent the next few years living more in Prydain than I did in Denver, Colorado," where she was born and raised. Fantasy has been one of her favorite genres ever since, along with science fiction, and so far, whenever she has an idea for a story, it turns into one or the other—or both—of these genres. B. works part time as a reference librarian for a mid-sized public library in Denver, where she lives with her mother, brother, sister-in-law, niece, and dog. Her favorite thing to do is camping with her mother; they do "no unnecessary work" and spend all day reading, hiking, and reading more. B. also enjoys board games and fantasy games.

B. calls herself "the poster child for persistence" as the first novel she sold, *Songs of Power* (2000), was the fifth novel she'd written; she was working on novel #13 at the time. B.'s 2001 *A Matter of Profit* was reviewed by *Booklist* as "a dynamic combination of sf, thriller, and MYSTERY that will draw readers in from the start." B. says, "there will always be mystery and suspense in any novel I write, because novels are pretty boring without them." *The Goblin Wood* (2003) is about young hedgewitch Makenna, who has written off the entire human race as "the enemy," and Tobin, a young knight who is a compassionate protector, trying to protect even his enemies. B. said that this book grew out of her anger at the prevailing attitude during the 1990s Gulf War, "that only the American casualties mattered. They never even considered the Iraqi dead, because after all, they were just Arabs . . . I can't tell you how much I hate that attitude." Her interest in the Middle East continues, with Persian mythology influencing *Flame* (2003), the first installment of her new SERIES, The Book of Sorahb. Shortly after *Flame* was released, the publisher decided to change the name of this work to *Fall of a Kingdom* and issue it as The Forsala Trilogy, Book I, to be followed in short order by *Rise of a Hero,* Book II, the new name for *Wheel, The Book of Sorahb,* Book II. The second volume in the trilogy, *Wheel,* was released in 2004, and B believes it is even better than *Flame.* She says that she's read many trilogies in which the second book was weaker than the first, so her goal with *Wheel* was to "raise the emotional stakes and the plot tension all around, and I think I've succeeded." *The Wizard Test* (forthcoming March 2005) is about a young knight who learns that his side of a war is in the wrong.

AWARDS: American Library Association-YALSA Best Books for Young Adults 2002 for *A Matter of Profit,* 2004 for *The Goblin Wood.* Bank Street College of Education Best Children's Books of the Year 2001 for *Songs of Power,* 2002 for *A Matter of Profit.* ALA-Booklist Editors' Choice: Books for Youth 2001 for *A Matter of Profit.* School Library Journal Book Review Stars October 2001 for *A Matter of Profit,* November 2003 for *Flame.* Publisher's Weekly Book Review Stars March 24, 2003 for *The Goblin Wood.*

FURTHER WORK: *Navohar,* 2000.

BIBLIOGRAPHY: Author's website, www.sfwa.org/members/bell; Publisher's interview, www.harpercollins.com; *Readers Read* interview, www.readersread.com

COLLEEN P. GILRANE

BELL, Ruth
Author, teen counselor, n.d., n.p.

With a degree from the University of California at Berkeley, a Masters Degree in Education from Harvard University, and a career that includes TEEN counseling in Boston and Los Angeles, it was a natural fit for B. to coauthor *Our Bodies, Ourselves,* and *Ourselves and Our Children* (1978). B. also helped to establish the Boston Women's Health Book collective and wrote *Talking with Your Teenager: A Book for Parents* (1984), *Number Jugglers: Math Card Games*

(1998), *Changing Bodies, Changing Lives: A Book for Teens on Sex and Relationships* (1990), and *Fraction Jugglers: Game and Work Book and Math Game Cards* (2001).

B.'s books encourage open and honest discussion between parents and teens about the emerging issues of the teenage years by helping to create a forum for such discussions. B.'s books deal not only with the physical changes that adolescence brings, but also with other changes in social interactions. Her work on sexuality embraces both heterosexual and homosexual alternatives within the framework of adolescent self-respect. She also details the importance of adolescents looking after themselves emotionally; she probes the causes and solutions for eating disorders, substance abuse, and physical abuse. Her books provide facts on many of the rituals of adolescence and also offer ways for parents and teens to communicate about delicate topics.

Currently residing in the Pacific Northwest, B. has two children.

BIBLIOGRAPHY: www.amazon.com; www.ourbodiesourselves.org/changing.htm; www.numberjugglers.com/aboutus.html

JEANNE MARIE RYAN

BELL, William
Author, b. 27 October 1945, Toronto, Ontario, Canada

B., who has taught English at both the secondary and post-secondary level since 1970, holds an M.A. in literature from the University of Toronto (1969) and an M.Ed. from the Ontario Institute for Studies in Education (1984). This provided a strong background in literature and writing before publishing his first novel, *Crabbe,* in 1986.

In this first novel, B., a member of Amnesty International and Greenpeace, used journal entries to relate the story, a technique he would use again later in YA novels. B.'s YA books are most often based in Canada, though he has also used China as the background for novels and PICTURE BOOKS. His interest in China may be from the time he spent teaching there. No matter the setting of the YA novel, the issues B. tackles are important—illiteracy, homosexuality, broken families, prejudice, and indiscriminate logging practices. Furthermore, "B.'s central characters [are] adolescent males involved in some aspect of self-discovery, a discovery which is usually related to their developing value structures."

In addition to his novels and picture books, B. edited *Contours,* an anthology of Canadian drama (1993) and contributed two essays on education in the field of writing to *Indirections,* a Canadian journal.

AWARDS: Ruth Schwartz Award for Excellence in Children's Literature, Belgium Award for Excellence in Children's Literature, and Ontario School Librarians' Award for Excellence, all 1990, all for *Forbidden City;* Manitoba Young Readers' Choice Award, for *Five Days of the Ghost;* Young Adult Canadian Book Award, Canadian Library Association, 2002, for *Stones.*

SELECT FURTHER WORKS: *Metal Head,* 1987; *The Cripples' Club,* 1988; *Death Wind,* 1989; *Five Days of the Ghost,* 1989; *Forbidden City,* 1990; *No Signature,* 1992; *Speak to the Earth,* 1994; *The Golden Disk,* 1995; *River, My Friend,* 1996; *Zack,* 1999; *Stones,* 2001; *Death Wind,* 2002.

BIBLIOGRAPHY: *Contemporary Authors Online,* 2002; *Contemporary Authors Online,* 2003, reproduced in *Biography Resource Center,* 2003, http://www.gale net.com/servlet/BioRC; "William Bell," *St. James Guide to Young Adult Writers,* 2nd ed., 1999, reproduced in Biography Resource Center, 2003, http://www.galenet.com/servlet/BioRC

SARA MARCUS

BENNETT, Cherie
Author, playwright, b. 6 October, 1960, Buffalo, New York

B. grew up in a writer's environment. Her father, Bennett Berman, wrote for television shows such as *The Twilight Zone* and *Route 66.* Her first novel, *With a Face like Mine,* was published in 1980 while she was studying religion at the University of Michigan. After college, B. worked in New York as a singer and dancer for several years before she focused seriously on writing. B.'s first SERIES of YA novels, Sunset Island, was introduced in 1991 and is set on an island off the coast of Maine. The series follows the efforts of three teens trying to find time for fun while working as au pairs during their summer break. A companion trilogy, Club Sunset Island, focuses on first-time pre-teen romances. B.'s Surviving Sixteen trilogy has been praised by reviewers for its humor and lively style. The 1993 novel *Did You Hear about Amber?* was inspired by B.'s personal experience and focuses

on a teen whose dreams of becoming a dancer are dashed when she is diagnosed with rheumatoid arthritis. *Good-Bye, Best Friend* (1993) about a girl with cystic fibrosis received several awards after it was produced for the stage as a play called *John Lennon and Me.* In 1994, B. debuted the *Wild Hearts* series that follows a teenage girl who moves to Nashville and with three friends forms a country music group that shares the series name. The Teen Angels series began in 1996 and was the first project created and co-authored with her husband, Jeff Gottesfeld. The series focuses on three older teens who meet untimely deaths and work to help people on earth deal with difficult life situations. B.'s Hope Hospital series carries a similar theme as three thirteen-year-old hospital volunteers learn about life, death, and boys. In her 1998 novel, *Life in the Fat Lane,* B. focuses on the unrealistic standards of beauty that affect teenagers. The story follows a former homecoming queen who must come to terms with an incurable metabolic disorder that causes her to gain one hundred pounds. *Searching for David's Heart* (1998) chronicles the life-changing journey of a pre-teen girl who goes searching for the recipient of her older brother's transplanted heart. *Zink* (1999) is based on the true story of a pre-teen who is fighting leukemia and her relationship with a herd of mystic zebras in Africa. *Anne Frank and Me* (2001), also co-authored with her husband, was originally produced as a play about modern American teens who come to better understand the HOLOCAUST. *A Heart Divided* (2004) follows a teen romance between a girl in Nashville and a boy in New York set against a controversy over the Confederate Flag in the boy's high school. B. has also written many of the Dawson's Creek novels based on the popular television series and is also working with her husband on the spin-off novels to the WB Network's *Smallville.* B. also writes a weekly newspaper column for teens called "Hey, Cherie!"

AWARDS: First Night award for best new play, RCI Festival of Emerging American Theater award, and Wing Walker Award, all 1993, and first place, Jackie White Memorial National Competition, 1995, all for *John Lennon and Me;* Children's Choice designation, Children's Book Council, and American Library Association distinction, both 1994, both for *Did You Hear about Amber?;* Dallas Shortfest! award, 1994, for *Sex and Rage in a Soho Loft;* Sholem Aleichem Commission award, 1994, and Bonderman Biennial award and First Night award, both 1995, all for *Anne Frank and Me;* New Visions/New Voices award, Kennedy Center for the Performing Arts, 1996, for *Cyra and Rocky;* New Visions/New Voices award, Kennedy Center for the Performing Arts, 1998, for *Searching for David's Heart;* first place, Jackie White Memorial Children's Playwriting Competition, 1998, for *Zink: The Myth, The Legend, The Zebra.*

FURTHER WORKS: *Girls in Love,* 1996; *Bridesmaids,* 1996; *Horror Ink* (America Online's first online reader-written young adult novel), 1997; *Trash* (with Jeff Gottesfeld), 1997–98; *Pageant,* 1998–99; *Searching for David's Heart: A Christmas Story,* 1998; *Love Him Forever,* 1999; *The Haunted Heart,* 1999; *And the Winner Is,* 1999; *The Wedding that Almost Wasn't,* 1999; *Mirror Image* (with Jeff Gottesfeld), 1999–2000; *University Hospital* (with Jeff Gottesfeld), 1999–2000; *Hot Trash,* 2004; *Trash Talk,* 2005. Other plays: *Honkey Tonk Angels, Sex and Rage in a Soho Loft, Cyra and Rocky, Zink and the So-Called Zebra, Searching for David's Heart.*

BIBLIOGRAPHY: *Contemporary Authors,* online, 2001; *Cherie Bennett.com,* online, 2003; Hipple, Ted, *Writers for Young Adults,* 1993; *Something about the Author.*

KRISTINE BULLER

BENNETT, James W.
Author, b. 1942, n.p.

B.'s interest in writing developed during an internship with a local newspaper during his college years in Illinois. He then taught creative writing at a community college until 1976. In 1975, however, B. was hospitalized with an emotional breakdown. During his recovery at a psychiatric hospital, B. began to write as an emotional outlet. B.'s experience with patients suffering from mental and emotional disorders resulted in his increased awareness of such disorders.

B.'s first novel, written years later, evolved from his acquaintance with a female patient who was withdrawn. B. worked on the novel for three years, researching female adolescents and recreating the patient's speech and mannerisms. The resulting novel, *I Can Hear the Mourning Dove* (1990), probes deeply into the mysteries of mental illness and has become a classroom curriculum choice in many high schools. *I Can Hear the Mourning Dove* tells the story of a gifted, sixteen-year-old girl named Grace who has suffered from periods of depression for years. Grace moves back and forth between school and the hospi-

tal, where she receives unexpected support from an antisocial delinquent named Luke.

B.'s next two novels were also successful. *Dakota Dream* (1994) is the story of Floyd, a teenage boy who finds himself lost among foster families, group homes, and social workers. Floyd persuades himself that he is really a misplaced Dakota Indian and embarks on a long journey to the Dakota tribe's Pine Ridge Reservation. In *The Squared Circle* (1995), a teenage boy uses basketball as an escape from his emotional problems. The novel received praise from critics for its insight into the character's emotional and intellectual awakening.

B.'s success with a TEEN audience led him to complete several more novels focusing on troubled youth. In addition, B. co-authored *Old Hoss* (2002), a fictional baseball biography of Charles Radbourn. Since 1990, B. has worked full time writing and making author visits to schools.

AWARDS: *I Can Hear the Mourning Dove*: ALA Best Book Young Adults, *Publisher's Weekly's* 1990's Ten Best Young Adult Books list; *Dakota Dream:* ALA Best Book for Young Adults and Best Books for Reluctant Readers: 1995 *Voice of Youth Advocate's* Finest Young Adult Novel, *The Squared Circle.*

FURTHER WORKS: *The Flex of the Thumb,* 1996; *Blue Star Rapture,* 1998; *Plunking Reggie Jackson,* 2001; *Faith Wish,* 2003.

BIBLIOGRAPHY: *Contemporary Authors,* vol. 158, 1998; www.jamesbennett.com

JODI PILGRIM

BERG, Elizabeth
Author, b. 2 December 1948, St. Paul, Minnesota

B. began to write as soon as she could hold a pencil and has been writing ever since. However, the rejection of her first submission at the age of nine caused her to wait twenty-five years to submit her next piece. She worked as a waitress, singer, chicken washer, information clerk, and registered nurse before her writing career began to take off when she entered and won a *Parents* magazine essay contest.

B.'s award-winning first novel *Durable Goods* (1993) follows the life of "army brat" Katie, a twelve-year-old whose mother died of cancer, leaving her to cope with an abusive father. In a *School Library Journal* review, Susan Woodcock states, "Katie is an endearing and persistent heroine, and Berg's prose borders on the poetic. This is an easy read, but its haunting images of coming of age are sure to remain with young adults." Although B. did not intend to write a sequel to *Durable Goods,* she missed the original characters and consequently wrote *Joy School* (1997), in which Katie experiences her first romantic fantasies and relationships and *True to Form* (2002), in which Katie lives with her dad and new stepmother and struggles with difficult choices characteristic of adolescence.

B. is known for giving life to the voices of women and for her honesty. Her novels take on numerous real-life issues, from challenging parent-child relationships to a woman's love for a gay man, to struggles with marriage, family, and illness. In *Book Magazine* (1999), B. says, "I didn't set out to write about anything other than to try to put out what was in my heart and soul, but it seems as though the focus is always on relationships and women's issues. And I guess if I had to be categorized, I wouldn't mind that."

In an interview with *The Book Report* (2000), B. stated that she believes writers are born with a fire in them creating a need to write. She writes most every weekday for up to four hours and feels as if she becomes the characters that she writes about in a process that is as much acting as writing. She describes her writing of dialogue as typing what she hears, as though she were eavesdropping on conversations. B. draws from her own experiences. For example, she used her nursing experience when writing about a coma patient in *Range of Motion* (1995) and says that there is a lot of herself in the character of Katie in *Joy School.* While B. occasionally has several ideas simultaneously, she focuses on writing one novel at a time. As a full-time writer, she describes her participation in a writer's group as a way to socialize, to hear her work read aloud by someone else, and to gain support. B. describes writing as the best job in the world—she works whenever she feels like it and the process is more like play than work.

AWARDS: ALA Best Books for YA 1994 for *Durable Goods;* ALA Best Books for YA 1998 for *Joy School;* ALA Best Books of the Year for *Durable Goods* (1993) and *Joy School* (1997). New England Book Award for Fiction for her body of work (1997). Finalist for the American Booksellers Book of the Year for *Talk Before Sleep* (published 1994, finalist 1996).

FURTHER WORKS: *Family Traditions: Celebrations for Holidays and Everyday,* 1992; *The Pull of the Moon,* 1996; *What We Keep,* 1998; *Escaping into the Open: The Art of Writing True,* 1999; *Until the Real Thing Comes Along,* 1999; *Open House,* 2000; *Never Change,* 2001; *Ordinary Life: Stories,* 2002; *Say When,* 2003; *The Art of Mending,* 2004; *The Year of Pleasures: A Novel,* 2005. Contributor to periodicals including *Good Housekeeping, Ladies' Home Journal, New York Times* magazine, *Parents, Redbook,* and *Woman's Day.*

BIBLIOGRAPHY: *Contemporary Authors Online,* Gale, 2002, www.galenet.com; *The Book Report,* August 18, 2000 interview, www.bookreporter.com; "Elizabeth Berg's Writing Life—How Sweet It is," *Book Magazine,* September/October 1999, www.bookmagazine.com; Meet the Writers—Elizabeth Berg, www.barnesandnoble.com

PATRICIA BRICKER

BERRY, James
Author, b. 1925, Jamaica

B.'s lyrical writing celebrates the Caribbean way of life and melodic language; it promotes pride and pleasure for one's culture. The author, reared in a coastal town in Jamaica, was exposed to a world in which a person's worth was deemed by the color of his skin. He grew up reading books about the lives of children in the UK, never encountering positive literature about West Indian people and their heritage. After spending time working at a comprehensive school in London, B. realized the need for books that promote Caribbean culture positively without a sense of inferiority.

The award-winning author lived in America for four years during World War II and was horrified by the country's attitude towards blacks. Although he returned to Jamaica for a few years, B. eventually immigrated to England because of the lack of career opportunities. He worked in London to educate himself and remained in the field of telegraphy until his job was eliminated. The money he received from his state pension allowed B. to devote himself wholeheartedly to his writing. It was not until he completed several volumes of POETRY for adults that the writer decided to focus on works that would expose West Indian heritage to young readers.

A Thief in the Village and Other Stories (1987), his first book for teenage readers, captures the literary merit of the commonplace in West Indian life, demonstrating that there were stories to be told within these people's experiences. The main themes throughout these SHORT STORIES are acceptance and fear of rejection, although B. gives them a special Caribbean twist. He reveals the lifestyles and speech patterns of his people in works such as *The Girls of Yanga Marshall* (1987) and *The Future-telling Lady and Other Stories* (1993). Taking information from B.'s childhood experiences, the books embrace local speech patterns and share, with pride, both folklore and local life. The inclusion of words from the Creole language adds to the cadence of B.'s writing, which has been praised by *School Library Journal* as both "poetic" and "onomatopoeic."

In 1992, B. wrote *Ajeemah and His Son,* his first novel, in which he explores the slave trade between Africa and Jamaica. B. says that, up until this publication, his work did not address how the black West Indian culture came to exist; such an explanation was essential to both his heritage and the historical literature of the Caribbean. In the novel, a son and his father are kidnapped by slave traders and transported in shackles to Jamaica. After their permanent separation, father and son experience differing outcomes of their captive lives. Their emotions and painful reactions to their new stations as sugar plantation workers are recounted, an impressive feat considering that B.'s story "cover[s] thirty-three years [in] a mere eighty-eight pages." Once again, B.'s treatment of West Indian history features the poetic prose for which he is often praised.

In both poetry and prose, B. uses the beautiful rhythm of words to represent his Caribbean home and people. Music infuses his poetry, as can be seen by the rap influences in *Everywhere Faces Everywhere: Poems* (1997). His gift with language captures the attention of readers from childhood to maturity.

AWARDS: 1981 National Poetry Competition Award, "Fantasy of an African Boy; *A Thief in the Village and Other Stories:* 1987 Grand Prix Smarties Prize for Children's Books, 1988 Coretta Scott King Honor Book; 1989 Signal Poetry Award, *When I Dance;* 1990 Chomondeley Award for Poetry; *Ajeemah and His Son:* 1993 Coretta Scott King Honor Book, 1993 Boston Globe–Horn Book Award.

SELECT FURTHER WORKS: *Fractured Circles,* 1979; *Chain of Days,* 1985; *Anancy-Spiderman,* 1988; *Spiderman-Anancy,* 1989; *When I Dance,* 1991; *Rough Sketch Beginning,* 1996; *Hot Earth Cold Earth,* 1996; *Don't Leave an Elephant to GO and Chase a Bird,* 1996; *First Palm Trees,* 1997; *Isn't My Name Magical?: Sister and Brother Poems,* 1999; *Around the World in 80 Poems,* 2001; *A Nest Full of Stars: Poems,* 2004.

BIBLIOGRAPHY: Miller-Lachman, Lyn, review of *The Future-Telling Lady and Other Stories, School Library Journal,* February 1993; Review of *Everywhere Faces Everywhere, Kirkus Reviews,* March 15, 1997; *Something about the Author,* vol. 110, 2000.

RACHEL WITMER

BETHANCOURT, Ernesto
Author, b. 2 October 1932, Brooklyn, New York

Born Thomas Ernesto Passailaigue, B. changed his name to Tom Paisley. After attending The City College and serving in the U.S. Navy (1950–54), B. worked at a variety of jobs, including singer, musician, composer, lyricist, actor, critic and in the 1950s as an undercover claims investigator for the New York office of Lloyd's of London. Since 1957, B. has fulfilled his dream of avoiding a 9 to 5 job, except for thirteen months, during which time he held a position he hated as an assistant copy chief at an advertising agency. His best-known and most successful display of creative energies is in the field of YA LITERATURE, with over twenty novels published as T. Ernesto Bethancourt between 1975 and 1984.

The birth of B.'s daughter led B. to write his first novel. "When my first daughter was born, I thought, 'My G-d, she could get to be a teenager and, if for some reason we couldn't talk or I was dead or something equally fascinating, she might wonder what I was all about,' and I started an AUTOBIOGRAPHY" he recalled. His work as a musician led indirectly to his first submission being published as the novel *New York City, Too Far from Tampa Blues* (1975).

"Just as B. did not set out to be a novelist, neither did he set out to write literature for young adults. However, because he was writing his first work for his daughter to read when she became a teenager, B. naturally wrote it in a style which a teenager would find easy to read and enjoyable." The success of this "mistake" led him to write more in the same genre. Despite the success of his first, second, third, and fourth novels, it was not until he moved to California in 1977 that B. changed his career path. "Until I came out here, my primary living was as a performer/entertainer. But I came out to California and found that what people pay outrageous money to hear in New York City, they wouldn't go around the corner to hear in California. . . . if I was to survive, I had better write more books."

B. discovered another advantage to writing novels—he could "present his political belief and values without doing so in a condescending manner." B. "defines the essential themes which form the basic structure for his work as 'basic values'—among these are honesty, belief in truth, and belief in working through the system. 'And if the system doesn't work, demanding to know why instead of attempting to destroy it—that's tied to belief in the system.'" In all of his novels these sentiments are expressed—sometimes subtly and sometimes overtly "in the form of direct elements of the plot." Despite his strong political beliefs, "B. does not set about to convert anyone to his political doctrine through his writing. In fact, he insists that the most important thing he hopes his readers will get out of his novels is 'a good time.'"

Two of B.'s works have been adapted for television: *New York City, Too Far from Tampa Blues* by NBC in 1979 and *The Dog Days of Arthur Cane* (1976) by ABC in 1984.

AWARDS: *Tune in Yesterday* was one of 100 YA titles selected for the second YALSA Best of the Best List: The Best of the Best Books (selections from 1960 to 1974).

FURTHER WORKS: *The Mortal Instruments,* 1977; *Tune in Yesterday,* 1978; *Dr. Doom: Superstar,* 1978; *Instruments of Darkness,* 1979; *Nightmare Town,* 1979; *Doris Fein: Superspy,* 1980; *Quartz Boyar,* 1980; *Phantom of the Casino,* 1981; *The Mad Samurai,* 1981; *Where the Deer and the Canteloupe Play,* 1981; *Deadly Aphrodite,* 1982; *Murder Is No Joke,* 1982; *T.H.U.M.B.b.: The Hippest Underground Marching Band in Brooklyn,* 1982; *Dead Heat at Long Beach,* 1983; *The Tomorrow Connection,* 1984; *The Great Computer Dating Caper,* 1984; *Legacy of Terror,* 1984; *The Me Inside of Me,* 1985.

BIBLIOGRAPHY: "Tom Paisley." U*X*L Junior DIS-Covering Authors. U*X*L, 1998. Reproduced in Discovering Collection. Farmington Hills, Mich.: Gale Group. October, 2001. http://galenet.galegroup.com/servlet/DC

RACHEL WITMER

BEYOND HARRY POTTER: MORE WIZARDS, WITCHES AND MAGIC SPELLS

Harry's back—much to the delight of readers of all ages all over the world. J. K. ROWLING hasn't lost her

magic touch. She continues to challenge and delight her readers with the further adventures of Harry and friends. But be advised. Harry is getting older. He's now fifteen and he acts like it. He's got TEEN ISSUES and concerns at the same time he has to continue using his magical abilities to survive.

If you have not yet read Volume 5—*Harry Potter and the Order of the Phoenix*—you're in for a treat. If you have, you know exactly how young fans feel who just can't get enough Harry.

NoveList has already provided Harry fans with some excellent resources. Check out Deanna Hanson's wonderful introduction to the Harry Potter SERIES: "Hurray for Harry Potter!" Why are we so wild about Harry? And where can Harry Potter fans turn to get their magic fix while they wait for the next Harry Potter book to appear? Many wonderful series and fun-filled individual titles are annotated here (with grade levels).

Still want more Harry? Then be sure to read Katherine Bradley Johnson's excellent article: "The Wide Appeal of Harry Potter." She shows you how to find "Harry-like" books in three different categories:

(1) Family Readalikes that adults will enjoy reading to their kids or with them.
(2) Titles for adults and young adults that might extend the pleasure of reading Harry.
(3) Adult FANTASY stories which go beyond, i.e., are truly not children's books yet offer similar kinds of pleasure for adult readers.

From *Bed-Knobs and Broomsticks* to *The Once and Future King,* here are potential Potter-pleasing read-alikes for all ages. Last but most certainly not least, don't pass up Sally Estes's annotated list of Harry Potter read-alikes, "Wizards in Training." So many HARRY POTTER read-alikes to explore—thank heavens! And there's always Harry to reread—as many times as you like, followed, of course, by the opportunity to indulge in some of these "Wizardly treats."

So what's left? Why a fourth article for *NoveList* on the theme of Potter Mania? Well, why not? There are old classics and new fantasies that are not covered by these articles. Harry is getting older; his adventures are getting darker—understandable, since he's started losing friends in his struggles against the forces of Lord Voldemart. So Harry fans are ready to handle some darker, edgier fantasies.

What has Harry Potter done for those of us who love fantasy? Revived fantasy as a popular genre. Encouraged new authors to contribute to this genre. Revitalized fantasy series with new contributions by authors who had gone on to other works. Resurrected out-of-print titles—much to the delight of those of us who were unable to pass favorites on to the next generation.

So, thank you, Harry. And thank you J. K. Rowling. Who will truly be forever with us—in so very many ways. And thank you to all the other wonderful authors out there who are creating rich, complex, fun-filled fantasies or dark, threatening, deliciously scary battles between good and evil. We turn from the latest Harry Potter and cry, "More. We want more." And you're there with us, with titles like the ones on the following list. And last but not least, a very special thank you to all fantasy readers everywhere. You have taken Harry Potter and the fantasy genre to your hearts. Supply and demand is alive and well in the fantasy realm right now. Long may that special Harry Potter spark continue. Long may the forces of good battle the forces of evil and prevail. Long may we enjoy the benefits of this publishing phenomenon that is—Harry Potter.

And now for the list of Harry Potter read-alikes:

AVI.
The author of the 2003 Newbery-winning *Crispin: The Cross of Lead* gives us the reality of the Middle Ages, not the magic. For magical elements, try:
Bright Shadows (Grades 3–7)
Morwenna has five wishes. After using four on behalf of the citizens of her country, she strikes out on her own, while she tries to decide what to do with that last wish.
Poppy, Poppy and Rye, and *Poppy's Return.* (Grades 3–7)
For animal-fantasy fans, the adventures of a young deer mouse.

L. Frank Baum. *The Wizard of Oz series* (Grades 3–7). Who says the classics can't be fun? We've all watched "The Wizard of Oz" movie over and over again. But this is just the tip of the iceberg in Baum's fantasy opus. The adventures of Dorothy and Toto, the Tin Woodman, the Scarecrow, and the Cowardly Lion don't stop with *The Wonderful Wizard of Oz.* Find out what happens next in the following: *The Marvelous Land of Oz, Ozma of Oz, Dorothy and the Wizard in Oz, The Road to Oz, The Emerald City of Oz, The Patchwork Girl of Oz, Tik-Tok of Oz, The Scarecrow of Oz, The Lost Princess of Oz, The Tin Woodman of Oz, The Magic of Oz.*

John Bellairs. Lemony Snicket and *Artemis Fowl* fans should enjoy the threat to the world in these darker fantasy series.
The Dark Secret of Weatherend (Grades 3–7).
There's a diary that contains mysterious writings. A young boy discovers these are plans to turn the world into an icy wasteland. And now someone has activated these plans. Sequel: *The Mansion in the Mist*
The House with a Clock in Its Walls (Grades 3–7).
An orphan boy comes to live with his Uncle, who is a witch determined to save the world from destruction. Sequels (by Brad Strickland): *John Bellair's Lewis Barnavelt in The Specter from the Magician's Museum, The Beast under the Wizard's Bridge, The Tower at the End of the Road, The Whistle, The Grove and the Ghost.*

L. M. Boston *The Children of Green Knowe.* (Grades 4–7).
Another classic to delight a new generation. Green Knowe is an ancient house inhabited by three children, who were alive in the 17th Century.

Grace CHETWIN. *Tales of Gom in the Legends of Ulm* (Grades 5–8).
Gom is the son of a poor woodcutter who raised him alone after his wizard mother abandoned her family. Old enough to strike out on his own, Gom discovers he has his own special powers, which make him the key to saving the world of Ulm from destruction. *Gom on Windy Mountain, The Riddle and the Rune, The Crystal Stair, The Starstone.*

Climo, Shirley. *Magic and Mischief: Tales from Cornwall* (Grades 3–7).
Before it was inhabited by humans, Cornwall was home to a host of mysterious creatures: giants, Spriggans, Knackers, and changelings. This collection of shivery tales introduces these denizens of the moors, mountains, and seacoasts of Cornwall.

Colfer, Eoin. *Artemis Fowl Series* (Grades 5–8).
The adventures of an evil genius and mastermind criminal, who takes on the world of Faerie, and he's

only 12 years old. *Artemis Fowl, Artemis Fowl: The Arctic Incident, Artemis Fowl: The Eternity Code, Artemis Fowl: The Opal Deception.*

COOPER, Susan. *The Boggart* (Grades 4–7). The author of the acclaimed *Dark Is Rising* series brings a Boggart, a mischievous spirit that had lived in an ancient castle in Scotland for centuries, to modern-day Toronto, with explosive results. Sequel: *The Boggart and the Monster.*

COVILLE, Bruce. *Unicorn Chronicles* (Grades 5–8). What can be more magical than a series about unicorns, and the young girl sent by her grandmother to protect them? *Into the Land of the Unicorns, The Song of the Wanderer.*

DAHL, Roald. *James and the Giant Peach: A Children's Story* (Grades 3–7). First, James escapes from his two wicked aunts. Then he embarks on a series of adventures, accompanied by six giant insects he meets inside a giant peach. Sound fantastic enough?

FLETCHER, Susan. *Dragon Series* (Grades 5–9). The dragons are in danger, and it's up to a few young people with special talents to save them: *Dragon's Milk, The Flight of the Dragon Kyn, Sign of the Dove.* If you enjoyed this author's dragon books, try her retelling of the story of Shahrazad. *Shadow Spinner* (Grades 5–9). Seen through the eyes of crippled Marjan (13), whose passion for collecting stories leads her to the Sultan's harem and a chance to save the life of his lovely wife.

Furlong, Monica. *Wise Child* (Grades 5 +). After her parents abandon her, Wise Child (9) goes to live with the witch woman Juniper and receive instruction in the use of herbs and magic. Sequels: *Juniper* and *Colman.*

Garner, Alan. *The Weirdstone of Brisingamen* (Grades 7 +). Susan and Colin are plagued by goblins, witches, and other ghastly creatures, until their connection to the stone in her bracelet becomes known. Susan possesses the magical Firefrost which must be returned to the good wizard Cadellin to protect the world from evil powers.

HADDIX, Margaret Peterson. *Just Ella* (Grades 7–9). FAIRY-TALE retellings are always fun. And this one is no exception. So much for living happily ever after! Ella discovers that Prince Charming's proposal ensnares her in a suffocating tangle of palace rules and royal etiquette from which she absolutely must escape.

Ibbotson, Eva. The author of the immensely popular *The Secret of Platform 13* continues to please young fans with magical works like the following: *Dial-a-Ghost* (Grades 3–6). A young British orphan is protected from the diabolical plans of an evil guardian by a family of ghosts. *Island of the Aunt* (Grades 4–8). Several sisters decide they need to kidnap children to bring to their secluded island home. Extra hands are needed for all the work involved with caring for their unusual assortment of sea creatures. *Which Witch* (Grades 5–9). The Great Wizard Arriman needs a child to follow in his footsteps of Loathing Light and Blighting the Beautiful. But which witch will he select to be his wife?

JARVIS, Robin. *The Deptford Mice Trilogy* (Grades 6 +). Daring mice battle evil, including the Dark God worshiped by enemy rats. *The Dark Portal, The Crystal Prison, The Final Reckoning.*

Jones, Diana Wynne. She writes of Enchanters and minstrels and alternate worlds and magic and mayhem and marvels galore. And don't forget humor—so much humor. *The Chronicles of Chrestomanci* (Grades 5 +). These are the adventures of the Enchanter Chrestomanci, who uses his nine lives to control the practice of magic in infinite parallel universes: *Charmed Life, The Lives of Christopher Chant, Witch Week, The Magicians of Caprona.* When their father, a traveling minstrel, is killed, his three children inherit a lute-like instrument, the cwidder, that has more than just magical powers. The adventures of *The Dalemark Quartet* (Grades 7 +): *Cart and Cwidder, Drowned Ammet, The Spell Coats, Crown of Dalemark.*

Polly, nineteen, has two sets of memories, one real-life of her school days and her parents' divorce, the other of heroic adventures after she meets the cellist Thomas Lynn. Her story is told in *Fire and Hemlock* (Grades 7 +). Sophie was just trying to live a peaceful life selling hats. She didn't mean to get on the wrong side of a wicked witch. Suddenly she's an old woman with nowhere to turn, except Wizard Howl in *Howl's Moving Castle* (Grades 6 +). Sequel: *Castle in the Air.*

Lemony Snicket. *See* Snicket, Lemony.

LEVINE, Gail Carson. *The Princess Tales* (Grades 3–6.) More humorous fairy-tale retellings: *The Fairy's Mistake.*

   Perrault's tale of the fairy Ethelinda and the twin sisters: *The Princess Test.* What else could it be, but Hans Christian Andersen's *The Princess and the Pea? Princess Sonora and the Long Sleep:* you guessed it—*Sleeping Beauty.*
The Princess Tales: Cinderellis and the Glass Hill, For Biddle's Sake, The Fairy's Return: Volume Two.

Levy, Robert. *Clan of the Shape-Changers* (Grades 6–8).
Susan, sixteen, can change into any kind of animal. Now she must battle a greedy shaman attempting to steal this secret from her people and then destroy them.

LUBAR, David. *Wizards of the Game* (Grades 5–8).
The humorous adventures of a middle-school boy who is obsessed with a fantasy role-playing game, until some real wizards show up needing his help.

Machale, D. J. *Pendragon Book One: The Merchant of Death* (Grades 5–8). First in a series, in which a fourteen-year-old boy is swept into an alternate world at war, and he does not know how to fight. Sequels: *The Lost City of Fear, The Never War, The Reality Bug, Black Water, The Rivers of Zadaa.*

MCKILLIP, Patricia A. *The Forgotten Beasts of Eld* (Grades 7 +). A wizard, used to the company of legendary beasts, must cope with the sorrows and delights of the human world when a baby comes into her care.

MORRIS, Gerald. *Arthurian Legends* (Grades 5–8). The adventures of Sir Gawain and some of his peers, with a distinctly humorous slant: *The Squires Tale, The Squire, His Knight and His Lady, The Savage Damsel and the Dwarf, Parsifal's Page, The Ballad*

of Sir Dinadan, The Princess, the Crone, and the Dung-Cart Knight, The Lioness and her Knight.

NICHOLSON, William. *The Wind on Fire Trilogy* (Grades 5–8). Kestrel and her brother Bowman have their hands full trying to save the people of Amaranth, from stifling rules and regulations to invasion and enslavement, before they travel in search of their promised homeland: *The Wind Singer: An Adventure; Slaves of the Mastery; Firesong.*

Nimmo, Jenny. *Midnight for Charlie Bone* (Grades 4–6). Since he can hear people in photographs, Charlie is sent to Bloor's Academy for gifted children and must say farewell to his happy, ordinary life. Sequels: *Charlie Bone and the Time Twister; Charlie Bone and the Invisible Boy; Charlie Bone and the Castle of Mirrors.*

NIX, Garth. *Abhorsen Trilogy* (Grades 7 +). The adventures of Sabriel, daughter of the Abhorsen, a Necromancer who can raise the dead and control them with his bells. Evil is loose in her world, and she will need the help of a Daughter of the Clayr to survive: *Sabriel, Liraiel: Daughter of the Clayr, Abhorsen.*

Paolini, Christopher. *Eragon* (Grades 7 +). Young Eragon finds a blue stone that hatches into a dragon. And so his adventures begin. Sequel: *The Eldest.*

PIERCE, Meredith Ann. *The Firebringer Trilogy* (Grades 7 +). The prince of the unicorn goes on a quest for fire in a distant land of two-footed creatures, hoping in this way to achieve his destiny and save his people from their enemies: *The Birth of the Firebringer, Dark Moon, The Son of Summer Stars.*

PIERCE, Tamora. This prolific author writes in quartets for the most part, full of strong young women and magic and mythical creatures and knights and daring deeds and an occasional dab of romance: *The Circle Opens* (Grades 6–10). This sequel quartet to *Circle of Magic* continues the adventures of Sandry, Tris, Daja, and Briar, now teenagers and still practicing magic: *Magic Steps, Street Magic, Cold Fire, Shatterglass.* Daine, thirteen, discovers that she has more than just a special bond with animals, which is why the Mage Numair enlists her help in the battle against the immortal creatures attacking the kingdom of Tortall. Her adventures can be found in *The Immortals* (Grades 6–10): *Wild Magic, Wolf Speaker, Emperor Mage, The Realm of Gods.* Keladry of Mindalen wants more than anything in the world to become a knight. But Keladry is a girl—a girl not willing to give up her dream in *The Protector of the Small* seires (Grades 6–10): *First Test, Page, Squire, Lady Knight.* Alanna, determined to become a knight in spite of the fact that she is a girl, disguises herself as a boy and begins the training that will eventually make her the first female knight in the kingdom. This was the author's first quartet: *Song of the Lioness.* (Grades 7 +): *Alanna: The First Adventure; In the Hand of the Goddess; The Woman Who Rides like a Man; Lioness Rampant.* And don't miss the adventures of Alanna's teenage daughter: *Trickster's Choice* and *Trickster's Queen.*

Pope, Elizabeth. *The Perilous Gard* (Grades 5–9). In 1558, while imprisoned in a remote castle, a young girl gets involved with the people in an underground labyrinth who are the last practitioners of druidic magic.

Sherman, Josepha. The world of Faerie combined with romance—how could that be anything but a winning combination? *Child of Faerie, Child of Earth* (Grades 7 +). Percinet, half-human son of the Queen of Faerie, falls in love with a human girl and must leave his home in the realm of magic to protect her from her stepmother, a cruel sorceress. *Windleaf* (Grades 7 +). In 1510 Thierry, the Count of Foretterre, falls in love. Unfortunately, his beloved is the daughter of the cold-hearted Lord of Faerie.

Snicket, Lemony. *A Series of Unfortunate Events* (Grades 4–7). The adventures (or rather misadventures) of the three Baudelaire children, orphaned at an early age and in constant danger from the plots and schemes of the dastardly Count Olaf, who will do anything to get his hands on their fortune: *The Bad Beginning, The Reptile Room, The Wide Window, The Miserable Mill, The Austere Academy, The Ersatz Elevator, The Village, The Hostile Hospital, The Carnivorous Carnival, The Slippery Slope, The Grim Grotto.*

SPRINGER, Nancy. *Red Wizard* (Grades 4–7). Ryan is accidentally whisked away from his seventh-grade

life by a wizard trying to find the perfect color red. Which gets him away from his demanding father just when the wizard is facing a crisis with a rebel warlock.

Strickland, Brad. *Dragon's Plunder* (Grades 5–8). Kidnapped by pirates because of his ability to whistle up the wind, Jamie, fifteen, must help their leader, a living corpse, find the dragon of Windrose Island—or else.

Travers, P. L. Mary Poppins series (Grades 3–7). The adventures of that wonderful English nanny, who can slide up banisters and introduce her young charges to people and experiences they would never have imagined in their wildest dreams: *Marry Poppins, Mary Poppins Comes Back, Mary Poppins Opens the Door, Mary Poppins in the Park, Mary Poppins in Cherry Tree Lane, Mary Poppins and the Home Next Door.*

Ure, Jean. *The Wizard in the Woods* (Grades 4–6). Ben-Mussy is a second-class junior wizard who bungles a spell during his Junior Wizard exams. Now he's lost in a wood somewhere, and his adventure is just beginning.

VANDE VELDE, Vivian. *Heir Apparent* (Grades 6–9). Giannine, fourteen, is trapped in a virtual-reality game in which she must fight dragons and ghosts in a quest to find the ring and the stolen treasure. If she doesn't succeed, she will die—both outside the game as well as inside.

Winthrop, Elizabeth. *The Castle in the Attic.* William's gift of a toy castle, complete with silver knight, leads to an adventure involving magic and a quest. Sequel: *The Battle for the Castle*

YEP, Laurence. Dragon series (Grades 7 +). Shimmer, the dragon, joins a monkey wizard, a reformed witch, and two humans on a quest to mend the magic cauldron needed to repair the dragon's home and winds up in the war against the evil Boneless King: *Dragon of the Lost Sea, Dragon Steel, Dragon Cauldron, Dragon War.*

YOLEN, Jane. *The Dragon's Boy: A Tale of Young King Arthur.* (Grades 3–7). Artos is a young orphan boy being raised by Sir Ectos. One day he stumbles into the cave of a lonely dragon who takes the boy under his wing and makes him the Pendragon, the son of the dragon, first step on a path he never dreamed could be his.

BONNIE L. KUNZEL

BIBLIOTHERAPY

Bibliotherapy is the practice of using literature to help people cope with and better understand their problems. There are different types of bibliotherapy and different levels of application. When the term was coined around the turn of the century, it typically referred to using literature as a way to elicit a reaction from the reader, whether positive or negative. Modern bibliotherapy tends to be more interactive, asking readers to reflect on the text through activities such as journal writing or group discussions. The educational and scientific communities often separate bibliotherapy into two different applications: clinical and developmental. Clinical bibliotherapy is utilized by trained therapists to help individuals with serious social or mental problems. Developmental bibliotherapy is used by teachers and librarians working with young people who are grappling with typical childhood and adolescent issues.

The practice of trying to instruct children and teens through books is as old as the genre of youth literature itself. Before the 1850s, books for youth consisted of didactic primers and pamphlets, often religious in nature, that emphasized strong moral convictions and severe punishment for transgressors. Literature for youth took a more light-hearted turn in the latter half of the 19th century with the publication of such adventurous and sentimental books as *Ivanhoe, The Wizard of Oz,* and *Little Women.* While more secular than their predecessors, these books still highlighted the importance of morals and glossed over the real-life problems of children and teens. It was only in 1950, with the publication of J. D. Salinger's *The Catcher in the Rye,* that books for young people tackled the messiness of life in a morally ambivalent way. Following Salinger's example, YA LITERATURE began exploring such previously taboo topics as peer pressure and drug use, divorce, and gender issues. This embracing of issue-propelled plotlines, often in a coming-of-age format, made YA literature a perfect candidate for bibliotherapy.

TEENAGERS can benefit a great deal from bibliotherapy. When adolescents interact with quality YA literature, they gain insight and perspective about their own problems. Bibliotherapy in the classroom or library creates a supportive medium for discussing those problems among peers. If a student is having a problem similar to that of a character in the book being discussed, they can safely comment on that problem by attributing it to the character instead of themselves. Teens can also learn to emphathize with others by realizing that their personal problems are not entirely unique. Bibliotherapy is also a powerful preventive tool. By modeling themselves on fictional teen protagonists, students can become better equipped to recognize similar problems in their own lives and make more informed choices about how to resolve them.

There is a consensus among experts that there are three steps to the bibliotherapeutic process for the reader: identification, catharsis, and insight. Identification occurs when the similarities between the character and the reader are clearly evident to the reader. Once readers identify with, and develop empathy for, the characters, they can begin to express their emotional response to the text. Catharsis comes about through this expression and can be communicated verbally, in group discussions or in journal entries, or in non-verbal ways, such as creating an art project based on the book, or performing a skit taken from a particular scene. Finally, by using discussion or feedback to further explore reader's emotional response, the educator can gain further insight in the issues raised by the text.

The most essential part of any bibliotherapeutic process is the selection of the book. Needless to say, practitioners of bibliotherapy must be familiar with a broad range of authors and topics covered in YA LITERATURE. There are many scholarly journals, articles, and books that include annotated booklists for educators new to bibliotherapy and unsure where to begin. For example, *The Journal of Adolescent and Adult Literacy* frequently carries articles about literature that teachers and librarians find helpful. They show that students will report that their friend has a problem, as shown in Mel Glenn's *My Friend's Got this Problem, Mr. Candler.* When selecting a book for either a group or individual bibliotheraputic project, the educator should consider several factors, including the reading level of the text, the quality of solutions that are offered, how realistically the issues in the novel are depicted, and, finally, the overall tone of the book. It is important that students feel that the chosen text is objective and not judgmental about issues close to their own experiences. After selecting the book, the educator will want to lead the students in guided reading, or through reading aloud. This allows the class or the individual to experience the book together with their peers or with the educator. The educator is also available if any of the students should have a strong emotional response to the text during the reading. Finally, the teacher or librarian will want to facilitate a follow-up discussion or activity centered on the text. This is often considered by the scientific community to be the one factor that separates bibliotherapy from reader's advisory, the recommending of books based on a reader's interest or reading level. This follow-up step insures that students have experienced the intended emotional response to the book and have expressed it through discussion, writing, or art.

Although bibliotherapy can be helpful in assisting teens with the common problems of adolescence, it has limitations. Teenagers may become defensive—projecting their own motivations onto characters thereby justifying their own behavior. Or they may fail to empathize with the characters altogether. The facilitator of the process may not have a sufficient grasp on the range of literature available to make an informed recommendation or may not be equipped to lead a discussion due to a lack of knowledge about the developmental stages of adolescence. Trained therapists and counselors are often wary of teachers and librarians undertaking bibliotherapy, fearing that these educators are not prepared for the range of emotional responses that a text may elicit from a group of teens. Therefore, it is best for educators to avoid topics that may induce traumatic responses they are not trained to deal with, such as abuse, rape, or violent crime. Common adolescent problems such as relationships, physical appearance, peer pressure, race, class, and economic issues are more appropriate for the classroom or library.

Bibliotherapy can be a powerful tool for teachers and librarians as they seek different ways of mining the rich subject material provided by young adult literature. This genre, with its thoughtful explorations of teenage feelings and motivations, is the perfect medium with which to discover the benefits of bibliotherapy with adolescents. As long as teachers and librarians keep in mind the limitations of bibliotherapy, the process can be a satisfactory one for both students and educators.

BIBLIOGRAPHY: Abdullah, Mardziah Hayati. "Bibliotherapy." *ERIC Clearinghouse on Reading, English and Communication* 177 (December 2002) eric.indiana .edu/ieo/digests/d177.html; Bettelheim, B. *The Uses of Enchantment,* 1976; Dixey, Brenda and Andrea D'Angelo. "Using Literature to Build Emotionally Healthy Adolescents. *Classroom Leadership Online* 3 (March 2000); www.ascd.org/readingroom/classlead/ 0003/1march00.html; Forgan, James W. "Using Bibliotherapy to Teach Problem Solving." *Intervention in School & Clinic* 38 (November 2002): 75–82; Hebert, Thomas P. "Meeting the Affective Needs of Bright Boys Through Bibliotherapy." *Roeper Review* 13 (June 1991): 207–212; Hebert, Thomas P. and Richard Kent. "Nurturing Social and Emotional Development in Gifted Teenagers Through Young Adult Literature." *Roeper Review* 22 (April 2000): 167– 171; Myracle, Lauren. "Molding the Minds of the Young: The History of Bibliotherapy as Applied to Children and Adolescents." *The ALAN Review* 22 (Winter 1995); Pardeck, Jean A. and John T. Pardeck. *Young People with Problems: A Guide to Bibliotherapy,* 1984; Pardeck, John T. "Using Literature to Help Adolescents Cope with Problems." *Adolescence* 29 (Summer 1994): 421–427; Schafer, E. D. *Exploring Harry Potter,* 2000.

JENNIFER HUBERT

BILLINGSLEY, Franny

Author, b. 3 July 1954, n.p.

B. grew up traveling all over the world, from Washington, D.C., to Yokohama, Princeton, Chicago, Copenhagen, and then back to Chicago. She spent a year attending the Cambridge (England) College of Arts and Technology, before coming back to the U.S. to attend the University of New Mexico. She took courses at the Institute of European Studies in Paris before finishing college at Tufts University. After getting her law degree from Boston University, B. did not settle down for long. After five years of practicing law, B. accepted the fact that she wasn't happy in her job while on a trip to visit her sister in Barcelona. Deciding to move there, B. brought all of her favorite books with her and while "reading and eating tapas," she realized her lifelong dream of becoming a writer. Upon returning to Chicago, B. began a twelve-year career as the children's book buyer for 57th Street Books, while continuing to write and teach fiction at the University of Chicago's Graham School and Columbia College in Chicago.

Focusing primarily on FANTASY novels, B.'s first book, *Well Wished* (1997), tells the story of a wishing well with mysterious powers that causes more problems than it solves. B.'s second novel, *The Folk Keeper* (1999), continues her tradition of writing strong female characters in hierarchical societies. Told in journal form, it is the story of a special young girl named Corinna Stonewall, who must disguise herself as a boy in order to be trained as a keeper of the mischievous folk creatures. Along the way, Corinna learns about herself, comes to understand her powers, and is able to find a place for herself in the world.

B. currently lives in Chicago with her husband Richard Pettengill and their two children, Miranda and Nathaniel.

AWARDS: *School Library Journal* Best Book of the Year (1997) for *Well Wished; Boston Globe–Horn Book Award* (2000) for *The Folk Keeper.*

BIBLIOGRAPHY: *Authors and Artists for Young Adults,* vol. 41, 2001; *Contemporary Authors,* online, 2001; *Something About the Author,* vol. 132, 2002; *Book Report,* vol. 19, 2001.

MEGAN PEARLMAN

BIOGRAPHY AND AUTOBIOGRAPHY FOR YOUNG ADULTS

Bio-graphy—the written story of a life. *Auto-biography*—the story of life written by the book's subject. From early in the history of the printed word, we have been endlessly fascinated with one another. The term *biography* was first used by John Dryden in a 1683 edition of *Plutarch's Parallel Lives,* which paired tales of famous Greeks and Romans and served as a model for biographical tales of heroes to admire and emulate. Contemporary biography and autobiography for teens tend to rely less on providing uplifting moral tales of instruction on the right way to behave; instead they layer the subject's story with details that reveal their sometimes flawed humanity—and because we can make a connection with these more realistic images, we can admire them more honestly and clearly.

"Every life has a story"—the tagline for the popular Biography cable channel—truly identifies the appeal of biography and autobiography for teen readers, the chance to walk in someone else's shoes and experience a life other than our own, to get answers to questions about the ways that people have navigated the passages of life, made choices, built character, and left a mark on the world. When they choose biography and autobiography, readers nurture their own seeds of potential, a yearning to make a connection outside of themselves and touch something of another person's inner life. These reading experiences expand views of diversity, make connections with another time and place, with circumstances, choices, consequences that impacted the subject's own time—and perhaps ours. Writing in *School Library Journal* Ed Sullivan said "the notion of becoming involved in the life of a real person always held more appeal for me than reading about a made-up character." He goes on to say that reading biographies allow teens to get to know a person, not just know about a person.

How do we evaluate biography and autobiography—look for a subject with enough depth to interest both author and reader; documented sources and further reading resources; accuracy of factual material, and clear indicators of an imagined dialogue; character development that reveals how the subject shaped his or her own life, demonstrating that things didn't "just happen" to them; less valuable and lasting biographies focus on current subjects of passing interest or impact; rather than original research, their content may be based on previously published works or publicist-produced materials; these works tend to sensationalize circumstances or adopt an adulatory tone that reveals no human flaws or imperfections (Nilsen and Donelson).

The importance of reading life stories is demonstrated in the number of titles recognized on recommended reading lists from the American Library Association, the International Reading Association, and the National Council of Teachers of English, as well as the number of such books that win literary awards, for example, Marc ARONSON's *Sir Walter Raleigh and the Quest for El Dorado* (2002), Elizabeth PARTRIDGE's *This Land Was Made for You and Me: The Life and Songs of Woody Guthrie* (2002), and Jack GANTOS's *Hole in My Life* (2002).

TEENS want to learn about someone admirable, for the struggle with all-too-human traits and flaws, to have an opportunity to live for a while in the subject's time, and recognize universal truths about what it means to be human. A good biography reveals its subject in depth—emotional and psychological, to reveal the essence of spirit and character.

There is a difference between biography and memoir—biography has a broad scope. It looks at the subject's entire life (or at least up to the time of publication for living subjects)—and biographies of living persons are often revised—Michael Jordan is a case in point, coming out of retirement from basketball several times. Despite the Library of Congress CIP (cataloging in publication) designation of "Authors, American, 20th century, biography" for Gary PAULSEN's *The Beet Fields* (2000), his fictional account of one unnamed character's sixteenth summer may build on incidents from Paulsen's own life, although it is not truly biographical. Jack Gantos's *Hole in My Life* (2002), an account of the adolescent mistakes that led to his writing career, contains biographical elements that fall short of a full autobiography by stopping at the time he took a new direction. Readers who first meet Anne FRANK through her diary entries can read more about her in full-length biographies like Mirjam Pressler's *Anne Frank: A Hidden Life* (1999) and Magdalena Alagna's *Anne Frank, Young Voice of the Holocaust* (2001). Couple these with Irene Gut Opdyke's powerful story of her experiences as a HOLOCAUST rescuer when she was not much older than the teens reading her story, *In My Hands: Memories of a Holocaust Rescuer* (1999).

Autobiography, like memoir, often allows young adults to identify with the subject's struggle to overcome adversity, make choices, and deal with consequences, a kind of survival story to which many teen readers can relate. Their powerful and often moving personal voice and perspective, telling details and anecdotes, and introspective point of view offer a level of intimacy that biography may not. Teen readers devour books like Dave Pelzer's *A Child Called It* (1995) and its sequels *The Lost Boy* (1997), *A Man Named Dave* (1999), *The Privilege of Youth* (2004), and Antwone Fisher's *Finding Fish* (2001), about living as a foster child who struggles with eating disorders and mental illness like Lori Gottlieb's *Stick Figure: a Diary of My Former Self* (2000) and Susanna Kaysen's *Girl Interrupted* (1993).

Many teen readers look for books about current pop-culture icons, who may not be much older than their fans. It's fun to learn more about Katie Holmes, Eminem, Salma Hayek, and other celebrities. These can be a mixed bag, some a little more thoughtful and researched, while others feel as though they are cobbled together from press releases and tabloid headlines. These pop-celeb books, though, tend to focus rather narrowly on the subject's current life and fame; they are as much fun to read and as ephemeral as an issue of *Teen People.*

In these days of reality television, the quality of reality reading in biography and autobiography for young adults is an antidote to the superficial and banal. Beyond these high-, if momentary-, interest titles, the world of biography should include outstanding biographies where authors are enthusiastic about their subject, whose research turns up interesting details that inform and involve readers through a lively narrative and careful choices. They may include additional material such as illustrations, photographs, and sidebars that complement and deepen the work (Sullivan). The increasing use of primary-source material like diaries, letters, journals, anecdotes and interviews, or facsimiles of notes and drawings, serve to personalize and deepen the reader's connection. Often a teen reader first looks for biography when it's connected to a school assignment, perhaps for AFRICAN AMERICAN History Month, Women's History month, or for reports on world leaders, explorers, scientists, inventors, or musicians. Beyond *The Miracle Worker,* teens can read about the wide-ranging social impact of Helen Keller's later life in Laurie LAWLOR's *Helen Keller, Rebellious Spirit* (2001). Today's "wired" teens can learn about online movers and shakers in Suzan Wilson's *Steve Jobs: Wizard of Apple Computer* (2001). It's fun to discover little-known heroes by reading books like Richard Maurer's *The Wright Sister, Katharine Wright and Her Famous Brothers* (2003), Thomas Goodhue's *Curious Bones: Mary Anning and the Birth of Paleontology* (2002), or Albert Marrin's *Terror of the Spanish Main: Sir Henry Morgan and His Buccaneers* (1999).

Heroes embody virtues and values of a culture. Their stories show us people whose lives make them worth admiring. Faulkner said "humanity will not only endure, it will prevail" by dint of individuals who live their lives consciously and productively. As teens struggle to define for themselves such concepts as integrity, dignity, values, and beliefs, good biographies can provide a vision.

Athletes have often been such heroes—and today's biographies of sports figures show more diversity than ever before. Books about Tiger Woods, Alan Iverson, Michael Jordan, Omar Vizquel, Michelle Kwan, Muhammed Ali, and Tony Hawk connect with teens involved in sports and competition, and speak to them about one's personal best, character building, team effort, and the price of glory and its sometimes transitory nature.

Powerful life stories come from times of war and conflict. In U.S. history we can read Russell FREED-MAN's *Lincoln: A Photobiography* (1987); Afghanistan—*Zoya's Story: An Afghan Woman's Struggle for Freedom* (2002); ethnic cleansing in Eastern Europe—Zlata Filipovic's *Zlata's Diary* (1994); facing times of personal crisis, illness and death (John Gunther *Death Be Not Proud* (1949); Lance Armstrong *It's Not about the Bike* (2001), or Andi Dominck's account of living with diabetes, *Needles* (1998).

Biography encompasses and clarifies social movements that show the clear, unflinching facts about what it's like to live with the effects of racism, sexism, or gender discrimination, in books like *The Last Time I Wore a Dress* (1997) by Daphne Scholinski, *Ditchdigger's Daughters, A Black Family's Astonishing Success Story* (1995) by Yvonne S. Thornton, or Adeline Yen Mah's moving *Chinese Cinderella: The True Story of an Unwanted Daughter* (1999), and *Young Black and Determined: A Biography of Lorraine Hansberry* (1998) by Patricia C. and Frederick L. MCKISSACK, renowned for their illuminating biographies of the African American experience. The immigrant experience is also explored in works like Esmeralda Santiago's *When I Was Puerto Rican* (1993) and Mawi Asgedom's *Of Beetles and Angels: A True Story of the American Dream* (2001).

Young adults can read about the lives of the writers they admire, about what makes someone artistic and creative, both the person and the process, and what elements in that life enabled their self expression. Notable recent titles include Chris CRUTCHER's amusing *King of the Mild Frontier* (2003), and Walter Dean Myers's *Bad Boy* (2001).

Collective biographies provide an easy entrée into the world of real people. Look for engaging informative reads like Cheryl Harness's *Rabble Rousers: 20 Women Who Made a Difference* (2003), or Kathleen KRULL's rollicking SERIES of famous lives that includes *Lives of the Artists: Masterpieces, Messes (and What the Neighbors Thought)* (1995) and *Lives of the Presidents: Fame, Shame (and What the Neighbors Thought)* (1998).

As young adults create the stories of their own lives, let's offer them the opportunity to step into an-other life and try it on for size with great biographies, autobiographies, and memoirs.

BIBLIOGRAPHY: Donelson, Kenneth L. and Alleen Pace Nilsen. *Literature for Today's Young Adults,* 4th ed., 1993; Sullivan, Ed. "A Librarian Makes the Case that Biographies Can Be Great Reads, Too," *School Library Journal,* February 1, 2001, p. 38.

MARY ARNOLD

BISHOP, Gavin

Illustrator, author, b. 13 February 1946, Invercargill, New Zealand

A steam train is traveling across a golden tussock plain. Inside its freight van is a family with their furniture. Seated on the sofa, the family look out through the van's open doors at the mountain scenery. This could be a scene from one of B.'s books, but in fact it is one of his earliest memories, as his family moved from Invercargill to Kingston. At five, he rode to the eleven-pupil school on horseback, sandwiched between two other boys, and he discovered that his favorite subject was art.

Following training at the Canterbury University School of Fine Arts, with Russell Clark as a tutor, B. became a high-school art teacher in Christchurch. Learning in 1978 that a publisher wanted New Zealand PICTURE BOOKS, B. wrote and illustrated *Bidibidi* (1982). Revision of the ink-and-watercolor pictures and "paring down" the text were B.'s apprenticeship in the craft of the picture book. The story of a sheep's quest for the secret of the rainbow, *Bidibidi* introduced many of the features associated with B.'s work: the South Island hill country landscape, carefully observed wildlife, exuberant humor, and touches of both the sinister and the spiritual.

B.'s first published book, *Mrs. McGinty and the Bizarre Plant* (1981), winner of the Russell Clark Award, named for his mentor, further demonstrated B.'s sharp eye for telling detail, especially in the use of architecture and furnishings to reflect characters' personalities.

Heavily influenced by his childhood reading of *Cole's Funny Picture Book,* a 19th-century AUSTRA-LIAN anthology of pictures, jokes and stories, B.'s humor often has a dark edge, as in *The Horror of Hickory Bay* (1984) where a headland comes to life, threatening to eat everyone. B. says, "Children find it enthralling because it's a wee bit scary and thrilling."—*NZ Listener,* 4 Feb. 1991, p. 80.

This scary aspect is also present, along with wit, in B.'s retelling of such classics as *Chicken Licken* (1984) and *The Three Little Pigs* (1989). Typically, B.'s animals are both realistic and highly expressive, while clever details, such as the turnip motif in the pig's house, delight young readers. Visual quotations in his pictures show B.'s awareness of illustrators from Hogarth to Sendak.

B. sees PICTURE BOOKS as works of literature in which the pictures tell a story in combination with the text. "The pictures and the words should be inseparable." This is exemplified in *Tom Thumb* (2001) where the narrative, framed in an 18th-century theatre, has its text woven into many of the complex illustrations. In illustrating Jeffrey Leask's *Little Red Rocking Hood* (1992) B. ensured that, when Red danced, everything in the book rocked, even the lampposts.

B. also makes dramatic use of color, nowhere more effectively than in *The Wedding of Mistress Fox* (1994), with its late Victorian architecture, where the dark shadows of mourning are dispelled by golden sunlight beating into the hallway as Master Fox arrives to propose.

B. distinguishes two types of books: his New Zealand books, such as *Hinepau* (1993), and those aimed at a larger market. U.S. publishers offer larger print runs but also require "an American voice" as well as changes in B.'s spelling, idiom, and pace. The American editor of *Stay Awake Bear!* (2000), for example, asked for brighter colors and had some art deco detail replaced with a plain background for the text.

B. is also aware of the importance of New Zealand readers being able to recognize their own country in their books, not just in the distinctive mountains of *The Three Billy Goats Gruff* (2003) but also in the presence of a Maori family in *The Video Shop Sparrow* (1999). B.'s fresh retellings of the Maori legends are deservedly popular. B.'s tribal links are to Ngati Mahuta and Ngati Pukeko, and he has drawn on his family's experiences in *Katarina* (1990), a warm account of his great-aunt's adventurous life. Many of his picture books are available in Maori language editions.

An important landmark in B.'s work is *The House that Jack Built* (1999), where the illustrations build a rich metaphorical account of the relations between colonial New Zealand's Maori inhabitants and the European settlers (symbolized by Jack) through set-tlement, trade and war. This magnificent book reflects B.'s belief that an increased awareness of things Maori makes for a richer and more stimulating society.

New challenges have always interested B. He was commissioned by the Royal New Zealand Ballet to write and design two ballets, *Te Maia and the Sea Devil* (1987) and *Terrible Tom* (1985), based on his youth in Invercargill. In the 1990s he wrote a SERIES of short beginner-readers, relishing the challenge of whittling words to produce such seven-sentence books as *Spider* (1995). For the dramatic illustrations for Robert Sullivan's retelling of Maori legends *Weaving Earth and Sky: Myths and Legends of Aotearoa* (2002), B. used the monoprint method on sheets of glass.

In 2003 B. wrote and illustrated *Giant Jimmy Jones,* the world's first three-dimensional animated children's pop-up book, prepared to demonstrate the eyeMagic 3D virtual picture book system developed by HITLabNZ in Christchurch, NEW ZEALAND. Although this book may never be commercially available, it paves the way for exciting developments. B. says, "The first time I saw Giant Jimmy Jones walk was extraordinary . . . I am really excited by this technology, not so much by what we have done this time, but by what we could do in the next book."

Married to fellow artist Vivien, B. lives in Christchurch. Having left teaching to become a full-time illustrator in 1999, he is now New Zealand's leading illustrator, at the peak of his imaginative and creative powers.

AWARDS: 1982 Esther Glen Medal, *The Year of the Yelvertons,* ill Gavin Bishop; 1982 Russell Clark Award, *Mrs McGinty and the Bizarre Plant;* 1983 HIT LabNZ Government Printer Award, Picture Book of the Year, *Mr Fox;* 1984 UNESCO Noma Concours Grand Prix winner, *Mr Fox;* 1994 AIM Children's Book Awards, *Hinepau;* 2000 Margaret Mahy Medal; 2000 NZ Post Children's Book Awards, *The House that Jack Built;* 2003 NZ Post Children's Book Awards Winner & Book of the Year, *Weaving Earth and Sky.*

FURTHER WORKS: *The Year of the Yelvertons,* by Katherine O'Brien, illus. Gavin Bishop, 1981; *Mr Fox,* 1982; *The Hungry Fox,* 1985; *Mother Hubbard,* 1986. *Katarina,* 1990; *The Lion and the Jackal,* 1992; *Maui and the Sun,* 1996; *Little Rabbit and the Sea,* 1997; *Maui and the Goddess of Fire,* 1997; *The Wolf in Sheep's Clothing,* 1999; *Woodchuck's New Helper,*

1999; *Stay Awake, Bear!,* 2000; *Pip the Penguin,* text by Joy COWLEY, 2001; *Tom Thumb,* 2001; *The Three Billy Goats Gruff,* 2003.

BIBLIOGRAPHY: Barley, Janet Crane. *Winter in July: visits with children's authors down-under,* 1995; *Contemporary Authors,* 121; Darnell, Doreen. "An Interview with Gavin Bishop," *Talespinner* 8 (Sep 1999): 23–29; Fitzgibbon, Tom and Spiers, Barbara, *Beneath Southern Skies: New Zealand Children's Book Authors & Illustrators,* 1993. 16–7; Gaskin, Chris, *Picture Book Magic: Chris Gaskin interviews nine leading New Zealand children's illustrators,* 1996; Hebley, Diane, "Bishop, Gavin." *The Oxford Companion to New Zealand Literature.* Ed. Roger Robinson and Nelson Wattie, 1998. 587–8; McKenzie, John L, "The Use (and abuse?) of History: A Response to Gavin Bishop's The House that Jack Built," *Magpies NZ Supplement* 13:4 (Sep 1999): 1–3; McKenzie, John L, "The Spectator Gaze and the Other in Gavin Bishop's Tom Thumb," *Talespinner* 13 (May 2002): 14–20; Nagelkerke, Bill, "Know the Author: Gavin Bishop," *Magpies NZ Supplement* 13:5 (Nov 1998): 4–6; http://www.gavinbishop.com/; http://library.christchurch.org.nz/Childrens/Childrens Authors/GavinBishop.asp/; http://wwwbookcouncil .org.nz/writers/bishopgavin.htm/; http://www.hitabnz .org/index.php?page = proj-smash-palace/; http://www .hitlabnz.org/pdf/Interface 2003-07-30Small.pdf/

TREVOR AGNEW

BLACK, Holly

Author, b. 10 November 1971, Long Branch, New Jersey

B. grew up in a decrepit Victorian house with a fear of the dark and a fascination with fairies, spooky dolls, and hats. After spending her formative years immersed in role-playing games and punk-rock music, B. attended Temple University and Trenton State College, where she majored briefly in Secondary Education and graduated with a B.A. in English Literature. She married painter Theo Black in 1999.

While continuing her education at Rutgers University (pursuing an M.A. in Library and Information Science), B. worked on her first novel, *Tithe: A Modern Faery Tale* (2002). This horrific FANTASY features Kaye, a changeling who grew up thinking she was human: Kaye is drawn into the battle between the Seelie and Unseelie courts after she rescues a handsome Black Knight named Roiben. A very dark tale of intrigue and betrayal in the Faerie Courts, *Tithe* received starred reviews from *Booklist* and *Publishers*

Weekly and was a finalist for the Mythopoeic Fantasy Award for Children's Literature.

B.'s next works were the first entries in the *Spiderwick Chronicles* SERIES (illustrated by Tony DiTerlizzi), beginning with *The Field Guide,* and *The Seeing Stone* (both 2003) which deal again with the faerie realm. The story is centered on the three Grace siblings and their discovery of "Arthur Spiderwick's Field Guide to the Fantastical World around You," a book that introduces them to a host of magical creatures. Instant bestsellers, film rights to the *Spiderwick Chronicles* have been optioned by Paramount Pictures and Nickelodeon Films.

AWARDS: 2002 ALA Best Book for Young Adults, *Tithe;* 2005 ALA Popular Paperbacks.

FURTHER WORKS: "The Night Market" in *The Faerie Reel,* ed. Ellen Datlow & Terri Windling, 2004; *Valient, A Modern Tale of Faerie,* 2005; *Notebook for Fantastical Observations,* 2005.

BIBLIOGRAPHY: wwwblackholly.com; *Publishers Weekly,* 28 Oct. 2002, v.249, i.42, pg. 74.

JULIE BARTEL

BLACK, Jonah, a.k.a. BOYLAN, Jennifer Finney/Boylan, James Finney
Author, b. 1951, Valley Forge, Pennsylvania

In addition to a wonderful comic voice, B. brings a unique point of view to the sexual and personal angst that grips seventeen-year-old diarist Jonah Black and his peers; until 2001, transgendered B. walked through life as James Finney Boylan. A recurring theme in B.'s often humorous work is people's everyday ability to cope with unusual problems. Playwright Edward Albee described B.'s wit as "levitating," noting that she "observes carefully, and with love."

B. grew up in Newtown Square and Devon, Pennsylvania. She is the second daughter of J. Richard Boylan, a trust banker, and Hildegard S. Boylan, a bookseller. In 1980, she graduated from Wesleyan University in Middletown, Connecticut. In New York, B. worked until 1982 as managing editor of *American Bystander* humor MAGAZINE, as editorial assistant to the managing editor of Viking/Penguin, and (until 1985) as fiction production editor for E. P. Dutton. The Writing Seminars of the Johns Hopkins University in Baltimore, Maryland, admitted her into a master's program in 1986 and later hired her to teach. She is now a full professor and, through July 2004, co-chaired the English department at Colby College, Waterville, Maine. She teaches Introductory and Advanced Fiction Workshops, Screenwriting, and Imaginative Writing. B. resides with her partner, Deirdre Finney, and their sons, Zachary and Sean.

B.'s success with *Getting In,* a comic quest for four under-achieving, over-reaching high-school seniors determined to enter New England's finest colleges, drew attention from 17th Street Productions (packager/publisher of "Sweet Valley High" and more), which conceived the Black Book diaries and its characters. In four fictional journals, Jonah Black—a dreamy diver possessed of a vivid imagination—tantalizes readers by never quite revealing why he was expelled and sent from his father's Pennsylvania home to live in Pompano Beach, Florida, with his Harvard-bound, wicked kid sister, his mother (a best-selling teen sex therapist), his horn-bug best friend, some drug-addled peers, and a mysterious bevy of never-quite-consummated loves. In the end, Black strikes a balance between what could be and what must be.

B. is enthralled that YA groups generate much Web chatter debating the authenticity of Black and the outcome of his perhaps imaginary dilemmas, and the publisher's marketing cleverly reinforces their drama.

AWARDS: ALA-YALSA: Quick Picks for Reluctant Young Adult Readers for *Girls, Girls, Girls* and *Stop, Don't Stop* (2002. ALA-YALSA: Quick Picks for Reluctant Young Adult Readers for *Girls, Girls, Girls* (2002). For *Getting In:* ALA-Adult Books for Young Adults Task Force Alex Award (1999), ALA BOOKLIST—Editor's Choice: Adult Books for Young Adults (1998), and *Wilson's Senior High Library Catalog, 16th ed.*

WORKS: as Jonah Black—*The Black Book (Diary of a Teenage Stud)* SERIES: *vol. 1, Girls, Girls, Girls,* 2001; *vol. II, Stop, Don't Stop,* 2001; *vol. III, Run, Jonah, Run,* 2001; *vol. IV, Faster, Faster, Faster,* 2002. *The Black Book* series is also available in Microsoft Reader digital format. German translations (2003) by Stephanie van Selchow are *Mmm . . . , Mädchen! Die intimen Bekenntnisse des J. B. 02. Salto Amore.* cbt.; *Liebe auf Umwegen,* and *Herz ist Trumpf.*

FURTHER WORKS: as Jennifer Finney Boylan, James Finney Boylan—*Remind Me to Murder You Later,* 1988; *The Planets,* 1991 (also on cassette, 1993); *The Constellations,* 1994; *She's Not There: a Life in Two Genders,* 2003.

BIBLIOGRAPHY: 17th Street Productions/Alloy Online, Inc.: postcard. Amazon.com database, 4 June 2004. Author homepage: http://www.colby.edu/personal/j/ jfboylan/author.htm, 9 June 04. E-mail with author: jfboylan@colby.edu, 10 June 2004. Children's Literature Comprehensive Database, 3 June 2004. E-mail with author's agent, Kristine Dahl of International Creative Management, Inc.: KDahl@icmtalent.com, 9 June 2004. The Grouchy Café's "Favorite Teenage Angst Books" discussion board—Is Jonah Black Real?: www.ezboard.com, 5 June 2004. OCLC First-Search WorldCat Database, 9 June 2004. Harper-Teacher.com: wwwharperchildrens.com/teacher/cata log/wwwharperteen.com.www.jonahblack.com

CLAUDIA L. BENNETT

BLEAK YA BOOKS: DARKEST BEFORE DAWN: HEALING LIGHT OF BLEAK YA BOOKS

As the new millennium overtook the old, a debate was still raging among young adult literature experts, authors and enthusiasts. *Bleak* had become a common descriptive for many works published for readers twelve and up. Some wondered if heavy-hearted fiction was good for the TEENAGE soul. "Judging from what teenagers are reading," said former *New York Times Book Review* editor Sara Mosle in the summer of 1998, "they're growing old before their time."

What was the source of Mosle's discontent? In 2004, YA media specialists at Michigan's Plymouth District Library called the subgenre, "Realistic Fiction." Beneath that banner, readers find books by authors such as Chris CRUTCHER, E. R. FRANK, Robert CORMIER, and Laurie Halse ANDERSON that realistically tackle the brutality of human evil from a distinctively teenage point of view.

Crutcher's most recent novel, *Whale Talk* (2001), has stirred up controversy in more than a dozen states, including Oregon, Texas, and Michigan. The natural son of a drug addict who gave him up because he was of color when his mother and father were decidedly white, Crutcher's likeable but realistic protagonist TJ faces racism and violence and, predictably, uses language many high-school students hear or use on any given school day.

And that's the point, said Michigan parent Olivia Verfaillie in October of 2003 when she challenged the book's use in the curriculum at Fowerville High School. "My daughters are not reading *Whale Talk* because I call this novel immoral and profane, further desensitizing our youth to obscenity."

"You're asking our children to sin," said Verfaillie's husband Ken to the teachers and school board at a public hearing. "Shame on you." Parents like the Verfaillies want the world described in safe terms consistent with their sometimes-hopeful religious convictions.

For Crutcher, their statements and others like them—one Oregon mother called *Whale Talk* "complete filth," based on perusing a two-page excerpt out of context—simply stiffens his resolve.

"It is the job of a fiction writer to reflect the world as she or he sees it rather than to depict it in some wishful way," he said in response to the Fowlerville challenge. "If I have done my job well, readers will not see Chris Crutcher influencing teenagers on how to act or talk, but rather TJ telling his story."

The real sin, he says, is any roadblock to human communication and survival in a rough, rough world. "In my job as a therapist I commonly hear the language you read in this book coming from the mouths of four and five year old children," he says. "It is the language of their lives, and as a therapist I would no more take it away from them, take away the language of their expression, than I would vote Republican."

Simon & Schuster editor Richard Jackson supports realistic, sometimes-depressing plotlines. "Hope is not necessarily part of the human condition," he says, "so why fake it? It's like prescribing that the genre must deliver this particular medicine, and that's a hardship for literature."

Statistics may be in realistic fiction's corner. According to a national study, one in three girls is sexually molested before reaching the age of eighteen. The same study suggests one in seven boys suffers the same fate. But some experts believe the accurate figure for boys is closer to one in five, citing the fact that boys under-report sexual assaults due to even harsher social stigmas. Add untold instances of physical abuse, neglect, and emotional abuse to those tallies, and the implications are staggering.

Should such a huge population of victimized young people make realistic fiction more than acceptable for readers twelve and up? It should, according to Dr. Joan Kaywell, Professor of English Education at the University of South Florida and the author of *Using Literature to Help Troubled Teenagers Cope*

with Family Issues. In fact, Kaywell believes edgy literature can actually save lives.

"Students who are being sexually abused, for example, won't go to the library to check out books on the topic because they know that they will become suspect," Kaywell says. In other words, if nonfiction points to a specific problem, fiction about people with similar life challenges provides emotional support without the critical glare.

Even without horrifying statistics, editor and author Marc ARONSON wonders how realistic fiction in books can be perceived as radical or dangerous when television has gone to obvious extremes. "It normalizes everything," he says. "FAMILY secrets, sexual orientation. . . . It would be the odd teenager who hasn't heard something about this sort of thing on TV."

It is about telling the truth, Crutcher insists, whatever your truth might be, "because if a kid finds out it's true for me and for him, there's the connection. There are kids who have engaged in something horrendous, because it was less painful than any alternative they could imagine. They know the very details of what it's like to be treated badly; and when they see themselves in a book, they know they're not so alone.

"They think, 'Chris Crutcher might know what I'm talking about; so maybe there are other people out there who know this, too. Maybe if I find someone that likes Chris's books, they'll understand this too.' That's the piece that's therapeutic. If a kid comes to me and says, 'God, read this,' we can start talking about that story, but we are just one step away from talking about what's real. It gives kids and adults a place to begin."

BIBLIOGRAPHY: Crutcher's website, Censorship page; *Detroit News*, 10/03/03, Banned book awaits vote. by Steve Pardo; *Daily Press & Argus,* 10/5/03, Two thumbs-up for Whale Talk by Christopher Nagy; *The ALAN Review,* Volume 26, No. 1 1998; Publisher's Connection Potpourri by Jerry M. Weiss; *The New York Times Magazine* 8/2/98, The Outlook's Bleak: Judging from what teenagers are reading by Sara Mosle; *Booklist,* January 1 and 15, 1998, Publishing on the Edge, by Ilene Cooper and Stephanie Zvirin; *The ALAN Review,* Winter 1994, Vol. 20, No. 2, Using Young Adult Problem Fiction and Nonfiction to Produce Critical Readers by Joan Kaywell; TeenReads.com Interview with Chris Crutcher by Kelly Milner Halls.

KELLY MILNER HALLS

BLOCK, Francesca Lia

Author, b. 3 December 1962, Hollywood, California

B. was reared in West Hollywood, California, by two artistic parents who influenced and encouraged her writing. Throughout her TEEN years, B. and her friends traveled around the San Fernando Valley (where she moved later on in childhood and attended North Hollywood High School) to visit the city of Hollywood, which always appeared enchanted and exotic to her and her friends. It was during these trips that B. started unconsciously collecting material for her future books.

Her father, a renowned artist, Irving Alexander Block, and her mother, a poet, read to her as a child, whether it was FAIRY TALES or Greek MYTHOLOGY. In high school she and her friends made up magical lands and secret words. B.'s love of literature, especially FANTASY and poetry, led her to attend the University of California, Berkeley, where she majored in English Literature. She wrote her thesis on Hilda Doolittle and Emily Dickinson.

During this time in college B. wrote her first book, *Weetzie Bat,* out of fun and a longing to return to Los Angeles. She did not take the book seriously, since it was a mere collection of memories from her travels with high-school friends. Shortly after she graduated from college, a family friend sent the book off to HarperCollins, where Charlotte Zolotow offered to publish it as a YA novel. This started B.'s career; she continued by writing the rest of the *Weetzie Bat* SERIES, now available in a single volume entitled *Dangerous Angels: The Weetzie Bat Books,* as well as other books for YA as well as adults.

When *Weetzie Bat* first hit the scene, it was loved and despised. Many people found the content too racy for young adults. B. deals with many difficult issues, such as drugs, sex, homosexuality, and abuse. Critics at first stated that B.s books promoted the sexually active drug-induced lifestyle that many of her characters lead. Upon closer look, however, B. gives a strong commentary upon these lifestyles, by both recognizing them as a part of today's society, but also showing the negative consequences.

In her 1996 collection of SHORT STORIES *Girl Goddess #9: Nine Stories,* B. tells the stories of nine different females of varying ages and lifestyles. All of these girls, according to the book's title and the overall theme of the book, are considered goddesses. One wouldn't think this at first when approaching these stories. One young girl is facing the loss of her mother with a little blue "jiminy cricket" creature who lives in her closet, while another high-school girl goes out and parties all night with rock stars. In the last story, a girl with two mothers goes out on a search for her father. She discovers that one of her mothers was really a man, who after impregnating the other mother, got a sex change.

B.'s writing style is self proclaimed as Pop Magic Realism. Her stories are all fairy tales in one sense, because of the magical things that occur. The scenery is almost always the bright colorful multiethnic land of Los Angeles. The characters prance around in a variety of costumes, from rugged cowboy boots with pink 1950s prom dresses, to feathers, glitter, and sequins. Behind all this beauty lie the harsh realities of today's world. Her morals are true to life and inspiring for young readers of any shape, size, age, or color.

Los Angeles is the scene of many of B.'s books. She describes fluidly the tastes, sounds, and smells that mix on the streets and in the homes. Everything is 1950s vintage, from the convertible cars to the flashy outfits. Even the music is a mix of old, new, and a variety of cultures. Many scenes are based on actual places in L.A. The exotic flowers really do exist in commonplace; the monuments and houses that are described really do exist.

The Weetzie Bat series tells the story of Weetzie Bat and her unusual FAMILY. Through love, loss, and angst-ridden teenage years, her family is held together by love. B.'s fresh and poetic voice weaves the series through Weetzie's children, husband, and friends, through their happy and sad times. B. gives the novel a flair with her made-up street slang, which is not actual street slang on purpose, because then she would outdate herself. B. lives with musician and writer Ted Quinn, a cat named Muriel, and a dog named Vincent van GoGo Boots in the San Fernando Valley, close to the heart of Los Angeles.

AWARDS: University of California, Berkeley, short fiction award, 1986; Emily Chamberlin Cook Award, 1986; *Weetzie Bat* ALA Best Book for Young Adults and Recommended Books for Reluctant Readers; ALA Margaret Edwards Award, 2005.

SELECT FURTHER WORKS: *Witch Baby,* 1992; *Cherokee Bat and the Goat Guys,* 1993; *The Hanged Man,* 1994; *Missing Angel Juan,* 1995; *Baby Be-Bop,* 1997; *I Was a Teenage Fairy,* 1998; *Violet and Claire,* 1999;

The Rose and the Beast, 2001; *Echo,* 2002; *Guarding the Moon,* 2003; *Wasteland,* 2003; *Goat Girls,* 2004; *Beautiful Boys,* 2004; *Necklace of Kisses,* 2005.

BIBLIOGRAPHY: Children's Books in Print, 2003; Contemporary Authors, 1991; Writers for Young Adults, Volume 1, 1993; http://www.harperchildrens.com; http://www.teenreads.com; http://www.dailycelebra tions.com; http://www.atombooks.co.uk.

SARAH M. KATZ

BLOOR, Edward
Author, b. 12 October 1950, Trenton, New Jersey

B. was born and reared in New Jersey where, like Paul, his protagonist in *Tangerine* (1997), he played soccer in high school and college. He received a B.A. from Fordham University in 1973. While teaching in south Florida, B. met his wife, Pam. They married in 1984 and have two children, Amanda and Spencer. After three years of teaching, B. took a position with Harcourt Brace School Publishers in Orlando where he is a senior editor. He and his family reside in central Florida.

B.'s first YA novel, *Tangerine,* has "something for everyone," from sibling rivalry (in the extreme) to environmental issues. As if avoiding his brother Eric and surviving natural disasters such as sinkholes and lightening strikes aren't enough, the protagonist Paul Fisher fights against biases and prejudices to play soccer (his favorite sport). Paul also deals with a vision handicap and must forge relationships as he comes of age. Vivid characterization and interwoven plots keep even the most reluctant readers turning the pages.

B. uses details from both his past and present life in his writing. For example, he modeled some of Paul's soccer-team members after some of his own teammates. B. stated that "we won the state championship two years in a row; however, I can't say it was my playing that won." The wooden portable buildings at Paul's overcrowded school are similar to the ones in his teaching experience in Ft. Lauderdale. And in his words, he and his family live in a "world of themed housing developments, homeowners' associations, and deed restrictions" much like Lake Windsor Downs in *Tangerine.* His wife's teaching partner lives in an orange grove owned by her brothers who provided information about the citrus industry, particularly the business of how to fight a freeze. B. draws from his experience of working in two different South Florida malls to capture mall culture for

the setting of his second novel, *Crusader* (1999). The main character, Roberta, a fifteen-year-old girl with a quiet strength and wisdom beyond her years, struggles to maintain her grades at school and work at her father and uncle's failing business. At the same time she searches for the truth to questions surrounding her mother's murder seven years earlier. In his third book, *Story Time* (2004), B. spins a tale of two students who find themselves at a school where they are victims of the overuse and abuse of "teaching to the test." B., who helps to develop school tests for his publisher, says, "*Story Time* is a bit of a roman a clef." In his novels to date, B. has developed believable, well-defined characters capable of dealing with problems and tragedies in their lives. His work also questions contemporary issues such as educational testing practices, environmental concerns, and prejudice.

AWARDS: Pick of the List, American Bookseller's Association (1997) Books in the Middle, Outstanding Titles of 1997, *Voice of Youth Advocates, Horn Book* Fanfare Selection (1997), 100 Titles for Reading and Sharing, New York Public Library (1997), Top Ten Best Books for Young Adults and Best Books for Young Adults Citations, ALA (1998), IRA's Young Adults' Choices (1999), all for *Tangerine,* Garden State Teen Book Award, Grade 6–8.

FURTHER WORKS: *Tangerine,* 1997; *Crusader,* 1999; *Story Time,* 2004.

BIBLIOGRAPHY: Bloor, Edward. E-mail interview. Feb. 29, 2004; *Contemporary Authors,* vol. 166, 1998. *Something about the Author,* vol. 98, 1999.

CATHY DENMAN

BLUM, Ralph
Author, b. 1932, n.p.

B. has written for several popular magazines, including *The New Yorker* and *Cosmopolitan.* He wrote SCIENCE FICTION novels in the 1970s, a nonfiction title on UFO sightings, and has more recently focused on nonfiction titles regarding the history and use of runes.

Having attended the University of Leningrad and worked in the drug research field, B. applied his experiences in *The Simultaneous Man* (1970). Using powerful chemicals, a government researcher's mental history is superimposed upon a convict, whose own memory has been erased. Before the researcher can

DOUGLAS ADAMS

DAVID ALMOND

LAURIE HALSE ANDERSON

BRENT ASHABRANNER

AVI

T. A. BARRON

JOAN BAUER

MARION DANE BAUER

JUDY BLUME

meet his mental twin, he is exiled from the military compound. The two finally meet in the USSR, where the researcher becomes the subject for future experimentation.

B. and his wife, Judy, share credit for the creation of *Beyond Earth: Man's Contact with UFOs* (1973). It chronicles many of the claimed UFO encounters of the previous hundred years, and includes several documents and newspaper articles, verbatim. While acknowledging that there is little hard evidence, the couple believes that, with so many sightings, the existence of UFOs will inevitably be confirmed.

The Book of Runes (1982) offers a modern understanding of the ancient practice of consulting marked sticks or stones as an oracle. B. advocates the study of runes in personal meditation, noting that many are quite serious about this practice. B. also published a set of runecards and other related texts.

BIBLIOGRAPHY: *Miami Hrald,* May 8, 1974; *The Encyclopedia of Science Fiction,* 1993.

MYRON A. MYKYTA

BLUME, Judy
Author, b. 12 February 1938, Elizabeth, New Jersey

B. is one of the most well-known and at the same time controversial authors of YA LITERATURE. TEENS have reached for her novels to help uncover the difficulties of growing up, while educators and parents have often shied away from them. B.'s novels are controversial because the topics are too difficult for many adults to speak about among themselves, let alone with their teenagers. Her novels deal with topics of concern for readers, such as menstruation (*Are You There God? It's Me, Margaret,* 1970), wet dreams (*Then Again, Maybe I Won't,* 1971), masturbation (*Deenie,* 1973), divorce (*It's Not the End of the World,* 1972; *Just as Long as We're Together,* 1987), DEATH (*Tiger Eyes,* 1981), friendship (*Here's to You, Rachel Robinson,* 1993, *Just As Long as We're Together,* 1987), moving (*Then Again, Maybe I Won't,* 1971) and first sexual experience (*Forever,* 1975). Criticism of these themes stems from a feeling that young adults do not need to be exposed to these issues through literature. However, it is addressing these sensitive issues that enhances B.'s popularity. Because her books have often been subject to censorship, she has become a powerful speaker and writer on the issue. As editor of *Places I Never Meant to Be*

(1999), B. presented her struggles with censorship, as well as her desire to maintain a world where young adults can read books that are honest and true while addressing concerns they have about growing up.

Sex is a topic often deemed inappropriate for YA novels; however, in 1975 B. took on the topic of teenage sex with her novel *Forever.* She wrote the novel for her daughter, who was fourteen at the time, and wanted a book about adolescents who have sex without horrible repercussions. In this honest novel Michael and Katherine fall in love and believe their love is destined to last forever, until a separation during the summer makes Katherine question their relationship. *Forever* contains characters that feel comfortable talking about sex and birth control. Although the novel was written before the AIDS epidemic, B. addresses the issue in introduction to recent editions of the book. She explains how Katherine's visit to the clinic to discuss her first sexual experience would be different today. The topic is controversial and the content straightforward; however this is a love story, one that has endured the test of time.

Realism is the key to B.'s popularity. As in life, problems are not always resolved in her novels. The protagonist learns to understand and cope with the issue at hand. The characters learn how to use their strengths to overcome or deal with adversity. B. leaves her readers thinking about what the characters will do next. For example, in *Tiger Eyes* (1981), Davey's family decides to return to New Jersey to deal with the death of her father. The reader is left wondering how the family will cope with life once they return home. This questioning about life and where it will take the reader is an important part of B.'s novels. She does not present characters that know all the answers; her protagonists have to sort through feelings of frustration. Her characters are presented as survivors of real situations.

B.'s novels deal effectively with issues that interest her teen readers. Through the use of the first person, B. gains an intimate relationship with her protagonist and allows the reader to make a new friend. The use of familiar syntax and language allows the reader to relate to the story with the intimacy of a friend's diary or a conversation in the lunchroom. In *It's Not the End of the World* (1972), Karen deals with her parents' divorce by desperately trying to get them back together, despite advice from friends that she is impotent in this situation. In *Just as Long as We're*

Together (1987) B. tackles the issue of friendship and divorce. Not only does Stephanie learn that her parents are separating but that her friendship with her best friend Rachel is struck a blow when Stephanie befriends Allison, a new girl in town. In *Deenie* (1973), B. continues to address issues important to young teens. Deenie has always been told that she is beautiful and that she will become a model. However, when she discovers that she has scoliosis and has to wear a brace, her life changes dramatically. B.'s use of first person demonstrates the value that she places on the content and its personal effect on the characters, as well as the reader.

FAMILY relocation is a common theme in many of her novels. The child's lack of control over this traumatic change is vital in how they deal with the dilemma. In *Are You There God? It's Me, Margaret* (1970), Margaret has moved to New Jersey and some of her self-discovery concerns deal with fitting in and finding new friends. *Then Again, Maybe I Won't* (1971) shows Tony dealing with the stress of changing neighborhoods and social class. As a way of dealing with the death of her father, Davey's family in *Tiger Eyes* (1981) moves from New Jersey to New Mexico. B.'s discussions of the unsettling factors young people have to deal with when they move help readers connect to the characters in her novels.

B.'s novels deal with sensitive issues. She chooses to write about these issues, because despite having a positive relationship with her family, she could not talk about her concerns. As a child she loved to read and make up stories inside her head while she was practicing piano, bouncing a ball, or playing with paper dolls. B. started writing when her children were in preschool. She would write stories while washing dishes. B.'s novels are enduring because the protagonists are trying to discover their place in the world, a role that despite the decade teens have been facing for years.

AWARDS: *Are You There God? It's Me, Margaret,* 1970 *New York Times* Best Books for Children list, 1975 Nene Award; *Tales of a Fourth Grade Nothing:* 1972 Charlie May Swann Children's Book Award, Pacific Northwest Library Association Young Readers Choice Award, and Sequoyah Children's Book Award of Oklahoma, both 1975, Massachusetts Children's Book Award, Georgia Children's Book Award, and South Carolina Children's Book Award, all 1977, Rhode Island Library Association Award, 1978, North Dakota Children's choice Award, and West Australian Young Readers' Book Award, both 1980, United States Army in Europe Kinderbuch Award, and Great Stone Face Award, New Hampshire Library Council, both 1981; *Blubber* 1977 Arizona Young Readers Award, 1977 Pacific Northwest Library Association Young Readers Choice Award, 1983 North Dakota Children's choice Award, 1978 South Carolina Children's Book Award; *Otherwise Known as Sheila the Great; Superfudge:* 1980 Texas Bluebonnet List, 1981 Michigan Young Reader's Award, 1982 First Buckeye Children's Book Award, 1982 Nene Award, 1982 Sue Hefley Award, 1982 United States Army in Europe Kinderbuch Award, 1982 West Australian Young Reader's Book Award, North Dakota Children's Choice Award, 1982 Colorado Children's Book Award, 1982 Tennessee Children's Choice Book Award, 1982 Utah Children's Book Award, 1983 Northern Territory Young Readers' Book Award, 1983 Pacific Northwest Library Association Young Readers Choice Award, 1983 Garden State children's Book Award, 1983 Iowa Children's Choice Award, 1983 Arizona Young Readers' Award, 1983 California Young Readers' Medal, and 1983 Young Hoosier Book Award; *Tiger Eyes:* 1983 Dorothy Canfield Fisher Children's Book Award, 1983 Buckeye Children's Book Award, 1983 California Young Readers Medal; Golden Archer Award, 1974; Today's Woman Award, 1981; Eleanor Roosevelt Humanitarian Award, Favorite Author—Children's Choice Award, Milner Award, and Jeremiah Ludington Memorial Award, all 1983; Chicago Public Library's Carl Sandburg Freedom to Read Award, 1984; Atlanta American Civil Liberties Union's Civil Liberties Award, and Center for Population Options John Rock Award, both 1986; D.H.L. Kean College, 1987; South Australian Youth Media Award for Best Author, South Australian Association for Media Education, 1988; *Forever:* ALA Margaret A. Edward Award.

FURTHER WORKS: *Freckle Juice,* 1971; *Tales of the Fourth Grade Nothing,* 1972; *Blubber,* 1974; *The Pain and the Great One,* 1984; *Fudge-a-Mania,* 1990; *Wifey* (adult), 1977; *The Judy Blume Diary,* 1981; *Smart Women* (adult), 1984; *Letters to Judy: What Your Kids Wish They Could Tell You,* 1986; *The Judy Blume Memory Book,* 1988; *Summer Sisters* (adult), 1998; *Double Fudge,* 2003.

BIBLIOGRAPHY: *Contemporary Authors, New Revision Series* v. 66 pages 57–62; *Contemporary Literacy Criticism* v. 12 pages 44–48; *Contemporary Literacy Criticism,* v. 30, pages 20–25; *Something About the Author* v. 79 page 20–26; Harris, L. L., *Biography Today,* 1992, pages 22–27; Weidt, M. N., *Presenting Judy Blume,* 1990.

NANCE S. WILSON

BOAS, Jacob
Historian, author, b. 1 November 1943, Westerbrook, Netherlands

Born in the same concentration camp that once held Anne Frank and her family, B. was born to Barend and Anna (de Haas) in 1943. B. immigrated to Canada in 1957 and became a naturalized citizen in 1962. A concentration camp survivor, B. has become a leading scholar on the Jewish HOLOCAUST.

B. earned his undergraduate degree from McGill University and both his masters and his doctorate from the University of California at Riverside. He married Patricia Miller, an artist, in 1983: they have two children. B. has spent much of his life as a teacher of history, as a high-school teacher in Quebec as well as a university professor. Additionally, B. has been a director of several Holocaust museums and research centers, including the Holocaust Center of Northern California and the Oregon Holocaust Research Center.

Although B. has written and spoken about the Holocaust in a variety of formats, it is his book, *We Are Witnesses: Five Diaries of Teenagers Who Died in the Holocaust,* which has had universal impact. The book not only includes writings of Anne Frank, but also those of four other TEENAGERS: David Rubinowicz, Yitzhak Rudashevski, Moshe Flinker, and Eva Heyman. Through these five teenagers, B. shows the world how the Holocaust affected these young adults. B. takes the reader on a journey of humility, fear, loss, confusion, and also hope, humanity, and dreams. *We Are Witnesses* is a powerful book that appears on reading lists for teaching and learning about the Holocaust.

B. is foremost a historian, but uses writing to bring that history to life and add meaning for his readers.

AWARDS: BBYA 1996 for *We Are Witnesses.*

SELECT FURTHER WORKS: *Boulevard des Misères: The Story of Transit Camp Westerbork* (1985).

BIBLIOGRAPHY: Devereaux, Elizabeth and Diane Roback. "Children's books—'We Are Witnesses: The Diaries of Five Teenagers Who Died in the Holocaust'," *Publishers Weekly,* June 26, 1995. *Contemporary Authors.* vol. 120; *Best Books for Young Adults,* 2000.

TINA HERTEL

BODANIS, David
Author, b. n.d., Chicago, Illinois

B. grew up in Chicago and studied mathematics, physics, and economics at the University of Chicago. He moved to Europe in 1977 to work for the *International Herald Tribune.* He has lived in Britain since the late 1980s, developing several careers. In 1990, after B. became a Senior Associate Member at St. Antony's College, Oxford, he began teaching a course called "An Intellectual Tool-Kit: Selected Topics in Social Enquiry, Aristotle to Complexity Theory." This course was the main postgraduate social science survey at Oxford for a number of years.

During the 1990s, B. became known in the business community for developing the concept of "mini-scenarios," which aids the fast-changing technology fields. In addition, B. has been involved in writing reports on the future of the world's energy industry. He has served as analyst and writer for companies such as General Motors and Shell. B. has spoken on global trends in science and has published articles in *The Guardian, The London Times, Reader's Digest, New Scientist, Smithsonian Magazine, The Observer,* and others.

Although B. is known worldwide as a leading business thinker and writer, he is also considered a successful author for YA. *The Secret House,* published in 1986, became a bestseller with its publication in the U.S. Like B.'s other novels, *The Secret House* delves into the world of science. B. cleverly describes an average day around a house, demonstrating the science beneath the surface such as bacteria in showers and on toothbrushes. His novels *The Secret Garden: Dawn to Dusk in the Astonishing Hidden World of the Garden* (1992) and *The Secret Family: Twenty-four Hours inside the Mysterious World of Our Minds and Bodies* (1997) provide more interesting scientific facts in a similar format. B. also used *The Secret Family* as the basis of a one-hour award-winning documentary he presented and co-wrote for the Discovery Channel and the CBC.

B. is best known for his most recent novel, $E = mc^2$ (2000), which enjoyed overnight success. The book was purchased by publshers in over twenty countries before its first release and reached the top ten on Amazon.com's bestseller list in the U.S. $E = mc^2$ is the story of Einstein's famous equation—the equation that eventually changed the understanding of the world. In the novel, B. demonstrates his skills as a teacher as he expertly describes what the equation means and why the equation is so important. The story covers the theory from the time it was just a concept to the events that led to the building of the atomic bomb.

FURTHER WORKS: *The Body Book: A Fantastic Voyage to the World Within,* 1985; *The Secret House: The Extraordinary Science of an Ordinary Day,* 1986; *The Secret Garden: Talking Beatles and Signaling Trees,* 1993; *Electric Universe: The Shocking True Story of Electricity,* 2005.

BIBLIOGRAPHY: www.davidbodanis.com

JODI PILGRIM

BODE, Janet

Author, b. 14 July 1943, Penn Yan, New York; d. 30 December 1999, New York City

The author of numerous nonfiction books for TEEN-AGERS dealing with such difficult subjects as juvenile crime and incarceration, eating disorders, rape, and teen pregnancy, B.'s career was cut short when she lost a battle with breast cancer. A testament to the chord B.'s books struck with her audience is the fact that her books have been among the most frequently stolen from public and school libraries.

B. attended school in London during the 1950s when her father served in the United States embassy there. Upon returning to the U.S., B. graduated from high school and the University of Maryland, from which she earned an undergraduate degree. After college, B. taught school in Europe, Mexico, and Florida and later worked in public relations.

In 1972, B. published her first book for young people, *Kids School Lunch Bag.* That same year, B. was gang raped in the woods of Kansas. After the attack, she found writing therapeutic. Her painful experience as a rape victim would lead her to write several highly acclaimed books on the subject for teenagers, including: *Fighting Back: How to Cope with the Medical, Emotional, and Legal Consequences of Rape* (1978); *Rape: Preventing It* (1979); and *The Voices of Rape* (1990), a book considered groundbreaking for its time because it represented the voices of both the perpetrators and victims. B. was also co-author of *Women against Rape,* a 1975 television documentary.

Teenage pregnancy was another topic B. addressed in several of her books. *Kids Having Kids: The Unwed Teenage Parent* (1980) traces the difficulties and responsibilities of teenage parenthood. A sequel, *Kids Still Having Kids: People Talk about Teen Pregnancy* (1992), expands the scope of the earlier book by concentrating on feelings and attitudes about sexuality.

B. continued her no-nonsense approach to difficult subjects with books like *Death Is Hard to Live With: Teenagers Talk about How They Cope with Loss* (1993). For the book, B. interviewed teens about the DEATHS of friends and relatives. The book frankly explores ways of making peace with the shock, guilt, and tragedy of death. B. shows teens how they can constructively make loss a part of their lives and still live life to the fullest.

Heartbreak and Roses: Real Life Stories of Troubled Love (1994) is one of the few and very best nonfiction books ever written about young adults and romance. A series of twelve SHORT STORIES, again drawn from interviews with teens, tells about the turbulence of romantic relationships—obsessive love, violent love, and tormented love leading to suicide. The stories are meant to both comfort and disturb the reader, and also to help readers gain insight into their own romantic relationships.

Hard Time: A Real Life Look at Juvenile Crime and Violence (1996) features interviews with teens who were incarcerated for crimes they committed and with teens who were victims of crime. A shocking, often depressing book, *Hard Time* reveals how much violence touches the lives of many teenagers. For many, it is an ever-present reality. As in many of B.'s other books, *Hard Time* features illustrations by her partner, cartoonist Stan Mack.

B.'s books were consistently recognized for excellence by organizations like the National Council for Social Studies and the Young Adult Library Services Association. She was also lauded by librarians and teachers for her consistently fair-minded approach to controversial topics, her use of young adults' own words as a primary source, and her approach of leaving her readers to draw their own conclusions about the information she presented. All of B.'s books are rooted in the idea that young adults, armed with appropriate information and knowledge, will be able to find ways to confront the problems they face and gain control over their own lives. Her ability to communicate honestly and openly with young adults was a unique gift.

AWARDS: ALA Best Books for Young Adults in 1995 for *Heartbeat and Roses: Real-Life Stories of Troubled Love* (with Stan Mack); ALA Best Books for Young Adults in 1997 for *Hard Time: A Real Life Look at Juvenile Crime* (with Stan Mack).

FURTHER WORKS: *Different Worlds: Interracial and Cross-Cultural Dating,* 1989; *New Kids on the Block: Oral Histories of Immigrant Teens,* 1989; *Truce: Ending the Sibling War,* 1991; *Trust and Betrayal: Real Life Stories of Friends and Enemies,* 1996; *Food Fight: A Guide to Eating Disorders for Pre-Teens and Their Parents,* 1997.

BIBLIOGRAPHY: Bode, Janet, "Course Correction," *The ALAN Review* 26.3 (Spring 1999): 13–15; Quattlebaum, Mary. "Janet Bode's Real Life Stories." *VOYA: Voice of Youth Advocates* 21.3 (August 1998): 187–188; *Something about the Author,* vol. 96, pp. 30–35; *Something about the Author,* vol. 118, p. 127.

EDWARD T. SULLIVAN

BOOCK, Paula

Author, editor, publisher, b. 6 April 1964, Dunedin, New Zealand

B. writes almost instinctively from the young person's perspective, working from their level. Her protagonists (not all of them female) are URBAN TEENS, on the cusp of adulthood, developing their ideas, groping for self-awareness and often kicking against the system. They use their personal strengths to cope with new challenges, parental expectations, macho males, and a world that is more complex than expected. B.'s work is always fresh and often humorous, with witty dialogue. It is also firmly founded in the Otago landscape, especially Dunedin.

Born into a well-known sporting and retail family, B. was a keen writer from childhood, producing poems, SHORT STORIES, and plays. Nevertheless B. refused to take the usual "literary" options of journalism or teaching. Instead, after an English degree at Otago University, a stint in the family shop, and a creative writing course, she became an editor. In this role B. learned about writing books that people want to read, and also learned to analyze her own work.

Her award-winning first novel *Out Walked Mel* (1991), completed in eight weeks, describes how Mel, frustrated at home and school, runs away from home on what becomes a journey of personal discovery, where she finds herself and her place in her family. The carefully constructed plot takes Mel along the path followed by the spirits of the dead in Maori traditional belief, as part of her journey of heart and spirit.

Teenage readers felt they recognized B.'s characters such as Mel, or Win and Sasscat, the delightful letter-writing sisters of *Sasscat to Win* (1992). Many teens dream of being adopted, but Win finds she really is and travels to Britain to meet her "real" mother. The parallel of NEW ZEALAND's relationship with Britain is not ignored: *Sasscat to Win* is literally about young New Zealanders' search for identity, but it also provides a warm, funny, and moving story. It is one of the few humorous novels about the frustrations and fears of being fifteen years old.

It is a mark of B.'s recognition as a respected writer and publisher that the launch of *Dare, Truth or Promise* (1997) produced almost no controversy despite it being the first New Zealand young adult novel with a lesbian theme. B. regards this story, of two young Dunedin women who fall in love, as her most significant novel, reflecting her own experiences. Louie and Willa encounter family resistance, emotional stress and near-tragedy, but with B.'s skillful writing and high quality characterization, this novel has been both a popular and critical success, noted for its themes of acceptance and honesty. As Louie's parish priest, Father Campion says, "How lucky you are to love and be loved in return." *Dare, Truth or Promise* took the awards for Best Senior Fiction and Supreme Award at the 1998 *NZ Post* Children's Book Awards, as well as being short-listed for the Esther Glen Medal.

Her only SCIENCE FICTION work, *The Tribe: Power and Chaos* (2000), is a powerful and atmospheric novel, written as background for the cult TV series, The Tribe. B. creates a sympathetic portrait of the young gang leader, Zoot, as well as charting vividly the collapse of society when a virus kills all adults, leaving packs of young people to scrabble for existence in the ruined cities.

In 1995 B. was one of three Dunedin business partners who set up Longacre Press, which now includes a strong range of YA writers, such as Bernard BECKETT and Jack LASENBY, in its list. B. believes that her work as an editor helps sharpen and refine her own writing. Currently B. is working on a historical novel set in Otago in the 1920s.

AWARDS: 1992 AIM Children's Book Awards, *Out Walked Mel;* 1994 Esther Glen Medal: *Sasscat to*

Win; 1998 NZ Post Children's Book Awards, *Dare, Truth or Promise*; 1998 NZ Post Children's Supreme Award, *Dare, Truth or Promise.*

FURTHER WORKS: "Song of the Shirt." In *Song of the Shirt: Three One-Act Plays for Young Actors,* 1993, *Home Run,* 1995.

BIBLIOGRAPHY: Ansley, Bruce. "Dare to be Different." *Listener* (NZ) 1 November 1997: 25–6. Darnell, Doreen. "Interview with a publisher: Paula Boock of Longacre Press, Dunedin." *Talespinner* 4 (Sep. 1997): 37–42. Fountain, Christine. "Know the Author: Paula Boock." *Magpies NZ Supplement* 13:1 (Mar. 1998): 2–3. Harper, Julie. "Longacre Press." *Magpies NZ Supplement* 16:2 (May 2001): 3–4. Fitzgibbon, Tom and Spiers, Barbara. *Beneath Southern Skies: New Zealand Children's Book Authors & Illustrators,* 1993. 18. Hebley, Diane. "Boock, Paula." *The Oxford Companion to New Zealand Literature.* Ed. Roger Robinson and Nelson Wattie, 1998. 63. http://www.bookcouncil.org.nz/writers/boock.htm/

TREVOR AGNEW

BOOK CLUBS AND BOOK-DISCUSSION GROUPS

Book discussion groups have been a feature in public library adult programming for many years. Over the past decade there has been a tremendous increase in the number of book discussion groups for young adults. The idea of a book discussion group was popularized in part due to the Oprah Winfrey television show with its monthly book discussion. Book groups are no longer limited to small groups with common socioeconomic bonds. It is no surprise that young adults are part of the trend. In 2001, a survey of TEEN readers commissioned by the National Education Association found that 87 percent of all teens say they find reading relaxing; 85 percent view it as rewarding and satisfying; and 79 percent consider it stimulating and exciting. A recent search of the terms "young adult book discussion" and "teen book discussion" drew over 1,000 hits in a major search engine. Clearly, there is an audience of YOUNG ADULT readers who want to share their thoughts and perceptions about their reading.

Starting a book discussion group for young adults is similar to organizing a book group for adults. Rachel Jacobsohn's *The Reading Group Handbook* (1998) is a primer for librarians or discussion facilitators, whether they are seasoned veterans or just starting out. The key elements, such as number of partici-

pants or the schedule of the meetings, are similar to those of adult groups. Limiting the number of participants is critical in maintaining the flow of the discussion: too many participants could stifle the less vocal members while too few could limit the entire discussion.

Finding book titles that are both appropriate for young adult readers and good discussion titles can be rewarding. Book award titles, such as the Michael L. Printz Award or book lists, such as the Best Books for Young Adults, are an excellent source of discussion titles. Many states or regions sponsor a young adult book award, and the list of past winners or current nominees provides a wide variety of choices. Genre book discussions overlap with adult discussion, and older teens might be drawn to a more adult selection. Book availability should always be a concern for book groups. But while many adults have the means to purchase their book group selections, teens have limited income for such purchases. Finding titles that are in libraries or can be purchased in a used bookstore will ease some concerns over cost. Local organizations often sponsor book groups and fund the purchase of the books.

Traditionally, book discussion starter questions have been developed by the facilitator. Today, while the facilitator still creates questions, many publishers have developed book discussion guides for titles identified as good for discussion groups. These guides are available on publisher websites or in print at many large bookstores. Publishers have also begun to include book group guides in some of their mass market and trade paperback editions.

The scheduling of book discussions is driven by the availability of the facility, the discussion leader, and the participants. Summer reading programs incorporate book discussions for young adults, though the group is more likely to be under the age of 16, since older teens often work at summer jobs. Attracting older teens creates a challenge for discussion leaders, in both scheduling and title choices. Age spread in teen participants often means older teens need a more adult-like group, while younger teens might need games or contests. Time of day and day of week might vary during the school year, particularly if the library serves several schools or school districts.

Food and beverages, if permitted in the library, can become an important component of the book group program. Coffeehouses and coffee shops have traditionally hosted formal and informal book groups; many libraries now incorporate this service into their book groups. Candace Fiore's *Running Summer Library Reading Programs* (1998) highlights the Tampa-Hillsborough County (Florida) Public Library System's *Booknic* program, where younger teens bring their lunch and books to discuss to the library (books and picnic = booknic). Other libraries appeal to local businesses or friends groups to support the food-service component. The Mukilteo (Washington) Library sponsors a *Brunch Bunch* series of discussions every summer, with donuts and juice for the attendees. They meet in mid-morning, during the week, for a series of five book discussions.

Mother–daughter book groups sprang up in the early 1990s and Shireen Dodson's book, *The Mother-Daughter Book Club: How Ten Busy Mothers and Their Daughters Came Together to Talk, Laugh and Learn through Their Love of Reading* (1997) serves as both an inspiration and a template for those interested in forming such a group. Multi-generational book groups, such as Mother–Daughter, Father–Son, offer the challenge of selecting titles that appeal to a broad age range. Dodson's book provides a wide range of suggested titles and discussion ideas.

Book groups are a part of the extracurricular activities at many high schools. Evanston Township High School (Illinois) began *Books R Us,* a forum for teens to discuss books and issues. The group does not limit their discussion to books, but includes plays and attends local stage performances to enhance the reading experience.

The Internet has brought about new types of book discussion. Online discussions, using a "chat" interface, allow the readers to exchange thoughts and discuss the book from remote corners of the world. Since most teens are familiar with chat groups, this has great potential for real-time book discussions. Users who find the chat process too cumbersome can subscribe to e-mail lists that allow them to share books and comments via e-mail. Major online booksellers provide the reader with an opportunity to comment on books or create lists of suggested titles that are then shared with other readers. Many libraries have added features to their websites that allow teens to submit book reviews or comments. And some libraries, such as Roselle Public Library (Illinois), have turned to a web-based service that allows readers to post comments online and then share these comments on the library website.

Great Books, sponsored by Britannica, has been a leader in book discussions of classic literature. They now provide an online classroom, where students participate in the discussion using software that is provided as part of the subscription. This is a fee-based service that targets home schools and charter schools in its advertising. http://www.greatbooksdiscussions .org/index.html.

As the book discussion/book group trend continues to expand, librarians will seek to build on traditional book groups and perhaps to experiment with electronic groups. The fundamental purpose is still to share the joy of literature with others, in whatever format the future brings.

BIBLIOGRAPHY: Berger, Allen and Elizabeth A. Shafran, *Teens for Literacy: Promoting Reading and Writing in Schools and Communities,* 2000; Braun, Linda W., *Teens.library: Developing Internet Services for Young Adults,* 2002.; Minkel, Walter, *"Time to Join the Club,"* School Library Journal, 2003; Slezak, Ellen, ed, *The Book Group Book,* 3rd ed., 2000.

TERRY BECK

BOOKTALKING FOR TEENS

Amelia Munson, an early advocate and promoter of YA Services at the New York Public Library, described ways to select and supply books for TEENAGERS in her classic, *An Ample Field* (1950). Her extensive list of "promotional devices" included such techniques as displays, discussions, and booktalks. Regarding the latter, Munson believed in training her young librarians to learn booktalking skills, devoting a chapter to it in *An Ample Field.* Booktalking was and is a proven way to promote books to teens, share enthusiasm for reading, and demonstrate the accessibility and friendliness of libraries.

Elinor Walker, who had been the coordinator of young adult services at the Carnegie Library in Pittsburgh for more than twenty-five years, was another early proponent of booktalking as a way to connect teens, books, and reading. The landmark titles she worked to produce, *Book Bait* (1957, 1967, 1979) and *Doors to More Mature Reading* (1964, 1981), listed high-interest adult titles of appeal to teens, gave a synopsis of each, mentioned ideas for booktalks and sections on which to focus in developing them, and recommended related titles.

In 1967, John T. Gillespie and Diana Lembo followed suit with *Juniorplots: A Book Talk Manual for Teachers and Librarians.* Instead of focusing only on adult books, which previously had been almost all that was available for a teen audience, this resource was able to concentrate more on books specifically written for young adults, an emerging field of literature in the 1960s. *Juniorplots* gave recommended titles, plot analysis, thematic material, booktalk ideas, and related book suggestions. In their Introduction, Gillespie and Lembo said: "There is an unfortunate lack of published material that can serve as a guide for those who give book talks to a young adult audience." At the time, that was true. However, Gillespie went on to author and co-author an entire SERIES of guidebooks with the purpose of assisting teachers and librarians in planning booktalks for teenagers.

Elaine Simpson, in *More Juniorplots* (1977), aptly defined booktalking. She says it is that part of a librarian's visit to a classroom or during a class visit to the library devoted to presenting two or more books to the group. It is an art and a device by which the librarian tries to interest young people in all books in general and in some books in particular through a talk so carefully prepared as to seem spontaneous, in which he or she gives the subject, the flavor and the appeal of each book presented. Indirectly through booktalks we are able to show the teenager that he or she is welcome in the school or public library, and that he or she has a place there. We are also able to identify ourselves as friends.

Margaret Edwards, author of the classic, *The Fair Garden and the Swarm of Beasts: The Library and The Young Adult* (1969) and a strong advocate of booktalking from the time she served as the young adult librarian at the Enoch Pratt Free Library in Baltimore, compares a book being shared through a booktalk to "a little piece of pie so good it tempts one to consume the whole concoction."

Amelia Munson in *An Ample Field* states, "The book talk falls into place between storytelling and book reviewing, partakes of both and is unlike either." Booktalks should foster the audience's curiosity to read the books and be so carefully prepared as to seem natural.

With these definitions in mind, there are some recognized techniques for preparing successful booktalks. They include reading widely and keeping a record of favorite fiction and nonfiction titles teens would enjoy; utilizing print, nonprint and online resources that teach how to develop and hone the craft; never giving away the ending of a title that is presented; preparing by writing, practicing, and memorizing booktalks in a comfortable and effective style; keeping a file of original and adapted booktalks; and having books, notes and handouts reading for the presentation. Expert booktalkers maintain good eye contact with their teen audience; employ appropriate performance techniques; avoid reading from the books themselves unless the reading is very brief and enhances the booktalk; provide booklists and information about library programs for teens; and incorporate a variety of books in their talks.

Teachers can also use booktalking effectively in promoting books and reading to their students. They may also choose to teach their students the craft of booktalking and encourage them to consider preparing booktalks for their classmates in lieu of traditional book reports and other reading-related assignments. In similar fashion, some school and public librarians instruct their young adult library advisory group members on how to booktalk, and these teens in turn may be asked to share their booktalks with other teens at school through in-person visits, by being videotaped, or on the school or local educational television cable channel.

In addition to the fact that young adult literature has become a prolific field, providing an abundance of titles to choose from, today's prospective booktalkers have an array of resources available to help learn and develop the craft. The most notable contributing expert is Joni Bodart, who broke ground with her *Booktalk!* series of guidebooks beginning in 1980. They provide a philosophical base for booktalking, instruction on writing, practicing and presenting booktalks, advice for connecting with teens in schools for booktalking performances, and an abundance of sample booktalks. Bodart encourages readers to use and adapt the booktalks contained in the guides. Bodart also produced an instructional video on booktalking in 1985 and manages a listserv specifically for booktalkers.

Likewise, articles, other guidebooks, videos, and websites are available to introduce budding booktalkers to the craft and aid them in becoming proficient booktalk writers and presenters. Sessions on booktalking are frequently offered at professional workshops and conferences for librarians and teachers, adding to interest and skill building.

Booktalks are fun, informative, and exciting; they are a great way to connect teenagers and reading. Through the years, preparation and presentation methods have not changed very much, but the resources and opportunities at hand to learn how to present successful booktalks have greatly increased, resulting in a better appreciation for and usage of this effective technique.

BIBLIOGRAPHY: **Articles:** Bromann, Jennifer. *The Toughest Audience on Earth.* School Library Journal. October 1999: 60–63; Chelton, Mary K. *Booktalking: You Can Do It.* School Library Journal. April 1976: 39–43; Guevara, Anne and John Sexton. *Extreme Booktalking: YA Booktalkers Reach 6,000 Students Each Semester!* Voice of Youth Advocates. June 2000: 98–101; Overmyer, Elizabeth. *Booklegging: Community-Wide Booktalking through Library-Trained Volunteers.* Journal of Youth Service in Libraries. Fall 1987; 82–86; Rochman, Hazel. *Booktalking the Classics. School Library Journal.* February 1984: 44; Roggenbuch, Mary Jane. *Booktalking as a Library Connection.* ALAN Review. Spring 1986: 48–50; Sacco, Margaret. *The Many Ways of Booktalks.* Emergency Librarian. March–April 1986: 17–18; Tuccillo, Diane. *First Step on the Bridge: Preparing a YA Spring Booktalking Program for 6th Graders.* Emergency Librarian. November–December 1986: 9–10.

Books: Baxter, Kathleen A. *Gotcha!: Nonfiction Booktalks to Get Kids Excited about Reading,* 1999; *Gotcha Again! More Nonfiction Booktalks to Get Kids Excited about Reading.* Englewood, 2002; Bodart, Joni Richards. New York: *Booktalk!* v. 1–5., 1986–92; *Booktalking the Award Winners.,* 1992–98; Bromann, Jennifer. *Booktalking That Works,* 2001; Edwards, Margaret A. *The Fair Garden and the Swarm of Beasts; the Library and the Young Adult,* 1969; Gillespie, John Thomas and Diana Lembo. *Juniorplots,* 1967; Gillespie, John Thomas. *Juniorplots 3,* 1987; *Juniorplots 4,* 1992; *More Juniorplots,* 1977; *Seniorplots,* 1989; *Teenplots: A Booktalk Guide to Use with Readers Ages 12–18,* 2003; Jones, Patrick. *Connecting Young Adults and Libraries: A How-To-Do-It Manual,* 2nd ed., 1998; Munson, Amelia H. *An Ample Field: Books and Young People,* 1950; Schall, Lucy. *Booktalks Plus: Motivating Teens to Read,* 2001; *Booktalks Plus II,* 2003; Walker, Elinor, compiler. *Book Bait: Detailed Notes on Adult Books Popular with Young People,* 1988; Walker, Elinor, et al. *Doors to More Mature Reading: Detailed Notes on Adult Books for Use with Young People.* 2nd ed, 1981.

Websites:
Joni Bodart's booktalking listserv registration. http:www.egroups.com/group/booktalking
Nancy Keane's Booktalks—Quick and Simple. http://www.nancykeane.com/booktalks
Novelist: http://novelst4.epnet.com/novel/default.asp
Videos:
Booktalking with Joni Bodart. H. W. Wilson, 1985. Approx. 30 min. ½ inch VHS.
Tales of Love and Terror: Booktalking the Classics, Old and New with Hazel Rochman.
ALA Video, 1987. 25 min. ½ inch VHS.

DIANE TUCCILLO

BORLAND, Hal
Author, b. 14 May 1900, Sterling, Nebraska; d. 22 Feb. 1978, Sharon, Connecticut

Following in his father's footsteps, B.'s career began in the newspaper business. At just eighteen years of age, B. was a reporter for the *Denver Post.* Several journalism jobs followed, including associate editor of *Flagler News* (his father's newspaper), publisher of *Stratton Press* in Colorado, and a job with Curtis Newspapers in Philadelphia. While working as a freelance writer for the *New York Times,* B. became well known for his nature-oriented essays. He wrote "outdoor editorials" for the Sunday paper from 1941 until just before his death in 1978.

B., an American naturalist, is noted for his nonfiction books. Novels such as *An American Year* (1946), *Hill Country Harvest* (1967), *Sundial of the Seasons* (1964), *Seasons* (1973), and *Hal Borland's Book of Days* (1976), are essays that bring to life nature's cycle of seasons. Through imagery, B. paints pictures with words.

B. was also the author of YA novels. *When Legends Die* (1963), *The Amulet* (1957), *The Seventh Winter* (1960), and *King of Squaw Mountain* (1964) all integrate the theme of man and his relationship with nature. For example, B.'s most famous work of fiction, *When Legends Die,* tells the story of a Ute Indian boy who is raised in the wilderness by his parents. After his parents' DEATH, the boy struggles in his relationships with both Caucasians and his fellow Ute people. He finds peace when he rediscovers his roots in the mountains. This popular novel, which became a *Reader's Digest* Book Club Selection, was adapted and made into a motion picture. B. wrote many MAGAZINE articles, poems, essays, and stories for children and adults. Although B. died in 1978, his eloquent words on nature are still appreciated and widely quoted today. B.'s work inspired the National Audubon Society to present the Hal Borland Award each year to an artist making significant contributions in topics pertaining to nature.

AWARDS: *High, Wide and Lonesome:* 1957 Westerners Buffalo Award for best nonfiction and the Secondary Education Board annual book award; 1968 John Burroughs Medal for distinguished nature writing.

FURTHER WORKS: *Rocky Mountain Tipi Tales,* 1924; *America is Americans,* 1942; *High, Wide, and Lonesome,* 1956; *This Hill, This Valley,* 1957; *The Enduring Pattern,* 1959; *The Dog Who Came to Stay,* 1961; *Beyond Your Doorstep,* 1962; *The Youngest Shepherd,* 1962; *Countryman,* 1965; *Our Natural World,* 1965; *Homeland: A Report from the Country,* 1969; *Country Editor's Boy,* 1970; *Borland Country,* 1971; *Penny,* 1972; *How to Write and Sell Nonfiction,* 1973; *This World of Wonder,* 1973; *A Place to Begin: The New England Experience,* 1976; *The Golden Circle: A Book of Months,* 1977; *Hal Borland's Twelve Moons of the Year,* 1979; *A Countryman's Woods,* 1983.

BIBLIOGRAPHY: *Something about the Author,* vol., 5, 1973; www.naturewriting.com

JODI PILGRIM

BOSSE, Malcolm (Joseph)

Author, b. 6 May 1933, Detroit, Michigan; d. 3 May 2002, New York City

B.'s experiences abroad for military service and lectures influenced the settings of many of his novels. His first two novels, set in Vietnam, were targeted at an adult audience and created a solid reputation for B. However, it was with the publication of *The Seventy-nine Squares* (1979) that the author branched over into the world of YA LITERATURE. According to the author, the only true difference between his writing for adults and adolescents is that in his young adult writing, he "leav[es] out the worst of [his] philosophical reflections or distortions"; B. does not patronize his young readers, nor does he suffocate them.

As in his adult works, B. uses diverse time periods and locations as backdrops to his stories of self-discovery and personal growth. In *The Seventy-nine Squares,* his protagonist, fourteen-year-old Eric Fisher, is given the gift of true sight from Mr. Beck, a dying eighty-two-year-old recently released from prison. Mr. Beck teaches Eric how to examine, study,

and moreover, see the world around him. *Cave beyond Time* (1980) is also set in modern times; while on an archaeological dig, Ben, a cynical TEENAGER, is attacked by rattlesnakes and rendered unconscious. In his stupor, he is transported back into prehistoric time and, through the help of wise companions, achieves the wisdom of a mature individual. B. revisits Southeast Asia in *Ganesh* (1981), setting his work in India and America. Born and raised for fourteen years in India, American teenager Jeffrey finds acceptance hard to come by when he moves to the American Midwest. *The New York Times Book Review* and *Booklist* both praised these first three young adult works.

Captives of Time (1987) and *The Examination* (1994) use historical settings as the stage for self-realization, medieval Europe and 16th-century China respectively. *Captives of Time* discusses chauvinist suspicion of female intelligence and determination. In a review from the *Los Angeles Times,* B. was applauded for creating characters that are firmly based in medieval Europe while being "emotionally contemporary." In *The Examination,* a journey taken by two brothers, Chen and Hong, deepens the respect and love felt between the two. Discovery is once again B.'s theme in *Deep Dream of the Rain Forest* (1993). Set after World War I, a British teenager is taken into the jungles of Borneo by a young Iban tribesman and an Iban girl who are on a dream quest; through the journey, the young boy learns the falsities of his white imperialistic views.

B.'s final work for young adults, *Tusk and Stone* (1995), uses the Indian caste system to prompt his protagonist's education and maturation. When Arjun, a Brahmin, is sold into slavery after witnessing his uncle's murder and his sister's abduction, his life is forever altered. B. creates different experiences and hardships for Arjun, making him stronger and braver with each incident. The journey that Arjun takes, from Brahmin teenager to stone carver slave, is another example of B.'s skillful craft.

At the time of B.'s death, this graduate of Yale University (B.A., 1950), the University of Michigan (M.A., 1956) and New York University (Ph.D., 1969) was highly respected for his literature, which merges a vast knowledge of Asian cultures and intelligently intricate plots.

AWARDS: *The Seventy-nine Squares:* 1979 ALA Notable Book, 1980 Library of Congress Best Books of the Year; *Cave beyond Time:* 1981 ALA Notable Books Award, 1981 National Council of Social Studies Teachers award; 1982 ALA Notable Book Award, *Ganesh;* Voice of Youth Advocates outstanding book: 1994 for *Deep Dream of the Rain Forest,* 1996 for *Tusk and Stone.*

SELECT FURTHER WORKS: *Journey of Tao Kim Nam,* 1959; *The Incident at Naha,* 1972; *The Man Who Loved Zoos,* 1974; *The Barracuda Gang,* 1982; *The Warlord,* 1983; *Fire in Heaven,* 1986; *Stranger at the Gate,* 1989; *Mister Touch,* 1991; *The Vast Memory of Love,* 1992; *Deep Dream of the Rain Forest,* 1993.

BIBLIOGRAPHY: *Contemporary Authors New Revision Series,* Vol. 49, 1995; Review of *Captives of Time, Los Angeles Times,* January 23, 1988; Review of *Ganesh, Booklist,* April 15, 1981; Review of *Ganesh, New York Times Book Review,* August 9, 1981.

RACHEL WITMER

BOVA, Ben(jamin)

Author, b. 8 November 1932, Philadelphia, Pennsylvania

Often described as a moral and socially responsible SCIENCE FICTION writer, B. is also a provocative and stimulating science fiction writer. Born during the Great Depression in a tough, working-class Philadelphia neighborhood, B. was an ardent reader, especially of science fiction. His love of science, astronomy, and space grew from his frequent trips to a local planetarium.

B.'s passion for learning and writing about the benefits of space exploration, scientific advancements, and humanity's responsible use of science is evidenced by more than one hundred books, numerous articles, commentaries, and interviews. B earned a B.S. from Temple University (1954), an M.A. from the State University of New York, Albany (1987), and a Ph.D. from California Coast University (1996).

The Star Conquerors (1959) was B.'s first novel for YA and was followed by his first nonfiction work, *The Milky Way Galaxy: Man's Exploration of the Stars* (1961). Whether it is fact or fiction, B. makes science and the possibilities of scientific advances an enjoyable and readily understandable experience for his readers.

B. tackles a variety of issues that show how science and society can affect each other. In *The Multiple Man* (1976), B. looks at cloning when a dead body too closely resembles the President of the United States. Love, adventure, theology, humanity, moons, glaciers, and time travel are all intertwined in the *Orion* SERIES of science fiction novels (1984, 1988, 1990, 1994, 1995). Space travel, culture clashes, and prejudices are themes in *Mars* (1992). Colonizing the moon and nanotechnology are combined with murder and greed in *Moonrise* (1996). B.'s series, *Asteroid Wars* (2001, 2002, 2004), shows how industrializing the solar system may be a solution to the greenhouse effect on earth.

B. summarizes his work best: "My work is usually marketed as science fiction, but I regard my novels as explorations of the near future, stories that show how science and government are shaping our lives, tales of real human beings at the frontiers of knowledge."

AWARDS: American Library Association citations for best science books of the year: *The Milky Way Galaxy* (1961), *The Fourth State of Matter: Plasma Dynamics and Tomorrow's Technology* (1971); *Welcome to Moonbase!* (1988), *The Beauty of Light* (1988); citation for best science fiction novel of the year for *Moonrise* (1996); six Hugo Awards for best editor (*Analog* editor); E. E. Smith Memorial Award for Imaginative Fiction (1974); Balrog Award (1983); Inkpot Award (1985); Isaac Asimov Memorial Award (1996); Fellow of the American Association for the Advancement of Science (2001).

SELECT FURTHER WORKS: *The Weathermakers,* 1967; *Brothers,* 1996; *Return to Mars,* 1999; *Venus,* 2000; *Jupiter,* 2001; *Exiles* series (1971, 1972, 1975); *Voyagers* series (1981, 1986, 1990); Nonfiction: *Planets, Life, and LGM,* 1970; *Starflight and Other Improbabilities,* 1973; *Man Changes the Weather,* 1973; *Workshops in Space,* 1974; *Through Eyes of Wonder: Science Fiction and Science,* 1975; *Assured Survival: Putting the Star Wars Defense in Perspective,* 1984; *Immortality: How Science Is Extending Your Life Span—and Changing the World,* 1998; *The Story of Light,* 2001; The Asteroid Wars series; *Tales of the Grand Tour,* 2004.

BIBLIOGRAPHY: *Contemporary Authors, New Revision Series,* vol. 94; *Dictionary of Literary Biography Yearbook* (1981); *Something About the Author,* vol. 133; *Best Books for Young Adults,* 2000; www.benbova .net; www.benbova.com

TINA HERTEL

BRADBURY, Ray

American, b. 22 August 1920, Waukegan, Illinois

B. is recognized as a leading writer of SCIENCE FICTION and a master of the SHORT STORY; additionally, he is an important author of POETRY, plays, and screenplays. Among the members of his vast audience are young readers described by one source as, "intellectually ambitious teenage boys," who become lifetime readers of a variety of science fiction and other literary works. Many young adults have encountered B. in middle and high school literature classes in *The Martian Chronicles* (1950). Although this book established B. as a leading writer of science fiction, it is questionable whether or not this is science fiction in its truest form. He is acknowledged for weaving moral and social/political themes throughout *The Martian Chronicles* that reflect America's anxieties in the early 1950s: the threat of nuclear war, the longing for a simpler life, reactions against racism and censorship, and the fear of foreign political powers. Called "cautionary tales of where we were and where we were going," *The Martian Chronicles* appeal even to those who are not science fiction fans; B. is not as concerned with Mars as with human reactions upon arriving there. His work has been described as simple, poetic, uncomplicated, and direct. Held in highest regard by writers of all experience levels, B.'s books are histories that are more relevant with each passing year and are legends upon which future legends are based.

There were many influences on B.'s creativity. B. said, "Jules Verne was my father, H. G. Wells was my wise uncle. Poe was the batwinged cousin we kept in the attic. Flash Gordon and Buck Rogers were my brothers. And Mary Shelley was my mother. There you have my ancestry." Readers, however, cannot discount the influence of his childhood experiences. As a young child of three, he went to movies with his mother and was "weaned on comic books, magic shows, Jules Verne, [and] circuses." B. spent his early years in Waukegan and Tucson before the family moved to Los Angeles when he was twelve. There he loved the big city and frequently collected autographs from individuals such as W. C. Fields, George Burns, and Gracie Allen. He planned to be an actor; however, two teachers are credited with realizing his talent and encouraging his writing career. He also received encouragement from the authors in the Los Angeles Science Fiction League.

Writing stories at the age of eleven, B. published his first work in 1938. This was the same year he finished high school, the end of his formal education. He sold papers to help support himself during these early years, and by the age of twenty-three, he was writing full time for pulps in such PERIODICALS as *Weird Tales* and *Detective Tales* each week. His first story collection, *Dark Carnival,* was published in 1947, the year he married. He later said his philosophy of life included, "Go to the edge of the cliff and jump off. Build your wings on the way down" (*Brown Daily Herald.* March 24, 1995), and his early plunge into authorship evidences this notion. By 1950 his first novel, *The Martian Chronicles,* was published.

The Illustrated Man (1951), a series of short stories about the scenes on one tattooed individual's skin, brought further success for B. Only a few years later, *Fahrenheit 451* (1954), a SERIES of five short stories, raised B.'s concern with censorship. The title, the temperature at which book paper burns, is set in a future society where the written word is forbidden and firemen are given the task of burning books. A professional book burner begins to question his duties when he learns of a time when people did not fear reading, and he begins to steal books marked for destruction. *Dandelion Wine* (1957) is another of B.'s most enjoyed works, full of autobiographical reflections and the search for meaning behind his childhood experiences.

B. continued to work throughout his life. However, his work in the late 1960s is more introspective, with more whimsy—less dark FANTASY than his early career. His work still, however, is acknowledged for its beauty, power, and succinct brilliance of prose. B.'s belief that writing has changed the way people think is evident in the realm of possibilities that he offers to readers of all ages, genders, and walks of life.

With over five hundred published works, B. is said to be timeless and have constant appeal as a classic author. However, his other creative involvements also speak to young readers about the source and role of imagination in life. He was a consultant for the U.S. pavilion at the 1964 World's Fair as well as serving as a creative consultant for architects, Disney, and others. Many of his works have been adapted to film and television programs such as *The Twilight Zone, Night Gallery,* and, of course, *Ray B. Theater.* His works have become symbolic within the work of others, such as Elton John's "Rocket Man," created around B's story of the same name. Dandelion Crater on Earth's moon was named in honor of B.'s *Dandelion Wine* collection.

Stating that "Science fiction is the most important literature in the history of the world, because it's the history of ideas, the history of civilization birthing itself . . . Science fiction is central to everything we've ever done," B. has been said to express universal human truths by slightly displacing them so they ambiguously resonate into the past and future. And in so doing, B. has fulfilled a philosophy stated in a speech in 1995 at Brown University, "Recreate the world in your own image and make it better for your having been here."

AWARDS: O. Henry Award: 1947 "Homecoming," 1948 "Powerhouse"; 1968 Aviation-Space Writers Association Award, "An Impatient Gulliver Above Our Roots"; 1970 Science Fiction Hall of Fame, "Mars Is Heaven"; 1977 World Fantasy Award for Lifetime Achievement; 1979 Balrog Award; 1980 Grandmaster of Fantasy Gandalf Award; 1984 Prometheus Hall of Fame Award, *Fahrenheit 451;* 1988 Grand Master Nebula Award; 1989 Bram Stoker Award: *The Toynbee Convector,* "The Thing at the Top of the Stairs," Bram Stoker Award for Lifetime Achievement; 2000 Medal for Distinguished Contribution to American Letters from the National Book Foundation.

SELECT FURTHER WORKS: *Switch on the Night,* 1955; *A Medicine for Melancholy,* 1959, (reissued 1998); *Something Wicked This Way Comes,* 1962; *The Ghoul Keepers,* 1961; *R Is for Rocket,* 1962; *S Is for Space,* 1966; *I Sing the Body Electric!,* 1969 (reissued 1998); *The Halloween Tree,* 1972; *The April Witch,* 1987; *Fever Dream,* 1987; "When Elephants Last in the Dooryards Bloomed," 1973; *Death Is a Lonely Business* 1985; *A Graveyard for Lunatics,* 1990; *Quicker Than the Eye,* 1996; *Dogs Think that Every Day,* 1997; *From the Dust Returned: A Family Remembrance,* 2001; *Let's All Kill Costance,* 2002; *The Cat's Pajamas,* 2004.

BIBLIOGRAPHY: Berner, Jason, 1999. "Ray Bradbury," *Encyclopedia of American Literature,* ed. Steven R. Serafin, New York: Continuum Publishing; Donelson, K. & Nilsen, A. 1989, *Literature for Today's Young Adults.* New York: Harper Collins; Ray Bradbury Online, www.spaceagecity.com/bradbury/quotes.htm; *Something About the Author,* 123, 2001; Cullinan, B. & Person, D. 2000, *The Continuum Encyclopedia of Children's Literature;* Timberg, S. 2003, "Mars in Apogee," *Los Angeles Times Book Review,* August 3, 2003; Ray Bradbury, BIO, www.teenreads.com/authors/au-bradbury-ray.asp

JANELLE B. MATHIS

BRADLEY, Marion Zimmer

Author, b. June 3 1930, Albany, New York; d. Sept. 25 1999, Berkeley, California
Robert Bradley 1949, 1 son. Divorced 1964.
Walter Breen 1964, 1 son, 1 daughter. Div 1990.
Pen-names:
Lee Chapman, John Dexter, Miriam Gardner, Valerie Groves, Morgan Ives.

A keen SCIENCE FICTION enthusiast all her life, B. published her first fan MAGAZINE at the age of seventeen, pointing out that science fiction fans are not escapists, but are politically and intellectually engaged. B. was educated at the New York State College for Teachers, (1946–8) and the Hardin-Simmons University, Abilene, Texas (B.A. 1964), carrying out graduate work at the University of California, Berkeley from 1965 to 1967. She then made her home in Berkeley, and lived there until her death in 1999.

B. moved to professional writing in the early 1950s to help support her family. She wrote in the mornings while her children were at school. In the poorly paid world of true-confession and science fiction magazines, B. began as a "high-output" writer. Her first SF sale was the story "Centaurus Changeling" in the Magazine of FANTASY and Science Fiction in 1954, while a space opera, *The Door through Space* (1961), was her first published SF novel.

In 1958, *Amazing Stories* serialized B.'s first Darkover novel, later published as *The Planet Savers* (1962), launching an evocative SERIES which established her reputation and evolved into over twenty volumes, now seen as a major work. Each Darkover novel stands alone, and B. advised new readers to follow the published order, rather than the internal chronology, so they could appreciate her expanding concept of Darkover. Basically, Darkover, an isolated planet with a dim red sun, becomes host to two distinct human cultures after the crash of a spaceship: the Terran people with their community-based reliance on shared technology and the Darkovan people with their independent, self-reliant anti-technological approach. (Darkover's parallel to the split between science fiction and fantasy genres has been noted.) Some characters, like Lew Alton in *The Sword of Aldones* (1962)—revised as *Sharra's Exile* (1981)—have mixed ancestry and face complex dilemmas.

Although B. always claimed to be a science fiction writer, the Darkover saga carries a strong fantasy element as the Darkovans develop their psychic talents, including telepathy. Communication is a recurring theme in the series, as in *Hawkmistress* (1982) where Romilly is able to speak with hawks and horses. In *Stormqueen* (1978) Dorylis can control the weather with her mind, but has to learn how to control her powers. Talents carry obligations on Darkover.

Furthermore, all fighting is face-to-face on this feudal planet; there are no armies, and conflict comes in many forms. While *The Spell Sword* (1974) has strong physical action, it was followed by *The Forbidden Tower* (1977) where the conflict is almost entirely psychological. B's early involvement in what Brian Aldiss has called the "loin-cloth and luxury" school of writing delayed the recognition of her Darkover series as a ground-breaking portrayal of an entire culture, with strong characterization and original plotting.

Although B. was an Episcopalian, she has been credited with popularizing the Earth Goddess concept and wiccan beliefs. In fact B. often used her wide knowledge of religious history and spiritual issues in her fiction, particularly when examining the place of women in society. An example is reflected in the tenth Darkover novel, *The Shattered Chain* (1976), where the limitations imposed by traditional sex roles are challenged as Lady Rohana sets aside her physical and mental bonds, an issue further developed with the exploits of the Free Amazons and the Renunciates in two sequels *Thendara House* (1983) and *City of Sorcery* (1984). *The Ruins of Isis* (1978), by contrast, depicts a matriarchy where men are brutally mistreated. *Firebrand* (1987) is centered on the women of the Trojan War, particularly Cassandra.

B. found that her created worlds enabled her to write about controversial issues with a far greater freedom than traditional novels would have allowed. B. stated, "I write fantasy because it is the only way I can tell the absolute, unvarnished truth." [Quoted in *Feminist Writers,* ed. Pamela Kester-Shelton, St. James Press, Detroit, 1996, page 61.]

In her youth B. read *The Boy's King Arthur* (1880) by Sidney Lanier and Hal Foster's Prince Valiant comic strip, engendering her life-long interest in Dark Age Britain. She believed that Malory had diminished the role of women in the Arthurian legends. Drawing on her wide reading of comparative religions, B. wrote a "reconstructionist" account, restoring women to their rightful place. *The Mists of Avalon* (1982), her single most successful novel, was her first best-seller and her first story to achieve mainstream critical notice.

B.'s version of the Arthurian legend is told by a female narrator, Morgaine, with events centered around female characters, often empowered by their religious role. The spiritually powerful Glastonbury and the legendary Avalon occupy the same mist-cloaked space on different planes of existence. Igraine, Viviane (the Lady of the Lake), and Gwenhwyfar play key roles, while the male characters are mainly seen through their eyes. The Avalon series introduced a wide-ranging and receptive female readership to the formerly male-dominated world of Arthurian legend, particularly in universities. B. had the good fortune to be writing readable novels about female spirituality, patriarchal societies, and the empowerment of women at a time when there was high interest in these issues. Three sequels completed the Avalon quartet, and further developed her vision of the conflict between the Druidic and Roman views of spirituality.

B.'s interests included composing and singing. *Night's Daughter* (1985) was based on Mozart's opera *The Magic Flute*. She greatly admired J. R. R. TOLKIEN, who was the inspiration for her *The Jewel of Arwen* (1974), and she set thirteen of his songs to music. B also wrote a children's book, *The Colors of Space* (1973).

B. edited the annual Swords and Sorceresses anthology for 16 years. In 1988 B. launched *Marion Zimmer Bradley's Fantasy Magazine,* a recognition of the wide audience for her style of writing. She edited it until her death, creating a platform for a wide range of fantasy writers, before it ceased publication at Issue 50 in 2000, a year after her death.

B. produced more than fifty novels and anthologies, helping make fantasy a popular genre. She was a trailblazer, establishing independent female characters in male-dominated genres. She used science fiction and fantasy to write (and enable others to write more freely) about colonization, gender, sexuality, hierarchical societies, human relationships, and the role of women.

AWARDS: 1984 Locus Award Best Fantasy Novel, *The Mists of Avalon;* 2000: World Fantasy Award: Life Achievement.

SELECT FURTHER WORKS: Darkover series: *The Bloody Sun,* 1964; *Star of Danger,* 1965; *The Winds of Darkover,* 1970; *Darkover Landfall,* 1972; *Heritage of Hastur,* 1975; *Two To Conquer,* 1980; *Heirs of Hammerfell,* 1989; *Rediscovery,* 1993 (with Mercedes Lackey); *The Shadow Matrix,* 1988; Exile's Song trilogy, 1996; Avalon series: *The Forest House,* 1993 [*Forests of Avalon*]; *The Lady of Avalon,* 1997; *Priestess of Avalon,* 2001; Other: *Seven from the Stars,* 1962; *Hunters of the Red Moon,* 1973; *Survey Ship,* 1980; *The House between the Worlds,* 1981; *The Inheritor,* 1984; *Warrior Woman,* 1985; *Dark Satanic,* 1988; *Black Trillium,* 1990 (with Andre NORTON & Julian May) *Witch Hill,* 1990; *Lady of the Trillium,* 1995; *Tiger Burning Bright,* 1995. (with Andre Norton & Mercedes Lackey); *Ghostlight,* 1995; *Witchlight,* 1996; *Gravelight,* 1997; *The Gratitude of Kings,* 1997 (with Elisabeth Waters); The Clingfire Trilogy, 2001; *The Fall of Atlantis,* 2008.

BIBLIOGRAPHY: Clute, John & Grant John, *The Encyclopedia of Fantasy,* 1997; Hildebrand, Kristina, *The Female Reader at the Round Table,* 2001; Jesser, Nancy, *Marion Zimmer Bradley in Feminist Writers,* ed Pamela Kester-Shelton, St James Press, Detroit MI, 1996: 60–63; *Contemporary Literary Criticism,* Vol 30, 1984: p. 26–32; Marion Zimmer Bradley Literary Works Trust website: http://mzbwork.home.att.net/bio.htm

TREVOR AGNEW

BRADSHAW, Gillian (Marucha)
Author, b. 14 May 1956, Washington, D.C.

B. re-creates the life and times that Arthurian legends are made of, as well as life in early medieval times, in ancient Egypt, Greece, and Rome. Carefully researching her topic, B. has the ability to weave imaginative and historical events together, mixing fiction with truth, creating characters that she brings to life so realistically that one thinks they actually played a role in history. Most recently, she incorporates the magic of FANTASY within the historical events in her writing. B. is the daughter of an American Association Press newsman and a British embassy confidential secretary who met in Rio de Janeiro. The second of four children in this family of readers and writers, she has lived in Santiago, Chile, and two areas of Michigan. Graduating from the University of Michigan with honors, she received her B.A. in English and Classical Greek in 1977. Two years later, majoring in Greek and Latin literature, B. earned her M.A. from Newnham College, Cambridge University. After graduation, B. stayed in Cambridge, using this time to write and to decide what kind of a "real job" she

was suited for. B. discovered two very important things: authors can earn their living by writing no matter where they live, and marriage was definitely in her future. On June 27, 1981, she married Robin Christopher Ball, a Ph.D. research physicist. During their first years of marriage, they lived in Paris and California, later moving back to Cambridge "where my husband taught and researched for many years. Eventually he was offered a chair at the University of Warwick, and we moved to Coventry." They have three sons, Christopher, Michael, and Neville, one daughter, Jennifer, and a dog. They live near Cambridge and spend time exploring the ruins in Greece and Italy. Set in 7th-century Constantinople, *The Alchemy of Fire* is her most recent historical novel.

AWARDS: Jule and Avery Hopwood Award for Fiction (1977), *Hawk of May;* ALA Alek List, *The Sand-Reckoner.*

FURTHER WORKS: *Hawk of May,* 1980; *Kingdom of Summer,* 1981, and *In Winter's Shadow,* 1982, combined into *Down the Long Wind: The Magical Trilogy of Arthurian Britain.* Historical Novels: *Beacon at Alexandria,* 1986; *The Bearkeeper's Daughter,* 1987; *Imperial Purple,* 1989; *The Colour of Power,* 1989; *Horses of Heaven,* 1992; *Beyond the North Wind,* 1993; *The Beacon at Alexandria (Hera),* 1994; *Island of Ghosts,* 1998; *The Sand-Reckoner,* 2002; *The Somers Treatment,* 2003; *Cleopatra's Heir,* 2003; *Render unto Caesar,* 2003. Fantasy Novels: *The Dragon and the Thief,* 1991; *The Land of Gold,* 1992; *Beyond the North Wind,* 1993; *The Wolf Hunt,* 2002 based on the 12th century *Lai de Bisclavret* (a medieval SHORT STORY about Bisclavret, the noble baron who was a werewolf). SCIENCE FICTION: *Dangerous Notes,* 2001; *The Wrong Reflection,* 2003.

BIBLIOGRAPHY: Personal Interview, *Contemporary Authors,* vol. 103, p. 54

VALERIE A. PALAZOLO

BRAITHWAITE, E. R. (Eustace Edward Ricardo)
Author, b. 27 June 1920, Georgetown, British Guyana

B. is renowned for his AUTOBIOGRAPHY, *To Sir, with Love* (1959), relating his experiences as a British high-school teacher in a depressed area of London, where lives change, injustices and racism are challenged, and respect is earned and given. These tenets transcend the ages. Many works that followed were based on his experiences in Guyana. Attending

Queen's College in British Guyana and The City College of New York, he graduated with a B.S. in 1940, and later attended Gonville and Caius College, Cambridge University, receiving a Masters of Science Degree in Physics in 1949. Between these two degrees, B. served as a fighter pilot in the Royal Air Force (1941–45) during World War II. He furthered his studies at the Institute of Education in London. B. received honorary doctoral degrees from Oxford University and The Sorbonne in Paris. As a schoolmaster in London (1950–1957) he worked for the London County Council, Department of Child Welfare as a welfare officer and consultant on affairs of blacks (1958–1960). As a human rights officer (1960–62) he worked for the World Veterans' Foundation in Paris. Here he also worked for UNESCO as an educational consultant and lecturer for the next five years. In 1967, B. became the representative for Guyana to the United Nations in New York City; then he became the Guyanan Ambassador to Venezuela until 1969. B. became a Professor of English at his alma mater, New York University. As a writer in residence in the English Department at Howard University in Washington, D.C., he teaches the first-year Composition for Honors class. Under his tutelage the *Faces & Voices Anthologies of Verse and Prose,* written by his students, is published by Howard University. In referring to his class, B. states, "Composition for Honors is a challenge, a clear though unspoken challenge to use words as imaginatively and artistically as our intelligence will allow, and because we may ever plumb the ultimate of our intellectual capacity, there will always be plenty of room for improving our ability to compose, in thought, in speech and in writing." To "develop and maintain any capacity to form opinions and judgments, one must first develop the habit of reading, for one's own pleasurable satisfaction," B. is, first, last and always, a teacher. In addition to teaching and writing, B. enjoys playing tennis and dancing.

FURTHER WORKS: *A Kind of Homecoming,* 1962; *Paid Servant,* 1968; *Choice of Straws,* 1967; *Reluctant Neighbors,* 1972; *"Honorary White": A Visit to South Africa,* 1975; *Faces and Voices 5: An Anthology of Verse and Prose (Conversation Piece; Language, the Essential Birthright; and Nicole),* Howard University, Washington, D.C., and contributing author to *Time* magazine.

BIBLIOGRAPHY: *Contemporary Authors Online,* Gale, 2003. Reproduced in *Biography Resource Center.* Farmington Hills, Mich.: The Gale Group, 2003. http://www.galenet.com/servlet/BioRC and *Faces & Voices 4* at http://www.howard.edu/library/Faces Voices4/BraithwaiteER.htm

VALERIE A. PALAZOLO

BRANCATO, Robin F.
Author, b. 19 March 1936, Reading, Pennsylvania

In B.'s literary world, there are no solutions for the hardships of adolescence; instead, the author offers methods for coping with the uncontrollable events of life. Her YA books often end without a concrete conclusion, much like in reality. B. does not pretend to offer answers for her readers; on the contrary, she hopes to create new questions for them to contemplate and new concepts to aid them in life.

Fortunately, B.'s childhood was not full of the trials that she creates for her characters. In fact, she received much of her exposure to the outside world through books. The author confesses that "[her] entrance into adolescence was gradual and relatively untraumatic," her time filled with friends, athletic activities, and of course, her literary work. She graduated from University of Pennsylvania in 1958 and received her master's degree in 1976. During this period, B. became a mother and worked as a textbook copy editor and a teacher of English, journalism, and world literature. However, the author did not feel satisfied with her writing, which was limited to several poems and short stories that had been published in small newspapers and magazines. At the recommendation of a fellow author, B. experimented with novel writing; the final product, *Don't Sit under the Apple Tree* (1975), was completed in the summer of 1973.

B. fills her characters with fears of the uncontrollable, such as mortality, mental illness, and thoughts of suicide. The characters in *Something Left to Lose* (1976) and Gary in *Winning* (1977) struggle with the worth of their existence and the need for their existence. Rebbie believes that her life, which includes an uncaring father and an alcoholic mother, has no real worth and that she therefore has nothing to lose through her careless lifestyle. Alternatively, Jane Ann obsessively embraces structure, believing it to be the only way to keep her sanity. The two friends are able to find a middle ground between damaging hedonism and compulsive self-control, and begin to understand the true finality of death. In *Winning,* Gary Madden is a paralyzed ex-football player who receives emotional support from his recently widowed English teacher. Without being saccharine, his teacher uses literature to jolt Gary's sense of self-worth and make him realize the potential his life still holds.

B. warns against the promise of idealistic bliss in *Blinded by the Light* (1978). Gail Brower investigates a religious cult that has captivated the mind and heart of her older brother, only to find herself being brainwashed along with the cult. While Gail's boyfriend eventually gets her to see the truth behind the serenity of the cult, Gail is unable to do the same for her brother.

B.'s work from the 1980s, including *Sweet Bells Jangled out of Tune* (1980) and *Uneasy Money* (1986), continue to place teenagers in difficult situations and present interesting methods of survival. Her inclusion of literary works such as *Our Town, Death of a Salesman,* and *Antigone* in her novels indicates her belief in learning and growing from literature. The concepts learned by B.'s fictional characters from these works equip them with tools with which to survive adolescence; similarly, B.'s young adult novels offer support to her young readers, struggling with their own maturation.

AWARDS: ALA Best Book: 1977 for *Winning,* 1980 for *Come Alive at 505,* and 1982 for *Sweet Bells Jangled out of Tune;* New Jersey Institute of Technology's New Jersey Authors Award: 1988 for *Uneasy Money,* and 1990 for *Winning.*

SELECT FURTHER WORKS: *Come Alive at 505,* 1980; *Facing Up,* 1984.

BIBLIOGRAPHY: *Children's Literature Review,* Vol. 32, 1994; *Contemporary Literary Criticism,* Vol. 35, 1985; DeSalvo, Louise A., "The Uses of Adversity," *Media and Methods,* April 1979, pp. 16, 18, 50–51; Gallo, Donald R., *Speaking for Ourselves: Autobiographical Sketches by Notable Authors of Books for Young Adults,* 1990; Review of *Winning, Booklist,* September 1, 1977, p. 30; *Something About the Author,* vol. 97, 1998.

RACHEL WITMER

BRANDENBURG, Jim

Author, b. 23 November 1945, Luverne, Minnesota

After graduating from the University of Minnesota Duluth with a degree in studio art, B. began work as a picture editor at the *Daily Globe* in southern Minnesota. In 1978, he became a contract photographer for *National Geographic* magazine. His photographs have been featured in dozens of *National Geographic* articles, and have also been published in many other MAGAZINES, including *Life, Time,* and *BBC Wildlife.* In addition, B.'s work has also been featured in several books and documentary films; he was commissioned by the U.S. Postal Service to design and photograph a set of ten stamps in 1981. He currently works as a freelance photographer.

B. has traveled throughout the world capturing images on film, ranging from the frozen Arctic to the desert of Southern Africa. He is the author of several best-selling books featuring his critically acclaimed photographs. B.'s books appeal to both adults and young people, but the combination of straightforward, clear text and arresting images makes many of his books especially popular with reluctant readers. *To the Top of the World: Adventures with Arctic Wolves* (1993) and *Sand and Fog: Adventures in Southern Africa* (1994) have both been praised for appealing to reluctant young adult readers. Although not necessarily intended for research purposes, his books are excellent for browsing, and offer readers a glimpse into the exciting world of natural history.

AWARDS: Two-time winner of the Magazine Photographer of the Year award from the National Press Photographers Association (1981 and 1983); Kodak Wildlife Photographer of the Year (1988); *To the Top of the World:* ALA Best Book for Young Adults and Recommended Book for the Reluctant YA Reader, both 1994; *Sand and Fog:* ALA Reluctant Young Adult Reader Award, 1995 Parents' Choice Award.

FURTHER WORKS: *White Wolf: Living With an Arctic Legend,* 1988; *Minnesota: Images of Home,* 1990; *To the Top of the World: Adventures with Arctic Wolves,* 1993; *Brother Wolf: A Forgotten Promise,* 1993; *Sand and Fog: Adventures in Southern Africa,* 1994; *An American Safari: Adventures on the North American Prairie,* 1995; *Chased by the Light: A 90-Day Journey,* 1998; *Looking for the Summer,* 2003.

BIBLIOGRAPHY: "Best Books for Young Adults," *Booklist* 90, 14 (15 March 1994): 1356; "Books for Young Adults," *Booklist* 85, 8 (15 December 1988): 699; Hester, Denia, Review of *To the Top of the World: Adventures with Arctic Wolves. Booklist* 90, 9 (1 January 1994): 820; "Recommended Books for the Reluctant Reader," *Booklist* 91, 15 (1 April 1995): 1412; Review of *White Wolf: Living With an Arctic Legend, Booklist* 85, 8 (15 December 1988): 670; Rochman, Hazel, Review of *Sand and Fog: Adventures in Southern Africa, Booklist* 90, 13 (1 March

1994): 1260; *Something about the Author,* Vol. 87, 1996; http://www.jimbrandenburg.com

KATE ADAMS

BRANFORD, Henrietta
Author, b. 12 January 1946, India; d. 23 April 1999, Southampton, England

B. trained to become a youth and community worker, worked as a nanny, in shops, and tried many other different jobs. After raising three children, she decided to write professionally. B. began her writing career about age forty.

B. believed that her work is for all ages and that it expresses the values of love and courage. B.'s stories can be cruel; her protagonists need courage in order to deal with the harsh realities they face.

In *Fire, Bed, and Bone* (1998), a historical tale set in 1381, the reader sees the British feudal system and the peasant revolts through the eyes of a hunting dog. The dog remains nameless throughout the story; at the start of the story, he is living comfortably with a family of serfs, but his life is disrupted when his family is arrested for attending a revolutionary rally. The dog becomes a hero when he finds a home for two of his master's children and brings the baby's bonnet to his imprisoned master and mistress to inform them of their children's safety. Through the dog's eyes, one sees the cruelty of the effects of evil wrongdoing. *Fire, Bed, and Bone* won the Bronze Award (1998) and was on the Carnegie Medal shortlist (1997).

In memory of B., and her Walker Books editor, Wendy Boase, The Branford Boase Award for a first novel was established in 2000.

AWARDS: Smarties Book Prize, Book Trust, 1994 for *Dimanche Diller; Guardian* Children's Fiction Award, 1998 for *Fire, Bed, and Bone;* Books in the Middle: Outstanding Titles, Voice of Youth Advocates, 1998, both for *Fire, Bed, and Bone;* Best Books for the Teen Age, 2000, for *White Wolf.*

FURTHER WORKS: *Royal Blunder* (SHORT STORIES), 1990; *Clare's Summer,* 1993; *Dimanche Diller,* 1994; *Dimanche Diller in Danger,* 1994; *Royal Blunder and the Haunted* House (short stories), 1994; *Birdo* (PICTURE BOOK), 1995; *Someone Somewhere* (picture book), 1995; *Nightmare Neighbours,* 1995; *The Theft of Thor's Hammer,* 1996; *Dimanche Diller at Sea,* 1996; *The Fated Sky,* 1997; *Spacebaby,* 1996; *Ruby Red: Tales from the Weedwater* (short stories), 1998;

Hansel and Gretel, 1998; *A Change of Safety,* 1998; *White Wolf,* 1999.

BIBLIOGRAPHY: *Contemporary Authors,* vol. 175; *Something about the Author,* vol. 106.

SUSAN E. MORTON

BRAUTIGAN, Richard Gary
Author, poet, b. 30 January 1935, Tacoma, Washington; d. September 1984, n.p.

Though not known primarily as a YA author, B.'s twenty-plus titles (ten novels, nine books of POETRY, two collections of SHORT STORIES, and various others) have long enjoyed a reading popularity with young adults seeking an alternative writing style. Called by many the "last of the Beats," B.'s writings range from the first books of poetry, which include *The Galilee Hitch-Hiker* (1958), *The Pill Versus the Springhill Mine Diaster* (1968), and *Loading Mercury with a Pitchfork* (1976), to the more famous novels *A Confederate General from Big Sur* (1965), *Trout Fishing in America* (1967), and *The Hawkline Monster: A Gothic Western* (1974), and finally to the inimitable short-story anthologies, which include *Revenge of the Lawn: Stories 1962–1970* (1971) and *The Tokyo-Montana Express* (1980).

B.'s popularity with young people is easy to understand: he has remained a writer the younger set has "discovered" again and again. Indeed, between 1967 and 1977, B.'s fiction and poetry ran through printing after printing, with *Trout Fishing in America* selling over three million copies. In the 1990s, several years after B.'s death in 1984, nine of the author's twenty-plus books had been brought back into print and could be found on college campuses everywhere. Indeed, B.'s concise use of language blends with his outrageous comedy and easy irony to move generation after generation of readers, renewing his popularity into the new millennium.

Before attempting to write his first novel, B. told an interviewer that he wrote poetry for seven years so that he could learn to write a sentence. This overstatement of fact is representative of B.'s prose-poem writing style. From *Trout Fishing in America,* B.'s narrator reports that the canyon was so narrow that the stream gushed out from the mountainside ". . . like water from a faucet. You had to be a plumber to fish that creek."

Often B.'s writing contains melancholic meaderings and statements on life itself or aspects of life, which lean heavily toward sentimentality yet are miraculously saved by a clever use of exaggerated figures of speech and highly metaphorical language, trademarks of B.'s style. Take the following lines from *The Tokyo-Montana Express* story/vignette "One Arm Burning in Tokyo" (the protagonist of this short fiction has lost an arm in an auto accident and leapt out of his hospital room window, thus ending his life): "When my friend told me the story, she said, 'It was a big waste. Why did he have to do that? A man can learn to live with one arm.' *Well, he couldn't,* and the end was just the same, anyway: a one-armed corpse burning in a crematorium. Where the other arm should be burning, there was nothing." B. committed suicide in his Bolinas, California, home in September of 1984.

FURTHER WORKS: *The Return of the Rivers,* 1957; *Lay the Marble Tea,* 1959; *The Octopus Frontier,* 1960; *All Watched Over by Machines of Loving Grace,* 1967; *Please Plant This Book,* 1968; *Rommel Drives on Deep into Egypt,* 1970; *June 30th June 30th,* 1978. *In Watermelon Sugar,* 1968; *The Abortion: An Historical Romance 1966,* 1971; *Willard and His Bowling Trophies: A Perverse Mystery,* 1975; *Sombrero Fallout: A Japanese Novel,* 1976; *Dreaming of Babylon: A Private Eye Novel 1942,* 1977; *So the Wind Won't Blow It All Away,* 1982; *An Unfortunate Woman: A Journey,* 2000.

BIBLIOGRAPHY: *Dictionary of Literary Biography, Volume 2: American Novelists Since World War II, First Series* (The Gale Group); *The Edna Webster Collection of Undiscovered Writings,* 1999; *The Tokyo-Montana Express,* 1980; *The Brautigan Bibliography* website: <www.eaze.net/~jfbarber/brautigan/index.html>; "Old Lady" *The San Francisco Poets,* 1971.

JOHN C. BAKEN

BRIDGERS, Sue Ellen

Author, b. 20 September 1942, Greenville, North Carolina

B. is considered a literary giant in the field of YOUNG ADULT LITERATURE, with themes of the importance of place and family running through each of her novels. B. is no stranger to the complexities of FAMILY— she grew up in small North Carolina towns where generations often remained and families were linked through various kinships. Family and friends knew each others' histories as well as their current situations. She realized through experience the difficulties and joys of living where many folks had expectations and concern. However, she states during an interview in *Something about the Author* AUTOBIOGRAPHY that "we learned to be proud of our heritage; we knew the unyielding, powerful hold of family." This insight she shares through the complex relationships that surround the challenges faced by her main characters. She also has shared her realization that fiction has at its origin much memory whether intentional or not and that much of her work is actually truth framed within fiction.

B.'s first novel, *Home before Dark* (1976), was immediately popular and evidences these themes of family and sense of place. Fourteen-year-old Stella and her family return to North Carolina after many years as migrant workers. The small tenant home is the first permanent house she can remember. After her mother's death and her father's decision to remarry, Stella initially will not leave the cabin that represents her first experience establishing "roots," although by the end of the novel she matures as she realizes a new sense of family. The novel is praised for attention to character and theme through profound imagery. Family relationships are also woven throughout *All Together Now* (1979), as twelve-year-old Casey spends the summer in her grandmother's small town while her own mother works and father is fighting in the Korean War. In this story about love and caring, Casey works with others to prevent a man from having his developmentally disabled brother institutionalized. Another difficult situation is faced by a teen in *Permanent Connections* (1987) in which seventeen-year-old Rob must stay in North Carolina with his grandfather and agoraphobic aunt while his uncle recuperates from a broken hip. This story is noted for its fine, realistic characterizations as a young person and his elders work through emotional attitudes toward understanding. Again, B.'s ability to portray these emotional relationships is exceptional. B. states that, "Technically the characters always come first and then the kind of people they are dictates what they do, just as you and I are products of heredity and environment."

FURTHER WORKS: *Notes for Another Life,* 1981; *Sara Will,* 1985; *Keeping Christina,* 1993; *All We Know of Heaven,* 1996.

BIBLIOGRAPHY: Hipple, Ted, *Writers for Young Adults,* Vol. 1, 1993; *Something About the Author Autobiography Series; St. James Guide to Young Adult Literature,* 1999.

JANELLE MATHIS

BRIDGING THE LITERARY-ACHIEVEMENT GAP: GRADES 4–12: ISSUES AND CHALLENGES

Twelve-year-old Chelsea Strickland is an avid lover of books. An independent reader since her preschool years, her love of books and stories was nurtured on the laps of the adults in her family. We asked Chelsea about her current favorite books and authors. She mentioned Eva Ibbotson's book *Which Witch?* Sharon CREECH's *Chasing Redbird* and *Walk Two Moons,* and J. K. ROWLING's Harry Potter SERIES, Amy Brashard's *The Sisterhood of the Traveling Pants,* and Georgia Byngs's *Molly Moon.* Chelsea had very definite opinions about why she liked particular books and authors. For example, the appeal of Creech's books is their symbolic and sensitive nature. Brashard is very imaginative, yet her books seem so real. *Molly Moon,* a book borrowed from her younger sister Rebecca, was fun because it was quick, easy, and humorous.

Obviously, Chelsea is a very lucky girl. Like many good readers she has a wide range of interests. She likes sports, riding her bicycle, using the computer to communicate with her friends and check information on the internet, watching the limited amount of television her parents allow, and reading books for pleasure. She has developed personal literary tastes and the ability to talk about books in a literate way.

Unfortunately, too many pre-adolescents and adolescents are not enjoying positive experiences with literature. Some lack assistance from adults to help them balance the many interests in their lives, so that reading becomes and remains a key part of what they choose to do. Others lack the skills required to read fluently enough to make reading the pleasure it should be. The following chapter offers a comprehensive overview of the major issues and challenges faced by today's educators as they attempt to develop proficient pre-adolescent and adolescent readers who know and love literature and view reading as an important part of their lives.

This article is divided into four sections. First, after a brief word about definitions, we outline what we con-sider to be key issues related to improving literacy learning among pre-adolescents and adolescents. Second, we describe how these issues become magnified in importance when working to alleviate the achievement gap among youth who, for a variety of reasons, are not achieving as well as educators, policymakers, and their parents expect. Third, we argue that these issues urgently need addressing if the goal is to close the achievement gap by improving literacy learning among youth from low-income minority neighborhoods. Finally, we outline key points in the forthcoming chapters to provide our readers with both a preview and a bridge to what is to come.

A Brief Word about Adolescence as a Concept

Until recently the term *adolescence* drew little critique from scholars interested in studying the physical, emotional, intellectual, and social development of youths ranging in age from roughly ten to eighteen. Its unquestioned acceptance rested largely on the notion that adolescence was a developmental stage through which youngsters passed on their way to becoming adults, or as Appleman (2000) has wryly described it, "a kind of purgatory between childhood and adulthood" (p. 1). Although this concept of adolescence is by no means obsolete, it has been tempered by work that questions the distinctions thought to separate the adolescent world from the adult world.

For example, the normative view of adolescents—as "not-yet" adults and thus less competent and less knowledgeable than their elders—is one that is increasingly being critiqued in the professional literature. Like others (Amit-Talai and Wulff, 1995; Lesko, 2001) before us, we do not subscribe to this view. Instead, we like to think of adolescents as knowing things that have to do with their particular life experiences and the particular spaces they occupy both in and out of school in a quickly changing world. This situated perspective in youth culture recognizes that school literacy, though important, is but one among multiple literacies that young people use daily.

Because they are particularly adept at multi-tasking, it is not uncommon for students as young as ten years of age to use their knowledge of traditional print, the Internet, and various forms of multimedia simultaneously. Picture, for example, a youth seated at her computer searching the Internet for information that she can use in writing a report that is due in social studies class tomorrow. Note how she switches her attention momentarily from the class assignment to instant messaging her friends about a newly released music CD. Note, too, how quickly she refocuses her attention on the assignment as she performs the necessary keystrokes for downloading a visual image that can be inserted into the report she is writing, all the while listening to her favorite music playing in the background.

Key Issues in Improving Young People's Literacy Learning

Granted, there are problems with the foregoing picture, not the least of which is the issue of access to the Internet, a problem commonly referred to as the *digital divide,* which can lead to inequity in opportunities for youth living in economically depressed conditions. There are also questions concerning students' attention spans and the quality of the homework that they complete while multitasking. These concerns stem primarily from the fact that much of what is known about exemplary literacy instruction for preadolescents and adolescents assumes an equal playing field, one in which attention is duly focused on constructing meaning from and with texts of various kinds by applying common background knowledge. That this assumption is rarely the case, especially given the increasing diversity of students in U.S. schools, will come as no surprise. Nevertheless, it is important to know what is expected of literacy learners at the intermediate, middle, and high school levels *as a group* before considering how these expectations may or may not play out for different subgroups of students. It is also important to understand the issues behind these expectations, several of which are spelled out here.

Expectation #1—Students Will Use Effective Text-Processing Skills and Strategies

The issue here is that regardless of a research base summarized by the National Reading Panel (2000) and the RAND Reading Study Group (2002) that shows comprehension monitoring, using graphic organizers, generating self-questions, using text structure as an aid to remembering, and summarizing are effective strategies and lead to improved comprehension, too few students possess these basic skills.

In the U.S. according to one source, the Carnegie Foundation (http://www.carnegie.org/sub/news/sns.html), close to 50 percent of all incoming ninth graders in this country's comprehensive, public high schools cannot comprehend the texts that their teachers expect them to read in order to complete class assignments. Students who do not comprehend adequately not surprisingly end up failing their courses and eventually dropping out of school. Even those who manage to stay in school often have a history of reading difficulties that prevent them from acquiring the requisite background knowledge, skills, and specialized vocabulary needed for learning in the subject areas. Their teachers understandably become frustrated and sometimes resort to what Finn (1999) calls a "domesticating" education. That is, they expect less of these students in exchange for the students' good will and reasonable effort in completing assignments that typically require little, if any, reading. It's an unfortunate case of less leading to less.

Instruction that is effective is embedded in the regular curriculum and makes use of the new literacies (Lankshear and Knobel, 2003), including multiple forms of texts (print, visual, aural, and digital) that can be read critically for multiple purposes in a variety of contexts. For this to become a reality, it will be important to teach students how to use relevant background knowledge and strategies for reading, discussing, and writing about a variety of texts. It will require the support of administrators and policy makers who buy into the idea that all students, including those who struggle to read in subject area classrooms, deserve instruction that is developmentally, culturally, and linguistically responsive to their needs (Alvermann, forthcoming).

Expectation #2—Students Will Be Motivated and Engaged

The cognitive demands of text processing, such as those described in the previous paragraph, are only part of the story, however. At issue here is the additional expectation that students will be motivated to participate in subject matter learning despite the fact that such learning often requires a long-term engagement with difficult concepts that on the surface may seem to have little relevance to adolescents' everyday lives. This expectation is heightened further when factors related to feelings of competency, or self-efficacy, are taken into account.

In adolescence as in earlier and later life, it is the belief in the self (or lack of such belief) that makes a difference in how competent a person feels. Perceptions of one's competencies are central to most theories of motivation, and the research on self-efficacy bears out the hypothesized connection between feeling competent and being motivated to learn something new. For example, providing adolescents who are experiencing reading difficulties with clear goals for a comprehension task and then giving feedback on the progress they are making can lead to increased self-efficacy and greater use of comprehension strategies (Schunk & Rice, 1993). Likewise, creating environments that make use of multimedia and newer forms of information communication technologies can heighten students' motivation to become independent readers and writers. This in turn can increase their sense of competency as readers (Kamil, Intrator, & Kim, 2000).

What is less clear from the research, however, is why students' motivations to read decline over time. Although decreases in intrinsic reading motivation have been noted as children move from the elementary grades to middle school, explanations vary as to the cause, with a number of researchers attributing the decline to differences in instructional practices (Eccles, Wigfield, and Schiefele, 1998; Oldfather and McLaughlin, 1993). Other researchers (e.g., Wade and Moje, 2000) attribute pre-adolescents' and adolescents' declining interests in subject matter reading to the transmission model of teaching. This model, with its emphasis on skill and drill, teacher-centered instruction, and passive learning is viewed as inferior to a participatory model of instruction that actively engages students in their own learning (individually and in small groups) and that treats texts as tools for learning rather than as repositories of information to be memorized and then all too quickly forgotten.

Expectation #3—Students Will Adopt Normative Ways of Reading and Writing

The academic struggles of pre-adolescents and adolescents who can read but all too frequently choose not to do so is an issue that bears close scrutiny. These individuals are commonly referred to as aliterate, but their situation is no less worrisome than that of readers who struggle to read for lack of adequate skills. Unlike the rather straightforward definition for aliteracy (having the capacity to read but electing not to), the term struggling reader is a contested one. A cursory analysis of the reading research literature reveals that struggling is used to refer to youth with clinically diagnosed reading disabilities as well as to those who are English learners, "at-risk," low-achieving unmotivated, disenchanted, or generally unsuccessful in school-related reading.

A smorgasbord of descriptors, these labels when applied to either an aliterate student or a struggling reader tell little or nothing about the sociocultural construction of such students. They also provide little guidance to teachers in terms of how to instruct individuals who can read but won't, or who want to read despite the struggle. According to anthropologists, McDermott and Varenne (1995), it is society at large that produces the conditions necessary for some individuals to succeed, others to struggle, and still others to fail outright. Applied to education, one could interpret this to mean that for some adolescents who have turned their backs on a version of reading and writing commonly referred to as academic literacy, it is the traditional school curriculum that is contributing to their difficulties.

Why might this be the case? One of us has argued elsewhere (Alvermann, 2001) that in an effort to raise the bar by implementing higher standards—a noteworthy goal in most people's minds—some schools are promoting certain normative ways of reading texts that may be disabling some of the very students they are trying to help. The possibility that schools are constructing certain types of readers as "aliterate" or "struggling" is even more problematic when one considers that certain normative ways of reading and writing are losing their usefulness, and perhaps to some extent their validity, in a world increasingly defined by the Internet, hypermedia, e-mailing, instant messaging, and the like (Bruce, 2002). If instruction is to benefit both aliterate and struggling readers, it should take into account their personal and everyday literacies in ways that enable them to use those literacies as springboards for engaging actively in academic tasks that are challenging and worthwhile. It should also make use of the new literacies (Lankshear and Knobel, 2003), including multiple forms of texts (print, visual, aural, and digital) that can be read critically for multiple purposes in a variety of contexts.

Finally, rather than expecting all students to adopt normative ways of reading and writing, preference might be given to rethinking current intervention programs, perhaps along the lines of what Luke and Elkins (2000) have alluded to as re/mediating adolescent literacies. *Re/mediation,* not to be confused with the older term, *remediation* without the slash, involves rethinking or reframing the way we think about intervening in adolescents' reading lives. It calls for moving beyond fruitless searches for some method or "magic bullet" that purportedly will fix their so-called deficits in reading. Re/mediation, in the sense that Luke and Elkins (2000) use the term, involves refashioning instructional conditions so as to enable students to use their out-of-school literacies and knowledge of various media forms to learn in the classroom. In a metaphoric sense, re/mediation involves fixing the conditions in which students learn rather than attempting to fix the students per se.

The Achievement Gap

The issues, already discussed in this chapter, regarding pre-adolescent and adolescent learners, are compounded when the students come from low-income and low-income minority homes. Specifically, these issues become demonstrably acute when students are members of families that are poor and African American or Hispanic. Such students are likely to attend schools with high mobility rates, inadequate resources and facilities, and large numbers of children with challenging learning needs. Even when their teachers try hard to make the best of the challenges before them, Knapp (1995) suggests that "many wonder why it seems so hard to engage and maintain children's attention to learning tasks, communicate what often appears to be common sense, and show demonstrable achievement gains on conventional measures of learning (p. 1). On the other hand, Knapp also offers what are likely to be the thoughts and feelings of many of the students these teachers are trying to reach, "From their point of view, it is not always obvious what they have to gain from being in school or from going along with what schools ask of them" (p.1).

Despite efforts by educators and policymakers during the last several decades, achievement gaps between certain groups of students stubbornly persist. Surveys of student achievement by the National As-

sessment of Educational Progress (NAEP) (2000) between 1973–1999 showed a persistent although slightly narrowing gap between white and black students. The score gap between white and black fourth-graders was smaller in 2002 than in 1994 and the gap between white and Hispanic fourth-graders narrowed between 2000 and 2002 but neither was found to differ significantly from 1992. At grades eight and twelve, no significant change in either gap was seen across the assessment years. It is important to note that overall NAEP results for reading in 2002 were not encouraging. The fourth-grade average score in 2002 was higher than in 1994, 1998, and 2000, but was not found to be significantly different from 1992. Among eighth-graders, the average score in 2002 was higher than in 1992 or 1994. The twelfth-grade average score in 2002 was lower than in 1992 and 1998 (National Center for Education Statistics, 2003).

In 2001, the reauthorization of the Elementary and Secondary Education Act, known as the No Child Left Behind Act, brought greater attention to this problem by requiring individual states, districts, and schools to be accountable for eliminating the achievement gap by the year 2014. States and districts are required to assess all students annually from grades three to eight and disaggregate the results to show adequate yearly progress for their total student population as well as for different demographic groups.

Although a great deal of serious attention has been given to this problem, it is safe to say that, as an educational community, we are far from final answers. The emerging concerns faced by educators and policymakers are extremely complex. Contributing factors rarely stand alone. More often, they are interactive and interdependent and include issues of socioeconomic status, home and linguistic background, and quality of instruction. A brief discussion of these follows.

Socioeconomic Status

Family income and reading achievement are closely linked. Socioeconomic differences are generally indexed by such variables as household income and parents' education and occupation, alone or in some weighted combination. Families rated low in SES are not only less affluent and less educated than other families but also tend to live in communities in which the average family SES is low and tend to receive less adequate nutrition and health services. In their discussion of SES as a risk factor, Snow, Burns, Griffin (1998) describe low SES as both an individual risk factor and a group risk factor. As individuals, poor children attending the same schools as more affluent children are more likely to become poorer readers than children from high-income families. Also as a group, low SES children from low-income communities are likely to become poorer readers than children from more affluent communities. However, when achievement scores and SES are measured individually for all children in a large sample, the strength of the association between SES and achievement is far lower. A low-status child in a generally moderate or upper-status school or community is far less at risk than that same child in a whole school or community of low-status children (Snow, Burns, and Griffin, 1998, p. 124). The effect of SES is strongest when it is used to indicate the status of a school, a community, or school district, rather than the status of the individual.

School funding plays an important role in the socioeconomic status of schools and communities. Recent studies have reanalyzed the research on school funding and its influence on the SES of schools and school districts. Biddle and Berliner (2003) analyzed the average annual expenditures per student for each of the states and the variation among districts in total revenues per student within each state. They found that while the disparities in funding differ sharply among the states, they were greater within some states than among the states as a group. Some U.S. students who live in wealthy communities or neighborhoods within states that have high levels of funding for public schools now attend public schools where funding is set at $15,000 or more per student per year, whereas other U.S. students, who live in poor communities or neighborhoods within states that have low levels of funding, must make do with less than $4,000 in per student funding in their schools for the year (p.3). Unlike the Coleman Report (1972), in which school quality (and level of school funding) had little-to-no impact once home and peer factors were taken into account, Biddle and Berliner state that funding inequities do make a difference and suggest that there were methodological flaws in the Coleman Report. For example, according to Biddle and Berliner, "The study included no measures for classroom size, teacher qualifications, classroom procedures, aca-

demic press, or sense of community associated with schools" (p. 8).

Home Background

Research indicates that the achievement gap is already in place before children enter kindergarten. The U.S. Department of Education's Early Childhood Longitudinal Study (ECLS-K) (2000) for the kindergarten class of 1998–99 is a compilation of data from a nationally representative sample of 20,000 children (and their parents and teachers) who entered kindergarten in the fall of 1998. In addition to numerous family background variables, the data include measures of cognitive skills and knowledge. The ECLS shows that by the time children are five years old, there is a gap in school-related skills and knowledge between African American and European American children, even when their mothers have equal years of schooling. Of course, as Ferguson (in press) points out, "equal years of schooling is not the same as equal quality of schooling. There is no measure in this data of parents' own test scores or the quality of the schools that the parents attended" (footnote #2). Nevertheless, the ECLS survey reveals differences in home-learning activities between children whose mothers have different amounts of schooling and also differences between blacks and whites within each mother's schooling category. In general, whites across categories buy more books, records, tapes, and CDs and engage more with their children in reading and academic enrichment activities than do blacks. Though the study also indicates that blacks play and sing with their children more than whites, these activities may not have the long-term benefits for beginning reading achievement that reading to children provides.

Phillips (2000) analyzed several achievement gap related surveys in an attempt to describe age-related changes in the black–white gap as children move through the grades. According to Phillips, "Taken together, we estimate that at least half of the black-white gap that exists at the end of twelfth grade can be attributed to the gap that already existed at the beginning of first grade. The remainder of the gap seems to emerge during the school years" (p. 136). While less is known about the child-rearing practices that may affect children's school performance during the middle school and high school years, it may be safe to say that differences (not deficits) in child-rearing practices may contribute to the gap. Explanations such as that offered by Ogbu (2002), who attributed much of the problem to black youth cultural patterns and behaviors that are counterproductive for academic success, have been disputed by other researchers. Ferguson (as reported in the *New York Times,* November 30, 2002) speculates that what Ogbu observed was "a clumsy attempt by Black students to search for a comfortable racial identity." Indeed, as adolescents attempt to find their place in society, their personal goals and behaviors often diverge from what the school expects and demands. When these students come from cultural backgrounds that differ greatly from that of the school, their attempts to "find their place" may be seen as even more divergent and may put them at risk of missing out on important educational experiences offered by the school and expected by society.

Linguistic Background

An increasing number of children enter school speaking either a language or a dialect that is other than standard English. Many of these children and their families immigrated from other countries in order to seek a better life. For a variety of social and economic reasons, these families usually remain within their new communities, thus helping to maintain existing similarities in culture and language. Educators have expressed growing concern about the disparities that exist between home and school language and culture in some communities. The concerns are often expressed in terms of deficits rather than differences. Yet, it is clear that students come to the classroom with varied linguistic abilities and educational backgrounds. This is especially true of pre-adolescent and adolescent learners.

The low achievement of poor African American and Hispanic children, in particular, has often been associated with their dialect or language. During the 1960s, linguists looked closely at language diversity as a cause of school failure. Those studies revealed key principles of language learning that remain helpful to teachers and curriculum developers: all language varieties are equally valid; all language varieties can accommodate all levels of thought; and any variety of standard English is not intrinsically better than any nonstandard dialect (Gopaul-McNicol, Reid,

and Wisdom, 1998, p. 7). Similarly, research in the language development of children for whom English is a second language supports the belief that the learner's home language should be valued and accepted as part of second language acquisition and learning. In the highly influential report, *Preventing Reading Difficulties in Young Children* (Snow, Burns, & Griffin, 1998) contend that research has shown that being able to read and write in two languages has cognitive, social, and economic benefits and should be supported whenever possible.

None of this denies the fact that the form language takes has economic, social, and political importance. Nor does it suggest that helping students achieve competence in standard English is not an important goal of the school. It does suggest that much of the low achievement of language-minority students may be pedagogically induced or exacerbated and therefore amenable to change (Rueda, 1991). Perhaps most important is the need to keep in mind that all children learn the language to which they have been exposed. As educators, we must resist the tendency to equate the use of language other than standard English with incompetence or a lack of intelligence (Strickland, Ganske, & Monroe, 2002).

The intermediate grades provide an excellent time in which to guide children in an exploration of various languages and dialects. Pre-adolescents are capable of comparing and contrasting various ways to express ideas, both orally and in writing. They can also begin to make judgments about when certain forms of language may be more appropriate than others. The notion of expanding children's language repertoires to accommodate a wider range of situations and linguistic capability should be the ultimate goal.

Quality of Instruction

Many researchers have turned their attention to what is increasingly considered to be a key contributing factor to the achievement gap—the differences in the quality of instruction that students receive. According to Haycock (2001), rather than focus on poverty and parental education, we should begin to concentrate on what takes place in the classrooms that minority students attend. The problems listed by Haycock include: students in high-poverty and high-minority schools are not being challenged; minority students are placed in low-level classes with a curriculum that does not prepare them for college; no provision is made for students who require more time and instruction to get on grade level; teachers are often not qualified in the subjects that they teach; schools with 90 percent greater enrollment of minority students have a higher percentage of under qualified teachers than predominantly white schools.

Other researchers (Darling-Hammond & Hudson, 1989; Ferguson & Brown, 1998) have linked teacher quality with student achievement and called for a look at both teacher quality, and teaching quality. Teacher quality pertains to distinct characteristics of teachers that are believed to predict teaching quality. Teaching quality refers to the effectiveness in teaching students to learn. Poor minority students appear to be at risk for both. High quality, ongoing professional development geared to the specific needs of the teachers and students in particular schools is a solution offered by many researchers (Haycock, 2001). Special incentives for teachers who work in high-risk schools is another (Christie, 2002).

In summary, recent research in adolescent literacy has shifted away from a primary focus on issues of cognitive processes and teacher instructional practices to acknowledge the importance of the complex intersections among adolescent learners, texts, and contexts (Payne-Bourcy & Chandler-Olcott, 2003). In particular, the importance of multiple literacies has been emphasized and the impact of cultural and societal trends on the students' literacy development has become an important aspect of what educators consider as they tackle hard questions about engaging these learners and keeping them engaged. There is also a growing awareness that these issues begin to surface well before adolescence. For many students, the upper elementary grades may provide the last opportunity to address the prevention of continued failure in reading and writing.

BIBLIOGRAPHY: Alvermann, D. E. (forthcoming), exemplary literacy instruction for adolescents: What counts and who's counting? In J. Flood & P. Anders (eds.). [Title of book forthcoming]. Newark, DE: International Reading Association; Alvermann, D. E. 2001, Reading adolescents' reading identities: Looking back to see ahead. *Journal of Adolescent and Adult Literacies, 44,* 676–90; Amit-Talai, V., and Wulff, H. (Eds.). (1995). *Youth cultures: A cross-cultural perspective;* Biddle, B. J. and Berliner, D. C. 2003, *What research says about unequal funding for schools in America: Policy perspectives.* San Fran-

cisco, CA: WestEd; Bruce, B. C. 2002, Diversity and critical social engagement: How changing technologies enable new modes of literacy in changing circumstances. In D. E. Alvermann (ed.), *Adolescents and literacies in a digital world* (pp. 1–18); Christie, K. 2002, States address achievement gaps. *Phi Delta Kappan, 84,* 102–3; Coleman, J. S. 1972, The evaluation of equality of educational opportunity. In F. Mosteller and D. P. Moynihan (eds.)., *On equality of educational opportunity: Papers deriving from the Harvard University Faculty Seminar on the Coleman Report,* pp. 146–67; Darling-Hammond, L., Hudson, L. 1989, Teachers and teaching. In R. J. Shavelson, L. M. McDonnell & J. Oakes, (eds.). *Indicators for monitoring mathematics and science education.* Santa Monica, CA: The Rand Corporation; Early Childhood Longitudinal Study (ECLS-K), 2000, Washington, D.C.; U.S. Department of Education, Office of Educational Research and Improvement; Eccles, J. S., Wigfield, A., and Schiefele, U., 1998, Motivation to succeed. In N. Eisenberg (ed.), *Handbook of child psychology: Vol. 3, Social, emotional and personality development* (5th ed., pp. 1017–95); Ferguson, R. F. (in press), *Why America's Black–White Achievement Gap Persists;* Ferguson, R. F., (2002), as reported in *New York Times,* November 30, 2002, p. B11; Ferguson, R. F. and Brown, J., 1998, Certification test scores, teacher quality, and student achievement. *The Black-White Test Score Gap,* 160–83; Gopaul-McNicol, S., Reid, S., and Wisdom, G., 1998, The psychoeducational assessment of Ebonics speakers: Issues and challenges. *Journal of Negro Education 67,* 16–24; Haycock, K., 2001, Closing the achievement gap. *Educational Leadership, 58* (6), 6–11; Kamil, M. L., Intrator, S. M., and Kim, H. S., 2000, The effects of other technologies on literacy and literacy learning, in M. L. Kamil, P. B. Mosenthal, P. D. Pearson, and R. Barr (eds.), *Handbook of reading research* (Vol. 3, pp. 771–88); Knapp, M. S., 1995; *Teaching for meaning in high-poverty classrooms;* Lankshear, C., and Knobel, M., 2003; *New literacies: Changing knowledge and classroom learning;* Luke, A., & Elkins, J., 2000, Re/mediating adolescent literacies. *Journal of Adolescent & Adult Literacy, 43,* 396–98; McDermott, R., and Varenne, H., 1995, Culture *as* disability. *Anthropology & Education Quarterly, 26,* 324–48; National Center for Education Statistics, 2003, *The Nation's Report Card: Reading highlights 2002.* Washington, D.C.: U.S. Department of Education; National Reading Panel, 2000; *Report of the National Reading Panel.* Washington, D.C.: National Institute of Child Health and Human Development; No Child Left Behind Act of 2001, Public Law No. 107–10, 115 Stat. 1425, 2002; Ogbu, J. U. (2002). as reported in *New York Times,* November 30, 2002, p. B11; Oldfather, P. and McLaughlin, J., 1993,

Gaining and losing voice: A longitudinal study of students' continuing impulse to learn across elementary and middle school contexts. *Research in Middle Level Education, 3,* 1–25; Phillips, M., 2000; Understanding ethnic differences in ethnic achievement: Empirical lessons from national data. In D. W. Grissmer, and J. M. Ross (eds.). *Analytic issues in the Assessment of Student Achievement,* Washington, D.C.: National Center for Education Statistics; RAND Reading Study Group (2002). *Reading for Understanding: Toward an R & D Program in Reading Comprehension;* Rueda, R., 1991; Characteristics of Literacy Programs for Language-Minority Students, in E. H. Hiebert, ed., *Literacy for a Diverse Society: Perspectives, practices, and Policies;* Schunk, D. H. and Rice, J. M., 1993; Strategy fading and progress feedback: Effects on self-efficacy and comprehension among students receiving remedial reading services, *Journal of Special Education, 27,* 257–76; Snow, C., Burns, M. S., and Griffin, M., 1998; *Preventing Reading Difficulties in Young Children,* Washington, D.C., National Academy Press; Strickland, D. S., Ganske, K., and Monroe, J., 2002; *Supporting Struggling Readers and Writers: Strategies for Classroom Intervention 3–6;* Wade, S. E. and Moje, E. B., 2000; The role of text in classroom learning, in M. L. Kamil, P. B. Mosenthal, P. D. Pearson, and R. Barr, (eds.), *Handbook of Reading Research,* vol. 3, pp. 609–27).

DOROTHY S. STRICKLAND
AND DONNA E. ALVERMANN

BRIN, David
Author, b. 6 October 1950, Glendale, California

B. loved to read and write stories as a young boy. Although B. enjoyed and respected the arts, he sought to be more grounded by reality. His pursuit of science led him to earn his Ph.D. in astrophysics in 1981 at the University of California. However, his writing hobby has dominated his career. Since the publication of his first novel in 1980, B. has gained fame as a SCIENCE FICTION writer. B. successfully uses his knowledge of science and his skills at writing to create science fiction books that explore topics ranging from evolution to the World Wide Web.

B.'s first novel, *Sundiver* (1980), was the beginning of a trilogy. The futuristic murder mystery was set in the Progenitous Universe, which contains various galaxies and inhabitants. Characters such as dolphins and apes believe they were "uplifted" by humans, which gave them capabilities to become intelligent citizens (hence, the "Uplift Trilogy"). B.'s second novel, *Startide Rising* (1983), is set two centu-

ries later in the Progenitous Universe. These first two novels are B.'s most commended, and critics praise his vision of evolution. B. has written more than twenty science fiction novels, SHORT STORIES, and a nonfiction novel.

B. is working on a third trilogy set in the famed Star Trek Universe, featuring characters from *Star Trek: The Next Generation.* B. speaks publicly on a variety of topics, many of them relating to the future. B. admits that he attempts to create stories and tales that deal with issues of honesty, even if the act of writing the story is itself an act of making stuff up.

AWARDS: Hugo Award: 1983 for *Startide Rising,* 1987 for *The Uplift War;* 1983 Nebula Award, *Startide Rising;* Locus Awards: 1983 for *Startide Rising,* 1987 for the *Uplift War,* and 1994 for *Otherness;* 1984 Balrog Award, *The Practice Effect.*

FURTHER WORKS: *Heart of the Comet,* 1986; *The River of Time,* 1986; *Dr. Pak's Preschool,* 1988; *Project Solar Sail,* 1990; *Glory Season,* 1993; *Infinity's Shore,* 1996; *Heaven's Reach,* 1998; *Transparent Society,* 1998; *Foundation's Triumph,* 1999; *Secret Foundations,* 1999; *Star Trek Forgiveness,* 2001; *Contacting Aliens: An Illustrated Guide to David Brin's Uplift Universe,* 2002; *Kiln People,* 2002; *Tomorrow Happens,* 2003; *The Life Eater,* 2003; *King Kong Is Back,* 2005.

BIBLIOGRAPHY: Jones, Daniel and Jorgenson, John D. (eds.), *Contemporary Authors,* vol. 70 (1999); www .kithrup.com; Olendorf, Donna (ed.), *Something about the Author,* Volume 65, 1991.

JODI PILGRIM

BROOKE, William J.
Author, b. 28 November 1946, Washington, D.C.

What if Cinderella's foot did not fit the fabled glass slipper? This is just one of the zany variations found in B.'s *A Telling of the Tales: Five Stories* (1990), which was named a Notable Book by the American Library Association in 1991. Known for his "fractured fairy tale" style of writing, B.'s canon of children's books also includes a comical folktale foray into prehistoric times in *A is for Aarrgh!* (2000), an introduction to "Little Well-Read Riding Hood" and other FAIRY TALES in the touching *Teller of Tales* (1994), and a story in which a boy's paintings come to life in *A Brush With Magic; Based on a Traditional Chinese Story* (1993). More twists on familiar stories appear such as a role reversal of *Beauty and the Beast* in *Untold Tales* (1992).

As an accomplished actor and singer, B. has performed a variety of roles with the New York Gilbert and Sullivan Players, Light Opera of Manhattan, Village Light Opera Group, and the New York Grand Opera. His musical experience may well contribute to the rhythm and musicality of his stories.

FURTHER WORKS: *Operantics: Fun and Games for the Opera Buff,* 1986.

BIBLIOGRAPHY: *Contemporary Authors Online,* 2000; *Eighth Book Of Junior Authors and Illustrators,* 2000; *St. James Guide to Children's Writers,* 5th ed., 1999; *Writers Directory,* 18th ed., 2002.

KRISTIN PEHNKE

BROOKS, Bruce

Author, b. 23 September, 1950, Washington, D.C.

B. moved to North Carolina at the age of six, following his parents' divorce. Much of his childhood was spent shuttling between his mother's home in North Carolina and his father's home in Washington, D.C. The experience made it difficult for B. to develop close friendships. Peers in North Carolina looked at him as the Yankee boy, while children in Washington, D.C., saw him as the kid from the South. When he had an opportunity to make a new, lasting friend, B. would tell that child stories to pique his interest. This helped develop B.'s storytelling skill, which has become his career. His experiences also drew the future author to books, where he found a constant in a world that was always changing around him.

B. graduated from the University of North Carolina in Chapel Hill in 1972 and went to work as a letterpress printer and journalist. Although he had always wanted to become a writer, B. understood the need for a career that would guarantee a paycheck. He wrote both before and after work, perfecting his craft. In the late 1970s, B. had the opportunity to attend the Iowa Writer's Workshop, a program that provided B. with two years to simply write. He graduated from the University of Iowa in 1982 with an M.F.A.

B.'s first novel, *The Moves Make the Man* (1984), has adolescent protagonists and B. was therefore advised to send the manuscript to the children's divisions of potential publishers. B., who had never written with a particular audience in mind, was surprised. He comments that he writes for "intelligent people. I

write *about* kids because my own childhood is still something that I am very much wondering about."

His first novel deals with school desegregation in 1950s southern America. Jerome, the only black boy in his junior high school, develops a friendship with Bix, an emotionally troubled white boy. Their different skin colors are of no concern to them, and the two loner boys become fast friends. Jerome and Bix start spending time on the basketball court, where Jerome teaches his new friend how to play the game. Bix builds confidence and strikes a deal with his stepfather: if he beats him at a game of one-on-one, he can see his hospitalized mother, who has suffered a nervous breakdown. The stepfather accepts the challenge, and Bix wins the game. Jerome comes with Bix to visit his mother, but the reunion is not a happy one. Bix runs away, leaving Jerome without a friend. *The Moves Make the Man* was named a Newbery Honor book and won critical acclaim. The success of this novel afforded B. the opportunity to leave his job and become a full-time writer.

B.'s second novel, *Midnight Hour Encores* (1986), received equally enthusiastic praise from reviewers. Sib, the sixteen-year-old protagonist, is a child of parents who separated after her birth. She lives with her father in Washington, D.C., and she has never met her mother. A musical prodigy who considers herself very independent, Sib decides that the time has come to meet the woman who had given her up at birth, and she asks her father to drive her to California. The trip is filled with self-discovery, as well as the discovery of a parent that she thought she knew. As a child of divorced parents, B.'s predilection to this topic of single-parent households seems obvious. But when commenting on this book, B. notes, "To me, *Midnight Hour Encores* is about being a father. I wrote that book in the year after my son was born. The most important thing in my life was being a father . . . My curiosity about the future—of what you get when you invest certain things in the very early days of your child's life—inspired my imagination to come up with those characters and that story."

B. returns to a sports theme in his first SERIES, the Wolfbay Wings hockey books. The twelve books in this series were written between 1997 and 1999. Each book in the series is titled after and focuses on a different member of the Wolfbay Wings hockey team. B.'s first series received positive reviews, and many critics note that B.'s love and knowledge of sports comes through in his writing.

Another of B.'s interests is nature and wildlife, and he has written several nonfiction books that demonstrate his knowledge of the subject matter and his ability to insert humor into nonfiction works. *Boys Will Be* (1993) is a nonfiction collection of essays about boyhood and fatherly concerns.

B. has succeeded at writing a veritable spectrum of books, and continues to work on both fiction and nonfiction. He currently lives in Silver Spring, Maryland, with his wife, Penelope, and their son, Alexander.

AWARDS: *The Moves Make the Man: School Library Journal* Best Books, *New York Times* Notable Book (1984), Newbery Honor and *Boston Globe–Horn Book* Award (1985), and ALA Notable Books; *Midnight Hour Encores: School Library Journal* Best Books, ALA Best Books for Young Adults, (1986), *Horn Book* Fanfare Honor List, National Council of Teachers of English teacher's choice, 1987, IRA young adult choice, (1988), and ALA/*Booklist* Best Books for Young Adults of the 1980s; *No Kidding:* ALA Best Books for Young Adults, ALA/*Booklist* young adult editor's choice, *School Library Journal* Best Books; *Everywhere: School Library Journal* Notable Books/ALA and Best Books; Best Books for Young Adults, ALA (1990) for *On the Wing;* Best Books for Young Adults, ALA (1992) for *Predator!;* John Burroughs Award (1992) for *Nature By Design; What Hearts:* Newbery Honor Book, Notable Books, and Best Books for Young Adults, all ALA, and Fanfare book, *Horn Book,* all 1993; *All That Remains:* ALA BBYA Award (2002).

FURTHER WORKS: *No Kidding,* 1989; *What Hearts,* 1992; *Asylum for Nightface,* 1996; *Vanishing,* 1999; *Throwing Smoke,* 2000; *All That Remains,* 2001; *Dolores,* 2002.

BIBLIOGRAPHY: *Authors and Artists for Young Adults,* volume 8; Marcus, Leonard. Interview with Brooks for *Publishers Weekly,* July 29, 1990, pp. 214–15; *Something about the Author,* volume 112; http://www.teenreads.com/authors/au-brooks-bruce.asp.

CARRA E. GAMBERDELLA

BROOKS, Kevin

Author, b. 30 March 1959, Exeter, Devon, England

B., whose controversial debut, the YA BOOK, *Martyn Pig* (2002), garnered him a lot of attention, has taken many detours on his road to becoming a full-time writer. He currently lives in Manningtree, Essex, the smallest town in the U.K., and was educated in psychology and philosophy at Ashton University in Birmingham and in cultural studies in London. His job experiences include gas pump attendant, crematorium handyman, Civil Service executive officer, zoo refreshment vendor, typist, post office clerk, railway ticket office clerk, and customer service representative.

In addition to writing books, B. composes and records music, paints, and sculpts. In addition to these hobbies, B. enjoys taking walks with his wife and dog and reading anything "from westerns to quantum physics." As a child he especially enjoyed adventures. He credits his writing inspiration to life's experiences—"reading, watching, listening, thinking, and just being alive."

B.'s first book, *Martyn Pig,* was nominated for the 2003 Sheffield Children's Book Award, Lancashire Children's Book of the Year Award, and the Carnegie Medal. B. also published several SHORT STORIES including: "The Small Cowboy," published in *Story Cellar* MAGAZINE; "The Day of the Bluebottle," published in *Philosophy Now;* and "Goodnight," published in *Original Sins,* a Canongate Prize Anthology.

AWARDS: 2000 Canongate Prize for New Writing, "Goodnight"; ALA BBYA 2004, *Lucas.*

FURTHER WORKS: *Lucas,* 2003; *Kissing the Rain,* 2004; *Candy,* 2005.

BIBLIOGRAPHY: Brooks, Kevin, email correspondence, 2003.

ERIN BOYD

BROOKS, Martha

Author, creative writing teacher, jazz vocalist, lyricist, b. 15 July 1944, Ninette, Manitoba, Canada

B.'s writing enjoys an international readership. Her works have been translated into Danish, Japanese, French, and German.

As a TEENAGER, B. attended boarding school at St. Michael's Academy, Brandon, Manitoba, but she grew up living on the grounds of the rural tuberculosis sanatorium where her father, a surgeon, was the medical superintendent. B's self-education in literature began during her prolonged stays in bed, the result of a congenital chest condition for which she later underwent surgery. Listening to her father reading

Huckleberry Finn, B. recalls realizing "that words shake the world." The sanatorium exposed B. to a multicultural, economically diverse community with the life-affirming focus of battling disease. She formed friendships with some of the patients, like art teacher, Gwen Parker, "who taught me . . . that the world does not have to be lost to us forever; we can reach out and find it again," a lesson that B. has many of her fictional characters discovering.

B.'s first published novel was the AUTOBIOGRAPHICAL fiction, *A Hill for Looking* (1982), but with the publication of *Paradise Café and Other Stories* (1988), she acquired a wider audience. The collection's fourteen stories emphasize B.'s interest in the importance of nurturing relationships, particularly for young people on the cusp of adult identity. The collection won numerous awards, including the *Boston Globe–Horn Book* Honor Book Award for Fiction in 1991 and the Vicky Metcalf Award.

In *Two Moons in August* (1991), B.'s interest in the theme of love and loss focuses on Sidonie who, as she anticipates turning sixteen, grieves for the mother who died on her birthday a year earlier. Through her family relationships, and her growing involvement with the strange Kieran, Sidonie comes to realize that the movement from love to loss is reversible.

In *Traveling on into the Light and Other Stories* (1994), B. looks at relational difficulties from various adolescent perspectives, both male and female. Problems with peers figure in some of the stories, but B.'s interest in parental loss continues as Sidonie and Kieran are the focus of the final stories. In several others, B. foregrounds parental absence through physically, emotionally, and psychologically abandoned children. In "The Kindness of Strangers," B. recounts the meeting of teen-age Laker and eighty-two-year-old Henry which was B.'s third published novel, *Being with Henry* (1999), winner of several awards including the Mr. Christie's Book Award.

The natural world's influence on B.'s early life, through the sanatorium's idyllic setting, resonates strongly in her fiction; her Icelandic grandparents encouraged her belief in "the immense mystery of the life force that seeps through plants and rocks—and . . . our binding relationship with all living creatures." Pelican Lake and its surroundings become the fictional lake in several of her novels perhaps most dramatically in *Bone Dance* (1997), where the natural landscape is a presence as central as the human characters that inhabit it. Her two young Native protagonists appear well-equipped to invoke the landscape's spirit world in their spiritual journey toward self-definition, while B.'s adept handling of their alternating points of view conveys her sensitive appreciation of Native culture. Among other recognitions, *Bone Dance* won the Ruth Schwartz Award.

After three previous nominations, *True Confessions of a Heartless Girl* (2002) was awarded the 2002 Governor General's Award for Children's Literature in Canada for Text. As previously, B. dramatizes the power of human generosity to redeem lives, but she signals a shift in direction, for, through her finely conceived adult characters, who evoke sympathy and interest in their own right, the novel seems to blur the distinction between young adult and adult fiction.

B.'s dramatic writings include the adaptation of *A Prairie Boy's Winter* (with Sandra Birdsell and David Gillies); *I Met a Bully on the Hill* [co-authored with Maureen Hunter (1995)]; and *Andrew's Tree* (1995), winner of the Chalmers Canadian Children's Play Award.

As a jazz singer, B. earned the 2002 Prairie Music Award for Outstanding Album of the Year for her first CD, *Change of Heart.*

The effectiveness of B.'s writing comes from her careful attention to ordinary details. In vivid, precise diction, she expresses the beauty of both the powerful Manitoba landscape and the haunted inner spaces of her characters as they negotiate their complex social realities. Her writing places the potential for sadness that informs ordinary human lives next to the compassion and love that dispel it. She emphasizes the value of a caring community with its capacity to redeem the individual through acceptance and forgiveness.

AWARDS: *Paradise Café and Other Stories: School Library Journal* Best Book of the Year, 1991 *Boston Globe–Horn Book* Honor Book for Fiction; Vicky Metcalf Award; 1991 ALA Best Book for Young Adults, *Two Moons in August; Traveling on into the Light:* Hungry Mind Review Children's Books of Distinction Award Young Adult, *School Library Journal* Best Book of the Year, 1994 ALA BBYA and Best Books for the Reluctant YA Reader, 1996 IBBY honor book; 1995 Chalmers Canadian Children's Play Award, *Andrew's Tree; Bone Dance:* 1997 ALA Best Book of the Year, Ruth Schwartz Award (Young Adult), the Canadian Librarian Association Book of the Year Award for Young Adults; *Being with Henry:*

2000 Mr. Christie's Book Award and the McNally Robinson Book of the Year for Young People; 2002 Governor General's Literary Award for Children's Literature, *True Confessions of a Heartless Girl.* This work, like the other four titles listed above, was also selected for ALA's Best Books for Young Adults list.

FURTHER WORKS: Brooks, Martha, "Surviving the Journey: Literature Meets Life," *The ALAN Review,* 28, No. 2 (Winter 2001); Shields, Carol and Marjorie Anderson, eds., *Dropped Threads: What We Aren't Told,* (2001).

BIBLIOGRAPHY: Archer, Cheryl, Review of *Bone Dance, CM Magazine* IV, Number 4 (October 17, 1997), www.umanitoba.ca/cm/vol4/no4/bonedance .html; Branch, Jennifer L. Review of *Being With Henry, CM Magazine* VI, Number 17 (April 28, 2000), www.umanitoba.ca/cm/vol16/no17/beingwith henry.html; Cherland, Meredith Rogers, "A Postmodern Argument Against Censorship: Negotiating Gender and Sexual Identity through Canadian Young Adult Novels," *CCL* 80 (1995): 41–53. Deakin, Andrea, "Martha Brooks," *ACHUKA* Children's Books UK, http://www.achuka.co.uk/can/brooks.htm; Gibson-Bray, Sarah, "Unmasking the Bully and other Schoolyard Games" (review of *I met a Bully on the Hill), CCL* 85 (1997): 73–77; Manitoba Writer's Guild, "Martha Brooks Profile," http://www.mbwriter .mb.ca/mapindex/; Ryan-Fisher, Bonnie, "The Book of Changes" (review of *Traveling On Into the Light), CCL* 80 (1995): 81–82; *Something About the Author,* Vol. 134 (2000); Steffler, Margaret, "Dancing With the Past" (review of *Bone Dance), CCL* 94 (1999).

RITA BODE

BROOKS, Polly Schoyer

Author, illustrator, b. 11 August 1912, South Orleans, Massachusetts

B. is best known in the world of YOUNG ADULT LITERATURE for *Beyond the Myth: The Story of Joan of Arc,* which appears on YALSA's 100 Best Books for Young Adults List. This carefully crafted BIOGRAPHY is considered the quintessential young adult biography of the French heroine. B.'s Joan is a character whose piety and strength form her spiritual basis.

B. began her writing, with Nancy Zinsser Walworth, with *The World Awakes: The Renaissance in Western Europe* (1962). This portrait of eight major Renaissance figures places their lives in the context of economics, politics, and history. Brooks's recent biography, *Cleopatra: Goddess of Egypt, Enemy of Rome* (1995), was written in the same lively but infor-

mative style as her earlier works. Often choosing strong feminist figures for her biographies, she balances historical facts with an approachable writing style. Her bibliographies indicate a high level of research, and her choice of illustrations demonstrate her ability to connect with young adults.

FURTHER WORKS: *World of Walls: The Middle Ages in Western Europe,* 1966. *Queen Eleanor, Independent Spirit of the Medieval World,* 1983.

BIBLIOGRAPHY: Reif, Rita, *Housewives Write Book on History, New York Times* (1857-current file); December 3, 1962, ProQuest Historical Newspapers, The *New York Times. Contemporary Authors Online,* 2002.

TERRY BECK

BROOKS, Terry
Author, b. 8 January 1944, Sterling, Illinois

With a B.A. from Hamilton College, followed by a law degree from Washington and Lee University, it was not necessarily evident that B. would eventually become one of the best-known FANTASY writers of the late 20th century. Greatly enamored of J. R. R. TOLKIEN's work, especially *The Lord of the Rings,* B. realized that his own writing might have an audience.

With B.'s publication of *The Sword of Shannara* (1977), a world that would entice many visitors emerged. The tale of Shea Ohmsford, the half elf, and the Warlock Lord, the quest for the sword of Shannara, and the perils faced by Shea and company, are only the beginning of the story. Wil Ohmsford takes center stage in *The Elfstones of Shannara* (1982) when he must work with Elven Amberle against the demons to clarify the destiny of the Four Lands. The *Wishsong of Shannara* (1985) finds Brin Ohmsford and the Druid Allanon facing the Mord Wraiths and Ildatch. These three works make up The Original Shannara Trilogy, although an interlocking quartet followed shortly with the Heritage of Shannara set (1993), comprised of *The Scions of Shannara, The Druid of Shannara, The Elf Queen of Shannara,* and *The Talismans of Shannara.* The sword of Shannara is once again needed, and with Allanon dead, Coll Ohmsford must take over the quest with the uncertain help of Par. Evil dominates the Four Lands in *The Druid of Shannara,* as Walker Boh struggles to do right with the Black Elfstone and meet the desires of Druid Allanon, who although dead lingers as a shade.

111

The shade of Druid Allanon is still a presence in *The Elf Queen of Shannara,* as is a descendent of Shea Ohmsford—Wren. On her unlikely shoulders falls the responsibility for finding the Elves of the Westland, some of whom she played with as a child. With the help of Garth Rover, she sets out, with not only her own destiny, but that of the Four Lands, in her hands. In *The Talismans of Shannara,* that destiny is shared by Wren with Walker Boh and Par, as they are targeted by various entities, ranging from The Four Horsemen to false friends, as the Shadowen try to work their dark magic against the will of the shade of Druid Allanon. The *First King of Shannara* (1988), although actually a prequel to Shea's tale, was not published until after The Original Shannara Trilogy and The Heritage of Shannara Quartet, and should not be read before that septet is completed. In it the groundwork for the SERIES is laid as in the Four Lands, Bremen, and the Warlock Lord Brona struggle to establish themselves and, in so doing, establish a pattern that remains for years to come. Shannara is revisited in *The Voyage of the Jerle Shannara: Ilse Witch* (2002), which focuses on the meeting of the last of the Druids, Walker Boh, with the Ilse Witch, as they struggle over the map that will lead them to magic. It was followed by *The Voyage of the Jerle Shannara: Antrax* (2002), in which Walker, separated from the airship and its inhabitants, struggles in the ruins of Castledown pursued by Antrax. The Ilse Witch imprisons Bek Rowe as she ponders his claims of kinship.

In his set of books centered on the Magic Kingdom of Landover, B. may be poking a bit of fun at himself as he chronicles the adventures of Ben Holiday, who like B. is an attorney who decides to chuck it all; however, Ben decides to buy himself a kingdom. In *Magic Kingdom for Sale—Sold!* (1986), Chicago lawyer, Ben Holiday, beguiled by an ad for a kingdom and tired of his current life, decides to buy Landover, only to discover that his troubles have just begun. Intrigued, however, by Willow, and helped by Questor Thews and Abernathy, a talking dog, Ben decides to try to make the best of the questionable deal that he had made with Meeks the Wizard. *The Black Unicorn* (1987) sees Meeks magically switching identities with Ben, after deciding that perhaps Ben actually got the better part of the deal. Although Ben manages to outwit Meeks yet again, peace is brief at best in Landover, as evidenced by *Wizard at Large*

(1988), Questor Thew tries to turn Abernathy back into a human being, by undoing the spell that accidentally turned him into a dog. The next bit of trouble that faces the Kingdom of Landover comes from Chicago, as Horris Kew reappears in Ben's life and entwines him in *The Tangle Box* (1994). In *Witches Brew* (1995), High Lord of Landover, Ben Holiday, must rescue his and Willow's daughter, Mistaya, as he meets one of his greatest hazards yet.

The Word and Void trilogy is representative of much more serious fantasy. Set in and around Sinnissippi Park, near where B. was born, *Running with the Demon* (1977), *A Knight of the Word* (1998), and *Angel Fire East* (1999), take place in contemporary times, pitting demons of the Void against Knight of the Word, John Ross, and Nest Freemark.

B. also wrote a novelization of *Star Wars Episode I: The Phantom Menace* (1999). The Shannara books are currently being broken into parts and released as young adult bestsellers by Del Rey. In his latest work, *The High Druid of Shannara: Jarka Ruus* (2003), B. returns to Shannara, where it all began, to create a new series of adventures taking place in that world. At least two more titles will be forthcoming in that series. B., a *New York Times* best-selling author, currently resides in the Pacific Northwest and Hawai'i. He and his wife, Judine, enjoy visits from their children in between book tours.

FURTHER WORKS: "Introduction" to *Myths and Magic: The Complete Fantasy Reference* (1999), *Star Wars Episode I: The Phantom Menace* (1999), "Introduction" to *The Complete Fantasy Reference* (2000), *The World of Shannara* (2001), *Sometimes the Magic Works: Lessons From a Writing Life* (2003); *Tanequil: High Druid of Shannara,* 2004; *Straken,* 2005.

BIBLIOGRAPHY: www.amazon.com; www.barnes andnoble.com/writers; www.novelst4.epnet.com; www.terrybrooks.net.

JEANNE MARIE RYAN

BROWN, Claude
Author, b. 23 February 1937, New York City; d. 2 February 2002, New York City

Contributor of articles to *Idssent, Esquire,* and other PERIODICALS, B. has published two works, *Manchild in the Promised Land* (1965) and *The Children of Ham* (1976), and won a Metropolitan Community Methodist Church grant (1959), and the *Saturday Re-*

view Ansfield-Wolf Award for furthering intergroup relations.

Both of B.'s works are realistic, depicting life in Harlem. "Often cited as the first book to describe the experience of urban AFRICAN AMERICANS in a truly effective manner," his AUTOBIOGRAPHY *Manchild in the Promised Land* "gives a grim picture of life for families who had moved from the plantations of the South, dreaming of a golden future and ending up in a Harlem slum, surrounded by thieves and drug addicts."

In response to his parents' deferential attitude towards whites, B. became a rebel, learning to steal before he began his school career. After a two-year stint at Wiltwyck School for Boys, B. went back to rebellious and truant ways. A shot in the stomach at age thirteen by an irate "homeowner whose bedspread he had stolen" began the process that would eventually change his life. B. survived the shooting and was sent to Warwick, another reform school, for nine months. Upon his return home, B. "found so little to do that he voluntarily returned to school."

Wondering if he would end up on the road to ruin, B. found himself saved by two things: his own strength of character and the help he received from the staff of the reform schools. The books loaned to him by the superintendent's wife at Warwick were a significant influence on B.—encouraging him to break free of Harlem and get an education—a B.A. from Howard University in 1965 and law studies at Stanford and Rutgers University.

AWARDS: *Manchild in the Promised Land* was one of 100 Young Adult titles selected for the first YALSA Best of the Best List: Still Alive (selections from 1960 to 1974).

BIBLIOGRAPHY: "Claude Brown." DISCovering Authors. Gale Group, 1999. Reproduced in Discovering Collection. Farmington Hills, Mich.: Gale Group. October, 2001. http://galenet.galegroup.com/servlet/DC/ "Claude Brown." U*X*L Biographies. U*X*L, 1999. Reproduced in Discovering Collection. Farmington Hills, Mich.: Gale Group. October 2001. http://galenet.galegroup.com/servlet/DC/

SARA MARCUS

BROWN, Dee Alexander

Author, librarian, historian, b. 2 February 1908, Stephens, Arkansas; d. 12 December 2002, n.p.

B. has written or been involved in the creation of more than thirty works of fiction and nonfiction, dealing primarily with the American West and its history. B.'s best-known work, *Bury My Heart at Wounded Knee* (1970), gave a voice to American Indians and altered the white American and European perception of these cultures in the West. Criticized by many as being a revisionist historian, B. completed careful research for his works and had a marvelous gift for storytelling that conveyed the history of Western America.

B. credits many sources for his love of reading, his captivating storytelling and his concise writing: his grandmother who taught him to read, a librarian who introduced him to the expedition of Lewis and Clark, the newspaper owners who helped him become a better writer, and a professor who expanded his love of history. Growing up among American Indians greatly impacted his desire to show readers a more complete picture of these misrepresented people.

B. was born in Louisiana and spent his childhood in Arkansas. He was reading Robert Louis Stevenson and Mark Twain before he went to first grade. He was introduced to printing at a local print plant where he learned about type setting. He was able to meet many of the characters and people of his town through his mother's job; she was the local postmistress, and he assisted her by delivering letters. His first publication came in high school when his stories appeared in *Blue Book* MAGAZINE.

B.'s early works with Martin F. Schmitt include *Fighting Indians of the West* (1948), *Trail Driving Days* (1952), and *The Settlers' West* (1955); these pieces provide a pictorial history of the West based on photographs the authors uncovered in the National Archives.

B. wrote part-time while working as an academic librarian at the University of Illinois. He was a librarian and faculty member there until 1975, during which time he wrote over half of his books.

B. wrote several works of nonfiction and historical fiction that discuss events surrounding the Civil War and the expansion of the American West. *Bury My Heart at Wonded Knee* is the book for which B. will be most remembered, as he reconstructed Hollywood's image of Native Americans. Told from the viewpoint of an American Indian, the book highlights the unflattering and unpleasant history behind the white settler and invalidates the myths of savage natives that white Americans had traditionally been taught.

B.'s work extends over six decades, from the 1942 *Wave High the Banner*, based on the life of Davy Crockett, to *The Way to Bright Star* (1998), a book the author completed at the age of ninety. This book tells the story of a young fifteen-year-old boy, Ben Butterfield, who must leave his home in Arkansas and bring two camels to a farm in Indiana. Set during the Civil War, *The Way to Bright Star* depicts the many adventures and dangers that Ben faces during his journey.

B. provided gripping portrayals of history. He was a prolific author who wrote from the point of view of real people in real times, and a historian who gave America stories that needed to be told.

AWARDS: 1971 American Library Association's Clarence Day Award, *The Year of the Century;* 1971 Christopher Award; 1971 New York Westerners' Buffalo Award, *Bury My Heart at Wounded Knee;* 1972 Illinois News Broadcasters Asociation Illinoisan of the Year; 1981 Western Writers of America's Best Western for Young People award, *Hear that Lonesome Whistle Blow: Railroads in the West;* 1984 Western Writers of America's Saddleman Award.

FURTHER WORKS: Fiction—*Wave High the Banner,* 1942; *Yellowhorse,* 1956; *The Girl from Fort Wicked,* 1964; *Creek Mary's Blood,* 1980; *Conspiracy of Knaves,* 1986. Nonfiction—*Grierson's Raid,* 1954; *The Gentle Tamers: Women of the Old Wild West,* 1958; *The Galvanized Yankees,* 1963; *The Year of the Century: 1876,* 1966; *Action at Beecher Island,* 1967; *Andrew Jackson and the Battle of New Orleans,* 1972; *The Westerners,* 1974; *Hear That Lonesome Whistle Blow: Railroads in the West,* 1977; *American Spa: Hot Springs, Arkansas,* 1982; *Wondrous Times on the Frontier,* 1993; *When the Century Was Young: A Writer's Notebook,* 1993; *The American West,* 1994; *Best of Dee Brown's West: An Anthology,* 1997; *Dee Brown's Civil War Anthology,* 1998.

BIBLIOGRAPHY: D. Martin, "Dee Brown, 94, Author Who Revised Image of West," *New York Times,* December 14, 2002; *Authors and Artists for Young Adults,* vol. 30; *Contemporary Authors New Revision Series,* vol. 60; *Something About the Author,* vol. 5, 110; Best *Books for Young Adults,* 2000.

TINA HERTEL

BRUCHAC, Joseph

Author, b. 16 October 1942, Saratoga Springs, New York

B. was born to Joseph E. Bruchac II, a taxidermist, and Flora (Bowman) Bruchac. But he was reared by his maternal grandparents in Greenfield Center, New York. He now lives with his wife, Carol, in the same house in which his grandparents raised him. B. is the author of fiction and nonfiction books for children, YOUNG ADULTS, and adults. The predominant theme of his writings comes from his Abenaki American Indian heritage. B., along with his wife, their two sons James and Jesse, and his sister, Margaret, works to educate young people about the cultural heritage of Native Americans, particularly that of his ancestors, the Abenaki. In his autobiography, *Bowman's Store: A Journey to Myself* (2001), B. tells of life in rural New York, of growing up in his grandparents' home with a mixture of Abenaki and American cultures, and of decisions he made because of his early life.

B. earned a B.A. in English from Cornell University (1965), an M.A. in Literature and Creative Writing from Syracuse University (1966), and a Ph.D. from the Union Graduate Institute in Ohio (1975). In the late 1960s the family lived in Ghana, West Africa, where he taught English and literature. B. taught at Skidmore College in Saratoga Springs while doing graduate work. B. and his wife are the founders of the Greenfield Review Literary Center and The Greenfield Review Press. B. has published articles, stories, and POETRY in over five hundred publications as well as over seventy books for young adults and children. These works are the results of oral histories and traditions that are passed from Abenaki elders and family. B. is a professional storyteller as well as an author, sharing traditional tales of the Native Americans of the Northeast U.S. around the world.

AWARDS: IRA Young Adults & Teachers Choice, *Thirteen Moons on a Turtle's Back,* 1993; Parent's Choice Honor Award, ALA Best Books for Young Adults, *Dawn Land,* 1994; Woodcraft Circle Storyteller of the Year award for traditional Native stories, *Bowman's Store,* 1998; Parent's Choice Honor Award, *Dog People,* 1995; ALA Notable Books for Young Adults, *Keepers of the Animals;* Association of Booksellers for Children Choice Award *Keepers of the Earth;* ALA Best Books for Young Adults, *Keepers of the Night; Skeleton Man:* ALA Notable Children's Books, 2002.

SELECT FURTHER WORKS: *The Faithful Hunter,* 1988; *Turtle Meat and Other Stories,* 1992; *The First Strawberries,* 1993; *The Native American Sweat Lodge,* 1993; *Flying With the Eagle,* 1993; *Dawn Land,* 1993; *A Boy Called Slow,* 1994; *Native Plant Stories,* 1995; *The Earth Under Sky Bear's Feet,,* 1995; *Chil-*

dren of the Longhouse, 1996; *Between Earth & Sky,* 1996; *Eagle Song,* 1997; *Many Nations: An Alphabet of Native America,* 1997; *Arrow Over the Door,* 1998; *The Waters Between,* 1998; *No Borders,* 1999; *Crazy Horse's Vision,* 2000; *How Chipmunk Got His Stripes,* 2001.

BIBLIOGRAPHY: *Authors & Artists for Young Adults,* Gale, vol. 19, 1996; *Something About the Author,* Gale, vol. 131, 2002; *An Interview with Joseph Bruchac,* E. T. Dresang http://www.soemadison.wisc.edu/ccbc/bruchac.htm; *Joseph Bruchac* III, http://www.nativepubs.com/nativepubs/Apps/bios/0124Bruchac Joseph

NAOMI WILLIAMSON

BUJOLD, Lois McMaster
Author, b. 1949, Columbus, Ohio

B.'s interest in books began at the age of nine. Her father was an Ohio State University professor who had doctorates in physics and engineering, as well as an affinity for SCIENCE FICTION, SF MAGAZINES and PAPERBACKS that he shared with his daughter. The author of the Vorkosigan Saga, one of the most beloved SERIES in science fiction, B. attended Ohio State University part time, majoring in English. In 1995, she and her children, Anne and Paul, moved to Minneapolis, Minnesota, from Marion, Ohio. A voracious reader all her life, B. began writing in junior high, but her first professional sale did not come until she had a story published in *Twilight Zone Magazine* in 1984. In 1986, she published her first three novels: *Shards of Honor, Warrior's Apprentice,* and *Ethan of Athos.*

B.'s novels, while having fascinating plots, are truly character driven. Her characters, in particular Miles Vorkosigan, take on lives of their own and become very real to readers. *Shards of Honor* is the tale of Cordelia Naismith, a scientist from the progressive planet of Beta, whose survey party is attacked by a force from the barbaric planet of Barrayar. She is captured by Barrayaran officer Aral Vorkosigan, sometimes known as "the Butcher of Komarr," who has been attacked by his own men. Cordial relations, much less romance, seem impossible for this couple from worlds with such opposing views, but as they work together to survive, they discover that they share the same values and high standards and begin to admire each other in spite of themselves. In *The Warrior's Apprentice,* seventeen-year-old Miles, the son of Cordelia and Aral, turns washing out of the Barray-

aran military academy (due to physical disabilities) into a triumph when he visits his grandmother on Beta and ends up assembling an unbeatable mercenary fleet. *Ethan of Athos* is the story of an obstetrician from an all-male world who must venture off planet, where he will undoubtedly encounter women (something no one he knows has ever done). B.'s fine crafted galactic civilization is world building at its finest.

Humor is also apparent in her novels. Readers who have read *A Civil Campaign: A Comedy of Biology and Manners* (Baen, 1999) erupt into laughter whenever the infamous dinner party is mentioned. In addition to science fiction, B. has also written four FANTASY novels: *The Spirit Ring* (1993), a historical fantasy; *The Curse of Chalion* (2001) which won the Mythopoeic award and explores religion as well as the conflict between good and evil in a magic-laced world; and the Hugo Award–winning *Paladin of Souls* (2003), a sequel to *Curse of Chalion* that features a heroine in her forties who demonstrates considerable teen appeal. Her next novel set in this fantasy world is *The Hallowed Hunt.*

B.'s fiction has been translated into at least fifteen other languages.

AWARDS: "The Mountains of Mourning" (novella) Hugo and Nebula Awards; *Falling Free*—Nebula Award; *Vor Game*—Hugo Award; *Barrayar*—Hugo Award; *Mirror Dance* Hugo and Locus Awards; *The Curse of Chalion*—Mythopoeic Award; *Komarr*—Minnesota Book Award for science fiction. Primio Italia Award (Italy); *A Civil Campaign*—Sapphire Award; *Paladin of Souls*—Hugo Award

FURTHER WORKS: *Falling Free,* 1988; *Brothers in Arms.* Baen, 1989; *Borders of Infinity,* 1989; *The Vor Game,* 1990; *Barrayar,* 1991; *Mirror Dance,* 1994; *Cetaganda,* 1995; *Memory,* 1996; *Young Miles,* 1997; *Komarr,* 1998; *Diplomatic Immunity,* 2000; *Miles, Mystery and Mayhem,* 2001; *The Hallowed Hunt,* 2005.

BIBLIOGRAPHY: The Bujold Nexus—the official Lois McMaster Bujold Homepage AUTOBIOGRAPHY. http://www.dendarii.com/biograph.html; Hennessey-DeRose, Christopher and Ryan Timothy Grable, "Award-winning author Lois McMaster Bujold is a slush-pile survivor," *Science Fiction Weekly* http://www.scifi.com/sfw/issue291/interview.html; "Women Who Rock the World—Meet Lois McMaster Bujold Science Fiction Writer Eyes on the Future" A Girl's

World.com http://www.agirlsworld.com/amy/pajama/
wmhistory/careers/lois/index.html

DIANA TIXIER HERALD

BULL, Emma
Author, b. 13 December 1954, Torrance, California

An early fascination with her parents' black Royal manual typewriter and a love of books were clear indications that B. would find a career in words. Her father worked in the sales department of a steel company, a job that caused him to relocate his family often. B. spent her childhood in various states, including California, New Jersey, and Wisconsin. During car rides from one home to another, B. would read. Her mother read to her as well, to soften the blow of having to ask her daughter to do something otherwise dreadful, like taking a bath or going to sleep.

B. nurtured her interest in words by majoring in English literature at Beloit College in Wisconsin. Some friends encouraged her to read *Babel-17,* a "New-Wave SCIENCE FICTION" novel that B. says "changed my life." Also, in college B. discovered her interest in music.

Upon graduation, B. moved to Minneapolis where she worked as a freelance journalist, editor, and graphic designer. There, she joined the Minnesota Science Fiction Society (Minn-stf) and later formed a writers' group with college friend Will Shetterly and several other members of Minn-stf. They called themselves the "Scribblies," and met once or twice a month to review one another's manuscripts. Within four years, all seven original members of this group had had at least one book published.

B. married Will Shetterly in 1981, and in 1983, the couple founded SteelDragon Press, a small publishing house specializing in COMIC BOOKS and limited-edition quality hardcovers. In 1987, B. published her first novel, *War for the Oaks.* In this contemporary FANTASY set in Minneapolis, the high courts of Faerie draft a rock musician to defeat an evil enemy using her musical talents. This novel was a finalist for the Mythopoeic Society Award. Since its publication, B. and Shetterly have written a movie script and created a trailer in the hope of someday making the story into a film.

B.'s second novel, *Falcon* (1989), is classic science fiction. It follows the title hero, who is a member of the royal family on the fictional planet Cymru. *Bone Dance* (1991) has been described as "a fantasy for technophiles." This novel is set in post-nuclear holocaust Minnesota, and tells the story of a teenaged androgynous character named Sparrow.

When she wasn't writing, B. turned to music. She was part of a Minnesota-based psychedelic folk-rock band, "Cats Laughing," which produced two albums, *Bootleg* and *Another Way to Travel.* B. also partners with "The Fabulous" Lorraine Garland and together they are the "Flash Girls." B. sings and plays guitar; Garland sings and plays the fiddle. As the "Flash Girls," B. and Garland have produced three folk albums, *The Return of Pansy Smith and Violet Jones, Maurice & I,* and *Play Each Morning Wild Queen.*

B. and Shetterly now live in Bisbee, Arizona. Together, they conduct writing workshops and continue to work on their own projects.

AWARDS: Selection, Three Hundred Best Books for Young Adults, New York Public Library, 1987, and Best First Novel, *Locus* MAGAZINE Poll, 1987, for *War of the Oaks;* Nebula Award nomination and Hugo nomination, both for *Bone Dance; Finder: A Novel of the Borderlands;* Best Books for Young Adults, 1995.

FURTHER WORKS: "A Bird That Whistles," *Hidden Turnings: A Collection of Stories through Time and Space,* 1990; "Silver or Gold," *After the King: Stories in Honor of J.R.R. TOLKIEN,* 1992; *Double Feature* (with Will Shetterly), 1994; *The Princess and the Lord of Night,* 1994; *Finder: A Novel of the Borderlands,* 1994; also a contributor to anthologies, including *Sword and Sorceress,* 1984; *Liavek: The Players of Luck,* 1986; *Bordertown,* 1986; *Life on the Border,* 1991; *The Armless Maiden and Other Tales for Childhood's Survivors,* 1995; *Freedom and Necessity,* 1997; *War for the Oaks,* 2004; *Nightspeeder,* 2004.

BIBLIOGRAPHY: *Something About the Author,* vol. 103; *Something About the Author,* vol. 99; http://www.qnet.com/~raven/emma.html; http://www.player.org/pub/flash/people/emma_biblio.html; http://www.player.org/pub/flash/people/emma.html; http://www.player.org/pub/flash/people/emma.html.

CARRA GAMBERDELLA

BUNN, Alan
Author, b. 20 July 1944, Kent, England

A high-school teacher for many years, B. retired early in order to focus on writing and travel. However, he still teaches children and young adults at the School for Young Writers in Christchurch, New Zealand.

B.'s keen interest in outdoor sports is reflected in his first two novels which are full of authentic action and suspense as well as containing solid characterization. The first, *Water in the Blood* (1990), focuses on surfing and kayaking; the second, *Driving Force* (1991), concentrates on a coast to coast endurance race. In the two books, landscape, physical effort, theme, and character development are inextricably linked. B. himself has said that he respects "those authors whose work has a wider awareness of the social implications of personal actions." Thus Liam, in *Water in the Blood,* chooses new challenges and new friends at a critical point in his life. This immensely popular book has been reprinted half a dozen times. Some of the characters from this novel reappear in *Driving Force,* a story in which a group of friends face the trials of friendship, difficult circumstances, and a terminal illness.

B.'s third novel, *Road Warriors* (1993), while still revolving around sport, specifically a triathlon, is also something of a departure from his earlier work; here is a fast-moving action comedy in which the arts, sports, and gangster motifs collide, creating, as the narrator of the book says, "a time-space capsule of experiences." B.'s latest novel for young adults, *Eyes in the Shadows* (2003), is a more sparse, understated story that is sharply written. It focuses on a young model who is stalked by a stranger, and a photography student whose powerful images capture various layers of bullying at his school. The author's long-time interest in drama was marked by the publication of a play, *A Time to March,* in 2003.

AWARDS: AIM Children's Book Award, Best First Book Award (1991) for *Water in the Blood.*

FURTHER WORKS: "Life's a laugh" in *Nearly Seventeen: New Zealand stories.* (Tessa Duder, ed), 1993; "The Woolsack," in *Zig Zag.* (William Taylor, ed.), 1993; *Re-draft 2001: new teenage writing in New Zealand.* (Alan Bunn, ed.), 2001; *Re-draft 2002: new teenage writing in New Zealand.* (Alan Bunn, ed.), 2002.

BIBLIOGRAPHY: Fitzgibbon, Tom, *Beneath Southern Skies: New Zealand Children's Book Authors & Illustrators.* 1993. http://library.christchurch.org.nz/Childrens/ChildrensAuthors/AlanBunn.asp

BILL NAGELKERKE

BUNTING, Eve

Author, b. 19 December 1928, Maghera, Northern Ireland

B. was born to Sloan Edmund and Mary Bolton, a merchant and housewife. B. was an avid reader as a child, reading anything in print. She attended Methodist College in Belfast, Ireland, from 1936–45 and Queen's University, Belfast, from 1945–47. On April 26, 1951, she married Edward Davison Bunting, a business executive. The couple has three children, Christine, Sloan, and Glenn. The family moved to the U.S. in 1958 where they settled in California. B.'s first book, *The Two Giants,* was published in 1972 after she took a college creative writing course.

B.'s books present difficult subjects such as homelessness, teenage suicide, DEATH, FAMILY issues, poverty, peer pressure, and other social and cultural issues to which young adults can relate. Moreover, the contemporary issues she includes in her works are ones that are applicable on a global level. Much of her subject matter comes from her personal encounters with immigration and discrimination.

Even in PICTURE BOOKS that are appropriate for YA, B. does not shy away from serious subject matter; racism, violence, and homelessness are some of the social issues in her books. Such books as *Smoky Night* (1994), *Fly Away Home* (1991), and *Going Home* (1996) introduce children who encounter great adversity and sadness in their young lives. *Dandelions* (illus. by Greg Shed) (1995) shows the barrenness and the isolation of life on the prairie. However, B. humanizes her characters so that they are identifiable to young readers.

In addition to YA appropriate picture books, B. has books specifically meant for the YA group, such as *Is Anybody There?* (1988) and *Spying on Miss Muller* (1995). Readers can gain personal insight about her writing by reading B.'s memoir *Once Upon a Time* (1995). By using factual information combined with fiction, B. has developed a writing style which conveys the heartaches of actual human experience.

AWARDS: Golden Kite Award, *One More Flight, Ghost of a Summer, December* (Honor); *New York Times* Top Ten Books, *The Big Barn, Goose Dinner, The Waiting Game, The Valentine Bears, The Mother's Day Mice, Sixth Grade Sleepover, Winter's Coming;* state reading awards: Hawaii Association of

School Librarians and the Hawaii Library Association, 1987, for *Karen Kepplewhite Is the World's Best Kisser;* South Carolina Young Adult Book Award, 1988–89, California Young Readers Medal, 1989, for *Face at the Edge of the World;* Sequoyah Children's Book Award, Oklahoma Library Association, Mark Twain Award, State of Missouri and Sunshine State Young Readers Awards, Florida Association for Media in Education, 1989, for *Sixth-Grade Sleepover;* Nebraska Golden Sower Award, 1992, for *Is Anybody There?* ALA Popular Paperbacks, 2003, for *Blackwater.* Bunting received the PEN Special Achievement Award, PEN International in 1984, for her contribution to children's literature and in 1997 the Regina Medal for her body of works.

SELECT FURTHER YA WORKS: *The Cloverdale Switch,* 1979; *The Haunting of Safe Keep,* 1985; *If I Asked You Would You Stay?,* 1987; *Face at the Edge of the World,* 1988; *Terrible Things: An Allegory of the Holocaust,* 1989; *A Sudden Silence,* 1988; *SOS Titanic,* 1995; *Blackwater,* 1999; *Dreaming of America: An Ellis Island Story* (1999); *Jumping the Nail,* 2000. SERIES include: *Magic Circle, Dinosaur Machine, No Such Things?, Eve Bunting Science Fiction, Eve Bunting Young Romance, Page Turners, Evelyn Bolton Horse Book* (using the name Evelyn Bolton), and *High Point* (written under the name A. E. Bunting).

BIBLIOGRAPHY: "Eve Bunting: She Loves to Tell a Story," *School Library Media Activities Monthly,* vol. 15, no. 1, September 1998; *Authors & Artists for Young Adults,* Gale, vol. 5, 1990; *Something about the Author,* Gale, vol. 110, 2000; "Talking With Eve Bunting: From the Titanic to ancient Egypt," *BookPage* Children's Interview: Eve Bunting Interview, May, 1997 retrieved June 4, 2003; *Children's Literature Review,* Gale, vol. 82, 2003.

NAOMI WILLIAMSON

BURGESS, Melvin

Author, b. 1954, Twickenham, Surrey, England

A TEEN girl with a love of sex is magically transformed into a dog, able to follow her desires and live freely sexually. A teenage couple runs away from home and joins a group of punks, gaining both initial freedom and a taste for heroin. Teenage boys explore their sexuality, contemplating the possibilities of having sex with a homeless woman. Taken individually, these story concepts have the potential to arouse controversy; taken together, these stories in their full treatments—*Lady: My Life as a Bitch* (2001), *Junk* (1996), (*Smack* in the U.S.), and *Doing It* (2003)—have stimulated ardent debate over the limits of YA

LITERATURE. In the process, B. has become an authorial symbol for edgy, honest, provocative literature for young people.

B. was born into a middle-class family and spent his childhood in Sussex. He describes himself as shy, lazy, and a poor student, someone who was miserable throughout his adolescence. B. did enjoy reading the works of authors such as Brecht, Orwell, Peake, Durrell, and had a talent for writing, particularly creative writing. With no concrete plan after graduating from secondary school, B. took a training course in journalism in which his father enrolled him, but quit the accompanying job as soon as the course was finished.

Throughout the next fifteen years, B. tried his hand at writing, but met with little success. He worked at various jobs including bricklaying, and he owned a marbling business for a time. At the age of thirty-five, B. decided to make a concerted effort to write full time. That year, his first novel for children *Cry of the Wolf* (1989) was published and short-listed for the prestigious Carnegie Medal. This book, an ecological thriller about a deranged hunter determined to slay the last wolves in England, has the same elements of darkness and rawness that characterize his subsequent works.

B.'s literary output has been notable, having had seventeen books published in little more than a decade. FANTASY is an important element in many of his titles, as can be seen in *The Baby and Fly Pie* (1993) and *Bloodtide* (1999); both novels have strong dystopian perspectives. B. has explored ecological themes in *Kite* (1998) and *Tiger, Tiger* (1996). Historical settings are incorporated in his works, some of which include the witch trials of the 17th century in *Burning Issy* (1992), Victorian London in *The Copper Treasure* (1998), and World War II–era rural England in *An Angel for May* (1992).

His more recent titles such as *Lady: My Life as a Bitch* (2001), *Junk* (1996), and *Doing It* (2003) mined the teenage psyche and the withdrawn uncompromising views of contemporary adolescent life. While B.'s depictions are tempered with honest consequences of characters' behavior, the author does not intend to be a moralist. Instead, B. says that he intends his works to speak frankly to and reflect candidly the lives of real teenagers; this is a group B. feels is largely neglected even in the literature that alleges to be for them. While his ventures have roused the ire of many adults who fear what messages young readers might take from these books, B. has been rewarded with loyal young readers and critical acclaim, as his Carnegie Medal and *Guardian* Prize for *Smack* attest.

AWARDS: *Junk:* 1996 Carnegie Medal, 1997 *Guardian* Prize for Children's Fiction; *Smack:* 1999 ALA Best Books for Young Adults.

FURTHER WORKS: *Loving April,* 1995; *Earth Giant,* 1997; *Old Bag,* 1999; *The Ghost behind the Wall,* 2000; *The Birdman,* 2000; *Billy Elliot,* 2001; *The Ghost Behind the Wall,* 2003.

BIBLIOGRAPHY: Burgess, Melvin (n.d.) Personal webpage. http://web.onetel.net.uk/~melvinburgess/; "Melvin Burgess." *Authors and Artists for Young Adults, Volume 28,* 1999, reproduced in *Biography Resource Center,* 2003. http://www.galenet.com/servlet/BioRC

CAROL TILLEY

BURNETT, Frances Hodgson

Author, b. 24 November 1849, in Manchester, England; d. 30 October 1924, Plandome, New York

B. was the highest paid woman author of her time, hugely popular on both sides of the Atlantic. No publisher ever turned down her work after she began writing for publication at the age of eighteen. Although she is best known now for several books read by young adults, she wrote primarily for adults and was the author of fifty novels and produced thirteen plays based on her work in London and New York. Best known today for her books *The Secret Garden* and *A Little Princess,* in her own time it was her novels *Little Lord Fauntleroy* (1886), *A Lady of Quality* (1896), and *The Dawn of a To-morrow* (1906) that topped the best-seller lists. Whether writing for adults or YOUNG ADULTS, B.'s work follows several themes that are reflected in her own life as well as in her work: the rags to riches story; the loss of parents; regeneration or transformation; movement from one country to another.

B. was the third child, and oldest girl, of five children, the last one born after the death of their father Edwin Hodgson in 1853. Their mother, Eliza Boond Hodgson, attempted for more than ten years to support her family by carrying on the family business of supplying Manchester households with brass fittings, chandeliers, and other domestic furnishings. It was a tenuous enterprise at best, and resulted in a series of moves into less expensive neighborhoods. When the American Civil War cut off the supply of cotton upon which Manchester's textile industry depended, businesses such as hers were the first to suffer. Finally, in 1865, Eliza Hodgson accepted her brother's offer and took her family to join him in Knoxville, Tennessee, where he kept a shop and ran a gristmill. The family arrived in the last months of the war, to a state ravaged by repeated occupations of both Union and Confederate armies, and found that their home was little better than a log cabin in New Market, a tiny outpost where the family nearly starved. They lived there for a year before moving to Clinton Pike, a bucolic area closer to Knoxville, where the children reveled in their first experience of a lush countryside after the gloomy and dirty industrial city where they had spent their early lives. It was here that B. grew to appreciate nature.

After a struggle to get by, B. tried her hand at running a school modeled after the young people's seminaries where she and her siblings had been educated and where she had been a great favorite because of her storytelling ability. That lasted only a year when, encouraged by the letters she discovered in popular MAGAZINES, she submitted a story with the expressed desire for payment. This came back with positive comments but no check, so unsure of what that meant she sent it out again, this time to *Godey's Lady's Book.* Puzzled by her obviously English approach and setting, the editors asked to see something else. She immediately wrote a second story and sent it in, and both were immediately accepted. The family was now able to move into Knoxville. However, with the death of their mother and the marriages of her brothers, B. needed more than ever to earn a living. From that time on, she lived by her pen, supported others, and nearly ruined her health in the process. By 1872 she had earned enough to finance a long visit to her Manchester relatives, leaving behind Swan Burnett, a young medical student from New Market, whom she promised to marry upon her return.

B. and Swan married in 1873, and their first child, a boy named Lionel, was born the next year. Knoxville felt very small to the ambitious young couple, so with B.'s writing to support them they moved to Paris for a year where Swan studied eye-and-ear medicine and young Lionel was cared for by an ex-slave named Prissie. B. became pregnant again and their second son, Vivian, was born in France. They returned after a year and set up housekeeping in Washington, D.C. where B. published her first novel, *That Lass o' Low-*

rie's, which was an immediate success in England and America and set her on her path to international fame. Her earlier serial stories began to be published, often without her permission, as novels, and by the 1880s there were seventeen published books of her work, all of them for adults. Then, after four years of nervous exhaustion and no writing, she published the book that put her permanently on the map of major authors: *Little Lord Fauntleroy.* The book began a craze that swept the country, and with it B. became not only famous but financially comfortable. When this book was pirated for an English play, she took the author to court and won a landmark decision that still protects the work of British authors.

The marriage between B. and Swan was not a happy one, and she began spending more and more time away from home, in Boston and Hartford and the seaside, with new friends. As she produced more books and became increasingly independent, she began to return to England nearly annually. Often her sons would join her for the summer in England or Italy, and she would winter in Washington. She and Swan spent years refuting rumors of a divorce, and whenever she returned from Europe she was met at the docks by crowds of reporters and gossip columnists who wanted to know about her private as well as her literary life. They were particularly interested in the amount of money she earned, much of it spent on her wardrobe and houses. Her time away from her family increased, and by 1889 she was living in England and had been away from the family for a year when news came of her son Lionel's tuberculosis. Extremely ill herself with a concussion suffered after being thrown from a horse cart, she nevertheless rushed home and took him to a series of spas, finally settling in Paris where he died in her arms in 1890. She was never again the same, suffering from guilt and regret from that time on, and throwing herself into philanthropy and children's causes.

By 1900, B. had divorced Swan and remarried an English doctor turned actor, Stephen Townesend, who was ten years her junior. Even though she was now able to live in a grand London house and a beautiful country home, Maytham Hall in Kent, this was a short-lived and unhappy marriage. Her sister Edith, now remarried after losing a husband and child, came to live with her; her husband and two sons often joined them. Maytham was the home of B.'s heart, and she created beautiful gardens there, but after los-

ing the lease on the hall, she returned to America and built a house in Plandome, on Long Island, where her son Vivian and his family also had a small home built on her property. Spending summers in Bermuda with Edith, B. threw herself into gardening, writing, and producing plays, several of which were also made into early films. It was in this house that she wrote *The Secret Garden* (1910). Despite its Yorkshire setting, the story, the first young readers' serial to be published in an adult magazine, was based in part on her gardens and robin at Maytham Hall. She died in Plandome in 1924, of colon cancer, with her family at her side.

FURTHER WORKS: In B.'s time, there was no firm demarcation between books for young adults and for older adults. Dickens, Twain, and ALCOTT all expected their novels to be read by both young people and their parents. B. wrote very long novels for adults, often breaking up her work by writing shorter novels for younger readers, generally publishing them in time for the Christmas market. Following is a list of B.'s books that might today be considered suitable for young adults. Because her books were published first as magazine serials, the dates reflect their first publication as books. *Little Lord Fauntleroy,* 1886; *A Little Princess* (first published in 1887 as a story, "Sara Crewe," which was both a novella and a play; later expanded into the full-length novel in 1905); *Little Saint Elizabeth and Other Stories,* 1890; *Giovanni and the Other,* 1892; *The One I Knew the Best of All,* 1893 (memoir of her childhood); *Piccino and other Child Stories,* 1894; *Two Little Pilgrims' Progress,* 1895; *In the Closed Room,* 1904; *The Secret Garden,* 1911; *The Lost Prince,* 1915; *The Little Hunchback Zia,* 1916.

BIBLIOGRAPHY: All material in this essay comes from Gretchen Holbrook Gerzina's BIOGRAPHY of Burnett, *Frances Hodgson Burnett: The Unexpected Life of the Author of "The Secret Garden,"* 2004, the first full biography of Burnett in thirty years, drawing upon full family cooperation and materials never before available to previous biographers.

GRETCHEN HOLBROOK GERZINA

BURNFORD, Sheila
Author, b. May 1918, Scotland; d. 1984, n.p.

At the time of her DEATH in 1984, B.'s lasting fame was mostly attributable to her first published book. *The Incredible Journey: A Tale of Three Animals* (1961) which became a classic almost immediately. It follows a bull terrier, a golden Labrador, and a Siamese cat, who are determined to return to their family and travel two hundred and fifty miles through Canada to accomplish that goal. The characters in the story are supposedly based on the author's pets and the way they cooperated, although the journey itself is a work of fiction.

The Incredible Journey was also named by The Free Public Library of Philadelphia in the third edition of *Modern Classic*. The story was enhanced even farther by Carl Burger's illustrations, and received a further boost towards immortality when it was made into a movie by Disney Studios in 1963. The Disney movie was remade and titled *Homeward Bound: The Incredible Journey* in 1993, and generated a sequel, *Homeward Bound II: Lost in San Francisco* which appeared in 1996.

Her other books were adult nonfiction—and none of them ever achieved the fame of *The Incredible Journey. The Fields of Noon* (1964) was a collection of essays, one of which told about her daughter's canary. Next was *Without Reserve* (1969), tales of Cree and Ojibwa Indians found on Ontario Province reservations and *One Woman's Arctic* (1973), which chronicled the lives of the Eskimos of Baffin Island. *Mr. Noah and the Second Flood* (1973) dealt with ecological issues. In *Bel Ria*—which was released in 1977—a dog's story is told after its owner's death.

B.'s work also appeared in *Canadian Poetry, Glasgow Herald,* and *Punch.* However, none of her other work achieved the fame of *The Incredible Journey,* which has a multigenerational following.

AWARDS: *Incredible Journey:* 1963 Canadian Library Association Book of the Year Award for Children; 1964 Young Reader's Choice Award; 1964 William Allen White Children's Book Award.

BIBLIOGRAPHY: Breckenridge, Kit. "Modern Classics," *School Library Journal,* April 1988, pp. 42–43; www.abebooks.com; www.imdb.com; www.novelst4.epnet.com; www.track0.com/ogwc/authors/burnford_s.html; www.tomfolio.com/bookssub.asp?catid=4&subid=15

JEANNE MARIE RYAN

BUTLER, Octavia E.

Author, b. 22 June 1947, Pasadena, California

B. is a highly acclaimed SCIENCE FICTION writer, the first to be awarded the prestigious MacArthur Foundation Fellowship, or "genius grant," in 1995. B. is also one of the first AFRICAN AMERICAN women to successfully break through the gender and genre barrier. B. has been the recipient of all of science fiction's top literary prizes. Her visionary fusion of FEMINISM, MYTHOLOGY, history, and spiritualism has created extraordinarily complex and powerful tales that expand the boundaries of contemporary SCIENCE FICTION.

B. earned an A.A. degree in 1968 from Pasadena City College, and also attended California State University at Los Angeles, and the University of California, at Los Angeles. In 1969 B. participated in the Open Door Program of the Screen Writers Guild of America, and studied under science fiction master Harlan Ellison, who encouraged her to pursue a writing career. After attending the Clarion SF Writer's Workshop in 1970, her first short story, "Crossover" debuted in their 1971 anthology, but it was several years before her first novel, *Patternmaster* (1976), established her ability to create provocative heroines and plausible aliens.

Patternmaster spawned the Patternist SERIES, stories of rivalry among an elite society of telepaths vying for control of a superhuman telepathic race. *Mind of My Mind* (1977), was written as a "prequel," and features Mary, a young "active" bred to detect latent telepaths and control the extrasensory community created by her tyrannical father. In *Survivor* (1978), an enslaved member of a human colony established on an alien planet must teach her prejudiced captors tolerance for different species.

B. incorporates historical elements of the African American experience as the basis for profound insights about the darker side of human nature. *Kindred* (1979) transports Dana, a young black heroine, back to an antebellum plantation in Maryland, where she must protect the life of her slave-owning ancestor in order to ensure her own birth. The next novel of the series, *Wild Seed,* takes readers on impressive time travelling of its own; it is actually the third in the chronology, and although written in 1980, the book won a retrospective James Tiptree Award in 1996 for classic science fiction. *Wild Seed* traces the origins of the Patternists, back to 17th century Africa, and pits two immortal beings in a battle of wills that ultimately creates a telepathic race. *Clay's Ark* (1984) is the final book of the Patternist series in which B. continues to explore themes involving genetically mutated humans in hostile environments. B.'s novelette, *Bloodchild* (1984) garnered a triple-crown of science fiction, winning multiple awards. *Bloodchild,* is the story of human male slaves who must bear the children of an insectlike alien race, in exchange for their species' survival. The author's deconstruction of feminine reproductive roles reflected a powerful trend in science fiction.

Dawn: Xenogenesis (1987), the first book of B.'s Xenogenesis trilogy, introduces Lilith Iyapo, a young widow rescued by aliens after nuclear war destroys the Earth. She awakens centuries later and finds herself a reluctant liaison between the two races, and gives birth to the first half-*Oankali* half-human child. Lilith's baby, Akin, is kidnapped in the next novel, *Adulthood Rites* (1988). His experiences with violent and illogical humans alter his development, and foster a new future neither race had envisioned. In *Imago* (1989), one of Lilith's hybrid children belongs to the special third Oankali gender, or *ooloi,* and has the ability to alter all forms of life.

The Earthseed cautionary tales began with *Parable of the Sower* (1993), the genesis of a humanist theology in a dystopian Earth. This fictional autobiography of the charismatic empath Lauren Olamina and the second installment of the series, *Parable of the Talents* (1998), both received honors. In the second novel, Lauren's journals provide her daughter Larkin with answers about her mother's devotion to the religion she believes will change humanity.

In keeping with her futuristic vision, B.'s most recent SHORT STORY, "Amnesty" (2003) can only be found on the internet at www.scifi.com. It is a masterful tale befitting one of the most evocative writers in science fiction today.

AWARDS: Hugo Award, 1984, for *Speech Sounds,* 1985; Nebula Award, 1984, Locus Award, 1985, Hugo Award, 1985, *Bloodchild,* 1987; MacArthur Foundation Fellowship, 1995; James Tiptree Award, Nebula Award, *Parable of the Talents,* 1999; Pen Center West Lifetime Achievement Award, 2000.

FURTHER WORKS: *Bloodchild and Other Stories,* 1995; *Xenogenesis: 3 vols. in 1,* 1989.

BIBLIOGRAPHY: Contemporary Authors, Vol. 38, p. 74–76. *Newsday,* March 22, 1973; *New York Times Book Review,* March 25, 1973, July 2, 1978; *New York Times,* March 27, 1973; *Newsweek,* April 9, 1973; *Milwaukee Journal,* May 20, 1973; July 9, 1978; *Washington Post,* April 15, 1990; *Los Angeles Times,* May 1, 1990; *Tribune Books,* August 12, 1990.

PAT PAYNE

C

CABOT, Meg(gin)
(Jenny Carroll and Patricia Cabot)
Author, b. 1 February 1967, Bloomington, Indiana

Having a writing style that connects easily with the way TEENS think and talk, C. has quickly become a popular author with YOUNG ADULTS. Using a DIARY or first-person narrator as her primary novel format, C. easily conveys the everyday challenges of adolescence in her books.

The Princess Diaries (2000) launched C. into the young adult spotlight. Written in novel-as-diary form, the book offers a funny and engaging look at what teenager Mia must face: boys at school, her mother dating her algebra teacher, and Mia's finding out that she is, in fact, a princess. C. credits her ability to be in touch with the inner teenage voice with the fact she herself was once a teenager and from having been a college dormitory manager for ten years. Growing up, C. always liked princesses and is quick to point out that she shares the same birth date with Princess Stephanie of Monaco, only C. is two years younger. For *Something about the Author* (vol. 127), C. wrote a diary about writing *The Princess Diaries,* stating she really was keeping a journal and reacting to her mother's dating one of her teachers and thought it would make a good book. However, her editor felt she should write a book about a princess instead; so she included a princess aspect in her story, but still kept the mother and teacher plot. The success of this book launched a SERIES of *Princess Diaries* book, as well as a popular Disney movie.

Writing had originally been a hobby for C., but she was often encouraged to get published. However, C. did not want to have her work rejected. When her father died, she realized that time is short and one should not worry about rejection. C. received numerous rejection letters, except one, so she asked that person to be her agent. C. has written other young adult books under the pseudonym Jenny Carroll, as well as ADULT FICTION under Patricia Cabot. Now that she has one publisher, all her books are published under her given name.

Along with the Princess Diaries series, C. has also written The Mediator series and the 1-800-WHERE-R-YOU series, both under her Jenny Carroll pseudonym. Both series deal with the supernatural, and have strong appeal for teen girls. Being able to communicate with the dead is not an easy thing for a teenager to deal with, as seen in The Mediator series. Suze is a mediator who helps the dead deal with unresolved issues so they may move on to the next world. There was a popular TV series on the Lifetime Channel called *1-800-Missing* and later changed to *Missing*; it is based on the 1-800-WHERE R-YOU series, where Jessica Mastriani gains psychic abilities after being struck by lightning. This allows her to find missing children, although some people want her to use her new gift in other ways.

All-American Girl (2002) shows how life as an average middle child can suddenly change when you save the President's life. This is yet another quick, easy, and delightfully funny read from C.

AWARDS: American Library Association Top Ten Quick Picks for Reluctant Readers selection and Best Book for YA for *Princess Diaries* (2001); Edgar Allan Poe Award nominee for *Safe House*-written under Jenny Carroll (2003).

FURTHER WORKS: *Princess in Love,* 2002; *Princess in the Spotlight,* vol. 2, 2002; *Princess in Waiting,* 2003; *The Haunted,* 2003; Mediator series.

BIBLIOGRAPHY: *Contemporary Authors,* vol. 197; *Something About the Author,* vol. 127; Dennan, Cathy L. "Review of *The Princess Diaries." Journal of Adolescent & Adult Literacy,* November 2002; Book Reviews in *Publishers Weekly,* October 9, 2000, November 6, 2000, July 9, 2001, and June 24, 2002; www .megcabot.com

TINA HERTEL

CADNUM, Michael

Author, b. 3 May 1949, Orange, California

C. is the author of more than twenty novels, fifteen of which have been published by children's divisions and marketed to young adults. His first published works were poems and adult horror novels. He has also written SHORT STORIES and a children's book. C. received his BA at the University of California and his M.A. at San Francisco State University. He and his wife Sherina reside in Albany, California.

C.'s interest in writing about flawed, even disturbed, characters is evident in his first novel published for TEENS, *Calling Home* (1991). The reader is shocked when Peter, a high-school senior, accidentally kills his friend in a drunken, momentary fit of pique, and then impersonates his victim in a series of phone calls. Realistic, psychologically frightening, and dark, this story is based on an actual incident. Stylistically typical of C.'s work, it paints an exacting, meticulous, and unsettling portrait of a character that is not particularly likeable, but thoroughly recognizable. *Breaking the Fall* (1992) continues in this vein, exploring teenage Stanley's dangerous acquiescence to the peer pressure exerted by Jared. Challenged by Jared, Stanley breaks into occupied homes, even into bedrooms in which the homeowners are sleeping, to steal inconsequential, personal items. *Taking It* (1995) tells of Anna, who pretends to shoplift for kicks, but gradually finds she's losing control and in need of help.

C. features characters who make poor moral choices and then must deal with the ambiguous con-

sequences that result in *Edge* (1997) and *Rundown* (1999). In the former, Zachary's father is shot and permanently disabled by an unknown gunman. Bent on revenge, Zachary literally gets the person he thinks is the perpetrator in his sights and there—balanced between two vastly different futures—must decide whether or not to pull the trigger. In the latter, sixteen-year-old Cassandra feels invisible in her family as her older sister's wedding approaches. While jogging she fakes an assault and files a false report of having been raped. While she gains the attention she craved, the growing burden of guilt—and the evidence—eventually force her to come clean. And in *Heat* (1998), Bonnie, a talented platform diver, quickly regains consciousness after cracking her head on the platform, but only slowly comes to understand that her beloved father, an attorney, is a crook.

An interesting shift to historical fiction began with the publication of *In a Dark Wood* (1998) in which C. sympathetically portrays one of the most villainous men in English literature, the Sheriff of Nottingham. Teen readers who appreciate C.'s deliberate attention to laser-sharp detail and precise interior monologue will revel in his historically accurate depictions that include the violence and grit of ages past while still focusing on the psychological aspects of his protagonists. C. revisits this setting in *Forbidden Forest* (2002), which again examines the Robin Hood myth from an unexpected perspective, that of Little John and a woman, Margaret Lea, who by separate paths join the band hiding out in mighty Sherwood Forest.

The Book of the Lion (2000) further illuminates a dark age in the character of Edmund, who is thrust by circumstance into the role of squire to a knight journeying to war for King Richard during the Crusades. In *The Leopard Sword* (2002), the same troop journey home via Rome and other stops only to find their homeland under political siege at the hands of Prince John.

Raven of the Waves (2001) portrays the innocence and inexperience of seventeen-year-old Lidsmod on his first Viking raid against medieval English villages. His initial bewilderment gives way to some understanding of that foreign culture that juxtaposes strongly with the equal possibility of sudden and violent death. Wiglaf, thirteen-year-old captive, counterposes with his gentle life of learning and healing.

C.'s meticulous word choice and precise attention to the inner voice of his protagonists never speaks down to teen readers, but rather challenges them to perceive nuance and subtle shifts in mood, tone, and scene. Whether inspired by contemporary news, a historic setting, scene, character, or traditional tale, C.'s novels intimately propel the reader into the mind of the protagonist. As in the best art of any medium, the reader may be left with conflicted feelings about difficult moral issues, disturbed and enlightened by the "what if's"—the questions and the choices they have confronted.

AWARDS: *In a Dark Wood,* 1998, was a finalist for the *Los Angeles Times* Book Prize for young-adult fiction; Poetry Northwest's Helen Bullis Prize and the Owl Creek Book Award.

SELECT FURTHER WORKS: Poetry—*The Morning of the Massacre,* 1981; *Invisible Mirror,* 1984; *Foreign Springs,* 1985; *Long Afternoons,* 1986; *By Evening,* 1992; *The Cities We Will Never See,* 1993; *The Woman Who Discovered Math,* 2001; *Illicit,* 2001. Novels—*Nightlight,* 1990; *Sleepwalker,* 1991; *Saint Peter's Wolf,* 1992; *Ghostwright,* 1993; *The Horses of the Night,* 1993; *Skyscape,* 1994; *The Judas Glass,* 1996; *Zero at the Bone,* 1996; *Daughter of the Wind,* 2003; *Ship of Fire,* 2003. Theater—"Can't Catch Me" was staged as a dramatic monologue by WNEP Theater, Chicago, in March, 2003, along with plays by David Mamet and Billy Aronson, and was also staged by the Aurora Theater, Berkeley, California, in September, 2002.

- POETRY appears in many anthologies, including several editions of the *Bedford Introduction to Literature* (Michael Meyer, Editor); *Poets for Life: 76 Poets Respond to AIDS* (Crown, Michael Klein, editor), and many others.
- Short stories appear in many anthologies, including "Wolf at the Door" and "The Green Man."
- Hundreds of poems and dozens of short stories are published in PERIODICALS, including *Virginia Quarterly Review, Georgia Review, America, Rolling Stone,* and *Commonweal.*

BIBLIOGRAPHY: Cadnum, Michael. *The Eye under Oath: Why Stories Are Alive.* ALAN Review, Vol 26 Winter 1999, pp. 5-8; Campbell, Patty. *The Sand in the Oyster.* Horn Book, Vol 70 May/June 1994, 358 + ; Cockett, Lynn and Jones, Patrick. *Real Terror.* Booklist, Vol 92 November 1995, 546; Jones, Patrick. *People Are Talking About . . . Michael Cadnum.* Horn Book, Vol. 70 March/April 1994, 177 + ; Shoemaker,

Joel. *An Interview With Michael Cadnum.* Voice of Youth Advocates, Vol 22 June 1999, 97–99.

JOEL SHOEMAKER

CALHOUN, Dia
Author, b. 4 January 1959, Seattle, Washington

After spending her growing-up years studying ballet, C. decided to forego a career in dance to attend Mills College, where she studied Book Arts and English Literature and graduated Phi Beta Kappa. As a freelance artist, she designed the logo for Alaska Airlines. Her first published novel, *Firegold* (1999), is a lyrical tale of a boy who does not look like everyone else in the apple-growing valley where he lives, so is blamed when blight hits the apple crop. In *Aria of the Sea* (2000), Cerinthe goes from her rustic island home to attend the Queen's dance academy and must come to terms with the guilt she feels over the loss of her mother and the question of what to do about her own powerful healing talents.

In 2003, with *White Midnight,* she returned to the world of *Firegold* but at a time four hundred years ago. What at first appears to be a "Beauty and the Beast"–type story takes an unexpected twist. When asked why she writes FANTASY she stated, "Fantasy is a way of talking about serious issues while being removed from them at the same time" and "I feel that fantasy provides more scope for the imagination, and it allows more use of the sub-conscious." C.'s books have been translated into French and German.

C. currently lives in Tacoma, Washington; her studio overlooks Puget Sound.

AWARDS: *Firegold:* 2000 ALA Best Books for Young Adults; *Aria of the Sea:* 2001 Mythopoeic Fantasy Award for Children's Literature, 2001 ALA Best Books for Young Adults; *White Midnight:* 2004 ALA Best Books for Young Adults.

FURTHER WORKS: *The Phoenix Dance,* 2005.

BIBLIOGRAPHY: AuthorChats (http://www.authorchats .com/archives/view Archive.jsp?id = 20011016Dia Calhoun.jsp); Winslow Press (http://www.winslow press.com/firegold/dia.cfm); Children's Literature (http://www.childrenslit.com/home.htm)

DIANA TIXIER HERALD

CALVERT, Patricia
Author, b. 22 July 1931, Great Falls, Montana

Growing up in the mountains of Montana in an old cabin with few amenities, C. listened to stories her mother would read or tell to her and her brother.

These stories were not the usual children's stories but anything that their mother could find to read or memories from her own childhood.

From the age of two, C. lived in the wilds of Montana where she grew to appreciate the beauty of the mountains and their inhabitants. When she was six, her family moved to more settled areas of Great Falls, Montana, so that the children could attend public school, but they returned to the mountains each summer. At this time it was discovered that she was dyslexic. Because of this disability she became a problem in the classroom. When it was suggested that she repeat first grade, her mother diligently worked with C. until her reading skills improved. By the time C. was in fourth grade, she had learned to read quite well and had begun to write her own stories.

Even though she planned to be a writer, C. studied to be a medical technologist. She attended the University of Montana and married George Calvert in 1950, joining her Air Force husband in Georgia. When he left the military they moved to Minnesota where C. worked at the Mayo Clinic in Rochester as an editorial assistant. She earned a B.A. in 1976 at Winona State University. During this time she continued writing stories for children's MAGAZINES.

C.'s first book, *The Snowbird,* a novel set in the 1880s, was published in 1980 with *The Money Creek Mare* following a year later. C. writes historical and modern novels using real-life experiences and problems that affect TEENS. In her AUTOBIOGRAPHY she says that she writes about, "struggle, failure, isolation, and being a jealous misfit."

AWARDS: *The Snowbird:* ALA Best Book Award, Society of Midland Authors Juvenile Fiction Award, Friends of American Writers Juvenile Award, YWCA Award for Outstanding Achievement in the Arts; *Yesterday's Daughter:* 1986 ALA Best Book for Young Adults; 1987 William Allen White Award, *Hadder MacColl;* The Christopher Award *Glennis, Before & After.*

FURTHER WORK: *Hadder MacColl,* 1985; *Yesterday's Daughter,* 1986; *Stranger, You & I,* 1987; *Picking up the Pieces,* 1993; *Bigger,* 1994; *Writing to Richie,* 1994; *Glennis, Before & After,* 1996; *The American Frontier,* 1997; *Sooner,* 1998; *Michael Wait for Me,* 2000; *Daniel Boone,* 2001; *Robert E. Peary,* 2001; *Betrayed,* 2002; *Standoff at Standing Rock,* 2001; *Sir Ernest Shackleton,* 2002; *Hernando Cortez,* 2002; *Lost in the Rockies,* 2004; *Vasco de Gama,* 2004.

BIBLIOGRAPHY: *Authors and Artists for Young Adults,* volume 18; *Contemporary Authors,* volume 105; *Something about the Author, Autobiography Series,* volume 17.

M. NAOMI WILLIAMSON

CAMPBELL, Patty

C. has been a critic, author, teacher, and librarian in the field of YA literature for the past thirty years. During the formative years of the genre, she was the Assistant Coordinator of Young Adult Services for the Los Angeles Public Library system, and she has taught adolescent literature at UCLA and Denver University. Her critical writing has appeared in the *New York Times Book Review* and many library journals. Currently she writes "The Sand in the Oyster" for *Horn Book* magazine, a column on controversial issues in books for teens, and is one of the two YA editorial reviewers for Amazon.com online bookstore. Campbell is the author of six books, among them *Two Pioneers of Young Adult Library Services* (Scarecrow) and the forthcoming *Daring to Disturb the Universe: The Life and Work of Robert Cormier* (Delacorte). Two series of literary criticism have been shaped by her as editor: Twayne's Young Adult Authors, and, currently, Scarecrow Studies in Young Adult Literature. She has served on the Board of Directors of both the Young Adult Library Services Association of ALA and the Assembly on Adolescent Literature of the National Council of Teachers of English. In 1989, she was the recipient of ALA's Grolier Award for distinguished service to young adults and books, and in 2001 NCTE chose her the winner of their ALAN Award. Campbell lives on an avocado ranch in California and writes and publishes books on van travel abroad with her husband David Shore.

PATTY CAMPBELL

Originally published in *The Horn Book Magazine,* September/October 2004. Reprinted by permission of The Horn Book, Inc., Boston, MA, www.hbook.com.

CANADIAN BOOKS FOR YOUNG ADULTS

In 1907 Lucy Maud Montgomery published *Anne of Green Gables* which has since become the most internationally recognized Canadian book for young readers. The irrepressible "auburn-haired" orphan captured hearts around the world and made readers aware not only of Prince Edward Island, but also of Canada. Montgomery followed earlier successful writers such as Margaret Marshall Sanders (*Beautiful Joe,* 1894) and Ernest Thompson Seton (*Wild Animals I Have Known,* 1884), and initially published her books in the U.S. Early English Canadian books needed American or British publishers.

Few books for young readers were published by Canadian authors during the first half of the 20th century. A notable exception was Farley Mowat who published (in 1956), a TEEN survival story, *Lost in the Barrens,* that still resonates with today's readers. Mowat's story of seventeen-year-old Jamie McNair and his aboriginal friend Awasin's two-week hunting trip for caribou—a riveting first-hand account of survival during a winter in the Canadian arctic—captured international attention. Mowat, along with Grey Owl and Roderick Haig-Brown, celebrated and respected the Canadian landscape and weather in their writings.

It was not until Canadians embraced national pride during the centennial year, 1967, that the need for indigenous publishing for children and youth was seriously considered within Canada's boundaries. Young energetic publishers, assisted by government grants, started operations in Canada. Groundwood Books, Kids Can Press, and Annick Press were among the first publishers to introduce Canada to the wealth of talent within its borders. *The Canadian Children's Book Centre* (established in 1976 with federal funds as well as publisher, educational, and librarian support) promoted Canadian books for children and young adults both nationally and internationally.

Kevin MAJOR was one of the first Canadian young adult authors to create an international stir with his debut novel *Hold Fast* in 1978. The immediacy of Major's forthright language, strong characters, and the uncompromising reality of the Newfoundland landscape and community make this a forceful account of an adolescent's struggle against unfair, domineering authority. *Hold Fast* not only established Major as an international figure in the world of literature for youth, but also presented Canada as a vivid setting for teen fiction.

The success of Major's work and a multitude of other authors' children's books (including Dennis Lee's *Alligator Pie*) provided a climate within Canada that was conducive both to the creative spirit of Canadian writers and to entrepreneurial publishers.

Brian DOYLE's *Hey Dad!* was one of the first titles published by Groundwood Books, and since that first publication readers have anxiously awaited each one of his subsequent novels. Groundwood quickly established itself as a publisher of important, relevant, and necessary books for young adult readers. Their writers, and other Canadian YA authors, moved away from the tales of landscape, wilderness, and struggles against the weather to complex stories of love, loss, FAMILIES, and relationships. Groundwood's authors include: Tim WYNNE-JONES whose many teen novels and SHORT STORY collections explore the complex lives of modern teens; Martha BROOKS with her arresting stories and novels written with compassion and psychological depth; and Diana WIELER, known for her powerful writing for teen males including *Bad Boy* (1989). Recent additions to the Groundwood collection of powerful writers for young adults are Deborah Ellis, with her Parvana trilogy recounting the struggles of a young girl in war-torn Afghanistan, and Mary SHEPPARD whose edgy *Seven for a Secret* reveals an empowering story of family secrets set in Newfoundland. Groundwood's early novels and stories published for young adults in Canada were written for young teens, but in recent years the age range has been extended with more complex and challenging material for older teens.

Canada can boast of many excellent publishers in addition to Groundwood Books. Annick Press, Fitzhenry and Whiteside, Kids Can Press, Orca Books, Red Deer College Press, and Tundra Books publish significant titles for young adults each year. International publishing houses including Penguin Books, Scholastic Press, and HarperCollins produce additional titles for this age group.

Though many of Canada's best-known authors have explored Canadian regions and historical events in their books, the universal themes of self-discovery, family dynamics, social experience, and the difficulties encountered when growing through the teen years have made their books popular not only within Canada, but throughout the world. Publishers successfully market their books throughout the United States and Europe.

Janet Lunn, Julie JOHNSON, James HENEGHAN, Iain LAWRENCE, Janet MCNAUGHTON, Suzanne Martel, Kit Pearson, and Troon Harrison have introduced the struggles of youth in compelling historical fiction set in a variety of times and places, including many locales far from Canadian soil. The late Monica HUGHES remains one of the foremost SCIENCE FICTION writers for this age group. Canadian FANTASY writers such as Michael BEDARD, Welwyn Katz, Martine Leavitt, Kenneth OPPEL (with his internationally successful Silverwing trilogy), and Arthur SLADE provide fantasy reading with an intriguing dark edge to young adults.

The trials of today's youth are explored in the novels of Beth GOOBIE, Linda Holeman, Katherine Holubitsky, Graham MCNAMEE, Teresa Toten, and Michele Marineau. The issues explored in their books include self-esteem, sexual, physical and psychological abuse, and the ever-important issue of finding one's way and place in the world.

Canadian aboriginal writers have not produced a large body of work for this age range; however there are a few notable exceptions including Ruby Slipperjack and Shirley Sterling.

One of the strengths of Canadian writing for young adults is the rich collection of short stories, both fiction and nonfiction. Budge Wilson burst onto the scene in 1990 with her stunning portraits of young women in *The Leaving*. Since that time, a variety of authors including Sarah Ellis, W. D. Valgardsen, Rick Book, and Gillian Chan have intrigued readers with their collections of short stories. Martha Brooks and Tim Wynne-Jones (both previously mentioned) have short story collections that are among the best published, both nationally and internationally, for this age group.

Susan Musgrave, a well-established Canadian adult author, has recently turned her hand to collecting true stories for teenage girls. Her first collection *Nerves Out Loud* provides stories of emotional impact that strike a chord with young teen girls.

Anne of Green Gables may still be Canada's best-known book, but the growth in Canadian publishing during the last thirty years has made it possible for a wide variety of other Canadian–authored books to entertain, intrigue, and inspire not only Canadians but young adult readers around the world.

FURTHER WORKS: Bedard, M. *A Darker Magic* (1987), *Redwork* (1992); Book R. *Necking with Louise* (1999); Brooks, M. *Two Moons in August* (1991), *Travelling on into the Light* (1994), *Bone Dance* (1997), *Being with Henry* (1999), *True Confessions of*

a Heartless Girl, (2002); Chan, G. *Golden Girl and other Stories* (1994), *A Foreign Field* (2002); Ellis, S. *Out of the Blue* (1994), *Back of Beyond* (1996); Goobie, B. *Before Wings* (2000); Haig-Brown, R. *Starbuck Valley Winter* (1944); Harrison, T. *A Bushel of Light* (2000); Heneghan, James. *Wish me Luck* (1997); Holeman, L. *Mercy's Birds* (1998), *Search of the Moon King's Daughter* (2002); Holubitsky, K. *Alone at Ninety Feet*, (1999), *Last Summer in Agatha* (2001); Hughes, M. *The Keeper of the Isis Light* (1980); Johnson, J. *Hero of Lesser Causes* (1992), *Adam and Eve and Pinch-Me*, (1994), *The Only Outcast* (1998), *In Spite of Killer Bees* (2001); Katz, W. W. *Witchery Hill* (1984); Lunn, J. *The Hollow Tree* (1997); Marineau, M. *The Road to Chilfa* (1992); McNamee, G. *Hate You* (1999); McNaughton, J. *To Dance at the Palias Royale* (1996), *Make or Break Spring* (1999); Pearson, K. *The Sky is Falling* (1989), *Awake and Dreaming* (1997); Slade, A. *Dust* (2001), *Tribes* (2002); Sterling, S. *My Name is Seepeetza* (1992); Toten, T. *The Game*, (2001); Valgardon, W. D. *The Divorced Kids Club and Other Stories* (1999); Wieler, D. *Ran Van: The Defender* (1993), *Ran Van: A Worthy Opponent* (1995), *Ran Van: Magic Nation* (1997), *Drive* (1998); Wynne-Jones, T. *Some of the Kinder Planets* (1993), *The Book of Changes* (1994), *The Maestro* (1995), *Stephen Fair* (1998), *Lord of the Fries* (1999), *The Boy in the Burning House* (2000).

BIBLIOGRAPHY: Baker, D. F. & Setterington, K. H., 2003, *A Guide to Canadian Children's Books;* Toronto: McClelland & Stewart. Egoff, S. A. & Saltman, J., 1990. *The New Republic of Childhood: A Critical Guide to Canadian Children's Literature in English;* Egoff, S., Stubb, G., Ashley, R. and Sutton, W., eds., 1996, *Only Connect: Readings on Children's Literature;* Toronto: Oxford University Press. Jones, R. E. and Stott, J. C. 2000. *Canadian Children's Books: A Critical Guide to Authors and Illustrators; Writing Stories, Making Pictures: BIOGRAPHIES of 150 Canadian Children's Authors and Illustrators,* 1994. *Children's and Young Adult titles*—Doyle, B. *Hey Dad!* 1978; Ellis, D. *The Breadwinner,* 2001; Lee, D. *Alligator Pie,* 1974; Major, K. *Hold Fast,* 1978; Montgomery, L. M. *Anne of Green Gables,* 1908; Mowat, F. *Lost in the Barrens,* 1956; Musgrave, S. (ed.) *Nerves Out Loud,* 2001; Oppel, K. *Silverwing,* 1997; Sanders, M. M. *Beautiful Joe,* 1894; Seton, E. T. *Wild Animals I Have Known,* 1898; Sheppard, M. C. *Seven for a Secret,* 2001; Wieler, D. *Bad Boy,* 1989; Wilson, B. M. *The Leaving,* 1990.

KEN SETTERINGTON

CANNON, A(nn) E(dwards)
Author, newspaper columnist, n.d., n.p.

C. is an author "with remarkable insights into the concerns of young people," though remarkably little is known of her personal life. Beginning in 1988 with *Cal Cameron by Day, Spider-Man by Night,* C. has created characters who "are sensitively drawn, prompting readers to identify with their anxieties and fears while applauding their successes."

C. creates characters whose surroundings cause them to mature at a rapid speed. *The Shadow Brothers* (1990) is the story of a Navajo TEEN as told by his adoptive (non–American Indian) brother. Henry Yazzie has been sent to live with his father's white friend's family so that he can attend good schools. An excellent student and athlete, the arrival of a second American Indian boy to the school has Henry questioning his identity as a Navajo. *Amazing Gracie* (1991) is a study of dysfunctional FAMILY life. Gracie's mother suffers from chronic depression, causing a great deal of responsibility to fall prematurely on the shoulders of Gracie. When her mother remarries and the family is relocated to Salt Lake City, Utah, Gracie must work ferociously to keep her mother from slipping deeper into a pit of depression. *Charlotte's Rose* (2002) explores a Mormon experience of 1856. Charlotte and her widowed father have recently emigrated from Wales and are preparing to cross to the American West as members of a Welsh handcart company. Because of their poverty, they are forced to push carts from Iowa City to Zion, Utah. Charlotte shoulders an additional burden when she takes responsibility for an orphaned infant. As she struggles with the task of caring for the baby, Charlotte finds herself falling in love with her charge. She finds great maturity while crossing the Mormon trail.

C. is also the author of PICTURE and easy to read children's books. She currently writes a column for the *Deseret News* and teaches writing YOUNG ADULT LITERATURE and other creative writing classes at Brigham Young University.

AWARDS: 1988 Association for Mormon Letters Literary Awards in The Novel, *Cal Cameron by Day, Spider-Man by Night;* American Library Association Best Books for Young Adults, 1990 for *The Shadow Brothers* and 1991 for *Amazing Gracie; Amazing Gracie* was also selected as one of the best 100 books of the last 20 years by the ALA.

SELECT FURTHER WORKS: *Cal Cameron by Day, Spider-Man by Night,* 1988.

BIBLIOGRAPHY: "A(nn) E(dwards) Cannon." *U*X*L Junior DISCovering Authors,* 1998, reproduced in Discovering Collection, 2001, http://galenet.gale group.com/servlet/DC/; http://www.amazon.com

RACHEL WITMER AND SARA MARCUS

"THE CANON": Introduction to Secondary School Reading

Authors featured in these entries are frequently assigned as part of the literary canon in schools across the nation. An informal survey of librarians and teachers identifies which authors are most often studied. A survey by the Online Computer Library Center (OCLC) reported in the February/March, 2005 issue of *IRA Reading Today* shows which books are judged most worthy to read. These lists were combined to determine which authors are in the literary canon.

The following selection provides authors and works of significant depth and quality that have enriched different generations in their relevance and meaning as part of units of study for TEENAGERS of varying abilities in American high schools.

Works are read in full or excerpted (depending on the course, time, and student ability), nevertheless, these authors inspire new thoughts, communication, writing and exchange of questions and debate among YOUNG ADULT readers.

Although thousands of additional authors and titles can be identified as significant sources of contemporary interest including best sellers, nonfiction, and other genres such as essay, POETRY and SHORT STORY, these works can be thematically linked through outside reading, student-teacher selection as part of a longer unit of study, an independent reading program, mini-course, or creative writing action research activity. However, the basic list provided represents authors and titles of classic nature usually found in quality comprehensive high school English Departments which are addressing state standards and preparing students with a rigorous language arts program as a foundation for further study in college.

Because some of these texts contain adult situations or moral issues, these titles are usually previewed by a teacher and provided with teacher-led instruction. (For example, issues of racism as evident in Richard Wright need to be addressed and open to mature discussion among students challenged to look at the significance of the text by the teacher.) Needless to say, books should not be recommended to a student if the teacher or librarian has not read the book. Many long-time favorites may contain adult issues as in *Native Son,* the infidelity scene of *Death of a Salesman,* or the alleged rape for which a man is on trial in *To Kill a Mockingbird.*

Horatio Alger (1832–98) graduated from Harvard Divinity School in 1852 and became a social worker in New York in 1864. This work inspired his American Dream, Rags-to-Riches themes in over 130 dime novels meant to motivate young street boys (newsies and bootblacks) hoping to develop a successful future. *Ragged Dick* SERIES. (1867)

Julia Alvarez (27 May 1950) born in New York City and reared in the Dominican Republic. She attended Connecticut College and received her M.F.A. from Syracuse University and the Bread Loaf School of English. She is Professor of English at Middlebury College. Poem collections include: *Old Age Ain't for Sissies* and *The Other Side/El Otro Lado. In the Time of the Butterflies* (1995) and American Library Association Notable New Book, *How the García Girls Lost Their Accents* (1992).

Maya ANGELOU See entry in this encyclopedia.

Jane Austen (1775–1817) born in Hampshire, England, as the second daughter and seventh of eight children. At age twenty-five, her family moved to Bath. Jane tutored and published some of her work anonymously since publication of women's writing was rare during her lifetime. Her main theme was love and marriage. Through plot and strong characterization, Austen's novels provide a thorough picture of society (social norms and social class) in the eighteenth-century English countryside. Austen's work is celebrated for her wit, irony, and outstanding detailed storytelling: *Pride and Prejudice* (1797), *Sense and Sensibility* (1811), *Emma* (1815).

Charlotte Brontë (1816–55), born in northern England countryside with two sisters and a brother. She was the daughter of an Anglican clergyman and attended a school for clergymen's daughters. The Brontë family is one of the most famous in English literature since two sisters, Charlotte and Emily, simultaneously wrote two of the most well-loved and read novels of the nineteenth century. Married in 1854 and died during pregnancy in 1855. *Jane Eyre* (1847), *Shirley* (1848), *The Professor* (published posthumously in 1857).

Emily Brontë (1818–48), born into a family that engaged in writing as a pastime and source of joy and amusement. Her most famous work, *Wuthering Heights,* portrays an intense love story in the English countryside. Both Emily and her famous sister Charlotte wrote significant English novels and published them about the same time. Emily's career was short-lived due to an untimely death of tuberculosis at the age of thirty.

Olive Ann Burns (17 July 1924–4 July 1990) Reared in Macon, Georgia, B. graduated from college (1946) and worked for the *Atlanta Journal* as a reporter. B. married a fellow journalist and wrote an advice column as Amy Larkin from 1960 to 1967. With responsibilities for an ailing mother, B. began gathering stories for a novel based on her family. This developed into *Cold Sassy Tree* (1984). The novel became an overnight classic. It colorfully details the life of a town on the brink of the leap into the 20th century with new inventions, styles, and, especially, changing social mores. An incomplete sequel, *Leaving Cold Sassy,* was published posthumously. *Cold Sassy Tree* has been developed into a TV movie and an opera.

Joseph Campbell (1904–87) Born in New York, Joseph Campbell became fascinated with Native American totems and rituals as a young boy, which led to a lifetime of study of world cultures, symbols, archetypes, rituals, and MYTHS. He received his B.A. and M.A. from Columbia University, then studied at the University of Paris and the University of Munich. He traveled throughout the world and across the United States before settling into an academic life at Sarah Lawrence, which enabled him "to follow his bliss," one of the key messages in all of his lectures. He studied "primal" people's created understanding of nature and beliefs, and developed lectures for all types of audiences. He received a National Institute of Arts and Letters Award for Contributions to Creative Literature for *The Hero with a Thousand Faces* (1949). In 1985, he was awarded the National Arts Club Gold Medal of Honor in Literature. In the 1980s, after writing many articles and books about world cultures, Joseph Campbell consulted with George Lucas on the *Star Wars* story ideas and subsequently developed a brilliant and inspiring series of interviews with Bill Moyers entitled "Joseph Campbell and the Power of Myth," which was broadcast posthumously in 1988. Campbell's books, articles, and interviews provide a rich resource for any literature or writing program.

There also is *The Portable Jung* (1972), *Myths to Live By* (1972), *The Inner Reaches of Outer Space: Metaphor as Myth and as Religion* (1986).

Albert Camus (1913–60) born in Algeria. His father was killed in World War I. In 1923, Camus was awarded a scholarship to the Lycee in Algiers (1924–32). From 1935 to 1939, he took on a variety of jobs for the Communist Party. He developed tuberculosis, from which he suffered throughout his later adult life. Nevertheless, during World War II he was a member of the French Resistance. He divorced his first wife, remarried, continued his writing career, and eventually died in a car accident in 1960. His novels are often read in conjunction with a study of existential philosophy. Camus was awarded the Nobel Prize for Literature in 1957. *L'Etranger—the Stranger* (1942) *La Peste—The Plague* (1947).

Lewis Carroll (1832–1898) Born Charles Lutwidge Dodgson, C. was the third of eleven children. He was a natural mathematician who enjoyed puzzles and wordplay. At the age of eighteen, he arrived at Oxford as a student and never left. He wrote two whimsical and symbolic texts frequently favored by creative-writing students. *Alice's Adventures in Wonderland* (1865) and *Through the Looking Glass* (1872) are colorful stories with shifts in perception, power, size, shape, and form—all of which can be delightful to young readers and challenging to older students who like to peer "through the looking glass" and beyond. Some favorite characters created by C. in these texts are: the Mad Hatter, the Queen of Hearts, Humpty Dumpty, and Twiddle Dee and Twiddle Dum. The nonsense language Jabberwock is another gift from Lewis Carroll's imagination.

Geoffrey Chaucer, born in London, the son of a wine merchant. He could read Latin, Italian, and French. Between 1378 and 1400, C. wrote *The Canterbury Tales*—a classic collection about citizens and religious people traveling with a spiritual purpose. The tales are cynical, humorous, satirical, and complex in their rich range of characterizations and story-telling techniques. Dante's example led C. to write in English. All of his surviving work dates from the 15th century. *The Canterbury Tales* (1378).

Joseph Conrad (1857–1924), named Josef Teodor Konrad Korzeniowski. C. was the son of an aristocrat

and translator—a Polish–born English novelist and short-story writer. Due to politics, as a child he was exiled to Volgada in northern Russia in 1861. During the mid-1870s, C. joined the French Merchant Marine and, later, the British Merchant Navy. This work gave him the opportunity to travel to the West Indies and Africa, which became a reference source for *Heart of Darkness* set in Africa near the Congo River, *Lord Jim* (1900) *Heart of Darkness* (1902).

Pat Conroy (1945) was the first of seven children born to a military officer and mother in Atlanta, Georgia. The family moved often, and C.'s books parallel his family history and career. Most noted for his gifts as a writer of distinguished prose and narrative, his themes deal with education, racism, child and spouse abuse, family conflict, harsh discipline in families and institutions, and love. He spends his life between San Francisco and South Carolina. Major works include *Prince of Tides* (1986), *Water Is Wide* (1972), *The Great Santini* (1976), *Lords of Discipline* (1980), *Beach Music* (1994).

Charles Dickens (1812–70) Born to a clerk who was imprisoned twice for debt, D.'s experiences as a result of his family's challenges influenced his themes, compassion, and compelling characters. Set in cities with poor living conditions for workers, D.'s novels often depict the contrast between the luxury of the wealthy class and harsh life of the lower classes. His plots reveal the elements in society that contribute to this inequity. As famous as a contemporary rock star in his time, D. wrote novels published in serial form for his fans to enjoy. His sensitivity to the working poor began when he was twelve years old and experienced three years of employment at a boot-blacking factory while his father was in jail for debt. Many of his novels were written in weekly serial form and appealed to all levels of society. D. toured Europe with other literary colleagues throughout his career. In 1842, he traveled to America and made a firm plea to the U.S. to join the newly forming International Copyright Law initiative to prevent literacy piracy. The concept was not well received although his illegally published texts were widely read in the U.S. He also spoke out against slavery when he visited the U.S. Titles often selected by high-school readers include: *Great Expectations* (1860–61), *A Tale of Two Cities* (1859), *Hard Times* (1854), *Oliver Twist*

(1837–39), *A Christmas Carol* (1843), and *David Copperfield* (1850).

Frederick Douglass (1818–95), born as a slave, D. escaped slavery yet risked his freedom to become an antislavery lecturer, publisher, and writer. D. published his inspiring, highly articulate, and graphic AUTOBIOGRAPHY documenting his experiences as a slave in 1845. This unusual event revealed his talent and intelligence, and inspired audiences to listen. He met with presidents Abraham Lincoln and Andrew Johnson. He later became President of the Freedman's Savings and Trust Company (1874), U.S. Marshall (1877), Recorder of Deeds (1880), and U.S. Consul General to Haiti (1889). *Autobiography of Frederick Douglass* (1845).

F. Scott Fitzgerald (1896–1940) was reared in St. Paul, Minnesota. He graduated from Princeton University and served in the U.S. Army in World War I. He fell in love with and later married Zelda Sayre, daughter of an Alabama Supreme Court judge who had a strong influence on him and his writing. In 1920, with the publication of his first novel, *This Side of Paradise,* F. became an overnight success at the age of twenty-four. Due to his popularity, lifestyle, and timely writing, F. became a successful short-story writer for weekly MAGAZINES. He had a strong influence on young people, the flappers of that time. The F.s were a beautiful, stylish, couple usually identified with The Jazz Age. F. traveled to Europe, met Hemingway and other artists of the time period, and eventually went to Hollywood. *This Side of Paradise* (1920), *The Great Gatsby,* (1925), *Tender Is the Night* (1934).

Ernest J. Gaines (1933) was born in Louisiana and reared by an aunt. G. was first recognized for his novel *The Autobiography of Miss Jane Pittman* (1971). He studied creative writing at Stanford University and received many honorary doctorates from U.S. universities. Gaines shared his professional time between California and Louisiana. He was nominated for a Pulitzer Prize in 1994 when he did receive the Fiction Award by the National Book Critics Circle, the Southern Writers Conference, and the Louisiana Library Association. *A Gathering of Old Men* (1983), *A Lesson Before Dying* (1993).

Robert Frost (1874–1963) born north of Boston, Massachusetts, F. attended Dartmouth and Harvard College but left without a degree. He became a teacher and newspaper reporter, then left for England to pursue his writing career. In 1915, he returned to New York City as a published poet with his first volume complete. He was a four-time winner of the Pulitzer Prize and the poet invited to read at JFK's inauguration. Frost's best known poems include: "The Road Not Taken," "Mending Wall," "Stopping by the Woods on a Snowy Evening," "Birches," and "The Death of the Hired Man."

William Golding (1911–93) (Sir William Gerald Golding) was born in the village of St. Columb Minor in Cornwall. He had a schoolmaster father with strong political convictions and beliefs in science. In 1939, he became an English teacher. When his most famous writing was published with popular acclaim, G. retired from teaching. He was awarded the Nobel Prize for Literature in 1983 despite the fact that *Lord of the Flies* (1954) had been rejected over twenty times before its publication.

Edith Hamilton (1867–1963) Born in Germany of American parents, H. began to learn Latin, Greek, French, and German as a child. She graduated from Bryn Mawr with a Masters degree in 1894. In 1896, she became headmistress of Bryn Mawr. Because of her life's work of researching and writing about the classics, Hamilton was made an Honorary Citizen of Athens in 1957, at the age of ninety. She was also elected to the American Academy of Arts and Letters. Most popular resource texts: *The Greek Way* (1930), *The Roman Way* (1932), *The Prophets of Israel* (1936), *Mythology* (1942).

Lorraine Hansberry (1930–65) was the first female AFRICAN AMERICAN to have a drama produced on Broadway. Born in Chicago, she was the daughter of a Howard University professor. *A Raisin in the Sun,* whose title derives from a poem by Langston Hughes, is loosely based on her autobiographical experience of racism when her family purchased a home in a predominantly white neighborhood. She died prematurely of cancer. *A Raisin in the Sun* (1959), New York Drama Critics Award, "Best Play of the Year." *To Be Young Gifted and Black* (1969), a play produced posthumously, was adapted from her writings.

Nathaniel Hawthorne (1804–1864) was born in Salem, Massachusetts, and became an outstanding American novelist and short-story writer. His father, a sea captain, died when H. was four years old. At age fourteen, he and his mother moved to a lonely farm in Maine. He attended Bowdoin College (1821–25) and soon returned to the farm to devote himself to his writing. His first novel, *Fanshawe,* was published anonymously in 1829 and did not receive good notices. H. collected his short stories in *Twice Told Tales* (1837) and again (1842). In 1842 he married Sophia Peabody, and they settled in Concord. H. wrote *Mosses from an Old Manse* (1846) and served as surveyor of the port to maintain a livelihood. *The Scarlet Letter* (1850) delves deeply into the human heart and presents moral conflict through the themes of love, sacrifice, compassion, and rigid Puritanical society. *The House of the Seven Gables* (1851) is set in New England, and also deals with problems of Puritanism. H. wrote *A Wonder Book* (1852) based on Greek mythology and *Tanglewood Tales* (1853) while he lived at Tanglewood near Lenox, Massachusetts. Other books include *The Blithedale Romance,* (1852), *The Marble Faun* (1860), and *Our Old Home* (1863). His numerous short stories are widely read.

David Haynes (1955) born in St. Louis, Missouri, a former sixth-grade teacher, H. has written numerous children's books in addition to his six novels, which have earned recognition by the American Library Association. He is the Director of Creative Writing at Methodist University in Dallas, Texas. *Right by My Side* (1993) *Somebody Else's Mama* (1995), *Live at Five* (1996), *Heathens* (1997), *All American Dream Dolls* (1997), *Retold African American Folktales* (1997), *Welcome to Your Life: Writings for the Heart of Young America* (ed. Haynes and Julie Landsman, 1998), *The Peon Book* (2004), and *The Full Matilda* (2004).

Ernest Hemingway (1898–1961) born in Oak Park, Illinois. His father taught him a love of the outdoors, but tragically committed suicide in 1928. H. began his writing career as a reporter for the *Kansas City Star* and also worked for the *Toronto Star.* He joined a volunteer ambulance corps in Italy after World War I and suffered a severe leg injury. He then lived in Spain, Paris and Cuba. He also had a home in Key West, Florida. During World War II, he served as a war correspondent. Although he is acclaimed for his novels, H. also wrote many short stories. His original character, Nick Adams, is the protagonist in a series of short stories. Known for his clear, simple-yet-significant language, H. received the Nobel Prize for Literature in 1954. His life came to a tragic end when he committed suicide in 1961. The novels include *The Sun Also Rises* (1926), *A Farewell to Arms* (1926), and *For Whom the Bell Tolls* (1940).

Herman Hesse (1877–1962) novelist and poet, left Germany to go to Switzerland at the outbreak of World War I and eventually became a Swiss citizen (1923). His pacifist beliefs caused him to be spiritually lonely and disengaged with the modern world as reflected in the themes of his novels. His books include *Peter Camenzind* (1904, tr. 1961), *Unterm Rad* (1905, tr. *The Prodigy* 1957), *Rosshalde* (1914), and *Demian* (1919, tr. 1923). One of his most famous novels, *Steppenwolf,* (1927, tr. 1929) deals with the dual nature of man. H. continues that theme in *Narziss and Goldmund* (1930, tr. *Death and the Lover,* 1932). His book frequently taught as part of the canon is *Siddhartha* (1922). Also widely read is *Das Glasperlenspiel,* (1943, tr. 1969 as *The Glass Bead Game*). H. received the Nobel Prize in 1946.

Homer (n.d., n.p.—some say Chios or Smyrna) Modern scholars generally agree that there was a poet named Homer who lived before 700 B.C.E. probably in Asia Minor; they also believe that the poet's work developed out of older legendary matter. *The Iliad* and *The Odyssey,* two epic poems attributed to H., form the heart of Greek literature. The two poems constitute the prototype of all epic poetry. Scholars generally believe that each is the work of one person. Some assign the author of *The Odyssey* to a poet who lived slightly after the author of *The Iliad. The Iliad* tells of the wrath of Achilles and subsequent tragic consequences in the Trojan War. *The Odyssey* begins nearly ten years after the fall of Troy when Odysseus begins his eventful and lengthy journey home.

Langston Hughes (1 February 1902–22 May 1967) born in Joplin, Missouri, to an abolitionist family, Hughes began his studies at Columbia University as an engineering student. He left to pursue his writing career. In 1923, he traveled to Africa and Europe and returned to New York City to become a significant figure of the Harlem Renaissance. He wanted to develop the body of African American literature by editing seven anthologies. His work includes editorials, documentaries, newspaper and magazine articles, scripts for radio, television, and opera. In 1950, H. developed a series of books featuring a kind, simple, witty, and natural character, Jesse B. Simple, who focused on the everyday issues faced by black Americans. *Not without Laughter* (1930), *"The Negro Mother" and Other Dramatic Recitations* (1931), *Selected Poems* (1959), *The Best of Simple* (1961), *Poems from Black Africa* (1963), *New Negro Poets* (1964), and *The Best Short Stories by Negro Writers* (1967) are many of his works.

Zora Neale Hurston (1891–1960) was born in Alabama as the fifth of eight children. The family moved to Florida where H.'s father had two leadership roles, as minister and mayor. Hurston's mother died when she was thirteen. A few years later, Hurston left home having heard lots of stories at the town general store. She traveled with a theater group, returned home to complete high school (while in her twenties), then attended Howard Academy and Howard University. Hurston was also one of the so-called new voices of the Harlem Renaissance. Works include *Their Eyes Were Watching God* (1937) and *The Complete Stories* (1995).

Aldous Huxley (1894–1963) lost his mother to cancer at the age of fourteen. At sixteen, while studying at Eton, illness affected his eyesight. H.'s interest in science became manifest in his SCIENCE FICTION writing. Huxley studied at Oxford and wrote over forty books throughout his life. He is best known for *Brave New World* (1931), which long preceded the rise of Hitler and Stalin. In 1938, he went to Hollywood to become a screenwriter. He later wrote *After Many a Summer Dies the Swan,* a literary comment on California life. In the 1950s, H. experimented with mescaline and LSD in supervised environments. *Doors of Perception* (1954), *Island* (1962), *Brave New World Revisited*—a book of essays examining abusive government techniques, written in 1958—all emerged. In contrast to his most famous novel, Huxley remained optimistic about the future of society.

John Knowles (1926–2001) attended Phillips Exeter Academy, which changed his life since it inspired his most well-known writing. Because K. was in school between the two World Wars, he had intense feelings about education and school traditions. Friendship, athletics, and loyalty were highly valued and became important themes in his writing. After high school, he entered the U.S. Army–Air Force Cadet Program from which he graduated, at Yale, in 1949. Knowles became a magazine writer, lecturer, and writer-in-residence at Princeton University and the University of North Carolina. His most popular book is *A Separate Peace* (1959).

Jerome Lawrence (1915) and *Robert E. Lee* (1918–94) were both born in Ohio and collaborated on many plays after they co-founded the Armed Forces Radio as part of their World War II experience (1943–44). In 1990, these talented dramatists were named Fellows of the American Theater at the Kennedy Center in Washington, D.C. Their most famous play was based on the Scopes Trial ("The Monkey Trials"). It is well-loved and relevant to high school students of many generations. The main plot, the challenge of teaching the theory of evolution in U.S. public schools, continues to be discussed in communities throughout the U.S. *Inherit the Wind* (1955): Donaldson Award, Outer Critics Circle Award, *Variety*—New York's Drama Critics Poll Award, Critics Award for Best Foreign Play, nominated for numerous Tony Awards. *Auntie Mame* (1956), *The Gang's All Here* (1959), *A Call on Kuprin* (1961), *Dear World* (1969), *The Night Thoreau Spent in Jail* (1971), *Jabberwock* (1972).

Harper Lee (26 April 1926) was born in Alabama, attended Huntingdon College, and the University of Alabama Law School. With one year at Oxford, she began work as an airline reservation clerk in New York City during the 1950s. Rejected by the J. B. Lippincott Company as a series of vignettes in need of revision, *To Kill a Mockingbird* was revised and published as a novel in 1960. It is safe to say that no U.S. high-school English curriculum would be complete without this favorite novel of significance.

Carson McCullers (1917–1967), was born in Columbus, Georgia, and studied at Columbia University. The prevailing theme in her work is the spiritual isolation that underlies the human condition. Her characters are outcasts or misfits who long for love that is never fulfilled in *The Heart Is a Lonely Hunter* (1940), her first novel, and frequently in others. *The Member of the Wedding* (1946), her best-known work, describes the life of a tender, lonely adolescent girl who searches for love and acceptance. M.'s other books include *Reflections in a Golden Eye* (1941), *The Ballad of the Sad Cafe* (1951), and *The Square Root of Wonderful* (1958). While M. was in her twenties, she suffered a series of strokes that left her partially paralyzed; during her last years she was confined to a wheelchair. A collection of her stories published posthumously, *The Mortgaged Heart* appeared in 1972. Her short story "Sucker" is an outstanding choice for its theme of male adolescent development and self awareness.

Arthur Miller (1915–2005) was the son of a ladieswear manufacturer who worked in a warehouse to earn money for his education at the University of Michigan. Influenced by Ibsen, he focused on social issues, distortions of the American Dream and success, and social injustice. One of his major goals and themes in his writing is the common man as tragic hero. Miller enjoyed the success of his works during his lifetime and was awarded three Tony Awards, the Pulitzer, the New York Drama Critics Circle Award, and many others. *Death of a Salesman* is often assumed to be somewhat autobiographical given his father's occupation. *The Crucible,* a play about injustice in the Puritan society, was written to focus attention on the similarities between the Army–McCarthy hearings in the U.S. Senate. M.'s relevant themes attract audiences of all ages, and his plays are often performed in local and Broadway productions. Most popular among high-school students: *Death of a Salesman* (1949), *The Crucible* (1953), and *All My Sons* (1947).

Toni Morrison, born Chloe Anthony Woffard (1931) to sharecroppers who moved the family to the midwest to provide a better future. She attended Howard University and Cornell University. In 1987, Morrison was named Goheen Professor of the Humanities at Princeton University. Morrison won the Pulitzer Prize for Literature (1988) and the Nobel Prize for Literature in 1993. M. is the first African American to win this award. Also popular are *The Bluest Eye* (1970), *Song of Solomon* (1977, winner of National Book Critics Circle Award), *Tar Baby* (1981), and *Beloved* (1987).

Tim O'Brien (1 October 1946), born in Minnesota, was against the Vietnam War but served when he was called (1969–70). Upon his return, O'Brien attended Harvard University then left to pursue a career as a newspaper reporter. He won the National Book Award for Fiction for *Going after Cacciato* (1978), and was a finalist for the Pulitzer Prize and National Book Critics Circle Award for *The Things They Carried* (1990). College students and readers of all ages turn to O'Brien and his novels for ways to discuss personal questions and confusion about war and the impact of war on individuals. Published books: *If I Die in a Combat Zone, Box Me Up and Send Me Home* (1973), *Nuclear Age* (1985), and *In the Lake of the Woods* (1994, National Book Award, *Time* Magazine Best Novel of the Year, James Fenimore Cooper Prize).

O. Henry, born William Sydney Porter (1862–1910) was reared by his grandmother and aunt after his mother died when he was three-years old. At the age of fifteen, he went to Texas to work and eventually married. He was accused of taking money from a bank where he had been employed and left for South America. In 1897, his wife became ill, and O. returned from Mexico only to find himself in the Ohio Penitentiary in 1898. He wrote in prison to make money to support his family. From 1903 to 1906, he wrote a weekly story for *New York World.* O., who is best known as a prolific New York City short-story writer with clever plots filled with irony, coincidence, and a twist in the tale is said to have taken his pen name from the uniform of a prison guard. O.'s stories are collected in many volumes and are part of innumerable short-story anthologies. Favorite stories include: "A Christmas Carol," "The Ransom of Red Chief," "The Furnished Room," "Springtime a la Carte," "After Twenty Years," "A Retrieved Reformation," and "The Last Leaf."

George Orwell, pseud. Eric Blair (1903–50) reared in India and Great Britain, won a scholarship to Eton. In 1922, he joined the Indian Imperial Police Force and resigned to develop his writing career five years later. The experience as a law enforcer influenced his major themes of social structure in our society. His work is often paired with Aldous Huxley's *Brave New World* although Orwell had more insight into the impact true totalitarian states could effect given the time in which he was writing. In 1938, he became ill with tuberculosis yet managed to write two of the most brilliant novels of political commentary of the century. Educators often pair events in the development of the Soviet Union with events in the brief-yet-brilliant allegory *Animal Farm* (1943) when presenting this work of significance to students. Also studied is *Nineteen Eighty-Four* (1946).

Edgar Allan Poe (1809–1849) was born in Boston. A U.S. poet and short-story writer recognized as one of the most talented writers in world literature. P.'s writing conveys a passionate intensity that becomes mysterious and dreamlike. P. is recognized as the father of the modern detective novel. Both of P.'s parents died before he was three-years old, and he was taken into the home of his godfather, John Allan, a wealthy Richmond merchant. The Allans took P. to school in Scotland and England. When he returned to the United States, he enrolled in the University of Virginia. Life was not easy, however; his foster mother died, John Allans remarried, and P. was faced with a dishonorable discharge from West Point. His first book, *Tamerlane and Other Poems* (1827) was followed by two more volumes (1829 and 1831) but none were praised as outstanding literature during his lifetime. Stories like "The Telltale Heart" and poems like "Annabel Lee" are widely assigned.

J. D. SALINGER (1919) born in New York City, went to military school and Columbia University. He served in the U.S. Army in World War II. Salinger prefers to live the life of a recluse. He wrote over thirty short stories and is best known for his novel of an American teenager who sees the hypocrisy of the adult world and recognizes the clarity and goodness of childhood. Works include *A Perfect Day for Bananfish* (1948), *Uncle Wiggly in Connecticut* (1948), *The Catcher in the Rye* (1951), *Nine Stories* (1953), *Franny and Zooey* (1961), *Raise High the Roof Beam, Carpenters* (1963). See also S.'s entry in this encyclopedia.

William Shakespeare (1564–1616) Tradition has it that S. was born and died on the same date in Stratford-on-Avon. He is recognized as the greatest writer

of all time. Little is known of his childhood although scholars have inferred that he attended school, where he would have studied Latin grammar, Roman comedy, ancient history, and classical mythology. S. married Anne Hathaway in 1582. Their first born, Susanna, arrived in 1583, and twins, Hamnet and Judith, were born in 1585. Little is similarly known about S. until he achieved fame as a playwright in London. There, he joined Lord Chamberlain's Men, later called the King's Men. S. played the roles of older men, such as Old Adam in *As You Like It* and the ghost in *Hamlet*. In 1597, he bought the ten-room mansion New Place in Stratford, which he saved for his retirement. In 1599, he became a partner in ownership of the Globe Theater built on the banks of the Thames River. The Globe was burned in 1613 due to an accident during a performance of S.'s own *Henry V*. It was rebuilt but subsequently closed down and destroyed by the Puritans in 1642. In 1989, as a gesture of international friendship, an American, Samuel Wanamaker, helped build a replica that stands today on the same site. Shakespeare's most popular plays read by high-school students include *Romeo and Juliet, Macbeth, Hamlet, A Midsummer Night's Dream, Julius Caesar, Othello, As You Like It, Richard III, The Taming of the Shrew, The Merchant of Venice,* and *Two Gentlemen of Verona.*

Mary Wollstonecraft Shelley (1797–1851) born in London to professional parents, S. lost her mother ten days after her birth. Her father's literary circle included Percy Bysshe S. At the age of sixteen, she ran away to Switzerland and France with S., and they married in 1816. *Frankenstein* (1818) was conceived as a ghost story for friends and subsequently developed into a novel with their encouragement. Upon the death of her son in 1819, just one year after the death of her daughter, S. had a nervous breakdown. In 1822, Percy Bysshe S. drowned in a storm near Cinque Terre, Italy. Their one surviving child, Percy Florence Shelley, survived into adulthood. S. was able to support herself and her son with profits from *Frankenstein* and continued her career devoted to social issues and education.

Sophocles (ca. 496–405 B.C.E.) was born near Athens as the son of a wealthy merchant. He studied all of the arts and became a great playwright of the Golden Age. At twenty-eight, he competed at the

Theater of Dionysus and took first prize. He wrote 120 plays and took 18 first prizes. He is credited with making each tragedy a complete play instead of a series of plays. Only seven of his plays survive, most popular are *Oedipus the King, Electra,* and *Antigone.*

John Steinbeck (1902–68) born in Salinas, California, to a family of modest means. His father was county treasurer, and his mother was a teacher. An avid reader, S. always hoped to be a writer. He worked his way through Stanford University but never finished. After work as a reporter in New York City, he returned to California and took on many manual labor jobs. These jobs provided a background for his fiction. His many novels focus on themes of social issues and life closely involved with nature and the soil. He was a champion of the underdog, especially those who did manual labor and suffered as outsiders with economic challenges. In 1962, he received the Nobel Prize for Literature. His works include *Tortilla Flat* (1935), *Of Mice and Men* (1937), *The Red Pony* (1937), *The Grapes of Wrath* (1939), *The Pearl* (1947) *East of Eden*, (1952), *Winter of Our Discontent* (1961), and *Travels with Charley* (1962).

Harriet Beecher Stowe (1811–96), born in Litchfield, Connecticut, to an intellectual family with many opportunities to sit in on conversations with her father's colleagues. She attended a seminary and became an assistant teacher. In 1936, S. married a professor, took care of a large family, remained active in the intellectual community of the U.S., and continued her writing. *Uncle Tom's Cabin* (1851, 1852) was first published in the antislavery newspaper the *National ERA*. It was an instant bestseller and classic, cited by Abraham Lincoln as the work behind the Civil War. She continued her writing career, focusing on social life in America.

Amy Tan (19 February 1952) born in Oakland, California, the daughter of Chinese immigrants. After both her father and brother died of brain tumors, Amy's family moved to Switzerland where she continued her education. She graduated from San Jose State University in English and Linguistics and worked as a business writer. In 1987, she visited China with her mother and developed ideas for a novel based on her mother's life forty years before in China. Popular are: *The Joy Luck Club* (1989), *The*

Hundred Secret Senses (1998), and *The Bonesetter's Daughter* (2001). Two children's books include *The Moon Lady* and *The Chinese Siamese Cats.*

Henry David Thoreau (1817–62) born in Concord, Massachusetts, and studied at Concord Academy and Harvard University. T. is an essayist, poet, and philosopher famous for his thoughts on what it means to live a natural life and be an independent thinking, yet responsible, American. He wrote "Civil Disobedience" as an essay on the right to follow one's conscience. Walden was designed as an experiment in living well in nature. T. opened a school in 1838. Widely read are *Walden* (1854), *Letters* (1865), and posthumously edited by Ralph Waldo Emerson, *Poems of Nature* published in 1895.

Mark Twain (Samuel Clemens) (1835–1910) born in Missouri and developed a career as one of America's most famous writers of the nineteenth century. He published over thirty works of satire, historical fiction, short stories, and social commentary. T. lived in Europe from 1890 to 1900, and lived in New York from 1901 to 1907. Important works include "The Celebrated Jumping Frog of Calaveras County" (1867), *The Adventures of Tom Sawyer* (1875), *The Prince and the Pauper* (1881), *Adventures of Huckleberry Finn* (1885), *A Connecticut Yankee in King Arthur's Court* (1889).

Alice Walker (1944) was born as the last of eight children. At the age of eight, she lost her sight in one eye. She began her college studies at Spellman College and received her B.A. in 1965 from Sarah Lawrence. W. established a reputation as an activist. She worked for civil rights, women's rights, against Apartheid, and on antinuclear projects among others. W. wrote numerous essays and articles, and in 1984 she established her own publishing company. She received the Rosenthal Award from the National Institute of Arts and Letters, the Lillian Smith Award from the National Endowment for the Arts, a Guggenheim Fellowship and a Radcliffe Institute Fellowship, and the Pulitzer Prize for *The Color Purple* (1983).

Walt Whitman (1819–92) born as one of nine children in New York City, and his family lived in Brooklyn and Long Island. In the 1820s and 1830s, W. worked as a printer providing him with access to a broad range of reading. He worked as a teacher, founded a newspaper, and eventually wrote for the *Brooklyn Eagle* and the *New Orleans Crescent.* During the Civil War, he went to Washington, D.C., and volunteered to help wounded soldiers. *Leaves of Grass,* first edition (1855), was revised throughout his life. *Leaves of Grass,* final edition, was published in 1891.

Elie Wiesel (30 September 1928) born in Rumania, survived Auschwitz, Buna, Buchenwald, and Gleiwitz. Wiesel spent his professional life devoted to education about the HOLOCAUST. He received the Nobel Peace Prize and the Congressional Gold Medal of Achievement. In 1978, he was appointed as Chair of the U.S. Presidential Commission on the Holocaust. He is the writer of poems, plays, and lectures, including the work *Night* (1958).

August Wilson (27 April 1945) set himself a task of writing a ten-play cycle for each decade of black history in the 20th century. He collaborated with the Yale School of Drama for the first production of *Ma Rainey,* winner of the New York Drama Critics Circle Award 1984–85. He is the best-known living African American playwright for *Fences* (1987, Pulitzer Prize winner), *Joe Turner's Come and Gone* (1988, Best New Play, New York Drama Critics Circle), and *The Piano Lesson* (1987, second Pulitzer Prize for Drama, Drama Desk Award).

Richard Wright (1908–60) born in Mississippi. When his parents separated, his mother and he lived with his grandmother. W. wrote and published stories while working in a menial job. His unique treatment of characters and point of view especially in regard to race relations made his writing influential and significant. In 1927, he went to Chicago and later in 1937 to New York City, where he became the Harlem editor of the *Daily Worker,* a communist party newspaper. In 1944, Wright ended his affiliation with the Communist Party. His novel *Native Son* is a compelling and shocking story of two families separated by race and social class. It is usually read in upper grades (11–12) with the support of a teacher to develop the rich and controversial discussions that will inevitably ensue. Also studied are *Uncle Tom's Children* (1938), *Native Son* (1940), and *Black Boy* (1945).

JOIE GAVIGAN HINDEN

CARBONE, Elisa Lynn
Author, b. 2 January 1954, Washington, D.C.

C.'s first book, *My Dad's Definitely Not a Drunk* (1992) (rereleased as *Corey's Story: Her Father's Secret* in 1997) was both controversial and well received. C. wanted to explain to children that alcoholism is a disease, and help them understand their relatives who were alcoholics. She later wrote REALISTIC FICTION for children and realistic and historical fiction for children and TEENS.

In *Stealing Freedom* (1998), a young slave girl from Maryland endures cruel conditions and escapes on the Underground Railroad to Canada while disguised as a boy. This story, based on the life of a real slave Ann Maria Weems, uses material from actual slave narratives. In *Storm Warriors* (2001), C. explores an unusual and little-known piece of history. This historical novel tells the story of a 19th-century AFRICAN AMERICAN boy who wants to join the all-black crew at the Pea Island life-saving station. This novel is also based on real events, and the story is filled with real characters and actual shipwrecks. *The Pack* (2003), a suspense story inspired by the Columbine school shootings, is given an unusual twist. A strange boy is befriended by several other students who wonder about the scars on his body and his odd behavior in class. He tells them that he is being studied by the National Institutes of Health, but refuses to say why. After swearing his friends to secrecy, the boy finally reveals the truth (that he was raised by wolves) in order to prevent a violent crime at his school.

AWARDS: 1998 ALA Best Book for Young Adults, *Stealing Freedom;* 2002 Virginia Library Association's Jefferson Cup Award, *Storm Warriors.*

FURTHER WORKS: *Last Dance on Halladay Street,* 2005.

BIBLIOGRAPHY: *Contemporary Authors,* online, 2003; *Something About the Author* Vol. 81, 1995.

ANDREA LIPINSKI

CARD, Orson Scott
Author, b. 24 August 1951, Richland, Washington

As a child, C. moved from state to state, living in Washington, California, and Arizona, before finally settling in Utah. C. enrolled at Brigham Young University at the age of sixteen, and after taking time off to serve a Mormon mission in Brazil, he graduated with honors in 1975. In the years that followed, C. worked as an editor and proofreader and in 1981 graduated with a Master's degree from the University of Utah. C. founded a theater troupe, operated a repertory company, and wrote many plays during this period, producing his first play, *The Apostate,* when he was just nineteen. This early training in drama (which he continues to write) allowed C. to experiment with different storytelling techniques and to sharpen his sense of dramatic presentation, skills he later put to use in numerous novels, novellas, and SHORT STORIES.

When it came to writing fiction, C. found that SCIENCE FICTION gave him the greatest freedom to tell the dramatic stories he wanted. His first short story, "The Tinker," was met with an encouraging rejection. C. followed it with a second submission to *Analog,* the short story "Ender's Game," which was published in 1977 and which earned C. the World Science Fiction Convention's John W. Campbell Award for best new writer. In 1978 C. released his first book, *Capitol,* and in 1980 he published *Songmaster* which, like *Capitol,* was well received by critics. C.'s next works—*Hot Sleep* (1979), *A Planet Called Treason* (1979), and *Unaccompanied Sonata and Other Stories* (1981)—did not fare quite as well; critics found them dark and gratuitously violent, though skillfully written. Shortly thereafter, however, C.'s best-known work, *Ender's Game* (1985) and its sequel *Speaker for the Dead* (1986) were released. C. became the first writer ever to win both the Hugo and the Nebula with consecutive novels in a SERIES.

The seven-book Ender series begins when Andrew "Ender" Wiggin is chosen to enter Battle School at the age of six. Trained to command his own army in the upcoming war with the Buggers, Ender is a tactical genius whose spirit and psyche are pushed to the limit by the demands of Battle School. *Speaker for the Dead* is set three thousand years after the first book, and tells the story of an adult Ender, still alive and trying to atone for his unwitting massacre of the Buggers. Ender's story continues in *Xenocide* (1991), with Ender working to save his adopted planet of Lusitania from a virus spread by the native "piggies."

Billed as the final volume in the Ender Quartet, *Children of the Mind* (1996) involves the continued attempt to save Lusitania, threatened, as a result of the colonists forbidden interaction with the piggies, with destruction by Starways Congress. Almost fif-

teen years after the original volume was published, however, C. returned to Ender's story, though from a different perspective. The remarkable *Ender's Shadow* (1999) retells the story of *Ender's Game* from the viewpoint of Bean, a not altogether minor character from that book. Shifting to Bean as the central protagonist, C. released *Shadow of the Hegemon* (2001), which recounts the events on Earth directly after Ender's original victory over the Buggers. *Shadow Puppets* (2002) continues the dramatic political maneuvering of Bean and the other Battle School graduates who are caught up as they decide whose vision of the future to support.

The Tales of Alvin Maker series is more FANTASY than science fiction, though it too concerns the growth and development of a young protagonist with astonishing capabilities. Set in an alternate early America inhabited by exiled witches, *Seventh Son* (1987) begins the story of Alvin Miller, a "Maker" whose magical powers stem from his birth as the seventh son of a seventh son. In this America, where the British Restoration never happened and where folk magic is the norm, Alvin is still unusual; his ability to bend reality makes him stand out, even in his magic-infused community. *Red Prophet* (1988) tells of Alvin's kidnapping in an attempt to stir up racial unrest. Readers learn about his relationship with Ta-Kumsaw, a Shawnee who resents the intrusion of the white people, and Ta-Kumsaw's brother Lolla-Wossiky, the Red Prophet, who preaches racial harmony. In *Prentice Alvin* (1989) Alvin is apprenticed to a blacksmith, though he finds his real work is in learning how to unlock the full power of his "making" ability. *Alvin Journeyman* (1995) continues the tale with a troubled Alvin adjusting to life after his apprenticeship. Forced to leave his home after being falsely accused of improprieties, Alvin returns to his birthplace, Hatrack River, to defend himself in court, and to battle the sinister Unmaker. Traveling further afield in *Heartfire* (1998), Alvin treks to New England with John James Audubon, attempting to put an end to the Puritan anti-witch laws. *The Crystal City* (2003) of Alvin's dreams is finally begun in the sixth book of the series, with Alvin continuing his quest to bring peace and equality to America and to avert the looming civil war foreseen by his increasingly powerful wife Peggy.

C.'s notable stand-alone works range from science fiction to fantasy to contemporary HORROR, in addition to numerous works of nonfiction, historical fiction, and PLAYS. Two works of special interest to young adults, however, are *Pastwatch: The Redemption of Christopher Columbus* (1996) and *Enchantment* (1999). *Pastwatch* tells the story of the future scientific group Pastwatch, whose members go back in time to 1592 to Christianize America and save the world. *Enchantment* is certainly a unique retelling of Sleeping Beauty, which blends Russian folklore with the traditional FAIRY TALE and is set in modern times.

Since his first short story, C. has written over sixty works of science fiction, fantasy, historical fiction, suspense, nonfiction, and religious fiction. His work in any genre is characterized by his close attention to moral complexities, offering readers no black-and-white choices, no actions without consequences. C. pays special attention to spiritual and moral concerns, integrating philosophical discussions and debate over controversial social and cultural issues into the narrative. He focuses on the role of the individual in society, and uses the moral development of children to explore the idea that people have the power to redeem both themselves and their society. C.'s ability to portray children as complex individuals has made him popular with both juveniles and adults, and his ability to infuse the most entertaining story with moral consequence is an indication of his tremendous talent.

AWARDS: John W. Campbell Award, best new writer or 1977 for "Ender's Game"; Hugo nominations 1978, 1979, and 1980 for short stories and 1986 for novelette *Hatrack River;* Nebula Award nominations 1979 and 1980 for short stories; Utah State Institute of Fine Arts prize 1980 for epic poem "Prentice Alvin and the No-Good Plow"; Nebula Award 1985 and Hugo Award 1986 for *Ender's Game;* Nebula Award 1986 and Hugo Award 1987 and Locus Award 1987 for *Speaker for the Dead;* World Fantasy Award 1987 for novelette *Hatrack River;* Hugo Award and Locus Award nomination 1988 for novella *Eye for Eye;* Locus Award for best fantasy and Hugo nomination and World Fantasy Award nomination 1988 for *Seventh Son;* Mythopoeic Fantasy Award 1988 for *Seventh Son;* Locus Award 1989 for *Red Prophet;* Hugo Award 1991 for *How to Write Science Fiction and Fantasy;* Alvin Journeyman Locus Award for best fantasy novel 1996; Israel's Geffen Award for Best Science Fiction Book 1999 for *Pastwatch: The Redemption of Christopher Columbus;* Grand Prix de L'Imaginaire 2000 for *Heartfire.* ALA's Best Books for Young Adults list: *Ender's Game* (1985 list) *Pastwatch* (1997 list) *Seventh Son* (1987 list) *Speaker for*

the Dead (1986 list) *Ender's Shadow* (2000 list) *Shadow of the Hegemon* (2002 list).

SELECT FURTHER WORKS: *Hart's Hope* (novel), 1983; *A Woman of Destiny* (novel) 1983, also published as *Saints,* 1988; *Wyrms* (novel), 1987; *Character and Viewpoint* (nonfiction) 1988; *The Folk of the Fringe* (novel), 1989; *How to Write Science Fiction and Fantasy* (nonfiction) 1990; *Maps in a Mirror: The Short Fiction of Orson Scott Card* (short stories), 1990; *The Worthing Saga* (omnibus volume incorporating *The Worthing Chronicle,* most of *Capitol,* and several previously unpublished or uncollected stories from the same future history), 1990; *Treason* (revised edition of *A Planet Called Treason* with new material), 1990; *The Memory of Earth* (novel), 1992; *The Call of Earth* (novel), 1992; *The Ships of Earth* (novel), 1994; *Earthfall* (novel), 1995; *Earthborn* (novel), 1995; *Stone Tables* (novel), 1997; *Magic Mirror* (PICTURE BOOK), 1999; *Sarah* (novel), 2000; *Rebekah* (novel), 2001; *First Meetings in the Enderverse* (novellas), 2003; *Robota* (illustrated novel with Doug Chiang), 2003.

BIBLIOGRAPHY: "Orson Scott Card." *Authors and Artists for Young Adults.* Vol. 11. Gale Research, 1993. Reproduced in *Biography Resource Center.* The Gale Group. 2003. http://www.galenet.com/serv let/BioRC; "Orson Scott Card." *Authors and Artists for Young Adults.* Vol. 42. Gale Research, 2002. Reproduced in *Biography Resource Center.* The Gale Group. 2003. http://www.galenet.com/servlet/BioRC; "Orson Scott Card." Contemporary Authors Online, Gale 2003. Reproduced in *Biography Resource Center.* The Gale Group. 2003. http://www.galenet.com/servlet/BioRC; "Orson Scott Card." *St. James Guide to Science Fiction Writers,* 4th ed. St. James Press, 1996. Reproduced in *Biography Resource Center.* The Gale Group. 2003. http://www.galenet.com/serv let/BioRC; "About Orson Scott Card." Author's website, Hatrack River. http://www.hatrack.com/osc/about.shtml; "Orson Scott Card: according to this science fiction writer, it is impossible to tell a story that does not involve moral choices." *Publishers Weekly.* 30 November 1990, Vol. 237 Issue 48, Pg. 54; "PW Talks with Orson Scott Card." *Publishers Weekly.* 20 November 2000. Vol. 247 Issue 47, 51.

JULIE BARTEL

CAREER NOVELS

Novels allowing, even encouraging, young adults to examine careers were hardly new in the 1940s. Edward Stratemeyer's Working Upward SERIES, published by W. L. Allison in 1897, had four novels about young people involved in specific careers—*The Young Auctioneer or, The Polishing of a Rolling Stone; Bound to Be an Electrician or, Franklin Bell's Success; Shorthand Tom, the Reporter or, The Exploits of a Bright Boy;* and *Fighting for His Own or, The Fortunes of a Young Artist.* All were plot-ridden with tidbits about careers tossed in as needed.

Francis Rolt-Wheeler's twenty-volume series of books about different boys in the services of the U.S. Government ran from 1909 to 1929. Unlike Stratemeyer's protagonists and their incidental comments about careers, Rolt-Wheeler's major characters were molded by their choice of careers. From the first of the series, *The Boy in the U.S. Survey* to the last, *The Boy with the U.S. Aviators,* all published by Lothrop, Lee, and Shepard, Rolt-Wheeler established the rules for the series—readers were given information about the specific service, its history and purpose, what qualifications were needed to be accepted into this branch of the government, and what kind of future was there for a young person entering this service, all this mixed with realistic accounts of the protagonist learning the ropes. Extensive illustrations, usually photographs, tied the plot to reality.

But the deluge of vocational books sugar-coated with fiction began in the 1930s and carried over to the next twenty years. As G. Robert Carlsen described these novels, the story follows the events of the first year as the major character enters and adjusts to a career: "All information about salary, the working conditions, and activities are documented. The intent was to give vocational information painlessly. But as in most stories written for ulterior purposes, characterization and plot patterns tended to be highly stereotyped." ["Forty-Years with Books and Teen-Age Readers," *Arizona English Bulletin* 18 (April 1976): 3].

The accuracy of career books varied from publisher to publisher. Dodd, Mead set the standard by announcing in *Publishers Weekly* for August 26, 1939, (p. 642) that the careers in its novels must have plenty of opportunities to offer, that the authors "should be professional people who have successfully and enthusiastically lived the careers which they are picturing," and that these authors "must be able to write interestingly." Other publishers were less discriminating.

Emma Bugbee's *Peggy Covers the News* (Dodd, Mead, 1936) set the tone of what was to follow. Bugbee was an experienced journalist who was hired in 1911 by the *New York Tribune* (later the *New York Herald Tribune*) and had her own byline three years later. She interviewed Eleanor Roosevelt, covered London for her paper, and was highly regarded by other journalists. Her five books about Peggy realistically convey the ambivalent excitement and boredom of getting and writing news.

Almost every career was covered. Helen Boyston's "Sue Barton" series was an exceptionally popular series on nursing from *Sue Barton, Student Nurse* (Little, Brown, 1936) to *Sue Barton, Staff Nurse* (Little, Brown, 1952). Helen Wells's "Vicki Barr, Flight Stewardess" series covered Vicki's flying mysteries in sixteen novels from *Silver Wings for Vicki* (Grosset and Dunlap, 1947) through *The Brass Idol Mystery* (Grosset and Dunlap, 1964). Diving was covered by Henry Gregor Felsen in *Navy Diver* (Dutton, 1942), years before *Hot Rod,* just as he took up engineering in *Jungle Highway* (Dutton, 1942). Stephen Meader wrote of farming in *Blueberry Mountain* (Harcourt, 1941) while Sarah L. Schmidt wrote about ranching in *Shadow over Winding Ranch* (Random House, 1940).

Kathryn A. Haebich compiled lists of books, fiction and nonfiction, aimed at YOUNG ADULTS in *Vocations in BIOGRAPHY and Fiction* (American Library Association, 1962). While the usual careers were there—nursing, journalism, teaching—the list contained surprises as well—architect, poet, caterer, fisherman, psychiatrist, horticulturist, hunter, miner, realtor, minister, and so on.

Whatever freshness the career novel once had, by the 1950s it had developed a formula and little more. Four or five characters were certain to appear: an attractive if sometimes shy heroine/hero just graduated and eager for a career; one or two friends of different temperaments; a villain or at the least a crotchety older person who puts temporary obstacles in the professional path of the protagonist; and an older and wiser person who helps the protagonist advance. Early in the book, the insecure hero/heroine suffers a mixture of minor setbacks—and a couple of major ones, but, undaunted, the protagonist wins the final struggle and a place in her/his profession. The book almost certainly passes rapidly and lightly over the job's daily grind, focusing instead on the high points, the excitement and events that make any job potentially, if rarely, dramatic.

KEN DONELSON

CARLSON, Lori Marie

Author, editor, translator, b. 21 June 1957, Jamestown, New York

"I try to be inspirational in my work," C. told an interviewer for the *Arizona Republic* (Leach, 2002). Although C. was speaking specifically about her ADULT novel, *The Sunday Tertulia,* this goal is motivation for each of the four anthologies for YOUNG ADULTS edited by her. C.'s primary contribution to YA literature is her work in the area of LATINO literature. Her anthologies celebrate the diversity of American life through the voices and eyes of Latino writers, artists, and poets.

C. began learning Spanish at age nine at Fletcher Elementary School. In her introduction to *Cool Salsa,* C. describes how she and a small group of friends met twice a week in the school library to learn "the basics of this roller-coaster, fast-beat language that would open up a world of wonder, travel, friendships" for her (*Cool Salsa,* 1994).

In the 1970s, when C. was growing up, there were few Latinos living in her hometown. The majority of the population in Jamestown was of Northern European ancestry and Protestant (*Barrio Streets, Carnival Dreams,* 1996). In her seventh grade Spanish class, C. became close friends with a girl who had moved to Jamestown from Puerto Rico. The friendship seems to have been the beginning of C.'s interest in understanding and bridging differences between cultural traditions. In several of her books, she mentions this friendship as the crucial turning point for her interest in Spanish.

C., who holds a B.A. in Spanish Literature and Linguistics from the College of Wooster, Ohio, and an M.A. in Hispanic Literature from Indiana University, Bloomington, speaks of her dreams as a young teenager in her introduction to *Barrio Streets, Carnival Dreams.* "I had Technicolor visions of a future in which a mature version of myself socialized with diplomats, artists, scholars, led a life of independence, all the while communicating in this magic tongue." Speaking Spanish was a means for her to see outside of her own cultural traditions and to experience the world.

In each of C.'s books, she hopes to understand other cultures through the words of the people of those cultures. Carlson's first young adult book, *Where Angels Glide at Dawn: New Stories from Latin America* (1990), contains ten stories by leading Latin American writers. Many of the stories are translated by C. or her co-editor Cynthia L. Ventura.

C.'s second book is the critically acclaimed *Cool Salsa: Bilingual Poems on Growing Up Latino in the United States.* In his introduction to *Cool Salsa,* the Pulitzer Prize-winning author Oscar Hijuelos writes that the book "opens doors to possibilities of thought and feeling in a way no book could do for me when I was growing up, because there were no books that addressed our world back then. Hearing one language on the streets, another at home, and a third at school, I had to make my own way—secretly yearning for a key to the future—which I did by writing my own words, my own rhythms, my own story" (*Cool Salsa,* 1994).

American Eyes: New ASIAN-AMERICAN Short Stories for Young Adults (1994) continues C.'s exploration and celebration of differences in American life. The ten stories, introduced by Cynthia Kadohata, 2005 Newbery Medal winner for *Kira-Kira,* focus on the tension that occurs when different cultural traditions meet. The stories are written by Asian Americans of Filipino, Chinese, Japanese, Korean, and Vietnamese descent.

C.'s most recent anthology is *Barrio Streets, Carnival Dreams: Three Generations of Latino Artistry.* This collection of poems, art, stories, essays, and memoirs is divided into three sections that roughly cover the experience of Latinos in 20th-century America. C. continues to explore the power of language in *Barrio Streets, Carnival Dreams.* She writes in her introduction that "more than any other ethnic group in this country, Latinos have drawn attention to the issue of whether or not one should keep one's language of origin, and they have fought to keep their values—familial, social, and religious—intact." Nowhere is C.'s theme better expressed than in the first poem of *Barrio Streets,* "Beautiful Spanish," by Magdalena Hijuelos. "I want to dedicate / a love song / to my beautiful Spanish Language / so natural / it flows/ as a breeze from the sea."

C. has taught in the Spanish Departments of Indiana University, Columbia University, and New York University. She is the former Director of Latin American Literature at the Americas Society. In addition to her four young adult anthologies, C. has written two adult novels, coedited an anthology of stories for adults, and edited and written three children's books.

AWARDS: *Cool Salsa: Bilingual Poems on Growing Up Latino in the United States:* Best Book for Young Adults, American Library Association; *Bulletin of the Center for Children's Books* Blue Ribbon Book; Notable Children's Trade Books, Social Education; *School Library Journal* Best Book of the Year. *American Eyes: New Asian-American SHORT STORIES for Young Adults:* Best Books for Young Adults, American Library Association; 2000 Popular Paperbacks for Young Adults: 25 Short Takes, American Library Association.

FURTHER WORKS: *You're On! Seven Plays in English and Spanish,* 1999.

BIBLIOGRAPHY: Curley, Suzanne, "Children's Bookshelf," *Los Angeles Times,* Jan. 29, 1995, p. 8; Estes, Sally, review of *Cool Salsa: Bilingual Poems on Growing Up Latino in the United States, Booklist,* Nov. 1, 1994, p. 488; Fader, Ellen, review of *Where Angels Glide at Dawn: New Stories from Latin America, Horn Book Magazine,* March–April 1991, p. 197; Leach, Anita Mabante, review of *The Sunday Tertulia, Arizona Republic,* June 11, 2000, p. J4; Lesesne, Teri S., Rosemary Chance, and Lois Buckman, review of *Cool Salsa: Bilingual Poems on Growing Up Latino in the United States, Journal of Adolescent & Adult Literacy,* Feb. 1995, p. 38; Martinez, Miriam and Marcia F. Nash, review of *Where Angels Glide at Dawn: New Stories from Latin America, Language Arts,* April 1991, p. 68; Roback, Diane and Richard Donahue, review of *Where Angels Glide at Dawn: New Stories from Latin America, Publishers Weekly,* Sept. 28, 1990, p. 103; Rochman, Hazel, review of *American Eyes: New Asian-American Short Stories for Young Adults, Booklist,* Jan. 1, 1995, p. 814; Sullivan, Edward T., review of *Cool Salsa: Bilingual Poems on Growing Up Latino in the United States, Book Links,* Nov. 1998, p. 15; Terrell, Nena, review of *Where Angels Glide at Dawn: New Stories from Latin America, Americas (English Edition),* July–August 1991, p. 61; "Lori Marie Carlson" *Contemporary Authors Online,* Gale, 2002.

R. PANDYA

CARSON, Rachel Louise

Author, editor, scientist, b. 27 May 1907, Springfield, Pennsylvania; d. 14 April 1964, Silver Spring, Maryland

Considered by *Time* MAGAZINE as one of the most influential people of the 20th century, C. opened the world's eyes to the hazards of chemical pesticides in the environment. C. had a fondness for the natural environment and realized how human beings are an integral part of that environment. Her love of nature was fostered by her mother; she made a career by combining that love with her other strong interest, writing.

C. earned her B.A. from Pennsylvania College for Women (now Chatham College) in 1929. She received an M.A. in zoology from Johns Hopkins University in 1932; she also studied at the Woods Hole Marine Biological Laboratory in Massachusetts. C. worked for the U.S. Bureau of Fisheries (now Fish and Wildlife Service) as an aquatic biologist and wrote radio scripts during the Depression. She eventually became editor-in-chief for all their publications from 1949–1952.

C. was able to retire from her position as editor-in-chief and commit her time fully to writing with the success of her book, *The Sea around Us* (1951). With this book, C. presented the complexity of the sea in an easy and flowing way understandable to the public. This book not only was number one on the nonfiction bestseller list in 1951 but also became an Academy Award–winning documentary by RKO in 1952.

C.'s best-known work, *Silent Spring* (1962), is also considered her most influential and most controversial. She brought the dangers of chemical pesticide use to the forefront and demanded people change the way they see the living environment around them. Although others had become aware of the problems with pesticide use, in *Silent Spring* C. painted a bleak picture of what the environment would become if we continued to use this destructive substance. She was able to bring to light not only the damaging effect on nature, but also on humans and their health. Many large chemical corporations launched verbal attacks and threats of litigation against C. saying she was unqualified to write such an account, even referring to her as crazy and hysterical. But through it all, her desire to protect the natural world that she held so dear gave her the strength to continue fighting for the environment and the way we treat that environment. C.'s strong and persistent voice helped launch changes, and also fostered new perspectives on the environment.

Silent Spring is still a part of the high-school CANON for reading; it has struck a spark with several generations of TEEN activists.

AWARDS: George Westinghouse Science Writing Award (1950), National Book Award (1951) for *The Sea Around Us,* Guggenheim fellowship (1951–52), John Burroughs Medal (1952), Henry G. Bryant Gold Medal (1952), Page-One Award (1952), National Council of Women in the U.S. book award (1956), American Library Association Best Young Adult Book (1962) for *Silent Spring,* Conservationist of the Year Award from National Wildlife Federation (1963), *Time*'s 100 Most Influential People of the Century.

FURTHER WORKS: *Under the Sea-Wind* (1941), *The Edge of the Sea* (1955), *The Sense of Wonder* (posthumous, 1965). *Lost Woods: The Discovered Writing of Rachel Carson,* ed. Linda Lear (1998).

BIBLIOGRAPHY: Lear, Linda. *Rachel Carson: Witness for Nature,* 1997. *Contemporary Authors New Revision Series,* vol. 35; *Something About the Author,* vol. 23; www.time.com/time/time100/; www.rachelcarson .org/

TINA HERTEL

CART, Michael

Author, critic, educator, b. 6 March 1941, Logansport, Indiana

C.'s contributions to all areas of YA LITERATURE are almost too numerous to list. He is acknowledged as an expert on, and an advocate for, the YA population, and has served on or presided over most committees dealing with the assessment of literature of YA.

C. and his twin sister Marcia were born in Logansport. From a very early age, he was a constant visitor to the public library and a compulsive collector of books, practices he continues to this day. As a young reader, C. was drawn to the FANTASY genre. He devoured the Raggedy Ann and Andy SERIES, Winnie the Pooh, and the Freddy the Pig books. The fascination with fantasy never left him. He was *particularly* enchanted with the Freddy the Pig stories and is currently at work on a biography of Walter R. Brooks, the author of *Freddy the Pig.*

Reading his articulate monthly column "Carte Blanche" in *Booklist,* it comes as little surprise that he received a B.S. in journalism from Northwestern University's Madill School of Journalism. He later earned an M.S. in Library Science from Columbia University and worked as a professional librarian from 1967 to 1991. C. served in the Army from 1964 until 1967 and was awarded the Army Commendation Medal.

C.'s interest in YA literature came later in his career. When he was between the ages that eventually have come to be known as *young adult,* there was no literature labeled "YA"; it had yet to emerge as a popular field of publication. C. was a book reviewer for *School Library Journal* and was aware that books targeted for the YA audience existed. He received an appointment to serve on the Young Adult Library Services Association (YALSA) Best Books for Young Adults committee in 1988, and had a "Road to Damascus experience a la St. Paul and became an instant convert . . . to young adult literature". He eventually became the president of YALSA, and instrumental in establishing the MICHAEL L. PRINTZ AWARD. This prize is given to a book that exemplifies literary excellence in YA literature. C. began to write books in this new developing field. He is the author of *My Father's Scar* (1996), a novel that became a Best Book for Young Adults in 1997, as well as the anthologies *Tomorrowland* (1999) and *Love and Sex: Ten Stories of Truth* (1999), also a Best Book and a Quick Pick for Reluctant Young Adult Readers, among many others. He is the recipient of the 2000 Grolier Foundation Award presented to a librarian for his "unusual contribution to the stimulation and guidance of reading by children and young people."

Actively involved in the American Library Association (ALA), C. has served on numerous book committees, including the Margaret A. Edwards Award, Best Books for Young Adults, the Alex Award, the Caldecott Medal, and the Printz Committee, Notable Children's Committee. He was also a judge for the National Book Award. C. has written prolifically for the professional literature about YA. He described the historical development in *From Romance to Realism: Fifty Years of Change in Young Adult Literature* (1996) and did an earlier in-depth study of Freddy the Pig's author in *What's So Funny? Wit and Humor in American Children's Literature* (1994). In addition, he writes regular columns in *Booklist* and numerous other places.

Not all of C.'s accomplishments deal with ALA. He is the co-producer and host of *In Print,* a nationally syndicated cable interview program. His most recent undertaking is a MAGAZINE called *Rush Hour,* published by Random House. Each issue contains original works of short fiction, POETRY, graphics, creative nonfiction, and personal essays all dealing with a single theme. The title of the magazine refers to the accelerated pace kept up by the young people of today.

C. moved to Chico, California, leaving the Los Angeles area following an earthquake. He packed 250 boxes of cherished books and moved them, as well as himself, to safer surroundings. He relocated again in 2003 to San Diego. This move forced him to downsize his massive book collection, which was now contained in 400 boxes. The collection is earmarked for California State University, Fresno, when C. has gone "to that Carnegie Library in the sky."

C.'s love for books is clearly evident in a story he tells about a friend who found a $100 bill in a book. He bemoaned the fact he had never found anything left inside a book before realizing that what he gained from a book was much more valuable: "enlightenment, entertainment, escape, and the enjoyment of art."

AWARDS: 1997 Best Book for Young Adults, *My Father's Scar; Love and Sex: Ten Stories of Truth:* 2000 Best Book for Young Adults and a Quick Pick for Reluctant Young Adult Readers; 2000 Grolier Foundation Award.

FURTHER WORKS: *Presenting Robert Lipsyte,* 1995; *In the Stacks: Stories about Libraries and Librarians,* 2002; *911: The Book of Help,* 2002; *The Art of Freddy,* 2002; *The Best American Nonrequired Reading,* 2002; *Necessary Noises: Stories about Our Families as They Really Are,* 2003; *The Heart Has Its Reasons: Homosexuality in Young Adult Literature,* 2003.

BIBLIOGRAPHY: Bean, Joy, "A Fresh Look at YA Literature," *Publishers Weekly,* July 2003, p.1; C., Michael, "From Insider to Outsider: The Evolution of YA Literature," *Voices from the Middle.* December 2001. pp. 95–98; C., Michael, *From Romance to Realism; Fifty Years of Growth and Change in Young Adult Literature,* 1996; C., Michael, *My Father's Scar,* 1996; Fitch, Katherine, interview with Michael C., March 11, 2003; E-mail interview http:www.houghtonmifflinbooks.com.

KATHIE FITCH

CARTER, Alden R.
Author, b. 7 April 1947, Eau Claire, Wisconsin

"[Eau Claire] was a good place to grow up: quiet, good schools, a very pretty town," C. said in an interview with Don Gallo. Flanked by an older brother and a younger sister, C. was an average student with a talent for language. As an eight-year-old, he realized he was a natural writer. He wrote for and edited his high-school newspaper, but it took a quarter of a century for him to turn his yearning into his profession.

C.'s childhood was somewhat clouded by his father's alcoholism. "Children of alcoholics almost always blame themselves for their parent's alcoholism," the author told Gallo, and he was no exception. Regardless, C.'s father was a nice man, a romantic who loved books; losing him as a sixteen-year-old left many of C.'s questions unanswered until maturity, making his self-discovery in many ways a little easier. While his novel *Up Country* (1989) is not autobiographical, C. admits that it helped him come to terms with the impact that alcoholism had on his own adolescent life.

After graduating from Eau Claire Memorial High School in 1965, C. received a Navy ROTC scholarship to the University of Kansas, where he met his future wife and earned a bachelor's degree in English in 1969. His service to the Navy came next; he honored his commitment as an officer for five years. C. did not remain in the Navy, largely due to his drive to be a writer. However, he is proud of the years he spent serving his country.

His marriage to Carol Shadis, a woman he had met nine years before their wedding day in 1974, was the next turning point in C.'s life. Earning his teaching certificate from Montana State was another. He believed teaching would provide a source of income and allow plenty of time to write. Subsequently, C. and his wife moved back to Wisconsin where he taught English and journalism in Marshfield for several years.

Working with young people was rewarding, but the time to write never materialized. In 1980, when he could no longer ignore the need to write with focus, C. quit teaching (with his wife's blessing) to write full-time and soon produced his first published novel, *Growing Season* (1984). This book is an ALA Best Book for Young Adults, inspired by the couple's rented farmhouse and their hard-working neighbors.

Many of C.'s novels for young readers have dealt with DEATH and diseases such as diabetes, cancer, and mental illness. He resists having his books classified in stereotypical categories; he simply writes about topics that interest him, and because he also writes nonfiction for several markets, detailed research is a natural part of his work.

C.'s mother, Hilda Carter Fletcher, has been one of his primary readers throughout his writing career. Her editorial punch has helped him to fine tune his manuscripts. A literary agent, however, guided C. into YA literature.

An idea usually sparks C.'s creative process. He follows that flash of inspiration with a rough outline and extensive research. By the time he gets his editor's suggestions for revisions, months later, he is sometimes "bored" with the story; yet he presses forward with a deep trust for his editor's wisdom, and completes the tedious corrections.

Holding the final book in his hands, even after writing more than forty published titles, is still a thrill for the Wisconsin author. Knowing his readers connect on so many personal levels is also rewarding. Regular school visits and conference speaking engagements assure that the energy flows in both directions.

C. still lives in Marshfield, Wisconsin, with his wife Carol, their son Brian, and daughter Siri. He maintains an office at the Marshfield Airport where a retired terminal has been converted into commercial space. He enjoys many outdoor activities including canoeing, hiking, and bicycling. He also loves to travel and spend time with his family. C. frequently collaborates with his wife, a photographer on PICTURE BOOKS, and their projects have received many awards and accolades. Despite this success, C. says fiction for older readers is his heart and his true passion.

AWARDS: Arthur Tofte Juvenile Fiction Book Award; Heartland Award for Excellence in Young Adult Literature; The Best of the Best: The 100 Best Young Adult Books of the Last 25 Years; Oppenheim Toy Portfolio Gold Seal Award.

FURTHER WORKS: *Wart, Son of Toad,* 1985; *Sheila's Dying,* 1987; *Dancing on Dark Water,* 1990; *Dogwolf,* 1994; *Between a Rock and a Hard Place,* 1995; *Bull Catcher,* 1997; *Crescent Moon,* 1999; *Love, Football and Other Contact Sports,* 2005.

BIBLIOGRAPHY: Alden R. C. website: http://www .aldencarter.com/; Interview by email, November 2003; Alden R. C. Interview with Don Gallo, Greenwood; UW-Eau Claire BIOGRAPHY: HTTP://WWW .UWEC.EDU/LIBRARY/SPCOLL/CARTER.HTML.

KELLY MILNER HALLS

CARY, Lorene
Author, b. 29 November 1956, Philadelphia, Pennsylvania

C. was one of the first AFRICAN AMERICANS to attend the prestigious St. Paul's school in Concord, New Hampshire. She later became a teacher there. Her memoir, *Black Ice* (1991), tells of her time at St. Paul's. ALA named *Black Ice* a Notable Book of the Year in 1992. C. continued her education at the University of Pennsylvania, receiving both a B.A. and an M.A. in 1978. She attended the University of Sussex in England as part of an exchange program and received another M.A. in 1979.

C. continues to write. She also teaches creative writing and actively supports the arts and her community.

AWARDS: Notable.

FURTHER WORKS: *The Price of a Child: A Novel,* 1995; *Pride: A Novel,* 1998.

BIBLIOGRAPHY: *Contemporary Authors Online,* Gale, 2003, reproduced in *Biography Resource Center,* 2003, http://www.galenet.com/servlet/BioRC

SHANNON CUFF

CASELEY, Judith
Author, illustrator, b. 17 October 1951, Rahway, New Jersey

Well-known for her self-illustrated PICTURE BOOKS, C. also writes novels for middle-grade readers and young adults. After receiving a B.F.A. from Syracuse University, C. worked in London as an aspiring artist, even illustrating greeting cards. Her early works in the 1980s were mostly picture books. In 1990, her first novel, *Kisses,* was published. It focuses on a main character, Hannah Gold, who, although a self-confident violinist, struggles with self-confidence when it comes to her love life. Hannah dates regularly but cannot compete with her best friend, Deirdre, for whom everything comes easily. Hannah's grandparents play a central role in her self-discovery, and C. does a good job of creating a REALISTIC TEENAGE character who is struggling with typical teenage problems. More recently, C. published *Losing Louisa* (1999) and *Praying to A.L.* (2000). *Losing Louisa* introduces the reader to Lacey Levine, another strong female protagonist, who is dealing with the aftereffects of her parents' divorce as she struggles to find her way through adolescence. When Lacey's older sister, Rosie, turns up pregnant, C. does a delicate job of handling the difficult issues involved, creating a realistic view of the relationship between two sisters facing such a challenge. In *Praying to A.L.*, thirteen-year-old Sierra confronts the impending death of her father from Alzheimer's disease. Sierra, who is grieving for her father, remembers fondly a shared interest in Abraham Lincoln. C. presents strong, realistic female characters, most of whom are Jewish, and creates situations of interest to YA readers.

AWARDS: *Kisses* (1990) American Library Association Best Book, *My Father the Nutcase* (1992) American Library Association Best Book.

FURTHER WORK: *My Father the Nutcase,* 1992.

BIBLIOGRAPHY: Caseley, Judith. "Judith Caseley—Author/Illustrator." Available [Online] http://www.judithcaseley.com; Contemporary Authors Online; Silvey, Anita, ed. *Children's Books and Their Creators.* New York: Houghton Mifflin, 1995, 124.

JANET CIARROCCA

CASTANEDA, Carlos
Author, b. 25 December ca. 1925, Cajamarca, Peru; d. 27 April 1998, Los Angeles, California

Best known for his first publication, an academic work entitled *The Teachings of Don Juan: A Yaqui Way of Knowledge* (1968), C.'s life, like his writing, remains something of a mystery. Reared by his grandparents on a chicken farm, C. attended a boarding school in Buenos Aires, Argentina, before moving to Los Angeles at the age of sixteen to live with a foster family and attend high school. At least this is what C. states. Immigration records show that he was born Carlos César Salvador Arana Castañeda on Christmas Day 1925, in isolated Cajamarca, Peru, and was educated at the Colegio Nacional de Nuestra Senora and the National School of Fine Arts in Lima. The official account says he immigrated to the U.S. in 1951 and later attended the University of California at Los Angeles. He graduated from college in 1962, received a master's degree from UCLA in 1964, and was granted a doctoral degree in 1970, after he wrote his thesis on Don Juan Matus.

Inspiring a resurgence of interest in the culture of the Southwest and Native Americans, as well as the 1960s counterculture, C. followed his success with *Don Juan* (1971) and *Journey to Ixtlan: The Lessons of Don Juan* (1972). *Tales of Power* (1974) and *The Eagle's Gift* (1981) marked a further turn in Casteneda's development, toward the purely visionary. In all, C. wrote ten works while shunning the spotlight, mostly refusing to be recorded or photographed. However, there is controversy over whether he really studied with Don Juan and if his recordings are accurate or completely of C.'s imagination—or somewhere in between.

AWARDS: *Journey to Ixtlan: The Lessons of Don Juan* was one of 100 Young Adult titles selected for the first YALSA Best of the Best List; *Still Alive* (Selections from 1960 to 1974).

FURTHER WORKS: *The Second Ring of Power,* 1977; *The Fire from Within,* 1985; *The Power of Silence: Further Lessons of Don Juan,* 1987; *El Arte de Ensonar,* 1995; *Magical Passages,* 1998; *The Active Side of Infinity,* 1999.

BIBLIOGRAPHY: "Carlos Castaneda." DISCovering Authors. Gale Group, 1999. Reproduced in Discovering Collection. Farmington Hills, Mich.: Gale Group. October, 2001. http://galenet.galegroup.com/servlet/DC/; "Overview of Carlos Castaneda." In DISCovering Authors. Gale Group, 1999. Reproduced in Discovering Collection. Farmington Hills, Mich.: Gale Group. October, 2001. http://galenet.galegroup.com/servlet/DC/; "Carlos Castaneda." Newsmakers 1998, Issue 4. Gale Group, 1998. Reproduced in Discovering Collection. Farmington Hills, Mich.: Gale Group. October, 2001. http://galenet.galegroup.com/servlet/DC/.

SARA MARCUS

CATRAN, Ken
Author, b. 16 May 1944, Auckland, New Zealand

Reared in an Air Force family in Auckland and Wellington, C. was always keen to write. His ambitions were encouraged when working as a radio journalist and, in the 1970s, he began writing scripts for NEW ZEALAND television and films. His young people's TV series such as *Hunter's Gold, Star Runner, Children of the Dog Star, Steel Riders, Space Knights, The New Adventures of Black Beauty* and Maurice GEE's *Under the Mountain* were screened around the world. *Hanlon* was nominated for an Emmy in 1986.

By 1992, C. decided he preferred the challenge and diversity of YOUNG ADULT fiction to screenwriting. Already widely respected, and even regarded with awe, because of his industry, wide reading, detailed research, and eclectic range of interests, C. burst onto the junior fiction field, producing two remarkable SCIENCE FICTION SERIES in three years.

The Solar Colonies trilogy (1993–4) shows young people facing the challenge of settling the planets beyond Earth. Themes of discrimination and colonial attitudes are explored in C's typically imaginative style. The Deepwater trilogy (1992–4) gives a small group of TEENS the responsibility for saving the human race, in a genetic ark travelling for half a million years across the universe. *Deepwater Black* (1992) was later televised in the U.S. although the script weakened C's key element of having young people meeting desperate situations without adult help.

Other lively science fiction novels followed. *Taken at the Flood* (2001) explores survivors' responses after a cataclysmic tidal wave, with thought-provoking parallels to New Zealand land rights issues. Vividly convincing, *The Tribe: Mall Rats* (2001), sets the background for the cult TV series The Tribe (filmed in New Zealand). A world with no adults proves a teenage nightmare, rather than a dream, with typhoid, looting, slavery, and gangs fighting for survival in the wreckage of the cities. Yet C. also offers his young characters hope for the future.

Many of C.'s novels reflect his interest in the potential effects of technology, ranging from the power that a cell phone gives to a serial killer in *Talking to Blue* (2000), through the potential of virtual reality in *Dream-Bite* (1995), to the electronic surveillance of *The Onager* (1996). *Fire Gods* (1997) presents an unexpected cultural exchange between space-faring dinosaurs and stone-age humans raising the issue of what really constitutes intelligent life in an often witty way. Humor is the most difficult form of writing but C. has produced many funny stories, including *Fries* (2002) which gives the lowdown on fast food, and *Something Weird About Mr Foster* (2002) in which a student finds that his teacher is an alien with unusual abilities.

History is C.'s great love. Inspired by his admiration for the work of Rosemary SUTCLIFF and Henry TREECE, he single-handedly proved that young readers of the 21st century enjoy historical novels. A turning point in his career came with the success of *The Golden Prince* (1999), C's own favorite among his novels. The detailed research and heightened realism bring readers directly into the tension and violence of the Trojan Wars, as the teenager Pyrrhus, son of Achilles, faces his first battle and tries desperately to prove himself. "We destroyed Troy, and Troy destroyed us," muses Pyrrhus, the classic lone outsider, a type that so often recurs in C.'s work.

C.'s interest in the classics, first manifested in the short novel *Neo's War* (1995), was a prelude to *The Golden Prince,* then led him to *Voyage With Jason* (2000), which brought the Argonauts convincingly to life. There can be few grimmer scenes in junior fiction than the closing pages of *Voyage With Jason,* where all but Jason avert their eyes while Medea hacks chunks of flesh from her brother's corpse and hurls them into the sea, to delay the pursuing galleys of Colchis. C., whose reading ranges from Mesopotamian archaeology to the campaigns against Napoleon, sees history providing a perspective on human nature across the board. His enthusiasm for the past led C. to take on the mantle of Elsie LOCKE and revitalize the historic novel for young New Zealand readers.

C. and his wife Wendy (also a writer) live in Waimate, South Canterbury, New Zealand.

AWARDS: 1983 NZ Best Script Award, *Children of the Dog Star,* 1999 CBCA Notable Book, *Golden Prince; Voyage with Jason:* 2001 NZ Post Children's Book Award, NZ Post Children's Book of the Year; 2002 Children's Literature Foundation of NZ Notable Book, *Road Kill;* 2003 NZ Post Children's Book Awards Shortlist, *Something Weird about Mr Foster;* 2003; NZ Post Children's Book Awards Shortlist, *From the Coffin Trenches;* 2003 NZ Post Children's Book Awards Shortlist, *Tomorrow the Dark.*

FURTHER WORKS: *Steel Riders,* 1987; "Solar Colonies" trilogy (*Doomfire on Venus,* 1993; *The Ghosts of Triton,* 1994; *Shadow of Phobos,* 1994); "Deepwater" trilogy (*Deepwater Black,* 1992; *Deepwater Landing,* 1993; *Deepwater Angels,* 1994); *Space Wolf,* 1994; *Focus and the Death-Ride,* 1994; *The Secret of Boomer Lake,* 1994; *Neo's War,* 1995; *Running Dogs,* 1998; *Black Sister,* 1999; *Blue Murder,* 2001; *Road Kill,* 2001; *Letters from the Coffin-Trenches,* 2002; *Tomorrow the Dark,* 2002; *Artists Are Crazy and Other Stories,* 2003; *Dawn Hawk,* 2003; *Jacko Moran, Sniper,* 2003; *Bloody Lizzie,* 2004.

BIBLIOGRAPHY: Catran, Ken. "History is Bunk." *Magpies* 17:2 (May 2002) 18–20; Edwards, Denis. "Watch Out Wilbur Smith." *Sunday.* 12 August 1990, pp. 10–13; Harper, Julie. "Know the Author: Ken Catran." *Magpies NZ Supplement* 15:3 (Jul. 2000): 4–6; Hebley, Diane. "Catran, Ken." *The Oxford Compan-*

ion to New Zealand Literature. Ed. Roger Robinson and Nelson Wattie. Auckland: Oxford University Press, 1998. 94; http://library.christchurch.org.nz/ Childrens/ChildrensAuthors/KenCatran.asp/; http:// www.vuw.ac.nz / nzbookcouncil / writers / catranken .htm/

TREVOR AGNEW

CENSORSHIP

Censorship: A definition

Censorship is any attempt by an individual or organization to remove books and other materials from the shelves of a school or public library. Censorship is not simply an action that requests books and materials be removed or restricted in use by one TEEN reader. Rather, censorship seeks to remove or restrict a book for *all* young adult readers. It differs from selection, the process by which most teachers, librarians, and other educators decide to include books and materials in a classroom or library, in that censorship seeks to exclude books and materials. Censorship is a growing problem in the field of YA LITERATURE.

How Censorship Affects the Field of Literature for YA

YA literature has not been without controversy. Censorship has long been an issue in this field. From the earliest novels for adolescents, such as *The Outsiders, The Pigman,* and *The Chocolate War,* all the way to contemporary titles such as *Speak* and *Doing It,* the content of YA literature has met with challenges from many fronts. Recent statistics indicate the size of the censorship problem in the United States. Between 1990 and 2000, 6,364 challenges were reported to, or recorded by, the Office for Intellectual Freedom of the American Library Association (see ALA OIF website at http://www.ala.org/bbooks/challeng.html #backgroundinformation for details). The nature of the challenges to books covers a wide range, as evidenced by the following statistics:

- 1,607 were challenges to "sexually explicit" material
- 1,427 to material considered to use "offensive language"
- 1,256 to material considered "unsuited to age group"

- 842 to material with an "occult theme or promoting the occult or Satanism"
- 737 to material considered to be "violent"
- 515 to material with a homosexual theme or "promoting homosexuality" and
- 419 to material "promoting a religious viewpoint." (Lesesne and Chance, 2002)

The vast majority of the challenges were to materials in schools or school libraries and were brought by parents.

Books Frequently Challenged

An examination of the most frequently banned books from 1990–2000 (access this list at: http://www .ala.org/ala/oif/bannedbooksweek/bbwlinks/100most frequently.htm) includes books that are considered classics of juvenile literature, such as Katherine PATERSON's *Bridge to Terabithia* (1977), *Forever* (1975) by Judy BLUME, and *The Chocolate War* by Robert CORMIER (1974). Adult titles that are required reading in many classrooms also appear on the list. *I Know Why the Caged Bird Sings* (1969) by Maya ANGELOU and Mark Twain's *Adventures of Huckleberry Finn* (1885) appear, as do *A Day No Pigs Would Die* (1972) by Robert Newton PECK and John Steinbeck's *Of Mice and Men* (1937).

Some books appear on the list due to references about ghosts, witches, magic and spirits, such as the classic trilogy of books from Alvin Schwartz, beginning with *Scary Stories to Tell in the Dark* (1981), and *Harry Potter* by J. K. ROWLING (1998). References to homosexuality and/or sexual situations can also be problematic, as evidenced in challenges against books such as J. D. SALINGER's *The Catcher in the Rye* (1951) and *It's Perfectly Normal* by Robie Harris (1994). Offensive language, often a target for books such as *Fallen Angels* (1984) by Walter Dean Myers, or violent content, as in a challenge for *The Outsiders* (1967) by S. E. HINTON, are additional reasons offered by censors who have challenged books.

Some Tips for Dealing with Censorship

Dealing with censorship begins *before* a challenge ever arises. The following suggestions may help to create a strong defense by having a strong offense.

- All schools and libraries should have in place a selection policy, a policy that guides the acquisition of materials to ensure that they are appropriate for the population of the community.
- Educators should be aware of the types of issues that would likely be the target of censors in the community.
- Educators should know the policy of the school when it comes to dealing with challenged materials. Generally, that policy is placed in the school or public library. Be familiar with the process and follow it closely.
- Educators should be aware that there are professional organizations that have the resources available for dealing with censorship. Contact the American Library Association's Office of Intellectual Freedom to report a challenge or to ask for help (www.ala.org). The National Council of Teachers of English (NCTE) also can help in dealing with challenges (www.ncte.org). The National Coalition Against Censorship (NCAC) is another a good resource.

Once a challenge has occurred, it is essential that educators strictly follow the procedures outlined for their library. Passive censorship, where books and materials are "lost" or simply removed without due process, remains problematic. Educators must see that the process is adhered to. Guidelines for establishing such a process can be found at various websites and in some of the publications listed in the bibliography.

BIBLIOGRAPHY: Doyle, R. P., *Banned Books,* 2001; Heins, M., *Not in Front of the Children,* 2001; *Intellectual Freedom Handbook,* 6th ed., 2001; Karolides, N. J., M. Bald and D. B. Sova, *100 Banned Books: Censorship Histories of World Literature,;* Lesesne, T. S. and Chance, R., *Hit List for Young Adults,* Chicago, IL: American Library, 2002; *Limiting What Students Shall Read: Books and Other Learning Materials in Our Public Schools: How They Are Selected and How They Are Removed. Report on a Survey Sponsored by Association of American Publishers.* American Library Association, 1981; *Newsletter on Intellectual Freedom,* Judith F. Krug, ed., American Library Association, Intellectual Freedom Committee, published bimonthly; *Places I Never Meant to Be: Original Stories by Censored Writers,* J. Blume, ed., 1999; *Rationales for Challenged Books,* National Council of Teachers of English in partnership with International Reading Association, 2000; Reichman,

H. *Censorship and Selection: Issues and Answers for Schools,* 3rd ed., American Library Association, 2001.

TERI S. LESESNE

The following books were the most frequently challenged in 2003 at www.ala.org/ala/oif/ bannedbooks.week

1. Alice SERIES, for sexual content, using offensive language, and being unsuited to age group.
2. Harry Potter series, for its focus on wizardry and magic.
3. *Of Mice and Men* by John Steinbeck, for using offensive language.
4. *Arming America: The Origins of a National Gun Culture"* by Michael A. Bellesiles, for inaccuracy.
5. *Fallen Angels* by Walter Dean Myers, for racism, sexual content, offensive language, drugs and violence.
6. *Go Ask Alice* by ANONYMOUS, for drugs.
7. *It's Perfectly Normal* by Robie Harris, for homosexuality, nudity, sexual content and sex education.
8. *We All Fall Down* by Robert Cormier, for offensive language and sexual content.
9. *King and King* by Linda de Haan, for homosexuality.
10. *Bridge to Terabithia* by Katherine Paterson, for offensive language and occult/satanism.

As compiled by the Office for Intellectual Freedom, American Library Association. The Office for Intellectual Freedom does not claim comprehensiveness in recording challenges. Research suggests that for each challenge reported there are as many as four or five which go unreported.

Other reasons for challenges included "nudity" (317 challenges, up 20 since 1999), "racism" (267 challenges, up 22 since 1999), "sex education" (224 challenges, up 7 since 1999), and "anti-FAMILY" (202 challenges, up 9 since 1999).

Please note that the number of challenges and the number of reasons for those challenges do not match, because works are often challenged on more than one ground.

Seventy-one percent of the challenges were to material in schools or school libraries. Another twenty-four percent were to material in public libraries (down two percent since 1999). Sixty percent of the challenges were brought by parents, fifteen percent by patrons, and nine percent by administrators, both down one percent.

The Most Frequently Challenged Authors of 2003

The most frequently challenged authors in 2003 were Phyllis Reynolds Naylor, J. K. Rowling, Robert Cormier, Judy Blume, Katherine Paterson, John Steinbeck, Walter Dean Myers, Robie Harris, Stephen KING, and Louise RENNISON.

The most frequently challenged authors in 2002 were J.K. Rowling, Judy Blume, Robert Cormier, Phyllis Reynolds Naylor, Stephen King, Lois DUNCAN, S.E. Hinton, Alvin Schwartz, Maya Angelou, Roald DAHL, and Toni Morrison.

The most frequently challenged authors in 2001 were J.K. Rowling, Robert Cormier, John Steinbeck, Judy Blume, Maya Angelou, Robie Harris, Gary Paulsen, Walter Dean Myers, Phyllis Reynolds Naylor, and Bette GREENE.

The most frequently challenged authors in 2000 were J.K. Rowling, Robert Cormier, Lois Duncan, Piers ANTHONY, Walter Dean Myers, Phyllis Reynolds Naylor, John Steinbeck, Maya Angelou, Christopher PIKE, Caroline Cooney, Alvin Schwartz, Lois LOWRY, Harry Allard, PAUL ZINDEL, and Judy Blume.

Please note that the most frequently challenged authors may not appear in the list of most frequently challenged books. For example, if every one of Judy Blume's books was challenged—but only once—not one of her books would make the top 10 list, but she herself would make the most challenged author list. Five of Judy Blume's books are on the list of *The 100 Most Frequently Challenged Books: Forever* (8), *Blubber* (32), *Deenie* (46), *Are You There, God? It's Me, Margaret* (62), and *Tiger Eyes* (78).

Top Ten Challenged Authors 1990 to Present

1. Alvin Schwartz
2. Judy Blume
3. Robert Cormier
4. J. K. Rowling
5. Michael Willhoite
6. Katherine Paterson
7. Stephen King
8. Maya Angelou
9. R. L. Stine
10. John Steinbeck

CHAMBERS, Aidan
Author, critic, editor, publisher, b. 27 December 1934, Chester-le-Street, England

C.'s involvement in the field of children's literature has gained him an international reputation. With his wife Nancy, he is the co-publisher of the internationally acknowledged journal *Signal*.

C. admits that going to school was not a happy experience. He was bad at mathematics and had difficulties in learning to read; his teachers described him as "slow" and it was not until he was nine that he could read fluently. At thirteen, he was transferred from a secondary modern school to Queen Elizabeth I Grammar School in Darlington with some other "late developers." There he met Jim Osborn, the school's head of English who introduced him to literature and the world of reading and who, he says, changed his life. Soon after his encounter with the pleasures of literature, C. realized that he wanted to be a writer.

After two years of compulsory military service in the Royal Navy, during which he spent most of his time reading books that he bought from a secondhand bookshop across from his office, C. studied at London University. It was there he found time to write his first play and receive his certification as an English teacher, graduating in 1957. Soon after, he was appointed to Westcliff High School for boys in Southend-on-Sea where he was in charge of drama. At the same time, he met a group of Christian teachers. Not long after this encounter in 1960, he joined a religious community and became a monk for about seven years. As a monk, he took another job as English teacher at Archway Secondary Modern School in Stroud, Gloucestershire (where he still lives) where he was in charge of the library and drama. Here he published his first stories and PLAYS written for the pupils he was teaching. Among these are *Johnny Salter* (1966) and *The Chicken Run* (1968). His reputation as teacher and librarian grew, and he was often invited to conferences to give talks, as well as to write articles for specialists' MAGAZINES. In 1967, he decided to leave his monastic life to become a full-time writer.

In 1978, C.'s *Breaktime* was published, followed by *Dance on My Grave* (1982), *NKI: Now I Know* (1987), *The Toll Bridge* (1992) and *Postcards from No Man's Land* (1999) which compose The Dance Sequence. These books gained C. an international reputation as a novelist. His skillful breaking of narrative conventions is often praised and his books are often described as postmodern and metafictive. The narrators of C.'s novels are male adolescents going through various experiences, and the narratives are centered on their coming to terms with these. Sexuality, spiritual beliefs, and homosexual relationships are issues one finds at the heart of adolescence. Chambers manages to deal with them with vivid awareness and accuracy. *Breaktime,* he says, is "preoccupied with physical experience"; *Dance on My Grave* with "emotions and personal obsessions"; *NIK: Now I Know* "dwells on the dramatic clash of belief and rational thought"; *The Toll Bridge* is about friendship; *Postcards from No Man's Land* "constantly crosses boundaries." C.'s novels are often associated with those of Robert CORMIER in the U.S.A.

C.'s work as an educator has been highly praised. Among his most influential publications are *The Reluctant Reader* (1969), *Booktalk* (1985), *The Reading Environment* (1991), *Tell Me: Children, Reading and Talk* (1993), and *Reading Talk* (2001). C.'s preoccupation in these pedagogical essays is the reader, and very often, the "slow" reader. His reflections on literature and teaching practices have had a great impact in the UK, as well as in the U.S., especially after the publication of *Tell Me* in which C. and a group of teachers develop a critical approach (the "Tell Me" approach) giving the child a much more important role in teaching. Throughout C.'s essays, the value of literature is emphasized as is the importance of interaction between the teacher, the child, and the book.

AWARDS Eleanor Farjeon Award, 1982, *Signal* (international journal); Dutch Silver Pencil Award, 1993, *The Toll Bridge;* Carnegie Medal, 1999, *Postcards from No Man's Land;* Hans Christian Andersen Award, 2002, from International Board of Books for Young People (IBBY); the YALSA Printing Award and BBYA 2003.

SELECT FURTHER WORKS: *The Car,* 1967; *Cycle Smash,* 1967; *Marle,* 1968; *Seal Secret,* 1980; *The Dream Cage,* 1982; *The Present Takers,* 1983; *Shades of Dark,* 1986.

BIBLIOGRAPHY: 'Aidan Chambers' in *Something About The Author: The Autobiographical Series,* Vol. 12, 1991, pp.37–55. http://www.aidanchambers.co .uk/bio.htm; Hipple, Ted. Writers for Young Adults, vol.1, 1993; Contemporary Authors, vol. 31, 1990; Contemporary Literary Criticism, vol. 35, 1985.

SEBASTIEN CHAPLEAU

CHARNAS, Suzy McKee
Author, b. 22 October 1939, New York City

C., oldest child of artists, has written numerous works of award-winning FANTASY, HORROR, and SCIENCE FICTION. She worked as a teacher before becoming a professional writer and has served as an instructor of both the Clarion and Clarion West Writers Workshops. She is most prominently known for a SERIES of FEMINIST science fiction novels begun in her first book *Walk to the End of the World* (1974). The rest of the series includes *Motherlines* (1978), *The Furies* (1994), and *The Conqueror's Child* (1999). Her highly original vampire fiction which includes the SHORT STORY "The Unicorn Tapestry" and the novel *The Vampire Tapestry* (1980) are among her most acclaimed works.

C.'s four novels for YOUNG ADULTS include *The Bronze King* (1985), *The Silver Glove* (1988), and *The Golden Thread* (1989), a trilogy about the fantastic adventures of Valentine Marsh and her friends. C.'s other young adult novel is *The Kingdom of Kevin Malone* (1993). More recently, C. has published *My Father's Ghost: The Return of My Old Man and Other Second Chances* (2002), a memoir about her father.

AWARDS: Nebula Award (1980); Hugo Award (1990); Gilgamesh Award (1990); Aslan Award: James Tiptree Jr. Retrospective Award (1996); James Tiptree Jr. Award (2000).

FURTHER WORKS: *Stagestruck Vampires and Other Phantasms,* 2004.

BIBLIOGRAPHY: *Authors and Artists for Young Adults* 2002; *Contemporary Authors Online* 2003; author website: http://www.suzymckeecharnas.com

JAMES GAHAGAN

CHBOSKY, Stephen (Steve)
Author, screenwriter, filmmaker, actor, b. 22 January 1970

C. was reared in Pittsburgh, Pennsylvania, in the 1970s and early 1980s. After graduating from the

University of Southern California's Filmic Writing program, he wrote his first film, *The Four Corners of Nowhere.* C. wrote, directed, acted, and produced the film with the help of only one other producer and several actors. The film premiered at the 1995 Sundance Film Festival and appeared shortly thereafter at the Chicago Underground Film Festival, where it won Best Narrative Feature Honors. The film chronicles the adventures of Duncan, a curious hitchhiker who encounters an eccentrically bizarre assortment of characters in and around Ann Arbor, Michigan. The deeply social film explores depression, genius, idealism, pop culture, political correctness, unconventional relationships, therapy, and abuse while maintaining a veneer of humor and eventually allowing Duncan to change the lives of the other characters forever.

C.'s next work, *The Perks of Being a Wallflower,* catapulted him to fame. Published in 1999, this highly controversial coming-of-age novel has often been compared and contrasted to both J. D. SALINGER's *The Catcher in the Rye* and John KNOWLES's *A Separate Peace,* following as it does a young high-school adolescent struggling to grow up. The story's protagonist, Charlie, is a self-declared social wallflower with a penchant for social criticism. A high-school freshman, Charlie's story is told through a series of letters written to a person whose identity remains undisclosed. Through these letters, Charlie relates his struggles and accomplishments during his first year of high school. A social outcast, Charlie is befriended by step-siblings Samantha and Patrick, seniors who not only see that this young freshman is included in the ranks of their upper class group, but who also introduce Charlie to friendship, drugs, love, sex, dating, drinking, and the feeling of being infinite. Even Patrick's boyfriend eventually thanks Charlie for his presence. A social documentary similar to *Four Corners,* this work elicited violent reactions, both positive and negative. When a librarian in Massachusetts added the book to a suggested reading list, the local high-school officials removed the book due to its portrayal of sexuality in a first relationship. Despite this, the book remained popular with YOUNG ADULT readers and is becoming something of a cult classic among its devoted young audience.

C.'s next project was the WB television series *Brutally Normal,* which he co-wrote with Michael Goldberg. The quirky situational comedy series ran for only three weeks in early 2000 before it was removed from programming due to low ratings.

In August of 2000, MTV Books published *Pieces,* with an introduction by C. This anthology of young writers who entered MTV's "Write Stuff" contest was co-edited by C., and this edgy collection is aimed at much the same niche as *The Perks of Being a Wallflower.*

A recipient of the Abraham Polonsky Screenwriting Award for his screenplay *Everything Divided,* C. is also a participant in the Sundance Institute's filmmakers' lab for his most recent project, *Fingernails and Smooth Skin.* C. lives in New York and is working on the film of the smash-hit musical *Rent.*

AWARDS: ALA Best Books for Young Adults list in 2000 for *The Perks of Being a Wallflower.*

BIBLIOGRAPHY: http://www.iblist.com/book.php?id = 2225; http://www.iblist.com/author.php?id = 690; http://us.imdb.com/title/tt0113099/plotsummary; http://us.imdb.com/name/nm0154716/; http://www.schoollibraryjournal.com/article/CA231217

ANDREW WESTOVER

CHERIPKO, Jan
Author, b. 3 August 1951, West Point, New York

C. was born at the West Point Military Academy, West Point, New York. His father was in the Army for more than twenty years, serving in World War II and Korea. C. attended Orange County Community College in Middletown, New York (1970–72) and St. Thomas Aquinas College in Sparkill, New York (1972–74). Two high-school teachers, Robert Ciganek and Kevin McFadden, had a profound influence on his love of literature.

C. married Valray Wills in 1981; they have one daughter, Julia Christina. C. currently lives in Bethany, Pennsylvania. C. is a full-time educator who teaches English and philosophy to at-risk young adults at the Family Foundation School in Hancock, New York.

The first novel that C. wrote, *Imitate the Tiger,* is about a high-school football player who is battling a drinking problem. *School Library Journal* called it "a frank account of an at-risk TEEN fighting for his life." In *Rat* a high-school basketball player struggles with the decision about whether to tell the truth or to maintain his loyalty to friends.

Voices of the River: Adventures on the Delaware is a photo-journal that chronicles a 215-mile canoe trip from Hancock, New York, to Philadelphia that C. took with a fourteen-year-old boy. *Get Ready to Play Tee-Ball* is a how-to-play photo book for youngsters who want to learn to play tee-ball or to play it better.

Caesar Rodney's Ride: The Story of an American Patriot is about the man who rode eighty miles on horseback to cast his vote for independence as a member of the Second Continental Congress. This historic event established the roll call vote for independence. Congress adopted the official Declaration of Independence two days after the vote on July 4, 1776.

Brother Bartholomew and the Apple Grove is a simple message of generosity and respect for the wisdom of the elderly. C. has written several books that are well respected; his future promises many more.

AWARDS: The Joan Fassler Memorial Book Award for *Imitate the Tiger;* New York Public Library Best Book of the Year for the Teens for *Imitate the Tiger, Rat;* International Reading Association Young Adult Choices for *Imitate the Tiger;* International Reading Association Children's Choices for *Rat;* Society of School Librarians International Honor Book for *Imitate the Tiger;* American Booksellers Best Book for *Imitate the Tiger;* Carolyn Field Honor Book for *Rat,* Children's Book Council—International Reading Association Children's Choice for *Rat.*

FURTHER WORKS: *Voices of the River: Adventures on the Delaware; Get Ready to Play Tee-Ball; Rat; Brother Bartholomew and the Apple Grove; Caesar Rodney's Ride; Sun, Moon, Stars, Rain,* 2005.

BERNICE E. CULLINAN

CHERRYH, C. J. (Carolyn Janice Cherry)
Author, b. 1 September 1942, St. Louis, Missouri

A prolific author of over seventy SCIENCE FICTION and FANTASY NOVELS, C. puts her knowledge of language and history to use in her fiction, creating detailed and complex alien cultures and languages complete with invented vocabularies and grammatical forms. Her fiction is also known for its representation of powerful female characters. In the Chanur SERIES, for example, it is the females of the catlike Hani species who explore space while the violent males are confined to their home planet.

C. often considers themes of xenophobia and cross-cultural understanding, from one of her earliest

works, The Faded Sun trilogy, down to her widely respected Foreigner series, which explores the relationship between humans and the alien Atevi. Her fantasy books include a trilogy based on Russian MYTHOLOGY (*Rusalka,* 1989; *Chernevog,* 1990; *Yvgenie,* 1991) and the Fortress series. *Downbelow Station* (1981) and *Cyteen* (1988) are both set in C.'s Alliance-Union universe.

C. received a B.A. in Latin from the University of Oklahoma in 1964 and an M.A. in classics from Johns Hopkins University in 1965. She taught Latin and history in Oklahoma City public schools from 1965 to 1977.

AWARDS: Hugo Award for Best Novel: *Downbelow Station* and *Cyteen.*

SELECT FURTHER WORKS: *Gate of Ivrel,* 1976: *The Pride of Chanur,* 1982; *Chanur's Venture,* 1984; *Cuckoo's Egg,* 1985; *Chanur's Homecoming,* 1986; *Chanur's Legacy,* 1992; *Foreigner,* 1994; *Invader,* 1995; *Inheritor,* 1996; *Precursor,* 1999; *Defender,* 2001; *Explorer,* 2002.

BIBLIOGRAPHY: *Contemporary Authors New Revision Series,* volume 10; *International Authors and Writers Who's Who,* 17th edition; author website www.cherryh .com

MICHELE HILTON

CHETWIN, Grace
Author, n.d., Nottingham, England

C. is an award-winning author of SCIENCE FICTION and FANTASY books for YOUNG ADULTS. She is an honors graduate in Philosophy from the University of Southampton. She lived for a time in NEW ZEALAND where she taught English, French, and founded a modern-dance school. She has also produced amateur operas and plays.

C. has written a fantasy SERIES, which begins with *Gom on Windy Mountain* (1986), and has three other titles that follow. *Gom* was nominated for the North-West Pacific Young People's Choice Award. She has a particular talent for portraying exciting time-travel ADVENTURES involving young people, as evidenced in her books *Collidescope* (1990) and *Friends in Time* (1992). *Collidescope* won the first Lone Star book award, a Texas state prize for YA fiction.

C. started her own publishing company, Feral Press, Inc. in the mid-1990s. Through this company, she obtained the rights to her out-of-print titles. She redesigns the books, prints and binds them herself, and makes them available via the internet. She also makes many school presentations and attends literary conferences. C. is now in the process of recording her work to make it available on CD, as her audience has requested. She resides in North Carolina.

AWARDS: *Gom* nominated for Northwest Pacific Young People's Choice Award *Collidescope*—Lone Star Book Award.

FURTHER WORKS: *On All Hallow's Eve,* 1984; *Out of the Dark World,* 1985; *The Riddle and the Rune,* 1987; *The Crystal Stair,* 1988; *The Atheling,* 1988; *The Starstone,* 1989; *Mr Meredith and the Truly Remarkable Stone,* 1989; *Box & Cox,* 1990; *Child of the Air,* 1991; *The Atheling,* revised, 2nd edition, 1991; *The Chimes of Alyafaleyn,* 1993; *Jason's Seven Magical Night Rides,* 1994; *Rufus,* 1996; *Everychild and the Twelve Days of Christmas,* 1997; *Beauty and the Beast,* 1997; *Briony's ABC of Abominable Children,* 1997; *Gerrad's Quest,* 1998; *The Orborgon,* 1999; *Deathwindow,* 1999; *The Burning Tower,* 2000; *The Fall of Aelyth-Kintalyn,* 2002; contributor to *Battling Dragons,* a college textbook, 1995.

BIBLIOGRAPHY: *Contemporary Authors online,* 2002; feralpressinc.com, online, 2002; Grace Chetwin, e-mail communication, 2002.

ANN K. SEEFELDT

CHICK LIT (AND CHICK MOVIES AND TELEVISION SHOWS)

Although the term *chick lit* is a relatively recent phenomenon, the genre itself has been in existence for quite some time. Is *Jane Eyre* (appearing in the mid-nineteenth century) by Charlotte Brontë, which chronicles the ADVENTURES of Jane from governess to wife, really that different from tales of modern Manhattan au pairs and nannies? Jane Austen's works are the touchstone for many modern-day tales of matchmaking mayhem—including, but not limited to, the extremely successful 1995 movie *Clueless,* which in turn gave birth to a short-lived television series, and a series of how-to books and novelizations. Included among them are *Cher's Furiously Fit Workout, Cher's Guide to Whatever,* and *A Totally Cher Affair.* Austen's novel *Pride and Prejudice* also inspired Helen Fielding when she penned *Bridget Jones's Diary,* which also became a successful film in 2001. This work gave the term new meaning. Austen's own works have not only inspired other literary

works, but more than a century after her death are still encouraging the production of new film-and-television renditions of her works.

The beginning of the 20th century saw works aimed toward slightly younger women readers. Laura Dent Crane's Automobile Girls SERIES, first appearing in 1910, less than twenty years after Ford premiered the first gasoline-powered automobile, was c. for its times: a group of girls ride around to various glamorous locales—among them Newport, the Berkshires, Palm Beach and Washington—going to parties on yachts, playing in tennis tournaments, foiling jewel thieves, and having various other adventures. Jean Webster's books, which also appeared in the beginning of the 20th century, could be considered c. as well. *When Patty Went to College* (1903) and *Just Patty* follow a young woman's adventures in college, and then in life. These stories, however, were to serve as background works for Webster's *Daddy Long-Legs,* which traced the fortunes of plucky heroine, Judy Abbott, from an orphanage through four years of college, as well as various romantic entanglements. *Daddy-Long-Legs* was turned into both a play and a MOVIE. Eventually multiple film versions were made—each starring one of the top actresses of the time—among them, Mary Pickford, Janet Gaynor, and Leslie Caron.

The Ruth Fielding series (premiering in 1913 and actively published until 1934) also had the distinction of being c. for its time, as did the Judy Bolton series, which was launched just as the Ruth Fielding series was winding down. Both girl heroines had marvelous adventures that enlivened their existences. Of course, the reigning queen of c. from that time is the incomparable Nancy Drew, who from her first appearance in 1930 led a glamorous life filled with mystery, adventure, a housekeeper, and a convertible. With all of that, she was a natural fit for movies and television. Within a decade of her first appearance, her adventures had been turned into four films starring Bonita Granville. Later, there was a Nancy Drew television series, as well as a recent TV movie. The original series of books has appeared in multiple versions, as well as inspiring several new takes on the classic girl-detective's adventures. A new series featuring Nancy Drew has appeared in the spring of 2004. Although geared toward a slightly younger audience, they still contain intrigue, possible ROMANCE, and excitement, just as the original stories did seventy-five years ago.

155

C. from the 1940s and 1950s includes the work of Rosamund DuJardin, Janet Lambert, and Lenora Mattingly Weber. In general, many of the books produced by these women deal with dances, dates, and life in general. However, in Janet Lambert's work, Penny Parrish helped to catch a spy, Rosamund DuJardin's heroines shared a summer working on a showboat, and Lenora Mattingly Weber's Beany Malone joined a secret society. Betty Cavanna's heroines led quieter lives, but also were popular with TEEN girls.

The advent of television heralded a new age for both c. and chick media. Disney's Annette Funicello not only appeared on TV and in movies, but also became the star of a short series of MYSTERY-adventure books. The film *Gidget,* which appeared in 1959, inspired four more movies, as well as a television series starring Sally Field in the 1960s, and another television series which appeared in the 1980s. Frederick Kohner wrote a series of Gidget books that appeared at about the same time as the films.

More current examples of C. include many of Francine PASCAL's works, culminating with her multiple Sweet Valley series, which feature those ultimate California girls, twins Elizabeth and Jessica Wakefield, their family, friends, foes, and adversaries. Pascal also wrote for the Sweet Dreams line that was popular from the 1980s. Multiple authors contributed to the line that featured glossy-photo covers—and heroines facing every dilemma a girl could possibly imagine.

In the 1990s, Joan BAUER added to the field with her teen novels, *Squashed* and *Thwonk,* dealing with the romantic entanglements of her heroines. Lisa Fiedler's novels *Curtis Piperfield's Biggest Fan* and *Lucky Me* deal with a young girl's moving from having a crush to becoming involved—somewhat seriously—with someone. Dyan SHELDON wrote *Confessions of a Teenage Drama Queen,* which then became a successful movie. The movie and subsequent television show, *Buffy the Vampire Slayer,* offered its own supremely edgy brand of chick media, as well as spawning an ever-growing series of books. *The Gilmore Girls* television show also qualifies as chick media, as do the series of books that the show has inspired.

As the 21st century dawns, c. is flourishing. British imports include Louise RENNISON's hilarious Georgia Nicholson series, which debuted with *Angus, Thongs, and Full Frontal Snogging* (a PRINTZ AWARD

book), as well as various sequels. A more recent British c. offering is the Mates, Dates, series by Cathy Hopkins. Katie Maxwell's *The Year My Life Went down the Loo* also qualifies. Offerings by authors in the U.S. range from *Sisterhood of the Traveling Pants* and *Second Summer of the Sisterhood* by Ann Brashares; *The Princess Diaries* (which is also a movie) by Meg CABOT, as well as all the other Princess books; the LDB novels by Grace Dent; the Gossip Girl series by Cecily von Ziegsar; Zoey Dean's A-list series; Carolyn MACKLER's *The Earth, My Butt, and Other Big Round Things; The True Meaning of Cleavage* by Mariah Fredericks; and other works too numerous to mention.

The fascinating part of the c. phenomenon, besides the plethora of books available, is the concentrated marketing effort behind them. At this time in publishing history, the branding and marketing of c. has reached mammoth proportions. The money and effort exerted to create this niche market is remarkable. Whether it continues and where it leads is yet to be seen.

BIBLIOGRAPHY: http://specialcollections.vassar.edu/webster; www.seriesbooks.com

JEANNE MARIE RYAN

CHILDREN'S CHOICES PROJECT

C. and Young Adult Choices are projects of a joint committee supported by the International Reading Association (IRA) and the Children's Book Council (CBC). IRA is a non-profit educational organization whose members include classroom and reading teachers, school administrators and supervisors, parents, college/university faculty, and others who are dedicated to improving reading instruction and promoting literacy worldwide. CBC is a non-profit organization that encourages the use and enjoyment of books and related literacy materials for young people. Its members are U.S. publishers and packagers of trade books for children and young adults and producers of book-related materials for children.

Begun in 1974, C. has three goals:

- To develop an annual annotated reading list of new books that will encourage young people to read.
- To help teachers, librarians, booksellers, parents, and others find books that young readers will enjoy.

- To provide young readers with an opportunity to voice their opinions about the books being written for them.

How are these goals reached? Each year, 10,000 schoolchildren in grades K-6 read and vote on the newly published children's and YA trade books that they like best. About 700 books are sent to five review teams located in different regions of the U.S. Each team consists of a children's literature specialist who acts as the Team Leader and one or more classroom teachers or school librarians, plus 2,000 local schoolchildren.

Throughout the school year, the books are read to or by the children; their votes are tabulated in March by the Team Leaders and the Children's Book Council, and the approximately 100 most popular titles are announced at the International Reading Association Annual Convention.

Each year's annotated list of *Children's Choices* is published in the October issue of *The Reading Teacher,* a journal about preschool and elementary school reading published by IRA. The list is designed for use not only by teachers, librarians, administrators, and booksellers, but also by parents, grandparents, caregivers, and everyone who wishes to encourage young people to read for pleasure. Both the current list and several previous years' selections, are available online at: http://www.reading.org/choices/choices_download.html. Information for prospective Team Leaders is available at http://www.cbcbooks.org/html/choices_form.html

MOLLY KER HAWN

CHILDRESS, Alice

Author, playwright, actress, director, b. 12 October 1916, Charleston, South Carolina; d. 14 August 1994, New York City

An uncompromising and talented playwright, C. is perhaps best-known for her YOUNG ADULT novels of the 1970s and 80s. Her parents separated shortly after her birth in 1916. For the early years of her life, her mother, Florence, raised C. in Charleston, South Carolina. In 1924, Florence and C. relocated to Baltimore, Maryland, where C. attended third grade. C.'s third grade teacher, Miss Thomas, was responsible for the development of her reading skills. The following year, Florence, always busy with work and travel,

gave C. to her mother, Eliza White, who lived in Harlem. Life with her grandmother in Harlem in the 1920s influenced C. and guided her for the rest of her life. Her spare time was spent with her grandmother, visiting a variety of New York City neighborhoods, art galleries, and libraries. C. credited testimonial services on Wednesday nights at Salem Church in Harlem as helping her learn how to write. In addition to C.'s voracious reading habit, fueled by the library, it was time spent at home with her grandmother, playing what C. described as a game that developed her writing talents. C. and her grandmother would sit by the window and watch passersby. Grandmother Eliza would ask C. questions about the passersby, and C. would invent stories about them, which her grandmother then instructed her to write down. C. attended P. S. 81 in Harlem and the Julia Ward Howe Junior High School. She developed her love of acting and the theatre in school. After the deaths of her grandmother and mother early in the 1930s, C. was forced to drop out of Wadleigh High School after only two years and go to work. C. was employed in sales, insurance, and domestic work, as well as other jobs. Like many writers, C. incorporated her own life's experiences into her writing. However, her work experiences found their way into her plays more than her novels.

C. married Alvin Childress, an actor from Mississippi who had relocated to New York City to begin a career in the theatre. The marriage produced one daughter, Jean, in 1935.

In 1941, C. and Alvin Childress both joined the American Negro Theatre in Harlem, where C. studied acting for eight years. Like the other members, C. was committed to the theatre's work and to her craft. When not acting in a production, she worked on scenery, sold tickets, or did anything else that needed to be done. During her years with the American Negro Theatre, C. took on more challenging tasks, serving as an acting coach, director, personnel director, and board member. C.'s time with the American Negro Theatre ended in 1954, due to her desire to focus on her writing.

Despite appearing in the Broadway production of *Anna Lucasta* in 1944, C. was not happy with her life as an actress. After losing roles due to racially prejudiced casting decisions, C. decided to devote her time to writing dramatic plays. C. wrote her first play, *Florence,* in one night in 1949 on a dare from Sidney

Poitier, with whom she worked on *Anna Lucasta* from 1946 to 1949. Without formal training or writing classes, C. taught herself to write plays by reading plays, particularly the works of William Shakespeare, whose play-within-a-play structure was utilized by C. in her own play, *Trouble in Mind, 1955.* It was her experience with *Trouble in Mind* that demonstrated C.'s refusal to compromise her work. Although optioned for a Broadway production, C. refused to alter the script to make the play more acceptable to a general, predominantly white audience.

Alvin C. moved to California in the late 1940s because of his work. This move posed problems for C. for several reasons. First, the couple's relationship became bicoastal, which creates its own set of problems. In addition, Alvin C.'s move to California was to take the role of Amos in the television series *Amos 'n' Andy,* based on the radio program of the same name. *Amos 'n' Andy,* a radio program created and acted by two white males, portrayed AFRICAN AMERICANS in a stereotypical manner. The CBS television show did the same but employed an African American cast. The program continued for two seasons, despite protests by the NAACP regarding the show's portrayal of African Americans. C.'s play, *Trouble in Mind,* addresses some of these issues.

C. married Nathan Woodard, a musician, on July 17, 1957. The couple often collaborated on theatrical productions. As a result, music was incorporated in her works throughout the rest of C.'s career.

The 1960s found C. becoming part of the educational arena, as a guest lecturer and panelist, discussing the state of African Americans and the arts. These visits to colleges and universities in the UK and the U.S. led to a Harvard University appointment as playwright in residence at the Radcliffe Institute for Independent Study from 1966–68.

In the early 1970s, C.'s career went in another direction. Ferdinand Monjo, a children's book author and editor, encouraged her to begin writing novels for young adults. Her first novel, *A Hero Ain't Nothin' but a Sandwich* (1973), became a landmark book in young adult literature, detailing the heroin addiction of thirteen-year-old Benjie Johnson. Benjie's story is told from multiple points of view, including Benjie, his mother, his school principal, and a drug dealer. As with her plays, C.'s young adult novels were critically noted for their realism, strong characterizations, and use of dialect. C.'s use of multiple narratives in her young adult novels demonstrated the influence of the theatre and plays on her prose work. While writing her novels, C. visualized the action on a stage, with each character's narrative very similar to a monologue.

C. wrote the screenplay for the feature film of her novel, *A Hero Ain't Nothin' but a Sandwich,* which was released in 1978. The MOVIE starred Larry B. Scott as Benjie, with Bernard Cohen played by David Groh, Nigeria Greene played by Glynn Turman, Rose Johnson played by Cicely Tyson, and Butler Craig played by Paul Winfield. While several changes were made for the film, the most noticeable ones were the setting, which shifted from New York to Los Angeles, and the ending which was less ambiguous than that of C.'s book.

Her second young adult book, *Rainbow Jordan* (1981) uses the same narrative structure as her first book. Fourteen-year-old Rainbow is left at home alone as her mother travels farther and farther from their New York home for work as an exotic dancer. Rainbow's social worker places her with Miss Josie each time her mother leaves. In addition, Rainbow is dealing with her boyfriend, Eljay, and his constant pressure for them to have sex.

C.'s third and last young adult novel, *Those Other People* (1989) deals with issues of race, homophobia, and sexual abuse. Seventeen-year-old high school graduate Jonathan has known he was gay for years. His parents are somewhat accepting of his sexual orientation. Jonathan decides to get a job before college as a computer teacher at a high school. At Minitown High School, Jonathan becomes involved with his students' lives when Theodora is sexually assaulted by a teacher and the only students who can help her are a brother and sister, Tyrone and Susan, who are the only African American students at the school.

Just as her plays were often considered controversial, so were her young adult novels. *A Hero Ain't Nothin' but a Sandwich* has been banned from school and public libraries numerous times because of language and subject matter, which were deemed inappropriate for the young adult audience by censors. One of the most famous cases, *Board of Education, Island Trees Union Free School District v. Pico* (102 S. Ct. 2799), went to the U.S. Supreme Court for a decision. The Supreme Court's ruling in 1983 in favor of Pico reinstated *A Hero Ain't Nothin' but a Sandwich* to the school district's high-school library.

A decade after her death from cancer, C.'s works are still being read and discussed.

AWARDS: *A Hero Ain't Nothin' but a Sandwich: New York Times Book Review,* Outstanding Book of the Year (1973), Young Adult Services Division, American Library Association, Best Books for Young Adults list (1975); Pulitzer Prize nomination for *A Hero Ain't Nothin' But a Sandwich* was one of 100 Young Adult titles selected for three of the four YALSA Best of the Best Lists: *Still Alive* (Selections from 1960 to 1974), The Best of the Best Books (selections from 1970 to 1983), *Nothin' But the Best* (selections from 1966 to 1986). *Short Walk,* 1979: *Rainbow Jordan: School Library Journal,* Best Book (1981), Outstanding Books of the Year list, *New York Times Book Review* (1982), Coretta Scott King Author Award Honor Book, 1982.

FURTHER WORKS: *Wine in the Wilderness: a Comedy-Drama,* 1969; *Mojo and String: Two Plays,* 1971; *Plays by American Women, 1930–1960* (Includes C.'s play *Trouble in Mind*), 1994; *Like One of the Family: Conversations from a Domestic's Life,* 1956.

BIBLIOGRAPHY: Carter, Betty. *Best Books for Young Adults, Second Edition.* ALA, 2000; Childress, Alice & Elizabeth Brown-Guillory. "Alice Childress: A Pioneering Spirit." *Sage,* Vol. 4, No. 1, Spring 1987, pp. 66–8; *Contemporary Literary Criticism,* Online Edition, 2003; *Contemporary Authors Online,* 2003; *DISCovering Authors,* Online Edition, 2003; *DISCovering Biography,* Online Edition, 2003; Hatch, Shari Dorantes and Michael R. Strickland, eds., *African-American Writers: a Dictionary.* ABC-CLIO, 2000; Hill, Elbert R., "A Hero for the Movies," *Children's Novels and the Movies;* Maguire, Roberta S. "Alice Childress." *Dictionary of Literary Biography,* Volume 249, Gale Group, 2001. Pp. 30–39. from *Dictionary of Literary Biography.* Online Edition. Gale Group, 2003; "Overview of Alice Childress." *DISCovering Authors.* Gale Group, 1999, from *Student Resource Center.* Gale Group, 2003; *U*X*L Junior DISCovering Authors.* Online Edition. U*X*L, 2003.

ANDREW W. HUNTER

CHRISTOPHER, John
Author, b. 16 April 1922, Knowsley, Lancashire, England

Best known for his SCIENCE FICTION trilogies for YOUNG ADULTS, C. is a pseudonym for Christopher Samuel Youd. The British author has written for adults under five other pseudonyms: Hilary Ford, William Godfrey, Peter Graaf, Peter Nichols, and Anthony Rye. Each pseudonym is used for a different genre. C.'s writings are often apocalyptic science fiction, but they have been criticized for not focusing on technology and science. His works are more concerned with characterization and the interactions of the characters than scientific principles. In addition to novels, C. has written many SHORT STORIES. One, "A Few Kindred Spirits," received a nomination for Best Short Story for the Science Fiction and FANTASY Writers of America, Inc.'s Nebula Award in 1965.

In 1932, C.'s family relocated to Hampshire, England. He attended the Peter Symonds School in Winchester, England. As a teenager, C. began writing and submitting his work to MAGAZINES for publication. He published his own magazine, *The Fantast,* during this time. At sixteen, C. left high school to work for the local government. C. was a member of the British Army's Royal Signals during World War II and served from 1941–46. During the early war years, C.'s first short story was published in the publication *Lilliput.* C. continued writing and sending out his work for publication while serving in the Army. In 1946, he submitted part of a novel that was derivative of Aldous Huxley's work to the Rockefeller Foundation, which was sponsoring a grant for new writers. The foundation asked C. to submit another work. His submission, several chapters from a new novel, won him the grant in 1947. Those chapters became his first novel, *The Winter Swan* (1949).

Upon completion of military service, C. married Joyce Fairbairn on 23 October 1946. The couple had five children: Nicholas, Rose, Elizabeth, Sheila, and Margret. As his family grew, C. worked as a freelance writer, utilizing spare moments to increase his income. It was during this period that C. began using pseudonyms for the science fiction short stories that he submitted to genre periodicals. From 1949 to 1958, C. was employed by and eventually became head of the Diamond Corporation's Industrial Diamond Information Bureau. He continued to write in his spare time.

C.'s novel *The Death of Grass,* 1956, published in the U.S. as *No Blade of Grass,* was released as a feature film in 1970, using the American novel's title. *No Blade of Grass* was the runner-up for the 1957 International Fantasy Awards Best Fiction Book. (The winner was *The Lord of the Rings* by J. R. R. TOLKIEN.) In 1958, C. left the Diamond Corporation to write full time.

It was in the late 1960s that one of his publishers suggested he try writing for a younger audience. The publisher wanted science fiction, but C.'s increasing interest in history helped him go in a new direction. C.'s vision of the future contained robotic aliens controlling humanity via mind control in a medieval European feudal system. The Tripods Trilogy consists of *The White Mountains,* 1967, *The City of Gold and Lead,* 1967, and *The Pool of Fire,* 1968. In *The White Mountains,* the Tripods, three-legged robots, control humans by installing caps on their heads. Thirteen-year-old Will knows that his time to be capped is coming soon and rejects the notion of being a slave to the robotic Masters. He chooses to escape the ceremony and is joined by two other boys in an attempt to escape to the White Mountains of Switzerland. *The City of Gold and Lead* finds Will enslaved and learning the inner workings of the Tripods as he serves one of the Masters who controls Earth. In *The Pool of Fire,* Will has escaped from his Master and joined a group of other former slaves to conquer the Tripods and save the Earth from destruction.

C.'s second trilogy, The Sword Trilogy, consists of *The Prince in Waiting* (1970), *Beyond the Burning Lands* (1971), and *The Sword of the Spirits* (1972). The setting for this trilogy is a futuristic Winchester, England, which, due to a series of natural disasters, is similar to the Middle Ages in Europe. His third trilogy, The Fireball Trilogy, consists of *Fireball* (1981), *New Found Land* (1983), and *Dragon Dance* (1986). This trilogy is an alternative history in which North America is controlled by the Aztecs, and the Holy Roman Empire still rules Europe.

C.'s first marriage ended in divorce. On 24 December 1980, he married Jessica Valerie Ball, who died in 2001.

C.'s novels, *The White Mountains* and *The City of Gold and Lead,* were adapted for British television as a twenty-five-episode series The White Mountains (1984–86). After the television series renewed interest in the trilogy, C. wrote a prequel to The Tripods Trilogy, *When the Tripods Came* (1988).

C. returned to issues of freedom in society in his most recent YA novel, *A Dusk of Demons,* 1994. Fourteen-year-old Ben, now the ruler of his home island, must battle the Dark One and his demons who control the mainland and also want his island.

In April 2003, C.'s American publisher, Simon & Schuster, celebrated the 35th anniversary of The Tripods Trilogy by reissuing all three books in special hardcover editions. C. wrote a new preface for the trilogy and revised each book in the trilogy.

C. lives and works in England.

AWARDS: American Library Association, Notable Book list, 1967, for *The White Mountain:* The *Guardian* Newspaper's Children's Fiction Award Shortlist, 1969, for *The Tripods Trilogy;* Christopher Award, 1970, for *The Guardians;* The *Guardian* Newspaper's Children's Fiction Award, 1971, for *The Guardians;* Parents' Choice Foundation's Parents' Choice Award for *New Found Land,* 1983. *Empty World* was one of 100 Young Adult titles selected for the 2nd YALSA Best of the Best List: The Best of the Best Books (selections from 1970 to 1983).

FURTHER WORKS: *The Year of the Comet,* 1955; *A Wrinkle in the Skin,* 1965; *The Possessors,* 1965; *The Little People,* 1967; *Dangerous Vegetables,* 1998. edited by Keith Laumer (contains C.'s short story "Manna," 1955); *The Lodestar,* 2002 (as Peter Nichols); *Bad Dream,* 2003; *Evolution's Captain,* 2003 (as Peter Nichols); *Bad Dream,* 2003.

BIBLIOGRAPHY: *Contemporary Authors Online.* Gale, 2003; Fantastic Fiction website, http://www.fantastic fiction.co.uk/; *The Tripods* website, http://www.gnelson .demon.co.uk/Tripods.html; *U*X*L Junior DIS-Covering Authors.* Online Edition. U*X*L, 2003.

ANDREW HUNTER

CISNEROS, Sandra
Author, poet, b. 20 December 1954, Chicago, Illinois

C.'s highly acclaimed works, including fiction and POETRY, appeal to older as well as YOUNG ADULTS. Her SHORT STORIES and novels represent her LATINO culture and CROSS OVER to appeal to readers of all cultures. With a B.A. from Loyola University of Chicago in 1976 and an M.F.A. from the University of Iowa in 1978, she taught high-school dropouts in a Chicago barrio before becoming an administrative assistant. C.'s popularity grew to mainstream recognition with the publication of *Caramelo* (2002). Her poetry, novels, and short stories evolved from an attraction to female Chicanos and Latinos to all genders and cultures because of the intense emotions reminiscent of myriad FAMILY activities. C. acknowledges that her writings sprouted from her memories of family events, characters, and relationships. Much of her material is based on her family's frequent travels from Chicago to her father's homeland of Mexico;

her loneliness as the only girl in a poor, migrant family with six brothers; and her voracious reading when young. When she first decided to write, while in college, she tried to write what she thought others wanted to hear. Eventually, she realized that she must find her own voice. Once she made this discovery, she began to write what she knew to audiences she knew. Her goal changed to fill the void of the nonexistent barrios in mainstream literature. As in her life, the language of her writings is bilingual. She states that sometimes only Spanish words accurately satisfy the descriptions she creates. In *Caramelo* (2002), C. smoothly weaves Spanish words into her English writing. Currently, C. is relieved that her writing has progressed from her worry if anyone will read it to the luxury of knowing that many people are listening and reading. Her hope is that more Chicano writers will publish in the mainstream to help further fill the void.

AWARDS: National Endowment fellow in 1982 and 1987; Before Columbus Foundation Award, 1985, *The House on Mango Street;* PEN/West Fiction Award, and Lannan Foundation Award, 1991, *Woman Hollering Creek and Other Stories.*

FURTHER WORKS: *Bad Boys,* 1980; *Woman Hollering Creek and Other Stories,* 1991; *Hairs: Pelitos,* 1994; *Loose Women: Poems,* 1994; *We Are the Stories We Tell: The Best Short Stories by North American Women since 1945,* 1990. *The House on Mango Street,* 1988.

BIBLIOGRAPHY: Cisneros, Sandra, lecture to Second Annual Achievement Festival, La Cumba Santa Barbara Junior High School, October 22, 1986; Memmott, Carol, "Caramelo Weaves a Colorful Tale," *USA TODAY,* October 10, 2002, 9D; Sagal, Jim, "Sandra Cisneros," *Publishers Weekly,* March 29, 1991, vol. 238, no. 15; 74, "Sandra Cisneros Tells Teachers to Tap Unique Differences," *The Council Chronicle,* February, 2003, vol. 12, no. 3:3. www.engl.cla.umn.edu/lkd/vfg/Authors/SandraCisneros

NANCY SPENCE HORTON

THE CIVIL RIGHTS ERA

The C., which emerged in the 1950s and came to fruition in the 1960s, represents a tumultuous time in the history of the U.S. It was a time of protest and unrest, as AFRICAN AMERICANS struggled to attain the rights as citizens that free white men had enjoyed since the birth of the country. Segregated at almost every turn, especially in the South, blacks were faced with schools housed in decaying buildings, substandard housing conditions, overt discrimination in stores and restaurants, and restrictions when they attempted to vote.

It became obvious that changes were coming following the Supreme Court's decision in *Brown v. Board of Education* (1954), declaring that segregating students in public schools was unconstitutional. Although it would take decades before the decision was fully enforced, this was an important first step.

Three years later, the Civil Rights Act of 1957 established the Commission of Civil Rights and added a C. Division to the Department of Justice. These actions represented a serious intention to see that existing laws were carried out. Three years after that, the C. Act of 1960 focused on helping African Americans register to vote. In the same decade, poll taxes and literacy tests were abolished.

The C. Act of 1964 represented a piece of legislation that effectively changed the way life was lived in the U.S. President Lyndon Baines Johnson, with his signing of this landmark act, continued the work of President Kennedy and Attorney General Robert Kennedy. This piece of legislation prohibited any kind of discrimination, ranging from lodging to service in restaurants, to that practiced by potential employers. To add teeth to the legislation, federal funding could be denied if discrimination occurred. In 1968, legislation prohibiting housing discrimination was passed.

Dr. Martin Luther King Jr. and Medgar Evers were among the leaders of the civil rights movement. King espoused nonviolent protest, modeling himself on Gandhi. In the March on Washington, he encouraged people to follow his methods, despite all the violence they endured, including the church bombing that caused loss of life in Birmingham, Alabama.

There is a great deal of literature for youth that deals with these times, and with the struggle that preceded the C. Julius LESTER's *To Be a Slave* (1968) chronicled what life was like for slaves, while *The Planet of Junior Brown* by Virginia HAMILTON (1971) followed two African American youths in modern-day New York. *Philip Hall Likes Me, I Reckon Maybe* by Bette GREENE (1974) follows Beth, a young black girl in sixth grade, through a crush on the inestimable Philip Hall. Hamilton's books about *The House of Dies Drear* offer an interesting point and counterpoint between the times of the Underground Railroad and today, as Thomas explores his new home. In *Northern Fried Chicken* (1983) by Roni Schotter, a Jewish girl from the 1960s becomes possessed by the events of the times. Brenda Scott WILKINSON'S *Not Separate, Not Equal* (1987) explores the integration of a Georgia high school through the eyes of Malene, a young African American. *Freedom Songs* (1991) by Yvette Moore chronicles Sheryl's determination to find a way to aid her uncle and his fellow Freedom Riders. In Ossie Davis's *Just Like Martin* (1992), Isaac Stone practices nonviolence in the face of violence in 1963. Nothing is the same for the Watson family after *The Watsons Go to Birmingham, 1963* (1995), by Christopher Paul CURTIS, which was both a Coretta Scott King and a Newbery Honor Book. Vaunda Micheaux Nelson describes the sudden interest the town of Mayfield experiences in the civil rights movement when one of their own becomes a Freedom Rider. *Joseph's Choice, 1861,* by Bonnie Pryor (2000), serves as a precursor to some of the moral choices young people would face a century later, as Joseph is torn between the views held by the abolitionists versus those held by the slave owners. Ann M. Martin's characters must wrestle with everyday life as well as school integration in *Belle Teal* (2001). The Ku Klux Klan spars with supporters of civil rights in Mississippi and a young boy's loyalties are tested in John Armistead's *The Return of Gabriel* (2002). In Kristi Collier's *Jericho Walls* (2002) set in 1957, a new relationship makes a young girl confront the mores of the time. *Black Angels* by Rita MURPHY (2002) chronicles the effects that the civil rights movement has on one family through the eyes of Celli, who at eleven must face not only shifting attitudes but family secrets.

These titles are only some of the many absorbing books about a time that continues to reverberate in the U.S. To more fully understand racial dynamics in this country today, it may be helpful for young people to read about a time that was not so long ago in our country's history. The books above offer a sampling of characters that were impacted by the civil rights movement. The movement changes the lives of the people in each story, regardless of race and sex. Certain stories struggle with the philosophy of civil rights, while others experience the forces of the time more immediately, through protests, school integration, or personal losses. However, the changes that the civil rights movement brought about cannot be underestimated despite the imperfection of the implementation that followed. These stories offer a glimpse of that world through a panoply of characters' experiences and impressions.

BIBLIOGRAPHY: "Civil Rights," *World Book Encyclopedia,* vol. 4 (Ci-Cz), 2002; www.amazon.com; www.bccls.org; http://novelst4.epnet.com

JEANNE MARIE RYAN

CLAPP, Patricia

Author, playwright, b. 9 June 1912, Boston, Massachusetts

Involvement in a community theater prompted C. to become a playwright, after she was asked to produce a play and was unable to find an appropriate play for the children's theater group. As a result she began publishing her own manuscripts and continued to do so for over a decade.

Writing novels also began in the same unassuming way. After compiling genealogical research for FAMILY members, she began writing a story about one of the characters. *Constance: A Story of Plymouth* (1969) was her first novel, a very successful book, leading her to complete more historical writings. With the success of these novels, her writing became an enjoyable activity she could complete in accordance with her own schedule.

AWARDS: *Constance: A Story of Early Plymouth:* National Book Award runner-up and Lewis Carroll Shelf Award; *Witches' Children: A Story of Salem:* 1982 ALA Best Book for Young Adult citation.

FURTHER WORKS: NOVELS: *Jane-Emily,* 1969; *King of the Dollhouse,* 1974; *Dr. Elizabeth: The Story of the First Woman Doctor,* 1974; *I'm Deborah Sampson: A Soldier in the War of the Revolution,* 1977; *Witches' Children: A Story of Salem; The Tamarack Tree: A Novel of the Siege of Vicksburg,* 1986. PLAYS: *Peggy's on the Phone,* 1956; *Smart Enough to Be Dumb,* 1956; *The Incompleted Pass,* 1957: *Her Kissin' Cousin,* 1957; *The Girl Out Front,* 1958; *The Ghost of a Chance,* 1958; *The Curley Tale,* 1958; *Inquire Within,* 1959; *The Girl Whose Fortune Sought Her,* 1959; *Edie-across-the-Street,* 1960; *Never Keep Him Waiting,* 1961; *Red Heels and Roses,* 1961; *If a Body Meet a Body,* 1963; *Now Hear This,* 1963; *The Magic Bookshelf,* 1966; *The Other Side of the Wall,* 1969; *The Do-Nothing Frog,* 1970; *The Invisible Dragon,* 1971; *A Specially Wonderful Day,* 1972; *The Toys*

Take over Christmas, 1977; *Mudcake Princess,* 1979; *The Truly Remarkable Puss in Boots,* 1979.

BIBLIOGRAPHY: *Contemporary Authors Online,* 2002.

PATRICIA KEANE

CLARKE, Arthur C.

Author, b. 16 December 1917, Minehead, Somersetshire, England

C. is known not only for his SCIENCE FICTION, but also for his scientific and technical writing on a range of topics including underwater diving, space exploration, aeronautics, and scientific extrapolation. C.'s science fiction novels *Childhood's End* (1953) and *Rendezvous with Rama* (1973, adapted edition 1979) are widely recognized as classics of the genre. *Rendezvous with Rama* won four major awards.

In 1941, C. volunteered for the Royal Air Force where he became a radar instructor and taught himself mathematical and electronics theory. His only non-science-fiction novel, *Glide Path,* is based on this work. After the war he entered college and obtained a degree in physics and applied mathematics. After two years as an assistant editor for a technical journal, he published *Childhood's End* and then embarked on a full-time writing career. *The Exploration of Space* (1952), one of his first nonfiction titles, was the first science book ever chosen as a Book-of-the-Month Club selection.

In 1954, C. wrote to Dr. Harry Wexler, then chief of the Scientific Services Division, U.S. Weather Bureau, about satellite applications for weather forecasting. Of these communications, a new branch of meteorology was born. Dr. Wexler became the driving force for the use of rockets and satellites for meteorological research and operations.

2001: A Space Odyssey (1968), co-written with director Stanley Kubrick, has been celebrated as one of the most important science-fiction films ever made. C. and Kubrick worked for four years on the film version. The book, based on the movie, was actually written in collaboration with Kubrick, who was simultaneously filming it. The men received an Academy Award nomination for the film version of *2001: A Space Odyssey.*

During 1968–70 C. commented on the Apollo missions with Walter Cronkite on CBS television. He also hosted his own television series, *Arthur C. Clarke's Mysterious World* (1980), and *Arthur C.*

Clarke's World of Strange Powers (1984) that have been aired in many countries. Although he had insisted it was impossible to write a sequel to *2001,* he published *2010: Odyssey Two* in 1982, *2061: Odyssey Three* in 1988, and *3001: The Final Odyssey* in 1997. Buzz Aldrin, who made his historic Apollo XI moonwalk in 1969, says he couldn't put the book down. "It is a tour de force that finally answers the questions that sparked the imaginations of an entire generation."

In 2000, C. was presented the "Award of Knight Bachelor" at a ceremony in Colombo, Sri Lanka, where he has lived since 1956. He has been doing underwater exploration along that coast and the Great Barrier Reef.

AWARDS: Academy Award nomination for *2001: A Space Odyssey;* Award of Knight Bachelor, 2000.

SELECT FURTHER WORKS: *The City and the Stars,* 1956; *The Nine Billion Names of God,* 1967; many nonfiction works on space travel.

BIBLIOGRAPHY: Agel, Jerome, (Ed.), *The Making of Kubrick's 2001,* New American Library, 1970; McAleer, Neil, *Arthur C. Clarke: The Authorized Biography.* Chicago: Contemporary Books; 1992; Slusser, George Edgar, *The Space Odysseys of Arthur C. Clarke,* Borgo, 1978; *Something about the Author,* Gale Research: Detroit, Mich., 1971–, Vol. 115, 2000, pp. 26–37; The Arthur C. Clarke Institute for Technology and Information, http://www.clarkeinstitute .com/index.html

CHRISTINA MARIA WELTER

CLARKE, Judith

Author, b. 24 August 1943, Sydney, Australia

A former teacher and librarian, AUSTRALIAN author C. illustrates the intricacies of parent-child relationships in her award-winning SERIES of books featuring TEENAGE protagonist, Al Capsella. Praised for its humor and adept handling of serious issues, this series debuts with the book *The Heroic Life of Al Capsella* (1988). In this and subsequent titles *Al Capsella and the Watchdogs* (1990) and *Al Capsella on Holidays* (1992), C. presents comic scenarios in which the wry-voiced hero recounts his struggle for independence from his eccentric, loving parents, who he feels are overly protective and intrusive. Witnessing interactions between his mother and her parents provides Al with room to reflect on their relationship with a certain degree of empathy.

AWARDS: *The Heroic Life of Al Capsella: Booklist* Editors' Choice, 1990, and Best Book for Young Adults by American Library Association, 1990; Victorian Premier's Award for Young Adult Novel, (1998) for *Night Train.*

FURTHER WORKS: *The Boy on the Lake,* 1989; *Teddy B. Zoot,* 1990; *Luna Park at Night,* 1991; *Riff Raff,* 1992; *Friend of My Heart,* 1994; *Big Night Out,* 1995; *Panic Stations,* 1995; *Night Train,* 1998; *Angels Passing By,* 1999; *The Lost Day,* 1999; *Wolf On the Fold,* 2001.

BIBLIOGRAPHY: *Contemporary Authors,* online, 2001. *Something About the Author,* vol. 110, 2000.

ANNETTE MACINTYRE

CLEAVER, (Leroy) Eldridge
Author, b. 31 August 1935, Wabbaseka, Arizona; d. 1 May 1998 Pomona, California

A minister of information and unofficial ambassador of the militant Black Panthers Party, Cleaver "wrote about the need for change, he advocated that blacks use arms in their struggle for liberation, and he felt a black socialist state was needed." He later "converted to Christianity and continued to seek improvements to the black position through nonviolent means." Still later he became a Mormon minister after returning to the U.S. from exile to avoid prison for shooting a policeman and entered into a plea bargain with the FBI.

In 1954, following a conviction for marijuana possession, Cleaver "began a twelve-year cycle that saw him in and out of prisons at Soledad, Folsom, and San Quentin." This cycle ended in parole "only after a number of literary figures petitioned the government on his behalf." While in prison he earned his high-school diploma, and was inspired by books he read to write his first book, *Soul on Ice* (1968) for which he received the Martin Luther King Memorial Prize in 1970. Besides gaining an education while a prisoner at Soledad Prison from 1954–1957 and again from 1958–66, Cleaver owned a boutique in Hollywood from 1978–79, contributed to *Commonweal, National Review,* and other periodicals, and lectured at universities.

Cleaver was a presidential candidate for the Peace and Freedom Party (1968), an independent candidate for Congress in the 8th Congressional District, California (1984) and a lecturer at universities among other careers, including exile in Cuba, Algeria, and France from 1968–75. His works have appeared in anthologies, including *Prize Stories, 1971: The O. Henry Awards,* and he has contributed to *Ramparts.* C. is on many reading lists and has influenced numerous young passionate followers; he is still studied and discussed by TEENS.

AWARDS: Martin Luther King Memorial Prize, 1970, *Soul on Ice.*

SELECT FURTHER WORKS: *C: Post-Prison Writings and Speeches,* 1969; *C.'s Black Papers, 1969; and Soul on Fire,* 1978; *Target Zero: A Life in Writing,* 2006.

BIBLIOGRAPHY: *Contemporary Authors Online,* Gale, 2003. Reproduced in BIOGRAPHY *Resource Center.* Farmington Hills, Mich.: The Gale Group. 2003. http://www.galenet.com/servlet/BioRC; "(Leroy) Eldridge Cleaver." DISCovering Authors. Gale Group, 1999. Reproduced in Discovering Collection. Farmington Hills, Mich.: Gale Group. October, 2001. http://galenet.galegroup.com/servletDC/; "(Leroy) Eldridge Cleaver." *St. James Guide to* YOUNG ADULT *Writers,* 2nd ed. St. James Press, 1999. Reproduced in *Biography Resource Center.* Farmington Hills, Mich.: The Gale Group. 2003. http://www.galenet.com/servlet/BioRC; "Eldridge Cleaver." Newsmakers 1998, Issue 4. Gale Group, 1998. Reproduced in Discovering Collection. Farmington Hills, Mich.: Gale Group. October, 2001. http://galenet.galegroup.com/servlet/DC/; "Eldridge Cleaver." DISCovering Biography. Gale Research, 1997. Reproduced in Discovering Collection. Farmington Hills, Mich.: Gale Group. October, 2001. http://galenet.galegroup.com/servlet DC/; "Eldridge Cleaver." U*X*L Biographies. U*X*L, 1999. Reproduced in Discovering Collection. Farmington Hills, Mich.: Gale Group. October, 2001. http://galenet.galegroup.com/servlet/DC/

SARA MARCUS
AND DANIEL KATZ

CLEMENT-DAVIES, David
Author, b. 6 January 1964, England

C. enjoyed animal fantasies as a child. Reading books like *Watership Down* and *The Jungle Book* provided the groundwork to write animal fantasies himself. But he did not start out knowing he would be an author: "I was sort of wondering what to do, especially after leaving university. I wanted to write, but I wasn't sure how to set about that. Eventually I went on and became a TRAVEL journalist." C. has traveled the world, going on excursions involving scuba diving, mountain climbing, sky diving, sailing, dancing, and other ADVENTURES. He writes about his experiences for a variety of travel PERIODICALS.

C.'s first novel, *Fire Bringer* (1999 in the UK; 2000 in the U.S.), took approximately three years to write. He says, "I had spent far too long worrying about the purpose of writing, whether it was wrong to try and make money from a novel, whether I was any good at it and so on. So one day I simply sat down and got on with it." *Fire Bringer* is an epic animal FANTASY about deer in ancient Scotland. A herd of red deer is saved from a dominating military leader by Rannoch, a young deer with the prophetic oak-leaf mark on his forehead. After growing up in hiding, Rannoch has powers that enable him to overcome evil in this classic struggle. *Horn Book* reviewer Anne St. John wrote, "Although the animals think, speak, and make elaborate plans, otherwise they have the characteristics of wild deer; the descriptive details are obviously the fruit of careful research." C. says he chose deer "quite specifically for their mystery, grace, and nobility," noting that the cycle of the antlers and yearly ruts was "moving to me about the struggle intrinsic in all life."

Fire Bringer is much more than a story about deer in the wild. It is also a commentary on human behavior, with many parallels to 20th-century political figures and events. C. told *Preview Magazine*, "I did not set out to write a political allegory as such . . . but I do come from a political background . . . and a sense of history and politics naturally informed my story. Like no other century, the twentieth evokes in me a sense of horror and potential cataclysm, and if *Fire Bringer* could influence us even remotely to avoid such extremism in the next century, I would be proud."

C.'s second novel for YOUNG ADULTS, *The Sight* (2001), is about wolves in mythic Transylvania. Morgra, a lone wolf with the Sight, the power to see the future, heal, and control others, is shown that a newborn wolf pup has power even stronger than hers. She sets out to gain this power for herself. The pack she hunts will not give in easily, setting in motion a battle that involves all of nature.

In both of C.'s novels, strong female characters drive the stories. A *Publishers Weekly* review of *The Sight* comments, "Strong female characters also provide a refreshing change to the often male-dominated SCIENCE-FICTION/fantasy field." C. says he did not set out to write strong heroines, but instead found his female characters growing increasingly strong as he wrote.

"To entertain, move, or inspire a reader is, after all, why writers bother in the first place," C. told *Preview Magazine*, recalling a letter he received from a twelve-year-old saying she thought *Fire Bringer* was the best book she had ever read. C. is proud to be called a writer, crediting his agent, Gina Pollinger, with first stating the fact. He said, "When you begin to talk of yourself as a 'writer,' it gives you a kind of new authority. You don't feel such a sham anymore, going into a pub and saying, 'I'm a writer.'"

AWARDS: Best Books for Young Adults, American Library Association, 2002 for *Fire Bringer*.

FURTHER WORKS: The Nutcracker, 1999; *Trojan Horse*, 1999; *Zo-Zo Leaves His Hole*, 1999; *Spirit: Stallion of the Cimarron*, 2002; *Alchemist of Barbal*, 2005.

BIBLIOGRAPHY: *Contemporary Authors Online*, Gale, 2002; *Preview Magazine*, Putnam Penguin Books for Young Readers, V. 2, No. 3, Fall 2000; Pan MacMillan Author BIOGRAPHY, http://www.panmacmillan.com.au / resources / AP-DavidClement-Davies2002.pdf; Book Page Interview by Michael Sims, http://www.bookpage.com/0010bp/david_clement_davies.html; wwwbarnesandnoble.com

JENNA OBEE

COFER, Judith Ortiz
Author, b. 24 February 1952, Hormigueros, Puerto Rico

C. was born in Puerto Rico but moved to Paterson, New Jersey, as a young child. Her experiences, and therefore her writings, have been peppered with information from both of the worlds she has inhabited. When C. was a child, she was always seeking ways to express herself creatively. She says that she was always acting out plays that she had created and telling her father stories. C. earned her bachelor's degree in English from Augusta College in Augusta, Georgia, and her master's degree in English from Florida Atlantic University. Her writing didn't come to fruition until she began to write POETRY as a graduate student. C.'s first poem was published when she was twenty-eight years old. Since that time, C. has written poetry, essays and SHORT STORIES, novels and, nonfiction. She continues to set aside time every day to write.

C.'s first novel was *The Line of the Sun* (1991), a story close to her own experience, that involves a Puerto Rican family's adjustment to their new lives in the U.S.

C. received much acclaim for *An Island Like You: Stories of the Barrio* (1998), a book containing twelve stories from the points of view of Puerto Rican TEENS struggling with their LATINO culture in America. Again, C. explored Puerto Rican culture in *The Meaning of Consuelo: A Novel* (2003). This time, however, the action of the story takes place in Puerto Rico during the 1950s and involves a young girl's coming of age. Although published for adults, this book is appealing to teenagers. C. does a superb job of bringing Consuelo and her vibrant FAMILY members and friends to life.

C.'s anthology *Barrio Streets, Carnival Dreams: Three Generations of Latino Artistry* is a collection of poems, art, stories, essays, and memoirs, divided into three sections, that covers roughly the experience of Latinos in 20th-century America. C. continues to explore the power of language in this work, writing in the introduction that "more than any other ethnic group in this country, Latinos have drawn attention to the issue of whether or not one should keep one's language of origin, and they have fought to keep their values—familial, social, and religious—intact." Nowhere is C.'s theme better expressed than in *Barrio Streets'* first poem "Beautiful Spanish" by Magdalena Hijuelos. "I want to dedicate/a love song/to my beautiful Spanish Language/so natural/it flows/as a breeze from the sea."

C. has taught in the Spanish Departments of Indiana University, Columbia University, and New York University. She is the former Director of Latin American Literature at the Americas Society. In addition to her four YOUNG ADULT anthologies, C. has written two adult novels, co-edited an anthology of stories for adults, and edited and written three children's books. She lives in New York City with her husband. C. is currently the Franklin Professor of English and Creative Writing at the University of Georgia.

AWARDS: *Silent Dancing: A Partial Remembrance of a Puerto Rican Childhood* (1998) received a PEN/ Martha Albrand Special Citation in non-fiction; *The Latin Deli: Prose and Poetry* (1993) won the Anisfield Wolf Book Award. *An Island Like You: Stories of the Barrio* (1998) was named a YALSA Best Book for Young Adults and it was awarded the first Pura Belpre medal by REFORMA in 1996; *The Meaning of Consuelo* (2003) was named a YALSA Best Book for Young Adults in 2004.

FURTHER WORKS: *The Latin Deli: Prose and Poetry,* 1993; *"Reaching for the Mainland" and Selected New Poems,* 1997; *The Year of Our Revolution: Selected Poetry and Stories,* 1998; *Silent Dancing: A Partial Remembrance of a Puerto Rican Childhood,* 1998; *Riding Low on the Streets of Gold: Latino Literature for Young Adults,* 2004; *Love Story Beginning in Spanish,* 2004; *Call Me Maria,* 2004.

BIBLIOGRAPHY: Gordon, Stephanie, "An Interview with Judith Ortiz Cofer," *AWP Chronicle,* October/ November 1997, p. 1–9; The author's official website: http://parallel.park.uga.edu/~jcofer/ *Literature Resource Center* online database, Thompson/Gale Group, 2004.

KIMBERLY L. PAONE

COHN, Rachel
Author, b. 14 December 1968, Silver Spring, Maryland

C.'s voice reflects the influence of Judy BLUME, Ellen CONFORD, and Francesca Lia BLOCK. C.'s debut novel, *Gingerbread* (2002), chronicles the life of sixteen-year-old Cyd Charisse, whose mother and stepfather, in an act of desperation, send her to her biological father in New York City. Cyd's cynical, yet vulnerable, character and voice resonated with YOUNG ADULTS. *Gingerbread* was named to the 2003 YALSA Best Books for young Adults List, the Quick Picks for Reluctant Readers List, and several state book award lists. C.'s theme of blended families is taken to another level in *The Steps* (2003), where a daughter's wish to have her father return to her is juxtaposed with his new life and FAMILY in AUSTRALIA.

C. took a different path with her next novel, *Pop Princes* (2004). Wonder Blake and her family mourn the death of her sister, Lucky, whose music career was cut short by her DEATH. Wonder steps into her sister's shoes and learns that music careers are not as glamorous as she thought.

AWARD: *Gingerbread* was named to the 2003 YALSA Quick Picks Top Ten list.

FURTHER WORKS: *Shrimp,* a sequel to *Gingerbread* (2005).

BIBLIOGRAPHY: Rachel Cohn website http://www .rachelcohn.com

TERRY BECK

SUE ELLEN BRIDGERS

MARTHA BROOKS

MICHAEL CADNUM

MICHAEL CART

AIDAN CHAMBERS

ALICE CHILDRESS

JOHN CHRISTOPHER

BROCK COLE

COLE, Brock

Author, b. 29 May 1938, Pittsburgh, Pennsylvania

Although C. moved frequently as a child throughout Midwestern small towns, reading at local libraries was one of the pleasures in his childhood, along with the freedom to explore the many towns in which his family lived.

C., a former philosophy teacher, realized that teaching was not his primary passion and chose to become a writer of children's books. He later became an illustrator of children's books by studying the work of illustrators he admired. In his YOUNG ADULT work, C.'s protagonists are independent TEENAGERS constantly searching for self-identity and frequently having to cope with adult situations and immature adults.

C. wrote his first young adult novel *The Goats* in 1987, a story laced with moral principles. In this novel a boy and a girl of thirteen are sent to camp by their parents. The campers decide the two socially backward campers should be "Goats"; they strip them of their clothing and leave the two stranded on Goats Island overnight in hopes that the isolation somehow will spark attraction for the other sex. The two protagonists or "Goats," Laurie and Howie, decide to escape from the Island on a log. They realize the cruelty of the prank and begin their struggle against the world by stealing clothing, money, and lodging from others to survive. They manage to keep a strong sense of morality by recording the items they have stolen, knowing they will need to pay it all back.

Celine (1989), C.'s second novel, is about a sixteen-year-old artist living with her twenty-two-year-old stepmother. Celine's father left the two for a lecture tour of Europe in hopes that the two young women will somehow hit it off and become closer. Celine also finds herself the permanent babysitter for neighbor Jake Barker. His parents, who are going through a divorce, seem to have abandoned him. Celine is aware of the situation and shows her sense of humor throughout the touchingly heartbreaking scenes. *Celine* was listed as the *Booklist* Editor's Choice citation and Notable Children's Book of the Year citation from *Publishers Weekly*.

C.'s third novel, *The Facts Speak for Themselves* (1997), is written from the point of view of thirteen-year-old Linda, who is being questioned about a murder she witnessed. Linda discovers there are errors in her social worker's transcripts and decides to set the record straight by writing her own version. Linda is the elder of three children of a single mother, and all three have different fathers. Linda takes over looking after her younger siblings when her mother gives up that responsibility. Her mother marries an older man whom she leaves after he suffers a stroke. Linda is left to look after him and a bond develops between the two. Linda eventually returns to her mother who has a new boyfriend, Frank. Frank is jealous of another man's attention to Linda and eventually murders him and commits suicide. Although Linda's voice is flat, matter of fact and shows no emotion, she is as captivating as C.'s protagonists in his two previous novels. Linda speaks of the shocking situations in which she finds herself, and turns them into ordinary reality with her honest and straightforward speech, making the situations all the more poignant and compelling.

In C.'s novels, his heroes and heroines are often innocently involved with issues of power, manipulation, and victimization. C.'s adults are seen as infantile, crass, and incompetent. The author notes that sometimes the most powerful things in a book happen offstage.

C. received a B.A. from Kenyon College and a Ph.D. from the University of Minnesota. He is married to Susan Cole, a classical studies professor, and has two sons.

AWARDS: 1980 Juvenile Award, Friends of American Writers, *The King at the Door; The Indian in the Cupboard;* 1985 California Reading Association, California Young Reader Medal, and Pacific Northwest Library Association Young Readers' Choice Award; 1985 Smarties "Grand Prix" for Children's books, *Gaffer Samson's Luck;* 1986 Parent's Choice Award, Parent's Choice Foundation, *Giant's Toe; The Goats:* 1988 Carl Sandburg Award, *New York Times* notable book, ALA best book for young adults, ALA notable book, all 1987; *The Facts Speak for Themselves: School Library Journal's* Best Books of 1997.

FURTHER WORKS: (Illustrator) Lynne Reid BANKS, *The Indian in the Cupboard,* (Illustrator) Jill Paton Walsh, *Gaffer Samson's Luck,* 1984.

BIBLIOGRAPHY: *Authors and Artists for Young Adults,* vol. 15; *Beecham's Guide to Literature for Young Adults,* vol. 10; *Children's Literature Review,* vol. 18; *Contemporary Authors,* vol. 136; *Junior DISCovering Authors; Major Authors and Illustrators for Children and Young Adults;* Pendergast, Sara & Pendergast, Tom, eds., *St. James Guide to Young Adult Writers,* 1999; *Something about the Author,* vol. 72 and vol. 136.

SUSAN E. MORTON

COLES, William E., Jr.
Author, b. 30 January 1932, Summit, New Jersey

Unimpressed by most novels written for TEENAGERS due to their lack of authenticity, C. wanted to create YA fiction that would portray the teenage experience much more REALISTICALLY. His novels feature young people who learn how to be true to themselves, after an artistic or academic journey of self-discovery. In C.'s first novel *Funnybone* (1992, co-written with Stephen Schwandt), awkward teenager Christine deals with her brother's disappearance by writing in her journal. She creates a fictional court jester named Funnybone, who can express those parts of her personality that she normally keeps hidden. Eventually, however, she discovers the difficulties that arise when you disengage from the world around you.

C.'s next two novels revolve around the history of Pittsburgh, where C. has lived since 1974. In *Another Kind of Monday* (1996), C. combines elements of MYSTERY and ROMANCE as he presents the tale of Mark, a high-school student who finds $300 and instructions for a scavenger hunt hidden inside a library book. The secret quest leads him not only to obscure places connected with his city's history, but also into a burgeoning romance with a beautiful, intelligent girl named Zeena, whom he enlists to help with the search. A 1902 Pittsburgh prison break mentioned briefly in *Another Kind of Monday* provides the central story for *Compass in the Blood* (2001). College freshman Dee tries to uncover the truth behind the sensationalism and rumors surrounding a hundred-year-old scandal involving two incarcerated brothers and the prison warden's wife, Katherine Soffel, who helped them escape. C. uses bits of historical fact and primary documents related to the case to heighten the excitement and suspense of Dee's investigation.

C. has also published several books on the craft of writing. He is a strong advocate for the integration of personal experience into authors' works. Retired from the University of Pittsburgh, where he taught writing and English literature for almost thirty years, C. is working on a sequel to *Compass in the Blood.*

AWARDS: 1992 *Publishers Weekly* Pick of the Lists, *Funnybone;* 1996 American Library Association Best Book for Young Adults, *Another Kind of Monday.*

BIBLIOGRAPHY: *Contemporary Authors Online,* 2001; Schulman, John, "Compass in the Blood," *Pittsburgh Post-Gazette,* August 7, 2001; Steele, Bruce, "Compass in the Blood," *University Times* (faculty and staff newspaper of the University of Pittsburgh), April 4, 2002.

MICHELLE CROWELL FOSSUM

COLLIER, Christopher and James Lincoln
Authors, Christopher b. 29 January 1930, New York City. James L. b. 27 June 1928, New York City

The C. brothers "went into the family business" when they became writers. Their father wrote ADVENTURE fiction as well as some children's books, and they have several aunts, uncles, and cousins who are writers as well. Growing up surrounded by artists and intellectuals, hard work and the joys of accomplishment were stressed. The C.s have written hundreds of books and articles between them and have also collaborated on many books for young people, the most popular of which have been historical fiction.

C.C. is a professor who specializes in early American history. After writing several scholarly books, he approached J.C. with the idea of working together. He felt that their collaboration was both logical and "necessary," if they wanted to make learning history enjoyable. J.C.'s background as a writer of children's novels, hundreds of published MAGAZINE articles, and half a dozen books for adults made him the perfect partner. Together, C.C. conceives the ideas for their novels and does all of the historical research. J.C. then creates characters and plot lines that are both an exciting and interesting way to examine and think about the past and writes the stories.

My Brother Sam is Dead (1974) is the first product of their collaboration. A gripping story of the Revolutionary War, it follows the Meeker family as they battle, both in the WAR and at home, during this complex time. By humanizing these events, C.C. and J.C. are able to teach and inspire discussion while at the same time provide entertainment. This compelling story of a family torn apart by divided loyalties was followed by two sequels: *The Bloody Country* (1976) and *The Winter Hero* (1978). The C. brothers also collaborated on the Arabus family trilogy, which told the story of a black family during the American Revolution. This trilogy is made up of *Jump Ship to Freedom* (1981), *War Comes to Willy Freeman* (1983), and *Who is Carrie?* (1984).

The C. brothers have since written many novels as well as over two dozen nonfiction works in their "Drama of American History" SERIES.

AWARDS: Newbery Honor Book, Jane Addams Honor Book, and National Book Award finalist (both 1975) for *My Brother Sam is Dead;* Notable Children's Trade Book in the Field of Social Studies by the National Council for Social Studies and the Children's Book Council (1981) *Jump Ship to Freedom,* and (1982) for *War Comes to Willy Freeman.*

SELECT FURTHER WORKS: *The Clock,* 1992, *With Every Drop of Blood: A Novel of the Civil War,* 1994, *Drama of American History* series, 1998.

BIBLIOGRAPHY: *Children's Books and Their Creators,* 1995; *Contemporary Authors,* online, 2001; *Fifth Book of Junior Authors & Illustrators,* 1983; *St. James Guide to Young Adult Writers* (2nd edition), 1999; *Writers for Young Adults,* online, 1997.

MEGAN PEARLMAN AND ANDREA LIPINSKI

COLMAN, Penny (Penelope)
Author, b. 2 September 1944, Denver, Colorado

C. spent part of her childhood living on the grounds of a state-run psychiatric hospital in Pennsylvania where her father worked as a psychiatrist. Her parents—her mother was an artist—nurtured C.'s curiosity and sense of adventure. C., her brothers, and her parents performed music together at home, raised a variety of animals on their farm, visited historical sites, and played at all manner of outdoor sports. She recalls her childhood as noisy; this is an accurate description for her adult life as well, as her three sons are close in age.

C. earned degrees from the University of Michigan and Johns Hopkins University, but she devoted most of her attention in the first part of her adult life to raising her sons. Despite the demands of childrearing, C. found time to work as a freelance writer and editor. In addition, C. worked with various social service and religious agencies. In the early 1990s, C. launched herself as a full-time writer with a book on the reformer Dorothea Dix (*Breaking the Chains: The Crusade of Dorothea Lynde Dix,* 1992) and a second one on women spies of the Civil War (*Spies! Women and the Civil War,* 1992).

In addition to her mother, C. credits one of her junior-high school history teachers with encouraging her love of history. This affection for history and her interest in social reform and justice issues spurred C.

to write a number of historical works for young people, highlighting often neglected topics concerning women. In addition to Dix, C.'s BIOGRAPHIES have highlighted women such as Fannie Lou Hamer, the CIVIL RIGHTS activist: Frances Perkins, the first woman to serve as a cabinet secretary in the United States; Madame C.J. Walker, the AFRICAN AMERICAN entrepreneur, and Mother Jones, the labor reformer. Other works by C. examine women in unconventional roles (e.g., *Where the Action Was: Women WAR Correspondents in World War II,* 2002), general reform issues (e.g., *Strike!: The Bitter Struggle of American Workers from Colonial Times to the Present,* 1995), general women's histories (e.g., *Girls! A History of Growing Up Female in America,* 2000), and social histories (e.g., *Corpses, Coffins, and Crypts: A History of Burial,* 1997).

Whatever the subject matter C. takes on, she does so with a great respect for her topic and her craft. Critics laud her meticulous and extensive research that enables her to incorporate primary sources, meaningful photographs, and the voices of her subjects in the books she writes. Reviewers also single out C.'s ability to engage the reader through brisk, straightforward texts that avoid politicizing potentially charged issues. C. views her role as a writer as one in which she accompanies readers through her books, helping them negotiate information with solid organizational structures, sensitivity, and humor.

In addition to writing, C. teaches at Columbia University.

AWARDS: *Rosie the Riveter:* 1995 Orbis Pictus Honor Award and 1996 American Library Association's Notable Books for Children; 1997 American Library Association's Best Books for YOUNG ADULTS, *Corpses, Crypts, and Coffins;* 2003 American Library Association's Notable Books for Children, *Where the Action Was.*

SELECT FURTHER WORKS: *Fannie Lou Hamer and the Fight for the Vote,* 1993; *A Woman Unafraid: The Achievements of Frances Perkins,* 1993; *Madame C. J. Walker: Building a Business Empire,* 1994; *Mother Jones and the March of the Mill Children,* 1994; *Toilets, Bathtubs, Sinks and Sewers: The History of the Bathroom,* 1994; *Women in Society: United States,* 1994; *Rosie the Riveter: Women Working on the Home Front in World War II,* 1995.

BIBLIOGRAPHY: Colman, Penny (n.d.), Personal webpage, Retrieved from http://ourworld.compuserve.com/homepages/pennycolman/; Delisio, Ellen R,

"News from the Front: Women Reporters of World War II. Wire Side Chat," *Education World,* 2002; Retrieved from http://www.education-world.com/a_curr/curr405.shtml; "Penny Colman." *Authors and Artists for Young Adults,* Vol. 42, 2002; Reproduced in Biography Resource Center, 2003. http://www.galenet.com/servlet/BioRC

CAROL TILLEY

COMAN, Carolyn
Author, b. n.d., Evanston, Illinois

When C. was growing up, she moved around quite a bit, and found herself attending a wide array of private, parochial, and public schools in Maryland, Connecticut, Indiana, New York, and New Jersey. She wrote her first story in the fourth grade (about the Easter Bunny) and, ever since, dreamed of becoming a writer. C. attended Douglass College at Rutgers University in New Brunswick, New Jersey; she later transferred to Hampshire College in Amherst, Massachusetts, where she studied writing and earned a degree. For many years, C. practiced bookbinding, first as an apprentice with master bookbinder, Arnos Werner, then in her own bindery, and finally in partnership with Nancy Southworth. C. worked as an editor and a writing instructor at Harvard Extension and Harvard Summer School, but her ultimate goal was always to become a writer.

C. began her writing career with the publication of a work she edited, *Body and Soul: Ten American Women* (1988) and followed that with a children's PICTURE BOOK titled *Losing Things at Mr. Mudd's* (1992), but it wasn't until the publication of *Tell Me Everything* (1993) that C. began to write YOUNG ADULT novels.

In all four of C.'s young adult books to date, young people who have suffered great hardship in their lives are presented with unique, touching, relentless stories to tell. C. has talent for introducing her characters to readers in a sympathetic yet unsentimental light. Her candor and truthfulness is what makes her characters flawed yet irresistibly interesting.

In *What Jamie Saw* (1995), which earned C. a Newbery Honor award, nine-year-old Jamie witnesses a horrible act of violence as his stepfather hurls Jamie's baby sister across the room. Although the baby is rescued by her mother, Jamie is still traumatized. Jamie's fledgling family runs away from his stepfather in the middle of the night and takes refuge with his mother's friend, Earl. However, instead of starting over, Jamie and his mother enter a time of near-hibernation. Jamie stops going to school and his mother quits her job. The two continue on this dead-end track until Jamie's teacher intervenes; they are saved from themselves and are able to rejoin the world outside. C.'s unflinching storytelling makes this a riveting read. C. sees through Jamie's eyes and relates the events of his story with an honesty that seemingly only a child would be able to muster. One might wonder why this book would be labeled as YA given the protagonist's young age, however, it is written with the kind of subject matter and subtlety that only older, more advanced readers can appreciate fully.

C.'s next novel, *Bee + Jacky* (1998), tackled an even more sensitive topic—sexual abuse between a brother and a sister. Thirteen-year-old Bee and seventeen-year-old Jacky are left alone over a long weekend, and they take this opportunity to reenact a dark search-and-rescue game they played several years before. This game was based on their father's participation in the Vietnam War and ended with Jacky locating Bee, attacking and raping her. This reenactment brings back traumatic memories for Bee, and she snaps—she begins hallucinating, she propositions her brother, walks around outdoors in the nude—and the roles are reversed when Jacky has to then care for his sister and face the demons of what he has done. This is, once again, not a story for the very young, or the faint of heart. The issues discussed are difficult, and the raw emotion and obvious trauma experienced by this entire FAMILY are not something that can be taken lightly. However, C. once again manages to portray the humanity of all of her characters, even Jacky, and allows her readers a rare view into the psyche of these damaged people.

C.'s more recent novel, *Many Stones* (2000), was awarded a PRINTZ HONOR and received many other accolades. In it, C. shows her wide-ranging versatility once more, as teenager Berry Morgan travels to South Africa with her estranged father to memorialize her sister Laura at the site of her murder. The story was inspired by the real-life murder of Amy Biehl, a Fulbright scholarship recipient working in South Africa, and C. contacted the Biehl family to request permission to draw on their daughter's experiences in the book. While much of the post-apartheid climate and political realities of South Africa are included, the story is just as much about grief, the strained relationship between a father and his TEENAGE daughter, and the coming-of-age of a young person in an emotionally grueling situation. Finely wrought, *Many Stones* not only gives American teenagers the opportunity to experience vicariously the unrest in South Africa; it also affords them the experience of walking in the shoes of young Berry, with whom many would be able to relate easily and on many different levels.

C.'s solid contribution to young adult literature can certainly be credited for the enjoyment, education, and enlightenment of large numbers of young people. It is through her unforgettable characters that readers can see bits of themselves or their peers, learn from their mistakes, or recognize the horrors and redemption that can be found in human nature.

C. is currently a faculty member at Vermont College, teaching in its MFA Writing for Children program. She is the mother of two and lives in Massachusetts.

AWARDS: *Body and Soul: Ten American Women* (1988) was named a YALSA Best Book for Young Adults. *What Jamie Saw* (1995) received a Newbery Honor book, was a National Book Award finalist, and was on both the *Booklist* Editor's Choice and Children's Notables lists. *Many Stones* (2000) received a Printz Honor, was a National Book Award finalist, received the *School Library Journal* Best Books of the Year citation and *Booklist* Top of the List citation, and was named a YALSA Best Book for Young Adults.

FURTHER WORKS: *Tell Me Everything,* 1994; *Beyond the Textbook: Teaching History Using Documents and Primary Sources* [editor], 1996; *Inside the Classroom: Teaching Kindergarten and First Grade* [editor], 1996.

BIBLIOGRAPHY: *Authors & Artists for Young Adults,* vol. 41, 2001; *Something About the Author,* vol. 127, 2002; http://www.teenreads.com, interview: 1/14/2000.

KIMBERLY L. PAONE

CONFORD, Ellen
Author, b. 20 March 1942, New York City

C. is known for her children's books such as the *Annabel the Actress* and *Jenny Archer* SERIES and for her fast-paced, humorous, and entertaining stories for children. YA Characters in her YA novels are generally young girls dealing with problems of adolescence

such as ROMANCE, popularity, and peer pressure. Novels include *Dear Lovey Hart, I Am Desperate* (1975), *And This Is Laura* (1977), *Dear Mom, Get Me Out of Here* (1992), and *I Love You, I Hate You, Get Lost* (1994). *Crush* (1998) is a collection of SHORT STORIES about a group of high-school students planning for the Valentine's Day dance. A rare departure from C.'s usual themes can be found in *To All My Fans, With Love, From Sylvie* (1982), which deals with such topics as sexual abuse and running away. Several of C.'s books have been adapted for television, including *Dear Lovey Hart, I Am Desperate* and *And This Is Laura.*

AWARDS: Best Book of the Year Citation: Best Book of International Interest Citation, Best Book Of the Year for Children, Parents' Choice Award, Northwestern Young Readers Choice Award.

SELECT FURTHER WORKS: *The Alfred G. Graebner Memorial High School Handbook of Rules and Regulations,* 1976: *We Interrupt this Semester for an Important Bulletin,* 1979; *Anything for a Friend,* 1979; *Seven Days to a Brand-New Me,* 1981; *If This Is Love, I'll Take Spaghetti,* 1983; *You Never Can Tell,* 1984; *A Royal Pain,* 1986; *Diary of a Monster's Son,* 1999.

BIBLIOGRAPHY: *Children's Books and Their Creators,* 1995; *Contemporary Authors,* online, 2002; *St. James Guide to Young Adult Writers* 2d ed., 1999; *Twentieth-Century Children's Writers* 4th ed., 1995.

ANDREA LIPINSKI

CONLY, Jane Leslie
Author, b. 1948, Virginia

C. was born to a pair of writers and editors, Robert C. O'BRIEN and Sally (McCasin) and began writing stories in the first grade. In 1974, her father, author of *Mrs. Frisby and the Rats of NIMH,* realized he was dying and asked his daughter to complete his last novel, *Z for Zachariah.* This became a family effort—her mother edited the novel.

C. began writing two novels "based on the characters and situations first developed in her father's work." Both *Rasco and The Rats of NIMH* (1986) and *R-T, Margaret, and the Rats of NIMH* (1990) are narratives of the next generation of super-intelligent rats. However, C. adds two new dimensions to these novels—she includes people and a greater degree of human traits in the rats.

In 1993, C. departed from the NIMH SERIES with *Crazy Lady!* focusing solely on people. There is a similar theme, however, of a child feeling out of place in his life. Following her father's footsteps, C. earned a Newbery Honor Book citation for this novel. *Trout Summer* (1995) again deals with children who feel as if they are outsiders. As she did in *Crazy Lady!*, C. portrays adult characters in depth.

Mother of a boy and a girl, C. holds a degree from Smith College (1971) and graduated from the Writing Seminar Program at the Johns Hopkins University in 1974.

AWARDS: Newbery Honors Book Award, *Crazy Lady!*

FURTHER WORKS: *When No One Was Watching,* 1998; *While No One Was Watching,* 2000; *What Happened on Planet Kid,* 2002; *The Rudest Alien on Earth,* 2002; *In the Night, on Lanvale Street,* 2005.

BIBLIOGRAPHY: "Jane Leslie Conly." U*X*L Junior DISCovering Authors. U*X*L, 1998. Reproduced in Discovering Collection, October 2001. http://gale net.galegroup.com/servletDC/

SARA MARCUS

CONRAD, Pam
Author, b. 18 June 1947, New York City; d. 22 January 1996, Long Island, New York

With a belief that stories are channeled through writers and not from them, C. created characters that dealt sensitively with believable, though tragic situations. In both historical settings and current situations, her use of fresh, simplistic descriptions leave memorable insights for readers of all ages. Her artistry was first evident in *Prairie Songs* (1985), the story of a well-bred woman moving from New York to the West who, unable to adjust to pioneer life, eventually loses her sanity when her baby dies during childbirth. Told through the eyes of the child Louisa who lives in a sod house and admires this doctor's wife, the story uses powerful characterization to share the realities of prairie life. A later novel, *Prairie Vision: The Life and Times of Solomon Butcher* (1993), revisits the prairie as C. further describes pioneer life and Butcher's experiences as a photographer and homesteader in the late 19th century.

Strong adolescent characters also are part of C.'s more contemporary novels. *Holding Me Here* (1986) focuses on a fourteen-year-old girl coping with her parents' divorce and *What I Did for Roman* (1987) tells of another teen's search for the father she has

never seen. Both explore the emotional coping and resulting relationships that carry the plot.

My Daniel (1989), while written for a younger audience, skillfully weaves the past and present when a grandmother shares with her grandchildren a search for dinosaur remains in the late 19th century. The grandmother takes the children to a museum and points out the remains that she and her brother Daniel found during childhood on their Nebraska farm. In her narrative the reader is absorbed in the rich descriptions of prairie life. C. again uses the genre of historical fiction as she takes readers on a personal journey to view the discovery of the new world in *Pedro's Journal: A Voyage with Christopher Columbus, August 3, 1492–February 14, 1493* (1991). This account was praised as being vivid, concise, and pleasing when it appeared, along with numerous others, the year before the 500–year commemoration of Columbus's journey.

During a writing career that ended with her death in 1996, C. received numerous awards, including the ALA notable book and Best Book for YOUNG ADULT citations, NCSS and CBC notable trade books in the field of social sciences citation, and Teachers' Choices citation from IRA. Two daughters, Johanna and Sarah, survive C. Sarah writes and illustrates books for young people.

AWARDS: *Prairie Songs:* 1986 *Boston Globe–Horn Book* Award, IRA Children's Book Award; 1989 Parents' Choice Award for Children's Books Parents' Choice Foundation, *The Tub People: Stonewords: A Ghost Story:* 1990 *Boston Globe–Horn Book* Honor, 1991 Edgar Award; 1992 Orbitus Pictus Award, *Prairie Vision: The Life and Times of Solomon Butcher.*

FURTHER WORKS: *Taking the Ferry Home,* 1988; *Stonewords; A Ghost Story,* 1990; *Zoe Rising,* 1996; *Our House,* 2005.

BIBLIOGRAPHY: *Children's Literature Review, 18,* 1989; *Contemporary Authors on Line,* 2003; *Something about the Author* AUTOBIOGRAPHY Series, *19,* 1995; *St. James Guide to Young Adult Writers,* 1999.

JANELLE B. MATHIS

CONROY, Pat
Author, b. 26 October 1945, Atlanta, Georgia

In spite of—or perhaps because of—his violent father Donald's rampages, C. became one of the most respected novelists in America. Drawing heavily from his troubled upbringing, C. once said his abusive father's biggest mistake was allowing a novelist "who remembered every single violent act" to survive the turmoil. "My father's violence is the central fact of my art and my life," he says in his BIOGRAPHY. In fact, his father's brutality is documented in both *The Great Santini* (1976) and *The Prince of Tides* (1986).

C. is the oldest of seven children. His mother Peg, a southern belle who adopted the persona of Scarlett O'Hara and read *Gone with the Wind* to young C. as a bedtime story, was fragile and ineffective in harboring either her children or herself from her husband's abuse. A Marine Corps officer, C.'s father frequently moved his family from base to base, school to school.

The Citadel Military Academy in Charleston, South Carolina, became one of C.'s first tastes of stability. While at the Academy, C. wrote *The Boo* (1970), a tribute to a Citadel teacher who offered compassion and fair punishment for cadets in need of direction. "It is a book without a single strength," he said, "except for the passionate impulse which led me to write it in the first place." All was not well at the Citadel, as is reflected in *The Lords of Discipline* (1980). The book's brutally honest portrayal of the Citadel moved the school to bar C. from campus activities. He was considered a traitor of substantial merit until the ban was lifted and he was awarded an honorary doctorate in October 2000.

C. graduated from the Citadel and went on to teach impoverished children in a one-room schoolhouse on Daufuskie Island off the South Carolina coast. After the Peace Corps ignored his application, C. used the challenge of teaching to try to better the world, and found the experience both rewarding and discouraging. He was able to excite the poverty-stricken young people and help them learn, but was fired by a wary school board for his creative enthusiasm. *The Water Is Wide* (1972), an autobiographical work about the experience, was adapted to the big screen by director Martin Ritt as *Conrack* (1974), a film starring Jon Voight.

His next autobiographical study, *The Great Santini,* evoked personal chaos for C. and his family. Both C.'s parents and his own marriage crumbled in the aftermath of a book that exposed so many family secrets. The novel's indictment of his father was so powerful that his mother gave the judge a copy as evidence to support her application for divorce.

The Lords of Discipline received critical reviews and harsh responses from his alma mater. *The Prince of Tides* was written shortly after C. remarried and moved from Atlanta to Rome. Considered his most popular book, it has sold more than five million copies and secured C.'s status as a best-selling American storyteller.

While touring for his next novel, *Beach Music* (1995), two events set the wheels of change in motion. C.'s second wife served him with divorce papers, and former basketball team members from the Citadel Bulldogs drifted back into his life. With their support, he weathered the disintegration of his marriage and started what would become *My Losing Season* (2002), another autobiographical work of nonfiction based on his days as an awkward but determined young athlete. In *My Losing Season,* C. says, "Many of my teammates wish that year had never happened," but he admits it was one of the greatest years of his life. "The lessons I learned playing basketball . . . have proven priceless to me as both a writer and a man."

C. now lives on Fripp Island in South Carolina with his wife, novelist Cassandra (Sandra) King.

AWARDS: National Education Association Humanitarian Award; 2003 SEBA Book Award; 2003 Alex Award; 2003 International Scholar-Athlete Hall of Fame; 2002 Listen Up Award; 1998 CNIB Award; 1997 CNIB Award; 1996 Audie Award; 1986 International Book Award; 1981 Lillian Smith Book Award.

BIBLIOGRAPHY: Pat C.'s website: http://www.patconroy.com; "His Own Happy Ending," AP, November 17, 2000—CNN Book News; "I Was Raised by Scarlett O'Hara," February 4, 2000—CNN Book News; "Don't Destroy the State's Best School," *Charleston Post & Courier,* 10 January 1999; "Winning in a Losing Season," *Houston Chronicle,* 22 November 2002.

KELLY MILNER HALLS

CONTEMPORARY CLASSICS

In most determinations of so-called classic novels, whether children's or YOUNG ADULTS or adults, whether MYSTERY or SCIENCE FICTION or ROMANCE or any other category of literature, two criteria are commonly employed: the opinions of experts in the field and the test of time among readers. Using these criteria with respect to young adult works, few would argue that three books merit the label "classic": *The*

Outsiders by S. E. HINTON, *The Pigman* by Paul ZINDEL, and *The Chocolate War* by Robert CORMIER.

Opinion of Experts

In 1988 Ted Hipple conducted a survey among the leaders in young adult literature to solicit their judgments about what they believed were the six best young adult novels of all time. Most of his respondents had been or currently were officers in ALAN (the Assembly on Literature for Adolescents of the National Council of Teachers of English) or had written widely about the field or both. The three novels listed above led the field, with *The Chocolate War* number one. All three titles were mentioned by over 60 percent of the respondents. Clearly these novels are classics according to the experts in 1987 (*English Journal,* December, 1989).

Then, in 2004, Ted Hipple and Jennifer Claiborne surveyed a similar set of experts and asked them the same question: what are the best young adult novels of all time? *The Chocolate War* again led the field, *The Outsiders* was ranked fourth, and *The Pigman* was fifteenth, among a total count of 159 novels named by 79 respondents (*English Journal,* January, 2005).

The Test of Time

This criterion must be considered differently for young adult works than for those written for adults, with the standard being that novels must be read by succeeding generations after their publication. Most demographers consider an adult generation to be about twenty years and, thus, a novel such as *The Adventures of Huckleberry Finn* by Mark Twain, written in 1884, has been widely read for over six generations. Yet a generation of young adult readers is far different, usually considered to be about six years, from ages eleven to seventeen. *The Outsiders* was published in 1967, *The Pigman* in 1968, and *The Chocolate War* in 1973. The first two have been read by six generations of members of their intended audience, matching *Huck Finn,* and the third by five generations. All three continue to be widely read.

TED HIPPLE

(Ted Hipple is one of the three people to whom this encyclopedia is dedicated. He died late in 2004.)

THE BEST YA NOVELS OF ALL TIME
A 2004 SURVEY
prepared by
Ted Hipple and Jennifer Claiborne
University of Tennessee

In all, 149 different novels were named from 77 respondents. These led the list, with the parenthetic number representing the votes each received: *The Chocolate War* by Robert Cormier (27); *The Giver* by Lois LOWRY (22); *Speak* by Lori Halse Anderson (19); *The Outsiders* by S. E. Hinton (15); *Hatchet* by Gary Paulsen (13); *Holes* by Louis SACHAR (13); *Monster* by Walter Dean Myers (13); *Staying Fat for Sarah Byrnes* by Chris CRUTCHER (13); *Make Lemonade* by Euwer WOLFF (12); *Out of the Dust* by Karen Hesse (11); *The Pigman* by Paul Zindel (10); *Fallen Angels* by Walter Dean Myers (8); *Weetzie Bat* by Francesca Lia BLOCK (8); *Chinese Handcuffs* by Chris Crutcher (7); *The Watsons Go to Birmingham, 1963* by Christopher Paul CURTIS (7); *The Catcher in the Rye* by J.D. SALINGER (6); *I Am the Cheese* by Robert Cormier (6); *Stargirl* by Jerry SPINELLI (6); *After the First Death* by Robert Cormier (5); *Annie on my Mind* by Nancy GARDEN (5); *Ironman* by Chris Crutcher (5); *Roll of Thunder, Hear My Cry* by Mildred Taylor (5). Ted Hipple conducted a similar survey in 1987. The top three books in that survey were *The Chocolate War, The Outsiders,* and *The Pigman.*

COOK, Robin
Author, b. 4 May 1940, New York City

A practicing physician specializing in eye surgery, C. is the author of more than twenty medical thrillers. His novels are regularly described as "fast-paced" and "spine-tingling," thus he enjoys a myriad of fans from both the YA and adult audiences.

C.'s most commercially successful book to date is *Coma* (1977), where unsuspecting patients are rendered comatose until their organs can be harvested and sold on the black market. Although *Coma* was only C.'s second book, his success was by no means a matter of luck. In 1975, before beginning his blockbuster, C. spent six months reading and analyzing over one hundred bestsellers. Noting the varying formulas of most suspense-oriented novels, C. decided early on that he would write thrillers. What makes C.'s stories unique, though, is his ability to infuse his tales with his "behind-the-curtain" knowledge of the medical field.

C. is not the first physician to coalesce his medical expertise with an aptitude for writing. In this way, he stands in the company of William Carlos Williams, Oliver Sacks, and Richard Selzer. Michael Crichton is C.'s contemporary in the genre of medical thrillers, a genre which may be traced all the way back to Sir Arthur Conan Doyle. Doyle was the first physician to enjoy wide popularity with his stories of Sherlock Holmes, who solved crimes by employing a scientific approach.

What distinguishes C. from other physicians-turned-authors is the feverish pace with which he publishes his books, many of which become best-sellers. Since the publication of *Coma,* C. has produced a new book almost every year. Although some reviewers have criticized C.'s stories for being formulaic—the only works C. has written that do not employ the conventions of his medical thrillers are *The Year of the Intern* (1972), *Sphinx* (1979), and, at least to a certain extent, *Abduction* (2000)—no one can disparage his careful research or the ultimate entertainment inherent in his novels.

Lorena Stookey (1996) believes that C.'s contribution to literature and modern culture is significant in that his writing informs the public on medical issues that are otherwise unavailable to them. This is especially valuable in a time when the health-care industry bases so many of its decisions on the marketplace. Stookey writes, "His overviews of . . . social institutions such as medicine and law dramatically reveal many of the ways in which the self-interests of these professions impinge upon the public welfare" (p. 3).

When C. is not practicing medicine or writing another page-turner, he enjoys renovating houses and apartments as well as skiing, surfing, painting, cooking, playing tennis . . . to name a few of his other interests. He currently resides in Naples, Florida.

FURTHER WORKS: *Brain,* 1981; *Fever,* 1982; *Godplayer,* 1983; *Mindbend,* 1985; *Outbreak,* 1987; *Mortal Fear,* 1988; *Mutation,* 1989; *Harmful Intent,* 1990; *Vital Signs,* 1990; *Blindsight,* 1991; *Terminal,* 1992; *Fatal Cure,* 1994; *Three Complete Novels* (includes *Harmful Intent, Vital Signs,* and *Blindsight*), 1994; *Acceptable Risk,* 1995; *Contagion,* 1995; *Invasion,* 1997; *Chromosome 6,* 1997; *Robin Cook: Three Complete Novels* (includes *Terminal, Fatal Cure,* and *Acceptable Risk*), 1997; *Toxin,* 1998; *Vector,* 1999; *Shock,* 2001; *Seizure,* 2002; *Marker,* 2005.

BIBLIOGRAPHY: Godat, C. (1997). Robin Cook: Overview. In D. Mote (Ed.), *Contemporary popular writers: Vol. 14* (pp. 94–95). Detroit, MI: St. James Press; *Literature resource center-author resource pages: Robin Cook.* (n.d.) Retrieved February 25, 2004, from http://www.galenet.com; Stookey, L. L. (1996) *Robin Cook: A critical companion.* In K.G. Klein (Series Ed.), *Critical companions to popular contemporary writers.* Westport, CT: Greenwood Press.

SHANNON COLLINS

COONEY, Caroline
Author, b. 1947, Old Greenwich, Connecticut

Publishing since 1981, C. is the prolific author of dozens of popular YA novels. A master of many genres, C. has had success in writing ADVENTURE, historical fiction, HORROR, MYSTERY/SUSPENSE, REALISM, and ROMANCE. C. novels typically feature TEENAGE protagonists who struggle to come to terms with age-appropriate concerns relating to FAMILY, identity, school, and other issues. Fast-paced and entertaining, stories feature characters with whom her readers can easily identify.

The daughter of a teacher and a business man, C. grew up in Old Greenwich, Connecticut, where she enjoyed an ordinary, suburban childhood. Music and reading were passions growing up. C. enjoyed her high-school and teenage years but found the transition to college difficult. Briefly attending two colleges and nursing school, C. fell in love with a man she worked with and left college to get married and start a family. By the age of twenty-five, she was raising two children and managing a household. C. was inspired to begin writing while staying at home with her children. Writing between the children's naps, C. experimented with several different forms. She found success when *Seventeen* MAGAZINE accepted a humorous SHORT STORY. She enjoyed writing for teens and since she found success in it, decided to continue.

C.'s first novel for young people was a mystery, *Safe as the Grave* (1979). Her first novel for young adults was *An April Love Story* (1981), the first of several romances. Many of the novels C. wrote in the early and mid-1980s were inspired by requests from her editors. C. had her greatest success with a SERIES that began with *The Face on the Milk Carton* (Delacorte, 1990) the story of fifteen-year-old Janie who has only the worries of any average teenager until she sees her picture on the back of a milk carton listed as "missing." The book was adapted into a popular television movie in 1995 and C. wrote several sequels, including *Whatever Happened to Janie?* (Delacorte, 1993) and *The Voice on the Radio* (Delacorte, 1996). Another one of C.'s most popular novels is *Driver's Ed* (Delacorte, 1994), the tragic story of two teens who meet in their high-school driver education class. Caught up in their new romance, the couple find themselves involved in a senseless prank with a shady friend that leads to the death of a young mother. The novel is a poignant, unsettling treatment of young people wrestling with moral responsibility.

A church organist and lifelong Congregationalist, C's religious faith is reflected in *What Child Is This? A Christmas Story* (Delacorte, 1997), an emotionally moving novel that examines the difficulties of children living in nontraditional families. Matt, a teenager who has been bounced from one home to another all his life as a foster child, longs to see fulfilled the wish of his younger sister to have a family she can call her own. As the Christmas holidays approach, Matt and his friends are drawn close together as they work to see her wish come true. This inspiring, uplifting story reminds readers of the true meaning of Christmas.

Whether writing adventure, mystery, romance, or suspense, C. always manages to craft a novel that appeals to a wide audience of teen readers. Her unique insight into, and empathy with, adolescents enables her to create novels with characters and stories that resonate with young adults.

SELECT FURTHER WORKS: *Among Friends,* 1987; *Family Reunion,* 1989; *The Fire,* 1990; *The Party's Over,* 1991; *The Cheerleader,* 1991; *Twenty Pageants Later,* 1991; *Flight #116 Is Down,* 1992; *Emergency Room,* 1994; *Both Sides of Time,* 1995; *Flash Fire,* 1995; *Wanted!,* 1997; *The Terrorist,* 1997; *Burning Up,* 1999; *The Ransom of Mercy Carter,* 2001.

SOURCES: *Something about the Author,* vol. 113, pp. 42–49.

EDWARD T. SULLIVAN

COOPER, Louise
Author, b. 29 May 1952, Hertfordshire, England

C., author of HORROR-FANTASY books for adults and TEENAGERS, began her writing career as a young adult, with the publication of her first novel, *The Book of Paradox* (1973). C.'s interest in MYTH and philosophy lead her to create the Time Master trilogy (1985),

which was highly praised for both its moral themes and interesting characters.

C. developed a provocative title character in the Indigo SERIES who unleashes seven demons from the Tower of Regret. Indigo travels through the surreal world, fighting nightmarish demons in her quest to rid the world of evil; *Revenant* (1993) and *Aisling* (1994) continued the Indigo series.

C. continued exploring alternative realities with the publication of the Chaos Gate trilogy (1991). C. delved into the duality of chaos and order, contradicting some accepted moralizations. The Star Shadow trilogy (1994) includes the fantasy titles *Eclipse* (1994), *Star Ascendent* (1995), and *Moonset* (1995).

AWARDS: 1993 American Library Association Notable Book Award for Young Adults, *The Sleep of the Stone.*

FURTHER WORKS: *Blood Summer,* 1976; *In Memory of Sarah Bailey,* 1977; *Crown of Horn,* 1981; *The Blacksmith,* 1982; "Tithing Night," 1987; "Cry," 1989; *The Sleep of Stone,* 1991; Time Master trilogy, 1995; "His True and Only Wife," 1995; "The Birthday Battle," 1997; "Not Wisely, but Too Well," 1997; *Daughter of Storms* trilogy, 1997; *Creatures* series, 1998; "The Glass Slip-up," 1998; *Mirror, Mirror* series, 2000; "The Spiral Garden," 2000; *The Summer Witch,* 2000.

BIBLIOGRAPHY: *St. James Guide to Fantasy Writers,* online, 2003; *Contemporary Authors Online,* 2003; The Official Louise Cooper Bibliography, online, 2003.

TERRY HAUGER

COOPER, Susan (Mary)
Author, b. 23 May 1935, Burnham, Buckinghamshire, England

C.'s books are among the most popular children's FANTASIES produced during the 'second golden age' (mid-1950s–mid-1970s) of children's literature in the UK. Her quintet, composed of *Over Sea, Under Stone* (1965), *The Dark Is Rising* (1973), *Greenwitch* (1974), *The Grey King* (1975), and *Silver On The Tree* (1977)—published in a single volume as *The Dark Is Rising Sequence* (1984)—have won literary distinctions.

C. attended Slough High School before going to Oxford University (1953–1956) where she received an M.A. in English (1956). While at Oxford, she was very interested in journalism and became the first woman to edit the University MAGAZINE *Cherwell.* After graduating from Oxford, she worked as a reporter and feature writer for *The Sunday Times* in London. In 1963, she married an American scientist and moved with him to the U.S. Together, they had a son and a daughter. Feeling homesick and nostalgic for her native Buckinghamshire, she turned to reading about Britain, especially Arthurian legends. This is the way she gained inspiration for *The Dark Is Rising* SERIES.

Over Sea, Under Stone was initially written as a single book for a competition run by the publishing company Jonathan Cape (publisher of Edith Nesbit) which wanted a "FAMILY ADVENTURE." The story relies strongly on clichés characteristic of its genre. It starts with Simon, Jane, and Barney Drew going by train to Trewissick—where C. used to go as a child—a Cornish fishing village, to stay with their great-uncle Merriman over the summer holidays. They discover a parchment map with clues to the whereabouts of a hidden treasure, a golden grail hidden centuries before "over sea, under stone." Soon, it becomes apparent that their great-uncle is not there by accident and they learn about the timeless battle between the forces of the Light and those of the Dark. As C. explores Arthurian and Celtic myths, the adventure takes on the fantastic dimension which permeates the rest of the series.

The legendary battle between the Light and the Dark is at the heart of the entire sequence. *The Dark Is Rising* is very different in style from *Over Sea, Under Stone.* It sees Will Stanton, the seventh son of a seventh son, travelling through time to join Merriman who appears to be Merlin, the figure who links all five books. Meeting Merriman, Will learns of his part and his quest as an Old One of the Light; he is the last of the Old Ones, Merlin being the first. Will must seek and find the Six Signs crafted through the centuries which are needed to defeat the Dark, for it is rising and is beginning its final assault on the world. Centered around Will's coming to terms with his new responsibilities, *The Dark Is Rising* is representative of the bildungsroman genre.

In *Greenwitch,* the Drew children go back to visit Merriman. The grail they discovered in *Over Sea, Under Stone* has been stolen. As the boys and their uncle try to find it again, Jane—who is often said to have been given a central position in this book because a feminist criticized Cooper for making her too

passive in the previous adventures—discovers the location of the manuscript that will help them decipher the inscriptions on the grail.

The Grey King is often seen as a kind of "Wordsworthian narrative" focusing on landscapes at length. Will Stanton, being very ill, has forgotten most of the knowledge gained as the last of the Old Ones, including a prophetic rhyme which describes the quest for the Golden Harp of the Light. In order to convalesce, Will is sent to a relative in Wales where he meets the Drew children. The story is centered on a Golden Harp which they need to finally defeat the rising forces of the Dark in the last book of the series *Silver On The Tree.*

AWARDS: *Boston Globe–Horn Book* Award, 1973, *The Dark Is Rising;* Newbery Medal, 1976, *The Grey King;* BBYA for *King of Shadows,* 2000.

FURTHER WORKS: *Dawn Of Fear,* 1970; *Seaward,* 1983; *The Boggart,* 1993; *Dreams and Wishes: Essays on Writing for Children,* 1996; *The Boggart And The Monster,* 1997; *King Of Shadows,* 1998; *Green Boy,* 2002.

BIBLIOGRAPHY: Watson, Victor. *Reading Series Fiction,* 2000, pp. 153–169. Krips, Valerie. "Finding One's Place In The Fantastic: Susan Cooper's *The Dark Is Rising*" in Joe Sanders. *Functions of the Fantastic,* 1995, pp. 169–173. http://www.thelostland.com/biography.htm; http://www.lib.rochester.edu/camelot/intrvws/cooper.htm.

SEBASTIEN CHAPLEAU

CORMIER, Robert

Author, journalist, b. 17 January 1925, Leominster, Massachusetts; d. 2 November 2000

C. left an indelible mark in YA literature. Three of his award-winning novels, *The Chocolate War* (1974), *I Am the Cheese* (1977), and *After the First Death* (1979), not only changed the landscape of YA literature, but also established C. as a master of TEENAGE psychological turmoil. He created characters that are tragically defeated by evil, mastering the art of REALISM in fiction. C.'s books have been translated into more than a dozen languages, and three of his novels were made into motion pictures.

C. said he always wanted to be a writer, and continually tried to record his thoughts on paper. It wasn't until an encounter with a teacher in seventh grade that his attention was nudged. He had handed in a book report at St. Cecilia's Grammar School.

When his teacher, a nun, handed it back to him, she pointed her finger at him, jabbed him on the shoulder and said, "Robert, you are a writer!" He stared at her in disbelief and said, "I am?" In retrospect, he jokingly said he didn't want to make a liar out of a nun, and so began his future career.

After this, all C. wanted to do was write. His poems were published in the local *Leominster Daily Enterprise.* As a freshman at Fitchburg State College, in Massachusetts, C.'s SHORT STORY "The Little Things that Count" was published by a national Catholic MAGAZINE, *The Sign,* with the help of his professor, Florence Conlon. This publication established him as a professional writer. In 1946, after a year of college, he left school and began writing scripts and commercials at radio station WTAG in Worcester, Massachusetts. In 1948 he began working for the *Worcester Telegram,* a local newspaper, writing a weekly human-interest column aptly named "A Story from the Country." C. always said that there were lots of untold stories in his hometown. His award-winning career as a journalist continued in 1955 as a city hall and political reporter when he joined the Fitchburg *Sentinel,* which later became the Fitchburg-Leominster *Sentinel and Enterprise.* Later he became an associate editor and agreed to write a biweekly column under the pseudonym John Fitch IV. This cover was blown when he received the K. R. Thomason Award in 1974 for the best human-interest column. In 1974, he was also honored by the New England Associated Press Association for having written the best news story under the pressure of a deadline. Although C. published three novels for adults between 1960 and 1965, he did not retire from the newspaper until 1978.

The Chocolate War (1974) was a milestone in YA literature, changing the way YA books were viewed. This novel was inspired by his son who came home from school with two bags of chocolates to sell. While his son's refusal to sell them met with no consequences, C. began to wonder what would have happened if the school officials had insisted on his participation. *The Chocolate War* revolves around a high-school student's decision to refrain from selling chocolates for his school's fund-raiser. For this decision, he is harassed and physically beaten by his vindictive classmates. These characters were so realistic that C.'s audience wanted to know what became of them. The sequel, *Beyond the Chocolate War* (1985), provides a response. The book's harsh content had

critics debating its validity for young adults. More than two decades later, *The Chocolate War* was still on the bestseller list and was also made into a MOVIE (1988).

C.'s next novel, *I Am the Cheese* (1977), was quite different from *The Chocolate War.* Here, C. wove a story about a young boy desperately struggling with an identity crisis and trying to make sense of the unexplainable in his life. The conclusion of the book reveals the full psychological torture that Adam experiences. Because he included his home telephone number in *I Am the Cheese,* C. received numerous calls from young people. This book was made into a movie in 1983.

After the First Death (1979) is a combination of physical and mental sorrow. Here, the hijacking of a children's bus by a terrorist is seen from the perspectives of a hostage, an Army general, the general's son, and the terrorist. By this time, C. was noted for his brilliantly written books that had darker, troubling sides. He partially attributes this disturbing side to his own experiences. Though highly controversial, together these three novels were cited when C. was awarded the 1991 Margaret A. Edwards Award for lifetime achievement in writing works for young adults. Today they are considered classics in young adult literature. In 1982, C. was honored by the National Council of Teachers of English and its Adolescent Literature Assembly (ALAN) for his "significant contribution to the field of adolescent literature" and for his "innovative creativity."

C.'s novels have frequently come under attack by CENSORSHIP groups, for they do not shy away from the problems that young people encounter in a tumultuous world. C. wrote his novels for an intelligent audience that could grasp the subtleties in his work. While he traveled all over the world, speaking to students and educators from schools and universities, C. loved to return home; it was there that he spent his life and the place about which he wrote.

AWARDS: 1974 K.R. Thomason Award; 1974 New England Associated Press Association; *Chocolate War:* 1974 *New York Times* Outstanding Book of the Year Award, 1974 ALA Best Book for Young Adult Literature, School Library Journal "Best of the Best 1966–1978" list (1979), 1979 Lewis Carroll Shelf Award; *I Am the Cheese:* 1977 ALA Best Book for Young Adults, 1977 *New York Times* Outstanding Book of the Year Award, *Horn Book* Fanfare Honor Book,

1997 Children's Literature Association Phoenix Award; 1979 ALA Best Book for Young Adults, *After the First Death;* 1983 BBYA, *Bumblebee Flies Anyway;* 1988 BBYA, *Fade.*

FURTHER WORKS: *Now and at the Hour,* 1960; *A Little Raw on Monday Mornings,* 1963; *Take Me Where the Good Times Are,* 1965; *8 Plus 1,* 1980; *The Bumblebee Flies Anyway,* 1983; *Fade,* 1988; *I Have Words to Spend,* 1991; *We All Fall Down,* 1991; *Tunes for Bears to Dance To,* 1992; *In the Middle of the Night,* 1995; *Tenderness,* 1997; *Heroes,* 1998; *Frenchtown Summer,* 1999; *Other Bells for Us to Ring,* 2000; *The Rag and Bone Shop,* 2001.

BIBLIOGRAPHY: Hoffman, Laura B., *Beyond the Shadows of Robert Cormier,* 1996; http://www.random house.com/teachers/authors/corm.html; http://www .carr.lib.md.us/mae/cormier/corm-bks.htm; http:// www.randomhouse.com/kids/author/cormier.html; http://www.ipl.org/div/kidspace/askauthor/Cormier .html; http://www.edupaperback.org/authorbios/Cor mier_Robert.html; http://www.northern.edu/hasting w/cormier.html

MICHELLE A. CARRYL

COTTONWOOD , Joe
Author, b. 19 August 1947, Washington, D.C.

C. wrote two novels for ADULTS, *Famous Potatoes* (1976) and *Frank City (Goodbye)* (1977), in the early states of his professional writing career. He also produced a book of POETRY, *Son of a Poet.* His thoughts turned to books for YOUNG ADULTS as his own children began to grow up. He turned thought into action and authored a book intended for the middle-school audience, *The Adventures of Boone Barnaby.* The book was published in 1990 and is set in a small town in Northern California. (C. lives with his family in La Honda, California, a small town nestled in the Santa Cruz Mountains.) The plot traces the twists and turns of the friendship among three boys while posing philosophical questions about the world in which they live. The author enjoys writing about REALISTIC relationships between people, family values, and the forces of nature.

C.'s second young adult book, *Danny Ain't* (1992), is about growing up quickly without much parental support, making choices which have consequences and learning from nature, which in this case is represented by two coyotes. The book won the BABRA Award for Best Children's Book in 1992. C.'s next book is also grounded in realism, based on

the author's personal experiences during the Loma Prieta (California) earthquake on October 17, 1989. *Quake* (1995) is about changes, not only the changes in the landscape wrought by the earthquake but the relationship shifts between two girls who are friends during the crisis.

In addition to being a successful author, C. also works as an independent building contractor.

AWARDS: New York City Public Library Best Books for the TEEN Age selection: 1995 for *Quake,* and 1996 for *Babcock.*

FURTHER WORK: *Babcock,* 1996.

BIBLIOGRAPHY: "The best, the notable & the recommended; young adults' choices for 1997," *Emergency Librarian,* v. 25 no. 4 (March/April 1998) 18–19; *Something about the Author,* vol. 92, 1997; Joe Cottonwood's website: http://www.joecottonwood.com/ bio.htm

REBECCA VARGHA

COULOUMBIS, Audrey
Author, n.d., Springfield, Illinois

C. is best known for her first novel for young people, the Newbery Honor Book (2000) *Getting Near to Baby.* It portrays the heartbreaking effect of the death of a baby sister. Thirteen-year-old Willa Jo tries to carry the burden of care for the family but Aunt Patty insists that the two girls come to stay with her. Willa Jo climbs out on the roof to watch the sun rise and little sister follows her. Character is revealed in the struggle with heartache. *Getting Near to Baby* was followed by her novels *Say Yes* (2002) and *Summer's End* (2003).

C. grew up in Springfield, Illinois, where her grandparents had settled. She moved to New York City when she was fourteen to live with her father's family.

C. writes by listening to her characters. Her listening skills began when she was a youngster traveling throughout the U.S. with her father, and taking countryside rides on her bicycle. "The characters show themselves when they are ready to tell a story and she will be there to listen."

AWARDS: 2000 Newbery Honor Award, *Getting Near to Baby.*

FURTHER WORKS: *The Misadventures of Maude March,* 2005.

BIBLIOGRAPHY: Scholastic "Author's Studies" home-page, 2003; www.audreycouloumbis.com.

HEIDI L. SACCHITELLA

COVER ART

TEENS tend not subscribe to the adage "Don't judge a book by its cover." Cover art alone can determine whether or not a teen will choose to read a book. If a teen judges the cover art on a book to be unattractive and unappealing, all the booktalking in the world will not save that book from a fate of collecting dust on the shelf.

Librarians have long complained to publishers about the need for covers that will attract their intended audiences with art that is true to the content of the book. Publishers have always done a good job of producing appealing cover art for SERIES fiction because, after all, those titles are being marketed directly to YOUNG ADULTS. In the area of more literary fiction, however, publishers have been slower to respond. To their credit, publishers have been more responsive to librarians' pleas for better quality and more accurate cover art in recent years.

Typically, a YA novel will have two different covers, one for the hardcover edition and one for the paperback. The target audience for hardcover editions is adult buyers—librarians, teachers, and to a lesser extent, parents. Most teenagers cannot or will not pay $15.95 to $21.95 for a new hardcover novel. They are more likely, however, to pay $5.95 to $7.95 for a PAPERBACK edition, so the cover art for those books is deliberately made to appeal strongly to teen sensibilities. The cover art for hardcovers might feature darker, more abstract, or impressionistic artwork, whereas paperbacks will feature bolder colors and more realistic depictions of characters or action scenes.

To assess the importance teens place on cover art when selecting a book to read, two surveys were conducted among middle- and high-school students in two Staten Island branches of The New York Public Library. In the first survey, conducted in 1997, twenty-one young adults, ages twelve to fifteen, were asked to evaluate the cover art of fifteen hardcover editions of novels which were the top selections in that year's YA LIBRARY SERVICES ASSOCIATION Best Books for YA list. The survey revealed there was rarely a consensus among the participants on the overall quality of a cover, but they did all agree that cover art was a primary factor in whether or not they chose a book to read. The participants agreed that a book's cover is the reader's first impression. A bad first impression will turn off a potential reader, and it is unlikely there will be a chance for a second impression.

The survey also revealed that young adult readers do look closely at cover art and that they expect the cover to convey the contents of the book. The covers the participants surveyed represented a variety of art styles. The most unpopular among them were two that offered abstract and absurdist styles. The teens disliked those covers that were described as "too weird" and "ugly" because they did not give them clues to what the story would be about. Covers that were rated the most appealing by the participants were those they felt gave them a clear sense of what the story would be about. Covers give readers expectations that what they anticipate will be fulfilled. Young adult readers feel misled and disappointed when the expectations a cover creates are not realized in the story.

In a follow-up survey conducted in 1999, participants were asked to look at both the hardcover and paperback covers of fifteen recently published YA novels and decide which format was more appealing. Twenty-four young adults, ranging in age from eleven to sixteen, participated in the survey. The participants were asked to evaluate the books by their cover art only. The books used in the survey were chosen arbitrarily. The only criteria in selecting the books were the drastic differences between the hardcover and paperback covers and a recent (within five years) publication date.

Participants preferred the paperback cover to the hardcover because the colors were bolder and brighter. Paperback covers were also preferred because they were judged to have more details. Most participants said they preferred paperback covers because they gave them a better sense of what the story is about. Realism and a cover that offers an explanation of the book's contents were two criteria for evaluation that consistently emerged in the survey.

Both surveys revealed that young adults expect cover art to give them some idea of what the story is about and what kind (e.g., HORROR, MYSTERY, ROMANCE) of story it is. One interesting comment that was consistently made concerned the "realism" of the cover. A cover that "looked real" was an important factor to many of the participants in both surveys in their evaluation of its quality. The presence of action and emotion in the cover art was important to many participants. Covers featuring people doing something were more appealing. When covers provoked some emotion among participants, such as fright, humor, or sadness, they said they were intrigued enough to want to read the story.

The most important conclusion to draw from these surveys is that cover art is extremely important in helping young adults decide whether or not to read a book. They scrutinize every detail, and they have very definite expectations of what a good cover should convey. What this means to publishers is that, if they want teens to read their books, they need to produce covers that will grab them and entice them to read those particular stories.

BIBLIOGRAPHY: Sullivan, Edward T. "Judging Books by their Covers: A Cover Art Experiment." *VOYA: Voice of Youth Advocates* 21.3 (August 1998): 180–182; Sullivan, Edward T. "Judging Books by their Covers, Part II: Hardcover vs. Paperback." *VOYA: Voice of Youth Advocates* 23.4 (October 2000): 244–248.

EDWARD T. SULLIVAN

COVILLE, Bruce

Author, b. 16 May 1950, Syracuse, New York

This prize-winning author is one of the most popular authors in FANTASY and SCIENCE FICTION literature for children and YOUNG ADULTS today. C. is the recipient of many awards including the IRA-CBC Children's Choice Award for *The Monster's Ring* (1982) and *Jeremy Thatcher, Dragon Hatcher* (1991). Another of the Magic Shop Book SERIES, *Jennifer Murdley's Toad* (1992), was named to the MD Black-Eyed Susan Award Master List. C. has won children's choice awards in over fifteen states.

C. credits his sixth-grade teacher, Mrs. Crandall, for inspiring his thoughts of becoming an author when she gave him an opportunity to write a long story. He recognized early on his love for writing, but did not envision himself as a children's and young adult writer. By the age of seventeen, C. was committed to his future career. He attended Duke University in North Carolina for a year before returning to New York. He then attended the State University of New York at Binghamton and the State University College

at Oswego, and received a B.A. in Elementary Education in 1974.

C. brings a wealth of experiences to his writing, having previously held positions as toymaker, gravedigger, camp counselor, cookware salesman and assembly line worker. C. has also held jobs that are more closely associated to his writing career, such as actor, script writer and director. He was an elementary teacher for seven years at Wetzel Road Elementary School in Liverpool, New York, teaching second and fourth grade and, for his last three years there, specializing in gifted and talented education. It was not until 1977 that C., along with his wife, illustrator Katherine Coville, sold his first book, *The Foolish Giant.* He and Katherine went on to collaborate on two more books, *Sarah's Unicorn* (1979) and *The Monster's Ring* (1982). Decades later, they continue their collaboration.

The Monster's Ring (1982) was based on occurrences in C.'s classroom where he often masqueraded as his own "half-mad twin brother Igor." This book became a great success, garnering a spot on the Children's Choice List and winning the South Carolina's Children's Award. It was also nominated for literature awards in Arizona, Indiana, and Iowa.

C. is an amazingly versatile writer; his combination of science fiction, ADVENTURE, suspense, and fantasy into SHORT STORIES, novels, and PLAYS appeal to children and young adults alike. *Herds of Thunder, Manes of Gold: A Collection of Horse Stories and Poems* (1989) and *The Unicorn Treasury* (1988) are anthologies of stories and poems he compiled. C.'s readers journey to a world of beauty and magic with a third anthology, *A Glory of Unicorns* (1998). Coville has several successful series, including My Teacher stories, Camp Haunted Hills, Magic Shop Books, and the Nina Tanleven ghost series. His ghost stories also include *The Ghost in the Third Row* (1987) and *The Ghost Wore Grey* (1988). *The Unicorn Chronicles,* highly acclaimed by readers, transport them into a fantasy world filled with characters that are believable and realistic. These stories touch the emotions in readers of all ages. For *Goblins in the Castle* (1991), C. retreats back in time to the days he taught fourth grade, bringing back his "half-mad twin brother Igor" as a featured character. The story, filled with suspense and imagery, has readers following hidden passages, descending into the deep, dank dungeon, and encountering the creature Igor who resides there beneath a castle filled with mysterious moaning. C.'s comic science fiction titles have captured the interest of millions of readers. Rod Allbright, the hero of *Aliens Ate My Homework* (1993), is based closely on C. himself.

In the early 1990s C. returned to the Magic Shop, writing first *Jeremy Thatcher, Dragon Hatcher* (1991), and then *Jennifer Murdley's Toad* (1992). *The Skull of Truth* (1997) and most recently *Juliet Dove, Queen of Love* (2003) take readers once again back to the Magic Shop. These characters are not the superhero type, but rather those that most readers can relate to and empathize with.

C. has a special interest in the theater and enjoys every aspect of acting, directing, and writing. He has written several plays and has appeared as William Shakespeare in Bernard Shaw's *The Dark Lady of the Sonnets*. This experience may have been the influencing factor in his PICTURE BOOKS of Shakespeare retellings, beginning with *The Tempest* (1994). C. has also performed with the Syracuse Symphony in the two stories he wrote for its special concerts, "The Metamorphosis of Justin Jones" and "The Golden Sail." Both are included in *Odder than Ever* (1999). Again, showing his versatility as a writer and artist, *The Dragonslayers* (1994) was originally a musical in C.'s fourth-grade class. That school musical became a book and, later, the Syracuse Stage, a professional theatre company, produced the musical with C. as one of the cast members.

C. collaborated with his longtime friend the author Jane YOLEN for the groundbreaking YA novel *Armageddon Summer* (1998), a first-person story with Yolen writing the girl's voice and Coville writing the boy's voice. Through the authors' skillful portrayals, two TEENS examine their faith, beliefs, feelings, and depth of courage as they deal with the very real possibility that they are facing the end of the world.

C.'s re-told Shakespeare series includes *William Shakespeare's Twelfth Night* (2003). Coville brings one of the Bard's best-loved comedies to print with a combination of his own prose adaptation and quotations from the play. Though simplified, it offers younger readers an opportunity to follow and experience the play's plot.

C. captures humor, adventure, and emotion in his writing. He paints vivid images that transport his readers to unknown worlds. And as readers of all ages set down *The Unicorn Chronicles, A Glory of Uni-*

corns, or *Jeremy Thatcher, Dragon Hatcher,* for a moment, just a moment, they wonder if it is all real or fantasy.

AWARDS: Mythopoeic Fantasy Award for *Jeremy Thatcher, Dragon Hatcher;* 1998 Best Books for Young Adults by the YOUNG ADULT LIBRARY SERVICES ASSOCIATION, *Armageddon Summer;* A Book Link Best Book of the Year, *Armageddon;* Golden Duck Award for Best Science Fiction, *My Teacher Glows in the Dark;* Connecticut Nutmeg Award, *My Teacher Flunked the Planet.*

SELECT FURTHER WORKS: *Half-Human,* 2001; *The Monsters of Morley Manor,* 2001; *The Lap Snatcher,* 2001; *Bruce Coville's UFO,* 2000; *Song of the Wanderer,* 1999; *I Was a Sixth Grade Alien,* 1999; *William Shakespeare's Romeo and Juliet,* 1999; *A Glory of Unicorns,* 1998; *My Grandfather's House,* 1996; *William Shakespeare's A Midsummer Night's Dream,* 1996; *William Shakespeare's Macbeth; The World's Worst Fairy Godmother,* 1996; *The Search for Snout,* 1995; *Bruce Coville's Book of Nightmares,* 1995; *Bruce Coville's Book of Nightmares: Tales to Make You Scream,* 1995; *I Left My Sneakers in Dimension X,* 1994; *Oddly Enough,* 1994; *Into the Land of Unicorns,* 1994; *Bruce Coville's Book of Aliens: Tales to Warp Your Mind,* 1994; *Aliens Ate My Homework,* 1993; *My Teacher Flunked the Planet,* 1992; *The Ghost in the Big Brass Bed,* 1991; *The Dinosaur That Followed Me Home,* 1990; *The Ghost Wore Grey,* 1988; *How I Survived My Summer Vacation,* 1988; *The Ghost in the Third Row,* 1987: *The Eyes of the Tarot,* 1983.

BIBLIOGRAPHY: Coville, B., "The name game: How do you come up with good names for characters in your fiction?" *Writing* Feb./Mar. 2003, vol. 25 Issue 5, 2; McElmeel, S. "Author Profile," *Library Talk,* Jan./Feb., 1993; Pappas, B. "Itsy Bitsy Breathes Fire for 'Dragon,'" *Hollywood Reporter,* 7 March 2000, vol. 362 Issue 4, 10; Smith, C. "Spotlight on SF/Fantasy" *Booklist,* April 2003, vol. 99 Issue 16, 1485; Yolen, J. and Coville, B. "Two Brains, One Book; or, How We Found Our Way to the End of the World," *Book Links,* November 1998; website: www.bruceco ville.com

KRISTINE M. MICHELL

COWLEY, Joy
Author. b. 7 August 1936, Levin, New Zealand

C. is so productive and versatile that she has been labelled an unstoppable force in children's literature, born to tell stories to children. While she was only sixteen and a student at Palmerston North Girls' High

School, C.'s talent was recognized. She was made editor of the weekly children's page of *The Manawatu Daily Times,* writing much of the material herself. She later published SHORT STORIES and novels for adults in a career which still continues.

A turning point came in the 1960s, when C.'s son had reading difficulties at school. Examining his books, she became convinced that early readers must be easy, exciting, meaningful and humorous—a good analysis of her own work. Since then C. has written over six hundred beginner readers, such as *Mrs Wishy-washy* (1980), with worldwide sales. Working with young readers confirmed C.'s conviction that young people delight in word play, alliteration, rhythms, puns, and the general richness of language. This is also true of her PICTURE BOOKS and novels, where the use of imaginative language and the power of words are often themes, as when in *Captain Felonius* (1996) a pirate buries his swearwords.

C.'s success in the three fields of readers, picture books, and novels has made her books familiar to children of all ages around the world. Two of her earliest stories, the anti-WAR fables, *The Duck in the Gun* (1969) and *Salmagundi* (1985), remain popular. Her writing styles range from the mock-melodrama of *Brave Mama Puss* (1995) to the hard-boiled private-eye dragon of *Dragon Fire* (2000), always with the touch of humor that sets her work apart. There is a strong sense of place in C.'s writing, so that the appropriate myths and customs are as important as the landscape. Thus readers gain a powerful awareness of places as diverse as Wisconsin in *Starbright and the Dream Eater* (1998) and Antarctica in *Pip the Penguin* (2001).

Her first novel for YOUNG ADULTS was the complex and satisfying *The Silent One* (1981), where Jonasi, an adopted outsider in his own Fijian village, is doubly isolated by his deafness. Making friends with a white turtle, Jonasi faces hostility and violent death, after a fateful last journey to the sea where he joins the turtle, in a conclusion that is both full of the power of MYTHOLOGY and left intriguingly open.

Like most young people's authors, C. is aware of the power of myth and folk legends. She has re-told Maori myths, such as *Stolen Food* (1993), a trickster tale from the Te Arawa canoe, and has also created her own semi-mythical tales like *Te Tamahine a Te Moana* (2000), published in English as *The Sea Daughter* (2002), a story which explains the existence of seals. The award-winning epic *Tulevai and the Sea* (1995) shows a mother's powerful love defeating the sea's determination to make her son Tulevai a slave.

Mythical and spiritual matters are part of everyday life in C.'s masterpiece, the Shadrach trilogy, where an unlikely pair of draught horses has a powerful influence on a rural family. A trickster, even in death, Shadrach sired Gladly and as the children in the novel mature, experience loss and grief, gain spiritual awareness, and achieve friendship, trust, and love, their lives are linked to these two horses. The spiritual journey goes much further in *Starbright and the Dream Eater* (1998), where a young girl has the mission of saving all life on Earth, in a powerful story about the sacredness of life and the role of redemption in saving that life from eternal destruction. The strength of this SF novel is the lively personality of Starbright, a small-town tomboy with a gift for wordplay and the courage to use her unexpected powers.

Equally impressive was C's other science fiction ADVENTURE, *Ticket to the Sky Dance* (1997), which creates a sinister but recognizable future world where twin street kids, Jancie and Shog, offered a career as models, find they are really to be used in an experiment in star-travel. *The Video Shop Sparrow* (1999) is a story with scriptural resonances. Two boys spot a sparrow trapped in a shop during the holidays, and in order to save the bird they have to persuade people that the fate of one little bird matters. Their reward is "a special trusting look" from the sparrow.

Regular visits to schools in the U.S., where her books are widely used, have inspired C. to use some American settings. In *Big Moon Tortilla* (2002), set on a Tohono O'odham (Papago) Reservation in Arizona, Marta is inspired by her grandmother to face her problems. Dyanne Strongbow's sympathetic illustrations add another dimension to the story. A Puerto Rican family living in multicultural New York, delightfully depicted by Joe Cepeda, help Miguel to save his pet in *Gracias the Thanksgiving Turkey* (1996).

C. is always extending the frontiers of young adult writing; the picture book *Brodie* (illustrated by Chris Mousdale, 2001) depicts children dealing with the DEATH of a classmate.

AWARDS: 1982 NZ Government Printer Book of the Year, *The Silent One;* 1985 Russell Clark Award, *The*

Duck in the Gun (ill. Robyn Belton); 1990 NZ Commemoration Medal; 1992 Margaret Mahy Lecture Award; 1992 AIM Children's Book Awards, *Bow Down Shadrach;* 1996 AIM Children's Book Awards, *The Cheese Trap* (ill. Linda McClelland); 1996 Russell Clark Award, *The Cheese Trap* (ill. Linda McClelland); 1997 NZ Post Children's Book Awards, *Nicketty-Nacketty, Noo Noo-Noo* (ill. Tracey Moroney); 1998 NZ Post Children's Book Award, *Ticket to the Sky Dance;* 1999 *Boston Globe–Horn Book* Award, *Red-Eyed Tree Frog;* 1999 NZ Post Children's Book Award, *Starbright and the Dream Eater;* 2001 NZ Post Children's Book Award, *Shadrach Girl;* 2002 NZ Post Children's Book Award, *Brodie* (ill. Chris Mousedale).

FURTHER WORKS: *The Terrible Taniwha of Timberditch,* 1982; *Bow Down Shadrach,* 1991; *Gladly, Here I Come,* 1994; *The Screaming Mean Machine,* ill. David Cox, 1994; *Beyond the River: Stories,* 1994; *Along Came Greedy Cat,* 1994; *The Day of the Rain,* ill. Bob Kerr, 1994; *Papa Puss to the Rescue,* 1995; *The Hitchhikers: Stories,* 1997; *The Wild West Gang,* ill. Trevor Pye, 1998; *Agapanthus Hum and the Eyeglasses,* 1999; *What Does Greedy Cat Like?* ill. Robyn Belton, 1999; *The Wild Wests and Pong Castle,* 2000; *Shadrach Girl,* 2000; *Agapanthus Hum and Major Bark,* 2001; *Froghopper,* 2002; *Agapanthus Hum and the Angel Hoot,* 2003; *Where Horses Run Free: A Dream for the American Mustang,* ill. Layne Johnson, 2003; *The Wishing of Biddy Malone,* 2004; *Hunter,* 2004.

BIBLIOGRAPHY: Agnew, Trevor. "Know the Author: Joy Cowley: Toad in a Tiger Moth meets Icarus." *Magpies NZ Supplement* 14:1 (Mar 1999): 2–5; Cowley, Joy. "Biographical notes." *School Journal Catalogue* 1978–1993, 1994, 133–4; Fitzgibbon, Tom and Spiers, Barbara. *Beneath Southern Skies:* NEW ZEALAND *Children's Book Authors & Illustrators,* 1993. 35–7; Hebley, Diane and Wattie, Nelson. "Cowley, Joy." *The Oxford Companion to New Zealand Literature.* Ed. Roger Robinson and Nelson Wattie, 1998. 115–6; http://www.joycowley.com/; http://library.christchurch.org.nz/Childrens/Childrens Authors/JoyCowley.asp/; http://www.bookcouncil .org.nz/writers/cowleyjoy.htm/

TREVOR AGNEW

CRAVEN, Margaret
Author, journalist, b. 13 March 1901, Helena, Montana; d. 28 July 1980, California

After a fulfilling childhood in Bellingham, Washington, in the Cascade region of the northwest U.S., a turning point occurred in C.'s life when her lawyer father became ill and the family lost its income. With limited finances, C. nonetheless headed off to Stanford with her twin brother, at a time when a university education for women was rare. C. graduated Phi Beta Kappa and began her journalistic career on the San Jose *Mercury Herald.* Hired by the editor as his secretary, she was soon regularly writing his front-page column, for which he insisted that she take credit.

Continuing to support herself through newspaper work, C. began to find a steady market for her SHORT STORIES in MAGAZINES such as *Ladies Home Journal* and *Collier's,* and, starting in 1941, became a regular contributor to *The Saturday Evening Post.* Twenty-five stories, from 1942 to 1962, were collected and published posthumously as *The Home Front* (1981). Although acknowledging their technical competence, some critics see C.'s stories as formulaic, with predictable themes and resolutions; but while she writes about traditional values as a means of overcoming adversity, some of her stories, like her memoir, *Again Calls the Owl* (1980), are marked by a quiet awareness of the conflicts facing women in a shifting social world. In C.'s time, married women could not hold jobs, and after her father's death in 1925, she was her mother's financial support.

C. is best known today for her first novel, *I Heard the Owl Call My Name,* a creation of her later years— she was sixty-seven when it was published in Canada, seventy-two when it found an American publisher. While still in her twenties, C. had been in an accident that left her with limited vision. A second operation in her sixties, which improved her eyesight significantly, enabled her to travel to northern British Columbia, where Kingcome is situated, to research her novel; she lived in the isolated village for nearly four months.

I Heard the Owl tells the story of a young Anglican minister, Mark Brian, who, unbeknown to himself, is terminally ill. Aware of his condition, his bishop sends him to minister to the natives of Kingcome "to learn . . . enough of the meaning of life to be ready to die" (144). C.'s writing is stylistically straightforward with her symbols, such as the salmon "swimmer," emerging naturally out of the novel's setting. She does not presume to adopt a native perspective, but tells her story from Mark's, the white man's, point of view, as he grows to appreciate the Kwakiutl outlook on nature and the values of their culture, which are slowly being eroded by outside forces.

In its sensitive, unsentimental treatment of native life, C.'s novel has become a classic of YA literature and readers of all ages have found spiritual solace in its handling of DEATH and other kinds of loss. As one of the characters points out, it is sometimes harder to lose people to life than to death.

FURTHER WORK: *Walk Gently this Good Earth,* 1977.

BIBLIOGRAPHY: *Flint, Joyce.* "Craven, Margaret," *American Women Writers: A Critical Reference Guide from Colonial Times to the Present.* Vol 1. 2nd ed., Ed. Taryn Benbow-Pfalzgraf, 2000; Teal, David A. "Craven, Margaret," *The Oxford Companion to Women's Writing in the United States,* 1995; Reviews: Foote, Timothy." A Swimmer's Tale." Review of *I Heard the Owl Call My Name. Time* (28 January 1974): 73; Levin, Martin. Review of *I Heard the Owl Call My Name. NYTBR* (3 February 1974): 28; McLatchie, Ian B. "Subversive Form." Review of *The Home Front. CANADIAN Literature,* 93 (Summer 1982): 145–46; Shuey, Andrea Lee. Review of *The Home Front. Library Journal,* 106 (1981): 812. Welch, Robert D. Review of *I Heard the Owl Call My Name. Library Journal,* 99 (1974): 503. Review of *Again Calls the Owl. Atlantic Monthly* (April 1980): 128.

RITA BODE

CREECH, Sharon

Author, b. 29 July 1945, Cleveland, Ohio

C. hit American children's literature running with *Walk Two Moons* (1994), the novel that won that year's Newbery Medal from the American Library Association. Since then, she has published ten more books for YOUNG ADULTS, including one Newbery Honor book and two PICTURE BOOKS.

After earning a Master of Arts degree from George Mason University in Virginia, C. worked for several years as an editorial assistant and, later, as a researcher. Following a divorce, she moved herself and her two children, Rob and Karin, to England, where she accepted a position as a teacher of American and British literature at an American School. She married Lyle D. Rigg, a fellow Ohio native living abroad and longtime headmaster of the school. The couple has since returned to the U.S. and settled near Princeton, New Jersey.

By all accounts, although C. had written before, it was her father's stroke, the following six years of his living mutely, and his subsequent death that fueled C.'s passion for writing. During the year after his death, she wrote three novels, including *Walk Two Moons.*

C. credits her storytelling ability to her childhood. Her family was large, and frequent family gatherings would find many relatives gathered around the kitchen table for visiting and storyswapping. To get attention in the ensuing chaos, C. learned to exaggerate and embellish her tales.

C.'s novels often include journeys, metaphorical and actual, physical and emotional. Frequently, they involve painful issues, such as DEATH, loss, and grief as well as positive issues, such as FAMILY, relationships, and self-discovery. Her characters are often self-reliant and independent, but they learn the importance of strong relationships as they bravely face adversity. According to C., her own writing is often very much a journey, with her not knowing when she starts a book exactly where it will take her or what the final destination will be.

In *Walk Two Moons,* thirteen-year-old Salamanca Tree Hiddle travels cross-country with her grandparents in an attempt to bring home the mother who has deserted her. *Absolutely Normal Chaos* (1995), C.'s first book published in England, is the summer JOURNAL of Mary Lou Finney of Easton, Ohio. Mary Lou's summer is disrupted by the visit of her cousin Carl Ray to her home and her own journey to his. *Pleasing the Ghost* (1996) is the touching story of nine-year-old Dennis, who is visited in his bedroom by a parade of ghosts, including his Uncle Arvie. In *Chasing Redbird* (1997), Zinnia Taylor, while grieving the death of a close relative, becomes obsessed with a long, winding trail she finds near her home. As she works to clear the trail, she discovers markers of her ancestors and truth about family. In *The Wanderer* (2000), Sophie is the only girl on a six-person crew of uncles and cousins sailing a forty-five-foot sailboat from Connecticut to England to visit her grandfather. Similar to *Absolutely Normal Chaos,* this novel is a journal; here, Sophie's tale is interspersed with the entries of her cousin, Cody. In *Ruby Holler* (2002), twin orphans Dallas and Florida, having lived in many dreadful foster homes, are chosen by an older couple, Tiller and Sairy, to assist them in accomplishing what they have planned as their last big ADVENTURES. The journeys they take ultimately lead them all back to Ruby Holler and each other.

Fishing in the Air (2000), C.'s first picture book, examines the warm relationship between a child and his father. *A Fine, Fine School* (2001) takes a humorous look at what happens to children and their families when an overly enthusiastic principal insists that such a "fine, fine school" should have more and more of the student's time. C. admits that the well-intentioned principal is modeled on her husband, Lyle, an energetic educator.

Love that Dog (2001) is C.'s first fictional foray into a free verse poetic format. It is the story of Jack, who thinks poetry is confusing, off-putting, and strictly for girls until, at his teacher's behest, he begins writing it, setting his feet on the path of self-discovery.

AWARDS: Newbery Medal Book, *Walk Two Moons;* Newbery Honor Book, *The Wanderer;* BBYA for *Chasing Redbird,* 1998, and *The Wanderer,* 2001; C. is the first American to win the Carnegie Medal, 2003, she received it for *Ruby Holler.*

FURTHER WORKS: *Heartbeat,* 2004; *Granny Torrelli Makes Soup,* 2003; *Bloomability,* 1999; *The Center of the Universe: Waiting for the Girl* (PLAY), 1992; *The Recital* (as Sharon Rigg), 1990.

BIBLIOGRAPHY: Britton, J., "Everyday Journeys," *Publishers Weekly,* 248, 2001; Rigg, L. D., "Sharon Creech," *Horn Book Magazine,* 91, 1995; *Something about the Author,* vol. 94, 1997; *Children's Literature Review,* vol. 42, 1997.

CREW, Gary

Author, b. 23 September 1947, Brisbane, Queensland, Australia

C. is a four-time recipient of the prestigious AUSTRALIAN Children's Book of the Year Award, first winning for his HORROR novel, *Strange Objects* (1991). He was short-listed for the Edgar Allan Poe Mystery Fiction Award for *Strange Objects* (1994). This was C.'s first horror story, and he created a MYSTERY that set a TEENAGER against the backdrop of a shipwrecked vessel, the *Batavia,* which sank in 1629.

C. developed an intense reading habit as the result of poor health during childhood. This habit grew into an interest in illustrations and art, and he trained to become a draftsman at the Queensland Institute of Technology.

During this time, he married and became the father of two girls. His son, Joel, born in 1978, rounded out

the family. C. completed his education, receiving a Master of Arts degree from the Queensland University.

Despite C.'s love of art, he doubted his own drawing skill and began writing instead while working as an English teacher. C. initiated his career as a writer for children and teenagers with the publication of *The Inner Circle* (1985). Appreciating the skill of children's book illustrators, C. collaborated with the artists to make sure his story and the art worked together cohesively. *The Watertower* broke new ground in the PICTURE BOOK genre due to the mysteriously ominous tone set by author and illustrator. Set against the backdrop of a water tower, the slight text and mesmerizing pictures pull the reader into the macabre world of C.'s imagination.

Continuing with the horror genre, C. wrote *Caleb* (1996), a brooding, Gothic FANTASY about a child's obsession with entomology that slowly evolves throughout the story. The collaboration with Steven Woolman, the same artist that worked on *The Watertower,* created black-and-white and sepia illustrations that enhanced the mystery. *The Figures of Julian Ashcroft* (1996) is another novel of the horror genre with frightening undertones. *Strange Objects* (1991) is considered such a gripping novel that children, teenagers, and adults all appreciate the sinister edge to C.'s writing style.

C. experimented with the SHORT STORY genre with the publication of stories such as "Sleeping over at Lola's" (1992), "Face to Stone Face" (1994), "A Breeze off the Esplanade" (1995), "The Bent Back Bridge" (1985), "The Barn" (1996), and "The Well" (1996). He also worked as the editor of the Dark House SERIES (1995) and edited the stories of others.

C. currently runs writing workshops and gives lectures at Queensland University of Technology and the University of the Sunshine Coast. His latest works include a series of picture books, *I Was Nothing: The Extinction of the Thylacine; I Said Nothing: The Extinction of the Paradise Parrot;* and *I Did Nothing: The Extinction of the Gastric Brooding Frog*—all in 2003. These titles are based on C.'s deep concern for endangered species. He uses this new focus to enlighten youth about the danger of extinction that many species face. Another focus is on MYTHOLOGY with C's fascinating story, *Old Ridley,* based on the tragic myth of Tithonus and Eos. Horror, mystery, gothic, fantasy, mythology—C. creates exceptional works that enthrall young and old. His expertly written stories, full of symbolism and mystery, continue to showcase his many talents.

AWARDS: *Strange Object:* 1991 Australian Children's Book of the Year [older readers], 1991 Alan Marshall Prize for Children's Literature, and, 1991 New South Wales Premier's Award; *Angel's Gate:* 1994 Australian Children's Book of the Year [older readers], 1994 National Children's Book of the Year; 1994 Australian Children's Book of the Year, *First Light; The Watertower:* 1995 Australian Children's Book of the Year, 1995 Bilby Children's Choice Award; 1996 Ned Kelly Award for Crime Writing, *The Well.*

SELECT FURTHER WORKS: *The Inner Circle,* 1986; *The House of Tomorrow,* 1988; *Inventing Anthony West,* 1994; *The Memorial,* 2004.

BIBLIOGRAPHY: *St. James Guide to Horror, Ghost and Gothic Writers,* 1998, reproduced in BIOGRAPHY Resource Center Online, 2003; http://www.home.gil.com.au/~cbcqld/crew/biog.htm

TERRY HAUGEN

CREW, Linda

Author, b. 8 April 1951, Corvallis, Oregon

C. frequently writes about young women growing up in Oregon during different eras. C was born and grew up in Oregon where she currently lives.

C's most recent novel is *Brides of Eden: A True Story Imagined.* This historical novel gives a fascinating look at a true incident which occurred in Corvallis in 1903, when Joshua, a young firebrand preacher arrives in town, develops a devoted following, and in so doing turns families and FAMILY members against each other, turning everything upside down. It is both intriguing and fascinating; one feels both for the vulnerable followers as well as for the angry townspeople, as one senses that lives will be wounded and some may be ruined forever and ever. An Afterword provides an insightful look at what happened to the main characters of this story. C. includes photographs of the town and some of the people which make the tale even more heartrending, knowing that it did really happen.

Fire on the Wind is a historical novel set in Oregon in 1933. It is based upon an event that occurred during the dry summer of 1933 when a fire, known as the Tillamook Burn, destroyed an entire region. Against this backdrop is the story of Estora (Storce) who lives in a logging camp with her family and other loggers. Like of all C.'s stories it is interesting to see how the heroines notice the different way their fathers interact with them now that they are young women or in Storie's case have "bosoms." They no longer bounce them on their knees and really don't know what to do except to behave in a very protective manner where their daughters and boys are concerned.

Children of the River is C.'s first novel. It is a moving story of a very capable young woman, Sandora, who at the age of seventeen has already experienced a lifetime. Anyone who reads Sandora's story will feel empathetic to her plight because of the pain and sorrow she feels having been harshly uprooted from her home to flee without her parents and siblings to a foreign land: the USA. At the age of thirteen Sandora flees Cambodia with her mother's younger sister and family.

Sandora is entrusted with the care of her three-day-old cousin. Tragedy occurs on the boat to freedom which haunts Sandora in the new land as she struggles with a new culture, a new love, and her own traditions. Without recriminations or chastisements to either culture C. tells a story of what it might be like to be a refugee. She speaks from an individual's view and tells what they may think, what they see, and what they judge. It is a tale that hurts so much that it makes it almost unbearable to read sometimes. Yet, the story always finds the essence of human kindness and decency at the most unusual times.

It isn't the image of a heroic American doctor leaving his home to treat people in a refugee camp in a faraway land that leaves a lasting impression. Instead it is a fleeting image of a Khmer man on a bicycle literally fleeing from death who quietly saves a life, while placing his own life at risk. It is this picture that stays long after reading *Children of the River.*

AWARDS: International Reading Association Children's Book Award, Golden Kite Honor Book, Michigan Library Association Young Adult Honor Book, ALA Best Book for Young Adults for *Children of the River,* 1989.

FURTHER WORKS: *Someday I'll Laugh about This,* 1990; *Nekomah Creek Christmas,* 1994; *Long Time Passing,* 1997; Nekomah Creek, 2001.

BIBLIOGRAPHY: *Contemporary Authors,* vol. 19–20; vol. 29; vol. 109. *Delacorte Press. Dictionary of Literary BIOGRAPHY,* vol. 87. *HarperCollinsPublishers.*

SUSAN E. MORTON

CRICHTON, Michael

Author, b. 23 October 1942, Chicago, Illinois

As World War II was raging, novelist C. was born.

In a 1995 interview with *Time Online,* C. said, "My father was a journalist and I was always interested in writing; even at a very young age, second or third grade. But it's a hard job and I wasn't sure I could succeed at it." Several unconfirmed reports suggest C. had an article published in the *New York Times* as a fourteen-year-old in 1956: a thoughtful look at the meteor-scarred Arizona desert under the pen name of Gladwin Hill. As a fifteen-year-old, he still dreamed of following in his father's footsteps, according to *Time.*

Even his teachers were behind him. In an interview with journalist Jesse Kornbluth, C said, "I still remember them: Miss Fromkin in the third grade, Miss Bennett in ninth, Mr. McGrath in eleventh and twelfth. What they really did was read all my awful stuff for years and years. I wrote endlessly as a kid, mostly lovesick sorts of things (I had a pretty poor social life). And my teachers encouraged me . . . despite what they were reading.

C. entered Harvard University hoping to pursue his writing career, but grew discouraged. "I lasted about a year [in English]," C. said in a 1999 article in the *Yale Daily News.* "I was in class one day, and the lecturer said, 'In Romeo and Juliet, act follows act, scene, scene.' After that I said, 'I'm out of here,' and went into anthropology." The study of early civilizations appealed to C. and he excelled, graduating *summa cum laude* in 1964. After Harvard, C. became a Visiting Lecturer in Anthropology at Cambridge University in 1965. "I carried this interest in the history of human beings into my study of medicine," he says in his informational materials. He entered Harvard Medical School in 1969 and spent a memorable year studying at the Salk Institute for Biological Sciences in La Jolla, California.

Amid the blistering demands of academia, C. found time to write. He helped pay for medical school writing thrillers under the pseudonyms "John Large" and "Jeffrey Hudson." The first novel credited to C., *The Andromeda Strain* was published in 1969—the same year he studied with Dr. Salk. At the same time, he was working toward his medical degree, C. was dubbed, "the father of the techno-thriller."

Soon after the success of his first novel, C. left his medical career to write full time, and he has been prolific, crafting eighteen works of fiction and non-fiction, selling more than one hundred million books, directing films, creating television series—including the wildly popular *E.R.*—and raising a family, in just over three decades.

The dinosaur novel *Jurassic Park* (1990) launched C. into the realm of iconic authors and filmmakers and expanded his adults-only reader base to include TEENS. In fact, young people brought about the sequel, *The Lost World* (1995). "It all began with kids who wrote me, or sent me e-mail, asking about the sequel," C. told *Time.* "This was all before the movie even began. Kids assumed there would be a sequel."

YOUNG ADULT readers continue to correspond with C., and he respects their participation, but insists that he doesn't specifically write to that audience. "I've always had a lot of younger readers, and I hope they like this book, too," C. said as he discussed his 2002 book release, *Prey.* "But I don't really write with anybody in mind."

While he may not have specific audiences in mind, C. does write to a specific task or purpose. "Generally I am aware of trying to do one of two things," he says in an interview. "Either I am trying to solve a problem of narrative—for example, how can you make people believe in living dinosaurs, at least for a few hours? Or I am trying to understand a problem in the real world—what's the relationship between aggressor and victim in sexual harassment? And out of that effort may come a book, or a screenplay."

Once an idea is in place, each book decides its own period of gestation. According to C., *The Great Train Robbery* (1975) took three years to complete, *Sphere* (1987) required twenty years, *Jurassic Park* took eight years and *Disclosure* (1994) was done in five. "Usually, an idea 'cooks' in my head for a very long time before I write it," he says.

Even as he writes, C. continues to read. What are a few of his all-time favorite books? "*Lord of the Flies* by William Golding is the novel I most admire of any I've read," he says. "*Life on the Mississippi* by Mark Twain (I consider it a novel); *The Thirteen Clocks,* James Thurber; *Northanger Abbey,* Jane Austen; anything by Sigmund Freud, who is undoubtedly the greatest novelist of the 20th century. And some childhood favorites: *The Hound of the Baskervilles* by Arthur Conan Doyle; *The Woman in White* by Wilkie Collins; *The Mysterious Island* by Jules Verne."

AWARDS: Edgar Allan Poe Award, 1968 and 1980; 1970 Association of American Medical Writers Award; 1995 Academy of Motion Picture Arts and Sciences Technical Achievement Award; 1995 George Foster Peabody Award; 1995 Writer's Guild of America Award; 1996 Emmy.

FURTHER WORKS: *The Terminal Man,* 1972; *Eaters of the Dead,* 1976; *Congo,* 1980; *Rising Sun,* 1992; *Airframe,* 1996; *Timeline,* 1999; *Prey,* 2002; *State of Fear,* 2004.

BIBLIOGRAPHY: Interview with Michael C., *Chicago Tribune* May 1997; *Time Online,* September 22, 1995; *Yale Daily News,* February 10, 1999, http://www.yaledailynews.com/article.asp?AID = 686; HarperCollins Interview, 2002; *The Book Report Interview,* Jesse Kornbluth, December 20, 1996.

KELLY MILNER HALLS

CROSS, Gillian
Author, b. 24 December 1945, London, England

C. writes social realism for YOUNG ADULTS. Her works especially appeal to avid readers who are drawn to popular genres, such as her fast-paced humorous novels, historical fiction, and psychological thrillers. As a young girl, she loved to entertain her family and friends, and she faithfully kept a JOURNAL. Later, she studied accomplished writers at Oxford and Sussex Universities and was intimidated by all the details; however, while reading K. M. Peyton's *The Beethoven Medal,* she realized that a novel tells a story, and the flow of words in a well-crafted novel tells the story well. *On the Edge* (1984) is a psychological thriller that received critical acclaim. One aspect of C.'s appeal as a writer is her belief that humans are strong enough to encounter difficulty, survive, and grow from the experience; therefore, she is not hesitant to expose a malevolent side of life in her fiction. This is particularly evident in *Tightrope* (2001), whose TEENAGE protagonist looks after her invalid mother and is a good student during the day. But at night she walks a tightrope between the gangs in her neighborhood and her desire to tag local buildings, risking her life to leave graffiti on even the most inaccessible surfaces.

AWARDS: Carnegie Medal Highly Commended Book and Guardian Award runner-up for *The Dark behind the Curtain* (1982); American Library Association Best Book for Young Adults and Notable Book, the Whitbread Award runner-up, and the Edgar Allan Poe runner-up for *On the Edge;* Carnegie commended book in 1986 and an ALA Best Book for Young Adults in 1987 for *Chartbreak* (1986), titled *Chartbreaker* in the U.S.; 1988 Carnegie Medal runner-up for *The Map of Nowhere* (1989); Carnegie Medal in 1991 for *Wolf,* Smarties Prize and the Whitbread Children's Novel Award for *The Great American Chase* (1993). ALA Best Books for Young Adults list 2001 for *Tightrope.*

FURTHER WORKS: *The Iron Way,* 1979; *The Dark behind the Curtain,* 1982; *The Demon Headmaster,* 1982; *Chartbreak,* 1986; *Wolf,* 1991; *Tightrope,* 1999; *Phoning a Dead Man,* 2002; Dark Ground trilogy, 2004.

BIBLIOGRAPHY: Gallo, Donald R., ed. *Speaking for Ourselves too,* 1993; Hunt, Peter, ed., *Children's Literature: An Illustrated History,* 1995.

NANCY SPENCE HORTON

CROSSOVER READS—TWEEN TO TEEN

Demographers report that there are more than twenty-seven million "tweens" in the U.S., an audience that book publishers, among others, are anxious to tap into. When young readers are ready to move up and on to more challenging reading experiences, it often proves to be a fluid time period between old favorites in the children's collection and new authors and ideas in books marketed for upper elementary and middle school audiences. Readers in the years between nine and twelve or thirteen are both transitional and aspirational in their reading interests as they move along the continuum toward true YA literature. And with this age group, it's all about rapid changes, the desire to emulate someone older and a wide range of developmental characteristics. A twelve-year-old has experienced roughly 50 percent more life than an eight-year-old! And what defines "young" or "appropriate" varies just as widely, and is dependent on many factors, including family values and behaviors, emotional and psychological maturity, personal interests, and reading comprehension skills. Looking at the age-level designations publishers apply to books can be misleading, since they are hoping to reach as wide an audience range as possible. As young readers move toward young adult books, they need to develop the requisite understanding and experience of the world to make sense of the characters, themes, and stories. What about their abilities and skill level—is reading a struggle or a bore? Reluctant readers often emerge at this time, when being read to is no longer a given at school or at home, and a newly developing and wider range of personal interests requires a greater variety of reading formats and genres to capture their interest. Gender differences in reading can become more pronounced. In the tween years, boys will be boys, and girls may be boys, but will boys be girls as far as reading books with main characters of the opposite sex? Young readers will say they prefer to read about characters at least a year or two older than they are, anxious to experience being older, more independent, increase their self-esteem, and find new avenues of interest to excite and entertain them.

In these in-between years, kids can act like kids when they are alone, but tend to want to play it cool and appear older and more sophisticated in public. They often still look to trusted adults for advice on reading choices; however, one can still count on bumping up against the tween need to challenge the voice of authority from time to time, so offer lots of variety in reading possibilities and make it as self-service as possible.

Research into this age cohort is fascinating—today's tweens tend to be conventional, optimistic about the future, to feel pressured to know more, do more, "play well with others" and be team-oriented, prefer active methods of learning and have a relatively high technology skill set (especially boys). Many have experienced complex family structures, a world of fallen and fallible heroes, and, with the world at their fingertips, or keyboard, tend toward instant gratification. They tend to be more comfortable and accepting of a multicultural world, say they are environmentally conscious and believe it's important to volunteer and make a difference (Howe and Strauss). The tween years are an age of fads and obsessions (think about the popularity of Pokemon and Dragon Ball Z, or even a certain wizard named Harry). As consumers, they believe in brand loyalty, and that extends to favorite authors and book SERIES. As they move along their reading path, tweens are comfortable with quick starts that engage their interest, and short chapters with lots of action. Some appealing themes in books include the idea of rescue and revenge, family and friendship, and transformation and change. When connecting tweens and books, think about the Triple I effect: individuality—very personal and passionately held interests and a ten-

dency to hero worship; imagination—almost anything should still be possible; imitation—tweens can be an avid fan base for what inspires them to aspire.

Accelerated Reader programs and schools' summer reading lists help direct tweens to new reading pleasures by introducing authors and genres, or titles with a slightly older feel by trusted author friends like Judy BLUME, Jerry SPINELLI, and Gary PAULSEN. Media tie-ins are an important connection, where books about TV or movie characters are cross-marketed (Mary Kate and Ashley series for tweens spawns Mary Kate and Ashley Sweet 16; Tokyopop's Lizzie McGuire series of graphic novels).

One great way to hook this transitional audience is with the familiar PICTURE BOOK format, but all grown up in theme and execution. Curriculum connections are a natural with books like *Pink and Say* (1994) by Patricia Polacco (Civil War history); *Smoky Night* (1994, David Diaz) social studies and civil unrest in Los Angeles; Pam Munoz RYAN's *When Marian Sang* (2003) to introduce studies on AFRICAN AMERICAN or Women's history. The burgeoning market for GRAPHIC NOVELS, especially Japanese manga, has found a ready audience in tween readers, so identify those series especially aimed at them—Electric Girl (2000) by Michael Brennan, a girl and her mischievious gremlin; Peter David's *Spyboy* series of ADVENTURES starring a high school superhero with a curfew; and Jeff Smith's marvelous Bone adventures.

Other exciting new formats have emerged to capture this audience. Verse novels are popular, especially with reluctant readers. Try Karen HESSE's Newbery Award–winning *Out of the Dust* (1997) and Sharon CREECH's *Love that Dog* (2001). Tweens will read POETRY beyond childhood favorites such as Shel Silverstein and Jack Prelutsky. Introduce them to artists like Sara Holbrook (*Walking on the Boundaries of Change: Poems of Transition,* 1998); Naomi Shihab NYE (*This Same Sky: a Collection of Poems from Around the World,* 1992); or the PRINTZ AWARD-winning collection *Heart to Heart, New Poems Inspired by 20th Century American Art,* (2001). Genre reading continues to be a familiar hook. MYSTERY readers enjoy moving from Warner's *The Boxcar Children* to Joan Lowery NIXON's suspenseful thrillers. SCIENCE FICTION fans of Bruce COVILLE's *Aliens Ate My Homework* (1996) will enjoy Madeline L'Engle's trilogy beginning with *A Wrinkle in Time* (1962) and on to William SLEATOR's exciting *Interstellar Pig*

(1984). Historical fiction readers who loved the humor of *Catherine, Called Birdy* (1994, Karen CUSHMAN) will happily discover AVI's *Crispin: the Cross of Lead* (2002); or they can move through Ann RINALDI's many American history titles, starting with the *Quilt Trilogy* (1994). And then there's FANTASY, where Harry Potter broke down any boundaries about who would read what, as well as resistance to big, fat books! Fans who can't wait for the next ROWLING opus are happily devouring books by Cornelia Funke (*Thief Lord,* 2001; *Inkheart,* 2003); planned trilogies from Jonathan Stroud (*Amulet of Samarkand,* 2003), Zizou Corder (*Lion Boy,* 2003), and Christopher Paolini (*Eragon,* 2003), this last having the bonus of a fifteen-year-old author! Add in the runaway hit *A Series of Unfortunate Events* by Lemony Snicket and the 2003 Newbery award-winning *The Tale of Despereaux* by Kate DiCamillo, and fantasy has an unbeatable track record with tween readers. Young adult readers have enjoyed the many FAIRY TALE retellings published for them, and books like *Ella Enchanted* (1997) by Gail Carson LEVINE and *The Prince of the Pond, Otherwise Known as deFawg Pin* (1992) by Donna Jo NAPOLI capture the tween audience and entice them into Meg CABOT's adventures of a modern-day princess in her *Princess Diaries* (2000), the basis of a popular MOVIE.

Publishers have capitalized on this in-between group with several series, including Scholastic's *Dear America* and *Royal Diaries,* Tyndale's *Left Behind: The Kids,* a junior version of Tim LaHaye's popular apocalyptic series, and Pleasant Company's *Girls of Many Lands.* Another interesting development has been the entry of adult authors like Carl Hiaasen (*Hoot,* 2002) and Neil GAIMAN (*Coraline,* 2002) into the field of juvenile fiction.

Think again about the tween characteristic of enjoying active methods of learning and connect them with high interest non-fiction from authors like David MACAULAY (*Pyramid,* 1975; *Mosque,* 2003), the developmental issues books from Free Spirit Press that answer tween questions about physical and emotional changes of puberty, *Chicken Soup for the Preteen Soul* (2000) or fun craft projects like making wallets and corsages from, of all things, duct tape (*Got Tape?* 2002) by Ellie Schiedermayer.

Looking for more crossover authors for readers moving from children's books to young adult reading? Stock lots of copies of Phyllis Reynolds NAY-LOR's popular Alice series, so readers can follow Alice through her own middle-school years and beyond. And keep a display of books by Christopher Paul CURTIS, Jerry SPINELLI, Kimberly Willis HOLT, Avi, Richard PECK, Lois LOWRY, Katherine PATERSON, and E. L. KONIGSBERG, whose most recent book, *The Outcasts of 19 Schuyler Place* (2004), brings to the forefront of the story a younger character from her award-winning *Silent to the Bone* (2000). Which books appeal across gender lines? You can't beat Louis SACHAR's *Holes* (1998), Edward BLOOR's *Tangerine* (1997), or any of Jack GANTOS' Joey Pigza books. Bookmark author John Scieszka's website, which encourages boys to read at www.guysread.com.

There are wonderful transition books for this wonderful transitional time of life, as children become young adults and begin to actively shape their own reading lives. Great writers, keep 'em coming.

BIBLIOGRAPHY: Dresang, Eliza, *Radical Change: Books for Youth in a Digital Age,* 1999; Howe, Neil and William Strauss, *Millennials Rising: The Next Great Generation,* 2000; Smith, Michael W., *Reading Don't Fix No Chevys: Literacy in the Lives of Young Men,* 2002.

MARY ARNOLD

CROWE, Chris
Author, n.d., n.p.

The IRA Children's Book Award recognizes the early work of an author who shows great promise. C.'s first novel for YA readers, *Mississippi Trial, 1955,* won the award in 2003. This novel is a historical story that centers on the real-life murder of Emmett Till, a black TEEN who was killed for allegedly flirting with a white woman in a small Mississippi town in 1955. When C. won the award, he joined the ranks of previous winners such as Christopher Paul CURTIS, Lois LOWRY, and Philip PULLMAN.

C. followed the success of *Mississippi Trial, 1955,* with a nonfiction account of the slaying of Till entitled *Getting Away with Murder: The True Story of the Emmett Till Case.* That book was a unanimous choice for the 2004 Best Books for YA (BBYA) list from the YA Library Services Association (YALSA) of the American Library Association.

The germ for the two books on Till originated with an interview C. conducted with Newbery-winning author Mildred Taylor. Taylor mentioned that the Till case was a pivotal one in the CIVIL-RIGHTS MOVEMENT. Intrigued, C. began to dig into the case. Soon, he realized that there was a story that needed telling. First, however, he completed his critical analysis of Taylor's work in *Presenting Mildred Taylor.* C. is also the author of *More than a Game: Sports Literature for Young Adults.*

A past president of the Assembly on Literature for Adolescents(ALAN), and editor of the YA literature column in *English Journal,* a publication of the National Council of Teachers of English (NCTE), C. is the author of many articles and chapters on YA literature. Sports literature for YA is a primary area of interest and research for him.

AWARDS: ALA Best Books for YA, 2003, *Mississippi Trial, 1955;* ALA Best Books for YA list, 2004, *Getting Away with Murder: The True Story of the Emmett Till Case.*

BIBLIOGRAPHY: Lesesne, Teri S., "History as Story: An Interview with Chris C.," *Teacher Librarian,* 31:4, pp. 58–60.

TERI S. LESESNE
AND EDWARD R. SULLIVAN

CRUTCHER, Chris
Author, b. 17 July 1947, Dayton, Ohio

Known widely as an author who tells the tough truths in his intense works of fiction, Crutcher's novels present adolescents struggling against seemingly insurmountable problems in their lives. Despite these obstacles, C.'s protagonists manage to survive, even to come out of their struggles in some sense stronger. From his first novel for YOUNG ADULTS, *Running Loose* (1983) to *Whale Talk* (2001) and beyond, the novels of C. have received critical acclaim. C.'s lifetime of work in the field of YA literature was acknowledged with the 2000 Margaret A. Edwards Award from the Young Adult Library Services Association (YALSA), a division of the American Library Association (ALA). Additionally, each of his books has been named to the Best Books for Young Adults (BBYA) list by YALSA. C. also received the California Young Readers Medal for two books, *Ironman* (1995) and *Staying Fat for Sarah Byrnes* (1993). His novels have appeared on numerous state reading lists.

C.'s work as a family therapist no doubt informs his writing. For many years, C. has worked with trou-

bled adolescents and their families. It should be no surprise, then, that each of his novels has a sensitive, caring adult who helps the protagonist deal with the problems he faces. Max in *Stotan!* (1986) and Mr. Nak, as well as Bo's school counselor (a grown Lionel from *Stotan!*) in *Ironman* (1995), for example, offer much-needed advice to the young protagonists. In *Whale Talk* (2001), T. J. routinely sees a psychologist and even helps her deal with a younger client.

C.'s novels examine what happens when a young man has to face tremendous loss. Sometimes the loss is literal: Louie Banks's girlfriend dies unexpectedly from a brain aneurysm in *Running Loose* (1983); Dillon witnesses his brother's suicide in *Chinese Handcuffs* (1989), and Lionels parents are killed in a boating accident in *Stotan!* (1986). The losses, however, can be more difficult to pin down. Sarah Byrnes in *Staying Fat for Sarah Byrnes* (1993) seems to have lost her power of speech. In *The Crazy Horse Electric Game* (1987), Willie loses his athletic prowess due to a head injury. He has also lost a sister to Sudden Infant Death Syndrome. Whether the loss is immediately apparent or not, each character struggles to find something to fill the void. Each of C.s main characters shares another common trait: he is an athlete. Willie Weaver in *The Crazy Horse Electric Game* (1987) plays baseball. *Stotan!* (1986), *Staying Fat for Sarah Byrnes* (1993), *Ironman* (1995), and *Whale Talk* (2001) focus on swimming, either as an individual sport or as part of the triathalon. Louie Banks in *Running Loose* (1983) plays football, and Dillon in *Chinese Handcuffs* (1989) is also a gifted athlete. Though sports figure prominently in each of C.'s novels, it would be a disservice to label his writing "sports fiction." Rather than focusing on the play-by-play of the individual sports, though there are plenty of details to make the competitions authentic, C. focuses on the individual athlete on and off the field.

C. penned a collection of stories in 1991. *Athletic Shorts* featured some characters from C.'s novels in stories sometimes set before the events of the novel and sometimes after the novel from which the character originated had ended. One of the stories, "A Brief Moment in the Life of Angus Bethune," became the basis for the movie "Angus." C. has also written a novel for adult readers entitled *The Deep End* (1994). In 2003, C. published *King of the Mild Frontier: An Ill-advised* AUTOBIOGRAPHY.

In addition to his works of YA literature, C. has written extensively about topics related to education, most notably CENSORSHIP and school violence. His column, "A Hand Up," is a regular feature of *Voices from the Middle,* the journal for middle-level educators from the National Council of Teachers of English. Each column addresses an issue of importance for TEENS and those who work with them in the classroom. C. was honored by NCTE in 1998 with its Intellectual Freedom Award for his efforts to combat censorship. A final characteristic of C.'s work may seem paradoxical considering the intense subjects he addresses in his books. Although C.'s novels deal with DEATH, suicide, violence, incest, and abuse, they are also marked with great good humor. Even in the midst of tragedy, that glimmer of humor provides a beacon of hope for the characters and those who read C.'s books.

AWARDS: *Running Loose,* BBYA 1983; *Stotan!,* BBYA 1986; *Crazy Horse Electric Game,* BBYA, 1987; *Chinese Handcuffs,* BBYA 1989; *Athletic Shorts,* BBYA 1991; *Staying Fat for Sarah Byrnes,* BBYA 1994, California Young Readers Medal; *Ironman,* BBYA 1996, California Young Readers Medal 1995; *Whale Talk,* 2002 BBYA; *King of the Mild Frontier: An Ill-Advised Autobiography,* BBYA 2004; Crutcher has three titles on the Best of the Best List: *Athletic Shorts: Six Short Stories* was one of 100 YA titles selected for the 4th YALSA Best of the Best List: Here We Go Again . . . 25 Years of Best Books (Selections from 1967 to 1992); *Running Loose* was one of 100 YA titles selected for the 3rd YALSA Best of the Best List: Nothin' but the Best (Selections from 1966 to 1986); *Stotan!* was one of 100 YA titles selected for two of the four YALSA Best of the Best Lists: Nothin' but the Best (Selections from 1966 to 1986), Here We Go Again . . . 25 Years of Best Books (Selections from 1967 to 1992).

FURTHER WORKS: *The Sledding Hill,* 2005.

BIBLIOGRAPHY: www.Authors4Teens.com; www.aboutcrutcher.com

TERI S. LESESNE

CURTIS, Christopher Paul

Author, b. 10 May 1953, Flint, Michigan

C. has a gift for creating books containing real-life characters that readers feel they know. These dynamic characters are prevalent in *The Watsons Go to Birmingham—1963* (1995) which received both a Newbery Honor and Coretta Scott King Honor in 1996. The Watson family is an AFRICAN AMERICAN family from Flint, Michigan, dealing with Byron, a boisterous and creative son. They decide that only Grandma Sands in Birmingham can teach Byron the self-discipline he needs. The book describes the family's drive south and the ADVENTURES that await them when they arrive during this troubled time in history.

C.'s family has been a dominant force in his writing. Each family member has played a significant role in his development as a writer. It began with his parent's supportive encouragement. Whenever his mother would read his school newspaper article, she would always heap praise on him. That positive feedback helped mold the individuality he expresses today in his writing. Shortly after high-school graduation, much to his mother's chagrin, C. began working on the assembly line of Flint's Fisher Body Plant, where he hung doors on cars. For thirteen years C. kept busy during his breaks by keeping a JOURNAL of things that happened at the plant. He never really thought he would be a writer; it was simply a way to make work at the factory more tolerable.

This was followed with the key role his wife Kaysandra played in developing his successful writing career. Impressed by his knack of getting to the essence of his topic, she encouraged him to pursue a writing career. Taking a year off to write full time on his first novel, *The Watsons Go to Birmingham—1963* (1995) was her idea. Their two children, Steven and Cydney, also contributed in their own ways: Steve was his first reader of *The Watsons Go to Birmingham—1963* while Cydney supplied artistic talent as the composer of the song "Mommy Says No" in *Bud, Not Buddy* (1999).

C.'s characters are a composite of important people in his life. Kenny Watson in *The Watsons Go to Birmingham—1963* is a combination of Curtis and his brother Kenny. Some of the incidents in the book are taken from actual events. The pictures on the front cover of *The Watsons Go to Birmingham—1963* are of Curtis's family. C. lived his stories. Many of his characters came from his heritage such as his grandfather Earl "Lefty" Lewis, a Negro Baseball League pitcher, and his grandfather Herman E. Curtis Sr., 1930's bandleader of "Herman Curtis and the Dusky Devastators of the Depression."

Search for identity is a powerful theme for the YA reader because it evokes sympathy for the protagonist. In *Bud, Not Buddy,* the protagonist is ten-year-old Bud Caldwell, who is frantically searching for information about a man who might be his father. Throughout his journey to the other side of the state, he encounters many setbacks that drive the plot. The book includes dynamic characters with realistic dialogue that help the reader connect with the story. Other themes prevalent in his novels are survival, hope, FAMILY, and racism.

Music is a common thread winding through C.'s books. In *The Watsons Go to Birmingham—1963,* the family purchases a radio to entertain them on their long car trip. In *Bud, Not Buddy,* the flyers of Herman E. Calloway and his famous band expose Bud to the music scene of the 1930s.

Threads intertwined in both his novels are C.'s family heritage and events in American history. Good historical fiction enables readers to connect with events and people in history. To accomplish that, C. does extensive research so that the setting of each novel is accurate. He not only researches historical events, but the way people acted, spoke, and the fears they had. Set in the 1930s, *Bud, Not Buddy* deals with Bud's journey to see if the man is indeed his father. In *The Watsons Go to Birmingham—1963,* C.'s realistic setting allows the reader to envision the past clearly. In both novels, C. provides the reader with a sense of historical time and place that gives focus to the novels. The detail he includes helps intensify the emotions of the eras.

Today C. is a full-time writer living in Ontario, Canada with his wife and two children. He is currently working on several YA books, one of which is a contemporary novel for young adults and another which might be a sequel to *Bud, Not Buddy.* C. is enthusiastic about informing young people about what a "wonderful, empowering, fun art writing is."

AWARDS: *The Watsons Go to Birmingham—1963:* 1996 Newbery Honor Book, 1996 Coretta Scott King Honor book, 1995 Bulletin Blue Ribbon, 1995 Golden Kite Award Book, *Horn Book* Fanfare, ALA Top Ten Best Book/Quick Pick, ALA Best Book for Young Adults, ALA Notable Book for Children, *Booklist* Top 25 Black History Picks for Youth, IRA Young Adult Choice, NCSS-CBC Notable Children's Trade Book in the Field of Social Studies, Bank Street Child Study Association Children's Book Award, *New York Times* Book Review Best Book, *Publishers Weekly* Best Book, *Publishers Weekly* Flying Start Author, and Notable Book for a Global Society; *Bud, Not Buddy:* 2000 Newbery Medal, 2000 Coretta Scott King Award, Golden Kite Award for Fiction, 1995 Golden Kite Honor Book, Sugar Maple Awards Winner Grades 4–6, and Young Reader's Choice Award, ALA Best Books for Young Adults list, 2000; *Bucking the Sarge:* 2004, *Publisher's Weekly* Best Children's Book, 2004 *SLJ* Best Books for Children, 2004 Parents' Choice Gold Award, 2004 *Booklist* Editor's Choice Award, 2005 ALA BBYA, 2005 ALA Notable Children's Books, 2004 Golden Kite Award.

BIBLIOGRAPHY: "Christopher Paul Curtis Bio information," NothingButCurtis.com, http://christopherpaulcurtis.smartwriters.com; Curtis, Christopher Paul, "Newbery Acceptance," *Horn Book Magazine* Vol. 76 Issue 4, Jul/Aug 2000, p. 386; Green, Michelle Y., "An eye for talent," *Reading Today* Vol. 21 Issue 1, Aug/Sep 2003, p. 20; Lamb, Wendy, "Christopher Paul Curtis," *The Horn Book Magazine.* Boston: July/Aug. Vol. 76, Iss.4; 397–402; Lesesne, Teri, "Writing the stories brewing inside of us," *Teacher Librarian* Vol. 27 Issue 4, Apr 2000, 60; Scott Smith, Russell & Grisby, Lorna, "His True Calling," *People* Vol 53 Iss. 15 4/17/2000, 113–115; Weich, Dave. "Christopher Paul Curtis Goes to Powell's," http://www.powells.com/author/curtis.html

KATHY A. VANSTROM

CUSHMAN, Karen
Author, b. 4 October 1941, Chicago, Illinois

C. is a Newbery Medal–winning author of historical fiction. C.'s interest in writing began when she read YA novels with her daughter. Long after her daughter progressed to adult novels, C. continued reading YA literature. C. holds degrees in English and Greek from Stanford University, human behavior and museum studies from U.S. International University, San Diego, and museum studies from John F. Kennedy University, Orinda, California. Early in her adult life she was discouraged from writing because conference speakers encouraged only trendy topics, whereas C. was interested in historical fiction and themes of responsibility, compassion, and coming of age. As C. listened to author Ray Bradbury tell the conference attendees to write from their hearts, she found the inspiration to write.

At this time in her life, C. pursued her interests in the medieval world, researching and writing for three years, and then publishing her first novel, *Catherine, Called Birdy* (1994). Her eleven years of teaching in the museum studies department of a San Francisco Bay area university gave the author background in everyday life of historical eras. C.'s experience of moving from Chicago to Tarzana in Southern California as an eleven-year-old provided the emotions of the title character in *The Ballad of Lucy Whipple* (1996). This work focuses on the few females who were involved in the California Gold Rush. In *Matilda Bone* (2000), C. takes her readers back to medieval England, but to a far different protagonist than Brat in Newbery winner *The Midwife's Apprentice* (1995). Matilda is as much in need of care and attention as Brat, but their lives are very different.

C. does most of her historical research in what she calls "old libraries that have books left over from the 1920s and 1930s"; she finds that newer sources do not contain the kind of information she needs. When asked why she thinks that her writing appeals to young adults, she answers that she can relate to their developmental phase because she is stuck in that same adolescence. C. states that her themes of identity and sense of place are issues that young readers typically experience. As an author, she believes in facing these issues through literature.

AWARDS: 1996 Newbery Medal, *The Midwife's Apprentice* and ALA Best Books for Young Adults list, 1996; *Catherine, Called Birdy;* Newbery Medal Honor Book, Carl Sandburg Award for Children's Literature, Golden Kite Award, *School Library Journal* Best Book, and Parents' Choice Foundation Ten Best Books list. Also, ALA Best Books for Young Adults list, 1995.

BIBLIOGRAPHY: Cushman, Philip, "Karen Cushman," *The Horn Book Magazine,* vol. 72, no. 4, 420–424; Lodge, Sally, "A Talk with Karen Cushman," *Publishers Weekly,* vol., 243, no. 35, 46; http://www.achuka.co.uk/special/cushman.htm

NANCY SPENCE HORTON

DAHL, Roald

Author, b. 13 September 1916, Llandaff, Wales; d. 23 November 1990

D., born to Norwegian parents, was the only son of a second marriage. His father died when D. was just three years old, leaving his mother to care for two stepchildren and her own four children. As a child, D. loved books and writing. He kept a secret DIARY hidden in a tin box and tied to a branch at the top of a tree in his garden. Every day, he would climb to the top of the tree, uncover his diary, and write that day's entry. His idiosyncratic tendency to write in secret places continued into adulthood; he often retreated to a hermitage in his backyard to concentrate on his work.

When D. was nine, he left home to board at St. Peter's Prep School where he was often homesick. To pass the time, D. wrote a letter to his mother every week. This began a tradition which lasted thirty-two years, until his mother's death. In these letters, D. chronicled both his school days and his childhood, two subjects which would resonate in later, published works.

At age eighteen, D. joined an expedition to Newfoundland, and later worked as an oil salesman. WAR broke out in 1939, and D. signed up with the Royal Air Force in Nairobi, Kenya. After a crash in Libya, D. was sent home to Wales as an invalid, but he was later transferred to Washington as an air attaché. There, he met the writer C. S. Forester, who published

D.'s first story, "Shot Down Over Libya," in the *Saturday Evening Post.*

D.'s first book, *The Gremlins* (1943), was a PICTURE BOOK that was a favorite of Eleanor Roosevelt's. D.'s early career, however, focused on SHORT STORIES for adults, and many of these stories contained D.'s characteristic macabre, devilish twists. These stories were published in widely read MAGAZINES, including *The New Yorker, Harper's,* and *Atlantic Monthly.*

In 1953, D. married actress Patricia Neal, with whom he had five children. D.'s career as a children's author took off in the 1960s, when he began writing the bedtime stories he told his children. *James and the Giant Peach* (1961), one of D.'s best-loved books, is the story of a sad little boy who lives with his wicked aunts after the tragic DEATHS of his mother and father. When James spills magic crystals on his aunts' peach tree, a magnificent, giant peach grows. James climbs into the enlarged piece of fruit, and the ADVENTURE begins.

Matilda (1988) is one of D.'s best-selling books for children. When it was first published, it broke all previous records for children's fiction when over half a million PAPERBACKS were sold in the UK alone in the first six months. Matilda is a smart little girl whose intelligence is greatly underappreciated. She has a particular knack for practical jokes, too, and can fool most everyone. The only person who can seemingly evade her is the mean school principal, or can she?

D. has said, "I'm probably more pleased with my children's books than with my adult short stories.

Children's books are harder to write. It's tougher to keep a child interested because a child doesn't have the concentration of an adult. The child knows the television is in the next room. It's tough to hold a child, but it's a lovely thing to try to do."

After a divorce, D. married Felicity "Liccy" Crosland in 1983. In 1990, he succumbed to a rare blood disorder. His books, however, have maintained their popularity with readers young and old. Over one million titles by D. are sold worldwide every year.

AWARDS: New England Round Table of Children's Librarians Award (1972) and Surrey School Award (1973) for *Charlie and the Chocolate Factory;* Surrey School Award (1975) and Nene Award (1978) for *Charlie and the Great Glass Elevator;* Surrey School Award (1978) and California Young Reader Medal (1979) for *Danny, Champion of the World;* Federation of Children's Book Groups Award (1982) and Good Book Guide "Best Books of the Past 20 Years" (1997) for *The BFG;* Massachusetts Children's Award (1982) for *James and the Giant Peach; New York Times* Outstanding Books Award, Federation of Children's Book Groups Award, and Whitbread Award (all 1983) for *The Witches;* World FANTASY Convention Lifetime Achievement Award (1983); *Boston Globe–Horn Book* nonfiction honor citation (1985) for *Boy: Tales of Childhood;* Federation of Children's Book Groups Award (1988) for *Matilda;* Smarties Award (1990) for *Esio Trot;* Millennium Children's Book Award and Blue Peter Book Award (2000) for *Charlie and the Chocolate Factory.*

FURTHER WORKS: *Charlie and the Chocolate Factory,* 1964; *The Magic Finger,* 1966; *Twenty-nine Kisses from Roald D.,* 1969; *Fantastic Mr. Fox,* 1970; *Selected Stories,* 1970; *Charlie and the Great Glass Elevator,* 1972; *The Witches,* 1973; *Danny, Champion of the World,* 1975; *The Wonderful Story of Henry the Sugar and Six More,* 1977; *The Complete Adventures of Charlie and Mr. Willy Wonka,* 1978; *The Enormous Crocodile,* 1978; *Tales of the Unexpected,* 1979; *Taste and Other Tales,* 1979; *The Twits,* 1980; *George's Marvelous Medicine,* 1980; *The BFG,* 1982; *Roald D.'s Revolting Rhymes,* 1982; *Roald D.'s Book of Ghost Stories,* 1983; *Two Fables,* 1983; *Dirty Beasts,* 1983; *Rhyme Stew,* 1983; *Boy: Tales of Childhood,* 1984; *The Giraffe and the Pelly and Me,* 1985; *Two Fables,* 1986; *Going Solo,* 1986; *Ah, Sweet Mystery of Life,* 1989; *Esio Trot,* 1990; *The Minipins,* 1991; *The Vicar of Nibbleswick,* 1991; *My Year,* 1993; *Vile Verses,* 2005.

BIBLIOGRAPHY: www.roalddahl.com; http://www.kirjasto.sci.fi/rdahl.htm; www.amazon.com

CARRA E. GAMBERDELLA

DALKEY, Kara M.
Author, b. 1953, Los Angeles, California

D., a writer of FANTASY novels for adults as well as YOUNG ADULTS, studied anthropology at the University of California at Los Angeles. She then went on to study fashion design at the Fashion Institute of Design and Merchandising. In the late 1970s, D. moved to Minneapolis where she joined a writer's group called Scribblies. This group work led to D.'s publication of FANTASY SHORT STORIES in the mid-1980s. D. then began writing fantasy novels set within historical settings for the adult market. After acquiring much acclaim for her numerous short stories and novels for adults, D. published her first novel for young adults, *Little Sister* (1996). The success of *Little Sister* led to the publication of a sequel, *The Heavenward Path,* and to the publication of a trilogy for the young adult market.

AWARDS: Children's Literature Association of Utah Young Adult Book (2000) for *Little Sister.*

SELECTED FURTHER WORKS: *Little Sister,* 1996; *The Heavenward Path,* 1998; *Ascension,* 2002; *Reunion,* 2002; *Transformation,* 2002.

REFERENCES: *Authors and Artists for Young Adults,* online, 2002; *Contemporary Authors,* online, 2001, *St. James Guide to Fantasy Writers,* online, 1996.

HOLLY E. MAY

DALY, Maureen
Author, b. 15 March 1921, County Tyrone, Ulster, Ireland

D. was born to Joseph Desmond and Margaret Daly. She attended Rosary College in River Forest, Illinois, and received her degree in 1942. She submitted her own work to a *Scholastic* MAGAZINE SHORT STORY contest when she was only fifteen years old, and won third prize for her efforts with "Fifteen." The following year, her English teacher encouraged her; she submitted "Sixteen," and took first prize. Her first novel, *Seventeenth Summer,* was published when she was only twenty-one years old. This book is still in print, and has sold over a million copies all around the world. When it was published, there was no "YOUNG ADULT" category for books, and the book was reviewed as an adult selection. Today, it has come to define the quintessential adolescent story of young love, romantic yearning, and what it is like to grow up female. D. became known through this important work as the Mother of Modern Young Adult Literature.

D. had three sisters; the daughters in *Seventeenth Summer* were patterned after her own FAMILY. Her father, Joseph Daly, left Ireland and journeyed to Fond du Lac, Wisconsin, where the author grew up. D. met her future husband, writer William McGivern, at a book signing. They married in 1946 and moved to Europe a few years later. They had two children, a daughter, Megan and a son, Patrick. Megan passed away from cancer in 1983. D. endowed a library in her daughter's memory at the Barbara Sinatra Children's Center, Eisenhower Medical Complex, Rancho Mirage, California.

D.'s literary career included working as a freelance writer and journalist from 1938 on. She was a reporter for the Chicago City News Bureau in the early 1940s and later became associate editor of *Ladies' Home Journal* from 1944–49. When she was in Europe, D. continued writing and developed a particular affinity for life in Malaga. The Spanish theme is reflected in many of her works at that time, particularly *Spanish Roundabout* and *Spain: Wonderland of Contrasts.*

When their daughter and son became teenagers, the D.s returned to live in the U.S. and moved to a farm in Pennsylvania. They later moved again—this time, to Palm Desert, California. D.'s husband passed away from cancer in 1982. Her grief in the years that followed led her to seek solace in her writing, this time focusing on young adult titles such as *Acts of Love* (1986) and *First a Dream* (1990).

AWARDS (1936) *Scholastic* magazine short story contest awards, third prize for "Fifteen"; (1937) *Scholastic* magazine short story contest awards, first prize for "Sixteen"; (1938) O. Henry Memorial Award for "Sixteen"; (1942) Dodd, Mead Intercollegiate Literary Fellowship Novel Award for *Seventeenth Summer;* (1952) Freedom Foundation Award for "humanity in reporting" for "City Girl"; (1962) Gimbel Fashion Award; (1969) Lewis Carroll Shelf Award for *Seventeenth Summer;* (1987) *Acts of Love* selected as one of *Redbook*'s Ten Great Books for Teens.

FURTHER WORKS: *The Ginger Horse,* 1964; *Spain: Wonderland of Contrasts,* 1965; *The Small War of Sergeant Donkey,* 1966; *Rosie, the Dancing Elephant,* 1967; *A Matter of Honor,* 1984 (with William P. McGivern); *My Favorite Suspense Stories,* 1968; *The Seeing,* 1980 (with William P. McGivern); "The Gift" in *God and Me,* 1988 (ed. Candida Lund); *More than Words,* 2004.

BIBLIOGRAPHY: Hipple, Ted, Ed. *Writers for Young Adults.* Vol. 1, 1997; Contemporary Authors Online, 2002.

SANDRA KITAIN

DANZIGER, Paula
Author, b. 18 August 1944, Washington, D.C.; d. 8 July 2004, New York City

Reared in Manhattan, D. knew by second grade that she wanted to be a writer. D. grew up in a dysfunctional family. Although her parents were caring, her father was an angry man and her mother was fearful of the imagined dangers on the farm where they lived for a time. When her father yelled at her, D. remembered his words, telling herself that someday she'd use them in a book. Neither was school a positive experience for D.; she was not a strong student, as her creative interpretations of assignments were not what her teachers had in mind. Additionally, D. struggled with weight problems that led to social vulnerability. D. escaped at her local library. With the help of a librarian there, she read and delighted in creating imaginary characters that she could control.

Despite her dislike of school, D. went on to earn a B.A. in English from Montclair State College in 1967. Upon graduating, D. spent many years with junior-high, high-school, and college students as a teacher and counselor. She preferred working with junior-high students, as they most appreciated her creative, flamboyant style. D. also spent many summers with poet John Ciardi, who, as her mentor, strongly influenced her life and work. In 1970, two automobile accidents in two days left D. with orthopedic problems and a temporary inability to read or write. During this time, D. began thinking about her career and decided to get a Master's degree in reading. It was also at this point that D. decided to act upon her interest in writing.

D. published her first book, *The Cat Ate My Gymsuit* (1974), four years after her two serious car accidents. The protagonist, Marcy Lewis, has low self-esteem as a result of her obesity and her dysfunctional FAMILY. Marcy suffers through her entrance into adolescence, and readers sympathize with her character. This book is the most AUTOBIOGRAPHICAL of D.'s works. In *The Pistachio Prescription* (1978), thirteen-year-old Cassie learns that the answer to her problems is to like herself, rather than eat the pistachio nuts which always seem to make her feel better. D. has written over twenty-five books for children. Her YA novels are primarily concerned with adolescent issues, including social and family relationships, self-esteem, obesity, and first love.

In 1998, D. teamed up with friend and fellow author Ann M. Martin (*Babysitter's Club* SERIES) to write *P.S. Longer Letter Later: A Novel in Letters* (1998). This story of two friends who are separated when one moves to Ohio is told through an exchange of letters, with each woman writing as a different character. To write this book, D. and Martin first discussed their characters, and then began faxing letters back and forth in the voices of the two girls. Those faxes became the novel, and each author's voice is distinctly present. This novel was followed by a sequel, *Snail Mail No More* (1999). Here, the two main characters continue their correspondence through e-mail, discussing such topics as divorce, coming of age, and boys.

A more recent book, *United Tates of America* (2002), allows D. to showcase another talent: scrapbooking. The book's thirteen-year-old protagonist, Skate Tate, has mixed feelings about middle school, but finds comfort in the scrapbook club she's been in since third grade. The book's scrapbook insert was designed by D.

D.'s clear insight into the TEENAGE psyche is a result of her own childhood, her experiences as both a teacher and counselor, and her highly developed imagination. Through her writing, D. acknowledges her readers' emotions and assures them that they are not alone in the world. Critical response to D.'s books has been mixed, but the popularity of her work confirms that her target readership appreciates her well-developed characters and their realistic situations, all written with a dash of humor. These are the hallmarks of D.'s writing style. The Amber Brown Fund was established by her friends after D.'s death, in 2004. The fund will be used to support young writers.

AWARDS: INTERNATIONAL READING ASSOCIATION Children's Choices: 1979, *The Pistachio Prescription*, 1980 for *The Cat Ate My Gymsuit*, and *Can You Sue Your Parents For Malpractice*, 1981 for *There's a Bat in Bunk Five*, and 1983 for *The Divorce Express*.

FURTHER WORKS: *Divorce Express*, 1974; *Can You Sue Your Parents for Malpractice?*, 1979; *There's a Bat in Bunk Five*, 1980; *It's an Aardvark-Eat-Turtle World*, 1985; *This Place Has No Atmosphere*, 1986;

Remember Me to Harold Square, 1987; *Everyone Else's Parents Said Yes*, 1989; *Make Like a Tree and Leave*, 1990; *Earth to Matthew*, 1991; *Not for a Billion Gazillion Dollars*, 1992; *Thames Doesn't Rhyme with James*, 1994; *Amber Brown Is Not a Crayon*, 1994 and series.

BIBLIOGRAPHY: *The Continuum Encyclopedia of Children's Literature*, 2001; *Eighth Book of Junior Authors and Illustrators*, 2000; http://www.childrenslit .com/f_danziger.html; http://hosted.ukoln.ac.uk/ stories/stories/danziger/interview.htm.

CARRA GAMBERDELLA

DASH, Joan
b. 18 July 1925, New York City

D. completed a B.A. at Barnard College in 1946. She has written numerous nonfiction books, the majority about women (many of them notable Jewish women). Beginning as an article in *Mademoiselle*, her first book about extraordinary women became *A Life of One's Own: Three Gifted Women and the Men They Married* (1973) about Margaret Sanger, Edna St. Vincent Millay, and Maria Goeppert-Mayer.

D. followed *A Life of One's Own* with *Summoned to Jerusalem: The Life of Henrietta Szold*, (1979), *The Triumph of Discovery: Women Scientists Who Won the Nobel Prize* (1991), and *We Shall Not Be Moved: The Women's Factory Strike of 1909* (1997). In these books, D. continued to reveal her own discoveries about intelligent and inspiring women, writing about the heroines who were often omitted from or barely mentioned in the canon of history. *We Shall Not Be Moved* was named a Best Book for YOUNG ADULTS in 1997.

In 2000, D. returned to the area of science with her celebrated *The Longitude Prize*. In it, D. retells the story of John Harrison, English carpenter and clockmaker, who discovered the method for determining longitude while at sea. Susan P. Bloom for *The Horn Book* notes the "rich anecdotes" and calls the book a "well-handled BIOGRAPHY" (2000, pp. 767–68). D. received the *Boston Globe–Horn Book* Award for Nonfiction (2001) for the book.

D. acknowledges that in writing nonfiction "the writer's job is to tell a story" (*Contemporary Authors* 2003). "[In] fiction," she adds, "the writer has to make up the story she's telling[, but in] nonfiction, the writer must find the story within the material" (*ibid.*). It is for D.'s ability to do just that, clearly present the story that already exists, that she has been praised. Bloom comments that in telling Harrison's story in *The Longitude Prize,* D. "never attempts to invent" (2000, p. 767). Carolyn Phelan, a writer for *Booklist,* in commenting on *The World at Her Fingertips: The Story of Helen Keller* (2001), says, "Keller's story would be extraordinary in any telling, but D.'s straight-forward account seems closer to reality than the more idealized stories sometimes offered to children" (2001, p. 1129).

D. resides in Seattle, Washington, with her husband.

AWARDS: *The Longitude Prize:* 2001 Inaugural Robert F. Sibert Honor Books; *Boston Globe–Horn Book* Award for Nonfiction, 2001; Best Books for Young Adults (nominated); *We Shall Not Be Moved:* Best Book for Young Adults, 1997; *The Longitude Prize* and *The World at Her Fingertips:* Best Books for Young Adults (nominated).

BIBLIOGRAPHY: Bloom, S. P. (2000). [Review of the book *The Longitude Prize*]. *The Horn Book, 76,* 767–768; Phelan, C. (2001). [Review of the book *The World at Her Fingertips*]. *Booklist, 97,* 1129; *Contemporary authors online* (2003), http://www.galenet.com/servlet/LitRC?finalAuth = true.

MARY MCMILLAN TERRY

DAVIS, Jenny
Author, b. 29 June 1953, Louisville, Kentucky

A troubled adolescence and early struggle with mental illness provided inspiration for this writer's best-known and most controversial work, *Sex Education.* A family move to Pittsburgh, Pennsylvania, in the 1960s introduced D. to harsh neighborhood realities of gangs, racial tensions, and violence and had a critical effect on her life. With the loss of her early enthusiasm for learning and her frequent delinquency from school, D. sought escape from her high school's hostile environment in museums, parks and libraries, sanctuaries that allowed her to pursue her own interests. Her high-school years were interrupted when she entered a psychiatric hospital at the age of fifteen. She remained there for one year, trying to come to terms with the difficulties she faced in her TEENAGE years and learning how to cope with the realities of growing up in an urban environment.

D. found the stability she was seeking when she entered college. She graduated from the University of Kentucky, and decided to pursue a career in the field of education, with a concentration at the middle-school level. D. did not start out with aspirations of becoming a writer; it happened because she was teaching writing. Her philosophy of teaching is to have students do things in which they find value. After teaching writing for one year, D. began writing SHORT STORIES herself and then moved on to longer works. She uses writing, social activism, and teaching to convey her personal experiences and help teenagers survive their own adolescent years. In her novels, D. confronts many challenges that teenagers face, and teaches that loneliness, insecurity, DEATH, and violence are all a part of life and that parents are not always right.

D.'s life experiences are conveyed through Olivia, "Livvy," a sixteen-year-old patient in a psychiatric hospital in *Sex Education.* The title of the book is bold, and D. remained convinced it was the only title appropriate for the novel, even though her publisher strongly disagreed. Despite the daring title, *Sex Education* won high praise for its powerful story that describes the difficulties of caring for others.

D. wrote her first novel *Good-Bye and Keep Cold* (1987) during the two weeks her sons went to California with their father. She did not set out to write a full-length novel; she merely needed something to keep her company during her separation from her FAMILY. D. gained notoriety with this book for her ability to balance the personality of her protagonist and a detached, objective point of view that allows readers to judge the main character on their own.

D. is the mother of four children as well as a full-time teacher. Due to her full schedule, finding time to write is sometimes difficult, but she is able to devote her weekends to writing. The work D. produces has at times been difficult for publishers to classify due to its mature subject matter. She did not originally intend to write for a YOUNG ADULT audience, but her unique way of approaching subjects tests the boundaries previously established in the genre.

AWARDS: American Library Association Best Book for Young Adults: 1987 for *Good-Bye and Keep Cold,* and 1991 for *Checking on the Moon.*

SELECT FURTHER WORKS: *Good-Bye and Keep Cold,* 1987; *Sex Education,* 1988, (published as *If I'd Only Known,* 1995); *Checking on the Moon,* 1991; *Anchovy Breath to Zoo Food: One Hundred Seventy-Five Names I Call My Brother When I'm Mad,* 1994; *Dear Heart,* 1998.

BIBLIOGRAPHY: "Jenny D.," *Authors and Artists for Young Adults,* vol. 21, 1997.

RHONDA EL-SAID

DAVIS, Terry

Author, b. 10 October 1946, Spokane, Washington

Born to a car salesman father and a homemaker mother, D. believes he was brought up to be a story-teller. Without siblings to help entertain him, he slipped into imaginary scenarios as the only child of a frail and sometimes ailing mother who adored good books. The fertile imagination he developed under her direction and on his own still informs his fiction today.

D.'s experiences as a junior- and senior-high-school athlete also influence his writing. He insists he was not a natural jock, and yet he excelled in baseball, basketball, and wrestling. Basketball came more easily to D., but the mental and physical mysteries of wrestling became a quiet passion. "It's about balance," D. says. "Even a smaller athlete can excel in wrestling if he can find his focus and his sense of personal balance." That same ideology became the driving thread of D.'s first and, as yet, most critically acclaimed novel, *Vision Quest* (1979). Through the voice of Louden Swain, D. captured the heart and soul of adolescent determination and longing so skillfully that John Irving called it "the truest novel about growing up since *The Catcher in the Rye.*" It was named an American Book Award nominee in 1980.

D. earned a B.A. from Eastern Washington University, where he came to know fellow Spokane novelist Chris CRUTCHER. The praise he received from John Irving had great importance in his life. Before *Vision Quest* was even a rough draft, D. studied under Irving's direction at the University of Iowa's Writers' Workshop. He was awarded his Master of Fine Arts in 1973 from the University of Iowa and studied as a Stegner Fellow at Stanford University in 1974–75.

When D. began to put *Vision Quest* on paper, Chris Crutcher—then a teacher in Northern California—played a part. "D. and I would go for a run," Crutcher says, "and talk about his latest chapter. I learned about the writing process from D., about revision and structure, long before I was writing stories of my own." When Crutcher did finish his first novel, *Running Loose* (1982), D. was among its first readers and helped find it a publishing home.

In 1982, Hollywood adapted *Vision Quest* to film, with Mathew Modine as Louden and Linda Fiorentino as his love interest, Carla. The ending strayed from D.'s original storyline, but he insists that the heart of the film and the book were very much in sync. *Vision Quest,* the MOVIE, was also famous for launching the career of a little-known lounge singer known as Madonna; the movie has become a cult classic.

On the heels of first novel success, Davis went on to write two more novels and many SHORT STORIES for YA anthologies and literary collections. He has been a teacher in the MFA program at Mankato State University in Minnesota since 1986. His first edited anthology will be released by Simon & Schuster in the fall of 2005.

Davis has raised two children of his own (a son Pascal and a daughter Anissa) and two stepchildren (Josh and Steph). He loves dogs, cats, classic motorcycles, racquetball, and thoughtful fiction. He is currently single and lives in Mankato, Minnesota, during the school year and at a cabin on the shore of Loon Lake near Spokane, Washington, during the summer months.

AWARDS: *If Rock and Roll Were a Machine* was named an ALA Best Book for Young Adults in 1993; *Vision Quest* was one of 100 YA titles selected for the 4th YALSA Best of the Best List: Here We Go Again . . . 25 Years of Best Books (selections from 1967 to 1992); American Library Association Best Books for YA; New York Public Library, Books for the Teen Age; Distinguished Alumni Award, Eastern Washington University; Governor's Award for the Arts, State of Washington; American Book Award nomination; Wallace Stegner Literary Fellowship, Stanford University.

FURTHER WORKS: *Mysterious Ways,* 1984; *If Rock and Roll Were a Machine,* 1992; *Presenting Chris Crutcher,* 1996.

BIBLIOGRAPHY: A series of interviews with Terry Davis by Kelly Milner Halls; Chris Crutcher interviews by Kelly Milner Halls; Terry Davis's website, www.terrydavis.net

KELLY MILNER HALLS

DEATH AND DYING IN YA LITERATURE

In recent years, authors of YA fiction have confronted death and dying in their works with an honesty and realism that were rarely seen before. Many young people turn to such literature as sources of comfort and/or information. These readers may be dealing with grief in their personal lives or know someone who is. For others, such issues are a mysterious curiosity. Literature provides a portal through which these young adults can learn about death and dying through characters who have had real experiences.

Related literature for younger children explores death and dying in a very gentle manner, usually through the natural loss of a beloved grandparent or pet. Young adult literature, however, often deals with tougher issues, including terminal illnesses and accidental deaths. The relationships in such novels—including parent/child, sibling, and best friend—make the stories even more complex.

Much of the grief-based literature for young adults deals intimately with terminal illness. In *A Time for Dancing* (1997) by Davida Willis HURWIN, sixteen-year-old Juliana is diagnosed with histiocytic lymphoma, a deadly form of cancer. Juliana receives chemotherapy, makes many emergency trips to the hospital, and tries her hardest to fight back against a body that is quickly betraying her. Her best friend, Samantha, feels helpless as she watches Juliana decide to stop chemotherapy and then slowly die. The chapters alternate between Juliana's and Samantha's voices, a technique that provides the reader with perspectives from both sides of this powerful story.

Another young adult novel that deals with a friend's terminal illness in a realistic way is *Six Months to Live* (1995) by Lurlene McDaniel. In this novel, Dawn and Sandy quickly become best friends in the hospital, where they are both undergoing cancer treatment. Each girl goes into remission, but Sandy later relapses. Dawn finds herself dealing with particularly difficult emotions, wondering why she was spared. McDaniel is the author of several other young adult novels that deal with terminal illnesses, including *A Time to Die* (1992), *I Want to Live* (1995), *Don't Die, My Love* (1997), and *Now I Lay Me Down to Sleep* (1999).

Other authors have written novels that deal with the terminal illnesses of family members. In *With You and Without You* (1986) by Ann Matthews Martin, the twelve-year-old narrator introduces the reader to her life before and after her father's death to cardiomyopathy, a heart ailment. The father, knowing that he has a set amount of time before dying, urges his family to help him make his remaining time happy. His death, however, is still very difficult to accept. Adding to the

novel's realism are the different ways in which the characters grieve.

In *Saying It Out Loud* (2001), Joan ABELOVE tells the poignant story of Mindy, a sixteen-year-old girl at odds with her mother. When her mother is diagnosed with a brain tumor, Mindy experiences extreme grief and guilt. As she works through these complex emotions, the reader is provided with the insights of a young woman who is searching for solid ground. Mindy reaches many conclusions, including the realization that before her illness, her mother and she communicated in subtle ways that she hadn't before noticed.

Many authors have written novels that center around accidental deaths. In *Tears of a Tiger* (1996), Sharon DRAPER tells the story of Andy, a high-school basketball star who drinks, drives, and gets into a terrible accident. His best friend—trapped in the car—burns to death. Despite counseling and the support of those around him, Andy cannot rid himself of the memory, and eventually commits suicide. Though the devastating double tragedy is a difficult subject to tackle, Draper approaches it with an honesty that captivates her TEENAGE readers.

In *The Perks of Being a Wallflower* (1999), first-time author Stephen CHBOSKY writes about shy, awkward Charlie, a high-school freshman whose best friend has recently committed suicide. The depression he experiences is made more difficult by the stress of being a student—and an unpopular one at that. But coming to terms with his friend's death and his own coming-of-age make Charlie a likeable character from whom readers will surely learn, if not identify.

Blackwater (1999) by Eve BUNTING is the story of a prank gone too far. Fueled by jealousy, thirteen-year-old Brodie tips a boulder, sending two friends into a raging river. He tries to save them, but he is the only one pulled from the river by rescuers. One friend is later found dead. As the search for the second friend continues, Brodie's conscience troubles him. His grief, coupled with the story's suspenseful plot, makes this a chilling read that will provoke thought among teenage readers.

There are also many nonfiction books for teenagers to help them deal with grief in a healthy manner. In *Straight Talk About Death for Teenagers: How to Cope with Losing Someone You Love* (1993), Earl Grollman discusses "Accidental Death," "Self-inflicted Death," "Talking," "Crying," and "Going

Nuts." Each succinct entry answers questions that young adults often ask when they find themselves in difficult situations.

Laura Dower, author of *I Will Remember You: What to Do When Someone You Love Dies* (2001), encourages teen readers to keep their chins high in the wake of a terrible loss. One aspect of this book that sets it apart from similar titles is a section on what teens should not say when talking with a friend who is grieving. Readers are also urged to take comfort in the fact that although they may feel completely lost, they are never alone.

Young adults want and need to be heard and understood, yet they are proverbially reluctant to express themselves. When they are faced with situations involving death and dying, many are unsure how to appropriately deal with grief. They question whether their reactions are normal and need guidance as to how to begin the healing process. Recent literature addresses these needs in a realistic and comforting manner.

FURTHER WORKS (other works that deal with death and dying): FLEISCHMAN, Paul, *Whiligig,* 1999; McDaniel, Lurlene, *The Girl Death Left Behind,* 1999; *Reach for Tomorrow (One Last Wish),* 1999; PATERSON, Katherine, *Bridge to Terabithia,* 1987; RYLANT, Cynthia, *Missing May,* 1993; SOTO, Gary, *The Afterlife,* 2003.

BIBLIOGRAPHY: DeMinco, Sandrea, "Young adult reactions to death in literature and life," *Adolescence,* spring 1995, Vol. 30, Iss. 117, 179; Harvey, Carolyn and Dowd, Frances S., "Death and dying in young adult fiction," *Journal of Youth Services in Libraries,* Winter 1993, Vol. 6, No. 2, 141.

CARRA GAMBERDELLA

DEAVER, Julie Reece
Author, b. 13 March 1953, Geneva, Illinois

D. grew up in a FAMILY where creativity was both modeled and encouraged. Her father was a writer as well as an artist, along with her mother. As a result, D. became an artist herself, having illustrations published in MAGAZINES such as *Reader's Digest* and *The New Yorker.* At the age of seventeen, D. won an honorable mention in the *Seventeen* magazine annual fiction contest. In that SHORT STORY, she wrote about characters her own age. As she grew older, however, she found that her characters remained TEENAGERS. And D. continued to write for the YA age group.

Pursuing writing, along with her older brother who also writes, D. wrote another story. Intended for *Seventeen,* it became her debut novel, *Say Goodnight, Gracie* (1988). The story deals with Morgan's overwhelming loss and grief as she deals with the death of her best friend. Morgan reappears in *The Night I Disappeared* (2002), this time as a confidant of Jamie, a troubled teenager dealing with a new home and a terrifying secret. In *Chicago Blues* (1995), D. tells the story of a family torn apart by alcoholism, and how two sisters must rely on one another in order to survive.

Through realistic dialogue and compelling stories, D. is able to tackle complex issues in an entertaining way: "I don't like young adult books that try to teach a lesson . . . I'm just interested in telling what I hope will be a good story." Besides novels, D. has also written television comedies and has been a special education teacher's aide. One day she hopes to be able to combine her art and her writing; in the meantime, she does the illustrations for her brother Jeffrey's MYSTERY novels.

AWARDS: American Library Association Best Book for Young Adults (1988) for *Say Goodnight, Gracie; Booklist* Young Adult Editor's Choice Citation (1995) for *Chicago Blues;* Evergreen Young Adult Award (1994); Virginia State Reading Association Young Readers Award (1991) for *Say Goodnight, Gracie.*

FURTHER WORKS: *First Wedding, Once Removed,* 1990; *You Bet Your Life,* 1993.

BIBLIOGRAPHY: *Contemporary Authors,* online, 2003; *Lives and Works: Young Adult Authors,* vol. 2, 1999; *St. James Guide to Young Adult Writers* (2nd edition), 1999.

MEGAN PEARLMAN
AND ANDREA LIPINKSI

DE GOLDI, Kate
Author, b. 18 August 1959, Christchurch, New Zealand

D., who writes stories for adults under the pseudonym Kate Flannery, also has a high profile as a children's and YA book reviewer on national radio. In addition, she has fronted a television books program and tutored classes on children's and YOUNG ADULT literature.

D.'s stories and novels are noteworthy for being located in actual places, particularly her birth city Christchurch and also the lush West Coast of South

Island, NEW ZEALAND. The author has written that she "wanted the geographic particularities imprinted on me *named* in my stories." Furthermore, her books are memorable for their unflinching honesty in exposing buried pasts, particularly those within FAMILIES, whether it is the traumas inflicted by WAR, adoption, or religion. In her own words, the "emotional truth" of the narrative outweighs any imperatives for unrealistic happy endings. D.'s characters are incisively yet sympathetically portrayed through a carefully crafted use of language, a skill in which the author excels. She is adept at precisely capturing and transmitting individual voices.

D.'s first young adult story, "Kissing Cousins," was included in the anthology *Falling in Love* (1995), edited by Tessa DUDER. This story featured Christy and Sonny, characters who later appear in D.'s second novel *Love, Charlie Mike* (1997), in which two wars are catalysts for the revelations of family secrets. Her first young adult novel, *Sanctuary* (1996), was a stunning debut: Catriona (Cat) spirals downward into the hidden depths as she struggles to come to terms with the accidental DEATH of her little sister in a house fire. *Sanctuary* is a literary novel in the best sense of the word, finely honed and multilayered. The far-reaching implications suggested by its title, the image of a caged and restless panther, extend to the deliberate pun on the protagonist's name, the story-within-a-story construction, and the oxymoron of the words "truth lies"; all of the elements make for a masterful work of literary technique and prowess. The characters in this first novel are immediate; their voices, concerns, and relationships authentic and integral.

Similarly genuine people appear in *Closed, Stranger* (1999), a term encapsulating the secrecy surrounding adoption in New Zealand until the early 1980s. Literary strength is particularly apparent through friends Max and Andy and the devastating impact on Andy when he meets his birth mother. D. has suggested recently that *Closed, Stranger* may be her final contribution to the young adult genre as she focuses more on writing for children. Even if that were the case, with these three works she has established an enduring reputation.

AWARDS: Esther Glen Award (1996) for *Sanctuary*. Shortlisted for this award in 1998 for *Love, Charlie Mike. New Zealand Post Children's Book Awards, Senior Fiction Award (1997) for Sanctuary*. Shortlisted for this award in 1998 for *Love, Charlie Mike*.

Shortlisted for this award in 2000 for *Closed, Stranger*. Arts Foundation of New Zealand Laureate (2001).

FURTHER WORKS: *Like You, Really,* 1994; "Cliff Minestrone," *Another 30 Stories for New Zealand Children,* (Barbara Else, ed), 2002; "A Fair Bit of Biff," *It Looks Better on You,* Jane Westaway and Tessa Copland, eds, 2003.

BIBLIOGRAPHY: Robinson, Roger and Nelson Wattie, eds. *The Oxford Companion to New Zealand Literature.* 1998. De Goldi, Kate. "Fiction made me," in *The New Zealand Children's Book Foundation Year Book.* 1999. http://library.christchurch.org.nz/Childrens/ChildrensAuthors/KateDeGoldi.asp; http://www.bookcouncil.org.nz/writers/degoldikate.htm.

BILL NAGELKERKE

DE LINT, Charles (Henri Diederick Hoefsmit)
Author, b. 22 December 1951, Bussum, Netherlands

Often described as a pioneer of contemporary FANTASY (or mythic fiction, as he prefers), D. is a World Fantasy Award–winning author who has penned over fifty works and who enjoys both devoted readers and wide critical acclaim. D. immigrated with his family to CANADA shortly after his birth, and spent much of his childhood moving as a result of his father's job with a surveying company. He lived in Western Ontario, Quebec, Turkey, and Lebanon, before finally settling outside Ottawa, Ontario. Leaving high school two credits shy of graduation, D. worked as a clerk in a record store and played Celtic music gigs on the weekends.

Though he wrote continuously for his own enjoyment, D. never considered trying to make a career of it until, at a friend's suggestion, he sold several stories to a small press MAGAZINE. During the next six years D. had limited success, until his novella *The Fame of the Grey Rose* (later expanded into the novel *The Harp of the Grey Rose*) was puchaed for inclusion in the fantasy SERIES *Swords against Darkness*. D. married the artist MaryAnn Harris in 1980 and, at her urging, began writing full time in 1983. That same year he sold three novels, and though he continued pursuing music (playing in bands Wickentree and then Jump at the Sun) D. devoted his professional life to writing.

As a teen, D. was a voracious reader whose tastes ran to MYTHOLOGY, folklore, and fantasy. Early favorite authors included Thomas Mallory, E. B. White,

J. R. R. TOLKIEN, Lord Dunsany, and Thomas Burnett Swann, as well as the heroic ADVENTURE fiction of Robert E. Howard and the HORROR tales of H. P. Lovecraft. D.'s debt to these classic works of fantasy is evident in his early work, most notably *The Riddle of the Wren* (1984), his first published novel. Though he completed a few more secondary world novels (*The Harp of the Grey Rose* [1985], *Wolf Moon* [1988], *Into the Green* [1993], D. moved away from traditional high fantasy. He credits his wife for the idea to set his novel *Moonheart* (1984) in an urban environment. A seminal work in the field, *Moonheart* is often credited as being one of the first successful blendings of mythological and folkloric elements with contemporary settings and characters. Using elements from Celtic and Native American folklore (as in so many of his later works), D. tells the story of an Ottawa manor house which serves as a doorway between the human world and a magical otherworld inhabited by creatures out of myth—such as the manitou—and figures out of legend—such as the Welsh bard Taliesen. *Spiritwalk* (1992) (collecting D.'s stories "Ascian in Rose," "Westlin Wind," and "Ghostwood") is a companion novel which offers readers another chapter in the continuing story of Tamson House and its eclectic inhabitants.

Dreams Underfoot (1993) marks the first appearance of "Newford," D.'s famous "everycity" which he created to free himself from the constraints of actual geography and location. This volume of SHORT STORIES was followed by further Newford collections *The Ivory and the Horn* (1995), *Moonlight and Vines* (1999), and *Tapping the Dream Tree* (2002), D.'s fiftieth book. The collections are some of D.'s best work, and earned a number of accolades, including World Fantasy Award nominations for *Dreams Underfoot* and *The Ivory and Horn* and the 2000 World Fantasy Award for Best Collection for *Moonlight and Vines*. D. further explored Newford and its denizens in perhaps his finest work, *Forests of the Heart* (2000), which features the Gentry ancient spirits of Ireland stranded in the new world. D.'s most recent work, *Spirits in the Wires* (2003), is another novel based at least partly in Newford, though much of the story takes place in a fantastic cyberspace where imagination fuels reality.

The Dreaming Place (1990) is D.'s only novel written expressly for YOUNG ADULTS. Native American folklore—in the form of a vampiric manitou—again plays a role in this story of a rebellious TEEN whose anger attracts the manitou's unwanted atten-tion. A recent collection *Waifs and Strays* (2002), nominated for a World Fantasy Award, gathers stories written throughout D.'s career and features all teen protagonists and a variety of settings—from Newford to Ottawa to the streets of cult-favorite Bordertown.

Preferring to interpret the mythical "battle between good and evil" on a smaller, personal, and very realistic scale, D. uses small stories to convey larger ideas and to illuminate the magic of everyday life and of the natural world. His work often centers around characters on the fringes of society—runaways, alienated teens, artists, abuse survivors, and his accurate and sensitive depictions of their lives allow him to ground his mythic sensibilities in hard reality. A truly unique vision, vivid characterization, and non-didactic messages have earned him a wide and loyal readership, as well as critical raves.

AWARDS: 1982 Small Press and Artists Organization Award for Fiction; First annual William L. Crawford Award for Best New Fantasy Author of 1984; 1988 Canadian SF/Fantasy Award (formerly known as the Casper; now called the Aurora), *Jack, the Giant-Killer;* 1989 Readercon Small Press Award, "The Drowned Man's Reel"; 1992 New York Public Library's Best Books for the Teen Age, *The Little Country;* 1997 Prix Ozone, "Timeskip"; numerous books cited on various YALSA and ALA "best of" lists; *Trader:* 1998 ALA BBYA; *The Blue Girl:* 2005 ALA BBYA.

FURTHER WORKS: *Mulengro,* 1985; *Yarrow: An Autumn Tale,* 1986; Jack, the Giant-Killer, 1987; *Greenmantle,* 1988; "The Drowned Man's Reel," 1988; *Svaha,* 1989; *Angel of Darkness* (as Samuel M. Key), 1990; "Berlin," reprinted in *Life on the Border,* 1991; *From A Whisper to A Scream* (as Samuel M. Key), The Little Country, 1991; 1992; *The Wild Wood* (Brian Froud's Faerielands, novel, illustrated by Brian Froud), 1994; *Memory and Dream,* 1994; *I'll Be Watching You* (as Samuel M. Key), 1994; *Jack of Kinrowan,* 1995; "Timeskip," 1996; *Trader,* 1997; *Someplace to Be Flying,* 1998; *Triskell Tales* (collection) 2000; *The Onion Girl,* 2001; *The Road To Lisdoonvarna,* 2001; *Seven Wild Sisters,* 2002; *A Handful of Coppers: Collected Early Stories,* vol. 1: *Heroic Fantasy* (collection) 2003; *A Circle of Cats,* illustrated by Charles Vess, 2003; *Medicine Road,* 2004; *The Blue Girl,* 2004; *Quicksilver and Shadow,* 2004.

BIBLIOGRAPHY: "Charles de Lint," *Authors and Artists for Young Adults,* vol. 33, 2000. Reproduced in *Biography Resource Center,* 2003; http://www .galenet.com/servlet/BioRC; "Charles (Henri Diederick Hoefsmit) de Lint," *St. James Guide to Fantasy*

Writers, 1999; "Charles de Lint," *St. James Guide to Young Adult Writers,* 2nd ed., 1999. Reproduced in *Biography Resource Center,* 2003; http://www .galenet.com/servlet/BioRCContemporary Author Online, 2003; "Charles de Lint: Mythic Fiction," *Locus Magazine.* June 2003. 7, 73–74; "PW Talks with Charles de Lint," *Publishers Weekly,* October 22, 2001, 53. Author's homepage: http://www .charlesdelint.com

JULIE BARTEL

DENENBERG, Barry
Author, b. 22 September 1946, Brooklyn, New York

D. describes books as his first love; he worked in a variety of bookstores. After being fired from a book company in 1986, he discovered that he hated being involved in the business aspect of books. He then pursued his second love, that of writing. D. studied history at Boston University; his interest in history is evident in his books. D. has written several BIOGRAPHIES as well as some popular historical fiction.

D. was given his first professional writing opportunity from Jean Feiwel, a publisher and editor-in-chief for a major children's publishing house. He later married her and they have one daughter, Emma, who shares this name with one of D.'s characters.

D.'s biographies cover a variety of interesting people, including Jackie Robinson, Charles Lindbergh, Muhammad Ali, John F. Kennedy, and Elvis Presley. D. not only captures the popular successes of the individuals in his biographies, but also the essence of their lives, their weaknesses, and personalities. D. portrays these legendary people with a great deal of accuracy, and provides necessary context, as well as essential background information. With *Nelson Mandela: No Easy Walk to Freedom* (1991), D. educates the reader not only of the life, jail time, and release of Nelson Mandela, but about apartheid and the events that touched both white and black South Africa. In *All Shook Up: The Life and Death of Elvis Presley* (2001), D. examines music and culture before, during, and after Elvis and shows parts of Elvis's rocky life.

Probably his most acclaimed and recognized work to date is *Voices from Vietnam* (1994) which presents an oral history of his experience in Vietnam during the WAR. In a work that is referenced in many curriculum guides to the Vietnam War, D. includes quotes from notable people such as former president Lyndon

Johnson, as well as Walter and Jane Cronkite. The book's greatest strength lies in the words and stories of those who experienced Vietnam firsthand.

D. is the author of several books in the popular SERIES "Dear America," "My Name is America," and "The Royal Diaries." He has written five books to date for the "Dear America" series, in DIARY format, from the perspective of girls growing up during various periods of history. D.'s books range from the 1840s in *So Far From Home* (1997) through Pearl Harbor in 1941 with *Early Sunday Morning* (2001) and covers the Civil War, the 1930s and World War II.

In "My Name is America," the counterpart series whose main characters are boys, D. highlights the American Revolution in *Journal of William Thomas Emerson* (1998) and Japanese internment camps in *Journal of Ben Uchida* (1998).

Through all of these works, D. brings the past to life and makes various aspects of history enjoyable reading for today's YOUNG ADULTS. Always thorough and never one to shy away from the controversial aspects of his characters or periods in history, D.'s books are both educational and entertaining.

AWARDS: ALA Best Books for Young Adults and New York Public Library Books for the Teenage for *Voices from Vietnam* (1996) and *An American Hero: The True Story of Charles A. Lindbergh* (1997); ALA's Top Titles for Adult New Readers, *Voices from Vietnam.*

FURTHER WORKS: *John Fitzgerald Kennedy: America's 35th President,* 1988; *The Story of Muhammad Ali,* 1989; *True Story of J. Edgar Hoover and the F. B. I.,* 1993; *An American Hero: The True Story of Charles A. Lindbergh,* 1996; *When Will This Cruel War Be Over?: The Civil War Diary of Emma Simpson, Gordonsville, Virginia, 1864,* 1996; *Stealing Home: The Story of Jackie Robinson,* 1997; *One Eye Laughing, the Other Weeping: The Diary of Julie Weiss, Vienna, Austria to New York, 1938,* 2000; *Mirror, Mirror on the Wall: The Diary of Bess Brennan: The Perkins School for the Blind 1932,* 2002; *Elisabeth of Austria: The Princess Bride,* 2003.

BIBLIOGRAPHY: www.scholastic.com *(Authors and Books Homepage section); Publishers Weekly* and *School Library Journal* book reviews.

TINA HERTEL

DESSEN, Sarah
Author, b. June 1970, Evanston, Illinois

Bursting onto the YOUNG ADULT LITERATURE scene in 1996, D. took off running and never looked back.

Her first five novels were all selected to the Best Books for Young Adults lists by the American Library Association and received numerous other awards and honors. D.'s writing is notable for its strong, believable characters facing difficult but unique and realistic situations during the tumultuous time of adolescence.

Although she was born in Illinois, D. grew up in Chapel Hill, North Carolina, with her parents, both professors at the University of North Carolina, and brother; she still resides there. She lives in the country with her husband, some lizards, and two dogs. D. finds that living in the area where she spent her TEEN-AGE years helps her keep in touch with the situations and feelings of that time in her life, which in turn helps her to emphatize with contemporary teenage lives as she writes.

In 1993, D. earned her B.A. in English with Highest Honors in Creative Writing at the University of North Carolina, where she presently teaches. After graduation, she decided to continue her job as a waitress and concentrate on her writing. Working as a waitress provided time for her to write in the afternoons and make a good living while giving her the opportunity to observe people who inspired her creativity.

In 1996, three years after graduating from college, her first book was published. *That Summer,* a unique sister-of-the-bride story, received starred reviews in *Publishers Weekly, Booklist,* and *Kirkus.* In addition, it was translated into four languages.

Two years later, *Someone Like You* followed. It is the story of two friends, one pregnant, whose boyfriend has just been killed in an accident, one falling in love with the wrong guy who is pressuring her for sex. *Keeping the Moon* (1999) features a teenage girl who loses weight and then learns that positive self-esteem comes from the inside, not the outside. Dealing with the frightening and difficult situation of a girl whose boyfriend physically and emotionally abuses her, *Dreamland* (2000) became D.'s most serious book to date. *This Lullaby* (2002) presents a unique character whose mother has married numerous times and, because of this family history, is terrified to commit to a romantic relationship herself. All four of these books have been awarded significant honors in the young adult literature field.

Besides her novels, D. has written SHORT STORIES that have appeared in anthologies. Her story, "Umbrella," was featured in *This Is Where We Live*

(2000). *One Hot Second: Stories about Desire* (2002) included her story, "Someone Bold."

Combining elements of D.'s first two novels, *Someone Like You* and *That Summer,* New Line Cinema produced a screenplay and feature-length MOVIE, *How to Deal* (2003). Tapping from two novels by one author to make a film is an unusual concept. *Someone Like You* provides the three main characters, while *That Summer* inspires the FAMILY life situations infiltrating the story. Popular actress Mandy Moore plays the lead character in the film. Although she did not write the screenplay, D. has written a novelization, *How to Deal* (2003).

D. did not set out to be a young adult writer, but her agent noticed the strong teenage voice in her works and submitted her first novel to a publisher who decided to publish it as a work for YOUNG ADULTS. Although D. enjoys writing for an older audience as well, time and again she is brought back to the stories of high school.

AWARDS: *Someone Like You:* 2001 South Carolina Young Adult Book Award; 2001 Missouri Gateway Book Award; Maryland Library Association Black-Eyed Susan Award; named "best" book by School Library Journal and ALA; ALA Quick Pick for Reluctant Readers. *Keeping the Moon:* 2000 ALA Best Books for Young Adults and Quick Picks for Reluctant Readers; Best Book of the Year by School Library Journal; New York Public Library Books for the Teen Age list. *Dreamland:* 2001 ALA Best Books for Young Adults; New York Public Library Books for the Teen Age list; YALSA Popular PAPERBACKS for Young Adults list. *This Lullaby:* Best Books for Young Adults and New York Public Library Books for the Teen Age lists; *Los Angeles Times* Book Prize Finalist.

FURTHER WORKS: *That Summer,* 1998.

BIBLIOGRAPHY: Dessen, Sarah. Home page. 1 May 2003 http://www.sarahdessen.com/bio.html; "Dessen, Sarah." In *Something About the Author,* v. 120, Gale, 2001, 82–86; Sarah Dessen.authors4teens.com 2 May 2003; http://greenwood.scbbs.com/servlet/A4Tstrat?source = bibliogrphy&authorid = sdessen

DIANE TUCCILLO

DEUKER, Carl
Author, b. 26 August 1950, San Francisco, California

D. is the son of John and Marie (Milligan) Deuker. Having lost his father when he was three years old, D. was raised by his compassionate and understanding single mother. As an only child growing up in Redwood City, California, he spent a great deal of time alone playing with his toys while fueling and developing his imagination. Manipulating his darts, marbles, and tinkertoys, D. created and acted out imaginary game plays and strategies for games of basketball and baseball. He later looked back on these to include in his work. While he enjoyed playing sports, D. was never a star athlete. By his senior year in St. Francis High School, located in Mountain View, California, D. opted out of team sports and concentrated on honing his skills in golf. It was during his years in high school that he also began writing SHORT STORIES and POETRY. His writing at this time was influenced by the lyrics of Bob Dylan, the Beatles, and the Rolling Stones. These artists' lyrics demonstrated to D. how powerful words could be.

D. went on to college and graduated with an Bachelor of Arts degree in English from the University of California at Berkeley in 1972. Two years later, he earned his M.A. in English from the University of Washington. Moving to Los Angeles, his first job was writing for the *Daily Journal*. One year later he enrolled in UCLA and earned his teaching certificate and credentials in 1976. Within the next year he met and married his wife, Anne Mitchell, also a teacher. Settling in Seattle Washington, D. has taught middle grade and junior high-school students since 1977. D. taught in the Saint Luke School in Seattle, Washington, from 1977–1990. During this time, from 1980 through 1985, he was also a film and book critic for the daily newspaper, the *Seattle Sun*.

Carl's and Anne's daughter, Marian, was born on January 23, 1989. That same year his first YOUNG ADULT novel was published after having been rejected at first by three or four publishers. From 1991 through the present time, D. has been working for the Northshore School District in Bothell, Washington, near Seattle. He is presently teaching all subjects in a sixth-grade honors program and enjoys the "variety of his day." His students have not been required to read his works, but those who have respond favorably and express pride in their teacher. Since it is difficult to get rich by writing, unless an author is very prolific, writing at least one published work each year, D. believes he will most likely continue teaching until his daughter finishes college, after which he will write "until he dies."

Spending his summers reading and writing, D. writes about what he knows best, sports, while bringing bits and pieces of different young people's personalities together to create his characters. These characters appear so true to life that often readers see their friends as the prototype for the character's personality and actions. Readers, especially boys, seem to be hooked on D.'s work. He attributes this to the fact that as an author, he is able to "deliver on what the book cover and title seems to promise—a solid sports story." When writing, D. draws his inspiration from some "events from his own life; some from people he knows; and some from his imagination."

His formula or "trick" for successful writing is the "combining of all those elements into a coherent story." D. is frequently told by his readers that his work "is the first book I've ever finished in my life."

D. writes with the assistance of his pet rats, which sit next to him on the sofa as he writes. Rats are his favorite type of pets, after his family discovered how nice they really are. They are mentioned in his book dedications, along with his wife and daughter. His family's favorite pet rat was named E-Kat.

Until recently his works were centered on the team sports of baseball and basketball; they appealed to young adult males and females who wanted to learn about the game. Themes in his books include team sports as important events in the life of the main character as he grows up. Emotions, challenges, and decisions are made both on and off the courts and can be easily identified by the youth of today.

Humble and generous, D. would like to be remembered for treating all people with respect, and if possible, he would like to give everyone the gift of patience. He strongly believes that "Everybody has a creative side. It's important to develop that side, whether it be through art or dance or music or writing. We aren't born just to go to work." For those interested in writing as a career, D.'s advice is that it is important to "Start small. Write stories and poems. It is discouraging to write hundreds of pages and then not have your work published. It's much less discouraging to write ten pages. Also, write every day—but don't think you have to write for hours. Even thirty minutes counts!"

In D.'s 2005 novel, the main character's name is Chance. The main character's name and the novel's title were chosen by readers who accessed D.'s website and cast their votes online. The book is an outgrowth of the events of September 11th. "I just didn't have the heart to write a sports book. I live near the waterfront, and as I was jogging there one day the germ of the story came to me. Basically, the new novel is about someone who gets caught up in a terrorist plot due to his poverty. This plot came to me much more quickly than any other."

Shakespeare is D.'s favorite author and *Moby Dick* his favorite book. D. is a longtime San Francisco Giants fan who also enjoys watching his other favorite team, the Seattle Mariners, play on Saturday afternoons.

D. continues to play a "good game of golf" and especially enjoys doing this on Sunday mornings. He enjoys answering letters and e-mail from his readers. His website is http://www.members.authorsguild.net/carldeuker/

AWARDS: *On the Devil's Court* (1988)—South Carolina Young Book Award in 1992; *On the Devil's Court* was one of 100 Young Adult titles selected for the 4th YALSA Best of the Best List: Here We Go Again . . . 25 Years of Best Books (Selections from 1967 to 1992); *Heart of a Champion* (1993) and *On the Devil's Court* (1988) were named to the American Library Association's Best Books for Young Adults List; *Painting the Black* (1997)—An ALA Best Book for the Young Adults in 1998 A New York City Public Library Book for the Teen Age; *Night Hoops* (2003)—Winner 2003 Golden Sower (Nebraska) Young Adult Award (2003); ALA Best Books for Young Adults in 2001.

FURTHER WORKS: *High Heat* (2003); *Runner* (2005).

BIBLIOGRAPHY: *Contemporary Authors Online.* The Gale Group, 2001; personal interview via e-mail.

VALERIE A. (HARTMAN) PALAZOLO

DIARIES, JOURNALS, AND LETTERS

Some novels are told through letters, diaries, and journals; they offer readers private expeditions through another's world. There is a sense of immediacy that is sometimes lacking in a more conventional narration and one has the intriguing sensibility of being given a personal key to another person's world.

A classic epistolary YOUNG ADULT novel is *Daddy-Long-Legs* (1912) by Jean Webster. Written at the beginning of the 20th century, these letters of Judy Abbott, an orphan girl, are primarily directed to her unseen guardian as they chronicle the four years of the college education that he is munificently paying for. She is the recipient of his largesse due to the fact

she is a ward of the orphanage of which he is a trustee. Ignorant of his actual identity, she blithely addresses him as Daddy-Long-Legs, since the only glimpse she has ever caught of him is his shadow on a wall. A companion novel, *Dear Enemy,* chronicles Judy Abbott's roommate, Sallie MacBride, as she struggles to remake the orphanage and deal with the ornery Scottish doctor who is the physician for the orphanage.

John Marsden's *Letters from the Inside* (1991) is a world away from Jean Webster's books. Taking place nearly a century later, it chronicles the lives of two sixteen-year-old AUSTRALIAN girls, Mandy and Tracey. As more letters are exchanged, honesty begins to replace make-believe: one of the girls is in prison, the other a victim of violence within her own home. Far lighter is Paula DANZIGER's and Ann M. Martin's *P.S. Longer Letter Later* (1998). Although Tara Starr and Elizabeth are not without problems in their lives, humor is evident throughout, and all in all, this is a much less harrowing read than the ambivalent *Letters From the Inside. P.S. Longer Letter Later* (a YALSA Quick Pick for Reluctant Young Adult Readers in 1999) is followed by *Snail Mail No More* (2000), which continues the correspondence of Tara Starr and Elizabeth through the medium of E-mail.

The diary format has been used quite often recently in a variety of SERIES books. These include the Diary of a Real TEEN series, The Royal Diaries, and the California Diaries by Ann M. Martin. The California Diaries are particularly memorable because of their graphics; the text is ostensibly written and sketched as if by the character whose diary is being read, giving an intimate feel to the diary. Adding to the illusion is that the series chronicles the lives of five characters, Dawn (formerly of The Baby-Sitters Club series), Sunny, Maggie, Amalia, and Ducky. Each character has a set of three diaries with a distinctive graphic style. *The Brimstone Journals* (2001) by Ron KOERTGE include individual musings from assorted members of the senior class, giving an overall portrait of the graduating class of 2001. It was an American Library Association Best Book for Young Adults in 2002.

Norma JOHNSTON chronicles a simpler time in her Keeping Days series. Broken into two parts, the first part was comprised of the original quartet of books: *The Keeping Days* (1974), *Glory in the Flower* (1974), *The Sanctuary Tree* (1977), and *A Mustard*

Seed of Magic (1977). Set in the years from 1900–1902, it records the events of the Sterlings of West Farms, Bronx, and their friends and neighbors, relayed through the journal of Tish, the second-oldest daughter. The second part of the series is set from 1917–1919 and is covered in *A Nice Girl Like You* (1981) and *Myself and I* (1981). The Sterling FAMILY is still at the center of the story, but now it is told through the eyes of the oldest grandchild, Saranne Albright. Old situations and challenges intrude on the present, as do the new issues that the First World War helps bring to a head. An incredibly powerful novel done in journal form is Margaret Peterson HADDIX's *Don't You Dare Read This, Mrs. Dunphrey* (1996), as a young girl records dual entries for a class assignment—one reflecting the life she dreams of, and the other which chronicles a life of abandonment and increasing desperation. The intimacy of the diary format allows the reader an immediacy that is unique.

JEANNE MARIE RYAN

DICKINSON, Peter

Author, b. 16 December 1927, Livingstone, Northern Rhodesia (Zambia)

Author of fiction and nonfiction for children and YOUNG ADULTS, as well as detective fiction for adults, D. is known for his versatility, breadth of subject matter, and originality. He knew in childhood that he was a writer and acknowledges among his chief influences *The Bird of Dawning* by poet John Masefield, who was a family friend, and Kipling. When D. was seven, his father, a civil servant, decided to move the family to England so that his four sons might attend school there; his father died within four months of their relocation. D. attended Eton and Cambridge, receiving a B.A. in 1951, and confesses he was an indifferent scholar. His first job was with the MAGAZINE *Punch;* he stayed for seventeen years, writing verse and book reviews, mainly of detective fiction, but also of children's books. He served in the British Army between 1946 and 1948 in World War II. With his first wife, Mary Rose Barnard, an artist, he had two daughters and two sons; he is now married to author Robin MC-KINLEY.

D. began his first novel for young readers as a means of unblocking his first adult detective novel. *The Weathermonger* (1968), inspired by a nightmare, became the first of The Changes trilogy, which imag-

ines a future England in which technology is demonized and abandoned. The trilogy continues with *Heartsease* (1969) and *The Devil's Children* (1970). D.'s SCIENCE FICTION has attracted considerable critical acclaim, including the book for which he is best known in the U.S., *Eva* (1988). Thirteen-year-old Eva wakes up after a car accident to discover that, to save her from an irreversible coma, scientists have transplanted her consciousness into the mind of a chimpanzee. In Eva's world, overpopulation has led to the extinction of most animals; champanzees are kept in zoos and used for research. D. imagines in detail Eva's life in a chimpanzee's body and the implications of this transformation for both herself and her world.

Other novels by D. combine historical content with ADVENTURE. Some of these novels, including *The Dancing Bear* (1972), *The Blue Hawk* (1975), and *Tulku* (1979), began as stories told in the car to his sons, who demanded stories with battles in them. *Tulku* is the story of Theodore, son of a missionary killed in the Boxer Rebellion, who journeys from China to Tibet with the eccentric Mrs. Jones and her companion Lung. In Tibet the Christian Theodore is confronted with the different beliefs and rituals of Buddhism, and the irreverent Mrs. Jones has the chance to achieve genuine enlightenment.

D.'s imagination has returned to Africa for several of his books, imagining Africa as it might have been and might become. D. is interested in pre-history and the earliest origins of humanity, which he imagines in Africa in *A Bone from a Dry Sea* (1992) and *The Kin* (1998). *The Kin* is meant to be a single volume, but has also been published in sections as four separate titles, *Suth, Noli, Po,* and *Mana. AK* (1990), imagines the life of Paul Kagomi, a child warrior in the African country of Nagala. The exploration of the colonial roots of WAR and the ongoing problems in central Africa demonstrates D.'s profound social conscience. Two alternate endings represent both hopes and fears for Africa's future.

D.'s versatility also extends to high FANTASY. *The Ropemaker* (2001), a PRINTZ Honor Book, began as a story told to his wife on walks with their three whippet dogs.

AWARDS: *Tulku,* 1979, Carnegie Medal, Whitbread Prize; Guardian Award, BBYA 1993; (*The Blue Hawk*); *AK,* 1990, Whitbread Literary Award; Printz Honor Book, *The Ropemaker,* 2001; 2001 Phoenix

CAROLYN COMAN

CAROLINE B. COONEY

SHARON CREECH

CHRIS CRUTCHER

ROALD DAHL

SARAH DESSEN

CARL DEUKER

PETER DICKINSON

Prize, *The Seventh Raven; Boston Globe–Horn Book* Prize for non-fiction, *Chance, Luck and Destiny;* Carnegie Medal and German Catholic Bishops' Prize, *City of Gold;* Crime Writers Association Golden Dagger Award, *The Glass-Sided Ants' Nest,* 1968, and *The Old English Peep Show,* 1969; *Bone from a Dry Sea* BBYA 1990; Here We Go Again: 25 Years of Best Books (1967–1992); *Eva,* BBYA 1990; *Tulka,* BBYA 1979.

FURTHER WORKS: *Emma Tupper's Diary,* 1970; *The Gift,* 1973; *Chance, Luck and Destiny,* 1975; *Annerton Pit,* 1977; *The Flight of Dragons,* 1979; *City of Gold,* 1980; *The Seventh Raven,* 1981; *Healer,* 1983; *Merlin Dreams,* 1988; *Shadow of a Hero,* 1993; *Touch and Go,* 1999; *The Lion Tamer's Daughter,* 1999; *Water: Tales of the Elemental Spirits* (with Robin MCKINLEY), 2002; *Tears of the Salamander,* 2003; *Inside Grandad,* 2005.

BIBLIOGRAPHY: Contemporary Authors CD-ROM; author website; (www.peterdickinson.com); interview with ACHUKA; (www.achuka.co.uk/guests/dickinson/int02.htm)

MICHELE HILTON

DOHERTY, Berlie

Author, b. 6 November 1943, Knotty Ash, Liverpool, England

A prolific British writer, D. has written more than forty books as well as plays, POETRY, and SHORT STORIES. Her books often deal with parent–child relationships, FAMILY life, and YOUNG ADULTS' development of identity. D.'s books are notable for her characterizations, in particular her well-developed adult characters. She was born in Liverpool, England, and attended private school. D. later attended the Upton Hall Convent School on a scholarship.

As a child, D. enjoyed writing and was encouraged in her interest by her father, also a writer. She wrote stories and poems, which her father typed for submission until she learned to type. These early stories and poems were published in the *Liverpool Echo* and the *Hoylake News and Advertiser,* two local newspapers. At age fourteen, the newspapers rejected D.'s submissions because they considered her too old to be published on their children's pages. During her high-school years, D. pursued her interest in music and she sang with one of her boyfriends in local clubs.

D. attended the University of Durham, where she continued to pursue her musical interests. She earned a B.A. degree from the University of Durham in 1965. Next, she attended the University of Liverpool, where in 1966, D. earned a certificate for postgraduate work in Social Science. She married fellow University of Durham student Gerard Doherty in 1966. From 1966 to 1967, D. was a social worker for the Leicestershire Child Care Services in Leicester, England. She was a homemaker from 1967–78, busy raising three children. Marital problems arose during this period and D. needed a source of income. In 1978, D. earned a certificate for postgraduate work in Education from the University of Sheffield. She became a classroom teacher because it fit her schedule as a mother with young children. A creative writing component in her postgraduate program reminded D. of her interest in writing.

In 1980 D. left the classroom and became a writer of radio plays for British Broadcasting Corporation (BBC) Radio-Sheffield. Her first two books, published in 1982 and 1983, consisted of D.'s BBC Radio plays in short-story form. She has been working as a full-time writer since 1983 and credits her experience as a writer of radio plays for schools as the main influence for her style of writing. D.'s third book, *White Peak Farm* (1990), is about Jeannie, a TEENAGE Derbyshire farm girl, and the hopes, dreams, secrets and love in a family lacking in communication skills.

D. received her first Carnegie Medal for *Granny Was a Buffer Girl* (1988). In this novel, seventeen-year-old Jess learns about love from her grandparents through reminiscences and family life. Her second Carnegie Medal-winning book, *Dear Nobody* (1992), was well received in the U.S. In *Dear Nobody,* one night of unprotected sex changes the lives of two high-school seniors, Chris and Helen, resulting in Helen's pregnancy. Helen is pulled in different directions: Chris wants to marry her and Helen's mother wants her to have an abortion. Helen copes with her pregnancy as well as her changing relationships with Chris and her mother by writing letters to Nobody, her unborn child. In *The Snake-Stone* (1995), a fifteen-year-old Olympic diving hopeful, James, decides to look for his birth mother. His journey takes him to his birth mother and back to the home of his adoptive parents, whom he now considers his real parents.

Twice, D. has won the Writer's Guild of Great Britain Award for her television adaptations of two of her own novels, *Dear Nobody* and *Daughter of the Sea.* She travels the world speaking at schools and conferences, but makes her home in the Peak District in England. In 2002, D. was awarded an honorary doctorate from the University of Derby. In 2004 the Children's Literature Association awarded the 2004 Phoenix Award for *White Peak Farm* (1990).

AWARDS: Writers Guild of Great Britain Award for *Dear Nobody* and *Daughter of the Sea;* Phoenix Award for *White Peak Farm;* Carnegie Medal, 1986, *Granny was a Buffer Girl* and 1991 for *Dear Nobody;* ALA Best Book for Young Adults, 1991, *White Peak Farm* and 1993 for *Dear Nobody.*

FURTHER WORK: *Holly Starcross,* 2002.

BIBLIOGRAPHY: Berlie D. website, http://www.berlie doherty.com/ (November 30, 2003); *Contemporary Authors Online,* 2001; Contemporary Writers in the UK website, http://www.contemporarywriters.com/authors/ (November 30, 2003); David Higham Associates website, http://www.davidhigham.co.uk/html/Clients/Berlie_Doherty (November 30, 2003); Shadowing the Carnegie and Greenaway Medals homepage, http://www.carnegiegreenaway.org.uk/index.html (November 30, 2003); *U*X*L Junior DIS-Covering Authors,* online Edition, 2003.

ANDREW W. HUNTER

DONNELLY, Jennifer
Author, b. 1963, Port Chester, New York

Jennifer Donnelly was born in Port Chester, New York and currently lives in Brooklyn. She attended the University of Rochester, graduating in 1986 with degrees in English literature and European history. Donnelly has received critical acclaim both in the United States and in the United Kingdom for her first YA novel, *A Northern Light* (2003). Not only was it selected as an Honor Book for the 2004 Michael L. PRINTZ AWARD but also the 2003 Carnegie Medal, making Jennifer D. only the second American ever to receive this award. In this multi-layered historical novel, Donnelly interweaves the murder of Grace Brown by Chester Gillette on the 11 of July, 1906 at Big Moose Lake in the Adirondacks into the story of sixteen-year-old Mattie Gokey, employed at Glenmore Hotel when Grace's body is found.

Through Mattie's first-person narrative, it is shown how Grace's murder and the content of letters written by Grace and Chester contribute to Mattie's thoughts regarding her own life and choices. Mattie's narrative weaves backward and forward as she tells about the hard life on the farm with her father and

sisters after the death of her mother, her romance with Royal, the son of a neighboring farmer, and her friendships with Weaver, a young black man who wishes to be a lawyer, and the local schoolteacher, Miss Wilcox—a writer of poetry—who introduces Mattie to literature. Mattie's dream of being a writer is emphasized in a text that is rich both with the vocabulary that Mattie learns every day and with references to literary works.

Based on her research and knowledge of the Adirondacks, Donnelly vividly describes Mattie's environment, dealing forthrightly with poverty, hardships, and sexual abuse but also showing how, despite differences, neighbors support one another in times of need. Embedded in Donnelly's novel are themes of class differences, racial discrimination, and the prejudice against educated women. In an interview with Karen Bell, Donnelly hoped that *A Northern Light* would "reinforce for girls the importance of self-determination." Mattie's strong voice is heard as she struggles with her choices: a scholarship to Barnard College or to settle for marriage to Royal.

A Northern Light was named a 2003 Printz Honor book by the American Library Association, and the title frequently appears in the list of contenders for top youth book choices by other organizations as well. The ALA recognition, though, is "particularly meaningful," D. notes, because of its connection with libraries. "The library was one of my favorite places as a child. Because books were to be found there, and because kind, lovely people who took an interest in me, and helped me to further my own interests, were also to be found there. I loved that they were serious and thoughtful and spoke to me as an equal. And they not only had the keys to the kingdom, they were willing to share them!" she explained.

Young readers of *A Northern Light* have in turn shared their responses to the story with D. She said, "They tell me that Mattie's story has inspired them in their own literary endeavors, that she's taught them it's important to pursue their dreams, even if that pursuit is difficult. That means the world to me. There is nothing as rewarding as having a positive impact on a child's life. Especially when the child is a TEENAGER, making the transition between childhood and adulthood and maybe making the first tentative steps in following her own dream, and finding her own unique voice." In Mattie, then, D. offers a character who was not available to her in the fiction she read as a young person. She has said, "There were some books, like Jane Wagner's awesome J.T., that made me see that stories could be about real kids with real problems, but titles like *Joey Pigza Swallowed the Key* weren't around yet, never mind *Speak* or *Feed*. I wish they had been."

Described by critics as "riveting" and the "perfect coming-of-age novel," *A Northern Light* has its origins in historical fact. More than one review notes the use of the 1906 Chester Gillette murder case, which also formed the basis for Theodore Dreiser's *An American Tragedy,* as a framework for this story. D. has explained to interviewers her passion for research; "Research is a big, fat field day for me," she said. This enthusiasm for historical detail led her to read everything from news accounts and tax records to trial transcripts in preparation for writing *A Northern Light.* D. also acknowledges the stories told by her grandmother as sources for this narrative. This blend of source material results in a novel with "hints of ROMANCE, MYSTERY, and historical fiction," in the words of one critic.

This combination is also evoked in D.'s first novel for adults, *The Tea Rose.* In an interview about this book, D. observed, "When I was growing up, books like *The Shell Seekers* or *The Thorn Birds* were *it.* My mother and aunt had piles of these books and I started reading them when I was 13. I had to sneak a few, though, because there were racy bits." In the same article, D. proclaimed her interest in popular fiction: "I'm at home holed up watching *Titanic* and reading the latest Danielle Steel. And I think that's what most of the rest of the world is doing, too."

D. has also written a children's PICTURE BOOK, *Humble Pie,* which was illustrated by Stephen Gammell who had been honored with a Caldecott Honor for an earlier book. Following the success of *A Northern Light,* D. is working on two new book projects and raising her young daughter with her husband in Brooklyn, New York.

AWARDS: Printz Honor Book, 2003.

BIBLIOGRAPHY: Jennifer Donnelly, personal communication, 2004; www.jenniferdonnelly.com, 2004; www.bhny.com/pow/POW032.html#bio, online, 2003; www.bookfinder.us/review5/0152167056.html, online, 2003; http://www.roadtoromance.ca/reviewnorthern light.htm/, online, 2003; Best Children's Books 2003, *Publishers Weekly,* November 10, 2003; First Fiction Finds for Fall, *Publishers Weekly,* August 12, 2002.

JENNIFER PIERCE AND HILARY S. CREW

DOYLE, Brian

Author, b. 12 August 1935, Ottawa, Ontario

Born and raised in Ottawa and the Gatineau Hills, D. has demonstrated his affection for CANADA by setting all of his novels there. Through this regionalism, D. "impregnated with the Irish culture of the people who settled in one hundred years earlier . . . he picked up his love of stories and anecdotes." Beginning to write at the age of ten, D. was once nominated for Head Boy in school but was removed from consideration by his Vice Principal, who said that D. would never amount to anything.

Graduating from Carleton University in 1957, D. worked various jobs as everything from a journalist to a taxi driver to a jazz singer. Eventually settling into teaching in 1960, D. spent the next thirty-three years teaching English at various high schools. Never willing to write just to be published, D. has said, "I have to write for myself or for a friend or for a family member. That's the only way it works." D. published his first piece of fiction, a short story, while trying to get his students to write in class.

In an attempt to capture the understanding and closeness he had with his daughter, Megan, D. wrote his first novel for her. *Hey Dad!* (1978) was a moment in time where D. felt, "I don't think I ever knew anybody as well as I did my daughter when she was that age." Never patronizing young readers, D. deals with issues of mortality, FAMILY, and growing up.

Once D.'s son reached the same age as Megan had been when he wrote *Hey Dad!,* D. wrote a novel for him. *You Can Pick Me Up at Peggy's Cove* (1979) was written for and about Ryan. Again dealing with the topic of a child's relationship with his or her father, D. kept the story small. "Doyle's emphasis is not on the ADVENTURES the children have but on their psychological states of being." Realism was important for D., as he ultimately wanted to entertain his children, but it was as D. was reading his work to the neighborhood kids and "they started asking about what was going to happen next, I realized the story went beyond family interest."

While writing about his children, D. kept his novels contemporary, but after *You Can Pick Me Up at Peggy's Cove,* D. went back in time to his own childhood for his next books. In *Up to Low* (1982), D. creates a TEENAGER named Tommy who seems to be the only sane person in an eccentric world. This witty and loving character translates beautifully into D.'s next novel, where Tommy returns in a much more turbulent time. *Angel Square* (1981) is a story of ethnic conflict in the Lowertown section of Ottawa in 1945, and the likeable Tommy makes "an appealing hero—resourceful and courageous."

D. has also written plays for children and contributed articles and short stories to newspapers and magazines. His works have been translated into French and published in Braille editions, widening the "audience of his books." Also widening that audience were the film adaptations of *You Can Pick Me Up at Peggy's Cove,* directed by Don McBrearty, and *Angel Square,* directed by Ann Wheeler.

Married since 1960 to his wife Jacqueline, D. left teaching in 1994, with the hope that he could establish a good writing routine and be more available to conduct readings across Canada.

AWARDS: Winner of the Canadian Author's Association's Vicky Metcalf Award for a Body of Work, 1991, for Brian D.; Canadian Library Association Book of the Year for Children Award, 1983 for *Up to Low,* 1996 for *Uncle Ronald,* 1988 for *Easy Avenue;* Mr. Christie's Book Award, 1996 for *Uncle Ronald,* 1990 for *Covered Bridge;* Books for the Teenage Selection from the New York Public Library, 1997 for *Spud in Winter,* 1999 for *Easy Avenue;* ALA Notable Children's Book 2005 and CLA Book of the Year 2005 for *Boy O'Boy.*

FURTHER WORKS: *Easy Avenue,* 1988; *Covered Bridge,* 1990; *Spud Sweetgrass,* 1992; *Spud in Winter,* 1995; *Uncle Ronald,* 1996; *The Low Life: Five Great Tales from up and down the River,* 1999; *Mary Ann Alice,* 2001.

BIBLIOGRAPHY: *Contemporary Authors,* online, 2001; *Something About the Author,* vol. 67, 104; *CM Magazine,* March 1991; Groundwood Books, online, 2002; "Brian Doyle." U*X*L Junior DISCovering Authors. U*X*L, 1998. Reproduced in Discovering Collection. Farmington Hills, Mich: Gale Group, October, 2001.

MEGAN PEARLMAN

DRAPER, Sharon M. (Sharon Mills)
Author and educator, b. 21 August 1948, Cleveland, Ohio

D. is an award-winning teacher and author whose books are noted for their appeal to reluctant readers and their honest portraits of TEENAGE life. Her novels depict courageous AFRICAN AMERICAN teens in dramatic, high-interest situations. All of her novels to date are set in Cincinnati, where D. taught English at Walnut Hills High School. Her awards as a teacher include Ohio Outstanding High School Language Arts Educator, Ohio Teacher of the Year, the Milken Family Foundation National Educator Award, and 1997 National Teacher of the Year.

D.'s first novel, *Tears of a Tiger* (1994), emerged as an immensely successful novel. In the story, Hazelwood High basketball star Robbie Washington dies in a car crash caused by drunk driving. The effect of his death on other students, especially Andy Jackson, the driver of the car, is explored. The story is told through a variety of narrative means, including the students' letters, DIARY entries, conversations, prayers, and English homework, including poems. D. probes the responses and thought processes of her teen characters while also demonstrating the ability of adults to have positive or negative effects on teen lives by going out of their way to help or failing in their responsibilities.

Forged by Fire (1997), the second book in the Hazelwood High trilogy, builds on the SHORT STORY "One Small Torch." This novel is a further indictment of the failure of adults in their responsibility to youth and the sad consequences of that failure, as well as a demonstration of the strengths and potential of youth. Gerald, who nearly died in a fire after his drug-addicted mother left him alone when he was younger, must attempt to keep his family going and protect his younger sister, Angel, from abuse by his stepfather.

The final novel in the Hazelwood High trilogy, *Darkness Before Dawn* (2001), focuses on another of the friends in Robbie Washington's circle, Keisha Montgomery. As the relationships of other characters in the trilogy develop, Keisha becomes involved with a predatory track coach, Jonathan Hathaway. Again, the novel demonstrates the importance of self-reliance, the difficulty of deciding which adults are trustworthy, and the importance of knowing when to ask for help. The first two books in the trilogy were listed as ALA Best Books for Young Adults.

Romiette and Julio (1999) is an interracial version of Shakespeare's star-crossed lovers. The romance between Romiette Cappelle, who is African American, and Julio Montague, who is Hispanic, attracts the animosity of the school gang, the Devildogs, who persecute the pair and put their lives in danger. In terms of technique the novel returns to *Tears of a Tiger* in its use of intertextuality and in offering a variety of narrative forms, including transcriptions of chat-room sessions between Romiette and Julio.

In *Double Dutch* (2002), Delia, Charlene, and Yolanda are part of a winning double dutch team, but Delia's participation on the team is in jeopardy just as the world double dutch championships approach. A state test, which she must pass to stay on the team, threatens to expose her secret: she cannot read. At the same time, Delia's friend Randy is keeping a secret of his own: his father, a long-distance trucker, has not returned from his last journey, and Randy struggles to pay bills and buy food himself, afraid that he will be placed in foster care.

In *The Battle of Jericho* (2003), D. returns to some of the themes of *Tears of a Tiger:* poor choices and unwise peer group activities lead to tragedy. Jericho is an excellent trumpet player, but wants more than anything to be part of a powerful, fraternity-like club, The Warriors of Distinction, whose hazing rituals are growing out of control. The interesting cast of Douglass High students includes Dana, a strong young woman who decides to seek initiation into the all-male Warriors and must prove that she is the equal of the men.

AWARDS: 1995 Coretta Scott King/John Steptoe Award for New Talent, *Tears of a Tiger;* Gertrude Williams Johnson Literary Contest, "One Small Torch"; 1998 Coretta Scott King Award, *Forged by Fire;* ALA Best Books for Young Adults: *Tears of a Tiger,* and *Forged by Fire;* 2004 Coretta Scott King Award: *The Battle of Jericho.*

FURTHER WORKS: *Ziggy and the Black Dinosaurs,* 1994; *Ziggy and the Black Dinosaurs: Lost in the Tunnel of Time,* 1995; *Ziggy and the Black Dinosaurs: Shadows of Caesar's Creek,* 1997; *Teaching from the Heart,* 1999; *Jazz Imagination: A Journal to Read and Write,* 2000; *Not Quite Burned Out, but Crispy around the Edges,* 2001; *Before the Dawn,* 2001; *Double Dutch,* 2002; *The Battle of Jericho,* 2003.

BIBLIOGRAPHY: African American Publications Biography Resource Center (http://www.africanpubs.com/Apps/bios/0519DraperSharon.asp); author website (http://sharondraper.com); Library of Congress Authority Files (http://authorities.loc.gov).

MICHELE HILTON

DUDER, Tessa
Author, b. 13 November 1940, Auckland, New Zealand

D.'s first published children's story appeared in an anthology called *The Magpies Said* (1980), edited by

NEW ZEALAND's doyenne of children's literature, Dorothy Butler. "The Violin" in some ways set the pattern for the novels that followed—stories about young people succeeding against the odds in difficult and competitive fields of endeavor. A musical theme is elaborated upon in D.'s second novel *Jellybean* (1985), which the author herself has described as "quite a strange little book about a girl whose mother is a professional musician."

The theme of finding oneself led naturally to the "Alex Quartet," four novels about TEENAGE swimmer Alexandra Archer. A smattering of enthusiastic reviews gives an indication of the high esteem in which the books were held, as does the plethora of awards individual titles received. Alex was a significant milestone in New Zealand literature for YOUNG ADULTS, offering gripping and sophisticated writing, a well-realized and evocative historical setting (Auckland late 1950s), a strong female character and a timely feminist perspective. From the sporting perspective, the books chronicle Alexandra Archer's quest for Olympic Games nomination and selection, beginning with her rivalry with Maggie Benton. The following book progresses to the Rome 1960 Olympics where, in a convincing mix of fact and fiction, Alex comes up against Australia's Dawn Fraser. The SERIES concludes with Alex's cynicism about, and eventual retirement from, professional competition and her increased involvement in acting. Woven into these plot lines are strands of Alex's personal life, equally tense and dramatic: the illness of Alex's beloved Gran while Alex is away in Rome, and the general skepticism shown, mainly by men, toward the sporting and intellectual abilities of young women in narrow-minded 1950s New Zealand. The stories have dated hardly at all since their first publication. They remain, as they were then, historical novels whose histories are delivered with a passionate authenticity and are layered with D.'s keen retrospective sensibility; the gender stereotyping, for example, is unmistakably portrayed as narrow-minded parochialism. Their themes are channelled through such a convincing main character who, at face value, remains the most self-absorbed teenager in New Zealand's YA literature. Read singly or together, the Alex Quartet showcases the best work of one of New Zealand's best writers; the books, classics of New Zealand YA literature, continue to deliver powerful and relevant stories.

D. has gone on to write several more interesting and innovative novels for young adults including *Hot Mail* (co-writer William Taylor, 2000), a novel written solely in e-mails. Her most recent trilogy is about another young woman, Tiggie Tompson, set squarely in contemporary New Zealand but blending present-day events (including the America's Cup competition) with an early immigration story.

A former champion swimmer and journalist, D. has lived and worked in countries as distinctively different as England and Pakistan. In addition to writing and lecturing, D. has been a guiding force in the New Zealand Children's Literature Foundation, particularly in the establishment of its annual Storylines Festival.

AWARDS: 1985 Choysa Bursary, *Jellybean;* ALA notable Books: *Jellybean; In Lane Three, Alex Archer;* Esther Glen Award: 1989 for *Alex,* 1990 for *Alex in Winter,* 1992 for *Alex in Rome;* 1990 AIM Children's Book of the Year, *Alex in Winter;* 1993 AIM Children's Book Awards, Senior Fiction Award, *Songs for Alex;* 1994 OBE; 2000 New Zealand Post Children's Book Awards, Senior Fiction Award, *The Tiggie Tompson Show;* 1994 O.B.E.; 1996 Margaret Mahy Medal; 2003 Meridian Energy Katherine Mansfield Memorial Fellowship.

FURTHER WORKS: *Night Race to Kawau,* 1982; *The Book of Auckland,* 1985; *Alex,* 1987. (Published in the United States as *In Lane Three, Alex Archer*); *Alex in Winter,* 1989; *Alex in Rome,* 1991; *Songs for Alex,* 1992; "The Runaway," in *Nearly Seventeen : New Zealand stories* (Tessa D., ed), 1993; "Not Just a Pretty Face," in *Zig Zag* (William Taylor, ed), 1993. "White daffodils," in *Crossing: New Zealand and Australian* SHORT STORIES (Tessa D. and Agnes Nieuwenhuizen, eds), 1995; "Tuesdays," in *Falling in Love* (Tessa D., ed), 1995; "Sea changes," in *Ultimate Sports* (Donald R. Gallo, ed), 1995; *Mercury Beach,* 1997; *The Tiggie Tompson Show,* 1999; *Tiggie Tompson, All at Sea,* 2001; *In Search of Elisa Marchetti: A Writer's Search for her Italian Family,* 2002; *Tiggie Tompson's Longest Journey,* 2003.

BIBLIOGRAPHY: Robinson, Roger and Nelson Wattie, eds. *The Oxford Companion to New Zealand Literature.* 1998. Barley, Janet Crane. *Winter in July : visits with children's authors down under.* 1995. Fitzgibbon, Tom, *Beneath southern skies : New Zealand children's book authors* & illustrators. 1993. http://library.christchurch.org.nz / Childrens / Childrens Authors/TessaDuder.asp; http://www.bookcouncil.org.nz/writers/duder.htm

BILL NAGELKERKE

DUNCAN, Lois

Author, educator, b. 28 April 1934, Philadelphia, Pennsylvania

D. grew up in Sarasota, Florida, the daughter of internationally known MAGAZINE photographers, Joseph and Lois Steinmetz. She has one younger brother. From early childhood, she knew she wanted to be a writer. She submitted her first story to a magazine at the age of ten and made her first sale at thirteen to the magazine *Calling All Girls.* Throughout her high-school years she wrote regularly for young people's magazines, particularly *Seventeen.*

In 1962, D. moved to Albuquerque, where she taught in the journalism department of the University of New Mexico and continued to write for magazines. Over three hundred of her articles and SHORT STORIES appeared in such publications as *Ladies Home Journal, Redbook, McCall's, Good Housekeeping,* and *Reader's Digest,* and for a number of years she was a contributing editor for *Woman's Day.*

D. is also the author of forty-eight books, ranging from children's PICTURE BOOKS to adult novels, but she is best known for her YA SUSPENSE novels. Many of those have been chosen as American Library Association "Best Books for Young Adults" and Junior Literary Guild Selections, and they have won Young Readers Awards in sixteen states and three foreign countries.

The most difficult book D. ever had to write was nonfiction. *Who Killed My Daughter?* (1992) is the true story of her search for the truth behind the brutal murder of the youngest of her five children, eighteen-year-old Kaitlyn. This book has been featured on such national TV shows as *Good Morning, America, Larry King Live, Unsolved Mysteries,* and, more recently, *Inside Edition.* Although it was written for adults, it was named a *School Library Journal* "Best Book of the Year" and an American Library Association Best Book for Young Adults and has been nominated for Young Reader Awards in nine states. It has also been condensed by Time-Life Books; was an alternate selection of the Literary Guild; and has been recorded for the blind. Her daughter's death eerily mirrored D.'s book *Don't Look Behind You* (1990), written two years before her personal tragedy. Since then, D. has become interested in the paranormal and ESP.

The critically acclaimed TEENAGE suspense novel, *Gallows Hill* (1997), is a winner. The *School Library*

Journal hails this book as "an exciting, suspenseful tale that will certainly be welcomed by D.'s many fans." One of those fans, Jeniece Lewis, an eighth-grader at Thompson Middle School, gave *Gallows Hill,* a modern-day witch who has to fight for her life, a 4-star rating in a student review for the *Richmond Times-Dispatch.* "This book is the bomb," she wrote. "Almost anyone who likes MYSTERY and suspense would love the story. Just don't get too caught up in it and read it in the bathtub like I did. You might drop it." *Killing Mr. Griffin* (1978) is one of D.'s most popular novels. A high-school English teacher mysteriously disappears but only a few students know the reason for his disappearance—his death.

D. is a mastermind of suspense with an imagination as bottomless. Her fans adore her, and new fans are constantly popping up. When her book, *I Know What You Did Last Summer,* was made into a MOVIE (1997), D.'s fans all over resurrected old copies of classic D. novels and new fans ran out to buy them. However, the movie was very loosely based on her novel. D. has expressed extreme displeasure concerning the movie. In the film, the person the kids hit is an adult, and after they injure him the kids deliberately kill him. The screenwriter also moved the location from the mountains of New Mexico to a seaside village on the East Coast so one character after another can be decapitated with boat hooks. One character (who was not in the book) gets shoved into a vat of boiling water while he's cooking lobsters. Most of the action takes place on a fishing boat; there was no boat in the book. D. said, "As a mother of a teenage girl who had her brains blown out while driving home from a girlfriend's house, there is no way I want to be part of desensitizing kids to violence and turning murder into a game. I am especially embarrassed by this travesty, because *I Know What You Did Last Summer* was one of the books that earned me the *SLJ/* YALSA MARGARET A. EDWARDS AWARD for a distinguished body of literature that provides young adults with a window through which to view the world and which will help them to understand themselves and their role in society. I won't let my grandchildren see the movie."

D. is married to Don Arquette, and two of their five children are also authors. Kerry Arquette writes children's books—the most recent two are *Daddy Promises* and *What Did You Do Today?*—and Brett Arquette is the author of an adult novel, *Deadly Perversions.* D.'s oldest daughter, Robin Arquette, is a singer-songwriter, who has collaborated with D. on a series of music tapes and CDs "Songs of Childhood." She is a quick read and the recipient of countless awards in writing. D. is recommended for young adult as well as adult readers.

AWARDS: *My Growth as a Writer,* BBYA, 1982; *Don't Look Behind You,* BBYA 1990; *Killing Mr. Griffin,* BBYA, 1978; Best of the Best Books, 1970–1983; Nothin' But the Best, the Best Books, 1966–1986; Here We Go Again; 25 Years of Best Books, 1967–1992; *Stranger with My Face,* BBYA, 1981; Best of the Best Books; *Who Killed My Daughter? The True Story of a Mother's Search for her Daughter's Murderer,* BBYA, 1993; ALA Popular Paperback, 2004; The Margaret A. Edwards is a lifetime achievement award for D.'s contribution to the YA field. *Killing Mr. Griffin* and *I Know What You Did Last Summer* were referred to in the Award citation: "Whether accepting responsibility for the death of an English teacher or admitting to their responsibility for a hit-and-run accident, D.'s characters face a universal truth—your actions are important and you are responsible for them."

SELECT FURTHER WORKS: *The Twisted Window,* 1987; *Wonder Kid Meets Evil Lunch Snatcher,* 1988; *The Circus Came Home,* 1994.

BIBLIOGRAPHY: Commire, Anne, ed, Something About the Author, vol.36, 1986; Sutton, Roger, A Conversation with Lois D., June 1992, pp. 20–24.

WILLIAM MARIANO

DUNNING, Stephen
Author, b. 31 October 1924, Duluth, Minnesota

It might seem strange for a college professor to write books directed at the adolescent reader, but D. has had first-hand experience with them. After graduating from Carleton College in 1949 and the University of Minnesota in 1951, the author taught secondary school in St. Paul, Minnesota for three years, then in Los Alamos, New Mexico for two years and Tallahassee, Florida, for five years.

In 1960, a year after graduating from Florida State University with his Ph.D., D. co-edited his first book with Dwight Burton, a volume called *Courage.* Soon after he began teaching at Duke University, leaving in 1963 to join the faculty at Northwestern University, and finally, settling into a career at the University of Michigan in 1964, from which he retired in 1988.

During that time, D. edited and wrote more than thirty books, some with others, some alone. His two most popular works are *Reflections on a Gift of Watermelon Pickle . . . and Other Modern Verse* (co-editor with Edward Lueders and Hugh L. Smith, 1966) and *Getting the Knack: 20 Poetry Writing Exercises* (co-author with William Stafford, 1992). Poet Doug Tanoury, who contributes exclusively to online literary MAGAZINES AND JOURNALS, such as *Outsider Ink* (http://www.outsiderink.com), keeps a copy of *Reflections on a Gift of Watermelon Pickle* from his seventh-grade English class at his writing desk and writer/school-teacher Tracie Vaughn Zimmer believes that *Getting the Knack* is "[t]he MOST useful book for the classroom."

Readers then might be surprised to learn that D. himself didn't consider POETRY of primary importance until 1975, when he made a promise to himself to practice poetry everyday: "Until 1975, I'd written mainly to publish. It seemed natural to send these early poems out to magazines. After I published forty or fifty, without noticeably changing the world, I realized that the energy going into the effort to publish was misdirected. It was the poems, not their publication! So publishing became more a casual thing. Then I liked the doing of it—the actual writing time—even more."

In 1997–1998, D. temporarily stopped writing poetry due to physical manifestations of Parkinson's disease. "My hand is too shaky to write, and I haven't worked out a method using a dictating machine," he explained. D. currently lives with his wife in Ann Arbor, Michigan.

AWARDS: 1977 Panhandler Award; 1978 Alumni Achievement Award, Carleton College; 1976 Fries Award, Michigan Council of Teachers of English; 1983 Michigan Council for the Arts Grant.

FURTHER WORKS: (co-editor with Carol Lee) *Frontiers*, 1961; (co-editor with Robert Smith and Jane Sprague) *Small World*, 1964; (editorial chairman) *Scholarly Appraisals of Literary Works Taught in High Schools*, 1965; *Teaching Literature to Adolescents: Poetry*, 1966; (co-compiler) *Poems from Reflections on a Gift of Watermelon Pickle . . . and Other Verse*, 1967; editor of series of long-playing records, "Today's Poets: Their Poems/Their Voices," Volumes I–V, Scholastic Records, 1967; *Teaching Literature to Adolescents: Short Stories*, 1968; (co-editor with Lueders and Smith) *Some Haystacks Don't Even Have Any Needle, and Other Complete*

Modern Poems, 1969; (editor) *English for the Junior High Years*, 1969; (with Ruth Clay and Andrew Carrigan) *Poetry*, 1970; (editor) *Mad, Sad and Glad*, Scholastic Book Services, 1970; (with Henry Maloney) *Superboy/Supergirl*, 1971; Supervising editor of twelve literature units published by Scholastic Book Services, 1961–64, revisions, 1972–; (with Lahna Diskin and Maloney) *Short Story*, 1973; (with M. Joe Eaton and Malcolm Glass) *Poetry II*, 1974; (with Alan B. Howes) *Literature for Adolescents: Teaching Poems, Stories, Novels, and Plays*, 1975; *Who Am I?*, 1978; *Dreams*, 1978; *Handfuls of Us*, 1980; *Walking Home Dead*, 1981; *Do You Fear No One*, 1982; *Good Words*, 1991.

BIBLIOGRAPHY: *Contemporary Authors Online*, 2000. *Outsider Ink;* http://outsiderink.com/01/summer/bios .php; Zimmer, T. *Poetry Resources*. Accessed 9/30/03 http://www.tracievaughnzimmer.com/teacher_resour ces.htm

JULIE SHEN

DURRELL, Gerald M.

Author, b. 7 January 1925, Jamshedpur, India; d. 30 January 1995, Jersey, Channel Islands, England

Author of more than thirty books for both children and adults, D. devoted his life to the study of animal behavior and the protection of endangered species throughout the world. His numerous expeditions to places such as Argentina, Paraguay, Sierra Leone, Mexico, Mauritius, and Madagascar formed the basis of both his nonfiction and fiction; they are characterized by a combination of humor and vivid description of wildlife. D.'s childhood with his family (older brother Lawrence achieved success as author of *The Alexandria Quartet*) on the Greek island of Corfu and his early preoccupation with zoology are chronicled in *My Family and Other Animals* (1956) and *Birds, Beasts and Relatives* (1969). In these amusing memoirs D. keenly focuses on the human species that was his own family, as much as upon his natural surroundings. At the outset of World War II, D. and his family relocated to Britain, where he was employed as an assistant zookeeper. He would later become a collector of animals, supplying a number of zoos with new species, and then eventually establishing his own zoo in Jersey in the English Channel Islands. D. recounted his 1953 animal-collecting adventures in Cameroon in *The Overloaded Ark* (1953) and *A Zoo in My Luggage* (1960). In later years, D. was committed to education efforts through his radio and docu-

mentary television programs about wildlife conservation. In 1959 he founded the Jersey [England]
Zoological Park and in 1964 established the Jersey
Wildlife Preservation Trust, which continues to operate today.

AWARDS: *Birds Beasts & Relatives,* Nonfiction BBYA,
1969; *Rosy Is My Relative,* BBYA, 1968; *Two in the
Bus,* BBYA, nonfiction BBYA, 1966; *Amateur Naturalist* Nonfiction BBYA 1984.

SELECT FURTHER WORKS: *The Overloaded Ark,* 1953;
The Drunken Forest (1954); *A Zoo in My Luggage,*
1960; *The Talking Parcel* (re-issued as *The Battle for
Castle Cockatrice*) (1974); The Whispering Land
(1975); *The Amateur Naturalist: A Practical Guide to
the Natural World,* 1982; *The Aye-Aye and I,* 1994.

BIBLIOGRAPHY: *Contemporary Authors.* Gerald Durrell obituary, *The Times* (London), January 31, 1995.

CHERYL WOLF

EDELMAN, Bernard

Author, editor, b. 14 December 1946, Brooklyn, New York

A veteran of the U.S. Army (1969–71), E. is best-known for his first book, *Dear America: Letters Home from Vietnam,* which he edited in 1985. He was also the associate producer of an HBO cable television special of the same name in April, 1988. *Dear America,* awarded a Best Books for Young Adults, is a firsthand account of the WAR seen through the eyes of the men and women who served in Vietnam. In this collection of more than two hundred letters, these witnesses share their impressions of the rigors of life in Vietnam, their longing for home and family, their emotions over the conduct of the war, and their despair over the casualties of war. E. himself served as a broadcast specialist/correspondent in Vietnam.

E. began his career after his time in the armed forces, working as an editor, freelance photographer, journalist, director of veterans' affairs, and curator. E. holds a B.A. from Brooklyn College of the City University of New York (1968) and an M.A. from John Jay College of Criminal Justice of the City University of New York (1983). He is also a "contributor of photography and articles to periodicals, including *Police Magazine* and New York *Sunday News Magazine.*"

AWARDS: *Dear America,* 1986, BBYA.

FURTHER WORKS: *Vietnam Photo Book* (with Mark Jury), 1986 edition; *Letters from Vietnam,* 1987; *Cen-*

tenarians: The Story of the 20th Century by the Americans Who Lived It, 1999.

BIBLIOGRAPHY: *Contemporary Authors Online,* 2001.

SARA MARCUS
AND RACHEL WITMER

EISNER, Will

Cartoonist, author, b. 6 March 1917, Brooklyn, New York; d. 3 January 2005, Fort Lauderdale, Florida

E. was a pioneering force in comics for over sixty years. His career spans groundbreaking work in early newspaper comics to the mature GRAPHIC NOVELS. The son of Jewish immigrants, E.'s early life and experiences growing up in New York tenements became the inspiration for much of his graphic novel work. At DeWitt Clinton High School in the Bronx, Eisner's budding interest in art was fostered, and his first work was published in the school newspaper. His interest in drawing was spurred by his father, who painted scenery in New York's Yiddish theaters.

E.'s first comic work appeared 1936 in *WOW What a Magazine!* He created two features for *WOW*—"Harry Karry" and "The Flame." When the MAGAZINE folded after four issues, E. formed a partnership with friend Jerry Iger, and the Eisner-Iger studio was born. The studio was a veritable comics factory, churning out strips in a variety of genres in the hope of placing them with American newspapers. Toward this end, Eisner–Iger recruited a number of young artists who would go on to become comics legends in their own right: Bob Kane, Lou Fine, and Jack

Kirby. The most enduring of E.'s work to come out of this period is "Hawks of the Seas," an ADVENTURE strip that had begun as "The Flame." The partnership ended in 1939 when E. joined the Quality Comics Group to produce a syndicated 16-page newspaper supplement. It was for this supplement that he created his most famous character, The Spirit.

Creating the Comic Book Section for Quality Comics gave E. the opportunity to reach a wide audience in newspapers across the country. The supplement contained three four-color features. The lead feature, "The Spirit," was a detective adventure entirely scripted and drawn by E. This story of a masked detective who protects Central City from the criminal element with no more than fists, cunning, and an unbelievable tolerance for punishment quickly became the most popular feature of the section. The supplement was renamed "The Spirit Section," and became E.'s proving ground for some of the most innovative work in the genre. Even in these early stories, the presence of cinematic camera angles, atmospheric lighting effects and creative storytelling techniques distinguished "The Spirit."

E.'s work was interrupted in 1942 when he was drafted into the Army for service in World War II. The Army took advantage of his skills as a cartoonist, and during the war he produced posters, illustrations, and strips for the troops. After the War, E. returned to a much diminished "Spirit," who had faltered in less able hands during his absence. In December 1945, he reintroduced the strip with a retelling of the Spirit's origin, and the Spirit was quickly back on track. Now with the support of other artists such as a young Jules Feiffer and later Wally Wood, E. continued the weekly installments of the Spirit until 1952. Never content to stay within the narrow confines of the detective genre, E. used the Spirit to explore a wide variety of stories, from simple tales of ordinary people to wild flights of fancy verging on SCIENCE FICTION.

During this period, E. attempted to foster several other projects for publication as newspaper strips or newsstand comics, including Kewpies, Baseball, Nubbin the Shoeshine Boy and John Law. None of these were successful, but some of the material created for them ended up in "The Spirit."

E. founded the American Visuals Corporation, a commercial art company dedicated to creating comics, cartoons, and illustrations for educational and commercial purposes. E. resurrected Joe Dope, a bumbling soldier he had created during the War, for a feature in P*S Magazine, an Army publication. His other clients included RCA Records, an oil filter company, the Baltimore Colts, and New York Telephone. This work soon occupied most of his time, and "The Spirit" was abandoned in favor of this more profitable work, which continued until the late 1970s.

In the mid-1960s, several articles renewed popular interest in the Spirit, and the strips were reprinted in a variety of forms that continue to this day. E. was persuaded to create a small amount of new Spirit material at this time, but despite the growing fans' insistence for more, E. did not have much taste for revisiting what he saw as the heroic fantasies of his youth. Seeking a more mature expression of the form, E. spent two years creating four short stories of "sequential art" that became *A Contract with God,* first published by Baronet in 1978. In this book, with its 1930s Bronx tenements and slice-of-life moral tales, E. returned to his roots and discovered new potential for the comics form—the graphic novel. E. followed *A Contract with God* with a SERIES of graphic novels published by the alternative comics publisher Kitchen Sink Press. With subject matter ranging from semi-AUTOBIOGRAPHICAL (*The Dreamer* and *To the Heart of the Storm*), keen observations of modern life (*The Building* and *Invisible People*) and science fiction parable (*Life on Another Planet*) E. helped break comics away from the juvenile ghetto of SUPERHEROES and "funny books."

In addition to producing a legacy of work, E. taught cartooning at the School of Visual Arts in New York, and is the author of two definitive works examining the creative process, *Comics and Sequential Art* and *Graphic Storytelling.* The Eisner Awards was established in 1988. His work gained even wider recognition when it was showcased in the Whitney Museum in 1996: the "NYNY: City of Ambition" show. E. has been cited as an inspiration by comics' creators from all corners of the genre. He influenced the work of Art SPIEGELMAN, Chris Ware, Harvey Pekar, Daniel Clowes, Max Allan Collins, and Joe Kubert, some of whom worked with E. during his comic-book days.

AWARDS: Established and received Eisner Award.

SELECT FURTHER WORKS: *Name of the Game,* 2001; *Fagin the Jew,* 2003; *The Spirit Archives,* 2004–2005.

BIBLIOGRAPHY: E., Will. *School Library Journal,* 1984; Freedman, S. G. "School Codifies a Literary

Form that Started in the Funny Pages," *New York Times,* October 6, 2004, p. B7.

KENNETH SEEMAN GINIGER

ELFMAN, Blossom

Author, n.d., n.p.

E.'s first published work was *The Girls of Huntington House* (1972), stories about being an English teacher of girls. It is probably natural that her next two works, *A House for Jonnie O* (1976) and *The Sister Act* (1978), also deal with TEENAGE pregnancy. This was a topic not usually dealt with openly at the time of publication and reflected the lessening restrictions on previously taboo subjects.

E. later wrote *The Butterfly Girl* (1980) and *The Return of the Whistler* (1981). In *The Return of the Whistler,* Arnie learns to survive despite his lack of ability in certain areas. *The Strawberry Fields of Heaven* (1983), was geared toward an adult audience. A woman stays with her husband rather than attempt life on her own. Next was another teen novel, *First Love Lives Forever* (1987).

E. then segued into writing a MYSTERY SERIES about Mike and Ally, teens from Martindale. *Love Me Deadly* (1989) is the first in the series. The school's secretary is killed and Mr. Emerson, an English teacher, is taken into custody; these events contribute to the unlikely partnership of brainy Mike and Ally the athlete as they struggle to find the real perpetrator. *Tell Me No Lies* (1989) is the second pairing of Mike and Ally to solve a mystery. In a departure from the Mike and Ally series, E.'s next work was *The Haunted Heart* (1989). Rachael is less than excited about her mother's remarriage but tries to make the best of it, even when events take an unexpected turn. Returning to Mike and Ally in *The Ghost-Sitter* (1990), E. explores the possibility that Martindale may be home to a ghost in the third book in the series.

The Curse of the Dancing Doll (1991) is the final Mike and Ally mystery to date. It is also the last YOUNG ADULT novel E. has published; after a hiatus of almost a decade, she published *The Case of the Pederast's Wife: A Novel* (2002). An adult historical novel, it chronicles the attempts of Dr. Martin Frame to help Constance Wilde, wife of Oscar Wilde.

E. is the matriarch of an extremely creative family which includes sons, Danny and Richard, grandson Bodhi, and his wife, Jenna. Her two sons are musi-cians, and her grandson and his wife are both actors. E. also won an Emmy award for her writing on the television movie project, *I Think I'm Having a Baby.*

AWARDS: 1972 ALA Best Book for Young Adults, *The Girls of Huntington House;* 1976 ALA Notable Book *A House for Jonnie O.*

BIBLIOGRAPHY: Eaglen, Audrey B. "Writing the Teen-Age Soap Opera." *School Library Journal,* April 1979; www.amazon.com; www.bccls.org; www.msu .edu/user/perrinet/elfman/bio/; www.novelst4.epnet .com

JEANNE MARIE RYAN

EMERGENCE OF YOUNG ADULT LITERATURE IN THE TWENTIETH CENTURY

The emergence of YA LITERATURE in the 20th century, although neither has recognized nor marketed as such, probably began with dime novels. Dime novels often had TEEN protagonists, as well as stories themed to capture a young reader's attention with ADVENTURE, MYSTERY, travel, and hard work. Horatio Alger Jr. penned countless tales with the theme that hard work would ensure future success. With the establishment of the STRATEMEYER SYNDICATE, an industry was born, as Edward Stratemeyer, the founder, developed characters for series that many writers then contributed to under whatever pseudonym Stratemeyer had assigned to that series. SERIES FICTION is a set of stories that share characters or settings, or a combination of both. Many credit Stratemeyer, as founder of the Stratemeyer Syndicate, with the creation of many notable characters—among them the Hardy Boys, Nancy Drew, Tom Swift, the Blythe Girls, the Moving Picture Girls, the Outdoor Girls, the Dana Girls, and Dave Porter—which cannot be argued. Yet there were many others who also contributed to the emergence of young adult literature in the first half of the 20th century.

Among them were A. T. Dudley, author of the Phillips Exeter books and Arthur M. Winfield who wrote the Putnam Hall stories. Lucy Maud Montgomery published *Anne of Green Gables,* which not only had several sequels but generated collections of vignettes set in and around Avonlea. *Daddy Long Legs* was published by Jean Webster, who had also authored *When Patty Went to College,* and a companion novel to *Daddy Long Legs, Dear Enemy.* L. M. Montgomery introduced a new character, Emily Starr, in 1922, which was also the year that two separate series entitled the Radio Boys appeared. Gerald Breckenridge penned ten adventure tales, while the Stratemeyer Syndicate produced thirteen titles authored by Allen Chapman. Meanwhile, Howard Pease had introduced Tod Moran, an adventurous teen who joins a ship's crew and has multitudinous adventures. The Stratemeyer Syndicate produced the Ted Scott Flying Stories under the name of Franklin W. Dixon. The Ted Scott Flying Stories reflected the country's excitement about Lindbergh's flight as did the Bill Bolton, Navy Aviator series, by Noel Sainsbury. The Linda Carlton books by Edith Lavell are supposed to be based on the female aviator, Amelia Earhardt.

Being a pilot was not the only career that was possible though, and many of the YA books of this time did focus on careers. The G-Men series by William Engle and Laurecne Dwight Smith had first appeared in 1926, and generated three stories over the course of fourteen years. Another popular career was nursing, exemplified by the Sue Barton books by Helen Dore Boylston. Appearing from 1936 to 1952, they follow Sue from her student-nursing days to her work at the Henry Street Settlement. Her marriage to a country doctor and growing family do not end her career, first as a superintendent of nurses, and then as a neighborhood nurse and staff nurse. The Cherry Ames series by Helen Wells and Julie Tatham, appearing in 1943, chronicles the career of another young nurse from her student days. The twenty-seven books follow Cherry through many different nursing jobs, and are focused more on the different possibilities that nursing offers. Helen Wells and Julie Tatham also wrote the Vicki Barr, Stewardess series, which appeared from 1947 to 1964 with a total of sixteen titles. Many of these career-centered books owe at least a small debt to Alger's work.

World Wars I and II had served as a backdrop to many stories geared toward young people at the time, including the Grace Harlowe books by Josephine Chase, writing as Jessie Graham Flower. First appearing in 1910 and ending in 1924, they follow Grace through high school and college, as well as the battles of World War I in Europe, before she returns to the U.S. for other adventures. The Aeroplane Boys by Ashton Lamar, appearing between 1910 and 1914, an early series about flying, also reflected the impending onset of United States involvement in World War I.

The approaching WAR is also reflected in many of the books published in the 1940s. The Don Winslow series by Frank V. Martinek, which starts in 1940, showcases Don joining the Navy and the adventures he has there. Janet Lambert set many of her first novels in an Army setting, using her background as an Army wife. The Penny and Tippy Parrish books, which kick off with *Star Spangled Summer* in 1941, start before World War II, but by the third book reflect the world of the U.S. at war. The characters are followed through the conclusion of World War II to the midst of the Vietnam War. Her stories about the Jordon family debut at about the same time, focusing on a large and motherless family surviving when their soldier father goes off to war. Her Kane series also uses World War II as a background—when a reservist decides to become active, his society wife and two daughters must adjust to Army life. *Meet the Malones* by Lenora Mattingly Weber is also set against the background of World War II, although it is mostly seen from a civilian point of view.

There were also plenty of fun books available for young adults, focused on characters who were about their age, but seemed to have a great deal of freedom of mobility and countless adventures. Solving MYSTERIES was all in a day's work in many of these stories, including the Beverly Gray mysteries by Clair Blank, the Judy Bolton mysteries by Margaret Sullivan, and of course, the Stratemeyer Syndicate's Hardy Boys and Nancy Drew mysteries. The Trixie Belden series by Julie Campbell and Kathryn Kenny began in 1948 and ended nearly forty years later in 1986. Through the thirty-nine titles, Trixie and her friends, known as the Bob-Whites, solve a multitude of mysteries as well as work to help their families and communities.

Sports stories were often nearly as popular as mysteries, including the Phillips Exeter stories from early in the century, which centered on sports, as did the Scranton High Chums by Donald Ferguson. Popular college coach Clair Bee penned the Chip Hilton books following a young athlete through the different sports seasons from the time of his high school career through his college career. The twenty-three titles feature baseball, football, and basketball stories.

Although better known for the Tarzan series, Edgar Rice Burroughs introduced the John Carter of Mars series in 1912. The eleven novels concluded in 1942, but also gave rise to comic books, where the adventures of John Carter continued. Tom Swift and Tom Swift Jr. also enjoyed all kinds of interplanetary adventures. Star Trek, originally a television show, would also generate a plethora of novelizations through the years. The Lone Ranger books by Fran Striker, which lasted for twenty years, also had a media tie-in.

The Betsy-Tacy series by Maud Hart Lovelace debuted in 1940. One of the offshoots of the series, *Carney's House Party,* pays homage to the Little Colonel books from the beginning of the century. Many of Janet Lambert's books in the 1950s are about teenagers and their family life in the suburbs, as are the Rosamund DuJardin books. Yet in sharp contrast to these is J. D. SALINGER's *Catcher in the Rye.* Published in 1951, Holden Caulfield was a different kind of teen protagonist—sharp, edgy, and filled with angst. The raw language in the book was groundbreaking at the time and a prophecy of things to come.

Many of the more literary books of the 1960s and 1970s began to touch on edgier topics, and reflect the times in which they were written. Madeleine L'Engle's *The Young Unicorns* transplants the Austin family to New York City, where they encounter a gang. S. E. HINTON's *The Outsiders* with its poignant sense of teen isolation appeared, as did *Rumble Fish.* Self-assessment, and eventual self-acceptance, are keynotes for Paula DANZIGER's protagonist, Marcy Lewis. Overweight, and miserable, a new teacher helps her find herself, and Marcy, in turn, finds the courage to defend the teacher against the anger of the community. Marcy's reluctant evolution is chronicled in *The Cat Ate My Gymsuit* and *There's a Bat in Bunk Five.*

The edginess would continue throughout the next two decades. Brock COLE's *The Facts Speaks for Themselves* was heart rending in its depictions of the abuse a young girl suffers, as was the abuse portrayed in *When Jeff Comes Home* by Catherine Atkins. Laurie Halse ANDERSON's *Speak* also showed a teen protagonist dealing with a really difficult situation. The protagonist of *Swallowing Stones* by Joyce MCDONALD learns to deal with his own moral culpability, while the protagonist of *Stone Water* by Barbara Snow GILBERT must test his moral fortitude. *Don't You Dare Read This, Mrs. Dunphrey* by Margaret Peterson HADDIX deals with abandonment. *Give a Boy a Gun* by Todd STRASSER and *Monster* by Walter Dean Myers spotlights teenage violence. In Ann M. Mar-

tin's California DIARIES series, characters try to deal with eating disorders, prejudice, and bad grades, among other topics. Even Francine PASCAL's Sweet Valley High series, and the other series that were generated from the original, began to deal with fairly weighty topics.

The recognition within the publishing industry of the economic power wielded by young adults, and their desire to be part of that, generated a plethora of work being published that was geared to the young adult market. The American Library Association, with its creation of the PRINTZ AWARD to honor outstanding YA literature, also helped to promote the genre, furthering the work done with the Margaret A. Edwards and Best Books for Young Adults Awards.

In the 21st century, teen literature has exploded. Series novels abound, as do single titles. No topic is forbidden, as the literature strives to meet the expectations of its sophisticated audience. GRAPHIC NOVELS have merely added another layer to the choices that are available to today's teens.

BIBLIOGRAPHY: Billman, Carol. The Secret of the Stratemeyer Syndicate: Nancy Drew and the Hardy Boys, and the Million Dollar Fiction Factory, 1986; www.lib.msu.edu / coll / main / spec_col / nye / juven .htm; www.seriesbooks.com.

JEANNE MARIE RYAN

ETHICAL DECISIONS AND THE YA NOVEL

The YA novel genre is full of ethical decisions that often drive the plots. Especially since the rise of the "problem novel," issues dealt with in YA literature have become increasingly more complex and difficult. However, at the heart of almost all young adult novels is the greatest ethical issue of all—how the protagonists can develop in a responsible way as they embark upon the journey to adulthood.

Although it might seem that the 1960s marked the beginning of explorations of the effects of major problems on protagonists in novels, the reality is that even the most seemingly innocuous YA works often dealt with some kind of moral issue. Although the books of yesteryear might not have the rawness or grittiness seen in Brock COLE's *The Facts Speak for Themselves* or Walter Dean MYERS's *Monster,* nonetheless they often dealt with characters that were at some type of a moral crossroad. Janet Lambert, in her multiple SERIES for adolescent girls, created various characters that dealt with envy of a friend's wealth, jealousy over a boyfriend's apparent interest in other girls, and conflicting demands between their own desires and the needs of their families. Lenora Mattingly Weber's heroines grappled with their own fears and hesitations, as well as how far they were willing to go to fit in with the crowd. How to respond to all sorts of serious issues is a hallmark of both her series, though in the end her heroines usually choose to take the right path even if they take a few steps down the wrong path. Clair Bee's Chip Hilton sports series often presented Chip in a difficult moral position—torn between doing the right thing and appearing to be a tattletale. Although both the resolutions and the problems may seem simplistic in today's world, they are no less heartfelt.

But, as the world became an edgier place, so did the literature dedicated to a young adult audience. Madeleine L'Engle's book *The Young Unicorns* showed the Austin family coping with a year in New York and facing gangs and urban violence. Later in the FAMILY's history, Vicky Austin must deal with the fact that a boy to whom she is attracted caused the DEATH of a family friend by his own carelessness in a suicide attempt. Another part of *A Ring of Endless Light* shows Vicky Austin also dealing with her beloved grandfather's death and his request that she let him know when it is time to let go. That request is mild compared to the grandfather's request to his grandson in Barbara Snow GILBERT's *Stone Water*. In this story, the grandfather asks far more of his grandson than just telling him when to let go—this grandfather wants his grandson to hasten his death. Joyce Sweeney deals with the pain of two brothers who have inadvertently caused their sister's death in *Free Fall*. Interwoven with the ADVENTURES of the two brothers and their two friends as they go spelunking and get trapped in an underground cave is the subtext and history that is destroying the relationship between the brothers. They are not the only ones who have secrets though, and the truth proves to be their one chance at survival—if the four of them can stand to face it. As the boys grapple with the physical dangers and their own emotional frailties, their only hope for salvation lies in their finding the fortitude to face their demons.

Facing demons is not an uncommon peril in YA literature, although some demons are more literal than others. Both the Buffy the Vampire and Angel series of books (based on the popular television shows) deal with fighting actual demons on a regular basis with the express purpose of saving the world. Often the price for saving the world demands a great deal of sacrifice on the part of the heroine and hero, and on the part of their assorted colleagues. Although neither show is on prime-time television any longer, the book series are quite popular. They have even generated nonfiction books, including *What Would Buffy Do?: The Vampire Slayer a Spiritual Guide*.

Rob THOMAS often has characters who deal with hard moral choices. The protagonist in *Satellite Down* struggles to accept what he has learned about the television business, and himself, before he reaches some glimmering of self-acceptance. Steve York, the unforgettable protagonist of the seminal *Rats Saw God*, starts by trying to deal with his heroic father. Yet it soon becomes obvious that his relationship with his dad is the least of his problems, when he discovers his girlfriend sleeping with their teacher. This sends Steve on a downward spiral that engulfs him—caught in a swirling vortex of drugs and defeat—his grades plummeting and his life coming apart. Only the intervention of a guidance counselor and a special senior project offer Steve a shot at redemption—but will he find it within himself to take a chance and start trusting again? And will he ever be able to trust his own instincts again?

Laurie Halse ANDERSON's heroine faces a similar conflict about trusting herself again after she is traumatized in *Speak*. Her attempt to cope with what has happened causes her to become silent as she immerses herself in the pain of what she has experienced. To transcend that pain requires great courage—a courage that she is no longer sure that she has.

Conflicts and problems abound in YA novels, but so does the promise of redemption if the protagonists have the courage to embrace the possibilities. As Holden Caulfield, J. D. SALINGER's hero in *The Catcher in the Rye*, muses upon the possibilities offered by the world, he acknowledges the pain that they can cause. The question that many of the protagonists of YA novels face is whether the hurt the world offers is offset by the potential of happiness of that same world. Believing in those unclear potentialities is perhaps the greatest risk any human being can take—yet how these protagonists choose to deal with the world determines how they live their lives. It is, in many ways, the greatest ethical decision that they can make.

                                        JEANNE MARIE RYAN

EXPLORING THE WORLD FROM HOME

One of the amazing things about literature is the ability it gives readers to enter worlds of which they might otherwise have never been a part. When a story is well told, readers become participants in that world, and return to it even after the book has been closed. Well-done stories are an opportunity to explore different cultures and situations that one might otherwise never be exposed to in any format. Novels offer portals to worlds perhaps unheard of. Also, since a book can be closed at any time, the reader's comfort level is disturbed, it offers an opportunity to insulate oneself that is not as readily available in other media formats. A book truly is a time-travel machine. With the simple act of opening a book to its first page, we are transported—sometimes the book was written about a different time or place, but other times, it actually was written in another time and place, and opening its pages takes us back to that time and that place.

Through reading, I have ridden with D'Artagnan and his Musketeers, shared the fears of the young Elizabeth before she became the Queen of Britain and experienced the banishment of her young handmaiden, and with her learned the many lessons of the Fairy Folk. I have disembarked at Jamestown, a stranger, only to be brought not only into the home of the Spragues, but into their hearts as well. With Meg Murry, I have traveled through time and space to rescue my father and then my little brother, only to have to travel into my brother's body to save him again, and then in a different adventure, to try and save the world. With Alexander Hero, I have visited country houses to try to detect a paranormal presence. It is a paranormal presence that is found, although not by Alexander Hero, in a lovely Federal home in Georgetown, and again in a vintage-clothing store in Virginia. I have traveled back to World War II, and helped Penny Parrish discover a spy at Fort Knox. As World War I looms on the horizon, I have breathlessly flown over the English countryside, in the relatively new *aeroplane*. I have consulted with my attorney father and helped him resolve a problem with my well-known detecting skills. My adventures are unique to what I have read.

Yet, countless people could tell of similar experiences. Perhaps that it is one of the greatest gifts of literature. . . . It helps us not only explore and understand different worlds from the security of our own homes, but to learn to appreciate them. When that happens, we learn that what draws us together as human beings is under our surface differences, far greater than the forces that would tear us apart. Such knowledge gives us both an empathy and a sympathy, useful both within our homes and outside them.

                                        JEANNE MARIE RYAN

FAIRY TALE RETELLINGS

Ask anyone to name their favorite fairy tale and you are likely to get as many answers as there are versions. Scholars agree that fairy tales are a part of folklore literature but that folktales are not necessarily fairy tales. Nor do fairy tales need to include fairies. In his essay "On Fairie Stories" reprinted from *Meditations on Middle Earth,* J. R. R. TOLKIEN states that, "fairy tales are stories about Fairy, or Faerie, the twilight realm where fairies exist."

Fairy tale comes from the French "contes des fée" and many fairy tales were written in 17th-century France. Most are even older in origin and were changed when written down by such writers as Charles Perrault, Hans Christian Andersen, and the Brothers Grimm. Jacob and Wilhelm Grimm collected folktales from German peasants and changed them to suit their audiences. The German term for "fairy tales" is Märchen, a word that does not have an equivalent in English but means a story or tale, and has come to mean a story of wonder and enchantment. In 17th-century France, each tale ended with a moralistic verse; the stories were often gruesome, cruel and not intended for children. Women rebelling against society's rigid constraints created many of these tales. They did not always end happily ever after as many do now. In the traditional Cinderella tale, she triumphs over her life of drudgery and servitude by using her wits, not with the help of magical fairy creatures.

During the Victorian Era, the idea of the idyllic childhood was romanticized and fairy tales were relegated to children and the lower classes. Their original intent was diluted and their darker, more violent, and frightening images eliminated. The focus of the fairy tale plot changed from the female to the male as the strong, heroic figure.

In the 20th century, writers began to create new works by adding their own ideas and imaginings to these traditional fairy tales. *Don't Bet on the Prince: Contemporary Feminist Fairy Tales in North America and England,* edited by Jack Zipes, is a collection of contemporary tales with a feminist slant that includes critical essays. Both *Ella Enchanted* by Gail Carson LEVINE and the stories in *Rose and the Beast: Fairy Tales Retold* by Francesca Lia BLOCK defy "expected" fairy tale endings. Cinderella runs off with her fairy godmother in one story in the revisionist fairy tale collection *Kissing the Witch: Old Tales in New Skins* by Emma Donoghue. Many fairy tales are also told from the secondary characters' perspectives. Author Donna Jo NAPOLI insightfully reinterprets the story of Hansel and Gretel from the witch's point of view in her beautifully written book *The Magic Circle.* In *Zel,* based on Rapunzel, she alternates the characters' points of view, sets the story in 16th century Switzerland, and makes Rapunzel's mother the witch. The Beast's point of view is featured in *Beauty,* a Beauty and the Beast retelling, set in Persia. David Henry Wilson's *The Coachman Rat* is a dark retelling of the Cinderella story from the coachman's perspective.

Many fairy tale retellings have restored the dark and disturbing elements traditionally found in fairy tales. Angela Carter's adult book *The Bloody Chamber* is full of dark, violent, and sensual images as it recalls many traditional fairy tales, including Bluebeard. *Truly Grim Tales* by Priscilla GALLOWAY contains gloomy tales told from the viewpoints of the villains. Robin MCKINLEY tackles incest in her powerful book *Deerskin,* a retelling of the fairy tale "Donkey Skin." Juliet MARILLIER's trilogy *Daughter of the Forest, Son of the Shadows* and *Child of the Prophecy,* begins with a retelling of the Celtic tale The Six Swans and vividly details the despair and suffering typically endured by characters in classic fairy tales. Tanith Lee's *White as Snow,* from the Fairy Tale series for adults edited by Terri Windling, is a scary version of Snow White that is definitely not a child's bedtime story.

The authors in this Fairy Tale SERIES, all based on familiar stories, have chosen to change the period or place where the story occurs. Charles DE LINT's *Jack of Kinrowan* (also known as *Jack the Giant Killer*) places his main character in a modern CANADIAN city. Kara DALKEY's version of Hans Christian Andersen's *The Nightingale* has become a historical novel set in Japan. *Briar Rose* by Jane YOLEN is a short novel that is set during THE HOLOCAUST, with allusions to Sleeping Beauty woven into it. The last example of a book from that series is *Tam Lin* by Pamela Dean, in which the Scottish ballad (and fairy tale) is set on a modern Minnesota college campus. Adele Geras's book *Watching the Roses* from her Egerton Hall trilogy, moves Sleeping Beauty to modern times, an eighteen-year-old English boarding school girl's sleep is the result of the trauma of being raped. The other books in the series, featuring three roommates in an English boarding school in the 1960s consist of *The Tower Room,* based on Rapunzel and *Pictures of the Night,* based on Snow White. Sheri S. TEPPER's adult book *Beauty* explores the life of a faerie girl as she ages from sixteen to 116 and journeys into the future in search of her destiny. *Sleeping Boy,* written for children by Sonia Craddock, takes the Sleeping Beauty tale and transforms it into a story about a German boy at the turn of the century, cursed to go to WAR when he turns sixteen. Instead, at sixteen, he falls asleep, destined to remain asleep until peace comes. *Kindergarten* by Peter Rushford is another contemporary tale that weaves a scary version of Hansel and Gretel

into the story of the Holocaust. Gregory Maguire has written many adult novels that also appeal to young adults, using themes from fairy tales including *Mirror, Mirror* (Snow White); *Wicked: The Life and Times of the Wicked Witch of the West;* and *Confessions of an Ugly Stepsister* (Cinderella).

Not all modern fairy tale retellings are grim and forboding. Many authors have written parodies of traditional tales in the form of "fractured fairy tales." Vivian VANDE VELDE has written numerous books that make fun of classic tales like *Tales from the Brothers Grimm and the Sisters Weird* and *The Rumpelstiltskin Problem.* James Finn Garner's *Politically Correct Bedtime Stories* and its sequel is a hilarious look for all ages at what fairy tales would look like if their sexual suggestiveness, excessive violence, and offensive stereotypes were eliminated. *A Telling of Tales, Untold Tales,* and *Teller of Tales* are all fractured fairy tale collections written by William J. BROOKE that use wordplay to examine human nature. Rebecca Lickiss's book *Never After* parodies "The Frog Prince" and the "Princess and the Pea," among other tales. *The Ordinary Princess* by M. M. Kaye subverts the idea of all princesses being blessed with beauty by making the main character ordinary. Patrice KINDL's *Goose Chase* is a lighthearted, original story with themes from Rapunzel, Cinderella, and other tales woven into its plot.

Most common are retellings of traditional fairy tales, often novel-length adaptations of shorter fairy tales. Young adults only familiar with the Walt Disney book and film versions of fairy tales may be surprised after reading these retellings. Cinderella is one of the most recognizable fairy tale characters, and she stars in many books and collections, including Margaret HADDIX's *Just Ella,* Shirley Rousseau Murphy's *Silver Woven in My Hair,* and Philip PULLMAN's *I Was A Rat.* The characters of Beauty and the Beast appear in *The Fire Rose* by Mercedes LACKEY and in Robin MCKINLEY's books *Beauty* and *Rose Daughter.* Rumpelstiltskin is represented in *Straw Into Gold* by Gary SCHMIDT, Eleanor Farjeon's *The Silver Curlew,* and *Spinners* by Donna Jo Napoli. Snow White is another popular character found in many retellings, including *Snow White and Rose Red* by Patricia C. WREDE (from the Fairy Tale series), Mercedes Lackey's *The Serpent's Shadow,* and Tracy Lynn's novel *Snow.* Cameron Dokey prominently features the character of Sleeping Beauty in the young adult book *Beauty*

Sleep, as does Mercedes Lackey in *Gates of Sleep* and Robin McKinley in *Spindle's End.* Versions of the Tam Lin tale include *The Perilous Gard* by Elizabeth Marie Pope, Patricia MCKILLIP's *Winter Rose,* Janet MCNAUGHTON's *An Earthly Knight* and *Fire and Hemlock,* by Diana Wynne JONES, a combination of tales of Tam Lin and Thomas the Rhymer. Scheherazade from the Arabian Nights appears in Susan FLETCHER's *Shadow Spinners* and Cameron Dokey's *Storyteller's Daughter.* Other notable books with familiar fairy tale characters include Robin McKinley's *The Door in the Hedge,* a retelling of the tales "The Frog Prince" and "The Twelve Dancing Princesses." Author Donna Jo Napoli features Jack and the Beanstalk in the young adult book *Crazy Jack* and the Pied Piper of Hamelin in *Breath.* Another tale from the Fairy Tale series called *Fitcher's Brides* by Gregory Frost focuses on Bluebeard. Berlie DOHERTY's *Daughter of the Sea* is based on Hans Christian Andersen's The Little Mermaid. Other tales of mermaids and water sprites are prominent in Donna Jo Napoli's *Sirena* and *Haunted Waters* by Mary Pope Osborne (the tale of Undine). Tales influenced by the Brothers Grimm are found in many fairy tale retellings for young adults. A few examples include Gillian Cross's *Wolf,* about a girl with a mother named Goldie, who has nightmares about wolves; Philip Pullman's *Clockwork: Or All Wound Up* and *The Green Man: Tales from the Mythic Forest,* a collection edited by Ellen Datlow and Terri Windling.

There have been many anthologies that retell fairy tales. Some of the most prominent ones are those edited by Datlow and Windling. Some of their numerous adult collections include: *Snow White, Blood Red; Ruby Slippers, Golden Tears; Black Thorn, White Rose; Silver Birch, Blood Moon; Black Swan, White Raven; Black Heart, Ivory Bones;* and several written for young adults including, *A Wolf at the Door* and *Swan Sister: Fairy Tales Retold.* Another anthology that contains stories based on fairy tales is *Firebirds: An Anthology of Original Fantasy and Science Fiction,* edited by Sharyn November. Young adult readers will also enjoy *Not One Damsel in Distress: World Folktales for Strong Girls;* and *Mirror, Mirror: Forty Folktales for Mothers and Daughters to Share,* both edited by Jane Yolen. Gail De Vos and Anna Altmann have written a book called *New Tales for Old: Folktales as Literary Fictions for Young Adults* that is full of lists of fairy tale retellings. H. Person

and D. Person show how contemporary children's books are based on stories from the Bible in *Stories of Heaven and Earth* (2005).

Authors have also written modern fairy tales in the form of POETRY. *Transformations,* by Anne Sexton and *Trails of Stones* by Gwenn Strauss are both collections of fairy tale poetry that will appeal to older young adults.

Although PICTURE BOOKS are written to appeal primarily to young children, there are those that appeal to readers of all ages. Jon Scieszka and Lane Smith's works are perfect examples. They have written many hilarious fairy tale retellings including: *The Frog Prince Continued; The Stinky Cheese Man and other Fairly Stupid Tales,* and *The True Story of the 3 Little Pigs.* Neil GAIMAN has written a book illustrated by Dave McKean, *Wolves in the Walls,* that recalls the tales of Little Red Riding Hood and the Three Little Pigs. *Recycling Red Riding Hood* by Sandra L. Bechett (2002) reviews hundreds of books that are based on early versions of Little Red Riding Hood.

Another book format that is tremendously appealing to young adults is the GRAPHIC NOVEL. *Fables: Legends in Exile* by Bill Willingham is a fractured fairy tale written in a comic-book format where the Big Bad Wolf is a hard-boiled detective in human form investigating the murders of characters from fairy tales and fables. The second volume in the series is *Fables: Animal Farm,* in which rebellion breaks out at the "Farm" where fables who cannot pass as human are forced to live. Several versions of Grimms' fairy tales written in graphic novel format are *The Big Book of Grimm* by Jonathan Vankin and Douglas Wheeler's *Fairy Tales of the Brothers Grimm.*

Fairy tales continue to fascinate readers because, as Terri WINDLING and Ellen Datlow state in the introduction to their book *Black Thorn, White Rose,* "they speak to us about our own lives here and now, using rich archetypal imagery and a language that's deceptively simple, a poetry distilled through the centuries and generations of storytellers."

BIBLIOGRAPHY: Bechett, Sandra L. *Recycling Red Riding Hood,* 2002. Block, Francesca Lia. *Rose and the Beast: Fairy Tales Retold,* 2000. Brooke, William J. *A Telling of the Tales: Five Stories,* 1990; *Teller of Tales,* 1994; *Untold Tales,* 1993. Carter, Angela. *The Bloody Chamber and Other Stories,* 1989. Craddock, Sonia. *Sleeping Boy,* 1999. Cross, Gillian. *Wolf,* 1986. Dalkey, Kara. *The Nightingale,* 1988. Datlow, Ellen and Terri Windling, eds. *A Wolf at the Door: And Other Retold Fairy Tales*, 2001; *Black Heart, Ivory Bones*, 2000; *Black Swan, White Raven*, 1997; *Black Thorn, White Rose*, p. 2, 1994; *The Green Man: Tales From the Mythic Forest*, 2002; *Ruby Slippers, Golden Tears*, 1996; *Silver Birch, Blood Moon*, 1999; *Snow White, Blood Red*, 1993; *Swan Sister: Fairy Tales Retold*, 2003; Dean, Pamela. *Tam Lin*, 1992. de Lint Charles. *Jack of Kinrowan*, 1995. de Vos, Gail and Ann Altmann, eds. *New Tales for Old: Folktales as Literary Fictions For Young Adults*, 1999. Doherty, Berlie. *Daughter of the Sea*, 1997. Dokey, Cameron. *Beauty Sleep*, 2002; *Storyteller's Daughter*, 2002. Donoghue, Emma. *Kissing the Witch: Old Tales in New Skins*, 1997. Farjeon, Eleanor. *The Silver Curlew*, 1954. Fletcher, Susan. *Shadow Spinner*, 1998. Frost, Gregory. *Fitcher's Brides*, 2002. Gaiman, Neil and Dave McKean. *Wolves in the Walls*, 2003. Galloway, Priscilla. *Truly Grim Tales*, 1995. Garner, James Finn. *Once Upon a More Enlightened Time: More Politically Correct Bedtime Stories*, 1995; *Politically Correct Bedtime Stories: A Collection of Modern Tales of Our Life and Times*, 1994. Geras, Adele. *Pictures of the Night*, 1993; *The Tower Room*, 1992; *Watching the Roses*, 1992. Haber, Karen, ed. *Meditations on Middle-Earth*, p. 216, 2001. Haddix, Margaret. *Just Ella*, 1999. Jones, Diana Wynne. *Fire and Hemlock*, 1985. Kaye, M.M. *Ordinary Princess*, 1984. Kindl, Patrice. *Goose Chase*, 2001. Lackey, Mercedes. *Fire Rose*, 1995; *Gates of Sleep*, 2002; *Serpent's Shadow*, 2001. Lee, Tanith. *White as Snow*, 2000. Levin, Gail Carson. *Ella Enchanted*, 1997. Lickiss, Rebecca. *Never After*, 2002. Lynn, Tracy. *Snow*, 2003. Maguire, Gregory. *Confessions of an Ugly Stepsister*, 1999; *Mirror, Mirror*, 2003; *Wicked: The Life and Times of the Wicked Witch of the West*, 1995. Marillier, Juliet. *Child of the Prophecy*, 2002; *Daughter of the Forest*, 2000; *Son of the Shadows*, 2001. McKillip, Patricia. *Winter Rose*, 1996. McKinley, Robin. *Beauty: A Retelling of the Story of Beauty and the Beast*, 1978; *Deerskin*, 1994; *Door in the Hedge*, 1982; *Rose Daughter*, 1997; *Spindle's End*, 2001. McNaughton, Janet. *An Earthly Knight*, 2004. Murphy, Shirley Rousseau. *Silver Woven in My Hair*, 1983. Napoli, Donna Jo. *Beast*, 2000; *Breath*, 2003; *Crazy Jack*, 1999; *The Magic Circle*, 1993; *Sirena*, 2001; *Spinners*, 1999; *Zel*, 1996. Osborne, Mary Pope. *Haunted Waters*, 1994. H. E. Person and D. G. Person. *Stories of Heaven and Earth: Bible Heroes in Contemporary Children's Literature*, 2005. Pope, Elizabeth Marie. *Perilous Gard*, 1974. Pullman, Philip. *Clockwork*, 1998; *I Was A Rat*, 2000. Rushford, Peter. *Kindergarten*, 1980. Schmidt, Gary. *Straw Into Gold*, 2001. Scieszka, Jon and Lane Smith. *The Frog Prince Continued*, 1991; *The Stinky Cheese Man and Other Fairly Stupid Tales*, 1992; *The True*

Story of the 3 Little Pigs, 1989. Sexton, Anne. *Transformations*, 1971. Strauss, Gwenn. *Trail of Stones*, 1990. *Sur La Lune Fairy Tales.* ed Heidi, Anne Heiner. 3 Dec. 2003. 7 Dec. 2003. http://www.surlalunefairytales.com. Tepper, Sheri S. *Beauty*, 1991. Vankin, Jonathan. *The Big Book of Grim*, 1999. Velde, Vivian Vande. *The Rumpelstiltskin Problem*, 2000; *Tales From the Brothers Grimm and the Sisters Weird*, 1995. Wheeler, Douglas. *Fairy Tales of the Brothers Grimm*, 2003. Willingham, Bill. *Fables: Animal Farm;* 2003; *Fables: Legends in Exile*, 2003. Wilson, David Henry. *The Coachman Rat*, 1989. Wrede, Patricia C. *Snow White and Rose Red*, 1989. Yolen, Jane. *Briar Rose*, 1992; ed. *Mirror, Mirror: Forty Folktales for Mothers and Daughters to Share*, 2000; and *Not One Damsel in Distress: World Folktales for Strong Girls*, 2000. Zipes, Jack, ed. *Don't Bet On the Prince: Contemporary Feminist Fairy Tales in North America and England*, 1986; *When Dreams Came True: Classical Fairy Tales and Their Tradition*, 1999.

SHARON RAWLINS

FAMILY IN YOUNG ADULT LITERATURE

The *Merriam-Webster Online Dictionary* lists twenty-one definitions of the word *family*. The definition that one might assume to be most likely to be listed first is "a group of persons of common ancestry," but interestingly enough, it is preceded by "a group of individuals living under one roof and usually under one head." This definition does not involve blood, mothers, fathers, two-point-five children, white picket fences, or dogs. Since American families are not held to these parameters, it is not surprising that families in YA literature are even more loosely defined.

In defining YA LITERATURE, many experts in the field allude to the fact that the norm in YA books is to tell a story with absent or only peripherally involved parents. This is often true since TEENAGERS are certainly more interested in reading about their peers than about their parents. However, many YA books have tackled the frequently strained, sometimes painful, often loving relationships between teens and their parents or other family members. Families of all shapes and sizes, blood-related and not, functional and dysfunctional, appear throughout the pages of YA literature.

It would be remiss to begin with a book other than the pioneer YA novel, *The Outsiders* (1967). S. E. HINTON, a teen herself at the time of the book's publication, wrote the quintessential family story. A group of teenage boys, largely living on their own due to parental neglect or absence, look to one another for support, financial help, advice, and brotherly love. Three of the characters are related, but the others are bound together by friendship. This makeshift family falls into *Merriam-Webster's* third definition: "a group of people united by certain convictions or a common affiliation." This kind of family situation is evidenced once again in the more recent *33 Snowfish* by Adam RAPP (2003). Rapp's three main characters, Boobie, Curl, and Custis have all escaped horrendous situations at home and find themselves on the run with Boobie's baby brother. Individually, they have never known what it is like to be part of a healthy family environment, but as they come to care for each other, they create a new family in which the four of them can finally feel somewhat safe. At the end of the novel, Custis forges an unlikely relationship and yet another family is born. Similarly, in Melvin BUR-GESS's *Smack* (1997) and in Ineke Holtwijk's *Asphalt Angels* (1998), groups of runaways and street children come to rely upon their comrades as family.

Many YA novels feature families with only one parent or with young people being raised by a grandparent or sibling. Since these situations are so prevalent in today's society, it is no surprise that this would be translated to the pages of YA literature. In Meg CABOT's *The Princess Diaries* (2000), teenage Mia lives with her divorced mother in Manhattan while her father, the Prince of fictional Genovia, lives in his home country. Fourteen-year-old Mattie lives with her widowed mother and her grandfather in Laurie Halse ANDERSON's historical fiction work, *Fever 1793* (2000). In *Summerland* by Michael Chabon (2002), young Ethan Feld lives with his widower father. Raven in *Spellbound* by Janet MCDONALD (2001) has a single mom, as does Chad in *Dunk* by David LUBAR (2002). Hope in *Hope Was Here* by Joan BAUER (2000) has been raised by her aunt; Em in *When She Was Good* by Norma Fox MAZER (1997) has to endure living with her abusive older sister after their parents' deaths.

Of course, there are YA books that feature two parents and their offspring living under the same roof, but the white picket fence and dog are usually optional. Cherie BENNETT's *Life in the Fat Lane* (1998) features Lara who has a disorder that makes her gain large amounts of weight and two parents who don't

deal particularly well with their now-fat, former beauty queen daughter. Jonas' parents in *The Giver* by Lois LOWRY (1993) are married and live together but are a product of their community's futuristic rituals and laws. Chris CRUTCHER's *Whale Talk* (2001) features two parents and an adopted, multi-racial son, T.J.

One of the healthiest, if not exactly normal, families in YA literature can be found in *Surviving the Applewhites* (2002) by Stephanie TOLAN. While they are certainly an eccentric bunch, the Applewhites are also a loving, intelligent, happy, and fully functional family. It is interesting to note, however, that this book is most appealing to middle-school students, and there are few, if any, books featuring this kind of family that would appeal to older teens.

The most interesting families in YA literature can undoubtedly be found in SCIENCE FICTION. In *The House of the Scorpion* by Nancy FARMER (2002), Matt, the protagonist, is a clone; therefore, his only real family, El Patron, is also the person who plans to harvest Matt's organs if he needs them. In *The Exchange Student* by Kate GILMORE (1999) Daria's family brings an alien into their home and makes him part of the family.

Other non-human beings have also been made a part of the family in YA Literature. In Donna Jo NA-POLI's *Beast* (2000), Orasmyn has been turned into a lion and Belle has no choice but to reluctantly accept him as part of her family. In *Straydog* by Kathe Koja (2002), Rachel's collie Grrl becomes more important to her than family and basically replaces them in her heart. In Joan BAUER's *Squashed* (1992), Ellie's enormous prize-winning pumpkin, Max, fills a large hole in her family.

Also prevalent in YA literature are books in which the main character is in search of family. This topic is portrayed in many different ways. In *America* by E. R. FRANK (2002), the title character is shuffled from foster home to foster home, suffers abuse and neglect, and is on a seemingly endless search for family despite the fact that he is surrounded by blood relatives much of the time. In AVI's *Crispin: The Cross of Lead* (2002) Crispin suffers many travails before discovering his true origins and what his family means to him.

Creating one's own family is, of course, a hot subject in Young Adult literature. There are many books pertaining to teenage pregnancy and teen parenthood.

In *Someone like You* by Sarah DESSEN (1998), Scarlett finds herself pregnant after her boyfriend is killed in a motorcycle accident and has to rely on her flighty mother and her best friend to help her through this trying time. Several books have been published recently that feature the teenage father as the primary caregiver. Two examples are *Hanging on to Max* by Margaret Bechard (2002) and *The First Part Last* by Angela JOHNSON (2003).

Merriam-Webster's eighth definition of family is "a unit of a crime syndicate (as the Mafia) operating within a geographical area" and even that example can be found in YA literature. Gordon Korman's *Son of the Mob* (2002) tells the story of a teenage boy named Vince whose father is a mob boss. Vince relates humorous stories about his "uncles" throughout the book.

YA books contain characters of various races, colors and religious beliefs, and span every possible genre. They also feature families of all types, so that teenagers are able to find a book with a story similar to their own experience. However family is defined, it is certain that nearly every possible example can be found in YA literature.

KIMBERLY L. PAONE

FANTASY

Since the 1960s and 1970s, when YA fiction came to be recognized as a distinct category, the term has been used mostly to describe realistic stories about teenage characters, typically dealing with previously taboo subject matter and previously ignored segments of society. While these honest, earnest problem books were devoured by young readers, another type of story became popular, a type that moves far beyond the personal and the real. Fantasy novels, instead of showing close-up views of a familiar world, offer broad, startling perspectives on an unknown world, or maybe several worlds. All stories, fantasy or realism, distort the world people live in, but fantasies—which include something impossible, some breach of natural law as we know it—do so openly. Before the 1960s, young adults might read children's fantasy writers such as Lewis Carroll and George MacDonald and adult authors such as Edgar Rice Burroughs and H. G. Wells.

As the 21st century begins, fantasy is a huge and growing field, with books at all levels of complexity.

Frequently, the same books are popular with children, young adults, and adults. At the moment, YA fantasy is particularly creative and prolific, and for the most part features books aimed at YA and those with YA characters. Compared with earlier periods, fantasy books now include more TEENAGE heroes and fewer younger children; they describe more complex plots and places. The tone is more serious, often pessimistic; characters are more deeply analyzed. Adult fantasy continues to include formulaic, escapist works; thus fantasy for YA can be more dense and more complex than many of those intended for adults.

Realistic novels address an adolescent's concern with identity, acceptance, personal growth. Yet adolescence is not only a time of self-absorption: teenagers also look outward. They develop ideals and ideas; learn to translate values into action; search for what it all means; and question everything, especially authority. Reading fantasy offers an example of making sense of a confusing, perhaps threatening world. According to Jean Piaget, children develop in predictable stages, moving toward rational, logico-scientific thinking and ultimately leaving behind any interest in fantasy and imaginative pursuits. But Jerome Bruner argues persuasively that throughout people's lives, for true wisdom and wholeness, the rational mode of thinking must be accompanied—and strengthened—by a narrative, imaginative mode. Fantasy helps readers realize that the universe is complicated and various, encompassing unusual perspectives; it encourages them to try out unusual perspectives themselves.

YA readers have grown beyond childhood fantasy books about cheerful utopias, small intrusions of magic into everyday life, exciting but safe shifts in time, space, and size; they seek darker, denser kinds of fantasy. HORROR tales (such as Stephen KING's and Caroline B. COONEY's) allow them to delve into extreme emotions that fascinate them—fear and rage. Retellings of FAIRY TALES offer new insights into old, resonant stories. Robin MCKINLEY's *Beauty* (1978) untangles "Beauty and the Beast," while her grim, beautiful *Deerskin* (1993) tells the "Donkeyskin" story of incestuous rape. T. H. White's *The Once and Future King* remains a poignant re-living of Arthurian legends.

Two kinds of fantasy are particularly important to teenagers: narrow-focus tales that explore deeply some piece of a dangerous world (such as Peter DICK-

INSON's *Eva,* 1988), and broad epic narratives such as J. R. R. TOLKIEN's *The Lord of the Rings* about conflicts between good and evil, between weak individuals and powerful systems. Characters in these deep or broad fantasies do not, as a rule, travel from primary worlds resembling ours into created Secondary Worlds, as Tolkien called them. Instead of the children's fantasy convention of leaving a "real world" behind—by flying to Oz in a cyclone or crawling into Narnia through a cupboard—these characters struggle to meet challenges in their own chaotic worlds. In these books young adult readers, who are entering into actual strange worlds in their own changing lives, practice making sense of a world and discovering its rules and patterns. The design of a fantasy world is as important as the plot, characters, and supernatural activities—flying on a broomstick, for instance, cutting a window between worlds, or turning oneself into a wolf.

One type of story is set in a place that is a recognizable version of the modern world but permeated by the impossible or the supernatural, often by something from the past. Alan Garner's *The Owl Service* (1967) explodes an old legend of jealousy and murder into the relations among three Welsh teenagers. In Louis SACHAR's *Holes* (1998), a hundred-year-old curse works itself out through the actions of ordinary kids. In Virginia HAMILTON's *Sweet Whispers, Brother Rush* (1982), a ghost reveals family secrets to a resentful young girl, and in William Mayne's *Earthfasts* (1966), an 18th-century drummer boy bursts out of an English hillside, roiling the connection between past and present.

The protagonist who travels to a different, astonishing world has not totally disappeared. Daniel PINKWATER's *Alan Mendelsohn, the Boy From Mars* (1979) is a wildly comic version. Mayne's *The Game of Dark* (1971) explores the tormented psychological state of its hero as he shifts between a sad home and a sad magic land where he must slay a monster. Clive Barker's *Abarat* (2002) presents a quest and grotesque creatures in a dreamlike mode. Hamilton's Justice Cycle (1978–81) combines the rich, subjective mode of fantasy with the overwhelming alien quality of SCIENCE FICTION. Young adults continue to feast on scientific themes and speculations of true science fiction (a kind of fantasy). They read classic adult authors such as Isaac ASIMOV, Frank HERBERT, and Robert A. Heinlein, along with newer writers such as

Orson Scott CARD, who can be found on both adult and YA shelves. Plots and concepts in Card's stark, futuristic *Ender's Game* (1985) and its sequels are convoluted but they are also riveting, even to middle-school students.

Countless fantasy authors have invented whole new worlds where the entire action takes place, with no transition from "reality." Many are fresh and compelling, clearly unlike our world or any literary worlds we have seen, though others are tediously derivative. One type offers an alternative world that feels like a distorted version of a real place or time: Jill PATON WALSH's lyrical *Torch* (1987) and Megan Whalen TURNER's intense stories, *The Thief* and *The Queen of Attolia* (1996, 2000), have a classical Greek texture; Robin MCKINLEY's *The Blue Sword* and *The Hero and the Crown* (1982, 84) take place in a desert and mountain world that might be a magic-infested part of the British Empire under Victoria. Card's Alvin Maker SERIES, starting with *Seventh Son* (1987), creates a vivid alternative frontier America of the early 19th century.

The invented world may be a satirical one, casting light on human behavior indirectly, through the actions of live toys or animals: Russell Hoban's *The Mouse and His Child* (1967), for instance, and Richard ADAMS's *Watership Down* (1983). Some of the most memorable books are the dystopias, typically presented as a local segment rather than a whole world. Peter DICKINSON's *Eva,* in which the mind and memories of a dying teenage girl are transferred into the body of a chimpanzee, takes place in a terminally overpopulated land of the future. Lois LOWRY's *The Giver* (1993) describes a pleasant, numb society where choices, emotions, and colors have been programmed out of human experience with deadly results. Similarly, in John CHRISTOPHER's Tripods books (1967–88), human initiative has been destroyed by a controlling group, this time from another planet. Robert C. O'BRIEN's *Z for Zachariah* (1974) presents the painful story of a surviving girl in a poisoned world after a nuclear holocaust.

The best-known fantasies are epic series that create complex societies, with histories, geographies, sometimes languages; groups of inhabitants are defined by race or species or location or supernatural abilities. Well-loved series by Tamora PIERCE and Patricia WREDE are enjoyable but not as ambitious as works by LE GUIN, Wrightson, PULLMAN, and others.

Some authors emphasize the role of history in their created worlds. In Patricia A. MCKILLIP's Riddlemaster trilogy (1976–79), Prince Morgon roams the eight kingdoms using traditional riddle-lore to seek the truth about the past and future of his ghost-ridden world. In *Sister Light, Sister Dark* and *White Jenna* (1988, 1989), Jane YOLEN offers intriguingly different accounts of the same events: the myth, the legend, the song, the garbled scholarly history written long afterward—and the real, moving story of women warriors and their shadow sisters. Cynthia VOIGT's splendid quartet about the feudal Kingdom (1985–99), sometimes considered fantasy though its invented world contains no supernatural elements, follows young heroes in different generations.

Tolkien's *The Hobbit* (1937) and The Lord of the Rings trilogy, with their bitter but joyous struggles between good and evil forces, provide the standard against which other epic fantasies are measured. Tolkien is a master of panoramic action and of intimate scenes as well. The elaborate fantasies of the later 20th century are descended from Tolkien—tired, unoriginal copies as well as imaginative works that take off in new directions. Le Guin suggests the difference between cliché and creation when she says, "I kept on pushing at my own limitations. That is what the practice of an art is, you keep looking for the outside edge. When you find it you make a whole, solid, real, and beautiful thing; anything less is incomplete."

Le Guin's own works are unquestionably whole and beautiful. Especially popular with young adults are her Earthsea books, the first three (1968–72) followed by two equally fine sequels (1990, 2000). The wizard Ged fights to contain the Land of the Dead and maintain balance and harmony for the people and dragons of Earthsea's island world. J. K. ROWLING's best-selling HARRY POTTER series (1997–2005) consists of six books thus far, with one more to come. These stories are popular because they welcome all levels of readers, and because the Potter world has overlapping layers: Magical Hogwarts School, nurturing and liberating, must coexist with the bland society of non-magical Muggles and with the menacing evil realm of Lord Voldemort. Today's readers cannot believe in a benign "school-story" universe, and they cannot deny the existence of horrible, threatening forces and dreary, deadening conventional life; so they appreciate this generous, energetic series that acknowledges all three layers.

In William NICHOLSON's trilogy The Wind on Fire (2000–03), which explores themes of cruelty and love, the Hath family leads a pilgrimage through surprising and moving adventures to their promised homeland. In Patricia Wrightson's Book of Wirrun trilogy (1977–81), a young Australian aborigine must defeat efforts of ancient earth spirits to disturb the balance of nature, which allows natives, white people, and earth spirits to live together on one continent. In Garth NIX's Abhorsen books (1995–2003), a girl with special powers can move among all three realms—a feudal kingdom riddled with magic, an industrial nation, an underworld river of the dead. In the Dalemark quartet (1975–93), Diana Wynne JONES describes a warring medieval society intertwined with its pre-history and with its urban future.

Other works explore not just layers of a world but parallel worlds. In her Chrestomanci quartet (1977–88), the prolific Diana Wynne Jones sends her sorcerer hero on missions to many worlds. In Diane Duane's So You Want to Be a Wizard series (1983–90), two Long Island teenagers travel in a ruined Manhattan, under the sea, and through the galaxies. Philip PULLMAN's His Dark Materials trilogy (1995–2000) combines dazzling action taking place on many worlds with complex insights into characters and ideas.

The words of fiction, Francis Spufford says, "help form the questions we think are worth asking; their potent images dart new bridges into being between our conscious and unconscious minds, between what we know we know, and the knowledge we cannot examine by thinking." Terry Pratchett proposes, "Here's to fantasy as the proper diet for the growing soul. All human life is there: a moral code, a sense of order and, sometimes, great big green things with teeth."

BIBLIOGRAPHY: Bruner, J., *Actual Minds, Possible Worlds,* 1986; Inhelder, Barbel and Piaget, Jean. *The Growth of Logical Thinking,* 1962. LeGuin, U. K., *The Language of the Night,* 1979; Pratchett, T., *Only Connect,* ed. S. Egoff, 3rd ed., 1996; Spufford, F., *The Child That Books Built,* 2002.

DEBORAH O'KEEFE

FANTASY GAMING IN YA LITERATURE

Although video games were invented in the 1950s, they did not become wildly popular until the 1980s, with the invention of PacMan, Donkey Kong, Final

Fantasy, and Super Mario Brothers. This phenomenon led to movies about gaming, such as *Tron* (1982), *War Games* (1983), and *The Last Starfighter* (1984). Not to be left out, authors began to take notice.

In the late 1980s, authors began to publish books with teens playing video games. However, the 1990s are when the FANTASY gaming genre took off, with the majority of them based on the theme of virtual-reality gaming. The most current books, from 2000–2004, seem to be continuing the virtual reality theme, as well as introducing fantasy role-playing games as another common theme.

As technology itself continues to move forward, no doubt the next generation will grow up with books about internet gaming, based on the rising popularity of playing video games on the Internet on either a Nintendo, X-Box, PlayStation, or computer. Here are a few titles for TEENS, categorized by type of game.

Video Games

In *Space Demons* by Gillian RUBINSTEIN (1988), Andrew becomes obsessed with a mysterious new Japanese computer game. The game, which thrives on the anger of the player, has the power to zap him and his friends into a dangerous world of menacing space warriors. They must learn how to control their anger and "love their enemies" in order to escape the game.

Video game genius Darryl is an orphan who is adopted by software guru Keith Masterly in Tor Seidler's *Brainboy and the Deathmaster* (2003). Unfortunately, Darryl is locked in a "think tank" with a few other teens to breed ideas for Mr. Masterly, whose plan is to kill them when his ultimate goal, creating an elixir of youth, is realized. Their only access to the outside world is through a video game.

Will WEAVER's *Claws* (2004) centers around two high-school students, Jed and Laura, whose lives are shattered when they discover that each has a parent who is having an affair with the other. Jed is able to come to grips with reality after he has played a game like The Sims and realizes that even in video games, life cannot be perfect.

Eagle Strike (2004), by Anthony HOROWITZ, has teenage spy Alex Rider chasing after famous pop star Damian Cray. The two meet at the unveiling of Cray's new video game that Alex has no problem beating. The invention of this new technology hides Damian's real motive, which involves hijacking Air Force One

to launch numerous nuclear missiles aimed at countries involved in drug trades.

Virtual Reality Games

The students of Dinsmore find out that the new video arcade is more than a video arcade in *Game Over* (1993) by Joseph Locke. The violent characters in the games portray real people, causing teens who play the games to commit violent acts in real life. Joe and Lorinda, the main characters, learn that they must literally fight the demon owner in the game to destroy the evil that is happening in the town.

In *Invitation to the Game* (1993), by Monica HUGHES, Lisse and seven friends find themselves facing a bleak future of unemployment post-graduation until they are invited to play "The Game," a mysterious computer simulation of a paradise. They find themselves working as a unit to win the ultimate goal: their heart's desire. Ultimately, they discover that they have been secretly training for a government project to colonize a planet.

In Michael SCOTT's *Gemini Game* (1994), Liz and BJ, teenage owners of a computer games company, must rescue players of their new virtual reality game who have fallen into a coma while playing. After evading the police, they successfully locate a copy of their game and isolate an "intelligent" virus, thus allowing the comatose players to be revived.

Rodomonte's Revenge (1994) by Gary PAULSEN begins with the opening of a new virtual reality arcade in town. Brett and Tom are the first to play but something goes wrong. The game downloads into their brains and the boys find themselves swept into the game they must win in order to return to real life.

In Gillian CROSS's *New World* (1995), Miriam thinks she is going to have the easiest job in the world: testing a new computer game. It turns out that it is a top secret virtual reality game made to identify your fears and scare you. The game proves to be so dangerous that Miriam, with the help of a few friends, persuades the makers to take it off the market.

A computer program is set up to allow high-school students the opportunity to see themselves at their ten-year reunion in E. M. GOLDMAN's *The Night Room* (1995). The simulation exercise is meant to teach them how to apply themselves and improve their self-esteem; however someone hacks into the system, causing one of the students to be shown as having died during high school. This sets the group of students into motion to ensure that the suicide doesn't happen in real life.

The Virtual War (1997) by Gloria SKURZYNSKI is about a future world where global contamination has necessitated limited human contact. In this world three young people with unique genetically engineered abilities are teamed up to wage a war in virtual reality. After spending their entire lives training for this war, they realize that there is more to life than living in their own private bubble.

In *Virtual World* (1997), by Chris WESTWOOD, teenager Jack North finds himself literally drawn into the frightening world of a new virtual reality game. However, the more time he spends in the game, the harder it is for him to distinguish between reality and fantasy. After realizing that he is trapped and lost in the game, the Maker comes to him in the game and lets him leave it.

Fantasy Role-playing Games

Marnie, a student at a New England prep school, is kidnapped by a teacher, who is a crazed fan of Marnie's deceased mother, in *Locked Inside* (2000) by Nancy Werlin. One of her co-players from an online fantasy game comes to her rescue, but gets locked in the cell with Marnie instead. After her captor commits suicide in front of Marnie, and new disturbing facts about Marnie's mother are revealed, Marnie is able to face the world again by using the courage and determination of her character from the game.

In *User Unfriendly* (2001), by Vivian VANDE VELDE, Arvin, his friends, and his mother play a fantasy game on a computer, where they actually become the characters and roam through a medieval landscape on a quest. Unfortunately, since the game has been pirated, new and unpredictable events go wrong, keeping the players frustrated. This includes a strange sickness which the character played by Arvin's mom develops, putting her life at risk outside the parameters of the game.

In *Heir Apparent* (2002), also by Vande Velde, Giannine gets a gift certificate from her father to a virtual reality arcade. She chooses the game Heir Apparent and, while she is in the midst of the game, someone hacks into the system, making it impossible for her to leave the fantasy game until she wins.

Mercer, who loves playing a fantasy role-playing game, hopes to bring a gaming convention to his middle school as a fundraiser in *Wizards of the Game* (2003) by David LUBAR. When public outcry crushes his hope of this ever happening, four real wizards ask for his help in returning to their world. Things get out of control when the wizards' world crashes in on Mercer's world, showing Mercer that his game is just a game and that he doesn't really have magical powers.

BIBLIOGRAPHY: *History of the Video Game:* http://www.sciencedaily.com/encyclopedia/history_of_the_video_game

CONNIE REPPLINGER

FARMER, Nancy
Author, b. 9 July 1941, Phoenix, Arizona

F. is the highly acclaimed author of children's PICTURE BOOKS, juvenile and YA novels, and adult FANTASY fiction. She has been the recipient of many awards, including three Newbery Honor Books, ALA's Top Ten Best Books for Young Adults, and a National Book Award.

Born in Phoenix and now residing in northern California, F. was raised in the small community of Yuma on the border of Arizona and Mexico, in a hotel managed by her father. Her experiences living at the hotel provided a unique opportunity to observe interesting characters and listen to their stories, as the patrons were predominantly cowboys, railroad men, rodeo wranglers, and circus performers.

As a girl, school did not interest her and she was often truant. However, she earned an A.A. degree from Phoenix College and a B.A. from Reed College in Portland, Oregon. She enlisted in the Peace Corps and served in India from 1963–65. After traveling for two years, F. studied chemistry at Merritt College in Oakland, California and the University of California at Berkeley from 1969–71. From there, F. traveled to Africa and worked at a variety of jobs, including lab technician. During this time, she met Harold Farmer, a poet and an English professor at the University of Zimbabwe. They married in 1976 and have one son, Daniel.

When her son was four years old, F. was suddenly inspired to begin writing, and she composed her first short story. She spent the next four years examining the works of other authors and developing her writing skills. College Press in Zimbabwe published her first books, novels for children, *Lorelei: The Story of a Bad Cat* (1987) and *Tapiwa's Uncle* (1993), and a picture book entitled *Tsitsi's Skirt* (1988).

After her family moved to the U.S. from Africa, F.'s novel for young readers, *Do You Know Me?* (1993), became her first book published in the U.S. It was well received and praised for its characterizations and humor. *The Ear, the Eye and the Arm* (1994) followed as her first YA novel, and was translated into German and Italian. Revised from its original publication (1989) in Zimbabwe for its American debut, the SCIENCE FICTION story takes place in Zimbabwe in the year 2194, telling of three young people kidnapped by criminals and being pursued by three highly unconventional private eyes.

The Warm Place (1995) was F.'s next novel for young readers. In this book, a giraffe escapes from the San Francisco zoo and journeys home. It was praised for its creative events and characters, quality of action, and outstanding dialog, and named Best Children's Book, Zimbabwe at the International Book Fair in 1996.

Another YA novel, *A Girl Named Disaster* (1996), is set in modern Zimbabwe and Mozambique, and follows a girl, Nhamo, who runs away to escape an arranged marriage in her traditional village, finding herself at first surviving in the wilderness, then struggling in the urban life of Zimbabwe.

After publishing two more picture books, *Runnery Granary* (1996) and *Casey Jones's Fireman: The Story of Sim Webb* (1998), F. published her third YA novel. *House of the Scorpion* (2002) is a futuristic science fiction story about a young clone who escapes the clutches of an evil drug lord in the nation of Opium.

F. contributed stories to the *Writers of the Future Anthology, #4* (1988) for Bridge Publications, and *Best Horror and Fantasy of 1992* (1993) for St. Martin's Press. She is working on a novel for adults, a science fiction story titled *VaiDoSol.*

As a YA novelist, F. has become an example of exceptional talent and skill. Her books bring to life other cultures and future worlds, and provide an opportunity for TEENS to contemplate what has been and what might be. Her unique writing style, outstanding characters, and interesting perspectives assure her a permanent star on the YA literature walk of fame.

AWARDS: *The Ear, the Eye, and the Arm,* 1995: Newbery Honor Book, ALA Best Books for Young Adults, SCBWI Golden Kite Award; *A Girl Named Disaster,* 1996: Newbery Honor Book, National Book Award finalist, ALA Best Books for Young Adults; *House of the Scorpion,* 2002: Newbery Honor Book, National Book Award winner, ALA Best Books for Young Adults, PRINTZ Honor Book; *The Sea of Trolls: Kirkus Reviews* Editor's Choice, 2004; *Publisher's Weekly* Best Children's Books, 2004; *Horn-Book* Fanfare, 2004; *SLJ* Best Books for Children, 2004; Parents Choice Gold Award, 2004; ALA BBYA, 2005.

BIBLIOGRAPHY: "Farmer, Nancy." *Something About the Author,* v.117, 2000, pp. 56–59; Horning, Kathleen T. "The House of Farmer." *School Library Journal* 1 Feb. 2003. 1 May 2003; <http://slj.reviewsnews.com/index.asp?layout = article&articleid = CA272673 &publication = slj>; *Meet the Writers: Nancy Farmer.* Barnes & Noble.com (1 May 2003) <http://barnesandnoble.com/writers/writersdetails.asp?cid = 1033958>

DIANE TUCCILLO

FAST, Howard Melvin

Author, b. 11 November 1914 in New York City; d. 13 March 2003, Old Greenwich, Connecticut

The son of an ironworker and a homemaker, F. grew up in a low-income area but later attended the National Academy of Design in New York and married Bette Cohen, an artist, in 1937. During the 1930s, F. worked as a page in the New York Public Library; he then began his career as a writer, working as a foreign correspondent for MAGAZINES including *Esquire* and *Coronet.* When World War II broke out, F. worked with the U.S. Office of War Information and with the Army Film Project in 1944. In 1945, F. was deployed as a WAR correspondent to the Chinese-India-Burmese front.

F. taught at Indiana University in Bloomington during the summer of 1947; he rose among the ranks to become an American Labor Party candidate for the U.S. Congress in the 23rd New York District in 1952. His writing skills became more diversified as the years went on; he branched out to become a film writer and chief news writer for the Voice of America from 1982–1984. F. wrote more than eighty books during his lifetime, and he also became a lecturer and was a frequent guest on radio and television programs. His first book, *Two Valleys,* was published in 1933, and his prolific writing career continued through the year 2000, with the publication of his last work, *Greenwich.*

F. believed in writing about topics of social importance, and his 1943 book *Citizen Tom Paine* was a pivotal work in F.'s gaining stature and credence in the field of historical writing. *Citizen Tom Paine* is widely read by students who value its insights on the Revolutionary War and its powerful story line. *Conceived in Liberty* (1939), *The Unvanquished* (1942), *The Last Frontier* (1941), and *Freedom Road* (1944) all contributed to his status as a writer of historical significance and a social conscience. F. thought that all writing should be a parable in the form of literature; his personal and political beliefs shaped his writing and ultimately, his career.

F. was blacklisted in the 1950s when it was revealed that he had been a Communist Party member, from 1943 to 1956. His refusal to cooperate with the House Un-American Activities Committee led to his imprisonment in 1947 for three months, for contempt of Congress. F. had refused to submit the records of the Joint Anti-Fascist Refugee Committee. His novel *Spartacus,* 1951, was an outgrowth of his experience in jail, and he was forced to self-publish the title under his Blue Heron imprint because of the effects of blacklisting on his career. Many other political titles followed, including *The Passion of Sacco and Vanzetti* (1953), *Silas Timberman* (1954), *The Story of Lola Gregg* (1956), *The Winston Affair* (1959), and *The Naked God* (1957). F. also was the Founder of the World Peace Movement and a member of the World Peace Council from 1950 through 1955. Maintaining his politically active stance, F. joined the Fellowship for Reconciliation.

F.'s interests and causes were threads in his books, and they were far-reaching as F. championed causes important to him: Jewish philosophy of social justice, cold-war Stalinism, and Zen Buddhism. No genre was off limits for F.; he wrote novels, PLAYS, film scripts, SHORT STORIES, critical essays, SCIENCE FICTION stories, satire, historical novels, contemporary novels, BIOGRAPHIES, POETRY, and thrillers. He wrote under the penname of E. V. Cunningham and the pen name Walter Ericson for his own pleasure and to further the cause of the women's movement. F. was the author of a weekly column in the *New York Observer* from 1989 through 1992. His columns also appeared in *Greenwich Time* and the *Stamford Advocate* in Connecticut.

F. was honored numerous times for his work: he received an Emmy Award for outstanding writing in a drama series, the National Jewish Book Award, The Bread Loaf Literary Award, the Schomburg Award for Race Relations, and the International Peace Prize from the Soviet Union. *Spartacus,* based on his book, became an Oscar-winning film in 1960.

F.'s works have been translated into eighty-two languages and his books have sold millions of copies around the world. His legacy of literature and social consciousness lives on through his words and through his considerable abilities as a storyteller.

AWARDS: Bread Loaf Literary Award, 1937; Schomberg Award for Race Relations, 1944, *Freedom Road;* Newspaper Guild Award, 1947; National Jewish Book Award, Jewish Book Council, 1949, *My Glorious Brothers;* International Peace Prize from the Soviet Union, 1954; Screenwriters Annual Award, 1960; Secondary Education Board Annual Book Award, 1962; National Association of Independent Schools, 1962; American Library Association "notable book" citation, 1972, *The Hessian;* BBYA 1972 Emmy Award Sciences, 1975, "The Ambassador"; Literary Lions Award, New York Public Library, 1985; Prix de la Policia (France), E. V. Cunningham works.

SELECT FURTHER WORKS: *Freedom Road,* 1944; *April Morning,* 1961; *The Crossing,* 1971; *The Legacy,* 1980; *The Magic Door,* 1980; *Max,* 1982; *The Outsider,* 1984; *The Immigrant's Daughter,* 1985; *The Dinner Party,* 1987; *The Call of Fife and Drum: Three Novels of the Revolution,* 1987; *The Pledge,* 1988; *The Confession of Joe Cullen,* 1989; *Being Red: A Memoir,* 1990; *The Trial of Abigail Goodman: A Novel,* 1993; *War and Peace: Observations on Our Times,* 1993; *Seven Days in June: A Novel of the American Revolution,* 1994; *The Bridge Builder's Story,* 1995; *An Independent Woman,* 1997; *Redemption,* 1999; *Greenwich,* 2000; *Masuto Investigates,* 2000; *Masuto,* 2001; *Samantha,* 2004.

BIBLIOGRAPHY: *Contemporary Novelists,* 5th edition, 1991; Wilson Kathleen, ed. *Twentieth-Century Writers,* 2nd edition, vol. 2, 1999; *Contemporary Authors Online,* 2003; Rothstein Mervyn, the *New York Times* obituary of Howard Fast, March 13, 2003.

SANDRA KITAIN

FEELINGS, Tom (Thomas)

Illustrator, author. b. 19 May 1933, Brooklyn, New York; d. 25 August 2003, n.p.

F.'s artist career began at a young age. When his kindergarten teacher showed one of his drawings to other teachers, F. knew that he would be an artist. He spent a great deal of time at home or at school working on comic-book drawings to avoid the gang activity in his neighborhood. Not far from his home, he met his first mentor, Mr. Thipadeaux, a black artist of Creole descent, who encouraged F. to create art that represented the world around him.

F. has spent his life bringing the stories of AFRICAN AMERICANS and African culture to life through his remarkable illustrations. He has illustrated several books for children and YOUNG ADULTS and has written an AUTOBIOGRAPHY entitled *Black Pilgrimage* (1972). One of the key figures from the Black Arts Movement in the 1960s, F. did not stop when the movement diminished in the 1970s. F. continued to embrace his African heritage, portrayed through his remarkable artwork.

In his work, F. expresses the beauty, strength and resilience of various black people despite the many years of hardship and suffering they have endured. Having grown up with little or few black cultural images in his childhood books, F. knew the importance of bringing black heroes to American youth. In one of his early projects, *Tommy Traveler in the World of Black History* (1991), F. creates those heroes and invites the reader to dream along with Tommy and become part of those histories.

F. collaborated with Julius Lester in *To Be a Slave* (1968). He created powerful, soulful paintings to visually express the words and truth of the slaves that Lester wrote about. This is one of the rare accounts of life as a slave told through the words of actual slaves, rather than through second-hand accounts by others. This book not only brings validity to the past, but may help America heal from painful truth.

F. often worked with African American writers to produce works with powerful words and vivid illustrations. These writers include Muriel Feelings (his former wife), Nikki GRIMES, Joyce Carol Thomas, and Maya ANGELOU. In a collaborative effort with Angelou, *Now Sheba Sings the Song* (1987) he gives female readers a book that shows the extraordinary strength of average black women. F. shows the fluid energy and rhythmic movement of these beautiful women while Angelou provides a lyrical poem for the heart and soul.

The Middle Passage: White Ships/Black Cargo (1995) provides some of the most visually stunning work of F.'s career. In this wordless book, F. provides sixty-four paintings depicting the Middle Passage of the slave-trade voyage; the first part of the journey is from Europe to Africa, the Middle Passage is from Africa to the New World, and the final part is the ship's return to Europe. Painfully real and visually expressive, these paintings artfully narrate the story of the millions of men, women, and children who were torn from their homelands to be sold in a strange, distant land. Although they portray the horror of this dark period in American history, these paintings also show the hope and spirit of those survivors of the Middle Passage.

F. died in August of 2003. The cause was cancer. His illustrations and paintings will continue to express both the strength and the pain of the African American and other black people.

AWARDS: 1969 Newbery Honor Book, *To Be a Slave* (Julius Lester, editor); Caldecott Medal Honor Book: 1972 for *Moja Means One* (Muriel Feelings, author) and 1975 for *Jambo Means Hello* (Muriel Feelings, author); 1972 *Horn-Book* magazine Honor list, *Black Pilgrimage;* ALA Notable Book: 1972 for *Black Pilgrimage,* 1979 for *Something on My Mind,* and 1982 for *Daydreamers;* 1974 *Boston Globe–Horn Book* Award for Illustration, *Jambo Means Hello;* 1977 Children's Book Showcase Award for *From Slave to Abolitionist;* Coretta Scott King Illustrator Award: 1994 for *Something on My Mind* (Nikki Grimes, author), 1994 for *Soul Looks Back in Wonder,* and 1996 for *The Middle Passage; Middle Passage*: ALA Best Books for Young Adults, 1996; *Soul Looks back in Wonder*: ALA Best Books for Young Adults, 1994.

FURTHER WORKS: *When the Stones were Soft: East African Folktales* (Eleanor Heady, editor, 1968), *Tales of Temba: Traditional African Stories* (Kathleen Arnot, 1969), *Black Folktales* (Julius Lester, editor, 1969).

BIBLIOGRAPHY: *Contemporary Authors New Revision Series,* vol. 25; *Something About the Author,* vol. 69; Vincent Steele. "Tom Feelings: A Black Arts Movement," *African American Review,* Spring 1998; www.tomfeelings.com.

TINA HERTEL

FEMINIST FAIRY TALES FOR YA

Women have long been associated with fairy tales, both in their writing and in their telling. Criticism, however, is frequently leveled at the representation of women and girls in traditional tales. Feminist literary criticism has been influential in bringing attention to the representation of passive young girls waiting to be awakened into life by the kiss of a prince, the equation of beauty with goodness, misogyny embedded in representations of wicked witch and crone figures (Lieberman, 1986). The Brothers Grim, particularly, are noted for encoding patriarchal values and ideologies into their edited tales. Some argue that fairy tales have been major vehicles of socialization (Zipes, 1988); and express concern about their influence on the acculturation and socialization of young girls (Lieberman, 1986, Lehr, 2001).

Part of the tradition of story-telling includes the re-visioning and re-telling of tales so that they accord with different cultural and time contexts (Hearne, 1989, Zipes, 2000). Writers of fairy tales are, therefore, changing the conventions used in telling traditional tales and challenging sexist discourses and stereotypical representations of female and male characters in order to create stories that are relevant to young people. Jarvis (2000) notes that fairy tales, identified as feminist, have been organized into three categories: anthologies of older tales featuring active and resourceful female protagonists to counter the representation of passive adolescent females in traditional tales; adaptations of traditional tales; and re-telling original tales using familiar fairy tale motifs (157).

Anthologies of traditional tales featuring resourceful heroines that are eminently appropriate for YA collections include: Ethel Johnston Phelps' collections, *The Maid of the North: Feminist Folktales From Around the World* (1981) and *Tatterhood and Other Tales* (1978); and *Fearless Girls, Wise Women, and Beloved Sisters* edited by Kathleen Ragan (1998). Appropriate for older TEENS is Angela Carter's *Strange Things Sometime Still Happen: Fairy Tales from around the World* (1993). Collections of original tales written from a feminist perspective that are appropriate for teens include Barbara Walker's original *Feminist Fairy Tales* (Harper, 1996), and Jack D. Zipes's *The Outspoken Princess and the Gentle Knight* (1994) which contain modern fairy tales written "for both young and adult readers." Many of Walker's tales represent older traditions of Goddess worship and deities, each tale embodying a "feminist message of some kind" (x). Walker writes that her tales are written to combat "misogynous messages, for example the message that: "Girls without beauty

are automatically also without virtue, happiness, luck, or love" (ix).

There have been an increasing number of re-tellings, as well as original novels, in which girls and women are represented as defying traditional roles that are marketed for YOUNG ADULT readers. Collections of retold tales for older teens include Francesca Lia BLOCK's *The Rose and the Beast: Fairy Tales Retold* (2000), Priscilla Galloway's *Truly Grim Tales* (1995), and Emma Donaghue's retellings in *Kissing the Witch: Old Tales in New Skins* (1997) in which Donague re-visions the relationship of heroines with witch figures as well as with princes. Novels for young teens that incorporate motifs and plot elements from traditional tales and which feature resourceful, active rather than passive princesses, include Margaret HADDIX's *Just Ella* (1999), Patrice KINDL's *Goose Chase* (2001), and *Ella Enchanted* by Gail Carson LEVINE (1998). Selected novels for older teens include Cameron Dokey's *Beauty Sleep* (2002) and Adele GERAS's recently reissued Egerton Hall trilogy: *The Tower Room* (2001), *Pictures of the Night* (2002), and *Watching the Roses* (2001). Donna Jo NAPOLI, particularly, has re-visioned fairy tales for young adults from a feminist perspective. These include: *Beast* (2000), *Crazy Jack* (1999), *The Magic Circle* (1992, 1993), *Zel* (1996), and *Spinners* with Richard Tchen (1999).

Varied criteria are used to define and select fairy tales characterized as feminist texts. The usual criterion cited is the representation of courageous, resourceful females who are given a central and active role in story plots. Phelps writes that "a women's right to freedom of will and choice" is an "underlying theme" linking the twenty-one folktales that represent different ethnic cultures in *The Maid of the North*. Novels for younger teens such as Levine's *Ella Enchanted*, Haddix's *Just Ella*, and Kindl's *Goose Chase* do not go beyond creating witty, clever, heroines who overcome obstacles through their own actions and seek their independence and freedom from the constraints of the traditional princess role. Power relationships among the protagonists are changed on a surface plot level; heroines achieve equality in their relationships with young men who, although of royal lineage, are not representatives of the traditional prince figure.

In collections for older teens, girls and women are represented as exhibiting a toughness that goes beyond the construct of passive to resourceful heroine often cited as the sole criterion of a "feminist" fairy tale. David Russell writes that Block's heroines in *The Rose and the Beast* are "gritty feminine heroes who do not have to sacrifice what it means to be feminine" and who "face the world head on, to construct their lives on their own terms" (2002). This is equally true of some female protagonists in Galloway's *Truly Grim Tales.* Carter's collection includes stories, told with humor and ribaldry, that celebrate older women who use their cunning and wiles to gainsay attempts by husbands to put women in their place. In reworking the traditional plots of Rapunzel, Snow White, and Beauty and the Beast to accord with contemporary contexts, Geras creates vibrant, sexy, female protagonists. Geras's Bella is the antithesis of Snow White. In *The Roses,* she describes herself as looking like Carmen in the beautiful scarlet dress that her stepmother, Marjorie, has bought for her (145).

Feminist retellings of fairy tales are characterized by changes in narrative strategies in telling stories. Recovering women's voices—so often silenced—has been a major objective of feminist writers. In selecting tales for her collection, *Fearless Girls, Wise Women, and Beloved Sisters,* Ragan's criteria include "narrative style" in which she considers stories in which a woman "has her own voice." In her introduction to Carter's collection of tales in *Strange Things Still Happen,* Marina Warner comments that the "issue of women's speech, of women's noise . . ." was a key feature of Carter's own fairy tales (x). Fracturing the anonymous, authoritative narrator of fairy tale is another narrative practice frequently used by feminist writers. Writers frequently give voice and agency to women whose motives are masked and whose voices are silenced in traditional tales.

In "A Taste for Beauty," for example, the woman who becomes the mother to "Snow" explains how she worked her way from working at an abatoir to becoming a model and tells about the bargain she made in order to become the wife of the king. Napoli uses first-person narrative and plural narratives in her retellings in order to present other sides of the story than those usually presented. In *The Magic Circle* and *Zel,* witch figures tell their own story in first-person narrative—a narrative strategy that invites readers to emphatize with these vilified figures in traditional versions of the Hansel and Gretel and Rapunzel tales, respectively. In Dokey's *Beauty Sleep,* the self-aware voice of Aurore informs readers in a "Preamble" that she tells her story in the way she wants it told. It is her "truth," her "way," her "story" (3). In this revision of the Sleeping Beauty tale, Aurore's father tells her that she has proven to him that she is his "true heir" to the kingdom because of her wish to know the world beyond the palace walls (51).

Revisions of fairy tales that are based on the reversal of gender roles and the change of passive princess to active heroine may, however, still be composed from discourses that encode patriarchal gender ideologies. To what extent a retelling of a fairy tale can be termed "feminist" also depends to what extend it goes beyond the mere reversal of sex roles at a surface level of the plot. In her choice of folk tales, Ragan, for example, uses a definition of a heroine that goes beyond the usual qualities associated with a hero. This "category of 'feminine heroic' qualities" includes women who use lateral thinking, kind women, persevering women, and protective women" and women who "keep family relationships alive in a family or community" (xxvi). Feminist writers construct their novels through feminist discourse that espouses alternative values to those voiced in traditional tales.

Frequently, feminist texts encode a valuing of interpersonal relationships, including the mother-daughter relationship, often devalued in selected traditional roles edited by the Brothers Grimm. In contrast to her story, "A Taste of Beauty," Galloway places value on the mother-daughter relationship in another story in the same collection, "Bed of Peas." In this re-telling of the Rapunzel tale a birth mother "retreats into madness" and, when recovered, cannot rest until she has found her daughter, Letitia, given away while she lay delirious after a difficult childbirth. Napoli especially places value on interpersonal relationship in her re-tellings of fairy tales. Loving bonds are constructed between mothers and daughters in *The Magic Circle* and *Zel;* emphasis is placed upon the love between fathers and sons in *Beast* and *Crazy Jack.* Geras plays with the wicked stepmother and daughter relationship in her re-visioning of the Snow White tale. While the pretext of the traditional version is tightly woven into Geras's novels, the relationship between Belle and her stepmother is represented as a changing dynamic full of nuances and contradictions.

Value systems and themes present in feminist writings are also reproduced in the texts of feminist revisions of fairy tale. For example, the value of community and interdependence is found in Napoli's novel, *Crazy Jack*. In Galloway's story, "The Good Mother," Galloway deconstructs the concept of the beast/wolf figure. Red Riding Hood, her grandmother, and "Beast" band together in nurturing Beast's babies and fend off the hunters. Whereas in the traditional tale of Rumpelstiltskin, spinning is associated with gold and greed, in Napoli and Tchen's retelling of the tale in *Spinners,* spinning is associated, among other connotations, with beauty and artistry. The description of Saskia's yarn as "Soft like a mother's breast" is another example of how imagery and metaphors can signify a different value system than that encoded in the brothers' Grimm version of Rumpelstiltskin.

One can speculate that feminist writers of fairy tales have drawn from feminist discourses that have been disseminated by books such as Carol Gilligan's *In a Different Voice: Psychological Theory and Women's Development* (1982), Lyn Mikel Brown and Carol Gilligan's *Meeting at the Crossroads: Women's Psychology and Girls' Development* (1992), and other studies conducted under the auspices of the Harvard Project on Women's Psychology and Girls' Development. These studies have been particularly instrumental in developing new constructions of female adolescence. Similarly, the stereotypes of masculinity in Freudian accounts of boys' adolescence have also been revised and made popularly available through such books as Dan Kindlon and Michael Thompson's *Raising Cain: Protecting the Emotional Life of Boys* (1999) and *Real Boys' Voices* by William Pollock with Todd Shuster (2000).

Writers of feminist fairy tales represent gender and gendered relationships differently from those in traditional tales. They encode in their tales values associated with feminist discourses and give voice to those frequently silenced in traditional tales. Above all, feminist writers play with different ways of representing their protagonists in order to resist stereotypical representations of gender and gendered relationships found in traditional tales. They are creative in the way they re-imagine these tales and make them relevant for a contemporary audience of teen readers. Their stories offer opportunities for young people to engage in critical dialogue about gender and values.

There has been research on how young people respond to feminist fairy tales, although this research tends to focus on younger readers and pre-adolescents rather than teen readers. Ann Trousdale's and Sally McMillan's study, "Cinderella Was a Wuss" (2003) compares the responses of a twelve-year-old girl to three stories from Phelps's collections and to one of the Grimm tales to the girl's responses to the same stories when she was eight years of age. Although Trousdale's and McMillan's findings are restricted to one girl's responses, they note that at twelve years of age, she was more aware of the social restrictions and narratives that limited females than at an earlier age and this affected her responses to the story. Trousdale and others working with students in the classroom suggest that alternative narratives to those in the traditional canon are made available to young people. Certainly, feminist fairy tales have the potential to offer teen readers different ways of knowing about gender and power but they also offer magic and delight as folk and fairy tales have always done.

BIBLIOGRAPHY: Hearne, Betsy. *Beauty and the Beast: Visions and Revisions of an Old Tale,* 1989; Jarvis, Shawn. "Feminism and Fairy Tales." In *The Oxford Companion to Fairy Tales,* 2000: 155–159; Lehr, Susan, ed. *Beauty, Brains, and Brawn: The Construction of Gender in Children's Literature,* 2001; Lieberman, Marcia K. "Some Day My Prince Will Come: Female Acculturation through the Fairy Tale" in *Don't Bet on the Prince: Contemporary Feminist Fairy Tales in North America and England,* ed. Jack Zipes, 1986: 185–208; O'Keefe, Deborah. *Good Girl Messages: How Young Women Were Misled by Their Favorite Books,* 2000; Russell, David. "Young Adult Fairy Tales for the New Age: Francesca Lia Block's *The Rose and the Beast,*" *Children's Literature in Education,* 33.2, June 2002: 107–115; Trousdale, Ann M. and Sally McMillan, Sally. "'Cinderella Was a Wuss': A Young Girl's Responses to Feminist and Patriarchal Folktales," *Children's Literature in Education,* 34.1, March 2003: 1–28; Zipes, Jack. *Fairy Tales and the Art of Subversion: The Classical Genre for Children and the Process of Civilization,* 1988; Zipes, Jack. ed., introduction." *The Oxford Companion to Fairy Tales,* New York: 2000: xv–xxxii.

HILARY CREW

FERRIS, Jean

Author, b. 24 January 1939, Fort Leavenworth, Kansas

Daughter of Jack, an Army officer and surgeon, and Jessie (Wickham) Schwartz, a homemaker, F. and her family moved frequently while she was growing up.

Her efforts to get to know her new neighborhoods, included listening to the conversations of those around her and looking into the windows of their homes as well as the surrounding neighborhoods. She also kept a DIARY/journal of her observations, thoughts and emotions. She grew up to earn both a B.A. (1961) and an M.A. (1962) from Stanford University.

In 1962, F. started working at the Veterans Administration Hospital in San Francisco, California, as a clinical audiologist and on September 8 married Alfred G. Ferris, an attorney. They have two daughters who both grew up to be teachers. F. continued working as a clinical audiologist from 1963–1964 for the San Diego Speech and Hearing Association in San Diego. After a hiatus in which she gave birth to Kerry Ordway and Gillian Anne, Ferris again worked as a clinical audiologist from 1975–1976 in a San Diego doctor's office, until she started freelance writing in 1977. As a secretary and office assistant from 1979–1984, Jean continued writing. She had saved her girlhood journals and drew on this early writing as she wrote her books. F. also saved all of her stories and kept them neatly in boxes under her bed. At her husband's urging, F. decided to submit some of these stories to publishers, keeping in mind a five-year plan. She decided to write a great deal for five years and then submit her work. If she "didn't have any success" she would "just go back to writing for" herself. After the attempted suicide of one of her daughter's friends, she "wanted to write about what would make a fourteen-year-old decide that there would never ever be anything worth living for." Three publishers requested full manuscripts of this work and two of these offered her contracts. F.'s first novel for YOUNG ADULTS, *Amen, Moses Gardenia,* was published in 1983 (the four-and-a-half-year mark of her five-year plan) as a message of hope for young adults. This was no easy task for a writer without an agent.

Her writing for young adults comes from her heart and reflects her belief that while young people face different challenges today than she did when she was growing up, the emotional issues remain the same and are ageless. Themes in her books parallel those emotions that all young people have at various stages as they grow toward adulthood. She writes the kinds of books she needed to read as she grew up and that were timely in offering thought-provoking choices, potential solutions and support, meeting the needs of her readers while also being entertaining. Her female characters possess a variety of qualities, as do real teenaged girls. Different story lines are supported by main characters that are true to life and possess many different characteristics as they sort through their needs and find solutions to challenges. Young adult girls can find themselves in any of her characters and find emotional support as they read her work. She believes that "the basic challenges of young people (today) are the same as they were when I was young: school, friends, parents, making big life choices." It is these choices that have changed some (sex, drugs, crime, etc.) but the "emotional truths have remained the same."

F. routinely writes each weekday to keep up "momentum" and saves her weekends for her other interests. She likes to write one good book a year and hopes to continue writing for a long time. *To Kill a Mockingbird* is her all-time favorite book.

When asked what she would most like to be remembered for F. states: "Maybe just that I tried to make a difference for young people who were struggling with hard things in their lives—whether through serious books that tried to address a particular problem, or through less serious books that just tried to offer a good time." If she could leave a gift to others it would be the "knowledge that everybody has hard things to deal with in life and it's attitude and will that see you through. Giving up is not an option, it is a bedrock truth for managing life." F. also wants to remind everyone to "have fun every time you get an opportunity to!"

The book, *Why My Mother is Green,* co-authored with an artist friend was never published as it became too costly to print. Her book, *Music from the Moon,* became the three books of the American Dream SERIES: *Into the Wind; Song of the Sea;* and *Weather the Storm* (Avon). F. is presently working to get these books reissued.

In addition to reading, F. enjoys going to plays and movies, traveling with her husband, taking long walks with her friends, volunteer work as time permits, and decorating her new condo in uptown San Diego.

AWARDS: *Once Upon a Marigold* (2002) has won the following: The Teens Top Ten List, Junior Library Guild Selection 2002; *Of Sound Mind* (2001) has won the following: ALA Best Book for Young Adults 2002 and 2003, New York Public Library List of Books for the Teen Age 2002; *Eight Seconds* (2000) has won the following: ALA Best Books for Young Adults 2002, New York Public Library Books for the Teen Age 2001 Winner, San Diego Book Award for Juvenile Fiction; *Bad* (1998) has won the following: ALA Best Book for Young Adults, New York Public Library Young Adult Services Books for the Teen Age (1999); *Love among the Walnuts* (1998) has won the following: ALA Best Books for Young Adults 1999; ALA 1999 Quick Pick for Reluctant Young Adult Readers; *All that Glitters* (1996) won the following in 1998: American Library Association Best Books nomination; Junior Library Guild selection, Texas Library Association selection for high school reading; *Signs of Life* (1995) won the following in 1997: Junior Library Guild selection; New York Public Library's Books for the Teenage selection; *Relative Strangers* (1993) won the following in 1995: Utah Children's Book Award nomination; South Carolina Young Adult Book Award nomination; *Looking for Home* (1991) won the following in 1991: American Library Association's Recommended Book for Reluctant Young Readers; International Reading Association Young Adults Choice; *Across the Grain* (1990) won the following in 1992: American Library Association's Best Book for Young Adults; California Young Readers Medal nomination 1992–1993; *Invincible Summer* (1987) won the following in 1987: Award for Outstanding Work of Fiction for Young Adults from the Southern California Council on Literature for Children and Young People; American Library Association's Best Books for Young Adults; A School Library Journal's Best Book of the Year; Booklist Editor's Choices for Young Adults.

FURTHER WORKS: *Relative Strangers,* 1993; *The Stainless Steel Rule,* 1986; *Amen, Moses Gardenia,* 1983.

BIBLIOGRAPHY: "Jean Ferris." St. James Guide to Young Adult Writers, 2nd ed. St. James Press, 1999. Reproduced in *Biography Resource Center.* Farmington Hills, Mich.: The Gale Group. 2004. http://galenet.galegroup.com/servlet/BioRC

VALERIE A. PALAZOLO

FIENBERG, Anna
Author, b. 23 November 1956, Canterbury, England

F.'s career began as an editor of a MAGAZINE in AUSTRALIA, where she reviewed contemporary children's fiction and wrote stories and plays. Her debut YOUNG ADULT novel, *Borrowed Light,* was first published in Australia in 1999 and in the U.S. in 2000. This story of Callisto May chronicles a young girl's pregnancy and its impact on her family and friends. Imagery

takes this novel beyond the stereotypical "teenage pregnancy" tale. It was named to the YALSA Best Books for Young Adults List in 2000. F.'s background in psychology is reflected in her depiction of Callie's struggles and eventual decision to terminate her pregnancy.

F.'s next young adult novel, *The Witch in the Lake* (2002), is a FANTASY full of magic, sorcery, and supernatural powers, all reflective of F.'s love of C. S. LEWIS' *Chronicles of Narnia.* Quite unlike *Borrowed Light,* this novel is set in the 16th century, though it is not considered historical fiction.

F. returned to children's fiction after her foray into YA fiction. She collaborates with her mother, Barbara Fienberg on several SERIES, most notably Tashi and Minton.

AWARDS: *Borrowed Light*: Canadian Broadcasting Corporation (CBC) Honour Book: 2000 Older Readers' Book of the Year; ALA BBYA 2001.

BIBLIOGRAPHY: *Contemporary Authors Online,* The Gale Group, 2000; http://www.allen-unwin.com.au/authors/annafienberg.pdf.

TERRY BECK

FINE, Anne
Author, b. 7 December 1947, Leicester, England

Coming from a large FAMILY gave F. the insight to handle family problems with understanding and humor. She wrote her first novel because she was trapped at home during a snowstorm and could not get to the library. Initially she wrote for herself, finding a publisher as an afterthought. F. writes primarily for children and YOUNG ADULTS, writing what she would want to read when she was her target age.

F.'s first novel for young adults was *Summer-House Loon* (1978), in which Ione Muffet, the narrator, tells of her attempts at matchmaking. The sequel, *The Other, Darker Ned* (1979), describes Ione's attempts at organizing a charity ball to benefit famine victims. Thus F. started her reputation for examining social issues with a keen and humorous eye. *The Stone Menagerie* (1980) is the story of a homeless couple living on the grounds of a mental institution who are found by a boy who visits frequently. *The Granny Project* (1983) is about four siblings who take over caring for their dying grandmother rather than send her to a home.

LOIS DUNCAN

WILL EISNER

NANCY FARMER

JEAN FERRIS

PAUL FLEISCHMAN

E. R. FRANK

RUSSELL FREEDMAN

NEIL GAIMAN

F. also examines family relationships in her novels. *Round the Ice-House* (1981), F.'s personal favorite of her published works, explores the relationship between twins Tom and Cass as they grow up and apart. *Madame Doubtfire* (1987, published in the United States as *Alias Madame Doubtfire,* 1988), a comedy about a father who pretends to be a female housekeeper so he can spend time with his children in his ex-wife's house, has been made into a popular MOVIE starring Robin Williams and Sally Field. Young TEENS dealing with their mother's new boyfriend after the divorce is the topic of *My War with Google-Eyes* (1989) (published in England as *Goggle-Eyes,* 1989). *The Book of the Banshee* (1992) shows how children may deal with divorce, as the narrator describes the horrible behavior of his sister, until the family reaches their breaking point. *Step by Wicked Step* (1996) uses a mysterious DIARY to allow the characters, all teens from broken homes, to discuss their own lives and fears.

Flour Babies (1994) looks at the family situation from a different angle. Simon and his classmates, borderline delinquents, are each given a six-pound sack of flour to care for as if they are babies. While his friends make a joke of the assignment, Simon learns about himself and his parents. *Flour Babies* won the Carnegie Medal and enthusiastic praise from the critics.

The Tulip Touch (1996) is likely F.'s darkest novel, lacking the wry humor of her other works. It is the story of Natalie, the only child in her parent's hotel. She makes friends with Tulip, a local farm girl, who leads her on increasingly dangerous adventures. That Tulip is from an abusive family comes through, even though F. only hints at the situation. *Up on Cloud Nine* (2002) also examines a darker subject, teen suicide. Stol is found on the ground with a concussion below an open window. His friend Ian doesn't believe Stol tried to kill himself, and writes his memories of their friendship while sitting with Stol in the hospital.

Throughout most of her novels, F. uses humor to soften what are otherwise intense subjects, without detracting from the story. Critics have commented frequently that F. is able to capture the humor of a situation while still providing useful insights into the social issues she explores. F. told Hazel Rochman, *Booklist* (1998), that readers can see in her stories that, "yes, things are bad, but you yourself can make the decision both to go forward and make something of your own life and also to hold sympathy and responsibility for the ones that fall."

AWARDS: Carnegie Medal, 1992, and Whitbread Children's Novel award, 1993, for *Flour Babies;* Carnegie Medal high commendation, 2003, for *Up on Cloud Nine* and ALA Notable Children's Book, 2003.

SELECT FURTHER WORKS: *Very Different and Other Stories,* 2001, *The True Story of Christmas* 2003; plus numerous titles for children and adults.

REFERENCES: *100 More Popular Young Adult Authors,* Bernard A. Drew, 2002; *Contemporary Authors Online,* Gale, 2003; *Authors and Artists for Young Adults,* Thomas McMahon, Ed., 1997; Anne Fine's website, http://www.annefine.co.uk/questions.html.

JENNA OBEE

FINNEY, Jack

Author, b. 2 October, 1911, Milwaukee, Wisconsin; d. 14 November 1995

Born Walter Braden Finney, F. attended Knox College in Illinois and later moved to New York City to work in advertising. He began writing SHORT STORIES for MAGAZINES such as *Collier's* and *The Saturday Evening Post.* In 1954 his first novel, *Five Against the House,* was published. A year later he wrote *The Body Snatchers* (later reissued as *Invasion of the Body Snatchers*), which was made into a film in 1956 and remade twice more. While some saw the chilling tale as an allegory of the cold war, F. always insisted it was nothing more than entertainment. F.'s interest in time-travel first surfaced in his collection of short stories entitled *The Third Level* (1957), a theme he would revisit many times with great success. His *Assault on a Queen* marked a return to the thriller genre, and *Good Neighbor Sam* (1963) was a humorous look at his experiences in the advertising industry that was made into a successful film starring Jack Lemmon. In 1968, he returned to his favorite theme of time travel in *The Woodrow Wilson Dime,* but it was for his time-travel novel *Time and Again,* published in 1970, that F. won the most attention and critical praise, unusual for a book of that genre. It also developed a loyal cult following. In 1995 F. published a sequel to his most popular novel, entitled *From Time to Time.* F. also explored the idea of time travel in a short story called *"The Love Letter,"* adapted after his death into a well-received television movie in 1998.

AWARDS: Lifetime Achievement, World FANTASY Awards (1987); Best Short Story Collection, *Infinity SCIENCE FICTION* for *The Third Level* (1958); Special Prize, *Ellery Queen Mystery Magazine* contest for "The Widow's Walk" (1946)

FURTHER WORKS: *The House of Numbers,* 1956; *Marion's Wall,* 1973; *The Night People,* 1977.

BIBLIOGRAPHY: *Something About the Author,* Vol. 109; Grimes, William, "Jack Finney, 84, Sci-Fi Author of Time-Travel, Dies." *The New York Times,* 17 Nov. 1995.

HEIDI SANCHEZ

FLAKE, Sharon G.
Author, b. n.d., Philadelphia, Pennsylvania

F., born and reared in North Philadelphia, relocated to Pittsburgh in her late teens. First a student, who graduated with a degree in English in 1978, and became an employee of the University of Pittsburgh, F. did publicity for her alma mater at the School of Business. F. tries to write for about three hours a day. F. has also counseled young people at the Center for the Assessment and Treatment of Youth in Pittsburgh.

F. is a single mother. Her daughter is a runner, and F. attends many of her track meets. Other activities she enjoys include television viewing, going to plays and movies—especially romantic ones, and reading. Langston Hughes is a particularly inspirational author in her opinion.

Her first published book is *The Skin I'm In* (1998), featuring Maleeka Madison. It explores the difficulties Maleeka endures and ultimately triumphs over. They include a mother overcome by grief over the loss of her husband and the banes of a TEENAGE girl's existence—a mean clique of girls, nontrendy clothing, and worst of all, her extremely dark skin color. When a teacher new to the school challenges her, Maleeka must decide which way she wants her life to go. *The Skin I'm In* has also appeared in a French language translation and won the 1999 Coretta Scott King-John Steptoe Award, given to emerging writers. F. also won the August Wilson Short Story Contest in 1994 for "The Luckiest Sister" and a scholarship from the *Highlights for Children* Writers Conference.

Her next work, *Money Hungry,* (2001) received a Coretta Scott King Honor Award. Its protagonist, Raspberry Hill, thinks that money is the surefire way to guarantee that she'll always have the home and security that have been lacking in her life, and the thought of how to get more of it haunts her. In 2001, F. was also awarded a Pennsylvania Council for the Arts Fellowship. *Begging for Change* (2003) follows Raspberry as she deals with a vicious attack on her mother, as well as the return of a father who exemplifies everything that Raspberry does not want to be. Is she going to be forced by circumstances to follow her father's path instead of her mother's? As always, Raspberry's struggles pull the reader in as we root for her to find her way.

Her most recent work, *Who Am I Without Him?: Short Stories About Girls and the Boys in Their Lives* (2004) garnered another Coretta Scott King Honor Award for her in 2005. This is a collection of ten SHORT STORIES that run the gamut from pathetic—a girl allows her boyfriend to beat her—to humorous. In these, as in all F.'s other work, she captures the essence of what life is about for some very memorable AFRICAN AMERICAN girls, and in the short story collection, boys. F. tells their stories as they are, and in doing so, shows lives full of their own dignity and struggle for meaning. Her determination to show people in all of their flawed yet generous humanity is part of what adds such resonance to her work.

AWARDS: *Money Hungry,* Coretta Scott King Honor Award, 2002. *The Skin I'm In,* ALA Best Books for Young Adults, 1999; Coretta Scott King-John Steptoe Award for new author 1999. *Who Am I without Him? Short Stories about Girls and the Boys in Their Lives,* ALA Best Books for Young Adults 2005; Coretta Scott King Honor Award 2005.

BIBLIOGRAPHY: http://www.discover.pitt.edu/media/pcc010625/flake.html; http://www.sharonflake.com; www.amazon.com

JEANNE MARIE RYAN

FLEISCHMAN, Paul
Author, b. 5 September 1952, Monterey, California

F. is noted as an artisan of sounds and words in his many works that span genre and topics. It is through his attention to the sound of language accompanying his imagery that he invites the reader to experience his stories through more than one sign system. Listening to classical music influenced the language forms that F. creatively uses. Perhaps of greatest importance, however, is the influence of F.'s father, Sid Fleischman, on his son. F. gives his father credit for developing his own insights and appreciation of the importance of sound in stories and recognizes his father's attention as a writer to dialect, forgotten phrases, and unique character names. Additionally, Sid Fleischman's love of the past was inherited by F. and sets the context for much of his son's writing.

F. wrote in *Horn Book*, "Since I think the sense of my stories out in some detail before I put them into words, the spontaneous, joyful, serendipitous, and mostly satisfying side of writing for me is trying to do exactly that: moving this clause to take advantage of that rhyme, finding a four-syllable word for slender, playing with the length of sentences. Giving the sense a sound." Perhaps most evident of this creative process are *I Am Phoenix: Poems for Two Voices* (1985) and *Joyful Noise: Poems for Two Voices* (1988). This celebration of nature through choosing just the right words to represent the songs of birds, in the first book, or insects, in the second, is designed to be read by two alternating voices or groups of voices. In *Joyful Noise,* fourteen insects use words that imitate their various humming and buzzing noises as they describe themselves in first person free verse. For this memorable book, F. won the Newbery Award in 1989.

F.'s use of language also serves to introduce characters who are unique in the depth of personality they share throughout various situations. Just as F. is creative with language, he also plays with format. In some cases, this format presents alternative perspectives that lead to enriching dialogue and thinking around his books. *Bull Run* (1993) is told from many perspectives representative of characters who were involved in this one battle. Each chapter is actually a monologue from history that reveals the events leading up to the battle and how each prioritized his/her concern—a doctor, photographer, horseman, colonel, mother at home—sixteen characters in all. This book can be presented as reader's theater or simply read and contemplated from the various perspectives. It powerfully points to the diverse effects of war on all citizens. *Seedfolk* (1997) also represents an excellently crafted story focusing on a garden that evolved and its many sharecroppers in the middle of inner-city Cleveland. The voices of diverse people in the community invite readers to critically consider the meaning of the garden for each and the value of a sense of community for all individuals.

Other books for adolescents include *Coming and Going Men: Four Tales of Itinerants* (1985) which again brings together to a central point the lives of four individuals in the early 1800s as they travel through a town in Vermont. Once again, F.'s love of history and wordsmithing create a distinctively clear picture of this era and characters to which readers connect. *The Borning Room* (1991) takes place in one location, a room in an Ohio home in the 1800s that was commonly set aside for births, illnesses, and deaths. Georgina Lott tells an artist who is to paint her picture before she dies that her involvement in historical events must be recorded. Set in more contemporary times, *Whirligig* (1998) and *Seek* (2001) focus on high-school students dealing with personal situations that demand their introspection. *Whirligig* focuses on a TEEN accident in which a young man, while trying to kill himself, accidentally kills a high-school-senior girl. His journey to fulfill the task set him by her mother forms the plot of this multi-layered novel. *Seek* concerns a high school senior who finds the voice of the father he has never met, and turns the AUTOBIOGRAPHY he is supposed to write into an oral portrait of his life.

F. has also used his talents of weaving together language and the arts to create PICTURE BOOKS such as *Shadow Play* (1990) and *Lost! A Story in String* (2000). Besides the Newbery Award and a Newbery Honor award, F. won the Scott O'Dell Award for *Bull Run*.

AWARDS: Newbery Award, *Joyful Noise: Poems for Two Voices,* 1988; Scott O'Dell Award, *Bull Run,* 1993; Newbery Honor Award. *Borning Room,* BBYA 1992; *Bull Run*, BBYA 1994 and Scott O'Dell Award; *Dateline Troy*, BBYA 1997; *Joyful Noise: Poems for Two Voices,* nonfiction BBYA, 1988; *Seedfolk,* BBYA 1998; *Whirligig,* BBYA 1999; *Mind's Eye,* BBYA 2000.

FURTHER WORKS: *Path of the Pale Horse,* 1983; *Rear-View Mirrors,* 1986; *Rondo in C,* 1988; *A Fate Totally Worse than Death,* 1995; *Mind's Eye,* 1999; *Big Talk: Poems for Four Voices,* 2000.

BIBLIOGRAPHY: *Authors and Artists for Young Adults,* 35, 2000; Contemporary Authors Online. The Gale Group, 2000. Gallo, Donald R., compiler and editor, *Speaking for Ourselves, Too,* 1993; *Something About the Author, Autobiography Series,* 20, 1995. St. James *Guide to Young Adult Writers,* 1999.

JANELLE B. MATHIS

FLETCHER, Ralph

Author, b. 17 March 1953

F. resides with his wife and children in New Hampshire. Learning early the ups and downs of FAMILY life, he was one of nine children and had parents who each had seven siblings. In 1975 F. completed his undergraduate degree at Dartmouth College and his Masters of Fine Arts at Columbia University in 1983. Although he grew up surrounded by words and stories, carrying paper and pencils around to capture any ideas, he began his career in New York City as a consultant, teaching teachers how to teach writing. As he visited schools, he used books as models for the children. These experiences helped F. realize words and stories were inside of him. While not his first book, *I Am Wings: Poems About Love* (1994) brought recognition. It is a book of thirty-three love poems written from an adolescent boy's viewpoint. It was proclaimed Best Book of the Year by the School Library Journal and received a Children's Choice Award from the International Reading Association. The ALA recognized it for reluctant readers. The YA POETRY in *Buried Alive* (1996) presents young love in its various forms and uncertainties.

F. did not stop at writing poetry. His fiction for elementary students is equally engaging. *Fig Pudding* (1995) follows the day-to-day life of the Abernathey family. Filled with hilarious adventures of the six children, this book also shares the grief of losing one of them. It is thought that this book was inspired by F.'s own experiences of growing up in a large family and losing a brother. A more recent movel, *Flying Solo* (1998), appeals to upper-elementary students because it chronicles a day in the life of a sixth-grade class when the substitute does not show up. When the students decide not to tell anyone they are alone and to run the class themselves, they do not realize all the personal issues that will arise as the day evolves. The consensus among reviewers and readers is that F. takes the reader through a gamut of emotions in his books as his characters tackle the difficult issues of trust, forgiveness, and DEATH. His fiction strives to push readers to examine their own feelings about absent parents, first loves, family alcoholism, beloved grandparents, serious illnesses, and their own innocence.

Whereas many authors stick to one kind of writing, F. found success writing nonfiction for young writers and teachers as well. In *Poetry Matters: Writing a Poem From the Inside Out* (2002), F. shares his love of writing. He professes that poetry is about the feelings it conveys and not the elements of language and correctness of meter or lines. Several of his non-fiction books were written with his wife, Joann Portalupi. As they work together, they hope to inspire teachers to teach writing in meaningful ways, so that they and their students can find their voice in their work.

AWARDS: *I am Wings: Poems About Love,* 1994; SLS Best Book of the Year; CBC & IRA Children's Choices; ALA Reluctant Readers.

SELECT FURTHER WORKS: *Walking Trees: Teaching Teachers in the New York City Schools,* 1990; *Water Planet: Poems About Water,* 1991; *What a Writer Needs,* 1993; *Walking Trees: Portraits of Teachers and Children in the Culture of Schools,* 1995; *A Writer's Notebook: Unlocking the Writer Within You,* 1996; *Ordinary Things: Poems from a Walk in Early Spring,* 1996; *Breathing In, Breathing Out: Keeping a Writer's Notebook, 1996; Twilight Comes Twice,* 1997; *Spider Boy,* 1997; *Room Enough for Love,* 1998; *Craft Lessons: Teaching Writing K–8,* 1998; *Live Writing: Breathing Life into Your Words,* 1999; *Relatively Speaking: Poems About Family,* 1999; *How Writers Work, 2000; How Writers Work. Nonfiction Craft Lessons: Teaching Information Writing K–8,* 2001; *Writing Workshop: The Essential Guide, 2001; Have You Been to the Beach Lately?,* 2001.

BIBLIOGRAPHY: *Something about the Author,* vol. 105, 1993. *School Library Journal,* July, 1995. *School Library Journal,* May, 1996. *School Library Journal,* May, 1997. *Booklist,* June 1, 1997. Various book reviews in *Booklist.* http://www.ralphfletcher.com/about.html.

CAROL WICKSTROM

FLETCHER, Susan (Clemens)
Author, b. 28 May 1951, in Pasadena, CA

F. knew at a young age that she wanted to be an author. In third grade, her teacher told her about Mark Twain, whose real name was Samuel Clemens and whose daughter was named Susan. F.'s maiden name is Clemens as well. "It was fate, I thought," F. said, "I decided not to become the daughter of a famous author (which is impossible to arrange), but to become a famous author myself (which is difficult enough)." F. earned a bachelor's degree in English at the University of California at Santa Barbara and a Master's degree in English from the University of Michigan. F. has moved frequently in her life and is currently living in Oregon. She worked in a variety of jobs before having her daughter and staying home to write children's stories and MAGAZINE articles.

F.'s primary work is a FANTASY trilogy about dragons, *Dragon's Milk* (1989), *Flight of the Dragon Kyn* (1993), and *Sign of the Dove* (1996). The idea for the main characters came out of F.'s desire to read FAIRY TALES with strong female protagonists. F. told *Something about the Author Autobiography Series*, "I began to be troubled by [fairy-tale] messages for girls. It seemed to me that the typical fairy-tale heroine . . . would sit around being beautiful, singing nicely, and being kind to birds and animals until her boyfriend—the Prince—came along and solved all her problems for her." She used her babysitting experience to create the "draclings"—baby dragons—that her characters nurtured.

In the first book of the trilogy, *Dragon's Milk*, Kaeldra babysits a dragon's infants while the mother goes to find food. The mother is killed and Kaeldra is left to care for the draclings, protecting them from men who want to kill them as well. *Dragon's Milk* has been described as a "blend of action, suspense, magic, and romance." In the sequel, *Sign of the Dove*, Kaeldra's sister Lyf continues working with the draclings when she becomes a teenager. This novel is a personal statement of the author: the transformation of Lyf echoes F.'s own battle against cancer. The final book in the trilogy, *Flight of the Dragon Kyn*, gives background to both of the previous books. It focuses on Kara, a teen with the natural gift of calling birds down from the sky. The king asks Kara to call down the dragons, and she realizes too late that she is bringing those dragons to their deaths. Fighting both the king and his people, Kara flees with the dragons and their kyn, or family, to help them find a safe home away from humankind.

In 1998, F. published *Shadow Spinner*, a retelling of the traditional 1001 Arabian Nights tale. Marjan, handmaiden to the princess Shahrazad, is the source of the stories the princess tells every night. Marjan risks everything to get the ending of the perfect story. *Horn Book* reviewer Mary M. Burns commented, "F. puts her own spin on the source material, telling a tale in which the pace is consistent, the characters interesting, and the plot impelling."

F. creates her works from her home office. She begins a book with research, using the real world to find experiences to put in her novels. For instance, when writing about working with birds and dragons, F. visited a local zoo and worked with raptors. She then writes a very rough draft, allowing herself to write as

badly as necessary. Several other drafts follow until she feels the words are right. Parts of her life appear in her works, including her daughter and her love of birds.

AWARDS: ALA Best Books for Young Adults, 1995, for *Flight of the Dragon Kyn*. Best Books *School Library Journal* (1998); Blue Ribbon Award, *Bulletin of the Center for Children's Books* (1998); ALA Best Books for Young Adults, 1999, for *Shadow Spinner*.

FURTHER WORKS: *The Haunting Possibility*, 1988; *The Stuttgart Nanny Mafia*, 1991; *Walk Across the Sea*, 2003; *Eve Green*, 2004.

BIBLIOGRAPHY: *100 More Popular Young Adult Authors*, Bernard A. Drew, 2002; *Contemporary Authors Online*, Gale, 2001; *Authors and Artists for Young Adults*, Thomas McMahon, Ed., 1997; *Something About the Author*, Alan Hedblad, Ed. 2000.

JENNA OBEE

FLINN, Alex
Author, b. 23 October 1966, Glen Cove, New York

By the time F. saw her first novel, *Breathing Underwater*, published in 2001, she had been collecting rejection slips for almost thirty years, beginning at the ripe old age of seven. F. was a natural storyteller. As a five-year-old, she started putting her words on the page. Two years later, her mother helped her submit them to *Highlights for Children* and *Cricket*.

If F. was an early writer, it follows that she was also an early reader. "*A Little Princess* by Frances Hodgson Burnett was my favorite by far," she says. "I read it maybe 20 to 30 times. I've heard it described as 'too dark' but I never thought so and I still don't. Every child is different."

F. also read Beverly Cleary books, Judy Blume books, and *National Velvet* by Enid Bagnold. "Oh," she remembers, "and I went trick-or-treating as both Pippi Longstocking and Laura Ingalls WILDER."

Dramatic flair and a move to Florida led F. to another early passion—singing. "From a very early age, I wanted to be in musical theater," she said. "I studied acting and singing, but my lack of ability as a dancer and my operatic voice inspired me to switch from theater to opera."

After an academic career in gifted early education programs including a performing arts magnet high school, F. studied opera at Florida State University. Backbiting and relentless competition convinced F.

her future was not in opera performance. She entered law school and also polished her college manuscript, which would eventually become *Breathing Underwater*.

Based on F.'s experience interning with the Florida State Attorney's Office and volunteering with battered women programs, early drafts of her first novel were a far cry from the finished book. She did not refine the story until after she was married and the mother of her first daughter. Inspired by a Key West Literary Seminar with Richard PECK and her friendship with YA author Joyce Sweeney, F. revised her college manuscript and sold it.

A year later, F. published *Breaking Point* (2002), the story of outsiders and school violence. *Nothing to Lose,* a powerful look at domestic violence from a son's helpless point of view, followed in 2004.

F. is maried to Gene Flinn, an attorney and mayor of a Miami suburb and is the mother of two daughters. She continues to write YA novels inspired by the diversity of her past and with an eye to the future.

AWARDS: ALA Best Books for Young Adults list, 2002, for *Breathing Underwater. Breaking Point:* ALA Quick Picks for Reluctant Young Adult Readers, 2003.

FURTHER WORKS: *Breathing Underwater,* 2001; *Breaking Point,* 2002; *Nothing to Lose,* 2004; Fade to Black, 2005.

BIBLIOGRAPHY: Interview with author; www.alex flinn.com.

KELLY MILNER HALLS

FORD, Vince
Author, b. 12 April 1970, Eltham, Taranaki, New Zealand

F.'s "wonderful childhood" on a hill-country farm at Mangamingi is reflected in his cheerful novels of rural life. After working as a jackaroo on an AUSTRALIAN sheep-station and producing agricultural videos, F. made a dramatic entry onto the teenage literature scene with the award-winning *2MUCH4U* [Too Much For You] (1999).

Davin, the enthusiastic eleven-year-old hero of *2MUCH4U* destroys his mother's truck in a farm accident very similar to one in which F. destroyed a $16,000 fertiliser truck in Western Australia. The boy sets up a job service to raise money, doing anything from feeding pig-dogs to plucking dead sheep. The

mood of self-confidence, displayed by Davin and his friends is maintained in the equally boisterous *SOMUCH2DO* [So Much to Do] (2001), where they try worm farming and eel selling. The strong role of female characters, such as Davin's mother and his friend Dessy, continues in *POSSUMS2U* [Possums to You] (2002). A storm adds danger to a possum-trapping holiday, but Davin's positive attitude helps his friends triumph over misadventures.

F.'s best book, to date, is *A Handful of Blue* (2003). Young Germ (Jeremy) feels powerless as the family farm is about to be sold and a school of whales is stranded on the beach. Out of the resulting tragedy, Germ achieves a mature understanding with his father and sister, and helps save the farm. As always in F.'s work, FAMILY and friends are vital.

Sport and humor are two other common characteristics of the work of one of the promising NEW ZEALAND writers of the 21st century.

AWARDS: *2MUCH4U:* 1998 Tom Fitzgibbon Award, 2000 NZ Post Children's Book Award, 2000 NZ Post Children's Best First Book Award; 2003 NZ Children's Literature Foundation Notable Book, *POSSUMS2U.*

FURTHER WORKS: *It's a Try,* 2000; *The Dare Club,* 2002.

BIBLIOGRAPHY: Harper, Julie. "Know the New Authors." *Magpies NZ Supplement* 15:2 (May 2000): 2–3; Agnew, Trevor. "Know the Author: Vince Ford: *SOMUCH2READ.*" *Magpies NZ Supplement* 18:2 (May 2003) 1–4; http://library.christchurch.org.nz/ Childrens / ChildrensAuthors / VinceFord.asp /http: / / wwwbookcouncil.org.nz/writers/fordvince.htm/

TREVOR AGNEW

FOREMAN, James Douglas
Author, b. 12 November 1932, Mineola, New York

F. is an author and lawyer who graduated from Princeton University and Columbia University and is past president and member of the Lightning Fleet 142. Interests include photography, travel, and antique arms of the 18th century. One of his best known young adult works is *Becca's Story* (1992), based upon letters and DIARIES of his ancestors. In his novel, Becca Case, from Michigan, must decide between two suitors, but the Civil War breaks out making her choice between Alex Forman and Charlie Gregory quite complicated.

AWARDS: *Becca's Story*: ALA Best Books for Young Adults, 1993.

FURTHER WORKS: *Islands of the Eastern Mediterranean* (1959—in collaboration with his wife, Marcia Forman); *The Skies of Crete*, 1963; *Ring the Judas Bell*, 1965; *The Shield of Achilles*, 1966; *Horses of Anger*, 1967; *The Cow Neck Rebels*, 1969; *My Enemy, My Brother*, 1969; *Ceremony of Innocence*, 1970; *So Ends This Day*, 1970; *Song of Jubilee*, 1971; *Law and Disorder*, 1971; *People of the Dream*, 1972; *Capitalism: Economic Individualism to Today's Welfare State*, 1972; *Communism: From Marx's Manifesto to 20ᵗʰ Century*, 1972; *Socialism: Its Theoretical Roots and Present-Day Development*, 1972; *The Life and Death of Yellow Bird*, 1973; *Code Nam Valkyrie*, 1973; *Follow the River*, 1975; *Fine Soft Day*, 1978; *A Ballad for Hogskin Hill*, 1979; *Freedom's Blood*, 1979; *The Pumpkin Shell*, 1981; *Cry Havoc*, 1988; *Doomsday Plus Twelve*, 1984; and *Prince Charlie's Year*, 1991.

BIBLIOGRAPHY: *Something about the Author*, vol. 8, 1976.

VALERIE A. PALAZOLO

FOX, Paula

Author, b. April 22, 1923, New York City

The daughter of a roving American writer and a Cuban mother, F. was moved about as a child from home to home, raised first by a kindly minister until age six, briefly by her parents, and then for a longer period by her Cuban grandmother. Her location changed from Cuba to New York. After her parents divorced, F. occasionally lived with her father. She attributes to her early years with the minister—poet, historian, and inveterate reader—her fascination with language and her desire to be a writer. Her experiences in Cuba, life with her mother's extended family in New York, and her interaction with her alcoholic father appear directly in *Borrowed Finery: A Memoir* (1999) and in refracted form in her YOUNG ADULT and adult novels.

F. began writing fiction as a career at age thirty-nine, while in Greece for six months with her second husband and her two sons. F.'s first book, the children's novel *Maurice's Room* (1966), examines a boy's conflict with his parents over the room-filling collections that they perceive as junk and time-wasters. Her later novels for children and young adults explore the disparities between parents' and

children's points of view, usually validating the child's perspective even when tempering it.

In *Western Wind* (1993), an eleven-year-old spends a summer getting to know her eccentric grandmother, whom she does not realize is dying. In *Lily and the Lost Boy* (1987), Lily is troubled by her older brother's fascination with a delinquent boy with a drinking father, yet to some degree befriends the boy herself. Somewhat less compelling is *A Place Apart* (1980), about a grieving girl's friendship with a manipulative actor at school. *One-eyed Cat* (1984) believably portrays a boy's first major act of disobedience, firing a prohibited rifle, as well as his anguish over the secret deed and the cat he is sure he has injured.

F. has a gift for writing from inside a child's or TEEN's head, showing the consciousness of her protagonists as intelligent, thoughtful, and human; she never dismisses the perspective of her youthful characters. As F. has said, ". . . children know about pain and fear and unhappiness and betrayal. We do them a disservice by trying to sugarcoat dark truths."

Blowfish Live in the Sea (1970) explores twelve-year-old Carrie's involvement in the tensions between her nearly nineteen-year-old half-brother Ben and her parents. Ben stops bringing friends home, drops out of school, and wears a ponytail. His moodiness culminates in a bus ride to Boston with Carrie to meet his long-absent father. F.'s portrayal of Ben's alcoholic father is particularized and convincing. Alcoholics who make grand promises and lie to their children appear repeatedly in F.'s fiction and resemble the frequently absent father described in her memoir. In *The Moonlight Man* (1986), Catherine spends a summer with her drunken father, finally understanding her parents' divorce and recognizing her own rage at and love for the charming, lying man. In *The Village by the Sea* (1988), ten-year-old Emma lives for two weeks with an alcoholic aunt whose bitter self-absorption takes all the attention of Emma's kind uncle; the story climaxes when Emma's aunt destroys a miniature village that the girl and a friend had painstakingly constructed of seashells and other beach discoveries. F.'s gift is showing her protagonists' inner confrontation with these damaged adults.

Working primarily in realistic fiction, F. writes what might be considered the problem novel if she allowed her characters easy solutions or uncompromising doom. However, her presentation of homelessness in *Monkey Island* (1991), homosexuality and AIDS in *The Eagle Kite* (1995), and alcoholism in the above-mentioned work usually avoids reductive explanations or simple solutions.

Her one historical novel, *The Slave Dancer* (1973), won the Newbery Medal and has been acclaimed for its portrayal of a boy sickened by his involuntary involvement in the slave trade. It has been criticized for seeming to absolve its well-realized sailor characters from their culpability for slave trading and for presenting the slaves as passive victims. Critics Margaret Rustin and Michael Rustin say of the novel, "[Jessie's] questions continue to reveal both the natures of his companions and the way in which the inhumanity and irrationality of the slave trade is rationalized. . . . It is an amazing achievement." Many of F.'s books have been translated into Chinese, Croatian, Danish, Dutch, French, German, Korean, Persian, Spanish, and Swedish.

AWARDS: ALA Best Books for Young Adults (1984) for *One-eyed Cat*. ALA Notable Children's Books, *How Many Miles to Babylon?* (1967; reissued 1980), *The Stone-Faced Boy* (1968), *Portrait of Ivan* (1969), *The Slave Dancer,* (1986), *One-eyed Cat, The Moonlight Man.* American Institute of Graphics Arts Children's Books (1970), *The King's Falcon.* American Book Award, for Children's Fiction PAPERBACK (1983) for *A Place Apart. Boston Globe–Horn Book* Award for fiction (1989) for *The Village by the Sea. Boston Globe–Horn Book* Honor Book (1994) for *Western Wind.* Brandeis Fiction Citation (1984). Bank Street College of Education's Child Study Children's Book Award (1984) for *One-eyed Cat*. Child Study Association of America's Children's Books of the Year (1969), *Portrait of Ivan,* (1970) for *Blowfish Live in the Sea,* (1973) for *The Slave Dancer,* (1987) for *The Moonlight Man.* Christopher Award (1985) for *One-eyed Cat*. Empire State Award (1994) for her body of children's works. Guggenheim Fellowship (1972). Hans Christian Andersen Medal for her children's books (1978). Hans Christian Andersen Special Honor List (1979) for *The Slave Dancer.* IBBY (USA) Honor List for Writing (1986) for *One-eyed Cat*. National Endowment for the Arts Grant (1974). National Institute of Arts and Letters Award (1972). New York Public Library's Books for the Teen Age (1981) for *A Place Apart.* Newbery Honor Book (1985) for *One-eyed Cat*. Newbery Medal (1974) for *The Slave Dancer. New York Times* Notable Books (1984) for *One-eyed Cat,* (1986) for *The Moonlight Man. New York Times* Outstanding Books (1980) for *A Place Apart.* Rockefeller Foundation Grant (1984).

School Library Journal's Best Books of the Year (1973) for *The Slave Dancer,* (1980) for *A Place Apart,* (1986) for *The Moonlight Man.* University of Southern Mississippi Silver Medallion (1987). *Monkey Island,* BBYA, 1992. *One-eyed Cat* BBYA, 1984. Nothing but the Best: Best of the Best BYA, 1966–86. Here We Go Again: 25 Years of Best Books: Selections from 1967 to 1992.

FURTHER WORKS: "The Virtues of Madame Douvay," an episode of the ABC television show *The Naked City,* 1962. *A Likely Place,* 1967. *Poor George,* 1967, reprt. 2001. *Dear Prosper,* 1968. *The Stone-Faced Boy,* 1968. *Hungry Fred,* 1969. *The King's Falcon,* 1969, reprt. 1991. *Desperate Characters,* 1970, reprt. 1980, 1999 (Paramount film, 1970). *Good Ethan,* 1973. *The Western Coast,* 1972, reprt. 2001. *The Widow's Children,* 1976. *The Little Swineherd and Other Tales,* 1978, newly illustrated, 1996. *A Servant's Tale,* 1984. *In a Place of Danger,* 1989, reprt. 1997. *The God of Nightmares,* 1990. *Amzat and His Brothers: Three Italian Tales Remembered by Floriano Vecchi,* 1993. "On Language," *School Library Journal,* 1995 [Reprt. from *Ohio Review* 1994]. *The Gathering Darkness,* 1995. *Radiance Descending,* 1997; *The Coldest Winter,* 2005.

BIBLIOGRAPHY: "F., Paula 1923–," *Contemporary Authors* Vol. 62. 1998. "F., Paula 1923–." *Something about the Author* 60. 1990. Estes, Glenn E., ed., "Paula F.," *Dictionary of Literary Biography,* Vol. 52: *American Writers for Children Since 1960: Fiction.* 1986. Jones, Sydney J., "F., Paula 1923–." *Something about the Author* vol. 120. 2001. Mercier, Cathryn M., "F., Paula." *Twentieth Century Young Adult Writers* 1994. Moss, Anita, "Varieties of Children's Metafiction," *Studies in the Literary Imagination.* 1985. Rustin, Margaret, and Michael Rustin, *Narratives of Love and Loss: Studies in Modern Children's Fiction.* 1987. Zitlow, Connie S. "Paula F." *Writers for Young Adults.* 1997.

LAUREEN TEDESCO

FRADIN, Dennis Brindell
Author, b. 1945, Chicago, Illinois

F. is a prolific writer who sometimes coauthors with his wife, Judith. F. is well known for hundreds of books written for young people about U.S. historical events, places and famous people, science and contemporary issues. Living in Evanston, Illinois, F. is careful to ensure that these books are factual and unbiased; he often travels to investigate his subjects first hand. Majoring in creative writing, F. graduated from Northwestern University in 1967 with a B.A.; he attended the University of Illinois for graduate study in 1998. He married Judith Bloom, a high-school English teacher, on March 19, 1967. They have three children: Anthony, Diana, and Michael. F., an elementary school teacher in a Chicago public school from 1968 to 1979, started writing children's books in 1976. He has a written SERIES of books on each of the states in the U.S. *From Sea to Shining Sea* (1991–1995), his favorite, the colonial period, in the Thirteen Colonies Series (1986–1992); and sharing celebrations with his Best Holiday Book series. F. has written BIOGRAPHIES of famous colonial Americans in the series Colonial Profiles, as well as biographies of Samuel Adams and Benjamin Franklin. His book, *Bound for the North Star* (2000), takes the reader on the journey to freedom through narrative accounts from escaped slaves and those who helped them escape. The subject of his most widely acclaimed book is Ida B. Wells-Barnett, a journalist, public speaker for CIVIL RIGHTS, suffragist, and crusader against lynching who helped give birth to the National Association for the Advancement of Colored People (NAACP). His well-known series for younger readers on the planets is widely read. His works are now being published in Spanish. F. and his family continue to make their home in Evanston where he enjoys writing, baseball, and astronomy.

AWARDS: *Planet Hunters,* nonfiction entry BBYA 1998. Riverbank Review's 2001 Children's Books of Distinction Award, Flora Stieglitz Straus Award for fiction, Bank Street College of Education, given for a nonfiction work that exemplifies the ideals of generosity of spirit and serves as an inspiration to young readers (2001) and Smithsonian Book of the Year (2002) for *Ida B. Wells: Mother of the Civil Rights Movement* (2000) co-authored with his wife. Nonfiction Children's Book of the Year Award, Society for Midland Authors (2001), *Bound for the North Star: True Stories of Fugitive Slaves* (2000).

SELECT FURTHER WORKS: *Words and Picture* Series, 1976–1981; *Disaster!* Series, 1982; *My Family Shall Be Free!: The Life of Peter Still,* 2001; Children's Fiction: *Cara,* 1977; *Cave Painter,* 1978; *Bad Luck Tony,* 1978; *North Star,* 1978; *Beyond the Mountain, Beyond the Forest,* 1978; *The New Spear* (1979) and *How I Saved the World* (1986); *The Republic of Ireland* (1984) and *The Netherlands* (1994); *The Planet Hunters: The Search for Other Worlds* (1997); *Fight On! Mary Church Terrell's Battle for Integration* (with J.B. Fradin), 2003.

BIBLIOGRAPHY: "Dennis Brindell Fradin." *Authors and Artists for Young Adults,* Volume 49. Gale Group, 2003. Reproduced in *Biography Resource Center.* Farmington Hills, Mich.: The Gale Group. 2003. http://www.galenet.com/servlet/BioRC

VALERIE A. PALAZOLO

FRANCO, Betsy
Author, b. 15 August 1947, Shaker Heights, Ohio

F. received a B.A. in studio art from Stanford University and an M.Ed. from Lesley College in Cambridge, Massachusetts. Her preferred art medium, painting, was something F. continued to do after graduation, until the birth of her second son when she found less and less time to devote to setting up her paints. Writing, though, required only a pencil and allowed F. to express herself creatively.

F.'s works run the literary gamut. She has published over fifty books for children and YOUNG ADULTS, including PICTURE BOOKS, nonfiction books, and POETRY anthologies. In addition, she has created various educational toys (Inchworks, TexTiles, and Attribute Socks).

Many of F.'s books explore mathematics, linking various concepts with other subjects and finding math in everyday life. *Unfolding Mathematics With Unit Origami* (1999) is one such book. To write it, F. drew on her experience of having lived as a child in Japan where an elderly neighbor taught her the country's ancient paper-making art. *Fourscore and 7: Investigating Math in American History* (1999) links geometry, factors and primes, fractions, and decimals to such historical events as the Boston Tea Party, the Gold Rush, and the struggle for voting rights.

F. has authored several professional books. *Thematic Poetry: All About Me!* (2000) contains many of F.'s original poems about neighborhood helpers, the community, and transportation. F. also includes activities for teachers to tie into the poems. *Word Families: Guess-Me Poems and Puzzles* (2003) teaches the concepts of word families to young readers through hands-on activities.

More recently, F. has worked as an editor, compiling anthologies of other writers' works. She finds that this experience provides a nice balance with her own writing, and also allows her the opportunity to work with interesting, talented people. *You Hear Me? Poems and Writings by Teenage Boys* (2000) is an uncensored collection of POETRY. F. advertised for writers in creative writing journals, by linking to classrooms via the Internet, and collecting poetry from both organized writing projects and individual boys. F.'s purpose in compiling these works is to let TEENAGE boys speak for themselves. While working on this book, F. was surprised and inspired by the openness of the writers.

F. also served as editor of a collection of poetry by teenage girls titled, *Things I Have to Tell You: Poems and Writings by Teenage Girls* (2001) and of an anthology featuring works by Native American teenagers and YOUNG ADULTS, *Night Is Gone, Day Is Still Coming: Poems and Stories by American Indian Teens and Young Adults* (2003). On editing these three anthologies, F. comments, "Any human being likes to be heard and wants to be treated with respect. People can sense when someone values what they have to say. Being an editor was a very privileged position to be in."

F. has been married for over thirty years to Douglas, and together they have three sons. They make their home in Palo Alto, CA.

AWARDS: 2001 ALA Best Books for Young Adults for *You Hear Me? Poems and Writings by Teenage Boys* (2000) and *Things I Have to Tell You: Poems and Writings by Teenage Girls* (2001); 2002 ALA Best Books for Young Adults.

SELECTED FURTHER WORKS: *Quiet Elegance: Japan Through the Eyes of Nine American Artists* (1997); *Counting Caterpillars and other Math Poems* (1998); *Clever Calculator Cat* (1999); *Grandpa's Quilt* (1999); *20 Marvelous Math Tales* (2000); *201 Thematic Riddle Poems to Build Literacy* (2000); *Caring, Sharing, and Getting Along* (2000); *Creepy Crawlies* (2000); *Math in Motion: Wiggle, Gallop, and Leap with Numbers* (2000); *Shells* (2000); *Why the Frog Has Big Eyes* (2000); *Adding Alligators and Other Easy-to-Read Math Stories* (2001); *Funny Fairy Tale Math* (2001); *Whatever the Weather: Thematic Poetry* (2001); *Amazing Animals* (2002); *Bat Named Pat, A* (2002); *Jake's Cake Mistake* (2002); *Pocket Poetry Mini-Books* (2002); *Silly Sally* (2002); *Six Silly Seals and Other Read-Aloud ABC Story Skits* (2002); *Going to Grandma's Farm* (2003); *Guess Me Poems and Puzzles: Alphabet* (2003); *Mathematickles* (2003); *Counting Our Way to the 100th Day!* (2004).

BIBLIOGRAPHY: www.betsyfranco.com; www.teenreads.com/athors/au-franco-betsy.asp; www.authorsontheweb.com/features/0204-poet/id-poet-authors-asp; www.keypress.com/authors/franco_betsy.html; www.amazon.com

CARRA GAMBERDELLA

FRANK, Anne(lies) Marie

Diarist, b. 6 June 1929, Frankfurt am Main, Germany; d. March 1945, near Bergen-Belsen, Germany

F. is known worldwide for her DIARY, *Het Achterhuis (Anne Frank: The Diary of a Young Girl),* the story of her early adolescence spent in hiding in Nazi–occupied Holland.

Eight people shared a group of hidden rooms that F.'s father, Otto, had constructed on the top floors of his office. They were often restricted, without water, toilet usage, or anything else that might reveal their presence. F. recorded the circumstances of going into hiding, the mundane events of daily life, and the hardships suffered by all persons involved.

Although the diary is a unique historical document, it is also an amazing window into the thoughts and feelings of a quickly maturing young woman. F. refers to the period as "the unbosomings of a thirteen-year-old schoolgirl."

After two years, the group was discovered by Nazis and relocated to concentration camps. Only Otto Frank survived. After finding the diary and sharing it with friends, Otto realized that it was a "meaningful human document" and should not be kept from the outside world.

The diary was adapted into an award-winning play and several films. F. also wrote SHORT STORIES, essays, and a partial novel. Commentators have noted the engaging style of F.'s writing and praised her wit, intelligence, and emotional development. In perhaps her most fitting epitaph, the courageous and inspiring F. wrote, "If God lets me live, . . . I shall work in the world for mankind."

AWARDS: ALA Best Books for Young Adults list, 1996, for *Diary of a Young Girl: The Definitive Edition.*

FURTHER WORKS: *Anne Frank's Tales from the Secret Annex,* 1983.

BIBLIOGRAPHY: *Twentieth-Century Literary Criticism,* vol. 17, 1985; *Contemporary Authors,* vol. 133, 1991.

MYRON A. MYKYTA

FRANK, E. R.

Author, b. 8 April 1968, Bethesda, Maryland

Though author and social worker F. was born to parents of East Coast sensibilities, she was whisked away to Evanston, Illinois, when she was three months old.

Then, just after her first birthday, her neuropathologist father took a job at the Medical College of Virginia and moved the family again, to Richmond this time.

Growing up the youngest of three children in the South provided a colorful but conflicted existence for the energetic child. Athletic and socially conscious, F. was hungry for justice, but aware of its absence. Many southern households employed black maids during that era, and F. was disturbed by their self-diminishing tone in addressing her and her friends. She asked them not to call her "Miss Emily," but habit and expectations made them refuse. Those and other rascist indicators—including the segregation of her neighborhood swimming pool—made a lasting impression.

Injustice took on a more personal slant when F. was denied the chance to play competitive soccer. Until the seventh grade, she played with the boys' teams at a modified Montessori school. But when she switched to traditional public schools, co-ed play was denied. Devastated, F. didn't play soccer again until she rediscovered it as an adult. Social cliques were another reality F. discovered in public school. By the time she understood the wardrobe that popularity required, she had to convince her mother why it was important—a conviction she didn't really embrace. "I knew it was crucial for my social acceptance, and I knew it was stupid, but there it was." Reading, however, was a passion Frank was never denied, though she had dark leanings. "I went for the books about DEATH, divorce, the HOLOCAUST, racism and all those tough topics," she said in one interview. Ugly was the counterbalance to beauty, Frank decided. And loss could spark the survivor in us all.

Those same themes, influenced by her work as a clinical social worker, are mirrored in F.'s critically acclaimed realistic fiction. Her early English teachers were not impressed with F., nor were they setting *her* creative energies on fire. She had no journalistic inclination and found no passion for academic writing she found "unbelievably dry."

F.'s editor at Simon & Schuster eventually dubbed both styles of writing in a language the writer could embrace. The writing that left her cold in middle school he called "thought writing"; the key to F.'s impressive talents he called "writing felt."

Unlocking F.'s creative options produced *Life Is Funny* (2000), a first novel with eleven different char-

acter points of view and an unconventional and sometimes emotionally painful series of plotlines. Both, she says, were unintentional; again, because her prose comes from a place felt, rather than thought out.

Her second novel, *America* (2002), centers on one central character—a TEEN all but shredded by the sometimes harmful foster care system. Just as emotionally compelling, comedian and talk show host Rosie O'Donnell promptly bought the film rights and took the project into pre-production.

Social work, a profession F. has in common with her mother and still performs part time, inspires the torturous, gritty characterizations. And the characters speak in their native tongues, which can be colorful and salty.

Why use expletives in a novel written for teens? Following in YA master Chris CRUTCHER's able footsteps, F. insists it's a matter of honesty. ". . . in order to write truly convincing characters," she says, "it's crucial to write the dialogue that feels as real to life as possible."

Her third novel, *Friction* (2003), also features troubled characters, but was originally written as a screenplay—a format she says negatively impacted the final product.

From an eighty-year-old colonial house in the tree-lined suburbs of New York, she continues to craft her reality-based fictional manuscripts. Like her characters, the B + student from Richmond has finally come of age, but she'll reach back into her sense of awkward adolescence whenever the storyline demands it.

AWARDS: *Life Is Funny:* ALA's Top Ten Quick Pick for the Reluctant Reader (2001) and Outstanding Books for the College Bound, Teen People Book Club NEXT Award 2000; *America:* 2003 ALA Best Book for Young Adults, 2002 *New York Times* Notable Book of the Year; Junior Library Guild Selection 2003.

BIBLIOGRAPHY: Greenwood Interview with Don Gallo, 2003; Simon and Schuster Interview, 2003; Interview notes.

KELLY MILNER HALLS

FRAUSTINO, Lisa Rowe
(S. L. ROBEL, a joint pseudonym)
Author, b. 26 May 1961, Dover-Foxcroft, Maine

F. has impressive credentials, including a B.A. from the University of Maine, an M.A. from the University of Scranton and a Ph.D. in English from Binghamton University. She is an award-winning children's writer and teacher. Her book *Ash: A Novel* (1995) won critical acclaim as an ALA Best Book for Young Adults, realistically portraying the impact of an older brother's mental illness on his family, especially his younger sibling. The popular novel has been translated into Italian and Danish. F. authored an award-winning PICTURE BOOK, *Hickory Chair* (2001), which sketches the story of a visually impaired boy and his deep, loving relationship with his wise grandmother. The story embraces strong FAMILY ties, visual DISABILITY, and the power of memories, beautifully illustrated by Benny Andrews. The plot is so skillfully crafted that it could stand alone. As a writer, F. weaves a tapestry within her stories about somber subjects like mental illness or blindness. The picture book was designated a Notable Children's Book in 2002 by ALA. The author writes and teaches extensively, including YOUNG ADULT and children's literature, plus creative writing classes. F. often publishes SHORT STORIES and articles. She is a talented editor as well as an author of short stories. In 2002, a published short story collection titled *Shattered: Stories of Children and War,* included one of F.'s short stories. Her column, "Dr. Lisa's Class," is a regular feature of the MAGAZINE, *Once upon a Time.*

AWARDS: Notable Children's Books ALA, 2002, for *The Hickory Chair;* Quick Picks for Reluctant Readers ALA, 1999, *Dirty Laundry: Stories about Family Secrets;* Best Books for Young Adults, 1996, *Ash: A Novel; Highlights for Children* Fiction Contest Winner, 1992.

FURTHER WORKS: *Grass and Sky,* 1994; *Dirty Laundry: Stories about Family Secrets,* 1998; *Soul Searching: Thirteen Stories About Faith and Belief,* 2002, ed. Lisa R. Fraustino.

BIBLIOGRAPHY: "ALA's Book Picks 2002: Notable Children's Books," *School Library Journal* 48 no 3 62-5 Mar. 2002; *Something about the Author,* vol. 84, 1996.

REBECCA B. VARGHA

FREEDMAN, Russell (Bruce)

Author, b. 11 October 1929, San Francisco, California

The winner of an astonishing number of major literary awards, F. is among the most critically lauded of all YA authors. His nonfiction work is frequently praised for its careful research, straightforward prose, and talented integration of period photographs into the text.

Born in San Francisco to parents who loved books and reading, F. became fascinated with the topics of animal behavior and history at a young age, reading extensively in both areas. He began his college education at San Jose State College (now San Jose State University), graduating from the University of California at Berkeley with a bachelor's degree in 1951. After college he entered the U.S. Army Counterintelligence Corps in Korea. He next embarked on a career as a newspaper reporter and editor, working for the Associated Press from 1953 to 1956. This early stint as a journalist prepared him for the thorough research that his "photobiographies" and other youth nonfiction would later require. In 1961, F. joined the staff of *The Columbia Encyclopedia.* During that same year, he published his first book, *Teenagers Who Made History.* After working as an editor for the Crowell-Collier Education Corporation, he moved to full-time freelance writing in 1965.

Many of F.'s early titles, such as *Animal Architects* (1971) and *How Animals Defend their Young* (1978), deal with the subject of animal behavior. However, F. has gained the most recognition for his photo-illustrated BIOGRAPHIES and collective biographies of historic American figures. He won a Newbery Medal for one such title, *Lincoln: A Photobiography* (1987), and Newbery Honors for three others: *The Wright Brothers: How They Invented the Airplane* (1991), *Eleanor Roosevelt: A Life of Discovery* (1993), and *The Voice that Challenged a Nation: Marian Anderson and the Struggle for Equal Rights* (2004). The period photographs in these books tell much of the story and strengthen the impact of the accompanying text. *Indian Chiefs* (1987) and *An Indian Winter* (1992) enriched the field of study about early America.

F.'s photobiographies have profiled a range of historical figures, from U.S. Presidents to inventors to arts figures. Perhaps most representative of this style is *Lincoln: A Photobiography* (1987). F. portrays Lincoln, not as a one-dimensional hero, but as a complicated man who suffered from lifelong depression and self-doubt while maintaining a witty and jovial public facade. Photographs taken throughout Lincoln's tenure as President highlight the emotional and physical toll he suffered as a result of the stress and uncertainty of his position during the Civil War.

F.'s equally compelling *Martha Graham: A Dancer's Life* (1998) portrays Graham as a woman who, after discovering relatively late her interest in dance, dedicated the rest of her life to artistic, psychological, and sociopolitical expression through movement, becoming one of the most significant figures in the development of modern dance. Energy-charged photos of the dancer at work enable the reader to glimpse the beauty and innovation of Graham's unique style.

F. has also published a number of collective biographies about people whose celebrity is not apparent. For example, *In the Days of the Vaqueros: America's First True Cowboys* (2001), he traces the origins of cowboys to the vaqueros (cow herders) in Mexico during the 16th century and documents their spread north to the U.S. Color reproductions of Western art and period photographs illustrate the text.

In addition to creating an outstanding body of work, F. has influenced the field of nonfiction publishing for youth or young people. The recent increase in photographic and other illustrative material in various INFORMATIONAL books can be credited in part to F.'s innovative work.

AWARDS: 1984 *Boston Globe–Horn Book* Award Honor, *The Children of the Wild* West; *Lincoln: A Photobiography*: 1987 Golden Kite Award Honor, 1988 John Newbery Medal; 1988 Golden Kite Award Honor, *Buffalo Hunt*; *Franklin Delano Roosevelt*: 1990 Golden Kite Award Honor, 1991 Orbis Pictus Award; *The Wright Brothers: How They Invented the Airplane*: 1991 Golden Kite Award, 1991 *Boston Globe–Horn Book* Award Honor, 1992 Newbery Honor; 1992 *Washington Post*–Children's Book Guild Nonfiction Award; 1992 Golden Kite Award Honor, *An Indian Winter*; *Eleanor Roosevelt: A Life of Discovery*: 1993 Golden Kite Award, 1994 Newbery Honor, 1994 *Boston Globe–Horn Book* Award; *Kids at Work: Lewis Hine and the Crusade against Child Labor*: 1994 Golden Kite Award, 1995 Orbis Pictus Award Honor; 1997 Orbis Pictus Award Honor, *The Life and Death of Crazy Horse;* 1998 Laura Ingalls Wilder Medal; *Martha Graham: A Dancer's Life*: 1998 Golden Kite Award, 1998 *Boston Globe–Horn Book* Award Honor; 2003 Orbis Pictus Award Honor, *Confucius: The Golden Rule.*

FURTHER WORKS: *In Defense of Liberty: The Story of America's Bill of Rights*, 2003.

BIBLIOGRAPHY: *Authors & Artists for Young Adults,* vol. 24, 1998; *Meet the Authors and Illustrators,* vol.

2, 1993; *Something about the Author,* vol. 123, 2001; *Twentieth Century Young Adult Writers,* 1994.

DENISE E. AGOSTO

FRENCH, Albert
Author, b. 5 July 1943, Pittsburgh, Pennsylvania

F. is the stepson of Harry King (a retired government employee) and son of Martha King (a housewife). He attended three different high schools but graduated from Penn Hills in 1962. Having joined the Marines following his graduation from high school, F. served as a corporal and infantryman in Vietnam. Wounded in service as a U.S. Marine during a tour of duty in Vietnam (1963–67), F. returned home, having been shot in the throat and struggling with depression.

After two decades of failed attempts at employment as photographer or editor, even attempting, unsuccessfully, to publish his own women's magazine, *Pittsburgh Preview,* F. became severely depressed. He spent three years in an apartment, emerging only occasionally for cigarettes. After viewing a television talk show about children on death row, F. holed up with "a one-page outline, an old typewriter and some whiteout," to emerge six weeks later with a start of his first novel, *Billy,* published later in 1993. The success of this novel caused F. to become a literary celebrity; he was interviewed extensively on radio and television and sold the film rights to Phillip Hoss. Hoss encouraged F. to write more novels, and to eventually publish his memoirs. "Whether he is describing racial prejudice and injustice, combat, or premature death, none of F.'s works are completely fictional."

AWARDS: *New York Times Book Review* Notable Book of 1994, for *Billy; New York Times Notable Book of 1997* for *Patches of Fire; Billy,* BBYA, 1995. *Holly,* which was published in 1995 was also nominated for the BBYA list. The general consensus of committee discussion was that this novel did not have the same appeal that *Billy* did. *Billy* is a young AFRICAN AMERICAN who accidentally kills a Caucasion girl (to stop her from hitting him). He is only twelve but is chased down by the law, tried, found guilty and executed.

FURTHER WORKS: *Holly,* 1995; *Patches of Fire: A Story of War and Redemption,* 1997; *I Can't Wait on God,* 1998; *Anchor,* 1998.

BIBLIOGRAPHY: "Albert French." *Contemporary Black Biography,* Volume 18, 1998. Reproduced in *Biography Resource Center,* 2003; http://www.galenet.com/servlet/BioRC; *Contemporary Authors*

Online, 2000; *Contemporary Authors Online,* Gale, 2003, Reproduced in *Biography Resource Center,* 2003, http://www.galenet.com/servlet/BioRC; "Anchor." *Publishers Weekly,* Dec. 13, 1999, p. 44; "Holly." *Publishers Weekly,* Feb. 27, 1995, p. 85(1); Loeb, Jeff. "Patches of Fire: A Story of War and Redemption," *African American Review,* Summer 1999, vol. 33, i2, p. 372(3).

SARA MARCUS

FREYMANN-WEYR, Garret
Author, b. n.d., New York City

Although F. was born and raised in New York City, she left the city to earn a bachelor's degree at the University of North Carolina at Chapel Hill. F. then returned to Manhattan to earn an MFA in Film at New York University.

F. cites her love of books and typewriters as her reason for pursuing writing. She has always loved the noises a typewriter makes—the bang of the keys and the "ding" when the carriage moves back.

F.'s most acclaimed book is *My Heartbeat* (2002). In it, the story's main character, Ellen, is forced to examine her intense feelings for her brother and his best friend, and is struck by the intense feelings between the two young men as well. The social, emotional, and sexual identities of all three young people are explored. F. sensitively portrays Ellen's growth and changing levels of understanding, and readers are drawn into the story by the intelligent characters and their moving plight to realize themselves.

F. says that she is deeply interested in people who are "headaches." She has found that people who are odd are fun to know and spend time with; therefore, in F.'s writing, she starts with a character and then focuses on his or her idiosyncracies.

In *The Kings Are Already Here* (2003), a TEENAGE girl training to be a ballerina and a teenage boy who is striving to become a chess champion meet. Their friendship evolves as the two decide what their real priorities are. Again, F.'s flair for writing about smart teens in interesting situations is demonstrated through these characters. The wonderful European locales add a unique flavor to the story. F. currently lives in Baltimore, Maryland, with her husband.

AWARDS: *My Heartbeat* was named a 2003 Michael L. PRINTZ Honor Book. It was also included on the *Booklist* Editor's Choice "Top of the List," the *School Library Journal* Best Books of 2002 list, the

ALA 2003 Best Books for Young Adults list, and was selected as one of the *Publishers Weekly* Best Children's Books of 2002.

FURTHER WORKS: *When I Was Older,* 2000.

BIBLIOGRAPHY: http://www.mindspring.com/~rhoda garret/freymannweyr.html; E-mail interview.

KIMBERLY L. PAONE

FRIEDMAN, Myra
Author, b. 1940 (?), St. Louis, Missouri

In addition to articles on music, arts, and contemporary cultural and social movements, F. wrote *Buried Alive: The Biography of Janis Joplin* (1973). F. studied music at Northwestern University, worked with Decca Records and wrote for five years at Columbia Records. In 1968, she began working for Janis Joplin's manager Albert Grossman, and was Joplin's publicist until the singer's death in October 1970.

The close friendship that developed between Joplin and F. provided the author with a great deal of exclusive material. Joplin hoped F. would write a profile on her and wished for it to be written with complete honesty and candidness. F. complied with this request and wrote an intensely personal BIOGRAPHY providing insight into Joplin's genius and the chaotic fame of the legendary queen of rock.

Critics of *Buried Alive* have hailed the book as both electrifying and self-indulgently autobiographical; strong opinions and reactions to the biography were plentiful. *Buried Alive* was revised and republished in 1992 with an added foreword and epilogue by the author.

AWARDS: *Buried Alive: The Biography of Janis Joplin*: ALA Best Books for Young Adults, 1973; YALSA Best of the Best 1960–1974.

BIBLIOGRAPHY: Friedman, Myra, *Buried Alive, The Biography of Janis Joplin,* 1973; *Entertainment Weekly* # 140, Oct. 16, 1992; *Notes,* vol. 51 (1) Sept. 1994.

AVIVA R ROSEMAN

FRIESEN, Gayle
Author, b. 18 September 1960, Chilliwack, British Columbia

F. grew up reading *Little Women* and *Anne of Green Gables* and loved to write, but she never thought that it was a realistic career path. Convinced that she would come across something that would inspire her career, F. eventually got a degree in English literature from the University of British Columbia but still did not feel as though she had found her true passion. It was only after having two children, working various jobs, and returning to school that she realized that she could, in fact, become a writer.

While traveling home one weekend with her daughter, F. came up with the idea for her first novel, *Janey's Girl* (1998). F. believed that the character of Janey came from "deciding that my story wasn't very interesting, and so wouldn't it be interesting if . . ." Letting the story emerge with no specifics, F. wrote a novel about a mother returning to her hometown with her daughter and the family secrets that would be revealed.

Interested in YA literature, thanks in part to her children, F.'s next novel is told in the voice of a young boy. *Men of Stone* (2000) is a story of oppression, presented historically through the character of Aunt Frieda and her experiences in Stalin's Russia. The story is told through young Ben's voice and includes troubles with a school bully.

F.'s imperfect characters and honest dialogue are examples of her free form, unplanned writing style; F. simply lets the story go where it feels most natural, allowing it to surprise even her.

AWARDS: CLA Young Adult Book Award, Canadian Library Association (1999) both for *Janey's Girl;* ALA Best Books for Young Adults list, 2000.

FURTHER WORKS: *Losing Forever,* 2002; *The Isabel Factor,* 2005.

BIBLIOGRAPHY: *Contemporary Authors,* online, 2000; *Something About the Author,* vol. 109, 2000.

MEGAN PEARLMAN

FRIESNER, Esther
Author, b. 16 July 1951, New York City

F. is a FANTASY writer who often combines humor with fantasy. She is known for her POETRY, SHORT STORIES, novels, and articles on humorous fantasy and SCIENCE FICTION writing. F. sold her first short story to *Isaac Asimov's Science Fiction Magazine,* the first publication to give her encouraging rejection slips.

F.'s contemporary fantasy novel *New York by Knight* (1986) was cited by Voice of Youth Advocates on their Best Science Fiction/Fantasy Titles list. F.'s Gnome Man's Land trilogy features a high-school

student from a single-parent home as its main character. In these three books, *Gnome Man's Land* (1991), *Harpy High* (1991), and *Unicorn U* (1992), Tim faces "little people" and monsters, as well as his own adolescent problems. This trilogy also features characters drawn from literature, myths, and FAIRY TALES.

F. edited several irreverent fantasy short story collections, including *Alien Pregnant by Elvis* (1994). F. has become well known for the SERIES of CHICKS books she edited which includes *Chicks in Chainmail* (1995), *Chicks N Chained Males* (1999), and *Did You Say Chicks?!* (2002). F.'s collection of twelve short stories *Death and the Librarian and Other Stories* (2002) includes all of her Nebula Award winners and finalists. This collection includes humorous stories like "How to Make Unicorn Pie" and "Jesus at the Bat," as well as the somber post-9/11 story "Ilion."

F. is a member of the Science Fiction Writers of America (SFWA), and makes appearances at science fiction conventions across the country.

AWARDS: 1995 Nebula Award for Best Short Story, "Death and the Librarian;" 1996 Nebula Award for Best Short Story, "A Birth Day;" Romantic Times Award for Best New Fantasy Writer (1986).

SELECT FURTHER WORKS: Chronicles of the Twelve Kingdoms series; Demons series; Majyk trilogy.

BIBLIOGRAPHY: *Contemporary Authors,* online, 2000; *Something about the Author,* vol. 71, 1993.

ANDREA LIPINSKI

FROST, Helen
Author, b. 1949, South Dakota

As a child, F. remembers learning to draw and write on the seemingly endless supply of "shiny" paper her parents kept available. As she became aware of both the physical act of making words into letters and the inventive nature of the mind, especially as revealed through her father's stories, it is only natural that writing and the teaching of writing formed the fabric of F.'s career. A writer of fiction, POETRY, plays and INFORMATIONAL books, F. is perhaps best known for her poetry writing, which has been ongoing for more than thirty years. Having lived in Scotland, Alaska, Massachusetts, Oregon, California, and Indiana, her national and international connections are evident in the material she writes. She won the Women Poets Competition with a book of poetry entitled *Skin of a Fish, Bones of a Bird* (1993). This title contains poetry on a variety of topics that reflects the culture of the small Athabaskan community of Telida, where she taught. FAMILIES, love relationships, survival, the intersections of the natural world and humanity, the impact of contemporary civilization all bring us in touch with individuals and a society about which not much is written. Both universal themes and the unique culture of everyday life are shared from F.'s perspective.

Her advice to young writers, "Stay open—to what you read, to what you and those around you are thinking, dreaming, feeling, to all the possibilities of life and language," reflects the blend of reality and possibilities within F.'s recent book, *Keesha's House* (2003). This novel is told through sestinas and sonnets and realistically reflects the dreams and feelings as well as life's possibilities for seven young people. F.'s first YA novel, *Keesha's House* was one of four books to receive the highly regarded PRINTZ AWARD Honor Book recognition in 2004. Given to books that exemplify literary excellence in young adult literature, this novel uniquely uses a poetic format to weave the stories of seven TEENS into a novel. Each of these teens faces a problem—pregnancy, addiction, homosexuality, abuse, delinquency, and abandonment. Each, however, reaches out to support others who have come to this safe haven, a house owned by a man who realizes the need at times for a place of refuge. Through alternating voices, the reader becomes privileged to understand the formation of this community following the death of Keesha's brother. Frost creatively combines the romance of sonnets and sestinas with the often stark reality of the issues in the character's lives, thus giving voice to these young people through the poetic form. Not only do the characters and events come alive, but the significance of poetry is vivid as a communication form that combines both affective and cognitive expressive modes. The reader discovers, to use the words of Ralston (2003), "Characters drawn with aching realism, who speak poetry in ordinary words and make connections."

Another book in which poetry is the format for creating a novel is *Spinning through the Universe: A Novel in Poems from Room 214* (2004). The setting, in a fifth-grade classroom, is compelling for an audience younger than that of *Keesha's House*. Additionally, F. has written a resource for teachers of writing, *When I Whisper, Nobody Listens: Helping Young People Write about Difficult Issues* (2001). Based on her work in schools and youth-serving organizations, this book had its roots in an anthology of student writing and a play entitled "Why Darkness Seems So Light."

With an interest in history, F. adds to her list of published books: *Russian Immigrants, 1860–1915* (2002) and *German Immigrants, 1820–1920* (2001). Both of these titles are part of a SERIES of books on immigration, *Coming to America*. Also, to her credit, are earlier published books for very young readers that focus on various countries, the food pyramid, and mechanical concepts of pulleys and levers.

In addition to her writing and work with the Fort Wayne Dance Collective in an interdisciplinary artistic violence prevention program, F. often gives poetry readings and speaks at conferences. She also teaches writing in schools and provides in-service programs for teachers. She is married and has two sons.

AWARDS: Printz Honor 2004 and ALA Best Books for Young Adults 2004 for *Keesha's House;* Women Poets Winner for *Skin of a Fish, Bones of a Bird,* 1993.

FURTHER WORKS: *A Look at Canada,* 2002; *A Look at France,* 2002; *A Look at Russia,* 2002; *A Look at Vietnam,* 2005; *A Look at Egypt,* all part of Our World Series.

BIBLIOGRAPHY: Frost, H. *When I Whisper, Nobody Listens: Helping Young People Write About Difficult Issues,* Heinemann, 2001; *Keesha's House, Journal of Adolescent and Adult Literacy* November 2002, vol. 46(3), p. 275; *Kirkus Reviews* 3/15/2003, 71(6), p. 467; Ralston, J., *Keesha's House,* Oct. 2003, *School Library Journal* 49(10), p. 99; Roback, D., Brown, J., Bean, J., Zaleski, J., *Publishers Weekly,* 4/21/2003, vol. 250 (6), p. 63; Rochman, H., *Keesha's House, Booklist,* 3/1/2003, vol. 99(13), p. 1192; Rochman, H. "Top 10 Youth First Novels" *Booklist,* 11/15/2003, Vol. 100 (6), p. 610; Jones, T., Toth, L., Charnizon, M., Grobarek, D., Larkins, J., Reynolds, A., *Keesha's House, School Library Journal,* March 2003, vol 49(3), p. J232; http://home.att.net/~frost-thompson/; http://capa.conncoll.edu/frost.sfbb

JANELLE MATHIS

G

GAIMAN, Neil

Author, b. 10 November 1960, Portchester, England

For more than two decades, the creative genius of G. has been widely spotlighted through *The Sandman,* his GRAPHIC NOVEL series from DC Comics.

Vastly popular, the saga began with the 1989 publication of *Preludes and Nocturnes,* the first monthly installment of G.'s mature-reader comic. When a gathering of individuals sought to capture Death, but instead freed the King of Dreams, G.'s otherworldly journey through hell and back was launched. Literally millions of G.'s loyalists have taken the journey with him.

"What do you need to know to enjoy the SERIES?" G. asks on his website, www.neilgaiman.com. "Only that there are seven brothers and sisters that have been since the beginning of time, the Endless. They are Destiny, Death, Dream, Desire, Despair, Delirium who was once Delight, and Destruction, the one who turned his back on his duties."

He simplifies the complexities with precision, but his followers would not dare imagine it. It is the intricate, intellectually gripping storylines that turned G. into a bankable writing entity. His readers mourned when he ended the series in 1996, after concluding installment #75. Happily, he revived the series in September 2003 with *Endless Nights,* and readers rejoiced.

The figure Death, described by amazon.com reviewer Jim Pascoe as "a perky, overly cheery, cute goth girl" is among G.'s most popular characterizations. The older sister of Dream, Death is transformed visually, evolving with each shift in the talent for illustration G. tapped for series installments. According to Sandman fans, however, the voice, which is the character's essence, generally remains the same.

As the series has matured, it has gathered a staunchly devoted following, both in the U.S. and abroad. Many believe G. and *The Sandman* single-handedly put graphic novels on library shelves and reading lists of YOUNG ADULTS, validating it as a legitimate literary format.

Endless Nights (2003), a more recent addition, marks the return of *The Sandman* with stories devoted to "The Endless"—one tale from each of the seven immortal siblings (Destiny, Death, Dream, Desire, Despair, Delirium, and Destruction). G. apparently hit this mark, for *Booklist* said *Endless Nights* was, "everything his fans could have hoped for."

Coraline (2002) has a more personal point of inspiration. "I was looking for books with cool, smart 4-year-old girls," Gaiman told the *St. Louis Dispatch,* "and I didn't find any. I decided that I'd write some. And that's where *Wolves,* and to some extent where *Coraline* came from. Two powerful, cool, sensible girls that I could give to my girls and give to other girls." *The Wolves in the Walls* (2003), a graphic novella for the nine-to-twelve-year-old audience may only marginally appeal to YA, but *Coraline,* illustrated by Dave McKean of *Sandman* fame, has fascinated both older TEENAGERS and adults.

In both books, the distracted parent figures remind G. of himself. "I'm always the one that would be writing in my office, typing with my kids coming up and saying, 'Why don't you play with us instead of writing.' 'Because if I don't write we don't eat so . . . go do something . . . learn to tap dance!'"

What is behind the creations of an imaginative author capable of such expansive storytelling? According to G., it was the personal freedom of his childhood. Raised the first of three children in Sussex, he was the self-proclaimed "weird" son of a vitamin company owner and a pharmacist. FANTASY transported young G. into the world of the literary masters. At seven, he obsessively alphabetized his books, fretting over the dual surname of writers like Roger Lancelyn Green—should his work fall in the ranks of the "L" or the "G." As a ten-year-old, G. began to fantasize about not just reading great writers, but joining their ranks and writing his own fiction. He pictured kidnapping G. K. Chesterton and Geoffrey Chaucer and their contemporaries just to tell the stories he imagined. "I plotted this 12-volume giant epic about these people going off to collect rocks from all over the universe," he says on his website, "in order to justify my daydreams of *creating* stories."

Today, G. needs no justification for his writing; his internationally acclaimed work stands on its own. He, his wife Mary, and their three children have made their home in the U.S.—a gothic Minneapolis house with "wolves in the walls"—since 1992. Nestled in suburbia, except when he's touring to promote his books, G. enjoys being able to avoid the public spotlight. "I don't particularly like being a personality," he told CNN. "I like being about the story I'm telling, I like being about the books."

SELECT AWARDS: Eagle Award: Best Graphic Novel, *Violent Cases* (1988), Best Writer of American Comics (1990); 1990 and 1991 Harvey Award, Best Writer and Best Continuing Series; 1991 World Fantasy Award, Best Short Story; 1993 Austrian Prix Vienne, Best Writer; 1993 Diamond Distributors "Gem" Award; 1994 International Horror Critics' Guild Award, *Angels and Visitations;* 1996 GLAAD Award, Best Comic; 1997 Lucca Best Writer Prize; 1997 Defender of Liberty Award; 1998 Macmillan Silver PEN Award (UK), *Smoke and Mirrors: Short Fictions and Illusions;* 2002 Nebula Award, *American Gods;* 1999 Mythopoeic Award, *Stardust;* Bram Stoker Award: Best Illustrated, *The Dream Hunters* (1999), Best Novel, *American Gods* (2002), Best Work for Younger Readers, *Coraline* (2003); Hugo Award: Best Science Fiction/Fantasy Novel, *American Gods*

(2002), Best Novella, *Coraline* (2003). ALA Best Books for Young Adults list, *Stardust,* 2000 list, *Coraline,* 2003 list.

SELECT FURTHER WORKS: *Don't Panic: The Official Hitch-hiker's Guide to the Galaxy Companion,* 1988; *Good Omens: The Nice And Accurate Prophecies Of Agnes Nutter, Witch,* 1990; *Angels and Visitations,* 1993; *The Sandman Book of Dreams,* 1996; *Neverwhere,* 1997; *The Day I Swapped My Dad for Two Goldfish,* 1997; *Day of the Dead,* 1998; *Smoke and Mirrors,* 1998; *Stardust,* 1999; *The Sandman Companion,* 1999; *The Quotable Sandman,* 2000; *American Gods,* 2001; *Murder Mysteries,* 2001; *A Walking Tour of the Shambles* (with Gene Wolfe), 2002; *Adventures in the Dreamtrade,* 2002; *Anansi Boys,* 2005; *Mirrormask,* 2005.

BIBLIOGRAPHY: CNN Feature, I Enjoy Not Being Famous, by Porter Anderson, July 30, 2001; www.neil gaiman.com; *St. Louis Post Dispatch,* November 18, 2003; *The Book Report* interview, June 29, 2001.

KELLY MILNER HALLS

GAINES, Ernest J.
Author, educator, b. 15 January 1933, River Lake Plantation, Pointe Coupée Parish, Louisiana

G.'s stories are often set in the South, in Louisiana where he grew up and worked. In a National Endowment for the Humanities (NEH) interview, G. states, "I can still write about [the South] because I left something there, you see. I left a place I could love. I left people there that I loved." That love is evident in his stories where he writes about the black culture and the rich storytelling traditions of rural Louisiana.

G. was born at River Lake Plantation, near New Roads, Pointe Coupee Parish. He was raised primarily by an aunt after his parents left for California during World War II. He worked in the cotton fields on a plantation when he was nine. He left Louisiana and the place he loved when he was fifteen. He joined his parents in California so that he could get the education his family wanted him to receive.

G. attended San Francisco State University and later earned a writing fellowship to Stanford University. He published his first short story in 1956.

The Autobiography of Miss Jane Pittman (1971), although often thought of as nonfiction, is indeed a work of fiction. G. did not interview any old women of the South, but absorbed a great deal through conversations with old people of Louisiana, reading slave narratives and interviews with slaves, BIOGRAPHIES, and histories. Once he took all that in, he let his imagination take over and the book flowed from there. G.'s books often have historical portions and come across as being very real, but all his works are fiction that carry the voice of his characters so genuinely. *Miss Jane Pittman* brings the reader the experiences of a woman who lived 110 years, through slavery and the CIVIL RIGHTS MOVEMENT, and can share those experiences vividly as a true storytelling master.

In the award-winning *A Lesson before Dying* (1993), G. takes the reader on an exploration of racial struggles, prejudices, racial identity, injustice, pride, growth, and strength. Grant Wiggins, a college-educated black man who feels trapped by societal norms and expectations, finds his only job is teaching at a small plantation church school. He wants to leave Louisiana and escape his career, his resentment, and the racial injustice of the South. But before he leaves, Miss Emma, the grandmother of a convicted man sentenced to die, asks him to teach her grandson, Jefferson, about pride, so he can die like a man. Jefferson, wrongly convicted of a murder, is guilty of being an illiterate black man in the wrong place at the wrong time in rural Louisiana. As these two men explore their lives and reflect on the situations and experiences, there is more than one lesson to be learned before dying.

G.'s characters and storytelling skill make his novels enjoyable and real. They expand one's knowledge by providing meaning, perspective, and truth to the history and facts that already exist.

AWARDS: Wallace Stegner fellow (1957), Joseph Henry Jackson Literary Award (1959), National Endowment for the Arts grant (1967), Guggenheim fellow (1971), Black Academy of Arts and Letters Award (1972), American Academy and Institute of Arts and Letters Award (1987), MacArthur Foundation fellow (1993), Langston Hughes Award (1994), National Book Critics Circle Award (1994), National Humanities Medal (2000), *The Autobiography of Miss Jane Pittman*, BBYA (1971), *Still Alive,* The Best of the Best (1960–1974), Here We Go Again: 25 Years of Best Books (1967–1992), *Gathering of Old Men*, BBYA (1983), *A Lesson Before Dying*, BBYA (1994) and National Book Critics' Circle Award for Fiction.

FURTHER WORKS: *Catherine Carmier,* 1964; *Of Love and Dust,* 1967; *Bloodline,* 1968; *A Long Day in November,* 1971; *In My Father's House,* 1978; *A Gathering of Old Men,* 1984; *Mozart and Leadbelly,* 2005.

BIBLIOGRAPHY: NEH Interview. "'I heard the voices . . . of my Louisiana people': A conversation with Ernest Gaines," *Humanities,* (July/August 1998); *Contemporary Authors New Revision Series,* vol. 75; *Something about the Author,* vol. 86; *Best Books for Young Adults* (2000); www.louisiana.edu/Academic/ LiberalArts/ENGL/Creative/Gaines.htm.

TINA HERTEL

GALLO, Donald R.
Author, b. 1 June 1938, Paterson, New Jersey

There are certain advocates in the world of YOUNG ADULT LITERATURE who are so passionate that they earn for themselves an outstanding place in the profession. Educator and anthologist G. is one such personality.

Dubbed the "godfather of the young adult SHORT STORY," by author and Brigham Young University professor Chris CROWE, G. remembers his teen years as being virtually book-free. Similar to Chris CRUTCHER and Jerry SPINELLI, his recreational reading was limited to light, relevant texts about Scouting or athletics.

G.'s parents were devout in their study of the Bible and read various newspapers, but never had the opportunity to enjoy a formal education. His mother, a telephone operator, entered into full-time employment when she dropped out of the tenth grade. His father, a laborer at Borden's Pioneer Ice Cream division, took a full-time job at thirteen to support his mother after his father passed away.

G. fondly remembers walking his father home from work on the ice cream loading dock, his bike in one hand, a Creamsicle in the other. He remembers his mother's over-protective supervision when it came to overnight campouts or wandering the neighborhood. He credits both strong relationships with making him the confident professional we see today.

Witnessing his parents' determined work ethic also convinced G. there was lifelong value in higher education. So he remained in school, even if he was slow to adopt adventurous reading or study habits. "I did what I had to, and I earned decent grades," Gallo says, "except for Latin, which I'd prefer not to discuss."

Even so, reading failed to set fire to G.'s imagination. English teachers saw potential in the bright student, but even their efforts were largely unfruitful. One of his teachers, Mr. Friedman, thought Hemingway's *The Old Man and the Sea* might touch G.'s nautical interests. But he found it as dull as any classroom assignment he'd been required to complete.

High-school athletics influenced G.'s early development, as did his continuous participation in the Boy Scouts of America. Quick and agile, he became one of East Side High's most valuable baseball and football players. He also worked hard to earn his Eagle Scout ranking, learning leadership qualities along the way.

Young G. sang in the Central Reformed Church choir in high school and even delivered guest sermons while in college. So successful were his orations that he was sent to Nebraska during his junior year to serve as assistant minister on the Omaha Indian Reservation.

Just months before graduating from Oberlin College, G. had a professional epiphany. After years of thinking he'd spend his life in the ministry, he became disenchanted with organized religion and decided to teach literature instead. After what he has called a "horrendous student teaching internship" and a stint in graduate school at Syracuse University, G. settled into "saving souls through literature instead of through Biblical teachings." G.'s choice was fruitful; his work as a teacher continued until 1997 when he retired to write and edit full time.

Even before retirement, G. had discovered his next calling—the compilation of exceptional YA short story anthologies. Though he acknowledged the importance of teaching a short-story unit in high-school and college literature classes, he could not deny there was a gap in teaching materials: very few stories about TEENS. G. set out to correct that.

After contacting authors he'd met at educational conferences, Gallo compiled and published *Sixteen* (1984), his first YA anthology. A dozen anthologies and many other book projects later, G. has become a prominent voice in the world of YA literature, speaking regularly at conferences and education meetings.

G. is a former President of the Assembly on Literature for Adolescents of the National Council of Teachers of English (ALAN), a former vice-chair of the Conference on English Education, a trustee of the NCTE Research Foundation, a member of the NCTE Editorial Board, and an editor of the *Connecticut English Journal*. He is an adjunct instructor of education at Cleveland State University and lives with his wife

C.J.—an English teacher—in the Cleveland suburbs. He has a son, Brian, and a stepdaughter Chris.

AWARDS: School Library Journal Best Book of the Year, 1984; American Bookseller Pick of the Lists, 1986; A Junior Library Guild Selection, 1992; VOYA Best Anthology/Collection of 1993; A Junior Library Guild Selection, 2003; Friend of OCTELA Award 2003; ALA Best Books for YA list for *No Easy Answers: Short Stories about Teenagers Making Tough Choices* (1998 list); *On the Fringe* (2002 list).

FURTHER WORKS: *Heard Word*, 1982; *Gaggle II*, 1981; *Living with Adolescent Literature*, 1980; *Poetry: Reading, Writing and Analyzing It*, 1979; *Connecticut English Journal: A Gaggle of Gimmicks*, 1978; *Sixteen: Short Stories by Outstanding Writers for Young Adults*, 1984; *Books for you: a booklist for senior high students*, 1985; *Visions: Short Stories by Outstanding Writers for Young Adults*, 1987; *Connections: Short Stories by Outstanding Writers for Young Adults*, 1989; *Presenting Richard Peck*, 1989; *Speaking for Ourselves*, 1990; *Center Stage*, 1990; *Author's Insights*, 1992; *Short Circuits: Thirteen Shocking Stories by Outstanding Writers for Young Adults*, 1992; *Join In: Multiethnic Short Stories by Outstanding Writers for Young Adults*, 1993; *Speaking for Ourselves, Too*, 1993; *Within Reach*, 1993; *Ultimate Sports: Short Stories by Outstanding Writers for Young Adults*, 1995; *From Hinton to Hamlet*, 1996; *No Easy Answers: Short Stories About Teenagers Making Tough Choices*, 1997; *Time Capsule: Short Stories About Teenagers Throughout the Twentieth Century*, 1999; *On the Fringe*, 2001; *Destination Unexpected*, 2003

BIBLIOGRAPHY: Greenwood Publishing interview; E-mail interviews; *Don Gallo, The Godfather of YA Short Stories* by Chris Crowe *English Journal;* Random House Spotlight on Don Gallo; OCTELA Spring Newsletter 2003.

KELLY MILNER HALLS

GALLOWAY, Priscilla
Author, educator, b. 22 July 1930, Montreal, Canada

G. is a teacher, writer, and grandmother. In addition to her books for YA, she has been honored for her career in education.

While still in high school, G. wrote a newspaper column and participated in a mentoring program that fed her dream of becoming a journalist. While in college in CANADA, she wrote for the *Queen's Journal*. There was no journalism program available at Queen's University, so she focused on English Language and Literature. After completing her studies in three years, she and her husband moved to northern Quebec, where she became a substitute teacher and had two children while working toward her education credentials. She faced discrimination as a young mother in the workforce, but eventually found teaching jobs in Toronto and then North York, where she worked until retirement. Although she had postponed her goal to be a writer, she continued to compose articles and POETRY.

Several changes occurred about midway through her teaching career: G. decided to pursue a Ph.D. at the University of Toronto, her first marriage began to dissolve, and she began writing seriously again. Under the wing of her dissertation advisor, G. began writing children's stories. While teaching a series of writing workshops, she developed the stories that became *Truly Grim Tales.* A collection of fractured FAIRY TALES, these stories for young adults offer a horrific perspective on familiar characters.

Her love of Greek MYTHOLOGY led her to re-tell several stories from the *Odyssey* and mythology for young readers. She writes with a fresh point about Daedalus and his son, Icarus, as well as strong female characters such as Atalanta. Another of her projects is a re-telling of Canadian author L. M. Montgomery's stories, *Emily of New Moon* in an adaptation for younger readers. She has written and translated children's books and written a nonfiction book for adults.

AWARDS: G.'s books have been finalists for the Canadian Library Association YA Book of the Year, the Mr. Christie's Award, and the Red Cedar Book Award; the Ontario Council of Teachers of English has named her Teacher of the Year; YALSA Best Book for Young Adults, 1996, *Truly Grimm Tales;* Bologna Ragazzi Award for YA non-fiction, *Too Young to Fight.*

FURTHER WORKS: *Aleta and the Queen: A tale of Ancient Greece,* 1995; *Atalanta: The Fastest Runner in the World,* 1995; *Courtesan's Daughter,* 2002; *Daedalus and the Minotaur,* 1997; *Snake Dreamer,* 1998; *Too Young to Fight: Memories from Our Youth during World War II,* 2000; *The Courtesan's Daughter,* 2002.

BIBLIOGRAPHY: *Contemporary Authors Online,* 2001; Galloway, Priscilla. *Priscilla Galloway.* http://www .priscilla.galloway.net *Something about the Author,* 1991: v. 66, pp. 83–5; *Resource Links,* August 1997 v2 i6 p. 247–50.

JENNIFER STILL

GANTOS, Jack
Author, b. 2 July, 1951, Mount Pleasant, Pennsylvania

For many years, G. has received acclaim as the author of the popular Rotten Ralph SERIES of PICTURE BOOKS. In the 1990s, G. moved into the field of YA literature with a series of novels about his own childhood. *Heads or Tails: Stories from a Sixth Grade* (1994) introduced readers to Jack and his rather unusual ADVENTURES with his parents and siblings. Starred reviews in *School Library Journal* and *Publishers Weekly* brought G. to the attention of older readers for the first time.

Since G. grew up with a father in the Navy, the family moved frequently. The one thing G. notes as a constant in his life was his journal, a practice he took up early in life and continues today. Those journals became an important source of material for the Jack books. Following the success of *Heads or Tails,* G. published a second book about Jack and his family of reprobates: *Jack's New Power: Stories from a Caribbean Year* (1995). This second book garnered rave reviews. *Jack's Black Book* (1997) was named to the New York Public Library's Books for the Teen Age in 1998. The following year, G. presented readers with a fourth Jack book, *Jack on the Tracks: Four Seasons of Fifth Grade* (1999). G. continued the Jack series with a fifth book *Jack Adrift: Fourth Grade Without a Clue.*

G.'s first truly YA novel, *Desire Lines* (1997), explores what happens when a young man exposes one of his classmate's secrets. The novel faced some challenges due to the tough issues G. tackles in the story. After *Desire Lines,* G. began another series of books. This series focused on the life of a young boy with A.D.D. named Joey Pigza. In *Joy Pigza Swallowed the Key* (1998), G. presents the inner turmoil of a young man who is unable to control many of his impulses even though he knows his behavior will result in trouble. Joey's saga continued in *Joey Pigza Loses Control* (2000), a book that won G. a Newbery Honor Medal. The trilogy that tells Joey's story concluded with *What Would Joey Do?* (2004). According to G., the first story in the Joey series tells of Joey's life with his mother. Part two explores Joey's life as he goes to spend a summer with his father. In the final installment, Joey finally has to learn to stand on his own and live his own life. G. recorded the audiobook versions of the Joey Pigza books, becoming one of the few authors to narrate his own writing.

In 2002, G. published a slice-of-life AUTOBIOGRAPHY entitled *A Hole in my Life* (2002) that told of his senior year living in a welfare hotel in Florida. His parents had moved to Puerto Rico, but G. wanted to stay behind and complete his senior year of high school. After graduation, G. agreed to help smuggle a load of hashish from the Virgin Islands to New York. G. was apprehended and sentenced to six years in a federal prison. Following an early release, G. went on to study writing at Emerson College. *A Hole in my Life* earned rave reviews and more than its share of awards.

Prior to entering the children's book field, G. was a Professor of Creative Writing and Literature at Emerson College. PRINTZ Honor Medalist Chris Lynch was one of G.'s students. G. also developed a course in writing picture story books while on the faculty of Emerson. Since leaving Emerson, G. has taught as part of the faculty of the MFA program at Vermont College. His knowledge of the field of children's and YA books fuels not only his own writing but the works of others.

AWARDS: *Heads or Tails,* 1994, starred review in School Library Journal and Publishers Weekly; *Jack's New Power,* 1995, starred review in SLJ; *Jack's Black Book,* 1997, NYPL Books for the Teen Age, 1998; *Joey Pigza Swallowed the Key:* ALA Notable Book, 1998, California Young Readers Medal, 2002; Newbery Honor Medal, *Joey Pigza Loses Control,* 2000; *A Hole in my Life, 2002*: Printz Honor Medal, Sibert Honor Medal, BBYA List by YALSA of ALA, New York Public Library's Books for the Teen Age.

BIBLIOGRAPHY: *Contemporary Authors,* New Revision Service, vol. 15, 1985; www.authors4teens.com

TERI S. LESESNE

GARDEN, Nancy
Author, b. 15 May 1938, Boston, Massachusetts

With an Italian father in the American Red Cross and a German mother, G. moved frequently as a child; she remembers moving to as many as five different cities in one year. G. was an only child born into a reading and storytelling family; her father told stories about pranks he played as a child and her mother told made-up household mysteries about a mouse trapped in a soup bowl. Her parents encouraged her to use her imagination; they frequently read books aloud to her

from early days. She naturally developed a love for reading; her favorites were Beatrix Potter's books, Robert Lawson's *Rabbit Hill,* Rudyard Kipling's Jungle books, Hugh Lofting's Doctor Doolittle books, Anna Seward's *Black Beauty,* and A. A. Milne's poems and Winnie-the-Pooh books. During her teenage years, she enjoyed the writings of Ernest Hemingway, John Dos Passos, and Thomas Wolfe. G.'s childhood hobbies developed into an adult passion for writing. G. has broken new ground and taken new roads in YOUNG ADULT literature.

G. attended Columbia University, received a BFA from the School of Dramatic Arts in 1961 and a Master's Degree from Teachers College in 1962. She began working at *Scholastic Magazines* as an assistant editor, became an associate editor, and later moved to Houghton Mifflin as an editor. G. also became a teacher of writing, a freelance writer, and a book reviewer. She worked in the theater as an actress and lighting designer. Through all of these experiences, she continued to sharpen her writing skills. While she was an actress, she wrote autobiographies of each character part she played.

G. is best known for her young adult novels dealing with the controversial topic of adolescent homosexuality. Unlike other authors who categorize homosexuality as morally wrong, G. integrates adolescent homosexuality into her storytelling in peaceful and acceptable ways. In doing so, she holds the attention of both homosexuals and heterosexuals and eases the heartache, tension and embarrassment among the two groups. She hopes that her novels can ultimately be instrumental in reducing the high incidence of suicide among adolescent homosexuals.

G. is successful as a writer of both fiction and nonfiction. Her realistic fiction for young adults includes *The Loners* (1972), *Annie on My Mind* (1982), *Peace, O River* (1986), *Lark in the Morning* (1991), *The Year They Burned the Books* (1999), *Dove and Sword* (1995), *Good Moon Rising* (1996), and *Meeting Melanie* (2003). Her best-known and most controversial work, *Annie on My Mind,* is a story of two TEENAGE girls, Annie and Liza, who meet while visiting a museum. They fall in love and eventually must come to terms with their homosexuality. When their relationship is discovered by school officials, it precipitates a crisis for Liza. The story is told in hindsight, when the girls are attending colleges on different coasts. The happy ending shows Liza and Annie reaffirming their feelings for each other. This book is beautifully written and is far above the typical problem novel.

G. also writes nonfiction books. *Berlin: City Split in Two* (1971) was her first published book. Later nonfiction included *Vampires* (1973), *Werewolves* (1973), *Witches* (1975), and *Devils and Demons* (1976).

G. began to write FANTASY with *Fours Crossing* (1981), the first of a SERIES of novels set in a modern-day New Hampshire town. Melissa, a thirteen-year-old whose mother has died, arrives to stay with her grandmother while her father travels. Melissa becomes friends with Jed, and the friends discover that something mysterious is preventing the spring season from coming to the town and gradually realize that a sinister hermit is the culprit. The friends decide to stop the culprit, but the hermit captures and imprisons them. Fortunately, they escape and save spring for the town. Three more books extend the Fours Crossing series: *Watersmeet* (1983), *The Door Between* (1987), and *The Joining* (1994).

G. deals with issues of homosexuality and homophobia in many of her novels. For this reason she and her books have often been the subject of controversy and banning. In an interview with a Teenreads.com editor, G. states that when she began to write, she used her characters as mouthpieces for her own personal views, instead of creating real, three-dimensional characters. She now avoids using characters to create a political statement; instead, she tells a good story about characters that seem real. Her readers empathize with characters that are harassed, brutalized or made to feel subhuman. Many teen readers also know what it is like to search for their identity as an individual and to deal with their emerging sexuality. G. strongly opposes attempts to censor and to ban books. It is a violation of the First Amendment, freedom of speech, which is a cornerstone of our democracy. G. believes that parents have the right to decide what their own children may or may not read, but they do not have the right to decide what other people's children may or may not read. G. also believes that it is important for teens and younger readers to have access to a wide range of ideas and viewpoints, so they can make up their own minds about their beliefs. Some adults, some very sincere ones, honestly disagree with that point of view.

The subject matter in G.'s novels is not restricted to homosexuality. She has also written about racial issues in *What Happened in Marston* (1971), inspired by the race riots of the 1960s and dramatized as an ABC Afterschool Special under the title "The Color of Friendship." Later G. wrote about drugs in *The Loners* (1972), and differing beliefs in various socioeconomic levels in *Peace, O River* (1986). G. did extensive research for her book, *Dove and Sword,* a historical novel about Joan of Arc's life.

G.'s ability to write well and discuss homosexuality in young adult novels has brought her much acclaim. She currently resides in Carlisle, Massachusetts, with her life partner.

AWARDS: 1982, *Annie on My Mind, Booklist* Reviewer's Choice, ALA Best Books; 1970–83, *Annie on My Mind,* ALA Best of the Best List; 1983–84, William Allen White Award Master List for *Four Crossings;* 2000, *Holly's Secret,* a Lambda Book Award finalist; 2000, Recipient of Robert B. Downs Intellectual Freedom Award; 2003, MARGARET A. EDWARDS AWARD for an author's lifetime achievement in writing for YA. One book was cited in the award announcement: *Annie on My Mind;* 2004 ALA Popular Paperbacks for *Dove and Sword.*

BIBLIOGRAPHY: Review of *Annie on My Mind, Bulletin of the Center for Children's Books.* December, 1982, p. 66; Chelton, Mary K., review of *Annie on My Mind, Voice of Youth Advocates,* August, 1982, p. 30; Dooley, Patricia, review of *Fours Crossing; School Library Journal,* May, 1981, p. 72; GARDEN, Nancy, essay in *Something about the Author Autobiography Series.* Vol. 8, Gale, 1989; Kaywell, Joan F. (2000); Nancy Garden (p. 59–99) in Ted Hipple (Ed.), Writers for Young Adults. Supplement 1. Cumulative Index. New York, Scribner's; Kerby, Mona. The Author Corner. http://www.carr.org/mac/garden/garden-.htm; Sutton, Roger D. review of *Annie on My Mind. School Library Journal,* August 1982, p. 125; Teenreads.com: Author Profile. Nancy Garden: http://www.teenreads.com/authors/garden-nancy.asp

KATELYN WOOTEN

GARLAND, Sherry
Author, b. 24 July 1948, McAllen, Texas

G. grew up in the Rio Grande Valley in Texas where she most enjoyed climbing trees and playing with farm animals. One of nine children born to tenant farmers, G. used her imagination to turn her surroundings into story settings. She credits her high-school teacher with inspiring her to write and to read literary classics. After finishing college, she raised a family and, fifteen years later, returned to writing, beginning with adult romance novels.

Just as G.'s home state of Texas would eventually provide characters and events for her books for young readers, so her work with Vietnamese families would become the focus of both INFORMATIONAL and fictional titles. As G. helped Vietnamese immigrant families adjust to life in Texas, she learned much about their culture. She extended her research to write *Vietnam: Rebuilding a Nation* (1990) to be used as a social studies text. The following titles sensitively share the awareness G. had developed about the people of Vietnam: *Song of the Buffalo Boy* (1992) is a novel about a young boy who is fathered by an American GI in Vietnam; *My Father's Boat* (1998) also shares a yearning for Vietnam by a father and son who are shrimping on the Gulf Coast amidst the father's stories about fishing in the South China Sea; *Why Ducks Sleep on One Leg* (1993) uses folklore to share Vietnamese culture and traditions.

Following the books about the Vietnamese culture, G. wrote *The Silent Storm* (1993) focusing on a hurricane that hit the coast of Texas in 1983. Research provided the detail needed for this story about a heroine faced with challenges in the midst of the storm. Additionally, *A Line in the Sand: The Alamo Diary of Lucinda Lawrence* (1998) shares the events leading up to th Battle of the Alamo, providing insight into Texas life in 1836.

AWARDS: *Song of the Buffalo Boy:* ALA Best Books for Young Adults, 1993; *Shadow of the Dragon:* ALA Best Books for Young Adults, 1994; *Indio:* ALA Best Books for Young Adults, 1996.

FURTHER WORKS: *Where the Cherry Trees Bloom,* 1991; *Best Horse on the Force,* 1991; *Indio,* 1995; *Cabin 102,* 1995; *The Last Rainmaker,* 1997; *Writing for Young Adults,* 1998; *Good Night Cowboy,* 1999; *Voices of the Alamo,* 2000; Valley of the Moon, 2001; *In the Shadow of the Alamo,* 2001; *Children of the Dragon: Selected Tales from Vietnam,* 2001.

BIBLIOGRAPHY: *Booklist,* April 1, 1992, p. 1438; November 15, 1993, p. 621 June 1, 1997, p. 1675; *Contemporary Authors Online.* The Gale Group, 2001; *Horn Book,* fall, 1993 p. 298, fall 1998, p. 292; *Somethng About the Author,* 114, 2000; *Voice of Youth Advocates,* October, 1992, p. 223; December, 1993, p. 290; December, 1995, p. 300.

JANELLE B. MATHIS

GEE, Maurice (Gough)
Author, b. 22 Aug. 1931, Whakatane, New Zealand

G. is not one important New Zealand writer but two. As well as being one of his country's best-read adult novelists, G. is also a respected writer for young adults. G. had been writing for twenty-five years, when a glimpse of Auckland's Mount Eden (a volcanic cone) inspired him to write his first novel for children. In *Under the Mountain* (1979), alien invaders work beneath Auckland's volcanic peaks to convert Earth's surface to a mud-like form in which they can settle. Eleven-year-old twins Rachel and Theo learn to use their latent psychic powers to defeat the aliens but not without cost. The impact of "real" settings and strong characters has made this powerful story a classic.

While writing a history of Nelson School, G. learned of a local arsonist and found the script of a patriotic pageant from World War I. The result was *The Fire-Raiser* (1986), a new phase of G.'s writing for young people: historical fiction. War fever grips a small town, already disturbed by mysterious fires. In hysterical mood, the townspeople burn a music-teacher's piano because it was made in Germany, while a socially disparate group of their children try to prove that a local farmer is the arsonist. *The Fire-Raiser* is notable for its accurate sketch of the national attitudes and class-consciousness of the times. The children are such strong characters that G. later wrote *Prowlers* (1987) about their adult lives.

The stream—so important in G.'s work, as "the stream one follows, with a new world opening up at every turning" flows through *The Champion* (1989), as well as G.'s masterwork, *The Fat Man* (1994). This dark study of bullying, revenge and guilt alarmed some critics but is now recognized as a brilliant account of a young boy's growing awareness of injustices in the adult world. Many features of G.'s FAMILY history are reworked in *The Fat Man.*

All of G.'s YOUNG ADULT novels combine strong characters (often female) and vivid storytelling with an awareness of evil and an acute understanding of human nature. After leaving his beloved Henderson (the setting of *The Fat Man* and *The Champion*) and living for many years in Nelson (the setting of *The Fire-Raiser*), G. now lives in Wellington. He is married with three children and two grandchildren.

SELECT AWARDS: 1983 NZ Government Printer Award: Children's Book of the Year, *The Halfmen of O;* 1986 Esther Glen Award, *Motherstone;* 1990 AIM Children's Book Awards, Second Prize and 1994 ALA Best Books for Young Adults, *The Champion;* 1995: Esther Glen Award, *The Fat Man;* 1995: AIM Children's Book Awards, Supreme Award, *The Fat Man;* 2002 Margaret Mahy Lecture Award.

FURTHER WORKS: *The World around the Corner,* 1980; *The Halfmen of O,* 1982; *The Priests of Ferris,* 1984; *Motherstone,* 1985; *The Champion,* 1989; *Orchard Street,* 1998.

BIBLIOGRAPHY: Fitzgibbon, Tom and Spiers, Barbara, *Beneath Southern Skies: New Zealand Children's Book Authors & Illustrators,* 1993. 67–9; Gee, Maurice, "Creeks and Kitchens," *The Inside Story: Children's Literature Foundation of New Zealand Year Book 2002,* 9–25.; Hill, David, *Introducing Maurice Gee,* 1981; Manhire, Bill, *Maurice Gee,* 1986; Nagelkerke, Bill, "Welcome Re-issues," *Magpies NZ Supplement* 12:4 (Sep 1997): 8; Nieuwenhuizen, Agnes, "Know the Author: Maurice Gee: Creek, kitchen and the art of language," *Magpies NZ Supplement* 12:1 (Mar 1997): 4–6.; Wattie, Nelson, "Gee, Maurice," *The Oxford Companion to New Zealand Literature,* Ed. Roger Robinson and Nelson Wattie, 1998, 197–9; http://library.christchurch.org.nz/Childrens/ChildrensAuthors/MauriceGee.asp/ http://www.bookcouncil.org.nz/writers/geemaurice.htm/

TREVOR AGNEW

GENREBLENDING: SCIENCE FICTION AND FANTASY CROSSOVERS

G. is a growing phenomenon in the publishing industry and the combinations of genres are endless. Some SCIENCE FICTION has strong elements similar to other genres, specifically FANTASY, Historical Fiction, MYSTERY and ROMANCE. Fantasy titles blend with the Mystery and Romance genres.

G. is not a trend limited to adult titles. YA examples can also be found in the categories of fantasy and mystery, fantasy and romance (in particular the ever-popular FAIRY TALE retellings), science fiction and historical fiction, science fiction and mystery and science fiction and romance. Noted critic and author David Hartwell has stated that "The Golden Age of Science Fiction Is Twelve," meaning that's the age when so many young readers first get hooked on science fiction. And when they do, it is frequently adult classics that draw them in: *The Lord of the Rings; Dune; 2001: A Space Odyssey;* the *Foundation Trilogy;* or MOVIE tie-ins like the numerous novels set in the *Star Wars* universe. But there is also growth in the field of publishing devoted to science fiction and especially fantasy titles for children and TEENS. The immense popularity of HARRY POTTER is generally regarded as being responsible for the publishing resurgence of these genres. All those who love the genres are really benefiting from this Harry fallout and proclaim "Blessings upon you, Harry Potter! And long may the influence of this young wizard-in-training continue!"

Why is there such interest in science fiction and fantasy? Because it's such a rich field. Since its inception, science fiction has included elements of other genres. *Frankenstein* is of course a HORROR classic, but Mary Wollstonecraft Shelley's creation is arguably the first science fiction novel. After all, her creature is the product of a scientific experiment.

Flash forward to contemporary times and the award-winning *Relic* and its sequel *Reliquary* by Douglas J. PRESTON and Lincoln Child. Those who love horror have got to love a book that features a monster in the bowels of the Museum of Natural History, a monster that surfaces periodically to scarf up museum visitors. Later, in the sequel, the monster stalks the tunnels of the New York City subway system. Again, this monster is a scientific creation, the product of major genetic changes.

Trees and Rivets

The question of whether a work is science fiction or fantasy continues to challenge readers trying to pigeonhole individual works. Some prefer Orson Scott CARD's definition that is popular with many fans. Look at the cover of the book. If it has trees on it, chances are good that it will be a work of fantasy. If it's got rivets, it's bound to be science fiction. But there are also fantasy and science fiction blends. The two most well known are the novels set on the planets of *Darkover* and *Pern.*

Darkover is the creation of Marion Zimmer BRADLEY. Before her death in 1999, she produced an incredible SERIES of novels set on this strange dark planet, a medieval-type world that can hold its own against the weapons and spaceships of Earth because of the strong extrasensory *laran* that some of its inhabitants possess. Time and again, the wielders of this *laran* (powerful mental ability) prove that the mind is mightier than the machine. The Darkover opus runs the gamut from *Hawkmistress!*, one of her earlier Darkover novels, to *The Fall of Neskaya,* one of her final Darkover novels, published shortly after her death. Fortunately, it was also the first in a trilogy that is being continued by her co-author Deborah J. Ross.

In *Hawkmistress!*, a teenage girl's *laran* shows that she has inherited the MacAran gift, the ability to communicate with and control animals. Because of this gift, she is able to flee an arranged marriage with a lecherous neighbor, only to wind up in the middle of a civil war in which her role is to fly huge Sentry Birds for the King.

The Fall of Neskaya, like *Hawkmistress!*, is set during the Age of Chaos, early in the planet's history. This time it's a young man who has *laran* so powerful he must be sent to one of Darkover's famous towers for training in how to use and control these incredible mental abilities—before they destroy him and those around him. Again he plays a pivotal role in a society on the brink of war. This may look like pure fantasy because of the sword-and-sorcery aspects of the society on this strange dark world, but it is science fiction too because this is a lost earth colony. Once earth rediscovers Darkover, its inhabitants have to contend with periodic efforts by the mother planet to regain control. Even the trappings of a modern interstellar civilization cannot stand against a society based on the powerful mental gifts possessed by the users of *laran.*

People who read science fiction and fantasy are familiar with Anne MCCAFFREY's *Pern.* This is a world where dragonriders bond with fire-breathing dragons, communicate telepathically with their bondmates, and teleport instantaneously anywhere on the planet to fight thread—long slender filaments that fall from the sky when the red star is near enough, filaments that consume anything living that they touch. They can be fought with fire, which is where the dragons and their riders come in. Again, this is a medieval-type world with a strong clan and guild structure. Some may believe that since there are dragons, these novels are fantasies—right? Wrong! Pern, like Darkover, is a lost Earth colony, and the dragons were created by the scientists among the original colonists. By using genetic manipulation on small indigenous fire lizards, they were able to create the dragons

that formed a biological line of defense against thread fall and its threat to all life forms on the planet.

One of the favorite subgenres of science fiction is time travel, and there are a lot of time-travel novels to choose from. But when you travel back in time to the early days of your own planet, you invite the blending of science fiction with historical fiction. Two favorites in this G. category involve time-travel organizations.

The first is Orson Scott Card's *Pastwatch.* The story is exactly like the title sounds. It involves a group of scientists who watch the past. They can observe, but not interface, with events in the past, until one scientist makes an incredible discovery. While standing on the sidelines watching an event in the past, the scientist realizes that the local person involved is watching back. This startling discovery, taken to the next step, leads to direct intervention. Because, if you can be seen by those who live in the past, then you can interact with them and even change the past. But to do so requires a sacrifice of monumental proportions: If you change the past, you will also change the future. Is there anything in the past worth sacrificing for the future? In this novel, the answer is yes—eradicating the institution of slavery. After careful study, the pivotal figure is identified—Christopher Columbus. The pivotal event is his discovery of America. The structure of the novel is fascinating. As the scientists study their subject, they develop a detailed picture of the life and times of Christopher Columbus, in addition to working up an analysis of when and how to intervene to stop slavery in its tracks.

Connie WILLIS won both the Hugo and the Nebula for *Doomsday Book,* a Time Travel novel that takes a researcher back to study the Middle Ages. Kivrin was supposed to appear in 1320, but the technician calibrating the drop was in the early stages of an influenza that would soon reach epidemic proportions in modern-day London. So Kivrin arrives in the wrong year, 1348, the year that the Black Death reached England. If that weren't bad enough, she arrives sick, fighting the same influenza that she left behind in London. Fortunately, she is rescued by a group of nobles who are themselves fleeing from the Black Death. The question is how can she ever get back home, since the research facility has been shut down because of the influenza. The result is a riveting look at life in the Middle Ages—the hardships, privations, dirt and disease that are a part of everyday life, and how this young researcher from the future will cope while she awaits rescue.

A Gumshoe by Any Other Name

Combining science fiction with the mystery genre can produce not only galactic policemen but also unique private eyes—human, alien, or mechanical. The best-known of the latter are probably Isaac Asimov's robot detective mysteries, featuring the robot hero named R. Daniel Olivaw and his human partner Lije Baley. Actually, Lije wasn't at all thrilled to be teamed up with a robot, at least not at first. However, he soon changes his mind, because now there's not one, but two first-rate brains (one organic and one positronic) to bring to bear on a case. When this detective duo appears on the scene, murderers don't stand a chance. The series begins with *The Caves of Steel.*

This next example is actually a triple genre blend, assuming humor is considered a separate category. This novel is a laugh-out-loud read as the characters solve the case. Jasper Fforde's *The Eyre Affair* is the first novel in a new series that features Special Operative Thursday Next, a literary detective who is in a battle to the death against Acheron Hades, evil genius and serial killer. It's bad enough that Acheron murders real people including police officers. But he takes it a step further and murders literary characters as well. Using a special prose portal device, he is able to enter works of fiction and murder literary characters. If he manages to enter the original edition of a work, the character he kills will disappear from every copy in the world. And horror of horrors, he's after Jane Eyre! Set in alternative England where time travel is a reality, and chock full of puns and literary allusions, this novel is a treat.

J. D. Robb is the pseudonym Nora Roberts uses for a police procedural series set in near future New York City. The first volume, *Naked in Death,* introduces supercop Eve Dallas and Roarke, the Irish billionaire businessman she meets when he is a suspect in a murder case she is investigating. After Eve proves that Roarke is not the one responsible for the bodies of naked call girls being found around the city, he becomes the love of her life—and vice versa. In subsequent volumes Eve continues to take out the bad guys while juggling the social commitments that come from being married to one of the wealthiest men on the planet, a man who has a background every bit as mysterious as her own.

Connie Willis won the Hugo again in 1999 for *To Say Nothing of the Dog; or, How We Found the Bish-op's Bird Stump at Last.* Ned Henry is a special operative for a time travel organization who has a next-to-impossible mission. He must travel back and forth in time looking for a hideous vase, the Bishop's Bird Stump, that disappeared the night Coventry Cathedral was bombed during World War II. Unfortunately, at the same time that he is busy with his pursuit of the Bishop's Bird Stump, the agency's newest member, Verity Kindle, is getting into serious trouble simply because she saves a cat from being drowned in the Victorian era and brings the animal home with her. This is a serious time travel breach. There are no cats left in the future, and now the timeline is beginning to slip as a result of this cat's being brought forward in time. Ned Henry must put his own case on hold and travel back to the Victorian era with her so that the cat can be returned to its own time, before it's too late. There's a lot of humor along the way, as well as romance as Ned falls in love with his fellow time-traveler.

All's Fair in Love and Space

There is a growing trend among romance writers to include the trappings of science fiction in their works. This is not the early pulp days of science fiction, with its emphasis on action and ADVENTURE and male heroes rescuing the damsel in distress. Instead, this is modern science fiction, characterized by the rise of female authors who, unlike Grand Master Andre NORTON, do not have to masculinize their names in order to be published. These are women who can write about WAR and conflict and alien encounters with the best of their male counterparts, but who can also write about characters in relationships. Romance readers who like science fiction should look for the "futuristics" label on their novels. They can also visit a Science Fiction Romance website for suggestions: http://members.aol.com/sfreditor/index.htm. Or they can check out award winners. The Romance Writers of America have a science fiction–fantasy award. The Prism Award was won by Catherine Asaro in 2000 for her novel *The Veiled Web,* in which a prima ballerina joins forces with one of the world's foremost computer programmers. He has created a cutting-edge artificial intelligence system that is coveted by international terrorists. When he and Lucia del Mar are kidnapped by these same terrorists, they manage to escape and flee to his home in Morocco, where an arranged marriage to protect her eventually leads to true love. It's not surprising that Catherine Asaro should win such an award, considering the quality of her writing and the ingenuity of her storytelling. She first burst on the science fiction scene with her novels of the Skolian Empire, beginning with *Primary Inversion* in 1996. This depiction of empires in conflict includes the struggle between sensitive empaths on one side and sensory-sucking sadists on the other. Not only is Sauscony Valdoria the potential heir to the Skolian Empire. She is also a Primary, leader of a four-person team that lands on the planet Delos for a period of well-earned rest and relaxation. Delos is a neutral planet in the war between the Skolians and the Traders, which is why it's possible for Sauscony to come face to face with a Trader. But Jabriol Qox is not just any Trader. He's the heir to the Trader Empire. And he's not a sadist like the other members at court. He's an empath, just like Sauscony. Could he be the soulmate she never thought she would find? Or is her enemy after all?

The other major science fiction and romance award is the Sapphire, sponsored by the *Science Fiction Romance Newsletter.* Both science fiction and fantasy works are eligible; it has been awarded annually since 1995. This is the award that Lois McMaster BUJOLD received in 1999 for *A Civil Campaign: A Comedy of Biology and Manners.* This author has created one of the most popular characters in science fiction today. Miles Vorkosigan is the son of the Prime Minister of Barrayar, a warlike planet that has little use for the weak and the defective. His mother is a scientist from the far more advanced planet of Beta. How his parents met and fell in love after his father captured his mother as part of a military action is told in *Shards of Honor,* an early novel in the series that also won a Romance Award. After they married, his parents were attacked in an attempted coup. Since poison gas was used, and his mother was pregnant with Miles at the time, the fetus was badly damaged. She refused to even consider an abortion, using the latest Betan technology to repair as much damage as possible. But Miles was born with brittle bones. He grows up to be very short in stature, but extremely long in brain power. The perpetual underdog, he's always getting into trouble, facing down impossible odds, and then miraculously coming out on top at the end—by the skin of his teeth. Finally, Miles meets a woman who is worthy of him and he has fallen in love. *A Civil Campaign* is the account of their courtship, sort of a Regency romance in space that is laugh-out-loud funny as Miles takes one wrong step after another, including hosting a dinner party at which bug feces is served. Thank heavens this comedy of errors has a happy ending.

Next in the series is *Diplomatic Immunity: A Comedy of Terrors,* the continuing adventures of Miles and his new bride. He and Lady Ekaterin are on their honeymoon, which of course means Miles has to solve a murder, stop an impending war, find a terrorist, and survive exposure to an Ebola-type virus, all of which he does in his usual, inimitable style.

It's a Mystery to Me

For a complete change of pace, there's the fantasy and mystery G. represented by the Meredith Gentry series. Laurell K. Hamilton's version of urban faerie appears in a sensual, dark, fantasy series featuring a half-faerie princess hiding out in Los Angeles. She has to hide to stay out of the clutches of her aunt, the Queen of Air and Darkness, but she also needs to support herself, so she gets a job working as an investigator on supernatural cases for the Gray Detective Agency. When her aunt finds her, she's given an ultimatum: get pregnant or die. Hamilton is up to her third book in the series and the princess is still trying to get pregnant, sleeping with the members of her bodyguard. Her sexual encounters are described in explicit detail, as are the battles she fights to survive when attacked by various creatures of the dark.

Hamilton is also the author of the Anita Blake, Vampire Slayer series, which is a pretty sexy series in its own right. Anita Blake wears a silver cross around her neck, carries a vial of blood for Voodoo ceremonies, and uses silver bullets in her gun. Why stake when you can shoot? She also has a problem: Jean-Claude, one of the most powerful vampire lords in the city, is in love with her. But she is not about to start sleeping with the undead—at least, not right away.

Nora Roberts, writing in her own name, sometimes adds a supernatural element to her romantic thrillers, as she does in her *Key Trilogy.* An art expert, a librarian, and a hairdresser join forces to find three keys that will restore the souls of three sleeping demigoddesses. Of course, each of these strong women winds up with a handsome male to help her on her quest.

Once upon a Time

The various facets of fantasy and romance can be seen in the following examples, beginning with Neil GAIMAN's *Stardust.* Based on his outstanding GRAPHIC NOVEL of the same name, this is the story of Tristan's quest into the world of Faerie to bring back a falling star. His quest leads him to a young girl with a broken leg (it was a long fall for the star—all the way down from the sky). With a witch on her trail who wants her heart for a special spell, Tristan faces a struggle to get this star maiden to safety.

Lian Hearn's *Across the Nightingale Floor,* the first of *The Tales of the Otori,* has lots of kung fu, court intrigue, assassins with supernatural powers, treachery, loyalty, and love, all set in ancient Japan. The sequel, *Grass for His Pillow: Tales of the Otori, Book 2,* is just as exciting and compelling to read, as is *Brilliance of the Moon,* a fitting conclusion to the trilogy.

Mercedes LACKEY is best-known for her novels of *Valdemar,* where riders are selected by telepathic, horselike companions to join them in their struggle against the forces of darkness. But she has also done some wonderful fairytale retellings: *The Gates of Sleep* (Sleeping Beauty), set in Edwardian England, featuring sorcerers possessed of varying degrees of elemental magic; *The Fire Rose* (Beauty and the Beast), set against the backdrop of the San Francisco earthquake of 1906; *The Black Swan* (Swan Lake) with ensorcelled Princesses, a Sorcerer who hates women, and the Sorcerer's talented daughter, whose magic he drains until she learns how to stand up for herself and the Swan maidens in her charge; and, *The Serpent's Shadow* (Snow White and the Seven Dwarfs) in 1909 London in the form of Hindu gods and goddesses.

Newcomer Juliet MARILLIER has created a marvelous fantasy in her *Sevenwaters* trilogy. The first volume is a re-telling of the fairy tale about the girl who takes a vow of silence and weaves jackets to save her brothers, who are ensorcelled as swans. Set against a backdrop of Druids and Fairies, the battle between the Britons and the Celts is part of a rich romantic fantasy.

Two of Patricia C. WREDE's fantasies are Regency romances set in England where magic is real. The first is the classic tale of the orphan girl who disguises herself as a boy to survive on the streets of London

but tries to rob the wrong man in *Mairelon the Magician.* He is a powerful magician, who just happens to need the help of a talented thief, so the orphan girl winds up working for him. At the end of the novel, she becomes his ward, and those who know Regency Romances, know what that means. Sure enough, in the sequel, *Magician's Ward,* Kim saves Mairelon from a magical attack and, of course, they fall in love.

There are more G. titles in the G. chapter of the reader's advisory guide, *Strictly Science Fiction.* Those who want to treat themselves to more of these diverting mixed-genre titles, will find plenty there to enjoy for a wide variety of reading tastes.

(*Submitted by Bonnie Kunzel, Youth Services Consultant, New Jersey State Library, author of two reader's advisory works on science fiction: First Contact: A Reader's Selection of Science Fiction and Fantasy* with Suzanne Manczuk, Scarecrow Press, 2001, and *Strictly Science Fiction: A Guide to Reading Interests* with Diana Tixier Herald, Libraries Unlimited, 2002.)

BONNIE L. KUNZEL

GEORGE, Jean Craighead
Author, b. 2 July 1919, Washington, D.C.

G. was born in Washington, D.C., but spent her summers with her identical twin brothers, Frank and John, at the family home in Craighead, Pennsylvania. She enjoyed the camping trips her family took on many weekends. A turkey vulture was her first pet. Her father was an entomologist and botanist for the U.S. Forest Service, and he was a great influence on her work. Her brothers are national experts known for their work concerning grizzly bears. They also were the first falconers in the U.S. Her naturalist father taught her how to "eat from the land" and how to enjoy wildlife and her natural surroundings.

G. credits poet Theodore Roethke as her mentor. She was his student when she attended Pennsylvania State College. She received her B.A. in 1941, with a major in Science and Literature. She did postgraduate work at Louisiana State University and at the University of Michigan. She says that her books are the result of three sources: her childhood, the books she has read, and the wild creatures she has raised. G. married John Lothar George in 1944, soon after the war. Her husband then completed his Ph.D. at the University of Michigan, and her first child was born there. She is the mother of three children, named Twig, Craig, and

Luke. In the early years of their marriage, the George family moved to Vassar College in Poughkeepsie, New York, where John taught ecology and conservation and Jean studied painting and began her writing career.

G.'s numerous works almost always are concerned with humans, animals, and the environment. She started out as a newspaper reporter for the International News Service in Washington, D.C., and for the *Washington Post* and *Times-Herald,* but she quickly realized that this was not her area of true interest. Then she started writing articles about animals for MAGAZINES and short nonfiction pieces about animals, many of which appeared in *Reader's Digest* magazine.

G.'s first children's novel, *My Side of the Mountain,* was published in 1959 and was awarded a Newbery Honor Award. It is the story of Sam Gribley, a twelve-year-old boy who leaves home to live in the Catskill Mountains of upstate New York for nine months. There he sets up house in a huge hollowed-out tree and gains the companionship of a falcon and a weasel. During his time in the mountains, Sam learns self-sufficiency and responsibility while living off the land. This story was made into a film in 1969.

In 1973, her novel *Julie of the Wolves* (1972) won the Newbery Medal. The book was based on research G. was completing. She learned that the wolves were friendly, lived in a well-run society, and had their own linguistic codes. She was inspired to further trace this discovery, and contacted some scientists who were studying this remarkable animal. *Julie of the Wolves* was conceived from this chance encounter. In 1994, G. wrote the sequel titled simply *Julie.*

From the tundra in Alaska to the tropical rain forest to the prairie, G. has explored and written over ninety books about animals and their habitats. Her success stems from the fact that she thoroughly researches her topics and experiences the environments she writes about, often joining scientists in the field and in their laboratories. She maintains a website where readers can find out more information about her writing and can correspond with her. She has most recently been collaborating with artist Wendell Minor to add full-color art to her work and with composer Chris Kubie to add the sounds of nature.

Over the years, G. is said to have taken care of 173 pets, not including dogs and cats, in her home in New York. Many of these animals have since returned to the wild. She wrote a book in 1996 documenting this endeavor entitled *The Tarantula in My Purse and 172 Other Wild Pets.* These animals included one screech owl, six ducklings, one weasel, one toad, three crows, one raccoon, three salamanders, one goose, seven sunfish, one skunk, and one tarantula.

G.'s hobbies include painting, going on field trips to universities and laboratories of natural science, modern dance, and white-water canoeing. She was a teacher in Chappaqua, New York from 1960–1968. G. is the grandmother of five children named Rebecca, Katie, Luke, Sam, and Hunter. She often pursues outdoor activities with them, including camping, hiking, and canoeing. Her children are now grown and daughter Twig is the author of three children's books—*A Dolphin Named Bob, Swimming with Sharks,* and *Jellies.* G. presently lives in Chappaqua, New York, with an African gray parrot, Tocca, and an Alaska husky, Qimmiq (Inuit for dog). She will always be known as the writer who brought nature and ecology to the forefront of children's literature, as well as the environmentalist children's book author whose legacy stressed the importance of the harmony of humans and their natural surroundings.

SELECT AWARDS: 1956 Aurianne Award, *Dipper of Copper Creek; My Side of the Mountain:* 1960, Newbery Medal Honor Book Award, 1965 Lewis Carroll Shelf Citation, 1969 George G. Stone Center Award; 1962 International Hans Christian Andersen Award Honor List; 1969 Woman of the Year, Pennsylvania State University; 1970 Eva L. Gordon Award, American Nature Study Society; 1971 Book World First Prize, *All upon a Stone; Julie of the Wolves:* 1972 Cotable Children's Book, 1973 Newbery Medal, 1973 National Book Award Citation, 1973 German Youth Literature Prize; 1973 Silver Skate Award, Children's Literature Association Top Ten Best American Children's Books in the past 200 years; 1988, Library of Congress Books for Children, for *Water Sky;* 1989 IRA/CBC Children's Choice, *Shark Beneath the Reef;* 1991 Knickerbocker Award; de Grummond Award, University of Southern Mississippi, for body of work.

SELECT FURTHER WORKS: *The Summer of the Falcon,* 1962; *Gull Number 737,* 1964; *Hold Zero!,* 1966; *All upon a Stone,* 1971; *Who Really Killed Cock Robin? An Ecological Mystery,* 1971; *The Cry of the Crow,* 1980; *The Grizzly Bear with the Golden Ears,* 1982; *Journey Inward,* 1982; *One Day in the Desert,* 1983; *How to Talk to Your Dog,* 1986, reprinted 2000; *How to Talk to Your Cat,* 1986, reprinted 2000; *The Talking*

Earth, 1987; *The Big Book for Our Planet,* Ed., 1993; *A Guide for Using Julie of the Wolves in the Classroom* (with Philip Denny), 1993; *Everglades,* 1995; *The Case of the Missing Cutthroats: An Ecological Mystery,* 1996; *Julie's Wolf Pack,* 1997; *Arctic Son,* 1997; *Rhino Romp,* 1998; *Frightful's Mountain,* 1999; *Snow Bear,* 1999; *Winter Moon,* 2001 (reprint); *Summer Moon,* 2002. (reprint); *Spring Moon,* 2002. (reprint); *Autumn Moon,* 2002. (reprint); *Cliff Hanger,* 2002; *Tree Castle Island,* 2002; *Frightful's Daughter,* 2002; *Galapagos George,* 2003; *Fire Storm,* 2003.

BIBLIOGRAPHY: Fuller, Muriel, Editor, *More Junior Authors,* 1963; Hipple, Ted, Ed. *Writers for Young Adults,* Vol. 2. 1997; Hopkins, Lee Bennett, *Pauses: Autobiographical Reflections of 101 Creators of Children's Books,* 1995; Rockman, Connie C., Ed. *Eighth Book of Junior Authors and Illustrators,* 2000; Silvey, Anita, Ed, *Children's Books and Their Creators,* 1995; *Contemporary Authors Online,* 2002; www .jeancraigheadgeorge.com

SANDRA KITAIN

GERAS, Adele Daphne
Author, b. 15 March 1944, Jerusalem

Because her father was employed in the British Colonial Service, G. lived her childhood in a number of locales, including Nigeria and Cyprus, before attending boarding school in England. G. graduated from Oxford in 1966 where she studied modern languages. After college, she tried to find employment as a singer and actress; having no success, she embarked on a career as a French teacher.

After deciding to write full time, G. spent two years trying to have a PICTURE BOOK published. Her first publication was *Tea at Mrs. Manderby's* (1976), and since then, G. has had more than 80 books published. While many of her books are clearly aimed at younger readers, G. is perhaps best known for her books for middle-grade and YA readers. Some of these works draw on her Jewish heritage, such as the historically cast *The Girls in the Velvet Frame* (1979) and *Voyage* (1983). In her Egerton Hall SERIES—*The Tower Room* (1990), *Watching the Roses* (1991), and *Pictures of the Night* (1993)—G. reinvents the stories of Rapunzel, Sleeping Beauty, and Snow White, setting them in a 1960s-era English girls' boarding school. It is *Troy* (2000), G.'s bawdy, feminist retelling of the last months of the Trojan War, which has captured the most critical acclaim. Besides the

awards that it won, *Troy* was on the shortlist for the Whitbread Children's Book Prize (2000) and was highly commended as part of the Carnegie Medal shortlist (2000).

G. is also the author of a book of poetry for adults.

AWARDS: 2001 *Boston Globe–Horn Book* Honor Book and ALA BBYA, *Troy.*

FURTHER WORKS: *Other Echoes,* 1983; *Letters of Fire, and Other Unsettling Stories,* 1984; *Snapshots of Paradise: Love Stories,* 1984; *Happy Endings,* 1986; *Daydreams on Video,* 1989; *A Lane to the Land of the Dead,* 1994; *Stagestruck,* 2000.

BIBLIOGRAPHY: "Adele Geras," *Authors and Artists for Young Adults,* Volume 48, 2003. Reproduced in *Biography Resource Center,* 2003. http://www.gale net.com/servlet/BioRC; "Author Profile: Adele Geras," (n.d.). Retrieved from WordPool at http://www.word pool.co.uk/ap/geras.htm; Geras, Adele (2002), Personal website, retrieved from http://adelegeras.com/

CAROL TILLEY

GIBBONS, Kaye
Author, b. 1960, Nash County, North Carolina

To create her highly acclaimed and best-selling fiction, G. draws upon her difficult childhood spent as the daughter of an alcoholic father and a suicidal mother, who killed herself when G. was ten. An avid reader and library patron, G. lived with relatives before winning a scholarship to North Carolina State University. She left college before graduating, however, to write full time.

Imitating the first Southern poet to, in her words, "make art out of everyday language," James Weldon Johnson, G. soon completed her first novel, *Ellen Foster* (1987). Using the voice of a young child to describe "life, death, art, eternity," she says she wrote the book about her own experiences of being bounced from one home to another during childhood. She enriched the story with humor, describing the protagonist's strengths in the face of great adversity. *Ellen Foster* was later produced by Hallmark Hall of Fame for CBS-TV, starring Emily Harris and Jenna Malone.

G.'s masterful use of colloquial speech in realistically lean dialogue also contributed to the success of her second novel, *A Virtuous Woman* (1989). Here, her husband and wife protagonists testify to the value of marriage, faced with the difficult awareness of the wife's impending death. Her third novel, *A Cure for*

Dreams (1991), is a multigenerational FAMILY saga, centered on a trio, granddaughter, daughter, and mother, whose poor treatment by the men in their lives is rendered irrelevant by their close bonds with each other. Two national bestsellers followed: *Charms for the Easy Life* (1993) and *Sights Unseen* (1995).

Critics have compared her writing to William Faulkner's. G., of course, has a much more personal take on her craft: "You see, I love what I do. I raise three human beings, and I do language for a living—it's only as terrifying as it is lovely."

SELECT AWARDS: *Ellen Foster:* Sue Kaufman Prize for First Fiction, American Academy and Institute of Arts and Letters, citation from Ernest Hemingway Foundation, Louis D. Rubin Writing Award, ALA Outstanding Books for the College Bound; National Endowment for the Arts Fellowship, *A Virtuous Woman;* 1991 *Chicago Tribune* Nelson Algren Heartland Award for Fiction and PEN/Revson Foundation Fellowship, both for *A Cure For Dreams;* 1996 Chevalier de l'Ordre des Arts et des Lettres; *Charms for an Easy Life:* ALA Best Books for Young Adults list, 1994

FURTHER WORKS: *On the Occasion of My Last Afternoon,* 1996; *Divining Women,* 2004

BIBLIOGRAPHY: *Contemporary Authors, GaleNet online,* 2003; *Wilson Biographies online,* 2003; Kaye Gibbons Official website: http://www.kayegibbons.com/biography.htm

CATHERINE GIVEN

GIBLIN, James Cross
Author, editor, b. 8 July 1933, Cleveland, Ohio

G. has been a highly influential force in youth publishing for more than four decades, both as an editor and as a writer of nonfiction for young people. G.'s love of books began in his childhood, a time during which his mother introduced him to the magic of literature, and he became an avid reader. His successful editing career can be traced back to the ninth grade, when he served as editor of his junior-high-school newspaper.

G. has always been curious about the world around him, and both literature and personal discovery have helped to shape his life and work. G. began his college education studying drama at Northwestern University in 1951, later transferring to Western Reserve University (now Case Western Reserve University),

where he completed a bachelor's degree in 1954. The following year he received an M.F.A. in creative writing from Columbia University. After an unsuccessful attempt at television script writing and playwriting, G. took a job as a clerk at the British Book Centre (a publishing company).

Over the following years, G. moved from publisher to publisher as he rose through the ranks. He became the editor-in-chief for the children's division of Seabury Press (later Clarion Books) in 1967 and was promoted to editor and publisher in 1979. He published his first book for children, *The Scarecrow Book* (written with Dale Ferguson), in 1980. As his writing career flourished, the demands of his editorial position prevented him from spending satisfactory time on his writing; accordingly, he retired from the full-time job to the position of contributing editor at Clarion in 1989.

When G. looks for a topic for a new book, he often attempts to find a gap in the publishing field. This has led to his selecting a number of unusual topics, such as the subject of chairs, detailed in *Be Seated: A Book about Chairs* (1993), and the history of chimney sweeps, examined in *Chimney Sweeps: Yesterday and Today* (1982).

G. tackled another uncommon topic in *When Plague Strikes: The Black Death, Smallpox, and AIDS* (1995). It presents a chilling yet fascinating examination of social conditions surrounding three pandemics. Through careful explanation, documentation, and factual storytelling, G. shows that although pandemics have come and gone throughout history, human reactions to their carriers have not altered considerably over the centuries. In the 14th century, carriers of the bubonic plague were feared and ostracized, just as carriers of the AIDS virus were dreaded and vilified in the late 20th century. And in both cases, the public sought to blame marginalized populations for the diseases, blaming Jews for the bubonic plague and homosexuals for AIDS.

More recently, G. has turned his attention to BIOGRAPHY. In his books, G. does not include unsubstantiated information or dialogue of his own invention; rather, he is meticulous in his research and will not include any vignette unless its accuracy has been confirmed. Research for *Charles Lindbergh: A Human Hero* (1997), which brought to light Lindbergh's sympathies toward Hitler, led to G.'s researching and writing *The Life and Death of Adolf Hitler* (2002).

The Life and Death of Adolf Hitler presents a multi-faceted view of the infamous dictator and the times in which he lived, as the author attempts to understand how Hitler came to believe that his evil objectives, which contradict all standard views of human morality, could be beneficial to his regime and therefore desirable. G. conducted two years of extensive original research for the book and used photographs from Eva Braun's personal photo albums (now owned by the National Archives) to illustrate much of the text.

As an editor, G. has worked with a number of respected authors, including Marion Dane BAUER, Russell FREEDMAN, and Jane YOLEN. To date G. has published more than twenty titles for children and YOUNG ADULTS. Garnering a number of major awards, this body of work represents the finest in youth nonfiction. G. has taught at the City University of New York and the Chautauqua Writers Workshop. He also writes about writing for young people in literary MAGAZINES.

SELECT AWARDS: 1982 Golden Kite Award, *Chimney Sweeps: Yesterday and Today;* 1983 American Book Award for children's nonfiction, *Chimney Sweeps: Yesterday and Today;* 1984 Golden Kite Award, *Walls: Defenses throughout History;* 1986 *Boston Globe–Horn Book* nonfiction honor, *The Truth about Santa Claus;* 1988 Golden Kite Award, *Let There be Light: A Book about Windows;* 1996 *Washington Post*–Children's Book Guild Award for his entire body of work and ALA Best Book for Young Adults for *When Plague Strikes: The Black Death, Smallpox, AIDS*; 1998 Orbis Pictus Award Honor and ALA Best Book for Young Adults, *Charles Lindbergh: A Human Hero;* 2001 Orbis Pictus Award Honor, *The Amazing Life of Benjamin Franklin;* 2003 Robert F. Sibert INFORMATIONAL BOOK Award, *The Life and Death of Adolf Hitler.*

FURTHER WORKS: *Fireworks, Picnics, and Flags,* 1983; *Let There Be Light,* 1987; *The Riddle of the Rosetta Stone: Key to Ancient Egypt,* 1990; *The Mystery of the Mammoth Bones: And How It Was Solved,* 1999; *Writing Books for Young People,* 1990; *The Century that Was: Reflections on the Last One Hundred Years,* 2000; *The Amazing Life of Benjamin Franklin,* 2000; *Secrets of the Sphinx,* 2004.

BIBLIOGRAPHY: *Authors & Artists for Young Adults,* vol. 39, 2001; *Children's Literature Review,* vol. 29, 1993; *Something about the Author,* vol. 122, 2001; James Cross Giblin, *Writing Books for Young People,* 1990; *The Continuum Encyclopedia of Children's Literature,* 2001.

DENISE E. AGOSTO

GIBSON, William (Ford)

Author, b. 17 March 1948, Conway, South Carolina

Prominent SCIENCE FICTION author G. graduated from the University of British Columbia in 1977 with a BA in English. It was here that he began writing science fiction. His first novel, *Neuromancer* (1984), was the first novel to win the Hugo, Nebula, and Philip K. Dick Awards in the same year. *Neuromancer,* acknowledged by many to be the seminal cyberpunk novel, also won the Ditmar Award of the Australian National Science Fiction Convention. The novel describes the fortunes of Case, a "console cowboy" who is hired by an Artificial Intelligence expert named Wintermute to hack into the systems of its owners, the wealthy Tessier-Ashpool clan, so that Wintermute can merge with another AI called Neuromancer. In describing the computerized reality that Case directly accesses with his mind, Gibson coined the term "cyberspace."

Critics consider *Neuromancer, Count Zero* (1986), and *Mona Lisa Overdrive* (1988) a trilogy, dubbed the Cyberspace trilogy, or the Sprawl trilogy after its futuristic urban setting. The term "cyberpunk" was used to describe the combination of advanced computer and biomedical technologies with a tough, street-wise "punk" aesthetic in these three novels and other contemporary science fiction.

Three subsequent novels, *Virtual Light* (1993), *Idoru* (1996), and *All Tomorrow's Parties* (1999), are also considered a trilogy. *Virtual Light* marked a departure from the earlier novels by describing have-not characters in San Francisco in the near future, when the poor have occupied the unused Bay Bridge and remade it into an unauthorized, ad hoc community of outsiders.

G. is popular with TEENS who read this genre of science fiction. David Hartwell, noted author and editor, has stated that twelve-year-old boys read and discuss *Neuromancer,* a book that is a challenge to many adult readers not familiar with the genre. His influence continues on authors such as Bruce Sterling and Neal Stephenson who write in the cyberpunk realm.

Gibson's financial world is consistently presenting dystopias in which technological advances serve a powerful corporate elite, exacerbating social problems and widening the gap between rich and poor. He moved to Canada in 1967 and resides in Vancouver, British Columbia.

AWARDS: *Neuromancer* (1984): Hugo Award, Nebula Award, Philip K. Dick Award, Ditmar Award of the Australian National Science Fiction Convention.

FURTHER WORKS: *Burning Chrome* (with Bruce Sterling), 1986; *The Difference Engine,* 1990; *Pattern Recognition,* 2003.

BIBLIOGRAPHY: Contemporary Authors, New Revision Series, vol. 90; author website (www.william gibsonbooks.com); Encyclopaedia Britannica; International Authors and Writers Who's Who, 17th edition.

MICHELE HILTON

GIFF, Patricia Reilly
Author, b. 26 April 1935, Brooklyn, New York

G. worked as a reading teacher in public schools on Long Island, New York, for twenty years and was in her forties before beginning her career as an author of children's fiction in 1979 with *Fourth-grade Celebrity.* G. has many degrees to her credit, receiving a B.A. from Marymount College in 1956, an M.A. in history from St. John's in 1958, a Professional Diploma in reading from Hofstra University in 1975, as well as an Honorary Doctorate of Humane Letters from Hofstra University in 1990. G. credits a lifelong love of reading as her inspiration for wanting to write. She held the dream of becoming an author for her whole life.

G. is known for her humorous stories that serve to help children cope with everyday problems of growing up. She has written numerous SERIES books as well as books that assist children in learning Spanish. After writing over sixty children's books, G. tried her hand at writing YA fiction and achieved success with books such as *Lily's Crossing* (1997) and *All the Way Home* (2001). *Lily's Crossing* is an acclaimed novel of historical fiction aimed at older readers. It tells the story of a young girl's journey across Europe during World War II. It was named a Newbery Honor book by the American Library Association in 1998. G. has also written numerous nonfiction works, including *Mother Teresa, Sister to the Poor* (1986); *Diana: 20th Century Princess* (1991), and *Louisa May Alcott* (1999).

G. currently lives in Connecticut. She has three children and four grandchildren. Besides writing, which she does every single day, she has also served as a reading consultant and an editorial consultant for Dell Publishing. In 1994, along with other members of her family, she opened The Dinosaur's Paw, a children's bookstore, in Fairfield, Connecticut. The bookstore houses books for children exclusively, and G. hopes that it will provide the means to bring books to an increasing number of children.

SELECT AWARDS: *Lily's Crossing:* 1997 Newbery Honor award, ALA Notable Book for Children, *Boston Globe-Horn Book* Award Honor Book; *Nory Ryan's Song:* 2000, ALA Notable Book, Best Book for Young Adults, *School Library Journal* Best Book of the Year, Society of Children's Book Writers and Illustrators Golden Kite Honor Book; *Pictures of Hollis Woods,* 2002, Newbery Honor Award, Best Book for Young Adults, 2003.

SELECT FURTHER WORKS: *Nory Ryan's Song,* 2000; *All the Way Home,* 2001; *Pictures of Hollis Woods,* 2002; *Maggie's Door,* 2003.

BIBLIOGRAPHY: *Contemporary Authors,* vol. 99, 2001; Children's Book Council online, 2003.

NANCY A. BUGGÉ

GILBERT, Barbara Snow
Author, b. 9 April 1954, Oklahoma City, Oklahoma

G. has held a wide variety of jobs in her life, including attorney, mediator, and writer. G. has worked on the political staffs of the Speaker of the U.S. House of Representatives and of the Governor of Oklahoma.

Interested in controversial social issues, G. found that she liked writing about younger characters because the burdens of life often seemed much more significant for them. G. is known for introspective books in which TEEN characters often have to make difficult decisions. In her first YA novel, *Stone Water* (1996), she chose to focus on the moral and legal complexities of assisted suicide. This quietly compelling book about an agonizing decision provokes much contemplation and discussion among its readers. In *Broken Chords* (1997), musical prodigy Clara is a finalist in a competition in which she could win a scholarship to Julliard. But she is torn between her dream of being a concert pianist and her desire to be an ordinary teenager.

G. was so affected by the Oklahoma City Bombing that it helped inspire *Paper Trail* (2000). It tells the story of a boy who grows up in a fundamentalist anti-government militia group called the Soldiers of God. When his father is revealed to be an FBI agent, the Soldiers of God turn against his family. Much of the story is told from the boy's point of view as he flees into the woods, putting all of his survival skills to the test and reflecting back on his life so far. Fact merges with fiction as chapters called "scraps" filled with facts and statistics about the militia movement are scattered throughout the book.

G. currently resides in Oklahoma with her husband and two children.

AWARDS: *School Library Journal* Best Book (1996) for *Stone Water;* New York Public Library Book for the Teen Age (1997); Oklahoma Book Award (1997) for *Stone Water;* Oklahoma Book Award (1999) for *Broken Chords.*

BIBLIOGRAPHY: *Contemporary Authors,* online, 2001; *Something about the Author,* vol. 97, 1998; *Teenreads .com,* online, 2000.

ANDREA LIPINSKI and MEGAN PEARLMAN

GILES, Gail
Author, b. 24 September 1947, Galveston, Texas

G. has been writing since fourth grade, when a teacher, desperate to keep her entertained while the rest of the class caught up, asked her to write a description of a family having dinner from the viewpoint of an ant. "I was hooked," G. said. As she matured, her writing took on an edgier style. When reading as a teen, G. "liked trying to figure out what happened next rather than have the author tell me everything." This enjoyment of SUSPENSE and MYSTERY influences her current works for TEENS.

In *Dead Girls Don't Write Letters* (2003), Sunny's older sister, who died suddenly a few months before, sends a letter saying she did not die and was coming home. But when she comes, Sunny realizes the girl is not her sister. A *Kirkus* reviewer writes, "Lies pile upon lies, and secrets upon secrets, in a twisty narrative that turns in on itself so often that the reader is left not knowing quite what is real." Beyond the delicious suspense are the interactions between Sunny and her family, showing that Giles truly understands the mind of a teen.

Shattering Glass (2002), G.'s debut YOUNG ADULT novel, is a visit to the "dark hell of high-school cliques," also according to *Kirkus*. The story begins, "Simon Glass was easy to hate . . . we each hated him for a different reason, but we didn't realize it until the day we killed him." In her most recent book, *Playing in Traffic* (2004), G. continues to ex-

amine high-school cliques and the outcasts who move among them.

"Why do I write such dark and edgy stuff?" G. asks. "I want the reader to come up and sneak a peak at violence and darkness, check out the edge of the abyss and decide it is a trip not to be taken." Many reviewers mark G. as a new author to be watched.

AWARDS: ALA Best Books for Young Adults, ALA Quick Pick, and Booklist Top Ten Mysteries for Youths for *Shattering Glass*. ALA Quick Pick, Teen Top Ten 2003 for *Dead Girls Don't Write Letters.*

FURTHER WORK: *Breath of the Dragon* (1997); *Playing in Traffic* (2004).

REFERENCES: Gail Giles' website, http://gailgiles .com; "Interview with Young Adult Author Gail Giles," Cynthia Leitich Smith Children's Literature Resources, http://www.cynthialeitichsmith.com/auth-ill GailGiles.htm; personal correspondence with Gail Giles, February 14, 2004.

JENNA OBEE

GILMORE, Kate
Author, b. 2 May 1931, Milwaukee, Wisconsin

G. has approached different subjects with each of her novels. Her first, *Of Griffins and Graffiti* (1986), tells the story of a group of TEENAGERS who decide to create a mural on the side of a jet plane that flies internationally. *Remembrance of the Sun* (1986), set in Iran during the late 1970s, is based on G.'s personal experiences. It is the story of Jill, an American teenager who falls in love with Shaheen, an Iranian classmate, just as he becomes involved in the revolutionary movement. Shaheen helps Jill's family escape Iran, but Jill lives with the question of what happened to Shaheen afterward. *Kirkus* called *Remembrance of the Sun* an "intelligent, multi-layered novel . . . that should keep any reader spellbound." *Enter Three Witches* (1991) follows the adventures of a teenage boy who tries to keep his girlfriend from discovering he lives with a group of witches. *Jason and the Bard* (1993) follows a high-school student who discovers the history of theatre during an apprenticeship with a summer Shakespeare festival.

Because of the vastness and importance of the subject matter, G. calls *The Exchange Student* (1999) her most challenging effort yet. It is one hundred years in the future when an exchange student comes to Earth from another planet. With the help of a famed zoologist and a teenage girl who keeps a small zoo in her home, the exchange student develops a plan to re-populate his home (where higher species have become extinct).

In addition to being a writer, G. has also worked as a legal secretary and as co-director for Arboretal Artifacts, an organization that makes unique topiaries and wreaths. G. resides in Astoria, New York, with her husband John.

AWARDS: *The Exchange Student:* 2000 YALSA Best Books for Young Adults and Dorothy Canfield Fisher Award list (2000–2001)

BIBLIOGRAPHY: *Kirkus* Reviews, October 1, 1986; *Contemporary Authors,* 2001, retrieved March 19, 2003 from Gale Literary Databases; *2000–2001 DCF Books,* 2001, retrieved March 23, 2003 from http://www.mps.k12.vt.us/msms/dcf/2001/2001.htm.

KRISTINE BULLER

GILSTRAP, John
Author, b. ca. 1957

G. holds a B.A. from the College of William and Mary (1979) and an M.S. from the University of Southern California. He is both a screenwriter and a novelist, and commutes daily to his workplace—his basement. He has worked as a journalist and founded an environmental compliance consulting company. Additionally, he has associated with Big Brothers, worked with disadvantaged boys, and is a volunteer fireman. He writes fast-paced thrillers that feature lots of action; these are written for adults but garner teen fans.

It was not until twenty years had passed, and twenty-seven refusals, that G., an expert on explosives safety and hazardous waste disposal, published his first novel, *Nathan's Run,* the story of a boy on the run, in 1996, written in his spare time. Later this "story of Nathan Bailey, age 12, fleeing the law for the murder of a juvenile detention center guard" was produced as a motion picture by Arnold Stiefel with Stiefel-Phillips and Silver Pictures. G.'s second novel, *At All Costs* (1998), about two FBI Most-Wanted fugitives for fifteen years "struggling to prove their innocence as mass murderers before their pursuers can find and arrest them," has been optioned for a feature film.

Although *Even Steven* is thought to be his most personal novel, all three of G.'s novels are "fast-paced thrillers about ordinary Americans caught by chance in deadly intrigue," and revolve around the theme of escape.

AWARDS: *Nathan's Run,* BBYA, 1997; *At All Costs,* Alex Award List, 1998.

FURTHER WORKS: *Scott Free,* 2003.

BIBLIOGRAPHY: *Contemporary Authors Online,* 2001; *Contemporary Authors Online,* 2003. reproduced in *Biography Resource Center,* 2003; http://www.gale net.com/servlet/BioRC; Lambert, Pam. "Punctuation and Pretzels." *Publishers Weekly,* March 4, 1996 v45 n4 p41(1); Nathan, Paul. "Case in Point." *Publishers Weekly,* April 10, 1995 v242 n15 p17(1); "Scott Free." *Publishers Weekly,* Dec 23, 2002 v249 i51 p45(2).

SARA MARCUS

GIOVANNI, Nikki (Yolande Cornelia Giovanni, Jr.)
Poet, author, lecturer. b. 7 June 1943, Knoxville, Tennessee

G. and her writings reflect a life fully lived from a child to woman, from naive college student to CIVIL RIGHTS and black power activist, from spirited daughter to caring mother. She holds strong connections with her AFRICAN AMERICAN heritage, which were reinforced by a family that excelled in the art of storytelling. Her POETRY is a reflection of her passions, from racism, civil rights, growing up, motherhood, and love. Her poems have a natural speaking rhythm or cadence, other than those of everyday life; she writes as she speaks with a strong sure voice that appeals to TEENS. G. writes poetry as if it is conversation and that makes her poems readily accessible.

G.'s early work shows her revolutionary poetry, such as *Black Feeling, Black Talk* (1968) and *Black Judgement* (1968). These works reflect G.'s political, spiritual, and personal growth. Her strong-willed character as a child was further evident in her activism and her writings.

My House (1972) explores many of the social issues of the outside world as well as issues of the self. This book is more personal than her previous works. The poems are divided into two sections—the inside of the house for her own reflections and the outside of the house for those issues that touch others. She writes of childhood memories, being a mother, the African nation, black leaders, and through it all, writes with spirit, warmth, love, and wit. G. continues her personal reflections and coming of age in *The Women and the Men* (1975).

Gemini: An Extended Autobiographical Statement on My First Twenty-Five Years of Being a Black Poet (1971) is a collection of her AUTOBIOGRAPHICAL reminiscences. It is a journey of G.'s own internal conflicts and struggles. It includes stories about her grandmother, her family, being a single mother, and how change in one's self can affect change in others.

G. continues to write and speak with her usual candor, openness, vigor, and is still as outspoken, engaging and entertaining now as she was in her earlier works.

AWARDS: National Endowment for the Arts, 1968; Harlem Cultural Council, 1969; named one of ten 'Most Admired Black Women' *Amsterdam News*, 1969; Prince Matchabelli Sun Shower Award, 1971; National Book Award nomination for *Gemini: An Extended Autobiographical Statement on My First Twenty-five Years of Being a Black Poet*, 1973; American Library Association 'Best Books for Young Adults' citation for *My House*, 1973; *Gemini*, Nonfiction entry BBYA, 1972; *My House: Poems,* Nonfiction entry, BBYA 1973, *Women and the Men,* Nonfiction entry BBYA 1975. Post-Corbett Award, 1986; Woman of the Year, National Association for the Advancement of Colored People, 1989; Ohioana Book Award, 1988; Jeanine Rae Award for the Advancement of Women's Culture, 1995; Langston Hughes Award, 1996; National Association for the Advancement of People Image Award for *Love Poems*, 1998 and *Blues: For all the Changes,* 2000.

FURTHER WORKS: *Ego-Tripping and Other Poems for Young People*, 1973; *Cotton Candy on a Rainy Day,* 1978; *Those Who Ride the Night Winds*, 1983; *Racism 101,* 1994; *Grand Mothers,* 1996; *Shimmy Shimmy Shimmy like My Sister Kate: Looking at the Harlem Renaissance through Poems*, 1995; *Love Poems*, 1997; *Grandfathers: Reminiscences, Poems, Recipes and Photos of the Keepers of Our Traditions,* 1999; *Blues: For All the Changes: New Poems,* 1999; *Quilting the Black-Eyed Pea: Poems and Not Quite Poems,* 2002; *The Collected Poems of Nikki Giovanni,* 2003.

BIBLIOGRAPHY: *Contemporary Authors New Revision Series,* vol. 91; *Something About the Author,* vol. 107; *Twentieth-Century Young Adult Writers*, 1994; Virgina C. Fowler. *Nikki Giovanni,* 1992, Best *Books for Young Adults,* 2000. nikki-giovanni.com.

TINA HERTEL

GLENN, Mel

Author, poet, b. 10 May 1943, Zurich, Switzerland

G., a former high-school English teacher, observed carefully the antics, conversations, and characteristics of the students who sat in his classroom year after year; from these keen observations came books. The book *Class Dismissed: High School Poems* (1982) examined the thoughts, feelings, sorrow, and joys of all types of students. *Class Dismissed II* (1986), *Back to Class* (1988), and *My Friend's Got This Problem, Mr. Candler* (1991) continue the strategy begun in the first collection: to show high-school students not as stereotypes but as real individuals with many of the same hopes and dreams and fears.

G. chose POETRY as his main format of expression. Accompanying these poems were stark black-and-white photographs provided by G.'s then-colleague Michael Bernstein. The pairing of text and photographs creates an attractive and interesting concept for readers; instead of thinking that G. had written the poetry, they believe that the poems had been penned by the students in the photographs.

After his SERIES of books set in "Anyhighschool," his next book of poetry, *Who Killed Mr. Chippendale?* (1996), forged new territory; it was a murder MYSTERY in poetry form. Set at fictional Tower High School, *Chippendale* relates the story of a high-school English teacher killed by a sniper's bullet. Reactions from students and staff are mixed. Some students loved Mr. Chippendale while others harbored animosity toward him. Was their hatred sufficient to kill him? The mystery is engrossing with plenty of red herrings to throw readers off the trail. G.'s willingness to push the envelope was rewarded when *Chippendale* was listed as a finalist for the Edgar Allen Poe Award for Best YA Mystery.

More books of poetry that tell stories followed. *The Taking of Room 114* (1997) tells of a history teacher taking his class hostage at the end of the school year. For this collection, G. created poems about each member of the class which spanned their high-school career; this conceit created realistic characters. Additionally, the voice of the teacher is included so readers could understand the teacher's motives for taking the class captive. Poems from the point of view of other teachers and the administration of Tower High School round out the story, once again permitting readers an inside look at the inner workings of the school. *Jump Ball: A Basketball Season in Poems* (1997) revealed the inner workings of a high-school team bound for the state championships. It is told through flashbacks, opening with a reporter on the scene of an accident involving a school bus that has slid off an icy road. Again, G. creates the backgrounds for the coach, the team members, the managers, cheerleaders, and others involved with the basketball team. Readers know from the outset that not all those on the bus have survived the crash. G. takes readers into the lives of the players off the court, proving that there are more precious aspects to life than basketball. *Split Image* (2000) tells of a young ASIAN AMERICAN girl caught between her two competing cultures. Laura Li tries her hardest to please her parents by being the perfectly demure Asian daughter. At school, however, Laura has a reputation as a party girl. The two halves of her personality are constantly in conflict, making Laura Li a prime candidate for a nervous breakdown.

G.'s ability to push beyond the traditional boundaries of YA literature and YA poetry has garnered critical praise. His unorthodox use of poetry has expanded the genre and opened doors for young writers tempted to wander into uncharted territory.

AWARDS: Best Books for Young Adults list: *Class Dismissed,* 1982; *My Friend's Got This Problem, Mr. Candler,* 1991; *Who Killed Mr. Chippendale?,* 1996; *Jump Ball,* 1997; *The Taking of Room 114,* 1997; *Split Image,* 2001. 1986, Christopher Award, *Class Dismissed II.* Edgar Allen Poe Award Finalist, *Who Killed Mr. Chippendale;* YALSA QuickPicks, Popular PAPERBACKS, New York Public Library Books for the Teen Age, *Class Dismissed! High School Poems*—Nonfiction entry BBYA 1982, The Best of the Best Books: 1970–1983; Pacific Northwest Young Reader's Award for *The Taking of Room 114,* 2000.

FURTHER WORKS: *One Order to Go,* 1984; *Play by Play,* 1986; *Squeeze Play,* 1989; *Foreign Exchange,* 1999.

TERI S. LESESNE

GOING, Kelly L.
Author, b. 21 August 1973, Rhinebeck, New York

G. remembers reading extensively as a child and young adult. Her childhood memories include reading books aloud with her parents, while growing up in New York. Although inspired by no single author, G. especially enjoys the works of J. D. SALINGER, Susan COOPER, and J.R.R. TOLKIEN.

Although G. continuously wrote for pleasure as a child and young adult, she did not intend to become a writer. G. attended Eastern College of Pennsylvania to study sociology, graduating with a Bachelor's degree in 1995. She spent two and a half years serving with the Mennonite Voluntary Service and then worked with an adult literacy program in New Orleans. G. worked several odd jobs before going to work at Curtis Brown, Ltd., a literacy agency in New York City. G. enjoys plentiful reading as a part of her job, assisting two agents at the literacy agency. G. plans to write on a full-time basis in the near future.

G.'s break-out novel, *Fat Kid Rules the World* (2003), was met with immediate success and gained recognition after being named a Michael L. PRINTZ Honor Book. The idea for *Fat Kid Rules the World* came to G. as the first line in the book—"I'm a sweating fat kid standing just over the yellow line. . . ." G. reports that her stories usually start with a very small idea, such as a single scene, character, or a line. She builds from the initial idea without the aid of an outline or a plan. This YA novel features the main character, Troy Billings, as a 6′1″, 296-pound kid who is contemplating suicide when he meets Curt MacCrae, a homeless dropout who is a legend at Troy's high school. Curt, a guitarist, quickly recruits Troy to play drums in his new punk-rock band. However, Troy does not know how to play the drums! The two memorable characters both need rescuing from their internal conflicts.

G. is praised for her powerful, eccentric characters. The inspiration for the character of Curt came from Nirvana lead singer Kurt Cobain. She wanted to create characters that were larger than life. She envisioned Troy as being physically larger than life and Curt musically larger than life. G. admits that the most challenging literary aspect of the construction of her story was making Troy and Curt lovable enough to be sympathetic without cleaning them up; Troy was to be obese and sweaty while Curt was to be a vulgar thief and liar. G. believes that it is important that the reader come to love their unlovable qualities.

The story, based on a punk band, required extensive research into punk music and into the art of drum playing. G. worked to make her novel true to punk music, in form as well as content. She created short chapters that parallel short punk songs. She intentionally incorporated imaging that is "in-your-face" and tried to play with language in the same way punk musicians play with language. For example, after the main character, Troy, encounters Curt's abusive step-father, G. writes, "I am the walrus, perched upon the muddy slope when the ground disappears below him." With intense research and writing, G. completed her novel in just six months.

G. is enthusiastic about contributing to the wealth of YA literature, for it is her personal favorite genre to read. G. currently resides in Beacon, New York, and is working on two novels.

AWARDS: *Fat Kid Rules the World* (2003) is a Michael L. Printz Honor Book and an ALA Best Books for Young Adults 2004.

BIBLIOGRAPHY: www.cynthialeitischsmith.com; www .klgoing.com; author interview.

JODI PILGRIM

GOLDEN, Christopher
Author, b. 15 July 1967, Framingham, Massachusetts

G. graduated from Tufts University in 1989 with a B.A. *cum laude* and lives in Massachusetts. Primarily an author of HORROR and SUSPENSE novels for YOUNG ADULTS, G. also writes COMIC BOOKS and novels based on comic-book characters. Among his original SERIES, the Body of Evidence thrillers involve a college student, Jenna Blake, who solves murders; in the Prowlers series, teenager Jack Dwyer sees the ghosts of the victims of the Prowlers, werewolves who disguise themselves as humans, and helps fight the predators. The Shadow Saga, a vampire series, includes *Of Saints and Shadows* (1994), *Angel Souls and Devil Hearts* (1995), *Of Masques and Martyrs* (1998), and *Gathering Dark* (2003).

G. is a major contributor to the Buffy the Vampire Slayer series of novels, authoring books such as *Sins of the Father* (1999), *Spike and Dru: Pretty Maids All in a Row* (2000), the four-part serial novel *The Lost Slayer* (2001), and *The Wisdom of War* (2002). He has written novels, GRAPHIC NOVELS, or comics based on the comic-book characters Daredevil, X-Men, Gen13, Hellboy, the Crow, Batman, and others.

AWARDS: Bram Stoker Award, 1992, *CUT!: Horror Writers on Horror Film.*

SELECT FURTHER WORKS: *Beach Blanket Psycho,* 1995; *Bikini,* 1995; *Sanctuary,* 1996; *Strangewood,* 1999; *Straight on 'til Morning,* 2001; *The Ferryman,* 2002.

BIBLIOGRAPHY: *Contemporary Authors,* vol. 150; author website, www.christophergolden.com

MICHELE HILTON

GOLDING, William
Author, b. 19 September 1911, St. Columb Minor, Cornwall, England; d. 19 June, 1993, n.p.

Perhaps because of his relatively solitary childhood, G. developed an interest in reading and writing early on. Although his first work would not be published until his college years, and his first novel not until he was forty-three years old, G. began writing when he was just twelve years old. From the publication of his first novel through the last fifty years of his life, this acclaimed author wrote a host of fablelike novels that established him as one of the most important British novelists of modern times and a winner of the Nobel Prize for Literature.

G.'s father, Alec Golding, was a distinguished British schoolmaster, as was his grandfather. This influenced not only G.'s own choice of profession, but also, ultimately, his choice of subject matter for his books. The influence of G.'s mother, Mildred Agatha Golding, can also be felt in G.'s work. She endowed her child with a sense that the world is, as G. explained, an "exhilarating but risky place" ("Before the Beginning," *Spectator,* 1961). G.'s parents may have had a particularly strong effect on their child because of his sheltered upbringing; before attending school, G. had little or no knowledge of people outside his family.

G.'s childhood reading included children's classics by Robert Michael Ballantyne, Jules Verne, Robert Louis Stevenson, Johann Rudolf Wyss, and Edgar Rice Burroughs. He also enjoyed Greek MYTHOLOGY and adult classics. The imprint of these works can be seen in G.'s writing.

G.'s love of reading translated into a love of writing early on. His first, unpublished novel, written as G. was on the cusp of adolescence, was an ambitious work that would include as background the rise of the trade union movement. That work was ultimately abandoned, but G. kept writing. In 1934, while at Brasenose College, Oxford, after he switched from studying science to studying English literature, G. published *Poems*. Later, he would disavow the work, but some critics suggest that G.'s prose is poetic in nature.

After college, G. married and became a schoolmaster at Bishop Wordsworth's School in Salisbury, Wiltshire. He taught there from 1939 to 1940, then again between 1945 and 1961; he served in the Royal

Navy during the intervening years. During this time, G. was also active in theatre, radio, and film. In a variety of ventures, he was writer, actor, and/or producer. Ultimately, it was his writing that brought him fame. In 1954, after being submitted to fifteen (by some accounts, twenty-one) publishing houses, *Lord of the Flies* was accepted by Faber & Faber in London.

Inarguably, *Lord of the Flies* is the book for which G. has received the widest acclaim. G. admitted that World War II had a tremendous impact on the book, as the faith he had in social man before the war was wiped out by "the vileness that went on, year after year" during this period, replaced by a sense that "the condition of man was to be a morally diseased creation." The war marked a crisis of faith for G—the son of an atheist, he began to believe that man is born to sin. In writing *Lord of the Flies,* G. started with a scene that may have been drawn from the island ADVENTURE stories of his youth—a group of schoolboys marooned on a deserted island—and turned it on its head—the boys show themselves to be, at heart, barbaric savages.

A classic that is popular in high-school English classes and on college campuses, *Lord of the Flies* explores, metaphorically, the nature of evil as it is revealed even by the youngest of people—two of the boys-turned-savages are barely pre-schoolers. At the start of the novel, a plane evacuating schoolchildren from England during a war crashes on a deserted island. The adult guardians are killed in the crash, and the children are left to their own devices. Initially, at the suggestion of intellectual Piggy, the children establish a democracy. They elect Ralph, a charming and popular boy, to be their chief. Jack, leader of the black-robed choirboys, suggests that his group function as the hunters for the group, and Ralph accepts this suggestion to placate him. However, the group's plans for their society degenerate quickly. When Jack, pursuing a wild boar, allows the signal fire to go out as a ship is passing, Ralph attempts to restore order. Instead, Jack leads his ever-increasing group of followers away from the group. Later, a military plane is shot down over the island. The dead pilot lands on the mountain, his parachute billowing in the wind. Boys who see it believe it is a "beast," and Jack argues that they must placate the beast by sacrificing pigs to it. Ralph, meanwhile, believes they must not abandon the mountain, an important location for their signal

fire. Jack leads most of the other boys to search for pigs and ultimately seizes control of the island and isolates Ralph and Piggy on the beach. The book culminates in savage attacks on several main characters before a British navy officer arrives to rescue the boys. Ironically, what they really need to be rescued from is themselves.

In 1955, G. was made a fellow of the Royal Society of Literature. G. was named a Commander of the British Empire in 1966. He won the Booker Prize in 1980 for *Rites of Passage* and the Nobel Prize for literature 1983. In 1988, he was knighted.

G.'s second book *The Inheritors* (1955)—a book G. himself considered to be his best work—delved into some of the same themes as his first: the nature of humankind, destruction of a people, and survival. G. explores a prehistoric world where Neanderthals live. In this novel, the Neanderthals, a vivid people who think in pictures rather than words, are eradicated by arguably evil Homo sapiens.

G. wrote an additional nine novels between 1956 and 1989. These, too, frequently touched on issues of human nature, destruction, and survival, as well as related themes such as faith, evil, and redemption. While they address the same topics, they do so in different times (*The Inheritors* takes place in prehistoric times, *The Spire* (1964) in the medieval period, and *Pincher Martin* (1956) during World War II and from different points of view.

AWARDS: Royal Society of Literature, fellow, 1955; Commander of the British Empire, 1966; Booker Prize for *Rites of Passage,* 1980; Nobel Prize for Literature, 1983; knighted, 1988.

FURTHER WORKS: *Fire down Below,* 1989; *Close Quarters,* 1987; *Rites of Passage,* 1980; *Darkness Visible,* 1979.

BIBLIOGRAPHY: Feeney, J. J., "William G. (1911–93): Lord of Horror, Lord of Awe." *America,* 169, July 31–August 7, 1993, pp. 6–7; Forbes, J. T. "William G.," *Dictionary of Literary Biography,* vol. 100, 1990; Friedman, L. S., *William G.,* 1993; Gindin, J. *William G.,* 1988; Oldsey, B. "William G." *Dictionary of Literary Biography,* vol. 15, 1983.

HEIDI HAUSER GREEN

GOLDMAN, E(leanor) M(aureen)
Author, b. 14 November 1943, Oakland, California

G. is the author of books for middle grade and YOUNG ADULT readers. In *Money to Burn* (1994), two friends stumble upon a suitcase containing $400,000, and decide to keep it, with exciting and humorous consequences. *Getting Lincoln's Goat: An Elliot Armbruster Mystery* (1995) involves a fifteen-year-old boy named Elliot who has always dreamed of being a private eye. He finds the opportunity to do an investigation of his own when the school's mascot, Lincoln the goat, disappears.

Shrinking Pains (1996) tells the story of a fountain of youth discovered in the backyard of Doug's new house. Doug, his friend Milo, and his cousin Cassandra explore the possibilities of magical water that can halve the age of anyone who drinks it for three hours. While the fountain has benefits (such as being able to get them into the movies for half price), the plot takes a sinister turn when it's discovered that a villain knows about their secret. *The Night Room* (1995) is a MYSTERY with a darker side for an older audience. A group of high-school juniors is given the opportunity to participate in a virtual reality program that will project them into their tenth high-school reunion. As each of the students goes into the *Night Room,* they see the predicted successes and failures in their careers, relationships, and lives. A virus injected into the program causes chaos when the participants learn at the runion that one of their number is supposed to have died eleven years earlier.

AWARDS: 1996 American Library Association Best Book for Young Adults, *Getting Lincoln's Goat.*

BIBLIOGRAPHY: Contemporary Authors, online, 2001; *Something about the Author,* vol. 103, 1999.

ANDREA LIPINSKI

GOLDSTEIN, Lisa
Author, b. 21 November 1953, Los Angeles, California

G. is a 1975 graduate of the University of Southern California. She co-owned the Dark Carnival Bookstore in Berkeley, California, from 1975–1982. In 1982, G. published her first novel, *The Red Magician,* the award-winning, coming-of-age FANTASY set in Europe just prior to World War II.

Two of G.'s other novels make strong use of historical facts overlaid with fantasy elements. *The Dream Years* (1985) combines time travel and faeries with Paris of the 1920s and 1960s. *Strange Devices of the Sun and Moon* (1993) is set in Elizabethan England, where events in the world of the faeries mirror events in the human royal court.

G. also makes use of mythological elements in several of her books such as *Summer King, Winter Fool* (1994), *Walking the Labyrinth* (1996), and *Dark Cities Underground* (1999). Many of G.'s best SHORT STORIES are collected in *Daily Voices* (1989) and *Travelers in Magic* (1994). *The Alchemist's Door* (2002), is a fantasy in which alchemist John Dee and Rabbi Judah Loew work to protect 16th century Prague.

AWARDS: *The Red Magician:* American Book Award (1983) and Porgie Award (1983).

FURTHER WORKS: *A Mask for the General,* 1989; *Tourists,* 1989.

BIBLIOGRAPHY: *Contemporary Authors Online,* 2003; *St. James Guide to Fantasy Writers,* 1996; *St. James Guide to Science Fiction Writers,* 1996; Author website: http://www.brazenhussies.net/goldstein/

JAMES GAHAGAN

GOOBIE, Beth
Author, b. 1959, Canada

G., a CANADIAN writer of POETRY and fiction for TEENS and adults, is also an accomplished pianist who (besides writing stories) taught piano lessons throughout high school. After working as a nanny in Holland for a year, G. attended the University of Winnipeg, where she earned a B.A. in English in 1983; at the same time, G. earned a second degree from the Mennonite Brethren Bible College in religious studies. She spent the next six years working with abused children and teens, before turning to writing again in 1987.

As an abuse survivor herself, G. continues to be a strong advocate for children and YOUNG ADULTS, and many of her works reflect her concern for the powerlessness of those under legal age. For example, *Scars of Light* (1994), a poetry collection and G.'s second book, describes the physical, emotional, and sexual abuse she endured as a child, a period she explores again—with a slightly different perspective—in *The Girls Who Dream Me* (1999). *Group Homes from Outer Space* (1992), G.'s first book for young adults, continues the theme with the tale of a girl who longs to be rescued from her abusive parents by space aliens, and *Who Owns Kelly Paddick?* (1993) recounts the struggles of a young teen running away from her sexually abusive father.

Not all of G.'s work centers on abuse, though most of it does focus on the travails and trials of being a teen. A teen plagued with guilt after hitting a pedestrian while driving drunk is at the center of *Hit and Run* (1994). A more familiar scenario is given new life in *Sticks and Stones* (1994) which features a girl unfairly labeled promiscuous by her school. *Mission Impossible* (1994) tells the story of a student who protests the school pageant by refusing to shave her legs, and *The Good, the Bad, and the Suicidal* (1997) involves another high-school protest—this time against a citywide curfew—which brings members of the Jocks (who have money), the Irregulars (who don't), and the Leftovers together to fight for their rights. On a more serious note, *The Dream Where the Losers Go* (1999) depicts the struggles of a young girl who is sent to lockup after a failed suicide attempt.

G.'s most celebrated work to date, *Before Wings* (2000), tells the story of an overprotected teen whose parents smother her in an attempt to keep her safe. After suffering a brain aneurysm at thirteen, fifteen-year-old Adrien feels as though all she can do is sit around and wait to die. During a working vacation at her aunt's summer camp, however, she forms a close relationship with Paul—a boy haunted by premonitions of his own death—and learns the importance of living every day as if it were your last.

AWARDS: Shortlisted, Alberta Fiction Award, for *Could I Have My Body Back Now, Please?;* American Library Association Quick Picks (for Reluctant Teen Readers) for *Sticks and Stones;* 1994 R. Ross Annett Juvenile Fiction Award for *Mission Impossible;* Shortlisted, Governor General's Award for Children's Literature for *Mission Impossible;* Shortlisted, Gerald Lampert Award for *Scars of Light;* 1995 League of Canadian Poets' Pat Lowther Award for *Scars of Light;* Our Choice Award, Canadian Children's Book Center, 1995 for *Mission Impossible,* 1998 for *The Good, the Bad, and the Suicidal,* 1999 for The Colours of Carol Molev, 2000 for *The Dream Where the Losers Go,* and 2001 for *Before Wings;* Joseph J. Stauffer Award for Literature, Canada Council, 1998; Canadian Library Association Young Adult Book Award for *Before Wings;* Sunburst Award for *Before Wings;* American Library Association Best Books for Young Adults, 2002, for *Before Wings;* American Library Association Best Books for Young Adults 2003 and Quick Picks 2003 nominee for *The Lottery.*

SELECT FURTHER WORKS: *Could I Have My Body Back Now, Please?* (SHORT STORY and poetry collection) 1991; *Kicked Out* (novel) 1995; *I'm Not Convinced* (novel) 1997; *The Colours of Carol Molev* (novel) 1998; *The Only-Good Heart* (adult novel) 1998; *The Lottery* (novel) 2002.

BIBLIOGRAPHY: "Beth G." *Contemporary Authors Online,* Gale, 2004. Reproduced in *Biography Resource Center.* The Gale Group. 2004. http://galenet .galegroup.com/servlet/BioRC; "Beth G." *Contemporary Authors Online,* Gale, 2004. Reproduced in *Literature Resource Center, Author Resource Pages,* the Gale Group, 2004. http://galenet.galegroup.com/ servlet/BioRC; "Before Wings," the *Horn Book,* March 2001, v. 77 no. 2, pg. 207; "Before Wings," *Booklist,* 15 March 2001, v. 97 no. 14, pg. 1391; "The Lottery," *Publishers Weekly,* 28 October 2002. v. 249 no. 43, pg. 73; "The Lottery," *Kliatt,* November 2002, v. 36 no. 6, pg. 10; "Sticks and Stones," *Kliatt,* July 2002, v. 36, no. 4, pg. 19. "Beth G." National Library of Canada website. http://www.nlc-bnc.ca/3/ 11/t11-6038-e.html

JULIE BARTEL

GORDON, Ruth I.

Editor, school librarian, reviewer, lecturer, b. 13 May 1933, Chicago, Illinois

G., a Sonoma County, California resident, compiles anthologies of POETRY for TEEN readers. She selects international poets, both ancient and modern, whose themes are more serious than humorous. In *Pierced by a Ray of Sun: Poems about the Times We Feel Alone (1995),* her themes include loneliness and uncertainty.

Previous works for younger readers, such as *Peeling the Onion* (1993), include themes of animals, nature, families, and sports. For older readers, her previous works include poems in *Under All Silences: Shades of Love* (1987) and *Time is the Longest Distance* (1991).

Her involvement in the American Library Association includes membership on committees for children's books, most notably chair of the Newbery and Notable Children's Books committees. She was a member of the Board of Directors of the Assn. for Library Services to Children (ALSC), and served on the ALSC Distinguished Service Award committee.

G. holds an A.B. degree from Tufts University, an M.A. from Brown University, and an M.L.S. and Ph.D. from the University of California at Berkeley.

She reads, writes, and speaks Italian and French and reads German and Hebrew.

Formerly a school teacher in northern California and Italy, G. went back to school to earn a degree in order to pursue a career in school librarianship. She continues to consult in librarianship for youth.

AWARDS: 1987 Best Book for Young Adults, *Under All Silences: Shades of Love; Peeling the Onion: Booklist* Books for Youth Editors' Choices and New York Public Library's 1994 Books for the Teen Age. 1996 Best Book for Young Adults, *Pierced by a Ray of Sun.*

BIBLIOGRAPHY: *Who's Who of American Women,* 18th ed., 1993–1994; *Directory of Library and Information Professionals,* 1988.

LANETTE GRANGER

GORDON, Sheila
Author, b. 22 January 1927, Johannesburg, South Africa

G.'s award-winning novels depict the influence of apartheid on the lives of young black and white South Africans. *Waiting for the Rain: A Novel of South Africa* (1987) features Frikkie, a white Afrikaaner, and Tengo, a black youth, whose relationship is strained by the oppressive social regime of their country. When the two young men confront each other on opposite sides of a riot, they are forced to make an emotionally difficult decision in the face of political unrest. *The Middle of Somewhere: A Story of South Africa* (1990) is the story of a nine-year-old South African named Rebecca, whose home is threatened by a white-biased government policy. When her father is imprisoned for his vocal opposition to this policy, her mother is forced to serve in the house of a wealthy white family in order to provide for her own family. G.'s novels have been translated into many languages.

AWARDS: *Waiting for the Rain:* Jane Addams Children's Book Award (1988), Preis der Leseratten (Germany), Blauer Brillenschlage (Germany), Prix d'Honneur, Academie de Grenoble (France), and Le Bouquine Prix des Lecteurs (France) (all 1989); 1991 Jane Addams Children's Books Honor: *The Middle of Somewhere;* Bancarellino Prize, Union of Pontremoli Booksellers (Italy), 1993. Best Books for Young Adults list, 1987.

FURTHER WORKS: *A Monster in the Mailbox,* 1978; *A Modest Harmony: Seven Summers in a Scottish Glen,* 1982; *Unfinished Business: A Novel of South Africa,* 1987.

BIBLIOGRAPHY: *Contemporary Authors,* online, 2001; *Something About the Author,* vol. 88, 1997.

ANNETTE MACINTYRE

GOULD, Steven
Author, b. 1955, n.p.

G.'s first piece of short fiction, "The Touch of Their Eyes," was published in the September 1980 issue of *Analog.* This publication was followed by many others, until G.'s writing shifted directions. *Jumper* (1992) was G.'s transition from SHORT STORIES to novels. At age seventeen, the protagonist of the book, David Rice realizes he has teleported only after it happens. Delighted with his new ability, he uses it to stay away from his father, who hurt him, and try to find his mom, currently missing in action. Surviving in New York City entails robbing a bank, which of course leads to new complications. G.'s next novel, *Wildside* (1997), features another TEENAGE protagonist, Charlie Newell. On the land he inherits is vast potential for untold wealth—not to mention a portal to an alternate universe—until his activities bring unwanted attention and danger from the government.

With the publication of *Greenwar* in 1997, G. and his wife, Laura Mixon, combined their expertise, his in oil and diving and hers in corporate environmentalism. Together they produced the story of Emma Tooke, her work at Gulf Stream, and Keith Hellman, who is not quite who he seems, as they battle natural disasters and human enemies. In *Helm* (1998), G. published a space FANTASY work. Leland de Laal, by trying on the Helm, a piece of technology not meant for his use, changes his fate and winds up at a school for Aikido. G. is an expert in martial arts—he has a Black belt in Aikido, the Japanese martial art. This knowledge served him well as he details Leland's training. *Blind Waves* (2000) is set in a not-too-far-distant future. When a flood spreads from Antarctica to encompass a great deal of the planet, citizens needing relocation create a vast problem. Patricia Beenan is drawn into it when in the course of her work, recovery from the ocean, she finds evidence of a human smuggling ring, and joins Immigration and Naturalization Commander Thomas Beckett to solve the crime and bring the perpetrators to justice. The crime turns out to have greater implications than it first appears, but the daring duo is up to the challenge.

A computer consultant since 1983, websites that G. designed have won awards. Aikido was the third martial art that G. tried, having tried Judo in his teenage years and moving on to Karate (where he focused on Shotokan). He currently lives in Texas with his wife and their two children.

AWARDS: 1985 Hugo Best Short story nominee, "Rory"; "Peaches for Mad Molly": 1988 Nebula Best Novellette nominee, 1989 Hugo Best Novellette niminiee; 1991 Locus Award nominee, "Simulation Six"; 1997 Goldenduck Award; American Library Association Best Book for Young Adults: *Jumper* (1992) and *Wildside* (1997).

FURTHER WORKS: "Gift of Fire," 1981; "Wind Instrument," 1981; "Rory," 1984; "Mental Blocks," 1985; "The No License Needed, Fun to Drive, Built Easily with Ordinary Tools, Revolutionary, Guaranteed, Lawnmover Engine Powered, Low Cost, Compact, and Dependable Male Order Device," 1986; "Poppa Was a Catcher," 1987; "Peaches for Mad Molly," 1988; "Simulation Six," 1990; "The Session," 1995; "Reflex," 2004.

BIBLIOGRAPHY: www.amazon.com; www.digitalnoir .com; www.digitalnoir/s&l.htm; www.novelst4 .epnet.com; www.sfsite.com/11a/sllm115.htm

JEANNE MARIE RYAN

GRANT, Cynthia D.

Author, b. 23 November 1950, Brockton, Massachusetts

The dauhter of Robert C. and Jacqueline (Ford) Grant, red-haired and freckled G. began writing at an early age. She loved the way sounds were put together to make words which had a "power to create worlds on paper," so she was highly motivated. She was writing POETRY and stories by the time she was eight. Thanks to her grandmother's position as a stringer, G. was first published in the local newspaper, the *Brockton Enterprise* at this young age. She grew up loving to read as much as she loved to write. Her favorite books were Carolyn Keene's Nancy Drew MYSTERIES. G. admits that Nancy was her role model: independent, resourceful and self-confident. She also enjoyed reading BIOGRAPHIES of famous women and dreamed of being famous herself one day. Moving west, G. attended high school in Palo Alto, California.

G. knew in high school that she wanted to be a famous writer and did not opt for college upon graduation. She entered the writer's real world of publishing by writing and submitting her works. Fame did not come immediately but rejections did, so G. had to work as a file clerk in an insurance office and later as a waitress. When not working, G. wrote and submitted her work to journals such as the *Atlantic Monthly* and the *New Yorker.* She was first published in a FEMINIST magazine. In spite of her rejections, G. continued writing and submitting her work to try to get it published. Later, trying her hand at the YOUNG ADULT audience, for young people twelve-years old and up, G.'s first realistic fiction young adult novel, *Hard Love,* was published in 1983. It appeared that she had found her writing niche.

Her realistic fiction is about young adults growing up in the real world. Situations dealing with and surviving homelessness, death of a loved one, child abuse and alcoholism are presented through a combination of despair intertwined with hope and optimism. For inspiration, she draws on her own experiences growing up during junior-high school as she painfully remembers the meanness of others to those students who were not good looking and/or who were different in any number of ways or who were smart and nerdy. Young adult readers identify with her realistically portrayed characters. Dialogues and conversations between these characters carry the realistic themes and define the support that friends and family give the main young adult character. Noted for not stereotyping, but rather individualizing, her characters have unusual, yet true-to-life characteristics with whom TEENAGERS can identify. Serious situations and events are laced with humor and both combine to make a point. The message that runs through all of G.'s books is that there is hope, and that it is possible to endure and survive growing up. As young adults read about the same types of events that happen in their real world, and read how G.'s characters in her stories work through these same problems and challenges, G. hopes that teenagers learn they do not have to be alone. She wants them to realize that there are family and friends to provide support as they share common feelings and experiences in growing up. In writing another of her books, *Phoenix Rising: Or How to Survive Your Life,* G. again drew on her own tragedy, the DEATH of one of her nineteen-year-old friends who died from cancer. Through this book, G. immortalized and "captured her (friend) on paper" for all time. This fitting memorial complements G.'s words about young adult authors, "most of us who write for children or young adults know that they read books not only to be entertained, but to be enlightened and encouraged." G. makes her home in California.

SELECT AWARDS: *Joshua Fortune* (1981) won the Annual book award from Woodward Park School; *Phoenix Rising* has won the following: Best Book of the Year Award, Michigan Library Association's Young Adult *Caucus* (1990), PEN/Norma Klein Award (1991), Author Day Award, Detroit Public Library (1992). One of 100 YA titles selected for the fourth YALSA Best of the Best list. Here we go again . . . 25 years of Best Books (selections from 1967 to 1992): *Shadow Man,* ALA Best Books for YA, 1994; *Uncle Vampire,* ALA Best Books for YA, 1994; *Mary Wolf,* ALA Best Books for YA, 1996.

FURTHER WORKS: *The Cannibals,* 2002; *The White Horse,* 1998; *Mary Wolf,* 1995; *Uncle Vampire,* 1993; *Shadow Man,* 1992; *Keep Laughing,* 1991; *Phoenix Rising; or, How to Survive Your Life,* 1989; *Kumquat May, I'll Always Love You,* 1986; *Hard Love,* 1983; *Big Time,* 1982; *Summer Home,* 1981; *Joshua Fortune,* 1980.

BIBLIOGRAPHY: *Authors and Artists for Young Adults,* Vol 23. "Grant, Cynthia D." Gale Research, 1998. Reproduced in Biography Resource center. Farmington Hills, Mich.: The Gale Group, 2004. http://gale net.galegroup.com/servlet/BioRC; *Contemporary Authors.* "Grant, Cynthia D." Reproduced in Biography Resource Center, Farmington Hills, Mich.: The Gale Group, 2004. http://galenet.galegroup.com/serv let/BioRC; *Something about the Author,* Vol. 77. Ed. by Kevin S. Hile and Diane Telgen. © 1994 P. 75–77.

VALERIE A. PALAZOLO

THE GRAPHIC NOVEL

In 1978, Baronet published *A Contract with God and Other Tenement Stories* by Will EISNER. In order to characterize itself and give identity to its singularity, the book described itself as a graphic novel. It sought a readership outside of the COMIC-BOOK audience and acceptance as a literary work. It was produced in hard cover and PAPERBACK and distributed to the standard book stores as well as comic shops. It was composed of four related stories about tenement life in the Bronx during the mid 1930s. It employed sequentially arranged images and dialogue held in balloons that was traditional to comic books, but it departed from the story line common to the comics of the time; instead, it was addressed to adults and dealt with sub-

ject matter more closely associated with the human condition. It told its story with an impressionistic style, in a package that was similar to conventional novels, and claimed to be inspired by earlier efforts at books of visual narrative by creators like Lynd Ward.

The term "graphic novel" was first used in 1976 to describe a compilation of an underground newspaper strip *Beyond Time and Again* by George Metzger. There were earlier attempts to find a dignified term, like Charles Biro's "illustories"; this failed to catch on because the comic-book content did not support the pretension. Earlier examples of this kind of storytelling in book form were produced by a Belgian wood engraver, Frans Masereel, who published *Die Sonne* (1927) in Germany. In 1930 Otto Nuckel, a German, published *Destiny,* a "novel in pictures" in the U.S. Later, Lynd Ward, the American woodcut artist and illustrator, produced a number of "wordless books," among which were *Silver Pony* and *Vertigo,* both published in 1937. The newspaper strip humorist, Milt Gross, published a comic satire of ROMANCE novels entitled *She Done Him Wrong,* and some romance novella paperbacks written in Spanish appeared in New York.

In the 1940s, comic-book adaptations of standard classics were widely circulated as *Classics Illustrated.* In 1945, a series of photographic narratives using movies stills were published in Italy under the title *Grand Hotel.* In 1955 Jules Feiffer's *Passionella* was published as a paperback. In the late 1960's, the underground cartoonist Jack Jackson produced a historical series about frontier life and American Indian legends. None, however, labeled themselves graphic novels; at that time no attempt was made to define stories rendered in sequential art as literary endeavor nor did comics presume any relationship with serious literature.

Shortly after *A Contract with God*'s publication, other books addressed to a similar audience appeared. *Maus* (1984) by Art SPIEGELMAN, and *Tantrum* (1979) by Feiffer found adult readers. While they did not label themselves as graphic novels, they certainly helped to further the acceptability of this form; indeed, *Maus,* Volume II, received a Pulitzer Prize in 1992. As the audience for this kind of book grew, the publishers in the diminishing market for standard comics adopted the term "graphic novel" as a generic description for comics that adapted traditional book binding and longer, more complex stories. This movement was a trade response to a reading phenomenon in Western popular culture. With the rise in mid-century of film and telecast movies that began to deal with the fast outpouring of information, customary printed text as the dominant format came under siege. Illustrated stories became widespread, photographic picture MAGAZINES proliferated, and the employment of imagery to speed up the absorption of ideas and information increased.

Toward the latter third of the century, portable computerized games began to compete for young reader's attention. Indeed, by then the schools had already found students becoming "reluctant readers" by the sixth grade. While academics involved in popular culture devoted much more attention to cinema, there was little available in acceptably constructed graphic literature to evaluate or consider as a potential solution to the literacy problem. Nevertheless, this medium that employed sequential art as a language was responding to a new literacy that involved a combination of words and images.

In 1974, "Comics in the Library," an article by Will Eisner, appeared in *School Library Journal,* making the case for the inclusion of comics in public and school libraries as a way of encouraging a higher standard of quality in this burgeoning medium. There appeared little or no response from librarians and the proposal languished until 2001. At this time, an article by Steve Weiner appeared in the *Library Journal* addressing the contribution to literacy that graphic novels and comic books were making. By this time, American schools were using the genre to prompt reading, and many universities included graphic novels in their curriculums. Library shelves now carried graphic novels and reported strong patronage.

With the beginning of the 21st century, mainstream book stores face competition with comic shops and have begun to include graphic novels in their inventory. Works by Neil GAIMAN (*Sandman 1,* 1991), Allen Moore, and Harlan Ellison were followed by newer author-artists like Chris Ware, Ben Katchor, and Joe Sacco. Despite the trend of collaborations, the solo author who undertakes all the aspects of creation continues. Artists such as Frank Miller, Scott McCloud, Jame and Gilbert Hernandez, Chris Ware, P. Craig Russel, and Robert Crumb continue to produce significant, innovative works. Outside the U.S. the genre has found wide acceptance and is a reflection of national culture. European author-artists like Mobieus, Hugo Pratt, Jacques Tardi, Mezieries, Vittorio Giardino, and Lorenzo Mahotti have produced enduring works that have been translated into many languages.

Whereas the graphic novel persisted as a generic description of the form that dealt in a significant variety of subject matter, the genre had an identity problem. Publishers seizing a marketing opportunity began to use the "graphic novel" term for collections of ADVENTURE stories and stories that pursued the same vengeance and pursuit plots of the standard comic books. "Graphic novel" is now used to describe FANTASY, HORROR, SCIENCE FICTION, and SUPERHERO stories. The popularity of stories in a classic Japanese style of art and rhythm of graphic narrative has added yet another form to the Western societies' library of picture-story literature. *Manga,* as they are called, enormously popular in Japan, presumably because of a basic relationship to the language's use of ideograph. Led by Tezuka, a number of Japanese author-artists, such as Tanaka, Koike, and Kojima have become popular worldwide. The classic Gen that deals with the atomic bombing of Hiroshima has a wide Western audience. Graphic novels began to engage in reportage by graphically narrating social tumult in various regions of the world. "Palestine" by Joe Socco initiated this genre to great acclaim. Ben Katchor's "Jew of New York," a satire introducing a form of social reporting, attracted wide adult readership.

The endurance of the graphic novel as a term is quite probable because the public has often demonstrated a reluctance to abandon a product's familiar description. For example, the word "comics" has long since failed to accurately describe a medium that no longer devotes itself only to comical situations, but nonetheless remains as a common description of the form. So, while visual literature may be a better description than the sometime pejorative character of the word "graphic," BIOGRAPHIES as well as histories and works of social value will gradually broaden its scope and the term graphic novel may well prevail.

As the level of talent in the field rises, the skill involved will increase its acceptance by critics and teachers. This and the need for rapid communication will continue to be the engine of its growth. Book sales and income to artist and author involved in this medium, buttressed by their rising status in the cultural community, will expand its position in the world of publishing. Furthermore, whereas the earliest graphic novels were written and drawn by the same person, the need for greater productivity has led the comic book to become the work of a script writer, a penciller, an inker, letterer, and colorist. As for technology, the print medium can now accommodate art of greater complexity, such as painting, photography, and computer-generated images.

Finally, because of the construction of a graphic novel demands a sophisticated assembly of images and words as well as a knowledge of the disciplines involved, it is taught and studied in the academies of the world.

WILL EISNER

Note: Will Eisner helped us in many ways; he was always willing to answer questions and guide us. He died January 3, 2005, as we were completing this book, which in part is dedicated to him. The cover of A Contract with God *graces our book.—The Editors*

GRAPHIC NOVELS IN LIBRARIES

The term "GRAPHIC NOVEL" means a story told in words and pictures ordered sequentially, in book form. Will EISNER is credited with coining the term in the late 1970s, although some comics aficionados have disputed this. Whoever invented the term, the graphic novel format has become part of the popular culture and literary landscape and has become a popular part of many library collections. The graphic novel is a book-length COMIC BOOK, and the comic book, as most people know it, is a stapled pamphlet which is published at regular intervals (monthly, bimonthly, or quarterly); some people call them all "comics."

Comic books were not always welcome in libraries; Allen Ellis and Doug Highsmith traced the attitudes of library professionals toward comics in their article "About Face: Comic Books in Library Literature," published in *Serials Review* (2000). According to their research, library literature began covering comic books in the 1940s, with articles that were mostly negative and denigrated the format. In 1968, Bill Katz's "Magazines" column in *Library Journal* recommended adding comics to library collections. In the 1980s, more librarians and educators began to promote the use of comic books in education, and Libraries Unlimited published *Cartoons and Comics in the Classroom: A Reference Guide for Teachers and*

Librarians, edited by James L. Thomas (1983). In 1988, *Voice of Youth Advocates (VOYA)* published an article by Patrick Jones, "Getting Serious About Comics," which discussed some of the graphic novels and trade PAPERBACK collections that were available then and advocated their inclusion as books in the library. In the 1990s more articles appeared in *Booklist, Library Journal,* and *School Library Journal,* and in 1994 *VOYA* began regular coverage of graphic novels with a column in the magazine (it didn't get its name, "Graphically Speaking," until December 1994, but began in February 1994); it's the longest-running graphic novel review column in library literature.

The 1992 Pulitzer Prize awarded to *Maus, Volume II,* by Art SPIEGELMAN, marked the recognition by the general culture that graphic novels can possess high literary quality. Graphic novels appeared on the Quick Picks for Reluctant Young Adult Readers lists (chosen by committees selected by the Young Adult Library Services Association—YALSA) beginning in the early 1990s, and on the Best Books for Young Adults lists in 1999. The Popular Paperbacks lists included "Going Alternative: Graphic Novels and PICTURE BOOKS" in 1997, and "Graphic Novels: SUPERHEROES and Beyond" in 2002. The 2004 lists include a number of graphic novel titles in the various subject lists, and more are on the 2005 nomination lists.

Graphic novels "arrived" in the library world in 2002. YALSA's preconference for the 2002 ALA Annual Conference was called "Getting Graphic @ the Library"—it proved to be the most popular YALSA preconference ever. That fall, the annual Teen Read Week theme was also "Getting Graphic @ the Library." The one listserv devoted to discussing graphic novels and comics in libraries, Graphic Novels in Libraries (GNLIB-L), was started in 1999; in 2002 the membership doubled in size after the ALA Annual Conference. That year, both *School Library Journal* and *Library Journal* started review columns devoted to graphic novels. In 2003 *Booklist* started publishing a Graphic Novels Spotlight in the February 1 issue; they did it again in the February 1, 2004 issue and again on February 1, 2005. Book distributors also began graphic novel purchasing programs for their library customers; Ingram, Baker and Taylor, Book Wholesalers, Inc., and Brodart all carry graphic novels and market them to libraries. Diamond Comics

Distributors started its Bookshelf program for libraries several years ago, then added reviews in 2001.

The G. is not a genre, but a format which embraces just about every fictional genre one can think of, as well as nonfiction. Most people associate superheroes with graphic novels—almost everyone can identify Spider-Man, Batman, and Superman. But there are lots of graphic novels with no superheroes: the aforementioned *Maus,* the AUTOBIOGRAPHICAL *Persepolis* by Marjane Satrapis depicting her life as a girl in Iran of the late 1970s and early 1980s; *The Tale of One Bad Rat* by Brian Talbot, about an abused TEEN who runs away and finds hope; Judd WINICK's *Pedro and Me* which depicted his friendship with young AIDS victim and advocate Pedro Zamora; Craig Thompson's autobiographical *Blankets,* about his senior year in high school with his first love and wrestling with questions about faith; the nine-volume *Bone* by Jeff Smith, an epic adventure with humor, ROMANCE, battles with evil and memorable characters; Neil GAIMAN's *Sandman,* a SERIES which encompassed classical literature, world MYTHOLOGY, religion, and HORROR; and many more.

One type of G. which is phenomenally popular is manga (pronounced "mah-n-gah"—bury the "n" at the back of the throat), or Japanese comics. Manga covers all genres (except superheroes); there are titles which appeal to teen boys, to teen girls, to children, and to adults. In libraries, manga especially appeals to teen girls, who embrace all kinds of titles, from *Sailor Moon* to *Ranma ¹⁄₂* to *Peach Girl, Mars, Marmalade Boy, Fruits Basket, Basara;* boys enjoy *Dragonball Z,* the various *Gundam* titles, *Yu Yu Hakusho, Trigun, Ruruouni Kenshin,* and many more. Manga is related to anime (pronounced "ah-nee-meh" with no emphasis on any syllable)—Japanese animation; manga is the book and anime is the film. Most manga titles also become anime series. Some libraries have successfully used the popularity of these forms to create vital and exciting library programs for teens which invite teen participation; anime and manga clubs are forming in many libraries and showcase the creative talents of the teens involved.

Since manga is translated from the Japanese (and, increasingly, from Korean and Chinese), the stories reflect the cultures that produce them. Sometimes this can create a dilemma for American librarians; casual nudity and coarse bathroom humor appear even in titles written for children; in the U.S. some people find this objectionable. Anime appears on television, on networks such as Nickelodeon and Cartoon Network; the shows are edited for American audiences, but the manga of the same titles are not, so sometimes parents become upset when they see the books their children bring home. Librarians need to know more about manga in order to make appropriate choices for their communities. On the other hand, manga can be used to discuss different cultural mores.

G. and manga appeal both to reluctant readers and to highly gifted readers alike. The limited text and highly visual appeal of the art make them nonthreatening to reluctant and inexperienced readers, while the stories and artwork appeal to other readers. The market for G.s is still growing, and the great variety of titles means there's something for every kind of reader, for every kind of reading taste.

BIBLIOGRAPHY: Ellis, Allen and Highsmith, Doug. "About Face: Comic Books in Library Literature," *Serials Review,* 2000, Vol. 25 Issue 2, p21 (23 pages). Gaiman, Neil. *Sandman* [series], 1993– . Satrapis, Marjane. *Persepolis: The Story of a Childhood,* 2003. Smith, Jeff. *Bone* [series], 1996–2004. Talbot, Brian. *The Tale of One Bad Rat,* 1995. Winick, Judd. *Pedro and Me: Friendship, Loss, and What I Learned,* 2000.

KATHARINE KAN

GRAVELLE, Karen

Author, editor, photographer, b. 22 July 1942, Alexandria, Virginia

G. is an award-winning author who is well known for her issue-related works for YOUNG ADULTS. As a former social worker and therapist, she saw a need for resources that addressed difficult questions teenagers face in their lives everyday. Through the *Simon & Schuster Interview Series* she demonstrates that her knowledge of the issues and topics that are important to young people is vast. She has many popular INFORMATIONAL books to her credit.

G. has written several books and articles for young adults including *Teenage Fathers: An Inside View,* which won the Young Adult Library Services Association/American Library Association Best Book Award in 1993. Her first work of fiction is her 1985 children's book *Feather.* A freelance writer and photographer since 1982, G.'s curiosity and interest in the world around her are showcased in the books she enjoys writing to help young people understand the world around them.

AWARDS: ALA BBYA 1993 for *Teenage Fathers: An Inside View.*

FURTHER WORKS: *Growing up in a Holler in the Mountains: An Appalachian Childhood,* 1997; *Growing up Where the Partridge Drums Its Wings: A Mohwak Childhood,* 1997; *Growing up in Crawfish Country,* 1998; *What's Going on Down There?: Answers to Questions Boys Find Hard to Ask,* 1998; *Five Ways to Know About You,* 2001.

BIBLIOGRAPHY: *Contemporary Authors,* online 2003; *Something about the Author,* vol. 78, 1994.

LAURIE M. ALLEN

GRAY, Dianne
Author, n.d., York, Nebraska

While earning an M.A. in liberal studies at Hamline University, in St. Paul, Minnesota, G. began to write in earnest. Her writing is infused with a deep sense of place she acquired while growing up on the Nebraska prairie and from where she now lives in Winona, Minnesota. In her website, she details the place in which she nows lives: "[My] home is at the crest of a Mississippi River bluff, . . . [The] road is steep, narrow, and winding. . . . Our back yard is wooded and wild." (Gray, http://prairievoices.com). Gray concludes the lengthy description with, "As you can tell, I think this is a really cool place to live." (*ibid.*). In her works, as well, there is a sense of celebration of place.

Cyndi Giorgis and Nancy J. Johnson note, "Gray has drawn from her own life to write *Holding Up the Earth,*" set on the Nebraska prairie (2001, p. 307). In the novel (2000), G.'s first for young people, fourteen-year-old Hope discovers a heritage of women who have lived before her on the prairie; she gains strength from their lives. Hope, who lost her mother in a car accident, finds, through reading DIARY entries and hearing stories, many heroic matriarchs who inspire her to live, as they did, in that hallowed place. For its study on the role of "place," Giorgis and Johnson (2001) include *Holding Up the Earth* in their bibliography about children's books that deal with "discovery of place, creation of place, places that present obstacles, and setting out for new places."

As an author concerned with place and the people who live in it, G. actively participated in the Family Reading Time program at Winona Middle School. "I wanted to . . . have families reading [*Holding Up the Earth*]," G. said, commenting on her participation in the program and the selection of her book as a work for discussion (Anderson 2002, p. 14).

Together Apart (2002), G.'s second novel for young people, is also set in the Nebraska prairie. The action of the novel begins a few months after the historical "School Children's Blizzard" of January 1888, named because it struck during the school day, resulting in the DEATHS of many children. Similar to *Holding Up the Earth,* female strength—found in Eliza, the judge's widow—influences the actions of the main characters of the novel. The free-thinking Eliza provides Hannah and Isaac a place of freedom where they can live and grow safely, a temporary respite from the world of brutal blizzards and oppressive parents.

AWARDS: All for *Holding Up the Earth:* Willa Award, Women Writing the West (Young Adult), 2001; Best Books for Young Adults, 2001; Golden Sower Nominee, 2002–2003 (Nebraska Library Association); and Mark Twain Nominee, 2002–2003 (Missouri Association of School Librarians).

BIBLIOGRAPHY: Anderson, M. A. (2002). Family reading time = quality reading time. *Book Report, 21* (2), 14–16; Giorgis, C. & Johnson, N. (2001). Finding a place. *The Reading Teacher, 55,* 304–311; Prairie voices: the website of author Dianne Gray (n.d.); http://www.prairievoices.com/

MARY MCMILLAN TERRY

GREEN, Hannah. See GREENBERG, Joanne.

GREENBERG, Jan
Author, b. 29 December 1942, St. Louis, Missouri

G. was born to Alexander and Lillian Schonwald, a manufacturer and an advertising executive. She married Ronald Greenberg August 31, 1963, and the couple has three daughters, Lynne, Jeanne, and Jacqueline. G. received a B.A. from Webster University in 1964 and an M.A.T. from Webster University in 1971. She taught creative writing and art appreciation in the St. Louis Public Schools from 1969–72, Forest Park Community College, St. Louis, from 1973–75, and served as director and instructor of an aesthetic-education master's degree program 1974–79 at Webster University. She reviewed books for the *St. Louis Post-Dispatch,* 1974–80, served on the Missouri Arts Council, literature committee (1984) and was a member of the Daniel Webster Society Board, Webster

University. G.'s husband is an art dealer in St. Louis and New York, specializing in Post-World War II American paintings and sculpture.

G. grew up loving to read and with a desire to write. She began writing a journal when she was ten and continues to keep notes of her thoughts. The library in her childhood home was filled with books, ranging from the classics to modern fiction that helped G. develop what she calls "my eclectic tastes in literature." Her fiction writing deals with topics of FAMILY concerns relating to TEENAGERS such as illness, family rivalries, and problems with friends and parents. In an interview for *Something about the Author* G. said, "I'm attempting to present an honest expression of human emotion. . . . Stimulated by the ever-present concerns I have as a mother and a participant observer in a strong family life." She believes that writing is a way to share in part of herself and that it is a "process of discovery."

G.'s first book, *A Season In-Between* (1979), was followed by *An Iceberg and Its Shadow* (1980). G. continued writing novels dealing with difficult relationships and family problems for teens, but by the 1990s she shifted to books about art and artists. Her passion for art led G. to collaborations on INFORMATIONAL and BIOGRAPHICAL books with Sandra Jordan, an editor and photographer. Their efforts resulted in *The Painter's Eye: Learning to Look at Contemporary American Art* (1991), *The Sculptor's Eye: Looking at Contemporary American Art* (1993), and *The American Eye: Eleven Artists of the Twentieth Century* (1995). These books provide readers with a glimpse into the world of art through interviews with contemporary artists; they include biographies and glossaries. G. and Jordan have also written engaging biographies of individual artists, including Vincent van Gogh, Chuck Close, Frank O. Gehry, and Jackson Pollock. Their work has been described by *School Library Journal* as "knowledgeable, eminently readable [and] visually enticing" accomplished "through solid research" which "reaches across the ages and cultures and challenges children." The books serve to educate children in the appreciation of art, to encourage them to look at art more closely, and to learn to express their appreciation in words. In a *Booklist* interview G. said, "Arts education is really about creating people who will take part in our culture." In a *Book Report* review (2002) for *Vincent van Gogh: Portrait of an Artist* (2001), the book is called author-

itative, unbiased, and one that readers will find "absorbing enough to read just for pleasure." According to a *Publishers Weekly* review (2003), G.'s biography of Romare Bearden is cited as a "dynamic portrait" of the AFRICAN AMERICAN artist where the "narrative reinforces the inviting artwork."

For her book *Heart to Heart: New Poems Inspired by Twentieth-Century American Art* (2001), G. asked well-known poets to write about their impressions of various forms of twentieth century art. In the introduction of *Heart to Heart,* G. talks of the influence art has had on her from an early age. She remembers visiting the St. Louis Art Museum with her mother who would sit and study the sculpture titled *Little Dancer of Fourteen Years* by Degas. Her mother encouraged G. to write down her impressions and thoughts about the sculpture but it was only as she got older that G. learned to appreciate the artist's style and to write down how she felt when she looked at the artwork. G. says, in *Heart to Heart,* "My first poems were inspired by art." During college G. began to understand how poetry and art have been tied together throughout history. The reviewer in *School Library Journal* praised *Heart to Heart* for being a "gorgeous, thoughtful, stimulating collection of art and poetry that turns the standard poetry/art book on its head." In the introduction G. describes the book as "celebrating the power of art to inspire language."

SELECT AWARDS: 1984 American Library Association Best Books for Young Adults citation, *No Dragons to Slay; Chuck Close Up Close:* Norman A. Sugarman Biography Award, ALA Notable Book, *Boston Globe–Horn Book* Honor Book, *School Library Journal* Best Book of the Year, Parenting Best Book of the Year; *Heart to Heart: New Poems Inspired by Twentieth Century American Art:* 2001 PRINTZ Honor Book, ALA Best Books for Young Adults; 2001 Sibert Honor Book, *Vincent Van Gogh: Portrait of an Artist; Action Jackson:* 2002 *Booklist* Best Books, 2002 *School Library Journal* Best Books, 2002 *Publishers Weekly* Best Books.

FURTHER WORKS: *The Pig-out Blues,* 1982; *No Dragons to Slay,* 1983; *Bye, Bye, Miss American Pie,* 1985; *Exercises of the Herat,* 1986; *Just the Two of Us,* 1988; *Chuck Close up Close* (with Sandra Jordan), 1998; *Frank O. Gehry: Outside In* (with Sandra Jordan), 2000; *Action Jackson,* 2002; *Runaway Girl: The Artist Louise Bourgeois* (with Sandra Jordan), 2003; *Romare Bearden: Collage of Memories,* 2003.

BIBLIOGRAPHY: *Jan Greenberg's Web Page,* Missouri Writes for Kids, retrieved June 4, 2003; *Something about the Author,* Vol. 61, 1990; *True Blue:* Jan G. and Sandra Jordan, *The Bulletin of the Center for Children's Books,* September, 2000; *Frank O. Gehry: Outside In* (Book review), *School Library Journal,* vol. 46, no. 9, Sept. 2000; *Heart to Heart* (Book review), *Book Report,* Nov/Dec 2001, vol. 20, no. 3; *Something About the Author,* vol. 125, 2002; *Story Behind the Story: From Images to Words, Booklist,* vol. 97, no. 4, March 15, 2001; *Heart to Heart* (Book Review), *School Library Journal,* vol. 47, no. 4, April 2001; *Vincent van Gogh* (Book Review), *Book Report,* vol. 20, 2002; *Runaway Girl* (Book review), *Contemporary Authors,* Vol. 196, 2002; *School Library Journal,* vol. 49, no. 5, May, 2003; *Runaway Girl* (Book review), *Horn Book Magazine,* vol. 79, no. 4, Jul/Aug, 2003; *Romare Bearden: Collage of Memories, Publisher's Weekly,* August, 2003.

NAOMI WILLIAMSON

GREENBERG, Joanne (Hannah Green)
Author, b. 24 September 1932, Brooklyn, New York

G. pursued her undergraduate degree at American University in Washington, D.C., majoring in anthropology and English literature. She studied at the University of London and at the University of Colorado. G. married Albert Greenberg in 1955 and had two sons, David and Alan. She has served as adjunct professor of Anthropology at the Colorado School of Mines since 1983.

G.'s interest in Native American culture led her to spend time on a Navajo reservation. She wrote short stories while she lived there, and these have been used for anthropological studies. G. is also a former member of the fire-fighting and emergency-rescue team near her home in Lookout Mountain, Colorado.

G.'s first book, *The King's Persons* (1963), dealt with the massacre of Jewish people in England in the 12th century. Her best-known work, however, was her second novel, written under the pseudonym *Hannah Green. I Never Promised You a Rose Garden* (1964) tells the story of a young girl suffering from schizophrenia. She based this on her own experience with mental illness, and she wrote it under the pseudonym to protect her children at the time. She claimed authorship of the book during the 1970s.

G.'s work as a vocational rehabilitation counselor inspired her keen interest in deaf patients and led to her writing *In This Sign,* which became a television movie.

G. continues to write and also tutors students in Latin and Hebrew. She maintains an active public speaking schedule at writers' seminars, workshops, and at schools.

AWARDS: (1963) Harry and Ethel Daroff Memorial Fiction Award from the National Jewish Welfare Board for *The King's Persons;* Community Grange Award for Citizenship; (1964) William and Janice Epstein Fiction Award from the National Jewish Welfare Board for *The King's Persons;* (1971) Marcus L. Kenner Award from the New York Association of the Deaf; (1971) Christopher Book Award for *In This Sign;* (1977) Frieda Fromm-Reichman Memorial Award from Western Maryland College; (1979) Frieda Fromm-Reichman Memorial Award from Gallaudet College; (1983) Rocky Mountain Women's Institute Award; (1990) Denver Public Library Bookplate Award; (1991) Colorado Author of the Year.

FURTHER WORKS: *The King's Persons,* 1963; *I Never Promised You a Rose Garden* (under pseudonym Hannah Green), 1964; *The Monday Voices,* 1965; *Summering: A Book of Short Stories,* 1966; *In This Sign,* 1968; *Rite of Passage,* 1971; *Founder's Praise,* 1976; *I Never Promised You a Rose Garden* film adapted, 1977; *High Crimes and Misdemeanors,* 1979; *A Season of Delight,* 1981; *The Far Side of Victory,* 1983; *Simple Gifts,* 1986; *Age of Consent,* 1987; *Of Such Small Differences,* 1988; *With the Snow Queen and Other Stories,* 1991; *No Reck'ning Made,* 1993; *Where the Road Goes,* 1998.

BIBLIOGRAPHY: *Contemporary Authors Online,* 2000; Magill, Frank, Ed. *Cyclopedia of World Authors,* Revised 3rd Edition, Vol. 2, 1989; www.mines.edu/fac_staff/senate/dist_lecturegreenberg_bio.shtml; www.narpa.org/greenberg.htm

SANDRA KITAIN

GREENE, Bette
Author, b. 28 June 1934, Memphis, Tennessee

G. was born in Memphis and raised in a small town in the Arkansas Delta, a town called Parkin. During World War II, she was considered lucky because her parents owned a country store stocked with gum and candy, items being rationed at the time. She, however, felt alienated because of her Jewish religion. It is not surprising that G.'s work for YOUNG ADULTS reflects those who feel alienated from society.

G. attended the University of Alabama, Memphis State University, Columbia University, and Harvard University, spanning the years from 1952 to 1965, but she never actually received a degree. Her various jobs included newspaper reporting, working as an information officer for the American Red Cross, and working in a hospital for psychiatric patients.

Her AUTOBIOGRAPHICAL book *Summer of My German Soldier* (1973) takes place in a small Arkansas town during World War II. Patty, a Jewish girl, helps an escaped prisoner of war named Anton. The novel explores the prejudice that Patty and Anton endure. She is targeted because of her religion, and he is stereotyped as a German soldier. However, he actually opposes the Nazis. Domestic violence is dealt with in this novel as well because Patty's dad is physically abusive. This story was eventually filmed as a television movie, winning an Emmy Award.

Morning is a Long Time Coming is G.'s sequel to *Summer of My German Soldier*. In that book, the main character, Patty, graduates from high school, goes on a trip to Europe, and falls in love with a Frenchman.

G. married Dr. Donald Greene in 1959 and has two children. She has received many honors for her writing, including a nomination for the National Book Award for *Summer of My German Soldier*. She also received the Golden Kite Award in 1974 for *Summer of My German Soldier*. The *New York Times* book award in 1974 was given to her book *Philip Hall Likes Me, I Reckon Maybe*. That book received Newbery Honor Book status in 1975. *Philip Hall Likes Me, I Reckon Maybe* received the *New York Times* outstanding book and outstanding title awards, the ALA Notable Children's Book Award, the Child Study Association Children's Book Award, and the *Kirkus* choice award, all in 1974.

G.'s book *Philip Hall Likes Me, I Reckon Maybe* focuses on the conflicts between Beth and Philip, two high-achieving black sixth graders. The characters appear again in the book's sequel *Get On Out of Here, Philip Hall!* In that book, the two eventually become friends.

AWARDS: Newbery Honor Book (1975) for *Philip Hall Likes Me, I Reckon Maybe*. *Summer of My German Soldier* won the *New York Times* outstanding book award in 1973, the National Book Award in 1974, the Golden Kite Society children's book writer's award in 1974, and was named as an ALA Notable Book in 1973. *Philip Hall Likes Me, I Reckon Maybe*, the *New York Times* outstanding Book award and outstanding title award, ALA Notable Children's Book Award, *Kirkus* Choice award in 1974.

FURTHER WORKS: *Summer of My German Soldier*, 1973; *Philip Hall Likes Me, I Reckon Maybe*, 1989; *Morning Is a Long Time Coming*, 1978; *Get on out of Here, Philip Hall!*, 1981; *A Writer's Survivor Kit*, 1981; *Them That Glitter and Them that Don't*, 1981; *The Drowning of Stephen Jones*, 1991; screenplay for *Summer of My German Soldier*, n.d.; *I've Already Forgotten Your Name, Philip Hall!*

BIBLIOGRAPHY: Commire, Anne. *Something About the Author*, Vol. 4. Gale, Detroit, MI., 1973. *Contemporary Authors Online*. The Gale Group, 2001. Silvey, Anita, Ed. *Children's Books and Their Creators*. Houghton Mifflin, NY, 1995.

SANDRA KITAIN

GREENFELD, Howard
Author, b. n.d., New York City

G. is the author of over twenty books for YOUNG ADULTS. He attended the University of Chicago and New York University before earning a Master's degree from Columbia University. He lived in France and Italy for many years, working as an English teacher, and then as a publisher. While in Europe, G. founded Orion Press, which he later sold, to publish English language translations of the European writers including Italo Calvino, Primo Levi, Albert Memmi, and Jean Piaget. G. is the author of many BIOGRAPHIES of people in the arts, including two books from the "First Impressions" SERIES—*Marc Chagall,* and *Paul Gauguin,* as well as biographies on Enrico Caruso, Puccini, *Gertrude Stein: A Biography* (1973 *Kirkus Reviews* Recommended Juvenile of the Year), F. Scott Fitzgerald, and Ben Shahn. His critically acclaimed book for young authors *Books: From Writer to Reader* has been used as a text in college courses. This book was chosen for: 1976 ALA Notable Children's Books, 1976 Best Books of the Year *School Library Journal*, *Kirkus* Choice, *Horn Book* Fanfare, and the AIGA Book Show. In 1993, G. wrote his first book on the HOLOCAUST, *The Hidden Children,* about heroism and survival, followed in 2001 by *After the Holocaust,* describing the adjustment and recovery of the many thousands of Jewish children and TEENAGERS. He has also written a critically acclaimed Jewish holiday series. G. currently resides with his family in the New York City area.

ROSE F. HAGAR

GREGORY, Kristiana

Author, b. 12 June 1951, Los Angeles, California

Books have always been a significant part of G.'s life. Encouraged by her father, an inventor, and her mother, a recreation supervisor, she developed a love for research, history, and writing. She has said "the historical things I write remind me of my childhood and the excitement of exploring something and finding out about it." G. is married and lives in Boise, Idaho, with her husband and two sons.

G. is an author of historical fiction stories set in the 18th, 19th, and 20th centuries; the books are written for juvenile and YA readers. Her protagonists are young people set in period-story ADVENTURES facing pivotal situations. G.'s stories deal with universal issues and the struggles of young people. She creates sympathetic characters in identifiable situations that are not unique to the time period of the story. Her writing is based on meticulous and detailed research.

G.'s first professional writing experience came during the 1970s when she became a freelance writer for newspapers; she subsequently wrote a children's book column for the *Los Angeles Times Book Review.* Her first choice of topics in writing fiction for children has been Native American history and culture, a part of her upbringing. Having lived in New Mexico, she became acquainted with the Mescalero Apache Indians. When her children were in school she began tutoring at the Pocatello High School, where she became acquainted with several Native Americans from Fort Hall. Having recognized how little was written about Native American culture, this experience inspired her to write *Jenny of the Tetons* and other stories about Native Americans. *Jenny of the Tetons* is written in honor of a Shoshone woman who G. wanted to memorialize. G. continued with Native American themes in her second book, *The Legend of Jimmy Spoon,* the tale of a young white boy who goes to live among the Shoshone. It was based on the memoirs of a 19th-century pony-express rider. Both books are accurate in detail and carefully researched.

Inspiration for the award-winning *Earthquake at Dawn* (1992), came while G. sat in an orthodontist's waiting room, reading a 1990 issue of *National Geographic* about the 1989 San Francisco earthquake. A sidebar in the article contained first-time published photographs taken by a young woman at the scene,

and included a brief story and letter describing what yet another woman had seen in the 1906 earthquake. Detailed descriptions about looters being shot and babies being born in the parks set her on the path of photographer Edith Irvine, the story's central character. The themes of survival, hope, and community of spirit permeate her story.

G. continues to write books, primarily with historic American themes, including several titles in the Dear America SERIES, in which periods of American history are illustrated through the fictional DIARIES of young people. She brings to life the American Revolution in this series with such titles as *The Winter of the Red Snow: The Revolutionary War Diary of Abigail Jane Stewart* (1996), *Five Smooth Stones: Hope's Diary, Philadelphia, Pennsylvania, 1776* (2001), and *We Are Patriots: Hope's Revolutionary War Diary* (2002).

G. has written other journals of U.S. history: *Across the Wide and Lonesome Prairie: The Oregon Trail Diary of Hattie Campbell* (1997) which is set in 1847, *The Great Railroad Race: The Diary of Libby West* (1999) which follows the construction of the transcontinental railroad in 1868, and *Seeds of Hope: The Gold Rush Diary of Susanna Fairchild* (2001) and *Orphan Runaways* (1998) which are centered around the California Gold Rush of 1849.

Cleopatra VII: Daughter of the Nile (1999) of the Royal Diaries series deviates from her usual themes and transports the reader through time and place to Egypt and Rome, telling the story of an adolescent Cleopatra.

G.'s works are parables for our time. She creates strong adolescent characters that are faced with extraordinary circumstances and forced to make difficult choices. The outcome is not always easy or happy, but leaves the reader with a sense of hope and greater understanding of the human condition.

AWARDS: *Jenny of the Tetons:* 1989 Golden Kite Award for Fiction, 1989 Notable Children's Trade Book in Social Studies citation, 1989 National Council for the Social Studies/Children's Book Council (NCSS-CBC); *Earthquake at Dawn:* ALA Best Book for Young Adults, 1992 National Council for the Social Studies/Children's Book Council (NCSS-CBC) list.

FURTHER WORKS: *Jimmy Spoon and the Pony Express,* 1994; *The Stowaway: A Tale of California Pi-*

rates, 1995; *Eleanor of Aquitaine,* 2002; *Prairie River* volumes 1–4.

BIBLIOGRAPHY: *Something about the Author,* Volume 74, 1993; *Something about the Author,* Volume 136, 2003; *Contemporary Authors: New Revision Series,* Volume 115, 2003; *Contemporary Authors Online,* 2003; http://kgregorybooks.com/

CLARA HUDSON

GRIFFIN, Adele
Author, b. 29 July 1970, Philadelphia, Pennsylvania

A relative newcomer to the field of YOUNG ADULT literature, G. is an outstanding and productive author. She attended the University of Pennsylvania and graduated with B.A. in English (1993). She was an assistant editor, 1996–1998, and has been a freelance manuscript reader since 1996.

G. writes three types of fiction: realistic, FANTASY, and historical. The majority of her realistic fiction focuses on the dysfunctional family and problem home. Her first book, *Rainy Season* (1996), portrays a pre-teen whose grief-stricken parents forbid the mention of the older deceased sibling. In her second book, *Split Just Right* (1997), a TEENAGER comes to realize that life is just right without her missing father. *Sons of Liberty* (1997), an award-winning book, depicts a home where the abusive father wakes up his two sons at midnight to repair the leaking roof, abuse which escalates until flight is the only solution. In *The Other Shepards* (1998) two teenage girls live in the shadow of three older siblings who died before the two girls were born. This last book has won the greatest number of awards and honors among her novels. *Dive* (1999) is written in second person as the monologue of an eleven-year old addressed to his older self-destructive stepbrother.

G. shifts her focus from dysfunctional families to problem adolescents in *Amandine* (2001). Delia, a new girl in the high school, is attracted to Amandine, an eerie, manipulative, and deceptive classmate, who enjoys painting grotesque pictures of the ugliest things and putting on skits to mimic classmates and teachers. Besides realistic fiction, G. is also skillful at creating fantasy. Published in 2002, *Witch Twins* and *Witch Twins at Camp Bliss* are about ten-year-old twin girls who use their magic powers to disrupt their father's wedding and cause confusion at a summer camp. Hannah, in *Hannah Divided* (2002), is a teen-

age math whiz with obsessive-compulsive behaviors who is selected to attend an elite school in Philadelphia; she faces the struggle and conflict between the rich and the poor, the city and the country. In *Overnight* (2003), G. addresses an adolescent clique, the power struggle among its members and its damaging effects on them.

G. creates strong characters who struggle to establish themselves in spite of authoritative and abusive fathers or of aloof parents. With keen insight, G. describes vividly FAMILY relationships and teenage relationships, as well as behaviors and interactions at school and home. Her novels are intriguing, engrossing, and fast-paced. As a young author whose writing career spans just eight years, G. can be expected to offer many more books in the future.

AWARDS: *The Other Shepards,* BBYA, 1999; *Sons of Liberty,* BBYA, 1998; ALA Notable Book citation, School Library Journal Best Books, YALSA Best Books for Young Adults, *Parent* Magazine Award, Kentucky Bluegrass Award, Pennsylvania Young Reader's Choice Award, Children's Literature Review. [Online]; *Amandine,* BBYA, 2002.

FURTHER WORK: *Shimmer,* 2001.

BIBLIOGRAPHY: Available: http://clcd.odyssi.com/cgi-bin/member. Novelist. [Online] Available: http://novest3.epnet.com/novel. Something about the Author, vol. 105, 1999.

SHU-HSIEN L. CHEN

GRIMES, Nikki
Author, b. 20 October 1950, New York City

Growing up as a foster child from a dysfunctional family, G. claims to have been fascinated with books at an early age. She later became aware that these books did not reflect her life experiences as an AFRICAN AMERICAN faced with challenging FAMILY situations. As a result, G. is known for her themes of friendship, family, relationships, and survival set among characters who have deep insights about life through facing its problems, joys, and everyday occurrences. Having twice earned the Coretta Scott King Honor Book award, G. won the Coretta Scott King Award in 2003 for *Bronx Masquerade* (2002), an intricate meshing of POETRY and narrative through the voices of eighteen TEENAGERS sharing their personal stories and discovering their self-worth. Additionally, she is the author of *Talkin' About Bessie:*

The Story of Aviator Elizabeth Coleman (2002) that won the award for illustration that same year.

G. writes in several genres but she is best known for her poetry. In *Meet Danitra Brown* (1994), the reader discovers both the theme of friendship that G. often employs and her energetic use of poetry to reveal the contemplations and questionings of the young. Friendship is also at the heart of *My Man Blue* (1999), a story told in fourteen poems about Damon, who has only his mother, and Blue, his mother's friend who has lost a son to the inner-city struggles that many youth face. The focus of this touching story, excellent for older readers, is the building of a relationship of trust through shared experiences and wisdom. Another collection of poems around building relationships is that of *Goin' out with Grandma Mac* (2001) in which a unique, independent-spirited grandmother is described through her granddaughter's eyes and heart. Again, G.'s use of language is drawn from the questioning innocence of the young; this language invites the readers to see those around them realistically and without the distorted perception that time and age brings. G. enjoys both fabric and bead work, and blends this interest in her poetry in *Aneesha Lee and the Weaver's Gift* (1999). In this unique story, the reader learns about Aneesha, who is metaphorically described in the process of weaving a tapestry.

Besides themes of friendship and family relationships, G. also uses the urban environment in which she grew up for settings in her poetry and prose. With a passion for travel, G. has visited Sweden, where she lived for six years, as well as China, Russia, Austria, Trinidad, and Tanzania. This latter country is the setting for *Is It Far to Zanzibar?* (2000).

Over fifty books by G. include prose as well as poetry in such titles as a BIOGRAPHY, *Malcolm X: A Force for Change* (1992), which focuses on the contribution of this black leader. *Jazmin's Notebook* (1998), a novel about a young Harlem girl in the 1960s who uses journaling to deal with life's difficulties, offers numerous connections to teen readers. Jazmin is a strong character who pursues academic achievements, contemplates religion, relationships, and boys, and provides a model of resiliency as a young foster child in an urban environment.

Drawing from her own experience and well-developed artistry, G. provides excellent models of perception, insight, characterization, and language

use for readers and writers. Additionally, her books provide excellent additions to the growing body of multiethnic literature for all readers.

SELECT AWARDS: Two Coretta Scott King Honor Book awards; (2003) Coretta Scott King Award, *Bronx Masquerade* (2002); (2003) Coretta Scott King Award for Illustration, *Talkin' About Bessie: The Story of Aviator Elizabeth Coleman* (2002); Bronx Masquerade, BBYA 2003.

SELECT FURTHER WORKS: *Something On My Mind*, 1978; *A Dime a Dozen*, 1998; *What Is Goodbye?*, 2004; *Tai Chi Morning*, 2004.

BIBLIOGRAPHY: *Children's Literature Review*, Volume 42, 1997. *Contemporary Authors Online*, 2003; Grimes, Nikki, "The Power of Poetry," 2000, *Book Links*, 9, pp. 32–36.

JANELLE B. MATHIS

GRISHAM, John Jr.
Author, publisher, b. 8 February 1955, Jonesboro, Arkansas

John Grisham Jr. was born February 8, 1955, in Jonesboro, Arkansas, the second of five siblings. His was a family of modest means, his father moving them frequently from job to job in construction and cotton farming. Settling, finally, in Southaven, Mississippi, G. graduated from Southaven High School in 1973 and enrolled in Northwest Junior College in Senatobia, Mississippi. There he played baseball and envisioned it as his career. Upon transferring to Delta State University in Cleveland, Mississippi, G. found tougher competition and realized that his future was not to be in baseball.

G. completed a degree in accounting at Mississippi State University in 1977. While studying there, G. began to keep a journal, a practice that would later pay off in his writing career. After finishing a law degree at the University of Mississippi in 1981, he married Renee Jones and returned home to Southaven to establish a law practice, specializing first in criminal law and more successfully in civil law. His near decade in law practice would prove quite useful in his future publications.

In 1983, G. was elected to the Mississippi State House of Representatives where he served until 1990. In his spare time, he began to write a novel. *A Time to Kill* was published in June of 1988 with only 5,000 copies printed. He immediately began writing a second book, the 1991 bestseller *The Firm,* which sky-rocketed in America, England, Italy, and Germany, spending forty-seven weeks on the *New York Times* best-seller list. The success of *The Firm* launched a career that would see G. named the best-selling author of the 1990s with over 60,000,000 copies of his works sold in some thirty-six languages. Several MOVIES have been based on his novels.

In spite of international acclaim, G. regards his spiritual life a high priority, involving himself in missionary trips and giving financial gifts to churches, missions, and charities. He considers himself an ordinary guy with strong moral values and a steadfast faith in God.

John, Renee, and their two children, Ty and Shea, reside either in their Victorian home and farm outside Oxford, Mississippi, or on their plantation near Charlottesville, Virginia.

AWARDS: ALA BBYA, 1993, *The Pelican Brief.*

FURTHER WORKS: *The Pelican Brief,* 1992; *The Client,* 1993; *The Chamber,* 1994; *The Rainmaker,* 1995; *The Runaway Jury,* 1996; *The Partner,* 1997; *The Street Lawyer,* 1998; *The Testament,* 1999; *The Brethren,* 2000; *The Painted House,* 2000; *Skipping Christmas,* 2001; *The Summons,* 2002; *The King of Torts,* 2003; *Bleachers,* 2003; *The Last Juror,* 2004.

BIBLIOGRAPHY: http://www.retirementwithapurpose .com / johngrisham.html; http:// www.olemiss.edu / depts/english/ms-writers/dir/grisham_john/; http:// www.randomhouse.com/features/grisham/author.html; http://www.randomhouse.com/features/grisham/; http:// en.wikipedia.org/wiki/John_Grisham

DEBORAH A. WOOTEN

GUEST, Judith
Author, b. 29 March 1936, Detroit, Michigan

G. was born in Detroit and attended the University of Michigan (B.A., 1958). Her experience as a public school teacher served her well in her career as a writer of books about adolescent angst. G. also drew upon her parenting experiences raising three sons with her husband Larry, a data-processing executive. While she was moving from Michigan to Minnesota she received a phone call from a publisher saying that her manuscript for *Ordinary People* was the first unsolicited work they had accepted in twenty-six years.

A Cinderella story for G. ensued, because *Ordinary People* became a bestseller, was selected by four book clubs, and became the 1980 Academy Award-winning best picture. She also won the Janet Heidinger Kafka Prize from the University of Rochester for *Ordinary People.* A stage version of *Ordinary People* was published in 1983.

Her writing career continued, always concentrating on the rhythms of FAMILY life and the brooding behavior with which adolescence is often associated. Her book *Second Heaven* (1982) also concentrates on the relationship between adults and TEENAGERS and what can go wrong. G.'s novels often help people reflect upon relationships with adolescents in their own lives.

Not content to rest on her success, G. continued to explore family relationships with her essay *The Mythic Family* (1988) and *Killing Time in St. Cloud* (with Rebecca Hill) in the same year. In 1997, *Errands,* a piercing look at husbands and wives, parents and children, and sibling rivalry, was published. She describes in great detail what happens to a family when the father dies from cancer. This book was chosen as a main selection of the Literary Guild and an alternate selection of another book club. G.'s books have a powerful influence on and importance to teen readers; she deals with topics that appeal to both adults and teens. Readers cannot ignore the power of her writing.

G. writes of the human experience, and she has adapted several of her works into screenplays, including *Second Heaven* and *Rachel River.* The MOVIE TIE-IN always increases her popularity with teens. G. has been a contributor to several periodicals including *The Writer.* She collaborated with Natalie Goldberg in 1986 to publish *Writing Down the Bones: Freeing the Writer Within.*

AWARDS: *Ordinary People,* BBYA, 1976; the Best of the Best Books, 1970–83; Nothin' but the Best: Best of the Best Books for YA, 1966–86; Here We Go Again: 25 Years of Best Books (1967–92); 1977 Janet Heidinger Kafka Prize, University of Rochester, *Ordinary People;* 1980 Best Picture, *Ordinary People.*

FURTHER WORKS: *Errands,* 1999; *The Tarnished Eye,* 2004.

BIBLIOGRAPHY: *Contemporary Authors Online,* 2001; *Major Twentieth Century Writers,* 2nd edition, vol. 2, 1999.

SANDRA KITAIN

GURNEY, James

Author, Illustrator, b June 14, 1958, Palo Alto, California

G. is the son of a mechanical engineer. As a youngster, he visited a nearby museum that exhibited the remains of an allosauras. This first encounter with a theropod triggered a lifelong fascination with prehistoric creatures, which, the author notes, ". . . just won't stay dead."

Studying anthropology at the University of California-Berkeley, G. received a B.A. in 1979. He attended the Art Center College of Design in Pasadena in 1980 where he studied drawing and painting. G. is married to the artist, Jeanette Lendino, has two children, Daniel and Franklin, and resides in New York's Hudson Valley. He is a member of the Association of Science Fiction Artists, Authors Guild, and Phi Beta Kappa.

G. is best known as the writer and illustrator of the three-volume *Dinotopia* SERIES, which received critical acclaim in 1992. *Dinotopia* began as a book about a lost island shared by humans and dinosaurs, and represents a determination to introduce realism to art depicting dinosaurs. G. convincingly accomplishes this with the help of 19th century travel journals, current scientific literature, and renowned paleontologists; through these sources, he is able to incorporate information about the dinosaurs' appearances and behavior. The volumes are a manifestation of a professional career that includes sixteen years as a historical and archaeological illustrator at the National Geographic Society, seven years of freelance illustrating for PAPERBACK SCIENCE FICTION and FANTASY books and a short stint as an animation background artist. Most recently, G. worked with other authors to create a series of sixteen youth novels and two adult novels that "expand his vision of a peaceful land of humans and dinosaurs." His books can be found in GRAPHIC NOVEL collections as well.

G.'s work has received attention beyond the publishing industry. In 2002, *Dinotopia* became a six-hour television mini-series. In 1988, the U.S. Postal Service commissioned G. for a postal card and, in 1997, a commemorative dinosaur stamp series. A Dinotopia float was featured in the Macy's 2001 Thanksgiving Day parade and later appeared in an exhibit at the Smithsonian in Washington, D.C. which showcased more than thirty original oil paintings from Dinotopia books.

AWARDS: Chesley Award, Association of Science Fiction and Fantasy Artists, 1991, 1992, 1995, 2000; Abby Award nomination, World Science Fiction Convention, 1992, and Hugo Award for best original artwork, World Science Fiction Convention, 1993, both for *Dinotopia;* Judges' Art Award, World Science Fiction Convention, 1993, for painting Garden of Hope; Locus Award, *Locus* magazine, 1993; World Fantasy Award, World Fantasy Association, 1993; Silver Medal, Society of Illustrators (New York), 1999; *Dinotopia: A Land Apart from Time,* BBYA, 1993.

FURTHER WORKS: *The Artist's Guide to Sketching* (with Thomas Kinkade), 1982; *Dinotopia: A Land apart from Time,* 1992; *Dinotopia: The World Beneath,* 1995; *The World of Dinosaurs* (With Thomas Holtz), 1998; *Dinotopia: First Flight,* 1999; *The Hand of Dinotopia,* 1999. Dinotopia Digest Novels: *Windchaser; River Quest; Hatchling, Lost City; Sabertooth Mountain; Thunder Falls; Firestorm; The Maze; Rescue Party; Sky Dance; Chomper; Return to Lost City; Survive; The Explorers; Dolphin Watch; Oasis.*

EXHIBITIONS: Various group shows at museums, universities, and other venues, including the Cleveland Museum of Natural History; Delaware Art Museum; Society of Illustrators (New York); Park Avenue Atrium (New York City); Words and Pictures Museum; Bruce Museum (Connecticut); Explorer's Hall (Washington, DC); University of Maryland; Norman Rockwell Museum (Stockbridge, MA); and Field Museum (Chicago, IL). *Dinotopia* solo shows in various locations, including L.A. County Museum of Natural History; Cleveland, OH; Buffalo, NY; Albuquerque, NM; and Richmond, CT.

BIBLIOGRAPHY: *Contemporary Authors Online,* 2001; *Rocks & Minerals,* Mar/Apr 2000, Vol. 75 Issue 2, p 133; http://www.rggallery.com/jgbio.php; "'DINOTOPIA' COMES TO THE SMITHSONIAN," Cox News Service, April 23, 2002.

GABRIELLA L. RADUJKO

GUY, Rosa

Author, playwright, b. 1 September 1925, Trinidad and Tobago, West Indies

G. was born on the twin-island republic of Trinidad and Tobago, and immigrated in 1932 with her sister to the U.S. to join her father and mother. Shortly after their arrival, their mother became ill; G. was sent with her sister to live with a cousin who followed the teachings of Marcus Garvey. Upon their mother's death in 1934, the girls returned to Harlem to live with their father. After his death in 1937, the girls lived in a succession of foster homes. G. left school at the age of fourteen to work in a brassiere factory in the garment district, where she met her future husband. She began studying with the American Negro Theatre.

G. eventually divorced her husband and joined the Committee for Negroes in the Arts and formed the Harlem Writers Guild with John Killens in 1951. She attended New York University where she studied theatre and writing. Her early writing years consisted of SHORT STORIES, and her first two stories were published in a Trinidadian newspaper. A visit to Haiti after the violent murder of her husband in 1962 caused G. to begin work on her first novel. *Bird at My Window* was completed in 1966, a year after the assassination of her good friend Malcolm X. The violent, senseless loss of life was portrayed by the protagonist Wade Williams who, worn down by the forces of poverty and racism, kills his own sister. This theme of social turbulence was extended to the publication of *Children of Longing* (1970), which is a collection of essays, interviews, and personal commentary following the assassination of Dr. Martin Luther King Jr. in 1968.

The next three books by G. made up a trilogy that began with *The Friends* (1973). This poignant coming-of-age story chronicles the dynamic development of two friends from distinct and separate cultures, classes, and languages. Phylissia Cathy is fourteen years old and Harlem born, while Edith Jackson is fifteen, struggling to adjust in her new environment, and coping with pressures from her oppressive West Indian father. The initial attempt at friendship between the two girls falters due to the trappings of physical, emotional, and social insecurities; G. captures these experiences while allowing the idea and hope for self-reconciliation to manifest itself as this unlikely friendship develops. *Ruby* (1976) invoked some controversy due to the lesbian overtones of the love affair between the two young women. The novel is moved along through G.'s development of the two protagonists who are driven apart by their cultural backgrounds but brought together by their need for love and acceptance. This love affair expounds the importance of relationships outside the family. It also shows the growth of an individual through the influence of personality traits, family interaction, and cultural background, all from the female perspective. *Edith Jackson* (1978) is a culmination of the story; the trilogy comes to an end, assuming an imagery of Edith's invisibility as the ravages of poverty are explored. Edith's life and

the world in which she lives erodes into a "faceless," "shadowed" existence as she had been rejected based on color, class, race, sexual abuse, and teen pregnancy. G. interweaves the problematic issues that young women face in their development. The characters come of age owing much to, and recognizing the importance of, their experiences.

G. introduces Imanu Jones in *The Disappearance* (1979) as a streetwise TEENAGER from Harlem, sent to live with a foster family in Brooklyn. This MYSTERY novel progresses as Imanu is the main suspect in the disappearance of the family's daughter; he embarks on a fast-paced, dynamic journey to clear his name. The title belies the theme of the gradual subjugation of poverty and racism faced by the characters. The sequel, *New Guys around the Block* (1983), again features Imamu Jones in a deteriorating neighborhood in Harlem. Imamu believes that the dilapidated buildings and depressed conditions will prevent the recovery of his mother, deep in an alcohol-induced coma. He promises to paint the apartment but gets sidetracked when a string of robberies of affluent apartments bring the police to Harlem. This novel is somewhat more optimistic, as Imamu is aware of life's possibilities and the limitations of his environment.

In addition to her young adult work, G. is the author of a one-act play, *Venetian Blind* (1954), and a documentary film about *The Friends*. While G.'s protagonists are usually black and female, the topics that they encounter hold universal appeal. Author Katherine PATERSON applauded G. for being able to "peel back society's labels and reveal beneath them highly individual men and woman."

AWARDS: 1979 Best Books for Young Adults, *The Disappearance;* 1988 first prize at Cabourg, France Festival, *My Love, My Love, or the Peasant Girl; The Music of Summer,* 1993 Best Books for Young Adults.

FURTHER WORKS: *Mirror of Her Own,* 1981; *Mother Crocodile,* 1981; *A Measure of Time,* 1983; *My Love, My Love, or The Peasant Girl,* 1985; *And I Heard a Bird Sing,* 1986; *The Ups and Downs of Carl Davis III,* 1989; *The Music of Summer,* 1992; *The Sun, the Sea, a Touch of the Wind,* 1995; *Bird at My Window,* 2001.

BIBLIOGRAPHY: Norris, Jerrie, *Presenting Rosa Guy,* 1988; www.classzone.com/lol/litcons/authors/guy, 2001; www.geocities.com/ronemrit/profiles/guy; *Contemporary Authors,* vol. 34, 1991.

DEXTER BRAITHWAITE

HADDIX, Margaret Peterson

Author, b. 9 April 1964. Washington Court House, Ohio

The wide variety of genres written by H. are a surprise to some, but given her background one better understands the versatility of this award-winning author. Growing up on a farm in Ohio, she was involved in a busy schedule of extra-curricular activities. An excellent student (National Honor Society president), she was also a member of the marching band, symphonic band, and pep band, as well as the orchestra. In addition, H. was a member of the American Field Service, Quill and Scroll (school newspaper), Drama Arts Club, the track team, and an academic-bowl team. Outside of school, she was active in 4-H and her church youth group. Throughout her busy school years H. maintained her love of reading and writing, wanting to become a writer. In college, she majored in journalism and creative writing.

After receiving a B.A. in English *summa cum laude* from Miami University in 1986, H. began her career in journalism as a copy editor in Fort Wayne, Indiana. She then became a reporter in Indianapolis. As a general assignment reporter, H. reported on stories ranging from community issues and news to politics and crime, and enjoyed the variety of stories and the interesting people she met. Taking snippets of time on the weekends and any other time available from reporting, H. continued to explore writing styles. Married to Doug Haddix, a newspaper editor in 1987, H. left newspaper reporting when he took a new job in Danville, Illinois. She worked at part-time jobs, including teaching English at a community college, and used the extra time to devote to writing.

While working as a reporter, H. persuaded her editor to let her write a story on a "living history" village in Indiana; this experience was the background for her first novel, *Running out of Time,* (1995). In an interesting use of time-travel, this story is set in the 1840s and 1990s. Jessie, a thirteen-year-old girl living in a pioneer settlement in 1840, is thrust into modern society in the 1990s when the children in her village and her family are stricken with diphtheria. Jessie's mother reveals that they, in fact, live in the 1990s and Jessie needs to escape their village to bring back modern medicines to save the children. *Don't You Dare Read this, Mrs. Dumphrey* (1996) is the story of Tish, a teenage girl struggling to keep her life together. This story found its beginnings in a series of newspaper articles H. wrote with two other reporters on child welfare. Borrowing from her experience teaching English and reading student journal entries, H. chose to give Tish a voice in the form of a journal. As she deals with the loneliness and despair, she feels as if her world were coming apart. Although the story grew out of a newspaper article H. wrote about a local church accused of being a cult, her third novel *Leaving Fishers* (1997) came about through "backward design." Picturing the main character, Dorry, as a young girl who had just left a cult-type religion, H. went backward to find out what had drawn Dorry to the group in the first place.

What began as a discussion between H. and her husband about having a third child led to questions and thoughts that grew into her most popular book to date, *Among the Hidden* (1998). From this novel a SERIES has grown, with plans for a total of seven. Set in the future when population police spend their time in search of illegal third children, the characters are in constant danger and unsure of who they can trust. Between the second book, *Among the Imposters* (2001), the third, *Among the Betrayed* (2002), and fourth, *Among the Barons* (2003) books in this series, H. wrote *Just Ella* (1999) a continuation of a Cinderella story where she discovers life is not as once imagined with her not-so-quite Prince Charming. A year later, *Turnabout* (2000), takes her readers back to the future with a story of two very elderly women who take an experimental drug to reverse aging. The story begins with them searching for answers about what the future holds as they spiral down to zero in a world nothing like their first time around. In *Takeoffs and Landings* (2001) H. tells the story of a FAMILY through the perspectives of the mother, her TEENAGE son and her teenage daughter as they struggle to regain their sense of family after the loss of their father.

H. and her husband live in Columbus, Ohio with their two children, Meredith and Connor. She enjoys walking her children to school each day and begins her creative writing process in thoughts on her walk home. A versatile and skillful author, H. continues to share her wide range of interests, knowledge, and experiences with her readers.

AWARDS: American Bookseller Pick of the Lists for *Running Out of Time* (1995) *Leaving Fishers* (1997) *Just Ella* (1999) *Turnabout* (2000) *Among the Imposters* (2001) A YALSA Best Book for Young Adults for *Running Out of Time* and *Don't You Dare Read This, Mrs. Dunphrey* (1997) *Leaving Fishers* (1998) *Among the Hidden* (1999) *Just Ella* (2000) A YALSA Quick Pick for Young Adults for *Running Out of Time* and *Don't You Dare Read This, Mrs. Dunphrey* (1997) A YALSA Quick Pick for Reluctant Young Adult Readers for *Among the Hidden* (2000) *Just Ella* (2000) *Among the Imposters* (2001) *Among the Betrayed* (2002) A YALSA Top Ten Quick Picks for Young Adults for *Among the Hidden* (2000) IRA Young Adults' Choice Award for *Just Ella* (2001) *Among the Imposters* (2003) Junior Library Guild Selection for *Running Out of Time* (1995) *Takeoffs and Landings* (2001) *Escape from Memory* (2003).

FURTHER WORKS: *Escape from Memory,* 2003; *The Girl with 500 Middle Names,* 2001; *Because of Anya,*

2002; "Fine" in *On the Edge: Stories at the Brink* (Lois DUNCAN, ed.), 2000; "Going through the Motions" in *I Believe in Water: Twelve Brushes with Religion* (Marilyn SINGER, ed.), 2000; "My People" in *Destination Unexpected* (Donald GALLO, ed.), 2003; "Escape" in *Shelf Life: Stories by the Book* (Gary Paulsen, ed.), 2003; *Among the Brave,* 2004; *The House on the Gulf,* 2004.

BIBLIOGRAPHY: *authors4teens.com,* Greenwood Publishing Group. Feb. 6, 2004, *Contemporary Authors,* New revision Series, Vol. 102.2001. *Something about the Author,* vol. 125, 2001.

CATHY DENMAN

HAHN, Mary Downing
Author, b. 9 December 1937, Washington, D.C.

Highly acclaimed in the field of literature for young people, H. has written twenty-one books for middle-grade readers and YOUNG ADULTS. Among them, eleven books have been chosen as book award winners in several states, including California, Indiana, Iowa, Georgia, Maine, Maryland, South Dakota, Texas, and Utah.

H. showed an early interest in writing and drawing in her childhood. To pursue her interest, she attended the University of Maryland, majoring in fine arts and English. After graduating in 1960 with a B.A., she became an art teacher at a junior high school for a year. She received an M.A. in 1969 and continued to study English in the doctoral program at the University of Maryland from 1970–1974. Besides being an art teacher, she has worked at various jobs: bookstore sales person, information specialist at a phone company, part-time college instructor; freelance artist for a reading program called "Cover to Cover," and a librarian in a public library in Maryland. After 1991, she devoted herself full time to writing.

H.'s first book, *The Sara Summer* (published in 1979 after three years of repeated revising and rewriting), is about a twelve-year-old girl who often feels awkward. In her second book, *The Time of the Witch* (1982), Laura, the protagonist, unknowingly seeks help from a witch in getting her parents back together. *Daphne's Book* (1983) portrays the friendship growing between two girls until one finds out about the problem home life of the other. In *The Jellyfish Season* (1985), a work of realistic fiction, H. looks at the adolescent problems and FAMILY stress that result from their father's unemployment. *Wait Until Helen*

Comes (1986) is a powerful and frightening ghost tale, characterized with well-defined characters, absorbing story line, and convincing supernatural elements. The book won many awards and honors. In her next two books, *Tallahassee Higgins* (1987) and *December Stillness* (1988), H. addresses contemporary issues regarding one's value system, the homeless, and Vietnam veterans. *The Dead Man in Indian Creek* (1989), also an award-winning book, recounts the story of a drug-related death and the possible involvement of a boy's mother. *The Doll in the Garden* (1989) and *Time for Andrew* (1994) are both ghost stories with an element of time travel; they are very popular among middle-school readers.

H. also writes historical fiction. A SERIES of books *Stepping on the Cracks* (1991), *Following My Own Footsteps* (1996), and *As Ever, Gordy* (1998), all set in World War II, tells the story of school bully Gordy, his deserter brother, and his grandmother. In *Stepping on the Cracks*, H. raises the question of moral conflicts related to a pacifist deserter. *The Gentleman Outlaw and Me-Eli* (1996) takes place in 1887 and portrays the adventures of a twelve-year-old girl; disguised as a boy, this character travels to Colorado to look for her prospecting father. In another historical novel, *Promises to the Dead* (2000), H. spins an intriguing tale of runaway slaves during the Civil War.

H.'s writing is versatile; in addition to MYSTERY, realistic fiction, and historical fiction, she is the author of a vampire story. *Look for Me by Moonlight* (1995) portrays a teenager's attraction to a charming and mysterious guest staying at her father's inn. The book has won many awards and honors including those given by ALA and IRA.

Although she has written a few chapter books for younger readers, H. writes primarily for middle-grade readers and young adults. Most of her protagonists are twelve-year-olds who deal with troubling subjects. Some face problems of parental separation, missing fathers, and abusive or alcoholic fathers; others, portrayed as orphans, are mistreated by relatives. The characters, whether they are children or young adults, are believable, interesting, and filled with humanity. The plots are engaging, well paced, and filled with considerable suspense. Her ghost stories are scary without being gory or violent. H.'s novels are rich with her skillful and lively use of language and vibrant imagery. Perhaps because of these characteristics, most of her books are quick reads and page-turners.

AWARDS: Scott O'DELL Historical Fiction Award, Mark Twain Award, Sequoyah Book Award, Maud Hart Lovelace Book Award, Rebecca Caudill Young Reader's Choice Book Award, Dorothy Canfield Fisher Children's Book Award, and Society of School Librarians International Book Award. ALA has listed some of her works in Notable Children's Books, YALSA Popular Paperbacks for Young Adults, and YALSA Quick Picks for Reluctant Young Adult Readers. *The Wind Blows Backward*, BBYA, 1994.

FURTHER WORKS: *Following the Mystery Man*, 1988; *The Spanish Kidnapping Disaster*, 1991; *The Wind Blows Backward*, 1993; *Anna All Year Round*, 1999; *Anna on the Farm*, 2001; *Hear the Wind Blow*, 2003; *The Old Willis Place*, 2005.

BIBLIOGRAPHY *Children's Literature Review*. [Available]: http://clcd.odyssi.com/cgi-bin/member; *Following the Mystery Man* (1988); *Novelist*. [Online] Available: http://novelst3.epnet.com/novel; *Something about the Author*, vol. 50, 1988; *Something about the Author*, vol. 81, 1995; *Something about the Author Autobiography Series*, vol. 12, 1991.

SHU-HSIEN L. CHEN

HALEY, Alex(ander) Murray Palmer

Journalist, essayist, historical novelist, b. 11 August 1921, Ithaca, New York; d. 10 February 1992, Seattle, Washington

An important figure in journalism and the AFRICAN AMERICAN community, H. received recognition for *The Autobiography of Malcolm X* (1965) and *Roots: the Saga of an American Family* (1976).

H. grew up listening to FAMILY history from his grandmother and aunts, learning of an enslaved African ancestor. H. joined the Coast Guard and began his literary career ghostwriting love letters for his shipmates. After leaving the service, he struggled as a writer for several years before his breakthrough, an interview with jazz great Miles Davis in *Playboy* (1962). This led to co-authoring the *Autobiography of Malcolm X*, which told of Malcolm Little's difficult early life, imprisonment, conversion to Islam, and subsequent adoption of the name Malcolm X, signifying his belief that American blacks had been deprived of their true identities. This title is regularly found on college reading lists.

H. began his own search for family identity and history soon after, spending twelve years completing *Roots*, the history of seven generations of descendants of Kunta Kinte, a Mandinkan from the village of Juf-

fure Gambia in West Africa. In compiling this historical novel, H. combined family lore with historical
documents and his skills as a storyteller. H. traveled
to Africa, visiting Juffure and taking an uncomfortable boat ride to the U.S. to help recreate the "Middle
Passage" slave route of his ancestors' time. *Roots*
won at least 270 awards, most notably the Pulitzer
Prize, but it was also the object of two separate
charges of plagiarism. Soon after its print publication,
Roots was adapted into a television mini-series
(1977), which 130 million Americans watched, ushering the format into mainstream popularity. *Roots: the
Next Generation* aired in 1977, bringing the history
into the present. *Roots* affected a wide range of people, breaking social, cultural, and racial boundaries,
and inspired many, particularly African Americans
and slave descendants, to begin their own family histories.

AWARDS: *Pulitzer Prize* committee special citation for
Roots (which won at least 270 other awards).

FURTHER WORKS: *A Different Kind of Christmas,*
1988; *Alex Haley's Queen: the Story of an American
Family* (with D. Stevens), 1993; *Mama Flora's Family: a Novel* (with D. Stevens), 1998.

BIBLIOGRAPHY: *Contemporary Literary Criticism,*
vol. 76; *Contemporary Authors,* vol. 61 (1998; *Afro-
American Writers after 1955: Dramatists and Prose
Writers,* 1985.

MYRON A. MYKYTA

HALL, Barbara

Novelist, screenwriter, b. 1960, Danville, Virginia

H. is best known for her work in television, notably
as story editor for network television series such as
Newhart, Moonlighting, and *A Year in the Life.* In addition to television screenwriting and production
work, H. is a notable YOUNG ADULT author. H.'s love
of writing turned from hobby to profession when her
first poem was published at the age of fifteen in *Teen*
MAGAZINE.

H. carefully crafts her young protagonists with a
thoughtfulness that brings them to life, with all their
faults and glories. Her novels play out the complexities of life for a young adult. From her first novel,
Skeeball and the Secret of the Universe, to *Dixie
Storms,* she draws upon the South to bring her readers
stories that are as grand as the place in which she
grew up. Commenting on her love of FAMILIES and

the South, she says "[t]he combination always results
in something colorful, humorous, and larger than
life."

The colorful and humorous can also be seen in the
TEEN protagonists and the adventures they face in her
two award-winning YA novels, *Dixie Storms* and
Fool's Hill. Dutch has to cope with drought and the
arrival of a sophisticated older cousin in the former.
Libby must cope with the perils of popularity when
she gets into a convertible with two new girls and is
taken for a ride down *Fool's Hill* in the latter.

AWARDS: Best Books for Young Adults list, 1991, for
Dixie Storms. Best Books for Young Adults list, 1993,
for *Fool's Hill.*

FURTHER WORKS: *Playing It Safe Away from the City:
Summer Smart Activities for Children,* 1986; *Skeeball
and the Secret of the Universe,* 1987; *Dixie Storms,*
1990; *Fool's Hill, 1992; A Better Place,* 1994; *The
House across the Cove,* 1995; *Close to Home,* 1997;
A Summons to New Orleans, 2000.

BIBLIOGRAPHY: *Contemporary Authors Online.* The
Gale Group, 2000.

REBECCA OSA MENDELL

HALL, Lynn

Author, b. 9 November 1937, Lombard, Illinois

H. was a secretary for eleven years before becoming
a full-time writer in 1968. Her work in a veterinarian's office heightened her early love of animals, a
love that is reflected in many of her children's books
featuring dogs and horses. However, H.'s writing for
young adults also focuses on fellow teenagers dealing
with hardships.

H.'s childhood was peppered with frequent moves
and the resulting struggle to find her niche in life.
After an unsuccessful marriage and a bout of unful-
filling jobs, H. embarked on her path to becoming a
writer of animal books. Her second manuscript turned
out to be her first published book, *The Shy Ones*
(1967). Other books ensued, several with story lines
taken directly from H.'s own experiences with animals as a child: *The Stray* (1974) recounts her memory of offering herself up for adoption to a farm family to remain close to her beloved animals; *The Horse
Trader* (1981) is based on the purchase of H.'s first
horse.

Through her writing for YA, H. has tackled serious
subject matter such as TEEN rage in *Fair Maiden*

(1990), homosexuality in the military in *Sticks and Stones* (1972), and child molestation in *The Boy with the Off-white Hat* (1984). Other of her YA books have elements of the detective novel about them, as in *Murder in a Pig's Eye* (1990) and *The Tormentors* (1990).

H. encourages other young dreamers to follow their childhood passions; quoting from H.'s interview in *Something about the Author Autobiography Series,* "They . . . hold the keys to our real needs."

SELECT AWARDS: Charles W. Follet Award, 1971, *A Horse Called Dragon;* ALA Best Young Adult Books: *Sticks and Stones* (1972), *The Leaving* (1980), *Uphill All the Way* (1984); *The Leaving:* 1981 *Boston Globe–Horn Book,* 1981 and 1982 New York Public Library's books for teenagers; Golden Kite Award Honor Book, 1986, *The Solitary;* Johnson Brigham Award from the Iowa State Historical Society, 1989, *The Secret Life of Dagmar Schultz.*

SELECT FURTHER WORKS: *Ride a Wild Dream,* 1969; *Too Near the Sun,* 1970; *Gentle Touch the Milkweed,* 1970; *To Catch a Tartar,* 1973; *Just One Friend,* 1985; *A Horse Called Dragon,* 1971; *The Whispered Horse,* 1980; *The Leaving,* 1980; *Denison's Daughter,* 1983; *Uphill All the Way,* 1984; *Tazo and Me,* 1985; *The Giver,* 1985; *Just One Friend,* 1985; *If Winter Comes,* 1986; *The Solitary,* 1986; *Danger Dog,* 1986; *A Killing Freeze,* 1988; *The Secret Life of Dagmar Schultz,* 1988; *Halsey's Pride,* 1990; *Dagmar Schultz and the Green-Eyed Monster,* 1991; *Windsong,* 1992; *Love Returns,* 1996.

BIBLIOGRAPHY: *Something about the Author,* vol. 79, 1995; *Something about the Author Autobiography Series,* vol. 4, 1987.

RACHEL WITMER

HAMBLY, Barbara

Author, b. 28 August 1951, San Diego, California

H., a master storyteller, made her mark in the world of words as a top-notch writer of FANTASIES but has cast her well-woven net out further into the world of literature and penned historical fiction, ROMANCE, SCIENCE FICTION, and MYSTERIES as well. Her works are written for adults, but they have great appeal for YOUNG ADULTS.

She first fell in love with fantasy as a child when she read *The Wizard of Oz.* J. R. R. TOLKIEN's *The Lord of the Rings* also influenced her (she named two of her characters in her *Darwath* SERIES, Ingold and Inglorian, after creatures of Middle Earth). Attending the University of California at Riverside, she earned an M.A. in medieval studies. While she has spent time working as a research assistant, a high-school teacher and a karate instructor, she always wanted to earn her living as a writer. As she says on her website, www.barbarhambly.com, "I always wanted to be a writer but everyone kept telling me it was impossible to break into the field or to make money. I've proven them wrong on both counts."

In 1982 Del Ray published *Time of the Dark,* the first of the *Darwarth* books, which garnered favorable reviews in *Science Fiction and Fantasy Review* and *Library Journal.* These were quickly followed by the sequels *The Walls of Air* (1983) and *The Armies of the Night* (1983). The two additional titles, *Mother of Winter* (1996) and *Icefalcon's Quest* (1998) were published later. With this series, H. created a fantasy world where eyeless "Dark Ones" love to fly and feast on human flesh.

One of her most enduring fantasies, the Dragonsbane quartet, *Dragonsbane* (1986), *Dragon Shadow* (1999), *Knight of the Demon Queen* (2000), and *Dragonstar* (2002), brings into vivid focus the lives of the wizard Jenny and her husband John, the dragonsbane. They are called upon first to defeat a dragon and then a demon queen. Both quests are perilous and gripping.

In addition to writing a number of her own series, H. has contributed novels to several media-related series, including *Star Trek, Beauty and the Beast,* and *Star Wars.* Whether she is writing TV stories, fantasies, mysteries, or vampire sagas, H.'s use of lush language creates riveting plots that take place in detailed worlds, filled with intriguing characters.

AWARDS: 1988 Locus award for *Those Who Hunt the Night;* 1996 Lord Ruthven for *Traveling with the Dead;* 1999 nominated for a British Fantasy Society Best Novel Award for *Dragonshadow*; ALA BBYA 1995 for *Stranger at the Wedding.*

FURTHER WORKS: The *Sun Wolf and Starhawk* trilogy: *The Ladies of the Mandrigyn,* 1994; *The Witches of Wenshar,* 1987; *The Dark Hand of Magic,* 1990; the *James Asher Vampire* series; *Those Who Hunt the Night,* 1988; and *Traveling with the Dead,* 1995; *A Free Man of Color,* 1997; *Sisters of the Night,* 1998.

BIBLIOGRAPHY: *Something about the Author,* vol. 108, 1999, Hedbled, Alan, ed.; *Library Journal,* May 15, 1982, p. 1014; *Science Fiction and Fantasy Book Review,* September, 1982, pp. 30–31. Current Authors

database; www.barbarahambly.com; www.locusmag
.com; and www.fantasticfiction.co.uk.

SUSAN FICHTELBERG

HAMILTON, Virginia

Author, b. 12 March 1936, Yellow Springs, Ohio; d.
19 February 2002, Dayton, Ohio

One of the most renowned AFRICAN AMERICAN authors in the field of children's literature, H. has received over seventy-five notable awards including the
National Book Award, the John Newbery Medal, the
Edgar Allan Poe Award, the Coretta Scott King
Award, the *Boston Globe–Horn Book* Award, the
Laura Ingalls WILDER award, and, most prestigious of
all, the Hans Christian Andersen Medal. H. was the
first African American author to receive the Newbery
Award and also the first author of YA literature to receive the MacArthur Genius Fellowship. A prolific
writer before her early death in 2002, H. wrote over
thirty-nine books in thirty-five years in almost every
genre for children. H.'s ability to write in various
genres, including BIOGRAPHIES, realistic fiction, FAN-
TASY, historical fiction, legend, MYTH, folk tale, PIC-
TURE BOOKS, and essays on her life and work, while
openly discussing social, political, and historical issues.

H. was surrounded by a family of storytellers. Especially from her mother's family, H. learned storytelling as a vehicle to attain personal, social, and cultural knowledge. The mixture of story with
"rememory," which H. describes as an "exquisitely
textured recollection, real or imagined, which is otherwise indescribable," is seen in much of H.'s
writing.

After ten years of writing while living in New
York City, H.'s first acknowledged success came with
the publication of *Zeely* (1967). Hailed as a "writer
who speaks for the black child," H. presented multiple narratives within the story, additionally creating
an unreliable narrator to provide a complex experience for the reader. In *The House of Dies Drear*
(1968), H. combined myth and MYSTERY for the passing on of cultural heritage while dealing with historical issues.

H.'s first John Newbery Honor Book was *The
Planet of Junior Brown* (1971). By carefully balancing two protagonists, H. allowed the reader to view
the seldom-acknowledged social problem of home-

less children. H. returned to this larger-than-life type
of protagonist in *M.C. Higgins the Great* (1974),
which received ten different awards, including the
Newbery. H. brought attention to social, racial, and
generational issues as well as environmental problems. H. also presented a view of so-called parallel
cultures. Much of H.'s writing returned to this theme
of different cultures being parallel to one another, one
not more worthy than another, but simply different
and able to coexist.

In the next ten years, H. wrote stories using psychic realism. These books include *Arrilla Sun Down*
(1976), *Sweet Whispers, Brother Rush* (1982), and the
Justice Trilogy: *Dustland* (1980), *The Gathering*
(1981), and *Justice and Her Brothers* (1981). All five
novels have African American female protagonists
and resemble each other in various ways. Each child
possesses a cultural ability that enables her to be
clairvoyant. While under the influence of strong male
siblings, each must struggle for selfhood. While processing unrealistic abilities such as mind travel, H.'s
characters are perceived to be realistic to the reader.
H. presents a multilayered text, and has allowed her
characters to explore beyond "ancestral time and cultural space."

H.'s collections of biographies and folklore collections were her personalized attempt to free African
American people from their struggles through story
and retellings. *Anthony Burns: The Defeat and Triumph of a Fugitive Slave* (1988) was not just a biography according to H. but a "narrative history of events
surrounding Anthony's life as well as a biography."
Slave narratives as plainly set forth in *Many Thousand Gone: African Americans from Slavery to Freedom* (1992), deemed as "liberation literature" by H.,
give a realistically painful view of the plight of the
slave. H.'s retellings and creations of folktales (notably *The People Could Fly* (1985), and *Her Stories:
African American Folktales, Fairy Tales, and True
Tales* (1995)) also serve as cultural indicators, echoing the early tales told by the African diaspora and
connecting this ethnic group with its past.

H. remains one of the most honoured writers of
our time. Her daring and creative ways of approaching previously unexplored themes and issues paved
the way for not only future African American writers,
but also all writers of YA LITERATURE, regardless of
race or religion. Future authors and readers of H.'s

books will be able to see H.'s manuscripts and papers, which will soon be housed in Library of Congress.

AWARDS: Coretta Scott King Author Honor Awards, ALA Popular Paperbacks, John Newbery Honor Books, *NY Times* Best Illustrated Books, National Book Award, *Boston Globe–Horn Book* Award, ALA BBYA, and *Booklist* Editor's Choice.

FURTHER WORKS: *W. E. B. DuBois: A Biography,* 1972; *The Time-ago Tales of Jadhu,* 1973; *Time-Ago Lost: More Tales of Jadhu,* 1973; *Paul Robeson: The Life and Times of a Free Black Man,* 1974; *Jadhu,* 1980; *The Magical Adventures of Pretty Pearl,* 1983; *Willie Bea and the Time the Martians Landed,* 1983; *A Little Love,* 1984; *Junius over Far,* 1985; *The Mystery of Drear House,* 1987; *A White Romance,* 1987; *In the Beginning: Creation Stories From Around the World,* 1988; *The Bells of Christmas,* 1989; *The Dark Way,* 1990; *Cousins,* 1990; *The All Jadhu Storybook,* 1991; *Drysolong,* 1992; *Plain City,* 1993; *When Birds Could Talk and Bats Could Sing,* 1996; *A Ring of Tricksters,* 1997; *Second Cousins,* 1998; *Bluish,* 1999; *Wee Winnie Witch Skinny,* 2001; (posthumously) *Time Pieces: A Book of Times,* 2002.

BIBLIOGRAPHY: *Children's Literature Review,* vol. 11, 1986, pp 54–95; *Contemporary Literary Biography,* vol. 26, 1993; Egoff, S. A., *Thursday's Child: Trends and Patterns in Contemporary Children's Literature,* 1981; Mikkelsen, Nina, *Virginia H.,* 1994; *Something about the Author,* vol. 123; Townsend, J. R., *A Sounding of Storytellers: New and Revised Essays on Contemporary Writers for Children,* 1979; Wheeler, J. C., *Virginia H.,* 1997.

TAMMY L. MIELKE

HANAUER, Cathi
Author n.d., n.p.

The relationship-advice columnist for *Seventeen* MAGAZINE for seven years, and the author of articles, essays, fiction, and reviews for such publications as *Elle, Glamour, McCall's Mirabella,* and *Mademoiselle,* H. broke into the YA literature field with *My Sister's Bones* (1996), a stunning debut novel. The story of Billie Weinstein, a New Jersey TEENAGER coping with an anorexic sister, bickering parents, identity struggles, teen angst, and raging hormones, the novel is a stellar example of outstanding young adult realistic fiction. Although published by Delacorte's adult division, the novel was cited a 1997 Best Book for Young Adults by the YOUNG ADULT LIBRARY SERVICES ASSOCIATION and has been widely embraced by teen readers and young adult librarians.

AWARDS: ALA BBYA for *My Sister's Bones.*

EDWARD T. SULLIVAN

HANDLER, Daniel. See SNICKET, Lemony.

HANSEN, Joyce
Author, b. 18 October 1942, New York City

H. was born and reared in New York City by her photographer father, Austin Victor, and her mother, Lillian (Dancy) Hansen. Her mother, who once aspired to become a journalist, passed her appreciation for books and reading on to her only daughter, who referred to her mother as "my first teacher." H. lived with her parents and her two younger brothers in the Morrisania section of the Bronx, where they were surrounded by an extended family that included aunts, uncles, cousins, and grandparents.

After graduating from New York City public schools, H. took night classes at Pace University and worked at various secretarial jobs during the day. She received a bachelor's degree in 1972 and began her teaching career where she had already spent so many years: in the New York City public school system. H. worked as a special education instructor for adolescents with reading disabilities. Most of her students were black and Hispanic, and H. understood the importance of providing them with literature featuring characters with which they could identify. H. went on to receive a Master's degree from New York University in 1978.

H. has published a number of SHORT STORIES and books for YOUNG ADULTS. Her works are both fiction and nonfiction and have been praised by reviewers for their authenticity in depicting black children in modern-day and historical times. H. credits her success as a young-adult novelist to her students. Without her teaching experience, H. notes, "I wouldn't have been moved to write some of the stories I've created thus far."

Her first novel, *The Gift-Giver* (1980), was inspired by her childhood in the Bronx and her experiences as a teacher. The protagonist is a caring foster child who exerts a positive influence on those around her. In this novel, H. dispels the notion that urban areas are filled with strife. She comments, "We forget that there are many people in our so-called slums or ghettos that manage to raise whole and healthy families under extreme conditions. Not every story coming out of the black communities of New York City is a horror story."

H. followed her first novel with two more novels set in New York City, *Home Boy* (1982) and *Yellow Bird and Me* (1986), which is a sequel to *The Gift-Giver*. Her next two novels were historical. *Which Way Freedom?* (1986) is set during the American Civil War and tells the story of a young slave named Obi who escapes, joins a black Union regiment, and soon finds himself in a bloody battle. Along the way, he meets a young girl named Easter. In the confusion of wartime, the two friends are separated. Its sequel, *Out from This Place* (1988), is set during Reconstruction. The war is over and the slaves are free, and Obi's friend Easter sets out to find her old friend and take control of her life. The success that H. found with these two works of historical fiction encouraged her to explore nonfiction, as well as other forms of writing.

In 1995, H. retired from teaching. She lives in South Carolina with Matthew Nelson, her husband of twenty-one years, and writes full time. H. understands the responsibilities that come with writing for a young audience, based on the fact that young adults are constantly looking to understand an increasingly complicated world. Of this responsibility, H. writes, "I still work very hard on my writing and try to make each book better than the last. I am still learning."

AWARDS: Parents Choice Citation (1986) for *Yellow Bird and Me;* Coretta Scott King Honor, American Library Association (1987) and (1995) for *Which Way Freedom?* and *The Captive;* Coretta Scott King Award (1998) for *I Thought My Soul Would Rise and Fly;* Children's Book Award, African Studies Association (1995) for *The Captive.*

SELECT FURTHER WORKS: *Between Two Fires: Black Soldiers in the Civil War,* 1993; *The Captive,* 1994; *I Thought My Soul Would Rise and Fly: The Diary of Patsy, a Freed Girl,* 1997; *Breaking Ground, Breaking Silence: The Story of New York's African Burial Ground* (with Gary McGowan), 1997; *Women of Hope: African Americans Who Made a Difference,* 1998; *The Heart Calls Home,* 1999; *One True Friend,* 2001; *African Princess,* 2004.

BIBLIOGRAPHY: *Something about the Author,* volumes 15 and 101; www.joycehansen.com

CARRA E. GAMBERDELLA

HARDMAN, Ric Lynden
Author, 8 November 1924, Seattle, Washington

When the former Columbia Pictures film producer began to write professionally in 1960, he launched YOUNG ADULTS into different historical periods through his many works. H.'s interest in the American West is evident. His screenplay *The Rare Breed* (1965) met success when it was made into a film starring Jimmy Stewart and Maureen O'Hara. Stewart's character is a cowhand in this light-hearted western romance.

H.'s most recent book, *Sunshine Rider, the First Vegetarian Western* (1998), is an unusual and humorous coming-of-age novel about a young man on a cattle drive in Texas during the 1800s. H. uses his mother's name, Purple, for one of the more colorful characters in this raucous but charming story. In the lengthy novel *Fifteen Flags* (1968), he brings to life the forgotten involvement of Americans in the protection of the Trans-Siberian Railroad during the Russian Revolution. Published in 1965, *The Chaplain's Raid,* a story about the conflict in Vietnam was published in England under the title *The Virgin War.*

H. married Kathleen Keifer and they have two children, Christopher Lynden and Regan Lynden. He was a member of the United States Marine Corps and earned a B.A. from the University of Washington, Seattle in 1949 and an M.A. from the University of California, Los Angeles in 1951.

AWARDS: ALA BBYA 1999 for *Sunshine Rider.*

FURTHER WORKS: *No Other Harvest,* 1962; and author of television scripts and several motion pictures.

BIBLIOGRAPHY: *Contemporary Authors Online,* 2001; "State Board of Equalization of the State of California," online posting, 1975.

DEBORAH LINDSTROM FINK

HARNETT, Cynthia M.
Author, illustrator, b. 22 June 1893, London, England; d. 24 October 1981

H., remembered for her meticulous attention to the details of everyday life in medieval England, was a pioneer of modern historical novels for young people. H. believed every detail in her novels must be scrupulously accurate because teachers relied on these historical novels to supplement their textbooks. She also thought it was important to document the lives of ordinary people in history, rather than the extraordinary. In her first book, *The Great House* (1949), H. tells the story of children born to 17th-century architects. In her last book, *The Writing on the Hearth* (1971), H. describes the destruction that results from the War of the Roses, by telling it through the words of a young schoolboy.

H.'s most prestigious book, *The Wool Pack,* also known as *Nicholas and the Woolpack* (1951), tells about the son of a wool merchant in 15th-century England, who uncovers a plot to ruin his father's business. As part of H.'s effort to endure historical accuracy and re-create authentic atmosphere, H. provided her own illustrations for her historical novels showing minute details of dressing and eating, and aspects of daily life. H. studied at the Chelsea School of Art and early in her career produced a SERIES of PICTURE BOOKS about life in the country. *David's New Life* (1937), about a boy and the animals he sees in the country, was produced with her artist cousin, Vernon Stokes.

AWARDS: Carnegie Medal (1951) for *The Wool Pack.*

FURTHER WORKS: *Ring out, Bow Bells!,* 1953; *Stars of Fortune,* 1956; *The Lord of Unicorn,* 1959; *The Writing on the Hearth,* 1971.

BIBLIOGRAPHY: Chevalier, Tracy, ed., *Twentieth Century Children's Writers.* 1989.

DENISE P. BEASLEY

HARRIS, Marilyn (Springer)
Author, b. 3 June 1931, Oklahoma City, Oklahoma

H. is the pseudonym for Marilyn Springer, author working in a wide variety of genres including the occult, historical, ROMANCE, contemporary realism, literary works, and books for young readers. H. published her first book, *King's Ex,* a compilation of SHORT STORIES, in 1967. Her early career weathered criticism with the publication of a novel called *The Peppersalt Land* (1970), which contained unpopular racial issues. The novel was reportedly removed from many libraries and retail stores for being too "integrated and racially aware" during the early 1970s. H.'s writing demonstrates the benefits of equality as well as the difficult social changes and mindsets that must change in order to achieve equality. The book was not well received by parents and other concerned groups.

H. soon gained well-deserved recognition with the publication of *Hatter Fox* (1973), which CBS adapted and presented as Movie of the Week in October 1978. In addition, *The Diviner* (1983) was anthologized and published in *Prize Stories: The O. Henry Awards* (1968). H., popular on an international level, has sold over nine million copies of her books. Among her bestsellers are *Hatter Fox* (1973), *Bledding Sorrow* (1976), *The Last Great Love* (1981), and the popular Eden SERIES. The Eden series is a planned series of six historical romance novels that runs from the 19th century to the present. *This Other Eden* (1977), set in England during the French Revolution, is the first in the successful series and tells the saga of the Eden and Locke FAMILIES.

H. enraptured her devoted readers and was considered by some to be among the most popular writers of fiction in the late 1980s.

AWARDS: Lewis Carroll Shelf Award, 1973, *The Runaway's Diary* (1971); Media & Methods Maxi Award, 1975, *Hatter Fox* (1973); Women in Communication By-liner Award, 1975; Oklahoma Writers Hall of Fame Award, 1980; Cottey College Distinguished Alumna Award, 1981; *Hatter Fox,* BBYA, 1973; Still Alive Best of the Best 1960–74; Best of the Best Books, 1970–83.

FURTHER WORKS: *In the Midst of Earth,* 1969; *The Conjurers,* 1974; *The Prince of Eden,* 1978; *The Eden Passion,* 1979; *The Portent,* 1980; *The Women of Eden,* 1980; *Eden Rising,* 1982; *The Diviner,* 1983; *Warrick,* 1985; *Night Games,* 1987; *The American Eden,* 1987; *Eden and Honor,* 1988; *Lost and Found,* 1991.

BIBLIOGRAPHY: biblio.com; Commire, Anne, ed., *Something about the Author,* vol. 47, 1987.

JODI PILGRIM

HARRISON, Sue
b. 29 August 1950, Lansing, Michigan

H. was born the daughter of Charles Robert, a high-school teacher, and Patricia Ann McHaney, a musician. She married Neil Douglas Harrison, a computer specialist, on August 22, 1969; they had three children: Neil Douglas, Krystal Faith, and Koral (deceased). H. received her B.A. degree summa cum laude from Lake Superior State University in 1971. She worked as a public-relations writer 1985–1988 and as an adjunct instructor in writing 1988–1990.

H. worked for nine years researching and writing her first book, *Mother Earth Father Sky* (1990). Set in 7056 BC, during the Ice Age on the Aleutian Islands, this book focuses on a newly married Aleutian girl, Chagak, who returns from berry picking to find that her entire village has been massacred by an enemy tribe. Heartbroken, she takes her surviving infant brother in a kayak and starts out for her grandmother's village. Instead of her grandmother's village, her boat lands on an island inhabited by a wise old shaman who becomes her friend and mentor. The book was nominated for the Reader's Choice Award in the states of Michigan and Washington and was one of ten books chosen for "Battle of the Books " in a statewide reading competition in Alaska. Reviewers describe her writing as richly textured, strong, elegant, and poetic.

H., who grew up in the town of Pickford in Michigan's Upper Peninsula, where numerous Native Americans live, says that she wanted to write something that was a historically correct realistic portrayal of Native American life nine thousand years ago. She also wanted the story to be a good, engaging read. She studied five languages (Aleut, Dakota Sioux, Cree, Tsimshian and Ojibway) to understand and write her authentic story.

H. is a thorough researcher; she immediately began to study the Athabaskan languages in preparation for writing her second book, *My Sister the Moon* (1992). Her third book, *Brother Wind,* (1995) completed her first trilogy, the Ivory Carver Trilogy. Later, she completed another trilogy, The Storyteller Trilogy. She is recognized as a critically acclaimed international best-selling author.

H.'s books have been published in Canada, Great Britain, Australia, New Zealand, The Netherlands, Belgium, Sweden, Germany, Italy, Spain, Iceland, Denmark, Norway, Austria, Portugal, Japan, France, Korea, Finland, and South America. Her writing is described as spellbinding, gripping, touching, and emotional; it has been compared to the writing of Jean AUEL.

AWARDS: 1983, Julian Ocean Literature Award, Triple "P" Publications International; 1991, ALA Best Books for Young Adults for *Mother Earth Father Sky;* 1992, Lake Superior State University Distinguished Alumni; 2001, Literary Guild for *Call Down the Stars.*

FURTHER WORKS: The Ivory Carver Trilogy: *Mother Earth Father Sky,* 1990; *My Sister the Moon,* 1992; *Brother Wind,* 1994. The Storyteller Trilogy: *Song of*

the River, 1997; *Cry of the Wind,* 1998; *Call Down the Stars,* 2001. *SISU,* 1997.

BIBLIOGRAPHY: Interview with Contemporary Authors, November 16, 1990. Harrison, *Contemporary Authors,* vol. 135, pp. 204–7; Daniel Morrison, designed site for *SISU,* biography, FAQ, links.

BERNICE E. CULLINAN

HARRY POTTER: Not Just for Kids Anymore

It all started when Ron Weasley's hand-me-down pet rat turned out to be the Animagus Peter Pettigrew, the man who betrayed Harry Potter's parents to Lord Voldemort.

On page 348 (U.S. edition) of *Harry Potter and the Prisoner of Azkaban,* J. K. ROWLING showed millions of readers that she was not only a culturally literate storyteller, but also one with a gift for hiding the truth in plain sight and for crafting complex mysteries in seemingly simple terms, leaving clues for readers who wouldn't learn the true nature of the information for hundreds of pages. Suddenly, readers of Rowling's books found themselves questioning everything she wrote, wondering if seemingly insignificant details in the third book were in fact clues to a larger mystery that would be exposed in upcoming volumes. The climax of discovery and conspiracy, which Rowling presents over the final seven chapters of the book, sets a precedent for themes of hidden and mistaken identities, the fight between good and evil and more importantly, the gray areas in between, and making distinctions between rules and law versus what is right morally and ethically. These ideas, along with the Harry Potter SERIES' classical elements of YA literature, pushed the book from a children's novel to one for young adults.

Though it is still marketed as a children's book series by Scholastic, Inc., the Harry Potter series bears many marks of the YA novel. The series is a bildungsroman in seven books and as it progresses, Harry and his two best friends, Ron Weasley and Hermione Granger, move through adolescence, gaining awareness of themselves and of the imperfect world around them. Edmund M. Kern writes of Harry's "higher moral sensibility," in *The Wisdom of Harry Potter: What Our Favorite Hero Teaches Us about Moral Choices:* "Rowling reveals this growth gradually. *The Sorcerer's Stone* makes plain that Harry must respond to circumstances beyond his control. *The Chamber of Secrets* goes a step further and makes clear that he did not choose his own strengths and weaknesses. *The Prisoner of Azkaban* shows how he becomes more conscious of both of these constraints: the contingent nature of life and the extent of his own abilities. It also asks tougher questions of him by portraying competing claims to what is true and what is right" (p. 75).

Harry and his friends encounter several of these "competing claims" consciously. Sirius Black, Harry's godfather and the title character of *Prisoner of Azkaban*, has a discussion with Harry, Ron, and Hermione in *Harry Potter and the Goblet of Fire* in which Ron makes it clear that the three are not "too young" to hear Sirius speak of troubled times in the wizarding world. This argument that Harry, Ron, and Hermione make—that despite their age they can handle difficult truths—is present in both *Goblet of Fire* and *Order of the Phoenix*. As they grow older, the three become more aware of this "contingent nature of life" and their capabilities, challenging those who believe that they still have not gained the maturity to deal with the truth of the dark side of the wizarding world. Together, they conspire to subvert authority, a classic trait of adolescence, because they discover that not all authority figures have the best interests of others at heart. As Sirius Black tells them in *Order of the Phoenix*, "The world isn't split into good people and Death Eaters" (p. 302). ("Death Eaters" is the self-proclaimed title of the followers of Lord Voldemort.)

This theme of moral ambiguity has been present since *Sorcerer's Stone*. For example, Potions teacher Severus Snape, who despises Harry, saves his life and doesn't explain why. (Harry does not learn why until *Prisoner of Azkaban*.) However, it is in *Order of the Phoenix* that Harry, Ron, and Hermione come face-to-face with the idea that not everyone they know fits into the category of either good or evil. One of the first incidents of this occurs when Harry learns that Ron's older brother Percy has split from the Weasley family. Percy believes that Albus Dumbledore, headmaster of Hogwarts and head of the Order of the Phoenix (a group of wizards banded together to fight Lord Voldemort's forces) is dangerous. Unlike FAIRY TALES and literature for younger children, where the roles of good and evil are clearly defined, *Order of the Phoenix* includes characters like Dolores Um-

bridge, a Ministry worker and current Defense Against the Dark Arts teacher, whose sweet personality belies unmitigated cruelty toward Harry. At the end of the book, Harry finds out that Albus Dumbledore has kept a secret of his birth from him for fifteen years, shattering Harry's idea that Dumbledore always knows what to do and always does the right thing. While not all the adults in Harry's life have this gray area in their personalities, he is able to see with the wisdom he gained in the past four years that often people can do the wrong thing for the right reason, a distinction he would not have been able to make as a child or pre-adolescent.

In addition to presenting the ideas of Harry, Ron, and Hermione adapting, growing, and becoming independent people with a multifaceted view of the world around them, the *Harry Potter* books fit the seven criteria of the best young adult literature according to Alleen Pace Nilsen and Kenneth L. Donelson in *Literature for Today's Young Adults*:

1. Young Adult Authors Write from the Viewpoint of Young People

Rowling tells the books from a third-person perspective limited to Harry's point of view. His closest friends, the ones he confides in, are also his age. While he respects many adults like Sirius Black, former (in *Goblet of Fire*) Defense Against the Dark Arts professor Remus Lupin, and Ron's parents, Arthur and Molly Weasley, he goes to Ron and Hermione with his problems once he decides to share them. At Hogwarts School of Witchcraft and Wizardry, Harry both takes classes and lives with people his own age. As Harry matures and becomes more aware of the imperfect world that surrounds him, Rowling's writing becomes more intricate, with an expanded vocabulary and backstories on wizarding families and history in addition to Harry's fight against Voldemort.

2. "Please Mother, I Want the Credit!"

"With formula fiction for young readers, one of the first things an author does is to figure out how to get rid of the parents so that the young person is free to take credit for his or her own accomplishments" (Nilsen p. 26).

Harry's fame in the wizarding world came because Lord Voldemort, who killed his parents, could not kill him, and according to Hogwarts' gamekeeper Rubeus Hagrid in *Harry Potter and the Sorcerer's Stone,* "No one ever lived after he decided ter kill 'em, no one except you, an' he'd killed some o' the best witches and wizards of his age . . ." (p. 56). Harry is alone from the time he is a year old, and learns at the end of *Harry Potter and the Order of the Phoenix* that a prophecy made before his birth says that he "was born with the power to vanquish the Dark Lord" but "neither can live while the other survives" (p. 841). Harry is always assisted in his fights against Voldemort by either Ron or Hermione or both, whose parents are absent because the three attend boarding school.

3. Young Adult Literature is Fast-Paced

Even though Harry's coming of age is spread over the course of seven books, the adventures in the individual books are fast-paced. Rowling's technique, best showcased in *Chamber of Secrets* and *Prisoner of Azkaban,* is to build a mystery that comes to an action-filled conclusion in the final chapters. It is at this point, when the mystery (usually involving identity) is revealed, that all the clues come together. *Goblet of Fire*'s pacing is a little different from the first three books. The action is spread evenly throughout the book, from the Quidditch World Cup to the three tasks of the Tri-Wizard Tournament to the climax, where Lord Voldemort returns to a corporeal body. *Order of the Phoenix* returns to the structure of clues that lead to a slow build to a climactic fight and discovery.

4. Young Adult Literature Includes a Variety of Genres and Subjects

The primary genre of the *Harry Potter* series is FANTASY, because it takes place in a world where extraordinary things happen because of magic. Harry receives his mail by owl at his boarding school and learns to take care of hippogriffs and Blast-Ended Skrewts. After firmly establishing the fantastic world, Rowling adds MYSTERY and adventure, starting with Harry, Ron, and Hermione's quest to protect the powerful Sorcerer's Stone from Severus Snape, the Potions teacher whom they believe to be serving Lord Voldemort.

5. The Body of Work Includes Stories About Characters from Many Different Ethnic and Cultural Groups

Harry's classmates at Hogwarts have surnames that include Patil, Finnigan, Goldstein, Malfoy, Chang, and Macmillan, representing a wide variety of cultures and countries. His fellow Gryffindor, Dean Thomas, is described in *Sorcerer's Stone* as "a Black boy even taller than Ron" (p. 123, U.S. edition). In *Goblet of Fire,* students from two other wizarding academies are invited to participate in a tournament at Hogwarts, and Harry competes against two foreign students named Fleur Delacour and Viktor Krum. International wizarding relations are an important part of society, and the Ministry of Magic, the governing body of wizards in the United Kingdom, has an entire department devoted to international magical cooperation.

Instead of showing racial or ethnic strife between wizards, Rowling invented her own form of discrimination: While it doesn't matter where a wizard was born or what language he speaks, the importance of wizarding heritage and bloodlines is a constant source of strife. Draco Malfoy, Harry's school nemesis, believes that because he is a pureblood, someone whose parents were both wizarding, he is superior to witches and wizards born to non-magic parents (Muggle-borns, whom Malfoy refers to as Mudbloods). Not all purebloods agree with the Malfoy point of view, however; Ron Weasley's family is pureblooded but because of Arthur's fascination with Muggles and the family's lack of money, they are called "blood traitors" by some.

6. Young Adult Books are Basically Optimistic, with Characters Making Worthy Accomplishments

Harry made a de facto accomplishment as a child, surviving Lord Voldemort's attack. However, he is not one to be lazy and let his legacy get him through life. Though he is not a good student, Harry is a loyal friend who always does the right thing when faced with a difficult situation. It is this trait that makes many readers identify with Harry, because Rowling sends the message that a person can still have intelligence and talent even if he isn't the sharpest student. Ron and Hermione, though they fight with each other and with Harry, as typical TEENS do, support Harry through his tough endeavors and round out his personality. While Harry is the brave, impetuous one with a talent for sports, Hermione is Hogwarts' top student, solving her problems with books, and Ron, though Hermione says he has "the emotional range of a teaspoon" (*Order of the Phoenix,* p. 459), functions as the group's caretaker. Harry fights Lord Voldemort several times and comes away alive, even rescuing Ron's younger sister Ginny at the end of *Chamber of Secrets.* Ron and Hermione have their own accomplishments as well. Both are named to prefect positions and Ron earns a spot on the Gryffindor house Quidditch team. They also join Harry on his trip to the Ministry of Magic at the end of *Order of the Phoenix,* where they fight with Harry against the Death Eaters until both become incapacitated.

Even though Harry's world becomes darker and more complex through the books, he always triumphs over Lord Voldemort and has a support system of adults, including Minerva McGonagall, the Gryffindor Head of House, who give him advice when he needs it. While optimism can run low at times throughout the Harry Potter books, Rowling makes sure that the side of light triumphs as a whole.

7. Successful Young Adult Novels Deal with Emotions That are Important to Young Adults

Growing up with his horrid aunt, uncle, and cousin and forced to sleep in a cupboard under the stairs, Harry never had any real friends and was deprived of love until he went to Hogwarts. Ron became Harry's first real friend at Hogwarts and in defending Ron, Harry also made his first enemy, Draco Malfoy. Harry's range of emotions grows as the books progress. He experiences many of the same emotions that readers do, including but not limited to loss (of his parents and later of Sirius Black), joy, friendship, anger, worry, love, and frustration. Though he doesn't always acknowledge his emotions consciously, through his actions he proves himself to be a complex character, imperfect yet resolute and determined to protect his friends. Harry's first moment of true hopelessness comes near the end of *Order of the Phoenix,* when he resigns himself to death during a battle with Lord Voldemort. When Lord Voldemort takes over his body in the same book, it is thoughts of Sirius Black, of the godfather he loves, that enable him to regain control of his body and to fight.

Part of Rowling's appeal to YA readers, who want to read books with realistic characters, is that she shows Harry's emotions through his actions rather than explaining how he feels. When Ron is kidnapped in *Goblet of Fire* as part of the second task Harry must accomplish in a wizarding tournament, we see Harry panicking and using his wits in an attempt to rescue Ron. Through this, we can deduce that Ron means a great deal to Harry, but Rowling keeps true to a fourteen-year-old boy's point of view by showing the actions he takes rather than exposing his emotions. Along with the anger and fighting, Harry also develops his first crush and experiences his first kiss in *Order of the Phoenix,* an experience common to many teens, but not to many children.

Harry's first kiss is one of many examples of elements that are common to YA novels, but not to children's. Very few, if any, books where the main character receives his or her first kiss are categorized as children's novels, but the *Harry Potter* series is. Characters in the series are seen making out in bushes, smoking, cursing, and beating younger children. Some characters are tortured during detention by Professor Umbridge in *Order of the Phoenix.* If this were any other book, it would be assigned to the YA section of the library. While children can appreciate Harry's adventures, his friendships, and the way good always triumphs over evil, acknowledging only these aspects of the book does a great disservice to Rowling's intentions and her teen readers, who can strongly identify with Harry's struggles, triumphs, and discovery of his morally ambiguous world. The sixth book, *Harry Potter and the Half-Blood Prince* continues the exciting adventures.

FURTHER SUGGESTED READING ON THE HARRY POTTER SERIES: Colbert, David, *The Magical Worlds of Harry Potter: A Treasury of Myths, Legends, and Fascinating Facts,* 2001; Heilman, Elizabeth, ed., *Harry Potter's World: Multidisciplinary Critical Perspectives,* 2003; Lovett, Charles, *J. K. Rowling: Her Life and Works,* 2003; Nel, Philip. *J. K. Rowling's Harry Potter Novels: A Reader's Guide,* Group. 2001.

RECOMMENDED HARRY POTTER WEBSITES: Warner Brothers's official Harry Potter site: http://www.harrypotter.com; J. K. Rowling's official site: http://www.jkrowling.com; Harry Potter for GrownUps: http://www.hpfgu.org.uk; The Harry Potter Lexicon: http://www.hp-lexicon.org; FictionAlley Park: http://www.fictionalley.org/fictionalleypark; Godric's Hollow: http://www.godrics-hollow.net/; Mugglenet:

http://www.mugglenet.com; DarkMark: http://www.darkmark.com.

HARRY POTTER CONVENTION SITES: Nimbus—2003; A Harry Potter Symposium: http://www.hp2003.org; Convention Alley, 2004: A Harry Potter Fan Convention: http://www.conventionalley.org/; The Witching Hour, 2005: http://www.witchinghour.org; Lumos 2006: A Harry Potter Symposium: http://www.hp2006.org.

WORKS CITED: Donelson, Kenneth L., and Nilsen, Aileen Pace, *Literature for Today's Young Adults,* 2001; Kern, Edmund. *The Wisdom of Harry Potter: What Our Favorite Hero Teaches Us about Moral Choices,* 2003; Rowling, J. K. *Harry Potter and the Chamber of Secrets,* New York: Scholastic Books. 1999; Rowling, J. K. *Harry Potter and the Goblet of Fire,* 2000; Rowling, J. K. *Harry Potter and the Order of the Phoenix,* 2003; Rowling, J. K. *Harry Potter and the Prisoner of Azkaban,* 1999; Rowling, J. K. *Harry Potter and the Sorcerer's Stone,* 1997.

CARLISLE KRAFT WEBBER

Herman by Kyle Fox, age sixteen

I've been clean for about a month now.
After about three therapists,
fifteen kinds of pills
and a good twenty-four hours of shock therapy,
I can finally say that I am clean.

It hasn't always been like this though.
It got bad, I mean really bad.
It came to the point where I hid myself in my room
and did it by myself.

I was so consumed
that people started to notice.
I was in denial and just assumed that it was a social
    thing.
that I didn't have the problem, everyone else did.

But like they say, admitting is the first step.
So here we go:
My name is Herman Walker
and I am addicted to HARRY POTTER.

It all started when I was hanging out with my
    friends one day.
We were at school and my friend Bryan pulled it
    out, the very first book.

I had heard what it was
but I had never really thought about it.
Bryan gave me the book and told me I had to read
    it;
everybody was.
I was a little hesitant at first
but I thought the first one wouldn't be so bad.

I read that night.
It was two o'clock in the morning,
and I was on the last chapter.
I finished it right before I had to go to school.

It was amazing!
I had never felt that rush,
that total body immersion.
I was flying.

I gave the book back to Bryan and asked him
where I could find more.
He had the whole collection,
had read them,
and was willing to give me both books II and III.
I read them over the weekend.

This was only the beginning of my descent.
It started out little at first.
I bought the movies,
collected some cards,
and even bought a few action figures.

It started to get heavier as the fifth book came out.
I had decided I was going to sleep outside the
    bookstore
two days before it came out.
I told my Mom I was sleeping over at a friend's
    house,
then hitched a ride to Barnes & Noble's and
    pitched my tent.

It rained that night, but I didn't care.
I was going to be the first boy in town to have the
    book.
It was all mine!!!

The thing about Potter books
is that you drop your old friends
and make new ones.
You think that the old friends have problems,

DONALD R. GALLO

NANCY GARDEN

JAMES CROSS GIBLIN

ROSA GUY

VIRGINIA HAMILTON

JAMES HASKINS

NAT HENTOFF

KAREN HESSE

and you'll just have to find new ones.
Luckily, I had great friends to show me the right
     way.

One Friday night, I came home from my Harry
     Potter book club, of which I was the president,
to find my parents, my sister, and my friend Bryan
     sitting in the living room.
They sat me down and told me I had a problem.
I squirmed and cried but I listened.
I realized they were right.
I had fallen.

So my mother took me to some doctors and they
     really helped.
They showed me that there was life outside of
     Harry, Ron, Hermione, and Hogwarts.
Slowly, they weaned me off the books and movies.
My cards and action figures were thrown away.
It was hard, but now that I look back, it was for
     the best.
I mean they're just books, right?

HASKINS, James S. (Jim)
Author, b. 19 September 1941, Demopolis, Alabama;
d. 6 July 2005, New York City

"I have always liked true stories better than made-up
ones," wrote H., the distinguished AFRICAN AMERI-
CAN author of over one hundred BIOGRAPHIES and informational books for young people. Dance and theater, the Harlem Renaissance, jazz, rap music,
magicians, segregation, slave trade, the Underground
Railroad, and the CIVIL RIGHTS MOVEMENT are among
the wide range of subjects about which H. has written. In addition, H. has written scores of biographies
about prominent African Americans in entertainment,
the fine and performing arts, government, literature,
politics, and science.

H. grew up in the Deep South in the time of strict
segregation. He attended a segregated school where
all of his classmates and teachers were black. The
books, equipment, and resources were inferior to
what the white school had, but H. recalls that his
teachers were exceptional. For them, teaching was not
a job but a calling.

H. lived with his family in one of several all-black
neighborhoods in Demopolis. His neighborhood was
considered "middle class" because it contained one
of the major black churches in town, as well as the
black elementary and high schools. The majority of
people in the neighborhood owned their own homes

and worked hard to maintain them. Small for his age
and not very athletic, H. preferred the company of
adults to his peers. He enjoyed listening to grownups,
soaking up the information he heard. H. learned to
read early, and his mother encouraged his love of
reading as best she could.

When H. was growing up, the Demopolis Public
Library was for whites only, but his mother found
other ways to feed her son's voracious appetite for
reading. H. recalls that some of his earliest reading
material was *The World Book Encyclopedia.* A local
supermarket had a special offer that gave customers
one volume of the encyclopedia if they spent a certain
dollar amount. His mother acquired the entire set that
way. H. recalls that while the other neighborhood kids
were outside playing, he sat at the kitchen table reading his encyclopedia.

After high school, H. earned two undergraduate
degrees, one from Georgetown University and another from Alabama State University. He earned a
master's degree from the University of New Mexico
and pursued further graduate study at the New School
for Social Research and Queens College in New York
City. After working briefly as a stock trader, H. went
to work for the New York City Board of Education,
teaching special education at Public School 92 in
Harlem. H.'s colleagues encouraged him to keep a
diary and it was from this ongoing habit that he produced his first book, *Diary of a Harlem Schoolteacher* (1969). *Diary* was highly praised by reviewers, and its success impressed publishers who
proposed that H. write a SERIES of books for young
people. H.'s career as an author was born.

The civil rights movement is a subject H. has written about throughout his career. *Separate, But Not
Equal: The Dream and the Struggle* (1997) is an excellent account of segregation and the Jim Crow era
in the south. Other titles include *I Have a Dream: The
Life and Words of Martin Luther King* (1992), *The
March on Washington* (1993), and *The Freedom
Rides: Journey for Justice* (1995). In 1992, H. coauthored with Rosa Parks her autobiography for YA.

H. has written about a wide range of topics relating to African American history. *Black, Blue, and
Gray: African Americans in the Civil War* (1998) examines the contributions black soldiers made to the
national strife. *The Geography of Hope: Black Exodus from the South after Reconstruction* (1999)
chronicles the westward migration of over twenty

thousand blacks in search of a better life in the newly opened frontiers in Kansas and Oklahoma. Other titles include *Get on Board: The Story of the Underground Railroad* (1993), *Bound for America: The Forced Migration of Africans to the New World* (1999), and *Building a New Land: African Americans in Colonial America* (2001).

H.'s many books about black culture and entertainment include *Black Theater in America: A History through Its People* (1982), *Black Music in America: A History through Its People* (1987), *Black Dance in America: A History through Its People* (1990), *One Nation under a Groove: Rap Music and Its Roots* (2000), *One Love, One Heart: The Story of Reggae* (2001), and *Conjure Times: Black Magicians in America* (2001). The biographies H. has written profile activists, artists, authors, entertainers, entrepreneurs, explorers, government leaders, scientists, and people from a wide range of other fields. His subjects include Muhammad Ali, Ella Fitzgerald, Langston Hughes, Jesse Jackson, Barbara Jordan, Spike Lee, Bayard Rustin, Carter G. Woodson, Malcolm X, and Andrew Young.

H.'s books consistently reflect thorough and insightful research, a lucid and engaging style, and great enthusiasm for the subject matter. His many awards and honors include being the multiple recipient of the Carter G. Woodson Award from the National Council of Social Studies and a multiple recipient of the Coretta Scott King Honor Award from the American Library Association.

AWARDS: Coretta Scott King Honor for *Black Dance in America*, 1991, and *Bayard Rustin*, 1998; 1993—ALA Best Books for Young Adults for *One More River to Cross: Stories of Twelve Black Americans* and *Rosa Parks: My Story*, by Rosa Parks with H; John and Patricia Beatty Award for *Cecil Poole*, 2004.

FURTHER WORKS: *Outward Dreams: Black Inventors and Their Inventions*, 1991; *The Scottsboro Boys*, 1994; *Black Eagles: African Americans in Aviation*, 1995; *Bayard Rustin: Behind the Scenes of the Civil Rights Movement*, 1997; *Power to the People: The Rise and Fall of the Black Panther Party*, 1997; *Spike Lee: By Any Means Necessary*, 1997; *Champion: A Biography of Muhammad Ali*, 2002; and *Cecil Poole: A Life in the Law*, 2002; *Against All Opposition: Black Explorers in America*, 2003; *Freedom Rides*, 2005.

SOURCES: *Something about the Author*, vol. 132, pp. 84–101.

EDWARD T. SULLIVAN

HAUTMAN, Pete
Author, b. 29 September 1952, Berkeley, California

H.'s family moved to Minnesota when he was five. Following high school, H. attended both the Minneapolis College of Art & Design and University of Minnesota during the 1970s. Before beginning a professional writing career, he worked at several jobs including sign painting, illustration, graphic design, advertising, and marketing. For a time he owned and operated Hautman Marketing Services in Minneapolis. After working in various capacities in marketing and design for almost twenty years, H. devoted himself to writing full time in 1993.

Under the pseudonym Peter Murray, H. began his writing career by writing juvenile nonfiction books for a Minnesota–based publisher; he has currently written over sixty titles on numerous topics. H. has also written several popular adult crime novels that critics often compare to the books of author Elmore Leonard.

It was not until 1996, when H. published his first YOUNG ADULT novel, *Mr. Was*, that he included elements of SCIENCE FICTION, MYSTERY, and thriller genres in his writing. In the book, Jack Lund finds a metal door that allows him to travel back and forth in time. As the story evolves, death, murder, jealousy, love, and an overwhelming sense of destiny all become factors that influence Jack's decisions.

Stone Cold (1998), H.'s next book, bears the closest resemblance to the content of his adult novels. In *Stone Cold*, Dennis Doyle slowly becomes addicted to gambling, with a special compulsion for playing poker. Critics and readers alike appreciated the novel's realism and brisk first person narration as well as H.'s non-judgmental treatment of addiction.

In *A Hole in the Sky* (2001), H. once again combines genres like science fiction and action with spirituality. By 2038, only 38 million people are left after the "Flu" kills a majority of the Earth's population, and people in the U.S. live in small communities. Ceej Kane lives with his grandfather and sister near the Grand Canyon where he meets a Hopi girl who is searching for the Sipapuni, a mystical portal that leads to another world. As Ceej's small world deteriorates, he believes the portal is the only way out of this world. Like H.'s other young adult novels, *A Hole in the Sky* deals with a teenaged protagonist who has to make decisions that affect not only his adolescence but also ultimately his adulthood.

Spirituality gives way to teenage rebellion against organized religion in his next work, the National Book Award–winning *Godless* (2004). The TEEN protagonist decides to found his own religion and chooses the town water tower as its deity, with all kinds of complications ensuing when the town bully gets involved.

AWARDS: *Mr. Was:* ALA Best Book for Young Adults (1997); nominated for the Edgar Allan Poe Award (1997) by the Mystery Writers of America. *Stone Cold:* ALA Quick Pick for Reluctant Young Adult Readers (1999). *Godless:* 2004 National Book Award. *Booklist* Editor's Choice Award, ALA BBYA.

FURTHER WORKS: *Sweetblood,* 2003; *No Limit,* 2005; *Invisible,* 2005.

BIBLIOGRAPHY: *Contemporary Authors, New Revision Series,* vol. 72, 1999; *Something about the Author,* vol. 128, 2002; *The Writer's Directory,* 18th ed., 2003; *Pete Hautman website,* http://www.petehautman.com

STEPHANIE SCHOTT

HAWES, Louise
Author, b. 1943, Colorado

H., who majored in art history and English literature, is a founding faculty member of the Vermont College MFA in Writing for Children Program. She is also the author of more than fifteen books for YA. She has lectured at colleges and universities across the U.S. and is dedicated to teaching and guiding other writers in the perfection of their craft. She is committed to helping new writers who want to write for children. In addition, she also visits middle- and junior-high schools to encourage young writers in their creative writing endeavors.

H.'s SHORT STORIES have been published in MAGAZINES and anthologies in the U.S. and CANADA. Her YA novels deal with themes that appeal to adolescents. Her YA novel, *Rosey in the Present Tense* (1999), a poignant story of TEENAGE grief and loss, has received various accolades. The story deals with the agony and loss felt by Franklin after his girlfriend dies in a car accident. The narrative effectively alternates between Franklin's first-person journal of his interactions with Rosey, who comes back to him as a spirit after her DEATH, and the third person narrative of his life without her. *Waiting for Christopher* (2002) deals with child abandonment and abuse, and tells the story of a young girl who kidnaps a child she sees being abused. It has been honored as one of the Top Ten Books of Summer by *Girl's Life* magazine and has been selected as one of the New York Public Library's Best Books for the Teen Age.

Well-defined characters dealing with adult issues from an adolescent viewpoint characterize the YA novels by H. Her books offer well-crafted depictions, written with realism and compassion, of the often turbulent lives of adolescents. H. also authored The Mercy Hospital SERIES and several titles for middle-school readers (The Nelson Malone Stories, Tales from the Cafeteria, and several titles in the Sweet Valley Twins series).

AWARDS: New Jersey Author's Award; *Rosey in the Present Tense:* Center for Children's Books Best Book of 1999, ALA Popular PAPERBACKS for 2002.

SELECTED FURTHER WORKS: *Nelson Malone Saves Flight 942,* 1989; *Nelson Malone Meets the Man from Mush-Nut,* 1990; *The Best Medicine,* 1993; *Don't Tell the Patient,* 1993; *Doctor Cute,* 1993; *Tales from the Cafeteria #1: Spaghetti and Spooks,* 1995; *Tales from the Cafeteria #2: Things That Go Bump in Your Soup,* 1995; *Willem de Kooning: The Life of an Artist,* 2002; *The Vanishing Point,* 2004.

REFERENCES: *ForeWord Magazine,* May 1, 2002; Author's website: http://www.louisehawes.com/.

KAREN PRAEGER

HAYDEN, Torey L(ynn)
Author, special education teacher, educational psychologist, b. 21 May 1951, Livingston, Montana

H. not only has a unique tenderness in working with emotionally disturbed and abused children, but she is able to share that tenderness through her experiences in poignant and inspiring books.

H.'s writing career began when she was eight years old and was caught by her teacher writing a story rather than reading her workbook. The teacher returned the story several weeks later and H. recalled the excitement she felt in rereading it.

H. finds inspiration for her stories in the children with whom she has worked over the years. These children have touched H.'s heart, and love and tenderness is evident in her writings. Working with emotionally DISABLED children brings about frustrations, challenges, and few successful outcomes, but H. is able to highlight the joy and hope that these children bring to her.

One Child (1980), H.'s first book based on her experiences, was described by the *New York Times Book Review* as having "sheer emotional impact." H. not only brings her own emotions and familiarity to the story, but makes the emotions and situations of six-year old Sheila real to the reader. H. takes her audience into the life of Sheila, an autistic, abused child, deemed a hopeless case. In working with Sheila, H. brings forth hope, strength, and love, and discovers the hidden genius of this child.

H. continues her story of Sheila in the sequel, *The Tiger's Child* (1995). Even with the breakthroughs and progress made in *One Child,* Sheila continues to live a difficult and troubled life. Although highly intelligent, Sheila does not go to college but works at McDonald's instead. This book gives readers a look at what has become of the small child in H.'s first book, showing them that through it all, Sheila displays an incredible amount of courage.

In her latest nonfiction book, *Beautiful Child* (2002), H. takes the reader into the life of a young girl, Venus Fox, who is electively mute. This is yet another beautifully written and emotionally moving story with H. as a teacher working with Venus and several other children in Venus' class. H. connects the reader with each of the characters and draws the reader into the feelings and events of each individual's life. Told from H.'s perspective, the reader not only sees the struggles of the children, but also of the adults who care for them.

H.'s book *The Mechanical Cat* (1998) has become a bestseller in Japan, Sweden, Finland, and Italy. It has not been printed in English as of this publication. Additionally, two MOVIES have been made based on H.'s books. Many of H.'s books have been translated into foreign languages and are enjoyed worldwide.

H. now spends her time in North Wales with her family. She continues to work and grow with her very special students. Her daughter was born with cerebral palsy which allowed H. to see the parental side of children with special needs.

AWARDS: 1981 Christopher Award, *One Child;* 1981 New York Public Library Book for the Teen Age, *One Child;* 1982 New York Public Library Book for the Teen Age for *Somebody Else's Kids;* 1983 American Library Association's Best Young Adult Book and School Library Journal Best Young Adult Book, *Murphy's Boy.*

FURTHER WORKS: *The Sunflower Forest,* 1984; *The Very Worst Thing,* 2003. Nonfiction: *Somebody Else's Kids,* 1981; *Murphy's Boy,* 1983; *Just Another Kid,* 1988; *Ghost Girl,* 1991; *Twilight Children,* 2005.

BIBLIOGRAPHY: J. Greenfield. "One Child (Book Review)," *New York Times Book Review,* May 4, 1980. *Contemporary Authors New Revision Series,* vol. 82; *Something about the Author,* vol. 65; *Best Books for Young Adults* (2000).

TINA HERTEL

HAYES, Daniel
b. 17 April 1952, Troy, New York

H. was reared on a working dairy farm with his two brothers and two sisters. In school, H. cared more for sports and other school activities than his schoolwork. In addition to developing a liking of sports and other outdoor activities, H. became a reader, particularly of MYSTERIES, to escape his isolated country life. After graduating from high school, H. attended the State University of New York-Plattsburgh, where he studied English and writing. By pushing himself, H. completed his studies in three years and earned a B.S. degree (1973) in English literature.

To pursue his career as a writer, H. moved to Hollywood, where he tried to find work as a screenwriter. Although he was unsuccessful as a screenwriter, he did write some freelance articles for a martial-arts magazine. Disillusioned with Hollywood, H. moved back to Troy and did some substitute teaching. In 1975 he found full-time employment as a junior-high English teacher at Waterford Central Catholic School in Waterford, New York. H. returned to school himself at the State University of New York in Albany, where in 1982 he completed a master's degree.

In 1984 H. returned to his alma mater, Troy High School, as an English teacher. Drawing inspiration from a magazine article and his experience working with students, H. began work on his first novel. He spent six years writing *The Trouble with Lemons* (1991): eighth graders Tyler and Lymie become involved in a mystery related to the murder of the high-school janitor. Along the way, Tyler deals with his low self-esteem, adjusting to a new school, coping with feeling ordinary in a family of movie stars, the DEATH of his father, and allergies and asthma. This is all accomplished with H.'s trademark humor, which is inspired by The Three Stooges and the interaction of adolescent boys. During this six-year process, H. met with editors who suggested that he write either a problem novel or a mystery, and not try to combine elements of both. H. remained true to his own writing process; he explored and developed his characters, and created a character-driven novel rather than plot-driven one.

H. followed the success of his first book with two sequels. In *Eye of the Beholder* (1992), Tyler and Lymie create fake sculptures as a joke, which are then deemed genuine and cause an uproar in their small town. *No Effect* (1993) finds the eighth-grade boys trying out for the high-school wrestling team and Tyler in love with their new science teacher.

H.'s fourth book, *Flyers* (1996), deals with fifteen-year-old Gabe Riley's attempt to deal with his father's alcoholism and make a horror movie using his friends in costume as monsters, which are thought to be real monsters by town residents. H.'s humorous novels are noted for their realistic characterizations and dialogue.

AWARDS: ALA Best Book for Young Adults: 1992 for *The Trouble with Lemons,* 1995 for *No Effect,* and 1998 for *Flyers.*

BIBLIOGRAPHY: Carter, Betty, *Best Books for Young Adults, Second Edition,* 2000. *Contemporary Authors Online,* 2001; Daniel Hayes home page, http://www.danielhayes.com/ (November 29, 2003); *Horn Book Magazine,* January–February 1993, p. 91; March–April 1994, p. 205; January–February 1997, p. 56; *Publishers Weekly,* March 22, 1991, p. 80; November 30, 1992, p. 56.

ANDREW W. HUNTER

HEAD, Ann (pseud. Anne Christensen Morse)

Author, b. 30 October 1915, Beaufort, South Carolina

During the past half-century, H. has written SHORT STORIES and novels that explore the intricacies of human relationships. Born Anne Christenson, H. grew up in Beaufort, South Carolina, where she still lives. She embarked on her writing career after spending three years at Antioch College in Yellow Springs, Ohio; her work gained almost immediate success, due in large part to its readability, breezy style, and meticulous attention to detail. During the 1940s and 1950s, H. had a prolific career as a writer of short fiction, serials, and novelettes, and was published in many popular women's MAGAZINES of the time, including *Ladies' Home Journal, Saturday Evening Post, Mc-Call's, Redbook, Good Housekeeping,* and *Cosmo-*

politan. She worked across genre lines, writing everything from ROMANCES to MYSTERIES, all of which focused on the complications surrounding the love between good friends, husband and wife, or mother and child.

By the late 1950s, H. expanded upon the themes of these shorter pieces and began writing full-length novels that offered snapshots of middle-class life in the late 1950s and early 1960s. These early novels, including *Fair with Rain* (1957), *Always in August* (1961), and *Everybody Adored Cara* (1963), feature adult female protagonists who spend much of the story learning how to navigate the various relationships in their lives. These works, while of interest to YA, were really written for a more mature female audience. Still, they represent H.'s light, captivating style and descriptive talents, which would have undoubtedly hooked some younger readers.

As the sexual revolution and various other social and cultural changes swept the United States in the late 1960s, H. wrote her first novel geared specifically to young adults. The groundbreaking publication of *Mr. And Mrs. Bo Jo Jones* (1967) spoke directly to a young adult population that, for the first time, openly discussed issues such as TEENAGE sexuality and pregnancy. The novel follows the story of a teenage couple facing an unplanned pregnancy, and all of the fear, confusion, and wary excitement that surround their decision to get married and raise their child together. While sometimes stereotypic in her depiction of the main characters—July is the intelligent daughter of a well-to-do family while Bo Jo is the football star and son of working-class parents—H. provides details and insights into their personalities that add depth and complexity. As the two young parents (and newlyweds) face the disappointment of their families and the uncertainty of their friends, they must look to themselves and the family that they have created for the answers. Overall, H. presents an optimistic portrayal of teenage pregnancy, ending the story with the happy family going off to college. While not giving the reader a totally realistic view, H. does create a compelling story that easily captures the attention of young adult readers. Even with somewhat dated language and cultural references, *Mr. And Mrs. Bo Jo Jones* continues to be hugely popular with contemporary teenage readers, and has remained in print since its original publication. *Good Dog! Educating the*

Family Pet was published in 1988, and H. continues to write from her home in Beaufort.

BIBLIOGRAPHY: http://faculty.leeu.edu/~dsummerlin/anne_Christensen_morse.htm; *Contemporary Authors Online*, 2000.; *St. James Guide to Young Adult Writers*, 1999.

MICHELLE CROWELL FOSSUM

HEINLEIN, Robert A(nson)

Author, b. 7 July 1907, Butler, Missouri; d. 8 May 1988, Carmel, California

H. is also known as Anson MacDonald, Lyle Monroe, John Riverside, Caleb Saunders and Simon York. H. attended the University of Missouri in 1925, graduated from the United States Naval Academy in 1929, and studied physics and mathematics at the graduate level in 1934 at the University of California, Los Angeles. He has owned a silver mine, been a candidate for California State Assembly (1938), worked as a real-estate agent, and served in the armed forces. When he died, he was cremated and his ashes were scattered at sea with military honors.

After contracting tuberculosis, which ended his Naval career as a gunner, H. experimented with various vocations "before discovering an ad in *Thrilling Wonder Stories* which offered a fifty dollar prize for the best piece of amateur fiction." Though H. wrote a story, "Life-Line," he considered it too good for the contest; instead, he submitted it to John W. Campbell at *Astounding Science Fiction* where it was ultimately published.

H. became a major figure in SCIENCE FICTION from the late 1930s until his death in 1988. His innovative ideas and stylistic approach earned him great popularity with both his readers and his peers. Perhaps his most significant contribution to the genre was, according to Peter R. Weston in *Contemporary Novelists*, the attitudes his pieces contained. H. credits others with strongly influencing him, especially his grandfather, "a horse and buggy doctor."

H.'s science fiction was innovative, according to Frank Robinson in the Locus obituary: "No other writer in the history of science fiction had written about the future in such as way as to make it as believable as the present." In many of his earlier stories, such as his two-part serial "If this Goes On—" (1940), "H. centered on a particular type of science fiction—logically extrapolating current science into the near future."

H.'s earlier novels, according to H. Bruce Franklin writing in *Robert A. Heinlein: America as Science Fiction*, were written to challenge and never underestimate readers. After time spent in the late 1950s working on a television series, *Tom Corbett: Space Cadet*, based on his novel, *Space Cadet* (1958), H. focused on writing for adults, focusing "on ideas, on changes in society, rather than on heroic adventures in alien places." The turning point was his novel *Starship Trooper* (1959) about a militaristic society. His next novel became his best known work; *Stranger in a Strange Land* (1961) was his third Hugo Award. His fourth Hugo Award was for *The Moon Is a Harsh Mistress* (1966). His novels, *Tunnel in the Sky, Starbeast, Have Spacesuit, Will Travel, Citizen of the Galaxy* et al. are still read and enjoyed by adults as well as by young people. They have held up amazingly well over time with lots of action strong plots to support the action.

AWARDS: Guest of Honor, World Science Fiction Convention, 1941, 1961, and 1976; Hugo Award, World Science Fiction Convention, *Double Stars* (1956), *Starship Troopers* (1960), *Stranger in a Strange Land* (1962), *The Moon is a Harsh Mistress* (1966); Boy's Club of America Book Award, 1959; Sequoyah Children's Book Award of Oklahoma, Oklahoma Library Association, 1961, *Have Space Suit—Will Travel* (1958); Nebula Award, Grand Master, Science Fiction and Fantasy Writers of America, 1975; Inkpot Award, 1977; L.H.D., Eastern Michigan University, 1977; Distinguished Public Service Medal, National Aeronautics and Space Administration (NASA), 1988 (post-humously awarded); Rhysling Award of the Science Fiction Poetry Association is named after the character in Heinlein's story "The Green Hills of Earth."

FURTHER WORKS: *Rocket Ship Galileo*, 1947; *Beyond This Horizon*, 1948; *Space Cadet*, 1948; *Red Planet*, 1949; *Sixth Column*, 1949; *The Man Who Sold the Moon*, 1950; *Farmer in the Sky*, 1950; *The Green Hills of Earth*, 1951; *Between Planets*, 1951; *The Day After Tomorrow*, 1951; *Universe*, 1951; *The Puppet Masters*, 1951; *The Rolling Stones*, 1952; *Revolt in 2100*, 1953; *Assignment in Eternity*, 1953; *Starman Jones*, 1953; *The Star Beast*, 1954; *Tunnel in the Sky*, 1955; *Time for the Stars*, 1956; *The Door into Summer*, 1957; *Citizen of the Galaxy*, 1957; *Waldo; Genius in Orbit*, 1958; *Methusaleh's Children*, 1958; *The Menace from Earth*, 1959; *The Unpleasant Profession of Jonathon Hong*, 1959; *Podkayne of Mars: Her Life and Times*, 1963; *Glory Road*, 1963; *Farnham's Freehold*, 1964; *The Worlds of Robert A. Hein-*

lein, 1966; *The Past Through Tomorrow: Future History Stories*, 1967; *A Robert Heinlein Omnibus*, 1966; *I Will Fear No Evil*, 1973; *Time Enough for Love: The Lives of Lazarus Long*, 1973; *Destination Moon*, 1970; *The Number of the Beast*, 1980; *Expanded Universe: The New Worlds of Robert A. Heinlein*, 1980; *Friday*, 1982; *Job: A Comedy of Justice*, 1984; *The Cat Who Walks Through Walls: A Comedy of Manners*, 1985; *To Sail beyond the Sunset: The Life and Loves of Maureen Johnson, Being the Memoirs of a Somewhat Irregular Lady*, 1987; *Grumbles from the Grave*, 1989; *Requiem*, 1992; *The Fantasies of Robert A. Heinlein*, 1999; *For Us, The Living*, 2004.

BIBLIOGRAPHY: "Robert (Anson) Heinlein." U*X*L Junior DISCovering Authors, U*X*L, 1998. Reproduced in Discovering Collection, 2001; http://galenet.galegroup.com/servlet/DC/; "Robert A(nson) Heinlein." DISCovering Authors, 1999; http://www.galenet.com/servlet/DC/.

SARA MARCUS

HELLER, Joseph

Author, b. 1 May 1923; d. 12 December 1999, Long Island, New York

H. attended the University of Southern California and graduated Phil Beta Kappa from New York University (B.A. in English, 1948). He received his master's degree from Columbia University in 1949 and was a Fulbright Scholar at Oxford University from 1949 to 1950. H. married Shirley Held in 1945; they had two children, Erica and Theodore, before their divorce in 1982. Nurse Valerie Humphries became his second wife in 1987 after he was diagnosed with the neurological disorder Guillain-Barre syndrome.

During World War II, H. was a B-25 wing bombardier, flew sixty missions and became a first lieutenant. It was these experiences in World War II that directly shaped his writing. His seminal work, *Catch-22* (1961), which achieved bestseller status, was made into a film directed by Mike Nichols in 1970. It is also on Modern Library's list of the One Hundred Best Novels of the 20th Century. As relevant today as when it was first published, the main character of this antiwar novel, John Yossarian, is a bombardier who does anything he can to be excused from combat. The title refers to the ridiculous regulations of military exemptions: anyone who is named insane must be excused from flying combat missions; however if you show fear of flying in the face of danger, then you must be sane and therefore, are able to fly. The phrase

catch-22 has become part of the vernacular in the English language, indicating a no-win situation. *Catch-22* has over ten million copies now in print and is considered to be one of the most important novels of the 20th century.

In addition to being a novelist, H. was an English instructor at Pennsylvania State University from 1950 to 1952, and he was employed by several MAGAZINES as an advertising writer during the late 1950s. He worked for *Time, Look,* and *McCall's.* In later years, he returned to the university setting and taught fiction and dramatic writing at Yale University in New Haven, The City College in New York, and at the University of Pennsylvania in Philadelphia. He remained a Distinguished Professor of English at CCNY until 1975. H. also wrote for the theater, and he adapted material for MOVIES and television. His SHORT STORY work was published in anthologies and magazines such as *Esquire, New Republic, Atlantic Monthly,* and *Cosmopolitan.*

H.'s sardonic bent continued to appear in his later works, most specifically in *Good as Gold* (1979), in which he satirizes life in the White House, and *Something Happened* (1974), in which he focuses on the absurd aspects of the American businessman and his alienating environment. In 1984, H. published *God Knows,* narrated by the biblical King David. It was hailed as a successful comic work and was followed up by *Picture This* in 1988, a novel in which his disdain for institutions and his sardonic humor shine through.

In 1986, when H. was diagnosed with Guillain-Barre syndrome, his experiences with this illness resulted in his nonfiction book *No Laughing Matter,* coauthored with his friend Speed Vogel. His second marriage came about because Valerie Humphries, one of his nurses, became his companion.

Closing Time was published in 1994 as a sequel to *Catch-22.* The novel brings many of the characters into the 1990s in H.'s trademark darkly humorous style. *Now and Then: From Coney Island to Here* (1998) was H.'s AUTOBIOGRAPHICAL work, recalling growing up in the 1920s and 1930s. His final masterpiece is *Portrait of an Artist, as an Old Man,* in which he reflects upon his life as a cultural icon and examines the results of having achieved success so early. It is H.'s testament to a life through letters, which he completed just before his death. Published in 2000, this book provides a rare glimpse into the creative mind of a literary giant.

AWARDS: 1949–1950 Fulbright Scholar, Oxford University; 1963 National Institute of Arts and Letters Grant in Literature; *God Knows:* 1985 Pix Intrallie, 1985 Prix Medicis Etranger.

FURTHER WORKS: *Nelson Algren's Own Book of Lonesome Monsters,* 1960. (Contributor); *Catch-22,* 1961; *Sex and the Single Girl,* Screenplay (with David R. Schwartz), 1964; *Casino Royale* (Screenplay based on Ian Fleming's novel), 1967 (Uncredited); *We Bombed in New Haven* (two-act play), 1968; *Dirty Dingus Magee* (Screenplay), 1970 (with Tom Waldman and Frank Waldman); *Catch-22,* (Film), 1970; *Catch-22: A Dramatization (One-Act Play),* 1971; *Clevinger's Trial* (Play), 1973; *Something Happened,* 1974; *Good as Gold,* 1979; *God Knows,* 1984; *No Laughing Matter,* 1984; *Picture This,* 1988; *Closing Time,* 1994; *Now and Then: From Coney Island to Here,* 1998; *Portrait of an Artist, as an Old Man,* 2000; *Catch as Catch Can,* 2003.

BIBLIOGRAPHY: *Contemporary Novelists,* Fifth Edition, 1991; *Contemporary Authors Online,* 2001; Glossbrenner, Alfred and Emily. *About the author,* 2000; www.nytimes.com/books/specials/author.html; Heller, Joseph. *Portrait of an Artist, as an Old Man,* 2000; Ruderman, J. *Joseph H.,* 1991.

SANDRA KITAIN

HENDRY, Frances Mary
Author, n.d. b. Glasgow, Scotland

H., author of children's books with a marvelous sense of humor, became a teacher similar to twenty-three other members of her family over the last three generations. Earning an M.A. in English and French, H. taught Secondary and Remedial English, Form I–V (eleven–seventeen year olds) for twenty years in Clydebank, Glasgow, and Naim, Scotland, where she makes her home with her husband. Her well-researched historical fiction and FANTASY books take place in Scotland. H. attributes the success of her books to the fact that she never writes those parts into her books that children would just skip over and not read: lengthy descriptions of scenery and characters, believing in "Show, don't tell." In addition to writing pantomimes for the local drama group, H. is presently working on a trilogy set in A.D. 60–68 entitled *Gladiatrix.* Autographed copies of her books can be ordered through her website: http://www.francesmary hendry.btinternet.co.uk.

AWARDS: *Quest for a Kelpie* (1986) the first children's book to win the SCOTTISH ARTS COUNCIL LITERARY AWARD. *Quest for a Maid* (1988) received the S.A.C. and was one of the 100 Best Children's Books of New York Libraries and of the Association of Children's Book Groups. *Chandra* (1995) earned THE WRITER'S GUILD and LANCASHIRE BOOK AWARDS.

FURTHER WORKS: *Quest for a Babe,* 1990; *Quest for a Queen Trilogy: The Lark,* 1992; *The Falcon,* 1989; *The Jackdaw,* 1993. *Jenny,* 1991; *The Seers Stone,* 1996; *Atlantis,* 1997; *Atlantis in Peril,* 1998; *Chains,* 2000; *The Crystal Palace,* 2001; *The '45 Rising,* 2001; *Mystery Kids Series*—pseudonym Fiona Kelly.

BIBLIOGRAPHY: Personal Interview.

VALERIE A. PALAZOLO

HENEGHAN, James
Author, b. 7 October 1930, Liverpool, England

H.'s career as a writer came after his career as a policeman in Liverpool, England, and as a fingerprint specialist in Vancouver, British Columbia. In his writing, realism mixes with history, ADVENTURE, and FANTASY. *The Grave* (2000) is a most unusual time-travel novel, beginning in 1974, when a young orphan boy leans into a grave and is sent back in time to 1847, at the height of the Irish Potato Famine. H.'s depiction of the squalor and living conditions at that time make history alive for the reader. The perilous voyage to America is realistically portrayed, with disease and death at every turn. Though some critics felt the ending was contrived, it is ultimately uplifting. *The Grave* was named to YALSA's Best Books for Young Adults List in 2002. His next book, *Flood,* follows a young boy whose mother and stepfather are killed in a horrible flood, but the boy is saved by a group of Sheehogues, or Little People. A mix of Celtic MYTHOLOGY, humor, and adventure make it a coming-of-age tale that will appeal to a younger audience. The book that followed, *Hit Squad* (2003), is part of a reluctant-reader series by Orca Publishing. He draws on his experience as a high-school teacher, as he depicts life in a CANADIAN high school. Though the SERIES is written for a younger audience, the appeal of the story is in its characters and gripping plot.

AWARDS: Geoffrey Bilson Historical Fiction for Young People Award, Arthur Ellis Crime Writing Award for Juvenile Fiction (all for *The Grave*); 2002 ALA BBYA for *The Grave.*

FURTHER WORKS: *Blue,* 1991; *Torn Away,* 1994; *Wish Me Luck,* 1997; *Waiting for Sarah* (with Bruce McGay), 2003.

BIBLIOGRAPHY: *Contemporary Authors Online,* Gale, 2003; Author website: http://www.jamesheneghan.com (accessed 5/18/2004)

TERRY BECK

HENKES, Kevin
Author, 1960, n.p.

For many, H. conjures up images of little mice dealing with the problems children face in their day-to-day lives. In books such as *Chrysanthemum, Lilly's Purple Plastic Purse, Wemberly Worried, Owen,* and *Julius the Baby of the World,* H. tackles issues such as sibling rivalry, fear of the unknown, taunting by peers, and other topics of interest to young readers. However, H. is also a writer of novels for older readers. His chapter books, notably short but poignant, deal with the issues faced by these older readers such as friendship, DEATH, desires, and FAMILY.

Words of Stone (Greenwillow, 1992) explores the unusual friendship between Blaze and Joselle. Blaze is quiet and reserved, perhaps more so after the death of his mother. Joselle is Blaze's opposite in personality, outgoing and demonstrative. Even though their friendship is a difficult one, both gain from the relationship. The nature of friendship is carefully navigated by *Words of Stone.*

Twelve-year-old Fanny yearns for a dog in *Protecting Marie* (Greenwillow, 1995), another of H.'s books for intermediate readers. Marie is a tiny paper figure that Fanny continues to protect in many ways. Most importantly, Fanny does not want anyone to discover Marie's existence for fear of scorn. *Protecting Marie* deals with family issues as well as the longing for a pet.

Sun and Spoon examines the life of a ten-year-old boy after the death of his beloved grandmother. Spoon is searching for the perfect memento by which to remember Gram. He finds that memento in an unexpected place. *Sun and Spoon* tackles one of the toughest times in a child's life: what happens after a loved one has died.

In *The Birthday Room* (Greenwillow, 1999), ten-year-old Ben receives a gift he is unsure he really wants. His parents create a special room for Ben to use to create art. Ben, though gifted artistically, feels undue pressure from this presentation of a special room. A summer spent with his Uncle Ian helps Ben decide how to proceed. *The Birthday Room* holds a mirror up to strained family relationships while also taking a closer look at how sometimes a present is actually perceived differently from giver to recipient.

Olive's Ocean (Greenwillow, 2003) was awarded a Newbery Honor Medal in 2004. The story of Olive and her summer at the shore visiting her grandmother revisits some familiar territory for H. Olive is determined that this summer will be different. For one thing, Olive resolves to find some way to commemorate the death of a classmate she did not know well. Olive also falls in love for the first time and finds out the hard way that hearts can be broken all too easily. It is her strengthening relationship with her grandmother that allows Olive to grow and mature through these tough times.

H.'s reflections on the topics and issues of interest to children in those important intermediate- and middle-school grades provide readers not only with satisfying reading experiences; readers also are able to feel empowered by the resiliency of the heroes and heroines who people these remarkable novels.

AWARDS: *Olive's Ocean:* Newbery Honor, 2004; Best Books for Young Adults list, 2004; ALA Notable Children's Books, 2004.

BIBLIOGRAPHY: http://www.kevinhenkes.com/ http://www.bbb.com/Library/author/Henkes.htm

TERI S. LESESNE

HENTOFF, Nathan Irving
Author, b. 10 June, 1925, Boston, Massachusetts

H., commonly known as *Nat,* is the son of Russian-Jewish immigrants, Simon (a traveling salesman and haberdasher) and Lena (Katzenberg) Hentoff (a housewife and cashier). They lived in the Jewish neighborhood of Roxbury, near Boston, where H. grew up during the wave of anti-Semitism in the late 1930s and early 1940s. When he was ten-years old, H. attended the Boston Latin School along with students from diverse ethnic backgrounds. It was at the Boston Latin School that each student's ability earned them a seat in the school, and not their social standing. If students did not achieve, they had no choice but to leave the school.

H. spent his childhood visiting the public library every weekend. It was in the library that he dreamed of being a famous author and being able to prove this success by locating the author's card with his name on it from the library's card catalog. H. would also go to the movies every Saturday. At this young age he developed a love for jazz and when older, often sneaked into Boston's bars and clubs to hear his favorite jazz musicians, such as Charlie Parker and Duke Ellington, play. During these times he included being a sideman for a jazz band in his dreams.

H. graduated from Boston Latin School and went on to college. As a student at Northeastern University, H. was a staff writer for the student-run newspaper, *Northeastern News.* He became its editor during his junior year. During an in-depth investigation by the paper's staff writers, a corruption scandal was uncovered which strongly suggested that the trustees of the university were funding anti-Semitic publications. Before the story went to press, the university president presented the newspaper staff with two distinct choices. All members of the newspaper chose to resign rather than not publish the findings of their investigation, including H.

Graduating with highest honors and receiving a B.A. from Northeastern University in 1946 H. continued his graduate studies that same year at Harvard University and later at the University of Paris, the Sorbonne in 1950.

H. married and divorced his first wife, Miriam Sargent in 1950. He married his second wife, Trudi Bernstein, on September 2, 1954, from whom he was later divorced in 1959. Their marriage produced two children, Jessica and Miranda. After their divorce, he married Margot Goodman, a writer whose work appears frequently in the *New York Review of Books.* Together they have two children, Nicholas and Thomas.

Beginning in 1943, while still in college and until 1953, H. was a writer, producer, and announcer for Boston radio station WMEX. Here he used the venues of live personal interviews and innovative musical programming to bring contemporary jazz and its musicians to the listening audience.

H.'s writing skills and abilities as a jazz critic were evident throughout his career as associate editor of *Downbeat* in New York City from 1953 to 1957. During this time, H. was adamant and vocal in his belief that black writers should be working on *Downbeat,* since jazz was primarily a musical venue for black artists. Instead, the magazine employed an all-white

staff. H. was fired for these ideas and gave up writing about jazz. H. was then a contributing columnist who initially worked for free for the New York City's new and fledging weekly publication, the *Village Voice,* beginning in 1958. His writing covered such current topics as education, politics, the Supreme Court, civil liberties, and corporal punishment. He was now no longer known as solely a jazz writer. H. became a staff writer for the *New Yorker,* beginning in 1960 and ending in 1986, and later a columnist for the *Washington Post,* beginning in 1984 and ending in 2000, and for the *Washington Times,* beginning in 2000. He has also written reviews in the following magazines: *New York Herald Tribune Book Week, Reporter,* and *Peace News.* H. has written novels and nonfiction works for adults. A strong advocate for CIVIL RIGHTS, H. has edited nonfiction works, written introductions to several books, and co-authored additional adult works.

H.'s experiences growing up, in radio, and as a contributor to prestigious MAGAZINE and newspapers, prepared him for his toughest audience: the TEENAGER. In 1960, H. was encouraged to write for YOUNG ADULTS by Ursula Nordstrom, the head of the Harper and Row young reader's division. H.'s writing for young adults focuses on story lines that include: civil liberties; the importance of education, hard work, effort and maintaining the discipline needed for achieving success; censorship; the military draft; authority, friendship, truth, personal decision making and developing an ability to take responsibility for maintaining the hard-won freedoms guaranteed by our Constitution and the Bill of Rights. Because more than fifteen publishers turned down his subsequent book for young adults, which focused on pockets of isolation and separatism among ethnic groups of students (Asian Americans, blacks, whites) as they attend high school and college, H. ceased writing for young adults, by choice, with his final publication in 1987. He has since written for adult audiences.

In addition to lecturing at colleges and schools, H. has served as an adjunct associate professor at New York University and as a member of the faculty at the New School of Social Research in New York City. His hobbies include reading, tennis, politics, music, and reading his name next to "author" in a library's cataloging system.

AWARDS: *The Day They Came to Arrest the Book* (1982)—American Library Association Notable

Book; *Jazz Country* (1965) won the following in 1966: Nancy Bloch Memorial Award New York Herald Tribune Spring Book Festival Award; *American Heroes: In and out of School* was one of 100 Young Adult titles selected for the 4th YALSA Best of the Best List. Here We Go again . . . 25 Years of Best Books (selections from 1967 to 1992).

FURTHER WORKS: YA Fiction: *The Day They Came to Arrest the Book,* 1982; *Does This School Have Capital Punishment?,* 1981; *This School Is Driving Me Crazy,* 1976; *In the Country of Ourselves,* 1971; *I'm Really Dragged but Nothing Gets Me Down,* 1971; *Jazz Country,* 1965, YA Nonfiction: *American Heroes: In and out of School,* 1987; *The First Freedom: The Tumultuous History of Free Speech in America,* 1980; *Journey into Jazz,* 1968.

BIBLIOGRAPHY: "Nat(han) (Irving) Hentoff," *Authors and Artists for Young Adults,* Vol. 42., 2002; *Contemporary Authors Online,* 2003; *Something about the Author,* Volume 42. p. 69.

VALERIE A. PALAZOLO

HERBERT, Frank Patrick

Author, b. 8 October 1920 in Tacoma, Washington; d. 11 February 1986, Port Townsend, Washington

H., one of America's most influential SCIENCE FICTION writers, was born in Tacoma, Washington, the son of a highway patrolman. On his eighth birthday, H. announced, "I wanna be a author," and throughout his writing career perceived himself as primarily a storyteller. He read H. G. Wells, Jules Verne, and the planetary romances of Edgar Rice Burroughs. Growing up on the Olympic and Kitsap Peninsulas, H. credited his rural upbringing with his improvisational, problem-solving approach to technology. After working as a reporter, he served in the wartime U.S. Navy as a photographer, from 1942 to 1943. After the war he studied at the University of Washington, Seattle, and was a journalist and editor on several West Coast newspapers, including the San Francisco *Examiner.* H. sold his first story in 1945 and his first science fiction story in 1952, but did not become a full-time novelist until 1969.

After a brief wartime marriage ended in divorce, H. married Beverly Stuart in 1946 and had two sons.

The rich texture and detail in H.'s writing reflect his careful research and wide experience as a radio news commentator, oyster diver, jungle survival instructor, and judo teacher. He traveled widely and was interested in jungle botany, navigation, psychology, religion, and undersea geology.

As well as science fiction stories and novels, H. wrote nonfiction about computers and ecology. His first bestseller was *The Dragon in the Sea* (1956). Originally serialized in *Astounding* MAGAZINE in 1955 as *Under Pressure* (his preferred title), this is the claustrophobic and exciting account of a psychologist's search for a traitor among the four-man crew of a nuclear subtug during a World War III secret mission. The story was published shortly after the first atomic submarine began operations. Although he had never been near a submarine, H.'s treatment of submarine technology and human psychology under pressure is both highly technical and convincing.

H.'s wide interest in religions is reflected in such novels as *The God Makers* (1972), while his interest in the effects of science on society can be seen in *The White Plague* (1982) and *The Dosadi Experiment* (1977). H.'s use of ecological concepts captured the enthusiasm of young readers in the 1960s. Set in a future Brazil, *The Green Brain* (1966) evoked the expanding intelligence of a hive-mind of millions of insects in an intense account of a mutating jungle ecology. By contrast, *Hellstrom's Hive* (1973), also known as Project 40, depicts human minds merging in an ant-like hive-mind to take control of the planet. The expansion of intelligence was a constant theme in H.'s work. *The Eyes of Heisenberg* (1966) is an early exploration of implications of genetic engineering.

Dune (1965) raised H.'s writing to cult status. Set on the parched planet of Arrakis, *Dune* pits a hardy tribe of desert warriors, the Fremen, against the technical resources of a vast space empire. The utter reality of the hostile alien environment, coupled with vigorous action, exotic settings, interplanetary intrigue and spiritual depth, made this novel an international success. Its ecological message—*Dune* is dedicated to the world's dryland ecologists—captured the enthusiasm of college readers, while the Fremen use of a spice-drug to enhance their vision of time and space echoed another interest of the 1960s. (Nor was the Arrakis-Earth parallel between the control of water and oil overlooked.) *Dune* won the two highest awards of science fiction: the Hugo and the Nebula (the first novel to be awarded the latter).

Dune Messiah (1971) developed further the links between the giant sandworm of Arrakis and the prophetic vision of his hero Paul Atreides (descendant of the Mycenaean kings Menelaus and Agamemnon), while the powerful *Children of Dune* (1976) brought the next generation, the twins Leto and Ghanima (psychically aware of the memories of all their ancestors) into the vast complexities of generations of breeding for psychological and spiritual power. To many readers, this was the logical end of the Dune epic. Each of the three subsequent novels in this six-millennia saga proved more dense, complex, and subtle. They require effort but reward careful reading.

Part of H.'s storytelling genius was his ability to bring together unrelated ideas and to cause them to resonate. He had always been impressed by his strong-minded Catholic maternal aunts. Then in the 1950s he had studied an attempt to halt Oregon's spreading sand dunes. From seeds like these came Arrakis and the Bene Gesserit Sisterhood.

Dune was filmed by David Lynch in 1984, creating a new wave of enthusiasm for the epic SERIES, especially in Europe and Asia. Television adaptations were made in 2000 and 2003. *Dune* has now sold over three million copies and H. remains one of the influential giants of 20th-century science fiction.

H. collaborated with his elder son Brian Herbert (b. 1947) on *Man of Two Worlds* (1986). Since H.'s death, Brian Herbert has also written the Prelude to Dune series (with Kevin J. Anderson), introducing the great families whose conflicts generate the events of Dune. Based on H.'s notes and conversations about the genesis of Dune, these are interesting novels but lack the power and passion of the original.

True to his convictions, H. lived with his wife and children, in homes—in Hawaii and Port Townsend, Washington—which were constructed on ecological principles, using wind and sun power. H died of cancer at age 65.

AWARDS: 1965: Nebula Award: Best Novel: *Dune.* [Science Fiction Writers of America]; 1966: Hugo Award: Best Novel: *Dune.* [World Science Fiction Convention].

FURTHER WORKS: Dune series: *God Emperor of Dune*, 1981; *Heretics of Dune*, 1984; *Chapter House Dune*, 1985 [later retitled *Chapterhouse: Dune*.]; *The Santaroga Barrier*, 1968; *Whipping Star*, 1970; *The Worlds of Frank Herbert* (short stories), 1971; *Soul Catcher*, 1972; *The Dosadi Experiment*, 1977; *The Jesus Incident*, (with Bill Ransom) 1979; *Direct Descent*, 1980; *The Lazarus Effect*, (with Bill Ransom) 1983; *The As-*

cension Factor, (with Bill Ransom) 1988. Prelude to Dune series: All by Brian Herbert and Kevin J. Anderson: *House Atreides*, 1999; *House Harkonnen*, 2000; *House Corrino*, 2001; *The Butlerian Jihad*, 2002; *The Machine Crusade*, 2003; *The Battle of Corrin*, 2004.

BIBLIOGRAPHY: Herbert, Brian, *Dreamer of Dune: the biography of Frank Herbert*, 576 pages, 2003; McNelly, Willis E. Comp, *The Dune Encyclopaedia*, 1984; O'Reilly, Timothy, *Frank Herbert*, Ungar Publishing, 1981, o.p. [see websites]; O'Reilly, Tim[othy]. Ed., *The Maker of Dune: Insights of a Master of Science Fiction*, 1987.

INTERNET SITES: www.dunenovels.com; http://tim .oreilly.com/sci-fi/herbert/

TREVOR AGNEW

HERRERA, Juan Felipe
Author, b. 27 December 1948, Fowler, California

H. describes his birthplace as one of the raisin capitals of the world and tells the story of his life as part of a migrant worker family in *Calling the Doves*, a book that has received numerous awards.

H. became a teaching fellow at the University of Iowa (1990) and taught at New College of San Francisco and Stanford University. H. received a B.A. in social anthropology from the University of California, a Master's degree in social anthropology from Stanford, and a Master's degree in Fine Arts in creative writing from the University of Iowa. H. began teaching at California State University Fresno in 1990, became a full professor in 1998, and was elected Chair of the Department in 2001.

Inspired by his mother, Lucha Quintana Herrera and the Latino CIVIL RIGHTS MOVEMENT of the 1960s. H. began working toward some very specific goals. He saw El Teatro Campesino in San Francisco in 1968 and immediately began organizing student and community theater programs directed toward social change. The troupes included ensembles such as El Teatro Chichimeca (1968), El Teatro Tolteca poetry, jazz theater (1969–72), Troka Percussion and Spoken Word Ensemble (1980–84), Teatro Zapata (1990–2000), Manikrudo Raw Essence Poetry in Performance Workshop (1994–2002) and the Teatro Ambulante de Salud, a Rural Health Education program in the San Joaquin Valley (2003–2004).

H. has written more than one hundred published collections of poems, articles, reviews as well as books of POETRY, prose, SHORT STORIES, YOUNG ADULT novels, and PICTURE BOOKS for children. Much of his work appropriate for young adults and published since 1990 is cited immediately below.

SELECT FURTHER WORKS: *Cabeza,* 2000; *Thunderweavers,* 2000; *Giraffe on Fire,* Poems, 2001, *Grandma & Me at the Flea / Los Meros Meros Remateros,* 2002; *Notebooks of a Chile Verde Smuggler,* 2002; *Cilantro Girl / La Superniña del Cilantro,* 2003; *Coralito's Bay / La Bahía de Coralito,* 2004; *Featherless / Desplumado,* 2004.

SELECT AWARDS: 1995, BABRA Award Poetry Nomination for *Night Train to Tuxtla* (Univ. of Az. Press); 1996, Hungry Mind Review—Award of Distinction Winner—for *Calling the Doves* (San Francisco Children's Books); 1996, IRA Teachers Choice for 1996 (*Calling the Doves*); 1996, Smithsonian Notable Children's Book (*Calling the Doves*); 1996, Cooperative Children's Book Center Choice (*Calling the Doves*); 1997, Ezra Jack Keats Award for *Calling the Doves;* 1998, FOCAL Award (Friends of Children & Literature) for *Calling the Doves.* 2000, Pura Belpre Award Honors for *Laughing Out Loud, I Fly* (HarperCollins: Joanna Cotler Books); 1999, Americas Award for *Crashboomlove (UNM Press).* Center for Latin American and Caribbean Studies, University of Wisconsin, Milwaukee; 2000, New York Public Library Winner for Books for the Teen Age, for 1999. (*Crashboomlove* [UNM Press]); 2000, Latino Literary Hall of Fame—Poetry *(Crashboomlove);* 2000, Smithsonian Notable Book of the year—*The Upside Down Boy;* 2001, Texas Libraries Master List—*The Upside Down Boy;* 2001, Cuatrogatos Bilingual Book of the Year Award. The Upside Down Boy; 2001, The New York Public Library: *Thunderweavers* outstanding book for high school students; 2002, Nomination for Poet Laureate of California, California Arts Council; 2002, Latino Literary Hall of Fame in Poetry for *Giraffe on Fire,* (Co-winner first place) New York: 2003, Charlotte Zolotow Honors for Top Ten Books of 2002 (*Grandma and Me at the Flea*). Cooperative of Children's Book Center, School of Education, UW-Madison; 2003, Skipping Stones Honor Award. *Grandma and Me at the Flea.* Children's Book Press; 2003, Americas Honor Award. *Grandma and Me at the Flea.* Children's Book Press.

BIBLIOGRAPHY: Cavallari, Mario. La muerte y el deseo: notas sobre la poesia de Juan Felipe Herrera, *La Palabra* Vol. 4, no. 1–2 (Spring–Fall, 1982–1983). P. 97–106; Colaboradores. In: *Revista Chicano-Riquena* Vol. 6, no. 3 (Summer, 1978), p. 77; Cullinan, Bernice, Conversation with author, April 30, 2004; Flores, Lauro. Auto/referencialidad y subversion: observaciones (con)textuales sobre la poesía de Juan Felipe Herrera. In: *Critica,* vol. 2, no. 2 (Fall, 1990), pp. 172–81; Flores, Lauro. Converging languages in a world of conflicts: code-switching in Chicano poetry. In: *Visible Language,* vol. 21, no. 1 (Winter, 1987), pp. 130–52; Foster, Sesshu. From Logan to the Mission: riding north through Chicano literary history with Juan Felipe Herrera, *The Americas Review,* vol. 17, no. 3–4 (Fall–Winter, 1989), pp. 68–87; Herrera, Juan Felipe. [Interview with] Juan Felipe Herrera, *Partial autobiographies: interviews with twenty Chicano poets,* edited by Wolfgang Binder, Erlangen, W. Germany: Verlag 1985, pp. 95–108; Herrera, Juan Felipe, Papers (1970–1998), call no. M1043, repository: Stanford University Libraries, Dept. of Special Collections and University Archives, 42 linear feet. (1998); "Reflections on the Ezra Jack Keats Award: From Words to World," *Library Journal,* Pp. 51–56; Spring 2000; Villagran, Nora, *El Sueno americano = The American Dream,* in, *Arts and Books, San Jose Mercury News,* March 12, 1989, p. 16.

BERNICE E. CULLINAN

HERRIOT, James (James Alfred Wight)

Author, veterinarian, b. 3 October 1916, Sunderland, England; d. 23 February 1995, Yorkshire, England

H. began writing about his experiences as a veterinarian in 1966 and has been a beloved author ever since. H. graduated from Glasgow Veterinary College in 1939 and joined the Yorkshire practice with J. Donald Sinclair (dubbed Siegfried Farnon in H.'s books) in 1940. He married Joan Catherine Danbury in 1941 and spent two years in the Royal Air Force. He and Joan had two children. H. was a man who thoroughly enjoyed his work and shared that joy in light, witty stories based on the experiences of his veterinary practice and his love of animals.

Described as a kindly animal doctor, H. wrote a collection of memoirs of a country veterinarian in *All Creatures Great and Small* (1972). The stories reflect on H.'s new practice and his fears and expectations about his new career. The stories bring to life his encounters with humans, cows, dogs, and cats with humor, warmth, compassion, and H.'s obvious zest for life. This book launched H. into literary fame and made him one of the most beloved authors of our time. His newfound fame did not change this kind man; he continued to care for animals for fifty years and wrote when he could in his spare time. H. was completely astounded by the success of this first book. He merely hoped it would be published and that perhaps a few people might enjoy his stories; instead, millions continue to read his work.

H. followed with *All Things Bright and Beautiful* (1974) and continued to make readers laugh and cry as he continued to recount his tender animal stories. The success of H.'s works transformed the image of veterinary medicine and helped increase the popularity of the profession.

AWARDS: ALA Best Young Adult Book: *All Things Bright and Beautiful* (1974) and *All Creatures Great and Small* (1975); American Veterinary Medical Association's Award of Appreciation (1975); Order of the British Empire (1979); Royal College of Veterinary Surgeons fellow (1982); Chiron Award (1992); James Herriot Award established by Human Society of the United States.

FURTHER WORKS: *All Things Wise and Wonderful*, 1977; *James Herriot's Yorkshire*, 1981; *The Lord God Made Them All*, 1981; *Every Living Thing*, 1992; *James Herriot's Dog Stories*, 1993; *James Herriot's Cat Stories*, 1994; *The Best of James Herriot: Favourite Memories of a Country Vet*, 1998.

BIBLIOGRAPHY: *Contemporary Authors New Revision Series,* vol. 40; *Something about the Author,* vol. 135; http://www.jamesherriot.org/

TINA HERTEL

HERZOG III, Arthur

Author, b. 6 April 1927, New York City

The very private and humble H., the son of Arthur Jr. and Elizabeth Lindsay (Dayton) Herzog, is most noted for his suspenseful disaster novels. This is quite a different genre from the writing done by his father, the well-known blues song that Billie Holiday made famous, "God Bless the Child."

After attending Arizona University for a short period of time, Herzog served in the U.S. Navy from 1945–1946. He went on to earn a B.A. from Stanford University in 1950 and an M.A. from Columbia University in 1956. He and his wife, now divorced, have one son, Matthew. In addition to his novels Herzog has been a contributing writer to several publications including the *New York Times, Esquire,* and *Harper's.*

Successful MOVIE adaptations have been made of two of his novels, *The Swarm* (same name—1978, using real bees and not computer animations) and *Orca* (Orca: The Killer Whale—1977).

H. is an avid reader and enjoys traveling. His website can be accessed at the URL; http://arthurherzog .com

AWARD: *Swarm* was one of 100 Young Adult titles selected for the 1st YALSA Best of the Best List: Still Alive (selections from 1960 to 1974).

FURTHER WORKS: *Gone but Not Forgotten*, 1998—co-authored with Patricia Fox-Sheinwold; *The Woodchipper Murder*, 1989; *How to Write Almost Everything Better*, 1987; *Vesco: From Wall Street to Castro's Cuba, the Rise, Fall and Exile of White Collar Crime*, 1987—Non-fiction work; *L.S.I.T.T.*, 1984, reprinted as *Takeover*, 1987; *The Craving*, 1982; *Aries Rising*, 1980; *Glad to Be Here*, 1979; *Make Us Happy*, 1978; *I.Q. 38*, 1977; *Heat*, 1989; *Orca*, 1976—Media Adaptation by Paramount, 1977; *Earthsound*, 1975; *The Swarm*, 1975—Media Adaptation by Warner Brothers, 1978; *The B.S. Factor*, 1973; *McCarthy for President*, 1969; *The Church Trap*, 1968; *The War-Peace Establishment*, 1965; *Smoking and the Public Interest*, 1963—co-authored.

VALERIE A. PALAZOLO

HESSE, Karen
Author, b. 29 August 1952, Baltimore, Maryland

H. grew up with her parents and a brother in an urban neighborhood of row houses in Baltimore. In pursuit of her interest in dramatics, H. attended Towson State College to study theater. There she met her future husband Randy; they eloped in 1971. After Randy was sent to Vietnam, H. resumed her undergraduate work at the University of Maryland. During that time, she wrote poems, gave readings, and gained a reputation as a poet. Before becoming a writer, H. worked as a teacher, librarian, advertising secretary, typesetter, and proofreader. Raising two small children sapped her energy and time for creating POETRY, so poetry was temporarily put on hold. While reading children's books for her young daughters, she came upon *Of Nightingales that Weep* by Katherine PATERSON, which had a profound impact on her literary career; she has considered Paterson her mentor since then.

H.'s first book, *Wish on a Unicorn* (1991), tells the story of a girl who feels burdened by her retarded younger sister; it takes a crisis to make her realize how special and important her sister is. In her next book, *Letters from Rifka* (1992), a series of letters describes a Jewish girl's flight with her family from

Russia to America in 1919. The book was highly acclaimed, and given several awards and honors. In the following year, three books for younger readers, *Lavender, Lester's Dog,* and *Poppy's Chair* were published.

H. uses a nuclear-power accident as a backdrop to tell a story of love, loss, and death in *Phoenix Rising* (1994). In *The Music of Dolphins* (1996), she raises the question of "what it means to be human" by telling the tale of a feral child's return to her dolphin family after her disappointment in human society.

H.s literary reputation grew when she received the Newbery Medal and the Scott O'DELL Historical Fiction Award for *Out of the Dust* (1997). In free-verse format, H. tells a compelling story of a thirteen-year-old girl's isolation and hardship on an Oklahoma farm during the dust bowl years of the Depression, and of the love, strength, courage, and forgiveness that led to her growth and acceptance. The narrative is written in DIARY entries from the girl's perspective, spanning the months from January 1934 to December 1935, H. describes the plight of the local farmers, the tragic house fire, her coping with her mother's death and her father's withdrawal, and the healing of the family. The relentless heat, drought, and dust are vividly portrayed through her powerful use of images and adroit use of words. Plain and unembellished language describes the protagonist's emotional nuances ranging from desolation, guilt, and pain to longing and hope. The candid narration, using the common language of daily life, strikes a resonant chord with readers. The free-verse poems flow eloquently, and the sparse text appeals to many young adults who are not inclined to read long, detailed descriptions of settings and events. The rhythms, in particular, sustain their reading interest and carry them through the book.

Besides *Out of the Dust,* H. also uses free-verse poems in two other books, *Witness* (2001) and *Aleutian Sparrow* (2003). The story of historical events in *Witness* is told in five acts through the voices of eleven people living in a small town in Vermont after the arrival of the Ku Klux Klan in 1924. The bigotry of white supremacists and the suffering of victims are conveyed through the voices of these people, including an African American girl, a young Jewish girl, a high-school student, several professionals, and some storekeepers. *Aleutian Sparrow,* also in free verse, depicts the removal of five Aleut villages by the government to a camp in the southeast of Alaska when the Japanese began to attack the Aleutian Islands during World War II. The poetic images and careful choice of words are powerfully woven into a tale of Aleutian traditions, the bleak landscape of the Aleutian Islands, the harsh conditions of camp life, and the suffering, illness and death of the Aleutians during three years of relocation in an alien environment.

Despite certain similarities in the unrhymed free verse of these three historical stories, the text in *Witness* and *Aleutian Sparrow* is much briefer than that in *Out of the Dust. Witness* is portrayed through the viewpoints of eleven people while the other two use only the voice of one teenage girl. The protagonist in *Out of the Dust* is fully developed as compared to the main character in *Aleutian Sparrow* and the eleven characters in *Witness,* who seem to lack depth of characterization. Nevertheless, all three poignant works of historical fiction end with some trace of hope and happiness. The social, political, and environmental issues brought out by H. will linger in readers' mind long after they close the books.

Stowaway (2000), *A Time of Angels* (1995), and *A Light in the Storm* (1999) are other works of historical fiction by H. who conducted thorough and detailed research for months before the writing process began. Her works convey a vivid and strong "sense of place," regardless of different locales such as Oklahoma and Russia. Her characters are generally based on real people in her life; for example, the protagonist in *Letters from Rifka* is modeled on her great-aunt. Several characters in her books are named Hannah after an elderly woman who was a childhood neighbor. H. portrays strong female characters who endure adversity, separation, and isolation, and who eventually gain strength and courage. The family love and sense of family powerfully sustains the characters during their sufferings. Her style is versatile; she uses prose, diary, letters, and free verse to tell stories that deeply engage readers. H.'s works are well liked by children as well as young adults.

AWARDS: Children's Book of Distinction Award from the *Hungry Mind Review, Wish on a Unicorn; Letters from Rifka:* Christopher Award, International Reading Association Children's Book Award, ALA Best Books for Young Adult, ALA Notable Children's Book, 1993, *School Library Journal* Best Book; 1997 IRA Young Adults' Choices, *Time of Angels; Music of the Dolphins:* 1996 YALSA Best Books for Young

Adults, 1996 *School Library Journal* Best Books for Young Adults, 1997 Golden Kite Honor Book by the Society of Children's Book Writers and Illustrators; *Phoenix Rising,* Charlotte Award, 1998 Heartland Award for Excellence in Young Adult Literature *Out of the Dust:* 1998 Newbery Medal, 1998 Scott O'Dell Historical Fiction Award; Notable Books for Children, 1998; *Stowaway:* 2000 YALSA Best Books for Young Adults, *School Library Journal* Best Book.

FURTHER WORKS: *Sable* (Marcia Sewall, illustrator), 1994; *Just Juice* (Robert Andrew Parker, illustrator), 1998; *Come on, Rain!* (Jon J. Muth, illustrator), 1999.

BIBLIOGRAPHY: Beck, Cathy et al., "Talking about Books: Karen Hesse," *Language Arts,* 79, Jan. 1999; *Children's Literature Review.* vol. 54, 1999, pp. 26–32; Karen Hesse, *kidsreads.com* [Online] Available: http://aolaol.kidsreads.com/authors/au-hesse-karen; Karen Hesse's interview transcript [Online] available; http://www.2.scholastic.com/teachers/authorsandbooks/authorstudies; Hesse, Karen. "Newbery Medal Acceptance," *Horn Book,* 74, July–Aug., 1998, pp. 422–27; Novelist, http://novelst3.epnet.com/novel; *Something about the Author.* vol. 103., 1999. pp. 80–86; *Something about the Author.* vol. 113, 2000. pp. 67–82.

SHU-HSIEN L. CHEN

HESSER, Terry Spencer
Author, b. 16 February 1954, Cicero, Illinois

As the older of two girls growing up in the Chicago suburbs, H.'s primary childhood interest was in stories—oral, written, and filmed. Yet she held jobs that tapped other interests. H. worked as a secretary, a hearing coordinator, and a clothing salesperson. She also held positions in marketing, public relations, and advertising. Almost twenty years ago, though, H. returned to stories. She now makes her living as a television producer and writer.

Kissing Doorknobs (2000) is H.'s fictionalized account of her own experience with obsessive-compulsive disorder (OCD). As an adult, H. discovered that the "undiagnosed mystery" in her childhood was, in fact, OCD. She investigated the disorder, and decided to turn her personal story into a work of fiction because, she writes, "It was so alienating to have had such terrible thoughts and worries and I had been so afraid to tell anyone the crazy thoughts in my head." *Kissing Doorknobs* tells the story of Tara Sullivan, a fourteen-year-old girl who suffers from increasingly strange compulsions, including counting cracks on

the sidewalk, obsessive prayer rituals, and the need to touch the doorknob then kiss her fingers thirty-three times before leaving the house. Here loved ones react in different ways. Tara's mother expresses increasing violence toward her daughter, while Tara's sister beats up anyone who makes fun of her sister. Tara's friends are sometimes accepting of her obsessive compulsions; at other times, they are extremely frustrated. H. also weaves other adolescent issues, including anorexia, shoplifting, drugs, and sex, into this debut novel.

H.'s interest in OCD resonates in a more recent documentary, "Worried Sick," which she wrote, produced, and directed for the Public Broadcasting Service. "Worried Sick" follows ten people of various ages who all suffer from OCD. Their personal stories are revealed as their jobs, relationships, freedom, and faith are all placed in jeopardy. This documentary also features interviews with several prominent researchers and clinicians and examines recent research on the disorder, including what may cause it. "Worried Sick" offers an in-depth view of this puzzling disorder, and provides a message of hope for those who suffer from, or know someone who suffers from, OCD.

H. received a bachelor's degree from Northwestern University. She is currently working on two books. The first is a YA novel about a girl boxer. The second is a memoir of her hometown—Cicero, Illinois—and of her family. H. lives in Chicago and has a nineteen-year-old daughter from a previous marriage.

AWARDS: American Library Association Best Books for Young Adults (1999), Bank St. College of Education the Best Children's Books of the Year (1999), and American Library Association Best of the Best Revisited (100 Best Books for Teens) (2000) for *Kissing Doorknobs.*

BIBLIOGRAPHY: "Terry Spencer Hesser." *The Complete Marquis Who's Who TM,* 2003; www.amazon.com; Personal interview with Ms. Hesser.

CARA GAMBERDELLA

HEWETT, Lorri
Author, n.d., n.p.

H. was born in Fairfax, Virginia and grew up in Littleton, Colorado. Writing her first novel at nine-years old, H. demonstrated the power of her imagination if not of her facts. However, the ballet classes H. attended helped to teach her the power of practice and perseverance that would also aid her with her writing. She continued writing throughout junior high and high school, although for a time she became involved with a fairly rebellious group of kids, who by sharing their problems with her became a way for her to experience a harder world than the one she lived in with her family. To open herself up to more of the black experience, H. joined the Shorter African Methodist Episcopal Church in Denver. H. wrote her first published novel *Coming of Age* (1991) during her senior year of high school, and learned that it would be published during her freshman year at Emory University, where she had received a merit scholarship that covered tuition, room, and board.

Winning the undergraduate fiction contest as a freshman, and having *Coming of Age* published during her sophomore year, helped H. decide to focus on writing instead of majoring in political science, followed by law school. H. continued to dance throughout college and joined many other organizations. She traveled throughout Europe during the summers of her last two years at college and did graduate studies in English at the University of St. Andrews, which she attended as a Robert Jones fellow.

In H.'s first two novels, *Coming of Age* and *Soulfire* (1996), she explores the housing projects of Denver, and the conflicts and challenges that TEENS growing up there face. H. set *Dancer* (1999) outside the inner city of Denver. The author's ballet experiences influenced this novel. In the book, Stephanie's will to dance is challenged by her ethnicity, her parents, and just by being a teen. She learns what she really wants after encountering Vance and his Aunt Winnie, who at one time danced with George Balanchine. In *Lives of Our Own* (2001), H. shifts the setting for her story from Denver to Georgia. Shawna Riley is from Denver originally and finds the South a far cry from what she is used to. The fact that segregation is still overt comes as a surprise to her and brings her into conflict.

H.'s highlights of the conflicts that AFRICAN AMERICAN teens face, regardless of their families and socioeconomic backgrounds, offer a much needed voice, and hopefully will be heard even more through the coming years. H. currently is a resident of Decatur, Georgia, and is a writer in residence at the Lovett School in Atlanta.

AWARDS: *Dancer:* 2000 ALA Best Books for Young Adults; 2000 New York Public Library Books for the Teen Age.

BIBLIOGRAPHY: www.amazon.com; www.novelst4.epnet.com; www.penguinputnam.com.

JEANNE MARIE RYAN

HICYILMAZ, Gaye
Author, b. 5 May 1947, Surbiton, Surrey, England

H., author of several novels for TEENS and the mother of four, grew up in Surrey and worked during the 1970s in Ankara, Turkey for several years as a British Council teacher. She moved with her family to Switzerland and now lives in Pembrokeshire, England.

H. is interested in adult attitudes toward youth and believes being a young adult in itself is a huge drama, whether it is expressed or not. Her stories involve young people who seem ordinary yet undergo great difficulties. H.'s protagonists frequently come from different places; she acknowledges her love of moving from place to place and getting to know the sense of a place.

H. is the winner of the Silver Pen Award (1992) for *Against the Storm* (1990) about a young boy named Mehmet whose family moves from the country to Ankara to become rich and instead find themselves living a shantytown existence. H. was inspired to write this story by an incident reported in the Turkish press.

H.'s novels have also been shortlisted for the Smarties Book Prize, The *Guardian* Children's Fiction Award, and The Whitbread Children's Book of the Year.

H. has written two novels: *Smiling for Strangers* (1998) and the historical novel *And the Stars were Gold* (1997) under the pseudonym Annie Campling.

AWARD: Writer's Guild Award, *The Frozen Waterfall.*

FURTHER WORKS: *The Frozen Waterfall,* 1993; *Watching the Watchers.* 1996; *Coming Home,* 1998; *In the Flame,* 2000; *Girl in Red,* 2000; *Pictures from the Fire,* 2003.

BIBLIOGRAPHY: *Contemporary Authors,* vol. 133; *Something about the Author,* vol. 77; *Schoolsnet* on line www.schoolsnet.com

SUSAN E. MORTON

HIGGINS, Jack
Author, b. 27 July 1929, n.p.

Born in England as Harry Patterson, H. is an internationally best-selling novelist, considered a "master of suspense." He has written more than sixty novels.

H. grew up in Belfast, Ireland, in a political environment that often proved to be stressful and somewhat dangerous. An early memory of H. features a Feinian demonstration in which his mother threw herself over him as bullets flew by their heads. H.'s mother had great influence on his life as she encouraged him to read at an early age. He attributes his success as a writer to this early start as an avid reader. Throughout his life, H. maintained the predominant goal of becoming a successful writer. After dropping out of school at the age of fifteen, he held many jobs including a circus tent-hand, a clerk, a tram-conductor, a soldier, a schoolteacher, and a lecturer. H. earned an honors degree in sociology at Bradford, England in 1962. While working as a teacher, he wrote during summer holidays and in his spare time. He published books one after another, under several pseudonyms, in order to bring in more money to supplement his job as a schoolteacher. In addition to the pseudonym H., he has published works under James Graham, Hugh Marlowe, and Martin Fallon.

Not until age forty when H. wrote *The Eagle Has Landed* (first published in 1975), did his first novel become an internationally best-selling novel. This highly original, action-packed WAR story launched him into literary fame. As in *The Eagle Has Landed,* many of H.'s experiences and contacts from his own army service are often reflected in his writings. He was promoted as a noncommissioned officer (N.C.O.) and served on the East German border during the Cold War. H.'s novels are often driven by a mix of fictional and nonfictional characters set during World War II. For example, *The Eagle Has Landed* features Nazi paratroopers landing in Britain in 1943 with orders to capture Prime Minister Winston Churchill. This H. novel was made into a film in 1976 starring Michael Caine, Donald Sutherland, Robert Duvall, and Jenny Agutter.

Critics from various opinions applaud H. for his irresistible novels, full of honor, bravery, and intrigue. His novels are often described as having a proclivity for suffering heroes. He once explained that characters come first when writing, not the plot, although fans describe his plots as ingenious. H. says that the key to a good plot is to incorporate a significant object or document which creates a race against time.

H. resides in London, England, with his wife Denise. He has four children from a previous marriage.

FURTHER WORKS: *Sad Wind from the Sea,* 1959; *The Savage Day,* 1972; *Storm Warning,* 1976; *Exocet,* 1983; *The Whitehouse Connection,* 1999; *Midnight Runner,* 2002; *Bad Company,* 2003.

BIBLIOGRAPHY: The University of Tennessee Literature Resource Center: http://www.galenet.com; Jack Higgins homepage: http://scintilla.utwente.nl/users/gert/higgins

ELIZABETH ANDERSON

HIGHWATER, Jamake Mamake (J. Mark, J. Marks-Highwater)

Author, choreographer, lecturer, b. date and p. unknown, most sources list b. 14 February 1942, Montana; d. 3 June 2001, n.p.

H. was one of the most important Native American writers for adults and YOUNG ADULTS of the 20th century. When he was seven, H. was adopted, and his origins have been kept private at his foster family's insistence. His natural mother, a woman of Blackfeet and Cherokee ancestry, was a storyteller who instilled in him a sense of identity and pride in his Native American heritage. H. wrote essays, poems, criticism, choreography, and novels for adults and young adults on Native American culture. H. took tales known traditionally through the spoken word and wrote them down. His books have a timeless appeal for readers of all ages.

H. won a Newbery Honor Award for *Anpao: An American Indian Odyssey* (1977), one of his best-known works. He did not intend for it to be a young adult book, but his publisher labeled it as a "FANTASY" geared for young adults. The book uses traditional and contemporary Native American legends to tell the story of a Native American boy's coming of age. Anpao meets a beautiful girl, Ko-ko-mik-e-is, who will only marry him if he gets permission from the sun. Amana, one of the characters from *Anpao,* is the main character in several of H.'s SERIES novels for young adults, the Ghost Horse cycle. It includes *Legend Days* (1984), *The Ceremony of Innocence* (1984), *I Wear the Morning Star* (1986), and *Kill Hole* (1988).

Many of H's novels are autobiographical, stemming from his own experiences as an Indian in America. H. was both praised and criticized for his harsh treatment of whites in some of his works. Some critics even refuted his claim of having been of Native American ancestry. Regardless of their criticisms, most reviewers and readers agree that H. was a unique and versatile writer who had the ability to present familiar themes in new ways and to include different cultural points of view in his works.

AWARDS: Newbery Honor Award (1978); *Boston Globe–Horn Book* Award (1978) and Best Book for Young Adults (American Library Association) citation (1978), all for *Anpao: An American Odyssey;* Best Books for Young Adults from *School Library Journal* (1980) for *The Sun, He Dies;* Notable Children's Book Award and Best Books for Young Adults (ALA) citation and Best Books of 1984 award from *School Library Journal* (1984) all for *Legend Days;* Best Books for Young Adults (ALA) citation (1986) for *Legend Days* and *The Ceremony of Innocence.* Received best film of the year, National Educational Film Festival, 1986, and CableACE Award, National Cable Television Association, 1990, both for the documentary he created based on his book *The Primal Mind: Vision and Reality in Indian America.*

FURTHER WORKS: *Anpao: An American Indian Odyssey,* 1977; *The Sun, He Dies: A Novel About the End of the Aztec World,* 1980; *The Primal Mind: Vision and Reality in Indian America,* 1981; *Moon Song Lullaby* (poems), 1981; *Eyes of Darkness,* 1983; *Legend Days* (first book of Ghost Horse cycle), 1984; *The Ceremony of Innocence* (second book of Ghost Horse cycle), 1984; *I Wear the Morning Star* (third book of Ghost Horse cycle), 1986; *Kill Hole* (fourth book of Ghost Horse cycle), 1988; *Songs for the Seasons* (poems), 1995; and *Rama: A Legend,* 1997; *Dark Legend,* 1999. OTHER: Music critic and contributor to *New Grove Dictionary of American Music.* Contributor of articles and critiques to literary journals, including *The New York Times, The Chicago Tribune; Archaeology, Commonweal, Esquire, Dance Magazine, Saturday Review* and *American Book Review.* Contributing editor, *Stereo Review,* 1972–79, *Indian Trader,* 1977–80, *New York Arts Journal,* 1978–86, and *Native Arts/West,* 1980–81; classical music editor, *Soho Weekly News,* 1975–79 and *Christian Science Monitor.*

BIBLIOGRAPHY: *Authors and Artists for Young Adult,* vol. 7, 1991; *Contemporary Authors—New Revision Series,* vol. 84, 2000; *Contemporary Authors,* vol. 199, 2002.

SHARON L. RAWLINS

HILL, David
Author, b. 1942, Napier, Hawke's Bay, New Zealand

One of the most esteemed writers for YOUNG PEOPLE IN NEW ZEALAND, H. was educated in Napier and at Victoria University, Wellington (M.A. in English, 1964). H. worked as a truck driver, soldier, and bartender before teaching English in high school for fourteen years. After producing some popular textbooks, and writing plays and short stories for the School Journal, he was inspired in 1979, by Margaret MAHY and Joy COWLEY, to take the financially perilous step of writing full time. While his articles, columns and reviews now appear widely in New Zealand papers and magazines, his main thrust has been in fiction for young people.

In the deceptively simple *See Ya Simon* (1992), Nathan's best friend Simon is fourteen, witty, intelligent, and keen on electronic games. He also has less than a year to live. Nathan's account of Simon's last months of life is simple and unsentimental; in fact it is often very funny. Although confined to his wheelchair by muscular dystrophy, Simon makes an impact in every aspect of Nathan's life from soccer to the school cross-country team. The final section, Simon's death and Nathan's reflection on their friendship, is brilliantly written. *See Ya, Simon* is H.'s much-beloved masterpiece.

H.'s over-modest formula for most of his novels is that he writes about things he did when he was a kid: playing sports (badly), trying to impress girls (unsuccessfully), and belonging to clubs and teams (vaguely). This certainly sounds like Ben in *Fat, Four-Eyed and Useless* (1997), a boy who finds refuge and then self-confidence in a school writing group, but H. always avoids stereotypes or else turns them upside down. In *Give It Hoops* (1998) a school basketball team comes from a small town in decline, the local meat works has closed, some players' parents are on drugs, others have separated, and the team's tattooed coach is there as part of his Community Service sentence. This is no rural idyll, but a very funny and readable account of their team-building and training techniques.

H. enjoys writing about teams because they contain different types of people—"there's always the chance for unexpected, brilliant or disastrous things to happen." He has covered numerous sports including soccer in *Good Move* (1995), cricket in *Seconds Best* (1996), tae kwan do in *Kick Back* (1995), and hockey in *Boots 'n' All* (1999). An entertaining writer, H. packs every page with small delights. (". . . sweating players wiped faces on their green-and-gold singlets, revealing an interesting variety of belly buttons"—*Give It Hoops.*) Team members are well characterized, while parents and teacher are recognizable too.

H. says he looks at situations and asks himself, "What if. . . ." Thus, as one who lives close to it, H. asks what would happen if the volcano Mount Taranaki-Egmont were to erupt again, in *The Sleeper Wakes* (2001). As a keen tramper, H. asks, in *Take It Easy* (1995) what would become of a school bush-walking party if their leader died in rugged country? Whether two self-centered young people can take responsibility and achieve survival, after a helicopter crash in the mountains, is the issue in *Cold Comfort* (1996).

The High Wind Blows (2001), where religious extremists try to sabotage a satellite launching, reflects H.'s personal interest in astronomy and black holes, while a parallel-universe story *Time Out* (1999) explores other possibilities postulated in astro-physics. These reach a logical and chilling conclusion in the appropriately named *Where All Things End,* 2002, set in 2040, during the death of science.

Recently, as publishers agreed with Ken CATRAN that historical fiction had a future, H. has been able to publish books which combine his own memories with careful research into significant events. *The Name of the Game* (2001) evokes the national anguish in 1981, as love of rugby conflicted with protests against South Africa's apartheid laws. Two of New Zealand's worst disasters are brilliantly recreated in their historical context, with the sinking of the Wahine in *No Safe Harbour* (2003) and the wreck of the Christmas Eve express train in *Journey to Tangiwai* (2003).

H. lives in New Plymouth, Taranaki, New Zealand, where his wife Beth is a language teacher.

AWARDS: *See Ya Simon:* 1994 Times Educational Supplement Award for Special Needs (UK), 2002 Silver Quill Award (Germany), 2002 Gaelyn Gordon Award; 1998 Esther Glen Medal, *Fat, Four-eyed and Useless.*

FURTHER WORKS: *Get in the Act: Three One-Act Plays,* 1985; *Ours But To Do: Plays,* 1986; *A Time to Laugh: Plays,* 1990; *The Games of Nanny Miro,* 1990; *A Day at a Time: Plays,* 1994; *Curtain Up,* 1995; *Help Yourself,* 1995; *Kick Back,* 1995; *The Winning Touch,* 1995; *Comes Naturally,* 1998; *Treasure Deep,* 1997; *Easy Does It,* 1999; *Impact,* 1999; *Just Looking, Thanks,* 1999; *Time Out,* 1999; *Afterwards,* 2000; *Last Minute,* 2000; *Right Where It Hurts,* 2002; *No Big Deal,* 2003.

BIBLIOGRAPHY: Chilwell, Jan. "Mr Hill the Writer." *Listener (NZ)* 8 Nov. 1986: 37; Fitzgibbon, Tom and Spiers, Barbara. *Beneath Southern Skies: New Zealand Children's Book Authors & Illustrators,* 1993. 88; Goldsmith, Susette. "Know the Author: David Hill." *Magpies NZ Supplement* 12:5 (Nov 1997): 2–4; Hebley, Diane. "Hill, David." *The Oxford Companion to New Zealand Literature.* Ed. Roger Robinson and Nelson Wattie, 1998. 236; Hill, David. "Biographical notes." *School Journal Catalogue 1978–1993,* 1994: 138–9; Hill, David. "Get 'em While They're Young." *Magpies NZ Supplement* 14:3 (Jul 1999): 5–6. http://library.christchurch.org.nz / Childrens / ChildrensAuthors / DavidHill.asp /; http://www.bookcouncil.org.nz/writers/hilldavid.htm/; http://www.bookcouncil.org.nz/writers/hilldavid.htm#kaphill/

TREVOR AGNEW

HILLERMAN, Tony
Author, b. 27 May 1925, Sacred Heart, Oklahoma

An award-winning author whose MYSTERIES are widely recognized for their depiction of Navajo culture and Southwest settings, H.'s novels have consistently been included in recommended reading lists for young adults. In addition to his career as a novelist, H. has farmed, served with distinction in the Army during World War II, and worked as a news reporter and editor. He worked in a variety of journalist positions from 1948 until 1962, and served as English department chair at the University of New Mexico from 1976–81. His third mystery, *Dance Hall of the Dead* (1973), was awarded an Edgar by the Mystery Writers of America. This title and others have been recognized by the Young Adult Library Services Association's committee on Popular PAPERBACKS for Young Adults, including a 2004 nomination for *Coyote Waits* (1990). H.'s writings, which include nonfiction journalism, have been incorporated in anthologies for young adults, such as *The Serpent's Tongue: Prose, Poetry and Art of the New Mexico Pueblos* (1997) edited by Nancy Wood. More often, though, H. is cited as an adult author whose mysteries are accessible to young adult readers.

AWARDS: 1974 Edgar Award, *Dance Hall of the Dead;* 1986 Western Writers of America Spur Award, *Skinwalkers;* 1987 Special Friends of the Dinee Award by the Navajo Nation; 1988 Anthony Award, *Skinwalkers;* 1989 Macavity Award, *Thief of Time;* 1989 Mystery Writers of America Grandmaster Award; 1990 Public Services Award of the Department of the Interior; 1990 National Media Award of the American Anthropological Association; 1991 Arrell Gibson Lifetime Award of the Oklahoma Center for the Book; 1992 Macavity Award, *The Talking Mysteries;* 1995 Anthony Award, *The Mysterious West;* 1997 Oklahoma Hall of Fame Inductee; 1998 Jack D. Rittenhouse Award of the Rocky Mountain Book Publishers Association; 2002 Agatha Award; *Seldom Disappointed.*

FURTHER WORKS: *The Blessing Way,* 1970; *Listening Woman,* 1978; *People of the Darkness,* 1980; *The Dark Wind,* 1982; *The Ghost Way,* 1984; *Skinwalkers,* 1986; *A Thief of Time,* 1988; *Talking God,* 1989; *Sacred Clowns,* 1993; *The Fallen Man,* 1997; *The First Eagle,* 1998; *Hunting Badger,* 1999; *The Wailing Wind,* 2002; *The Sinister Pig,* 2003; *Skeleton Man,* 2004.

BIBLIOGRAPHY: Charles J. and Morrison, J., "Clueless? Adult Mysteries with Young Adult Appeal," VOYA 20.5, 1997; Estes, S., *Booklist,* 1997; Hillerman, T., interview, *Profiles,* KQED, San Francisco, 2003; Hillerman, T., *Seldom Disappointed,* 2002; Hillerman, T. and Bulow, E., *Talking Mysteries: A Conversation with Tony Hillerman,* 1991; Pederson, J., *St. James Guide to Crime & Mystery Writers,* 4th ed., 1996; www.tonyhillermanbooks.com; www.ala.org; Literature Resource Center, online, 2003.

JENNIFER BUREK PIERCE

HI/LO BOOKS FOR YA READERS

Starting around the time of World War I, many American jobs began to demand a high-school education or specialized training, thus turning the national spotlight on general secondary educational practices. This advanced education and training involved reading, which illuminated a serious situation: many adolescents, new to high schools, training programs, or the armed forces, were neither completing nor comprehending the written material required of them. The thinking of the time was that these TEENAGERS were not proficient readers, so educators working within school systems, or for businesses and government, began producing text material, often in the form of comics or as manuals stripped of all tangential information, expressly for them.

By the 1960s and 1970s, nonreading adolescents, or YOUNG ADULTS as they were now called, still comprised a noticeable segment of school populations. Typically they were defined as remedial or disabled readers, again suggesting that they lacked the skills to read proficiently. Yet, true to their chronological ages

and social interests, these adolescents rejected reading material developmentally appropriate for younger children. So again, writers began producing materials, textbooks, and supplemental readers earmarked for classroom instruction as well as library (trade) books intended for pleasure reading.

By this time, however, reading researchers had developed several methods for simplifying prose. Edward Fry produced one of the most popular; one could count the number of syllables and sentences in a segment of text, plot those points on a graph, and determine a grade level readability score. Prose containing long sentences and multisyllabic words was considered more difficult, and thus at a higher grade level, than text with shorter sentences and words.

Concurrently, standardized tests, which purported to determine a youngster's reading acuity and translate that measure to a corresponding grade level, became a routine assessment instrument in many American schools. Now adults, armed with an adolescent's reading level and the reading level of a piece of prose, could make a seemingly exact match, giving teenagers texts that appeared to correlate with their reading skills.

A flood of trade books, with reading levels ranging from first to fifth grade and written specifically for young adult remedial readers, hit the marketplace. Mainstream publishers, such as Watts, Dutton, and Lippincott, designated such books with the anagram hi/lo, signifying high interest on the part of the reader and low readability on the part of the text. In all too many cases, however, the reverse was true.

Clearly the lower the grade level of a book, the greater the potential market, so writers manipulated texts in order to create the lowest possible Fry levels. The resulting books contained choppy, short sentences; an overabundance of pronouns; and imprecise, albeit simple, vocabulary. Probably the most serious issue raised about formula-driven text comes from the evidence that longer sentences which offer connectives are often easier to understand than shorter ones which require the reader to imply relationships (Pearson, 1974–75; Davidson and Kantor, 1982).

All too often these hi/lo volumes introduced cardboard characters confronting a full plate of trendy problems, including drug use, teenage pregnancy, and gang warfare; simplistic plots; and didactic messages. There were, of course, notable exceptions, and professional organizations, such as the National Council of the Teachers of English (NCTE) and the American Library Association (ALA), produced books and lists that highlighted the best of the genre.

Young adults never adopted these books as their overwhelming favorites. Instead, if they read for pleasure, they, like many of their avid reading peers, turned to young adult literature, reading and re-reading books such as Paul ZINDEL's *The Pigman* and S. E. HINTON's *The Outsiders.* Consequently, educators began questioning the basic assumptions behind these H. books. Perhaps, they suggested, young adults were indeed able to read these texts and simply chose not to. NCTE dropped its H. book committee and the ALA began recommending books not for remedial readers, but instead for reluctant ones.

Once readers were redefined, the books recommended for them were also. No longer were books judged through mechanical methods of counting syllables and sentences, but instead they were evaluated through a complex set of criteria. First of all, experiences with many hi/lo titles proved that young adults would not read just anything; they demanded fine stories or interesting content in order to continue reading. AVI's *Wolf Rider,* a compelling MYSTERY with a sophisticated theme, set the literary standard.

Second, these books needed a hook, such as an enticing jacket (see Michael Capuzzo's white shark swimming straight toward the reader in *Close to Shore*) or a tantalizing opening that would draw readers toward them. Again, books such as *Wolf Rider* immediately plunge readers into the action: "The kitchen phone rang three times before Andy picked it up. 'Hello?' he said. A voice replied, 'I just killed someone.'" (Avi, 1986, 1)

Third, format became a prime consideration. Reluctant readers frequently selected books containing short and discrete chapters, stories, poems, or segments that allow natural stopping points in the reading. Fine illustrations, relevant to the content and interspersed throughout the text, such as those in *The DK Encyclopedia of the Cat,* also make text appear less daunting.

These books, as well as GRAPHIC NOVELS and adult page-turners, are not written expressly for reluctant readers. They are, instead, read by them. And while nonfiction H. works still comprise a noticeable segment of children's and young adult publishing, they are generally geared towards classroom use and pro-

duced by publishers (Rosen and Capstone, for example) who target this market exclusively. While they may appear in school and public libraries, their critical reception is limited. Pat Ryan's *Extreme Snowboarding,* a dry H. title, for example, failed to garner much professional enthusiasm, while Cindy Kleh's *Snowboarding Skills,* a complex adult book that employs well-designed photographs that complement and expand the prose, received an ALA endorsement in 2004.

Quick Picks, the ALA's annual recommendations of books for reluctant young adult readers, are listed at http://www.ala.org/ala/yalsa/booklistsawards/booklistsbook.htm. These suggestions will include a few titles that fit traditional hi/lo patterns (such as *Navy SEALs: Special Operations for the U.S. Navy*), but the bulk of selected books come from all segments of adult and young adult publishing.

BIBLIOGRAPHY: Carter, Betty, "Formula for Failure," *School Library Journal* 46 (7) (July, 2000), pp. 34–37; Carter, Betty and Richard F. Abrahamson, "The Best of the Hi/Lo Books for Young Adults: A Critical Evaluation," *Journal of Reading* 30(3) (November/December, 1985), pp. 204–211; Davidson, Alice and Robert N. Kantor, "On the Failure of Readability Formulas to Define Readable Texts: A Case Study from Adaptations," *Reading Research Quarterly* 17 (2) (1982), pp. 187–209; Fry, Edward, "Fry's Readability Graph: Clarifications, Validity, and Extension to Level 17," *Journal of Reading* 21(3) (December, 1977), pp. 242–52; Mason, George E, "High Interest-Low Vocabulary Books Their Past and Future," *Journal of Reading* 24 (8) (April, 1981), pp. 603–07; Pearson, P. David, "The Effects of Grammatical Complexity on Children's Comprehension, Recall, and Conception of Certain Semantic Relations," *Reading Research Quarterly* 10 (2) (1974–75), pp. 155–193.

WORKS CITED: Avi, *Wolf Rider,* 1986; Capuzzo, Michael, *Close to Shore,* 2003; Fogle, Bruce, *The DK Encyclopedia of the Cat,* 1997; Hinton, S. E., *The Outsiders,* 1968; Kleh, Cindy, *Snowboarding Skills: The Back-to-Basics Essentials for All Levels,* 2003; Paument, Simone, *Navy SEALs: Special Operations for the U.S. Navy,* 2003; Ryan, Pat, *Extreme Snowboarding,* 1998; Zindel, Paul, *The Pigman,* 1969.

RICHARD F. ABRAHAMSON AND BETTY CARTER

HINTON, S. E. (Susan Eloise)
Author, b. 22 July 1948, Tulsa, Oklahoma

At times referred to as the Voice of Youth, H. revolutionized writing for YOUNG ADULTS with the publication of her first book, *The Outsiders* (1967). This realistic portrayal of the life of a young adult began a period in young adult literature called "The New Realism" in which young adult authors were not afraid to write about the real-life issues TEENAGERS were facing. H. has been awarded the ALA Best Books for Young Adults Award for four of her works. She was the first recipient of the American Library Association's and *School Library Journal*'s MARGARET A. EDWARDS AWARD in 1988, which acknowledged the impact her books have had on young adults and her ability to offer books that can reach into their lives.

As a young child H. loved to read. She dreamed of being a cowboy and began writing short stories about her love for horses. As she reached young adulthood, H. was not content with the reading selections available for her age group. She therefore began writing her own stories to read. At the tender age of fifteen she began her first draft of *The Outsiders* (1967). While she was writing the book her father died of a brain tumor. The loss of her father led H. to seek comfort in her writing. As with most of her books, she drew upon information from her own life to create *The Outsiders*. The town of Tulsa, as well as the school she attended, Will Rogers High School, were used as part of the book's setting. H. felt like an outsider in high school and disliked the social inequality that young adults experienced; she used this as the basis for *The Outsiders*. She finished the book at the age of seventeen and after graduating high school she enrolled in the University of Tulsa. H. submitted the manuscript to a friend's mother who was an author and it was passed along to a publisher who was interested. In April of 1967 *The Outsiders* was published as a novel under the name S. E. Hinton, a decision made by the publishers who feared that readers would not read the book knowing a woman wrote it. This as well as the fact that her books are written from a male perspective has often led to the confusion of her gender. *The Outsiders* was a huge success and still to this day is read by many young adults; it is acknowledged as a classic in young adult literature.

The success of *The Outsiders* put a lot of pressure on H. to produce a second book just as good if not better than her first. These expectations proved too much for her to handle and led to three years of writer's block. She was fearful that her first book was a mistake and that she was not a skillful writer. During this time she read a lot of literature hoping to sharpen her writing skills. She focused on college and switched her area of studies from journalism to education. At college she met her future husband, David Inhofe, who was instrumental in the writing of her second book, *That Was Then, this Is Now.* David pushed H. to write two pages a day until she finished. After graduating from college in 1970 she and David were married. In 1971, *That Was Then, this Is Now* was published. It told a story of friendship and like her previous work, it, too, is written in first person from a male's point of view. The critics gave positive reviews stating that this book was more mature and disciplined than her first.

Prior to the publication of *That Was Then, this Is Now* (1971) H. wrote a short story "Rumble Fish" which was published in *Nimrod,* a literary supplement of the *University of Tulsa Alumni Magazine.* Although a short novel, H. published it as a book in 1975. The critics gave mixed reviews but this did not discourage her. In 1979, H. published *Tex.* Critics praised the novel and acknowledged the maturation of her writing skills.

After the publication of *Tex,* H. took a nine-year break. It was during this time that her four novels were released as MOVIES. In September of 1982 *Tex* was released; *The Outsiders* and *Rumble Fish* followed in 1983. That same year her son Nicholas David was born. In 1985, *That Was Then, this Is Now* was released. In July of 1988, H. received the first annual YASD/SLJ Margaret A. Edwards Award, which honored her ability to speak to the young adults and reach them through her writing. The following October she published *Taming the Star Runner* (1988). Unlike her previous novels this was written in the third person. H. explained that she was busy with her personal life and could not be consumed by a new character.

In recent years, H. has left young adult literature and made a switch to writing for children. As with her previous books, she wrote about what she knew at the time and at this point in her life she was raising her son. In 1995, she published *Big David, Little David,* a picture book for kindergarten-age children. H. has continued on this path and published *The Puppy Sister* (1995) for elementary school children.

Although her recent works are not for the young adult population (e.g., *Hawkes Harbor* [2004]), she will be remembered for her contribution to the world of young adult literature. H. was an integral part of the transition of young adult novels into a reality-based writing mode. She gave teenagers an outlet where they could identify with the problems or issues that occurred in the books. She wrote about life as it was and appealed to teenagers around the world. Her novels are truly timeless classics and will continue to be read.

AWARDS: *Rumble Fish,* BBYA, 1975; *Taming the Star Runner,* BBYA, 1988; *Tex,* BBYA 1979, Best of the Best Books 1970–83 Nothin' but the Best BBYA 1966–86; *That Was Then, this Is Now,* BBYA, 1971; Still Alive: Best of the Best, 1960–1974; Nothin' But the Best BBYA 1966–86; First Margaret A. Edwards 1988.

FURTHER WORKS: "Teen-Agers Are for Real," 1967; "Rumble Fish" (short story), 1968

BIBLIOGRAPHY: Daly, Jay, *Presenting S.E. Hinton,* 1989; S.E.Hinton.com/bio; www.randomhouse.com/teachers/authors/sehi.html; http://www.edupaperback .org/authorbios/Hinton_SE.html

SARA HEANEY

HITE, Sid
Author, n.d., n.p.

With the publication of *Dither Farm: A Novel* in 1992, H. began the reinvention of his childhood, imbuing it with a different kind of magic than that he had known growing up. Great Aunt Emma's magical carpet proves too tempting for the children in the Dithers family, but when they use it without her consent, more trouble than they know what to do with encompasses the family. Set in 1969, the protagonists of *It's Nothing to a Mountain* (1995) all must cope in different ways with the losses of their parents. In *Answer My Prayer* (1995), both Lydia and her angel are surprised at how much happens when her angel decides to answer her prayer and how much it will involve the whole nation of Korasan. The Dither children, parents, family, friends, and neighbors, return for an encore appearance in *Those Darn Dithers* (1996). *The Distance Of Hope* (1998) which is not set in contemporary time follows Yeshe as he seeks to discover the White Bean Lama, who may be able to cure what ails his eyesight.

The 1999 release of *Cecil in Space* marks H.'s return to a contemporary setting as he chronicles the seventeenth summer of Cecil Rowe. Bricksburg, Virginia seems akin to Bowling Green, Virginia, where

H. himself passed many less than eventful small-town summers playing sports, fishing, and reading, and this novel may be an outgrowth of those times, as Cecil, the protagonist, reads, writes, and falls in love. Another retrospective on small-town life, *An Even Break* (1999), follows Frisk Tilden, the twelve-year-old manager of the town pool room, as he learns to play pool, hold his own, and help out his single mom with household expenses. Although set in the 1970s, the story works well and its issues are contemporary. *Stick and Whittle* (2000) follows the title characters, otherwise known as the Melvins, who despite the twelve-year difference in their age forge a partnership in the post–Civil War West. Paul Shackleford can't believe that the price of one lie is to be sent to stay with relatives on a farm in Virginia, but in 2001's *A Hole in the World,* he learns a lot from the Vallenports, and even more from stories about the recently dead Hennley Gray. He begins to reflect on what he would like to become in between learning to farm, and spending time with Gray's dog, Einstein. H. joins the roster of talented authors writing for the My Name Is America SERIES with the *Journal of Rufus Rowe: A Witness to the Battle of Fredericksburg* (2003).

Although H. currently lives in Sag Harbor, New York, his small-town childhood in Virginia plays a part in most of his work. His fantastical flourishes inform almost all of his work and add to the uniqueness of his voice. H. enjoys travel, and is a great reader as well. He grew up as the only boy in a family of five children, and novels were a great escape for him.

AWARDS: *It's Nothing to a Mountain:* ALA Best Books for Young Adults, 1995; *Stick and Whittle:* Florida Sunshine State Young Reader Award, 2004.

FURTHER WORKS: *The King of Slippery Falls,* 2004.

BIBLIOGRAPHY: www.amazon.com; www.henryholt childrensbooks.com/ authordetails.asp?ID = Hite; www.novelst4.epnet.com.

JEANNE MARIE RYAN

HO, Minfong
Author, b. 7 January 1951, Rangoon, Burma

Daughter of an economist and a chemist, H. was born in Burma, grew up in Thailand and Singapore, and presently lives in Ithaca, NY. Her educational background includes attendance at Tunghai University, Taichung, Taiwan (1968–69), a B.A. with honors in history and economics from Cornell University in 1973, and an M.F.A., also from Cornell, in creative writing in 1980. Fluent in Chinese, Thai, and English, she has worked as a journalist, lecturer, nutritionist, relief worker, and workshop presenter in both Asia and the U.S. She is married to John Value Dennis, Jr, a soil scientist, and has three children, Danfung, MeiMei, and Christopher. Her hobbies include swimming, hiking, and "growing things."

H.'s works, which include novels for YOUNG ADULT readers and middle graders as well as picture books for children, present realistic depictions of her native Southeast Asia. While many writers have tended to approach the subject with romanticism, H. has been lauded for including poverty, violence, and DEATH among the harsh issues she addresses. She has also been recognized for her sensitivity and understanding toward her characters' feelings, and has a penchant for strong female protagonists and stable family relationships. In her own words, H. has described her writing process as a form of "political expression," providing truth in opposition to the historical misrepresentations of Southeast Asia by white writers, many of whom wrote out of "condescension and ignorance."

H. achieved acclaim with her first young adult novel, *Sing to the Dawn* (1975). The full-length work began as a short story written during cold winter days at Cornell, a climate which made H. homesick for Thailand. After submitting it for the Council for Interracial Books for Children's annual short story contest, H. won the award for the Asian American Division of unpublished Third World Authors, and was then encouraged to enlarge the story into a novel. Her subsequent works have been well received internationally, and many of them have been anthologized and translated into Chinese, French, Japanese, Tagalog, and Thai.

AWARDS: 1975 first prize from the Council of Interracial Books for Children, *Sing to the Dawn; Rice Without Rain:* 1988 first prize from the National Book Development Council of Singapore, 1990 Parents Choice Award, 1991 ALA Best Books for Young Adults, and 1991 *Booklist* Editor's Choice; *The Clay Marble:* 1991 National Council on Social Studies/ Children's Book Council Notable Children's Book in the Field of Social Studies, 1991 *Parents Magazine* Best Books selection, 1992 American Booksellers Association "Pick of the Lists," and 1992 Notable

Children's Trade Books in the Language Arts, ALA Popular Paperbacks, 2003.

FURTHER WORKS: *Rice without Rain,* 1986; *The Clay Marble,* 1991; *Maples in the Mist: Children's Poems from the Tang Dynasty,* 1996; *First Person Fiction: Gathering the Dew,* 2003.

BIBLIOGRAPHY: *Contemporary Authors Online,* 2001; *Interracial Books for Children Bulletin,* Volume 8, No. 7 (1977), pp. 5, 21; *Twentieth-Century Young Adult Writers,* 1994, pp. 292–93.

ANDREA WONG

HOBBS, Valerie
Author, b. 18 April 1941, Metuchen, New Jersey

H. was born into a close-knit family. The name Valerie was given to H. after it was drawn from a hat filled with suggestions contributed by extended family members. Her early memories include family celebrations, animals, and the natural world that surrounded her New Jersey home.

In 1956, her world changed completely when her parents announced that they were moving to California. Struggling with poor finances, H.'s father hoped to open his own restaurant and relocated the family to Ojai, CA. This pivotal event became the source of her debut novel, *How Far Would You Have Gotten If I Hadn't Called You Back?* Bronwyn, the novel's sixteen-year-old protagonist, deals with her FAMILY's move by socializing with a wild crowd. As she falls behind in school, becomes involved in drag racing, and has a sexual encounter with an older man, Bronwyn learns that some of life's lessons must be learned the hard way. This first novel was a quick success, garnering an ALA Best Books for Young Adults citation in 1995.

H. did not become a writer herself until she had spent a number of years guiding young writers as an English teacher. Always a good student, H. attended the University of California, Santa Barbara, and graduated with a degree in education in 1968. She taught in Oahu, Hawaii, after separating from her first husband. In 1974, she and her daughter Juliet returned to Santa Barbara to be closer to her family. She met Jack Hobbs, and they married in 1978. She returned to UCSB to pursue her Master's degree, and in 1981 she began a twenty-year career as a writing instructor at her alma mater.

The same year, H. became a fellow in the South Coast Writing Project and first began to think of herself as a writer. She began writing and publishing SHORT STORIES. "Ojai, 1959," a short story published in *California Childhoods* (1987), grew into her successful first novel. H. did not initially write with a YOUNG ADULT audience in mind, but her agent saw the potential and marketed it accordingly; consequently, H. discovered that she enjoyed writing for young adults. Her second novel, *Get It While It's Hot. Or Not* (1996), focuses on the friendships of four teenage girls and the complicated sexual relationships and problems they face. Her contemporary themes and strong realistic characters earned H. a "Flying Starts" citation from *Publishers Weekly* in 1996. She was also honored with the PEN/Norma Klein Award for "emerging voice of literary merit in American children's literature" in 1999.

Frequently, H. addresses the issues of lifestyle changes and choices; she often draws from some of her own experiences. She drew upon memories of her brother's time in Vietnam to write *Sonny's War* (2002). This story centers on a TEENAGER who has a brother in the WAR while she attends anti-war protests at home. H. recently retired from teaching in order to devote all of her time to her writing, beginning with *Letting Go of Bobby Jones, or, How I Found Myself of Steam by Sally Jo Walker* (2004).

AWARDS: *How Far Would You Have Gotten If I Hadn't Called You Back?:* ALA Best Books for Young Adults, 1996; *Letting Go of Bobby James, Or How I Found My Self of Steam:* ALA Quick Picks for Reluctant Young Adult Readers, 2005.

FURTHER WORKS: *Carolina Crow Girl*, 1999; *Charlie's Run*, 2000; *Tender*, 2001; *Stephan's Story*, 2003; *Defiance*, 2005.

BIBLIOGRAPHY: *Something about the Author*, vol. 145, pp. 100–103; *Something about the Author*, Autobiography Feature, vol. 145, pp. 104–115.

DEDE SMALL

HOBBS, Will

Author, b. 22 August 1947, Pittsburgh, Pennsylvania

H.'s books appeal to a wide variety of TEEN readers, including those often-hard-to-reach male teens. He is best known for fast-paced outdoor adventure stories with strong environmental themes that appeal to YOUNG ADULT readers. Often based on personal experience (rafting, hiking, and camping in remote places), H.'s writing is also informed by research in

fields such as geology, archeology, and paleobotany. His settings are particularly vivid, functioning almost as an additional character in the development of the plot. H. is a constant presence on state award lists and all of his books are still in print. Thirteen of his novels (all but the recently published *Jackie's Wild Seattle*) have been recorded as audio books.

Reared in an Air Force family, H. traveled extensively before attending Stanford University, where he earned a B.A. in 1969 and an M.A. in 1971. He taught reading and English at Colorado junior high and high schools before becoming a full-time writer in 1990. His first published book, *Changes in Latitudes,* (1988) may also be his most angst-ridden: Travis, sixteen, vacationing with his mom and younger brother, Teddy, in Mexico, discovers his mother is having an affair. Meanwhile, he and Teddy become involved with efforts to save endangered sea turtles. In the conclusion, Teddy dies, leaving Travis to ponder what went wrong.

The Weminuche Wilderness in the San Juan Mountains near Durango is prominent in *Bearstone* (1989) and the sequel *Beardance* (1993). Cloyd, a troubled Ute Indian youth, is sent to live and work with Walter, a crusty old rancher/gold miner; the two eventually ride into the high country together. In these two adventures involving grizzlies and gold, Cloyd undergoes a mythic/spiritual epiphany as he risks everything to save Colorado's last grizzly bears.

H.'s love for and knowledge of river rafting are showcased in *Downriver* (1991) and its companion novel, *River Thunder,* (1997). In *Downriver,* a group of teens in trouble with the law (aka "hoods in the woods") are sent into the wilderness with the hope that they will emerge having built feelings of trust and positive self-worth. Instead, they impulsively steal the van, rafts, and equipment and launch themselves on a harrowing survival adventure that pits the protagonist's romantic interest against her own better judgment. H. has rafted the Colorado through the Grand Canyon ten times, so the setting is fully realized, authentic, and vividly described. *River Thunder* reunites most of the same characters for another trip down the canyon as they confront the duplicitous nature of the manipulative Troy amid the dangers of record-high water roiling the canyon.

Far North (1996) is set along the South Nahanni River in the remote Northwest Territories of Canada. Boarding school roommates Gabe, who is Caucasian, and Raymond, who is Dene, are stranded with Johnny Raven, a Dene elder, when their float plane is swept over Virginia Falls (twice as high as Niagara). Facing one disaster after another, they must learn to work together to survive the brutally cold winter and overcome their cultural differences.

As an author of exciting books that are infused with a love for and appreciation of the outdoors, H. successfully fuses his understanding of teens with his concerns about the environment in his skillfully crafted novels that reveal strength of spirit as well as appreciation of wild places.

SELECT AWARDS: BBYA by YALSA/ALA *Bearstone, Downriver, The Big Wander, Beardance, Far North, The Maze, Jason's Gold;* YALSA's "100 Best Young Adult Books of the 20th Century," *Far North and Downriver.* BBYA 1992: Here We Go Again: 25 Years of Best Books: Selections from 1967–92.

FURTHER WORKS: *The Big Wanderer,* 1992; *Kokopelli's Flute,* 1995; *GHOST CANOE,* 1997; *The Maze,* 1998; *Jason's Gold,* 1999; *Down the Yukon,* 2001; *Wild Man Island,* 2002; *Jackie's Wild Seattle,* 2003; *Leaving Protection,* 2004.

BIBLIOGRAPHY: Blasingame, James, *Interview with Will Hobbs, Journal of Adolescent & Adult Literacy,* Vol. 46, #5, Feb, 2003, pp. 444–45; *Something about rthe Author,* Vol. 127, 2002; James, Helen Foster, "Talking with Will Hobbs," *Book Links,* Vol. 9, #4, March, 2000, pp. 56–59; Shoemaker, Joel, "Interview with William Hobbs," *Voice of Youth Advocates,* Vol. 21, June, 1998, pp. 99–102; Lesesne, Teri S., Buckman, Lois, Beers, Kylene, "Interview with Will Hobbs," *Journal of Adolescent & Adult Literacy,* Vol. 41, #3, November, 1997, pp. 326–40; Thompson, Edgar H, "Interview with Will Hobbs," *Journal of Youth Services in Libraries,* Vol. 8, #3, Spring, 1995, pp. 243–49; Hobbs, Will, "On the Beautiful Trail We Go: The Story Behind The Big Wander," *The ALAN Review,* Vol. 22, #1, Fall, 1994, pp. 5–9; http://www.willhobbsauthor.com.

JOEL SHOEMAKER

HODGE, Merle
Author, essayist, b. 1944, Curepe, Trinidad

The daughter of an immigration officer, H. attended elementary and high school in Trinidad before winning the Trinidad and Tobago Girls Island Scholarship in 1962, which allowed her to study French at University College, London. H. received B.A. and M.Phil. degrees, focusing her studies on the poetry of French

Guyanese author Leon Damas. She returned to Trinidad in the early 1970s, where she taught French at the junior secondary level, before accepting a position in the French Department at the University of the West Indies, Jamaica. In 1979, H. went to Grenada, where she joined the regime of Prime Minister Maurice Bishop and was put in charge of developing a socialist education program. Bishop was assassinated in 1983, forcing H. to leave Grenada and return to Trinidad. H. is currently a lecturer in English and creative writing at UWI in Trinidad.

H.'s Caribbean childhood provides the basis for her two novels, *Crick, Crack, Monkey* (1970) and *For the Life of Laetitia* (1993). *Crick Crack* is the story of a young girl, Tee, as she leaves a rural Trinidadian life for a more anglicized existence; *Laetitia* follows a young Caribbean girl through her first year away at school. H. has also written numerous essays and SHORT STORIES and given seminars on Caribbean life, women's issues, and education.

AWARD: BBYA list, 1994, *For the Life of Laetitia.*

REFERENCES: Hughes, Michael, *A Companion to West Indian Literature,* 1979; *Merle Hodge Biography,* Emory University, online, 1998; University of the West Indies, St. Augustine, online, 2003.

KRISTINE S. WICKSON

HOFFMAN, Alice
Author, b. 16 March 1952, New York City

"There are people who write fiction to come to terms with their own lives. I'm much more interested in creating alternate universes, not everyday reality." This quote from H. sums up many of the themes and tones of her novels. Readers are transported into different worlds where deer weep, winter ice turns blood-red, and where the air carries the smell of roses even though it is mid-January and everything is dead. And yet, readers do not question these paradoxes as they are written in such a realistic, matter-of-fact tone of voice.

H. was born in New York City on March 16, 1952 and grew up on Long Island. After graduating from high school in 1969, she attended Adelphi University, where she received a B.A. and then received a Mirrellees Fellowship to the Stanford University Writing Center, which she attended in 1973–74, receiving an M.A. in creative writing. She lives outside Boston and is married with two sons.

As a child, H. read Mary Poppins, the Brothers Grimm, and Ray Bradbury. "I loved anything that could remove me from reality and make me see possibilities," she said. This love is shown in her first novel, *Property Of,* written when she was twenty-five; on the Avenue, at one of the frontiers where New York City blends into suburbia, street gangs—the Orphans, the Pack—engage in deadly, intricately structured games of street combat. Boys and young men explode in spasms of grotesque, horrifying violence, redeemed, in their minds, by codes of honor, by chivalrous intentions, by courage, and the purity of their struggle for power, dominance, and territory. Meanwhile, others cynically manipulate these rivalries to advance their own fortunes in the drug trade.

This novel shows real life, which is sometimes hard. H.'s books tend to feature outsiders: strong women, single women, struggling women, children facing dangers. Readers are surprised when they come across such harsh reality when it seems the least possible. A recent novel, *Blue Diary,* shows a happily married couple until the wife finds out that her husband committed a brutal rape fifteen years before.

Harsh reality showed up in H.'s own life in 1998 when she learned that she had breast cancer. Writing helped her through the long months of treatment, and she has been healthy ever since.

Aside from life's hardships, H.'s novels have elements of magic and the power of nature. Another novel, *Second Nature,* is a modern FAIRY TALE based on a beauty and a beast, at least on the outside. Inside, the reader will be lost in a powerful story of innocence and wickedness.

H. writes so much about nature that it almost comes across as a character of its own. H. believes that nature affects people intensely and adds an emotional dimension to things. The magical elements surround the main themes of love and loss. "I feel more influenced in my own work by dreams than I do by other writer's works. Or by popular culture, movies—what else is there to write about than love and loss?" Ironic, since her novel *Practical Magic* was made into a MOVIE.

H.'s novel, *Blackbird House,* was released July 2004.

AWARDS: ALA BBYA, 1993, *Turtle Moon,* 2000, *Local Girls; PW* Best Children's Books, 2003.

FURTHER WORKS: *The Drowning Season,* 1979; *Angel Landing,* 1980; *White Horses,* 1980; *Fortune's*

Daughter, 1985; *Illumination Night,* 1987; *At Risk,* 1988; *Archives of Memory,* 1990; *Here on Earth,* 1990; *Seventh Heaven,* 1990; *Turtle Moon,* 1992; *Practical Magic,* 1995; *Fireflies: A Winter's Tale,* 1997; *Local Girls,* 1999; *Horsefly,* 2000; *The River King,* 2000; *Aquamarine,* 2001; *Indigo,* 2002; *Green Angel,* 2003; *The Probable Future,* 2003; *Moondog,* 2004; *The Ice Queen,* 2005; *The Foretelling,* 2005.

REFERENCES: H. official website: www.alicehoffman .com; www.bookpage.com

JENNIFER CLAIBORNE

HOFFMAN, Nina Kiriki

Author, b. 20 March 1955, San Gabriel, California

H. is a unique voice among authors of contemporary FANTASY and SCIENCE FICTION literature for YOUNG ADULTS. Her stories often have ordinary settings but are wonderfully quirky and strange at the same time, reminiscent of Rod Serling. H. has also been compared to Ray Bradbury and Charles DE LINT because of her ability to combine magical elements with urban realism in an original, imaginative, and often wryly humorous way. H.'s best-known work, *The Thread that Binds the Bones,* is about a janitor who magically prevents the suicides of two TEENAGERS. H.'s World Fantasy Award–nominated novella *Unmasking* and Nebula and World Fantasy Award–nominated story "Home for Christmas" is about a woman who can talk to inanimate objects and witness people's dreams. In the novel, *A Red Heart of Memories,* Matt meets Edmund, another psychic, and helps him to understand his past and his powers. Its sequel, *Past the Size of Dreaming,* continues their quest to combat the darkness within themselves as they track down Edmund's childhood friends. *A Stir of Bones* is a standalone prequel to *A Red Heart of Memories* and *Past the Size of Dreaming.* H.'s works are noted for their whimsical humor and unusual plot twists. *A Fistful of Sky* recounts the trials of a young woman with the power to curse things. Hilarious results unexpectedly ensue as she tries to find insignificant objects to curse. H. has also written novels for R. L. Stine's Ghost of Fear Street SERIES and for the Star Trek Voyager series.

AWARDS: Third place, Writers of the Future Award (1985) for Short Story "A Step into Darkness," Bram Stoker Award for Superior Achievement in a First Novel (1993) for *The Thread that Binds the Bones;* ALA BBYA, 2004, *A Stir of Bones.*

FURTHER WORKS: *Legacy of Fire* (SHORT STORIES), 1990, *Courting Disasters, and Other Strange Affinities: Short Stories,* 1991, *Child of an Ancient City* (with Tad Williams), 1992, *Unmasking,* 1992, *The Thread that Binds the Bones,* 1993, *Common Threads,* 1995, *A Handful of Twist Ties,* 1995, *The Silent Strength of Stones,* 1995, *Body Switchers from Outer Space* (Ghosts of Fear Street series, 14), 1996, *Why I'm Not Afraid of Ghosts* (Ghosts of Fear Street series, 23), 1997, *Echoes* (with Kristine Kathryn Rusch and Dean Wesley Smith) (Star Trek Voyager series, 15), 1998, *I Was A Sixth-Grade Zombie* (with R. L. Stine) (Ghosts of Fear Street series, 30), 1998, *A Red Heart of Memories,* 1999, *Past the Size of Dreaming,* 2000, *A Fistful of Sky,* 2002, *Time Travelers, Ghosts, and Other Visitors,* 2003, *A Stir of Bones,* 2003. Contributor of over 200 short stories to MAGAZINES and journals, including *Fantasy and Science Fiction, Amazing Stories and Weird Tales,* and such anthologies as: *The Year's Best Fantasy and Horror: Ninth Annual Collection,* 1996, *Otherwere,* 1996, *Twists of the Tale,* 1996, *Tarot Fantastic,* 1997, *The UFO Files,* 1997, *Wizard Fantastic,* 1997, *Black Swan, White Raven,* 1997, *Alien Pets,* 1998, *Black Cats and Broken Mirror,* 1998, *Whitley Strieber's Aliens,* 1998, *Alien Abductions,* 1999, *Twice Upon a Time,* 1999, *Bruce Coville's Strange Worlds,* 2000, *Warrior Fantastic,* 2000, *Graven Images,* 2000, *Past Imperfect,* 2001, *Redshift: Extreme Visions of Speculative Fiction,* 2001, *The Green Man: Tales from the Mythic Forest,* 2002, and *Firebirds: An Anthology of Original Fantasy and Science Fiction,* 2003.

BIBLIOGRAPHY: *Authors and Artists for Young Adults,* Vol. 52, Gale, 2003. *Contemporary Authors Online,* Gale, 1992; *Science Fiction & Fantasy Literature,* 1975–1991, Gale, 1992.

SHARON L. RAWLINS

HOGAN, James P.
Author, b. 1941, London, England

Born to a German mother and an Irish father, H. was reared near Portobello Road in London. His feet were misshapen at birth, and the operations to fix them took place over several years. Although H. hiked and camped in Scotland and Wales in his teens, his years of inactivity made him quite a reader. His enjoyment of reading, however, did not translate into him being a good student; his formal education ended at sixteen. H.'s mother convinced him to take a scholarship exam, which led him to the Royal Aircraft Establishment at Farnborough and an engineering course. An early first marriage produced twins by the time H.

was twenty. H. married twice more and now is the father of three daughters and three sons.

H.'s career has included design engineering, sales engineering, and eventually being in charge of a sales training program in Massachusetts. With the publication of *Inherit the Stars* in 1977, H. not only won an office bet, but also embarked on a new career. By 1979, H. was writing full time. *Inherit the Stars* is the first book in the Giants SERIES, followed by *The Gentle Giants of Ganymede* (1978) and *Giants' Star* (1981). (These three books were then published as a Book Club edition titled *The Minervan Experiment* (1982) and *The Giants Novels* (1991)) and *Entoverse* (1991). H. also wrote *Mind Matters: Exploring the World of Artificial Intelligence* (1998), a work of nonfiction, as is *Truth Under Tyranny: Science's Impermissible Thoughts* (2004).

However, H.'s contributions to the YOUNG ADULT field rest primarily in the following works: *Bug Park* (1997), *Star Child* (1998), and *Outward Bound* (1999). *Bug Park* is an exciting action tale in which corporate intrigue, FAMILY loyalty, and life itself are at stake for TEENS Kevin and Taki, as they ultimately triumph with the help of some mechanical contrivances. In *Star Child,* Taya's assumptions about her world are challenged, as is her belief in the omniscience of her friend Kort. Linc Marani's assumptions about himself are challenged when he is sent to a new space colony in *Outward Bound.*

H. is also the author of a comprehensive collection of comic books, novellas, and short fiction. He currently has residences in both Pensacola, Florida and Bray, located in Wicklow, a coastal town in Ireland.

AWARDS: *Bug Park:* 1998 YALSA Best Books for Young Adults, 1998 YALSA Quick Pick for Reluctant Young Adult Readers.

FURTHER WORKS: *The Genesis Machine,* 1978; *The Two Faces of Tomorrow,* 1979; *Thrice Upon a Time,* 1980; *Voyage from Yesteryear,* 1982; *Code of the Lifemaker,* 1983; *The Proteus Operation,* 1985; *Endgame Enigma,* 1987; *The Mirror Maze,* 1989; *The Infinity Gambit,* 1991; *The Multiplex Man* 1992; *The Immortality Option,* 1995; *Realtime Interrupt* 1995; *Paths to Otherwhere,* 1996; *Cradle of Saturn,* 1999; *The Legend That Was Earth,* 2000; *The Anguished Dawn,* 2000; *Martian Knightlife,* 2001.

BIBLIOGRAPHY: www.amazon.com; www.jamesphogan.com; www.novelst4.epnet.com

JEANNE MARIE RYAN

HOLLAND, Isabelle (Christian)

Author, b. 16 June 1920, Basel, Switzerland; d. 9 February 2002, New York City

H. was born into a family native to Tennessee, although she spent most of her childhood outside of America. Her father, Philip, was in the diplomatic service of the U.S., allowing H. to live in Switzerland, Guatemala, and England. Her mother, Corabelle, frequently entertained H. with stories from a variety of sources, including the Bible. While in England, she was educated at boarding schools. H. sold her first story, "Naughty Betty," to the English children's MAGAZINE, *Tiger Tim,* when she was thirteen.

H. lived outside the U.S. until she was twenty years old. When World War II broke out, she left the University of Liverpool and returned to the United States where she attended Tulane University (B.A., 1942). H. worked for the U.S. War Department for a short time before moving to New York City and attaining a job as a secretary for *Life* magazine. She was also employed by several magazines and publishing houses, including *McCall's,* Crown, Lippincott, *Harper's,* and Putnam, where she served as a copywriter, publicist, and novelist. H. also wrote under the name Francesca Hunt. As a publicity director for Lippincott, she crossed paths with Harper LEE who was working on *To Kill a Mockingbird.* H. continued to write stories for magazines after she moved to New York, receiving many rejections, and in 1948 she sold "The Professor's Butterfly" to *Country Gentleman.*

While working at Lippincott, H. started writing a novel. In her autobiography she states that her writing career began with *Cecily,* a young adult novel which "contained, of course, a large autobiographical element," Holland's experiences in English boarding schools. Published by Lippincott in 1967, *Cecily* received excellent reviews and was considered a change from the books written for YA at that time.

H.'s fiction for TEENS often focuses on controversial issues such as rape, DEATH, FAMILY problems, and emotional and psychological difficulties and have strong moral themes. The characters in these books are children or adolescents dealing with the emotional ups and downs of their relationships with adults. In *Heads You Win, Tails I Lose* (1973), the protagonist's parents are too distracted by their own marital problems to notice their daughter's severe weight loss. *The Man without a Face* (1972) encounters Charles, a fourteen year-old boy desperate to leave his turbulent home and attend boarding school. He recruits Justin McCloud, a local man whose face is severely disfigured and whose past is mysterious, to tutor him for the entrance exams; the result of this situation is a complex love relationship between the two men.

H. wrote more than twenty adult gothic and romantic suspense novels and thirty-one young adult and children's books, many of which have been translated into several languages. Reviews of H.'s work repeatedly speak of her realistic characters with their insecurities and problems who learn to be survivors. Original materials from H.'s writings are located in the deGrummond Collection at the University of Southern Mississippi and in the Children's Literature Research Collection in the Elmer L. Andersen Library at the University of Minnesota. H. taught creative writing at New York University School of Continuing and Professional Studies and "How to Write a Children's Book" at New York University School of Education.

AWARDS: *Of Love and Death and Other Journeys,* National Book Award nomination, 1976; *The Man without a Face:* 1972 ALA Best Books for Young Adults, ALA Best of the Best Books (YA) 1970–1983, NYT Outstanding Children's Books of 1972; *Abbie's God Book* and *God, Mrs. Muskrat, and Aunt Dot,* Church and Synagogue Library Association Ott Award, 1983.

FURTHER WORKS: *Kilgaren,* 1974; *Trelawny,* 1974; *Moncrieff,* 1975; *Of Love & Death & Other Journeys,* 1975; *Darcourt,* 1976; *Grenelle,* 1976; *Alan and the Animal Kingdom,* 1977; *Hitchhike,* 1977; *Tower Abbey,* 1978; *Now Is Not Too Late,* 1980; *Abbie's God Book,* 1982; *A Horse Named Peaceable,* 1982; *God, Mrs. Muskrat, and Aunt Dot,* 1983; *Perdita,* 1983; *A Death at St. Anselm's,* 1984; *Green Andrew Green,* 1984; *Henry and Grudge,* 1986; *The Christmas Cat,* 1987; *Toby the Splendid,* 1986; *Thief,* 1988; *Bump in the Night,* 1988; *The Journey Home,* 1990; *The Unfrightened Dark,* 1990; *The House in the Woods,* 1991; *Love and Inheritance,* 1991; *Behind the Lines,* 1994; *Family Trust,* 1994; *The Promised Land,* 1996; *Paper Boy,* 1999.

BIBLIOGRAPHY: *Authors and Artists for Young Adults,* vol. 11, 1993; *Something about the Author,* vol. 132, 2002; Drew, B. A., *The 100 Most Popular Young Adult Authors, Biographical Sketches and Bibliographies,* Rev. 1st ed., 1997. Autobiographical essay, *Contemporary Authors,* vol. 181, 2000.

M. NAOMI WILLIAMSON

HOLM, Jennifer L.
Author, b. June 1968, California

When H. discovered her great-aunt's DIARY from the early 1900s, it not only sparked an interest in exploring her FAMILY history, but led to a career in writing books for children and YOUNG ADULTS. After extensive research of her ancestors' emigration from Finland to their settlement in the Nasel River Valley in the Washington Territory, the scene was set for her first historical fiction novel *Our Only May Amelia* (1999). H. returned to the Washington Territory with a new female protagonist in her second historical fiction novel: *Boston Jane: An Adventure* (2001). The first in an exciting trilogy, it is the story of a remarkable young lady who gives up high society of Philadelphia for a challenging, arduous life as a pioneer woman out west. According to a starred *Booklist* review, "Strong characterization, meticulous attention to historical details and a perceptive understanding of human nature makes this a first rate story not to be missed."

Before writing, H. was a broadcast producer, creating commercials for companies such as Hershey, Nickelodeon, and American Express. Now a full-time writer, she attributes her success as an author to avid reading. H. is currently writing a companion book to *Our Only May Amelia* (working title *My Brother Wilbert*). H. and her husband are also writing a comedy/spy SERIES about a cat called The Stink Files: *Dossier 001: The Postman Always Brings Mice* and *Dossier 002: To Scratch a Thief* (both 2004); and *Dossier 003: You Only Have Nine Lives* (2005).

AWARDS: *Our Only May Amelia:* 2000 Newbery Honor Book Award, Silver Award, Parents' Choice, Best Books of the Year, 2000 ALA Notable Book; 2002 ALA BBYA for *Boston Jane.*

FURTHER WORKS: *Boston Jane: Wilderness Days,* 2002; *Boston Jane: The Claim,* 2003; *The Creek,* 2003.

BIBLIOGRAPHY: Contemporary Authors Online, 2001. New Entry: 08/31/2001. "Jennifer Holm." June 1, 2003. <Http://www.jenniferholm.com>. H. E-mail to the author, June 1, 2003.

KIMBERLY DESTEFANO

HOLMAN, Felice
Author, b. 24 October 1919, New York City

H. is a novelist and poet who writes for children and YOUNG ADULTS. Although her best-known young adult novel, *Slake's Limbo* (1974), was written over two decades ago, her work continues to attract literary audiences, demonstrating her writing's timelessness. The social issues that H. includes in her writing are just as captivating today as when they were originally discussed.

H. acknowledges her parents for instilling in her a love for storytelling. She fondly recalls times during the Depression when the exchange of stories boosted her family's spirits. The young H. was a shy student and was sent to boarding school at fifteen in order to improve her social skills. After graduating from Syracuse University in 1941, she married fellow student Herbert Valen and later moved to Westport, Connecticut.

H.'s early work was comprised of children's books, partially based on the doings of her daughter Nanine. *Elisabeth, the Birdwatcher* (1963), *Elisabeth, the Treasure Hunter* (1964), and *Elisabeth and the Marsh Mystery* (1966) were all well received by literary critics who found the tales humorous while containing important messages. *Horn Book* praised books such as *Professor Diggins' Dragons* (1966) and *Victoria's Castle* (1966) for being naturally amusing and inventive.

After writing several middle-grade novels, such as *A Year to Grow* (1968) and *The Future of Hooper Toote* (1972), and a few books of POETRY, H. turned to her young adult audience with *Slake's Limbo.* The book wrestles with survival and the lengths to which one TEENAGE boy goes in order to live. Artemis Slake, H.'s protagonist, flees from his aunt's house and his abusive peers, and travels into the depths of the New York City subway tunnels. In the course of 121 days, Artemis flourishes in the life he forms for himself, living in a cave below Grand Central Station and completing odd jobs for food and money. Surprisingly, it is the kindness of strangers that reaffirms Artemis' faith in civilization. H. uses metaphoric descriptions of her teenage survivor and his entire experience, creating a novel that *Horn Book* calls "a paean to the indomitable human desire to live."

H. followed her award-winning *Slake's Limbo* with several other young adult novels, including *The Murderer* (1978), *The Wild Children* (1983), and *Secret City, U.S.A.* (1990). *The Murderer,* set in the 1930s, depicts a thirteen-year-old Jewish boy who, while waiting for his bar mitzvah, questions the turbulent world that surrounds him. *School Library Journal* responded positively to this story of Pennsylvanian Hershy Marks, and gave similar approval to the latter two works. In them, H. revisits her theme of survival; in *The Wild Children,* youngsters are left homeless after the Russian Revolution in 1917, while in *Secret City, U.S.A.,* inner-city youths Benno and Moon discover an abandoned house and decide to turn it into a haven for children. Both works were criticized for their overly optimistic and clean-cut endings, yet they received largely positive reviews from literary critics.

H.'s books for middle readers and young adults, including the more recently published *Real* (1997), are known for containing poetic prose, strong characterizations, and intricate plots. While the majority of her work is intended for younger readers, the notoriety of *Slake's Limbo* has carved out a place for H. in young adult literature.

AWARDS: *Slake's Limbo:* Austrian Book Prize, Lewis Carroll Shelf Award, ALA Best Book for Young Adults, ALA Notable Book, all 1978, the 1994 list "101 Best Books for Young Adults written since 1966"; 1979 ALA Notable Book, *The Murderer;* 1985 ALA Best Book for Young Adults, *The Wild Children;* 1991 Child Study Association Book, *Secret City, U.S.A.*

SELECT FURTHER WORKS: *The Witch on the Corner,* 1966; *The Cricket Winter,* 1967; *The Blackmail Machine,* 1968; *At the Top of My Voice and Other Poems,* 1969; *The Holiday Rat and the Utmost Mouse,* 1969; *The Future of Hooper Toote,* 1972; *I Hear You Smiling and Other Poems,* 1973; *The Escape of the Giant Hogstalk,* 1974; (with Nanine Valen) *The Drac: French Tales of Dragons and Demons,* 1975; *The Song in My Head,* 1985; *Terrible Jane,* 1987; *Brothers of the Heart: A Story of the Old West, 1837–1838,* 1999.

BIBLIOGRAPHY: Heins, Ethel L., review of *Professor Diggins' Dragons, Horn Book,* October 1966, p. 59; Langford, Sondra Gordon, "A Second Look: *Slake's Limbo," Horn Book,* November–December 1987, pp. 778–79; *Something about the Author,* vol. 82, 1995; Viguers, Ruth Hill, review of *Victoria's Castle, Horn Book,* August 1966, p. 426.

RACHEL WITMER

THE HOLOCAUST

The European H. was not the first mass genocide of an entire people, nor would it be the last. It does, however, stand out from other genocides in history for a multitude of reasons. No other genocide before or since has been perpetrated on such a grand scale. Jews and other "enemies of the state" were persecuted from the moment that Adolf Hitler seized power in 1933, but the wholesale, systematic killing of Jews was not begun until the early 1940s. The architects of the so-called Final Solution planned the elaborate infrastructure enabling them to exterminate human beings at an unprecedented rate on an unprecedented scale. The majority of the six-million Jews and the millions of Romany homosexuals, mentally and physically disabled, Jehovah's Witnesses, political enemies, and other people were exterminated within a time frame of only three years from 1942 to 1945. Hitler came very close to achieving his goal of a Jew-free Europe. Nothing has surpassed the Nazis' efficiency in organized, wholesale murder. The sheer magnitude of the event ensured that it would be remembered long after it occurred. The Nazis were also scrupulously efficient about keeping records, and their failure to destroy a good deal of them before capture leaves historians with plenty of documentary evidence. The H. also occurred in the midst of a global conflict. A good part of the Western world was present to bear witness when the WAR ended. Consider also the scores of H. survivors who have devoted their lives to ensuring the memory stays alive by speaking to audiences and writing and recording their experiences for posterity. More has been written about the H. than any other genocide. For young adults, there are hundreds of outstanding BIOGRAPHIES, INFORMATIONAL books, and novels on the subject.

Despite this vast, ever-increasing canon of outstanding H. literature available for young adults, it seems that if students do read anything about the H. in school, it is Anne FRANK's *Diary of a Young Girl.* It is the standard text to teach students about the H. Cole (1999) notes that: ". . . Anne Frank is ubiquitous. . . . Since the 1950s Anne Frank's name has been attached to a day, a week, a rose, a tulip, countless trees, a whole forest, streets, schools and youth centres, and a village. Her DIARY has been translated into more than fifty-five languages, has sold over twenty-four million copies worldwide and is *the* canonical 'Holocaust' text" (23). There is a lot more to the H. than Anne Frank's *Diary of a Young Girl.* The work has its merits, but it does not fully convey the horrors of the H., such as death camps and savage physical brutality inflicted upon victims. *Diary of a*

Young Girl offers little insight into the catastrophic proportions of the H. and does not describe the unspeakable horrors people suffered. The book is more a coming-of-age story of a precocious young adolescent than an insightful look into the horrors of the H. Because Anne Frank has become an international icon, a symbol of what was lost in the H., students and teachers alike mistakenly think that reading her diary will convey all one needs to know about the H. The sad truth is that Frank's story is only one of millions of stories from the H. Her experience is not representative of all, or even most, of the other people who suffered and perished. All that we need to know about the H. will not be learned from reading *Diary of a Young Girl.*

To see a larger, more realistic picture of the event, young adults should be exposed to the many other personal narratives, novels, poems, and other works from the vast canon of H. literature. They need to read the perspectives of those who perished and those who survived, those who hid in and out of sight, those who were persecuted and rescued, those who escaped and resisted. The H. is far too significant an event in human history to be relegated to the perspective of one thirteen-year-old girl.

Writing about the H. is not an easy task for any author. For those who experienced the horrors of it firsthand, it is particularly painful to relive those memories. Fiction writers who choose the H. as their subject are faced with the immense challenge of making the experience true for readers—not only to be accurate in depicting historical details, but also in conveying the intense emotional power needed to bring authenticity to these stories. The best novels about the H. are those that are far more than historical fiction. The best H. fiction are those stories which make real for readers the inexplicable horrors of this dark moment in human history, bringing those experiences to vivid life through characters and circumstances with which readers can empathize, enabling them to experience vicariously what it could be like to live in a world in which one's very existence is enough to warrant oppression, torture, and extermination.

CANADIAN author Carol MATAS has successfully brought these kinds of stories to life several times over. *Lisa's War,* Matas's first H. novel originally published in 1987, is about what is now one of the more familiar stories from the H.—the largely suc-

cessful attempt by the Danish Resistance to save its Jewish compatriots from deportation to the extermination camps. *Kris's War,* originally published in 1989 as *Code Name: Kris,* a sequel to *Lisa's War,* is a fast-paced, action-packed story that also depicts a strong, courageous adolescent protagonist who risks his life to make a difference. Commissioned by the U.S. H. Memorial Museum in Washington, D.C. Matas's third H. novel, *Daniel's Story,* published in conjunction with an exhibit at the museum called "Daniel's Story: Remembering the Children," tells the story of a FAMILY forced from their home and sent to live in the Lodz Ghetto. Later, they are sent to the Auschwitz death camp. In *After the War,* Matas explores a subject entirely overlooked in books written for young people. What became of survivors immediately following their liberation from the camps? In *Greater than Angels,* Matas returns to the subject of "Righteous Gentiles" risking their own lives to save Jews. Matas tells the story of the citizens of Le Chambon-sur-Lignon in Vichy France who courageously risk their lives to save the many Jews who took refuge there during the Nazi occupation. Matas's *In My Enemy's House* explores a darker dimension of the H. Marisa is a Polish–Jew whose blond hair, blue eyes, and fair complexion enable her to pass as an "Aryan." When the Nazis invade Poland, Marisa poses as a Gentile and travels to Weimar to work as a house servant for the Reymanns, a wealthy farm family whose patriarch is a high-ranking Nazi official.

Informational books on the H. for young adults are plentiful. Two excellent historical overviews of the Holocaust are Milton MELTZER's *Never to Forget: The Jews of the H.* and Barbara ROGASKY's *Smoke and Ashes: The Story of the H.* Outstanding stories of "Righteous Gentiles," individuals who helped Jews escape extermination at the risk of their own lives, include *Darkness Over Denmark: The Danish Resistance and the Rescue of the Jews* by Ellen LEVINE, *Rescue: The Story of How Gentiles Saved Jews in the H.* by Milton Meltzer, and *In My Hands: Memories of a H. Survivor* by Irene Gut Opdyke with Jennifer ARMSTRONG. Exceptional survivor memoirs include Ana Novac's *The Beautiful Days of My Youth: My Six Months in Auschwitz and Plaszow, I Have Lived a Thousand Years: Growing up in the H.* by Livia Bitton-Jackson, and Yehuda Nir's *The Lost Childhood: A World War II Memoir.* For more recommendations of over five hundred H. titles appropriate for

349

young adults, consult Edward T. Sullivan's annotated, bibliographic guide, *The H. Literature for Youth.*

WORKS: Bitton-Jackson, Livia. *I Have Lived a Thousand Years: Growing up in the H.* 1997; Frank, Anne. *The Diary of a Young Girl: The Definitive Edition,* 1995; Levine, Ellen, *Darkness Over Denmark: The Danish Resistance and the Rescue of the Jews,* 2000; Matas, Carol, *After the War,* 1996; Matas, Carol, *Daniel's Story,* 1993; Matas, Carol, *Greater than Angels,* 1998; Matas, Carol, *In My Enemy's House,* 1999; Matas, Carol, *Kris's War,* 1992 (originally published as *Code Name: Kris,* 1989); Matas, Carol. *Lisa's War,* 1991 (originally published 1987); Meltzer, Milton, *Never to Forget: The Jews of the H.,* 1976; Meltzer, Milton. *Rescue: The Story of How Gentiles Saved Jews in the H.,* 1988; Nir, Yehuda, *The Lost Childhood: A World War II Memoir,* 2000; Novac, Ana, *The Beautiful Days of My Youth: My Six Months in Auschwitz and Plaszow,* 1997; Opdyke, Irene Gut with Jennifer Armstrong, *In My Hands: Memories of a H. Survivor,* 1999; Rogasky, Barbara. *Smoke and Ashes: The Story of the Holocaust* (revised and expanded ed.), 2001.

BIBLIOGRAPHY: Cole, Tim. *Selling the H.* New York: Routledge, 1999. Sullivan, Edward T. "Beyond Anne Frank: Recent H. Literature for Young People." *The New Advocate* 15.1 (Winter 2002): 49–55; Sullivan, Edward T. *The H. Literature for Youth: A Guide and Resource Book.* Lanham, MD: Scarecrow, 1999.

EDWARD T. SULLIVAN

HOLT, Kimberly Willis
Author, b. 9 September 1960, Pensacola, Florida

H. grew up in various parts of the world but claimed her grandmother's home in Forest Hill, Louisiana as her own. H.'s father was a chef for the Navy; this led to national and global life experiences at busy Navy bases. As a result, H. chose to focus on Southern small-town life in her writing. The small-town settings provide realistic contexts for the development of unique characters recognized for their rather eccentric qualities. In fact, when H. was asked about her characters, she replied that she finds it "a high compliment when people say that they think my characters are eccentric or quirky, because I guess that's what I love about life." As a reader, H. was drawn to the power of realistic characters often in isolated circumstances, such as those she found in the writings of Carson McCullers.

At the age of twelve, H. considered becoming a writer but says she was discouraged by a teacher who failed to nurture her efforts. So her life's work began with being a news director for a local radio station and was followed by six years as an interior designer. She decided to begin writing for young readers following a move with her husband and young daughter to Amarillo, Texas.

My Louisiana Sky (1998) was the first of various novels that begin with a memorable character drawn from H.'s own life and placed within the backdrop of small-town relationships. One of the characters, Tiger Ann Parker, lives in Saitter, Louisiana. Tiger Ann has parents who are developmentally challenged and as a YOUNG ADULT becomes increasingly aware of the perspectives of townspeople who observe her FAMILY's situation. Her grandmother lives with them and tries to provide insights to help the young girl cope with the situation. When the grandmother dies, however, an aunt arrives to help. The aunt offers to take Tiger home with her to Baton Rouge. Tiger must make significant life decisions, and, amidst other crises, realizes the strength of her family ties as well as her own fortitude of character. This award-winning book has its roots in a conversation H. shared with her parents about a "strange-looking lady" she saw while they traveled through rural Louisiana. Her mother's brief description of this person as being "mentally retarded and having a husband who was mentally retarded and lots of kids" stayed with her.

H. continues to portray small-town realities in *Mister and Me* (1998), the story of Jolene, a young AFRICAN AMERICAN girl in the South during the 1940s. This book for young adults uses a setting with family connections to H.'s grandfathers, that of a Louisiana logging town. This story shows a young girl accepting into her fatherless family a man courting her mother. Love and persistence help this well-developed character through a realistic situation.

When Zachary Beaver Came to Town (1999) again reflects a character that left an impression on H. as a young girl. H. bought a ticket to see the "fattest boy in the world," and as a result of lasting impressions of her brief conversation with him, Zachary Beaver was created. The protagonist of the story is Toby, who lives in the town of Antler. Toby's driving curiosity about the six-hundred-pound boy, Zachary, who arrives in a trailer results in many unanswered questions. Toby and his friend set out to find answers, especially when Zachary is left alone in Antler. At the same time Toby must deal with the end of his parents' marriage and the DEATH of his friend's popular older brother in Vietnam.

Other young people in more recent novels by H. also face dilemmas that lead to changes in their lives and perceptions of the small-town environments in which they live. *Dancing in Cadillac Light* (2001) introduces Jaynell. When her widowed, eccentric grandfather comes to live with her family, Jaynell is frequently his companion and ultimately learns about social responsibility. After his death, his kindness toward a poverty-stricken family creates issues in the 1960s small-town setting; the issues require readers to contemplate social class and compassion.

Keeper of the Night (2003), set in Guam, tells of a young girl whose mother committed suicide and whose family is dealing with the aftermath in various ways. In short poetic vignettes as chapters, Isabel describes her family's struggles to survive. Using the tropical setting to enhance this book, H.'s mastery of character connects readers to the resilient Isabel; unique secondary characters provide support in her time of loss.

SELECT AWARDS: *Boston Globe–Horn Book* Award for Fiction, ALA's Notable Books, Top Ten Best Books for Young Adults for *My Louisiana Sky; My Louisiana Sky,* BBYA, 1999; *When Zachary Beaver Came to Town,* National Book Award, 1999.

BIBLIOGRAPHY: Horning, Kathleen T., "Small Town Girl," *School Library Journal,* March 2001, pp. 43–45; Rochman, Hazel, review of *My Louisiana Sky,* 1998, p. 1438; *Contemporary Authors Online,* 2001.

JANELLE B. MATHIS

HOMES, Amy Michael
Author, b. 1961, Washington, D.C.

H. attended American University and is a graduate of Sarah Lawrence College (1985). She is the author of several books for adults, but made her debut as a YA author with a novel about a young boy's coming of age. *Jack* (1989) tells the story of a TEENAGE boy growing up and coming to terms with his parents' divorce and his father's homosexuality. H. was applauded for her accurate portrayal of a teenage boy and the way in which he realistically deals with those circumstances.

H. books for adults often feature teenage characters and focus on the stranger side of human existence. Her collection of SHORT STORIES, *The Safety of*

OBJECTS (1990), was adapted into a feature film in 2001.

FURTHER WORKS: *In a Country of Mothers,* 1993; *The End of Alice,* 1996; *Appendix A: An Elaboration on the Novel The End of Alice,* 1996; *Music for Torching,* 1999; *Cecily Brown,* co-author, 2000; *Things You Should Know,* 2002; *Los Angeles: People, Places, and the Castle on the Hill,* 2002.

BIBLIOGRAPHY: *Contemporary Authors Online,* 2003, reproduced in *Biography Resource Center,* 2003. http://www.galenet.com/servlet/BioRC.

SHANNON CUFF

HOOBLER, Dorothy and Thomas
Authors, Dorothy; b. 1940, Philadelphia, Pennsylvania; Thomas, b. 1941, Cincinnati, Ohio

The H.s, married since 1971, have formed a prolific writing team well-known for their nonfiction, BIOGRAPHY, and most recently historical fiction titles for young people. While they have written many stand-alone titles, many of their most popular nonfiction titles have been SERIES. The *Images Across the Ages* series of collective biographies includes portraits of famous Chinese, Indian, and African people. The *Family Album* series provides an overview of domestic life of various ethnic groups using material from journals, letters, and oral histories. Titles in this series include *The Mexican-American Family Album* (1994) and *The Irish-American Family Album* (1995). Many of the H.s' nonfiction books have been selected as Notable Trade Books in the Field of Social Studies.

More recently, the H.s have gained fame with their historical fiction titles. *The Ghost in the Tokaido Inn* (1999) and its sequel *The Demon in the Teahouse* (2001) tell the story of a young boy in eighteenth-century Japan who dreams of being a samurai and who finds himself solving several mysteries. This combination of MYSTERY and historical fiction has been very popular among readers and critics alike. *The Ghost in the Tokaido Inn* was named to the American Library Association's Best Books for Young Adults in 2000.

AWARDS: ALA Popular Paperbacks 2004 for *The Ghost in the Tokaido Inn;* Edgar Allen Poe Award 2005 for *In Darkness, In Death.*

FURTHER WORKS: *An Album of World War I,* 1976; *Vietnam: Why We Fought,* 1990; *Mandela: The Man,*

The Struggle, The Triumph, 1992; *In Darkness, In Death,* 2004.

BIBLIOGRAPHY: *Contemporary Authors,* online, 2001; *The Eighth Book of Junior Authors and Illustrators,* 2000; *Something about the Author,* vol. 109, 2000.

ANDREA LIPINSKI

HOOSE, Phillip M.
Author, songwriter, musician, b. 31 May 1947, South Bend, Indiana

H. is best known for his works about the participation of children and young adults in American history and society. His first children's book, *It's Our World, Too!: Stories of Young People Who Are Making a Difference, How They Do It, How You Can Too!* (1993, rev. 2002), is a collection of stories about young people in the U.S. who took active roles to initiate social change. In this book, H. gives his readers motivating accounts of children and TEENS who work to improve their communities.

H.'s *We Were There Too!: Young People in U.S. History* (2001) is a compilation of captivating accounts of children and teens who experienced or took part in various events in America's four-hundred-year history. The book stresses little-known achievements of children and teenagers in American history, from the Revolutionary War to more modern struggles. By including stories of young men and women from many ethnic, cultural and religious backgrounds, H. allows his readers a new point of view of U.S. history. Both books were named Notable Books by the American Library Association.

H. is a founding member of the Children's Music Network, a nonprofit association established in 1986, so that parents, teachers, musicians and others with interests in music for young people could network and share inspiration and information.

AWARDS: 1994 Christopher award, *It's Our World, Too!, We Were There, Too!:* 2002 ALA Best Books for Young Adults, 2002 Notable Social Studies Trade Book; ALA Notable Children's Books, 2002; *The Race to Save the Lord God Bird:* Orbis Pictus Honor; 2005, ALA Best Books for Young Adults, 2005, *Kirkus Reviews* Editor's Choice, 2004, ALA Notable Children's Books, 2005, Parents' Choice Gold Award, 2004, *Publisher's Weekly* Best Children's Books, 2004.

FURTHER WORKS: *Hey Little Ant,* 1998; *The Race to Save the Lord God Bird,* 2004.

BIBLIOGRAPHY: Children's *Book Council, Archives,* online. *Library of Congress,* online.

SARAH SPINK DOWNING

HOOVER, H(elen) M(ary)
Author, b. 5 April 1935, Stark County, Ohio

SCIENCE FICTION author H. cannot recall a time during which books did not factor into her life. Her parents, both of whom were educators, were a guiding force in their daughter's introduction to literature. By the time H. entered elementary school, her reading level was so advanced that she found the material offered to her in the classroom rudimentary and dull. It is perhaps this dissatisfaction with textbook material that led the author to later make her own contribution to YA literature through novels and textbooks.

After H.'s long struggle to establish herself as an author, *Children of Morrow* (1973) was published. She found that publishers took her work more seriously after she abbreviated her given names to initials, leaving the gender of her name unspecified. *Children of Morrow* is the first of H.'s dystopian novels, exploring the future ecological repercussions due to the carelessness of the present. Both this science-fiction work and *The Lions Club* (1974), a historical fiction piece, began H.'s career as a young adult novelist, presenting readers with protagonists that are unique yet worthy of emulation.

The themes of responsibility and awareness of others repeatedly emerge in H.'s work. *The Shepherd Moon* (1984) and *Only Child* (1993) both present characters whose perception of the world is altered through eye-opening events. In the former, Meredith Ambrose, a young member of an elite class in forty-third century Earth, is introduced to the injustices that the lower social castes suffer and realizes the imbalance between her life and the rest of the planet. Cody, the main character in *Only Child,* is also subjected to unpleasant truths about his people and the effects of their colonization of another species. After being kidnapped and held as a hostage by this species, he learns that his people are responsible for their needless slaying, and must decide where to place his loyalty. In turn, the boys in *Orvis* (1987) discover humanity within a robot previously thought to be without emotion. *Winds of Mars* (1995) once again centers around an aristocratic teenaged girl who finds her perception of truth shattered when her father proves to be a cruel exploiter of those less powerful.

In addition to numerous awards, all of H.'s works have been honored by the Dorothy Canfield Fisher list, the Oglethorp Award list, and the Maud Hart Lovelace list. They are intricate enough to prepare young readers for more challenging works while holding the interest of mature science-fiction aficionados.

AWARDS: *The Lion's Club:* ALA Best Book for Young Adults and *New York Times* Pick of the Lists, both 1974; Another Heaven, Another Earth: ALA Notable Book and Best Book for Young Adults, both 1981, and 1994 ALA's 101 Best of the Best Books of the Past Twenty-four years; The Shepherd Moon: American Booksellers Best Pick of 1984, New York Times Pick of the List, junior Literary Guild selection; 1987 Parents' Choice Children's Gold Media Award for Literature, Orvis; The Dawn Palace: ALA BBYA, Parents' Choice Silver Media Award, both 1988; 1989 Library of Congress best books for children list; *Winds of Mars:* ALA Popular Paperbacks, 2004.

FURTHER WORKS: *Treasures of Morrow,* 1976; *The Delikon,* 1977; *The Rains of Eridan,* 1977; *The Lost Star,* 1979; *The Return to Earth,* 1980; *The Time of Darkness,* 1980; *Another Heaven, Another Earth,* 1981; *The Bell Tree,* 1982; *The Dawn Palace: The Story of Medea,* 1988; *Away Is a Strange Place to Be,* 1990; *The Whole Truth . . . And Other Myths,* 1997.

BIBLIOGRAPHY: Review of *Winds of Mars, School Library Journal,* www.amazon.com, Accessed 12/04/03; *Something about the Author Autobiography Series,* Vol. 8, 1989; *Something about the Author,* Vol. 83, 1996; *Twentieth-Century Science Fiction Writers,* 1991.

RACHEL WITMER

HOPKINS, Lee Bennett

Poet, anthologist, b. 13 April 1938, Scranton, Pennsylvania

H. has had a firm dedication to POETRY for most of his life. He grew up in Scranton, Pennsylvania and Newark, New Jersey in housing developments. His parents divorced before he reached the age of ten and his single mother used devious means to provide her children with what they needed. These early experiences helped H. develop a special empathy for at-risk youth; he advocates using poetry to help disadvantaged youth reach their academic potentials. He describes his life poetically in *Been to Yesterdays: Poems of a Life* (1995) and living with his mother

in prose in *Mama* (1992) and *Mama and Her Boys* (1993).

H. attended Newark State Teachers College (now Kean College, 1960), teaching sixth grade after graduation and received a master's degree from the Bank Street College of Education (1966). Later he received a Doctor of Laws degree from Kean University (1980). As a teacher, he used poetry in all areas of the curriculum.

In 1968, H. moved from teaching to become a curriculum and editorial specialist at a children's publishing house. At the same time, he became a frequently published writer himself, including a number of poetry anthologies. Since 1976, he has been a full-time poet, anthologist, and writer, publishing over eighty books in all areas of the curriculum for children and young adults.

Continuing his efforts to promote poetry for children and young adults, H. established and funds two awards: The Lee Bennett H. Poetry Award and the Lee Bennett H./International Reading Association Promising Poet Award. The LBH award is for a book of poetry, either an original collection or an anthology. This award is administered by the Pennsylvania State University and has been presented annually since 1993. The Lee Bennett H./International Reading Association Promising Poet Award is for a poet who has published no more than two books of poetry. It has been presented every three years since 1995.

H. served on the National Council of Teachers of English (NCTE) Board of Directors (1975–78), Commission on Literature (1982–85), and Children's Literature Assembly (1984–87). He chaired the NCTE Poetry Award for Children twice—in 1978 and 1991. He currently serves on the University of Southern Mississippi Medallion Recipient Committee, the Augusta Baker's Dozen Committee of Columbia, SC, and the National Center for Children's Illustrated Literature, Abilene, Texas.

H. has been quoted as saying that YA literature began with the writing of Robert CORMIER and S. E. HINTON.

AWARDS: 1972 Outstanding Alumnus in the Arts; 1980 Phi Delta Kappa Educational Leadership Award; 1983 Manhattan Council (IRA) Literacy Award; CBC Children's Book Week Poet; *Been to Yesterdays:* 1966 Christopher Award and 1996 Golden Kite Honor.

FURTHER WORKS: *Pass the Poetry, Please!*, 1972; *Side by Side: Poems to Read Together* (editor), 1988; *Good Books, Good Times!*, 1990; *Hand in Hand: An American History through Poetry*, 1994; *Blast Off!*: *Poems About Space* (editor), 1995; *Been to Yesterday*, 1995; *Good Rhymes, Good Times!*, 1995; *Marvelous Math* (editor), 1997; *Lives: Poems About Famous Americans* (editor), 1999; *Spectacular Science: A Book of Poems*, 1999; *Yummy: Eating through a Day*, 2000; *My America, A Poetry Atlas of the United States* (editor), 2000; *Alphathoughts*, 2003.

BIBLIOGRAPHY: *The Writing Bug*, 1993; *Children's Books and Their Creators*, 1995; *Something about the Author*, vol. 125, 2002.

DENISE E. AGOSTO

HOROWITZ, Anthony

Author, b. 1955, North London, England

H. is an immensely popular author of children's books, especially the Alex Rider SERIES which chronicles the adventures of a fictional TEENAGE spy for M16. The author himself is an avid fan of James Bond movies; from an early age one of his favorite rituals around the Christmas holidays was viewing the latest big-screen films adapted from the novels of Ian Fleming. His adventure series featuring the character Alex Rider are clearly influenced by the intrigue, action, and gadgets that H. saw at an early age. In his most recently published Alex Rider book, *Eagle Strike* (2003), Alex's girlfriend is aptly named Sabina Pleasure. There are characters named Sir David Friend and Dr. Grief in *Point Blank* (2002), also in the Alex Rider Series. As the reader might expect, Dr. Grief is a mad scientist intent on ruling the entire world through a twisted genetic cloning experiment gone awry. As the teenage hero, Alex has the requisite hi-tech tools which no self-respecting spy would be without, such as a bulletproof ski suit, infrared goggles, and a portable CD player equipped with a built-in satellite transmitter and buzz saw, handy for sawing through iron bars.

The books in this series are tightly plotted, thrilling, and full of action. Because the audience level is young adult, Alex Rider is often in peril and encounters his fair share of evil villains. The spy parallels to James Bond end there and the young hero packs no gun. Alex Rider is schooled in martial arts so he figures out other ways to conquer the bad guys.

In real life, H. has two sons, one of whom helps with research in terms of what it is really like to ski or snowboard. His wife, Jill Green, is a television producer. The YA level of detail gives his books an authenticity which speaks to young people who enjoy rollicking, spy thrillers with a main character close to their own age. The author has climbed to the top of a high crane and sat in a car crusher for the experience of adding realistic details and feeling to his books.

As a young child H. grew up in a wealthy, upper-class environment; unfortunately, his childhood was quite miserable. His father traveled often on business and was simply unavailable to the young child. His mother was a rather unusual parent and, on his thirteenth birthday, presented H. with an authentic human skull per his request. At age eight, he was sent to a boarding school in Harrow (England). His childhood experiences were akin to a story out of "Charles Dickens or Roald Dahl," according to a newspaper interview (*Straits Times-Singapore*) with the author on November 8, 2003. The impact of his childhood is directly reflected in his writing. He began to write books for children in 1979 and since that time has more than twenty-five to his credit. H. had a rocky relationship with his grandmother in particular. He portrays her in a most unfavorable light in the fictional work titled *Granny* (1995) about a child who lives in a wealthy family.

Early in his career, H. quickly established his reputation as a successful writer for screen and television. His most widely known works for television include Agatha Christie's sleuth Hercule Poirot (starring David Suchet), Midsomer Murders, Murder in Mind, and Foyle's War.

H. is a gifted versatile writer with a range that is truly amazing. He published his first children's book *Enter Frederick K. Bower* in 1979. The author is also extremely productive, penning children's books from FANTASY stories about a boarding school for wizards and witches, *Groosham Grange* (1988) to thrilling spy stories. He has a penchant for puns and his books are excellent for reluctant readers.

AWARDS: Red House Children's Book Awards (2003); ALA Quick Picks for Reluctant Readers (2002–2005); ALA BBYA (2003).

FURTHER WORKS: *Devil's Door-Bell*, 1983; *Night of the Scorpion*, 1984; *Silver Citadel*, 1986; *Adventurer*, 1987; *Just Ask for Diamond*, 1986; *Day of the Dragon*, 1989; *Starting Out*, 1990; *Complete Adventures of Robin of Sherwood*, 1990; *Groosham Grange II: the Unholy Grail*, 1991; *Public Enemy Number 2:*

Starring the Famous Diamond Brothers, 1991; *The Falcon's Malteser: Starring the Famous Diamond Brothers,* 1991; *Death walks tonight: horrifying stories* edited by H., 1995; *The Switch,* 1996; *South by South East,* 1997; *Public Enemy Number Two,* 1997; *The Devil and his Boy,* 1998; *Horowitz Horror,* 1999; *More Horowitz Horror: Eight Sinister Stories You'll Wish You'd Never Read,* 2000; *Stormbreaker,* 2000; *Mindgame,* 2001; *I Know What You Did Last Wednesday,* 2002; *Point Blank,* 2002; *Eagle Strike,* 2003; *Skeleton Key,* 2003; *Myths and Legends,* 2003; *Scorpia,* 2005.

BIBLIOGRAPHY: M. Hobson, J. Madden., *Children's Fiction Sourcebook: A Survey of Children's Books for 6–13 years olds,* 1995; R. Reginald, *Science Fiction & Fantasy Literature, 1975–1991: a bibliography of science fiction, fantasy, and horror fiction books and nonfiction monographs.* 1993.

REBECCA VARGHA

HORROR IN YA LITERATURE

Alfred Hitchcock said, "I aim to provide the public with beneficial shocks . . . we're no longer able to get our goose bumps instinctively." Although Hitchcock was talking about film, his statement is certainly true for horror books as well. There is a parallel between the rise of horror film and books; at present, the number of books has far surpassed the films. Known by a variety of names—horror, thriller, creep and gore, mystery-horror, terror, the fantastic, gothic fiction, and/or weird tales—this genre is popular with TEENS. Noel Carroll (*The Philosophy of Horror*) defines horror as "contain[ing] a monster who is "threatening" and producing "disgust or repulsion" in the reader."

According to the "Mood of American Youth" survey, 41 percent of the teens report reading horror/thrillers. This ranks second only to mystery/murder at 45 percent. This survey also found that girls are significantly more likely to read horror/thrillers than boys.

There has always been horror in literature, but the genre exploded in the late 1980s and early 1990s and rapidly became the subject of debate about its benefits and harmful effects. While parents, librarians, educators, and journalists made their cases against the genre, teens embraced the books and read voraciously. Christopher PIKE, R. L. Stine, and Richie Tankersley Cusick led the way and others followed. What is it about these books that made them so popular in the beginning?

- The books follow a predictable plot with short, suspense-filled, cliff-hanging chapters. Every word is calculated to have impact on the reader. The mood and tone are sustained throughout the book, with little pause for reflection or critical thought.
- The teen characters are smart, resourceful, popular, and engage in teen-related activities. Adult characters are peripheral, ineffectual, or oblivious.
- The settings are familiar teen places such as schools, malls, and other local "hangouts," or they are set in places teens want, such as a teen-only school or resort.
- The books "speak" to teens' concerns about popularity, being different, rejected, personal slights and revenge, and growing sexual awareness.
- The gore/grossness factor is fascinating to teens who are dissecting frogs in biology class and who love food fights in the cafeteria. It's a "cheap thrill."
- The books allow teens to be scared while feeling safe. The world-at-large can be an uncertain and scary place and teens can safely control their fears in the pages of a horror/thriller book.

Publishers recognize the potential gold mine of the horror genre for teens and continue to create and expand these offerings, developing different SERIES for younger and older teen readers. R. L. Stine's *Fear Street* led the way with the Point Thriller, Horror High, and Starfire Horror series quickly following. Each year brings new contributions to the genre; most recently horror series are focusing on witches, vampires, and shape-shifters. There is often an ongoing struggle of one group of characters such as a coven of witches with developing powers.

Both established and new authors write for this genre. This growth and development is moving the genre to new heights and different directions; with more complicated plot lines, enhanced character development, and richer language, teen readers are urged to ponder the larger moral questions created by the events and struggles in the books. Horror series were once available only in PAPERBACK but are now being published in hardcover as well. Amelia ATWATER-RHODES, Annette Curtis KLAUSE, Vivian VANDE VELDE and others are changing, shaping and deepening this genre to a new maturity. Teens are irrepressible in their right to choose what they read. They ignore the fact that Stephen KING writes for adults; they like his work and they read it. Their sense of entitlement leads them to Dean KOONTZ and John SAUL, authors they read enthusiastically. Teens, horror, and freedom to read go together.

Where sexual awareness was once implied, it is now being explored and integrated into characterization and plot. Attraction between a young witch and warlock explores not only the physical and emotional appeal but also the result of combined powers. While the couple engages in hand holding, hugging, gazing into each other's eyes, and tender embraces, authors writing in this genre still stop short of sexual intercourse. Rather, they use this "love" as a mechanism for two characters to come together to overcome evil.

Debate about the value of the teen horror genre follows the pattern of most series. Comments such as "It isn't good literature," and "At least they (teens) are reading something," are argued by significant adults in teens' lives. Meanwhile, teens ignore this debate as their predecessors ignored the criticism of Nancy Drew. While everyone, even teens, agree that this genre is not "great literature" the fact remains that these books in some way speak to teens.

Recognizing that teens were going to read horror series, despite (or maybe because of) the issues and opinions raised, librarians began to promote horror fiction. In 1993, The Young Adult Library Services Association produced the "Horror Genre List." A committee selected twenty paperback titles that had proven or potential appeal to teens. In cooperation with Baker and Taylor, this list contained short, snappy annotations, posters, and tip sheets with display and program ideas. Since then, this separate book list has been discontinued and the horror genre has been integrated into YALSA's ongoing, yearly lists, thereby establishing this genre as a recognized and important component in the larger body of literature for young adults.

There is little doubt that the horror genre for young adults is here to stay. Its evolution is as ongoing as its readers developing maturity. Horror holds us in the spell of fascination, gratifying some psychological need; many of us enjoy being scared within a safe environment. We are captivated with the possibilities of the unique characters and their abilities. We are repulsed by the "creep and gore" and thrilled when good triumphs over evil.

AWARDS: *Firestarter* (Stephen KING), BBYA 1980; *Night Shift* (Stephen King), BBYA 1978; Nothin' but the Best; Best of the BBYA 1966–86.

BIBLIOGRAPHY: Campbell, Patty, "Should Kids Read Goosebumps?" Horn Book Magazine, March/April 1994; Carroll, Noel, The Philosophy of Horror, 1990; Dickson, Randi, "Horror to Gratify, not Edify," Language Arts, November 1998; Gehring, Wes, "Frankenstein and Friends," USA Magazine Today, September 1999; "Mysteries, Thrillers Are Top Choices for Pleasure Reading Among Teens, Reading Today, February/March 1997; "New Paperback Book Lists," Emergency Librarian, March/April 1993.

MOLLY KINNEY

HOTZE, Sollace
Author, educator, b. 1932, Gates Mills, Ohio

H. enjoyed reading growing up, which influenced her to write books for young people. She began writing toward the end of a twenty-year teaching career, and is best noted for her historical novels for YA. Her first work, *A Circle Unbroken* (1988), in which the young heroine is captured during an Indian raid, befriended, and taken in by a Sioux chief and his FAMILY and then unsuccessfully reunited with her white family, won acclaim and was named a Notable Book by the American Library Association and a Notable Social Studies Tradebook by the National Council for the Social Studies.

H.'s novels, which show great attention to detail in plot, character, and setting, are well written and compelling. Along with others at the Barrington (Illinois) Area Arts Council, she is instrumental in the creation of *Whetstone,* a literary MAGAZINE, serving as editor for four years.

AWARDS: ALA Best Books for Young Adults, 1988, 1992, Friends of Chicago Library's Carl Sandburg Award for *A Circle Unbroken*; ALA BBYA, 1993, for *Acquainted with the Night.*

FURTHER WORKS: *Summer Endings,* 1991; *Acquainted with the Night,* 1992.

SARAH SPINK DOWNING

HOUSTON, James A.
Author, illustrator, b. 12 June 1921, Toronto, Ontario, Canada; d. 17 April 2005, Stonington, Connecticut

H. is best known for his illustrated novels depicting human life and wildlife in Arctic settings. He studied art at the Ontario College of Art and later studied in Paris and Tokyo. He lived in the Arctic among the Inuit from 1948 to 1962, enabling him to craft his artwork and tales with insider knowledge of Inuit culture. He next moved to New York, where he began his career as a YA books illustrator and author with the publication of *Tikta'liktak: An Eskimo Legend* (1965). His editor, Margaret McElderry, encouraged him to tell the stories he learned from the native Inuit.

H.'s preferred illustration media include pencil, ink, woodcuts, and dry point (an acid-less form of etching). His Inuit-influenced style is characterized by bold lines and a spare use of color. H.'s most recent books have included adult novels as well as nonfiction titles, such as *Fire into Ice* (1998), a nonfiction juvenile title about glassmaking.

AWARDS: CANADIAN Library Association Book of the Year Award for Children (1966) for *Tikta'liktak;* Canadian Library Association Book of the Year Award for Children (1968) for The *White Archer;* Vicky Metcalf Award for a Body of Work (1977); Canadian Library Association Book of the Year Award for Children (1980) for *River Runners;* Max and Greta Ebel Memorial Award for Children's Writing for *Whiteout,* (1989).

FURTHER WORKS: *Akavak: An Eskimo Journey,* 1968; *Ghost Paddle: A Northwest Coast Indian Tale,* 1972; *Frozen Fire: A Tale of Courage,* 1977; *Long Claws: An Arctic Adventure,* 1981; *Black Diamonds: A Search for Arctic Treasure,* 1982; *Ice Swords: An Undersea Adventure,* 1985; *Running West,* 1990; *Drifting Snow: An Arctic Search,* 1992; *Confessions of an Igloo Dweller, 1996;*

BIBLIOGRAPHY: *Something about the Author,* vol. 74, 1993.

DENISE E. AGOSTO

HOWE, James
Author, b. 2 August 1946, Oneida, New York

H. grew up in a family filled with clever wordsmiths. By his own admission, he began using puns and wordplay to gain attention. As a young boy, he wrote plays, short stories, and created his own newspaper. He graduated with a Bachelor of Fine Arts from Boston University in 1968. In 1977 he received an M.A. from Hunter College of the City University of New York. Prior to his writing career, he spent four years as a freelance actor and director and five years as a

literary agent. His first wife, Deborah, encouraged him to write his first books.

H. is a prolific children's author. His love of words is depicted in his ability to challenge the reader of fiction with double meanings and inventive spellings. *Bunnicula: A Rabbit-Tale of Mystery* (1979, co-authored with Deborah Howe) introduces readers to an engaging cast of characters: Chester, a condescending cat, and Harold, a clumsy dog, team up to protect their owners, the Monroes, from their newly adopted family member, Bunnicula, a rabbit. Chester and Harold are convinced that Bunnicula is a vampire, who has been sent to terrorize the family. This book led to a SERIES that proved to be humorous and suspense-filled with titles such as *Howliday Inn* and *The Celery Stalks as Midnight. Bunnicula* was produced on videocassette, while *The Celery Stalks as Midnight, Howliday Inn,* and *Nighty-Nightmare* have been produced as sound recordings. In *Bunnicula Strikes Again!* (2001) H. continues to combine FANTASY and reality to explore FAMILY relationships and friendships. H. takes great delight in knowing that some of his works have been translated into other languages.

In addition to *Bunnicula,* H. is responsible for other series. In the Pinky and Rose Series, H. captures comical situations and provides entertaining language, while addressing serious subject matter. In the Sebastian Barth series, H. fashions MYSTERIES that are dangerous and droll while underscoring serious issues such as homelessness and moody TEENAGERS.

Recognizing that a good series will keep kids reading, H. has begun "Tales from the House of Bunnicula" with *It Came from Beneath the Bed!* (2002). He brings his clever wit to the page with more antics of Bunnicula as the characters fight stuffed animals, aliens, and whatever comes their way.

H. has also produced notable works that are not part of a series. His most noted nonfiction book, *The Hospital Book* (1981), was praised for its accurate depiction of hospital proceedings from a child's point of view. In *A Night without Stars* (1996) H. created a fiction story around a young patient's fear of having open-heart surgery. In his early-adolescent book, *The Misfits* (2003), we find a story of stereotyping that typifies this age group. Again, H. deals with a turbulent time in such a way that it reminds us all to be ourselves.

AWARD: *The Watcher,* BBYA, 1998: *The Color of Absence:* ALA Best Books for Young Adults, 2002; *The Misfits:* ALA Popular Paperbacks, 2005.

FURTHER WORKS: *Annie Joins the Circus,* 1982; *The Case of the Missing Mother,* 1983; *How the Ewoks Saved the Trees: An Old Ewok Legend,* 1984; *Morgan's Zoo,* 1986; *Mister Tinker in Oz,* 1985; *The Secret Garden* (adaptation), 1987; *Carol Burnett: The Sound of Laughter,* 1987; Bunnicula Series: *Nighty-Nightmare,* 1987; *The Misfits,* 2001; *My Life as a Babysitter,* 1992; Sebastian Barth Mystery Series: *What Eric Knew,* 1985; *Stage Fright,* 1986; *Eat Your Poison,* 1986; *Dew Drop Dead,* 1990; *Invasion of the Mind Swappers from Asteroid 6!,* 2002. *Howie Monroe and the Doghouse of Doom, 3.* 2002; *13: Thirteen Stories That Capture the Agony and Ecstasy of Being Thirteen,* 2003; *Totally Joe,* 2005.

BIBLIOGRAPHY: *Something about the Author,* vol. 29, 1982; *Something about the Author,* vol. 71, 1993; *Twentieth-Century Children's Writers,* 1989; various editorial reviews from *Booklist.* http://www.bepl online.org/kidspage/kids_howe.html.

CAROL WICKSTROM

HOWE, Norma

Author, b. 7 February 1930, San Jose, California

H. grew up loving to read and to write. H. wrote for her high-school newspaper and majored in English in college but, it being the 1950s, her main focus was being a good wife and mother. In working various jobs while raising her family, H. began to write and sell confession stories to MAGAZINES such as *True Story* and *Modern Romance.*

H.'s novels for young readers delve into popular topics such as ROMANCE and peer pressure as well as more cerebral subjects such as faith and free will. While H.'s husband was working for the California State Department of Education, he was called to testify at the "Scopes Two" trial, the ongoing battle between evolutionists and creationists over which version of the origin of life should be taught in schools. This experience inspired her first full-length novel, *God, the Universe, and Hot Fudge Sundaes* (1984). Seeing the opportunity to write about some of the philosophical questions that intrigued her, H. wrote about a sixteen year-old girl who attends a trial between evolutionists and creationists. With humor and insight, H. explores the conflict between faith and reason.

In her first novel H. took the time to explore issues of peer pressure and individualism in TEENAGE life with *In With the Out Crowd* (1986). Always able to identify with young adults, H. has said, "I have the feeling I have never really grown up." In her Blue Avenger SERIES of *The Adventures of Blue Avenger* (1999), *Blue Avenger Cracks the Code* (2000), and *Blue Avenger and the Theory of Everything* (2002), H. was able to tell a story that dealt with another philosophical question, free will versus determinism. A boy mourning the DEATH of his father seeks solace in the comic book hero, Blue Avenger, and on his sixteenth birthday decides to change his name and officially become Blue Avenger. (This was inspired in part by a friend of H.'s son who changed his name to that of a cartoon character.) The rest of the book (and the series) explore how Blue Avenger uses his abilities to fix big problems like saving his principal from killer bees and small problems like creating a recipe for dripless lemon meringue pie. Through an omniscient point of view, H. was able to tackle serious issues with a "light touch."

Besides writing, H. loves to travel with her husband, especially to Italy where several of her books have been set.

AWARDS: University of Iowa Books for Young Adults Program (1985) for *God, the Universe, and Hot Fudge Sundaes;* Recommended Book for Reluctant Readers, American Library Association (1988) for *In with the Out Crowd;* California Young Reader Medal nomination (2001–2002) for *The Adventures of Blue Avenger.* Also, the Best Books for Young Adults list, 2000.

FURTHER WORKS: *The Game of Life,* 1989; *Shoot for the Moon,* 1992.

BIBLIOGRAPHY: *Authors and Artists For Young Adults,* vol. 41, 2001; *Contemporary Authors,* online, 2001; *Something about The Author,* vol. 126, 2002.

MEGAN PEARLMAN and ANDREA LIPINSKI

HRDLITSCHKA, Shelley

Author, b. 22 July 1956, Vancouver, British Columbia, Canada

H. started her career teaching elementary school, during which she discovered her love of children's literature. While on a parenting leave she started writing, but waited ten years for her first contract, for *Beans on Toast* (1998).

In H.'s first novel, the protagonist, Madison, is a thirteen-year-old girl confronted with her parents' divorce and her own insecurities about her social acceptance at Band Camp. She continually finds herself on the outside of life, facing the possibility of being sent home. In the two weeks of camp, Madison finds herself challenged and realizes the extent of her resiliency. H. treats the "ugly duck" syndrome sensitively in the uncommon setting of Band Camp.

Dancing Naked (2001) is a story of TEENAGE pregnancy that is told alternatively through a third-person narrative, clinical inserts of fetal development, journal entries and e-mails. Sixteen-year-old Kia's pregnancy is followed through the nine months and her final decision to put her child up for adoption. H. has been praised for creating a book in which the character's decision to keep her baby does not exclude abortion as an option. Kia feels that abortion was wrong for her but does not pass an overriding judgment on the procedure. In addition to the topic of pregnancy, H. involves prejudices against gay men and relationships between young people and the elderly in her novel. It does not focus solely on teenage pregnancy, but rather weaves in other aspects of adolescent life; for this reason, *Dancing Naked* is about the entire world surrounding Kia. Pregnancy marks a key moment in Kia's life, but it also creates a new path to adulthood that is full of curves and twists. It begins a new road that produces entirely new choices.

Though H. has written in many forms and genres, she now focuses solely on fiction for YOUNG ADULTS, inspired in part by ideas from her three daughters.

AWARDS: 1998 Canadian Children's Book Centre Our Choice Award, *Beans on Toast; Dancing Naked:* 2003 ALA Quick Pick; CLA YA Honour Book; 2002 White Pine Award, 2002 Canadian Children's Book Centre Our Choice Award; *Kat's Fall:* ALA Quick Pick, Popular Paperback, 2005.

FURTHER WORKS: *Disconnected,* 1998; *Tangled Wed,* 2000; *Kat's Fall,* 2004; *Sun Signs,* 2005.

BIBLIOGRAPHY: *Contemporary Authors Online,* 2002; http://www.canscaip.org/bios/hrdlitschkas.html; http://members.shaw.ca/shelleyhrdlitschka.html.

RACHEL WITMER
AND SARA MARCUS

HUDSON, Jan

Author, b. 27 April 1954, Calgary, Alberta, Canada; d. April 1990, n.p.

H. will be remembered for her two well-researched novels featuring Native Americans and her graphic depiction of past events on the North American prairie.

H. grew up in Alberta, Canada, daughter of a librarian professor and school teacher. H. married a Native American and adopted his daughter Cindy Linn. H. was pursuing a law degree when she came across historical records of the Blackfoot nation, her stepdaughter's heritage. H. was moved to write her first novel *Sweetgrass,* based upon records of the smallpox epidemic that greatly weakened the Blackfoot Tribe of Alberta.

Although *Sweetgrass* was completed in 1979, it was not published until 1984. *Sweetgrass* won the CANADIAN Library Association (CLA) award and a place on the 1986 International Books for Young People (IBBY) Honour List for writing from Canada.

H.'s second novel, *Dawn Rider* (1990), about a sixteen-year-old Blackfoot girl, Kitfox, whose love and skill with the first horse of her tribe allows her to save her people from slaughter. Although *Dawn Rider* is not rated as highly as *Sweetgrass,* it is certainly captivating, especially to girls who love horses. *Dawn Rider* won the 1991 R. Ross Annet award sponsored by the Writers Guild of Alberta.

H. wrote of what it might have been like to be a Native American during the 18th century during the migration of Europeans to the Plains.

Hudson was at work on her third novel at the time of her sudden death. She was thirty-five years old.

AWARDS: Children's Literature Prize, Canada Council also known as The Governor General Literary Award, Best Children's Book of the Year, Canadian Association of Children's Librarians, 1984 and Notable Book and Best Book for Young Adults Citations, American Library Association, 1989 all for *Sweetgrass,* 1984, ALA BBYA list, 1991, *Dawn Rider.*

BIBLIOGRAPHY: *Authors and Artists for Young Adults,* vol. 22; *Children's Literature Review,* vol. 40; *Contemporary Authors,* vol. 136; *Junior DISCovering Authors;* Pendergast, Sara & Pendergast, Tom, eds., *St. James Guide to Children's Writers,* 1999; *Something about the Author,* vol. 77.

SUSAN E. MORTON

HUGHES, [James] Langston

Author, b. 1 February 1902, Joplin, Missouri; d. 22 May 1967, New York City

H. was an influential, renowned, and sometimes controversial poet, author, playwright, and lecturer, descended from a family of notable people. His grandmother was the first black woman admitted to Oberlin College, and his grandfather was an abolitionist. H.'s great-uncle, John Mercer Langston, was the first AFRICAN AMERICAN elected to public office. H.'s father was determined to live in a society where race was not an issue and blacks were not denied any privileges, so he took his family from the U.S. and moved them to Mexico. H.'s time in Mexico, however, was short. Soon after he and his family arrived, there was a huge, damaging earthquake. That was warning enough for H.'s mother, who promptly took the family back to Kansas. His father remained in Mexico.

Growing up without his father physically present, H. was often shifted among his mother, his grandmother, and his Auntie Reed (a friend of his grandmother's). As a result, he spent time in many areas of the Midwest. It was during his childhood of solitude and instability that H. became enamored with books and developed a love of reading that provided him both companionship and solace. He was also fascinated by the stories that his grandmother told him about the Civil War and the freeing of slaves. Eventually he and his mother settled in Cleveland, and he graduated from high school there. It did not take long for H. to become a published writer. Shortly after high school, he wrote the poem "The Negro Speaks of Rivers," published in 1921 in *Crisis Magazine,* a publication of the NAACP. H. gained a great deal of recognition from this poem, and it is still one of his better-known works today.

H. had a love for learning, but a wanderlust spirit took him away from college. H. attended Columbia University from 1921–22, but soon left to travel to Africa by working as a steward on a freighter. After touring Africa, he went on to tour Russia and Europe while working menial jobs. He developed a love for the popular musical movement of the time, jazz, and began writing poems that complemented rhythmic jazz sounds.

After traveling the world, H. returned to what would become known as his favorite part of the city, Harlem, in 1924. Inspired by his travels, H. had by now written numerous works, which were quickly published in a number of MAGAZINES and newspapers. He eventually received a scholarship to Lincoln University in Pennsylvania. His first two books of POETRY were published in 1926 *(The Weary Blues)* and 1927 *(Fine Clothes to the Jew)* while he was still in college. The latter book brought H. much criticism for being harsh and portraying African Americans in a less than favorable light. H. graduated from college in 1929.

After college, H. began work on his first novel. H.'s writings reflect his belief in sharing his life experiences as he saw them: good, bad, or indifferent. He felt he had to be himself, rather than uphold a façade to please the white world or to make African Americans look like they were something they were not. He found beauty in the truth of daily life.

His first novel, *Not without Laughter,* was published in 1930. He soon began reading his poetry on university campuses to college students, which marked the beginning of his lecturing career. He once again toured abroad, writing SHORT STORIES while in Russia, and eventually covering the Spanish Civil War from Madrid for the *Baltimore African American* newspaper in 1937.

H. was extremely versatile and wrote in many genres. His foray into the world of YA literature resulted in books and poetry, such as *Popo and Fifina* (1932), *The First Book of Negroes* (1952), and *The First Book of Jazz* (1955). He wrote nonfiction as well, including *The Sweet Flypaper of Life* (1955) and *Fight for Freedom: The Story of the NAACP* (1962). He was also involved in theatre. He wrote his first play in 1935 and founded the Harlem Suitcase Theater in 1938, the New Negro Theater in Los Angeles in 1939, and the Skyloft Players in Chicago in 1943.

H. wrote extensively about race, segregation, and race relations. He often used humor to express serious feelings on the subject of race. One of his most popular characters, Jesse B. Semple, known as "Simple," was featured in weekly newspaper columns for the *Chicago Defender* and later published in five books.

H. enjoyed a long and prolific career. His work resonated with the average person. He was known as an influential figure in the Harlem Renaissance of the 1920s and is credited as being the first African American to support himself solely through his writing. H. died in 1967 in Harlem, due to complications from cancer.

AWARDS: Witter Bynner, First place, undergraduate poetry contest, 1926; Harmon Gold Medal for Literature, 1931; Guggenheim fellowship for creative work, 1935; Spigarn Medal, NAACP, 1960.

FURTHER WORKS: *Popo and Fifina: Children of Haiti* (1932); *The First Book of Rhythms* (1952); *Famous*

American Negroes (1954); *The First Book of the West Indies* (1956); *Famous Negro Heroes of America* (1958); *The First Book of Africa* (1964); *The Sweet and Sour Animal Book* (1994).

BIBLIOGRAPHY: Berry, F., *Langston H.: Before and beyond Harlem,* 1992; A. Rampersad, *The Life of Langston H.,* 2001.

NANCY A. BUGGÉ

HUGHES, Monica

Author, b. 3 November 1925, Liverpool, England; d. 2003

H., a productive author for young adults and children, is known for her well-crafted books of SCIENCE FICTION. She has also written historical fiction and many contemporary novels for all ages. Although born in England, she has traveled extensively since she was quite young. Settling in CANADA, she is one of Canada's finest writers for children and young adults.

Originally, H. set out to write for adults, but with her book *Gold-Fever Trail: A Klondike Adventure,* she began to write primarily for young adults. In 1974, after the publication of *Crisis on Conshelf Ten,* she began an extensive career in the science-fiction genre for young adults. Her most famous science-fiction works are part of her Isis trilogy. In *Alan Review,* she said "the writing science fiction is full of magical moments . . . it can help explicate today's world and tomorrow's possibilities for young people."

H. uses her native Canada as a backdrop for her books, often including the Native people of her country for authenticity. She includes current topics such as scientific progress, environmental issues, and child abuse, giving her novels a legitimacy that make them welcome additions to good YA literature.

AWARDS: 1988 Alberta Achievement Award; 1987 Boeken Leeuw Book Lion Award; 1988 City of Edmonton Cultural Creative Arts award; Phoenix Award, 2000.

FURTHER WORKS: *Sandwriter,* 1985; *The Dream Catcher,* 1986; *Invitation to the Game,* 1991; *The Crystal Drop,* 1993; *The Golden Aquarians,* 1995; *What If . . . ? Amazing Stories,* 1998; *The Other Place,* 2000.

BIBLIOGRAPHY: *Alan Review,* Vol. 19, No. 3, Spring, 1992, pp. 2–5, *Something about the Author,* v. 119, 2001.

LAURIE M. ALLEN

HUNTER, Mollie

Author, b. 30 June 1922, Scotland

H. is a prolific, multiaward-winning author for adults and YOUNG ADULTS. A native and resident of Scotland, she seeks to entertain her readers with stories from her heritage but also to speak to people from all cultures. Her love of history, theatre, and music is apparent in her work and helps define her characters as they struggle with good and evil in everyday life. A gifted storyteller, she is known for historical fiction, FANTASY, folktales, and realistic novels for all ages. *The Kelpie's Pearls* (1964) was named as an American Library Association Notable Book and was on the *Horn Book* Honor List. *The Ferlie* (1968), a fantasy, was chosen as a Child Study Association of America Book of the Year. H. contributes articles and essays for newspapers, MAGAZINES and anthologies.

AWARDS: Children's Books of the Year (1968, 1970, 1971, 1974, 1975, 1976, 1978, 1987); Outstanding Book of the Year, *New York Times* (1972); Best Books, *School Library Journal,* (1975); Best Books For Young Adults, American Library Association (1986); *The King's Swift Rider;* ALA Popular Paperback, 2002.

SELECTED FURTHER WORKS: *The Three Day Enchantment,* illustrated by Simont, 1985; *The Mermaid Summer,* 1988; *Talent Is Not Enough: Mollie Hunter on Writing for Children,* 1990; *The King's Swift Rider,* 1998. *The Pied Piper Syndrome and Other Essays,* 1992; *Day of the Unicorn,* illustrated by Donna Diamond, 1994; *Gilly Martin the Fox,* illustrated by Dennis McDermott, 1994.

BIBLIOGRAPHY: *Contemporary Authors,* 2001; *Something about the Author,* vol. 106, 1999.

LAURIE M. ALLEN

HURWIN, Davida Wills

Author, b. 1950, San Francisco, California

H. grew up in Mill Valley, California, but she now lives in Southern California. Since her main passion is dancing, it is only natural that she heads the Dance/Drama department at a private school. H. is married, with a daughter. H. continues to dance as well as to write.

A Time for Dancing (1995) is based on a true incident in the writer's life; when H. met a dancer who was dying at age seventeen from cancer, she felt the need to share this story. High school is a time of seeming immortality, and Julie and Samantha seem singularly blessed. Their friendship could not be closer, and it is natural that they are dancing partners as well. Life is golden the summer after their junior year in high school, until Jules is diagnosed with cancer. The story is unfolded by the two girls in turn, each sharing her point-of-view a chapter at a time. Julie must deal with treatments and her growing weakness, but Sam faces a different kind of powerlessness when she realizes that Jules is going somewhere that she cannot follow.

The sequel to A Time for Dancing, The Farther You Run (2003), follows Sam during the year after Julie's death. Without Jules, Sam has lost her desire to dance, or to go to college, or to do any of the things that she and Julie had planned to share together. A new friend, Mona, motivates her enough so that she gets a job, and Sam and Mona decide to move into an apartment in San Francisco. Still, Sam has a long way to go before she heals, and Mona has demons of her own.

H.'s first book, with its heartfelt portrait of loss, created immortal characters. Julie's spirit lingers in the second book, even though she is no longer physically present. Whether or not Sam and Mona will be able to handle that is at the crux of the sequel. These two works explore the grief and sadness not only of dying young, but of being the one who has to go on living, themes that often engross YOUNG ADULTS.

AWARDS: ALA, BBYA, A Time for Dancing, 1996; ALA Popular Paperbacks, 2005.

BIBLIOGRAPHY: www.amazon.com; www.edithere .com/atfd/stories/storyReaders$104; http://endeavor .med.nyu.edu / lit-med / lit-med-db / webdocs / webdes crips/hurwin1024-des.html; http://endeavor.med.nyu .edu / lit-med / lit-med-db / webdocs / webauthors / hur win548-au-.html; www.novelst4.epnet.com.

JEANNE MARIE RYAN

HURWITZ, Johanna
Author, b. 9 October 1937, New York City

H. is best known for her light-hearted, realistic school stories which often feature recurring characters. For instance Rory, Derek, and Bolivia are showcased in the outstandingly humorous books The Hot and Cold Summer (1984), The Cold and Hot Winter (1988), The Up and Down Spring (1993), and The Up and Down Fall (1996). Her written work extends beyond

this genre, however, and includes historical fiction, PICTURE BOOKS, YOUNG ADULT novels, and BIOGRAPHIES of such figures as Helen Keller, Leonard Bernstein, Astrid Lindgren, and Anne Frank.

H. dreamed of becoming a writer from an early age. She participated in a reading club for 5th- and 6th-grade girls when she attended school in the Bronx, often sharing her own stories with the members. Her family, however, encouraged her to pursue a profession that would provide financial stability. While still attending high school in Queens, she began working at the New York Public Library. She graduated from Queens College in 1958 and, the following year, received a degree in Library Science from Columbia University. It was then that she began her career as a children's librarian at the New York Public Library, serving at twenty different branches before leaving in 1963. It was during this time that H. published her first story in 1961. After her children were born, H. was a librarian at the Calhoun School in Manhattan and, some years later, on Long Island. She also taught library science courses at Queens College.

Once her children were enrolled in school, H. began to write down the stories she developed for them years earlier. It took four years from the time H. submitted her first manuscript of Busybody Nora until it was published in 1976. This book is loosely based on the adventures of her daughter. H. continued to work two days a week at the Great Neck Library and write at home during her remaining time. She eventually became a full-time writer and since has published more than sixty books.

H. first wrote for the seven- to nine-year-old audience, simply because this age group is so excited by the little things in daily life. Her topics were selected from the events her children, Nomi and Beni, had experienced firsthand. The fictional characters were based upon herself or members of her family. Once I Was a Plum Tree (1980) is the most autobiographical. Ten-year-old Gerry Flan, whose parents are nonobservant Jews, searches for her own ethnic and religious identity in postwar America. The Rabbi's Girls (1982) is based upon the life of H.'s mother. The Law of Gravity (1978) was prompted by an incident with a pail of paint.

A Word to the Wise and Other Proverbs (1994) is a gathering of some of the most recognizable American proverbs. Along with Robert Rayevsky, they bring some of the wit and wisdom of an age gone by to their readers. The idea for this book was sparked by H.'s visit to Belvoir Castle in July, 1989. In *Leonard Bernstein: A Passion for Music* (1993), H. introduces her readers to the energetic life of Bernstein as pianist, teacher, composer, and conductor. Though good fortune impacted Bernstein's life, H. illustrates how his talent and determination shaped his career.

Birthday Surprises: Ten Great Stories to Unwrap (1995) was different from her previous books. H. edited the anthology of ten stories contributed by well-known children's authors. The single premise for all the stories is that a beautifully wrapped birthday gift is found to be an empty box. The stories range from humorous to poignant, but in the end, leave the reader with a lot to think about.

In *Faraway Summer* (1998), H. introduces modern-day readers to the Fresh Air Fund, which provides free rural vacations for inner-city children, through the experiences of a young Jewish orphan girl in 1910. Hadassah "Dossi" Rabinowitz journeys to a Vermont farm where she spends two weeks. H. balances two different cultures as the young characters develop a friendship. *Dear Emma* (2002) is a sequel to *Faraway Summer* in which Dossi continues her relationship with the Vermont family through letters. Dossi faces multiple tragedies during this period, including her involvement in the great Triangle Shirt-

waist Factory fire. Hurwitz presents her readers with images of early 1900 New York City and reveals the struggles that many immigrants and poor faced during this time.

Today when H. is not traveling to far corners of the world, she divides her time between Great Neck, New York, and Vermont.

AWARDS: 1987 Texas Bluebonnet Award, *The Hot Cold Summer;* 1994 Garden State Children's Choice Award, *School's Out;* 1989 Kentucky Bluegrass Award, *Class Clown;* SLJ Best Book of the Year for *Class Clown.*

FURTHER WORKS: *Hurricane Elaine,* 1986; *Even Steven,* 1996; *Ozzie on His Own,* 1995; *Tough Luck Karen,* 1982; *Anne Frank: Life in Hiding,* 1988; *Astrid Lindgren: Storyteller to the World,* 1989; *Helen Keller: Courage in the Dark,* 1997.

BIBLIOGRAPHY: Musleah, R., "A Magical Pursuit: The Satisfying Art of Writing Children's Books," *Jewish Woman,* winter, 2002, p. 30; Marcus, L., ed., *Author Talk: Conversations with Judy* BLUME, *Bruce* BROOKS, *Karen* CUSHMAN, *Russell* FREEDMAN, *Lee Bennett* HOPKINS, *James* HOWE, *Johanna* HURWITZ, *E. L.* KONIGSBURG, *Lois* LOWRY, *Ann M. Martin, Nicholasa* MOHR, *Gary Paulsen, Jon Scieszka, Seymour Simon, and Laurence* YEP, 2000; website: johannahurwitz .com.

KRISTINE M. MICHELL

I

INFORMATIONAL BOOKS: AN AUTHOR'S POINT OF VIEW

What defines a YA informational book? Is it a 256-page tome about the life of George Washington, or a 96-page photo essay about September 11, 2001, or perhaps a beautifully illustrated PICTURE BOOK BIOGRAPHY of Queen Cleopatra? In the contemporary book world, the definition is likely to include all three.

As an author, I've delved into several types of YA nonfiction and found the switch from one form to another immensely stimulating. When I wrote picture book biographies of George Washington, I thought they would be read by seven-to-ten-year-olds, and they were. But I also got fan letters from thirteen and fourteen-year-olds telling me how much they had liked the books.

While planning my next picture book biography, *The Amazing Life of Benjamin Franklin,* I deliberately aimed it toward audiences of older as well as younger readers. In an age when TEENS are accustomed to getting so much of their information from television and the Internet, I realized that a picture book format is no impediment, as it was to earlier generations of young adults. This broader audience presents the author with a problem though: How do you create a portrait of meaning and substance for both children and young adults? The problem was compounded with the Franklin biography because he lived such an extensive life, and one that included so many different accomplishments. At various times and in various places he was a printer, a businessman, a writer, an

inventor, a diplomat, and a statesman. How could I possibly embrace them all in one short book?

I found the answer to that question when, in the course of research, I came across references to Franklin's tumultuous relationship with his son William—the only son who lived to maturity. While Franklin was an ardent patriot, William remained loyal to the British throne and became an exile in London after the Revolutionary War. This estranged Franklin from his son, and they were never able to mend the breach. Once I discovered this emotional spine for the book, everything else seemed to fall into place.

Another challenge was finding ways to convey Franklin's love of life—and of wine and women—in ways that would be understandable to younger as well as older readers, and acceptable to the adults who buy books for them. Here, for example, is how I described Ben's first trip to England as a youth of eighteen: "He found work with a London printer and spent his free time exploring the great city and reading all the latest books. He had his share of fun, too, going to pubs with friends and flirting with the pretty girls he met." Much later in the book, when Ben travels to Paris to serve as America's ambassador to France, I found a way to show, with few words, that he had not changed much over the years: "At seventy-two, Ben still had an eye for the ladies. He even fell in love with one, Madame Helvetius. She was a brilliant widow who entertained all the leading writers, scientists, and politicians in her home. Ben went so far as to propose marriage, but the widow wasn't ready for that. However, she remained a good friend for the rest of his life."

When a text is short, like the one for *Franklin,* I like to flesh it out with supplemental information at the back of the book. More mature readers can delve into this material to extend their knowledge of the subject, while teachers can use it with students who may not be able to read it by themselves. At the back of *Franklin,* for example, there is a timeline of major events in his life, descriptions of some of his useful inventions, a guide to historic sites associated with the man, and a selection of his sayings from "Poor Richard's Almanac."

Compression is obviously a major concern when one is writing a picture book biography. But it is also a problem in a biography for young adults, like the ones I have done of Charles A. Lindbergh and Adolf Hitler. Where adult biographers may spend eight hundred or a thousand pages delving into the most minute details of their subjects' lives, the biographer for young people must often pick and choose. In the end, there may be room in a 192- or 224-page book for only those incidents and anecdotes that seem essential to give a complete and honest picture of the person.

When friends learned that I was researching a biography of Hitler, some were nonplussed. Why would I want to write about such a monster? they asked. Truthfully, I had been curious about the Nazi leader since I was a boy (and incidentally, I believe that the best nonfiction books usually spring from the author's curiosity about a given subject and an intense desire to explore it). I grew up during World War II, when Hitler's face and voice were everywhere—on magazine covers, in movie newsreels, and on posters urging people to "Buy a War Bond and Fight the Führer." In the decades that followed, there were references to him in countless books and movies, but my curiosity was not satisfied. I wanted to understand who he was and why he committed such terrible crimes against humanity. That dissatisfaction made me investigate him further and eventually led to my writing his biography.

The research took me first to respected adult biographies by such writers as John Toland, Ian Kershaw, and Joachim Fest. Next I read biographies of other Nazi leaders such as Joseph Goebbels and Hermann Goering, histories of the period by authorities such as William L. Shirer and Klaus P. Fischer, and the autobiographies of Albert Speer and Hitler himself. I

should offer a word of warning about the latter. Whereas it is always desirable to work from primary source material whenever possible, the writer must bear in mind that such material may be slanted or edited in a self-serving way. That is certainly the case with Hitler's *Mein Kampf.* I also viewed documentary films of the period like Leni Riefenstahl's *Triumph of the Will* and the marvelous British television series *The World at War* to refresh my memory of Hitler's appearance, his voice, the way he walked, and his characteristic gestures. While I did not make a trip to present-day Germany for onsite research, I did draw extensively on memories of two bus tours I took across Western and Eastern Europe in the 1960s. Having seen the ruins of Hitler's Reichstag in Berlin, the burned-out shell of the former city hall in Warsaw's Jewish ghetto, and the war memorials to the Russian dead in Minsk and Moscow, I was better able to describe Hitler's wartime atrocities and the terrible damage he inflicted on the people of Europe.

Teachers and librarians today demand more solid source notes in young adult nonfiction than ever before. When it came to attributing my research sources for the Hitler biography, I employed a variety of methods. Wherever possible, I tried to work the origin of the material into the text proper since, as a reader, I hate to have to turn constantly to the back of the book to locate sources. In my opinion, there is no better way to lose the momentum of the narrative. At the back of *Hitler,* I wrote a bibliographical essay that describes my major sources and traces the path I followed in the course of the research. My hope is that essays like this will be helpful to young readers when they have to construct their own research paths for term papers and other classroom writings. Following the essay, I compiled a chapter-by-chapter list of specific sources for each topic discussed, in the order in which it appeared in the chapter.

In order to maintain reader interest, most writers of informational books try to bring out the dramatic potential of their material. In *Hitler,* for example, I highlighted the scene in the bunker near the end of the war when the Führer finally realized the end of the war was near. However, I did so without resorting to any invented dialogue, a literary tactic which is frowned upon by librarians and teachers alike. Instead, I relied on excerpts from the memoirs of Hitler's associates who were down in the bunker with him and observed his behavior firsthand.

Many people think a writer's work on an informational book for young adults is done when the manuscript is finished. But an important stage still lies ahead: researching and selecting the prints and photographs that will be used as illustrations. In our highly visual age, the impact a YA nonfiction book makes on reviewers and readers depends to a greater degree than ever on the excellence of its illustrations and design. Photo research can be frustrating when you cannot find what you want, but it can also be full of rewarding discoveries. That is what happened when I made a trip to Washington in search of pictures for *Hitler.* At the National Archives, I came across a real treasure trove—the photo albums of Eva Braun, Hitler's longtime mistress. At the end of World War II, U.S. Army men found the albums in one of Eva's residences, and sent them to the Archives, where they remain today.

It gave me an eerie feeling to leaf through photostatic copies of all thirty-five albums and study the snapshots in them, each with a caption handwritten by Eva. Before my eyes were photos of Hitler beaming at Eva's little niece, and bending down to kiss Eva's hand, and posing with her and their pet dogs on the terrace of the Berghof, his Alpine retreat. I ordered prints of all three for use in the book, examples—as a friend of mine put it—of "the banality of evil," the phrase Hannah Arendt coined in her book about SS leader Adolf Eichmann.

It may sound stuffy, but I firmly believe that all I. writing ought to educate the reader in one way or another. I know that when I sit down to read a newspaper or magazine article, or a nonfiction book, I hope I shall learn something I did not know before. I think that is doubly true of children and young adults; they are eager to find out everything they can about the world and its people, past and present.

All the best writers of I. for young adults—from Russell FREEDMAN to Jim MURPHY to Susan Campbell BARTOLETTI—are aware of their readers' hunger for facts and insights. They work hard to satisfy that hunger with books that extend the readers' knowledge and stimulate the imagination. These too have been my chief goals in the informational books I have written thus far. And, with the encouragement of my readers, I hope to do an even better job of achieving them in the future.

JAMES CROSS GIBLIN

Reproduced, with permission, from *School Library Journal.* Copyright © by Reed Business Information, A Division of Reed Elsevier, Inc.

INGOLD, Jeanette
Author, b. n.d., New York City

I. was born and reared in New York but the family moved frequently and settled in Missoula, Montana. She began her writing career as a newspaper reporter in Missoula and received a B.A. in psychology and an M.Ed. in secondary education from the University of Delaware. She worked as an educator after her marriage to Kurt Ingold. They lived in Kansas, Texas, and Delaware before moving to Missoula. As a reporter, she had learned to do careful research.

An avid reader as a small child, I. read to her children, Carrie and Kurt Jr. As her children got older and no longer wanted their mother to read to them, I. found she wanted to maintain her connection to children's literature. She drew upon her childhood experiences, remembering her family's travels from New York to Texas, and recalling stories she heard from her parents and grandparents. With these memories in hand, she began writing books.

I.'s books are historical in nature and set in the first half of the 20th century. She uses old maps, newspapers, telephone directories, pictures, and interviews to write about characters that have strong personalities and realistic traits. Her first books, *The Window* (1996) and *Mountain Solo* (1996) were followed by *Pictures, 1918* (1998), *Airfield* (1999), and *The Big Burn* (2002). This last book was inspired by devastating 1910 forest fires in Montana and Idaho. This event changed the way that wildfires are fought, and I. felt it important to bring the story into the YA literary world.

Some of I.'s books were selected by Texas Library Association for their Tayshas List. These books are of special historical interest to young adults in Texas; they are high-quality books that stimulate thoughts, fire imaginations, and promote vigorous conversations. Similar to the Texas Bluebonnet Award for elementary students, the Tayshas award is directed to high-school students. The award takes its name from the Caddo Indian word meaning friends or allies; it is written as "Texas." The word was applied to the Caddos by the Spanish in eastern Texas who regarded them as friends and allies against the Apaches.

AWARDS: *The Window:* ALA Best Book for Young Adults: 1997 IRA Young Adults' Choice; *Pictures, 1918:* New York Public Library Book for the Teen Age; *Airfield:* New York Public Library Book for the

Teen Age; *The Big Burn:* Montana Book Award Honor Book, Texas Tayshas list selection.

FURTHER WORKS: *Hitch*, 2005.

BIBLIOGRAPHY: *Authors and Artists for Young Adults,* volume 43; *Contemporary Authors,* volume 198; *Something about the Author,* volume 128; Stepping into Other Lives, Other Times: An Interview with Jeanette Ingold, R. J. Vaillancourt, *Public Libraries,* March/April, 2002. www.jeanetteingold.com; An Interview with Jeanette Ingold and Teri Lesesne, *Teacher Librarian* October/November 1999; Dan Darigan and Mary Louise Woodcock, *Writer: Time Travel* March 1999; "Teaching The Window: Imagination and Fact in the World of a Blind Teenager." Spring 1997 *Oregon English Journal.*

NAOMI WILLIAMSON

INSPIRATIONAL YA FICTION

Perhaps the prevalence of inspirational fiction in the U.S. is not unusual considering the country's Puritan roots. The constant need for self-improvement is a particularly American theme, although in recent years it has begun to be one of the country's chief exports. Inspirational fiction often has as its cornerstone the propagation of themes found in specific organized religions. Often referred to as Christian fiction, this is a misnomer, since there are other religions that also seek to inspire through novels that highlight their religion and beliefs and are targeted at a YA audience. There is also fiction that is inspiring without any type of religious overtones and has a far greater reliance on secular humanism. Inspirational fiction for young people, however, has been present for centuries.

Sunday School books, although not exactly inspirational fiction, were prominent in the early 19th century. Their themes emphasize the importance of living a morally upright life. With such an emphasis on living righteously in everyday life, it seems a natural transition that popular fiction would echo these moral injunctions. Margaret Farquharson, writing as Margaret Finley, was an especially prolific contributor to the field with the twenty-eight title Elsie Dinsmore SERIES, which made its first appearance in 1868. These books continued to appear until 1905, spreading their moralistic piety through multiple generations. To put this in context, however, it should also be remembered that Louisa May ALCOTT's classic *Little Women,* first published in 1868–1869, opens with the March girls, under the encouragement of Marmee, giving up their Christmas dinner to a family even poorer than themselves. Although their selflessness is ultimately rewarded, a somewhat prevalent theme in inspirational fiction, it is the fact that they sacrifice that makes them able to reap a greater reward later. Horatio Alger, Jr. was to take a slightly more secular approach to the theme of self-improvement, with his books for boys promoting the idea that hard work would garner great wealth.

In the 20th century, two of the great FANTASY series are J. R. R. TOLKIEN's classics, *The Hobbit, The Fellowship of the Ring, The Two Towers,* and *The Return of the King,* and C. S. LEWIS's Chronicles of Narnia. These may be considered inspirational fiction because of their classic themes of good versus evil. This theme resonates in much of the fiction of the 20th century, although often in a less overt way than the work of these two members of the Inklings, the group of writers who met often.

Many of the SPORTS series that appeared throughout the century strove to be inspirational in a different way—promoting the ideals of good sportsmanship and fair play. These include the Phillips Exeter series by A. T. Dudley, the Baseball Joe series by Lester Chadwick, the Baseball Series by Christy Mathewson and Everett Scott, the Basketball Series by Harold Sherman, the Football Eleven by Ralph Henry Barbour, and the Chip Hilton Sports stories by Clair Bee.

Bethany House Publishers has carved a definitive niche in the contemporary Christian fiction market for TEENS. The company offers Robin Jones Gunn's Christy Miller series and its continuation, the Christy & Todd, College Years series, as well as the Sierra Jensen series, also written by Robin Jones Gunn. Patricia Rushford writes the prolific Jennie McGrady MYSTERY series, while Shirley Brinkerhoff offers the Nikki Sheridan series, and Elaine Schulte writes the Becky books for younger and soon-to-be teens. The Holly's Heart series by Beverly Lewis are also geared towards young teens—as are the Accidental Detective series by Sigmund Brouwer. For both boys and girls, the historical Promise of Zion offers thrilling adventures as do the books in the contemporary Bloodhounds, Inc. series by Bill Myers. The Golden Filly and High Hurdles series, both by Laraine Snelling, are meant to attract horse lovers who may also enjoy the Summerhill Secrets series by Beverly Lewis set in Pennsylvania Amish country. The Brio Girls series offers stories for slightly older teens. Other offerings include more historical fiction series for teens of both sexes. Multnomah Publishers, another publisher of Christian books of all kinds, offers relatively little in the way of inspirational fiction, except for the Diary of a Teenage Girl series that presents struggles faced by girls maintaining their faith amid the usual challenges of the teen years. However, Zondervan, another Christian fiction publishing company, offers even less—their big offering appears to be a boxed set of Elsie Dinsmore. The ultimate fate of the world is the subject of contemporary treatment by Jenkins and LaHaye in their Left Behind series. The Clearwater Crossing series by Laura Peyton Roberts also contains overtones of Christian fiction.

However, it is not only those who practice Christianity who seek inspirational YA fiction. Many observant Jews also seek characters that reflect their daily practice of their faith and find it difficult. The Vivi Hartman series by Harriet Feder incorporates her heroine's Judaic beliefs into her work. Carol MATAS also has books that show characters with a strong Jewish faith, as does Kenneth Roseman with his The You Do-It-Yourself Jewish Adventure Series.

It should be noted that in fiction written to conform to a certain philosophy, sometimes the theme overpowers the story and characterization. Although this is certainly not true in all cases, it is worth checking. If the reader's main goal, however, is simply to have the underlying structure of whichever belief system is being propagated in the book, it becomes less of a concern.

The search for inspirational fiction is common to all cultures. It is not only in books that put forth specific religious beliefs that inspiration can be found. Marilyn LEVY's novel, *Run for Your Life,* a fictionalized account of a group of girls whose running ability helps them escape the projects, is very inspiring—in a humanistic way.

BIBLIOGRAPHY: www.amazon.com; www.bethany house.com; http://www.lib.msu.edu/coll/main/spec_col/nye/index.htm; www.multnomahpubl.com; www.seriesnovels.com; www.zondervan.com

JEANNE MARIE RYAN

IRWIN, Hadley
Author, pseudonym

IRWIN, Ann(abelle) (Bowen)
Author, b. 8 October 1915, Peterson, Iowa

HADLEY, Lee
Author, b. 10 October 1934, Earlham, Iowa; d. 22 August 1995, Madrid, Iowa

"Ann Irwin and Lee Hadley have been writing books together as I. since 1979. The duo noted in the ALAN *Review* that I. is 'over a hundred and twenty-five years old' and has 'taught for 75 or 80 years, everything from kindergarten through graduate school.'"

Also known as one half of I., Annabelle Irwin earned a B.A. from Morningside College (1937) and an M.A. from the University of Iowa (1967). Before co-authoring popular books for TEENS with Lee Hadley, Irwin co-authored two books about the history of Iowa with Bernice Reida: *Hawkeye Adventure* (1966) and *Hawkeye Lore* (1968), as well as two fiction books for children, *Moon of the Red Strawberry* (1977) and *Until We Reach the Valley* (1979). Irwin also published two plays, *And the Fullness Thereof* (1962) and *Pieces of Silver* (1963) and one novel, *One Bite at a Time* (1973) on her own.

Also known as the other half of I., Hadley coauthored thirteen books with Irwin. The two women dealt with real-life issues relevant to adolescents of the time.

With a B.A. from Duke University (1956), an M.A. from the University of Wisconsin-Madison (1961), and a trip to Europe behind her, the voracious reader Hadley decided on a career in teaching. After working nine years at a high school, Hadley moved back near her parents and took a job at Iowa State University. It was at Iowa State that Hadley and Irwin crossed paths.

After co-authoring department reports and a scholarly article, the two women were reluctant to cease their collaborations. They began to write for young adults, and a new author was born. I.'s first book, *The Lilith Summer,* was published in 1978 and later adapted into both a film and teachers' guide in 1984. Their 1985 book, *Abby, My Love,* was adapted into a *CBS Schoolhouse* special in 1988. Although they deal with issues relevant to teenagers, I. does not see a difference between writing for their teenage audience or an adult reader. I.'s second novel, *We Are Mesquakie, We Are One* (1980), was distinguished with the Jane Addams Peace Association Honor Book designation.

SELECT AWARDS: 1981 Jane Addams Peace Association Honor Book Award, *We Are Mesquakie, We Are One;* 1982 Society of Midland Authors Award, *Moon and Me;* ALA Best Young Adult Book Award: 1982 for *What about Grandma?,* and 1985 for *Abby, My Love;* 1986 Children's Book Council and International Reading Association Children's Choice Book Award and Children's Book Award, *Abby, My Love;* 1987 Library of Congress Children's Books of the Year list, *Kim/Kimi.*

SELECT FURTHER WORKS: *Bring to a Boil and Separate,* 1980; *Moon and Me,* 1981; *What About Grandma?,* 1982; *I Be Somebody,* 1984; *Kim/Kimi,* 1987; *So Long at the Fair,* 1988; *Can't Hear You Listening,* 1990; *The Original Freddie Ackerman,* 1992; *Jim Dandy,* 1994; *Sarah with an H,* 1996.

BIBLIOGRAPHY: "Ann(abelle) (Bowen) Irwin," *U*X*L Junior Discovering Authors,* 1998, reproduced in Discovering Collection, 2001, http://galenet .galegroup.com/servlet/DC/ Accessed 05/15/2003; "Irwin-Hadley," *Authors and Artists for Young Adults,* vol. 13, 1994, reproduced in Biography Resource Center, 2003, http://www.galenet.com/servlet/BioRC Accessed 09/10/2003; "Lee Hadley." *U*X*L Junior DISCovering Authors,* 1998, reproduced in Discovering Collection, 2001, http://galenet.galegroup.com/ servlet/DC/ Accessed 05/15/2003.

SARA MARCUS

HADLEY, Irwin. See IRWIN, Ann(abelle).

ISAACS, Anne
Author, b. 2 March 1949, Buffalo, New York

I. read voraciously as a child and had two poems published in a city-wide children's MAGAZINE by the time she was ten. In college she was especially interested in reading 19th-century novels and poetry, while as an adult she began to read extensively in children's literature. Oftentimes, she experienced a book for the first time while reading it to her own children.

I.'s first book, *Swamp Angel* (1994), a tongue-in-cheek style PICTURE BOOK illustrated by Paul O. Zelinsky, was heralded by the critics as a visually exciting and wonderful read-aloud story. In a more serious work, *A Bowl of Soup* (2004), I. deals with the experiences of a young woman interned in a Nazi labor camp in Czechoslovakia during the 1940s. In a later novel, *Torn Threads* (2002), I. tells the story of two TEENAGE sisters who manage to survive a Nazi work camp although their entire family is murdered.

I. is currently working on a historical fiction novel.

SELECT AWARDS: *Swamp Angel:* 1995 Caldecott Honor, *School Library Journal* Best Book, *Publishers Weekly* Best Book, 1995 *Boston Globe–Horn Book* Honor Book, NCTE Notable Trade Book in Language Arts, *Torn Threads:* 2001 ALA Best Books for Young Adults list.

FURTHER WORKS: *Treehouse Tales,* 1997; *Cat up a Tree,* 1998.

BIBLIOGRAPHY: *Something about the Author,* 1997; Electronic Resources Public Library, 2003.

AVIVA ROSEMAN

J

JACKSON, Shirley

Author, b. 14 December 1919, San Francisco, California; d. 8 August 1965, North Bennington, Vermont

A master of modern Gothic fiction, J. wrote numerous SHORT STORIES and several novels, delving into the darker side of human nature. Her works tend to show the effects of a cold and uncaring society, particularly on female protagonists who often suffer from emotional or psychological disturbances. Although much of J.'s work is meant for adult readers, several of her works feature younger female characters, and her famous and critically acclaimed short story "The Lottery" (1948) has appeared in countless high-school literature anthologies.

Born in San Francisco, J. retreated into a disciplined world of writing at a very young age. After attending the University of Rochester for a short time, she eventually matriculated with a B.A. degree from Syracuse University in 1940. At Syracuse she met her husband, Stanley Edgar Hymen, who eventually became a well-known literary critic. While in college, J. was heavily influenced by anthropological studies, particularly by James Frazier's *The Golden Bough*, which gave her insight into ancient scapegoat rituals—the sins of a society were thought to be expurgated through the sacrifice of one of its members.

Although J. returned to this theme repeatedly throughout her life, the best example is her short story "The Lottery." Originally published in *The New Yorker*, the story takes place on a beautiful day in a seemingly peaceful town. Only in the final paragraphs does the true horror become clear; the citizens have gathered together for a macabre lottery in which the "winner" of the black-marked ballot gets stoned to death as a ritual sacrifice.

During her relatively short life, she had a remarkably eclectic writing career, penning radio and television scripts, and numerous MAGAZINE stories for such varied publications as *The Yale Review* and *Good Housekeeping*. In contrast to her darker fiction, her magazine pieces are short, humorous pieces of domestic fiction drawn largely from her own life. She also wrote a nonfiction children's book, *The Witchcraft of Salem Village* (1956), which featured themes such as the power of mass hysteria and the capability of human nature to turn dark and cruel. Many of her stories have also been translated into film and stage versions; the most notable example is *The Haunting of Hill House* (1959), which inspired the 1963 film "The Haunting" starring Julie Harris. J. died of heart failure in 1965.

AWARDS: Edgar Allan Poe Award (1965), "The Possibility of Evil," 1961, "Louisa, Please Come Home"; Parents Pioneer Medal for Outstanding Achievement, Syracuse University, 1965.

FURTHER WORKS: *The Road Through the Wall,* 1948; *Hangsaman,* 1951; *Life Among the Savages,* 1953; *The Bird's Nest,* 1954; *Raising Demons,* 1957; *The Sundial,* 1958; *The Bad Children: A Play in One Act for Bad Children,* 1959; *We Have Always Lived in the Castle,* 1963.

BIBLIOGRAPHY: Oppenheimer, Judy. *Private Demons: The Life of Shirley J.* 1988. Ragland, Martha. "Shirley

Jackson," *The Dictionary of Literary Biography,* vol. 6. 1980. "Shirley Jackson," *Contemporary Literary Criticism Online.* 1996.

MICHELLE CROWELL FOSSUM

JACQUES, Brian

Author, b. 15 June 1939, Liverpool, England

Say the name "Brian Jacques" in a roomful of literate twelve-year-olds and you'll hear the response, "Redwall," before your lips have stopped moving. The British author's following is extensive and devout. J.'s personal thread of truth has hit a powerful chord with his audience of young readers. "In the book *Mossflower,*" he says, "there is a little mouse called Gonff, the prince of mouse thieves. He's a good thief, full of fun with a good heart. He's probably the most like me, as a child. A survivor, that's what he is. And I was a survivor too."

Born in Liverpool, J. says he was "a ducker and a weaver," a blue-collar kid who grew up in the city and worked at the docks after school. "I wasn't an egghead," he says. "I used to box and swim, but I loved to read and movies were a big thrill, especially anything with cowboys and Indians." Even as a ten-year-old, J. reportedly had a mind for creative fiction. So vivid were his early stories that he was accused of plagiarism as a boy. He finished school at fifteen and set out to see the world as a merchant seaman. Once landlocked, he worked as everything from fireman to folksinger (with the Liverpool Fisherman) to playwright. His Redwall stories began as volunteer outreach for the visually impaired.

J. had a friend who ran the Royal Wavertree School for the Blind in Liverpool, so he frequented the classrooms. He sought to entertain the young students with lively stories, intricately told to bring to life settings they could not see except with their visual imagination. "I'd even get dressed up as Father Christmas in me cowboy boots and me big ten gallon hat to do it," he says. J.'s friend, the late Alan Durban (an English teacher), encouraged him to publish the tales. Finally, filmmaker Willie Russell *(Educating Rita)* submitted the manuscripts to a British publishing house, where they were accepted and published in 1986—a year later in the U.S. Pleased, but not overwhelmed, J. assumed the life of Redwall would follow his seven books of published poetry's quiet pattern of success. "I thought, 'Nice, but small,'" J. says. "Then it turned out to be like Topsy. It just sort of [grew]."

Today, the Redwall adventures are bestsellers with a following that grows as young readers do—often passed down generation-to-generation, sibling-to-sibling. Framed by the classic battle between good and evil, J. never spares the violence or consequences of such a struggle in his Redwall titles. He makes no apology for his realism, and his readers consistently thank him. "They're real," says fourteen-year-old Vanessa, who discovered Redwall thanks to her eighteen-year-old cousin Doug's fervent recommendations. "And the female characters are as smart and tough as the boys." Mariel, a favorite from *Mariel of Redwall* (1991), is a feisty female mousechild who survives being cast overboard while shipbound and sets out to exact her revenge.

Beyond violence, J. infuses his stories with loyalty, bravery, kindness, greed, and other human strengths and weaknesses, page after page after page. Indeed, his creations frequently exceed four hundred pages. But his faithful readers do not complain: "More swashbuckling to love," they readily answer.

J. has stepped beyond Redwall in some recent endeavors, including *Castaways of the Flying Dutchman* (2001) and *The Angel's Command* (2003)—tales that follow young Ben and his dog Ned across the high seas. But his Redwall tales remain his most enduring offering to date.

J. lives in his beloved Liverpool with his own dog, Teddy. His sons and granddaughter live nearby and regularly listen to the author's weekly radio program, Jakestown, on BBC Radio. His website, www.redwall.org, is one of the most popular online forums for young readers, worldwide.

AWARDS: 1987 ALA Best Book for Young Adults; 1987 School Library Journal Best Book; 1987 Parents' Choice Honor Book for Literature; West Australian Young Readers Book Awards; (1990, 1991, 1992, 1997); 1998 Audie Award for Audio books.

FURTHER WORKS: *Mossflower,* 1988; *Mattimeo,* 1989; *Salamandastron,* 1992; *Martin the Warrior,* 1993; *The Bellmaker,* 1994; *The Outcast of Redwall,* 1995; *Great Redwall Feast,* 1996; *Pearls of Lutra,* 1996; *The Long Patrol,* 1997; *Marlfox,* 1998; *The Legend of Luke,* 1999; *Lord Brockree,* 2000; *Taggerung,* 2001; *A Redwall Winter's Tale,* 2001; *Triss: A Tale from Redwall,* 2002; *Loamhedge: A Tale from Redwall,* 2003; *The Ribbajack and Other Curious Yarns,* 2004; *Rakkety Tam,* 2004; *High Rhulain,* 2005.

BIBLIOGRAPHY: Brian Jacques official website: http://www.redwall.org/dave/jacques.html; A Conversation with Brian Jacques Random House UK Interview; Personal interview with Brian Jacques for Kids Reads; Penguin Putnam, Face-To-Face with Brian Jacques.

KELLY MILNER HALLS

JANECZKO, Paul

Poet, anthologist, b. July 1945, Passaic, New Jersey

A former high-school English teacher, J. turned his enthusiasm for POETRY into a full-time job as poet and anthologist. His first collection, *Crystal Image* (1977), came from the sheaves of mimeographed poems J. had shared with his English classes. A wide array of other anthologists followed quickly. J. found time along the way to write books of poetry, some nonfiction books about a variety of subjects, plus some professional books about teaching poetry to children and young adults. J.'s aim is to provide TEENS with poems that speak to them and to their world; he wants each poem in his collection to be within the experience of the adolescent. Including poems with humor is another goal J. has for his volumes. J. is knowledgeable about adolescents through teaching and parenting.

Following *Crystal Image*, (1977) J. produced several other anthologies of poetry. *Postcard Poems* (1979) was recognized in 1980 as one of the New York Public Library's Books for the Teen Age. J.'s next collection, *Don't Forget to Fly: A Cycle of Modern Poems* (1981), was also named to this list. Additionally, the book was added to the Best Books for Young Adults (BBYA) list from YOUNG ADULT LIBRARY SERVICES ASSOCIATION of the American Library Association. J. produced a nonfiction book *Loads of Codes and Secret Ciphers* (1981) next, showing readers how codes have been used to communicate secretly as well as to send messages when other forms of communication were not possible (i.e., flag code used to communicate between ships, Morse Code, etc.).

Poetspeak: In their Words, about Their Work (1983), *Strings: A Gathering of Family Poems* (1984), and *Pocket Poems: Poems Selected for a Journey* (1985) were also BBYA winners. *Poetspeak* marked a bit of a departure for anthologies; in addition to using contemporary poems, J. added a new dimension to the collection by including photographs of the contributors and inviting the poets to comment on their works. Readers could see some of the inspiration for the poems; they could catch a glimpse of the creative process.

Going Over to Your Place: Poems for Each Other (1987) and *The Music of What Happens: Poems that Tell Stories* (1988) were also named to the BBYA list. His next two works, an original collection *Brickyard Summer* (1989) and *The Place My Words are Looking For: What Poets Say about and through their Work* (1990), both received many literary honors. In 1993, J.'s second book of original poetry, *Stardust Otel,* was published. A collaboration with fellow poet and anthologist Naomi Shihab NYE led to *I Feel a Little Jumpy Around You* (1996). This anthology presented readers with pairs of poems about the same topic, one each from the male and female perspective. *That Sweet Diamond: Baseball Poems* (1998) was the third of J.'s original collections to be published.

J. has also written several volumes for teachers and students about writing, reading, and understanding poetry. *Poetry from A–Z* (1994) and *How to Write Poetry* (1999) deal with writing poetry in many forms. *Seeing the Blue Between* (2002) presents a collection of poems from contemporary poets. Following the poem(s) is a letter of advice from the poet to the reader interested in learning more about writing poetry. *Opening a Door: Reading Poetry in the Middle School* (2003) presents lessons on using poetry with adolescents in a classroom setting.

All of J.'s writing mirrors his passion in life: making poetry accessible to all readers. J. spends about fifty days each year in classrooms conducting poetry workshops with children of all ages. Additionally, he makes presentations about the power of poetry to gatherings of educators across the country.

SELECT AWARDS: *Postcard Poems* (1980): New York Public Library Books for the Teen Age; *Don't Forget to Fly* (1981): New York Public Library Books for Young Adults, YALSA BBYA; *Poetspeak* (1983), *Strings* (1984), *Pocket Poems* (1985), *Going Over to Your Place* (1987), *The Music of what Happens* (1988): YALSA BBYA; *Brickyard Summer* (1989), Lupine Award for the Maine Library Association; *The Place My Words are Looking For* (1990): IRA/CBC Children's Choices (1990), Horn Book Fanfare Award, Best of the BBYA lists; *I Feel a Little Jumpy Around You* (1996), 1996 BBYA list; *Stone Bench in an Empty Park* (2001), NYPL Books for Teen Age 2000, 2001.

FURTHER WORKS: *This Delicious Day,* 1987; *Preposterous: Poems of Youth,* 1991; *Looking for your Name,* 1993; *Poetry from A–Z: A Guide for Young Writers,* 1994; *Wherever Home Begins: 100 Contemporary Poems,* 1995; *Home on the Range: Cowboy Poems,* 1997; *Very Best (Almost) Friends: Poems of Friendship,* 1999; *Dirty Laundry Pile: Poems in Different Voices,* 2001; *Blushing Expressions of Love in Poems and Letters,* 2004; *Worlds Afire,* 2004; *Top Secret: A Handbook of Codes, Ciphers and Secret Writing,* 2004; *A Kick in the Head: An Everyday Guide to Poetic Forms,* 2005; *A Poke in the I: A Collection of Concrete Poems,* 2005.

BIBLIOGRAPHY: www.authors4teens.com; http://www.authorsontheweb.com/features/0204-poet/kid-poet-authors.asp

TERI S. LESESNE

JARVIS, Robin

Author, b. 1964, Liverpool, England

J. writes spine-tingling tales of magic, HORROR, adventure, and FANTASY, with a sprinkling of MYTHOLOGY. It never occurred to him that he would be an author, but, since 1988, his time has been occupied writing and illustrating novels for children and young adults.

As a child in England, J. avidly read and re-read books by Lucy Boston, author of *The Green Knowe* SERIES, Alan Garner who wrote *The Weirdstone of Brisingamen,* and J. R. R. TOLKIEN's *Lord of the Rings.* He received a degree in Graphic Design from Newcastle Polytechnic and later worked as a model maker in television and advertising. He was working on a model of a huge, furry, green alien and began doodling pictures of small mice during his break. Encouraged by a friend, he showed his sketches to a publisher who inquired if he had a story to go with them. J. decided to give writing a try and wrote *The Dark Portal; Book One of the Deptford Mice Trilogy.* Published in England in 1989, it was a thrilling success and became runner-up for the Smarties Award given to an outstanding children's book. J.'s full-time career as an author and illustrator was launched.

Two more novels completed his animal-fantasy trilogy and he also wrote *The Deptford Histories.* The series of three prequels explore the events and characters that lead up to the Deptford Mice stories. Through this experience J. realized that drawing was as important as inspiration for his stories because by sketching he was better able to understand and know the personalities of his characters.

The Whitby Witches, a sophisticated trilogy, never ceases to surprise the reader. It involves two orphans, a mysterious black dog, dark forces, and fantastical creatures called Aufwaders. One of the characters, Miss Boston, is named in honor of J.'s favorite childhood author, Lucy Boston. J.'s drawing of his childhood teddy bear wearing dog tags was the inspiration for *The Woven Path; Book One of the Wyrd Museum Trilogy.* In this tale of time travel, a young boy, a sinister and magical museum, and a trio of aging mysterious sisters, interact with a teddy bear possessed by the soul of a deceased World War II U.S. airman. In real life, J. is afraid of spiders, wood lice, and other crawling creatures; he seems to confront his fears by creating Belial, a giant cockroach as another character. The story is continued in two more suspenseful novels, and undoubtedly he will write more in this series.

A deep forest is the setting for another series that begins with the book *Thorn Ogres of Hagwood.* Creatures called werlings practice the art of "wergling" or shape shifting. Celtic mythology, a golden casket, a hideous queen called Frightie Aggie, and monstrous Thorn Ogres blend to create a fantasy of adventure and horror. *The Dark Waters of Hagwood* continues the series.

SCIENCE FICTION and fantasy combine in *Deathscent; Intrigues of the Reflected Realm.* J. creates a stunning world of floating isles high in the sky where animals do not exist and simple machine-like creatures service humans.

J. creates all the illustrations for his books. In the UK, covers are done collaboratively with a graphic designer and, in the U.S., by another illustrator. J. believes that everyone deserves to escape the real world once in awhile and hopes his suspenseful books provide a retreat for the reader. He resides in Greenwich, London.

AWARDS: Nominated for Smarties Book Prize, 1989, and Booklist Editor's Choice, 2000, *The Dark Portal;* Lancashire Libraries Children's Book of the Year Award, *The Whitby Witches;* Lancashire County Libraries Children's Book of the Year Award Runner-up, and nominated for Young Telegraph/Fully Booked Children's Paperback of the Year, both 1996, West Australia Young Readers Book Award, *The Woven Path;* 100 Best Books 1998, *The Raven's Knot.*

FURTHER WORKS: *Alchymist's Cat,* 1989; *A Warlock in Whitby,* 1992; *The Oaken Throne,* 1993; *The Whitby Child,* 1994; *Thomas,* 1995; *The Raven's Knot,* 1997; *The Fatal Strand,* 1998; *Deathscent,* 2001; *The Crystal Prison,* 2001; *The Final Reckoning,* 2002; *Thorn Ogres of Hagwood,* 2002; *Dark Waters of Hagwood,* 2004.

BIBLIOGRAPHY: Jarvis, Robin. Robin Jarvis.com; 1989–2003. 07 Apr. 2003; http://www.robinjarvis.com/homepage.html; Paskins, Stella. "Authors . . . An Interview With Robin Jarvis." 2003; http:www harpercollins.co.uk/Authors/Interview.aspx?id = 54& aid = 2914; "Robin Jarvis; Author of Woven Path." 2003; http://www.troll.com/product/features/woven path.html.

KATE NAGY

JENKINS, A.M. (Amanda McRaney)
Author, b. 16 December 1961, Fort Worth, Texas

Authors such as S. E. HINTON and J. K. ROWLING likely use initials at their publishers' request, so that their books would attract male readers. J. purposely requested using only initials so that the writer's gender would not be obvious from the book cover. J. had often watched boys bypass books because they were not written by a male.

J. was born and raised in Texas and currently resides with three sons and a host of animals, including dogs, cats, fish, and gerbils.

J. had just about given up on her dream of writing when she learned she had won the Delacorte Press Award for a First Young Adult Novel, *Breaking Boxes* (1997). In *Breaking Boxes,* J. captures the raw language and emotions of a male adolescent, as she also does in her other books. The story is told in the first person by Charlie, a sixteen-year-old, who has boxed up his feelings of anger, loss, and TEENAGE angst. Charlie's father left long ago, his mother died of alcoholism, and his older, homosexual brother, Trent, is now raising him. Charlie makes friends with Brandon at school, only this friendship is challenged when Brandon finds out Trent is gay. These young men must learn how to deal with their emotions, anger, friendships, relationships, and other typical teenage issues.

J. writes in the second person for her next novel, *Damage* (2001). Still taking on tough issues such as homosexuality, J. addresses depression and suicide in this novel. Austin should have it all—he's popular, a

football player, has good friends, and also has a beautiful girlfriend. Austin, however, suffers from depression and struggles to make it day-to-day. Although he lost his father at a young age to cancer, J. deftly shows that depression does not result from a single event. Austin's girlfriend, Heather, is also dealing with depression, but when Austin reveals his desire to kill himself, she leaves him. J. once again captures typical high-school struggles and relationships.

J. continues with high-school struggles in *Out of Order* (2003), with Colt, a baseball star who has problems in school. Colt hates high school but likes its social order, where he feels he is at the top of the social circle. He loves baseball and his very intelligent girlfriend, Grace. When his mother decides he can only play baseball if he brings his grades up, Colt asks Corinne, a green-haired outcast, to tutor him in English. Readers will enjoy and probably relate to this story of fitting in.

Readers have taken to the raw, but poetic, writing of J. and have much to look forward to in future YA novels. A forthcoming novel, *Beating Heart: A Ghost Story* will be part third-person novel and part prose. One of main characters is a teenage male, and another is a girl who is no longer living.

AWARDS: Delacorte Press Prize for First Young Adult Novel for *Breaking Boxes* (1997); California Young Readers Medal and ALA Popular Paperbacks for *Breaking Boxes* (2000); ALA Best Books for Young Adults for *Damage* (2002) and *Out of Order* (2004).

BIBLIOGRAPHY: Interview with J., June 2004; *Publishers Weekly, VOYA, Kirkus Reviews, School Library Journal.*

TINA HERTEL

JIANG, Ji-li
Author, b. 3 February 1954, Shanghai, China

A daughter of actors and the eldest of three children, J. grew up surrounded by books, music, and movies, and was an accomplished student with a promising future in Chairman Mao's New China. However, with the advent of the Cultural Revolution in 1966, J. and her family fell out of favor with government officials when their status was changed from "red" (meaning "good") to "black" (meaning "evil"). Because one of her grandfathers—already dead thirty years—had been a landowner, J. and her family were subjected to persecution, terror, arrest, and public humiliation. J. was no longer able to attend her prestigious school and participate in events, and was asked to publicly renounce her parents, which she refused to do. The ordeals of her difficult adolescence were later detailed in her award-winning AUTOBIOGRAPHY, *Red Scarf Girl: A Memoir of the Cultural Revolution* (1997).

After the Cultural Revolution ended in 1976, J., harboring dreams of becoming an actress, applied to the Shanghai Drama Institute, but was denied an audition because of her family's background. Following this disappointment, J. attended and graduated from Shanghai Teachers' College and Shanghai University. Arriving in the U.S. in 1984, she lived with an American family in Hawaii, who inspired her interest in autobiography when they gave her a copy of *The Diary of Anne Frank*. J. earned a B.A. from the University of Hawaii at Manoa in 1987, and in the process of building a successful career in hotel management, she "realized then how little some Americans knew about China and the Chinese people. [She] made up my mind to write [her] story immediately."

Published in 1997, *Red Scarf Girl* has been praised for its "undidactic approach," vivid and lively writing style, and "heart-pounding" rendering of a horrifying event with which many Americans are unfamiliar. The novel was awarded several top literary prizes and has been translated into five foreign languages.

J. is the founder and current president of East West Exchange Inc. Located in Emeryville, California, where J. resides, the corporation promotes and facilitates cultural and business exchanges between China and Western countries. A popular speaker at schools, conferences, and conventions, J. has been invited to share her story throughout the U.S.

AWARDS: *Red Scarf Girl:* 1997 Notable Children's Trade Book in the Field of Social Studies from the National Council for the Social Studies, 1997 *Booklist* Books for Youth Editors' Choice, 1997 *Publishers Weekly* Best Book, 1997 *Voice of Youth Advocates* Books in the Middle: Outstanding Title, 1997 *VOYA* Nonfiction Honor List, 1997 Bay Area Book Reviewers Association Award for Children's Literature, 1998 Parents' Choice Gold Award, 1998 Judy Lopez Memorial Award, 1998 ALA Notable Children's Book, 1998 ALA Best Book for Young Adults, 1997 ALA Book Links Lasting Connections Book, 1998; *The River Bank Review* Book of Distinction; ALA Popular Paperbacks, 2003.

BIBLIOGRAPHY: *Booklist*, Oct. 1, 1997, p. 331; *Contemporary Authors*, online, 2001; Ji-li Jiang's personal website at www.jilijiang.com; *Publishers Weekly,* July 28, 1997, pp. 75–76; *Publishers Weekly,* Nov. 10, 1997, p. 28

ANDREA WONG

JIMENEZ, Francisco
Author, b. 29 June 1943, San Pedro Tlaquepaque, Mexico

J. is the author of children's books, YOUNG ADULT literature, and scholarly works. Groundbreaking drama unfolds concerning his family's migration to California when J. was four-years old. Their compelling quest to overcome extreme poverty throughout his childhood and young adult life has produced inspiring fiction. His ever-present worry over discovering that some family members were illegal immigrants was expressed as, "I lived in constant fear for ten long years, from the time I was four until I was fourteen years old" (CCBC Choices, 2001).

His inability to understand English resulted in failure in first grade. With the help of teachers and a vocabulary notebook in his pocket for memorizing words, J. overcame the language barrier. He received a B.A. at Santa Clara University, M.A. and Ph.D. from Columbia University in 1969 and 1972. He is a professor of modern languages and literature at Santa Clara University and served as director of the university's Division of Arts and Humanities in the College of Arts and Sciences. He taught at Harvard, Stanford, and Notre Dame.

J. published textbooks on the Spanish language and edited anthologies of Latin writers before chronicling his own experiences. His collection of eleven stories became the multiple award-winning book, *The Circuit: Stories from the Life of a Migrant Child.* The sequel, *Breaking Through,* has also won numerous awards. With these works, J. realized his desire to give voice to the experiences of a large sector of our society that had been underrepresented. He writes "with simplicity about a harsh world seldom seen in children's books" (*Booklist* 2001).

AWARDS: 1997 Americas Award, for *The Circuit;* and 1998 John & Patricia Beatty Award; 1999 *The Circuit Stories from the Life of a Migrant Child,* ALA Best Books for Young Adults; 2001 Tomas Rivera Mexican American Children's Book Award; 2001 Americas Award for Children's and Young Adult Literature; 2001 Smithsonian Magazine's Notable Books for

Children; 2002 ALA-YALSA Best Books for Young Adults; 2002 Pura Belpre Award Honor Book; *Booklist* Editor's Choice for Older Readers; CCBC (Cooperative Children's Book Center) Choices Award.

FURTHER WORKS: *Chicano Literature: Sources and Themes,* 1974; (editor) *Identification and Analysis of Chicano Literature,* 1978; (editor) *Poverty and Social Justice: Critical Perspectives: A Pilgrimage Toward Our Own Humanity,* 1997; *La Mariposa ("The Butterfly"),* 1998; *Cajas de Carton* (with Luis Leal), 2002.

BIBLIOGRAPHY: CCBC (Children's Cooperative Book Center Choices), 2002; Rochman, Hazel, *Booklist,* Sep. 1, 2001 (Vol. 98, No. 1). Children's Literature Comprehensive Database: http://clcd.odyssi.com/member/csearch.htm Retrieved 11/2/03; *Something about the Author,* volume 108, 2002.

JANET MARTHA DUSCHACK

JOHNSON, Angela
Author, b. 18 June 1961, Tuskegee, Alabama

J. is a versatile AFRICAN AMERICAN author who has achieved great success writing PICTURE BOOKS, POETRY, SHORT STORIES, and novels. J.'s main contribution to YOUNG ADULT literature is her many outstanding novels. J.'s novels stand out for their distinct characterizations and emotional power. Her realistic FAMILY stories deal with tough issues such as adoption, caring for elderly family members, coping with the DEATH of a loved one, and TEEN parents. She addresses these topics sensitively and thoughtfully, in ways that are believable, hopeful, and sometimes humorous.

Born in Tuskegee, Alabama, J. grew up in Ohio in a multigenerational family in which storytelling was a popular activity. J. attended Kent State University and later worked in child development with Volunteers in Service to America. She published her first picture book, *Tell Me a Story, Mama* in 1989. She decided that year to pursue writing as a full-time career.

J. wrote six more picture books before publishing her first novel *Toning the Sweep* (1993). This novel tells the story of three generations of African American women trying to cope with the inevitable death of a beloved grandmother who has terminal cancer. Told through the eyes of the fourteen-year-old narrator Emmie, the novel is a poignant, powerful story of love, loss, and the importance of family. *Toning the Sweep* was one of the first of many novels in which J. demonstrated her outstanding skill in depicting the rich and deep complexities of family dynamics.

Humming Whispers (1995) tells the story of fourteen-year-old Sophy, an aspiring dancer who fears she will become like her older sister Nicole who suffers from schizophrenia. *Songs of Faith* (1998), tells the story of thirteen-year-old Doreen who desperately misses her divorced father and is struggling to come to terms with disturbing changes in her family life. In 1999, J. became only the second author to win the Coretta Scott King Author Award and Author Honor Award in the same year. J. received the Author Award for *Heaven* (1998), a coming-of-age story about fourteen-year-old Marley whose seemingly perfect life in the small town of Heaven is disrupted when she discovers her father and mother are not her real parents. *The Other Side: Shorter Poems* (1998), the King Honor Book, is a collection of AUTOBIOGRAPHICAL poems about life in a small rural community, an affectionate recollection of childhood, family, and community.

In 2004, J. was awarded both the Coretta Scott King Author Award and the Michael L. PRINTZ Award for Excellence in Young Adult Literature for her novel, *The First Part Last* (2003), the story of Bobby, an African American teenage boy who copes with the changes that come to his life when he becomes a father and must care for his baby daughter. The story is particularly notable for the way it shatters societal stereotypes of African American teenage fathers. Instead of abandoning responsibility, Bobby embraces it and works hard to be a good father to his baby daughter.

In 1993, J. became one of a handful of authors of children's and young adult books to receive a prestigious MacArthur Foundation Fellowship.

SELECT AWARDS: ALA BBYA 1994, 2004, 2005; ALA Popular Paperbacks, 2003.

FURTHER WORKS: *Gone from Home: Short Takes* (1998); *Running Back to Luddie* (2001); *Looking for Red* (2002); *A Cool Moonlight* (2003); *Bird* (2004).

BIBLIOGRAPHY: Smith, Henrietta, ed. *The Coretta Scott King Awards Book, 1970–1999; Something about the Author,* volume 102 (1999), pp. 124–128.

EDWARD T. SULLIVAN

JOHNSON, Julie
Author, n.d., n.p.

J.'s first book, *Hidden Victims: An Eight-Stage Healing Process for Families and Friends of the Mentally Ill* (1988), and her second book, *Understanding Mental Illness: For Teens Who Care about Someone with Mental Illness* (1989), both make use of her M.S.W. degree. Her background as a psychotherapist would also come into play with her next titles, *Celebrate You: Building Your Self-esteem* (1991) and *Making Friends Finding Love* (1992). *Celebrate You: Building Your Self-esteem* draws on both J.'s own problems as a TEEN, as well as her counseling experiences.

J. seeks knowledge from many cultures, and has been to Bali and Australia on her quest. She has meditated since she was in her own teens, and includes that as one of her suggestions in *The Thundering Years: Rituals and Sacred Wisdom for Teens* (2001). Drawing on a variety of passage rituals, she seeks to guide teens through a tumultuous time in their lives. The book won the 2002 Independent Publisher Book Award for Multicultural Juvenile Nonfiction. The *I Ching for Teens: Take Charge of Your Destiny with the Ancient Chinese Oracle* (2001) represents more of J.'s attempts to connect teens with various cultures and rituals. *Teen Psychic: Exploring Your Intuitive Spiritual Powers* (2003) encourages teens to use their intuition fully as she shares tales of intuition throughout the ages.

J. spent her childhood and YA years in Madison, Wisconsin, and lived in Minneapolis, Minnesota, before moving to where she currently resides in Spring Green, Wisconsin, with her partner and their daughter. She does sessions on Intuitive Empowerment, Opening up to the Teen Psyche, the Unleashed Writer (Creative Writing), and Meditation.

BIBLIOGRAPHY: www.amazon.com; www.circlesanctuary.org/circle/articles/miscellaneous/ZenofTeen.html.

JEANNE MARIE RYAN

JOHNSON, Scott
Author, b. 23 November 1952, Chicago, Illinois

Graduating with honors, J. earned a B.A. from Indiana University in 1974. He then went on to graduate with a M.F.A. in 1978 from the University of Massachusetts. He uses his twenty-four years of experience as a high-school English and creative writing teacher in Pleasantville, New York to fine-tune his ability to understand and write about adolescents. As he writes, J. reflects on his own life and events that happened during his adolescence. He is able to examine these memories and share his insights and lessons he has learned with today's youth.

J. grabs his readers' interest, bringing them into the story as they identify and emphasize with the characters' thoughts, feelings, and emotions. Each main character must overcome adversity and learn some tough lessons in life. Friends and family members are naturally affected by these experiences as well. Sometimes, making the right decision and following the right path is as close as meeting the nearest stranger; in *One of the Boys* (1992), the main character, Eric, must overcome peer pressure and evaluate the meaning of true friendship. In deciding what his moral beliefs are, he affects future decisions that must be made. In J.'s book, *Safe at Second* (2001), all future major-league career goals for the main character, Todd Bannister, appear to be eliminated when a line drive causes him to lose an eye. His injury and gradual adjustment to his glass eye causes Todd's relationships with everyone to change dramatically. He gradually discovers his newfound inner strength and courage, learning to see his world through a different outlook of overcoming obstacles.

In addition to writing, J. enjoys the outdoors as a member of the Sierra Club and Nature Conservancy. This love of nature and care for the environment complements his enjoyment of backpacking, hiking, and bicycling. In his free time, he plays acoustic guitar and mandolin. J., the father of three boys, lives with his wife, Susan, in Mahopac, New York.

AWARDS: ALA "Best Books for Young Adults" (1993) for *One of the Boys;* ALA "Best Books of 1999," School Library Journal's "Best Books for Young Adults" (1999), ALA "Best Books for Young Adults" (2000) and "Quick Picks for Reluctant Young Readers" (2000) for *Safe at Second.*

FURTHER WORK: *Overnight Sensation,* 1994.

BIBLIOGRAPHY: *Contemporary Authors Online,* Gale, 2003. Reproduced in *Biography Resource Center,* 2003. http://www.galenet.com/servlet/BioRC.

VALERIE A. PALAZOLO

JOHNSTON, Julie
Author, b. 21 January 1941, Smiths Falls, Ontario

J. studied physical and occupational therapy at the University of Toronto and worked in that field in the

1960s. Settling in Peterborough, Ontario, J. attended Trent University, where she received a B.A. in Honors English (1984) and an Honorary Doctorate of Literature (1996). She began her formal writing career in 1978, concentrating on articles, essays and SHORT STORIES that were published in various CANADIAN and British MAGAZINES. Her plays, *There's Going to be a Frost* (winner of The Canadian Playwriting Competition in 1979) and *Lucid Intervals,* both won awards in the Sears Festival. J. completed her first novel, *Hero of Lesser Causes,* in 1986; it was published in 1992 and was awarded the Governor General's Award. When J.'s equally popular and successful second novel, *Adam and Eve and Pinch-Me,* was also awarded the Governor General's Award in 1994, she became the first writer to have both a first and second novel receive this top award. J.'s third novel, *The Only Outcast,* published in 1998, was followed in 2001 by *In Spite of Killer Bees.*

Hero of Lesser Causes depicts narrator Keely Connor's attempts to encourage her brother, Patrick Connor, when he contracts polio during a summer heat wave in 1946. J.'s education and experience in the field of physio-occupational therapy provide the background that establishes this novel so firmly in an accurate emotional and physical context. Inspiring and believable, Keely's determination is set in an Ottawa Valley conveyed by J. as having "more to it than geography." Sara Moone, the narrator of *Adam and Eve and Pinch-Me* and another inhabitant of J.'s evocative Ontario landscape, shares with Patrick feelings of anger and resentment for the events in her life that have left her withdrawn and suspicious. J.'s inclusion of humor establishes a tone that works well to depict the sorrow and bitterness of these young characters. Making use of a historical DIARY of a sixteen-year old boy's 1904 summer visit to Rideau Lake, *The Only Outcast* follows Fred Dickinson as he struggles with the loss of his mother and the presence of an intolerant father. In *Love Ya Like A Sister: A Story of Friendship* J. edited the journals, letters and e-mails written by Katie Ouriou, a sixteen-year old from Calgary, who died of leukemia while living in France with her family.

J.'s adolescent characters suffer more extreme losses and misfortunes than most of her young readers will ever experience. The emotional suffering, perseverance, and recovery, however, are credible; J. is willing to deal honestly and directly with the psy-chological results of the situations endured by her characters. Readers respond to the characters' determination and compassion because these qualities are not inherent but are realistically gained in the midst of feelings of defeat and hopelessness. J.'s adept use of humor and her accurate depictions of Ontario landscapes and towns provide the tone and the space that render her characters and their feelings both familiar and universal.

AWARDS: *There's Going to be a Frost:* Canadian Playwriting Competition, 1979, Sears Festival; *Lucid Intervals,* Sears Festival; Governor General's Literary Award for Children's Literature in English, (1992) *Hero of Lesser Causes,* (1994) *Adam and Eve and Pinch-Me;* Joan Fassler Memorial Book Award (USA), the National Chapter of Canada IODE Violet Downey Book Award, Canadian Library Association Young Adult Honour Book, 1993, *Hero of Lesser Causes;* Ruth Schwartz Children's Book Award (Young Adult/Middle Reader category), Young Adult Canadian Book Award (Canadian Library Association), 1995 for *Adam and Eve and Pinch-Me;* The Globe and Mail's Selection of the Best Young Adult Book, 1998, *The Only Outcast;* Society of School Librarians' International Honour Book, Mr. Christie's Silver Seal Book Award Winner, Manitoba Young Readers' Choice Award, 2002, *In Spite of Killer Bees;* Vicki Metcalf Award, 2003.

FURTHER WORKS: Screenplay of *Hero of Lesser Causes,* 1994; "Sorry for the Delay," *Books in Canada,* 1994; "Mirrors," *Blue Jean Collection,* 1992; "The Interior of Pots," *Matrix,* 1992; *In Spite of Killer Bees,* 2000; *Susanna's Quill,* 2004.

BIBLIOGRAPHY: *Canadian Who's Who,* 2002; Baker, Deirdre and Ken Setterington, *A Guide to Canadian Children's Books,* 2003; Little, Jean, "Julie J.: An Exciting New Voice," *Canadian Children's Literature* 77(1995): 33–38; CANSCAIP Member page http://www.canscaip.org/bios/johnstonj.html; Writers Union of Canada Member page http://www.writersunion.ca/j/johnston.htm; National Library of Canada's entry on Julie J. http://www.nlc-bnc.ca/read-up-on-it/t11-6043-e.html; Canadian Children's Book Centre's entry on Julie J. http://collections.ic.gc.ca/ggawards/johnsto2.htm; Trent University English Department Alumni Comments http://www.trentu.ca/english/alumni.html#johnston.

MARGARET STEFFLER

JOHNSTON, Norma

Author, n.d., Ridgewood, New Jersey

Nicole St. John is known as J., as well as by the pseudonyms Lavinia Harris, Kate Chambers, Pamela

Dryden, Catherine E. Chambers, Elizabeth Bolton, and Adrian Robert. Although her full-time writing career started in 1972, J. has had a variety of other careers. These include a lingerie buyer for the family shop, a member of a fashion trade newsletter staff, a buyer's assistant in Boston, and the owner of a fashion boutique. She has also been an acting student at the American Theatre Wing in New York, a producer's assistant, and an actress in summer theater. She also spent time as an English teacher, a drama teacher, a writing teacher, an editor for a religious book publisher, and a youth counselor—which led to being producer and director of an interfaith drama company. J. holds a teaching certificate from Montclair State College.

J.'s first published novel, *The Wishing Star* (1963), which she wrote at sixteen, was named a Junior Literary Guild selection. A historical novel set in 1899, it was to be the first of her many historical novels. Drawing on her rich FAMILY history, with ancestors on both the maternal and paternal side who had been in the country over one hundred years before the U.S. was a separate country, was natural. J. used her paternal family tree for the Carlisle Chronicles characters, who were related to characters from the Keeping Days SERIES.

The Keeping Days series had two parts. The first is comprised of the original quartet of books: *The Keeping Days* (1974), *Glory in the Flower* (1974), *The Sanctuary Tree* (1977), and *A Mustard Seed of Magic* (1977). Set in the years from 1900–1902, it records the events of the Sterlings of West Farms, the Bronx, and their friends and neighbors, chronicled through the eyes of the second-oldest daughter, Tish, in her journal. The second part is set from 1917 to 1919 and is covered in *A Nice Girl Like You* (1981) and *Myself and I* (1981). The Sterling family is still at the center of the story, but now it is told through the eyes of the oldest grandchild, Tish's niece, Saranne Albright. Old situations and challenges intrude on the present, as do the new issues that World War I helps bring to a head. The Carlisle Chronicles (*Carlisle's Hope, To Jess, With Love and Memories,* and *Carlisles All*) (1986) deal with the complexities of family and friends, though in a more contemporary setting. Jess Carlisle grapples with the true meaning of her heritage over the course of the series.

Strangers Dark and Gold (1975), *Pride of Lions* (1979), and *The Days of the Dragon's Seed* (1982)

are a myth-based trilogy set in ancient Greece and Rome. In 1992, J. published *Louisa May: The World and Works of Louisa May Alcott.* She followed this with another BIOGRAPHY, *Harriet: The Life and World of Harriet Beecher Stowe* (1994) and in 1995 *Remember the Ladies: The First Women's Rights Convention.*

J. served as the first president of the Mid-Atlantic Chapter of Sisters in Crime, belongs to the International Sisters in Crime, the Mystery Writers of America, and the Authors Guild, and founded and chairs The Ngaio Marsh Society International. She has served as a chair of Rutgers University Council on Children's Literature. Her travels include Canada, England, Istanbul, and Mexico. Some of her travels are reflected in her books, as is the fact that she is a MYSTERY lover from a family of mystery lovers. J. lived in Ridgewood, New Jersey as a child—and still lives in the area. The houses in *Shadow of a Unicorn* and *Ready or Not* are based on her childhood home.

FURTHER WORKS: *The Wider Heart,* 1964; *Ready or Not,* 1965; *The Bridge Between,* 1966; *Of Time and Seasons,* 1975; *A Striving After Wind,* 1976; *The Swallow's Song,* 1978; *If You Love Me, Let Me Go,* 1978; *The Crucible Year,* 1979; *Timewarp Summer,* 1982; *Gabriel's Girl,* 1983; *Watcher in the Mist,* 1986; *Shadow of a Unicorn,* 1987; *Whisper of the Cat,* 1988; *Return to Morocco,* 1988; *The Potter's Wheel,* 1988; *The Delphic Choice,* 1989; *The Time of the Cranes,* 1990; *The Dragon's Eye,* 1990; *The Image Game,* 1994; *Lotta's Progress,* 1997; *Over Jordan,* 1999; *Feather in the Wind,* 2000.

BIBLIOGRAPHY: www.amazon.com; www.chipmunk crossing.com/aboutauthor/author.html; www.novelst4 .epnet.com; www.scils.rutgers.edu/~kvander/nicole .html

JEANNE MARIE RYAN

JONES, Diana Wynne
Author, b. 16 August 1934, London, England

J.'s early life was surprisingly influential on her future career as a FANTASY writer. Her childhood was disrupted by the outbreak of World War II, first as she and her sister were evacuated to Wales, later as the family moved again to the Lake District. After yet another brief move to Yorkshire, the family returned to London in 1942. In 1943, her parents moved the family again to Thaxted in Essex where they ran a residential school and are said to have ignored their own three daughters (J. was the oldest). Despite her dyslexia, J. found reading to be a source of escape and comfort during the bombings. At the age of eight, she announced her intention of becoming a writer, much to the amusement of her parents. With a dearth of reading material, J. was restricted mainly to the MYTHOLOGY and legend books available on the shelves of her parents' school. At Christmas, their father allowed the three sisters to choose one volume from a set of Arthur Ransome books, which was to be shared between them for the next year. The numerous relocations, the distant and unsympathetic father figure, and the need for self-sufficiency are all repetitive themes in J.'s work.

J.'s excellent grades gained her acceptance to St. Anne's College, Oxford in 1953. Here she was exposed to the Inklings, namely C. S. LEWIS and J. R. R. TOLKIEN. She attended lectures by both literary figures and was undoubtedly influenced by their ideas. She received a B.A. in 1956, and married John A. Burrow, a scholar of Middle English. Together they have three sons. Her desire to give her sons the books for which she had longed in her own childhood prompted J. to write. After ten years of rejected manuscripts, *Wilkin's Tooth* was published in 1973.

Alienated children and unpleasant fathers appear in both *Wilkin's Tooth* (published as *Witch's Business* in the U.S.) and *The Ogre Downstairs* (1974). Adults make life difficult for children by eliminating allowances or remarrying; although fathers may eventually be revealed to be misguided rather than evil, the children are forced to save themselves.

The "Dalemark Quartet" is distinctive for J.'s increased use of high-fantasy conventions. *Cart and Cwidder,* the first of the SERIES, appeared in 1975. The royal kingdom, which is saved and liberated by a combination of adventure and derring-do, is not J.'s normal territory. However, her self-sufficient street urchins and young royals who must learn to help themselves are recognizable as the distant relatives of the neglected or mishandled children in her previous books. *Drowned Ammet* (1978), The *Spellcoats* (1979), and *The Crown of Dalemark* (1995) revisit the characters and situations of *Cart.*

One of the distinctive characteristics in J.'s writing is her quirky sense of humor. The balance between comedy and tragedy is distinctly the violent orientation of late childhood. Giggles and terror are often juxtaposed, and a character in a ridiculous hat may move the reader to tears. Although sometimes off-putting to adults, TEEN readers recognize and identify with the manic emotions. It is the humorous elements that frequently keep the story rooted in the mundane world. In *Dogsbody* (1975), the exiled celestial being is forced to inhabit the body of a dog. The foibles of this character are lovably familiar and hilarious to any dog owner. This very familiarity serves to heighten the reader's sympathy for the pain of the exile; how could one not feel for one's silly family friend? Likewise, the Goon in *Archer's Goon* (1984) who lounges in the kitchen like any gigantic, thuggish teenaged brother is both funny and sad, and emphasizes the oddity of wizardly doings. Sophie supplies comic contrast to the spirit Calcifer and the wizard Howl in Howl's *Moving Castle* (1986) and *Castle in the Air* (1990). Sophie is condemned to care about silly hats. After she crosses the Witch of the Waste, Sophie receives a terrible punishment and is turned into an old woman. The situation is horrifying yet laughable. This trademark mix is perhaps best displayed in *Charmed Life* (1977) and *The Lives of Christopher Chant* (1988), in which principal character Chrestomanci embodies these contradictions and alternates between being exasperating, charming, manipulating, and victimized. Although *The Homeward Bounders* (1981) and *Fire and Hemlock* (1985) deal with more desperate and frightening situations, there are flashes of the same sense of humor.

More recently, J. returned to FAMILY dynamics with *Dark Lord of Derkholm* (1998) and *Year of the Griffin* (2001). Both involve the dynamics of a family in which a somewhat careless father provided himself with human and griffin children. By recognizing and using their disparate abilities, the siblings survive while saving their (ultimately) loving father. While neither of her other recent works, *Deep Secret* (1997) and *The Merlin Conspiracy* (2003) are intended solely for the YA audience, they feature TEENAGED protagonists who discover their place in sometimes bewildering, often frightening, magical worlds. Their lot is bearable due to the hilarity of their absurdly prosaic interactions with parents and guardians.

J. is a powerful writer who disguises her frightening psychological insights with an unusual sense of humor. Readers who have the pleasure of discovering her work will be rewarded by unexpected plot twists, unlikely characters, unanticipated laughter, and tantalizing thematic depths.

SELECT AWARDS: 1977 *Guardian* Award for Children's Books, *Charmed Life;* 1999 Mythopeic Award, Children's section; 1999 Karl Edward Wagner Award (British Fantasy Society).

SELECT FURTHER WORKS: *Charmed Life;* 1977; *The Magicians of Caprona,* 1980; *Witch Week,* 1982; *A Sudden Wild Magic,* 1994; *A Tale of Time City,* 2002; *Stopping for a Spell,* 2004; *Conrad,* 2005.

BIBLIOGRAPHY: *Dictionary of Literary Biography, Volume 161: British Children's Writers Since 1960, First Series,* 1996, pp. 225–32.

CATHY CHAUVETTE

JORDAN, June

Poet, essayist, activist, b 9 July 1936, New York; d 14 June 2002, Berkeley, California

At the time of her DEATH, J. was one of the most widely published AFRICAN-AMERICAN writers of her time. Her literary contributions, which include several dozen books of POETRY, plays, nonfiction, and children's literature, reflected her fervent drive to persevere in the face of racism and sexism.

Born in Harlem to West Indian parents Granville and Mildred Jordan, J.'s childhood after age five was spent in the Brooklyn neighborhood Bedford-Stuyvesant. Her father's physical abuse set the tone for her home life and later made its way into much of her adult writing. Between the years of 1953 and 1957, J. attended Barnard College and the University of Chicago. Her marriage to her white husband ended in 1965, leaving her to care for her son as a single working mother.

J.'s first poetry collection, *Who Look at Me,* was published in 1969. Some of her subsequent works are *Some Changes* (1971), *Thing That I Do in the Dark* (1977), *Living Room* (1985), and *Naming Our Destiny* (1989). As a both a poet and journalist, J. wrote about feminism and the struggles against racism, for freedom of choice, and the opportunity for minorities. Her essays are collected in the books *Civil Wars* (1981), *On Call* (1985), *Moving Towards Home* (1989), and *Technical Difficulties: African-American Notes on the State of the Union* (1992).

J. also made significant contributions to children's and YA literature during the 1970's. *His Own Where* (1971) drew on her personal childhood experience and was also a vehicle for her campaign for the recognition of the legitimacy of Black English. This work embraced Black English as a form of black cultural

expressionism. Among her other children's works are the BIOGRAPHY *Fannie Lou Hamer* (1972), *Dry Victories* (1972), and *New Life: New Room* (1975). J.'s refusal to sugarcoat the truth about racism and social injustices translates into honest and powerful literature for young people.

Starting in 1967 and up until her death in 2002, J. held academic positions at over seven universities, including City College of New York, Yale University, Sarah Lawrence College, and the University of California at Berkeley. Her work was published in numerous periodicals, namely the *Village Voice, New York Times, Ms., Essence,* and the *American Poetry Review.* Her work was also spotlighted on the stage, specifically in her play *The Issue* and *Bang Bang Uber Alles,* a musical for which she wrote the libretto.

AWARDS: 1969–1970 Rockefeller grant for creative writing; 1982 National Endowment for the Arts fellowship; 1984 Achievement Award for International Reporting from the National Association of Black Journalists; 1991 PEN Center USA West Freedom to Write Award; 1994 the Ground Breakers-Dream Makers award from The Woman's Foundation; Lila Wallace Reader's Digest Writers Award (1995–1998).

FURTHER WORKS: *SoulScript,* 1970; *The Voice of the Children* (co-edited by J.), 1970; *New Life: New Room,* 1975; *Passion, New Poems 1977–1980,* 1980; *Kimako's Story,* 1981; *Living Room,* 1985; *I Was Looking at the Ceiling and then I Saw the Sky,* 1995; *Kissing God Goodbye,* 1997; *Soldier: A Poet's Childhood,* 2000; *Some of Us Did Not Die,* 2002; *SoulScript: A Collection of Classic African American Poetry,* 2004.

BIBLIOGRAPHY: *Contemporary Literary Criticism* (2 vols.), 1976 and 1983; "June Jordan," in *Afro-American Writers After 1955: Prose Writers and Dramatists,* vol. 38 of *Dictionary of Literary Biography,* 1985; www.junejordan.com/bibliography.html.

RACHEL WITMER

JORDAN, Robert (pseud.)

Real name: James Oliver Rigney.
Other pseud.: Reagan O'Neal, Jackson O'Reilly, Chang Lung.
Author, b. 1948, Charleston, South Carolina

J.'s love affair with books began when his brother helped him learn to read at the age of four. After serving with the U.S. Army in Vietnam, where he earned the Distinguished Flying Cross and the Bronze Star,

J. studied at The Military College of South Carolina. Gaining a degree in physics, he worked for the U.S. Navy as a nuclear engineer. Hospitalized after a traffic accident, J. took up a long-held ambition of writing, first as a journalist and critic. Writing as Reagan O'Neal, he wrote the Fallon historical SERIES, as well as producing seven sequels to the Conan novels of Robert E. Howard, from *Conan the Invincible* (1982) to *Conan the Victorious* (1984). These proved an apprenticeship for J.'s major work.

With Mark Twain and Jules Verne among his favorite authors, J. has a keen interest in history, FANTASY, and SCIENCE FICTION. These enthusiasms come together in *The Eye of the World* (1990), the first volume of the Wheel of Time saga. The *New York Times* declared, "With the Wheel of Time, Jordan has come to dominate the world TOLKIEN began to reveal." Although this may be an overstatement, it accurately identifies J.'s readership.

While it may never achieve cult status, J.'s work offers a large cast engaged in sharply defined action against the forces of evil, in a world with a richly detailed history and MYTHOLOGY. Similar to Tolkien's Middle Earth, J.'s world has maps, its own calendar, and enough invented words and concepts to require a Glossary.

J. pits a seemingly undistinguished band of simple village folk against vast supernatural forces. Rand al' Thor first appears as a skinny boy shepherd declaring, "I'd like to be a king," to his friends Mat, Perrin, and Egwene. Then, even as monstrous Trollocs attack, Moraine of the Aes Sedai arrives to declare that Rand is the Dragon Reborn, the person who was born to save humanity. Their quest begins.

The great attraction of J.'s writing in the Wheel of Time saga is not his prose style (which is so bad that even his fans enjoy swapping awful examples) but the subtlety of the situation in which his characters find themselves. Good and evil are not easily distinguished, and motives are mixed within the battling groups. For example, the Children of the Light are certainly dedicated to the overthrow of the Dark Lord, but their arrogant belief that they alone are in the right, along with their brutal methods, has made them loathed as the Whitecoats. In another turn of time's cycle they may re-emerge as the Blackshirts.

The concept of time as cyclical and history as a repetition enables J. to incorporate aspects of many myths and legends, from Arthur to Atlantis. Celtic and Scandinavian influences are significant. In the past, humans like Lews Therin Telemon (the original Dragon) have defeated Shait'an, the Dark One, at great cost, but the source of evil has been unleashed again. J. believes that fantasy enables an author to deal directly with issues or right and wrong, good and evil.

The driving force of the True Source, which powers the Wheel of Time, can only be channeled by especially talented men and women. The Dark One has contaminated the "saidin" aspect of the power so that males who use it eventually become insane. This has tragic consequences for Rand, whose ability to be a unifying leader is undermined by his being constantly on the brink of madness.

The complementary power "saidar," used only by women, has enabled the creation of a powerful sisterhood of advisors, Aes Sedai, (similar to the Bene Gesserit Sisterhood of Frank HERBERT'S *Dune*) but some of them, the Forsaken, went over to the Dark One. Suspicion and distrust, therefore, limit the influence of the Aes Sedai. Threatened by invaders, magicians, monsters, and the lingering consequences of past wars, the kingdoms battle on, their desperate struggle to survive, making this a major fantasy epic.

The Wheel of Time may lack depth of characterization, the prose may be leaden and the story dragged out but J.'s narrative is powerful and readers' feelings are soon fully involved.

J. lives in an 18th-century house in Charleston with his wife Harriet and has declared his intention to continue writing until they nail shut his coffin.

FURTHER WORKS: CONAN SEQUELS: *Conan the Defender,* 1982; *Conan the Unconquered,* 1983; *Conan the Triumphant,* 1983; *Conan the Destroyer,* 1984; *Conan the Magnificent,* 1984; THE WHEEL OF TIME: *The Great Hunt,* 1990; *The Dragon Reborn,* 1991; *The Shadow Rising,* 1992; *The Fires of Heaven,* 1993; *Lord of Chaos,* 1994; *A Crown of Swords,* 1996; *The Path of Daggers,* 1998; *Winter's Heart,* 2000; *Crossroads of Twilight,* 2003; *New Spring,* 2004; FALLON SERIES (as Reagan O'Neal): *Fallon Blood,* 1980; *Fallon Pride,* 1981; *Fallon Legacy,* 1982.

BIBLIOGRAPHY: Clute, John and Grant John, *The Encyclopedia of Fantasy,* 1997; Jordan, Robert & Patterson, Teresa, *The World of Robert Jordan's The Wheel of Time,* 1997; [also bio notes from *The Path of Daggers* (1998).].

TREVOR AGNEW

JORDAN, Sherryl

Author, illustrator, b. 8 June 1949, Hawera, New Zealand

Known for her FANTASY and PICTURE BOOKS, J., a New Zealand author, has created gripping fantasy books for adolescents in addition to picture books for children. She has been a recipient of various awards and honors including those given by American Library Association and International Reading Association.

J. attended Taurange Girls' College in 1962–1964, and had two years of nursing training from 1967 to 1968. She was an illustrator for children's books (1980–1985), a part-time teacher's aide in primary schools, and worked with severely hearing impaired children (1979–1987). She began full-time writing in 1988. In 1993, she was invited to the University of Iowa as writer-in-residence.

J. showed a strong interest in writing and drawing since age ten. She started her literary career with picture books. *The Silent One* (1981) won a national competition for illustrations. Afterward, she gave up successful illustration work for writing. However, the road to success in publishing her books was torturous. After numerous picture books and novels were rejected, she was on the verge of giving up. When working on her 13th novel, she decided it would be a turning point for her to continue or leave writing. Fortunately, *A Time of Darkness* was not only published in 1990 but also given Virginia State Young Readers' Award. The debut novel, published in New Zealand as *Rocco,* portrays a TEENAGE boy's time travel to a prehistoric society.

In her second book, *The Juniper Game* (1991), J. tells the story of two teenagers' experiments in communicating through telepathic powers, with an unexpected connection with a young woman in the medieval age. In 1992 she published two books, *Wizard for a Day* and *Winter of Fire.* The former, part of the Denzil SERIES, is about wizards trapped in the past. In the books about time travel, J. explores the concept that time is not what it seems to be. *Winter of Fire* depicts a warrior-soul slave girl Elsha delivering her downcast race from the Chosen, the ruling class, in a frigidly cold world where the sun has vanished. Before working on this novel, she was incapacitated with Occupational Overuse Syndrome (OOS). Inspired by Elsha's unyielding spirit, J. took up the pen despite her doctor's advice to do otherwise. Her painful struggle of learning how to use her hands again parallels Elsha's grueling battle to improve her people's servile life as they toil endlessly in the coalfield.

J. writes other genres besides fantasy. *Wolf-woman* (1994, published in New Zealand as *Tanish*), delineates a feral child's longing for the wolves and her choice between staying with the warlike clan or returning to the wolf pack. In 1996, J. published *Secret Sacrament,* an absorbing story about Gabriel, whose witness of a tragic event at age seven influences his decision to become a healer and later to sacrifice himself to save a dying neighbor nation.

J. is also adept at crafting historical fiction. *The Raging Quiet* (1999) describes the friendship between a young widow and a deaf youth evolving into love amid the prejudice of cruel villagers. Her most recent book, *The Hunting of the Last Dragon* (2002), is about a young peasant's adventurous journey with a young Chinese noblewoman in 14th-century England.

Most of J.'s novels are fantasy, dealing with such themes as time travel, medieval ages, ancient society, and primitive people. The setting may be a distant place in an ancient time, yet her novels have rich details of the period and flavor of the place. As she states, most of her stories have been mysterious gifts to her, and they appear clearly, like movies in her head, sometimes scene-by-scene. J. has been inspired by these memory-like images of ancient time and place while creating all her novels since *The Juniper Game.*

AWARDS: *A Time of Darkness,* 1990, Virginia State Young Readers' Award; *The Raging Quiet,* 1999: IRA/CBC Young Adult Choice, YALSA, School Library Journal Best Books, Pacific Northwest Young Readers Choice Award, Bank Street School of Education Children's Book of the Year. All of her books published in the U.S. have made BBYA lists. *Winter of Fire,* 1994, BBYA; *Wolf-Woman,* 1995, BBYA ; *The Raging Quiet,* 2000, BBYA; *Secret Sacrament,* 2002, BBYA; *The Hunting of the Last Dragon,* 2003, BBYA.

FURTHER WORKS: *Telltale* (Joy *Cowley,* author), 1982; *Mouse* (Joy Cowley, author), 1983; *The Firewind and the Song* (self-illustrated), 1984; *Mouse Monster* (Joy Cowley, author), 1985; *Matthew's Monsters* (Dierdre Gardiner, illustrator), 1986; *No Problem Pomperoy* (Jan van der Voo, illustrator), 1988; *Kittens,* Short-lands, 1989; *The Wobbly Tooth,* 1989; *Babysitter Bear* (Trevor Pye, illustrator), 1990; *The Wednesday Wizard,* 1991; *Denzil's Dilemma,* 1992; *The Other Side of Midnight* (Bryan Pollard, illustrator), 1993; *Sign of the Lion,* 1995.

BIBLIOGRAPHY: *Author Profile: Sherryl Jordan.* [Online] Available: http://www.teenreads.com/authors; *Children's Literature Review.* [Online] Available: http://clcd.odyssi.com/cgi-bin/member; *Novelist.* [Online] Available: http://novest3.epnet.com/novel; *Something about the Author,* vol. 71, 1993; *Something about the Author,* vol. 122, 2001; *Something about the Author Autobiography Series,* vol. 23, 1997.

SHU-HSIEN L. CHEN

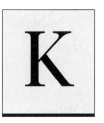

KARR, Kathleen
Author, b. 21 April 1946, Allentown, Pennsylvania

K. was born to Stephen and Elizabeth Csere, a mechanical engineer and a homemaker. The family lived on a chicken farm in New Jersey, where she learned the meaning of work. During free time from her chores, she found that reading and writing were perfect entertainment. K. also learned to rely upon her own imagination.

K. began submitting articles for publication while still in high school. While attending the Catholic University of America she became interested in film and film history. K. received a B.A. in 1968 from the Catholic University of America. She married Lawrence F. Karr, a physicist and computer consultant, on July 13, 1968. The couple has two children, Suzanne and Daniel. K. earned an M.A. in 1971 from Providence College and attended Corcoran School of Art in 1972. A brief attempt at teaching English proved that she did not want to have a career as a teacher. K. chose to work in film production, writing many articles on film history.

K. taught film and communications prior to beginning her career as an author of children's and YA books. She wrote her first adult novel, *Light of My Heart,* after her husband dared her to write something that she would enjoy. Eventually her children asked her to write a book for them. This first book was *It Ain't Always Easy,* published in 1990.

K.'s novels vary in time and location but always include humor, adventure, and suspense, as well as characters whose activities are filled with excitement and whose lives draw the reader into the story through the use of authentic details and well-rounded characterizations. K. says that she feels at home in other times and places, and she uses this to distinct advantage when she places her characters, plots, and settings in times past. Reviews of K.'s work emphasize and confirm her use of details to weave stories that are fast-paced and satisfying.

K. currently lives in Washington, D.C.

SELECT AWARDS: New York Public Library Books for the Teen Age, *The Cave; The Great Turkey Walk:* Notable Children's Trade Book in the Field of Social Studies, 1999 National Council for the Social Studies/ Children's Book Council, 1999 National Council of Teacher of English Notable Children's Book in the Language Arts; 2000 American Library Association Best Book for Young Adults selection, *Man of the Family; The Boxer:* Golden Kite Award, Notable Children's Trade Book in the Field of Social Studies, New York Public Library Books for the Teen Age selection, 2001 ALA Best Book for Young Adults.

SELECTED FURTHER WORKS: *Oh, Those Harper Girls! or, Young and Dangerous,* 1992; *Gideon and the Mummy Professor,* 1993; *The Cave,* 1994; *In the Kaiser's Clutch,* 1995; *Go West! Young Women,* 1996; *Phoebe's Folly,* 1996; *The Great Turkey Walk,* 1998; *Oregon, Sweet Oregon,* 1998; *Gold-Rush Phoebe,* 1998; *Spy in the Sky,* 1998; *The Lighthouse Mermaid,* 1998; *Man of the Family,* 1999; *The Boxer,* 2000; *It Happened in the White House: Extraordinary Tales from America's Most Famous Home,* 2000; *Skullduggery,* 2000; *Playing with Fire,* 2001; *Bone Dry,* 2002;

385

Mama Went to Jail for the Vote, 2000; *Dear Mr. President, Dwight D. Eisenhower: Letters from a Schoolgirl during the Red Scare,* 2002; *Fishing Day,* 2003; *Gilbert & Sullivan Set Me Free,* 2003; *The 7th Knot,* 2003; *Exiled: Memoirs of a Camel,* 2004; *Worlds Apart,* 2005.

BIBLIOGRAPHY: *Authors and Artists for Young Adults,* Gale, vol. 144, 2002; *Something about the Author,* vol. 127, 2002; *Our Member Pages,* The Children's Book Guild of Washington, D.C., retrieved June 4, 2003.

M. NAOMI WILLIAMSON

KATZ, Jon
Journalist, novelist, b. 1947, New Jersey

K. has a vast array of experience working with the written word. A reporter and editor for the *Washington Post, Boston Globe, Philadelphia Inquirer,* and *Dallas Times–Herald,* he was also the executive producer of *CBS Morning News* from 1983 to 1985, as well as a media critic for national MAGAZINES, including *New York, Rolling Stone,* and *Wired.* But K.'s projects that are most notable for younger audiences include his thrilling MYSTERIES. K.'s sleuthing protagonist, Kit Deleeuw, is described as a "sensitive male inversion of the hardened, booze-and-dames detective . . . an attentive father to his two kids while finding time for some private investigating on the side."

In his Kit Deleeuw SERIES, K. uncovers a dark, distressing side of suburban life, which includes murder, suicide, divorce, adultery, betrayal, and financial ruin. K.'s novels are rooted in hard-hitting topics, including media-and-information control. Although both criticized and praised, K.'s *Virtuous Reality: How America Surrendered Discussion of Moral Values to Opportunists, Nitwits, and Blockheads like William Bennett* (1999) has been credited by Mary Carroll in *Booklist* as a work that "offers sensible advice to media producers and consumers, especially parents and kids."

K. is also well known in the YA arena for a work of nonfiction. *Geeks: How Two Lost Boys Rode the Internet out of Idaho* (2000) is the true story of two nineteen-year-old boys who do exactly what the title says and go from societal outcasts—computer nerds—to masters of cyberspace and their own destiny. This work made the 2001 Best Books for Young Adults list and received starred notices from *Kliatt* and *Booklist.* At the time of the Columbine shooting (April 20, 1999), these two young men were trying to make it on their own in Chicago. They had paid their own price for being different, had managed to survive high school, and now saw a chance to jump start their lives, leaving dead-end jobs behind and trusting that "the net" would provide—and it did. This is a true-life coming-of-age story that found a large audience in TEEN readers who could understand and relate.

AWARDS: *Geeks: How Two Boys Rode the Internet out of Idaho:* ALA Best Books for Young Adults list, 2001.

FURTHER WORKS: Novels: *Sign Off,* 1991; *Death by Station Wagon,* 1993; *The Family Stalker,* 1994; *The Last Housewife,* 1995; *The Fathers' Club,* 1996. Other: *Media Rants: Postpolitics in the Digital Nation,* 1997; *Death Row: A Suburban Detective Mystery,* 1998; *Running to the Mountain: A Journey of Faith and Change,* 1999; *The New Work of Dogs: Tending to Life, Love, and Family,* 2003; *The Dogs of Bedlam Farm,* 2004.

BIBLIOGRAPHY: *Contemporary Authors Online,* 2003.

REBECCA OSA MENDELL

KAUFMAN, Bel
Writer, educator, b. 1911, Berlin, Germany

K., who spent her childhood in Moscow, Russia, is the granddaughter of the famous Jewish writer Sholom Aleichem, on whose stories *Fiddler on the Roof* is based. K. has her B.A. (magna cum laude) from Hunter College, her M.A. (with first honors) from Columbia University, her Doctorate of Letters, Nasson College, Maine, and a Doctorate of Humane Letters from Hunter College.

K. began teaching English in New York City high schools. She continued teaching as an adjunct and assistant professor at The City University of New York. She also served as a lecturer at The New School for Social Research and several other universities.

K. is the author of *Up the Down Staircase* (1964), a nationwide bestseller for 64 weeks and number one in the nation for over five months. More than six million copies of the book have been sold. It has been translated into sixteen languages. Currently in its forty-seventh printing, *Up the Down Staircase* was made into a film (Warner Brothers) and a television play (20th Century-Fox) as well as a play for students. As a representation of American films, it was selected for the Moscow Film Festival.

K. is also the author of *Love, Etc.,* a novel published in hardcover in 1979 and in PAPERBACK in 1980. She is the author of numerous articles in *Satur-*

WILL HOBBS

KIMBERLEY WILLIS HOLT

B. JACQUES

SHERRYL JORDAN

BEL KAUFMAN

M. E. KERR

DAVID KLASS

ANNETTE CURTIS KLAUS

day Review, McCall's, Today's Education, Esquire, Ladies Home Journal, the *New York Times,* and many other periodicals.

K. translated lyrics from Russian into English and has written "Sholom Aleichem in America" in *Abroad in America* (1976), published by Smithsonian Institute.

K. has received numerous academic and humanitarian awards for her writing and public speaking. In addition to two honorary doctorates, she is the recipient of the P.E.N. Short Story Award (1983); Woman of the Year Brandeis University (1980); Best Articles on Education by the Educational Association of America (1976 and 1979); the Anti-Defamation League Plaque; National Human Resource Award; Woman of the Year Award (Histadrut); United Jewish Appeal Plaque; Box Office Blue Ribbon award; the State of Israel Bonds Plaque; Paperback of the Year Fiction Award; Hall of Fame Hunter College; the Screenwriters' Annual Award; UJA Women's Division Citation; Certificate of Merit, D.I.D.; Two Thousand Women of Achievement; National Register Prominent Americans; National School Bell Award; National Treasure Award; and more.

Currently, K. is working on a theater piece, lyrics for a musical, and numerous delightful literary projects. One of her writing goals, learned from her illustious grandfather, is to bring a humorous touch to any situation. She keeps readers reading by keeping them laughing.

BERNICE E. CULLINAN

KEHRET, Peg
Author, b. November 11, 1936, LaCrosse, Wisconsin

K. is the daughter of Arthur, an executive of the Hormel Co. and Elizabeth, a homemaker. K. attended the University of Minnesota from 1954 to 1955 and married Carl E. Kehret, a player-piano restorer, on July 2, 1955. The mother of two children, Bob and Anne, K. is a member of the Authors Guild, the Society of Children's Book Writers, and Illustrators and Mystery Writers of America.

K. is an author of children's novels of suspense and danger as well as plays and books for adults who began her writing career as a child. Her grandfather paid her three cents a story and this inspired her to publish her own newspaper about the dogs in her neighborhood. K. contracted polio in the seventh

grade and was paralyzed from the neck down. Although told that she would never walk again, H. made an almost complete recovery. She says, "I vividly remember the time when I got sick and my months in the hospital and my eventual return to school. Maybe that's why I enjoy writing books for young people; I recall exactly how it felt to be that age. When I write, it is easy for me to slip back in my imagination and become twelve years old again." Her autobiography, *Small Steps: The Year I Got Polio* (1996), was a great success and won K. many awards.

In the 1970's, K. began her professional writing career as an adult, spurred on by continued work in community theatres. She sold over three hundred MAGAZINE stories before producing lengthier works. She wrote one-act and full-length plays, including the award-winning *Spirit!,* before she began writing books for young people. Her first juvenile title, *Winning Monologs for Young Actors,* was released in 1986 and was followed by her first YA novel, *Deadly Stranger* (1987).

K. creates characters that find themselves in exciting situations and use their wits to solve their problems.

SELECT AWARDS: *Spirit!:* Forest Roberts Playwriting Award, Northern Michigan University, 1978, Best New Play of 1979, Pioneer Drama Service; *Deadly Stranger:* Young Reader's Choice Awards in Nevada and Oklahoma 1989 Recommended Books for Reluctant Young Adult Readers; 1992 Books for the Teen Age, New York Public Library, *Cages and Winning Monologs for Young Actors: 65 Honest to Life Characterizations to Delight Young Actors and Audiences of All Ages;* 1995 Maud Hart Lovelace Award, *Nightmare Mountain;* 1992 IRA Young Adult's Choice Award, *Sisters, Long Ago; Cages:* Recommended Books for Reluctant Young Adult Readers, Books for the TEEN Age, New York Public Library Young Adult's Choice, Maud Hart Lovelace Award; 1992 Pacific Northwest Writer's Conference Achievement Award; *Terror at the Zoo:* IRA Young Adult's Choice, Pacific Northwest Young Reader's Choice Award; Sequoyah Award, *Horror at the Haunted House;* Quick Picks for Reluctant Young Adult Readers, *Danger at the Fair;* 1995 Children's Books of the Year, *The Richest Kids in Town; Small Steps: The Year I Got Polio:* 1996 Golden Kite Award, 1998 Dorothy Canfield Fisher Award, 1999 Mark Twain Award, 1998 Children's Crown Award, 1998–99 Mark Twain Award, *Earthquake Terror.*

FURTHER WORKS: *Winning Monologs for Young Actors: 65 Honest to Life Characterizations to De-*

light Young Actors and Audiences of All Ages, 1986; *Encore!: More Winning Monologs for Young Actors: 63 More Honest-to-Life Monologs for Teenage Boys and Girls,* 1988; *The Winner,* 1988; *Nightmare Mountain,* 1989; *Sisters, Long Ago,* 1990; *Cages,* 1991; *Acting Natural: Monologs, Dialogs, and Playlets for Teens,* 1991; *Terror at the Zoo,* 1992; *Horror at the Haunted House,* 1992; *Night of Fear,* 1994; *The Richest Kids in Town,* 1994; *Danger at the Fair,* 1995; *Don't Go Near Mrs. Tallie,* 1995; *Desert Danger,* 1995; *Cat Burglar on the Prowl,* 1995; *Bone Breath and the Vandals,* 1995; *Backstage Fright,* 1996; *Earthquake Terror,* 1996; *Screaming Eagles,* 1996; *Race to Disaster,* 1996; *Searching for Candlestick Park,* 1997; *The Volcano Disaster,* 1998; *The Blizzard Disaster,* 1998; *I'm Not Who You Think I Am,* 1999; *Shelter Dogs: Amazing Stories of Adopted Strays,* 1999; *The Flood Disaster,* 1999; *Don't Tell Anyone,* 2000; *The Hideout,* 2001; *Saving Lilly,* 2001; *My Brother Made Me Do It,* 2001; *The Stranger Next Door,* 2002; *Spy Cat,* 2003; *Escaping the Giant Wave,* 2003; *Abduction!,* 2004.

BIBLIOGRAPHY: *Contemporary Authors Online,* 2000. *Contemporary Authors Online,* 2003. Reproduced in *Biography Resource Center,* 2003. "I'm Not Who You Think I Am," *Publishers Weekly,* March 22, 1999 v246 il2 p. 93(1). *Authors and Artists for Young Adults,* Volume 40, 2001. Reproduced in *Biography Resource Center,* 2003.

SARA MARCUS

KELLEHER, Victor (Michael Kitchner)
Author, b. 19 July 1939, London, England

K. was born into a large, poor family with strong Irish roots. At the age of fifteen, K. moved with his parents from London to Africa. There he quit school and worked as a miner and hunter. By age eighteen, K. decided that killing wild animals was inherently wrong and he became an advocate of both wildlife and the environment. He also became, and remains today, a vegetarian.

He graduated from the University of Natal in 1961 with a degree in English. Later, K. earned advanced degrees from the University of St. Andrews (Diploma in Education, 1963), University of the Witwatersrand (B.A., 1969), and the University of South Africa (M.A., 1970; D. Litt. Phil., 1973). He taught at various universities in South Africa, New Zealand, and AUSTRALIA. In 1976, K. settled in Australia with his South African wife, Alison Lyle. For some time, he taught at the University of New England, Armidale. K. then moved to Sydney to pursue his writing full-time.

K.'s fiction is dominated by his experiences in Africa, and he includes aspects of FANTASY and SCIENCE FICTION in his novels. One of K.'s early novels, *The Forbidden Paths of Thual* (1979), follows Quen, a TEEN protagonist. Quen is on a dangerous, yet straightforward, search for a token that would free his people from an army of ruthless soldiers that are terrorizing the village. Norman Culpan, writing a review for *School Librarian,* noted that this YA read is, "interesting, refreshing, worthwhile."

K. continues to write for teens as well as adults. On his writing for teens, he remarks, "I try to write exciting, adventurous stories because those are the kinds of stories I appreciated as a child; and, like many writers, I enjoy recapturing the feelings and response of my childhood . . . I suppose one of the many advantages of writing for children is that it enables me to pursue certain ideas that the majority of adults simply don't take seriously."

AWARDS: Patricia Hackett Prize for Short Fiction (1978) for *The Traveller;* West Australian Young Reader's Special Award (1982) for *Forbidden Paths of Thual,* (1983) for *The Hunting of Shadroth;* Australian Children's Book of the Year from the Children's Book Council of Australia (1983) for *Master of the Grove;* Australian Science Fiction Achievement Award from the National Science Fiction Association (1984) for *The Beast of Heaven;* Honor award from the Children's Book Council of Australia (1987) for *Taronga;* Australian Children's Book Honor award (1991) for *Brother Night.*

FURTHER WORKS: *Papio: A Novel of Adventure,* 1984; *The Green Piper,* 1984; *The Makers,* 1986; *Bailey's Bones,* 1988; *The Red King,* 1989; *Brother Night,* 1900; *Del-Del,* 1991; *To the Dark Tower,* 1992; *Micky Darlin',* 1992; *Where the Whales Sing,* 1994; *Parkland,* 1994; *Earthsong,* 1995; *Fire Dancer,* 1996; *Slow Burn,* 1997.

BIBLIOGRAPHY: *Biography Resource Center.* Farmington Hills, MI: The Gale Group, 2004; http://galenet.galegroup.com/servlet/BioRC.

CARRA E. GAMBERDELLA

KELTON, Elmer
Author, b. 29 April 1926, Andrews, Texas   Pseudonyms Alex Hawk, Lee McElroy

K., son of a cowman, has written about his native West Texas in forty novels that have been published over a span of more than fifty years. K. attended the

University of Texas at Austin from 1942 to 1944 and 1946 to 1948 and earned a B.A. degree in journalism. He served two years in the U.S. Army (1944–46), including combat infantry service in Europe. K. and his wife Ann, a native of Austria, have been married for fifty-four years. He is a newspaperman, writing his novels and SHORT STORIES only evenings, weekends and holidays.

K. grew up around cowboys who talked constantly about the old days: the range wars and cattle drives and the struggles of those who settled West Texas. He writes about his native West Texas history in fictionalized form, but not in the stereotypical format of Old West lawlessness. K.'s novels are crafted to develop his characters while exploring controversial historical topics. His second novel *Buffalo Wagons* (1957) was about the bison hunters in Comanche territory in 1873. With this novel, K won his first Spur Award. In *The Day the Cowboys Quit* (1971), the leader of the men during the Canadian River cowboy strike of 1883 is portrayed honestly, even though he is torn between loyalty and friendship. The cowboy strike is a little-known event in Western history. *The Smiling Country* (1998), set in 1910, is the story of the technological change facing the protagonist. Fences and motorized vehicles forever changed the cowboy way of life, as reflected in this novel.

Quoting K., from *Twentieth-Century Western Writers,* "The better we understand history the more likely we are to understand the present and to be able to cope with the future." K. once told *Contemporary Authors,* "With fiction we are able to stir the senses and emotions and, by personalizing history, give it a reality the reader might otherwise never experience." K. also writes under the pseudonyms Alex Hawk and Lee McElroy.

AWARDS: Spur Award from Western Writers of America: 1957 for *Buffalo Wagons,* 1971 for *The Day the Cowboys Quit,* 1973 for *The Time it Never Rained,* and 1981 for *The Eye of the Hawk;* Western Heritage Award from the National Cowboy Hall of Fame: 1978 for *The Good Old Boys,* 1987 for *The Man Who Rode Midnight;* 1987 Barbara McCombs/ Lon Tinkle Award from the Texas Institute of Letters; 1990 Distinguished Achievement Award from the Western Literature Association; 1998 Lone Star Award for lifetime achievement from the Larry McMurtry Center for Arts and Humanities; Lifetime Achievement Award from the National Cowboy Symposium; 1998 ALA BBYA for *Cloudy in the West.*

FURTHER WORKS: *The Good Old Boys,* 1978; *Wolf And The Buffalo,* 1980; *Barbed Wire,* 1984; *Wagontonue,* 1986; *The Man Who Rode Midnight,* 1987; *Stand Proud,* 1990; *Slaughter,* 1992; *Manhunters,* 1994; *Cloudy in The West,* 1997; *Buckskin Line,* 1999; *Badger Boy,* 2001; *Bitter Trail,* 2002; *Ranger's Trail,* 2003; *Texas Vendetta,* 2004; *Jericho's Road,* 2004.

BIBLIOGRAPHY: *Author Bio,* http://www.elmerkelton .net/author_bio.htm, 2002; *Authors in the News,* vol. 1, 1976; *Contemporary Authors, New Revision Series,* vol. 85, 2000; Twentieth-century Western Writers, 1982.

KAREN L. DENNISON

KERNER, Elizabeth
Author, b. 1958, Florida

K. was born into a Navy family and subsequently led a peripatetic existence. She read voraciously as a child, which fueled her interest in becoming a writer. In 1976, she attended St. Andrews University in Scotland, earning an M.A. in English Language (Philology).

K.'s first published FANTASY novel, *Song in the Silence: The Tale of Lanen Kaelar* (1997), tells the story of a young heroine whose dreams lead her on a quest to find the mythical Dragon Isle and its inhabitants. In the sequel, *The Lesser Kindred* (2001), Lanan Kaelar must battle her archenemy to save both human and dragonkind. This inventive fantasy trilogy comes to a rousing conclusion in volume three, *Redeeming the Lost* (2004).

AWARDS: Selection, ALA BBYA (1998) for *Song in the Silence;* Selection, New York Public Library "Best Books for the TEEN Age" (1998) for *Song in the Silence.*

BIBLIOGRAPHY: *Contemporary Authors,* online, [2002/2003]; Elizabeth Kerner Official website, http://www.elizabethkerner.com

SANSANEE S. GRAVES

KERR, M. E.
Author. b. 27 May 1927, Auburn, New York

K. is a pseudonym for Marijane Meaker. As a writer with a penchant for pseudonyms, Meaker has also been published under the names of Ann Aldrich, Mary James, M. J. Meaker, Vin Packer, and Laura Winston. Her father, Ellis, owned a factory that produced mayonnaise and her mother, Ida, was a homemaker. K credits her parents as early influences in her development as a writer. Her father was an avid reader of the classics as well as popular fiction of the time, in addition to many magazines and newspapers. Neither of K.'s brothers was interested in reading or literature, so her father lavished his attention on her by reading aloud to her and introducing her to the public library. As her father was an avid reader, K.'s mother, Ida, was an avid gossip. Ida would take K. out on Saturday nights to drive around town and observe the townspeople. Ida would return home, call all her friends, and relate what she had observed around town.

K.'s life in Auburn changed dramatically in 1939 and 1940. Her older brother left for military academy and her younger brother was born. K. became depressed and spent time alone in her room listening to music, writing stories, and dreaming of romance. As she became a teenager, K. also became a middle child. In an effort to get her daughter out of the house and socializing, Ida enrolled K. in ballroom dance at the local dance school. K. had already studied tap dancing at this same school and had realized she lacked the coordination and rhythm to be an accomplished dancer.

When K. did not respond to the ballroom dance lessons, she faced greater life changes as her parents sent her to Stuart Hall, an all-female Episcopal boarding school in Staunton, Virginia. Although she always thought her family was wealthy, K. encountered girls from wealthier families. It seems that this experience developed K.'s understanding of class differences and of what it is like to be an outsider.

While home for the summer in 1944, K.'s parents purchased a summer cottage in the country on Owasco Lake. K., still isolated from her old friends in Auburn, spent the summer baby-sitting her younger brother and writing and submitting stories to publication, using her first pseudonym. She chose Erick Ranthram McKay so that she could use her father's monogrammed E. R. M. stationery. Using *Writer's Digest* as her guide, K. submitted stories to women's magazines and received many rejections.

Upon her return to boarding school, K.'s rebellious streak increased. In February of her senior year, K. was expelled for playing darts, using faculty photos as dartboards. After spending two months working for a defense plant, K.'s mother worked with Stuart Hall's administration and got her daughter re-admitted

to the boarding school so that she could graduate with her class.

K. attended Vermont Junior College. In her short tenure, she was the editor of the school newspaper and had her first short story published in that same paper. K. transferred to the University of Missouri. While she had enjoyed her freedom at the junior college, Columbia, Missouri, offered greater opportunities for her. She joined a sorority, continued writing short stories, and accumulating rejection slips, dating, and volunteering at the local mental hospital.

In 1949, K. graduated from the University of Missouri with a B.A. in English. She moved into an apartment in New York City with some of her sorority sisters. Not yet able to work from home as a full-time creative writer, K. went to work for Dutton, a publishing house, as an assistant file clerk in 1949. She lasted for a short while being fired from this job and many others for working on her writing during work hours. Unable to get a literary agent, K. became her own agent. K. used different pseudonyms for different genres and even began using the names of her roommates.

In 1949, K. was able to become a full-time writer through an arrangement with her roommates. They would work and, in exchange for her board, she would cook for them. In 1951, K. sold her first story, "Devotedly, Patrick Henry Casebolt" to *Ladies Home Journal* under the name of Laura Winston.

A publisher had noticed her story for *Ladies' Home Journal.* Based on sample chapters and an outline, K. was offered an advance of $2,000. K. began writing MYSTERY and suspense novels after she learned that this genre would be reviewed in the mystery section of the *New York Times,* but that her PAPERBACK originals would not because the newspaper did not review such books. Combining the names of two friends, she came up with the pseudonym Vin Packer for her mystery and suspense novels. K. had a long and successful career writing mysteries as Packer.

Her second book as Vin Packer was a hit. *Spring Fire* (1952), a book about lesbianism and sorority sisters sold nearly 1.5 million copies. The income from this novel enabled K. to travel and rent an apartment on her own. Between the years 1950 to 1964, K. had twenty books published using two pseudonyms. Her friend, author Louise Fitzhugh, began to encourage K. to write for young adults. Fitzhugh's novel, *Har-*

riet the Spy, based in part on K.'s childhood, had been published as a YA novel, a type of book she was not aware existed. In addition to writing full time, K. attended the New School for Social Research, where she studied anthropology, child psychology, and sociology.

In 1968, K. was a volunteer writing teacher at Commercial Manhattan Central High School. This setting and its students, combined with encouragement from Fitzhugh as well as reading of Paul ZINDEL's *The Pigman,* gave K. the push she needed to write her first YA novel, *Dinky Hocker Shoots Smack!* Fitzhugh insisted that K. try writing for young adults because many of her most well-developed characters in her mystery novels were in their TEENS. In choosing a pseudonym for her young adult novels, K. chose to adapt her real last name Meaker into her new persona, M. E. Kerr.

For this novel, K. found inspiration in one of her students, an overweight girl who ate and watched TV while her mother worked with troubled adults at their church. In K.'s version, Dinky is a middle-class, overweight girl whose mother is a lawyer working with drug addicts. In an attempt to get her mother's attention, Dinky paints graffiti "Dinky Hocker Shoots Smack!" on the building where her mother works. The graffiti could not be further from the truth. Dinky's drug of choice is food.

The success of *Dinky Hocker Shoots Smack!* gave K. the impetus to reevaluate her work and the courage to make changes in her life. In her mid-forties, K. had found the sort of success that she had not realized with her adult mystery writing. Based on this and the ease at which she was able to come up with story ideas for YA novels, she left behind murderers to explore serious societal issues in what are commonly referred to as "problem novels." While most "problem novels" focus on the problem and solution, reviewers have noted that K.'s works contain fully developed characters, often ostracized, who deal with serious issues through humor and love. K. is also known for her strong characterization of the adults in her YA novels.

For her fourth young adult book, *Gentlehands* (1978) K. again used young people in her life for inspiration. Her seventeen-year-old middle-class neighbor was in love with a rich girl whose family visited the area each summer. K.'s listening ear provided her with another story idea that she combined with her reading of a book on Nazi war criminals. K. used the middle-class boy, Buddy, in love with the rich girl, Skye Pennington, as the basis for *Gentlehands.* During the course of the novel, Buddy spends time with his grandfather and uses his grandfather to impress Skye, when much to Buddy's dismay, he discovers that his beloved grandfather is a Nazi war criminal.

In 1979, *Dinky Hocker Shoots Smack!* was adapted as *"Dinky Hocker"* for an *ABC Afterschool* special, starring Wendy Jo Sperber as Dinky and June Lockhart as Helen Hocker. Despite this presentation, K. does not feel suited to television or film writing because of the amount of collaboration with others to develop a finished product. K. prefers to work alone.

K. followed up *Gentlehands* with *Little Little,* which features two teenage dwarves, Little Little and Sidney Cinnamon, in a love story. The major conflict is that Little Little's mother attempts to arrange a marriage for her daughter with another dwarf, Little Lion, an evangelist.

In the mid-1980s, K. chose very difficult subject matter in what was to become a landmark in young adult literature. *Night Kites* (1986) was the first young adult book to deal with AIDS. As with many of her books, this one also came about due to personal observation. K. began working on *Night Kites* in 1984. A family in the town where she lives was caring for a son with AIDS. K. saw the reactions of some townspeople and the ostracism that family faced. While K. intentionally avoids most pop-culture references in her novels, she allowed herself to use them in *Night Kites,* in her belief that AIDS would be cured quickly as many previous diseases had been.

In *Night Kites,* Erick, a high-school senior, falls in love with his best friend's girlfriend and has sex for the first time. Erick and his family are trying to deal with his older brother's announcement to the family that he has AIDS. In the end, Erick loses his girlfriend when he tells her of his brother's illness.

K.'s *Deliver Us from Evie,* 1994, is about eighteen-year-old Evie's romance with the daughter of a wealthy family in rural Missouri, told from the point-of-view of Evie's brother. That same year, K.'s short story "We Might As Well All Be Strangers" was published in *Am I Blue? Coming out from the Silence,* a collection of SHORT STORIES about homosexuality written by YA authors.

The Books of Fell (2001) was a reissue of the Fell Trilogy (*Fell,* 1987; *Fell Back,* 1989; *Fell Down,*

1991). In the trilogy, K. returned to her mystery/suspense roots by writing about a teenager hired by his girlfriend's neighbor to impersonate his son at a private school and to infiltrate a secret society.

K. continues to write for young adults. When not working, she enjoys reading, walking, and networking with other writers.

AWARDS: *Dinky Hocker Shoots Smack!*: American Library Association (ALA) Notable Books list (1972), *School Library Journal* (SLJ) Best Books of the Year list (1972); *New York Times'* Outstanding Books of the Year list, 1973, *If I Love You, Am I Trapped Forever?*; *SLJ* Best Books of the Year list, 1974, *The Son of Someone Famous*; *Is That You, Miss Blue?*: ALA Notable Books list (1975), ALA Best Books for Young Adults list (1975), *New York Times'* Outstanding Books of the Year list (1975); *SLJ* Best Books of the Year list, 1977, *I'll Love You When You're More Like Me; Gentlehands*: Christopher Award (1978), *SLJ* Book of the Year Award (1978), *New York Times'* Outstanding Books of the Year list (1978); *Little Little:* Society of Children's Book Writers, Golden Kite Award (1981), *SLJ* Best Books of the Year list (1981); *SLJ* Best Books of the Year list, 1982, *What I Really Think of You*; ALA Best Books for Young Adults list, 1983, *Me, Me, Me, Me, Me: Not a Novel*; ALA Best Books for Young Adults list, 1985, *I Stay Near You*; ALA Recommended Books for the Reluctant Young Adult Reader list, 1986, *Night Kites*; ALA and *SLJ*, MARGARET A. EDWARDS AWARD for Lifetime Achievement in Young Adult Literature, 1993, for *Dinky Hocker Shoots Smack!, Gentlehands, Me, Me, Me, Me, Me: Not a Novel,* and *Night Kites*; *Deliver Us from Evie*: ALA Best Books for Young Adults list (1995), ALA Recommended Books for the Reluctant Young Adult Reader list (1995). Three of Kerr's books were selected for the 3rd, and 4th YALSA Best of the Best lists: 2nd The Best of the Best Books (Selections from 1970 to 1983): *Dinky Hocker Shoots Smack!,* 3rd Nothin' but the Best (Selections from 1966 to 1986): *Gentlehands* and *Night Kites* 4th Here We Go Again . . . 25 Years of Best Books (Selections from 1967 to 1992): *Gentlehands.*

FURTHER WORKS: *Blood On the Forehead: What I Know about Writing,* 1998; *The Books of Fell,* 2001; *Highsmith: A Romance of the 1950s,* 2003, as Marijane Meaker; *Shockproof Sydney Skate,* 1972, as Marijane Meaker; *Shoebag,* 1990, as Mary James; *Slap Your Sides,* 2001; *Spring Fire,* 1952, as Vin Packer.

BIBLIOGRAPHY: *Authors & Artists for Young Adults,* Vol. 2., 1989; Bernstein, Robin. "Marijane Meaker." *Gay and Lesbian Literature.* Vol. 2., 1998; Carter, Betty. *Best Books for Young Adults, Second Edition,* 2000; *Contemporary Authors Online,* 2003; Contemporary Literacy Criticism. Vol. 35., 1985; Nilsen, Alleen Pace. "M. E. Kerr." *Writers for Young Adults.* Vol. 2., 97. pp. 177–185; *U*X*L Junior DISCovering Authors.* Online Edition. U*X*L, 2003; *Writers for Young Adults.* Vol. 2., 1997.

ANDREW W. HUNTER

KESEY, Ken (Elton)

Author, b. 17 September 1935, La Junta, Colorado; d. 10 November 2001, Eugene, Oregon

K. was a champion athlete in his youth, winning a scholarship for outstanding wrestler in the northwest. He earned a B.A. from the University of Oregon in 1957, majoring in speech and communications. He enjoyed acting in high school and college, and later studied creative writing at Stanford University. It was there in the early 1960s that he began to explore Eastern mysticism and experiment with psychedelic drugs, both hallmarks of early hippie culture. His interests in altered states of consciousness led him to take part in drug experiments conducted at the Veterans Administration Hospital in Menlo Park, California. He later worked there as a night attendant in the psychiatric ward. These experiences set the scene for his best-known novel, *One Flew Over the Cuckoo's Nest* (1962).

K.'s portrayal of Randle J. McMurphy, the patient who challenges the corrupt authority of Big Nurse Ratched, struck a chord with 1960s American youth. The novel has since made its way into the American literary canon. *One Flew Over the Cuckoo's Nest* inspired an Academy-award-winning film, a Broadway play, and is taught in classrooms to this day. The success of this first novel established K. as an icon of the counterculture.

K.'s second book, *Sometimes a Great Notion* (1964), is viewed as his attempt to write "the great American novel." Although stylistically more challenging than *Cuckoo's Nest,* it did not receive the same critical success. *Great Notion* portrays a logging family in a conservative northwestern community. Rugged-individualist Hank Stamper is at odds with both his intellectual half-brother Lee and his community as he stands against a union strike. The author has said that the clashing half-brothers represent two sides of himself.

Just after the publication of *Great Notion,* K. set out on his now-famous travels with a group of followers known as the Merry Pranksters. "You're either on the bus or you're off the bus," is their oft-repeated refrain in Tom Wolfe's account of their exploits, *The Electric Kool-Aid Acid Test* (1968). Crossing the country in a 1939 Day-Glo-painted International Harvester bus, their destination was noted simply as "Further." K. would later give his own account of this trip in *The Further Inquiry* (1990). He is arguably as famous for these exploits as for his novels.

AWARDS: Saxton Fund fellowship, 1959; Distinguished Service award, State of Oregon, 1978; Western Literature Association annual award for Distinguished Achievement in Writing, 1988; 1991 *Los Angeles Times* Robert Kirsch Award

FURTHER WORKS: *Kesey's Garage Sale,* 1973; *Demon Box,* 1986; *Little Trickster the Squirrel Meets Big Double the Bear* (juvenile), 1990; *Caverns* (coauthor), 1990; *Sailor Song,* 1992; *Sea Lion* (juvenile), 1992; *Last Go Round,* 1994.

BIBLIOGRAPHY: Leeds, B. H., *Ken K.,* 1981.

JUDY SILVA

KESSLER, Cristina
Author, n.d., Modesto, California

K. grew up in Los Altos, California, but has traveled in ninety-eight countries—living for nineteen years in Africa—and has learned nineteen languages. She is a self-proclaimed "fanatic traveler" (book jacket of *Konte Chameleon Fine, Fine, Fine!,* 1997). In her writing—both fiction and nonfiction about Africa—she, "[likes] to get the good news out about Africa" (Kessler, http://www.cristinakessler.com).

Her colorful books (sometimes by virtue of her own photography—as in *All the King's Animals,* 1995—or with dramatic illustrations by Stammen in *Jubela,* 2001, or Schoenherr in *One Night,* 1995) are filled with pictures and descriptions of the land and folklore, dialects, and indigenous animals of the continent. Many of her children's books have received awards and honors (*Jubela, One Night, All the King's Animals,* and *My Great-Grandmother's Gourd* [2000]).

Beginning with the publication of *All the King's Animals,* K. started to explore topics of global importance, in this case endangered animals. With *No Condition is Permanent* (2000), Kessler's first YA novel, the author proves herself unafraid of dealing with the controversial topic of female circumcision. In the novel, the young American protagonist, Jodie, is a Californian transported to Africa. (K., also a California native, worked as a Peace Corps volunteer from 1981–1983 in Sierra Leone, the setting of the novel.) Through Jodie's fourteen-year-old eyes, readers see, hear, and smell Africa and learn about the culture as she becomes accustomed to African life. As an outsider, Jodie, at first secretly, hears about and then must come to terms with the reality of a secret society (into which her close friend, Khadi, is being inducted) that practices female circumcision. Stanlie M. James, with the Afro-American Studies Department at the University of Wisconsin (Madison) says, "Kessler has made a sincere attempt to treat the customs and traditions of another culture with respect," (2001, http://www.h-net.org/~afrteach/).

As the topic of female circumcision is controversial, so has been the reception of K.'s book. Yulisa Amadu Maddy and Donnarae MacCann (2002) find many problems in K.'s tale and place it in the category of an "anti-African mindset" (p. 92). In the overall degradation of African social culture and tradition that Maddy and MacCann read in *No Condition Is Permanent,* they note that though Jodie experiences a change of heart "[curbing] her chauvinism and self-righteousness, . . . The focus is on what Khadi learns. Readers are led to consider how Khadi discovers the evils of circumcision, the evils of juju," essentially, what is "wrong" with Sierra Leonean culture (p. 93).

Her next work, *Our Secret, Siri Aang* (2004), also addresses female circumcision as one of the subplots. The twelve-year-old protagonist is a Masai girl who befriends a black rhinoceros and her baby (one secret). Her family is traditional, but she would like to get an education and delays the coming-of-age ceremony, which includes female circumcision, by not revealing the fact that she has begun to menstruate (more secrets). When poachers kill the mother rhino, she follows their tracks into the bush country, determined to do everything possible to save the baby rhinoceros. Her dangerous quest becomes a journey of self-discovery in this survival novel that is also a fascinating examination of Masai culture.

K. lives in St. John in the Caribbean with her husband, Joe.

AWARDS: *No Condition is Permanent*: Best Books for Young Adults 2001; The Best Children's Books of the Year, 2001; Lasting Connections, 2000; *Jubela*: The Best Children's Books of the Year, 2002 (Bank Street College of Education); *One Night*: The Children's

Literature Choice List, 1996; *My Great-Grandmother's Gourd*: The Best Children's Books of the Year, 2001 (Bank Street College of Education).

BIBLIOGRAPHY: James, S. M. (2001). [Review of the book *No condition is permanent*]. *H-Afrteach: An H-net Network for Teaching About Africa*. Retrieved on June 24, 2004, from the World Wide Web: http://www.h-net.org/~afrteach/; K. C. (n.d.) *Cristina Kessler* (home page). Retrieved June 24, 2004, from the World Wide Web: http://www.cristinakessler.com/; K. C. (1997). *Konte chameleon, fine, fine, fine!*. Honesdale, PA: Boyds Mills Press; Maddy, Y. A. & MacCann, D. (2002). Anti-African themes in 'liberal' young adults novels. *Children's Literature Association Quarterly, 27* (2), 92–99.

MARY MCMILLAN TERRY

KEYES, Daniel

Author, b. 9 August 1927, Brooklyn, New York

At the age of seventeen, from 1945–1947, K. went into Maritime Service as a senior assistant purser. Graduating from Brooklyn College in 1950 with a B.A. in psychology, K.'s fascination with the "complexities of the human mind" began early. Working various jobs as everything from an associate fiction editor to an English teacher in the New York City school system, K. earned an M.A. at night school at Brooklyn College, studying English and American literature. Later going on to become an English professor at Ohio State University, K. spent his time "teaching days and writing weekends."

This focus not just on storytelling but on the mind of characters manifested itself in a SHORT STORY K. wrote that was published in *The Magazine of Fantasy and Science Fiction* in 1959. "Flowers for Algernon" (1966), arguably K.'s most famous and highly regarded work, started out simply as the fifth short story that K. was submitting for publication to *Galaxy* MAGAZINE. However, this story of a mentally disabled man who temporarily is able to achieve extraordinary intelligence became an instant classic.

After "Flowers for Algernon" won the Hugo award in 1959, K. expanded the story into a novel that has never gone out of print. Going on to win the Nebula award in 1967, *Flowers for Algernon* (1966) was also adapted into the film "Charly," for which Cliff Robertson won an Academy Award for his performance, a television play for CBS Playhouse titled "The Twin Worlds of Charlie Gordon" (1961), the stage play *Flowers for Algernon* (1969), and a musical, *Charlie and Algernon,* that was produced on both Broadway and London's West End. K. had said about these many incarnations, "They tried to change the ending—nobody has ever been able to change the ending, and I'm happy for that!"

K.'s ability to combine sensitivity and a sense of reality in his work lent itself to his nonfiction writing as well. Always intrigued by people's minds, it seemed a natural progression for K. to go on to write books such as *The Fifth Sally* (1980) and *The Minds of Billy Milligan* (1981). Both deal with multiple personality disorder, and in *The Minds of Billy Milligan,* K. was able to tell the true story of the first person in U.S. history to be acquitted of a felony by reason of multiple-personality disorder. As it turned out, *Flowers for Algernon* was a favorite of Billy's many personalities, and K. was able to obtain permission from his subject to write a book, thanks to his earlier work.

K. wrote *The Milligan Wars: A True-Story Sequel* (1994) that was published in Japan and will be released in the U.S. once the MOVIE version of the original *Billy Milligan* is filmed. K. lives in southern Florida with his wife Aurea Vazuez and continues to write both fiction and nonfiction. K.'s most recent work is *Algernon, Charlie and I: A Writer's Journey* (2000), which chronicles the path that was taken in the creation of his most famous novel.

AWARDS: Hugo Award, World Science Fiction Convention, 1959, for "Flowers for Algernon" (short story); Nebula Award, SCIENCE FICTION Writers of America, 1966, for *Flowers for Algernon* (novel); special award, MYSTERY Writers of America, 1981, for *The Minds of Billy Milligan*; Kurd Lasswitz Award for best book by a foreign author, 1986, for *Die Leben des Billy Milligan* (German translation); Edgar Allan Poe Award nomination, Mystery Writers of America, 1986, for *Unveiling Claudia: A True Story of a Serial Murder.*

FURTHER WORKS: *The Touch,* 1968, *The Contaminated Man,* 1973, *Daniel K. Collected Stories,* 1993, *Daniel Keyes Reader,* 1994, *Until Death Do Us Part: The Sleeping Princess,* 1998.

BIBLIOGRAPHY: *Contemporary Authors,* online, 2000; *Something About the Author,* vol. 37, 2001; *Locus Magazine,* June 1997; "Daniel K." DISCovering Authors. Gale Group, 1999. Reproduced in Discovering Collection. Farmington Hills, Mich.: Gale Group. October, 2001.

MEGAN PEARLMAN

KINCAID, Jamaica
Author, b. 25 May 1949, St. Johns, Antigua

In her nearly forty years in the U.S., the former Elaine Potter Richardson has gained critical acclaim as Jamaica K. Her writing is infused with autobiographical references which take the reader into the mind and emotions of a young woman dealing with her mother, as well as with her anger and frustration over the colonialism in her home country, Antigua.

K.'s work has gained a large following among YA readers, many dealing with similar identity struggles and issues in their own lives. The writing style is sparse, simple, and descriptive. Her works include the novels *Lucy* (1990) and *Annie John* (1985), a SHORT STORY collection *At the Bottom of the River* (1984), a nonfiction book *A Small Place* (1988), and a more recent work, set on the island of Dominica in the West Indies, *The Autobiography of My Mother* (1990).

K. was a product of the Antiguan version of the British educational system, one she detested but in which she completed her secondary education. She later studied photography at the New School for Social Research [now New School University] and studied for a year at Franconia College in New Hampshire.

This author recently left a long-time position as a staff writer for *The New Yorker*. She lives in Bennington, Vermont, with her husand, the composer Allen Shawn, a professor at Bennington College, and their two children.

FURTHER WORKS: *Among Flowers: A Walk in the Himalayas,* 2005.

BIBLIOGRAPHY: Ferguson, M., *Jamaica Kincaid: Where the Land Meets the Body,* 1994; Simmons, D., *Jamaica K.,* 1994.

SUSAN L. MARINOFF

KINDL, Patrice
Author, b. 16 October 1951, Alplaus, New York

When K. was three years old, her family moved into a wonderful Victorian house full of wasted space, rooms with no purpose, and a cellar deep enough to hide a Minotaur. When the family moved into a modern house five years later, K. admits she "spent the next decade sulking." Luckily, the new house had an abandoned cabin in the woods behind it to replace the wonders of the Victorian house. K. spent many hours of her childhood following creative endeavors alone in that cabin. She writes, "Now that I am grown up I write for children because I am still that child, fond of reading, animals, and solitude. I wouldn't know how to write for grown-ups. I wouldn't know what to say." As soon as her son Alex finished high school, K. found a replacement for her childhood home. She says her current house even has a giant crypt in the basement suitable for keeping a Minotaur, just in case she gets one.

K.'s fondness for animals has continued into her adult life. She and her husband raised two Capuchin monkeys to become aids to quadriplegics as part of a program called Helping Hands. Her monkeys are very much involved in her writing process; one sits on her shoulder while the other is on her lap. K. dedicated *Owl in Love* (1993) to Kandy, one of her monkeys, "without whom this book would have been written in half the time."

K. has found the solitude and dramatic home to facilitate her writing. She did not always consider herself a writer, despite a childhood of practice. She never finished college, working in New York City while trying to succeed as an actress. After failing at that endeavor, K. worked for her father's engineering company, where she met her husband, Paul Roediger. After years of secretarial training, K. left her father's business in hopes of becoming a writer. K. complains that her pleasant family life is a "great handicap to a professional writer, as marital bliss and a happy childhood are not productive of much copy."

Owl in Love (1993), a FANTASY ROMANCE, was K.'s debut novel. The heroine, Owl, is a shape-shifter, a high-school girl by day and an owl by night. She has a crush on her science teacher and follows him home, where she sees a boy hiding in the woods behind his house. Owl discovers that the boy is also a wereowl and in dire need of her help. Behind the supernatural plot line, the story examines the range of emotions that TEENAGERS encounter. K. says, "It's an age when you try on masks of different personalities and can change your personality quite deliberately."

This theme continues in her second book, *The Woman in the Wall* (1997). The main character of this book is Anna, an agoraphobic who has literally hidden herself in the walls of her home for seven of her fourteen years. She finds herself growing into a woman, and her lifestyle is threatened when she develops a crush on one of her sister's friends. Anna is forced to rebuild her life outside of the walls while finding herself from within.

Goose Chase (2001) features another odd heroine, Alexandria, a goose girl/princess who has been blessed (or is it cursed?) with great beauty and the abilities to shed gold dust and diamond tears. Alexandria's FAIRY-TALE story is full of wit and charm and even a handsome prince.

K. combines excellent characterization with a strong talent for pacing and plot. While her stories portray real teenage characters with which young readers can easily identify, despite their peculiarities, they are pure escapism. Jeannette Hulick, Reviewer and Editorial Assistant of *The Bulletin of the Center for Children's Books,* writes, "the novelty of K.'s characters and their situations serves to make her stories all the more riveting, and, as with any good fantasy, the circumstantial differences from everyday life only highlight and sharpen readers' sense of their own lives while simultaneously allowing them to escape (albeit temporarily) reality."

AWARDS: *Owl in Love*: Golden Kite Honor Book, Mythopoeic Award; Crawford Award, ALA BBYA 1995, ALA Quick Pick, 1995; *School Library Journal* best book, *Bulletin of the Center for Children's Books* blue ribbon, New York City Public Library's Books for the Teen Age; *The Woman in the Wall*: AUSTRALIAN National Book Award Honor, New York City Public Library's 100 Best Children's Books, New York Public Library's Books for the Teen Age, ALA Best Books for Young Adults 1998; *Goose Chase*: *Booklist*'s 10 Best Youth Romances, *Booklist*'s 10 Best Fantasies, *Booklist*'s Editor's Choice, *VOYA*'s Best Fantasy, New York City Public Library's Books for the Teen Age, New York Public Library's Books to Read and Share.

FURTHER WORKS: *Lost in the Labyrinth,* 2002; *The Baby's Dilemma.*

BIBLIOGRAPHY: *Something about the Author,* 2002; *Contemporary Authors,* 1996; Winkler, L.K. *The ALAN Review,* 1999; The Bulletin of the Center for Children's Books, online, 2002; Patrice K.'s Web page, http://www.patricekindl.com, 2003; Personal correspondence (2003).

JENNA OBEE

KING, Laurie R.
Author, b. 19 September 1952, Oakland, California

Although she was born across the bay from San Francisco and has lived in the area most of her life, K. has never lived in—and in fact, rarely visits—the city she vividly describes in her SERIES of MYSTERIES focused on the character of Kate Martinelli. The fact that she can write about contemporary San Francisco, early twentieth-century England, and feminist theology with a credibility and vigor that leaves readers and critics wanting more is testament to K.'s abilities as a writer.

By her own admission, K. was a mediocre student in high school. Her family viewed education as primarily a male endeavor; this coupled with their frequent moves likely contributed to her early lack of engagement. Given their views on education, K.'s family was surprisingly encouraging of her love of reading, and books were preferred over television as the primary source of entertainment throughout her youth.

K. returned to the San Francisco area on her own for her senior year of high school. She enrolled in a junior college after graduation, working full time for her education. Eventually K. transferred to the University of California-Santa Cruz, graduating with a degree in religious studies. K. then enrolled in the Graduate Theological Union at Berkeley where she earned a master's degree focusing on feminist theology.

The Beekeeper's Apprentice (1994), which introduced the indomitable fifteen-year-old Mary Russell, was K.'s first novel, written in a period of twenty-eight days. She had only recently begun to experiment with fiction once her children's attendance at pre-school permitted her some spare time. Copyright concerns regarding her use of the Sherlock Holmes character kept the book out of publication for a while; K.'s first published work was actually her second novel *A Grave Talent* (1993), the first in her series to feature Kate Martinelli, a lesbian police detective. Reviewers and readers alike met both novels with praise.

K. has continued both the Russell and Martinelli series, along with writing several independent mystery novels (e.g., *A Darker Place,* 1999). Critics have lauded her lively characterizations, feminist perspectives, and intricate plots that draw upon the power of setting. K. is able to effectively integrate her theological expertise in a number of her works—e.g., the goddess theology in *Night Work* (2000), god as feminine in *A Monstrous Regiment of Women* (1995)—due to her constructed parallels between mystery writing and the storytelling of the Old Testament. Critics and readers have also praised K. for her non-stereotypical portrayal of homosexuality through Martinelli, a character that comes across as functional and real, her sexual orientation integrated without handicap.

AWARDS: *A Grave Talent:* 1994 Edgar Award for Best First Novel, 1993 John Creasey Dagger award; 1994 ALA Best Books for Young Adults, *The Beekeeper's Apprentice;* 1995 Nero Wolfe award, *A Monstrous Regiment of Women;* 1996 ALA Notable Book, *With Child;* 1998 *School Library Journal* Best Books of the Year, *The Moor;* 2001 Macavity Award, *Folly;* Honorary doctorate (1997) from the Church Divinity School of the Pacific.

SELECT FURTHER WORKS: Mary Russell novels: *The Beekeeper's Apprentice,* 1994; *A Monstrous Regiment of Women,* 1995; *A Letter to Mary,* 1997; *The Moor,* 1998; *O Jerusalem,* 1999; *Justice Hall,* 2002. Kate Martinelli novels: *A Grave Talent,* 1993; *To Play the Fool,* 1995; *With Child,* 1996; *Night Work,* 2002. Other novels: *A Darker Place,* 1999; *Folly,* 2001; *Keeping Watch,* 2003; *The Game,* 2004; *Locked Rooms,* 2005.

BIBLIOGRAPHY: K., Laurie (n.d.), personal Web page, retrieved from http://www.laurierking.com/; "Laurie R. K." *Authors and Artists for Young Adults,* vol. 29, 1999, reproduced in Biography Resource Center, 2003, http://galenet.galegroup.com/servlet/BioRC

CAROL L. TILLEY

KING, Stephen (Edwin) (Richard Bachman)

Author, b. 21 September 1947, Portland, Maine

K. has for decades been acknowledged as one of the best HORROR writers the world over. K. has also worked in a knitting mill, as a janitor, and as a laundry worker. He was an English teacher at the Hampden Academy (high school) in Hampden, Maine from 1971–1973; a writer-in-residence in 1978–1979 at the University of Maine at Orono. K. is a member of the Authors Guild and Authors League of America. K. is a writer of countless novels, SHORT STORIES, nonfiction works, and MOVIE adaptations, as well as under the pseudonym Richard Bachman. K. wrote his first novel, *Carrie,* which made the School Library Journal's Book List in 1974. Then came *Salem's Lot* in 1975, *The Shining* in 1977, *The Stand* in 1978, all receiving prestigious awards. Later they would all become good "scare the skin off your bones" movies as well. Then came his first four books with another publisher, *The Dead Zone* in 1979, *Firestarter* in 1980, *Cujo* in 1981 and *Different Seasons* in 1982. Then came *Creepshow* (a movie) in 1982, *Pet Sematary* in 1983, *Christine* in 1983, *The Talisman* (with Peter Straub) in 1984, *The Eyes of the Dragon* in 1984, *Cycle of the Werewolf* in 1985 and also a new edition titled *Silver Bullet* in 1985. *Bare Bones, It,* and *Maximum Overdrive* were all released in 1986. Then came *Misery* and *The Tommyknockers* in 1987 and *Nightmares in the Sky* and *Night Visions* in 1988. He wrote two short stories, "Night Shift" in 1978 and "Skeleton Crew" in 1985. A nonfiction work appeared in 1981—*Stephen King's Danse Macabre.* He is also the author of screenplays, "The Shining," "Creepshow," and "Silver Bullet." The prolific author has written short stories, contributed to periodicals, including *Fantasy and Science Fiction, Gallery, Startling Mystery Stories, Cavalier, Ellery Queen's Mystery Magazine, Oui, Rolling Stone, Adelina, American Bookseller* and *Playboy.*

Two years after his birth in 1947 K.'s father, a merchant seaman, went out for a pack of cigarettes and never returned. His mother was left to raise two boys in near-poverty conditions, holding jobs as a laundry presser as well as a doughnut baker. As a child K. was often picked on because he was overweight and uncoordinated. His nightmares as a child he says, "were always inadequacy dreams. Dreams of standing up to salute the flag only to have his pants fall down." As an adolescent he became terrified and preoccupied with death—death in general and his own in particular. He was convinced he would not live past twenty. He often fantasized about dark deserted streets as well as strange figures leaping at him from behind bushes. As a youth he would spend countless Saturdays at the theatre watching horror and SCIENCE-FICTION movies. After getting into trouble for writing a small satiric newpaper as a sophomore in Libson High School in Maine called "The Village Vomit"; it was this "sophomoric thing" that he did that changed his life. As part of his detention a guidance counselor thought he was better suited to write sports for the Libson Enterprise, a twelve-page weekly, contingent upon the editor's approval. This editor K. admits, "taught me everything I know about writing in ten minutes." His name was John Gould." Gould told K., "Writing can be your ticket to the promised land. Something you can do for a living." K. has made and is still making quite a living with his writings and screenplays. He has that uncanny ability to make you relive your childhood nightmares. Most who read his writings say they could not put the book down from start to finish. The only time you do find yourself putting his books down is to check under the bed or in a closet to be sure the boogeyman is not lurking there. He is married for thirty-two years to Tabitha Jane Spruce and they have three children. They live in a Victorian mansion in Bangor, Maine.

WILLIAM MARIANO

KINGSOLVER, Barbara
Author, b. 8 April 1955, Annapolis, Maryland

K. was born in Annapolis, Maryland, but grew up in rural Kentucky. She earned a B.A. in biology from DePauw University in Indiana and an M.S. in biology and ecology from the University of Arizona. Much like her character, Taylor, in *The Bean Trees* (1988), K. left Kentucky and ended up living in Arizona. Although often asked if her writing reflects her life, K. feels she better serves readers by not writing about herself but rather by making up complex and interesting characters and plots. She does, however, feel it is important to write about social and political issues. Influenced by Doris Lessing, she realized that important issues could be written about in a subtle, yet intriguing, manner. K. does not write about social and political issues in a preachy way, but rather these issues are woven into her stories, characters, and plots. Although considered an adult writer, many of K.'s works appeal to YA readers for their poetic flow, humor, and contemporary issues. K.'s novels offer a strong tie to social and political issues that may be in a school's curriculum.

The Bean Trees was K.'s first novel and was received with positive critical reviews. It is the story of a woman, Taylor Greer, and the relationships she forms as she leaves Kentucky and settles in Arizona. Along the way, she unexpectedly becomes a mother to a Native American girl called Turtle. In Arizona, she develops relationships with two other women, Mattie and Lou Ann. The story is engaging and often humorous but also comes across with a strong sense of realism.

Animal Dreams (1990) also has themes of Native American culture, being an outsider, developing relationships, as well as issues of environmental pollution and political activism. This story focuses on Codi Noline as she returns to her hometown of Grace, Arisona, to care for her father who has Alzheimer's Disease.

K. wrote a sequel to *The Bean Trees,* her novel *Pigs in Heaven* (1993). This award-winning novel takes readers back into Taylor and Turtle's lives several years later. Turtle has witnessed an accident and her insistence and Taylor's belief in her lead to a rescue which puts Turtle in the media spotlight. This added attention calls into question Taylor's adoption of Turtle, especially since Turtle is Native American and being raised by a white woman. More interesting characters are introduced into this funny and compassionate plot.

Another popular adult work that was also nominated for the American Library Association's Best Book for Young Adults is *The Poisonwood Bible* (2000). Prior to this, K. wrote stories set in America. *The Poisonwood Bible* takes readers to African Congo, as a missionary FAMILY struggles to survive the country and each other. The story unfolds over several decades and is considered by many as one of K.'s most provocative works.

K. not only expresses her commitment to social and political issues through her novels, but also in an award she established and funds, the Bellwether Prize for Fiction. It is awarded for "a Literature of Social Change" in even-numbered years. The winner receives an award of $25,000 in cash and guaranteed publication by a major publisher. The award was established in 1997 and the first award was presented in 2000.

AWARDS: American Library Association's Best Books for Young Adults *The Bean Trees* (1988) and *Animal Dreams* (1992); American Library Association's Notable Book for *The Bean Trees* (1988), *Homeland and Other Stories* (1990), and *Animal Dreams* (1991); *New York Times* Notable Book for *The Bean Trees* (1988), *Animal Dreams* (1991), and *Pigs in Heaven* (1994); citation of accomplishment from United Nations National Council of Women (1989); PEN fiction prize for *Animal Dreams* (1991); Edward Abbey Ecofiction Award for *Animal Dreams* (1991); Woodrow Wilson Foundation/Lila Wallace fellow (1992–93); *New York Times* "Ten Best Books of 1998" for *The Poisonwood Bible* (1999); Book Sense Book of the Year Award for *The Poisonwood Bible* (2000); National Book Prize of South America for *The Poisonwood Bible* (2000); National Humanities Medal (2000).

FURTHER WORKS: *Homeland and Other Stories,* 1989; *Holding the Line: Women in the Great Arizona Mine Strike of 1983,* 1989; *Another America/Otra America,* (poetry), 1992; *High Tide in Tucson: Essays from Now or Never,* 1995; *Prodigal Summer,* 2000; *Small Wonder* (essays), 2002; *Last Stand: America's Virgin Lands,* 2002.

BIBLIOGRAPHY: *Contemporary Authors; Contemporary Novelists; Publishers Weekly;* www.kingsolver .com (author website); www.bellwetherprize.org (award website).

TINA HERTEL

KITCHENER, Michael. See KELLEHER, Victor.

KLASS, David

Author, b. 8 March 1960, Bennington, Vermont

Born to an anthropology professor father and a family of writers, K. has grown into a distinguished author of novels for young readers such as *You Don't Know Me* (2001), and major motion picture screenplays such as the adaptation of James Patterson's *Kiss the Girls.* His mother, uncle, and two siters are also published authors. His teachers at Yale included novelist Richard Price, poet John Hollander, editor Gordon Lish, and playwright Ted Talley, each with a great deal of practical information to offer. "I tried to learn as much as I could," K. told Don Gallo in a 2003 interview.

After spending a year in India due to his father's scientific assignments, K. experienced the rest of his childhood in Leonia, New Jersey (15 minutes by car from Manhattan). It is from this period that K. draws much of his fictional inspiration. "I loved SPORTS and would play until it got dark," he says in his publisher's biography, "baseball, soccer, basketball, tennis, bowling, and golf." In short, his world revolved around sports.

Baseball and soccer were K.'s roads to glory until he graduated from Leonia High School in 1978. Basketball, wrestling, track, tennis and bowling became college passions. Strong impressions, both good and bad, lingered from his competitive endeavors. The full spectrum often resurfaces in his fiction for TEENS.

Even so, K.'s literary potential was as obvious as his competitive nature. His sister Perri, an accomplished writer even as a teenager, entered and won *Seventeen* MAGAZINE's short fiction competition twice. "I had a bit of sibling rivalry with my older sister," he says in his publisher's profile. "I decided that I would win it, too, even though I had never read an issue of the magazine in my life." To his delight, he did exactly that as a senior in high school in 1978. "My winning entry, 'Ringtoss,' was my first published short story," he recalls.

Relatively fresh from his academic base, K. started writing fiction in his late twenties. Capturing the wonders and woes of those years was only natural. "I still had vivid memories," he told Gallo. The seasonal nature of high-school sports provided a manageable time frame against which K. would work.

But sports weren't the first topic K. broached as a first-time author. Instead, he turned to his experience teaching English in a Japanese school from 1983 to 1985 to craft *The Atami Dragons* (1984). Traveling the Japanese countryside and learning some of the language, K. became enchanted with the people and the environment. As a result, the book came together quite easily. Living an adventure brought energy to his fictional text.

That same first novel also introduced K. to the world of MOVIE making. After producer Paul Maslansky optioned the story for film, he asked K. to give him a tour of Atami, the resort town where he was teaching. Maslansky urged K. to come to Hollywood as a screenwriter when his teaching contract was fulfilled, and he did exactly that.

Instant fame was not attained, but knowledge certainly was. A decade later, as he was considering medical school on the East Coast, a promising script caught the attention of a prominent agent and paying screenwriting jobs came more consistently.

Even while writing for films, K. held to his desire to write YA novels. Fearless in his approach, K. tackled sports and the controversial allegations of the use of a performance-enhancing drug by high-school athletes in *Wrestling with Honor* (1989). When a straight (but gifted) athlete tests positive for drugs but is innocent, he takes a stand and refuses to test again or to compete. K. admits the plot line drew considerable fire, but when a good book shines light on a serious problem, he believes it is a positive thing. He has ferociously defended student rights to personal privacy.

Environmental issues proved just as powerful in *California Blue* (1994). Called "beautifully rendered" by *Publishers Weekly,* the story follows John Rogers' struggle with his father's terminal illness, his

399

uphill battle to protect an endangered butterfly species, and the attraction that develops between him and his youthful high-school biology teacher, Miss Merrill.

Ten years in Los Angeles convinced K. to take a fictional look at the battered local environment. Critically acclaimed, *California Blue* became one of K.'s most popular books, in part because he offered no easy answers. He acknowledged that while the butterfly was endangered, so were the people who might be unemployed by its protection. K.'s portrayal of the sexual attraction between student and teacher stirred the pot of literary controversy. But he makes no apology, sighting his own teenage crush on a high-school teacher as evidence of the plot point's authenticity. "Young adult novels cannot and should not shy away from realistic situations, even if they make some teachers and librarians and parents uncomfortable," he told Don Gallo.

In subsequent novels, K. proved just as courageous, tackling racism in *Danger Zone* (1996), the casting couch in *Screen Test* (1997), and child abuse in *You Don't Know Me* (2001). Humor was as crucial to *You Don't Know Me* as violence, K. insists, in order to maintain a readable balance. But the sacrifice of algebra, he says, was personal.

Though each of K.'s novels are distinctive, they have at least one thing in common. They jump into the action of the story just before a chain of events that will leave the main character changed and much more aware begins to unfold. It's habit for K.—and intention.

That change, he says, the evolution, is what touches readers, binding them emotionally to the book and the writer. He gauges his success, in part, by the letters he receives from young readers. When they tell him his work has touched them, has made a difference, he says "it's a truly wonderful feeling."

K. lives near Central Park in New York City today with his wife and two children.

SELECTED AWARDS: 1990 Southern California Council Fiction for Young Adults Award, *Wrestling with Honor; Danger Zone:* 1998 Nebraska Golden Sower Award and 1999 Oklahoma Library Association Sequoia Award; 2003–2004 South Carolina Young Adult Book Award Nominee, *You Don't Know Me;* ALA Best Books for Young Adults: *Wrestling With Honor,* 1990; *Danger Zone,* 1997; and *You Don't Know Me,* 2002.

FURTHER WORKS: *Breakaway Run,* 1986; *A Different Season,* 1988; *Home of the Braves,* 2002; *Dark Angel,* 2005.

BIBLIOGRAPHY: Farrar, Strauss & Giroux Author Profile: http://www.fsgkindsbooks.com/authordetails.asp?ID = Klass; Don Gallo Interview/*Authors4Teens;* Scholastic Biography: http://www2.scholastic.com/teachers/authorsandbooks/authorstudies/authorhome.jhtml?authorID = 1790&collateralID = 10718&displayName = Biography.

KELLY MILNER HALLS

KLASS, Sheila Solomon

Author, educator, b. 6 November 1927, Brooklyn, New York

K. is a teacher and author of PLAYS, novels, and SHORT STORIES. Growing up she attended P.S. 16, Eastern District High School, Brooklyn College, and later earned her M.A. (1951) and a M.F.A. (1953) from the State University of Iowa. Best known for her children's and YA-fiction books, K. uses realistic events as background for her characters' development as they overcome adversity through a combination of their personal characteristics, which include resourcefulness, courage, humor, and their abilities to strategize and plan thus leading to a successful conclusion and outcome of events. Her writings range from modern realistic novels to most recently, historical and fictionalized BIOGRAPHIES of famous women when they were young girls growing up, such as Louisa May ALCOTT in *Little Women Next Door* (2000) and Annie Oakley in *Shooting Star: A Novel About Annie Oakley* (1996).

K. is the mother of three children, professionals who have followed in her footsteps and are renowned writers in their own right: a daughter, Perri, a pediatrician and best-selling novelist and essayist; David, a YA writer and screenwriter *(Kiss the Girls);* and her youngest, Judy, a playwright who also writes SCIENCE FICTION novels *(The Cry of the Onlines—*a *Star Trek* novel), and has published three books of POETRY.

K. has traveled with her children and Morton, her husband, for forty-eight years (d. April 28, 2001), (and an expert in the anthropology of religion in South Asia as well as former professor of anthropology at Barnard College and Columbia University for over thirty years), as he conducted research in Trinidad, West Indies, and West Bengal, India.

K. has taught junior-high-school English as well as creative writing at Manhattan Community College. She has still found time to participate in the New York City Learning Leaders Program, reading aloud to students in the public schools and discussing her works.

AWARDS: Drue Heinz Literature Prize Finalist, *In An Open Field: A Novel,* 1997. ALA Recommended Book for Reluctant Young Adult Readers, *Rhino,* 1993. ALA BBYA, *Page Four,* 1987.

FURTHER WORKS: *To See My Mother Dance,* 1981; *Nobody Knows Me in Miami,* 1981; *Alive and Starting Over,* 1983; *The Bennington Stitch,* 1985; *Page Four,* 1986; *Credit-Card Carole,* 1987; *Kool Ada,* 1991; *Rhino,* 1993; *Next Stop: Nowhere,* 1995; *The Uncivil War,* 1997; *In a Cold Open Field: A Novel,* 1997.

BIBLIOGRAPHY: *Contemporary Authors Online,* 2001; *Eighth Book of Junior Authors and Illustrators,* pp. 271–73. H. W. Wilson.

VALERIE A. PALAZOLO

KLAUSE, Annette Curtis

Author, b. 20 June 1953, Bristol, England

The innovative works of K. have changed the tone of young adult SCIENCE FICTION and FANTASY. Vampires have become sensuous as well as scary, and aliens from outer space can be funny and have legitimate problems.

When K.'s father, a radiologist, was offered a temporary assignment in Washington, D.C., he moved his family from England to the U.S. By this time, red-haired K. was in her teens. The temporary assignment became a permanent one, and the family remained in the Washington area.

K. was intrigued by the supernatural, favoring ghost and HORROR stories. Once she stumbled across a box of science-fiction MAGAZINES her father had discarded, and the stories mesmerized her. She pursued her fascination and discovered the works of Robert HEINLEIN, C. S. LEWIS and Andre NORTON; science fiction was not "rubbish" as suggested by her mother but rather viable literature. She tried her hand at this form of writing and produced "The Blood Ridden Pool of Solen Goom," a SHORT STORY filled with blood and gore. She next turned her attention to POETRY; the shorter format appealed to the impatient adolescent.

K. entered the University of Maryland in 1976. Upon graduation, she discovered that a degree in En-

glish Literature was not sufficient to begin a career, so she returned to school, earning a Master's of Library Science. She worked for commercial companies in D.C. before finding employment as a children's librarian in the public library system of Montgomery County, Maryland. When asked in an interview whether her career as a librarian or writing for children came first in her life, she replied, "Many of my reasons for becoming a writer and becoming a children's librarian were pretty much the same: to be connected to literature, to bring others the joy of reading that I experienced as a child and to tell stories. My writing always seemed to be directed at children and TEENS even after I grew up." Once she had finished with her schooling and had a secure job, she began to submit poems and short stories to magazines, many of which remain unpublished. She joined a writing workshop at this time and was encouraged to write professionally. To this day, K. continues to meet with this group to discuss works in progress.

K.'s first YOUNG ADULT novel, *The Silver Kiss* (1990), presented vampires in a new light. Zoë, a teenager struggling with loneliness and her mother's terminal illness, meets Simon, an attractive three hundred-year-old vampire who is tracking his evil brother, Christopher. Their relationship helps Zoë deal with her life and sustains Simon during his final confrontation with Christopher. The sensual, tender love story between Zoë and Simon is totally different from any YA vampire/horror story previously written.

Alien Secrets (1993) introduces the character Puck who, after being expelled from boarding school, journeys on a space ship to meet her parents on the planet Shoon. She is asked to befriend Hush, an alien also traveling to Shoon and also in disgrace. Together they solve the mystery of a missing statue and are hailed as heroes. K.'s love of science fiction is clearly evident in this work for young teens.

In *Blood and Chocolate* (1997), K. returns to her horror theme with Vivian, a sixteen-year-old werewolf. She slides easily between her human and werewolf forms; she lives the life of a normal teenager with a human boyfriend by day, but becomes a member of a wolf family at night. Vivian lacks the warmth and tenderness of Zoë in *The Silver Kiss,* but the sensual, supernatural theme occurs in both novels.

The novels written by K. have received numerous awards and accolades. Both her strong female heroes that convey sensuality and her fast-paced plots make

K.'s voice a strong one in the field of young adult literature.

AWARDS: Best Book of the Year Honor Book; Booklist Best Books 1990, 1993; *School Library Journal* Best Books of the Year 1990, 1993, 1997; 1991 ALA Best Books for Reluctant Readers; ALA Best Books for Young Adults 1991, 1998; South Carolina Young Book Award 1993, 2000; 1993 California Young Reader Medal; 1993 Maryland Black-eyed Susan Award; 1993 Sequoyah Young Adult Award; 1997 *Booklist* Editor's Choice.

FURTHER WORKS: *Freaks*, 2006.

BIBLIOGRAPHY: "Authors Among Us—Children's Writers Who are or Have Been Librarians." (Online) http//ravenstonepress.com/klause.html, March 15, 2003; Hipple, Ted, *Writer for Young Adults*, supplement 1, 2000; McMahon, Thomas (ed.), *Authors & Artists for Young Adults*, vol. 27, 1999.

KATHIE FITCH

KNOWLES, John

Author, b. 16 September 1926, Fairmont, West Virginia; d. 30 November 2001, Fort Lauderdale, Florida

When K. wrote his coming-of-age masterpiece, *A Separate Peace* (1960), he sealed the fraternal love and loyalty of his own prep-school experience in a time capsule. While his years at Philips Exeter Academy were not peppered with the raging competition and jealousy that existed at the fabricated Devon Academy, K. wound his love for his former school into his most celebrated work. Such was its popularity that he was thought potentially to become the "next J. D. SALINGER." However, he never received equal accolades for subsequent works.

A Separate Peace, both hailed in the high-school English classroom and among adult literary circles as a novel of "exceptional power and distinction," explores various aspects of male adolescence in the summer prior to World War II. Like *A Separate Peace*'s protagonist, Gene Forester, K. was not part of the American Northeastern elite, yet his parents insisted on a more traditional education for their son. As a result, K. examined a brochure of Exeter and enrolled at the school at age fifteen. Following the completion of his B.A. from Yale University (1949), an experience which K. professed to be uninspiring after his time at Exeter, he worked as both reporter and drama critic for the *Hartford Courant*, experi-

mented with the freelance writing world, and served in the U.S. Army Air Force.

At the time of K.'s death, many devotees of *A Separate Peace* were left still questioning the purpose behind Phineas's pinnacle accident: did Gene intentionally cause Finny's downfall? The staying power of the novel has been proven, as high-school students have delved into this question for more than three decades.

The success of *A Separate Peace* allowed the author to embrace the profession of full-time writer with no need to rely on other means of income. The sequel, *Peace Breaks Out* (1981), revisits Devon Academy through the eyes of alumni and teacher Peter Hallam. Although critics admired K.'s prose and appreciated his intricate observations of adolescent male behavior, *Peace Breaks Out* did not achieve the literary recognition of its predecessor.

The American elite was studied further by K. in *Indian Summer* (1966) and *The Paragon* (1971), weighing conservative Northeastern lifestyle against a more individualistic and honest path. *A Stolen Past* (1983), another book based upon reflective characters and tragic events, is a commentary on the life of a writer. It is centered on Allan Prieston, a successful writer haunted by his own good fortune; the book explores his source of inspiration and his guilt over its exploitation. K.'s final novel, *The Private Life of Axie Reed* (1986), was formulated while the author recovered from an automobile accident, and is yet another example of his use of memory as a literary tool.

During the 1960s, K. served as writer-in-residence at the University of North Carolina and Princeton. He relocated to Florida in the mid-1980s and taught creative writing at Florida Atlantic University.

AWARDS: *Separate Peace,* 1960, Richard and Hinda Rosenthal Foundation Award, American Academy and Institute of Arts and Letters, and William Faulkner Foundation Award; one of 100 Young Adult titles selected for the 1st YALSA Best of the Best List: Still Alive (Selections from 1960 to 1974); *Peace Breaks Out,* ALA BBYA, 1981.

FURTHER WORKS: *Morning in Antibes,* 1962; *Double Vision: American Thoughts Abroad,* 1964; *Phineas,* 1968; *Spreading Fires,* 1974; *A Vein of Riches,* 1978.

BIBLIOGRAPHY: Review of *A Separate Peace, Times Literary Supplement,* May 1, 1959, p. 262; *Something about the Author,* vol. 89, 1997; Valby, Karen, "John

Knowles: 1926–2001: Rest in Peace," *Entertainment Weekly,* December 14, 2001, Issue 630.

RACHEL WITMER

KOERTGE, Ronald

Author and poet, b. 22 April 1940, Olney, Illinois

K. has been a professor at Pasadena City College since 1965. As a teenager, K. found he had a knack for both the written and the spoken word. He often used his ability to shock and to get attention. It wasn't until graduate school, though, that he began to take his writing seriously and sought publication for his work. His POETRY was well-received, and a novel for adults, *The Boogeyman,* was published in 1980. When K.'s two subsequent adult novels were rejected, a friend suggested the author's irreverent tone might be well-suited to YA literature. One of his rejected novels became *Where the Kissing Never Stops* (1986), and K.'s career as a young adult novelist began. Since that time, K. has written a number of novels for young adults, as well as two novels in poetic form.

K.'s stories are typically humorous and touching coming-of-age stories about male TEENAGERS. The books are sometimes controversial, as K. is both frank and realistic in his portrayal of sexual encounters. His believable, awkward characters wrestle with issues common to youth, including identity, peer pressure, insecurity, relocation, problems with parents, and sexual feelings. What might be called "dysfunctional" or "outrageous" is accepted as "normal" in the experiences of K.'s teenage protagonists.

Where the Kissing Never Stops details the concerns of seventeen-year-old Walker, whose mother has taken a job as a stripper, whose girlfriend recently left town, who seems unable to control his addiction to junk food, and who has recently begun a ROMANCE with a girl very different from himself. Through the course of the story, Walker reconciles these competing concerns and comes to some level of peace with his chaotic adolescence.

Billy, the main character of *The Arizona Kid* (1988), faces similar issues. He, too, falls in love, and deals with adult sexual behavior, this time in the form of his Uncle Wes's gay lifestyle. Set against the backdrop of horseracing, this realistic teen novel was included on ALA's 100 Best of Best list. K.'s first two novels established a framework for some of his later writing. *The Boy in the Moon* (1990) addresses a trio

of friends and changes in their relationship brought about by romance and conflict with parents. *Mariposa Blues* (1991) returns to the world of horse racing, this time as an important element in the main character's stormy relationship with his father. *The Harmony Arms* (1992) also takes a strong look at the teen-father relationship, while *Tiger, Tiger Burning Bright* (1994) expands the lens of FAMILY conflict outside of K.'s usual teen-parent focus, to examine intergenerational relationships through the experiences among Jesse, his mother, and his grandfather.

In *Confess-o-Rama* (1996), Tony gains a new circle of friends when he and his mother relocate after his stepfather's death. The teenager finds relief from the pressures of youth by calling an anonymous teen hotline, until he realizes that the hotline is not as innocuous as it initially seems. *The Brimstone Journals* (2001) blends K.'s love of poetry and experience with storytelling in a controversial novel. Fifteen narrative voices participate in this compelling, complicated story about an event of school violence.

K. returns to a single protagonist and revisits a poetic novel format in *Shakespeare Bats Cleanup* (2003). Fourteen-year-old Kevin, sidelined from his beloved game of baseball while recovering from mono, borrows his father's book of poetry. He begins to write haiku and sonnets mockingly, but as time passes, Kevin's wordplay becomes a useful device in helping him sort through a variety of teen issues.

AWARDS: *The Arizona Kid* (1988): ALA's 100 Best of Best list, ALA Best Books for Young Adults; National Endowment for the Arts Fellowship (1990); California Arts Council Grant for Poetry (1993); Arts Fellowship in 1990 and a California Arts Council Grant for Poetry in 1993; *The Arizona Kid,* 1988 Best Books for Young Adults List Also: Selected for "Here We Go Again: 25 Years of Best Books: Selections from 1967 to 1992"; *Boy in the Moon,* 1991 Best Books for Young Adults List; *The Brimstone Journals,* 2002 Best Books for Young Adults List; *Harmony Arms,* 1993 Best Books for Young Adults List; *Stoner and Spaz: A Love Story,* 2003 Best Books for Young Adults List; *Tiger, Tiger Burning Bright,* 1995 Best Books for Young Adults List; *Where the Kissing Never Stops,* 1986 Best Books for Young Adults List.

FURTHER WORKS: *The Heart of the City,* 1998; *Stoner and Spaz,* 2002; *Margaux with an X,* 2004.

BIBLIOGRAPHY: "Ronald Koertge." *Dictionary of Literary Biography,* vol. 105, 1991; "Ron K." *Authors and Artists for Young Adults,* vol. 43, 2002; "Ronald

K." *Contemporary Authors Online,* 2001; "Ron(ald) K." *St. James Guide to Young Adult Writers,* 2nd ed., 1999.

HEIDI HAUSER GREEN

KOLLER, Jackie French
Author, b. 8 March 1948

Reared in Derby, Connecticut, K. spent much of her childhood and young adult years weaving stories for her own pleasure and her friends' enjoyment. She attended the University of Connecticut, where she studied interior design and received a B.A. in 1970. She married George Koller that same year. George went on to graduate school, and K. supported them by taking a job with an insurance company. Her love of storytelling grew as she raised a daughter, Kerri, and two sons, Ryan and Devin.

K. credits her becoming a published author to the attendance at many writers' conferences and the help and support of her family and friends. Her first children's story appeared in an anthology in 1986. After working for six years and receiving numerous rejections from publishers, her first chapter book, *Impy for Always,* was published in 1989. Her first book for young adults, *Nothing to Fear,* was published in 1991. That book was followed in 1992 with K's *The Primrose Way,* a YA work of historical fiction.

Her first novel for YAs, *Nothing to Fear,* was based on K.'s mother's life during the Great Depression. Margaret French led a difficult life because of her abusive, alcoholic father; she had to work full time and leave school to help support her family. She met K.'s father, Ernest, after the start of World War II, when K. became an officer in the U.S. Navy.

K. was an excellent student, always receiving top grades, but she was very tall for her age and branded as "a giant and a brain." Somewhat of an outcast, she retreated into the world of books, daydreaming and communing with nature. She didn't think she could actually become a writer; however, she thought she might be able to work as an animator.

K. blossomed during her years at the University of Connecticut, no longer feeling singled out for her height, now being praised for her intellect. Still not thinking she could become a published writer, K. started by telling stories to her family and friends, and was encouraged by her husband's gift of a brand-new electric typewriter. K. always searched her background as the basis for her books, whether it was her father's infatuation with boats and the sea, which served as her inspiration for *The Last Voyage of Misty Day* (1992) or her experience with an alcoholic grandfather in *A Place to Call Home* (1995).

Whether writing for the beginning reader or for adolescents, K. tries to create an in-depth relationship with the character she is writing about. She says that sometimes she thinks a book will be for a younger audience, but in the end, after examining the subject, she realizes it should be re-written for a different audience. K. has also written poems and short stories; she has been regularly published since 1989. K. now lives in Western Massachusetts with her husband and her Labrador Retriever named Casse. K. maintains a website, which features her studio and her interest in gingerbread houses at www.geocities.com/jackie koller/novels.html. Her other hobbies include hiking, painting, and reading.

AWARDS: *If I Had One Wish,* 1991: 1992 YALSA Recommended Book for Reluctant Young Readers, 1992 NYPL Book for the TEEN Age; *Nothing to Fear,* 1991: 1992 NYPL Book for the Teen Age, 1992 IRA Teachers' Choice, 1993 IRA Young Adults' Choice, 2000 & 2001 Popular PAPERBACK for Young Adults; *The Primrose Way,* 1992: An ALA BBYA, 1993 NYPL Book for the Teen Age; *Last Voyage of Misty Day,* 1992: 1992 Junior Library Guild Selection, 1993 YALSA Recommended Book for Reluctant Young Readers, 1993 NYPL Book for the Teen Age; *A Place to Call Home,* 1995: 1995 American Bookseller Pick of the Lists, 1996 American Library Association Notable, 1997 IRA Teacher's Choice; Bulletin for the Center for Children's Books Blue Ribbon Award; Bank Street College Annual Book Award-Honor Book.

FURTHER WORKS: *If I Had One Wish . . . ,* 1991; *The Primrose Way,* 1992; *The Falcon,* 1998; *The Promise,* 1999; "Brother Can You Spare a Dream?," *Time Capsule Anthology,* 2000; *Someday,* 2002.

BIBLIOGRAPHY: Contemporary Authors Online, 2001; Jackie@aol.com; www.geocities.com/jackiekoller/novels.html.

SANDRA KITAIN

KONIGSBURG, E(laine) L(obel)
Author, b. 10 February 1930, New York City

One of the most distinguished writers of literature for young people, K. is the only author to have two books on the prestigious Newbery Award list at the same time. Often self-illustrating her books, K. is known for writing complex, witty stories that frequently come from personal experience, but also setting novels in the medieval world and the Renaissance. Praised by critics and scholars for her experimentation and innovation, many of K.'s sophisticated novels are better suited for YA audiences than younger children, although she is widely recognized as a children's author.

Born in New York City in 1930, K. grew up in small mill towns in Pennsylvania. An avid reader of all kinds of literature, she was a good student with a talent for drawing. She graduated high school as valedictorian and enrolled at Carnegie Mellon University in Pittsburgh, earning a degree in chemistry. While working as a bookkeeper to help pay for college, K. met her future husband David who was studying to become an industrial psychologist. After graduate study at the University of Pittsburgh, K. married David and moved to Florida where she taught science in an all-girls school. Teaching gave K. insight into the lives of young people that she would use with great skill in her writing.

K. left teaching in 1955 when her first child was born. By 1959, K. was a full-time mother raising three children, although she did take time to pursue painting. When her children all reached school age, K. started her writing career. She drew from her FAMILY life experiences for her books. She used her children as her first audience, reading them her work and revising based upon their reactions.

K.'s writing career was an immediate, astonishing success. Her first novel *Jennifer, Hecate, Macbeth, William McKinley, and Me, Elizabeth* (1967) was followed with the now-beloved classic *From the Mixed-up Files of Mrs. Basil E. Frankweiler* (1967). In 1968, K. received the Newbery Medal for her second novel and Newbery Honor Award for her first, the first and only time an author has achieved this dual distinction. For both of these novels, K. drew from observations she made of her own children. K.'s next two novels, *About the B'nai Bagels* (1969) and *George* (1970), were not as well received.

K.'s fascination with medieval times led her to write the historical FANTASY *A Proud Taste of Scarlet and Miniver* (1973), the life of Eleanor of Aquitaine told through the perspective of historical characters in heaven. Another historical novel, *The Second Mrs. Giaconda* (1975), tells the story of Leonardo da Vin-

ci's middle years. The MYSTERY *Father's Arcane Daughter* (1976) further revealed K.'s interest in experimenting with narrative.

K. received her second Newbery Medal in 1997 for *The View from Saturday* (1996), an innovative novel using a series of first-person narratives to tell the story of four members of a championship quiz-bowl team and the paraplegic teacher who coaches them. K. followed that novel with the edgy, provocative *Silent to the Bone* (2000), the story of thirteen-year-old Branwell who loses his power of speech when he is wrongly accused of injuring his baby sister. K. showcases her talent for creating odd, quirky stories with *The Outcasts of 19 Schuyler Place* (2004) about twelve-year-old Margaret Rose Kane who, upon leaving an oppressive summer camp, spearheads a spirited campaign to preserve three unique towers her great uncles built in her backyard over the course of forty years.

SELECT AWARDS: ALA BBYA, 1976, 2001, 2005; *Kirkus Reviews* Editor's Choice, 2004; *PW* Best Children's Books, 2004; SLJ Best Books for Children, 2004.

FURTHER WORKS: *The Dragon in the Ghetto Caper,* 1974; *Throwing Shadows,* 1979; *Journey to an 800 Number,* 1982; *Up from Jericho Tel,* 1986; *T-Backs, T-Shirts, COAT, and Suit,* 1993; *Blood Relation,* 2005.

BIBLIOGRAPHY: *Something about the Author,* vol. 126, pp. 127–33; *Talk Talk: A Children's Book Author Speaks to Grown-Ups* (Atheneum, 1995).

EDWARD T. SULLIVAN AND
WILLIAM AND MARY MARIANO

KOONTZ, Dean

Author, b. 9 July 1945, Everett, Pennsylvania

K. was born and reared in Pennsylvania. He had a difficult childhood, marked by poverty and violence. This was due in large part to his father's alcoholism and his mother's long bouts of illness. Books became a positive outlet for him as he grew. Today K. is a prolific author with many bestsellers to his credit and a huge fan base. His writing career began early in his life as a student at Shippensburg State College. By the time he graduated in 1966, he had already sold some of his work and won a fiction contest in the *Atlantic Monthly.* He continued writing part time while working as a teacher and counselor with underprivileged children in the Appalachian Poverty Program as a high-school English teacher. After three years, he focused on writing as his sole career.

It was not until 1980 that K. achieved success with mainstream readers, with the publication of his novel *Whispers*. While the book received mixed reviews, K. left his mark as a master of suspense and MYSTERY. K.'s works are sometimes referred to as HORROR novels, but he does not label them as such. Rather, he considers his novels to be representative of good triumphing over evil, and therefore, optimistic about life. His novels contain elements of various genres including horror, suspense, SCIENCE FICTION, and ROMANCE. He tackles tough issues facing modern society, such as the dangers of technology, the struggle between emotion and thought, and the supernatural. His plots often contain explicit violence, murder, and other dark elements. The influence of science fiction and the supernatural in K.'s novels has drawn many YA readers to his books. *Watchers* (1987) is credited as the first of K.'s books to attract a large YA following, and his YA audience continues to grow. In addition to his mainstream novels attracting young adults, K. has also written specifically for YA audiences, with *Oddkins* (1988) and *Santa's Twin* (1996).

K. is known as a best-selling author who delivers one suspenseful page-turner after another, including *The Bad Place* (1990), *Dragon Tears* (1992), *Mr. Murder* (1993), *Strange Highways* (1995), and *Sole Survivor* (1996). He has written under numerous pseudonyms such as Deanna Dwyer, K. R. Dwyer, Brian Coffey, Leigh Nichols, and Owen West. Many of his novels have been adapted into films, MOVIES, and television miniseries (*Demon Seed, Shattered, Watchers, Hideaway, Phantoms,* and *Intensity*). K. is responsive to his large and loyal fan base. He published an e-book, *The Book of Counted Sorrows* (2001) in response to his fans' urging. K. often quoted this fictitious book throughout his many novels. After years of his fans searching for *The Book of Counted Sorrows* to no avail, K. decided to publish it. K. currently lives in southern California with his wife of over thirty years.

AWARDS: 1987 ALA Best Books for Young Adults, *Watchers;* 1988 Daedalus Award, *Twilight Eyes.*

SELECT FURTHER WORKS: *The Vision,* 1977; *Twilight Eyes,* 1985; *Lightning,* 1988; *Oddkins: A Fable for All Ages,* 1988; *Cold Fire,* 1991; *Dark Rivers of the Heart,* 1994; *Santa's Twin,* 1996; *Watchers,* 1987; *Fear Nothing,* 1998; *By the Light of the Moon,* 2002; *The Face,* 2003; *The Paper Doorway,* 2003; *Odd Thomas,* 2003; *The Taking* 2004.

BIBLIOGRAPHY: *Something about the Author,* vol. 92, 1999; *Contemporary Authors,* vol. 95, 2001.

NANCY A. BUGGÉ

KORMAN, Gordon
Author, b. 23 October 1963, Montreal, Quebec

K. wrote his first published book when he was twelve years old and in the seventh grade, but, he says, it wasn't on purpose. That year the track coach was assigned to teach language arts, a subject he neither knew nor liked. The coach assigned a year-long writing project to write a book, telling the students they could write about anything they chose. K. decided to write his autobiography because there would be no need to do any research. Students were told to create an outline during the first week and submit a chapter each month. K. met the requirements but says the final document had no relation to the outline. At the end of the year, K. mailed his manuscript to Scholastic Inc. because that was the only publisher he knew; he had been in charge of collecting money from other students to pay for their weekly *Scholastic News.* Surprisingly, they published *This Can't Be Happening at MacDonald Hall* (1978) and continued to publish his work for the next twenty books.

The MacDonald Hall SERIES contains characters based on K.'s classmates and, not surprisingly, he understands them wholly. Readers laugh at the same jokes that made K. and his classmates laugh, and they speak the same language that the characters in his books speak. There is a tremendous overlap between the author and audience, which accounts for the vivid authenticity of K.'s work.

K. focused on the characters Bruno and Boots for six more titles. He began to feature more sophisticated slapstick as he, his characters, and his audience matured. Tired of reading books where the dog character always dies, Wallace Wallace refuses to write a favorable book report on "Old Shep, My Pal" for his English class in *No More Dead Dogs* (2000). In *The Toilet Paper Tigers* (1993), baseball fans cheer for the lighthearted romp. *The Chicken Doesn't Skate* (1996) creates a blast on ice hockey. The Slapshots series is packed around super-sports, and the action is hilarious.

When people ask K. how he writes his books, he says that he always starts off with something real, but then he unleashes his imagination to make it funnier, more interesting, or a better story. He says by the time he finishes a book, you can hardly recognize much of the real-life part. *The Son of the Mob* (2002), in which the Chief of Police's daughter becomes emotionally involved with the son of a Mafia boss has been partially described as Romeo and Juliet meet the Sopranos.

K.'s books are uproariously funny; he says that he wrote *The Zucchini Warriors* (1988) to keep his readers awake. While he has a special talent for humor, K. is expanding his typical approach into adventure, MYSTERY, and suspense with the Island trilogy: *Shipwreck, Survival,* and *Escape* (all 2001). Here six young adults are sent on a character-building boat trip that evolves into a fight for survival. K. comments on his shift in tone: "Here were six shipwrecked kids who were in real danger of dying every minute. That's not the time to be cracking jokes. So it's not humor that keeps the reader turning pages; it's suspense and fear." K. also has an Everest trilogy (*The Contest, The Climb,* and *The Summit,* all 2002) in which a group of TEENAGERS compete to become the youngest kids ever to climb Mt. Everest. Whatever genre he selects, K. knows how to create tension and hold the attention of his readers.

K. is an outstanding example of a young writer who seems likely to continue to make a significant contribution to the field of YA literature. He lives on Long Island with his wife and two children.

AWARDS: IRA Children's Choice Award: 1986 for *I Want to Go Home,* 1987 for *Our Man Weston;* 1987 Markham Civic Award for the Arts, for body of work; *A Semester in the Life of a Garbage Bag:* ALA Best Book List, 1987 and Editor's Choice, 1988; 1991 Air Canada Award, for body of work; *Losing Joe's Place:* ALA Best Book for Young Adults and Quick Pick for Reluctant Young Readers, both 1991; 1992 Manitoba Young Readers' Choice Award, *The Zucchini Warriors;* ALA Best Book for Young Adults: 2003 for *Son of the Mob,* 2004 for *Jake, Reinvented.*

SELECTED FURTHER WORKS: *Go Jump In The Pool,* 1979; *Beware The Fish,* 1980; *I Want To Go Home,* 1981; *Who Is Bugs Potter,* 1980; *Our Man Weston,* 1982; *Bugs Potter LIVE at Nickaninny,* 1983; *The War With Mr. Wizzle,* 1982; *No Coins Please,* 1984; *Don't Care High,* 1985; *Son Of Interflux,* 1986; *A Semester in the Life of a Garbage Bag,* 1987; *Radio 5th*

Grade, 1989; "A Reasonable Sum," *Connections* (ed Donald R. Gallo), 1989; *Losing Joe's Place,* 1990; *MacDonald Hall Goes Hollywood,* 1991; *The D-Poems of Jeremy Bloom,* 1992; *The Twinkie Squad,* 1992; *Why Did The Underwear Cross The Road,* 1994; *Something Fishy At MacDonald Hall,* 1995; *The Last-Place Sports Poems of Jeremy Bloom,* 1996; "Hamish Mactavish is Eating a Bus," *From One Experience to Another* (ed. M. Jerry Weiss & Helen S. Weiss), 1997; *The Sixth Grade Nickname Game,* 1999; *Nose Pickers From Outer Space,* 1999; *Planet Of the Nose Pickers,* 2000; *Invasion Of The Nose Pickers,* 2001; *Maxx Comedy: The Funniest Kid in America,* 2003; *Jake, Reinvented,* 2003; "Dive" Trilogy, 2003; *Son of the Mob,* 2004.

BIBLIOGRAPHY: Scholastic Author Fact Sheet; http://millennium.scholastic.com/wconnect/wc.dll?fc_bio ~factsheet~0000000093; Gordon K. Web page: www.gordonkorman.com.

BERNICE E. CULLINAN

KOSS, Amy Goldman
Author, b. 26 January 1954, Detroit, Michigan

K. turned to her passion for writing and illustrating after many varied but uninteresting jobs. She began her new career with the publication of several drawings, poems, articles and short stories. Following these successes, K. wrote and illustrated several PICTURE BOOKS with rhyming text.

After having children of her own, K. shifted her writing towards middle-school readers. Her work for this age group has won considerable praise for realistically capturing the problems of pre-adolescents. K. is able to clothe serious issues in sensitive and humorous text. *The Ashwater Experiment* (1999) appears on the School Library Journal's 1999 Best Books of the Year list. *The Girls* (2000) was a YALSA (Young Adult Library Services Association, a Division of the American Library Association) Best Book for Young Adults in 2001.

AWARDS: 1998 Bank Street College Children's Books of the Year in the special interest category, *How I Saved Hanukkah;* 1999 School Library Journal's Best Books of the Year, *The Ashwater Experiment; The Girls:* 2001 YALSA Quick Picks for Reluctant Young Adult Readers, 2001 YALSA Best Books for Young Adults.

SELECTED FURTHER WORKS: *The Trouble with Zinny Weston,* 1998; *How I Saved Hanukkah,* 1998; *Smoke Screen,* 2000; *Stolen Words,* 2001; *Gossip Times*

Three, 2001; *A Stranger in Dadland,* 2001; *Strike Two,* 2001; *The Cheat,* 2003; *Gossip Times Three,* 2003.

BIBLIOGRAPHY: School Library Journal website: http://slj.reviewsnews.com/ *Something about the Author,* v. 115, 1999; YALSA website: http://www.ala.org/yalsa.

LAURA CHARRON

KOTLOWITZ, Alex
Author, n.d., New York City

K. came to writing naturally since his father is also a writer. A graduate of Wesleyan University, at one time he wanted to major in zoology. A native of New York City, he relocated to Lansing, Michigan, and worked for *The Lansing Star.* After freelancing for about five years, he reported for the *Wall Street Journal* from 1984–1993.

The publication of *There Are No Children Here: The Story of Two Boys Growing up in the Other America* in 1991 was a heartbreaking testimony about the lives of two boys growing up in Chicago's Henry Horner Housing Project. The Rivers brothers, Lafayette and Pharoah, are portrayed as they try to survive conditions that would easily overcome almost anyone. Written with the cooperation of both boys and their mother, LaJoe Rivers, it is an eye-opening portrait that many citizens of this country would prefer never to see. It was expanded from an article K. did for the *Wall Street Journal.* Eventually named as one of the one hundred and fifty books of the 20th century by the New York Public Library, it is a terrifying look at the conditions some children in the U.S. live in. Oprah Winfrey appeared in a television film of the book in 1993 that premiered on ABC.

The Other Side of the River (1998) traces the response when a drowned black TEEN's body floats to the surface of the St. Joseph River in Michigan. His drowning is a subject of speculation in towns on two sides of the river, predominantly black Benton Harbor and predominantly white St. Joseph. The death of Eric McGinnis in 1991 remains unsolved despite K.'s diligent attempts to discover the truth—yet the other truths he discovers are riveting. K.'s work has also brought him the Robert F. Kennedy Journalism Award, as well as the George Polk Award.

K. is not only a former *Wall Street Journal* reporter, but during college was active in the Big Brother Program; he has also worked at an Atlanta settlement house. His career includes speaking engagements, as well as a stint as a writer-in-residence at Northwestern University. He is also a Distinguished Visitor at the John D. and Catherine T. MacArthur Foundation. K. lives near Chicago with his family.

FURTHER AWARDS: *Never a City So Red: A Walk in Chicago,* 2004.

AWARDS: *There Are No Children Here: the Story of Two Boys Growing Up in the Other America:* Helen B. Bernstein Award for Excellence in Journalism, Christopher Award, Carl Sandburg Award.

BIBLIOGRAPHY: www.amazon.com; http://lnf.uoregon.edu/notablc/kotlowitz.html; http://journalism.nyu.edu/pubzone/race_class/thiercernese/speaker1.htm.

JEANNE MARIE RYAN

KOZOL, Jonathan
Author, educator, b. 5 September 1936, Boston, Massachusetts

K. was born into a family of means. His father was a physician; his mother was a social worker. K. attended a private secondary school and then attended Harvard University where he graduated in 1958. As a Rhodes scholar, K. studied at Oxford. Concluding that education was something that extended beyond the academic world, he resigned his scholarship and moved to Paris into a working-class community where he tried his hand at writing. By the time K. returned to the U.S. in 1963, the country was in a state of turmoil because of the issue of race relations. The murder of three Freedom workers by the KKK served as a conduit for K; he began teaching in a summer program in Roxbury, Massachusetts, a predominately black community. This led to a teaching position in the Boston public school system.

K's experiences as a fourth-grade teacher were the basis of his first book *Death at an Early Age.* At the time it was written, public schools in Boston had not been desegregated. It was K.'s contention that what passed for teaching in the Roxbury schools was of poor quality, repressive, and deficient in imagination and creativity. Its net effect compromised the opportunities for success. *Death at an Early Age* was well received and received the National Book Award in 1968.

K.'s next book, *Free Schools,* was published in 1972. It can best be described as a "how to" guide for the creation of alternative schools by both parents and teachers. Other books by K. include *Illiterate America,* which focuses on adult illiteracy and the ensuing problems that it creates, particularly in the workplace. *Rachel and Her Children: Homeless Families in America,* set amidst the backdrop of New York's Fifth Avenue, provided the reader with an in-depth, personal look at the daily struggles faced by homeless families. *Rachel and Her Children* was widely acclaimed and was the recipient of the Robert F. Kennedy Book Award in 1989, as well as the Conscience in Media Award.

Savage Inequalities: Children in America's Schools (1991) was the result of K.'s visits to a wide range of public schools in different communities, both urban and suburban. Those schools located in urban areas are often dirty, overcrowded, and with limited resources and supplies for the students they serve; the suburban schools are physically appealing, well equipped, and appropriately staffed. As K.'s publisher noted in a letter to then–President Bush, *Savage Inequalities,* addresses the disparities that exist in public schools because of "the inequitable distribution of public funds" (Collier). In addition to receiving the New England Book Award for nonfiction in 1991, *Savage Inequalities* was the subject of a PBS special that focused on schools in America.

Starting in 1993, K. again spent time in an impoverished inner-city area, talking with children, parents, and community leaders who live there. *Amazing Grace: The Lives of Children and the Conscience of a Nation* is a collection of the hopes, aspirations, and thoughts of the children who live in the Mott Haven section of the Bronx, noted for its violence. The book was widely praised and became a bestseller. K. continues to be an advocate and voice for America's inner-city children.

AWARDS: National Book Award in Science, Philosophy and Religion (*Death at an Early Age*), 1968; Robert F. Kennedy Book Award, The Conscience in Media Award, ALA BBYA (*Rachel and Her Children*), 1989; Finalist, National Book Critics Circle Award, The New England Award in Non-fiction (*Savage Inequalities*), 1992 ALA BBYA (*Amazing Grace*), 1997. K. has also been a Rockefeller Foundation fellow and has received fellowships from the Field and Ford Foundations.

BIBLIOGRAPHY: Collier, Laurie (ed.) *Authors and Artists for Young Adults.* Vol. 46. Farmington Hills: Gale Research press, 2002; http://www.albany.edu/writers-inst/kozol.html; http://myhero.com/myhero/hero .asp?hero = jkozol

ALICE R. LEONE

KRAKAUER, Jon
Author, b. 1954, Brookline, Massachusetts

K. turned his outdoor hobbies into a profession by writing articles and nonfiction books. As an ardent reader, K. always had a secret fantasy about being a writer, but it was not until a friend quit his job to become a writer that K. began to seriously consider making writing a profession. An accomplished climber, K. got his first writing job for *American Alpine Journal.* Parlaying his interests into articles for everything from architectural magazines to *Smithsonian,* K. became a professional writer in 1983.

K.'s first book was a collection of essays on mountain climbing, *Eiger Dreams: Ventures Among Men and Mountains* (1990). K. was then commissioned to write an article on Christopher McCandless, a unique young man who chose to live his life as a modern-day Thoreau. This story of a man who died of starvation in the woods of Alaska was troubling to K., and became more troubling as parallels between McCandless's life and his own became apparent. After the article was completed, K. expanded the article into the book *Into the Wild* (1996). For the most part, it was the story of McCandless's life, but it also included chapters about K.'s life that described the lure of the outdoors, risks he had taken, and thoughts on how his own life might have turned out differently if luck had not been on his side.

K.'s next novel, which came about quite literally due to a force of nature, was also a commissioned work. While on a Mt. Everest expedition, during which he was working on an article on the commercialism of Everest climbing expeditions, K. and several others were caught in a surprise winter storm that killed eight climbers. K.'s reflections on this harrowing experience led to the compelling bestseller *Into Thin Air: A Personal Account of the Mount Everest Disaster* (1997). Adapted for television in 1997, *Into Thin Air* is a complex story that does not place blame. Saying he will quit writing before he ever quits climbing, K. argues that climbing matters: it is where "actions have real consequences."

AWARDS: American Library Association's Best Books For Young Adults (1998) for *Into Thin Air: A Personal Account of the Mount Everest Disaster* and (1997) for *Into the Wild.*

FURTHER WORKS: *Under the Banner of Heaven: A Story of Violent Faith,* 2003.

BIBLIOGRAPHY: *Authors and Artists for Young Adults,* vol. 24, 1998; *Contemporary Authors,* online, 2001; *Something about the Author,* vol. 108, 2000, *Boldtype,* online, 2000.

ANDREA LIPINSKI
AND MEGAN PEARLMAN

KREMENTZ, Jill

Author, photojournalist, b. 19 February 1940, New York City

Having begun her trailblazing career as a MAGAZINE writer and a reporter, as well as an award-winning photojournalist, K. published her first photo book, *Sweet Pea: A Black Girl Growing Up in the Rural South,* in 1969. Filled with K.'s intimate photographs of life inside the girl's school, church, and home, it included K.'s eloquent narrative, written as if by nine-year-old Sweet Pea herself. The book was endorsed by anthropologist, Margaret Mead, who praised it for bringing much-needed multicultural awareness to readers outside Sweet Pea's experience of the lingering discrimination against southern AFRICAN AMERICANS.

Moving on between 1976 and 1991 to develop a wide-ranging series of documentary-style books about children, K. photographed and wrote the A Very Young SERIES: *A Very Young Dancer, A Very Young Rider, A Very Young Gymnast, A Very Young Circus Flyer, A Very Young Skater, A Very Young Skier, A Very Young Actress, A Very Young Gardener,* and *A Very Young Musician.* She began her How It Feels series, which included *How It Feels When a Parent Dies, How It Feels When Parents Divorce, How It Feels to be Adopted* and *How It Feels to Live with a Physical Disability,* published between 1981 and 1992. K.'s husband, author Kurt VONNEGUT Jr., whom she married in 1979, wrote the preface to her book of penetrating photographs of over a thousand famous writers, *The Writer's Image* (1980). Another of her photographic projects, titled *The Writer's Desk* (1999), captures some of her 1,500 subjects at work.

AWARDS: American Institute of Graphic Artists Fifty Books of the Year List; *School Library Journal* Best

Books of the Year List and *The New York Times* Best Seller List of Children's Books, for *A Very Young Dancer,* all 1976; *A Very Young Rider* and *A Very Young Gymnast, School Library Journal* Best Books of the Year List 1978; Garden State Children's Book Award, 1980; *Washington Post*/Children's Book Guild Nonfiction Award, 1984. ALA Best Book for Young Adults: 1983 for *How It Feels to Be Adopted,* 1990 for *How It Feels to Fight for Your Life,* 1981 for *How It Feels When a Parent Dies.*

BIBLIOGRAPHY: *Contemporary Authors Online, Gale,* 2002; *Fifth Book of Junior Authors and Illustrators, WilsonWeb online,* 2003.

CATHERINE GIVEN

KRISHER, Trudy

Author, b. 22 December 1946, Macon, Georgia

K. grew up in southern Florida where, during her childhood, she acquired an awareness of the social dynamics between the races. It is out of this awareness that her first novel for young adults, *Spite Fences* (1994), emerged. "[*Spite Fences*] has its roots in my childhood," K. told *Contemporary Authors* (2002), "in the Jim Crow South at the beginning of the modern CIVIL RIGHTS MOVEMENT."

K. majored in English at the College of William & Mary and earned an M.A. at Trenton State College. In 1992 her first book, *Kathy's Hats,* was published. The book came at a time, notes Connie S. Zitlow (1997), when K. "and her children had faced so many struggles that she didn't think she would ever write again" (p. 156). Born not out of a sense of social injustice but out of a personal issue—Trudy's daughter's struggle against cancer—the book was the first of five published since 1992. In this children's book, Kathy's love of hats diminishes when she has to wear one after losing her hair during chemotherapy treatments, but revives when she is told about the most special hat of all, the thinking cap. In the "Author's Note," K. acknowledges the "special courage that lives in the hearts of all young cancer patients" (*Kathy's Hats,* 1995).

Spite Fences, published in 1994, has been acknowledged by various sources for its literary value and critical depth. For this novel K. won the Cuffie Award from *Publishers Weekly* for the Most Promising New Author of 1994. *Spite Fences* is an exploration of self in society, specifically, a white girl in Jim Crow society. Maggie Pugh, the protagonist, witnesses (in her racist community) and endures (from her abusive mother) the brutal effects of racism in the 1960s South. However, through the use of her camera—a gift from Zeke, her black friend—Maggie is able to capture, reveal, and accept the truth of her community and to learn who she is. Roberta Seelinger Trites (1999) writes about the empowering force photography holds in this novel. "For Maggie," Trites says, "the perspective the camera provides her is more than a matter of feeling a sense of agency—it is a matter of expressing truth" (p. 140). Eventually Maggie wins a *Life* magazine contest, and her photographs are published; thus, she becomes, through the exhibition of her photographs, a truth teller in the struggle for civil rights.

Kinship (1997), set in the same community as *Spite Fences,* deals with the concept of FAMILY. Yet it, too, is about a self in society, as Pert Wilson struggles to understand who she is and who her family is in terms of the society in which they live. "Pert . . . understands more about herself," says Zitlow (1997), "when she looks at others and is honest with herself about her family" (p. 161).

In *Uncommon Faith* (2003) K. continues the theme of human rights but sets the action of this novel in Millbrook, Massachusetts, in 1837–38. The novel, which deals with the rights of women and slaves and issues of religion, is told through the many voices of the community, but Faith Common, the spirited heroine, vocally and tacitly challenges many of the mores of her community. Elizabeth Bush (2004), for *The Bulletin of the Center for Children's Books,* says, "K. takes Faith well beyond the spunky, proto-feminist gal role of much of historical fiction by infusing her questioning spirit with religious as well as social motivation" (p. 284).

K. lives in Ohio where she is an assistant professor of Extended Learning and Human Services at Sinclair Community College.

AWARDS: *Spite Fences:* Best Books for Young Adults, 1995; ALA International Reading Association Children's Book Awards, Winner 1995 Older Readers International; Jefferson Cup Award Honor Book, 1995. *Kinship:* ALA Best Books for Young Adults, 1998; The Best Children's Books of the Year, 1998 (Bank Street College of Education). *Uncommon Faith:* Amelia Bloomer Project, 2004; ALA Best Books for Young Adults, 2004; Best Children's Books of the Year, 2004 (Bank Street College of Education); Capital Choices, 2003.

FURTHER WORKS: "We Love Lucy," *Time Capsule: Short Stories About Teenagers Throughout the Twentieth Century,* 1999; *Writing for a Reader: Peers, Process, and Progress in the Writing Classroom,* 1995.

BIBLIOGRAPHY: Bush, E. (2004). [Review of *Uncommon Faith*]. *The Bulletin of the Center for Children's Books, 57,* 283–84; Contemporary authors online, 2002, http://www.galenet.com/servlet/LitRC?final Auth = true; Retrieved June 18, 2004, from the World Wide Web; K., T., 1992, *Kathy's Hats: A Story of Hope.* Trites, R. S., 1999, "Narrative Resolution: Photography in Adolescent Literature, *Children's Literature: Annals of the Modern Language Association Division on Children's Literature and the Children's Literature Association, 27,* 129–49; Zitlow, C., 1997, "Trudy K.," T. Hipple, ed., *Writers for Young Adults,* pp. 155–63.

MARY MCMILLAN TERRY

KRULL, Kathleen

Author, b. 29 July 1952, Fort Leonard Wood, Missouri

K. was born in Missouri and attended Lawrence University where she earned a B.A. in 1974. She was employed as an editorial assistant at Harper & Row in Evanston, Illinois, moving on to the position of associate editor for Western Publishing in Racine, Wisconsin. She was promoted to managing editor at Raintree Publishers, Milwaukee, and later became senior editor at Harcourt in San Diego.

From 1984 on, K. began her freelance writing career, which included writing reviews. She taught at the University of Wisconsin-Milwaukee as well as at the University of California at Los Angeles and San Diego, and at San Diego State University. K. has been a speaker at numerous Writers' and Teachers' conferences and workshops.

K. has a broad knowledge of music since she played different instruments while growing up; she also minored in music at Lawrence. At the age of twelve she began playing her church organ. This interest developed into her music-themed books.

Several of K.'s excellent BIOGRAPHIES for young readers are very popular among students. Her book *Lives of Extraordinary Women: Rulers, Rebels (and What the Neighbors Thought)* (2000) features the stories of famous women such as Cleopatra, Joan of Arc, Harriet Tubman, and Eleanor Roosevelt. *Lives of the Presidents: Fame, Shame (and What the Neighbors*

Thought) (1998) features interesting information about Presidents, spanning from George Washington (no, he did not have wooden teeth) to Bill Clinton's favorite foods, pastimes, and the scandals of his presidency. Another popular book by K., *They Saw the Future: Oracles, Psychics, Scientists, Great Thinkers, and Pretty Good Guessers* (1999), features fascinating information about the Ancient Mayan civilization, Leonardo da Vinci, Nostradamus, and Jeane Dixon, the modern soothsayer.

Lives of the Musicians: Good Times, Bad Times (and What the Neighbors Thought) (1993) tells the stories of numerous composers, including Vivaldi, Mozart, and Beethoven. *Lives of the Artists: Masterpieces, Messes (and What the Neighbors Thought)* (1995) uncovers the secret of Van Gogh's ear, and reveals the lives of Michaelangelo, Frieda Kahlo, and Andy Warhol to eager readers. *Lives of the Writers: Comedies, Tragedies (and What the Neighbors Thought)* (1994) introduces Shakespeare, Poe, Twain, and Isaac Bashevis Singer as real people with peccadilloes. *Lives of the Athletes: Thrills, Spills (and What the Neighbors Thought)* (1997) deals with the lives of twenty athletes, on and off the playing field. *Lives of the Musicians, Lives of the Writers,* and *They Saw the Future* were all nominated for the Best Books for Young Adults lists (ALA).

K. lives in San Diego where she pursues interests in gardening, quilting, and traveling. She is a member of the Society of Children's Book Writers and Illustrators, Allied Authors of Wisconsin as well as The Chicago Children's Reading Roundtable. She writes reviews of children's books for *L. A. Parent Magazine,* and the *Los Angeles Times Book Review.* Publications in which her work appears include the *New York Times Book Review, Publishers Weekly,* and the *Chicago Tribune.* Her book *The Boy on Fairfield Street: How Ted Geisel Grew up to Become Dr. Seuss* has been named to the 2005–6 Master List for the Texas Bluebonnet Award.

AWARDS: *Gonna Sing My Head Off!:* Notable Book in the Field of Social Studies citation, American Library Association (ALA) Best Books citation, New York Public Library Children's Choice citation, and International Reading Asociation (IRA)-Children's Book Council, all in 1993; *Lives of the Musicians: Boston Globe–Horn Book* Honor Book in Nonfiction, ALA Notable Book Citation, IRA Teacher's Choice citation, all in 1994; Southern California Council on Lit-

erature for Children, and Young People, 1993; Golden Kite Honor Book award for nonfiction; Society of Children's Book writers and Illustrators, 1993; PEN Wet Children's Literature Award, 1994; "Celebrate Literacy" Award, Greater San Diego Reading Association, 1994.

FURTHER WORKS: (as Kathleen Cowles): *The Seven Wishes,* 1976; *Golden Everything Workbook Series,* 1979; *What Will I Be?/A Wish Book,* 1979. (as Kathryn Kenny): *Trixie Belden and the Hudson River Mystery,* 1979; *The Mystery of the Antique Doll,* 1984; *The Mystery of the Memorial Day Fire,* 1984; *The Indian Burial Ground Mystery,* 1985; *The Mystery of the Headless Horseman,* 1985; *The Mystery of the Mississippi,* 1985; *The Pet Show Mystery,* 1985; *The Black Jacket Mystery,* 1986; *The Mystery of the Galloping Ghost,* 1986; *The Mystery of the Vanishing Victim,* 1986; *The Mystery of the Velvet Gown,* 1986. (As Kevin Kenny): *Sometimes My Mom Drinks Too Much,* 1980; *It Only Hurts When I Grow,* 1988; *The Christmas Carol Sampler,* 1983; *Songs of Praise,* 1988; *Twelve Keys to Writing Books That Sell,* 1989; *Alex Fitzgerald's Cure for Nightmares,* 1990; *Alex Fitzgerald, TV Star,* 1991; *Gonna Sing My Head Off! American Folk Songs for Children,* 1992; *It's My Earth, Too: How I Can Help the Earth Stay Alive,* 1992; *Maria Molina and the Days of the Dead,* 1994; *City Within a City: How Kids Live in New York's Chinatown,* 1994; *The Other Side: How Kids Live in a California Latino Neighborhood,* 1994; *Bridges to Change: How Kids Live on a South Carolina Sea Island,* 1995; *One Nation, Many Tribes: How Kids Live in Milwaukee's Indian Community,* 1995; *Presenting Paula Danziger,* 1995; *Calafia; The Queen of California,* 1995; *V is for Victory: America Remembers World War II,* 1995; *Wish You Were Here: Emily Emerson's Guide to the 50 States,* 1997; *Wilma Unlimited: How Wilma Rudolph Became the World's Fastest Woman* (contributor), 2000; *The Book of Rock Stars: 24 Musical Icons That Shone Through History,* 2003; *A Woman for President: The Story of Victora Woodhull,* 2004.

BIBLIOGRAPHY: The Gale Group, "Contemporary Authors Online." 2001. *Something about the Author,* Vol. 80, 1995.

SANDRA KITAIN

KUKLIN, Susan
Author, photographer, b. 6 September 1941, Philadelphia, Pennsylvania

Blending her outstanding photo-journalistic talents with a penchant for dramatic storytelling, K. is the author of over twenty books, many of which tackle controversial and difficult subjects for TEENS. Her works for young adults range from suicide to AIDS, from prejudice to human-rights activists. K.'s books are notable for her ability to find human drama behind the statistics, making them both informative and pleasurable to read.

Majoring in drama at New York University, K. complemented her formal education with acting classes at the Herbert Berghof Studio. In graduate school K. found herself losing interest in an on-stage career in favor of directing. After graduating from NYU, she supplemented her meager theater income by working as an English teacher and curriculum specialist with New York City schools. Stressing drama in her curriculum, K. found particularly rewarding her success in helping inner-city students learn how to appreciate Shakespeare. During these years, K. traveled widely and took up photography, first as a hobby to record the trips she made.

K. did not turn to writing books until she was living in Knoxville, Tennessee, where, working with Planned Parenthood, she produced a photo-essay of mountain families in the region. Editors took notice of her work and commissions followed. K. honed her photographic skills, immersing herself in further study and also learning printing and other darkroom techniques. Once back in New York, she showed her portfolio around to publishers. She was soon contributing photographs to children's books. K. contributed photographs to eight children's books before writing and publishing one of her own, *Mine for a Year* (1984). Her books for YOUNG ADULTS are aimed at both middle- and high-school audiences. Many of her books have incorporated her lifelong interest in the theater and the performing arts.

AWARDS: ALA Best Book for Young Adults: 1995 for *After a Suicide: Young People Speak Up;* 1990 for *Fighting Book: What Some People Are Doing about AIDS;* 1987 for *Reaching for Dreams: A Ballet from Rehearsal to Opening Night;* 1992 for *What Do I Do Now? Talking about Teenage Pregnancy.*

FURTHER WORKS: *Fighting Back: What Some People are Doing About AIDS* (1988); *What Do I Do Now: Talking About Teenage Pregnancy* (1991); *Speaking Out: Teenagers Talk on Race, Sex, and Identity* (1993); *After a Suicide: Young People Speak Up* (1994); *Irrepressible Spirit: Conversations with Human Rights Activists* (1996); *Iqbal Masih and the Crusaders Against Child Slavery* (1998); *Hoops with Swoopes* (with Sheryl Swoopes) (2001); *Trial: The Inside Story* (2001).

SOURCES: www.susankuklin.com; *Something about the Author,* vol. 95, pp. 105–108; Personal assessment of books; book flyleaves.

EDWARD T. SULLIVAN

LACKEY, Mercedes Ritchie
Author. b. 24 June 1950. Chicago, Illinois

L. is one of the most prolific FANTASY authors of the last decade. She describes herself primarily as a storyteller, though she is also an accomplished musician, a federally licensed bird rehabilitator, and an amateur dollmaker. Reared in Indiana, L. graduated from Purdue University in 1972 with a degree in biology. After graduation, she worked as an artists' model and computer programmer until a new job took her to Tulsa, Oklahoma, where she worked for American Airlines from 1982 until 1990. She left to write full time. During this period, L. wrote numerous stories for SCIENCE FICTION and fantasy fanzines publishing imitations of Andre NORTON (one of her greatest influences as well as later collaborator) and the first Diana Tregarde stories, which appeared in *Shadowstar*. L. attended conventions where she shared her work and met established writers like C. J. CHERRYH, who encouraged L. to send her work to professional markets. Following that advice, L. submitted a novel to DAW Books, and in 1987 they published her first novel, *Arrows of the Queen,* followed quickly by sequels *Arrow's Flight* (1987) and *Arrow's Fall* (1988).

At the center of that trilogy is perhaps L.'s best-known creation, the fantastic land of Valdemar, site of a host of intertwined series—which span over 600 years of history. Home to both humans and intelligent nonhuman species, Valdemar features some of L.'s most memorable characters such as the birdlike Gryphons and the Companions, godlike psychic horses

who bond with exceptional humans, elevating the human to the status of Herald of Valdemar. The Mage Winds Trilogy, beginning with *Winds of Fate* (1991), takes up where *Arrow's Fall* leaves off. The story features Elspeth, who is not only heir to the throne, but also a Herald, and who must find a way to renew the magic that protects Valdemar. Her story, continued in *Winds of Change* (1992) and *Winds of Fury* (1993), is told from a different point of view in *By the Sword* (1991), a separate novel set during the same time period as the books in the Mage Winds Trilogy, but told from the point of view of Kerowyn, Elspeth's arms instructor.

The last Herald-Mage SERIES takes place six hundred years before the events of the previous two series. In *Magic's Pawn* (1989), Vanyel is the Last Herald Mage and heir to the throne, but yearns to be a Court Bard instead. He discovers his talent for magic in *Magic's Promise* (1989) and becomes the most powerful mage in Valdemar. Vanyel is a complex character, alienated from his parents (who disapprove of his homosexual relationship) and haunted by dreams of his own death. The third book, *Magic's Price* (1990), unites Vanyel and his parents, but true to his dreams he loses his life defending Valdemar from its enemies. The remaining Valdemar series are equally intertwined and cover various periods during Valdemar's history. The Mage Storms trilogy, which includes *Storm Warning* (1994), *Storm Rising* (1995), and *Storm Breaking* (1996) tells of violent magical storms that threaten Valdemar. The Owl Mage trilogy, written with husband Larry Dixon, takes place in the aftermath of those storms and includes *Owlflight* (1997), *Owlsight* (1998), and *Owlknight* (1999). Also written with her husband, the volumes in the Mage Wars trilogy—*The Black Gryphon* (1993), *The White Gryphon* (1994), and *The Silver Gryphon* (1996)—take place a millennia before the other Valdemar novels, and tells the story of the legendary Gryphon Skanandron.

Set in a world radically different from Valdemar, L.'s Bedlam Bard, SERRAted Edge, and Diana Tregarde series are urban fantasies that combine some of L.'s most-often recurring themes: abused or alienated TEENS with magical abilities, elves, evil mages, and music. The Bedlam Bard series includes *Knight of Ghosts and Shadows* (with Ellen Guon, 1990), *Summoned to Tourney* (with Ellen Guon, 1992), *Spirit's White as Lightning* (with Rosemary Edghill, 2001) *Beyond World's End* (with Rosemary Edghill, 2001), and *Mad Maudlin* (with Rosemary Edghill, 2003) and tells the stories of Bard Eric Banyon, Julliard–caliber musician and frequent hero in the battle between the less-savory Unseleighe Sidhe and the modern world.

The gritty SERRAted Edge books are a collaborative, shared world series that feature the South Eastern Road Racing Association (SERRA), a group of elves who enchant the cars that they race. The first book in the series, *Born To Run* (with Larry Dixon, 1992), deals with child pornography and prostitution. *Wheels of Fire* (with Mark Shepherd, 1992) takes it even further, with a central plot involving parental kidnapping, a religious cult, intolerance, racism, violence, and abuse. The main character of *When the Bough Breaks* (with Holly Lisle, 1993) is a young girl with an abusive past and *Chrome Circle* (with Larry Dixon, 1994) deals with interracial (or in this case, interspecies) relationships. In keeping with L.'s focus on misunderstood and abused youth, each volume includes phone numbers that readers can call to help in the search for missing children and helpline numbers for youth in abusive situations. Though the subject matter is often difficult, the series is not as gloomy as it may seem, offering hope and optimism with the outcome of each volume. Similar in tone, the Diana Tregarde Investigations novels mix HORROR, fantasy, and private investigation, telling the story of a psychic investigator and Guardian—Diana Tregarde, a witch whose duty is to oppose and curtail the misuse of Magick, and whose cases, as a result, often involve

supernatural and occult forces. *Burning Waters* (1989) features a series of ritualistic murders committed by devotees of dark magic; *Children of the Night* (1990) is a vampire MYSTERY with a twist; and *Jinx High* (1991) centers on the dark power sleeping beneath Tulsa, Oklahoma, and the high-school girl (or is she?) who wants to wake it.

Along with elves, music, and a concern for youth, collaborations are another L. staple. As evinced above, L. frequently writes tandem, and claims she can imitate anyone else's style. Some of L.'s more successful stand-alone collaborations are based on video and computer games: *Freedom Flight* (with Ellen Guon, 1992) is based on the video game *Wing Commander,* and *Castle of Deception* (with Josepha Sherman, 1992) is based on the popular *Bard's Tale* computer game. But her best-known partnership is with Andre Norton. The Halfblood Chronicles, all written with Norton, includes *The Elvenbane: An Epic High Fantasy of the Halfblood Chronicles* (1991), *Elvenblood* (1994), *Elvenborn* (2002), and *Elvenbred* (2004), and tell the story of elves who control the world and keep humans as slaves.

AWARDS: *Arrows of the Queen:* ALA Best Books for Young Adults, 1987; *Magic's Price* won 1991 Lambda Award; *Magic's Pawn* nominated in 1990 and *Storm Warning* nominated in 1995 for Lambda Awards; Science Fiction Book Club Book of the Year Award 1991 for *The Elvenbane* (novel with Andre Norton); *Bardic Voices: The Lark and the Wren:* ALA Best Books for Young Adults, 1993.

FURTHER WORKS: *The Oathbound* (novel), 1988; *Oathbreakers* (novel), 1989; *Lark and the Wren* (novel), 1992; *The Ship Who Searched* (novel with Anne MCCAFFREY), 1992; *Fortress of Frost and Fire* (novel with Ru Emerson), 1993; *If I Pay Thee Not in Gold* (novel with Piers ANTHONY), 1993; *Prison of Souls* (novel with Mark Shepherd), 1993; *Rediscovery* (a *Darkover* novel with Marion Zimmer BRADLEY, 1993; *The Robin and the Kestrel* (novel), 1993; *A Cast of Corbies* (novel with Josepha SHERMAN), 1994; *The Eagle and the Nightingales* (novel), 1994; *Sacred Ground* (novel), 1994; *The Fire Rose* (novel), 1995; *The Sword of Knowledge* (anthology), 1995; *Tiger Burning Bright* (novel with Marion Zimmer Bradley and Andre Norton), 1995; *Firebird* (novel), 1996; *Four and Twenty Blackbirds* (novel), 1997; *Sword of Ice and Other Tales of Valdemar* (anthology), 1997; *Fiddler Fair* (SHORT STORY COLLECTION), 1998; *Oathblood* (novel), 1998; *The Black Swan* (novel), 1999; *Flights of Fantasy* (anthology), 1999; *The Riv-*

er's Gift (novel), 1999; *Werehunter* (short story collection), 1999; *Brightly Burning* (novel), 2000; *The Serpent's Shadow* (novel), 2001; *It Takes a Thief* (novel), 2001; *Exile's Honor* (novel), 2002; *Gates of Sleep* (novel), 2002; *Shadow of the Lion* (novel with Dave Freer and Eric Flint), 2002; *Joust* (novel), 2003; *The Outstretched Shadow* (novel with James Mallory), 2003; *This Rough Magic* (novel with Dave Freer and Eric Flint), 2003; *Exile's Valor: A Novel of Valdemar* (novel), 2003; *The Fairy Godmother,* 2004; *This Scepter'd Isle,* 2004; *Alta,* 2004; *The Wizard of Karres,* 2004.

BIBLIOGRAPHY: L., *St. James Guide to Fantasy Writers,* 1996, reproduced in Biography Resource Center, 2003, http://www.galenet.com/servlet/BioRC; L., *St. James Guide to* YA *Writers,* 2nd ed., 1999, reproduced in Biography Resource Center, 2003, http://www.galenet.com/servlet/BioRC; L., *Authors and Artists for YA,* vol. 13, reproduced in Biography Resource Center, http://www.galenet.com/servlet/BioRC; http://www.greenmanreview.com/mercedes.lackey.omnibus.htm; http://www.mercedeslackey.com.

JULIE BARTEL

LAIRD, Elizabeth
Author, n.d., New Zealand

Her parents were from Scotland and New Zealand, but L. is a world citizen. She left her New Zealand homeland to become a teacher in Malaysia in a girls' school. She taught in Ethiopia and was a disc jockey on Radio Voice of Gospel that broadcast throughout Africa and India. She met her husband-to-be David McDowell while flying through India, and lived in Baghdad where he was employed by the British Council; L. worked as a violinist in the Iraq Symphony Orchestra. McDowell's work next took them to Beirut in the midst of the country's civil war. Their second son was born in Vienna, where they had been sent in the midst of the crisis in Beirut.

L. does not consider herself an issue writer, although her books tend to tackle subjects of some seriousness. *Red Sky in the Morning* (1988), recommended for the Carnegie Medal and on the short list for the Children's Book Award, and *Kiss the Dust* (1994) were based on personal experiences. In *Red Sky,* L.'s brother who was disabled and died influenced the author's portrait of Anna and her own ill brother, Ben; observing the Kurds in Iraq provided material for *Kiss the Dust. Jake's Tower,* on the short-list for the 2001 Carnegie Medal, was not necessarily based on any of her life experiences. *The Garbage King* (2003) follows Ethiopian street children as they struggle to survive.

L. traveled to Africa to collect stories based on African oral traditions. She has traveled to Ethiopia, Kenya, New Zealand, India, and China, as well as other locations and speaks some Amharic. When at home in Richmond, Britain, L. gardens and likes to watch movies. According to the author, reading and writing are important ways for writers to hone their craft.

AWARDS: *Loving Ben:* ALA Best Books for Young Adults, 1990; *Red Sky in the Morning:* Carnegie Medal nominee, shortlist for Children's Book Award; *Kiss the Dust:* 1992 Children's Book Award, Dutch Royal Geographical Society Glass Globe Award; ALA Best Books for Young Adults, 1993; Shortlist for 2001 Carnegie Medal, *Jake's Tower.*

FURTHER WORKS: *The Garden,* 1979; *Clara,* 1988; *Anna and the Fighter,* 1989; *Simon and the Spy,* 1990; *Hiding Out,* 1993; *Stinker Muggles and the Dazzle Bug,* 1995; *Secret Friends,* 1996; *Anita's Big Day,* 1997; *Graffix: the Listener,* 1997; *Dead Man's River,* 1998; *Eddy and the Movie Star,* 1999; *Sugar and Candy,* 1999; *The House on the Hill,* 1999; *Secret Friends,* 1999; *The Storm,* 1999; *The Christmas Gift,* 2002; *The Ice Cream Swipe,* 2003; and the Wild Things SERIES (ten novels set in Africa—series deals with conservation).

BIBLIOGRAPHY: www.amazon.com; www.jubileebooks.co.uk/jubilee/magazine/authors/liz_laird/liz_laird_profile.asp; www.jubileebooks.co.uk/jubilee/magazine/authors/liz_laird/liz_laird_interview.asp; www.novels4.epnet.com

JEANNE MARIE RYAN

LANDAU, Elaine
Author, b. 15 February 1939, Lakewood, New Jersey

A prolific author of well-researched and well-written nonfiction, L. has over two hundred books to her credit. Always an aspiring writer, L. wrote her first book when she was nine-years old. She was in her mid-twenties when *Black in America: A Fight for Freedom* (1973), co-authored by CIVIL RIGHTS activist Jesse Jackson, was published. Before pursuing writing full time, L. worked as an editor, journalist, and librarian.

Frequently praised by reviewers for her careful research and engaging writing style, L. covers a wide range of topics in her books, including diseases, drug abuse, feminism, the HOLOCAUST, paranormal phenomena, sexual harassment, slavery, and white supremacy. L. is also the author of numerous BIOGRAPHIES about such figures as John F. Kennedy Jr., Osama bin Laden, and Prince William. A recent biography is *Heroine of the Titanic: The Real Unsinkable Molly Brown* (2001).

Many of L.'s books address issues that are of particular interest to contemporary TEENAGERS, such as alcoholism and drug abuse, dating, eating disorders, relationships, and sexuality. Typically concise, engaging, and accessible to a variety of reading levels, L.'s books are frequently used by students for researching homework assignments and by reluctant readers who find more in-depth INFORMATIONAL books too difficult.

SELECT FURTHER WORKS: *Teenage Drinking* (1994); *The Beauty Trap* (1994); *Breast Cancer* (1995); *Hooked: Talking about Addiction* (1995); *Fortune Telling* (1996); *Near-Death Experiences* (1996); *Standing Tall: Unusually Tall People* (1997); *The Sumerians* (1997); *Living with Albinism* (1998); *Tourette Syndrome* (1998); *Air Crashes* (1999); *Parkinson's Disease* (1999); *John F. Kennedy, Jr.* (2000); *Land Mines: 100 Million Hidden Killers* (2000); *Autism* (2001); *Slave Narratives: The Journey to Freedom* (2001); *Osama Bin Laden: A War Against the West* (2002); *Veterans Day: Remembering Our War Heroes* (2002); *Cocaine* (2003); *A Healthy Diet* (2003); *American Icons: Nike, McDonalds, Coca Cola, Levi Strauss,* 2003; *Alcohol,* 2003; *Dyslexia,* 2004; *Wild West Outlaw,* 2004; *Schizophrenia,* 2004; *Jesse James: Wild West Train Robber,* 2004.

BIBLIOGRAPHY: www.elainelandau.com; *Something about the Author,* vol. 94, pp. 135–39.

EDWARD T. SULLIVAN

LANTZ, Francess
Author, b. 27 August 1952, Trenton, New Jersey

L. attended Dickinson College, completing a B.A. in 1974 and an M.L.S. at Simmons College in 1975. She has written and published over thirty books, many of which are serial books: Varsity Coach SERIES (1986, 1987), Swept Away series (1986, 1987), Sweet Valley Twin books (1988, 1989), and You're the One! series (2000).

L. creates a good rapport with her young readers. She is interested in what interests them. In an interview she told *Contemporary Authors,* "I was a consumer of popular culture (rock 'n' roll, fashion, mov-

ies, etc.) as a teenager and I still enjoy it," (2001). L. understands her readers and can relate to them. "For some reason," L. told *Contemporary Authors,* "I find it very easy to remember my pre-teen and teenage years" (2001). Given her keen memory of her TEEN experience and her knowledge of contemporary fashions, music, and concerns, L. is able to create stories that are readily accessible to young readers. This is evidenced by Disney's decision to make her book *Stepsister from Planet Weird* (1997) into a MOVIE.

Another way L. connects with her readers is through her visits to schools, opportunities that give her delight. In an interview with Jo Ellen Misakiam (2002), L.'s enjoyment in meeting her young readers is evident as she describes her emotions after meeting and talking to students who were enthusiastic about her visit: "Back in my hotel room [at the end of the day] I'm still buzzing from my day. I made the kids laugh, and I made them think. I inspired them to be creative, to question the world, to write, and to read. I feel like . . . a success!" (p. 24).

L. has found success in terms of the quantity and quality of her books. *Someone to Love* (1997) has received positive critical feedback. In this novel, fifteen-year-old Sara must struggle with her parent's decision to adopt a baby. "My novels are about contemporary kids trying to discover who they are and what they believe in," L. told *Contemporary Authors* (2001). In *Someone to Love,* Sarah must do just that. She meets and befriends the baby's young mother, and this makes her anxious for the freedom that she has not known in her suburban life. After running away with the young mother, Sara must decide for herself what she will ultimately do. Anne O'Malley, writing for *Booklist,* says, "the novel explores all sides of adoption very well" (1997, p. 1420).

L. lives in Santa Barbara, California, with her husband and son.

AWARDS: *On the Fringe:* Best Books Best Books for Young Adults, 2002; Los Angeles' 100 Best Books, 2001 (IRA Children's Literature and Reading SIG and the Los Angeles Unified School District) *Someone To Love:* Best Book for Young Adults, 1998; Young Adults' Choices, 1999 (International Reading Association).

FURTHER WORKS: *Good Rockin' Tonight,* 1985, 1982; *The Truth about Making Out,* 1990; *Dear Celest, My Life is a Mess,* 1992; *Mom, There's a Pig in My Bed!,*

1992; Boys' School Girls series: *Randy's Raiders,* 1994; *Be a Star!,* 1996; *Neighbors from Outer Space,* 1996; *Someone to Love,* 1997; series books: In the Avon Flare Book series: *Fade Far Away,* 1998; The New Adventures of Mary-Kate and Ashley series: *The Case of the Missing Mummy,* 1998; You're the One! series: *Love Song,* 2000; *A Royal Kiss,* 2000; *Lights! Camera! Love!,* 2000; *Letters to Cupid,* 2001; *Stepbaby from Planet Weird,* 2001; *On the Fringe,* 2001; *On Her Way: Stories and Poems About Growing Up Girl,* 2004; Luna Bay series.

MARY MCMILLAN TERRY

LARSON, Gary

Cartoonist, b. 14 August 1950, Tacoma, Washington

L. is known for *The Far Side,* his syndicated daily comic-strip feature that ran from 1979 until his retirement in 1995. It has been collected into several bestselling compilations and numerous cartoon-a-day calendars.

After working in various settings, including for the Humane Society, L. sold his first comic strips to nature MAGAZINE *Pacific Search.* His first regular comic strip, "Nature's Way," began running in the *Seattle Times* in 1978; it was canceled within a year due to its "unnatural selection of . . . subject matter." The *San Francisco Chronicle* hired L. and introduced *The Far Side* as a daily in 1979. It featured often absurd takes on common and farfetched situations. The subjects were frequently any one of a variety of anthropomorphized creatures (particularly cows, dinosaurs, and pets), usually portrayed as more intelligent than their human counterparts. When humans were featured, they were often portrayed as foolish or insignificant.

Critics have described *The Far Side* as "radically dependent on twists of perception" and "hooking deeply into the psyches of the susceptible." Critical acclaim did come, with several awards following. *The Far Side* was often controversial, a trait for which L. strove: "If you start doing cartoons that are too universal, you end up with something . . . uninteresting. I'd rather be misunderstood." Popular collections include *The Far Side* (1982), *Beyond "The Far Side"* (1983), various years of *"The Far Side" Gallery* (1984–1995).

His first work after retiring from writing *The Far Side* strip was a PICTURE BOOK with great appeal for TEENS and adults. *There's a Hair in My Dirt: A*

Worm's Story provides an ecological lesson on the dangers of nature in a story a father worm tells his son. The result is a work that is full of irreverant, laugh-out-loud humor, the L. way.

AWARDS: National Cartoonists Society Award, Best Humor Panel, 1986; Reuben Award (National Cartoonists Society), Outstanding Cartoonist of the Year, 1991; Max and Moritz Prize (International Comics Salon), Best International Comic Strip Panel, 1993; ALA Best Book for Young Adults for *Prehistory of the Far Side: A Tenth Anniversary Exhibit* (1991) and *There's A Hair in My Dirt: A Worm's Story* (1999).

FURTHER WORKS: *Prehistory of "The Far Side": A 10th Anniversary Exhibit,* 1989; *Complete "Far Side,"* 2003.

BIBLIOGRAPHY: *Contemporary Authors,* New Revision Series, vol. 60, 1998. *Something about the Author,* vol. 57, 1989.

MYRON A. MYKYTA

LASENBY, Jack

Author, b. 9 March 1931, Waharoa, Eastern Waikato, New Zealand

L. is the honored bard of past and future in literature in New Zealand. Although he attended Matamata District High School and Auckland University, L. feels the most important part of his education was in the wilderness of the Urewera Mountains. He was in a group of trainee deer-cullers, who listened at night to the brilliant storyteller Ted Rye; six of these young men later became published authors.

For most of his life, L. has worked with men who told stories: on the wharves, in freezing work and bush camps. Later he was a teacher, then an editor of the *NZ School Journal* (an important training ground for many NZ writers, such as Margaret MAHY), before lecturing at Wellington Teachers' College.

L. was nine when he was paid half-a-crown (twenty-five cents) for an anecdote in a women's MAGAZINE. POETRY and children's books, like *Charlie the Cheeky Kea* (1974), followed but L. did not become a full-time writer until after the publication of *The Lake* in 1987. *The Lake,* a watershed in New Zealand books for YOUNG ADULTS, is a dramatic story of a young woman's survival in the bush (introducing females into New Zealand's literary tradition of "man alone"), as well as one of the first young person's novel to discuss the issue of sexual abuse within a FAMILY.

Although most of L's childhood reading came from overseas, his own writing recognizes the New Zealand spirit. For twelve-year-old Ruth, in *The Lake,* it is Maui, not Prometheus, who steals the secret of fire. Maori myths are told around the campfire. She uses her dead father's copy of *Plants of New Zealand* to whisper their secret names to the plants in the bush. Finally, Ruth's hard-earned sense of self-confidence gives her the ability to return to her family to demand answers.

L. claims no special insight into modern TEENAGERS and suggests he has overcome this problem by setting stories in the past or the future. L.'s memories of summer holidays on the Coromandel Peninsula are recreated in *The Mangrove Summer* (1988), with the chilling addition of wartime fears of Japanese invasion. Jill takes the children to hide in scrub country where they survive, but Jill's experience of power over others also has tragic consequences. As in all L.'s work, there are references to classic children's stories. *The Conjuror* (1992) is a remarkable novel about the importance of knowledge. A future slave-based society imposes a strict hierarchy on the color of people's eyes. The sinister rulers, The Sisters, hold power through fear and ignorance. Books are banned. Only the forbidden knowledge—including reading and ancient myths—passed on to Johnny can save him from the cruelty and violence. L.'s belief in the power of MYTHOLOGY, the value of skills, and the importance of passing them on are important aspects of his fiction.

L. struck out in a new direction with *Because We Were the Travelers* (1997), the first volume of a quartet, in which a handful of survivors try to cope in a future dystopian New Zealand that is almost destroyed by climatic disasters. Ish, cast out from his nomadic tribe, saves an old woman, Hagar, who proves to be a repository of knowledge. They try to build a better life, in the midst of savagery. The SERIES is rich in literary and mythical connotations: Ish is an outcast like Ishmael in *Genesis,* while Hagar echoes the wise crone of Innuit/Eskimo mythology. Subtle references to myths and literary works, from *Kim* to *Great Expectations,* add extra depth, as Ish battles enemies and the elements to keep alive such features of civilization as reading and healing.

L.'s fabulist Uncle Chris, who regularly brought him messages from the bull on his farm, is immortalized in *Uncle Trev* (1991) and its sequels. Uncle Trev tells amazing yarns to cheer up his convalescent niece and outrage her mother. Yodeling eels, a travelling asparagus bed, the Waharoa Women's Institute Cavalry, bathtub tomato sauce, vanishing stockyards, and a dog-scoffing boar pig are typical.

With her scorn for reality and habit of swigging Old Puckeroo Horse Liniment until smoke comes out her ears, Aunt Effie is another narrative delight. In *Aunt Effie* (2002), tales of her wild youth carry her twenty-six nieces and nephews off her giant bed into a world of pirates, cannibalism, bigamy, and giant trees. As with *Mary Poppins,* the children are swept from safety to peril and back, gaining vividly funny experiences of life, and some new skills, along the way.

AWARDS: 1989 Esther Glen Award, *The Mangrove Summer;* 1991 Frank Sargeson Fellowship; 1993 AIM Children's Book Honour Award, *The Conjuror;* 1996 AIM Children's Book Awards, *The Waterfall;* 1997 NZ Post Children's Book Awards, *The Battle of Pook Island;* 1998 NZ Post Children's Honour Book, *Because We Were the Travellers;* 1999 NZ Post Children's Book Awards, *Taur;* 2001; NZ Post Children's Honour Award, *The Lies of Harry Wakatipu;* 2003 Margaret Mahy Lecture Award.

FURTHER WORKS: *Rewi the Red Deer,* 1976; *Uncle Trev and the Great South Island Plan,* 1991; *Uncle Trev and the Treaty of Waitangi,* 1992; Seddon St Gang trilogy: *Dead Man's Head,* 1994. *The Waterfall,* 1995. *The Battle of Pook Island,* 1996; Travellers Quartet: *Because We Were the Travellers,* 1997. *Taur,* 1998. *The Shaman and the Droll,* 1999. *Kalik,* 2001; *Uncle Trev's Teeth,* 1997; *The Lies of Harry Wakatipu,* 2000; *Harry Wakatipu Comes the Mong,* 2003.

BIBLIOGRAPHY: Darnell, Doreen. "An Interview with award-winning New Zealand writer Jack L." *Talespinner* 3 (May 1997): 22–27; Darnell, Doreen. "Looking Back, Looking Forward—Jack L.'s contribution to New Zealand children's Literature." *Talespinner* 3 (May 1997): 18–21; Huber, Raymond. "Know the Author: Jack L." *Magpies NZ Supplement* 15:4 (Sep 2000): 4–6; McNaughton, Iona. "Outlook NZ Writers 1: Jack L." *The Dominion* 9 Feb. 1993; 6; Fitzgibbon, Tom and Spiers, Barbara. *Beneath Southern Skies: New Zealand Children's Book Authors & Illustrators,* 1993. 103–4; Holloway, Judith. "Jack L.: Fabulist." *Listener (NZ)* 27 Jan. 1992: 48–9; L., Jack. "Biographical notes." *School Journal Catalogue 1978–1993,* 1994. 140; Neale, Pauline. "L., Jack." *The Oxford Companion to New Zealand Literature.* Ed. Roger Robinson and Nelson Wattie, 1998. 300; http://library.christchurch.org.nz/Childrens/Childrens

Authors/JackLasenby.asp/; http://www.bookcouncil
.org.nz/writers/lasenby.htm/.

TREVOR AGNEW

LASKY, Kathryn

Author, b. 24 June 1944, Indianapolis, Indiana

L. is acknowledged for precise attention to detail, vivid imagery and characterizations, and a rich blend of well-researched fact and natural storytelling in her work. She began imaginative writing when still a child; she recalls that she was a compulsive story maker and, while initially secretive about these stories, eventually shared them with her parents and husband. She credits these people with her decision to write professionally. L. stated in a *Horn Book* article, "I really do not care if readers remember a single fact. What I do hope is that they come away with a sense of joy—indeed celebration—about something they have sensed of the world in which they live." Her works written prior to 1985, when she made this statement, as well as the many that have followed speak for her efforts to achieve this goal.

L. writes both historical and realistic fiction as well as INFORMATIONAL BOOKS for readers of all ages. Her books for various ages contain strong characters often challenged by issues of their time. In her nonfiction books, detail and imagery bring topics such as monarch butterflies, doll making, ships and sailing, paleontology, the beginning of the Audubon Society, and cultural celebrations to life for readers. From her own experiences and discoveries uncovered through her research, L. recreates these experiences tempered with a sense of mystery and awe. At times, she works with her husband who is a photographer.

L.'s Jewish heritage is the basis for several books for YOUNG ADULTS. *The Night Journey* (1981) is framed within Rachel's grandmother's storytelling. Great-grandmother Nana takes Rachel and the reader back to the time when her family fled persecution in Czarist Russia. This title won the National Jewish Book Award. In *Prank* (1984), Birdie researches the World War II treatment of the Jews and develops an awareness of anti-Semitism following her own brother's desecration of a synagogue. *Pageant* (1986) is a coming-of-age story about a Jewish TEEN, Sarah, who flees to New York from her home town of Indianapolis where she experiences bigotry. This occurs in tandem to President Kennedy's assassination, and, ac-

cording to some critics, is connected to Sarah's experience; L. communicates the complexity of the national attitude during these events.

Historical eras and events are brought to life in titles such as *Beyond the Great Divide* (1983), *Bone Wars* (1988), and *A Journey to the New World: The Diary of Remember Patience Whipple, Mayflower, 1620* (1996). *Beyond the Great Divide* takes place during 1849 and focuses on a young Amish girl who is aided by Native Americans when she is separated from her family on a Westward Trail. This survival story is authentically and sensitively told and reflects the difficulties and resiliency of the early settlers. *Bone Wars* tells of the search for dinosaur artifacts during the Sioux and Indian Wars (late 1800s). Amidst competition between researchers to find these bones, a boy hired to assist one team joins a friend to search for bones and place them where a larger number of people would benefit from them; as a result, dinosaur bones are protected in museums today. This book has been highly acclaimed for both its representation of the archaeological discoveries as well as Native American history at the turn of the century. *A Journey to the New World* is one contribution to Scholastic's Dear America SERIES and covers the journey on *The Mayflower* and the year following their arrival to the new world. L. uses her personal experiences at sea and her vivid character descriptions to tell about the journey and those individuals involved through the eyes of a young girl.

L. does not shy away from sensitive topics as seen in *Prank,* a focus on anti-Semitism; *Traces of Life: The Origins of Human Kind* (1989), the history of research of humans and evolution; and *Memoirs of a Book Bat* (1994). In *Memoirs of a Book Bat,* teenaged Harper travels with her fundamentalist parents who organize opposition movements against what they perceive as evil. Harper loves books and her parents' work in a censorship conflict causes her to oppose their efforts and eventually run away to her grandmother.

L. has also written adult books under the name Kathryn Lasky Knight.

AWARDS: *Sugaring Time: Boston Globe–Horn Book* Award, Newbery Honor Book (1984); *The Night Journey:* National Jewish Book Award and Association of Jewish Libraries Sydney Taylor Book Award; *Washington Post*/Children's Book Guild Nonfiction Award, 1986; CBC–IRA Children's Choice, *She's*

Wearing a Dead Bird on Her Head; Phoenix Award Honor Book, *The Night Journey*; Sydney Taylor Book Award (1981); *Beyond the Divide:* ALA Best Books for Young Adults, 1983; *Prank:* ALA Best Books for Young Adults, 1984; *Pageant:* ALA BBY, 1986; *Beyond the Burning Time,* ALA BBY, 1995; *Star Split:* ALA Popular Paperbacks, 2004; various ALA notable book citations and Best Books for Young Adults citations.

FURTHER WORKS: *I Have Four Names for My Grandfather,* 1976; *Tugboats Never Sleep,* 1977; *The Dollmaker: The Eyelight and The Shadow,* 1981; *The Weaver's Gift,* 1981; The Night Journey, 1981; *Sugaring Time,* 1983; *Monarchs,* 1993; *Beyond the Burning Time,* 1994; *The Librarian Who Measured the Earth,* 1994; *Days of the Dead,* 1994; *She's Wearing a Dead Bird on Her Head!,* 1995; *True North: A Novel of the Underground Railroad,* 1996; *Marven of the Great North Woods,* 1997; *Hercules: The Man, the Myth, the Hero,* 1997; *Dreams in the Golden Country: The Diary of Zipporah Feldman, A Jewish Immigrant Girl,* 1998; *Elizabeth I, Red Rose of the House of Tudor,* 1999; *Vision of Beauty; The Story of Sarah Breedlove Walker,* 2000; *Interrupted Journey,* 2001; *Born in the Breezes: The Voyages of Joshua Slocum,* 2001; *Mary, Queen of Scots: Queen without a Country, France, 1553,* 2002; *Jahanara: Princess of Princesses, India 1627,* 2002.

BIBLIOGRAPHY: *Contemporary Authors Online,* 2001; *Horn Book,* Sept.–Oct. 1985, p. 527; *Author and Artists for Young Adults,* 19, 1996; *Children's Literature Review,* 11, 1986; *St. James Guide to Young Adult Writers,* 1999.

JANELLE B. MATHIS

LATINO/A YA LITERATURE

The unprecedented growth of the L. population in the U.S. has created an awareness of the richly complex heritage that weaves a unique tapestry of intercultural literary traditions. U.S. L. is a category of its own, reflecting the diversity of Latin cultures represented in the U.S.—Mexican, Puerto Rican, Central and South American, and European. Despite the extraordinary growth of the Latina/o population in the U.S., the literature that depicts this culture is disproportionately represented in the number of YOUNG ADULT books published yearly. Changing demographics that represent the projections of the U.S. Census Bureau (2000), project that in 2020 Latinos will represent 17 percent of the population. Demographics also tell us that the number of Latinos in the U.S. under age eighteen increased 59 percent between 1990 and 2000. The Cooperative Children's Book Center states that only 42 of the approximately 5,250 children's books published in 2000 were about Latinos and less than half of those were by Latino authors and illustrators. This is in contrast to 88 published in 1997.

The history of L. for children and adolescents in the U.S. is rich, beginning with the oral tradition of numerous Hispanic cultures that settled in Florida, Mississippi, and the states bordering Mexico. The earliest L.–American author is Cabeza de Vaca, the early explorer who combined memoir and chronicle in *The Account.* As immigrants moved to this country from Puerto Rico, Cuba, and South America, new stories became part of this heritage. The beginning of Latin American children's literature is considered to be *La Edad de Oro* or *The Golden Age.* This literary MAGAZINE was written by José Marti and published in 1898 in four issues; it is still in print today in the form of a book. Pura Belpre, a Puerto Rican storyteller in New York, published in 1932 one of the earliest recognized books for L. young people. Today, there is an award given in her honor by the American Library Association for children's books written and illustrated by L.s. In 1940, George Sanchez called for linguistically and culturally relevant materials for L. students. In California, as Nancy Larrick was calling attention to the need for literature that represented the voices of those groups outside the Anglo-American experience, Ernest Galarza self-published *Colección Minilibros* (1974), a SERIES of books written in both English and Spanish. Additionally, in 1976 the International Association for Children's Literature in Spanish was founded. As other events recognized and encouraged L. as to write for young readers, the demand for such literature has increased; in addition to valuing the life experiences of L. readers, it is "helping to shape a wider, shared history and experience among various cultural groups," according to A. F. Ada. Ada is a recognized author, scholar, and advocate of L. literature for children and young adults and acknowledges the variety of nationalities represented in emerging authors, themes reflecting the realities of Latino life, and genres, of which memoir is a favorite for all ages of readers.

The current status of Latina/o literature in the U.S. continues to be reflected by the needs reported earlier by Barrera and Garza de Cortes: an increase in numbers of titles, the promotion and encouragement of

Latina/o authors as well as authentic content and themes, and a realization of the need and market for such literature. Seeking L. voices to join in celebrating and sharing this rich heritage through literature, author Pat Mora addresses the need for L. writers for young readers. "I tell all new writers and illustrators of color how much their voices and stories are needed, as I know how difficult their journey will be . . . I remember being told that if Latinos had submitted anything worthy of being published, it would have been published already." Lulu Delacre, a Puerto Rican author, states that publishing books with Latino themes gets harder in that she must find stories with broad appeal. Additionally, books often go out of print quickly. Publisher Philip Lee, in an interview with Glenna Sloan, addresses challenges faced at his publishing company; there are not enough stories about people of color published and there are few choices actually submitted in order to select books. He also mentions that there is a lack of diversity among those working in the publishing field itself. Harriet Rohmer relates that her company goes into communities to discover what should be shared in books and works with artists and authors who write for adults as potential children's authors.

In that way, Rohmer discovered Juan Felipe HER-RERA, author of *Calling the Doves,* a winner of the Ezra Jack Keats Award. Despite the need for more literature that speaks to the experiences of Latino young people, there are significant writers and illustrators who work in a variety of genres to provide rich cultural images for Latina/o youth while addressing universal themes and issues. Gary SOTO, a Mexican-American author from California, writes about both the universal experiences of love and friendship as well as topics specific to his own cultural background. *Living up the Street: Narrative Recollections* (1985) is a collection of twenty-one short essays about growing up in the barrios of Fresno, while *Baseball in April* (1990), *Crazy Weekend* (1994), and *Buried Onions* (1997) are good examples of Soto's appeal to adolescents. Another autobiographical work is Victor MARTINEZ's *Parrot in the Oven: Mi Via* (1996); this author's universality does not abandon the unique feelings and insights of Latino youth growing up in the barrios. This book won a National Book Award, Pure Belpre Award, and Americas Book Award. Yet another life experience shared is that of Francesco JIMINEZ, whose works for young adults are highly

recognized. Receiving the 1998 *Boston Globe–Horn Book* Award for *The Circuit: Stories from the Life of a Migrant Child* (1997, 1999), Jimenez wrote its sequel, *Breaking Through* in 2001. Rudolfo Anaya, a strong advocate for multicultural material in the curriculum, is the author of *Bless Me Ultima* (1972) about a young boy growing up in a small New Mexico town and *The Anaya Reader* (1995), a collection of fiction, SHORT STORIES, essays, and PLAYS.

Sandra CISNEROS provides forty-four vignettes in *The House on Mango Street* (1984) that introduce individuals in a Latin neighborhood of Chicago. This collection is often used in high-school classrooms as it provides numerous opportunities for understanding oneself and the L. culture. Pat Mora, a poet who creates images of the Southwest and the Mexican-American experience, compiled a book of POETRY for young adults that shares Mexican traditions, historical figures, memories of growing up and hopes for the future in *My Own True Name: New and Selected Poems for Young Adults* (2000).

Julia Alvarez shares her experiences as an immigrant to the U.S. from the Dominican Republic in *How the García Girls Lost Their Accents* (1991). The isolation felt by the girls living in New York is but one issue presented among others such as racism and anorexia. *Before We Were Free* (2002) tells of the struggle for democracy in the Dominican Republic as witnessed by a female protagonist who learns of the sacrifices made and risks taken by people for freedom. This book won the Americas Award, given by the National Consortium of Latin American Studies Programs.

Other writers have used strong female protagonists to address social issues faced by the diverse groups who comprise the Latina/o culture in the U.S. Pam Muñoz RYAN in *Esperanza Rising* (2000) shares the injustices and poverty of migrant workers during the Depression Era. Ophelia Dumas Lachman in *The Girl from Playa Blanca* (1995) uses MYSTERY as the framework to tell an immigrant story about two young people who come to California from Mexico in search of their father. Judith Ortiz COFER's *An Island Like You: Stories of the Barrio* (1995) and *The Year of Our Revolution: New and Selected Stories and Poems* (1998) share a Puerto Rican neighborhood in New Jersey in the 1960s. Diane Gonzales Bertrand's *Sweet Fifteen* (1995) shows a young girl coming to understand the value of cultural traditions, and *White*

Bread Competition (1997) by Jo Ann Yolanda Hernandez provides understanding of growing up as a Chicano ninth grader in the contemporary Southwest.

Among adult writers who provide rich portrayals of the Latina/o experience for mature young adult readers are Arturo Islas, Gabriel García Márquez, Isabel Allende, and Victor Villasenor. Numerous PICTURE BOOKS by authors and illustrators such as Alma Flor Ada, Francesco X. Alacorn, Juan Felipe Herrera, Enrique Valasquez, Carmen Lomas Garza, David Diaz, George Ancona, and others are also significant additions to the young adult reading experience within the rich traditions and complexities of the L.-American experience.

BIBLIOGRAPHY: Ada, A. F. and Campoy, F. I., *The Continuum Encyclopedia of Children's Literature,* ed. B. E. Cullinan and D. G. Person, 2000; Algebraum, H. and Olgas, M. F. U. S. *L. Literature,* 2000; Anderson, N. "The Need for L. Children's Literature," *The Florida Reading Quarterly,* 2002; Barrera, R. B., & de Cortez, O. G. "Mexican-American Children's Literature in the 1990s: Toward Authenticity," *Using Multiethnic Literature in the K–8 Classroom,* ed. V. Harris, 1990; Barrera, R. B., Quiroa, R. E., and West-Williams, C., "Poco a Poco: The Continuing Development of Mexican American Childrens Literature in the 1990s," *New Advocate,* 1999; Battle, J. "A Conversation with Rudolpho Anaya," *New Advocate,* 2001; Carger, C. L. "Harriet Rohmer on New Voices and Visions in Multicultural Literature," *New Advocate,* 2001; Garcia, G. E. "How Will Bilingual/ESL Programs in Literacy Change in the Next Millennium?," *Reading Research Quarterly,* 2000; Mathis, J. "Literacy Possibilities and Concerns for Mexican-American Children's Literature: Readers, Writers, and Publishers Respond," *Celebrating the Faces of Literacy, The 24th Yearbook of the College Reading Association,* ed. P. Linder, M. B. Sampson, J. R. Dugan, and B. Brancato, 2002; Mora, P. "Confessions of a Latina Author," *New Advocate,* 1998; Samuels, B. G. "Somewhere Over the Rainbow: Celebrating Diverse Voices in YA LITERATURE," *Young Adult Literature in the Classroom,* ed. J. B. Elliott and M. M. Dupuis, 2002; U.S. Census website.

JANELLE B. MATHIS

LAUBER, Patricia
Author, b. 5 February 1924, New York City

L. is an author whose repertoire ideally suits the young mind eager to explore the world. From dinosaurs to floods to trees to planets, L. has addressed the topic in a way that makes nonfiction appealing and interesting.

L. began her writing while in college, as the editor-in-chief of the *Wellesley College News.* After introducing young readers to *Clarence the TV Dog* and four Clarence sequels, L. focused on revealing the world's scientific secrets to young readers. She is the author of over eighty books, among them many award winners.

In addition to her success in writing books, L. has served the field of education as editor of *Junior Scholastic,* editor-in-chief of *Science World,* and chief editor in math and science for the *New Book of Knowledge Encyclopedia.*

When not writing, L. enjoys sailing, hiking, traveling, reading, cooking, and listening to music. She and her husband, Weston, live in Connecticut.

SELECT AWARDS: 1983—*Washington Post* Children's Book Club Guild Award for contribution to the field of children's literature; *Journey to the Planets and Seeds: Pop, Stick, Glide* were nominated for American Book Awards in the nonfiction category; *Seeing Earth from Space:* ALA Best Books for Young Adults, 1991; 1998—*Painters of the Caves* honored by the National Geographic Society; 1999—*Painters of the Caves* received the Maine Lupine Award

SELECT FURTHER WORKS: *Volcano: The Eruption and Healing of Mount St. Helens,* 1986; *Tales Mummies Tell,* 1985; *Hurricanes: Earth's Mightiest Storms,* 1996; *Flood: Wrestling with the Mississippi,* 1996; *Painters of the Caves,* 1998; *Who Came First?: New Clues to Prehistoric Americans,* 2003.

BIBLIOGRAPHY: *Contemporary Authors, New Revision,* vol. 38, 1993; A. Silvey, ed. *Childrens Books and Their Creators,* 1995; *Something about the Author,* vol 75, 1994.

SUSAN L. MARINOFF

LAWLOR, Laurie
Author, b. 4 April 1953, Oak Park, Illinois

L. decided to become a writer while in the third grade. She went to journalism school at Northwestern University in Evanston, Illinois and worked for many years as a freelance writer and editor before committing herself to writing full time: fiction and nonfiction for children and YOUNG ADULTS.

L. writes in many categories and genres. She enjoys writing historical fiction, particularly the history of settling the American West in the 19th century.

L.'s vivid description brings to life events that occurred over a hundred years ago.

L's historical stories were inspired by her family's folklore. L's great grandparents were pioneers in South Dakota, traveling in covered wagons with five children; letters from her great-aunt inspired the climax in Addie Across the Prairie SERIES.

In L.'s BIOGRAPHIES of real-life legends such as *Daniel Boone* (1989) and Johnny Appleseed in *The Real Johnny Appleseed* (1995) are meticulously researched, showing her subjects' struggles as well as their triumphs. The biographies teach about the social, political, and cultural environments these legends lived in and also try to make sense of their lives.

The biography *Shadow Catcher: the Life and Work of Edward S. Curtis* (1994) explores the life of the American photographer. L. chronicles his life and passion for collecting and preserving the North American Indian culture using photographs and text. The urgency and tireless work of Curtis is evident throughout this biography along with the personal and health sacrifices that he made to pursue his ambition. *Shadow Catcher* won the Carl Sandburg award for Children's Literature, Golden Kite Book Award, 1994, sponsored by the Society of Children's Book Writers and Illustrators (SCBWI) and Hungry Mind Review *Children's Book of Distinction Award,* 1995.

L. presents an interesting and sometimes unique look at the history of the shoe in *Where Will This Shoe Take You?: A Walk Through the History of Footwear* (1996) which chronicles the shoe from tree bark to the popular jogging shoe. L. discusses footwear as an indicator of social and economic status, cultural differences, social movements, political trends, and power gauge.

L. provides thorough bibliographies for each of her nonfiction books; useful resources for all ages.

Lighter fare can be found in her Heartland Series, whose heroine Moe (actual name: Madeline Genevieve McDonough), a high-spirited youth with good intentions, finds herself always in the midst of trouble. Even in this light-hearted story L. provides an accurate portrayal of the history of town life on the prairies in early 20th century. *Take to the Sky* (1996), set in 1908, L. mirrors the events of the Wright Brothers' first flight with Moe's desire to be the first woman aeronaut!

AWARDS: Children's Literature Award (Utah), 1989, Nebraska Golder Sower Award, 1989, Rebecca Cau-

dill Young Reader's Book Award nomination, 1990, and Iowa Children's Choice Award, 1990, all for *Addie across the Prairie;* KC Three Award, 1990–91, for *How to Survive Third Grade;* Nebraska Golden Sower Award nomination, Iowa Children's Choice Award, and North Dakota Picker Tale Award, all 1992, all for *Addie's Dakota Winter; Shadow Catcher: The Life and Works of Edward S. Curtis:* ALA Best Books for Young Adults, 1995; *Helen Keller: Rebellious Spirit:* ALA Best Books for Young Adults, 2002; ALA Notable Children's Books, 2002.

FURTHER WORKS: *How to Survive Third Grade,* 1989; *Second-Grade Dog,* 1990; *Little Women* (novelization of the movie based upon the novel by Louisa May ALCOTT), 1994; *Gold in the Hills,* 1995; *Come Away with Me* ("Heartland" series), 1996; *The Biggest Pest on Eighth Avenue,* 1997; *The Worst Kid Who Ever Lived on Eighth Avenue,* 1998; *Window on the West: The Frontier Photography of William Henry Jackson,* 1999; *Wind on the River,* 2000; *Helen Keller: Rebellious Spirit,* 2001; *Old Crump: The True Story of a Trip West,* 2002; *Magnificent Voyager: An American Adventurer on Captain Cook's Last Expedition,* 2002; *"American Sisters" Series; "Addy Across the Prairie" Series.*

BIBLIOGRAPHY: *Something about the Author,* vol. 80 & vol. 137; www.laurielawlor.com

SUSAN E. MORTON

LAWRENCE, Iain
Author, b. 22 February 1955, Sault Ste. Marie, Ontario

L. grew up in various parts of CANADA—his family moved eleven times before he left school. His passion for writing began through a love of reading. He recalls his father reading bedtime stories such as *Stuart Little, Treasure Island* and *Moonfleet,* to his brother and him when they were growing up. L. left school for a while and when he returned, he had decided to become a writer. He became a newspaper journalist and spent ten years writing articles and reporting. After that, he left journalism to devote time to his two favorite activities, writing and sailing.

L. originally wrote for adults, but an agent convinced him to rework his one novel into a YA story. The result was a well-received book *The Wreckers* (1998), the first in the High Seas trilogy. Reminiscent of his childhood bedtime stories and Robert Louis Stevenson, L. spins a captivating tale of shipwrecks, pirates, and MYSTERY. L. introduces us to John Spencer, the fourteen-year old survivor of a shipwreck. As

John tries to find his missing father, he learns the coastal community is luring ships in to wreck on their rocky shore so they can loot their cargo. John must escape these wreckers, find his father, and perhaps even prevent other wrecks. L. continues John's high-sea adventures in *The Smugglers* (1999), when John and his father purchase a wondrous new ship called the Dragon; the ship, however, may not be as wonderful as it appears. L. finishes the trilogy with *The Buccaneers* (2001), where John takes his first voyage to the West Indies without his father on the Dragon. Along the way he encounters pirates, cannibals, storms, and a mysterious stranger. Although readers would like to have more John Spencer adventures, L. feels John's sailing days are over.

In his next book, L. leaves the 1800s sea adventures behind for the circus in the American West after World War II. In *Ghost Boy* (2000), he creates a compelling character who calls himself Harold the Ghost because he is an albino. Always feeling like an outcast from his community, Harold runs away to the circus, where he hopes to find himself and lose his sense of isolation.

Lord of the Nutcracker Men (2001) takes place during World War I and is set back in England again. Johnny receives a set of wooden toy soldiers that his father had carved before he leaves for the war. While fighting in the trenches, his father sends Johnny letters, each with a newly carved toy soldier. Johnny must confront his feelings that he may somehow be controlling his father's fate in the way that he plays with his toy soldiers.

L. returns to an ocean setting for his next book *The Lightkeeper's Daughter* (2002), but with a female as the main character. Elizabeth (Squid) McCrae returns to her hometown of Lizzie Island, located off the coast of British Columbia, where her father is the island's lightkeeper. Squid and her daughter return home, and she must come to terms with some of the memories of her childhood there, especially of her brother's death.

B for Buster (2004) is another of L.'s captivating stories. Once again his protagonist is involved in a WAR, only this time it is World War II, in which underage Kak enlists in the Canadian Air Force. Kak begins his bomber adventures in the plane called *B for Buster,* but soon realizes his adventure is filled more with fear than with heroic endings.

AWARDS: American Library Association's Best Books for Young Adults for *The Wreckers* (1999), *The Smugglers* (2000), and *Ghost Boy* (2001); Geoffrey Bilson Award for Historical Fiction for Young People for *The Wreckers* (1999); Edgar Allan Poe Award nominee for Best Children's Mystery for *The Wreckers* (1999); New York Public Library Books for the Teen Age citation for *The Wreckers* (1999), *The Smugglers* (2000), and *Ghost Boy* (2001); *Booklist* Editor's Choice for *The Wreckers* (1999); *School Library Journal* Best Books of the Year citation for *The Wreckers* (1999); *Bulletin of the Center for Children's Books* Blue Ribbon Book for *The Wreckers* (1999), *The Smugglers* (2000), and *The Lightkeeper's Daughter* (2004); American Library Association's Notable Children's Books for *Ghost Boy* (2001), *School Library Journal* Best Books citation for *Ghost Boy* (2001); *Publishers Weekly* Best Books citation for *Ghost Boy* (2001); *Publishers Weekly* Best Children's Books citation for *Lord of the Nutcracker Men* (2001); American Library Association's Best Books for Young Adults for *The Lightkeeper's Daughter* (2003); American Library Association's Best Books for Young Adults for *B for Buster* (2005).

FURTHER WORKS: *Far-Away Places: Fifty Anchorages on the Northwest Coast* (1995); *Sea Stories of the Inside Passage: In the Wake of the Nid* (1997).

BIBLIOGRAPHY: *Authors and Artists for Young Adults,* v. 51; *Contemporary Authors; Publishers Weekly* book reviews. www.randomhouse.com/features/iain lawrence/books.html.

TINA HERTEL

LEARNING AND TEACHING LITERACY IN GRADES 4–12: ISSUES AND CHALLENGES

A view of adolescents—as "not-yet" adults and thus less competent or less knowledgeable than their elders—is one that is increasingly being critiqued in the professional literature. Like others (Amit-Talai and Wulff, 1995; Lesko, 2001) before us, we prefer to think of adolescents as knowing things that have to do with their particular life experiences and the particular spaces they occupy both in and out of school in a constantly changing world. This view of youth culture is supported in the research on young people's literacy learning, and especially in the expectations we have for them.

Expectation #1—Students Will Use Effective Text-Processing Strategies

Findings from two major research syntheses produced by the National Reading Panel (2000) and the RAND

425

Reading Study Group (2002) indicate that comprehension monitoring, using graphic organizers, generating self-questions, using text structure as an aid to remembering, and summarizing are effective strategies that lead to improved comprehension. Instruction in the use of these strategies must be embedded in the regular curriculum, and it must provide students with opportunities to read critically so that a text's unexamined assumptions are open for discussion. Being literate in today's world entails reading strategically to comprehend multiple forms of texts (print, visual, aural, and digital) in a variety of contexts (Alvermann, 2003; Lankshear and Knobel, 2003).

Expectation #2—Students Will Be Motivated and Engaged

It is the belief in the self (or lack of such belief) that makes a difference in how competent a person feels. Perceptions of one's competencies are central to most theories of motivation, and the research on self-efficacy bears out the hypothesized connection between feeling competent and being motivated as a learner. Providing adolescents who are experiencing reading difficulties with clear goals for a comprehension task and then giving feedback on the progress they are making can lead to increased self-efficacy and greater use of comprehension strategies (Schunk and Rice, 1993). Learning environments that support the use of multimedia and newer forms of information communication technologies can heighten students' motivation to become independent readers and writers (Kamil, Intrator, and Kim, 2000).

Expectation #3—Students Will Adopt Normative Ways of Reading and Writing

In an effort to raise the bar by implementing higher standards—a noteworthy goal in most people's minds—some schools are promoting certain normative ways of reading texts that may be disabling some of the very students they are trying to help (Alvermann, 2001; Bruce, 2002). Rather than expecting all students to adopt conventional modes of reading and writing (mostly print-based), preference might be given to re/mediating literacy instruction (Luke & Elkins, 2000). *Re/mediation,* not to be confused with the older term, *remediation* without the slash, involves reframing the way we think about intervening in adolescents' reading lives. It calls for moving beyond fruitless searches for some method or "magic bullet" that purportedly will fix their so-called deficits in reading. Re/mediation, in the sense that Luke and Elkins use the term, involves refashioning instructional conditions so as to enable students to use their out-of-school literacies and knowledge of various media forms to learn in the classroom. In a metaphoric sense, re/mediation involves fixing the conditions in which students learn rather than attempting to fix the students per se.

The expectations outlined above are predicated upon a student's ability to read and comprehend a variety of types of texts—a prerequisite to the enjoyment of literature. Unfortunately, large numbers of adolescents are unable to experience the joys of literature and the satisfaction that comes from using books for personal purposes. Many of these children are low-income, minority students. Although a great deal of serious attention has been given to this problem, it is safe to say that, as an educational community, we are far from final answers. Contributing factors rarely stand alone. More often, they are interactive and interdependent and include issues of socioeconomic status, home and linguistic background, and quality of instruction. A brief discussion of each follows.

Socioeconomic Status

Family income and reading achievement are closely linked. Socioeconomic differences are generally indexed by such variables as household income and parents' education and occupation, alone or in some weighted combination. Families rated low in SES are not only less affluent and less educated than other families but also tend to live in communities in which the average family SES is low and tend to receive less adequate nutrition and health services. However, a low-status child in a generally moderate or upper-status school or community is far less at risk than that same child in a whole school or community of low-status children (Snow, Burns and Griffin, 1998, p. 124).

Home Background

Research indicates that the achievement gap is already in place before children enter kindergarten (U.S. Department of Education's Early Childhood

Longitudinal Study, 2000). While less is known about the child-rearing practices that may affect children's school performance during the middle school and high school years, it may be safe to say that differences (not deficits) in child-rearing practices may contribute to the gap.

Linguistic Background

The low achievement of poor AFRICAN AMERICAN and Hispanic children, in particular, has often been associated with their dialect or language. During the 1960s, linguists looked closely at language diversity as a cause of school failure. Those studies revealed key principles of language learning that remain helpful to teachers and curriculum developers: all language varieties are equally valid; all language varieties can accommodate all levels of thought; and any variety of standard English is not intrinsically better than any nonstandard dialect (Gopaul-McNicol, Reid and Wisdom, 1998, p. 7). Similarly, research in the language development of children for whom English is a second language supports the belief that the learner's home language should be valued and accepted as part of second language acquisition and learning.

None of this denies the fact that the form language takes has economic, social, and political importance. Nor does it suggest that helping students achieve competence in standard English is not an important goal of the school. It does suggest that much of the low achievement of language-minority students may be pedagogically induced or exacerbated and therefore amenable to change (Rueda, 1991; Strickland, Ganske, and Monroe, 2002).

Quality of Instruction

Many researchers have turned their attention to what is increasingly considered to be a key contributing factor to the achievement gap—the differences in the quality of instruction that students receive. According to Haycock (2001), rather than focus on poverty and parental education, we should begin to concentrate on what takes place in the classrooms that minority students attend.

In summary, recent research in adolescent literacy has shifted away from a primary focus on issues of cognitive processes and teacher-centered instructional practices to acknowledge the importance of the complex intersections among adolescent learners, texts, and contexts. In particular, the importance of multiple literacies has been emphasized and the impact of culture and societal trends on the students' literacy development has become an important aspect of what educators consider as they tackle hard questions about engaging these learners and keeping them engaged.

BIBLIOGRAPHY: Alverman, D. E. (2003). Exemplary literacy instruction for adolescents: What counts and who's counting? In J. Flood and P. Anders (eds.). *Urban education: Issues and policies.* Newark, DE: International Reading Association; Alvermann, D. E. (2001). Reading adolescents' reading identities: Looking back to see ahead. *Journal of Adolescent & Adult Literacies, 44,* 676–90; Amit-Talai, V., and Wulff, H. (eds.). (1995). *Youth cultures: A cross-cultural perspective.* New York: Routledge; Bruce, B. C. (2002). Diversity and critical social engagement: How changing technologies enable new modes of literacy in changing circumstances. In D. E. Alvermann (ed.), *Adolescents and literacies in a digital world* (pp. 1–18). New York: Peter Lang; Gopaul-McNicol, S., Reid, S., and Wisdom, G. (1998). The psychoeducational assessment of Ebonics speakers: Issues and challenges. *Journal of Negro Education 67,* 16–24; Haycock, K. (2001). Closing the achievement gap. *Educational Leadership, 58* (6), 6–11; Kamil, M. L., Intrator, S. M., and Kim, H. S. (2000). The effects of other technologies on literacy and literacy learning. In M. L. Kamil, P. B. Mosenthal, P. D. Pearson, and R. Barr (eds.), *Handbook of reading research* (Vol. 3, pp. 771–788). Mahwah, NJ: Erlbaum; Lankshear, C., and Knobel, M. (2003). *New Literacies: Changing Knowledge and Classroom Learning.* Buckingham, UK: Open University Press; Lesko, N. (2001). *Act Your Age! A Cultural Construction of Adolescence.* New York: Routledge Falmer; Luke, A., & Elkins, J. (2000). "Re/mediating Adolescent Literacies," *Journal of Adolescent and Adult Literacy, 43,* 396–98; National Reading Panel. (2000). *Report of the National Reading Panel,* Washington, D.C.: National Institute of Child Health and Human Development; RAND Reading Study Group (2002). *Reading for Understanding: Toward an R & D Program in Reading Comprehension.* Santa Monica, CA: Science & Technology Policy Institute, RAND Education; Rueda, R. (1991). "Characteristics of Literacy Programs for language-minority students," E. H. Hiebert, (ed.). *Literacy for a Diverse Society: Perspectives, Practices, and Policies.* New York: Teachers College Press; Schunk, D. H., and Rice, J. M. (1993). "Strategy Fading and Progress Feedback: Effects on Self-Efficacy and Comprehension among Students

Receiving Remedial Reading Services. *Journal of Special Education, 27*, 257–76; Snow, C., Burns, M. S., and Griffin, M. (1998). *Preventing Reading Difficulties in Young Children*. Washington, D.C.: National Academy Press; Strickland, D. S., Ganske, K., and Monroe, J. (2002). *Supporting Struggling Readers and Writers: Strategies for Classroom Intervention 3–6*. Newark, DE: International Reading Association; U.S. Department of Education. (2000). "Early Childhood Longitudinal Study" (ECLS-K). Washington, DC: National Center for Education Statistics.

DOROTHY S. STRICKLAND
AND DONNA E. ALVERMANN

LEE, (Nelle) Harper

Author, b. 28 April 1926, Monroeville, Alabama

L. was born to Frances Finch L., a lawyer, and Amasa Coleman L. The youngest of their five children, L.'s early life has all the aspects of a Southern classic.

"This was my childhood," she told interviewer Roy Newquist in his book *Counterpoint* (1964). "We devised things; we were readers, and we would transfer everything we had seen on the printed page to the backyard in the form of high drama. Did you never play Tarzan when you were a child? Did you never tramp through the jungle or re-fight the battle of Gettysburg in some form or fashion?" she continued. "We did. Did you never live in a tree house and find the whole world in the branches of a chinaberry tree? We did."

According to her eldest sister, Alice, L. was a "feisty tomboy" whose imagination knew no limits. Fed by the unusual activities of small-town Alabama, she grew up next door to a boy also destined for literary greatness—Truman Capote. Together they absorbed the rhythms of life and language that would inspire, among other works, L.'s legendary novel *To Kill a Mockingbird* and Capote's *In Cold Blood* (a book L. helped him research years later).

An able student, L. went to Huntington College in Montgomery for a year in 1944, then followed in her father and her sister Alice's footsteps, studying law at the University of Alabama in Tuscaloosa. In 1948, L. was offered and accepted an opportunity to study at Oxford University for one year. According to Alice, it was here that she "fell in love with England."

Once her year abroad had ended, L. returned to Tuscaloosa to finish law school, but left before her studies had concluded; the drama of law touched L.'s soul but technicality did not. Besides, New York was calling, according to Alice, and L. was listening.

Like her friend Truman Capote, L. took an inexpensive flat in Manhattan in 1949 and set out to explore her inner novelist. At twenty-three, she took a job as an airline clerk at Eastern to pay the bills, and wrote—mostly SHORT STORIES—as her off-time would allow.

Thanks to the generosity of friends who believed in her talent, Lee was able to quit her job and write full-time in the late 1950s. Though the funds were intended as a gift, L. called it a loan, promising to repay the debt and at the same time live up to their expectations.

Literary agent Maurice Crane saw promise in one of her short stories and encouraged her to expand it into a novel. One publisher agreed with Crane's assessment, but insisted the work needed revision. Two years later, *To Kill a Mockingbird* was published in July of 1960. L. was thirty-four.

Widely heralded as a work of genius, the author's tale of prejudice and injustice told through the tender young voice of tomboy Scout won a Pulitzer Prize for Literature in 1961. L. was further honored in 1966, when President Johnson appointed her to the National Council of the Arts (along with artist Richard Diebenkon, Jr.).

L. was blissfully pleased with the film adaptation starring Gregory Peck, released in 1962. During the film's production, L. and Peck formed a lifelong friendship. "I can tell you we have loved her and admired her ever since we met," Peck's wife Veronique told the *Chicago Tribune* in 2003. In deference to L., Peck's daughter, Cecilia, named her son Harper in honor of the beloved family friend.

On the whole however, the spotlight never appealed to L. "There were so many demands made on her," Alice Lee said in the *Chicago Tribune* interview. "People wanted her to speak to groups. She would be terrified to speak." So L. simply declined the trappings of fame. Because she seldom grants interviews, she has been called reclusive for decades, but her friends and family cannot agree. She is warm and friendly, says her sister Alice and her close circle of intimate friends. She is fully engaged by and involved with her world in New York and Alabama, they say. She simply lives a vibrant life for herself and not for the media buzz.

L., who never married, splits her time between Manhattan and Monroeville, between ball games and fishing dates. And contrary to popular belief, she does write, though she has submitted very little for further publication, as least not under the name of Harper Lee.

Why has L. declined to publish a second novel? Her sister Alice offers an equally compelling question in response. "When you have hit a pinnacle, how would you feel about writing more?" she said in the *Chicago Tribune.* "Would you feel like you're competing with yourself?"

But longtime friend Reverend Thomas Butts is yet hopeful in an interview with the *Chicago Tribune.* "I tell her that after she dies, Alice is going to come to clean out her apartment and find [manuscripts] under the bed."

BIBLIOGRAPHY: Mills, Marja, "A Life Apart," *Chicago Tribune,* September 13, 2002; ThinkQuest Harper Lee Biography; Jane Kansas + 2040 Creighton Halifax NS B3K 3R2 Canada, Harper Lee website: http://mockingbird.chebucto.org/; Roy Newquist interview in Counterpoint, 1964 Rand McNally.

KELLY MILNER HALLS

LEE, Marie G.

Author, b. 25 April 1964, Hibbing, Minnesota

Being the only Asian teenager in her small Northern Minnesota town definitely influenced L.'s portrayal of the characters in her YA novels. Hibbing, Minnesota is known for being Bob Dylan's hometown, a quintessential all-American town. L. considered herself an all-American teenager as she was growing up. She read *Seventeen* MAGAZINE, was a hockey cheerleader, and even was lucky enough to win a makeover from *Seventeen.* Ironically, it was this makeover by an American TEEN magazine that brought L.'s Korean heritage home to her. To enhance all of her features, the makeover specialists played up her Asian looks, which really upset L. who had always considered herself to be just like her friends, most of whom were of Nordic heritage. L. graduated from Brown University in 1986 and worked for an economics research firm after college.

By basing her first novel, *Finding My Voice* (1992), on the experiences she lived through as a teen, L. clarified her feelings about her heritage, as well as creating a character in Ellen who struggled with many of the same identity issues L. had. Beyond the normal things that teens deal with—grades, college acceptance, time management versus wanting to hang out—Ellen faces those who are cruel to her because she doesn't look like them.

Learning to deal with one's heritage is also a part of *If It Hadn't Been for Yoon Jun* (1993). A white couple adopts a Korean child and it is not until she is in middle school when she encounters a Korean boy that identity issues are raised. *Saying Goodbye* (1994), a sequel to *Finding My Voice,* finds Ellen at college with a Korean boyfriend and an African American roommate with whom she does not get along. L. uses the backdrop of SPORTS in her 1996 book, *Necessary Roughness.* Football player Chan deals with moving from the big city of Los Angeles to Minnesota, but finds that is the least of his problems as the year unfolds. In *F Is for Fabuloso,* Jin-Ha, who has recently arrived from Korea with her family, is challenged both by math class and prejudices—although with some aid from Grant Hartwig learns to face both, as well as facing her family.

L. contributed many of her papers to the University of Minnesota where they can be found in the Children's Literature Research Collection and contain a variety of production materials, including holographs, typescripts, notes, front matter, galleys, page proofs, clippings, research material, and one letter from Judy Blume to L. Her work "Dead and Gone" appears in the anthology *On the Wings of Peace* published in 1995; she has also been published in *The Kenyon Review* and *The New York Times.* L. helped to found the Asian American Writer's Workshop.

AWARDS: *Finding My Voice:* 1992 Friends of American Writers Best Book Award, ALA Best Book for Reluctant Readers; *Necessary Roughness:* 1997 New York Public Library Best Books for the TEEN Age, 1998 ALA Best Books for YA.

FURTHER WORK: *Night of the Chupacabras* (1998)

BIBLIOGRAPHY: www.amazon.com; www.novelst4.epnet.com; http://scholar.lib.vt.edu/ejournals/ALAN/winter95/Lee.html; http://special.lib.umn.edu/findaid/html/clrc/clrc0158.html

JEANNE MARIE RYAN

LEE, Stan

Author, editor, media executive, b. 28 December, 1922, New York City

Growing up poor in New York City, Stanley Martin Lieber dreamed of success as a writer of great novels.

Therefore, when he was first published for pay, for a short story written to fulfill Post Office regulations in 1941's *Captain America Comics #3* published by Timely Comics, he opted to use the pseudonym name "Stan Lee," saving his full name for the great novels that were sure to be in his future. At the time, L. was working on staff at Timely, which would later become Marvel, as assistant to the editor and art director.

But great responsibility was soon thrust upon the teenaged L. Joe Simon and Jack Kirby, who in addition to creating Captain America were also editor and art director of Timely, resigned abruptly. This left assistant editor L. temporarily in charge while publisher Martin Goodman (a distant relative of L.'s) searched for replacements. Apparently, Goodman was satisfied with L.'s performance because, with the exception of several years spent in the Army during World War II, L. was editor-in-chief of the Marvel line until 1972, when, after Goodman's sale of his publishing company (which included MAGAZINES as well as comic books), L. became Publisher of Marvel Comics. At present, L. is employed by Marvel as Chairman Emeritus, by far the longest-tenured employee at that, or almost any other, company. L.'s stint as Marvel's editor went through different phases. During the SUPERHERO craze of the 1940s, the company published the adventures of such characters as Captain America, Bill Everett's Sub-Mariner and Carl Burgos' Human Torch. In addition to editing and art-directing many comics, including the ones that contained these superheroes' stories, L. also wrote adventures of a plethora of characters.

After helping innovate the superhero genre in the 1940s, in the late '40s and early '50s, Timely (also known as Atlas) settled into a routine of imitating whatever genres were popular in other comics, which in turn often reflected what was current in novels, movies, radio, and television. This was a predictable but not especially exciting way of doing business. The years marched on and L. was approaching middle age.

In the late 1950s, Goodman's attempts to distribute his own publications, instead of relying on established distributors, backfired. The Atlas line was cut back drastically. The only comic staff member left was L., who employed freelancers and used backlogged inventory to put out the few comics Atlas could distribute.

As the company was emerging from this period, L. hired some new artists, including Jack Kirby and Steve Ditko. Together, they put out a limited line of ROMANCE, western, and especially monster comics. To L., it was uninspiring. Comics were just coming out of the chaos of the 1950s, the period when Dr. Frederic Wertham, among other self-styled social reformers, blamed comics, especially, but not exclusively, HORROR comics, for the rise of juvenile delinquency. After that unpleasant time, most comics were now governed by content restrictions that were often arbitrary and frustrating to creators. L. felt as if it were finally time for him to move on. At the same time, DC Comics had been having success with its superhero revival, especially *Justice League of America,* a team comic that joined together their most popular heroes.

Goodman asked L. to come up with something to compete with *Justice League.* L.'s wife suggested that if L. were going to quit anyway, why not do this new SERIES the way he thought a comic should be done, not just copying what others were doing. With that in mind, L. and Kirby in 1961 created *The Fantastic Four,* a radical departure from superhero comics that had preceded it. The FF had stories that were character-driven. While the plots were certainly action-packed, they were also showcases for the relatively complex personalities of the heroes and villains. Sales were good and kept going up. L. and Marvel had a hit on its hands.

In short order, L. and his artist-collaborators/co-creators were using this style of storytelling to create and chronicle the adventures of a pantheon of characters. With Kirby, L. created the Hulk, Thor, and the X-Men. With Ditko, L. created Spider-Man, the Marvel icon. Success led to success and Marvel Comics was on its way to becoming the industry leader.

Instead of leaving the company, L. now dug in and was the prime mover in putting Marvel—and comics in general—on the cultural map. In addition to editing the line and writing most of it, L. established rapport with readers in the letters and special announcements pages of the comics. He was able to make fans feel that he (and the artists) were the readers' good friends, and that creators and consumers alike were members of a special club. This double bond between readers and characters and readers and creators was a change in the way comics were perceived. It led to reader involvement and loyalty such as had never been seen on a sustained level before. It is a dynamic that drives the comics industry to this day.

L. continued this brand building, giving interviews to the television and radio shows and newspapers and magazines that were now interested in comics, and lecturing extensively on the college circuit. L. appeared on nationwide CBS-TV *Sunrise Semester,* which Bernice Cullinan moderated for New York University. Because the comics themselves were more sophisticated, the readership grew to encompass intelligent, educated TEENAGERS and YOUNG ADULTS as well as children. Even after L. had given over editing and publishing to other hands, he was still the public face of Marvel, and as such, to many the public face of comics in general.

In recent years, L. has occupied himself with promoting Marvel's fortunes in Hollywood, including serving as executive producer of the *Spider-Man* and *X-Men* MOVIES, as well as of many other Marvel-based movies and television series. He has also launched several media businesses of his own. He continues to write the *Spider-Man* syndicated newspaper comic strip, which is drawn by his brother, Larry Lieber.

Long ago, L. legally changed his name to Stan Lee. The FANTASY had eclipsed the reality, which somehow seems appropriate. After all, L.'s fantasies transformed an entire popular culture.

DANNY FINGEROTH

LEE, Tanith
Author, b. 19 September 1947, London, England

Born and reared in London, L. has earned a huge following for her writing, which includes a wide variety of genres, including FANTASY, SCIENCE FICTION, HORROR, mainstream juvenile novels, SHORT STORIES, and historical fiction (*The Gods are Thirsty,* 1996). Although L. wrote her first story at the age of nine, she remembers being unable to read until her father taught her when she was almost eight-years old. She also remembers being told fairy stories created by her mother. A FAIRY-TALE element remains an important aspect in many of L.'s stories. For example, her first published novel, *The Dragon Hoard* (1971), tells the story of Prince Jasleth, who receives an evil birthday gift from the witch Maligna. Jasleth goes in search of the Dragon Hoard to end the spell cast on him. *The Dragon Hoard,* written in just two weeks, was the

first of many fantasy novels which eventually led L. to fame.

As an adult, L. studied art and worked as a librarian while trying to succeed as a writer. Although L. began her career publishing books for children, the publication of *The Birthgrave* (1975), an adult novel, enabled her to quit work and focus completely on her writing career. L. is well known as an author of adult novels such as *The Silver Metal Lover* (1982) and the Flat Earth books. L. has been appealing to a wide range of audiences ever since, publishing more than 60 novels and short stories. L. receives praise for her portrayal of strong female characters. In *Red as Blood* (1983), L. twists the tales from the Brothers Grimm, telling them from the point of view of the Sisters Grimmer, transforming the formerly passive female protagonists into proactive females.

Though an eclectic writer, L. remains best known for her fantasy novels such as *Black Unicorn* (1991) and *Gold Unicorn* (1994). Currently, L.'s Claidi Chronicles are popular with TEENS. The Chronicles include *Wolf Tower* (2000), *Wolf Star* (2001), *Wolf Queen* (2002), and *Wolf Wing* (2002), featuring a sixteen-year-old slave named Claidi. The novels are structured as a series of journal entries written by Claidi, an orphan who serves as a lady's maid until she escapes from the Wolf Tower where she has been imprisoned. L.'s most recent novel, *Piratica* (2004), sold out within three weeks after publication. In *Piratica,* L. narrates a story of a girl's adventure on the high seas. The story, set in the early 1800s, is based on historical tales of Molly Faith, who was a female pirate nicknamed Piratica. The protagonist in the story plays the role of Molly's daughter longing for the adventures of her deceased mother.

L. continues to live in London and is currently working on many novels, producing them at an amazing rate. The film industry is eager to obtain her scripts.

AWARDS: L. received the British Fantasy Society's August Derleth Award in 1980 for *Death's Master* (1979). She earned the World Fantasy Award for best Short Story in 1983 for "The Gorgon." In addition, *Black Unicorn* (1992) and *Red as Blood, or, Tales from the Sisters Grimmer* (1983) both made the BBYA list; *Wolf Tower:* ALA Popular Paperbacks, 2003.

FURTHER WORKS: *Princess Hynchatti and Some Other Surprises,* 1972; *Animal Castle,* 1972; *Companions on the Road,* 1975; *The Winter Players,* 1975; *East of Midnight,* 1977; *The Castle of the Dark,* 1978; *Shon the Taken,* 1979; *Prince on a White Horse,* 1982; *Madame Two Swords,* 1988; *Red Unicorn,* 1997; *Islands in the Sky,* 1999; *Biting the Sun,* 1999; *White as Snow,* 2000; *A Bed of Earth,* 2002; *The Vampire Sextette,* 2002; *When Darkness Falls,* 2003; *Ultimate Dragon,* 2003; *The Dragon Quintet,* 2004; *Thirty-Four,* 2004; *Fatal Women,* 2004.

BIBLIOGRAPHY: Peacock S., ed., *Something about the Author,* vol. 134, 2003; www.locusmag.com; www.tabula-rasa.info; www.tanithlee.com.

JODI PILGRIM

LE GUIN, Ursula K.
Author, b. 21 October 1929, Berkeley, California

L. was her parents' first and only daughter, the fourth child of anthropologist Alfred Kroeber and writer Theodora (Kracaw) Kroeber. Her childhood was a happy one, and her beautiful redwood home had "lots of visitors, lots of talk and argument and discussion about everything, lots of books around, lots of music and story-telling. The life of the mind can be a very lively one. I was brought up to think and to question and to enjoy." Her inspiration to become a writer was, she notes, "learning to write, at five."

Her parents encouraged L. to work hard at any talent she might have, and L. identified that talent as writing. She adds, "My parents never encouraged me in the sense of making a fuss about what I wrote or praising my determination to write." L. graduated from Radcliffe College in 1951 with a bachelor's degree in French. Of that point in her life, she notes, "I never thought I wanted to be a writer. I always thought I was one. The big question was how could I earn a living at it? My father wisely suggested I get some training in a moneymaking skill so that I would not have to live off my writing. . . . With this in mind, I decided to work toward a higher degree in Romance languages and teach."

In 1953, L. received her master's degree from Columbia University, and then began working on her Ph.D. in French and Italian Renaissance Literature. She received a Fulbright Fellowship to study in France, and onboard the Queen Mary she met Charles Le Guin. Six months later, in December 1953, they married. When the couple returned to the U.S., L. decided to stop pursuing her doctorate. Instead, she taught French, worked various part-time jobs, and

continued to write. Her husband encouraged her talent; L. writes, "My husband never questioned my right to write. This is fairly rare, especially in husbands. My advice to young writers is, if you can't marry money, at least don't marry envy."

During the next eight years, L. had POETRY published and also completed five unpublished novels. Then L. came across the works of SCIENCE FICTION writers such as Philip K. Dick and Cordwainer Smith. She knew that her work was in the same vein. Her first science-fiction novel, *Rocannon's World,* was published in 1966. This novel also contains elements of FANTASY. In order to separate the fantasy and science-fiction genres in her own mind as well as in future works, L. went on to write *A Wizard of Earthsea* (1968) and *The Left Hand of Darkness* (1969). At this point L. notes that she "finally got my pure fantasy vein separated from my science fiction vein . . . and the separation marked a large advance in both skill and content."

Today, L. is widely recognized as one of the most significant authors of science fiction and fantasy. She has written poetry and novels, as well as novellas, SHORT STORIES, PLAYS, essays, reviews, and texts for musical compositions. In addition, she has served as the editor of various science-fiction collections. Her work is geared toward a wide audience: children, YOUNG ADULTS, and adults. It is notable that few American writers have done work of such high quality in so many genres and for so many different audiences.

Among L.'s books for young adults, *Catwings* (1988) is a classic. This story begins with the birth of four kittens, each of whom has wings. At first their mother is at a loss for an explanation. She then realizes that the wings will allow her kittens to fly away from the dreary, dangerous city in which they live. What the mother cat does not anticipate is the adventure and hazards that await her kittens in the country. *Catwings* was followed by *Catwings Return* (1989), *Wonderful Alexander and the Catwings* (1994), and *Jane on her Own: A Catwings Tale* (1999).

L.'s earlier work, *A Wizard of Earthsea* (1968), led to several more novels, all of which are collectively called The Books of Earthsea. They include *The Tombs of Atuan* (1970), *The Farthest Shore* (1972), *Tehanu* (1990), *Tales from Earthsea* (2001), and *The Other Wind* (2001). In these books, the wizard Ged is followed from childhood to old age in various locations on Earthsea, a "rural archipelago complete with its own anthropology, geology, and language." In the fictional world of Earthsea, language is a powerful force.

In her writing, L. stresses the importance of knowledge of oneself and how that knowledge relates to the outside world. The Books of Earthsea also characterize L.'s style in regard to the important humanitarian issues she explores through her writing, including relationships, communication, power, identity, and DEATH. The books that make up this SERIES are often regarded as the most important achievements in L.'s vast bibliography. They are often compared to great classics of both fantasy and children's literature, such as The Lord of the Rings by J. R. R. TOLKIEN and The Chronicles of Narnia by C. S. LEWIS.

L. and her husband have lived in Portland, Oregon since 1958, and are the parents of three children: Elisabeth, Caroline, and Theodore. They also have three grandchildren. L. leads a private life, and her public appearances are limited mostly to the West Coast.

AWARDS: 1968 *Boston Globe–Horn Book* Award, *A Wizard of Earthsea;* Nebula Award: 1969 for *The Left Hand of Darkness,* 1975 for "The Day Before the Revolution," 1975 for *The Dispossessed,* 1990 for *Tehanu,* and 1996 for "Solitude"; Hugo Award: 1969 for *The Left Hand of Darkness,* 1973 for *The Word for World Is Forest,* 1974 for "The Ones Who Walk Away from Omelas," 1975 for *The Dispossessed,* and 1998 for "Buffalo Gals"; 1972 Newbery Silver Medal Award, *The Tombs of Atuan;* 1972 National Book Award for Children's Books, *The Farthest Shore:* Locus Award: 1973 for *The Lathe of Heaven,* 1984 for *The Compass Rose;* 1979 Lewis Carroll Shelf Award, *A Wizard of Earthea;* 1979 Gandalf Award Grand Master of Fantasy; 1991 American Academy & Institute of Arts & Letters Harold Vursell Award; Locus Readers Award: 1995 for "Forgiveness Day", 1996 for *Four Ways to Forgiveness,* 2002 for *The Telling,* and 2002 for "The Bones of the Earth" and "The Finder" in *Tales from Earthsea;* 1998 International Fantasy Award, "Buffalo Gals"; 2002 Endeavor Award, *The Telling;* 2004 MARGARET A. EDWARDS AWARD for Lifetime Achievement, writing YA lit: for the Books of Earthsea trilogy: *A Wizard of Earthsea, The Tombs of Atuan, The Farthest Shore,* and *Tehanu, Dispossessed:* ALA Best Book for Young Adults, 1974; *Very Far Away from Anywhere Else:* ALA Best Books for Young Adults, 1976; Selected for "The Best of the Best Books: 1970–1983";

Beginning Place: ALA Best Book for Young Adults, 1980.

SELECT FURTHER WORKS: *Very Far Away from Anything Else,* 1976; *The Beginning Place,* 1980; *The Telling,* 2000; *The Birthday of the World and Other Stories,* 2002.

BIBLIOGRAPHY: *Something about the Author,* Volume 99; www.ursulakleguin.com.

                                          CARRA E. GAMBERDELLA

LEITNER, Isabella
Author, b. 28 May 1924, Kisvarda, Hungary

A child survivor of Auschwitz, L. has dedicated her life to educating her TEENAGE readers about the HOLOCAUST. After losing most of her family in World War II, she married and began raising her two sons whom she calls her "greatest triumph over Hitler." She has written several books for adults and children recounting the horrors of the Holocaust. Her first book, *Fragments of Isabella* (1978), was nominated for a Pulitzer Prize, translated into fourteen languages and made into a film by Ronan O'Leary (1989). Her story is continued in *Saving the Fragments: From Auschwitz to New York* (1985), journeying from the concentration camps to America where she and her two sisters met their father in New York City. She retells her heartbreaking story for school children in the book *The Big Lie: A True Story* (1992). With a simple but powerful use of language she infuses her books with haunting and moving images of the survivors and of those who perished.

AWARDS: *Fragments of Isabella* was nominated for the Pulitzer Prize and received a Best Books for Young Adults citation, American Library Association, 1978.

FURTHER WORKS: *Isabella: From Auschwitz to Freedom,* 1994.

BIBLIOGRAPHY: *Contemporary Authors Online,* 2001; *Center for Holocaust Genocide Studies Online Biographies,* 2003.

                                          LAURIE M. ALLEN

LEMIEUX, A(nne) C(onnelly)
Author, journalist, b. 1954, Bridgeport, Connecticut

L. once commented that her writing is "a process of finding connections." L. has created many connections with young people through frank novels about troubled TEENS. Young people can find solace and the beginning of a path to understanding issues such as teen depression and suicide with novels such as *The TV Guidance Counselor.* With novels that delve into more than heartache, L. craftily and playfully connects to her readers with novels such as *Fruit Flies, Fish, and Fortune Cookies* and its sequel, *Dare to Be, M.E.!* She is recognized for her easy-reader Super Snoop Sam Snout MYSTERY SERIES and her FANTASY trilogy of the Fair Lady.

L. was strongly influenced by Harper LEE's *To Kill a Mockingbird,* evolving over time into characters with the moral depth found in L.'s stories. From Michael Madden struggling with his desire to commit suicide to Mary Ellen's discovery of her friend's bulimia, L. finds a way to connect to her readers through many avenues of adolescent development. Most importantly, L. explains the goal of her writing in *ALAN Review:* "My foremost aim is to write with honesty, and without condescension, with humor which encompasses the paradoxes, incongruities, and even absurdities of life. My hope is that my characters' voices will catch kids' attention, and connect with their hearts, and that my stories might help expand their emotional vocabularies. I believe a writer can be an agent of connection."

AWARDS: *The TV Guidance Counselor:* ALA Best Book for Young Adults, American Library Association, 1994.

FURTHER WORKS: *The TV Guidance Counselor,* 1993; *Super Snoop Sam Snout: The Case of the Yogurt Poker,* 1994; *Super Snoop Sam Snout: The Case of the Stolen Snowman,* 1994; *Super Snoop Sam Snout: The Case of the Missing Marble,* 1994; *Fruit Flies, Fish, and Fortune Cookies,* illustrated by Diane de Groat, 1994; *Do Angels Sing the Blues?,* 1995; *Dare to Be, M.E.!,* 1997; *Fairy Lair: A Special Place,* 1997; *Fairy Lair: A Hidden Place,* 1998; *Fairy Lair: A Magic Place,* 1998; *All the Answers,* 2000. Contributor to anthologies, including a poem to *Food Fight,* 1996, a short story, "Just Say . . .," to *New Year, New Love,* 1996, and to *My America: A Poetry Atlas of the United States,* Simon & Schuster, 2000. Contributor to *Family Issues* ("Using Literature to Help Troubled Teens" series), edited by Joan Katwell, 1999. Works in Progress: *Jester's Quest, Lovespeed,* and *Brewtopia,* YA novels, *Sea-Sar Salad,* a POETRY collection, and *Being and Becoming: Journeying Through Life with a Special Child,* adult nonfiction.

BIBLIOGRAPHY: *Contemporary Authors Online.* The Gale Group, 2001.

REBECCA OSA MENDELL

LEMONY Snicket. See SNICKETT, Lemony

L'ENGLE, Madeleine
Author, b. 29 November 1918, New York City

A recipient of the MARGARET A. EDWARDS AWARD for a lifetime achievement in writing YOUNG ADULT literature, L. has shown herself to be a master of the pen and the imagination. She is a staunch believer in truth and is fascinated by what the world has to offer. L. is known as a writer in many genres; she has delved into the world of SCIENCE FICTION, MYSTERIES, POETRY, autobiographies, FAMILIES, and Christian literature. L.'s characters are so engaging that the reader feels as if they are real. L. allows the reader to become connected with her characters by putting them into new stories and allowing them to grow up. The reader is able to follow every step of the character's journey and become enveloped by it.

L. turned to the art of writing at the young age of five to amuse herself. After graduating from Smith College *cum laude,* L. got a job working in the theater. She wrote her first novel, *Small Rain* (1945), while on tour for the play "Uncle Harry." When L. left the theater, she moved to Connecticut where she wrote her first YA novel. *Meet the Austins* (1960) is about a happy family whose lives are disrupted and forever changed one day by a recently orphaned girl named Maggy.

In 1962, L. discovered the world of particle physics. It was at this time that she wrote one of her most famous novels, *A Wrinkle in Time,* which won the Newbery Award (1963), the Sequoyah Children's Book Award (1965), and the Lewis Carroll Shelf Award (1965). It has also been made into a television MOVIE. This novel is about a young girl named Meg Murry who embarks on an adventure through space with her brother Charles Wallace to find her father.

The Moon by Night (1963) is about sixteen-year-old Vicky Austin who, while traveling cross-country with her parents, meets two boys who later become each other's rivals. *The Young Unicorns* (1968) takes the reader on another adventure with the Austin family. In this book, Suzy and Rob Austin are put in great danger when they learn of an evil plot to rule New York City.

In *A Wind in the Door* (1973), Meg Murry and Charles Wallace return as protagonists. The tale is about a cherub, Proginoskes, who has come to save Charles Wallace from a serious illness. Further following the journey of Charles Wallace is *A Swiftly Tilting Planet* (1978); Charles is now fifteen and his mission is to go back in time to change history in order to stop a mad dictator from declaring nuclear WAR. In *A Ring of Endless Light* (1980), a Newbery Honor Book, Vicky Austin is back, in a tale about her dealing with life and death and her complicated involvement with three boys. *An Acceptable Time* (1989), the sequel to *A House like a Lotus* (1984), is about a young woman named Polly who visits her grandparents in a remote town in Connecticut and gets transported back in time when the town was populated by Druids.

Biblical references flood L.'s novels, but her writing as a whole does not stop there. It continues to make leaps and bounds into dimensions much greater than anyone has ever imagined. *Many Waters* (1986) follows the Murry family's twin boys, Sandy and Denny, as they are transported back in time to meet with the biblical Noah; they must find a way to get back before the flood comes.

L.'s novels illustrate how passionately she views life and the art of writing. The journeys she takes readers on through space and time are poignant. Even though a character might leave planet Earth, the words of wisdom and the lessons that are taught and learned are all relevant to life on any planet and in any time. People of all ages and all walks of life are drawn to L.'s novels.

Today L. lives in Connecticut and New York City. She served as a librarian and writer-in-residence at the Cathedral of Saint John the Divine for many years. Her son, Bion, died in December 1999. L. has two living daughters, five grandchildren, and four great-grandchildren.

AWARDS: *A Wrinkle in Time,* 1962: Newbery Award (1963), the Sequoyah Children's Book Award (1965), and the Lewis Carroll Shelf Award (1965); *The Moon by Night,* 1963, Austrian State Literary Prize (1969); *A Swiftly Tilting Planet* (1978), American Book Award; *A Ring of Endless Light* (1980), Newbery Honor Book; Sophie Award (1984), Regina Medal (1984), Adolescent Literature Assembly Award (1986) for her incredible writing accomplishments; Madeleine L'Engle was named the 1998 recipient of the Margaret A. Edwards Award, honoring her life time contribution in writing for teens. She was cited in the award for the Austin Family series, which in-

cludes *Meet the Austins* and *A Ray of Endless Light,* and the Time Fantasy series, which includes *A Wrinkle in Time* and *A Swiftly Tilting Planet.*

FURTHER WORKS: *Ilsa,* 1946; *And Both Were Young,* 1949; *Camilla Dickinson,* 1951; *A Winter's Love,* 1957; *The Arm of the Starfish,* 1965; *The Love Letters,* 1966; *The Other Side of the Sun,* 1971; *A Circle of Quiet,* 1972; *The Summer of the Great Grandmother,* 1974; *Dragons in the Waters,* 1976; *The Irrational Season,* 1977; *A Severed Wasp,* 1982; *Two-Part Invention,* 1988; *Certain Women,* 1992; *Troubling a Star,* 1994; *A Live Coal in the Sea,* 1996; *A Full House,* 1999.

BIBLIOGRAPHY: Bonastra: The Madeleine L. WWW Resource; http://www.geocities.com/Athens/Acropolis/8838; http://www.madeleinelengle.com; http://www.randomhouse.com/teachers/authors/leng.html; The Tesseract: A Madeleine L. BIOGRAPHY in 5 Dimensions; http://hometown.aol.com/Kfbofpq/Lengl/html; http://mle_project.tripod.com. Zarin, Cynthia "The Story Teller: Fact, fiction and the books of Madeleine L." *The New Yorker,* April 12, 2004, pp. 60–67.

TRILBY WILDE
AND LENA ROY

LESTER, Julius
Author, b. 27 January 1939, St. Louis, Missouri

One of the first male AFRICAN AMERICAN writers in the field of YOUNG ADULT literature, L. has been active in political and literature circles since the 1960s. L.'s books have received a Newbery Honor Medal, ALA's Notable Book Award, The *New York Times* Outstanding Book Award, a Caldecott Honor medal, and the *Boston Globe–Horn Book* Award. While often dealing with cultural issues, L. uses humor mixed with the brutalities of truth to paint a realistic picture of life, presenting it in a storyteller's way.

L. knows about brutal realities having been raised in the Southern U.S. Born in 1939 in St. Louis, L.'s family moved to Kansas when he was two years old. As a teenager, he lived in Nashville, Tennessee, spending most of his summers with his grandmother in Arkansas. L. was the son of a Methodist pastor in the South during the 1940s and 1950s; through his father, he was exposed to Southern segregation and its results. In 1960, L. graduated from Fisk University with a B.A. in English, but chose to pursue a career in music while also becoming politically active in the CIVIL RIGHTS MOVEMENT. In the mid-1960s, he joined

SNCC, the Student Non-Violent Coordinating Committee, eventually becoming the head of its photo department. L.'s photography from this era is held in collections at the Smithsonian Institute and at Howard University. L. and folksinger Pete Seeger co-authored *The 12-String Guitar as Played by Leadbelly* (1967), which was published when L. was twenty-eight. In the late 1960s, L. hosted and produced a radio show in New York for eight years and also hosted a live television show for two years. During this time, he also wrote for adults.

On the advice of his publisher, L. started writing young adult books. His first book for YA was *To Be a Slave* (1968)—through the use of slave narratives collected in the 1800s and narratives given by ex-slaves in the 1930s, L. painted a picture of slavery as viewed by those subjected to it. L. received much praise for this effort and many books followed in the same vein, presenting African American history in straightforward historical fashion.

L. combines his interest in African-American history, folklore, and politics within a storytelling format. But while L. is a very entertaining author, he aims to educate the African American child and other readers about their cultural heritage. *The Knee-High Man, and Other Tales* (1972) is a collection of six black folktales, including Brer Rabbit. L. returned to this character in *The Tales of Uncle Remus: The Adventures of Brer Rabbit* (1987), *More Tales of Uncle Remus* (1988), *Further Tales of Uncle Remus* (1990), and *The Last Tales of Uncle Remus* (1999). L. shows his storytelling ability by writing these stories with every bit of the edge they had in previous retellings but in a language style which makes them accessible for today's audience while respectful of the African American folklore. L.'s *Sam and the Tigers* (1996) is a retelling of one of the most historically debated books which prompted Virginia HAMILTON to comment that L.'s "Sam is revolutionary in its re-visioning of *Little Black Sambo.*"

L.'s *John Henry* (1994) and *Othello: A Novel* (1999) are new versions of old stories. Working again with illustrator Jerry Pinkney, L. gives the legend of John Henry hero status and explains that today's children need such role models. Retelling Shakespeare's play *Othello* as a novel, L. changes the setting to London and makes two of Shakespeare's original characters black. L. makes race a central theme yet keeps the focus on the weakness of the human soul and the difference between what is perceived and what is real, staying true to Shakespeare's play in a unique way.

L. writes for a specific reason: to educate his readers and to provide a cultural context for African American children. Known as the "spokesman of the black revolution" during the 1960s, L. is now a professor of Near Eastern and Judaic Studies at the University of Massachusetts in Amherst. L. presents the African American perspective through stories that are relevant to African American children, enabling them to approach their culture through their own language and psyche.

In L.'s *When Dad Killed Mom* (2001), he acknowledges violence in other sectors of America, discussing the aftermath of domestic violence when an affluent, white, college professor in a small, New England town shoots his wife in broad daylight. Jenna and Jeremy alternate their point of view to explain the story; they must deal with the action of their father and cope with their new life without their mother. While the ethnicity of the characters is white, the story touches audiences from all cultures. L.'s work has been translated into eight languages, indicating its worldwide appeal.

SELECT AWARDS: Newbery Honor Medal, *To Be a Slave* (1968); *Long Journey Home* (1998): National Book Award Finalist, Caldecott Honor; *John Henry* (1994): 1995 *Boston Globe–Horn Book* Award, 1994 Aesop Prize Winner, 1995 Randolph Caldecott Medal Honor Book; Coretta Scott King Author Honor Books: 1983 for *This Strange New Feeling,* 1988 for *The Tales of Uncle Remus;* and numerous citations on ALA lists.

FURTHER WORKS: *The Angry Children of Malcolm X,* 1966; *The Mud of Vietnam: Photographs and Poems,* 1967; *Look Out Whitey! Black Power's Gon' Get Your Mama!,* 1968; *Black Folktales,* 1969, 1998; *Search for the New Land: History as a Subjective Experience,* 1969; *Revolutionary Notes,* 1969; *The Long Journey Home: Stories from Black History,* 1972; *Two Love Stories,* 1972; *This Strange New Feeling,* 1982; *Falling Pieces of the Broken Sky,* 1990; *And All Our Wounds Forgiven,* 1994; *How Butterflies Came to Be,* 1997; *What a Truly Cool World,* 1998; *From Slave Ship to Freedom Road,* 1998; *When the Beginning Began: Stories about God, the Creatures, and Us,* 1998; *Shining,* 2000; *Pharaoh's Daughter,* 2000; *The Autobiography of God,* 2000; *Why Heaven Is Far Away,* 2002; *On Writing for Children and Other People,* 2004.

BIBLIOGRAPHY: *Children's Literature Review,* vol. 2, 41, 1997, pp. 91–115; L. Julius, *Lovesong: Becoming a Jew,* 1988; MacCann, Donnarae, "Julius L.," *Twen-*

tieth-Century Children's Literature Review, vol. 2, 41, 1997, pp. 575–76, *Something about the Author,* vol. 112, 2000, pp. 112–17; eds. Pendergast, Tom and Sara Pendergast, *St. James Guide to YA Writers,* 1999.

TAMMY L. MIELKE

LEVENKRON, Steven

Author, psychologist, b. 25 March 1941, New York City

Born to Joseph and Florence, L. attended Queens College and Brooklyn College. He and his wife, Abby Rosen, and their two children, Rachel and Gabrielle, now live in New York City. L. studied psychotherapy in college and worked as a clinical consultant in several New York hospitals such as Montefiore Hospital and Medical Center and the Center for the Study of Anorexia and Bulimia. At the present time L. is a member of the advisory board of the National Association of Anorexia and Associated Disorders in Highland Park, Illinois.

L. is most widely known for his work about anorexia nervosa. He has published three YA books including his first and most widely known, *The Best Little Girl in the World* (1978). Through the fictional story of Francesca, L. illustrates and communicates the problems and hardships of anorexia to YA. In 1981 L.'s book was made into an ABC-TV MOVIE, which brought his already successful book more recognition. L. was recognized for his literary accomplishment and was applauded for bringing anorexia to public attention with an annual award from the National Association of Anorexia Nervosa and Associated Disorders.

L. continues the story of Francesca in a sequel, *Kessa* (1986). He develops Francesca's life experiences and sends her down a path of saving others battling anorexia while continuing with her ongoing battle.

L. also focuses on other serious illnesses such as self-mutilation and obsessive-compulsive disorders. In his most recent YA publication, *The Luckiest Girl in the World* (1997), Katie Roskova, a beautiful, smart, and talented figure skater, resorts to "cutting" in order to ease the tension and stress in her early TEENAGE life. L. addresses obsessive-compulsive disorders in his book *Obsessive-Compulsive Disorders: Treating and Understanding Crippling Habits* (1991).

As a distinguished author and psychologist, L. has brought anorexia nervosa to public awareness. He ac-

complished this by using his scholarly background in psychotherapy to make anorexia more understandable for young adults. His award-winning books have impacted YA literature and have shed light on psychological topics.

AWARDS: 1998 ALA BBYA for *The Luckiest Girl in the World;* 1978 ALA BBYA for *Best Little Girl in the World* was one of 100 YA titles selected for the 2nd YALSA Best of Best List: The Best of the Best Books (Selections from 1970 to 1983).

FURTHER WORKS: *Cutting: Understanding and Overcoming Self-Multilation,* 1998; *Anatomy of Anorexia,* 2000.

BIBLIOGRAPHY: The University of Tennessee Resource Center: http://www.galnet.com; Time Warner Bookmark: http://www.twbookmark.com/authors/22/1210/

KATELYN WOOTEN

LEVINE, Ellen

Author, n.d., n.p.

L. is the author of several INFORMATIONAL BOOKS for YOUNG ADULTS that explore civil and human rights subjects. *Freedom's Children: Young Civil Rights Tell Their Own Stories* (1993) is a collection of interviews of thirty AFRICAN AMERICANS who as children and TEENAGERS were CIVIL RIGHTS activists in the 1950s and 1960s, participating in sit-ins, protest marches, and other events. *A Fence Away from Freedom: Japanese Americans and World War II* (1995) chronicles the internment of Japanese Americans during World War II following the bombing of Pearl Harbor. *Darkness Over Denmark: The Danish Resistance of the Jews* (2000) is an account of people in Denmark who risked their lives to protect and rescue their Jewish neighbors from the Nazis during World War II.

AWARDS: Jane Addams Award (1994) and ALA Best Books for Young Adults (1994) for *Freedom's Children;* Carter G. Woodson Award (1996) for *A Fence Away from Freedom; Darkness over Denmark:* ALA BBYA, 2001; Dorothy Canfield Fisher Children's Book Award, 2002.

FURTHER WORKS: *The Journal of Jedidiah Barstow: An Emigrant on the Oregon Trail,* 2002.

EDWARD T. SULLIVAN

LEVINE, Gail Carson

Author, artist, b. 17 September 1947, New York City

L. became interested in writing at an early age, and she was urged to express herself creatively. As an elementary grade student, L was a charter member of the "Scribble Scrabble Club." During her TEEN years, her POETRY was published in an anthology of high-school writers. Despite her interest in writing, her early career ambitions focused on becoming an artist or actress. After the completion of a B.A. from City College of the City of New York in 1969, L.'s concern for others took precedence over her artistic impulses and she became a social worker. L. began writing again while collaborating with her husband on a children's musical, *Spacenapped*. It was her interest in painting, however, that led her to take courses in writing and illustrating children's books; it was there that she discovered her gift for writing children's fiction.

A devoted reader of fairy tales as a child, L. used the plot line of Charles Perrault's *Cinderella* as inspiration for a class assignment—the result was *Ella Enchanted* (1997). While possessing all the elements of Perrault's story, including a fairy godmother, prince, pumpkin, glass slipper, *Ella Enchanted*'s heroine is different; Ella's obedience, unlike Cinderella's, whom L's felt was too "goody-two-shoes," is caused by a spell placed upon her as a baby by a well-meaning fairy. Ella uses her inner resources to break the curse and find happiness.

Not all of L.'s self-reliant characters are female. In *Dave at Night* (1999), a story loosely based on her father's childhood in a Jewish orphanage during the 1930s, we meet a scrappy and capable eleven-year-old boy named Dave. Despite the break-up of his family and the hardship of life as a resident of the Hebrew Home for Boys, Dave needs no one. Fearless, Dave escapes at night into the rich world of the Harlem Renaissance. Dave comes to recognize, however, that he cannot find happiness alone and accepts the love and support of friends.

In *The Wish* (2000) and *The Two Princesses of Bamarre* (2001), one once again sees the theme of independence, coupled with the need for community. A modern tale centered on a pre-teen's longing for social acceptance, *The Wish* blends fairy-tale elements with the real world of New York City. When Wilma Sturtz is granted a wish for giving up her seat on the subway to a fairy in disguise, she wishes for popularity. When the spell ends, she discovers that it does not change who she really is or who her real friends are. In *The Two Princesses of Bamarre*, L. returns to the FANTASY world of fairy tales. The heroine, Addie, is strong and capable, but crippled with self-doubt. By

trusting herself and others, Addie breaks a curse that has haunted her kingdom for generations.

Betsy Who Cried Wolf (2002) is a shift for L. It is her first PICTURE BOOK, as well as her first reworking of a folktale. It is the story of a shepardess who refuses to be talked out of her claim that she has seen a wolf. Betsy soon discovers that what the wolf, Zimmo, really wants is a helping hand and that by helping him she gains a valuable friend and assistant.

An author of warmth and imagination, the appeal of all of L.'s work will be lasting. Perhaps her greatest achievement is her ability to update fairy tales and folk tales to reflect the modern values of self-reliance and cooperation while adding to the genre's original charm. L.'s playful, witty novels and stories have not only made her a favorite of both children and parents, but have also won her critical acclaim.

AWARDS: *Ella Enchanted,* 1998 Newbery Honor Book, ALA Notable Book, ALA Best Book for Young Adults; *Dave at Night,* 1999 ALA Notable Children's Books, ALA Best Book for Young Adults, 2000.

FURTHER WORKS: *The Princess Tales: Volume 1,* 1999; *Cinderellis and the Glass Hill,* 2000; *For Biddle's Sake,* 2002; *The Fairy's Return,* 2002.

BIBLIOGRAPHY: *Book Report,* 16, Jan.–Feb. 1998, pp. 34–35; *Christian Science Monitor,* 92, Jan. 2000, pp. 18–19; *Contemporary Authors,* vol. 166, 205–6; *Eighth Book of Junior Authors and Illustrators,* 2000; *Horn Book,* 76; Jan.–Feb. 2000, pp. 76; *School Library Journal,* 46, Nov. 2000; *Something about the Author,* 98, 97–8.

JOY MORSE

LEVITIN, Sonia (Wolff)
Author, b. 18 August 1934, Berlin, Germany

The scope of L.'s writing is remarkable, ranging from PICTURE BOOKS to historical and SCIENCE FICTION for YA. L., the prolific author of over forty books for young people, has garnered numerous honors and acclamations for her work. However, despite her many local and national awards, her novels earn mixed reviews from critics.

L.'s early childhood was shadowed by the rise of Hitler's power preceding World War II. Sensing the horror that was to come, her family fled L.'s Berlin for the U.S. in 1938, settling permanently in California. During those first difficult years in the U.S., her father struggled to sustain a small garment business,

RON KOERTGE

E. L. KONIGSBURG

KATHRYN LASKY

MADELEINE L'ENGLE

JULIUS LESTER

GAIL CARSON LEVINE

SONIA LEVITIN

C. S. LEWIS

ROBERT LIPSYTE

while her mother suffered from poor health. The youngest of three children, L. spent most of her childhood in the care of her older sister. Her hobbies included taking care of the family's numerous pets, playing the piano, and, of course, writing.

L. attended the University of California at Berkeley from 1952 to 1954, and graduated from the University of Pennsylvania with her B.S. in Education in 1956. L. married in 1953, and after graduation, the couple settled in California. After her first child was born, L. taught a variety of junior high and adult education classes from 1956 to 1972. From 1957 to 1960, L. also attended graduate school at the San Francisco State College, where one of her professors was Walter Van Tilburg Clark, author of the classic *The Ox-Bow Incident* (1940). It is probable that Clark's influence, the rich historical lore of L.'s home state, and her experiences with immigration helped shape the direction of her future writing, most of which incorporated historical and autobiographical elements.

With the exception of a few MYSTERY books, L.'s body of work for young adults generally falls into two categories: historical fiction and fiction that explores Jewish culture. Perhaps her best-known work is her trilogy about an immigrant Jewish family, whose troubles and joys start in *Journey to America* (1970) and are further explored in *Silver Days* (1989) and *Annie's Promise* (1993). The story of the fictional Platt family is clearly autobiographical, and critics responded warmly to the emotional story. *Booklist* declared in a 1993 review of the PAPERBACK reissue of *Journey to America:* "L.'s fine prose has not dated in the years since the book's first appearance."

L.'s other historical works touch on a myriad of topics, several of which include historical California settings. She explored a puzzling history mystery in *Roanoke: A Novel of the Lost Colony* (1973); documented the trials of the first woman to travel on a wagon train to California in 1841 (*The No-return Trail,* 1978); and recorded the pitfalls and triumphs of a TEENAGER on a cross-country search for his father in 1860 (*Clem's Chances,* 2001).

L. also delves into Jewish culture, both past and present. Besides the Journey to America trilogy, L. looked into the ancient exodus of the Jewish people from their land of slavery with *Escape from Egypt* (1994), and the more complex problems of Jewish teens growing up in a modern Jerusalem in *The Singing Mountain* (1998). Her novel, *The Return* (1987),

is about the 1984 secret airlift of hundreds of refugee Ethiopian Jews from Africa to Israel and received a starred review in *School Library Journal.* Her more recent science fiction novel about a futuristic being that travels back in time to learn about anti-Semitism in medieval Europe (*The Cure,* 1999) was labeled unique.

In an autobiographical statement for the Educational Paperback Association's Web page, L. commented, "I like to write stories about ordinary people pitched into unusual or startling situations, about people of courage and ingenuity." Indeed, L.'s everyday heroes, whether cowboys or refugees, inspire and educate teen readers by providing them with the sense that heroes don't have to be exceptional to become super. Her large and varied body of work has made a tremendous impact on YA literature.

AWARDS: 1981, "Distinguished contribution to the field of children's literature," Southern California Council for Children and Young People; *The Return:* Sydney Taylor Book Awards, 1987, ALA Best Books for Young Adults, 1987; *Silver Days:* ALA BBYA, 1990; *Escape from Egypt:* ALA BBYA, 1995.

FURTHER WORKS: *Rita the Weekend Rat,* 1971; *Who Owns the Moon?* 1973; *Jason and the Money Tree,* 1974; *A Single Speckled Egg,* 1975; *The Mark of Conte,* 1976; *Beyond Another Door,* 1977; *Reigning Cats and Dogs,* 1978; *A Sound to Remember,* 1979; *Nobody Stole the Pie,* 1980; *The Fisherman and the Bird,* 1982; *All the Cats in the World,* 1982; *The Year of Sweet Senior Insanity,* 1982; *Smile Like a Plastic Daisy,* 1983; *A Season for Unicorns,* 1986; *The Man Who Kept His Heart in a Bucket,* 1991; *The Golem and the Dragon Girl,* 1993; *Adam's War,* (Vincent Nasta, illustrator) 1994; *Evil Encounter,* 1996; *A Piece of Home,* (Juan Wijngaard, illustrator) 1996; *Nine for California,* (Cat Bowman Smith, illustrator) 1996; *Boom Town,* (Cat Bowman Smith, illustrator) 1997; *Yesterday's Child,* 1997; *Incident at Loring Groves,* 1998; *Taking Charge,* 1999; *Dream Freedom,* 2000; *Clem's Chances,* 2001; *Room in the Heart,* 2003. Also *What They Did to Miss Lily,* 1981, under the name Sonia Wolff.

BIBLIOGRAPHY: Cooper, Ilene. "The Cure," *Booklist,* 1, June 1999, p. 1814; Kellman, Amy. "The Return," *School Library Journal,* May 1987, p. 115; L., Sonia. "Autobiographical Statement," Educational Paperback Association, http://www.edupaperback.org, 3, May, 2003; L., Sonia. "Sonia L.'s Homepage," http://www.bol.ucla.edu/~slevitin/, 26, Apr. 2003; Marinucci, Ron. "The Cure," *Book Report,* Sept./Oct. 1999; "Sonia L.," Contemporary Authors Online,

2001; "Sonia L.," *Lives and Works: Young Adult Authors,* vol. 6, 1999; "Sonia L. Papers," University of Southern Mississippi de Grummond Collection, http:// www.lib.usm.edu / ~degrum / findaids / levitin .htm, 3, May, 2003; Weisman, Kay. "Journey to America," *Booklist,* 1, Sept. 1993, p. 61.

JENNIFER HUBERT

LEVY, Marilyn
Author, screenwriter, n.d., n.p.

L., screenwriter of *Bride of the Wind* (2001), has also written for theatre having her PLAY, *Dangerous Perceptions* produced in New York City. As a feminist, psychotherapist, and former English teacher, this author has also written seventeen YA books. These novels explore cultural differences, YA issues and their experiences while growing up. Some of her books are out-of-print, but they may be purchased, used, online. Her books include: *The Girl in the Plastic Cage,* 1982; *Life is Not a Dress Rehearsal,* 1984; *Love is a Long Shot,* 1986; *Keeping Score,* 1987; *Touching,* 1988; *Love Is Not Enough,* 1989; *Sounds of Silence,* 1989; *Summer Snow,* 1989; *Remember to Remember Me,* 1989; *No Way Home,* 1990; *Rumors and Whispers,* 1990; *Fitting In,* 1992; *The Last Goodbye,* 1992; *Putting Heather Together Again,* 1992; *City Girl, Country Girl,* 1993; *Run for Your Life,* 1997; *Is That Really Me in the Mirror?,* 1999.

L. is currently working on writing screenplays for *Sabina* and her novel, *Run For Your Life.*

AWARDS: *Run for Your Life:* ALA Best Book for Young Adults, 1997; ALA Popular Paperbacks, 2002.

REFERENCES: www.cinema.com/article/item.phtml? ID = 1790

VALERIE A. PALAZOLO

LEWIS, C. S.
Author, b. 29 November 1898, Belfast, Ireland; d. 22 November 1963

L., born Clive Staples, published under the initials "C. S.," and called "Jack" by family and friends for much of his life, was a man of many different roles. A well-respected literary scholar renowned for his work in medieval and Renaissance English literature whose academic writing has stood the test of time, L. is better known for his non-academic writing. Although he is acclaimed for his Christian apologetics, there can be no question that the most memorable and

well-known of L.'s work is The Chronicles of Narnia SERIES.

Perhaps it is appropriate that a man who himself had a painful childhood should write one of the most influential contributions to children's literature, especially in the genre of FANTASY. L.'s father, Albert James L., was a solicitor, and his mother, Flora Augusta Hamilton Lewis, was a mathematical scholar. However, she died when L. was just nine-years-old. Almost immediately, L. and his brother Warren were sent away to boarding school, a change which L. found particularly upsetting. He attended several schools in Belfast and England and felt that the best part of this time was the two and a half years he spent as a private student of W. T. Kirkpatrick, whose intellectual training L. greatly admired.

In 1917, L. entered Oxford, but he left the university after joining the army and served in France with the Somerset Light Infantry. He was wounded in 1918 and returned to Oxford the following year. After college, L. was elected a Fellow of Magdalen College at Oxford, as a tutor in English language and literature. He held the position for nearly thirty years, until he accepted the position of chair of medieval and Renaissance literature at Magdalen College, Cambridge in 1954.

Although his early years were filled with religious doubt, L. felt he experienced a religious awakening during his early thirties. His efforts thereafter were, to a great extent, influenced by this experience. He was deeply involved in the Oxford Socratic Club, founded in 1942 "to sponsor weekly debates on 'the pros and cons of the Christian religion'" (McGovern, 1983). In addition to a long reign as the group's president, L. was a frequent speaker. L., with J. R. R. TOLKIEN and Charles Williams, formed "The Inklings," an informal group that gathered weekly for reading and criticism of works in progress.

L. wrote in a wide variety of genres. His first two published volumes were POETRY (*Spirits in Bondage,* 1919; *Dymer,* 1926). His first novel, *Out of the Silent Planet* (1938), was SCIENCE FICTION. It was followed by a sequel (*Perelandra,* 1943), and the trilogy was completed with *That Hideous Strength* (1945). His first substantial scholarly work, *The Allegory of Love: A Study in Medieval Tradition* (1936), was awarded the Gollancz Memorial Prize for Literature in 1937. His religious writing included *The Screwtape Letters* (1942), a series of essays published weekly in the

Guardian purported to be letters of advice from Screwtape, an experienced devil to a Wormwood, a novice devil, and *The Great Divorce* (1945).

In 1950, *The Lion, the Witch, and the Wardrobe,* the first of the Narnia books was published. Each year through 1956 would see the publication of another book in the series including: *Prince Caspian* (1951), *The Voyages of the Dawn Treader* (1952), *The Silver Chair* (1953), *The Horse and His Boy* (1954), *The Magician's Nephew* (1955), and *The Last Battle* (1956). The final book in the series received the Carnegie Medal.

The books are designed for reading by and to children. As McGovern explains, the books have simple vocabulary and the chapters are uniform length for ease when reading them aloud. Further, the stories are action-packed, many of the main characters are children, and the fantasy world in which the books are set can only be reached by children. Yet the books are also enjoyed by adults, especially those who return to the books with a new, more experienced perspective years after enjoying them as children.

L.'s own childhood reading included fairy tales; his adult work included medieval and Renaissance literature. He eschewed modern writing and preferred classical themes. The influence of these works can be seen in the Narnia series, with its witches and royalty, magic and symbolism, heroes and quests.

The influence of L.'s religious faith is readily evident in the tales. L. explained that his inspiration for the stories in his essay collection *Of Other Worlds* (1966) and admitted that his modeling of the stories on the New Testament was deliberate. L. believed that stories for children "could steal past a certain inhibition that had paralyzed much of [his] own religion in childhood" and that by portraying "God and the sufferings of Christ . . . into an imaginary world, stripping them of their stained-glass and Sunday school associations, one could make them for the first time appear in their real potency."

The Narnia tales are not intended to directly mirror the New Testament. L. explained that it was his hope that the stories might open the reader to the Gospel, but that he did not intend them to be a retelling of the Bible itself. According to L., Aslan, the Christ-like lion of the fantasy series, does not do what Christ did on earth; he does what Christ would do in a place like Narnia.

Since their publication, the Narnia books have been controversial, receiving praise from critics such as Madeleine L'ENGLE, and scorn from others, such as L.'s own friend and fellow fantasy writer, J. R. R. Tolkien. Nevertheless, the books continue to attract a broad, diverse audience of both children and adult readers.

L., a longtime bachelor, married late in life. His 1952 BIOGRAPHY, an account of his earlier religious awakening, was titled *Surprised by Joy: The Shape of My Early Life;* "Joy" would also shape the last years of L.'s life. Joy Gresham, an American novelist, had long admired L.'s religious writing, which had been influential in her conversion from Judaism to Christianity. The pair met in 1952 and married in April of 1956 in a civil ceremony to prevent Joy's threatened deportation. In December, a religious ceremony was performed at the hospital where Joy was receiving treatment for terminal bone cancer. Miraculously, the couple enjoyed four years together before she succumbed to the disease. The following year, L. published *A Grief Observed* under a pseudonym.

L. died of a heart attack on the same day that John F. Kennedy was assassinated and Aldous Huxley died. It was also a week before L.'s sixty-fifth birthday.

FURTHER WORKS: *Of Other Worlds: Essays and Stories,* 1966; *Surprised by Joy: The Shape of My Early Life,* 1956; *Till We Have Faces: A Myth Retold,* 1966.

BIBLIOGRAPHY: Christopher, J. R. *C.S. L,* 1987; Coren, M. *The Man Who Created Narnia: The Story of C.S. L.,* 1996; Green, R.L. and Hooper, W. *C.S. L: A Biography,* 1974; Lindskoog, K. *Journey into Narnia,* 1997; McGovern, E. *"C. S. L" Dictionary of Literary Biography,* vol. 15, 1983; Vander Elst, P. *C.S. L.,* 1996.

HEIDI HAUSER GREEN

LIBRARIANS AND STORYTELLING

Librarians enjoy a proud heritage of storytelling. The exact date of the first library story hour is uncertain, but librarians have been telling stories to children for over a century. As early as 1896, Anne Carroll Moore (1871–1961) had given storytelling a place in the children's room of the new Pratt Institute Free Library in Brooklyn, New York. By 1899 both the Carnegie Library of Pittsburgh and the Buffalo Public Library had established the story hour as a regular part of library service to children. Storytelling was already practiced in schools, hospitals, playgrounds, and settlement houses when librarians began to recognize its potential for introducing children to literature.

In 1900 Marie Shedlock (1854–1935) came to the U.S. from England to lecture on Hans Christian Andersen and tell his tales. Shedlock was a teacher of young children for many years before becoming a professional storyteller in 1890. Her lectures on storytelling formed the basis of a book, *The Art of the Storyteller* (1951) which became a classic. Mary Wright Plummer, director of the School of Library Science at Pratt Institute in Brooklyn, heard Shedlock and invited her to tell stories to the trustees, directors, and faculty of Pratt. When Anne Carroll Moore, head of the children's room at Pratt, heard Shedlock, she knew the children must hear her too. At the children's program, held on a snowy Saturday morning in January 1903, a little girl asked Miss Moore, "Is she a fairy, or just a lady?" In later years Moore wrote, "There was never any doubt in my mind after that morning that a children's library should have a regular story hour."

It was Shedlock's inspiration, as she traveled around the U.S. telling stories and lecturing on storytelling, that gave impetus to the idea of storytelling as a true art. Shedlock emphasized simplicity, careful selection, and reliance on the human voice alone to convey the nuances of the story. Anna Cogswell Tyler (1859–1923), Moore's assistant at Pratt, was inspired by Shedlock to become a storyteller and later developed the storytelling program at the New York Public Library, following Moore's appointment as the first Supervisor of Work with Children at the New York Public Library in 1907. Others who fell under Shedlock's spell and became well-known library storytellers during the first half of the century included Mary and John Cronan and Ruth Sawyer.

Gudrun Thorne-Thomsen (1873–1956) also had a great influence on the development of library storytelling. Thorne-Thomsen was the daughter of the Norwegian actress Fredrikke Nielsen, known for her portrayal of the women in Henrik Ibsen's plays. She came to Chicago in 1888 at the age of fifteen to live with her mother's sister and to train as a teacher at Cook County Normal School. There she came under the influence of Colonel Francis W. Parker, whom John Dewey called "the father of progressive education." On completion of her studies, Thorne-Thomsen

joined the faculty of the University of Chicago where she taught children's literature, storytelling, and reading.

Library storytelling has always been associated with books and reading, and it was Gudrun Thorne-Thomsen who early on recognized the connection between listening to stories and learning to read. Story listening is not a passive activity; listeners are required to create images or pictures in their minds from the words of the teller. Similarly, to comprehend the meaning of printed material, the child must understand oral language patterns and see images that the printed words represent.

The first library story hours were planned for children of age nine and older. By that age, children were expected to have mastered the mechanics of reading. Librarians thought of storytelling as a form of reading guidance. By telling a story and indicating the book from which it came and pointing out that hundreds of other wonderful tales could be found in books, the librarian was introducing reading as a source of enjoyment throughout life.

It is interesting to note that library storytelling developed during a period of heavy immigration. Approximately a million immigrants entered the U.S. each year from 1900 to 1913. Librarians looked on storytelling as a way of integrating many diverse heritages and of teaching English and the English language orally.

Attendance at library story hours for children of school age peaked in the 1920s. In 1920 Alice Jordan estimated that the Cronans were telling stories to 1,800 library listeners per week as well as to 4,000 classroom pupils in auditorium groups. At the Carnegie Library in Pittsburgh nearly 150,000 children attended story hours in 1924.

Picture-book hours for children ages five to seven began as early as 1902, but did not reach their peak in popularity until decades later, following the influx of artists from Europe after World War I and improved methods of reproducing art in books; these set the stage for the flowering of the American PICTURE BOOK.

In 1935 the Detroit Public Library began picture-book hours for preschoolers three to five years old. Other libraries soon followed. Storytelling programs for school-age children were scheduled less frequently as organized activities competed for the children's attention and greater administrative demands on children's librarians left less time for story-hour preparation.

An even greater change in library storytelling programming occurred in the 1960s. Results from research demonstrate the importance of interaction between children and their caregivers during the first three years of life. That interaction impacts on language development, cognitive functioning, personality, and social behavior. In response to the growing evidence that young children were capable of responding to stories on a more sophisticated level than formerly thought, children's librarians began experimenting with storytelling programs designed for children from eighteen months to three years of age, accompanied by a caregiver. Today infant and toddler pograms are offered by almost every library in the U.S., often with long waiting lists.

Only a small number of libraries now offer story hours for children over eight years of age on a regularly scheduled (weekly, semimonthly, or monthly) basis. The tendency is to invite a professional storyteller to perform on a special-occasion basis. Librarians continue to use storytelling techniques in book talks, to tell stories during class visits, and to offer workshops on storytelling to older boys and girls, YOUNG ADULTS and teachers. The whole-language movement made teachers more aware of children's literature and eager to learn effective ways of sharing it with children.

Through the outstanding contributions of such librarians as Augusta Baker (1911–98) and Pura Belpre, librarians and teachers came to realize the power of storytelling in preserving the traditions of a culture for the foreign-born child and of building appreciation of one's own or another's culture for the native-born child. Enjoying a story together creates a sense of community. It draws people closer to one another, adult to child, child to child.

Storytelling continues to be a vital part of library work with children in the U.S. and librarian-storyteller ambassadors, such as Caroline Feller Bauer, Anne Pellowski, and Spencer Shaw are spreading the tradition all over the world.

BIBLIOGRAPHY: Alvey, Richard G. *The Historical Development of Organized Storytelling to Children*, p. 16, 1981. Bauer, Caroline Feller. *Caroline Feller Bauer's New Handbook for Storytellers*, 1993. Greene, Ellin. *Storytelling: Art and Technique*, 3rd ed., 1996. See "Festschrift for Augusta Baker," pp. 186–256. Hamilton, Martha and Mitch Weiss. *Children Tell Stories: A Teaching Guide, 1990.* Hernandez-Delgado, Julio L. "Pura Teresa Belpre, Storyteller and Pioneer Puerto Rican Librarian." The Library Quarterly 62 (October 1992): 425–40. Jeffery, Debby Ann. *Literate Beginnings: Programs for Babies and Toddlers*, 1994. Jordan, Alice M. "The Cronan Story Hours in Boston." The Horn Book Magazine 26 (November–December 1950), pp. 460–64. Moore, Anne Carroll. *My Roads to Childhood: Views and Reviews of Children's Books*, 1939, p. 145. Pellowski, Anne. *The World of Storytelling, 1990,* Sawyer, Ruth. *The Way of the Storyteller,* rev. ed., 1977. Sayers, Frances Clarke. *Anne Carroll Moore: A Biography,* 1972. Shedlock, Marie. *The Art of the Story-teller,* 3rd ed., 1951.

ELLIN GREENE

LIFE AMONG THE CHALLENGED

Mark Haddon's bestselling success with his quirky and extraordinary work *The Curious Incident of the Dog in the Nighttime* (2004) focuses attention on the challenges met by his teenage protagonist, Christopher John Francis Boone, an autistic savant. However, Christopher John Francis Boone is only one of many TEEN characters in fiction who must either overcome or at least try to cope with their own physical or mental challenges, or deal with a close friend or family member who is faced with that type of situation and, in so doing, bring strongly individual voices to their worlds. Some of the teen novels that deal with physical struggles examine cerebral palsy, paralysis or crippling, deafness, blindness, amputation, cleft lips, epilepsy, polio, and muscular dystrophy, among other conditions. The novels that deal with mental struggles investigate mental slowness, Down syndrome, autism, Asperger's syndrome, obsessive-compulsive disorders, and attention deficit disorder (ADD)—and their effects not only on those who have the problems, but the loved ones who surround them. There is also, beyond the works of fiction, narrative nonfiction, such as Marie Killilea's *Karen* (1952) and *With Love from Karen* (1963), that deal with her FAMILY's coping with her daughter's cerebral palsy. Each of these works lends a glimpse into a world that not everyone may be familiar with, yet offers needed insights.

One of the first YA fiction books of the 20th century to deal with physical problems was Frances Hodgson BURNETT's *The Secret Garden* (1911). The orphaned Mary takes it upon herself to rehabilitate not only her dead aunt's garden, but the woman's hunchbacked husband and her invalid son. In Jean Webster's *Dear Enemy* (1915), socialite Sally Mac-Bride finds herself dealing with a variety of physical and mental challenges faced by her charges when she takes on the job of being the head of an orphanage. These are only two examples of how long such topics have been of interest to authors.

Yet, it is how each author brings his or her own voice and individual circumstance to these works that distinguishes them. In *Listen for the Fig Tree* (1974) by Sharon Bell MATHIS, an AFRICAN AMERICAN girl copes with her blindness against the backdrop of experiencing her initiation into the rituals of Kwanzaa. Isabelle HOLLAND's *The Unfrightened Dark* (1990) chronicles Jocelyn's response when her seeing-eye dog is taken in a tale of MYSTERY and suspense. Mandy must learn to cope with her blindness in Jeannette INGOLD's *The Window* (2003). Despite her blindness, Kelly assists fearful Alison in Hope Ryden's *Wild Horse Summer* (1997). In *Things Not Seen* (2002) by Andrew Clements, Bobby finds some solace in his sudden invisibility when he meets and befriends a young blind girl and begins to question what vision and sight truly mean. Although he is not quite blind—except legally—Paul manages to fashion a place for himself on the soccer team when his family relocates to Florida in Edward BLOOR's *Tangerine* (1997). Beverly Butler traces the story of a young woman as she first must adjust to her blindness in *Light a Single Candle* (1962) and then fights to go on with her life and plans for her future in *Gift of Gold* (1972).

In *Mind's Eye* (1999) by Paul FLEISCHMAN, Courtney learns to come to terms with her paralysis through the help of her elderly roommate in the nursing home. Told in PLAY form, the two take an imaginary journey through Italy and in so doing Courtney learns how to live the life she now has. Annie is determined to find out the truth about what happened to her fiancé despite being tied to her wheelchair, so she sets off with his teenage sister, Haley, to find out in *Phoning a Dead Man* (2002) by Gillian CROSS. *Sarah's Dilemma* (1995) by Judy Baer shows its young heroine coping with being wheelchair-bound in this entry. After being paralyzed in an accident, a former football star must come to terms with his circumstances in Robin F. BRANCATO's *Winning* (1997). Wendy Orr's *Peeling the Onion* (1997) documents what happens when a karate champion suffers a broken neck. Both injury

and rehabilitation are themes in Chris CRUTCHER's *The Crazy Horse Electric Game* (1987). Rocky learns to see herself in a new way, in spite of the leg braces she wears, when an artist comes to town in Gary Paulsen's *The Monument* (1991). Despite being in a wheelchair, the title character in *Stefan's Story* (2003) by Valerie HOBBS, wants to save a forest tract and pursue a friendship.

In Marilyn Gould's *The Twelfth of June* (1986), Janis deals not only with her cerebral palsy, but with her friend Barney's bar mitzvah. Clarence comes to grips with a cleft lip as well as union organizers in West Virginia in *Up Molasses Mountain* (2002). Both Katie and her horse have physical problems in *Willow King* (1998) and its sequel, *Willow King: Race the Wind* (2000) but that does not mean that the Kentucky Derby is beyond their dreams in these two books by Chris Platt. In *Annie's World* (1990), a deaf girl adjusts to a public high school. Published by Gallaudet University Press, Gallaudet is primarily a school for the deaf.

Not only in contemporary times are such issues faced however, but in times past. Meghan's losses seem too much to bear in *Postcards to Father Abraham* (2000), by Catherine Lewis—she becomes an amputee due to cancer, and her brother is in Vietnam. In *Izzy, Willy-Nilly* (1986) by Cynthia VOIGHT, the protagonist must also learn how to deal with an amputated leg. When Jeanne Marie meets Kit, in the course of her volunteer work at the local hospital, he has polio—yet he is also determined to return to the climbing that he loved before he became paralyzed. Their continuing relationship as each reaches toward their goals makes for fascinating reading in *Wings and Roots* (1982) by Susan Terris. *A Bright Star Falls* (1959) by Lenora Mattingly Weber also deals with a polio victim and the effect she has on all with whom she comes in contact. In the early 1950s, two boys deal with a mystery despite the deafness of one of them in *The Boys of San Joaquin* (2005). One of the Dear America SERIES books, *Mirror, Mirror on the Wall: The Diary of Bess Brennan* (2002) by Barry DENENBERG, chronicles life at the Perkins School for the Blind in 1932. Norma JOHNSTON's heroine in *Myself and I* (1981) deals with a leg that is injured, and for some reason becomes persistently worse, against the background of World War I. In spite of his epilepsy, a young boy joins the fighting in 1746 Scotland in Jane YOLEN's *Prince across the Water* (2004). In

Bridget Crowley's historical novel set in the 13th century, *Feast of Fools* (2003), a choir member who is crippled gets caught up in intrigue. Only an ability to tell tales stands between her queen and death in the crippled Marjan's harem world of ancient Persia in Susan FLETCHER's *Shadow Spinner* (1998). Kira, the heroine of Lois LOWRY's SCIENCE FICTION and FANTASY tale of an alternate world, *Gathering Blue,* is almost stoned to death due to her lameness, although she has another unique gift that saves her in the end.

Sometimes, these challenges cause unusual relationships to be formed—for the mutual benefit of the parties involved. This is the case in W. R. Philbrick's *Freak the Mighty* (1993) where Max, a slow learner, teams up with the physically challenged Freak. Another such partnership can be found in *Stoner and Spaz* (2002) by Ron KOERTGE when a drug addict and a victim of cerebral palsy form a friendship.

At times, though physical challenges may be more apparent to observers, mental challenges can also cause those they afflict a great deal of peril. This is certainly the case in Terry Spencer HESSER's *Kissing Doorknobs* (1998) when the protagonist struggles against spiraling obsessive-compulsive disorder. Alexandra Eden's mystery series featuring Verity Buscador who suffers from Asperger's syndrome but solves mysteries in spite of it in *To Oz and Back* (2003) and *Holy Smoke* (2004) also demonstrates the difficulties in such disorders. The protagonist in Virginia Euwer WOLFF's *Probably Still Nick Swansen* (1988) deals with the stigma of being learning disabled, as does Emily in Susan Goldman Rubin's *Emily Good as Gold* (1993) and *Emily in Love* (1997). Richard also has to deal with being a slow learner in *Keep Stompin' till the Music Stops* (1977) by Stella PEVSNER.

Yet, it is not only those who actually suffer from physical or mental disabilities who may be challenged. There are also those who care for them, be they family or friends. Sometimes, the challenges that they face may seem even greater than the person who has the disability. This is certainly strongly and movingly portrayed in Terry TRUEMAN's work—especially *Stuck in Neutral* (2000), in which Shawn McDaniel worries that his father wants to end his suffering and is unable to communicate the joy he experiences due to the severity of his cerebral palsy. Coping with a family member's CP is also the theme in Trueman's *Cruise Control* (2004), wherein a boy

must become the man of the house when his father leaves, and also deal with his ill brother. Bridget must come to terms with her sister's mental slowness and unplanned pregnancy when her sister is raped during the Civil War era in Norma Johnston's *Of Time and of Seasons* (1975) and *A Striving after Wind* (1976). Siblings who are struggling to accept the disabilities of family members is a common theme in YA literature. Peg KEHRET's protagonist must figure out how to save his paralyzed sister in the aftermath of an earthquake when there are just the two of them and their dog in *Earthquake Terror* (1996). Betsy Byars chronicled it in *The Summer of the Swans* (1970), as did Sarah Lamstein in *Hunger Moon* (2003), William Mayne in *Gideon Ahoy!* (1999), Lynn McElfresh in *Can You Feel the Thunder?* (1999), Lois Metzger in *Barry's Sister* (1992) and *Ellen's Case* (1995), Randy POWELL in *Tribute to Another Dead Rock Star* (1999), S. L. ROTTMAN in *Head above Water* (1999), and D. B. Beard in *The Babbs Switch Story* (2002). Sometimes it is not a sibling, but other family members with whom the protagonist must come to terms. This is the case in *Of Sound Mind* (2001) by Jean FERRIS when a TEEN struggles to come to terms with his deaf family. Tiger Ann must also deal with her slow parents in *My Louisiana Sky* (1998) by Kimberly Willis HOLT. Life is different as Shar's dad changes because of his aneurysm in Alden R. CARTER's *Robodad* (1990). Kady must deal with the senility of her grandma as well as a mentally slow neighbor in Beth Nixon WEAVER's *Rooster* (2001). Sometimes, a friend is affected as is the case with Cathy when she tries to help her friend Mark, who has muscular dystrophy, by finding him a horse in *Under the Shadow* (1983) by Anne Knowles. Friendship can turn to something more as it does in the following two historical novels: *Mary Mehan Awake* (1997) by Jennifer ARMSTRONG and Sherryl JORDAN's *The Raging Quiet* (1999) when Marnie discovers a young man is deaf instead of crazy. Last but not least, people are changed by random exposure to other people's lives, as happens to Kirk, when he reads to a blind woman and finds his own focus in Peter Moore's *Blind Sighted* (2002) and to the students of a paraplegic teacher who come together as a team in E. L. KONIGSBURG's *The View from Saturday* (1996).

None of the disabilities in any of these books is the same—as no one's life is quite the same as anyone else's. Yet, each one offers insight on experiences that touch the humanity that lies within everyone and encourages readers to think about what brings human beings together in the deepest possible sense. Often, the first perceptions of a situation have little to do with reality.

JEANNE MARIE RYAN

LIPSYTE, Robert

Author, 16 January 1938, Bronx, New York

An accurate look at the work of L. requires a wide-angle lens. On staff at the *New York Times* since he turned nineteen in 1957, the accomplished SPORTS journalist has covered some of the most provocative stories in athletic history. From the Islamic evolution of Muhammad Ali to the sexual revelations of Greg Louganis, L. has regularly claimed a ringside seat. With his place in nonfiction undeniably secured, he wandered into the realm of fiction to master yet another writer's challenge. Success jumped genres with him, as his novels were both popular and critically acclaimed.

What environment nurtured such a versatile wordsmith? The firstborn Jewish son of two teachers (his sister was born seven years later), L. started life in the cradle of education. He was reared in the Rego Park section of Queens and played both the accordion and the piano. His skill with words became obvious as early as the 3rd grade when he wrote for the elementary school literary magazine; soon after he discovered the admirable social conscience of John Steinbeck.

"By junior high school it was clear to me I wanted to write," he told Don Gallo in a 2001 interview. "There was never a specific event that I can remember, but rather the realization that I had found something where the process was the reward."

Spurred by academic and family encouragement, L. wrote a column for the high-school paper before his early enrollment in a special post-Korean War program at Columbia University. A college graduate by nineteen, he needed a summer job to fund graduate school in California, where he hoped to get his Ph.D. in romantic English poetry. Under these circumstances, he answered a classified ad for an editorial assistant at the *New York Times*.

Hired as the kid-in-training to write stories no one else wanted to cover, L. cut his journalistic teeth on the Mets first spring training and a boxing match no one at the *Times* could take seriously—Olympic gold medalist Cassius Clay's young-pup challenge of the heavyweight champion of the world, Sonny Liston. The champ was down and out by the seventh round. Lipsyte—"the kid"—broke the staggering front-page news. English poetry would have to wait.

By the time he turned twenty-nine, L. had his own column in one of America's top newspapers and had published his first novel, *The Contender* (1967), the story of a seventeen-year-old Harlem boy Albert Brooks's determined drive toward championship boxing. "I was out to rewrite King Lear, not Kid Lear," L. admitted. Under the skilled editorial direction of Ursula Nordstrom and Charlotte Zolotow, the novel became a YA title. L. didn't produce a second novel until nearly a decade had passed, but *One Fat Summer* (1977), L.'s somewhat autobiographical novel about fourteen-year-old fat boy Bobby Marks, was also a critical success.

"I had been a fat kid, hated my body," L. said in a 2001 interview, "and found solace in creating a comfortable universe with words." After playful fictitious romps where thin people died horrible deaths, L. tapped into the reality of his own painful memories to produce a novel of sheer honesty and a character he and his readers loved.

A year later, and again in 1991, testicular cancer forced L. to face his fiercest personal battle in a war he refuses to say he has won. *The Chemo Kid* (1992), L.'s fictional response to an authentic cancer challenge, proved cleansing and therapeutic. His destiny was uncertain, but he could control the outcome for high-school cancer victim Fred Bauer.

Fiction has shored up L.'s emotional and professional well-being, but he admits that he has learned a great deal from the monumental celebrities he has interviewed along the way. Three stand out as most memorable: Onondaga tribal Chief Oren Lyons became L.'s spiritual mentor and longtime friend; former football star Ed Gallegher, the "queer quad," who tried to take his own life when he realized he was gay, but survived as a quadriplegic to find his soul; and Dick Gregory, who, "took a parochial white boy and made him Catholic."

SELECT AWARD: 1967 Child Study Association Wel-Met Children's Book Award; 1977 *New York Times* Outstanding Children's Book of the Year; 1999 ALAN Award for Contribution to Young Adult Literature; 2001 MARGARET A. EDWARDS Lifetime Achievement

Award; ALA Best Book for Young Adults: 1992 for Brave; 1977 for *One Fat Summer;* selected for "The Best of the Best Books: 1970–1983."

FURTHER WORKS: *Summer Rules,* 1981; *Jock and Jill,* 1982; *The Summerboy,* 1982; *The Brace,* 1991; *The Chief,* 1993; *Warrior Angel,* 2003.

BIBLIOGRAPHY: Sports Literate interview by William Meiner, 2000; L.'s website, www.robertlipsyte.com; Interview by Don Gallo, 2001/2003.

KELLY MILNER HALLS

LITERATURE LINKS: BOOK PAIRS TO SHARE

Those familiar with the saying "Truth is stranger than fiction" can add another truth and fiction statement to their list. Fact enriches fiction and fiction makes fact memorable. Think about it. Facts enrich fiction by providing information about such things as history, places, scientific concepts, or people. Adding this information enriches the story because the reader becomes more familiar with facts used in the story. Fiction makes historical events come to life and paints word pictures of animals, places, and things within an interesting story. Why not use more book pairs? For example, Paul FLEISHMAN's collection of myths, *Dateline Troy,* with its connecting contemporary photographs showing the same social/political situation, demonstrates the power of pairing. It's almost required to pair *Stowaway,* by Karen HESSE, with a BIOGRAPHY of Captain Cook; A good story makes readers want to learn more facts and vice versa. Well-written books delight and entertain even as they teach.

As we consider the literary interests of readers, particularly those in the intermediate grades and middle schools, we note they are beginning to sense their place in time and better understand the chronology of past events. They are interested in problems of the world, therefore historical fiction and fact provide the opportunity to examine issues from different viewpoints. Pairing fiction and nonfiction books together, or other complementary texts, builds upon reader interests, presenting multiple invitations to engage with story, and expands ways of knowing.

A great way to start is with a favorite author. *How Angel Peterson Got His Name* (2003) by Gary Paulsen is full of the adventures the author and his friends participated in—their version of extreme

SPORTS for that era. Not only do you learn how Angel got his name, but of other daredevil jumps, twists, and tricks the boys tried. A great SERIES just out— Extreme Sports (2003, various authors)—includes mountain biking, rock climbing, and snow sports that challenge gravity. These books extend the interest kids have in their own participation and they learn some successful techniques as well as other information. They may avoid being called Angel themselves.

Gary Paulsen fans will enjoy his latest outdoor adventure, *Brian's Hunt,* as Brian, now sixteen, takes a break from school to return to the wilderness, content to be hunting and camping alone, but thinking about a family he knows. Near their home, he finds an injured dog, and goes in pursuit of the animal that hurt the dog and caused other damage. In this quick read, with little dialogue and absorbing narrative, Paulsen captures the mind of youth in the happenings of the natural world.

Another book boys in particular will like is *Warriors,* by Joseph BRUCHAC. The author, who knows the challenges of the American Indian, earned a four-star review. *Children of Native America Today,* (Dennis and Hirschfelder) that references the Haudenosaunee (Iroquois) Confederacy, provides important background information that increases understanding of the turn of events in this well-written realistic fiction.

In *Safely to Shore: America's Lighthouses* by Iris Van Rynebach (2003), the author suggests each lighthouse has a story to tell, and the text does just that— from live-in caretakers to computer-oriented structures, the history of protecting ships and their crews is told, and answers questions such as "What makes the light?" and "How are lighthouses used today?" Descriptions of famous lighthouses are included, with detailed illustrations done in watercolor by the author. To bring in Robert Munsch's *Lighthouse: A Story of Remembrance* (2003) enriches the factual information by telling of a young boy's visits to the lighthouse where the grandfather was the keeper of the light in a poignant intergenerational story.

The Same Stuff as Stars by Katherine PATERSON tells of a young girl finding solace by observing space, and in the book she turns to *Starry Messenger* by Peter Sis as a companion text. Many readers may not have seen this unusual biography of Galileo. To put these two books together enhances both fact and fiction. For older readers, teachers might introduce

The Tree of Life by Peter Sis (2003) which depicts the life of Charles Darwin, 19th-century naturalist, geologist, and thinker, in a DIARY format vividly illustrated by Sis with charts, maps, and a gatefold spread.

Historical fiction is a natural for pairing with information text. A well-written book, *Adaline Falling Star* by Mary Pope Osborne (2000) is a legendary tale about an Arapaho girl, supposedly fathered by Kit Carson, who is sent to live in St. Louis while Carson is off exploring. Providing readers with the biography *Kit Carson,* from the American Lives series (2003) makes an interesting blend of fact and fiction. History themes for children are becoming increasingly popular. We agree with Ilene Cooper, children's book editor for the American Library Association's *Booklist,* who said, "There's been this amazing leap in the quality and breadth of the topics." (*Newsweek,* February 2, 2004).

One of the dependable authors of historical fiction, Ann RINALDI, has a book, *Or Give Me Death,* about the personal life of Patrick Henry. While Rinaldi tells how Henry's children raised themselves during his long absences advocating independence for the American colonies, readers can quickly turn to the brief biography of this important leader in *Scholastic Book of Outstanding Americans: Profiles of More Than 450 Famous and Infamous Figures in U.S. History* by Sheila Keenan (2003). For more detailed information about this critical time in American history, Russell Freedman's book, *Give Me Liberty! The Story of the Declaration of Independence* (2000) provides an excellent, well-written resource.

Richard PECK continues his wonderful historical fiction in *The River Between Us,* a Civil War story in which a family in Illinois takes in two mysterious racially mixed ladies from New Orleans who become the center of speculation and controversy. However, as readers continue to enjoy the FAMILY chronicle in *A Year Down Yonder,* they may wish to learn more about that era in history with books such as *Witness to History: The Great Depression* (2003) part of a series published by Heinemann written by varied authors. This book provides photographs, news clippings, and a timeline to help readers put events into perspective, including national and global impact. Providing facts about the Depression stimulates classroom discussion and adds to the understanding of the award-winning narrative.

Awarded many honors, *Esperanza Rising* by Pam Munoz RYAN has helped readers learn of the plight of immigrant families when Esperanza and her mother flee their privileged lives in Mexico and find refuge in the migrant camps of Southern California during the Great Depression. Because the story also addresses the conditions of migrant camps and the beginning of labor issues, pair this book with *Harvesting Hope: The Story of Cesar Chavez* by Kathleen KRULL. On a more light-hearted note, a title that combines both the facts and narrative text is *How Do You Raise a Raisin?* also by Pam Munoz Ryan (2003). Supported by Craig Brown's clever art, this book describes the history of the nutritious treat and other information related to its harvest and many uses. We find this a tasty treat for readers everywhere.

In *Through My Eyes,* Ruby Bridges tells her own story of a pivotal event in history. Surrounded by racial turmoil, Ruby is the only student in a classroom with a compassionate teacher. An inspiration to us all, Ruby's words, dramatic photographs, and quotations may be paired with the classic, *The Story of Ruby Bridges* by Robert Coles. The Caldecott honor book, *Martin's Big Words: The Life of Dr. Martin Luther King Jr.* by Doreen Rappaport, stimulates more discussion. Two new PICTURE BOOKS that complement each other are *Papa's Mark* (2003) about an AFRICAN AMERICAN's first voting experience, and *America Votes: How Our President is Elected* (2003). In *Defense of Liberty* (Freedman) references the constitutional right to representation.

My America: A Poetry Atlas of the United States, selected by Lee Bennett HOPKINS, is a wonderful collection of fifty poems, grouped by geographic regions that sing not only of landmarks but also of daily life across the nation. The text is enhanced by maps of the regions and fascinating facts for each state. Pair it with Woody Guthrie's *This Land is Your Land.*

These books support U.S. geography and history curriculum but do so in an eloquent and artistic manner. A picture book to add to this group is *The Journey of Oliver K. Woodman* by Darcy Pattison (2003), the story of a wooden man with a backpack that takes a trip across the country and includes a postcard and a map to follow his adventures. *I Am America, and America is Me* by Charles R. Smith, Jr. (2003) is a unique photographic essay with bold rhyming text that celebrates the many faces of children growing up in America today. Both pictures and prose capture the spirit of our nation.

The abundance of biographical editions related to Meriwether Lewis and William Clark could be paired with other stories celebrating the anniversary of westward exploration. Joseph BRUCHAC's *Sacajawea: The Story of Bird Woman and the Lewis and Clark Expedition* is written as if it were Sacajawea's own journal of this history-making event. *The Captain's Dog* by Roland SMITH, tells the story of the Lewis and Clark expedition from the perspective of the pet dog that accompanies the explorers. The events are accurate but interesting from the dog's point of view. Pair it with factual accounts of the expedition.

A beautiful picture book, *Sacagawea* by Lise Erdrich (2003), illlustrated by Julie Buffalohead, captures the life of this woman who was translator, peacemaker, caretaker, and guide for the expedition. Exploring the topic through different genres and multiple texts expands our comprehension.

Because of many requests, Patricia Reilly GIFF has written a sequel to *Nory Ryan's Song,* titled *Maggie's Door* (2003) which is the story of the journey from Ireland to America told both by Nory and her neighbor Sean Red Mallan. The ship's passage is harrowing but the characters are pulled onward by a single dream: to reach Nory's sister Maggie in Brooklyn. *We Are Americans: Voices of the Immigrant Experience* by Dorothy and Thomas Hoobler (2003) is an excellent source, with photographs, as these Irish immigrants describe what it was like to become part of their new country. Readers will want to revisit *Nory Ryan's Song* which details the horrors of the Irish potato famine and this young girl's struggle to keep her family alive as they await the return of their Da, a story of courage and the will to survive. Pair this book with a factual history of the potato famine, such as *Black Potatoes: The Story of the Great Irish Famine 1845–1850* (Susan Campbell BARTOLETTI) which won both the Seibert and Orbis Pictus awards for best INFORMATIONAL book.

Another excellent resource that extends the immigrant experience is *Shutting Out the Sky: Life in the Tenements of New York,* 1880–1924 by Deborah Hopkinson (2003). In this book, accompanied by photographs, five young immigrants remember their struggles and dreams. Although needing no extension of information, readers may want to refer to these books with specific interest in those who immigrated from

Italy as they enjoy reading the popular new book by Sharon CREECH, *Granny Torrelli Makes Soup.* As she prepares zesty Italian cooking, Granny Torrelli offers simple wisdom to Rosie about boy/girl friendships by telling tales of her own childhood.

WAR also displaces people, and one of the little-known experiences of groups being forced to evacuate their communities is recounted in the poetic text *Aleutian Sparrow* by Karen Hesse (2003). As with her award-winning book, *Out of the Dust,* which spurred further reading to understand both the setting and the times, this story of people who lived in the Aleutian Islands being uprooted to southeast Alaska during World War II as the Japanese were threatening their villages also generates study about this part of the globe. There is a natural curiosity about the history of Alaska and these island inhabitants, who might have numbers as many as 25,000 at one time, and then reduced to one-tenth of that by circumstances over which they had no control. Such research gives even more power to the history of a strong people who survived this government edict. Many publishers have series devoted to the geography and history of states.

When students read *A Single Shard,* the Newbery winner by Linda Sue PARK, encourage investigation into the Korean classic art of celadon pottery, which adds so much to the story. Dealing with international conflicts, it would be an incomplete understanding of the Japanese occupation of Korea in the late 1930s if one only read the wonderful historical fiction, *When My Name Was Keoko* by Park and then failed to do some research into the sequence of events that affected so many Korean people. Another powerful book reflecting discrimination and restricted rights to the original occupants of a country is *Out of Bounds: Seven Stories of Conflict and Hope* by Beverley NAIDOO. The author's reputation for haunting stories of the struggles for freedom and dignity of her people has been recognized with several awards. This book takes us through different eras of the apartheid movement in South Africa, and demands further research into the painful steps toward equality. *South Africa in Pictures,* one of the Visual Geography Series, Web enhanced is one available source.

As intermediate readers learn about children in other countries, they are often surprised by the challenges of those who face a lifestyle quite unfamiliar. However, the leaders of tomorrow are those readers today, and they need to know about the global society—both rich and poor. One of the best recent chapter books is *Colibri* by Ann Cameron (2003). This is the story of a twelve-year old girl who was kidnapped as a youngster by an unscrupulous man who forced her to beg on the streets in Guatemalan villages—a captivating tale of survival and resilience, even as Colibri is taught signs of hope by one who rescues and returns her to her parents. Although this well-written novel easily stands alone, interest in the conditions that mirror the poverty in this country are well documented in *Out of the Dump: Writings and Photographs by Children From Guatemala* (edited by Kristine Franklin and Nancy McGirr (1996). Given cameras, children living in a garbage dump were asked to photograph and write about their lives. "The result: Soulful photos of haunted faces and loving families, . . . essays and poems full of pain—and humor and youthful optimism." (*U.S. News and World Report,* April 1, 1996, p. 71).

Breadwinner by Deborah Ellis is a fascinating fictional story based on fact that tells of a young girl in Afghanistan who must get money to sustain her ill mother and infant sister. She dresses as a boy so she can go into the city and sell bread, something a girl could not do. Ellis has followed up with two other titles set in contemporary Afghanistan, *Parvannah's Journey* and *Mud City.* The three books form the Breadwinner Trilogy and provide a picture of the poverty, politics, and physical reality of life in this country. The new, completely revised and redesigned editions of the highly acclaimed Visual Geography Series includes *Afghanistan in Pictures,* Young people must become knowledgeable about the Middle East. The series is one of the best to provide up-to-date, accurate information about these countries.

If You Could Be My Friend: Letters of Mervet Akram Galit Fink presented by Litsa Boudalika. This actual two-year correspondence between two girls in war-torn Israel, sharing hopes and concerns, shows how much alike they are even though they are separated by the conflict that grips their country. Pair this book with information from newspapers and the Internet on the current political situation and violence in the Palestinian region. Another book related to children trying to understand the conflict, *Samir and Yonatan* by Daniella Carmi is the story of a Palestinian boy spending time in an Israeli hospital for war injuries and who learns the personal stories of four

other children he considered the enemy at first—a story of anger and reconciliation important for today's students to consider.

FANTASY and fact make interesting literature links. For those enchanted with AVI's *Crispin,* another Newbery winner, learning about life in the Middle Ages is fun in a spin-off from the ever-popular Magic School Bus Series titled *Mrs Frizzle's Adventures in a Medieval Castle* by Joanna Coles. Or bring in *Life in a Medieval Castile* by Tony McAleavy, one of the new books in the English Heritage series (2003).

Vendela in Venice by Christina Bjork and Inga-Karen Eriksson provides a picture book travel guide about the city that is the setting for *The Thief Lord* by Cornelia Funke. How about pairing a new book by the same author but with a different setting and characters such as *Inkheart* (Funke, 2003)? In *Inkheart,* a young girl and her father risk their lives to fight a vicious gang of criminals who have escaped from the print in a book. Typical of so many stories set in different countries a book like this creates an interest in maps, globes, and atlases, and a new one, *The Children's World Atlas,* is an excellent source.

Anyone leaving the theater well satisfied with the film version of *Holes,* the Newbery winner by Louis SACHAR, would also be amused at hearing a youngster comment, "That was a good MOVIE, maybe they will make a book out of it!" An obvious literature link is pairing a book with the film, *Maldanado's Miracle* by Theodore TAYLOR, the story of a twelve-year old Mexican boy crossing the border and finding an accidental "miracle" threatens his new life. This interesting story has just been reissued and inspired a made-for-TV movie. *Whale Rider* is another chapter book that readers can see as a box-office hit at the local cinema. This Maori tale of the inheritance of tribal leadership and a young girl's ability to communicate with whales is enhanced by the interpretation on film. The characters, setting, and story come alive.

A person's first visit to an art museum may yield interesting observations—some indicating minimal appreciation for famous paintings as in *The Shape Game* by Anthony Browne. For great fun, bring in *Babar's Museum of Art: An Original Laurent de Brunhoff Book* (2003). This Babar book builds upon the original framework of the author's father and is witty in its elephant-inspired versions of Michelangelo's work and other celebrated paintings. Or consider *Math-Terpieces* by Greg Tang.

Some of the best connections occur in a well-liked series, particularly when they are written by a well-liked author. In *Chose of Cutler Creek,* by Cynthia DeFelice, Allie is contacted by the ghost of a dog, which causes her to investigate the surly new boy at school and his father to see if they are involved. A quote from a previous book by DeFelice seems appropriate here in celebrating literary links. As the main character was preparing to write, ". . . she marveled that only twenty-six letters could be put together in so many ways and for so many reasons, forming words that had the power to make a person laugh or cry, imagine a different world, think a new thought. . . ." (*The Strange Night Writing of Jessamine Colter*).

A caution: Just introduce and make the paired information text available for readers, not an assigned task, or you may miss the reward. Some authors may not like the idea of pairing fact and fiction, or even fact with fact presented in different genre or literary forms. Librarians, teachers, and parents must exercise wisdom and only provide the opportunity for young readers to extend their learning if they wish. We might ruin some wonderful literacy events by trying to do too much with a book. As someone once commented after reading twenty suggested activities to do with an award-winning novel, ". . . trying to drain too much out of a book leaves it lifeless."

Recognizing that teachers, librarians, and parents often seek complementary books to share with young people and that readers often want more—more information on a topic, more books like the one they have just read, or another perspective or context to help them understand a topic, person, or event more clearly—consider the following variations of paired text: (1) *Fiction/Fact:* One fiction and one informational work that addressed the same subjects; (2) *Complementary Fiction:* Two works of fiction about the same topic or events; (3) *Folktale Versions:* Works that comprise variations of the same folktale theme; (4) *Information Matches:* Two nonfiction works that address the same topic, perhaps one being a picture encyclopedia or another resource book; (5) *Biographical Duos:* Two biographies about the same person or different people that share something in common; (6) *Poetry Partners:* A book of poetry paired with another book, either poetry, fiction, or nonfiction; (7) *Different Reading Levels:* Two or more books, fiction

or nonfiction, that address the same or complementary subjects in order to access the information for readers of varied reading abilities. This is very important as standards-based education requires opportunities to learn subject matter content through a variety of resources.

NANCY LIVINGSTON

LOBEL, Anita

Author, b. 3 June 1934, Krakow, Poland

Born Anita Kempler, L. survived the HOLOCAUST with her brother and was reunited with her parents in Sweden after the war. The family emigrated to New York in 1952. She attended Pratt Institute on a scholarship, and there she met Arnold Lobel, whom she married in 1955, the same year she graduated from Pratt with a B.F.A. degree. She began her career as a fabric designer, and her detailed and intricate illustrations reflect her experience with fabrics and patterns. In 1965, L. wrote and illustrated her first children's book, *Sven's Bridge,* for which she was honored by the *New York Times Book Review* as one of the year's ten best children's book illustrators. She received this recognition again in 2000 for *One Lighthouse, One Moon.* L. illustrates a wide range of themes, both for her own writings or for other authors, from fairy tales and comical stories to serious topics such as parental neglect and war. Her most autobiographical work is the acclaimed *No Pretty Pictures: A Child of War,* the true story of her family's horrific experiences during the Holocaust. When selected for the 1999 ALA Best Books for Young Adults list, TEEN readers could hardly believe that the illustrator of light-hearted PICTURE BOOKS they had read and enjoyed as children could have experienced such a childhood—and survived.

L. collaborated on four books with her husband, Arnold L., before his death in 1987. One of those collaborations, *On Market Street,* was named a Caldecott Honor Book in 1982. L. has been an actress and a singer; these interests shape her work. L. says it is the "drama" in a picture book that most interests her and that she likes to stage a book the way a director would stage a play. She notes that advances in printing technology have allowed her to create more complicated and colorful illustrations than she could in the past.

AWARDS: Orbis Pictus Award (1999), National Book Award Finalist (1999), ALA Best Books for Young

Adults (1999) for *No Pretty Pictures;* Children's Book Showcase Award for *A Birthday for Princess* (1974) and *Peter Penny's Dance* (1977); *Boston Globe–Horn Book* Award for *On Market Street* (1981) and *The Rose in My Garden* (1984).

FURTHER WORKS: *The Black Bull of Norroway: A Scotish Tale; Princess Furball; Toads & Diamonds;* written by Charlotte Huck, illustrated by Anita L.; *Potatoes, Potatoes,* 1967; *How the Tsar Drinks Tea,* 1971; *Alison's Zinnia,* 1990; *All the World's a Stage,* 2003; with Arnold L.: *How the Rooster Saved the Day,* 1977; *A Treeful of Pigs,* 1979; *The Rose in My Garden,* 1984.

BIBLIOGRAPHY: *Something about the Author,* vol. 96; anitalobel.com.

HEIDI SANCHEZ

LOCKE, Elsie

Author, historian, b. 17 August 1912, Hamilton, New Zealand; d. 8 April 2001, Christchurch, New Zealand

L. (née Farrelly) was proof that small packets contain valuable goods. While tiny in the physical sense, she crammed several lifetimes of campaigning for women's rights and young people's access to their history, raising an achieving family, writing novels and history, outdoor activities, gardening and community issues into her eighty-eight years. Most New Zealanders, however, will remember L. as the person who introduced them to their own history.

From a family of six, L. was inspired by her enlightened mother to seek higher education at a time when few girls did so. After Waiuku District High School, L. put herself through Auckland University (B.A., 1933), working in the University Library. Marrying Jack Locke in 1941, she moved with him to Christchurch, her base for the next sixty years. L. never had Virginia Woolf's £500 a year but she always made sure she had a room for writing.

Although L. began writing at school and had articles published in Auckland, her most significant early writing was for the *NZ School Journal.* Several special historical issues brought history alive for young readers. L.'s historical vignettes, carefully researched, reflected her deep interest in how New Zealand's people, Maori and Pakeha, perceived events around them. Warriors and whalers, miners and seamstresses, all spoke through L.'s history bulletins, which were widely used in schools in the 1960s

and 1970s. They provided L. with the basis for later history books, *The Kauri and the Willow* (1984) and *Two Peoples, One Land* (1988). These books opened history to young people and helped them understand how their society had been formed.

The Runaway Settlers (1965) was L.'s first novel for children; a real woman, Mary Small fled from her brutal drunkard of a husband in Australia, to raise her six children in the new colony of Canterbury. Regularly reprinted, *The Runaway Settlers* was regarded by feminists as a manifesto, but L. insisted she was more interested in telling a story. Her combination of narrative talent and historical accuracy makes the young family's adventures, including a cattle drive through the mountains to the goldfields, an exciting story. This classic was the first chosen for the Gaelyn Gordon Award for a Much-Loved Book.

L. was one of the first to write for young New Zealanders without feeling the need to insert explanations for overseas readers. As well as giving a specifically New Zealand dimension to historical writing for young people in fiction and nonfiction, L. turned her discerning eye upon prejudices and injustices of the past. Thus it is no surprise in *The Runaway Settlers,* either that the autocratic runholder, "the nabob," is scandalized when he is rebuked by Mrs. Small for breaking his contract with her son, or that their encounter is historically accurate. "No one ever spoke to him in this way!"

For many young readers, L.'s writings were the first indication that Maori had their own view of history. L. had studied the Maori language in order to appreciate the Maori viewpoint better. *The End of the Harbour* (1968) creates a dual perspective of events by using two boys living in Waiuku, one English, one Maori, to illuminate relations between Maori and Pakeha as war threatens. The issues and opinions of a crucial moment in the nation's history are given human features, and the reality of the events behind the invasion of the Waikato is well captured.

Another controversial moment in New Zealand history was the land dispute which led to two dozen deaths at Wairau in 1843. L. wrote the richly detailed *Journey under Warning* (1983) using her own great-grandfather's eyewitness account. L. unravels the issues and shows the importance of understanding and patience between different cultures.

LOIS LOWRY

JOYCE McDONALD

FRED AND PATRICIA McKISSACK

MARGARET MAHY

CAROL MATAS

HARRY MAZER

While giving a vivid account of the catastrophic Tarawera volcanic eruption of 1886, *A Canoe in the Mist* (1984) also brings together a range of Maori and Pakeha characters (most of them female), in a struggle for survival from the ash showers. L. puts the eruption into its Maori context, introducing the reader to Maori spiritual values, legends, and attitudes to the exploitation of the landscape. Like all of L.'s historical novels, this story has a resonance for the present and the future.

L. became a treasured Christchurch citizen, a tiny figure cycling through city traffic, active in community affairs, no stranger to controversy, and a tireless worker for young people's literacy and libraries. Her memory is honored by a bronze plaque outside Christchurch's central library, and the Elsie Locke Park. In 2001 LIANZA's annual award for young people's nonfiction became The Elsie Locke Medal.

AWARDS: 1958 Katherine Mansfield Award for Nonfiction; 1992 Children's Literature Association Award for Service to Children's Literature; 1992 Nada Beardsley Literacy Award (Canterbury Reading Association); 1995 Margaret MAHY Lecture Award; 1996 AIM Children's Honour Award: *Joe's Ruby;* 1999 Gaelyn Gordon Award for a Much-Loved Book, *The Runaway Settlers.*

FURTHER WORKS: *A Land Without a Master,* 1962; *Six Colonies in One Country: New Zealand, 1840–1860,* 1965; *Maori King and British Queen,* 1974; *Look under the Leaves,* 1975; *Moko's Hideout,* 1976; *The Boy With Snowgrass Hair* (with Ken Dawson), 1976; *Explorer Zach,* 1978; *The Gaoler,* 1978; *A Land Without Taxes,* 1978; *Joe's Ruby,* 1995.

BIBLIOGRAPHY: Agnew, Trevor. "New Zealand Fiction: A Teacher-Librarian's Perspective." *Magpies NZ Supplement* 13:1 (Mar. 1998): 4–6; Ansley, Bruce. "A Bird in the Hand." *Listener* (NZ) 20 Apr. 1996: 40; Locke, Elsie. "Biographical notes." *School Journal Catalogue 1978–1993,* 1994. 141; Noble, Jo. "Elsie Locke, 1912–2001" *Magpies NZ Supplement* 16:4 (Sep. 2001): 4–5; Fitzgibbon, Tom and Spiers, Barbara. *Beneath Southern Skies: New Zealand Children's Book Authors & Illustrators,* 1993. 105–6; Gilderdale, Betty. *A Sea Change: 145 Years of New Zealand Junior Fiction,* 1982; Hebley, Diane. "Locke, Elsie." *The Oxford Companion to New Zealand Literature.* Ed. Roger Robinson and Nelson Wattie, 1998. 309; http://library.christchurch.org.nz/Childrens/FamousNewZealanders/Elsie.asp/; http://www.bookcouncil.org.nz/writers/lockeelsie.htm/.

TREVOR AGNEW

LOGUE, Mary

Author, poet, editor, b. 16 April, 1952, Minneapolis, Minnesota

L. has made a variety of contributions to the literary world. She has been active in the publishing industry as an editor and poet. Her first book was an anthology of POETRY which featured the work of the NorHaven Poetry Collective in the Minneapolis area. Called *The Thief of Sadness* (1979), this book included the work of several mentally challenged women authors from the area. Her book of poetry, *Discriminating Evidence* (1990), won the First Book of Poetry Award from Mid-List Press. She has also published several very popular MYSTERY novels for adults, including *Dark Coulee: A Claire Watkins Mystery* (2000), which was awarded the Minnesota Book Award for Best Popular novel. It is one in the SERIES of mysteries featuring detective Claire Watkins. L.'s books for young people include nonfiction accounts of the lives of Mahatma Gandhi, Elizabeth Barrett Browning, Helen Keller, and Walt Disney. She has also written two mysteries for young adults: *The Missing Statue of Minnehaha* (1993), and *The Haunting of Hunter House* (1993). One of L.'s books for young people, *Dancing With an Alien* (2000), is a SCIENCE FICTION novel and TEEN romance that made the 2001 Best Books for YA list. Many of her books are set in the upper Midwest, where she resides with fellow author Peter Hautman. L. has also translated works including a recent book *The Wolf Who Loved Music* (2003) by the Swiss author Christophe Gallaz. Her book *Bone Harvest* was released in 2004. L. currently works as a writer and editor at a children's press in Mankato, Minnesota.

AWARDS: First Book of Poetry Award for *Discriminating Evidence* (1990). Minnesota Book Award for Best Popular Novel for *Dark Coulee: A Claire Watkins Mystery* (2000); ALA Best Books for Young Adults (2001) for *Dancing with an Alien.*

FURTHER WORKS: *Forgiveness: The Story of Mahatma Gandhi,* 1996; *Elizabeth Barrett Browning: Love,* 1996; *Trust: The Story of Helen Keller,* 1999; *Imagination: The Story of Walt Disney,* 1999; *Red Lake of the Heart,* 1987; *Still Explosion: A Laura Malloy Mystery,* 1993; *Blood Country: A Claire Watkins Mystery,* 1999; *Glare Ice: A Claire Watkins Mystery,* 2001; *Believing Everything: An Anthology of New Writing* (editor), 1980; *Halfway Home: A Grand-*

daughter's Biography, 1996; *Settling,* 1997; *Over the Waves* (coeditor), 1999; *Bone Harvest: A Claire Watkins Mystery,* 2004.

BIBLIOGRAPHY: *Something about the Author,* vol. 112, Gale Research, *Contemporary Authors, New Revision Series,* vol. 114, Gale Research.

LIZ HANE

LORD, Bette Bao
Author, b. 3 November, 1938, Shanghai, China

At the time of L.'s birth, her father was a nationalist Chinese government official. After immigrating to the U.S. in 1946, she graduated from Tufts University in 1959 and earned a Master's Degree from the Fletcher School of Law and Diplomacy in 1960.

L.'s writing career began when she chose to tell the story of her younger sister who had been forced to stay behind in China during the Revolution. L.'s nonfiction book *Eighth Moon* (1964) was her attempt to share with the world the harsh conditions of her sister's life in China under the totalitarian regime. L. returned to studying, teaching, and performing dance, her first love. She then made her first return visit to her native land in twenty-seven years. This trip sparked her next book, a historical novel called *Spring Moon,* the story of five generations of a Chinese FAMILY as they weather the difficult social changes wrought by Communist rule. In *Spring Moon* (1981). L. provides sharply contrasting details of old ways, such as the tradition of girls' feet being bound, versus the new, such as women's participation in Communist revolutionary marches. Events over forty years of Chinese history that led to the bloodbath at Tiananmen Square were described in a work of nonfiction, *Legacies: A Chinese Mosaic,* a work with sufficient appeal to earn it a place on ALA Best Books for YA list, 1991.

L. also wrote a children's book, *In the Year of the Boar and Jackie Robinson,* 1984, about an immigrant Chinese girl's difficulties and eventual acceptance in the U.S. *Legacies* (1990) is a compilation of true stories of Chinese government brutality against citizens. Another novel, *The Middle Heart,* followed in 1996.

AWARDS: National Graphic Arts prize, 1974, for photo essay; American Book Award nomination for *Spring Moon;* Woman of the Year, Chinatown Planning Council, 1982; Distinguished Americans of Foreign Birth Award, 1984; Distinguished American Award, International Center, 1984; honorary doctorate, University of Notre Dame, 1985; Jefferson Cup Award, ALA, 1987, both for *In the Year of the Boar* and *Jackie Robinson;* American Women for International Understanding Award, 1988; USIA Award for Outstanding Contributions, 1988; inducted into International Women's Hall of Fame, 1989; *Legacies: A Chinese Mosaic:* one of the ten best nonfiction books named by *Time* magazine, 1990; ALA Best Books for Young Adults, 1991; Exceptional Achievement Award, Women's Project and Productions, 1992; Literary Lion citation, New York Public Library, 1992.

BIBLIOGRAPHY: *Contemporary Authors Online,* Gale online, 2003; *Current Biography Electronic; World Authors 1990–1995,* WilsonWeb online, 2003.

CATHERINE GIVEN

LOWRY, Lois
Author, b. 20 March 1937, Honolulu, Hawai'i

L. is a two-time Newbery Award–award winning author of books for YA. Her first book, *A Summer to Die* (1977), enthralled readers everywhere. L. is able to depict life realistically while writing about topics such as futuristic societies, cancer, mental illness, adoption, the Holocaust, and other topics of interest to a YA audience.

L.'s stories are infused with sensitivity arising from personal experiences. The setting for *Autumn Street* (1980) was taken from her maternal grandparents' home in Carlisle, Pennsylvania. She spent time there while her father was stationed in Japan during World War II. L. passed her time in her grandfather's library immersed in the books she loved. It was a great way for the introverted young girl to spend her time. She became an avid reader, a trait she possesses to this day.

L. was deeply affected by World War II. She was an "Army brat," following her father to bases all over the world. Many of her topics developed from what she experienced as a girl, living through those turbulent times. Newspapers and newsreels were full of the atrocities occurring in the death camps in Germany, and they had deep emotional impact. L. wrote about this period in *Number the Stars* (1989).

L. possesses the ability to navigate her characters through a labyrinth of humorous situations. One of her lighthearted stories eventually became the first chapter of the novel *Anastasia Krupnik* (1979). The Anastasia novels appeal to many YA because of the evolution of the witty and precocious Anastasia. In spite of the nature of the books, readers can find a serious thread running through each of them, starting with the death of Anastasia's grandmother in the first volume. The title character is based on L.'s daughters, Alix and Kristin. Other Anastasia novels followed: *Anastasia Again!* (1981), *Anastasia at Your Service* (1982), *Anastasia, Ask Your Analyst* (1984), *Anastasia on Her Own* (1985), *Anastasia Has the Answers* (1986), *Anastasia's Chosen Career* (1987), *Anastasia at this Address* (1991), and *Anastasia Absolutely* (1995). At the request of her readers, L. started another series with Sam, Anastasia's young brother, as the protagonist. *All About Sam* (1988) is based on L.'s son Grey and his interest in airplanes. Other books about Sam's adventures include *Attaboy, Sam!* (1992), *See You Around, Sam!* (1995), and *Zooman Sam* (1999).

L. is able to vary her writing style, a testament to her versatility as a writer. She frequently alternates between humorous and serious themes. After her skillful handling of humor in the Anastasia series, she tackled a contrasting theme in *Autumn Street* (1980), one of her darker novels. When thirteen-year-old Elizabeth must live with her grandparents while her father is overseas during the war, she learns how to face the realities of the adult world. Once again, the author translates events from personal experiences into her fictional work.

L.'s two Newbery Medal award books *Number the Stars* (1989) and *The Giver* (1993) embrace more somber subject matters. *Number the Stars* is based on the personal experience of a friend, Annelise, who grew up in Copenhagen during German occupation. It brings to life historically realistic characters and events during the Holocaust through the eyes of ten-year-old Annemarie Johansen. When the Danish population defies the Nazis and attempt to save the Jewish community, Annemarie is faced with protecting the family of her Jewish friend, Ellen Rosen. L. has the ability to draw the reader into each story and form connections to the characters. Her protagonists show sensitivity and intelligence when involved in unthinkable situations.

Often considered L.'s most controversial novel, *The Giver* also examines the dark aspects of human behavior. In her Newbery Awards acceptance speech, the author explains the role her father played in her conception of the utopia where the past is deliberately forgotten. L. imagines the flaws that might exist in

such a perfect place when her father was ill and lost most of his long-term memory. Much to the dismay of many readers, the ending of *The Giver* is inconclusive; readers can develop their own ideas of the continuing story.

One reason that L. is such an effective writer is that she encourages her readers to make connections to her novels. In *Gathering Blue* (2000), Kira is left orphaned and DISABLED in a society where the weak are destroyed. This is the story of a brave girl who takes on society and fights for her existence, a theme to which most young people can relate. Readers are also encouraged to reflect after reading. L.'s later book, *The Silent Boy* (2003), explores an unusual friendship between fourteen-year-old Katy and Jacob, the boy who never spoke. When problems erupt, Katy becomes aware of how actions can have disturbing consequences. The reader is once again left to ponder at the conclusion of the book.

L.'s autobiography *Looking Back: A Book of Memories* (1998), is composed of written memories interspersed with photographs of significant events in her life.

FURTHER WORKS: *A Summer to Die*, 1977; *Find a Stranger, Say Goodbye*, 1978; *The One Hundredth Thing about Caroline*, 1983; *Taking Care of Terrific*, 1983; *Us and Uncle Fraud*, 1984; *Switcharound*, 1985; *Rabble Starkey*, 1987; *Your Move, J.P.!*, 1990; *Stay! Keeper's Story*, 1997; *Gooney Bird Green*, 2003.

KATHY A. VANSTROM

LYNCH, Chris
Author, b. 2 July 1962, Boston, Massachusetts

As a young boy growing up in the Jamaica Plains section of Boston, L. had an early introduction to the rough-and-tumble setting that he uses in many of his works. L. was the fifth of seven children, and his father died when L. was only five. L.'s mother struggled to raise her children on her own; despite the circumstances, the author never felt deprived.

He had a positive elementary school experience, but once L. got into high school, he was discouraged. He enjoyed SPORTS, often playing street hockey and baseball as a young boy, but the athletic mentality at his high school was not healthy. L. notes, "Sports has a tremendous potential for channeling energy. But instead it mostly encourages the macho ethos and schools let athletes run wild. This carries through life. . . . People who were never told what they could not do." L. dropped out of high school, and then went on to Boston University, where he took a news-writing course. L. transferred to Suffolk College, changed his major from political science to journalism, and graduated in 1983.

For the next six years, L. held a variety of jobs, including house painter, moving-van driver, and proofreader. L. slowly but surely came to realize his calling, and in 1989 he enrolled in a master's program in professional writing and publishing at Emerson College in Boston. There, he met Jack Gantos, a children's book writer and, at the time, a teacher at Emerson College. L. took a children's writing class from Gantos; because of this class, L. completed what eventually became his first published novel, *Shadow Boxer* (1993). In this story, two brothers growing up in the outskirts of Boston must learn to deal with their father's death. George, the older brother, understands that his father's career, boxing, ultimately cost him his life. George's younger brother, Monty, is certain that boxing is in his blood. Monty begins training, and George tries in earnest to steer his brother away from the ring. Sibling rivalry escalates, but George eventually succeeds.

Shadow Boxer introduced L.'s style as one of short, hard-hitting paragraphs. L. found it liberating that his style was accepted in literary circles. Reviewers, in fact, have commented that the brief vignettes L. writes are more accessible to reluctant readers who may not have the attention span for long, drawn-out novels.

L. followed *Shadow Boxer* with *Iceman* (1994). This is the coming-of-age story of a disturbed young boy who uses his time in the hockey rink to surface his aggressions, in turn shutting out his teammates, friends, and family members. The novel is divided into three sections, much like the three periods of a hockey game. During its course, the protagonist learns to face his fears and control his anger.

In 1996, L. published his Blue-Eyed Son trilogy: *Mick, Blood Relations,* and *Dog Eat Dog.* Like his earlier works, these stories are set on the tough streets of Boston, and fifteen-year-old Mick is the reader's tour guide. Mick is slowly coming to the realization that the cultures outside his tight-knit Irish-American neighborhood should not be discriminated against, and he begins to make new friends. The change is not easy, however, and Mick becomes an outcast in both his family and social circles. The second book in the trilogy, *Blood Relations,* finds Mick a little older and a little wiser.

The racial tension and hatred are still rampant, but Mick is surer of himself. In *Dog Eat Dog,* the final book in the trilogy, Mick leaves his tough Irish-Boston neighborhood and rises above his upbringing to discover who he truly is.

In 1997, L. created another SERIES, The He-Man Women Haters Club, comprised of *Johnny Chesthair* (1997), *Babes in the Woods* (1997), *Scratch and the Sniffs* (1997), *Ladies' Choice* (1997), and *The Wolf Gang* (1998). In the first book the reader is introduced to Lincoln, aka Johnny Chesthair. He starts a club in his uncle's garage and invites four friends to join, each an adolescent boy with some peculiarity. Each novel in the series is narrated by one of these boys, and the humorous stories revolve around the spirit of getting strong and learning how to deal with women.

L. does not shy away from the realities of TEENAGE life and of urban areas in his literary works. L. writes, "I want to tell realistic stories, which I think come with their own messages built into them without my having to preach. . . . The only way I can contribute anything is merely to chronicle the facts of lives as I see them." L. currently lives in Scotland with his wife, Tina, and their two children, Sophia and Walker.

AWARDS: ALA Best Books for Young Adults and Quick Picks for Reluctant Young Adult Readers citations: 1994 for *Shadow Boxer,* 1995 for *Iceman* and *Gypsy Davey,* and 1996 for *Slot Machine;* 1993 *School Library Journal* Best Book of the Year List, *Shadow Boxer;* 1994 *Bulletin of the Center for Children's Books* Blue Ribbon Award, *Iceman* and *Gypsy Davey;* 1994 *Booklist* Editors' Choice award for *Gypsy Davey;* 1995 *Hungry Mind Review* Book of the Year award, *Slot Machine;* 1997 International Reading Association Young Adults' Choices citation, *Slot Machine; Gold Dust:* ALA Best Books for Young Adults, 2001; ALA Notable Children's Books, 2001; Dorothy Canfield Fisher Children's Book Award, 2002; *Freewill:* ALA Best Books for Young Adults, 2002; Michael L. Printz Honor, 2002.

FURTHER WORKS: *Gypsy Davey,* 1994; *Slot Machine,* 1995; *Political Timber,* 1996; *Extreme Elvin,* 1999; *Whitechurch,* 1999; *Gold Dust,* 2000; *Freewill,* 2001; *All the Old Haunts,* 2001; *Who the Man,* 2002; *The Gravedigger's Cottage,* 2004.

BIBLIOGRAPHY: *Authors and Artists for Young Adults,* Volumes 19 and 44; *Something about the Author,* Volume 131; www.ChrisLynchBooks.com; http://www.teenreads.com/authors/au-lynch-chris.asp

CARRA E. GAMBERDELLA

McCAFFREY, Anne (Inez)

Author, b. 1 April 1926, Cambridge, Massachusetts

Noted science fiction author since the late sixties, M. was the very first SCIENCE-FICTION author to earn a spot on the *New York Times* Best Sellers List, in 1978 for *White Dragon.* M. combines fantasy with science fiction as exemplified in her Dragonriders of Pern SE-RIES. In addition to science fiction/FANTASY, she has also written romantic novels with strong female characters. M. has contributed to the following genres: SHORT STORIES, novellas, novels, fantasy, science fiction and ROMANCES.

M. was born in Cambridge, MA, daughter of George Herbert McCaffrey, a city administrator and U.S. Army colonel and Anne D. (McElroy) McCaffrey, a real estate agent. She graduated from Radcliffe College with a B.A. in Slavonic languages in 1947. She has pursued graduate study at the University of Dublin. She also studied voice for nine years. She was married to H. Wright Johnson from January 14, 1950, until their divorce in 1970. She has three children: Alec Anthony, Todd (who has followed in her footsteps and is also writing novels set in Pern) and Georgeanne. Her current residence is Dragonhold-Underhill, in County Wicklow, Ireland. Her early career was spent as a copyright/layout designer/secretary for Liberty Music Shops (1948–50) and Helena Rubenstein (1950–52). She is director of Fin Film Productions (1979–present), and Dragonhold, LTD. Additionally, she also runs Dragonhold Stables on her land in Ireland.

Weyr Search won M. the Hugo Award (World Science Fiction Society) for best novella in 1968; she was the first woman to receive this prestigious award. *Dragonrider* also won the Nebula Award (Science Fiction Writers of America) in 1968 as best novella of the year. These two award winners were released as *Dragonflight* (1968) and were the beginnings of the World of Pern. This is a world in which humans ride dragons and protect their world from Threads, destructive spores that fall from a neighboring planet when its irregular orbit brings it close enough. The dragonriders communicate telepathically with their mounts. *Dragonquest* (1971) continues the saga of Pern with the clash of preserving past traditions and using new scientific insights to control the spores. *Dragonsong* (1976), *Dragonsinger* (1977), and *Dragondrums* (1979) are a trilogy targeted at a young adult audience. Over a dozen Pern novels round out the SERIES, creating a world that has been compared to TOLKEIN's Middle Earth and LE-GUIN's Earthsea. Christopher Swann characterizes M.'s Pern as having "gained a depth and significance far outweighing other fictional settings found in fantasy and science fiction." However, the technological elements of science fiction are subordinate to the fantasy setting, since Pern and all the worlds M. creates are based on solid scientific principles. Her dragons, after all, were created from genetically engineered fire lizards on Pern, not from myth or fantasy.

Another novel of note is *The Ship who Sang* (1969). It was an emotional release for her, written after her father's death. In her own words, "*Ship* taught me to use emotion as a writing tool . . . And I do, with neither apology nor shame, even though I am writing science fiction . . ." M.'s themes include bonding, birth, adolescent emergence and adult transformation, according to Mary Turzillo Brizzi, along with concerns over loss, disfigurement, and recompense. Brizzi also states that M. draws her imagery from "music, Irish and other folklore, cuisine, classical MYTHOLOGY and . . . natural and human flight."

Her first published story, *Restoree* (1967), was written in protest against the clichés of the standard space opera, particularly the unrealistic portrayal of women. According to Edra Bogle, most of her protagonists are women or children, whom she treats with understanding and clarity. M. views injustices imposed on women and children by powerful men and the social system as the basis of many of her stories. Lessa from *Weyr Search* has faults engendered by her early experiences, making her selfish and demanding at times, but no less memorable. Menolly in *Dragonsong* is compared by Marleen Barr to feminist writers Helene Cixous and Tillie Olson in that her female artist's creativity is being subverted by her family and society. Through self-exile from her family home, she finally defines herself as an artist, rather than by the women's chores she might otherwise have to perform. M. has brought the characterization of active women characters into the world of science fiction.

M. has also collaborated in "shared universes" with Margaret Ball and Elizabeth Ann Scarborough to create the world of a unicorn girl called Acorna. And she has dabbled in Arthurian legend with *Black Horses for the King* (1996), the story of imported horses and a boy who becomes their farrier. With the publication of *Dragon's Kin* (2003), one of the more recent books in the Pern series, she introduced her many fans to a new co-author, her son Todd.

SELECT AWARDS: 1968 World Science Fiction Society Hugo Award for best novella, "Weyr Search"; 1968 Science Fiction Writers of America Nebula Award for best novella, "Dragonrider"; 1975 E. E. Smith Award for fantasy; ALA notable book citations: 1976 for *Dragonsong* and 1977 for *Dragonsinger;* Selected here for "Here We Go Again . . . 25 Years of Best Books: Selections from 1967 to 1992"; 1977 Horn Book Fanfare Citation, *Dragonsong;* 1979 Gandalf Award, *The White Dragon;* 1981 Golden Pen Award; Science Fiction Book Club awards: 1986 for *Killashandra,* 1989 for *Dragonsdown,* 1990 for *The Rene-*

gades of Pern (first place) and *The Rowan* (third place), 1991 for *All in Weyrs of Pern,* 1993 for *Damia's Children,* and 1994 for *The Dolphins of Pern;* 1992 ALA Best Books for Young Adults: *Pegasus in Flight;* 1999 MARGARET A. EDWARDS Lifetime Achievement Award for Outstanding Literature for Young Adults, American Library Association's YALSA, *School Library Journal;* 2000 British Science Fiction Association Cthulu Award.

FURTHER WORKS: *Decision at Doona,* 1969; *The Kilterman Legacy,* 1975; *Get Off the Unicorn,* 1977; *White Dragon,* 1978; *Moreta, Dragonlady of Pern,* 1983; *The Girl Who Heard Dragons,* 1985; *Nerilka's Story,* 1986; *Dragonsdawn,* 1988; *The Renegades of Pern,* 1989; *All the Weyrs of Pern,* 1991; *The Chronicles of Pern,* 1992; *The Dolphins of Pern,* 1994; *Dragonseye,* 1997; *A Gift of Dragons,* 2002; *Dinosaur Planet,* 1978; *Crystal Singer,* 1982; *The Rowan,* 1990; *Crystal Line,* 1992; *Damia,* 1992; *Damia's Children,* 1993; *Lyon's Pride,* 1994; *Power Play,* 1995; *Freedom's Landing,* 1995; *Pegasus in Space,* 2000; *Acorna's World,* 2000; *The City and the Ship,* 2004.

BIBLIOGRAPHY: Barr, Marleen, "Science Fiction and the Fact of Women's Repressed Creativity: Anne McCaffrey Portrays a Female Artist." *Extrapolation* 23, Spring 1982; *Children's Literature Review,* vol. 49, 1998; *Contemporary Popular Writers,* 1997; *Dictionary of Literary Biography,* vol. 8, 1981; *Major Artists and Illustrators for Children and Young Adults,* vol. 4, 1993; *St. James Guide to Science Fiction Writers,* 4th ed., 1996; *Something about the Author,* vol. 8, 1976; vol. 70, 1992; vol. 116, 2000; *Something about the Author: Autobiography Series,* vol. 11, 1991; *Twentieth Century Young Adult Authors,* 1994.

JOANN C. JANOSKO

McCALL, Nathan
Author, b. 1955, Portsmouth, Virginia

Holding a B.A. (with honors) from Norfolk State University, M. has worked as a reporter for the *Virginian-Pilot,* the *Atlanta Journal-Constitution,* and the *Washington Post.* His two works were published late in his career—*Makes Me Wanna Holler: A Young Black Man in America* (1994) and *What's Going ON* (1997).

"A former felon who spent three years in the Virginia prison system for armed robbery, M. used his period of incarceration to educate himself and to begin an ongoing process of self-determination and success in the white man's world—without compromising his defiance of racist America." "The story of his rise from street thug to respected journalist is chronicled in his memoir *Makes Me Wanna Holler: A Young Black Man in America.*" Using stark language and unsparing honesty, M. tells of "his past and the debt he had to pay to right his wrongs."

Despite a promising beginning in a middle-class Southern town, "M. began to resent his status in a racist society." A bungled burglary led to a twelve-year prison sentence. Knowing he would be eligible for parole in three years, M. "adopted a regimen of discipline and good behavior." Part of this was a beneficial chance—working in the prison library where he was led "to literature that spoke to his condition as a black American." While in jail, M. studied literature and philosophy independently, and kept a journal. Though in his third year, M. learned printing and design layout at a minimum-security facility, M. knew he wanted to be a journalist. After returning to Norfolk State University and graduating from college, M. became a journalist. However, it was not until his third position, at the *Washington Post,* that M. revealed his dubious past.

AWARDS: *Makes Me Wanna Holler: A Young Black Man in America*: ALA Best Books for Young Adults, 1995.

BIBLIOGRAPHY: "Nathan McCall." *Newsmakers 1994,* Issue 4. Gale, 1994. Reproduced in *Discovering Collection,* 2001. http://galenet.galegroup.com/servlet/DC/.

SARA MARCUS

McCAUGHREAN, Geraldine (Jones)
Author, b. 6 June 1951, Enfield, London, England

M. (surname is pronounced "mc-cork-ran") says she "hanker[s]" for the age when an entire village gathered round an itinerant storyteller to hear adventurous tales about "things that really matter: about love and death and why the world isn't perfect and how it came to be the way that it is." Those who dwell in the modern world are fortunate that the "silver-tongued" M. is one such storyteller, with more than 120 works published.

M. is the youngest of three children born to Leslie Arthur (a fireman) and Ethel (a teacher; neé Thomas) Jones. She married John McCaughrean, now a retired naval officer, in 1988, and in 1989 gave birth to daughter Ailsa (Allie) Joy. The family lives in Berkshire with a white golden retriever named Daisy. M.

writes full time. Her stories have been translated into twenty-seven languages. M. attended Southgate Technical College in Middlesex (1969–70) and graduated with honors from Christ Church College in Canterbury (1977, B.Ed.). She worked in London as a secretary for Thames Television (1970–73); as assistant editor (1977–80), subeditor (1978–79) and staff writer (1982, 1983–88) for Marshall Cavendish Ltd., and as editorial assistant (1980–81) for Carreras-Rothman Ltd. in Aylesbury. She became an editor for *Banbury Focus* (1981–82) and subeditor and writer for *Storyteller* and *Great Composers.*

M. was an extremely timid child. Her dreams of being a knight, spy, or detective helped her discover that writing provided a comfortable means of expression and a pleasurable means of indulging FANTASY. M.'s style echoes influences of *The Ship that Flew* by Hilda Lewis, a childhood favorite. M.'s motto is: Write about what you'd like to know. She reveals a keenly curious, well-educated mind; her topics range through time and geographic space, frequently weaving similar traditions from different cultures. Her adventurous, often historical novels and retellings are carefully researched, although some reviewers take exception to the accuracy of her biblical retellings. M., critical of her fiction for adults, is more satisfied with the tales she writes for younger adults. Her retellings of myth and CLASSICAL stories receive rave reviews, lauding her ability to conjure magic through words. Those lyrical books, though rated for upper-division youngsters, are complex enough to be solid material for middle and high-school classrooms, particularly if they are to be read orally or enacted. M. has written fifty short plays for schools.

The same may be said of those novels suitable for ages nine and up: their fascinating subjects, masterful language, and adventurous pace hook readers of all ages, making M. a good choice for older struggling readers. The stories are set in medieval England, in a British antiques shop, in Argentina, on the high seas near Madagascar in 1717, in a boardinghouse where it's always Christmas, in England during World War I, in thirteenth-century China, and on the Oklahoma frontier in 1893. The young adult category includes: *A Little Lower than the Angels* (1987), *A Pack of Lies: Twelve Stories in One* (1988), *Gold Dust* (1993), *Plundering Paradise* (1996; retitled *A Pirate's Son* in the U.S., 1998), *Forever X* (1997), the disquieting *The Stones are Hatching* (1999), *The Kite Rider* (2001),

Stop the Train! (2001), and its sequel novella written for World Book, *Show Stopper!* (2003).

AWARDS: United Kingdom: All London Literary Competition (1978) for short story *"The Pike,"* Whitbread Children's Book Award (1987) for *A Little Lower than the Angels*; Library Association Carnegie Medal and Guardian Prize (1989) for *A Pack of Lies;* Smarties Book Prize Bronze Award (1996) for *Plundering Paradise*; United Kingdom Reading Association Book Award (1998) for *Forever X*; Blue Peter Book of the Year Award and 'Book to Keep Forever' Award (2000) for *Pilgrim's Progress*; Blue Peter 'Best Book to Keep' Award (2001) and Smarties Book Bronze Award (2001) for *The Kite Rider*; CILIP Carnegie Medal 'Highly Commended' (2001) and Smarties Book Bronze Award (2002) for *Stop the Train!*.

United States: Parenting Reading Magic Award for *Greek Myths* (1993) and for *The Bronze Cauldron* (1998); ALA Notable Children's Book, ALA Best Book for Young Adults, and Center for Children's Books Blue Ribbon Book (1998) for *The Pirate's Son*; ALA Notable Children's Book and ALA Best Book for Young Adults (2003) for *The Kite Rider*; School Library Journal Best Books for 2003 for *Stop the Train!*

Germany: Katholischen Kinderbuchpreis (1991) for *Gabriel und der Meisterspieler*.

FURTHER WORKS: *Saint George and the Dragon*, 1989; *The Maypole*, 1989; *Fire's Astonishment*, 1990; *Vainglory*, 1991; *Stories from Shakespeare*, 1994; *Lovesong*, 1996; *The Ideal Wife*, 1997; *Little Angel*, 1995; *The Random House Book of Stories from the Ballet*, 1995; reissued as *The Orchard Book of Stories from the Ballet*, 2004; *God's People*, 1997; *Unicorns! Unicorns!*, 1997; *Never Let Go*, 1998; *Beauty and the Beast*, 2000; *The Nutcracker*, 1999; *God's Kingdom*, 1999; *Princess Stories*, 2000; *Grandma Chickenlegs*, 2000; *How the Reindeer Got their Antlers*, 2000; *My Grandmother's Clock*, 2002; *One Bright Penny*, 2002; *Gilgamesh the Hero*, 2003; *Jalopy!*, 2003; *The Jesse Tree*, 2003; *Dog Days*, 2003; *The Oxford Treasury of Fairy Tales*, 2003; *Odysseus*, 2004. Other genres: PLAYS: *Britannia on Stage: 25 Plays from British History*, 2000; *Greeks on Stage: 25 Plays from Greek Mythology*, 2002; POETRY: in *Hello New!: New Poems for a New Century*, 2000; John Agard, comp., "The Seventy-Five O'Clock News," "The Bare Bones of Dinosaurs," "Roses Round My Door," in *On a Camel to the Moon*, 2001; Valerie Bloom, comp., "Carried Away." Radio: *Last Call* (a play), adaptations of *A Little Lower than the Angels, The Kite Rider, Stop the Train.* SHORT STORIES: "Thoughts of a Drought Dragon" in *Fire and Wings: Dragon*

Tales from East and West, Marianne Carus, and Misty Nilesh, eds., 2002; a variety of work in over 40 anthologies published since 1978. In Wales: *Da Was (Good Dog), Mali Me (Baabra Lamb), Iarlles (Gregorie Peck), Glesni (Blue Moo)*—(all 1994).

BIBLIOGRAPHY: Children's Literature Reviews on Children's Literature Comprehensive Database, http://www.childrenslit.com/; NovelList database; *Book Review Digest* (1999, 2002); *Something about the Author*, vol. 139, 2003, vol. 87, 1996; RealPlayer video clips and other links, http://www.channel4.com/learning.

CLAUDIA L. BENNETT

McCORMICK, Patricia
Author, b. 1956, Washington, D.C.

A former crime reporter and children's movie reviewer, M. cut to the core with her quiet, disturbing character Callie in her well-known and well-praised young adult novel *Cut*. After reading an article in *New York Times Magazine* about young women who cut themselves in order to deal with the stress in their lives, M. found herself thinking about these young women. Eventually a fictional character, whom she'd grown to think of often, was given a voice in *Cut*.

M. once commented: "We all do self-destructive or at least self-defeating things—usually at the very times when we need to take the best care of ourselves. Most times, the actions are relatively harmless: locking ourselves out of the house, forgetting an assignment, overdosing on Ben and Jerry's. They hurt us more than they hurt anyone else.

"It was at a time of great stress in my life that I began this book. I didn't cause myself bodily harm with a blade—I did do some stupid, panicky things— but all of a sudden a young girl appeared in my writing—a girl so lost she was seriously hurting herself. Obviously, I deeply identified with her.

"When I read stories, I see, or hope to see, aspects of my life reflected in them. I'm always looking for answers in the books I read; if not answers, at least somebody who has the same question. I hope my book will be that kind of book for some reader."

AWARDS: ALA Quick Pick for Reluctant Young Adult Readers, 2001, for *Cut;* American Library Association (ALA) 2002 for *Cut;* Best Book for Young Adults (ALA) 2002 for *Cut.*

FURTHER WORKS: With Steven Cohen, *Parents' Guide to the Best Family Videos*, 1999; contributor of articles to periodicals, including *Parents* magazine and the *New York Times*.

BIBLIOGRAPHY: *Contemporary Authors Online*, 2002.

REBECCA OSA MENDELL

McDONALD, Janet
Author, attorney, n.d., Brooklyn, New York

M. was born in Brooklyn and grew up in public housing projects. She had a difficult childhood, living in a dangerous neighborhood and a crowded apartment. She escaped her circumstances by using her intelligence to get into college. She attended Vassar as an undergraduate. While she excelled academically, M. encountered trouble due to her drug use. She continued her education at New York University Law School, but again faced adversity. She was arrested for arson, was raped, and suffered a mental breakdown. Fortunately, M. was able to overcome her troubled past and use her experiences in her writing. Her education also included a stint at Columbia University's School of Journalism.

Her memoir, *Project Girl: An Inspiring Story of a Black Woman's Coming-of-Age* (1999), was named a *Los Angeles Times* Best Book of 1999. She has gone on to write novels for YOUNG ADULTS.

M. continues writing and works as an attorney in Paris, France.

AWARDS: *Spellbound:* ALA Best Book for Young Adults, 2002. Her young adult novel *Chill Wind* (2002) received the Coretta Scott King/John Steptoe New Talent Award; *Twists and Turns:* ALA Quick Picks for Reluctant Young Adults, 2004.

FURTHER WORKS: *Twists and Turns*, 2003; *Brother Hood*, 2004.

BIBLIOGRAPHY: *Contemporary Authors Online*, 2003. Reproduced in *Biography Resource Center*, 2003. http://www.galenet.com/servlet/BioRC; www.project girl.com.

SHANNON CUFF

McDONALD, Joyce
Author, educator, b. 4 August 1946, San Francisco, California

M. has had many careers that attest to her love of writing—among them production assistant and editor at publishing houses, publisher of children's authors, and teacher of writing and literature. She has found that her diverse experience has enriched her own work, enabling her to examine her writing from the perspective of an editor, a marketer, and a critic. However, her books are also rooted in a profound sense of place, drawing on her childhood in Chatham, New Jersey, and the wild, wooded region of rural New Jersey where she makes her home.

M. produced her first handwritten, crayon-illustrated book at age six. Always a voracious reader and growing up in a book-loving family, she wrote her first novel at age ten and continued to write stories throughout elementary school and high school. Although her high-school work was praised by her teachers, she began college as an art major because, as she admits, she had never thought of writing as a career but as a necessary element of life, "like eating or breathing." She eventually earned both bachelor's and master's degrees in English at the University of Iowa, and today her art background finds its main outlet on her lovingly maintained website.

M. moved to New York City and, in 1976, began a professional career in publishing. She continued to write adult novels and SHORT STORIES but had no luck finding interested publishers. She had always done a huge amount of reading for pleasure and one day found herself browsing the shelves in the children's section at the county library. She fell in love with the work of Lois LOWRY, Barbara Park, and Betsy Byars and became an avid reader of authors for young people. In 1984, she founded her own publishing company, which specialized in the work of New Jersey children's authors.

In 1988, M. published her first children's book, *Mail-order Kid*, which was warmly received by reviewers. Its ten-year-old narrator, Flip, is rather offended that his parents have adopted a six-year-old Korean orphan. Flip's efforts to adapt to this new family member are portrayed in tandem with his efforts to acclimate his inappropriate new pet, a wild fox, to domestic life.

Homebody, M.'s first PICTURE BOOK, was illustrated by Karl Swanson and published in 1991. Drawn from a real-life experience and illustrated with evocative watercolors, it depicts an abandoned cat that lurks near her old home as it is renovated by new owners. The simple, powerful story is based on M.'s love of animals, especially cats—she and her husband Mac own six.

M. sold her publishing business after she returned to academia, teaching writing classes and earning a

461

Ph.D. at Drew University in 1994. During this period, she found time to write another children's novel, *Comfort Creek,* which was published in 1996. *Comfort Creek* was inspired by stories that M.'s husband told about his Florida childhood and is rich in atmospheric detail. The protagonist, spunky sixth-grader Quinnella Ellerbee, is a vivid and often hilarious character who copes with an absent mother and unemployed father.

Swallowing Stones, M.'s first YOUNG ADULT novel, followed in 1997 and garnered positive notices, including being named an ALA Top Ten Book for Young Adults. As with much of M.'s other work, the novel was inspired by a true story. In *Swallowing Stones,* a TEENAGE boy fires a single gunshot into the air on the Fourth of July and learns the next day that, when the bullet fell to earth, it killed the father of a girl who goes to his high school. The novel explores their interconnected stories as the boy ensnarls himself in a tangle of lies in an effort to escape responsibility for his act.

In 2000, M. stopped teaching at Drew University to devote herself full time to writing and published her second YA novel. Four troubled, marginalized, angry teens are the focus of *Shadow People.* Although they have little in common, they form an unlikely gang and plot ways to get revenge on all the adults who have been tormenting them. They progress from violence against property to endangering the life of a girl who has unknowingly gained the enmity of some of the gang. M. did not flinch from showing all the rage and disaffection of the post–Columbine youth culture, and she did not supply a happy ending.

In *Shades of Simon Gray* (2001), M. experimented with a blend of FANTASY and suspense, weaving the MYSTERY of a 1798 lynching with a present-day high-school cheating scandal. It is an impressive example of M.'s fascination, in her own words, "with the complexities and duality of human nature, and the choices we make in our lives."

M.'s next novel, *Devil at My Heels* (2004), is set in Florida in 1959 and deals with a fifteen-year-old girl who fears that the Ku Klux Klan may be threatening the migrant workers in her father's orange groves. In March 2004, M.'s short story, "Transfusion," appeared in a collection edited by Lisa Rowe Fraustino entitled *Don't Cramp My Style: Stories About That Time of the Month.*

AWARDS: *Swallowing Stones:* ALA Top Ten Best Book for Young Adults, ALA Best Books for Young Adults, 1998; ALA's 100 Best Books for Teens (1966–2000), New York Public Library Book for the Teen Age, *VOYA* Outstanding Title of the Year, Children's Book Committee Best Children's Book of the Year, ALA/YALSA Popular PAPERBACKS for YA 2003; New York Public Library Book for the Teen Age. *Shadow People; Shades of Simon Gray*: 2002 ALA Best Book for Young Adults, New York Public Library Book for the Teen Age, 2001 *VOYA* Best SCIENCE FICTION, FANTASY, and HORROR Book.

FURTHER WORKS: *The Stuff of Our Forebears: Willa Cather's Southern Heritage,* 1998.

BIBLIOGRAPHY: http://www.amazon.com/exec/obidos/show-interview/m-j-cdonaldoyce/ref%3Dpm%Fdp%5Fl%5Fb%5F8/103-1620401-1591034; *Contemporary Authors Online,* 2003; Interview with Debbi Michiko Florence, 2002, available online at http://debbimichikoflorence.com/index.2ts?page = joycemcdonald; http://www.joycemccdonald.net

MARY MENZEL

McFADDEN, Kevin. See PIKE, Christopher.

McINTYRE, Vonda N(eel)
Author, b. 28 August 1948, Louisville, Kentucky

Daughter of H. Neel (an electrical engineer) and Vonda Keith (a volunteer worker), M. earned a B.S. in biology from the University of Washington, Seattle, in 1970, and studied genetics at the graduate level from 1970 to 1971. M. has worked as a conference organizer and a riding and writing instructor, as well as being a member of The Authors Guild, Authors League of America, Science Fiction Writers of America, Planetary Society, Space Studies Institute, National Organization for Women, Cousteau Society, Nature Conservancy, and Greenpeace. M. focuses her writing on SCIENCE FICTION, bringing her background in biology and genetics to her works. "A hallmark of M.'s writing is her theme of physical transformation, either through genetic engineering or mechanical means." In her SHORT STORIES, novellas, and novels, M. uses biocontrol as an essential technique for her characters.

Also reflected in M.'s writing is her sense of feminine equality. M. frequently shows the danger of making assumptions by choosing ambiguous names and by carefully not mentioning a character's gender until function and personality are well established. Another feminist element is M.'s portrayal of nontraditional sexual partnerships and individual freedom of choice in sexual preferences.

The Moon and the Sun (1997) is one of M.'s most recent and successful works. The story is set in Versailles, France, in 1693, and tells the story of Marie-Josephe, a lady-in-waiting to the niece of Louis XIV, and her brother, Father Yves de la Croix, the Sun King's philosopher and explorer. Father Yves presents Louis XIV with a living sea woman and a dead man captured on a sea voyage, a science fiction that recounts a meeting between alien and human races, as well as intermingling history and science. M.'s story is captivating because it develops a new history based on science, a story that is independent from unknown presumptions of the future.

The relationship between the sea woman and Marie-Josephe explores the issue of communication despite language barriers. While vying for the sea woman's life with the king, Marie-Josephe creates images evoked from the sea woman's entrancing songs. Another barrier depicted in the story is the division of women from arts and science. Although Marie-Josephe is the superior scientist, she is considered second to her brother and regarded as his assistant. Another composer steals the credit for her musical composition. She is squashed under the thumb of misogyny, her brilliance thwarted. Marie-Josephe is internally conflicted about her abilities in life and the appropriateness of her endeavors. M.'s story tries to provide a reasonable explanation for why the accomplishments of women have not always survived in history. Marie-Josephe is able to succeed partly because she has the support of the king of France, but her situation is exceptional and overly ideal. Considering the number of women who lacked powerful allies in their struggle for acceptance, M. raises the question: "How much has been lost to our world, throughout history, because women have been denied, either explicitly or through social strictures, the chance to realize their potential?"

M.'s work goes beyond science fiction and inspires young adults to question history and realize its repercussions on the future.

AWARDS: 1974 Nebula Award, "Of Mist and Grass and Sand"; 1979 Hugo Award and 1979 Nebula Award, ALA Best Books for Young Adults, 1978, selected for "The Best of the Best Books, 1970–1983"

and "Nothin' But the Best: Best of the Best Books for Young Adults, 1966–1986; *Dreamsnake;* 1997 Nebula Award, *The Moon and the Sun.*

FURTHER WORKS: *The Exile Waiting,* 1975; *Aurora: Beyond Equality* (editor with Susan Janice Anderson), 1976; *Dreamsnake,* 1978; *Fireflood and Other Stories* (includes novelettes "Of Mist, and Glass, and Sand" and "Aztecs"), 1979; *Interfaces* (contributor), 1980; *The Entropy Effect,* 1981; *Star Trek II: The Wrath of Khan,* 1982; *Superluminal,* 1983; *Star Trek III: The Search for Spock,* 1984; *Enterprise: The First Adventure,* 1986; *Star Trek IV: The Voyage Home,* 1986; *Barbary,* 1986; *Starfarers,* 1989; *Screwtop,* 1989; *Transition,* 1991; *Metaphase,* 1992; *Nautilus,* 1994; *Star Wars: The Crystal Star,* 1994; *The Moon and the Sun,* 1997; *Curve of the Earth,* 2000; *Nebula Awards Showcase,* 2004; *Duty, Honor, Redemption,* 2004.

BIBLIOGRAPHY: Asaro, Catherine. "A Review of *The Moon and the Sun.*" http://www.sfsite.com/01b/moon49.htm; *Contemporary Authors Online,* 2003. Reproduced in *Biography Resource Center,* 2003. http://www.galenet.com/servlet/BioRC; "Vonda N(eel) McIntyre." *DISCovering Authors,* 1999. Reproduced in *Discovering Collection,* 2001. http://galenet.galegroup.com/servlet/DC/; "Moon and the Sun." *Publishers Weekly,* July 28, 1997; "Star Wars: the Crystal Star." *Publishers Weekly,* October 24, 1994.

RACHEL WITMER
AND SARA MARCUS

McKILLIP, Patricia A(nne)
Author, b. 29 February 1948, Salem, Oregon

M. began her storytelling career as a child helping to raise her younger siblings. She started her first novel, *The House on Parchment Street* (1973), when she was just fourteen years old. She started writing, she says, "during one of those 'moody' periods teenagers have when they know they want something, but don't know quite what it is." Writing stories and reading them to her siblings gave her the feeling that she had found that thing she didn't know she wanted. Her parents supported her writing habit. M. says, "They let me grow at my own speed, which strikes me now as an extraordinary way for modern parents to behave."

M.'s first books, including *The House on Parchment Street,* were written for children. Her first adult novel was *The Forgotten Beasts of Eld* (1974), the first in the FANTASY *Riddle of Stars* trilogy. M. was soon recognized as a "top notch fantasy writer," according to Roger C. Schlobin in *Science Fiction and Fantasy Book Review.*

In an attempt to break away from fantasy, M. wrote *Stepping from the Shadows,* an AUTOBIOGRAPHICAL novel for TEENS, the story of a young girl who learns to be an author by telling stories to her imaginary friend. M. followed this title with other stories for young adults, including two SCIENCE FICTION novels, *Moon-Flash* (1984) and *The Moon and the Face* (1985). The switch to science fiction was a surprise to fans. M. draws a definite line between science fiction and fantasy, saying, "If I'm writing fantasy I use elements of epic, fantasy, myth, legend . . . When I write science fiction . . . I try to turn my back on traditional fantasy elements and extrapolate a plot from history, or daily life, or whatever science happens to stick in my head."

M. continues to publish both fantasy and science fiction for all age groups. She uses either genre, selecting the one that best suits the specific story. *Contemporary Authors* (2002) notes "her ability, regardless of the genre in which she is writing, to touch on basic human traits and themes." M. creates believable characters in extraordinary settings, giving her readers the chance to escape their lives and still learn about themselves.

AWARDS: *The Forgotten Beasts of Eld:* 1975 World Fantasy Award for best novel and American Library Association notable book selection; *Fool's Run*: ALA Best Books for Young Adults, 1987.

FURTHER WORKS: *The Throme of the Erril of Sherill,* 1973; *The Night Gift,* 1976; *Heir of Sea and Fire,* 1977; *Harpist in the Wind,* 1979; *Fool's Run,* 1987; *The Changeling Sea,* 1988; *The Sorceress and the Cygnet,* 1991; *The Cygnet and the Firebird,* 1993; *Something Rich and Strange,* 1994; *The Book of Atrix Wolfe,* 1995; *Winter Rose,* 1996; *Song for the Basilisk,* 1998; *Tower at Stony Wood,* 2000; *Ombria in Shadow,* 2002; *In the Forests of Serre,* 2003; *Alphabet of Thorn,* 2004.

BIBLIOGRAPHY: *Contemporary Authors Online,* 2002; *Authors and Artists for Young Adults,* 1995; *The Encyclopedia of Fantasy,* 1997; *Supernatural Fiction Writers: Fantasy and Horror,* 1985.

JENNA OBEE

McKINLEY, (Jennifer) (Carolyn) Robin

Author, b. 16 November 1952, Warren, Ohio

M. has written fantasy for all ages, but is best known for her young adult novels and SHORT STORIES that feature strong female protagonists. For more than two decades, M. has contributed to the development of YOUNG ADULT LITERATURE, capturing her readers' imaginations with beautiful prose and magical settings. From the landscape of archetype she breathes life into maidens, villains and beasts. She also deals with epic themes of good and evil, as well as audience-appropriate questions of identity. In particular, she has created a place for the female hero in the realm of high FANTASY and literary folktale retellings.

As an only child in a military family, M. spent much of her time traveling and reading; her love for J. R. R. TOLKIEN's *Lord of the Rings* would later influence her writing. She majored in English, graduating *summa cum laude* in 1975 from Bowdoin College. Since the 1978 debut of her first novel, *Beauty,* she has remained a regularly published author. M. has also worked as an editor and transcriber, research assistant, bookstore clerk, teacher and counselor, editorial assistant, barn manager, and freelance editor. In 1992, she married fellow fantasy writer, Peter DICKINSON, and now lives in Hampshire, England, with three whippets, a horse, and over four hundred rose bushes.

M has founded much of her work on traditional folktales and legends. Her most widely recognized novel, *Beauty: A Retelling of Beauty and the Beast* (1978), has won several awards and citations. Others include: *The Outlaws of Sherwood* (1988, based on "Robin Hood"), *Deerskin* (1993, "Donkeyskin"), *Rose Daughter* (1997, "Beauty and the Beast"); and *Spindle's End* (2000, "Sleeping Beauty"). She also writes short stories; "The Twelve Dancing Princesses" appears in *The Door in the Hedge* (1981). M.'s great strength with this genre lies in her ability to balance between remaining true to the structure, spirit, and integrity of the traditional stories while, at the same time, retelling them as unique, literary pieces.

M.'s other works, known as the Damarian Cycle, are set in an evocative landscape very similar to the human world in terms of social structure, flora and fauna. However, Damar is also a place filled with magic, wonder, dragons, and fairies. M.'s first novel in the cycle, *The Blue Sword* (1982), tells of a young protagonist who discovers both her heroism and the legendary Gonturan, a sword that also appears in *The Hero and the Crown* (1984). This prequel earned M. the 1985 Newbery Medal for its powerful characterization of Aerin, the hero responsible for championing her country. Other Damar writings include three short stories: "The Stone Fey" appeared in *Imaginary Lands* (1985), an anthology that M. edited. In 1998, this story was also published as an illustrated book. "The Healer" and "A Pool in the Desert" are found respectively in *A Knot in the Grain and Other Stories* (1994) and *Water: Tales of Elemental Spirits* (2002).

A number of common elements and themes occur in M.'s body of work. Her writing style is rich, dense and poetic. Notably, M. has received much acclaim for her female protagonists or, as she calls them, "Girls Who Do Things." They are adventurous, intelligent and active; they also represent the ordinary girl who is awkward, introverted and plain-looking, but who matures into a successful, attractive young woman. M.'s great fondness for the barn, especially the horse stables, also finds its way into her writing. Her protagonists often prefer the companionship of an animal that becomes an important friend and ally. Finally, while not all of M.'s stories involve mythic journeys and high fantasy, they all contain the themes of hope and heroism.

SELECT AWARDS: *Horn Book* Honor List citations: 1978, *Beauty: A Retelling of the Story of Beauty and the Beast;* 1985, *The Hero and the Crown;* 1988, *The Outlaws of Sherwood;* 1995, *Knot in the Grain;* Best Books for the TEEN AGE citation: New York Public Library, 1980, 1981, and 1982, 1978 ALA Best Books for Young Adults, *Beauty; The Blue Sword:* 1982 ALA Best Books Young Adult, 1983 Newbery Honor Book; selected for "The Best of the Best Books: 1970–1983," 2003 ALA Popular Paperbacks; 1985 Newbery Medal, 2004 ALA Popular Paperbacks, 1985 ALA Best Books for Young Adults, *The Hero and the Crown;* 1986 World Fantasy Award for best anthology, *Imaginary Lands;* 1994 Best Books for the Teen Age and Best Adult Book for the Teen Age, 1994 ALA Best Books for Young Adults, 2005 ALA Popular Paperbacks, *Deerskin;* Notable Book selection, *The Hero and the Crown*; *Rose Daughter*: ALA Best Books for Young Adults, 1998.

FURTHER WORKS: *Deerskin*, 1993; *The Stone Fey,* 1998; *Sunshine,* 2004.

BIBLIOGRAPHY: *Authors and Artists for Young Adults,* Vol. 4, 1990, Vol. 33, 2000; *Best Sellers,* January 1985, p. 399; *Children's Literature Review,* Vol. 10, 1986; *Dictionary of Literary Biography,* Vol. 52: *American Writers for Children since 1960: Fiction,* 1986; "(Jennifer) (Carolyn) Robin McKinley." *Contemporary Authors Online,* 2003. *Magazine of Science Fiction and Fantasy,* January 1998, 28–33;

April 1998, pp. 36–37; March, 2001, p. 108; *Junior Bookshelf,* June 1984, pp. 141–42; Robin McKinley's Official Home Page, http://www.robinmckinley.com; Rytting, Jenny Rebecca. *Famous in Legend and Story: Robin McKinley's Portrayal of Heroes; St. James Guide to Fantasy Writers,* 1996; *St. James Guide to Young Adult Writers,* 2nd ed., 1999; *Twentieth-Century Children's Writers,* 3rd ed., 1989.

GINGER MULLEN

McKISSACK, Patricia and Fred

Author, b. 9 August 1944, Smyrna, Tennessee

A writer of historical fiction and BIOGRAPHIES that focus on AFRICAN AMERICAN themes, M.'s writing has been described as bringing subjects to life by capturing unique and noteworthy events, possessing energy and passion, and weaving well-crafted and well-researched tapestries. The roots of her love for stories are found in family experiences involving her grandfather. This love of literature continued throughout her school years and was shared by her husband, Frederick M. As part of the first generation of African Americans to integrate schools and restaurants, they experienced firsthand the tremors of change throughout the South, and ultimately these experiences enriched their writing. Both the greater opportunities for African Americans in the 1960s as well as personal experiences with the injustice of segregation provided impetus for her writing. As a teacher of writing at the secondary level, she is highly regarded for both her individual contributions to literature for young adults and the collaborative works with her husband that extend across genres.

M.'s first book came out of necessity when she could not find biographical material about Paul Laurence Dunbar to present to her junior-high-school class. This aroused her interest in writing biographies about numerous African Americans such as Langston Hughes, James Weldon Johnson, Marian Anderson, Ralph Bunche, Sachel Paige, Madame C. J. Walker, and others. Written with her husband, these biographies include both those created as part of a SERIES as well as those published individually. They are noted for their presentation of individuals with strong convictions and purpose. One of these, *Sojourner Truth: Ain't I a Woman?* (1992), was named a Coretta King Honor Book.

Accounts of African American history that are not as well known have been brought to life by M.

Achievements of significant individuals in their fields, despite issues of racism and segregation, are documented in works such as *Black Diamond: The Story of the Negro Baseball Leagues* (1994); *Red Tail Angels: The Story of the Tuskegee Airmen of World War II* (1995); and *Black Hands, White Sails: The Story of African-American Whalers* (1999). These histories have been praised as "Impeccably documented, handsomely designed, and thoughtfully executed . . . ," according to Burns (1996) in a review of *Red Tail Angels*.

M.'s outstanding contribution in yet another genre is found in the Newberry Honor book *The Dark-Thirty: Southern Tales of the Supernatural* (1992). African-American folklore and culture accompany the readers as they enter *The Dark Thirty*. This is literally the half hour before night in which children were still allowed to play outside, a period in which they experience ghost tales retold in a captivating way.

Historical fiction is another significant area of writing for M., as can be seen in the fictionalized diaries, *A Picture of Freedom: The Diary of Clotee, A Slave Girl* (1997) and *Color Me Dark: The Diary of Nellie Lee Love, The Great Migration North* (2000). One reviewer comments that M. creates sophisticated content, weaving suspense and historical details that are "tuned to the understanding of a middle-school audience" (Burns, 1997). This supports M.'s concern that all young people be reached at this crucial time in their development. *Christmas in the Big House, Christmas in the Quarters* (1994), describes the extensive plantation preparation for Christmas in the year prior to the Civil War. The M.s articulately create a contrast between the grandeur of the "big house" that was filled with talk and fear of war and rebellion and the humble slave quarters where hope and optimism for freedom filled the air.

M. is highly regarded because of her numerous significant and often award-winning contributions to literature reflecting the African American culture in a variety of genres. In addition to a Newbery Honor and a Caldecott Honor, she has also received several Coretta Scott King Awards, the Jane Addams Children's Book Award, and a *Boston Globe–Horn Book* Award, among others. Included in her writings, that already number over 100, are also PICTURE BOOKS for younger readers. She explains what she does by saying, "Writing has allowed us to do something positive with our experiences, although some of our experiences have been very negative. We try to enlighten, to change attitudes, to form new attitudes—to build bridges with books." Her comments reveal the potential of her influence on young readers who are invited to engage in this body of artistic yet scholarly authentic historical accounts.

SELECT AWARDS: Coretta Scott King Award: 1990 for *A Long Hard Journey: The Story of the Pullman Porter*, 1993 for *Sojourner Truth: Ain't I a Woman?*, 1995 for *Christmas in the Big House, Christmas in the Quarters*; 1993 *Boston Globe–Horn Book* Award, ALA Best Books for Young Adults, 1993, *Sojourner Truth: Ain't I a Woman?*; *The Dark-Thirty: Southern Tales of the Supernatural*: 1993 Coretta Scott King Award, 1993 Newbery Medal Honor Book United States; YALSA Best Books for Young Adults: 1996 for *Red-Tail Angels: The Story of the Tuskegee Airmen of World War II*, 1997 for *Rebels Against Slavery: American Slave Revolts*; Coretta Scott King Honor Books: 1997 for *Rebels Against Slavery*, 2000 for *Black Hands, White Sails: The Story of African-American Whalers*, 2004 for *Days of Jubilee*.

SELECT FURTHER WORKS: *Martin Luther King, Jr.: A Man to Remember*, 1984; *Mirandy and Brother Wind*, 1988; *Jesse Jackson: A Biography*, 1989; CIVIL RIGHTS MOVEMENT in America from 1865 to the Present, 1991; *Marian Anderson: A Great Singer*, 1991; *Mary Church Terrell: Leader for Equality*, 1991; *Paul Robeson: A Voice to Remember*, 1992; *Royal Kingdoms of Ghana, Mali, and Songhay: Life in Medieval Africa*, 1994; *Rebels Against Slavery: American Slave Revolts*, 1996; *Let My People Go: Bible Stories of Faith, Hope, and Love, As Told by Price Jefferies, A Free Man of Color, to His Daughter, Charlotte, in Charleston, South Carolina, 1806–1816*, 1998; *Ma Dear's Aprons*, 1997; *Young, Black, and Determined: A Biography of Lorraine Hansberry*, 1998; *Nzingha: Warrior Queen of Matamba, Angola, Africa, 1595*, 2000; *Goin' Someplace Special*, 2001; *Days of Jubilee: The End of Slavery in the United States*, 2003.

BIBLIOGRAPHY: Burns, Mary. Review of *Red-Tail Angels*. *Horn Book*, March–April, 1996; Burns, Mary, Review of *Run Away Home*. *Horn Book*, November–December, 1997; *Contemporary Authors Online*, 2001; M., Patricia. *Can You Imagine?*, 1997; *Something about the Author* vol. 117, 2000.

JANELLE B. MATHIS

McLAREN, Clemence

Author, b. 3 November 1938, New Jersey

M., known as *Clemi* to those who visit her user-friendly website, has been a fan of Greek MYTHOLOGY since she was a young girl growing up with her grandparents in New Jersey. On cold nights nothing was better for M. than wrapping herself about a book, and it wasn't long until the legendary stories became familiar friends. So dear were these stories and characters that M. soon found herself wondering about the intimate lives of her imaginary confidantes. Through her writing, M. has been able to satisfy her curiosity and share her findings, as well as the drama and adventure of mythology, with a whole new group of young readers. Not only does M. bring classical literature to modern audiences, but she lends a strong voice to female characters previously lost in the mists of time.

M.'s critically acclaimed *Inside the Walls of Troy* (1996) retells the story of the Trojan War from the viewpoint of two women at the forefront of the action, Helen and Cassandra. M. returned to this formula with her *Waiting for Odysseus* (2000) a novel that rejuvenates Homer's *The Odyssey*. The work of antiquity is infused and revitalized by an array of fresh voices as it is retold from the view of, among others, Odysseus' wife Penelope, the goddess Athena, and the sorceress Circe. M. used her penchant for taking her own life and interests and fleshing them out in her writing to tell a modern story with a thoroughly modern heroine. In *Dance for the Land* (1999), twelve-year-old Kate finds herself in a new and sometimes combative world when her family relocates to Hawaii. Kate must find a place for herself among a strange but ultimately beautiful culture. M. herself lives and teaches in Hawai'i.

AWARDS: New York Public Library, Best Books for the TEEN AGE (1997) for *Inside the Walls of Troy;* American Library Association, Best YA Books (1998) for *Inside the Walls of Troy.*

FURTHER WORK: *Aphrodite's Blessing: Love Stories from the Greek Myths,* 2002; *Dance for the Aina,* 2003.

BIBLIOGRAPHY: M. Clemence. *Everyday Life with Clemi,* June 19, 2004. http://members.aol.com/runpaddle/aboutclm.htm; http://www.buffalostate.edu/library/databases/

MOLLY ROSE ZEIGLER

McNAMEE, Graham
Author, b. August 1967, Toronto, Ontario, Canada

M., author of books for children and young adults, began his writing career when he entered a competi-

tion to write a young adult novel. The result, which came in second place, was *Hate You* (2000), the compelling story of seventeen-year-old Alice Silvers who writes songs that she cannot sing. Her voice is damaged because as a child trying to defend her mother from her father's abuse, she got in the way and her father choked her, damaging her voice permanently. She is embarrassed by what she calls her Frankenstein voice, "all cracked, scratched, and broken." Both her love and her hatred for her father resurface when she learns that he is dying in a nearby hospital and that he wants to see her again. The strength and authenticity of Alice's voice, along with her struggles as she attempts to deal with the people around her, have made this a popular book among readers and critics.

In *Acceleration* (2003), seventeen-year-old Duncan discovers a small leather book among other unclaimed items while working at his summer job in the lost and found department of the Toronto subway system. The book turns out to be the explicit journal of a potential serial killer. Reading the journal, Duncan learns that the writer has already tortured animals and committed arson and has begun to stalk women on the subway. When the police do not take him seriously, Duncan and his friends decide that they will try to discover the author's identity and trap him before he kills someone—if he hasn't already.

AWARDS: *Hate You:* Honor Book in the fifteenth annual Delacorte Press Contest for a First Young Adult Novel and 2000 ALA Best Book for Young Adults; 2001 PEN/Phyllis Naylor Working Writer Fellowship, *Sparks;* Edgar for Best Young Adult Mystery, 2004, ALA Best Books for Young Adults and ALA Quick Picks for Reluctant Young Adult Readers, 2004, *Acceleration.*

FURTHER WORKS: *Sparks,* 2002.

BIBLIOGRAPHY: Graham McNamee Author Spotlight, November 14, 2003. http://www.randomhouse.com/author/results.pperl?authorid=20115

ANDREA LIPINSKI

McNAUGHTON, Janet
Author, b. 29 November 1953, Toronto, Ontario, Canada

M., who grew up in Toronto, attended York University (Honours B.A.) and holds an M.A. and Ph.D. in folklore from Memorial University in St. John's, Newfoundland; she has lived there since 1979. Influenced by Edith Fowke at York University, M. was drawn to Newfoundland and Memorial University because of the graduate program in folklore. She uses her academic knowledge and folklore expertise in her creative writing.

M. began her writing career as a book reviewer. Her first piece of creative writing was a draft that was eventually published as *To Dance at the Palais Royale,* a story based on the experiences of her mother's family in Toronto during the 1920s. While trying to get this work published, she began a second novel, *Catch Me Once, Catch Me Twice.* For this project she relied on her doctoral dissertation on developments in medicine, midwifery, and childbirth in Newfoundland for the creation and portrayal of her characters. The book was successfully published in 1994 and was followed by *To Dance at the Palais Royale* in 1996.

Make or Break Spring (1998), set in St John's in 1945, continues the wartime and immediate postwar story of the main character, Evelyn McCallum, from *Catch Me Once, Catch Me Twice.* M.'s fourth novel, *The Secret Under My Skin* (2000), is set in a dark Terra Nova (Newfoundland) in the twenty-fourth century. *An Earthly Knight* (2003), set in twelfth-century Scotland, marks a return to historical fiction with a touch of FANTASY. For younger children, M. has written and published *The Saltbox Sweater* (2001), set during the moratorium on cod fishing in Newfoundland in the 1990s.

Gathering the oral history of her mother's family and an interest in fairies are related to M.'s graduate work; her early research is clearly seen in the historical and supernatural elements in her fiction. M.'s historical research and comfortable use of fantasy combine in a balanced way to both inform and enchant the readers of her fiction, carrying them to distant times and places.

AWARDS: *To Dance at the Palais* Royale: Violet Downey National Chapter IODE Book Award, 1997; Nova Scotia Library Association's Ann Conner Brimer Award for Children's Literature in Atlantic Canada, 1997; Geoffrey Bilson Award for Historical Fiction for Young People, 1997; Canadian Library Association's Young Adult Honour Book. *Make or Break Spring:* Ann Connor Brimer Award, 1999; Writers' Alliance of Newfoundland and Labrador/NewTel Children's Literature Award, 1998–99. *The Secret Under My Skin:* Ruth Schwartz Award, 2001; Mr. Christie Award, 2001; Ann Connor Brimer Award, 2001; Newfoundland and Labrador Book Award in

the Bruneau Family's Children's Literature Award category, 2002.

FURTHER WORKS: Reviews, articles, and columns in *Quill and Quire, Canadian Bookseller, Books in Canada, Canadian Gardening, Today's Parent, Tree House Family* MAGAZINE.

BIBLIOGRAPHY: Baker, Deirdre, and Ken Setterington, *A Guide to Canadian Children's Books,* 2003; Profile of Janet M. by Dave Jenkinson in *Canadian Review of Material* http://www.umanitoba.ca/cm/profiles/mcnaughton.html; Janet M.'s homepage, http://www.avalon.nf.ca/~janetmcn/; Writers Union of Canada Member page, http://www.writersunion.ca/m/mcnaught.htm; CANSCAIP Member page, http://www.canscaip.org/bios/mcnaughtonj.html; Newfoundland Writers, in *Canadian Literature Archive,* http://www.umanitoba.ca/canlit/authorlist/newfoundlandwriters.shtml

MARGARET STEFFLER

MacDOUGALL, Ruth Doan
Author, b. 19 March 1939, Laconia, New Hampshire

Daughter of author Daniel Doan, M. was exposed to the life of an author from a very young age; at the age of six, she had already written her first story. Holding a B.Ed. from Keene Teachers College (1961), M. began her published writing career in 1965 with *The Lilting House,* and soon followed with more works.

M.'s reputation soared after the publication of the national bestseller *The Cheerleader* (1973). It was one of the first novels to paint an accurate portrait of an American TEENAGE girl during the 1950s. M.'s use of language and attention to the idiosyncrasies of high-school behavior create the realistic world of cheerleader Henrietta Snow. At the culmination of high school, M. opts to have her protagonist break away from the traditional world to which her high-school friends belong and pursue alternative opportunities. This work has been praised in numerous literary reviews for being the essential depiction of 1950s America through the eyes of a maturing adolescent girl. Henrietta's adult life is later explored in *The Cheerleader's* sequel, *Snowy* (1993).

Continuing a tradition of assisting her father that began with the publication of his novels, M. began updating his hiking guidebooks in 1991. Upon Doan's death in 1993, M. assumed the authorship of the new editions of his work while continuing to write for her literary audiences. Currently, M. resides with her husband Don in New Hampshire, and is a member of the New Hampshire Writer' Project.

AWARDS: *The Cheerleader,* selected for "The Best of the Best Books: Selections from 1970 to 1983," selected by librarians for this Young Adult Library Services Association (YALSA) list.

FURTHER WORKS: *The Cost of Living,* 1971; *One Minus One, Wife and Mother,* 1976; *Aunt Pleasantine,* 1978; The Flowers of the Forest, 1981; A Lovely Time Was Had By All, 1982; *Henrietta Snow,* 2004.

BIBLIOGRAPHY: *Contemporary Authors Online,* 2001; author's Web page, http://www.ruthdoanmacdougall .com/author/index.html

RACHEL WITMER

MacGREGOR, Rob
Author, n.d., n.p.

Best known for his seven Indiana Jones novels, M. originally attended college intending to become an archaeologist. Instead, he switched his major to journalism and began his career as a reporter. M.'s interest in archaeology and adventure never faded; between jobs, he traveled and visited ruins in England, Greece, Mexico, and Peru. By the time M. became involved with Indiana Jones, he had traveled to all the places that his protagonist visits in his adventures. The author's firsthand knowledge and personal passion for the world that Indy inhabited produce a captivating writing style.

M.'s interest in archaeology and love of travel provided the impetus for his Indiana Jones novels: *Indiana Jones and the Last Crusade* (1989), *Indiana Jones and the Dance of the Giants* (1991), *Indiana Jones and the Peril at Delphi* (1991), *Indiana Jones and the Seven Veils* (1991), *Indiana Jones and the Unicorn's Legacy* (1992), *Indiana Jones and the Interior World* (1992), and *Indiana Jones and the Genesis Deluge* (1992). Other novels that M. adapted from scripts include *Private Eye* (1988), *Private Eye: Flipside* (1988), *The Phantom* (1996), and *Spawn* (1997).

M.'s writing skills are not limited to novels; he has also written six nonfiction books: *The Making of Miami Vice,* co-authored with Trish Janeshutz (1986); *The Rainbow Oracle,* co-authored with Tony Gorsso (1989); *The Everything Dream Book* (2000) and *The Lotus and the Stars: The Way of Astro-Yoga,* co-authored with wife Trish MacGregor (2001); *Dreams: The Running Press Pocket Guide,* written as Robert MacGregor (2003); and *Star Power: Astrology for Teens,* co-authored with daughter Megan MacGregor (2003).

M. wrote two TEEN MYSTERIES set out west on an Indian reservation—along the lines of Tony Hillerman for teens. He won an Edgar Allan Poe Award for the first: *Prophecy Rock.* A teenage boy spends the summer with his divorced father, a Navajo policeman on the reservation, and helps him solve a mystery. In the sequel, boy is back home with his mother (in civilization). When the boy is accused of killing his girlfriend, his father leaves the reservation and comes to help clear his son.

M. is a self-proclaimed chameleon; in describing his writing career, the author says that he changes his "colors" to reflect his environment.

AWARDS: 1996 Edgar Allan Poe award in the Young Adult category for *Prophecy Rock,* 1995.

FURTHER WORKS: *The Crystal Skull,* 1991; *Hawk Moon,* 1996; *PSI/Net* (with Billy Dee Williams), 1999; *JUST/In Time* (with Billy Dee Williams), 2000; *Amazon: The Ghost Tribe,* 2001; *Dream Power for Teens: What Your Dreams Say about Your Past, Present, and Future,* 2004.

BIBLIOGRAPHY: Booktalk: All the Buzz about Books, online, 2003; *The Indy Experience.com,* The Ultimate Guide to Indiana Jones, online; New Page Books, online, 2003; http://www.booktalk.com/robmacgregor/ robbiography1.html.

VALERIE WAETZIG WILLIAMS

MacLACHLAN, Patricia
Author, b. 3 March 1938, Cheyenne, Wyoming

M.'s childhood experiences are inspiration and fodder for her novels and PICTURE BOOKS. Moving from Wyoming to Minnesota at an early age, interacting with all generations, and being exposed to art in all forms gave her experiences that served her well as a writer later in life. It wasn't until she had children of her own, however, that her early reading experiences turned into writing. A student of Jane YOLEN, she blossomed as a writer. Her first book for middle-school readers was *Arthur for the Very First Time* (1980), followed by the popular *Sarah, Plain and Tall* (1985). M.'s exposure as an author is increased because her works have been translated into many languages and transformed into filmstrip/cassettes, audio cassettes, and television productions. M.'s works provide readers of all generations a glimpse into families who tell comforting stories about struggles and stability through the changes of life. Along these lines, her novel, *Baby,* appealed to TEENS and adults as a FAMILY, struggling to cope with the loss of a newborn, finds an abandoned baby in a basket at their door with a note. "This is Sophie. She is almost a year old and she is good . . . I will come back for her one day. I love her." The one day turns out to be a year away, at the end of which the healing power of love has helped all the members of the family come to terms with their grief. Teen appeal due to the subject matter and the presence of a twelve-year-old girl in the family is validated by this novel's selection for the 1994 Best Books for YA list.

AWARDS: Newbery Medal, 1986, Scott O'DELL Historical Fiction Award for *Sarah, Plain and Tall;* ALA Best Book for YA 1994 for *Baby* and 1992 for *Journey.*

FURTHER WORKS: *The Six Day,* 1979; *Cassie Binegar,* 1982; *Unclaimed Treasures,* 1984; *The Facts and Fictions of Minna Pratt,* 1988; *Journey,* 1991; *Baby,* 1993; *Skylark,* 1994; *All the Places to Love,* 1994; *What You First Know,* 1995; *Painting the Wind,* 2003.

BIBLIOGRAPHY: Broadwater, Lisa. "Remembering Her Roots." *Dallas Morning News,* October 10, 1995, 4C; *Something about the Author,* vol. 62, 1990.

MAAS, Peter
Journalist, Author, b. 27 June 1929, New York City; d. 23 August 2001, New York City

M.'s determined writing career began while he was attending Duke University. He scooped an exclusive interview in the hospital room where labor leader Walter Reuther was recuperating from an assassination attempt; that story was later sold to the Associated Press.

M. was writing investigative pieces for MAGAZINES and newspapers when he stumbled onto the identity of Joseph Valachi, a mob hitman who had become a government informer. The U.S. Department of Justice hired M. to edit Valachi's account of life in the Cosa Nostra, entitled *The Real Thing,* but later sought an injunction to block publication. After prevailing in court, *The Valachi Papers* (1969) was rejected by twenty publishers but then became an international bestseller. *Serpico* (1973) was the basis of a hit MOVIE, and other bestsellers followed. At the same

time he was doing research for his books, M. continued writing articles for the *New York Times, Parade* magazine, and other news sources.

M.'s final book, *Terrible Hours* (1999), depicts the heroic triumph of the inventor of submarine rescue. This topic contrasted with the majority of his primarily nonfiction books, which feature organized crime figures, corrupt police officers, and psychopathic killers. The brilliance, determination, and courage of engineer Swede Momsen shine through the parallel descriptions of the submarine Squalus's crew, the naval hierarchy, and the families of the missing men.

AWARDS: *Rescuer:* ALA Best Books for Young Adults, 1967; *Serpico:* ALA Best Books for Young Adults, 1973, selected for "Still Alive: The Best of the Best: 1960–1974"; School Library Journal's Best Adult Books for Young Adults, 2000, for *Terrible Hours;* Christopher Awards, Books for Adults, 1994, for *Marie: A True Story.*

FURTHER WORKS: *The Rescuer,* 1968; *King of the Gypsies,* 1975; *Made in America,* 1979; *Marie: A True Story,* 1983; *Manhunt,* 1986; *Father and Son,* 1989; *In a Child's Name: The Legacy of a Mother's Murder,* 1990; *China White,* 1994; *Killer Spy: The Inside Story of the FBI's Pursuit and Capture of Aldrich Amos, America's Deadliest Spy,* 1995; *Underboss: Sammy the Bull Gravano's Story of Life in the Mafia,* 1997; *The Terrible Hours: The Man Behind the Greatest Submarine Rescue in History,* 2000.

BIBLIOGRAPHY: *Contemporary Authors Online,* 2002; *New York Times,* August 24, 2001, A17; *New York Post,* August 24, 2001, 6.

BARBARA J. HAMPTON

MACAULAY, David
Author, illustrator, b. 1946, Burton-on-Trent, England

M. was born in England and moved to the United States in 1957 when his father, a machine technician, relocated for a job. M. attended the Rhode Island School of Design (B.F.A., architecture, 1969). After working as an interior designer, a junior-high-school teacher, and a teacher at RISD, he began to experiment with creating books.

M.'s first book, *Cathedral* (1973), details the construction of a gothic cathedral in black-and-white line drawings. His lifelong fascination with the mechanical workings of the world is expressed in whimsical yet mechanically accurate monochromatic pen-and-ink drawings. He produced several more works discussing different architectural pieces: the construction of a Roman city in *City* (1974); the erection of the monuments to the pharaohs in *Pyramid* (1975); the building of medieval fortresses in *Castle* (1977); and the secret of a city's hidden support system in *Underground* (1976).

In *The Way Things Work* (1988), the internal mechanisms of both simple, everyday objects and complex machinery are explained through detailed illustrations, accompanied by humorous text. In 1998, *The Way Things Work* was updated (*The New Way Things Work*) to include a section called "The Digital Domain," which illustrates the inner workings of robots, virtual reality, modems, digital cameras, compact disks, and computer bytes.

Even M.'s fiction—such as *Motel of the Mysteries* (1979), a FANTASY about an archeological excavation of twentieth-century society two thousand years in the future, or *Unbuilding* (1980), a story about the demolition of the Empire State Building—is informed by meticulous research and a deep understanding of history and the laws of physics.

M.'s elaborate show-and-tells have made him beloved by adults and young people throughout the world. *Time* magazine once noted, "What he draws, he draws better than any other pen and ink illustrator in the world." His books have sold more than two million copies in the U.S. alone, and his work has been translated into a dozen languages. Five of his titles (*Cathedral, Castle, City, Pyramid,* and *Mill*) have been adapted for PBS television programs. M. lives and works in Rhode Island.

AWARDS:: *New York Times* Ten Best Illustrated Books, 1973; Caldecott Medal Honor, 1974 for *Cathedral,* 1978 for *Castle*; American Institute of Architects Medal, 1978; *Way Things Work*: ALA Best Books for Young Adults, 1980; Hans Christian Andersen Illustrator Medal, 1984; Caldecott Medal, 1991, for *Black and White*; *Building Big*: ALA Notable Children's Books, 2001; *Motel of the Mysteries*: ALA Best Books for Young Adults, 1979; *Mosque: Publisher's Weekly* Best Children's Books, 2003. ALA Notable Children's Books, 2004. SLJ Best Books for Children, 2003.

FURTHER WORKS: *Great Moments in Architecture,* 1978; *Mill,* 1983; *BAAA,* 1985; *Why the Chicken Crossed the Road,* 1987; *Ship,* 1993; *Shortcut,* 1995; *Rome Antics,* 1997; *Building the Book "Cathedral,"* 1999; *Building Big,* 2000; *Mosque,* 2003.

BIBLIOGRAPHY: *Contemporary Authors Online,* 2001; *Dictionary of Literary Biography,* 61; American Writers for Children Since 1960, 1987; *Major Authors and Illustrators for Children and Young Adults,* 1993; http://www.houghtonmifflinbooks.com/authors/macaulay/macaulaybio.shtml.

CHERYL WOLF

MACKLER, Carolyn
Author, B. 1973

With a writing resume that includes articles on sexuality for *Ms.* and *Glamour,* a SERIES of lighthearted personal reflections for *Shape,* and several contemporary SHORT STORIES for *Girl's Life,* M. found her narrative niche in YOUNG ADULT novels. Her debut novel, *Love and Other Four-Letter Words* (2000), her PRINTZ Honor–winning *The Earth, My Butt, and Other Big Round Things* (2003), and *Vegan, Virgin, Valentine* (2004) combine honest explorations of adolescent girls' physical and emotional transformations with a witty, fluid style and immediately recognizable contemporary settings.

M. grew up in New York state. Stories—those she heard from her parents, those she read in young adult novels (Judy BLUME was a favorite), and those she began writing—were a key part of her youth. By her own account, she was boy crazy, but her academic performance was strong enough to earn her admission to Vassar; she graduated in 1995. Since graduaton, M. has worked full time as a writer contributing to magazines and fiction collections. In addition, she edited a *George* magazine book project (*250 Ways to Make America Better,* 1999) and authored an eBook (*The Class of 2000: A Definitive Survey of the New Generation,* 2000) in conjunction with a special CBS News project. She lives in New York City.

M. draws on memories of her own adolescence, along with gleanings from eavesdropping and her continued reading of young adult literature, to write about female characters who triumph over fears and concerns about body image and sexuality as well as other common adolescent concerns. In an interview for her alumni magazine, M. said, "You have these characters who are experiencing things for the first time. Their sense of independence, of their bodies, of their voices, of sex—they're all brand new; what could be better to write about? It is so dynamic, and so vital . . . I'm absolutely fascinated with adolescence. I love transitions, and change is really the signature thing that happens in the TEEN years."

Critics and readers praise M.'s novels for their honest characters and fresh approach. For example, in *The Earth, My Butt, and Other Big Round Things,* the protagonist, Virginia, is a plus-sized teen with clueless parents, an absent best friend, a maybe-boyfriend, and a brother who has fallen from her pedestal of adoration. Eschewing conventional solutions to her dilemmas, Virginia cashes in her savings account to celebrate Thanksgiving in a way she needs to, has her eyebrow pierced, dyes her hair purple, and embraces with zest those things about herself, her family, and her life that she had been avoiding. M. deals with serious issues—including date rape—with humor. In an interview with the British trade publication *Book seller.com,* M. said, "As a writer, you know that you will only have a teenager's attention for a few hours between everything else they do, so you have to make it enjoyable for them to read, but also address really important issues."

Her frank depictions of teen sexuality—in which sexual activity is not condemned, but even portrayed as pleasurable—are likely to be a touchstone for adults who are concerned with the content of young adult literature. M.'s novel *Love and Other Four Letter Words* has already been removed from at least one library collection because of its sexual content. The popularity of *The Earth, My Butt, and Other Big Round Things* with both critics and readers is likely to position that book for challenges as well, given its inclusion of scenes depicting masturbation and adolescent sexual experimentation.

AWARDS: American Library Association's Quick Picks for Young Adult Readers and International Reading Association's Young Adult's Choice, 2001, for *Love and Other Four Letter Words;* 2004 Michael L. Printz honor award; New York Public Library Best Book for the Teen Age, and American Library Association's Best Books for Young Adults, 2004, for *The Earth, My Butt, and Other Big Round Things*; *Vegan Virgin Valentine*: ALA Quick Picks for Reluctant Young Adult Readers, 2005.

FURTHER WORKS: *Vegan Virgina Valentine,* 2004.

BIBLIOGRAPHY: "Author Profile: Carolyn M." AOL TeenReads.com, August 2003. http://aol.teenreads.com/authors/au-mackler-carolyn.asp; Goldberg, Beverly (2001). "Censorship Watch," *American Libraries* 32 (11), 25; Mackler, Carolyn (n.d.). Personal Web page. http://www.carolynmackler.com/index.htm; "Novels for Testing Readers." *The Bookseller.com.* March 18, 2004. http://www.thebookseller.com/?pid=84&did=11524; Sgarro, Amy. "Love is a Four Letter Word." *Vassar Online: The Alumnae/I Quarterly,* Winter 2000. http://www.aavc.vassar.edu/vq/winter2000/BkLove.html.

CAROL L. TILLEY

MACY, Sue
Author and editor, b. May 13, 1954, New York City

M., who grew up in Clifton, New Jersey, was unusually active as a child, playing games such as catch and "Cowboys and Indians." She professes to have been a true tomboy, never having the patience for quiet, indoor games.

The author graduated from Princeton University (B.A. in history and American studies, 1976) and gained her first writing practice as a newspaper intern. She then worked as an editor and news MAGAZINE writer in New York City, where she expanded her research skills and her style. Eventually, she gave up the publishing world to pursue a career as a full-time writer.

M's work reflects her admiration for female athletes. Her 1993 *A Whole New Ball Game: The Story of The All-American Girls Professional Baseball League* received praise for its thorough research and insights into the lives of league members, placing the league in a historical and sociological context. She researched the All-American Girls Professional Baseball League extensively for more than ten years. This included interviews with players, attending the team's reunions, and building an archive of this almost forgotten era in sports history.

M. edited a number of other books about women's athletes. *Play like a Girl: A Celebration of Women in Sports* (1999) and *Girls Got Game: Sport Stories and Poems* (2001) were recognized for drawing parallels between the struggles women faced in both SPORTS and society. The celebration of female athletes, as well as her focus on minority athletes, is highly inspirational for young readers.

In *Bull's-Eye: A Photobiography of Annie Oakley* (2001), M. also focuses on women's attempts to empower themselves. Annie Oakley, a beloved icon of American history who traveled with the Buffalo Bill Wild West Show, comes to life in this readable, attractive BIOGRAPHY based on Oakley's unpublished autobiography and family members' stories; historical photos, a chronology, and a bibliography are included.

AWARDS: ALA Best Books for Young Adults: 1994 for *A Whole New Ballgame* and 1997 for *Winning Ways; Bull's Eye*: ALA Notable Children's Books, 2002.

FURTHER WORKS: *Winning Ways: A Photohistory of American Women in Sports*, 1997; *Barbie: Shooting Hoops*, 1999; *Swifter, Higher, Stronger: A Photographic History of the Summer Olympics*, 2004.

BIBLIOGRAPHY: *Something about the Author*, 2003; *Booklist*, November 2001; Sue M. website http://www.suemacy.com.

CHRISTINE MARIA WELTER

MADARAS, Lynda
Author, b. 11 July 1947, New Jersey

M. began publishing novels after earning a bachelor's degree from Carnegie-Mellon University in 1969. M. has received considerable recognition for her books about growing up and going through puberty. Her first puberty book, *The "What's Happening to My Body?" Book for Girls* (2000), was a collaboration with her daughter Area. The partnership worked well—Area's contributions as an adolescent provided an appropriate point of view for the intended audience. The two went on to write other books on the topic, including *My Body, My Self for Boys* (2000), *My Body, My Self for Girls* (2000), and *My Feelings, My Self* (2000). Their workbooks, such as *My Body, My Self for Girls*, contain quizzes, games, and fun activities for girls going through this challenging stage of life.

M. has published eleven books on health, childhood, and parenting, including novels in the *What's Happening to My Body* SERIES. She addresses young teens with a unique, nonthreatening style, providing excellent oganization and a thorough coverage of the adolescent experience. Her most recent novel, *Ready, Set, Grow!: A "What's Happening to My Body?" Book for Younger Girls* (2003), applies to a younger audience than her previous books, due to an earlier onset of puberty in many children today. The book includes actual questions and comments from young girls.

More than twenty years as a sex and health education teacher in Pasadena and Santa Monica, California, has provided M. with expertise in the area of adolescent TEENS. She is well known by librarians, nurses, and teachers. M. has made numerous appearances on Oprah, Today, Good Morning American, CNN, and PBS. In addition, she is quoted in newspapers and magazines. Currently, M. resides in California and continues to write informative novels for young adults. She also teaches puberty classes and workshops.

AWARDS: *The "What's Happening to My Body?" Book for Boys: A Growing up Guide for Parents and Sons*, 2000, and *The "What's Happening to My Body?" Book for Girls: A Growing Up Guide for Parents and Daughters*, 2000, were selected for "Here We Go Again: Twenty-five Years of Best Books: Selections from 1967–1992"; ALA Best Books for Young Adults: 1983 for *"What's Happening to My Body?" Book for Girls: A Growing Up Guide for Parents and Daughters* and 1988 for *Lynda Madaras Talks to Teens about AIDS*.

FURTHER WORKS: *Child's Play*, 1978; *The Alphabet Connection*, 1979; *Great Expectations*, 1980; *Womancare*, 1981; *Mother/Daughter*, 1983; *Autobiography of Jane Patterson*, 1983; *Lynda Madaras' Growing Up Guide for Girls*, 1986; *What's Happening to My Body?* 1987; *Lynda Madaras Talks to Teens about AIDS, an Essential Guide for Parents, Teachers and Young People*, 1988.

BIBLIOGRAPHY: May, H., ed. *Contemporary Authors*, vol. 107 (1983); scholar.lib.vt.edu; www.kidsreads.com; www.newmarketpress.com.

JODI PILGRIM

MAGAZINES AND PERIODICALS

M. for TEENS are a relative newcomer in the periodical market. The first magazine actually published with teenagers in mind was *Seventeen* (1944). Following the huge popularity that this magazine engendered, other periodicals emerged in the teen magazine arena, most notably *MAD* (1952) and *YM* (1953). During the 1960s and 1970s, the push was on to publish magazines that related to the teen customs and society of those eras. Publications such as *Rolling Stone* (1967), *Tiger Beat* and *Teen Beat* (1976), and *Right on!* (1971) found that teens responded to specialty-style magazines. And yet the "old favorites" survived. As the decade of the 1990s came to an end, publications that focused on teens and their culture became a marketing focal point.

Today's teens are completely different as an age group. They are the fastest growing population segment and they have enormous spending power. Teenagers have a major influence on household spending and teenagers who read magazines are the most influential. Contrary to the common stereotype, many YOUNG ADULTS do enjoy reading in their spare time. Teens look to their magazines for guidance in a lot of areas. Teens are really obsessed with what they look like and with their relationships. They're also interested in all kinds of role models. So by combining celebrities with fashion, romance, beauty, and advice on all sorts of "problems," you have an almost certainly popular magazine. Periodicals such as *Teen, Sassy, Teen Vogue, Cosmo Girl, Elle Girl,* and *Twist* cater to savvy teenage girls.

Teenage boys, however, have provided a challenge to magazine publishers until the beginning of 2000, when periodicals that cater to boys' interest emerged. Now *Gampro and Nintendo Power* attract computer gamers. *Thrasher, Transworld Skateboarding, SLAP,* and *Skateboarder* are popular with skateboarding enthusiasts. *Spin, Vibe,* and *Source* are aimed at the music-minded young adult. Other SPORTS such as snowboarding, inline skating, BMX biking, and surfing have specialty periodicals that are available.

Entertainment magazines draw readers from both sexes. *Teen People* tops the charts and is one of the most widely read M. *TeenInk* and *Teen Voices* are among several periodicals that offer an opportunity to publish teen-generated POETRY, SHORT STORIES, articles, and more. Another market that publishers are breaking ground in is the Hispanic teen market. *Teen People en Español, Latin Girl,* and *Latina* are a few examples of what is available today. Today's teenager is more Internet savvy, and current magazine publishers have begun to design and offer online M. similar to their paper counterparts. *Seventeen, Teen People,* and *TeenInk* are but a few. And original online "e-zines" or "zines" are growing in popularity. Examples of current sites are *Cyberteen* (www.cyberteen.com) and *Teens Hangout* (www.studentcenter.org). Another phenomenon that has begun to emerge is the "magalog or catazine"—hybrids of magazines and direct mail pieces (Merrill, 3). *MXG* and *Alloy* are two of the more prominent in this market.

The vast majority of teenagers who have money to spare subscribe to their own choice of M. But what about those teens who can't afford the luxury of buying magazines off the rack, let alone through a subscription? Schools and public libraries try to provide a variety of teen-oriented M. for these patrons as well as for others who may utilize the resources of the library. Many libraries house most of the "youth" periodicals in the children's room. But more and more libraries are finding a physical niche/area for their teenage clientele and are placing the magazines that would attract that specific age group in the niche. Those teens that frequent the library find their favorites with no problem. But in order to attract nonusers and bring them inside the library's walls, library staffs who work with teens find different ways to publicize their collection. Having a display of "new" titles is easy to do. Printing up a bookmark or small flier that might appeal to the teens and passing the material out in school, recreation centers, youth organizations, and teen-related businesses can get the attention of the young adults who may not frequent the library. Designing a Web page that is "cool" and having a link on the library's homepage can be an effective way to lure teens to the library to check out the magazine collection. Designing a contest for the community or planning a program that would link to the magazine collection are other ways to promote the teen magazine collection. One example would be to have a "fashion fair," with beauty advisers, fashion consultants, or representatives from local clothing stores in the library along with the magazines that promote the topic on display. Another idea would be to hold in-line or skateboarding clinics with M. nearby so that teens could look at the periodicals or even check them out. Once it starts being used, the collection will grow in popularity, as word-of-mouth is also a great resource for librarians.

If you have an excellent collection of M. for teens, then you are in touch with your patrons' needs and wants. But if starting a collection is on your mind and you are in a quandary as to which magazines to choose, ask the people who will read them—the teens themselves. Survey them on their favorite M. titles. If you have a teen board/committee, ask members what they would like to see, or even have the group prepare a list for inclusion on the shelves. Make sure that you have a variety of specialty magazines as well as general periodicals.

So what might constitute a core collection of M. for teens? Here is a suggested list for possible inclusion in a public or school setting: General Interest and

Celebrities: *Teen People, Teen People en Español;* Girls: *CosmoGirl, Seventeen, Twist, YM, LatinGirl, Jump;* Guys: *MH-18;* News: *Newsweek, Time;* Business: *Teenpreneur;* Music: *Vibe, Source, Spin, Alternative Press, Right on!, Word Up;* Sports: *ESPN, Sports Illustrated;* Inline skating: *Daily Bread;* Skateboarding: *Thrasher, Transworld Skateboarding, SLAP;* Snowboarding: *Transworld Snowboarding;* Professional Wrestling, *WWE, Pro Wrestling Illustrated;* Computer Gaming: *GamePro, PC Gamer, Computer Games;* SCIENCE FICTION/FANTASY: *Starlog, Realms of Fantasy;* Fashion: *Teen Vogue, Elle Girl.* Humor: *MAD;* Literary: *TeenInk, Cicada, Merlyn's Pen;* Entertainment: *J-14, Entertainment Weekly.*

BIBLIOGRAPHY: Bennett, Jo. "Beyond Games and Sports: New Service Titles Target Male Teens." *Folio,* May 1, 2000. http://foliomag.com/ar/marketing_beyond_games_sports/; Carr, David. "Media; Coming Late, Fashionably, Teen Vogue Joins a Crowd." *New York Times,* January 13, 2003. http://query.nytimes.com/search/restricted/article?res = FA0611FF3F550 C708DDDA80894DB404482; Fine, Jana. "M. and Webzines for the Way Cool Set." *School Library Journal* (November 1996): 34; Fine, Jon, and Katie Johnson. "Teen Title Crush Leads to Circ Cuts." *Advertising Age,* July 7, 2003, 21; Harvey, Mary. "Let's Hear it for the Boys." *American Demographics,* August 2000, 30; Merrill, Christina. "Keeping up with Teens." *American Demographics,* October 1999, 27; Scarlett, Stephanie. "Magazines for Teens." *The Journal Gazette,* April 27, 2002; http://www.fortwayne.com; Steil, Jennifer. "Youth Market Bustling: Teen Buying Power Fuels Girl Titles," *Folio,* February 1, 2001. http://foliomag.com/ar/marketing_youth_market_bustling/; "Study Demonstrates That Teens Read: Young People Who Read Have a Heavy Influence on Family Spending." *Chain Drug Review,* February 18, 2002, 53; "Who Are These Kids?" *Promo,* July 1, 1999. http://www.promomagazine.com/ar/marketing_kids/.

JANA FINE

MAHY, Margaret
Author, b. 21 March 1936, Whakatane, New Zealand

Few YA authors have provoked as much serious literary criticism as M. It is a tribute to the author that her novels are immensely readable and well written. Magical elements blend with ordinary reality to depict a world immediately recognizable to TEENAGER readers—one in which the fantastic, bewildering truth lurks beneath the mundane, everyday reality.

M. is a native of NEW ZEALAND, but has said in interviews that her early reading experience was largely in books by English authors with settings in England. In the 1989 Arbuthnot lecture, M. suggests that this may have influenced her fluid vision of the truth; because it helped her to see that it is possible for Christmas to be both a time of beach vacations and of "dark firs on snowy hillsides." The child of Frances George, a builder and May, a teacher, M. earned a B.A. from the University of New Zealand in 1958. She also attended the New Zealand Library School and worked as a LIBRARIAN before becoming a full-time writer. The ambition to be a writer inspired her to progress from a "listener" to a "teller, then a reader, and then a writer." Her early work included POETRY and PICTURE BOOKS with a heavy mix of young adult novels. She continues to produce books for readers of all ages.

M.'s career was given an unexpected jump-start forward when Helen Hoke Watts visited her in New Zealand in 1968. Publisher Watts admired the variety and quality of M.'s projects; she purchased every single manuscript M. had written with a promise that she would have first chance at any other forthcoming manuscripts.

The Haunting (1977), M.'s first book for young adults, embarks on several themes that continue to play a part in her work. FAMILY relationships, the shifting nature of truth, and a dense prose alert to the poetry of the everyday remain hallmarks of her work. In *The Haunting,* Barney struggles to come to terms with the family inheritance of magic that he feels is a curse rather than a blessing. His extended family both empowers and threatens his self-determination. In *The Changeover* (1984), M. parallels Laura's changing perceptions of self, her relationships with her divorced parents, and her ordinary adolescent confusion with her new perception of herself as a "sensitive" and potential witch. In the course of the novel, M. follows Laura's relationships with the Carlisle family (and theirs with one another) and the new realities that Laura discovers when she makes the changeover. *Catalogue of the Universe* (1985) abandons the overtly supernatural elements of *The Haunting* and *The Changeover*; nevertheless, the mysteriously slippery nature of teen reality, convincingly rendered, leaves the reader with a similarly dislocated sense of hyper-reality. Angela's search for her father and Tycho's unhappy love for her send the two on a reeling voyage of discovery that eventually leads them to a safe haven.

Memory (1987) is another story set in an alternate reality. Here, Johnny's belief that loss of memory would provide him relief from the self-accusations left by a childhood tragedy clash with the experience of Sophie's Alzheimer's disease. Sophie's perceptual confusion eventually helps Johnny to clarify his emotional chaos.

Anthea retreats from the terrifying new reality of her status as an orphan into a dangerous supernatural world inhabited by a ghost in *Dangerous Spaces* (1991). Her practical cousin Flora fights to drag Anthea back from the drug-like beauty of this dream reality. Anthea needs to come to terms with Flora's bumptious family; her ability to abandon the seduction of the supernatural is tied to accepting the tragedy in her past and bonding with her new family. The most dangerous aspect of Anthea's situation is her ability to see reality as sliding from one version to another. The dangerous nature of uncertain reality is explored from another perspective in *Underrunners* (1992); what starts as a FANTASY game between two friends shifts by imperceptible degrees to a frightening actuality. Elements of fantasy and reality combine to present the characters and the reader with an awareness of the fragile nature of the truth. Many of the stories in M.'s collection, *The Door in the Air and Other Stories* (1988), explore this same idea; in "The Bridge Builder," for example, bridges become a variety of objects other than bridges—musical instruments and bird cages. Their primary purpose is unclear—what role are they meant to serve? This question, which resonates for young adult readers; implict in much of M.'s work.

A more recent novel, *Alchemy* (2003), makes powerful use of the central metaphor of transformation in the lives of teens. Roland's life appears to be ideal on the surface, but his inner self is a mass of insecurities, making him easy for an unscrupulous teacher to exploit. Jess's life appears to be in disarray, but her social ineptitude conceals a strong sense of personal integrity. Small wonder that Roland finds her attractive. When the two become embroiled in a magical battle for control, it mirrors their inner struggles to become themselves. This is the true alchemical transformation of the book, because Roland and Jess combine to be-

come a stronger and purer substance together than either was before they became friends.

M. is a powerful writer who will not please every reader's taste. Her message of "slippery" reality, brought under control by the power of relationships and truth to one's self, is not a message every teen wants to hear. The poetic language requires an attentive audience, able to tolerate subtlety. For the right reader, M. is an intoxicating glimpse of possibility and truth.

AWARDS: Carnegie Medal, British Library Association: 1982 for *The Haunting*, 1986 for *The Changeover: A Supernatural Romance*, and 1987 for *Memory*; *The Changeover*: International Board on Books for Young People, 1986, ALA Notable Children's Book, 1984, and *Boston Globe–Horn Book* Award Honor book, 1985, selected for "Here We Go Again: 25 Years of Best Books: Selections from 1967 to 1992"; ALA Best Books for Young Adults: 1986 for *The Changeover*, 1987 for *The Tricksters*, and 1988 for *Memory*; 1985 Esther Glen Award, *The Changeover*; 1993 AIM Children's Book Award, *Underrunners*; 2003 New Zealand Post Award, *Alchemy*; *Catalogue of the Universe*: 1986 ALA Best Books for Young Adults.

FURTHER WORKS: *The Tricksters*, 1986; *The Other Side of Silence*, 1995; *Don't Read This: and Other Tales of the Unnatural*, 1998; *24 Hours*, 2000.

BIBLIOGRAPHY: *Contemporary Authors Online*, 2001; Kelly, Patricia, "Margaret M.," *Writers for Young Adults*, Ted Hipple, ed., 1997.

CATHY CHAUVETTE

MAJOR, Kevin (Gerald)
Author, b. 12 September 1949, Stephenville, Newfoundland, Canada

To understand M.'s importance to CANADIAN young adult literature, compare him to American counterparts Robert CORMIER and Judy BLUME. He was as influential on the burgeoning Canadian YOUNG ADULT level in the late 1970s as these two writers were in its U.S. development. It was namely these American authors who increased M.'s awareness of young adult literature and Canada's growing need for a comparable type of realism. M. has since become one of Canada's premier authors for young adults, introducing his native province, Newfoundland, to a wide literary audience.

While substitute teaching, M. observed the literature his students favored and realized that there was a need for realistic literature that dealt with adolescence in Newfoundland. In M.'s own words, he "wanted to capture the Newfoundland way of life" and convey the way "the young are caught between the old traditional values of Newfoundland outport society and the onslaught of American popular culture."

In such novels as *Hold Fast* (1978) and *Far from Shore* (1980), M. creates characters that struggle to find their identity under distressing circumstances. *Hold Fast,* a novel frequently compared to Twain's *Huckleberry Finn,* is M.'s first attempt at conveying adolescence in Newfoundland. Fourteen-year-old Michael, orphaned by the DEATH of his parents, is forced to move from his rural village to the comparatively large city where his oppressive uncle and cousin reside. M.'s descriptions of Michael's connection to nature and his bewilderment by the artificial city are peppered with authentic dialect that closely connects the book to Newfoundland. In his debut novel, M. produced a work that explores national pride, social prejudice, and adolescent confusion about identity. *Far from Shore* once again presents a Newfoundland TEENAGER, one who allows his life to deteriorate when his father's alcoholism damages familial harmony. The lesson of personal responsibility for one's mistake is, however, a universal message that transcends geographic borders. Multiple voices tell M.'s story through different perspectives and different opinions, although some critics found the various voices to be disjointed and confusing.

Alternative narratives are taken further in *Thirty-six Exposures* (1984), a compilation of thirty-six disconnected chapters that are themselves the incomplete exposures of a complex story. While a *School Library Journal*'s reviewer believed that the exposures leave characters incompletely developed, *Booklist* commented that they give the story momentum.

With these first three novels, M. gained a reputation for the explicit sexual content and street language in his writing, a reputation that caused his books to be banned in several school libraries. M. retaliated against this censorship by making it a topic in his 1991 publication, *Eating between the Lines.* Through humor, the novel contains "a serious message about the importance of allowing children and young adults to experience literature in all its richness."

M. creates honest portrayals of characters that reside in atypical environments as he exposes the anxi-

ety and fears that accompany adolescence. This combination, along with his experimental styles of multiple narratives, has made M. a strong voice for both Newfoundlanders and outsiders alike. M. is also the author of children's PICTURE BOOKS and a strong contributor of adult fiction and nonfiction books based on his Canadian roots.

AWARDS: *Hold Fast:* Canada Council Children's Literature Prize, Canadian Library Association Book of the Year Award, Ruth Schwartz Children's Book Award, all 1979, and Hans Christian Andersen Honor List citation, International Board on Books for Young People, and *School Library Journal* Best Books of the Year citation, both 1980; *Far from Shore:* Young Adult Caucus of the Saskatchewan Library Association Canadian Young Adult Book Award, and *School Library Journal* Best Books of the Year citation, both 1981; *Eating between the Lines*: Nova Scotia Library Association Ann Conner-Brimer Award and Canadian Library Association Book of the Year Award, both 1992; 1992 Canadian Author Association Vicky Metcalf Award for breadth of work; *The House of the Wooden Santas*: Mr. Christie Book Award and Nova Scotia Library Association Ann Conner-Brimer Award, both 1998; Newfoundland and Labrador Arts Council Artist-of-the-Year Award.

SELECTED FURTHER WORKS: *Dear Bruce Springsteen,* 1987; *Blood Red Ochre,* 1989; *Diana: My Autobiography,* 1993; *No Man's Land,* 1995; *Gaffer,* 1997; *House of Wooden Santas,* 1997; *Ann and Seamus,* 2004.

BIBLIOGRAPHY: Beaton, Virginia. "Onward and Upward." *Books in Canada,* October 1993; *Children's Literature Review,* vol. 11, 1986; *Contemporary Authors Online,* 2002; *Contemporary Literary Criticism,* vol. 26, 1983; Estes, Sally. Review of *Thirty-six Exposures, Booklist,* November 1, 1984; Fecher, Ellen M. Review of *Thirty-six Exposures, School Library Journal,* February 1985; Noyes, Stacey. *Writing Stories, Making Pictures,* 1994; *Something about the Author,* vol. 82, 1995.

RACHEL WITMER

MARGARET A. EDWARDS AWARD

Administered by the Young Adult Library Services Association (YALSA), a division of the American Library Association (ALA), the annual Margaret A. Edwards Award recognizes authors who over time have made major contributions to YOUNG ADULT literature in their writing. The award usually honors an author for several exceptional books from his or her body of work, but there have been occasions when authors are recognized for a singular important achievement. In 1996, Judy BLUME received the award for her novel *Forever,* which revolutionized the way TEEN sexuality was depicted in young adult fiction. Nancy GARDEN received the award in 2003 for *Annie on My Mind,* a groundbreaking novel depicting the ROMANTIC love between two teenage girls. Garden's novel was the first young adult novel to depict a homosexual relationship as "normal."

By the mid-1980s, young adult literature had established itself as a serious body of literature and a respected field of study. In 1986, Neff A. Perlman, publisher of *School Library Journal,* approached editor-in-chief Lillian N. Gerhardt with a proposal to establish an award to recognize young adult authors with a distinguished body of work. Gerhardt decided it was more appropriate for *School Library Journal* to sponsor the award, so she asked YALSA (then called the Young Adult Services Division) to develop the criteria for the award and administer it.

The Young Adult Services Division's then Past-President Joan Atkinson, Vice-President/President-Elect Vivian Wynn, and President Marian Hargrove worked with a special committee to develop the guidelines for what would initially be called the *School Library Journal* Young Adult Author Award/ Selected and Administered by the American Library Association's Young Adult Services Division. The *ALA Handbook of Organization, 2003–2004* states that the charge of the committee is: "To select a living author or coauthor whose book or books, over a period of time, have been accepted by young people as an authentic voice that continues to illuminate their experiences and emotions, giving insight into their lives. The book or books should enable them to understand themselves, the world in which they live, and their relationship with others and with society." In addition to these broad goals, specific criteria were established for selecting a recipient and the particular book or books for which the recipient would be cited. When choosing an author and naming specific books honored in the award, the committee must consider the following: "Does the book(s) help adolescents to become aware of themselves and to answer their questions about their role and importance in relationships, society and in the world?; Is the book(s) of acceptable literary quality?; Does the book(s) satisfy the curiosity of young adults and yet help them thought-

fully build a philosophy of life?; Is the book(s) currently popular with a wide range of young adults in many different parts of the country?; Do the books serve as a 'window to the world' for young adults?" Originally establish as a biennial honor, the award is now given annually. In 1990, the name of the award shortened to the Margaret A. Edwards Award.

A committee of five, three elected and two appointed, is responsible for the selection of the award recipient, who receives a cash prize of $1,000 and a citation. *School Library Journal* is the donor of the award and also funds the administrative costs. The award is presented to the author at a luncheon held during the American Library Association annual conference. The winner is required to attend the event to accept the award and to make a brief acceptance speech.

The award was named in honor of a pioneering LIBRARIAN who worked for the Enoch Pratt Free Library in Baltimore. Assigned to work with adolescents and their recreational reading in the 1930s, Edwards found her true calling. Her approach to working with adolescents was groundbreaking. Among her many unorthodox methods was the then unheard of practice of soliciting recommendations and suggestions from teenagers to inform her collection development. Another revolutionary practice of Edwards was going into high schools to present book talks to students. Edwards set the foundations for outreach, programming, reader's advisory, youth participation, and many other facets of contemporary young adult library services.

In 1988, the first Margaret A. Edwards Award was awarded to S. E. HINTON. The recipients who have followed are: Richard PECK (1990), Robert CORMIER (1991), Lois DUNCAN (1992), M. E. KERR (1993), Walter Dean Myers (1994), Cynthia VOIGT (1995), Judy BLUME (1996), Gary Paulsen (1997), Madeleine L'ENGLE (1998), Anne MCCAFFREY (1999), Chris CRUTCHER (2000), Robert LIPSYTE (2001), Paul ZINDEL (2002), Nancy GARDEN (2003), Ursula K. LE GUIN (2004), and Francesca Lia BLOCK (2005).

BIBLIOGRAPHY: *ALA Handbook of Organization 2003–2004;* Carter, Betty. "Who Is Margaret Edwards and What Is This Award Being Given in Her Honor?" *The ALAN Review* (Spring 1992): 45–48; www.ala.org/yalsa/booklistsawards/margaretedwards.

EDWARD T. SULLIVAN

478

MARILLIER, Juliet
Author, b. 27 July 1948, Dunedin, New Zealand

M., who didn't start writing until her children were grown, vowed to become a published author by the age of fifty or to give up the idea altogether. Before that, she studied music and languages at Otago University, working her way through college as a LIBRARIAN's assistant. After graduation, M. taught music students and lectured on music history, performed as a professional singer, worked in a children's library and at a local theater, married, and had four children. Having moved from NEW ZEALAND to AUSTRALIA in 1976, M. was living in Perth, western Australia, when she sold her first novel; she got the call from her publisher on her fiftieth birthday.

M. credits her affinity for the stories and music of Scotland and Ireland to her upbringing in an area with strong Scottish roots. The celtic influence of the people around her sparked an early and lasting fascination with the history, music, and folklore of those isles, an appreciation evident in each of her novels to date. M.'s styles, which she calls "magical history," integrates history, ROMANCE, adventure, and magic into works thick with folklore, myth, and archetypal—though often historically based—characters. Though often dealing with harsh subjects such as rape, murder, betrayal, FAMILY loyalty, and teachery, M.'s use of the shared body of myth and folklore give her books a mythic core through which horrific events and emotions may be interpreted.

For example, the Sevenwaters Trilogy, set in the ninth century during Ireland's Dark Ages, describes a period in Irish history rife with political machinations and religious upheaval, but also illuminates everyday mysteries and deep-seated beliefs that look much like magic to today's readers. The SERIES begins with *Daughter of the Forest* (2000), a retelling of the Grimms' tale of the "Six Swans." Sorcha, youngest of seven children (and the only girl), endures unspeakable hardships—and a vow of silence—while trying to undo a curse placed on her brothers by the evil Lady Oonagh. *Son of the Shadows* (2001) continues the story as seen through the eyes of Sorcha's daughter, Liadan. After inadvertently meeting and falling in love with a mercenary (who is a personal enemy of her family), Liadan learns to use her healing powers to mend the rifts between warring kingdoms and between her husband and father. The final book

in the trilogy, *Child of the Prophecy* (2002), concludes the story of Sorcha's family. Fainne, Sorcha's niece, must travel to Sevenwaters to reclaim their heritage, but both her journey and her life are threatened by her evil fairy grandmother, whose plotting goes deeper than anyone in the family suspects.

M.'s next book, *Wolfskin* (2003), tells the story of Eyvind and Somerled, blood brothers whose choices place them on opposite sides of a bloody conflict. Set in Norway and the Orkney Islands, the novel depicts the fascinating life of Thor's warriors—called Wolfskins—who dedicate their entire existence to his service. When Eyvind, a young but revered Wolfskin, accompanies Somerled to the Light Isles in the hope of forming a new Viking community, he is forced to see his boyhood friend in a new light and to choose between his oath to his blood brother and his desire to protect the island's folk. The Saga of the Light Isles duology continues in *Foxmask* (2004).

AWARDS: *Romantic Times* Readers' Choice Award for Best FANTASY Novel, 2000, for *Daughter of the Forest*; 2001 American Library Association Best Books for Young Adults for *Daughter of the Forest*; 2001 American Library Association Alex Award for *Daughter of the Forest*; 2000 Aurealis Award for Fantasy Novel for *Son of the Shadows*.

FURTHER WORKS: "Otherling," *Realms of Fantasy,* April 2001, and *Andromeda Spaceways Inflight Magazine,* June 2003, Issue 7; "In Coed Celyddon," in *The Road to Camelot,* ed. Sophie Masson (short story) 2003; *Foxmask* (novel, sequel to *Wolfskin*) 2004; *The Dark Mirror* (novel) 2005.

BIBLIOGRAPHY: Author website: http://www.vianet .net.au/~marill/default.htm; *Contemporary Authors Online,* Gale 2004. Reproduced in *Biography Resource Center.* 2004. http://galenet.galegroup.com/ servlet/BioRC; "Juliet M." *Authors and Artists for Young Adults,* vol. 50, 2003. Reproduced in *Biography Resource Center,* 2004: http://galenet.galegroup .com/servlet/BioRC; *Contemporary Authors Online,* Gale 2004. Reproduced in *Literature Resource Center, Author Resource Pages,* 2004. http://galenet.gale group.com/servlet/BioRC; *Library Journal,* May 15, 2000, *Publisher's Weekly,* April 16 2001; *Kliatt,* July 2002; *Kirkus Reviews,* May 15 2003; *Booklist,* May 15 2003.

JULIE BARTEL

MARINO, Jan
Author, b. 1936, Boston, Massachusetts

The author of numerous YA problem novels, M. began writing at an early age by making up new conclusions to traditional stories, giving them her own original "happy endings." When she was nine, M.'s brother Robbie died. Wanting to keep his memory alive when no one in her family would talk about him, M. began to write stories about Robbie. Later, this experience of the DEATH of a sibling became the basis for *Eighty-eight Steps to September* (1989) and enabled M. to finally accept the loss of her brother. With *The Day that Elvis Came to Town* (1991), M. once again drew upon her FAMILY's history for the setting and characters. While she never lived in the South or in a boarding house, M.'s aunt in Massachusetts owned a boarding house with varied and interesting boarders. Some of the more colorful boarders and the aunt appear in *The Day that Elvis Came to Town* (1991).

M. offers no easy answers to her characters or her readers, but rather offers them the wisdom and courage to believe in themselves. The young adults in M.'s novels are developed with exceptional compassion for the characters and their unique predicaments. Considering the happy endings that M. added to her stories as a child, it is not surprising that many of her young-adult novels are resolved with a positive, affirming, and hopeful message for her audience. M. says that much of her personal reward for writing comes from hearing the insightful voices of her characters. With their message of hope, M.'s YA novels have a universal appeal and have been translated and published in England, France, and Italy.

AWARDS: *The Day That Elvis Came to Town:* New York Public Library Book for the Teen Age, *Booklist* Editor's Choice, *School Library Journal* Best Book, and Alabama Reading Incentive Award, all 1992; 1993 New York Public Library Book for the Teen Age, *Like Some Kind of Hero*; 1999 Rocky Mountain Women's Institute grant for workshops encouraging TEEN development of crisis management through writing.

FURTHER WORKS: *Like Some Kind of Hero,* 1992; *For the Love of Pete,* 1993; *The Mona Lisa of Salem Street,* 1995; *Searching for Atticus,* 1997; *Letter to my Dad,* 1997; *Write Me a Happy Ending,* 2001.

BIBLIOGRAPHY: *Children's Books and Their Creators.* Edited by Anita Silvey, 1995; *Contemporary Authors Online,* 2003. Reproduced in *Biography Resource Center,* 2003. http://www.galenet.com/servlet/BioRC; "Jan M." *Authors and Artists for Young Adults,* 2001. Reproduced in *Biography Resource Center,* 2003. http://www.galenet.com/servlet/BioRC; "Jan M." *Young Audiences: A Bright Idea in Education,* 2003.

http://www.youngaudiencescolorado.org/residency/jan_marino.htm

SARA CATHERINE HOWARD

MARRIN, Albert
Author, b. July 24, 1936, New York City

M., professor and chairman of the history department at Yeshiva University in New York City, has successfully made the past accessible to young readers in more than two dozen books devoted to subjects in both United States and world history. Prior to becoming a university professor, M. worked for nine years as a social studies teacher in a New York City public junior-high school. A lifelong New Yorker, M. earned his undergraduate degree from the City University of New York and his Ph.D. in history from Columbia University. M.'s many years of experience teaching young adults is reflected in the respect he shows for his audience in his books.

Superior to most INFORMATIONAL books for YA and in league with literature by such authors as Russell FREEDMAN, Milton MELTZER, and Jim MURPHY, M.'s works challenge readers to understand historical events and figures in both the cultural and social contexts of all human history. Scrupulously researched and skillfully written with a scholar's sensibilities, M. makes abundant use of primary sources to bring history to life for young people, retelling it in a way that they find accessible and appealing.

Typically focusing on dramatic moments and famous personalities to tell the story of a pivotal historical event, M.'s books cover a wide span of U.S. history, from the colonial period through the late 20th century. The Civil War is a subject that M. has repeatedly visited in books like *"Unconditional Surrender": U.S. Grant and the Civil War* (1993), *Virginia's General: Robert E. Lee and the Civil War* (1994), and *Commander in Chief: Abraham Lincoln and the Civil War* (1997). The history of the native Indians of the Great Plains is another subject M. has explored in several works: *War Clouds in the West: Indians and Cavalrymen, 1860–1890* (1984); *Cowboys, Indians, and Gunfighters: The Story of the Cattle Kingdom* (1993); *Plains Warrior: Chief Quanah Parker and the Comanches* (1996); and *Sitting Bull and His World* (2000). M. has also explored the fate of indigenous civilizations under Spanish colonialism, including *Aztecs and Spaniards: Cortes and the Conquest of*

Mexico (1986), *Inca and Spaniard: Pizarro and the Conquest of Peru* (1989), and *Empires Lost and Won: The Spanish Heritage in the Southwest* (1997). Other subjects M. has revisited in his books are piracy, tyrants from history, and World War II.

Reviewers consistently praise M.'s books for their documentation, dramatic writing style, historical insight, readability, and unbiased treatment of controversial subjects. M.'s books have been consistently recognized for their excellence by such organizations as the American Library Association, the Children's Book Council, the National Council for Social Studies, and the Western Writers of America. In 1995, M. received the Washington Children's Books Guild and *Washington Post* Non-Fiction Awards for "outstanding lifetime contribution [that] has enriched the field of children's literature."

AWARDS: *Boston Globe–Horn Book* Honor in 1985 for *1812: The War Nobody Won*; *Boston Globe–Horn Book* Honor in 1994 for *"Unconditional Surrender:" U.S. Grant and the Civil War*; *Boston Globe–Horn Book* Honor in 2000 and Carter G. Woodson Book Award in 2001 for *Sitting Bull and His World*; and numerous citations on ALA lists.

FURTHER WORKS: *1812: The War Nobody Won*, 1985; *The Yanks are Coming: The United States in the First World War*, 1986; *The War for Independence: The Story of the American Revolution*, 1988; *Stalin: Russia's Man of Steel*, 1988; *Napoleon and the Napoleonic Wars*, 1990; *The Spanish-American War*, 1991; *The Sea King: Sir Francis Drake and His Times*, 1995; *Terror of the Spanish Main*, 1999; *George Washington and the Founding of a Nation*, 2001; *Dr. Jenner and the Speckled Monster: The Story of the Conquest of Smallpox*, 2002; *Empires Lost and Won*, 2004; *Old Hickory*, 2004.

BIBLIOGRAPHY: *Something about the Author*, vol. 126, pp. 146–51.

EDWARD T. SULLIVAN

MARRIOTT, Janice
Author, b. 1946, Coventry, England

M. came to NEW ZEALAND as a child of eleven and has since lived and worked in the United States, CANADA, and England. Currently she works as an audio producer for one of New Zealand's leading publishers of reading materials for the national and international market, for which she also writes children's fiction and nonfiction. While M.'s stories for adults have appeared in various MAGAZINES and on radio, her writing for young adults began with a trilogy of humorous novels featuring the very individual Henry Jollifer. The first was *Letters to Lesley* (1989), a lively first person narrative in which Henry tries to marry off his mother. It was followed by *Brain Drain* (1993), in which Henry decides to go overseas, and was concluded by *Kissing Fish* (1997), where Henry's romantic side is developed.

M. is one of the few writers to have successfully contributed to the genre of humorous fiction for New Zealand young adults. The impressive and award-winning (but, since, sadly neglected) *Crossroads* (1995) is an altogether more serious novel, which, as its title suggests, looks closely and incisively into the lives of TEENAGERS at a privotal point; William on the run from memories of his mother's death and the part he played in that, and Ellie, who falls in love with him but is at the same time beginning to assert her individuality. The novel concludes with the bittersweet realisation that the different roads William and Ellie must inevitably travel will mean that "they had all today, and some other days, but maybe not forever."

M. has said in connection with her writing for teenagers that theirs is "a very extreme world . . . you're either full on or totally switched off. I think I enjoy that. I empathise with strong emotions." M.'s more recent work has been for younger readers, although she was awarded the first "Foxton Fellowship"—a writer's residency—in 2001 to work on another novel.

AWARDS: *Crossroads*, 1996 Esther Glen Award; 1996 AIM Senior Fiction and Supreme Wards.

FURTHER WORKS: "Natural Selection" in *Nearly Seventeen: New Zealand Stories*. Edited by Tessa Duder, 1993; *I'm Not a Compost Heap!*, 1995; *Hope's Rainbow*, 1996; *Alien on Wheels*, 1997; *The B4 Battle*, 1997; *The Big Bug Blast*, 1997; *Green Slime Dinner Time*, 1997; *Yates Gardening for Kids: Growing Things to Eat*, 2003.

BIBLIOGRAPHY: Robinson, Roger, and Nelson Wattie, eds. *The Oxford Companion to New Zealand Literature*. 1998; http://www.bookcouncil.org.nz/writers /marriott.htm

BILL NAGELKERKE

MARTIN, Ann Matthews
Author, b. 12 August 1955, Princeton, New Jersey

M. loved books as a child. Her father, *New Yorker* cartoonist Henry Martin, and her mother Edie Martin, a former school teacher, encouraged M. and her sister to read; the parents would often read aloud to them. M.'s favorite books included the classics such as Frances Hodgson BURNETT's *The Secret Garden,* L. Frank Baum's *Wizard of Oz,* and Lewis Carroll's *Alice in Wonderland,* as well as the more contemporary Roald DAHL's *Charlie and the Chocolate Factory* and Astrid Lindgren's *Pippi Longstocking.* M. says, "Reading aloud drew our family together." M.'s teachers noticed her ability to write as early as the fourth grade.

M. graduated from Smith College in 1977; in 1978, she entered the publishing field as an editor of children's books. In 1980, M. began to work on her first book, *Bummer Summer* (1983), which describes a young girl getting acquainted with her stepmother.

M.'s early passion for babysitting started when she was about nine years old. While working in publishing, a colleague suggested that she turn her memories of babysitting into a novel. She followed her memories in creating the book, basing characters and plot lines on actual events. The first book in the Baby-sitters Club SERIES, *Kristy's Great Idea,* was published in 1986; the series that followed has sold nearly 150 million copies to date. The characters in the books come from homes of blended families, single-parent homes, and homes in which grandparents live; besides relating to children who love babysitting, the books also include alternative home lives to the traditional two-parent structure.

Over more than a decade, the members of the club have changed slightly. By the time the series ended in 1999 with *The Fire at Mary Anne's House* (BSC #131), the roster of the club had undergone some changes: Stacey, an original member of the club, moves back to her native city of Manhattan in *Goodbye, Stacey, Goodbye* (BSC#13, 1988) but returns to Stoneybrook after her parents' divorce (#28: *Welcome Back, Stacey,* 1992); Dawn, a member who joined during *Dawn and the Impossible Three* (BSC#5, 1987), left the club to live with her father in California in *Farewell, Dawn* (BSC#88, 1995); Mallory and Jessi join the club around the same time in *Hello, Mallory* (BSC#14, 1988) and *Jessi's Secret Language* (BSC#16, 1989); Abby replaces Dawn (#90: *Welcome to the BSC, Abby,* 1995) and remains in the series until the final book.

This series affected YA LITERATURE in a great way: it got children interested in both reading and babysitting, and provided them with older, albeit a bit too unrealistically wholesome, role models. Children who did not classify themselves as readers found themselves entranced by the world of these teenaged girls. While on tours to promote the series, M. has met readers who dress up like Kristy, Claudia, and other characters in the Baby-Sitters Club.

When the Baby-Sitters Club series ended, M. began a new series that confronts her original characters (Kristy, Claudia, Mary Anne, Stacey) with more contemporary issues. Baby-Sitters Club Friends Forever lasted through twelve books and two super specials. With the final super special *Graduation Day* (2001), M.'s characters graduate from junior-high school and, symbolically, from their childhood. The books, in addition to MOVIES and live action videos based on Baby-Sitters Club characters, have generated more than 30,000 fan club members. The original series has been the framework for three additional series: Little Sister, Baby-Sitters Club MYSTERIES, and California DIARIES. These books have been translated into nineteen languages, indicating their worldwide appeal.

M. is also the author of numerous books outside her popular series. Once Baby-Sitter books began to conclude, the author had more time for outside endeavors. M. and Paula DANZIGER began an E-mail correspondence that resulted in *P. S. Longer Letter Later: A Novel in Letters* (1998) and *Snail Mail No More* (1999), two books about a long distance friendship. M.'s *A Corner of the Universe* explores the fragile bonds of FAMILY and received the 2003 Newbery Honor Book Award.

Because of the wonderful success of M.'s BSC products, she was able to give back to the community in a significant way. In 1990, M. created the Ann M. Martin Foundation to help provide financial support to causes benefiting children, education, literacy programs, homeless people and animals. She says, "[W]hen you're making up a story, you're in charge. You can solve problems the way you wish they could be solved in real life." The foundation is M.'s effort to aid other people with their problems. While she, as one person, can only do so much, her foundation has the means to reach a great number of people and help in the quest to educate all children. Small programs that would otherwise be brushed aside are the foundation's number one target, and money is given to programs both in the United States and foreign countries.

Both through her literary and philanthropic efforts, M. is a paramount figure in YA literature.

AWARDS: 2003 Newbery Honor Book Award, ALA Notable Children's Books, 2003, Dorothy Canfield Fisher Children's Book Award, 2004, *A Corner of the Universe;* numerous Children's Choices; *The Doll People*: ALA Notable Children's Books, 2001, Dorothy Canfield Fisher Children's Book Awards, 2002; *The Meanest Doll in the World*: SLJ Best Books for Children, 2003, *Publisher's Weekly* Best Children's Books, 2003; *Here Today: Booklist* Editor's Choice, 2004.

FURTHER WORKS: *Stage Fright,* 1986; *With You and Without You,* 1986; *Missing Since Monday,* 1987; *Me and Katie (The Pest),* 1987; *Slam Book,* 1987; *Just a Summer Romance,* 1987; *Ten Kids, No Pets,* 1989; *Ma and Pa Dracula,* 1991; *Eleven Kids, One Summer,* 1991; *Leo the Magnificent,* 1996; *The Complete Guide to the Baby-sitters Club,* 1996; *Belle Teal,* 2001; *The Meanest Doll in the World,* 2003; *Here Today,* 2004. SERIES: The Baby-Sitters Club, The Baby-Sitters Club Mysteries; The Baby-Sitters Club Portrait Collections; Baby-Sitters Little Sister; California Diaries; The Kids in Ms. Colman's Class.

BIBLIOGRAPHY: "About Ann M. Martin." Scholastic Biographical sheet.

BERNICE E. CULLINAN AND RACHEL WITMER

MARTINEZ, Victor
Author, poet, b. 1954, Fresno, California

M. grew up in Fresno where he attended California State University. Later he received a postgraduate fellowship to Stanford. Throughout his life M. has worked at a number of different occupations: "as a field laborer, welder, truck driver, firefighter, teacher, and office clerk" (book jacket of *Parrot in the Oven: Mi Vida,* 1996). Yet amidst the list of different things he has "been," M. has been hesitant to call himself a writer. He noted this in his acceptance speech for the National Book Award for Young People's Literature (1996): "I would like to thank . . . some of my teachers that convinced me that I was a writer, even though I doubted it" (National Book Award, 2004). After *Parrot in the Oven,* few critics doubted it; the book has received scores of accolades.

A poet initially, M. wrote *Caring for a House* (1992) and *A la Conquista del Corazon* (with Juan Antonio Diaz, 1993). *Parrot in the Oven: Mi Vida* was M.'s first novel. The novel is about Manny's tough decisions and struggles with love, FAMILY, and

personal identity, about his efforts to grow up and out of the low opinion his father has of him. The widely celebrated novel received much attention for its contemporary and multicultural relevance—the story of a Mexican-American boy's coming of age—and its critical depth.

Rafael Pérez-Torres (2003) notes the importance of the Mexican culture and family history in Manny's self-development. "The narrator is seeking to make sense of [himself] within an alien space," notes Pérez-Torres, and it is his Mexican past that aids Manny in this process. "The calling up of the past," says Pérez-Torres, "helps the [narrator] understand [himself] in a process of growth and transformation."

M. lives in San Francisco. He is a contributor to the *Iowa Review* and *Bloomsbury Review* (*Contemporary Authors,* 2004).

AWARDS: *Parrot in the Oven:* National Book Award for Young People's Literature, 1996; Pura Belpre Author Award, 1998; Americas Award for Children's and YA LITERATURE, 1996; Books for the TEEN Age, 1997, New York Public Library.

REFERENCES: The National Book Award, 2004. http://www.nationalbook.org/nbaacceptspeech_vmartinez.html; *Contemporary Authors Online,* 2004. http://www.galenet.com/servlet/LitRC?finalAuth = true; Pérez-Torres, R. 2003. Placing Loss in Chicano/a Narrative. *Literature and Psychology 49,* 110–27.

MARY MCMILLAN TERRY

MASON, Bobbie Ann
Author, b. 1 May 1940, Mayfield, Kentucky

SHORT STORY writer and novelist, M. says she appreciates the chaos and the meaningless coincidences that occur in everyday life. Having been born and having lived in rural Kentucky, her colorful stories depict working-class "New South" characters with often pathetically low expectations. Delving into her characters' spiritual malaise, she searches for its causes. She is intrigued by the cookie-cutter encroachment of asphalt and plastic commercial districts upon rural landscapes and by the suburban sprawl/mall sameness that has given them a new common language of corporate brand names. Known for her humor, her characters' realistically nuanced speech and the trueness of their tiniest gestures, M. is equally praised for her ability to probe their inner workings.

M.'s first novel, *In Country* (1985), follows Sam, a seventeen-year-old Kentucky girl, on her pilgrimage to the Vietnam Memorial, searching for the meaning behind the DEATH of the father she never knew. In her Kentucky world, replete with the 20th–21st century accoutrements that one critic termed "hick chic," M.'s Sam masterfully conveys the adolescent's ambivalence about confronting and reacting with mature integrity to the truth. The novel was adapted into a HOLLYWOOD FILM in 1988. The quality of the book was recognized by YALSA Preconference members, who chose it for the Nothin' But the Best List— selections from 1970 to 1983.

M.'s short stories, *Shiloh and Other Stories* (1982) and *Love Life: Stories* (1989), have also won much critical acclaim. Her third novel, *Feather Crowns,* set in the Kentucky farm country of the early 1990s, deals with the American way of fame. M.'s *Clear Springs: a Memoir* gave readers a sense of the key formative elements of her writing.

AWARDS: National Book Critics Circle Award nomination, American Book Award nomination, PEN-Faulkner Award for fiction nomination and Ernest Hemingway Foundation Award, all 1983, all for *Shiloh and Other Stories;* American Academy and Institute of Arts and Letters Award, 1984; National Book Critics Circle Award nomination and Southern Book Award, both 1994, both for *Feather Crowns;* Southern Book Award for fiction, Southern Book Critics Circle, 2002, for *Zigzagging Down a Wild Trail.* ALA Best Book for Young Adults, 1985, *In Country.* Selected for "Nothin' but the Best: Best of the Best Books for Young Adults, 1966–1986."

FURTHER WORKS: *Nabokov's Garden: A Guide to Ada,* 1974; *Spence and Lila,* 1988; *Love Life,* 1989; *Girl Sleuth,* 1995; *Midnight Magic: Selected Stories of Bobbie Ann Mason,* 1998; *Zigzagging Down a Wild Trail: Stories,* 2001; *Elvis Presley,* 2002

BIBLIOGRAPHY: *Contemporary Authors Online,* 2003; *World Authors 1980–85, WilsonWeb* online, 2003.

CATHERINE GIVEN

MATAS, Carol

Author, creative writing instructor, b. 14 November 1949, Winnipeg, Manitoba, Canada

M. is one of CANADA's most popular and prolific writers of YA fiction. Her works have been translated into Danish, French, Swedish and Spanish.

After receiving a B.A. in English from the University of Western Ontario (1969), M. studied acting at the Actor's Lab in London, England. Following the birth of her first child, her interest in writing increased greatly. Her first four published novels are works of SCIENCE FICTION, with twelve-year-old Rebecca (named after her daughter) as the protagonist; they explore the threatening implications of contemporary tensions gone awry, from genetic engineering to a futuristic world run by big business. While they are all different, *The D.N.A. Dimension* (1982), *The Fusion Factor* (1986; reissued in 1991 as *It's Up to Us*), *Zanu* (1986), and *Me, Myself and I* (1987) introduce M.'s enduring preoccupation with how one person can make significant changes in the world.

Inspired by her Danish husband's FAMILY stories of World WAR II, M. established herself as a writer of historical fiction for young people with *Lisa* (1987; *Lisa's War,* 1989, U.S. release) and *Jesper* (1989; *Code Name Kris,* U.S. release). Both novels explore the courage and the price paid to save much of the Jewish population in Denmark during Hitler's invasion. Other of M.'s WWII novels deal specifically with the HOLOCAUST: *Daniel's Story* (1993) was published in conjunction with Washington's Holocaust Memorial Museum exhibit, Daniel's Story: Remember the Children. In *After the War* (1996) and *The Garden* (1997), M. tells the story of fifteen-year-old Polish Jew, Ruth Brandenburg, who survives the death camps and arrives in Israel, only to find herself confronted by further threats of violence and aggression in the struggle for a Jewish homeland.

Through compelling stories, characterized by the meticulous research and accurate detail that define her achievement, M.'s other historical fiction also addresses controversial topics: *Sworn Enemies* (1993) looks at the injustices perpetrated by Jews against fellow Jews under Tsar Nicolas II in 19th-century Russia; *The Burning Time* (1994), with its strong feminist stance, tells the story of the wrongfully persecuted women during the witch hunts in 16th-century France; *The War Within* (2000), set during the American Civil War, addresses discrimination against both blacks and Jews; *Rebecca* (2000; *Sparks Fly Upward,* 2002, U.S. release) explores discrimination in 1912 Winnipeg through the crosscultural friendship between the title's Jewish character and Sophie, who is Ukrainian and Christian.

M. uses settings in contemporary times to confront difficult moral issues. For example, *The Race* (1991), *Cloning Miranda* (1999), and *The Second Clone* (2001) look at the complex decision making frequently forced on adolescents by the ethical inadequacy of adults. M.'s most controversial book, however, *The Primrose Path* (1995), is published only in Canada. In taking on the subject of a Jewish Orthodox rabbi who molests children, M. strongly asserts her belief in literature's capacity to empower children with knowledge and recognition rather than denying difficult issues.

In her Mind SERIES, *Of Two Minds* (1994) and three subsequent novels, co-written with Perry Nodelman, M. returns to her early FANTASY interests, a legacy of her literary hero, L. Frank Baum. Her other collaboration has been with her husband Per Brask to adapt *Lisa* and *Jesper* to the stage. She has also created dramatic adaptations of *Sworn Enemies* and *Telling* (1998). M's latest venture is the Rosie series: *Rosie in New York: Gotcha!; Rosie in Chicago: Playball!,* and *Rosie in L.A.: Action!*

M. is a writer who takes risks. Her novels probe intense, serious issues, challenging her audience to recognize the complex variables at the heart of moral truths. The interest that she elicits for her characters and their stories prevent any hint of didacticism. She uses the young adult fiction convention of first-person narration to give broad ethical dilemmas a human face, and her emphasis on dramatic presentation through dialogue, with narration focusing on the descriptions of the scene's physical details, has a special appeal to young readers. Despite her dark themes, her works fulfill her own stated purpose in writing: to impart "the pleasure of reading."

AWARDS: *Lisa,* 1987: Sydney Taylor Book Award, Geoffrey Bilson Award, Fiction for Young Readers, Young Adults' Choices by the International Reading Association; *Jesper,* 1989: Sydney Taylor Book Award; *After the War* (1996) and *The Garden* (1997): Jewish Book Award; *After the War:* 1997 ALA Best Book of the Year for Young Adults; *Sworn Enemies* (1993): Sydney Taylor Award

FURTHER WORKS: *Adventure in Legoland,* 1991; *Safari Adventure in Legoland,* 1993; *The Lost Locket,* 1994; *More Minds,* 1996; *The Freak,* 1997; *Greater Than Angels,* 1998; *In My Enemy's House,* 1998; *Out of Mind,* 1998; *Meeting of Minds,* 1999; Dear Canada series: *Footsteps in the Snow: The Red River Diary of*

Isobel Scott, Rupert's Island, 1815, 2002; *Devorah,* Toronto, WW2, forthcoming.

BIBLIOGRAPHY: Caie, Graham, "*Jesper:* A Danish Thriller." *CCL* 59 (1990): 85–87; Jenkinson, Dave, Review of *The Primrose Path, CM Magazine,* September 29, 1995. http://www.umanitoba.ca/cm; M., Carol, website, http://home.earthlink.net/~carol matas/cmbib.htm; *New York Times Book Review,* May 21, 1989, September 5, 1993; Nelson-McDermott, "Minds on Fast Forward" (review of *A Meeting of Minds*). *CCL* 105–6 (2002): 181; Nodelman, Perry, "Good, Evil, Knowledge, Power: A Conversation Between Carol M. and Perry Nodelman." *CCL* 82 (1996): 57–68; Odegard, Sandra, "A Hope for Change" (reviews of *Zanu, The Fusion Factor and Lisa*). *CCL* 50 (1988): 79–80; *Something About the Author,* vol. 112, 2000; Violetta, Noreen Kruzich, "Interview with Carol M." http://www.scbwicanada .org/interview2.htm

RITA BODE

MATCHECK, Diane
Author, b. 15 September 1964, Ypsilanti, Michigan

M. was born and reared in Michigan. While growing up, she often spent vacations visiting various national parks throughout the country. As a result, M. cultivated a true appreciation of nature and an interest in Native American history. She attended Michigan State University where she studied psychology. After college M. eventually moved to Palo Alto, California, where she currently resides. She is an active community member and library supporter.

This talented author has only written one novel, which debuted in April 1998. Titled *The Sacrifice* (1998), it is a YOUNG ADULT book of historical fiction that tells the story of a fifteen-year-old Native American Indian girl in the 18th century. This young member of the Crow tribe sets out to prove her true destiny and has a pivotal adventure that tests her survival skills. She begins as an arrogant outcast and grows into an inspiring heroine during an adventurous trip. While trying to be strong, she grows to care about a Pawnee boy and experiences romantic feelings for the first time, though the emotion is fleeting.

M.'s psychology background has proven beneficial to her, and shows in her wonderful character development skills and her emotional portrayals. The story's setting is Yellowstone National Park and Scotts Bluff National Monument, home of the Pawnee and the Crow tribes. Her love of nature inspires graphic landscape descriptions, easy for readers to relate to. M. is a very thorough researcher and her novel is both geographically and culturally educational. *The Sacrifice* is recommended on young adult book lists both nationally and internationally.

AWARDS: 1998 ALA Best Book for Young Adults and *Booklist:* Top Ten First Novels of 1998 for *The Sacrifice.*

BIBLIOGRAPHY: Cooper, Ilene, *Booklist,* June 1998, p. 1757; Farrar Straus Giroux, telephone interview, 16 October 2003; Roy, Loriene. *School Library Journal,* October 1998, p. 140; Personal information provided by author's publishers: Deutscher Taschenbuch Verlag in Germany and Farrar Straus Giroux in the United States.

CHRISTINE GERLOFF

MATHIS, Sharon Bell

Author, b. 26 February 1937, Atlantic City, New Jersey

Highly acknowledged as a writer who realistically and optimistically writes for African-American readers, M. thoughtfully crafts stories whose heroes experience disability, aging, DEATH, poverty, and other harsh realities of urban life. These young protagonists, however, are also surrounded by powerful FAMILIES and community relationships that affirm and support their developing self-respect and responsibility through infinite love. M. gives credit to her family for their creativity and strength as sources of inspiration and insight. Growing up in Brooklyn, M. was exposed to a variety of literary works through reading and attending plays with her parents, Alice Mary Frazier Bell and John Willie Bell. A student in a parochial school, she was influenced by Richard Wright and Frank Yerby.

After graduation from Morgan State College in 1958, M. married Leroy Franklin Mathis and moved to Washington, D.C. She began a teaching career and entered the world of writing by publishing a SHORT STORY. Later, she joined the Black Writers Workshop in 1969, where she created a children's literature section and won a fellowship to the Bread Loaf Writer's Conference. Her concern for her students supported her professional writing interest as she decided to write a high-interest, low-level vocabulary novel for those struggling readers she was teaching. At a time when Martin Luther King Jr.'s assassination dominated the social and emotional tones of the community, African-American children needed even greater affirmation of their identities, strengths, and ability to deal with love and death. *Brooklyn Story* (1970) focuses on two TEENAGERS who, while reconciling the abandonment of their mother, experience grief and empowering love as they work to reunite their family.

Teacup Full of Roses (1972) focuses on the struggles of a teenager who is responsible for a motley group of family members: an exceptionally talented younger brother, a blindly protective older brother addicted to drugs, a disabled father, and a mentally challenged great aunt. *Listen for the Fig Tree* (1973) tells of Muffin, a blind teenager coping with her father's murder and her mother's alcoholic dependencies. Her search for self-respect is supported by caring friends. In *The Hundred Penny Box* (1975), Mike develops insight into the importance of family history when his senile great-aunt comes to live with them. Simply told, this story speaks to all generations, while *Cartwheels* (1977) focuses on the dreams of three girls, each vying to win a gymnastic competition and its fifty dollar prize. In each book, M.'s sensitivity and understanding of black children's challenges and strengths tell compelling stories to which young readers can connect—whether affirming their identity or finding insights into diverse life experiences.

While her books draw from the experiences found in black communities, M.'s clear, artistic style speaks universal messages to all young people as they deal with life's responsibilities and frustrations; these are messages of hope, determination, and dignity.

AWARDS: 1971 and 1986 Council on Interracial Books Award, *Sidewalk Story;* 1974 Coretta Scott King Award, *Ray Charles* (1973); 1976 Newbery Honor Book, *The Hundred Penny Box* (1975); ALA Best Books for Young Adults: 1972 for *Teacup Full of Roses* and 1974 for *Listen for the Fig Tree.*

FURTHER WORKS: *Running Girl: The Diary of Ebonee Rose,* 1997; *Red Dog, Blue Fly: Football Poems,* 1991.

BIBLIOGRAPHY: *Dictionary of Literary Biography 33: Afro-American Fiction Writers after 1955,* 1984; *Something about the Author,* vol. 3, 1987; Gallo, Donald R., comp. and ed., *Speaking for Ourselves,* vol. 1, 1990; *St. James Guide to Young Adult Writer's,* 1999.

JANELLE B. MATHIS

MAXWELL, Robin
Author, b. 1923, Tientsin, North China

M., born Desmond Power, is a CANADIAN of Irish descent. She began her writing career after retiring from the data processing field and published her first book in 1990, *Merry-Go-Round.* Most of her novels are historical works.

FURTHER WORKS: *Little Foreign Devil,* 1996; *The Secret Diary of Anne Boleyn* 1998; *Flambard's Canadian Capers,* written as Desmond Power, 2000; *The Queen's Bastard: A Novel,* 2000; *Virgin: A Novel,* 2001; *Virgin: A Prelude to the Throne,* 2002; *The Wild Irish,* 2003.

VALERIE WILLIAMS

MAY, Karl
Author, b. 25 February 1842, Hohenstein Ernstthal, Germany; d. 30 March 1912, Dresden, Germany

M. was born into a family of poor weavers and was blind for the first six years of his life. Despite early disabilities, he became a successful writer of popular fiction. M. wrote 82 books that have sold more than 100 million copies in 39 languages, including Chinese and Japanese.

M.'s novel *Winnetou* (1892) became his most famous book. It is the story of a young Apache chief told by his white friend and bloodbrother, Old Shatterhand. Set in the American Southwest, the Indian way of life is threatened by the construction of the first transcontinental railroad. Winnetou is the only Native American chief who could have united the various quarreling tribes and reached an equitable settlement with the settlers. Tragically, Winnetou is murdered by gold-seeking thugs. His DEATH also foreshadows the death of his people.

It is unlikely that M. ever visited the United States, which nonetheless captured his imagination. Winnetou became the most beloved of all of M.'s heroes, and for more than thirty years (1875–1909) the author returned to him again and again, in various novels and SHORT STORIES. M.'s interest in Native Indians was prompted by his compassion for victims of violence and injustice. He admired Harriet Beecher Stowe (*Uncle Tom's Cabin,* 1852), and like her tried not to entertain but to inform his readers about justice.

M.'s stories left lasting impressions on their readers. Herman Hesse called M.'s stories fiction as wish fulfillment and described his work as mythical-allegorical daydreams of discovery, strife, and redemption. Ironically, M. was a favorite author of Adolf Hitler as well as Albert Einstein—such was M.'s universal appeal.

With the advent of films, M.'s popularity spread. Even today, modern scriptwriters use M.'s well-described characters and write new scripts for them. Many of M.'s STORIES transferred to MOVIES can still be viewed on late-night television. It is rare that a publishing company publishes only one author. Karl-May-Verlag, has been maintained for three generations.

BIBLIOGRAPHY: Novak, Ben, "Cowboys and Indians: Karl M.'s Teutonic American West," *Weekly Standard,* December 25, 2000

(*From* The Continuum Encyclopedia of Children's Literature)

BERNICE E. CULLINAN

MAZER, Anne
Author, b. 2 April 1953, Schenectady, New York

M., the daughter of youth novelists Harry MAZER and Norma Fox MAZER, studied art at Syracuse University's School of Visual and Performing Arts and French language and literature at the Sorbonne in Paris. She turned to writing youth literature only after her first child was born. She is now known as a writer of PICTURE BOOKS, juvenile novels, and YOUNG ADULT novels, as well as for being an editor of SHORT STORY anthologies for young adults.

Two of her anthologies for young adults include *Working Days: Stories about Teenagers and Work* (1997) and *Going Where I'm Coming from: Memoirs of American Youth* (1999). The fifteen stories in *Working Days* depict the lives of TEENAGERS, from working in the fast-food industry to picking crops. As is typical of most of the anthologies edited by M., the teenage protagonists in *Working Days* represent diverse cultural backgrounds, from Mexican American to Greek American to AFRICAN AMERICAN. *Going Where I'm Coming From* combines fourteen nonfiction essays in which adult and youth writers representing a variety of ethnic and racial groups reminisce about growing up in the U.S. The personal nature of these AUTOBIOGRAPHICAL stories highlights the similarities and differences of the immigrant experience in the U.S. As is true of all of her anthologies, these stories serve to celebrate adolescent life and spirit.

As for her own writing, many of M.'s most recent books are entries in her juvenile fiction SERIES, The Amazing Days of Abby Hayes. M. is also an accomplished SHORT STORY writer, as evidenced in A Sliver of Glass and other Uncommon Tales (1996), a collection of HORROR short stories. Many of her anthologies also include stories that she herself has written.

AWARDS: 1998 ALA Best Book, Working Days: Short Stories about Teenagers at Work; A Walk in My World: ALA Popular Paperbacks, 2003.

FURTHER WORKS: Moose Street, 1992; The Oxboy, 1993; America Street: A Multicultural Anthology of Stories, ed., 1993; A Walk in my World: International Short Stories about Youth, ed., 1998.

BIBLIOGRAPHY: Something about the Author, vol. 105, 1999.

DENISE E. AGOSTO

MAZER, Harry
Author, b. 31 May 1925, New York City

Inspired by a TEEN's inquiry in an advice column, M. wrote his first novel for young people, Guy Lenny (1971), is about a twelve-year-old boy dealing with divorced parents. Consequently, M. became one of the first contributors to the fledgling field of YOUNG ADULT fiction. His next book, Snowbound (1973), the story of two teenagers battling to survive a blizzard, was produced as a 1978 NBC After School Special. The Dollar Man (1974), featuring outsider Marcus seeking the father he has never known, became a Kirkus Choice pick.

M.'s relationship with his wife, Norma Fox M., was a writing partnership as well as a marriage. Together, the couple wrote three young adult novels. The Solid Gold Kid (1977) was the first. It was named a YALSA 100 Best of the Best Books, 1967–92, among other honors. More than ten years later, they collaborated again, on Heartbeat (1989), followed by Bright Days, Stupid Nights (1992), which also received honors. The M.s found writing together challenging, often frustrating due to differing styles, and yet worthwhile learning experiences.

M. later wrote The War on Villa Street (1978), which was named a Best Book for YA by ALA. In it, Willis from The Dollar Man deals with a gang, FAMILY problems and a desire to be a runner. The Last Mission (1979) is M.'s highly acclaimed semi-AUTOBIOGRAPHICAL novel about a young U.S. Army Air

Corps gunner who survives being shot down over Europe during World War II. Another notable survival story, The Island Keeper (1981), features emotionally scarred Cleo stranded on a remote Canadian island with winter descending.

I Love You, Stupid! (1981), a BBYA, reintroduces Marcus from The Dollar Man, who is preoccupied with sex but discovers real love and friendship. Hey, Kid! Does She Love Me? (1984), about a boy who dreams of ROMANCE and a filmmaking career, was named to the New York Public Library Books for the Teen Age and IRA/CBC YA Choice lists. When the Phone Rang (1985) chronicles three teens' adjustment to their parents' DEATH in a plane crash. Among other awards, it was selected as a BBYA.

The Girl of His Dreams (1987) reintroduces the character Willis, still pursuing running and finding love. City Light (1988), featuring a teen hoping to fulfill his own life dreams and not his father's, was named a YALSA Best Book for Reluctant Young Adult Readers. In Someone's Mother Is Missing (1990), two sisters find themselves parentless when their father dies and their mother disappears. Another BBYA, Who Is Eddie Leonard? (1993), places the title character in a new FAMILY where he poses as their long missing 15-year-old son.

In addition to Guy Lenny, M. wrote other books for younger teens. In The Wild Kid (1998), a School Library Journal Best Book and a Horn Book Fanfare choice, a troubled teen rescues a lost boy with Down syndrome. Cave under the City (1986) follows two parentless brothers struggling in New York during the Great Depression, and Dog in the Freezer: Three Novellas (1997) offers an unusual collection about boys and their dogs.

M. and his wife have made a lasting contribution to the body of young adult literature. It is for this outstanding contribution that the Adolescent Literature Assembly of the National Council of Teachers of English selected them to jointly receive the ALAN Award in 2003.

AWARDS: Snowbound: 1984 Booklist Contemporary Classic, 1970–73 Best of the Best Books by ALA; "Here We Go Again: 25 Years of Best Books: 1967–1992"; Solid Gold Kid; The Last Mission: New York Times Best Book, New York Public Library Books for the Teen Age, ALA Popular Paperbacks, 2002, YALSA "Nothin' but the Best: Best of the Best Books for Young Adults, 1966–86"; ALA Best

Books for Young Adults: *The War on Villa Street*, 1978, *Last Mission*, 1979, *I Love You, Stupid!*, 1981, *When the Phone Rang*, 1986, *Girl of His Dreams*, 1994, *Who is Eddie Leonard?*, 1994, *Hey Kid! Does She Love Me?*: New York Public Library Books for the Teen Age, IRA/CBC Young Adult Choice lists; *The Girl of his Dreams*: Recommended Book for Reluctant Readers, BBYA New York Public Library Book for the Teen Age; YALSA Best Book for Reluctant Young Adult Readers, *City Light; Boy at War*: VOYA Top Shelf Fiction for Middle School Readers, New York Public Library Best Books for the Teen Age.

FURTHER WORKS: *Boy at War: A Novel of Pearl Harbor*, 2001; *A Boy No More*, 2004.

BIBLIOGRAPHY: *Harry M.* authors4teens.com. http://greenwood.scbbs.com/servlet/A4TStart?authorid = hmazer&source = introduction; Reed, Arthea J. S. "Norma and Harry: Relationship, Romance and Writing." *Norma Fox Mazer: A Writer's World*, 2000, pp. 55–70; Reed, Arthea J. S. *Presenting Harry M.*, 1996; *Something about the Author*, vol. 105, 1999, pp. 144–50.

DIANE TUCCILLO

MAZER, Norma Fox

Author, b. 15 May 1931, New York City

A prolific contributor to the body of outstanding young adult literature, M. has been a National Book Award nominee, the recipient of numerous national and international book awards, and has had nine books selected for the Best Books for YA lists from YALSA, including three Best of the Best Books. She has also written SHORT STORIES for a variety of YA anthologies and co-edited two adult POETRY collections.

M. grew up in Glens Falls, New York, the daughter of Jewish immigrants and the second of three sisters. As she was growing up, she was inquisitive and developed an appreciation for FAMILY stories of joy and tragedy that were shared by relatives. Her writing has often paralleled aspects of her family experiences and relationships. Early on, M. knew she wanted to be an author and wrote for her school newspaper. She attended Antioch College from 1949 to 1950, and married Harry M., also a popular young adult author, on February 12, 1950. Together they have four children, Anne, Joseph, Susan, and Gina; daughter Anne has followed in her parents' writing footsteps. During the challenging years of parenting, M. and Harry managed time to write, although not the novels to

which they aspired. To earn money for their family, they wrote fictionalized first-person scenarios for the "women's true confessions" market.

After ten years, M. finally wrote her first novel for a young TEEN audience, *I, Trissy* (1971), considered one of the groundbreaking books in the relatively new field of young adult literature. Her subsequent novels, *A Figure of Speech* (1973), nominated for the National Book Award, and *Saturday, the Twelfth of October* (1975), a time-travel FANTASY to an ancient matriarchal society, gave evidence to M.'s growing skills as a writer. Her short-story collection, *Dear Bill, Remember Me?* (1976), gave M. the confidence to believe she was at last a truly competent author, and she began writing for a more mature adolescent audience.

In 1977, M. coauthored *The Solid Gold Kid* with Harry. It was selected as one of YALSA's 100 Best of the Best Books, 1967–92. *Heartbeat* (1988) and *Bright Days, Stupid Nights* (1992) were additional collaborations. Through the more than fifty years of their marriage, M. and Harry have supported and encouraged each other in their individual writing endeavors. Because they found authoring novels together challenging because of different writing styles, these three novels have been their only collaborations.

M. has been praised for her frank portrayal of teenage sexuality. She does not sugarcoat the truth, nor does she shy away from more graphic descriptions of teenage experimentation: *Up in Seth's Room* (1979) portrays a romantic relationship between a boy expecting sexual intercourse with his inexperienced and unready girlfriend; *When We First Met* (1982), a sequel to *A Figure of Speech*, is a ROMANCE about a girl who falls in love with the son of the drunken driver who killed her sister; *Someone to Love* (1983) chronicles the intimate romance of two vivid characters, a lonely college freshman and her dropout boyfriend. *Three Sisters* (1986) features a strong main character attracted to her sister's fiancé.

M. does not use the theme of sexuality exclusively in her writing. One of her most touching and successful books is *After the Rain* (1987), which is about a different kind of love. Written for M.'s father and reflecting her family history, it tells of the developing heartfelt relationship between a dying old man and his granddaughter. This Newbery Honor Book gleaned additional awards. It was followed by *Silver* (1988), featuring strong and sensitive Sarabeth Silver, who also appears in the sequel, *Girlhearts* (2001).

Although not written as a MYSTERY, *Taking Terri Mueller* (1981) was given a prestigious Edgar Allan Poe Award by the Mystery Writers of America in 1982. *Summer Girls, Love Boys, and Other Short Stories* (1982), M.'s second collection, receiving similar critical acclaim as her first, was produced as a 1984 HBO film.

Babyface (1990) introduces Toni, a young teen who discovers a long-held parental secret. *Out of Control* (1993) is the story of smart, artistic, outsider Valerie, who is attacked by three popular boys at school. It was honored with numerous awards, including selection as a BBYA, and received critical acclaim. *Missing Pieces* (1994) chronicles a girl's search for the father who abandoned her.

Unusual, sad, and powerful, *When She Was Good* (1997) was a work in progress for years. It is M.'s darkest and most mature novel, a psychological study of the extremely dysfunctional relationship between two orphaned sisters: gentle, loving Em, and disturbed, abusive, terrifying Pamela. It received great critical acclaim and was selected as a BBYA. *Good Night, Maman* (1999), a sibling Nazi escape story, also received a great deal of attention.

Besides *I, Trissy*, M. wrote *Mrs. Fish, Ape, and Me, the Dump Queen* (1980), *Supergirl* (1984), *A, My Name Is Ami* (1981), *B, My Name is Bunny* (1987), *C, My Name Is Cal* (1990), *D, My Name Is Danita* (1991), and *E, My Name Is Emily* (1991), for a younger adolescent audience.

Through the years, M.'s talents and skills have grown tremendously, and she has become a master of the young adult novel. Her contributions to the literature were acknowledged in 2003 when the ALAN Award from the Adolescent Literature Assembly of the National Council of Teachers of English was mutually bestowed on her and husband, Harry.

SELECT AWARDS: 1982 Edgar Award from the Mystery Writers of America, *Taking Terri Mueller;* ALA Best Books for Young Adults, Someone to Love; *Downtown: New York Times* Best Book, New York Public Library Best Book for the Teen Age, YALSA Best Book; Newbery Honor Book, *After the Rain;* 1967–92 YALSA 100 Best of the Best Books, *Silver;* 2000 *Booklist*'s Best Book in HOLOCAUST Literature, *Good Night, Maman*; and numerous citations on ALA lists.

FURTHER WORK: *Downtown,* 1984.

BIBLIOGRAPHY: Holtz, Sally Holmes. *Presenting Norma Fox M.,* 1987; *Norma Fox M.* authors 4teens.com. http://greenwood.scbbs.com/servlet/A4T start?authorid = nmazer&source = introduction; *Norma Fox M.* teenreads.com. http://www.teenreads.com/authors/au-mazer-norma.asp; Reed, Arthea J. S. *Norma Fox M.: A Writer's World,* 2000; *Something about the Author,* vol. 105, 1999, pp. 150–56.

DIANE TUCCILLO

MEAD, Alice

Author, b. 11 January 1952, Portchester, New York

M. earned her B.A. from Bryn Mawr College in 1973, her M.Ed. from Southern Connecticut State University in 1975, and an additional B.S. in art education from the University of Southern Maine in 1985. She married Larry Mead (a recreational director) in November 1983, and is the mother of Jeffrey and Michael. M. worked as an art teacher in Connecticut and Maine from 1974 to 1992, and as a preschool teacher in Maine from 1980 to 1983. Because of a chronic illness, M. was forced to retire from teaching; the time that she was required to rest gave her the incentive to focus on her writing. Her first piece was *Tales of the Maine Woods,* a storybook about nature.

M. depicts childhood in her writings as a time filled with extreme emotions and unparalleled hope for the future. Her experience as an art teacher for children from low-income FAMILIES inspired M. to write about children whose futures are not planned out for them. She explains, "In America, wealth abounds yet a large proportion of American children are poor. Everyone tells poor kids to have hopes, to dream—but how do you go about it? We have a society that sees children in very negative ways. I like to celebrate the intensity and steadfastness of kids, their creativity and fresh energy." As a teacher, M. wanted to foster a place where these children were safe to explore their imaginations. This desire to provide safety and refuge for unprotected children is reflected in her writing.

M.'s novels for young adults often feature young people coping with dire circumstances. With ingenuity, determination, and the aid of helpful adults, these characters are able to make positive, if small, changes in their own lives and in the lives of those around them. In *Crossing the Starlight Bridge* (1994), nine-year-old Rayanne is forced to adjust immediately to life in the city, her grandmother, a new school, and the disintegration of her parents' marriage. It is through her artistic abilities that she finds aid in the transition.

M.'s attention to the turmoil in Bosnia and the one million brutally oppressed Albanian children there motivated her to write about the struggles of the Balkan people. *Adem's Cross* (1996) portrays a fourteen year old Albanian who struggles between his personal hostility and the mandates of his people. The Albanians have adopted a policy of nonviolent resistance against the Serbs, but Adem wants nothing more than to retaliate against his oppressors. Trying to find his place in this WAR-torn country is Adem's cross to bear. This novel is not a plug for M.'s personal belief in pacifism; rather, it is a defense for children in uncontrollable situations, such as cultural crossfire.

M. is a member of the Maine Writers and Publishers Alliance and Maine Art Education Association. She is active in efforts to aid children in Kosovo and a board member for Project Co-Step, an organization for developmentally delayed preschoolers.

AWARDS: *Adam's Cross*: ALA Best Books for Young Adults, 1997, ALA Popular Paperbacks, 2002.

SELECT FURTHER WORKS: *Walking the Edge,* 1995; *Junebug,* 1995; *Journey to Kosovo,* 1995; Ed., with Arnold Neptune, *Giants of the Dawnland: Ancient Wabanaki Tales,* 1996; *Junebug 2,* 1997; *Junebug and the Reverend,* 1998; *Soldier Mom,* 1999; *Billy and Emma,* 2000; *Girl of Kosovo,* 2001; *Year of No Rain,* 2003.

BIBLIOGRAPHY: "Adem's Cross." *Publishers Weekly,* Oct. 21, 1996 vol. 243, no. 43, p. 84(1); *Contemporary Authors Online,* 2003. Reproduced in *Biography Resource Center,* 2003. http://www.galenet.com/servlet/BioRC; "Crossing the Starlight Bridge." *Publishers Weekly,* April 18, 1994; "Girl of Kosovo." *Publishers Weekly,* March 19, 2001; "Soldier Mom." *Publishers Weekly,* December 6, 1999; "Year of No Rain." *Publishers Weekly,* May 19, 2003; Alice M.'s homepage: http://home.maine.rr.com/alicemead/All%About%Alice%Mead%20Page.htm#AllAbout Alice.

RACHEL WITMER AND SARA MARCUS

MEAKER, Marijane. See KERR, M. E.

A MEDITATION ON WRITING LANDSCAPE

"The ultimate concern of the artist is not to paint mountains and clouds and trees but the air between them."—Wang Wei
(From a forthcoming book to be published by Writer's Digest Books in 2006. Used with permission.)

Too many writers ignore landscape, to their peril. Perhaps the problem is their lack of visual acuity. We are unpracticed in the art of looking.

Nobody has taught us to *see*. Except in art courses, we are never told the value of looking at what is all around us. Oh, if something big moves—a bear, a truck, a train, a moose—we will notice. And get out of the way. But most of us miss the little things or the immovable objects. Or if we notice, it is a fleeting moment, then gone.

For the majority of people, landscape is simply just *there*. It exerts no gravitational pull on our senses. We walk through it, slap at it, step over it, break off a piece. But observe it carefully? That takes too long.

Many authors know this about landscape: that it can be a simple setting or background for their characters. But the better authors realize much more. Place can be shorthand (or longhand) to explain a hero or villain: think of the difference between the living green forest of ents and the orc-made desert of Mordor in *Lord of the Rings.*

Better writers also know that landscape can be metaphor, can be a parallel to their characters' lives, can become central to the action, can even be a character in itself.

Think of Robert Louis Stevenson's Davey Balfour, striding across the harsh Highland countryside, becoming a man. The territory he treads helps shape him.

Think of the uncompromising sea through which Captain Ahab plows and how it defines him, creates him just as the whale Moby Dick "tasks" him and "heaps" him.

Or how the rough island on which Robinson Crusoe is marooned is the making of his soul.

How Mary Lennox is changed by her secret garden, how she blossoms and grows strong within its stone walls.

Think of the cozy familiarity of the March girls' landscape, how the careful plantings, the warm comfortable house, emphasizes their domesticity as they grow from little women into mature ones.

Then consider Catherine Earnshaw and Heathcliff, as wild and untamable as their wind-swept moors.

Sometimes, as in the Dune SERIES, the arid desert through which the sand worms tunnel, becomes a metaphor for the life lived. Sometimes, as in the island on which Ratty and Mole find the living Pan in

Wind in the Willows, landscape is the beating heart of the book. And just see what the variety of landscapes do to poor Gulliver in his travels or Alice in her Wonderland.

In the stories written about King Arthur there are many characters: Arthur, who is the king despite himself, valourous and trusting and true. Merlin, the magic maker, who unmakes himself through love. Guinevere, married to a king, loved by a knight, trying to remain true to both and to herself as well. Lancelot, the perfect knight, whose perfection is a trap for all. And the others: Morgan le Fey, Mordred, Bors, Gawaine, the Green Knight, the Lady of the Lake, Elaine . . . characters who live on and on.

But the character that interests me the most is Camelot itself. Whether it is a place of turrets and ballrooms shining on a hill, or a rough turf-and-timbered fortress surrounded by a stone shell wall; whether we call it Camelot or Camlann or something else entirely, that castle focuses our attention. It tells us that within this place magic, MYSTERY, adventure, and ROMANCE will happen. It is a spot that is both within time and without.

So when I wrote my YA novel about King Arthur—*Sword of the Rightful King*—the castle became a character on its own.

However, it's not just Arthurian stories that demand that kind of landscape. All novels work best when they have a landscape that seems real, alive, purposeful, important.

Phillipa Pearce writes in her lovely FANTASY novel for children—*Tom's Midnight Garden*—"There is a time, between night and day, when landscapes sleep." It is a lovely line, full of the promise of magic. And magic is what happens. Tom goes through the back door of the flat, though he's been told it only leads to an alley strewn with garbage cans. And there, magically, a garden appears, a Victorian garden from the 1880s, with broad sweeps of lawn and yew hedges, and a water tank filled with the flash of goldfish.

Pearce's description of the garden echoes her own love of landscape, and her words truly are magical: "At first <Tom> took the outermost paths, gravelled and box-edged, intending to map for himself their farthest extent. Then he broke away impatiently on a cross-path. It tunneled through the gloom of yew-trees arching overhead from one side, and hazel nut stubs from the other: ahead was a grey-green triangle of light where the path must come out into the open

again. Underfoot the earth was soft with the humus of last year's rotted leaves. . . ." and a few sentences later . . . "His path came out by the asparagus beds of the kitchen-garden—so he found them later to be. Beyond their long, grave-like mounds was a dark oblong—a pond. At one end of the pond, and overlooking it, stood an octagonal summer-house with an arcaded base and stone steps up to its door. The summer-house, like the rest of the garden, was asleep on its feet."

Already the reader is as enchanted as Tom. But the description of the garden—walled on three sides, a lawn, a fir tree wound with ivy, a hedge with a hole in it just the size for a boy to squeeze through, then a meadow with cows, and geese in the long grasses— the description goes on for another three pages.

Just so lovingly, Robin MCKINLEY describes the Beast's garden in *Beauty*. A keen gardener herself, McKinley's visual sense of the garden is word perfect. She writes: "Beauty's father" was distracted from his pleasant musings by a walled garden opening off the path to his right; the wall was waist-high, and covered with the largest and most beautiful climbing roses that he had ever seen. The garden was full of them; inside the rose-covered wall were rows of bushes: white roses, red roses, yellow, pink, flame-colour, maroon; and a red so dark it was almost black.

"This arbor of roses seemed somehow different from the great gardens that lay all around the castle, but different in some fashion he could not define. The castle and its gardens were everywhere silent and beautifully kept; but there was a self-containment, even almost a self-awareness here, that was reflected in the petals of each and every rose, and drew his eyes from the path.

"He dismounted and walked in through a gap in the wall, the reins in his hand; the smell of these flowers was wilder and sweeter than that of poppies. The ground was carpeted with petals, and yet none of the flowers were dead or dying; they ranged from buds to the fullest bloom, but all were fresh and lovely. The petals he and the horse trampled underfoot took no bruise."

In Alice HOFFMAN's *The Probable Future,* the Sparrow family of magical women are all intimate with the landscape. Hoffman, too, knows such things, describing spring this way: ". . . the smell of the laurel, so spicy just before blooming, the way everything turned green, all at once, as though winter itself were a dream, a fleeting nightmare made up of ice and heartlessness and sorrow." As well as this: ". . . the yearly flight of returning cowbirds and blackbirds and sparrows, flocks whose great numbers blocked out the sun for an entire day every year, a winged and breathing eclipse of the pale, untrustworthy sky."

The generous literary landscape—whether garden or mountainside, forest or copse, moor or plain—is as much a part of these stories as the plot, the characters, the theme.

Still, the problem comes down to this: How to visualize a landscape well enough that the reader is truly there? I can take a friend by the hand and lead him around my garden in Massachusetts or along the St. Andrews coastline in Fife. But how does a writer lead a reader?

Perhaps it would be helpful to think of landscape as coming in three parts.

First, find the large shapes. Some are immovable and in human terms, immutable. Ask yourself how the mountains are defined against the sky. Are they so far away they are fuzzy and muzzy around the edges. Are they lumpy, which makes them older, or sharp and pointed which means they are younger and have not yet been worn away. Read some good books on geology and construct your mountain ranges accordingly, because a mountain landscape made by volcanic action will be different from one that has been carved out by eons of rivers meandering down their sides.

Water—rivers, streams, oceans—certainly move within their banks and sometimes in fierce storms or in the aftermath of run-offs even break over those banks. How to describe them that the reader actually sees the shifting blues and greens, the foaming spume of white water, the tumble of waves. What about the shadows of fingerlings darting along the sandy bottoms, or the whale that humps out of the blue-black water.

Some large shapes are mobile and shifting. What about the clouds? Are they streamers or plump cumulus? Are they white as ibis feathers or gray as stone? (And by the way, do you see a difference in the colors gray and grey?)

Do the trees rise up like fists or spread out like fingers? Does the mountain wear a stubble of small trees on its face?

With such depictions of landscape, the writer can set a mood, background music for the eye. Or can set

up the landscape to act contra-puntally against (or with) the hero.

Second, there are singular features: a rock, flower, vine, bird against the slate of sky. These individuals are punctuations of landscape, used instead of an exclamation point.

Perhaps you could place a solitary gnarled tree to stand defiantly upon a hill. Or place a blood-colored flower near the outstretched hand of a dead knight. As your hero treads up a hill, heedless of the pine needles underfoot or the wuthering of the wind tangling his/her hair, the reader sees the character in motion. By watching his or her actions upon the landscape or in concert with it, the reader does not need to be told how they are feeling. Editor Patricia Gauch calls it "floating" when a character seems to be disconnected or unconnected with the landscape. *Where is he?* she asks her authors. *How strong is the wind? How hot is the sun? What color are the rocks? Do the shadows tell us the time of day?*

Third, know that landscape well enough to individualize the features: grey porous rock, spikes of yew, eruptions of red poppies in a green field, blue morning glories straining for the sun, a hawk in a perilous stoop taking its living from the sky.

Go outside and walk about. Don't take notes, but let yourself truly see what is in front of you, above you, below you. Sit still for a half-hour, for an hour, and watch what goes on around you. Life happens. Busy, mobile, life. If you do not move, you will not affect it. You will be an eye only. A careful, studious, sometimes startled eye.

What might you see? Ants and beetles scurrying by your boots, a woodpecker flecking the bark behind you, a squirrel stopping to gaze at you with its black button eyes, a butterfly resting on your shoulder with a tremor of wings.

If you are luckier, a rabbit will skitter by your feet, a fox with its flagged tail will stalk by, a deer might find its way to a stream and stand drinking with its long tongue, a flash of trout might ripple the water.

In the city, though the buildings take the place of the large shapes of mountains, there is still a great deal to see: birds, beetles, green shoots springing up through the cracks in the pavement, wallflowers perching precariously atop stone abutments, gargoyles that wink in the rain, the changing shape of shadows gray on gray.

The trick is that the details of the landscape must be precise. It is as if the author has been there, not just a visitor but a native of the place.

Henry James has said about the novel that its supreme virtue is its "solidity of specification." And award-winning children's book author Lloyd ALEXANDER echoes this when talking about his own novels. "What appears gossamer is underneath as solid as pre-stressed concrete."

Some authors get to that specificity by making lists, writing out travelogues, drawing maps, researching seasons/flora/fauna in books. But first of all, the author must become an observer: of nature as well as of character.

If you do not look, you cannot see. If you cannot see, how can you write well enough to make others see? How can you write well enough to keep your characters from floating?

And after you see, you must learn to hear: unseen frogs chorusing in the fading light, the weeping cry of a screech owl, the long fall of a coyote's voice.

And after that the smells: the sharp brine of ocean, the pong of rotting seaweed, the crisp mountain air scented lightly with pine.

And how—I hear you ask—to keep all of this in your head? You don't, unless you are a wildlife expert, a rare gardener, a butterfly fancier as fine as Nabokov, a fly fisherman extraordinaire, or live (as I do) with a birding expert. Actually, none of us can keep it all in our heads. I bet even Peter Matthiesen has to do his homework.

So, on your research shelves, close at hand, you will store bird books and mushroom identification books, books about animal tracks and seashells and the changing face of forests. Buy secondhand Audubon guides and when you go on vacation bring home all the pamphlets you can find. These go right next to your thesaurus and dictionary and books of time lines and rhyming dictionary and encyclopedias and *Strunk and White*.

But first and most important, go outside. Sit in a shadow. Become part of the tree. Watch the world. Drink it in.

And then write it. All of it. As much as you can get down. Landscape as character, as metaphor, as background and foreground, as counterpoint to your hero, as villain, as friend. Become that better writer who knows the worth of landscape and can set down what is seen to illuminate what is not seen. Draw that

world with your words and you will draw the readers in.

JANE YOLEN

MELTZER, Milton
Author, b. 8 May 1915, Worcester, Massachusetts

M. has written over one hundred books, and has earned a number of awards for his well-researched and well-written texts. He is a strong advocate for nonfiction writing, especially works that inform YOUNG ADULTS about issues in social justice and are balanced portrayals of American history.

M. was born and reared in Worcester by Austro-Hungarian–immigrant parents who wanted to assimilate into American society. He was a serious student and an avid reader from the time he was a small boy. Beginning in junior high school, M. held a series of jobs to help support his family: delivering newspapers, canned goods, and milk, often in the early hours before school started. His income became increasingly important as the Depression worsened. M.'s *Brother, Can You Spare a Dime? The Great Depression, 1929–1933* (1969), *Violins and Shovels: The WPA Arts Projects* (1976), and *Dorothea Lange: Life Through the Camera* (1985) arose from his personal experiences during the Depression, as did several volumes on economic injustice, including works on slavery, labor struggles, and poverty.

During his high-school years, M. was introduced to the works of Henry David Thoreau and other American authors. M.'s *A Thoreau Profile* (1962) was the first of several BIOGRAPHIES of American writers including Emily Dickinson, Herman Melville, Edgar Allan Poe, Carl Sandburg, Mark Twain, and Walt Whitman. His high-school study of American history prompted him to create engaging books on that subject for young adults. *The American Revolutionaries: A History in Their Own Words* (1987) and *Voices From the Civil War: A Documentary History of the Great American Conflict* (1989) use original sources and present personal and public perspectives on these events. Biographies of George Washington, Benjamin Franklin, Thomas Jefferson, Andrew Jackson, Thomas Paine, and Theodore Roosevelt, and his collection of POETRY, *Hour of Freedom: American History in Poetry* (2003), show his continuing interest in American history. As M. studied American literature and history, he also became increasingly interested in his own family's history. In his AUTOBIOGRAPHY, *Starting from Home: A Writer's Beginnings* (1988), M. talks about how the Great Depression and the suffering of Jews at the hands of the Nazis shaped his growing insights into his ethnic background and his abiding concern for social justice.

M. has spent nearly all of his adult life as a writer. He attended Columbia University, then became a staff writer for the Works Progress Administration from 1936 to 1939. He married his wife Hilda on June 22, 1941. He served in the U.S. Army Air Force from 1942 to 1946. M.'s experiences during World War II perhaps influenced him to write about both WAR and peace. His works include several books on the HOLOCAUST, books on the American Revolution, the Seminole War, and the Mexican War, *Weapons and Warfare: From the Stone Age to the Space Age* (1996), and *Ain't Gonna Study War No More: The Story of America's Peace Seekers.* (1985). To help readers understand what appears to be a recent phenomenon, M.'s *The Day the Sky Fell: A History of Terrorism* (2002) discusses the long history of international terrorism and its causes and consequences, connecting these to the events of September 11, 2001.

After WWII, M. wrote for radio, for a political campaign, for a pharmaceutical company, and for a scientific and medical publishing company. While working at these other positions, M. also began writing his own books. He collaborated with his friend, poet Langston Hughes, to produce his first book, *A Pictorial History of the Negro in America,* (1956), most recently revised as *A Pictorial History of African-Americans* (1995). Biographies of Frederick Douglass, Mary McLeod Bethune, and Langston Hughes, and a history, *There Comes a Time: The Struggle for Civil Rights* (2001), indicate his continuing interest in AFRICAN AMERICAN history.

M.'s first book for young people, *A Light in the Dark: The Life of Samuel Gridley Howe* (1964), was written at the request of his own two daughters. Since 1968, he has written for young people full time. M. pioneered the use of documentary history in his writing for young people. In addition to works on American history, he has created documentary histories of *The Jewish Americans: A History in Their Own Words, 1650–1950* (1982), *The Hispanic Americans* (1982), and *The Chinese Americans* (1980). Books about his own Jewish background include *World of Our Fathers: The Jews of Eastern Europe.* (1974) *The*

Jews in America: A Pictorial Album (1985), *Never to Forget: The Jews of the Holocaust* (1976), and *Rescue: The Story of How Gentiles Saved Jews in the Holocaust* (1988).

A continuing fascination with CIVIL RIGHTS led to *The Bill of Rights: How We Got It and What It Means* (1990), in addition to books on human rights issues around the world, women's rights, and more than one biography of notable women who fought for them. Along with these titles, M.'s curiosity about a wide range of subjects has resulted in, among others, books on horses, gold, potatoes, food, names, the printing press, the cotton gin, and trains. All of his books are refreshingly clear, balanced presentations of INFORMATION, filled with both the broad sweep of history and the small facts and events that provide insight into our shared humanity.

SELECT AWARDS: Thomas Alva Edison Mass Media Award for *In their Own Words: A History of the American Negro, Volume 2,* 1966; Christopher Award for *Brother, Can You Spare a Dime? The Great Depression, 1929–1933,* 1969; Jane Addams Peace Association Children's Honor Book Award for *The Eye of Conscience: Photographers and Social Change,* 1975; Association of Jewish Libraries Book Award, *Boston Globe–Horn Book* Award, Charles and Bertie G. Schwartz for Jewish Juvenile Literature, Hans Christian Andersen Honor List, American Library Association Best of the Best Books, 1970–83 for *Never to Forget: The Jews of the Holocaust,* 1977–83; National Council for the Social Studies Carter G. Woodson Award for *The Chinese Americans,* 1980; Christopher Award and National Council for the Social Studies Carter G. Woodson Award for *All Times, All Peoples: A World History of Slavery,* 1980; *Boston Globe–Horn Book* Award for *The Jews in America: A History in Their Own Words, 1650–1950,* 1983; Olive Branch Award from the Writers and Publishers' Alliance for Nuclear Disarmament, New York University Center for War, Peace, and the News Media, Child Study Children's Book Committee, and Jane Addams Peace Association Children's Book Committee Award for *Ain't Gonna Study War No More: The Story of America's Peace Seekers,* 1986; Catholic Library Association John Brubaker Memorial Award, Society of Children's Book Writers' Golden Kite Award for *Poverty in America,* 1986–7; Jane Addams Peace Association Children's Book Award for *Rescue: The Story of How Gentiles Saved Jews in the Holocaust,* 1989; Laura Ingalls WILDER Award for substantial and lasting contribution to literature for children, 2001; Children's Book Council, Social Studies Association Best Book of the Year for *Hour of Freedom: American History in Poetry,* 2004, and numerous citations for ALA Lists.

FURTHER WORKS: *Crime in America,* 1990; *Witches and Witch Hunts: A History of Persecution,* 2001; *The Amazing Potato,* 1992; *Gold,* 1993; *Cheap Raw Material: How Our Youngest Workers Are Exploited and Abused,* 1994; *Ten Queens: Portraits of Women of Power,* 1998; *Food: How We Hunt and Gather It . . .,* 1998; *Ten Kings: And the Worlds They Ruled,* 2002; *North Across the Border: The Story of the Mexican-Americans,* 2002; *The Printing Press,* 2003, *The Cotton Gin,* 2003, *Hear That Train Whistle Blow: How the Railroad Changed the World,* 2004.

BIBLIOGRAPHY: M. "Where Do All the Prizes Go? The Case for Nonfiction." In P. Heins, ed., *Crosscurrents of Criticism: Horn Book Essays, 1928–1977,* 1977, pp. 51–57. M. "Beyond the Span of a Single Life." In B. Hearne and M. Kaye, eds., *Celebrating Children's Books: Essays On Children's Literature in Honor of Zena Sutherland,* 1981, pp. 87–96; M. "A Common Humanity." In B. Harrison and G. Maguire, eds., *Innocence and Experience: Essays and Conversations on Children's Literature, 1987,* pp. 490–497; M. *Starting From Home: One Writer's Beginnings,* 1988; Chatton, Barbara. "Profile: Milton Meltzer: A Voice for Justice." *Language Arts,* vol. 79 no. 5, 2002.

BARBARA CHATTON

MERTZ, Barbara. See MICHAELS, Barbara.

MEYER, Carolyn

Author, b. 8 June 1935, Lewistown, Pennsylvania

M. has experienced success and has earned many awards and honors through her insightful writing ability that ranges across a wide variety of styles. She has written nearly fifty works, both nonfiction and fiction, for children and YOUNG ADULTS. M.'s accomplished writings span the gamut from how-to books to historical fiction, including several books that depict characters from diverse cultural backgrounds as well as a SERIES with high school students who staff a counseling hotline.

M. earned a B.A., *cum laude,* from Bucknell University in 1957. In addition to her career as a freelance writer, she has worked as an instructor for the Institute of Children's Literature, an Alpha Lambda Delta lecturer for Bucknell University, and a guest lecturer at various schools and organizations.

M.'s novel-writing debut occurred after one of her SHORT STORIES was printed in a secretarial MAGAZINE. Though her short story was printed in shorthand and her family members were unable to read it, the writing bug bit, and M.'s first book, *Miss Patch's Learn-to-Sew Book,* was published in 1969.

Following this first nonfiction publication, M. wrote and published several other sewing, baking, and craft how-to books for children. M.'s nonfiction writing trend switched gears slightly in 1976 with her *Amish People: Plain Living in a Complex World,* a publication that earned M. an American Library Association notable book citation. The novel's creation was spurred by a trip to her childhood home in Pennsylvania. M. wrote other nonfiction books about characters with a variety of cultural backgrounds, including *Eskimos: Growing Up in a Complex World* (1977), which was chosen as a *New York Times* Best Book in 1977, *Voices of South Africa: Growing up in a Troubled Land* (1986), which earned a Best Book for Young Adults citation in 1986, and the *Voice of Youth Advocates,* YASD Best Book citation in 1988, and *Voices of Northern Ireland: Growing up in a Troubled Land* (1987). Bernadine Larsen, a Caucasian woman who married into an Alaskan Eskimo FAMILY, worked with M. on *Eskimos: Growing up in a Complex World.* Additionally, M. spent weeks in both South Africa and Europe researching and interviewing people for the latter two books.

In 1978, M. ventured into the world of fiction writing with the publication of *C. C. Poindexter.* M. used some of her own emotions and struggles as a TEENAGER in creating C.C.'s character. Real-life events and people inspire many of M.'s fiction and nonfiction works, including her second novel, *Eulalia's Island* (1982), which was partly motivated by one of M.'s sons. *Eulalia's Island* recounts the story of thirteen-year-old Sam's family vacation to the Caribbean, where he meets Eulalia and learns to appreciate his FAMILY as well as himself. Additionally, M. has used the Southwest region as the setting for several young adult novels. While living in New Mexico and now Texas, she was inspired to write *The Luck of Texas McCoy* (1984), *Elliott and Win* (1986), and *Wild Rover* (1989).

Most recently, M. has been praised and acknowledged for her young adult works of historical fiction. *Mary, Bloody Mary* (1999), the first book in her Young Royal series, follows the life of Mary Tudor, the daughter of King Henry VIII of England. Two other books that are centered around King Henry VIII's reign, *Beware, Princess Elizabeth* (2001), which was chosen as the 2001 best book of historical fiction by the readers of Disney's *Adventure* magazine, and *Doomed Queen Anne* (2002), reveal more of the mystery and intrigue from that time period. Her contributions to the Royal DIARIES series include three novels so far: *Anastasia: The Last Grand Duchess, Russia, 1914* (2000), *Isabel: Jewel of Castilla, Spain, 1466* (2000), and *Kristina: The Girl King, Sweden, 1638* (2003).

AWARDS: 1990 Pennsylvania School LIBRARIANS Association Author of the Year; *White Lilacs:* ABA's Pick of the Lists, ALA Best Book for Young Adults, IRA Young Adults' Choice, all 1993; ALA notable book citations (1971 and 1979); Best Book for Young Adults citations (1980, 1980, 1992, 1993, 1995, and 1996). *Mary, Bloody Mary:* Top Ten Best Books for Young Adults, 2002 Pacific Northwest Librarians Association Young Readers' Choice Award; and numerous citations on ALA lists.

SELECT FURTHER WORKS: *A Voice from Japan: An Outsider Looks In,* 1988; *Killing the Kudu,* 1990; *White Lilacs,* 1993; *In a Different Light: Growing Up in a Yup'ik Eskimo Village,* 1996, *Gideon's People,* 1996; *Jubilee Journey,* 1997; *My Sister, My Enemy: The Story of Queen Elizabeth,* 2001. M.'s Hotline Series for Young Adults includes *Because of Lissa,* 1990; *The Problem with Sidney,* 1990; *Gillian's Choice,* 1991; *The Two Faces of Adam,* 1991.

BIBLIOGRAPHY: "Carolyn (Mae) M." *Contemporary Authors Online,* 2001, *Gale Group Databases,* accessed 6 June 2003, http://www.infotrac.galegroup.com; website of Carolyn M., accessed 29 June 2003, http://www.readcarolyn.com

HEATHER A. SHUMAKER

MICHAELS, Barbara (pseud. Barbara Mertz)

Author, b. 1927, Illinois

M. graduated from the University of Chicago and continued to study there until she received her doctorate from the world-famous Oriental Institute in 1952. Her Egyptology degree helped a great deal in her writing career—as a matter of fact, her first published work was a nonfiction book of Egyptology—*Temples, Tombs, and Hieroglyphs, A Popular History of Ancient Egypt* (1978). Written while she was still married to Richard Mertz and rearing two young children,

Elizabeth and Peter, she then wrote *Red Land, Black Land, Daily Life in Ancient Egypt* (1978).

M.'s first published work of fiction, *The Master of Blacktower,* appeared in 1966 under her first pseudonym, Barbara Michaels. It proved to be the opening foray in a remarkable career that spans numerous books, and a second pseudonym, Elizabeth Peters. Under the Barbara Michaels pseudonym, M. writes mostly stand-alone books that range from historical gothics to paranormals. An exception to this is the trilogy containing *Ammie, Come Home* (1968); *Shattered Silk* (1986); and *Stitches in Time* (1995), which starts with paranormal elements. These are not present in the second book, but the third shifts back to the paranormal. Many of the novels written under M.'s name feature young heroines in exotic locales, making them fun to read for the TEEN reader. *Be Buried in the Rain* (1985), although set in Maryland in contemporary times, is an extremely effective ghost story.

Under the pseudonym Elizabeth Peters, M. writes primarily SERIES, although there have been some stand-alone books. In the Amelia Peabody series, which starts in the late Victorian Age and is currently at the end of World War I, M. makes great use of her Egyptology degree, tracing the excavations of the Radcliffe entourage in Egypt, although occasionally they do return to England. The main characters in this series include Amelia Peabody Emerson, her husband Radcliffe Emerson, their son, Walter Peabody Emerson (aka Ramses), and their ward, Nefret, along with multiple other friends and family members. The Vicky Bliss series has a modern day setting and features art curator Vicky Bliss, her lover John Smith, and her boss Schmidt, as well as the many villains the trio manages to meet. The Jacqueline Kirby series is also set in modern times and features Jacqueline Kirby, LIBRARIAN, and later, ROMANCE writer. Some of the stand-alone books under this pseudonym include *Devil-May-Care* (1977) and *The Love Talker* (1980).

M.'s work is distinguished by her meticulous attention to detail. She approaches each novel with the same intensity that would be bestowed on a scholarly book, and that attentiveness causes the books to have a depth that often transcend their genre. Her humor, combined with her keen appreciation of world affairs, makes reading her works a pleasure. She has been on the editorial board of *The Writer,* belongs to the Egypt

Exploration Society, the James Henry Breasted Circle of the Oriental Institute, and the National Organization for Women. She was named the Grandmaster of the MYSTERY Writers of America in 1998, as well as receiving the Malice Domestic Lifetime Achievement Award in 2003.

AWARDS: ALA Best Books for Young Adults: 1969 for *Ammie, Come Home*, 1971 for *Dark on the Other Side*; 1973 for *Witch*; 1985 for *Be Buried in the Rain*.

FURTHER WORKS: *Sons of the Wolf*, 1967; *Prince of Darkness*, 1969; *Dark on the Other Side*, 1970; *The Crying Child*, 1971; *Greygallows*, 1972; *Witch*, 1973; *House of Many Shadows*, 1974; *The Sea King's Daughter*, 1975; *Patriot's Dream*, 1976; *Wings of the Falcon*, 1977; *Wait for What Will Come*, 1978; *The Walker in Shadows*, 1979; *The Wizard's Daughter*, 1980; *Someone in the House*, 1981; *Black Rainbow*, 1982; *Here I Stay*, 1983; *The Grey Beginning*, 1984; *Search the Shadows*, 1987; *Smoke and Mirrors*, 1989; *Into the Darkness*, 1990; *Vanish With the Rose*, 1992; *Houses of Stone*, 1993; *The Dancing Floor*, 1997; *Other Worlds*, 1998. As Elizabeth Peters: *The Jackal's Head*, 1968; *The Camelot Caper*, 1969; *The Dead Sea Cipher*, 1970; *The Night of Four Hundred Rabbits*, 1971; *Legend in Green Velvet*, 1976; *Summer of the Dragon*, 1979; *The Copenhagen Connection*, 1982; *Guardian of the Horizon*, 2004.

BIBLIOGRAPHY: http://www.amazon.com; http://www.autopen.com/elizabeth.peters.shtml; www.mpmbooks.com; www.novelst4.epnet.com; http://www.fantasticfiction.co.uk/authors/Barbara_Michaels.htm

JEANNE MARIE RYAN

MIKAELSEN, Ben
Author, b. 24 November, 1952, La Paz, Bolivia

M. spent his childhood as an American in Bolivia and his high-school years in the U.S. as a former Bolivian resident. As a teenager, M. wrote and performed outdoor feats to counteract his feeling of isolation while growing up. M. combines his love of writing and outdoor adventure in his YOUNG ADULT novels. In preparation for writing them, he conducts applied research, visiting and camping out in the novels' settings, trying to live the experiences of his characters: going undercover with narcotics agents and spending three days living on the streets of Mexico for *Sparrow Hawk Red* (1993); volunteering for marine rescue for *Stranded* (1995), which follows a twelve-year-old girl's efforts to save a dying pilot whale and her calf;

raising an orphaned bear cub, Buffy, as background for *Rescue Josh McGuire* (1991).

M.'s books are MULTICULTURAL, challenging readers to care about those outside their world. In *Petey* (1998), M. writes with compassion and humor about a child with cerebral palsy at a time when no one knew what the disease was or how to treat it. Petey was confined to an insane asylum in the 1920s; at this time, doctors equated cerebral palsy with mental deficiency. By the end of the novel, an eighth-grade boy learns to appreciate the now seventy-year-old Petey's strengths of comedy and joy. In *Red Midnight* (2002), twelve-year-old Santiago and his four-year-old sister escape Guatemala by kayak after soldiers burn their village and kill their family. They make the perilous ocean journey to Florida in order to survive tell their story.

M.'s adventure novels, though often didactic, are fast-paced and absorbing. In his first novel, *Rescue Josh McGuire,* a thirteen-year-old hides in the Montana mountains with a bear cub his father has orphaned; he plans to stay until hunting laws change to prohibit bear hunting while mother bears are raising cubs. *Sparrow Hawk Red* sweeps readers into the fast-paced, dangerous street world of Mariposa, Mexico, where thirteen-year-old Ricky poses as a "street rat" and attempts to steal a drug cartel's plane for the U.S. Drug Enforcement Agency. The novel relies on an unlikely set of qualifications for its boy hero, but Ricky's ultimate victory seems to justify the illegal risk taking that could have resulted in his death or torture at the hands of the drug lord.

M.'s novels often explore environmental concerns, suggesting a cooperative rather than an exploitive relationship with nature. *Touching Spirit Bear* (2001) and *Countdown* (1996) particularly develop this theme. In the former, a hardened delinquent learns to know himself and develops respect for the forces of nature when he is sentenced to spend a year alone on a remote Alaskan island. The Native American overseers of this alternative sentencing, and his encounter with a mysterious white bear that first mauls and then watches over him, give Cole lessons in treating wildlife and humans with reverence. In *Countdown,* an African boy, appalled at the erosion of his land's natural resources, blames self-centered American practices. He vents his anger to the first American junior astronaut, who communicates with him by radio from space.

AWARDS: ALA Best Book for YA, 2002, Sunshine State Young Reader Award Winners, 2004, *Touching Spirit Bear*; ALA Notable Books for Children, 1999, *Petey;* California Young Reader Medal, 1995, *Rescue Josh McGuire,* 1997, *Sparrow Hawk Red,* 2003, *Touching Spirit Bear*; IRA Award, 1992, *Rescue Josh McGuire;* Maryland Children's Choice Book Award, 1998, *Stranded;* NAPRA Nautilus Award for YA Literature, 2002, *Touching Spirit Bear;* Nebraska Golden Sower Award, 1995, *Rescue Josh McGuire;* North Dakota Flicker Tale Children's Book Award, 1998, *Rescue Josh McGuire,* 2002, *Touching Spirit Bear;* Western Writers of America Spur Award, 1992, *Rescue Josh McGuire,* 1999, *Petey;* Wyoming Indian Paintbrush Book Award, 1995, *Rescue Josh McGuire,* 1997, first runner-up, *Stranded;* Best Books for Young Adults, 1999, ALA Popular Paperbacks, *Petey,* 2002.

FURTHER WORKS: "Bear in the Family," *Voices from the Middle,* 1998; *Tree Girl,* 2004.

BIBLIOGRAPHY: "Ben M.: About Ben/An Interview with Ben." http://benmikaelsen.com/about_ben_int erview.htm; "Ben M.: About Ben/Awards." http://benmikaelsen.com/about_ben_awards.htm; Benson, Sonia. "M., Ben(jamin John) 1952–." *Contemporary Authors,* vol. 139, 1993. "M., Ben(jamin John) 1952–." *Something about the Author,* vol. 107, 1997.

LAUREEN TEDESCO

MIKLOWITZ, Gloria D.
Author, b. 18 May 1927, New York City

M. has amazingly filled the roles of writer, filmmaker, secretary, and mother. Equally adept at writing for young children and YOUNG ADULTS, she thoroughly researches her subjects and has earned praise throughout her career for dealing with tough topics. Her books for young adults deal with issues as diverse as drug abuse, rape, nuclear holocaust, racism, sexual abuse, the use of steroids, and cults as well as historical issues like the Spanish Inquisition.

M. received her B.A. from the University of Michigan in 1948, and married Jules Miklowitz, a college professor, that same year. After she graduated from college, she moved to New York to pursue a career in the publishing field. She was employed by a publisher as a secretary, and at night she pursued her graduate degree at New York University. After her marriage, she moved to Pasadena, California. She accepted a secretarial position with the Navy while her husband was working as a researcher at the Naval Ordnance Test Station. Her job developed into a filmmaking position, and she was subsequently trained as a writer, developing scripts. She continued with this position until the birth of her second son, David.

While caring for her sons, Paul and David, M. enrolled in a class on how to write for publication. Through her own interest and her experience reading to her young boys, M. began her publishing career with a Beginning to Read book entitled *Barefoot Boy* in 1964.

That year M. and her husband spent eight months in Rome, Italy, and Rehovoth, Israel, on a National Science Foundation fellowship. M. has shared her talent for writing with others, as a writing instructor for Pasadena City College and for the Writers Digest School. She has won numerous awards and honors for her work; her name is recognized for quality in both fiction and nonfiction. She admits that many of her female characters are semi-AUTOBIOGRAPHICAL and that the reader will usually find an aspect of her past in each book she writes.

M. has continuously added to her resume, with books published during the years 1964 through 2005. In addition to writing her own books, M. has been a contributor to anthologies of stories for children and to professional MAGAZINES such as *Publishers Weekly, Writer,* and *Hadassah.* She has also written for children's magazines such as *American Girl* and *Seventeen.*

The De Grummond Collection at the University of Southern Mississippi houses representative samples of M.'s work. Her career spans forty years, and she has written over forty books. Her work has appeared on television in *After School* specials and *Schoolbreak* specials. M. currently resides in La Canada, California, where she is often invited to be a guest speaker at conferences and schools. Both sons are college professors, and M. is the proud grandmother of two granddaughters.

AWARDS: National Council for Social Studies and CBC (Children's Book Council): *Earthquake!,* 1977, *Save That Raccoon!,* 1977; New York Public Library's Books for the TEEN Age Selection: *Did You Hear What Happened to Andrea?* (1978), *The Love Bombers* (1981), *The Young Tycoons* (1982); 1980 Western AUSTRALIA Young Reader Book Award, *Did You Hear What Happened to Andrea?;* 1987, Recommended Books for Reluctant YA Readers selection for *Goodbye Tomorrow, Secrets Not Meant to Be Kept;*

1989 International Reading Association YA Choices selection, *Secrets Not Meant to Be Kept;* 2002 Notable Book for Older Readers from the Association of Jewish Libraries, *Secrets in the House of Delgado;* 2002 ALA Popular Paperbacks, *Masada: The Last Fortress.*

FURTHER WORKS: *The War Between the Classes,* 1985; *After the Bomb,* 1985; *Anything to Win,* 1989; *Past Forgiving,* 1995; *Camouflage,* 1998; *Masada: The Last Fortress,* 1998; *Secrets in the House of Delgado,* 2001; *The Enemy Has a Face,* 2003.

BIBLIOGRAPHY: Commire, Anne, *Something about the Author, vol. 4,* 1973; *Contemporary Authors Online,* 2002; Hipple, Ted, ed. *Writers for Young Adult,* vol. 2, 1997; M. *Past Forgiving,* 1995; M. "Writing the Juvenile SHORT STORY." *Writer,* March 1994, pp. 13–16.

SANDRA KITAIN

MILLER, Frances A.
Author, b. 15 October, 1937, New York City

Mother of four children, M. began her career in 1966 as a tutor and volunteer in public schools, turning to teaching reading and English for a year before following her husband to AUSTRALIA for six years. While in Australia she began publishing her writings, which she had begun in 1974, starting with *The Truth Trap* in 1980.

Sequels soon followed, as well as "five BIOGRAPHIES of Americans for high school students" and contributions to *Collection Building.*

AWARDS: *The Truth Trap* was chosen Best Book for Young Adults by the American Library Association and won the California Young Reader Medal in 1985; It was also selected for "Here We Go Again: 25 Years of Best Books: Selections from 1967 to 1992."

BIBLIOGRAPHY: *Contemporary Authors Online,* 2001.

SARA MARCUS

MOERI, Louise
Author, b. 30 November 1924, Klamath Falls, Oregon

M. has written numerous stories, several of which were published for young adults, including *A Horse for XYZ* (1977), *The Girl Who Lived on the Ferris Wheel* (1979), *First the Egg* (1982), and *The Forty-third War* (1989). *The Devil in Ol' Rosie* (2001), set in the early 1900s, is based on stories M.'s father told her about his childhood on a remote ranch in central Oregon. It has been described as "a kind of medita-

tion on the meaning of manhood and responsibility" (*Booklist,* 2001). M.'s stories impart thoughtful messages with the wisdom one gains from experiencing challenges in life and making the best possible use of the opportunities presented by those challenges.

M. writes stories that are "crashingly down to earth, and revolve around the life-and-death struggles of simply staying alive in the world. She has always seen life for young people as it really is, without dramatic rescues, heroic players, sweeping happy endings. "My theme—if I could be said to have one is that life presents you with a mixed bag of conditions—and the human spirit achieves greatness by attacking those given conditions and making something out of them" (personal correspondence, 2003).

M. is an expert on such situations; the daughter of a farmer, she grew up during the Great Depression and her family moved several times. In her words, she "was born into a troubled FAMILY and into troubled times. My childhood was lived against a background of fear and worry . . . It was many years before I realized that life without scars is not possible, and the important thing is not what happens to you, but what you do with it." (*SAA,* vol. 24, p. 151). Her tales of pioneer life, such as *The Devil in 'ol Rosie,* come from the stories and memories passed on from her parents' pioneer upbringing.

Her books reflect the lessons she has learned in her life. In *The Forty-Third War,* the "story of a twelve-year-old boy involuntarily conscripted into rebel forces in a fictitious Central American country . . . They are taught a new awareness of their country's problems, loyalty to their fellow soldiers, and a premature passion for life and its treasures. There are no neat answers, no pat solutions here" (*SLJ,* 1989), but this ALA Best Book for Young Adults and ALA Recommended Book for the Reluctant YA Reader will hold readers' attention and would be useful for discussions about Central America's WARS and nationalistic priorities in general.

M. has lived in the same home since 1963 and continues to write every day. She married in 1946, had three children, and today has several grandchildren she has helped raise. She also received a B.A. in 1946 from the University of California, Berkeley. M. has always been a writer, but it was her involvement with children's literature during her nineteen years of work in the Manteca Public Library that gave her the desire to write her own stories. Accustomed to challenges, M. shares the lessons learned in her life and keeps on writing.

AWARD: ALA Best Book for YA, 1990, for *The Forty-Third War.*

FURTHER WORKS: *Star Mother's Youngest Child,* 1975; *How the Rabbit Stole Moon,* 1977; *Save Queen of Sheba,* 1981; *Unicorn and the Plow,* 1982; *Downwind,* 1984.

BIBLIOGRAPHY: Moeri, Louise. Personal correspondence, November 25, 2003; *Something about the Author,* vol. 24, 1981; van Sonnenberg, Catherine. "The 43rd War." *School Library Journal,* 1989; Wilms, Denise. "The Devil and 'ol Rosie." *Booklist* 97, March 15, 2001.

LAURENE MADSEN

MOHR, Nicholasa

Author, illustrator, 1 November 1935, New York City

M. was the youngest of seven children and the only girl born to parents who had immigrated to New York from Puerto Rico during the Depression. Her father died when she was eight-years old, leaving her mother in a precarious financial situation.

M.'s artistic tendencies revealed themselves at an early age. As a way of keeping her busy, her mother frequently supplied her with paper, pencils, and crayons; this venue became an outlet for her inner feelings and was a source of comfort to her.

By the time M. was ready to enter high school, her mother had died and she was left in the care of an aunt who was cold and distant towards her orphaned niece. Although her artistic talents had been noticed by her teachers, M.'s plan to attend an academic high school were nearly railroaded by a guidance counselor who recommended that she attend a vocational high school to learn sewing because she believed "Puerto Rican women were by nature good seamstresses" (Zarnowski). After completing high school, M. enrolled in New York City's Arts Students League. She found herself attracted to the artwork of Mexican artists such as Diego Rivera and Jose Clemente Orozco and subsequently traveled to Mexico City to study Hispanic art in depth. According to M., the work of these artists "spoke to me and my experiences as a Puerto Rican woman born in New York. The impact was to shape and form the direction of all my future work" (Collier). After returning to New York, M. enrolled at the New School for Social Research (now New School University) and then at the Brooklyn Museum of Art School. The vibrancy of M.'s artwork caught the attention of a publishing executive who asked her to produce some SHORT STORIES. However, her initial efforts were rejected because her writings did not contain violence, gangs, or criminal activity, and thus were deemed not to be an authentic representation of the Puerto Rican community. This stereotyping angered M., who felt that the editor's interest lay in a "Puerto Rican female protagonist who would be featured in a sensational book" (Collier). Fortunately, another editor offered M. a contract to produce a novel; the result was *Nilda.* M. herself stated that "I found a medium where I was really comfortable. I could draw a picture with words" (Collier).

Nilda, which is set against the backdrop of WWII, tells the story of a young girl trying to bridge the gap between the close-knit world of FAMILY and familiar friends and the harsh realities of the outside world. This was followed by *El Bronx Remembered,* a collection of short stories dealing with a wide range of topics and issues. The characters in these stories span all ages, thus adding to their appeal. M.'s second novel *Felita* and its sequel, *Going Home,* are more suited to a younger audience. However, many of the themes and situations that appear in M.'s earlier works are present in these novels. It is interesting to note that M. does not view herself as a writer solely for young people; instead, she would rather be viewed as a writer for all people, regardless of their age. M. has been the recipient of numerous awards for both her writings and her illustrations. She lives in Brooklyn.

AWARDS: For *Nilda: New York Times* Outstanding Book Award in Juvenile Fiction, 1973, Jane Addams Children's Book Award, Jane Addams Peace Association, 1974; Society of Illustrators, Citation of Merit for book jacket design, 1975; *School Library Journal* Best of the Best citation, 1966–78. For *El Bronx Remembered: New York Times* Outstanding Book Award in TEENAGE Fiction, 1975; *School Library Journal* Best Book Award, 1976; National Book Award finalist for Most Distinguished Book in Children's Literature, 1977. For *In Nueva York: School Library Journal* Best Book Award, 1977; American Library Association and Notable Trade Book Award: Best Book Award in Young Adult Literature, 1977; Joint Committee of National Council for the Social Studies and Children's Book Council, 1977. For *Felita:* Notable Trade Book Award from Joint Committee of National Council for the Social Studies and Children's Book Council, 1980; American Book Award before Columbus Foundation, 1981. Also: Commendation from the Legislature of the State of New York, 1986; Honorary Doctorate of Letters, SUNY-Albany, 1989.

BIBLIOGRAPHY: Collier, Laurie, ed. *Authors and Artists for Young Adults,* vol. 8. Detroit: Gale Research Press, 1992; Zarnowski, Myra. "An Interview with Author Nicholasa Mohr." *Reading Teacher,* October 1991; http://voices.cla.umn.edu/newsite/athors/MO HRnicholasa.htm

ALICE R. LEONE

MOORE, Martha

Author, b. 17 August 1950, Canyon, Texas

M., who comes from a long line of English teachers, always knew she was headed in the same direction. Writing has been a part of her life for many years, although she did not publish her first novel, *Under the Mermaid Angel,* until 1995. She wrote many stories and poems that she shared with her classes. She is a disciplined writer, spending much time perfecting her work. She works early in the morning, working hard to achieve her goal of depicting the "ageless human heart and soul."

Being a high-school English teacher gives M. an insight into the often tumultuous feelings of TEENAGERS (and also a testing ground for new writings). Influences on her writing have been the many teenagers in her life, as well as her own FAMILY and her experiences in raising a family and also having a career. She focuses on writing stories that depict the heart and soul of youth coming of age. Strong, memorable, frequently eccentric characters are a highlight of her works.

A sense of community is evident in her work, as she strives to introduce characters of all ages. She develops plots that show the experiences and emotions that can evolve when young and old learn from one another. Her books often feature out-of-the-ordinary settings, such as a trailer park, a junkyard, a derelict town museum, or a small-town home filled with bird carvings.

The award-winning *Under the Mermaid Angel* (1995) was originally published as a SHORT STORY in a MAGAZINE and is the first novel written by M. It depicts a young teenager, Jesse, and the unlikely friendship she develops with her flamboyant thirty-year-old neighbor, Roxanne. Jesse comes to learn that

outward appearances are not important—it's what's inside the heart of a person that counts.

AWARDS: *Under the Mermaid Angel,* Delacorte Press Prize for a First Young Adult Novel, 1994; Notable Book by the American Library Association in 1995; Best Book for Young Adults (ALA), 1996.

FURTHER WORKS: *Angels on the Roof,* 1997; *Matchit,* 2002.

BIBLIOGRAPHY: *Contemporary Authors Online,* 2001; *The ALAN Review,* 1996.

KAREN PRAEGER

MORI, Kyoko

Author, b. 9 March, Kobe, Japan

M is a Japanese-American poet, novelist, and nonfiction writer who provides a strong voice for women of all cultures. She was raised in Japan, where she learned to write in Japanese and English, and moved to the United States in 1977 to complete her undergraduate studies at Rockford College in Illinois. M. became a naturalized citizen of the U.S. in 1977. She went on to obtain her master's and Ph.D. in English from the University of Wisconsin-Milwaukee. In addition to being a writer, M. has taught creative writing at S. Norbert's College in De Pere, Wisconsin, as a Brigg-Copeland lecturer at Harvard University, and speaks on various aspects of MULTICULTURAL LITERATURE. The DEATH of her mother, who committed suicide in 1969, motivated her to become independent. This independence served her well in her adult life, as she was able to write about her reactions to her mother's suicide, which was the foundation of the critically acclaimed *Shizuko's Daughter* (1993). Her experience with art and writing in her early years also set her on the path of a profession in literacy. M. perceives fiction and reality as colliding, "Often when I write fiction, I find that the things I make up open doors for me and allow me to write about the truth in a different way." In *Polite Lies: On Being a Woman Caught Between Cultures* (1997), M. compares and contrasts the differences in the American and Japanese cultures and how she strives to find a balance between the two. *Stone Field, True Arrow: A Novel* (2000), M.'s first publication in the category of adult literature, further examines the emotions of FAMILY and independence, with the added dynamic of marriage.

AWARDS: American Library Association, *New York Times,* and *Publishers Weekly,* Council of Wisconsin, and the Elizabeth Burr Award for *Shizuko's Daughter,* 1993; ALA Best Book for Young Adults, 1994 for *Shizuko's Daughter,* 1996 for *One Bird.*

FURTHER WORKS: *Fallout,* 1994; *One Bird,* 1995; *The Dream of Water: A Memoir,* 1995.

BIBLIOGRAPHY: http://www.jcu/edu/pubaff/eyeonjcu/kyoko_mori.htm; http://www.marquette.edu/library/information/news/colloq/kyoko.html; http://www.us-japan.org/mori.html

NANCY SPENCE HORTON

MORIARTY, Jaclyn
Author, b. October 8, 1968, n.p.

Besides writing, M. likes to spend her time at the beach or the movies. She grew up in Sydney with her four sisters and brother, along with numerous animals. M. studied English and law at the University of Sydney, got her master's degree at Yale and her Ph.D. at Cambridge. It was while she was studying in England that she wrote her first novel. She is married to a Canadian and works as a media and entertainment lawyer. Her book *Feeling Sorry for Celia* (2000) is an epistolary novel that tells the story of one TEENAGE girl's attempts to come to terms with her wild friend Celia. Its sequel, *Finding Cassie Crazy* (2003), also known as *The Year of Secret Assignments,* continues in the same vein.

AWARDS: ALA Best Books for Young Adults: 2002 for *Feeling Sorry for Cecilia*; 2005 for *The Year of Secret Assignments.*

BIBLIOGRAPHY: www.panmacmillan.com.au/pandemonium/jaclyn.

CHRISTINA MERCEDES KRUGER

MORPURGO, Michael
Author, b. 1943, St. Albans, England

M. never dreamed he would become a writer. After a stint in the army, he went into teaching. As a teacher, M. began to encourage his students to write and was eventually encouraged to write himself. He left teaching to set up Farms for City Children; M. and his wife now have three farms in the UK, where inner-city children can come spend a week working with animals in the countryside. Farm life, he has found, is quite compatible with a career as an author. M.'s en-

tire adult life has been devoted to children, whether it is through his teaching, his farms, or his writing.

Although M. has been a leading figure in the field of YOUTH LITERATURE IN THE UK for some thirty years, many of his earlier works are not available in the United States. This prolific writer has written well over fifty books. M.'s book *Why the Whales Came* (1985) was adapted for a MOVIE entitled *When the Whales Came* (1989). He researches each story extensively, since many of them take the reader to a different time or place. Most importantly, M. writes to tell a good story, whether of adventure or of courage. And above all, moral dilemmas often ensue.

AWARDS: *Wombat Goes Walkabout,* 1982; *War Horse,* 1982; *Waiting for Anya,* 1990; *The War of Jenkins' Ear,* 1993; *The Dancing Bear,* 1994; *Wreck of the Zanzibar,* 1995; *The Butterfly Lion,* 1996; *Robin of Sherwood,* 1996; ALA Best Book for Young Adults, 1992, *Waiting for Anya,* 1996, *War of Jenkins' Ear*; ALA Notable Children's Books, 2004, *Kensuke's Kingdom.*

SELECT FURTHER WORKS: *King of the Cloud Forests,* 1988; *Twist of Gold,* 1993; *Ghostly Haunts,* 1995; *The Butterfly Lion,* 1997; *Farm Boy,* 1999; *Kensuke's Kingdom,* 2003; *Private Peaceful,* 2004.

BIBLIOGRAPHY: *Booklist.* http://www.ala.org/booklist/; BBC Radio 2003. http://www.bbc.co.uk/radio4/gfi/story/authors/michael_morpurgo.shtml; Harper Collins Publishers 2002. http://www.collinseducation.com/Extract/SP009_MorpurgoBiog.pdf; *Something about the Author,* vol. 93, 1997; YALSA. http://www.ala.org/yalsa

LAURA CHARRON

MORRIS, Gerald Paul
Author, b. 29 October 1963, Riverside, Wisconsin

M. was born in the U.S. but reared in Singapore. Both of his parents were missionaries in the Chinese church. He married Rebecca Hughes in 1986, and has three children, two boys, William and Ethan, and a daughter, Grace. M. is currently a practicing Baptist pastor in Wisconsin. He has been a professor of biblical studies, a landscaper, a substitute teacher, a contract laborer, and a crème-pie baker. As a child he read voraciously, but he called the books "terribly bad Western novels" (Houghton Mifflin). He began writing when he was in 8th grade, and in fact it was those horrible Westerns that he tried to emulate. Years later he discovered the King Arthur tales and uses them today for inspiration for his novels. M. has reworked some of the ancient tales by adding plenty of action, humor, and even satire. He prefers writing for children and adolescents because "they see their world with clearer eyes." (SAA). His first book, *The Squire's Tale* (1998), retells the adventures of Sir Gawain, one of Arthur's Knights of the Round Table, and Terence, an orphan he befriends who becomes his squire. Sir Gawain and Squire Terrance are on another quest in M.'s second book, *The Squire, His Knight & His Lady* (1999). M. also has a very dry wit that is not only evident in his novels, but also carries over into his everyday life: M. says, "I write children's novels as an antidote to my own sermons." M. has written six Arthurian novels to date, all based on medieval times and usually based on CLASSIC tales.

AWARDS: *The Squire, His Knight and His Lady*: ALA Best Books for Young Adults, 2000, ALA Popular Paperbacks, 2003; *The Savage Damsel and the Dwarf*: ALA Best Books for Young Adults, 2001, Dorothy Canfield Fisher Children's Book Award, 2002; *Parsifal's Page*: Dorothy Canfield Fisher Children's Book Award, 2003.

FURTHER WORKS: *The Savage Damsel and the Dwarf,* 2002; *Parsifal's Page,* 2001; *The Ballad of Sir Dinadan,* 2003; *The Princess, the Crone, and the Dung-Cart Knight,* 2004.

BIBLIOGRAPHY: *Something about the Author,* vol. 107, 1999; Houghton Mifflin website, 2004; Children's Literature Network online, 2004.

                                    MARISA KAMMERLING

MORSE, Anne Christensen. See HEAD, Ann

MOVIES

At first glance, films and books look like creative opposites. One is based on the visual arts, one is visible only in the mind. One is crafted in techno-color across the expanse of a massive white screen, the other is made of tiny black-and-white words on a string of small, but literary pages.

But at the core of both art forms there is one very crucial piece of common ground—there is *story*. And whereas a book can exist without its theatrical counterpart, the play or M., a film could not and would not get made without at least a preliminary script or treatment in hand.

One script type of growing popularity is the coming-of-age story. Translation: stories like those found in the hands of YA readers. More and more, Hollywood producers are seeing the emotional and economic potential in telling a story nearly everyone over the age of thirteen can understand on one level or another.

So how does a YA novel go from the written page to the silver screen? And how often does that creative union translate into creative bliss? Seven successful YA authors, who have made the celluloid transition, share their insights here.

In 2002, *Life in the Fat Lane* authors Cherie BENNETT and Jeff Gottesfeld joined the writing staff of *Smallville,* the WB network's TEENAGE look at Superman's coming-of-age. But they were no strangers to the entertainment industry.

Meg CABOT knew her reluctantly royal was distinctive protagonist when she wrote *The Princess Diaries* for HarperCollins. But she never imagined Disney and Julie Andrews would so wholeheartedly agree.

Coming-of-age author Chris CRUTCHER has written nine, an autobiography, and one SHORT STORIES COLLECTION for Greenwillow, an imprint of Harper-Collins. Almost every page he has written has been optioned for motion-picture production. But only one project, *Angus,* has actually been captured on film.

Vision Quest starring Matthew Modine as Louden Swain was novelist Terry DAVIS's first big screen endeavor. It forever linked him with Madonna—she made her film debut alongside Louden—and launched his academic direction as a screenwriting professor.

Dying young scenarios have made Random House novelist Lurlene McDaniel a healthy living for the past two decades. But a made-for-television translation of *Don't Die, My Love* (retitled *A Champion's Fight* at NBC), helped frost her literary cake.

Writing novelizations for films such as *Addam's Family Values, Free Willy,* and *Ferris Bueller's Day Off* certainly helped make Todd STRASSER a successful, full-time writer. But selling the rights to his original story, "Drive Me Crazy," may have been a more cost-effective order.

With literally dozens and dozens of titles to her credit, few could dispute author Jane YOLEN's status as a children's-book diva. But seeing actress Kirsten Dunst bring *The Devil's Arithmetic* protagonist Hannah to life in the Showtime production added a new layer to her accomplishments.

Are movie scripts true to young adult novels?

Bennett/Gottesfeld: So many things can go wrong. Script problems, director problems, actor problems, notes-from-studio problems . . . the list of book-to-film adaptations that actually work beautifully, as well as or better than the underlying material, is pretty short. *One Flew Over the Cuckoo's Nest,* is an example of an adaptation that knocked it out of the park. But there, everything came together magnificently. From our standpoint, the script is the bedrock on which everything else is built.

Cabot: People are surprised when they pick up the second book in the Princess Diaries SERIES without having read the first, and find that Mia's father, who was killed off in the film, is still alive.

Crutcher: I wasn't around for any of it, but I think *Angus* got pushed off track when they decided to make only one set of parents gay, then edited that out; and when they decided to make Angus younger.

Davis: For *Vision Quest,* the filmmakers wanted to make a commercial feature aimed at a young audience, and this is what they did with really phenomenal success. I mean, good God, the thing has been on TV every week for almost twenty years. The book, though, is richer, especially thematically and in terms of character. And I am proud of the work I did in the conclusion of the book, whereas the film featured another concluding scene, which they surely had to do in view of their goals for the movie.

Strasser: From what I've seen, it is almost trying to replicate the book story on the screen. I just don't think it can be done that way. To be successful you have to take the idea of the book, or even one idea in the book, and make a movie story out of it. One of my favorite movies is *McCabe and Mrs. Miller* by Robert Altman. At some point, I noticed that it was based on a book called *McCabe* by a writer named Edmund Naughton. For years I poked around used bookstores and libraries for the book. Finally, a very kind LIBRARIAN from Denver lent it to me. In the movie, the first three-quarters of the story is about how McCabe builds this town out of almost nothing. The last quarter is about how it is taken away from him. The book was almost the opposite. A little bit

about how he built it, but mostly about how it was taken away.

Yolen: First, I have to say that the movie is *not* the book. They made many changes in *The Devil's Arithmatic.* Some because their star (Kirsten Dunst) was four years older than my main character, and the difference between not-quite-fourteen and over seventeen is enormous. Second, because the growth of character needs to be shown in outward action. And third, because moviemakers like to put their own stamp on a film. I think the movie works on its own terms. And I hadn't read the book myself carefully in ten years when the movie came out. So many kids who were more recently invested in the story didn't like it as well as I did.

Are any of your other books being considered as film projects?

Bennett/Gottesfeld: Over the last several years, many different books and plays have been optioned. Here are some: Teen Angels series (Avon), first by Universal Family Television, then this past season by Spelling Entertainment for a UPN show. It went to pilot script for UPN, but alas, was not picked up. The University Hospital SERIES (Berkley) was optioned by Tollin-Robbins Productions. Our Wild Hearts series (Pocket Books) optioned by Lantana Productions. We wrote the script, they loved it. But the financing for the project fell apart at the last minute. *Good-bye, Best Friend* (HarperPaperbacks, 1993), was optioned by Jane Seymour's production company. *Life in the Fat Lane* is currently under option to Storyopolis, and *Anne Frank and Me* to Gullane Entertainment.

Cabot: My teen paranormal series 1-800-WHERE-R-U is optioned by Lion's Gate, but not in production.

Crutcher: Yes, three.

Davis: None of my other books is optioned; none in production. I do believe, however, that *Mysterious Ways,* which came out in September, will be optioned. I am also trying to interest ESPN films in *If Rock and Roll Were a Machine.*

Strasser: I have a feeling it's two, but I'm really not sure. Due to some unfortunate contractual glitches, a number of my books are locked up even without an option.

Yolen: Briar Rose, Commander Toad books, *Wizard's Hall,* are all optioned. Others have been optioned and fallen through.

How common is it for books to be optioned, but never produced?

Bennett/Gottesfeld: It happens more often than not. In fact, *far* more often than not. As an example, according to a recent story in *Variety,* one of the major TV networks heard 1,200 pitches last year for shows for their upcoming season. They commissioned approximately 75 pilot scripts. They decided to shoot about 20 pilots. They'll choose maybe four hours of programming from those twenty pilots. This isn't exactly the same thing as book options turning into films, I know, but it's close enough in its principles. Just think of all the major YA blockbusters that haven't become films, and have incredibly powerful titles: *Walk Two Moons, Staying Fat for Sarah Byrnes, Out of the Dust.* Walter Dean MYERS's *Monster* is even written as a film script!

Davis: It is hugely common, most, most, most common, for books to be optioned but not produced. I've read that something like only twenty percent of books optioned are ever produced. My guess is that the percentage is lower.

McDaniel: Very common. I know of optioned books that have languished for years without ever going to production. So many factors, including focus groups and detailed market research often occur before a book is actually filmed or taped. If it doesn't test well, it's scrapped, but still tied up with option clause wording via a contract.

Strasser: I hear it's pretty—no, check that—very common. Ironically, I've had four out of seven produced, but three were for TV. I generally assume the thing's not going to get made.

How long does it take the average produced book to move from page to screen?

Bennett/Gottesfeld: Forrest Gump took ten years. Things *can* happen fast, a la Harry Potter. But there tends to be a driving reason for the process to get accelerated like that.

Cabot: The Princess Diaries took almost exactly a year. But that was fast-tracked by the studio. *All American Girl* is looking like it will be the same.

Crutcher: There is no set time. There are too many things that can hurry production up, and *way* too many things that can slow it down.

Davis: A lot of books take many years from option to production to premier. I was astonishingly lucky with *Vision Quest.*

Strasser: I'm told mine (*Drive Me Crazy*) was done in record time—like a year or something. It showed in the final product.

Yolen: The Devil's Arithmetic took over ten years. How long does it take to make this transition? It takes as long as it takes. A bestseller can go quicker.

Have you tried to retain any degree of creative control? Should that matter to an author?

Bennett/Gottesfeld: Yes and no. Because we also write for the screen, and, depending on the circumstances, we sometimes are the ones to do the adaptation. In that case, we'd have a lot of creative input. We're pretty much reconciled to the fact that when we're not writing the script, we have a voice, but not a veto. And even when we are writing the script, there are going to be a lot of other voices, and the veto will be with the persons shelling out the millions of dollars it'll take to get the project made. That's just the way the business works.

Cabot: The producers kept in touch with me, and I certainly offered my advice, but when it comes to making movies, I know zero, so I felt comfortable letting the project go.

Davis: I wish I'd retained some creative control when *Vision Quest* was made. I didn't have the personal maturity or the wisdom about story. I do now, however, and hope to be some part of the team if another book of mine is ever filmed.

KELLY MILNER HALLS

MOWRY, Jess
Author, b. 27 March 1960, Starkville, Mississippi

Born in the South but reared by his father in Oakland, California, M. grew up a voracious reader, largely self-educated. He worked as a mechanic, truck driver, tugboat engineer, and scrap-metal collector before deciding to work with young people at a community center in the neighborhood where he grew up. Inspired by this work and frustrated by the lack of books written for or about black children, M. began writing fiction and was first published in 1988. In addition to writing novels, stories, and PLAYS, he continues to work with youth at the community center and also mentors young writers of color.

M. is best known for his second novel, *Way Past Cool* (1992), which features a thirteen-year-old boy named Gordon, the leader of a West Oakland gang called The Friends. Gang members are bonded together in the struggle to remain alive despite the challenges that poverty, absent parents, plotting drug dealers, and friction with a rival gang The Crew has thrust upon them. Reviewers of the novel praise M. for his ability to realistically capture dialogue and his talent for creating vivid characters that subvert stereotypical portrayals of urban TEENS of color. In addition to its best-selling U.S. release, *Way Past Cool* has been published in nine other countries, translated into eight languages, and has been made into a feature film based on M.'s screenplay.

M. has also written adventures, MYSTERIES, and ghost stories with black children protagonists, and he has published a number of SHORT STORIES in anthologies and MAGAZINES.

AWARDS: Society of School Librarians International Book Awards, *Ghost Train,* 1997; ALA BBYA, *Way Past Cool,* 1993; PEN Oakland/Josephine Miles Award, *Rats in the Trees,* 1990; 2002 ALA Popular Paperbacks: *Babylon Boyz.*

FURTHER WORKS: *Children of the Night,* 1991; *Six Out Seven,* 1993; *Ghost Train,* 1995; *Babylon Boyz,* 1997; *Bones Become Flowers,* 1999.

BIBLIOGRAPHY: Author's homepage, http://members .tripod.com/~Timoun/index-2.html; *Children's Literature Review,* http://www.childrenslit.com; Spencer, Pam, *What Do Young Adults Read Next? A Reader's Guide to Fiction for Young Adults,* 1994.

REBECCA LASSWELL

MULTICULTURAL LITERATURE

Booklist's Hazel Rochman presented the 2000 May Hill Arbuthnot lecture on April 16, 2000, at the Thomas J. Dodd Research Center, University of Connecticut. The following essay is excerpted from her lecture, which appears in full (with bibliography and notes) in *JOYS* (Summer 2000). It was also published in *Booklist,* February 15, 2001. Reprinted with permission.—Eds.

Reading, writing, talking, and arguing about books have helped me find a home in a strange place. I don't feel I belong in any country. I was never at home in South Africa, where I was born and raised under apartheid. In fact, until the astonishing changes of the last decade, I was always ashamed to say I came from South Africa. And I feel out of place here in the U.S., where I have lived since 1972. I came without papers or a passport. I was granted citizenship, eventually, and I'm grateful for that, but national anthems and flags and borders don't mean a thing to me. I've never felt rooted in any place. What I do love about this country is that there's room for all kinds of restless people like me. There's space here for strangers and for our stories.

Hearing Strangers' Voices

In my work at *Booklist,* I'm thrilled to see a great outpouring of children's books about strangers, voices that for too long have gone unheard, books that open up new worlds for this new millennium. Many of these books, both fiction and nonfiction, draw on DIARIES and letters and interviews and personal accounts; slave narratives, refugee and survivor testimonies, stories about immigrants, about kids at work, about growing up gay. These books reflect the present change in how we look at our history and ourselves, the new awareness that women and children and men from everywhere have played crucial roles, that all our stories matter. These exciting new books won't replace the CLASSICS we know and love but add to them and make us reread the familiar books in a new light.

As we open up to the stories of strangers everywhere, our view of the mainstream is changed and enriched and complicated. The writer Christopher Bram says we get to see around corners we didn't even know were there. The apartheid government said the opposite. Where I grew up, by law each group had to stay in its own box with its own kind. There was to be no connection between us. And to institutionalize that apartness, the police state enforced total CENSORSHIP. They had to. It would be dangerous for us to see around corners, to read stories that showed the humanity of strangers. No black child ever saw herself in a book. And I never saw her either, except as local color.

Mark Mathabane, as a child in his slum in Alexandra Township near Johannesburg, was told that he was Tsonga and he should learn everything in Tsonga. He did love the marvelous traditional stories his mother told him, but later, when he got hold of some old junk copies of children's books, he was also enthralled by Grimms' fairy tales and by *Treasure Island,* with its gripping tale of buried treasure and mutiny on the high seas. He says: "My heart ached to explore more such worlds, to live them in the imagination in much the same way as I lived the folktales of my mother and grandmother."

Barely ten miles from Mark Mathabane's home, I lived in a Johannesburg suburb, a totally separate world. I also read *Treasure Island.* Like Mathabane, I loved the adventure stories, and I loved all that drumbeat, British-colonial rhyming kind of stuff; hearing my dad recite POETRY like that is what first made me a reader. One of our favorites was Sir Walter Scott's "Breathes there the man with soul so dead / Who never to himself hath said / 'This is my own, my native land?'"

I never thought about what it meant. What native land? I didn't know Mathabane's mother's stories; never heard the voices of the people in my country. They were total strangers. Their languages, their poems, were noises in the background. I knew nothing of our story or our homeland.

When Richard Rodriguez spoke at the California State Library Association a few years ago, he talked about what libraries meant to him as a child: "What you gave me, LIBRARIANS, was a library that was so confusing," he said. "It was not separated by ethnicities and race. You gave me James BALDWIN when I was about 9 years old. I remember reading *Nobody Knows My Name.* I remember reading about growing up in Harlem, and I thought to myself, 'This life is so different from mine. But why is it that my gut feels so tight with it. Why do I feel connected to this man?' And I remember reading *My Ántonia* by Willa Cather and thinking to myself, 'Hell, I've never even seen snow, and I'm standing there on a train station on a snowy night with these immigrants from a place called Bohemia. What is this? Who is she? And why do I care so much about her? Why is her life mine?'"

The best stranger stories are often told through the eyes of a child, and they possess the power to shake up what seems cozy and familiar. Louise Erdrich's *Birchbark House* does just that with a story based on a letter she found from one of her ancestors. *Birchbark House* is the first of a cycle of novels set at the time of the Laura Ingalls WILDER classics, and Er-

drich makes us imagine what it was like for an Ojibwa Indian child when the non-Indian white people were "opening up" the land. Why has no one written this story before? Why are there so few good children's books about the people displaced by the little house in the big woods? *Little House* readers will discover a new world, a different version of an American story they thought they knew. I interviewed Louise Erdrich about this book [BKL Ap 1 99], and she spoke affectionately about the classic Little House novels, despite their limitations. "Certainly those books were formative for me," Erdrich said. "I read them as a child and in rereading them as an adult, I was shocked to recognize that, not only was there no consciousness about the displaced people whose land the newcomers were taking, but also that there was a fair amount of racism. In the Little House books, there are always these moves from place to place. The fact is that any time land was opening up, it was land from which native people were displaced, and in every Ojibwa FAMILY there's a similar series of moves."

Truth and Reconciliation

The same thing happened in South Africa. The whites came from Europe, and they "discovered" the country. That means they came with their guns and they took the land and the rich gold and diamond mines and everything else. They built cities and they lived very well, but blacks had to get special permission to come to white areas to work. The whites made up one-fifth of the population, but they took more than four-fifths of the land. Only the whites could vote. Only the whites could use the "public" library, only the whites could go to a decent school. The police and the army forcibly removed black people from their homes, bulldozed their communities, and resettled them far away in barren wastelands the government called *homelands.* It was a trail of tears. Under apartheid, that word *homeland* meant exactly the opposite of home. It meant exile. And the word *native* was an insult, a generic word for black people. Again, it meant exactly the opposite. "Native" meant "stranger."

There was no work in the homelands. So parents had to leave to find work in the towns. Beyond all the rhetoric, that was the central fact of apartheid cruelty: it broke up family life. What was it like to leave your "homeland" as a TEENAGER and come to the city, a stranger in search of work? To have to produce your pass on demand to any policeman? To see your parents cower to the police or run for their lives? To fall in love with someone of another color and go to jail for it? To leave the country secretly and be trained as a soldier and return to fight a guerilla war? To see Nelson Mandela walk free after 27 years in prison? Young people were at the forefront of the rebellion, especially the Soweto children's uprising in 1976. Their protest against their inferior education started the great upheaval that eventually ended the apartheid regime. Between 1960 and 1990 some 15,000 young people under the age of eighteen were detained without trial. Torture was commonplace. We've heard about some of it in the last few years in the heartwrenching evidence before the Truth and Reconciliation Commission. As the court moved around the country, people came forward to tell what happened to them. I once heard a cabinet minister in Nelson Mandela's government say that the commission had given a voice to those who had been told by the police that they could scream as loud as they liked, and no one would hear. The head of the Commission, Archbishop Desmond Tutu, prayed at the opening of the hearings "that we may have the strength to listen to the whispers of the abandoned, the pleas of those afraid, the anguish of those without hope." They did listen, and ordinary people came forward to tell what happened to them, people who once were strangers with no voice.

Through all the apartheid years, a few great writers, black and white, continued to write with honesty and passion. Their books reached a world audience. At home nearly all of them were censored: banned, banished, imprisoned.

Listening to the Young

Today's young people will tell it. They're going to school. You have no idea how moving it is to go back to South Africa now and see young people of all races going to school together. To see parents bringing their own children to school. The apartheid legacy is still overwhelming. They have to transform the classrooms that were once supposed to train children for menial labor. They need books from everywhere for their libraries. They want access to the Internet. They're learning their history. And as the new artists

and writers among the people find their voices, as they find room of their own, we're going to have a renaissance of stories by those who once were told that no one would ever want to know.

In this country, too, there are people whose stories we do not hear. Francisco JIMÉNEZ's great book *The Circuit* is based on his life as a child in a migrant farmworker family, from the time they leave Mexico to enter the U.S. "under the wire," through the years of moving from place to place, picking cotton, picking grapes, picking strawberries, thinning lettuce, tapping carrots, always moving. Like Steinbeck's classic *Grapes of Wrath,* Jiménez's stories combine stark social realism with heartrending personal drama. The language is simple and it is music.

It is a book for all of us. One of the great things about *The Circuit* is that the characters aren't idealized: though the family is warm, their bitter struggle creates anger and jealousy as well as love. Some teachers are kind; some classrooms and playgrounds are ugly.

There's the same honesty in Anita Lobel's memoir *No Pretty Pictures: A Child of War.* We have heard many moving HOLOCAUST stories, but Lobel's is among the best, especially on the issue of "home." It's strength is in the truth of the child's viewpoint, told with physical immediacy and no pride of victimhood. Barely five years old when the Nazis came to her comfortable home in Poland, she spent the next five years in hiding and on the run; then she was captured and transported to concentration camps. Through the marches, hunger, mud, stench, and corpses, her younger brother was nearly always with her, disguised as a girl to hide his circumcision. Looking back, she avoids sermonizing and analysis. She remembers how it was.

When I interviewed Lobel [BKL Ag 98], she had some very surprising things to say about her "homeland." She was adamant that she would not in any way sanctify herself as a victim. And no, she does not feel uprooted, she said. She does not miss Poland or Sweden. From the time she came here she said she wanted to be "normal." "I love being a New Yorker," she said. "I don't want to be anywhere else. I want to belong, but on my own terms, not to be set apart by race or place. I wouldn't say that I have any roots. What has that got to do with anything? Me, I start all over every day."

Primitives in Paradise

In contrast to the honesty of Lobel, too many stories of childhood upheaval—whether due to immigration or racism or political oppression—long for a paradise that never was. Everything before was perfect. Everybody was always happy and good. Louise Erdrich attacks that sort of romantic portrayal of the Native American past, what she calls those "Edward Curtis sepia-toned" images of native people.

We get that misty romanticism about the past whether it's the shtetl in Eastern Europe or Ireland in pastoral bliss. With Africa, the idyllic isn't just the past. It continues, with images of primitive innocence, reverential images of animals and savages untouched by modern pollution: rhythmic, exotic, dramatic, generic. It's exactly that unspoiled native nonsense that the apartheid leaders tried to invent. They pretended to honor roots, but that meant that innocent savages needed white care and control, to be kept apart, except for menial labor. Math and science weren't part of their culture. Natives could teach us about nature, about getting in touch with our instinctive selves.

I get a "primitive" children's book like that to review every season. In a recent title the mysterious African warrior could communicate not only with the lion and the elephant, but also with the polar bear. It's strangers who write those kind of condescending stories, tourists who drop in for a short time, make some contacts, take some photos of the sweet children and endangered animals, and then leave for the next stop.

These aren't stories about strangers; they are stories by strangers posing as something else. You end up with Africa as Tarzan, with Hiawatha's paint and feathers, with exotic strangers like "them," not individuals like "us."

Both Sides of the Border

I've grumbled a lot about romanticism, false nostalgia, strangers who write tourist exotica, who write about what they don't know. And yet with the best writers, the opposite may be true. Some of the great stories have been written out of longing, homesickness, rootlessness; stories that come from both sides of the border, stories by newcomers that take readers where they never imagined.

There are even writers who love something so much they can invent it. Robert Frost wrote some of his best poems—"After Apple-Picking," "Birches," "Mending Wall"—when he was in London, away from New England. He wrote them out of homesickness. But in his case the amazing thing is that he was homesick for a home that he'd created.

When I first came here, Robert Frost always seemed to me so much the elemental New England voice. I loved the casual, ordinary words of the plain Yankee farmer. How I envied Frost his roots. Then I discovered just last year, reading Jay Parini's great new BIOGRAPHY of Frost, that it's all a myth, that Frost grew up in San Francisco. He came to rural New England as an outsider, a stranger, and he so fell in love with the place that he made it his own and transformed it for all of us.

And yet—there's always another "and yet"—some of the best stories are about those who want to leave, who feel like strangers at home. In Allen Say's recent PICTURE BOOK *Tea with Milk,* he tells the American immigrant story in reverse. His mother, Masako, grew up in a Japanese-American family in California. When she finished high school, her restless, homesick father took the family back to live in his village in Japan. Masako became a foreigner in her parents' country, longing for home in San Francisco, unable to be a "proper" Japanese lady. When she rebels and breaks away, like many foreigners everywhere, like me, she discovers her home in the city. She finds work, opportunity, and a husband from an even more diverse background than her own. This is an "ugly duckling" romance and a universal story about everyone who feels they don't belong at home.

The point is we are all part of many places, many homelands—whether the community is defined by ethnicity or language or sexual orientation or age or place or religion or work or sport or hobby or whatever. And the best books take us up close and show how diverse each homeland is.

The 2001 National Book Award winner, Kimberly Willis HOLT's *When Zachary Beaver Came to Town,* captures the sense of being stuck at home. It's 1971 in Antler, Texas, a place too small and boring for thirteen-year-old Toby Wilson's mom, who has left to try and be a country music star. Then a stranger comes to town. He's Zachary Beaver, a 600-pound teenager, "the fattest boy in the world," who never leaves his trailer. At first Toby and his friend Cal come to gape at the freak-show, but eventually they help Zachary step outside. Not that he's sweet and grateful. He's a mean liar, rude and angry, as well as achingly vulnerable. They all are. Through Toby's eyes, you get to know that small place in all its neon particulars and its gentleness. You see how you can shut yourself in too tight a space. We've all known places like this. In the tradition of many southern writers, Holt reveals the freak in all of us, and the power of redemption.

I read this book and it took me back to reading Carson McCullers' *Ballad of the Sad Café* when I was a teenager in Johannesburg; I remember how that story just swept me away; it was about me. The British writer Aidan CHAMBERS says that "When you write about what you think is most private—just about you—you discover everybody's like that."

He's talking about the stranger in all of us. When I was first asked to give this lecture, several people wondered if I would be talking about MULTICULTUR-ALISM. I wanted to say, "Well, yes." But I knew that if I so much as mentioned that word, I'd be met either with pious rhetoric or weary irony—you know, that sneering comment, "It's so P.C.," that everyone thinks makes them sound cool and sophisticated. Until, of course, you touch their special territory. They know quality, and quality is the mainstream, and the mainstream is them. Then there are those who treat multiculturalism as "other": a special unit in the curriculum or a separate place in the library or a unifying theme for an anthology. I often get asked for suggestions for multicultural children's books. Well, what would you leave out? Multiculturalism is all our stories. That is what I've been talking about: multiculturalism, not as a slogan or as a sermon or as a sneer, not as role models or as exotica, and not as bland universalism, but as unsettling stories that transcend the apartheid barriers and connect us with strangers and bring us home.

And yet, just as the best books bring us home, they also help us stray. You know that old story about the hero who searched for treasure all over the world and then found it right there in his own backyard? What that story is really saying, mythologist Wendy Doniger believes, is that it's only because you've traveled that you can find treasure at home. You need the stranger. You are the stranger. When you get lost in a story, when you get to care about a character, you find yourself in a new world that makes you look at

yourself in a new way. You imagine other people's lives, and that makes you discover your own.

HAZEL ROCHMAN

MURPHY, Jim
Author, b. 25 September 1947, Newark, New Jersey

M. is a master of writing nonfiction for children and young adults, as well as an accomplished novelist of works for young people. He is especially interested in the roles they have played throughout American history, and many of his nonfiction titles feature firsthand historical accounts of children and young adults.

M. passed a relatively happy childhood growing up in northern New Jersey, spending much of his leisure time outdoors. Beginning at the age of twelve, he became an avid reader of both fiction and nonfiction. He graduated from Rutgers, the State University of New Jersey, in 1970, and worked as a construction worker immediately after completing college. Meanwhile, he applied for a variety of positions in the publishing industry, hoping to find an entryway into the field of children's publishing. Within a year he joined the staff of Seabury Press (now Clarion) as an editorial secretary with both clerical and editing duties, and eventually worked his way up to managing editor. It was there that he developed a mastery of children's writing, acquired largely through his editing experiences. In 1977, he left the company to become a full-time freelance writer, although he continued to accept some editing work.

His earliest titles were nonfiction works describing unusual inventions (i.e., *Weird and Wacky Inventions,* 1978) and vehicles (i.e., *Two Hundred Years of Bicycles,* 1983; and *The Custom Car Book,* 1985). As his career progressed, he began to focus on American history, beginning with *The Boys' War: Confederate and Union Soldiers Talk about the Civil War* (1990) and *The Long Road to Gettysburg* (1992).

M.'s most famous book is the Newbery Honor Book *The Great Fire.* While researching another book a few years before writing *The Great Fire,* he chanced upon a letter written by a young girl who had survived Chicago's great fire of 1871. The girl's vivid first-person account and incredible bravery left a strong impression on M. This experience later inspired him to research and write *The Great Fire* with a focus on excerpts from first-person survivor accounts. In writing *The Great Fire,* M. sought to write nonfiction as if it were fiction, with a beginning that lays out the conflict and "characters," a middle that builds to a climax, and an ending that concludes the conflict and the stories of the major "characters" in the book. *The Great Fire* also features other literary devices more common to fiction than nonfiction, including chapters that end with cliff-hangers, first-hand personal narrative excerpts that serve as "dialogue," and an action-driven plot. Perhaps most unusual is M.'s presentation of the fire itself; it is handled as if it were one of the characters in the story, a character driven to destroy life and property. The result of these literary devices is a gripping nonfiction work that reads almost like a novel.

Another nonfiction title of particular note is *Blizzard! The Storm that Changed America* (2000). It recounts the events surrounding and during the New York City blizzard of 1888. In M.'s hallmark style, he fills his narrative with first-person eye-witness accounts, emphasizing the youth point of view. M. also considers the long-term effects of the blizzard, showing that the disaster led to the creation of city emergency procedures across the country and even helped to bring about the construction of the New York City subway system.

Although best known as a nonfiction writer, M. has also published a number of fiction titles, including entries in two historical fiction SERIES, the *Dear America* series (*My Face to the Wind: The Diary of Sarah Jane Price, a Prairie Teacher, Broken Bow, Nebraska, 1881,* 2001) and the *My Name Is America* series (*The Journal of Brian Doyle: A Greenhorn on an Alaskan Whaling Ship,* 2003). As in his nonfiction work, these books contain the same strong characterization, emphasis on period details, and vivid plot construction.

SELECT AWARDS: 1990 Golden Kite Award, *The Boys' War: Confederate and Union Soldiers Talk About the Civil War;* 1992 Golden Kite Award, *The Long Road to Gettysburg;* 1994 Orbis Pictus Award, *Across America on an Emigrant Train; The Great Fire:* 1995 *Boston Globe–Horn Book* Award Honor, 1996 Newbery Honor, 1996 Orbis Pictus Award; 2001 Washington Post–Children's Book Guild Nonfiction Award; 2001 Robert F. Sibert INFORMATIONAL Book Award Honor, Dorothy Canfield Fisher Children's Book Award, 2002, *Blizzard! The Storm that Changed America*; and numerous citations on ALA lists.

FURTHER WORKS: *Guess Again: More Weird and Wacky Inventions,* 1985; *An American Plague: The True and Terrifying Story of the Yellow Fever Epidemic of 1793,* 2003; *Gone A-Whaling: The Lure of the Sea and the Hunt for the Great Whale,* 2004.

BIBLIOGRAPHY: Authors & Artists for Young Adults, vol. 20, 1997; *Something about the Author,* vol. 124, 2002.

DENISE E. AGOSTO

MURPHY, Pat
Author, b. 9 March 1955, n.p.

M. began her career as a SHORT STORY writer of SCIENCE FICTION in 1976. Her first novel was *The Shadow Hunter* (1982), in which a Neanderthal man is transported into the future. In her second novel, *The Falling Woman* (1987), she uses her fascination with anthropology to write about themes such as how different cultures deal with the world and how the past affects the future. She uses FANTASY, ghost stories, and science fiction to fashion characters that may shift and change as their roles in the narrative change.

M. received widespread critical acclaim for *The City, Not Long After* (1989). This futuristic love story reveals a sense of humor as the main characters defend their world with courage and cunning.

Along with her fiction works, M. also writes nonfiction science books for The Exploratorium, San Francisco's art, science, and human perception museum. She has taught science fiction writing at Stanford University and at the University of California at Santa Cruz.

AWARDS: 1987 Nebula Award for best novel, Science Fiction Writers of America, *The Falling Woman;* 1987 Nebula Award for best novella, *Rachel in Love;* 1987 Theodore Sturgeon Memorial Award; 1991 Philip K. Dick Award, best original PAPERBACK, *Points of Departure;* 1991 World Fantasy Award, *Bones.*

FURTHER WORKS: *Nadya: The Wolf Chronicles,* 1996, *There and Back Again* (reworking of J. R. R. TOLKIEN's *The Hobbit*), 1999, *Wild Angel,* 2000.

BIBLIOGRAPHY: *Contemporary Authors Online,* 2003; rebeccasreads.com

LAURIE M. ALLEN

MURPHY, Rita
Author, n.d., n.p.

M. combines rites of passage with a touch of magic. Her first book, *Night Flying* (2000), was the winner of the Delacorte Press Contest for a First Young Adult Novel, awarded annually by Random House to encourage the writing of contemporary young adult fiction. "[A]n auspicious debut," according to *Publishers Weekly,* it tells the story of fifteen-year-old Georgia Hansen. All of the women in her FAMILY can fly, but none were allowed to fly solo until age sixteen. On the eve of her sixteenth birthday, Georgia learns a few things that aid her in making difficult decisions.

M.'s second book, *Black Angels* (2001), is set in the segregated South during the CIVIL RIGHTS MOVEMENT. When eleven-year-old Celli begins to see little black angels appear on her family's property in rural Mystic, Georgia, her long-lost grandmother arrives in town with the famed Freedom Riders and a family secret. The story weaves a volatile piece of American history with Celli's emerging consciousness.

In *Harmony* (2002), fifteen-year-old Harmony McClean finds it hard growing up in the Tennessee mountains; as a baby, she was found next to a meteor that had crashed through the roof of a chicken coop. Things don't get any easier as she develops telekinetic abilities. When a logging company threatens to cut down an old growth forest, Harmony uses her new gift to save her giant friends and in the process comes to terms with herself. *Horn Book* calls it an "engaging" tale that "will speak to readers on the cusp of adolescence" (January/February 2003).

AWARDS: 1999 Delacorte Press Prize for First Young Adult Novel, 2001 ALA Best Books for Young Adults, 2002 Dorothy Canfield Fisher Children's Book Award, 2003 ALA Popular Paperbacks, *Night Flying.*

BIBLIOGRAPHY: Brown, J., Devereaux E., Frederick, H. & Maughan, S, "Flying Starts." *Publishers Weekly* 247, no. 51, 26–29, 2000; *Horn Book* magazine, 79, no. 1, 82–83, 2003

JULIE SHEN

MUSIC IN TEEN FICTION

Music plays an important role in the lives of TEENS. Teenaged musicians and dancers have a formalized relationship with music and are active participants in school or community orchestras, bands, ensembles, or dance troupes. Other teens create music in a less formal setting, playing instruments in their basements and garages or dancing just to have fun. While some teens enjoy a creative relationship with music, countless other teens avidly listen to and enjoy the music that surrounds them in their everyday lives as they listen to the radio, attend concerts, and listen to their ipods. The music that teens listen to serves as a backdrop for their lives. Teens form associations with particular songs and events in their lives. They may go through phases of listening to a particular artist or style of music. That style will always remind them of certain times and places.

Some authors play with music to convey a sense of time and place. Rob THOMAS in *Rats Saw God* (1996) tells the story of Steve York, who must write a one hundred-page paper about his experiences in high school to make up for his failing grade in English and graduate from high school. *Rats Saw God* chronicles Steve's fall from top student to near dropout and is *filled* with references to music. His love of grunge music lends realism to the story, setting it firmly in the early 1990s. Steve is a music-obsessed teen, so the first-person narrative is filled with references to music. Steve describes a raucous rendition of "Kum Ba Yah" on the beach. He relates the tale of inviting Allison (who "looked like a girl in an AC/DC video—*before* the innocent hears Angus play") to a Pearl Jam concert and discussing favorite bands. Rob Thomas uses music to create a setting for the novel, lending authenticity to the voice of the main character.

Another book that successfully employs music in the creation of a setting is Stephen CHBOSKY's *The Perks of Being a Wallflower* (1999). Charlie, the wallflower of the title, tells his story through a sequence of open letters. His is the quintessential high-school experience—he's a geeky loner who struggles with social interactions. Charlie steps into the limelight when he is forced to play the role of Rocky at a midnight viewing of the "Rocky Horror Picture Show." Charlie, normally shy and retiring, actually enjoys the pantomiming, strutting, dancing, and acting that the part requires. References to music are sprinkled throughout the novel; for example, Charlie listens to *The White Album* while drinking and playing Truth or Dare with friends. One particularly moving reference to music is Charlie's list of songs on a mix tape that he had made for his friend Patrick. Charlie merely lists the songs and artists on the tape (including "Landslide" by Fleetwood Mac, "Dear Prudence" by the Beatles, and "Daydream" by Smashing Pumpkins) but indicates that he selected "Asleep" by the Smiths as the first and final song of the mix tape. The lyrics of the song are not written out, but Chbosky infers that the song is of particular importance to Charlie due to its double exposure on the tape. Readers are left to hear Morrissey's plaintiff lyrics ("Sing me to sleep / Sing me to sleep / I'm tired and I / I want to go to bed . . . I don't want to wake up on / my own anymore . . . Don't feel bad for me / I want you to know / Deep in the cell of my heart / I really want to go") perfectly capture the mood of the book and Charlie's tiredness in the face of coping with the loss of his brother.

Music could almost be considered a character in Nick Hornby's *High Fidelity* (1995). The ADULT novel, which appeals to teen readers, focuses on Rob, who lives and breathes music. Rob owns a record store with an amazing selection and a music-snob staff. Rob is obsessed with music and list-making. He only realizes that he has made a mess of his life when his long-time live-in girlfriend, Laura, dumps him at the novel's start. Rob rearranges his record collection again and again while mulling over the choices he has made, contacting old girlfriends in the hopes of finding out what went wrong with their relationships, and practically stalking Laura. Rob's trek down memory lane is lined with memories of people, places, and music.

Francesca Lia BLOCK also uses music to set the scene in her acclaimed novel *Weetzie Bat* (1989). Weetzie dances her heart out while being jostled and bashed in the pit at a Fear concert. In the second book of the SERIES, *Witch Baby* (1991), the title character holes up in a shed and drums like no one has drummed before. Witch baby and her sibling, Cherokee Bat, team up with their friends to form a band in *Cherokee Bat and the Goat Guys* (1992) and then face the in-fighting so common among bandmates. Block also wrote about siblings in a band in her FANTASY novels for adult readers, *Ecstasia* (1993) and *Primavera* (1994), in which Greek MYTHOLOGY and music fiction meld to present the story of Calliope and Rafe, who travel to the underworld to see their dead parents.

Dogbreath Victorious (1999) by Chad Henry offers a lighthearted comedic look at a group of slackers who wish to win a local battle of the bands. One problem: none of them has any real ability as a musician.

Tim and his friends form Dogbreath, a band that struggles through each practice session (they struggle just to make it *to* the practice sessions!). The boys are distressed to hear that a rival band, The Angry Housewives, has formed and created quite a buzz, and are even more upset when they learn that the band is fronted by Tim's mom in this fun tale of intergenerational musical rivalry.

Another humorous title that highlights the importance of music and concert-going in the lives of teens is *LBD: It's a Girl Thing* (2003) by Grace Dent. Three fourteen-year-old friends, known amongst themselves as Les Bambinos Dangereuses, are forced to start their own music festival, Blackwell Live, when their parents deny them their God-given right to attend the Astlebury Music Festival.

In Dyan SHELDON's *Confessions of a Teenage Drama Queen* (1999), attending a concert takes on epic importance in the life of Lola Cep, a New York City girl who has been transplanted to suburban New Jersey against her will. Lola has already battled with her nemesis, Carla Santini, for the lead role in their school's rendition of *Pygmalion*. Now she has plans to attend the final performance of Siddharta, her favorite band, and the after-party that everyone is talking about. Unfortunately, Carla Santini has scored tickets to the event and Lola has not, which means that Lola and her close friend Ella must crash the events.

The extreme pressures faced by young musicians are explored in *Mountain Solo* (2003) by Jeanette INGOLD. Tess, a sixteen-year-old violinist with a promising career, falters at an important concert in Germany. Shaken by her failure, Tess retreats to Montana to spend time with her father and his second wife while rethinking her career. Tess' stepmother is an archaeologist who is searching for clues about pioneers in the region, and Tess discovers the mysterious life of Frederick Bottner, another violinist who lived in Montana during frontier times. Tess eventually realizes that she truly loves playing the violin and will continue on her path as a violinist, but that she must determine her own fate rather than having her life decided by her mother.

The Mozart Season (1991) by Virginia Euwer WOLFF is another story of the pressures faced by young musicians. Allegra has been selected as a finalist in a violin competition in Oregon and must practice Mozart's Fourth Violin Concerto all summer in order to be ready. Allegra's preparatory period is filled with hope and fear as she struggles with doubts about her abilities and uncertainties about who she is and how she fits in the world.

Blueprint (2000) by Charlotte Kerner also deals with the stresses faced by young musicians of great talent. Kerner's novel, originally published in Germany, is the story of Iris, a famous pianist, and her clone/daughter, Siri. Iris made the decision to clone herself when she learned that she suffered from multiple sclerosis. Siri, left alone after her mother's DEATH, struggles with grief at the loss of her parent but also with anger and resentment because of the pressures she feels Iris foisted upon her. The book examines both the extreme pressures and expectations placed on a child prodigy by a parent and the ethical implications surrounding cloning.

David Bowler's *Firmament* (2004) is the story of a young man coming to terms with his musical talents and with his father's death. Luke's dad was a concert pianist and Luke has the talent to follow in his path. As Luke's grades drop and his relationships with people (including his mother and piano teacher) falter, Luke feels that music is the only stable thing in his life. Luke is also a skilled climber and he is bullied into taking part in a robbery during which his ears lead him to a shocking discovery.

Siblance T. Spooner is a sixteen-year-old cello prodigy who goes in search of the mother who abandoned her in Bruce BROOKS's *Midnight Hour Encores* (1986). Siblance and her father, Taxi, set off across the country to find her mom. As they travel, their conversation flows through music of all types and a remembrance of the 1960s, when Siblance's parents were together.

While he isn't a prodigy, John, the fourteen-year-old protagonist of David KLASS's *You Don't Know Me* (2001), is another teen who is strongly affected by the pressures facing young musicians. John plays the tuba in the high-school band. His tuba is inclined to emit croaking noises, and John has creatively developed a frog-like persona for his tuba. John's tuba playing is just one element of the novel, in which a young man struggles in an abusive home environment but manages to find areas of light and happiness through friendships, love, and tuba playing.

CATHY DELNEO

MYERS, Anna
Author, b. n.d., White Face, Texas

M. wrote her first story the summer before first grade. Growing up in a large FAMILY in which everyone was a storyteller, M. remembers going to the library on Saturdays and her five older siblings reading aloud to her. After graduating from the University of Central Oklahoma, M. taught high-school English in Tulsa and in Norman, Oklahoma, before moving to New York to teach. After marrying Paul Myers, a poet, M. moved back to Oklahoma and continued teaching until her eldest child was born. As a teacher, M. found that she only read books that were aimed at young people. As M.'s children got older, M. realized she had to get serious about writing in order to pay for college tuitions. M. decided on historical fiction because, as a former student once said, "If you don't know where you have been, you can't know where you are going."

M.'s first book was *Red-dirt Jessie* (1992), and since its publication M. has written a book a year. Perhaps the most difficult book to write was *When the Bough Breaks* (2000), because it was written right after the DEATH of her husband. The novel deals with desperation and loss as two generations of woman come together to share their pain in a dark story of secrets revealed.

Graveyard Girl (1995) takes place during the yellow fever epidemic in Memphis in 1876. Grace the "graveyard girl," so called because she tolls the cemetery bell for those who have died, befriends Eli, who has lost his mother and sister to the epidemic. In *The Keeping Room* (1997), British general Cornwallis takes over the home of Colonel Joseph Kershaw. The story is seen through the eyes of Kershaw's son, Joey, and the readers share his frustration over being unable to protect his family.

Tulsa Burning (2002) is a novel that chronicles the real-life events of the Tulsa race riot of 1921. M. wanted to tell the story of a boy struggling with anger and hatred who in the end has the courage to overcome those emotions because as a teacher M. has encountered many children with the same struggles. M. still lives and teaches in Oklahoma and enjoys traveling and speaking with children about her work.

AWARDS: Oklahoma Book Award for *Red-dirt Jessie,* 1993, for *Graveyard Girl,* 1995, American Bookseller's Pick of the Lists for *Graveyard Girl,* 1995; American Library Association's Quick Picks for Reluctant Young Adult Readers for *Ethan Between Us,* 1999; New York Public Library's Book for the TEEN Age for *When the Bough Breaks,* 2001, and for *Tulsa Burning,* 2003.

FURTHER WORKS: *Rosie's Tiger,* 1994; *Fire in the Hills,* 1996; *Spotting the Leopard,* 1996; *Ethan Between Us,* 1998; *Monster,* 2000; *Captain's Command,* 2001; *Stolen by the Sea,* 2001; *Flying Blind,* 2003; *Hoggee,* 2004.

BIBLIOGRAPHY: *Children's Literature Resources,* online, 2002; Walkeryoungreaders.com, online; Anna myers.info, online.

MEGAN PEARLMAN

AND ANDREA LIPINSKI

MYERS, Walter Dean

Author, b. 12 August, 1937, Martinsburg, West Virginia

M.'s mother died when he was three, and his father brought him from West Virginia to Harlem where the Deans, his foster parents, adopted him. M. received love from the Deans that ultimately strengthened him. M.'s father and his grandfather used to tell him stories. His father told him scary stories while his grandfather told him stories from the Hebrew Bible, "God's-gonna-get-ya kind of stories." When he was young, M. read a lot of comic books or any sort of literature he could find. One day a teacher grabbed his comic book from him and tore it up. M. was distraught, but the teacher then gave him a pile of books from her own library; this event was, according to the author, the best thing that could have happened to him. The public library became M.'s most treasured place; he couldn't believe his luck that the thing he enjoyed most, reading, was free.

M. had a severe speech impediment that prevented many people from understanding him. One of M.'s teachers thought that writing would help him pronounce certain words more clearly; she thought that if he wrote something, he would use words he could pronounce. She offered him the chance to write anything he could imagine, and he began writing little poems that helped him because of the rhythms. He began to write SHORT STORIES, too. His writing was the only thing he was praised for in school. By the time he was in high school, he defined himself as an intellectual because he couldn't speak well and had a

limited social life; he reasoned that intelligence was something hidden from most people. He knew his family could not afford college for him, so high school became of little importance to him.

After time in the Army, M. felt he could not do anything besides menial jobs. He started loading trucks and then worked in the post office for a while. All this time, M. spent his nights writing. He won the contest sponsored by the Council on Interracial Books for Children for black writers of children's books; this was to be his first published book, *Where Does the Day Go?* (1969). The publication gave the author validation; despite his meager education, he had been able to create something of substance. He decided to pursue writing as a full-time career, setting up disciplined work conditions for himself.

M. became a YA novelist quite accidentally. An editor mistakenly thought that a short story M. had submitted was the first chapter of a novel. M. made up the rest of the plot off the top of his head, realizing that the opportunity to have a published YA novel was too good to pass up. This fluke became *Fast Sam, Cool Clyde, and Stuff* (1975), a book which depicts inner-city TEENAGERS' quest for fun and activity in a optimistic light. This novel presents a much more positive view of Harlem than M.'s later YA books. Here the backdrop of Harlem and the realism of drugs and poverty is compounded by the turmoil and peril of city life. In *Hoops* (1981), *Motown and Didi: A Love Story* (1984), *Scorpions* (1988), *The Mouse Rap* (1990), and *Slam!* (1998), the protagonists all strive for something beyond their surroundings; they must overcome the challenges of their tumultuous families and the neighborhood at large.

M.'s books are formed from his own background. He writes about places he has lived, hobbies he has had, and interests he has wanted to pursue. For instance, his curiosity about history and major historical figures has impelled him to write historical BIOGRAPHIES. Both *Malcom X* (1994) and *The Greatest: Muhammad Ali* (2001) are tributes to men whom M. finds absolutely riveting. The author says, "Muhammad Ali is the first AFRICAN AMERICAN about whom almost every young man could say, 'That's who I'd like to be!' When Ali burst upon the scene in the early sixties, he was a fascinating blend of youth, daring, conviction, and charm." M. feels honored to be able to write about a man so worthy of emulation. In addition to his personal experience, M. stumbles across other concepts for plots. One specific idea was hatched when a used-book dealer in London handed M. a packet of letters concerning an African princess who had been a protégée of Queen Victoria. After more background research, the princess, Sarah Forbes Bonetta, became the subject of *At Her Majesty's Request: An African Princess in Victorian England* (1999). M. wants to educate readers about figures and topics that he feels are neglected.

Of his career, M. pronounces: "Ultimately, what I want to do with my writing is to make connections—to touch the lives of my characters and, through them, those of my readers." Because M. has the ear of a teenager, his books speak openly and honestly to his adolescent readers. M.'s son Christopher joined his father in YA literature, creating enhancing illustrations for M.'s books.

SELECT AWARDS: Coretta Scott King Award: 1980 for *The Young Landlords,* 1985 for *Motown and Didi,* 1989 for *Fallen Angels,* 1992 for *Now is Your Time!,* 1997 for *Slam!;* Coretta Scott King Honor Books: 1989 for *Scorpions,* 1993 for *Somewhere in the Darkness,* 1994 for *Malcolm X: By Any Means Necessary,* 1998 for *Harlem,* 2000 for *Monster; Harlem:* 1998 Caldecott Honor Book, 1997 *Boston Globe–Horn Book* Award Honor Book; 2000 Michael L. Printz Award, *Monster; At Her Majesty's Request:* Orbis Pictus Honor Book, IRA Notable Book for a Global Society; 1993 Newbery Honor Book, *Somewhere in the Darkness;* and numerous citations on ALA lists and Best of the Best.

SELECT FURTHER WORKS: *Fallen Angels,* 1984; *The Legend of Tarik,* 1991; *Now is Your Time for Freedom,* 1991; *The Righteous Revenge of Artemis Bonner,* 1992; *Somewhere in the Darkness,* 1992; *Shadow of the Red Moon,* 1995; *The Glory Field,* 1996; *Harlem* (illus. Christopher Myers), 1997; *Amistad: A Long Road to Freedom,* 1998; *The Journal of Joshua Loper: A Black Cowboy, the Chisholm Trail, 1871,* 1999; *The Journal of Scott Pendleton Collins: A World War II Soldier, Normandy, France, 1944,* 1999; *Monster* (illus. Christopher Myers), 1999; *145th Street: Short Stories,* 2000; *The Journal of Biddy Owens, Birmingham, Alabama, 1948,* 2001; *Bad Boy: A Memoir,* 2001; *Crystal,* 2002; *The Beast,* 2003; *A Time to Love* (illus. Christopher Myers), 2003.

BIBLIOGRAPHY: "About Walter Dean Myers," *Scholastic Biographical Sheet; The Bulletin of the Center for Children's Books,* vol. 55, July/August 2002, p. 412;

Cullinan, Bernice and Person, Diane, eds. *The Continuum Encyclopedia of Children's Literature,* 2001.

BERNICE E. CULLINAN
AND RACHEL WITMER

MYSTERY NOVELS

Most scholars of Western literature agree that Edgar Allan Poe deserves credit for the first detective story. His "Murders in the Rue Morgue" (1841) introduced moody, intellectual C. Auguste Dupin, whose brilliant analytical mind solves a bizarre locked-room mystery by making the impossible possible. Works by Wilkie Collins and Arthur Conan Doyle followed, along with cheaply produced, formulaic, escapist "dime novels" or "penny dreadfuls," quite sensational for the times, which were widely read during the mid-to-late nineteenth century. Many of the dime novels were detective stories. Their heroes, less sophisticated than Doyle's or Poe's, often used chase and disguise rather than deductive reasoning or intuition to bring villains to justice.

Young people got their own version of detective novels in the early 1900s, thanks to the STRATEMEYER SYNDICATE, the inspiration of shrewd businessman and prolific children's book author Edward Stratemeyer. Under Stratemeyer's direction, a stable of ghostwriters churned out a host of popular children's SERIES, including the Hardy Boys, which appeared in 1927, and Nancy Drew in 1930, both of which featured TEEN amateur detectives: Frank Hardy was eighteen years old in the original SERIES; Nancy, sixteen. Although criticized as simplistic, formulaic, and poorly written, the books were extremely popular at the time, and remain so even today. Both have produced spin-offs obviously intended to appeal to young, contemporary teens looking for lightweight whodunits. In the Hardy Boys Case Files series, for example, Frank and Joe are globetrotting investigators who carry weapons; the twenty-five-book Nancy Drew on Campus series turned the intrepid River Heights teen into a college coed who trades homespun cases for campus conundrums and romance.

Young adults not satisfied with the Stratemeyer detective blueprint more often than not went directly to adult books, where they could find sophisticated, clever plots, characters with more depth, social commentary, and even humor to extend the mystery. In addition to Poe and Doyle, YA became huge fans of

Agatha Christie (Miss Marple and Hercule Poirot), Mary Roberts Rinehart, Josephine Tey, Ellery Queen, Dorothy Sayers, G. K. Chesterton (Father Brown), and Erle Stanley Gardner (Perry Mason).

An expanding YA LITERATURE that encouraged genre fiction helped win back teen mystery fans. Many of the books portrayed teens as lonely fighters against evil, an appealing picture for teen readers who often see themselves as outsiders. Jay Bennett (*Birthday Murderer* and *Dangling Witness*) began writing teen mysteries in the late 1960s and continued writing them into the 1990s. Willo Davis Roberts (*View from the Cherry Tree*), who started out writing for adults, wrote a number of mysteries with teen protagonists during the 1970s. Lois DUNCAN's *I Know What You Did Last Summer* (1973) and her *Killing Mr. Griffin* (1978), both with ensemble teen casts, garnered enough attention to be turned into MOVIES. And Joan Lowery NIXON's 1980 Edgar Award winner *The Kidnapping of Christina Lattimore* was just one of many teen mysteries she penned over two decades.

In 1961, mysteries written specifically for young people had sufficiently evolved to be acknowledged by the Mystery Writers of America. The organization, which had recognized outstanding adult mystery writing since 1946 with the prestigious Edgar Allan Poe Mystery Awards, established a youth category, Best Juvenile Mystery Book. A number of the early awards went to writers whose work was read by adolescents—among them, Phyllis A. Whitney, who won the first Juvenile Award for *Mystery of the Haunted Pool*. An award for Best Young Adult Mystery was finally added in 1989, with Sonia LEVITIN receiving the first one for *Incident at Loring Groves,* in which partying teens face exposing their own illegal behavior when a classmate is murdered.

Though not as prevalent for teens as for younger children, series mysteries are still plentiful and popular today. Many are published only in PAPERBACK. Certainly more graphic than their Stratemeyer counterparts, they still hook readers with their predictability and empowered teen protagonists who flirt with danger. Christopher GOLDEN's *Body of Evidence* stars contemporary college student Jenna Blake in stories that combine crime solving with the paranormal. R. L. Stine's extensive *Fear Street,* which mixes HORROR and mystery, has been popular enough to generate several offshoots, among them *Fear Street: Seniors,* which center on teen boys and teen girls in a

variety of unrelated mystery-suspense stories. In 2001, the late Paul ZINDEL, winner of the MARGARET A. EDWARDS AWARD for his lifetime contribution to YA literature, inaugurated the P. C. Hawke Mysteries, an updated Hardy Boys–like series, in which a contemporary fifteen-year-old high-school student and his sidekick sleuth their way through eleven lightweight adventures.

Suspense and mystery fiction for teens is more than locked rooms, red herrings, and catching criminals these days. Psychological thrillers have claimed an enthusiastic teen readership. AVI's *Wolf Rider* (1986), *Calling Home* (1991) by Michael CADNUM, *Tenderness* (1997) and the *Rag and Bone Shop* (2001) by Robert CORMIER, *Killer's Cousin* (1998) by Nancy WERLIN, E. L. KONIGSBURG's *Silent to the Bone* (2000), *Shattering Glass* (2002) by Gail GILES, and *Acceleration* (2003) by Graham MCNAMEE blend mystery with complicated, provocative issues of importance to teens without sacrificing suspense or the credibility of the protagonist. These books are as much about the character as they are about the situation; the reader "investigates" both.

Teens in search of historical mysteries can travel back to Victorian London in Philip PULLMAN's excellent Sally Lockhart trilogy, which melds creativity with scholarship, or join teenagers living in places in America's past in the History Mystery books, published by Pleasant Company/American Girl. Hilari Bell's *A Matter of Profit* (2001) and *Mary Hoffman's Stravangza: City of Masks* (2002), and J. K. ROWLING's HARRY POTTER books are fine examples of mystery folded into SCIENCE FICTION and FANTASY. And Anthony Horowitz's Alex Rider Adventures turn a "typical" teen into a crime-stopping super spy.

Of course, teen mystery lovers still enjoy books by adult writers. Scott Turow, Tony Hillerman, Dick Francis, Dorothy Gilman, Elizabeth Peters, Ruth Rendell, Sarah Paretsky, Dana Stebenow, Sue Grafton, and Rita Mae Brown continue to attract teen readers. Lindsay Davis's books set in ancient Rome, Eric Garcia's hard-boiled detective stories featuring a dinosaur gumshoe, and Jacqueline Winspear's novel *Maisie Dobbs,* in which a nurse turned P.I. tracks wrongdoers in London in the 1920s, are fun as well. Whether teen mystery readers want the formulaic or the familiar, challenging subjects, methodical reasoning, or breakneck suspense, they do not have to look far.

STEPHANIE ZVIRIN

MYTHIC FICTION

Coined by authors Charles DE LINT and Terri WIND-
LING to more accurately describe their own work, the
term M. has become widely recognized in recent
years. The term is often used interchangeably with
URBAN FANTASY or contemporary fantasy, though it
has a much different meaning. Not all mythic fiction
takes place in an urban setting, and not all mythic
fiction is set in contemporary times; further, not all
M. could realistically be called fantasy. In fact, it was
their unhappiness with the imprecision of "fantasy,"
a term both too broad (because it includes work not
based on myth or folklore) and not broad enough (because it connotes only books published in the fantasy
and SCIENCE FICTION genres, usually set in imaginary
worlds), that inspired de Lint and Windling to label
their work M. In retrospect, their attempt to more
faithfully reflect the spirit of their writing and to appeal to a broader audience has given us a much-
needed term with which to define a large, coherent,
though somewhat amorphous body of literature.

The simplest and best definition of M. is fiction
that draws essential substance from myth, folklore,
fairy tale, and legend. The conscious use of mythic
themes and tropes—that is, elements and language
that reflect either the figurative or literal use of images, symbols, and metaphors from myth and folklore—is the key ingredient, and allows the exploration of realistic themes on a symbolic level. As in the
best fantastic literature, the strength of M. lies in the
metaphorical foundations of the story and in the writer's use of timeless motifs to comment on contemporary life. Drawing upon material that has inspired
readers for thousands of years gives writers a voice in
the continuing conversation that tries to make sense
of the human experience; it resonates with depth in M.

The concept of M. encourages examination of the
notions of "literary" versus "popular" literature, or
"mainstream" versus "genre," and challenges readers to look beyond the publisher's label and judge
quality and content for themselves. Working from the
premise that what is good can also be popular and
that work that appeals to the masses can also have
a critical merit, de Lint, Windling, and others who
champion the term use M. as a label that bridges the
perceived gap between mainstream and genre literature, between quality work and popular work. Intentionally challenging the artificial distinctions of the
publishing industry, M. encompasses the whole range
of literary works, crossing genre boundaries to include everything from high fantasy to historical fiction to HORROR.

Secondary or imaginary world fiction that uses
mythic themes and tropes to tell us something about
the world we live in could be considered M., even
though its imaginary setting and subsequent fantasy
label may seem contrary to the concerns that inspired
the term. However, rather than removing us from our
world for a time—the respectable aim of much fantasy literature—secondary world fantasy, which uses
mythic tropes, metaphors, and symbols, allows the
author to comment on the real world and readers to
examine it—albeit from a bit of a distance. While the
majority of imaginary or secondary world fantasy
does not fall within the scope of mythic fiction, some
works, such as J. Gregory Keyes' *The Briar King*
(2003) or Patricia MCKILLIP's *In the Forests of Serre*
(2003), most certainly do. *The Briar King* takes place
in a wholly imaginary realm, but the mysterious and
frightening creature at its core is surely inspired by
the archetypal Green Man. Moreover, one of the
book's central themes—that the behavior and beliefs
of its inhabitants are reflected in their relationship
with the natural world—is an old idea that has been
examined through story for thousands of years. In a
similar vein, while the myriad mythological references in McKillip's book are clearly Russian, the
world itself is emphatically not, which identifies the
work as mythic secondary world fiction.

There need not be literal magic or obvious fantastical elements, however, for a work to be considered
M. McKillip's aforementioned *In the Forests of Serre*
features characters out of legend, mystical creatures
such as the Firebird and Baba Yaga, and a magical
blend of Russian mythic imagery; it is certainly fantasy, with all the requisite elements of magic and AD-
VENTURE. At the same time, it is unequivocally
mythic fiction, utilizing themes and tropes of myth
and legend to comment on timeless concerns such as
hope and hopelessness, loss, love, and FAMILY. On
the other hand, works such as Alice HOFFMAN's
Green Angel (2003) or, for adults, *The Probable Future* (2003), are more subtle in their offerings, using
evocative language, the occasional fantastic event or
character, and hints of something deeper bubbling
below the surface to create an atmosphere of magic.

519

Hoffman's Green, the girl who can make anything grow, is less overtly fantastic than the obviously enchanted Firebird, but no less powerful a mythic character.

A similar distinction must be drawn between M. and magic realistic literature, often associated with Latin American writers but increasingly popular across the globe as a way to express specific ideas through story. Though they share a number of similar qualities, works of magic realism are not always mythic, utilizing, as they may, any and all kinds of imagery to create their magic. The use of surrealist imagery or other random fantastical elements sets much magic realism apart from mythic fiction, though their literary ambitions are often the same. While many works with young adult appeal, such as Laura Esquivel's *Like Water for Chocolate* (1995) and Arundhati Roy's *The God of Small Things* (1998), do indeed fit nicely into both categories, much magic realist literature uses imagery too random to be labeled M.

In actual practice, some M. is easy to identify, using myth and folklore in obvious ways such as FAIRY TALE RETELLINGS—*The Goose Girl* (2003), Shannon Hale's lyrical retelling of the story of the same name, and Robin MCKINLEY's *Spindle's End* (2002), based on the story of Sleeping Beauty. Books based on myths, either forthrightly such as *Quiver* 2002), Stephanie Spinner's account of Atalanta, or as INSPIRATION such as Cynthia VOIGT's *Orfe* (2002), which transplants the story of Orpheus and Eurydice to the modern day world of rock music, are also readily identifiable as M.

Some works, however, are more subtle, using images, language, and symbols, rather than the story itself to create a mythic sensibility. Charles DE LINT's *Someplace to be Flying* (1999) does not reflect a particular myth or legend, but uses mythic tropes and archetypes to comment on real-world relationships, the idea of FAMILY, the grace of forgiveness. Drawing on images from native Indian mythology, *Someplace to Be Flying* features Raven (whose pot starts all the trouble), Coyote (the Trickster), and the Crow Girls (more dangerous than they look), and First People who have walked the earth since its creation and who still involve themselves in the affairs of men. Even beyond the more obvious archetypal characters, the novel creates a feeling of mythic depth by incorporating scenes and images that rely on myth for their reso-

nance and power. For example, after his beloved is killed while trying to fly (a disturbing scene with its own mythic echos), Jack Daw takes violent revenge on the Cuckoo clan in a bloody massacre that evokes a myriad of similar images. The fantastic elements are not just trappings, but are crucial to the substance of the novel, and de Lint skillfully selects from the rich store of mythic material to add potency and wisdom to the story he tells.

A number of classic young adult SERIES can truly be called M., including Susan COOPER's Dark Is Rising series, Madeleine L'ENGLE's Time Quartet, the Tales of Alvin Maker series by Orson Scott CARD, and His Dark Materials trilogy by Philip PULLMAN. Infused with folkloric reference and mythic resonance, each of these authors used traditional material to add additional layers of meaning to their work. M. novels aimed at or suitable for young adults are becoming increasingly popular of late, ranging across the genre spectrum from ghost stories, to historical fiction, to epic fantasy. Authors such as Charles de Lint, Alan Garner, Robert Holdstock, Jane Lindskold, Juliet MARILLIER, Patricia MCKILLIP, Robin MCKINLEY, Tim Powers, and Terri Windling produce consistently excellent mythic work for TEENS, but there are also a number of other mythic novels that may not spring so readily to mind.

Ghosts play a pivotal role in both *Tamsin* by Peter BEAGLE (2001) and *A Stir of Bones* by Nina Kiriki HOFFMAN (2003). *Tamsin* tells the story of Jenny, recently transplanted from New York City to the haunted moors of Dorset, and vocally unhappy about the change. Distracted from her own problems by her new friend, Jenny must confront the ghostly Tamsin, the Wild Hunt, free her lost love, and reconcile herself to the past. *A Stir of Bones* features another tragic ghost, Nathan, who killed himself after learning of the death of his entire family. This YA prequel to adult novels *A Red Heart of Memories* (2000) and *Past the Size of Dreaming* (2002) tells the story of troubled teen Susan's abusive father, her relationship with Nathan, the new "real" friends she makes after meeting him, and the preternaturally sentient house that takes in the group.

Authors better known for their adult work, for example, Michael Chabon and Alice Hoffman, have both written M. for younger teens (Hoffman's magical adult fiction is increasingly popular with older teens). *Summerland* by Michael Chabon (2002) takes its inspiration from stalwarts such as LEWIS and TOL-KIEN, but also owes a great deal to American folklore. Entwining baseball, the trickster Coyote (who has decided to end the world), and Native American lore, *Summerland* recounts the adventures of Ethan Feld, the worst player in the history of baseball, after he is chosen by a band of fairies to put together a team of fantastic creatures and play in a series of games, the outcome of which will determine the fate of the world. Hoffman's *Green Angel* (2003) takes on a more serious topic, echoing as it does the terrorist events of September 11, 2001. Green, known as such for her uncanny abilities with plants, is forced to stay at home when the rest of the family travels across the river to the city. When the city is destroyed by fire, Green must learn to survive on her own, to replant her garden, to connect with people, and to hope again. As with much of Hoffman's work, the magic is subtle but unmistakable, a trademark she repeated in the two watery tales *Aquamarine* (2002) and *Indigo* (2003).

Aficionados of contemporary fantasy will enjoy the myth-steeped adult novel *American Gods* by Neil GAIMAN (2002), which posits that the gods of old countries and old religions are at war with the new American gods of television, credit cards, the Internet, the telephone. Shadow, released from prison and grieving for his recently deceased wife, embarks on a cross-country road trip with the creepy Mr. Wednesday, unwittingly gathering up players for the final epic battle between old gods and new. (Gaiman's incomparable *Sandman* comic, published in a series of ten GRAPHIC NOVELS, also offers more sophisticated readers an astounding epic of mythic fiction.) One of the first novels to be labeled urban fantasy, *War for the Oaks* by Emma BULL (2001) is also the rock 'n' roll novel that inspired a new subgenre. The novel tells the story of Eddi McCandry, a musician who's just lost her boyfriend and her band when she's drafted, not altogether willingly, into the never-ending war between the Seelie and Unseelie Courts. Alternately pursued and guarded by the fantastic phouka, Eddi must battle the evil Unseelie Queen of Air and Darkness, rebuild her life, and find a new band.

In contemporary fiction, the historical *House of the Winds* by Mia Yun (2000) is narrated by the youngest child of a family living in Korea in the 1960s. As their less than desirable life proceeds, moving from house to house, each more shabby than the last, the narrator's mother, Young Wife, tries to give her children magic in the form of stories about Korea in a happier time. *Truth and Bright Water* (1999) by Thomas King, who is of Cherokee and Greek descent, explores the relationship of two young men, Tecumseh and Lum, who live in towns separated by the Shield river Truth in Montana and Bright Water on an Ottawa Indian reservation. Steeped in mystery and Native American lore, the story begins when the two boys watch a young woman dump the contents of a suitcase over a cliff and then jump off herself.

Besides the growing number of collections of retold fairy tales for teens such as *Swan Sister: Fairy Tales Retold* and *A Wolf at the Door: And Other Retold Fairy Tales* (2001), both edited by Ellen Datlow and Terri Windling, collections of myth-based tales like *Green Man: Tales from the Mythic Forest* (2002), also from Datlow and Windling, are becoming popular. Taking its theme from the mythic Green Man, the book includes stories that evoke various incarnations (some traditional, some most definitely not) of that mythic being. Finally, *Firebirds: An Anthology of Original Fantasy and Science Fiction,* edited by Sharyn November (2003), includes many stories that could be considered M., including Delia Sherman's "Cotillion," a re-telling of the ballad "Tam Lin"; Kara DALKEY's reworking of Hans Christian Andersen's "The Snow Queen" in "The Lady of the Ice Garden"; and Garth NIX's "Hope Chest," about an innocent girl who must save her family from evil.

BIBLIOGRAPHY: The Endicott Studio. www.endicott-studio.com; "Charles de Lint: Mythic Fiction." Interview with Charles de Lint. *Locus,* June 2003; "Terri Windling: Border Coyote." Interview with Terri Windling. *Locus,* October 2003.

FURTHER READING: *The Talisman* and *Black House* by Peter Straub and Steven King, 1984 and 2003; *The Porcelain Dove* by Delia Sherman, 1994; *Waking the Moon* by Elizabeth Hand, 1996; *The Ghost Country* by Sara Paretsky, 1999; *Galveston* by Sean Stewart, 2001; *The Antelope Wife* by Louise Erdrich, 2001; *Daemonomania* by John Crowley, 2001; *Swim the Moon* by Paul Brandon, 2002; *Fudoki* by Kij Johnson, 2003; *The Salt Roads* by Nalo Hopkinson, 2003.

JULIE BARTEL

MYTHOLOGY AND LEGEND

The word *myth* is often used to imply a story which is false or untrue, but that definition is inaccurate and somewhat misleading. Derived from the ancient–Greek word *mythos,* which means a spoken story, M. take place in time apart from historical time, and often feature deities, mortals heroes, semi-divine beings, and fantastic creatures. These sacred stories have no specific author, were passed orally from generation to generation, and most importantly, were (or are) believed to be literally true by the societies that produced them.

M.s explore the human condition and explain the world around us, making comprehensible both the origin and state of the natural world, and the existence and behavior of humans and animals. As M.s were passed down through the ages they were often written down, fixed in a permanent form as dictated by each author, transcriber, or translator, each with his (usually) or her own bias and cultural background. In reading M.s today, there are many ways to approach them; some think they should be taken literally, meaning just what they say—whereas others approach them looking for symbolic content or allegory. In any case, M. the world over tends to resonate with us, to speak to some universal experience of question shared by all humans, and whether told straightforwardly or used as the basis for a newer story, M. adds depth and insight to YOUNG ADULT LITERATURE.

M.s attempt to explain different phenomena and different parts of the human experience, and are fairly universal. Creation M.s tell how the world began, how the people in it came to be, and why it is the way it is. *In the Beginning: Creation Stories from around the World* by Virginia HAMILTON (illus. Barry Moser, 1988) and *The Four Corners of the Sky: Creation Stories and Cosmologies from around the World* by Steven J. Zeitlin (illus. Christopher Raschka, 2000) are two books that retell various international stories. Nature M.s explain the seasons, animals, the earth, the sky, and connect people to their environment. *Dictionary of Nature Myths: Myths of the Earth, Sea, and Sky* by Tamra Andrews (2000) is a good source of nature M. retellings. *Giants, Monsters, and Dragons: An Encyclopedia of Folklore, Legend, and Myth* by Carol Rose (2001) is an illustrated work that describes various beasts and also discusses commonalities across cultures. *Zoo of the Gods: The World of Animals in Myth and Legend* by Anthony S. Mercatante (1999) features both real and imaginary animals, and discusses the M. and cultural importance of

each. Hero M.s recount the exploits of those exceptional people who fought monsters or gods, or accomplished impossible tasks. *The Kingfisher Book of Mythology: Gods, Goddesses, and Heroes from around the World* by David Bellingham (2001) gives an overview of gods, goddesses, and heroes.

Legends (the word is derived from a Latin word meaning *to gather, select, read*) are similar to M.s in that they are anonymous tales passed down orally from generation to generation. Unlike M.s, however, legends feature someone who was—or was believed to have been—historical rather than divine, but whose deeds and exploits have been embellished or dramatized, resulting in fantastic, larger-than-life stories. Legends are associated with a specific place and particular time in history, and although they are not necessarily believed to be literally true by those who tell them, they are regarded as being at least partly historical, though perhaps not verifiable.

A folktale is, again, an anonymous oral narrative passed on from one generation to another, this time intended to entertain or instill community values. These tales are acknowledged never to have happened at all, and unabashedly feature fantastic elements and generalized characters such as the Queen, Youngest Son, or Witch. Fables are similar to folktales, but they usually feature talking animals and definite moral messages.

Collections of M., legend, and folklore, especially for YAs, often do not distinguish between the three distinct types of stories, either including different types in one volume, or labeling specific types erroneously. Though definitions and distinctions between types are not essential, it is helpful to understand how and why stories are created, in what circumstances they were told, and for what purpose. Understanding these differences gives context to the tales and adds meaning and vitality. Still, collections of M. or legends, however they're labeled, are increasingly popular, and offer YA readers an array of topical arrangements. Edith Hamilton's *Mythology,* which offers classic retellings of Greek M.s, is still a standard work, as is *Bulfinch's Mythology: Complete and Unabridged.* Thomas Bulfinch collected not only Greek, Roman, and Celtic stories, but Scandinavian and Eastern as well, grouping them into "The Age of Fable or Stories of Gods and Heroes, The Age of Chivalry," which tells the tales of King Arthur and of the Mabinogion, the medieval Welsh epic, and "Legends of

Charlemagne or Romance of the Middle Ages." A more recent classic, Jane YOLEN's excellent *Favorite Folktales from around the World* (1988), also includes stories from different cultures in one volume, dividing them into categories such as "The Very Young and the Very Old," "A True Loves and False," and "A Tricksters, Rogues, and Cheats."

Increasingly popular today are collections that revolve around a theme such as *Mightier than the Sword: World Folktales for Strong Boys* (2003) and *Not One Damsel in Distress: World Folktales for Strong Girls* (2000), both by Jane Yolen, *Wisdom Tales from around the World: Fifty Gems of Story and Wisdom from Such Diverse Traditions As Sufi, Zen, Taoist, Christian, Jewish, Buddhist, African, and Native American* by Heather Forest (1996) or *Gray Heroes: Elder Tales from around the World* (1999), also by Yolen. The Discovering Mythology SERIES from Lucent Books features myths and legends from across the globe, divided by theme into separate volumes, including *Gods and Goddesses* by Wendy Mass (2002), *Death and the Underworld* by Michael J. Wyly (2001), *Heroes* by Don NARDO (2001), *Quests and Journeys* by Nardo (2001), and *Monsters* by Nardo (2001).

Collections of M. are often grouped by geographical region, and thankfully the usual collections of Greek and Roman M. have been supplemented of late by a myriad of series and collections dedicated to myths and legends around the globe. *The Norse Myths* by Kevin Crossley-Holland, *Japanese Tales* by Royall Tyler (2002), and *American Indian Myths and Legends* by Richard Erdoes and Alfonso Ortiz (1985) are just some of the volumes in the Pantheon Fairytale and Folklore Library. These consistently outstanding collections of various traditional stories, always include notes on historical context and the origins of particular versions, and are suitable for good YA readers. The Mythology series from Enslow, which includes *Celtic Mythology* by Catherine Bernard (2003), *African Mythology* by Linda Jacobs Altman (2003), *Mayan and Aztec Mythology* by Michael A. Schuman (2001), *Inuit Mythology* by Evelyn Wolfsan (2001), *Chinese Mythology* by Irene Dea Collier (2001), and *Egyptian Mythology* by Nardo (2001) is similar, and is aimed specifically at a YA audience.

YA novels that retell in a straightforward, though unique, manner, the story of a particular M. or legend, or which use M. as the basis or background of a story have become increasingly popular, and novels based on Greek and Roman M. are particularly plentiful. *Troy* by Adele Geras (2002) re-creates the Trojan War of Homer's *Iliad* as seen through the eyes of four TEENS trapped in the city. *Goddess of Yesterday* by Caroline B. COONEY (2002) uses the same material to tell the story of Anaxandra, unwilling companion of Helen. Retelling the legend of Theseus and the Minotaur, *Lost in the Labyrinth* by Patrice KINDL (2002) offers an unusual narrator in Xenodice, sister of the feared and misunderstood beast. *The Great God Pan* by Donna Jo NAPOLI (2003) tells the story of the half man, half goat Pan, a cursed god in love with a young princess. *Quiver* by Stephanie Spinner (2002) recounts the story of Atalanta, the fastest mortal runner, and her efforts to keep the promise of chastity she made to the goddess Artemis. Radically different and set in the modern day world of popular music, *Orfe* by Cynthia VOIGT (2002) is a lyrical and tragic retelling of the story of Orpheus and Eurydice.

Celtic M. offers another frequently-mined treasure of classical material for modern writers. Perhaps the best known, and a classic in its own right, is Lloyd ALEXANDER's Prydain Chronicles, which use Welsh myth to tell the story of Taran, assistant Pig-Keeper in *The Book of Three, The Black Cauldron, The Castle of Llyr, Taran Wanderer,* and *The High King* (all reissued in 1999). A very faithful and slightly more sophisticated version of *The Mabinogion* may be found in Evangeline Walton's retelling, collected in the *Mabinogion Tetralogy* (2003) which includes *The Prince of Annwn, The Children of Llyr, The Song of Rhiannon,* and *The Virgin and the Swine*. Moving from Wales to Ireland, *The Red Branch* by Morgan Llywelyn (1990) uses the heroic Irish tales from the Ulster Cycle to tell the story of legendary warrior Cuchulain. For older readers, Stephen R. Lawhead's Song of Albion trilogy—*The Paradise War* (2002), *The Silver Hand* (2002), and *The Endless Knot* (2002)—uses a modern setting to frame the story of two young graduate students, and the pivotal roles in Celtic M. they take on after being transported through a cairn back to ancient Ireland.

Little Sister by Kara DALKEY (1998) and its sequel *The Heavenward Path* (1998) uses elements of Asian M. as well as Buddhist and Shinto folklore to tell the story of Mitsuko as she travels through the netherworld in search of her sister's soul. The Master Li series by Barry Hughart (*Bridge of Birds: A Novel of*

Ancient China that Never Was, The Story of the Stone, Eight Skilled Gentlemen) does not retell a specific story, but uses traditional Asian lore to populate a fantastic "ancient China that never was." Kij Johnson offers spectacular adaptions of Japanese legend, suitable for older teens, in *The Fox Woman* (2000), the story of a fox who falls in love with a Japanese nobleman, and *Fudoki* (2003), the tale of a cat who survives a fire, is given a new shape, and earns a name as a formidable female warrior.

The M. of various so-called First Peoples, the original inhabitants of lands across the globe, offers a wealth of material for YA authors. *The World before this One: A Novel Told in Legend* by Rafe Martin (2002) is a collection of Seneca tales bound together by the story of Young Crow, the world's first storyteller. *Anpao: An American Indian Odyssey* by Jamake HIGHWATER (1992) tells the story of the eponymous character's quest for permission to marry his beloved, a woman who belongs to the sun, and the many mythical creatures he battles along the way. M. is blended with harsh reality in *The Whale Rider* by Witi Ihimaera (2003), the story of Kahu, granddaughter of the Maori in New Zealand, who must overcome the prejudices of her people in order to save them.

The most famous and most frequently mined cycle of legends are certainly the tales of King Arthur. The legend has proved to be an almost inexhaustible source of material. Classics such as Mary Stewart's Arthurian Saga, which includes *The Crystal Cave, The Hollow Hills,* and *The Last Enchantment* (all reissued in 2003) and Marion Zimmer BRADLEY's *The Mists of Avalon* (1982) have been joined by numerous series aimed specifically at YA. Younger teens will be drawn to the Young Merlin trilogy by Jane Yolen, made up of *Passager* (1996), *Hobby* (1996), and *Merlin* (1997) or Gerald Morris's Arthurian ADVENTURES *The Squire's Tale* (2000), *The Squire, His Knight, and His Lady* (2001), and *The Savage Damsel and the Dwarf* (2000). Nancy SPRINGER's *I Am Mordred: A Tale From Camelot* (2002) and *I Am Morgan Le Fey* (2002) both re-create the familiar story from the point of view of traditionally villainous characters. *The Sword of the Rightful King* by Jane Yolen (2003) offers a wholly unusual take on the familiar tale, as someone else manages to pull the sword from the stone before young Arthur.

Legends of Robin Hood, his band of Merry Men, and their adventures in Sherwood Forest are another source of literary fascination, and the basis of many YA novels. *In a Dark Wood* by Michael CADNUM (1999) tells the story of Geoffrey, Sheriff of Nottingham, and offers an interpretation suitable for more sophisticated teens. Its sequel, *Forbidden Forest: The Story of Little John and Robin Hood* (2002), again focuses on an overlooked character, telling the story of why and how Little John joined the band of thieves. Another nontraditional retelling, this one for younger teens, comes from *Rowan Hood: Outlaw Girl of Sherwood Forest* by Nancy Springer, who offers Robin's daughter, Rowan, as heroine. Sequels *Lionclaw* (2002) and *Outlaw Princess of Sherwood: A Tale of Rowan Hood* (2003) both feature unusual main characters while still focusing on the tale of Robin Hood. More conventional retellings are available in Roger Lancelyn Green's fine *The Adventures of Robin Hood* (1995) or in *Robin Hood of Sherwood Forest* by Ann MCGOVERN (2001).

There are many other well-known legends that either form the basis of, or offer, inspiration for YA novels. The legend of Scheherezade forms the backdrop for Susan FLETCHER's *Shadow Spinner* (1999), a tale of ancient Persia, and the same tale is told with a slightly different twist in *The Storyteller's Daughter* by Cameron Dokey (2002). The Sumerian legend of Gilgamesh is excellently retold in *Gilgamesh the Hero* by Geraldine MCCAUGHREAN (illus. David Parkins, 2002). Part of the fine Oxford Myths and Legends series, this volume retells perhaps the oldest-known recorded story, that of the young King Gilgamesh and his heroic friend Enkidu. When Enkidu dies, Gilgamesh sets out on a quest for immortality, enduring many trials and earning much wisdom along the way. *Innana: From the Myths of Ancient Sumer* (2003) is Kim Echlin's retelling of the recently discovered stories of Gilgamesh's sister, the goddess Innana, as she learns to create and destroy, falls in love, and, like her brother, seeks everlasting life. Moving from Sumer to ancient Mexico, *The Legend of Lord Eight Deer: An Epic of Ancient Mexico* by John M. D. Pohl (2001) presents the legendary story cycle of Lord Eight Deer, greatest of the Mixtec leaders. Crossing both time and space again, the Russian legend of the Firebird is central to the story of an outcast teen who tries to save a new friend in *Feather Boy* by Nicky Singer (2002). The fantastic bird also drives the action in Patricia MCKILLIP's wondrous *In the Forests of Serre* (2003), a more lyrical tale involving a princess, the mad prince she is betrothed to, the Mother of All Witches, and the mystical firebird.

Many GRAPHIC NOVELS, exceedingly popular with teens, use myths and legends as source material. *The Age of Bronze: A Thousand Ships* by Eric Shanower (2001), volume one of a projected seven-volume series, retells the story of the Trojan War. *The Ring of the Nibelung: The Rhinegold and the Valkyrie* by P. Craig Thompson (2002) and its sequel *The Ring of the Nibelung: Siegfried and Götterdämmerung: The Twilight of the Gods* (2002) tell the story of Siegfried, which Richard Wagner retold in his grand Ring Cycle, and the Ragnarok series by Myung-Jin Lee (2002) tells a manga version of the Norse M. Perhaps the most successful graphic-novel series ever, Neil GAIMAN's extraordinary Sandman (beginning with *Preludes and Nocturnes,* 1993) features a number of characters and events inspired by M. from around the world and throughout history. Suitable for more ma-

ture teens, the series is fairly dark and occasionally violent, but of impeccable quality.

Over thousands of years, stories have been used to teach, to entertain, to provoke thought and introspection. Mythological tales are transformed by popular culture, changing shape in order to hold their appeal, while retaining the knowledge and insight they offer. Traditional tales, in any form, can remain relevant and fascinating, offering much-needed direction, especially to YAs as they negotiate their own labyrinths, battle their own monsters, and make their own heroic journeys.

BIBLIOGRAPHY: *Encyclopedia Mythica, An Encyclopedia on Mythology, Folklore, and Legend,* http://www.pantheon.org; T. Bulfinch. *Bulfinch's Mythology,* http://www.bulfinch.org; A. S. Mercadante, *The Facts on File Encyclopedia of World Mythology and Legend,* 1988; A. Cottrell, *The Macmillan Illustrated Encyclopedia of Myths and Legends,* 1989.

JULIE BARTEL

NA, An
Author, b. 17 July 1972, Korea

N. is an author of considerable promise within the field of YOUNG ADULT LITERATURE. Born in Korea, her family moved to America when she was four years old, just as her character Young Ju does in *A Step From Heaven* (2001). N. grew up in San Diego, California, and can easily relate to the challenges a different culture can bring to one's sense of self and personal growth.

N. earned her B.A. at Amherst College and then went on to earn her M.F.A. in writing from Norwich University. She taught middle school but now dedicates her time fully to writing. She divides her time between Oakland, California, and Warren, Vermont.

A Step From Heaven chronicles the life of a young Korean girl and her experiences as she comes to America at the age of four through her high-school years. It uniquely captures the challenges, fears, and joys of balancing a young life and journeying through two very different cultures. Although N. drew from some of her own experiences of being an immigrant in America, the characters are more extreme in her novel than many of the people in her own life. N. is the winner of the Michael L. PRINTZ AWARD for *A Step From Heaven*. She won it the same year a Korean-American won the Newbery: Linda Sue PARK for *A Single Shard*.

Not only is diversity an important aspect of N.'s first novel, it also deviates from the traditional narrative form of writing. N. takes us through her character's life by offering us snapshots. Although written chronologically, time varies and each event is vividly painted through images created with N.'s words and the context. Through this, N. carefully constructs the characters, the places, the cultural differences, and the interactions between FAMILY and other people in her character's life.

N.'s next novel will also be about a Korean American family. This family will run a dry-cleaning business and the daughter will fall in love with one of their workers, a Mexican-American young man. This promises to be yet another insightful and intriguing read for young adults.

AWARDS: *A Step from Heaven,* 2002; Michael L. Printz Award (2002); Booklist Editors' Choice selection (2002); National Book Award finalist (2002); ALA Best Books for Young Adults, 2002; ALA Notable Children's Books, 2002; *New York Times* Notable Children's Books, 2001; Dorothy Canfield Fisher Children's Book Award, 2003; Asian Pacific American Award for Text in Children's and YA Literature.

BIBLIOGRAPHY: Lodge, Sally. "Flying Starts: An Na." *Publishers Weekly,* June 25, 2001; Adams, Lauren. "Disorderly Fiction." *Horn Book* magazine, September/October 2002; Nilsen, Alleen Pace, Ken Donelson, and James Blasingame Jr. "2001 Honor List: A Vote for Diversity." *English Journal,* November 2002. Rochman, Hazel. "The Booklist Interview: An Na." *Booklist,* March 15, 2002.

TINA HERTEL

NAIDOO, Beverley

Author, b. 21 May 1943, Johannesburg, South Africa

N. was born to a father who was a composer and music copyright manager and a mother who was a broadcaster and theater critic. N. married Nandhagopaul Naidoo, an attorney (solicitor); they have two children.

N. worked as a field worker for a nutrition company; she was a primary and secondary teacher in London, England, as well as a writer and a researcher. In 1963, N. received her B.A. from the University of Witwatersrand, South Africa. In 1964, she was detained under the "ninety days" solitary confinement law. At the age of twenty-two she moved to England to study at the University of York, where she received her certificate of education in 1968. She received honorary doctorates from The Open University (2003) and the University of Southampton (D.Litt.), (2002).

When N. went to university during the 1960s, she met people who challenged her to open her eyes. She had always lived in communities where white people had privileges that black people did not have. Her upbringing had led her to believe that white people were superior and it was natural for them to have the best of everything. When people at the university helped N. to realize how false this belief was, she became aware and angry at all the injustice around her. She wanted to write stories that would challenge narrow ways of seeing. The African National Congress was banned and Nelson Mandela went "underground" before he was captured. N. became involved in the resistance movement to apartheid; her resistance caused her to spend eight weeks in solitary confinement in jail.

As a white child in South Africa, N. literally had two mothers: one her birth mother and the second the black cook-nanny who cared for her every need. N. was taught to consider the black mother as a servant and to call her "Mary." One day Mary received a telegram and she collapsed in front of N. Two of Mary's small daughters had gotten diphtheria and died. N. could not have gotten diphtheria because white children had been inoculated whereas black children were not. The first book N. wrote is dedicated to the memory of those two young children and their mother.

N. wanted to present an authentic picture of the interaction between blacks and whites; her first book,

Journey to Jo'burg: A South African Story (1984), did that and took the young adult audience by storm. Readers could not believe that white people treated black Africans so thoughtlessly. She wrote the text simply and read the pages to her own children (ages six and ten at the time) to see if it sounded like spoken language and if they could understand it. The book was banned in South Africa.

In 1985, N. published *Censoring Reality,* a study of the image of South Africa presented to British and American YAS in nonfiction. Before she began her book, N. conducted research with a local anti-apartheid group in South Africa. She found that any child who went to school or public library shelves to look for factual material would be finding and reading books that either omitted or largely distorted the reality of apartheid. N. knew that she must present an authentic picture of interaction between blacks and whites.

N. says, "I was brought up with the usual conceptions most white South Africans have, completely taking for granted the services of our cook-cum-nanny, whose own three children lived more than 300 kilometers away, cared for by . . . I don't know."

In *No Turning Back: A Novel of South Africa* (1997), N. wrote about a twelve-year-old boy (Sipho) who ran away to the dangerous streets where he joined "malunde"—street children who live rough and survive, if they are lucky. In *The Other Side of Truth* (2000), N. moved away from South Africa because she wanted to explore what would happen to children who were thrown from a comfortable family in Lagos to becoming—overnight—refugees alone in London. When asked if everything she writes is "true," N. said that everything she writes could happen, although she creates a story and characters that are fictional. She did most of her research in England by spending a few months finding out about the experiences of refugee children in London.

N. agrees that her books allow readers to look through the windows to see what is really happening in South Africa. She continues to pursue her goal to present an honest picture of South Africa.

AWARDS: 1999, Arts Council Writer's Award for work-in-progress, UK. Awards for *The Other Side of Truth:* 2000, Carnegie Medal, UK; 2000, Smarties Book Prize Silver Medal, UK; 2001, Notable Trade Book in the Field of Social Studies, USA;

2002, Best Book for Young Adults, ALA, USA; 2001, ALA Booklist Top of the List, USA; 2002, Jane Addams Book Award (older children category) USA; 2002, International Board on Books for Young People Honor Book; 2003, Sankei Children's Book Award, Japan. Awards for *Out of Bounds:* 2003, Parents' Choice Silver Honor Award, USA; 2004, Riverbank Review Children's Book of Distinction; 2004, Best Book for Young Adults, ALA. Awards for *No Turning Back:* 1995, Smarties Prize for Children's Books, UK shortlist; 1996, The Guardian Children's Fiction Award, UK shortlist; 1998, Notable Children's Trade Book in the Field of Social Studies, USA; 1998, Josette Frank Award (Child Study Children's Book Committee Award), USA; 1998, International Reading Assoc. Awards for *Journey to Jo'burg: A South African Story:* 1985, Other Award from Children's Book Bulletin; 1986, Children's Book Award, Child Study Book Committee, Bank Street College of Education; 1987, Child Study Association of America's Children's Books of the Year; 1988, Parents' Choice Honor Book, Parents' Choice Foundation; *Chain of Fire*, ALA Best Books for Young Adults, 1991.

FURTHER WORKS: *Censoring Reality: An Examination of Books on South Africa,* 1985; *Chain of Fire,* 1989, 1990; *Out of Bounds,* 2003; *Web of Lies,* 2004; *Free as I Know* (Editor), 1987; *Through Whose Eyes?,* 1992.

BIBLIOGRAPHY: Blatchford, Roy, ed. *That'll Be the Day,* 1986; *Children's Literature* Review. vol. 29, 1993; *Fiction, Folklore, Fantasy and Poetry for Children,* 1876–1985, vol. 1, 1986; N., "The Story behind *Journey to Jo'burg.*" *School Library Journal,* May, 1987; N. *Censoring Reality.* ILEA Centre for Anti-Racist Education and the British Defence/Aid Fund for Southern Africa, 1985; Bulletin of the Center for Children's Books, May 1986; *School Library Journal,* April 1987; *Something about the Author,* vol. 36, 1991.

BERNICE E. CULLINAN

NAMIOKA, Lensey

Author, b. 14 June 1929, Peking, China

N.'s father helped develop the current system of Chinese writing and bestowed upon his daughter a completely original name. "Lensey" is the result of a father who liked to experiment with language. N. immigrated to America when she was nine; the memory of moving to a new country has peppered N.'s literature for children and young adults. The author did not know any English upon her arrival in the U.S., and the only common language she found in school was math.

N. attended Radcliffe College from 1947 to 1949 and completed her B.A. (1951) and M.A. (1952) from the University of California, Berkeley. She was a mathematics college instructor and translator before deciding to concentrate on professional writing. Her new career was established with the publishing of *The Samurai and the Long-nosed Devils* (1976). She is best known for two genres: exciting, ADVENTURE-MYSTERY books about sixteenth-century Japanese samurai warriors and humorous juvenile novels about young Chinese immigrants living in Seattle. N.'s work draws heavily on her Chinese cultural heritage and her husband's Japanese background.

April and the Dragon Lady (1994) has done for the understanding of Chinese-American culture in YA LITERATURE what Amy Tan's *The Joy Luck Club* did for adult literature. April Chen, a sixteen-year-old Chinese American, and her grandma belong to entirely different cultural and generational worlds. Grandma's ideas about a woman's place clash with April's more Westernized views. She objects to April's Caucasian boyfriend and challenges her plans to attend college away from home. N.'s characterizations are particularly strong, for both Amy and her grandmother alternatively appear sympathetic and accountable for their actions.

Ties that Bind, Ties that Break (1999) is a thoughtful exploration of the ways cultural pressures can alter both personal values and physical appearance. Ailin, the protagonist, resists the Chinese tradition of having her feet bound, and is caught between the modern world of 1911 and time-honored customs. While her father is progressive enough to educate Ailin at as she enters adolescence, Ailin finds that her FAMILY is no longer willing to support her. Following her father's death, Big Uncle forbids the continuation of education and gives his niece the choice of becoming a nun or a peasant's wife, the only alternatives left for an unmarried Chinese woman with unbound feet. Instead, Ailin finds work as a nanny for American parents and comes to America with their emotional and financial support. With the gracious help of others, Ailin is able to carve out a new path for herself in life.

N.'s success is based, at least in part, on two philosophies: to give the same pleasure through reading to young people today that she had as a child, and to provide messages about the need for understanding and tolerance without being preachy and dull.

AWARDS: Washington State Governor's Award: 1976 for *While Serpent Castle*, 1996 for *April and the Dragon Lady;* 1995 Parent's Choice Gold Award, *Yang the Third and her Impossible Family;* Parenting Magazine Reading Magic Award, *Yang the Youngest and His Terrible Ear*; *April*: 2003 ALA Popular Paperbacks; ALA Best Books for Young Adults: 1981 for *Village of the Vampire Cat*, 1990 for *Island of Oeyes*, 2000 for *Ties that Bind, Ties that Break.*

FURTHER WORKS: *White Serpent Castle*, 1976; *Valley of Broken Cherry Trees*, 1981; *Village of the Vampire Cat*, 1981; *Who's Hu?*, 1981; *The Phantom of Tiger Mountain*, 1986; *Island of Ogres*, 1989; *The Coming of the Bear*, 1992; *Yang the Youngest and His Terrible Ear*, 1992; *Yang the Third and Her Impossible Family*, 1995; *Den of the Fox*, 1997; *Yang the Second and Her Secret Admirers*, 1998; *Yang the Eldest and His Odd Jobs*, 2000; *An Ocean Apart, a World Away*, 2002.

BIBLIOGRAPHY: "Lensey Namioka," U*X*L Junior DISCovering Authors, 1998. Reproduced in DISCovering Collection, 2001. http://galenet.galegroup.com/servlet/DC/; "Lensey Namioka," *Contemporary Authors*, 2000. http://galenet.galegroup.com/servlet/LitRC/; Author's website. http://www.lensey.com/index.html/

RACHEL WITMER
AND SARA MARCUS

NAPOLI, Donna Jo
Author, b. 28 February 1948 in Miami, Florida

N. was the last of four children born to hard-working parents in Miami. She has said her world was relatively small during childhood, but she learned English from a mother and father who spoke Napoletano, an Italian dialect. Her grandmother spoke to her mother in Calabrese, a dialect even older. Thanks to the melting pot that was Miami, she heard a swirl of Hebrew, Yiddish, and Spanish in the neighborhood where she lived. So even if her geographic reach was limited, her audible exposure went far beyond it.

Vision problems went undetected until N. was nearly ten. But once that barrier was lifted, she fell in love with books and reading. "I began doing research almost as soon as I learned to read, because I was as hungry for nonfiction as for fiction," she told Downhome Books in September of 2003. "I loved finding out about things and then trying to do experiments on my own to verify what I had read."

Both time and money were tight in the N. household. As a result, she has no memory of being read to at home. "We had no books in my house," she said. "I never saw my mother read." Growing up in a financially challenged household, N. learned to value elements of the spirit rather than earthly wealth. She shopped for second-hand clothes and did without nonessentials as a matter of habit. Even today, she is a thrift-store maverick who cares little about how she looks in terms of public perception. According to N., some people call these traits "crazy." N.'s father read the newspaper and, on rare occasions, bought his youngest daughter a 50-cent book when he did the grocery shopping. But N.'s real introduction to the wonders of books came by way of thoughtful LIBRARIANS.

BIOGRAPHIES, *A Tree Grows in Brooklyn*, and author Mary Renault's SERIES on Ancient Greece were among N.'s early favorites. She credits those books and her high-school Latin teacher, Mrs. Margaret Reynolds, with fostering her love for MYTHOLOGY and its influence in her own fiction, including *Sirena* (1998) and *The Great God Pan* (2003). Her learning challenges completely behind her, N. went from high school to stellar university endeavors. She received her B.A. in mathematics in 1970 and her Ph.D. in romance languages and literature in 1973, both from Harvard. She went on to MIT to do postdoctoral study in linguistics. She has demonstrated her expertise as a teacher and lecturer at a dozen universities around the world, including Swarthmore College in Pennsylvania, where she is currently tenured.

N.'s reputation as a strong young adult writer is exemplified by support provided to her by the National Endowment for the Humanities, a grant from the Mellon Foundation, another from the Sloan Foundation, and with many other awards from various organizations. Some adults have called N.'s sexual honesty in *Zel* (1996) and *Sirena* and *The Great God Pan* obscene, but thousands of faithful young readers reject those judgments. N. herself takes such parental panic with a grain of salt and a dash of humor. "I've gotten criticism for the main character cursing in *When the Water Closes over My Head* (1994)," she told Downhome Books. "A reading teacher in New Hampshire once wrote to me and said she'd had her class go through the book whiting out all the [bad] 'language.' Think of all those poor little children defacing books." N. admits her personal conversations occasionally include a few choice words but insists her fictional dialogue is not about her habits or the moral judgments of adult readers. It's about the intellectual honesty of her fiction; if a curse word fits the nature of the character, the curse word is included.

N. carries the same honesty over into difficult personal situations, like divorce or heartbreak or DEATH. "There is nothing soft and gentle about a divorce from the point of view of the child," Napoli says in a September 2003 interview. "To pretend otherwise is, to me, despicable. We must honor our children's feelings, good and bad feelings—and being truthful is the only way to do that."

N. is proud of her academic and professional accomplishments, but she is also proud of her husband and family. She married her husband Barry in 1968 after meeting him her freshman year at Harvard. He courted her with the poetry of e.e. cummings, and the poems remain her favorites even today, 35 years later. Together, they have produced five intelligent children as they've traveled and pursued their dreams as individuals and as a couple. She dedicated her book *Crazy Jack* (1999) to her husband and college sweetheart, saying, "To Barry, who always stands by his crazy woman."

N. continues to tell her stories as honestly as she can, from her home outside of Philadelphia. She promises much more is yet to come.

AWARDS: 1995 Leeway Foundation Grant for Excellence in Fiction; 1997 Jerry Weiss Book Award given by the New Jersey Reading Association; 1998 Golden Kite Award given by the Society of Children's Book Writers and Illustrators; 1998 Sydney Taylor Book Award given by the National Association of Jewish Libraries; 1998 Drexel University and Free Library of Philadelphia Children's Literature Citation; 2003 Kentucky Bluegrass Award; ALA Best Book for Young Adults: 1994 for *The Magic Circle*, 1997 for *Song of the Magdalene*, 1998 for *Stones in Water*, 1999 for *Serena*, 2004 for *Breath*; 2004 ALA Popular Paperbacks for *Breath*; *Bound*: Kirkus Reviews Editor's Choice, 2004, *Publisher's Weekly* Best Children's Books, 2004, SLJ Best Books for Children, 2004.

FURTHER WORKS: *The Magic Circle*, 1995; *Songs of the Magdalene*, 1996; *Stones in Water*, 1999; *Spinners*, 1999; *For the Love of Venice*, 2000; *Beast*, 2000; *Daughter of Venice*, 2002; *Breath*, 2003; *North*, 2004; *Bound*, 2004.

BIBLIOGRAPHY: http://www.donnajonapoli.com/; Downhome Books interview, September 2003; Leeway Foundation Biography; Penguin Biography.

NAYLOR, Phyllis Reynolds
Author, b. 4 January 1933, Anderson, Indiana

Realizing the significance of life experiences as the threads that connect a story to its various readers, N. draws upon her own experiences as she writes and is identified as a prolific and versatile author. N. authentically develops her characters so that the complexity of challenges and joys they face are depicted with insight into the emotional journeys of each character. Her adolescent characters appeal to young readers who often are faced with similar situations, such as single parent homes, mental illness, moral choices; these characters often have struggles to understand growing up, especially when they have no one to depend on except themselves. N.'s writing also crosses genre from realistic fiction and FANTASY to INFORMATIONAL books.

As N. was growing up, her parents read aloud to her every night, inspiring the creative juices within her. N. says that she paid more attention to the story at hand rather than to the author's background. What was paramount was the story. By the time the author had reached fifth grade, she was, as she says, "writing books" by recording plots that raced through her head at school. At college, N. studied clinical psychology, but earned the money for her tuition by relying on her writing and selling her stories. Instead of graduate school, N. decided it was time to devote her time to a career in writing.

N. has won numerous awards; she is well known for creating *Shiloh* (1991), which won the John Newbery Medal in 1992. Marty rescues a dog from its abusive master and then must decide whether to return Shiloh or disobey his parents and try to protect him. Marty works through this problem after much soul searching and is allowed to work for the dog's owner to pay for Shiloh. Two sequels followed *Shiloh* as well as a MOVIE adaptation. N. confides that this story had its beginnings during a visit to Shiloh, West Virginia. While staying with friends, N. was followed home from a walk by a stray dog. N. wrote the novel in response to her thoughts about the dog; the dog was later adopted.

NORMA FOX MAZER

MILTON MELTZER

CAROLYN MEYER

BEVERLY NAIDOO

PHYLLIS REYNOLDS NAYLOR

GARTH NIX

JOAN LOWRY NIXON

HAN NOLAN

Other books by N. also have AUTOBIOGRAPHICAL roots. *The Keeper* (1986) details the story of an adolescent boy coping with his father's mental illness. Having experienced schizophrenia through her first husband's own illness, N. wrote of a thirteen-year-old's strength to survive this situation. In *A String of Chances* (1982), a sixteen-year-old girl reaches a point in her life where she must confront religious doubts, a first romance, and the DEATH of an infant in the FAMILY. Evie and her family have genuine, caring reactions to richly portrayed situations and relationships. As in many of N.'s novels, no final resolution is reached; rather, the reader is filled with hope that the protagonist's strength of character will prevail. J. D. Stahl states, "Willing to present complex religious, ethnical, and psychological issues in her fiction, N. does so without a hidden—or, for that matter, obvious—agenda, but with simple honesty and sensitivity."

In her humorous Alice SERIES, N. describes a young girl entering adolescence without a mother figure; she must depend on advice given by her father and older brother. Alice is quite an individual, yet she copes with universal problems that confront all adolescents. *Alice in April* (1993) tackles the frightening task of a doctor visit during adolescence. Alice is faced with a full body checkup, her first one since the onset of puberty. Horrified by the judgments the doctor will make when he sees her body, Alice faces extreme anxiety. After all her worrying, Alice is relieved and somewhat baffled to find that her body is perfectly normal. This is only one example of the issues that Naylor brings to light in a very open style of writing; in the series of over ten books, Alice's ordeals are presented often through the use of comedy and always with insight.

N. has also written nonfiction books, many of which give advice to young readers: *How I Came to Be a Writer* (1978), *Getting Along with Your Friend* (1980), *Getting Along with Your Teachers* (1981). Her contributions, however, are most abundant in the area of fiction, and N. has been acknowledged with numerous literary awards.

N. credits a good deal of her happiness in life to her ability to write; she explains it as a pressure building up inside of her all day that must be released through writing. She lives in Bethesda, Maryland, with her husband and enjoys hiking and swimming.

AWARDS: *How I Came to Be a Writer*, IRA/CBC Children's Choice; *Night Cry*, Edgar Allan Poe Award; *All but Alice:* ALA Notable Children's Book, ALA Quick Pick for Reluctant Young Adult Readers; *Shiloh:* 1992 Newbery Medal, ALA Notable Children's Book, IRA Young Adult Choice; *Alice in April:* ALA Quick Pick for Reluctant Young Adult Readers; *Keeper*, 1986 Best Books for Young Adults List; *Jade Green*, ALA Quick Pick for Reluctant Young Adult Readers, 2001, ALA Popular Paperbacks, 2003. 1966–86; 'Nothin' but the Best: Best of the Best Books for Young Adults"; *Outrageously Alice*, 1998 Best Books for Young Adults; *Send No Blessings*, 1991 Best Books for Young Adults; *String of Chances*, 1982 Best Books for Young Adults; *Unexpected Pleasures*, 1987 Best Books for Young Adults; *Year of the Gopher*, 1987 Best Books for Young Adults.

FURTHER WORKS: *The Mad Gasser of Bessledorf Street*, vol. 1 in Besseldorf series, 1983; *Night Cry*, 1984; *The Agony of Alice*, 1985; *Beetles, Lightly Toasted*, 1987; *Alice in Rapture, Sort Of*, 1989; *Reluctantly Alice*, 1991; *All but Alice*, 1992; *Alice In-Between*, 1994; *Alice the Brave*, 1995; *Alice in Lace*, 1996; *Ice*, 1996; *The Fear Place*, 1996; *I Can't Take You Anywhere*, 1997; *Sang Spell*, 1998; *Outrageously Alice*, 1998; *Sweet Strawberries*, 1999; *Walker's Crossing*, 1999; *Danny's Desert Rats*, 1999; *Alice on the Outside*, 2000; *Jade Green*, 2000; *The Great Chicken Debacle*, 2001; *Alice Alone*, 2001; *The Grooming of Alice*, 2002; *The Picnic*, 2002; *Faces in the Water*, 2002, *Simply Alice*, 2003; *Patiently Alice*, 2003; *Alice in Bunderland*, 2003; *Including Alice*, 2004.

BIBLIOGRAPHY: Stahl, J. D. *St. James Guide to Young Adult Writers*, 1999; Naylor, P. R. *How I Became a Writer*, 1978; N. "The Writing of 'Shiloh.'" *The Reading Teacher*, 46, 1992, pp. 10–12; *The Seventh Book of Junior Authors and Illustrators*, 1996; *Contemporary Authors Online*, 2001.

JANELLE B. MATHIS

NELSON, Marilyn
Author, poet, b. 26 April, 1946 Cleveland, Ohio

N. comes from a long line of creative individuals; her mother was a teacher and her father, an Air Force officer, wrote POETRY and PLAYS. As an elementary school student, N. began to write poetry, completing her first poem at age eleven. Her interest in literature continued and, after receiving degrees from the University of California, Davis (B.A.), the University of Pennsylvania (M.A.), and the University of Minnesota (Ph.D.), N. taught creative writing (poetry) and ethnic literature courses at the University of Connecticut, Storrs. An accomplished author and poet, N. has received two creative writing fellowships from the National Endowment for the Arts, a Fulbright teaching fellowship, and a Guggenheim fellowship. She is also the recipient of an honorary doctorate from Kutztown University in Pennsylvania.

N. is a prolific author who has written six books of poetry, two children's collections, and several chapbooks. Her work has appeared in numerous anthologies and literary collections. Her works include *The Homeplace* (1990), a moving collection of poems inspired by the FAMILY stories told by her mother on her deathbed. *The Fields of Praise: New and Selected Poems* (1997), powerful and life-affirming poems that reflect the AFRICAN AMERICAN experience. Her sixth work, *Carver: A Life in Poems* (2001), eloquently blends verse with BIOGRAPHY and history as she tells the story of botanist and inventor George Washington Carver.

In recognition for her work, N. became Poet Laureate of Connecticut on June 28 2001, a position that she will hold for five years. According to her nominator Susan Holmes, artistic programs director at the University of Connecticut, "she is a vital American voice speaking of our past and present from her multiple perspectives of daughter, mother, wife, artist, teacher, friend and African-American."

Known as a poet of stunning power, in her spare time N. enjoys another creative endeavor, quilting.

AWARDS: Pushcart Prizes; 1990 Connecticut Arts Award; 1992 Annisfield-Wolf Award, *The Homeplace;* 1998 Poet's Prize, *The Fields of Praise: New and Selected Poems; Carver: A Life in Poems:* 2001 *Boston Globe–Horn Book* Award, 2001 Flora Stieglitz Straus Award; 2002 Newbery Honor Book, 2002 Coretta Scott King Honor Book, ALA Best Books for Young Adults, 2002; ALA Notable Children's Books, 2002; *Fortune's Bones; The Manumission Requiem*: Kirkus Review's Editor's Choice, 2004; Coretta Scott King Author Honor Books, 2005, ALA Notable Children's Books, 2005.

FURTHER WORKS: *Magnificat,* 1994; *Mama's Promises,* 1985; *For the Body,* 1978; *The Cat Walked through the Casserole and Other Poems for Children* (with Pamela Espeland), 1984; *Halfdan Rasmussen's Hundreds of Hens and Other Poems for Children* (Translated from Danish with Pamela Espeland), 1982; *Fortune's Bones: The Manumission Requiem,* 2004.

BIBLIOGRAPHY: "Connecticut Poet Laureate Marilyn N." http://www.ctarts.org/PoetLaureate.htm, November 12, 2002; "Marilyn N.," http://frontstreetbooks.com/all_writers.htm; "Marilyn N., *The Fields of Praise.*" http://www.lsu.edu/lsupress/catalog/spr-sum-97/nelson; "Marilyn N. Waniek, The Homeplace." http://www.lsu/edu/lsupress/catalog/1990/Waniek_Homeplace.htm; "Marilyn's N.'s Labyrinth." http://www.ucc.uconn.edu/~waniek/; "Marilyn N." http://www.poets/org/poets/poets.cfm?prmID = 98, 1997–2003

KRISTEL FLEUREN

NELSON, Theresa
Author, b. 15 August 1948, Beaumont, Texas

The author of seven award-winning novels for young adults, N. has been critically acclaimed for her portrayal of the harsh social realities that affect adolescents, including WAR, abuse, and AIDS.

Born one of eleven children in southeast Texas, N. has written that "dreaming, reading, imagining—they've always been almost interchangeable in my head." Heavily influenced by her childhood experiences in a large FAMILY headed by a tap-dancing, calf-roping, ex-Marine father and a mother whose promise in ballet was topped only by her storytelling prowess, N. inevitably grew to love books and the ADVENTURES to be found at home. Inspired by such fictional role models as Jo from *Little Women* and Anne of Green Gables, she began writing stories at a very young age.

Eventually, writing stories led N. into the world of drama, and she followed in her parents' footsteps by taking singing and dancing lessons as well. "Theater," N. said, "offered endless worlds to explore." These explorations had profound effects both on her professional and her personal life. The theater introduced her to her future husband, actor Kevin Cooney, when they happened to be cast in the same college production of *Little Mary Sunshine.* They would eventually have three children. After their marriage and her husband's tour of duty in Korea, N. settled in Houston where the couple remained active in the local theater scene and continued their interrupted schooling. N. received her B.A. in English magna cum laude from the University of St. Thomas in Houston in 1972, but it wasn't until the early 1980s that she returned to writing. In 1984, she published *The 25 Cent Miracle,* which told the story of Elvira

Trumbull, a girl whose vivid imagination and dreams were inspired by N.'s memories of growing up in a small Texas town. Like her other works, this novel merged elements of hope and imagination with a harsh reality—the experience of living with an unemployed, alcoholic father.

In the novels that followed, N. continued to confront serious topics, but always with an underlying hope expressed through magical or imaginative elements. *Devil Storm* (1987), based in part on her recollection of stories of the deadly Texas Hurricane of 1990, incorporates magical realism embodied in the character of Tom, a mysterious ex-slave, to heighten the sense of wonder in her readers.

Taking place over a half-century later, *And One for All* (1989) focuses on the experiences and ambivalence of adults during the Vietnam War as seen through the eyes of twelve-year-old Geraldine, who watches her brother and his friend work through their differing views of the war. N. drew from her own experiences during the Vietnam War era; she grew up with a military father and her husband's best friend died in the war.

N.'s other novels center on less global and more personal tragedies. *Beggar's Ride* (1992) tells the story of Claire, a twelve-year-old runaway who has been sexually abused by her mother's boyfriend. The novel spotlights the world of troubled TEENS who find themselves in the no-man's-land between dysfunctional families and a sometimes even more dysfunctional justice and social welfare system. In *Earthshine* (1994), N. uses humor and the magical elements present in everyday experiences to chronicle a girl's process of dealing with her father's battle against AIDS and his failing health. *Ruby Electric* (2003) also weaves together threads of magic and FANTASY in the story of Ruby, an aspiring twelve-year-old screenwriter, who uses her lush fantasy life to compensate for the uncertainties that surround her, specifically, the disappearance of her policeman father.

N. calls each of her novels "a miracle," and she continues to write them from her home in Sherman Oaks, California, outside Los Angeles.

AWARDS: ALA Best Book for Young Adults: 1990 for *And One for All,* 1992 for *The Beggar's Ride,* 1995 for *Earthshine;* ALA Notable Children's Book: 1989 for *And One for All,* 1992 for *The Beggar's Ride,* 1994 for *Earthshine; School Library Journal* Best Book of the Year: 1986 for *The 25 Cent Miracle,* 1989

for *And One for All,* 1992 for *The Beggar's Ride,* 1994 for *Earthshine;* 1994 *Boston Globe–Horn Book* Fiction Honor Book, *Earthshine;* 1987 National Council on Social Studies/Children's Book Council: Notable Children's Trade Book in the Field of Social Studies, *Devil Storm;* 1986 Washington Irving Children's Choice Award, *The 25 Cent Miracle;* 2004 ALA Notable Children's Books, *Ruby Electric.*

BIBLIOGRAPHY: *Contemporary Authors Online,* 2001; "Theresa Nelson." http://www.teresanelson.net

MICHELLE C. FOSSUM

NEUFELD, John (Arthur)

Author, b. 14 December 1938, Chicago, Illinois

N. began writing on young adult themes before the onslaught of young adult books in the 1970s. He was a maverick; in his work, TEENAGERS fill the roles of protagonists while the adults play peripheral parts. His first book, *Edgar Allan* (1968), was written to be a simple, easily understood story. The concept of the failed adoption of a black child by a white family was not intended to be specifically for younger readers; N. wanted to create a piece of literature that could hold a reader's attention firmly and be completed within a few readings. The issues that arose from this work led him into the YA LITERATURE genre.

N. read throughout his childhood, advancing to adult titles at a young age. By the time he attended Phillips Exter, he had read the works of Ernest Hemingway, Albert Camus, and Federico Garcia Lorca. He began to think of himself as a writer while attending Yale, and thought he would eventually like to work in all genres. After graduation, N. spend some time in London and Paris before being drafted into the U.S. Army and spending six months in the service. By 1962, the author decided it was time to develop a career, and made his way into the publishing world of New York. Although he never achieved the status of editor, the years that N. spent in publishing gave him time to further exercise his own writing skills and introduced him to people invaluable to his future career.

By drawing on stories from experiences told to him, N. created two highly successful first novels, both of which helped create the young adult genre. *Lisa Bright and Dark* (1969), a story of mental illness, came from a dinner conversation with a psychiatrist. N. emigrated upon Nixon's presidential election and wrote his third book, *Touching* (1970), while in England. Based on his stepsister, the book explains cerebral palsy through the character of Twink, discussing disease and the limitations it causes.

As the young adult classification was becoming an accepted field of literature, N. crusaded for books that were not considered high quality literature. He expressed the need for novels that describe teenagers with all their questions, doubts, errors, and desires. We need books about "a girl curious about sex yet frightened by rumors of pain, or a boy worried about his inability to perform sexually"; these are viable characters in life, and N. knew the importance of their representation in literature for young adults. He was certainly practicing the writing that he preached with the publication of *Freddy's Book* (1973), the story of a young boy's quest to understand the meaning of the "F-word."

Though the fear of being pigeonholed as an issues writer made N. step away from the young adult genre, he returned in the 1980s with revitalized ideas. CENSORSHIP is discussed in *A Small Civil War* (1982), while *Sharelle* (1983) shines a light on the truths of teenage parenthood. N.'s experience in a day-care center for the homeless children fueled *Almost a Hero* (1995), the story of a twelve-year-old boy who volunteers at a similar place.

While N. has written a few books for adults, he returns to his young adult books to arm his readers with something substantive, believing that publishing a fictional work that depicts difficulties, is the way to prepare readers for difficulties encountered in life.

AWARDS: 1968 *Time* magazine Book of the Year, *Edgar Allan; New York Times* Best Book of the Year, children's division, and ALA Notable Book, 1968 for *Edgar Allen* and 1969 for *Lisa, Bright and Dark*

FURTHER WORKS: *Sleep, Two, Three, Four!*, 1971; *For All the Wrong Reasons*, 1973; *Sunday Father*, 1975; *Trading Up*, 1975; *The Fun of It*, 1977; *A Small Civil War*, 1982; *Family Fortunes*, 1988; *Gaps in Stone Wall*, 1996.

BIBLIOGRAPHY: *U*X*L Junior DISCovering Authors*, 1998. Reproduced in Discovering Collection, 2002. http://galenet.galegroup.com/servlet/DC/; Kalkhoff, Ann. "Innocent Children or Innocent Librarians?" *School Library Journal*, October 1972, pp. 88–92; *Something about the Author*, vol. 81, 1995; *Wilson Library Bulletin*, October 1971.

RACHEL WITMER

NEWTH, Mette
Author, b. 31 January 1942, Oslo, Norway

As an adult whose writing and illustrations are geared primarily toward young adults, N. concedes that her insight is limited. "My only consolation," she explains, "is that writing convincingly from outside of one's own personal (not *private*) experience is a problem shared by all writers, though not all have to face it, or want to face it."

Married to British-born author Philip Newth, with whom she has three children, N. was educated at the National College of Art and Design and the National Academy of Fine Arts, both of which are located in Oslo. N. had her first book published in 1969, and she now has twenty novels and PICTURE BOOKS to her credit, some of which were created in conjunction with her husband. N.'s works have been translated into seventeen languages.

N.'s most recent foreign publication is *The Transformation* (2000). This novel tells the story of an Irish monk and an Inuit woman in fifteenth-century Greenland. Together, they battle the elements, conflicting beliefs, and each other before realizing that they are meant to be together.

N. also writes nonfiction, and has published over forty essays and articles on art and society issues in Norwegian and Nordic papers and MAGAZINES. In addition, her artwork has been displayed in collective and single exhibitions, both in Norway and around the world.

N. has held various occupations related to her passions for art and literature. From 1989 to 1993, she was principal of the National College of Art and Design in Bergen, Norway. She then worked as the administrator of the Norwegian Forum for Freedom of Expression. Currently, N. is the head of the National College of Art in Oslo.

AWARDS: American Library Association Best Books for Young Adults and School Library Journal Best Book of the Year, *The Abduction*, 1990; Parent's Choice Foundation Silver Honor, *The Dark Light*, 1998; Pick of the List, American Booksellers Association and Young Adult's Choice, New York Public Library, *The Transformation*, 2000; Best Books for Young Adults, *Abduction*, 1990; Best Book for Young Adults, *The Dark Light*, 1999.

FURTHER WORKS: *Lille Skrekk*, 1975; *Nora og ordene*, 1975; *Benjamins borg*, 1976; *Ballsprett*, 1980; *Mammaen min er så høy som stjernene*, 1980; *I bakgården til Rosa og Fred,* 1983; *Oppdagelsen: en fabel fra virkeligheten,* 1984; *Soldreperen,* 1985; *The Abduction,* 1989; *The Dark Light,* 1995; *Under huden,* 1999.

BIBLIOGRAPHY: *Contemporary Authors Online,* 2003. Reproduced in Biography Resource Center, 2003; www.newth.nt/mette/; www.teenreads.com

CARRA GAMBERDELLA

NEWTON, Suzanne
Author, b. 8 October 1936, Bunnlevel, North Carolina

Creator of characters "who stand up to difficult situations," N. earned an A.B. from Duke University in 1957 and published her first work, *Purro and the Prattleberries* in 1971. "Besides writing, N. has participated in the Poetry-in-the-Schools project in North Carolina, where poets and writers spend a week in school classrooms helping children to find a voice of their own through POETRY." The daughter of Hannis T. and Billie (O'Quinn) Latham, N. married Carl R. Newton (a civil servant) on June 9, 1957, and is the mother of four children, Michele, Erin, Heather, and Craig. N. is a member of the North Carolina Writer's Conference, Authors Guild, and Authors League of America, and lives in Raleigh, North Carolina, with her family.

Besides working full time as an author, N. has also been a writer-in-residence at Meredith College, from 1984 to 1985, and has contributed SHORT STORIES, poems, and articles to *Home Life, Parents' Magazine, Human Voice Quarterly, Southern Poetry Review,* and *Long View Journal.*

N.'s numerous awards include American Association of University Women (North Carolina branch) award for juvenile literature, 1971, for *Purro and the Prattleberries,* 1974, for *Care of Arnold's Corners,* 1977, for *What Are You Up to, William Thomas?,* 1978, for *Reubella and the Old Focus Home,* and 1981, for *M. V. Sexton Speaking. I Will Call It Georgie's Blues* was named an American Library Association Notable Book and Best Book for Young Adults and *New York Times* and *New York Times Book Review* Best Book of the Year, all 1983. It was also selected for "Nothin' but the Best: Best of the Best Books for Young Adults, 1966–1986" and the 2004 ALA Popular Paperbacks.

SELECT FURTHER WORKS: *Care of Arnold's Corners,* 1974; *What Are You Up To, William Thomas?,* 1977; *Reubella and the Old Focus Home,* 1978; *M. V. Sex-*

ton Speaking, 1983; *I Will Call It Georgie's Blues,* 1983; *An End to Perfect,* 1984; *A Place Between,* 1986; *Where Are You When I Need You?,* 1991.

BIBLIOGRAPHY: "Suzanne Newton," U*X*L Junior DISCovering Authors. U*X*L, 1998. Reproduced in Discovering Collection, 2001. http://galenet.gale group.com/servlet/DC/; *Contemporary Authors Online,* 2003. Reproduced in *Biography Resource Center,* 2003. http://www.galenet.com/servlet/BioRC

SARA MARCUS

NICHOLSON, William
Author, b. 12 January 1948, Tunbridge Wells, England

Although N. was a well-known film, theater, and TV writer for years before publishing fiction, he has since become a great FANTASY writer of the 21st century. He is not to be confused with Sir William Nicholson (1872–1949), an artist and illustrator.

N., who grew up in Sussex and Gloucestershire, attended a Roman Catholic boarding school and Cambridge University. In the seventeen years that he worked for the BBC, he wrote, directed, and produced over forty documentaries. His screenplays include *Shadowlands* and *Gladiator;* for each he was nominated for an Academy Award. N. lives in Sussex with his wife, son, and two daughters.

N.'s trilogy for young people, *The Wind on Fire,* is set in an imaginary world that includes Aramanth, a city-state where residents are controlled through endless exams; feuding tribes whose cities are huge land-ships traveling the plains; and the underground village of a happy people who live covered with mud. The Morah's evil army is an enormous marching band of beautiful, murderous TEENAGERS in white uniforms. N. invents original motifs, MYTHOLOGIES, and magic, while suggesting familiar archetypes. The style is appealing and accessible to younger children, yet the themes are subtle enough to challenge teenage and adult readers. N.'s plots are exciting; characters develop surprisingly; the narrating voice is witty and warm. Fantastic and realistic elements are blended dexterously.

The trilogy, which includes *The Wind Singer* (2000), *Slaves of the Mastery* (2001), and *Firesong* (2002), follows the ADVENTURES of the brave, loving members of the Hath FAMILY. They fight against several totalitarian societies and journey toward the peaceful land promised by their ancestor, prophet of

535

the Manth people. Hanno, the father, does badly on the exams that assign each family to a rigid tier in Aramanth society. Ira protects her children and rails against the system. When the ten-year-old twins, empathetic Bowman and rebellious Kestrel, are threatened with horrible punishment for defying a teacher, they escape and set out on a quest for the silver device that will make the ancient Wind-Singer tower sing again and free Aramanth from the tyrannical Morah.

Five years later, another cruel kingdom seizes citizens of Aramanth to serve as slaves for the Master. The society that the Master has created seems beautiful and harmonious; the system, however, is based on fear; slaves are controlled by being forced to view their caged relatives burned alive. The Hath family members use their different talents to bring down the Master. By the third book, readers understand the vast pattern: as the prophet had predicted, his descendents and their comrades must struggle through an age of brutality before the new time of kindness can start. The Haths, helped by magical Singer people, defeat the Morah's evil and create a new community.

The Wind on Fire trilogy is well designed, and individual scenes are moving, suspenseful, and funny. The young characters find their way in a chaotic universe and learn that cooperation, intelligence, and sacrifice can overcome pride and greed. N.'s books, until now better known in the UK, are making their way in the U.S. as well, as young readers discover their magic and their humanity.

AWARDS: *The Wind Singer,* Nestle Smarties Gold Medal, 2000; *The Wind Singer* and *Slaves of the Mastery,* American Library Association Notable Children's Books, 2001 and 2002.

BIBLIOGRAPHY: "William N." Achuka.com, March 10, 2002; *Booklist,* October 15, 2000 and October 15, 2001; Jones, J. Sydney. "William N." *Authors and Artists for Young Adults,* vol. 47, 2003; *Publishers Weekly,* August 28, 2002; *School Library Journal,* December 2000 and December 2001.

DEBORAH O'KEEFE

NIVEN, Laurence Van Cott
Author, b. 30 April 1938, Los Angeles, California

N. was drawn to SCIENCE FICTION, and left the California Institute of Technology in 1958 without receiving a degree; according to N., his attention was drawn to a used-book store jammed with science-fiction

MAGAZINES. After earning a B.A. in mathematics from Washburn University in 1962, N. used a trust fund set up for him by his great-grandfather to spend the year writing. The result was *World of Ptavvs* (1966), his first novel from his popular Known Space SERIES.

The Tales of Known Space provide an explanation for humans venturing into space. In this history, humanity shares the solar systems nearest to Sol with several alien species. According to background in *World of Ptavvs,* alien races have dominated Known Space for eons, beginning with the Thrintun, which have been extinct for a billion years. The novel finds the exception of this extinction to be one deadly Thrint that has been held in a stasis field and released once again. *A Gift from Earth* (1968), *Neutron Star* (1968), *The Shape of Space* (1969) and *The Protector* (1973) continue the expansion of Known Space's history, while *Ringworld* (1970), *Ringworld Engineers* (1979), and *Ringworld Throne* (1996) conclude the saga. In these latter books, alien Puppeteers flee the explosion at the galaxy's core that makes the space uninhabitable, and enlist human aid to explore what N. has entitled the "Big Dumb Object." In addition to these listed titles, *Known Space* is the home of over thirty SHORT STORIES and novels.

In the mid-1970s, N. began a collaboration with author Jerry Pournelle, which resulted in another literary success. The combination of these authors' talents—Pournelle's skill for developing intricate plots and N.'s ability to form thoroughly original concepts—make for well-rounded and entrancing stories. One of their most intelligent works is *Inferno* (1975), a spin on the original title by Dante Aligheri. The novel reworks the theological explanation of evil, blaming God for sadism, and places antinuclear power propagandists in hell.

N.'s collaborations with Steven Barnes resulted in The Dream Park SERIES, which includes *Dream Park* (1981), *The Barsoom Project* (1989), and *Dream Park: The California Voodoo Game* (1992). These novels are set in a 21st-century virtual reality, specifically a game world environment. The ruling corporation runs complex role-playing games and projects in both the real world and on Mars. Collaborations such as these outweigh N.'s solo work; the author has created only four works outside the *Known Space* genre.

N. deals with human-alien relations and the division between FANTASY and science fiction. He writes about the future of science and technology in a positive light and with incredible conceptual flare.

AWARDS: Hugo Awards: 1967, *Neutron Star,* 1971, *Ringworld,* 1972, *Inconstant Moon,* 1975, *The Hole Man,* 1976, *Borderland of Sol;* Nebula Award: 1970, *Ringworld;* Locus Award: 1970, *Ringworld,* 1980, *The Convergent Series,* 1984, *The Integral Trees,* 2001, *The Missing Mass;* Dimitar Award: 1972, *Ringworld,* 1973, *Protector; Mote in God's Eye:* ALA Best Books for Young Adults, 1997.

SELECT FURTHER WORKS: *The Flying Sorcerers,* 1971; *The Mote in God's Eye,* 1974; *A World Out of Time,* 1976; *The Magic Goes Away,* 1978; *The Patchwork Girl,* 1980; *Oath of Fealty* (with Pournelle), 1981; *The Descent of Anansi* (with Barnes), 1982; *The Integral Trees,* 1984; *Footfall* (with Pournelle), 1985; *The Smoke Ring,* 1987; *The Legacy of Heorot* (with Barnes and Pournelle), 1987; *The Man-Kzin Wars* (with Poul Anderson and Dean Ing), 1988; *Man-Kzin Wars II* (with Ing and S. M. Stirling), 1989; *Man-Kzin Wars III,* 1990; *Achilles' Choice* (with Barnes), 1991; *Fallen Angels* (with Pournelle and Michael Flynn), 1991; *Man-Kzin Wars IV,* 1991; *Lantern: Ganthet's Tale,* 1992; *Man-Kzin Wars V,* 1992; *The Gripping Hand* (with Pournelle), 1993; *Crashlander,* 1994; *Man-Kzin Wars VI* (co-author), 1994; *Beowulf's Children* (with Pournelle and Barnes), 1995; *Man-Kzin Wars, VII,* 1995; *Three Books of Known Space,* 1996; *Destiny's Road,* 1997; *Rainbow Mars,* 1999; *Saturn's Race,* 2001; *Fallen Angels,* 2002; *Scatterbrain,* 2003.

BIBLIOGRAPHY: "Laurence Van Cott N." *DISCovering Authors,* 1999. Reproduced in *Discovering Collection,* 2001. http://galenet.galegroup.com/serv let/DC; "Larry N. Biography." http://larryniven.org/ biography.htm

RACHEL WITMER
AND SARA MARCUS

NIX, Garth
Author, b. 1963, Melbourne, Australia

About a year after N.'s birth, his family left Melbourne and settled in Canberra, AUSTRALIA (the capital of Australia), where he happily grew up. Bright and creative, N. inherited his parents' love of good books and their ability to write. His father wrote scientific works, full of facts and precision. His mother wrote about the fine art of crafting paper. While both parents focused on topics distant from those N. would eventually master, the gift of written communication permeated his life.

His passion for reading exploded when he entered school and discovered the wonders of the public library. There he says he met the authors—not in physical form, but through their stories and within their pages. Late in his seventeenth year, N. joined the Australian Army Reserve to see if a military career was his destiny. Though he served part time in the Reserve for the next five years, he knew it was not his truest calling. He briefly took a government job that eventually gave him the time and money to travel and write.

Thrilled by his good fortune, at age twenty he decided to become a professional writer, but earned his university degree—a B.A. in professional writing—as an extra precaution. As part of his degree requirement, he started a novel that would become *The Ragwitch,* published in Australia in 1990, and in the United States in 1994. Though little known in the United States, readers herald the book as realistic FANTASY with characters so endearing they invoke laughter and tears.

A year as a clerk at Canberra's Dalton Bookstore gave N. the chance to finish his novel before he moved to Sydney to work in the Australian publishing industry in 1987, where he stayed for six years. During this fruitful time, N. fell in love, traveled extensively to retrace the steps of Alexander the Great, and continued to write. Neither the romance nor the work in the publishing industry lasted, but the fiction survived. He finished *Sabriel* in 1994 and then started a job in marketing and public relations. Unhappy with his new professional direction, his fiction took on a new tone and texture. *Shade's Children* (1997) was inspired and influenced by that sometimes unhappy period.

Even if written during a time of challenge, *Shade's Children* won international loyalty from N.'s growing fan base and praise from the American press. Called compelling and chilling, the dark story of a futuristic world where all people who reach the "sad birthday" of their fourteenth year are dismantled and made into battling machines, opened the door for more popular works yet to come.

During his last days at the public relations and marketing firm, N. crossed paths with Anna, the woman who would become his wife. "We had actually met five years before," N. says on his website.

"She started work at the last publishing company I was at on the same day I left." They were married in April 2000 in the village of Bawley Point in New South Wales.

Though his career was going quite well, thanks in part to the stellar success of *Sabriel* (1996) (called "rousing, charming and slyly funny" by the *San Francisco Chronicle*), N. resisted the draw of becoming a full-time writer. He worked as a literary agent to add balance to his professional life. However, after the release of *Sabriel's* companion novels, *Lirael* (2001) and *Abhorsen* (2003)—not to mention the wildly popular Seventh Tower SERIES—the demands of fiction could no longer be ignored, so N. settled into a full-fledged, full-time writer's world.

Until the summer of 2002, stories were N.'s proudest creations, but on July 11, 2002, Thomas Henry Nix was born to parents Garth and Anna; once again, a whole new world was magically born. But the author is sure the blending of old with new will create a peaceful coexistence. He is just as certain there are many, many Garth N. stories yet to be told.

AWARDS: *Sabriel:* 1995 Aurealis Award for Best FANTASY Novel and Best YA Novel, ALA Notable Book and Best Book for Young Adults, ALA Popular Paperbacks, 2003, CBCA Notable Book, LOCUS MAGAZINE Recommended Fantasy novel, 1997 New York Public Library Books for the TEENAGE; 2002 Adelaide Festival Award for Children's Literature; ALA Best Book for Young Adults: 1997 for *Sabriel,* 1998 for *Shade's Children* 2002 for *Lirael: Daughter of the Clay*; *Shade's Children*: ALA Popular Paperbacks, 2004.

FURTHER WORKS: *X-Files: The Calusari,* 1997; "From the Lighthouse," 1998; "Hansel's Eyes," 2000; *The Fall,* 2000; *Castle,* 2000; *Aenir,* 2000; *Above The Veil,* 2001; *Dark Revelation,* 2001; *The Violet Keystone,* 2001; *Mister Monday,* 2003; *Grim Tuesday,* 2003; *Drowned Wednesday,* 2005.

BIBLIOGRAPHY: Interview with Garth N.; Teen Reads; Garth N. website: http://members.ozemail.com.au/~garthnix/.

KELLY MILNER HALLS

NIXON, Joan Lowery (Jaye Ellen)

Author, educator, b. 3 February 1927, Los Angeles, California; d. 28 June 2003, Houston, Texas

It has been noted that N. is the undisputed mistress of crime fiction and MYSTERIES for YAS. Over the course of a career spanning almost four decades and comprising more than a hundred books, N. has proved time and again that she has what it takes to attract and hold readers of many ages. Mary Lystad said it best in the *St. James Guide to Young Adult Writers,* "N.'s skillful writing and boundless imagination make young readers want to read on, to find out what surprises wait on the next page and discover if their solutions to her never-ending puzzles would be the correct one." "In a field of YA MYSTERY writers, a field crowded with authors," stated Melissa Fletcher Stoeltje in the *Houston Chronicle* MAGAZINE, "she is by all accounts the Grande Dame."

As a child, N. wrote poems in ninth grade and was editor of her school newspaper. This was in 1941, the year of the attack on Pearl Harbor. She tried to volunteer as a writer of propaganda for the Red Cross, but her offer was ignored. Instead, while at Hollywood High School she would write letters to lonely servicemen and helped serve breakfast to them in the school cafeteria. It was also at Hollywood High that she met her favorite and most influential teacher. Miss Bertha Standfast would be her English teacher the next three years as N. enrolled in every one of her classes. "I treasured the direction Miss Standfast gave me," she would say. "You have the talent, your going to be a writer," Miss Standfast would tell her. It was she who insisted that N. major in journalism when she went to college. At the age of seventeen N. wrote her first article for a magazine, selling it to the *Ford Times.*

It only took one week after high school for N. to enter the University of Southern California as a journalism student. "My training as a child in journalism taught me discipline," she says. "For one thing, I learned to create at the typewriter. We took our exams on the typewriter." She also notes, "Journalism taught me to focus because I had to sit down and write, whether I felt like it or not—no waiting for inspiration. I learned the skill of finding the important facts in a story, and how to isolate them from all the unnecessary details." While at USC, N. met her future husband, Hershell "Nick" N., a student majoring in naval science. After earning her degree in journalism, she could not find a job in her field due to all the correspondents returning from the WAR. The Los Angeles area was in need of teachers, so she found work as a substitute for kindergarten through the third grade.

After moving to Billings, Montana, because of her husband's job, N. would later say she shed many tears about moving. She says, "All I knew about the state of Montana was that it was full of cattle and cactus, and I didn't want to leave my family, my friends, and my beautiful state of California." The move was a blessing in disguise for N. and all lucky readers who have benefited from her works. It was in Montana that she read an announcement for the upcoming Southwest Writers Conference. This is when she became enthusiastic about writing for children. "I had children, I had taught children, and I have a vivid kind of memory which enables me to remember all the details I saw and the emotions I felt when I was a child," she reminisced. "I made a mental note to myself. Maybe I'd try writing something for children." She would write in her mind for weeks at a time, tending to every detail in her story. Every day after school, she would get to her typewriter and write what she remembered. N. would also read to her children her day's work and often take their suggestions—making it funnier or sadder. N. would even join groups of fellow writers to read and critique each other's manuscripts.

For an author so vast in writing skills it is noteworthy that her first book, *The Mystery of Hurricane Castle* (1964), was rejected twelve times by different publishers before Criterion finally accepted it. The story tells of the Nickson sisters, Maureen and Kathy and their younger brother Danny who seek shelter during a hurricane in a stone castle occupied by a ghost. From this debut book right to this day, N. is at the pinnacle when it comes to YA Adult mystery writers of our time. From mysteries in haunted castles, to kidnap victims, to her Ellis Island SERIES, and the ever-popular Claude and Shirley series, N. is a real pro at delivering likable, true-to-life characters and intriguing plots. Over her many years of writing (she still publishes an average of two books per year), N. has covered the gamut and then some. She is a must read for all YAs and adults as well.

WILLIAM MARIANO
AND MARY MARIANO

NOLAN, Han

Author, b. 25 August 1956, Birmingham, Alabama

The road N. traveled on her way to becoming an award-winning writer has been a winding and occasionally rocky one. From an early career as a dance teacher to a disappointing debut novel that only hinted at her talent, she currently reigns as one of the most highly praised authors in the field today. Her effervescent stories, full of unusual characters in compelling situations, have earned her both a National Book Award and consistently starred reviews.

From an early age, N. studied the art of dance. She earned her B.S. in dance education from the University of North Carolina in 1979, and her M.A. in dance from Ohio State University in 1981. After she and her husband adopted three children in 1985, N. wanted to work from home, and she began to explore the possibilities of a career in fiction writing. After studying numerous books on writing technique and publishing markets, N. began to write and submit SHORT STORIES that were consistently rejected. Undaunted, she continued to polish her craft, and was finally rewarded in 1994 with her first published novel, *If I Should Die before I Wake*. The book tells the story of a hospitalized neo-Nazi TEENAGER who somehow obtains telepathic memories about the HOLOCAUST from her roommate, a dying Jewish woman. The reviews were mixed; critics found the story implausible and the teenage character shallow, although many praised her description of the horrors of the death camps and the complex characterization of Chana, the Holocaust survivor.

N.'s next novel, *Send Me Down a Miracle* (1996), was, in some ways, much lighter than her first work. The story of a Southern teenager torn between her loyalty to her strict religious father and her admiration for a local performance artist who claims to have received messages from Jesus came straight from N.'s firsthand knowledge of the American South. The book combined offbeat humor with the more serious subject of religion, and the critics loved it. Consequently, N. received her first National Book Award nomination.

It was the novel *Dancing on the Edge* (1997) that really brought N.'s name to the forefront of YA LITERATURE and fiction. The story of a mentally disturbed teenager whose dancing talent is at the heart of a terrible FAMILY secret was described as having "a set of elaborately drawn characters that will surprise readers at every turn." N. won the National Book Award that year, the only writer up to that point to have been nominated two years in a row.

N. continues to expand her now trademark eccentric characters and settings with her most recent works, *A Face in Every Window* (1999) and *Born Blue* (2001). *A Face in Every Widow* features teenager James Patrick (JP) and his immature "Mam," who wins a shabby old country house in a contest. Mam proceeds to fill the house with all manner of oddball personalities until JP feels like the only normal person left. His journey to acceptance of his Mam's new life is both funny and poignant. One reviewer proclaimed, "Only a writer as talented as Han N. could make this improbable story line and bizarre cast of characters not only believable, but also ultimately uplifting, intriguing, and memorable."

Born Blue, on the other hand, while just as well-received, painted a much darker picture of the coming of age experience. After much abuse from her heroin-addicted mother, blond-haired, blue-eyed foster child Janie decides that her father whom she never met must have been black like the soul singers she admires. To reflect this heritage, Janie changes her name to Leshaya. The events that follow create a riveting tale of a child-woman whose self-destructive behavior always keeps her dreams just beyond her grasp. Arguably N.'s most challenging and controversial novel to date, the writing of *Born Blue* was heralded as "superb; like the blues, it bores down the soul."

In an interview with YA expert Don Gallo, the former creative-movement teacher remarked that writing isn't much different from dancing: "Dance, like writing, requires discipline, training, faith, confidence, and thick skin." Like a dancer, N.'s lyrical prose arcs elegantly over the page, imbuing her remarkable characters with a dynamic inner life. While the world of dance may be poorer in her absence, this quiet and unassuming writer has brought her abundant gifts to a truly fortunate young adult literature community.

AWARDS: *Dancing on the Edge,* 1997, ALA Best Books for Young Adults, 1998; National Book Award 1998; *Born Blue,* 2002; ALA Best Books for Young Adults, 2002, ALA Popular Paperbacks, 2004.

FURTHER WORK: *When We Were Saints,* 2003.

BIBLIOGRAPHY: Bradburn, Frances. "A Face in Every Window." *Booklist,* November 1999, Cooper, Ilene. "Dancing on the Edge." *Booklist,* October 1997; Follos, Alison, "Born Blue." *School Library Journal,* November 2001. Gallo, Don. "Han N." authors4teens.com; "Han N." *Contemporary Authors Online,* 2001.

JENNIFER HUBERT

NORTON, Andre

Author, b. 17 February 1912, Cleveland, Ohio; d. 17 March 2005, n.p.

N. was born Mary Alice to parents Adalbert Freely and Bertha (Stemm) Norton in Cleveland, Ohio, from American pioneer stock. She had her name changed legally to the gender-neutral "Andre" in 1934 to make her writing more marketable to publishers of boy's ADVENTURE stories, her first professional endeavors. She also wrote under pseudonyms, Andrew North and Allen Weston. She attended what is now Case Western Reserve University from 1930 to 1932 with the intention of becoming a history teacher. The Great Depression forced her to abandon her education in favor of employment. She worked at Cleveland Public Library from 1930 to 1951, beginning as a checkout clerk and advancing to children's LIBRARIAN except for a short period in 1941–42, when she spent a short time in the Washington, D.C., area as owner of a bookstore, at the Library of Congress, and as a special librarian for a citizenship project. Because of poor health, she retired from the library and became a full-time freelance writer in 1950, and continues today. She suffers from agoraphobia, which, though controlled with medication, precludes her from traveling. She is currently director of the High Hallack Genre Writers Research Library in Murfreesboro, Tennessee, a resource for writers and scholars of popular fiction, established in 1999. Her works include animal tales, FANTASY fiction, SCIENCE FICTION, historical fiction, and children's literature.

Her first published work was *The Prince Commands* (1934), an adventure story. However, N. wrote her first story while still in high school. Reformatted, it was published as *Ralestone Luck* in 1938. N. brought the research skills of a librarian to her early writings, as exemplified by *Scarface* (1948), a historical novel about the pirates of Tortuga. In 1952, she wrote her first science fiction book, *Star Man's Son, 2250 A.D.,* which has sold over one million copies. She states that she was "drawn to the science fiction genre because it poses no limit on [her] imagination." However, her writings also are concerned with the excesses of "uncontrolled progress and malevolent science"; her villains are countered by "talismans, magic, and the rhythms of the natural world." In her own words, she characterizes herself as "a very staid teller of old-fashioned stories with firm plots and morals." Her main characters are usually young loners, outcasts and misfits looking for a place in society while they attempt to discover who they are. Many of her stories depict telepathic animals with human-like intelligence and emotions, including dolphins, horses, bears, and especially cats. Her later works have strong female protagonists, such as those in the Witch World SERIES, considered by many to be her finest works.

N. has written more than one hundred books. However, since much of her work was classified as YOUNG ADULT LITERATURE, N. may not have received all the recognition she deserved. However, she has won many awards, beginning with an award from the Dutch government for her historical novel about the Dutch underground, *The Sword is Drawn* (1944). She was nominated for Hugo awards for various science fiction works. She was the first woman awarded the Gandalf Master of Fantasy Award (1977). She was recipient of the Andre Norton Award (1978) established by the Women Writers of Science Fiction. She received both the Nebula Grand Master Award and the Jules Verne Award in 1984. *The Elvenbane* (1991), written with Mercedes LACKEY, won the Science Fiction Club Readers Award in that year.

AWARDS: Award from Dutch government, 1946, for *The Sword Is Drawn;* 1950 Ohioana Juvenile Award honor book, *Sword in Sheath;* 1965 Child Study Association Book of the Year award, *Steel Magic;* 1976 Phoenix Award for overall achievement in science fiction; 1977 Gandalf Master of Fantasy Award (lifetime achievement); 1978 Orlando Science Fiction Society Life Achievement Award; Balrog Fantasy Award, 1979; 1983 Fritz Leiber Award for work in the field of fantasy; 1983 E. E. Smith Award; 1984 Nebula Grand Master Award (lifetime achievement); 1984 Jules Verne Award for work in the field of science fiction; 1986 Daedalus Award (lifetime achievement); 1987 Second Stage Lensman Award (lifetime achievement); 1991 Science Fiction Book Club Readers' Award, *The Elvenbane;* named to Science Fiction and Fantasy Writers Hall of Fame, 1996; World Fantasy Convention Life Achievement Award, 1998.

SELECT FURTHER WORKS: *The Stars Are Ours!,* 1954; *Beast Master,* 1959; *Ride Proud Rebel,* 1961; *Key Out of Time,* 1963; *Witch World,* 1963; *Web of Witch World,* 1964; *Three Against Witch World,* 1965; *Warlock of the Witch World,* 1967; *Golden Trillium,* 1993; *The Warding of Witch World,* 1996; *Queen,* 2003; *Beast Master's Circus,* 2004.

BIBLIOGRAPHY: *Something About the Author,* vol. 1, 1971; vol. 43, 1986; vol. 91, 1997; *Children's Literature Review,* vol. 50, 1986; *Major Authors and Illustrators for Children and Young Adults,* vol. 4, 1993; *Dictionary of Literary Biography,* vol. 8, 1981; vol. 52, 1986; Boyer, Robert H., *Fantasists on Fantasy: A Collection of Critical Reflections,* 1984; *The Andre Norton website,* http://www.andrenorton.org

JOANN C. JANOSKO

NYE, Naomi Shihab
Author, b. 12 March 1952, St. Louis, Missouri

N. is best known for her POETRY, which excels in bringing together the voices and experiences of diverse people. As she shares unique communities within a global society, N. focuses on what might be considered mundane in everyday life, her eloquent use of descriptive words transforms the ordinary into priceless images.

N. was born to a Palestinian father and an American mother of German descent. She spent most of her childhood in St. Louis before her family moved to Jerusalem, at that time still part of Jordan. During high school she returned to live in San Antonio, Texas. Both her Arab heritage and the community of San Antonio, where she still resides with her husband and son, are prominent in her writing.

In an interview with Paula Graham, N. discusses her use of journals to collect ideas: "snatches of things," such as signs, details from travels in other countries, notes about her grandmother, and other thoughts and observations. She shares that she always collects many more treasures than she would ever use, in various journals for different purposes, and advises students to do the same. N. believes that extensive reading and keeping a notebook, which make people alert to all the messages, signs, and images around them, are the two most useful things a writer can do.

Numerous collections of poems around universal themes highlight N.'s career as a poet. *This Same Sky: A Collection of Poems from Around the World* (1992) consists of the work of 129 poets from 68 countries. As a MULTICULTURAL resource, this collection highly regards the ordinary life experiences of these poet voices from a global perspective. "Poetry has always devoted itself to bringing us into clearer focus—letting us feel or imagine faraway worlds from the inside," N. states in the introduction. Her response to any concern that much might be lost in translating poetry from one language to another is, "Perhaps, but how much is gained!"

In a similar vein, *The Tree Is Older than You Are* (1995) celebrates the Mexican culture. With richly colored paintings by Mexican artists throughout, this book captures the spirit of the people through N.'s detailed imagery and bilingual text. In *Hugging the Jukebox* (1999), N. paints realistic images of everyday life in poetic celebration of diverse individuals and perspectives. *What Have You Lost* (1999), with photographs by Michael Nye, is a collection of poetry that focuses on the universal experience of loss; it includes those things that are missed only momentarily when lost and the ones that are monumental and can never be reclaimed. Poems that focus on wallets, time, FAMILY, friends, happiness, pets, keys, and other topics eloquently share the ways people cope and understand loss and the difficulties they experience because of it. N. reminds us, however, "The things that cause you friction are the things from which you might make art." Two of her collections for young people are *Come with Me: Poems for a Journey* (2000), illustrated by Dan Yaccarino, and *Salting the Ocean: 100 Poems by Young Poets* (2000), illustrated by Ashley Bryan.

N. has always maintained connections to her Arabian culture and says in the introduction to *Varieties of Gazelle, Poems of the Middle East* (2002) that she has always written down little things that later connected her to other Arab writers in sharing their heritage. This collection of poems takes readers into aspects of a culture often considered unfamiliar despite the growing population of Arab-Americans. Regarding the complexity of emotions that surrounded society following September 11, 2001, N. turned to poetry and stated, "We need poetry for nourishment and noticing, for the way language and imagery reach comfortably into experience, holding and connecting it more successfully than any news channel we could name."

Habibi (1996), N.'s first YA novel, tells the story of Liyana Abboud, an Arab-American TEEN who experiences the violence in Jerusalem in the 1970s after moving there with her family. Filled with emotion and imagery, the complexities of growing up in an angry adult society are autobiographically described through Liyana's love of language. Additionally, *Sitti's Secret* (1992), a PICTURE BOOK about a young Arab-American girl and the relationship she builds with her grandmother in Palestine, adds to the wealth for readers.

AWARDS: *Habibi:* ALA BBYA, 1998, ALA Notable Children's Book 1998, ALA Popular Paperbacks, 2002; *I Feel a Little Jumpy Around You:* ALA BBYA, 1997; *Sitti's Secrets:* SLJ Best Book of the Year; ALA Notable Children's Books; *Space Between our Footsteps:* ALA BBYA, 1999; *What Have You Lost?:* ALA BBYA, 2000; *The Tree is Older than You Are:* ALA BBYA, 1996; Voertman Poetry Prize, Texas Institute of Letters, I. B. Lavan Award, Academy of American Poets, Jane Addams Children's Book Award, Paterson Poetry Prize. *Nineteen Varieties of Gazelle:* BBYA, 2003, ALA Notable Children's Books, 2003, Nominated for National Book Award.

FURTHER WORKS: *Different Ways to Pray,* 1980; *Yellow Glove,* 1986; *Never in a Hurry,* 1996; *The Flag of Childhood: Poems from the Middle East,* 2002.

BIBLIOGRAPHY: *Contemporary Authors Online; Contemporary Women Poets,* 1997; *Dictionary of Literary Biography,* 120, 1992; Graham P. W., ed. *Speaking of Journals,* 1999, pp. 198–207.

JANELLE B. MATHIS

OATES, Joyce Carol

Author, educator, b. 16 June 1938, Lockport, New York

O. is one of the most prolific writers of our time, having produced a variety of works spanning five decades. Much of O.'s works involve working-class themes, reflecting her upbringing in rural New York in Erie County. O. has been a storyteller practically all her life. Before she could write, she told stories through drawings and paintings. She had written her first novel before she was fifteen, although it was not published. That did not deter her, however, as she went on to publish at least one work every year since 1963. Additionally, her work is not limited to any particular form or genre. O. has written fiction, nonfiction, POETRY, SHORT STORIES, essays, criticism, and PLAYS. The majority of her work has been considered adult literature; however, in the new millennium, O. has also written juvenile and YA stories.

Although O. has written many books and short stories that could be enjoyed by YAs, *Big Mouth and Ugly Girl* (2002) was the first book written specifically for that audience. Characteristic of much of her work, O. includes elements of FAMILY and relationship dynamics. Matt is Big Mouth, who often uses his 'big mouth' to win approval of others. One of Matt's jokes gets him accused of wanting to blow up the high school he attends. Ursula, who calls herself Ugly Girl, goes to his defense and a relationship develops between these two unlikely characters. FAMILY dynamics play into the story around this plot—Ursula's mother does not attend her basketball games, but goes to her sister's dance recitals instead. Ursula's mother discourages her from getting involved in Matt's situation, and Matt's family decides to sue the school.

Her next novel for YAs was *Freaky Green Eyes* (2003), which again looks at the dynamics of family relationships as well as at violence and coming-of-age. Franky is in awe of her father, a famous former football player and now a sports broadcaster. She struggles when her mother begins to separate herself from the family. *Freaky Green Eyes* represents Franky's inner strength and came about when she had to fight off a rape at a party. When Franky's mother disappears completely, she calls on her strong Freaky Green Eyes ego; she learns that her father is abusive and may have murdered her mother. She testifies against her father and then struggles as her older stepbrother feels she has betrayed the family. This story keeps the reader interested all the way through.

O. has also written a short story collection geared toward YAs, especially females. O. takes twelve very different TEENAGE girls and presents twelve very powerful stories in *Small Avalanches: and other stories* (2002). O. takes the reader into the girls' lives as they deal with becoming adults, with changing family relationships, and with ways their behavior affects others. Some stories are quite complex—the collection is geared more for advanced teen readers.

When not writing, O. is a writer in residence and a Roger S. Berlind Distinguished Professor at Princeton University.

AWARDS: Mademoiselle college fiction award for "In the Old World," 1959; National Endowment for the Arts grants, 1966, 1968; Guggenheim fellowship, 1967; O. Henry Award for "In the Region of Ice," 1967, "The Dead," 1973, and "My Warszawa," 1983; Rosenthal Award for *A Garden of Earthly Delights,* 1968; National Book Award for *them,* 1970; O. Henry Special Award for Continuing Achievement, 1970, 1986; Lotos Club Award of Merit, 1975; Pushcart Prize, 1976; Rhea Award for "Dungannon Foundation," 1990; Alan Swallow Award for fiction, 1990; co-winner, Heidemann Award for one-act plays, 1990; Bobst Award for Lifetime Achievement in Fiction, 1990; Bram Stoker Lifetime Achievement Award for HORROR fiction, 1994; Bram Stoker Award for Horror and Fisk Fiction Prize for *Zombie,* 1996; *Freaky Green Eyes: Publisher's Weekly* Best Children's Books, 2003; O. Henry Prize National Book Award for *Blonde,* 2001; Best American MYSTERY Stories designation for "High School Sweetheart," 2002; 2003 American Library Association Best Books for Young Adults, ALA Popular Paperbacks, 2005, for *Big Mouth & Ugly Girl.*

SELECT FURTHER WORKS: *them* (1969), *The Wheel of Love and Other Stories* (1970), *Wonderland* (1971), *Do with Me What You Will* (1973), *The Assassins: A Books of Hours* (1975), *Childwold* (1976), *Angel of Light* (1981), *American Appetites* (1989), *Because It Is Bitter and Because It Is My Heart* (1990), *Black Water* (1992), *Foxfire: Confessions of a Girl Gang* (1993), *We Were the Mulvaneys* (1996), *Man Crazy* (1997), *Blonde* (2000), *I'll Take You There* (2002), *The Tattooed Girl* (2003), *The Falls: A Novel* (2004).

BIBLIOGRAPHY: *Authors and Artists for Young Adults* (v. 52); *Contemporary Authors; Contemporary Novelists.*

                                                    TINA HERTEL

O'BRIEN, Robert C. (pseud. Robert Leslie Conly)

Author, b. 11 January 1918, Brooklyn, New York; d. 5 March 1973, Washington, D.C.

O. was born Robert Leslie Conly. He wrote his novels under a pseudonym because his employer, *National Geographic,* discouraged its authors from publishing anything outside the MAGAZINE. O. grew up in Amityville, New York, as the difficult middle child of an Irish family. He was often ill as a child and was fearful of attending school. It was during his childhood that O. found his niche in the arts. He enjoyed singing and playing the piano. A voracious reader and writer, O. wrote POETRY and a novel. His active imag-

ination and FANTASY world was set aside during his high-school years. At this time, O. began his early morning regimen of music practice, study, and solitary walks at 4 a.m. each day. He also edited the school paper and developed his writing skills at Amityville High School.

After high school, O. attended Williams College from 1935 to 1937. Leaving during his second year due to stress, O. moved back home and returned to studying music, specifically the piano. During the year O. took off, he studied concurrently at Columbia University and music at Julliard School of Music. After the year, he returned to college. While he studied music again at Eastman College, O. decided to become a writer and completed his B.A. in English at the University of Rochester in 1940. After earning his degree, he worked his way up from an entry-level position to staff writer for *Newsweek.* During his employment at *Newsweek,* O. met Sally McCaslin and the two married in 1943. From 1944 to 1951, O. worked at the *Times-Herald* newspaper in Washington, D.C. During this period O. and his wife had four children: a son and three daughters. In 1951, O. went to work for *National Geographic* as a writer and editor. While employed at *National Geographic,* he traveled internationally for his work. O.'s assignment in Northern Ireland in 1964 formed a deep and lasting impression on him.

O. gave serious consideration to writing fiction. His novels are apocalyptic coming-of-age tales that contain elements of fantasy and SCIENCE FICTION. O.'s first novel, *The Silver Crown,* was published in 1968 to mixed reviews. This coming-of-age tale concerns ten-year-old Ellen, whose family dies in a fire after she receives a silver crown for her birthday. O.'s second book, *Mrs. Frisby and the Rats of NIMH,* is an animal fantasy about a widowed field mouse who must rely on a group of intelligent rats from a research facility to help her move her home and save her dying son. In 1982, MGM/United Artists released animator Don Bluth's feature film adaptation of O.'s *Mrs. Frisby and the Rats of NIMH* (1971). The MOVIE, *The Secret of NIMH* (1982), was well received despite the renaming of Mrs. Frisby to Mrs. Brisby. It was popular with children in the 1980s and continues to be popular as those children are now adults who are sharing the film with their children. O.'s third novel, *A Report from Group 17* (1972), is about a girl who discovers too much about a research institute that is developing biological weapons. His final novel, *Z for Zachariah* (1975), is the DIARY of sixteen-year-old nuclear WAR survivor Ann Burden. She is discovered by Mr. Loomis, an ungrateful scientist, whom she nurses back to health from radiation poisoning.

O. died of a heart attack in 1997 in Washington, DC. His daughter, Jane Leslie Conly, has continued O.'s literary legacy. She is the author of seven novels for young people, including *Rasco and the Rats of NIMH* (1986) and *R–T, Margaret and the Rats of NIMH* (1990), which continue the story of the characters of *Mrs. Frisby and the Rats of NIMH*.

AWARDS: 1972 Newbery Medal, *Mrs. Frisby and the Rats of NIMH;* ALA Best Book for Young Adults: 1972 for *A Report from Group 17* and 1975 for *Z for Zachariah;* 1976 Edgar Allan Poe Award for Best Juvenile MYSTERY, *Z for Zachariah.*

FURTHER WORKS: *The Silver Crown,* 1968.

BIBLIOGRAPHY: Carter, Betty. *Best Books for Young Adults.* 2nd ed., 2000; *Contemporary Authors Online,* 2000; *U*X*L Junior Discovering Authors,* 2001; Jane Leslie Conly official website, http://www.childrens bookguild.org/conly.html; Mystery Writers of America website, http://www.mysterywriters.org; National Book Award website, http://www.national book.org/

ANDREW W. HUNTER

O'BRIEN, Tim (William Timothy O'Brien)
Author, b. 1 October 1946, Austin, Minnesota

O. grew up in a small Minnesota town, a chubby loner intrigued by the firsthand accounts written by his father—an insurance salesman—about serving at Iwo Jima and Okinawa; these accounts were published in the *New York Times.* O. put his own writing ambitions on hold during college and opted to study political science with the hopes of prompting progressive political change. Immediately following graduation from Macalester College in 1968—a full scholarship to Harvard for graduate study awaiting him—O. was drafted as an infantry soldier during the height of the Vietnam War. The writer who defined the Vietnam War in American literature was a peace activist who, on learning of his draft, considered deserting to Canada; O. served his term.

On returning from Vietnam, O. renewed his academic career, beginning doctoral study at the Harvard School of Government. *Playboy* had already pub-

lished a story of his about Vietnam experiences when he completed his semi-AUTOBIOGRAPHICAL work *If I Die in a Combat Zone, Box Me up and Ship Me Home* (1973). He abandoned his graduate studies and took a position as a reporter for the *Washington Post.* The job fueled his ambition to write creatively, and he quit after a year to pursue writing full time. The decision proved wise; *Going after Cacciato* (1978) was awarded the National Book Award in 1979, and *The Things They Carried* (1990) was short-listed for both the Pulitzer Prize and the National Book Critics Circle Award.

O. views his relationship with Vietnam as being like Faulkner's with the South; it is his territory, his essence. The harshness and grit of WAR are never disguised in O.'s works, nor is the continuum of humanity—from savagery to heroism—disavowed. While the Vietnam War is central to his works, O. is also concerned with storytelling and the boundaries between truth and fiction. The fantasized journey in *Cacciato,* the importance of story in *The Things They Carried,* the deception and uncertainty in *In the Lake of the Woods* (1994), and the decaying façade of character in *Tomcat in Love* (1998) exemplify this concern.

Although O. does not intentionally write for young adults, many of his works have attracted a TEENAGE audience. They are drawn into works such as *The Things They Carried* by the realistic depiction of the Vietnam War and the soldiers who served. This book and others by O. are increasingly being included in high-school curricula as contemporary literacy classics.

AWARDS: *If I Die in a Combat Zone, Box Me up and Ship Me Home:* 1973 *New York Times* Outstanding Book and 1973 American Library Association's Best Books for Young Adults; 1978 National Book Award, *Going After Cacciato; The Things They Carried:* 1990 Melcher Book Award and 1991 ALA Best Books for Young Adults; 1995 James Fenimore Cooper Prize for Historical Fiction, *In the Lake of the Woods.*

FURTHER WORKS: *Northern Lights,* 1975; *The Nuclear Age,* 1985; *July, July,* 2002.

BIBLIOGRAPHY: Coffey, Michael. "Tim O.; inventing a new form helps the author talk about war, memory and storytelling." *Publishers Weekly* 237, no. 7, pp. 60–61; Karp, Josh. "The What-If Game." *Atlantic [Monthly] Unbound,* October 30, 2002, http://www

.theatlantic.com/unbound/interviews/int2002-10-30 .htm; Lee, Don. "About Tim O." *Ploughshares* 21, no. 4, pp. 196–201; "Tim O." *Contemporary Authors Online,* 2003. Reproduced in Biography Resource Center, 2003. http://galenet.galegroup.com/servlet/ BioRC

CAROL L. TILLEY

O'DELL, Scott

Author, b. 23 May 1898, Los Angeles, California; d. 15 October 1989, Mount Kisco, New York

Curiously, Scott O. was born Odell Gabriel Scott. When he was a young man, his name was mistakenly transposed by an editor in an article byline, and O. had his name legally changed.

The son of Bennett Mason and May Elizabeth (Gabriel) Scott, O. was a young explorer in the then-frontier town of Los Angeles. His family moved often, but never far. This allowed O. to learn about many different cultures—the Spaniards who first settled in the Claremont region, and the Mexican and Diegueno Indian cultures, which were prominent in the town of Julian, in the heart of the Oriflamme Mountains on the Mexican border. He enjoyed discovering the nature and culture around him. Not surprisingly, the sea and the frontier, as well as Native Americans, Spaniards, and Hispanics, found their way into O.'s later writing. O. also hunted animals for sport as a young boy, an act that would cause him remorse during adulthood, when his writing would express contempt for hunters and for his boyish antics.

O. never enjoyed school, but he loved to read. One of his favorite authors, Sir Walter Scott, was his great-grandmother's first cousin. After finishing high school in 1918, O. enlisted in the U.S. Army and was sent to Occidental College in Los Angeles for training. One month later, an armistice was issued and O. was discharged. He decided to continue his studies at Occidental College, but he never completed a degree. O. later studied at the University of Wisconsin, Stanford University, and the University of Rome, but a college degree eluded him.

In 1925, O. began to write articles for a local newspaper. He also worked as a technical director for Paramount Studios, as a Technicolor cameraman for Metro-Goldwyn-Mayer, and he taught a mail-order course in photoplay writing. His first novel, *Women of Spain: A Story of Old California,* was published in

1934. But O.'s first novel for TEENS, and inarguably his most famous work, didn't appear until 1960. That novel is *Island of the Blue Dolphins.*

O. did not set out to write a novel for children. In fact, his primary intention for writing *Island of the Blue Dolphins* was to protest hunting. This historical novel tells the story of a Native Indian girl named Karana who is left on an uninhabited island off the California coast after a pack of wild dogs kill her brother. Slowly, Karana learns to respect the land and the animals with which she shares her home. She even learns to forgive Rontu, the dog who killed her brother. O. based the story of Karana on the true story of a girl who lived alone on a California island for eighteen years. *Island of the Blue Dolphins* won O. critical acclaim, including the coveted Newbery Medal and Hans Christian Andersen Award for lifetime achievement.

Island of the Blue Dolphins was the first of O.'s many novels for YA, several of which are based on historical events, including *The King's Fifth* (1966). This is the story of a young mapmaker who goes on a quest for gold in southwestern America. In *The Black Pearl* (1967), a sixteen-year-old boy battles with a devilfish that guards a rare and giant pearl in an underwater cave. *Sing down the Moon* (1970) is another work of historical fiction for young adults that chronicles the experiences of a young Navajo girl during the enslavement and forced migration of her people. These three books each won O. a Newbery Medal.

O. is also the author of novels for young adults that deal with present-day issues. *Child of Fire* (1974) deals with gang wars. In this novel, a parole officer tries to keep the violence and heroics of two Hispanic teenagers under control. *Alexandra* (1984) tells the story of a young girl diver. While helping her grandfather on the family boat, she discovers that someone is using their sponges as a hiding place for smuggled cocaine.

O. enjoyed fan letters, and often responded to them. O. once wrote, "Letters from children, these acts of friendship, help make all the work worth doing." O. died of prostate cancer in 1989, leaving two unfinished novels. Before his DEATH, he had asked his wife, Elizabeth Hall, to finish the novels for him, which she did; *Thunder Rolling in the Mountains* was published posthumously in 1992, and *Venus Among the Fishes* was published posthumously in

1995. An award named in his honor is given to a writer each year.

After his ashes were, at his request, scattered over the Pacific Ocean off the coast of La Jolla, California, a pod of dolphins emerged from the water. The dolphins accompanied the boat of mourners back toward land, leaving only when the boat entered San Diego Bay.

O. left a lasting legacy in the world of literature. His skill at entwining current dilemmas with historical background is unmatched. Furthermore, he has been praised for raising the social awareness of his readers on topics ranging from enslavement and forced migration to the human strength of endurance and the power of survival. O.'s writing expresses his concern for nature as well as his sensitivity toward the human spirit.

AWARDS: *Island of the Blue Dolphins:* 1961 American Library Association (ALA) John Newbery Medal, 1962 International Board on Books for Young People Hans Christian Andersen Award of Merit, American Library Association Notable Book citation; *The King's Fifth:* 1967 Newbery Honor Book and *Horn Book* Honor citation; *The Black Pearl:* 1968 Newbery Honor Book, ALA Notable Book citations, and *Horn Book* Honor citation; *Sing down the Moon:* 1971 Newbery Honor Book, ALA Notable Book citation, *Horn Book* Honor citation, Children's Book of the Year citation; 1972 Hans Christian Andersen Medal for lifetime achievement.

FURTHER WORKS: *The Dark Canoe,* 1968; *Journey to Jericho,* 1969; *The Treasure of Topo-el-Bampo,* 1972; *The Cruise of the Arctic Star,* 1973; *The Hawk That Dare Not Hunt by Day,* 1975; *Zia,* 1977; *The 290,* 1976; *Carlota,* 1977; *Kathleen, Please Come Home,* 1978; *The Captive,* 1979; *Sarah Bishop,* 1980; *The Feathered Serpent,* 1981; *The Spanish Smile,* 1982; *The Castle in the Sea,* 1983; *The Amethyst Ring,* 1984; *The Road to Damietta,* 1985; *Streams to the River, River to the Sea,* 1986; *The Serpent Never Sleeps,* 1987; *Black Star, Bright Dawn,* 1988; *My Name Is Not Angelica,* 1989.

BIBLIOGRAPHY: *Something about the Author,* vol. 134; http://www.suite101.com/article.cfm/840/43435; www.scottodell.com

CARRA E. GAMBERDELLA

O'KEEFE, Susan Heyboerf (a.k.a. Alexandra Canarsie)
Author, b. 17 April 1953, Englewood, New Jersey

O. received her B.A. in literature and psychology at a New York State college. She also obtained her master's in creative writing from The City College of New York. Her first employer hired her to write direct-mail advertising copy. O. is married and the mother of a son who has named the family's two pet parrots Wallace and Gromit. O. makes her home in Edgewater, New Jersey.

O.'s first published book is titled *One Hungry Monster* (1989). Her books reflect her interest in sharing the power of prayer; her ability to make these books nondenominational give them wide appeal. She has written a dozen children's books and in 2001 expanded her repertoire to include YA material.

O. maintained an author's website in the past and offered advice to up and coming writers of children's literature. "Keep trying and don't give up, no matter what anyone says. This does NOT mean that you should stubbornly consider yourself always right and critics always wrong. No matter who you are and no matter how well you write, you need to learn how to rewrite—every piece, every time, usually multiple times. What this DOES mean is not to take literary criticism personally. If a piece is rejected, IT is rejected, not you. Even if a piece really stinks, IT stinks, not you. If you want to be a writer, you CAN be—but you must be willing to do the work."

O. now lives in the house in which she grew up, but resides in the apartment underneath her parents' residence. She has two sisters, one of whom lives in Connecticut and another in California. O.'s husband is a counselor who specializes in the treatment of substance abuse. She is now the mother of a college-aged son; she is employed by a publishing company.

AWARDS: TAYSHAS List, the recommended high-school reading list published by the Texas Library Association, for *My Life and Death by Alexandra Canarsie.*

FURTHER WORKS: *My Life and Death by Alexandra Canarsie,* 2001; *Death by Eggplant,* 2004.

BIBLIOGRAPHY: *Something About the Author,* vol. 133, 2002; www.susanokeefe.smartwriters.com.

SANDRA KITAIN

OKIMOTO, Jean Davies
Author, b. 14 December 1942, Cleveland, Ohio

O. draws from her professional and personal experiences as a psychotherapist and a twice-married woman of a biracial family to write realistic novels for YA. Her protagonists encounter and resolve situa-

547

tions commonly faced by modern TEENAGERS, including divorce, fear of failure, loss of friends, and conflict with stepsiblings. Her work has been praised for being "fresh and real," her characters "well-drawn," and solutions "viable."

The themes of FAMILY relationships and biracialism are common to many of her works. Married to Joseph T. Okimoto, a Japanese-American psychiatrist, O.'s family includes his Asian sons and her daughters from her first marriage, who are white. Wanting to represent herself "honestly" as a writer of MULTICULTURAL literature, O. chooses to use a double-barreled name to avoid confusion: "My maiden name is there just so I'm not misrepresenting myself."

While O. has also written PLAYS, SHORT STORIES, and children's PICTURE BOOKS, and is considering a venture into adult fiction, she will "always write for teenagers because [she likes] them." Her fiction has tended to feature teenage male characters, even though she admits that books about boys typically do not sell as well; she offers the explanation: "I just think they're so funny."

The daughter of a businessman and a homemaker, O. grew up in Ohio, attended DePauw University (1960–63) and the University of Washington (1971–72), and received her M.A. from Antioch College in 1977. O. married Peter C. Kirkman, an Air Force officer, in 1961; they have two daughters, Katherine and Amy. O. and Kirkman divorced in 1971. She married Okimoto in 1973 and became a stepmother to his sons, Stephen and Dylan. O. has worked as a high-school teacher of remedial reading, as a University of Washington, Seattle, editorial consultant in child psychiatry, and as the chair of the Mount Baker Youth Service Bureau in Seattle. She has been practicing psychotherapy privately in Seattle, where she currently resides, since 1975. Her hobbies include swimming, sailing, and painting.

AWARDS: 1982 Washington State Governor's Writers' Award, *It's Just Too Much: Jason's Women:* 1986 American Library Association Best Book for Young Adults and 1987 International Reading Association Choice Book.

FURTHER WORKS: *My Mother Is Not Married to My Father,* 1979; *It's Just Too Much,* 1980; *Norman Schnurman, Average Person,* 1982; *Who Did It, Jenny Lake?,* 1983; *Jason's Women,* 1986; *Take a Chance, Gramps!,* 1990; *Molly By Any Other Name,* 1990;

Talent Night, 1995; *The Eclipse of Moonbeam Dawson,* 1997; *To Jaykae: Life Stinx,* 1999.

BIBLIOGRAPHY: *Contemporary Authors,* 2001, online; *January* magazine, November 1998, online.

ANDREA WONG

ONEAL, Zibby (Elizabeth)
Author. b. 17 March 1934, Omaha, Nebraska

O. developed a love of reading and stories from her mother and an artistic awareness from her father. These traits helped O. portray adolescence as a complex and trying period of growth and change. O. grew up in a traditional nuclear FAMILY and had what many would consider an easy childhood. O. was able to draw on her own adolescent experiences, emotions, and issues to lay the foundation for her YA novels even though the main characters are primarily troubled TEENAGERS trying to find their way in life.

O. always felt that adolescence was a self-absorbed world and would use islands in her writings to illustrate this metaphor. Moving out of childhood into adolescence and maturity takes teens from a place where they may like to stay but must realize they cannot stay in forever.

In her first young adult novel, *The Language of Goldfish* (1980), O. portrays Carrie Stokes in the conflict between holding on and letting go of her childhood. Carrie must learn to use her inner strength to move forward. She must deal with becoming a unique individual and must begin to separate herself from her parents. O. boldly brings the difficult issues of a mental breakdown and suicide into this novel, showing how delicate and intricate growing up can be.

O. continues to show the struggle of dealing with confusing feelings and becoming a complete individual. In *A Formal Feeling* (1982), Anne Cameron learns to integrate herself in a world that seems very different. Her mother has died, her father has remarried, and now Anne must reconcile conflicting feelings she has about her mother as well as herself. She is a child becoming an adult, still in need of a lot of love but not revealing the necessity for it.

In her third key novel for YA, *In Summer Light* (1985), O. brings us yet another young woman struggling to find direction in her life. Kate Brewer admired her father as a child, but now as a teenager, with her own goals and desires, she sees her father in a much different light. The book shows the challenges of evolving parental relationships, life ambitions, and rejected love.

These three novels are true and beautiful reflections of the difficult period of growing up. Yet O.'s words paint flowing, light, and easy pictures that reveal each character's ability to rise above her own struggles and become a clear-thinking, independent, young woman.

AWARDS: Friends of American Writers Award for *War Work,* 1972; American Library Association's Notable and Best Books for Young Adults citations and Best of the Best 1970–1983 for *The Language of Goldfish,* 1980, *A Formal Feeling,* 1982, and *In Summer Light,* 1985; *New York Times* Best Book of the Year list for *A Formal Feeling,* 1982; Christopher Award, 1983; *Horn Book* Honor Book, *Boston Globe–Horn Book* Award, 1986, and Best Book for Young Adults, 1985, for *In Summer Light.*

FURTHER WORKS: *War Work,* 1971; *The Impossible Adventures of Marvelous O'Hara Soapstone,* 1972; *Grandma Moses: Painter of Rural America,* 1986; *A Long Way to Go,* 1990.

BIBLIOGRAPHY: *Contemporary Authors New Revision Series,* vol. 84; *Something about the Author,* vol. 82; *Writers for Young Adults,* vol. 2 (1997); *Best Books for Young Adults* (2000).

TINA HERTEL

OPPEL, Kenneth
Author, b. 31 August 1967, Port Alberni, British Columbia, Canada

When O. was only fourteen, he wrote *Colin's Fantastic Video Game Adventure.* A family friend took the handwritten manuscript to Roald DAHL, who was an old friend. The famous author endorsed the work to his literary agent, who subsequently took on the TEEN's book. By the time O. was in eleventh grade, the book was accepted; it was published before he graduated from high school in 1985.

O. knew he would go on to university and expected he might become a professor, writing on the side. He graduated from the University of Toronto with a B.A. in English and cinema in 1989, and by this time had penned and sold a PICTURE BOOK, *Cosimo Cat* (1990), as well as a junior novel, *The Live-Forever Machine* (1990). After graduating, he worked briefly as an editor at Scholastic Canada, but left after a few months to allow more time for writing.

He worked as a temp for a year and then got married.

Moving to England with his wife Phillipa, where she would earn her Ph.D. at Oxford, O. worked as a typist and wrote prolifically. During this time, he wrote several of his middle readers, the Bad Case SERIES, as well another picture book, *Follow That Star,* (1994) and his futuristic thriller, *Dead Water Zone* (1993).

The Bad Case books are a bridge between picture books and junior novels, featuring a trio of children who get into scrapes, solve MYSTERIES and survive various mishaps with their wacky inventions. O. seems intent on challenging gender stereotypes in these books by assigning mathematical and scientific abilities to female characters while the male characters are concerned with feelings and social situations. At the same time, the values of compassion and sensitivity are prioritized over detached logic and ultimately lead to successful resolutions.

The YA novel *Dead Water Zone* is an eerie cautionary tale that takes place in a Dickensian slum where the water has been poisoned by a biomedical disaster, causing the inhabitants of Watertown to become altered and addicted. The book provides much insight into moral dilemmas and the complexities of sibling relationships, while creating suspense and action.

After spending two years in Newfoundland from 1993 to 1995, O. accepted the position as a children's literature editor for the review journal, *Quill and Quire.* Once again, he was driven to write and left this position after one year in order to have more time for his creative works. In addition to prose, he had also begun writing screenplays, an occupation he balances with writing children's books. While writing screenplays can be more lucrative than children's books, O. enjoys both but prefers the latter. Many of his screenplays were purchased but never produced. Moreover, screenplays that are eventually developed are merely a blueprint for a work that will be further interpreted and altered by many artists including directors and actors. On the other hand, O. gains much satisfaction from the creative control and achievement of writing a book.

Of O.'s greatest and most noteworthy achievements are undoubtedly his highly celebrated FANTASY works about bats. *Silverwing* (1997), *Sunwing* (1999) and *Firewing* (2002) are a series of novels that richly detail the sweeping landscapes and complete mythologies belonging to the worlds of bats. Told from the point of view of the bat heroes, these densely plotted stories are packed with action, honour, revenge, and redemption. Competing ideologies of rival bat colonies evoke complex and open-ended inquiries into religion and belief systems that prove the books' value to readers of all ages up to adult. Relying on traditional mythical plot elements such as journeys to the underworld, and borrowing from ancient and current religions, these stories are grand in scale and tempered with touching humour. With a fourth book likely to round out the works, O. has earned a place as a leading writer of action FANTASY.

AWARDS: Air Canada Literary Award, CANADIAN Authors Association, 1995, for outstanding promise demonstrated by a young (under thirty years) Canadian author. Mr. Christie's Book Award, 1998; Red Cedar Book Award, 1999–2000; Ontario Library Association's Silver Birch Award (1998), Hackmatack Atlantic Readers' Choice Award (1999–2000), Manitoba Young Readers' Choice Award, 2000; Blue Heron Award, 1998; Canadian Library Association Book of the Year for Children Award, 1998, all for *Silverwing*. Mr. Christie's Book Award, 2000; Ruth Schwartz Children's Book Award, 2000; Rocky Mountain Book Award, 2003; Red Cedar Award, 2001–2002; Manitoba Young Readers' Choice Award, 2001; and Canadian Library Association Book of the Year for Children, 2000, all for *Sunwing*.

FURTHER WORKS: *Cosmic Snapshots,* 1993; *Galactic Snapshots,* 1993; *A Bad Case of Ghosts,* 1993; *A Bad Case of Magic,* 1993; *A Bad Case of Dinosaurs,* 1994; *A Bad Case of Robots,* 1994; *Emma's Emu,* 1995; *A Bad Case of Super-Goo,* 1996; *Peg and the Whale,* 2000; *Airborn,* 2004.

BIBLIOGRAPHY: Evans, Gwyneth. "A Bad Case of Robots." *Quill and Quire* 61, no. 5, 1995, p. 48; Jenkinson Dave. "Ken O." *Resource Links* 2, no. 5, 1997, pp. 199–202; Jones, Raymond E., and John C. Stott. *Canadian Children's Books: A Critical Guide to Authors and Illustrators,* 2000; Little, Jean. "A Distinctive and Successful Canadian Fantasy." *Canadian Children's Literature* 23, no. 2, 1997; Peters, John. "Firewing (Book)." *School Library Journal* 49, no. 1, 2003; *Something about the Author,* vol. 99, 1999; *Writing Stories, Making Pictures:* BIOGRAPHIES of 150 Canadian Children's Authors and Illustrators, 1994.

KIRSTEN ANDERSEN

ORLEV, Uri
Author, b. 24 February 1931, Warsaw, Poland

After O.'s mother was killed by the Nazis and the rest of his family perished in World War II, he and his younger brother were hidden from the Nazis by Polish families until 1943, when they were sent to a concentration camp. Together, they immigrated to Palestine (now Israel) two years later.

O. began writing his first books for children and adolescents in 1975. Four of his YA novels have been translated into English: *The Island on Bird Street* (1984), *The Man from the Other Side* (1991), *Lydia, Queen of Palestine* (1993), and *The Lady with the Hat* (1995). His first book for children, *The Beast of Darkness* (1976), received the Ze-ev Prize from the Israel Ministry of Education in 1977 and was designated an Honor Book in 1979 by the International Board on Books for Young People (IBBY). In *The Island on Bird Street,* O. tells the story of a Jewish boy whose circumstances and challenges are similar to those he endured during the WAR, surviving by his wits in a ruined Warsaw house. *The Man from the Other Side* depicts the friendship that grows between a troubled TEENAGER and the bright and gentle young Jewish man whom he hides from the German soldiers occupying his grandparents' own home.

Reviewers have praised O.'s writing for his high-spirited and balanced characters, whose depth of development by the author impresses upon the reader the duality of human nature. Each of O.'s nearly two dozen novels has received numerous awards.

SELECTED AWARDS: Honor Award, Ministry of Youth, Family, Women and Health of the Federal Republic of Germany and West Berlin, 1987; first recipient of Janusz Korczak International Prize (Poland), 1990, Sydney Taylor Book Awards, 1984, *The Island on Bird Street;* 1995 Honor Award, Jane Addams Peace Association and Women's International League for Peace and Freedom; Hans Christian Andersen Award for body of work, 1996; ALA Best Book for Young Adults and Batchelder Award, 1992, for *Man from the Other Side.*

FURTHER WORKS: *Run, Boy, Run,* 2003.

BIBLIOGRAPHY: *Contemporary Authors Online. Gale,* 2002; *Magill on Literature, EBSCO Host online,* 2003.

CATHERINE GIVEN

ORR, Wendy
Author, b. 19 November, 1953, Edmonton, Alberta, Canada

O. lived in many different places throughout her childhood and holds dual citizenship in CANADA and AUSTRALIA. She was born in Canada where her father, Anthony M. Burridge, served as a pilot for the Royal Canadian Air Force. Just before her third birthday, the family moved to France, where she started school. When she was in the second grade, they moved back to Canada (Red Deer, Alberta). From that point on, the family lived in various parts of Canada as well as in the U.S., in Colorado.

After graduating from high school, O. studied animal husbandry for a year in Kingston, Ontario. A vacation in England during that year made her decide to move to London. There she attended the London School of Occupational Therapy, earning her diploma in 1975. During the three years she spent in London, she traveled extensively; on a short trip to Wales, O. met an Australian farmer, Thomas Orr (Tom), whom she married six months later. O. moved to Australia after finishing her degree in occupational therapy. From 1975 to 1980, she worked as an occupational therapist in Albury Community Health (Albury, Australia). She then studied at La Trobe University (Australia), earning a bachelor's of applied science and postgraduate certificate. Upon finishing her studies, she worked as an occupational therapist at the Language and Development Clinic of Shepparton, Australia.

O. had written an article, "Living in Wheelchairs," and done some creative writing in her spare time while in school. She had cherished stories and language since childhood and had always dreamed of becoming a writer. However, it was not until late 1985 that she began writing for publication. O. has published mostly works of fiction for children, including PICTURE BOOKS and novels for beginning readers, but she has also published a novel for YOUNG ADULTS and one for adults. Her children's books are best known for their imaginative, adventurous, and humorous plots and characters, and she has won awards in both Australia and the U.S.

O.'s vibrant and honest novel for young adults, *Peeling the Onion* (U.S. publication, 1999), chronicles the struggles of an Australian TEENAGER named Anna Duncan who is severely injured in a car accident on the way home from a karate tournament. Anna, an outstanding athlete who was about to obtain her black belt, must adjust to the limitations to mobility that her injuries have imposed on her. Facing physical as well as neurological impairments, Anna finds that she has to redefine herself and her relationships with friends and FAMILY and reframe her career goals as she recovers from the accident. In writing *Peeling the Onion,* probably more than in any other of her works, O. drew from her own life experiences. In 1991, she was seriously injured in a car accident; her resulting DISABILITIES forced her to leave her career in occupational therapy.

O. and her husband owned a dairy farm in northeastern Victoria for almost twenty years; in 1999, they sold the farm and moved to Mornington Peninsula (Victoria). Their two children, James and Susan, are college students in Melbourne. O.'s hobbies in daily life include animal care, gardening, travel, and reading.

AWARDS: *Peeling the Onion:* 1997 Australian Family Therapy Association high commendation, 1997 Children's Book Council of Australia honor book for Older Readers, 1998 American Library Association's Best Books for Young Adults, and Best of the Best; 1998 New York Public Library Books for the Teenage award; 1987 Ashton Scholastic PICTURE BOOK Awards, *Amanda's Dinosaur;* 1995 Books of the Year for Junior Readers, *Ark in the Park;* 1995 Australian Family Therapy Association recommendation, *Ark in the Park.*

FURTHER WORKS: *Leaving it to You,* 1992; *The Laziest Boy in the World* (illus. Fabio Nardo), 1994; *A Light in Space* (illus. Ruth Ohi), 1994; *A Light in Space Dirtbikes,* 1995; *Paradise Palace* (illus. David Mackintosh), 1997; *Paradise Gold* (illus. David Mackintosh), 1999; *Nim's Island* (illus. Kerry Millard), 1999; *Poppy's Path* (illus. Ritva Voutila), 2001; *The House at Evelyn's Pond,* 2001; *Spook's Shack* (illus. Kerry Millard), 2003.

BIBLIOGRAPHY: *Contemporary Authors Online,* 2002; *Something about the Author,* vol. 90, 1997; *Marquis Who's Who in the World 2001,* 18th ed., 2000; personal website of Wendy O., http://www.wendyorr .com/

EMILY M. L. SEITZ

OUGHTON, Jerrie (Preston)
Author, b. 13 April 1937, Atlanta, Georgia

O. was the child of educators, and chose that field for her own career. She has worked in public education for many years, beginning as a teacher in Raleigh, North Carolina, in 1963. She was educated at Meredith College and married William Paul Oughton on November 28, 1963. They have five children. O. lists her hobbies as "writing, writing, and writing" and currently lives in Lexington, Kentucky.

O.'s books tackle complex emotional situations in a sensitive way. Her work includes YA novels and two award-winning PICTURE BOOKS with illustrator Lisa Desimini: *How the Stars Fell into the Sky: A Navajo Legend* (1992) and *The Magic Weaver of Rugs: A Tale of the Navajo* (1994). O. admires the spirituality and oral tradition of the Navajo, and wants to help preserve their stories. Both books were recognized as Notable Books by the National Council for the Social Studies, and were selected as Best Children's Book by *Smithsonian Magazine* for their years of publication. O.'s novels for young adults have received many awards, among the more prestigious being the American Library Association's Best Book for Young Adults in both 1999, for *The War in Georgia* (1998), and in 2001, for *Perfect Family* (2000). These books are set in the mid-twentieth-century American South, and their characters are forced to make hard choices about serious issues such as bigotry and TEEN pregnancy. O. writes about these topics in an understated and realistic way, enhancing understanding without preaching, creating well-developed and engaging characters.

AWARDS: Notable Book, National Council for the Social Studies, 1992; California Children's Media Award for Excellence in POETRY, MUSIC and Legend, 1992; Best Children's Book, *Smithsonian Magazine,* all for *How the Stars Fell Into the Sky: A Navajo Legend* (1992). Notable Book, National Council for the Social Studies, 1994; Best Children's Book, *Smithsonian Magazine,* both for *The Magic Weaver of Rugs: A Tale of the Navajo* (1994). Best Book for Young Adults, American Library Association, 1999, for *The War in Georgia* (1998); Best Book for Young Adults, American Library Association, 2000, for *Perfect Family* (2000).

FURTHER WORKS: *Music from a Place Called Half Moon* (1995).

BIBLIOGRAPHY: *Something about the Author,* vol. 131, 2002. Paul Oughton, Author Illustrator Source, www.author-illustr-source.com/jerrieprestonoughton.htm.

LIZ HANE

THE OUTCAST IN YA LITERATURE

An O. is defined in the dictionary as "one who is cast out from home, friends, etc. or by society." Examine the many factors that can cause such a negative response: prejudice, illness, social stigma, depression, confusion. The TEEN years are so tumultuous that perhaps every teenager at one point or another identifies himself as an O. One's identification as an O. can be an outgrowth of someone's own personal outlook, or it can be imposed upon him or her by society.

Because this experience is quite normal among teenagers, the role of the O. is prominent in YA literature. When one feels isolated and alone, as teenagers often do, reading about characters that are experiencing similar feelings can be cathartic. Izzy's growth as she learns to become an individual in Cynthia VOIGT's *Izzy, Willy-Nilly* and Piggy's methods of dealing with mockery in William Golding's *Lord of the Flies* provide the best kind of BIBLIOTHERAPY for young adults searching for answers and coping with their own feelings of isolation.

According to the article "Teen Reading: Gross Is Good," which appeared in *ALA Cognotes:* "Teens seek stories that are real and relevant to their lives. This is especially true for reluctant readers. . . ." Melodrama suits the natural mode of adolescence, states A. O. Scott in his article, "Pimples Are the Least of this Girl's Worries." "Adolescence is a sloppy, ungainly, awkward time," he reminds us. He mentions novels by Sarah DESSEN, such as *Someone like You* and *That Summer* as YA books sympathetic to the plights of teenagers.

Although there seems to be more suicide, incest, and divorce in YA novels than in YA life, the highly dramatic nature of the written works appears to young readers. It can either assist adolescents who are unfortunate enough to have encountered the situations or provide examples of characters that have problems greater than the readers can ever imagine. Whichever is the case, young readers are attracted to characters that face extreme obstacles in their lives.

Most problem novels follow a model whereby a character is in a predicament or comes to a realization and then seeks to solve it. Authors Chris CRUTCHER and Chris LYNCH are known for using SPORTS themes to develop this formula. "The one constant in almost all YA fiction," says author Patrick Jones, "is that the problem resolves, the protagonist grows, and life is good."

The theme of O.s is traced to the important role peer groups play as teenagers drift from total dependence on their parents and move into inexperienced social situations. In these groups, the adolescents are discovering where they fit and what role they fill the best; it is here that the conformists and the nonconformists emerge. Alleen Nilsen and Kenneth Donselson recognize the importance of Young Adult literature when it allows teenagers to participate vicariously in more relationships than are feasible in life. *Tiger Eyes* by Judy BLUME, *Remembering the Good Times* by Richard PECK, and *The Friends* by Rosa GUY explore what happens when all teenagers do not automatically find their niche in a social circle.

The classic work about teenage O., written by S. E. HINTON, is simply titled *The Outsiders*. This work pits the greasers ("dirt heads") against the socs ("the society kids"). Taking Nilsen's and Donelson's theories further, Tom Reynolds examines misfits and free spirits in an article for *Novelist* (EBSCO Publishing). He states that a teenager's desire to break free from his parents and to be liked and respected by his peers represents two sides of the same situation. "But what happens," he questions, "to the individual teenager, boy or girl, who never seems to fit in?"

Reynolds recommends Robert CORMIER's *The Chocolate War* and Jerry SPINELLI's *Stargirl* as two examples of YA fiction dealing with these issues. "*The Chocolate War* is a benchmark work on this subject against which subsequent works of YA fiction are often judged," Reynolds writes. In this work, he asserts, teens pay a terrible price for being different.

Stargirl is a somewhat lighter treatment of a similar topic. "Susan's behavior marks her as being different. She is the worst kind of O., a free spirit," Reynolds explains. Spinelli's point is to assert that "teenagers, like adults, need to resist the temptation to label the non-conformist as weird, strange, or a loser. Such people may actually have something to offer that no one else can." This is a valuable lesson capable of being learned at any age. Reynolds concludes his article by stating that "in the end, most teens who don't seem to fit in are really not much different from their peers."

Teens would be well-advised to look for the works of Carol PLUM-UCCI, Robert Cormier, Walter Dean MYERS, Julie Anne PETERS, Todd STRASSER, David LUBAR, JAMES HOWE, Ellen Wittlinger, Gary Paulsen, and Jerry Spinelli to find well-written books about teenagers in the throes of identity crises.

In 2001, Donald GALLO edited a collection of stories about the outsider experience. Important YA writers such as Joan BAUER, Alden R. CARTER, Chris Crutcher, Jack GANTOS, Angela JOHNSON, M. E. KERR, Ron KOERTGE, Frances LANTZ, Graham SALISBURY, Will WEAVER, and Nancy WERLIN are represented in the book, *On the Fringe*. In his introduction to the anthology, Gallo writes, "We hope these stories provide glimpses into the minds of teenagers who are different from their more popular peers and will offer you thought-provoking experiences that may result in greater understanding and tolerance of others."

Perhaps there will someday come a time that O.s will consider themselves to be incasts, included in part of teenage culture.

BIBLIOGRAPHY: Bay Area Kids, *Books We Love Best: A Unique Guide to Children's Books,* 1991; Gallo, Donald R., *On the Fringe,* 2001; Gillespie, John T., *Best Books for Young Teen Readers, Grades 7–10,* 2000; Halsted, Judith Wynn, *Some of My Best Friends Are Books,* 1994; Jones, Patrick, *Connecting Young Adults and Libraries, A How-to-Do-It Manual,* 2nd ed., 1998; Nilsen, Alleen Pace, and Donelson, Kenneth L., *Literature for Today's Young Adults,* 6th ed., 2001; Rowlson, Dawna, *Teen Reading: Gross is Good,* ALA Cognotes, 2003; Reynolds, Tom, *Misfits and Free Spirits: Teen Fiction Looks at the Nonconformist,* 2002; Reynolds, Tom, *Heartbreaks Waiting to Happen: Urban Youth and YA's Fiction of Tough Choices,* 2002; Reynolds, Tom, *Beyond Happy Endings—The Fiction of Robert Cormier,* 2001; Rochma, Hazel, "Walter Dean Myers," *The Booklist,* 2002; Scott, A. O., "Pimples Are The Least of This Girl's Worries," *New York Times,* July 2003; Udovitch, Mim, "Mandy Moore's Nonblond Ambition," *New York Times,* July 2003.

SANDRA KITAIN

P

THE PAPERBACK EVOLUTION

Toward the middle of the 19th century, as paper became more readily available and improved mechanics made it possible to print books, the dime novel became commonplace. A forerunner to the current P., these novels were inexpensive to print and often known as pulp fiction, due to how they were produced as well as to their content. They were also known as dime novels, and often contained tales of different places filled with MYSTERY and ADVENTURE. Some of the dime novels geared toward YA included the stories of Horatio Alger Jr., with their promise of wealth if a code of conduct was followed. The Frank Merriwell stories were also geared toward YA, and eventually those serial stories actually were reproduced in a hardcover format.

The beginning of the 20th century saw a great increase in publishing, and a fair share of that was generated toward the youth market, but most of the books were produced in a hardcover format. This remained the case through several decades. Allen Lane changed the publishing market dramatically in 1935, when he put out his Penguin paperbacks. Books once found mostly in libraries and bookstores were much more widely available as P.s. Relatively inexpensive to manufacture thanks to mass production (made possible by technological advances), they were also more economically accessible to people, as well as being omnipresent.

Delayed perhaps by World War II, in the middle 1940s, quality P.s for youth began to be produced.

The Teen-Age BOOK CLUB, begun in 1945, had a great deal to do with that. By 1974, Scholastic Book Club Services could lay claim to twelve million members. Although it would seem that the popularity of classroom book clubs was inarguable, it was not until 1974 that P. publishing for youth became widespread when at least seventy publishers, inspired by the classroom book clubs, began generating their own P.s for youth. Perhaps they were also encouraged by a study of P. use among the young made in 1964, by the New Jersey Department of Education. The study showed that 68.5 percent of the youth surveyed preferred P.s to read. The American Library Association had also published *Paperback Books for Young People* in 1972, but it was only another small step in the ongoing evolution of legitimizing P.s. Much more telling was the bottom line, which proved to be quite profitable. The fact that TEENS had increased buying power added to this success.

P.s are popular with teens for a variety of reasons. They are extremely portable and are often bright and attractive. Due to the low cost of producing them, the topics that they cover are often timelier than that of hardcover books; they may be more transient, yet they are very important to the teenage market. Part of marketing to the teen demographic is appealing to whatever currently appeals to them, which can change rather quickly. Being able to satisfy that need in an economical way makes the teen market much more appealing to publishers than it would have been decades ago. The fact that their disposable income has increased dramatically in the last thirty years also makes them a much more attractive audience. The appeal to the teen demographic group is popular not only with publishers, but also with advertisers of a multitude of products.

BIBLIOGRAPHY: Cox, J. Randolph. *The Dime Novel Companion: A Source Book,* 2000; Larrick, Nancy. "The P. Opportunity." *School Library Journal,* April 1975, pp. 21–22; "Publishing, History of." *Encyclopedia Britannica,* 2003. Encyclopedia Britannica Premium Service. http://www/britannica.com/eb/article?eu = 117359 www.seriesnovels.com.

                                            JEANNE MARIE RYAN

PARK, Linda Sue
Author, b. 25 March 1960, Urbana, Illinois

In a very short time, P. experienced success in the publishing world the likes of which most writers only dream. Who would have thought that her unsolicited manuscript to a publisher would later win her the Newbery Award after just three novels? Her editor, Dinah Stevenson, calls it "an amazing true publishing success story," because P. apparently did "a number of things wrong." P. did not follow the protocol of aspiring children's book writers, even coming across as unprofessional at times. However, Stevenson spotted the quality of P.'s work and signed her on to publish her first book, *Seesaw Girl* (1999). It is about a girl from a well-to-do FAMILY in 17th-century Korea who seeks to know life outside the walls of the compound that she has never left. Similarly, her next two books, *The Kite Fighters* (2000) and the Newbery winner *A Single Shard* (2001), are set in traditional ancient Korea, while *When My Name Was Keoko* (2002) is set from 1940 to 1945 during the Japanese occupation of Korea.

This quickly established career in writing for children was not something directly related to P.'s education or previous careers. Her extensive education included a B.A. from Stanford University in 1981 and a higher diploma in Anglo-Irish literature from Trinity College, Dublin, Ireland. She then went on to pursue an M.A. at Birkbeck College in London, England, which she finished in 1988, the year she married Irish journalist Ben Dobbin. Writing for children was a completely new undertaking for P. who previously had a writing career as a food journalist in London, England, from 1985 to 1990. Later, she became a teacher of English as a second language in London, in Brooklyn, and Rochester, New York.

It was not until she had her own children that she realized she wanted them to understand their Korean heritage. This was an endeavor that required much research for P., who had been raised in the Midwest to be "more American than Americans." However, since she was the daughter of Korean parents, Eung Won Ed (a computer analyst) and Susie Kim (a teacher), P. began to realize that she could glean ideas from her own childhood. The idea for *The Kite Fighters* came from P.'s father, who told her when she was a child about kite fighting as a sport in Korea a long time ago. The more she did research for her books, the more P. got in touch with her Korean heritage and saw how aspects of her upbringing were framed in the context of Korean tradition. Her research skills as well as her clear writing style combined to create detailed, accurate settings and memorable characters. In *A Single Shard,* Tree-ear, the main character, is an orphan, and while nothing is known about Tree-ear's parents, his good character seems to have been nurtured by the care of Crane-man, who was also an orphan from birth. Although P.'s research on traditional pottery techniques is itself tremendous and well-written, her construction of character and relationships upholds the value of friendship.

When My Name Was Keoko is written in an unusually fresh style in which two story lines run parallel. Sun-hee and her brother Tae-yul are the eyes that P. writes through, alternating between each point of view a chapter at a time. Again, readers will find interesting background information in P.'s customary author's note. She used stories her parents told about the Japanese occupation in Korea to write the book.

Although her stories are fictional, P. has an indelible personal connection to her own stories that makes North American readers feel at home learning about the Korean culture.

SELECT AWARDS: *SeeSaw Girl:* Texas Bluebonnet Award, West Virginia State Children's Book Award, South Carolina State Children's Award, 2001–2002; *The Kite Fighters:* Notable Books for a Global Society Award, 2001, Master list Vermont Dorothy Canfield Fisher award 2001–2002, Indiana Young Hoosier Award, Tennessee Volunteer State Book award, 2002–2003; 2002 Newbery Medal, *A Single Shard;* 2002 Jane Addams Children's Honor Book, *When My Name Was Keoko,* and numerous citations on ALA lists.

BIBLIOGRAPHY: *Contemporary Authors Online,* 2002; Stevenson, Dinah. "Linda Sue P." *The Horn Book Magazine,* July/August 2002.

CAROLYN KIM

PARKS, Gordon (Roger Alexander Buchanan)

Photographer, author, director, composer, musician, b. 30 November 1912, Fort Scott, Kansas

P. overcame the impeding poverty and racism of his childhood to become one of the most versatile artists of the twentieth century. In addition to writing the YA classic, *The Learning Tree* (1963), P. is an accomplished author, photojournalist, and musician who also ventured into uncharted territory in the American film industry. Out of the sheer desire to "keep moving" and resist the clutches of failure, P. has experimented with numerous forms of creative expression and has met with success in every undertaking.

P. was born to Andrew Jackson and Sara Ross Parks, whom he later credited as being models of hard work, clemency, and empathy. After his mother died when he was fifteen, P. left Kansas for Minneapolis and supported himself by working as a pianist, busboy, basketball player, and Civilian Conservation Corpsman. At the age of twenty-five, he began to seriously consider photography as a career direction. While flipping through a MAGAZINE one day, he came across an article with photographs of migrant farm workers that captured his interest. According to P., these "stark, tragic images of human beings caught up in the confusion of poverty" triggered a new creative outlet in P.'s life. He began to freelance work for *Vogue* and *Life* magazines, on staff at *Life* for more than two decades. Additionally, he also busied himself photographing the tenement dwellers on the South Side of Chicago, depictions that earned him a Julius Rosenwald Fellowship in 1941.

Eager to experiment with other forms of expression, P. produced his first literary piece, the semi-autobiographical novel *The Learning Tree.* Now a book that appears in many junior high and high-school English classes, *The Learning Tree* is an inspiring story of a TEENAGED boy whose entrance into adulthood is hampered by societal and economic circumstances. The success of P.'s novel led to the silver screen, where P. not only was hired to direct the MOVIE version of his work, but also became the first

AFRICAN AMERICAN to direct a major Hollywood film. In addition to being the director, the multitalented man wrote the screenplay adaptation, composed the movie's score, and produced the film.

P. has further demonstrated his life in several other written works, including *A Choice of Weapons* (1966), *To Smile in Autumn* (1979), and *Voices in the Mirror* (1990). In discussing *A Choice of Weapons,* P. described how this book is meant to strengthen the young people who find themselves struggling against boundaries erected by racism and poverty. He said, "I have a right to be bitter, but I would not let bitterness destroy me. As I tell young black people, you can fight back, but do it in a way to help yourself and not destroy yourself."

Looking back on their lives, most people experience satisfaction knowing that they have excelled in their one chosen career; P., however, has distinguished for himself places in the literary, photographic, musical, and cinematic worlds, and has achieved a standard of excellence in every one.

SELECT AWARDS: Photographer of the Year by the American Society of Magazine Photographers (1960); Philadelphia Museum of Art Award and the Art Directors Club Award (1964); ALA Notable Book Award, *A Choice of Weapons* (1966); Nikon Photographic Award for promotion of understanding among nations of the world (1967); Emmy Award, *DIARY* of a Harlem Family (1968); Black Film Makers Hall of Fame (1973); Christopher Award, *Flavio* (1978); Frederick Douglass Gold Medal (1984); the American Society of Magazine Photographers Award (1985); Governor's Medal of Honor from the State of Kansas (1985); Commonwealth Mass Communications Award and a National Medal of Arts, both 1988; American Library Association Best Book for Young Adults: 1966 for *A Choice of Weapons,* 1971 for *Born Black,* 1991 for *Voices in the Mirror.*

FURTHER WORKS: *Flash Photography,* 1947; *A Poet and His Camera,* 1969; J. T. (photographer), 1969; *Born Black,* 1971; *Gordon P.: Whispers of Intimate Things,* 1971; *In Love,* 1971; *Shaft* (screenplay writer and director), 1971; *Shaft's Big Score* (director), 1972; *The Super Cops* (director), 1974; *Flavio,* 1978; *Shannon,* 1981; *Arias in Silence,* 1994; *Glimpses Towards Infinity,* 1996; *Half Past Autumn: A Retrospective,* 1997; *The Sun Stalker,* 2003.

BIBLIOGRAPHY: Smith, Dr. Jessie Carney, ed. *Notable Black American Men,* 1998; *Something about the Author,* vol. 108, 2000.

RACHEL WITMER

PARTRIDGE, Elizabeth
Author, n.d., California

P. grew up in a large family of artists and photographers in the San Francisco Bay Area. Her grandmother is the acclaimed photographer Imogen Cunningham, and her father, Rondal Partridge, apprenticed with photographer Dorothea Lange. P.'s and Lange's family later became quite close, and Lange would become the subject of two of P.'s young adult nonfiction books. In 1974, P. was the first student to graduate with a degree in women's studies from the University of California at Berkeley. She then went on to study Chinese medicine in Great Britain. P. returned to the Bay Area to practice acupuncture and herbal medicine.

In the early 1990s, P. began writing for children and YA, specializing in BIOGRAPHIES, historical fiction, and PICTURE BOOKS. P.'s first book, *Dorothea Lange: A Visual Life* (1993), was followed by *Clara and the Hoodoo Man* (1996), a middle-grade novel set in rural Appalachia. *Restless Spirit: The Life and Work of Dorothea Lange* (1998), a remarkable biography of the celebrated photographer who documented the Great Depression, the internment of Japanese-Americans, and other important 20th-century events, received numerous accolades, including the Golden Kite Honor Award for Nonfiction and the Jane Addams Honor Book award. *This Land Was Made for You and Me: The Life and MUSIC* of Woody Guthrie (2002) was a finalist for the National Book Award and won both the *Boston Globe–Horn Book* Award for Nonfiction and the Golden Kite Book Award for nonfiction.

AWARDS: Jane Addams Honor Book Award, 1998, Golden Kite Honor Award for Nonfiction, 1998, ALA Best Books for Young Adults, 2000, for *Restless Spirit: The Life and Work of Dorothea Lange;* National Book Award Finalist, 2002, *Boston Globe–Horn Book* Award for Nonfiction, 2002, and Golden Kite Book Award, 2002, ALA Best Books for Young Adults, 2003, ALA Notable Children's Books, 2003, Dorothy Canfield Fisher Children's Book Award, 2004, all for *This Land Was Made for You and Me: The Life and Music of Woody Guthrie.*

BIBLIOGRAPHY: *Something about the Author,* vol. 134, pp. 140–42; www.elizabethpartridge.com.

EDWARD T. SULLIVAN

PASCAL, Francine
Author, b. 13 May, 1938, New York City

P. was born in New York City, but her family moved from Manhattan to Jamaica, Queens, when she was five-years old. As a child, one of P.'s favorite pastimes was reading, which she viewed as a retreat. Her active imagination also found an outlet in her DIARY entries and later at the age of eight in POETRY. P. was strongly influenced by her oldest brother Michael, also an aspiring writer, who would later become a successful playwright. She was also encouraged by teachers and classmates with whom she shared her work. She often wrote plays and put on performances with her friends for neighborhood audiences. After attending the New York City public schools, P. graduated from New York University with a bachelor's degree in 1958. There she met her future husband, John Pascal, a journalist. He would become both her mentor and her writing partner, and together they would rear daughters Laurie, Susan, and Jamie.

After developing her own writing, first with magazines such as *True Confessions, Modern Screen, Ladies' Home Journal* and *Cosmopolitan,* P. and her husband worked together as second writers for the soap opera *The Young Marrieds* in 1965. They were given a basic plot that they would then flesh out with dialogue and detail. In 1968, along with her brother Michael Stewart, P. and her husband wrote the words for the musical *George M!* It was a hit on Broadway, and the couple later wrote a television special based on the musical (1970). They continued to collaborate, and worked together on the nonfiction work, *The Strange Case of Patty Hearst* (1974).

After working as a freelance writer and journalist, P. wanted to expand her range and, with her husband's encouragement, set to work on an idea she had about a thirteen-year-old girl's troubled relationship with her mother. The result became P.'s first YA novel, *Hangin out with CiCi* (1977). Sending it to only three publishers, she sold the publication rights to this first novel in only two weeks. Set in the Jamaica, Queens, neighborhood where P. grew up, it is about Victoria, a selfish young girl who believes that she travels back in time to 1944, where she unwittingly becomes friends with her own mother. *Hangin' out with CiCi* was praised for its humor and realism, was adapted as "My Mother Was Never a Kid," and was aired as an ABC *Afterschool Special*. P.'s second novel for YAs,

557

My First Love and Other Disasters (1979) was named a Best Book for Young Adults by the American Library Association. P.'s next novel, *The Hand Me down Kid* (1980) looked at the issue of sibling rivalry and was also adapted as an ABC *Afterschool Special.*

P.'s greatest recognition came with her creation of the Sweet Valley High SERIES, set in idyllic and sunny Sweet Valley, California, and featuring Jessica and Elizabeth, beautiful and popular identical twins with quite different personalities. What began as an idea for a television soap opera aimed at TEENS, instead became an immensely popular series of teen novels. First published in 1983, there are more than one hundred titles in the Sweet Valley High series alone, in addition to series spin-offs. Recognizing the popularity of the series, which is written at the middle-school reading level, P. adapted *Sweet Valley High* to different audiences. *Sweet Valley Kids* is aimed at lower-elementary students, whereas *Sweet Valley Twins* is aimed at upper-elementary students. *Sweet Valley University,* which picks up where *Sweet Valley High* leaves off, is geared toward middle- and high-school students, as is *Sweet Valley High—Senior Year.* In all, more than 450 Sweet Valley titles have been published with over 100 million copies sold and translations into more than 20 languages. In 1985, P. made publishing history when the first Sweet Valley High super edition, *Perfect Summer,* became the first YA novel to appear on the *New York Times* Best-Seller list. In 1994, *Sweet Valley High* became what P. had first envisioned: a syndicated television series.

In the late 1990s, P. started working on a new series, Fearless. Markedly different from the Sweet Valley series, Fearless focuses on Gaia Moore, a seventeen-year-old high school student living in New York City. The daughter of a covert terrorist agent and an international journalist, Gaia lacks the "fear gene" and finds herself having many adventures, often ending up in deep trouble. Although not yet on the scale of the Sweet Valley collection, there are already more than 30 titles in the Fearless series.

With so many series in progress, it is impossible for P. to do all the writing herself, but she oversees a number of authors and maintains artistic control of each novel. Next from P. is a YA novel, *The Ruling Class* (2004). When not writing, P. enjoys reading and traveling, often splitting her time between her apartment in New York City and her home in the south of

France. P. also remains involved in the theater world through the American Theatre Wing.

AWARDS: 1979 Best Book for Young Adults by the American Library Association, *My First Love and Other Disasters; Hand Me Down Kid;* 1982 Dorothy Canfield Award and 1988 Versele Award.

FURTHER WORKS: *Love and Betrayal and Hold the Mayo!,* 1985; *If Wishes Were Horses,* 1994.

BIBLIOGRAPHY: *Something about the Author,* v. 80, pp. 171–78; *Something about the Author,* v. 51, pp. 142–48; *Fifth Book of Junior Authors and Illustrators,* 1983, pp. 235–36; *Biography Today: Profiles of People of Interest to Young Readers—Author Series,* 2000, vol. 6, pp. 124–35; *The 100 Most Popular Young Adult Authors: Biographical Sketches and Bibliographies,* 1996, pp. 373–91.

DEDE SMALL

PATERSON, Katherine

Author, b. 31 October 1932, Qing Jiang, Jiangsu, China

Highly revered as an artist, P. writes from the heart about the complexity of life's challenges that interrupt the idealism of childhood. Her characters are young people who, while facing difficult situations, learn to rise above their problems and give of themselves as they hopefully face the future. P.'s characters deal with issues such as DEATH AND DYING, jealousy, guilt, child abuse, mental illness, racism and poverty. For her well-honed craftsmanship and compassionate portrayal of the characters, she has won almost every award possible for writers of adolescent literature, including two Newbery Medals and two National Book Awards. P. claims that there are three influences on her development as a writer: her birth in China and later years in Japan as a missionary and teacher, the American South, and her biblical heritage.

P.'s writing reflects her personal experiences, as well as the places she has called home. Born to missionary parents, P. and her FAMILY were forced to return to the U.S. at the beginning of World War II and subsequently moved eighteen times during her school years. P. received her B.A. from King College and masters' degrees from both the Presbyterian School of Christian Education and Union Theological Seminary, where she met her husband, a Presbyterian minister. With two biological sons and two adopted daughters, P. shares her love of children and her insight into their lives in many of her books.

P.'s first three novels reflect her experiences and keen insights into the values and history of Japan. In *The Sign of the Chrysanthemum* (1973), Muna, the thirteen-year-old illegitimate son of a peasant woman and a Samurai, sets out in search of his father and his true name. *Of Nightingales that Weep* (1974) has a female protagonist who rejects her stepfather and, through her musical talents, learns to overcome intolerance. Both novels are set in the 12th century. *The Master Puppeteer* (1975) is a MYSTERY set in 18th-century Japan. Using the art of puppetry, P. weaves a story that eloquently depicts how hope for society lies within people willing to give of themselves. *The Master Puppeteer* received numerous awards and citations, including a National Book Award.

Perhaps P. is best known for *The Bridge to Terabithia* (1977), a story written after the death of P.'s son's best friend. Jesse, an artist at age ten, and Leslie, a well-read, imaginative girl who moves in next door, become friends and create a secret world of Terabithia in the woods behind their houses. Leslie's death, from attempting to swing across the flooded creek to Terabithia, is a turning point in Jesse's life. P.'s skill in creating this unique relationship, as well as her realistic and compassionate portrayal of death, was recognized when the book received the Newbery Award.

The Great Gilly Hopkins (1978) had its roots in P.s experience as a foster mother and reflects a young person in search of his/her parent and identity, a theme often found in P.'s work. Gilly is eleven and, having already been in several foster homes, resists any affection offered by Maime Trotter. Lying and sometimes swearing, she convinces herself that her mother is eventually returning to get her. At the end of the story, Gilly realizes that she loves Trotter but that she will be returned to her biological grandmother. Although her mother is not planning to reunite with Gilly, the girl has matured and can face her situation.

Jacob Have I Loved (1980) is considered complex, compassionate, and fresh. Weaving together themes and motifs from the biblical story of Jacob and Esau, this novel is the story of sibling rivalry between twin sisters. Sarah Louise is physically stronger and the firstborn of the twins, while frail Caroline is beautiful and musically talented. Set on an imaginary, isolated Chesapeake Bay island, the story weaves a complex plot of rivalry between the twins and their developing relationships involving family and friends. Often cited as her best book, this title won a Newbery Award.

Lyddie (1991), a work of historical fiction with superb characterization, takes place in 1840s New England. Determined to earn money to reunite her family, the title character endures grim mill conditions with determination and experiences an awakening to her own potential. A novel set in more contemporary times, *The Same Stuff as Stars* (2002), again introduces a resilient young female, abandoned and faced with the responsibility for the care of her brother and great-grandmother. Despite her situation, she discovers hope in the various individuals of this small Vermont town. In *Park's Quest* (1988), Park goes in search of information about his father, a pilot killed in the Vietnam War. *Come Sing, Jimmy Jo* (1984) tells of a musically gifted, soft-spoken mountain boy, also in search of his family and home.

P. has said that her goal is to create stories that engage her readers' senses, imagination, intellect, and emotions. *Contemporary Authors Online* states: "P. is regarded as a major writer whose honesty, compassion, literary skill, and themes of freedom and unification show sincere respect for young people while demonstrating her knowledge of and faith in, humanity as a whole."

SELECT AWARDS: *Bridge to Terabithia*, 1978 Newbery Medal; *The Great Gilly Hopkins*, 1979 Newbery Award Honor Book, National Book Award; *Jacob Have I Loved*, 1981 Newbery Medal; *Lyddie*, ALA Best Books for Young Adults, 1992; *Jip, His Story*, ALA Best Books for Young Adults, 1997; *Here We Go Again*, 25 Years Best Book of the Year Award, 1967–1992; *Preacher's Boy:* Charlie May Simon Children's Book Award, 2002.

FURTHER WORKS: *Rebels of the Heavenly Kingdom*, 1983; *Consider the Lilies: Flowers of the Bible* (with husband, John P.), 1986; *The King's Equal*, 1992, 1999; *Flip-Flop Girl*, 1994; *A Midnight Clear: Stories for the Christmas Season*, 1995; *Jip, His Story*, 1996; *Parzival: The Quest of the Grail Knight*, 1998; *Celia and the Sweet, Sweet Water*, 1998; *Preacher's Boy*, 1999; *The Invisible Child: On Reading and Writing Books for Children*, 2001.

BIBLIOGRAPHY: *Children's Literature Review* 7, 1984; *Contemporary Authors Online; Contemporary Literary Criticism* 12, 1980; *Continuum Encyclopedia of*

Children's Literature, 2001; *Dictionary of Literary Biography*, vol. 52: *American Writers for Children Since 1960: Fiction*, 1986, pp. 296–314; P., K. *A Sense of Wonder: On Reading and Writing Books for Children* (includes *Gates of Excellence* and *The Spying Heart*), 1995; Gallo, D. *Speaking for Ourselves: Autobiographical Sketches by Notable Authors of Books for Young Adults*, 1990; *St. James Guide to Young Adult Writers*, 1998.

JANELLE B. MATHIS

PATON WALSH, Jill (pseud. Gillian Bliss)
Author, b. 29 April 1937, London, England

Having studied at Oxford, where she attended lectures by J. R. R. TOLKIEN and C. S. LEWIS, P. has followed the examples of these writers and scaffolds her own works with philosophy, religion, and the high arts. Her works are built on engaging plots and frequently have historical settings tinged with magic. She has earned the respect of critics and readers as a literary writer whose style matches her substance.

P.'s works for young people include *The Emperor's Winding Sheet* (1974), which examines the decaying Byzantine Empire from the perspective of a young English boy, and *Knowledge of Angels* (1994), an adult novel accessible to bold YA readers that uses the story of a feral child to explore faith in God. In other works, P. takes readers to a plague-infected English village (*A Parcel of Patterns*, 1983), industrial-era Victorian England (*A Chance Child*, 1978), and London during World War II (*Fireweed*, 1969).

P. has said that young people make the best characters—from the heroic and besieged Grace Darling (*Grace*, 1991) to Vrethiki, the Emperor Constantine's companion in *The Emperor's Winding Sheet* (1974). She also believes that young people make the best readers, and P. is unafraid to reward them with complex and sometimes dark themes—including WAR, DEATH, faith, human rights, and free will. Her work during the past decade has been primarily for adults and includes completing a MYSTERY novel by Dorothy Sayers left unfinished at her death (*Thrones, Dominations*, 1998) and a SCIENCE FICTION book that examines an alternative history of Eastern Europe following the Second World War (*A Desert in Bohemia*, 2000).

P. and fellow writer for young people John Rowe Townsend founded and co-own a small press.

AWARDS: Whitbread Literary Award (1974) for *The Emperor's Winding Sheet; Boston Globe–Horn Book* Award (1976) for *Unleaving;* Booker Prize (shortlist) (1994) for *Knowledge of Angels;* Phoenix Prize (1988) for *A Chance Child;* Commanders of the Order of the British Empire (1996) for services to literature; ALA BBYA (1984) for *Parcel of Patterns.*

FURTHER WORKS: *Hengest's Tale*, 1966; *The Dolphin Crossing*, 1967; *Goldengrove*, 1972; *Toolmaker*, 1973; *The Dawnstone*, 1973; *Crossing to Salamis*, 1977; *The Walls of Athens*, 1977; *Persian Gold*, 1978; *The Green Book*, 1981; *Babylon*, 1982; *Gaffer Samson's Luck*, 1984; *Torch*, 1987; *The Wyndham Case*, 1993; *A Piece of Justice*, 1995.

BIBLIOGRAPHY: *Authors and Artists for Young Adults*, vol. 47, 2003. Reproduced in Biography Resource Center, 2004. http://galenet.galegroup.com/servlet/BioRC; *Contemporary Authors Online*, 2004. Reproduced in Biography Resource Center, 2004. http://galenet.galegroup.com/servlet/BioRC; P., Jill (n.d.). Personal Web page, http://www.greenbay.co.uk/jpw.html

CAROL L. TILLEY

PATTOU, Edith
Author, b. 12 July 1953, Evanston, Illinois

Growing up in Chicago and its suburbs, P. was an avid reader who particularly enjoyed the Narnia books by C. S. LEWIS. Her lifelong ambition was to be an author. As a TEEN, she spent a summer in Ireland living with a family in Dublin. The Irish culture and stories provided inspiration for her Song of Eirren SERIES. She earned a B.A. in English literature from Scripps College in California, a master's in literature from Claremont Graduate School, and a master's in library science from UCLA. She has worked in bookstores, for public television, as an editorial assistant, and as a children's LIBRARIAN. She has also done screenwriting and written a PICTURE BOOK for children, *Mrs. Spitzer's Garden*. She has lived in Columbus, Ohio, since 1995, with her husband Charles and daughter Vita. She formerly lived in Colorado and North Carolina.

P.'s epic FANTASY novel *East*, a beautiful RETELLING of the Norwegian FAIRY TALE *East of the Sun, West of the Moon*, captivated teens with its lush descriptions and multidimensional characters. P., who had first encountered the tale in one of the Andrew Lang Fairy Books when she was a child, wrote: "I loved the strength and tenacity of the heroine, as well as the role reversal from the usual fairy tale in that the girl undertakes a grueling journey in order to rescue the prince."

AWARDS: *East:* ALA Best Books for Young Adults (Top 10), 2004, ALA Notable Children's Book, 2004, Book Sense 76 List, New York Public Library Books for the Teen Age, *School Library Journal* Best Books for Children, 2003; *Hero's Song: The First Song of Eirren:* IRA Young Adults' Choice, *Fire Arrow: The Second Song of Eirren:* Booklist Top 10 Fantasy Novel.

FURTHER WORKS: *Hero's Song,* 1991; *Fire Arrow,* 1998.

BIBLIOGRAPHY: Harcourt Publicity Department; Authors and Illustrators for Young People homepage from the Upper Arlington City School District website. http://green.upper-arlington.k12.oh.us/ohioauthors/pattou,edith.htm

DI HERALD

PAULSEN, Gary

Author, b. 17 May 1939, Minneapolis, Minnesota

P.'s simple and direct writing has taken many a YA on ADVENTURES from the CANADIAN wilderness, the Alaskan Iditarod, the Pacific Ocean, the Civil WAR, and into the future. His writing is realistic, yet fanciful, partly because P.'s life has been a SERIES of one adventure after another.

P.'s childhood was a solitary one. He did not fit in at school and did not do particularly well there. He spent a lot of time in the Minnesota wilderness trapping and hunting animals. P. went into the local library one night to get warm. The LIBRARIAN came up to him and asked him if he wanted a library card. Soon, she not only handed him a library card but a book. P. read every night before going to bed, "reading as a wolf eats." P. attributes his success to his introduction to books.

P. left home at the age of fourteen to travel with a carnival, beginning a series of adventures that would become his life. P. has experienced life as a farm hand, an engineer, a construction worker, a truck driver, a soldier, a sailor, and a competitor in two rounds of the 1,180-mile Alaskan dog-sled race, the Iditarod. These experiences provided him with the background from which to write his compelling stories.

When P. realized while working as a technician that he wanted to be a writer, he walked off the job in the middle of his shift. P. then created a fake resume and got a job as a MAGAZINE proofreader, working on his own writing in the evenings. Eventually he left California for northern Minnesota where he completed his first novel, *The Special War* (1966), in one winter. P. wrote his first book for YA in 1968, *Mr. Tucket.*

The publication of *Mr. Tucket* (1968) was the first in a series of Western adventures taking place from 1847 to 1849. The Tucket series begins with Francis Tucket, a fourteen-year-old boy heading West with his FAMILY on the Oregon Trail when he is captured by Pawness. It takes wild horses, hostile tribes, and a mysterious one-armed mountain man named Mr. Grimes to help him escape. Once he has escaped, Mr. Grimes teaches him how to survive in the wilderness. Eventually he leaves Mr. Grimes in search of his family. P. continues the adventure of Francis Tucket in *Call Me Francis Tucket* (1995), *Tucket's Ride* (1998), *Tucket's Gold* (1999), and *Tucket's Home* (2000). Throughout all the books, P. captures the reader's attention with a character that finds it important to do what is right while facing a fast-paced and exciting adventure.

P. presents another protagonist with strength and courage in the face of adventurous adversity with Brian in *Hatchet* (1987). In this Newbery Honor Book, P. presents Brian's struggle after he is the sole survivor of a plane crash in the far northern wilderness of Canada. Through his ordeal, Brian learns to respect nature while gaining a greater understanding of the world. P. continues to present Brian's adventure with *The River* (1991), *Brian's Winter* (1996), and *Brian's Return* (1999). Each of the stories presents Brian's survival in the wilderness as a central theme. In *Hatchet,* Brian is rescued at the end of the summer, but what would it have been like to survive the winter? This is the story presented in *Brian's Winter.* In *The River,* the government wants to learn how Brian survived, so he is asked to return to the wilderness to show what he learned; however, living in the wilderness is unpredictable and things don't work out as neatly as planned. After being rescued, Brian finds it hard to live in the civilized world; in *Brian's Return,* he decides to return to the wilderness to discover where he truly belongs. A new Brian book is in the works. The use of a powerful protagonist with a difficult situation to overcome is common to many of P.'s books. His straightforward portrayal of these positive characters makes his books enjoyable for young adults who equate reading with hard work.

P.'s presentation of strong characters also makes his historical fiction come alive for the reader. *Soldiers Heart* (1998) takes place during the Civil War P. shows the reader the war through the eyes of a boy who signed up only because he did not want to miss the great adventure. *Nightjohn* (1993) is a beautifully researched tale about a slave who had escaped to the North but returns South to teach reading. This tale is told from the point of view of a young slave girl, Sarny, who decides to risk her life to learn to read. Sarny was such a powerful character that in response to readers who wanted to know what happened to her, P. wrote her story in the sequel, *Sarny* (1997).

In addition to his novels, P. has also written numerous nonfiction books on SPORTS and nature, as well as slightly fictionalized experiences from his own life. His nonfiction books on sports include *Dribbling, Shooting, and Scoring—Sometimes* (1976), *Riding, Roping, and Bulldogging—Almost* (1977), and *Going Very Fast in a Circle—If You Don't Run out of Gas* (1979). He writes about nature and survival in *Father Water, Mother Woods* (1996). P. shares his love for dogs and a little bit of his life in *My Life in Dog Years* (1998) and *Puppies, Dogs, and Blue Northerns* (1998). In *Harris and Me: A Summer Remembered* (1993), *Woodsong* (1990), and *Guts: The True Stories behind Hatchet and the Brian Books* (2001), P. presents stories from his own life filled with insights about nature and survival.

P.'s books have garnered him critical acclaim throughout the world of YOUNG ADULT LITERATURE. His success is due to his honest and straightforward characters struggling to make their way in the world. His books display his belief that young people care about the world around them. His ability to tap into the human spirit and present characters of all ethnic groups with sensitivity and understanding has brought him enormous popularity among readers, critics, and publishers.

SELECT AWARDS: ALA Best Books for Young Adults: *Dancing Carl* (1983), *Tracker* (1984), *Cookcamp* (1992), and *The Beet Fields* (2001); Newbery Medal Honor Books: *Dogsong* (1986), *Hatchet* (1988) and *The Winter Room* (1990); American Library Association Notable Books: *Dogsong* (1985), *The Crossing* (1987), *Hatchet* (1987), *The Winter Room* (1989), *The Haymeadow* (1992), *Harris and Me: A Summer*

Remembered (1993), and *Nightjohn* (1993); 1985 Society of Midland Authors Book Award, *Tracker;* 1985 Parents' Choice Award, Parents' Choice Foundation, *Dogsong; Hatchet:* 1988 *Booklist* Editor's Choice citation, 1989 Dorothy Canfield Fisher Children's Book Award, 1991 Maud Hart Lovelace Book Award, 1990 Flicker Tale Children's Book Award, 1990 Sequoyah Children and YA Book Awards; 1988 ALA Best Book, *The Island;* 1990 Parents' Choice Award, *The Boy Who Owned the School; The Voyage of the Frog:* 1990 Teachers' Choice Award from International Reading Association, 1990 Best Books of the Year citation from *Learning* Magazine, 1989 ALA Best Book, 1989 *School Library Journal* Best Book of the Year; Western Writers of America Spur Award: *Woodsong* (1991) and *The Haymeadow* (1993); *The Winter Room:* 1990 Judy Lopez Memorial Award, 1990 *Parenting* Magazine Best Book of the Year; *The River:* 1991 IRA/Children's Book Council, 1991 *Parents* Magazine Best Book of the Year; *Woodsong:* 1991 *Booklist* Editor's Choice citation, 1991 Society of Midland Authors Book Award, 1993 *Booklist* Books for Youth Top of the List citation, *Harris and Me: A Summer Remembered;* IRA/Children's Book Council, *Dogteam* (1994) and *Nightjohn* (1994); *Soldier's Heart:* ALA BBYA, 1999; Sunshine State Young Reader Award Winner, 2001; *Brian's Return:* Charlie May Simon Children's Book Award, 2002; 1997 Margaret A. Edwards Award for lifelong contribution on writing books for teens.

SELECT FURTHER WORKS: *The Night White Deer Died,* 1978; *Popcorn Days and Buttermilk Nights,* 1983; *Sentries,* 1986; *The Island,* 1990; *The Crossing,* 1990; *The Cookcamp,* 1991; *Canyons,* 1991; *Monument,* 1991; *The Car,* 1994; *A Christmas Sonata,* 1994; *The Tent: A Tale of One Sitting,* 1995; *Danger on Midnight River,* 1995; *Escape from Fire Mountain,* 1995; *The Rifle,* 1997; *The Transall Saga,* 1998; *Curse of the Ruins,* 1998; *The Schernoff Discoveries,* 1998; *Alida's Song,* 1999; *Canoe Days,* 1999; *The White Fox Chronicles,* 2002; *Brian's Hurt,* 2003; *The Quilt,* 2004;

BIBLIOGRAPHY: *Contemporary Authors New Revision Series,* vol. 54, 1997; *Something about the Author,* vol. 79, 1995; http://www.randomhouse.com/features/garypaulsen/index.html.

NANCE WILSON

PECK, Richard

Author, b. 5 April, 1934, Decatur, Illinois

P. states: "I never wrote a line of fiction until I was thirty-seven years old, and even then only because I'd been driven to this extreme by seventh-graders." P.

taught school for several years before he decided it was time to tell a few stories. He states in an essay that he was not born a writer, "But I was born listening," he says, "eavesdropping if you like."

Reared in Decatur P. had a great deal to listen to. Primarily, he listened to his mother who read to him before he could read for himself. She was not trying to teach him to read or to write but to become a successful first-grader. She taught him how to print the letters of the alphabet and required that he write a thank-you note for every gift from a grandparent. He had a table and a chair, his size, along the kitchen wall. From her station in the kitchen, his mother told him how to spell out words and leave spaces between. Surrounded by interesting real-life characters, including his father, a veteran severely wounded in World War I, and his father's lively uncle, an elderly dandy with an eye for the ladies, P. learned the impact of powerful characterization firsthand. He also learned about living in their legendary shadows. As his family thundered at the dinner table about World War II and Roosevelt, young P. listened to Edward R. Murrow on the radio and dreamed of an escape to Manhattan.

Though he began teaching in Chicago, P. never forgot his Big Apple dreams. He decided early on that he was not going to settle down anywhere until he had tried living in New York; he accepted a teaching job at Hunter College High School in order to experience life in Manhattan. P. thought he would only stay for a year or so, but he says, "That was in 1965, and I've been in New York ever since."

P. had not been in New York more than a year when he discovered the publishing industry, but he insists there was little cause for optimism in the early years. "In 1971, a very prominent author told me I could not make it in this field," P. remembers. "He said Johnson is not in the White House anymore so the Great Society money isn't raining in on schools. The Great Society days are over, dried up, finished." More than thirty years and thirty-five novels later, P. has proven his discouraging mentor wrong. Beginning with the publication of *Don't Look and It Won't Hurt* in 1972, he has written a book a year ever since. "If I'm not writing a book," P. says, "I'm thinking about writing a book." P. has a talent for capturing and reflecting everyday conversation and characters in his books. Some of his friends have been pleasantly surprised to find themselves described in his books.

Though experts vary when it comes to selecting P.'s finest manuscript, he himself offers a clear answer. "I believe *Remembering the Good Times* is the best work I can do," he says. "It centers on a subject I think needs to be considered by the young. It dramatizes the classic signs of suicide. I was glad teachers used that book in schools because I don't write them for me. I write them for young people."

Awards have been bestowed upon P. with heightened enthusiasm since the year 2001. The American Library Association's Newbery Award was announced in January of 2002 for *A Year down Yonder* (2000). Then, flanked by First Lady and former LIBRARIAN Laura Bush, the President of the United States George W. Bush named P. a National Humanities Medal Recipient in April 2002. In 1999 he received a Newbery Honor Book Award for its prequel, *A Long Way from Chicago*.

Although he has received nearly every prize possible, P. continues to challenge himself as a storyteller. When he recognizes a lack in educational passion for history, he decides to write books to foster historical interest. "We, as a species, don't like the idea of coming out of a vacuum," P. says, "So we are compelled to create an alternate set of memories, to replace those we don't have. If we want to convince our young people that history is not dry, we will need to turn it into a FAMILY story. Think of it. The Civil War wasn't just a series of battles. It was brother fighting brother. We must capture that on the page. Give history a human face."

Another of P.'s primary concerns is CENSORSHIP. "I am censored because I have written ghost stories. I wrote *Are You in the House Alone?*, which is about rape. What I learned from that is that every word you write could be censorable. So you have to give yourself permission not to self-censor. There is no way to write a book that might not be censored because parents who have failed in their responsibilities will find a scapegoat. Book burners never have happy home lives."

Devoutly opposed to both censorship and vulgar language, P. is exactly what his champions suggest he is—a true original, held in high esteem by both his peers and his readers. Teachers and librarians are grateful for his work; they share it happily and enthusiastically with students. On a personal level as well as in fiction, P. has countless stories yet to tell.

SELECT AWARDS: 2004 Scott O'DELL Award, 2003 National Book Award Nomination, 2001 National Humanities Medal, 2001 Newbery Medal, 2003 Charlie May Simon Children's Book Award for *A Year down Yonder,* 1999 Newbery Award Finalist, 1990 MARGARET A. EDWARDS AWARD for lifetime achievement in YOUNG ADULT literature, 1976 Edgar Allan Poe Award, Heart-land Prize—Chicago Tribune, 1996 ALA BBYA for *The Last Safe Place on Earth,* 1999 ALA BBYA and 1999 John Newbery Honor Book for *A Long Way from Chicago* and *Strays like Us,* 2001 ALA BBYA for *A Year Down Yonder,* 2002 ALA BBYA, 2004 Charlie May Simon Children's Book Award for *Fair Weather,* 2004 ALA BBYA for *The River Between Us,* 2005 ALA BBYA 2005 *Kirkus Reviews* Editor's Choice, 2005 Christopher Book Award for *The Teacher's Funeral: A Comedy in Three Parts.* Three of his works were selected for the YALSA Best of the Best Lists: *Are You in the House Alone?:* The Best of the Best Books (1970–83), Nothin' But the Best (1966–86), Here We Go Again . . . 25 Years of Best Books (1967–92); *Father Figure: A Novel:* The Best of the Best (1970–83); *Ghosts I Have Been:* The Best of the Best (1970–83), Nothin' But the Best (1966–86).

FURTHER WORKS: *Through a Brief Darkness,* 1973; *Dreamland Lake,* 1973; *Representing Super Doll,* 1974; *Secrets of the Shopping Mall,* 1979; *Princess Ashley,* 1987; *Father Figure,* 1988; *Those Summer Girls I Never Met,* 1988; *Voices after Midnight,* 1989; *Unfinished Portrait of Jessica,* 1991; *The Ghost Belong to Me,* 1991; *Bel Aire Bambi and the Mall Rats,* 1993; *The Last Safe Place on Earth,* 1995; *Strays like Us,* 1998; *Fair Weather,* 2001; *The River between Us,* 2003; *Past Perfect, Present Tense: New and Collected Stories,* 2004; *The Teacher's Funeral,* 2004.

BIBLIOGRAPHY: Richard P. *Invitations to the World: Teaching and Writing for the Young,* 1994; CWIM 2002, interview by Kelly Milner Halls; Educational PAPERBACK Association BIOGRAPHY; The Essential Guide to Children's Books and Their Creators, 2002.

KELLY MILNER HALLS

AND BERNICE E. CULLINAN

PECK, Robert Newton

Author, b. 17 February 1928, Vermont

P., author of the popular *A Day No Pigs Would Die* (1972), shares his childhood memories in many of his writings. He often describes ADVENTURES in nature that impacted his life, and many of his characters resemble FAMILY members and friends. For example, *A Day No Pigs Would Die* is based on his experiences on the hog farm where he grew up and where he helped his father; the plot includes the main character's coming-of-age experience when he must gather the courage to kill his pet pig on his family's Vermont farm. Additionally, the main character in P.'s Soup SERIES is based on his boyhood best friend. Besides being a writer and farmer, P. has worked in a papermill and as a lumberjack, a hog butcher, and a New York City advertising executive. P. furthered his education at Rollins College and Cornell University. He married Dorothy Anne Houston, a LIBRARIAN and painter, in 1958, and they are the parents of two children, Christopher Haven and Anne Houston. P.'s interests include playing ragtime piano and various SPORTS.

P.'s work includes fiction and nonfiction novels, SHORT STORIES, PLAYS, screenplays, POETRY, songs, jingles, and television commercials. In addition to his novels based on childhood memories, he has written coming-of-age novels that are set on ranches (*Spanish Hoof,* 1985) and several works of historical fiction set during colonial and Revolutionary WAR times, with Fort Ticonderoga serving as the setting for *Hang for Treason* (1976). P.'s various works contain shining characters that are strong, respected teachers because of the wonderful influence of his first teacher, Miss Kelly, whom he admired greatly.

AWARDS: *A Day No Pigs Would Die:* Selected for "Still Alive: The Best of the Best 1960–1974," 1973 ALA Best Book for Young Adults, 1973 *Book World* Spring Book Festival Award, 1975 Media & Methods Maxi Award, 1977 Colorado Children's Book Award, and 1980 and 1981 New York Public Library's Books for the TEEN Age; *Millie's Boy:* 1973 *New York Times* Outstanding Book Citation, 1975 Child Study Association of America Children's Book of the Year; Child Study Association of America Children's Book of the Year: 1975 for *Bee Tree and Other Stuff,* 1976 for *Hamilton,* and 1987 for *Soup on Ice;* New York Public Library's Books for the Teen Age: 1980, 1981, 1982 for *Hang for Treason,* and 1980 and 1982 for *Clunie.*

SELECT FURTHER WORKS: *Eagle Fur,* 1978; *Fiction is Folks: How to Create Unforgettable Characters,* 1983; *My Vermont,* 1985; *Hallapoosa,* 1988; *The Horse Hunters,* 1988; *My Vermont II,* 1988; *A Part of the Sky,* 1994; *Nine Man Tree,* 1998; *Cowboy Ghost,* 1999; *Extra Innings,* 2001; *Horse Thief,* 2002; *Bro,* 2004.

BIBLIOGRAPHY: "Robert Newton P." *Contemporary Authors Online,* 2001. http://www.infrotrac.gale

group.com; Locher, Frances Carol, ed. "P., Robert Newton 1928–." *Contemporary Authors,* vols. 81–84, 1979.

HEATHER A. SHUMAKER

PENMAN, Sharon Kay
Author, b. 13 August 1945, New York City

P. uses extensive research in her highly detailed historical novels, combining her love of medieval history and literature. P.'s first novel, *The Sunne in Spendour* (1982), focuses on the 15th century and King Richard III. *Here Be Dragons* (1985) is the first of a trilogy set in 13th-century England and Wales. The power struggle over Wales between King John I and Llewelyn, Prince of Northern Wales, is illuminated with violence and betrayal. The second novel, *Falls the Shadow* (1988), explores further political conflict involving King Henry III and Simon de Monfort. The final novel of the trilogy, *The Reckoning* (1991), focuses on King Edward I and a de Monfort descendent. A fight for the crown between the Plantagenet King Henry I's only legitimate child, his daughter Maude, and her cousin Stephen Blois is the basis for *When Christ and His Saints Slept* (1995). *Time and Chance* (2002) recounts the tumultuous marriage of Eleanor of Aquitaine and King Henry II.

P. has written two medieval MYSTERIES in which she uses a young squire, Justin de Quincy, to solve murders and uncover plots that involve royalty as well as peasants. *Queen's Man: A Medieval Mystery* (1996), set in 1193 and *Cruel as the Grave: A Medieval History* (1998) were nominated for Edgars. Both mysteries are replete with details, plots, and characters. The young protagonist and the page-turning plots of these two works have earned them a place on lists of adult books with considerable TEEN appeal.

P. received her B.A. from University of Texas in 1969, and her J.D. from Rutgers University in 1974.

AWARDS: *The Queen's Man:* ALA Best Books for Young Adults, 1998.

FURTHER WORKS: *Time and Chance,* 2002; *Dragon's Lair: A Medieval Mystery,* 2003; *Prince of Darkness,* 2005.

BIBLIOGRAPHY: *Contemporary Authors Online,* 2002; Sharon Kay P. website, http://www.sharonkaypenman.com.

LAURIE BERG

PENNEBAKER, Ruth
Author, b. November 25, 1949, Ponca City, Oklahoma

P. is a writer of various types of printed media—novels, newspaper articles, humor books. She holds a B.A. in English from Eckerd College and a J.D. with honors from the University of Texas School of Law.

As a columnist for newspapers and a commentator on radio, P. has demonstrated a quick wit and perceptive insights on current issues. She uses these attributes to write about life issues—birth, DEATH, love and laughter—in compelling and heartfelt ways in her works for YA. P. discusses real and relevant issues—TEEN pregnancy in *Don't Think Twice,* cancer in *Both Sides Now,* and the desire to be loved in *Conditions of Love.* And she does so with wit (sharpened in her column writing and humor books) and heart. Debbie Carton, for *Booklist,* calls P.'s cast of characters in *Don't Think Twice* (1996), for example, "entertaining [and] fully realized," while also noting that the author "presents a compassionate, many-layered look at the complexities of teen pregnancy."

Don't Think Twice, P.'s first novel, is a celebrated account of teenage pregnancy. Set in 1967 in a Texas home for unwed mothers, the novel is narrated by Anne. With her sarcastic voice—sarcastic about the situation that she and the other girls find themselves in—she works hard to maintain emotional distance from the other girls at the home, from the reality of her pregnancy, and from her decision to give her baby up for adoption. P. brings the action to life with funny moments involving the colorful and vivid residents of the home, and with appropriate emotional complexity surrounding the issue. Carton calls the novel "realistic and moving."

Conditions of Love (1999) is a first-person account of an adolescent girl's grappling with her life. "An insightful exploration of teenage neuroses, and the importance of reconciling truth with myth and appearances," says Shelle Rosenfeld of *Booklist* (1999, p. 1689). The story is about life and death, specifically, the life of Sarah (a high-school freshman) in the wake of her father's death. Sara lives somewhere between high morals (writing letters protesting the death penalty) and a very immediate and incessant desire to be popular. She must decide how she will live when faced with the hard truth about her father, with the difficult circumstances in the life of her friend, and with her own desires.

565

P. is close to the themes of her writing, many of which were born out of her own experiences. From her insights on life in Texas came *A Texas Family Time Capsule* (2002), a collection of her best newspaper columns. From her struggle with breast cancer came *Both Sides Now* (2000), a teenager's struggle to reconcile her desire to maintain a positive outlook (and her "perfect" life) with the reality of her mother's recurrence of breast cancer. Deborah Stevenson, writing for *The Bulletin of the Center for Children's Books,* maintains that this book "achieves the difficult feat of portraying a FAMILY dominated by a particular emotional convention, which is critically failing them" (2000, p. 370).

P. lives in Austin, Texas, with her husband and son. In addition to an adult novel, *The Ones You're With,* she has written for the *New York Times,* the *Dallas Morning News, Redbook,* and provides commentary for KUT, Austin's public radio station.

AWARDS: *Don't Think Twice:* Best Books for Young Adults, 1997; *Publishers Weekly* Book Review Stars, April 1996; *School Library Journal* Book Review Stars, May 1996; *Conditions of Love:* Bulletin Blue Ribbons, 1999 (*Bulletin of the Center for Children's Books*); *Both Sides Now: School Library Journal* Book Review Stars, July 2000.

FURTHER WORKS: *A Texas Family Time Capsule,* 2002; *Stork Realities: What No One Ever Tells You About Pregnancy,* 1985; *Parents: A Toddler's Guide,* 1986.

BIBLIOGRAPHY: Carton, D. "Review of *Don't Think Twice.*" *Booklist* 92, 1498; Homepage of Ruth P., http://ruthpennebaker.com/; Rosenfeld, S. "Review of *Conditions of Love.*" *Booklist* 95, 1689; Stevenson, D. "Review of *Both Sides Now.*" *Bulletin of the Center for Children's Books* 53 (2000), 370.

MARY MCMILLAN TERRY

PETERS, Julie Anne
Author, b. 16 January 1952, Jamestown, New York

P. earned a B.A. in elementary education and immediately failed as an elementary-school teacher. She continued her education, getting her B.S. in computer and management science, followed by a master's in business and computer science. She worked in a variety of education and computer-related positions before realizing they were not the careers for her. So she began to write stories for young people. Through those stories, P. recalls the crucial choices she made as a TEEN that have made an impact on her entire life.

P.'s books for teens include *Define "Normal"* (2000) and *Keeping You a Secret* (2003). In addition she has written numerous stories for younger children. *Define "Normal"* follows two very different teens as their personal values clash and intertwine in an attempt to figure out which one of them is the "normal" one. *Keeping You a Secret* is a love story between two girls who must deal with the pressure of high school as well as of being gay. P.'s novels explore the diversity of FAMILY relationships and self-identity issues with a healthy dose of humor. She is proud that reluctant readers enjoy her stories. She says, "The most gratifying aspect of writing for young people is discovering that your books transcend storytelling to make a difference in a person's life."

AWARDS: BBYA and Quick Picks for Reluctant Young Adult Readers 2001 for *Define "Normal;" Luna:* ALA Best Books for Young Adults, 2003.

FURTHER WORKS: *The Stinky Sneakers Contest,* 1992; *Risky Friends,* 1993; *B.J.'s Billion-Dollar Bet,* 1994; *How Do You Spell GEEK?,* 1996; *Revenge of the Snob Squad,* 1998; *Romance of the Snob Squad,* 1999; *Love Me, Love My Broccoli,* 1999; *A Snitch in the Snob Squad,* 2001; *Luna,* 2004. (NOTE: all of these further works are intended for children.)

REFERENCES: *Contemporary Authors,* New Revision Series (2002); *Authors and Artists for Young Adults* (2002); Julie Anne P. official website, http://www.julieannepeters.com

JENNA OBEE

PETERSEN, P.J.
Author, b. 23 October 1941, Santa Rosa, California

P. was born to Carl Eric and Alice (Winters) Petersen, who were California prune farmers. He married Miriam Braun on July 6, 1963; they have two children, Karen and Carla. P. received an A.B. from Stanford University in 1962, an M.A. from San Francisco State University in 1964, and a Ph.D. in American literature from the University of Mexico in 1972. P. taught English at Shasta College in Redding, California, from 1964 until he retired in 2000. He currently lives in Redding, with his wife, Miriam.

P. grew up wanting to be a writer and was a regular patron of the public library in Geyserville, California.

He was an avid reader who also spent time listening to the dramatic offerings of radio in the 1940s and 1950s. Living in a rural area, P. used radio and books to learn about the world and other people. He grew up reading Zane Grey, Carolyn Keene, and Mark Twain. He continued to read through his high-school years, moving on to John Steinbeck, Willa Cather, and James Thurber, rounding out his reading with comic books and *MAD* magazine. While in high school, he wrote SHORT STORIES.

P. wrote his first novel shortly after he graduated from Stanford; however, after numerous rejections, he put away his dream of being a writer and became a teacher instead. After receiving his master's degree in 1964, he began teaching at Shasta College. His first published book, *Would You Settle for Improbable?* (1981), was written for his daughter Karen, who was in the seventh grade at the time.

P. has said that he uses his personal approach to life as the basis for his stories. His books deal with serious, contemporary themes and problems that he tempers with humor and optimism. The books range from MYSTERIES to survival stories, with ROMANCE and ADVENTURE included. P.'s books usually explore relationships between young people and the various people in their lives. He writes of FAMILY and community life, stressing positive traits for young people while using real situations that are recognizable and that appeal to those dealing with problems in everyday life.

P.'s thought-provoking style allows his readers to emphathize or sympathize with the characters in his books. Not surprisingly, they have received positive reviews that acknowledge his ability to teach lessons without being didactic. His books are written with lighter themes that portray life's problems as having attainable solutions that young people understand. His first collaboration was with children's book author Ivy Ruckman on *ROB&SARA.COM* in 2004.

AWARDS: National Endowment for the Humanities fellowship, 1976–77; 1981 ALA Best Books for Young Adults, *Would You Settle for Improbable?;* 1992 American Bookseller Pick of the Lists designation, *Liars;* 1996 OMAR Award, *The Sub;* 2000 William Allen White Award, *White Water; Nobody Else Can Walk It for You:* ALA Best Books for Young Adults, 1982.

FURTHER WORKS: *Corky and the Brothers Cool,* 1985; *Going for the Big One,* 1986; *Good-bye to Good*

O'Charlie, 1987; *The Freshman Detective Blues,* 1987; *How Can You Hijack a Cave?,* 1988; *The Fireplug Is First Base* (with Betsy James), 1990; *I Hate Camping,* 1991; *Liars,* 1992; *The Sub,* 1993; *I Want Answers and a Parachute,* 1993; *I Hate Company,* 1994; *The Amazing Magic Show,* 1994; *Some Days, Other Days,* 1994; *White Water,* 1997; *Can You Keep a Secret?,* 1997; *My Worst Friend,* 1998; *I Hate Weddings,* 2000; *Rising Water,* 2002.

BIBLIOGRAPHY: *Contemporary Authors,* rev., vol. 30, 1990; *Something about the Author,* vol. 118, 2001; P. J. P.'s Web page, http://usawrites4kids.drury.edu/authors/petersen.

M. NAOMI WILLIAMSON

PEVSNER, Stella

Author, n.d., Lincoln, Illinois

P. is the author of nineteen books for children and young adults. She is best known for her humorous novels of everyday preteen and TEEN FAMILY life. Some of her books also deal with more serious issues, such as teen suicide and marital discord. Many of her novels appeal primarily to a preteen female audience.

Early in her professional career, P. worked as an ad writer in an advertising company. She later married and had children, only beginning to write books for young people after her son suggested that she try her hand at fiction.

P.'s most popular novels are light realistic comedies that depict everyday adolescents dealing with everyday problems. For example, *And You Give Me a Pain, Elaine* (1978), explores Andrea's feelings that her older sister's unruly behavior is consuming her parents' attention so completely that they are beginning to ignore her. *Me, My Goat, and My Sister's Wedding* (1985) relates Doug's problems as he tries to keep his family from finding out that he is caring for a friend's pet goat. In the somewhat more serious *Would My Fortune Cookie Lie?* (1996), thirteen-year-old Alexis struggles to cope with her parents' marital problems and to understand the relationship between a mysterious young man and her family.

A long-time resident of Illinois, P. was voted Illinois Children's Book Author of the Year in 1987. Many of her novels, first published in the 1970s, 1980s, and 1990s, are still available in PAPERBACK, a testament to their lasting popularity.

AWARDS: *And You Give Me a Pain, Elaine:* 1979 Golden Kite Award, 1979 Society of Midland Authors

Award, 1979 Omar's Award; 1974 Chicago Women Publishing Award, *Call Me Heller, That's My Name;* 1980 Carl Sandburg Award, *Cute is a Four-Letter Word;* 1996–97 Society of Midland Authors Award, *Would My Fortune Cookie Lie?; How Could You Do It, Diane?:* ALA Best Books for Young Adults, 1990.

FURTHER WORKS: *Cute is a Four-Letter Word,* 1980; *How Could You do it, Diane?,* 1989; *The Night the Whole Class Slept Over,* 1991; *Jon, Flora, and the Odd-Eyed Cat,* 1994; *Is Everyone Moonburned but Me?,* 2000.

BIBLIOGRAPHY: *Authors and Artists for Young Adults,* vol. 15, 1995; *Something about the Author,* vol. 131, 2002.

DENISE E. AGOSTO

PEYTON, K. M. (Kathleen Wendy)
Author, b. 1929, Birmingham, England

P., author of over fifty children's books, has also published using the pseudonyms of Kathleen Herald and Michael P. She wrote her first book at age nine and published *Sabre, Horse of the Sea* at age fifteen, P. loves the sea and is an avid sailor. Her books, rich in character development, are based upon her life experiences while growing up. Her plots are developed through her characters and their interactions with one another. P.'s art studies are evident in illustrations she has drawn for several of her books. Her home in Chelmsford, in Essex, England, demonstrates her love of horses.

AWARDS: *The New York Herald Tribune* Award for *The Maplin Bird,* 1965; The *Carnegie Medal for The Edge of the Cloud,* 1969; and the *Guardian* Award for the *Flambards Trilogy,* 1970; *Prove Yourself a Hero:* ALA Best Books for Young Adults, 1979.

FURTHER WORKS: *The Plan for Birdmarsh,* 1966; *Thunder In The Sky,* 1966; *The Team,* 1967; *Fly-by-Night,* 1969; *Flambards,* 1969; *Pennington's Last Term,* 1971; *The Beethoven Medal,* 1972; *Pattern of Roses,* 1973; *Pennington's Heir,* 1974; *Marion's Angels,* 1979; *The Right-Hand Man,* 1979; *Midsummer Night's Death,* 1981; *Dear Fred,* 1981; *Prove Yourself a Hero,* 1981; *Flambards Divided,* 1982; *Going Home,* 1982; *Who Sir? Me Sir?,* 1983; *Sea Fever,* 1983; *Free Rein,* 1983; *Flambards in Summer,* 1989; *Darkling,* 1990; *Poor Badger,* 1991; "The Old Corpse Road" from *Chilling Christmas Tales,* 1992; *The Wild Boy and Queen Moon,* 1995; *The Swallow Summer* (also illustrated), 1996; *Windy Webley,* 1997; *Plain Jack,* 1997; *The Pony That Went to Sea,* 1998;

Snowfall, 1998; *The Swallow Tale,* 2000; *Blind Beauty,* 2001.

VALERIE A. PALAZOLO

PFEFFER, Susan Beth
Author, b. 17 February 1948, New York City

Award-winning P. is a prolific figure in children's and YOUNG ADULT LITERATURE, having written over sixty books for both reading levels. She began her career in 1970 with the publication of her first YA book, *Just Morgan,* which she wrote during her last semester at New York University. This story about an orphaned girl was followed by *Better than All Right* (1972) and *Rainbows and Fireworks* (1973), two books that solidified P.'s role as a young person's writer.

P.'s childhood in the suburbs of New York City has made its way into much of her work, causing her to be called "a chronicler of adolescent middle-class America." The designation only emphasizes P.'s candid writing style and engaging storylines. While many of her titles for younger children are light and entertaining, such as *The Beauty Queen* (1974) and *What Do You Do When Your Mouth Won't Open?* (1981), P. has never been one to shy away from daunting subject matter in her young adult work. *About David* (1980) has been applauded for its treatment of TEENAGE suicide/murder and its aftermath. The focus of the book is on the people left behind and the questions that remain in the wake of tragedy, specifically on how David's best friend, Lynn, copes with what happened as she strives to empathize with David's earth-shattering act and return to her previous understanding of normality. A review of the book by *Best Sellers* states that *About David* presents an invaluable portrayal of grief for high-school students; so poignant is the book, it has been included in some school curriculums as a measure against suicide.

The Year Without Michael (1987) and *Twice Taken* (1994) both address the disappearance/abduction of children, although *Twice Taken* studies the victim's reaction, while *Michael* focuses on the families' sorrow and confusion. *Family of Strangers* (1992) examines a dysfunctional and estranged FAMILY whose defunct communication leaves the youngest daughter in shambles. *Horn Book* applauded P. for balancing "weighty adolescent issues with intriguing characters and an absorbing story." Despite the dark nature of these stories, P. manages to create engaging voices that make the stories manageable for impressionable readers.

Also the author of the younger level Portraits of Little Women SERIES, P. displays a sense of humor and realism in all of her writing. She professes to have more of an interest in creating identifiable characters, as seen in *Courage, Dana* (1983) and *The Pizza Puzzle* (1996), than in producing great literary works full of symbolism and intricate plot development; As P. told *Authors and Artists for Young Adults,* the pleasure of writing is found in "mixing a bunch of stuff together and creating people or families that you know really well."

AWARDS: Dorothy Canfield Award, 1979, *Kid Power;* South Carolina Young Adult Book Award, 1983, ALA Best Books for Young Adults, 1980, *About David;* Parent's Choice, 1983, *Courage, Dana; The Year Without Michael:* ALA Best Book for Young Adults, 1987, South Carolina Young Adult Book Award, ALA Best 100 Books for Teenagers (1968–93); ALA BBYA, 1993, *Family of Strangers;* selected for "Here We Go Again: 25 Years of Best Books: Selections from 1967 to 1992": *The Year Without Michael.*

SELECT FURTHER WORKS: *The Beauty Queen,* 1974; *Kid Power,* 1977; *Marly the Kid,* 1975; *Truth or Dare,* 1983; *Getting Even,* 1986; *Turning Thirteen,* 1988; *Darcy Downstairs,* 1990; *April Upstairs,* 1990; *Twin Surprises,* 1991; *Most Precious Blood,* 1991; *Twin Troubles,* 1992; *The Ring of Truth,* 1993; *The Riddle Streak,* 1993; *Nobody's Daughter,* 1995; *The Trouble with Wishes,* 1996; *Justice for Emily,* 1997; *The Pizza Puzzle,* 1999; *Revenge of the Aztecs,* 2004.

BIBLIOGRAPHY: Bennett, John Lansingh. Review of *About David. Best Sellers,* vol. 40, November 1980, p. 303; *Children's Literature Review,* vol. 11, 1986; Knoth, Maeve Visser. Review of *Family of Strangers. Horn Book* magazine, May 1992; Noah, Carolyn. *School Library Journal,* vol. 44, June 1998, p. 151; *Something about the Author,* vol. 83, 1996.

RACHEL WITMER

PHILBRICK, Rodman

Author, b. 1951, Boston, Massachusetts

P., the oldest of four children, was born to two avid readers in 1951. An aspiring writer from the sixth grade, P. wrote many of his early works in secrecy to avoid being ridiculed by his classmates. By the age of twenty-seven, P. had written between seven and nine unpublished novels while working as a carpenter, longshoreman, and boat builder. P. is a direct descendant of one of the oldest families in the seacoast region of New Hampshire; a few of his relatives are documented as drowning in a storm off the coast of New Hampshire in the mid-1600s. P. married Lynn Harnett in 1980; they have collaborated on more than ten PAPERBACK books. He divides his time between Maine and the Florida Keys. One of his favorite hobbies is fishing, and in his spare time P. is also a MOVIE reviewer for the *Portsmouth Herald.* P. currently travels and lectures; he teaches children and YA how to improve their writing skills. P. also writes books in which he explores aliens, genetic engineering, and technical mind control, under the pen names Willaim R. Dantz or W. R. Philbrick.

After numerous rejections by publishers in his late twenties, P. ventured into genre writing and wrote several MYSTERIES, detective, and SCIENCE FICTION stories for adults. P. entered children's literature by chance when his publisher transitioned to YA mysteries. This led P. to revise a story that he had written at sixteen, which became *Freak the Mighty* (1993), a bittersweet story of a boy with a convict father who befriends a boy suffering from Morquio's syndrome. *The Mighty* (1998), although a highly acclaimed film adaptation, did not draw a large audience: regardless the story is P.'s most outstanding work for YA to date. Despite this setback, P. went on to write several other stories for young people, including three SERIES, The Werewolf Chronicles, Visions, and The House on Cherry Street, in addition to a sequel to *Freak the Mighty* called *Max, the Mighty* (1998). P.'s eminent themes in his YA novels include an unwillingness to accept limitations, the determination to triumph over adversity, and the exploration of emotion. P. states that "everything is life or death to a twelve-year-old," and the most important thing is friendship. P. is an excellent role model for aspiring writers of all ages, having experienced both extremes of success and rejection in the literary field. Although P. writes for adults and adolescents simultaneously, he expresses a strong interest in continuing his writing for YA and has made it a personal mission to ensure that his students are taught not only to write well, but to be proud of their work.

SELECT AWARDS: Shamus Award, Best Paperback Detective Novel, 1993, *Brothers and Sinners;* Shamus Award, nomination for Best Paperback Detective Novel, 1988, *Crystal Blue Persuasion,* 1989, *Tough Enough;* Judy Lopez Honor Book, 1993, *Freak the*

Mighty; California Young Readers Medal Winner, 1993, *Freak the Mighty;* Arizona Young Readers Medal Winner, 1993, *Freak the Mighty;* ALA Best Book for Young Adults, 1994, *Freak the Mighty,* 2001, for *The Last Book in the Universe; The Young Man and the Sea;* SLJ Best Books for Children, 2004.

FURTHER WORKS: *The House on Cherry Street: The Haunting,* 1995; *The House on Cherry Street: The Horror,* 1995; *The House on Cherry Street: The Final Nightmare,* 1995; *The Werewolf Chronicles: Night Creature,* 1996; *Visitors: Strange Invaders,* 1997; *Visitors: Things,* 1997; *Visitors: Brain Stealers,* 1978; *Shooting Star,* 1982; *Children of the Wolf,* 1996; *The Wereing,* 1996; *Abduction* (with Lynn Harnett), 1998; *Dark Matter,* 2000; *The Last Book in the Universe,* 2000; *REM World,* 2000; *Coffins,* 2002; *The Fire Pony,* 1996; *The Journal of Douglas Allen Deeds,* 2003; *The Young Man and the Sea,* 2004.

BIBLIOGRAPHY: "A Mighty Interview with Rod P." http://www.seacoastnh.com/film/mihjty.html, 1997; "About Rodman P." http://www.rodmanphilbrick .com/info.html, 2000; "My Biography." http://www .teacher.scholastic.com/writeit/bookrev/bio.htm, 2000; "Finding a Voice." http://borg.lib.vt.edu/ejournals/ ALAN/spring96/philbrick.thml, 1996, 2001.

ILONA N. KOTI

PHILIP, Neil
Author, b. 1955, York, England

P. is a folklorist and mythologist who is prolific in retelling and creating anthologies of MYTHOLOGY and folklore from around the world. As he weaves historical insight with the oral traditions of many cultures, P.'s work appeals to all ages. Whether editing a volume from a particular culture such as the Native Americans, weaving together the work of various cultures on a single topic such as the role of women, or retelling individual tales of heroes as seen in *The Tale of Sir Gawain* (1999), *Robin Hood* (1997), or *Noah and the Devil: A Legend of Noah's Art from Romania* (2001), P. evidences a precisely researched involvement through his authentically detailed accounts of events, people, and the literature of his chosen subject.

P.'s focus on Native Indians is demonstrated in numerous books in which both his voice and that of others address their lore and culture. *In a Sacred Manner I Live* (1997) is a collection of speeches and wise insights by Native Americans that includes photographs, providing a perspective on the culture. A

Braid of Lives: Native American Childhood (2000) shares numerous stories of growing up in the latter part of the 19th century. The stories, from over twenty tribes, amuse, provoke compassion, and appeal to both young and old readers; they describe games, rites of passage, survival, education and other universal aspects of growing up. *The Great Mystery: Myths of Native America* (2003) presents the beliefs of various tribes as to how the world came to be as well as underlying themes and differences among these explanations. The introduction discusses the changing nature of myth and its significance in understanding culture; authentic photographs and a bibliography enhance the book. *The Great Circle: A History of Native Americans* (2003) is an authoritative weaving together of pre–Columbian history through contemporary times. Through their voices and archival photographs, Native Indian beliefs about land, religion, science, and history are considered. Native Indian resiliency in the face of misunderstanding with the whites and treaties lined with deception is described while stressing the positive continuing presence of these people and their heritage.

Additionally, P. is recognized for his work with ancient mythology and classical western European FAIRY TALES. Such titles as the *Illustrated Book of Myths: Tales and Legends of the World* (1995), *Annotated Guides: Myths and Legends* (1999), *Illustrated Book of Fairy Tales* (1998), and *The Complete Fairy Tales of Charles Perrault* (1983), are highly acknowledged, comprehensive collections for young readers.

Thematically, P. works with voices across cultures, frequently in poetic form, in titles such as *War and the Pity of War* (1998). This work uses seventy poems spanning various countries and centuries since 11 BC to describe the horrors, courage, and questions of WAR. In *It's a Woman's World, A Century of Women's Voices in POETRY* (2000), P. uses the voices of women from six continents across the 20th century in sixty poems that focus on war, love, women's rights, birth, growing up, and domestic life. He currently lives and writes in Cotswold, England.

AWARDS: ALA Best Book for Young Adults: 1998 for *In a Sacred Manner I Live: Native American Wisdom,* 1999 for *War and the Pity of War.*

FURTHER WORKS: *Arabian Nights,* 1994; *The Golden Bird,* 1996; *Adventures of Odysseus,* 1997; *The New Oxford Book of Children's Verse,* 1998; *Eyewitness:*

Mythology, 2000; *Stockings of Buttermilk: American Folktales,* 1999; *Best Loved Poems,* 2003; *Horse Hooves and Chicken Feet: Mexican Folktales,* 2003; *In the House of Happiness; A Book of Prayer and Praise,* 2003; *Mythology of the World,* 2004.

BIBLIOGRAPHY: Hurst, C. O. "Celebrate the Earth with Native American Books." *Teaching PreK–8* 28, no. 7, p. 62, 1998; Mills, R. "Review of *Noah and the Devil.*" *Library Talk,* 15, no. 1, p. 42, 2002; Mueller, M. "Review of *A Braid of Lives.*" *Book Report,* 19, no. 4, p. 74, 2001; Persson, L. "Review of *It's a Woman's World.*" *School Library Journal* 46, no. 5, p. 186, 2000; Philip, Neil. "The shared moment: Thoughts on children and poetry." *Approaches to Children's Books,* 88, pp. 3-15, 1999; Sushko, A. "Review of *The Great Mystery: Myths of Native America.*" *Book Report,* 20, no. 4, p. 72.

JANELLE MATHIS

PICTURE BOOKS FOR YA READERS

Picture story books (PSB), a fusion of text and illustration, offer unique opportunities for older readers. The best PSBs use words to elaborate the pictures and vice versa. The question that must cross skeptical readers' minds is: How are PSBs used effectively with older readers?

First, they serve to assist readers who have learning DISABILITIES that prevent them from adequately decoding and comprehending longer text materials. PSBs can appeal to these disabled readers by not only providing them with more readily decodable text, but by providing context clues within the illustrations. Students who are struggling to acquire language (i.e., second language learners) can also benefit from PSBs in the same way. For those working with older illiterates, PSBs can provide satisfactory and successful reading experiences very quickly.

However, PSBs are not simply the domain of struggling readers. Students who are interested in the field of visual literacy and art can also benefit from an examination of the PSB format. In a typical PSB, artwork is utilized to develop a sense of the character. One has only to note the subtle differences Maurice Sendak creates in Max in *Where the Wild Things Are* to see how character can be revealed in a seemingly simple manner. Illustrations can convey details about other elements of plot such as setting and conflict. *Blueberries for Sal* by Robert McCloskey, for example, tells one story in the illustration while a somewhat different story is being related in the text. Additionally the artist's use of monochromatic color, in this case the blue of the berries, can carry the story forward as well. Style and technique of illustrations as well as media are also fertile areas of study for art students who examine the PSB.

PSBs for older readers can be valuable for teaching literary devices as well. *Quick as a Cricket* by Audrey and Don Wood provides concrete examples of similes easily accessed by readers. Other PSBs would be useful for predictions, generalizations, and inferences. For example, Chris Raschka's *Yo! Yes?* and the sequel, *Ring!Yo?,* are excellent for reinforcing skills such as prediction and inference. Foreshadowing can be seen easily in *Where the Wild Things Are,* represented by the piece of art Max has hanging on the wall in the second illustration; the drawing is that of a wild thing. The caption on the drawing "by Max" indicates that what is to follow is Max's invention. The trip he takes, then, is in his imagination. Older readers begin to identify sophisticated literary devices in more easily comprehended PSBs, which provides them with a sense of confidence that they can transfer to more complex texts.

Using PSBs to teach various literary forms and genres is also a possibility. An examination of motifs such as magic numbers, simple rhymes, and magic transformations is easily accomplished in Tomie dePaola's *The Legend of the Bluebonnet* and applied to more CLASSICS later (i.e., there are three witches crooning a simple rhyme as "Macbeth" opens). The defining characteristics of BIOGRAPHY are present in the works of notable authors such as Diane Stanley. Her Orbis Pictus–winning *Leonardo da Vinci* accomplishes a great deal in forty-eight pages. Likewise, students can gain information from reading historical fiction in PSB format such as Jane YOLEN's thought-provoking *Encounter,* an examination of what it might have been like for the Taino people when Christopher Columbus appeared on their island.

Finally, PSBs appeal to older readers who are looking for some fun reading. Their presence on the Best Book for Young Adults lists is testimony to their wide appeal. *The Stinky Cheese Man and Other Fairly Stupid Tales* by Jon Scieszka and Gary LARSON's *There's a Hair in My Dirt* are two PSBs popular with TEENS and those who work with them.

Eliza Dresang's *Radical Change* explores how PSBs have begun to develop in new and interesting directions of the last few years. They now tackle controversial issues such as homosexuality, homelessness, aging, DEATH and dying, and suicide to name a few. Sherry GARLAND's *I Never Knew Your Name* presents the story of a young man who has committed suicide. The story is told from the point of view of a younger neighbor who saw the victim alone often. There is regret as the narrator returns to the refrain that he never even knew the name of the lonely boy. Perhaps they could have been friends, he ponders. *Patrol* by Walter Dean MYERS, set during the Vietnam War, explores the emotions of a young serviceman who has doubts and fears about his surroundings and the people he has been told are the "enemy." Certainly, these PSBs are intended for an older audience, one capable of discussing the topics presented in a deceptively simple format.

BIBLIOGRAPHY: Huck, Charlotte S., and Susan Hepler, Janet Hickman, Barbara Z. Kiefer, *Children's Literature in the Elementary School,* 2003; Jacobs, James S., and Michael O. Tunnell, *Children's Literature, Briefly,* 1996; Lukens, Rebecca J. *A Critical Handbook of Children's Literature,* 2003; Norton, Donna E., *Through the Eyes of a Child: An Introduction to Children's Literature,* 2003; Temple, Charles, and Miriam Martinez, Junko Yokota, Alice Naylor, *Children's Books in Children's Hands: An Introduction to Their Literature,* 2002.

TERI S. LESESNE

PIERCE, Meredith Ann

Author, b. 5 July 1958, Seattle, Washington

P., a FANTASY author, recognizes a connection between the impenetrable strength of her fictional protagonists and her own bravery as a child. When faced with the irrational rage of an alcoholic and abusive relative, the young author refused to be threatened or intimidated. The rebuff of the relative killed any threat that this menace posed to P. Consequently, there is a continual theme of bravery in the midst of peril in the author's award-winning books.

P. centers her novels around heroes and heroines who fight against evil through the help of love, fulfilling their destined paths. The Darkangel trilogy follows the quest of courageous Aeriel, a servant girl set to destroy the White Witch's rule. Through the installments of *The Darkangel* (1982), *A Gathering of Gargoyles* (1984) and *The Pearl of the Soul of the World* (1990), Aeriel falls in love with the vampire Irrylath, sacrifices her heart to release him from the

dominion of the witch, and finally faces her nemesis in an ultimate struggle between good and evil. P.'s Darkangel SERIES, with its poetic language and seamless storylines, established the author as a master of "credible" fantasy. The Firebringer trilogy, which includes *The Birth of the Firebringer* (1985), *Dark Moon* (1992), and *The Son of the Summar Stars* (1996), takes place amidst a civilization of unicorns. Over the course of the books, Jan, son of the Prince of Unicorns, is transformed from an impetuous youth into a strong and loving father who reclaims the unicorns' ancestral home.

P. was additionally successful with the publication of two independent works, *The Woman Who Loved Reindeer* (1985) and *The Treasure at the Heart of Tanglewood* (2001). The legends of Earth Mother are celebrated in *Tanglewood* through the mysterious healer Hannah, an immortal being from whose head blooms flowers and whom a wizard controls. In *Reindeer,* a young woman wins the trust of a changeling and saves her people from its potential danger. In the fantasy genre, it is essential that the author weave an alternate world with no cracks through which the readers' attention may slip; once the reader questions the credibility of the author's world, they awake from "dream," as P. refers to her stories. The totality of her worlds and her imaginative interpretations of fantasy archetypes make P. "one of the foremost young authors of fantasy today."

P. writes first and foremost for herself, using the language she feels necessary to craft her story. To the critics who question her use of ornate language, the author counters, "Should I dumb [my work] down? Should I pretend that I don't speak English? . . . I can't change the way I think and I can't change my vocabulary and pretend that I don't know words that I know." P. compares her work to the realization of a dream: "If somebody wants to sneak up while you're asleep . . . and see what dream is running around inside your head, that's fine." She will not tamper with her "dream" in order to market her work to a specific audience. Nevertheless, her stories of evolution and character "metamorphosis" have a special connection with YA readers, as they too enter the unknown world of adulthood.

SELECT AWARDS: *The Darkangel:* 1982 American Library Association Best Books for Young Adults, American Library Association Best of the Best Books 1970–1982 citation, 1982 *New York Times* Notable

Children's Book, 1983 IRA Children's Book Award, 1986 California Young Reader Medal, and *Booklist* Best Books of the Decade (1980–89); *The Woman Who Loved Reindeer:* 1985 American Library Association Best Books for Young Adults, 1985 Parents' Choice for Literature, and 1986 New York Public Library Books for the TEEN Age exhibit; 1991 American Library Association Best Books for Young Adults, *The Pearl of the Soul of the World.; Treasure of the Heart of Tanglewood;* ALA Best Books for Young Adults, 2002.

FURTHER WORKS: *Where the Wild Geese Go,* 1988; "Rampion," *Four from the Witch World,* ed. Andre NORTON, 1989; *Waters Luminous and Deep: Shorter Fiction,* 2004.

BIBLIOGRAPHY: *Children's Literature Review,* vol. 20, 1990; Nist, Joan. Review of *The Woman Who Loved Reindeer.* ALAN Review (Winter 1985), p. 31; *Something about the Author,* vol. 67, 1992; Willard, Nancy. "Vampire on the Moon." *New York Times Book Review,* April 25, 1982.

RACHEL WITMER

PIERCE, Tamora

Author, b. 13 December 1954, Connellsville, Pennsylvania

P., the prolific creator of FANTASIES featuring strong female protagonists, has authored five complete quartets, as well as a set of volumes, *Trickster's Choice* and *Trickster's Queen* (both 2004), that are companions to her first quartet, *The Son of the Lioness* (1983–88). Growing up, she loved reading (*Yertle the Turtle* by Dr. Seuss and *Winnie the Pooh* by A. A. Milne were two of her favorite books) and telling stories. When she was in sixth grade, her father encouraged her to write these original stories down and she followed his advice. The next year, her teacher introduced her to J. R. R. TOLKIEN's *The Lord of the Rings.* Enchanted by Middle Earth, she became an avid reader of fantasies, but found there were not many stories where girls embarked on the heroic ADVENTURES. When she began to pen her own sword-and-sorcery tales, she envisioned female heroes. Her writing career almost ended before it began when, in tenth grade, writer's block struck. She did not write fiction again until the summer before her junior year of college.

P. attended the University of Pennsylvania, studying psychology. When she finally agonized her way through her writer's block, she wrote and later sold a

SHORT STORY, "Demon Chariot." With that success, she decided, in her senior year, to take a course in writing fiction. Her professor challenged her to write a novel. Mulling over ideas for her first venture into a longer work of fiction, she recalled the things she wrote about as a child and began her first fantasy. She graduated in 1976 with a B.A. in liberal arts and tried her hand at several different jobs, including: tax data clerk, tax clerk, social worker and house mother, secretary, assistant to a literary agent, radio producer, and freelance editor. All the while she occasionally sold stories and articles and worked on her full-length novel for adults, *The Song of the Lioness.*

She moved to Manhattan to focus on getting her novel published and found an agent who suggested that *The Song of the Lioness* was not really one novel for adults but four separate novels for YA. Agreeing, she rewrote the story as a quartet and in 1983, her first book, *Alanna the First Adventure,* was published. This first fantasy received generally positive reviews and was quickly followed by the sequels, *In the Hand of the Goddess* (1984), *The Woman Who Rides Like a Man* (1986), and *Lioness Rampant* (1987). Each book takes Alanna further along in her quest to become the first Lady Knight of Tortall, during a time when women weren't allowed to be warriors. The books garnered more critical praise, and P. was well on her way to a successful career as a full-time writer. During this period, she met and later married Tim Liebe.

Her books gradually developed a loyal following. By 1992, P. was able to support herself with her writing. She began visiting schools and later went on both national and international tours to promote her books and to stay in touch with her audience. She enjoys meeting her readers and says on her website, "My success is due to my readers, adults and kids, and I love being able to thank them in person." Although some critics have given one of her recent works, *Trickster's Choice* (2004), mixed reviews, her fans remain undeterred.

For her forays into imagined realms, P. mines everything around her, from the people in her life to history and current events. She figures out character names from combing through baby-name books and websites, maps, language books, and her own notebooks, in which she jots down interesting names and ideas whenever she stumbles across them. Although her works inhabit places that never were, she does as much research as she can to make the setting and the experiences of her characters as real as possible. For *Magic Steps* (2000) she learned how to spin on a drop-spindle so that she would understand the problems her main character would encounter. Combining all of these efforts with extensive rewrites, P. creates novels that are set in vividly imagined realms where magic lurks anywhere from castle to battlefield. They are peopled by characters that do extraordinary things, who nevertheless are plagued with many of the same foibles and challenges as their readers. Her plots are well paced and leave readers both with a sense of satisfaction and a desire for more. She is adept at constructing coming-of-age fantasies where young women as well as young men experience adventure. Her books have earned a place in the hearts of fans and on library shelves.

AWARDS: Author's Citation, Alumni Association of the New Jersey Institute of Technology, 1984, 2003 ALA Popular Paperbacks, for *Alanna: The First Adventure;* Schüler-Express ZDF Preis (Germany), 1985, and South Carolina Children's Book Award nomination, 1985–86, both for *In the Hand of the Goddess;* Children's PAPERBACKS Bestseller, *AUSTRALIAN Bookseller and Publisher,* 1995, for *Wolf-Speaker;* Best Books for Young Adults list, Hawaii State Library, Best SCIENCE FICTION, Fantasy and HORROR list, *Voice of Youth Advocates,* both 1995, and Best Books for Young Adults list, American Library Association, 1996, all for *The Emperor Mage;* Best Science Fiction, Fantasy and Horror list, Voice of Youth Advocates, 1996, and Best Books for the TEEN Age list, 1996, New York Public Library, 1997, both for *The Realms of the Gods;* The Circle of Magic SERIES nominated for the Mythopoetic Award for Children, 2000; *First Step* nominated for the Nevada Young Readers Award, 2002, and the Pennsylvania Young Reader's Choice Award, 2002; *Lady Knight* nominated for a Colorado Blue Spruce Young Adult Book Award, 2003; *Squire* nominated for a Washington Evergreen Youth Adult Book Award, 2004; ALA Best Books for Young Adults, 2002; *Trickster's Choice:* ALA BBYA, 2004.

FURTHER WORKS: The Immortals quartet: *Wild Magic,* 1992, *Wolfspeaker,* 1994, *The Emperor Mage,* 1995, *The Realm of Gods* 1996; The Magic Circle quartet: *Sandry's Book,* 1997, *Tris's Book,* 1998, *Daja's Book,* 1998, *Briar's Book,* 1999; The Protector of the Small quartet: *First Test,* 1999, *Page,* 2000, *Squire,* 2001, *Lady Knight,* 2002; The Circle Opens quartet: *Magic Steps,* 2000, *Street Magic,* 2001, *Cold Fire,* 2002, *Shatterglass,* 2003; *Trickster's Queen,* 2004.

BIBLIOGRAPHY: *Something about the Author,* vol. 96, 1998; *Horn Book,* vol. 80, no. 1, p. 90; *School Library Journal,* vol. 30, no. 6, p. 84, vol. 31, no. 4, p. 94, vol. 32, no. 10, p. 105, vol. 49, no. 12, p. 158; *Contemporary Authors Online;* www.tamora-pierce.com; www.kidsread.com; www.powells.com/authors/pierce.html; http://www.randomhouse.com/teachers/awards/state/html

SUSAN FICHTELBERG

PIKE, Christopher (Kevin McFadden)
Author, b. November 1954, Brooklyn, New York

When P. produced his first novel, *Slumber Party,* in 1986, the TEEN publishing world was revolutionized. How could anyone resist teen ski bunnies who were being hunted? His sequels to *Slumber Party, Weekend* and *Chain Letter,* only added to his luster as a trendsetting HORROR writer for YAS. His writing, featuring teen heroes and heroines, is recognized for the way P. treats teen life as it really is on a daily basis, while at the same time incorporating HORROR, ghosts, murder, and mayhem.

In November 1954, Kevin McFadden arrived in the world. Born in Brooklyn, McFadden opted out of college to work in computer programming. However, since he was simultaneously trying to break into the adult publishing market, McFadden decided to take a pen name. Christopher Pike was the name of the Captain of the Starship U.S.S. Enterprise on *Star Trek* prior to Captain Kirk, and just one more thing to which Kevin McFadden would eventually give new life.

However, P.'s attempts to break into the adult market were meeting with little success. By chance, P.'s work was perused by a young adult editor–and both a career and a genre were revitalized! P. currently has millions of copies of his various books in print. His SERIES, Remember Me, poses large philosophical questions that are interwoven throughout an engrossing trilogy. Perhaps it is this mix of both the large and the small, as well as the regular and the out-of-the-ordinary in most of his work, that have led to P.'s extraordinary success.

His fans are dedicated and range in age beyond teenagers. P. himself is especially devoted to his young fans, recognizing that adolescence is a tumultuous time for many teens, leading to more intense situations than are often found at other stages of life. His realistic approach to teen life in all of its facets is part of the enduring value of his work, although his tight pacing and adventurous tales should not be underrated.

P. is an avid reader and runner who also has an interest in astronomy. Currently residing in Santa Barbara, California, P. is a surfer who also finds time to meditate. He tries hard to protect his privacy, and relatively little is known about his personal life.

FURTHER WORKS: *Bury Me Deep,* 2001; *Witch,* 2001; *Monster,* 2001; *Die Softly,* 2001; *Road to Nowhere,* 2002; *Alosha,* 2004.

BIBLIOGRAPHY: http://www.geocities.com/sastra2/pike.html; www.fortunecity.co.uk/library/poetry/94/chris5.html; www.hycyber.com/HF/pike_christopher.html.

JEANNE MARIE RYAN

PINKNEY, Andrea Davis
Author, b. 25 September 1963, Washington, D.C.

P. has made her mark in children's literature as both an author and editor. With a degree in journalism, she started out writing and editing MAGAZINES. She then switched to editing children's books, holding prestigious positions with various publishers. At Hyperion, she established a popular imprint known as *Jump at the Sun,* with the purpose of recognizing children's books that celebrate black culture. With the encouragement of her husband, award-winning illustrator, Brian Pinkney, P. went on to write her own children's books. P. and Brian have collaborated on many PICTURE BOOKS. Her work was also influenced by her mother, a former school teacher, and her father, a gifted storyteller, both of whom were active in the CIVIL RIGHTS MOVEMENT. Writing both fiction and nonfiction, P. creates stories for a wide audience, ranging from board books for toddlers to novels for YA. With her nonfiction work, she upholds quality standards through extensive research on her topics. In addition to reading as much as possible on her subjects, she seeks out primary source information (interviews, visits to museums, etc.) Her BIOGRAPHIES, featuring Alvin Ailey (1993), Benjamin Banneker (1994), Bill Picket (1996), Duke Ellington (1998), and Ella Fitzgerald (2002), give readers great insight into the lives of famous AFRICAN AMERICANS and their contributions to society. Through her ability to write and select notable books, P. has played an important role in filling a gap in YA and children's literature.

AWARDS: Best Arts Feature award, Highlights for Children Foundation, 1992; *Parenting* Publication award, 1993; Pick of the List designation, American Booksellers, 1993, for *Seven Candles for Kwanzaa;* Notable Children's Trade Book in the Field of Social Studies, NCSS–CBS, 1994, for *Dear Benjamin Banneker;* Notable Book citations, Society of School Librarians International and American Library Association, both 1996, both for *Bill Picket: Rodeo Ridin' Cowboy;* Coretta Scott King Award, 1999, for *Duke Ellington; Let It Shine!; Stories of Black Women Freedom Fighters* selected as a King Author Honor Book, Coretta Scott King Awards competition, 2001; Carter G. Woodson Book Award, middle-level category, National Council for the Social Studies, 2001, ALA Notable Children's Books, 2001, for *Let It Shine!*

FURTHER WORKS: *Seven Candles for Kwanzaa,* 1993; *Hold Fast to Dreams,* 1995; *I Smell Honey,* 1997; *Pretty Brown Face,* 1997; *Solo Girl,* 1997; *Shake Shake Shake,* 1997; *Watch Me Dance,* 1997; *Raven in a Dove House,* 1998; *Silent Thunder: A Civil War Story,* 1999; *Let it Shine! Stories of Black Women Freedom Fighters,* 2000; *Abraham Lincoln: Letters from a Slave Girl (Dear Mr. President),* 2001; *Mim's Christmas Jam,* 2001; *Ella Fitzgerald: The Tale of a Vocal Virtuoso,* 2002.

BIBLIOGRAPHY: "Andrea Davis P." *St. James Guide to Children's Writers,* 5th ed., 1999. Reproduced in *Biography Resource Center,* 2003; http://www.galenet.com/servlet/BioRC; *Contemporary Authors Online,* 2003. Reproduced in *Biography Resource Center,* 2003. http://www.galenet.com/servlet/BioRC; "Voices From the Gaps: Women Writers of Color." June 1, 2003, http://voices.cla.umn.edu/authors/PINKNEYandreadavis.html

KIMBERLY DESTEFANO

PINKWATER, Daniel Manus
Author, illustrator, b. 15 November 1941, Memphis, Tennessee

In an interview with Marilyn Wann on the Fat!So? website, YA author P. describes his family as highly dysfunctional: his father, Philip Pinkwater, was a hold-up man in Poland and worked as a bootlegger in New York City and rag seller in Memphis; his mother Fay, the daughter of a rabbi, was a dancer. He credits an elder half-brother and half-sister with his upbringing.

P. spent four years at Bard College studying art and sculpture. After finishing college, he relocated to Hoboken to begin his art career. He was not very successful as an artist and "sort of fell upon" writing children's books after an editor he met at a party suggested he try it. Since then, he has written and illustrated over eighty books for children, YA, and adults. He married Jill Miriam Schutz—an author and illustrator, in 1969—the same year he began his writing career. They both have won numerous awards for their work, and over the years she has illustrated many of her husband's works. P. is also known for his regular contributions to National Public Radio's news show *All Things Considered,* and he appears on *Weekend Edition Saturday* to discuss books with Scott Simon.

P.'s books have been described as wacky, outrageous, and real, as well as completely imaginary. His first success came with the publication of *The Terrible Roar* (1969), a book that is wonderful to read out loud. Each time the little lion opens his mouth, he roars, and each roar causes something to disappear. His eccentric plot summaries speak for themselves: in *Blue Moose* (1975), a man who runs a restaurant meets a talking blue moose that moves in and spends the winter serving as head waiter; in *The Hoboken Chicken Emergency* (1977), Arthur Bobowicz is sent out to bring home the family's Thanksgiving turkey but returns instead with Henrietta—a 266-pound chicken with a mind of her own; in *Lizard Music* (1976), eleven-year-old Victor becomes involved with a community of intelligent lizards who tell him of a little-known invasion from outer space.

Five Novels: Alan Mendelsohn, the Boy from Mars; Slaves of Spiegel; The Last Guru; Young Adult Novel; The Snarkout Boys and the Avocado of Death was released in 1997 and combines five of the author's favorite works in a thick PAPERBACK. The original copyrights of these novels range from 1979 to 1982, and some had been out of print. Each of the novels pokes fun at the ordered ordinariness of the world. Using TEENAGERS as protagonists and the voices of reason, P. plays on the foibles and habits of adults, opening his readers' eyes to the inherent strangeness around us. *The Snarkout Boys and the Avocado of Death* features alienated teenagers, avocado-obsessed mad scientists, and a plot to replace all of the world's realtors with aliens. Walter Galt and Winston Bingo are typical outcasts at Genghis Kahn High School. While sneaking out in the middle of the night to go to an all-night movie theater, they meet the usual assortment of weird P. characters. *The Last Guru* reads as a social satire. Harold Blatz, a young boy whose only dream is to bet on a horse race, is used to show how ridiculous social trends and popular culture can become. He saves his allowance money for years before he can get his Uncle Roy to place a bet for him. Roy tries to teach him a lesson by betting on a long shot, but Harold wins anyway. Consequently Harold becomes the third richest person on the planet, then a recluse in a Tibetan village, then the leading spiritual guru in the world, and finally returns to being an ordinary teenager.

The Education of Robert Nifkin (1998), a YA novel, has been interpreted as one of Pinkwater's autobiographical works. Set in the 1950s in Chicago, Robert Nifkin describes highly unorthodox high-school experiences in the form of a college application essay. In his first week at Riverview High, Robert is accused of being either a commie or a fairy by his homeroom teacher, informed of an international Jewish conspiracy by his English teacher, spends hours copying dreary blackboard essays into a notebook, and finds himself sitting at the geek table at lunch. Robert eventually stops attending and convinces his parents to send him to private Wheaton School. Here anarchy rules and instruction includes sessions at Maxie's Bookshop, crowded with "loonies, lonelys, speakers, listeners, debaters, radicals, beatniks, artists, insomniacs, and chess players." The irreverent descriptions of high-school life and Robert's sardonic observations will delight individualists and those who suffered under uptight parents and educators.

In *Chicago Days, Hoboken Nights* (1991), a collection of AUTOBIOGRAPHICAL essays, P. recalls his school days: "I used to be a jerk, a wimp, and a weenie. I was a sissy. And a big fat sissy to boot. I was so shy and uncomfortable that my very presence inflicted agony on everyone I met, adults especially." He listened to the radio, watched television, played the flute, and discovered writing. He remembers writing one-page parodies when he was in fifth grade. "I was highly inspired by *MAD* magazine," he recalls. "I bought the first issue off the newsstand." In school, young P. used to write funny notes "that I would pass around the classroom to try to make my friends laugh out loud and get in trouble." When he won a SHORT STORY contest and was given a subscription to National Geographic, he was exhilarated: "That's how I first learned that you could get things by writing."

When P. is not writing YA LITERATURE, he enjoys commenting on National Public Radio's *All Things Considered* and *Car Talk*. For National Public Theater, he also created and co-hosted Chinwag Theatre, a storytelling, theme-exploring, family-friendly radio program. The main idea of the show is to treat children the way they should be treated—with respect. In Chinwag (slang for talking), P. and his co-host spin yarns, make points, and laugh at each other's silly offerings. The show was syndicated on fifty stations throughout the United States.

In today's fast-changing publishing world, P.'s books continue to fascinate readers as they have for over thirty years. He uses his bizarre characters to highlight the underlying silliness of routine life. At the same time, these characters connect with the reader and make us appreciate them while recognizing our own shortcomings and difficulties.

SELECT AWARDS: American Library Association Notable Book, *Lizard Music*, 1976; *New York Times* Outstanding Book, *The Last Guru*, 1978; Parents' Choice Award, *Roger's Umbrella*, 1982.

FURTHER WORKS: Nonfiction: *Superpuppy: How to Choose, Raise, and Train the Best Possible Dog for You* (with Jill Pinkwater), 1977; *Young Adults*, 1985; *Fish Whistle: Commentaries, Uncommontaries, and Vulgar Excesses*, 1989; *Chicago Days, Hoboken Nights*, 1991; *The Afterlife Diet*, 1995. Fiction: *Wizard's Crystal*, 1973; *Magic Camera*, 1974; *Three Big Hogs*, 1975; *Around Fred's Bed*, 1976; *The Blue Thing*, 1977; *Fat Men from Space*, 1977; *The Last Guru*, 1978; *Return of the Moose*, 1979; *Alan Mendelsohn, the Boy from Mars*, 1979; *Yobgorgle, Mystery Monster of Lake Ontario*, 1979; *The Worms of Kukumlima*, 1981; *Young Adult Novel*, 1982; *Slaves of Spiegel: A Magic Moscow Story*, 1982; *Roger's Umbrella*, 1982; *Devil in the Drain*, 1984; *Ducks!*, 1984; *The Frankenbagel Monster*, 1986; *Guys from Space*, 1989; *Borgel*, 1990; *The Phantom of the Lunch Wagon*, 1992; *Spaceburger: A Kevin Spoon and Mason Mintz Story*, 1993; *Ned Feldman, Space Pirate*, 1994; *At the Hotel Larry*, 1997; *Wolf Christmas*, 1998; *Big Bob and the Halloween Potatoes*, 2000; *The Lunchroom of Doom*, 2000; *Uncle Boris in the Yukon, and Other Shaggy Dog Stories*, 2001; *The Werewolf Club Meets the Hound of the Basketballs*, 2001; *The Werewolf Club Meets Dorkula*, 2001; *The Werewolf Club Meets Oliver Twit*, 2002; *Mush's Jazz Adventure*, 2002; *Fat Camp Commandos Go West*, 2002; *The Picture of Morty and Ray*, 2003; *Bad Bears in the Big City*, 2003; *Looking for Babowicz: A Hoboken Chicken Story*, 2004.

BIBLIOGRAPHY: *Contemporary Authors New Revision Series,* vol. 89, 2000, pp. 327–31, P., Daniel Manus. "Interview with Deborah Kovacs and James Preller." *Meet the Authors and Illustrators,* vol. 2, 1993; *Something about the Author,* vol. 114, 2000; P.'s website: http://www.pinkwater.com.

CHRISTINE WELTER

PLATH, Sylvia

Author, b. 27 October 1932, Boston, Massachusetts; d. 11 February 1963, London, England

Also known as *Victoria Lucas* when publishing *The Bell Jar* (1963), which discusses the circumstances and consequences of her breakdown during the summer of her junior year at Smith, P., a member of Phi Beta Kappa, earned a B.A. *summa cum laude* from Smith College (1955) on a scholarship, attended Harvard University in the summer of 1954, Newnham College in Cambridge as a Fulbright Scholar from 1955 to 1957, and earned an M.A. in 1957.

Though she wrote many works, and published POETRY in periodicals at an early age, only a single volume of her poetry *The Collosus* (1960) was published during P.'s lifetime before she committed suicide after dealing with depression for a long time. Her husband, poet Ted Hughes, whom she separated from after learning of his infidelities, edited many of the posthumous publications of P.'s works.

The sudden death of her father "in 1940 devastated the eight-year-old P., and many commentators note the significance of this traumatic experience in interpreting her poetry, which frequently contains both brutal and reverential images of her father as well as sea imagery and allusions to bees."

Two of P.'s works have been adapted. "A film version of *The Bell Jar* was produced by Avco-Embassy in 1978; *Letters Home* (1975) was adapted into a play by Rose Leiman Goldemberg and staged in 1979. Gwyneth Paltrow starred in a P. bio-picture released in 2003, forty years after P.'s suicide.

P.'s awards include the Mademoiselle College Board contest winner in fiction, 1953; Irene Glascock Poetry Prize, Mount Holyoke College, 1955; Best Hokin Award, *Poetry* MAGAZINE, 1957; first prize in Cheltenham Festival, 1961; Eugene F. Saxon fellowship, 1961; Pulitzer Prize, 1982, for *Collected Poems*.

AWARDS: *The Bell Jar*: ALA Best Books for Young Adults, 1971; various citations on the Best of the Best lists.

SELECT FURTHER WORKS: *Uncollected Poems,* 1965; *Ariel,* 1965; *Three Women: A Monologue for Three Voices,* 1968; *Wreath for a Bridal,* 1970; *Crossing the Water: Transitional Poems,* 1971; *Crystal Gazer and Other Poems,* 1971; *Lyonnesse,* 1971; *Million Dollar Month,* 1971; *Winter Trees,* 1971; *The Bed Book,* 1976; *Johnny Panic and the Bible of Dreams: Short Stories, Prose, and Diary Excerpts,* 1979; *Collected Poems,* 1981; *Stings,* 1983; *The Journals of Sylvia Plath,* 1983; *Aerial: The Restored Edition,* 2005.

BIBLIOGRAPHY: "Sylvia Plath," DISCovering Authors, http://galenet.galegroup.com/servlet/DC/

SARA MARCUS

PLATT, Kin
Author, b. 8 December 1911, New York City

P. was born in New York City, and during his school days, he would always draw funny cartoons. This led to his employment as a caricaturist for the *Brooklyn Daily Eagle.* In the 1930s, he worked as a radio comedy writer prior to joining the U.S. Army Air Forces in 1943. He served in the Chinese-Burmese-Indian theatre of World War II and was the recipient of a Bronze Star for his wartime service.

P. was interested in drawing cartoons as well as writing, and his comic strip, *Mr. & Mrs.,* which ran from 1947 to 1963, was quite popular. His later comic strip, *The Duke and Duchess,* was published between 1950 and 1954. These comic strips appeared in the *New York Herald Tribune* syndicated papers. *The Village Voice* and *The Los Angeles Times* published his theatrical caricatures, along the lines of Hirschfeld. P. also expressed himself artistically through painting and sculpting. His talents include writing for young children as well for an older readership.

P.'s books often focus on the emotional issues young people face. *The Blue Man,* his first juvenile book, was published in 1961. This was a thriller geared toward a male readership. MYSTERY writing was also his forte, with titles such as *mystery of the Witch Who Wouldn't* and *Big Max in the Mystery of the Missing Moose.* The Big Max SERIES (easy-to-read books) starred a very young detective. P. continued to write for over thirty years. He also served as editor of several books published by Pendulum during the 1970s.

P's book *The Boy Who Could Make Himself Disappear* (1968) was made into a film in 1973 under the title *Baxter, Sinbad and Me.* His 1966 mystery, was awarded the Mystery Writers of America Edgar Award for juvenile mysteries. *Chloris and the Creeps,* written in 1973, won the Southern California Council on Literature for Children and Young People Award.

P. is known for his high-interest, low vocabulary books, which are natural attractors for reluctant readers. P. enjoys playing golf and devotes his time between New York and Los Angeles. Christopher Platt is his only son.

AWARDS: 1967 Mystery Writers of American Edgar Award, *Sinbad and Me;* 1974 Southern California Council on Literature for Children and Young People Award, *Chloris and the Creeps;* ALA Best Books for Young Adults, 1971, selected for "The Best of the Best Books: 1970–1983" for *Headman.*

FURTHER WORKS: *Flames Going Out,* 1980; *Frank and Stein and Me,* 1982; *Crocker,* 1983; *Murder in Rosslare,* 1986; *Darwin and the Great Beasts,* 1992.

BIBLIOGRAPHY: *Contemporary Authors Online,* 2002; Hipple, Ted, ed. *Writers for Young Adults,* 1997; Holtze, Sally Holmes, ed. *Junior Authors and Illustrators,* 5, 1983; P., Kin, *Hey, Dummy,* 1971.

SANDRA KITAIN

PLATT, Randall Beth
Author, b. 1948, Seattle, Washington

A native of the Pacific Northwest which she uses as the setting for most of her works, P. is best known for the Fe-As-Ko SERIES of "humorous Westerns." As a child, P.'s desire to become an actress inspired her to write scripts for her favorite TV Westerns, such as *Bonanza* and *Gunsmoke.* This experience influenced *The Four Arrows Fe-As-Ko* (1991), which was made into the film *Promise the Moon* (1997), *The Royalscope Fe-As-Ko* (1997), and *The 1898 Base-Ball Fe-As-Ko* (2000). P. has tackled a number of different genres in YOUNG ADULT LITERATURE in works such as *The Likes of Me* (2000), a coming-of-age tale about a half-Caucasian, half-Chinese albino girl, and *Out of a Forest Clearing: An Environmental Fable* (1991). P. received the Keystone State Reading Award in 1999.

AWARDS: *The Likes of Me:* ALA Best Books for Young Adults, 2001.

FURTHER WORKS: *Honor Bright* (1997); *The Cornerstone* (2000).

REFERENCES: *Writers Review* online 2001; *Amazon.com* online, 2003; *Plattbooks.com* online, 2003.

KRISTINE S. WICKSON

PLAY IS WORK: PRETEND PLAY AND STORYTELLING

For young children, play *is* work, *their* form of work. Work, then, as adults—parents, educators—typically think of it, is not an unwanted regime that is imposed and forced upon a child, but is, in actuality, the natural progression of childhood and development. It would follow, that the way one works—whether it is a stringent, matter-of-fact, external-to-self system of simply accomplishing a set goal; or a relevant, evolving, integrating process of expressing what is internal—is an instrumental factor in governing one's perception of what work is, and consequently how it is taught. The methodology of work, therefore, is what is imposed on a child, and not the idea of work itself.

P. has long been recognized as central to the cognitive development of children. "P. provides a natural context for beginners to experiment with literacy" (Vacca, et al., 2000). Storytelling has also emerged as a key cognitive skill in the process of intellectual development. Children's P. can be used as a tool for assessing children's symbolic competence and narrative structure. "One reason for this relationship is that pretend play reflects children's emerging representational abilities and thus provides valuable information about their social and cognitive development" (Lyytinen, 1995).

Piaget views P. as an early form of work, a child's play of externalizing the internal, thereby assimilating what may be difficult to cognitively process, understand and express. He "theorized that children do not internalize knowledge directly from the outside but construct from inside their heads, in interaction with the environment, (Kamii, 1991)" (Vacca et al., 2000). Symbolic P. then becomes more and more reflective of reality, developing in the direction of constructive ability or work.

Hanline, (1999), maintains that "P. gives children opportunities to understand the world, interact with others, express and control emotions, develop symbolic capabilities, attempt novel or challenging tasks, solve problems, and practice skills." P., then, should be encouraged, so that the subsequent, inevitable *emergence of*—and not necessarily *transition to*—work, in that play *is* work, will be realized.

Storytelling and P. provide a motivating context for literate behavior, as children communicate through narration to themselves in solitary P. and to their peers in social P. In some preschools and kindergartens, story-playing is a regular activity. Children have the option each day to dictate a story play to a teacher, while observing and participation in its translation into written language. Later it is enacted by their friends during circle-time activity. "Story playing helps children organize their experience, both verbal and nonverbal, that fulfill the fundamental purpose of communicating the child's needs, interests, and desires. For the young child, these larger purposes of language provide the motivation and framework for later literacy development" (Kim, 1999).

"Although young children with disabilities may exhibit a limited repertoire of P. skills (Lender, Goodman, and Linn, 1998; Skellenger, Rosenblum, and Jager, 1997), there is a lack of evidence to suggest that children with DISABILITIES should be excluded from P.-based settings" (Hanline, 1999). For all children, therefore, regardless of level of development, P. is strongly advocated. Three- to five-year-old preschoolers, in particular, "should have access on a daily basis to three types of P.—*construction play:* P. that allows children to represent an idea through a media or to use objects to build something; *symbolic P.:* imaginative role-playing that involves the transformation of persons, objects, or events into make-believe or pretend persons, objects, or events; and *sensorimotor P.:* learning about the world through the senses and physical interaction with the environment" (Hanline, 1999).

Children will better appreciate the idea of work if their concept of P. is valued and underscored. With this argument in mind, P.-based methods of teaching and learning should be advocated, as opposed to the staunch view that learning is simply the absorption of what is said or acknowledged to be true. Piaget says it best: "When the active school requires that the student's effort should come from the student himself instead of being imposed, and that his intelligence should undertake authentic work instead of accepting pre-digested knowledge from outside, it is therefore simply asking that the laws of all intelligence should be respected."

BIBLIOGRAPHY: Hanline, Mary F. (1999), "Developing a Preschool Play-based Curriculum," *International Journal of Disability, Development, and Education,* 46 no. 3 289–305; Kamii, C. (1991), "What Is Constructivism?," C. Kamii, M. Manning, and G. Manning, eds., *Early Literacy: A Constructivist*

Foundation for Whole Language, Washington D.C., National Education Association; Kim, Sook-Yi. (1999), "The Effects of Storytelling and Pretend Play on Cognitive Processes, Short-term and Long-term Narrative Recall," *Child Study Journal,* 29 no. 3 175–91; Lender, W. L., Goodman, J. F., and Linn, M. (1998), "Repetitive Activity in the Play of Children with Mental Retardation," *Journal of Early Intervention,* 21, 308–22; Lyytinen, P. (1995), "Cross-situational Variation on Children's Pretend Play," *Child Care, Health and Development,* 17, 9–25; Vacca, J. L., Vacca, R. T., Gove, M. K., Burkey, L., Lenhart, L. A., McKeon, C. (2000), *Reading and Learning to Read,* Pearson Education, Inc.

AURALEE DALEY

PLAYS FOR ADOLESCENTS

Traditionally, plays for TEEN audiences resided primarily in junior and senior high-school productions of light comedies (*Our Hearts Were Young and Gay*), the occasional serious play (*The Effect of Gamma Rays On Man-in-the-Moon Marigolds*), or versions of Broadway musicals such as *The Music Man* and *Bye Bye Birdie.* Most representations avoided controversial subject matter or complex characters. A few exceptions, *The Miracle Worker* and *The Diary of Anne Frank,* for example, came from the adult stage to win popularity in hundreds of school productions. Until recently, the reading of drama in secondary classrooms largely consisted of analyses of Shakespearean texts and of established modern works such as *Our Town* by Thornton Wilder, *The Crucible* by Arthur Miller, or *A Raisin in the Sun* by Lorraine Hansberry. But beginning in the 1980s, plays written expressly for younger audiences began increasingly to constitute a body of dramatic literature that was free of origins in the commercial theatre. Aurand Harris asked his audiences to confront and to accept the inevitable DEATH of his hero in *The Arkansaw Bear.* Suzan Zeder in *Step on a Crack* guided viewers through her heroine's hard-won struggle to accept a stepmother as a replacement for her deceased parent. While David Saar based *The Yellow Boat* on his own son's death from complications related to AIDS, he affirmed the courage of FAMILIES in times of crisis and the power of art in our lives. Such works arrived in professional regional theatres for young audiences throughout the country, in university productions, and on tour; the published texts of these plays soon burst forth on library shelves in a number of anthologies.

Because the original play, however well written and received by commentators, still faces the almost insurmountable obstacle of having little name recognition at the box office or in bookstores, the last ten years has witnessed a notable increase in stage adaptations of popular novels. Robert CORMIER's *The Chocolate War* and Patricia MACLACHLAN's *Sarah, Plain and Tall,* both adapted by Joseph Robinette, are examples, along with John Gardner's *In the Suicide Mountain,* dramatized by James Still under the title *A Village Fable. Dragonwings,* adapted by its author Laurence YEP, and *The Pinballs* of Betsy Byars, as dramatized by Aurand Harris, are others.

Among the dozens of established playwrights now addressing adolescents (each writes for younger audiences as well), six must be singled out, in alphabetical order. Laurie Brooks deals with adolescent issues in her award-winning *The Wrestling Season,* which explores the affects of peer pressure upon individual identity; in *Deadly Weapons* she exposes the reckless behavior of TEENAGE friends. Others of her "forum" plays include *The Tangled Web* and *Everyday Heroes,* after which the characters discuss with audiences questions raised in the action. Max Bush dramatizes the possible meaning of adolescent dreams in *Wildboy* and the conflict of a teenage girl in dealing with the death of her sister in *Sarah.* His prize-winning *Ezigbo, the Spirit Child* is based on a Nigerian story of a mother's attempt to keep her child from being stolen from the human world to that of the spirits. Jose Cruz Gonzales focuses upon issues such as illiteracy in his comedy *Salt and Pepper* and conservation in *The Highest Heaven.* His highly theatrical *Harvest Moon* chronicles four generations of a Mexican-American farming family; in *Earth Songs* he experiments with imagery, mime, and MUSIC to create a compelling world vision. James Still in *Hush: An Interview with America* scrutinizes the relationship of a father and his daughter's roller-coasting adolescent development; in *Just Before Sleep,* he inspects the subject of homelessness as seen in a family's embattlements with bureaucratic social agencies. His widely produced *Amber Waves* concentrates on a family's attempt to save their farm from financial disaster and each other from spiritual despondency. Y York demonstrated her mastery as a playwright when she adapted Janet Taylor Lisle's *Afternoon of the Elves* and when she dramatized Rudyard Kipling's *The Garden of Rikki Tikki Tavi.* Her recent plays include original works such as *The Forgiving Harvest,* a comic drama looking at the encroachments of the city upon a farm and the heroine's desperation to save her pet steer, and *Nothing is the Same,* about four childhood friends of different ethnic backgrounds living in Hawaii on the eve of Pearl Harbor. In *Mother Hicks,* Suzan Zeder tells the stories of three outsiders: a foundling girl, a deaf boy, and Mother Hicks, who some think is a witch, and how they come to protect each other. *The Taste of Sunrise,* a bilingual work in American Sign Language and spoken English, is a prequel to *Mother Hicks.*

Other notable playwrights, each with numerous scripts, include Sandra Fenichel Asher, Ric Averill, Cherie BENNETT, Caleen Sinnette Jennings, Carol Korty, Joanna Halpert Kraus, Brian Kral, John Urquhart, Pamela Sterling and Mary Hall Surface. A number of dramatic authors, most identified with adult theater, also sometimes write tellingly for youth: Alan Ayckbourn *(Gizmo),* Horton Foote *(The Actor),* Wendy Kesselman *(Maggie Magalita),* Bryony Lavery *(More Light),* David Mamet *(The Poet and the Rent),* and Wole Soyinka *(Travel Club and Boy Soldier).*

Encouragement to write for this age group is found in three programs dedicated to the development of new plays: New Visions/New Voices, sponsored by the Kennedy Center for the Performing Arts, Washington, D.C., the Bonderman Symposium held at the Indiana Repertory Theatre in Indianapolis, and New Plays for Young Audiences at the Provincetown Playhouse, produced by New York University. Most of the playwrights mentioned here have had one or more plays first emerge from these series.

Notable anthologies that include many texts of plays described here are *All the World's A Stage: Modern Plays for Young People,* edited by Lowell Swortzell (1972); *Around the World in 21 Plays: Theatre for Young Audiences,* edited by Lowell Swortzell (1997); and *Theatre for Young Audiences,* edited by Coleman A. Jennings (1998). A world view of theatre for young audiences may be found in *The International Guide to Children's Theatre and Educational Theatre,* edited by Lowell Swortzell (1990). Important publishers of plays are Anchorage Press, www.applays.com; New Plays Incorporated, www.newplaysforchildren.com; Dramatic Publishing, www.dramaticpublishing.com; Samuel French, www.samuelfrench.com

LOWELL SWORTZELL

PLUMMER, Louise
Author, n.d., Netherlands

P. writes YA novels about TEENAGE girls that vary from humorous and sarcastic to deep and introspective. *My Name is Sus5an Smith, The 5 is Silent* (1991) tells the story of a young artist who wants to reconnect with her uncle. Sus5an loves and idolizes him, even though he abandoned her aunt ten years earlier. When she meets him again during the summer she spends in Boston, she decides to prove her love to him. When he betrays her trust, even Sus5an realizes that his reputation was well-deserved. *The Unlikely Romance of Kate Bjorkman* (1995) is about a teenage girl who hopes for romance with her older brother's friend who comes to stay with their family over Christmas vacation. The story is told in the form of Kate's ROMANCE novel (written with the help of *The Romance Writer's Phrase Book*). In a unique format, chapters of the book alternate between Kate's novel and her revision notes. *A Dance For Three* (2000) is the story of a girl whose life changes when she becomes pregnant by her boyfriend. At first, she dreams of the three of them living happily ever after, but her dream is shattered when her boyfriend abuses her and then abandons her. Compounded by her father's DEATH and her mother's mental illness, this is too much for her and she has a nervous breakdown. While in the hospital, she takes the first steps towards putting her life back together.

The Mormon faith is a recurring theme in P.'s novels as well as in her nonfiction book *Thoughts of a Grasshopper: Essays and Oddities* (1992). P. has received literary awards in Young Adult Literature by the Association for Mormon Letters for several of her books.

AWARDS: Association for Mormon Letters Awards: 1991 for *My Name is Sus5an Smith, The 5 is Silent,* 1995 for *The Unlikely Romance of Kate Bjorkman,* and 2001 for *A Dance For Three; School Library Journal's* Best Books of 1995 for *The Unlikely Romance of Kate Bjorkman;* ALA Best Books for Young Adults: 1992 for *My Name is Sus5an Smith, the 5 is Silent,* 2001 for *A Dance for Three.*

FURTHER WORK: *The Romantic Obsessions and Humiliations of Annie Sehlmeier,* 1987.

BIBLIOGRAPHY: Louise P. Info Page, http://deseretbook.com/authors/author-info?author_id = 4841;

Louise P. BYU Faculty Homepage, http://english.byu
.edu/asp/webpages/mainpage.asp?netid = lp9.

ANDREA LIPINSKI

PLUM-UCCI, Carol
Author, b. 16 August 1957, Brigantine, New Jersey

P. writes emotionally intense tales—realistic MYS-
TERY thrillers with a touch of supernatural—that have
engaging, complex characters, gripping storylines,
and dramatic settings, in a voice that speaks to TEENS.
Growing up in a funeral home on a barrier island in
the Pine Barrens, New Jersey, she spent many sleepless nights waiting for a "guest" to come stalking up
the stairs and make a snack out of her. Her mother's
and father's ancestors settled in the Pine Barrens over
twelve generations ago—an area known for many
New Jersey legends such as the *Jersey Devil,* a creature who is half man and half beast.

P. earned a communications degree from Purdue
University, where she received the Kneale Award in
Journalism Excellence in Feature Writing. She is a
former staff writer for the Miss America Organization
who, at age twenty-six, began writing a novel by
adapting a SHORT STORY that took ten years to get
published. The woods and wild ocean of the New Jersey coast are essential to her mysteries, providing
chilling backdrops. She continues to live near the Pine
Barrens, which provide the wild, remote settings for
her novels.

P. decided to write for teenagers because she felt
she could speak to them better than she could to
adults; she feels she relates to younger people with a
carefree mind-set. While none of her novels are gruesome HORROR tales, P. does write dark stories with
compassionate yet realistic situations such as teenage
angst, prejudice, friendship, peer pressure, homophobia, suicide and even the supernatural. She gets her
ideas from situations that kids face everyday, where
someone may be ostracized, understood, beat up, or
suffering a wrong at the hands of others. Her stories,
perhaps embellished from those sleepless nights in
the funeral home filled with dark fantasies, build in
excitement, engage the reader, and are hard to put
down.

When asked on an online *AuthorChat* what elements of a good story she felt attracted readers, P.
responded: "First, I think you have to raise questions
that the reader wants the answer to . . . such as,

where's the body? Second, great characters, a character should feel like a new friend. When the story is
over, if a reader misses that character . . . feels like
they want more stories about that character . . . the
writer probably has a good thing going. Finally . . .
realism, especially with teenagers." (*AuthorChat* online, June 28, 2004)

Her books combine these elements in well-crafted,
exciting stories. She writes from an adult perspective
through the voice of a teenager and considers her
writing to be more for adults than for children, while
focusing on teenagers. She is not trying to teach a
lesson or a moral, but wants to tell a good story that
draws readers in and makes them think.

P.'s first published novel, *The Body of Christopher
Creed,* tells the story of the disappearance of a high-
school's geeky outcast, Christopher Creed, whose last
E-mail message to the principal suggested he would
commit suicide. Torey, the narrator, is a popular football player who has known Creed since childhood; his
conscience nags him for not being more tolerant and
accepting of Chris. While gossip and suspicion of
murder are cast towards the school's "bad kids,"
Torey befriends those from the boondocks—outsiders
with lousy homes and few breaks—in his search for
Chris, and realizes many truths about himself, his
friends, and Chris. This complex tale of alienation,
friendship, and the importance of FAMILY, set near an
Indian burial ground in the dark woods, is woven with
fine characterizations and with an open-ended conclusion, leaving the reader almost breathless.

P., mother of two children, stays involved with
worthy causes in her community. She has worked
with groups promoting literacy worldwide and has
raised money for refugee Afghani children through
UNICEF. She now teaches writing at Atlantic Community College in Mays Landing, New Jersey, close
to her home. She loves connecting with students and
the fact that they listen to her and take her advice. As
the youngest of her family, she was not accustomed
to being taken seriously. But with three successful
novels to her credit and four outstanding contracts
with publishers ahead of her, more exciting and suspenseful tales can be expected from this author of
taut, gripping mysteries.

AWARDS: Kneale Award in Journalism Excellence in
Feature Writing, Purdue University, *One Book New
Jersey Author,* 2004. *The Body of Christopher Creed,*
2000: Michael L. PRINTZ Award Honor Book, 2001;

Best Books for Young Adults, 2001; American Library Association Children's Choices, 2001; International Reading Association; Edgar Allen Poe Award Finalist for 2001 Best Young Adult Novel; South Carolina Young Adult Book Award Winner 2003; and nominated for nine other states' YOUNG ADULT reading awards. *What Happened to Lani Garver,* 2002: Best Books for Young Adults, 2003, American Library Association; New York Public Library Book for the Teen Age, 2003; Teen Top Ten List (voted #2) 2003, YALSA, American Library Association.

FURTHER WORKS: *What Happened to Lani Garver,* 2002; *The She,* 2003.

BIBLIOGRAPHY: Carol P. chat. AuthorChats.com, November 1, 2001, http://www.authorchats.com/archives / viewArchive.jsp?id = 20011101CarolPlumUcci.jsp&t = Carol + Plum-Ucci&jrunsessionid = 1086390358073248280; with author e-mail, August 6, 2004. *Town Topics,* June 23, 2004. "One Book New Jersey Author Is Inspired by Her Childhood." from http://www.towntopics.com / jun2304 / other4.html; Yount, Caroline. Writing her way to the top. *Rutgers Focus,* April 6, 2001, http://ur.rutgers.edu/focus/index.phtml?Article_ID = 701&Issue_ID = 89.

LAURENE MADSEN

POETRY FOR YA: A GOLDEN AGE

James Dickey said, "What you have to realize . . . is that P. is just naturally the greatest thing that ever was in the whole universe. If you love it, there's no substitute for it."

Getting teenagers to share Dickey's love affair with poems may just be easier today than ever before. The ubiquitous rhythm and rhyme of rap on the radio, the popularity of poetry slams, the ever-expanding number of websites where adolescents post and reach each other's creative writing, and the wonderful diversity of P. books published for YAS have all converged to place us in a golden age for TEENS and P. in the early 21st century.

The world of P. for young adults changed dramatically when teacher and poet Mel GLENN wrote his first book of poems for and about teenagers. *Class Dismissed! High School Poems* was published in 1982. The success of Glenn's collection of original poems featuring adolescent concerns and teens as main characters turned the spotlight bright green for publishers to speed ahead with books of poetry written especially for adolescents. Glenn's book was named a Best Book for Young Adults by the American Library Association. Glenn's collections of poems gradually evolved into novels told in poetic form. Perhaps because of fewer words on a page, format that demanded quick turning of pages, or the short length of the books, teen readers embraced this new kind of novel written for them.

Virginia Euwer WOLFF set a high standard with her poem–novel *Make Lemonade* (1994). It is about fourteen-year-old LaVaughn and her attempts to help an unwed mother and her FAMILY. Karen HESSE won the Newbery Award for *Out of the Dust* (1998), acclaimed as a poem cycle that reads like a novel. Three years later, *True Believer,* Wolff's sequel to *Make Lemonade,* received the National Book Award. Many other poetry–novels followed, most recently Kathy APPELT's *My Father's Summers: A Daughter's Memoir* (2004) and Paul JANECZKO's story of the Ringling Brothers & Barnum and Bailey Circus disaster of 1944, *Worlds Afire* (2004). Hesse calls *Worlds Afire* "a searing account . . . that readers will not easily forget."

Just as Mel Glenn played a pivotal role in P. for YA, so did Paul Janeczko. Building on his years of teaching adolescents, Janeczko continues to compile some of the most heralded anthologies of poetry for high-school readers. Janeczko's gifts include his network of contemporary poets, his knowledge of small presses that are the lifeline for keeping contemporary poetry alive, and his keen sense of what teenagers care about. His collections are not divided into the typical subsections of P. about love or death or nature, but rather are cycles of poems grouped to play off each other. This arrangement allows teen readers to create their own connections from poem to poem. More than any other person, Paul Janeczko is responsible for introducing new poets to YA and to the teachers and LIBRARIANS who work with teenagers. For twenty-five years Janeczko's books have been praised and earned him as many Best Books for YA citations as Robert CORMIER.

While Janeczko's collections introduced a different format for poetry anthologies aimed at high-school readers, format has changed in another way. Poetry presented in the PICTURE BOOK format has entered the world of books for young adults. Chestnuts such as Frost's "Stopping by the Woods on a Snowy Evening" and "Birches," Noyes's "The Highwayman," and Tennyson's "The Lady of Shalott" have been published in beautiful picture books.

Arguments against these books center around breaking up the careful structuring of the overall poem to fit the picture book format. A greater concern to some poets and educators is articulated by the late poet and commentator Myra Cohn Livingston. She writes that we ought to be encouraging youngsters "to make their own pictures" instead of "presenting them with an illustration for every set of words today. Thus like TV viewers they can no longer make their own" (Livingston, 1989). These arguments aside, a segment of adolescent readers embraces such books and appreciates the help the illustrations often give in understanding the poem. A few lines on a page seem easier to approach than seeing the whole poem without visual breaks. With such gifted illustrators as Ed Young, Ted Harrison, and Christopher Bing teaming up with wordsmiths Robert Frost, Robert Service, and Ernest Lawrence Sayers, today's readers can experience poetry visually as well.

What hasn't changed in poetry for young adults is what they like. Decades of poetry preference research yield the following findings: Narrative poetry is favored in grades 7–12 while the haiku form is most disliked; adolescents in grades 7–12 prefer humorous poems, including limericks. An appreciation of more subtle humor in poetry increases as teens move from middle school into the late high-school years; rhythm and rhyme are important attributes of favored poetry in early adolescence and are of less importance as students mature; In the early teen years, adolescents prefer modern P. over traditional or CLASSIC pieces; figurative language often interferes with junior-high students' attempts to understand poetry. As teenagers mature, this becomes less of a stumbling block (Abrahamson 2002).

When teens are free to choose what they like, the humor of Jack Prelutsky, Shel Silverstein, and Judith Viorst still touch the funny bone and stand in stark contrast to the poems typically found in literature textbooks for teenagers—poems by such writers as Shakespeare, Dickinson, and Wordsworth.

The good news is that at the dawn of the 21st century, YA have more books of P. aimed at them than ever before. From exceptional compilations of contemporary poems that speak to adolescent concerns to collections of original poems written especially for teens to novels told in poetry form to picture book versions of a single poem, a cornucopia of poetic possibilities is available to help convince young adults

that, "poetry is just naturally the greatest thing that ever was in the whole universe."

BIBLIOGRAPHY: Abrahamson, Richard F. "Poetry Preference Research: What Young Adults Tell Us They Enjoy." *Voices from the Middle* 10, no. 2 December 2002, p. 22; Appelt, Kathy. *My Father's Summers: A Daughter's Memoir,* 2004. Livingston, Myra Cohn. Letter to *School Library Journal* 35, no. 6, 1989: 60; Hesse, Karen. *Out of the Dust,* 1998. Janeczko, Paul. *Worlds Afire,* 2004; Glenn, Mel. *Class Dismissed! High School Poems,* 1982. Wolff, Virginia Euwer. *Make Lemonade,* 1994; Wolff, Virginia Euwer, *True Believer,* 2001.

RICHARD F. ABRAHAMSON
AND BETTY CARTER

PORTER, Connie Rose
Author, b. 1959, New York City

P. grew up in Lackawanna, New York (near Buffalo). She began writing POETRY when she was fourteen years old, making use of the typewriter her parents bought her for Christmas (Maughan, 2004). After completing a B.A. from the State University of New York, Albany, in 1981, and an M.F.A. in creative writing from Louisiana State University in 1987, she began teaching creative writing.

Her first novel, *All-bright Court* (1991), received many notable acknowledgments. "P. has written a beautiful and profound first novel," says Anne Whitehouse, reviewer for the *New York Times Book Review* (1991). Set in the 1960s and 1970s, the book deals with the hardships faced by a community of black FAMILIES who move from the South to the North to work in a steel mill outside Buffalo, New York.

Because of the success of this first novel, Pleasant Company, the publishers of the American Girls books, asked P. to write the Addy books, notes Lan Elliott (1994). Since 1993, P. has written at least ten titles for the American Girls' Addy SERIES. The books, beginning in the final year of the Civil War, follow an AFRICAN-AMERICAN girl, Addy, from the tobacco fields in North Carolina, through a riveting escape to freedom in the North, and into and out of many subsequent ADVENTURES. The books have been praised for the "honest" picture of slavery they present (Sutton 1993, p. 69) and the "good balance of emotion, historical facts, and suspense [that] keep readers interested" (Soltan 1994, p. 67).

Amid the popular Addy books, P. published the "beautifully realized novel" (Higbie, 1999, p. 17)

Imani All Mine in 1999. The novel relates the story of an intelligent young black woman who is raped and her subsequent decision to keep the baby and raise her in the violent Buffalo neighborhood in which she lives. "P. goes beyond the TEENAGER mother stereotype," says Lyn Miller-Lachmann, writing for *MULTICULTURAL Review,* "to present a heroine full of courage and love for her child and ready to face the difficulties and responsibilities of her life" (1999, p. 79).

P. has taught creative writing at the high-school (Milton Academy in Massachusetts) and college (Emerson College and Southern Illinois University, Carbondale) levels. She now lives in Virginia Beach, Virginia.

AWARDS: *All-bright Court: New York Times* Notable Book; Editors' Choice, Adult Books for Young Adults, 1991 (American Library Association-*Booklist*); Notable Books, 1991 (American Library Association-RASD); *Imani All Mine:* Alex Awards, 2000 (American Library Association-YOUNG ADULT LIBRARY SERVICE ASSOCIATION-Adult Books for Young Adults Task Force); Best Books for Young Adults, 2000, Top ten (American Library Association); Editors' Choice, Adult Books for Young Adults, 1999 (American Library Association-*Booklist*).

BIBLIOGRAPHY: *Contemporary Authors Online,* 2002, http://www.galenet.com/servlet/LitRC?finalAuth = true; Elliot, L. "Connie P.: Telling It the Way It Was." *Teaching PreK–8,* 25 (1994), 40–42; Maughan, S. "Author: Connie P." http://aol.kidsreads.com/authors/au-porter-connie.asp; Soltan, R. "Review of *Addy Saves the Day: A Summer Story.*" *School Library Journal,* 40 (1994), 106; Sutton, R. "Review of *Meet Addy: An American Girl.*" *Bulletin of the Center for Children's Books,* 47 (1993), 55.

MARY MCMILLAN TERRY

POTOK, Chaim (Herman Harold)

Author, educator, rabbi, b. 17 February 1929, New York City; d. 23 July 2002, Merion, Pennsylvania

P., the eldest of four siblings, was brought up in an Orthodox Jewish home in the Bronx. Since his FAMILY was too poor to purchase toys, P. amused himself by reading.

P. received his B.A. in English literature in 1950 from Yeshiva University. Four years later, he received his M.H.L. from the Jewish Theological Seminary of America. P. entered the United States Army in 1955 to serve as a chaplain in the Korean War, helping both a front-line medical battalion and an engineer combat battalion. In 1957, P. was employed as an instructor at the University of Judaism in Los Angeles, California. He also was the director of Camp Ramah in Ojai, California. After his marriage to Adena Mosevitzsky in 1958, P. spent four years as a scholar-in-residence at Har Zion Temple in Philadelphia. In 1964, he became managing editor of *Conservative Judaism* and, the following year, he became editor-in-chief of the Jewish Publication Society of America, a post he continued to hold through 1974. P. received his Ph.D. in philosophy from the University of Pennsylvania in 1965; he later returned to the University of Pennsylvania in 1983 and during 1992–98 as a visiting professor. He also served as visiting professor at Bryn Mawr College in 1985 and at Johns Hopkins University from 1995–98.

P. was an ordained rabbi as well as a scholar of Judaic texts. His devotion to both the religious and the secular world resulted in opposing demands that provided him with themes for his writing such as cultural conflicts and, ultimately, cultural choices. *The Chosen* was published in 1967, and to this day is one of P.'s most beloved and potent works. The author probes into the American Jewish Hasidim and Orthodox subcultures in the 1940s, a critical point in history for Jews. Reuven Malter, an Orthodox Jewish boy from Williamsburg, Brooklyn, becomes a friend to Danny Saunders, the son of a Hassidic *tzaddik.* Unbeknownst to Reuven at the time of their meeting, his scholarly father has been Danny's introductory guide to scientific and philosophic literature. As the friends grow older, Danny's struggle between the limits of Hasidism and the intellectual wealth of the secular world threatens his fragile relationship with his father, Rebbe Saunders. Reuven becomes the intermediary for Rebbe Saunders and Danny and discovers how complicated the promise of friendship can be. The story is constructed around the end of World War II and the rise of the Zionist movement in the United States. Intellectualism and spiritualism are the grounds for clashes between fathers, between each son and his own father, and between the two young men. Both belief methods are used to explore the love between fathers, sons, and the most loyal of friends.

The Chosen gains immense literary strength through symbolism such as a baseball game, Reuven's friends in the hospital, and P.'s constant references to sight, which run throughout the novel. In the story, the baseball game is simply a contest between schools and that brings Reuven and Danny together. Symbolically, the game represents two groups of Jews playing the "greatest American past-time," baseball; they, as Jews, can be as American as everyone else. Published two years later, *The Promise* continues with the lives of Reuven and Danny during their post-college years. Reuven pursues his rabbinical ordination at the Hirsch Yeshiva while Danny, no longer a Hasidic Jew, studies psychology at Columbia. Once again, P. brings to the pages of his work the clash of differing schools of Jewish religious thought, and textual critical versus literalist study of the Talmud.

P. credited the books *Brideshead Revisited* by Evelyn Waugh and *A Portrait of the Artist as a Young Man* by James Joyce as the two most influential novels in his decision to become a writer. P. achieved the status of novelist and scholar, and he was also known as a professor, historian, rabbi, editor, and playwright. During his lifetime, he divided his time between the Philadelphia area and Jerusalem. His writing has been translated into every major language in the world. P. also wrote SHORT STORIES and contributed articles to the following publications: *TriQuarterly, Commentary, Reconstructionist, Moment, Esquire, American Judaism, Forward, Saturday Review, New York Times Book Review, Kenyon Review, American Voice,* and *New England Review.*

P.'s children, Rena, Naama, and Akiva, have followed their father's interest in literature and in photography. His hobbies included oil painting and photography.

SELECT AWARDS: 1967 Edward Lewis Wallant Award, *The Chosen;* 1969 Athenaem Prize, *The Promise;* 1997 Honorary Doctorate in Humane Letters from La Sierra University; 1997 National Foundation for Jewish Culture Achievement Award; 1997 National Jewish Book Award for Fiction, *The Gift of Asher Lev;* 1997 Honorary Doctorate in Humane Letters from La Sierra University; 1999 O. Henry Award, "Moon"; 2000 Distinguished Arts Award from the Pennsylvania Council on the Arts; ALA Best Books for Young Adults: *The Chosen,* 1967; *Promise,* 1969; *My Name is Asher Lev,* 1972, *Zebra and Other Stories,* 1999.

FURTHER WORKS: *Jewish Ethics,* pamphlet series, 14 vols., 1964–69; *The Jew Confronts Himself in American Literature,* 1965; *My Name is Asher Lev,* 1972; *In the Beginning,* 1975; *Wanderings: Chaim Potok's History of the Jews,* 1978; *The Book of Lights,* 1981;

Davita's Harp, 1985; *Ethical Living for a Modern World,* 1985; *Theo Tobiasse: Artist in Exile,* 1986; *The Gift of Asher Lev,* 1990; *I Am the Clay,* 1992; *The Tree of Here,* 1993; *The Sky of Now,* 1995; *The Gates of November: Chronicles of the Slepak Family,* 1996; *Zebra and Other Stories,* 1998; *Isaac Stern: My First Seventy-nine Years,* 1999; *The Chosen* (PLAY) (with Aaron Posner), 2001; *Old Men at Midnight,* 2001.

BIBLIOGRAPHY: Krementz, Jill. *The Jewish Writer,* 1998; Magill, Frank, ed. *Cyclopedia of World Authors,* rev. 3rd ed., 1989; Walden, Daniel, ed. *Conversations with Chaim Potok,* 2001; Wilson, Kathleen, ed. *Major 20th Century Writers,* 2nd ed., vol. 4., 1999; *Contemporary Authors Online,* 2002.

SANDRA KITAIN

POWELL, Randy
Author, technical writer, educator, b. 26 August 1956, Seattle, Washington

P.'s teaching background at an alternative school for junior high and high-school dropouts has given him valuable insight into TEENAGERS' psyches, particularly adolescent males. He is also a former faculty member of the Vermont College Master of Fine Arts Program in Children's Literature.

P. uncannily portrays the uncertainty and confusion many teenagers feel during their high-school years in his novels. P. loves SPORTS, particularly tennis, and this love of many types of sports is always a theme present in his books and helps explain why his novels have such great appeal for teenagers. Despite this, the game of baseball, although a major part of the story, is not even played in the baseball-themed novel *Dean Duffy* (1995). His main focus in all of his books is on teenagers who are adrift and trying to find their place in the world. All of P.'s books are about characters that have some kind of problem to solve. P uses humor to reveal his multidimensional characters' vulnerabilities and flaws with great accuracy and compassion. His knack for using humor to examine the lives of teens is evident in clever novels such as *Is Kissing A Girl Who Smokes like Licking an Ashtray?* (1992), *My Underrated Year* (1988), or *Tribute to Another Dead Rock Star* (1999). He has been compared at times to Ron KOERTGE and Chris CRUTCHER.

All of P.'s novels focus on the importance of FAMILY relationships and most contain a bit of ROMANCE as well. Unlike other YOUNG ADULT novels, adults play a pivotal role in many of his novels and frequently act as mentors or role models. P.'s novels reflect reality by having ambiguous endings that allow a reader to decide for him or herself what happens. *My Underrated Year* (1988), P.'s first novel, features a teenage boy whose success as a football and tennis player is threatened when new team members threaten his superior status. P. considers *Is Kissing A Girl Who Smokes like Licking an Ashtray?* (1992) his most quirky and one of his most memorable novels. It portrays the relationship between a shy, ex-pinball addict who's attracted to his polar opposite: the niece of friends of the family, an outspoken, wisecracking cigarette smoker with an irresistible talent for trouble. *Dean Duffy* (1995) is about a teen struggling to deal with the loss of his ability to play baseball, the major focus of his life. A teenage girl struggling with a slump in her tennis career and her lifelong best friend, a teenage boy who works as her tennis coach, face similar career struggles in P.'s funny novel *The Whistling Toilets* (1996), one of P.'s admittedly more AUTOBIOGRAPHICAL books. Idolization of dead rock stars is featured in *Tribute to Another Dead Rock Star* (1999), detailing a teenage boy's conflicted feelings for his dead rock star mother and those she left behind, including his mentally disabled younger half-brother. Families that have dysfunctional relationships are a staple of young adult literature, but P.'s description of Louie, the mentally disabled half-brother, is an excellent portrayal of someone with this affliction. *Run if You Dare* (2001) realistically portrays an unmotivated teenager forced to turn his life around or face repeating the same disappointing life choices that his father has. Three guys are forced to reexamine their prejudices and long-held beliefs when, while looking to replace a flag football team member; they discover that the best candidate is a girl with unshaven legs, in the witty *Three Clams and an Oyster* (2002).

P. prefers writing for teens instead of adults about what interests him. His honest and humorous character portrayals and situations are the reasons his novels are so appealing to teens. One young reader was reportedly inspired to try playing tennis after reading *The Whistling Toilets*. All of his books have a strong sense of place and are set in Seattle, where he was born and grew up. He says he doesn't have a favorite novel. There are certain things that make each one his favorite in a different way. He rewrote *Dean Duffy* (1995) the most times. The one that he's the most

sentimental about is his debut novel, *My Underrated Year* (1988). P. thinks the one that has the best characterizations is *Tribute to Another Dead Rock Star* (1999), while *Run if You Dare* (2001) is the most unappreciated. *Tribute to Another Dead Rock Star* (1999) has been optioned for a film and his novels have been nominated for several state reading awards.

AWARDS: Best Books for Young Adults American Library Association citation and Pen West Award for Children's Literature, 1993, for *Is Kissing A Girl Who Smokes Like Licking An Ashtray?;* Best Books for Young Adults and Quick Picks for Young Adults (American Library Association citations, 1996, for *Dean Duffy;* Junior Literary Guild selection, 1999, Best Books for Young Adults (American Library Association) citation, 2000, ALA Popular Paperbacks, 2004, for *Tribute to Another Dead Rock Star;* Best Books for Young Adults (American Library Association) citation, 2003, for *Three Clams And An Oyster.*

BIBLIOGRAPHY: *Authors and Artists for Young Adults,* vol. 35, 2000; *Contemporary Authors,* vol. 190, 2001; e-mail from Randy P., May 25, 2004; *Something about the Author,* vol. 118, 2001; Randy P. website, http://www.randypowell.com

SHARON L. RAWLINS

PRATCHETT, Terry
Author, b. 28 April 1948, Beaconsfield, Buckinghamshire, England

P., Britain's most-popular living fiction writer, has never received a rejection slip. His first SHORT STORY was published in *Science FANTASY MAGAZINE* when he was fifteen and his first novel, *The Carpet People* (1971, rev. ed. 1993)—an epic saga of microscopic people living deep in the pile of a carpet—was accepted when he was only seventeen.

Educated at the Beaconsfield Public Library (by giving himself multiple borrowing privileges while a volunteer helper), P. took up journalism, which gave him "an accelerated course in human nature." As a reporter, he learned the power of a person armed only with notebook and pencil. A spell in public-relations work for several nuclear-power stations helped hone his sense of humor. Writing in his spare time, P. published several novels before *The Colour of Magic* (1983) launched the Discworld fantasy SERIES, whose success (some thirty novels by 2004), enabled him to become a fulltime writer.

Married to Lyn, with one daughter Rhianna, P. lives "behind a keyboard" near Salisbury in Wiltshire, and raises carnivorous plants. All other information about P.'s private life is kept confidential but his Discworld series has created a worldwide army of dedicated fans who pack his public-speaking tours, the best after-sales service offered by any writer.

Although the Discworld books are regarded as adult, they have a wide following among adolescents, and several main characters are very young, including Susan and Imp in *Soul Music,* Mort in *Mort,* and Eskarina in *Equal Rites.* P. impishly explains, "I write for both adults and kids. It's good to write about DEATH, love, hope, and immortality but I have to simplify things a bit when I write for adults."

P.'s stories for young people are in the long tradition of intelligent children's literature. The Bromeliad Trilogy began with *Truckers* (1990) where a nome (gnome) civilization lives secretly within a department store. These four-inch people have created their society around their shop, complete with customs, MYTHS (Sun and Rain are ancient legends), and religious beliefs (they worship Arnold Bros Est 1905). It takes the plucky rat-hunting outsider, Masklin, to get the nomes to come out of the woodwork, when he realizes the store is to be demolished. Their epic escape in a hi-jacked truck is a very funny highlight. Later volumes, *Diggers* (1990) and *Wings* (1990), continue the exodus, describing in droll detail, the nomes' ADVENTURES in a quarry, Masklin's trip to Florida by Concorde, the capture of a satellite and their space-faring destiny.

In *Only You Can Save Mankind* (1992) Johnny Maxwell is the sort of twelve-year-old boy that nobody notices, an outsider's outsider. Johnny, who lives in Blackbury (the setting of *Truckers*), plays a space-aliens computer game and learns that life is not a game. He and the highly intelligent Kirsty find that they are responsible for saving an entire alien civilization of blue-blooded alligators. With typically Pratchettian references to films (such as *Alien*), TV news, pop MUSIC, and myths, *Only You Can Save Mankind* holds a witty distorting mirror up to society.

In the sequel, *Johnny and the Dead* (1994), Johnny meets the long-dead inhabitants of the Blackbury Cemetery. He and his friends try to thwart attempts "to develop" the graveyard, but the real charm of this book lies in the colorful personalities of the ghosts. With their rivalry, guilty secrets, disputes, and snobbery, the dead are the liveliest feature of a witty story. *Johnny and the Bomb* (1997) is equally vivid, but this time Johnny and Kirsty are drawn into a time-travel paradox, switching between their own familiar Blackbury and the one that was (or is going to be, or may not be) bombed in 1941. Their efforts to prevent disaster are exciting, the period detail is painfully accurate (deeply offending Kirsty), past and present interlock superbly, and P.'s skillful combination of tragedy and humor is as effective as ever. Best of all, the reader gradually realizes that there are fewer characters in this novel than there seem to be.

In 2001 P. broke new ground (and won the Carnegie Medal) by writing a Discworld novel for young readers, *The Amazing Maurice and His Educated Rodents.* P. insists that he worked harder on *Maurice* than he ever worked before, and the result is a graceful modern CLASSIC. The eponymous Maurice, a highly intelligent cat, is working a crafty plague-of-rats swindle with the help of a group of even more intelligent rats, when they discover that the town of Bad Blintz conceals some evil secrets. Younger readers enjoy the spoof on the Hamlin legend and the bold humor (such as rats doing synchronized-swimming in the cream) but, as always with P.'s writing, there are extra rewards concealed in the text. For example, the rats (who gained their high IQs due to exposure to toxic cauldron waste in a wizards' dump) are fascinated by a saccharine children's story called *"Mr. Bunnsy Has an Adventure."* "There's no sub-text, no social commentary," complains Malicia, who represents the non-rat aspect of the girl-power in this story.

There is plenty of girl-power in *The Wee Free Men* (2003), P.'s second "young" Discworld novel. Although the Mac Nac Feegle (the Wee Free Men of the title) surge through the story like Smurfs from a Glasgow slum, the tale is dominated by an equally courageous but utterly unprepossessing heroine, Tiffany Aching, aged nine. When her little brother is kidnapped by the Queen of the Fairies, Tiffany sets out to rescue him, armed only with a frying pan. Although Tiffany clearly has the potential to be a witch (a combination of shrewd woman, psychologist, shaman, and cow-doctor in P.'s cosmology) it is her bond with her dead grandmother that enables her to save the world and rescue the handsome prince. As always, P. takes every accepted belief and turns it neatly upside down.

Tiffany's future as a witch with a virtual pointy hat is developed in the sequel, *A Hat Full of Sky* (2004).

NAOMI SHIHAB NYE

KATHERINE PATERSON

RICHARD PECK

TAMORA PIERCE

DANIEL PINKWATER

RANDY POWELL

PHILIP PULLMAN

LOUISE RENNISON

Despite his O.B.E. (Order of British Empire) for "services to literature," P. says that his novels are neither literature nor SCIENCE FICTION. "I feel like a guy who went to the Wars of the Roses wearing a pink rose." Intelligent, witty, sentimental, cynical and perceptive P. remains about the most refreshing writer in the world.

SELECT AWARDS: 1996, Nestle Smarties Book Prize: Silver Award Winner: *Johnny and the Bomb;* 1997, Carnegie Medal: Shortlist: *Johnny and the Bomb;* 1998, O.B.E. for Services to Literature; 1999, Hon. D. Litt, University of Warwick; 2002, Carnegie Medal: Winner: *The Amazing Maurice and his Educated Rodents;* ALA Best Books for Young Adults: *The Amazing Maurice and His Educated Rodents,* 2002, *The Wee Free Men: A Story of Discworld,* 2004, *A Hat Full of Sky,* 2005.

SELECT FURTHER WORKS: *Truckers,* 1990; *Diggers,* 1990; *Wings,* 1990; *Only You Can Save Mankind,* 1992; *Nightwatch,* 2004; *Going Postal,* 2004.

BIBLIOGRAPHY: Stone, Grant. "Terry P." *Magpies,* 8:1, March 1993, 15–19; Baise, Jennifer. Ed. *Children's Literature Review,* vol. 64, 2000, pp. 17–48; P., Terry and Briggs, Stephen. *The Discworld Companion,* Victor Gollancz, London, 1994; *Authors and Artists for Young Adults,* vol. 19; *Contemporary Authors,* vol. 143; *Something about the Author,* vol. 82; www.nl.lspace.org; www.turtlesalltheway.com.

TREVOR AGNEW

PRESTON, Douglas, and Child, Lincoln

Authors, publishing executive, P. b. 20 May 1956, Boston, Massachusetts; C. b. 13 October 1957, Westport, Connecticut

C., an editor at St. Martin's Press, decided to commission a book about the American Museum of Natural History in New York City. P., a museum employee, was chosen to write the book based on articles he had written about the history of the museum. The result of this commission is *Dinosaurs in the Attic: The Behind-the-Scenes Story of the American Museum of Natural History* (1986).

After this project was completed, P. and C. came up with the idea for their first collaboration, *Relic* (1995), a suspense novel that was set in part in a natural history museum. What appears to be a cursed statue of a half-human, half-reptile god is sent from the Amazon to the museum, leaving a trail of death in its wake. This collaboration was so successful that

P. and C. began writing more suspense novels, including *Mount Dragon* (1996), *Reliquary* (1997), and *The Cabinet of Curiosities* (2002).

In each of their books, P. and C. mix science with suspense. Many of their characters make appearances in several books, giving fans yet another reason to eagerly anticipate their next collaboration. *Still Life With Crows* (2003), for example, features the popular and enigmatic Special Agent Pendergast as its main protagonist. *Mount Dragon* and *Reliquary* were both included on the New York Public Library's Books for the TEEN Age list, and *Relic* was adapted into a major motion picture.

AWARDS: *Relic:* ALA Best Books for Young Adults, 1996; Garden State Teen Book Award Winner, 1998; *Mount Dragon:* Garden State Teen Book Award Winner, 1999.

FURTHER WORKS: *Thunderhead,* 1999; *The Ice Limit,* 2000; *The Cabinet of Curiosities,* 2002; *Still Life with Crows: A Novel,* 2003; *Brimstone,* 2004.

BIBLIOGRAPHY: *Contemporary Authors Online,* 2001; *Something about the Author,* vol. 113, 2000.

ANDREA LIPINSKI

PRESTON, Richard

Author, b. 5 August 1954, Cambridge, Massachusetts

With a spotty high-school academic record that included a suspension for assaulting a teacher, P. was rejected from every college to which he applied. Undeterred, P. placed a collect call to the dean of admissions at Pomona College in California every week until he was admitted. He eventually received his Ph.D. in English from Princeton University in 1983 before beginning a career as a professional writer.

Best known for his highly readable, engrossing accounts on scientific subjects, P. has written many articles for periodicals such as *Discover, Science Illustrated,* and *The New Yorker.* One such article inspired *The Hot Zone* (1994), a best-selling nonfiction book about the deadly Ebola virus. *The Cobra Event* (1997), a suspense novel about bioterrorism, followed. In 2002, P. documented the devastating effects of smallpox and anthrax in *The Demon in the Freezer: A True Story.* This brother of author Douglas Preston also has an asteroid named in his honor.

AWARDS: Science-Writing Award in Physics and Astronomy by a Professional Writer, American Institute of Physics, 1988; Eugene McDermott Award in the

Arts, Massachusetts Institute of Technology, 1992; Westinghouse Award, American Association of Arts and Sciences, 1993; *Hot Zone:* ALA Best Books for Young Adults, 1996.

FURTHER WORKS: *First Light: The Search for the Edge of the Universe,* 1987; *American Steel: Hot Metal Men and the Resurrection of the Rust Belt,* 1991.

BIBLIOGRAPHY: *Literature Resource Center,* online database, 2003; *The Official Richard P. website,* http://www.randomhouse.com/features/richard preston/, 2003

KAREN ALGEO KRIZMAN

PRICE, Susan

Author, b. 8 July 1955, Oldbury, England

"Born and raised in the Black Country" is the proud claim of P., who still lives in the West Midlands, where she grew up. Her family's rented house was in a slum, with mice, cockroaches, and a shared toilet. When P. was four they moved to a council house closer to Dudley. This part of Britain is where the Industrial Revolution began. The Titanic's anchor chain was forged in Dudley and the Netherton Canal tunnel actually ran beneath P.'s childhood home. (In 1975 P. recreated a strike from the region's industrial past in *Twopence a Tub.*)

Educated at Tividale Comprehensive, P. hated school, an experience mirrored in *From Where I Stand* (1984), and turned to reading, particularly Rudyard Kipling's *Jungle Book* and the fairy tales of Hans Christian Andersen. She had told stories and written from an early age, often winning prizes. Her first novel, *The Devil's Piper* (1973), was accepted for publication when she was only sixteen (so that her father had to sign the book contract) and was published before she left school. This tale of children kidnapped by a "luchorpan" (leprechaun) already shows P.'s skillful use of dialect and confident adaptation of mythical materials.

After supporting herself as a dishwasher, museum guide, and supermarket check-out worker—experiences reflected in *Sticks and Stones* (1976)—P. was able to become a full-time writer in 1981.

Her Carnegie Medal–winning novel *The Ghost Drum* (1986), with its strongly Slavic atmosphere, reflects P.'s intereset in Russian fairy stories and Polish folklore, inspired by her Polish uncle. At midwinter eve, a slave's wish is granted and her baby is taken away by a shaman to be raised as a "woman of power." *Ghost Dance* (1992) and *Ghost Song* (1994) complete the Ghost World SERIES, maintaining the same mixture of original storytelling within the authentic atmosphere of northern folktales.

Odin's Monster (1986) draws on Icelandic traditions in its narration and mood, while many of P.'s stories are in the style of Scandinavian myths, legends, and sagas. An interesting feature of P.'s writing is her subtle use of narrators within stories: anything from a cat *(Ghost Drum)* to a lopped-off head found on a battlefield *(The King's Head).*

An important aspect of P.'s fiction is the inclusion of OUTCAST figures, such as homeless Joe in *The Sterkarm Handshake* and bereaved Zoë and unemployed Duncan in *The Bearwood Witch* (2001).

A recurring figure in P.'s fiction is the Shaman, the one who "knows all the magics." With the power to talk to animals and ghosts, change shape (like the "ancient woman in Lappish clothes" in *The Ghost Drum*) or even to summon the dead (like Mrs. Beckerdyke in *The Bearwood Witch*), the Shaman is in touch with the other side of life: "Cold, dark, disease, DEATH, WAR, discord."

P. has retold traditional nursery stories in The Kingfisher Treasury of Nursery Stories, (illus. Colin and Moira McLean) (1990) and in PICTURE BOOKS like *Goldilocks and the Three Bears* (1999), but she has also shown great originality in adapting some stories. *The Runaway Chapati* (ill. Stephen Waterhouse) (1999), for example, has a little Indian girl baking a chapati, which runs away pursued by a monkey and a crocodile, until a tiger provides the fate usually reserved for the Gingerbread Man. *In a Nutshell* (1983), the story of two tiny people, was illustrated by her sister, Alison Price.

P.'s sense of humor appears in witty junior novels like *Hairy Bill* (2002). Her SHORT STORIES—many of them with ghostly themes, such as the memorable "Overheard In A Graveyard"—appear in such collections as *Nightcomers* (1997) and *Here Lies Price* (1987). P. also writes superb HORROR stories, such as *The Wolf-Sisters* (2001), where a Saxon warrior encounters werewolves with terrifying consequences.

P.'s masterpiece is *The Sterkarm Handshake* (1998), a richly atmospheric picture of the 16th century reivers (raiders) of the Scottish-English border country. When FUP, a 21st century corporation, builds a time tunnel to exploit the area's resources, its staff use aspirins as trade goods and pose as Elves with magic powers. Andrea—a sympathetic anthropologist—experiences the warmth of life in the Sterkarm family, but her love for Per, the chief's son, is doomed as conflict develops between the two groups.

P. is skillful in showing the different perceptions of her characters. Thus Windsor, an insensitive executive, despises the Sterkarms as savages, their tower as cramped and dirty, and Andrea as fat. Per is appalled by the roads of the future but exhilarated by the skirmishes and violence that so disturb Andrea. Per sees Andrea as bonny and desirable, "all plump warm curves," knowing that a thin woman might be ill or infertile. In addition, P. has integrated ballads and folktales so smoothly into her narrative that the reader experiences their emotional power as strongly as the borderers do. The conclusion, where the Sterkarms launch a raid into the 21st-century corporation headquarters, is both exciting and moving.

The sequel, *A Sterkarm Kiss* (2003), where the corporation tries to organize marriage bonds between feuding families to pacify the border, is equally powerful. Andrea (now working as a barmaid) encounters a Per, seemingly identical to the one she loved in the 16th century, but, since FUP has entered a parallel universe, the new Per is disturbingly different, even driving a car in the 21st century.

The Sterkarm novels succeed as SCIENCE FICTION, action ADVENTURES and historical novels as well as ROMANCES, and a third volume is planned.

P. lives in Dudley, with her Scottish partner and her cat.

SELECT AWARDS: The 1976 Other Award, *Twopence a Tub;* 1987 Carnegie Medal, *The Ghost Drum;* 1999 Guardian Children's Fiction Prize, 2004 ALA Popular Paperbacks, *The Sterkarm Handshake.*

SELECT FURTHER WORKS: *Home from Home,* 1977; *Ghosts at Large,* 1984; *Ghostly Tales,* 1987; *Master Thomas Kat,* 1988; *The Bone Dog,* 1989; *Phantom from the Past,* 1989; *Thunder Pumps,* 1990; *A Feasting of Trolls,* 1990; *Knocking Jack,* 1992; *Head and Tales,* 1993; *Foiling the Dragon,* 1994; *Coming Down to Earth,* 1994; *Elfgift,* 1995; *Hauntings,* 1995; *The Saga of Aslak,* 1995; *Horror Stories,* 1995; *Pedro,* 1997; *The Collector's Stories,* 1998; *A True Spell and Dangerous,* 1998; *The Ghost's Wife,* 1998; *Ghosts and Lies,* 1998; *Telling Tales,* 1999; *The Wolf's Footprint,* 2003.

BIBLIOGRAPHY: Locher, Frances C., ed. *Contemporary Authors,* vol. 105, 1982, 388; *Something about the Author,* vol. 25; Susan P. website (run by her cat) includes a FUP section for the Sterkarm novels: www.susanprice.org.uk

TREVOR AGNEW

MICHAEL L. PRINTZ AWARD

Established in 2000 by the Young Adult Library Services (YALSA), a division of the American Library Association (ALA), the Michael L. Printz Award for Excellence recognizes the best YA book from the previous year's publications. "Best" is defined solely in terms of literary merit. The committee is composed of nine members, four elected and five appointed. The award-winning book may be fiction, nonfiction, POETRY, or an anthology. To be eligible, a title must have been designated by its publisher as being either a young adult book or one published for the age range that YALSA defines as young adult—ages twelve to eighteen. Works of joint authorship or editorship are eligible. In addition to the award-winning book, as many as four honor titles may also be selected. Eligible books must have been published between January 1 and December 31 of the year preceding the announcement of the award. Books previously published in another country are eligible as long as the American edition is published during the period of eligibility. The committee has the option of not giving an award if no title is deemed meritorious.

Since 1966, YALSA has produced an annual list called Best Books for Young Adults, which honors books selected by a committee. This is a list of the best books for young adults, not the best young adult books, so the result is a mix of adult and children's books with crossover appeal and genuine young adult titles. The list does not afford an opportunity for singular young adult titles to receive recognition. There are also several criteria for selecting a book for the list. Literary excellence is one, but popularity is another, and sometimes popularity without much quality is enough to make it. In an attempt to appeal to the wide age range of twelve to eighteen that YALSA serves, the list has grown very long over the years, to a point where eighty-plus titles have made the list in some years.

Until the creation of the P. Award, there was no means by which to distinguish individual works of young adult literature for literary excellence. There were a few half-hearted attempts to put something together. One notable and controversial attempt was the so-called "Walden Award." In 1971, Amelia E. Walden, the author of dozens of novels for young adults published between 1946 and 1977, offered YALSA $25,000 to establish an annual book award that would bear her name. Controversy erupted when Walden attached three conditions, requiring the selection committee to: choose a book relevant to TEENS and that it preferably be fiction; give equal consideration to both literary merit and popularity; and choose a book that reflects a positive approach to life. It was the last criterion, especially, that caused the most controversy. Among other problems would be trying to decide what exactly a "positive approach" means.

In 1998, YALSA then-president Michael CART formed a YA Book Award Feasibility Task Force to try again at establishing an award for literary excellence in young adult literature. Composed of academics, public and school librarians, and representatives of the publishing industry, the task force was able to compromise on individual differences and quickly reached a consensus. The first awards committee was formed in 1999 so that the first award could be announced at the American Library Association midwinter conference in January 2000.

The award was named in honor of Michael L. P., a high-school LIBRARIAN in Topeka, Kansas, and a much-loved, much-respected, longtime member of YALSA who died at age fifty-nine in 1996. He had a great passion for books and reading and always looked for innovative ways of instilling that same passion in teens. It is for that reason the award was named for him.

The first recipient of the P. was *Monster* by Walter Dean MYERS, a gritty, innovative story about a sixteen-year-old convicted murderer who records his prison experiences in the form of a MOVIE script. The second recipient of the award was David ALMOND's *Kit's Wilderness,* a novel about a young boy who returns with his FAMILY to their northern England town where generations of his family have worked and died. Korean-American author An Na won the third award for her novel *A Step from Heaven,* the story of a young Korean girl and her family struggling to adjust to a new life in America. The 2003 P. went to *Postcards from No Man's Land* by Aidan CHAMBERS, a complex, mature novel that alternates between two stories—one contemporary and one historical. A recent winner of the P. is Angela JOHNSON's novel *The*

First Part Last, the story of an AFRICAN AMERICAN teenage boy who copes with the changes that come to his life when he becomes a father and must care for his baby daughter.

BIBLIOGRAPHY: Almond, David. *Kit's Wilderness,* 2000; Chambers, Aidan. *Postcards from No Man's Land,* 2002; Johnson, Angela. *The First Part Last,* 2003; Myers, Walter Dean. *Monster,* 1999; Na, An. *A Step from Heaven,* 2000; www.ala.org/yalsa/printz/

EDWARD T. SULLIVAN

PULLMAN, Philip

Author, lecturer, b. 19 October 1946, Norwich, England

One of Britain's most beloved children's authors, P. has won international acclaim. As a child, P. spent much time traveling with his parents (his father and stepfather were both in the Royal Air Force). He lived in Africa and Australia, where his interest in the power of story was sparked by comic books; to this day, P. remains a proponent of the inclusion of comics and GRAPHIC NOVELS under the heading of literature. After returning to the UK as a teenager, P. discovered the English poets, including Milton, Blake, and Keats, whose later influence on *His Dark Materials* is evident. He then won a scholarship to Oxford to study English, became a middle-grade English teacher, and worked as a part-time lecturer at Westminster College in Oxford. In 1970, P. married Judith Speller; the couple has two sons.

In 1978, P. published his first novel, *Galatea,* which was marketed towards adults and became "a cult classic among aficionados of SCIENCE FICTION and FANTASY." His first children's book was *Ancient Civilizations* (1978), a nonfiction work that explored cultures of the past. *Count Karlstein* (1982), his first fictional work for children, was adapted from a school play he had written for his students. In 1985 he published his first award-winning work, *The Ruby in the Smoke* (U.S., 1987), the first of a trilogy that introduced the daring yet feminine Sally Lockhart. Set in Victorian England, the trilogy is replete with images of opium dreams, British colonialism, and Dickensian squalor. The story is continued and concluded in *The Shadow in the Plate* (a.k.a. *The Shadow in the Moon*) (1987/88 UK/U.S.) and *The Tiger in the Well* (1990). Characters from the trilogy also appear in *The Tin Princess* (1994).

In addition to writing historical fiction, P. has also published realistic fiction: *The Broken Bridge* (1990/92) and *The White Mercedes* (1993) (reissued as *The Butterfly Tattoo*); the "New Cut Gang" SERIES books: *Thunderbolt's Waxworks* (1994) and *The Gas-Fitter's Ball* (1995); fantasy: *The Firework Maker's Daughter* (1996), *Clockwork, or All Wound Up* (1996/98) and *I Was a Rat!* (2000); and edited *Detective Stories* (1985).

P. is, however, best known for the epic His Dark Materials (HDM) trilogy, including *Northern Lights* (published in the U.S. as *The Golden Compass,* 1995), *The Subtle Knife* (1997), and *The Amber Spyglass* (2000). This richly layered modern fable follows Lyra Belacqua and Will Parry through half a dozen universes in a quest for the source of Dust, a mysterious substance that is at the center of much fear and suspicion. Compared by some critics to *Paradise Lost,* HDM has gained fame and, especially within the Catholic Church, notoriety for its alternative version of the Christian creation story. P. has gained similar attention for his criticism of C. S. LEWIS, whose Chronicles of Narnia are recognized as pro–Christian fables, and for his notion of the Republic of Heaven—the idea that people should build paradise in the here-and-now rather than expect it beyond the grave.

SELECT AWARDS: *The Ruby in the Smoke:* International Reading Association Children's Book Award, the Preis der Leseratten, German TV, and the Lancashire Libraries Children's Book Award, all 1988; ALA Best Books for Young Adults List: *The Ruby in the Smoke* and *Shadow in the North,* 1988; *The Golden Compass,* 1997; *The Subtle Knife,* 1998, *The Amber Spyglass,* 2002. *Northern Lights:* 1996 Carnegie Medal, *Guardian* Children's Fiction Award, and the British Book Award; 1996 Smarties Gold Award, *The Firework-Maker's Daughter;* 1997 Smarties Silver Award, *Clockwork;* the United Kingdom Reading Award and the International Reading Association Children's Book Award, 1998; 2001 Whitbread Book of the Year Award, *The Amber Spyglass* (first work for young people to win the award); 2002 Author of the Year Nibbies Awards; 2002 Eleanor Farjeon Award.

FURTHER WORKS: *Sherlock Holmes and the Adventure of the Sumatran Devil* (PLAY), 1984; *The Three Musketeers* (play, adapted from Alexandre Dumas), 1985; *Frankenstein* (play, adapted from Mary Shelley, 1987); *How to Be Cool,* 1987; *Spring Heeled Jack: A Story of Bravery and Evil,* 1989 UK/1991 U.S.; *Penny Dreadful,* 1989; *The Wonderful Story of Aladdin and the Enchanted Lamp* (retold from the traditional), 1995; *Puss in Boots* (play), 1997; *Mossycoat,* 1998; *Tiger in the Well,* 1991, *Broken Bridge,* 1993, *Lyra's Oxford,* 2003.

BIBLIOGRAPHY: *Achuka,* http://www.achuka.co.uk (11 June 2001), interview with P Alderice, K. "*PW* talks with Philip P.," *Publishers Weekly* 247, September 25, 2000, p. 119; *Artists and Authors for Young Adults,* vol. 41, 2001; *Contemporary Authors Online,* 2003; Interview, http://www.powells.com/authors/pullman.html (August 31, 2000); P., P. "The Republic of Heaven." *Horn Book* 77, November/December 2001, pp. 655–67; Townsend, J. R. "Paradise Reshaped." *Horn Book* 78, July/August 2002, pp. 415–21.

CHRISTINE E. S. BORNE

QUALEY, Marsha

Author, b. 27 May 1953, Austin, Minnesota

An avid reader, Q. also wrote articles for her high school's publications. From 1971 to 1972, Q. studied at MacAlester College in St. Paul, Minnesota. In 1972, she transferred to the University of Minnesota where her studies focused on American history and literature. It was during her college years that Q. began writing regularly, although she did not study creative writing. She earned her B.E.S. in 1976, the same year she married David Qualey. From 1978 to 1989 she was a homemaker and volunteer while raising four children. In 1995, Q. and her family moved to Cloquet, Minnesota, as a result of her husband's work-related transfer. She and her family now live in St. Paul.

Q.'s professional break came when she submitted a SHORT STORY to *Seventeen Magazine*. Although the MAGAZINE was not interested in publishing the story, *Seventeen*'s fiction editor wrote to Q. with some suggestions. In 1990, Q. became a full-time writer and turned the rejected short story into her first book, *Everybody's Daughter* (1991). Sixteen-year-old Beamer is the daughter of the book's title. She grew up on a commune and, as the first child born there, is parented by all the adult commune members. Even after the commune disbands, Beamer still has to deal with all these parental figures, who are the town's primary residents. This novel is the first in a group of interrelated novels that incorporate the same characters. Although not sequels, both *Come in from the Cold* (1994) and *Hometown* (1995) feature protagonists who were secondary characters in *Everybody's Daughter* (1991). Q.'s second novel, *Revolutions of the Heart* (1993), details the experiences of seventeen-year-old Cory Knutson, as she attempts to cope with the grief of her mother's DEATH and the racial prejudice she faces after she begins dating a young Native American man.

Q.'s most AUTOBIOGRAPHICAL novel, *Come in from the Cold* (1994), focuses on Maud and Jeff, characters from *Everybody's Daughter* (1991). Set in 1969–70, Jeff's involvement in the peace movement grows after his brother is killed in the Vietnam War. Maud's sister, an underground radical, was also involved in the antiwar movement and dies during a bombing at a university. Maud and Jeff meet at a peace march, fall in love, marry, and join the Woodlands commune of *Everybody's Daughter* (1991). The other related novel, *Hometown* (1995), takes place during the Persian Gulf War of 1991. Gumbo, a friend of Jeff in *Come in from the Cold* (1994), moved to Canada to avoid the draft during the Vietnam War. Gumbo moves back to his hometown, Red Cedar, with his sixteen-year-old son, Border, who feels the backlash of Gumbo's actions during the previous WAR from his high-school classmates during a period of patriotic fervor.

With her fifth novel, Q. began writing MYSTERIES. In *Thin Ice* (1997), seventeen-year-old Arden Munro searches for answers to her old brother's disappearance. Next came *Close to a Killer* (1999) and *One*

Night (2002); both share the same setting: fictional Dakota City, Minnesota, based on the Minneapolis-St. Paul area. In *Close to a Killer* (1999), another mystery, Barrie Dupre works at her ex-con mother's beauty shop, Killer Looks, which is at the center of a murder investigation.

Popular with YOUNG ADULTS, teachers, and LIBRARIANS, Q.'s books are known for their strong characterizations, particularly female, and their believable dialogue.

AWARDS: American Library Association Best Books for Young Adults: 1994 for *Revolutions of the Heart,* 1995 for *Come in from the Cold,* and 2000 for *Close to a Killer;* ALA Popular Paperbacks, 2004 for *Close to a Killer.*

FURTHER WORK: *One Night,* 2002; *Too Big a Storm,* 2004.

BIBLIOGRAPHY: Barron, Ronald. "Marsha Q.: "One Writes What One Would Read." *The ALAN Review,* vol. 25, no. 1, Fall 1997, http://scholar.lib.vt.edu/ejournals/ALAN/fall97/barron.html; Carter, Betty. *Best Books for Young Adults, Second Edition,* 2000; *Contemporary Authors Online,* 2001; Marsha Q.'s YA Novels website, http://www.marshaqualey.com/; *U*X*L Junior DISCovering Authors,* online edition, 2003.

ANDREW W. HUNTER

QUARLES, Heather
Author, n.d., n.p.

A Door Near Here (1998) is Q.'s thesis for her M.F.A. degree. The novel tells the story of a fifteen-year-old girl named Katherine who is doing everything she can to keep her FAMILY together. Katherine's mother is an alcoholic; when she becomes depressed after losing her husband and her job, she succumbs to her disease and is incapable of taking care of her family. As the days turn into weeks in which her mother won't leave her bed, Katherine tries to take care of her three younger siblings. Simple tasks like getting to school on time, paying bills, and food shopping become huge problems without an adult's supervision. The pressure on the children to conceal their problem from the rest of the world is increased by the threat that the youngest member of the family, eight-year-old Alisa (whose father is unknown), might be taken away and placed in foster care. Alisa, who has always been imaginative, spends more and more time looking for the fictional world of Narnia. Actually, she is looking for the door to Narnia (the "door" of the title), convinced that if she can just find and go through that door, Aslan will come back with her and heal her mother. When one of Katherine's teachers suspects that the children are being neglected and offers to help, the TEEN is driven by fear to make a decision that will have near-disastrous consequences. Katherine's struggle with her role in the family and her attempts to keep her siblings together are poignant and heartfelt. Readers will strongly identify with her character and sympathize with her being forced to assume the position of adult in her family.

AWARDS: Delacorte Press Prize for Best First Young Adult Novel, 1997, ALA Best Books for Young Adults, 1999, for *A Door Near Here.*

BIBLIOGRAPHY: Heather Quarles Author Spotlight, 14 November 2003 http://www.randomhouse.com/author/results.pperl?authorid = 24704

ANDREA LIPINSKI

R

RANDLE, Kristen Downey

Author, b. 8 May 1952, n.p.

A former English teacher, R. grew up all around the United States, including California, New York, and Texas. She attended Brigham Young University and eventually earned a master's degree. R. married a musician with whom she has four children. They live in Utah where they own and operate Rosewood Recording Studio. R. is a member of the Church of Jesus Christ of Latter Day Saints. In her free time, she likes to bead, quilt, cook, and hike.

R. is the author of four YA novels. Two of her novels have been named to the American Library Association Best Books list. The most well known of these is *The Only Alien on the Planet* (1994), which was also awarded the California Young Readers' Medal and was nominated for numerous other awards, and *Breaking Rank* (1999). Her books are filled with well-developed characters that face tough situations and emotional conflicts.

AWARDS: ALA Best Books for Young Adults: *Only Alien on the Planet*, 1996, *Breaking Rank*, 2000.

FURTHER WORKS: *Home Again*, 1981; *One Song for Two*, 1984; *The Morning Comes Singing*, 1986; *On the Side of Angels*, 1989; *Slumming*, 2003; and the PICTURE BOOK *Why Did Grandma Have to Die?*, 1988.

BIBLIOGRAPHY: www.kristen.randle.com; *Something about the Author,* vol. 24, 1997, pp. 197–215; Cuthbertson, Ken. *Authors & Artists,* vol. 34, pp. 171–75.

CHRISTINA MERCEDES KRUGER

RAPP, Adam

Author, playwright, b. 1968, Chicago, Illinois

A prolific playwright, R. is also known for five YA novels that deal graphically and unflinchingly with the darkest aspects of American society. His young protagonists must cope with authority figures who abuse their power, grossly dysfunctional FAMILIES, and all kinds of physical and emotional violence.

R. was raised in a single–parent family in Joliet, Illinois; his mother worked as a prison nurse. R. attended college in Iowa on a basketball scholarship and discovered an immediate affinity for fiction writing. He moved to New York City soon after graduation to write (and to play street basketball, he claims) and his debut novel, *Missing the Piano,* was published in 1994. Living with his actor brother Anthony eventually drew him into writing for the stage as well. R. finds the camaraderie of producing PLAYS a welcome contrast to the seclusion he undergoes when writing a novel.

Many of R.'s books are based on episodes from his own troubled youth, which included stints in a military academy and at reform school. *Missing the Piano* explores the secret hierarchies, racism, and cruelty of military school. *The Buffalo Tree* (1997) portrays reform school as an unrelenting ordeal of brutality and dehumanization. In *The Copper Elephant* (1999), R. creates a hellish futuristic world in which children are used as slave labor and pursued by an evil government called the Syndicate. *Little Chi-*

cago (2002) and *33 Snowfish* (2003) portray children who are runaways, prostitutes, and victims of sexual abuse. In R.'s world, the best that a young person can hope for from an adult is to be ignored. The alternatives are to be betrayed, abused, or murdered.

Reception of R.'s work by adult reviewers tends to be guarded; the language of his books is blunt, the subject matter is grim, and often the protagonist is left facing a BLEAK future. But in general, R.'s honesty and distinctive voice have won him critical praise, and his books can be a helpful starting point for discussion of the difficulties faced by children and TEENS.

AWARDS: 1995 American Library Association Best Book for Young Adults and Best Book for Reluctant Readers, *Missing the Piano;* 2004 ALA Best Books for Young Adults, *33 Snowfish.*

FURTHER WORK: *Under the Wolf, Under the Dog,* 2004.

BIBLIOGRAPHY: *Contemporary Authors Online,* 2003; BIOGRAPHY of R. at Front Street Books website, http://www.frontstreetbooks.com; *American Theatre* interviews, October 2002 and January 1997.

MARY MENZEL

READ, Piers Paul
Author, b. 1941, Beaconsfield, England

Educated by monks in a Catholic school in rural Yorkshire, R. studied history and philosophy before publishing his first novel, *Game in Heaven with Tussy Marx,* in 1966. Three novels followed: *The Junkers* (1968), *Monk Dawson* (1969), and *A Married Man* (1979), all of which were HORROR stories.

Throughout his writings, R. promulgates his theory that Roman Catholicism is the only route to spiritual salvation. Social hypocrisy is one of R.'s favorite themes, as explored in his novels *The Upstart* (1973), *The Professor's Daughter* (1971), and *A Season in the West* (1989). In 1973, *Alive: The Story of the Andes Survivors,* about the survivors' choice to cannibalize each other after their plane crash, won R. a substantial income in royalties. Not surprisingly, considering the subject matter, this book was extremely popular with TEEN readers and was selected for the ALA Best Books for Young Adults list for 1974. Some 250,000 hardcovers and over 4 million copies sold upon the book's publication.

Explaining that he had written the nonfiction work simply to earn enough to enable him to write more

fiction, his first love, R. proclaimed his interest in continuing to explore philosophical and moral ideas through his novels. He worked as adjunct professor of writing at Columbia University in 1980. In 1993, *Ablaze: the Story of Chernobyl,* his second nonfiction work, was published—ten years after the tragic event in the Soviet Union. In this book, R. explores the instantaneous deaths by radiation poisoning due to the explosion and fire, as well as the likely cancer DEATHS in years to come. R.'s two other nonfiction books, *Polonaise* (1977) and *A Free Frenchman* (1986), deal with World War II loyalty issues among Polish and French FAMILIES.

AWARDS: Ford Foundation fellow in Berlin, 1963–64; Harkness fellow in New York and Lexington, MA, 1967–68; Geoffrey Faber Memorial Prize, 1969, for *The Junkers;* Hawthornden Prize, 1970, for *Monk Dawson;* Maugham award, 1980; Thomas More Association medal, 1974; Enid McLeod award, 1988; James Tait Black Memorial prize, 1988; *Alive: The Story of the Andes Survivors:* ALA Best Books for Young Adults, 1974, selected for "Still Alive: The Best of the Best, 1960–1974."

BIBLIOGRAPHY: *Contemporary Authors Online,* 2003.

CATHERINE GIVEN

READING: TEXT CONNECTIONS

"Meaning does not reside in the text alone, waiting for a reader to unearth it; meaning is created in the transaction that occurs between a text and a reader" (Cullinan and Galda, 2002, p. 306). Brian Cambourne (2002) states that the degree to which learners make sense of a learning situation is an indicator of the degree to which they can place it in a context that helps them make connections. Students who infuse their own experiences and background knowledge with newly encountered text are better able to organize that information. Learning takes place as students reconstruct what they already know in relation to the new ideas. This learning involves the active construction of a personal network of interrelated knowledge. For example, Lisa wrote, "In *Encounter,* when the strange ships arrived in San Salvador in 1492, a young boy living on this island prayed to his idol. This was the perfect moment in the story to connect to because the book that I had just finished reading was *Cleopatra's Diary* where I learned that she also prayed to an idol. Reading *Cleopatra's Diary* helped me write my connection to *Encounter.*" Lisa linked information from a read-aloud to a self-selected book, which added to her understanding of the world of literature. In making connections to text, comprehension is deepened, understanding of life and the world is broadened, oral and written language are expanded, and most importantly, reading becomes an enjoyable experience (Fountas and Pinnell, 2001).

Text-to-self, text-to-world, and *text-to-text* are three ways in which students connect to text (Keene and Zimmerman, 1997). Text-to-self connections are made when students link their own personal experiences to the ideas they are reading about. In text-to-world connections, students relate their reading in a global sense as they move beyond personal experiences. Text-to-text connections are made when readers link the material they are reading to another text they have read or with which they are familiar.

Text-to-self connections are made when students use their own life experiences and background knowledge to understand what they are reading. Just as each reader lives a different life and has different experiences, reading evokes highly individual, personal feelings and mental images for each student. As students read a text, they construct meaning (Goodman, 1985). They imagine how a character might feel or they identify with the character in some specific way. In addition, the experiences students read about in books help them to better understand themselves. When students think about the ways they differ from or are similar to a character or an experience in a story, they learn about themselves and, in turn, make reading meaningful. Thinking about these connections helps students interpret and judge elements of text, which leads to new insight (Beach, 1987).

Jaime made a text-to-self connection while reading the book *How to Make an Apple Pie and See the World* by Marjorie Priceman, "This book reminds me of my mama and I making pumpkin pie because the book is about making apple pie. We only make pumpkin pie on Halloween." In writing this connection, Jaime uncovered a personal relationship with the text as she associated an event in the story she heard to a FAMILY tradition she shares with her mother on Halloween. Text-to-self connections often act as "stepping stones," they lead to text-to-world and text-to-text connections.

Students make text-to-world connections when they think more expansively about the world around them. When interacting with text, students develop a less egocentric view as they think about issues and characters from a local, national, global, moral, MULTICULTURAL, and/or historical point of view. The inspiring story *Wilma Unlimited* by Kathleen KRULL is an example of a PICTURE BOOK that fosters broad-based responses and viewpoints. In the story, Wilma Rudolph overcomes crippling polio and becomes the first female to win three gold medals in the Olympics. From a local point of view, readers connect to the fact that she was from their state, Tennessee. Students think nationally when they recall that she represented the United States in the Olympics. They think globally when they realize that the Olympics involves many countries and nationalities. Students make text-to-self connections when they relate to Wilma's self-confidence to achieve her dream. Students connect from a multicultural point of view when they recognize that Wilma is an AFRICAN-AMERICAN hero; they relate historically when they connect her to presidents, to diseases, and to SPORTS of that time. Readers look at different worlds and begin to identify and understand their own values (Schmidt and Pailliotet, 2001).

For example, after hearing the story of the Olympic runner Wilma Rudolph in *Wilma Unlimited,* Sean made the following connection: "This story reminds me of Jesse Owens because of the way he ran and did the long jump. I think Hitler accused America of making a cyborg (which is a bionic human). Jesse won a few gold medals. I don't know why they accused us of making a cyborg. I think it was the way he did his events. Jesse Owens is one of my favorite African Americans." Sean's connection shows evidence that he comprehended the story. It is apparent that he is thinking globally as he is reminded of an event in which a famous African-American athlete captures the attention of leaders around the world. After hearing Sean's connection, other students in the class made an additional connection between Wilma Rudolph and President Roosevelt, who was in office when she was born. President Roosevelt, the 32nd president, was in a wheelchair due to polio and Wilma overcame polio as a child.

In another example, Amy made a text-to-world connection after hearing the story *Tower to the Sun.* Amy used her imagination to fuse a futuristic FANTASY story with a landmark built in 1175 in Italy. She made the following text-to-world connection: "*Tower to the Sun* reminds me of a building in Italy because the top of the tower is leaning over. The tower in Italy is called the Leaning Tower of Pisa." Amy reveals her background knowledge of history when she recalls the Tower of Pisa. *Tower to the Sun* is another example of a picture book that evokes different responses from a local, national, global, multicultural, and/or historical point of view. Students make connections from a local point of view when they recycle cans and paper weekly in their school. Nationally, students make connections by preserving landmarks and respecting the property of others. Students connect from a global perspective when they recognize the ozone depletion problem. Students connect morally and multiculturally when they realize that everyone is responsible for the earth's present and future condition. Historically, just as Amy's connection reflects, students can connect this book to different landmarks located around the world.

Students make text-to-text connections, or intertextual connections, when they connect one book to another through character, plot, theme, or setting. According to Wooten (2000), connections to other pieces of literature are especially prized. Connecting books to other books adds dimension to students' understanding of the world of literature. By intertwining the stories they encounter, students understand literature at a deeper level. They move from thinking about stories as individual, disconnected pieces to understanding that literature is a connected body of work.

After hearing the story *Nettie's Trip South* by Ann TURNER, Angie made the following connection: "This story reminds me of a book that I read called *Meet Addy*. This story reminds me of the days of slavery." In this text-to-text connection, Angie linked a read-aloud to a self-selected book. By relating two pieces of literature set in the same time period, she is also constructing her own historical timeline. This type of connection help to scaffold her thinking in order to construct a clearer understanding of this time period.

Hayley made another text-to-text connection to the imaginative story *Tower to the Sun,* stating, "It reminds me of a book called *Where Does The Garbage Go?* because in the book it tells how we pollute, and in *The Tower to the Sun* the air was really polluted." Like Angie, Hayley related her self-selected book to a read-aloud, this time incorporating knowledge she obtained from the science curriculum. It is evident through her connection that Hayley constructed

meaning of the story *Tower to the Sun* when she associated it with *Where Does the Garbage Go?*

One book can relate to a variety of books, including read-alouds and self-selected books. For example, after reading aloud, *Abe Lincoln Remembers* by Ann Turner, fifth graders made connections to six different books; *Pink and Say* by Patricia Polacco, *Nettie's Trip South* by Ann Turner, *Meet Felicity: An American Girl: 1774* by Valerie Tripp, *My Brother Martin* by Christine King-Farris, *Ruby Bridges* by Robert Coles, and *Addy Learns a Lesson* by Valerie Tripp. Students connected *Pink and Say* to *Abe Lincoln Remembers* because both books are about the Civil War; *Pink and Say* is also a true story about the author's great-great-grandfather who shook the hand of Abraham Lincoln. *Nettie's Trip South* and *Addy Learns a Lesson* were also connected to *Abe Lincoln Remembers,* but from different points of view during the Civil War time period. *My Brother Martin* and *Ruby Bridges* were connected to *Abe Lincoln Remembers* because the main characters believed in justice and fought for that right either for themselves or for others who were mistreated. When a reader makes a book connection, the teacher is given a glimpse through a window into the child's mind, gaining insight into his/her literature background knowledge.

Teachers can facilitate text-to-text connections by grouping stories, poems, and nonfiction works based on a common theme or topic that is important to students' understanding of history or literature. An example of a possible grouping on aviation could include: *Wright Brothers* by Pamela Duncan Edwards, *Brave Harriet* by Marissa Moss, *Fly High! The Story of Bessie Coleman* by Louise Borden, and *Wingwalker* by Rosemary Wells. Through these books, students are able to experience different opinions, viewpoints, and ideas about flight and create connections among the various texts. Another thematic book grouping could focus on the Civil War. *Blue and Gray* by Eve BUNTING, *Mr. Lincoln's Whiskers* by Karen Winnick, *Drummer Boy* by Ann Turner, and *Follow the Drinking Gourd* by Jeannette Winter are all excellent books that reflect various perspectives from the Civil War time period. These books invite text-to-text connections and assist students in formulating their own historical timelines.

When they make connections among stories, students develop an awareness of similarities and differences across genres. Connections can link POETRY to realistic fiction, or possibly FANTASY to nonfiction. The possibilities are endless. Students are also better able to bridge the gap that often exists between the content areas. Math, social studies, science, and other content areas become intertwined in one learning situation. Comprehension continues to be widened and deepened when genres and content are thoughtfully brought together.

Students benefit from making, sharing, and listening to book connections. Students with different backgrounds, ethnicities, and disabilities are all able to find some way to connect to text. Molly, a Korean-American student, often makes connections to her native heritage after listening to historical fiction in the classroom. In addition to diversity, students of various age levels are also able to thoughtfully connect to text. For example, Jake, a first-grader, related the character Junie B. Jones to his own mischievous first-grade experiences. Katie, a high-school student, connected *Native Son* by Richard Wright to *Richard Wright and the Library Card* by William Miller. She realized that the book *Richard Wright and the Library Card* is a true story about the author of *Native Son*. She also recognized that the two YA stories are connected on a deeper level. Both books incorporate similar events, and the author, Richard Wright, projects aspects of his life in the novel *Native Son*.

A nurturing environment that accounts for and celebrates individual differences is conducive to students making text connections. Louise Rosenblatt (1978) further explains that it is important to create an atmosphere in the classroom that is receptive to students' unique, authentic responses. Recent brain research shows that when teachers create a safe environment, students are able to interact with text and construct meaning in a comfortable social context. There are no wrong answers when connections to text are created, because each student's connection is individual and personal. As connections to text are shared, voices are heard and ideas validated. Students gain more confidence when they know they are being heard, and they realize that they are making some of the same connections as other students in the class. In such an environment, meaning of text is amplified and comprehension is reinforced.

There must be numerous opportunities for students to explore, listen to, read, and share literature. Books groupings, time-period studies, and read alouds are examples of ways that teachers can culti-vate students' connections to text. When students have time to "play" with literature, they make numerous and thoughtful connections that lead to a deeper understanding of and an appreciation for literature. It is important for teachers to make a conscious effort to thoughtfully link children to books in order for them to make connections to text, which then results in comprehension. Students can journey to places they have never been before as they go beyond one literal meaning of a text.

BIBLIOGRAPHY: Beach, R. "Strategic Teaching in Literature." In B. F. Jones, A. S. Palinscar, D. S. Ogle, and E. G. Carr, eds. *Strategic Teaching and Learning: Cognitive Instruction in the Content Areas,* 1987; Cullinan, B., and Galda, L. *Literature and the Child,* 5th ed. 2002; Farstrup, A. E., and S. Jay Samuels. *What Research Has to Say About Reading Instruction;* Fountas, I. C., and Pinnell, G.S. *Guiding Readers and Writers Grades 3–6,* 2001; Goodman, K. S. Transactional Psycholinguistics Model: Unity in Reading. In H. Singer and R. B. Ruddell, eds., *Theoretical models and processes of reading,* 3rd ed. 1985; Harvey, S., and Goudvis, A. *Strategies That Work: Teaching Comprehension to Enhance Understanding,* 2000; Keene, E. O., and Zimmerman, S. *Mosaic of Thought: Teaching Comprehension in a Reader's Workshop,* 1997; Rosenblatt, L. *The Reader, the Text, the Poem: The Transactional Theory of the Literacy Work,* 1978; Schmidt, P., and Paillotet A. *Exploring Values through Literature, Multimedia, and Literacy Events,* 2001; Wooten, D. *Valued Voices: An Interdisciplinary Approach to Teaching and Learning,* 2000.

CHILDREN'S LITERATURE BIBLIOGRAPHY: Borden, Louise and Kroeger, Mary Kay, 2001, *Fly High! The Story of Bessie Coleman;* BUNTING, Eve, *Blue and the Gray;* Edwards, Pamela Duncan, *The Wright Brothers;* Coles, Robert. (1995). *Ruby Bridges.* Scholastic; Gregory, Kristiana, 1999, *The Royal Diaries: Cleopatra VII: Daughter of the Nile;* King-Farris, Christine, 2003, *My Brother Martin;* KRULL, Kathleen, 2000, *Wilma Unlimited: How Wilma Rudolph Became the World's Fastest Woman;* Miller, William, 1997, *Richard Wright and the Library Card;* Moss, Marissa, 2001, *Brave Harriet;* Polacco, Patricia, 1994, *Pink and Say;* PORTER, Connie, 1993, *Meet Addy;* Priceman, Marjorie, 1996, *How to Make an Apple Pie and See the World;* Showers, Paul, 1994, *Where Does the Garbage Go?;* Thompson, Colin, 1999, *Tower to the Sun;* Tripp, Valerie, 1991, *An American Girl: Meet Felicity: 1774;* Turner, Ann, 1987, *Nettie's Trip South;* Turner, Ann, 1998; *Drummer Boy;* Wells, Rosemary, 2002, *Wing Walker;* Winnick, Karen B., 1996, *Mr. Lincoln's Whiskers*; Winter, Jeannette, 1992, *Follow the Drinking Gourd*; Wright, Richard, 1940, *Native Son*; YOLEN, Jane, 1992, *Encounter.*

ELIZABETH ANDERSON

AND SARAH LOYD RAYMER

REAVER, Chap (Herbert)

Author, b. 1935, Cincinnati, Ohio; d. 1993, n.p.

R. got his nickname when his dad said what a cute "little chap" he was. A former chiropractor and long time part-time writer, R. found his place among appreciative aficionados of good MYSTERIES. After writing his first novel, *Mote,* for which he received the Edgar Allen Poe Award, he quickly went from underdog to champion—a self-described regular guy who wrote a book, tried to get it published, and won an award for it.

Mote's main character Chris investigates the murder of one of his teachers. Chris works together with a black police detective named Steinert. His amateur yet skillful detective work leads him to a white supremacist group called Equal Rights for White Americans and its AFRICAN-AMERICAN counterpart, the Black Brigade, making racism one of the main focal points of the novel. R. himself was very active in the NAACP, and eventually became the national vice president. While recognizing the gravity of racism, R.'s stories often deal with the ridiculous and absurdity of racism in a humorous way. And while *Mote* focuses on grave and serious issues, R. also believed that at its core, it was a coming-of-age story about the bonds of friendship. This theme was picked up in his next novel as well, a Western in which the friendship between two TEENS begins when the one saves the other, a Native American, from being lynched.

AWARDS: Delacorte Press Prize for an Outstanding First Young Adult Novel, 1990; Edgar Allan Poe Award for Best Young Adult Mystery, Mystery Writers of America, 1991, both for *Mote;* Hugo Award nomination for SHORT STORY, World SCIENCE FICTION Society, 1992, for "Feel Good Stuff"; Edgar Allan Poe Award for Best Young Adult Mystery, Mystery Writers of America, and ALA Best Book for Young Adults 1993, for *A Little Bit Dead.*

FURTHER WORKS: *Mote,* 1990; *A Little Bit Dead,* 1992; *Bill,* 1994. Contributor of articles and short stories to periodicals, including *Amazing Stories* and several humor publications.

BIBLIOGRAPHY: *Contemporary Authors Online,* 2003.

REBECCA OSA MENDELL

RECENT TRENDS IN YA LITERATURE

I consider YA books to be those published specifically for readers between twelve and eighteen, although TEENS read books published for children and for adults also. Readers between ages twelve and eighteen often seek the same adult bestsellers their parents are reading. Teen novels have changed in recent years and treat subjects that would not have been considered suitable in the past. Since the use of street language and the depiction of sex have increased on television shows, in film, and in popular MUSIC, it is not surprising that the language in fiction would change. Dialogue reflects the conversations one hears in the hallways of American high schools. Terrible events such as rape are part of some excellent books for teens.

Rita WILLIAM-GARCIA has written a poignant novel, *Every Time a Rainbow Dies* (2001), which begins with a teenage boy, Thulani, on his rooftop witnessing a rape taking place in the alley below. When he tries to help Ysa, she rebuffs him at first, but he becomes fascinated by her and a love story begins. The gritty urban realism of the novel contrasts with the emotional story of the relationship between a boy and a girl. Laurie Halse ANDERSON's *Speak* (1999) concerns the plight of a victim who was raped at a party. After the attack, Melinda loses the ability and the desire to speak. Her recovery is slow and painful, but eventually she is strong enough to speak out and deal with her attacker at school. These are outstanding examples of new novels which portray sexual violence.

With an abundance of high quality books available for teens, it was time to create a special award for these titles. The MICHAEL L. PRINTZ AWARD recognizes the wealth of good books written for teens by selecting one award book and up to four honor books annually. The first winner, *Monster* (1999) by Walter Dean MYERS, tells the story of a teen accused of participating in a holdup. Events are revealed through the boy's journal and through a screenplay he is writing. Readers must decide just what happened in Myers's skillful, original work. Since the Newbery Award is for books for readers up to age fourteen and the Printz Award is for books for readers ages twelve and older, the same book could possibly win both awards, but the Printz committees have looked for more mature works so far. Books originally published abroad may also win the Printz Award. The 2003 committee selected *Postcards from No Man's Land* (2002) by Aidan CHAMBERS, which was first published in Great Britain. It is a many-layered novel featuring a British boy who visits Holland to learn about his grandfather's WWII experiences. The grandfather's story is told in moving flashbacks while the boy gradually finds his own self-confidence and a ROMANCE of his own.

Well-known adult authors are writing successfully for younger adults. Perhaps the increased publicity about books for teens inspired them. Joyce Carol OATES's novel *Big Mouth and Ugly Girl* (2002) is a realistic work about an unusual friendship that develops when one high-school student stands up for another who is in trouble. Carl Hiaasen drew upon an event from his own Florida youth to tell the amusing and involving story of young people trying to save owls in *Hoot* (2002). It is wonderful to see such talented writers creating books for teens.

The phenomenal success of the HARRY POTTER SERIES by J. K. ROWLING has led to a demand for more FANTASY. Not long ago, fantasy readers were considered rather special, but now teens who enjoyed *Harry Potter and the Sorcerer's Stone* (1997) and its sequels ask for other recommendations. Phillip PULLMAN's trilogy, His Dark Materials (1995), appeals to many young adults. The sophisticated excellence of his writing has captivated many readers. The final volume is the first book by a writer for young people to win the overall Whitbread Award in Great Britain. Old fantasy favorites are being reprinted and new authors are writing exciting stories. It is a marvelous era for imaginative fiction.

Books by authors from different ethnic backgrounds are more common now. Immigrants' stories are reaching the main stream and enriching the knowledge of teens about others. *A Step from Heaven* by An NA (2001), which won the 2002 Michael L. Printz Award, tells of a Korean girl's adjustment to tremendous changes for her FAMILY when they settle in the United States. *Born Confused* by Tanuja Desai Hidier (2002) introduces Dimple Lala, who at seven-

teen is not sure whether she wants to be a New Jersey girl or an exotic Indian. The publication of new authors who can share their worlds with teens is a fine new development. AFRICAN AMERICAN authors continue to write books that are important not only to black teens. Jacqueline WOODSON's novel *Hush* (2002) explores the plight of a family in the witness protection program. Every reader can relate to the loss of friends, work, and a happy home.

Nonfiction continues to be popular with teens. Fortunately, there is a special new award to recognize outstanding books: The Robert F. Sibert Informational Book Award. Although it is administered by the Association for Library Service to Children, the books recognized are also enjoyed by young adults. Individual titles are read for pleasure rather than for homework. The SERIES books tend to be heavily used for assignments, although the widespread availability of electronic resources has led readers away from the utilitarian books. A new trend is for authors of adult works to edit and rewrite for a younger audience. For example, Nathaniel PHILBRICK shortened his National Book Award–winning work *In the Heart of the Sea* (2000) for younger readers who might be daunted by its original length. Gail Buckley edited *American Patriots* (2001) for teen readers interested in the history of blacks in the military.

More teens are writing POETRY today. Many have been inspired by poetry slams and workshops while others simply work alone. Collections of poems by teens can be very good. *Movin': Teen Poets Take Voice,* edited by Dave Johnson (2000), is a good example of writing from poetry workshops at The New York Public Library. Poetry anthologies such as the beautiful *Heart to Heart* by Jan GREENBERG (2001) are a delight to many. Narrative verse is an ancient form made new again. *Bronx Masquerade* (2002) by Nikki GRIMES is a good recent example. Eighteen students in a Bronx high school tell their stories during open mike Fridays in English class. Many authors are finding success with this format during a period of popularity for poetry.

The traditional concerns of young adults continue to be the most important themes in work written for them. Young adults who feel alone, outside the mainstream, can find solace reading about other teens. Coming of age is the eternal problem for young people. When is one fully an adult? What is true love? How can one solve problems while being a teen? No matter what the format of the work in any era, the dilemmas of youth endure.

KARLAN SICK

REES, Celia
Author, educator, b. 17 June 1949, Solihull, England

Born and reared in England, R.'s novels for young adults have been translated into twelve languages and published around the world. After attending Warwick University, earning a B.A. with honors in history and politics, R. decided to pursue a teaching career and earned postgraduate degrees in education. It was while she was teaching in a secondary school that some students told her they wanted to read exciting, thrilling stories like those of Lois DUNCAN, Caroline B. COONEY or R. L. Stine, but that were set in England and contained British characters. This inspired R. to begin writing YA fiction, most of which has been set in her home country.

Her first novel, *Every Step You Take,* was published in Great Britain in 1993. Writing in the juvenile HORROR fiction genre, R. often uses graphic violence and descriptions to support her stories of maniacal killers, believable ghosts, and murderous schoolyard bullies, all specters that can have a terrifying effect on young readers. R. has also managed to expand the HORROR and supernatural genre; by drawing on her undergraduate education in history and politics, she weaves historical and sociological elements into her narratives, creating a multidimensional effect.

After writing numerous novels published in Great Britain, R. had her first American release with *The Truth Out There* (2000). The book delves into the repercussions of a long-held FAMILY secret and manages to incorporate UFOs and autism into the storyline. In 2001, R. published what would become one of her most popular books, *Witch Child,* which drew on her interest in early American history. An avid fan of museums and art galleries, R. became inspired to write this novel after visiting the American Museum near Bath, England. *Witch Child* tells the tale of Mary Newbury, the granddaughter of an accused witch who had to flee England in 1659. She finds herself in an uncertain refuge, to say the very least, a Puritan settlement rife with suspicion and fear. Told through Mary's DIARY entries, *Witch Child* and its sequel, *Sorceress* (2002), reveal the world of 17th-century witch persecution, religious intolerance, and Native

American spirituality. These attributes highlight the supernatural and historical influences that characterize R.'s work.

AWARDS: American Library Association Best Book for Young Adults, *Witch Child,* 2001, and *Pirates,* 2004.

FURTHER WORKS: (published in Great Britain): *Every Step You Take,* 1993; *The Bailey Game,* 1994; *Colour Her Dead,* 1994; *Blood Sinister,* 1996; *The Vanished,* 1997; *Ghost Chamber,* 1997; *Midnight Hour,* 1997; *Soul Taker,* 1997; H.A.U.N.T.S. (SERIES), 1998; *The Cunning Man,* 2000; *Pirates!,* 2003.

BIBLIOGRAPHY: *Something about the Author,* vol. 124, 2002; Witch Child, http://www.witchchild.com/author.asp

MICHELLE CROSWELL FOSSUM

REISS, Kathryn
Author, b. 4 December 1957, Cambridge, Massachusetts

R. grew up in Ohio. Following her graduation from Duke University, where she received B.A. degrees in English and German, she studied in Bonn, Germany, as a Fulbright-Hayes Scholar at Friedrich-Wilhelms-Universität. While in Bonn, she wrote the first draft of her first novel, on a day that she was immersed in Goethe's works and wanted to read something light, in English. Since she'd already read all of her English novels, she decided to write one herself rather than go to the bookstore in the pouring rain. After revisions taking several years, including time off to get married, attend graduate school, and have two children, the novel was eventually published as *Time Windows* in 1991. R., who received her M.F.A. in English and creative writing from the University of Michigan in 1988, currently lives in northern California with her husband and five children, and is a part-time assistant professor teaching creative writing at Mills College.

R. has said, "There are certain stories that simply beg to be told. I feel a kind of urgency to write when I have a good plot in mind." She does not talk about her stories before they are down on paper in some form, as talking about them causes them to lose energy for her. She has a special interest in writing for middle grade and young adult audiences, and tries to write the sort of books that she liked when she was that age, especially stories about magic and MYSTERY. Time, time travel, and ghosts of persons from previous times recur in her novels. In *Time Windows,* her first novel, thirteen-year-old Miranda finds a mysterious dollhouse in the attic of her new home that allows her to see into the past lives of the women who had lived in the house. Fifteen-year-old Miranda appears again in *Pale Phoenix* (1994), in which an orphan hopes to recapture her previous life in Puritan Salem. In *Paint By Magic* (2002), eleven-year-old Connor travels through time, attempting to find his mother and solve a mystery that has her trapped between times.

Ghosts of people from earlier times in history seem to influence the lives of characters in several of R.'s novels. The old song, "You are lost and gone forever / Dreadful sorry, Clementine" plays over and over again in Molly's head in *Dreadful Sorry* (1993) as she begins to see the world through the eyes of Clementine, a visitor to her house eighty years earlier. In *PaperQuake: a Puzzle* (1998), modern eighth-grader Violet, who is deathly afraid of earthquakes, keeps finding letters, DIARIES, and newspaper articles about the 1906 San Francisco earthquake that, along with her dreams, lead her to believe that she must act to prevent earthquake-related deaths in the present. A governess who died eighty years ago haunts *Sweet Miss Honeywell's Revenge,* (2004).

AWARDS: American Library Association—YALSA Best Books for Young Adults, 1993, *Time Windows;* American Library Association—YALSA Popular PAPERBACKS for Young Adults, 2001, *Time Windows;* International Reading Association Young Adults' Choices, 1995, ALA Popular Paperbacks, 2005 *Dreadful Sorry;* Society of School Librarians International Book Awards Honor Book, 2002, *Paint by Magic;* Edgar Allan Poe Best Young Adult Novel nominee, 1995, *Pale Phoenix,* 1999, *PaperQuake: A Puzzle,* also 2004 ALA Popular Paperbacks.

FURTHER WORKS: *The Glass House People,* 1992; Ghosts in the Dollhouse trilogy; two American Girls History Mysteries for younger readers.

BIBLIOGRAPHY: *Contemporary Authors Online;* Mills College website, www.mills.edu

COLLEEN P. GILRANE

RENNISON, Louise
Author, b. 1951, Leeds, England

R. worked as a standup comedian and a humor columnist for London's *Evening Standard* before becoming a popular YA author. One of her columns for the paper led to the development of *Angus, Thongs, and Full-Frontal Snogging* (U.S. release, 2000), her first book for young people. As R. tells the story, a humorous article she wrote about dating after age thirty-five led a publisher to approach her about writing a fictional TEEN girl's DIARY; apparently, her "self-obsessed and childish" tone was ideal for a female teen protagonist. The publisher, Brenda Gardner, tells the tale a little differently, citing the attraction of R.'s ability to "laugh at the female psyche" at any age. What resulted from R.'s frequently funny perspective on relationships is a SERIES of books, told via diary entries. They recount the life of a teenage girl learning to cope with the changes wrought by young adulthood and the circle of FAMILY and friends that revolve around her.

R. acknowledges a strongly AUTOBIOGRAPHICAL element in the diaries that chronicle Georgia Nicolson's teen angst and euphoria. In interviews, R. recounts her own orange cat, kissing lessons with a neighborhood boy, and efforts to dye her hair. "Most of the anecdotes are true," R. has said of the episodes in her first book. At the same time, though, some of the darker aspects of R.'s own life were omitted from the Georgia stories. These include her TEEN pregnancy which resulted in a daughter whom she gave up for adoption—but has since been reunited with—and her family's move to New Zealand, which caused her a great deal of unhappiness. R. has stated that she chose to omit these more difficult elements of her own adolescence to preserve an optimistic and even naïve persona for her narrator. "I wanted to concentrate on the comedy, the fun and light side," R. told one interviewer. "[Georgia]'s a bit innocent, really, like me when I was her age. I had a very fun childhood. . . . It was very free and happy."

Angus, Thongs, and Full-Frontal Snogging attracted both kudos and criticism. One awards committee cited the novel's handling of significant adolescent concerns like relationships and sexuality in a light, engaging manner. It focuses on fourteen-year-old Georgia's efforts to navigate school, friendships, and relations with the other sex, won awards and a following of teen readers. Favorable reviews of the work compare Georgia Nicholson to both Helen Fielding's Bridget Jones and Sue Townsend's Adrian Mole, though R. disclaims the influences. Reviewers, however, have gone so far as to say that the similarities to the adult works in the same genre make Georgia's story "seem less like writing and more like copying." R. also received criticism for derogatory remarks about lesbians, although it has been acknowledged as consistent with the teen character's worldview. Additionally, the books' references to underwear, sex, and female body parts have led some parents to protest the inclusion of R.'s works in school library collections. It is worth noting that there are some differences in recommended ages for readers of the fictional diaries; whereas *Angus* won the prestigious Smarties Award in England in the category of fiction for nine-to-eleven year olds, most U.S. reviews have identified R.'s books as ones for ages twelve and up.

While the books take the female perspective on teenage ROMANCE, R. says that she receives fan mail from readers of both sexes. The responses from American readers include enthusiasm for Georgia's use of idiomatic British expressions and their subsequent explanations.

Since the publication of *Angus,* R. has continued the teen diarist's ADVENTURES in a number of sequels: *On the Bright Side, I'm Now the Girlfriend of a Sex God* (originally titled *It's OK, I'm Wearing Really Big Knickers* when published in the UK) (2001), *Knocked Out by My Nunga-Nungas* (2002), followed by *Dancing in My Nuddy Pants* (2003). Plans to continue the SERIES are indefinite. As R. has explained, "I don't think Georgia or her friends would be quite as interesting grown up. But . . . I wouldn't mind hanging around with her a bit longer."

The books have been translated for publication in more than twenty-six countries. For American readers, British idioms, like the use of "snogging" for making out, have been explained via a glossary transcribed in Georgia's chatty, nonsensical, and irreverent style. Additionally, textual changes in the American edition cut some profanity and potentially controversial ethnic references.

AWARDS: 2001 PRINTZ Honor Book, 2001 Best Books for Young Adults, 1999 Nestle Smarties Book Award/ Bronze Award in the nine–eleven years category, all for *Angus, Thongs, and Full-Frontal Snogging.*

BIBLIOGRAPHY: Abbey, C. D., ed., *Biography Today Author Series: Profiles of Interest to Young Readers,* 2002; Andronik, Catherine M., *Book Report,* 2002; Ginn, Kate. *The Scotsman,* 2000; *Horn Book,* 2000; Kloberdanz, Kristin. *Book Magazine,* 2000; *Publisher's Weekly,* 2002; booktrusted.com, online; www .ala.org, online; www.georgianicolson.com, online

JENNIFER BUREK PIERCE

REVIEW JOURNALS

YA LITERATURE is widely reviewed in a number of professional journals. Some of these are devoted entirely to young adult literature; others include children's literature as well. Both the National Council of Teachers of English (NCTE) and the International Reading Association (IRA) have special interest groups on young adult literature that publish a journal dedicated to the promotion of young adult literature. NCTE's Assembly on Literature for Adolescents (ALAN) has been publishing *The ALAN Review* since 1973. IRA's Special Interest Group on Adolescent Literature (SIGNAL) has been publishing the *SIGNAL Journal* since 1978.

Both publications, which began as newsletters for a membership of teachers, LIBRARIANS, professors, publishers, and authors, have developed into refereed professional journals. They include news of interest to members of the special interest groups as well as articles and columns related to young adult literature. Each J. has a book-review column. *The ALAN Review*'s "Clip & File YA Book Reviews" section prints its reviews in a 3 × 5 card format; *SIGNAL* uses a column format. Reviews in both journals are unsolicited and written by teachers, LIBRARIANS, and university professors. Reviewers generally provide short summaries of the books accompanied by brief literary evaluations for the purpose of acquainting educators and librarians with new YA titles.

The *Voice of Youth Advocates (VOYA)* is a third J. devoted exclusively to YA literature. Established in 1977 by Dorothy Broderick and Mary K. Chelton and published by Scarecrow Press, *VOYA* describes itself as "the library magazine serving those who serve young adults." Although the J. contains articles and columns devoted to improving library programming, its book-review section comprises a substantial portion of the publication. Librarians review new YA titles by using the VOYA Book Review Code to rate them according to quality, popularity, and grade-level interest. *VOYA* is invaluable for YA librarians looking for the latest SCIENCE FICTION, or FANTASY, or HORROR title, not only because of the annual Best List of these genres that appears in the April issue, but also because reviews of SCIENCE FICTION, FANTASY, and HORROR titles appear in a separate section and include many PAPERBACK originals and adult titles with TEEN appeal.

Although the American Library Association (ALA) has a special interest group for YA literature, the Young Adult Library Services Association (YALSA), its J. *Young Adult Library Services (YALS)*—formerly both *Journal of Youth Services (JOYS)* and *Top of the News*—does not review books. Instead, ALA's *Booklist* provides a comprehensive reviewing source for YA librarians. In addition to its reviews of adult books, *Booklist* includes "Books for Youth" in each of its biweekly issues. In the "Books for Older Readers" portion of this section, professional staff members and contributing editors review fiction and nonfiction for grades seven to twelve. A review in *Booklist* constitutes a recommendation for library purchase; starred reviews indicate books that have particular merit.

School Library Journal for Children, Young Adult and School Librarians (SLJ) relies on a cadre of four hundred practicing librarians from across the country to review all new books published for children and young adults in this monthly publication. YA titles appear in the "Grades 5 & Up" section, which is divided into fiction and nonfiction. Individual reviews indicate more specific grade-level appropriateness of each title as well as provide summaries and evaluative comments intended to assist librarians as they make purchasing decisions. Books rated as exceptional are given starred reviews.

Whereas *SLJ* is generally considered the most comprehensive major reviewing source, the *Horn Book* magazine is deemed the most literarily critical J. focusing on books for children and YA. *Horn Book* staff members, who also contribute scholarly essays to this bi-monthly publication, write the reviews. The "Book Reviews" section is divided into categories for PICTURE BOOKS, fiction, folklore, POETRY, and nonfiction. YA titles are indicated by middle-school or high-school grade-level suggested designations. *Horn Book* does not usually review books it does not recommend. A starred review indicates a book the editors believe to be outstanding. Initiated in 1924, *Horn Book* represents a long tradition of quality reviewing.

Founded by Zena Sutherland in 1945 and now published monthly by the University of Illinois Press, the *Bulletin of the Center for Children's Books* includes reviews for titles identified as appropriate reading for grades nine to twelve along with reviews of books for younger children. Staff reviewers provide concise summaries and critical evaluations aimed at informing librarians about the book's content, reading level, strengths and weaknesses, and quality of format. They code each book as starred for "Special Distinction," R for "Recommended," M for "Marginal," NR for "Not Recommended," Ad for "Additional Title if Topic is Needed," SpC for "Special Collection," or SpoR for "Special Reader," and provide suggestions for curricular use.

Kirkus Reviews, Publisher's Weekly, and the *New York Times Book Review* are three additional comprehensive review sources for adult books that, like *Booklist,* include sections for children's and YA books. Published biweekly, *Kirkus* notices are written by "specialists selected for their knowledge and expertise in a particular field." *Publishers Weekly* prints both positive and negative reviews in its fall and spring special sections on books for children and YA. The *New York Times Book Review* also publishes a special fall and spring section featuring children's and YA books in addition to occasional reviews printed throughout the year. Reviews are written by authors and illustrators as well as by regular professional reviewers.

Booklist, SLJ, Horn Book, Bulletin of the Center for Children's Books, Kirkus, and *VOYA* are the main review sources used by many school and public librarians for collection development purposes. Teachers also find them useful, and although they are not considered major reviewing sources, *The ALAN Review* and *SIGNAL Journal* can also be beneficial for educators looking for YA literature to use with their students. In addition, IRA's *Journal of Adolescent and Adult Literary* and *English Journal* from NCTE both have review columns featuring recent YA titles recommended for use in the classroom.

BIBLIOGRAPHY: Galda, Lee, and Bernice E. Cullinan. *Literature and the Child,* 2002; Donelson, Kenneth L., and Alleen Pace Nilsen. *Literature for Today's Young Adults,* 2005.

ELIZABETH POE

REYNOLDS, Marilyn
Author, b. 13 September 1935, California

R. was reared in Temple City, California, where her father owned a meat market. After high school, R.

married and raised children, then returned to college at California State University to earn her B.A. in English in 1965 and her teaching certificate in 1967. She taught at-risk students in California schools for decades, gaining experience that would eventually be used to establish her second career as an author of YOUNG ADULT fiction.

R. found little time to write while raising three children and teaching full time. In 1978, while working on a master's in reading education, R. took a creative writing class. An assignment for that class turned into an op-ed piece, published in the *Los Angeles Times*. Encouraged by the publication of this article, R. continued to pursue a writing career.

R.'s love of reading influenced her desire to write for TEENS. In particular, R. sought to help reluctant readers develop lifetime reading habits. In an attempt to broaden her students' reading possibilities, R. wrote her first teen novel, *Telling* (1996), which narrates the account of a twelve-year-old girl who was being molested by a neighbor. With the publication of *Telling*, R. launched the first of her True-to-Life SERIES from Hamilton High, for which she has become well known.

Strong student responses to her novel led R. to write *Detour for Emmy* (1993), the story of a girl who gets pregnant at the age of fifteen. The following year, she addressed the same issue, but from the point of view of the teen father in *Too Soon for Jeff* (1994). *Baby Help* (1998) also involves a young teen mother who lives with her baby's teenage father and his mother. The main character, Melissa, must confront the fact that her boyfriend is exhibiting abusive behavior toward their child. R.'s True-to-Life series now numbers seven young adult novels and a collection of SHORT STORIES. R. takes on realistic and tough issues that conflict the lives of many of today's teens. Topics for her stories include abuse, teen pregnancy, racism, acquaintance rape, gay/lesbian harassment, bullying, and sexual abstinence. R. is praised for writing realistic and INFORMATIVE stories, the content and authentic dialogue of which appeal to reluctant readers.

R. and her husband Michael currently reside in northern California, where she continues her work with at-risk students. R. visits colleges, high schools, and public libraries. In addition to author visits, R. administers workshops where she guides teachers through classroom techniques designed for at-risk learners.

SELECT AWARDS: R.'s titles appear on many of ALA's Best Books lists as well as New York Public Library's lists of Best Books for the Teen Age. *Detour for Emmy* (1993) received several awards, including a Best Books for Young Adults citation in 1994, the South Carolina Young Adult Book Award in 1995–96, and the Best Books for the Teen Age designation. *Too Soon for Jeff* (1994) earned a Best Books for Young Adults citation and was on the Quick Picks for Young Adults list. In addition, R. earned a Daytime Emmy Award nomination in 1997 for Writing in a Children's Special for the ABC After School Special adaptation of *Too Soon for Jeff*. *But What about Me?* (1996) and *Beyond Dreams* (1995) were picked as Best Books for the Teen Age in 1996, while *Baby Help* (1998) was chosen in 1999 and *If You Loved Me* (1999) was chosen in 2000. *Telling* (1996) was honored as a Quick Pick for Young Adults, and *Beyond Dreams,* a collection of six short stories, was recognized in 2000 as an ALA Short Takes Selection.

FURTHER WORKS: *True-to-Life Series from Hamilton High Teaching Guide,* 1996; *Love Rules,* 2001; *I Won't Read and You Can't Make Me,* 2004.

BIBLIOGRAPHY: Peacock, S. (Ed.). *Something about the Author,* 2001; www.heinemann.com; www.morn ingglorypress.com.

JODI PILGRIM

RICE, Robert
Author, b. 1945, Wyoming

R., successful author of YA books, has had a career as a lawyer, driven a taxi, and worked in intelligence before fiction writing became his full-time pursuit. He has been able to draw upon his diverse experiences to write unique stories with persuasive detail. R. earned an M.A. in international affairs at American University and has also completed graduate work in American studies at the University of Florida. His first successful book, published in 1991, was *The Last Pendragon,* a FANTASY novel about King Arthur that received critical acclaim. His next book, *Agent of Judgement,* published in 2000, is a thriller about the future of genetic engineering and the dangers of right-wing Christian fundamentalism. His most recent book, released in 2003, is called *The Nature of Midnight.* R. has also had SHORT STORIES and poems published in various periodicals. He won the Oregon State POETRY Contest in 1990. R. currently lives in Southwestern Montana.

AWARDS: Oregon State Poetry Contest, 1990; ALA Best Book for Young Adults, 1993, *The Last Pendragon.*

FURTHER WORKS: *The Last Pendragon,* 1991; *Agent of Judgement,* 2000; *The Nature of Midnight,* 2003; various SHORT STORIES and poems published in periodicals.

BIBLIOGRAPHY: Robert Rice homepage, www.robert rice.com/bio.htm; Library of Congress, www.lcweb .loc.com.

TREVOR A. PROSS

RINALDI, Ann

Author, b. 27 August 1934, New York City

R.'s longing for a career as a writer was hindered during her youth by her unyielding father. Although a successful newspaper manager himself, he saw no reason to support his daughter's dreams of a career in writing or working in the newspaper industry. He did not allow R. to attend college, and so she became a secretary.

After marrying and rearing two children, R. decided she wanted to pursue writing professionally. She wrote four novels, but felt they were of low quality. To satiate her desire to write, R. asked to pen a weekly column for the *Somerset Messenger Gazette.* The paper accepted her, and this led to more frequent assignments with the *Trentonian* daily paper. The success of her newspaper career was gratifying, and R. won several awards for it, including the New Jersey Press Association's First Place Award in 1978 and 1989 for columns in the *Trentonian.* However, R.'s interest in writing novels remained.

In 1980, *Term Paper* became her first published novel. The story was one she had been working on for years; only after finishing it did she think it might be marketable as a YA novel. An engaging look at the struggles of Nicki, a TEENAGER who is coming to terms with both her father's DEATH and her changed relationship with her guardian older brother, R.'s book was accepted by the first publisher to read it. R. returned to these characters in her second book, *Promises Are for Keeping* (1982).

R.'s entry into writing historical YA literature was stimulated in large part by her son Ron. When he became involved in Revolutionary War reenactments, the whole family was drawn into the excitement and drama of the events. Inspired by a reenactment of an important day in the history of her beloved Trenton, R. resolved to write a good historical novel for YA. Following a year of extensive research, *Time Enough for Drums* was completed. However, R. had difficulty persuading publishers that historical fiction could interest young readers. Ten publishers later, *Time Enough for Drums* (1986), the first of R.'s many historical novels for young adults, was published.

Time Enough for Drums is the story of Jemima Emerson, a patriot whose loyalties are divided by an older sister who marries a British officer, a brother who becomes an officer in the Continental Army, parents with their own political activities, and grandparents who have differing political views. Jemima is conflicted about her own beliefs but, during the course of R.'s novel, achieves a new maturity, a sense of responsibility, and a strong resolve.

Not all of R.'s historical characters and settings are entirely fictional, a fact that has led to controversy for more than one of her works. *Wolf by the Ears* (1991) may be the most controversial example. It is the DIARY of Harriet Hemmings, daughter of Sally Hemmings and servant (a.k.a. slave) of Thomas Jefferson. R.'s Harriet struggles with abiding rumors that Jefferson is her father, rumors that historians still argue over today.

Although some readers have felt the portrayal of Harriet in *Wolf by the Ears* to be racist, R. has not stayed away from issues of race and parentage in her writing. *Cast Two Shadows: The American Revolution in the South* (1998) revisits these themes in the story of fourteen-year-old Caroline. Her FAMILY is devastated by WAR—her father imprisoned as a rebel, her brother fighting for the British, her sister now the companion of the pompous British officer occupying their house, and her mother forced to wait on them— but Caroline now has the opportunity to develop stronger family bonds. The daughter of her father and a slave she's never known, Caroline is able to become closer to her grandmother, Miz Melindy, and to learn more about her past—and herself—thanks to the relaxing of racial barriers during wartime.

R.'s passion for historical writing has continued throughout the course of her career. She has published more than two dozen young adult novels, the vast majority of them historical fiction. Like Jemima Emerson, the characters of her novels are not important people in terms of history. Rather, they are unknowns who face real-life events with courage and conviction. Adult and child characters alike deal with problems and conflict. Their lives and personalities are consistently changed by the events unfolding around them. By novel's end, R's protagonists are typically more resilient for dealing with the problems they encounter. They often raise important social themes, from race relations to feminist issues to family bonds and community responsibility. In recognition of the importance of R.'s contributions to historical fiction, the Daughters of the American Revolution awarded her their National History Award in 1991.

Although she enjoys writing about the American Revolution, R. has also covered the eras of the Civil War, the Salem witch trials, and World War II. Her topics range from poet Phillis Wheatley to the feud of the Hatfields and the McCoys, from Valley Forge to the Ohio territory.

SELECT AWARDS: ALA Best Books for Young Adults: *Time Enough for Drums*, 1986, *Last Silk Dress*, 1988, *Wolf by the Ears*, 1992, *A Break with Charity*, 1993, *In My Father's House*, 1994, *Hang on a Thousand Trees with Ribbons*, 1997, *An Acquaintance with Darkness*, 1998; *The Cotton Quilt:* ALA Popular Paperbacks, 2002.

FURTHER WORKS: *The Good Side of My Heart*, 1987; *The Fifth of March: A Story of the Boston Massacre*, 1993; *A Stitch in Time*, 1994; *Finishing Becca: A Story about Peggy Shippen and Benedict Arnold*, 1994; *Broken Days*, 1995; *The Secret of Sarah Revere*, 1995; *Hang a Thousand Trees with Ribbons: The Story of Phillis Wheatley*, 1996; *The Blue Door*, 1996; *Keep Smiling Through*, 1996; *Mine Eyes Have Seen*, 1997; *An Acquaintance with Darkness*, 1997; *The Second Bend in the River*, 1997; *My Heart Is on the Ground: The Diary of Nannie Little Rose, a Sioux Girl*, 1999; *Amelia's War*, 1999; *The Coffin Quilt: The Feud between the Hatfields and the McCoys*, 1999; *The Education of Mary*, 2000; *The Journal of Jasper Jonathan Pierce*, 2000; *The Staircase*, 2000; *Girl in Blue*, 2001; *Taking Liberty*, 2002; *Or Give Me Death*, 2003; *Sarah's Ground*, 2004; *Mutiny's Daughter*, 2004.

BIBLIOGRAPHY: "Ann R." *Contemporary Authors Online*, 2001; "Ann R." *St. James Guide to Young Adult Writers*, 2nd ed., 1999; "Ann R." *Something about the Author*, vol. 78, 1994.

HEIDI HAUSER GREEN

RITTER, John H.

Author, b. 31 October 1951, San Diego, California

R. is the son of a journalist and grew up near the Mexican border in a rural area of eastern San Diego County. His parents moved to California from Ohio after his father took the job of SPORTS editor for the *San Diego Union*. After his mother's DEATH when he was four, he and his brothers spent a large amount of time playing baseball. His love of baseball was to become a major theme in his writing. After high school, during which he became interested in song writing and was especially influenced by Bob Dylan, he attended the University of California at San Diego, where met his wife. He then decided to leave college, becoming a painter's apprentice, and setting aside time to write.

In the 1980s he joined a local fiction group and took writing classes. His interest in YOUNG ADULT LITERATURE was influenced by his own experiences with prejudice and bias. In his first book, *Choosing up Sides*, he used the theme of baseball as background because it was a topic he knew well; he also understood the game's metaphorical value. *Choosing up Sides* takes place in the 1920s in southern Ohio. It is the story of Luke Bledsoe, oldest son of a preacher, and the conflict between his love of baseball and his father's fundamentalist religious beliefs.

His second novel, *Over the Wall*, also a historical novel, deals with the Vietnam War. It is the story of a boy's discoveries about himself and his father. Baseball remains a theme in this book as well in his latest novel, *The Boy Who Saved Baseball*, which was published in 2003. His novels attempt to provide alternative solutions to injustices faced by the main characters.

AWARDS: July BLUME Award, Society of Children's Book Writers and Illustrators, 1994; Children's Book Award, International Reading Association (IRA), Best Book for Young Adults, American Library Association (ALA), and Blue Ribbon Book, Bulletin of the Center for Children's Books, all 1999, and Young Adult Readers Choices, IRA, 2000, all for *Choosing up Sides*; Books for the TEEN Age list, New York Public Library, Parents' Guide to Children's Media Award, Shenandoah University, and Texas State Lone Star Book designation, all 2001, for *Over the Wall*.

BIBLIOGRAPHY: *Contemporary Authors Online*, 2001; www.johnritter.com

JOAN PEARLMAN

ROBERSON, Jennifer

Author, b. 26 October 1953, Kansas City, Missouri

R. is a 1982 graduate of Northern Arizona University. In addition to writing, R. is also a professional dog trainer and breeder. She also publishes under the pseudonyms Jay Mitchell and Jennifer O'Green.

While in college, R. began her writing career with the FANTASY *Shapechangers* (1984). This book began R.'s Chronicles of the Cheysuli SERIES, which currently spans eight novels (1984–92), and involves the ADVENTURES of a race of shapechangers. R.'s other lengthy series, the Sword-Dancer Saga, is a fantasy series about a male sword-dancer named Tiger and a female sword-dancer, Del. Both of these series and many of R.'s other stories are noted for their strong female characters. R. has also written three historical novels: *Lady of the Forest* (1992), *Lady of the Glen* (1996), and *Lady of Sherwood* (2000). R. has also produced three anthologies: *Return to Avalon* (1996), *Highwaymen: Robbers and Rogues* (1997), and *Out of Avalon* (2001).

Many of R.'s short works have been collected in anthologies, including seven in Marion Zimmer BRADLEY's *Sword and Sorceress* (vol. 1–8). R.'s latest novel is the sixth tale of Tiger and Del, *Sword-Sworn* (2002). Her Karavans series is forthcoming.

AWARDS: 1984 *Romantic Times* Best New Fantasy Author, *Shapechangers;* 1994 YALSA Best Books for Young Adults List, *Lady of the Forest.*

BIBLIOGRAPHY: *Contemporary Authors Online,* (2003); *St. James Guide to Fantasy Writers,* 1996; Author's website, http://cheysuli.com/

JAMES GAHAGAN

ROBERTS, Willo Davis
Author, b. 28 May 1928, Grand Rapids, Michigan; d. 19 November 2004, n.p.

R. pursued writing at an early age in order to fill a social void caused by frequent moves and shyness. After high school, R. found little time to write, as she and her husband were struggling to succeed as dairy farmers. R. sold her first novel in 1955, an adult MYSTERY titled *Murder at Grand Bay.* When R. went to work at a hospital, she continued to publish suspense novels. Upon learning of the fad genre called "nurse novels," R. transformed many of her previously written novels to feature "nurse heroines." She published many titles before the trend faded.

Although originally an adult novelist, R. is best known as an author for young people. She published her first children's book in 1975 after her editor suggested she rewrite *The View from the Cherry Tree* as

a children's book. Initially reluctant, R. rewrote the novel, which became the first of her many successful books for children and YA. In this mystery, a boy named Rob witnesses a murder. Preparing for his sister's wedding, his FAMILY is too busy to be bothered, and Rob is on his own against a murderer.

R. demonstrated her skill at writing in other genres in works like *Don't Hurt Laurie!* (1977), the story of a young victim of parental abuse. The novel received both praise and criticism for its violent content and remains popular after many years. R. was particularly successful in writing entertaining novels that deal realistically with human relationships. R. continued to write as she traveled with her husband, often gathering information for her novels on site.

AWARDS: *Don't Hurt Laurie!* (1977); Notable Children's Trade Book in the Field of Social Studies, Young Hoosier Book Award, West AUSTRALIAN Young Reader's Award; Mark Twain Award: *The Girl with the Silver Eyes* (1980), *Baby Sitting Is a Dangerous Job* (1985); 1986 Pacific Northwest Writers Conference Achievement Award for body of work; *Sugar Isn't Everything* (1987) was named Outstanding Science Trade Book for Children; Edgar Allan Poe Award: 1989 for *Megan's Island* (1988), 1995 for *The Absolutely True Story of My Visit to Yellowstone with the Terrible Rupes* (1994), 1997 for *Twisted Summer* (1996); 1990 Governor's Award for body of work; *Twisted Summer*: ALA Popular Paperbacks, 2004.

FURTHER WORKS: *The Minden Curse,* 1978; *The Petsitting Peril,* 1983; *No Monsters in the Closet,* 1983; *Elizabeth,* 1984; *Caroline,* 1984; *Victoria,* 1985; *The Magic Book,* 1986; *What Could Go Wrong?,* 1989; *To Grandmother's House We Go,* 1990; *Scared Stiff,* 1991; *Dark Secrets,* 1991; *Jo and the Bandit,* 1992; *What Are We Going to Do about David?,* 1993; *Secrets at Hidden Valley,* 1997; *The Kidnappers: A Mystery,* 1998; *Hostage,* 2000; *Buddy Is a Stupid Name for a Girl,* 2001; *Undercurrents,* 2002; *Rebel,* 2003; *Blood on His Hands,* 2004.

BIBLIOGRAPHY: Peacock, Scot, ed. *Something about the Author,* vol. 133, 2002.

JODI PILGRIM

ROCHMAN, Hazel (Fine)
Author, editor, critic, b. 13 April 1938, Johannesburg, South Africa

R. is perhaps best known for her writings and speeches on the importance of diversity and the need to move beyond the stereotypical understandings of others. Her early life prepared her well for this undertaking.

R. was born into a Latvian Jewish family in South Africa. Her parents had escaped the escalating Nazi movement in Europe prior to the beginning of World War II, only to settle in a country that was increasingly embroiled in its own racial and ethnic conflicts. R.'s childhood was spent in a comfortable suburb of Johannesburg, where her father was a physician. Her love of language and books was nourished through reading ADVENTURE stories and listening to her father recite POETRY. Although R. describes her family as liberal, she notes that she grew up fairly ignorant of racial conditions in South Africa. Segregation was status quo; while she cared about people, R. has said that in her early life, "people" meant white people and not blacks or other people of color.

After completing secondary school, R. earned a B.A. from the University of Witwatersrand and began to work as a journalist. About the same time, she married Hyman Rochman. While R. was not involved in anti-apartheid politics, her husband was, and R.'s political interests grew. The two left South Africa on a one-way passport and settled for ten years in England, where R. taught English in a girls' high school. Because of their activism, R. and her husband were not allowed to return to South Africa until after the fall of the apartheid government in the 1990s.

In 1972, R. and her family moved to Chicago. At this time, she pursued a library science degree at the University of Chicago. She worked for eight years as the LIBRARIAN at the University of Chicago laboratory school. In 1982, R. became a United States citizen.

In 1984, R. began reviewing YA books for *Booklist*. (Currently, R. is editor of the Books for Youth section of *Booklist*.) A respected and outspoken commentator, R. has also chaired the National Book Awards Committee for Young People's Literature and the Scott O'DELL Award Committee for historical fiction for young people.

R.'s experiences in political activism, librarianship, and book criticism provided her with an opportunity to advocate for MULTICULTURALISM—a term she views as inclusive, not separatist—in a book titled *Against Borders: Promoting Books for a Multicultural World* (1993). *Against Borders* contains essays and themed bibliographies targeted at YA readers. For this book, R. won the 1994 G. K. Hall Award for Library Literature.

In several story collections that R. edited, she has been able to explore multiculturalism further. In *Somehow Tenderness Survives: Stories of Southern Africa* (1988), R. brings together ten stories by writers such as Nadine Gordimer and Marc Matabane. By representing the different sides of the South African color line, she emphasizes the human impact of apartheid. R. explores related themes in other story collections (all coedited by Darlene Z. McCampbell), including identity in *Who Do You Think You Are?: Stories of Friends and Enemies* (1993), hatred and survival in *Bearing Witness: Stories of the HOLOCAUST* (1995), and journeys of transformation in *Leaving Home: Stories* (1997). In each collection, R. selects stories from authors more frequently associated with adult literature—Amy TAN, Tim O'BRIEN, Toni Morrison, John Updike, and Ray BRADBURY, for example—and presents them to a YA audience. Reviewers have praised her insightful and scrupulous skills as editor of these collections, noting her ability to select stories that illuminate the theme.

AWARDS: 1989 Children's Reading Round Table of Chicago Award; 1994 G. K. Hall Award for Library Literature, *Against Borders: Promoting Books for a Multicultural World; Somehow Tenderness Survives: Stories of Southern Africa:* 1988 American Library Association Best Book for Young Adults and 1989 New York Public Library Best Book for the TEEN Age; *Who Do You Think You Are?: Stories of Friends and Enemies:* 1994 American Library Association Best Book for Young Adults and 1994 *School Library Journal* Best Book; 1996 American Library Association Best Book for Young Adults, *Bearing Witness: Stories of the Holocaust;* 1998 American Library Association Best Book for Young Adults, *Leaving Home: Stories.*

BIBLIOGRAPHY: "Hazel R." *Contemporary Authors Online,* 2003. Reproduced in Biography Resource Center, 2003. http://galenet.galegroup.com/servlet/ BioRC; R., Hazel. "Against Borders," *Horn Book* magazine 71, no. 2 (144–56); R., Hazel. "The 2000 May Hill Arbuthnot Honor Lecture: A Stranger Comes to You." *Journal of Youth Services in Libraries* 13, no. 4 (20–27).

CAROL L. TILLEY

RODOWSKY, Colby

Author, 1932, n.p.

R. resides in Baltimore, Maryland—on Norwood Road—across from the home where she lived as a child. When R. was ten, her family relocated to New York and from there moved again to Washington, D.C., but ultimately they returned to Baltimore. R. attended college in Maryland as well, graduating with a major in English from the College of Notre Dame of Maryland. As a teacher, R. always found time to read and write in between her elementary-school classes and then her special-education classes. Marriage to a lawyer resulted in a houseful of six children, five girls and a boy. All of R.'s children married, and she now has thirteen grandchildren. A published author of works since the 1970s, R.'s works span a wide range—some are for young children, while others are definitely written for TEENS.

Among the latter are *Spindrift* (2000) and *Not Quite a Stranger* (2003). In *Spindrift*, Cassie's exposure to marital infidelity within her FAMILY changes her perceptions of everything. Charlotte must deal with a new addition to the family in *Not Quite A Stranger*. In *Remembering Mog* (1996), an American Library Association Notable Book, Annie slowly comes to terms with living without Mog after his sister is the victim of a senseless crime, while in *Sydney, Invincible* (1995), Sydney realizes that high school is not the ideal time to become a big sister again, or to adjust to a parent's remarriage or the problems of a boy friend, all while being responsible for the production of the school paper. *Hannah in Between* (1994), another American Library Association Best Book for YA/International Readers Association-Children's Book Council Young Adult Choice/Quick Picks for Young Adults—chronicles Hannah's need to make difficult choices that a family member's addiction issues force. In *Lucy Peale* (1992), the title character must face not only being raped, but the fact that a child is coming as a result. Unable to confide in her fundamentalist family, she must work out her own destiny. In *Sydney, Herself* (1989), a class assignment leads Sydney into wild imaginings.

R.'s work includes historical and time-travel books, as well as books about everyday life.

AWARDS: *Hannah in Between:* 1995 ALA Best Book for Young Adults/IRA-CBC Young Adult Choice/Quick Picks for Young Adults; *Remembering Mog:* 1996 ALA Notable Book; *Julie's Daughter:* 1985 ALA Best Books for Young Adults.

FURTHER WORKS: *What about Me?*, 1976; *P.S. Write Soon,*, 1978; *Evy-Ivy Over,* 1978; *A Summer's Worth of Shame: A Novel,* 1980; *The Gathering Room,* 1981;

H, My Name Is Henley, 1982; *Julie's Daughter,* 1985; *Fitchett's Folly,* 1987; *Keeping Time,* 1988; *Dog Days,* 1990; *Jenny and the Grand Old Great-Aunts,* 1992; *The Turnabout Shop,* 1998; *Not My Dog,* 1999; *Jason Rat-a-Tat,* 2002; *Not Quite a Stranger,* 2003.

BIBLIOGRAPHY: www.amazon.com; www.childrens bookguild.org/rodowsky.htm; www.novelst4.epnet.com

JEANNE MARIE RYAN

ROGASKY, Barbara
Author, editor, b. 9 April 1933, Wilmington, Delaware

After working for many years as an editor for a variety of children's publishers, R. turned to a career of full-time photography and writing for young people. Her works include RETELLINGS of Grimm FAIRY TALES and Jewish folklore as well as collections of POETRY. *Smoke and Ashes: The Story of the HOLOCAUST* (1988) is a highly praised history for young people. Lauded as one of the finest books of its kind on the subject, an updated and expanded edition was published in 2002. Upon its publication in 1988, *Smoke and Ashes* was cited as a Best INFORMATIONAL Book for children by *Publishers Weekly, School Library Journal,* and both the children's and YA services divisions of the American Library Association.

FURTHER WORKS: *Winter Poems,* 1994; *The Golem: A Version,* 1996; *Leaf by Leaf: Autumn Poems,* 2001; *Gilgul,* 2002.

SOURCES: *Something about the Author,* vol. 86, pp. 201–3.

EDWARD T. SULLIVAN

ROMANCE IN YA LITERATURE

While educators encourage TEENS to read and wonder why they lose library users and readers at adolescence, it is important to think about how adults respond to their reading choices. Adult readers of the R. genre frequently feel they need to apologize for their reading interests. R.s have historically been treated as a lesser genre; yet over half of all PAPERBACKS sold are romances! According to Romance Writers of America, Inc., "seventy-one percent of romance readers say they read their first romance at age sixteen or younger." Clearly, teenagers read romance novels.

Teen readers are looking for the same things as adult R. readers: a good story, a satisfying emotional relationship between the hero and the heroine, and the promise of a happy-ever-after ending. These, in fact, are what define a romance. According to Romance Writers of America, a R. has two critical elements: "a central love story" and an "emotionally satisfying and optimistic ending." The R. may have many subplots, settings, and include a variety of plot elements, as long as those two criteria are met. The main plot must focus on two people falling in love and fostering a relationship. Any conflicts or climaxes must pertain to that love story.

There are other important reasons that teenage readers turn to R.s. Sexual development, romantic interests, and first crushes are crucial parts of adolescent development and are important steps to becoming an adult. It makes sense that R.s are of priority interest to adolescents as they experience these things for the first time. Reading R.s allows them to explore vicariously relationships for which they are not ready. R.s show examples of the different ways men and women interact and present teens with information about sex and sexuality. As teens begin relationships and experience the ups and downs of crushes and dating, R. novels, with their happy endings, are very reliable and comforting.

Before YA literature was considered a genre of its own, there existed the so-called junior novel. These early novels, specifically written for adolescents, were quite gender-specific. Thus, the novels for girls were about girls and boys and dating, and mostly R. A good example of these sweet, chaste, early romances is the classic *Seventeenth Summer* by Maureen DALY (1942). In the 1950s Beverly Cleary contributed *Fifteen* (1956) and *Jean and Johnny* (1959) to this genre. These junior novels were a precursor to the realistic young adult genre that emerged in the early 1960s.

The development of gritty realism in the late 1970s and 1980s can be seen in the R.s that came out of that period; these novels acknowledged the full development of adolescents, including their burgeoning sexuality. They maintain the required qualities of the R., but they address other issues as well, including interracial R., sex, and sexual orientation.

In 1975, Judy BLUME's *Forever* shocked many people with its frank dialogue involving two seventeen-year-olds who become lovers. Sexual responsibility is shown when Katherine goes to Planned Parenthood for birth control pills. Michael and Katherine are also represented as desiring to express their love for each other through sexual intercourse; their choice to become partners is not a flippant decision. Similarly, Annie and Liza in Nancy GARDEN's *Annie on My Mind* (1982) are teens falling in love, grappling with their complex feelings, and embarking on a relationship. This lesbian love story was a pivotal work in the young adult genre; its portrayal of physically and emotionally healthy homosexual teens falling in love was a real breakthrough. Since its publication, gay and lesbian characters and stories are being published more regularly.

Today, R.s for teens are found in the full range of adult R. subgenres, including SERIES, paranormal, historical, and mainstream fiction. Series R.s, like other series fiction, offer a reliable format as well as a consistent and steady supply of new books. A very popular subgenre is the R. that incorporates DEATH AND DYING and/or a paranormal encounter. Lurlene McDaniel is the most well-known writer of these stories. Her weepies often feature a teen with a terminal illness; whether the characters go into remission or die, they will surely find pure love. R. need not end with DEATH, either, as seen in Cherie BENNETT's Enchanted Hearts series. Ghosts and past life loves are tremendously appealing to those who enjoy tragic R.s. Time travel R.s, such as Caroline B. COONEY's Both Sides of Time series, also fit into this category. Paranormal R. has seen a surge in popularity in the 1990s. Vampires, werewolves, and shapeshifters can now enjoy falling in love, just like any other teen. Books such as Patrice KINDL's *Owl in Love* (1993) or Annette Curtis KLAUSE's *Blood and Chocolate* (1997) were notable standouts in their respective years. Historical R.s are a huge field in adult R. publishing. Many publishers have reached out to the teen market by creating their own line of teen historical R.s. For example, the Avon True R. books are quality R. for teens written by adult R. authors and set in a wide variety of time periods. They are similar to the adult lines of historical fiction but are far more chaste.

Patricia Cabot, author of historical adult R.s, is better known in the world of YA literature as Meg CABOT, author of The Princess Diaries series. Her YA novels, particularly *Princess in Love* (2002), are examples of mainstream teen fiction with strong romantic elements. These types of teen R.s are perhaps the most widely read, and they follow the trends of teen literature in general. For example, novels in verse became extremely popular, and Sonya Sones's *What My Mother Doesn't Know* (2001) was a R. told entirely in poems. YA literature has become more MULTICULTURALLY diverse, as can be seen in *Romiette and Julio* (1999) by Sharon DRAPER.

R.s for teens have developed consistently with YA literature. Teens today can read a wide variety of types of R.s featuring strong, independent young women in love. Although we might dismiss early R.s like *Seventeenth Summer* as simplistic and overly wholesome, R.s like the Sweet Dreams series as predictable and fluffy, R.s like Lurlene McDaniel's tearjerker novels as melodramatic, these R.s share something important that makes them valuable additions to a YA collection. R. novels depict teenagers dealing with feelings and emotions that are virtually universal during adolescence: Does he like me? Do I like her? What if my friends don't like him? Am I normal? Is it love? The ability to fall in love and have these feelings is what makes us human. Reading about these feelings and relationships connects, comforts, and entertains teens, making R. an ideal and important YA genre.

BIBLIOGRAPHY: R. Writers of America. www.rwanational.org; CART, Michael. *From Romance to Realism: 50 Years of Changes in Young Adult Literature,* 1995; Forman, Jack. "Young Adult Novels." *Children's Books and Their Creators,* 1995; *Horn Book Magazine; School Library Journal; Book Links.*

SARAH CORNISH

ROSENBERG, Liz

Author, b. February 3, 1958, Glen Cove, New York

R. says, "Reading children's books was a large part of how I survived childhood. . . . In writing for children, I remember that past and repay that debt."

R.'s stories vary from refugees fleeing WAR-torn countries and children grieving over a dead FAMILY member to alphabet books and books of nursery rhymes for even younger children. Her book *The Carousel* was a PBS Reading Rainbow feature book, and *Monster Mama* won the Children's Choice Award.

She also goes on to say, "[Children's books and POETRY] try to go directly to the heart of the matter." Her book of poems, *The Fire Music,* won the Agnes Starret Poetry Prize in 1986. Her poetry anthologies for YAS all include adult poems: *Earth-Shattering Poems,* the award-winning *Light-Gathering Poems,*

and *The Invisible Ladder: An Anthology of Contemporary American Poems for Young Readers,* which won the Claudia Lewis Poetry Prize and was selected for New York Public Library's Best Books for TEENS. She believes that "it's all right if you can only grab hold of one corner of it [the poem], because eventually that corner may be enough to pull you all the way through."

R's YOUNG ADULT novels include *Heart and Soul* and *Seventeen.* She has been an English professor at SUNY–Binghamton since 1979, teaching creative writing courses. She was awarded the Binghamton Excellence in Teaching Award for 1983–84, and she was a National Kellogg Fellow from 1982 to 1985.

AWARDS: *Monster Mama,* Children's Choice Award; *The Fire Music,* 1986 Agnes Starret Poetry Prize; *The Invisible Ladder: An Anthology of Contemporary American Poems for Young Readers,* Claudia Lewis Poetry Prize, New York Public Library's Best Books for Teens.

FURTHER WORKS: *Adelaide and the Night Train,* 1989; *The Scrap Doll,* 1992; *Children of Paradise,* 1993; *Moonbathing,* 1996; *Eli and Uncle Dawn,* 1997; *A Big and Little Alphabet,* 1997; *These Happy Eyes,* 1999; *On Christmas Eve,* 2000; *Roots and Flowers,* 2001; *We Wanted You,* 2002.

BIBLIOGRAPHY: http://english.binghamton.edu/faculty/lros; *Contemporary Authors: New Revision Series,* vol. 89, 2000; *Something about the Author,* vol. 129, 2002.

BRITT ANDERSON

ROSENBLATT, Louise

Educator, b. 23 August 1904, Atlantic City, New Jersey; d. 2005, Arlington, Virginia

A distinguished educator, R. continues to be a powerful influence in literary, theoretical, and pedagogical studies. R. has published numerous works including: her pedagogical study, *Literature as Exploration,* 1938, and her theoretical work, *The Reader, the Text, the Poem,* 1978, which are esteemed as her most notable contributions.

R. attended Barnard College at Columbia University, where she graduated with honors. During her sophomore year at Barnard, she roomed with Margaret Mead who triggered her interest in anthropological studies. She then pursued a doctorate in comparative literature at the Sorbonne. Her dissertation, entitled *L'lde del'art pour l'art dans la literature anglaid pendant la periode victoriemme,* focused on the nineteenth-century aesthetic movement in England and France, and was published in 1931 when R. was twenty-seven years old. Throughout her life, her thinking was influenced by great minds such as John Dewey, Albert Einstein, Horace, C. S. Peirce, and Mead. These influences, as well as studies in linguistics, ethnography, the arts, anthropology, philosophy, education and social sciences, have helped create a multidisciplinary lens through which she views and interprets the world.

Returning to New York, R. taught at Barnard and studied anthropology with professors Franz Boas and Ruth Benedict who influenced her understanding of how diverse cultures encourage the development of a democratic society. Democracy continued to be a paramount focus throughout R.'s life. She viewed education as the key to preserving and improving a democratic way of life in which original ideas are valued. From her viewpoint, readers experience literature personally, putting themselves in the place of others so that they can "envision the broader human consequences of political decisions." (Karolides, p. 169)

Since the first publication of *Literature as Exploration* in 1938, R.'s theories about the important relationship between text and the reader have endured. The New Criticism movement of the 1930s through the 1950s presupposed that the reader should approach a text passively, receiving the author's meaning. R.'s transactional theory introduced the idea that readers actively create meaning in a cyclical fashion by transacting with text. Her position has never disregarded nor negated the value of literary criticism, "I welcome any kind of effective classroom practice or combination of lecture and discussion methods, so long as it is productive interchanges with the teacher and among the students." (Karolides, pp. 161–62).

In 1978, R. published her second major work, *The Reader, the Text, the Poem,* in which she draws the distinction between the *efferent* and *aesthetic* modes of experiencing text. Within the efferent point of view, students are motivated by a need to acquire information (from the Latin *effere,* to carry away). On the other hand, from the aesthetic point of view, the focus is on the reader's lived-through experience. Efferent and aesthetic readings are not on opposite ends of the continuum but rather are a mixture of the two. Transacting with text recognizes the dynamic shifting

back and forth from one end to the other of this continuum. (Rosenblatt, 1978).

R. spent the majority of her teaching career at New York University (1948–1972). She also taught at Rutgers University, Michigan State University, University of Pennsylvania, Northwestern University, and others. R. was married to Sidney Ratner, scholar in history and philosophy, for more than sixty years. R. celebrated her one-hundredth birthday on August 23, 2004.

AWARDS: Franco-American Exchange Fellow 1925–1926; Commission on Human Relations of the Progressive Education Association 1935; Guggenheim Fellow 1942–43; Associate Chief of the Central Reports section of the Bureau of Overseas Intelligence of the Office of War Information 1943–45; NYU Great Teacher Award 1972; NCTE Distinguished Research 1980; Leland Jacobs Award for Literature 1981; Assembly on Adolescent Literature Award 1984; International Reading Hall of Fame 1992; Outstanding Educator in English Language, 1999.

FURTHER WORK: R., L., *Making Meaning with Texts: Selected Essays,* 2005.

BIBLIOGRAPHY: B. Cullinan and L. Galda, 2001, *Literature and the Child* (5th ed.); Karolides, N. J., 1999, "Theory and Practice: An Interview with Louise M. R.," *Language Arts,* 77, 158–70.

DEBORAH A. WOOTEN AND
ELIZABETH ANDERSON

ROSTKOWSKI, Margaret I.
Author, b. 12 January 1945, Little Rock, Arkansas

R. began her writing career relatively late, at the age of thirty-seven. An avid reader as a child, R. moved to Utah early in life. She received degrees from Middlebury College (B.A., 1967) and the University of Kansas (M.A.T., 1971). Beginning in 1974, R. taught languages and writing in Ogden, Utah, public schools, and she continues this work today. She has been an active member of the Friends of Weber County Libraries. R. was married to Charles Anthony R. in 1970 and has two sons.

R.'s books often deal with FAMILY relationships and the interaction between individuals and history. R. has studied history extensively, and each of her novels for young adults is tied to a period in the past. *After the Dancing Days* (1986), her most successful novel, is set in the aftermath of World War I. The book won several awards, including the Golden Kite

Award from the Society of Children's Book Writers in 1986. *The Best of Friends* (1989) takes place in the Vietnam War era, and *Moon Dancer* (1995), while contemporary, explores the ancient and mystical culture of the Anasazi in the American Southwest. R. credits much of her inspiration to her daily contact with TEENAGE students. She also draws from her own memories and experiences, such as the memory of visiting the hospital with her father, who was a doctor. R. extracts the feelings from these memories and reproduces them within her stories.

AWARDS: Golden Kite Award from the Society of Children's Book Writers, 1986; BBYA, 1986; Children's Book Award from the International Reading Association, 1987; Jefferson Cup Award from the Virginia Library Association, 1987, ALA Popular Paperbacks, 2002, all for *After the Dancing Days* (1986). Sequoyah Young Adult Book Award Masterlist, 1995; Texas Lone Star Reading List selection, 1995; New York Public Library Books for the Teen Age selection, 1995, all for *Moon Dancer* (1995).

BIBLIOGRAPHY: *Contemporary Authors, New Revision Series,* vol. 87, 2000; *Something about the Author,* vol. 59, 1990; *Twentieth Century Young Adult Writers,* 1st ed. 1994.

LIZ HANE

ROTTMAN, S(usan) L(ynn)

Author, educator, b. 12 July 1970, Albany, Georgia

R. started writing stories when she was in grade school. She continued writing through high school and college, and one of these early stories even won her a scholarship while she was a student at Colorado State University. After college, R. became a teacher. She had dreams of becoming a novelist but virtually stopped mentioning them after a colleague insinuated that all new, young English teachers shared that same unattainable wish. R. began teaching with enthusiasm at her first job, a junior high school in Colorado Springs. There she saw for the first time the frustration and lack of interest in her students' eyes. R. determined that she needed to capture the interest of her students in order to get them to improve their reading skills. She set out to write stories that were both interesting and of sufficient literary quality to use with her students, and she has succeeded in that goal several times over.

In all of R.'s books, she introduces TEENS to their peers—young people with whom others can easily relate and sympathize. The young people in her books are imperfect, realistically portrayed teenagers who are forced to deal with obstacles such as alcoholic parents, abuse and neglect, the burden of caring for a mentally challenged sibling, the DEATH of loved ones, runaways, crime, and so much more. These books have been critically acclaimed, widely accepted and are indeed read by teenagers.

In *Hero* (1997), R.'s first novel, ninth-grader Sean has had to endure a great deal of physical and emotional abuse from his alcoholic mother, compounded by the absence of his father. As a result, he has become difficult, angry, and distrustful. Being sentenced to a week's community service on a farm for fighting and breaking curfew helps Sean work through his anger and begin to trust people again. This book is a perfect choice for reluctant readers, especially those tough kids who share some of Sean's prickliness. R. has also made *Hero* appealing to average teens by presenting Sean as accessible and likeable, even to those with whom he has nothing in common.

R. takes another tack with *Head Above Water* (1999). Skye, R.'s only female protagonist to date, is saddled with much of the care of her brother Sunny, who has Down syndrome. At the same time, she is trying to juggle her schoolwork, her chores at home, her first boyfriend, and her spot on the swim team. Like Sean in *Hero,* Skye is a character who suffers, but the versatile R. creates a whole new world and a completely different set of circumstances for this character to inhabit. R. also reaches an entirely new audience of adolescent girls with *Head Above Water.*

R.'s multifaceted talent is evident in all of her books: some full of SPORTS and action; others quiet, yet just as powerful. R.'s observation of her students through the years has assisted her in her writing, and many of her former students have inspired the characters that have appeared in her books. R.'s experiences as a coach and sports enthusiast have also aided her commanding descriptions of swim meets and whitewater rafting expeditions.

R. currently has many projects in the works, including books for younger children and adults. She is married and has two children.

AWARDS: *Hero* (1997): Young Adult/Children's Oklahoma Book Award, Nevada Young Readers Award, New York Public Library Books for the Teen Age citation, ALA Best Book for Young Adults, 1999,

Rough Waters (1998): ALA Quick Pick for Reluctant Young Adult Readers, Young Adult Choice Winner by the International Reading Association; ALA Best Books for Young Adults, 2000, *Head Above Water* (1999); *Stetson* (2002): ALA Best Book for Young Adults, 2003, Texas Library Association TAYSHAS High School Reading List.

FURTHER WORKS: *Rough Waters,* 1998; *Stetson,* 2002; *Shadow of a Doubt,* 2003.

BIBLIOGRAPHY: *Something about the Author,* vol. 106, 1999; Carroll, Pamela Sissi. "An Interview with Author, Teacher, Mom, Coach (Whew!) S. L. R." *The* ALAN *Review,* n.d.

KIMBERLY L. PAONE

ROWLING, J(oanne) K(athleen)
Author, b. 31 July 1965, Chipping Sodbury, England

R. spent most of her childhood living in the countryside in the southwest of England. Before moving to Tutshill (on the border between England and Wales) at the age of nine, R. lived near Bristol, England. The strongest memory she has of Tutshill is her terrifying teacher, Mrs Morgan, from Tutshill Primary School, who, R. says, seated her pupils according to their marks. From there she went to Wyedean Comprehensive, where her favourite classes were English and foreign languages. Very early she realized that she wanted to be a writer, though she never really told anyone; her favorite pastime was to write stories to entertain her friends at lunchtime. In her final year at Wyedean, she became Head Girl.

R. went to the University of Exeter in Devon, England, where she studied French and Greek, and Roman Studies. As part of her degree, she spent a year in Paris as a teaching assistant. In 1986, she received her degree from Exeter and moved to Clapham, South London. She found a job as a secretary, using the office computer to type her stories. In 1990, she moved from London to Manchester with her boyfriend. One weekend, as she had been looking for a flat in Manchester, she took a train back to London and the idea of HARRY POTTER came to her. Six months later, Rowling's mother died at the age of forty-five. Saddened by this terrible loss, she decided to move to Oporto, Portugal (1991), where she taught English for a while and started writing the first Harry Potter book. In 1992, she married a Portuguese journalist and bore their child. As R. fell out of love with her husband, she moved to Edinburgh, Scotland, where, being a twenty-seven-year-old unemployed single mother, she lived on public assistance.

Following her sister's enthusiastic advice, R. applied for and won an £8,000 grant from the Scottish Arts Council that enabled her to finish *Harry Potter and the Philosopher's Stone* (1995). Not long after she finished the book, the publishing company Bloomsbury bought the rights in the United Kingdom and Scholastic for the U.S. market. In 1998, the first Harry Potter book was published, and very soon after that, R. became one of the most popular children's authors of all time.

As the writer of *Harry Potter and the Philosopher's Stone* (published as *Harry Potter and the Sorcerer's Stone* in the U.S.) (1997), *Harry Potter and the Chamber of Secrets* (1998), *Harry Potter and the Prisoner of Azkaban* (1999), *Harry Potter and the Goblet of Fire* (2000), and *Harry Potter and the Order of the Phoenix* (2003), R. has revolutionized the world of children's literature and brought it unprecedented critical attention. The Harry Potter books are the best-selling books in the history of children's literature, and they have been translated into more than sixty-one languages. As well as bringing R. financial success and international fame, the Harry Potter books have gained her some prestigious literary awards. In 1999, *Harry Potter and the Prisoner of Azkaban* was nominated for the Whitbread Prize event, which generated huge debate in the media. As the jury considered R.'s novel not "respectable" enough for such a prestigious award, the prize was finally given to Seamus Heaney for his translation of *Beowulf,* and R. received just the Whitbread Children's Book Award instead. In March 2001, R. received the Order of the British Empire, a medal of achievement awarded by the Queen of England. *Harry Potter and the Half-blood Prince,* published in 2005 had a record print run.

The Harry Potter SERIES, R. says, is to be composed of seven novels, covering the seven years Harry and his friends spend at Hogwarts School of Witchcraft and Wizardry. Since they are centered around the school, the Harry Potter books share many characteristics with other school story ADVENTURES. Rich in the MYTHOLOGY and archetypes of the FANTASY genre, it is no wonder the adventures of Harry and his friends, as they face the forces of evil embodied by the wizard Voldemort, who killed Harry's parents, are so popular with readers of all ages.

SELECT AWARDS: Smarties Gold Award: 1997, *Harry Potter and the Philosopher's Stone,* 1998, *Harry Potter and the Chamber of Secrets;* Children's Book of the Year by the British Book Awards in 1997, 1998; *Harry Potter and the Sorcerer's Stone,* ALA Best Books for Young Adults, 1999; *Harry Potter and the Chamber of Secrets,* Best Book for Young Adults, 2000; *Harry Potter and the Prisoner of Azkaban,* ALA Best Books for Young Adults, 2000; *Harry Potter and the Goblet of Fire,* Hugo Award.

BIBLIOGRAPHY: Nel, Philip. *JK Rowling's Harry Potter Novels,* 2001; "J. K. Rowling" in P. Hunt, *Children's Literature,* 2001, pp. 122–24; http:www.bloomsburymagazine.com/harrypotter/muggles_index.html

SEBASTIAN CHAPLEAU

RUBENSTEIN, Gillian M.

Author, b. 29 August 1942, Potten End, Berkhamstead, Hertfordshire, England

R. grew up in England and attended Oxford University where she studied languages. Now living in AUSTRALIA, R. is well known for her works of SCIENCE FICTION and FANTASY. R. began writing for YA when her TEEN son stopped reading due to the lack of interesting material. Her first novel *Space Demons* (1986) was written to compete with his love of computers. *Space Demons* won many awards, including Young Australians Best Book Award (1990). R. brings her life experiences into her novels; she drew on her schooling when she created her own language in *Galax-Arena* (1992). *At Ardilla* (1991) is based on summer holidays with her children. Her love of animals is captured in *Foxspell* (1994), *Answers to Brut* (1988), *Pure Chance* (1998), and her popular Jake and Pete SERIES. Even previous work experience, as in *Under the Cat's Eye* (1997), is drawn upon. R. has written over thirty books for children and young adults, eight plays and many SHORT STORIES as well.

AWARDS: Children's Book Council of Australia Book of the Year, 1989 for *Beyond the Labyrinth,* 1995 for *Foxspell.*

FURTHER WORKS: *Melanie and the Night Animal,* 1988; *Skymaze,* 1991; *Flashback, the Amazing Adventures of a Film Horse,* 1990; *Keep Me Company,* 1991; *Shinkei,* 1995; *Witch Music,* 1996; *Annie's Brother's Suit,* 1996; *The Mermaid of Bondi Beach,* 1999; *The Whale's Child,* 2003.

BIBLIOGRAPHY: *Authors and Artists for Young Adults,* vol. 22, 1997; Gillian R.'s website, 2003.

MARISA KAMMERLING

RUBY, Lois

Author, b. September 11, 1942, San Francisco, California

R. is an author of historical fiction, realistic novels, and stories with Jewish-American themes for YA and middle grade children. She grew up in San Francisco, where she walked to the library every Saturday to check out books. Her father, Philip Fox, was an artist, and her mother, Eva (Feldman), was an apartment manager. R. won a contest in the seventh grade with an essay entitled "Use Your Garbage Can," and while a sophomore in high school wrote a satire on students in her school that was published in *Teen Magazine.*

R. attended the University of Berkeley, receiving a degree in English and a master's degree in library science from San Jose State College. She worked as a YA LIBRARIAN at the Dallas Public Library. R.'s books mirror the lives of TEENS today. Her fiction addresses controversial and day-to-day adolescent issues such as religion, relationships, racism, and diverse cultures. She calls it "hard, contemporary fiction for mature teenagers." She also writes stories and historical fiction for young adults. R. lived in Wichita, Kansas, for thirty years and, as a result, her writing has been influenced by what she calls "Kansasisms."

R. attributes part of her writing style to the fact that as a small child she lived in the Dominican Republic at a time when that country was ruled by a dictator. She remembers those times more vividly than other times in her early years. She also spent a great deal of time with her grandmother, a Yiddish woman for whom R. would read and write letters. Her first book, *Arriving at a Place You've Never Left,* a collection of SHORT STORIES, was published in 1977.

R. presently lives in Albuquerque, New Mexico, with husband Tom, a psychologist, whom she married in 1965. The author has three sons, David, Kenn, and Jeff.

AWARDS: American Library Association Best Books for Young Adults: 1977 for *Arriving At a Place You've Never Left,* 1994 for *Miriam's Well; Two Truths in My Pocket:* Notable Children's Trade Book in the Field of Social Studies, National Council for the Social Studies, and 1982 Children's Book Council; 1995 Children's Book Council, *Steal Away Home;* New York City Public Library Books for the Teen Age: 1994 for *Miriam's Well,* 1995 for *Skin Deep,* and 1995 for *Steal Away Home.*

FURTHER WORKS: *What Do You Do in Quicksand?,* 1979; *Two Truths in My Pocket,* 1982; *This Old Man,* 1984; *Pig-Out Inn,* 1987; *Words on the Page, the World in Your Hands* (contributor), 1990; *The Voice of Youth Advocates Reader* (contributor), 1990; *Miriam's Well,* 1993; *Steal Away Home,* 1994; *Skin Deep,* 1994; *Soon Be Free,* 2000; *Swindletop,* 2000; *The Moxie Kid,* 2001.

BIBLIOGRAPHY: *Contemporary Authors,* vol. 183; *Something about the Author,* vol. 105; Lois R. website, http://www.loisruby.com

M. NAOMI WILLIAMSON

RYAN, Pam Muñoz
Author, b. 25 December 1951, Bakersfield, California

R. was born to Don Bell and Esperanza Muñoz in Bakersfield, California. As a child, R. rode a bicycle to the local air-conditioned library to escape the scorching heat of the San Joaquin Valley summers. The library became her favorite place to spend hot days, and the author credits it for the development of her love of books and reading.

R.'s favorite book in junior high was *Sue Barton, Student Nurse,* but she remembers also reading the CLASSICS *Treasure Island* and *Gone with the Wind.* In addition to the printed word, she heard stories told by her maternal grandmother, Esperanza Ortega, the real-life inspiration for the main character in the award-winning book *Esperanza Rising* (2000). That same grandmother was the "matriarchal hub" of her FAMILY. R. remembers many large celebrations with aunts, uncles, and other family members who lived nearby. She is the oldest of three sisters and the oldest of twenty-three first cousins on her mother's side.

R. knew she wanted to work with books and thought she might like to be a teacher. She attended college and received her bachelor's and master's degrees from San Diego State. After working in education as a bilingual teacher and an early childhood administrator, a professor convinced her to write stories. At age thirty-two, R. wrote *One Hundred Is a Family* (1994), a beginning concept book that uses numbers one to ten in various groupings to represent the diverse makeup of families today. One day while shopping, R. observed the misuse of the American flag. She was inspired to write her second PICTURE BOOK, *The Flag We Love* (1996), illuminating the history of the flag in verse form coupled with illustrations of events in American history.

After winning awards and successfully completing additional picture books, Pam wrote *Riding Freedom* (1998), historical fiction based on the true story of Charlotte Parkhust, a child who ran away from an orphanage in the 1800s to follow her dream of working with horses. Disguising herself as a boy in order to be a stagecoach driver in California, Charlotte survived on her own in a man's world as Charlie Parkhurst, and was the first woman in U.S. history to vote.

R.s Novel *Esperanza Rising* is a fictionalized account of her grandmother's childhood journey from a wealthy life in Aguascalientes, Mexico, to the tough labor camps and work farms of Southern California during the Great Depression. Written with honesty and clarity, *Esperanza Rising* presents a rich story of immigration, hardship, and the struggle to succeed in spite of all obstacles. It has won more than eleven awards, including the prestigious Pura Belpre Award given to LATINO/A writers.

R. uses personal experience for inspiration and the library for meticulous background research for first-person accounts and archival records. She is a full-time writer and has numerous picture books to her credit. She frequently works on a novel and a picture book at the same time. She is married, has four children, and resides in Leucadia, California.

SELECT AWARDS: *Riding Freedom:* Teacher's Choice Award, National Willa Cather Award for Best Young Adult Novel, both 1999; *Esperanza Rising:* 2000 *Smithsonian* Magazine Notable Children's Book, 2000 *Publishers Weekly* Best Book of the Year, 2001 Jane Addams Children's Book Award, 2001 Women's International League for Peace and Freedom Excellence in a Work of Fiction Award, 2001 American Library Association Top Ten Best Books for Young Adults, 2002 Pura Belpre Author Award, 2003 Charlie May Simon Children's Book Award; *When Marion Sang:* NCTE Orbis Pictus Award, *School Library Journal* Best Book of the Year, 2003 ALA Sibert Honor Award, ALA Notable Children's Books, 2003, and Parent's Choice Gold Award.

SELECT FURTHER WORKS: *Hello, Ocean!* 2001; *Mud is Cake,* 2002; *When Marion Sang: The True Recital of Marian Anderson,* 2002; *A Box of Friends,* 2003; *How Do You Raise a Raisin?,* 2003; *Becoming Naomi Leon,* 2004.

BIBLIOGRAPHY: Biography Resource Center, 2003; "Pam Munoz R.: Children's Author," http://www.pammunozryan.com/; "Pam Munoz R.'s Biography." Scholastic Author Studies homepage. http://www2.scholastic.com/teachers/authorsandbooks/authorstudies/authorhome.jhtml?authorID=1406&displayName=Booklist

KATE NAGY

RYAN, Sara

Author, b. November 13, 1971, Athens, Ohio

R. received her B.A. in medieval and renaissance studies from the University of Michigan and earned her master of information and library science degree in 1995, also from the University of Michigan. She was one of the founders of the Internet Public Library (www.ipl.org), where she worked until 1997 when she moved to Portland, Oregon. In addition to writing and keeping her Internet BLOG updated, she works full time as a School Corps LIBRARIAN for Multnomah County Library, Oregon.

R.'s first novel, *Empress of the World* (2002), a love story between two TEENAGE girls at a summer institute for gifted youth, received the attention of numerous literary critics. SLJ commented that "the character seem to breath in their realism and the setting . . . is evoked in sensual detail."

R. is active in the library world. She has served on the Young Adult Library Services Association board, YALSA's Teen website Advisory Committee, and Outstanding Books for the College Bound Committee. She was co-chair of YALSA's President's Program for the annual meeting of the ALA in Orlando and is a member of the Society of Children's Book Writers and Illustrators. R. was co-author of the Tag Team Tech column in *VOYA (Voice of Youth Advocates)* from 2000 to 2003, and has published articles in *School Library Journal* and *Journal of Youth Services in Libraries.*

AWARDS: *Empress of the World:* ALA Best Books for Young Adults, 2002 Oregon Book Award, and New York Public Library Books for the TEEN Age, all 2002.

FURTHER WORKS: *Me and Edith Head* (illus. Steve Lieber), 2001; "Launchpad to Neptune" with Randy POWELL in *Girl Meets Boy,* 2005.

BIBLIOGRAPHY: www.sararyan.com; http://raven stonepress.com/sараryan.html

SARAH E. NELSEN

RYLANT, Cynthia

Writer, educator, librarian, b. 6 June 1954 Hopewell, Virginia

R. is an author of fiction, nonfiction, and POETRY for children and YAs, as well as an author and author/illustrator of PICTURE BOOKS for children. R. is known the world over as a gifted writer who has contributed some of the most memorable works to several genres of young people's literature. Like many children's authors, she bases her works on her own childhood experiences, especially growing up in the West Virginia mountains. R., the creator of contemporary novels and historical fiction for YA, also has written books on FANTASY and middle grade fiction, as well as lyrical prose poems, collections of SHORT STORIES, beginning reader books, books of prayer and blessings, volumes of poetry and verse books, two AUTOBIOGRAPHIES, and even a BIOGRAPHY of three well-known children's authors. Several volumes of R.'s fiction and picture books are published in a SERIES, including the popular Henry and Mudge that takes you on wild adventures with a little boy named Henry and his very large dog, Mudge.

Perhaps most well known as a novelist, R. often portrays compassionate young people who live in rural settings or small towns. They tend to be set apart from their peers. Young protagonists, both male and female, meet the challenges in their lives with the help of FAMILY and friends as well as acquaintances from their communities. R. is praised for her sensitivity toward young people while understanding their feelings. Always stressing the importance of family and community in her works, R. is also noted for her characterizations of adults, especially the elderly, and for exploring themes such as DEATH and religion often not addressed in children's literature. Often focusing on relationships between young and old and between people and animals, she is a bold writer, who underscores her works with such themes as the act of creation, both by God and human artists. In her works, she stresses the importance of all living things, as well as the power of love and the need to let go.

A quote from Eden K. Edwards writing in *Children's Books and Their Creators* sums up R. best: "[she] demonstrates an inimitable ability to evoke the strongest of emotions from the simplest of words . . . In her work, R. gives depth and dignity to a litany of quiet characters and sagaciously reflects on some of life's most confusing mysteries. . . . All of R.'s stories, including her picture books marketed for younger readers, create memorable characters and places, and provide TEENS with a window on the world." R. attributes her writing style to many things, but especially to her sad childhood. Her father was a sergeant in the U.S. Army and fought in the Korean

War. Contracting hepatitis while in Korea, he later died when R. was thirteen. In her autobiography, *But I'll Be Back Again: An Album* (1989), she wrote, "I did not have a chance to know him or say goodbye to him, and that is all the loss I needed to become a writer."

She was also in love with the Beatles, especially Paul McCartney. When she was nine, she sat transfixed watching the Beatles on *The Ed Sullivan Show* along with the rest of the country. She notes, "the Beatles gave me a childhood of sweetest anticipation. Our country was falling apart with WAR and riots and assassinations, but the Beatles gave me shelter from these things in their music and in the dreams they caused me to dream." She added in *But I'll Be Back Again,* the title of which is taken from the song "I'll Be Back" by the Beatles, "I think that in a lot of ways Paul McCartney became for me my lost father. . . . Paul and the Beatles became more for me than just rock 'n' roll heroes. They became something for me to know, a dream I could see." R. concluded, I felt I knew them better than the father I could not find and the mother who did not speak of him."

With over one hundred published works and many awards, R.'s approach to teaching children and young adults is right on focus, and her genius for broaching areas not discussed in children's literature is second to none. From *When I Was Young in the Mountains,* (1982) and *The Relatives Came to Miss Maggie* (1983) and *The Troublesome Turtle* (1999) to *Puzzling Possum* (1999), not to mention the SERIES CLASSICS for generations to come, Henry and Mudge, Mr. Putter and Tabby, and the ever-popular The Everyday Books series, R. has become a constant in classrooms across America and the world. Educators use this wonderful author's insights and sometimes-twisted wit to mold YAS into daring yet abiding individuals. This is an author who is definitely a "must read" for young people of all ages.

SELECT AWARDS: Many, including *When I Was Young in the Mountains:* School Library Best Journal's Best Book of 1984, and Children's Book of the Year; Child Study Association of America: 1985 for *The Relatives Came*; *Missing May:* John Newbery Medal, 1993; and numerous citations on the ALA lists.

SELECT FURTHER WORKS: Over a hundred, including Everyday Books; self-illustrated board books for pets, children, garden, house, school, and town.

WILLIAM MARIANO

S

SACHAR, Louis

Author, educator, 20 March 1954, East Meadow, New York

S. was born in New York, but his family moved to Orange County, California, when he was nine. S. remembers their new rural life as one filled with orange groves, and the neighborhood kids would often have orange fights. The son of Robert, a salesman, and Ruth, a real-estate broker, S. did well in school; math was his favorite subject. S., however, did not become a devoted reader until high school.

S. went off to Antioch College in Yellow Springs, Ohio, but during his freshman year, his father died unexpectedly. S. moved back to California to be closer to his mother and continued his studies at the University of California at Berkeley. S. was initially an economics major with a penchant for Russian literature. He signed up for a Russian–language course so that he could read Russian novels in their original versions, rather than as translations. Looking back, S. writes, "After about a year, I realized that the only language I was ever going to be reasonably competent in was English. I soon dropped my Russian class and began searching for something to take its place."

That "something" was working as a teacher's aide in a local elementary school. In return, S. received three college credits to make up for his dropped Russian class. Although he did not realize it at that time, S.'s experience as a teacher's aide would help shape his career. He writes, "It became my favorite college class, and a life-changing experience. I found that I

didn't like any of the little stories that the children were reading, and as I had always wanted to write, I decided to try my hand at a children's book of my own." S.'s stint at Hillside Elementary School became the inspiration for his first book, *Sideways Stories from Wayside School* (1978).

S. graduated with a B.A. in economics in 1976 and worked for a year in a sweater factory in Norwalk, Connecticut. A year later, he began law school at Hastings College of the Law in San Francisco. During his first week in law school, S. learned that his first manuscript had been accepted for publication. This began a six-year internal struggle for S.: Should he become a lawyer or an author?

He continued law school, earned his J.D. in 1980, and passed the bar exam. But S. still had a decision to make. "Happily," he writes, "I passed, but I quickly realized that I wasn't as thrilled as I should have been. By now, it was clear that writing was my first career choice. Still, I needed a job, so after some procrastination, I began practicing law to finance my writing habit." In 1989, S.'s books sold well enough to enable him to leave the field of law and concentrate full time on writing.

One of S.'s most beloved books is *There's a Boy in the Girls' Bathroom* (1987). It is the story of a fifth-grade bully named Bradley who is smart and imaginative, but antisocial and without friends. To console himself, Bradley collects chipped and broken pieces of animal pottery. His need for acceptance is genuine, and is helped along by a new student and a caring school counselor. Through the course of the novel, Bradley transforms into a confident young man who learns to accept himself.

Of *Holes* (1998), S. writes, "It was the greatest challenge to write, and I feel like I met that challenge." *Holes* is an obvious departure from S.'s earlier works, most notably because of the dark and sometimes frightening side to the story. Additionally, when writing earlier works, S. began with characters and built the story around them. But when he sat down to write *Holes,* S. started with a place, Camp Green Lake.

Stanley Yelnats, the story's protagonist, is sent to Camp Green Lake when he is falsely accused of stealing a pair of sneakers. Stanley takes strange comfort in knowing that his FAMILY has been cursed by a long-gone relative and that his time at Camp Green Lake is just part of being a Yelnats. The mean female warden requires Stanley, as well as the other delinquent boys who have been sent there as punishment, to dig holes: five-feet wide and five-feet deep. It quickly becomes obvious to the boys that the warden is in search of something, and the holes, it is hoped, will uncover whatever it is.

Even though Stanley is not the typical ideal hero, his character resonates with many young readers. S. writes, "He's a kind of pathetic kid who feels like he has no friends, feels like his life is cursed. And I think everyone can identify with that in one way or another. And then there's the fact that here he is, a kid who isn't a hero, but he lifts himself up and becomes one. I think readers can imagine themselves rising with Stanley."

SELECT AWARDS: 1979 International Reading Association and Children's Book Council Children's Choice, *Sideways Stories from Wayside School; There's a Boy in the Girls' Bathroom:* 1987 Parents' Choice Foundation Parents' Choice Award and 1990 Mark Twain Award; 1989 Parents' Choice Award, *Wayside School is Falling Down; Holes:* 1998 National Book Award, 1998 *School Library Journal* Best Books, 1998 *Horn Book* Fanfare list, 1998 *Bulletin of the Center for Children's Books* "Blue Ribbon 1998" selection, and 1999 Newbery Medal, 1999 ALA Best Books for Young Adults; Sunshine State Young Reader Award Winners, 2003.

FURTHER WORKS: *Johnny's in the Basement,* 1981: *Someday Angeline,* 1983; *Sixth Grade Secrets,* 1987; *Sideways Arithmetic from Wayside School,* 1989; *The Boy Who Lost His Face,* 1989; *Wayside School Is* *Falling Down,* 1989; *Dogs Don't Tell Jokes,* 1991; *More Sideways Arithmetic from Wayside School,* 1994; *Wayside School Gets a Little Stranger,* 1995.

BIBLIOGRAPHY: *Something about the Author,* vol. 104; www.louissachar.com.

CARRA E. GAMBERDELLA

ST. GEORGE, Judith

Author, b. 26 February 1931, Westfield, New Jersey

S. was born to parents John and Edna Alexander. She received a B.A. from Smith College in 1952 and married Episcopal minister David St. George two years later. She now has four adult children and five grandchildren.

As a child, S. was enamored with reading and writing, along with sports such as skating, tennis and baseball. She recalls writing silly plays in elementary school that she produced with her friends. Her fascination with writing continued in college, where she signed up for all of the creative-writing classes that were available.

S. attributes her impassioned interest in history to the year she and her husband spent residing in the historic Longfellow House in Cambridge, Massachusetts, which also was George Washington's headquarters during the first year of the American Revolution. Much of S.'s historical writings and interest in the lives of presidents grew out of that pivotal year in Cambridge.

So You Want to Be President? is a fascinating book filled with intriguing tidbits of trivia about the presidents of the United States. The inspiration for *So You Want to Be President?* came from the idea that the position of President of the United States is the ultimate ambition in the eyes of children. She began to research the personalities and characters that have resided in the White House over the years. S.'s humorous and informative writing style appeals to readers: "Thomas Jefferson was top-notch in the brains department . . . In his spare time he designed his own house (a mansion), founded the University of Virginia, and whipped up the Declaration of Independence." The book closes with advice to those aspiring to become president, "If you want to be President—a good President—pattern yourself after the best." She also wrote *So You Want to Be an Inventor?,* both books illustrated by David Small.

Another fascinating book by S. is *In the Line of Fire: Presidents' Lives at Stake,* which describes assassinations, the careers of the assassins, and the lives of the vice presidents who had to step in. She describes numerous failed attempts to assassinate U.S. presidents as well.

S. is dedicated to her work and particularly enjoys doing the research that nonfiction books involve. She spends time in libraries and often travels to the settings of her books. Her research adventures have included trips to Panama, Mount Rushmore, and the White House.

Aside from historical books, S. also enjoys writing MYSTERIES. *Haunted* is an eerie tale that features sixteen-year old Alex as the protagonist hired to house-sit the Von Dursts estate. As the title indicates, the house is haunted with supernatural forces.

S.'s work has led her to represent New Jersey as a delegate to the White House Conference on Library and Informational Services. She has also served as a member of the Brooklyn Bridge Centennial Commission and as chairperson of its educational committee. She also helped to create a brochure about the Brooklyn Bridge for kids in New York City.

S. wishes to share her love of reading and history with others. "Above all, I want the people in my books to come alive for my readers the way they come alive for me."

SELECT AWARDS: American Book Award Honor Book, 1983; New York Academy of Science Award; Christopher Award, 1985; Golden Kite Award, 1990; Caldecott Medal in 2001 (with illustrator David Small); *So You Want to Be President?*: Randolph Caldecott Medal, 2001.

FURTHER WORKS: *The Chinese Puzzle of Shag Island,* 1976; *Shadow of the Shaman,* 1977; *Mystery at St. Martin's,* 1979; *The Brooklyn Bridge: They Said It Couldn't Be Built,* 1982; *Crazy Horse,* 1994; *To See with the Heart; The Life of Sitting Bull,* 1996; *John and Abigail Adams: An American Love Story,* 2001.

BIBLIOGRAPHY: *Contemporary Authors Online,* 2001; http://galenet.galegroup.com; Teachervision.com; http://www.teachervision.fen.com/lesson-6682.html

ELIZABETH ANDERSON

SALINGER, J(erome) D(avid)

Author, b. 1 January 1919, New York City

Although it continues to be CENSORED, S.'s *Catcher in the Rye* (1951), is still widely read in most American high schools today. This is perhaps, the work for which S. is most remembered. It has been translated into twelve languages. Holden Caufield, the main character, is frequently compared to Huck Finn in Mark Twain's *Adventures of Huckleberry Finn.* Both stories are coming-of-age novels with male protagonists who see much phoniness around them in society; both are written in colloquial language.

S. was born in New York City, to Sol and Miriam Salinger, who lived like most upper-middle-class families. S. began his writing career as a young man. His grades were average and the ability to remain in one school was not easy for him. He attended several high schools and was enrolled by his father in the Valley Forge Military Academy, which also became the model for Pencey Prep, the high school Holden Caufield attends. There, S. composed a three-stanza poem that was put to music, which became the school anthem.

S.'s work was first published in 1940 in *Story* MAGAZINE, a SHORT STORY entitled "The Young Folks," written when he took a writing course at Columbia University. The class was taught by Whit Burnett, an author and editor who founded *Story* magazine. As the 1940s rolled along. S. was publishing stories in *Collier's,* the *Saturday Evening Post, Esquire,* and *Cosmopolitan.* He served in both England and France during World War II, where he continued to write, though none of his stories written during this time were considered noteworthy.

During World War II, S. married a French woman named Sylvia. They returned to the U.S. but the marriage was short-lived and ended after eight months. Beginning in 1946, S. began writing almost exclusively for *The New Yorker,* a magazine for serious writers. He moved from Greenwich Village to Tarrytown, New York, where he made a rare appearance at a short-story class at Sarah Lawrence College. It was after this visit that S. became reclusive and avoided all public appearances.

Finally on July 16, 1951, *The Catcher in the Rye* was published. Though its popularity was slowly attained, it did, after several years, bring S. considerable critical praise and respect within the literary establishment. It was also a selection of the Book-of-the Month Club. His protagonist, Holden Caufield, has become an American icon with the likes of Jay Gatsby and the aforementioned Huck Finn.

S.'s next work was a collection of SHORT STORIES, originally published in magazines, entitled *Nine Stories* (1953). Here, S. focuses on the dilemmas both adults and children face in dealing with the emotional situations of their daily lives, sometimes making poor moral decisions. He offers his characters alternatives to the hostility of life with a spiritual approach instead. This was an outcome of S.'s deep interest of Zen Buddhism.

One of the stories published in *Nine Stories* (1953), "Uncle Wiggily in Connecticut," was made into a MOVIE by Goldwyn entitled *My Foolish Heart.* S. very much disapproved of what Hollywood made of his story and has since refused to sell screen or television rights to any of his other works.

In 1955 S. married again, this time to Claire Douglas. They had two children—a daughter, Margaret Ann, born in 1955 and a son, Matthew, born in 1960. The marriage ended in divorce twelve years later.

S.'s interest in Eastern philosophies becomes evident in his writings about the Glass FAMILY, including *Franny and Zooey* (1961), first published as short stories in *The New Yorker.* In 1963, more Glass family stories, *Raise High the Roof Beam, Carpenters, and Seymour: An Introduction* were published. The former title was the story of Seymour Glass's wedding day and the latter story is written from Buddy's point of view about his relationship with his brother Seymour, a troubled character. The final Glass family novella, *Hapworth 16, 1924* (1965), further delved into the character of Seymour and his philosophical digressions. It was published in *The New Yorker* in 1965. S. has not published any work since.

S. continued to live in seclusion until the 1980s, when biographer Ian Hamilton wanted to publish letters by S. found at the Firestone Library of Princeton University and the library at the University of Texas. S. protested the use of his letters and the US Court of Appeals confirmed that the letters were his property and could not be included in the BIOGRAPHY without permission. The biography by Hamilton *In Search of J.D. Salinger,* was finally published in 1988, but without the letters.

AWARDS: BBC's The Big Read voted *The Catcher in the Rye* (1951) one of Britain's twenty-one best loved novels, 2003.

FURTHER WORKS: "The Young Folks," 1940; "The Varoni Brothers," 1943; "I'm Crazy," 1945; "Slight Rebellion Off Madison," 1946; "A Young Girl in 1941 with No Waist at All," 1947; "The Inverted Forest," 1947; "A Perfect Day for Bananafish," 1948; "Just Before the War with the Eskimos," 1948; "A

Girl I Knew," 1948; "The Laughing Man," 1949; "Down at the Dinghy," 1949; "For Esme-with Love and Squalor," 1950; "Pretty Mouth and Green My Eyes," 1951; "Teddy" (1953); *The Complete Uncollected Stories of J.D. S.,* 1974, unauthorized edition.

BIBLIOGRAPHY: Lundquist, J., *J.D. S.,* 1979; *American Writers,* vol. 3, 1998; *Major 20th Century Writers,* vol. 4, 1991; *Contemporary Authors online,* 2004.

JOAN FENTON HENRY

SALISBURY, Graham
Author, educator, n.d., n.p.

Winner of the 2003 *Boston Globe–Horn Book* Award for *Lord of the Deep,* S. is a prolific author of YOUNG ADULT LITERATURE. S.'s family owned Hawaii's *Honolulu Advertiser* for a hundred years, but S. thought that writing fiction offered more possibilities. He spent a childhood on the Hawaiian islands of Oahu and Hawaii after losing his father on his first birthday in 1945 during World War II. To attend college, he moved to California and matriculated at California State University. Continuing his education on the East Coast, his next degree was an M.F.A. from Vermont College, Norwich University. His association with Vermont College continues to this day, since he serves on the faculty of the Writing for Children portion of the Master of Fine Arts program.

Beyond his work writing and teaching at the university level, S. also finds time to run a business, play rock 'n' roll, surf, and be a parent. He has also been in charge of a glass-bottom boat, served as a hand on a boat dedicated to deep-sea fishing, and, before teaching on the university level, taught at an elementary school. The Millennium, S.'s rock group, hit number one in the Philippines with one of their songs. Other ADVENTURES—some of which are reflected in his works—include having a shark join him while surfing, being attacked by both a moray eel and a Portuguese man-of-war, and living to tell the tale.

Now a resident of Portland, Oregon, S. still draws on his Hawaiian heritage (even though his family's missionary background has not yet been mined) for much of his work. *Island Boyz,* his collection of SHORT STORIES, received a trio of awards, among them a *Booklist* Editor's Choice Award; Best of the Best, 2002; New York Public Library Books for the TEEN Age, 2003; and the Chicago Public Library Best of the Best, 2003. Drawing heavily on his own experiences, S.'s work about deep-sea fishing, *Lord of the*

Deep, won a plethora of awards including the 2002 *Boston Globe–Horn Book* Award. S. decided to take a look at the aftermath of Pearl Harbor on two teens in Hawaii—one Japanese-American—in his historical young adult novel, *Under the Blood-Red Sun.* It became a 1994 *Booklist* Editor's Choice, a 1994 Parent's Choice Honor Award, and a 1994 winner of the Scott O'DELL Award for Historical Fiction. *Shark Bait* was named a Parent's Choice Honor Award winner, and *Jungle Dogs* was a Junior Literary Guild Pick (in January 1999), as well as a 1999 Best Book for YA according to the American Library Association as well as a New York Public Library Book for the Teen Age. S. also has many works that appear in various collections.

Far greater than the awards he receives is the ability S. has to engage the teenage reader. His gripping tales of action and adventure also encompass hard moral choices, and the dilemmas faced by compelling characters as they navigate their way a little closer to adulthood. Readers are absorbed by his storytelling and remain hooked, as his characters not only experience perilous outer journeys, but also the equally difficult internal ones. His work compels the reader to continue reading until the character finds a safe harbor.

SELECT AWARDS: *Lord of the Deep:* finalist in the *Riverbank Review's* 2002 Children's Books of Distinction, an American Library Association Best Book for Young Adults 2002, a Best of the Year Book award from the Cooperative Children's Book Center, a *School Library Journal* Best Book of the Year (as well as a starred review recipient), a *Horn Book* Fan Fare selection, 2001, a New York Public Library 2001 Title for Reading and Sharing, Dorothy Canfield Fisher Children's Book Award, 2003, and a *Booklist* Editor's Choice for 2001; *Blue Skin of the Sea:* 1992 Best Book of the Year by *School Library Journal,* 1993 Best Books for Young Adults by the American Library Association, a Parent's Choice Book Award for 1992; *Under the Red-Blood Sun:* ALA Best Books for Young Adults and a 1995 Notable Children's Book of the Year by the American Library Association; the Library of Congress awarded it a 1995 Notable Children's Books of the Year and it also received a 1995 Books for the Teen Age by the New York Public Library Award.

BIBLIOGRAPHY: http://scholar.lib.vt.edu/ejournals/ALAN/winter97/w97-03-Benton.html; www.amazon.com; www.grahamsalisbury.com.

JEANNE MARIE RYAN

SALZMAN, Mark Joseph

Author, educator, screenwriter, actor, b. 1959, Greenwich, Connecticut

S., a distinguished author, expert at martial arts and accomplished cellist, graduated Phi Beta Kappa, Summa Cum Laude from Yale in 1982 with a degree in Chinese Language and Literature. From 1982 to 1984, S. lived in China where he taught English at Hunan Medical College and continued to study martial arts.

Years spent in China provided the inspiration for his first book, *Iron and Silk* (1987), a memoir that provides insight into the Chinese culture, which was a finalist for the Pulitzer Prize for non-fiction, received the Christopher Award and the New York Public Library Literary Lions Award, and has since been translated into twelve languages. In addition, S. wrote the screenplay and starred in the critically acclaimed film version of *Iron and Silk,* which was shot entirely on location in China.

S.'s second book, *The Laughing Sutra* (1991), is a fictional account of a young man who escapes from China during the Cultural Revolution on a quest to find an ancient Chinese scroll in America. *The Soloist* (1994), a novel about a cello prodigy, was nominated for both the Pulitzer and Los Angeles Times book prizes. A second memoir *Lost in Place: Growing Up Absurd in Suburbia* (1995), recounts his growing up in Connecticut during the 1960's and 1970's.

Other works include *Lying Awake* (2000), which takes place in a Carmelite Monastery and is written from the point of view of Sister John of the Cross became a national bestseller, and *True Notebooks* (2003) which documents his experiences teaching writing at a maximum-security prison for juvenile offenders and won the 2004 Alex Awards. His power as a writer is such that his fiction and his non-fiction have been praised for a lyrical style, sagacious insight and uncanny honesty. He lives in Los Angeles with his wife, filmmaker Jessica Yu.

BIBLIOGRAPHY: www.rambles.net/salzmansutra.html; *St Charles Public Library—Short Bios,* www.stcharleslibrary.org/readers_service/bios/; *Headlines November 6 Literary Lunch,* www.usc.edu/isd/pubarchives/now/stories/ www.bookweb.org/news/btw/3999.html.

DEBORAH A. WOOTEN

SAMUELS, Gertrude
Author, photographer, n.d., Manchester, England

S. graduated from New York University with a B.A., and began her career as a staff member of a newspaper and MAGAZINES. Her position gradually moved up to staff writer and photographer, and eventually she ended up attaining the position of editor of a magazine. From 1943 to 1975, S. had the honor of being "the only staff writer for the *New York Times* Sunday magazine." S. then went on to work as a freelance writer and photographer and, in 1948, served as a Special United Nations observer for United Nations Children's Fund (UNICEF) in eight European countries. Additionally, she served as a WAR correspondent in Korea in 1952.

S. writes in a variety of genres—history, historical fiction, BIOGRAPHY, drama, as well as contributing articles and photographs to newspapers and magazines. Her political interests in countries of conflict such as Vietnam, Korea, and Israel permeate her writing for young people.

AWARDS: 1974 American Library Association Best Book, The Best of the Best, 1970–1983, *Run, Shelley, Run!*

SELECT FURTHER WORKS: *B-G, Fighter of Goliaths: The Story of David Ben-Gurion*, 1961; *Run, Shelley, Run!*, 1974; *Mottele: A Partisan Odyssey*, 1976; *Adam's Daughter*, 1977; *Yours, Brett*, 1988.

BIBLIOGRAPHY: *Contemporary Authors Online*, 2001; *Something about the Author*, vol. 17, 1979.

SARA MARCUS

SANCHEZ, Alex
Author, b. 12 April 1957, Mexico City, Mexico

S., author of the Rainbow SERIES, which currently includes *Rainbow Boys* (2001) and *Rainbow High* (2003), was born in Mexico City to parents of Cuban and German heritage. His family moved to the United States when he was five-years old. He graduated Phi Beta Kappa from Virginia Tech University in 1978 with a bachelor's degree in liberal arts and sciences, with concentrations in English, philosophy, and architecture. He earned a master's in guidance and counseling in 1985 from Old Dominion University.

S.'s Rainbow novels are especially notable because they help fill the gap in TEEN literature that features gay characters. His characters must not only face the experiences that are universal to most high-school-aged teenagers, such as peer pressure, academic achievement, and falling in love, but they must also face unique and complex challenges in discovering and, ultimately, accepting that they are gay. His vivid description of the challenges and experiences these characters face would be of great interest to teens both gay and straight.

S. was inspired to write through his own experiences and issues of coming out as well as his work as a counselor. *Rainbow Boys* is a book S. describes that he most wanted—and needed—to read himself when a teenager. This has been reflected in the hundreds of teens that have contacted S. to share with him their feelings—that they were encouraged by his books to help find the self-acceptance and the courage to come out.

Included in the back of *Rainbow Boys* is contact information for support and educational organizations that gay teens can utilize. Many teens have been inspired to start local or school support organizations for gay, lesbian, bisexual, transgender, or questioning (GLBTQ) teens.

AWARDS: 2002 YALSA Best Books for Young Adults, *Rainbow Boys*.

FURTHER WORKS: "If You Kiss a Boy," SHORT STORY included in *13: Thirteen Stories that Capture the Agony and Ecstasy of Being Thirteen*, 2003; *So Hard to Say*, 2004.

BIBLIOGRAPHY: Alex S. homepage, http://www.alexsanchez.com; Interview on Teen Reads homepage, http://www.teenreads.com/authors/au-sanchez-alex.asp, January 15, 2002; Pavao, K. "Flying Starts: Six First-Time Authors and Illustrators Talk about their Fall Debuts." *Publishers Weekly*, December 24, 2001.

KEVIN R. FERST

SANDERS, Dori
Author, peach farmer, b. 1934 or 1935, York, South Carolina

The date of S.'s birth is cited as both 1934 and 1935, depending on the source consulted. However, the place of her birth, York, South Carolina, is quite near where she grew up in Filbert, South Carolina. She lived on eighty-one acres, sharing a small house with her parents and nine siblings. Her grandparents, widowed aunt, and cousin lived in another house on her father's land.

Farming was part of S.'s life from the beginning. Crops grown by the family included sweet potatoes and peaches. S. not only helped her family grow produce, but also was active in selling it at a stand located by the side of the road near their property. As a matter of fact, it was while working at the stand that the idea came to her for *Clover*. Two separate funeral processions drove by, one black and one white. S. mused on what would happen if the participants in the two funerals were actually joined by one DEATH.

Much of the background for *Clover* (1990) was taken from S.'s own life, although it differs from her life in many key regards. Clover must learn to deal with her new white stepmother when her father dies suddenly. Its portrait is not just of Clover's struggles, though, but of life in the segregated South, a theme that is seen again in *Her Own Place* (1993). This novel reflects S.'s love of the land, as she tells the life story of a woman who struggles to raise her children alone as she also works her land. *Her Own Place* also reflects the changing times of the country, when women became self-supporting, working at factories that were producing goods for the WAR effort, as S. experienced during World War II. In *Dori Sanders Country Cooking: Recipes and Stories from the Family Farm Stand* (1996), S. shares FAMILY vignettes as well as great things to cook.

S. continues to be a resident of York County and has donated her manuscripts to the University of South Carolina. Despite the fact that she has become a renowned author, S. has remained committed to farming. She does most of her writing during the off-seasons. She also speaks at schools and libraries, encouraging children with her personal knowledge. On her professional life, S. says, "Farming is who I am. If someone asks me what I do, I say, 'I'm a farmer.' And only later do I say, 'Oh, and I also do some writing.' I grew up in a place and a time, and I'll never be able to get myself out of where I am. I'll never write about anything else."

AWARDS: 1990 Lillian Smith Award, 1991 Best Books for Young Adults, *Clover*.

BIBLIOGRAPHY: *Contemporary Authors Online*, 2003; www.amazon.com; www.sc.edu/library/socar/uscs/1994/addr94.html; www.oakridger.com/stories/032100/com_0321000016.html; www.novelst4.epnet.com; www.annistonstar.com/entertainment/2003/as-books-0806-0-3h06b4249.htm; http://scafricanamericanhistory.com/calendar.asp?month=1&year=1994.

JEANNE MARIE RYAN

SARGENT, Pamela
Author, editor, b. 20 March 1948, Ithaca, New York

Since publishing her first SHORT STORY as a college senior, S. has been active in the field of SCIENCE FICTION and FANTASY literature. She has described science fiction as a format that allows readers to ask questions about what they have been taught to believe. Her contributions to the genre have included novels, edited anthologies and periodicals, short stories, and book reviews. S. earned a B.A. and an M.A. in philosophy from the State University of New York at Binghamton, though she struggled with a speech impediment and undiagnosed nearsightedness as a child and often missed school as a TEENAGER.

She gained notice as an author with a YA readership in 1975 for *Women of Wonder,* her first anthology of science fiction written by women, and cemented this connection with the novel *Earthseed* (1983), both of which were recognized as ALA Best Books for Young Adults. In *Earthseed* young spacefaring colonists, who have grown up with only their ship's computer mind for a parent, are confronted with the harsh reality of learning to survive on their own, even as they discover that Ship has not been telling them everything it knows. S.'s other novels with YA protagonists have included the Watchstar trilogy (*Watchstar,* 1980; *Eye of the Comet,* 1984; *Homesmind,* 1984) and *Alien Child* (1988). A long-since depopulated future earth is the setting for *Alien Child,* where aliens accidentally cause the birth of two test-tube children, who must decide at an early age whether or not to revive the human race. With George Zebrowski, S. has written numerous titles in the Star Trek SERIES. She has also edited three editions of Nebula Awards anthologies.

AWARDS: Nebula Award for novelette "Danny Goes to Mars," 1992; BBYA, 1975, *Women of Wonder: Science Fiction Stories by Women about Women;* 1983 for *Earthseed*.

FURTHER WORKS: *The Shore of Women,* 1986; The Venus trilogy (*Venus of Dreams,* 1986; *Venus of Shadows;* 1988, *Child of Venus,* 2001); *The Best of Pamela S.,* 1987; *Ruler of the Sky,* 1990; *Women of Wonder, The Classic Years: Science Fiction by Women from the 1940s to the 1970s,* 1995; *Women of Wonder, The Contemporary Years: Science Fiction by Women from the 1970s to the 1990s,* 1995; *Climb the Wind: A Novel of Another North America,* 1999; *Behind the Eyes of Dreamers and Other Short Novels,*

2002; *Eye of Flame: Fantasies,* 2003; *Garth of Izar,* 2003.

BIBLIOGRAPHY: Elliot, Jeffrey M. *The Work of Pamela S.: An Annotated Bibliography and Literary Guide,* 1996; Hile, Janet L. *Authors and Artists for Young Adults,* vol. 18, 1996; Nakamura, Joyce, ed. *Contemporary Authors Autobiography Series,* vol. 18, 1993.

AMANDA WERHANE

SAUL, John

Author, b. 5 February 1942, Pasadena, California

Often incorrectly classified as a HORROR writer, S. is a master at writing psychological occult thrillers. With over 30 books and 80 million copies sold worldwide, S.'s claim to fame came after fifteen years as a struggling author. *Suffer the Children* (1977), S.'s first published novel, was the first PAPERBACK to reach the *New York Time's* bestseller list and also the first paperback to be advertised on television. S. admits that his writing in *Suffer the Children,* which he completed start to finish in 28 days, was not his best, but it was certainly his goriest; he toned down the more-macabre elements after realizing that his audience consisted primarily of children and YAS. *The Blackstone Chronicles* (1994), written in six installments, is one of S.'s most popular titles and has been adapted into a computer game. Several of S.'s books dwell on the topics of being a loner, which is a universal adolescent theme. S. himself acknowledges the type of audience he writes for: "I don't think that the kind of thing that I write appeals to the . . . adult mind." Unlike many of the ghoulish HORROR/thriller writers, S. is funny, dashingly handsome, and gay. S. married his partner, Michael Sack, in a Catholic Church in Oshkosh, Wisconsin, after only six months of dating, and they are still together after twenty-five years. Although S. has never made a special point about being gay, he wrote a novel about a gay man under the pseudonym S. Steinberg before becoming famous. *A Fairy Tale* was published in 1980. Prior to becoming a best-selling author, S. worked at a car rental dealership and was the first male Western Girl, where he filled in as a temporary typist. S. also dabbled in college, attending four universities in three states, during which time he constantly changed his majors. Though S. never earned a degree, his two primary majors were anthropology and theater. S. has also written several comic-murder MYSTERIES, and a few one-act PLAYS

that were produced in Los Angeles and Seattle; unfortunately, he is limited by his publishing contract to writing books within his "genre."

According to S., he conducts very little research when writing his books, as he is "paid to lie," which he says is the great thing about fiction, since "you make it up as you go along." S. spends about four hours per day writing and can finish a novel in approximately two to three months; apparently the faster S. writes, the better the novel is. Surprisingly, his seventh-grade English teacher suggested that he become a writer after S. cleverly combined twenty-word vocabulary assignments into one very long and articulate sentence for the duration of the school year. S. is an advocate of writers' conferences, but when lecturing or touring, he travels the country in a lavish bus, having lost all desire to stay in hotel rooms. With residencies in Maui, Seattle, and San Juan, S. is also an avid golfer. Without the grimness and gore of his books, S.'s own life is nevertheless a paradox. He is a whimsical man who loves musicals, plays bridge, and has a toy collection. But he's a writer of stories about demented, homicidal TEENS. Even though S. contractually cannot make us laugh, he still can frighten millions of readers.

AWARDS: 1975, Lifetime Achievement Award, Northwest Writers; 1990, Pacific Northwest Writers; 1990, American Library Association Best Books for Young Adults; 1991, New York Public Library Award; 1992, Evergreen Young Adult Book Award for *Creature;* 2002, Spotted Owl Award Runner Up for *Manhattan Hunt Club.*

FURTHER WORKS: *Punish the Sinners,* 1978; *Cry for the Sinners,* 1979; *Comes the Blind Furry,* 1980; *When the Wind Blows,* 1981; *God Project,* 1982; *Nathaniel,* 1985; *Brainchild,* 1986; *Hellfire,* 1986; *The Unloved,* 1988; *Creature,* 1989; *Second Child,* 1990; *The Unwanted,* 1990; *Darkness,* 1991; *Sleepwalk,* 1991; *Shadows,* 1992; *Guardian,* 1993; *The Homing,* 1994; *Black Lightening,* 1995; *The Blackstone Chronicles,* 1997; *The Presence,* 1997; *Right Hand of Evil,* 1999; *Nightshade,* 2000; *The Manhattan Hunt Club,* 2001; *Midnight Voices,* 2002; *Black Creek Crossing,* 2004

BIBLIOGRAPHY: http://www.johnsaul.com/bio.html, 2004; "John S." *January Magazine,* http://www .januarymagazine.com, 1999; "Fear and Loving in the Best-Seller Rack." *The Advocate,* http://www .advocate.com/html/stories/845/845_saul.asp, 2001; Paul Bail. *John S.: A Critical Companion,* 1996.

ILONA N. KOTI

SAVAGE, Deborah
Author, artist, b. 15 December 1955, Northampton, Massachusetts

S. is both an author and an artist, winning awards in both fields. She started writing young, moving to Provincetown, Massachusetts, just after finishing high school. She was only seventeen, but had every intention of becoming a writer and an artist. Before publication of her first novel, S. was a teacher of art and creative writing. She received her B.A. in 1987 from the University of Massachusetts. She continued to teach art and English while writing her first books. From 1980 to 1985, S. taught wood-cut printmaking in both Massachusetts and New Zealand. S. has exhibited her woodcut prints and watercolors in Massachusetts, Connecticut, and New Zealand. Her poster for the Cape Cod Museum of Natural History won the Award of Merit from the American Museum Association in 1984.

Her time spent in NEW ZEALAND has influenced her books thematically. Many of them include Maori characters and traditions. Her characters often must attempt to understand and reconcile the differences between races and classes while maintaining their friendships. S. also creates strong female characters, who frequently step beyond the limitations of traditional gender roles to seek ADVENTURE.

S.'s recent novel, *Kotuku* (2002), has been named one of the Best Books for Young Adults for 2003 by the American Library Association. In an author's note, S. writes, "In 1981 I moved to New Zealand and, although I lived there for only a few years, the experience had a profound impact on my life and writing. [. . .] Over the next decade I returned many times to New Zealand for extended visits, and my first three novels were set there. During those years I was torn between a love for my New England home and birthplace in Massachusetts and the strange, compelling connection I felt toward New Zealand, which I had grown to consider my spiritual home. *Kotuku* is an attempt to bridge these two worlds."

Summer Hawk (1999) is the story of Taylor, her rescue of a baby hawk, and the adventures that follow. In *A Rumour of Otters* (1986), Alexa defies her role as a girl and sets off in search of the otters seen by a Maori tribesman of the past. *A Rumour of Otters* was named a Notable Children's Book by the American Library Association. *School Library Journal* listed it

as a Best Book, and *Parents' Choice* magazine gave it a remarkable Book of Literature Award.

S. has been a guest author and workshop presenter for schools in New Zealand, Pennsylvania, New York, Massachusetts, Washington, and Connecticut. She was writer-in-residence at Hollins University (Roanoke, Virginia) in 1998. In addition, she has given presentations for the Northwest Corner Coalition for Nuclear Disarmament, the Massachusetts Association for Educational Media, the Boston Public Library Creative Writing Workshop, the International Federation of Teachers of English conference, and the American Association of University Women book-and-author luncheon. POETRY by S. has been published in such periodicals as *Dark Horse, Spectrum,* and *Cross Currents.* Some of her illustrations have also been printed in *Planning Quarterly* and *Cross Currents.*

AWARDS: 2000 Boston Authors Award for Young Adult Literature, 2000 ALA Best Books for Young Adults, *Summer Hawk;* 1986 American Library Association Notable Children's Book, *A Rumour of Otters;* 2003 ALA Best Books for Young Adults, *Kotuku.*

FURTHER WORKS: *Flight of the Albatross,* 1988; *A Stranger Calls Me Home,* 1992; *To Race a Dream,* 1994; *Under a Different Sky,* 1997.

BIBLIOGRAPHY: "Children's Literature Lectures at Hollins." *Roanoke Times & World News,* http://www.nexis.com/research; "Deborah S.," http://www.houghtonmifflinbooks.com/catalog/authordetail.cfm?authorID=1816; Olendorf, D., ed. *Contemporary Authors,* vol. 143, 1994; S., D. *Kotuku,* 2002.

CARA J. RANDALL

SCHMIDT, Gary D.
Author, b. April 1957, New York

Author of a variety of books for children and YAS, Schmidt's work is consistently thought provoking and engrossing. His first book, *Poetry for Young People: Robert Frost* (1994) is representative of how many of his books make cultural treasures more accessible to young readers. *"The Great Stone Face": A Tale by Nathaniel Hawthorne* (2002) and *"Pilgrim's Progress: A Retelling* (1994) further exemplify this talent. *Straw into Gold* (2001), a novel based on the Rumpelstiltskin FAIRY TALE, was named a Blue Ribbon Book by the Bulletin for the Center of Children's Books; *The Sin Eater* (1998) (based on the folk tale of the same name) won an American Library Association

Best Book award. S. has also written BIOGRAPHICAL and historical books: *Mara's Stories: Glimmers in the Darkness* (2001), a book dealing with the HOLOCAUST, was a *Horn Book* Fanfare Book for 2002 and an Association of Jewish Libraries' Notable Jewish Books for 2001. S. is currently a professor of English at Calvin College in Michigan.

SELECT AWARDS: Newbery Honor and PRINTZ Honor and 2004 SLJ Best Books for Children for *Lizzie Bright and the Buckminster Boy; Mara's Stories: Glimmers in the Darkness:* 2002 *Horn Book* Fanfare Book, 2001 Association of Jewish Libraries' Notable Jewish Books.

FURTHER WORKS: *The Blessing of the Lord: Stories from the Old and New Testaments,* 1997; *William Bradford: Plymouth's Faithful Pilgrim,* 1998; *Saint Ciaran: The Tale of a Saint of Ireland,* 2000; *Anson's Way,* 2001; forthcoming: *Losing Malaga, God's Hands, First Boy; Lizzie Bright and the Buckminster Boy,* 2004.

BIBLIOGRAPHY: E-mail correspondence with Gary S. 2003.

ANASTASIA NIEHOF

SCHULZ, Charles M(onroe)

Cartoonist, author, b. 26 November 1922, St. Paul, Minnesota; d. 12 February 2000, Santa Rosa California

Beloved cartoonist and creator of the *Peanuts* cartoon strip, S. connected to millions of people all over the world with his funny, yet slightly troubled characters and their everyday foibles. S. was connected to comic strips practically all his life: from his nickname, Sparky, given to him by an uncle based on Sparkplug (a horse in the Barney Google comic strip) to becoming the most widely syndicated comic strip artist in history. Even after his death, S. remains linked to his comic strip; he died just hours before his final comic strip was to appear, featuring a farewell letter signed by S.

Peanuts first was syndicated on October 2, 1950. This strip was originally *Li'l Folks,* which appeared in the *St. Paul Pioneer Press* from 1947. When the strip was sold to United Features Syndicate, the name was changed to *Peanuts,* much to S.'s disappointment. Yet, S. was drawing all his life and now a life-long dream had come true.

S. was able to make *Peanuts* appeal to everyone, especially TEENS, with his keen representations of ev-

eryday trials and tribulations—insecurity, inferiority, and loneliness to simple joys—friendship, community, and love. Charlie Brown, Lucy, Linus, Snoopy, and the whole gang each had unique personalities, and each dealt with the cruelties and wonders of life in a humorous way. S. was able to take his love of cartooning and his delightful characters and create a pop culture legacy that included over 2,600 newspapers in 75 countries, numerous book collections selling over 300 million copies worldwide, several animated TV specials earning four Emmy Awards and two Peabody Awards, and over 20,000 products based on the *Peanuts* characters.

S.'s comic strip can still be read in newspapers but the strip itself will never be drawn by another person—S. made that part of his contract. Good grief! No one could ever create *Peanuts* the way S. did.

AWARDS: Reuben Award, 1955, 1964; Yale Humor Award as Outstanding Humorist of the Year, 1956, School Bee Award, 1960; National Cartoonists Society Best Humor Strip of the Year, 1962; *Peanuts Treasury,* Best Books for Young Adults, 1968; International Cartoonist of the Year, 1978; Charles M. Schulz Award, 1980; Museum of Cartoon Art Cartoonist Hall of Fame, 1986; Commander of Arts and Letters from France, 1990; Order of Merit from the Italian Minister of Culture, 1992; National Cartoonists Society Milton Caniff Lifetime Achievement Award, 2000, posthumous; Congressional Gold Medal, 2001, posthumous.

FURTHER WORKS: *Peanuts,* 1952; *Happiness Is a Warm Puppy,* 1962; *A Charlie Brown Christmas,* 1967; *Peanuts Treasury,* 1968; *Be My Valentine, Charlie Brown,* 1976; *Happy Birthday, Charlie Brown,* 1979; *Charlie Brown, Snoopy, and Me,* 1980; *You Don't Look 35, Charlie Brown,* 1985; *Being a Dog Is a Full-Time Job: A Peanuts Collection,* 1994; *Schultz's Peanuts: A Golden Celebration,* 1999; *Peanuts Christmas,* 2002.

BIBLIOGRAPHY: *Contemporary Authors New Revision Series,* vol. 6; *Something about the Author,* vol. 10, 118; www.schulzmuseum.org.

TINA HERTEL

SCHWARTZ, Virginia Frances

Author, educator, b. 14 December 1952, in Stoney Creek, Ontario, Canada

S. grew up in CANADA, in a place that, as she told *Contemporary Authors,* provided her with "beauty, space, endless time to daydream, storytelling, and access to books" (2002). In this place she learned a love for storytelling.

After completing a B.A. from Waterloo Lutheran University (now Wilfrid Laurier University) and an M.S. from Pace University, she lived in New York, where she taught fourth and fifth grades (Red Cedar Book Awards, 2004). Yet after being trained to teach writing, she began doing that solely and loved it (*Contemporary Authors,* 2002). This is also when S.'s books began to appear.

In her novels, all of which are historical fiction, S. deals with the lives of marginalized people. This, she told *Contemporary Authors,* is because, "[slaves, immigrants, and Native Americans] have suffered tremendous hardships and injustices. In my novels I give them hope and a different life" (2002). The hope and different lives come through her characters' personal journeys—some are physical (along the Underground Railroad to freedom), others emotional (a mother's journey out of depression), or maturational (a brother and sister's journey into adulthood). All of these journeys have a spiritual element to them. S. observed, "Spirituality, or thinking about God, helps us recognize our true selves and develop our potential" (*Contemporary Authors Online,* 2002).

In 2000 her first book, *Send One Angel Down,* was published. The book was born when S. began teaching her students about slavery. "I had not experienced it," she writes in the "Author's Note" of her book; "How could I teach them about it?" The novel arose from a person she read about in Julius LESTER's *To Be a Slave.* S.'s story is about Eliza, a blue-eyed, light-skinned slave, fathered by the white plantation master. Abram, Eliza's cousin, tells the story about his efforts to protect and provide for his beautiful cousin, who is eventually freed and becomes a nanny in New York.

Send One Angel Down has been praised and honored for its truthful portrayal of slavery and the hope it inspires in humanity. Joanna Rudge Long, writing in 2000 for *Horn Book,* notes, "S. writes passionately of the privations and cruelties of the old South, and of the love and loyalty of the slaves for one another." Debbie Carton of *Booklist,* also in 2000, concurred: "This is a profoundly moving tale that is ultimately hopeful but never glosses over the horrific treatment of slaves."

In *If I Just Had Two Wings* (2001), another award-winning book, S. continues to utilize her knowledge from her research on slavery, specifically the Underground Railroad. In the "Author's Note" of *Send One Angel Down,* readers can hear the beginning of her second novel: "I discovered Eloise Greenfield's poem, 'Harriet Tubman,' from *Honey I Love.* The children were amazed to learn of the secret passage to Canada called the Underground Railroad, a trip Tubman traveled nineteen times. . . . We memorized and acted out that poem again and again." S. wrote a novel about it, one that Paula Rohrlick of KLIATT says is "full of details of the Underground Railroad, with actual names of conductors and stations and fascinating background on the many secret signals and songs" (2002, http://articles.findarticles.com).

In the novel, Phoebe, a thirteen-year-old slave who longs for freedom, runs away with an older girl and the girl's two children. They head for the Underground Railroad, following clues in songs and from people they encounter. They encounter many life-threatening obstacles on the road to the freedom they desire. Michael CART for *Booklist* calls the novel "a passionate, often stirring account of the human spirit's capacity to endure and triumph."

S. has written two more novels: *Messenger* in 2002 and *Initiation* in 2003. Both are historical fiction novels with deeply spiritual themes. The first is about a young girl born a week after her father's DEATH who is, as she sees it, his messenger, sent to free her mother from a life of drudgery. The other is based on a Kwakiutl—the Pacific Coast aboriginal tribe—transformation myth. S. told *Contemporary Authors* about the importance of spirituality in her own life: "I look to a higher place than just my own mind for everyday guidance."

AWARDS: *Send One Angel Down:* Best Books for Young Adults, 2001, ALA-YALSA; The Children's Literature Choice List, 2001; Top Shelf Fiction for Middle School Readers, 2000, Voice of Youth Advocates; Parents' Choice, 2000; Black-Eyed Susan Book Award, 2003 (nominee, Maryland); Charlotte Book Awards, 2002 (Nominee, New York); Garden State TEEN Book Awards, 2003 (nominee, New Jersey); Georgia Children's Literature Awards, 2003 (nominee, Georgia); Iowa Teen Award, 2002–2003 (nominee, Iowa); Maine Student Book Award, 2001–2002 (nominee, Maine); South Carolina Book Awards, 2003 (nominee, South Carolina). *If I Just Had Two Wings:* Red Cedar Book Award, 2003; Manitoba Young Readers' Choice Award, 2003; Geoffrey Bilson Award for Historical Fiction for Young People,

2002; Silver Birch Award, 2002; Young Adult Canadian Book Award, shortlist 2002; Rocky Mountain Book Award nominee, 2003.

BIBLIOGRAPHY: Carton, D. "Review of *Send One Angel Down*" *Booklist* 96, 1897–98, 2000; Cart, M. "Review of *If I Just Had Two Wings*" *Booklist* 98, 638, ,2001; *Contemporary Authors Online,* 2002, http://www.galenet,com/servlet/LitRC?finalAuth = true; Long, J. R. "Review of *Send One Angel Down*". *Horn Book* 76, 465, 2000; Red Cedar Book Awards, 2004, http://redcedar.swifty.com; Rohrlick, P. "Review of *If I Just Had Two Wings*". *KLIATT,* http://articles.findarticles.com/p/articles/mi_m0PBX; Schwartz, V. F. *Send One Angel Down,* 2000.

MARY MCMILLAN TERRY

SCIENCE FICTION

It has been said by science-fiction author and critic David Hartman that the Golden Age of science fiction is twelve. And indeed that seems to be the age at which the classification YA starts, according to the Young Adult Library Services Association. It is the age when young readers either abandon the imaginative titles that captivated them as children or become avid readers of SF, gobbling up every "what if" tale in sight.

Science fiction is the literature of wonder. It asks, *What if?* What if we could travel faster than the speed of light? What if computers were to become sentient? What if the climate of the earth were to change suddenly and drastically?

Definitions of science fiction abound. Peter Nichols, in his article on the history of SF in *The Encyclopedia of Science Fiction,* writes, "SF proper requires a consciousness of the scientific outlook, and it probably also requires a sense of the possibilities of change." As defined by Stanley Schmidt, the editor of *Analog,* it is those stories "in which some aspect of future science or technology is so integral to the plot that, if that aspect were removed, the story would collapse." John Clute, in *Science Fiction: The Illustrated Encyclopedia* (DK Publishing, 1995), wrote that SF (the accepted acronym for the genre) "is any story that argues the case for a changed world that has not yet come into being." In her essay "On Science and Science Fiction" in *The Ascent of Wonder: The Evolution of Hard SF* (Tor, 1994), Kathryn Cramer explained, "SF allows us to understand and experience our past, present, and future in terms of an imagined future." In simpler terms, science fiction deals with the impact of science, whether real or imagined, on individuals or society.

YAs were reading science fiction before the terms *science fiction* and *young adult* were even coined.

The term *science fiction* was coined by Hugo Gernsback in his MAGAZINE *Amazing Stories* in 1926, but young people had already been reading this type of genre in the works of Jules Verne and H. G. Wells. In fact, according to many experts, including Charles Sheffield, Brian Aldiss, and Peter Nichols, the first real science fiction was penned by TEENAGER Mary Shelley and published in 1818 under the title *Frankenstein, or The Modern Prometheus.* It extrapolated a story from the science of the day. The Tom Swift SERIES that started in 1910 captivated the imaginations of boys in the early 20th century with its inventions and travels to places that we did not have the technology to explore at the time. The 1940s and 1950s saw the publication of many titles aimed at teenage science fiction readers with Robert A. HEINLEIN's *Space Cadet, Rocket Ship Galileo, Farmer in the Sky, The Star Beast, Citizen of the Galaxy, Have Space Suit—Will Travel* and seven others, Isaac ASIMOV's *Lucky Starr* series, and series written by Gordon Dickson and others that have been long out of print. The 1960s saw young adults enthralled by the stories of Arthur C. CLARKE and Philip K. Dick.

In the July 1986 issue of *Isaac Asimov's Science Fiction Magazine,* Asimov wrote in an essay that there is no significant distinction in writing for adults and juveniles. Readers of SF tend to ignore age designations. YAs who read science fiction read ADULT BOOKS in the genre and always have.

Adolescent characters figure prominently in science fiction. As Bonnie Kunzel wrote in *Strictly Science Fiction,* "Perhaps more than in any other genre teenagers are acceptable protagonists for novels. It could be that in SF writers don't aim for an adult or young adult audience, they just aim for SF readers. The adventure of heading out for new frontiers is a young person's game and this is reflected in the youth of many characters in SF."

SF published for teens is of the same caliber as SF published for adults. Some of the best writing targeted specifically for the young adult audience has won major awards. In 2002 Nancy FARMER's *House of the Scorpion,* the tale of a clone raised to be the source of a drug lord's spare parts who escapes to make his own destiny, won a National Book Award as well as PRINTZ honor and a Newbery honor. In 1971, Sylvia Engdahl's *Enchantress from the Stars,* a story of politics and alien contact, won a Newbery honor; nearly twenty years later it won the 1990 Phoenix Award, given by the Children's Literature Association "from the perspective of time."

The best science fiction is timeless, relying on how science impacts people rather than on the gadgets and gizmos involved. Orson Scott CARD's *Ender's Game* won both Hugo and Nebula awards, and even though it wasn't originally marketed for young adults, it has become one of the novels most read by high school students. *Fahrenheit 451* by Ray BRADBURY is still popular and thought provoking with young adults as well as adults nearly half a century after its first publication.

Science fiction, FANTASY, and HORROR are inextricably linked by virtue of sharing editors, publishers, magazines, and even to some extent, fans. Those three genres are usually grouped together in a statistical analysis of the field. In the early years of the 21st century, the proportion of science fiction in relation to fantasy being published had decreased with the popularity of the HARRY POTTER books and interest in epic fantasy stirred by the films based on J. R. R. TOLKIEN's Lord of the Rings trilogy.

Science fiction has several subgenres and theme types that appeal to different readers.

ADVENTURE science fiction resounds with the clang of battle in titles such as Karin Lowachee's *Warchild* (2001) and its sequel *Burndive* (2003), where humans war with aliens and pirates in the tradition of *Ender's Game* and its many sequels. The scents of strange worlds come alive as protagonists explore other worlds either after traveling through space or by passing through a dimensional irregularity—like Charlie, who goes to a parallel world untouched by humans in Steven GOULD's *Wildside* (1886).

Hard science fiction focuses on the science in science fiction, creating well-thought-out extrapolations of what could be. Cloning, genetic engineering, virtual reality, space travel, and physics, as well as other scientific themes, appear in books by Charles Sheffield, Jerry Pournelle, David Brin, Robert Sawyer, Karl Schroeder, and others. Many YA readers have a highly developed sense of humor, making humorous classics like Douglas ADAMS's "increasingly mis-

named" five-volume *Hitchhikers Trilogy* (1980–92) popular with teens. David LUBAR's *Flip* (2003) puts an underachieving middle school boy into the personas of people as diverse as Spartacus, Einstein, and Queen Victoria after he determines how to activate entertainment disks lost by aliens in the nearby woods.

Time travel, using a scientific method rather than magic, has often appeared in science fiction popular with young adults. Michael CRICHTON's *Timeline* (1999), Orson Scott Card's *Pastwatch: The Redemption of Christopher Columbus* (1996), and *To Say Nothing of the Dog* (1997) by Connie WILLIS have all been named to ALA's Best Books for Young Adults lists.

Unusual powers including telepathy, teleportation, telekinesis, and precognition are an enticing subject seen in *Jumper* (1992) by Steven GOULD, *Hidden Talents* (1999) by David LUBAR, Robert CORMIER's *Fade* (1988), and Neal SHUSTERMAN's *Star Shards* trilogy (1995–2002). Alien beings are a fascinating idea in science fiction. When we do venture into space, will we encounter other civilizations? Have beings from other worlds already visited Earth? Hilari Bell explores the difference in outlook aliens could have in *A Matter of Profit* (2001), Barney meets aliens in William SLEATOR's Piggy SERIES (1984–2002), and Daria finds herself living with an alien in Kate GILMORE's *The Exchange Student* (1999). Joss is teamed up with a fascinatingly dual-natured alien in Alison Goodman's *Singing the Dogstar Blues* (2003) that combines aliens, time travel, and MYSTERY.

Some of the most memorable science-fiction novels written for YAs take place in either a utopian or a dystopian world. In M. T. ANDERSON's *Feed* (2002), teenagers are constantly hooked into a vast computer system through an implanted link in their brains. In Margaret Haddix Peterson's Shadow Children series (1998–2003) it is a capital offense to be the third child in a family. *The Giver* (1993) by Lois Lowry, a tale of a world where all is colorless and everyone is equal, won the Newbery Medal and was named one of YALSA's 100 Best Books for Young Adults.

One of the largest subgenres of science fiction is post-apocalyptic, which shows the world after life as we know it has ended. The *Fire-Us* trilogy (2002–2003) by Jennifer ARMSTRONG and Nancy Butcher follows the adventures of a group of children and teens who have survived a plague that killed off their memories as well as all the adults in the community. In *Shade's Children* (1997) by Garth NIX, an alien invasion has turned humans into either killing machines or food, and a band of runaway children under the direction of a computer program are the only ones fighting back. In Octavia E. BUTLER's *Parable of the Sower* (1993), empathic Lauren leads a small group of survivors to what one hopes would be a better life when the walls of her family's protected enclave fall in the chaos created by pollution and overpopulation. In Philip Reeve's *Mortal Engsine* (2003), great mobile cities roam Europe getting the resources they need by consuming other communities. It has often been said that it is the best and the brightest YAs who read science fiction. As long as there are inquisitive young readers, there will be a readership for the books that ask, *What If?*

DIANA TRIXIER HERALD

SCOPPETONE, Sandra (pseud. Jack Early)
Author, b. 1 June 1936, Morristown, New Jersey

S.'s writings run the gamut from PICTURE BOOKS to YA novels, from PLAYS to teleplays. She has also published novels under the pseudonym Jack Early. S. is known for her frank dealings with controversial topics in her work, including homosexuality, alcoholism, murder, and lesbianism. One can find her manuscripts in the Kerlan Collection at the University of Minnesota.

S. wanted to be a writer since she was a young girl, and her parents supported her decision not to attend college, but to move to New York City to pursue her dream of becoming a writer. Famed author Louise Fitzhugh *(Harriet the Spy)* worked with S. on her first published picture book, *Suzuki Beane* (1961). S. was proud to be a published author in her twenties and went on to write for television and film.

Her first young adult novel, *Trying Hard to Hear You* (1974), deals with homosexuality and is based on an actual situation which S. witnessed on Long Island. S. says her books for YA are successful because she creates the same quality material for adolescents as she does for adults. She is not condescending, her work shows maturity and genuine emotions. She followed this book with *The Late Great Me* in 1976, this time focusing on TEENAGE alcoholism. In *Happy Endings Are All Alike* (1978), S. describes a lesbian relationship between two adolescents; unfortunately, this book, like many others that push boundaries established in literature, was banned after its publication. Trying her hand at murder MYSTERIES, S. published *Playing Murder* in 1985, and she proved successful in that genre as well.

Some Unknown Person (1977) is an ADULT novel factually based on the murder of a playgirl named Starr Faithfull. S. followed this with a string of murder mysteries for adults starring a detective named Lauren Laurano, who is modeled after S. *Everything You Have Is Mine* (1991), *My Sweet Untraceable You* (1994), *Let's Face the Music and Die* (1996) reflect S.'s continued interest in writing adult mystery novels.

S. has also written three novels under the pseudonym of Jack Early about detective Fortune Fanelli. She tells these stories in the first-person male voice, and the name *Jack Early* creates the ultimate illusion of gender.

S. wants very much to have her work affect YA and make them feel good about themselves. Whether they are gay or lesbian or recovering alcoholics, S. has a message for them. She is hopeful that her books will help change people's lives for the better. S.'s hobbies include antiquing, watching classic films, and attending auctions. She lives in Greenport, New York, with her partner, writer Linda Crawford.

SELECT AWARDS: 1972 Eugene O'Neill Memorial Award, *Stuck;* Ludwig Vogelstein Foundation Grant, 1974; 1976 New Jersey Institute of Technology Award, *Trying Hard to Hear You;* 1974 Best Books for Young Adults, *Trying Hard to Hear You;* 1978 Best Books for Young Adults, *Happy Endings Are All Alike;* 1985 Shamus Award, Private Eye Writers of America, *A Creative Kind of Killer* (as Jack Early); 1985 Edgar Allan Poe Award nomination, *A Creative Kind of Killer* (as Jack Early); 1986 Edgar Allan Poe Award nomination, *Playing Murder;* various Best of the Best Books citations.

FURTHER WORKS: *Bang Bang, You're Dead,* 1968; *CBS Playhouse,* 1968; "Where the Heart Is," 1970; *Such Nice People,* 1980; *The Late Great Me,* 1982 (film); *Innocent Bystanders,* 1983; *A Creative Kind of Killer,* 1984 (Jack Early); *Long Time Between Kisses,* 1984; *Razzamatazz: A Novel,* 1985 (Jack Early); *Playing Murder,* 1985; *Donato and Daughter,* 1988 (Jack Early); *I'll Be Leaving You Always,* 1993; *Donato and Daughter,* 1993 (television) (Jack Early); *Gonna Take A Homicidal Journey,* 1998. Plays:

"Three One-act plays," 1964; "One-Act Play," 1965; "Two One-act Plays," 1968; *Home Again, Home Again Jiggity Jig,* 1969 (play); *Something for Kitty Genovese,* 1971 (one-act play); *Scarecrow in a Garden of Cucumbers,* 1972 (screenplay); *Love of Life,* 1972 (teleplay); *Stuck,* 1972 (play); *A Little Bit Like Murder,* 1973 (teleplay); *The Inspector of Stairs,* 1975 (screenplay).

BIBLIOGRAPHY: Commire, Anne. *Something about the Author,* vol. 9, 1976, *Contemporary Authors Online,* 2001.

SANDRA KITAIN

SCOTT, Michael (Peter) (pseud. Anna Dillon)

Author, anthologist, b. 1959, Dublin, Ireland

S. is recognized in Ireland as an accomplished writer whose anthologies, novels, and SHORT STORIES span a spectrum of genres that include Irish folklore and MYTHOLOGY, FANTASY, SCIENCE FICTION, contemporary and historical fiction, and HORROR. A prolific author and anthologist with over sixty titles to his credit, S. has written extensively for adults, YA, and children. S. has also written a SERIES of historical novels for adults under the pseudonym *Anna Dillon.*

S. was born and raised in Dublin and was educated at St. Aidan's. S.'s passion for Celtic folklore was inspired by his two favorite childhood authors, Mary Norton and Patricia Lynch. A true bookman, S. came to writing in 1982 after working in several Dublin bookstores and as an antiquarian-book seller. He was first published in 1983 and has since established himself as an authority on Irish history and mythology. Three of his anthologies—*Irish Folk and Fairy Tales* (3 vols., 1983–85), Irish *Myths and Legends* (1992), and *Irish Ghosts and Hauntings* (1994)—are definitive collections.

As the natural result of gathering and compiling traditional Irish stories for his anthologies, many of S.'s works for young adults and children are set in Ireland or are informed by Irish myths and legend. *October Moon* (1992), about an American TEENAGER whose family buys a 400-year-old farm in County Kildare, was the first HORROR novel published specifically for young adults in Ireland. *Ireland: A Graphic History* (1995), co-written with Morgan Llewellyn, is a GRAPHIC NOVEL that can make several thousands of years of Irish history accessible to reluctant readers. *19 Railway Street* (1996), also co-written

with Morgan Llewellyn, is an interesting blend of genres. This historically based time-travel horror novel, about a young girl from Dublin who meets a girl from the past, was chosen as one of the fifty best books for children in 1996 by Great Britain's Federation of Children's Book Groups.

S. has written about contemporary teens in *Judith and Spider* (1992) and *Good Enough for Judith* (1994). These titles are particularly popular in the Netherlands. S. is best known in the United States as a young adult writer for his 1993 virtual reality-based techno-thriller *Gemini Game* (1993), which was selected for the Young Adult Library Services Association's (YALSA) 1996 Quick Picks for Reluctant Young Adult Readers.

FURTHER WORKS: *Earthlord,* 1992; *Firelord,* 1994; "I Told You So," in *Don't Forget Your Spacesuit, Dear,* 1996; *Irish Hero Tales,* 1989; "The Kiss," in *Great Irish Tales of the Unimaginable,* 1994; "The Light in the Forest," in *Magic: the Gathering: Tapestries: An Anthology,* 1996; *The Piper's Ring,* 1992; the Tales of the Bard trilogy, published in omnibus form as *Culai Heritage,* 2000.

BIBLIOGRAPHY: Brady, Anne M., and B. Cleeve, eds. *A Biographical Dictionary of Irish Writers,* 1985; Pringle, David, ed., *St. James Guide to Horror, Ghost & Gothic Writers,* 1998; Reginald, Robert et al., eds. *Science Fiction and Fantasy Literature: 1975–1991,* 1992; Scott, Michael. "By Imagination We Live: Some Thoughts on Irish Children's Fantasy." *The Lion and the Unicorn* 21 no. 3 (1997): 322–29.

DAN H. LAWRENCE

SEBESTYEN, Ouida

Author, b. 13 February 1924, Vernon, Texas

S. developed a love for reading and writing early in her childhood. She participated in school plays and decided in high school that she wanted to be a writer. As a YA she worked various jobs, including doing maintenance on planes used in World War II. She wrote in her spare time and she finished her first novel at age nineteen, but had trouble finding a publisher. She spent several frustrating years trying to get her work in print. Her break came in 1950, when one of her stories was accepted for publication. She had other stories published as well, but still no luck in getting a book deal. S. finally decided to focus on YA literature when she realized that one of her stories, featuring a child as the main character, was generating a lot of interest. She fleshed out the story and reintroduced it as a novel. When S. was fifty-five years old, *Words by Heart* (1979, reprinted 1997) became her first published novel. This story of a young black girl won numerous awards and was made into an Emmy–nominated television show.

S. followed the success of her first novel with several other award-winning titles for young adults. *Far from Home* (1980) was named an American Library Association Best Book for Young Adults and a *School Library Journal* Best Book of the Year in 1980. *IOUs* (1982) was also an American Library Association Best Book for Young Adults as well as a Library of Congress Children's Book. *The Girl in the Box* (1988) is a breathtaking story told in first-person narrative, of a girl who has an argument with her good friend. She is kidnapped and locked in a dark basement. She fears she will never escape. During her lengthy, forced stay in the dark basement, she reflects on her own life. Readers never know for sure if she escapes, is rescued, or dies.

In addition to working odd jobs and pursuing her writing career, S. also attended the University of Colorado.

AWARDS: *Words by Heart:* 1979 *New York Times* Outstanding Book, *School Library Journal* Best Book, American Library Association Best Books for Young Adults, American Library Association Notable Book, 1980 International Reading Association Children's Book Award, 1982 American Book Award; ALA Best Books for Young Adults: *Far from Home*, 1980; *IOU's*, 1982.

FURTHER WORKS: *On Fire*, 1985; *The Girl in the Box*, 1988; *Out of Nowhere: A Novel*, 1995; anthologized in *Sixteen*, edited by Donald R. Gallo, 1984.

BIBLIOGRAPHY: *Contemporary Authors Online*, 2003. Reproduced in *Biography Resource Center*, 2003, http://www.galenet.com/servlet/BioRC.

SHANNON CUFF

SEGAL, Erich Wolf

Author, b. 16 June 1937, Brooklyn, New York

S., the son of a rabbi, earned his bachelor's degree from Harvard University in 1958, where he graduated as the school's first Latin salutatorian and class poet. He also pursued graduate studies in classics and comparative literature at Harvard, receiving his doctorate in 1956.

S.'s career has encompassed varied professional and intellectual activities. He started out on the faculty of Yale University, remaining there for eight years. Tel Aviv University, Wolfson College at Oxford University, and Princeton University are three of the seven esteemed institutions where S. has taught and researched since his time at Yale. He has also worked as a sports commentator for television, covering Olympic Games and other athletic events for ABC and NBC. In addition to these accomplishments, S. has written both screenplays and highly popular novels, which are primarily geared to an adult audience.

S. is best known for *Love Story*, a novel about a cross-class ROMANCE between a wealthy Harvard law student and a poor Radcliffe music major. The theme of romance and class differences appears again in S.'s *Acts of Faith*, a novel about the daughter of the Jewish rabbi, Rebecca, who falls in love with a Roman Catholic man. S.'s fiction is a popular success; over twenty million copies of *Love Story* have been printed, and the novel has been translated into more than thirty languages. However, generally critics have been lukewarm about S.'s writing, commonly assessing his prose as bland and his character development as weak. Several of S.'s works have been adapted for the screen, including *Love Story*.

AWARDS: *Love Story*: 1970 ALA Best Books for Young Adults

FURTHER WORKS: *Oliver's Story* (1977); *Only Love*, 1999.

BIBLIOGRAPHY: Dupler, D. "Erich Segal: Overview." In D. Mote, ed., *Contemporary Popular Writers* 1997, http://galenet.galegroup.com; *Contemporary Authors Online*, 2002.

JUDAH S. HAMER

SERIES FICTION

S. is a set of stories that share characters or settings, or a combination of both. It is an episodic genre, sometimes unveiling the tale in its entirety with the addition of each separate part, other times merely using the same characters or settings. In stronger S.s, the characters evolve through time as they face and resolve their problems and issues. Other characters remain much the same from episode to episode in the more formulaic S., without ever showing much of a change. This does not lessen the popularity of such

S.; it simply indicates that the character's growth is less of a draw than the ADVENTURES that the aforementioned character encounters.

S. first became popular with the rise of dime novels, which often portrayed the same character in ongoing adventures. However, it was really at the dawn of the 20th century that S. for YA came into its own. Although many credit Edward Stratemeyer, founder of the STRATEMEYER SYNDICATE, with the evolution of the genre into what is known today as S., he was not alone. That the Stratemeyer Syndicate created many notable characters—among them the Hardy Boys, Nancy Drew, Tom Swift and Tom Swift Jr., the Bobbsey Twins, the Blythe Girls, the Moving Picture Girls, the Outdoor Girls, and the Dana Girls—cannot be argued. However, as the 20th century began, so did an avalanche of S.

In the first decade of the new century, the Stratemeyer Syndicate launched the Dave Porter books by Edward Stratemeyer in 1905, the Larry Dexter books by Howard R. Garis (which eventually came to be known as The Young Reporter S.) and continued with the Rover Boys by Arthur M. Winfield, which had first appeared in 1899 and would continue until 1926. Other S. that appeared, without help from the Stratemeyer Syndicate, included the Phillips Exeter books by A. T. Dudley, which were SPORTS stories, the Putnam Hall stories by Arthur M. Winfield, as well as the first appearance of the Submarine Boys by Victor G. Durham in 1909. *Anne of Green Gables* by L. M. Montgomery appeared in 1908. The Yardley Hall novels by Ralph Henry Barbour also were published, as well as two S. about West Point. The West Point S. by Captain Paul B. Malone contained five titles and was published from 1904 to 1911, while the West Point S. by H. Irving Hancock continued the adventures of the Grammar School Boys in four titles that appeared in 1910–11. Oddly, the Grammar School Boys titles did not appear until 1911.

Another S. that emerged in the second decade of the twentieth century was the Grace Harlowe S. by Josephine Chase, writing as Jessie Graham Flower. They first appeared in 1910, as did the Stratemeyer Syndicate's Tom Swift titles and would encompass twenty-seven volumes before ending in 1924. In that time, the heroine goes through high school and college, as well as World War I in Europe, before returning to the U.S. for more adventures. The Tom Swift S. would last until 1941 and produce thirty-eight titles.

Edgar Rice Burroughs, better known for the Tarzan S., introduced the John Carter of Mars S. in 1912. The eleven novels concluded in 1942, but also gave rise to comic books, in which the adventures of John Carter continued. The River Motor Boat Boys by Harry Gordon had a fairly short run, with eight titles appearing in 1913–15. Nineteen thirteen was also the year that the Stratemeyer Syndicate introduced the Ruth Fielding S. by Alice B. Emerson. It would generate thirty titles before ending in 1934. Another Stratemeyer S., the Saddle Boys by Captain James Carson, only generated five titles in 1913–15. The Westerns were not unduly popular, a fate shared by another S. put forth by Stratemeyer, the YMCA Boys by Brooks Henderley, which produced three titles in 1916–17. *The Adventures of Tom Slade* by Percy Keese Fitzhugh began in 1915 and would encompass nineteen books, before ending in 1930. The Scranton High Chums by Donald Ferguson appeared in 1919 with four books centering on SPORTS.

Lucy Maud Montgomery introduced a new series chronicling the life of Emily Starr in 1922, which was also the year that two separate S. titled the Radio Boys appeared. Gerald Breckenridge wrote ten adventure tales, while the Stratemeyer Syndicate produce thirteen titles authored by Allen Chapman. The G-Men S. by William Engle and Laurence Dwight Smith appeared in 1926, and generated three stories over the course of fourteen years. The Tod Moran books by Howard Pease were first published in the 1920s and over the course of thirteen books follow Tod around the world as he solves MYSTERIES and has adventures. The Stratemeyer Syndicate had a banner year in 1927—the Ted Scott Flying Stories first appeared under the name of Franklin W. Dixon, as did the Hardy Boys. Leslie McFarlane was to guide the Hardy Boys through their first twenty years, and although the S. has had a variety of incarnations, the books are being published to this day. Although eclipsed by the Hardy Boys, the Ted Scott Flying Stories should not be underestimated. Twenty titles appeared from 1927 to 1943, tapping into the excitement about aviation that the country was feeling in the wake of Lindbergh's flight.

The Bill Bolton, Navy Aviator books by Noel Sainsbury in which all four titles appeared in 1933, also reflected the excitement about flying that was in the air. Lindbergh was not the only flying ace though, the Linda Carlton S. by Edith Lavell was supposed to be based on the adventures of Amelia Earhart and produced five titles between 1931 and 1933. The Sue Barton books by Helen Dore Boylston appeared from 1936 to 1952. They follow Sue from her student nursing days to her work at the Henry Street Settlement to her marriage to a country doctor and job, first as a superintendent of nurses and then as a neighborhood nurse and staff nurse. The Beverly Gray mysteries by Clair Blank ultimately produced twenty-six titles and were published from 1934 to 1955. The Judy Bolton mysteries first appeared in 1932 and enjoyed a publishing run of thirty-five years, with a total of thirty-eight books.

However, the queen of girl detectives for the decade and for many decades to come was from the Stratemeyer Syndicate. Nancy Drew made her debut in 1930 in *The Mystery of the Old Clock,* and proved to be a winner. Hiring authors to churn out stories with them had proved to be a marketing bonanza for Stratemeyer. The Nancy Drew S. proved that without the shadow of a doubt, even being turned into four movies in the 1930s: *Nancy Drew, Detective* (1938), *Nancy Drew and the Hidden Staircase* (1939), *Nancy Drew . . . Reporter* (1939), and *Nancy Drew . . . Troubleshooter* (1939). The actress who played Nancy, Bonita Granville, even had mystery books in which she was featured as the star. Both Hardy Boys mysteries and the Nancy Drew mysteries were turned into television shows in the nineteen seventies. The Hardy Boys also generated an animated television show in the 1960s. Nancy Drew reappeared on television as recently as 2002, proving that Mr. Stratemeyer had a good idea. The Lone Ranger books by Fran Striker, which lasted for twenty years, also had a media tie-in.

The Betsy-Tacy S. by Maud Hart Lovelace appeared in 1940. Based at the beginning of the century, the books start when the girls are five and follow them throughout their school years and until they have children of their own. The approaching World War II is reflected in many of the S. set in the 1940s. The Don Winslow S. by Frank V. Martinek, which starts in 1940, showcases Don joining the Navy and the adventures he has there. Janet Lambert set many of her first novels in an Army setting, using her background as an Army wife. The Penny and Tippy Parrish books, which kicked off with *Star Spangled Summer* in 1941, start before the WAR begins, but by the third book, they reflect the world of the United States

at war. The characters are followed through the conclusion of World War II to the Vietnam War. Lambert's stories about the Jordon FAMILY came out at about the same time, focusing on a large and motherless family surviving when their soldier father goes off to war. The Kane S. also uses World War II as a background—when a reservist decides to become active, his society wife and two daughters must adjust to Army life. *Meet the Malones* by Lenora Mattingly Weber is also set against the background of World War II, although it is mostly seen from a civilian point of view. The Malone S. chronicles the adventures of the Malone family through marriages, DEATHS, and births ranging over fourteen books and several years. The Cherry Ames S. by Helen Wells and Julie Tatham, starting in 1943, chronicles the career of a young nurse from her student days. The twenty-seven books follow Cherry through many different nursing jobs. Helen Wells and Julie Tatham also wrote the Vicki Barr, Stewardess S., which appeared from 1947 to 1964 with a total of sixteen titles. The Trixie Belden S. by Julie Campbell and Kathryn Kenny began in 1948 and ended nearly forty years later in 1986. through the thirty-nine titles, Trixie and her friends, known as the Bob-Whites, solve a multitude of mysteries as well as working to help their families and communities. Popular coach Clair Bee wrote the Chip Hilton books that follow a young athlete through the different sports seasons from the time of his high-school career through his college career. The twenty-three titles feature baseball, football, and basketball stories, although many have scenes set in the soda shop where Chip works to supplement his scholarship. Christie Drayton and her crowd hang out at the community drugstore in *Where the Heart Is* and *Treasure Trouble,* which appeared in 1948 and 1949, but the ascent of the corner drugstore as a TEEN hangout was just beginning.

The soda shop plays an important part in many of the S. books that appear in the 1950s. Janet Lambert has many of her teens hang out at a soda shop in the Cinda Hollister S. Rosamund DuJardin occasionally uses a soda shop as a setting in her Midge and Tobey Heydon books. DuJardin also wrote the popular Marcy Rhodes S. as well as the Pam and Penny Howard books. In the realm of fantastic adventure, the Tom Swift, Jr. S. appeared in 1954—and was published for another seventeen years, offering thirty-three new installments. The Tom Corbett books by

Carey Rockwell originated in another medium, but managed to generate eight titles.

The 1960s offered more media tie-ins, with Walt Disney's Annette S., which were supposedly the adventures of Annette Funicello from The Mickey Mouse Club. *Dark Shadows* offered another television tie-in. Although Alfred Hitchcock and the Three Investigators was not exactly a media tie-in, it did feature, however peripherally, famed director Alfred Hitchcock. The S. generated forty-three titles by a variety of authors from 1964 to 1987.

Appearing in 1966, the Blade books by Jeffrey Lord (really a pseudonym for a variety of authors) were published for nearly twenty years and generated over thirty-five titles. Considered fantasies, they joined other SCIENCE FICTION and FANTASY books of that decade, including the Mars Stories S. by Edward P. Bradbury. That trilogy followed the adventures of a human, Michael Kane, on Mars (the trilogy included *Warriors of Mars, Blades of Mars,* and *Barbarians of Mars).* Although these were not strictly geared towards young adults, they did reflect a trend toward exploring new worlds, as did the Star Trek S., based on the television show.

Some *may* call Madeleine L'ENGLE's books a S. since they follow the same characters. She had published *A Wrinkle in Time* in 1962, which followed Meg Murry on her interplanetary travels in her quest to rescue her father. Two years previously, L'Engle's novel *Meet the Austins* had appeared. Both would prove to be the foundations of two separate S. that would span decades and ultimately overlap. The Austin S. would produce three more books by the end of the decade: *The Moon by Night* (1963), *The Twenty-four Days before Christmas* (1964), and *The Young Unicorns* (1968). Meg Murry's daughter Polly world make her first appearance in *The Arm of the Starfish* in 1965. The Murry books are known as the Kairos S. since they take place out of chronological time.

The 1960s and 1970s also began to reflect the tumult of the times, offering more cutting-edge subjects in many contemporary YA novels. This also was reflected in S. books during that time, as edgier subjects began to seep into the characters' lives. The Austins, temporarily living in New York City in *The Young Unicorns* (1968) encounter gangs. Meg Murry reappeared in 1973's *The Wind in the Door* and 1978's *A Swiftly Tilting Planet,* in which she helped to save the world from devastation. Self-assessment and eventual self-acceptance, are keynotes for Paula DANZINGER's protagonist, Marcy Lewis. Overweight, and miserable, a new teacher helps her find herself, and Marcy, in turn, finds the courage to defend the teacher against the anger of the community. Marcy's reluctant evolution is chronicles in *The Cat Ate My Gymsuit* and *There's a Bat in Bunk Five.* The Anthony Monday S. by John Bellairs and Brad Strickland appeared from 1978 to 1992 with *The Treasures of Alpheus Winterborn, The Dark Secret of Weatherend, The Lamp from the Warlock's Tomb,* and *The Mansion in the Mist*— adventure stories geared for boys.

The Sweet Dreams S. appeared in the 1980s. Basically teenage ROMANCES, they occasionally dealt with weightier issues, as evinced by the debut book in the S., *P.S. I Love You* by Barbara Conklin, which had a dying hero. The Caitlin S., made up of three interlocking trilogies (the Promise, Love, and Forever sets), also dealt with DEATH. However, the jackpot series of the 1980s probably belonged to Francine PASCAL, with her Sweet Valley High books. That S. would eventually generate several others, including Sweet Valley Kids, Sweet Valley Twins, Sweet Valley Senior Year, Sweet Valley University, and Sweet Valley Superthrillers, which appeared over the next twenty years. Another S. from the 1980s that had a place in the spotlight was Ann M. Martin's Babysitters Club.

YA fiction in S. reached new heights in the 1990s. Some S. that appeared included the Georgia Nicholson S. by Louise RENNISON—an import from Great Britain—the Fearless titles by the prolific Francine Pascal, and a few S. that centered on witchcraft. Fantasy abounded, including S. by Tamora PIERCE and reissues from Patricia WREDE. The Love Stories S., which emerged in the middle of the 1990s, offer fairly typical romances, although the characters show some MULTICULTURALISM. Multiculturalism also played a big part in the Heart Beats books by Elizabeth Rees, as did the fusion of classical ballet and ballroom dancing. Ann Martin's S. for younger readers generated a spin-off: the California DIARIES books. Following the lives of five friends through each friend's diaries, the graphic layout of the diaries was done in each character's individual handwriting and included doodles and sketches, much as real journals might. These, too, were multicultural. The *Roswell* books by Melinda Metz were about a group of six friends, three of whom were aliens. The book S. actually generated its own television show. A multitude of television tie-ins included the Angel S., the Buffy the Vampire books, the Charmed books, the Sabrina the Teen-age Witch S., which generated its own spin-off, the Salem's Tail S., which focused on Sabrina's cat, and the Seventh Heaven S.

The 21st century continues the trend of television tie-ins with the debut of the Gilmore Girls as well as the continuation of many of the other S. Buffy the Vampire continues, although the television show no longer is in production. Other new S. appear on an almost weekly basis. Time will tell how popular they are.

BIBLIOGRAPHY: Billman, Carol. *The Secret of the Stratemeyer Syndicate: Nancy Drew and the Hardy Boys, and the Million Dollar Fiction Factory,* 1986; www.imbd.com; www.lib.msu.edu/coll/main/spec_col/ nye/juven.htm; www.madeleinelengle.com; www .seriesbooks.com

JEANNE MARIE RYAN

SHEFFIELD, Charles
Physicist, author, b. 25 June 1935, Hull, England; d. 2 November 2002, Rockville, Maryland

S. began his career as a physicist in the mid-1960s, serving as a consultant to NASA and later as chief scientist and board member for Earth Satellite Corporation. He produced over one hundred technical papers on various scientific topics. It was in the late 1970s at the age of forty that S. turned to fiction writing, initially as a distraction after the death of his first wife, but also as a response to what he perceived was the scarcity of SCIENCE FICTION grounded in hard science.

S. proved equally prolific as a fiction writer and often explored themes of interplanetary on interspecies conflict. His work drew comparisons to fellow novelist Arthur C. CLARKE, most notably with the publication of *The Web between the Worlds* (1979), in which he explored the idea of a "beanstalk," a space elevator based at the equator that would allow the easy launching of spaceships. By striking coincidence, this same concept was explored in Clarke's 1979 novel, *The Fountains of Paradise.*

S. wrote or co-authored more than two dozen novels, including *Sight of Proteus* (1978, later reprinted in 1994 as *Proteus Combined*), the first of several novels in the Behrooz Wolf SERIES. Other works include *My Brother's Keeper* (1982), *The Mind Pool* (1986), *Godspeed* (1993), *Tomorrow and Tomorrow* (1997), and *The Spheres of Heaven* (2001), as well as novels in the Heritage Universe and Jupiter series. This latter series is of particular interest to those who work with young adults. S. sought to revive the spirit and ADVENTURE of the early days of science fiction for today's TEEN readers. The novels in the Jupiter series were a deliberate paean to the early works of Clarke, ASIMOV, and HEINLEIN—teen characters engaged in a struggle to overcome adversity, using science and scientific principals to insure an optimistic outlook for the future. S. also published several SHORT STORY collections; in 1994 he won science fiction's highest honors, the Hugo and the Nebula, for the novelette "Georgia on My Mind."

S. served as past president of the Science Fiction and FANTASY Writers of America as well as of the American Astronautical Society. He was also a fellow of both the American Association for the Advancement of Science and the British Interplanetary Society. His second marriage ended in divorce. A third marriage, to fellow science fiction author Nancy Kress, lasted five years before S. succumbed to brain cancer in 2002.

AWARDS: Sei-un Award, 1991, for *The McAndrew Chronicles;* John W. Campbell Award, 1992, for *Brother to Dragons;* Hugo Award and Nebula Award, 1994, for *Georgia on My Mind.*

FURTHER WORKS: *Resurgence: A Novel of the Heritage Universe,* 2002; *The Lady Vanishes and Other Oddities of Nature,* 2002; *Dark as Day,* 2002, *The Amazing Dr. Darwin,* 2002.

BIBLIOGRAPHY: *Contemporary Authors Online,* 2003.

SANSANEE S. GRAVES

SHELDON, Dyan
Author, b. n.d, Brooklyn, New York

Born and educated in the United States, S. currently resides in London, England. Formerly an editor for a book publishing company, she is the author of books for adults and children, including *Whale's Song,* which won the British Library Association's Kate Greenaway Medal in 1991. She gained recognition for her works for YA *Confessions of a Teenage Drama Queen* (1999) won several honors and awards.

AWARDS: 1991 Kate Greenaway Medal, *Whale's Song; Confessions of a Teenage Drama Queen:*

American Library Association Quick Pick for Reluctant Readers, New York Public Library Books for the Teen Age, *Booklist* Editor's Choice distinction.

FURTHER WORKS: *You Can Never Go Home Again,* 1995; *Save the Last Dance for Me,* 1995; *The Boy of My Dreams,* 1997; *My Perfect Life,* 2002; *Planet Janet,* 2003.

JENNIFER ROY

SHEPPARD, Mary C.
Author, instructor, journalist, b. 15 March 1952, Corner Brook, Newfoundland, Canada

With a M.Sc in journalism from Columbia University in New York, S. has had a successful full-time career in the CANADIAN media. Based now in Toronto, she is currently chief producer for online news at CBC.ca. A two-year stay in Amsterdam in the mid-1990s allowed her time to pursue her interest in writing fiction. The result was her debut novel, *Seven for a Secret* (2001), which has won awards and received several notable citations. At this writing, S. is nearing completion of a second novel, tentatively entitled, *One for Sorrow.*

S.'s experiences growing up in Newfoundland provide a sense of authenticity to her depiction of the small isolated fishing village of Cook's Cove in *Seven for a Secret.* The sprightly Melinda, one of three fifteen-year-old cousins at the novel's center, narrates the story in her Newfoundland vernacular, effectively conveying the vitality of a vigorous community that creates its own joys amid limited opportunities and frequent hardships. The novel's plot revolves around the three cousins' discovery of FAMILY secrets that parallel discoveries about themselves, discoveries that usher them toward young womanhood. The setting in the not-so-distant past, the summer of 1960, facilitates S.'s exploration of challenging issues concerning decisions for young women that retain their relevance for a contemporary audience as well as exploring broader ethical dilemmas involving conflicts among individuals' needs.

AWARDS: *Seven for a Secret:* 2002 Ontario Ruth Schwartz Award, 2003 American Library Association Best Books for Young Adults list, International Library of Munich's selections for 2002

FURTHER WORK: *False Faces,* 2004.

BIBLIOGRAPHY: Reviews of *Seven for a Secret:* Sheppard, Philippa. *Quill and Quire* 67 (Summer 2001):

53; Thomas, Mary. *CM Magazine,* 8, no. 9, January 4, 2002, http:www.umanitoba.ca/outreach/cm/vol8/no9/seven4secret.html; Vogels, Josie. "Sex and the Modern Teen." *The Globe and Mail,* August 24, 2002, R9.

RITA BODE

SHERMAN, Josepha
Author, publisher, n.d., New York City

Today's television and MOVIE audiences are familiar with story characters such as Buffy, the Vampire Slayer; Star Trek's most famous Vulkan, Dr. Spock; the Highlander, and Xena, the Warrior Princess. Many of these FANTASY stories were crafted from the imagination of the prolific writer, Josepha S. Daughter of Nat, an employment manager, and Alice (née Altschuler), a screenwriter and teacher, S. is known for her fantasy novels. She is also a storyteller, folklorist, and editor–owner of S. Editorial Services. She has more than 42 books and over 125 stories and articles to her credit.

Integrating her knowledge of ancient Near Eastern archaeology with folklore and MYTHOLOGY, S. is able to create believable cultures, worlds, characters, and events within the pages of her books and within her stories. When asked, S. will tell you that TOLKIEN has had the biggest influence" on her work, which has expanded to include writing for a segment of the animated TV show *Adventures of the Galaxy Rangers.* At the other end of the spectrum, S. has written BIOGRAPHIES about Bill Gates, Venus Williams, Jerry Yang and David Filo, the cofounders of Yahoo, as well as the founder of amazon.com, Jeff Bezos. Her editorial projects include *Mythology For Storytellers* by M. E. Sharpe and *In Celebration of Lammas Night* by Mercedes LACKEY.

S. travels throughout the U.S. lecturing and storytelling. She has shared her knowledge at speaking engagements at the Library of Congress and American Folklore Society conferences. When writing, S. sits at a typewriter to work and if she encounters "writer's block" just stops writing, and goes to a different project. Her advice to anyone who would like to become a writer it to "Write what you WANT to write! Read. Everything."

A graduate of Hunter College, S. continues to make her home in the Riverdale section of the Bronx, in New York City. The New York Public Library has included many of her books on their lists for TEEN

Readers. S. loves horses and her hobbies include "horse whispering" and traveling. Memberships include SCIENCE FICTION Writers of America and the Society of Children's Book Writers.

AWARDS: *Trickster Tales: Forty Folk Tales from Around the World* (1996) Best New Book for New Adult Readers by the Adult Lifelong Learning Section of the Public Library Association; *Gleaming Bright* (1994), a Junior Library Guild Selection; *King's Son, Magic's Son* (1994), a New York Public Library Book for Teen Age; *Child of Faerie, Child of Earth* (1992), an ALA Best Books for Young Adults and a New York Public Library Book for the Teen Age; Compton Crook Award for best fantasy novel (1990) for *The Shining Falcon.*

FORTHCOMING: *Young Warriors Stories of Strength,* 2005; *Stoned Souls* with Mercedes Lackey, February 2006.

FURTHER WORKS: Series—Star Trek, Star Trek Pocket Unnumbered, *Vulcan's Forge* (1997) with Susan Shwartz; Bardic Voices, Bardic Choices, *A Cast of Corbies* (1994) with Mercedes Lackey; Unicorn, *Swept Away* (1988), *The Dark Gods* (1989); Prince of the Sidhe, *The Shattered Oath* (1995), Forging the Runes (1996); Bard's Tale, *Castle of Deception* (1992) with Mercedes Lackey—Set in the same universe as the computer game *The Bard's Tale IV, The Chaos Gate* (1994); Novels—*Golden Girl and the Crystal of Doom (Find Your Fate Junior, Golden Girl, No 3),* 1986; *The Shining Falcon,* 1989 Cc 1990; *The Horse of Flame,* 1990; *Child of Faerie, Child of Earth,* 1992; *Windleaf,* 1993, synopsis; *A Strange and Ancient Name,* 1993; *King's Son, Magic's Son,* 1994; *Gleaming Bright,* 1994; *Vulcan's Forge (Star Trek)* with Susan Shwartz, 1998; *Son of Darkness,* 1998, reviews; *Highlander: The Captive Soul: A Novel (Highlander),* 1998; *ALL I NEED TO KNOW I LEARNED FROM XENA: WARRIOR PRINCESS,* 1998; *Visitors* with Laura Gilman, 1999; *Twice upon a Time* with Denise Little, Jane YOLEN, Jane Lindskold and Sheila Gilbert, 1999; *Vulcan's Heart (Star Trek)* with Susan Shwartz, 2000; *Deep Water* with Laura Anne Gilman, 2000; *The Secret of the Unicorn Queen: Swept Away and Sun Blind* with Gwen Hansen, 2004; *Mage Knight 4: The Black Thorn Gambit,* 2004; *Gene Roddenberry's Andromeda: Through the Looking Glass (Gene Roddenberry's Andromeda)* with Tribune Entertainment, 2004; *Exodus: Vulcan's Soul Trilogy, Book 1 (Star Trek)* with Susan Shwartz, 2004, *Gene Roddenberry's Andromeda: Through the Looking Glass (Gene Roddenberry's Andromeda),* 2005; *Queen Lydia Liliuokalani, Last Ruler of Hawaii,* 2004. Anthologies—*Lammas Night* with Mercedes Lackey, 1996; *Lammas Night,* 1996; *Urban Nightmares* with Keith DeCandido, 1997. Short Fiction—*The Shrouded Sorceress,* 1981; *Vol'ka,* 1987; *The Ring of Lifari,* 1987; *Runaways,* 1988; *Heart of Ice,* 1988; *The Price of the Wind,* 1991; *City of the Singing Chimes,* 1991; *Stacked,* 1992; *Red Wings,* 1992; *Looking Forward: Excerpt from Castle of Deception* with Mercedes Lackey, 1992; *Shades of Light and Darkness,* 1993; *The Magic-Stealer,* 1993; *Dark Odds,* 1993; *Shani,* 1994; *Racehorse Predicts the Future,* 1994; *The Love-Gift,* 1994; *Ancient Magics, Ancient Hope,* 1994; *Witch-Horse,* 1995; *Teacher's Pet,* 1995; *Macha,* 1995; *The Defender of Central Park,* 1995; *The Case of the Purloined L'Isitek,* 1995; *A Song of Strange Revenge,* 1996; *One Late Night, with Jackal,* 1996; *Mother Knows Best,* 1996; *The Coyote Virus,* 1969; *The Captive Song,* 1996; *A Game of Mehen,* 1997; *Doggedly,* 1997; *Babysitter,* 1997; *A Matter of Honor,* 1998; *The Cat Who Wasn't Black,* 1998; *When Push Comes to Shove* with Susan Shwartz, 1999; *The Usurper Memos,* 2001. Essays/Articles—Introduction *(Lammas Night),* 1996; Introduction *(Urban Nightmares)* with Keith R. A. DeCandido. Folklore titles—*A Sampler of Jewish-American Folklore,* 1992; *Rachel the Clever and Other Jewish Folktales,* 1993; *Once Upon a Galaxy,* 1994; *Greasy Grimy Gopher Guts: the Subversive Folklore of Children* with T. K. F. Weisskiph, 1995; *Trickster Tales,* 1996; *Merlin's Kin: Tales of the Hero Magician,* 1998. Also, S is the contributor of stories and poems to magazines, including *Cricket, Image, Children's Digest, Fantasy Tales, Highlights for Children, Earthwise Quarterly, Starwind,* and *Child Life.*

BIBLIOGRAPHY: http://galenet.galegroup.com/servlet/ BioRC; http://www.twbookmark.com/authors/20/ 1307/; Fantastic Fiction, 2005, http://www.fantastic fiction.co.uk/authors/JosephaSherman.htm; *10 Questions with Josepha Sherman,* http://members.tripod .com/~geek_world/fantasy_interview_sherman.html.

VALERIE PALAZOLO

SHETTERLY, Will

Author, editor, publisher, b. 22 August 1955, Columbia, South Carolina

S. is a 1976 graduate of Beloit College. He has written novels, SHORT STORIES, screenplays, and comic books. With his wife Emma Bull, S. ran SteelDragon Press from 1984 to 1996. He has coedited with Bull a SERIES of five anthologies beginning with *Liavek* (1985) and ending with *Liavek: Spells of Binding* (1990). S.'s first novel, *Cats Have No Lords* (1985), is a fantasy involving the ADVENTURES of a cat named

Lady Lizelle. His second novel, *Witch Blood* (1986), tells the tale of characters tainted by magic in their blood. *Elsewhere* (1991) and *Nevernever* (1993) are stories about happenings in a borderland between magic and reality. S.'s favorite of his own novels is *Dogland* (1997), a story of racism set in Florida in the late 1950s. *Chimera* (2000) is a noir-styled detective tale about genetically altered creatures and the nature of humanity.

FURTHER WORKS: *The Tangled Lands,* 1989; *Double Feature,* 1999, with Emma Bull; *Thor's Hammer,* 2000.

BIBLIOGRAPHY: *Contemporary Authors Online* 2003; *St. James Guide to Fantasy Writers,* 1996; author's website: http://www.player.org/pub/flash/people/will .html.

JAMES GAHAGAN

SHILTS, Randy
Journalist, author, b. 8 August 1951, Davenport, Iowa; d. 17 February 1994, n.p.

S. began his career as a television reporter, but after moving to the *San Francisco Chronicle* in 1981 he soon became known nationally for his reporting on important issues in the gay community. His 1982 book, *The Mayor of Castro Street: The Life and Times of Harvey Milk,* garnered critical acclaim for its understanding of intricate San Francisco politics and its warm portrait of an unusual politician. In 1987, S. won international attention for his exhaustive look at the roots of the AIDS crisis, *And the Band Played On: Politics, People, and the AIDS Epidemic.* He is widely acknowledged as one of the major contributors to the general public's awareness of the AIDS epidemic, and the book was nominated for a National Book Award. Although he was beginning to suffer from AIDS symptoms, he was able to complete *Conduct Unbecoming: Gays and Lesbians in the U.S. Military, Vietnam to the Persian Gulf* (1993), a masterful overview of the hostility and discrimination faced by gay men and women in the military.

AWARDS: Special citations from San Francisco Board of Supervisors, 1982 and 1987, and from the office of San Francisco mayor, 1988; 1988 American Society of Journalists and Authors Outstanding Author Award; 1994 Lambda Literary Award for *Conduct Unbecoming*; *And the Band Played on*: ALA Best Books for Young Adults, 1987; selected for "Here We

Go Again: 25 Years of Best Books: Selections from 1967 to 1992."

BIBLIOGRAPHY: *Authors and Artists for Young Adults,* vol. 19, 1996.

MARY MENZEL

SHINN, Sharon
Journalist, author, b. 28 April 1957, Wichita, Kansas

S is a working journalist who also happens to be an award-winning author of novels that combine FANTASY, SCIENCE FICTION, ROMANCE, and MYSTERY. She has been a writer from childhood, but did not get published until her late thirties. By that time, she had written more than ten novels.

Certain themes crop up over and again in S.'s books: a person torn from her roots; opposites attracting; the search for self; the fight for justice; the triumph of love. Her stories involve class struggles, advanced technology, religious issues, faith and tolerance. Perhaps S.'s best-known work is her Samaria trilogy: *Archangel* (1996), *Jovah's Angel* (1997), and *The Alleluia Files* (1998). These books tell stories of humans and genetically engineered angels living in a world ruled by a technological "god." S. says she is drawn to writing science fiction and fantasy because these genres allow her to tell big, spectacular stories that still have small, everyday details within them.

S. has also said she likes writing in a variety of genres since she reads different kinds of books and it keeps her happy as a writer. She claims that the books she read as a child have remained as vivid to her as the day she read them. She contrasts them with the "adult" books she reads that do not have the same staying power. Perhaps this is why she is such a popular YA author. S. graduated with a degree in journalism from Northwestern University; in addition to writing novels, she works on various trade and association magazines.

AWARDS: 1995 William Crawford Award for Achievement in Fantasy; 1996 The International Association for the Fantastic in the Arts Award; 1995/1996 The Dell Award for Best New Science Fiction Writer.

FURTHER WORKS: *Shape Changer's Wife,* 1995; *Wrapt in Crystal,* 1999; *Heart of Gold,* 2000; *Summers at Castle Auburn,* 2001; *Jenna Starborn,* 2002; *Angelica: A Novel of Samaria,* 2003; *Angel-Seeker,* 2004; *The Safe-Keeper's Secret,* 2004.

BIBLIOGRAPHY: *Contemporary Authors Online,* 2001; *Books in Print Online,* 2003; Missouri Center for the

Book online, http://authors.missouri.org/q-s/shinn-s
.html, 2003; *Something about the Author, vol. 110,*
1999.

GERALDINE A. DIORIO

SHORT STORY COLLECTIONS

As instruction in English and reading classes begins
each fall, the first unit of instruction in many cases is
the S. S. can be used to teach all of the essential elements of plot, character, setting, theme, mood, tone,
and style. Because stories are, by definition, short,
they can be read and discussed quickly. However, in
the past, S. and story collections did not circulate well
in the library unless students were assigned the reading. S., though, offer many benefits for YA readers,
benefits not always available from the reading of
more classic selections in this genre.

More than twenty years ago, Don Gallo, a noted
scholar in the field of YA LITERATURE, commented on
the lack of S. for YA written by contemporary writers.
His idea was to solicit a collection of stories by leading authors in the field of YA literature and publish
them in a trade edition rather than in a traditional textbook format. Thus, *Sixteen* was born. *Sixteen* contains
S. written by award-winning authors including Richard PECK, Ouida SEBESTYEN, and M. E. KERR. The
stories were divided into four themes; Gallo included
some discussion questions at the end of the book as
well. More collections were to follow: *Visions* and
Connections. Short Circuits is a collection of HORROR
stories; *On the Fringe* examines issues of bullying
and marginalization of TEENS. *Destination Unexpected* has a journey theme, while *Ultimate Sports*
explored the world of athletics.

Others offered their own collections. Sometimes
an author wrote an original collection of his own stories. Chris CRUTCHER'S *Athletic Shorts* featured stories about characters from some of his novels situated
in a different point in their lives. *Paradise Café and
other Stories* by Martha BROOKS dealt with love in all
of its wonders and sorrows as its chief theme. Strange
phenomenon such as killer biscuits and stinky princesses form the basic theme for Bruce COVILLE'S
Odder than Ever. Stories about his childhood and his
FAMILY are at the core of *Oddballs,* a S. by William
SLEATOR. Chris LYNCH, Peter SIERUTA, Gary SOTO,
Rene Saldana, Carol Dines, and a host of others have
contributed story collections that appeal to YA
readers.

Other authors opted for an edited collection of the
works of others. Michael CART'S *Tomorrowland,* published at the beginning of the new millennium, asked
contributing authors to posit some guesses about what
might be in store for us in the future. *Necessary
Noise,* another of Cart's collections, examines the dynamics of the family in all of its permutations. *Love
and Sex: Ten Stories of Truth* has a rather self-descrip-
tive title. Judy BLUME edited a collection of stories by
authors whose works have been challenged or banned
in *Places I Never Meant to Be.* Marion Dane BAUER
tackled the tough issue of sexuality in *Am I Blue?
Coming out of the Silence.* Another critical issue, that
of guns in the hands of teens, became the focus of
Harry MAZER'S *Twelve Shots.* Lois DUNCAN, Jennifer
ARMSTRONG, James HOWE, and Helen and Jerry WEISS
have also contributed edited collections about a variety of themes.

Some of the collections published in recent years
have an additional feature: proceeds from their sales
are donated to organizations and charities. For *Sixteen,* Don Gallo donated some of the proceeds from
sales to the ALAN Foundation. The foundation, managed by the Assembly on Literature for Adolescents
of the National Council of Teachers of English
(ALAN), funds research into YA literature with grants
to educators each year. Proceeds from Gary
PAULSEN'S collections, *Shelf Life: Stories by the
Book,* are being donated to international literacy organizations.

One final interesting phenomenon bears noting.
Some of the stories from collections have been developed by their authors into full-length novels and into
other formats as well. Chris Crutcher's "A Brief Moment in the Life of Angus Bethune" became the basis
for the MOVIE *Angus.* Richard Peck's "Shotgun Chea-
tham's Last Night above Ground" ultimately became
a starting point for his Newbery Honor book, *A Long
Way from Chicago.* Likewise, "The Last Book in the
Universe" by Rodman PHILBRICK began as a story for
Cart's *Tomorrowland* and is now a novel. S. have become a popular format and outlet for contemporary
YA authors.

BIBLIOGRAPHY: Allen, Janet. *Yellow Brick Road:
Shared and Guided Paths to Independent Reading,
4–12,* 2001; Atwell, Nancie. *In the Middle,* 1987;
Beers, Kylene, and Barbara Samuels. *Into Focus: Understanding and Creating Middle School Readers,*
1998; Beers, Kylene. *When Kids Can't Read, What*

Teachers Can Do, 2002; Donelson, Kenneth, and Aileen Pace Nilsen. *Literature for Today's Young Adults,* 1999.

TERI S. LESESNE

SHOUP, Barbara
Author, b. 4 May 1947, Hammond, Indiana

S., author of both novels and books on education and learning, had always wanted to be a writer. However, it wasn't until she was a teacher at Learning Unlimited, an alternative-education program, did she realize that she was not living her childhood dream.

Her first book was *Living and Learning for Credit* (1978), followed by *New Roles for Early Adolescents in Schools and Communities* with Joan G. Schine and Diane Harrington and *Learning Unlimited: A Model for Options Education,* both published in 1981. Her first novel for adults, *Night Watch,* was published in 1982.

In 1994, S.'s first YA novel, *Wish You Were Here,* was published. This novel is a realistic look at a young man's life after his parent's divorce and the challenges that he must face. In 1997, S. published her second young adult novel, *Stranded in Harmony.* This novel explores the life of a confused high school senior, trying to escape from his small-town life. In 2000, S. published the adult novel *Faithful Women* and, in 2001, *Novel Ideas: Contemporary Authors,* a collection of twenty-three interviews of well-known authors on the artistic process.

S. married Steven Shoup in 1967; they have two children, Jennifer and Katherine.

AWARDS: *Wish You Were Here:* 1994 Bulletin for the Center for Children's Books Notable Young Adult Book, 1995 ALA Best Book for Young Adults; *Stranded in Harmony:* ALA Best Books for YA, 1998; *Vermeer's Daughter:* SLJ Best Adult Books for High School Students, 2003.

FURTHER WORK: *Vermeer's Daughter,* 2003.

BIBLIOGRAPHY: *Contemporary Authors Online,* 2003; *Something about the Author,* vol. 24, 1997.

KERRY J. GLEASON

SHUSTERMAN, Neal
Author, b. 12 November 1962, New York City

A graduate of the University of California, Irvine, in 1985 with B.A.s in both psychology and drama, S. has worked as a screenwriter, playwright, and novelist. After graduating from college, S. worked as a counselor for the summer camp of his youth, hoping "to try out his stories on youthful ears." In fact, some of the stories concocted at camp were, years later, expanded into award-winning novels. At age twenty-two, S. started his writing career, and became the youngest syndicated columnist in the country when Syndicated Writer's Group picked up his humor column. Today, he is known for his wide range of YOUNG ADULT LITERATURE, spanning genres from BIOGRAPHY to fantastic suspense.

S. earned a promising reputation in the young adult field after the publication of his first novel, *The Shadow Club* (1988). The novel draws on the common rivalries found in adolescent friendships and examines the resulting jealousy and its dangerous effects. Both *School Library Journal* and *Voice of Youth Advocate* gave positive reviews to this new novel, showing that critics and young readers both agree on its merit. Another excellent appraisal of S.'s work came from the *Horn Book* for *Speeding Bullet* (1990). According to the review, the account of TEENAGER Nick and his discovery of true heroism is "gritty, fast-paced, and, at times, funny." S. makes readers stop and reflect on parental relationships in *What Daddy Did* (1990), a true story that follows Preston through his anger, grief, and final forgiveness of his father for killing his mother. This story of a devastated FAMILY is intended to forge communication between generations and promote understanding between young adults and their parents. *The Eyes of Kid Midas* (1992) examines the pitfalls of complete wish fulfillment and absolute power. While these novels are only a sampling of S.'s work, they illustrate the breadth of the author's creations.

S. compares the writer in him to a vampire: both creatures must be invited in to have any power over their audiences, and once tampered with, the best writers and vampires "grab [their subjects] by the throat and [refuse] to let go." The result of this "attack" affects the subjects deeply and profoundly, leaving an indelible mark. S. believes that stories read during adolescence must be selected with great care, for the books he encountered during his teenage years impacted his life greatly. These stories are perhaps the most important that readers will encounter and should be works of substance.

S. has been married to Elaine Jones (a teacher and photographer) since 1987, and is the father of four children who all serve as inspiration. He is a member of PEN, Society of Children's Book Writers and Illustrators, and the Writers Guild of America (West). In addition to writing novels, S. has adapted numerous books for television, including *Night of the Living Dummy III* and *The Werewolf of Fever Swamp* for R. L. Stine's Goosebumps SERIES. He has also been a staff writer for the *Animorphs* television series, created educational films for the Learning Corporation of America, including *Heart on a Chain* and *What about the Sisters?,* and developed the "How to Host a Mystery" and "How to Host a Murder" games.

AWARDS: 1988 International Reading Association Children's Choice Award, *The Shadow Club; What Daddy Did:* 1992 American Library Association Best Book, 1992 IRA Children's Choice Award, 1992 Outstanding Fiction for Young Adults Award, 1993 IRA Young Adult Choice Award; 1992 New York Public Library Best Books for the Teen Age list, *Speeding Bullet;* 1993 ALA Best Books for Reluctant Readers, *The Eyes of Kid Midas;* 1997 New York Public Library Best Book for the Teen Age list, *Scorpion Shards;* 1997 ALA Best Books for Reluctant Readers, *MindQuakes: Stories to Shatter Your Brain;* ALA Quick Pick Top Ten List and Best Book for Young Adults, both 1998, ALA Popular Paperbacks, 2003, *The Dark Side of Nowhere*; *Downsiders*: ALA Best Books for Young Adults 2000, ALA Popular Paperback, 2002.

SELECT FURTHER WORKS: *It's Okay to Say No to Cigarettes and Alcohol,* 1988; *Dissidents,* 1989; (with Cherie Currie) *Neon Angel: The Cherie Currie Story,* 1989; *Kid Heroes: True Stories of Rescuers, Survivors, and Achievers,* 1991; *Darkness Creeping: Tales to Trouble Your Sleep,* 1993; *Piggyback Ninja,* 1994; *Scorpion Shards,* 1995; *Darkness Creeping II,* 1995; *The Dark Side of Nowhere,* 1996; *MindQuakes: Stories to Shatter Your Brain,* 1996; *Mindstorms: Stories to Blow Your Mind,* 1996; *MindTwisters: Stories to Play with Your Head,* 1997; *The Thief of Souls,* 1999; *Downsiders,* 1999; *MindBenders: Stories to Warp Your Brain,* 2000; *Shattered Sky,* 2002; *The Shadow Club Rising,* 2002; *Full Tilt,* 2003; *The Schwa Was Here,* 2004.

BIBLIOGRAPHY: "About Neal S.," http://www.storyman.com/st00008.htm; *Contemporary Authors,* vol. 133; Fader, Ellen. "Review of *Speeding Bullet.*" *Horn Book,* May/June 1991; "Full Tilt." *Publishers Weekly,* June 23, 2003, p. 68; Gale, David. "Review of *The Shadow Club,*" *School Library Journal,* May 1988; Holstine, Lesa M. "Review of *The Shadow Club,*" *Voice of Youth Advocates,* June 1988; *Major*

Authors and Illustrators for Children and Young Adults, 2nd ed., 2002: Reproduced in *Biography Resource Center,* 2003, http://www.galenet.com/servlet/BioRC; "Shattered Sky." *Publishers Weekly,* April 8, 2002, p. 210(1); *Something about the Author,* vol. 85, 1996; "A Word from the Author." http://www.storyman.com/st00009.htm

RACHEL WITMER

AND SARA MARCUS

SIERUTA, Peter, D.
Reviewer, author, n.d., n.p.

S. has been, as he notes in an article for the *Horn Book* magazine, "a [*Horn Book*] *Guide* reviewer for most of its history" (2002); as such, he has read and reviewed countless numbers of books. To his editor friends he is, as he says, like Life Cereal's Mikey, "He'll review anything!" (ibid.).

In 1989 S.'s *Heartbeats and Other Stories,* was published. Because of S.'s breadth of experience with varied literature, it is a collection of diverse SHORT STORIES told from different perspectives and for different reasons. "Assuming as many different voices as there are chapters in this collection," state Kimberly Olson Fakih and Diane Roback, writing for *Publishers Weekly,* S. proves himself an able student of the short story form" (1989, p. 92). Yet the collection is thematically unified as well, as Carolyn Noah indicates. Commenting for *School Library Journal,* Noah writes, "In each of these nine stories, a TEEN confronts an ordinary situation which has taken on an extraordinary dimension, and grows from it" (1989, p. 120).

Fakih and Roback add in their review, "[Tales like], 'Walking,' will whet readers' appetites and make them hope that S.'s next work is an expansion of any of the small universes in this first book" (1989, p. 92). Yet S. has not followed Heartbeats with other collections of stories or a novel, though his short story "Antaeus" was published in Anita Silvey's *Help Wanted: Short Stories about Young People Working* (1997). He is, as he says, a reviewer, filling pages with his opinions of the works of others.

As a reviewer of various works, S.'s responses to these works vary greatly. Sometimes his reactions are funny; he admits, "Okay, I laughed," (S, 2002) at the misadventures of the heroes in the Captain Underpants SERIES. And sometimes his opinions are angry. In an e-mail "review" of *Walk Two Moons,* a 1995

Newbery winner, S. notes, "I must admit that I AM quite angry about this year's selection. [My] strident tone . . . was probably due to the fact that my initial response to the book—both emotionally and critically—has not been confirmed by the majority of people who are posting" (1995, CHILDLITlisterv). His desire to promote literature of value is nonetheless apparent in both cases.

In addition to reviewing for *Horn Book,* S. works for the Wayne State University Libraries in Detroit.

AWARDS: *Heartbeats and Other Stories:* Best Books for Young Adults and Quick Picks for Reluctant Young Adult Readers, 1990.

BIBLIOGRAPHY: Fakih, K. O., and Roback, D. *Publishers Weekly* 23, no. 92, 1989; Noah, C. *School Library Journal* 35, no. 8, 120, 1989; S., P. D. *Horn Book* 13, no. 1, 2002; http://www.hbook.com/article_seiruta guide.shtml; S., P. D. http://www.fairrosa.info/disc/ walktwomoons.html, 1995.

MARY MCMILLAN TERRY

SILVERBERG, Robert
Author, b. 15 January 1935, New York City

S. had already begun his career as a prolific writer before graduating from Columbia University in 1956.

S. has written articles, fiction and nonfiction full-length works, and SHORT STORIES in various genres, experimenting with style and technique, focusing mainly on SCIENCE FICTION. He has written under a large number of pseudonyms, including Robert Arnette, T. D. Bethlen, Walker Chapman, Dirk Clinton, Roy Cook, Walter Drummond, Dan Eliot, Don Elliot, Franklin Hamilton, Paul Hollander, Ivar Jorgenson, Warren Kastel, Calvin M. Knox, Dan Malcolm, Webber Martin, Alex Merriman, David Osborne, George Osborne, Lloyd Robinson, Eric Rodman, Lee Sebastian, Hall Thornton, Richard F. Watson, Don Elliot, Ivar Jorgensen, Robert Randell, Gordon Aghill, Alexander Blade, Ralph Burke, Richard Greer, Clyde Mitchell, Robert Randall, Ellis Roberston, Gerald Vance, and Dan Elliot.

S.'s numerous awards include Hugo Awards, World Science Fiction Convention, 1956, for best new author, 1969, for best novella *Nightwings,* 1987, for best novella, *Gilgamesh in the Outback,* and 1990, for best novelette, *Enter a Soldier; Later: Enter Another; New York Times* Best Hundred Children's Books citation, 1960, for *Lost Race of Mars;* Spring

Book Festival Awards, New York Herald Tribune, 1962, for *Lost Cities and Vanished Civilizations,* and 1967, for *The Auk, the Dodo, and the Oryx: Vanished and Vanishing Creatures;* National Association of Independent Schools Award, 1966, for *The Old Ones: Indians of the American Southwest;* Nebula Awards, Science Fiction Writers of America, 1970, for story "Passengers," 1972, for story "Good News from the Vatican," 1972, for novel *A Time of Changes,* 1975, for novella *Born with the Dead,* and 1986, for novella *Sailing to Byzantium;* John W. Campbell Memorial Award, 1973, for excellence in writing; Jupiter Award, 1973, for novella *The Feast of St. Dionysus;* Prix Apollo, 1976, for novel *Nightwings;* Milford Award, 1981, for editing; Locus Award, 1982, for FANTASY novel *Lord Valentine's Castle;* ALEX 1999 for *Legends: New Short Novels* and ALA Best Books for Young Adults, 1980.

SELECT FURTHER WORKS: *Revolt on Alpha C,* 1955; *Starman's Quest,* 1959; *Lost Race of Mars,* 1960; *Regan's Planet,* 1964; *Time of the Great Freeze,* 1964; *The Mask of Akhnaten,* 1965; *The Gate of Worlds,* 1967; *The Calibrated Alligator and Other Science Fiction Stories,* 1969; *Across a Billion Years,* 1969; *World's Fair, 1992,* 1970; *Sunrise on Mercury and Other Science Fiction Stories,* 1975; *Project Pendulum,* 1987; *Letters from Atlantis,* 1990; *Roma Eterna,* 2003; *Phases of the Moon: Stories of Six Decades,* 2004.

BIBLIOGRAPHY: "Robert S.," DISCovering Authors, 1999, reproduced in Discovering Collection, 2001, http://galenet.galegroup.com/servlet/DC/.

SARA MARCUS

SINGER, Marilyn
Author, editor, b. 3 October 1948, Bronx, New York

S. grew up in North Massapequa, Long Island. She had to undergo heart surgery in 1956 and this was very traumatic for her since her parents and doctor did not share the facts about her illness with her.

S. attended the University of Reading (Junior Year Abroad) and then Queens College for her bachelor's degree in English and education. Marriage to Steven Aronson followed two years after her college graduation (1971). S. then received her master's degree from New York University. She was employed at the Daniel S. Meade Literary Agency in New York as an editor in 1967, and followed that with a position at *Where* MAGAZINE in New York as an assistant editor.

S. taught English and speech for the New York City Board of Education (high-school level) for five years beginning in 1969.

S.'s writing is varied and spans many areas of interest and many age groups. She writes for middle graders, juvenile level, MYSTERIES, YA FANTASIES, and books for young children. S. is proud to be hostess for the aol Children's Writers Chat. She is a member of the Society of Children's Book Writers and Illustrators, the Authors' Guild, American Library Association, Mystery Writers of America, Dog Writers Association of America, PEN American Center, Nature Conservancy, Staten Island Companion Dog Training Club, North American Dog Agility Council, Phi Beta Kappa, New York Zoological Society, Brooklyn Botanic Garden, and the American Museum of Natural History. S. has also written teacher's guides, catalogs, and program notes on films. She wrote scripts for the children's television show *The Electric Company* and was curator of "SuperFilmShow!" avant-garde films for children.

AWARDS: Children's Choice Award, International Reading Association (IRA) for *The Dog Who Insisted He Wasn't* (1977), for *It Can't Hurt Forever* (1979), for *Ghost Host* (1988), and for *Nine O'Clock Lullaby* (1991). Maude Hart Lovelace Award, Friends of the Minnesota Valley Regional Library (Mankato) for *It Can't Hurt Forever* (1983). American Library Association (ALA) Best Books for Young Adults citation for *The Course of True Love Never Did Run Smooth* (1983). Parents' Choice Award, Parents' Choice Foundation for *The Fido Frame-Up* (1983). *New York Times* Best Illustrated Children's Book citation and *Time* Best Children's Book citation (1989), Notable Trade Book in the Language Arts, National Council of Teachers of English (1990) and Texas Bluebonnet Award nominations (1992) for *Turtle in July.* South Carolina Book Award nomination for *Twenty Ways to Lose Your Best Friend* (1992–1993). Iowa TEEN Award nomination for *Charmed* (1993). Notable Children's Trade Book in the Field of Social Studies, National Council for the Social Studies and Children's Book Council for *Family Reunion* (1995). Notable Children's Trade Book in the Field of Social Studies and Children's Book Council for *On the Same Day in March* (2000). Washington Children's Choice PICTURE BOOK Award nomination for *Chester the Out-of-Work Dog* (1996). Dorothy Canfield Fisher Award nomination *For All We Needed to Say* (1997–98). Society of School LIBRARIANS International Best Books for *Deal with a Ghost* (1997–98). Dorothy Canfield Fisher Award Nomination for *Bottom's Up!* (1998–

99). Best Books for the Teen Age selection, New York Public Library for *Stay True: Short Stories for Strong Girls* (1998). Best Books for the Teen Age selection, New York Public Library for *I Believe In Water: Twelve Brushes with Religion.* Edgar Award nominee for *Deal with a Ghost* (1988). Taysha's List selections for *Deal with a Ghost* (1998–99). Taysha's List selection for *I Believe in Water: Twelve Brushes with Religion.* Popular PAPERBACKS for YAs selection, YA Library Services Association, for *Stay True: Short Stories for Strong Girls* (2000). Top Ten Science Books for Children selection, *Booklist,* for *On the Same Day in March* (2000).

FURTHER WORKS: *A History of Avant-Garde Cinema* (editor and author of introduction), 1976; *New American Filmmakers* (editor and contributor), 1976; *No Applause, Please,* 1977; *It Can't Hurt Forever,* 1978; *The First Few Friends,* 1981; *The Fanatic's Ecstatic, Aromatic Guide to Onions, Garlic, Shallots and Leeks,* 1981; *Tarantulas on the Brain,* 1982; *The Course of True Love Never Did Run Smooth,* 1983; *The Fido Frame-Up,* 1983; *Leroy Is Missing,* 1984; *The Case of the Sabotaged School Play,* 1984; *A Clue in Code,* 1985; *Horsemaster,* 1985; *The Case of the Cackling Car,* 1985; *A Nose for Trouble,* 1985; *Where There's a Will, There's a Wag,* 1986; *Lizzie Silver of Sherwood Forest,* 1986; *The Lightey Club,* 1987; *Ghost Host,* 1987; *Mitzi Meyer, Fearless Warrior Queen,* 1987; *Several Kinds of Silence,* 1988; *Minnie's Yom Kippur Birthday,* 1989; *The Case of the Fixed Election,* 1989; *The Hoax on You,* 1989; *Turtle in July,* 1989; *Storm Rising,* 1989; *Charmed,* 1990; *Exotic Birds,* 1990; *Twenty Ways to Lose Your Best Friend,* 1990; *The Golden Heart of Winter,* 1991; *California Demon,* 1992; *Big Wheel,* 1993; *Sky Words,* 1994; *Family Reunion,* 1994; *Please Don't Squeeze Your Boa, Noah!,* 1995; *The Morgans Dream,* 1995; *The Maiden on the Moor,* 1995; *In the Palace of the Ocean King,* 1995; *A Wasp Is Not a Bee,* 1995; *All that We Needed to Say: Poems about School from Tanya and Sophie,* 1996; *Deal with a Ghost,* 1997; *Bottoms Up!,* 1998; *Prairie Dogs Kiss and Lobsters Wave,* 1998; *Josie to the Rescue,* 1999; *The Circus Lunicus,* 2000; *I Believe in Water: Twelve Brushes with Religion,* 2000; *A Dog's Gotta Do What a Dog's Gotta Do: Dog's at Work,* 2000; *A Pair of Wings,* 2001; *Tough Beginnings: How Baby Animals Survive,* 2001; *Monster Museum,* 2001; *Footprints on the Roof: Poems about the Earth,* 2002; *The Company of Crows,* 2002; *Fireflies at Midnight,* 2003; *How to Cross a Pond: Poems about Water,* 2003.

BIBLIOGRAPHY: http://www.users.aol.com/writerbabe/singer; *Something about the Author,* vol. 125, Gale Group. Detroit, MI 2002; Ward, Martha E., Dorothy

A. Marquardt, Nancy Dolan, Dawn Eaton, *Authors of Books for Young People,* 3rd ed., 1990.

SANDRA KITAIN

SIS, Peter

Author, illustrator, b. 11 May 1949, Brno, Moravia, Czechoslovakia

S. (pronounced *seas*) grew up in a monolithic, monochromatic, communist-controlled world in which there was a scarcity of colors, paper, and freedom. S.'s mother, an artist, and father, a filmmaker and explorer, helped to ensure a nurturing childhood in spite of the ever-present dreary political climate. S.'s parents encouraged him to color his world with reading, writing, and drawing. He did so with childhood heroes that included George Mallory and Andrew Irvine (two mountaineers who vanished mysteriously on Mt. Everest), Vincent Van Gogh, Marco Polo, Galileo Galilei, and Charles Darwin, all of whom were independent, innovative thinkers who suffered consequences for their views and contributions.

During the mid-1950s, S.'s father was drafted into the army, ordered to China to make films and teach filmmaking. This two-month assignment turned into almost a full year of unimaginable experiences for his father. While in China, his father visited Tibet and met the Dalai Lama, a meeting which so changed his father that S. could no longer relate to him. Years later, S. turned this experience into a book, *Tibet Through the Red Box,* that had sufficient TEEN appeal to be nominated to American Library Association's Best Books for YA.

S. earned an M.A. from the Academy of Applied Arts in Prague in 1974, then attended the Royal College of Art in London (1977–79). A Ten-minute animated film he created while in school called *Mimikry* won the Golden Bear Award in the West Berlin Film Festival and opened doors for him to travel to America in 1982. He decided to stay in the U.S. and was later granted asylum. He decorated eggs and taught classes in order to generate an income. His unique style of precision art went unnoticed until he was fortuitously introduced to Maurice Sendak who, in turn, introduced S. to the world of children's literature. S. soon moved to New York City and made it his new home. He began illustrating for the *New York Times* and drawing illustrations for books by other authors. Over the years, S. has produced more than one thousand illustrations for the *New York Times.*

In 1989, S. became a U.S. citizen and began to follow his dreams. In 1991, S. wrote and illustrated *Follow the Dream: The Story of Christopher Columbus.* This PICTURE BOOK is filled with rich detail that reminds readers of the determination and sacrifice that exploration requires. In 1993, S. acquainted readers with Jan Welzl, one of his childhood homeland heroes, in *A Small Tall Tale from the Far Far North.* In this story of an explorer who is a free thinker much like its author, we are once again allowed to peek into S.'s life. The picture book is filled with maps, storyboards, panoramas, and even a MYTH told in pictographs.

The Three Golden Keys (1994) tells of the history of his home country through the eyes of a little boy (young S.) as he rides in a hot air balloon. This work is S.'s personal tribute to the collapse of the Iron Curtain and the rebirth of his country. A mystical, multi-layered allegory, *The Three Golden Keys* recaptures the wonder of his own lost childhood while providing readers with an understandable history of Prague. Like *Tibet through the Red Box,* this work also attracted teen readers and was nominated for the ALA best Books for YA list. Jacqueline Kennedy Onassis edited *The Three Golden Keys* shortly before her DEATH and called S. "a genius." Her words were repeated in 2003 when Sis became the first children's illustrator to receive the MacArthur Genius Fellowship Award.

In 1996's *Starry Messenger: Galileo Galilei* (1996), S. combines layers of illustrations and text to capture the mood of the Renaissance along with the fear of the Inquisition. *Tibet Through the Red Box* (1998) relates stories his father told him and the contents of the DIARY his father kept while serving in the military in Tibet. *The Tree of Life* (2003) is the story of the quintessential independent thinker, Charles Darwin. It took S. five years to complete this book. *Train of States* (2004) is also excellent.

S. colors our world with influences and experiences from his childhood that are reflected in his films and illustrations. His film work is in the permanent collection of the Museum of Modern Art. S. resides in New York with his wife Terry, daughter Madeleine, and son Matej.

SELECT AWARDS: *New York Times* Best Illustrated Children's Books: 1987 for *Rainbow Rhino* and 1990 for *Beach Ball; Boston Globe–Horn Book* Honor Book, 1994, *A Small, Tall Tale from the Far, Far*

North; Caldecott Medal Honor Book: 1997 for *Starry Messenger: Galileo and Galilei* and 1999 for *Tibet through the Red Box;* MacArthur Genius Fellowship Award, 2003; *Tree of Life*: ALA Best Books for Young Adults, 2004, ALA Notable Children's Books, 2004; SLJ Best Books for Children, 2003, *Publisher's Weekly* Best Children's Books, 2003.

FURTHER WORKS: 2002: *This Place I Know: Poems of Comfort* (poems selected by Georgia Heard); 2001; *The Hobbit Young Adult* edition, S. cover. Illustrator: 2000, *Faust, Part One;* 2000, *The Wind Singer;* 1997, *Many Waters;* 1989, *Halloween Stories and Poems;* 1989, *The Midnight Horse;* 1988, *The Ghost in the Noonday Sun;* 1987, *Scarebird;* 1986, *The Whipping Boy;* three Stories to Solve folktale collections, 1985, 1990, 1994.

BIBLIOGRAPHY: Erbach, Mary. "Peter S. on the Tree of Life." *Booklinks,* November 2003; S., Peter. "My Own Evolution." *School Library Journal,* September 2003; West, Jane. "Peter S." *The Continuum Encyclopedia of Children's Literature* 2001, pp. 724–25; http://www.zuzu.org/sisinterview.html; http://www.macfound.org/programs/fel/fellows/sis_peter.htm; http://www.sabeth.albert@fsgbooks.com; http://www.soemadison.wisc.edu/eebc/friends/sis.htm; http://www.petersis.com

DEBORAH A. WOOTEN

SKURZYNSKI, Gloria (Jean)
Author, b. 6 July 1930, Duquesne, Pennsylvania

Whether writing for children, preteens or YA, about worlds past, present, or future, S. embraces her mission to entertain, enlighten, and encourage her readers. Her characters are intelligent and resourceful, though not necessarily admirable. Having internalized the digital age, S. includes links to quality websites to help young readers of her vivid science and technology explorations remain knowledgeable about current technology and explore further. Her books are as much inspired by her hometown, where steel mills ran the economy, as by the aerospace industry which led S. to settle in Salt Lake City, Utah. A reverence for FAMILY life, nature, and cultural differences pervade even her most recent tales about virtual reality.

A child of second-generation immigrants, S. was a weekly habitué of the Carnegie Free Public Library in Duquesne. She graduated first in her class, turning down scholarships at three Pittsburgh universities to attend Mount Mercy College (now Carlow). Believing the school restricted her lively intellect, she left

after two years and became a statistical clerk; at this point, she had married an aerospace engineer from nearby Monessen. By 1959, S. was a busy mother of five daughters. Encouraged by correspondence with the Pulitzer poet Phyllis McGinley, a middle-aged S. began writing MAGAZINE articles and PICTURE BOOKS when her youngest child entered school. *Bionic Parts for People* (1978) and *Safeguarding the Land* (1981, detailing the careers of female public lands managers), are early examples of S.'s eagerness to address contemporary issues.

A novel for YAs, *The Clones* (2002), continues her futuristic saga begun in *Virtual War* in which Corgan, Sharla, and Brigg, genetically altered TEENAGERS, are chosen by the Western Hemisphere Federation to fight a virtual battle for the only habitable spot on earth. The historical novels *Rockbuster* (2001), *The Tempering* (1983, reissued 2000), and *Good-bye, Billy Radish* (1992) explore the lives of three young men during the early twentieth century. Each is beset by antiunionist, multi-ethnic, socioeconomic forces: Tommy Quinlan labors in a Utah coal mine; a Pennsylvania steel mill dictates life for young Ukrainian immigrant Bazyli Radichevych and his older neighbor, Karl Kerner.

In *Spider's Voice* (1999), S. recasts the ill-fated romance of 12th-century lovers Abelard and Heloise, telling the story through the deaf-mute shepherd boy employed by Abelard. *Manwolf* (1981) and *What Happened in Hamelin* (1979) combine legend and history with science to explain the medieval origins of stories about werewolves and the Pied Piper.

For middle-school readers, the MYSTERIES IN OUR NATIONAL PARKS plots (coauthored with S.'s daughter) are solved by siblings Ashley and Jack Landon, two teens routinely dazzled by nature but confounded by the antics of a recently acquired foster sibling. Each installment features a map and an afterword to explain environmental issues. FAMILY camping excursions in the Utah desert inspired a SERIES of survival thrillers, including *Lost in the Devil's Desert* (1982). *Cyberstorm* (1995) takes readers through a Virtual Reality Rent-a-Memory machine.

In all her work, S. embraces goals exemplified by Pittsburgh's late Fred Rogers: to encourage spiritual harmony and intellectual curiosity.

SELECT AWARDS: *Rockbuster:* Golden Spur Award, Western Writers of America, 2000, New York Public

Library's Books for the Teen Age, 2001; Best Books for Young Adults, 2000, *Spider's Voice; Virtual War:* ALA Popular Paperbacks, 2004, Best Books for Young Adults, 1998, Quick Picks for Reluctant Readers, New York Public Library's Books for the Teen Age, 1997, Junior Library Guild Selection; American Institute of Physics Children's Science Book Award, 1992, *Almost the Real Thing; Good-Bye Billy Radish;* Best Books of the Year, School Library Journal, Judy Lopez Memorial Honor Book; *What Happened in Hamelin:* Christopher Award, 1980, ALA Booklist Reviewer's Choice, 1979, *Horn Book* Honor List, 1979; *The Tempering:* Golden Kite Award of the Society of Children's Book Writers, ALA's Best Books for Young Adults, School Library Journal's Best Book of the Year, Library of Congress Children's Book of the Year, Child Study Association's Books of the Year; *Manwolf:* ALA's Best Books for Young Adults, 1981, and *Booklist* Reviewer's Choice, 1982 awards, Child Study Association Book of the Year; Golden Kite Honor Book from Society of Children's Book Writers, 1978, *Bionic Parts for People: The Real Story of Artificial Organs and Replacement Parts.*

SELECT FURTHER WORKS: *The Magic Pumpkin,* 1971; *The Remarkable Journey of Gustavus Bell,* 1973; *The Poltergeist of Jason Morey,* 1975; *In a Bottle with a Cork on Top,* 1976; adapter for *Two Fools and a Faker: Three Lebanese Folktales,* 1977; *Martin by Himself,* 1979; *Honest Andrew,* 1981; *Caught in the Moving Mountain,* 1984; *Swept in the Wave of Terror,* 1985; *The Minstrel in the Tower,* 1988; *Dangerous Ground,* 1989; *Here Comes the Mail,* 1992; *Caitlin's Big Idea,* 1995; *Waves, the Electromagnetic Universe,* 1996; *Discover Mars,* 1998; *On Time: From Seasons to Split Seconds,* 2000. With Alane Ferguson: *The Mystery of the Spooky Shadow,* 1996; *The Mystery of the Vanishing Creatures,* 1996; *The Mystery of the Haunted Silver Mine,* 1997; *The Mystery of the Fire in the Sky,* 1997; *Wolf Stalker,* 1997, 2001; *Rage of Fire,* 1998; *Cliff-Hanger,* 1999; *The Hunted,* 2000; *Ghost Horses,* 2000; *Over the Edge,* 2002; *Valley of Death,* 2002; *Escape From Fear,* 2002; *Out of the Deep,* 2002; *Running Scared,* 2002; *Buried Alive,* 2003; *Are We Alone?: Scientists Search for Life in Space,* 2004.

BIBLIOGRAPHY: *Authors and Artists for Young Adults,* vol. 38, 2001; *Contemporary Authors;* vol. 33–36, 1978; *Contemporary Authors: New Revision Series,* vol. 100, 2002, vol. 58, 1997, vol. 30, 1990, vol. 13, 1984; McElmeel, Sharron L. "Gloria S.: Author Profile." *Book Report,* November/December 1997; OCLC FirstSearch WorldCat database (1992–2003); S., Gloria. "Paper and Photons: The Future of Information, Children's Science Books versus the Internet." *School Library Journal,* October 10, 1998. S.

website, http://www.gloriabooks.com; *Something about the Author,* vol. 8, 1976, vol. 74, 1973, vol. 122, 2001; *Something about the Author Autobiography,* vol. 9, 1990.

CLAUDIA L. BENNETT

SLADE, Arthur G(regory)
Author, b. 9 July 1967, Moose Jaw, Saskatchewan, Canada

After earning a B.A. from the University of Saskatchewan in 1989, S. began his career as an advertising copywriter until he became a full-time writer in 1995. Publishing his first novel in 1997, *Draugr,* S. began writing for the YA audience. S. finished this first novel at the age of eighteen and went on to write approximately one novel a year since that first one, although not all have been published.

A voracious reader of Norse MYTHOLOGY, which he went on to study in college, S. based many of his novels on these Norse myths. Besides writing various SERIES for YA, S. is also the author of a comic book series, Hallowed Knight. In addition. S.'s stories have been recorded for the collection *Up There There Are Only Birds: Stones from the Edge.*

This CANADIAN author's best-known work to date is the award-winning *Dust* (2003) involving a crippling drought and the classic "stranger come to town plot," a stranger who is in this case definitely up to no good!

AWARDS: Governor General's Award for Children's Literature text, 2001, both for *Dust,* as well as the 2004 American Library Association's Best Books for Young Adult list.

FURTHER WORKS: *The Haunting of Drang Island,* 1999; *Loki Wolf,* 2000; *Tribes,* 2002; *Return of the Grudstone Ghosts,* 2005.

BIBLIOGRAPHY: *Contemporary Authors Online,* 2002.

SARA MARCUS
AND RACHEL WITMER

SLEATOR, William
Author, composer, and pianist, b. 13 February 1945, Harve de Grace, Maryland

Regarded as one of the most important American SCIENCE FICTION authors for young adults, S. has written about thirty books since he published his first book, *The Angry Moon* (1970), a Caldecott Honor book illustrated by Blair Lent.

S. is the son of William Warner, a physiologist and professor, and Esther, a physician. It is S.'s claim that he began writing at age six. In high school, he wrote poems, stories, and composed music, and was considered a genius when the school orchestra performed his composition. Since childhood, he has been fascinated by the grotesque and macabre, which is reflected in many of his works.

S. graduated from Harvard University in 1967 with a B.A. in English. Post-graduation, he spent one year in London, studying musical composition and working as an accompanist for the Royal Ballet School and Rambert School. From 1974 to 1983, he worked as a rehearsal pianist with the Boston Ballet Company and also composed ballets, touring all over Europe and the United States with dancers. After 1983, he left the company and devoted himself to full-time writing.

S.'s first YA novel, *Blackbriar* (1972), was created from his experiences in England while living in an ancient cottage in the forest. His second novel, *Run* (1973), was also set in a house where he had once lived. With no more real places to write about, he turned to his imagination and began to create science fiction works. 1974 marked the publication of his first science fiction novel. *House of Stairs* is the story of five orphaned TEENAGERS who are subjected involuntarily to an experiment on human behaviors while confined to a house of endless stairs. The exciting story was chosen in YALSA 100 Best Books, 1950–2000. S. explores time travel and sibling relationships first in *The Green Futures of Tycho* (1981) and later in *Strange Attractors* (1990), *Boltzmon!* (1999), and *Singularity* (1985). *Interstellar Pig* (1984) tells the story of a teenage boy struggling for his life and the fate of the world, as the board game he plays with his strange neighbors on the beach turns deadly. The book was followed in 2002 by a sequel titled *Parasite Pig*.

S.'s works have elements of suspense, weird creatures, space ADVENTURE, and bizarre happenings, as well as fast-paced and readable text, which appeal greatly to reluctant readers. By telling a story of a race of grotesque underground dwellers, S. raises the issue of forest conservation and sibling rivalry in *Beasties* (1997). In *The Boxes* (1998), the protagonist Annie opens two boxes, despite her uncle's repeated warning, and faces rapidly self-reproducing crablike creatures and a clock-like object able to slow down time. *Marco's Millions,* published years later in 2001, was the prequel to *The Boxes. Boltzmon!* (1999) tells the story of a remnant of a black hole that transports a preteen into an alternate universe where he foresees his imminent death; unless he can complete a quest to prevent it, an accident caused by his sister will destroy him. In addition, S. created two supernatural stories set in Thailand, *Spirit House* (1991) and *Dangerous Wishes* (1995).

Talented, prolific, and popular, S. has been continuously creating intriguing and interesting FANTASY and science fiction for young adults for the past thirty years. His works explore time travel, space adventure, extraterrestrial beings, fourth dimension, sibling rivalry, FAMILY relationships, alien intrusion, and psychic abilities. The fast-moving plots and outlandish adventures, along with readable text, truly motivate and engage YA readers. He divides his time between Boston and Bangkok, Thailand.

AWARDS: 1970 Caldecott Honor Book, *The Angry Moon* (illus. Blair Lent), *Interstellar Pig,* 1984; 1974 BBYA, *House of Stairs,* 1984, *Instellar Pig,* 1985, *Singularity,* 1987, *Duplicate,* 1988, *Boy Who Reversed Himself,* 1991, *Strange Attractors,* 1994, *Oddballs;* ALA Notable Children's Books, California Young Reader Medal Winners; YALSA Quick Picks for Reluctant Young Adult Readers 1997, *Beasties,* 1998, *The Boxes,* 1999, *Boltzmon!, Rewind;* Young Readers Choice Award, 1998, *The Boxes,* 1999, *Rewind;* YALSA Popular PAPERBACKS for Young Adults, 1993, *Strange Attractors,* 1998; 1993 ALA Notable and Best Book, *Oddballs.*

FURTHER WORKS: *Among the Dolls* (illus. Trina Schart Hyman), 1975; *Into the Dream* (illus. Ruth Sanderson), 1979; *Once Said Darlene* (illus. Steven Kellogg), 1979; *That's Silly* (illus. Lawrence DiFiori), 1981; *Fingers,* 1983; *The Boy Who Reversed Himself,* 1986; *The Duplicate;* 1988; *Others See Us,* 1993; *Oddballs,* 1993; *The Night the Heads Came,* 1996; *Rewind,* 1999; *The Boy Who Couldn't Die,* 2004.

BIBLIOGRAPHY: *Children Literature Review,* vol. 29, 1993, pp. 196–97; *Something about the Author,* vol. 118, 2001. pp. 201–6; "William S.," http://www.friend.ly.net/scoop/biographies/sleatorwilliam; "William S.—Master of Sci-Fi," http://www.angelfire.com/mi/willsleator; "Young Adults Meet Their Author," http://www.town.Arlington.ma.us/schools.

SHU-HSIEN CHEN

SMITH, Charles R.

Author, photographer, n.d., Los Angeles, California

Growing up in the Compton area of South Central Los Angeles, S. spent many hours reading anything he could get his hands on and making up his own stories. His grandmother did not like him to go out in what was frequently a dangerous neighborhood, so S. found himself with a lot of time on his hands after school. In addition to reading, S. entertained himself and friends and family by inventing his own stories. He also spent his time playing sports, basketball in particular, passing many hours perfecting his jump shot.

S. first became interested in photography and writing as a career while working on his high-school yearbook staff. He had been writing for many years, but it was during high school that he first picked up a camera. S. immediately became enamored with the medium, and decided he wanted to make a living as a photographer. After graduating from the Brooks Institute of Photography, S. headed for New York City with the goal of working as an assistant to a professional photographer to gain some experience before going out on his own. He gradually built a portfolio of professional photography assignments, including MAGAZINE layouts and book covers.

When an art director saw S.'s basketball pictures, she recommended that he do a full-length children's book. S.'s first book for middle-school readers was *Rimshots* (1999), a collection of photography and verse about basketball. His knowledge of and love for SPORTS, together with his talent for photography, have led him to write several highly regarded PICTURE BOOKS for middle-school readers that combine action photography and verse.

AWARDS: *Tall Tales: Six Amazing Basketball Dreams*: ALA Quick Picks for Reluctant Young Adult Readers, 2001.

FURTHER WORKS: *Tall Tales,* 2000; *Short Takes,* 2001; *Perfect Harmony,* 2002; *Hoop Queens,* 2003; *Hoop Kings,* 2004.

BIBLIOGRAPHY: www.charlesrsmithjr.com

EDWARD T. SULLIVAN

SMITH, Roland

Author, b. November 30, 1951, Portland, Oregon

S. wanted to be a writer even as a small child, spending hours working at an old manual typewriter his parents gave him. While at Portland State University, where he majored in English and biology, S. took a job at a children's zoo. After twice capturing escaped animals, he was given the job as full-time animal

keeper at the Portland Zoo. He moved to the Port Defiance Zoo and Aquarium in Portland, where he served in several capacities, including curator of mammals and birds, assistant zoo director, and senior research biologist. S. also worked with the red wolf reintroduction program in the Carolinas and Mississippi. While working for over twenty years at these zoos S. wrote and presented many scientific papers and lectures.

S. was encouraged to write his first children's book after talking with author D. Patent, who was interviewing him about the red wolf program for a book. His first book, *Sea Otter Rescue,* was published in 1990 and was illustrated with S.'s photographs taken during rescue efforts after the Exxon Valdez oil spill. Awarded the Outstanding Science Trade Book for Children in 1990, S. followed his first book with a SERIES on ZOOS: *Primates in the Zoo* (1992), *Snakes In the Zoo* (1992), *Whales, Dolphins, & Porpoises In the Zoo* (1994), and *Cats In the Zoo* (1994), as well as other science books for children.

S. spent time in Africa studying elephants for his nonfiction book, *In the Forest with Elephants* (1998). Using the knowledge gained from this research and his scientific background, S. wrote his first fiction book, *Thunder Cave* (1995), which was followed by sequels, *Jaguar* (1997) and *The Last Lobo* (1999). Smith's fiction books continue to be among the lists of nominations and winners for many state award books.

S. lives on a farm south of Portland with his wife, Marie.

AWARDS: 1990 Outstanding Science Trade Books for Children, *Sea Otter Rescue; Sasquatch*: 2002 Florida Sunshine State Young Reader Award Winner; *Jaguar:* 1999 Florida Sunshine State Young Readers Award, 1999 Nebraska Golden Sower Award, 2000 Florida Sunshine State Young Reader Award Winners; *Captains Dog:* 1999 Pacific Northwest Booksellers Association Children's Book Award, 2002 Beacon of Freedom Award; 2003 Nevada Young Readers Award, 2002 ALA Quick Picks for Reluctant Young Adult Readers, *Zach's Lie.*

FURTHER WORKS: *African Elephants,* 1995; *Amy's Missing,* 1996; *Journey of the Red Wolf,* 1996; *Vultures,* 1997; *Sasquatch,* 1998; *The Captain's Dog,* 1999; *Zach's Lie,* 2001; *B is For Beaver* (with Marie Smith), 2003.

BIBLIOGRAPHY: *Contemporary Authors,* vol. 179, 2000; *Something about the Author,* vol. 115, 2000;

Roland S. website, www.rolandsmith.com; Mc-Elmeel, Sharron L. "Roland S.: A Profile of an Eco-ADVENTURE Writer." *Library Talk* 12, no. 2, p. 6.

M. NAOMI WILLIAMSON

SMITH, Sherwood
Author, b. 28 May 1951, Glendale, California

S. has been writing FANTASY and SCIENCE FICTION for publication since the mid-1980s. She has a B.A. from the University of Southern California and an M.A. from the University of California, Santa Barbara.

S. taught elementary and high school and tutored children with learning DISABILITIES. When she was thirteen, she began submitting at least one novel a year to publishers, but stopped when she was twenty-one.

S. published novels under different pseudonyms (Robyn Tallis and Jesse Maguire) before becoming better known by works under her own name. Her first book as Smith, *Wren to the Rescue* (1990), introduced readers to Wren, an orphan with magical powers, and her daring ADVENTURE to rescue Princess Tess from the wicked wizard, King Andreus. The wicked wizard carried out his plot of revenge against Tess's father by kidnapping Tess. Wren, accompanied by the Magic School's best apprentice, Tyron, and its worst, Prince Connor, sets out to rescue Tess. Other works in this popular SERIES are *Wren's Quest* (1993) and *Wren's War* (1995). The protagonists in *Wren's Quest* face the growing pains of adolescence and the dangers, trials, and mysteries of S.'s fantastic world and mystical times. Wren takes time out from magician's school to search for clues to her parentage while one friend in the castle shape shifts into a dog to spy on a plot against the royal family. With *Wren's War*, S. forces the main characters into adulthood as they rely on one another to raise an army and overcome the evil ruler.

S. writes stories she would have loved as a young adult: adventurous stories with humor, MYSTERY, magic and joy, where individuals can make a difference. Her works are translated into Danish and sold in Israel and Russia.

AWARDS: Anne Spencer Lindbergh Prize in Children's Literature Honor Book, 1995–96.

FURTHER WORKS: *The Beginning* (as Jesse Maguire), 1989; *Fire in the Sky* (as Robyn Tallis), 1989; Exordium series with Dave Trowbridge: *The Phoenix in Flight* (1993), *Ruler of Naught* (1993), *A Prison Un-*sought (1994), *The Rifter's Covenant* (1995), *The Thrones of Kronos* (1997); *The Borrowers:* MOVIE TIE-IN, 1997; *Derelict for Trade* (with Andre NORTON), 1997; *A Mind for Trade* (with Norton) 1997; *Crown Duel*, 1997; *Court Duel*, 1998; *Echoes in Time* (with Norton), 1999; *Journey to Otherwhere*, 2000; *Augur's Teacher*, 2001; *Beyond the Last Star: Stories from the Next Beginning* (ed. With Jeffry (*sic*) Dwight), 2002; *Atlantis Endgame* (with Norton), 2002.

BIBLIOGRAPHY: *The* ALAN *Review*, Winter 1994; *Booklist*, April 1, 1993; Homepage of Sherwood S., http://www.sff.net/people/Sherwood/, 2003; Sherwood S. Bibliography, http://www.fantasticfiction .co.uk/authors/Sherwood_Smith./htm, 2003; *Something about the Author*, vol. 82, 1995.

KAREN L. DENNISON

SNICKET, Lemony (pseud. Daniel Handler)
Author, b. 1970, San Francisco, California

Lemony Snicket is the pseudonym of Daniel Handler, author of adult novels *The Basic Eight* (1999) and *Watch You Mouth* (2000 and 2002) under his own name. In *The Basic Eight,* critics deem Handler has created a novel that features five of the top adolescent issues—belonging, power, loyalty, drugs, and body image, and has spun a poignant, satirical novel. A graduate of Wesleyan University in Massachusetts, S. received an Academy of American Poets Prize in 1990 and an Olin Fellowship in 1992, which enabled him to write full time. The son of an accountant and a college dean, S. first wrote POETRY and then switched to fiction as he noticed his poetry become increasingly prose like. He also wrote comedy material for a syndicated radio program called The *House of Blues Radio Hour* in his native San Francisco.

"If you are interested in stories with happy endings, you would be better off reading some other book." So begins *The Bad Beginning* (1999), the first in a projected SERIES of thirteen gothic-style melodramatic novels under the collective name A Series of Unfortunate Events. S. is a master of the morose description, the gloomy, bleak archaic phrase and literary send-up, striking an even balance of delight and despair. He writes in the tradition of Charles Dickens, Roald DAHL, and Edward GOREY. Working in a serio-comic Victorian-gothic style, S. presents the evil Count Olaf, so thoroughly evil that he has no redeeming or virtuous characteristics. He is single-mindedly determined to get his hands on the Baudelaire orphans' fortune by any means available. His relentless pursuit follows Violet, Klaus, and baby Sunny through shade and darkness; the three being pursued retain their positive outlook on life, certain that good will triumph over evil despite the series' opening sentence and the hapless efforts of a collection of inept guardians, one of whom is eaten by monster-sized leeches in *The Wide Window* (2000). The others are similarly dispatched to comically grotesque violent ends.

S.'s series of novels intended for middle-grade readers, four of which appeared at the same time on the extended *New York Times* list of best-selling children's novels on July 23, 2000, make consistent use of wordplay, literary allusions, and stock characters from gothic novels. The young heroes are good, pure of heart, ever cheerful, and hopeful despite the number of unrelenting obstacles put in their path. Count Olaf is thoroughly evil, a composite of all such dreary characters from every second-rate B movie. He appears at each opportune moment that catastrophe overtakes the ever-happy orphans.

S.'s sophisticated humor is repeatedly dispensed as he interrupts the stories to define words and expressions: "Uncle Monty would often segue—a word which here means 'let the conversation veer off'" (*The Reptile Room,* 1999). Even the author's name is an allusion to the sly, suppressed laughter that fills the pages of each book. Sinister puns and literary allusions abound. One of their custodians, Uncle Monty, advisor about the handling of toads and snakes, councils them "to never, under any circumstances, let the Virginia Wolf-snake near a typewriter." The orphans, inveterate readers, find a library available to them at each macabre place to which they are sent to live.

Television, film, and audio rights to S.'s work have been purchased, and foreign-publishing right have been sold in many countries. Scenes from three books, *The Bad Beginning, The Reptile Room,* and *The Wide Window* were the basis for a motion picture released in December 2004.

AWARDS: *The Bad Beginning*: Colorado Children's Book Award Winners, 2003.

FURTHER WORKS: *The Wide Window: Book the Third,* 2000; *The Miserable Mill: Book the Fourth* (A Series of Unfortunate Events), 2000; *The Austere Academy: Book the Fifth* (A Series of Unfortunate Events), 2000; *The Ersatz Elevator: Book the Sixth* (A Series of Unfortunate Events), 2001; *The Vile Village: Book the Seventh* (A Series of Unfortunate Events), 2001; *The Hostile Hospital: Book the Eighth* (A Series of Unfortunate Events), 2001; *The Carnivorous Carnival: Book the Ninth* (A Series of Unfortunate Events), 2002; *The Slippery Slope: Book the Tenth* (A Series of Unfortunate Events), 2003; *The Grim Grotto: Book the Eleventh* (A Series of Unfortunate Events), 2004; *The Basic Eight,* 1999; *Watch Your Mouth,* 2000 and 2002; *The Lemony Snicket: The Unauthorized Autobiography,* 2002.

BIBLIOGRAPHY: Person, Diane. "L.S." In B. Cullinan and D. Person, eds., *Encyclopedia of Children's Literature,* pp. 733–34; http://eee.uci.edu/~dlp/daniel/index.html Welcome to DanielHandler.com.

DIANE G. PERSON
AND DEBORAH WOOTEN

SNYDER, Zilpha Keatley
Author, b. 11 May 1927, Lemoore, California

Best known for her children's books, S. has also authored YA and adult titles. *The Egypt Game* (1967) stemmed from both her experience as a teacher and recollections of her own childhood; it was the first of her books to garner several awards, including a Newbery Honor. This title is also recognized for its depiction of the young characters' interracial friendships. *The Headless Cupid* and *The Witches of Worm* also earned Newbery honors. Her other works for young adults are *A Fabulous Creature* (1981) and *The Birds of Summer* (1983).

AWARDS: ALA Best Books for Young Adults, 1981, *A Fabulous Creature; The Birds of Summer:* PEN Literary Award and the Parents' Choice Award: *Libby on Wednesdays*: ALA BBYA, 1991; *The Witches of Worm*: John Newbery Honor, 1973; *Cat Running*: John & Patricia Beatty Award, 1995; *The Egypt Game*: John Newbery Honor, 1968; *The Headless Cupid*: John Newbery Honor, 1972; *The Unseen*: SLJ Best Books for Children, 2004.

BIBLIOGRAPHY: Zilpha Keatley S., www.microweb.com/lsnyder/home.html, 2003; *Something about the Author,* 1985; *Contemporary Authors,* 1981.

JENNIFER BUREK PIERCE

SOTO, Gary
Author, poet, b. April 12, 1952, Fresno, California

S. was reared in working-class Mexican–American household. He was the second of three children born to Manuel and Angie (Trevino) Soto. FAMILY members often worked in the field at the nearby Sun-Maid raisin plant to help out at home, especially following the DEATH of S.'s father when S. was just five-years old. The family struggled to make ends meet. As a result, there was little money for books. S. notes, "I don't think I had any literary aspirations when I was a kid. In fact, we were pretty much an illiterate family. We didn't have books, and no one encouraged us to read. So my wanting to write POETRY was pretty much a fluke."

S. graduated from Roosevelt High School in 1970 and went on to study English at Fresno State College. It was when he was a twenty-year-old college student that S. first discovered contemporary American poetry by such poets as Edward Field, W. S. Merwin, Charles Simic, James Wright, and Pablo Neruda. After reading the works of novelist Gabriel García Márquez, S. writes, "I was hooked. I wanted to make writing my life."

S. transferred to California State University, where he studied under poet Philip Levine. Levine taught S. how to analyze and critique a poem, and also how to put one together. Upon graduating, S. married Carolyn Oda and then went on to the University of California at Irvine, from which he received an M.F.A. in creative writing in 1976. In 1977, his first book of poetry was published.

It was not until the early 1990s that S. began writing with a younger audience in mind. His first collection of stories for young readers, *"Baseball in April" and Other Stories,* was published in 1990. The male and female characters are all Mexican–American, and the collection was praised for both its cultural merit and its ability to reach all children. Reviewers were especially impressed by S.'s debut into YA LITERATURE since S. was able to remain entirely within the TEENAGERS' universe.

A Fire in My Hands (1991) was S.'s second work for young readers. This is a collection of twenty-three free-verse poems, some of which were taken from an adult collection that S. had published in 1985, *Black Hair.* Each poem somehow reflects S.'s youth as a Mexican–American boy in California, or his experiences as a father.

S.'s first YA novel, *Taking Sides* (1991), tells the story of Lincoln, a Hispanic eighth-grader who has recently moved from one community to a more affluent one. He now plays on the basketball team of his new school, which is composed of many white faces. When his new team is scheduled to play against his former-school team, Lincoln is unsure how to handle the uncomfortable situation. After all, he will be playing against some of his best friends from the old neighborhood. Ultimately, Lincoln learns how to deal with the situation the best he can, and Lincoln's good sportsmanship shines through. Reviewers commented on S.'s ability to deal with racial prejudice and the stress that it can place on minority children.

In S.'s second YA novel, *Pacific Crossing* (1992), Lincoln appears again, this time with his best friend, Tony. The two boys are sent to Japan to live as exchange students and to study the martial arts of *kempo.* Lincoln must again face cultural differences, albeit in a different light. His Japanese "brother," Mitsuo, helps Lincoln realize that outward differences do not change the fact that deep within, most people have common passions.

The Skirt (1992) is the story of a Hispanic girl who has lost her folkloric skirt on the school bus during a Friday afternoon. Her dance recital is on Sunday, and she is determined to find it before then. She enlists the help of a friend, and together the girls hatch a plan to break into the school bus and get the skirt back. Again, S.'s decision to use a Hispanic protagonist allows him to combine specifics of the Hispanic culture with themes that are common to all cultures—losing things for example. This helps make the novel accessible to all children, regardless of their cultural background.

S.'s favorite work is *Jesse* (1994). This coming-of-age novel is about two Mexican–American brothers in the early 1970s. The younger brother, Jesse, moves in with his older brother and they start taking classes at a junior college, both wishing to avoid the Vietnam–era draft. The two brothers work as field laborers, and hope that the education they are pursuing will allow them to break the family cycle of physical labor.

S. continues to write for both adults as well as for a younger audience. He writes prose and poetry, and has more recently written screenplays.

AWARDS: Best Book for Young Adults citation, American Library Association, John and Patricia Beatty Award (1991), and Pura Belpré Honor (1996) for *"Baseball in April" and Other Stories;* American Library Association Notable Book Selection and Parents' Choice Award (1995) for *Chato's Kitchen;* Literature Award, Hispanic Heritage Association (1999), Author-Illustrator CIVIL RIGHTS Award, National Education Association (1999), and PEN Center West Book Award (1999) for *Petty Crimes*; *Pacific Crossing*: ALA Popular Paperbacks, 2003; *The Afterlife*: ALA Quick Picks for Reluctant Young Adult Readers, 2004; *Buried Onions*: ALA Popular Paperbacks, 2002; ALA Best Books for Young Adults, 1998.

FURTHER WORKS: *Neighborhood Odes,* 1992; *Canto Familiar/Familiar Song,* 1955; *Local News* 1993; *The Pool Party,* 1993; *Crazy Weekend,* 1994; *Boys at Work,* 1995; *Summer on Wheels,* 1995; *Buried Onions,* 1997; *Novio Boy,* 1997; *Petty Crimes,* 1998; *Nerdlandia: A PLAY,* 1999; *Jessie De La Cruz: A Profile of a United Farm Worker,* 2000; *The Afterlife,* 2003.

CARRA E. GAMBERDELLA

SOUTHGATE, Martha Evelyn
Author, b. 10 December 1960, Cleveland, Ohio

Before publishing her first book, S. was a writer and editor for twelve years for many periodicals, including *Essence, Premiere, Rosie, O,* and *New York Times Magazine.* She also served as an editorial writer and entertainment reporter for the *New York Daily News.*

S.'s novels explore the complex issues of race, class, and identity, never offering easy solutions. Her first novel, *Another Way to Dance* (1996), won the Coretta Scott King Genesis Award for Best First Novel. Her personal experiences as a young AFRICAN-AMERICAN ballet dancer informed this novel about an aspiring ballerina who struggles with these issues.

The Fall of Rome (2002) was influenced by the challenges S. herself faced as one of the few African-American students at a predominantly white, wealthy prep school. Published as an adult novel, it is easily read as a YOUNG ADULT novel as well.

S. earned a B.A. from Smith College and an M.F.A. from Goddard College. She is a recipient of a 2002 New York Foundation for the Arts grant. She has also received fellowships from the MacDowell Colony and the Virginia Center for the Creative Arts.

AWARDS: ALA Best Book for Young Adults, 1997, *Another Way to Dance;* YALSA Alex Award for Adult Books for Young Adults, 2003, *The Fall of Rome.*

BIBLIOGRAPHY: *Contemporary Authors Online,* 2002; Martha Southgate website, http://www.marthasouthgate.com

ELLIE MEEK TWEEDY

SPARKS, Beatrice Mathews. See ANONYMOUS.

SPEARE, Elizabeth George
Author, b. 21 November 1908, Melrose, Massachusetts; d. 15 November 1994, Tucson, Arizona.

S., primarily a writer of historical fiction for young people, was born and raised in New England, where she lived most of her life. She attended Smith College from 1926 to 1927, and earned an A.B. at Boston University in 1930. While pursuing her graduate degree, she taught at a private school in Boston. After she earned an M.A. from Boston University in 1932, she taught as a high-school English teacher in Rockland, Massachusetts (1933–1935), and then as a high-school English teacher in Auburn, Massachusetts (1935–1936). Upon her marriage to industrial engineer Alden Speare in 1936, she moved to Connecticut and spent the next fifteen years rearing her two children, Alden Jr. and Mary Elizabeth. The experiences she had raising her family became the material for her first published works in the 1950s, articles about FAMILY living in *Better Homes and Gardens, Woman's day,* and *Parents.*

Once her children were raised, she had the time to pursue writing, which had remained one of her lifelong interests. She gravitated towards interests in history and received some success with an article on the Smith sisters of Glastonbury, Connecticut, who had gained notoriety for refusal to pay taxes in the 1870s. Further research on the history of Connecticut produced her first novel, *Calico Captive* (1957), based on the history of Susanna Johnson, a woman captured by American Indians during the time of the French and Indian Wars. Her next novel, *The Witch of Blackbird Pond* (1958), focused on sixteen-year-old Kit, who, after the DEATH of her uncle, must face tremendous adversity and culture shock when she relocates from Barbados to a Puritan community in Connecticut and joins her only living relatives. This book received the honor of being unanimously voted the Newbery Medal winner in 1959.

The Bronze Bow (1961), winner of the Newbery award in 1962, takes place during biblical times and features nineteen-year-old Daniel, whose family was murdered by Romans. Through his experiences, which include joining a rebel patriot group and witnessing the teachings of Jesus, Daniel's hatred of the

Romans and focus on vengeance is transformed. S. wished to make *The Bronze Bow* a book that would make the personality of Jesus accessible to students and demonstrate how Jesus' teachings could profoundly change lives wrought with anger. S.'s final major fiction work for children was *The Sign of the Beaver* (1983). This book features thirteen-year-old Matt, left alone in the Maine wilderness during the 1700s to guard his family homestead. When he is unexpectedly rescued by a Penobscot chief and his grandson, he develops a new understanding and respect of a foreign culture.

S. wrote two books of nonfiction, including *Child Life in New England, 1790–1840* (1961) and *Life in Colonial America* (1963). She also wrote one historical fiction for adults, *The Prospering* (1967).

AWARDS: *The Witch of Blackbird Pond:* 1959 Newbery Award, 1960 International Board on Books for Young People (IBBY) Honor list, 1960 American Institute of Graphic Arts Children's book; 1976 New England Round Table Children's LIBRARIAN's Award; *The Bronze Bow:* 1962 Newbery Award, 1964 IBBY Honor list; *The Sign of the Beaver:* 1984 Newbery Honor Book, 1984 Christopher Award, 1984 Scott O'DELL Award for Historical Fiction, 1983 Best Books for Young Adults, 1984 Teacher's Choice; Laura Ingalls WILDER Award, 1989.

FURTHER WORKS: *Calico Captive,* 1957; *The Witch of Blackbird Pond,* 1958; *The Bronze Bow,* 1961; *The Sign of the Beaver,* 1984; *Child Life in New England 1790–1840,* 1961; *Life in Colonial America,* 1963; *The Prospering,* 1967; *The Sign of the Beaver,* 1983.

BIBLIOGRAPHY: *St. James Guild to Young Adult Writers,* 2nd ed., 1999; *Almanac of Famous People,* 7th ed., 2000; *Something about the Author,* vol. 62, 1990; *Something about the Author,* vol. 83, 1996.

KEVIN R. FERST

SPIEGELMAN, Art
Author, illustrator, editor, b. 15 February 1948, Stockholm Sweden

A member of the underground-comics movement and a commercial artist, S. immigrated to the United States with his parents in 1951. Along with his parents, Vladek, a salesman, and Anja, a homemaker, S. became a U.S. citizen and grew up in Rego Park, Queens, New York. S.'s parents had relocated to Sweden after surviving the HOLOCAUST, during which they were inmates in the Auschwitz concentration camp. Unfortunately, their first son, Richieu, did not survive.

S. discovered his love of drawing early in life and spent his spare time copying the work of his favorite comic book and MAGAZINE artists. S. cites *MAD* magazine as a strong influence, which became evident in his commercial work. At thirteen, he worked as an artist for his junior high-school newspaper. The following year S. sold his first piece of artwork to the *Long Island Post* for its cover.

While his parents would have preferred he focus on science and become a doctor or a dentist, S. focused on his passionate love of art. He attended the High School of Art and Design in Manhattan, where he learned commercial art. S. had his work published in numerous underground comics and newspapers, publications that contained social commentaries, including existentialist and provocative comics that were often considered offensive by mainstream American society. Underground publications were usually self-published and had limited print runs, as 'zines do today. Before he finished high school, the United Press Syndicate offered S. his own comic strip based on some of his characters. He declined the offer, even then knowing that the general public would not always understand or appreciate his work.

From 1965 to 1968, S. attended Harpur College, currently the State University of New York at Binghamton, where he studied philosophy and art. Since 1965, S. has been a freelance writer and artist. The college's newspaper often published his work, as did an alternative newspaper, the *East Village Other.*

As a YA, S. had submitted one of his 'zines, *Blasé,* to The Topps Company in exchange for some baseball cards by one of their artists. Topps executives remembered S. and hired him for a summer job between his freshman and sophomore years in college. He impressed executives and was hired for a permanent position at the end of the summer. From 1966 to 1989, S. was employed in several capacities at The Topps Company. He served as artist, creative consultant, designer, and writer of two of Topps' most famous bubble gum and trading card/sticker packages: Wacky Packages and Garbage Pail Kids. While Wacky Packages mocked product packages, the Garbage Pail Kids was a parody of the Cabbage Patch Kid doll craze of the 1980s.

Just as all was going well, illness struck S.'s FAMILY. S. had a nervous breakdown in 1968 and recuperated in a sanatorium. His mother's brother died and his mother, who had suffered from chronic depression since the Holocaust, committed suicide. Soon after his recovery, S. moved to San Francisco and immersed himself in the underground comics scene.

While living in San Francisco, S. had his work published in numerous underground comics publications as well as in his own small press books. For most of his work, he used the pseudonyms Joe Cutrate, Al Floogglebuckle, and Skeeter Grant. In 1972, S. created the now famous piece, "Prisoner on the Hell Planet," about his mother's suicide for *Short Order Comix,* which was later reproduced as the only human illustration in *Maus.* The idea for *Maus* began to germinate that same year in a short strip done for the publication *Funny Aminals.* In 1972 S. also served as editor of *Douglas Comix.* From 1974 to 1975, S. taught a class on drawing comics at the San Francisco Academy of Art. S. coedited *Arcade, the Comics Revue* 1975 to 1976 with the creator of the Zippy the Pinhead character, Bill Griffith.

In the mid-1970s, S. moved back to New York. It was there that he met publisher Françoise Mouly. The couple was married on July 12, 1977, and now have two children, Nadja and Dashiell. From 1979 to 1987, S. taught a course on the historical development and aesthetic aspects of comics at the School for Visual Arts in Manhattan.

In 1978, S. began to interview his father about his life and experiences during the Holocaust. He taperecorded these conversations knowing that his father was ill. He also traveled to Auschwitz to study drawings done by those imprisoned there during World War II in order to develop *Maus.* It was during this period that he and Mouly began a publication called *RAW* (1980). *RAW* was a tabloid-sized comics magazine that gave exposure to emerging graphic artists and writers such as Daniel Clowes, J. Otto Seibold, Chris Ware.

RAW gave S. an opportunity to publish *Maus.* Sadly, S.'s father died in 1982 before *Maus* was complete. By the mid-1980s, S had finished his work and began to show *Maus* around to editors, who were not quite sure what to make of it. The first problem was S.'s use of the black-and-white comics format to tell a serious, AUTOBIOGRAPHICAL story. Secondly, the characters are anthropomorphized: animal characters represent each ethnic group (i.e., Jewish characters were represented by mice, Americans by dogs, Ger-

mans by cats, the Polish by pigs, etc.). S. received many rejections before Pantheon decided to take a chance on the work. *Maus: A Survivor's Tale, My Father Bleeds History,* was published in 1986. Whereas fans of underground comics were accustomed to social commentary in comics, the general public still held the opinion that stories in this format were expected to be humorous and lighthearted. The Pulitzer Prize committee, on the other hand, had no trouble recognizing the quality of this work and awarding *Maus* a Pulitzer Prize in 1992. With this award to what is essentially a GRAPHIC NOVEL in today's terms (a book written in comic book format), the way was opened for future works in graphic format and of literary quality, like Neil GAIMAN's awardwinning Sandman SERIES, to be recognized as works of art.

Mouly is art director for *The New Yorker* magazine. S. joined her there in the early 1990s, working as a contributing editor and artist. His controversial cover art during his tenure created a stir among the publication's readers.

Maus: A Survivors Tale II, And Here My Troubles Began, 1991, continues the story of S.'s father and S.'s experiences as a child of a Holocaust survivor. His work continued to accrue accolades. An exhibition, "Art S.: The Road to *Maus,*" ran through 1993 in Manhattan. In 1994, S. released a CD-ROM, *The Complete Maus,* that included transcripts of his interviews with his father and interviews with S. regarding his work on both parts of *Maus.*

For the past nine years, S.'s artwork has been included in art exhibitions in galleries in New York, Philadelphia, Baltimore, San Francisco, and Los Angeles. "Too Jewish? Challenging Traditional Identities" is a traveling exhibition that has consistently included S.'s artwork.

Citing political reasons, S. left the *New Yorker* magazine in 2003 to work on *In the Shadow of No Towers,* a SERIES of large-format panels expressing his thoughts as an American artist living mere blocks from the former site of the World Trade Center in Manhattan. All American magazines and newspapers he approached refused to run this new work. In addition to the political content critical of the war in Iraq, many publishers saw the large format of the work as problematic. S. took his latest work to Europe and found a more receptive audience from several publications, including *Die Zeit,* a German newspaper, and the *London Review of Books.* S.'s publisher, Pantheon, released a monographic version of *In the Shadow of No Towers* in 2004.

Currently, S. is busy with a variety of projects. He is writing the libretto and designing sets for a comics-based opera entitled *Drawn to Death: A Three Panel Opera.* He and Mouly are editing a children's comics anthology series called *Little Lit.* S. has updated his Comics 101 lecture, now called Comics 101.1, which he is presenting at universities and other venues. The lecture covers the history of comics and the importance of them.

AWARDS: American Library Association's Best Books for Young Adults list, 1986, for *Maus, A Survivor's Tale,* 1986; American Library Association's Best Books for Young Adults list, 1992, for *Maus: A Survivor's Tale II: And Here My Troubles Began,* 1991; Guggenheim fellowship for *Maus;* Joel M. Cavior Award for Jewish Writing, 1986, for *Maus: a Survivor's Tale, My Father Bleeds History;* Pulitzer Prize Special Award in Letters, 1992, for *Maus.*

FURTHER WORKS: *The Complete Maus: A Survivor's Tale,* 1996; *Jack Cole and Plastic Man: Forms Stretched to Their Limits,* 2001 with Chip Kidd.

BIBLIOGRAPHY: Carter, Betty. *Best Books for Young Adults, Second Edition.* American Library Association, 2000; *Contemporary Authors Online,* 2003; *Contemporary Literary Criticism,* online, 2003; *DISCovering Authors,* online, 2003; Fischer, Jack. "S.'s Not Kidding: Comic-Book Pioneer Is Preparing a New Graphic Novel about Sept. 11; He'll Speak Tuesday in Berkeley." *Mercury News,* Sunday, February 22, 2004; LAMBIEK.NET website, www.lambiek.net/spiegelman.htm; Morgan, Karen Ferris. "Art S.: Overview." *Twentieth-Century Young Adult Writers* 1994, from *DISCovering Authors,* online, 2003; *Newsmakers 1998* 3, 1998, from *Student Resource Center,* 2003; Smith, Christopher Monte. "Very Interesting People: Art S." *BookSense* website, www.booksense.com/.people/archive/spiegelmanart.jsp; The Steven Barclay Agency website, www.barclayagency.com/spiegelman.html

ANDREW W. HUNTER

SPINELLI, Jerry

Author, b. 1 February 1941, Norristown, Pennsylvania

S. is an award-winning author of books with dynamic characters and captivating plots for children and YAs. His childhood events and experiences are reflected in many of his novels. Growing up in a brick row house in the west end of Norristown, Pennsylvania, he rode his bike, played baseball, and skipped stones across Stony Creek. The details of his life that are included in his novels help readers feel that they are there. Vivid descriptions of settings help the reader to visualize the railroad tracks, red hills, creek, woods, and alleyways where kids love to play. Like many boys, S. loved sports and dreamed of becoming a major league baseball player. His love of SPORTS was the impetus for the start of his writing career, which began with a poem he wrote about an exciting football game that was published in a local newspaper.

S.'s quest to become a writer continued when he attended Gettysburg College, where he earned an undergraduate degree in 1963. He then enrolled in a writers course at Johns Hopkins University, where he eventually completed his master's degree. Although he worked as an editor for an engineering MAGAZINE, he wrote during his lunch hours, after-work hours, and at any other available time. His early works went unpublished, but he persevered. In 1977 he married fellow author Eileen Mesi. Together they have six children who have been a rich source of subject matter to incorporate into his writing.

S.'s personal experiences are intertwined into his novels in a way that readers are able to make connections to their own. His large FAMILY provided a plethora of real-life characters and situations that inspired his writing. His research library for his books generally came from his childhood memories. His gift for writing makes these events come to life for YA readers. One night before going to bed, he wrapped some fried chicken and put it in the refrigerator for work the next day. In the morning he went to get it and it was gone. Six children were sleeping upstairs. He knew one of them had snatched his lunch. This was the event that inspired him to write his first published novel, *Space Station Seventh Grade* (1982).

The main characters of his second novel, *Who Put that Hair in My Toothbrush?* (1984) were based on his own children. The views of the two main characters, ninth-grader Greg and his younger sister, Megin, are presented in alternating chapters, in which their sibling rivalry becomes apparent. One quality that helps young adults relate to S.'s books is that his novels are written from the point of view of young people. YA readers think that *Who Put that Hair in My Toothbrush?* is so humorous because most siblings can relate to the events and feelings that are portrayed.

S. also gets ideas for stories from newspapers and incidents that happen around him. One day he read a story about a girl who competed on her high-school wrestling team. That inspired the book *There's a Girl in My Hammerlock* (1991). A newspaper article about an annual event in a small town in Pennsylvania was the impetus for the novel *Wringer* (1997).*Wringer,* a Newbery Honor winner in 1998, is the story of Palmer LaRue, who is dreading his tenth birthday. He does not want to become "a wringer," a person who wrings the heads off pigeons, but he feels intimidated by his friends and is afraid to protest against this unusual rite of passage. This is the story of how Palmer learns to take a stand for what he believes.

The theme of courage is a powerful force in many of S.'s other novels. In *Crash* (1996), the protagonist, a star football player, addresses the issue of bullying when he goes from being a bully himself to defending Penn Webb, a puny, quiet boy. In *Maniac Magee* (1990), Jeffrey Magee is an orphaned boy who comes to Two Mills looking for a home. He's only twelve, but he can run faster than anyone, untie impossible knots, and perform other amazing athletic feats. The most courageous thing he does is try to unite the racially divided town. The escalating conflict that results instills the reader with a feeling of injustice. Hopefully the idea that people need to be treated equally will result. S. received the coveted Newbery Medal in 1991 for *Maniac Magee,* which also addressed the problem of homelessness and self-survival.

Like Maniac Jeffrey Magee, many of S.'s characters are sad, struggling boys with problems. *The Library Card* (1997) chronicles the effect a library card has on four young people, including two boys, Mongoose and Sonseray, who struggle to find their own identity and purpose in life. In *Loser* (2003), S. once again follows this pattern with Zinkoff, a character who is always picked last for games with his peers. Even though most of his peers consider him a loser, he has a positive attitude and big heart that will hopefully inspire others to be more understanding towards people like Zinkoff in the future. *Milkweed* (2003) also fits this profile. Once again the protagonist is a needy boy with no home or family. He sleeps in the cellar with a group of boys and tries to take care of them. Although most of S.'s novels take place in the present, this novel, *Milkweed* (2003), takes place in Warsaw, Poland, during World War II.

Stargirl (2000) addresses the feelings of adolescents who are unique and might not blend in with their classmates. The courage Stargirl exhibits when she arrives at Mica High School changes how other people think. Young adult readers can connect to S.'s characters who convey emotions many of them feel while struggling to understand the confusing time of adolescence.

Readers who are familiar with S.'s works will enjoy reading his AUTOBIOGRAPHY, *Knots in My Yo-Yo String: The Autobiography of a Kid* (1998), which describes the author's early life in Norristown and his emergence as a world-class writer. The pictures and personal ADVENTURES in this work give insight into the themes that are prevalent in his novels and give the reader further insight into S., the writer.

SELECT AWARDS: *Maniac Magee:* 1990 *Boston Globe–Horn Book* Award, 1991 Newbery Medal, 1992 D. C. Fisher Award; 1998 Newbery Honor Award, *Wringer;* 1999 ALA Best Books for Young Adults, *Knots in My Yo-Yo String; Stargirl:* ALA Top Ten Best Books for Young Adults, *Publishers Weekly* Best Book of 2000, ALA BBYA, 2001, Parents' Choice 2000 Fiction Gold Award, NAIBA Book Award for Children's Literature, Bank Street College of Education Best Book of the Year, New York Public Library Book for the TEEN Age, 2002 IRA Young Adults' Choices; ALA Best Book for Young Adults: 1991 for *Maniac Magee,* 1992 for *There's a Girl in My Hammerlock,* 1997 for *Crash,* 1999 for *Knots in My Yo-Yo String,* 2001 for *Stargirl*; 2004 for *Milkweed.*

FURTHER WORKS: *Night of the Whale,* 1985; *Dump Days,* 1986; *Jason and Marceline,* 1986; *Fourth Grade Rats,* 1991; *School Daze: Report to the Principal's Office,* 1991; *The Bathwater Gang Gets Down to Business,* 1992; *Do the Funky Pickle,* 1992; *Picklemania,* 1993; *Tooter Pepperday,* 1995; *Blue Ribbon Blues: A Tooter Tale,* 1998.

BIBLIOGRAPHY: Decandido, Graceanne A., Maholey, Alan. "Macaulay Wins Caldecott Medal, S. Gets Newbery." *School Library Journal,* February 91; Drew, Bernard A. "The 100 Most Popular Young Adult Authors," 1996; *Contemporary Authors,* vol. 45, 1995; Keller, John. "Jerry S." *Horn Book,* July/ August, 1991; McElmeel, Sharron L. "100 Most Popular Children's Authors"; *Libraries Unlimited,* 1999; Murphy, Susan. "Books for Adolescents—Stories That Reach the Kids: An Interview with Jerry," *Jour-*

nal of Adolescent & Adult Literacy, December 1991; *Something about the Author,* vol. 39, 1985, vol. 71, 1993; S., Jerry., *Knots in My Yo-Yo String: the Autobiography of a Kid,* 1998; S., Jerry. *Horn Book,* July/August 1991; S., Jerry. "Newbery Medal Acceptance," *Horn Book,* July/August 91.

KATHY A. VANSTROM

SPORTS IN YA LITERATURE

Contemporary Sports Fiction

As the portrayal of TEENS in YA fiction has grown more realistic, S. have taken on an increasingly large role in teen literature. Just as the schedules of America's teens are filled with school, homework, relationships, S., and the arts, so are the schedules of today's teen characters packed with activities. S. play a role in teen fiction even outside of the realm of S. fiction. Teens trying to stave off stress may go for a run, like Kate in Laurie Halse ANDERSON's *Catalyst* (2002). Groups of friends usually have at least one athletic member, such as soccer enthusiast Kate in *The Sisterhood of the Traveling Pants* by Ann Brashares (2001). The *absence* of S. has even become an important storyline in teen fiction: Wallace Wallace is forced to stay after school and help with the play during detention, thus missing football practice in Gordon Korman's *No More Dead Dogs* (2000); Paul isn't allowed to play soccer due to an eye condition in *Tangerine* (1997) by Edward BLOOR; Berry quits the swim team after her sister's murder in South Africa in *Many Stones* (2000) by Carolyn Coman; baseball player turns poet due to a bout of mononucleosis in Ron KOERTGE's *Shakespeare Bats Cleanup* (2003). Even FANTASY and SCIENCE FICTION books can include a sporting element, as do J.R. ROWLING's Harry Potter SERIES and Orson Scott CARD's Ender series.

Contemporary writers for teens continue to carry the torch in the creation of novels written with S. as the predominant theme. Many S. fiction authors choose to emphasize character development and relationships rather than focusing solely on S. The list below, categorized by S., touches on some of the significant S. fiction works for teens of the past twenty years.

Baseball and Softball

The popular Baseball Card Adventure series by Dan Gutman started with the 1997 *Honus and Me,* in which Joe Stoshack finds a rare Honus Wagner baseball card while cleaning a neighbor's attic. Joe's find is more valuable than he thinks: the card is his ticket to time travel. Joe is coached by and travels with Honus and ultimately gets to play in the 1909 World Series. Further books in the well-researched series introduce Babe Ruth, Shoeless Joe Jackson, Jackie Robinson, and Dorothy Maguire.

In Scott JOHNSON's *Safe at Second* (1999), Todd Banister is a pitcher destined for the majors until a freak accident blinds him in one eye. Encouraged by his best friend, Todd attempts a comeback. Paulie, Todd's best friend, also has to deal with broken dreams, as he had planned to ride Todd's coattails and manage him in the major leagues.

The Speed of Light (2003) by Ron Carlson is finely crafted tale of an era only recently gone by, when kids played outside and simple pleasures like baseball could keep three boys occupied for an entire summer. Larry and his best friends Witt and Rafferty create and play many permutations of baseball as they spend the summer sleeping outside, avoiding bullies, and just hanging out. Slightly reminiscent of the TV series *The Wonder Years,* this quiet story holds many secrets about the boys' FAMILIES and their town.

Summerland, by Pulitzer Prize–winning Michael Chabon, is one of the more unusual books about baseball written for young adults. The protagonist is a young man named Ethan Feld, a self-proclaimed awful baseball player, who must save the universe as we know it and his own father through a series of baseball games. Combining American folklore, baseball and its history, and magic, this is a tale of a reluctant hero and a band of friends.

In Virginia Euwer WOLFF's 1998 novel *Bat 6,* twenty-one distinct voices tell the story of a softball team that grapples with life in post-World War II America. The girls on the team play out some of the conflicts beneath the surface in the community when Shirley, the daughter of a soldier killed in Pearl Harbor, assaults Aki, a Japanese-American girl recently returned from an internment camp during a game.

Basketball

Bruce BROOKS's *The Moves Make the Man* (1984) is one of the most famous S. books written for teens. In this Newbery Honor-winning title, Jerome is a black teen who, through basketball, becomes friends with a white classmate from a troubled home. This story of an unlikely friendship raised eyebrows with its realistic use of language.

In his Coretta Scott King Award-winning title *Slam!* (1996), Walter Dean MYERS uses fast-paced urban language to tell the tale of a young man who sees basketball as his ticket to a better life. Slam's basketball style is in-your-face and in control. His off-the-court life, on the other hand, is a realm he feels he has no control over. Slam struggles as he learns to apply his basketball strategies to his life. Myers also wrote *Hoops* (1981), in which Lonnie, a young man with the potential to go pro, and his coach grapple with the pressures involved in high-stakes basketball. In *The Outside Shot* (1984), the sequel to *Hoops,* Lonnie plays basketball for a Midwestern college and struggles to keep his grades up and his nose clean.

The *Harlem Beat* series by Yuriko Nishiyama adds a whole new element to the S. fiction genre—visuals. Originally published in Japan in 1994, this manga was brought to the United States in 1999. The premise is simple: Nate Torres doesn't make the school basketball team but still wants the glory that playing basketball brings. His only option is to hone his skills through street ball.

Boxing

Fighting Ruben Wolfe by AUSTRALIAN Markus ZUSAK (2002) is the story of two brothers who become involved in an underground boxing. The boys' only training has been swapping punches with one another in their backyard. Thrown in the ring, younger brother Cameron flounders while his older sibling, Ruben, becomes a fighting machine. The edgy Australian dialect and gritty day-to-day details of a family whose finances are spiraling downward add meat to the story.

Two brothers also figure prominently in Chris LYNCH'S novel, *Shadow Boxer* (1993). After their father's boxing-related DEATH, George is determined to keep his younger brother, Monty, from the ring.

Football

Damage by A. M. JENKINS (2001) tells the story of Austin Reid, a seventeen-year-old still trying to come to terms with the death of his father to cancer. Austin,

a handsome star athlete with a pretty girlfriend and a nice mom, seems to have everything but suffers from depression and contemplates suicide. Jenkins distinctively presents all aspects of Austin's life—from football practice to sexual encounters—in the second person, lending immediacy to the work.

Chan Jung Kim is a Korean–American soccer player adjusting to life in a Midwestern football town in *Necessary Roughness* (1996) by Marie G. LEE. Chan joins the football team in an attempt to blend in, and suffers a major blow when his sister, Young, is killed in a car accident.

Soccer

In AVI'S *S.O.R. Losers* (1984) a team of seventh graders wishes they'd never been put on a soccer field. After losing their first game by thirty-two points, the boys are shocked to learn that school administrators and their parents expect them to keep on playing.

N 2 Deep (2001) by Laurie Lazzaro Knowlton is part of a series from a Christian perspective called TodaysGirls.com. Amber Thompson must look to God for help in coming to terms with the limitations of teen life when she finds her time spread too thin between school, soccer, and her new job as a webmaster. Another book in the series, *Stranger Online* (2003) by Carol Smith, deals with a student on the swim team.

In *Home of the Braves* (2002) by David KLASS, Joe Brickman expects to be the star of his school's soccer team when he returns to school in the fall of his senior year. Unfortunately, a new student from Brazil challenges Joe's supremacy on the field. When the new student starts dating the girl Joe has had a crush on, Joe has to learn to overcome life's disappointments.

Swimming

TJ, the main character in Chris CRUTCHER'S *Whale Talk* (2001), is a bright and athletic high-school student who does not conform to other people's ideals. But when TJ realizes that participation on a swim team would be a way for some of the school's outcasts to earn some respect—and a coveted letter jacket—he agrees to captain the team. The book is in part about swimming and the thrill of competition regardless of your level of ability, but the storyline also incorporates themes of domestic violence, bullying, and racism.

Fifteen-year-old Alex Archer competes for a place on the 1960 New Zealand Olympic team in Tessa DUDER's *In Lane Three, Alex Archer* (1984). As if fighting for a place on the team isn't enough, Alex also deals with the death of her boyfriend, the decline of her beloved grandmother, and societal expectations about females in sports.

Classic S. Fiction

Today's S. fiction for teens has evolved from a well-known and well-loved lineage penned by such authors as Thomas Dygard, Robert LIPSYTE, Matt Christopher, and R. R. Knudson. These authors created coming-of-age stories focused primarily on the excitement of the game and the thrill of competition.

Lipsyte, who received the MARGARET A. EDWARDS AWARD for lifetime achievement in literature for young adults in 2001, entered the S. fiction genre with a bang with his first novel *The Contender* in 1967. This groundbreaking work (contemporary with S. E. HINTON's *The Outsiders*) features Albert, a seventeen-year-old boy from Harlem who goes to a boxing gym in order to gain some respect and put an end to being bullied. Albert doesn't just learn about boxing, he learns about the act of becoming a boxer—and a man. Albert's story continues in Lipsyte's 1991 novel *The Brave,* where he has grown into a toughened member of the NYPD. Albert rescues Sonny Bear, a young man who was barely off the bus that carried him from his reservation to New York City before he got involved with drug pushers, from continued torment in a correctional facility. Albert brings Sonny to the same gym in Harlem where he learned to box in *The Contender,* then Sonny returns to the reservation to work with another mentor, his great-uncle, who imparts the wisdom of their tribes' Running Brave warriors. Sonny wins a citywide amateur boxing tournament, but is stripped of the title when it becomes apparent that he is not technically an amateur. Sonny faces yet another setback when Albert is shot. In the third novel of the series, *The Chief* (1993), readers resume the story of Sonny, who has been making a living as a professional boxer. Sonny gets a job as a sparring partner for a former champion in Las Vegas and then is noticed by Hollywood agents who want to make him a star. Sonny's rise to fame coincides with

a problem back at the reservation where a casino threatens the Moscondaga way of life. Complex plots and fast-paced writing characterize Lipsyte's work. His novels have had lasting appeal and have become a part of the cannon of young adult literature.

Like Lipsyte, Dygard had years of journalism under his belt before he wrote his first S. book. Dygard started his writing career as a sportswriter and reporter for a local paper in Little Rock, Arkansas, and eventually became a reporter and then bureau chief for the Associated Press in many cities including Tokyo. In spite of his success with the Associated Press, Dygard still had one dream: to write novels for young readers. His first work, *Running Scared,* the tale of a high-school quarterback with a fear of running the ball, was published in 1977. Since then, Dygard published nearly a book a year until his death in 1996. Dygard has contributed numerous compelling accounts of teen athletes—including a sports book with a female protagonist, *Forward Pass.* Published in 1989, *Forward Pass* delivers a timely tale of a high-school student Jill Winston, whose skills as a wide receiver are necessary to her team's success. Dygard's novel was published as female athletes were making news across the country by challenging rules that prohibited them from participating on teams traditionally comprised of males.

Although for a slightly younger audience, R. R. Knudson's novels about Zan Hagen are also noteworthy in their early contribution to the genre. Zan, a female student, is an incredible all-around athlete who starts an all-girl football squad from the members of her dance class in *Zanballer* (1974). Zan then fights to play on her school's mostly male baseball team in *Zanbanger* (1977), suffers a shoulder injury in *Zanboomer* (1978), and trains for the Olympics as a marathoner in *Zan Hagen's Marathon* (1984). Knudson portrays Zan as a well-rounded young woman with exceptional athletic ability and fills out the story with the inclusion of Arthur Rinehart, a likeable although thoroughly unathletic male friend. Arthur does get involved in the sport of weightlifting in *Rinehard Lifts* (1980), and in *Rinehart Shouts* (1987) the characters correspond while Zan is traveling to the Sports Hall of Fame with her family. The series of books focus on Zan's athletic abilities, but also on the friendship between the Zan and Arthur, which remains platonic. Knudson performed a great service in the creation of a smart, humorous female character who is able to compete with the boys.

An overview of S. fiction for young adults would be incomplete without mention of Matt Christopher, whose books have great appeal to die-hard S. fans. While Christophers books are not geared specifically at a teen market, they have quite a following among children grades four to seven and are a wonderful resource for reluctant readers who enjoy S. Christopher's first book, *Baseball Pals,* came out in 1956. Christopher was a prolific writer who aimed to bring S. alive for young readers. While the majority of his titles are about baseball, he also wrote about many other S., including hockey, basketball, football, and tennis.

BIBLIOGRAPHY: Steinberg, R. "Striking out Stereotype: Girls in S. Fiction." *School Library Journal,* June 90, p. 62; Hurlburt, Tom. "Slam Dunks and Strikeouts." *School Library Journal,* July 92, p. 30; Robert Lipsyte. *Authors and Artists for Young Adults,* vol. 45, 2002; Thomas Dygard. *Major Authors and Illustrators for Children and Young Adults,* 2nd ed., 2002; R. R. Knudson. *Authors and Artists for Young Adults,* vol. 20, 1997; Matt Christopher. *Major Authors and Illustrators for Children and Young Adults,* 2nd ed., 2002.

CATHY DELNEO

SPRINGER, Nancy

Author, b. 5 July 1948, Montclair, New Jersey

S. has made her life motto "Conform, Go Crazy, or Become an Artist." This motto describes her life from early childhood to her years as a housewife to her current role as a writer. S. describes her childhood as an unhappy one, and this made up her "conform" phase; being raised in the fifties translated to conforming. A shy and skinny child, S. was often picked on by others. Her family later moved to Gettysburg, where they owned a motel. Reading and her daydream fantasies served as escapes from this discontented life. Her daydreams helped her through her teenage years, and she eventually started to write these daydreams down.

S. continued her period of conformity as a housewife, married to a preacher and the mother of two children. With these roles, she entered her "go crazy" phase. Struggling with her emotions and unhappiness, she had thoughts of suicide, saw psychologists, and was medicated at various points, all in an effort to help her become content with being a housewife. S. finally decided to get rid of all the doctors and medications and concentrate more on herself and her writing. She no longer just conformed to being a wife and mother, but was able to break free and become a writer as well, thereby entering her "artist" phase. Writing is what S. prefers; she is able to easily write in a variety of formats and genres: nonfiction, fiction, SHORT STORIES, POETRY, SCIENCE FICTION, FANTASY, contemporary fantasy, and MYSTERIES.

S.'s first novel was *The Book of Suns* (1977), which is also part of her World of Isle SERIES. It was later rewritten and renamed *The Silver Sun,* corresponding to the color-themed titles in the series. In this book, S. weaves an enjoyable story involving MYTHOLOGY, ADVENTURE, and relationships. From her very first book, S.'s writing shows strong character development and the characters' intertwining relationships, as she does here with the brothers, Alan and Hal. These two face many challenges together as they try to overcome evil and meet their own destinies. The World of Isle series includes four other books, all dealing with Celtic mythology and CLASSIC heroic fantasy adventures.

S. left the World of Isle for her next two novels but remained within the world of fantasy. In *Wings of Flame* (1985), she builds a new world in the kingdoms of Deva and Vashti. This story revolves around the characters of Prince Kyrem of Deva, King Auron of Vashti, and Seda, an orphan born lower than a slave. In *Chains of Gold* (1986), the Winter-King Arlen and his bride Cerilla fall in love. In order to have a life together, Arlen's friend Lonn takes Arlen's place at the sacrifice, only to haunt Arlen and Cerilla as a ghost following their escape to the Mountains of Mystery.

With her success in writing fantasy novels, S. fulfilled a childhood dream of buying a horse. Her love of horses is carried over in her realistic fiction with the novel *A Horse to Love* (1987), which shows the rewards and the frustrations Erin, a young girl, experiences when she is given a horse. Taking care of the horse helps Erin to develop her self-confidence. S. uses horses in other YA novels to confront themes such as coming of age, peer pressures, race relations (*They're All Named Wildfire,* 1989), and DISABILITIES (*Colt,* 1991).

S. is also able to blend her horse themes with contemporary fantasy in *The Hex Witch of Seldom*

(1988), where TEENAGER Bobbi has psychic abilities and her grandfather gives her a horse that is not at all typical. Instead, this horse is actually a member of the Circle of Twelve and helps Bobbi develop her powers. Set in her current home state, Pennsylvania, S. also blends local folklore into this story.

Another contemporary fantasy that blends current issues, such as prejudice, homosexuality, and middle age, in a fantasy setting is *Larque on the Wing* (1994). Larque, an older heroine who is an artist with psychic abilities, is in somewhat of a midlife crisis. She is seeing the ghost of a young girl who appears to be her adolescent self. She is also transformed into Lark, a homosexual male.

S. crossed over to the MYSTERY genre with strong success, earning Edgar Awards for *Toughing It* (1994) and *Looking for Jamie Bridger* (1995). Tuff witnesses his brother's murder and seeks revenge in *Toughing It*. Living in a difficult and basically uncaring home, Tuff pairs up with Pen Leppo, who may be his biological father, to bring justice to his brother's murderer. In this emotional adventure, S. nicely ties together issues of poverty, self-identity, violence, mourning, and rage. In *Looking for Jamie Bridger*, Jamie is raised by her grandparents, who refuse to share any information with her when she expresses a desire to learn about her parents. When she decides to confront her grandfather on the issue, he dies of a heart attack. This allows Jamie to finally seek out the answers she needs, but her quest may have some surprise twists in this fine mystery.

In her Tale from Camelot SERIES, S. brings to life some fascinating Authurian characters from Camelot. *I Am Mordred* (1998) focuses on the son of King Arthur. Mordred must come to terms with who he is and who his father is. S. interprets the story of another Camelot adversary in *I am Morgan le Fay* (2001).

S. looks to another legend in her most current series, Rowan Hood, which follows the adventures of Robin Hood's daughter as she seeks out the father who does not know her.

S. has won numerous awards and continues to delight her readers with solid characters and intriguing plots in a wide range of genres. Young Adult readers are fortunate that S. did indeed decide to "become an artist"!

AWARDS: 1989 International Reading Association/ Children's Book Council Children's Choice, *A Horse to Love; The Hex Witch of Seldom:* New York Public Library Books for the Teen Age citation and American Library Association Best Books for Young Adults citation, 1988; 1992 Joan Fassler Memorial Book Award; *Colt:* 1993 IRA/CBC Young Adult's Choice citation, 1993 New York Public Library Books for the Teen Age citation; 1993 Pennsylvania Library Association Carolyn W. Field Award notable book citation for *The Friendship Song;* 1995 James Tiptree Jr. Memorial Award, *Larque on the Wing;* ALA Recommended Book for the Reluctant Young Adult Reader citation, *The Boy on a Black Horse;* 1995 Mystery Writers of America Edgar Allan Poe Award and Carolyn W. Field Award Honor Book, 1995 ALA Best Books for Young Adults, *Toughing It;* 1996 Mystery Writers of America Edgar Allan Poe Award, *Looking for Jamie Bridger;* 1997 Pennsylvania School Library Association Outstanding Pennsylvania Author Award; *I Am Mordred:* ALA Best Books for Young Adults, 1999, and Pennsylvania Library Association Carolyn W. Field Award, 1998; *I am Morgan Le Fay*: Vermont's Dorothy Canfield Fisher Children's Book Award, 2003; *Blood Trail*: ALA Quick Picks for Reluctant Young Adult Readers, 2004.

FURTHER WORKS: *The White Hart,* 1979; *The Sable Moon,* 1981; *The Black Beast,* 1982; *The Golden Swan,* 1983; *Madbond,* 1987; *Mindbond,* 1987; *Godbond,* 1988; *Not on a White Horse,* 1988; *Apocalypse,* 1989; *Red Wizard,* 1990; *The Great Pony Hassle,* 1993; *Stardark Songs* (poetry), 1993; *Music of Their Hooves* (poetry), 1993; *The Boy on a Black Horse,* 1994; *Fair Peril,* 1996; *Secret Star,* 1997; *Plumage,* 1999; *Sky Rider,* 1999; *Rowan Hood: Outlaw Girl of Sherwood Forest,* 2001; *Separate Sisters,* 2001; *Lionclaw: A Tale of Rowan Hood,* 2002; *Outlaw Princess of Sherwood: A Tale of Rowan Hood,* 2003; *Blood Trail,* 2003; *Wild Boy: A Tale of Rowan Hood,* 2004.

BIBLIOGRAPHY: *Authors and Artists for Young Adults,* vol. 32; *Contemporary Authors New Revision Series,* vol. 41; *Something about the Author,* vol. 65; *Publishers Weekly* and *Kirkus* book reviews.

TINA HERTEL

STANLEY, Diane

Author, b. 27 December 1943, Abilene, Texas

S.'s father was a Navy pilot, and her mother was a writer. Her parents divorced soon after she was born, and she and her mother moved to New York City. As an only child, reading was at the center of her life with her mother, and S. was interested in art from the very beginning. She drew frequently as a child, but she never took art seriously until a professor at Trinity

University in San Antonio recognized her talent, and she decided to become a medical illustrator.

While pursuing a graduate degree, she studied art at the University of Edinburgh and traveled to Russia. This was the beginning of her fascination with Russian history and literature. After she had children of her own, she discovered children's PICTURE BOOKS, and decided to use both her artistic talent and writing ability to create children's books herself. She became inspired to write a SERIES of BIOGRAPHIES for children on a Russian theme, the first of which was *Peter the Great.* She worked on picture book biographies and concentrated on a single man or woman. She not only studies the lives of her characters intimately, but she concentrates on the architecture and costumes of the period depicted, and uses something in the art or culture of the subject's country as a theme throughout the book. Other biographies include *Cleopatra, Leonardo da Vinci, and Michelangelo.* S. has also written several fiction books and writes and illustrates books researched by her husband, Peter Vennema.

AWARDS: William Allen White Children's Book Award, Emporia State University, 1988–89, *Peter the Great;* Carter G. Woodson Award, National Council for the Social Studies, 1992, *Siegfried;* Golden Kite Award for best picture book text, Society of Children's Book Writers and Illustrators, 1997, for *Saving Sweetness;* awards for *Leonardo da Vinci* include Orbis Pictus Award for Outstanding Nonfiction for Children from National Council Teachers of English and the *Boston Globe–Horn Book* Award Honor Book for Nonfiction. *A Time Apart*: ALA Best Books for Young Adults, 2000; *Saladin: Noble Prince of Islam* ALA Notable Children's Books, 2003. Works have been recognized on numerous notable book, pick of the lists, editor's choice, master lists, and best of the year lists, 1979–98.

FURTHER WORKS: *A Time Apart,* 1999; *Saladin: Noble Prince of Islam,* 2002.

BIBLIOGRAPHY: *Contemporary Authors Online, 2001;* www.dianestanley.com; www.eduplace.com/kids/hmr/mtain/stanley.html

JOAN PEARLMAN

STAPLES, Suzanne Fisher

Author, b. 27 August 1945, Philadelphia, Pennsylvania

S. had a deep love for books and writing from an early age. In her third-grade year, she and her sister started a newspaper. Her parents encouraged her early writing attempts, and her teachers pointed her to books that influenced her decision to write for children. ADVENTURE stories by Rudyard Kipling and Robert Louis Stevenson were among her favorites.

After graduating with a degree in English from Cedar Crest College in Allentown, Pennsylvania, S. had a number of writing-related jobs, working in both the United States and abroad for United Press International, *Smithsonian* magazine, the *Washington Post,* and other publications. By 1980 she had achieved the status of UPI Bureau Chief of New Delhi, India. In 1983 she accepted a part-time position as a foreign correspondent for the *Washington Post.* Her work as a correspondent and news editor for United Press International took S. to Afghanistan, Hong Kong, India, and Pakistan. Her many adventures included traveling with Indira Gandhi as she campaigned for Prime Minister and photographing Soviet troops fighting in Afghanistan. Most fortunate for all of her readers, however, was the opportunity posed to S. by USAID, the United States Agency for International Development, who asked her to conduct a research study on poverty in Pakistan, particularly focused on the plight of women. This research, according to S., became "the framework" for her novel, *Shabanu* (1989) and its sequel, *Haveli* (1993).

The United States Agency for International Development asked S. to participate in a study of poor rural women in Pakistan. The study focused on the objective of literacy training combined with job training to increase the chances of poor Pakistani women to earn greater income and break the cycle of poverty. The study took S. to the sparsely populated Cholistan Desert, home to a semi-nomadic people. She lived with these people and collected their stories. If any author should win recognition for opening a window to another culture, another set of standards and values, that author is S. Through her writing she has lifted a veil on the courage, strength, and humor of the Pakistani people. By lifting this veil, she helps shed light on the status of women in the Islamic world, a subject difficult to comprehend by Western standards.

The stories S. heard inspired her to write her first novel for YOUNG ADULTS, *Shabanu: Daughter of the Wind,* the story of a twelve-year-old spirited nomadic girl who is unwillingly betrothed to an older man by her parents in an arranged marriage. A series of unfortunate occurrences present Shabanu with the opportunity to choose between this arranged marriage to a wealthy landowner who already has three wives and her independence. S.'s debut story of a young woman who must balance her own desires against her obligations to her FAMILY and to centuries of tradition was highly acclaimed by reviewers and the recipient of numerous prestigious honors.

Haveli, S.'s second novel, continues Shabanu's story six years after the first novel ended. S. explores the intrigues among the four wives of the aging Rahim. The youngest and most beautiful of the wives, and the least cultured, Shabanu falls prey to the scheming of the elder wives and must use her wits to protect herself and her young daughter, Mumtaz. The idealistic Shabanu also tries to protect her best friend from an arranged marriage to her husband's mentally disturbed son. Shabanu loses both her husband and her friend to violent DEATHS and falls in love with Omar, a relative of her husband who returned from the United States.

The results of the research S. conducted are explained in her article in the 1995 *ALAN Review,* edited at the time by M. Jerry Weiss. In the article, S. reveals the philosophical stance she has taken in its title, "Different Is Just Different." It is this very philosophy, that different is to be viewed as an alternative, not as a value judgment, that makes her novels such rewarding reading for the young adult audience. S. summarizes her thoughts with her own hope, that "*Shabanu* and *Haveli* are all good books about people who are different from us . . . will inspire us to grow beyond our limits to learn understanding. And that this understanding will foster peace in the world by teaching us not to fear differences."

S.'s third novel, *Dangerous Skies* (1996), is a disturbing, powerful story that explores the racism that continues to pervade a small town on the shore of Virginia's Chesapeake Bay. Two twelve-year-old friends, white male Buck and black female Tunes, discover the body of their older friend Jorge Rodrigues floating in a creek. The friends suspect Jumbo Rawlins, a respected white landowner, but when Jumbo implicates Tunes in the murder, the friends are forced to face the racist world they inhabit. Many reviewers of the novel compare its sensitive treatment of the perils of racism to Harper LEE's *To Kill a Mockingbird.*

S. returns to an Asian setting in her fourth novel, *Shiva's Fire* (2000), the story of a young girl named Parvati who is known in her village for her extraordinary dancing ability. A great guru, a master of Indian classical dance, invites Parvati to study with him, and she commits herself to a rigorous program of dance, devotion, and study, but she finds the direction she takes drives a wedge between her and her family. S.'s novel *The Green Dog,* subtitled *A Mostly True Story,* is an AUTOBIOGRAPHICAL novel that draws heavily from her own childhood experiences. The funny, nostalgic story centers on a daydreaming loner named Suzanne who, during the summer before fifth grade, acquires a canine companion who has a nose for trouble.

AWARDS: Newbery Honor in 1990 for *Shabanu: Daughter of the Wind,* ALA Best Books for Young Adults: 1990 for *Shabanu,* 1994 for *Haveli,* 1997 for *Dangerous Skies.*

BIBLIOGRAPHY: Roe, Betty, and Mike. "Suzanne Fisher S.: A Woman Who Believes in the Power of Study." *Tennessee Reading Teacher* (Fall 1998): 14–15; *Something about the Author,* vol. 105, pp. 208–10; S., Suzanne Fisher. "Different Is Just Different." *The ALAN Review,* vol. 22, no. 2, Winter 1995; Watson, Jinx Stapleton. "Individual Choice and Family Loyalty: Suzanne Fisher S.' Protagonists Come of Age." *The ALAN Review,* vol. 27, no. 1, Fall 1999, 25–28.

EDWARD T. SULLIVAN
AND SUSAN MARINOFF

THE STAR WARS UNIVERSE—IN BOOKS: IN A GALAXY FAR, FAR AWAY. . . .

Some twenty plus years ago, a SCIENCE FICTION phenomenon opened at a theater near you—the first of the Star Wars MOVIES. *Episode IV,* or *A New Hope* as it was called, introduced us to a farm boy who longed to be a pilot and wound up a young Jedi Knight in training, Luke Skywalker, to a gruff, independent, down-on-his luck smuggler, Han Solo, and to beautiful, strong-willed kidnap victim and Rebel Alliance leader Princess Leia. Plus a Wookie, two robots (C3PO and R2-D2) and retired Jedi Master Obi-Wan Kenobi. These are stories that feature good versus evil, the underdog on the run from the minions of the evil Empire, the truly impressive array of armaments in the arsenal of the Empire, and the sublimely evil dweller on the Dark Side, Darth Vader. ADVENTURE piled on adventure as these characters reappeared in subsequent films—two sequels: *The Empire Strikes Back* and *Return of the Jedi*. Now, a generation later, we are returning to the world of Star Wars, but chronologically decades earlier. Here we have the early days of young Obi-Wan Kenobi and his Padawan apprentice who eventually gives in to the forces of the Dark Side during the Clone Wars, Anakin Skywalker (a.k.a. Darth Vader his pre-breathing mask days).

Star Wars fans can and have watched these movies over and over again. But they haven't had to stop there. The desire for all things Star Wars has spawned an industry, not only in theaters, but also on the shelves of bookstores and libraries all around the world. Old familiar characters, the tried and the true, are joined by new favorites, like the short-lived but extremely charismatic Darth Maul. Did anyone not sit up and take notice of this sinister Sith warrior, with his striking red paint job and double-sided light saber? Unfortunately, he died all too soon. Fortunately, he and other characters live within the pages of one or more books, part of a growing opus of science fiction adventures set within the Star Wars universe. Some are the stories of the movies; others relate adventure after adventure of various characters introduced in these movies, much to the delight of fans, who just can't get enough of all things Star Wars. So see the movies, read the books, and enjoy.

Various authors have taken the movies as a starting point and gone in different directions. It's a matter of personal preference. You can dip in anywhere and follow the adventures of favorite characters, or you can follow the internal chronology, beginning with the earliest adventures set within the Star Wars universe. The following is such a chronological list of Star Wars titles, annotated to help you decide which ones you'd like to read and in what order.

The Rising Force (Jedi Apprentice, Book 1) by Dave Wolverton. Long before he appeared in *Episode IV: A New Hope*, young Obi-Wan Kenobi was destined for the Jedi Agricultural Corps, until he was thrown together with Jedi Master Qui-Gon Jinn on a mission to the barren planet of Bandomeer.

The Dark Rival (Jedi Apprentice, Book 2) by Jude Watson. In this sequel to *The Rising Force*, Qui-Gon discovers that his mission to the planet Bandomeer is a trap, set for him by a former apprentice who has gone over to the Dark Side. In his struggles against his fallen Padawan, he comes to rely more and more on the willing assistance of young Obi-Wan Kenobi.

The adventures of Jedi Master Qui-Gon and his new Padawan Obi-Wan Kenobi continue in the other volumes of this SERIES, written for young people by Jude Watson: *3. The Hidden Past, 4. The Mark of the Crown, 5. The Defenders of the Dead, 6. The Uncertain Path, 7. The Captive Temple, 8. The Day of Reckoning, 9. The Fight for Truth, 10. The Shattered Peace, 11. The Deadly Hunter, 12. The Evil Experiment, 13. The Dangerous Rescue, 14. The Ties that Bind, 15. The Death of Hope, 16. The Call to Vengeance, 17. The Only Witness, 18. The Threat Within.*

Star Wars Episode One: The Phantom Menace by Terry BROOKS. The novelization of the movie that introduced young Anakin Skywalker and Darth Maul to the Star Wars universe. The events depicted here took place when Obi-Wan was still the Padawan apprentice of Master Jedi Qui-Gon Jinn, long before Luke met Leia and Han and a retired Obi-Wan in *A New Hope*.

Rogue Planet by Greg BEAR. Young Anakin Skywalker is now the Padawan apprentice to young Jedi Obi-Wan Kenobi. He gets restless at times and risks his life at games. He is also beginning to feel the stirrings of the rage that will later lead him to the Dark Side. But he is still young and excited at their latest mission, a trip to a planet where a Jedi has disappeared, where spaceships are grown, not made, and where their lives will depend on one of these ships.

The Approaching Storm by Alan Dean Foster. In the years following *The Phantom Menace*, the Republic continues to fall apart. It is the Jedi who are called upon to help maintain order. Which is why Obi-Wan Kenobi and young Anakin Skywalker were sent to the planet Ansion. Upon their return, they face a world on the brink of the Clone Wars.

Star Wars Episode Two: Attack of the Clones. Movie and book describe the battles that take place during the Clone Wars.

Star Wars Episode Three. Two years after the *Attack of the Clones*, Anakin Skywalker gives in to the call of the Dark Side and becomes Darth Vader.

The Han Solo Trilogy by A. C. Crispin: *1. The Paradise Snare, 2. The Hutt Gambit, 3. Rebel Dawn.* Ten years before he appeared in *A New Hope*, TEENAGE Han Solo left an unhappy adopted home and went off to become a pilot, both in and then out of the Imperial Navy. As a fugitive smuggler, con man, and thief, he befriends a former Wookie slave named Chewbacca and makes a deadly enemy of Jabba the Hutt.

The Adventures of Lando Calrissian by L. Neil Smith: *1. Lando Calrissian and the Mindharp of Sharu, 2. Lando Calrissian and the Flamewind of Oseon, 3. Lando Calrissian and the Starcave of Thonboka.* Meet Han Solo's friend Lando, gambler, rogue, con man, and all 'round good guy. These are his adventures leading up to his being at the right place at the right time, able to rescue Leia and Luke from Cloud City in *The Empire Strikes Back.*

The Han Solo Adventures by Brian Daley: *1. Han Solo at Star's End, 2. Han Solo's Revenge, 3. Han Solo and the Lost Legacy.* These adventures of Han and Chewbacca take place some five years before they rescued Luke and Obi-Wan from that infamous cantina. Here Han is involved in a rescue mission to the prison planet Star's End, gets revenge for being tricked into carrying slaves on his ship, and searches for a hidden treasure that leads to a desperate effort to recover the hijacked Millenium Falcon.

Episode IV: A New Hope. George Lucas gave us the movie and the book. Darth Vader captures Princess Leia. She sends a message to Obi-Wan Kenobi using two 'droids. R2D2 and C-3PO encounter Luke Skywalker in the quest for Obi-Wan. Han Solo and Chewbacca get involved in the rescue of the princess. And Luke first learns to use the Force.

Tales from the Mos Eisley Cantina, edited by Kevin J. Anderson. Sixteen stories by some of the leading writers of science fiction provide additional information about a variety of characters who were in Mos Eisley Cantina when there was a disturbance at the door and in walked a farm boy and Obi-Wan Kenobi.

Splinter of the Mind's Eye: From the Adventures of Luke Skywalker by Alan Dean Foster. A few years after Luke meets Leia in *A New Hope,* he follows her on a mission to the planet Circarpous. There he learns of the Kirburr crystal, a mysterious gem so strong in the force that its bearer becomes almost invincible. Which means that Luke has got to find that crystal— before Darth Vader does.

Episode V: The Empire Strikes Back by George Lucas. Movie and novelization, middle work in the original Star Wars trilogy. During the three years after the events of *A New Hope,* Luke flies off to meet and train with Master Jedi Yoda, while Han and Leia encounter old friends and enemies in Cloud City.

Tales of the Bounty Hunters, edited by Kevin J. Anderson. Five stories featuring the bounty hunters

that Darth Vader sent after Han Solo, including that perennial favorite among Star Wars fans, Boba Fett.

Shadows of the Empire by Steve Perry. The period between *The Empire Strikes Back* and *The Return of the Jedi* marks the appearance of a new villain, Prince Xizor of the Black Sun. While Luke continues his Jedi Knight training and Leia organizes a team to rescue a frozen Han Solo, the Prince is after vengeance. Darth Vader killed his family; now he plans to kill Vader's son—Luke.

Episode VI: Return of the Jedi by George Lucas. The movie and novelization take place four years after Han, Luke and Leia meet in "A New Hope." After his friends rescue a frozen Han from the clutches of Jabba the Hutt, they join forces to finally defeat the Emperor and the malevolent Darth Vader.

Tales from Jabba's Palace, edited by Kevin J. Anderson. The nineteen stories in this collection focus on different characters who were present when Jabba brought the helpless Han Solo to his palace.

The Bounty Hunter Wars by K. W. Jeter: *1. The Mandalorian Armor, 2. Slave Ship, 3. Hard Merchandise.* It's Prince Xizor, leader of a secret crime syndicate, versus Boba Fett, the galaxy's most successful bounty hunter. Guess who wins!

The Truce at Bakura by Kathy Tyers. Bakura, a terrestrial-type planet, is being invaded by deadly, lizard-like aliens. Fortunately, the Force is with Luke Skywalker, because he's the one who gets embroiled this time.

X-Wing Series: 1. Rogue Squadron by Michael Stackpole, *2. Wedge's Gamble* by Michael Stackpole, *3. The Kryptos Trap* by Michael Stackpole, *4. The Bacta War* by Michael Stackpole, *5. Wraith Squadron* by Aaron Alston, *6. Iron Fist* by Aaron Alston, *7. Solo Command* by Aaron Alston. Around six or seven years after the battle against the Death Star in *A New Hope,* Wedge Antilles, Luke's friend and flying partner, is asked to rebuild the legendary Rogue Squadron. He recruits the most skilled and daring of all the X-wing pilots. Now all they have to do is survive the various missions they are sent on by the New Republic.

The Courtship of Princess Leia by Dave Wolverton. Some eight years after they first met in *A New Hope,* Han realizes that he loves Leia and wants to marry her, but he may have waited too long. She is seriously considering another offer, that of dashing, wealthy young Prince Isolder, heir to a consortium of some sixty-three planets, who would be valuable allies in the New Republic's struggle against the Empire. Han is going to have to act fast if he hopes to win Leia back for himself.

X-Wing Series: 8. Isard's Revenge by Michael Stackpole. A year after Leia's courtship, Wedge Antilles, a general now, is still leading his famed X-wing fighters on seemingly impossible missions. This time they have to form an alliance with a former enemy to save captured friends. But how long will such an alliance last, and who will suffer when it dissolves?

The Thrawn Trilogy by Timothy Zahn: *1. Heir to the Empire. 2. Dark Force Rising, 3. The Last Command.* This trilogy continues the adventures of Luke, Leia and Han and represents the first Star Wars novels to be published in the wake of the movie phenomenon. And some fans still regard them as the best. Leia and Han are happily married and Leia is expecting Jedi twins. Luke has finally become a Jedi Knight, the first in a long time. But there is one surviving warlord who has taken command of the remnants of the Imperial Fleet. Grand Admiral Thrawn of the Empire is making plans to strike back, and when he does, the new Rebel Alliance could fall.

The Jedi Academy Trilogy by Kevin J. Anderson: *1. Jedi Search, 2. Dark Apprentice, 3. Champions of the Force.* Princess Leia's Jedi twins have been born and will play an important role in the ongoing battle between the scattered remnants of the Empire and the representatives of the New Republic. Focal point of the battle this time is Luke Skywalker's Jedi Academy and the talented young students who are being tempted by the forces of the Dark Side.

I, Jedi by Michael Stackpole. Corran Horn is the fighter pilot hero of Stackpole's X-wing novels. Here the battle against the Dark Side becomes close and personal after his wife disappears on a mission for the New Republic. Corran has inherited some latent powers over the Force from his grandfather, a legendary Jedi hero. But to learn how to use this power, he enrolls in Luke's Jedi Academy, the first step on a path that will eventually offer him the choice of his wife or his life, unless he chooses to surrender to the Dark Side.

Children of the Jedi by Barbara Hambly. An ex-smuggler's attack on Han Solo during a state visit sends Leia and Han on a quest to find the long-lost Children of the Jedi on the planet of Belsavis. At the same time, Luke struggles to deactivate an ancient Imperial Dreadnaught, whose artificial guidance system has set it on a deadly path towards the same planet.

Darksaber by Kevin J. Anderson. The Darksaber is a new planet-crushing device like the destroyed Death Star. Unfortunately, it has fallen into the hands of Durga the Hutt, criminal warlord on the planet Tatooine. Fortunately, Luke and Han are on the same planet.

Planet of Twilight by Barbara Hambly. Leia is now the New Republic's leader, and her life is in danger. Kidnapped by a sinister warlord on the barren backwater world of Nam Chorios, she has to rely on her own wits and developing Jedi powers to escape and be ready to continue the battle when her friends come for her.

X-Wing Series: 9. Starfighters of Adumar by Aaron Allston. General Wedge Antilles and his X-wing force are sent to the planet Adumar to represent the New Republic in a competition for that planet's support in the ongoing struggle against the Empire. But warriors, assassins, and a rogue Republic agent turn this diplomatic mission into a struggle to survive.

The Crystal Star by Vonda N. McIntyre. Leia's three children, Anakin and the twins Jaina and Jacen, are kidnapped. Accompanied by Chewbacca and R2-D2, she sets out to find them, a quest that leads her to an outpost of enslaved children, while Han, Luke, and C3PO encounter a crystal star near a black hole that puts them all in danger.

The Black Fleet Crisis Trilogy by Michael P. Kube-McDowell; *1. Before the Storm, 2. Shield of Lies, 3. Tyrant's Test.* At last the Empire has been destroyed and peace and prosperity have come to the New Republic on Coruscant, but not for long. Luke goes off to his mother's home world to find her people. Lando encounters a spacecraft with weapons of incredible power. And Leia faces the threat of a genocidal war at the hands of a ruthless new leader.

The New Rebellion by Kristine Kathryn Rusch. It's election time in the New Republic, and some of the candidates are former imperial officials. When a bomb injures Leia and leaves the imperials in charge of the senate, Han, Chewbacca, and Lando investigate and uncover a massive plot against the New Republic. At the same time Luke encounters a Jedi opponent who is in service to a would-be Emperor. Billions will die if this plot succeeds.

The Corellian Trilogy by Roger MacBride Allen: *1. Ambush at Corellia, 2. Assault at Selonia, 3. Showdown at Centerpoint.* When Han Solo arrives on the planet Corellia with Leia, their children, and Chewbacca for a trade summit, he finds a planet on the brink of civil WAR. Even worse, there is an incredibly powerful weapon that can destroy suns if it falls into the wrong hands.

The Hand of Thrawn Duology by Timothy Zahn: *1. Specter of the Past, 2. Vision of the Future.* Grand Admiral Thrawn was killed ten years ago. But now he's back, sending pirate ships staffed by clones to attack the New Republic. It's up to Han, Leia and Luke to stop him—again.

Junior Jedi Knights. Star Wars adventures, written for young readers, about the exploits of young Anakin, who gets his Jedi training at Uncle Luke's Academy: *1. The Golden Globe* by Nancy Richardson, *2. Lyric's World* by Nancy Richardson, *3. Promises* by Nancy Richardson and Rebecca Moesta, *4. Anakin's Quest* by Rebecca Moesta, *5. Vader's Fortress* by Rebecca Moesta, *6. Kenobi's Blade* by Rebecca Moesta.

Young Jedi Knights by Kevin J. Anderson and Rebecca Moesta. The adventures of Han and Leia's twins, fourteen-year-old Jaina and Jacen, as their studies at Uncle Luke's Jedi Academy bring them into battle against the forces of the Dark Side *1. Heirs of the Force, 2. Shadow Academy, 3. The Lost Ones, 4. Lightsabers, 5. The Darkest Knight, 6. Jedi under Siege, 7. Shards of Alderaan, 8. Diversity Alliance, 9. Delusions of Grandeur, 10. Jedi Bounty, 11. The Emperor's Plague, 12. Return to Ord Mantell, 13. Trouble on Cloud City, 14. Crisis at Crystal Reef.*

The New Jedi Order. The Jedi may have met their match in the new race of warriors that appears to challenge them. Not only are the Yuuzhan Vong incredibly strong, but they also use highly advanced organic devices, vehicles, and technology. It will be a long and dangerous struggle for the fate of the New Republic on the part of Han, Luke, Leia, their friends and children. The series includes: *1. Vector Prime* by R. A. Salvatore, *2. Dark Tide 1: Onslaught* by Michael A. Stackpole, *3. Dark Tide II: Ruin* by Michael A. Stackpole, *4. Agents of Chaol I: Hero's Trial* by James Luceno, *5. Agents of Chaos II: Jedi Eclipse* by James Luceno, *6. Balance Point* by Kathy Tyers, *7. Edge of Victory I: Conquest* by Greg Keyes, *8. Edge of Victory II: Rebirth* by Greg Keyes, *9. Star by Star* by Troy Denning, *10. Dark Journey* by Elaine Cun-

ningham, *11. Enemy Lines I: Rebel Dream* by Aaron Allston, *12. Enemy Lines II: Rebel Stand* by Aaron Allston.

So there you have it. Star Wars for the young. Star Wars for the old. Star Wars for all ages in between. The books enrich the world created by the movies. The movies stimulate and inspire the authors who are expanding the Star Wars universe in all directions in the books. Star Wars is alive and well and going strong. And I for one am absolutely delighted to see so many talented authors turning their attention to this movie creation in all its various aspects. For fans of SCIENCE FICTION, space opera, FANTASY, ROMANCE, military battles, aliens, robots, martial arts, biotechnology, et al., the Star Wars opus is the perfect choice for books that will take you away from your own life and into the worlds of a galaxy far, far away. Long may they endure and long may we have the opportunity to enjoy them.

BONNIE L. KUNZEL

STEIG, William

Author, illustrator, b. 1907, Brooklyn, New York; d. 2003, n.p.

The name S. brings immediate association with distinctive *New Yorker* covers, wry cartoons on the human condition, and award-winning PICTURE BOOK illustrations. But only to associate S. with his artwork is to sell the man short. S. proved himself to be a fine writer as well, evidenced by his novels *Dominic* (1972) and *Abel's Island* (1976) and the texts of his picture books, which offer a complexity rarely found in children's literature. It is this aspect that heightens the appeal of S.'s work in YA reading circles.

In writing about S.'s work shortly after the author/artist's death, Roger Angell commented on S.'s versatility in *The New Yorker*: "[S.'s] celebrated and beloved children's books, some aimed at the very young but most, or perhaps all of them (including some vigorous, straightforward novels for young TEENS), apparently intended to satisfy or explore the childlike spirit that he held onto so firmly." In the catalog for the S. exhibition at the Eric Carle Museum of Picture Book Art, Jane Bayard Curley also notes S.'s appeal to older readers with this observation: "In *Abel's Island* S. amused himself—and his adult audience—by naming his characters after the Impressionist Childe Hassam, the Surrealist Giorgio de Chirico, the English watercolorist Sir William Russell Flint, the Elizabethan court painter George Gower, and the Ashcan school painter William Glackens."

Interestingly, S. didn't begin writing until late in life. He was born in 1907 in the Bronx where early memories of street gas lights, neighbors exchanging gossip on front stoops, and kids harmlessly playing in the streets would surface in his later works. His parents, housepainter and seamstress, dabbled in the arts, and S. spoke of other influences from the Grimms' FAIRY TALES, Charlie Chaplin MOVIES, Humperdinck's opera *Hansel and Gretel,* and the Katzenjammer Kids comic strips.

Following high school and two years at The City College of New York, S. attended the National Academy of Design. At the time, his ambition was to be a beachcomber or go to sea like Herman Melville, but the Depression put him to work.

Drawing came naturally and at age twenty-three, S. began peddling his cartoons, eventually selling them to *The New Yorker,* where he gained a reputation of being one of the MAGAZINE's most popular cartoonists. His New York tenement background became fertile ground for his drawings, where FAMILY relationships and exchanges between blue-collar people provided a platform for his witty and sometimes caustic humor. S. was prolific: according to *New Yorker* essayist Roger Angell, S. had, at his death, produced 121 *New Yorker* covers and more than 1,700 drawings, some still awaiting publication.

In the 1960s, Robert Kraus, a *New Yorker* colleague, suggested to S. that he create a book for children; *Roland the Minstrel Pig* (1968) was the result. In this droll story, an innocent pig seeking fame and fortune in the wide world is nearly undone by a crafty fox until a kindly lion intervenes. From the beginning, S.'s lively storytelling captured readers, and soon his ever-increasing audience quickly discovered the thought-provoking themes subtly implanted in the stories. The theme of the world as a place filled with both wonder and evil, introduced in Roland, appears again and again, while Roland the character, whose curiosity about the world leads to better understanding of himself, became a prototype for several later portrayals.

The use of magical and transformational elements appears frequently in the author's writings, wrapped in various guises. *Sylvester and the Magic Pebble* (1969), for example, revolves around the rescue of the donkey Sylvester, an innocent protagonist, who is inadvertently turned into a rock; transformation back to his donkey self comes through good fortune and circumstance. The argumentative Caleb, in *Caleb and Kate* (1977), suffers the indignity of being metamorphosed into a dog; only after he defends his wife from would-be robbers is he returned to his human self. Magic is again a force in *Gorky Rises* (1980); the frog Gorky concocts a potion giving him the gift of flight, but is eventually and happily returned to solid ground. In *The Amazing Bone* (1976), the pig Pearl, dallying in the joy of springtime, astonishingly finds a talking bone, which comes to her rescue when she is accosted by a fox looking for supper. Transformation of all kinds, physical and emotional, underlines S.'s tales, and, combined with his gift for experiencing life through the eyes of a child, provides inspired and delightfully witty books.

Nowhere, however, does transformation play a larger role than in S.'s longest novel *Abel's Island* (1976). In this story, a mouse named Abel finds his secure life turned upside down when he is swept away in a hurricane and left marooned on an island. Separated from his beloved wife Amanda, he is forced to use his ingenuity to endure the privations of life on a deserted island and to reexamine his former easy way of life. In doing so, Abel re-creates himself, becoming survivor, philosopher, artist, and most of all a better mouse.

Two other favorite S. books are *Dr. DeSoto* (1982) and *Brave Irene* (1986). More realistically oriented, though *Dr. DeSoto* does feature talking animals, they too carry the theme of personal evolution. Dr. DeSoto, a dentist, and his assistant wife, are mice; their courage is challenged when a fox with a bad toothache begs for their services. In *Brave Irene* a young girl struggles through a blizzard to carry out her mother's wishes, finding rewards for her perseverance at the story's end.

Conclusions of S.'s tales are not only invariably happy but are presented in endearing and uplifting ways: Abel returns home to find his wife eagerly awaiting him; Pearl and the bone exchange happy songs at bedtime; Sylvester's family put the rock away for safekeeping and revel in his being a donkey again; and Gorky's family celebrates his return with a party.

A penchant for wordplay, rich, rhythmic use of language, and tongue-in-cheek naming of characters draws readers into the author's humorous, sophisticated view of the world. In *Abel's Island,* for example, S.'s urbane voice describes Abel: "The stubbornness of his character stood him now in good stead," and, later in misery: "rain caused one to reflect on the shadowed, more poignant parts of life—the inescapable sorrows, the speechless longings, the disappointments, the regrets, and cold miseries." Abel speaks of being in love "snout over claws" and describes an owl as a "sentinel of hell" and a "dealer of death."

Character names are sly but witty: In *Dominic,* for example, S. names a goose "Matilda Fox" and a mouse "Manfred Lyon." Ever mindful of the child reader, he includes the kind of weird language sounds that youngsters love, describing the thunder in *Farmer Palmer's Wagon Ride* (1974) as "dramberemboroomed bamBOMBED," but he also uses soulful phrases as in *The Amazing Bone,* "the warm air touched her so tenderly that she could almost feel herself changing into a flower."

S.'s prose, like his illustrations, are low-key, brisk, engaging, playful, skillful, only a few of the accolades that could be used to describe his books. They are, however, the reasons why S. will continue to be read by the young and the not so young for generations to come.

AWARDS: 1970 *Boston Globe–Horn Book* Honor Book and Caldecott Medal for *Sylvester and the Magic Pebble;* 1971 *New York Times* Outstanding Book of the Year for *Amos and Boris;* 1975 National Book Award Finalist for *Dominic;* 1977 Newbery Honor Book and *Boston Globe–Horn Book* Honor for *Abel's Island;* 1977 *Boston Globe–Horn Book* Honor and Caldecott Honor for *The Amazing Bone;* 1980 *New York Times* Outstanding Book of the Year for *Gorky Rises;* 1982 United States nomination for illustration, Hans Christian Andersen Medal; 1983 American Book Award, *Boston Globe–Horn Book* Honor Book, Newbery Honor Book for *Doctor DeSoto;* 1985 *Redbook's* Children's Picture Book Award for *Solomon the Rusty Nail;* 1986 *New York Times* Best Illustrated Book for *Brave Irene;* 1988 United States nomination, Hans Christian Andersen Medal for writing; 1990 *School Library Journal* Best Book of the Year for *Shrek!*

FURTHER WORKS: *CDB!,* 1968; *Tiffky Doofky,* 1978; *Solomon the Rusty Nail,* 1979; *CDC?,* 1984; *Yellow & Pink* 1984; *Rotten Island,* 1984; *The Zabajaba Jungle* 1987; *Spinky Sulks,* 1988; *Consider the Lemmings* (with Jeanne S.), 1988; *Shrek!,* 1990; *Zeke Pippin,* 1994; *Grown-Ups Get to Do All the Driving,* 1995; *The Toy Brother,* 1996; *Pete's a Pizza,* 1998; *Made*

for Each Other, 2000; *Wizzil,* 2000; *When Everybody Wore a Hat,* 2003; *Yellow and Pink,* 2003.

BIBLIOGRAPHY: Angell, R. "Postscript William S." *The New Yorker,* October 20, 2003, 69–72; Cullinan, B. and Person, D. *The Continuum Encyclopedia of Children's Literature,* 2001; Curley, Jane Bayard. Catalog essay, *Heart and Humor: The Picture Books Art of William S.* (exhibited at the Eric Carle Museum of Picture Book Art, February 8, 2004–April 25, 2004); Lorenz, L. *The World of William S.,* 1998; Silvey, A. *Children's Books and Their Creators,* 1995.

BARBARA ELLEMAN

STEVERMER, Caroline J.
Author, b. 13 January 1955, Houston, Minnesota

S. was the daughter of a dairy farmer and a teacher, growing up on the banks of the Mississippi in Minnesota. After graduating from Bryn Mawr College in Pennsylvania with a B.A. in the history of art, S. "tried like hell to live in New York City but found I had no aptitude." She returned to Minnesota where she is an editorial assistant for the Minneapolis *Star Tribune.* Although S. recognizes the need to earn money in other ways, she keeps on writing.

S. has written novels in a variety of genres and for a variety of ages. Her first works, *The Alchemist: Death of a Borgia* (1980), *The Duke and the Veil* (1981), and *The Serpent's Egg* (1988), were MYSTERIES set in historical England. *The Serpent's Egg* includes a FANTASY element as well. Then, in 1988, S. published *Sorcery and Cecelia* with Patricia C. WREDE, a well-known YA author. *Sorcery and Cecelia* is the story of cousins who correspond from country and city, unraveling a mystery centered on a mysterious chocolate pot. Wrede and S. each wrote the letters from their characters without planning the plot as they went. The result is an exciting and entertaining romp in Regency England.

S. continued to publish for young adults, finding a home in the fantastic. *River Rats* (1992) is SCIENCE FICTION for TEENS, a post–Apocalyptic story of teenagers running the Mississippi in a river boat. In her books *A College of Magics* (1994) and *When the King Comes Home* (2000), S. returns to her historical roots, including ROMANTIC and fantastic elements as well. Both are tales of discovery by young women who find they wield magical powers that bring extra responsibility as well. The books were each praised for their humor by reviewers.

AWARDS: 1995 Fantasy and Science Fiction, Minnesota Book Awards for *A College of Magics;* 2004 ALA Best Books for Young Adults for *Sorcery and Cecelia; River Rats:* ALA Best Books for Young Adults, 1993.

BIBLIOGRAPHY: *St. James Guide to Fantasy Writers,* 1996; *Contemporary Authors Online,* 2002; *Sorcery and Cecelia,* author's note, 1988.

JENNA OBEE

STOEHR, Shelley

Author, dancer, teacher, choreographer, b. 31 January 1969, Sellersville, Pennsylvania

S. creates gritty contemporary novels that speak to issues not usually addressed in fiction today. In her first novel, *Crosses* (1991) she deals with the subject of cutting oneself and mental illness. In her second novel, *Weird on the Outside* (1995), her main character leaves her divorcing parents to become a stripper in New York City. In her fourth book, *Tomorrow Wendy: A Love Story,* she approaches the subject of TEENAGE lesbianism with accuracy and realism.

S.'s main characters are complex and her use of language is explicit but effective. S. successfully creates a realistic atmosphere characterized by the use of drugs, explicit sex, and the emotional upheaval of adolescence. These works are difficult to call a "good read," but the author feels she is being honest in her writing; her themes of independence and growth through strife are well established.

AWARDS: 1990 Delacorte Press Prize for Best First Young Adult Novel Honor Book citation, and ALA Best Book for Young Adults, 1993, *Crosses.*

FURTHER WORKS: *Wannabe,* 1997.

BIBLIOGRAPHY: *Contemporary Authors Online,* 2001.

LAURIE M. ALLEN

STOLL, Cliff(ord)

Author, b. 4 June 1950, Buffalo, New York

S., a self-proclaimed skeptic, states that his skepticism of computers grew out of his love for technology. In 1980, S. received a Ph.D. in planetary science from the University of Arizona after presenting his dissertation, "Politarization of Jupiter at Large Phase Angles." Since then, S. has worked at space observatories in China, Hawaii, and the renowned Harvard-Smithsonian Center for Astrophysics. Particularly noteworthy is the fact that S. developed the world's leading software for a system that monitors asteroids near the earth's atmosphere. S.'s major claim to fame was catching a KGB spy after noticing a $0.75 computer accounting error in the mid-1980s. He later published an account of his ADVENTURES in solving this MYSTERY in *The Cuckoo's Egg: Tracking a Spy Through the Maze of Computer Espionage* (1990). This nonfiction best seller also had considerable TEEN appeal, which earned it a place on the ALA Best Books for Young Adults list in 1991. Despite S.'s academic prestige, his readers criticize him for exaggerating the worst aspects of technology and for basing his theories solely on personal opinion without incorporating supporting evidence or additional research. Regardless, his fans, which include Bill Gates, find S. to be an entertaining and thought-provoking author. S. has lectured for the CIA, the FBI, the U.S. Senate, and the House of Representatives on technological issues; he also appeared as a guest lecturer on MSNBC for several years. S. is currently a stay-at-home father and in his spare time runs his own company, Acme Klein Bottles, out of Oakland, California. Known for his large glasses, wild hair, and perpetual smile, S. is a distinct scholar and lecturer with a penchant for homemade chocolate chip cookies and an aversion to television. Still an active astrophysicist, S. continues to publish works on a regular basis, one of his latest being *Modeling Histories of Chrondrites* (1998).

A major theme in several of his works is the paradigm of data versus information and the question of how we extract knowledge from our educational system without overloading our youth with technology. *High-Tech Heretic: Why Computers Don't Belong in the Classroom and Other Reflections by a Computer Contrarian* (1999) is based upon this premise. S. quotes, "human kindness, warmth, interaction, friendship and FAMILY are far more important than anything that can come across my cathode-ray tube." Perhaps in his pursuit of truth, S. has realized that technology accelerates our lives, particularly that of our children's, who are faced with what S. likes to call "edutainment" rather than education in the public school system, an observation that transcends beyond knowledge into wisdom.

AWARDS: ALA Best Book for Young Adults: 1991 for *The Cuckoo's Egg: Tracking a Spy Through the Maze of Computer Espionage.*

FURTHER WORKS: *The KGB, the Computer and Me,* 1990; *Silicon Snake Oil: Second Thoughts on the Information Highway,* 1995.

BIBLIOGRAPHY: Cliff S. Homepage, http://www.ocf .berkeley.edu/~stoll/; "A Skeptical View of Computing," http://www.stanford.edu/class/ee380/9697fall/ node1.html; *Parker, Jeffrey.* "Editor's Comments on: High Tech Heretic," http://www.technology-teaching-research-humanities.com/high%20tech%20heretic.htm

ILONA N. KOTI

STOLZ, Mary
Author, b. 24 March 1920, Boston, Massachusetts

S., who was born in Boston, is the daughter of Thomas and Mary Slattery. Because of problems related to her father's alcoholism, S. and her sister spent considerable time with her maternal aunt and uncle in New York City. It was through them that S. developed her love of reading and fascination with the written word. S.'s ability was recognized and encouraged at the Birch Wathen School. After graduating from high school, she attended Columbia University/Teacher's College for a brief period and then a business/secretarial school. S. married in 1940 and motherhood soon followed.

S.'s writing career began in a most unusual way. While she was still in her twenties, she became quite ill with an unspecified ailment. After surgery failed to alleviate her discomfort, S. had a consultation with Dr. Thomas C. Jolenski, who recommended that she engage in some activity that would occupy her mind while she was recuperating. The result was her first novel, *To Tell Your Love,* which was published in 1950. (It should also be noted that S. married Dr. Jolenski.) The book was well received by critics, who commended S. for the realistic, respectful, and positive way she portrayed and presented her protagonists. She draws upon her memories, experiences, and recollections in her writings and is able to create her characters by drawing upon people she has known, as well as those she has imagined and/or dreamt about. Other titles that followed include *The Organdy Cupcakes; Ready or Not; Wait for Me, Michael; Leap before You Leap;* and *Ivy Larkin: A Novel.*

More of S.'s books are written for the YOUNG ADULT audience and are considered to be of high quality; however, in recent years, her books have been subject to criticism. In part, this is because some of the issues that TEEN readers face today are not always reflected in her books. S. herself is cognizant of this limitation. However, she also states, "You can't write about what you don't know" (Guica). She has also written for a younger audience with titles such as *The Bully of Barkham Street* and *The Noonday Friends.*

In recent years, S. has devoted considerable time to writing stories with characters and topics that interest AFRICAN-AMERICAN children. It is her contention that there is a shortage of appropriate materials written for this particular audience.

S. and her husband reside in Florida, where she is active in numerous social and environmental issues.

AWARDS: Junior Book Award, Boys' Club of America, 1964; Newbery Award Honor Book designation, 1965; Recognition of Merit Award, George G. Stone Center for Children's Books (for entire body of work), 1982; *Cezanne Pinto:* ALA Best Books for Young Adults, 1995. Additionally Mary S. has received numerous ALA Notable Book citations.

BIBLIOGRAPHY: Bryfonski, Dedria, ed. *Contemporary Literary Criticism,* vol. 12, *Young Adult Literature,* 1980; Collier, Laurie, ed. *Authors and Artists for Young Adults,* vol. 8, 1992, http://galenet.galegroup .com.

ALICE R. LEONE

STRASSER, Todd
Author, b. 5 May 1950, New York City

It took S. six years to write and publish his first novel for YAS, *Angel Dust Blues* (1979); he has written over one hundred novels and novelizations since. With characters that TEENS can readily relate to and issues that are core to adolescence, S.'s books continue to be popular reads for today's youth. Whether S. writes about using drugs in *Angel Dust Blues,* learning a friend has leukemia in *Friends till the End* (1981), being in a rock 'n' roll band in *Rock 'n' Roll Nights* (1982), or capturing the teen emotions of sex in *How I Spent My Last Night on Earth* (1998), S. is able to capture the true angst, joy, and humor teens experience while going through those trying adolescent years. There is also a decided shift in his books: although adolescent issues today are similar to years past, the issues seem more extreme or acute today.

In a more recent novel, *Give a Boy a Gun* (2000), S. bravely looks at the issue of gun violence in schools. The story is told in the second person as the characters try to come to terms with what went wrong with Gary and Brendan after they held their school hostage with semi-automatic weapons and pipe bombs. Although this is ripped-from-the headlines fiction, S. presents serious issues that beg to be examined in today's society: gun control, media influence, FAMILY structure, social rejection, SPORTS culture, school cliques, little adult supervision, and violence. This is not a book that one can just put down, but that will elicit talk, and perhaps some positive actions.

Give a Boy a Gun includes factual quotes throughout the narrative or footnotes at the bottom of the page. These drive home the hard, cold facts about the impact of guns on society and its youth.

CON-fidence (2002) also tackles the pressures of the social structures of school life. Lauren is a girl who desperately wants to be a member of the in-crowd. Celeste is a new girl who is instantly among the school's popular group. When she convinces Lauren to become class co-treasurers, Lauren is elated. However, when money is missing from the class account, Lauren must look within and draw on her own self-confidence to get through the situation. It is an enjoyable read on popularity, peer pressure, true friendship, truth, loyalty, and being true to one's values.

S. has connected with the teen mindset for over twenty years; hopefully, he will continue to do so for another twenty or more.

AWARDS: Best Books for Young Adults citations: *Friends till the End: A Novel* 1981, *Rock 'n' Roll Nights: A Novel* 1982; New York Public Library's Books for the Teen Age citations: *Angel Dust Blues* 1981, *The Wave* 1982, *Friends till the End: A Novel* (1982), *Rock 'n' Roll Nights: A Novel,* 1983, *Workin' for Peanuts,* 1984, *How I Changed My Life,* 1996; Edgar Allan Poe nominee, *The Accident,* 1988; New York State Library Association Award for Outstanding Children's Literature, 1995; American Library Association Notable Book, *Hey, Dad, Get a Life!,* 1997; BBTA, 1982 for *Rock 'n' Roll Nights.*

FURTHER WORKS: *Turn It Up!,* 1984; *The Complete Computer Popularity Program,* 1984; *A Very Touchy Subject,* 1985; *Wildlife,* 1987; *The Mall from Outer Space,* 1987; *The Accident,* 1988; *Beyond the Reef,* 1991; *The Diving Bell,* 1992; *Freaked,* 1993; *The Good Son,* 1993; *Hocus Pocus,* 1993; *How I Changed My Life,* 1995; *Thief of Dreams,* 2003; *Can't Get There from Here,* 2004; and several novelizations based on films.

BIBLIOGRAPHY: *Contemporary Authors New Revision Series,* vol. 47; *Something about the Author,* vol. 107;

Writers for Young Adults, vol. 3, 1997; *Best Books for Young Adults,* 2000; Sanner, Devon Clancy. "Give a Boy a Gun." *Journal of Adolescent and Adult Literacy,* March 2002.

TINA HERTEL

STRATEMEYER, Edward

Author, founder, of writing syndicate, b. 1861, Elizabeth, New Jersey; d. 1930, Newark, New Jersey

S created a plethora of the best-selling books for children ages eight to twelve; most young adult readers read them as they passed through that stage or as they later searched for easy reading material. S. became interested in writing and was aware of the success of the Horatio Alger SERIES, the Elsie Dinsmore series, and stories by G. A. Henty, a participant in major British historical events. Henty had developed a formula using a fifteen or sixteen-year-old boy who was physically fit, good hearted, and hot-headed. S. expanded Henty's formula and style; he wrote *Under Dewey at Manila* shortly after the Spanish-American War. The book sold well; S. enjoyed writing WAR stories, so he wrote several other books using American wars as the background. Sales for the American war stories increased and S. became an entrepreneur; he not only wrote fast-moving ADVENTURE stories himself, he also hired a team of writers to help write them. The S. Syndicate was established. S. would outline a plot, develop the character, and turn the draft over to one of his hired (hack) writers to complete. S. realized that books sold best if they were in a series; he published series. He also decided that the writer should use a pseudonym; no matter if the writer died, someone else could continue to use the same pseudonym. S. wanted the books to look as much like contemporary adult novels as possible; he used similar bindings and typefaces. He wanted the books to be a predictable length and to have the chapters end in the midst of a highly tense situation; that would increase the readers desire to turn the pages and continue reading. The series guaranteed that there was another book about the same characters or the situation. This formula worked.

The first series of books produced by the S. Syndicate was the Rover Boys written under the pseudonym Arthur M. Winfield. The Rover Boys appeared in thirty volumes written between 1899 and 1926. The next series was The Bobbsey Twins; it grew to seventy-two volumes beginning in 1904 and continuing until 1979. Legend says that S. himself wrote the first three books and then hired ghostwriters to write the remaining books, often from outlines he prepared. Newer information and analysis of the writing style suggests that he probably wrote only the first book (James Keeline at Keeline.com).

Tom Swift, and later a Tom Swift, Jr. series (attributed to Victor Appleton and Victor Appleton II) began in 1910; there were forty volumes when the series ended in 1941. The Hardy Boys attributed to Franklin W. Dixon produced eighty-five volumes from 1927 to 1985.

The S. Syndicate published the Colonial Boys series, the Mexican War series, and the Pan American series. S. and his syndicate developed other series, such as the Rover Boys, the Motor Boys, Tom Swift, the Hardy Boys (1927), ghostwritten by Leslie McFarlane, and the Bobbsey Twins (1904). The writers used the pseudonyms Arthur M. Winfield, Clarence Young, Victor Appleton, Franklin W. Dixon, and Laura Lee Hope.

After S. died in 1930, his daughter Harriet Stratemeyer Adams took over the massive operation that still produces books including the Nancy Drew series (1930) ghostwritten by Mildred Wirt Benson under the pseudonym Carolyn Keene. James Keeline says that vols. 4–28 of the Bobbsey Twins appear to be the work of Howard R. Garis, a close friend of S. and one of the syndicate's most prolific writers. Keeline also says that Garis wrote some, if not all, of the other series. Garis stopped writing for the syndicate around 1922/23 when he had several disagreements with Harriet S. Adams and her sister Edna C. S. who were running the syndicate. Each had their own ideas about who would be the controlling creative force for the syndicate. Edna showed little interest in the syndicate and sold her share to Harriet within a few years. Harriet took over the task and introduced other series such as the Dana Girls (1934) and Judy Bolton (1932). Over the years Harriet introduced the Happy Hollisters, Trixie Belden, Cherry Ames, and Vicky Barr. In the 1950s, Harriet began revising the old volumes in the Nancy Drew and Hardy Boys series to get rid of antiquated words (roadster) and to remove racial slurs and stereotypes.

In the 1980s Harriet S. Adams decided that Nancy Drew and the Hardy Boys should be published in PAPERBACK. Grosset & Dunlap did not want to lose the massive profits they had enjoyed and sued to retain control. The case let the world know that the syndicate existed. The syndicate had always insisted on privacy and the ghostwriters were contractually obligated to keep their authorship secret. Harriet S. Adams died at age eighty-nine in 1982; her protege, Nancy Axelrod, supervised the series until it was published under the editorial direction of Simon and Schuster. When Walter Karig, a well-known novelist, made sure that his name appeared on the Library of Congress cards for the various Nancy Drew books he had written, the cards disappeared. Grosset & Dunlap lost the suit. Simon & Schuster purchased the syndicate from Nancy Axelrod, Adams's protégé. The syndicate functions today much as it always has.

BIBLIOGRAPHY: Billman, Carol. *The Secret of the S. Syndicate: Nancy Drew, the Hardy Boys, and the Million Dollar Fiction Factory;* Cullinan, Bernice E. (2003) "Edward S." The Continuum Encyclopedia of Children's Literature, 2003; Galda, Lee, and Cullinan, Bernice E. "The History of Children's Literature." *Literature and the Child,* 5th ed., 2002; Keeline, James D., james@keeline.com; Nash, llana, and Farah, David. *Series Books and the Media: Or This Isn't All,* 1996.

BERNICE E. CULLINAN

STRATTON, Allan
Author, playwright, actor, b. 5 March 1951, Stratford, Ontario, Canada

S. was already an actor and award-winning playwright before entering the realm of YOUNG ADULT authors with the publication of *Leslie's Journal* (2000). After studying at Neuchatel Jr. College in Switzerland, he returned to Canada, where he earned both his B.A., 1973, and his M.A., 1974, at the University of Toronto. He spent the next few years acting, and published his first PLAY, *72 Under the O,* in 1977. After the success of *Nurse Jane Goes to Hawaii* (1980), S. devoted more time to writing plays. *Rexy!* (1981) won the Chalmers Award and the Dora Mavor Moore Award, both for best CANADIAN play. *Rexy!* also won the 1982 Canadian Authors' Association Award for best play. In 1995, his play *Papers* won the Chalmers Award for outstanding new play.

The American Library Association named *Leslie's Journal* one of the Best Books for Young Adults in 2002. It made the Our Choice 2001 list, Canadian Children's Book Center. In *Leslie's Journal,* S. takes the challenge of writing from the perspective of a tenth-grade girl. In her journal, she describes the progress of a manipulative, increasingly abusive relationship with the new boy in school. He is handsome, wealthy, and easily charms Leslie's mother, who is then lost as an ally. S. perfectly captures the adolescent feeling of being doomed and isolated in Leslie's language. Even when adults try to intervene, the end result does not help Leslie.

His first novel, *The Phoenix Lottery* (2000) won a Stephen Leacock Award of Merit and was staged as a play in 2001. The next young adult novel by S., *Chanda's Secrets,* published in 2004, was named a MICHAEL L. PRINTZ AWARD Honor Book.

S. is still actively involved in the local theatre community in and around the Toronto area.

AWARDS: 2001 Stephen Leacock Award of Merit, *The Phoenix Lottery;* 1985 Chalmer Award, *Papers: Rexy!;* 1981 Dora Mavor Moore Award, 1981 Chalmers Award; 1981 Canadian Club Award, *Nurse Jane Goes to Hawaii;* 2005 Printz Honor Book, *Chandra's Secrets*; ALA Best Books for Young Adults: 2002 for *Leslie's Journal,* 2005 for *Chanda's Secret.*

FURTHER WORKS: *The Rusting Heart* (a radio play), 1968; *Joggers,* 1982; *Friends of a Feather,* 1984; *The 101 Miracles of Hope Chance,* 1987; *Bingo!,* 1987; *A Flush of Tories,* 1990; *Bag Babies,* 1990; *Dracula: Nightmare of the Damned,* 1995.

BIBLIOGRAPHY: Encyclopedia of Canadian Theatre online, http://www.canadiantheatre.com/dict.pl?term =Stratton%2C%Allan; Authors and Illustrators, http://www.annickpress.com/ai/stratton.html; Author's homepage: http://www.allanstratton.com; http://www .playwrightsguild.ca/cgi-bin/puc/catalogue.cgi?function =detail&Authors_uid=322

CARA J. RANDALL

STRICKLAND, Dorothy S.
Educator, author, b. 29 September 1933, Newark, New Jersey

S. grew up in Union, New Jersey. She received her B.S. from Kean University (formerly Newark State College) in 1955. She earned her M.A. in 1958 and her Ph.D from New York University in 1971.

S. became a teacher in the New Jersey public schools—she taught six years as a classroom teacher and five years as a reading consultant and learning DISABILITY specialist. She joined the faculty at Rutgers University in 1990. S. is the Samuel DeWitt Proctor Professor of Education at Rutgers University. Formerly she was the Arthur I. Gates Professor at Teachers College, Columbia University and served on the faculties of Kean University and Jersey City State College.

S. is a past president of both the International Reading Association and the Reading Hall of Fame. She has held several positions in the National Council of Teachers of English and is an active member of the National Association for the Education of Young Children. She was a member of the panel that produced *Becoming a Nation of Readers* (1985) as well as the panel that developed *Preventing Reading Difficulties in Young Children* (1988). S. has been featured on national videotape series on literacy learning.

S. has published more than one hundred articles in major educational journals. A selection of books she has written, co-authored, and edited include: *Learning about Print in Preschool Settings* (2004); *Improving Reading Achievement through Professional Development* (2004), *Language Arts: Learning and Teaching* (2004), *The Administration and Supervision of Reading Programs,* 3rd ed. (2002), *Supporting Struggling Readers and Writers Grades* 3–6 (2002), *Families: Poems Celebrating the* AFRICAN AMERICAN *Experience* (1994), *Emerging Literacy and Language Literacy* (1989), *Listen Children: An Anthology of Black Literature* (1982). S. has worked with YOUNG ADULT LITERATURE and young adult learners. Most recently, she and Donna Alvermann edited *Bridging the Literacy Achievement Gap,* Grades 4–12 (2004), which is excerpted in this volume.

AWARDS: International Reading Association Outstanding Teacher Educator of Reading, 1985; National Council of Teachers of English Outstanding Educator in Language Arts, 1998; Rewey Bell Inglis Outstanding Women in the Teaching of English; New York University Distinguished Alumnus, 1990; Kean University Outstanding Alumnus, 1990; Bank Street College Honorary Doctorate of Humane Letters, 1991.

BERNICE E. CULLINAN

STRIEBER, (Louis) Whitley
Author, b. 13 June, 1945, San Antonio, Texas

S., best known for his HORROR novels, is also the author of cautionary tales and nonfiction works about extraterrestrials. After graduating with a B.A. from the University of Texas in 1968, he moved to New

York and began a career in advertising that lasted until 1977.

S.'s first book *The Wolfen* (1978) is about urban werewolves living in the South Bronx. The idea first came to him after so-called coydogs in Central Park followed him; "coydogs" are wild half coyote and half dogs living relatively unseen in urban areas. Three years later *The Hunger* (1981) described alien vampires living in modern-day New York City. Interestingly, the word *vampire* is not found in *The Hunger*. Both novels were made into MOVIES in 1981 and 1983 respectively. In the 1980s, S. joined James Kunetka to write two cautionary tales, one of which is *Warday: and the Journal Onward* (1984).

On December 26, 1985, S. reported being abducted by aliens from another world. He describes his experience in the controversial nonfiction book *Communion* (1987). He has been questioned and ridiculed for publishing *Communion* as nonfiction. He maintains that he submitted to a polygraph test to prove that he, at least, believes his account. Since *Communion*, he continues to write horror and nonfiction works on otherworldly visitors. He is the leading voice on the subject of UFOs and the phenomenon of aliens among us. He has a weekly online radio show and journal on his website of "daily news on the edge," Dreamland. The editor is Anne Strieber, his wife of thirty-two years. The policy of *Dreamland* is "to present the credible edge in science, religion and culture. We want to inform you about the real unknown—the world of genuine scientific mysteries and possibilities that the general media ignores."

AWARDS: Olive Branch Award for Writers and Publishers for Nuclear Disarmament, 1986; World FANTASY Best SHORT STORY Nominee for "Pain" in the Anthology *Cutting Edge*, 1987; *Wolf of Shadows*: ALA Best Books for Young Adults, 1985.

FURTHER WORKS: Novels: *Black Magic,* 1982; *The Night Church,* 1983; *Wolf of Shadows,* 1986; *Nature's End: The Consequences of the Twentieth Century* (with Kunetka), 1986; *Catmagic,* 1987; *Majestic,* 1990; *The Wild,* 1991; *Billy,* 1991; *Unholy Fire,* 1992; *The Forbidden Zone,* 1993; *Evenings with Demons,* 1997; *Nightman,* 1999; *The Last Vampire,* 2001; *Lilith's Dream: a Tale of the Vampire Life,* 2002. Nonfiction: *Transformation: The Breakthrough,* 1988; *Breakthrough: The Next Step,* 1995; *The Communion Letters* (with Anne Strieber), 1997; *The Secret School: Preparation for Contact,* 1997; *Confirmation: the Hard Evidence of Aliens among Us,* 1998; *Whitley Strieber's Aliens,* 1999; *The Coming Global Superstorm* (with Art Bell), 1999 (AUDIO), 2000 (print); *Casebook: Alien Implants,* 2000; *Dark Object: The World's Only Government Documented UFO Crash,* 2001; *The Path,* 2002.

BIBLIOGRAPHY: *Contemporary Authors, New Revision Series,* vol. 81, 1999, 405–9; McCarty, Michael. "Whitley S. Communes with Aliens, Werewolves, and the Creative Muse." *Science Fiction Weekly,* April 14, 2003, SciFi.com; S., Anne, and Whitley. *Unknown Country,* http://www.unknowncountry.com

SUSY MOORHEAD

SULLIVAN, Charles

Editor, educator, b. 1933, Boston, Massachusetts

S. has edited numerous anthologies that feature art and POETRY. Some of these focus on places (Ireland, America), concepts (as in *Loving: Poetry and Art,* 1992), or on people, as his celebrated *Children of Promise: AFRICAN-AMERICAN Literature and Art for Young People* (1991).

After attending Swarthmore College, S. achieved a Ph.D. in social psychology from New York University and an M.P.A. from the Pennsylvania State University. He has taught at numerous institutions and most recently served as the assistant dean of the Graduate School of Arts and Sciences at Georgetown University.

In *Children of Promise: African-American Literature and Art for Young People,* S. has collected a far-reaching and inspiring collection of works of art (*The Ride for Liberty—The Fugitive Slaves* by Eastman Johnson, 1862), literature (excerpts from *The Souls of Black Folk* by W. E. B. DuBois), and poetry ("To The Young Who Want to Die," Gwendolyn Brooks), to name merely a few. The collection relates the lives in art and artifact, song and poem of African-Americans. S. includes pertinent works of art and language to illustrate the history of African-Americans from the era of slavery through the CIVIL RIGHTS era and into the present. A reviewer from *Publishers Weekly* calls *Children of Promise* "a richly diverse and well-chosen introduction to African American culture" (1991).

S. remembers the era of slavery by including a public notice of an upcoming slave sale, excerpts from Frederick Douglass's writing, and folk songs. A photograph of *The Robert Gould Shaw Memorial* (1884–97) is included to commemorate the African-

Americans' role in the Civil War. Art with the theme of education ("Learning to Read" by Frances E. W. Harper) and work ("Southern Road" by Sterling A. Brown) indicate the struggle and injustice encountered by African-Americans trying to improve their lives. Numerous poems and an essay show the importance of Harlem as a cultural capital.

A penultimate sweep of photographs—from Jesse Owens in the Olympic Games (1936), through The March on Washington (1963), and Martin Luther King, Jr., in a Jefferson County Courthouse Jail Cell . . . (1967)—that decrescendos to a photograph of a girl with a microphone urging her friends to "Stop the Death of a Race," seems to reiterate the question, "Has hope [again] been deferred?"

A reviewer from *Ebony* says, "*Children of Promise* serves as an interesting educational tool for every member of the family" (1991). S.'s other anthologies for young people are educational and enlightening collections as well. Rudine Sims Bishop, writing for the *Horn Book* magazine, calls *Here Is My Kingdom: Hispanic-American Literature and Art for Young People* (1994) "[An] anthology that effectively combines visual and literary art to evoke a portrait of diversity under a common umbrella" (1995).

S.'s numerous anthologies for young people indicate his varied interests, but varied with a common thread of art, both visual and literary. In fact, as noted in "About the Author" in *Imaginary Gardens: American Poetry and Art for Young People* (1989), "He enjoys writing poetry on his houseboat, *Passages,* in the rivers of the Chesapeake Bay," a fitting pastime for an editor who has set scenes and people, images, and events to the tune of poetry.

AWARDS: *Children of Promise: African-American Literature and Art for Young People:* Best Books for YA, 1992, ALA-YALSA; ABC Children's Booksellers Choices Award Winner 1992 Collections; National Association of Parenting Publications Awards (NAPPA) Winner 1991. *Here Is My Kingdom: Hispanic-American Literature and Art for Young People:* Editors' Choice: Books for YA, 1994, ALA-*Booklist; Publishers Weekly* Book Review Stars, May 1994. *Imaginary Animals: Poetry and Art for Young People:* Best Book for YA, 1998, ALA.

FURTHER WORKS: *The Lover's Companion: Art and Poetry of Desire,* written with Dr. Ruth Westheimer, 2002; *American Folk: Classic Tales Retold,* 1988; *Ireland in Poetry,* 1995; *American Beauties: Women in Art and Literature,* 1993; *America in Poetry,* 1988.

BIBLIOGRAPHY: Bishop, R. S. "Review of *Here Is My Kingdom: Hispanic-American Literature and Art for Young People.*" *Horn Book* magazine 71, no. 315, 1995; "Review of *Children of Promise: African-American Literature and Art for Young People.*" *Ebony* 47, no. 18; "Review of *Children of Promise: African-American Literature and Art for Young People.*" *Publishers Weekly* 238 no. 49, 66; S. C., ed. *Imaginary Gardens: American Poetry and Art for Young People,* 1989.

MARY MCMILLAN TERRY

SUPERHEROES AND COMIC BOOKS OF THE 1960s

During and immediately after World War II, superheroes ruled the roost in the world of ADVENTURE comic books. With Jerry Siegel and Joe Shuster's Superman leading the way, the popular imagination was seized by the colorful FANTASY figures that flew through urban canyons and then across the ocean to hand humiliating setbacks to the Axis powers. That the superheroes were not real and had no actual ability to affect the outcome of the WAR was irrelevant. Apparently the morale-building and fantasy release they provided was significant enough.

Building on a tradition as old as Gilgamesh, Samson, Hercules, and Paul Bunyan, it seemed natural that superheroes came to dominate popular culture. When the pulp MAGAZINE began to decline, comic books came along to keep the publishers and printers in business. And in a world without seamless special-effects MOVIES and the ubiquity of cable television and video games, the hints of abilities above and beyond that of mortal men that superheroes displayed—and that readers' imaginations embellished—proved a winning recipe for commercial success.

Comic books were read by children, of course, but also by many adults, especially those serving in the armed forces, eager for a quick and nondemanding escape. The comics companies were all too happy to supply the GIs of World War Two with as many of the four-color magazines they could consume. And the Axis-fighting superheroes were the stalwarts that fought the same fight as the soldiers did, albeit in their own alternate fictional universe. The fact that if there really was a Superman the war would have ended in a week was never really a problem.

With the end of the war, comics retained their popularity, but the superhero fad proved to be just that.

Comics turned to other subject matter. Though it might seem hard to believe, given the ubiquitous nature of superheroes in today's popular culture, the superhero was fairly marginalized by the early 1950s. Superman, Batman, and Wonder Woman were appearing regularly in comic books, and the *Superman* television series was popular. But after an explosion of popularity in the 1940s, the superhero fad had pretty much receded.

There were still scores of comic books and television series, but there were other faddish concerns that ruled popular culture. The Western was supreme, and ROMANCES and jungle adventures were popular as were war stories and comedies of various sorts. Pop culture was not complex but it was varied. Moreover, while there had been several comic book-based movie serials and cartoons, most notably the Fleischer Studio's Superman cartoons of the early 1940s, there was no feature-length superhero-based film. The superhero was "kid's stuff," good for Saturday morning serials, but not for full-length treatment.

When superheroes faded, the genres that rose to the fore in comic books were HORROR and true crime, often indistinguishable from each other. Graphic-for-the-time depictions of violence and sexuality were the subject matter for many comics. The most artistically done were those produced by Entertaining Comics (EC). Publisher William M. Gaines and editor Al Feldstein both wrote many of the stories. They were aided and abetted by artists such as Jack Kamen, Bernard Krigstein, Graham Ingles, and Jack Davis. EC Comics set the standard for surprise endings, often with wittily gory punch lines and socially conscious messages. The comics were extremely popular and spawned a host of imitators that were neither as well done nor as concerned with social matters but were as—and often more—graphically violent.

Although there had always been suspicion of and even hostility toward comics from both well-intentioned and self-serving cultural gatekeepers, there had never been outright banning or policing of them. The major companies recruited experts of various types to be on advisory boards and that seemed to keep the most hostile critics at bay.

In the 1950s, legislators and social scientists looking for an explanation for the rise in what was called "juvenile delinquency" seized on the ubiquitous HORROR comic as one of its root causes. The most prominent voice in this assault on not just horror comics but on all comics was that of Dr. Frederic Wertham, a progressive psychiatrist who saw comics as a strong element in the forming of a delinquent personality, and, some say, as a convenient stepping-stone to advance his own career beyond the narrow world of psychiatry onto a more visible platform.

Whatever his and others' motivations, horror comics—and all comics not featuring adorable funny animals—were seen as too controversial for many distributors and retailers. Comics sales plummeted. Many comics companies went out of business or severely cut back on production. A code of acceptable content—administered by an industry-created Comics Code Authority—was adopted by most of the major publishers, with the notable exception of EC. Their entire line was considered too hot to handle by newsstands and drug stores. After trying to reinvent their line, with artistic success but low sales, EC ended up with one publication. That publication was *MAD* magazine, which essentially saved Gaines's operation.

However, the remaining comics were now restricted in what they could present, and sales were nowhere what they had been. There were romance comics, TEEN comics such as Archie, funny-animal comics, kid fantasy comics such as Richie Rich and Casper. There were SCIENCE FICTION comics and monster comics (featuring very tame monsters, indeed). But the only superheroes left were Superman, Batman, and Wonder Woman.

In 1956, DC attempted a revival of some of the superheroes it had been so successful with in the genre's heyday of the 1940s. If horror and true crime were to be avoided, maybe the straight-ahead adventures of costumed heroes would prove popular. The popularity of the Superman SERIES indicated this might be true.

Under the guidance of editor Julius Schwartz, DC published revamped versions of two of their popular heroes of the 1940s—The Flash and Green Lantern—and found there was indeed great interest in costumed superheroes again. Before long, Flash and Green Lantern had regular series, and Hawkman was reimagined for the new decade. So were Aquaman and The Atom. Before long, the publisher decided to team its most popular heroes in a single book called *Justice League of America*. A similar grouping—The Justice Society of America—had proven popular in the 1940s. The

JLA, as its readers knew it, proved successful. The superhero revival was in full swing.

This did not go unnoticed by DC's competitors, most notably Martin Goodman's Atlas Comics. Atlas was home to the popular Captain America, Human Torch, and Sub-Mariner comics in the 1940s. Goodman saw that the sales figures on Justice League were high and ordered his editor to come up with something that could compete with it.

His editor was a man named Stan LEE.

In response to his publisher's directive, Lee—not even forty-years old, but already a veteran of more than twenty years as an editor and writer—decided to take a gamble. Frustrated by the formulaic stories he was writing and editing for Atlas, Lee decided to try writing a comics series that would have more realism and depth than the typical superhero fare of the day. Most of the superhero stories of the time were plot driven. The plots were clever and often utilized real science, so they even had a somewhat educational aspect. Even when they did not, they were engrossing in the twists and turns of the stories, and though many of the twists and turns were ludicrous and skirted logic, the audience of mainly children accepted and enjoyed them. The characters, however, tended to be similar. Batman spoke—and thought—like Superman, The Flash and The Atom. Any personality traits could be described in a word: The Flash's alter ego, Barry Allan, was a slowpoke; Hal Jordan, who was secretly Green Lantern, was brave; Bruce Wayne (Batman) was wealthy.

Since Atlas—sometimes also known as Marvel Comics—had no current ongoing superheroes to team up, Lee came up with a comic called *The Fantastic Four* in response to the Justice League. With the artistic and creative collaboration of Jack Kirby—who had co-created Captain America among many other characters over the years—Lee delivered a comics series to Goodman unlike any ever seen before.

The Fantastic Four, in the course of its first few issues, was stylistically different from what comics had been. The series was character driven. The plots were simpler but the heroes and villains were deeper. Most notably, the group's Thing character was grotesque, a true monster, and though he had a heart of gold, it took some digging to get to. Becoming The Thing, despite the super-strength that went with it, led him to feel—and to truly be—alienated from other humans. He was ugly and angry about it.

In short order, Lee and his artistic partners—Kirby, Steve Ditko, Don Heck, among others—as well as his brother, Larry Lieber—created a roster of heroes who were, despite their powers and nobility, also fairly neurotic. The Mighty Thor, forever in oedipal conflict with his father Odin, couldn't bring himself to tell the woman who loved him that he was really the lame physician Don Blake. Iron Man, always a hair's breadth from DEATH due to a heart condition, could never allow himself to get too close to anyone. And, of course, Peter Parker—the amazing Spider-Man—just couldn't buy a break. No matter how many supervillains he defeated, it seemed like the entire world—from newspaper publisher Jonah Jameson to his own aunt—thought he was a no-good creep. And with his low self-esteem working overtime, Peter tended to agree with them a lot of the time.

These were heroes that no one had seen in a comic before. They had depth as you might find in a well-written movie or even a novel. They were people who seemed to act like an average person, blessed (or cursed) with superhuman powers would. And these were the *good guys.* The villains were often even more complex. Dr. Doom, Loki, Magneto—these were not characters whose idea of success was accumulating as many bags with dollar signs on them as they could. They had agendas, often involving revenge on the world for wrongs that could never be righted. They suffered loss that, in their eyes, no sum of money or material comfort could repay.

As what came to be known as the Marvel style evolved, Lee and Goodman saw sales skyrocket. More, they saw that their comics and characters were being sought out and enjoyed by older readers, college students to be specific. Without knowing it, they were changing the demographics of comics. Now that the content was relatively more sophisticated, it was being reflected in the readers. The superhero was now seen as a metaphor for the times.

Soon, the rest of the industry was scrambling to keep up with Marvel's innovations. Readers were no longer satisfied with simplistic storytelling and character delineation. Within ten years, Marvel had overtaken DC as the industry sales leader.

But the cultural import of the so-called Marvel Revolution—was more widespread than in simply making Marvel Comics more popular among readers. Similar to the way *MAD* magazine would come to redefine humor in America, Marvel Comics would become the dominant sensibility in American popular drama. Marvel readers grew up to become writers, producers, and directors of movies, TV shows, and popular novels. The Marvel "formula," so familiar today, demonstrated that action stories could be multifaceted.

One sees the fruits of this influence to the present day. Such cultural phenomena as Buffy the Vampire Slayer and HARRY POTTER owe their existence to the Marvel sensibility. The combination of soap-operatic elements (romance, extreme emotions, cliffhanging plots) with action adventure and science fiction tropes made for a paradigm shift in the idea of what popular entertainment could be. It could make you think and cheer, make you cry and transport you. It could make you feel as if, despite being part of a mass phenomenon, the stories were being told just to you by the creators. And the heroes of these stories were, whatever their outer trappings of power and glamour, a whole lot like you. The popularity of the Marvel Comics–based films of the 2000s—such as *Spider-Man, The X-Men,* and their sequels—only highlights the durability of the appeal of the Marvel approach to storytelling and character creation.

Like most great discoveries, this very modern approach to heroic adventure storytelling was there all the time. It just took Stan Lee and Marvel to find it.

DANNY FINGEROTH

SUTCLIFF, Rosemary

Author, b. 14 December, 1920, East Clanden, Surrey, England; d. July 23, 1992, England

S. is probably best known for her multibook saga of the Aquila FAMILY of Roman Britain, beginning in the second century with Marcus Flavius Aquila in *The Eagle of the Ninth* (1954) and continuing through *The Silver Branch* (1957), *Frontier Wolf* (1980), *The Lantern Bearers* (1959), and her adult novel *Sword at Sunset* (1963), to *Dawn Wind* (1961) in the sixth century. Readers who love the Aquila family recognize the flawed emerald ring, carved with the family dolphin symbol, as it reappears on the hands of even later descendants in *The Shield Ring* (1956), a novel of the Norman invasion in which the harper Bjorn possesses a ring that came to him from "a foremother out of Wales," and S.'s final novel *Sword Song* (1997), published posthumously.

In her AUTOBIOGRAPHY *Blue Remembered Hills* (1983), S. recalled a childhood afflicted and isolated

by severe rheumatoid arthritis, and the obsessive overprotection of her mother, enlivened only by the tales of MYTH and legend that were read to her. She remained ill all her life, and her characters often possessed some matching DISABILITY of body or temperament. S. lived with her parents until they died, at first moving often as the family followed her father's naval postings. Her first books were *The Chronicles of Robin Hood* and *The Queen Elizabeth Story* (both 1950), but she quickly discovered the Romano-British period and made it her own. In a 1986 interview she said, "I think that I am happiest of all in Roman Britain. I feel very much at home there. The Middle Ages I am not at home in. I am interested in them and love to read about them, but I can't write about them . . . I think it is because I can't take the all-pervasiveness of religion, which has a stranglehold on life. The more level-headed viewpoint of the Romans is nearer to our own way of looking at things. If I could do a time flip and landed back in Roman Britain, I would take a deep breath, take perhaps a fortnight to get used to things, and then be all right, for I would know what was making the people around me tick. But if I landed in thirteenth or fourteenth-century England, I'd be lost. I have a special "'ah, here I am again, I know exactly what they are going to have for breakfast' feeling when I get back into Roman Britain."

Perhaps because as a young woman she lived through World War II and the constant threat of invasion, many of her books deal with early invasions of the island. But all those successive invaders are absorbed by Britain and thereby changed into Britons. S.'s work conveys the sense of connectedness to the countryside that Rudyard Kipling evoked in *Puck of Pook's Hill* (S. complained in her 1960 monograph on Kipling that he had gone out of style) and her stories, like his, root her fictional families in the land as much as in their separate times and origins. In *The Lantern Bearers,* the Romano-British Aquila realizes, as his legion is being ordered home to try to salvage what is left of Rome, that it is the British countryside that has his heart; that his Roman family have become Britons over the three centuries they have lived there. He deserts, letting the ship sail without him, to fight for Britain instead of Rome.

The idea of sacred and sacrificial kingship, the king's connection to and representation of the land, is a parallel thread that runs throughout S.'s work. This theme is most strongly developed in *Sword at Sunset,* among the first Arthurian retellings to fix Arthur in a historical setting; and in *The Mark of the Horse Lord* (1965), in which Phaedrus the gladiator, hired to pose as the king of the Dalriadain (because the true king is maimed and thus cannot rule), becomes their king in truth when he becomes willing to die for them. This theme is reflected in S.'s fondness for the Arthurian cycle as well, and she returned to it in several other books.

S.'s work regularly appeared on the ALA Notable Books list, the Carnegie Medal commendations, and the *Horn Book* honor list. Her numerous awards include the Carnegie Medal, 1960, for *The Lantern Bearers;* the *Boston Globe–Horn Book* Award for outstanding text, and the Carnegie Medal runner-up, 1972, for *Tristan and Iseult;* the Order of the British Empire, 1975; and the Children's Literature Association Phoenix Award, 1985, for *The Mark of the Horse Lord.* In 1982 she was made a Royal Society of Literature fellow; and in 1992 a Commander, Order of the British Empire.

AWARDS: ALA Best Books for Young Adults: *Road to Camlann,* 1983, *Black Ships before Troy,* 1994.

FURTHER WORKS: *Outcast,* 1955; *Warrior Scarlet,* 1958; *Knight's Fee,* 1960; *The High Deeds of Finn MacCool,* 1967; *The Witch's Brat,* 1970; *Tristan and Iseult,* 1971; *Song for a Dark Queen,* 1978; *The Road to Camlann: The Death of King Arthur,* 1981; *Flame-Coloured Taffeta,* 1985; *The Shining Company,* 1990; *Black Ships before Troy: The Story of the Iliad,* 1993.

BIBLIOGRAPHY: Meek, Margaret. *Rosemary S.,* 1962; *Something about the Author,* vol. 44, pp. 188–97; Talcroft, Barbara L. *Death of the Corn King: King and Goddess in Rosemary S.'s Historical Fiction for Young Adults,* 1995; Thompson, Raymond H. "Interview with Rosemary S." *Avalon to Camelot,* 1987. Accessed through *Taliesin's Successors: Interviews with Authors of Modern Arthurian Literature,* http://www.lib.rochester.edu/camelot/intrvws/sutcliff.htm; London *Times,* July 25, 1992, p. 17.

AMANDA COCKRELL

SUTTON, Roger

Editor, author b. 26 October 1956, Manchester, Connecticut

S. is the editor-in-chief of *Horn Book* MAGAZINE, a position he has held since 1996. First published in 1924, *Horn Book* was the first magazine to deal exclusively with children's literature. It consists of book

reviews and editorials, many of which are authored by S., as well as a variety of feature articles and columns. S. also supervises the publication of the *Horn Book Guide,* a biannual rating guide of all children's books published. S. was previously the editor of *The Bulletin of the Center for Children's Books.*

Although he is the most noted for his editorial work, S. is also an author in his own right. He has written for numerous journals, most notably *Booklist, The New York Times Book Review,* and *School Library Journal.* He has also written the nonfiction YOUNG ADULT book *Hearing Us Out: Voices from the Gay and Lesbian Community* (1994). *Hearing Us Out* presents first-person narratives adapted from fifteen interviews with adults and TEENAGERS about their experiences growing up gay or lesbian. It was selected as an American Library Association Best Book for Young Adults. S. is also the co-author of *Evaluating Children's Books: A Critical Look* (1992), and the co-editor of *The Best in Children's Books 1985–1990: The University of Chicago Guide to Children's Literature* (1991).

S. has also served on numerous youth literature award committees, including the 2000 MICHAEL L. PRINTZ AWARD committee, the 1999 National Book Award for Young People's Literature committee, and the 1999 Newbery Medal committee. He holds a bachelor's degree from Pitzer College and a master's in library science from the University of Chicago. Before becoming an editor, he worked in public libraries as a young adult services LIBRARIAN, a children's librarian, and a branch manager.

AWARDS: *Hearing Us Out*: ALA Best Books for Young Adults, 1995.

BIBLIOGRAPHY: *Horn Book* magazine website: http://www.hbook.com/sutton.shtml; *Something about the Author,* vol. 93, 1997.

DENISE E. AGOSTO

SWARTHOUT, Glendon

Author, b. 8 April 1918, Pinckney, Michigan; d. 23 September 1992, Scottsdale, Arizona

S. earned a B.A. (1939) and an M.A. (1946) from the University of Michigan, and a Ph.D. (1955) from Michigan State University. Before beginning his prolific writing career in earnest, S. taught at numerous universities (1946–63) and served a tour of duty in the U.S. Army (1943–45), achieving the rank of sergeant.

Sixteen novels (eight of which were made into MOVIES), six books for young adults (co-authored with his wife Kathryn), one SHORT STORY collection, and one PLAY (co-authored with John K. Savacool) compose the literary dossier of Glendon S.

Bless the Beasts and Children (1970) is S.'s masterpiece. In the book, a group of adolescent boys from an Arizona camp for troubled TEENS unify on behalf of the buffalo, to save them from senseless slaughter by sportsmen. The novel has sold over two million copies and received numerous literary accolades. It is now in its 25th anniversary edition reprinting.

Apart from *Bless the Beasts and Children,* S. is known for his Westerns and the film adaptations of his novels (*Where the Boys Are,* 1960, MGM 1960 and 1984, for example). His two major contributions to the Western genre are *The Shootist* (1975, 1998), a Western on which the John Wayne movie by the same name was based, and *The Homesman* (1988, 1990), both of which have received literary praise.

His son, Miles, also a writer, has completed special introductions in recent reprintings of *Bless the Beasts and Children* and *The Shootist* and an afterword about his father's literary career in *Easterns and Westerns* (2001).

AWARDS: Overall Achievement: Winner of the O. Henry Prize for short stories, 1960; National Society of Arts and Letters Gold Medal, 1972; Owen Wister Award, 1991 (Western Writers of America). *Bless the Beasts and Children:* Nominated by Doubleday for the Pulitzer Prize, 1970, ALA Best Books for Young Adults, 1970; *Still Alive:* Selections from 1960–1974 Best Books for Young Adults; The Best of the Best Books, Selections from 1970 to 1983 (BBYA); Nothin' But the Best: Selections from 1966 to 1986 (BBYA); Here We Go Again . . . 25 Years of Best Books: Selections from 1967 to 1992 (BBYA) *The Shootist* (1975): chosen by the Western Writers of America as one of the best Western novels ever written; Spur Award Winner, Best Western Novel, 1975. *The Homesman* (1988): Spur Award Winner, Best Western Novel, 1988; Wrangler Award Winner, Best Western Novel, 1988. *Cadbury's Coffin* (1982): Edgar Allan Poe Awards, nominee 1983 Best Juvenile Novel.

FURTHER WORK: *Whichaway* (1966, 1992, 1997), young adult novel.

BIBLIOGRAPHY: The Official website of Glendon S., http://www.glendonswarthout.com/index.htm; *Contemporary Authors Online,* 2003.

MARY MCMILLAN TERRY

SWEENEY, Joyce
Author, b. 9 November 1955, Dayton, Ohio

S. focuses many of her stories around the relationships of younger characters and often takes the reader inside the mind of a typical TEEN. S. has said she may enjoy writing about FAMILY relationships because she came from a nontraditional family; her father died when she was very young. Her younger years were spent in a rural area near Dayton, Ohio, which helped develop her love for the outdoors and nature. Before she began school, her family moved to Dayton, where S. immediately felt like an outsider. She was a book-loving country girl and did not relate well with the children in the city.

S. knew very early on that she wanted to be a novelist. Her writing endeavors began in elementary school with poems because they were easy to finish. In high school a teacher helped shaped her writing career by encouraging her to write fiction and by teaching her about how the publishing world operates. In high school she also met the person who would later become her husband.

S. sold her first work of fiction, a SHORT STORY, to *New Writers,* and her second work to *Playgirl* while in college. This was the validation she needed to make a career of writing. After college she worked in advertising and as a legal secretary. Her husband helped her realize her lifelong dream by encouraging her to pursue writing on a full-time basis.

As a result of writing full time, S. was finally able to get a novel published, *Center Line* (1984), thanks to a new award being offered, the Delacorte Prize for Outstanding First Young Adult Novel. Her success in being published was also due to the efforts of her agent. S.'s agent had, in fact, submitted this novel and it had been rejected by over thirty publishers before deciding to enter it in this contest for first time writers for young adults. *Center Line* is the story of the Cunnigan brothers, who run away from an abusive father to make better lives for themselves. Each brother brings something into this new situation. Shawn, the oldest, is a leader; Steve is the sensitive one but leaves his family to marry; Chris is somewhat of a ladies man; Rick causes some trouble; and young Mark is a bit immature, but is able to earn some money for the family. When Rick and Shawn get into a fight one day, Rick decides to report his family. In the end, however, they remain together and beat the odds.

Inspired to write because of her own love of great novels, S. felt somewhat slighted when her first two novels were called young adult novels. Now, however, S. purposely writes for the young adult audience; she finds this group to be enthusiastic and receptive. S. also believes that tackling tough issues helps educate and prepare young adults to help work through difficult situations. This is evident in many of her novels, where she has touched on themes such as abuse, suicide, environmental issues, competitiveness in SPORTS, teenage pregnancy, young love, interracial dating, friendship, and even the paranormal and supernatural. She feels that she can make a difference with teenagers because critical life and social issues come into play.

In *The Dream Collector* (1989), Becky tries to figure out how to buy her family Christmas presents on her limited funds, so opts to buy a self-help book that will help them make their dreams come true. Of course, sometimes you have to be careful what you wish for!

S. tries a bit of the supernatural in *Shadow* (1994) in which Sarah is able to see the ghost of her dead cat. Sarah soon begins to realize that her cat is trying to warn her of impending danger.

Players (2000) shows how destructive competitiveness in sports can be if not kept in check. The story focuses on Corey, the captain of the basketball team at St. Philip's High School. This team has a good chance to go to the finals and become the city champions; they even have a great new player on the team, Noah. The team starts having some troubles and many of the troubles point to Noah's doings. Corey comes to realize that not everyone has good intentions and must try to bring the team together.

Sophie is in her third trimester of pregnancy in *Waiting for June* (2003). What complicates matters for Sophie, however, is that she is a high-school senior. Additionally, she is dreaming about whales, she wants to learn the identity of her own father, she will not let anyone know the father of her baby, and she is receiving death threats. There is plenty of drama in this novel and even some humor.

S. has written successfully for both male and female readers. She includes a variety of themes and characters in her novels to keep even reluctant readers interested. Many teenagers can easily relate to these realistic stories.

AWARDS: Delacorte Press Prize for Outstanding First YA Novel for *Center Line*, 1983; American Library Association Best Books in Young Adult category for *Center Line*, 1984, *The Tiger Orchard*, 1994, *Shadow*, 1995, *The Spirit Window*, 1999; American Library Association Best Books citation for Reluctant Readers for *The Dream Collector*, 1989, *Face the Dragon*, 1990, *Piano Man*, 1992, *Shadow*, 1994, *Free Fall*, 1996; New York Public Library Best Books List for *Shadow*, 1994 and *Free Fall*, 1996, ALA Quick Picks for Reluctant Readers for *Players*, 2001, *Takedown*, 2005.

FURTHER WORKS: *Right Behind the Rain*, 1987; *Face the Dragon*, 1990; *Piano Man*, 1992; *The Tiger Orchard*, 1993; *Free Fall*, 1996; *The Spirit Window*, 1998; *Takedown*, 2004.

BIBLIOGRAPHY: *Authors and Artists for Young Adults*, vol. 26; *Contemporary Authors New Revision Series*, vol. 86; *Something about the Author*, vol. 65, 68, 108; *Publishers Weekly* and *Kirkus* reviews.

TINA HERTEL

TAMAR, Erika
Author, b. 10 June 1934, Vienna, Austria

T., author of YA novels, middle-grade novels, and children's PICTURE BOOKS, came to the U.S. as a child with her physician father and homemaker mother. After attending New York University and graduating from the TV/Film Institute at Stanford University, T. dreamed of directing television or film, and began her career in the arts as a production assistant and casting director for the soap opera *Search for Tomorrow*. Afterward, she became involved in community theater on Long Island. Her work in the visual arts gave her a keen sense of character development.

T. says that she sees a strong correlation between acting and writing. Her ability to slip into character is what she relies on when working on a book. Her works for young people, many of which are set in the inner city, explore the unexpected truths of her characters. They are also unflinchingly honest in their treatment of tough issues. An example of this can be found in *Fair Game*, which tackles the controversial subject of gang rape. But this rape is set in an upper-class high school, the perpetrators are members of the athletic elite, and the victim is a mentally challenged TEEN who goes along with whatever is inflicted on her simply because she wants to feel accepted and to belong. This is a high price to pay, indeed, for what she thought was popularity. The ALA Best Books Committee recognized the power of this story and the tough situation faced by the young girl. They selected the title for the 1994 list. T. draws a great deal from personal experience when she writes about the inner city, having lived in Manhattan. She is a self-described extrovert and enjoys restaurants, theater, art galleries, walking, and swimming, although writing is her great passion.

Among other award-winning novels, T. has also contributed to the Party of Five: Claudia SERIES of books for YA.

AWARDS: *Fair Game:* 1994 ALA Best Books for YA, 1993 New York Public Library Books for the Teen Age list, Garden State Master List; 2001 Western Writers of America Spur Award for Best Western Juvenile Fiction, *The Midnight Train Home.*

FURTHER WORKS: *Blues for Silk Garcia,* 1983; *Goodbye, Glamour Girl,* 1984; *It Happened at Cecilia's,* 1989; *High Cheekbones,* 1990; *Out of Control,* 1991; *The Truth about Kim O'Hara,* 1992; *Fair Game,* 1993; *The Things I Did Last Summer,* 1994; *The Midnight Train Home,* 2000; *Amanda's Story,* 2004.

SARAH SLOTHOWER

TAN, Amy
Author, b. 19 February 1952, Oakland, California

Ever since T.'s childhood in Oakland, she knew she wanted to become a writer despite her parents' hopes that she would become a neurosurgeon. She received a B.A. in 1973 and an M.A. in 1974 from San Jose State University and then married Louis DeMattei. Later she worked as a language development consultant, directed programs for mentally disabled children, and moved into a freelance business, educational writing, before she turned to her true love, fiction writing, as an escape from her workaholic tendencies.

Called "one of the best-known American writers of ASIAN ancestry," T.'s FAMILY heritage has shaped her as a writer and a person. As the child of Chinese immigrants, she felt forced to assimilate into American culture but was also expected to respect Chinese tradition. Her parents wanted T. and her brothers to speak English perfectly so they could achieve the "American Dream," although they spoke to their children in a combination of Mandarin and English. T.'s career, however, was born through these Asian roots. In 1986 when her mother, Daisy, was hospitalized, T. realized that she knew very little about her mother's past, so she agreed to visit China with her. This trip gave T. a better understanding of her two cultures and inspired her to write her first novel in 1989, *The Joy Luck Club,* which quickly rose from being a bestseller to a "classic-in-embryo" and was made into a screenplay in 1993. The collage of characters and stories depicts the cultural and generational differences between a young Asian-American woman and her late mother's Chinese friends.

Her next book, *The Kitchen God's Wife* (1991), was inspired largely by Daisy's life in China. Like T.'s first novel, it also contains some AUTOBIOGRAPHICAL elements and explores mother-daughter relationships as it tells the story of a Chinese mother revealing the secrets of her tragic life in China to her daughter, who gains strength and insight from her mother's past. *The Hundred Secret Senses* (1995) shifts to a relationship between sisters and explores the supernatural. Her next novel, *The Bonesetter's Daughter* (2001), reflects her own experiences when Daisy was diagnosed with Alzheimer's disease and confronts the challenges of growing up as an Asian American.

AWARDS: *The Joy Luck Club:* American Library Association 1990 Best Books for Young Adults, Commonwealth Club Gold Award for Fiction, Bay Area Book Reviewers Award for Best Fiction, all 1989; 1991 *Booklist* Editor's Choice, *The Kitchen God's Wife;* Best American Essays Award, 1991.

FURTHER WORKS: *The Moon Lady* (juvenile), 1992; *The Chinese Siamese Cat* (juvenile), 1994; *The Best American Short Stories* (guest editor), 1999; SHORT STORIES, including "The Rules of the Game," published in *State of the Language,* 1989, and *Best Amer-*

ican Essays, 1991; Contributor to several periodicals, including *Atlantic Monthly, McCall's Threepenny Review, Grand Street,* and *Seventeen.*

BIBLIOGRAPHY: "Amy Ruth_Tan," *Contemporary Authors Online,* Gale, 2003; Gray, Paul and Sachs, Andrea. "The Joys and Sorrows of Amy T." *Time,* 157(7), 19 Feb. 2001; Huntley, E. D. *Amy T.: A Critical Companion,* 1998.

RUTH HITCHCOCK

TASHJIAN, Janet
Author, b. 29 June 1956, Providence, Rhode Island

T. earned a double major in journalism and philosophy at the University of Rhode Island. After trying a career in sales, she read O'Brien's *The Things They Carried,* which changed her life and prompted her to quit her job to become a writer. She enrolled in Emerson College's M.F.A. program and studied writing with such notable writers as National Book Award-winner James Carroll and children's author Jack GANTOS.

T.'s early books were for children whereas her later books have targeted older audiences. Her first novel, *Tru Confessions,* about a young girl and her mentally handicapped brother, is told in DIARY format through Trudy's computer journal. *Marty Frye, Private Eye,* a short children's chapter book, is a MYSTERY with a seven-year-old main character who rhymes his way through solving several petty crimes. *Multiple Choice* deals with a fourteen-year-old whose obsessive behavior leads to serious consequences. *The Gospel According to Larry* tells the story of Josh, the secret creator of a website devoted to antimaterialism that develops a national cult following. *The Gospel According to Larry* was named *Booklist* Editor's Choice in 2001 and one of YALSA's Best Books for Young Adults in 2002. Two young adult novels *Faultline* and a *Larry* sequel, are in progress.

T., who writes every day, believes that writing is both an art (inspiration and creativity) and a craft (structure and format). Her advice to aspiring writers is to read good books, learn from them, and keep writing until an individual voice emerges.

AWARDS: *The Confessions:* ALA Popular Paperbacks, 2003; *The Gospel According to Larry:* ALA Best Books for Young Adults, 2002; ALA Popular Paperbacks, 2005.

HAZEL ROCHMAN

J. K. ROWLING

GRAHAM SALISBURY

WILLIAM SLEATOR

ART SPIEGELMAN

SUZANNE FISHER STAPLES

THEODORE TAYLOR

CHRIS VAN ALLSBURG

BIBLIOGRAPHY: "Janet T." *Contemporary Authors Online,* 2001; Janet T. homepage, http://www.janet tashjian.com

TERRI SNETHEN

TAYLOR, Mildred D.

Author, b. 13 September 1943, Jackson, Mississippi

T., an acclaimed author of YOUNG ADULT novels, has based most of her work on the inspirational stories from her own FAMILY's history. She often heard these stories as a child, and has adapted them with a retained child's perspective. T. was raised in Toledo, Ohio, but often visited her birthplace for large, family gatherings. There she listened to stories passed along the generations about her great-grandparents' lives during and after slavery, focusing on their struggles to maintain their dignity and spirit. The stories she heard at home were a great contrast to the stories that T. heard in school, stories in which black Americans were represented with no pride.

Upon entering high school, T. knew that she wanted to be a writer. She also noticed the painful contradiction between the historical portrayals of black people in history books compared to the heroic, strong people found within the vibrant stories she heard orally. Desiring to combine the strong characterizations of black individuals and written history, T. used her family stories to prompt her own writing. These stories formed the historical context for her books, in which T. skillfully instills the dynamic events, the memorable characters, and the immeasurably proud heritage.

After she graduated from Scott High School in 1961, T. attended the University of Toledo and earned a B.A. in education in 1965. She then joined the Peace Corps and spent two years teaching English and history in Ethiopia. After returning to the United States, T. entered the University of Colorado, earning a Masters in journalism in 1969. During her graduate study, she was active in the Black Student Alliance; after completing her degree, she showed her appreciation to the university by working to improve the Black Studies program. In 1971, she relocated to Los Angeles to pursue her writing endeavors and worked for some time as an editor. She eventually returned to Colorado, where she still resides.

T.'s stories address the experiences of the Logan family. Their stories take place in rural Mississippi during the Great Depression, a time that still bore the scars of slavery and its racist effects on society. Her vivid use of imagery and details gives the story accurate historical context and molds well-developed characters; the dialogue breathes life into these characters and creates three-dimensional people. T. based this particular setting on the experiences of her father and his generation, people who were raised in the post–Reconstruction South and later helped create the CIVIL RIGHTS MOVEMENT of the 1960s.

The Logan family's story is begun in *Song of Trees* (1975). T. narrates the stories from the point of view of Cassie Logan, a spirited eight-year-old girl. Cassie is full of pride and determination, but her innocence slowly crumbles as she learns about the reality of racism. With such realistic detail, the reader can easily experience the feelings, sights, sounds, and thoughts of her characters through the perspective of a precocious girl. In 1974, T. entered her novel in the Council on Interracial Books for Children competition and won first prize in the AFRICAN-AMERICAN category.

T. writes about the Logan family's struggle to retain their dignity and pride in a society that tried to stifle such qualities in African-Americans. Ownership of land is of paramount importance to the Logan family, for it represents independence from the sharecropper life. The Logan's land is a primary source of pride; they are responsible for all their crops and the recipients of all the revenue. Half of the family's four hundred acres is mortgaged, so the Logans share ownership with the bank. T. uses the land as a symbol for all that the Logans cherish and must protect. The family stands up for themselves, their land, and their human rights; this is the point of view that T. learned from her family.

The Logan's story is continued in *Roll of Thunder, Hear My Cry* (1976). T. brilliantly paints the scenes and carefully crafts the dialogue that allow the reader to experience Cassie's revelations about racism in a prejudiced society. Her uncle sells his Packard in order to pay back the loan that the bank demands to be paid in full. She also experiences the double standards in the public school system, a system that presents its black students with abysmal textbooks and shoddy learning conditions. Cassie's parents try to explain when she should protest biased conditions and what she will have to learn to tolerate if she is to survive in contemporary society. Prejudiced children and adults squash her pride repeatedly, but she learns

691

what true damage the white community can inflict upon members of the black community. She also accepts the pride and power that is held in the Logan land. Additionally, *Roll of Thunder, Hear My Cry,* received the Newbery Award (1977) and was produced as a three-part television miniseries and broadcast by ABC in 1978. T. expands the story of the Logan family in a prequel, *The Land* (2001), in *Let the Circle Be Unbroken* (1981) and in *The Road to Memphis* (1990).

T. writes with the hope of providing a resounding voice for black people whose stories of struggle and joy, and whose heroic lives were absent from the history books when she was a child. These stories are vividly portrayed through the eyes and ears of a black child and her family, and represent the trials and tribulations and ultimate survival of this American family.

AWARDS: *Song of the Trees:* 1975 *New York Times* Outstanding Book, 1976 Children's Book Showcase Book, 1976 Jane Addams Honor Book; *Roll of Thunder, Hear My Cry:* 1977 Newbery Medal, 1977 *Boston Globe–Horn Book* Award Honor Book, 1977 Jane Addams Honor Book, 1985 Buxtehuder Bulle Award; *Let the Circle Be Unbroken:* 1981 American Library Association Best Book for Young Adults, 1982 Jane Addams Honor Book, 1982 Coretta Scott King Award; *Road to Memphis:* 1991 Coretta Scott King Award, 1991 Christopher Award, 1991 ALA Best Books for Young Adults; *The Gold Cadillac:* 1988 Christopher Award; *The Friendship:* 1988 *Boston Globe–Horn Book* Award, Coretta Scott King Award, 1988; *The Land:* ALA Best Books for Young Adults, 2002, Coretta Scott King Award, 2002, Charlie May Simon Children's Book Award, 2004; 1997 ALAN Award for Significant Contribution to YA Literature from the National Council of Teachers of English.

FURTHER WORKS: *The Gold Cadillac,* 1987; *The Friendship,* 1987; *Mississippi Bridge,* 1990; *The Well,* 1995; *The Land,* 2001; *Logan,* 2004.

BIBLIOGRAPHY: Cullinan, Bernice E., and Lee Galda, *Literature and the Child,* 5th ed, 2002; http://scholar .lib.vt.edu/ejournls/ALAN/spring98/taylor.html; http://www.africanpubs.com/Apps/bios/1198Taylor Mildred.asp; http://www.edupaperback.org/author bios/TaylorMildred.html; http://www.olemiss.edu/ mwp/dir/taylormildred/; http://www.penguinputnam .com/Author/AuthorPage/0,,0000025506,00.html

THERESA HAHN
AND RACHEL WITMER

TAYLOR, Theodore

Author, b. 23 June 1921, Statesville, North Carolina

T. has published over fifty works for children, YAs, and adults. He has been an editor, screenwriter, ghostwriter, journalist, publicist, producer, and director. His fiction and nonfiction address a wide variety of subjects and issues, reflecting his environmental, political, and social views.

He spent his boyhood in North Carolina with his parents and four sisters. At that time, T. enjoyed Old Testament "action" stories in an illustrated Bible. He was later introduced to the writings of well-known authors, John Steinbeck becoming his favorite.

Exploring nature in North Carolina fostered T.'s sense of adventure. At nine, his family moved to Johnson City, Tennessee. His father struggled to find work in the midst of the Great Depression; in order to assist his family, T. found the following odd jobs: delivering newspapers, dry cleaning, plucking chickens, selling scrap metal, crabbing, and working as "cornerman" for boxers.

In 1934, T.'s family moved to Cradock, Virginia, near Portsmouth. There his affinity for ships and the sea intensified. Achieving passing grades in high school was a challenge, but T.'s English teacher encouraged him to write. In 1935, T. accepted a 50-cent-a-week job composing a SPORTS column on the athletic events at his high school for the *Portsmouth Star;* later, he headed to Washington, D.C., and worked as a copy boy at the *Washington Daily News.* Eventually, he wrote entertainment features and reviews for the *Star* and became its sports editor in 1941. After the attack on Pearl Harbor, T. covered stories pertaining to the WAR. In 1942, he joined the Merchant Marines and was in the naval reserves. In 1944, he became a navy ensign on a cargo attack ship in the Pacific. After the war, he volunteered for duty at the nuclear bomb experiment on Bikini Atoll, Operation Crossroads, which became his inspiration for *The Bomb* (1995), recipient of the Scott O'DELL Historical Fiction Award.

T. attended the American Theatre Wing at Columbia University while considering becoming a playwright but never earned a college degree. In 1950, he returned to the Navy and served at the Pentagon. A friend's book contract, which was reassigned to him, resulted in T.'s first adult BIOGRAPHY, *Magnificent Mitscher* (1954).

After a variety of other jobs, T. became a publicist for three years in Hollywood, working with celebrities. After his first screenplay, he left Hollywood and made documentaries. T. later wrote a popular nonfiction book for young readers, *People Who Make Movies* (1967), based on the film industry.

T.'s first novel for young readers was *The Cay* (1969), a survival story of eleven-year-old Phillip who is rescued by Timothy, an old West Indian sailor, after Germans bomb their ship during World War II. Phillip, blinded, overcomes anger and prejudice while they are marooned on a Caribbean island. The popular novel received much critical acclaim and was given the Jane Addams Children's Book Award in 1970, which was returned in 1975 when the book was labeled as racist, an accusation heartily disputed by T.; critics have now developed a more accepting and unprejudiced view, and consider *The Cay* to be a modern children's CLASSIC. T.'s prequel/sequel, *Timothy of the Cay* (1993), interchanges the story of Timothy's boyhood at sea with Phillip's struggle to regain his sight.

T. has several films accredited to him before his retirement from the motion picture industry. He went on to publish his Cape Hatteras young adult trilogy: *Teetoncey* (1974), *Teetoncey and Ben O'Neal* (1975), and *The Odyssey of Ben O'Neal* (1977). T. later published *The Trouble with Tuck* (1981), about a girl who trains a blind dog to assist a retired Seeing Eye Dog, and its sequel, *Tuck Triumphant* (1991). Other YA books include *Sweet Friday Island* (1984), about a girl and her father surviving on a remote island off Baja, California; *Walking up a Rainbow* (1986), a clever Western; *The Hostage* (1987), an environmental rescue story; and *Sniper* (1987), a MYSTERY surrounding a California wildlife preserve.

T. married his first wife, Gweneth Goodwin, in 1946. They had three children, Mark, Wendy, and Michael, and divorced in 1979. In 1981, Flora Schoenleber became his second wife. Today, T. makes his home in Laguna Beach, California.

AWARDS: 1970 Jane Addams Children's Book Award, *The Cay;* 1990 BBYA, *Sniper; The Weirdo* (1991): Edgar Allan Poe Mystery Award, 1993 BBYA; 1994 BBYA, *Timothy of the Cay;* 1995 Scott O'Dell Historical Fiction Award, 1996 BBYA, *The Bomb.*

FURTHER WORKS: *The Weirdo*, 1991; *A Sailor Returns,* 2001; *Lord of the Kill,* 2002; *The Boy Who Could Fly without a Motor,* 2002.

BIBLIOGRAPHY: T., Theodore. Homepage, http://www.theodoretaylor.com/; T., Theodore. "Exploding the Literary Canon." *ALAN Review*, vol. 25, no. 1, Fall 1997, http://scholar.lib.vt.edu/ejournals/ALAN/fall97/taylor.html; "T., Theodore." In *Something about the Author,* vol. 128, 2002, pp. 220–30.

DIANE TUCCILLO

TAYLOR, William

Author, b. 11 October 1938, Lower Hutt, Wellington, New Zealand

T. is one of the most popular and prolific novelists for YA in New Zealand. He attended five different high schools in three years, an unsettling experience reflected in his first children's novel, *Pack up Pick up and Off* (1981). T. worked as a bank clerk before becoming a teacher, which he describes as "more a love affair than a job." He taught in a number of rural schools before becoming principal of Ohakune Primary School. After his very funny account of his teaching experiences, *Burnt Carrots Don't Have Legs* (1976), T. wrote several adult novels, and was also the Mayor of Ohakune. The Choysa Bursary for Children's Writers in 1985 enabled him to write full time.

Since then, T. has produced a stream of lively, often very funny novels for young people. Common factors are the rural settings, the convincing characters, and young males behaving like real young males rather than etiquette book examples. Hooligans are not unknown in T.'s oeuvre. In *My Summer of the Lions* (1986), boys steal hubcaps, and in *Possum Perkins* (1987) they are teasing girls, while Tom Costello, the main character of *Circles* (1996), is suspended for drinking and smoking in a girls' school dormitory. An irritating brat can also be a caring young man, a point frequently made in T.'s stories.

T. insists that the comic saga of the Greenhill Crowd was not supposed to be funny: it just turned out that way. Five unlikely friends (Lav, Griller, Maggie, Bogdan and Tom) do terrible things to SPORT in *The Worst Soccer Team Ever* (1987), (televised as *All for One* in 1991), theater in *Break a Leg* (1987), business enterprise in *Making Big Bucks* (1987), and high-school journalism in *Fast Times at Greenhill High* (1992).

Lively characters in unexpected situations are a staple of T's humor. T's best comic creation is *Annie & Co and Marilyn Monroe* (1995), a witty account of TEENS in a small town, defeating boredom by claiming to be Princess Di's long-lost sister or doing good works for the Bible Church of Rural Redemption. (Many of T.'s characters, whether comic or serious, have an interesting spiritual element.) In stories like *Beth and Bruno* (1992) (*Secret Lives* in UK) and *Circles* (1996), T. is aware of the social structure of rural towns, where society is small scale and people's interlocking lives are a writer's gift. In the introduction to his SHORT STORIES, *At the Big Red Rooster* (1998), T. described his themes as "those of relationships between people, the individual's perception of the world around them and how we see each other and, of course, how people deal with one another."

As a novelist T. is prepared to face difficult issues. *Possum Perkins* (*Paradise Lane* in the US) (1987) was, along with Jack LASENBY's *The Lake* (1987), one of the first New Zealand novels for young people to mention sexual abuse of children, a reflection of the two writers' concern as teachers. T. has written several books on gay themes. *The Blue Lawn* (1994) broke new ground and won awards but *Jerome* (1999) handles the theme of young people becoming aware of their sexuality more skillfully and with superior narrative technique. *Pebble in a Pool* (2003) is a more mature treatment of the dilemma of a young man openly declaring his gay nature in a small town. All three were published in the United States as well as in New Zealand.

T's strongest novels are about young men trying to come to terms with the world about them. In *Scarface and the Angel* (2000) it is Damon's facial (and emotional) scars that make him a loner until an old woman provides him with a reason for living. In *Spider* (2002) it is Matthew's musical talent that makes him feel separated from FAMILY and friends, while in *Circles* (1996) it is Tom's discovery that his rebellious nature is part of his family heritage that helps him take on new responsibilities. These are powerful, satisfying works.

T. now lives in retirement at Raurimu, near Mount Ruapehu, in New Zealand's King Country.

AWARDS: 1991 Esther Glen Award, *Agnes the Sheep;* 1995 AIM Children's Book Awards, *The Blue Lawn;* 1998 Premio Andersen Award (Italy), *Agnes the Sheep (O Che Beela Eridita);* 1996 Margaret MAHY Lecture Award.

FURTHER WORKS: *Shooting Through,* 1986; Greenhill Crowd quartet: *The Worst Soccer Team Ever,* 1987; *Break a Leg,* 1987; *Making Big Bucks,* 1987; *Fast*

Times at Greenhill High, 1992. *The Kidnap of Jessie Parker,* 1989; *I Hate My Brother Maxwell Potter,* 1989; *Agnes the Sheep,* 1990.

BIBLIOGRAPHY: Harper, Julie. "Know the New Authors." *Magpies NZ Supplement* 15, no. 2 (May 2000): 2–3; Duder, Tessa. "Know the Author: William T." *Magpies NZ Supplement* 14, no. 2 (May 1999): 1–4; Fitzgibbon, Tom, and Spiers, Barbara. *Beneath Southern Skies: New Zealand Children's Book Authors & Illustrators,* 1993, 145–47; Stafford, Jane. "T., William." *The Oxford Companion to New Zealand Literature,* 1998, 528–29; T., William. "Biographical Notes." *School Journal Catalogue 1978–1993,* 1994, 149; T., William. "A Strange Way for An Adult Male to be Making a Living!" *New Zealand Children's Book Foundation Inc. Year Book,* 1998, 9–31; http://library.christchurch.org.nz/Childrens/ChildrensAuthors/WilliamTaylor.asp/; http://www.bookcouncil.org.nz/writers/taylorwilliam.htm/

TREVOR AGNEW

THE TEACHER–LIBRARIAN PARTNERSHIP: A TEACHER–RESEARCHER'S VIEW FROM THE FIELD

"The library is the heart of our school," remarked the principal to the school visitor. "You can feel the pulse of our learning, right here." This rather small elementary school library housed, at that moment, about 12,000 volumes, 16 computers, 44 children from second and fifth grades, 2 teachers, and 1 LIBRARIAN. The BIOGRAPHY-alive projects were in their third day of exploration. Around the room, small groups of students worked together to find facts and the voice of their historical characters. Students were gleaning information from books, MAGAZINES, video tapes, and the Internet. They wanted to be historians in the style of Jean Fritz, who can bring her biographies alive.

The woven framework of that lesson had its beginning some two years before. As the newly hired teacher-librarian for an elementary school, I was ready to assume the multifaceted roles of the job. In 1987, Yesner and Jay popularized the metaphoric description of a librarian as the "heartbeat of the school." *Information Power* (AASL and AECT, 1998) divided the role of the librarian into three specialized areas: instructional consultant, teacher, and information specialist. The success of integrated content presented in a literature-based approach hinges on the collaborative efforts of the librarian's teacher role (Girogis, 1993). One of the benefits from partnerships developed through these roles provides leadership, instruction, and consulting assistance for classroom teachers (AASL, 2001).

During the first week in my new position as an elementary school librarian, I established full flexible scheduling and individual student responsibility for book check-out. The remainder of the year I tried different techniques to enhance partnerships with the teachers.

From my doctoral work (1994), I identify three ways that classroom teachers create instructional partnerships with the librarian. First, teachers created opportunities that were *purposeful* when they planned lessons that flowed from the classroom instruction into the library lessons and back to the classroom. Second, teachers created partnerships that were *springboards* when the librarian connected teachers of different classes to one another as they were studying the same information. The third way partnerships occurred was identified as *on-the-fly*. Teachers walking through the library on errands would stop and quickly plan a library lesson. On-the-fly partnerships also occurred when the teacher planned a future library lesson with the librarian at any site outside the library, signed up for time on the flexible scheduling board, or offered to the librarian an invitation to view classroom projects.

Anticipating partnership opportunities, I carried a notebook with me whenever I left the library so that if I could talk with a teacher about the next library visit, I would be ready to record it. I had my notebook always within reach when teachers signed up at the flexible scheduling board. Formal planning sessions were few because of the time involved from each member.

The biography-alive projects, however, were the result of purposeful planning sessions. The second grade teacher and fifth grade teacher had been working together on the school's technology committee when they said they needed to have their students do something together. As they reviewed their curricula, they linked the second grade study of biographies with the fifth grade study of American history. That is when I became involved in the planning; they needed to know what materials were available for their project. Since the biography resources would focus the learning, we started with a review of those resources first. Next, we looked at the end of the unit

performance assessments. Then we established group and individual expectations specific for each grade. Finally, project guidelines were written for students.

Over the next couple of weeks, student research flowed from their classrooms into the library and back to the classrooms. Library materials and art supplies blended into the reader-writer workshop in which these students completed their projects. Near the end of the planned project, the biographies-alive turned into a two-classroom community presentation in which question-and-answer scripts were written by the groups. With the stage set and the spotlights on, one member of each group wore a rented costume for his or her character and answered questions from his or her group. The final theater production was spectacular; a video tape was made for sharing the projects with other classes and schools.

Three-way springboard partnerships occurred more often. One such topic involved the study of space. A second grade teacher had taken special NASA coursework during the summer to prepare to work with her students as they studied the planets. During her lessons, students found facts about planets, wrote journals to record the information, hung planet models from the ceiling of their classroom, and constructed their own miniature moonrover out of candy.

This knowledge of the activities in the second grade classroom had not reached the sixth grade teachers on the other side of the campus. So when a sixth grade teacher announced that he was going to start a unit on space, I immediately suggested to him that he connect with the second grade teacher. To ensure that the springboard partnership was formed, I walked back to the teacher's classroom with him and explained my ideas as we walked. Then, leaving the sixth grade classroom, I went straight to the second grade classroom, where I informed the teacher of the previous conversation. Later that week, sixth grade students became the audience at a second grade "open house." Individually, second grade students partnered with sixth grade students to share all they knew about space. Building on the second grade students' projects, the sixth grade students expanded their learnings on space; a turnabout open house resulted.

On-the-fly partnerships became the mainstay of my collaborations with the teachers. From my doctoral study, I identified this partnership as that most often used by teachers and librarians. Only in post-doctoral longitudinal work did I identify the layering value of on-the-fly partnerships. Deep, rich under-standings occurred when these partnerships were compounded over time. Just as with any relationship, the longer the two members work together in the same community, the better the individuals' behaviors can be predicted (Hughes-Hassell & Wheelock, 2001). "An integrated instructional process where librarians and reading teachers respect the ability of each other and share in the instruction can go far in maximizing student learning" (Montgomery, 1991, p. 35).

By the third year working through the curriculum of this elementary school, I felt connected to the cur-riculum sequence taught by returning faculty. An ex-ample of the growth in on-the-fly partnerships oc-curred with a fourth grade teacher. She usually stopped on her way home to schedule class sessions. The first year in mid-November, she announced that the students were studying the rainforest and that I could do something on that. "Do you want general books on the rainforest?" She went on to state that she would just use this time as an introduction to the rainforest. After the lesson in the library, the class gathered up the books we had used in the introduction and checked them out. That was the end of my involvement for that year with the unit on rainforests.

The second year in mid-November, the same fourth grade teacher announced again that the stu-dents were studying the rainforest. By then I knew to ask this teacher to briefly explain to me what she planned to cover in the unit. She listed that the stu-dents needed to know about the global locations, plants, and animals of the rainforest. My response be-came, "So what are they going to write about?" When the topic of animals was the response, I knew I could be ready with our resources: books, magazines, videos, and the Internet. The library session went bet-ter, I was more richly connected to the teacher's planned curriculum. The introduction of the topic had occurred within the classroom, so in the library we could spend time investigating the rainforest. At the end of our time together, the class again gathered up the books and materials we had used and checked them out. When the teacher wanted a follow-up les-son four days later, I commented, "You have all our resources. Do you want a fiction book on the rainfor-est?" With fiction, the students identified the author's accuracy according to their learnings.

The third year in mid-November when the same fourth grade teacher again announced that the stu-dents were studying the rainforest, I went to the heart of the study, "Will the students be writing animal re-ports this year?" She responded, "Oh, yes, but this year I want each student to have a different animal." We quickly scheduled an introduction session and two animal research-report writing sessions. Then two days before their second class-visit, she gave me the names of the animals the students had selected for their reports. Now the students could research, orga-nize, and write like Joanna Cole. When November comes again, we will have ways to improve the study of the rainforest even more.

A similar type of three-year growth resulted with a fifth-grade teacher. In April, she was going to have the students do reports on the presidents. This teacher was very observant to what was happening in the li-brary. As per her regular daily schedule, she cruised through the library with lunch tray in hand. This day she stated that she wanted the little book, a folded step-book, that I had made with the second grade stu-dents for their dinosaur books. She wanted the book for her students to take notes on their individual presi-dents. In the scheduled library lesson, we made the books, introduced the materials, and researched the presidents. The teacher wanted the materials left in the library so students would not forget the resources at home. Two more sessions with researching and the projects were gone for another year.

In the second year, four months before these fifth grade lessons were taught, the fifth grade teacher ob-served that many teachers had written on the flexible scheduling board "six-traits" and then listed the trait, i.e., word choice. Our school had a significant interest in the methodology as the state writing assessment rubric was based on the six traits of writing. This year, the teacher asked if we could improve the writ-ing process by incorporating in the library lessons the six traits of writing. The first scheduled library lesson went like the year before; we made books for note taking, introduced library resources, and became en-gaged in the research. Each of the next two sessions, we highlighted a) organization and word choice, and b) sentence fluency and voice. Again, the teacher wanted the materials left in the library so they would not be forgotten at home. A final library session was scheduled for project completion, but during lunch for the next week, I had a few students finishing their projects.

The third year, the partnership became more involved but the planning session was brief. The on-the-fly partnership sounded like: "president report time," "ok, books?" "yes," "six-traits?" "yes, and could we get some help with editing?" "like what?" The fifth grade teacher indicated that we needed older students to come into the fifth grade classroom and help with the editing process of the final report. She reminded me that under my direction her students had helped second grade students edit their dinosaur projects. My answer led the teacher to believe I would arrange to have high school students from the school a half mile down the street come and help us. In the first scheduled library session, we made books for note taking, introduced library resources, and engaged in research. This year, the teacher allowed the students to make the decision about checking out the materials or leaving them in the library for return sessions; about two-thirds of the students checked out their materials.

The second and third sessions highlighted six traits of writing. A fourth work session was scheduled followed by a fifth session for editing. When the plans for high school editors did not work out, I had six senior citizens come to my rescue. For ninety minutes, the eight adults and thirty fifth grade students worked on editing. The projects were complete by the end of the week and no one was in for lunch to complete a project. I will purposefully plan to have high school student editors ready for next April. Through the layered value of on-the-fly partnerships, this quickly planned and easily enacted scenario recurred each year with richer results of learnings for the students.

Typical partnership constraints were evident even in this setting. The ever-present problem of funding for resources resurfaced every year. While I could order some new literature in weak areas of the collection, I never had enough funds to purchase three or four books per individual student topic investigated during the year.

Another constraint was when teachers did not schedule adequate visits to the library for their students. I purposefully sought to find the teacher. Then with flexible schedule clipboard in hand, I would ask what time was mutually convenient to bring the class to the library. Then I would sign up the class session on the spot. I found this partnership constraint to be one that I could monitor and overcome with professional diplomacy.

A final constraint that I had identified in previous research was the use of the library as a disciplinary tool for the classroom teacher. Only in the first year were students sent unexpectedly to the library with a note of discipline. The just-sit routine became the research-or-read routine. Students returned to their classrooms with notes of progress completed while they were in the library. Teachers wanting discipline assistance found other faculty members.

Through longitudinal research, I was able to identify that strong teacher-librarian partnerships enable the library to become the heart of the school. Partnership constraints can be minimized when school libraries are active learning centers, when the librarian is committed to effective teaching and is a dynamic teacher (Whelan, 2004). For an effective teacher-librarian partnership, one in which the heartbeat of the school comes alive, enthusiastic teachers, librarians, and students work together and learn through an immersion into the literature.

BIBLIOGRAPHY: American Association of School Librarians [AASL]. 2001. *Information Power: Building Partnerships for Learning* [brochure]. Chicago: American Library Association; American Association of School Librarians [AASL], & Association for Educational Communications and Technology [AECT]. 1998. *Information power: Guidelines for School Library Media Programs.* Chicago: American Library Association; Girogis, C. 1993. *Librarian as Teacher: Exploring Elementary Teachers' Perceptions of the Role of the School Librarian and the Implementation of Flexible Scheduling and Collaborative Planning.* Ph.D. diss., University of Arizona, Tucson; Hughes-Hassell, S., & Wheelock, A., eds. 2001. *The Information-Powered School.* Chicago: Public Education Network and American Library Association; Jones, J. R. 1994. *The Teacher-Librarian Partnership in a Literature-Based Approach.* Ph.D. diss., Arizona State University, Tempe; Montgomery, P. 1991. Library Media Literacy: Minding the Library Media and Reading Connection. In C. C. Kuhlthau, ed., *Information Literacy: Learning How to Learn* Chicago: American Library Association, (pp. 32–35); Whelan, D. L. 2004. 13,000 Kids Can't Be Wrong. *School Library Journal* 50 no. 2, 46–50; Yesner, B. L., and Jay, H. L. 1987. *The School Administrator's Guide to Evaluating Library Media Programs.* Hamden, CT: Library Professional Publication.

JOANNA R. JONES

TEEN ISSUES

According to the U.S. Department of Health and Human Services, one in every five girls is sexually molested before she reaches the age of twelve. According to the USDHHS, one in seven boys faces the same harsh reality, though it is known that boys underreport their traumas, so that figure is probably low.

That means at least two of every twelve young people sitting in an average American high school are hiding a brutal secret beneath a cloak of shyness or rage or obesity or obsessively stellar grades. And that figure does not include physical or emotional abuse. It does not include sheer neglect.

Enter the T. or "Problem Novel" subgenre of adolescent books—powerful works of fiction that, according to some experts, can help save lives.

Author and East Carolina University library science professor Dr. Jami Biles believes the trend began in the late 1960s with books like S. E. HINTON's *The Outsiders* (1967). But even before the movement was documented, literary entities were paving the way.

William GOLDING first published *The Lord of the Flies,* a dark survival tale of teenage boys stranded by a plane crash on a remote and uninhabited island in 1954. The brutality possible at the hands of teenage desperation is deftly explored in this relatively modern classic. In 1959, John KNOWLES wrote *A Separate Peace,* the reflective story of protagonist Gene Forrester's coming of age, including his complicated relationship with and attraction to his best male friend, the ultrasuccessful athlete Finny. Even Daniel Keyes's Hugo Award winning work of SCIENCE FICTION, "Flowers for Algernon," first published in 1959, foreshadowed problem novels yet to come as it examined a developmentally challenged young man's struggles with being strikingly different while yearning to fit in.

Storytellers who blazed the T. book trail were sometimes forced to approach controversial topics with caution and metaphoric facsimiles. Their new millennium counterparts—authors like Chris CRUTCHER, Robert CORMIER, E. R. FRANK and Angela JOHNSON—thunder past the censors without apology or regret. "Even though realistic problem novels have always been racy and edgy to some degree, they are more so now," Dr. Biles says in a feature on her website (www.askdrjami.com). "While this trend has led

to increased discomfort for LIBRARIANS who sometimes wonder if any 'happy books' featuring normal, well-adjusted kids are being written, it has paid off for publishers in a big way. Teen books are selling like hotcakes; they are one of the few growth areas in an otherwise dull publishing market."

Indeed it has. Consider these four successful examples.

In *The First Part Last,* (2003), Angela Johnson explores teen pregnancy from the young AFRICAN AMERICAN father's distinctive point of view. After his beloved girlfriend Nia slips into a coma during childbirth, Bobby chooses to rear baby Feather without her mom. As he tells his infant about heaven, readers cry for the boy with man-sized challenges and grief, in part since Johnson does not minimize his challenge or his pain. "Bobby is my favorite character in this novel," writes one male reader on amazon.com, "because he shows so much love toward Feather . . . this novel actually changed the way I think about life itself."

In *Tenderness* (1998), Robert Cormier steps into the mind of a psychopath who has gone from killing kittens to contemporaries in the course of just eighteen brutalized years. Charm and good looks at first mask his thirst for blood as he woos fifteen-year-old runaway Lori, who could be his next victim. But even after she discovers his deadly secret, she is drawn to him, moved by the contrast of his tenderness against a killing theme.

But the T. novel is not just a marketing ploy. It is, in many instance, a therapeutic outreach as well.

E. R. Frank's body of work is not yet extensive in numbers, but each novel written by this social worker captures the very heart of the subgenre—and its healing potential—with unflinching honesty. *America* (2002), the story of a sixteen-year-old boy trapped in the broken foster-care system for more than a decade—and standing on the brink of suicide because of it—is an indictment of help that hurts, through the eyes of one character that represents literally thousands of real kids.

Chris Crutcher, a child and FAMILY therapist in the Pacific Northwest, is perhaps the boldest and most successful of the modern breed. All but one of his nine novels reaches into the realm of the problem novel since his fiction is so heartily influenced by his work as a mental-health professional. But *Athletic Shorts,* a collection of SHORT STORIES, and *Whale Talk*

(2001) are books best known for their honesty and their propensity for being challenged. "I gather you are quite taken with yourself because you put dirty words and homosexual propaganda in books for young people," wrote one anonymous person in an E-mail to Crutcher in October of 2004. "I'm sure you consider yourself extraordinarily clever and courageous." The "homosexual propaganda" described in the letter was a short story from *Athletic Shorts* called, "In the Time I Get," about a teenage boy torn between showing compassion for a man dying of AIDS and protecting his image as a high-school jock in the wake of anti-gay community sentiment—clearly an issue most teens would understand. And Crutcher explains the story's origin this way. "When I wrote 'In the Time I Get,' I had recently experienced the grief of the DEATH of a client from AIDS. He was a guy who had been wreckless all his life; had three children he almost never saw, who were recently removed from their mother because of a drug addiction. The guy discovered what was happening and came back to work in therapy to get the kids back so they could stay together and not be farmed out into foster care. He did amazing work, went back into his own history and acknowledged every mistake and every careless action that put his kids at risk. The rest of the men in his men's group looked up to him for the courage to tell the truth. He was far more impactful to the group than I was as the therapist and group leader.

"Then he came to treatment one night and announced that he had some bad news. He had AIDS. It was full-blown and all his work was for nothing because it was taking over. You could *feel* the other men in the group backing away from him, as he spoke. Two days later, he was hospitalized and I visited him there. The disease was on fast forward. A week later I went again and when I asked how many of the other group members had been to visit him, he got tears in his eyes and said, 'None. It's OK, though. They're scared.' And then he gave me a line I used in the story. He said, 'You know, the tough part about this disease, beside the fact that it's killing me, is that no one will touch me. I haven't been touched since I entered the hospital.' Like Louie in the book, I touched him, and he cried like a baby. In another week he was gone.

"The other group members were a rugged bunch. Many of them had decided he was 'queer' and it was his own damn fault, though many of them had been intraveneous-drug users. And they were horribly misinformed about how the disease passes, which was another reason none of them went to visit. In the end, though many of them didn't know it, they lost a hero and he died alone.

"It is not OK in this country to be a bigot. It may be legal, but it's not OK."

Crutcher's words describe his story, but capture the heart of T. novels at their finest. They reach into the soul of humanity and sample a little truth, then share that essence with readers most likely to wonder what truth really means—teens struggling with coming-of-age (which constitutes ALL teens from ALL kinds of families).

Why defend using T. books in twenty-first century classrooms? "Because those kids exist," Crutcher says. "They cannot reveal anything that would point to those secrets, so their behavior may look opposite of what is bothering the student. Teachers need to embrace a classroom policy of inclusion. The more they understand about what it is to have and keep those dark secrets, the better they can structure their classrooms to be safe."

Can those books be "life saving" as some experts contend? "In baseball that question would be seen as a 'lob pitch,' he responds. "I don't know if they're life-saving or not. What they do is let kids know they are not alone and there are people to turn to. If that's life-saving, then the answer is yes."

KELLY MILNER HALLS

TEEN PERFORMANCE ARTS

At many colleges and universities, new and old theater buildings are part of the campus. Well-known, distinguished performers of the arts are teaching and passing on their expertise and skills. The same situation exists in other areas of the arts. Nearly every large or small city has one or more acting companies. Theatrical productions are brought to people everywhere: schools, camps, nursing homes, senior centers and villages. There is always a tour of young and older performers sharing their talent and enthusiasm for the stage, as well as teen arts festivals, camps, classes at recreation centers, and at the YMCA. Theater is a precarious profession. There are more performers auditioning for parts than there are parts; understandably, the field is very competitive.

The performing arts community or industry offers variety. You can be anything from an actor, singer or dancer to the producer of a major theatrical production. If you prefer to work backstage, your job can be stage manager, lighting designer, sound designer, director, make-up artist, hairdresser, wardrobe dresser or costume designer. You might aspire to be the general manager of a theater, a conductor, arranger, composer, orchestrator or librettist. Perhaps you want to use your skills as secretary, receptionist, fund-raiser or personal manager, working on the administrative side of an orchestra, opera or ballet company. The performing arts need critics, journalists and press agents, to communicate with the public and booking agents, managers and literary agents to spread the word. Those who want to incorporate education and the performing arts can teach drama, dance or music (Shelly Field. 1999. *Career Opportunities in Theater and Performing Arts.* 2nd ed.).

Today, there are many books, MAGAZINE, and newspaper articles as well as television and radio programs to help young people interested in working in this field but who haven't a clue as to what opportunities are out there, where to look for them, and what training is needed.

If you go to the theater today, you will see many young people attending as well as performing, whether you are attending a professional production or a local amateur one. Backstage you will likely see them there also as stage crew, dressers, lighting, and assistant of many kinds. Some are lucky enough to work as interns in a community theater or for a professional company that allows them to gain valuable experience. Today many young people are featured on the stage in theatrical productions or musical groups as well as on television and in the movies.

Many are called to the performing arts from the day they are born. Others are drawn to it by seeing a performance and wanting to have that experience for themselves. In SPORTS you don't have to talk. You just have to demonstrate your skill in the sport you are involved in and to act as if you are confident and focused when competing. If you want to learn everything about theater check out lots of books at the library and read magazine articles which tell you to watch your local newspapers for local theater company audition notices. The performing-arts world is a challenge, but it's a worthwhile one, as it builds self-esteem and confidence you can use in other areas of your life.

If you are interested in pursuing a career in the performing arts, you are encouraged by professional actors to look into camps; recreation centers, dance schools, music schools for voice, acting, and audition classes, theater companies for young people and school drama clubs. These places offer you the chance to learn the principles of acting through creative exercises and games, improvisations as ways to develop your concentration, communication skills, how to learn monologues, interpret and deliver them, audition preparation, and how to increase your knowledge of the theater, not only its history but the history of period productions. You learn the inner workings of the backstage theater where the audience is not admitted.

What will you learn if you follow this path? You will learn why actors have certain rituals, what those famous theatrical quotes that you always hear mean, how to build scenery, props, and many other behind-the-curtains aspects. Plus you'll make new friends and learn how to work as a team to put on really fantastic and high-quality productions.

So whether you want to perform in front of the curtain as an actor, musician, dancer, or behind the curtain as a composer, playwright, director, costume designer, dresser, coach or the usher, the first step is to get informed and get involved. The rest is up to you. Don't forget that in your searching you can use magazines and journals, as well as the Internet. One good source is *The Actors Guide to the Internet* by Rob Kozlowski, 2000.

BIBLIOGRAPHY: Ax, Barbara, ed., *Summer Theater Directory 2003: A National Guide to Summer Employment, for Professionals and Student: Performers (Equity & Non-Equity), Directors, Designers, Technicians, Management (Summer Theater Directory (Theater Directory),* 2002 (printed annually); Banham, Martin. *Cambridge Guide to Theater,* 1993, pp. 122–25; Caltron, Louis E. *Theatre Sources Dot Com: A Complete Guide to Online Theatre and Dance Resources,* 2001; Charles, Jill. *Directory of Theatre Training Programs: 2001–2003,* 8th ed; Ellis, Roger. *Audition Monologs for Student Actors II: Selections from Contemporary Plays,* 2002; Garrison, Gary. *Monologues for Men by Men,* vol. 2, 2002; Hill, Kimberly Mohne, *Monologues in Dialect for Young Actors,* 2002; Lane, Eric. *Leading Women: Plays for Actresses,* 2002; Milstein, Janet B. *The Ultimate Au-*

dition Book for Teens: 111 One-Minute Monologues, 2000; Narto, Don. World History Series: Greek and Roman Theater 1995, pp. 83–85, 89–95; Ratliff, Gerald Lee. The Theatre Audition Book: Playing Monologs from Contemporary, Modern, Period, Shakespeare and Classical Plays, 1998; Slaight, Craig. Great Monologues for Young Actors, 1999; Wehrum, Victoria. The American Theatre 1974, pp. 77–79; Wickham, Glynne. A History of the Theatre, 2nd ed. 1992, pp. 7–10; http://www.theatrehistory.com; http://www.aada.org; http://www.stellaadler.com; http://www.backstagecasting.com; http://www.performink.com

DAWNA L. MCCLENDON

TEMPLE, Frances (Nolting)
Author, b. 15 August 1945, Washington, D.C.; d. 5 July 1995, Geneva, New York

Though T. attended three universities, Wellesley College (1963–65), the University of North Carolina (B.A., 1969 in English and African studies), and the University of Virginia (M.Ed., 1976), she received her real education through her life experiences. The child of a diplomat, T. lived in a variety of locations and settings that would later play a part in her writings. From home schooling on an isolated farm in Virginia, sharing a bedroom with three sisters, to a convent school in France, to a two-year stint with the Peace Corps in Sierra Leone, these situations "provided T. not only with a big picture and a global view, but also established in her a sense of compassion and fairness—the ability to see the world's problems on the individual, human level."

T. did not plan to be a writer of fiction. Though she was an author of award-winning books of contemporary and medieval history, T. actually started by doing free-writing exercises she did while her primary-school students were doing their writing exercises. She never actually finished any of these scribbles. However, one day a student complained that T. never finished what she had started—unlike the rule that she preached to her students! Not expecting to be published, T. nevertheless sat down one summer and kept writing until she finished a book in 1987, The Ramsay Scallop (1994), which became an ALA Best Books for YA.

Writing and publishing her first book "transformed T.: she saw stories in the world around her and in quick succession wrote manuscripts dealing with contemporary life and young people living through extraordinary perils. . . . The realism was no accident:

T. blended meticulous research and familiarity with many parts of the world with a deep and abiding sense of fairness and belief in other humans."

Although The Ramsay Scallop was finished in 1987, T. wrote and published Taste of Salt: A Story of Modern Haiti (1992) during a work-study semester that she and her husband spent in the Dominican Republic in 1990. This novel told in heavy dialect of the timely occurrences in Haiti. It received a Jane Addams Children's Book Award and a Hungry Minds Books of Distinction Award. Grab Hands and Run (1993) followed, building on some work that T. had done previously. This too was based on her real-life experiences with a LATINO–refugee family on their way to Canada searching for freedom.

In Tonight by Sea (1995), T. returned to portraying conditions in Haiti as she had in Taste of Salt. Paulie experiences the repressiveness of the government firsthand and must decide how much she should risk to save someone else. This novel won a 1995 Americas Award, as well as being included in Great Books for Girls by Kathleen Odean (1997).

AWARDS: ALA Best Books for Young Adults: Grab Hands and Run, 1994, The Ramsay Scallop, 1995.

SELECT FURTHER WORKS: (adaptor and illustrator) Tiger Soup: An Anansi Story from Jamaica, 1994; The Beduin's Gazelle, 1996.

BIBLIOGRAPHY: "Frances (Nolting) T.," U*X*L Junior DISCovering Authors, U*X*L, 1998. Reproduced in Discovering Collection, http://galenet.galegroup.com/servlet/DC/; Smith, L., Children's Book Awards International, 1990–2000, 2003.

SARA MARCUS
AND JEANNE MARIE RYAN

TEPPER, Sheri S. (pseud. E. E. Hortak, B. J. Oliphant, A. J. Orde)
Author, b. 1929, Denver, Colorado

T. has written several FANTASY trilogies, creating magical worlds full of MYSTERY, danger, and ADVENTURE. T.'s first fantasy trilogy is set in a role-playing society where the rules and magic change to suit the players. King's Blood Four (1983), Necromancer Nine (1983), and Wizard's Eleven (1984) make up the first True Game trilogy. The second True Game trilogy (all 1985) features The Song of Mavin Manyshaped, The Flight of Mavin Manyshaped, and The Search of Mavin Manyshaped. Using her shape-shifting talents, Mavin leaves her tribe to go on adventures, finding a lost city and a lost friend. The third trilogy (1988) consists of *Jinian Footseer, Dervish Daughter,* and *Jinian Star-Eye.* Jinian, a young woman, must fight evil forces that are determined to bring an end to the Game and the entire world. T. guides us through a magical realm in a fourth fantasy trilogy: *Marianne, the Magus, and the Manticore* (1985), *Marianne, the Madame, and the Momentary Gods* (1988), and *Marianne, the Matchbox, and the Malachite Mouse* (1989). *The Awakeners* (1987), consists of two novels *(Northshore* and *Southshore)* about a priestess, a boatman, and their rebellion against the ruling powers of their planet. *The Revenants* (1986), a single novel, is a fantasy quest. *A Plague of Angels* (1994) mixes humans with dominant magical creatures. *Shadow's End* (1994) is a SCIENCE FICTION and MYSTERY adventure in which an investigator from earth seeks the answer to why all humans are disappearing from neighboring planets.

T.'s science fiction novels involve environmental and societal holocausts, oppression of women and other life forms, and religious fanaticism. *After Long Silence* (1987) introduces a colonized planet still inhabited by an alien intelligence. The controversial *The Gate to Women's Country* (1988) explores human nature and gender diversity following a holocaust that creates two societies, each dominated by one of the sexes. *Grass* (1989) studies how successfully two races can share a world with life-threatening problems. Considered to be one of T.'s best novels, *Raising the Stones* (1991) discusses religious fanaticism. It's sequel, *Sideshow* (1992), continues the religious theme when confronted with intolerance and faith-testing trials. America has been swept up in fundamentalism in *Gibbon's Decline and Fall* (1996), threatening the future of humanity. Seven women must uncover a sinister plot of world domination. In *The Family Tree* (1997) Dora, a police officer, investigates the connection between the murders of three geneticists and rampant flora that is making the city inhospitable for human life. Mouche uses his unique abilities to discover how to save his planet from the effects of the moons in the *Six Moon Dance* (1998). *Singer from the Sea* (1999) portrays a traditional, class-bound woman who embarks on a new destiny to save her world. Using the theme of change and renewal, *The Fresco* (2000) is an attempt to answer the questions of who the Pistach are and what the

sacred Fresco means to them. Hundreds of years earlier, in the twenty-first century, an asteroid hit the Earth. Now, in *The Visitor* (2002), a young woman, using a book left behind by a scientist, must search for the truth and reclaim the earth from superstition and oppression.

T. favorably explored the HORROR genre with *Blood Heritage* (1986), *The Bones* (1987), and *Still Life* (1989, as E. E. Hortak). T. also wrote mysteries under two pseudonyms, B. J. Oliphant and A. J. Orde.

AWARDS: Hugo Award nomination, 1990, and *New York Times* Notable Book citation, for *Grass;* Edgar Award nomination, Mystery Writers of America, 1990, for *Dead in the Scrub;* award for best fantasy of the year, *Locus,* 1991, ALA Best Books for Young Adults, 1992, for *Beauty.*

FURTHER WORKS: As B. J. Oliphant: *Dead in the Scrub,* 1990; *The Unexpected Corpse,* 1990; *Deservedly Dead,* 1992; *Death and the Delinquent,* 1993; *Death Served up Cold,* 1994; *A Ceremonial Death,* 1996; *Here's to the Newly Deads,* 1998. As A. J. Orde: *A Little Neighborhood Murder,* 1989; *Death and the Dogwalker,* 1990; *Death for Old Times' Sake,* 1992; all Jason Lynx novels, *Looking for the Aardvark,* 1993; *A Long Time Dead,* 1995; *Death of Innocents,* 1997; *The Companions,* 2003.

BIBLIOGRAPHY: Clute, J. and P. Nichols, *The Encyclopedia of Science Fiction,* 1993; *Contemporary Authors Online,* 2003; "Sheri S. T." *St. James Guide to Science Fiction Writers,* 4th ed., 1996.

LAURIE BERG

TERKEL, (Studs) Louis
Author, b. 16 May 1912, New York City

T., is a self-described "guerrilla journalist," known for his oral histories of Americans of all stripes. After working as a stage actor and movie house manager, T. began his broadcasting career in 1930s radio, playing gangsters and writing SPORTS news. Then, in the 1950s, he hosted a live interview program called "Stud's Place" on NBC television. He signed an anti-Jim Crow and anti-poll tax petition and consequently was fired by NBC. He credits this firing with his choice to become a Chicago radio station host and disc jockey, broadcasting daily for some forty-five years. On his WFMT show, he played Mahalia Jackson's gospel music, Woody Guthrie, operatic music, jazz, and blues. He also continued his interviewing on the show, known as *Wax Museum;* he also produced radio documentaries and SHORT STORY broadcasts. T.'s sympathetic listening was the basis of his fame, forming the core of his published works, which intimately show realities of the American experience in first-person narratives. In addition to his books, he wrote several PLAYS, including *Amazing Grace* (1967). His book *Working* was adapted into a Broadway musical in 1978; his books *American Dreams* and *Talking to Myself* were staged in 1987 and 1988, respectively. *Will the Circle be Unbroken?: Reflections on Death, Rebirth and Hunger for a Faith,* which was published in 2001, addresses people's attitudes toward DEATH, while it also focuses on the importance of talking about life and living it to the fullest.

AWARDS: Ohio State University award, 1959, UNESCO Prix Italia award, 1962, both for *Wax Museum;* University of Chicago Alumni Association Communicator of the Year award, 1969, National Book Award nominee, 1975, George Foster Peabody Broadcasting award, 1980, Society of Midland Authors award, 1982, for *American Dreams: Lost and Found,* and 1983, for best writer; Eugene V. Debs award, 1983, for public service; Pulitzer Prize in nonfiction, 1985, for *"The Good War": An Oral History of World War II;* ALA Best Books for Young Adults: *American Dreams: Lost and Found,* 1980, *"The Good War,"* 1984; Hugh M. Hefner First Amendment Award for Lifetime Achievement, 1990.

FURTHER WORKS: *Giants of Jazz,* 1957; *Division Street: America,* 1967; *Hard Times: An Oral History of the Great Depression,* 1970; *Working,* 1974; *Talking to Myself,* 1977; *American Dreams,* 1980; *"The Good War,"* 1984; *Envelopes of Oral Sound,* 1990; *The Neon Wilderness,* 1986; *Chicago,* 1986; *The Great Divide,* 1988; *RACE: How Blacks and Whites Think and Feel about the American Obsession,* 1992; *Coming of Age,* 1995; *My American Century,* 1997; *The Spectator,* 1999.

BIBLIOGRAPHY: *Literature Resource Center; Academic Search Premier; Ebsco Host,* 2001.

CATHERINE GIVEN

THESMAN, Jean
Author, n.d., n.p.

T. grew up in a family that valued storytelling, reading, and family history. From an early age, T. listened as her mother and her mother's friends recalled stories about their ancestors while sitting around the kitchen table. T. was invited to participate in this storytelling tradition at age fourteen, when the women deemed her mature enough to understand and join their discussion. Also a storyteller, T.'s father was a well-traveled man; he told T. of his exploits, often illustrating his tales with photographs from his trips. T. found his tales, which included "shipwrecks, battles, encounters with Chinese warlords, and even beheadings," both "fascinating as well as horrifying."

T. learned to read before starting school. She was taught by her mother, who did not want to leave such an important task to strangers. T.'s writing was also precocious; a newspaper published one of her poems during her first-grade year. T.'s decision to become a writer seems only natural—indeed, she feels that storytelling runs in her blood and considers writing books for TEENS to be the world's best job.

Since that first poem, T. has written over forty novels. They span many genres, including contemporary realism, FANTASY, historic ROMANCE, and suspense. In addition to books published under her own name, T. has also published several HORROR novels under the name T. J. Bradstreet.

Although she had published several earlier novels, T.'s writing rose to prominence in 1987 when she published *The Last April Dancers, Running Scared,* and *Who Said Life Is Fair?* In these novels, T. explores some of the themes prominent in her later books, such as FAMILY, responsibility, and romance.

In *The Last April Dancers,* sixteen-year-old Cat must cope with her father's suicide. With the romantic support of Cam, the boy next door, she disentangles the webs surrounding several family mysteries and in the process finds the courage to take control of her own life. In *Running Scared,* fifteen-year-old Caroline and her younger cousin Jasper struggle to survive after they are taken prisoner by a militant survivalist group. *Who Said Life Is Fair?* presents the dilemmas that Teddy, editor of the school newspaper, faces as she questions the school administration's interference in the school newspaper and tries to sort out her involvement with the classmate she admires and her childhood friend, Bill, who now admires her.

The Rain Catchers (1991), winner of the Golden Kite award, is possibly T.'s best-known novel. Fourteen-year-old Grayling, inspired by a group of her grandmother's friends who share their lives by weaving them into stories, seeks to understand her own story. She journeys from Seattle to San Francisco to trace her roots, eventually confronting her mother and learning about her heritage.

The inclusion of supernatural abilities or characters is another characteristic common to a number of T.'s novels. In the historical novel *Rachel Chance* (1990), for example, both fifteen-year-old Rachel and her grandfather's friend, Druid Annie, have the ability to occasionally "see true," allowing them glimpses into the future. Although Rachel relies on her own wits and determination to rescue her kidnapped younger brother, her glimpses of the future reassure her of her eventual success. Both *Appointment with a Stranger* (1989) and *Cattail Moon* (1994) feature ghostly characters. In *Between* (2002), T. weaves legends and mythical creatures into a 1941 setting. Fourteen-year-old Charlotte discovers that her younger brother, Will, is really a supernatural "Fair One," sent to save Darkwood, a nearby forest that is home to creatures such as griffins and dragons. Along with an ecological theme, T. again explores family bonds, relationships, and responsibility as Charlotte and Will struggle through their mixed emotions surrounding Will's dilemma of whether to remain with his human family or to save Darkwood.

T.'s most recent books continue to explore relationships. *Calling the Swan* (2000) recounts fifteen-year-old Skyler and her family's attempts to move on with their lives after the disappearance of Skyler's older sister, Alexandra. *In the House of the Queen's Beasts* (2001) describes how two fourteen-year-old friends, Emily and Rowan, learn from each other and begin to heal from their individual tragedies.

T.'s writing has been praised for its subtlety, lyricism, and sensuality. In addition to the Golden Kite award, she has received the Sequoyah YA Award and many American Library Association Best Book for YAs and Recommended Book for the Reluctant YA Reader designations, among others.

AWARDS: American Library Association Best Book for Young Adults: *The Other Ones*, 2000, *The Ornament Tree*, 1997, *When the Road Ends*, 1993, *The Rain Catchers*, 1992, *Rachel Chance, The Last April Dancers;* New York Public Library Books for the Teen Age: *The Ornament True;* International Readers Association Young Adults' Choices: *Cattail Moon, The Rain Catchers, Appointment with a Stranger, The Last April Dancers, Who Said Life is Fair?, Was It Something I Said?;* Teachers Choices Award: *Cattail Moon;* YALSA Quick Picks for Reluctant Young Adult Readers: *Summerspell;* Society of Children's Book

Writer's and Illustrators Golden Kite Award: *The Rain Catchers;* Sequoya Young Adult Award: *Appointment with a Stranger;* American Library Association Recommended Book for the Reluctant Young Adult Reader: *Appointment with a Stranger, The Last April Dancers, Who Said Life is Fair?, Running Scared, Erin.*

FURTHER WORKS: *New Kid in Town*, 1984; *Was It Something I Said?*, 1988; *Couldn't I Start Over?*, 1989; *Heather*, 1990; *When Does the Fun Start?*, 1991; *When the Road Ends*, 1992; *Triple Trouble*, 1992; *Mirror, Mirror*, 1992; *Molly Donnelly*, 1993; *Nothing Grows Here*, 1994; *Summerspell*, 1995; *The Ornament Tree*, 1996; *Wendy's Wish* (under T. J. Bradstreet), 1996; *The Storyteller's Daughter*, 1997; *Before She Wakes* (under T. J. Bradstreet), 1997; *The Moonstones*, 1998; *Meredith*, 1998; *Teresa*, 1998; *The Tree of Bells*, 1999; *The Other Ones*, 1999; *A Sea So Far*, 2001; *Rising Tide*, 2003.

BIBLIOGRAPHY: *Something about the Author*, vol. 74, 1993; *Seventh Book of Junior Authors and Illustrators*, 1996; www.jeanthesman.com

ALLISON RICHARDSON

THOMAS, Rob

Author, b. 15 August 1965, Sunnyside, Washington

T. received his B.A. and teaching certificate from the University of Texas at Austin in 1987. Upon graduating, he worked for five years as a journalism teacher at Reagan High School in Austin, and then moved to Los Angeles, where he worked at Channel One, a Los Angeles-area television network for teenagers. When he took the job at Channel One, T. was forced to leave the rock band he had been playing in for past nine years. Of this time in his life, T. notes, "Suddenly, I had this huge creative void in my life. I wasn't doing anything, so I started writing . . . a page a day that filled that hole in my life. Once I learned the discipline of that, I became what I wanted to be. I was a pretty mediocre bass player, and I had beat my head against the wall for nine years trying to make it in the band. It happened very quickly for me as a writer. It was a matter of finding the right niche."

On becoming a writer, T. knew it was just a matter of timing and discipline. "Writing a book," he has said, "was always sort of this mountain out there in my future that I was going to climb someday." Armed with the commitment to write one page of a manuscript each morning, his first novel, *Rats Saw God* (1996), was born. The novel is driven by TEEN angst issues, including divorce, identity, and teenage infidelity. The protagonist, Steve York, has lived his life in the shadow of his perfect, astronaut father. His parents divorce, and then his first love betrays him by having an affair with Steve's favorite teacher. Steve starts taking drugs and hanging out with the wrong crowd. He eventually drops out of school, only to return the following September to an interesting offer from his guidance counselor: He is given the opportunity to achieve academic redemption by writing a one-hundred-page story chronicling the events leading up to his current problems. The result is a story that gives readers personal insight into the mind of a teenager who is dealing with intensely complicated yet heartfelt issues.

The idea for T.'s second novel, *Slave Day* (1997), was inspired by a videotape he received while working at Channel One. The videotape showed a student slave auction that was conducted in the spirit of fundraising. T. set *Slave Day* in Texas, and the story plays out over a twelve-hour period of time during which teachers and student council members are auctioned off to the highest bidders. Keene Davenport, an AFRICAN-AMERICAN student, is outraged by this demeaning event and devises a plot to put an end to his high school's endorsement of it. He finds, though, that it is easier to tackle the problem from the inside, and this leads him to his decision to bid on the class president and star basketball player, Shawn Greeley. With Shawn as his slave, Keene creates intensely demeaning tasks, including picking up cotton balls and shining shoes.

In *Slave Day,* T. explores the issue of racism primarily through the first-person perspectives of two black students, Keene and Shawn. The inclusion of two African-American characters here allowed T. to contrast their views, and ultimately made the writing process smoother. T. observes, "I would have been much more nervous had I written from only one black character's perspective. Then, I'm afraid whatever that character was like, it would have been seen as my take on what all African Americans sound/behave like." In order to make *Slave Day* as authentic as possible, T. had some of his African-American students read the manuscript. He also passed his work to Trey Ellis, one of his favorite African-American authors, who told T. that the manuscript "sounded on to him." When *Slave Day* was published, it was immediately praised for its dialogue. A review in *Publishers Weekly* stated, "T. is so good at capturing teen lan-

guage and responses that the book will be welcomed by readers looking for a reflection of their own struggles."

T. gives voices to the depressed, cynical adolescent boys of today's world, and introduces into their worlds complex, real issues, including drugs, sex, cliques, divorce, and all the insecurities that come with being a teenager. His writing is fresh and modern, yet still reflects the characteristic teenage angst that has perpetually haunted adolescents.

T. has written song lyrics for bands including Hey Zeus and Black Irish. Additionally, he has written screenplays for television, including *Dawson's Creek* and *Cupid.*

AWARDS: *Rats Saw God:* American Library Association (ALA) Best Book for Young Adults, 1997 ALA Quick Pick for Reluctant Young Adult Readers, 2002 ALA Popular Paperbacks; YALSA Top Ten Best Books, School Library Journal Best Book of the Year, and New York Public Library Book for the Teen Age, 1996–97; ALA Quick Pick and Best Book, 1998, *Doing Time.*

FURTHER WORKS: *Doing Time: Notes from the Undergrad,* 1997; *Satellite Down,* 1998; *Green Thumb,* 1999.

BIBLIOGRAPHY: "Rob T." *Authors and Artists for Young Adults,* vol. 25, 1998; "Rob T." *St. James Guide to Young Adult Writers,* 2nd ed., 1999; *Something about the Author,* vol. 97.

CARRA E. GAMBERDELLA

THOMPSON, Julian F(rancis)

Author, b. 16 November 1927, New York City

A writer who persistently writes out his drafts in longhand and types his manuscripts on a typewriter, T. remains loyal to his YA audience, providing them with identifiable characters that become responsible yet naturally flawed human beings. Adults have complained that his writing covers too many issues with not enough substance, yet the fame of T.'s novels among young readers illustrates the author's importance to YA literacy.

The son of a playwright, T.'s affluent childhood came to an end with the DEATH of his father. He found great solace in SPORTS at Lawrenceville School, and his grief was slowly healed through work as a sports counselor for camps and intramural teams. Although T. does not consider himself to have been a spectacular student, he graduated from Princeton University in 1949 and received his M.A. from Columbia University in 1955. He returned to his former school, Lawrenceville, and filled the positions of teacher, coach, and housemaster from 1949 to 1962 and from 1965 to 1967. During and between these periods at Lawrenceville, T. was struggling to set his writing career in motion. It was not until his experience at an alternative school called Changes, Inc. that he made some headway in his personal writing. While teaching creative writing courses, T found a literary voice through which he could write, a language that could suitably narrate his stories. In 1978, T. married Polly Nichy, whom he met at Changes, and retired permanently from teaching; the two moved to Vermont, where T. placed his complete attention on his writing.

The author could finally celebrate in 1983, the year in which his first two books, *Facing It* and *The Grounding of Group Six,* were published. It was much to his surprise that his novels were classified under the young adult genre; he did not intentionally write for this age group, yet his experience with TEENAGERS had logically penetrated his writing. The classification of his work was not important, only the fact that he was being read. People could label his books whatever they pleased as long as his work found an eager audience of readers.

Perhaps T.'s literary success lay in the fact that his characters mirrored people encountered in his life. While a human being has many personality facets, fictional characters often fall short of being believable, three-dimensional people. With actual people as references, T. taps into all angles of human emotion. His protagonist in *Facing It* is an athlete who believes he has lost his identity with the amputation of three fingers; background information about this character came directly from the author as a boy, an athlete mourning the loss of his father and his known life.

In his subsequent works, T. incorporates in his writing issues such as nuclear war (*A Band of Angels,* 1986), monetary control (*The Taking of Mariasburg,* 1988), book CENSORSHIP (*The Trials of Molly Sheldon,* 1995), and child pornography (*Ghost Story,* 1997). While adult critics often view T.'s use of foul language, sexual explicitness, and graphic violence as gratuitous and a mere ploy for popularity among teenagers, obviously he strikes the right chord with his substantial audience of young adult readers. These are the issues that teenagers spend time thinking about, and T. "elaborates on or derives plots from character-istics of some of the students he knew as a teacher and as a teenager himself." Despite the discrepancy between adult criticism and teenage feedback on T.'s books, the author has received recognition for his work from young adult literary associations.

In a speech entitled "An Underutilized Resource: Values Education and the Older YA Novel," T. explains the necessity of novels in the classroom that contain accessible prose. When students encounter characters that talk the way they talk, they "become the experts" of the classroom and gain confidence in their ability to understand literature. Always the teacher, T. has brought his interactions with adolescents into his understanding of YOUNG ADULT LITERATURE, and, above all, knows the importance of turning skeptical teenagers into adult readers.

AWARDS: 1986 American Library Association Best Book for Young Adult, *Band of Angels;* 1987 *Booklist* Editor's Choice, *Simon Pure.*

FURTHER WORKS: *A Question of Survival,* 1984; *Discontinued,* 1985; *Simon Pure,* 1987; *Goofbang,* 1989; *Herb Seasoning,* 1990; *Gypsyworld,* 1992; *Shepherd,* 1993; *The Fling,* 1994; *Philo Fortune's Awesome Journey to His Comfort Zone,* 1995; *Brothers,* 1998; *Terry and the Pirates,* 2000; *Hard Time,* 2003.

BIBLIOGRAPHY: *Something about the Author,* vol. 99, 1999; *Major Authors and Illustrators for Children and Young Adults,* 2nd ed., 8, 2002; Thompson, Julian. "An Underutilized Resource: Values Education and the Older Young Adult Novel," http://scholar.lib .vt.edu/ejournals/ALAN/spring96/mbrshipcom.html

RACHEL WITMER

TIME TRAVEL: YESTERDAY, TODAY, AND TOMORROW

When I think of time travel, the first book that comes to mind is H. G. Wells' classic *The Time Machine.* The movie was wonderful, but the book is a time travel tour de force. Since it was written by H. G. Wells, this is a classic "science is the answer" scenario. But what an answer it provides as it takes the reader forward in time, to a future in which the gentle, vulnerable Eloi are at the mercy of the brutal Morlocks. And on beyond that—to the end of the world.

From this basic template time travel has gone in a multitude of directions. This article will explore some of these—in novels that challenge, provoke and above all entertain.

Way Back—Way, Way Back

Going back in time was a dream come true for a researcher enamored of the Middle Ages in *The Doomsday Book* by Connie WILLIS. But then her drop was miscalculated and she wound up in England, just when the Black Death was appearing, and she wasn't feeling too well. To make matters worse (as if that were possible), contemporary London was in the throes of an epidemic. As a result, the University was closed, so there was no one standing by to try and bring her home.

Connie Willis also went back in time to visit the Civil War in *Lincoln's Dreams*. The method of travel in this case is a psychic link with General Robert E. Lee or someone very close to him. The protagonists visit the sites of several major battles in an effort to find out whose dreams they are experiencing.

Michael CRICHTON leaves dinosaurs behind to visit fourteenth-century France in his time travel best seller, *Timeline*. Anthropologists have only dreamed of experiencing the past first-hand, until quantum technology in the twenty-first century makes it possible to actually go back and walk the streets of a feudal village. But that dream becomes a nightmare for the team sent back to the "feudal ages" when their guide is killed and they are stranded in time. As far as they know, their chances of returning to modern times are slim indeed.

Sam Magruder also goes way back in time, all the way back to the Cretaceous Period in George Simpson's *The Dechronization of Sam Magruder*. He was researching a quantum theory of time when he literally slipped through the cracks and wound up in a swamp inhabited by dinosaurs. As the only human on Earth and with no way back to the future, he observes dinosaur behavior carefully and leaves a record, chiseled onto stone slabs, for future scientists to decipher, thereby settling some of the major controversies of modern times about dinosaur behavior and appearance. The author, who died in 1984, was one of this century's most renowned paleontologists, and his expertise is clearly evident in this unusual novella, found among his effects.

Robert SILVERBERG's time traveling researchers visit the fabled halls of Atlantis in *Letters from Atlantis*. But they do not make the trip in their physical bodies. Instead, they share the minds of individuals who are involved in the final tragic days of the fabled island kingdom. And in the process they discover that even knowing what is going to happen in the future doesn't mean that you can change the past.

Pat MURPHY also has a protagonist who communicates with the past. In *The Falling Woman*, a middle-aged archeologist is not only able to see what is going on during the height of the Mayan civilization, but she can also communicate with individuals from this ancient epoch.

And finally Michael Bishop takes his protagonist way back in time, two million years back to be precise, to a time when African apes were evolving. In *No Enemy But Time*, a black American who travels back in time to study these apes gets so involved with them that he winds up marrying a beautiful hominid he names Helen.

Forward into the Future

What better guide to the challenges we can expect in the future than the renowned (and prolific, extremely prolific) Isaac ASIMOV. Time guardianship is the responsibility of Eternity, an organization that exists to better mankind, in his *The End of Eternity*. In this work the hero rebels against the boredom that results when mankind always takes the safest route through time.

Another Asimov hero is just a simple tailor who is catapulted forward into the future in *Pebble in the Sky*. This is a future in which the Earth is under the control of the Galactic Empire. This is also an Earth where the "year 60 rule" is in effect, used as a form of population control. People in their 60s are considered to have nothing further to contribute to society and so are expendable. Euthanasia is an acceptable form of population control, used to keep the planetary population down to approximately 20 million. There are no records to show that the 62-year-old tailor has passed the critical age, so he has an unprecedented chance to change things.

Another protagonist catapulted forward in time is a little Neanderthal boy, who suddenly finds himself in the twenty-first century in *The Ugly Little Boy*, by Isaac Asimov and Robert Silverberg. There he discovers that while the world he lives in has changed completely, human nature hasn't.

Into the future is also where Jaybee Corbell flees in Larry NIVEN's *A World Out of Time*. It began with his effort to survive cancer by having himself frozen.

But after 200 years society has changed, and he was awakened, not because he was safe from the disease but because he was needed to go on a mission to the stars, in someone else's body. But Corbell was not about to let someone else dictate to him. He headed his spaceship into the galactic core, where the fabric of time and space were distorted, giving him a chance to escape. Afterwards, he returned to Earth, only to discover that he had escaped too well. Three million years had gone by while he was away and everything had changed, except the fact that he was still in danger.

Bobbling into the future is what the characters in Vernor Vinge's *Marooned in Realtime* do to escape a depopulated Earth. A group of lonely survivors enter stasis bubbles, wait for a preset period of time to pass, and then stop and check to see if the scattered remnants of humanity are out there. But one of the leaders has been deliberately stranded in realtime and spends her life near the stasis bubble, waiting in vain for it to open and for her friends to come back to her. She dies before this happens, but she leaves behind journals that are studied by an investigator in his effort to solve what is essentially a case of murder.

Bobble technology was first introduced in the prequel, *The Peace War*. Not as a method of time travel, but as an instrument that is used for the execution of transgressors. How times have changed!

Recently re-released, *The Big Time* by Fritz Leiber demonstrates the fact that "You can't time travel through the time you time travel in when you time travel." Leiber's time travelers are humans who are being used to fight in a WAR between two groups of aliens, the spiders and the snakes. Wounded soldiers, doctors, and even entertainers are locked in a room that is outside the time stream. Unfortunately, an atomic bomb is locked in the room with them, and the bomb is ticking down.

And finally Robert Silverberg explores the possibilities of time travel, both past and future in his novel, *Project Pendulum*. In the year 2016, twins Sean, a math whiz, and Eric, a Paleontologist, take part in an incredible time travel experiment. They sit at opposite ends of a pendulum and swing back and forth in time, from 0 to 95 million years, into both the past and the future. Episodic vignettes describe what happens to them during the various pauses they make on their journey.

Superiority and Persecution

Even the HOLOCAUST can be the subject of a time travel adventure, as J. R. Dunn shows in his *Days of Cain*. Most of the researchers in the future have accepted the restrictions that limit them to watching, but not interacting with the past. But Alma Levine feels differently. As a result, she and her followers have taken a stand. They plan to wipe out the abomination that is the Holocaust. Alma is working from within, literally, as an inmate in an infamous DEATH camp. But it seems that our future prosperity depends on past suffering, or in this case, that millions must die in the ovens. So the Holocaust must not be tampered with—at all costs.

Orson Scott CARD also featured researchers who were studying the past in his *Pastwatch: The Redemption of Christopher Columbus.* In the Earth's heavily-polluted future, researchers discover that they are no longer limited to merely studying and observing the past; they can interact with it and even make changes. But if they do, they will change the future. Can anything be worth sacrificing the future for? After much deliberation and soul-searching, they decide that the institution of slavery is worth making such a sacrifice. Since all time lines intersect with one individual, Christopher Columbus, and one point in time, his arrival in the new world, someone from the future is going to have to make the trip back in time and be there to greet him and make the necessary changes.

And speaking of slavery, Octavia BUTLER, one of the major AFRICAN-AMERICAN authors writing SCIENCE FICTION today, has also gone back in time in her powerful *Kindred,* but with a twist. This time it is a modern African-American woman who suddenly finds herself transported back in time, not to study but to actually experience slavery—first hand.

The Twentieth Century

In a comparison novel to *The Doomsday Book,* time travel researchers are at it again. But in *To Say Nothing of the Dog, Or, How We Found the Bishop's Bird-stump at Last,* these researchers don't travel nearly as far back in time. Their mission, if they choose to accept it, is to try and find a hideous Victorian flower vase that disappeared the night Coventry Cathedral was bombed during World War II. And as if that weren't challenge enough, there's the problem of time beginning to shift because a new member of the team rescued a drowning cat and brought her forward in time. This is against the temporal laws; only inanimate objects can be transported back and forth in time. Transporting living creatures can cause time to slip. And if these time slips become too intense, the future will be changed. Which is why these same researchers are now visiting the Victorian era, trying to get the cat back to where she belongs—before it's too late.

There's more ROMANCE in the air in Jack FINNEY's *Time and Again*. This time it grows out of a romantic encounter that takes place during a government-sponsored time travel project. Si Morley is a commercial artist who is recruited to travel back in time to New York City. His target date is the winter of 1882. Once there, he makes sketches and takes photographs to bring back, as proof that he did indeed made the trip. He also falls in love, but as Jack Finney shows in *Time and Again,* the course of true love cannot run true when one party's presence in the past can alter the present and future. Further time travel ADVENTURES continue in the sequel, *From Time to Time.*

Lisa Mason, on the other hand, does not take her protagonist nearly as far back in time in her *Summer of Love*. Her goal is the summer of 1967, or the Summer of Love as it was called by those who were there, in Haight Ashbury. Her protagonist is a researcher from the future who has to go back to Haight Ashbury, right at the height of the Hippie movement. Chiron is this researcher and he has been entrusted with a extremely important mission, to find and protect the fetus of a man who is vital to the future. But the mother, Susan Stein, is a TEENAGE runaway who has totally bought into the message of personal freedom and independence of the swinging sixties. Chiron is willing to risk his own life to protect the mother and baby, but no one in the future warned him that having an abortion was one of the types of birth control practiced in the past. In the companion novel, *The Golden Nineties,* the researcher is a Chinese revolutionary who is sent back to 1895 San Francisco.

With the fate of the world in the balance, scientists in the future communicate with scientists in the past in Gregory Benford's *Timescape*. Environmental disasters have become so severe that a scientist in Cambridge, England, in 1998, manages to send a message back in time, warning the past of the future. And in 1962, a physicist in California gets the message.

Time travelers visit the next decade in *An Exaltation of Larks* by Robert Reed. Specifically, they visit the campus of a small college in the 1970s. One offers immortality, but only to a select few. The other works hard to try and undermine his efforts. And the students at the college are caught in the middle of this struggle.

Robert HEINLEIN presented his own unique vision of time travel in *The Door into Summer.* In that novel, the protagonist Dan Davis spends thirty years in suspended animation, tricked by his greedy fiancée and by his unscrupulous business partner. But when he wakes up in the year 2000, he discovers that he is not a helpless victim after all. He can actually travel back in time and get his revenge, if he wants to.

To Infinity and Beyond (Even to Mars)

Going back in time on the planet Mars is what Hanville Svetz does in Larry Niven's humorous and wildly-inventive *Rainbow Mars*. All the most dire predictions for Earth's polluted future have come true. Svetz, who works for the Institute for Temporal Research, is sent back in time by Waldemar the Tenth to recover extinct species for a sadly depleted Earth. But Waldemar the Eleventh is interested in space travel instead and sends him to find out why the Martian canals dried up. So back in time he goes, to the year 1500, at a time of working canals, hostile Martians, and a beanstalk that extends so far out into space it is used as a space elevator. But Svetz should have worked harder at discovering just what effect this plant was having on the red planet before working to bring it to Earth.

Andre NORTON's *Time Traders* SERIES chronicled the adventures of an intrepid band of time travelers: *The Time Traders, Galactic Derelict, The Defiant Agents,* and *Key Out of Time*. In collaboration with P. M. Griffin, she returned to this world in *Firehand.* That's the new name that Ross Murdoch of the Time Traders now goes by. This time he and his teammates have come to the planet Dominion to avert a tragedy in the past by helping the populace fight a guerrilla war against the Baldies.

Lots of time travel in lots of different time lines is the fate of Mark Strang, a private eye from Pittsburgh and the protagonist of John Barnes *Timeline Wars Series: Patton's Spaceship, Washington's Dirigible,* and *Caesar's Bicycle.* In all three, Mark is fighting the alien Closers, who are bent on enslaving the universe and are willing to take the battle across a million alternate Earths to do so.

In the *Time Scouts* series: *Time Scout, Wagers of Sin,* and *Ripping Time,* Robert Asprin and Linda Evans posit a future in which time travel has become possible as the result of a global disaster. So now even tourists can travel through time, but it's better for them to pass through the gates under the guidance of a qualified time scout. "Kit" Carson is one such scout, comfortably retired, until his granddaughter decides to become the first female time scout and he has to come to her rescue. In the second in the series, Skeeter Jackson has to deal with ripples in time and an Earth that is considerably changed as a result. And Jack the Ripper cuts up in the third.

Julian May takes a group of travelers back in time to Pliocene Europe in *The Saga of Pliocene Exile,* which consists of four novels: *The Many Colored Land, The Golden Torc, The Nonborn King,* and *The Adversary.* This is the struggle between the Tanu and Firvulag, the cruel versus the warrior mentality. The travelers are misfits from the Galactic Milieu, who have their hands full.

If you have the time, why not travel back and forth in it with some of these authors? They have shared their vision of a better (or possibly worse) past, present and future for mankind. All you need is the time—to enjoy, to contemplate and to read!

Timeless Titles on Time Travel

Asimov, Isaac. *The End of Eternity. Pebble in the Sky. The Ugly Little Boy.*

Asprin, Robert. *Time Scout Series: Time Scout—Wagers of Sin—Ripping Time.*

Barnes, John. *Timeline War Series: Patton's Spaceship—Washington's Dirigible—Caesar's Bicycle.*

Benford, Gregory. *Timescape.*

Bishop, Michael. *No Enemy But Time.*

Butler, Octavia. *Kindred.*

Card, Orson Scott. *Pastwatch: The Redemption of Christopher Columbus.*

Crichton, Michael. *Timeline.*

Dunn, J. R. *Days of Cain.*

Finney, Jack. *Time and Again* and sequel *From Time to Time.*

Heinlein, Robert A. *The Door into Summer.*

Leiber, Fritz. *The Big Time.*

Mason, Lisa. *Summer of Love* and *Golden Nineties.*

May, Julian. *Saga of Pliocene Exile: The Many-Colored Land—The Golden Torc—The Nonborn King—The Adversary.*

Murphy, Pat. *The Falling Woman.*

Niven, Larry. *Rainbow Mars. A World Out of Time.*

Norton, Andre. *Redline the Stars: A New Adventure of the Solar Queen. Firehand.*

Reed, Robert. *An Exaltation of Larks.*

Silverberg, Robert. *Letters from Atlantis. Project Pendulum.*

Simpson, George. *The Dechronization of Sam Magruder.*

Vinge, Vernor. *Marooned in Realtime* and prequel *The Peace War.*

Willis, Connie. *Doomsday Book. Lincoln's Dreams. To Say Nothing of the Dog.*

BONNIE L. KUNZEL

TINGLE, Rebecca

Author, n.d., Utah

T. grew up in Utah as the oldest child in quite a large FAMILY. She frequented the Orem Public library and enjoyed nature and childhood hobbies along with her siblings. After a short career in ballet, she obtained her B.A. in English at the University of Utah. Later she received her M.A. in English with a medieval specialization at Brigham Young University and studies at Oxford University as a Rhodes Scholar.

T. began writing her first novel, *The Edge on the Sword.* Sally Estes of *Booklist* describes T.'s novel as an "exciting, poignant first novel set in the late 800s." This medieval story tells the tale of the oldest daughter of King Alfred, who eventually became the most renowned queen of the Saxons. This warrior queen was a young woman who did indeed become the edge on the sword, using fighting techniques taught her by her faithful bodyguard to protect herself and her people against invaders. T. takes her readers through this mysterious old world into a wonderful coming-of-age ADVENTURE tale.

AWARDS: Best Books for Young Adults, 2002, for *The Edge on the Sword.*

FURTHER WORKS: *The Edge on the Sword,* 2003; *Far Traveler,* 2005.

REBECCA OSA MENDELL

TODD, Penelope
Author, editor, b. 1958, Christchurch, New Zealand

Currently working as an editor, T. is a relative new-comer to the YA novel scene in NEW ZEALAND. She has, nonetheless, quickly established herself as a major voice both in terms of literary quality and origi-nality of theme. In response to the question of why she ventured into writing, T. responded that she wanted "to say all the things that'd been composting for forty years."

T.'s first book for children, *Three's a Crowd* (under pseudonym Penelope Huber, 1999) was de-scribed by one reviewer as containing "finely honed prose and sensitive insights into character"; indeed, these two qualities have made T.'s subsequent novels for young adults prominent. *Peri* (2001) takes a quirky and insightful look at the complexities of first love, contrasting the complimentary viewpoints of high-school student Peri and her little brother Luke. Communication in its various forms is a dominant theme of the novel. In *The Boy Next Door* (2002), Hilary's relatively uncomplicated life is suddenly shifted when new inhabitants move into the neigh-bouring house; prickly and defensive Joe, a boy Hila-ry's age, and his rather flaky mother Margot bring color into Hilary's otherwise drab and ordered exis-tence. The story itself is not overly dramatic; it is the quiet, reflective minutiae of everyday life that stand out, illuminated by prose that is precise, imagery that is consistent, and characters who have depth and so-lidity.

T.'s fourth novel, *Watermark* (2003), is even more ambitious. Eighteen-year-old Zillah, whose name means "shadow," is caught in the "vortex of back-wash" between school and planned teacher training. En route to a holiday job, she abandons her friend Bridget, responding instead to a mysterious invitation to Roimata on the South Island's west coast. A re-mark from Zillah reveals that "[she] knew if [she] didn't go something would close up around [her] and seal [her] into a safe summer, a safe settled life." After negotiating a swollen river, Zillah finishes up in a small, provisioned hut where she fends for herself— "Look at me, reduced to a complete primitive in the course of a single day"—until meeting the source of the invitation, siblings Joss and Hep. *Watermark* is a story about losing and finding oneself, tackling diffi-cult and different options, and loosening the strait-

jacket of parental and societal expectations. "The real watermarks are made where the rain and the sea and the rivers get too big and surge over their bound-aries"; it's a compelling theme, and T. carries if off successfully. Her writing is top notch, her use of lan-guage vibrant and original. Zillah is a dynamic yet vulnerable character with whom young adult readers will easily identify.

AWARDS: 2000 New Zealand Post Children's Book Award, *Three's a Crowd*.

BIBLIOGRAPHY: http://library.christchurch.org.nz/Chil drens/ChildrensAuthors/PenelopeTodd.asp; http:// www.bookcouncil.org.nz/writers/toddpenelope.htm.

BILL NAGELKERKE

TOLAN, Stephanie S.
Author, b. 25 October 1942, Canton, Ohio

T.'s love for literature began during her childhood, a time when she would sneak books after bedtime and read underneath the covers with the aid of a flashlight. She genuinely believed that the black words on the pages contained magical powers that could transform the story into actuality. By the time she was in fourth grade, she had completed her first story and had de-cided on her future career as a writer.

Despite receiving her first rejection slips by the age of eleven, T. continued to write throughout junior- and senior-high school. Earning both a B.A. (1964) and an M.A. (1967) from Purdue University and be-coming a teacher at the academic level, T. put her writing on hold. In 1976 she began to write full time and participated in the National Endowment for the Arts POETS-in-the-Schools project in Pennsylvania and Ohio. In this program, she found a new genera-tion who shared her enthusiasm for reading. Of her students, T. says, "They brought back to me that spe-cial reading joy that most adults—even the readers among us—have lost, and I wanted to try my hand at writing for those kids, so like myself at their age and yet so different."

All of T.'s books deal with social issues that affect her audience of YA and middle-grade readers. She fo-cuses on social issues and the unheard voices of young people that are ignored by society. By writing about these problems in her books, T. feels she can do something to help change this trend. Her books are grounded in the belief that all young people have the right to be who they are, to be fully accepted for

711

themselves, and to be allowed to believe in themselves. These are the recurring themes in her novels, and T.'s life experiences have been the inspiration for these themes.

In her first novel, *Grandpa—and Me* (1978), T. explores aspects of aging. The central character, Kerry, learns to understand the changes taking place with her grandfather's strange behavior and also comes to a new understanding of her place within her FAMILY. *Plague Year* (1990) follows the hatred, fear, and harassment that originates in a small town high school and spreads throughout the community.

T. promotes the discussion of the changing world through her literature. Under the coat of humor, as in her Skinner SERIES of books, T. focuses on the problem of making money that many middle-class people face in times of changing technology. Her first Skinner book, *The Great Skinner Strike* (1983), deals with Michael Skinner's involvement in a nationally publicized strike, while *The Great Skinner Enterprise* (1987) centers around a home business. Outside the Skinner series, *Save Halloween!* (1993) provides the battleground for different ethical beliefs. Johanna Filkins, daughter of an evangelical Christian minister, clashes with her father over the issue of democracy. While he wishes to impose their church's belief on their town, Johanna understands this as a threat to the town's freedom.

T. also worked with Katherine PATERSON to adapt *Bridge to Terebithia* and *The Tale of the Mandarin Ducks* into musicals, first produced professionally by Stage One, Louisville, Kentucky. In addition, she and Paterson adapted *A Tale of Jemima Puddle Duck* by Beatrix Potter into a play that was produced by the same theatre company.

T. is an advocate for gifted children and their place in the world. She coauthored *Guiding the Gifted Child* and has written many articles about the challenges these children and adults face. She lectures throughout the country to audiences of parents and teachers attempting to meet their children's needs. Because of their different learning abilities, T. recognizes the special attention that must be paid to the education of these students. Her familiarity with exceptional children inspired her book *Welcome to the Ark* (1996), which follows the lives of four brilliant outcasts who live in an unstable world.

AWARDS: 1981 Ohioana Book Award, *The Liberation of Tansy Warner*; 1983 American Psychological As-

sociation Media Award, *Guiding the Gifted Child*; School Library Journal Best Book of 1988, *A Good Courage*; Notable Trade Book by the National Council of Social Studies, *Grandpa—and Me*; *Plague Year*: 1992–93 Virginia Young Readers Best Choices, 1993–94 Nevada Young Readers Award Winner; 2003 Newbery Honor Book, 2005 ALA Popular Paperbacks, ALA Notable Children's Books, 2003, Dorothy Canfield Fisher Children's Book Award, 2004, ALA Best Books for Young Adults, 2003, *Surviving the Applewhites*.

SELECT FURTHER WORKS: *The Ledge*, 1968; *Not I, Said the Little Red Hen*, 1971; *The Last of Eden*, 1980; *The Liberation of Tansy Warner*, 1980; *No Safe Harbors*, 1981; *A Time to Fly Free*, 1983; *Pride of the Peacock*, 1986; *The Great Skinner Getaway*, 1987; *A Good Courage*, 1988; *The Great Skinner Homestead*, 1988; *Marcy Hooper and the Greatest Treasure in the World*, 1991; *Sophie and the Sidewalk Man*, 1992; *The Witch of Maple Park*, 1992; *Who's There?*, 1994; *The Face in the Mirror*, 1998; *Ordinary Miracles*, 1999; *Flight of the Raven*, 2001; *Bartholomew's Blessing*, 2003.

BIBLIOGRAPHY: "Stephanie S. T." *U*X*L Junior DISCovering Authors*, 1998, reproduced in Discovering Collection, 2001; http://galenet.galegroup.com/servlet/DC/; Alvine, Lynne. "Stephanie S. T." *Writers for Young Adults*, ed. Ted Hipple, 2000; http://galenet.galegroup.com/servlet/LitRC; "Stephanie S. T." *Authors and Artists for Young Adults*, vol. 45, 2002. Reproduced in Biography Resource Center, 2003, http://www.galenet.com/serlet/BioRC; "Stephanie S. T." *Contemporary Authors*. Reproduced in Contemporary Authors Online, 2003, http://galenet.galegroup.com/servlet/LitRC; "Stephanie S. T." HarperCollins website, http://www.harpercollins.com/catalog/author_xml.asp?AuthorId=18819.

RACHEL WITMER
AND SARA MARCUS

TOLKIEN, J. R. R.

Author, b. January 3, 1892, Bloemfontein, South Africa; d. September 2, 1973, Bournemouth, England

John Ronald Reuel T. was born in South Africa, where his father worked as a bank manager. But when T. was only four-years old, his father died. T., his mother, and his younger brother, Hilary, returned to his mother's homeland, England, and settled near Birmingham. At that time, T.'s mother, Mabel, and her sister May, converted to Catholicism, and Mabel reared her two boys as such. Their parish priest,

Father Francis Xavier Morgan, often visited the family, and T. remained a devout Catholic all his life.

In 1896, Mabel died from diabetes, which was untreatable at the time. Her orphaned sons were sent to a boarding house but were cared for in many ways by Father Morgan. Under Father Morgan's watchful eyes, T. began showing a remarkable gift for language. In fact, T. made up several languages for the sheer pleasure of it. Then, at age sixteen, T. met Edith Bratt, another resident of the boarding house. When their friendship became something more than that, Father Morgan stepped in to forbid T. to see her until he was twenty-one years old.

He obeyed, and left for Exeter College in Oxford, where he studied CLASSICS, and then English Language and Literature. In 1914, T. wrote a poem entitled "The Voyage of Earendel, the Evening Star." The poem contained one of T.'s created languages and the related MYTHS. T.'s later work would draw on the same lines. Then, on the day that T. turned twenty-one, he wrote Edith a letter, in which he proposed marriage. A year later, in 1916, they wed.

Immediately following his marriage, T. was sent to battle in World War I. After four months in the trenches, he developed a typhuslike infection and was returned to his bride in England. In 1918, T. began working as an assistant on the *Oxford English Dictionary*. In 1920, he took a position as a reader in English at the University of Leeds. He was promoted to a professor of English at the University in 1924. In 1925, T. was appointed to the prestigious position of Rawlinson and Bosworth Professor of Anglo-Saxon at Oxford University.

At that time, T. was already the father of three children: John (1917), Michael (1920), and Christopher (1924). His last child, Priscilla, would come along in 1929. T. did not publish many scholarly works, but those he did publish were influential, including "Beowolf: The Monsters and the Critics" (1936). T.'s university life was unremarkable. In 1945, he received the Merton Professorship of English Language and Literature at Oxford University, and he held this post until his retirement in 1959.

T.'s social life, however, was busy. Together with various friends including C. S. LEWIS, T. helped found The Inklings, a group of friends who met regularly to drink, converse, and share writing. One of T.'s most famous lines, however, came at an unlikely moment. He was correcting exam papers, and was disheartened to find that one of his students had left an answer page blank. On this page, T. wrote, "In a hole in the ground there lived a hobbit." His own words intrigued him, and T. set out to discover everything he could about this creature. T. spun tales of the hobbit for his children, and eventually put it all in writing. *The Hobbit* was published in 1937. The publisher was so pleased with T.'s first novel that he asked him to write a sequel. During the next eleven years, T. worked on this task, which would come to be known as *Lord of the Rings*. This masterpiece was published in three volumes: *The Fellowship of the Ring* (1954), *The Two Towers* (1954), and *The Return of the King* (1955). *The Lord of the Rings* was an immediate success, and its popularity was revived in the mid-1960s by American university students, who developed a cultlike following to the work. By the end of 1968, almost three-million copies of *The Lord of the Rings* had been sold around the world.

In 1977, *The Silmarillion,* edited by Christopher T., was published. This work is particularly poignant, as the main characters were inspired by a moment that T. shared with his young bride. As they were walking through the woods one day, Edith danced for T. in a hemlock grove. This led T. to develop the tales of Beren and Lúthien. T. thought of himself as Beren, and of Edith as Lúthien. Although this novel was started in the 1920s, T. had difficulty finishing the work. It was not until his later years that he was able to do so.

Edith died in 1971, and T. died from complications resulting from a bleeding gastric ulcer and chest infection in 1973. On their gravestone, it reads:

EDITH MARY TOLKIEN, LÚTHIEN, *1889–1971*
JOHN RONALD REUEL TOLKIEN, BEREN,
1892–1973

AWARDS: *New York Herald Tribune* Children's Spring Book Festival award (1938) for *The Hobbit*; International FANTASY Award (1957) for *The Lord of the Rings*; *Locus* Award for best fantasy novel (1978) for *The Silmarillion.*

FURTHER WORKS: *The Reeve's Tale,* 1939; *Sir Orfeo,* 1944; *Farmer Giles of Ham* (1949); *The Adventures of Tom Bombaldi and Other Verses from the Red Book* (1962); *Tree and Leaf* (1964); *The Tolkien Reader* (1966); *Smith of Wootton Major* (1967); *The Road Goes Ever On: A Song Cycle* (1968); *Bilbo's Last Song* (1974); *Sir Gawain and the Green Knight,*

Pearl and Sir Orfeo (1975); *The Father Christmas Letters* (1976); *Unfinished Tales of Numenor and Middle-earth* (1980); *The Book of Lost Tales, Part I* (1983); *The Book of Lost Tales, Part II* (1984); *The Lays of Beleriand* (1985); *The Shaping of Middle-earth* (1986); *The Lost Road and Other Writings* (1987); *Sauron Defeated* (1992); *Morgoth's Ring* (1993); *The War of the Jewels* (1994); *The Peoples of Middle-earth* (1996)

BIBLIOGRAPHY: Crabbe, K. W., *J. R. R. T.,* 1981, 1988; www.tolkiensociety.org.

CARRA E. GAMBERDELLA

THE TOP DOZEN FAVORITE YA BOOKS

This year my English teacher seems clueless about the books she picks for us to read. The authors of these books are all dead and, trust me, we are hanging on for our lives while suffering through these "teacher selections." So I decided to think back about all of the great books that I have read over the years. I talked it over with my classmates and we came up with our list of the "drop dead" best books for YAS. The books on this list are perfect for bringing new life to a moribund YA reading program.

- *Harry Potter* SERIES by J. K. ROWLING: This is the top-rated book series of all time. Sometimes when I feel as though I am alone and need to escape, Harry and his ADVENTURES are the perfect safe way to leave home. Rowling takes us places we've never been before. I wish I had a "firebolt" and could fly into the story and compete and win just like Harry. When characters in these books face danger and even die, it's OK. But when the hippogriff (Buckbeak) was set free, I was really relieved. Thank you for not killing him.
- *A Series of Unfortunate Events* by Lemony SNICKET: I like this series of books because their unpredictable nature lures me into an imaginary torture chamber that makes me laugh. It is a quirky sort of humor and young adults like me just cannot get enough of it.
- *Holes* by Louis SACHAR: I like this book because of all the negative things in Stanley's life that turned out to work in his favor. It feels as though I am reading about the TV show *Survivor.*

- *The Tale of Desperaux* by Kate Dicamillo: I like this book because it shows connections between humans and animals. I really relate because sometimes the dreams I have for myself are ones that other people think are ridiculous.
- *Eragon* by Christopher Paolini: I like this book because it is full of magic and adventure. You can tell that it is written by a young adult because he relates to my imagination and desire to go to strange, perilous places. I hope that this book becomes a MOVIE soon.
- *The House of the Scorpion* by Nancy FARMER: I like this book because it is spellbinding and it keeps me on my toes. Parts of the book are shocking and gruesome; the scariest part is that it could really happen. I cannot quit thinking about the possibility of cloning people for body parts and wondering what would happen to our society if cloning for body parts was legal. It was a bit depressing, but once you start reading it you can't put it down.
- *Because of Winn-Dixie* by Kate Dicamillo: I like this book because Kate describes the characters with full detail, especially her dog Winn Dixie. This is one of my favorite books because one minute I am laughing and the next minute I'm thinking deeply about the people around me and wondering if I might be missing something.
- *Life of Pi* by Yann Martel: This is a survival book that makes me wonder how much pain and suffering a person can endure before they die. It makes me think about nature, loneliness, survival, God, and DEATH over and over again. The first time I read it, I had to talk this book out with someone because I could not get it out of my head. I felt like Pi, only I knew that I would have probably died because I did not have the life skills and self-control that he had. I wanted those skills. I wondered if he had ever wanted those skills as well. The way Pi takes a tiny topic such as what a turtle looks and tastes like and describes every detail is amazing.
- *Crispin* by AVI: All Crispin did was to be in the wrong place at the wrong time. Crispin's constant companion in the 14th century is fear that causes pain and agony complete with a lead cross necklace. I wonder if Pi and Crispin could have been friends.

- *Walk Two Moons* by Sharon CREECH: We have two favorite parts of this story. The marriage bed story is the girls favorite and the boys favorite is when Creech tells the story about not judging anyone until you have walked in their shoes.
- *Number the Stars* by Lois LOWRY: This is a wonderful and thrilling book about World War II that will keep you guessing. This book changed my thinking about how kids helped out during the war. Thank you, Lois Lowry.
- *The Joey Pigza Series* by Jack GANTOS: I like this series of books because it makes me laugh and sometimes makes me think of people that I know. Jack Gantos makes words fit together smoothly and naturally. It is like a voice in my head having a cool conversation.

MATT WOOTEN

TRAVEL IN THE TWENTIETH CENTURY: THE MODERN QUEST

The travel novel is usually a quest. Characters may be in search of missing relatives, hidden treasure, a sense of self, or something elusive that only reveals itself in the ending. In these novels, the journeys truly are the destinations, which are far more relevant than whatever the original purpose of the trip may have been.

Perhaps the best-known travel book of the twentieth century is Jack Kerouac's *On the Road*. It inspired generations of the young, and not-so-young, in their quests of self-discovery. Its title was even used as the foundation for a SERIES in the late 1990s, when a young girl chooses to delay college and travel throughout the U.S.

The Hobbit and *The Lord of the Rings* by J. R. R. TOLKIEN, although usually recognized as FANTASY novels and CLASSICS, are also travel novels. When Bilbo Baggins decides to go on a journey, he sets in motion a series of events that will take a second generation to resolve, as his nephew, Frodo, must set out on an excursion of his own, to resolve some of the issues that remain from Bilbo's trip. However, in both journeys, neither Bilbo nor Frodo, nor their traveling companions, come away from their travels without knowledge that is no less precious for being hard-earned.

The Testing of Tertius by Robert Newman is a genuine fantasy quest novel. Tertius and his companions must meet a variety of challenges on their journey, which ultimately will provide them with enough self-knowledge to meet their next tasks.

Meg Murry's journey encompasses interplanetary travel, as she learns to move through time by tesseracting, and rescues her father, and then her beloved younger brother, Charles Wallace, through the lessons she has learned in her excursions to different planets in Madeleine L'ENGLE's *A Wrinkle in Time*. Her ability to travel in unique ways stands her in good stead in the next two novels, as she rescues her brother again in *A Wind in the Door* by traveling inside his body. She is joined again by Calvin, but in *A Swiftly Tilting Planet,* she travels through time alone except for her unborn child.

Joan BAUER's *Rules of the Road* features an across-the-country trip—where all the terrain that is covered is not geographic. Jenna Boller needs to get her life in order, so a chance to spend the summer on the road is not to be easily dismissed. To get paid for it by the executive of the company that she currently works for is too good to be true—so she happily agrees to chauffeur Mrs. Gladstone. This is a modern-day quest for both characters—and they learn a lot more than just the rules of the road.

A car trip is at the center of Janet Lambert's *Myself and I,* as Susan Jordon is forced to postpone her own plans to help her sister-in-law and close friend drive from New York State to the midwest with her new baby. The journey persuades Susan that she needs to defend her own desires, but *The Stars Hang High* finds her on another excursion, as she gives into her father's urgings and joins him on a cruise. It is on this second expedition that Susan finally faces who and what she truly wants from life, when her father becomes gravely ill while they are in Hong Kong.

In *Beany and the Beckoning Road,* Beany Malone learns valuable lessons about trips when she and her brother set out from Denver to take their young nephew to California. Among them is the importance of setting out prepared for all the contingencies that may arise—and another is that one's unresolved problems come with a person, until he or she finds a way to come to terms with them.

These are just a few of the stories that center on journeys that YAS might enjoy. Each protagonist ultimately learns some lessons—while having a few ADVENTURES on the road—even if the road is a tesseract.

JEANNE MARIE RYAN

TREMBATH, Don
Author, b. 22 May, 1963, Winnipeg, Manitoba, Canada

Starting to write at the age of ten, T. would leave stories out for his FAMILY to read. With their encouragement, T. eventually began to believe that writing was an option. T. has said, "I think all young people should have the opportunity and encouragement to write." In keeping with that ethos, T. volunteers as a tutor and writing instructor in Alberta where he lives. Previously working as a photographer, reporter, and editor at the *Morinville Mirror,* T. has also written a biweekly column for the *Edmonton Journal* called "To Be a Dad." More than anything else T. considers himself to be a full-time father to his two children.

T.'s first novel, *The Tuesday Café* (1996), introduced the character of Harper Winslow, a troubled TEENAGER who sets a fire in his school. He is sentenced to write an essay entitled "How I Plan to Turn My Life Around" and to perform community service as punishment for the arson charges. In a fresh, authentic voice, Harper tells the story of participating in a writing workshop and working on his essay. In the process, Harper learns about himself and his relationship with his parents. A special projects coordinator at Prospects Literacy Association in Edmonton, T. clearly has a wealth of knowledge to draw upon in creating characters and stories. In *A Fly Named Alfred* (1997), *A Beautiful Place on Yonge Street* (1999), and *The Popsicle Journal* (2002), T. continues the story of his protagonist from *Tuesday Café.*

In *Lefty Carmichael Has a Fit* (2002), T. explores the difficult and often terrifying topic of LIFE AMONG THE CHALLENGED—epilepsy. T. tempers the serious subject material with the humor, warmth, and lively dialogue found in all of his books.

AWARD: 1997 R. Ross Annett Juvenile Fiction Award for *The Tuesday Café.*

FURTHER WORK: *Frog Face and the Three Boys,* 2001.

BIBLIOGRAPHY: *Contemporary Authors Online,* 2001; *Something about the Author,* vol. 96, 1998; *St. James Guide to Young Adult Writers* (second ed.), 1999.

ANDREA LIPINSKI
AND MEGAN PEARLMAN

TWOHILL, Maggie. See ANGELL, Judie.

TRUEMAN, Terry
Author, educator, b. 15 December 1947, Birmingham, Alabama

Birmingham was *Stuck in Neutral* (2000) author T.'s place of birth. But he was transplanted to Seattle before Southern memories could take root. His sister, Cindy, was born four years later to his mother, Jeanne Lapine, and his father, Sydney McDaniel Trueman, a Navy fighter pilot in World War II and a white-collar worker.

Life was good in Seattle, but not idyllic for a young T. His mother, a functional alcoholic, was loving but inconsistent. His father was gruff and difficult to please. And one of T.'s earliest memories was of his grandfather's DEATH by suicide. But in spite of those early emotional traumas, T. was popular and successful in school.

By the time he was sixteen, his high-school creative writing teacher suggested he might be a gifted writer. "Kay Keyes told me I had talent," he remembers. "It was the first time a teacher had ever said such a thing. But I didn't give writing a serious, professional consideration until I started writing *Stuck in Neutral* at the age of 48."

Teaching, on the other hand, he gave a vigorous try. After receiving a B.A. in creative writing at the University of Washington, T. went on to earn a master's in applied psychology and an M.F.A. in creative arts, both from Eastern Washington University near Spokane, where he has lived since 1974.

Though his parents divorced in 1973, T. continued to build adult relationship with them both until his mother died of cancer in 1988. His father is still living in Tucson, Arizona, with his second wife.

T. taught and was wildly popular as an instructor at Spokane Falls Community College for years before he put his skill for writing to truly lucrative use. Controversial for his desire to pull even struggling students into the creative writing fold, T. made many friends and many enemies.

While teaching, he had yet another life-altering experience. His firstborn son, Sheehan, suffered brain damage on delivery and was profoundly DISABLED by cerebral palsy, a disease that crippled baby Sheehan both physically and mentally. Devastated by grief and loss, T.'s relationship with Sheehan's mother did not survive, and they went their separate ways.

Haunted by the impact CP had on his son, he began to write what would become an epic poem named for his son. Gut-wrenching and brutally honest, *Sheehan* was a critical success, though published by a tiny, independent press. It never really eased T.'s guilt at not being able to "fix" his disabled child. But it did remind him of his dreams to be a professional writer.

T. and his next life partner adopted Jesse as an infant a few years after Sheehan was born. T. thrived as a father, and built a lasting, strong relationship with his second son. Though he and Jesse's mother didn't stay together, T. and Jesse are close to this day.

When T. met another Spokane author, Terry DAVIS, he decided to write a novel loosely based on his AUTOBIOGRAPHICAL poem about Sheehan. With help from Davis, who wrote *Vision Quest* (1981), a CLASSIC still in print today, T. crafted *Stuck in Neutral,* which became a PRINTZ Honor Book. His follow-up novel, *Inside Out* (2003), was named one of the American Library Associations Top Ten Quick Picks for Reluctant Readers in 2004. *Cruise Control,* a companion book to *Stuck in Neutral,* was released in October 2004. T. no longer teaches but writes full time and lives with his current wife Patti in Spokane.

AWARDS: ALA Best Book for Young Adults: 2001 for *Stuck in Neutral,* 2004 for *Inside Out;* Printz Honor Book, 2001; *Stuck in Neutral;* Kentucky Bluegrass Award, 2002; ALA Quick Picks for Reluctant Young Adult Readers: *Inside Out,* 2004, *Stuck in Neutral,* 2001.

FURTHER WORKS: *Swallowing the Sun,* 2003; *Cruise Control,* 2004.

BIBLIOGRAPHY: http://www.terrytrueman.com; interviews, 2002, 2003, 2004.

KELLY MILNER HALLS

TURNER, Ann Warren
Author, b. 10 December 1945, Northhampton, Massachusetts

T. describes her childhood as one full of books and reading: "I was one of those children who sniffed, slept on, and sometimes ate books. Once a week my father would go to the library and bring back seven books, one for each day of the week. I would open my mouth like a baby bird to devour food. I really think I would have died, had I not had books." When

she was eight years old, T. wrote her first story, which featured a dragon and a dwarf named Puckity. T. is now the author of over thirty novels, PICTURE BOOKS, and POETRY collections for children and YA.

T. attended the University of Manchester, Bates College (B.A.), and the University of Massachusetts (M.A.T.). She taught high-school English for one year, but quickly realized that she preferred writing books to teaching about them. She wrote her first book for children at her mother's suggestion. The pair wrote and illustrated a children's book together about vultures.

When asked about the writing, T. admits that it is not an easy process for her. She wrestles her way through stories, "punching out unnecessary words, arguing with self-important paragraphs, until [she] arrive[s] at the end thirsty, tired, but victorious." Sometimes, however, she has urges to flush a manuscript down the toilet or burn it in the driveway. T. advises writers to have faith in themselves and in their abilities because, she says, everyone has stories inside.

T. has written many books for young adults ranging from poetry to historical fiction. *Nettie's Trip South* is a picture book based on the DIARY of Turner's grandmother and tells the story of a young girl who journeys for the first time to the antebellum South. Nettie describes her encounter with slavery to her friend Addie: "Addie, I was so worried I was almost sick. Julia told me slaves are thought to be three-fifths of a person. It's in the Constitution. I'd never seen a slave and wondered, What were they missing? Was it an arm, a leg, a foot, or something inside?"

The Girl Who Chased Away Sorrow: The Diary of Sarah Nita, a Navajo Girl, New Mexico, 1864 is another historical fiction piece. This novel features thirteen-year-old Sarah Nita, a Navajo girl, telling the story of the Navajo's forced 400-mile walk from their homeland to Fort Sumner.

Learning to Swim (2000) is a powerful memoir about a dark period in T.'s past. Written in prose, the story describes sexual abuse encounters with a neighbor. "I am hiding in / Their garage, the oily one / With the dented car, / And Kevin is running past, / Looking for me / With hands that grab, / And Lonny is looking, too, / With his fat wavery lips / Like worms that want / To squish on my cheeks, / And they say it's a game / But I am shivery / In the garage / With the smell of oil / All around."

T. keeps writing because she feels as if she has been "called" to be a writer. Her liberal upbringing influenced her writing and instilled in her a concern about different people and cultures. This concern drives and inspires her to continue writing. "It's not always fun, it's certainly not easy, but when I am writing I feel totally and completely alive."

AWARDS: American Library Association notable book citation, 1980, for *A Hunter Comes Home;* American Library Association notable book citation, 1985, for *Dakota Dugout;* "Pick of the List" for *Nettie's Trip South;* Notable Children's Book in the Field of Social Studies for *Grasshopper Summer* and *Heron Street;* Reading Rainbow and NCSS Notable for *Through Moon and Stars* and *Night Skies;* Best Books of 1991, Notable, NCTE, for *Rosemary's Witch;* Best Book for Young Adults, 1999, and Quick Pick for Reluctant Young Adult Readers, 1999, for *A Lion's Hunger.*

FURTHER WORKS: *Dakota Dugout,* 1985; *Third Girl from the Left,* 1986; *Street Talk,* 1986; *Time of the Bison,* 1988; *Grasshopper Summer,* 1989; *Rosemary's Witch,* 1991; *Grass Songs,* 1994; *Elfsong,* 1995; *One Brave Summer,* 1995; *Finding Walter,* 1997; *Mississippi Mud,* 1997; *A Lion's Hunger,* 1999; *Sitting Bull Remembers,* 2004.

BIBLIOGRAPHY: *Contemporary Authors Online,* 2001, http://galenet.galegroup.com; http://www.annturnerbooks.com/home.html; http://www.scholastic.com/dearamerica/parentteacher/guides/dearamerica/lovethy.htm.

ELIZABETH ANDERSON

TURNER, Megan Whalen
Author, b. 1965, Fort Sill, Oklahoma

The mother of three, T. has written only two novels and a collection of SHORT STORIES. Her reputation, however, is commensurate with that of much more prolific authors, due to the intelligence, imagination, and ambition of her novels.

T. earned her B.A. in English language and literature from the University of Chicago, but her early attempts at writing children's books were difficult and frustrating. So she put aside any thoughts of being a published writer and worked for seven years as a children's book buyer for bookstores in Chicago and Washington, D.C. Her first published work was the FANTASY collection *Instead of Three Wishes* (1995), which was sent to Greenwillow Books by none other

than famed author Diana Wynne JONES. These seven stories were written at a middle-school level and were respectfully reviewed.

T.'s first novel, *The Thief* (1996), was greeted with rapturous reviews and marked the arrival of an important new author for YAS. *The Thief* is the first-person account of young Gen, latest in a long FAMILY line of thieves, who is forced to steal an ancient artifact for an unscrupulous king. Set in an imaginary land with many resemblances to ancient Greece, peopled with royalty and soldiers and scholars and gods, the novel was named a Newbery Honor Book for 1997 and put T. on the literary map. Young readers recognized themselves in clever, resilient, sarcastic Gen and eagerly followed him through a twist-laden tale of politics and ADVENTURE.

The Queen of Attolia (2000) continued Gen's adventures but was told in the third person, enabling T. to weave a more complicated story of intrigue, WAR, political alliances, and unexpected love. Although *The Thief* had not flinched from showing the hardships and brutality of war, *The Queen of Attolia* was even darker, put Gen through a great deal of suffering and disillusionment, and assumed a fairly high level of sophistication in its readers. The reviews were again stellar, with critics assuming that readers who enjoyed *The Thief* had now grown up enough to tackle its more complex sequel.

The biographical information in T.'s books indicates that her husband is a professor of English and that the family relocates whenever his work or research requires a move. T. also lists travel as one of her interests, and it is apparent that she brings a keenly observant eye to her family's travels, enabling her to evoke faraway mythical lands in compelling detail.

AWARDS: For *The Queen of Attolia, Booklist* Top 10 Fantasy Books for Youth; *Bulletin of the Center for Children's Books,* Blue Ribbon List, Best Books of 2000; New York Public Library Books for the TEEN Age, 2001; Parents' Choice 2000 Fiction Gold Award, Parent's Guide Honor Award, 2000; A Chosen Book of the Cooperative Children's Book Center, 2001. For *The Thief,* Newbery Honor Book Award, 1997; American Library Association List of Notable Books, 1997; Best Books for Young Adults, 1997, Young Adult Library Services Association; *Bulletin of the Center for Children's Books,* Blue Ribbon List, Best Books of 1996; *Horn Book* Fanfare List, Best Books of 1996; Books for the Teen Age, 1997, New

York Public Library; Selection of the Junior Library Guild; Dorothy Canfield Fisher Children's Book Award Master List, 1997–98; ALA Popular Paperbacks, 2003. For *Instead Of Three Wishes, Booklist* Editors' Choice List, Best Books of 1995; 1996–97 Dorothy Canfield Fisher Children's Book Award Master List.

FURTHER WORKS: "The Baby in the Night Deposit Box," in *Firebirds: An Anthology of Original FANTASY* and *SCIENCE FICTION*, ed. Sharyn, 2003.

BIBLIOGRAPHY: *Contemporary Authors Online,* 2001; http://home.att.net/~mwturner/; http://harpercollins .com

MARY MENZEL

URBAN LEGENDS

U., many specific to TEENS, are the oral history aspects of adolescent life and customs that have made their way into written and published format. Urban legends could be defined as stories constructed around events of modern life. Whether factual or not, the strength of the conviction has caused many of these legends to bing-bong back and forth across the country for many decades. The characteristic strong belief in the truth of the tale brought about the now famous phrase "F.O.A.F.," meaning that a Friend of a Friend related the particular story with the certainty that the events, no matter how terrible or strange, actually occurred. These stories have been collected by popular folklorists such as Daniel Cohen, Alvin Schwartz, James HASKINS, and most famously, Dr. Jan Brunvand.

Brunvand began collecting and studying urban legends between 1970 and 1980, with the goal of determining *why* and *where* these stories were being told. Brunvand notes in the first of several collections, *The Vanishing Hitchhiker* (1981), that many stories told by teens, in addition to giving that scary thrill, serve to identify areas of the transition to adulthood that cause anxiety to teens. Telling these stories around a campfire, at a church retreat, or on a sleepover with friends helps teens verbalize their fears about various aspects of becoming adults. Teens find comfort sharing their fears with friends in this roundabout way. For example, stories about dating and going to college are common.

While published collections of legends have gradually increased in popularity with teens, some of the stories have an even earlier history. In *The Vanishing Hitchhiker,* Brunvand notes that on November 8, 1960, the day John F. Kennedy was elected president, a letter from a teenager appeared in "Dear Abby" asking about the truthfulness of a story about a man with a hook instead of a right hand scaring some teenagers who were parked alone in a secluded spot. This famous urban legend has passed through several generations of teenagers and has become modified in various ways. For example, another version is that the boyfriend goes to get help for their car, which won't start. He doesn't return; the girl waits. In the morning when police rescue her, they find her now dead boyfriend hanging from the tree above the car where she had been waiting all night. The sound she'd heard throughout the night scratching the roof of the vehicle had been her boyfriend's fingernails sweeping across the roof of the car!

Other popular legends center around topics of prime interest to teens such as food, cars, and even shopping malls where teens congregate. Some of the legends about food have caused such widespread rumors that consumers actually stopped buying particular brands. For example, a rumor about spider eggs in a type of bubblegum caused a reduction in purchasing of that brand. The story "Southern fried rat," which tells of a dead rat that became accidentally fried with pieces of chicken, may have had a similar negative effect on fried chicken franchises. The story about a customer having to pay a major department store a huge sum of money for the store's recipe for red velvet cake also has been applied to a very famous cookie company.

U. are an area of YA literature that is international in scope and incorporates a variety of cultures. Telling and studying these stories can be a very successful curriculum-related classroom activity, since every culture on our planet has its scary stories. For example, the *Kwaidan* are famous Japanese ghost stories. W. D. Westervelt collected and published *Hawaiian legends of ghosts and ghost-gods.* The legend of the wailing "La Llorona" is well-known in Latin cultures. The Golem of Jewish folklore has even found its way into the popular works of TOLKIEN. Drawing on the commonalities of these stories can help to increase the understanding of diversity and improve cultural awareness among TEENS who might otherwise hang with their own racial groups.

While some teenage folklore has been passed along for many years in the traditional oral ways, the speed with which the stories pass throughout the world has been greatly enhanced with the coming of e-mail and websites such as www.snopes.com, where stories are recorded in a variety of categories.

In summary, U. enjoy wide popularity with teens; many teen stories have evolved around local cemeteries, empty houses, scary and isolated country roads, and other neighborhood landmarks. Sharing these stories and listening to the stories of local teens or teens visiting from other countries can be an enriching experience for teachers and LIBRARIANS. The exchange of stories among many ages can be a binding experience between generations and cultures. Telling these stories, which are grounded in the interests and reflect the anxieties of this age group, can often entice teens into becoming involved with the strong oral tradition of storytelling in a way that is esteem enhancing as well as entertaining for all ages involved.

FURTHER WORKS: Brunvand, Jan. *Too Good to Be True,* 1999; MCKISSACK, Patricia. *The Dark-Thirty,* 1992; Schwartz, Alvin. *Scary Stories to Tell in the Dark,* 1981; Young, Richard, and Judy Young. *Scary Story Reader,* 1993.

BIBLIOGRAPHY: Brunvand, Jan. *Encyclopedia of U.,* 2002; DeVos, Gail. *Tales, Rumors, and Gossip,* 1996; Horner, Beth. "To Tell or Not to Tell." *Illinois Libraries,* September 1983, pp. 458–64; Serchay, David. "Webwatch: U."*Library Journal,* January 1, 2002; Wilson-Lingbloom, Evie. "Storytelling Teenage Folklore." In *Hangin out at Rocky Creek,* 1995, pp. 144–56.

EVIE WILSON-LINGBLOOM

VAIL, Rachel
Author, b. 25 July 1966, New York City

V. never planned on becoming a writer. V. found the writing process daunting, and it was not until her time at Georgetown University that she became inspired. Encouraged through a theater class to focus on the characters and the details rather than on the whole story, V. found that bringing these things together "makes stories happen." V.'s emphasis on characters and realism have served her well; her books explore the ups and downs of the transition into adulthood. V.'s first novel, *Wonder* (1991), tells the story of a twelve-year-old girl who finds herself a social OUT-CAST. The title comes from her polka-dot dress being referred to as a "Wonder Bread explosion."

In *Ever After* (1994) and *Daring to Be Abigail* (1996), V.'s narrative technique changes as the stories are presented in DIARY and letter form respectively. Friendship is always a central topic for V., both the vulnerability of it and the responsibility that should come with it. While always keeping a sense of humor, V. captures the imperfection of growing up with a natural voice.

In V.'s popular Friendship Ring SERIES, the story of a group of friends is told through the eyes of each member of the group. The first three volumes, *If Only You Knew, Not That I Care,* and *Please Please Please* (all 1998), tell the stories of friends Zoe, Morgan, and CJ as they share their thoughts about themselves and each other and perform their creative writing assign-ment: to bring ten items to class that define them-selves.

Known for having a very good ear when it comes to TEENAGE dialogue, many have even drawn compar-isons between V. and popular children's author Judy BLUME. V. is commended for her, "remarkable talent for capturing so perfectly the pleasure and pain of being thirteen."

AWARDS: Editor's Choice, *Booklist,* 1991 for *Wonder* and 1992 for *Do-Over*; "Pick of the List," American Booksellers Association, 1991 for *Wonder*; Best Books designation, *School Library Journal,* 1996 for *Daring to be Abigail.*

FURTHER WORKS: *Do-Over,* 1992; *What Are Friends For?,* 1999; *Never Mind: A Twin Novel* (with Avi), 1994; *If We Kiss,* 1995.

BIBLIOGRAPHY: *Authors and Artists For Young Adults,* vol. 33, 2000; *Contemporary Authors Online,* 2001; *The Seventh Book of Junior Authors and Illustrators,* 1996; *Something about the Author,* vol. 94, 1998.

ANDREA LIPINSKI
AND MEGAN PEARLMAN

VAN ALLSBURG, Chris
Author, illustrator, b. 18 June 1949, Grand Rapids, Michigan

V. currently resides in Providence, Rhode Island, with his wife Lisa and their daughter Sophia. He grew up in Grand Rapids during the 1950s. His comfortable, idyllic surroundings as a child afforded him the plea-sures of a typical childhood that included catching tadpoles, sledding on nearby slopes, bike riding to school, and playing baseball. During the third grade he read a BIOGRAPHY of Babe Ruth virtually nonstop until completion, his motivation for doing so not entirely derived from interest in the story or the SPORT. He simply wanted to complete the task of reading an entire book. Over the following summer he borrowed a collection of Walt Disney comic books from a neighbor. With his red wagon fully loaded, he pushed and tugged them to his bedroom and started reading. It took him one week to read all the comic books cover to cover. He grew fond of the lively characters and missed them after returning the books to their owner. Not only were strong imaginative seeds planted during the act of reading, a commitment to complete a task was grounded in V.'s character. Putting aside an uncompleted book was never an option, and this type of obsessive reading behavior, manifested in various forms, followed him throughout his life.

Early in V.'s life he not only established good work habits but he also revealed his innate gift for art, his favorite subject in elementary school. The thought of missing art class was so unpalatable that he was known to go to school on art days even if he was sick. His abilities were being cultivated for writing and illustrating award-winning children's literature.

V. earned an undergraduate degree in the fine arts at the University of Michigan and a master's in sculpture at Rhode Island School of Design. Meanwhile, Lisa, his wife, had occasion to show some of V.'s artwork to author and illustrator David MACAULAY. Macaulay persuaded V. to submit his drawings to editors, which precipitated a relationship with Walter Lorraine of Houghton Mifflin.

V.'s unique artistic style skillfully and creatively employs perspective, point of view, and use of light to develop the strong narrative potential in each illustration. V.'s artwork is reflective of the techniques of famous artists: Jan Vermeer's use of light and Edgar Degas' craft of composition are reflected in V.'s works. These qualities moved him to the forefront with his first publication, *The Garden of Abdul Gasazi* (1979), winning him the Caldecott Honor Book Award. In this first offering, the world of illustration fused with magic entices readers to wonder and question whether or not a bull terrier has turned into a duck. This same bull terrier mysteriously appears in at least one illustration in each of V.'s subsequent PIC-

TURE BOOKS. The bull terrier was modeled on his nephew's dog, Winston. The dog died shortly after the release of the book. V. decided to honor Winston by including him in his subsequent books.

Jumanji (1981) and *The Polar Express* (1985) were both recipients of the Caldecott Medal and both have become the basis for MOVIES. V. says *Jumanji* grew out of a mental image of losing control of a situation in unsuspecting settings, such as a stampede in a living room. He added to this setting two bored children playing a recently discovered board game that comes to life. The idea behind the holiday CLASSIC *The Polar Express* (1985) was a daydream that felt like a lucid memory; it featured a solitary train in the woods waiting for a young boy to come aboard.

V.'s work has often been described as surrealistic FANTASY that has the propensity to lure the readers' imagination into uncharted territory. The target audiences for all the V.'s books include adults, YA, and children, because of the layers of fascination and depth found in the text and illustrations.

AWARDS: Caldecott Honor Book for *The Garden of Abdul Gasazi,* 1979; Caldecott Medal for *Jumanji,* 1982; Caldecott Medal for *The Polar Express,* 1986; the Regina Medal for lifetime achievement in children's literature; the *Boston Globe–Horn Book* Award; Children's Choices International Reading Association; Teacher's Choices International Reading Association.

FURTHER WORKS: *Swan Lake* (illustrations), 1989; *The Wretched Stone,* 1991; *The Widow's Broom,* 1992; *The Stranger,* 1986; *The Bad Day at Riverbend,* 1995; *The Z Was Zapped,* 1987; *Just a Dream,* 1990; *The Wreck of the Zephyr,* 1983; *The Mysteries of Harris Burdick,* 1984; *The Sweetest Fig,* 1993; *Two Bad Ants,* 1988; *Ben's Dream,* 1982; *Zathura,* 2002.

BIBLIOGRAPHY: Keifer, Barbara, selector. *Getting to Know You: Profiles of Children's Authors Featured in Language Arts, 1985–90,* 1991; Wooten, Deborah. "Chris V." In B. Cullinan and D. Person, eds., *The Continuum Encyclopedia of Children's Literature,* 2001 (pp. 795–96); http://www.eduplace.com/author

DEBORAH A. WOOTEN

VAN DRAANEN, Wendelin
Author, n.d., Chicago, Illinois

V., a former math and computer science teacher, is most renowned for her humorous SERIES of Sammy Keyes MYSTERIES. The first book, *Sammy Keyes and the Hotel Thief* (1998), introduces the character of Sammy (short for Samantha), a tomboy who has a penchant for getting into trouble. Throughout this series, Sammy finds herself entangled in various mysteries and uses her quick wits and sense of humor to solve the case. She faces such challenges as an abandoned baby, a stolen cross, a kidnapped dog, a burned-down cabin, and even a murder. Her tomboy character was inspired by V.'s own childhood and the mysteries came from growing up with TEEN sleuths such as Nancy Drew and Encyclopedia Brown.

Flipped (2001) is a humorous love story about friends Juli and Bryce who have lived across the street from each other since second grade. The story, told in alternating chapters from each character's point of view, traces the progress of Juli's unrequited love for Bryce to Bryce's unrequited love for Juli.

In *Swear to Howdy* (2003), Joey and Rusty spend the summer together filled with lots of pranks and ADVENTURES. When their pranks go awry, they're usually followed by a promise that begins with the line, "I swear to howdy, if you tell a soul . . ." and ends with them nicking their fingers and mixing blood. But when one of their pranks turns tragic and Joey's sister dies, both boys are traumatized by guilt and have to decide if they will hide the truth or break their pact of silence.

AWARDS: *Sammy Keyes and the Hotel Thief:* Edgar Award for Best Children's Mystery and Best Book for Young Adults, American Library Association, both 1999; *Shedderman #1: Secret Identity: Booklist* Editor's Choice, 2004, Christopher Book Award, 2005; *Flipped:* Florida Sunshine State Young Reader Award Winners, 2005, Dorothy Canfield Fisher Children's Book Award, 2003.

FURTHER WORKS: *How I Survived Being a Girl,* 1997; *Sammy Keyes and the Sisters of Mercy,* 1999; *Sammy Keyes and the Hollywood Mummy,* 2001; *Sammy Keyes and the Art of Deception,* 2003; *Sammy Keyes and the Psycho Kitty Queen,* 2004.

BIBLIOGRAPHY: *Authors and Artists for Young Adults,* vol. 36, 2000; *Contemporary Authors Online,* 2003; *Something about the Author,* vol. 122, 2001.

ANDREA LIPINSKI

VANCE, Susanna

Author, b. 10 September 1945, Independence, Missouri

A self-described daydreamer, V. recalls that she had a hard time paying attention in school because her head

was often crowded with stories. But although V. enjoyed writing, she pursued a number of other careers, including photography, before becoming a professional writer. V. began writing seriously while working as a journalist and photographer for the small Tennessee newspaper *Buffalo River Review.* V. found she enjoyed writing so much that she began working on a novel, and shortly thereafter quit her newspaper job to pursue her own writing.

A full-time writer since about 1994, V. has published a number of SHORT STORIES in literary MAGAZINES such as *Thema, Acorn,* and *El Dorado.* Her first short story, "The Big Favorite," was nominated for the Pushcart Prize. V. was inspired during her childhood by the stories of Hans Christian Andersen, and often incorporates aspects of magic realism and the fantastic into her work. For example, Baby Girl, the narrator of V.'s first novel, *Sights* (2001), believes that she can predict the future. In V.'s second novel, *Deep* (2003), one of the two narrators, Morgan, receives guidance from her drowned sister's spirit. The theme of resilience runs through both novels as well; in *Sights,* Baby Girl must overcome a very traumatic past, while Birdie and Morgan in *Deep,* both afflicted by different personal challenges, must escape from a psychopath who has imprisoned them.

V., who now resides in Oregon, comments that she enjoys writing for YAS because she views the TEEN experience as potent and powerful, a traumatic and glorious time that changes the way we see ourselves. She finds it a source of many "golden, magical" stories that are "worth listening to, worth writing down, and worth being read."

AWARDS: *Sights* 2002 American Library Association Best Book for Young Adults; Oregon Literary Fellowship, 2001; Edna Holmes Literary Fund of the Oregon Community Foundation Fellowship, 2001; 2001 *Publishers Weekly* Flying Starts; 2002 Pacific Northwest Writers Association Short Story Selection for Barnes and Noble Literary Night; *Deep:* ALA BBYA, 2004.

BIBLIOGRAPHY: Personal communication with Susanna V., 2003; "Flying Starts." *Publishers Weekly,* vol. 248, no. 26, 2001.

ALLISON RICHARDSON

VANDE, Vivian

Author, b. 1951, Rochester, New York

V. has always wanted to be a writer. Marriage to Jim Vande Velde, followed shortly by the birth of her daughter Beth left her with two options. Since she was no longer working outside the home as a secretary, V. decided she either needed to hone her skills as a housekeeper, or find a reason not to do that. Luckily for her legions of loyal fans, she decided on becoming a writer.

A Hidden Magic (1985) was V.'s first published work. V. thought writing was difficult until she tried to get her book published—that turned out to make writing seem like a stroll in the park. Thirty-two people turned her down until the thirty-third accepted her. On her website, V. details other writers who were initially turned down. Among them are: Stephen KING, Madeline L'ENGLE, Edgar Allan Poe, J. K. ROWLING, and Dr. Seuss. To help aspiring writers learn to deal with rejection, V. feels it is helpful to have other writers who help you through—in an organized group. Members of V.'s writing group include Tedd Arnold, M. J. Auch, Patience Brewster, Bruce COVILLE, Cynthia DeFelice, Robin Pulver, and Ellen Stoll Walsh.

V.'s TEEN books often deal with FANTASY or the paranormal; they include Alison; Who Went Away?; Being Dead; The Changeling Prince; A Coming Evil; Companions of the Night; The Conjurer Princess; Curses, Inc., and Other Stories; Dragon's Bait; Magic Can Be Murder; and Never Trust a Dead Man. Her awards range from American Library Association's Best Book for YA Awards (for Being Dead, Companions of the Night, Heir Apparent, Never Trust a Dead Man, and Tales from the Brothers Grimm and the Sisters Weird) to the IRA Young Adults' Choice Awards (for Being Dead, Curses, Inc. and Other Stories, Tales from the Brothers Grimm and the Sisters Weird, and There's a Dead Person Following My Sister Around). Many of V.'s books are also American Library Association's Quick Picks for Reluctant Young Adult Readers—Companions of the Night; Curses, Inc., and Other Stories; Dragon's Bait; Ghost of a Hanged Man; Never Trust a Dead Man; and Tales from the Brothers Grimm and the Sisters Weird.

The American Booksellers Association gave two of V.'s books special recognition by making them Pick of the List Books—Companions of the Night and A Hidden Magic. Recipient of an Edgar Award by the MYSTERY Writers of America for the Best Young Adult mystery in 2000 for Never Trust a Dead Man, V. was also awarded a Best Book of the Year for that

title by School Library Journal. Her books have been mentioned by the New York Public Library in their Books for the Teen Age five times: Being Dead; Companions of the Night; Curses, Inc., and Other Stories; Dragon's Bait; and Heir Apparent. Companions of the Night was named a YALSA Popular PAPERBACK for Young Adults.

V.'s blend of fantasy stories peopled by believable characters has won her a large audience. Her characters may find themselves in odd situations but their basic humanity is a large part of each of V.'s story's charm. V. says her stories start with a simple question, the idea of what if. . . . Her advice to aspiring writers is varied—although she feels reading is a key component, as is analyzing what you read. V. also suggests that people write about things that interest them and that one should try to write on a regular basis. If this is V.'s key to success, it seems well worth a good attempt on the part of others who want to write their own works, considering how well V.'s own career has done.

BIBLIOGRAPHY: www.amazon.com; www.vivianvandevelde.com.

JEANNE MARIE RYAN

VINGE, Joan D.

Author, b. 2 April 1948, Baltimore, Maryland

Born Joan Carol Dennison to engineer Seymour W. Dennison and executive secretary Carol Erwin, V. is partially of Native American decent. Although she initially planned to major in art, V. received a B.S. in anthropology from San Diego State University in 1971. She married Vernor Vinge, also a famous SCIENCE FICTION writer, in 1972, but they divorced in 1979. Shortly thereafter, V. married her editor, Jim Frenkel, and currently lives in Madison, Wisconsin, with her two children and assorted animals.

V. has received accolades from esteemed critics for her consistent quality and outstanding fabrication of alien civilizations in her novels; she is considered to be one of the most respected science fiction writers in the field. Female empowerment, genocide, gene mutation, the corruption of power, and cross-cultural cohabitation are some of the major recurring themes in V.'s works. Besides anthropology and archaeology, V. has a passion for MYTHOLOGY and FAIRY TALES, particularly the ubiquitous legend of the Earth Mother, which has been incorporated into several of her novels.

Greatly inspired by Hans Christian Andersen, V. went on to write a SHORT STORY, *Tin Soldier* (1974), and a major novel, *The Snow Queen* (1980), that bear both the title and the underlying themes of the fairy tales. *The Snow Queen*, perhaps V.'s most famous and impressive work, is the title of the first of four books in a SERIES also known as the Tiamant Cycle. *The Snow Queen* (1980–2000) series is possibly just as celebrated for the beautiful cover art, drawn by Michael Whelan, that depicts the ethereal masks of the Winter Queen and the Summer Queen.

Interesting enough, V. personally designed the cover art for some of her early novels. She has also written two other major series: *The Cat Cycle* (1982–96) follows the life of Cat, a telepathic street punk who struggles against a corrupt universe; *The Heaven Chronicles* (1976–78) is based on restarting a new world in an asteroid colony. V. is also known for her novelizations of many popular MOVIES such as *Willow* (YA version, 1988), *Ladyhawk* (1985), *Dune* (YA Version, 1984) and *The Return of the Jedi Storybook* (1983).

Although V.'s works are primarily classified as science fiction, her stories strongly border on FANTASY. The exemplary vocabulary and advanced ethical concepts make her books a challenge for many adults to read as well as adolescents. V.'s works could best be described as an amalgamation of Ray Bradbury and J. R. R. TOLKIEN; she exhibits the best of science and technology and perfectly intertwines it with an almost believable alien world. In her own words, V. stated, "writing is the anthropology of the future," and following her own mantra, V. relentlessly scribes a way to unearth otherworldly ADVENTURES that continue to delight and enchant her readers.

AWARDS: Hugo Award: 1976, *Dragonwings;* 1977, *Child of Owl;* 1978 *Eyes of Amber;* 1981, *The Snow Queen.*

FURTHER WORKS: "To Bell the Cat," 1977; "The Crystal Ship," 1976; "Mother and Child," 1975; "Voices from the Dust," 1980; "Exorcycle," 1982; "The Storm King," 1980; "Phoenix in the Ashes," 1978; "The Peddler's Apprentice" (with Vernor Vinge), 1975; "Latter Day Martian Chronicles," 1990; *Tarzan, King of the Apes,* 1983; *Mad Max III: Beyond Thunderdome,* 1985; *Return to Oz,* 1985; *Santa Claus the Movie,* 1985; *Willow* (with George

Lucas), 1988; *Lost in Space,* 1998; *World's End,* 1984; *Tangled up in Blue,* 2000; *Psion,* 1982; *Psiren,* 1981; *Catspaw,* 1988; *Dreamfall,* 1996; *The Outcasts of Heavens Belt,* 1978; *Legacy,* 1980; *Heaven Chronicles,* 1991; Afterward to "The Janus Equation," 1980; *An Open Letter to Andre* NORTON, 1986; Introduction to "The Left Hand of Darkness," 1992; *Death by Chocolate: A Murder* MYSTERY, 1996.

BIBLIOGRAPHY: "Joan D. V. BIOGRAPHY," http://www.bluewyrm.com/sibylnet/answer_vinge.html, 2000; "Joan V. Bibliographical Information," http://www.sff.net/people/jvinge/bio.htm, 2000; "Joan D. V.," http://www.fantasticfiction.co.uk/authors/Joan_D_Vinge.html, 2000.

ILONA N. KOTI

VOIGT, Cynthia

Author, b. 25 February 1942, Boston, Massachusetts

V. does not have strong memories of her own childhood, but her writing is filled with vivid impressions of youth. Although V. aspired to be a writer since high school, it wasn't until after the end of her first marriage that she committed herself to her craft. Since then, this widely acclaimed writer has written more than two dozen books for YAs and children.

V. was born to Elise Keeney and Frederick C. Irving, a corporate executive. She was the second child of four and grew up in southern Connecticut. V. received her B.A. from Smith College, completed graduate work at St. Michael's College, and later got teacher's certification at Christian Brothers College.

V. often laughs about the unexpected directions in which life has gone. She swore in her younger years that she would never become a teacher, but she eventually accepted a teaching position because she needed a job; this was a critical phase in V.'s process of becoming a writer. As a teacher of second, fifth, and seventh grade, V. decided she should be familiar with children's books if she was going to assign book reports. Checking out as many as thirty books at a time, she read through the school's library collection. During her voracious reading, V. became aware of the possibility of meaningful stories for children of all ages; as a result, she became familiar with the field of her future work.

For V., stories naturally develop, and they are written when she feels the time is right for them. *Homecoming* (1981), her first published book, was inspired by the sight of a car full of kids waiting at a grocery store. V. wondered what would happen if their parent never returned; from that simple question, the Tillerman FAMILY was born.

In *Homecoming,* the Tillermans' mother fails to return from the store, prompting TEENAGE Dicey to lead her three younger siblings to find their only known living relative, a great-aunt whom they have never met. The four children journey alone, by foot, car, bus, and boat, first from Pewauket to Bridgeport, Connecticut, and then to Crisfield, Maryland, a distance totaling over 400 miles. The Tillermans find a most unlikely home with their eccentric, hermit grandmother, and settle into Gram's life on the Chesapeake Bay. Dicey is also the focus of the Newbery Award-winning *Dicey's Song* (1982), in which she comes to terms with her mother's DEATH and changes in her family life. In Newbery Honor Book *A Solitary Blue* (1983), Jeff Greenbaum, Dicey's close friend, reconciles himself to his mother's earlier desertion and latest betrayal. Other Tillerman books have brothers James and Sammy attempting to track down the father who abandoned them (*Sons from Afar,* 1987), and Dicey learning through failure (*Seventeen against the Dealer,* 1989). Two books, *Come a Stranger* (1986) and *The Runner* (1985), deal with racism. The former explores the experience of Dicey's AFRICAN AMERICAN friend Mina as summer dance camp awakens her understanding of racism and a visiting minister inspires a new understanding of herself. The latter focuses on the compelling story of Dicey's uncle, "Bullet," a star high-school athlete with a troubled home life who comes to terms with his own racism before dying in Vietnam.

V.'s acclaimed Kingdom SERIES includes *Jackaroo* (1985), *On Fortune's Wheel* (1990), *The Wings of a Falcon* (1993), and *Elske* (2001). Each of these books takes place in a mythical land, and all involve love, journey, and ADVENTURE. In spite of that, these are by no means FAIRY TALES. The endings are more realistic than they are happy, and not every hero lives. However, each of V.'s characters has the strength to continue in spite of adversity, a recurrent theme of all of her complex stories.

While she often revisits the same places and themes in her writing, V. writes across a wide variety of genres. Her works include MYSTERY (*The Vandemark Mummy,* 1991), historical realism (*The Runner*), contemporary realism (*Dicey's Song*), and PICTURE BOOKS (*Stories about Rosie,* 1986). Her subjects have been involved in rock 'n' roll (*Orfe,* 1993), recovered from a traumatic amputation (*Izzy Willy-Nilly,* 1986), lived out a Robin Hood fantasy (*Jackaroo*), been sold into slavery (*On Fortune's Wheel*), served in Vietnam (*The Runner*), and survived sexual abuse (*When She Hollers,* 1994).

V.'s novels typically focus on themes of self-reliance, independence, and friendship. Her characters are often outsiders, have dysfunctional families, rely on their own strength, and learn about the importance of relationships with others. Her books are sometimes controversial, and she writes candidly about difficult issues such as racism, sexual abuse, disfigurement, anger, slavery, homosexuality, and abandonment.

V. has commented that she would ideally like to write from 8 a.m until noon, but life often cuts into her time. When the author writes, she first makes an outline of the plot and a map where she can separate every chapter. She likes stories based on fact and she enjoys developing characterization; the creation of plot, however, often gives V. trouble. She has lived a long time in Annapolis, and has spent the summers on an island in the Chesapeake Bay. She loves the sea and spends a great deal of time boating, crabbing, and swimming; these activities frequently appear in her work. Currently, V. makes her home in Deer Isle, Maine.

SELECT AWARDS: 1984 Newbery Honor Book, *A Solitary Blue;* 1984 Edgar Award, *The Callender Papers;* 1983 Newbery Medal, *Dicey's Song;* 1990 California Young Reader's Award, ALA Popular Paperbacks, 2002, *Izzy—Willy, Nilly; The Runner:* 1989 ALAN Award, 1988 Silver Pencil Award; Margaret Alexander Edwards Award, 1995; 1995 ALA BBYA for *When She Hollers;* 2000 ALA BBYA for *Elske.* In addition, four of V.'s books have been selected for the 3rd YALSA Best of the Best list: Nothin' But the Best (Selections from 1966 to 1986): *Homecoming, Izzy— Willy-Nilly, Runner, Solitary Blue. Izzy, Willy-Nilly* was also selected for the 4th YALSA Best of the Best list: Here We Go Again . . . 25 Years of Best Books (Selections from 1967 to 1992).

FURTHER WORKS: *Good Morning, Rosie,* 2003; *Bad Girls in Love,* 2002; *It's not Easy Being Bad,* 2000; *Bad, Badder, Baddest,* 1997; *The Bad Girls,* 1996; *David and Jonathan,* 1992; *Tree by Leaf,* 1988; *Stories about Rosie,* 1986; *Building Blocks,* 1984; *Tell Me If the Lovers Are Losers,* 1982.

BIBLIOGRAPHY: "Cynthia V." *Authors and Artists for Young Adults,* vol. 30, 1999; *Children's Literature Review,* vol. 48, 1998; Reid, S. *Presenting Cynthia V.,* 1995; Devereaux, E. "Cynthia V." *Publishers Weekly,* July 1994, pp. 225–26; Hile, Kevin S., ed. *Something about the Author,* vol. 79, 1995; Senick, Gerald J., ed. *Children's Literature Review,* vol. 13, 1987.

                                    HEIDI HAUSER GREEN

VONNEGUT, Kurt

Author, b. 11 November 1922, Indianapolis, Indiana

Much of V.'s writing focuses on the dangers of ignorant applications of technology. These concerns may be traced in part to his early experiences of automation during and immediately after the Great Depression, when he saw the jobs and self-worth of many workers destroyed by the factory machines that replaced them. Starting out as a school journalist, V. wrote humor columns and editorials for the *Cornell Daily Sun.* After leaving Cornell as a junior to enlist in the Army, he soon served as an infantryman in World War II. He was captured by the Germans and forced to work underground in a factory at Dresden. Allied Forces decimated Dresden, but V., working below ground, was unharmed. He was made a corpse carrier for what he terms "the largest massacre in European history." So great was the emotional impact of this experience that many consider much of his work an attempt to use his art as a means to process its horror. His work after the WAR and a brief stint at the University of Chicago brought him to General Electric as a research publicist where he witnessed firsthand the downside of capitalist technological development. He began writing SHORT STORIES and published his first novel, *Player Piano,* in 1952. *Mother Night* (1961) was followed by *Cat's Cradle* (1963); *God Bless You, Mr. Rosewater* (1965); *Welcome to the Monkey House* (1968); and *Slaughterhouse-Five* (1969). V.'s absurdist irony deliberately places the reader in the collaborative role of knowing more than the characters know.

AWARDS: Nominated for National Book Award, 1969 for *Slaughterhouse-Five;* National Institute of Arts and Letters grant, 1970; Guggenheim Fellowship, 1967; Honorary M.A. by the University of Chicago, 1971; elected Vice President of P.E.N. American Center, appointed member of the National Institute of Arts and Letters, both 1972; Awarded honorary L.H.D. by Indiana University; succeeded Anthony Burgess as Distinguished Professor of English Prose at City University of New York, 1973; received honorary Litt.D by Hobart and William Smith College, 1974; elected vice president of the National Institute of Arts and Letters, 1975; named State Author for New York, 2000.

FURTHER WORKS: Play, *Happy Birthday, Wanda June,* (1971); *Between Time and Timbuktu,* 1972; *Breakfast of Champions,* 1973; *Wampeters, Foma and Granfalloons: Opinions,* 1974; *Slapstick or Lonesome No More,* 1976; *Jailbird,* 1979; *Palm Sunday, An Autobiographical Collage,* 1981; *Deadeye Dick,* 1982; *Galapagos,* 1985; *Bluebeard,* 1987; *Hocus Pocus,* 1990; *Fates Worse Than Death: An Autobiographical Collage of the 1980's,* 1991; *Timequake,* 1997; *God Bless You, Dr. Kevorkian,* 2004.

                                    CATHERINE GIVEN

WALKER, Alice

Author, b. 9 February 1944, Eatonton, Georgia

W. is the youngest of eight children born to poor sharecropper parents in Eatonton, Georgia. Both her parents were storytellers. In *Our Mother's Garden,* she describes her mother, Minnie Tallulah Grant Walker, as "a walking history of our community." At age eight, W. was blinded in her right eye by a BB-gun bullet while playing "cowboys and Indians" with her brothers. The accident made a permanent impact on her, as she felt socially OUTCAST due to the facially disfiguring scar. Experiencing feelings of loneliness, she became absorbed in books and at an early age began to write POETRY. W. has said that while she was in high school, her mother gave her three important gifts: a sewing machine, which gave her the independence to make her own clothes; a suitcase, which gave her permission to leave home and travel; and a typewriter, which gave her permission to write. W. graduated from high school as class valedictorian in 1961 and went on to study on a scholarship at Spelman College in Atlanta, Georgia. After two years she transferred to Sarah Lawrence College, where she completed a B.A. in 1965. Subsequently, she spent time in the South registering voters and she worked at the New York City Welfare Department. She married white human rights lawyer and activist Mel Leventhal in 1967, and their daughter Rebecca was born in 1969. Life in segregated Mississippi was difficult for them. The couple divorced in 1977. During all this time, she continued to write.

Her first novel, *The Third Life of Grange Copeland,* was published in 1970 when she was 26 years old. Black tenant farmer Grange Copeland flees from his life in the South and heads to the North, leaving his wife and son behind in Georgia. When he returns years later, he finds his son in prison for the murder of his wife. As the guardian of his granddaughter, Grange Copeland grapples with his final chance to free himself from spiritual and social enslavement.

W.'s most famous work, her novel *The Color Purple* (1982), won the American Book Award, the National Book Award, and the Pulitzer Prize in 1983. *The Color Purple* portrays Celie, a Southern woman in an abusive relationship, during her struggle to find self-worth. The entire story is told in letters over the span of thirty years: Celie's simple letters to God, her letters to her lost sister Nettie in Africa, and Nettie's letters to Celie. Celie eventually triumphs over oppression. Critics interpret the story as a feminist novel about an abused and undereducated black woman's struggle. It was acknowledged for its eloquent use of black English vernacular. *The Color Purple* gained even further recognition when Stephen Spielberg adapted it into a MOVIE. Spielberg's approach made the film both controversial and a popular hit. Whoopi Goldberg and Oprah Winfrey made their screen debuts in this movie. Although the film was praised for its portrayal of AFRICAN AMERICAN heroines, the black community was fiercely critical of its negative depiction of black men.

In 1983. W. published her first collection of nonfiction, *In Search of Our Mothers' Gardens.* The theme of this influential essay collection is closely related to the theme of *A Color Purple*: black women in relation to their FAMILIES, their mothers, each other, black men, white society, and the world at large. The essays also discuss other writers and their writing, and reflect on the CIVIL RIGHTS MOVEMENT of the 1960s and the antinuclear movement of the 1980s. W. coined the term *womanism* as she explored the theory and practice of different versions of feminism. "Womanism" became a populist and poetic synonym for black feminism. W. explained in *The New York Times Magazine* in 1984, "I don't choose womanism because it is 'better' than feminism . . . Since womanism means black feminism, this would be a nonsensical distinction. I choose it because I prefer the sound, the feel, the fit of it; because I cherish the spirit of the women (like Sojourner) the word calls to mind, and because I share the old ethnic-American habit of offering society a new word, when the old word it is using fails to describe behavior and change that only a new word can help it more fully see. (. . .) Womanist is to feminist as purple is to lavender."

In *The Temple of My Familiar* (1989) and *Possessing the Secret of Joy* (1992), W. takes on the issue of female circumcision in Africa, which again brought both approval and controversy.

More recent publications include *Anything We Love Can Be Saved* (1998), an essay collection about W.'s life as an activist, the poetry collection *Absolute Trust in the Goodness of the Earth* (2003), and the novels *By the Light of My Father's Smile* (1999) and *Now is the Time to Open Your Heart* (2004). In her poetry, W. explores the fundamental beauty of existence in light of the frenzy that permeates modern life. She writes about grief, love, forgiveness, and acceptance in a deeply profound and spiritual language. W.'s books have been translated into more than two dozen languages. She has won numerous awards and honors. She is in high demand as a lecturer and lives in Mendocino, California.

AWARDS: Lillian Smith Award from the National Endowment for the Arts; Rosenthal Award from the National Institute of Arts and Letters; Fellowships from the Radcliffe Institute; Merrill Fellowship; Guggenheim Fellowship; O'Henry Award. ALA Best Book for Young Adults, 1984, selected for "Nothin' but the Best: Best of the Best Books for Young Adults, 1966–1986," for *In Search of Our Mothers' Gardens: Womanist Prose.*

FURTHER WORKS: *Meridian,* 1976; *The Same River Twice: Honoring the Difficult,* 1996; *The Way Forward Is with a Broken Heart,* 2000.

BIBLIOGRAPHY: Gates, Henry Louis Jr., and K. A. Appiah, eds. *Alice W.: Critical Perspectives Past and Present,* 1993; "Alice W." *African-American Writers,* ed. Lea Baechler, A. Walton Litz, and Valerie Smith, 1991; Banks, Erma D., and Keith Byerman. *Alice W.: An Annotated Bibliography,* 1989; *Alice W.,* ed. Harold Bloom, 1990.

CHRISTINE MARIA WELTER

WALKER, (Dianne Marie) Kate

Author, b. 10 January 1950, Newcastle, Australia

W. is a prolific writer of books for all ages. W.'s published titles include PICTURE BOOKS for children, adult nonfiction, and a YA novel. Her work has also appeared in anthologies and MAGAZINES. She was inspired to start a writing career after making up bedtime stories for her daughter. W. has received numerous awards in her native AUSTRALIA. Her picture book *Marty Moves to the Country* (1980) was named an Australian Children's Book of the Year in the Picture Book Section in 1981. *The Dragon of Mith* (1989) received a similar honor in the Junior Section in 1990.

W.'s young adult novel *Peter* (1993) tells the story of a young man struggling with his sexuality. She received awards in both Australia and the United States for *Peter.* It was named an Australian Children's Book of the Year Honour Book, Young Adult Section, 1991.

In addition to her writing career, W. also teaches writing workshops for teachers of children and high-school students and has written numerous books on the art of writing.

AWARDS: *Peter*: ALA 1994 Best Books Lists: Notable Books of the Year, Best Books for Young Adults, and Best Books for Reluctant Young Adult Readers.

SELECT FURTHER WORKS: *The Frog Who Would Be King,* 1989; *King Joe of Bogpeat Castle,* 1989; *The Alien Challenger,* 1983; *Suzie and the Pencil-Case Genie,* 1988; *The Letters of Rosie O'Brien: A Convict in the Colony of New South Wales, 1804,* 1988; *Tales from the Good Land,* 1988; *Burying Aunt Renie,* 1989; *Writing Games,* 1991; *Step By Step Stories,* 1991; *Story Writing: Teaching and Tapping Your Subconscious Mind,* 1993; *Writing Enrichment,* 1994; *Journal Writing,* 1994

BIBLIOGRAPHY: *Contemporary Authors Online,* 2003. Reproduced in *Biography Resource Center,* 2003, http://www.galenet.com/servlet/BioRC

SHANNON CUFF

WALLACE, Rich
Author, b. 29 January 1957, Hackensack, New Jersey

W.'s engagingly written novels combine high-school boys, SPORTS, and small-town Pennsylvanian life. This lifelong athlete was born to a family in which both parents had attended college; he grew up as one of seven children.

W. was not interested in school or reading, but often spent his spare time playing sports and writing stories. During high school, in addition to playing sports, W. wrote personal journals and articles for the high-school newspaper. W. attended Montclair State College but dropped out before completing his degree. While in college, he explored his interest in writing by taking creative writing classes, including one in which he wrote a novel.

A college internship led to a ten-year period of working for several New Jersey newspapers in a variety of reporting and editorial capacities. His internship at the *Herald-News* in Passaic, New Jersey, led to a position as an editorial assistant from 1978 to 1979 and later as sports reporter from 1979 to 1982. In 1980, W. returned to Montclair State College, finished his course work, and graduated with a B.A. degree. After five years at the Passaic *Herald-News,* W. worked for the *Daily Advance* in Dover, New Jersey, first as sports editor from 1982 to 1984 and then as news editor from 1984 to 1985. In 1985, he moved to the *Trenton Times* in Trenton, New Jersey, as copy editor from 1985 to 1986 and then as assistant city editor from 1986 to 1987. It was during this period that W. submitted the novel written for his creating writing class to publishers. Patricia Lee Gauch, then an editor, wrote him a rejection letter and shared other editors' comments, including those of staff member Tracy Gates.

W.'s next career move took him into MAGAZINE publishing. In the late 1980s he began working for the perennial childhood favorite, *Highlights for Children.* W. worked as copy editor from 1988 to 1990, assistant editor from 1990 to 1992, and coordinating editor from 1992 to 1998. It was during his tenure as coordinating editor for *Highlights for Children* that W.'s

first novel, *Wrestling Sturbridge* (1996) was published. When W. had a manuscript with which he was happy, he contacted Tracy Gates, who expressed an interest in his work. She liked it and later edited *Wrestling Sturbridge* for publication. Since 1998, W. has worked as senior editor for *Highlights for Children.*

W.'s novels and his collection of linked SHORT STORIES, *Losing Is Not an Option* (2003), are all set in the working-class town of Sturbridge, a darker and grittier version of Honesdale, Pennsylvania. Just as each of his books deals with sports, W.'s characters are all struggling to find themselves and their places in the world. W.'s *Wrestling Sturbridge* presents Ben, a senior who challenges his best friend for the top spot on the wrestling team. His second novel, *Shots on Goal* (1997), features Barry, also known as Bones, who does not enjoy coming in second to both Joey, his best friend on the soccer team, and his older brother at home. W. creates further plot tension between Bones and Joey when Joey begins dating Bones's love interest, Shannon.

W.'s novels are known for having realistic plots, well-developed characters, and exciting sports scenes. He admits to using sports as a metaphor for life in his books, and wants to be honest in his portrayal of TEENAGE boys' lives. Ultimately, W. hopes that readers will be inspired by characters such as Ben in *Wrestling Sturbridge* and Bones in *Shots on Goal* and realize their full potential in life.

AWARDS: *Wrestling Sturbridge,* 1997 American Library Association Best Book for Young Adults, 1997 Recommended Book for Reluctant Young Adult Readers; *Playing without the Ball*: 2002 ALA BBY.

FURTHER WORKS: *Playing without the Ball: A Novel in Four Quarters,* 2000; *Losing Is Not an Option,* 2003; *Restless: a Ghost Story,* 2003.

BIBLIOGRAPHY: Carter, Betty. *Best Books for Young Adults, Second Edition,* 2000; Comerford, Lynda Brill, Allison Stonce, Sally Lodge, Shannon Maughan, Julie Yates Walton, Heather Vogel Frederick. "Flying Starts: Six Children's Book Newcomers Share Thoughts on Their Debut Projects." *Publishers Weekly,* July 1, 1996, p. 34; *Contemporary Authors Online,* 2001.

ANDREW W. HUNTER

WALTER, Mildred Pitts
Author, b. 9 September 1922, Sweetville, Louisiana

As an AFRICAN AMERICAN growing up in rural Louisiana in the 1920s and 1930s, W. faced the twin obstacles of poverty and racial prejudice. Determined to get an education, she became the first of her FAMILY to earn a college degree when she graduated from Southern University.

W. spent many years teaching elementary school in Los Angeles and working as an activist in the California CIVIL RIGHTS MOVEMENT, most notably in the Congress of Racial Equality (CORE). As a teacher of black children, W. grew increasingly frustrated with the lack of books about and by black people. When W. shared her concerns with a book publisher, he persuaded her to write stories of her own. W.'s first book for children, *Lillie of Watts,* was published in 1971.

African American culture and history permeate W.'s work. *The Girl on the Outside* (1982) depicts the complex emotions involved in the integration of a southern high school in the 1950s. In *Because We Are* (1983), a girl is forced to transfer from an integrated high school to an all-black one. In *Justin and the Best Biscuits in the World* (1996), a Coretta Scott King Award-winning novel, a boy and his cowboy grandfather explore the family history of their "Exoduster" forebears, who left Tennessee in 1880 to start a ranch in Missouri. The INFORMATIONAL book *Mississippi Challenge* (1992) chronicles the complicated history of voting rights in Mississippi through the mid-1960s.

AWARDS: *Justin and the Best Biscuits in the World*: Coretta Scott King Author Award, 1987; *Mississippi Challenge*: Coretta Scott King Author Honor Books, 1993; *Trouble's Child*: Coretta Scott King Author Honor Books, 1986; *Because We Are*: Coretta Scott King Author Honor Books, 1984.

FURTHER WORKS: *Mariah Loves Rock,* 1988; *Mariah Keeps Cool,* 1990; *Second Daughter,* 1996; *Ray and the Best Family Reunion Ever,* 2001

BIBLIOGRAPHY: www.eduplace.com/kids/hmr05/mtai/walter.html

EDWARD T. SULLIVAN

WALTER, Virginia A.
Author, librarian, teacher, n.d., n.p.

W. was a career LIBRARIAN for twenty-four years and served as past president of the American Library Association before embarking on a publishing career. In the field of librarianship, she compiled and annotated bibliographies on WAR and peace issues and the human immunodeficiency virus (HIV) and acquired immune deficiency syndrome (AIDS). She conducted

a number of library-related studies, the results of which she presented in a handful of publications including *Strategic Management for Public Libraries: A Handbook* (1996) and *Output Measures and More: Planning and Evaluating Public Library Services for Young Adults* (1995).

W.'s experience as a children's librarian inspired her to write the PICTURE BOOK *"Hi, Pizza Man!"* (1995). Her first juvenile picture book centers upon a mother and toddler anxiously waiting for the surprise brought by the pizza deliveryman. W. wrote her second book, *Making up Megaboy,* for YAS. *Making up Megaboy* (1998) is a collection of first-person narratives detailing the troubling story of thirteen-year old Robbie Jones.

AWARDS: *Making Up Megaboy*: ALA Best Books for Young Adults, 1999.

FURTHER WORKS: *Output Measures for Public Library Service to Children: A Manual of Standardized Procedures,* 1992; *War and Peace Literature for Children and Young Adults: A Resource Guide to Significant Issues,* 1993; *HIV and AIDS: Information for Children: A Guide to Issues and Resources,* 1999; *Children and Libraries: Getting It Right,* 2000.

BIBLIOGRAPHY: *Contemporary Authors Online,* 2003; http://skipper.gseis.ucla/faculty/

MIMI O'MALLEY

WAR

The topic of W. is covered in multiple ways. Specific W.s may be referred to, from the Trojan W. to current world upheavals. The underlying philosophy of W. may be examined in FANTASY and SCIENCE FICTION novels. The themes of good versus evil is fairly consistent in W. novels, although whether W. is evil in and of itself is also examined.

Cast Two Shadows: The American Revolution in the South by Ann RINALDI and *Dawn's Early Light* by Elswyth Thane offer views on the Revolutionary War from women of the South. Choices must be made in James Lincoln COLLIER's *My Brother Sam Is Dead* between the Patriots and the Loyalists.

Different views of the Civil W. are seen in *Soldiers' Heart,* by Gary Paulsen, and *Across Five Aprils,* by Irene Hunt. The Williamsburg Chronicles by Elswyth Thane continue with *Yankee Stranger,* when Eden Day's world is torn asunder by the Civil W.—and falling in love with a Yankee. Further in the

SERIES, Eden's son, Bracken, serves as a correspondent during the Spanish–American War.

Erich Maria Remarque's CLASSIC *All Quiet On the Western Front* tells the story of World W. I through the eyes of a young German soldier. Set in the U.S., at about the same time, Norma JOHNSTON touches upon the reactions of a group of young boys when they find an abandoned dachshund, a reflection of the disdain many Americans at the time felt for all things German. K. M. PEYTON's historical Flambards books are partially set against a background of World W. I, as well as chronicling the fairly new field of aeronautics, as the aristocracy of Great Britain face the changes brought about by W. *Forgotten Fire* by Adam Bagdasarian chronicles conflict in Turkey during the time of the Great W..

Janet Lambert's books dealing with World W. II and the repatriation of Germany are told mostly from a strictly American point of view, although Tippy Parrish's sympathy for the defeated German citizens offers a slightly different angle. *Under the Blood-Red Sun* by Graham SALISBURY relates the trials of a Japanese–Hawaiian FAMILY has to deal with during World W. II. Miriam BAT-AMI's *Two Suns in the Sky* also offers an interesting view on World W. II. The American Catholic Christine Cook begins to fall in love with Adam Bornstein, who is a Yugoslavian Jew kept behind fences in the Emergency Refuge Shelter, in Cook's hometown of Oswego, New York. This creates conflict. *The Divine Wind: A Love Story* by Garry Disher deals with World W. II and its aftermath as a young AUSTRALIAN man must come to terms with the results of the W. and his feelings toward his Japanese first love. *The Upstairs Room* by Joanna Reiss is also a story of World W. II, told by a young Jewish girl, who spent it in one room, hiding from the Nazis. *Soldier Boys* by Dean Hughes tells the story of the Battle of the Bulge, from the viewpoint of a young American soldier and a young German soldier.

A company struggles to survive in Vietnam in *Fallen Angels* by Walter Dean MYERS, as does Army Nurse Rebecca Phillips in *The Road Home* by Ellen Emerson WHITE.

Novels focusing on more contemporary conflicts include *Girl of Kosovo* by Alice MEAD, which details the conflict between the Albanians and the Serbs in Kosovo. The author's *Soldier Mom* deals with Operation Desert Storm. *Gulf* by Robert WESTALL deals with a young boy who begins to channel an Iraqi sol-

dier. In another part of the world, *Taste of Salt: A Story of Modern Haiti* by Frances TEMPLE chronicles the conflicts that ravage the island nation.

The philosophy of W. is examined in *Virtual W.* and its sequel, *The Clones (The Virtual W. Chronogs, Book 2)* by Gloria SKURZYNSKI, placed in the future, which deal with a young warrior's skill, as well as his aversion, to the game of W. John Marsden's Tomorrow books (*Tomorrow, When the W. Began; The Dead Of Night; A Killing Frost; Darkness Be My Friend; Burning For Revenge; The Night Is for Hunting;* and *The Other Side of Dawn*) center on a group of Austrialian TEENS. Coming back from a campout in the bush, Ellie and her group find devastation. Their country has been taken over and their families captured. As the group struggles to survive and fight the enemy, what W. is receives a thorough examination. Orson Scott CARD also muses on the meaning of W. in his Ender novels.

W., what it is and what makes it potentially justified, varies from individual to individual. The above stories at least provide a starting point for thoughts about the topic and provide readers with various viewpoints and opinions—set in both historical and futuristic contexts. In light of the recent history of the U.S., the subject of W. has once again become an omnipresent shadow. Informed citizens, as always, will need to stand on the side of civilization instead of chaos.

JEANNE MARIE RYAN

WATSON, Larry
Author, b. 1947, Rugby, North Dakota

The culture and people of the western Midwest plains are explored throughout the novels and poems of W. As the son and grandson of town sheriffs in North Dakota, W. was an unmotivated student but loved to read. After junior college, W. entered the University of North Dakota. He enrolled in a writing class and began writing POETRY. With faculty encouragement, he abandoned pre-law and decided on teaching as a career. He wrote SHORT STORIES for his M.A., and moved to the University of Utah to pursue the flexible Ph.D. program in creative writing.

For his thesis at the University of Utah, he wrote *In a Dark Time*, a MYSTERY of sorts. This was his first published novel, which gained respectful reviews although it was not especially profitable. After leaving the University of Utah, W. has taught writing and literature at the University of Wisconsin/Stevens Point since 1978. His recent success has allowed him to cut his teaching time in half. W. has published short stories, poems, essays, and book reviews.

AWARDS: Milkweed National Fiction Prize, 1993; The Mountains and Plains Bookseller Association Regional Book Award; National Education Association creative writing fellowship, 1987; *Montana 1948*: ALA Best Books for Young Adults, 1994.

FURTHER WORKS: *In A Dark Time,* 1980; *Leaving Dakota,* 1983 (poetry collection); *White Crosses,* 1995; *Orchard,* 2003.

BIBLIOGRAPHY: *Contemporary Authors,* online, 2003; *Publishers Weekly,* Jan. 23, 1995.

MIMI O'MALLEY

WEAVER, Beth Nixon
Author, n.d., n.p.

W. made a major impact in the YA genre with her first novel. Set in Florida in 1969, *Rooster* (2001) is a coming-of-age story narrated by Kady, fifteen, who is frustrated by what she sees as her deprived life on a rundown orange grove, with an over-crowded house, semiliterate parents, and a senile grandmother. Rooster is the eponymous, poultry-obsessed, brain-damaged boy next door. who admires Kady as his godmother. When she catches the eye of Jon, a wealthy, popular boy, Kady's emotions overwhelm her, and she neglects Rooster.

Some have been concerned by the novel's candid account of Kady lying to her parents, partying, and experimenting with marijuana, but W.'s candid approach to TEENAGE emotions is convincing. After her carelessness leads to Rooster being injured, Kady has the courage to choose the right action. The realistic detail, epitomized by the dramatic climax of the fight to save the orange crop from frost, adds to *Rooster*'s impact.

Successful in capturing the mood of an era and creating an appealing and popular narrator, W. is a publicity-shy freelance writer and mother of four who lives in Orlando, Florida.

AWARDS: 2002 Children's Literature Choice List, 2002 Booklist Top Ten First Novels for Youth, and 2002 American Library Association Best Book for Young Adults for *Rooster.*

BIBLIOGRAPHY: http://winslowpress.com/rooster/rooster.cfm

TREVOR AGNEW

WEAVER, Will(iam) (Weller)
Author, b. 19 January 1950, Park Rapids, Minnesota

W. earned his B.A. from the University of Minnesota in English in 1972 and his M.A. from Stanford University's Stanford Writing Program in English and creative writing in 1979. After his father retired, W. returned home to operate the dairy farm while teaching writing part time. In 1981, W. relinquished the farm, dedicating himself to both a full-time professorship and a writing career.

W. credits his childhood on a remote farm in Minnesota for the development of his imagination; without the distraction of television, he was forced to play outdoors and have actual experiences. The American Midwestern farm is foremost in the author's work; he knows the experience of growing up isolated and feeling like an OUTCAST. The Midwest is the area with which he identifies, and it is the consistent setting of W.'s adult and YOUNG ADULT novels. While his professional writing career began with the publication of two adult works, his target audience was switched when W. realized the wealth of ideas available in his FAMILY. Wanting to spend more time with his two TEENAGE children, W. listened to their vignettes about school and created stories for them.

Striking Out (1993), the first work in W.'s Billy Baggs trilogy, met with critical success. The story of Billy, a thirteen-year-old boy from the rural Midwest, combines baseball with the typical adolescent difficulties, such as feeling like an outsider, coming to terms with DEATH, discovering sexual feelings, and clashing with one's parent. Although SPORTS played a significant role in *Striking Out,* W. managed to avoid being named a "sports writer." His wealth of characterization and strong storyline attracted reluctant readers, especially teenage boys whose entrance into adolescence had temporarily ended their independent reading.

Billy's teenage years are followed in *Farm Team* (1995) and *Hard Ball* (1998), two sequels that achieved similar success to *Striking Out.* The "rich kid/poor kid" conflict is more apparent in these latter two works as Billy and his town rival come to understand each other's hardships. A review of *Hard Ball* remarks, "Weaver gets this world exactly right, with the haves and have nots living separate lives, even in sparsely populated Minnesota farmland."

In a break from the Billy Baggs trilogy, W. branched out from the sports backdrop and tried his hand at a new genre of fiction writing. *Memory Boy* (2001) is set in the postapocalyptic future following the volcanic eruption of Washington's Mount Rainer. A resulting shortage of necessary goods impels a teenager from Minneapolis to use his extraordinary memory to bring his family to a place of refuge where there is a greater chance of survival. *Booklist* called W.'s departure from sports writing "an imaginative and plausible rendering of a futuristic society." *Claws* (2003), another novel wrought with suspence, tackled the issue of parental infidelity and its effect on the teenager.

With W.'s most recent work, he has moved further away from the category of sports writing. His marvelous characterizations and captivating storylines have earned him the title of "one of the strongest emerging voices in the field of young adult literature." As for W., the connection between his work for adults and young adults is apparent: "There are certain affinities for YA in my adult work, large parts of them that younger readers could enjoy as well."

AWARDS: *Striking Out:* 1993 American Library Association Pick of the Lists, 1994 ALA Best Books for Young Adults; *Farm Team:* ALA Best Books for Young Adults and IRA Distinguished Book Award, both 1996, and Best Books for Teens lists in Texas and Iowa; *Hard Ball:* South Carolina Best Books, Texas Lone Star List; ALA Best Books for Young Adults, 1999.

FURTHER WORKS: *Red Earth, White Earth,* 1986; *A Gravestone Made of Wheat,* 1989; "Stealing for Girls," in *Ultimate Sports* (ed. Don GALLO), 1995; "The Photograph," in *No Easy Answers* (ed. Gallo), 1997; "Bootleg Summers," in *Time Capsule* (ed. Gallo), 1999.

BIBLIOGRAPHY: Brown, Jean E. "Will W." *Writers for Young Adults,* 2000. Reproduced in Writers for Young Adults Supplement, http://galenet.galegroup.com/servlet/LitRC/; "Review of *Memory Boy,*" *Booklist,* www.amazon.com; Rosser, Claire. "Review of *Hard Ball,*" *Kliatt,* July 1998, p. 9; *Something about the Author,* vol. 109. 2000.

RACHEL WITMER

WEISS, M. Jerry

Author, editor, professor, b. 16 April 1926, Oxford, North Carolina

W. was born and grew up in North Carolina. He served in the Naval Reserve (1944–46), taught high school in Chase City, Virginia, and completed his B.A. at the University of North Carolina (1949). W. married Helen Weiss in 1950; they have four children. W. took a position with the New York City Board of Education, moving his family to New York. There he completed his M.A. (1951) and doctoral degree (1962) at Teachers College, Columbia University. W. held teaching positions at Defiance College, Defiance, Ohio; Pennsylvania State University, University Park; and Jersey City State College, Jersey City, New Jersey. He served as a consultant to several book publishers.

W. coedited several books with Helen W. including *The American Way of Laughing* (1977), *More Tales out of School* (1980), *From One Experience to Another: Award-Winning Authors Share Real-Life Experiences through Fiction* (1997), *Lost and Found: Award-Winning Authors Share Real-Life Experiences through Fiction* (2000), and *Big City Cool: SHORT STORIES about Urban Youth* (2002).

W. worked actively in numerous professional organizations; he was elected to positions at the local, state, regional, and national levels. In the College Reading Association (president, 1964–65), National Council of Teachers of English (president of Assembly on Literature for Adolescents, 1974–75), and American Association of University Professors (president of the Jersey City State College chapter, 1974–76), American Library Association and the International Reading Association (he was chair of the committee on adolescent literature 1976–78 and the committee on reading and the arts 1978–81).

AWARDS: 1973, Distinguished Service Award, the College Reading Association; 1976, Assembly on Literature for Adolescents, National Council of Teachers of English; 1977, The Elliot Landau Award; 1979, Distinguished Service Award, The New Jersey Reading Association; Established the M. Jerry W. Award.

FURTHER WORKS: *Guidance Through Drama,* 1954; *A Guide to Play Selection,* 1958 and 1975; *Reading in the Secondary Schools,* 1961; *Ten Short PLAYS,* 1963; *Books To Grow On: A PAPERBACK Library,* 1976; *An English Teacher's Reader,* 1961; *Man and WAR,*

1963; *The Unfinished Journey: Themes from Contemporary Literature* (compiled with Theresa Oakes), 1967; *Tales Out of School,* 1967; *Kaleidoscope,* 1970; *Man to Himself,* 1970; *New Perspectives on Paperbacks,* 1972; *From Writers to Students: The Pleasures and Pains of Writing,* 1979; *More Tales Out of School,* 1980; *Books I Read When I Was Young* (with Bernice Cullinan), 1980; *Lost and Found,* 2001; *Big City Cool: Short Stories about Urban Youth,* 2002; *The Signet Book of Short Plays,* 2004.

BIBLIOGRAPHY: *Contemporary Authors New Revision Series,* vol. 9, 1983; *Contemporary Authors Online,* 2003; conversation with Jerry and Helen W., 2004; Three Investigator'sBooks.com; International Reading Association Profile.

MIMI O'MALLEY
AND BERNICE E. CULLINAN

WELTY, Eudora Alice

Author, photographer, b. 13 April 1909, Jackson, Mississippi; d. 23 July 2001, Jackson, Mississippi

W. is best known for her novels and SHORT STORIES set in the Southern Delta region of the United States, especially in her home state, Mississippi. She was a prolific writer and explored many literary genres, including one children's book, *The Shoe Bird* (1964), numerous essays, critical reviews, and a BIOGRAPHICAL memoir, *One Writer's Beginnings* (1984). W.'s fiction is recognized for its realistic portraits of the ordinary inhabitants of Southern small towns. Intensely private about her personal life, the author revealed her inner world through her writings. *The Golden Apples* (1949), a SERIES of connected short stories depicting life within Morgana, a fictional town in Mississippi, plucks the fruit of her imagination. The National Center for Education and the Economy included this work in its *New Standards Reading List* (1997, 2001) for high-school students. W. is noted for respecting her characters' situations and honoring their strengths while humorously accepting their defects. As a photographer, she captured snapshots of rural Mississippians and Louisiana residents through her camera lens, as exhibited in the collection of pictures taken during the 1930s Great Depression and published under the title *One Time, One Place: Mississippi in the Depression; A Snapshot Album* (1971; rev. ed., 1996).

W.'s parents, Christian and Chestina W., met and married as schoolteachers in West Virginia. In 1904,

they moved to Jackson, Mississippi, where her father worked in the insurance business and her mother was a homemaker. Born in Jackson, W. was their only daughter and the oldest of three children. The W. family enjoyed reading, music, gardening, and photography. One of W.'s earliest memories was listening to her parents read aloud to each other. She learned to read before entering elementary school and became a voracious independent reader, particularly enjoying MYTHS, fables, and ADVENTURE stories. In her novella, *The Robber Bridegroom* (1942), W. drew on Mississippi folklore and FANTASY and created an original Southern fairytale of young Rosamond and her cruel stepmother, Salome, amid historical details of the infamous Natchez Trace and its notorious Mississippi River bandits.

As a child, W.'s emerging talents earned early recognition. At age eleven, her first publication was a drawing that appeared in *St. Nicholas,* a children's MAGAZINE. Shortly afterward, prior to entering Jackson Central High School, she won $25 for a poem in a jingle contest. Following in her father's footsteps, W. took up photography, a skill she applied in her job as publicity agent for the Works Progress Administration (WPA), one of Roosevelt's New Deal programs. W. incorporated her WPA experiences and exposure to rural Southern poverty into her last novel, *Losing Battles* (1970). In this major work, which took over a decade to complete, she explores the comedy and complexities of growing up, FAMILY relationships, and community, as young Jack Renfro returns home from prison to his bride, Gloria, his Granny's birthday, and their family reunion.

As a college junior, W. ventured north to complete undergraduate studies at the University of Wisconsin, majoring in literature and fine arts. In 1930, she attended Columbia University in New York City to study advertising on the advice of her father, who doubted that she could support herself financially by writing. In 1931, her father became ill and died. W. returned to Jackson, where she basically lived and worked the rest of her life, except for periodic travels. In her memoir, W. discussed her hometown roots, commenting that, for some, it takes courage to stay at home, and that "All serious daring comes from within." She recollected that as a young child she rode the train with her father and wondered about the residents of the illuminated houses she saw along the way. Through her writings, W. created characters, both ordinary and archetypal, through interior journeys of her imagination, although not far from Mississippi.

Lyrically narrating her stories with Southern dialect and cadences, W. painted picturesque Mississippi landscapes with their ever-present crape myrtle and chinaberry trees. Against this lush green backdrop, she explored the internal states and growth of human beings in the course of daily life and major events. In *Delta Wedding* (1946), W. examined individuals in the context of family relationships as motherless, nine-year-old Laura McRaven travels to the Shellmound Plantation for the wedding of her cousin, Dabney Fairchild. In this novel, W. humbly opened the door of her imagination to a pageant of characters, illuminating their interior lives, dealing with themes of isolation, rejection, maturation, and spiritual connection.

W. has been the recipient of many awards, including the Pulitzer Prize for *The Optimist's Daughter* (1972), six O. Henry awards, the National Medal of Arts, the Presidential Freedom Medal of Honor, and the Presidential Medal of Arts. She was inducted into National Women's Hall of Fame in Seneca Falls, New York. W. is the only author whose works were included in the Library of America series while she was living. She has been called the "Voice of the South." In 2002, approximately one year following Welty's DEATH, Jackson's Old Capitol Museum honored "the life and work of one of Mississippi's most famous literary figures" through the exhibit, "Remembering W."

AWARDS: O. Henry Award, 1942, 1943, 1968; National Institute of Arts and Letters Gold Medal for fiction writing, 1972; Pulitzer Prize in fiction, 1973, for *The Optimist's Daughter*; National Medal for Literature, 1980; American Library Association notable book, 1980, American Book Award, 1981, and National Book Award, Fiction, PAPERBACK, 1983, for *The Collected Stories of Eudora Welty*; American Book Award, 1984 for *One Writer's Beginnings*; National Medal of Arts, 1987.

FURTHER WORKS: *A Curtain of Green* (collection of short stories), 1941; *The Robber Bridegroom,* 1942; *The Wide Net, and Other Stories,* 1943; *Delta Wedding,* 1946; *The Golden Apples* (related short stories), 1949; *The Ponder Heart,* 1954; *The Bride of Innisfallen, and Other Stories,* 1955; *The Shoe Bird* (children's story), 1964; *Losing Battles,* 1970; *One Time,* *One Place: Mississippi in the Depression; A Snapshot Album,* 1971; *One Writer's Beginnings,* 1984.

BIBLIOGRAPHY: *Contemporary Authors Online,* 2002; *Eudora W. House.* Mississippi Department of Archives and History, http://www.mdah.state.ms.us/welty/weltymdah.html; Ford, Richard, and Michael Kreyling, eds. *Welty: Stories, Essays and Memoir,* 1998.

JOYCE ANN WHEATLEY

WERLIN, Nancy
Author, b. 29 October 1961 in Peabody, Massachusetts

W. has become a force in YA literature in the space of ten years and five novels. Her novels deal with complex topics ranging from autism, TEEN homicide, abduction, drug dealing disguised as charity work, and bioethics.

W. is the youngest of three sisters from a middleclass Jewish FAMILY. Her father worked as a computer programmer and an engineer and her mother was a stay-at-home mom. W. began reading at age three and has remained a voracious reader for life. At age ten, W. decided she would be a writer so that she could create her own stories. Although a good student, W. has admitted that school was not challenging to her. Her dislike of school increased during adolescence because of her feelings of social awkwardness. It was during middle and high school that W. began writing her own SHORT STORIES.

Despite her dislike for formal education, W. graduated from Yale with a bachelor's degree in English in 1983. In order to make herself more marketable upon graduation, W. began studying computer programming during her last year of college.

From 1983 to 1987, W. worked as a technical writer for several software companies in the United States and Germany. In 1987, W. began working as a technical writer for Thomson Investment Software in Boston, Massachusetts. W. worked part time in order to begin writing fiction. She continued with this company until 1997.

W.'s part-time work status paid off with the publication of her first novel, *Are You Alone on Purpose?*, published in 1994. *Are You Alone on Purpose?* focuses on fourteen-year-old Alison Shandling, whose twin brother, Adam, is autistic, and Harry Roth, the fifteen-year-old son of a rabbi who is a widower. Harry is a bully whose meanness and rudeness creates difficult situations for Alison at school and for her whole family at synagogue. Harry's anger regarding her mother's DEATH and his father's emotional distance are the cause of his acting out. When Harry is paralyzed as a result of a diving accident, Alison befriends him during Adam's preparation with Rabbi Roth for Adam's bar mitzvah. Alison not only makes a friend in Harry, but also a boyfriend, much to her family's surprise. Both Alison and Harry must learn to articulate their own needs to those around them. The novel also addresses spiritual questions surrounding God's will and tragic events in people's lives. W.'s first novel was praised for its strong characterizations of main and secondary characters, polished writing, and interesting plot.

With her second and subsequent novels, W. has found her strength in writing thriller/MYSTERY/suspense novels that are similar to Lois DUNCAN's YA novels, but push the boundaries of young adult literature with challenging, contemporary subject matter. *The Killer's Cousin* is the story of seventeen-year-old David Yaffe, who is sent to Cambridge, Massachusetts, to live with his aunt and uncle and their eleven-year-old daughter, Lily. David's parents send him away from Baltimore after a high-profile trial the previous year in which David was acquitted of the murder of his girlfriend, Emily. Lily's parents are still trying to recover from the apparent suicide of Kathy, their oldest daughter, four years ago. In addition to trying to leave behind the events of the previous year, David finds only one friend at St. Joan's Prep School: Frank Delgado. While David doesn't fit in since he is the new student with a past, Frank does not fit in since he dresses like a skinhead. Lily's open hostility to David's living in Kathy's third-floor apartment and other matters lead David to conclude that perhaps Lily had a part in Kathy's death. In addition to winning the highest honor for a mystery novel, W. was again lauded for plot and characterization as well as establishing herself as a presence as a writer of thriller/suspense books for young adults.

W.'s third novel, *Locked Inside,* is the story of sixteen-year-old Marnie Skyedottir, heir to the fortune of Skye. Marnie has distanced herself from her guardian, Max, and really only has a friend in Elf, one of her fellow players in the online game Paliopolis. Marnie spends so much time on the Internet that her grades suffer and the dean assigns her to Ms. Leah Slaight for tutoring during spring break. The delu-

sional Leah believes she is Marnie's half-sister. She kidnaps Marnie and locks her in her basement. Convincing Marnie that she is also Skye's daughter is more important to Leah than sharing Marnie's inheritance. After Marnie is missing from Paliopolis for several days, Elf, a.k.a. Frank Delgado of *The Killer's Cousin,* searches for Marnie. He finds her but is also trapped in the basement by Leah. Elf and Marnie use their gaming abilities to escape. Leah must then reconcile herself with Max and her classmates in addition to living in the real world instead of in Paliopolis.

The following year, W.'s fourth book, *Black Mirror,* was published. As the novel opens, sixteen-year-old Frances Leventhal is mourning her older brother Daniel's death by a heroin overdose. Although their father and grandmother live nearby, the siblings attend the Pettengill School, a boarding school in same town, on scholarships. Their mother, Sayoko, returned to Japan to study at a Buddhist monastery. While Daniel was deeply involved in the Pettengill School's chapter of the Unity Service organization, Frances refused to join. Unity, founded by Pettengill alumni Patrick Leyden, raises money to provide scholarships for students to live at the Pettengill School. Both Frances and Daniel were recipients of Unity scholarships. Having isolated herself from the other students, Frances copes with Daniel's death by spending time alone in her dorm room smoking the rest of Daniel's stash of marijuana. Finally, Frances decides to join Unity to work on a memorial project in Daniel's honor. Although the group does not welcome her, Frances forces her way into working with them. Frances's only friend is Pettengill's groundskeeper, Andy Jankowski, who is mentally challenged. Andy's negative comments regarding his work with Unity and Leyden's desire to use Frances in a letter-writing campaign to gain monetary support for the expansion of Unity to middle schools are indications to Frances that the charity group may not be legitimate. Frances must assert herself and become involved in the lives of others to uncover the truth about Unity with the help of Andy, her art teacher Ms. Wiles, and her crush, a rumored drug dealer named James Droussian. Throughout the book, Frances struggles with her identity as a biracial person and a young woman. The black mirror of the title refers to the Jewish symbol of covering a mirror with a black silk cloth while a person is in mourning. At the end of the book, Frances has grown and matured through her experiences. She removes the black cloth from the mirror and wears her white cashmere sweater, white being the Buddhist symbol for mourning. She is now ready to embrace all of herself and the woman she is becoming. In a nod to faithful readers, W. includes cameo appearances by Frank Delgado and Marnie Skydottir observed by Frances near the end of the book.

Her fifth novel, *Double Helix,* deals with questions related to bioethics and genetic engineering. After graduating from high school, eighteen-year-old Eli Samuels decides to take a year off before attending college to work and continue living at home with his father. Eli also wants to stay close to home because his mother is in a nursing home dying of Huntington's disease. Eli applies for a job as a laboratory assistant at Wyatt Transgenics working for the world-renowned Dr. Quincy Wyatt, a Nobel Prize-winning scientist. Dr. Wyatt hires Eli as a favor to his parents, whom he knew years ago. Eli's father is mysterious, but ada-mant that Eli not work for Dr. Wyatt. On a visit to Dr. Wyatt, Eli meets the beautiful young Kayla Matheson. During the course of his work, Eli finds a hidden elevator that appears to go to a subbasement floor. Later, when Mrs. Samuels dies, Kayla attends the funeral as Dr. Wyatt's representative. While sorting his wife's belongings, Mr. Samuels finds a photo of his late wife when she was in her early twenties. He gives the photo to Eli and they both realize that Kayla Matheson looks like Mrs. Samuels did at that age. Kayla and Eli join forces to investigate what lies in the subbasement and what role Dr. Wyatt played in the Samuels' family's past.

W. continues to gain critical praise as well as a popular readership for her novels, which are rich in characterization, sophisticated in plot, and challeng-ing in subject matter. In addition to writing fiction for young adults, W. works part time for several software companies.

AWARDS: ALA Quick Pick for Reluctant Young Adult Readers list, 1994, *Are You Alone on Purpose?*; ALA Best Books for Young Adults list, 1999, *The Killer's Cousin*; ALA Quick Pick for Reluctant Young Adult Readers list, 1999, *The Killer's Cousin*; Mystery Writers of America, Edgar Award, Best Young Adult Mystery, 1999, *The Killer's Cousin*; IRA Young Adult Choice, 1999, *The Killer's Cousin*; ALA Best Books for Young Adults list, 2002, *Black Mirror*; *Double Helix*: ALA Best Books for Young Adults,

2005; Booklist Editor's Choice, 2004; SLJ Best Books for Children, 2004; *Black Mirror*: ALA Popu-lar Paperbacks, 2005; *The Killer's Cousin*: ALA Pop-ular Paperbacks, 2003, NJ Garden State Teen Book Award Winners, 2001.

FURTHER WORKS: "Shortcut," *On the Fringe* (ed. Don GALLO) 2001; "WAR Game," *Twelve Shots: Outstand-ing Short Stories about Guns* (ed. Harry MAZER), 1997.

BIBLIOGRAPHY: Carter, Betty. *Best Books for Young Adults.* 2nd ed., 2001; *Contemporary Authors Online,* 2001; Nancy Werlin's website, http://www.nancy werlin.com

ANDREW HUNTER

WERSBA, Barbara
Author, b. 19 August 1932, Chicago, Illinois

Having earned a B.A. from Bard College, W. began writing at the age of twenty-six, starting with *The Boy Who Loved the Sea* (1961). W. enjoyed writing, though "it was not until *The Dream Watcher,* pub-lished in 1968, that she was able to develop any real characters." This novel was later adapted by W. as a play first produced in Westport, Connecticut, in 1975. W. drew on her theater background to write and pro-duce the PLAY, but later had to end a fifteen-year act-ing career due to hepatitis.

W. credits Carson McCullers as being her greatest inspiration. She extracts many of her accurately por-trayed characters from situations in her life: "W. is able to accurately portray the difficulties of youth in part because her childhood was touched with loneli-ness and pain." W.'s works are known for the way in which "the young protagonists find their way with the help of an older, often quite eccentric character." Though best known for her YA novels, W. has also written books and POETRY for children.

AWARDS: ALA Best Books for Young Adults: *Run Softly, Go Fast*: 1970, *Country of the Heart*: 1975, *Tunes for a Small Harmonica*: 1976, *Carnival in My Mind*: 1982, *Whistle Me Home*: 1998. *Run Softly, Go Fast* was selected for three Best of the Best lists: "The Best of the Best Books: 1970–1983," "Nothin' But the Best: Best of the Best Books for Young Adults, 1966–1986," "Here We Go Again: 25 Years of Best Books: Selections from 1967–1992."

FURTHER WORKS: *The Brave Balloon of Benjamin Buckley,* 1963; *The Land of Forgotten Beasts,* 1964; *A Song for Clowns,* 1965; *Do Tigers Ever Bite*

Kings?, 1966; *Run Softly, GO Fast,* 1970; *Let Me Fall Before I Fly,* 1971; *Amanda, Dreaming,* 1973; *The Country of the Heart,* 1975; *Tunes for a Small Harmonica,* 1976; *Twenty-Six Starlings Will Fly through Your Mind,* 1980; *The Crystal Child,* 1982; *The Carnival in My Mind,* 1982; *Crazy Vanilla,* 1986; *Fat: A Love Story,* 1987; *Love Is the Crooked Thing,* 1987; *Beautiful Losers,* 1988; *Just Be Gorgeous,* 1988; *Wonderful Me,* 1989; *The Farewell Kid,* 1990; *The Best Place To Live Is the Ceiling,* 1990; *You'll Never Guess the End,* 1992; *Life Is What Happens While You're Making Other Plans,* 1994; *Whistle Me Home,* 1997.

BIBLIOGRAPHY: "Barbara W." U*X*L Junior DIS-Covering Authors, 1998. Reproduced in Discovering Collection, http://galenet.galegroup.com/servlet/DC, 2001.

CATHERINE GIVEN

AND SARA MARCUS

WESTALL, Robert (Atkinson)

Author, b. 7 October 1929, Tynemouth, England; d. 15 April 1993, Cheshire, England

W., son of Robert, a foreman-engineer at an English gasworks, and Maggie Alexandra (Leggett), died at the age of sixty-three. Growing up, he had a happy childhood and attributes this to his relationship with his father. He would visit his father at the gasworks, often taking him his lunch. He observed the respect co-workers had for his father and learned that this respect was earned because of his father's mechanical abilities to create, troubleshoot, and repair machines. His father also possessed artistic abilities in drawing and toy making. W. was taught how to draw by his father, but preferred receiving and playing with the toys his father made especially for him. Each was unique and lovingly cherished because of the exceptional craftsmanship and care his father put into them, as well as everything he created.

W. admired men who represented unshakable truth and honesty and who possessed unwavering abilities to stand up for their beliefs, men such as Socrates, Oliver Cromwell, Martin Luther, Ralph Nader, and Martin Luther King Jr. W. maintained this same sense of integrity throughout his life and within his work. W. also had strong feelings about cats, as readers will discover in most of his books. W. has often been quoted as saying, "I like cats, because you have to earn their friendship."

In junior high school W. started writing, completing his first novel when he was twelve years old. This was never published, and during his high school years, W. had little time to write. He studied art and concentrated his efforts on sculpture. He continued these studies in college and also published his first short piece of work in his former high school's MAGAZINE. It was seven years later, when he was completing his graduate studies in London, that W.'s writing was again published. This time his work was published in his hometown newspaper.

W. graduated with first-class honors in 1953 with a B.A. in fine arts from the University of Durham. From 1953 to 1955, W. served in the British Army in the Royal Signals. After his tour of service, he went on to graduate from the Slade School, University of London with a D.F.A. in 1957. He then started teaching art to children in Birmingham. In 1958 he married Jean Underhill, an administrator. W. was the head of the art department and an art teacher at Sir John Deane's College in Northwich, England, beginning in 1960, and changed to head of careers guidance in 1970. He was the director of Telephone Samaritan of Mid-Cheshire from 1965 to 1975. From 1968 to 1971, W. was a staff writer for *Cheshire Life.* He was the critic for art and architecture for the *Cheshire Chronicle* from 1962, and worked for the *Guardian* as an art critic in 1970. W. worked as an antiques dealer from 1985 through 1987, after which he gave up this business to become a full-time writer. Starting as an art critic for the local newspaper, his skills and popularity grew as did the publication of his works into broader and better-known newspapers and magazines, including *Better Homes and Gardens.*

Writing for a YA audience came gradually and after he received an invitation to visit some of his son's friends, local gang members, in their secret clubhouse. The reason for the invitation? He was asked to fix a leak in their clubhouse roof, which he did. This visit clearly pointed out the differences between his adolescence and that of his son and his son's friends. In writing his first novel, W. used "authentic language" (street language) and included realistic details of violence. Although he waited two years before trying to publish this work, critics praised his accurate descriptions of adolescence during the WAR. W.'s career as a writer took off and he started producing new works almost yearly. He continued to write of sexuality, the reality of TEENAGE emotions as experienced by YA, FAMILY issues, and HORROR using characters that any young adult can easily identify with behaviorally, physically, emotionally, and so forth. Through different genres of SHORT STORIES, ghost stories, realistic fiction, FANTASY, and SCIENCE FICTION and traces of the supernatural and terror, W. created works that appeal to most teenagers and crosses all generations.

W.'s writing for young adults was drawn from personal experiences of his childhood and from the relationships he had with his son Christopher and especially with his father. W.'s father had a profound influence on his life and on his writing. Not only did he teach his son the importance of knowing how to do things, but he also emulated a strong ethics and was a positive role model of masculinity. These images are reflected in several of the characters W. has written into his books.

Tragedy struck when Christopher died in an accident at the early age of eighteen. Chris was his father's sounding board and critiqued his writing as only a son could. W. listened to and followed his son's suggestions about his writing, making sure to remove extraneous descriptions and details that slowed down the action. After his son's DEATH, writing became difficult for W.

Much of W.'s writing has been controversial because of the strong language and violence he used within his novels. Other reviewers believe that the events and struggles of the characters depicted within the storylines are clearly written.

Divorced in 1990, W. enjoyed designing, building, and sailing model yachts. He had a strong love for cats and enjoyed old clocks, watching people and birds, ruins, and the sea. W. lived in Northwich, England, until he died from pneumonia.

AWARDS: *The Machine-Gunners* (1975): The Carnegie Medal from the Library Association of Great Britain in 1976, The *Boston Globe–Horn Book* Award for fiction in 1977; *The Wind Eye*: American Library Association Best Book for Young Adults in 1978; *Devil on the Road* (1979): American Library Association Notable Book in 1979, Runner up for the Carnegie Medal from the Library Association of Great Britain; *The Scarecrows* (1981): the Carnegie Medal in 1982; ALA Best Books for Young Adults: *Future Tracks*, 1984, *Kingdom by the Sea*, 1992, *Stormsearch*, 1993, *Yaxley's Cat*, 1993, *Gulf*, 1997.

FURTHER WORKS: Novels for Young Adults—*Time of Fire*, 1997; *A Place for Me*, 1993; *Falling into Glory*,

1993; *Size Twelve*, 1992; *The Kingdom by The Sea*, 1990; *Stormsearch*, 1990; *Cat!*, 1989; *Urn Burial*, 1987; *The Witness*, 1985; *Break of Dark*, 1982; *Futuretrack Five*, 1980; *Fathom Five*, 1980; *The Watch House*, 1978; *The Wind Eye*, 1977. Fantasy Novels— *The Wheatstone Pont*, 1993; *Gulf*, 1992; *Yaxley's Cat*, 1991; *The Christmas Cat*, 1991; *The Promise*, 1990; *If Cats Could Fly . . . ?*, 1990; *Old Man on a Horse*, 1989; *Blitzcat*, 1989; *Ghost Abbey*, 1988; *The Creature in the Dark*, 1988; *Rosalie*, 1987; *The Cats of Seroster*, 1984; *The Devil on the Road*, 1978; *The Watch House*, 1977; *The Wind Eye*, 1977. SHORT STORY Collections—*Shades of Darkness: More of the Ghostly Best Stories of Robert W.*, 1994; *Christmas Spirit*, 1994; *Blitz*, 1994; *Demons and Shadows*, 1993; *A Trick of Light: Five Unnerving Stories*, 1993; *The Fearful Lovers*, 1992; *The Christmas Ghost*, 1992; *The Stories of Muncaster Cathedral: Two Stories of the Supernatural*, 1991; *The Christmas Cat*, 1991; *A Walk on the Wild Side*, 1989; *Echoes of War*, 1991; *The Call and Other Stories*, 1989; *Ghosts and Journeys*, 1988; *Rachel and the Angel and Other Stories*, 1986; *The Other: A Christmas Story*, 1985; *The Haunting of Chas McGill*, 1983; *Break of Dark*, 1981.

BIBLIOGRAPHY: *Authors and Artists for Young Adults*, vol. 12, 1994. Reproduced in *Biography Resource Center*, http://www.galenet.com/servlet/BioRC, 2004; *Contemporary Authors Online*, 2001. Reproduced in *Biography Resource Center*, http://www.galenet.com/ servlet/BioRC, 2004; *Fifth Book of Junior Authors and Illustrators*, 1983.

VALERIE A. PALAZOLO

WESTHEIMER, David (a.k.a. Z. Z. Smith)
Author, b. 11 April 1917, Houston, Texas

Reared in Texas and educated at Rice and Columbia Universities, W. read widely in everything from MYTHOLOGY to Edgar Rice Burroughs. Graduating with a B.A. in 1937, he was an editor at the *Houston Post* before joining the U.S. Army Air Force. The navigator of a B24 bomber shot down after an attack on Naples harbor in 1942, W. was a prisoner of WAR in Italy and Germany for twenty-eight months. Notes made shortly after his 1945 release formed the basis of his wartime memoir, *Sitting It Out: A World War II POW Memoir* (1992). He earned the Air Medal and Distinguished Flying Cross, retiring from the Air Force Reserve as a lieutenant-colonel.

After the war, W. moved to Los Angeles, writing novels and screenplays. He reworked his wartime experiences into a number of well-written ADVENTURE stories.

Rider on the Wind (1979) has the crew of a B24 learning about the realities of war in Palestine and the western desert while *The Olmec Head* (1974), later retitled *Delay en Route* (2002), told of a released POW's adventures in Paris. *The Song of the Young Sentry* (1968) evokes the tension and absurdities of prison camp life. W.'s greatest popular success, however, came with *Von Ryan's Express* (1964), about Allied prisoners in Italy escaping from the Germans.

Lighter than a Feather (1971), later retitled *Death Is Lighter than a Feather* (1995), is an alternate history of how the Allied invasion of mainland Japan might have developed without nuclear weapons.

W.'s best novel, *My Sweet Charlie* (1965), brings together two fugitives, a black Northern lawyer and a pregnant Southern girl, with poignant results. It was made into an Emmy-winning television drama in 1970.

W. is also a poet. *The Great Wounded Bird* (1999) is his prize-winning account of his war told in POETRY.

He lives with his wife Dody, whom he married in 1945, in the same Los Angeles apartment they moved to in 1961.

AWARDS: 1999 Texas Review Poetry award, *The Great Wounded Bird*; *My Sweet Charlie* and *Von Ryan's Express* were both selected for "Still Alive: The Best of the Best, 1960–1974."

FURTHER WORKS: *Summer on the Water,* 1948; *The Magic Fallacy,* 1950 (a.k.a. *Day into Night*); *The Long Bright Days,* 1950; *Watching Out for Dulie,* 1961; *A Very Private Island* (as Z. Z. Smith), 1962; *Days of Wine and Roses* (novelization of film script), 1963; *This Time Next Year,* 1963; *Over the Edge,* 1972; *Going Public,* 1973; *The Avila Gold,* 1974; *Rider on the Wind,* 1979; *Von Ryan's Return,* 1980; *The Amindra Gamble* (with John Sherlock), 1982.

BIBLIOGRAPHY: Biographical notes in W.'s books.

TREVOR AGNEW

WESTWOOD, Chris
Author, b. 1959, Yorkshire, England

Born and raised in a West Yorkshire mining village, W. studied film and television production at Bornemouth Film School. After he had worked for three years as a journalist, the success of his HORROR and FANTASY stories for YOUNG ADULTS enabled him to become a full-time writer.

W.'s first novel, *A Light in the Black* (later retitled *He Came from the Shadows*), was published in 1989. A small Yorkshire town, not unlike W.'s birthplace, is dying after its mine closes. An unsettling stranger, Mr. Stand, seems able to grant people's dearest wishes (even bringing a toy dog to life), but Jules is suspicious of his powers. The final confrontation, deep in a coal pit, gives a savage twist to this disturbing fantasy.

Typical of W.'s horror fiction, *Calling All Monsters* (1990) is set firmly in the present. Joanne visits a local horror writer, Martin Wisemann, for a school project, but finds him no longer able to write. Because Joanne believes so strongly in Martin's stories, the monsters from his books are achieving reality. Fearing the menace of their joint creations, Joanne and Martin plan a "final chapter."

In *Shock Waves* (1992), a surprising version of the vampire legend, Leigh, a lonely Bornemouth art student, meets Stephen through a dating service. Leigh's dream becomes a nightmare when friends are dying, "the life drawn out of them," and Stephen's behaviour becomes unsettling. Leigh, who provides an unusual conclusion, is typical of W.'s strong female characters.

Virtual World (1996) is set in a squalid, overcrowded future, where fourteen-year-old Jack escapes into a game that proves all too real: the Silicon Sphere.

W.'s masterpiece, *Brother of Mine* (1994), a remarkable examination of self-image and identity, is set in Wakefield, Yorkshire. Nick is resentful of his twin Tony, and his festering discontent explodes when Tony impersonates him. The TEENAGE brothers narrate alternate chapters, giving vivid first-person insights into their complex relationship. As in *Shock Waves,* art is an important feature of the story. Interestingly, the twins' reconciliation is achieved through a book; storytelling always generates great power in W.'s writing.

W. is published in the U.S. and the UK, and his SHORT STORIES, such as the classic "Closeness," are often anthologised.

FURTHER WORKS: *Dark Brigade,* 1991; *Virtual World,* 1996; *Personal Effects,* 1999.

TREVOR AGNEW

WHARTON, William

(Pseud. Albert W. DuAime)
Author, artist, b. 7 November 1926, Philadelphia,
Pennsylvania

Born Albert W. DuAime, W. used his uncle's name,
William Wharton, as his pen name. Reared in working-
class Philadelphia, an experience warmly evoked in
Birdy (1978) and *Pride* (1985), W. was selected for
the Army Specialized Training Program Reserve
(ASTPR) because of his high intelligence. After serving with the 87th Infantry Division in the gruelling
Ardennes Campaign, he recovered from a serious facial wound and left the Army in 1947.

He studied painting and later completed a Ph.D. at
the University of California, Los Angeles. With his
wife Rosemary, also a teacher, W. had four children
and taught for a time, living in Topanga Canyon, California, before moving to France in 1959. W. painted
professionally in Paris, living with his FAMILY in a
canal barge he converted, an experience described in
Houseboat on the Seine: A Memoir (1996).

W. calls himself "a painter who writes." In 1978
he wrote *Birdy,* an account of a battle-shocked soldier
in a military mental hospital who regains his sanity
through his mystical bonding with the canaries he
raised as a boy. A powerful statement of the human
ability to transcend suffering and despair, *Birdy* became a bestseller, translated into fifteen languages.
Birdy was nominated for the Pulitzer prize, named
Best First Novel at the National Book Awards, and, in
1985, transferred to the Vietnam War, was made into
a highly successful film.

Birdy's continuing cult status meant that there was
a ready market for W.'s later novels, each of which
transmuted aspects of his own experience into remarkable works of fiction. In *A Midnight Clear*
(1982), a squad of highly intelligent soldiers (who
like W. are all ex-ASTPR) encounters an enemy patrol equally reluctant to play the game of WAR, with
tragic results. The narrator is Sergeant Will Knott;
wordplay is important in this novel (and its successors), reflecting W.'s own fascination with words.

Pride (1985) develops several minor characters
from *Birdy* in the grim Depression–era story of a lion
that escapes from a carnival sideshow. Told almost
without dialogue, *Pride* contrasts the determined efforts of Dick, a shop steward, to preserve and protect

his family with the tragic failure of Cap, the lion's
owner, to keep his "family"—a motorcycle daredevil
act—together. The importance of family (pride in
lion terms) and the bond between animals and humans are recurring themes in W.'s work. W. was
deeply affected at the age of eleven by his encounter
with the actual lion depicted in *Pride.*

Dad: A Novel (1986) is a deeply emotional study
of the power of love through three generations of
males. Jack watches his ailing father (Dad) briefly regain independence of spirit when he is hospitalized.
Jack learns that Dad has created a fantasy wife and
family on the Jersey shore, and also reexamines his
own relationship with his son Billy. W.'s own father
had died in 1975. *Dad* was filmed in 1989; *A Midnight Clear* in 1992.

Scumbler (1984) concerns a sixty-year-old artist
in Paris, painting and creating living spaces as sanctuaries that he calls "nests." Although W. uses his own
self-portrait on the cover, it is a very different painter
who emerges among the hippies of the Latin Quarter,
raffish and gregarious but constantly in search of a
place of refuge and security for his family. *Last Loves*
(1991), also set in Paris, describes the unusual relationship between a homeless street painter and a blind
musician in Paris. Their brief ROMANCE brings them
both an expanded version of life. As in *Franky Furbo*
(1989), W. uses a range of typefaces to distinguish
characters.

Tidings (1987) creates a disunited American family whose divisions are accepted and bonds reaf-
firmed after a mystical Christmas experience in a
French millhouse.

Even more mystical was the fable *Franky Furbo*
(1989), a story within a story, based on tales W. told
to his children. William Wiley, an American writer
living in Italy, tells his children stories of Franky
Furbo, a magic fox who lives in a tree-house, and
uses his powers to bring two soldiers back from their
DEATH on a battlefield. One is William himself, although he may actually be Franky Furbo in human
form, striving to save foxes so they can mutate into
the future civilization that will produce Franky Furbo.

W. has always shunned publicity, but in 1988, a
year before the publication of *Franky Furbo,* his
daughter Kath, her husband, and their two children
were among those killed in a twenty-four-car collision in Oregon. W.'s campaign against the pasture

burning, which had caused the tragedy, is described in W.'s deeply moving *Ever After: A Father's True Story* (1995). Typically, W.'s account includes some spiritual experiences and a section where he writes as Kath. As W. noted in his epigraph to *Last Loves,* "believing is seeing."

AWARDS: 1979 National Book Awards Best First Novel, *Birdy;* ALA Best Book for Young Adults, 1979 for *Birdy* and 1982 for *Midnight Clear.*

FURTHER WORKS: *Wrongful Deaths,* UK, 1994 (U.S., *Ever After*); *Houseboat on the Seine: A Memoir,* 1996.

BIBLIOGRAPHY: *Contemporary Novelists,* 7th ed., 2001; Interview with William W.; http://www.robot wisdom.com/jorn/wharton.html/

TREVOR AGNEW

WHELAN, Gloria
Author, b. 23 November 1923, Detroit, Michigan

W. has been a storyteller since she was a toddler. A babysitter typed her stories before she could write them, and in elementary school she wrote POETRY. At ten years of age, W. was stricken with rheumatic fever. Bedridden for a year, viewing nothing but a brick building through her bedroom window, she welcomed the ADVENTURES she found in reading, especially fiction novels. Her favorites included *The Wind in the Willows, The Secret Garden,* and a nonfiction SERIES called the Wonder Books. *Little Women* was also a favorite of W. and gave her examples of rules at a time in life when she needed guidelines. In high school W. continued to write and was editor of the school paper. Her dream of someday writing a novel continued into college. She did write many SHORT STORIES and poems for adults, and graduated from the University of Michigan with a master's degree in social work.

In 1948, W. married Joseph L. Whelan, a physician, and began her first career as a social worker for the Minneapolis Family and Children's Service. While raising two children, Joseph and Jennifer, she became the supervisor of a day-care program. Eventually, tired of the busy city life, W. and her husband moved to a rustic cabin in northern Michigan, situated on a lake and surrounded by wilderness. She had frequented this area as a child with her father and was attracted to the quiet, peaceful life near woods, water, and wildlife.

In 1978, at age fifty-five, W.'s dream of writing a novel became a reality when her first book, *Clearing in the Forest,* was published and received an award from the Friends of the American Writers. This YA novel about a boy who works on an oil rig was inspired by an oil-drilling situation on W.'s rural property. The following year, she became an instructor in American literature at Spring Harbor College in Michigan and had her second book published, *A Time to Keep Silent* (1979). This is a sensitive story about a young girl who refuses to speak to anyone after the DEATH of her mother.

Since 1987, W. has written thirty-two books for children and YA, sometimes producing three books in a year. Many of her works are regional historical fiction with settings from favorite places such as Mackinac Island, Oxbow Lake, and the Au Sable River in her beloved Michigan. However, through meticulous research and "imaginary trips in her head," she has written novels with settings in China, India, Vietnam, and Russia, all places she has never visited. *Homeless Bird* (2000), for which she won the National Book Award, was inspired by a *New York Times* article highlighting a city in India where widows are abandoned by their in-laws. A thirteen-year-old widow mentioned in the article became the inspiration for Koly, the main character in her book.

Critics applaud her writing as sensitive, engaging, thought provoking, and full of richly detailed background. At age eighty, gifted storyteller W. continues to write every day.

SELECT AWARDS: Distinguished Achievement Award from the Educational Press Association of America, Juvenile Book Merit Award, Friends of American Writers, 1979, *A Clearing in the Forest;* 1994 Juvenile Fiction Award, Society of Midland Authors; 1996 Great Lakes Book Award, *Once on This Island,* 1998; Michigan Author of the Year, Michigan Library Association/Michigan Center for the Book; *Homeless Bird:* National Book Award and *School Library Journal* Best Books citation, both 2000; Best Books of the Year citation, selected for Best of the Best (selections from 1995 to 2004), Bank Street College of Education; Creative Artist Award, Michigan Council for the Arts; Citations for Texas Lone Star Reading List and International Reading Association Children's Choices List; Dorothy Canfield Fisher Award, 2002; Nominations for Georgia Children's Book Award, and Mark Twain Award.

SELECT FURTHER WORKS: *A Time to Keep Silent,* 1979; *Next Spring an Oriole,* 1987; *Silver,* 1988; *A*

Week of Raccoons, 1988; *The Secret Keeper,* 1990; *Hannah,* 1991; *Bringing the Farmhouse Home,* 1992; *Goodbye, Vietnam,* 1992; *Night of the Full Moon,* 1993; *That Wild Berries Should Grow: The* DIARY *of a Summer,* 1994; *The Indian School,* 1996; *Friends,* 1997; *The Miracle of Saint Nicholas,* 1997; *Shadow of the Wolf,* 1997; *Forgive the River, Forgive the Sky,* 1998; *Farewell to the Island,* 1998; *The Pathless Woods: Ernest Hemingway's Sixteenth Summer in Northern Michigan,* 1998; *Miranda's Last Stand,* 1999; *Welcome to Starvation Lake,* 2000; *Return to the Island,* 2000; *Angel on the Square,* 2001; *Rich and Famous in Starvation Lake,* 2001; *Fox Eyes,* 2001; *The Wanigan: A Life on the River,* 2002; *Are There Bears in Starvation Lake?,* 2002; *Jam and Jelly by Holly and Nellie,* 2002; *Fruitlands: Louisa May* ALCOTT *Made Perfect,* 2002; *The Impossible Journey,* 2003; *A Haunted House in Starvation Lake,* 2003; *Chu Ju's House,* 2003.

BIBLIOGRAPHY: *Contemporary Authors Online,* 2002; Isaacs, Kathleen T. "Flying High." *School Library Journal,* March 2001; Gloria W. homepage, http://www.gloriawhelan.com/; "The End of the World." *Book,* January 2001.

KATE NAGY

WHITE, Ellen Emerson (a.k.a. Nicholas Edwards, Zack Emerson)

Author, b. 1961, Georgia

Reared in New England, W. graduated from Tufts University and settled in New York City. Although keen on law, W. has always written, and her first novel, *Friends for Life* (1983), was accepted while she was eighteen and still in college. Although she began with adult ROMANCE and amateur sleuth novels, her major work has been in the YOUNG ADULT field.

W.'s nonfiction includes such popular athletic lives as *Shaquille O'Neal* (1994), *My Story: The Autobiography of Olga Korbutt* (1992), and *Tiger Woods* (2001), but her main effort has been in bringing history to life.

Writing as (the male-sounding) Zack Emerson, she produced the gritty Echo Company quartet, following the progress of an American unit in the Vietnam War, beginning with *Welcome to Vietnam* (1991). Fascinated by the character of Rebecca, W. then wrote *The Road Home* (1995) under her own name, recounting an Army nurse's grim experience of the Tet Offensive and her later difficulties in coming to terms with stateside life. The realistic account of Rebecca's problems and those of her G.I. friend, Michael of Echo Company, who lost a leg in the WAR, made this a CROSSOVER success, popular with adults as well as with young readers.

W. enjoys research for such titles as the *Voyage on the Great Titanic: The* DIARY *of Margaret Anne Brady: 1912* (1998) and *Kaiulani: The People's Princess: Hawaii, 1889* (2001), but although the historical facts are well presented, the personalities of the diarists are never captured. W. was more successful in creating the fictional war diaries of two Boston TEENAGERS. *The Journal of Patrick Seamus Flaherty: United States Marine Corps: Khe Sanh, Vietnam: 1968* (2002) follows the experiences of an eighteen-year-old besieged in Khe Sanh. His sister Molly, meanwhile, keeps her own diary in *Where Have All the Flowers Gone? The Diary of Mollie McKenzie Flaherty* (2002), recording her anxieties and fears, as well as mixed feelings over antiwar protests. Able to confide in Molly, Patrick writes letters to her more revealing than the cheerful ones he sends to their parents. Each diary complements the other, illuminating the tensions and sacrifices of a controversial era.

The President's Daughter SERIES is a realistic account of Meg, the teenage daughter of the United States' first woman president, and her efforts to lead a normal life. *Long Live the Queen* (1989) is the chillingly detailed account of the emotional and psychological toll when Meg is kidnapped.

W.'s most popular work has been the lighthearted *Santa Paws* (1996) and its sequels written for younger readers. Adopted by the Callahan FAMILY, a homeless puppy grows into an heroic but accident-prone dog. W. also continues to write adult novels, including novelizations of films such as *Arachnaphobia* (1990).

AWARDS: ALA Best Book for Young Adults, 1990 for *Long Live the Queen,* 1996 for *Road Home;* 2002 ALA Best Book for Young Adults, *Kaiulani: The People's Princess; Road Home:* Best of the Best (selections from 1995–2004).

FURTHER WORKS: *Life without Friends,* 1987; *Jennifer Capriati,* 1991; *Bo Jackson,* 1994; *Jim Abbott,* 1995; Echo Company Series (as Zack Emerson): *Hill 568,* 1991; *Tis the Season,* 1991; *Stand Down,* 1992; President's Daughter Series (2001): *The President's Daughter,* 1984; *White House Autumn,* 1985; Santa Paws Series (as Nicholas Edwards): *The Return of Santa Paws,* 1997; *Santa Paws to the Rescue,* 2000; *Santa Paws, Come Home,* 2000; *Santa Paws, Our*

745

Hero, 2002; *Santa Paws: the PICTURE BOOK* (with Deborah Schechter; illus. Robert Blake), 2003.

BIBLIOGRAPHY: http://www.hawkpub.com/emerson white.htm/

TREVOR AGNEW

WHITE, Robb
Author, b. 20 June 1909, Philippine Islands; d. 1990, Santa Barbara, California

W.'s birth marked the beginning of both a long life and an extremely prolific career. Born to Robb (a missionary) and Placidia Bridgers White, W.'s education was sparse until his arrival in high school in Virginia. He then attended the United States Naval Academy. There was no formal schooling in the areas where his father served as a missionary. He graduated with a B.S. degree in 1931, which was the precursor to his service in the United States Navy from 1941 to 1945. His time spent in administration and public information gave him material for his books, as did other aspects of his naval career. Besides his naval service, W. also worked as a clerk and an engineer. W.'s marriage to Rosalie Mason lasted from 1937 until 1964, when it ended in divorce. He later married Joan Gibbs. W. had three children—Robb, Barbara, and June.

W.'s first published work, *The Nub,* appeared in 1935. Although it was followed by multiple titles, W.'s work received little critical acclaim at first. W. had been publishing books for nearly forty years, for adult, YOUNG ADULT, and children's audiences, when an ADVENTURE tale he penned about a TEEN trying to earn extra money garnered all kinds of recognition. *Deathwatch* (1972) was named an Outstanding Book of the Year by the *New York Times.* Ben finds his very life at stake when he agrees to act as Madec's guide in the desert and finds himself enacting "The Dangerous Game." *The Frogmen* (1973) is a historical novel, telling tales of a young man's working as a frogman in World War II. It was a Junior Literacy Guild selection. Joining a circus is only the first step in a young woman's quest to fly on the trapeze in *The Long Way Down: A Novel* (1977). W.'s book *Fire Storm* (1979) also dealt with survival, as a ranger and a young boy must escape the fire that rages around them.

Many of W.'s earlier works for children are adventure tales, often having to do with the sea. His adult books are mostly travel memoirs—among them his

AUTOBIOGRAPHICAL *Two on the Isle: A Memory of Marina Cay* (1985). He also wrote for MOVIES and television. His screenplays include *Macabre, House on Haunted Hill, 13 Ghosts, The Tingler, Homicidal,* and *Deathwatch.* His television work includes episodes for *Men of Annapolis, Perry Mason,* and *Silent Service* among others.

At the time of his death, W. left behind an impressive body of work in a multitude of genres. He had the ability to shift his work to adjust to the changing tides and fashions of publishing, which accounts in no small part for his long and prolific career.

AWARDS: *The Nub:* YALSA Popular PAPERBACKS for Young Adults, YALSA's 100 Best Books (1950–2000); 1973 Edgar Award, *Deathwatch. Deathwatch:* Selected for five Best of the Best lists: Still Alive (Selections from 1960 to 1974), The Best of the Best Books (Selections from 1970 to 1983), Nothin' But the Best (Selections from 1966 to 1986), Here We Go Again . . . 25 Years of Best Books (Selections from 1967 to 1992), 100 Best Books for Teens from 1966–2000.

FURTHER WORKS: *Smuggler's Sloop,* 1937; *Run Masked,* 1938; *In Privateer's Bay,* 1939; *Three Against the Sea,* 1940; *Lion's Paw,* 1946; *Secret Sea,* 1947; *Sail Away,* 1948; *Candy,* 1949; *The Haunted Hound,* 1950; *Our Virgin Island,* 1953; *Midshipman Lee of the Naval Academy,* 1954; *Up Periscope,* 1956; *Flight Deck,* 1961; *Torpedo Run: Mutiny and Adventure Aboard a Navy PT Boat during World War II,* 1962; *The Survivor,* 1964; *Surrender: Action in the Philippine Islands during World War II,* 1966; *Silent Ship, Silent Sea,* 1967; *No Man's Land,* 1969.

BIBLIOGRAPHY: *Contemporary Authors Online,* 2002; www.abebooks.com; www.amazon.com; www.bccls .org; www.novelst4.epnet.com

JEANNE MARIE RYAN

WHITE, Ruth
Author, b. 15 March 1942, Whitewood, Virginia

W. is the award-winning author of several acclaimed novels for middle and high school age readers. Her stories are set in southern Appalachia, often in the impoverished coal-mining region of western Virginia where she grew up. W. is consistently praised for her characterizations, vivid depiction of settings, and sensitive treatment of difficult subjects like the DEATH of a parent, mental illness, and sexual abuse.

The fourth daughter of a coal miner who died when she was six years old, W. grew up during the

1950s. Too poor to afford television, W.'s family entertained themselves with reading aloud and performing music. This helped W. develop a strong imagination that would be a great asset in her writing career. W. pursued a career as a schoolteacher, later becoming a school LIBRARIAN.

W. chose to write for adolescents because of her particular interest in the many challenges TEENAGE girls face growing up. W. remembers her own adolescence as a time in her life when she was most confused and unhappy. She believes this is a universal experience that most adolescent girls go through, regardless of the time or the place. In her stories, W. tries to convey the pain of growing up and the struggle to find one's identity and individuality that adolescent girls experience.

In *Sweet Creek Holler* (1988), W.'s first novel for YOUNG ADULTS, six-year-old Ginny and older sister June must deal with the rumors that arise when they move to a new town and the people there learn that their father was shot to death, leaving them and their mother to fend for themselves. During the six years they live in the small mining town of Sweet Creek Holler, the girls witness the devastating effect gossip has on sensitive souls.

Weeping Willow (1992), set in 1956 in another small southern Appalachian town, tells the story of fourteen-year-old Tiny, the eldest child in her FAMILY. As she grows into adulthood, Tiny has to deal with her stepfather's unwanted sexual advances as well as the typical challenges a girl her age must face in high school.

W.'s most highly praised novel, *Belle Prater's Boy* (1996), set in Coal Station, Virginia, in the 1950s, is a beautifully crafted story that explores the nature of friendship, loss, and love. The novel revolves around twelve-year-old Gypsy, known for her long hair, and her father, who died tragically seven years earlier. When her cousin Woodrow, Belle Prater's boy, moves in next door after the mysterious disappearance of his mother, he and Gypsy develop a unique friendship that allows them to face tragedy and transcend it.

Memories of Summer (2000), also set in the 1950s, begins in the small coal-mining town of Glory Bottom, Virginia, but the majority of the story takes place in Flint, Michigan. Thirteen-year-old Lyric must move with her father, Poppy, and older sister Summer from their tucked-away holler in Virginia to the big city of Flint where Poppy hopes to find work at General Motors. Getting out of Glory Bottom is a "dream come true" for the girls. After a hopeful beginning up north, Summer, who always had "funny ways," starts exhibiting progressively more disturbing behavior. First she drops out of school and then from life altogether, descending into a psychotic world of delusions and extreme paranoa. Lyric, who loves her sister deeply, tries to cope with the increasing anger, embarrassment, and frustration she feels about Summer's disease.

AWARD: Newbery Honor in 1997 for *Belle Prater's Boy,* ALA Best Books for Young Adults: *Weeping Willow,* 1993, *Belle Prater's Boy,* 1997.

FURTHER WORKS: *Buttermilk Hill,* 2004; *Tadpole,* 2004.

BIBLIOGRAPHY: *Something about the Author,* vol. 117, pp. 193–96.

EDWARD T. SULLIVAN

WHITMORE, Arvella
Author, educator, b. 14 March 1922, n.p.

Born and raised in the Midwest during the Depression, W. received her associate degree from Christian College (now Columbia College) in 1942. She proceeded to graduate from Washburn University with her A.B., L.L.B. in 1944. She obtained her master's degree in speech and theater from the University of Iowa in 1947.

W. taught speech and wrote PLAYS, many of which were performed in the Minneapolis public school district. She married Page G. Whitmore in October 1953 and raised their four children before starting her career as a children's author. W. has written three novels for YOUNG ADULTS, each an unusual coming-of-age story in which a young person finds within himself or herself the courage to face down adversity. She resides in Minneapolis, Minnesota.

AWARDS: Notable Children's Trade Book in Social Studies, National Council for the Social Studies/Children's Book Council, 1990; ALA Best Book for Young Adults, 2000; Society of Midland Authors Young Adult Award, 2000; Minnesota Book Award for Young Adults, 2000.

FURTHER WORKS: *You're a Real Hero,* 1985; *The Bread Winner,* 1990; *Trapped between the Lash and the Gun,* 1999.

BIBLIOGRAPHY: *Contemporary Authors Online,* 2003.

MIMI O'MALLEY

WIELER, Diana (Jean)

Author, b. 14 October 1961, Winnipeg, Canada

A recognized author of SHORT STORIES, PICTURE BOOKS, and novels, W. is known as one of CANADA'S most distinguished authors of YA literature.

Despite a demonstrated interest in writing throughout her teenage years, W.'s early career interests were varied. She became interested in media, enrolling at the Southern Alberta Institute of Technology in Calgary, Alberta, after high school. There she completed one year of the two-year Cinema, Television, Stage and Radio Arts Program. W. admits that learning to write commercials was the best training she could ever have had as a writer. While working as an advertising copywriter in Calgary and Saskatoon, Saskatchewan, W. continued to work on her creative writing in the evenings and on weekends. In 1983, she published her first work, the picture book *A Dog on His Own*. The next summer she left radio to work as a creative features writer with the Saskatoon *Star Phoenix*.

W. continued her newspaper work for five years while pursuing her own writing interests in her spare time. Her first YA novel, *Last Chance Summer* (1986), about a twelve-year-old foster-home misfit, drew upon her experiences as a volunteer crisis worker with the Saskatoon Sexual Assault Centre. Her debut YA novel led to much anticipation of her second book, *Bad Boy* (1989). In the story, sixteen-year-old A.J. is shocked by the revelation that his best friend and hockey teammate is gay.

In 1990, W. decided to make a fulltime commitment to writing for young people, and has not shied away from difficult subject matters in her YA works. Since then, she has completed her Ran Van trilogy about a TEENAGE loner who turns into a superhero after adopting a video game alter ego. W. continues to work with YA, spending much of her time introducing her books and talking about her life as an author. She also conducts writing workshops with both teenagers and adults. W. admits that writing about teenagers for teenagers is very exciting; they are, after all, a tough audience.

SELECTED AWARDS: 1985 CBC Radio Literary Competition, first prize, *To The Mountains by Morning*;

Bad Boy: 1989 Governor General's Literary Award for Children's Literature, 1990 International Honor List selection, 1993 ALA Best Books for Young Adults, 1990 Young Adult Services Interest Group of the Canadian Library Association Young Adult Book of the Year Award; 1993 Mr. Christie's Book Award (Best English Book for Twelve Years and Up), *Ran Van the Defender*; McNally Robinson Young Adult Book of the Year Award: 1997 for *Magic Nation* and 1998 for *Drive*.

FURTHER WORKS: *To the Mountains by Morning,* 1987; *Ran Van the Defender,* 1993; *Ran Van: A Worthy Opponent,* 1995; *Ran Van: Magic Nation,* 1997; *Drive,* 1998; *Highway Blues,* 2002.

BIBLIOGRAPHY: W., Diana. "My BIOGRAPHY." Makers gallery.com, http://www.makersgallery.com/wieler /who.html; *Something about the Author,* vol. 109.

KRISTEL FLEUREN

WILDER, Laura E. Ingalls

Author, b. 7 February 1867, Pepin Wisconsin; d. 10 February 1957, Mansfield, Missouri

W. is best known for her Little House SERIES in which the central character is based on the author as a girl. These autobiographical books are a vivid picture of the overall experience of pioneer life.

W.'s life began in the woods of Wisconsin, where her father was a farmer and hunter, and her mother a former schoolteacher. During her childhood years, her life was dictated by the various moves her FAMILY made across the country; these migrations would later become the basis for W.'s writings. Her father Charles Ingalls, known as *Pa,* regularly entertained his wife and four daughters with his captivating stories and beautiful fiddle concerts. Pa once said that music "puts heart to a man," and provided interludes from the rigors of pioneer life; Pa's music is integral in W.'s description of home. W. continued the tradition of her father's storytelling with her own children. She was also able to add the ADVENTURES of her own experiences as a pioneer girl.

The Homestead Act of 1862 offered free land to those brave enough to forge into the West. The Ingalls family departed on a ten-year journey that covered the Midwest, searching for fruitful land and a permanent home. This traveling chapter of their lives is described throughout the Little House Books. The family traveled to the Indian Territory of Kansas in *Little House on the Prairie* (1935); Walnut Grove, Minnesota, in *On the Banks of Plum Creek* (1937); Burr Oak, Iowa; and finally established a permanent homestead at De Smet, South Dakota, in *By the Shores of Silver Lake* (1939). During these moves, W. developed her ability to transform images into words due to her elder sister. Mary was blinded by spinal meningitis (scarlet fever is the explanation for Mary's blindness in W.'s work) and depended on W.'s description of the world around them to replace her vacant eyes.

In 1885, W. married Almanzo James Wilder, who is portrayed in her writing as the dashing young hero who saves (the town) from starvation by facing a dangerous blizzard in search of supplies (*The Long Winter*, 1940). Their courtship developed when Laura began teaching school far away and Almanzo drove her home and back each weekend (*These Happy Golden Years*, 1943). In real life, the couple was plagued with diphtheria, crop failures, the DEATH of their first child, and a fire that destroyed their first home. Their second child, Rose, was born in 1886, and the three settled in the couple's final home at Rocky Ridge Farm in Missouri.

W.'s writing career began after an editor of a farming MAGAZINE heard a speech that she wrote. She was contacted to write for the magazine, and published her first piece, "Favors of the Small Farm Home," on February 18, 1911. Subsequent articles quickly followed the magazine pieces; with the help of her daughter Rose, W. began publishing in other journals and had a column called "As a Farm Woman Thinks" in the *Missouri Ruralist*. Both mother and daughter pursued individual writing careers, each writing in a direct and simplified style that gave insight into their lives. W.'s first book, *Little House in the Big Woods* (1932), was an immediate success and served as an integral part of the foundation of the series that followed.

W. wanted to share both the positive and disheartening perspectives of a life filled with a resilient family, frequent moves, land, and the pioneering spirit of Americans in the 19th century. She "wanted children to understand more about the beginning of things, to know what is behind the things they see—what it is that made America as they know it." Her books garnered great recognition from children and adults alike. It was the courage and decent human behavior involved in W.'s upbringing and writings that appealed to her original readers and children decades later.

The Laura Ingalls W. Award, named to honor W., is given to books considered worthy of sitting on the same shelf as W.'s books. The American Library Association established the award in 1954 and presented their first medal to W. herself.

AWARDS: 1943 *New York Herald-Tribune* Spring Book Festival Prize, *These Happy Golden Years.*

FURTHER WORKS: "Tuck'em in Corner," 1915; "The Farmer's Wife Says," 1919; "My Ozark Kitchen," 1925; *Farmer Boy,* 1933; *Little Town on the Prairie,* 1941; *On the Way Home,* 1962; *The First Four Years,* 1971; *West from Home,* 1974.

BIBLIOGRAPHY: Anderson, William T., ed. *A Little House Sampler,* 1988. Spaeth, Janet. *Laura Ingalls W.,* 1987.

RACHEL WITMER
AND AURALEE DALEY

WILHELM, Kate
Author, b. 1928, Toledo, Ohio

Literally a jack-of-all-genres, W. has written almost forty novels, over twenty-five SHORT STORIES, and has been published in multiple SCIENCE FICTION, FANTASY, and MYSTERY anthologies. W.'s primary genres were science fiction and fantasy until the late 1980s, when she began fervently writing mysteries—particularly detective fiction. According to her former editor, Gordon Van Gelder, W. is "one of the few people who has mastered both the novel and the short story."

Married to Damon Knight (1922–2002), also an award-winning science-fiction writer and anthology editor, W. and her husband taught the Clarion Workshop in fantasy and science fiction for nearly thirty years at Michigan State University; both received honorary doctorates from the university for their efforts. Additionally, W. has also lectured on writing technique at various universities in South America and Asia. Having had her works translated into over a dozen languages, W. has developed quite a following, particularly in England, France, and Germany, where she has received the Kurt Lasswitz Award and the Prix Apollo. W. is a fervent enthusiast of local libraries and regularly partakes in charities and fundraisers. Currently residing in Eugene, Oregon, with her family, W. coincidentally has her most famous character, attorney Barbara Holloway, based in the same town. W. has recently been inducted into the Science Fiction

Hall of Fame; however, her detective novel fans would more than likely appeal this verdict and arraign her as a great mystery writer.

AWARDS: Hugo Best Novel Winner, 1977, for *Where Late the Sweet Birds Sang*; Nebula Best Short Story Winner, 1968 *The Planners*, 1987 *Forever Yours, Anna*; Nebula Best Novelette Winner, 1986, *The Girl Who Fell into the Sky*; Hugo Best Novelette nominee, 1975, *A Brother to Dragons, A Companion of Owls*; Hugo Best Novella nominee, 1982, *With Thimbles, with Forks and Hope*; Hugo Best Short Story nominee, 1988, *Forever Yours, Anna*, 1995, *I Know What You're Thinking*; Nebula Best Novel nominee, 1965, *The Clone*, 1971, *Margaret and I*, 1976, *Where Late the Sweet Birds Sang*, 1981, *The Winter Beach*; Nebula Best Short Story nominee, 1967, *Baby, You Were Great*, 1970, *A Cold Night Dark with Snow, I Know What You're Thinking*; Nebula Best Novella nominee, 1970, *April Fool's Day Forever*, 1971, *The Plastic Abyss*, 1971, *The Infinity Box*, 1979, *Juniper Time*, 1985, *The Gorgon Field*, 1993, *Naming the Flowers*; Nebula Best Novelette nominee, 1972, *The Funeral*; World Fantasy Best Novella nominee, 1986, *The Gorgon Field*; 1976 ALA Best Books for Young Adults: *Where Late the Sweet Birds Sang*.

FURTHER WORKS: *The Hamlet Trap*, 1987; *The Dark Door*, 1988; *Smart House*, 1989; *Sweet, Sweet Poison*, 1990; *Seven Kinds of Death*, 1992; *A Flush of Shadows*, 1995; *The Case Book of Constance and Charlie vol. 1 and vol. 2*, 1999; *Death Qualified: A Mystery of Chaos*, 1991; *The Best Defense*, 1994; *For the Defense; or, Malice Prepense*, 1996; *Defense for the Devil*, 1999; *No Defense*, 2000; *Desperate Measures*, 2001; *The Clear and Convincing Proof*, 2003; *More Bitter than Death*, 1962; *The Mile-Long Spaceship*, 1963; *The Clone*, 1965; *Andover and the Android*, 1966; *The Nevermore Affair*, 1966; *The Killer Thing*, 1967; *Let the Fire Fall*, 1969; *The Year of the Cloud*, 1970; *City of Cain*, 1974; *The Infinity Box*, 1975; *The Clewison Test*, 1976; *Fault Lines*, 1977; *Listen, Listen*, 1981; *A Sense of Shadow*, 1981; *Oh, Susannah*, 1982; *Welcome, Chaos*, 1983; *Huysman's Pets*, 1985; *Crazy Time*, 1988; *Children of the Wind*, 1989; *Cambio Bay*, 1990; *And the Angels Sing*, 1992; *Justice for Some*, 1993; *The Good Children*, 1998; *The Deepest Water*, 2000; *Skeletons: A Novel of Suspense*, 2002; *The Hills are Dancing*, 1986; "The Last Days of the Captin," 1962; "The Man without a Planet," 1962; "A Time to Keep," 1962; "Jenny with Wings," 1963; "Countdown," 1968; "The Hounds," 1969; "The Encounter," 1970; "The Infinity Box," 1971; "Sister Angel," 1983; "The Dragon Seed," 1985; "And the Angels Sing," 1990; "The Day of the Sharks," 1962; "All for One," 1995; "Torch Song," 1995; "Forget Luck," 1996; "Merry Widow," 1996; *The Unbidden Truth*, 2004.

BIBLIOGRAPHY: "*Kate* Wilhelm." http://www.palm-digitalmedia.com/author/detail/1302, 2004; "Kate W. Biography," http://www.katewilhelm.com, 2003; "*Kate Wilhelm*," http://www.fantasticfiction.co.uk/authors/Kate_Wilhelm.htm, 2004.

ILONA N. KOTI

WILKINSON, Brenda

Author, b. 1 January 1946, Moultrie, Georgia

A member of Authors Guild and Authors League of America, W. portrays aspects of AFRICAN AMERICAN life that were previously neglected in YOUNG ADULT LITERATURE. For example, in the 1970s, the portrayal of urban life had overshadowed the depiction of the pre-CIVIL RIGHTS black community, prompting W. to write about this underexposed experience that she herself had lived.

W. was raised in the small town of Waycross, Georgia, and educated in the last of the segregated public schools. With her mother's encouragement, she left her hometown after high school and lived with relatives while attending Hunter College in New York City.

W. was published for the first time when her SHORT STORY appeared in *We Be Word Sorcerers*, an anthology edited by Sonia Sanchez. Later, she speaks of a need to recreate her childhood environment through literature; coming generations of children need to understand the experience of small town life in Georgia in the mid-1950s. She did not want this important historical period to be forgotten. Her first book, *Ludell* (1975), introduces W.'s protagonist who also grows up in Waycross, Georgia. The insufficient black segregated schools are illustrated as well as Ludell's poor living conditions, yet the young girl blossoms through the exchange of love in her community. Two more books, *Ludell and Willie* (1977) and *Ludell's New York Time* (1980), feature Ludell growing up, encountering romantic love, and relocating to Manhattan.

Not all critics approved of W.'s use of southern African American dialect, yet young readers find the dialect to be very natural. They are drawn to the various aspects of Ludell and the dilemmas she faces as an average preadolescent. Additionally, W.'s adult critics praise her strength in relating details of race with unpretentious emotion and honesty.

After her Ludell trilogy came to an end, she took time off from writing young adult novels, but returned in 1987 with *Not Separate, Not Equal.* She presents the tumult surrounding six black students who integrate a high school. The universal fears of peer rejection and attending a new school are compounded when these students face violent threats and community rejection. Once again, in *Definitely Cool* (1993), W. takes the universally experienced issue of entering junior high and tailors it to fit her unique character, Roxanne. This TEENAGER from a Bronx housing project attends a new school in a predominately white suburb and must weigh her desire for popularity against the consequences it would bring. W. masterfully selects conventional issues present in young adult literature and revitalizes them with new settings.

W.'s books have wide appeal and will continue to do so because they present stories to which young people relate. She does not, however, encourage conformity from her audience, and retains the black southern dialects in her writing as a way of telling her readers, "You don't have to be exactly like everyone else."

AWARDS: *Ludell and Willie:* Outstanding Children's Books of the Year by the *New York Times,* ALA Best Book for Young Adults, both 1977. Also selected for "The Best of the Best Books: 1970–1983."

FURTHER WORK: *Jesse Jackson: Still Fighting for the Dream,* 1990.

BIBLIOGRAPHY: "Brenda W." *U*X*L Junior DIS-Covering Authors,* 1998. Reproduced in Discovering Collection, http://galenet.galegroup.com/servlet/DC/, 2001; Bennett, Susan G. "Brenda W." *Writers for Young Adults,* ed. Ted Hipple, http://galenet.galegroup.com/serlet/LitRC, 1997; "Brenda W." *Contemporary Authors Online,* 2001; http://galenet.galegroup.com/servlet/LitRC; *Fifth Book of Junior Authors & Illustrators,* 1983; *Something about the Author,* 1997.

RACHEL WITMER
AND SARA MARCUS

WILLEY, Margaret
Author, b. 5 November 1950, Chicago, Illinois

When she was four, W.'s FAMILY moved from Chicago to southwestern Michigan. W. writes of her early years: "As a girl, I was both very shy and very strong. I did not know as a child that I would become a writer, but I loved to read and I made books into my friends, as all writers do." As the eldest daughter in a large family, W. watched many of her siblings struggle through their TEENAGE years. Much of what she witnessed—including depression, first loves, and rebellion—are adolescent issues that later found their way into her writing.

W. left home at age seventeen and went on to receive her B.A. and B.Ph. from Grand Valley State College in 1975 and her M.F.A. from Bowling Green State University in 1979. In 1980, W. married Richard Joanisse from Sault Ste. Marie, Canada, and together they have one daughter. Her husband's French-Canadian family has a very strong ethnic identity, and W. welcomed the opportunity to find her place in his world. The French-Canadian culture provided W. with rich ground for observation. Later, she started to work her notes into novels, SHORT STORIES, and a novella.

In 1983, W. published her first novel for teenagers, *The Bigger Book of Lydia.* This novel introduces the issue of body image through two characters, Lydia and Michelle. Lydia is very self-conscious about her small size, and keeps a journal in which she collects information on how to grow bigger and stronger. The journal is eventually lost. Then Michelle enters Lydia's life. Michelle has recently spent time in an eating disorder clinic, where she had been treated for anorexia. The girls become friends, sharing deep fears and secrets with each other. When Lydia's journal reemerges, the girls find comfort in its pages.

Following publication of this book, W. became a vocal advocate concerning issues that relate to young women. She and her husband teach a course on adolescent culture at Grand Valley State College. She also serves on many advisory boards to promote positive mental health in girls, including that of the magazine, *Daughters.* W. believes that "our media-saturated, advertising-infused culture creates special challenges for the mental health of girls that we are only just beginning to understand."

In *If Not for You,* published in 1988, W. tackles the issue of teen pregnancy. Of this novel, *Publishers Weekly* remarked, "Seldom has a new love between teens been expressed in terms so genuinely real." Divorce is another serious issue that W. addressed in her novel *The Melinda Zone* (1993). In this novel, fifteen-year-old Melinda's parents have decided to divorce, and the young girl finds herself caught between their demands. She spends the summer living with various relatives and slowly finds herself and the courage to confront her parents.

W. is also the author of several PICTURE BOOKS. *Thanksgiving with Me* (1998) tells the story of Thanksgivings past as a young girl waits for her six uncles to arrive on Thanksgiving Day. *Clever Beatrice* (2001) is a French-Canadian-inspired folktale set in Michigan's Upper Peninsula. W. wrote the story as a tribute to her husband's heritage.

AWARDS: American Library Association Best Books for Young Adults: *The Bigger Book of Lydia,* 1983, *Finding David Dolores,* 1986, *If Not For You,* 1988, and *Saving Lenny,* 1991; Creative Artist Grant, Michigan Arts Council, 1984, 1988, and 1995; Recommended Books for Reluctant YA Readers selection, *If Not For You,* 1989; Best of the Best for Children listing, American Library Association, *David Dolores,* 1993; Paterson Prize for Books for Young People and an American Library Association Quick Pick, *Facing the Music,* 1997; Charlotte Zolotow Award and American Library Association Notable book, *Clever Beatrice,* 2002.

FURTHER WORK: *Beatrice the Brave,* 2004.

BIBLIOGRAPHY: *Something about the Author,* vol. 86; www.margaretwilley.com; www.soemadison.wisc .edu/ccbc/friends/willey.htm.

CARRA GAMBERDELLA

WILLIAMS, Carol Lynch
Author, b. 28 September 1959, Lincoln, Nebraska

W.'s novels for children and YAS feature girls who rely on their minds and their inner strength, often in the face of adversity. W.'s first book was published when she submitted it to the Delacorte First YA Writing contest. W. was told that while she did not win, the publisher was interested in her book, which became *Kelly and Me* (1993). In this novel, two sisters have a summer full of ADVENTURES until a sudden tragedy impacts their lives.

The True Colors of Caitlynne Jackson (1997) tells the gripping story of half-sisters Caitlynne and Cara, victims of an emotionally and physically abusive mother. After their mother abandons them, their relief turns to fear when she doesn't return after several weeks and they have to fend for themselves. *If I Forget, You Remember* (1998), also deals with an uncomfortable subject, as a FAMILY is disrupted when their grandmother, who suffers from Alzheimer's disease,

moves in with them. *My Angelica* (1999) is a humorous romance in which George has a secret crush on his friend Sage, a writer who unfortunately doesn't realize how untalented she is. The story alternates between George's point of view, Sage's point of view, and excerpts from the unbelievably bad ROMANCE novel that Sage is writing. In *A Mother to Embarrass Me* (2002), twelve-year-old Laura thinks that her mother has changed "from cool to geek." Laura is mortified by her mother's singing, her cooking, and most importantly, her pregnancy.

W. is also the author of the Latter-Day Daughters SERIES, in which the faith of Mormon girls helps them overcome crises.

AWARDS: 1998 American Library Association Best Book for Young Adults, *The True Colors of Caitlynne Jackson.*

FURTHER WORK: *Carolina Autumn,* 2000.

BIBLIOGRAPHY: *Authors and Artists for Young Adults,* vol. 39, 2001; *Contemporary Authors Online,* 2000; *Something about the Author,* vol. 110, 2000.

ANDREA LIPINSKI

WILLIAMS, Lori Aurelia
Author, b. n.d., Houston, Texas

W.'s decision to take a creative writing class at the University of Texas set her on the track of pursuing a graduate degree in creative writing and becoming a writer. W.'s stunning debut novel, *When Kambia Elaine Flew in from Neptune* (2000), tells the story of the relationship between Shayla and her new neighbor Kambia Elaine. Shalya, an aspiring writer, is curious about her new neighbor, who seems to spend a lot of time in an imaginary world populated by Lizard People and Wallpaper Wolves. As the story unfolds, it is revealed that Kambia's wild stories hide a history of abuse that she cannot accept or comprehend. Shayla also has problems of her own: her older sister Tia leaves home, and she has to deal with the return of her long-absent father.

In the sequel, *Shalya's Double Brown Baby Blues* (2001), Shalya's story continues as she develops her writing skills and finds herself trying to reconcile the tension within her FAMILY. Her situation is made worse when her father has a child by his new wife, and the new child (named Gift) has the same birthday as Shayla. Several other characters make appearances, including Tia and her boyfriend, Shayla's old girlfriends, and a troubled boy named Lemm who is hiding a drinking problem. Kambia Elaine also returns, and her life is disrupted as a stranger begins sending her reminders of her traumatic past.

The characters in W.'s books speak with authentic voices, whether they use street slang or written words. Shalya's writing, especially, serves as a poetic thread that weaves its way through these books.

AWARDS: 2001 ALA Best Book for Young Adults, *When Kambia Elaine Flew In From Neptune;* PEN/ Phyllis NAYLOR Working Writer Fellowship (2002) for *Broken China, Falling Cherubs, and Aliens.*

BIBLIOGRAPHY: *Authors and Artists for Young Adults,* vol. 52, 2003; "Author Profile: Lori Aurelia W." http://www.teenreads.com/authors/au-williams-lori .asp, November 14, 2003; Miriam E. Drennan. "Lori Aurelia W. Gives Silenced Children a Voice." interviewer, http://www.bookpage.com/0004bp/lori_aurelia_ williams.html, November 14, 2003.

ANDREA LIPINSKI

WILLIAMS, Michael
Author, b. 24 June 1935, Swansea, Wales

W. always had a fascination with the visual landscape that more often than not is a product of human endeavor and transformation. Born in Wales, W. married a high school teacher, Eleanore Lerch, in 1955. They had two children. He received his B.A. from the University College of Swansea, University of Wales with first-class honors in 1956. He completed his Ph.D. in 1960 followed by a diploma of education from St. Catharine's College, Cambridge, in 1960; an M.A. from Oxford University in 1978; and D.Litt. from the University of Wales in 1990.

W. served as a lecturer and later professor of geography at University of Adelaide, Adelaide, Australia, between 1960 and 1996. This academic profile concentrated on specific landscape-forming processes, such as draining of wetland environments, forest clearing, and agricultural change. He was a part-time lecturer at the South AUSTRALIAN Institute of Technology (1963–70) and a lecturer at the University College in London (1966–67 and 1973).

Opportunities to work in Australia and the United States broadened the range of his work, so that *The Americans and Their Forests* is continental in scale and straddles transformations from pre-Indian times to the present. He has been a visiting fellow and lecturer at universities in England, Australia, and the United States.

AWARDS: John Lewis Gold Medal, Royal Geographic Society, 1974; Biennial Literary Prize, Adelaide Festival of the Arts, 1976; *Crocodile Burning*: ALA Best Books for Young Adults, 1992.

FURTHER WORKS: *South Australia from the Air* (editor), 1969; *The Draining of the Somerset Levels,* 1970; *The Making of the South Australian Landscape,* 1974; *Australian Space, Australian Time: Geographical Perspectives, 1788–1914* (with J. M. Powell), 1977; *The Changing Rural Landscape of South Australia,* 1977, rev. 1991; *Adelaide at the Census,* 1971, 1977; *The Americans and Their Forests: An Historical Geography,* 1989; *Wetlands: A Threatened Landscape,* 1990; *Planet Management* (editor), 1993; *Into the Valley,* 1994; *The Genuine Half-Moon Kid,* 1995; *Understanding Geographical and Environmental Education: The Role of Research* (editor), 1996; *The Landscapes of Lowland Britain,* 1999.

BIBLIOGRAPHY: *Contemporary Authors Online,* 2003.

MIMI O'MALLEY

WILLIAMS-GARCIA, Rita
Author, b. 6 September 1963, Avon, Connecticut

W. was born on the East Coast of the U.S. but grew up on the West Coast. Her family moved to Seaside, California, when she was very young; they eventually moved back east, first to Georgia, then to Jamaica, New York, and later, when she was twelve years old, to Far Rockaway, New York. W. graduated from Hofstra University on Long Island and pursued a master's degree at Queens College. She married Peter C. Garcia, a Desert Storm veteran; they have two daughters, Michelle and Stephanie.

W. says: "I learned to read at age two by looking at billboards, figuring out the sounds associated with the letters and putting it all together. My sister, who was in kindergarten used to slide her story books between the slats of my wooden playpen, lean her head against the bars while I read to her. (I had to make up some of the words, but many I figured out.) Words always had a particular attraction for me, even as a baby."

W.'s mother was an inspiration to her to use her imagination. W. says that her mother was the grand figure in her life "because she frightened me, made me laugh, and loved to paint things in weird colors— napalm orange, chartreuse and aqua. She encouraged me to be creative and to see objects and situations beyond their physicality."

W. says that she cannot think of a day that has passed since kindergarten that she hasn't written for her own pleasure. She made her first sale and published her first story in *Highlights* when she was fourteen-years old. She collected mounds of rejection letters both before and after this success. While attending Hofstra University, W. was awakened to the impact of black literature by Ntozake Shange's *for colored girls who considered suicide/when the rainbow is enuf.* W. says that it was not until after she left Hofstra that she fully realized her mentors to be Toni Morrison, Alice Walker, Zora Neale Hurston; these writers led her to her true cast of characters and her authentic audience.

In her senior year of college she says she wrote a draft of her next story (*Blue Tights,* 1987) out of necessity. "I was working with a remedial reading group that needed materials from their point of view. Such a book did not exist, so I wrote out little scenes, mostly taken from my students' lives, and we'd read them." She wanted to give a voice to black females in literature, as she had found no such voice in her own adolescent reading. At the same time, W. did not want Joyce, her protagonist, to be the poster girl for race; she wanted to develop a character that proceeded through life and struggled with her development as any other child who just happened to be black.

After *Blue Tights* was published nearly ten years later, W. promised her editor that she would not write another YA novel. "I didn't feel particularly encouraged by the glut of soulless TEEN novels that seemed to comprise Young Adult books. I didn't want to make true experience palatable for ten-year-olds, didn't want to construct the NAACP poster child in hopes of winning some award, and didn't want to kill the wonderful strangeness of fiction for the reader by explaining every little thing." However, her mind was continuously peppered with new ideas for YA books, and her career took off in the very definite direction of YA literature.

W. writes about AFRICAN AMERICAN teenagers in contemporary, realistic situations who deal with unique but universal problems. She insists that she does not write about issues; instead, she writes about characters' lives. For example, when she tells people that her third novel, *Like Sisters on the Homefront* (1995), is about a twice-pregnant fourteen-year-old, they conclude that it is about abortion and the plight of a teenage mother. Quoting W., "that's what After School Specials are for." Instead of a formula story,

this book is about teen-mother Gayle and her journey to get back what she didn't even know was missing from her life. The contrast between Gayle and her Southern relatives portrays the ironic collision of class and culture within.

W.'s great strengths are being able to write about real teenage boys and girls, and her effective use of authentic adolescent linguistic patterns of urban African American youth. Hazel ROCHMAN says in *Booklist* that the dialogue snaps and swings from raucous insults and jealous anger to painful lyricism.

AWARDS: 1991 PEN/Norma Klein Citation; 1992 ALA Best Book for Young Adult for *Fast Talk on a Slow Track; Like Sisters on the Homefront:* 1996 ALA Booklist Best Book of the Year, 1996 Coretta Scott King Honor Book Award, ALA Best Book for Young Adults; 1997 PEN/Norma Klein Award; *Every Time Rainbow Dies*: ALA Best Books for Young Adults, 2002; *No Laughter Here*: ALA Best Books for Young Adults, 2005. *Like Sisters on the Homefront* was selected for the Best of the Best (Selections from 1995 to 2004); *Fast Talk on a Slow Track*: ALA Popular Paperbacks: 2002.

FURTHER WORKS: *Fast Talk on a Slow Track,* 1991; *Catching the Wild Waiyuuzee,* 2000; *Every Time a Rainbow Disco,* 2001; *No Laughter Here,* 2004.

BIBLIOGRAPHY: Pais, Susan, Phyllis Brown, and Ann Gartner, with Kay E. Vandergrift. "Learning about Rita W.," scils.rutgers.edu/kvander/williamsgarcia .html, 1996; Rochman, Hazel. *Booklist,* vol. 92, 1996; Rowe, Beverly. "Interview with Rita W.," www .myself.com/haveyouheard/03/garcia.htm, 2003; W., Rita. *Autobiography.* Lodestar Books Publication; Yoder, Carolyn, ed. "Rita W. at Chautauqua," 2001.

BERNICE E. CULLINAN

WILLIS, Connie
Author, b. 31 December 1945, Denver, Colorado

W. is a SCIENCE FICTION writer who resides in Greeley, Colorado. After graduating from Colorado State College in 1967 with a B.A., and she was a schoolteacher before embarking on a writing career.

W. prefers writing short fiction and her SHORT STORIES and novellas have won numerous Hugo and Nebula awards; however, her novels are also award winning, beginning with *Lincoln's Dreams* (1988), which won the John W. Campbell Award of the World Science Fiction Convention. W. spent five years writing *Doomsday Book* (1992), which is set in 2054, when time travel is a new technology used for historical research. Oxford student Kivrin becomes the first historian to travel to the Middle Ages, a period thought too dangerous for travel; meaning to travel to 1320, she instead arrives in 1348 and must watch the Black Death decimate the Oxfordshire village whose inhabitants she has come to care about. *Doomsday Book* won both the Hugo and Nebula awards for best novel.

W. continued to explore time travel and English history in the Hugo Award-winning *To Say Nothing of the Dog; or, How We Found the Bishop's Bird Stump at Last* (1998), in which her protagonist, Ned Henry, travels to 1888 in his effort to rebuild Coventry Cathedral. In *Passages* (2001), medical researchers investigating near-death experiences discover a connection between those experiences and the Titanic. *Passages* was nominated for the Arthur C. CLARKE Award.

AWARDS: Hugo Award: 1982 for "Fire Watch," 1983 for "A Letter from the Clearys," 1988 for "The Last of the Winnebagos," 1993 for *Doomsday Book,* 1993 for "Even the Queen," and 1994 for "Death on the Nile"; Nebula Award: 1982 for "Fire Watch," 1982 for "A Letter from the Clearys," 1988 for "The Last of the Winnebagos," 1990 for "At the Rialto," 1992 for *Doomsday Book,* and 1992 for "Even the Queen"; 1988 John W. Campbell Award, *Lincoln's Dreams*; *To Say Nothing of the Dog*: ALA Best Books for Young Adults 1999.

FURTHER WORKS: *Water Witch* (with Cynthia Felice), 1980; *Fire Watch,* 1984; *Light Raid* (with Cynthia Felice), 1989; *Impossible Things,* 1993; *Uncharted Territory,* 1994; *Remake,* 1994; *Bellwether,* 1996; *Promised Land* (with Cynthia Felice) 1997; *Miracle, and Other Christmas Stories,* 1999.

BIBLIOGRAPHY: *Contemporary Authors New Revision Series,* vol. 91; Shindler, Dorman T. "Connie W.: The Truths of Science Fiction." *Publishers Weekly,* vol. 248, no. 21, pp. 76–77.

MICHELE HILTON

WILSON, Budge

Author, educator, journalist, b. 1927, Halifax, Canada

W. has worked as a teacher of English and arts, a filing clerk, artist, LIBRARIAN, fitness instructor, freelance editor, journalist, commercial artist, and photographer. She is best known for her work as a YA author. Her playful books are full of stories that entertain and teach. Since publishing her first book in 1984, she has published over twenty seven books,

with translations in ten languages in thirteen countries. After living in Ontario for over twenty five years, W. and her husband returned to Nova Scotia in 1989 and live in a small fishing village on the South Shore of the province.

In the decade after that move, W. published three collections of SHORT STORIES, subtle and beautifully written. One of these works, *"The Leaving" and Other Stories* (1992), is a powerful look at what it means to grow up female. For an author then in her sixties, W. had a remarkable grasp of TEEN emotions. Her masterful depiction of the roller-coaster ride her young protagonists experience, as a result, was recognized by the members of the ALA Best Books for Young Adults committee, who selected this work for the 1993 list. Additional awards are given below.

AWARDS: *The Best/Worst Christmas Present Ever* was chosen by the *Emergency Librarian* as one of the twelve Best PAPERBACK Children's Books of 1986; CLA YA Book Award, CANADIAN Library Association, 1991, ALA Best Books for Young Adults, 1993, for *"The Leaving" and Other Stories.*

FURTHER WORKS: *The Best/Worst Christmas Present Ever* (Blue Harbor SERIES), 1984; *A House Far from Home* (Blue Harbor series), 1986; *Mr. John Bertrand Nijinsky and Charlie,* illus. Terry Roscoe Boucher, 1986; *Mystery Lights in Blue Harbor* (Blue Harbor series), 1987; *Cordelia Clark,* 1994; *The Courtship* (stories), 1994; *"The Dandelion Garden" and Other Stories,* 1995; *Mothers and Other Strangers,* 1996; *The Long Wait,* 1997; *The Cat that Barked,* 1998; *Duff's Monkey Business,* 2000; *A Fiddle for Angus,* 2001. Short stories—"The Sale," 1977; "Three Voices," 1983; "The Metaphor," 1983; "Big Little Jerome," 1985; "The Leaving," 1985; "Mr. Manuel Jenkins," 1986; "The DIARY," 1987.

REBECCA OSA MENDELL

WILSON, Diane Lee

Author, n.d., Illinois

W.'s first novel, *I Rode a Horse of Milk White Jade* (1998), is a historical novel set in Mongolia and China in the fourteenth century. Oyuna, accompanied by her horse and cat, goes on a quest that takes her beyond the Gobi desert to Khan's court. Named a 1999 Best Book for Young Adults by the American Library Association, the novel was acclaimed upon its release, also receiving a silver medal from the Commonwealth Club of California. *To Ride the Gods' Own Stallion* (2000) is another historical story centered on horses. This book is set in seventh-century Assyria, and Soulai, not unlike Oyuna in *I Rode a Horse of Milk White Jade,* must fulfill a mission to change the luck that plagues his FAMILY.

Living in Escondido, California, W. shares her life with a husband and daughter. She is also an equestrienne.

BIBLIOGRAPHY: www.harpercollins.com/services/authorupdate; www.novelst3.epnet.com.

JEANNE MARIE RYAN

WILSON, Jacqueline
Author, b. 17 December 1945, Bath, England

W. wanted to be a writer since the age of six. By the time she was seventeen, she was making a living writing for TEEN MAGAZINES. This author, hugely popular in England, is finally becoming recognized in the United States as an excellent writer for younger readers. More of her works are now being published in this country.

W. has written books for adults, but for the past twenty years, her work has been directed toward young people. She has been a leader in social realism in YOUNG ADULT LITERATURE. Her books typically feature spunky girl protagonists, desperate situations, and a lot of humor. This blend of lively first-person narratives with serious subject matter captures even reluctant readers. Although she writes about girls, W. makes sure that her characters are also sympathetic to boy readers.

W. has been on countless British shortlists and award lists over the years. In 2002, she was awarded the prestigious Order of the British Empire by the Queen for her services to literacy in schools. In the United States, ALA *Booklist* and YALSA selecting her books.

AWARDS: *Girls in Love*: ALA Quick Picks for Reluctant Young Adult Readers, 2003.

SELECT FURTHER WORKS: *Bad Girls,* 2001; *Double Act,* 2001; *Vicky Angel,* 2001; *Girls in Love,* 2002; *Girls under Pressure,* 2002; *Girls out Late,* 2002; *Girls in Tears,* 2003.

BIBLIOGRAPHY: *The Guardian Online,* March 25, 2000, http://books.guardian.co.uk/departments/children andteens/story/0.6000.150645.00.html; *Kids at Random House,* http://www.kidsatrandomhouse.co.uk/jacquelinewilson/; *Something about the Author,* vol.

102, 1999; *Young Writer,* http://www.mystworld.com/youngwriter/authors/jacqwilson.html.

LAURA CHARRON

WINDLING, Terri
Editor, author, b. 1958, Fort Dix, New Jersey

Best known for her editorial prowess, W. is also a strong writer of mythic fiction, an inspired artist, and an advocate for genre-bending works in a variety of formats. After attending Antioch College, W. took a position at a publishing house in 1979, working as an editor until 1986. During her publishing tenure, W. paid close attention to literary tales based on MYTHOLOGY and folklore and promoted works of contemporary FANTASY, magic realism, and reworked FAIRY TALES. Her highly successful Fairy Tale SERIES of novels (continued at another publishing house) boasts some of the finest writers in the field, including Charles DE LINT, Patricia WREDE, Jane YOLEN, and Tanith LEE. W. edited her first anthologies with a joint author, including the *Elsewhere* trilogy (1982–1984). Compiled with Mark Alan Arnold, *Elsewhere* blurs the lines between mainstream and genre fiction and between genres themselves. The anthology won W. the first of many World Fantasy Awards.

Moving to another publisher in 1986, W. created (with Arnold) the Borderland series of anthologies and novels expressly for TEENS. A cult classic and critical favorite, the Borderland series take place in a mythical ruined city on the border between the real world and Faery. Featuring an eccentric array of misfits and outcasts—some human, some elven, and some a mixture of both breeds—Bordertown explores social, environmental, and psychological themes using its fantastic central metaphor to interpret real-world difficulties. W. further explores these themes, especially the plight of homeless and abused children, in the groundbreaking anthology *The Armless Maiden and Other Tales for Childhood's Survivors* (1995). The book's central essay recounts her story of growing up in an abusive home, leaving at fifteen, and surviving as a homeless teen while trying to graduate from high school.

Similar themes of feminism and survival mark much of W.'s editorial work, including Faerie Tale Anthologies series (1993–1999) of retold fairy tales for adults, created with Ellen Datlow. W.'s best known anthology series, *The Year's Best Fantasy and*

Horror (1988–), again co-edited with Datlow, has reached sixteen volumes and has gathered consistent critical acclaim. The 2003 collection includes an announcement of W.'s retirement from the series in order to focus on her own writing; this includes a sequel to her first adult novel, *The Wood Wife* (1996). A mythic story set in the desert outside Tucson, *The Wood Wife* won the Mythopoeic Award in 1996. W. continues her collaborations with Datlow, editing unique myth- and fairy tale-inspired anthologies, most notably *A Wolf at the Door* (2000) and *Swan Sister: Fairy Tales Retold* (2003) for younger readers, and *The Green Man: Tales from the Mythic Forest* (2002) and *Faery Reel* (2004) for teens; both works are illustrated by artist Charles Vess.

W. has had a pervasive and lasting influence on the fantasy field, discovering and fostering the work of an amazing array of writers, including Charles de Lint, Ellen Kushner, Sheri S. TEPPER, Patricia C. Wrede, Steven Brust, Emma BULL, Will SHETTERLY, Pamela Dean, Delia Sherman, Megan Lindholm, Midori Snyder, and Gregory Frost, among many others. As the founder of the Endicott Studio ("an interdisciplinary organization dedicated to the creation and support of mythic arts") and a founding member of the Interstitial Arts Foundation ("a group of literary, visual, and performance artists who have come together to celebrate art that crosses borders"), W. continues to champion mythic, genre-blending works in all formats, and to explore an ever-increasing number of avenues for her own creative expression. W.'s titles regularly appear on the American Library Association lists.

AWARDS: 1982 World Fantasy Award, *Elsewhere;* three World Fantasy Awards for volumes in the *Year's Best Fantasy and Horror* series; 1996 Mythopoeic Award, *The Wood Wife;* 1999 World Fantasy Award, *Silver Birch, Blood Moon;* World Fantasy Award nomination in 2003 for Best Anthology *(Green Man)* and a Special Professional Award for Editing.

FURTHER WORKS: *Faery* (anthology), 1984; *Changeling* (young adult novel), 1995; "The Color of Angels" (novella in anthology *The Horns of Elfland,* ed. by Kushner, Keller, and Sherman), 1997; ed. *Sirens* (collection), 1998; *The Raven Queen* (with Ellen Steiber, book 2 in the *Voyage of the Bassett* series), 1999; *A Midsummer Night's Faery Tale* (PICTURE BOOK with Wendy Froud), 1999; *The Winter Child* (picture book with Wendy Froud), 2001; *The Faeries of Spring Cottage* (picture book with Wendy Froud), 2003.

BIBLIOGRAPHY: *Contemporary Authors Online,* 2003. Reproduced in Biography Resource Center, 2003, http://www.galenet.com/servlet/BioRC; *St. James Guide to Young Adult Writers.* 2nd ed., 1999. Reproduced in Biography Resource Center, 2003, http://www.galenet.com/servlet/BioRC; MacDonald, Henry. "An Interview with Terri W.," http://www.endicott-studio.com/inttwhm.html; Keller, Donald G. "Into the Woods: The Faery Worlds of Terri W." *Legends Profile Series,* http://www.legends.dm.net/fairy/woods.html; Author's website, http://www.endicott-studio.com.

JULIE BARTEL

WINDSOR, Patricia (Colin Daniel, Katonah Summertree, Griselda Daniel)

Author. b. September 21, 1938, in New York City
m. Laurence Windsor Jr in 1959, 2 children, div 1978.
m. Steve Altman 1986. div 1987.

Born Patricia Frances Seelinger and reared in an apartment in New York, W. saw school as an intrusion into her reading, which included J. D. SALINGER and Dylan Thomas. W. began writing at the age of ten and had three dozen rejection slips from *Seventeen* MAGAZINE before her sixteenth birthday. Educated at Bennington College and New York University, she has held many positions in public relations, magazine editing, teaching creative writing, and voluntary work.

At twenty-one she married Laurence Windsor Jr. They have two children. After her marriage ended, W. moved to England for three years with her children—rather like the FAMILY in *Home Is Where Your Feet Are Standing* (1975). She has also lived in New York, Connecticut, and Georgia, making eleven moves in twelve years. W. notes that her settings often reflect her current surroundings.

W.'s first major success was inspired by reading Paul ZINDEL's *My Darling My Hamburger* and realizing that novels for YAs could concern "real people." She reacted by writing *The Summer Before* (1973) about Alexandra, a TEEN runaway overcoming her grief and depression after a friend's DEATH and learning to enjoy life again. It won an ALA Best Books for Young Adults Award and the German–language edition gained the Austrian State Award for Books for Children and Youth.

W.'s wry sense of humor is found in many of her novels, especially the Martha and Teddy SERIES, which began with *How a Weirdo and a Ghost Can*

Change Your Entire Life (1986). Martha's reluctant friendship with the quirky Teddy strikes a strong response with young readers as the unlikely pair brave school ridicule and encounter a series of supernatural MYSTERIES.

This ability to create plausible young characters in implausible situations has impressed commentators like Aidan CHAMBERS and is used to comic effect in *Just like the Movies* (1990). In a skillfully controlled double narrative, runaways Andy and Marvin find themselves involved with gangsters, kidnapping, and drug-running. With its strong (almost Runyonesque) characterisation, unexpected attitudes, and willingness to overturn stereotypes, *Just like the Movies* demonstrates the strengths of W.'s writing.

Her many HORROR stories, which combine traditional horror themes with teen perspectives, are exemplified by *The Blooding* (1996). Mavis is keen to prove herself to her mother. When her sinister employer proves to be a werewolf who offers to "transform" Mavis, her first thought is that her mother will never be able to belittle her again.

Inspired by a benign ghost in her Greenwich home, W. has written a number of novels with supernatural elements. Thus, in *Killing Time* (1980), Sam becomes involved in Druid blood rites, while in *The Hero* (1988), Dale uses premonitions of disasters in his dreams to save some young people but draws sinister attention to himself.

W.'s sardonic and scary thriller *The Sandman's Eyes* (1984), where Michael, suspected of murder, returns home to seek the real killer and, in a tightly plotted climax, finds more than he wants to know, won the Edgar Allan Poe Award for Best MYSTERY.

W. also writes SHORT STORIES and song lyrics. She now lives in Savannah, Georgia, claiming it has more ghosts than any other city.

AWARDS: 1973 *Chicago Tribune Book World* Honor Book Award, *The Summer Before;* 1973 ALA Best Books for Young Adults Award, *The Summer Before;* 1981 Austrian State Award for Books for Children and Youth, *The Summer Before* (German-language edition); 1985 Edgar Allan Poe Award Winner, *The Sandman's Eyes;* 1992 Edgar Allan Poe Award shortlist: *The Christmas Killer;* 1993 IRA Young Adults' Choice, *The Christmas Killer.*

FURTHER WORKS: *The Summer Before,* 1973; *Something's Waiting for You,* Baker D., 1974; *Home is Where Your Feet Are Standing,* 1975; *Diving for Roses,* 1976; *Mad Martin,* 1976; *Killing Time,* 1980; *The Demon Tree,* 1982 (as Colin Daniel); *The Sandman's Eyes,* 1985; *How a Weirdo and a Ghost Can Change Your Entire Life,* 1986; *The Hero,* 1988; *Just Like the Movies,* 1990; *Two Weirdos and a Ghost,* 1991; *A Very Weird and Moogly Christmas,* 1991; *The Christmas Killer,* 1992; *A Little Taste of Death,* 1992; *The Proof of the Pudding,* 1992; *Teeth,* 1993; *The Blooding,* 1996; *The House of Death,* 1996.

BIBLIOGRAPHY: *Major Authors and Illustrators for Children and Young Adults,* 2nd ed. 2002; *St James Guide to Young Adult Writers,* 2nd ed., 1999; *Authors and Artists for Young Adults,* vol. 23; *Contemporary Authors Online;* www.bornauthor.com/Bio.html.

TREVOR AGNEW

WINICK, Judd
Author, b. 12 February 1970, Long Island, New York

W. landed his first professional cartooning job with a single-panel comic strip he created, *Nuts & Bolts.* This comic strip ran weekly in regional newspapers around the New York metropolitan area. W. graduated from the University of Michigan, Ann Arbor in 1992; he majored in art. While there, he continued his *Nuts & Bolts* SERIES in *The Michigan Daily.*

Two years after graduating from college, W. was cast in the third season of *The Real World,* a television series produced by MTV and an early example of a series in the "reality TV" genre. *Nuts & Bolts* was published in the *San Francisco Chronicle* during the filming of the series. While a cast member of *The Real World,* W. befriended fellow cast member and AIDS activist Pedro Zamora. When health complications prevented Zamora completing an AIDS education lecture tour, W. took over, relating his experiences living with a person who has AIDS. Following Zamora's death in 1994, W. wrote a GRAPHIC novel entitled *Pedro & Me.* While W. has received critical praise for his comic book work since the publication of *Pedro & Me,* he is perhaps most known and notable for this graphic novel, which narrates W.'s friendship with Zamora.

W. has shown a continued commitment to social issues. As part of the creative team responsible for *The Green Lantern* comic book series, in 2002 he contributed to a storyline about a gay character who deals with coming-out and with being the victim of a hate crime.

AWARDS: *Pedro & Me:* GLAAD Media Award for Best Comic Book, 2000 *Publishers Weekly* Best

Book, 2000 EISNER Nomination for Best Original Graphic Novel, 2001 Robert F. Sibert INFORMATIONAL Book Honor Award, 2001 Notable Children's Book Selection, American Library Association, 2001 American Library Association Gay, Lesbian, Bisexual, Transgender Roundtable Nonfiction Honor Book. 2001 ALA Best Books for Young Adults, selected for Best of the Best (Selections from 1995 to 2004).

FURTHER WORKS: *The Adventures of Barry Ween, Boy Genius,* 2000; *The Adventures of Barry Ween, Boy Genius 2.0,* 2000; *The Adventures of Barry Ween, Boy Genius, Vol. 3,* 2001; *The Adventures of Barry Ween, Boy Genius, Vol. 4: Gorilla Warfare,* 2002; *Exiles,* 2002; *Exiles: A World Apart,* 2002; *Exiles, Vol. 3: Out of Time,* 2003; *Exiles, Vol. 4: Legacy,* 2003; *Frumpy the Clown: Freaking Out the Neighbors, Vol. 1,* 2001; *Frumpy the Clown: The Fat Lady Sings, Vol. 2,* 2001; *Green Lantern: New Journey, Old Path,* 2001; *Green Lantern: Circle of Fire,* 2002; *Green Lantern: The Power of Ion,* 2003; *Green Lantern: Brother's Keeper,* 2003; *Pedro and Me: Friendship, Loss and What I Learned,* 2000.

BIBLIOGRAPHY: Contino, Jennifer M. "Judd W." *The Pulse,* 2002, http://www.comicon.com; W., Judd. *The Worlds of Judd Winick,* http://www.frumpy.com/

JUDAH S. HAMER

WINTON, Tim
Author, b. 1960, Perth, Australia

W. has won accolades for novels featuring richly evoked settings and roundly drawn characters that embark on journeys of self-discovery. W. incorporates religious themes and imagery into his writings, underlying his characters' dilemmas with good and evil, humanity and brutality.

W. attended Curtin University in Perth but did not complete his degree. He embarked on a writing career, publishing several novels, film scripts, SHORT STORIES and books for children. *Shallows* (1984) was the first of his novels to find its way into American bookstores, appearing in 1984; that same year, it won AUSTRALIA's esteemed Miles Franklin Award for literature. *That Eye, The Sky* (1987) is the third of W.'s novels and the first of his works to explicitly explore religion.

W.'s *Lockie Leonard, Human Torpedo* (1991) was adapted by Paige Gibbs for stage and performed by the Perth Theatre Company; *That Eye, The Sky* was adapted for stage by Justin Monjo and Richard Roxburgh in 1994. *Cloudstreet* (1992) was adapted by Nick Enright and Justin Monjo in 2001.

W. has lived in Greece, France, and Ireland. He now lives in Western Australia with his wife and three children.

AWARDS: Vogel Award, Allen and Unwin Australia, 1981; Miles Franklin Award, 1984, 1992, and 2002; Deo Gloria Prize, 1991; Commonwealth Writers Prize: Southeast Asia and South Pacific section Best Novel, 1995; shortlisted for Booker Prize, 1995 and 20021 *Lockie Leonard, Human Torpedo*: ALA Best Books for Young Adults, 1993.

FURTHER WORKS: *An Open Swimmer,* 1982; *In The Winter Dark,* 1988; *The Riders,* 1995; *Blueback: A Contemporary Fable,* 1997; *Down to Earth: Australian Landscapes* (with Richard Woldendorp), 2000; *Dirt Music,* 2001; *Lockie Leonard, Legend,* 1997; *Lockie Leonard, Scumbuster,* 1999; *The Deep,* 2000; *Jesse,* 1988; *The Bugalugs Bum Thief,* 1991; *Scission and Other Stories,* 1985; *Minimum of Two,* 1988; *Blood and Water: Stories,* 1993.

BIBLIOGRAPHY: *Contemporary Authors Online,* 2003.

MIMI O'MALLEY

WISLER, G. Clifton
Novelist, b. 15 May 1950, Oklahoma City, Oklahoma

Shortly after his birth, W.'s family moved to Dallas, Texas. While attending Hillcrest High School, W. sharpened his journalistic skills as an assistant SPORTS editor of the award-winning *Hillcrest Hurricane.* He received his B.F.A. at Southern Methodist University in 1972 and proceeded to earn his M.A. there in 1974. During his postsecondary education, he taught journalism at Denton High School, Denton, Texas from 1972 to 1973. He switched curriculum and began teaching English for twelve years in the Garland and Plano, Texas, public school system. By 1987, he decided to pursue his writing career full time.

His first novel, *My Brother, the Wind* (1979), was nominated for the American Book Award in 1980 and has been translated into German and Swedish. W. has written five books under the pen name of "Will McLennan": *The Ramseys* (1989); *Matt Ramsey* (1989); *Ramsey's Luck* (1989), *Piper's Ferry: A Novel of the Texas Revolution* (1990), *Ramsey's Law* (1991).

W. is also deeply involved in working with Boy Scouts as an adult leader. He was an assistant scoutmaster for the 1985 National Boy Scout Jamboree, and served as contingent leader for the Mikanakawa Lodge's contingents to the National Order of the

759

Arrow conferences in 1983 and 1986. He annually takes his troop on a historical pilgrimage to Shiloh Battlefield. For his efforts, W. has received the Walker Award, the District Award of Merit, and the Silver Beaver Award (1985), the highest recognition a local council can grant to a volunteer leader. He currently resides in Plano, Texas.

AWARDS: Western Writers of America Spur Award finalist for Best Western Juvenile Fiction, 1983; Child Study Children's Book Committee Children's Book of the Year Award, 1986; International Reading Association's Children's Book Committee, 1987; Children's Book Council of National Council for Social Studies, 1987; Child Study Children's Book Committee Children's Book of the Year, 1988; *Red Cap*: ALA Best Books for Young Adults, 1992.

FURTHER WORKS: *A Cry of Angry Thunder,* 1980; *Winter of the Wolf,* 1981; *The Trident Brand,* 1982; *Thunder on the Tennessee,* 1983; *Buffalo Moon,* 1984; *The Chicken Must Have Died Laughing,* 1983; *A Special Gift,* 1983; *The Raid,* 1985; *The Antrian Messenger,* 1986; *The Wolf's Tooth,* 1987; *This New Land,* 1987; *The Seer,* 1989; *The Mind Trap,* 1990; *Red Cap,* 1991; *Jericho's Journey,* 1993; *Mr. Lincoln's Drummer,* 1995; *Caleb's Choice,* 1996; *The Drummer Boy of Vicksburg,* 1997.

BIBLIOGRAPHY: *Contemporary Authors Online,* 2003.

MIMI O'MALLEY

WITCHES AND WIZARDS AND DRAGONS, OH MY! GOOD THINGS COME IN THREES: FANTASY SERIES TO ENJOY AFTER YOU HAVE INDULGED YOURSELF IN HARRY POTTER AND THE LORD OF THE RINGS

After reading HARRY POTTER (all four books) and *The Lord of the Rings* (four if you count *The Hobbit*), most of us probably indulged ourselves by heading for the theatre to see the Harry Potter and Lord of the Rings MOVIES. We've gotten our Harry Potter and *Lord of the Rings* fix—for the time being. But now what? Of course, we can always reread—one of life's guilty pleasures. Rediscover old friends, immerse ourselves in familiar settings and scenarios, revisit old haunts, and experience the thrills of ADVENTURE and discovery—once removed. That's the joy of rereading. We've been here before, but it feels so good to be back again.

However, steeped in FANTASY as you may be, are you nevertheless in the mood for something new? Want to try one of the incredible fantasy trilogies written expressly for young readers? I know that the statement "The Golden Age of SCIENCE FICTION is twelve" applies equally well to fantasy; many fans of fantasy as well as science fiction discover the joys of reading these genres around the age of twelve. That's when they frequently begin reading works by adult authors, like the long-lasting, immensely popular Xanth SERIES by Piers ANTHONY, the Valdemar novels with their mind-reading, horselike companions by the prolific Mercedes LACKEY, those magnificent dragons in the Pern opus by Anne MCCAFFREY, the Wheel of Time cycle by Robert JORDAN (that goes on and on and is still nowhere near completion, much to the intense delight of his many fans), and the many hilarious visits to Discworld that Terry PRATCHETT has provided us.

In addition to the incredibly rich offerings available today in the adult fantasy market, there is a fantasy phenomenon taking place in the world of children and YA books. No doubt fueled by the explosive popularity of Harry Potter, more and more fantasies are being written or reprinted or added to by authors who are writing specifically for young readers. In the past year alone, Diane Duane has added new volumes to her So You Want to Be a Wizard series, and Meredith Ann PIERCE, author of the incredible Darkangel trilogy has finally returned to the fantasy fold with the remarkable *Treasure at the Heart of the Tanglewood.* I have also learned that plans are underway to reissue *The Spellkey Trilogy,* and that Ann Downer plans to add a fourth entry to that series. Good news, indeed! And I'm sure we've all heard the incredible good news that Philip PULLMAN has decided that he has not finished with the world of The Golden Compass. He still has more to add to the adventures of Lyra and Will. I know he writes slowly and carefully and exquisitely. So I know it will take him quite some time to finish the fourth in this extraordinary series. But I can't help it. I still can hardly wait!

So what to do to pass the time until we can expect more Harry? I have a suggestion. Why not try some of the other fantasy trilogies that are out there and popular with TEENS (and adults) today. It was easy to come up with a list of my favorite fantasy trilogies. The hard part was deciding what order to put them in. Should I go by subject matter, by recommended age level, by thematic complexity? Well, I'm a LIBRAR-IAN. So why not in alphabetical order—by author. If you are an adult, please don't stop reading now, thinking there won't be anything on this list you will enjoy. I promise you. I'm an adult. I've read and enjoyed these. There are some really wonderful, imaginative works that are being turned out today for fantasy readers—young or old. On the other hand, if you are a younger reader, look through the list and see which ones you've already read. Hopefully, not all of them, but you never know. If you find something new, dive right in. You'll find wizards, witches, shapeshifters, dragons, good and evil witchcraft, Arthurian sagas, and, I sincerely hope, lots and lots of fun!

So let's begin with a new Arthurian saga that has attracted many readers and gotten a lot of critical attention. Kevin Crossley-Holland is a British author who has taken a most unusual approach in his retelling of the adventures of King Arthur. His protagonist is a young boy, Arthur de Caldicot, who lives on the border between England and Wales in 1199. In *The Seeing Stone,* Arthur longs more than anything else to become a squire. He's worried, however, because his father has him studying his letters with the local priest. He doesn't want to become a scribe or priest, but he just can't seem to make his father understand. Arthur also has a friend and protector, the mysterious Merlin, who visits him periodically. On one visit, Merlin gives Arthur a shining black stone, a piece of obsidian, and tells the boy to keep it safely hidden away, only looking into it when he is alone. What Arthur sees when he does look into this "seeing stone" is his namesake, King Arthur, as a young boy. The more he learns about King Arthur, the more he begins to wonder about the similarities between their lives, especially when he finally recognizes the Hooded Man who advises and instructs King Arthur as his own Merlin. And you get all this in one hundred very brief chapters—lots of vivid scenes of what life in the Middle Ages was really like. One other thing to keep in mind while reading *The Seeing Stone:* it was on the shortlist for the Whitbread Award, won a Smarties Prize Bronze Medal, and has been nominated for the 2002 Los Angeles Young Adult Book Prize, the first year that a work by a British author has been among the finalists for this prestigious award.

Book 2 of his Arthur trilogy, *At the Crossing Places* is even longer—101 brief chapters, vignettes of the life of the now fourteen-year-old Arthur de Caldicot. At the end of *The Seeing Stone,* Arthur got his wish and became a squire. When Lord Stephen came to hold court at his father's castle, he was impressed by Arthur's courage, in particular by how the young boy spoke up at the trial of a local man accused of theft. Shortly afterward, Arthur was invited to come to Holt Castle and train as Lord Stephen's squire. His eventual goal is to go to Jerusalem and the Crusades. As he concentrates on his training, Arthur still consults his "seeing stone," continuing to follow the adventures of his namesake as he prepares to follow his lord into battle. His adventures when he does go on a later crusade will have to wait for book 3, which hopefully will be available in the very near future.

From Arthur, let's visit another medieval-type world, a world of kings and knights and battles. This world has something Arthur didn't face—dragons. But this is not a world in which humans live in fear of dragons. In the spin that Susan FLETCHER has given her trilogy, it is a world in which dragons live in fear of humans. It all started with *Dragon's Milk,* published in 1989. Young Kaeldra accidentally discovers that she has the ability to communicate with dragons the night there is a birthing—the first such in a hundred years. The ancient ones (dragons) left the land of men ages ago, but according to rumor, they left something important behind—clutches of eggs. The rumors must be true, because for the first time in what seems like forever, there is a hatching being guarded by a dragon mother. Then Kaeldra's younger sister comes down with a case of the dreaded vermilion fever. The only cure for it is dragon's milk. So Granmyr sends Kaeldra to find the dragon's cave. She does so, discovers she can communicate with the dragon, and then strikes a bargain. For enough dragon's milk to cure her sister, Kaeldra will babysit for the young dragons. And so she meets and falls in love with three wonderful babies: Embyr, Pyro, and Synge, who behave just like mischievous puppies and whose favorite word is "hungry." Everything is fine until a dragonslayer appears and kills the mother dragon on one of her sheep raids. Now Kaeldra is left with three baby draclings to guard and protect. Which won't be easy because most people want to kill dragons, not save them. I loved this book and kept hoping there would be more about these characters. Dragon lore abounds in a fast-paced, diverting page-turner—a fantasy with a heart!

In 1993 Susan Fletcher published another dragon book: *Flight of the Dragon Kyn.* I thought it would be a sequel to *Dragon's Milk,* but it's not. Instead, it's more of a prequel, set in the same northern, snow-covered world of the previous novel and explaining how dragons came to the hidden valley. Kara, fifteen, is called to the court of King Orrik. When she was a child of four, she contracted vermilion fever and was left near a dragon's lair to die. But she didn't die. Instead, the dragon mother nursed the young child back to health and then sent her home, with no memory of what had happened during her absence. King Orrik wants to wed Princess Signy and provide his kingdom with a much-needed heir. But she will not accept his offer of marriage until he has slain the dragons who killed her brother. That's where Kara comes in. Ever since her stay with the mother dragon, she has had the ability to call down birds from the sky. Legend has it that those who can call down birds can also call down dragons. Kara enjoys her stay at court until the dragon hunt begins. When she finally does call a dragon and it is slaughtered, she "remembers" it as the one who mothered her and saved her life so long ago. Afterward, she tries desperately to come up with a plan to save the remaining dragons, in spite of the King's command to the contrary. Once again there's a lot of action and a lot of dragon lore in a fantasy that covers the gamut from intrigue to rebellion to romance.

Three years later, in 1996, the third volume in Fletcher's dragon trilogy appeared, *The Sign of the Dove.* This is a sequel to *Dragon's Milk,* set once again in a world where only a few humans are willing to fight to save the lives of dragons. The sign of the dove is how these rebels identify each other. It's not an easy task because the Kargs want the dragons dead, especially after their deposed queen has offered incalculable wealth for dragon hearts, which are supposed to make warriors impervious to steel. Even some Elythians are willing to join the hunt, which unfortunately includes Kaeldra's brother-in-law. It is seven years since Kaeldra saved a clutch of dracling babies. The remaining dragons have all disappeared, but there is still a protector up north waiting for the final eggs to hatch so that she can lead the babies across the sea to a safe haven. When word arrives that the next-to-last dragon mother has been slain, a gal-

lant young harper and a girl with green dragon eyes join the quest to save the baby draclings and take them north to safety. More struggles to save the dragons, more struggles with these adorable (if rather sharp-toothed creatures), more fights, healing, fast-paced adventure, and fun. I was not the least bit disappointed with any of the books in this trilogy, taken individually or all together.

How about something a little darker? All right—how about something considerably darker? Then you're ready for another British import, the Deptford Mice trilogy by Robin JARVIS. I'm a longtime *Watership Down* fan, and I'm always looking for animal fantasies along those lines. I've read about deer, the Herla of *Fire-Bringer* by David CLEMENT-DAVIES, and about wolves in his newest animal fantasy, *The Sight.* I've read about ants in Robin Hawdon's incredible *A Rustle in the Grass.* I've read about the adventures of a young silverwing bat in Kenneth OPPEL's remarkable *Silverwing* and followed him as he seeks to rescue his father in the sequel, *Sunwing.* And I'm as excited as my TEEN readers when the prolific Brian JACQUES produces a new Redwall novel. I love those mice and all their animal friends (and enemies). So I was ready, willing, and able to tackle a new animal fantasy. I must admit, I didn't expect it to be quite so dark. On the other hand, look at the cover. Why wouldn't it be as dark as it is? The books in this SE-RIES might be dark, with a truly frightening villain, but they also riveting page-turners. I wound up reading them in one sitting. (By the way, that's the other advantage to these trilogies written for a younger audience. Most of them are not only fast-paced, but considerably streamlined, especially when compared to some of the hefty tomes being produced for the adult market. They're also so engaging that it's difficult to stop reading them. But I digress!)

The Dark Portal grabs you from the very beginning. The mice who live in Deptford have been warned to beware the grill and its malevolent influence. Behind it lies the sewers and the kingdom of the rats and the Dark Portal, entrance to the lair of their god Jupiter. But no matter how careful the mice are, they can't escape the evil call that comes to them every once in a while. Emanating from the Dark Portal, it calls them through the grill to their destruction. That's what happened to Albert Brown, whose daughter, Audrey, refuses to believe that her father is dead and goes into the sewers looking for him. Her only protection is a brand new Anti-Cat Charm, lucky for her. When she disappears, her friends come looking for her and wind up in the middle of a bloody, gruesome battle against seemingly impossible odds. In the end, the mice discover who and what Jupiter is. The question is, will they live to tell the tale?

The Crystal Prison, book two of The Deptford Mice Trilogy, continues the adventures of Audrey and her friends. In this novel, the power-hungry rats and the mystical bats that play such an important role in book one take a backseat to nature-loving mice. The ruler of the squirrels gives Audrey a special mission. The mouse-maiden is to accompany the young fieldmouse Twit back to his home, taking the fortune-teller rat, Madame Akkikuyu, with them. Madame survived the final battle against the evil Jupiter, but the elderly rat's memory is now as patchy as her fur. Even though the Starwife hasn't seen evil in the heart of this rat, she still doesn't trust her. And since their former foe thinks she is now friends with Audrey, the logical conclusion is to have Audrey take her far, far away. Audrey's brother insists on going as well, to see that they all arrive safely. At journey's end, Audrey and her companions discover that Madame Akkikuyu did not have any evil in her heart; it was in a tattooed face on her ear. The voice that comes from this tattoo leads to acts of murder, accusations of witchcraft against Audrey, and the return of Jupiter—just in time for book three, *The Final Reckoning.* It's back to London and a final showdown that involves lots of action, lots of gore, the DEATHS of friends and allies, the theft of the very stars from the sky, and a final stouthearted stand against one of the most villainous villains it has been my pleasure to encounter—thankfully, vicariously.

Time for a change of pace, and I have just the trilogy to recommend. Have you encountered The Wind on Fire Trilogy yet? If not, you're in for a real treat. *The Wind Singer,* Book One in The Wind on Fire Trilogy, is an example of a perfect world. At least, that's what the people in charge think. In fact, they are the only ones who think it is a perfect society, the members of the ruling class who enjoy all its amenities. Much as in today's test-driven society, wealth, status, and advancement depend on the individual's ability to perform well on standardized tests. But in this world, the entire FAMILY has to take the tests. The city of Amaranth has become a rigid, caste-bound society that is defined by these tests. Even the colors its citi-

zens are allowed to wear and the neighborhoods they live in depend on the outcome of these tests. Kestrel and her twin brother Bowman are different from everyone else. Their parents are individualists who think for themselves and are not impressed by the concept of taking tests to improve their station in life. Kestrel takes it one step further and rebels against the status quo. This leads to a secret meeting with the imprisoned emperor and a quest. Kestrel and Bowman are to leave the city and look for the missing key to the wind singer. If their quest is successful and the wind singer sings again after generations of silence, the stranglehold of the rigid caste system that has taken control of Amaranth will finally be broken. That's a lot of responsibility to put on the shoulders of two young children, but Kestrel and Bowman are strong and independent and more than capable of successfully completing such a mission—if they don't die trying.

Well, they do not die and they do succeed. In fact, they live to fight another day, as you'll find out when you read *The Slaves of the Mastery,* book two in The Wind on Fire Trilogy. (Talk about starting with a bang.) In the opening pages, the city of Amaranth is destroyed by the soldiers of The Mastery. Kestrel alone escapes being marched off to slavery. From her perch high on the smoking ruin of the wind singer, she watches as the Mastery's handsome leader, Marius Semeon Ortiz, destroys her home and marches the unresisting survivors off. Kestrel vows revenge, but then collapses among the fallen and is picked up by the forces of the Sovereignty of Gang. They hope for a truce with The Mastery by offering Princess Johdila in marriage to the ruler's son. So now Kestrel is on her way to The Mastery as the companion of Princess Johdila, with revenge never far from her mind. Meanwhile, Bowman has risen to a similar position, that of companion to the prospective groom, the leader Ortiz who destroyed Amaranth. Escape seems impossible because The Mastery punishes any act of disobedience by burning the friends and relatives of the rebels—alive. But then a strange being visits Bowman and gives him a message. He is the child of the prophet, the one sent to destroy and to rule. Only by accepting this role foretold for him can he save his sister's life and lead his people out of imprisonment. Their journey continues in *Firesong,* the third and final volume in the trilogy. What will happen next to the twins and their people?

Moving right along, let's talk about one of my favorite fantasy trilogies written for young people in many years. Garth NIX is an AUSTRALIAN author who has more or less swept the YA fantasy arena by storm with his fascinating account of the adventures of the daughter of a necromancer. Her name is Sabriel, and her adventures unsurprisingly begin in a novel of the same name, *Sabriel.* Sabriel's mother died giving birth, and the baby's infant spirit was already at the first Gate of Death when she was brought back to the land of the living by the Abhorsen. He's the necromancer, the one who can lay the dead to rest or bind them to his will. Now the Abhorsen has a daughter to follow in his footsteps. He sends her out of the old country to a boarding school where she can learn how to use her magical abilities in safety. He monitors her progress and visits her when he can. But then he fails to come to her graduation. Instead, a visitation appears, bearing her father's sword and the seven bells essential to his craft, the ones he uses for binding the dead. That's when she realizes that her father is in danger. If she wants to save him, she must cross over into the old country and begin practicing necromancy herself for the very first time.

In the sequel, *Lirael: Daughter of the Clayr,* Sabriel is the Abhorsen, practicing necromancy to protect her kingdom. She is married to King Touchstone, the young man she rescued in her quest to save her father. And she is the mother of two children. Her daughter is destined to follow in her father's footsteps and be the next ruler. Her son, Prince Sameth, is already in training to be the next Abhorsen. But his confidence is shattered in an encounter with a deadly enemy, making the young prince doubt whether he will ever have the skill to serve as the Abhorsen. In the meantime, Lirael, a daughter of the Clayr, has problems of her own. At fourteen she is much too old to continue wearing the blue tunic of a child. But since she still hasn't received the Clayr Gift of Sight, she is not entitled to wear the white tunic of an adult. She is pretty much in despair when she is given another option. A job opens up for her in the library. During the next four years she works her way up from the yellow tunic of a third assistant librarian to the red of a second. She also discovers that while she is still denied the Gift of Sight, she has other gifts that are even more powerful. As she explores the bowels of the library and is attacked by creatures of the dark, she fends them off with magic and a sword. (I ask

you—how can you not love a book about a sword-wielding librarian?) Lirael discovers that she can also combine Charter and Free magic to create an elemental creature, the Disreputable Dog, who helps her in her battles and in finding *The Book of Remembrance and Forgetting.* Now the Clayr have a Rememberer again, for the first time in years, and Prince Sameth has an ally to help him in his struggles against the forces of evil.

When you get to the end of *Lirael,* you will discover it is a cliffhanger. There's a reason for this. Garth Nix explained at the Young Adult Library Services Association SCIENCE FICTION and Fantasy Preconference in San Francisco in the summer of 2001 that he had not written a trilogy. He wrote *Sabriel,* and then he wrote a one-volume sequel, *Lirael.* But that book was so thick that his publisher insisted he cut it in half. So he did, literally. We had to wait over a year for the other half of *Lirael* to be published. Fantasy fans can rejoice in *Abhorsen.* At last we will discover what happens to Lirael and Prince Sameth in their battle against the evil threatening their kingdom. Stay tuned!

It's hard to find something new to follow the stellar fantasies produced by Garth Nix. So how about something old instead? I am delighted to announce that the Darkangel trilogy by Meredith Ann PIERCE is back!!! This trilogy has never been out of favor with my fantasy fans, and I lived in fear that one of the out-of-print volumes would fall apart. They didn't, and now I can relax. A PAPERBACK edition is available of all three. The adventures of Aeriel, the young slave girl who risks her life to confront a vampire, are readily available again. If this is your first encounter with this fascinating trilogy, you are in for a rare treat.

The Darkangel is the first volume of the trilogy. That's where we first meet Aeriel, a young slave girl who has to follow her beautiful mistress, Eoduin, up the mountain to gather hornbloom nectar for a wedding. Her mistress insists on going up the mountain, in spite of her old nurse's warning to beware the Darkangel, a vampire who steals maidens and drinks their souls. Who could believe such a story? But Eoduin's disbelief turns to terror when the Darkangel himself comes for her. Aeriel runs to a nearby village for help, but no one dares challenge the vampire. So she sets out alone up the mountain after the Darkangel. If she is too late to save her mistress, she can at least avenge her. But when she comes face to face with the Darkangel, Aeriel has the same helpless reaction to him that her mistress had. She too is swept away, but not to become his bride. She is far too ugly for that. Besides, he only takes one bride a year, and that honor (and fate) has already been bestowed upon her mistress. As with his other brides, he drank Eoduin's blood, ate her heart, and now wears her soul in a special necklace. Aeriel's fate is far different. She is to be a servant in his castle, caring for the thirteen "wraiths" who live there, all that is left of his brides. She also tends the garden and dares the vampire's wrath to feed his starving gargoyles. Like any woman who spends time with the Darkangel, she falls under the spell of his beauty. But Aeriel does more than just bask in his presence. She tells him stories, including the one about the king's son who was stolen by the Water Witch. This story gives the vampire nightmares. To get them to stop, he decides to kill Aeriel. She manages to escape and goes looking for the starhorse with the blade adamant that she can plunge into the Darkangel's breast. When her quest is successful and she returns to the castle, things have changed. She has grown and filled out and is much prettier than before, so pretty that the Darkangel selects her to be his fourteenth and final bride.

In the second volume of Aeriel's adventures, *A Gathering of Gargoyles,* Aeriel is indeed the bride of the Darkangel, but unlike his previous thirteen brides, she's still alive. She and Irrylath (the Darkangel) have left his castle and made it safely to the home of his mother, but he is still very much under the spell of the White Witch. To help her husband and protect the kingdom from the White Witch, Aeriel must go on a quest and fulfill a prophecy. She has to find the vanished wardens of the land and bring them back to serve as steeds for Irrylath's six brothers, who will need them in their battle against the White Witch. Along the way, she is joined by various companions, including the six gargoyles she freed when Irrylath was still the seventh Darkangel. They all help her on her quest, which is fortunate because she is threatened by bandits, other Darkangels, and anything else the White Witch can think of to throw in her way. More unrequited love for a soul in torment, but at least there is the beginning of hope that her love may win redemption for Irrylath after all.

The Pearl of the Soul of the World is the final installment of the adventures of Aeriel. In it, things are looking up for Aeriel and her world—at least at first.

Evil is on the run, the lovers are finally united, a bright future appears to be in store for the entire world, mysteries are revealed, and the White Witch is destroyed. General rejoicing for all concerned—right? Wrong! Because Aeriel has to make a choice. She can have her one true love or save her world—one or the other, not both! The battle is over, the wardens are ready to set about rebuilding their devastated lands, but Aeriel's work has only just begun should she choose to accept this mission and save the world. This beautifully written fantasy series is a favorite of teen girls, who rarely get all the way to the end with a dry eye.

Now that we're in the P's, it's time to consider one of the most remarkable fantasy trilogies to come along—ever. And the fact that it was specifically written for young people just makes it that much more remarkable. By now I imagine that just about everyone has heard the news that Philip PULLMAN accomplished the previously unheard-of feat of winning the Whitbread Award for *The Amber Spyglass.* This is not just the children's award. There are five Whitbread Awards given each year: adult fiction, first novel, POETRY, memoir, and children's work. The five winners are then stacked against each other and the overall Whitbread winner selected. For the first time ever a work for young people won the top award. All three volumes of this beautifully written work comprise an opus of significant literary quality. All three are extraordinarily compelling in their depiction of a world very much like ours, only different. A world in which babies are born bonded with shape-changing daemon companions. These daemons can take any shape until the child reaches puberty. That's when the daemon selects a permanent shape. But the two remain bonded for life. If for any reason the bond is broken, the connection severed, they both die. This is a world where mysterious dust particles or dark materials have appeared in the frozen north. Lyra, who lives at Jordan College and roams the nearby town at will, goes off to search for her missing father, Lord Asriel, after he disappears on a quest to investigate this mysterious dust. Children are disappearing from town as well, including a close friend. So Lyra sets off, hoping to rescue them as well as to find her father, not realizing that the opening battle in a war is about to begin. On her quest she takes the Golden Compass her father gave her before he disappeared, explaining to his daughter that it would tell her the truth, once she discovers how to use it. On her side are witches, an explorer, and an armor-wearing polar bear (my favorite character). Rallied against her are scientists conducting experiments on the missing children, trying to sever their bonds with their daemon companions while keeping them alive. Even her own mother enters the fray, against Lyra.

In book two, *The Subtle Knife*, Lyra meets Will, a boy from earth. His father disappeared years ago. Will's home was invaded by strangers looking for letters from his missing father. Will fought them off and then escaped through a gateway to an alternative world. This is a truly frightening world in which adults have fallen prey to specters. But Will meets a girl there, a fighter accompanied by a daemon companion. He and Lyra become friends. He is looking for his missing father. Lyra's Golden Compass tells her to help him in his quest, but then it is stolen. After a life and death struggle that results in the loss of two fingers, Will becomes the bearer of the Subtle Knife. The two are separated at the end of the novel, but not for long.

Lyra and Will complete their mission in *The Amber Spyglass* as the author brings his audacious revision of *Paradise Lost* to a conclusion that is both serene and devastating. We discover who captured Lyra at the end of *The Subtle Knife*. We learn that Will still has this blade that can cut between worlds and make it possible to travel back and forth at will. Will is joined by two tiny winged companions who are determined to escort him to Lord Asriel's mountain redoubt. But Will has a different goal. He is determined to rescue Lyra and return her Golden Compass to her. The armor-wearing polar bear is back, as is Dr. Mary Malone from the second volume. In fact, she is the one who invents the Amber Spyglass during her stay among the elephantlike mulefa. That's how she makes the horrifying discovery that dust is disappearing through the cuts made by the Subtle Knife, leaving death in its wake. Only Lyra and Will can stop it, but first there's the Church to avoid, since it's the Church that wants Lyra dead. Then there's the final battle against evil, an Armageddon involving polar bears, fallen angels, Lyra's mother and father, representatives of the Church, you name it. Will the world survive? Not without a supreme sacrifice (of course—there's always a sacrifice!) So moving, so incredibly well-written, so suspenseful, so hard to put down, and so very, very sad at the end. And I am absolutely delighted that the author has decided to revisit this world and add one more volume to the adventures of this resourceful young girl and her faithful friends and companions.

After you come down from the literary heights of the Pullman trilogy, you will probably be in the mood for something much lighter. How about another trip to an alternate world, featuring a young girl who does not have a shape-shifting companion. Instead, she does the shapeshifting herself. Sound intriguing? Then you're ready for Sherwood SMITH's Wren trilogy, beginning with *Wren to the Rescue*. Wren is a young orphan who discovers that her best friend is not what she appears to be. Instead of an orphan like Wren, Tess is a princess who has been in hiding from evil King Andreus since she was five-years old. Her parents have finally decided that it is safe for her to come home, which she does, bringing Wren along as her companion. But as it turns out, she came home too soon after all. The very first morning she is kidnapped by a servant of King Andreus and whisked away to his fortress. Wren goes to the rescue, accompanied by Tyron, a young magician or wizard in training. Her other companion is Connor, the youngest and clumsiest of Tess's uncles. He's a flop at working magic but was born with the ability to talk to animals, which comes in handy during their quest when Wren is turned into a dog. The three have adventures galore—riding on giant bird creatures, fighting against the minions of evil King Andreus, crawling through dark tunnels. Eventually they are captured and thrown into Andreus's dungeons, but not for long. The fantasy quest itself is quite good, including as it does elements of MYSTERY pertaining to Wren's birth and parentage. But the real strength here is the interaction of these three likeable young teens as they set out to rescue their friend.

Wren's adventures continue in *Wren's Quest*. Her mission this time is to find her own long-lost relatives. Prince Connor goes with her on her quest. He is not very skillful at magic, having failed to pass even the most basic test. But when they are pursued by enemies, he's the one who is able to call upon inner resources and control the weather in one case and work a little shape-changing magic in another. In the meantime, the kingdom is in danger—again. The princess is trying to find out what is going on at court. Tyron, the young journeymage, tries to help by taking the shape of a dog, with near-disastrous results—for him. But of course Wren and Connor arrive in time to help save the day. What fun!

In volume three, *Wren's War,* Wren and her friends are at WAR—and how! In the palace, the princess faces treachery and the murder of her mother and father by the minions of Andreus. She manages to escape and is soon rallying the people of her kingdom to stand with her against him. At the same time, she is trying to stay out of the clutches of her Uncle Fortian, who plans to keep her "safe" (i.e., a virtual prisoner) while he takes over the country as her regent. Fortunately, she is not alone. Helping her are Connor, Tyron, and of course Wren. Connor is loyal and faithful and level-headed enough to see that the country needs healing—the healing he can bring about if he can activate the land magic of his heritage. The talented journeymage Tyron becomes a master after he helps Connor remove the land-binding spell so that he can heal it. And Wren does a lot of shapeshifting, taking the form of a big mountain owl, courtesy of a magic necklace that a sorceress gave her. The struggle is won, finally, by the strong bonds of friendship and respect these four young people have for one another.

I really hated to say good-bye to Wren and her friends. But then I discovered another shapeshifting treat, the Switchers trilogy by Kate Thompson. More teens who can assume different animal shapes. More battles against the forces of evil. More fun! In the first book, *Switchers,* Kate, who lives in Dublin, discovers that she is different. She is a shapeshifter or switcher, able to switch back and forth between human and animal shapes. Which is why she likes to go for long walks and spend time all alone. She was seven or eight when she switched for the very first time. In the safety of her bedroom she suddenly became a bear. Ever since then she has understood that she doesn't have to be just Tess all the time. But now her family is moving and there's a strange boy at the bus stop who seems to want something from her. He has even told her, "I know about you," and "I know what you do." She soon discovers that Kevin is also a switcher. He prefers being a rat, of all things, and he wants Tess to help him—you guessed it—save the world! The weather has gone crazy. There are ice and snow storms building up in the arctic regions that are beginning to head south. An elderly woman, a former switcher herself, explains the problem to the children. The krools have been awakened from their icy slumber and are on the move, spreading ever-thicker ice

and snow storms to hide their progress. Kevin and Tess must hurry to confront them before it's too late because Kevin's fifteenth birthday is rapidly approaching. That's when switchers must decide which form they want to assume—permanently. Not only do the two teens battle the krools in the form of dragons, exhibiting amazing flights and pyrotechnic displays, but they also have to avoid fighter planes searching for the monsters who destroyed an expedition. Needless to say, the pilots are quite puzzled at the sudden appearance of dragons in the arctic skies! This clever fantasy features two strong teens who are so different that they are drawn to each other because of how different they are.

Tess and Kevin return in *Midnight's Choice,* except Kevin is no longer in human form. He has taken the form of a phoenix, the mythical golden bird that arises anew from its ashes. He had to assume this form or perish in his final battle against the krools in the previous novel. Only a phoenix could absorb a direct hit from flying napalm—and survive. After Tess switches to the shape of a phoenix and joins Kevin in the park, she has such a golden, rewarding, energizing time that she is seriously considering the phoenix for her permanent shape as well. But that's next year—when she turns fifteen. Then Kevin is captured and put in the zoo and the pet rat that belongs to Tess responds to a mysterious call and escapes. Tess takes the form of a rat herself and follows him. At journey's end she finds a teenage boy and his anemic mother. Martin is a vampire. To protect herself from his attack, Tess has to become one herself. But this puts her under his control and gives her a very different, much darker outlook on life. Tess remains under his control until Kevin escapes from the zoo and comes to rescue her. In the resulting battle, Tess becomes the catalyst for the transformation of both boys. Her desperate struggle to just be human again spills over and makes the boys human as well. Kevin is once again her red-headed best friend, while Martin the vampire finally has a chance at a normal life. When the excitement is over, Tess still has one last year to spend as a switcher. But then what?

In *Wild Blood,* the third in the Switchers trilogy, the big day is rapidly approaching. Tess will soon turn fifteen, and when she does, she will lose a very special part of her life. She will no longer be able to switch, to take the form of any animal, to fly with the birds or crawl through tunnels underground with the mice. What's worse—she must decide what shape she wants to assume when she turns fifteen—whether to remain human and lose the freedom of flight or scurrying around in dark tunnels, or to give up her humanity and enjoy the all-too-brief life of one of her animal forms. Then comes the final blow. She will not be able to stay at home with her family and friends as the final change approaches. Her parents are going on a trip, and she has to stay with cousins at their farm in Ireland, two boys who do a lot of the work on the farm, an asthmatic girl, a kind but rather retiring aunt, and a loud, abrasive, threatening uncle. Because he is determined to sell off some of the wild land, strange things start happening on the farm and in the woods around it. Kevin comes for a visit and plays Pied Piper to save some mice from poison. But then some children disappear and Kevin is blamed for leading them away as well. There's also a secret involving a mysterious uncle to be solved, and then Tess's birthday finally dawns. What's it to be? Will she choose to be an animal, opt to become a fairy, or will she decide to remain human after all? Inquiring minds want to know. Inquiring readers will not be disappointed—in this as well as in both of the previous entries in this extremely well-written series.

From shapeshifters back to dragons again—what could be more perfect? Especially when the dragons are those that inhabit the pages of Jane YOLEN's masterful Pit Dragon trilogy. For the past two decades teens (and adults) have been able to follow the adventures of young Jakkin Stewart as he works himself up from bondsman to dragon master. *Dragon's Blood* first introduces young Jakkin, who works on a "worm farm" where dragons are bred and raised to fight in the gaming pits. Jakkin has come up with a plan to gain his freedom. He will steal a dragon hatchling, raise it, train it to fight, and in that way leave his old life behind. He is taking a chance because there are severe penalties for anyone caught stealing a dragon. Also, not all dragons turn out to be first-class fighters, and not everyone who tries to train them has the gift for it, the ability to mind-bond with the "great worms," as the dragons are called. Jakkin manages to get his hatchling and in the process accidentally bonds with the baby dragon to a much higher degree than formerly seen between a dragon and his trainer. His former master even helps him with the training, as does a mysterious young girl, Akki, who knows far more than she should about the planet's ruling class

and the intricacies of the gaming system at the core of the planet's society. This fast-paced read has lots of action as well as a truly lovely relationship that develops between Jakkin and his magnificent dragon, Heart's Blood, with whom he communicates in glorious color.

The story of Jakkin and his dragon continues in the second volume of the Pit Dragon trilogy, *Heart's Blood.* When the novel opens, Jakkin is a pit master and Heart's Blood a successful contestant in the pits of Austar IV. She is also the mother of five hatchlings, baby dragons that Jakkin hopes to be able to imprint in the same way he did Heart's Blood. If he succeeds, he'll be able to communicate with them in the same special way that he does with their mother. His plans are changed when he gets drawn into the political turmoil on Austar IV. His beloved Akki has disappeared into a rebel group and an off-world politician urges Jakkin to infiltrate that group and find out what is going on, not only for Akki's sake but for the good of his world as well. When violence erupts, Jakkin and Akki are forced to flee for their lives, with only Heart's Blood standing between them and an angry mob that blames them for the destruction of the dragon pit. Jakkin has to face the death of Heart's Blood and the loss of everything he has worked so hard for, but in the end, as he and Akki flee for their lives, they still have each other and the baby hatchlings to help them survive.

In the final volume, *A Sending of Dragons,* Jakkin and Akki have managed to escape and are living in the wild with Heart's Blood's five young dragons. But Jakkin and Akki have changed. They can now communicate with each other mentally as well as with the baby dragons, a change caused by the time they spent hiding from their pursuers inside Heart's Blood's body. In addition to their enhanced communication skills, they can also more easily endure the planet's bitter cold. Fleeing from a helicopter, they enter the caverns of Auster and discover a deadly cult, a dangerous, bloody society of gray people and gray dragons who have developed a belief system based on metal and dragon's blood. It's touch-and-go for awhile, but in the end Jakkin and Akki manage to escape the deadly cult and start a whole new life together.

So does this give you a wide enough range of fantasy "threesomes" to explore while you wait for your next Harry Potter fix? Remember, these are trilogies.

I've deliberately stayed away from foursomes—and more. I could write another whole article on the fantasy treasures to be found in even longer series for young adults, and probably will—in the very near future. But for now, your mission, should you choose to accept it, is to give one or more of these trilogies a try. I've attempted to provide a broad spectrum of the fantastic and the fun, hoping that there will be something here to please just about everyone. Are you a King Arthur fan? Try David Crossley-Holland's very different take on the Arthurian legends. Are you into dragons in a big way? There are the adventures of dragons in peril in the works of Susan Fletcher and in the dragon pits on Austar IV, an intriguing world created by Jane Yolen that has attracted readers for the past twenty years. Do you prefer other types of animals? If you don't mind a little blood and gore, give the rats and mice that inhabit the world created by Robin JARVIS a try. Are you tired of rigidity and conformity? Want to experience the battles and turmoil of a society being forcibly recreated? Then take a look at what happens to the citizens of the city of Amaranth in the works of William NICHOLSON. If you like beautiful writing and are intrigued by the idea of a protagonist who has the dead on his (or her) side to help battle the forces of evil, then you should definitely give Garth Nix a lot of attention. On the other hand, if you are more intrigued by vampire adventures, turn your attention to the recently reissued works of Meredith Ann PIERCE—so gloriously dark, so incredibly well written, so difficult to put down once you have started reading them. Do you find literary fantasy to be more appealing? Want to spend time with a master of style, nuance, characterization, bold sweeping philosophical explorations—and have fun doing it? You don't have to go any further than Philip Pullman's fantasy masterpiece, acclaimed by critics and beloved by readers of all ages—a truly extraordinary accomplishment. Do you prefer more lighthearted fare? Then by all means let Sherwood Smith take you into Wren's world. You'll be glad you got to know these characters, who develop such strong bonds of friendship and respect as they struggle to survive—against treason and court intrigues. Or perhaps it is not the royal experience you're looking for. Want to know how a normal young girl manages to cope with the discovery that she's not so normal after all? Then spend some time in Kate Thompson's world, especially when her young protagonist has to decide how she will spend the rest of her life at age fifteen. Talk about the road not taken!

I hope you enjoy reading some of the titles in this article as much as I have enjoyed putting this list together for you. It's been a delightful trip down memory lane for me, a chance to call up old favorites and place them alongside newly discovered treasures in a forum where both will be appreciated (I hope) by a variety of readers. Here's a smorgasbord for your delectation, a pastiche for your pleasure, a fantasy sampler for the young—of all ages.

BONNIE L. KUNZEL

WITTLINGER, Ellen
Author, b. 21 October 1948, Belleville, Illinois

W.'s parents, Karl and Doris Wittlinger, lived in Belleville; her father was a grocer and her mother a grocer and secretary. W. earned a B.A. from Millikin University in 1970, where she studied art and sociology. She moved to Oregon where she worked on a small newspaper before being accepted into the Writers' Workshop at the University of Iowa; there she received an M.F.A. in 1973. W. then moved to Cambridge, Massachusetts, to pursue her writing career. She received fellowships from 1974 to 1976 to the Fine Arts Center, Provincetown, Massachusetts. W. married David Pritchard, an editor, in 1978. The couple has two children, Kate and Morgan. W. began her career as a children's LIBRARIAN at the Swampscott Public Library, where she worked from 1989 to 1992. She was also a writing instructor at Emerson College, Boston. W. currently lives in Swampscott, Massachusetts.

W. spent a great deal of growing-up time with her grandparents until she reached school age. She recalls that they were overly protective; she always felt that she was being watched. Around the time W. started school, her paternal grandmother died; because W. had spent so much time with her grandmother, she was "miserable and frightened" when she began school. As an only child, W. discovered books to fill her life while her parents worked. These books became her friends and provided adventure in her life. An article in *Authors and Artists* states that the public library became a refuge for W., a place where she could escape. Uncle Walter, her mother's younger brother, provided some of her most memorable times as a child. Uncle Walter traveled the country as a member of dance bands; when he visited W.'s family, he told stories about people he met during his travels or his work. In *Something about the Author,* W. says she thinks that her uncle's stories helped her to realize that there was more to the world than the small town of Belleville, Illinois. As she grew up, W. became more adjusted to school and made friends. In an article in *Authors and Artists,* W. said that when her parents opened their own market when she was about seven, she felt as if this gave her more of an "identity."

W. grew up wanting to be an artist and a writer. As a teenager she began writing POETRY. After her marriage, W. and her husband moved to Boston where in 1979 she published a book of poetry, *Breakers.* She also wrote two plays for adults, *One Civilized Person* (1982) and *Coffee* (1985), but found that it was very difficult to get plays produced.

When the couple's children were born, W. became a full-time mother. Her husband was working as an editor for a publisher in Boston, and the couple moved to Swampscott, Massachusetts. W. had worked as a librarian during her student days at the University of Iowa and at the Tufts University library in Boston. When her son started school, W. took a part-time job as a children's librarian at the Swampscott Public Library. As she read and learned more about children's books and authors of children's books, W. decided that she wanted to try her hand at writing for children. Her first YA book, *Lombardo's Law,* the story of two mismatched teenagers with common interests who find they have even more in common once they get to know each other, was published in 1993. W. has been attributed with the ability to send a "message of reassurance to young teens who feel out of step with their peers" (*Authors and Artists*). With positive reviews for her first novel, W. gave up her job and began writing full time. Her second YA novel, *Noticing Paradise,* was published in 1995.

W. says, in *Something about the Author,* that she finds that she is interested in "kids who are on the fringes, the slight oddballs and lovable misfits who aren't quite comfortable in their own skins." They find that being different makes people around them uncomfortable. W. says "that people have more in common than these differences of gender or sexual orientation, or even race . . . than they would have you believe" (interview with Ellen W). Her books deal with social problems such as homelessness, DEATH, family abuse, dysfunctional FAMILY life, and murder, issues that directly affect TEENS. W. is an advocate of gay and lesbian characters in books. In an interview for the *Voice of Youth Advocates,* W. says that she feels that there is a misunderstanding of homosexuality among teens. By reading about homosexuality in books written for them, teens might not see the differences as quite so large in real life. W. puts both a male and female protagonist in her books, and they usually contain a reference to art in some form. Art "gives them a way to express themselves and feel good about who they are" (*VOYA*).

AWARDS: 1994 ALA Best Young Adult Novels list, ALA Best Reluctant Reader list for *Lombardo's Law*; 2000 Michael L. PRINTZ Honor Book, 2000 Best Books for Young Adults selection, Lambda Book Award winner; Quick Picks for Reluctant Readers for *Hard Love*; selected for Best of the Best Selections from 1995 to 2004; Junior Library Guild selections for *What's in a Name* and *Gracie's Girl*; 2001 ALA Best Book for Young Adults, Massachusetts Book Award for *What's in a Name*; 2002 ALA Best Books for Young Adults selection, Junior Library Guild Selection, Patterson Prize for Books for Young People for *Razzle*; 2004 ALA Best Books for Young Adults selection, for *Zigzag. The Long Night of Leo and Bree*: ALA Quick Picks for Reluctant Young Adult Readers, 2003; *Razzle*: ALA Popular Paperbacks, 2005; *Gracie's Girl*: Florida Sunshine State Young Reader Award Winners, 2003; Dorothy Canfield Fisher Children's Book Award, 2002; *Hard Love*: ALA Popular Paperbacks, 2002.

FURTHER WORKS: *Lombardo's Law,* 1993; *Hard Love,* 1999; *What's In a Name?,* 2000; *Gracie's Girl,* 2000; *Razzle,* 2001; *The Long Night of Leo and Bree,* 2002; *Zigzag,* 2003; *Heart on My Sleeve,* 2004.

BIBLIOGRAPHY: *Authors and Artists,* 2001; Ellen W. homepage, http://www.ellenwittlinger.smartsriters.com; "Gracie's Girl" (book review). *School Library Journal,* November 2000; "How Art Can Save You: An Interview with Ellen W." *VOYA,* December 2003; "Interview with Young Adult Book Author Ellen W., http://www.cynthialeithchsmith.com/author-illEllen Wittlinger.htm; "The Long Night of Leo and Bree" (book review). *Horn Book,* March/April 2002; *Something about the Author,* 2002; "Zigzag" (book review). *School Library Journal,* August 2003.

N. NAOMI WILLIAMSON

WOLFF, Virginia Euwer
Author, b. 25 August 1937, Portland, Oregon

W. lives and writes in the rural woodlands of Oregon near Mt. Hood, in a place reminiscent of her childhood home in the same area. She has described the house in which she grew up as somewhat primitive but furnished with features that would become central to her life: "a log house—with bark left on inside and out . . . no electricity, a massive stone fireplace, a grand piano, and tons of books." Despite an idyllic location, W.'s childhood was not without its dark moments; her father died when she was five, and she struggled with his loss for many years, particularly through adolescence.

W. attributes her eventual emergence from this difficult time in part to playing the violin, an instrument she took up as a young child, which came to serve her as "a stabilizing thing." Books were also an important part of her childhood.

Despite the influence of the violin, W.'s adolescence was troubled. She describes herself as a slow and lackadaisical student, more interested in *MAD* magazine and J. D. SALINGER's angst-filled protagonists than her own education. Nonetheless, she was admitted to Smith College where she completed her bachelor's degree in English in 1959. Later W. would begin—though not complete—an M.F.A.

When she married after college, W. continued to live on the East Coast with her husband and two children. It was years later, following her divorce in 1976, that W. returned to Oregon.

Before becoming a full-time writer in her sixties, W. taught elementary and secondary school. Teaching remains part of her aim as a writer. W. told an interviewer, "We kid authors are not didacts. But I think we all have to step back and say we're trying to teach. I'm trying to teach that we learn only through pain, which is what I finally figured out in my life."

The problems of her own life, with their accompanying feelings of insecurity and weakness, play a role in the development of W.'s fictional TEENS. One of her characters, Allegra Shapiro (*The Mozart Season,* 1991), also plays violin, but W. sees her experiences coloring her character's development in other ways, too. *Probably Still Nick Swanson* (1988) for example, depicts a character with learning DISABILITIES challenged by school and YA society. The first two books in the Make Lemonade trilogy, *Make Lemonade* (1993) and *True Believer* (2001), feature characters that contend with poverty and endeavor to escape dangerous, downtrodden environments. A third book in this SERIES takes up the story of Jolly and her FAMILY. W. focuses attention on characters who share her

experience of not fitting in and not feeling able to succeed or to master concepts as quickly as one's peers.

While each of her young adult books has won critical recognition and several awards, the stories of Jolly and LaVaughn in the Make Lemonade trilogy have received the strongest praise. Reviewers enjoy the use of language in these books; in describing the beauty and power of the novels, they write about the "fierce originality that characterizes the best books" and "heart-stopping stream-of-consciousness."

W. acknowledges that these books involved risk taking on her part. "Fools rush in," she told an interviewer. "Everything I've written has been where angels fear to tread." The use of POETRY to create LaVaughn's unique and evocative perspective on adolescence concerned her as something that could be challenged as "presumptuous" and "arrogant." Yet W. persisted. She sometimes disclaims the effort as "daring," instead saying that the form resulted simply from persistence and an inability to tell stories in the ways other authors did.

A writer known for her exquisite use of language as well as her sensitive treatment of her characters, W. is quite attuned to language. In interviews, she describes how her adapted East Coast speech habits made her seem different and alien when she tried to re-assimilate into a Northwest community. W. also acknowledges the influence of CLASSIC literature on her writing; she reads literary greats to build "an accumulating sense of language" and "a layering of perception." "I won't settle for just any sentence," W. said in an interview, and "I don't bother to read people who do. I believe garbage in, garbage out. I can't contaminate my sense of language by reading sloppy, careless writers who don't know the difference." She wrote only one adult novel, *Rated PG* (1981), and remains most interested in writing for youth.

SELECT AWARDS: School Library Journal Best Book, 1988, 1993; ALA Best Books for Young Adults, 1988, for *Probably Still Nick Swanson,* 1992 for *Mozart Season,* 1994 for *Make Lemonade,* 2002 for *True Believer;* International Reading Association Children's Book Award, 1989; PEN-West Book Award, 1989; ALA Notable Books, 1991, 1999; ALA Best Books for Children, 1993; Jane Addams Book Award for Children's Books that Build Peace, 1999; National Book Award for Young People's Literature, 2001;

PRINTZ Honor, 2002; ALA Notable Children's Books, 2002, Best of the Best (1995 to 2004) for *True Believer; Probably Still Nick Swanson* was selected for Here We Go Again . . . 25 Years of Best Books (1967 to 1992).

BIBLIOGRAPHY: *Authors and Artists for Young Adults,* 1999; www.scholastic.com; "V. E. W. Interview," www.achuka.co.uk/features/features.htm, online; "V. E. W. Interview," *Publishers Weekly,* 2000; "V. E. W. Interview," *Booklist,* 1994; *Contemporary Authors Online,* 2003.

JENNIFER BUREK PIERCE

WOODSON, Jacqueline

Author, b. 12 February 1963, Columbus, Ohio

W. is highly recognized for her portrayal of characters that are often marginalized in society—young girls, ethnic minorities, homosexuals, and the poor. As she sensitively but realistically takes the reader into their various situations, W. writes from her own experiences of feeling powerless in her search for individuality and voice. W.'s stories are a celebration of differences. The issues at the heart of her writing reach within many ethnic communities; as a result, her work is a powerful addition to literature that is acclaimed as MULTICULTURAL. The genuineness of the characters and their situations invite readers to consider these issues through their own connections to the narrative rather than limiting the experience to the characters in question.

W. spent her childhood moving between South Carolina and New York City, and she states that as a young person she continuously felt like an "outsider." As an outsider, W. sensed an absence of democracy in her search for her own individuality; she challenged teachers and turned to writing POETRY and anti-American songs. W. received a B.A. degree in English from Howard University and worked as a children's drama therapist.

Early on she recognized her passion for writing and, with some encouragement from a teacher, began to write about topics that were not present in her childhood literature, such as communities of color, girls, and the complexities of friendships. Her empathy for girls with low self-esteem is evident in her early books, a trilogy about Margaret and Maizon. *Last Summer with Maizon* (1990), *Maizon at Blue Hill* (1992), and *Between Madison and Palmetto* (1993) are praised for the sensitive portrayal of two close friends and the community in which they search for self-esteem and identity. The first title focuses on

friendship as well as the loss of Margaret's father. *Blue Hill* reveals Maizon's unpleasant experiences with snobbery and racism at an exclusive all-white boarding school where she must deal with issues of self-esteem and identity. In *Between Madison and Palmetto,* the eighth-graders confront issues such as bulimia, integration, and the unavoidable testing of friendship.

W. is praised for the sensitivity with which she develops sexuality in her characters, including topics such as homosexuality and biracialism, as in *The Dear One* (1991), *The House You Pass on the Way* (1997), and *I Hadn't Meant to Tell You This* (1994). The third book is about the relationship between Marie, an affluent black girl, and Lena, a child from a poor white FAMILY. The reader learns that Marie's mother has abandoned her family and that Lena is being sexually molested. In a search for how she can help her friend, Marie decides she cannot do anything; Lena runs away and there is no simple resolution.

Autobiography of a Family Photo (1995) is W.'s first "adult novel," yet the voice in the book is a child's. A young girl is the narrator, and W. presents a vivid depiction of youth, specifically memories from her own. A series of intimate vignettes chronicle a young girl's experiences growing up, personal memories that W. shares openly with her readers. The novel is composed of brutally honest prose that beckons readers into W.'s world.

The resiliency of childhood is a theme in *Locomotion* (2003) in which two children are adopted into different homes following the death of their parents in a fire. The voice of eleven-years-old Lonnie is heard through poetry, the way his teacher has shown him to organize his thoughts and tell his story. W. compassionately lets readers experience his pain, acceptance, hope, and exceptional naive maturity in efforts to remain close to his sister. A similar theme of resiliency in adapting to a new home is found in *Our Gracie Aunt* (2002), the story of children who must leave their home to live with an aunt they hardly know. Their mother is hospitalized for substance-abuse rehabilitation. They thrive on the care and love Aunt Gracie bestows upon them, and the story ends with acceptance and hope that they will one day be reunited with their mother.

Even in her PICTURE BOOKS, W. presents situations that invite readers of all ages into personal contem-

VIVIAN VANDE

RUTH WHITE

RITA WILLIAMS-GARCIA

ELLEN WITTLINGER

JACQUELINE WOODSON

JANE YOLEN

TIM WYNNE-JONES

plation about the issues involved. *The Other Side* (2001) simplistically tells the story of two young girls, one black and one white, who become friends one summer despite the fence that separates their yards. The story questions why the "fences" exist anyway and who might remove them.

SELECT AWARDS: Coretta Scott King Honor Book: *From the Notebooks of Melanin Sun* and *I Hadn't Meant to Tell You This; Melanin Sun:* Jane Addams Peace Award, a Lambda Literary Award for Children's/Young Adult Fiction, American Library Association Best Book for Young Adults; Lambda Literary Award, *The House You Pass on the Way; Autobiography of a Family Photo: Kenyon Review* Award, Lambda Literary Award for Lesbian Fiction; *Locomotion*: ALA Notable Children's Books, 2004; SLJ Best Books for Children, 2003; Coretta Scott King Author Honor Books, 2004.

FURTHER WORKS: *Martin Luther King, Jr., and His Birthday,* 1990; *Book Chase,* 1994; *We Had a Picnic This Sunday Past,* 1997; *Lena,* 1998; *Sweet, Sweet Memory,* 2000; *Visiting Day,* 2002; *Hush,* 2002.

BIBLIOGRAPHY: Graham, P. W. *Speaking of Journals,* 1999, pp. 60–65; W. "A Sign of Having Been Here." *Horn Book,* November–December, 1995, pp. 711–15; W. "Who Can Tell My Story?" *Horn Book,* January–February, 1988, pp. 34–38; *Something about the Author,* vol. 94, 1998; *St. James Guide to Young Adult Writers,* 2nd ed., 1999.

JANELLE B. MATHIS

WORLD BOOK DAY ADULT LITERACY INITIATIVE

Since its launch in 1998, World Book Day has grown to be the biggest and most successful generic books campaign in the UK. Setting out to reverse a trend of declining children's books sales (these were pre–HARRY POTTER days), over the last seven years World Book Day has done much to encourage children to explore the joys of reading.

Every year, over 12 million World Book Day £1 book tokens are distributed through schools to all children in full-time education. They can exchange their tokens for a free £1 book, published specially for World Book Day, or get £1 off any other book of their choice. Well over a million of the £1 WBD children's books are printed, distributed, and sold.

The campaign is hugely successful. Thousands of book events take place in schools, bookshops, libraries, and arts centers across the country. Redemption

levels of the WBD book tokens are high and growing. Parents, teachers, and booksellers report hundreds of magical moments when children are given the opportunity to own and enjoy a book for the first time in their lives. But there remains a large part of the UK population that is, with one or two honorable exceptions, ignored by the British book industry.

Current statistics show that there are around 5 million adults in the UK who have limited literacy skills. They are effectively excluded from the pleasures that reading can bring—whether from a novel, a cook book, or a travel guide.

It's those people the publishers and bookseller supporters of World Book Day are turning to in 2006.

We plan to publish a series of books for new and reluctant adult readers, specially commissioned from high-profile authors, that will retail at a price lower than mass-market PAPERBACKS. The books will be both fiction and nonfiction with genuine mass-market appeal; best-selling novelist Ruth Rendell has already offered to contribute.

The government is supportive of the initiative and Arts Council England is funding the appointment of a project director to oversee the books' publication. The project director will be able to call on the professional expertise of agencies that work in the adult literacy field to ensure the books contain the appropriate levels of tone, readability, and, above all, quality.

The ability to read is a basic right of every citizen, and the recent drive for literacy in British schools must be mirrored by a drive for literacy in adults. Books for emergent readers need to be brought into the mainstream of the UK industry and, once launched, should be published regularly and well.

It is heartening to report that initial responses from publishers and booksellers have been overwhelmingly positive. We have a real opportunity in the UK to bring the pleasures and benefits of reading to a section of the British public previously ignored by the publishing industry.

BIBLIOGRAPHY: www.worldbookday.com

GAIL REBUCK

WREDE, Patricia Collins
Author, b. 27 March 1953, Chicago, Illinois

With the strong encouragement of her parents, W. started writing in the seventh grade and never really stopped, though she never expected it to be more than a hobby. She majored in biology at Carleton College in Minnesota and managed to avoid taking any English courses at all during her university years. After earning an M.B.A. from the University of Minnesota in 1977, W. worked for several years as a financial analyst and accountant, wrote in her spare time, and finished her first novel, *Shadow Magic,* in 1978. Early in 1980, W. formed a writer's group known as the Scribblies with fellow unpublished hopefuls Pamela Dean, Emma BULL, Will SHETTERLY, Steven Brust, and Nate Bucklin. In April of that year she sold her first novel. In 1985, W. quit her job shortly before her fifth book was published, concentrating on writing full time.

Beginning with that first novel, *Shadow Magic* (1982), the five books in the Lyra SERIES are loosely connected based on their shared setting, the fantastic world of Lyra, which features two moons and a TOLKIEN–like landscape. Shared by humans, fairies (called the Shee), and the Wyrd, forest-dwelling cat people, Lyra is also home to the Shadow-born, evil spirits that inhabit human bodies, and is the scene of violent territorial and spiritual disputes. In *Shadow Magic,* heroine Alethia finds that the FAIRY TALES she grew up with offer her more than just stories if she's willing to look more closely at her own magical abilities—as she tries to find allies to help keep her country from WAR. *Daughter of Witches* (1983) takes place in a different time period and in a different part of Lyra, but has a similar theme. Ranira, whose parents were burned as witches, is forced to come to terms with the power she has kept hidden when she meets a sorceress named Mist. One of W.'s few male protagonists is featured in *The Harp of Imach Thyssel* (1985), which concerns the quest for a magical harp and the man whose destiny it is to play it. Witches figure prominently again in *Caught in Crystal* (1987), which tells of the Sisterhood of Stars, a group of sorceresses who ask Kayl to rejoin them as they try to complete a dangerous quest. *The Raven Ring* (1994) continues the quest-based structure of the series in a tale of a magical ring that is lost and must be found.

W.'s other series, the Chronicles of the Enchanted Forest, began as a SHORT STORY, written for inclusion in an anthology. "The Improper Princess" was accepted, though editor Jane YOLEN, urged W. to expand it into a full novel; the result was *Dealing with Dragons* (1990). Playing with conventions and stereotypes, W. turns familiar fairy-tale motifs inside out

in this very humorous series, which begins when Princess Cimorene runs away from her stifling life at court and impending marriage to a handsome but boring prince to be the servant of the dragon Kazul. Though a number of well-meaning princes attempt to rescue her from Kazul, Cimorene stays and helps Kazul fight the evil wizards who wish to rule the dragon colony. *Searching for Dragons* (1991) continues Cimorene's story as she helps Mendanbar, young king of the Enchanted Forest, and again battles the evil wizards. Mendanbar is as unconventional a king as Cimorene is an unconventional princess and, in true fairy-tale style, the book ends with a wedding. The evil wizards attack the Enchanted Forest again in *Calling on Dragons* (1993), but this time, surprisingly, they succeed. The novel ends with the wizards taking over Mendanbar and Cimorene's castle and trapping Mendanbar in a dimensional warp. Cimorene has no choice but to wait for her infant son, the newborn prince to grow up and use the king's magic sword to free him and the castle, which is what happens in the final book in the series, *Talking to Dragons* (1993). Prince Daystar, finally grown, rescues his father and conquers the evil wizards for good. W.'s SHORT STORY collection *Book of Enchantments* (1996) contains a number of stories related to the Enchanted Forest, including "Utensile Strength," an especially funny tale where a wizard tries to create the ultimate weapon and ends up with the Frying Pan of Doom.

W. is also known for her romantic historical FANTASY, much of it set in an alternate Regency England where magic is part of everyday life. Written in a series of letters, *Sorcery and Cecelia; or, The Enchanted Chocolate Pot* (with Caroline Stevermer, 2003) is the tale of Katherine (Kate) and Cecelia (Cecy), friends forced to spend a season apart when Kate leaves the countryside for London. Kate is soon confronted by the possibly evil sorceress Lady Miranda, and Cecy becomes entangled with the possibly evil wizard Sir Hilary. Both girls become involved in the attempt to recover an enchanted chocolate pot belonging to the Marquis of Shofield. Set in a similar time, *Mairelon the Magician* (1991) tells a classic rags-to-riches story featuring Kim, a female pickpocket living on the streets of London. Disguised as a boy and taken on by a young magician as his apprentice, Kim is soon at the center of a race to collect a set of silver needed for an important spell, and finds along the way that she herself may have a talent for magic. Kim's magical training is explored in the sequel, *Magician's Ward* (1997), which finds her using her new-found talent to help Mairelon after his powers are stolen.

W.'s romantic and magical fantasies are soft and gentle rather than dark and gritty; they feature female characters who are resourceful and strong when required. Vivid characters with endearing personalities and individual quirks are her strength, even though she favors familiar fantasy "types" such as wizard, witch, princess, outlaw, and the thief with a heart of gold. W.'s trademarks are humor and light ROMANCE, stories where good and evil are easily discerned, and stories that, more often than not, end happily ever after.

AWARDS: 1984 Best Books for Young Adults Recommend Reading List, *Daughter of Witches;* 1985 Best Books for Young Adults Recommend Reading List, *The Seven Towers;* 1989 *Booklist* Editor's Choice, *Snow White and Rose Red; Dealing with Dragons:* 1991 Minnesota Book Award for Fantasy and SCIENCE FICTION, 1991 *School Library Journal* Best Book of the Year, 1994 YALSA Best of the Best list, and 1991 ALA Best Books for Young Adults; 1992 ALA BBYA, *Searching for Dragons;* 1993 ALA Notable Books for Young Adults, *Calling on Dragons*; *Dealing with Dragons*: 2 Best of the Best Lists: Here We Go Again . . . 25 Years of Best Books (Selections from 1967 to 1992) and 100 Best Books for Teens from 1966–2000; *Sorcery and Cecelia, or the Enchanted Chocolate Pot,* ALA Best Books for Young Adults, 2004.

FURTHER WORKS: *The Seven Towers,* 1984; *Snow White and Rose Red,* 1989; *Star Wars: Episode II, Attack of the Clones,* 2002; *The Grand Tour,* 2004.

BIBLIOGRAPHY: "Autobiography of Patricia C. W.," http://www.dendarii.co.uk/Wrede/; *Contemporary Authors Online,* 2003. Reproduced in Biography Resource Center, 2003, http://galenet.com/servlet/BioRC; "The Enchanted Chocolate Pot: A Page for Caroline Stevermer and Patricia C. W.," http://www.tc.umn.edu/~d-lena/Stevermer%20page.html; *St. James Guide to Fantasy Writers,* 1996; St. James Guide to Young Adult Writers, 2nd ed., 1999.

JULIE BARTEL

WYNNE-JONES, Tim

Author, b. 12 August 1948, Bromborough, England

One of CANADA's foremost authors for children and YAS, W. emigrated from England as a child. He earned a B.F.A. from the University of Waterloo in 1974 and an M.A. in visual art from York University in 1979 before beginning his career as a graphic designer in Toronto. Throughout the late 1970s, he taught visual art at the University of Waterloo and York University, in addition to co-founding a graphic design company, Solomon & Wynne-Jones.

Although noted for his work for children and young adults, W.'s writing career is wide, including the authorship of four novels for adults, numerous radio plays, lyrics for the television production *Fraggle Rock* (1983–87), and the children's opera *A Midwinter Night's Dream* (with Harry Somers, 1988). W. also edited *Boys' Own: An Anthology of Canadian Fiction for Young Readers* (2002), co-authored *Rosie Backstage* (1994) with his wife Amanda Lewis, illustrated a collection of POETRY, and worked as a children's book reviewer for the national newspaper the *Globe and Mail* from 1985 to 1988.

W.'s career as a writer was launched when he wrote *Odd's End* (1980), a novel for adults, and was awarded the Seal First Novel Award, worth $50,000. Since then, he has gone on to win numerous prestigious awards, including recognition for the entire body of his work when he received the Vicky Metcalf Award in 1997.

His first experience with children's literature took place when he and a group of sociology students from the University of Waterloo received a grant to examine racism and sexism in children's books. After investigating numerous children's books, W. thought he could write a better one, and wrote *Madelaine and Ermadello* (1977). He followed with the Zoom trilogy about an ADVENTURE-seeking cat, illustrated with gallery artist Ken Nutt's evocative black-and-white drawings. Beginning with *Zoom at Sea* (1983), the cat embarks on a mythic journey to a seascape that is magically contained in his friend Maria's house. The house becomes the site of more symbolic and mythic transformations as Zoom travels to the North Pole via Maria's attic in *Zoom Away* (1983), and to the basement ancient Egypt in *Zoom Upstream* (1993). The heroic-quest story pattern is common in W.'s PICTURE BOOKS, found even in the most simple storytelling. For example, the child protagonist of *I'll Make You Small* (illustrated by Maryann Kovalski, 1986) ventures to the house of his curmudgeonly neighbour and succeeds in softening the cranky man's heart. W.'s other picture books are just as varied and creative as his eclectic career would suggest.

W. has achieved noteworthy success as a writer of SHORT STORIES for adolescents. His first collection, *Some of the Kinder Planets* (1993), was met with considerable acclaim and captured the sense of wonder and emotional intensity that energizes W.'s work. Each story depicts a child in ordinary situations that become somehow extraordinary and sometimes supernatural, creating greater meaning for the character and reader alike. This particular book is perhaps W.'s most acknowledged work, earning three major awards. *The Book of Changes* (1994), another short-story collection, received less attention but was also very successful in exploring the transformations of its characters and the idea of thresholds, which would become important to the adolescent characters in his later novels for young adults.

In 1995, W. published *The Maestro*, the first of several novels that hold interest for TEENAGERS as well as older children. This novel, an adventure story of physical and emotional survival, was also very acclaimed and established W. as a writer for young adults. W.'s background in art and design is clearly influential in this novel that evokes many clear and lasting visual images for the reader. W.'s next young adult novel, *Stephen Fair* (1998), invites questions of identity that are specific to its title character as well as the broader and universal concerns of identity that arise during adolescence. *The Boy in the Burning House* (2000) is a dark MYSTERY demonstrating W.'s ability as a crime writer.

W.'s contributions to literature for children, young adults, and adults are varied, eclectic, and ambitious. Rich with images, W.'s stories are original and heartfelt, introducing believable characters in extraordinary circumstances.

AWARDS: 1979 Seal First Novel Award 1979 for *Odd's End;* 1983 Amelia Frances Howard-Gibbon Award, 1983 Municipal Chapter of Toronto IODE Book Award, 1984 Ruth Schwartz Children's Book Award, all for *Zoom at Sea;* 1987 ACTRA Award for Best Radio Drama for *St. Anthony's Man;* 1993 Governor General's Literary Award for Children's Literature for *Some of the Kinder Planets* and 1995 for *The Maestro;* 1994 Canadian Library Association Book of the Year for Children Award for *Some of the Kinder Planets* and 1998 for *Stephen Fair;* 1995 *Boston Globe–Horn Book* Award for Fiction for *Some of the Kinder Planets;* 1996 Canadian Library Association

Young Adult Canadian Book for *The Maestro;* 2002 Edgar Award from the MYSTERY Writers of America, ALA Popular Paperbacks, 2004, for *The Boy in the Burning House;* 1997 Vicky Metcalf Award for body of work.

FURTHER WORKS: *Mischief City* (illus. Victor Gad), 1986; *Architect of the Moon* (illus. Ian Wallace), 1988; *The Hour of the Frog* (illus. Catharine O'Neill), 1989; *Mouse in the Manger* (illus. Elaine Blier), 1993; *The Last Piece of Sky* (illus. Marie-Louise Gay), 1993; *On Tumbledown Hill* (illus. Dušan Petričić), 1998; *Lord of the Fries and Other Stories,* 1999; *Ned Mouse Breaks Away* (illus. Dušan Petričić), 2002.

BIBLIOGRAPHY: Evans, Gwyneth. "W., Tim(othy)." *Twentieth Century Children's Writers,* 1995; Jenkinson, Dave. "Tim W.—poet, playwright, song writer, teacher, critic and award winning author for children and young adults." *Emergency LIBRARIAN* 15, January/February 1988, pp. 56–62; Jones, Raymond E., and John C. Stott. *Canadian Children's Books: a critical guide to authors and illustrators,* 2000; *Something about the Author,* vol. 96, 1998; *Writing Stories, Making Pictures: biographies of 150 Canadian children's authors and illustrators,* 1994; Walker, Ulrike. "A Matter of Thresholds." *Canadian Children's Literature* 60, 1990, pp. 108–16.

KIRSTEN ANDERSEN

WYSS, Thelma Hatch

Author, b. 17 November 1934, Bancroft, Idaho

W.'s youth was spent on the FAMILY ranch with her parents A. Wilder Hatch and Agatha Pratt Van Orden Hatch. From there, W. went to college and graduated from Brigham Young University; later she earned an M.F.A. from Vermont College. She lives with husband, Lawrence Frederick Wyss, in Salt Lake City, Utah, and also has a son, David Lawrence Wyss, and two grandchildren.

Before becoming a published author, W. worked at *Glamour,* a fashion MAGAZINE, in New York City, and then taught English at the high-school level in Salt Lake City, Utah. W.'s first published work, *Star Girl,* appeared in 1967, and was followed by *Show Me Your Rocky Mountain!* fifteen years later in 1982. However, it was not until 1988, with the publication of *Here at the Scenic-Vu Motel,* and W. hit her full stride as an author.

Here at the Scenic-Vu Motel (1988) is about TEEN-AGERS who live too far from their school and must commute from the Scenic-Vu Motel. Jake and his group, which is composed of both males and females, stay at the motel while attending Pineville High School. Jake chronicles their experiences to fulfill a class assignment during his senior year. *A Stranger Here* (1993) was a Junior Literary Guild Selection. Jada, living in 1960, encounters Starr Freeman, a World War II ghost, who provides a change of company from her aunt and uncle. Over time, he also provides her with a different glimpse of who she is and who she has the potential to become. *Ten Miles from Winnemucca* (2002) follows Martin Miller on the road to Red Rock, Idaho, as he attempts to adjust to the changes wrought by his mother's new marriage. His frustrations about his new family were pushed too far when his obnoxious and wealthy new stepbrother violated his privacy after his mother left on a long European honeymoon. Martin's journey, which is both a physical and an emotional one, ultimately leads him back home. This work was also named a Junior Library Guild selection.

W. proves through her works for YAs that she has a deft ear for teen voices. This ear allows her to present quite different teens in diverse situations, using both humor and emotion to engage her readers in the lives of her characters. Her talent has drawn in the most reluctant readers who are compelled by W.'s characters and the decisions they make.

AWARDS: *Here at the Scenic-Vu Motel:* American Library Association Best Book for Young Adults, 1988 Recommended Book for Reluctant Young Adult Readers, Best of the Best Books for Young Adults; Selected for Here We Go Again . . . 25 Years of Best Books (1967–1992).

BIBLIOGRAPHY: www.amazon.com; www.novelst3 .epnet.com; "Thelma Hatch W." *Contemporary Authors Online,* 2003.

JEANNE MARIE RYAN

YA BOOKS IN THE UK

Young Adult literature—or TEEN ("teenage") literature, as it has been known in the UK until very recently—seems at first sight to date from the "second
golden age" of British children's books, beginning in
the 1950s. However, it can be argued that very many
books "for children" from around 1850 to 1900 were
shared by readers of all ages: the "empire-building"
colonialist books of G. A. Henty were read by boys
and men (and girls); the sensationalist ADVENTURES
by Robert Louis Stevenson like *Treasure Island*
(1883), and H. Rider Haggard's *King Solomon's
Mines* (1885) were not restricted in their readership
by age ranges (just as their 20th-century successors,
such as the Indiana Jones films have a wide audience).
The best-selling novels of Frances Hodgson BURNETT
were not, on their first publication, simple to classify.

Only with writers such as Edith Nesbit did a real
gap open up between children's books and adults'
books, and for the first fifty years of the twentieth
century, this distinction was maintained. The highly
influential Swallows and Amazons SERIES (1930–47)
by Arthur Ransome, for example, follows its characters well into their teens, but there is no mention of
any quasi-adult matters such as sexuality, complex relationships, or spiritual *angst*. How consciously or unconsciously protective this mode of writing was is
demonstrated by the imitation of Ransome written by
two teenage girls, Katherine Hull and Pamela Whit-
lock, *The Far Distant Oxus* (1937). This is a true forerunner of the teenage novel, with its authors, given the

mores of the period, occasionally dwelling directly on
sensuality.

The idea of a teenage novel only comes with a
concept of teenage, which emerged in the UK in the
1950s—but even then it was seriously questioned
whether there could be a market for such books. The
twelve-year-old reader was expected to move directly
on from Ransome or Enid Blyton to writers like Leslie Charteris (The Saint) or Ian Fleming (James
Bond), or, in the literary sphere, to Dickens or the
Brontës or George Orwell. Also, well into the 1960s,
childhood was seen as a time of innocence, to be protected, and it was only when this concept of childhood
was seriously eroded by television and methodical
commercial exploitation that the hybrid YOUNG
ADULT status could be written for.

YA books of the 1950s and 1960s sprang from a
period of cultural uncertainty: adults writers looked
back to a more stable prewar world, while their audience looked forward to an unstable future of major
social change. The same basic impulses that had led
the Religious Tract Society to produce the wholesome
Boys' Own Paper in 1879 (ironically, it closed in
1967)—adult fear of adolescent independence and
"premature" maturity—produced books that were
"safe"—that watered down reality, simplified consequences, and underestimated their audience. Some
early examples of "purpose-built" YA novels such as
Josephine Kamm's *Young Mother* (1965), or well-
meaning series such as The Bodley Head's Career
Novels for Girls, with titles such as *Pauline Becomes*

a Hairdresser (1958), had many of the solemnly educational characteristics of the evangelical novels of a century earlier.

Genuine YA books, those that readers grow with and through, rather than out of, came initially from writers such as K. M. PEYTON, who is distinguished for pioneering two of the major genres. Her Pennington trilogy, beginning with *Pennington's Seventeenth Summer* (1970), is essentially realist, following a rebellious antihero into young parenthood. At the other extreme, her Flambards sequence (1967–82) leans toward period ROMANCE; significantly, when it was adapted for television, it graduated to a prime-time slot.

The YA form also built on the strong tradition of British FANTASY, demonstrating that, far from being an escapist mode, fantasy engages with issues that can preoccupy adolescence. As series progressed, they tended to become deeper and darker; thus, the final books in series such as Mary Norton's *The Borrowers* (*The Borrowers Avenged* (1982)), and later books in Joan AIKEN's 19th-century series (for example, *Midnight is a Place,* 1974) move into the new category. Characteristic is Susan COOPER's *The Dark is Rising* sequence; the first book, *Over Sea, Under Stone* (1965) is in many ways a quintessential children's adventure, in which cosmic battles are made child-sized, while in the last, *The Silver on the Tree* (1977), the concerns have moved beyond the protected area of childhood. Like Ursula K. LE GUIN's Earthsea novels, Cooper's sequence is now marketed in the YA or even adult categories.

The form became commercially important with dozens of precisely targeted imprints—Scholastic Adlib, Penguin's Peacocks, Hodder Headline's Signature, and so on. The dominant influence has been from the U.S., with what became known as the "anorexic" novels, under the influence of Paul ZINDEL, Judy BLUME, and Robert CORMIER, and mass imports of Sweet Valley High and similar series. These have had their British imitations and adaptations, but there has also been a strong vein of serious mainstream work from writers such as John Rowe Townsend, James Watson, Robert WESTALL, Jan Mark, Nina Bawden, Bernard Ashley, and many distinguished others.

In many cases, such as Alan Garner's classics *The Owl Service* (1967), *Red Shift* (1973), and *The Stone Book Quartet* (1976–7), or Jill Paton Walsh's novels, such as *A Parcel of Patterns* (1983) or *Goldengrove* (1974), it is the pace and tone, the assumption that the audience is capable of reflectiveness and subtlety, that marks the books as YA. Perhaps the master of this form has been Aidan CHAMBERS, whose six-book sequence, beginning with *Breaktime* (1978), engages primarily with the minds of intensely articulate, intelligent, and reflective adolescents and only secondarily with the issues that preoccupy them.

The romance has flourished at the hands of writers like Michelle Magorian (for example, *A Little Love Song,* 1991), but the dominant branch of YA writing has been that which deals directly with the problems of growing up in an increasingly dysfunctional world. The most distinguished authors of these novels are Ann FINE, notably with the very black comedy *Madame Doubtfire* (1987) or the serious study of a disturbed child in *The Tulip Touch* (1996), and Gillian CROSS, whose *Wolf* (1990) is a postmodern view of the disintegration of society (the female hero's father is a terrorist). Through the 1990s, British YA books pushed at the boundaries of what was appropriate and, in doing so, reflected the shrinking of childhood itself. Melvin BURGESS's ultrarealism, notably *Junk* (1996), a story of adolescent drug-addiction that won the Carnegie Medal, marked the high, or low, point of this progression.

But the emergence of the HARRY POTTER phenomenon suggests that Burgess's ironically politically correct view of adolescence and the needs of adolescent readers were actually out of step with the culture. J. K. ROWLING's series, which gradually moves from children to YA, has unseated the conventional divisions between children's books, YA books, and adult books. Unashamedly regressive in terms of genre and gender, it takes us back to the 19th-century "shared" book. Similarly, Philip PULLMAN, after a series of YA semi-pastiches of Victorian thrillers (the Sally Lockhart books, beginning with *The Ruby in the Smoke* (1991)), produced a cross-audience triumph with the His Dark Materials trilogy (1995–99).

All this creative activity, which has extended to YA PICTURE BOOKS—such as Quentin Blake's *The Green Ship* (1998), or Raymond Brigg's *Fungus the Bogeyman* (1979)—has mirrored the limiting of childhood and the "children's book," just as the family film (the majority of Disney's output, for example) has aimed for a CROSSOVER audience. The presentation of the 2002 Carnegie Medal for the best British

779

children's book of the year to Terry PRATCHETT for *The Amazing Maurice and His Educated Rodents* sums up the trend. Pratchett has been at the top of the UK bestseller lists for many years with his Discworld books, which assume extensive intertextual knowledge in the audience.

And the future? If the book is to have a significant future, it is the YA book that is at the center of the battle. Thus far, the book has not taken on the implications of the IT revolution, although some, such as Malorie Blackman's *Hacker* (1993) or Caroline Plaisted's *e-love* (2001) acknowledges the new environment. The inertia in the publishing industry suggests that the YA novel has a secure future, even if the latest attempt, by the multinational Nestlé, to institute a prize for the teenage novel, has foundered on the opposition to Nestlé's baby-milk marketing policy by Pullman, Burgess, and others. The so-called teenage novel has always been controversial in the UK, and that seems set to continue.

PETER HUNT

YA CHOICES

Each year, thousands of YAs are afforded the chance to select their favorite recently published YA books to be included in the Y. annotated booklist from the International Reading Association. Approximately 4,500 students in grades 7 to 12 from different regions of the United States read and vote on their favorite books from a list of preselected titles. The thirty books that receive the most votes are placed on the final list, which is annotated. The annotated list is published annually in the November issue of the *Journal of Adolescent and Adult Literacy*. Offprints of the list are also available for purchase through the International Reading Association (www.reading.org).

Begun in 1987, the Y. program is one of three "choices" programs sponsored by the International Reading Association. Children's Choices focuses on those books deemed best by students in elementary schools in the United States. Teachers' Choices gives educators in the U.S. a chance to vote on those books that make good curricular companions. The Y. program grew from a desire to learn more about the needs and interests of TEEN readers. Encompassing students in grades seven through twelve, the Y. program seeks not only to place books in the hands of students but to ask those readers to evaluate the books as well.

The Y. project has three main goals. The primary goal of the project is to develop an annual annotated reading list of new books that will encourage young adults to read. Certainly asking students in middle and high schools across the country to select their favorite books ensures that the books on the final list are those that will motivate seventh through twelfth graders to read. Helping teachers, parents, booksellers, and others involved in adolescent literacy is another goal of the program. The annual list can serve to guide purchases of books for this population. Finally, the Y. project seeks to provide middle and secondary school students with an opportunity to voice their opinions about the books being written for them. Seldom do student evaluations count when award-winning books are announced.

The Y. program is highly structured to ensure that the books donated by American publishers get into the hands of the more than four thousand students across the United States. First, coordinators from various geographic regions of the United States are charged with locating cooperating schools, teachers, and students who will read books from the preliminary list. The regions from which the coordinators come are rotated on a regular basis, affording all states the chance to apply to be considered for involvement in the Y. program. Coordinators are charged with locating schools within their region to participate in the program. Coordinators must receive all the books from the preliminary list, inventory them, and ensure that the books are distributed to the participating schools.

Each year thousands of middle and high school students read books that have been selected from new publications donated by U.S. publishers. In order to be considered for the preliminary list, a book must receive at least two positive reviews in the standard reviewing journals. Once students read a book, they are asked to complete a brief ballot indicating their evaluation of the book. Students are asked to rate the books they read on a three-point scale by checking whether they really liked a book, whether it was simply okay, or whether they disliked the book. Regional coordinators collect and tally the ballots from their part of the country. The ballots are then tabulated at the national level by the International Reading Association. The top thirty vote getters appear on the final list published by IRA.

This annual list has become an important one for teens. These books, chosen by their peers, are regarded as the "the best of the year." Additionally, teachers and LIBRARIANS can utilize these lists to develop classroom and school library collections that reflect the needs and interests of the students. Publishers also find these lists instructive in terms of knowing more about what types of books teens find accessible and interesting. For more information about the Y. program, information sheets and application forms can be downloaded at the IRA website (www.reading .org). Lists of TAC winners from previous years are also available online in PDF format.

BIBLIOGRAPHY: International Reading Association website, www.reading.org.

TERI LESESNE

YA CHOICES AWARD

In 1987, the International Reading Association inaugurated its first annual YA Choices project. Aimed at students in grades seven through twelve, the Y. project had three goals. First, to provide middle- and high-school students with the chance to select their favorite books from a predetermined core collection of YA materials. Once the ballots were tabulated and the final list published, the other two goals of the Y. project were met: to develop a list of new books that encouraged reading by YA, and to assist those who worked with this population in identifying good books for students in grades 7 to 12.

The process for the Y. is simple, yet the project requires quite a bit of organization and coordination. Each year, publishers donate multiple copies of YA books that have received at least two positive reviews. Generally, somewhere between 250 and 300 books are distributed to schools across the U.S. through a system that divides the country into geographic sections. A team leader for each section is selected by the International Reading Association to coordinate the distribution of books in each region. Approximately 4,500 students across the U.S. read the books and complete ballots. The simple ballot asks students to rate the book as one they really liked, one that was OK, or one that they did not like. Ballots are collected and tabulated by each team leader. Totals are turned in to the IRA officials who then compile the final list of Choices.

Thirty books (occasionally there is some variation) comprise the final list. It is annotated by the team leaders and appears in the November issue of the *Journal of Adolescent and Adult Literacy,* the secondary journal of the International Reading Association. Offprints of the list are available from IRA. Additionally, the lists can be accessed at the IRA website, www.reading.org.

Educators selected as team leaders must be members of IRA, have knowledge in the field of YA LITERATURE, have access to large numbers of students in grades 7 to 12, and be willing to serve a two-year term as team leader. Team leaders for the project must also attend IRA conferences and meetings of the Y. committee. Duties include receiving and distributing the books to students, collecting and tabulating ballots, and writing some of the annotations for the final list. Applications for team leaders are also available at the IRA website. Rewards of serving on the teams include becoming aware of new high quality books for TEENAGERS and getting to keep the books in your classroom when the project is complete. Teachers who have used the trade books in their classrooms seldom return to total dependence on textbooks. They observe an increase in student enthusiasm, an increase in the time spent reading voluntarily, and an increase in scores on reading fluency tests.

TERI S. LESESNE

YA LIBRARY SERVICES ASSOCIATION (YALSA)

The Young Adult Library Services Association, also known as *YALSA,* a division of the Chicago-based American Library Association, focuses on issues relating to library services to adolescent patrons, ages twelve–eighteen. The mission of Y. is "to advocate, promote and strengthen service to young adults as part of the continuum of total library service, and to support those who provide service to this population." Y. began as the YA YA Services Division in 1957 as a result of massive reorganization within the American Library Association, which included the splitting of the Association of Young People's LIBRARIANS into two divisions, the Children's Library Association and YASD. In 1992, the name of the division was changed to the Young Adult Library Services Association.

Y. gained greater recognition with its new name, logo, and redefined identity and image. Mission and vision statements were developed to serve as a guide for the division's activities, as well as to provide direction for programming and services. Governed by a president who serves a one-year term and a board of directors elected by the membership, the division has launched many major national and international initiatives. Serving the Underserved, a project focusing on training public library generalists in good customer-service practices for young adults, has trained over ten thousand participants around the country. In 1993, Y. established the Excellence in Library Services for Young Adults project, which acknowledges the nation's top young programs in public and school libraries.

In 1997, Y. launched an initiative called TEEN Read Week, an annual event encouraging public and school libraries to focus on and celebrate teen reading through special events and programming. Typically designated for a week in October, Teen Read Week is centered around a theme, like a summer reading program, which is broad enough for libraries to adapt as they are able according to their means and size. To support the program, Y. develops programming suggestions and tip sheets for publicity and promotion that libraries can use for their own celebrations. ALA Graphics develops a variety of products tying into the theme that libraries can purchase. Teen Read Week themes have included "It's Alive @ Your Library," promoting HORROR literature; "Make Reading a Hobbit," promoting FANTASY literature; and "Reading Rocks."

The division administers several important awards for young adult literature and notable lists for young adult books and audiovisual materials. The MARGARET A. EDWARDS AWARD, named for a pioneering young adult librarian, recognizes an author's body of work. Recipients of the award include Robert CORMIER, Chris CRUTCHER, S. E. HINTON, Walter Dean MYERS, Gary PAULSEN, Richard PECK, and Paul ZINDEL. The Alex Awards recognize adult books that have great appeal and interest to young adult readers. The MICHAEL L. PRINTZ AWARD, named for a long-time active member of Y., recognizes distinguished literary achievement for books published specifically for young adults in a calendar year. Annual notable lists selected by committees include Best Books for Young Adults, Quick Picks for Reluctant Young Adult Readers, Popular PAPERBACKS for Young Adults, and Selected Videos and DVDs for Young Adults. An-

other important list, updated every five years, is Outstanding Books for the College Bound. These lists serve as important selection tools for public and school librarians serving young adults.

Y. publishes two periodicals for its membership: *Y. Young Adult Library Services Association,* a quarterly journal featuring articles by both scholars and practitioners, and *YAttitudes,* an online newsletter published for members only on the Y. website. Y. has also published many important books about young adult library services and literature, including *Bare Bones Young Adult Services: Tips for Public Library Generalists; Best Books for Young Adults: The Selection, the History, the Romance; Fair Garden and the Swarm of Beasts,* a revision of the pioneering work on young adult library services by Margaret A. Edwards; *Hit List: Frequently Challenged Young Adult Books for Young Adults; New Directions for Library Services to Young Adults; Young Adults Deserve the Best: Competencies for Libraries Serving Youth; Youth Participation in School and Public Libraries*; and *Youth Participation: A Training Manual.*

Y. maintains a strong electronic presence. Two important listservs the organization maintains are Y.-BK and Y.-L. The Y.-BK discussion list focuses on young adult literature appropriate for middle and high-school readers. The listserv is populated mainly by librarians and teachers, but authors and editors also frequently participate in discussions. Y.-L focuses more on the business of the organization and issues of library services. Other open listservs are TeachYAL, devoted to discussion of the teaching of young adult literature and library services on the college and university level, and YAL-OUT, which discusses issues relating to library outreach services for young adults. In addition to its extensive website open to both members and nonmembers offering information about all aspects of the organizations, Y. also maintains a "For Members Only" section that offers exclusive annotated lists of recommended books, videos and audio-cassettes, audio speeches, and special subject bibliographies.

Y. also annually offers to members grant opportunities exceeding $30,000. The grants include the Baker and Taylor Conference Grants, Book Wholesalers, Inc. Collection Development Grants, Frances Henne/*VOYA* Research Grant, Great Book Giveaway Competition, and the Sagebrush Corporation for a Young Adult Reading or Literature Program.

With a membership of over four thousand, Y. counts among its members authors, classroom teachers, college and university professors, public and school librarians, and publishers. Y. maintains strong ties with other professional organization that share its mission to advance young adult literacy, such as the International Reading Association and National Council for Teachers of English.

BIBLIOGRAPHY: www.ala.org/yalsa/.

EDWARD T. SULLIVAN

YA LITERATURE

Although the first golden age of children's literature dates to late Victorian England, the first golden age of young adult literature did not emerge until nearly a century later, and then, across an ocean. For the genre now conventionally called "young adult literature" is essentially an American contribution to world literature and—since it is defined by its intended readership—could not exist until the very idea of young adulthood as a separate and distinct part of life's progress from cradle to grave became part of the public consciousness, something that did not begin to happen until well into the Great Depression of the 1930s. Generally speaking, before that time people were regarded by society as either children or adults and the act that transformed child to adult was taking one's first job.

The decline of the job market in the decade of the 1930s resulted in a dramatic increase in high-school enrollment and, with it, the emergence of a new TEEN culture that would cast a long shadow over both American publishing and Madison Avenue, the home of American advertising, which quickly saw that teens represented a new consumer target.

As for publishers, they began to react cautiously as early as the mid-1930s by publishing a new kind of book that was too mature to be regarded as a traditional children's book but not sufficiently sophisticated for adults. Some early examples of this include Helen Boylston's *Sue Barton, Student Nurse* (1936) and John R. Tunis's *The Iron Duke* (1938), both of which have occasionally been dubbed the first Y. novels.

However, it was not until 1942 that a novel with a more legitimate claim to that title was published: Maureen DALY's semi-AUTOBIOGRAPHICAL *Seventeenth Summer,* which she began writing when she was, herself, seventeen. Though published as an adult book, the novel quickly became enormously popular with teenagers, demonstrating to publishers that there was now an avid readership for titles like Daly's that were told in the "authentic" first-person voice of a teenage protagonist and that focused on experiences that were a predictable part of most young adult lives. The result was a decade-long rush to publish similar novels of the joys and sorrows of first love. Their enormously successful authors—Janet Lambert, Betty Cavanna, and Rosamund DuJardin, among others—became brand names, and the titles of their books were homages to Daly: *Going on Sixteen, Practically Seventeen,* and so on. Unlike *Seventeenth Summer,* though, these paler imitations were published as "junior" novels, a patronizing term coined by publisher Longmans Green in the early 1930s. Their upper-middle-class white characters were largely interchangeable, their plots were formulaic, their settings were the small-town America familiar to readers of the *Saturday Evening Post,* and their endings were inevitably happy.

In the meantime the creation of *Seventeen* MAGAZINE in 1945 further evidenced the emergence of teen culture—and teen consumers. Indeed, by the end of the decade, Eugene Gilbert, founder of the Youth Marketing Company, proclaimed, "Our salient discovery is that within the past decade (i.e., the 1940s) teenagers have become a separate and distinct group in our society" (quoted in Palladino, Grace. *Teenagers: An American History.* New York: Basic Books, 1996, p. 104).

Teenagers are boys as well as girls, of course, and though the latter were the first to be targeted as readers and consumers, the former did not remain overlooked so long. In 1948, *Hot Rod* magazine was launched, ushering in a decade of boys' books about cars. Henry Gregor Felsen's classic *Hot Rod* was published in 1950, *Street Rod,* in 1953, and *Crash Club* in 1958. Meanwhile, "space" rods became another significant subject of male interest with the advent of SCIENCE FICTION, ushered in by the 1947 publication of Robert A. HEINLEIN's *Rocket Ship Galileo.*

Young adult literature does not exist in a vacuum; it is a reflection of the larger world—social, cultural, and economic—in which its readers exist. And so it is no surprise that the literature of the 1950s—famous as a decade of conformity and sober-minded seriousness—remained mired in the conventions of the

1940s. ROMANCE continued to be a staple of the literature; career novels were epidemic (and, indeed, had been inaugurated by the Sue Barton books a decade-and-a-half earlier); and—for boys—SPORTS and ADVENTURE stories also flourished.

But . . . "where is the reality?" author S. E. HINTON would ask a decade later in the immediate wake of the publication of her first young adult novel *The Outsiders* ("Teenagers Are for Real." *New York Times Book Review,* August 27, 1967, p. 26). The answer was to be found in the few anomalies of the 1950s: J. D. SALINGER's *Catcher in the Rye* (1951), for example, though published for adults, introduced, in the character of Holden Caulfield, the model of adolescent alienation and anomie that was replicated in the CLASSIC teen MOVIE *Rebel without a Cause* (1955) and would become a defining characteristic of young adult literature two decades later; similarly, *Two and the Town* (1952) by Henry Gregor Falsen, an anomalously honest look at teenage sexuality, was also twenty years ahead of its time. Otherwise, young adult literature remained an exercise in status quo until the turbulent social changes of the 1960s created a climate receptive to more realistic portrayals of adolescent life in America.

Though S. E. Hinton's 1967 novel *The Outsiders,* with its mean-streets urban setting and theme of class warfare, is widely regarded as the first authentic young adult novel, it was prefigured by such earlier titles as Frank Bonham's *Durango Street* (1965) and Nat HENTOFF's *Jazz Country* (1965).

As if by Y. we now mean a literature of contemporary realism that unsparingly examines the realities and vicissitudes of adolescent life in America, a second novel published in that same watershed year of 1967, Robert LIPSYTE's *The Contender,* remains the more authentic examplar of the then new genre. The next year another CLASSIC, Paul ZINDEL's *The Pigman,* was published, followed a year later by John Donovan's landmark *I'll Get There. It Better Be Worth the Trip,* the first young adult novel to examine homosexuality.

Clearly, the times were a-changin', and young readers were ready for a new kind of literature whose hallmarks were authenticity, authorial honesty, and relevance to readers' real lives. All of these elements came together in Robert CORMIER's landmark novel *The Chocolate War,* which, published in 1974, became the first novel to suggest that not all endings in

YA fiction needed to be happy. Cormier's sometimes stark worldview and deterministic philosophy remain controversial to this day, but the publication of his first YA novel was a defining moment for the genre, granting it literary legitimacy and helping to usher in the first golden age of literature for teens. A year earlier, the Young Adult Services Division of the American Library Association recognized the new literary viability of the genre by opening its annual Best Books for Young Adults list to young adult books for the first time. Until that date, ironically, the list included only adult titles. In addition to Cormier, other exceptional talents who began their young adult writing careers in the formative decade of the 1970s were M. E. KERR, Richard PECK, and Walter Dean MYERS.

Though Lipsytc, Bonham, and HENTOFF had all created AFRICAN AMERICAN characters in the 1960s, they were, themselves, white. Myers—along with Rosa GUY and Alice CHILDRESS—became the first to write from the black perspective and thus added a new depth of social realism and authenticity to the genre.

Further contributing to young adult literature's coming of age in the 1970s was the publication in 1975 of Judy BLUME's groundbreaking novel *Forever,* the first YA novel to acknowledge, in explicitly written scenes, that teens are sexually active. Aside from Felsen's anomalously early *Two and the Town,* YA literature before 1975 had a history of discreetly ignoring the place of sex in teen life, though the relentlessly dire consequences of sexual activity—unwanted teen pregnancy—had been the cautionary subject of Zoa Sherburne's *Too Bad About the Haynes Girl* (1967), Paul Zindel's *My Darling, My Hamburger* (1969), and Jeanette Eyerely's *A Girl Like Me* (1966) and *Bonnie Jo, Go Home* (1972). Blume, however, was the first to acknowledge that teens could have sex, enjoy it, and not suffer dire consequences. As a result, of course, *Forever* remains one of the most banned of all books for young readers.

Despite its contributions, the rise of realism in the 1970s offered some less salutary consequences, as well. In the hands of less-skilled writers, the newly relevant literature, as practiced by Cormier, Lipsyte, Hinton, Zindel, Myers, and others began to turn into the formulaic, didactic exercise that would come to be called the "problem novel." In these books, characterization, style, setting, and other literary considerations took a back seat to the ripped-from-the-headlines problem of the week, the more wretchedly excessive the better.

Perhaps in reaction to a surfeit of realism, young adult literature returned, in the 1980s, to its roots in romance, but with a significant difference. The brand name authors of the 1940s—Cavanna, DuJardin, Lambert, et al.—were replaced in the 1980s by brand name *SERIES,* original PAPERBACK publications with names like Wildfire, Young Love, Sweet Dreams and—most notably—Sweet Valley High.

The rise of paperback genre series (HORROR—led by such franchises as Goosebumps and Fear Street—joined romance as the subject *du jour* by the end of the decade) evidenced more than weariness with realism. It reminded observers that young adult literature is driven by economic as well as by social and cultural forces.

Historically, the market for Y. was an institutional one; that is to say, adult LIBRARIANS and teachers were the principal purchasers, not teens themselves. It was the shrinking of these institutional budgets, a hallmark of the 1980s driven by such tax-cutting measures as California's Proposition 13, which forced publishers to rediscover teens as consumers and led them to refocus their production on mass market paperbacks, a format both more affordable and more attractive to teens. Tacitly complicit in this change was another market phenomenon—the rise of shopping malls, which became American teens' home away from home, and the presence therein of national-chain bookstores such as B. Dalton, Crown, and Walden.

As a result, individual hardcover novels began to go into eclipse and, by the early 1990s, pundits were forecasting the imminent death of Y.

Such pronouncements were premature, but it is a fact that the chains' treatment of young adult books as children's books (by shelving them in the juvenile department), coupled with the rise of a new middle-school market, resulted in the radical "youthening" of YA literature. And by the late eighties, the average age of protagonists had begun falling from seventeen to as young as twelve.

In retrospect, there was another compelling reason for the decline of Y. in the 1980's and early 1990's: a corollary decline in America's teenage population that began in 1977 and continued to 1992.

Ironically, the very same market and demographic forces that had nearly been the death of young adult literature sparked its remarkable renascence in the mid-1990s.

For, beginning in 1992, a dramatic spike in the number of teens transformed this formerly stagnant segment of the American population into one of its fastest growing categories, one that demographers predict will continue to expand through the year 2010. Meanwhile, Madison Avenue has rediscovered teenagers as significant consumers and no wonder, since, according to the market research firm Teenage Research Unlimited, teens were spending an average of $104 a week by 2001 (cited in *The Best American Nonrequired Reading* 2002. Boston: Houghton Mifflin, 2002, p. vi). If anything, this phenomenon accelerated the market shift from institutional to retail as the chain bookstores—now morphed into gigantic superstores—began expanding their stock of young adult books and, by the end of the 1990s, even began creating separate young adult sections for the first time, featuring not only paperback series and paperback reprints of CLASSICS but also original trade paperbacks and individual hardcover titles as well.

Although the institutional market has never fully rebounded, it has recovered sufficiently that publishers now often issue books in simultaneous hardcover and paperback editions, the former targeted at libraries and schools and the latter at teen consumers themselves.

More importantly, however, ALA's YA Services Division—now renamed the YA Library Services Association (YALSA)—became a vigorous advocate in the early 1990s for the revival of a young adult literature that would rediscover and even expand its original high-school-age audience by becoming more relevant and risk-taking than at any time since the first golden age of the 1970s.

Coincidentally, a new generation of YA authors began publishing in the late 1980s, writers like Francesca Lia BLOCK, Bruce BROOKS, Chris LYNCH, and Brock COLE, whose venturesome work resonated with older teens. Block particularly, in her five-volume series of novels about her nontraditional heroine Weetzie Bat and her FAMILY of filmmakers and musicians, was the first to speak to what is now routinely called a "CROSSOVER" audience; i.e., readers ranging in age from fifteen to twenty-five. Coincidentally, this is the same demographic that MTV targets; its commercial success in cross-marketing itself and the products its advertisers purvey is, increasingly, a model the publishing industry strives to replicate.

As a result, the once-clear line between young adult and adult books has begun to blur. Adult writers with established literary reputations—authors like Joyce Carol OATES, Michael Chabon, Francine Prose, Isabel Allende, Emma Donoghue, Julia Alvarez, Edwidge Danticat, and others—have begun writing for YA readers. At the same time, publishers have begun publishing what are clearly YA books as adult titles. Examples include Stephen CHBOSKY's *The Perks of Being a Wallflower* (Pocket Books/MTV), Joseph Weisberg's *Tenth Grade* (Random House), and Alan Watt's *Diamond Dogs* (Little, Brown). At the same time, young adult books are being packaged to look like adult titles, and many of these are series being published as paperback originals; for example, Megan McCafferty's *Sloppy Firsts* and *Second Helpings* (Three Rivers Press, an imprint of Random House), Zoey Dean's A List and Cecily Von Ziegasar's Gossip Girls series (both from Little Brown).

In a further effort to expand the audience for Y., publishers have increasingly permitted, even encouraged, authors to push back the boundaries of what was once considered "suitable" for YA readers. The resulting product has been widely described as "edgy" literature—literature that has the freedom to explore the often hard-edged realities of contemporary YA life in creatively risk-taking ways. Further evincing this trend, publishers in the late 1990s began creating new imprints that specialized in this type of literature; for example, Scholastic's Push, HarperCollins' Tempest and Simon and Schuster's Pulse.

In its newly courageous candor and creative risk-taking, the field of young adult literature has finally—twenty years later—caught up with the visionary Robert Cormier, thus insuring his status as the single most important writer in the history of the genre.

And in the process the field came of age in the mid-1990s, a period that marked the beginning of a second golden age of young adult literature.

The tangible expression of this was YALSA's creation, at decade's end, of the MICHAEL L. PRINTZ AWARD, the first YA book prize to be awarded solely on the basis of literary merit. It is worth noting that not only fiction is eligible for award consideration but also nonfiction, POETRY, art (GRAPHIC NOVELS, for example), and anthologies. Also eligible are works first published in another country (provided an American edition has been published during the period of eligibility; i.e., the calendar year preceding the announcement of the award).

The extraordinary scope and variety of the kinds of books eligible is further evidence of the creatively dynamic and imaginatively expansive field that is Y. in the first decade of the twenty-first century.

It is a field rich in trends, among them: (1) The rise of literary and creative nonfiction pioneered by writers like Russell FREEDMAN, James Cross GIBLIN, Rhoda Blumberg, Jim MURPHY and, more recently, Marc Aronson. (2) The bold reimagining of books' visual aspect, expressed in lavishly illustrated nonfiction such as that pioneered by Dorling Kindersley in its Eyewitness Books; in the rise of the graphic novel (also called the adult picture novel or the novel of sequential art) that has its roots in the comic books of the 1930s and '40s but brought to new creative and artistic heights by Art SPIEGELMAN (*Maus*), Eric Shanower (*The Age of Bronze*), Chris Ware (*Jimmy Corrigan*), Daniel Clowes (Ghost World), and others; in the evolution of the PICTURE BOOK for young adults, "invented" by Jon Scieszka and Lane Smith in works like *The True Story of the Three Little Pigs by A. Wolf* and *The Stinky Cheese Man*. (3) The renaissance of the SHORT STORY and the related rise of a new kind of short story anthology—pioneered by Don GALLO—that is theme-driven and composed of original stories commissioned for the anthology. (4) The merging of the short story and the novel to form a new kind of episodic, character-driven fiction. An early example of the form is Bruce BROOKS's pioneering *What Hearts;* more recent examples are Chris Lynch's *Whitechurch,* E. R. FRANKS' *Life is Funny* and Ellen WITTLINGER's *What's in a Name?* (5) The appearance of new narrative strategies and techniques that employ text in the form of E-mail and instant messages, excerpts from letters, journals, 'zines, and e-zines. (6) The runaway popularity of another new narrative form is the novel in verse—a form pioneered by Virginia Euwer WOLFF (*Make Lemonade*), Karen HESSE (*Out of the Dust*), and Sonya Sones (*Stop Pretending*)—and a corollary renaissance of interest in all poetic forms, including theme-driven anthologies and collections of poetry by young adults themselves. (7) The sudden explosion of two literary genres—FANTASY and historical fiction—that had previously found little expression in Y. The new interest in fantasy derived, largely, from the international success of the HARRY POTTER books, but there seems to have been no single catalyst for the spate of excellent historical fiction that suddenly began appearing in the early twenty-first century, unless it might, in part, have been fuelled by the focus on the millennium and the enormous commercial success of Scholastic's Dear America books, a series of DIARIES by fictional adolescent immigrants.

Many of these trends have now come together in a new publishing venture that would not have been possible even five years ago and that further evidences the coming of age of young adult literature. *Rush Hour. A Journal of Contemporary Voices* is a semiannual literary publication for readers aged sixteen to twenty-two, which—founded by the author of this entry—is published each spring and fall by Random House in simultaneous hardcover and trade paperback editions. The former is targeted at the institutional market and the latter at the retail market. *Rush Hour* is rooted in the belief that readers in its target demographic range are eager to find creative material that reflects, with immediacy and innovation, the complex realities of their lives. To reflect that, the contents of each issue are purposely eclectic, including original short stories, excerpts from forthcoming novels, essays, creative nonfiction, poetry, graphics, art, and drama. Each issue also focuses on a theme. Themes for the first five issues, for example, are "Sin," "Bad Boys," "Face," "Reckless," and "Good Girls."

According to its publishing manifesto, *"Rush Hour* intends to change the way people think about young adult literature and the way it is published, to demonstrate that the very phrase 'young adult literature' is not an oxymoron but a descriptor, instead, of a place of remarkable creative energy and activity."

In addition to the trends already discussed and those manifested in *Rush Hour,* another of the most exciting may be the growing internationalization of the genre. Though, as noted earlier, young adult literature began as a largely American phenomenon, it has now become a vital literary form in every English-language-speaking country of the world, and an increasing number of titles from CANADA, England, AUSTRALIA, and NEW ZEALAND are now being published in American editions. Indeed, two of the first four Printz Awards went to British writers (David ALMOND and Aidan CHAMBERS).

Since its very earliest days, Y. has excelled at giving faces to YA who were, for whatever reason, outsiders. It is ironic, thus, that at a time of such extraordinary activity in the field, two groups of young people have remained too nearly invisible: one is gay, lesbian, bisexual, transgender, and questioning (GLBTQ) youth; the other is newly immigrant teens, especially LATINOS.

The pioneering young adult librarian Margaret A. Edwards tartly wrote, in her 1969 book *The Fair Garden and the Swarm of Beasts,* "Many adults think that if sex is not mentioned to adolescents, it will go away." That wishful thinking, which pervaded the early history of young adult literature, began to change in the 1970s—as noted above—with the publication of Blume's *Forever.* The novelist Norma Klein joined Blume as an early advocate of sexual truth-telling and, throughout the 1980s and early 1990s, a number of taboos generally fell by the wayside. One of the last major ones—incest—was finally treated in not one but three bold books published in 1994: Francesca Lia BLOCK's *The Hanged Man,* Jacqueline WOODSON's *I Hadn't Meant to Tell You This,* and Cynthia VOIGT's *When She Hollers.* (The subject had been treated more discreetly in Ruth WHITE's 1992 novel *Weeping Willow* and Cynthia D. GRANT's 1993 *Uncle Vampire*).

Nevertheless, homosexuality continued to receive only scant attention. From 1969, the year John Donovan's pioneering *I'll Get There. It Better Be Worth the Trip* was published, to the end of the 1990s, no more than one hundred novels for teens appeared that even tangentially skirted the issue, and many of those were compromised by stereotypical characters receiving melodramatic "punishment" for the transgression of being homosexual. Nevertheless, a few titles stood out: Nancy GARDEN's *Annie on My Mind* (1982) remains a classic treatment of the subject and the first novel to suggest that homosexuality embraced not only sex but also love. M. E. KERR's *Night Kites* (1986) was the first novel to deal—honestly and sensitively—with the relationship of homosexuality and AIDS, while Theresa NELSON's later novel, *Earthshine* (1994), did an equally caring job for slightly younger readers. In 1988 Ron KOERTGE's *The Arizona Kid* (1988) became the first to bring a refreshing candor and humor to its treatment of homosexuality. But it was not until 2000, when Ellen Wittlinger received a Printz Honor Award for her novel *Hard Love,* the emotionally engaging story of a boy who falls in love with a lesbian girl, that the tide began to turn, and by 2003, the first hints of a sea change appeared. That year Nancy GARDEN received the prestigious MARGARET A. EDWARDS AWARD, presented by YALSA for lifetime achievement in young adult literature. Aidan Chambers received the Printz Award for *Postcards from No Man's Land,* and Garret FREYMANN-WEIR received a Printz Honor for *My Heartbeat.* Both of these beautifully written novels brought rare insight, maturity, and sensitivity to the treatment of their characters' efforts to come to terms with the ambiguities of their sexual identities.

Of equal importance, David Levithan's *Boy Meets Boy* (also 2003) became the first "feel good" gay novel, the first in which characters are openly gay and almost universally accepted. In its blithe acceptance—indeed, celebration—of human differences, it represents a near revolution in social attitudes and the publishing of gay-themed books for adolescents.

Still another benchmark was achieved in 2004 with the publication of Julie Anne PETERS's *Luna,* the first YA novel to feature a transgender teen.

But what about the newly immigrant? Since the rise of the MULTICULTURAL movement of the 1980s, which accompanied the greatest wave of immigration to the United States since the nineteenth century, teens from other countries and cultures have fared slightly better in the scope and frequency of their treatment. The problem has been to find authors who could write authentically about their cultures from within the experience. This has been particularly true of the Latino world. Now estimated at 38.8 million, the Latino community has become the largest minority population in the United States (http://www.census .gov/Press-Release/www/2003/cb03-100.html). And yet, according to statistics compiled by the Cooperative Center for Children's Books at the University of Wisconsin, Madison, from 1994 to 2003, no more than 693 titles—a meager average of 77 per year—were published in the United States to give faces to this segment of the population, which is growing at a rate nearly four times that of the general population.

Other immigrant populations have fared somewhat better. *One Step from Heaven,* a luminous novel of the Korean–American experienced by An NA, received the 2002 Printz Award, for example, while Lawrence YEP has been writing with grace and eloquence about the Chinese–American experience for many years. In 2003 Orchard Books launched an impressive new series called First Person Fiction, featuring authors from a variety of backgrounds writing about the experience of coming to America.

Lastly, characters of mixed race are finally beginning to emerge as major characters in YA novels, a long overdue acknowledgement of what the 2000 U.S. census indicated—that these teens represent an increasingly large segment of the overall adolescent population of the U.S. Their faces, too, need to be seen.

The history of Y. has been an unremittingly dynamic one. And like young adults themselves, it remains an excitingly vital, rapidly growing and changing genre. It is—and for the foreseeable future promises to remain—one of the most intellectually exciting, creatively stimulating, and emotionally satisfying areas of publishing.

MICHAEL CART

YA LITERATURE IN NEW ZEALAND

N. has a rich and vital body of writing for YA. Contemporary authors are multifaceted, embracing a variety of writing and activities not only for youth, but also including children's PICTURE BOOKS, scripts, and performance. N. is an island country, a little smaller than Colorado, with a varied landscape from alpine mountains and volcanoes to plains, fjords, and myriad islands; a unique fauna—flightless birds, lizards, and no native land mammals—plus a culture that is a blend of indigenous Maori, colonial "English," and a diverse immigrant population. This variety lends the literature of this small nation a unique feel and idiom.

Recognizing the strength of N. literature for YAs are a number of awards, most given annually. The N. Post Children's Book Awards (from 1990 until 1996, with a different sponsor they were the Aim Children's Book Awards) include a senior-fiction section and is the leading prize, promoted nationally with activities, posters, and author visits. Many of the writers listed here have won, some more than once. The Esther Glen Award, named for one of the earliest and most prolific children's authors, is given by the Library and Information Association of N. (LIANZA) for the most distinguished contribution to N. literature for children and young adults. This award has been running since 1944. LIANZA also established the Elsie Locke Award (which since 2001 has been the Young

People's Non-Fiction Award) in 1986, recognizing works that make a distinguished contribution to non-fiction for young people. The Margaret MAHY Medal is awarded by the Children's Literature Foundation of N. "to a person who has made an especially distinguished and significant contribution to children's literature, publishing or literacy." Generally, the winner will be someone with an international reputation in the field of children's literature who has contributed substantially to the field over time. As part of this award, the recipient gives the Margaret Mahy lecture, on a relevant topic, usually in March of the year of the award. Other awards include the Gaelyn Gordon Award for a Much-Loved Book and the Betty Gilderdale award. Some of these awards carry a substantial financial prize, something beneficial for many of the winners given that they are writing for a small market with the consequent small returns.

There are a number of organizations supporting literature for YAs in N., through grants, prizes, tours, booklists, and so forth. The Children's Literature Foundation (CLFNZ) promotes "public awareness of the importance of reading and literature for all children" and their management committee consists of people with a background in and commitment to literature for children. In support of YA authors, the CLFNZ organizes author visits, discussion groups, and awards prizes. The government funded organization Creative N. gives grants in many areas of the arts, including YA writing. The N. Book Council runs a scheme called Writers in Schools, which, since 1972, has leading writers promoting reading and inspiring young writers: "each year, over one hundred thousands students have a chance to meet their writing heroes at schools around the country."

At the forefront of writing for N.'s TEENS is Margaret Mahy. Beginning her writing career in the 1970s with stories in the *School Journal* (a government-funded journal of writing supplied to all primary schools), some of which were adapted into picture books, Mahy has gone on to write many of the most popular books in N. and, with international publications, her works appear in over a dozen languages. *The Changeover* (1984) won the prestigious Carnegie Medal (as had her 1982 children's novel *The Haunting*). With an award named after her (Mahy presented the inaugural lecture in 1991) for children's literature, Mahy is at the pinnacle of contemporary N. writers. A winner of the N. Children's Book award in 2003,

the Esther Glen Award in 1983, 1985, 1993, and 2001, as well as receiving an honorary doctorate from the University of Canterbury (N.), the May Hill Arbuthnot Lecture in 1989, and in 1993 the Order of N. (N.'s highest award, given to only twenty living people), Mahy's reputation continues to grow.

Tessa DUDER represented N. as a swimmer, and her experiences with training and competition form the background to her quartet of novels about Alexandra Archer (*Alex* [1987], *Alex in Winter* [1989], *Alessandra: Alex in Rome* [1991] and *Songs for Alex* [1992]). Although not autobiographical, the stories have captured the imagination of N. readers, winning the N. Children's Book Awards Senior Fiction section (*Alex, Alex in Winter,* and *Songs for Alex*) and the Ester Glen Award (*Alex*). The first novel was adapted into a feature film (1993) for which Duder was a script consultant. *The Tiggie Tompson Show* (1999), featuring a TEEN with a famous mother, coping with school, peers, and a year of amazing events, also won the Senior Fiction Award and was followed in 2001 by *Tiggie Tompson, All at Sea.* Duder is an avid sailor and has written a number of books with this as the background. Also an editor, she compiled a collection called *Nearly Seventeen* (1993) for YAs, featuring many of N.'s foremost writers. Duder has been a writer in residence as Waikato University, and has won other awards including a N. Arts Council Writing Bursary, a Creative N. writing grant, and the Katherine Mansfield Memorial Fellowship. In 1996 she won the Margaret Mahy Medal and in 1994 was awarded an O.B.E. (Order of the British Empire) for services to literature.

A former school teacher, William TAYLOR has written more than thirty books, many of which are for young adults. In 2000, he collaborated with Tessa Duder, writing *Hot Mail,* an epistolary novel of E-mails between two teens. His novels for YAs tend to deal with serious themes—his novel *The Blue Lawn* (1994), winner of the Senior Fiction Award in 1995, is a confronting story about teens discovering their sexuality. His recent book *Spider* (2002), is a hard-edged story dealing with ambition and identity. *Spider* was chosen by the International Youth Library Munich for White Ravens 2002–Outstanding Books for Children and YAs. Taylor has won numerous awards in N. as well as the Italian Premio Anderson Award for best children's book of the year, and has held an Iowa Writing Fellowship. In 1998, he won the Margaret Mahy Medal.

Gaelyn Gordon (1939–97) wrote a range of books, including *Prudence M Muggeridge, Damp Rat* (1991) a fast-paced humorous thriller, the more serious *Stonelight* (1988), and *Mindfire* (1991) as well as the singularly humorous *Several Things Are Alive and Well and Living in Alfred Brown's Head* (1990) and its sequel *Take Me to Your Leaders* (1993). Gordon was at one time a teacher and was known for her close attention to the way teens interacted—her keen ear lends her fiction a degree of authenticity not often found in run-of-the-mill YA stories. Also enthusiastic about theater, especially children's theater, in the early 1990s she toured with William Taylor, Tessa Duder, and children's writer–illustrator Martin Baynton (1953) as Metaphor, a performing troupe, bringing a unique blend of slapstick and literature to audiences in schools and libraries around N. In 1999, the Children's Literature Foundation of N. established the Gaelyn Gordon Award for a Much-Loved Book, given annually for a book that is a favorite, which has not won a major award in N.—a fitting tribute.

Ken CATRAN is a writer with numerous credits. Penning many scripts for television, Catran has won N. awards and was nominated for an Emmy Award in 1986 for *Hanlon.* Beginning in the early 1990s, he wrote a number of SCIENCE FICTION novels for YAs such as *Deepwater Black* (1992) and *Space Wolf* (1994). In more recent years, he has written several novels with a historical basis, including the *Voyage with Jason* (2000) winner of the Senior Fiction and Book of the Year Award, and *Letters from the Coffin Trenches* (2002), a novel about seventeen-year-old Harry's experiences during World War I, told through letters between Harry and his girlfriend Jessica. Catran also cowrote the screenplay for *Alex.*

One of N.'s favorite authors is Jack LASENBY, whose Travellers SERIES (beginning with *Because We Were the Travellers* [1997], continuing with *Taur* [1998], *The Shaman and the Droll,* [1999] and *Kalik* [2002]) has made an impact in the YA science-fiction genre—all the books have been finalists in the N. Children's Book Awards, *Taur* winning the senior-fiction award. The stories are set in a tribal culture, existing in a post-apocalyptic N. Lasenby has been involved in literature for many years having taught English, and as an editor of *School Journal.* The Wellington Children's Book Association, of which La-

senby is a patron, established the Jack Lasenby Award in 2002 for winners of a biannual competition for children who write in the region.

David HILL was already an established N. writer when his first YA novel *See Ya, Simon* was published in 1992. The story follows the last year in the life of Simon, a teenager afflicted with muscular dystrophy, and is filled with humor and pathos. The book was shortlisted for several awards and in 1994 won the *Times Educational Supplement* Award for Special Needs and in 2002 won the Gaelyn Gordon Award for a Much-Loved Book. His subsequent books for YAs, varying in subject matter from SPORTS to tramping to school life have been well-received, and Hill continues to build a following.

Sherryl JORDON (1949–) began her involvement with the publishing world as an illustrator but decided to focus on writing, and after a few false starts won the Children's Book of the Year for *Rocco* (1990). Her teen fiction includes the FANTASIES *Winter of Fire* (1993), *Tanith* (1994), *The Secret Sacrament* (1996), and *The Hunting of the Last Dragon* (2002). Jordon has won or been shortlisted for N. and International Awards, winning, among others, the USA *School Library Journal* Best of (1999), the Buxtehulder Bulle Prize, a Fellowship to the International Writing Program of the University of Iowa and the Margaret Mahy Medal.

Winner of the 1997 Esther Glen Award and the *N. Post* Senior Fiction Award for *Sanctuary* (1996), Kate de Goldi (1959–) is another popular author. Her recent books include *Love, Charlie Mike* (1997), and *Closed, Stranger* (1999). Janice MARRIOT also won both the Esther Glen and Senior Fiction awards, in 1996, for her novel *Crossroads* (1995), a story about Ellie, a teen frustrated by her parents' unwillingness to allow her to get a driver's licence. Paula BOOCK won awards for *Sasscat to Win* (1993) and *Dare, Truth or Promise* (1997). Boock also contributed the title play to *Song of the Shirt: Three One-act Plays for Young Actors,* along with Renee (1929) and Fiona Farrell (1947), a volume aimed at fifteen-to-eighteen-year-olds.

Teenaged writers in N. have numerous creative outlets, mainly in the form of "teen-only" writing competitions run by such organizations as the School of Young Writers in Christchurch and the BNZ Young Writers Award. There is a growing recognition that young writers of N. need outlets and encouragement with their writing as they develop into the authors of the future.

SEAN MONAGHAN

YA LITERATURE IN THE TWENTIETH CENTURY

YOUNG ADULT LITERATURE emerged during the early twentieth century, although it was neither recognized nor marketed as such at the time. Perhaps it began with the dime novel. Dime novels often had TEEN protagonists, as well as stories themed to capture a young reader's attention with ADVENTURE, MYSTERY, travel, and hard work. Horatio Alger Jr. wrote countless tales with the theme that hard work would ensure future success. With the establishment of the STRATE-MEYER Syndicate, an industry was created, as Edward Stratemeyer, founder, developed characters for SERIES that many writers then contributed novels to under whatever pen name Stratemeyer had assigned to that series. Series fiction is a set of stories that share characters and settings or a combination of both. Many credit Stratemeyer, founder of the Stratemeyer Syndicate, with the creation of numerous notable characters—among them, the Hardy Boys, Nancy Drew, Tom Swift, the Blythe Girls, the Moving Picture Girls, the Outdoor Girls, the Dana Girls, and Dave Porter—which cannot be argued.

Many others also contributed to the emergence of young adult literature in the first half of the twentieth century. Among them were A. T. Dudley, author of the Phillips Exeter books, and Arthur M. Winfield, who wrote the Putnam Hall stories. Lucy Maud Montgomery published *Anne of Green Gables* (1908), which not only had several sequels but generated collections of vignettes set in and around Avonlea. *Daddy Long Legs* (1912) was published by Jean Webster, who also wrote *When Patty Went to College* (1903) and *Dear Enemy* (1916), a companion novel to *Daddy Long Legs*. L. M. Montgomery introduced a new character, Emily Starr, in 1922, which was also the year that two separate series titled the Radio Boys appeared. Gerald Breckenridge wrote ten adventure tales, while the Stratemeyer Syndicate produced thirteen titles authored by Allen Chapman. Meanwhile, Howard Pease had introduced Tod Moran, an adventurous teen who joins a ship's crew and has multitudinous adventures.

The Stratemeyer Syndicate produced the Ted Scott Flying Stories under the name of Franklin W. Dixon.

The Ted Scott Flying Stories reflected the country's excitement about Lindbergh's flight, as did the Bill Bolton, Navy Aviator series by Noel Sainsbury and the Linda Carlton books by Edith Lavell, supposedly based on female aviator Amelia Earhardt. Being a pilot was not the only career that was possible though, and many of the young adult books of this time did focus on careers. The G-Men series by William Engle and Laurence Dwight Smith first appeared in 1926 and generated three stories over the course of fourteen years. Another popular career was nursing, exemplified by the Sue Barton books by Helen Dore Boylston. Appearing from 1936 to 1952, the books follow Sue from her student nursing days to her work at the Henry Street Settlement. Her marriage to a country doctor and growing FAMILY do not end her career, first as a superintendent of nurses, and then as a neighborhood nurse and staff nurse. The Cherry Ames series by Helen Wells and Julie Tatham, appearing in 1943, chronicles the career of another young nurse beginning with her student days. The twenty-seven books follow Cherry through many different nursing jobs, and are focused more on the different possibilities that nursing offers. Helen Wells and Julie Tatham also wrote the Vicki Barr, Stewardess series, which appeared from 1947 to 1964 with a total of sixteen titles. Many of these career-centered books owe at least a small debt to Alger's work.

The two world WARS served as a backdrop to many stories geared toward young people at the time, including the Grace Harlowe books by Josephine Chase, writing as Jessie Graham Flower. First appearing in 1910 and ending in 1924, the books follow Grace through high school and college and on to the battles of World War I in Europe. She returns to the U.S. for other adventures. The Aeroplane Boys by Ashton Lamar, appearing between 1910 and 1914, an early series about flying, also reflected the impending onset of United States involvement in World War I. The approaching Second World War is also reflected in many of the books published in the 1940s. The Don Winslow series by Frank V. Martinek, which starts in 1940, showcases Don joining the Navy and the adventures he has there. Janet Lambert set many of her first novels in an Army setting, using her background as an Army wife. The Penny and Tippy Parrish books, which kick off with *Star Spangled Summer* in 1941, start before the Second World War, but by the third book reflect the world of the United States at war. The characters are followed from the conclusion of World War II to the midst of the Vietnam War. Lambert's stories about the Jordon family debut at about the same time, focusing on a large and motherless family surviving when their soldier father goes off to war. Her Kane series also uses World War II as a background—when a reservist decides to become active, his society wife and two daughters must adjust to Army life. *Meet the Malones* (1944) by Lenora Mattingly Weber is also set against the background of World War II, although it is mostly seen from a civilian point of view.

There were also plenty of entertaining books available for young adults, focused on characters who were about their age but who seemed to have a great deal of freedom of mobility and countless adventures. Solving MYSTERIES was all in a day's work in many of these stories, including the Beverly Gray mysteries by Clair Blank, the Judy Bolton mysteries by Margaret Sullivan, and of course, the Stratemeyer Syndicate's Hardy Boys and Nancy Drew mysteries. The Trixie Belden series by Julie Campbell and Kathryn Kenny began in 1948 and ended nearly forty years later in 1986. Through the thirty-nine titles, Trixie and her friends, known as the Bob-Whites, solve numerous mysteries while working to help their families and communities.

SPORTS stories were often nearly as popular as mysteries. The Phillips Exeter stories from early in the century centered on sports, as did the Scranton High Chums by Donald Ferguson. Popular college coach Clair Bee wrote the Chip Hilton books, following a young athlete through the different sports seasons from the time of his high-school career through his college career. The twenty-three titles feature baseball, football, and basketball stories.

Edgar Rice Burroughs, although better known for his Tarzan series, introduced the John Carter of Mars series in 1912. The eleven novels concluded in 1942, but the adventures of John Carter continued in comic books. Tom Swift and Tom Swift, Jr. enjoyed all kinds of interplanetary adventures. Star Trek, originally a television show, would also generate a plethora of novelizations through the years. The Lone Ranger books by Fran Striker, which lasted for twenty years, also had a media tie-in.

The Betsy-Tacy series by Maud Hart Lovelace debuted in 1940. One of the offshoots of the series, *Carney's House Party,* pays homage to the Little Colonel

books from the beginning of the century. Many of Janet Lambert's books in the 1950s are about teenagers and their family life in the suburbs, as are the Rosamund DuJardin books. Yet in sharp contrast to these is J. D. SALINGER's *The Catcher in the Rye.* Published in 1951, Holden Caulfield was a different kind of teen protagonist—sharp, edgy, and filled with angst. The raw language in the book was groundbreaking at the time, prophetic of things to come.

Many of the more literary books of the 1960s and 1970s began to touch on edgier topics, reflecting the times in which they were written. Madeleine L'ENGLE's *The Young Unicorns* (1968) transplants the Austin family to New York City, where they encounter a gang. S. E. HINTON's *The Outsiders* (1967), with its poignant sense of teen isolation, appeared, as did "Rumble Fish" (1968). Self-assessment and eventual self-acceptance are keynotes for Paula DANZINGER's protagonist, Marcy Lewis. Overweight and miserable, a new teacher helps her find herself, and Marcy, in turn, finds the courage to defend the teacher against the anger of the community. Marcy's reluctant evolution is chronicled in *The Cat Ate My Gymsuit* (1974) and *There's a Bat in Bunk Five* (1980).

The edginess continued throughout the next two decades. Brock COLE's *The Facts Speak for Themselves* (1997) is heart rending in its depictions of the abuse a young girl suffers, as is the abuse portrayed in *When Jeff Comes Home* (1999) by Catherine ATKINS. Laurie Halse ANDERSON's *Speak* (1999) also shows a teen protagonist dealing with a truly difficult situation. The protagonist of *Swallowing Stones* (1997) by Joyce McDonald learns to deal with his own moral culpability, while the protagonist of *Stone Water* (1996) by Barbara Snow GILBERT must test his moral fortitude. *Don't You Dare Read this, Mrs. Dunphrey* (1996) by Margaret Peterson HADDIX deals with abandonment. *Give a Boy a Gun* (2000) by Todd STRASSER and *Monster* (1999) by Walter Dean MYERS spotlight teenage violence. In Ann M. Martin's California series, characters try to deal with eating disorders, prejudice, and bad grades, among other topics. Even Francine PASCAL's Sweet Valley High series, and the other series that were generated from the original, began to deal with fairly weighty topics.

The publishing industry's recognition of the economic power wielded by young adults generated a plethora of work that was geared to the young adult market. The American Library Association, with the creation of the PRINTZ AWARD to honor oustanding young adult literature, also helped to promote the genre, furthering the work already done with its Best Books for Young Adults Awards.

In the twenty-first century, teenage literature has exploded. Series novels abound, as do single titles. No topic is verboten, as the literature strives to meet the expectations of an increasingly sophisticated audience. GRAPHIC NOVELS merely added another layer to the choices that are available to today's teens. YA literature is definitely here to stay.

BIBLIOGRAPHY: Billman, Carol. *The Secret of the Stratemyer Syndicate: Nancy Drew and the Hardy Boys, and the Million Dollar Fiction Factory,* 1986; www.amazon.com; www.imdb.com; www.lib.msu .edu/coll/main/spec_col/nye/juven.htm; www.series books.com.

JEANNE MARIE RYAN

YEP, Laurence Michael

Author, b. 14 June 1948, San Francisco, California

Y., the child of a second-generation mother and immigrant father, was torn between his Chinese heritage and American upbringing. In an effort to have their son adapt to American culture, Y.'s parents, Thomas Gim and Franche Lee Yep, chose not to teach him Chinese, for which he was ostracized by his classmates. Growing up in a primarily black neighborhood in California, Y. attended a Chinese Catholic grammar school. His language barrier did not help him assimilate with the Asian students, nor did he identify with the rest of the minority population. Y. experienced significant isolation during high school, which further instilled Y.'s sense of alienation and loneliness, a theme developed throughout most of his works.

As an avid fan of SCIENCE FICTION, Y. published a SHORT STORY at the age of eighteen and his first novel *Sweetwater* (1973), a book about humans living on an alien planet, five years thereafter. Y. has published many other sci-fi novels, which include a Star Trek book, *Shadow Lord: No. 22* (1985), that also embraces the topic of alienation and coming of age. Y. went on to receive a B.A. in 1970 from the University of California at Santa Cruz and, in 1975, a Ph.D. in English for a dissertation on William Faulkner's early novels from the University of New York at Buffalo. Since then, Y. has received praise for *Dragonwings*

(1975), *Child of Owl* (1977), and *Sea Glass* (1979), in which he depicts his Chinese heritage through adolescents seeking acceptance from both their peers and FAMILY.

Y. has established himself as a writer dedicated to creating quality literature that gives a voice to not only Chinese–American youth, but to any TEENAGERS who are seeking acceptance and striving to establish their own identity. Y. married Joanne Ryder, an editor and children's writer, and has taught writing as well as ASIAN-AMERICAN studies at the University of California, Berkley and Santa Barbara. Although Y. has been criticized for blurring Chinese history and losing the momentum of his plots, his well-crafted scenes, enchanting language, and strong characters capture the essence and imagination of young readers. Perhaps Y. described his technique best in an interview, when he stated that he writes based on a child's perspective of history rather than that of an adult; through a child's eyes, everything is fresh and new and alien. Y.'s style of writing imparts a genuine sense of a young adult's willingness to adapt and, like Y., overcome the loneliness and isolation of adolescence.

AWARDS: *Dragonwings:* 1975 *New York Times* Outstanding Book of the Year, 1976 Newbery Medal Honor Book, 1976 Jane Addams Children's Book Award Honor Book, 1976 Children's Book Award, 1976 Carter G. Woodson Book Award, 1979 Lewis Carroll Shelf Award, 1984 Friends of Children and Literature Award; 1994 Newbery Medal Honor Book, *Dragon's Gate; Child of Owl:* 1978 Jane Addams Children's Book Award Honor Book, 1977 *Boston Globe* Book Award Honor Book; 1979 Commonwealth of California Silver Medal, *Sea Glass,* 1994 ALA Best Books for Young Adults for *American Dragons: Twenty-Five Asian-American Voices; Dream Soul:* Charlie May Simon Children's Book Award, 2003.

FURTHER WORKS: *Seademons,* 1977; "Pay the Chinaman," in *Between Worlds: Contemporary Asian-American Plays,* 1990; *Dragonwings* (play), 1993; "Selchy Kids," in *World's Best Science Fiction 1969* (Donald A. and Terry Carr, ed.), 1969; "My Friend, Klatu," in *Signs and Wonders,* 1976; *Dragon of the Lost Sea,* 1982; *Kind Hearts and Gentle Monsters,* 1982; *The Mark Twain Murders,* 1982; *Liar, Liar,* 1983; *The Serpent's Children,* 1984; *The Tom Sawyer Fires,* 1984; *Dragon Steel,* 1985; *Mountain Light,* 1985; *Shadow Lord: A Star Trek Novel No. 22,* 1985; *Monster Makers,* 1986; *The Curse of the Squirrel,* 1989; *The Rainbow People,* 1989; *When the Bomb*

Dropped: The Story of Hiroshima, 1990; *Dragon Cauldron,* 1991; *The Star Fisher,* 1991; *Tongues of Jade,* 1991; *The Lost Garden,* 1991; *Dragon Wars,* 1992; *Dragon's Gate,* 1993; *The Butterfly Boy,* 1993; *The Man Who Tricked a Ghost,* 1993; *The Boy Who Swallowed Snakes,* 1994; *The Ghost Fox,* 1994; *The Junior Thunder Lord,* 1994; *Tiger Woman,* 1994; *The City of Dragons,* 1995; *Later, Gater,* 1995; *Tree of Dreams: Ten Tales from the Garden of Night,* 1995; *Hiroshima,* 1995; *Dragon Prince,* 1996; *Ribbons,* 1996; *The Case of the Goblin People,* 1997; *The Tiger's Apprentice,* 2003.

BIBLIOGRAPHY: *Children's Literature Review,* vol. 3 and vol. 17, 1978; *Children's Books and Their Creators 1995;* "Learning About Laurence Y." http://www.scils.rutgers.edu/~kvander/yep.html, 1996; "About the Author," http://www.scholatic.com, 2003.

ILONA N. KOTI

YOLEN, Jane
Author, b. 11 February 1939, New York City

Y. is a master of FANTASY and POETRY, and rightfully calls herself a storyteller. Using the tools of imagination and language, she evidences in each of her books the delicate craftsmanship that identifies a master storyteller. Inspired by a variety of folk literature, Y. goes beyond RETELLING the story by creating her own descriptions, situations, and events of fantastical characters and "once upon a time" contexts. Besides the genre of fantasy and poetry, Y. has also written in other genres for readers of all ages. Within her many titles are INFORMATIONAL books that include well-researched facts about animals, the environment, the Quaker people, and mysterious phenomena, while retaining a poetic quality of language. Her talents in the world of fiction and historical fiction are recognized as having a fluid, musical style of writing as well as evocative and moving plots.

Growing up in New York City, Y. came from a family of storytellers. Her father was a publicist and newspaperman and her mother, a social worker and unpublished writer. Y. was a frequent patron of the public library; she read all the folk fantasies she could find as well as history and ADVENTURE books. Attending a Quaker summer camp in Vermont, Y. nurtured her writer's background as she learned more about storytelling and passive resistance. Y. was involved in a myraid of high-school activities, and she later at-

tended Smith College. After graduation, she cultivated careers in journalism and freelance writing. Her work introduced Y. to both an editor, Frances Keene, a lifelong influence on her writing career, and to her future husband, David Stemple.

Y.'s passion for writing fantasy grew over time, as evidenced by her diverse stories spanning time and continents. *Neptune Rising: Songs and Tales of the Undersea Folk* (1982) contains stories centered on the relationships between sea folk and humans. In *The Mermaid's Three Wisdoms* (1978), a mermaid named Melusina teaches Jess, a human, the wisdom of the merfolk about living in the rhythm of the sea. Considering Arthurian legend to be the greatest story ever told, Y. retells the life of the young Merlin in the Young Merlin trilogy—*Passager* (1996), *Hobby* (1996), and *Merlin* (1997). Readers can follow the story of Jakkin on the distant planet Austar through the Pit Dragon trilogy—*Dragon's Blood: A Fantasy* (1982), *Heart's Blood* (1984), and *A Sending of Dragons* (1987). Additionally, Y. has created books of her poetry stories. Her thoughts about dragons as well as other mythical creatures are included in *Here There Be Dragons* (1993), *Here There Be Unicorns* (1994), *Here There Be Witches* (1995), *Here There Be Angels* (1996), *Here There Be Ghosts* (1998). With a continuous consideration for the female role in literature, Y. brings together tales of strong women in folklore from around the world in *Not One Damsel in Distress* (2000).

Autobiography and literary experiences are woven throughout Y.'s work, and she is motivated by her love of writing. In *Contemporary Authors,* she states, "I just want to go on writing and discovering my stories for the rest of my life because I know that in my tales I make public what is private, transforming my own joy and sadness into tales for the people." Her books reflect not only her love of folk story and passion to share her fantasy worlds with others but her desire to be a catalyst to inform and to invite thoughtful contemplation of issues and events. *The Devil's Arithmetic* (1988) has been described as compelling and graphic and Y. classified it as a "book that has to be written" in her speech for the Sydney Taylor Book Award. Crossing the genre of fantasy and historical fiction, this novel uses time travel to position the reader in a concentration camp and consider the atrocities there through the eyes of a young girl. Additionally, *Briar Rose* (1992), again drawing from Y.'s own Jewish heritage, metaphorically blends elements of *Sleeping Beauty* with Becca's grandmother's life in an internment camp. *Encounter* (1991) was considered controversial as it presented a reversed perspective of the first meeting of Columbus and the Native Americans through the memories of a Taino man. *The Gift of Sarah Barker* (1981) has been described as powerful and provocative in its depiction of the contradictions within the Shakers' lifestyle.

Y.'s books have won numerous major awards and numerous honors for her body of writing and have been included in the prestigious Kerlan Collection. Many of her books have been translated into other languages as well as adapted for various media forms. Y.'s ability to not only see into the hearts and imaginations of others and to share these insights through writing but also to fill the voids within through the universality of fantasy has made her an author for all times and all people.

AWARDS: Caldecott Medal: 1968 Honor Book for *The Emperor and the Kite*, 1988 for *Owl Moon;* Nebula Award: 1997 Best Short Story for "Sister Emily's Lightship," 1998 Best Novelette for "Lost Girls"; The Golden Kite: 1974 for *The Girl Who Cried Flowers & Other Tales*, 1975 Honor Book for *The Transfigured Hart*, 1976 Honor Book for *Moon Ribbon & Other Tales;* Sydney Taylor Book Award: 1988 for *The Devil's Arithmetic;* Christopher Medal: 1977 for *The Seeing Stick*, 2000 for *How Do Dinosaurs Say Goodnight?;* Mythopoeic Fantasy Award: 1985 for *Cards of Grief*, 1993 for *Briar Rose*, 1998 for the Young Merlin trilogy: *Passager, Hobby, Merlin;* World Fantasy Award: 1987 for *Favorite Folk Tales from around the World;* 1997 Maud Hart Lovelace Book Award, *The Devil's Arithmetic;* and numerous state, regional, and specialized awards (see http://www.janeyolen.com/janeawards.html for a complete list); also, 1993 ALA BBYA for *Briar Rose;* 1999 ALA BBYA for *Armageddon Summer* with Bruce COVILLE); 2001 ALA BBYA for *Queen's Own Fool* (Robert J. Harris); 2003 ALA BBYA for *Girl in a Cage* (with Robert J. Harris); 2004 ALA BBYA, Dorothy Canfield Fisher Children's Book Award, 2005, for *Sword of the Rightful King: A Novel of King Arthur;* 2005 ALA BBYA for *Prince across the Water; Vampires: A Collection of Original Stories* was one of 100 YA titles selected for the 4th Best of the Best List: Here We Go Again; 25 Years of Best Books (1967–92).

FURTHER WORKS: *Pirates in Petticoats*, 1963; *The Emperor and the Kite*, 1967; *The Minstrel and the Mountain: A Tale of Peace*, 1967; *World on a String: The Story of Kites*, 1968; *Greyling*, 1968; *The Seventh Mandarin*, 1970; *Writing Books for Children*, 1973; *The Girl Who Cried Flowers and Other Tales*, 1974; *Simple Gifts: The Story of the Shaker*, 1976; *The Hundredth Dove and Other Tales*, 1977; *Dream Weaver*, 1979; *How Beastly!: A Menagerie of Nonsense Poems*, 1980; *Dragon Night and Other Lullabies*, 1980; *Brothers of the Wind*, 1981; *Sleeping Ugly*, 1981; *Children of the Wolf*, 1984; *The Stone Silenus*, 1984; *Favorite Folktales from around the World*, 1986; *Piggins*, 1987; *Owl Moon*, 1987; *The Faery Flag*, 1989; *Guide to Writing for Children*, 1989; *Best Witches: Poems for Halloween*, 1989; *Wizard's Hall*, 1991; *Letting Swift River Go*, 1992; *Street Rhymes around the World*, 1992; *Weather Report: Poems*, 1993; *Among Angels: Poems*, 1995; *Camelot: A Collection of Original Arthurian Tales*, 1995; *The Haunted House: A Collection of Original Stories*, 1995; *Sacred Places*, 1996; *Armageddon Summer*, 1998; *Raising Yoder's Barn*, 1998.

BIBLIOGRAPHY: *Authors and Artists for Young Adults*, no. 4, 1990, pp. 229–41; *Contemporary Authors Online*, 2001; *Dictionary of Literary Biography*, 52: *American Writers for Children since 1960*, 1986, pp. 398–405; Drew, Bernard, A. *The One Hundred Most Popular Young Adult Authors*, 1996; Juhnke, James C., and Janey Olen. "An Exchange on Encounter." *New Advocate*, 1993, pp. 94–96; *St. James Guide to Young Adult Writers*, 1999; *Teaching and Learning Literature*, 1996, Hopins, Lee Bennett. "O, Yolen: A Look at the Poetry of Jane Yolen," pp. 66–68; Yolen, *Touch Magic: Fantasy, Faierie, and Folktale in the Literature of Childhood*, 1981; Yolen, *Writing Books for Children*, 1983; http://www.janeyolen.com/jane awards.html

JANELLE B. MATHIS

YOUNG, Karen R.
Author, b. 21 November 1959, Ithaca, New York

Y. began her writing career when she worked for news MAGAZINES from Scholastic in New York City. Y, who was studying to be a teacher, enjoyed writing and, abandoning her aspirations of becoming a teacher, began to write for other children's magazines to pursue her new-found career. While rearing her children, Y. began to assemble the beginnings of her novel *Beetle and Me: A Love Story* (1999), which was inspired by a PICTURE BOOK she wrote in high school called "The Blue Volkswagen." In a brief BIOGRAPHY Y. states that she enjoys the emotional clarity that adolescents show during their high-school years, and often uses them as the main characters in her works.

Beetle and Me is the story of a fifteen-year-old girl, Daisy Pandolfi, who grew up around an auto garage and racetrack. Now that she is almost old enough to drive, Daisy has a strong desire to have her own car. However, her hopes are set on the old purple 1957 Volkswagen Beetle her parents drove when she was little, a car full of memories and in need of a lot of work. Daisy works to persuade her parents that she is capable of bringing their FAMILY's old Beetle back to life. With her parents' cautious consent, Daisy spends most of her free time throughout the summer reconstructing her new car. To Daisy, the Beetle is a sign of independence and therefore she wants no fingerprints but her own on the vehicle into which she pours so much of her own work, love, and time.

Unexpectedly when away from her entrancing-car engine, Daisy falls in love at first sight with a handsome young musician named Daniel who has moved to her town. As much as Daisy feels romantically drawn to Daniel, she finds he dislikes cars and has little in common with her. Daisy finds another love when she decides to help with lighting for the school musical and meets Billy, a senior who is as much a car fanatic as herself.

Throughout Y.'s novel, Daisy battles to understand her love for the spirit-filled Beetle, her family, and Billy. As Daisy works on her car, she learns more about herself as a young woman and more about the newfound feelings of love within her life.

AWARDS: ALA Best Books for YA in 2000 for *The Beetle and Me: A Love Story*

FURTHER WORKS: *The Ice's Edge: The Story of a Harp Seal Pup,* 1996; *Guinness Record Breakers,* 1997; *Video,* 1999; *Artic Investigations: Exploring the Frozen Ocean,* 2000; *Outside In,* 2002; *Small Worlds: Maps and Mapmakers,* 2002; *Cobwebs,* 2004.

BIBLIOGRAPHY: About Me: Karen Romano Y. Websthetics.com; http://members.aol.com/wrenyoung/bio.html

EDWARD W. GRINEWICH

YOUTH THEATER

A typical Y. (in contrast with theatre for young audiences, which aspires to produce existing scripted plays or entertainments) involves a group of TEENS ranging from thirteen to nineteen and numbering from thirty to forty or more members who meet to create their own collaborative performances. They draw inspiration from contemporary issues, historical events, PLAYS, novels, and newspapers, as well as from their own daily lives. Facilitated by adult leaders, they improvise and develop selected themes, stories, and characters in biweekly meetings known as drama workshops. Operating in small groups, they periodically share their work with the entire gathering and find an appropriate framework or dramatic device by which to join their efforts in a single presentation.

Workshop techniques employed in the youth-theatre devising process may include warm-up theatre games, improvisation through role play, development of dialogue, showing and sharing, followed by analysis and reflection. The results are performed for audiences in schools, churches, social centers, and sometimes even in city streets (with the actors moving from one location to another, and audiences following). Although the intention is not to develop a traditional play, this can happen, as in the example of the popular British musical *Blood Brothers,* seen in London and New York after its creation by the Liverpool Youth Theatre. Philip PULLMAN served as a mentor to a nineteen-year-old playwright who had adapted his story, "I Was A Rat," which was successfully staged by the Junior Oxford Youth Theatre. Y.s sometimes build a presentation around their response to and interpretation of a particular author, such as Shakespeare, Moliere, Ibsen, Brecht, and Beckett. Or they may fashion their reactions to an avant garde playwright in an anthology of personal impressions.

The Y. movement first began to flourish in Great Britain after World War II. By the 1980s, it had spread to the Scandinavian countries with widespread popularity and productivity. Soon after, theatres emerged in Czechoslovakia, Germany, and Poland, with international festivals arranged in order to share ideas and inspiration through joint workshops. Today, the National Association for Youth Theatres (NAYT) offers training courses for leaders and directors.

In the United States, the Y. movement developed slowly and still does not approximate British and European activity but, even so, is not without significant contribution as seen in the work of the Creative Arts Team and its Y. operating in New York City, where their reactions to September 11, 2001, made powerful theater.

BIBLIOGRAPHY: Boal, A., *Games for Actors and Non-Actors*, 2000; Jackson, T., ed., *Learning through Theatre*, 1998; Neelands, J. and T. Goode., *Structuring Drama Work: A Handbook of Available Forms in Theatre and Drama*, 2000; Taylor, P., *Applied Theatre: Creating Transformative Encounters in the Community*, 2003.

NANCY AND LOWELL SWORTZELL

ZELAZNY, Roger

Author, b. 13 May, 1937 Euclid, Ohio

After receiving his M.A. from Columbia University, where he studied English, including Elizabethan and Jacobean drama, Z. took a job with the Social Security Administration. While holding this job, he would write a SCIENCE FICTION story one night and then refine it the next. In his first year of writing, he sold some twenty science-fiction SHORT STORIES. Then in 1969, he began to earn his living in full-time freelance writing. One of the most enduring authors of imaginative fiction, Z. has written hundreds of science-fiction and FANTASY short stories, novellas, novels, and story collections. His highly praised works are generally composed of mythically based, complex outer-space ADVENTURE stories or intricately literate tales infused with mysterious magic. Perhaps his greatest contribution to the genre of science fiction has been a writing style characterized by psychological depth, replete with poetic elements. He is known for his use of the theme of the highly intelligent and competent yet fallible hero whose lack of emotional maturity precipitates a breakdown that causes him to reflect on how his deficiencies have led him to lose in his life. Z.'s early works, including *Home Is the Hangman, This Immortal, Doorways in the Sand,* and *The Last Defender of Camelot,* are colorful, fast-paced science fiction, representing the best of the New Wave's work on the dehumanizing effects of technology. His book, *Damnation Alley,* 1969, was adapted as a film of the same title by 20th Century–

Fox in 1977. His Amber SERIES, featuring the struggles of Prince Corwin and the other children of King Oberon of Amber against the forces of Chaos, is especially popular with TEEN readers.

SELECT AWARDS: Numerous awards include a Nebula Award, Science Fiction Writers of America, 1965, for best novella, "He Who Shapes;" 1965, for best novelette, "The Doors of His Face, the Lamps of His Mouth," and 1975, for best novella, "Home Is the Hangman"; Hugo Award, World Science Fiction Convention, 1966, for best novel, *This Immortal;* 1968, for best novel, *Lord of Light;* 1975, for best novella, "Home Is the Hangman," 1983, for best novelette, "Unicorn Variations," 1986, for best novella, "Twenty-Four Views of Mount Fuji by Hokusai," and 1987, for best novelette, "Permafrost"; Prix Apollo, 1972, for French edition of *Isle of the Dead; Doorways in the Sand,* named one of the best young adult books of the year, 1976, ALA; Balrog Award, 1980, for best story, "The Last Defender of Camelot," and 1984, for best collection, *Unicorn Variations;* Locus Award, 1984, for collection *Unicorn Variations,* and 1986, for novel *Trumps of Doom;* nominated for Nebula Award, 1994, for *A Night in the Lonesome October.*

FURTHER WORKS: *The Dream Master,* 1966; *Lord of Light,* 1967; *Isle of the Dead,* 1969; *Creatures of Light and Darkness,* 1969; *Jack of Shadows,* 1971; *Today We Choose Faces,* 1973; *To Die in Italbar,* 1973; *Bridge of Ashes,* 1976; *Roadmarks,* 1979; *Changeling,* 1980; *The Changing Land,* 1981; *Madwand,* 1981; *Eye of the Cat,* 1982; *Dilivish, the Damned,* 1983; *A Dark Traveling,* 1987; the Amber Series—*The Chronicles of Amber* (contains *Nine*

Princes in Amber, The Guns of Avalon, Sign of the Unicorn, The Hand of Oberon, and *The Courts of Chaos,* 1970–79); *Frost and Fire: Fantasy and Science Fiction Stories,* 1989; (With Robert Sheckley); *Bring Me the Head of Prince Charming,* 1991.

BIBLIOGRAPHY: Krulik, T., *Roger Z.,* 1986.

CATHERINE GIVEN

ZINDEL, Paul

Author, b 15 May 1936, Staten Island, New York; d. 27 March 2003, New York, New York.

Z. was one of the first authors to write books directed specifically to young adults. *The Pigman* (1969) a story about two TEENAGERS, Lorraine and John, who tell the tale of their relationship with a lonely old man, departed from the traditional books written for young adults at the time. *The Pigman* resulted in Z. being considered one of the founders of the young adult literary genre. During his career his books spanned genres from realistic fiction to HORROR.

Z.'s turbulent childhood was influential in his writing. When he was two years old his father, a New York City policeman, left his FAMILY to live with a girlfriend, and then disappeared almost completely from Z.'s life. His mother quickly turned against men as the Z. family struggled to survive despite the numerous jobs she sought as a way to get rich quick. As the schemes brewed and the paranoia developed in Z.'s family; the lack of continuity of homes or friends instilled in him a powerful imagination. Although he never left Staten Island, he saw the world.

One move that stands out in Z.'s childhood memory was the move to Travis, Staten Island. It was here that he met his Pigman, the adult who helped him sort out the dilemmas of growing up. Z retells this experience in *The Pigman and Me* (1991). In this autobiography, readers find teenagers who are reminiscent of characters created in his other novels. They are normal kids who worry about social issues, resent their parents, and struggle to be themselves. Z.'s Pigman helped him to see writing as a possibility for his future. He received his first prize for writing in high school. When he was fifteen he contracted tuberculosis and was sent to upstate New York to recuperate. When he returned to school a year and a half later, he wrote his first play based on his experience. He entered the play in a contest sponsored by the American Cancer Society and won a Parker Pen as a prize.

Z. attended Wagner College on Staten Island where he majored in chemistry. During this time he took a creative writing class with famed playwright Edward Albee. Albee became Z.'s mentor and encouraged him to pursue writing.

Z.'s first career was an attempt to combine his two loves, writing and chemistry. He became a technical writer at Allied Chemical, but after a few months, Z. returned to Wagner to earn an M.S. in Education. For ten years, 1959–1969, Z taught chemistry in high school, and his experience with teenagers and his willingness to listen to them proved to be a valuable resource to his future writing. Z. continued to write plays while he was teaching, and in 1963, he wrote the *Effect of Gamma Rays on Man-in-the-Moon Marigolds.* The play was first produced on stage in 1965 and, in 1966, produced for television. In 1971, Z. was awarded a Pulitzer Prize for *Marigolds.* His realistic portrayal of young adults advanced Z.'s career as a young adult writer. Charlotte Zolotow, a Children's book editor for Harper and Row, was moved by the realistic dialogue and depictions of teenagers in *Marigolds;* she asked Z. if he would be interested in writing for young people.

Z.'s young adult literature revolves around basic themes of loneliness, self-deprecation and parental resentment. While in the classroom Z. took the time to listen and to learn about the students; as a result, he saw that the students frequently felt alone in the world. Because of this experience with former students, Z.'s characters often speak of their feelings of isolation. In *The Amazing and Death Defying DIARY of Eugene Dingman* (1987) Eugene struggles with feeling different from his peers. Z.'s characters exhibit the real emotions of adolescents who feel they are alone and struggling to sort out the confusing world.

As teenagers grapple with their understanding of the world, they often have a negative view of themselves. Z.'s characters reflect his readers; they question their physical appearance and mental capacities. Liz, Sean, Maggie and Dennis, characters from *My Darling, My Hamburger* (1969), constantly evaluate their physical and mental worth. In *A Begonia for Miss Applebaum* (1989) Henry and Zelda question their actions and analyze each other. Eugene Dingman's diary is filled with comments that reflect his self-doubts. The feeling of insecurity is common among Z.'s characters as it is among teenagers.

Parents displayed in Z.'s books are either incompetent or objects to be loathed. As children turn into teenagers they begin to see their parent's shortcomings. In *The Pigman* (1969) John and Lorraine's parents each have their faults. *A Begonia for Miss Applebaum* also presents parents whom the protagonists maneuver to accomplish their goals. In *My Darling, My Hamburger,* Liz acts out against her parents' pressures and makes the mistake of a life time. In *Loch* (1994), a book written for reluctant young adult readers, the father is portrayed as lacking self-confidence.

Z. attracts young adult readers through his use of slap stick humor and misfit characters. In *David and Della: A Novel* (1993) David suffers from depression and writer's block after his girlfriend's suicide and his parents' alienation. When David meets the extraordinary Della, his life becomes fast-paced and full of one liners as he writes a play in which Della will star. In *Pardon Me, You're Stepping on My Eyeball!* (1976), Louis and Edna, two misfit teenagers, meet in group therapy to help them deal with their troubled parents and lives. Z. wraps humor around these novels to make his characters interesting and the books fun to read.

Z. writes directly to his audience and grabs their attention. In *Doom Stone* (1996), *Reef of Death* (1999), *Rats* (2000), *Raptor* (1999), and *Night of the Bat* (2003) Z. attracts reluctant young adult readers with horror, gore, and suspense. Z. also created a SERIES in which P.C. Hawk and Mackenzie Riggs are two teen detectives, beginning with *P.C. Hawk Mysteries #1: The Scream Museum* (2001).

SELECT AWARDS: 1967 Ford Foundation Grant for drama; *The Pigman:* a 1968 Child Study Association of America's Children's Book of the Year, 1969 *Boston Globe–Horn Book* Award for text; *New York Times* Outstanding Children's Books of the Year: 1969 for *My Darling, My Hamburger,* 1970 for *I Never Loved Your Mind,* 1976 for *Pardon Me, You're Stepping on My Eyeball!,* 1978 for *The Undertaker's Gone Bananas,* and 1980 for *The Pigman's Legacy; The Effect of Gamma Rays on Man-in-the-Moon Marigolds:* Obie Award for Best American Play from the *Village Voice,* Vernon Rice Drama Desk Award for the Most Promising Playwright form the New York Drama Critics, and the New York Drama Critics Circle Award for Best American Play of the Year all 1970, and Pulitzer Prize in Drama and the New York Critics Award, both 1971; ALA Best Young Adult Books: 1971 for *The Effect of Gamma Rays on Man-*

in-the-Moon Marigolds, 1975 for *Pigman,* 1976 for *Pardon Me, You're Stepping on My Eyeball!,* 1977 for *Confessions of a Teenage Baboon,* 1980 for *The Pigman's Legacy,* and 1982 for *To Take a Dare; Media and Methods* Maxi Award, 1973, The Best of the Best Books (1970–1983), Here We Go Again . . . 25 Years of Best Books (1967–1992), Still Alive (1960–1974), *The Pigman;* New York Public Library's Books for the Teen Age: 1980 for *Confessions of a Teenage Baboon,* 1980, 1981, and 1982 for *The Effect of Gamma Rays on Man-in-the-Moon Marigolds,* 1981 for *A Star for the Latecomer,* and 1981 and 1982 for *The Pigman's* Legacy; MARGARET A. EDWARDS Award, 2002; ALAN Award, 2002; *Rats:* ALA Popular Paperbacks, 2003; *The Pigman and Me:* 100 Best Books for Teens from 1996–2000.

FURTHER WRITINGS: *And Miss Reardon Drinks A Little,* 1967; *I Never Loved Your Mind,* 1970; *The Secret Affairs of Mildred Wild,* 1972; *I Love My Mother,* 1975; *Ladies at the Alamo,* 1977; *The Girl who Wanted a Boy,* 1981; *Let Me Hear you Whisper* (play), 1966; *The Wacky Facts Lunch Bunch,* 1994, *P.C. Hawke Mysteries #2 Surfing Corpse,* 2001; *P.C. Hawke Mysteries #3 The E-mail Murders,* 2001; *P.C. Hawke Mysteries #4 The Lethal Gorilla,* 2001; *P.C. Hawke Mysteries #5 The Square of Murder,* 2002; *P.C. Hawke Mysteries #6 Death on the Amazon,* 2002; *P.C. Hawke Mysteries #7 The Gourmet Zombie,* 2002; *P.C. Hawke Mysteries #8 The Phantom of 86th Street,* 2002; *The Houdini Whodunit,* 2002; *Death by CD,* 2004; *The Petrified Parrot,* 2004.

BIBLIOGRAPHY: *Contemporary Authors, New Revision Series* v. 31 pages 481–484; *Contemporary Literary Criticism* v. 26 pages 470–481; D. L. Winarski, "Paul Z.: Flirting with the Bizarre" *Teaching K–8* v. 25 n. 3 page 47–49; L.L. Harris. "Paul Z." *Biography Today, Author Series* v. 1 1995, Page 169–179; *Something About the Author* v. 58 pages 198–210; http://www.randomhouse.com/teachers/authors/zind.html; http://www.bayarea.com/mld/mercurynews/news/local/5511948.htm

NANCE WILSON

ZUSAK, Markus
Author, educator, b. 1975, Sydney, Australia

Z. lives and writes in Sydney, AUSTRALIA. He was sixteen-years old when he first began writing, and by 1998 his first book, *The Underdog,* was published (1999 in the U.S.).

Z.'s life appears in his works. In an interview with Tammy Currier, he notes, "[*The Underdog*] most resembles actual events in my life" (2003). However, other aspects of Z.'s life aid him in his next book, the celebrated *Fighting Ruben Wolfe* (2000, 2001 in the U.S.). The boxing matches in it, the author notes, are not the outcome of extensive research: "I did enough fighting . . . with my brother and his friends . . . growing up [to write these scenes]." The Wolfe FAMILY, too, is reminiscent of his own. The son of emigrants to Australia, Z. notes the impact of his parents' lives on his own: "their hardships and struggle to live decent lives are probably the basis of everything I approach" (2003). Such a struggle is evident in the Wolfe family—an unemployed father and overemployed mother. The protagonist of three of the novels, Cameron, through his introspective writing, is similar to Z., as well.

Z.'s writing began through his love of story. He notes, "I always had stories in my head. So I started writing them." These SHORT STORIES have received much acclaim both in Australia and in the U.S.

Z.'s first novel, *The Underdog,* introduces the Wolfe family, the characters in three of his next four books. This first volume follows the two younger brothers, Ruben and Cameron, as they strive to be like their older brother Steve. In *Fighting Ruben Wolfe,* Ruben and Cameron become involved in an underground-boxing circuit. High in action but also introspection, the violence represents the struggles of the family. A reviewer for *Publishers Weekly* (2001) said, "Z. offers a lot of SPORTS action as well as a sensitive inspection of sibling relationships and family pride."

Z.'s most recent book, *Getting the Girl* (2003), follows the story of the Wolfe family and particularly Cameron in his desire for independence and love. Janet Hilbun, writing for *School Library Journal,* calls the novel, "a story of family dynamics and coming of age, interspersed with the protagonist's poi-

gnant poems and observations." The dynamics of the family become tense when Ruben drops his girlfriend, who, afterward, indicates interest in Cameron. "Z. explores," notes a writer for *Kirkus Reviews* in 2003, "the intersection between family loyalty and romantic affection; [the novel is] poignant yet unsentimental . . . [and] will touch the heart," as any good story does.

Z. lives in Sydney, Australia, where he continues to teach English on occasion. He also visits schools to talk to students, but his time is predominately spent writing. "I guess without stories we'd be empty," Z. notes to Currier, and this prolific writer (five novels in six years) is far from empty.

AWARDS: *Getting the Girl:* Choices, 2004 (Cooperative Children's Book Center); *The Messenger:* 2003 CBC Book of the Year for Older Readers, and the Ethel Turner Prize in the 2003 NSW Premier's Literary Awards; *When Dogs Cry:* Children's Books of the Year Awards, Honor 2002 Older Readers Australia; Young Adult Book of the Year in the BookQueensland Premier's Literary Awards; *Fighting Ruben Wolfe:* Best Books for Young Adults, 2002 (ALA-YALSA); The Best Children's Books of the Year, 2002 (Bank Street College of Education); Black-Eyed Susan Book Award, nominee 2003–2004 (Maryland); Kentucky Bluegrass Award, nominee 2003; Maine Student Book Award, nominee 2002–2003.

BIBLIOGRAPHY: Currier, T., 2003, Retrieved June 27, 2004, from the World Wide Web: http://www.teenreads .com/authors/au-zusak-markus.asp; Hilbun, J., 2003, *School Library Journal, 49,* 4, 171; Markus Z., n.d., Lateral Learning: Speakers' Agency, http://www .laterallearning.com/authors/zusak.html; *Publishers Weekly,* 2000, *248,* 9, 87; *Kirkus Reviews,* 2003, *71,* 402.

MARY MCMILLAN TERRY

Book Awards that Include YA Titles

Award websites:

The website www.ala.org/ala/yalsa/booklistsawards covers:

- Alex Awards
- Best Books for Young Adults
- Margaret A. Edwards Award
- Michael L. Printz Award
- Outstanding Books for the College Bound
- Popular Paperbacks for Young Adults
- Quick Picks for Reluctant Young Adult Readers
- Selected Audiobooks
- Selected DVDs and Videos
- Teens' Top Ten

YA Choices are available at: http://www.reading.org/resources/tools/choices_young_adults.html

THE AMERICAN LIBRARY ASSOCIATION www.ala.org

The American Library Association sponsors a number of book awards. These awards range from individual titles to lists of new and/or noteworthy books to the recognition of authors for their lifetime achievement in the field of YA literature. Since different divisions sponsor different awards, the list below is arranged by sponsoring division and then by awards in alphabetical order within that division. An E-mail address is provided for each award for ease in updating these lists.

ALSC (The Association for Library Service to Children) www.ala.org/alsc

ALSC is the sponsor of a number of literary awards, including the well-known Newbery and Caldecott awards. To access these and other litarary award, click "Awards and Scholarships" and then "Literary and Related Awards." The John Newbery Medal Home Page (Most Distinguished Contribution to American Literature for Children) is the first listing, followed by the Randolph Caldecott Medal Home Page (Illustrator Award), Laura Ingalls Wilder Medal (Author Award), Andrew Carnegie Medal (Video Award), Mildred L. Batchelder Award (Translation Award), Pura Belpré Award (Hispanic Authors), Robert F. Sibert Informational Book Medal (Non-Fiction), May Hill Arbuthnot Honor Lecture Award (Author). The Related Links at the bottom of the page are for: ALSC Children's Notable Media Lists (Video), Printz Award (YALSA) Home Page (Young Adult) and Coretta Scott King Book Awards Home Page (African American Authors).

JOHN NEWBERY MEDAL www.ala.org/ala/alsc/awardsscholarships/literaryawds/newberymedal/newberymedal.htm

The Newbery Medal honors the author of the most distinguished contribution to American literature for children. Established in 1922, it was named for eighteenth-century British publisher and bookseller John Newbery, the first to publish books for children. It is awarded annually by the Association for Library Service to Children, a division of the American Library Association.

NEWBERY MEDAL AND HONOR BOOKS, 1922 TO THE PRESENT

2002 Linda Sue Park. *A Single Shard.* Clarion Books/Houghton Mifflin

Honor Books:

Horvath, Polly. *Everything on a Waffle.* Farrar Straus Giroux
Nelson, Marilyn. *Carver: A Life in Poems.* Front Street

2003 Avi. *Crispin: The Cross of Lead.* Hyperion Books for Children

Honor Books:

Farmer, Nancy. *The House of the Scorpion.* Atheneum
Giff, Patricia Reilly. *Pictures of Hollis Woods.* Random House/Wendy Lamb Books
Hiaasen, Carl. *Hoot.* Knopf
Martin, Ann M. *A Corner of the Universe.* Scholastic
Tolan, Stephanie S. *Surviving the Applewhites.* HarperCollins

2004 Kate DiCamillo. *The Tale of Despereaux: Being the Story of a Mouse, a Princess, Some Soup, and a Spool of Thread.* Illustrated by Timothy Basil Ering. Candlewick

Honor Books:

Henkes, Kevin. *Olive's Ocean.* Greenwillow Books
Murphy, Jim. *An American Plague: The True and Terrifying Story of the Yellow Fever Epidemic of 1793.* Clarion

2005 Cynthia Kadohata. *Kira-Kira.* Atheneum Books for Young Readers/Simon & Schuster

Honor Books:

Choldenko, Gennifer. *Al Capone Does My Shirts.* G. P. Putnam's Sons/a division of Penguin Young Readers Group
Freedman, Russell. *The Voice that Challenged a Nation: Marian Anderson and the Struggle for Equal Rights.* Clarion Books/Houghton Mifflin
Schmidt. Gary D. *Lizzie Bright and the Buckminister Boy.* Clarion Books/Houghton Mifflin

For Newbery Medal Awards 1922–2001, see page 820 below.

LAURA INGALLS WILDER MEDAL
**www.ala.org/ala/alsc/awardsscholarships/
literaryawds/wildermedal/
wildermedal.htm**

The Wilder Medal honors an author or illustrator whose books, published in the United States, have made, over a period of years, a substantial and lasting contribution to literature for children. Established in 1954, it was named after its first winner, the renowned author of the *Little House* series, who wrote books about the country's people, rather than the country's leaders. Between 1960 and 1980, the Wilder Award was given every five years. From 1980 to 2001, it was awarded every three years. Beginning in 2001, it has been awarded every two years.

2003 Eric Carle
2005 Laurence Yep

For Laura Ingalls Wilder Medal winners 1954–2001, see page 830 below.

MILDRED L. BATCHELDER AWARD
**www.ala.org/ala/alsc/awardsscholarships/
literaryawds/batchelderaward/
batchelderaward.htm**

The Batchelder Award, established in 1966, is awarded to an American publisher for the most outstanding children's book originally published in a foreign language in a foreign country and subsequently translated into English and published in the United States. It is named after Mildred L. Batchelder, a former executive director of the Association for Library Service to Children who was a believer in the importance of good books for children in translation from all parts of the world. She spent 30 years with ALA, working as an ambassador to the world on behalf of children and books, encouraging and promoting the translation of the world's best children's literature and striving to eliminate barriers to understanding between people of different cultures, races, nations, and languages. Since 1979 the award has been given annually to a publisher for a book published in the preceding year. Before 1979 there was a lapse of two years between the original publication date and the award date. To make the transition to the new system, two awards were announced in 1979: one for 1978 and one for 1979. Beginning in 1994, honor recipients were selected and announced as well.

1994 Winner: Molina Llorente. *The Apprentice.* Translated from the Spanish by Robin Longshaw. Farrar, Straus and Giroux (Spain)

Honor Books:

Heymans, Annemie & Margriet. *The Princess in the Kitchen Garden.* Translated from the Dutch by Johanna H. and Johanna W. Prins. Farrar
Verhoeven, Ruud von der Rol & Rian. *Anne Frank Beyond the Diary: A Photographic Remembrance.* Translated from the Dutch by Tony Langham and Plym Peters. Viking

1995 Winner: Bjarne Reuter. *The Boys from St. Petri.* Translated from the Danish by Anthea Bell. Dutton

Honor Book:

Dalokay, Vedat. *Sister Shako and Kolo the Goat: Memories of My Childhood in Turkey.* Translated from the Turkish by Güner Ener. Lothrop, Lee and Shepard

1996 Winner: Orlev, Uri. *The Lady with the Hat.* Translated from the Hebrew by Hillel Halkin. Houghton

Honor Books:

Hoestlandt, Jo. *Star of Fear, Star of Hope.* Translated from the French by Mark Polizzotti. Walker and Co.

Van Dijk, Lutz. *Damned Strong Love: The True Story of Willi G. And Stephan K.* Translated from the German by Elizabeth D. Crawford. Henry Holt and Co.

1997 Winner: Kazumi Yumoto. *The Friends.* Translated by the Japanese by Cathy Hirano. Farrar, Straus & Giroux

No Honor Books

1998 Winner: Josef Holub. *The Robber and Me.* Edited by Mark Aronson and translated from the German by Elizabeth D. Crawford. Henry Holt

Honor Books:

Heidenrich, Elke. *Nero Corleone: a Cat's Story.* Translated from the German by Doris Orgel. Viking Publishing

Wassiljiewa, Tatjana. *Hostage to War: a True Story.* Translated from German by Anna Trenter. Scholastic Press

1999 Winner: Schoschana Rabinovici. *Thanks to My Mother.* Translated from the German by James Skofield. Dial

Honor Book:

Morgenstern, Susie. *Secret Letters from 0 to 10.* Translated from the French by Gill Rosner. Viking

2000 Winner. Anton Quintana. *The Baboon King.* Translated from the Dutch by John Nieuwenhuizen. Walker and Company

Honor Books:

Björk, Christina. *Vendela in Venice.* Illustrated by Inga-Karin Eriksson. Translated from the Swedish by Patricia Crampton. R&S Books

Buchholz, Quint. *Collector of Moments.* Translated from the German by Peter F. Neumeyer. Farrar, Straus and Giroux

Holtwijk, Ineke. *Asphalt Angels.* Translated from the Dutch by Wanda Boeke. Front Street

2001 Winner: Daniella Carmi. *Samir and Yonatan.* Translated from the Hebrew by Yael Lotan. Arthur A. Levine/Scholastic Press

Honor Book:

Lehmann, Christian. *Ultimate Game.* Translated from the French by William Rodarmor. David R. Godine

2002 Winner: Karin Gündisch. *How I Became an American.* Translated by James Skofield. Cricket Books/Carus Publishing

Honor Book:

Morgenstern, Susie. *A Book of Coupons.* Illustrations by Serge Bloch. Translated from the French by Gill Rosner for the U.S. edtion. Viking Press

2003 Winner: Cornelia Funke. *The Thief Lord.* Translated from the German by Oliver Latsch. The Chicken House/Scholastic Publishing

Honor Book:

Johansen, Hanna. *Henrietta and the Golden Eggs.* Illustrated by Käthi Bhend. Translated by John Barrett. David R. Godine

2004 Winner: Uri Orlev. *Run, Boy, Run.* Translated from the Hebrew by Hillel Halkin. Walter Lorraine Books/Houghton Mifflin Company

Honor Book:

Schyffert, Bea Uusma. *The Man Who Went to the Far Side of the Moon: The Story of Apollo 11 Astronaut Michael Collins.* Translated from the Swedish by Emi Guner. Chronicle Books

2005 Joëlle Stolz. *The Shadows of Ghadames.* Translated from the French by Catherine Temerson. Delacorte Press/Random House Children's Books

Honor Books:

Bredsdorff, Bodil. *The Crow-Girl: The Children of Crow Cove.* Translated from the Danish by Faith Ingwersen. Farrar Straus Giroux

Chotjewitz, David. *Daniel Half Human and the Good Nazi.* Translated from the German by Doris Orgel. Richard Jackson Books/Simon & Schuster's Atheneum division

For Mildred L. Batchelder Award winners 1968–93, see page 835 below.

THE PURA BELPRÉ AWARD
www.ala.org/ala/alsc/awardsscholarships/
literaryawds/belpremedal/belprmedal.htm

The Pura Belpré Award, established in 1996, is presented to a Latino/Latina writer and illustrator whose work best portrays, affirms, and celebrates the Latino cultural experience in an outstanding work of literature for children and youth. It is co-sponsored by the Association for Library Service to Children (ALSC), a division of the American Library Association (ALA), and the National Association to Promote Library and Information Services to Latinos and the Spanish-Speaking (REFORMA), an ALA Affiliate. The award is named after Pura Belpré, the first Latina librarian from the New York Public Library. As a children's librarian, storyteller, and author, she enriched the lives of Puerto Rican children in the U.S.A. through her pioneering work of preserving and disseminating Puerto Rican folklore. The awards are given biennially.

2002
Narrative Winner: Pam Munoz Ryan. *Esperanza Rising.* Scholastic

Honor Books:

Alarcón, Francisco X. *Iguanas in the Snow.* Illustrated by Maya Christina Gonzalez. Children's Book Press
Jimenez, Francisco. *Breaking Through.* Houghton Mifflin

2004
Narrative Winner: Julia Alvarez. *Before We Were Free.* Alfred A. Knopf

Honor Books:

Osa, Nancy. *Cuba 15.* Delacorte Press
Pérez, Amada Irma. *My Diary from Here to There/Mi Diario de Aquí Hasta Allá.* Children's Book Press

For Pura Belpré Award winners 1996–2001, See page 830 below.

THE ROBERT F. SIBERT AWARD
www.ala.org/ala/alsc/awardsscholarships/
literaryawds/sibertmedal/Sibert_Medal.htm

The Robert F. Sibert Informational Book Award, established by the Association for Library Service to Children in 2001, is awarded annually to the author of the most distinguished informational book published in English during the preceding year. The award is named in honor of Robert F. Sibert, the long-time President of Bound to Stay Bound Books, Inc. of Jacksonville, Illinois, and is sponsored by the company. ALSC administers the award.

2002 Medal Winner: Susan Campbell Bartoletti. *Black Potatoes: The Story of the Great Irish Famine, 1845–1850.* Houghton Mifflin

Honor Books:

Curlee, Lynn. *Brooklyn Bridge.* Simon & Schuster/ Atheneum
Greenberg, Jan and Sandra Jordan. *Vincent Van Gogh: Portrait of an Artist.* Delacorte
Warren, Andrea. *Surviving Hitler: A Boy in the Nazi Death Camps.* HarperCollins

2003 Medal Winner: James Cross Giblin. *The Life and Death of Adolf Hitler.* Clarion

Honor Books:

Blumenthal, Karen. *Six Days in October: The Stock Market Crash of 1929. A Wall Street Journal Book.* Atheneum
Gantos, Jack. *A Hole in My Life.* Farrar Straus & Giroux
Greenberg, Jan and Sandra Jordon. *Action Jackson.* Illustrated by Robert Andrew Parker. Roaring Brook Press/The Millbrook Press
Ryan, Pam Munoz. *When Marian Sang: The True Recital of Marian Anderson.* Illustrated by Brian Selznick. Scholastic

2004 Medal Winner: Jim Murphy. *An American Plague: The True and Terrifying Story of the Yellow Fever Epidemic of 1793.* Clarion Books/ Houghton Mifflin

Honor Book:

Cobb, Vicki. *I Face the Wind.* Illustrated by Julia Gorton. HarperCollins

2005 Medal Winner: Russell Freedman. *The Voice that Challenged a Nation: Marian Anderson and the Struggle for Equal Rights.* Clarion Books/ Houghton Mifflin Company

Honor Books:

Kerley, Barbara. *Walt Whitman: Words for America.* Illustrated by Brian Selznick, Scholastic Press/ Scholastic Inc.
Montgomery, Sy. *The Tarantula Scientist.* Photographs by Nic Bishop. Houghton Mifflin Company
Rumford, James. *Sequoyah: The Cherokee Man Who Gave His People Writing.* Translated into Cherokee by Anna Sixkiller Huckaby. Houghton Mifflin Company

See also page 830 below.

SRRT (SOCIAL RESPONSIBILITIES ROUND TABLE)

SRRT is a unit within the American Library Association. It works to make ALA more democratic and to establish progressive priorities not only for the Association, but also for the entire profession. Concern for human and economic rights was an important element in the founding of SRRT and remains an urgent concern today. SRRT believes that libraries and librarians must recognize and help solve social problems and inequities in order to carry out their mandate to work for the common good and bolster democracy. It is also the sponsor of the Coretta Scott King Award.

THE CORETTA SCOTT KING AWARD
http://www.ala.org/ala/srrt/corettascott king/corettascott.htm

The Coretta Scott King Award is presented annually by the Coretta Scott King Task Force of the American Library Association's Ethnic Multicultural Information Exchange Round Table (EMIERT). Recipients are authors and illustrators of African descent whose distinguished books promote an understanding and appreciation of the "American Dream." The Award commemorates the life and work of Dr. Martin Luther King Jr., and honors his widow, Coretta Scott King, for her courage and determination in continuing the work for peace and world brotherhood. Winners of the Coretta Scott King Award receive a framed citation, an honorarium, and a set of Encyclopaedia Britannica or World Book Encyclopedias. Coretta Scott King Award books are chosen by a seven-member national award jury. The CSK Award Jury also chooses the winners of the John Steptoe Award for New Talent Award winners. These books affirm new talent and offer visibility to excellence in writing or illustration at the beginning of a career as a published book creator. Prior to 1974, the Coretta Scott King Award was given to authors only.

2002
Author Award: Mildred Taylor. *The Land*. Phyllis Fogelman Books/Penguin Putnam

Author Honor Books:

Flake, Sharon G. *Money Hungry*. Jump at the Sun/Hyperion
Nelson, Marilyn. *Carver: A Life in Poems*. Front Street

2003
Author Award: Nikki Grimes. *Bronx Masquerade*. Dial Books for Young Readers

Author Honor Books:

Grimes, Nikki. *Talkin' About Bessie: the Story of Aviator Elizabeth Coleman*. Illustrated by E. B. Lewis. Orchard Books/Scholastic
Woods, Brenda. *The Red Rose Box*. G. P. Putnam's Sons

2004
Author Award: Angela Johnson. *The First Part Last*. Simon & Schuster Books for Young Readers

Author Honor Books:

Draper, Sharon M. *The Battle of Jericho*. Atheneum Books for Young Readers
McKissack, Patricia C. and Frederick L. *Days of Jubilee: The End of Slavery in the United States*. Illustrated by Leo and Diane Dillon. Scholastic
Woodson, Jacqueline. *Locomotion*. G. P. Putnam's Sons/Penguin Young Readers Group

2005
Author Award: Toni Morrison. *Remember: The Journey to School Integration*. Houghton Mifflin Company

Author Honor Books:

Flake, Sharon G. *Who Am I Without Him?: Short Stories about Girls and the Boys in Their Lives*. Jump at the Sun/Hyperion Books for Children
Moses, Shelia P. *The Legend of Buddy Bush*. Margaret K. McElderry Books, an imprint of Simon & Schuster
Nelson, Marilyn. *Fortune's Bones: The Manumission Requiem*. Front Street

For Coretta Scott King Award Winners 1970–2001, see page 826 below.

John Steptoe Award for New Talent

1995 Author Award: Sharon M. Draper. *Tears of a Tiger*. Simon & Schuster
1996 No Award Presented
1997 Author Award: Martha Southgate. *Another Way to Dance*. Delacorte
1998 No Award Presented
1999 Author Award: Sharon Flake. *The Skin I'm In*. Jump at the Sun/Hyperion
2000 No Award Presented
2001 No Award Presented
2002 No Author Award Presented
2003 Author Award: Janet McDonald. *Chill Wind*. Frances Foster Books/Farrar, Straus and Giroux
2004 Author Award: Smith, Hope Anita. *The Way A Door Closes*. Illustrated by Shane W. Evans. Henry Holt
2005 Author Award: Barbara Hathaway. *Missy Violet and Me*. Houghton Mifflin

YALSA (THE YOUNG ADULT LIBRARY SERVICES ASSOCIATION) BOOKLISTS AND BOOK AWARDS:
www.ala.org/yalsa/booklists

YALSA currently sponsors ten awards of individual titles or lists of books of note for young adult readers (ages 12 to

18). Each of the sections on the YALSA BOOKLISTS AND BOOK AWARDS website includes information on the award or list, a nomination form (if input from professionals in the field is encouraged) and links, not only to the winning titles or lists for the current year, but also to past winners.

YALSA 2005 LIST FOR TEEN READ WEEK

Fiction

The Year of the Hangman by Gary Blackwood (2002)
Pocahontas by Joseph Bruchac (2003)
Redemption by Chibbaro (2004)
Witches' Children: A Story of Salem by Patricia Clapp (1982)
The Ransom of Mercy Carter by Caroline B. Cooney (2001)
Betsy Zane, the Rose of Fort Henry by Lynda Durrant (2000)
Saturnalia by Paul Fleischman (1990)
Johnny Tremain by Esther Forbes (1998)
Early Thunder by Jean Fritz (1987)
The Lost Voyage of John Cabot by Henry Garfield (2004)
The Bell of Freedom by Dorothy Gilman Butters (1984)
Hope's Crossing by Joan E. Goodman (1998)
A Killing in Plymouth Colony by Carol Otis Hurst (1998)
Trouble's Daughter: The Story of Susanna Hutchinson, Indian Captive by Katherine Kirkpatrick (1998)
The Primrose Way by Jackie French Koller (1992)
Beyond the Burning Time by Kathryn Lasky (1994)
Just Jane: A Daughter of England Caught in the Struggle of the American Revolution by William Lavender (2002)
Roanoke: A Novel of the Lost Colony by Sonia Levitin (2000)
1776: Son of Liberty: A Novel of the American Revolution by Elizabeth Massie (2000)
The Serpent Never Sleeps: A Novel of Jamestown and Pocahontas by Scott O'Dell (1987)
Sorceress by Celia Rees (2002)
Witch Child by Celia Rees (2001)
A Break With Charity: A Story about the Salem Witch Trials by Ann Rinaldi (1992)
Or Give Me Death: A Novel of Patrick Henry's Family by Ann Rinaldi (2003)
The Secret of Sarah Revere by Ann Rinaldi (1995)
Weetamoo, Heart of the Pocassets, by Patricia Clark Smith (2003)
The Witch of Blackbird Pond by Elizabeth George Speare (2001)
Life, Liberty, and the Pursuit of Murder: A Revolutionary War Mystery by Karen Swee (2004)

Nonfiction

George Washington, Spymaster: How America Outspied the British and Won the Revolutionary War by Thomas B. Allen (2004)
Witch-hunt Mysteries of the Salem Witch Trials by Marc Aronson (2003)
To Conquer Is to Live: The Life of Captain John Smith of Jamestown by Kieran Doherty (2001)
Jamestown, John Smith, and Pocahontas in American History by Judith Edwards (2002)
Journal of a Revolutionary War Woman by Judith E. Greenberg (1996)
A Young Patriot: The American Revolution as Experienced by One Boy by Jim Murphy (1996)
An American Plague: The True and Terrifying Story of the Yellow Fever Epidemic of 1793 by Jim Murphy (2003)
Guns for General Washington: A Story of the American Revolution by Seymour Reit (1990)

This list was prepared for YALSA 2005 by the Teen Read Committee.

ALEX AWARDS (Adult Books for Young Adults) www.ala.org/yalsa/booklists/alex

The Alex Awards were established in 1998. Named for Margaret A. Edwards (whose nickname was Alex), this award selects the top ten adult books each year, both fiction and non-fiction, as well as genres that have special appeal for young adults. The books are selected from the titles published in the previous calendar year, must be well-written and very readable, and can include titles published in another country in English or in the U.S. in translation. Since Margaret A. Edwards is a major figure in the young adult field, who worked as a young adult librarian for many years at the Enoch Pratt Library in Baltimore and was known for her passionate support of adult books for young adults, it was a natural connection to use her nickname for this award. Field nominations are encouraged and a nomination form is available on the website.

2004

"From different perspectives and cultures, the universal questions surrounding the purpose of life, the pursuit of love, finding one's place in the world and accepting death are addressed within the pages of these titles (Judy Sasges, 2004 Committee Chair)

Davis, Amanda. *Wonder When You'll Miss Me.* William Morrow/HarperCollins
Haddon, Mark. *The Curious Incident of the Dog in the Night-time.* Doubleday
Hosseini, Khaled. *The Kite Runner.* Riverhead

Niffenegger, Audrey. *The Time Traveler's Wife*. MacAdam
    Cage
Packer, Z.Z. *Drinking Coffee Elsewhere*. Riverhead
Roach, Mary. *Stiff*. Norton
Salzman, Mark. *True Notebooks*. Knopf
Satrapi, Marjane. *Persepolis*. Pantheon
Winspear, Jacqueline. *Maisie Dobbs*. Soho
Yates, Bart. *Leave Myself Behind*. Kensington

2005

"These titles speak to realities that affect all of us: unconditional friendship and love, pushing or being pushed beyond one's limits, learning about society's norms and mores, dealing with adversity, and exploring the world that surrounds us." (Kimberley Hrivnak, 2005 Committee Chair)

Almond, Steve. *Candyfreak: A Journey through the
    Chocolate Underbelly of America*. Algonquin Books of
    Chapel Hill
Cox, Lynn. *Swimming to Antarctica: Tales of a Long-
    Distance Swimmer*. Knopf
Halpin, Brendan. *Donorboy*. Random House
Kurson, Robert. *Shadow Divers*. Random House
Meyers, Kent. *Work of Wolves*. Harcourt
Patchett, Ann. *Truth & Beauty: A Friendship*. HarperCollins
Picoult, Jodi. *My Sister's Keeper*. Atria
Reed, Kit. *Thinner Than Thou*. Tom Doherty Associates
Shepard, Jim. *Project X*. Knopf
Sullivan, Robert. *Rats: Observations on the History and
    Habitat of the City's Most Unwanted Inhabitants*.
    Bloomsbury

2005–1998 (available on the website)

BEST BOOKS FOR YOUNG ADULTS (BBYA) www.ala.org/yalsa/booklists/bbya

A committee of fifteen librarians from around the country selects the most significant books with teen appeal published for young adults and adults over a sixteen-month period of time—the year before the list is announced at ALA Midwinter and from September to December of the year before that. The winning titles are annotated by the committee members and the resulting list is published in the March issue of *Booklist* and is available to YALSA members on the Members Only website. The winning list without annotations is available at the website listed above. Both fiction and non-fiction titles of acceptable literary quality with proven or potential appeal to teens, ages 12–18, are included on the final list. This includes characterization and dialog in works of fiction that are believable within the context of the story and a readable text in an appealing format for works of non-fiction. Field nominations are accepted, but require a second from a committee member to be eligible for discussion. A nomination form is available on the website. Beginning in 1997, committee members have also been asked to select their Top Ten titles from the extensive Best Books for Young Adults list itself.

2004

The nominations list contained 207 titles. This list was narrowed to a list of 84 winning titles that includes graphic novels, adult books for young adults, books from small presses, science fiction and fantasy titles (two genres of particular appeal to young adults), and high-quality, works of non-fiction with considerable teen appeal.

Eleven books received a unanimous vote from the committee:

Crowe, Chris. *Getting Away with Murder: The True Story
    of the Emmett Till Case*. Penguin Putnam/Phyllis
    Fogelman Books
Donnelly, Jennifer. *A Northern Light*. Harcourt
Hearn, Lian. *Across the Nightingale Floor: Tales of the
    Otori, Book One*. Putnam Publishing Group/Riverhead
    Books
Johnson, Angela. *The First Part Last*. Simon and Schuster
    Books for Young Readers
Levithan, David. *Boy Meets Boy*. Random House/Alfred A.
    Knopf
Maynard, Joyce. *The Usual Rules*. St. Martin's Press
Meyer, L. A. *Bloody Jack: Being an Account of the Curious
    Adventures of Mary "Jacky" Faber, Ship's Boy*.
    Harcourt, Inc.
Murphy, Jim. *An American Plague: The True and Terrifying
    Story of the Yellow Fever Epidemic of 1793*. Houghton
    Mifflin Co./Clarion
Pattou, Edith. *East*. Harcourt Children's Books
Spinelli, Jerry. *Milkweed*. Random House, Inc./Alfred A.
    Knopf
Vance, Susanna. *Deep*. Random House/Delacorte

Top Ten Best Books for Young Adults for 2004 (by special vote of the committee)

Brooks, Martha. *True Confessions of a Heartless Girl*.
    Farrar, Straus & Giroux/Melanie Kroupa Books
Donnelly, Jennifer. *A Northern Light*. Harcourt
Haddon, Mark. *The Curious Incident of the Dog in the
    Night-Time: A Novel*. Random House/Doubleday
Johnson, Angela. *The First Part Last*. Simon & Schuster
    Books for Young Readers
Levithan, David. *Boy Meets Boy*. Random House/Alfred A.
    Knopf
Maynard, Joyce. *The Usual Rules*. St. Martin's Press
Pattou, Edith. *East*. Harcourt Children's Books
Rapp, Adam. *33 Snowfish*. Candlewick Press

Stroud, Jonathan. *The Amulet of Samarkand: Bartimaeus Trilogy, Book One.* Hyperion Books for Children/Miramax

Thompson, Craig. *Blankets: An Illustrated Novel.* Top Shelf Productions

2005

The 15-member committee narrowed its list of 214 official nominations to the final list of 86 significant adult and young adult titles recommended for ages 12 to 18. The 86 winning titles make up a diverse list that features science fiction and fantasy, nonfiction, novels in verse, cutting-edge contemporary fiction and graphic novels.

Fourteen books received a unanimous vote from the committee:

Bolden, Tonya. *Wake up Our Souls: a Celebration of Black American Artists.* Harry N. Abrams, Inc.

Fusco, Kimberly Newton. *Tending to Grace.* Alfred A. Knopf

Greenberg, Jan and Sandra Jordan. *Andy Warhol: Prince of Pop.* Delacorte

Hoose, Phillip. *The Race to Save the Lord God Bird.* Farrar, Straus and Giroux/Melanie Kroupa Books

Konigsburg, E. L. *The Outcasts of 19 Schuyler Place.* Simon and Schuster/Atheneum

Lawrence, Iain. *B for Buster.* Delacorte Press

Levithan, David. *The Realm of Possibility.* Alfred A. Knopf

Marchetta, Melina. *Saving Francesca.* Alfred A. Knopf

Oppel, Kenneth. *Airborn.* HarperCollins Children's Book Group/Eos

Rosoff, Meg. *how i live now.* Random House Children's Books/Wendy Lamb Books

Saenz, Benjamin Alire. *Sammy and Juliana in Hollywood.* Cinco Punto Press

Silverstein, Ken. *The Radioactive Boy Scout: The True Story of a Boy and His Backyard Nuclear Reactor.* Random House

Stratton, Allan. *Chanda's Secrets.* Annick Press

Updale, Eleanor. *Montmorency: Thief, Liar, Gentleman?* Orchard Books

Top Ten Best Books for Young Adults for 2005 (titles that showcase the quality and diversity of literature published for teens, by special vote of the BBYA Committee):

Braff, Joshua. *The Unthinkable Thoughts of Jacob Green.* Workman Publishing Co/Algonquin Books of Chapel Hill

Curtis, Christopher Paul. *Bucking the Sarge.* Random House Children's Books/Wendy Lamb Books

Hoose, Phillip M. *The Race to Save the Lord God Bird.* Melanie Kroupa Books

Levithan, David. *The Realm of Possibility.* Random House Children's Books/Alfred A. Knopf Inc.

Marchetta, Melina. *Saving Francesca.* Random House Children's Books: Alfred A. Knopf Inc.

Morpurgo, Michael. *Private Peaceful.* Scholastic

Oppel, Kenneth. *Airborn.* HarperCollins Children's Book Group/Eos

Rapp, Adam. *Under the Wolf, Under the Dog.* Candlewick Press

Saenz, Benjamin Alire. *Sammy and Juliana in Hollywood.* Cinco Puntos Press

Weeks, Sarah. *So B. It: A Novel.* HarperCollins Children's Books: Laura Geringer Books

2005–1996 (available on the website)

For BBYA 2000–2004, see page 840 below.

THE MARGARET A. EDWARDS AWARD
www.ala.org/yalsa/booklists

The Margaret A. Edwards Award, established in 1988, honors an author's lifetime achievement for writing books that have been popular over a period of time and are of acceptable literary quality. It also recognizes an author's work in helping adolescents become aware of themselves and addressing questions about their role and importance in relationships, society, and in the world. The books cited in the award must have been published in the United States five years or more prior to the first meeting of the Margaret A. Edwards committee and must be in print at the time of the award. Nominations from the field are accepted. A nomination form is available on the website.

2002 Paul Zindel

"Paul Zindel knows and understands the reality young adults deal with day-to-day," said Award Committee Chair Mary Long, a teacher-librarian at Wilson Middle School in Plano, Texas. "He has the ability to depict young adults in an honest and realistic way. The characters he developed nearly 40 years ago still speak to today's teens."

Five titles, published by Harper Collins and Bantam Dell Publishing, were cited in the award:

The Pigman. (1968)
The Pigman's Legacy. (1984)
The Pigman & Me. (1993)
My Darling, My Hamburger. (1969)
The Effect of Gamma Rays on Man-in-the-Moon Marigolds: A Drama in Two Acts. (1971)

2003 Nancy Garden

"Nancy Garden has the distinction of being the first author for young adults to create a lesbian love story with a positive ending," said Award Committee Chair Rosemary Chance, an assistant professor at The University of Southern Mississippi. "Using a fluid, readable style, Garden opens a window through which readers can find courage to be true to themselves."

One title was cited in the award: *Annie on My Mind*. Farrar Straus & Giroux

2004 Ursula K. Le Guin

"In her writing, as in her life, Ms. Le Guin takes on issues arising from the effort to live humanely in the natural world, exploring the tension between individuality and social norms," said Award Committee Chair Francisca Goldsmith. "In the Earthsea fantasy series, young protagonists mature not only physically, but also spiritually, as Ms. LeGuin's real world readers must in order to navigate young adulthood."

Titles cited in the award:

A Wizard of Earthsea (1968) originally published in 1968, now published by Bantam Spectra (a division of Random House); and sequels: *The Tombs of Atuan* (1971); *The Farthest Shore* (1972); *Tehanu* (1990) all published by Simon Pulse (pb) and Atheneum (hc) both imprints of Simon & Schuster
The Left Hand of Darkness (1969) an Ace Book published by the Berkley Publishing Group (a Division of Penguin Group USA Inc.)
The Beginning Place (1980) currently published by Tor

2005 Francesca Lia Block

"Block's work has been considered ground-breaking for its magical realism and bringing alive the L.A. scene," said Edwards Award Committee chair Cindy Dobrez. "Block takes traditional folklore archetypes and translates them for contemporary teens with her inventive use of lyrical language, transforming gritty urban environments into a funky fairy tale dreamworld."

Titles cited in the award (all published by HarperCollins):

Weetzie Bat (1989)
Witch Baby (1991)
Cherokee Bat and the Goat Guys (1992)
Missing Angel Juan (1993)
Baby Be-Bop (1996)

For Margaret A. Edwards Award winners 1988–2001, see page 831 below.

THE MICHAEL L. PRINTZ AWARD FOR EXCELLENCE IN YOUNG ADULT LITERATURE www.ala.org/yalsa/printz

The Michael L. Printz Award, established in 2000, is an award for a book that exemplifies literary excellence in YA literature. It is named for a Topeka, Kansas school librarian who was a long-time active member of the Young Adult Library Services Association and who was known for his passion for connecting teens and books. In addition to the single best work, published for young adults anywhere in the world, the committee may select up to four honor books. The award covers the books published in the calendar year prior to the announcement of the winners. Nominations from the field are accepted and a nomination form is available on the website.

2002 Winner: An Na. *A Step from Heaven*. Front Street

"Both intimate and universal, this powerful story of Young Ju's coming of age is rooted in the conflict between her traditional Korean immigrant family and the need to find her place in the United States," said Judith A. Druse, chair of the Printz Award Selection Committee. "Each chapter is a stirring story, and together these lyrical vignettes create a heartfelt account of every teen's struggle between family and self."

Four Honor Books Were Selected by the Committee:

Dickinson, Peter. *The Ropemaker*. Delacorte
Greenberg, Jan. *Heart to Heart: New Poems Inspired by Twentieth-Century American Art*. Abrams
Lynch, Chris. *Freewill*. HarperCollins
Wolff, Virginia Euwer. *True Believer*. Atheneum Books for Young Readers.

2003 Winner: Aidan Chambers. *Postcards from No Man's Land*. Dutton/Penguin Putnam

"The alternating narratives of Jacob and Geertrui make a story that is intense, sophisticated and surprising," said Suzanne Manczuk, acting chair of the Printz Award Selection Committee. "Jacob discovers that 'nothing in Amsterdam is what it appears to be.'"

Three Honor Books Were Selected by the Committee:

Farmer, Nancy. *The House of the Scorpion*. Simon and Schuster/Richard Jackson
Freymann-Weyr, Garret. *My Heartbeat*. Houghton Mifflin Company
Gantos, Jack. *Hole in My Life*. Farrar, Straus and Giroux

2004 Winner: Angela Johnson. The First Part Last. Simon & Schuster Books for Young Readers

"Bobby's voice comes strong and poignant, pulling readers into the heartache, confusion, and insecurity," said Pam Spencer Holley, Chair of the 2004 Printz Award Committee. "Angela Johnson's work never verges on sentimentality and brings readers close to the true meaning of parenthood."

Four Honor Books Were Selected by the Committee:

Donnelly, Jennifer. *A Northern Light.* Harcourt, Inc.
Frost, Helen. *Keesha's House.* Farrar, Straus and Giroux/ Frances Foster Books
Going, K. L. *Fat Kid Rules the World.* G. P. Putnam's Sons/ Penguin Young Readers Group
Mackler, Carolyn. *The Earth, My Butt and Other Big Round Things.* Candlewick Press

2005 Rosoff, Meg. *how i live now.* Wendy Lamb Books, an imprint of Random House

"Through Daisy's evolving voice, readers see a teen who moves beyond self-absorption to become a resourceful survivor, understanding the need to care for others," said Award Chair Betty Carter. "Meg Rosoff achieves balance in a story both darkly symbolic and bitingly funny."

Three Honor Books Were Selected by the Committee:

Oppel, Kenneth. *Airborn.* EOS, an imprint of HarperCollins
Schmidt, Gary D. *Lizzie Bright and the Buckminster Boy.* Clarion Books, a Houghton Mifflin Company Imprint
Stratton, Allan. *Chanda's Secrets.* Annick Press

For Michael L. Printz Award winners 2000–2001, see page 831 below.

OUTSTANDING BOOKS FOR THE COLLEGE BOUND AND LIFELONG LEARNERS www.ala.org/yalsa/booklists/obcb

A YALSA Committee of public, secondary school, and academic librarians, in collaboration with the Association of College and Research Libraries, selected the 2004 list. Revised every five years as a tool for several audiences—students preparing for college, educators, librarians, and parents—it offers opportunities for independent reading and lifelong learning and is helpful as students prepare for college entrance exams and courses, or read to strengthen their knowledge in a variety of subject areas and enhance their appreciation for different cultures and times. For the first time in 2004 the decision was made to organize the list into five academic disciplines: history, humanities, literature and language arts, science and technology, and social sciences.

It includes works of fiction, nonfiction, poetry, biography and drama, all of which were selected using a variety of criteria: readability, cultural and ethnic diversity, balance of view points, and variety of genres and title availability, with a focus on titles that have been published over the past five years.

Both the 2004 and the 1999 lists are available on the website. All titles are annotated.

The 1999 list, entitled simply Outstanding Books for the College Bound, is divided into five categories: Fiction, Non-fiction, Biography, Drama and Poetry.

POPULAR PAPERBACKS FOR YA
www.ala.org/yalsa/booklists/poppaper

Each year this committee, established in 1997, chooses up to five themes or genres and then selects and annotates ten to twenty-five popular titles, widely available in paperback and published either for young adults or adults (but with considerable teen appeal). Since the purpose of these booklists is to encourage teens to read for pleasure, popularity is more important than literary quality. Both fiction and nonfiction titles are eligible, but they must be in print and available in paperback. The lists are annotated by the committee members, but after 1999 the annotated lists are only available on the Members Only website. But all themes and accompanying titles can be viewed at the website listed above. A nomination form is also available on that website for field nominations.

2005

Fairy Tales
Heartbreak
Horror
Define "Normal"

2004

If It Weren't for Them: Heroes
On That Note . . . Music and Musicians
Guess Again: Mystery and Suspense
Simply Science Fiction

2003

Lock It, Lick It, Click It: Diaries, Letters and Email
Flights of Fantasy: Beyond Harry and Frodo
This Small World: A Glimpse at Many Cultures
I've Got a Secret

2002

Relationships: Friends and Family
War: Conflict and Consequences

Tales of the Cities
Graphic Novels: Superheroes and Beyond

2001

Humor
Paranormal
Poetry
Western

2000

Short Takes
Page Turners
Romance
Self-Help

1999

Good Sports
Teen Culture
Changing Dimensions
Different Drummers

1998

Adult Mysteries for Teens
Feel Good Books
Facing Nature Head On
Teens from Other Times: Historical Fiction

1997

Books for the Soul
Going Alternative: Graphic Novels and Picture Books
Lesbian/Gay Tales
Multicultural Fiction
The Stories of Our Lives

QUICK PICKS FOR RELUCTANT YOUNG ADULT READERS www.ala.org/yalsa/booklists/quickpicks

This committee is charged with preparing an annotated list of books for reluctant teen readers. This is not a high/low list for teens who have difficulty reading at grade level. Instead, it's for teens who can read but choose not to, until they are introduced to just the right book—like the page-turners on the Quick Picks list, books for recreational, rather than curricular or remedial reading. Unlike the books on the Best Books list, these are leisure-reading titles, chosen because of their subject matter, cover art, readability, format and style. Teen input is a vital part of the book selection process, with committee members consulting teen readers and sharing their responses during the discussion. Eligible books are those published for young adults and adults over

a sixteen-month period of time—the year before the list is announced at ALA Midwinter and from September to December of the year before that. The annual lists are available at the website, along with a nomination form for input from the field. After 2000 the full annotated lists are located on the Members Only section. In addition to the Quick Picks list itself, committee members now select a Top Ten list, also available on the Quick Picks website.

2004

79 titles were selected for this year's list; 30 fiction and 49 non-fiction.

Top Ten Quick Picks List for 2004 (by special vote of the committee):

Boards: the Art and Design of the Skateboard. Universe Publishing
Ashanti. *Foolish/Unfoolish: Reflections on Love.* Hyperion
Giles, Gail. *Dead Girls Don't Write Letters.* Millbrook Press/Roaring Brook Press
Horowitz, Anthony. *Skeleton Key: An Alex Rider Adventure.* Penguin Putnam Books for Young Readers.
Johnson, Angela. *The First Part Last.* Simon and Schuster Books For Young Readers
Macdonald, Andy. *Dropping In With Andy Mac: Life of a Pro Skateboarder.* Simon & Schuster/Pulse
Platt, Larry. *Only the Strong Survive: The Odyssey of Allen Iverson.* HarperCollins/ReganBooks
Schiff, Nancy Rica. *Odd Jobs: Portraits of Unusual Occupations.* Ten Speed Press
Seate, Mike. *Jesse James: The Man and His Machines.* Motorbooks International/MBI
Trueman, Terry. *Inside Out.* HarperCollins/Tempest

2005

80 titles on the list were published late 2003 through 2004 and represent over 30 different publishers. Thirty-three of the titles are non-fiction and forty-seven are fiction. Top Ten Quick Picks List for 2005 (by special vote of the committee):

Flake, Sharon. *Who Am I Without Him? A Short Story Collection About Girls and the Boys in Their Lives.* Hyperion
Gottlieb, Andrew. *In the Paint: Tattoos of the NBA and the Stories Behind Them.* Hyperion
Heimberg, Jason and Justin Heimberg. *The Official Movie Plot Generator: 27,000 Hilarious Movie Plot Combinations.* Brothers Heimberg Publishing
Kenner, Rob and Pitts, George. *VX: 10 Years of Vibe Photography.* Abrams/Vibe Books
Klancher, Lee. *Monster Garage: How to Customize Damn*

Near Everything. Motorbooks International/MBI
Publishing
Riley, Andy. *The Book of Bunny Suicides.* Penguin/Plume
Shaw, Tucker. *Confessions of a Backup Dancer.* Simon and
Schuster/Aladdin
Sleator, William. *The Boy Who Couldn't Die.* Abrams/
Amulet
Takaya, Natsuki. *Fruits Basket series. Vols. 1–5.* Tokyopop
Woods, Brenda. *Emako Blue.* Penguin Putnam

2005–1996 (available on the website)

AUDIOBOOKS FOR YOUNG ADULTS
www.ala.org/yalsa/booklists

The best recordings of books that are published for or appeal to young adults are selected and annotated by committee members. The list appears without annotations on the website after 2000. When the Members Only website was established, the decision was made to move all annotations to that site.

2004

Thirty-four titles were selected for the list from the preceding two years of spoken word releases. From a high-quality fantasy like *Abhorsen* by Garth Nix to the adult masterpiece *A Yellow Raft in Blue Water* these are quality recordings that not only appeal to teens but also enhance their appreciation of the written works on which they are based.

2005

The titles appearing have been selected from the past two years of spoken word releases. They have been selected for their appeal to a teen audience, the quality of their recording, and because they enhance the audience's appreciation of any written work on which they may be based. While the list as a whole addresses the interests and needs of YAs ranging in age from 12 to 18, individual titles may appeal to parts of that range rather than to its whole.

Barry, Dave and Ridley Pearson. *Peter and the Starcatchers.* Narrated by Jim Dale. Brilliance Audio, 2004, 7 discs, 9 hours
Barry, Max. *Jennifer Government.* Narrated by Michael Kramer, Books on Tape, 2003, 6 cassettes, 9 hours
Choldenko, Gennifer. *Al Capone Does My Shirts: A Novel.* Narrated by Johnny Heller. Recorded Books, 2004, 5 cassettes, 5.75 hours
Danziger, Paula. *The Cat Ate My Gymsuit.* Narrated by Caitlin Brodnick and the Full Cast Audio Family. Full Cast Audio, 2004, 3 discs, 2.75 hours
Davis, Donald. *Grand Canyons.* August House, 2004, 1 disc, 49 minutes

Draper, Sharon M.. *Battle of Jericho.* Narrated by J.D. Jackson. Recorded Books, 2003, 6 cassettes, 8.25 hours
Fink, Sam. *The Three Documents That Made America: The Declaration of Independence, The Constitution of the U.S.A. & The Bill of Rights.* Written and read by the author. Documents read by Terry Bregy. Audio Bookshelf, 2004, 2 discs, 1.5 hour
Frost, Helen. *Keesha's House.* Narrated by multiple readers, Recorded Books, 2004, 2 cassettes, 2.25 hours
Gletizman, Morris. *Girl Underground.* Narrated by Mary-Anne Fahey. Bolinda, 2004, 3 discs, 3.5 hours
Hesse, Karen. *Aleutian Sparrow.* Narrated by Sarah Jones. Listening Library, 2003, 1 cassette, 1.75 hours
Hoeye, Michael. *No Time Like Show Time.* Narrated by Campbell Scott, Listening Library, 2004
Johnson, Angela. *First Part Last.* Narrated by Khalipa Oldjohn and Kole Kristi. Listening Library, 2004, 1.75 hours, 1 cassette
Marnika, Dino. *The Dons.* Narrated by Bolinda, 2003, 4 discs, 4 hours
Martel, Yann. *Life of Pi.* Narrated by Jeff Woodman. HighBridge Audio, 2003, 7 cassettes, 11.5 hours
McCaughrean, Geraldine. *Kite Rider.* Narrated by Cynthia Bishop and the Full Cast Audio Family. Full Cast Audio, 2004, 6 discs, 6.75 hours
Myers, Walter Dean. *Shooter.* Narrated by Chad Coleman, Bernie McInerny, and Michelle Santopietro. Recorded Books, 2004, 3 discs, 3.75 hours
Nix, Garth. *Keys to the Kingdom Series.* Narrated by Allan Corduner, Listening Library. #1: *Mister Monday* 2003, 5 cassettes, 8 hours; #2: *Grim Tuesday* 2004, 4 cassettes, 7 hours
Peck, Richard. *The River Between Us.* Narrated by Lina Patel with Daniel Passer. Listening Lirary, 2004, 3 cassettes, 4 hours
Pratchett, Terry. *The Wee Free Men.* Narrated by Stephen Briggs, Harper's Children Audio, 2003, 7 cassettes, 9 hours. Sequel: *A Hat Full of Sky.* Narrated by Stephen Briggs, Harper Collins Audio, 2004, 8 discs, 9 hours
Pullman, Phillip. *Ruby in the Smoke.* Narrated by Anton Lesser. Listening Library, 2004, 4 cassettes, 6.5 hours Sequel: *The Shadow in the North* read by Anton Lesser. Listening Library, 2004, 6 cassettes, 9.5 hours
Peyton, K. M.. *Blind Beauty.* Narrated by Nicki Praull. Bolinda, 2003, 6 cassettes, 9 hours
Rees, Celia. *Pirates.* Narrated by Jennifer Wiltsie, Listening Library, 2004, 6 cassettes, 9 hours
Ryan, Pam Munoz. *Becoming Naomi Leon.* Narrated by Annie Kozuch. Listening Library, 2004, 3 cassettes, 4.25 hours
Simmons, Michael. *Pool Boy.* Narrated by Chad Lowe, Listening Library, 2004, 3 cassettes, 3.5 hours
Stroud, Jonathan. *Golem's Eye.* Narrated by Simon Jones. Listening Library, 2004, 10 cassettes, 16.5 hours

Swindells, Robert. *Abomination.* Narrated by Amanda
Hulme. Bolinda, 2004, 3 discs, 3.5 hours

Tashjian, Janet. *Fault Line.* Narrated by Clara Bryant and
Jason Harris. Listening Library, 2004, 3 cassettes, 4
hours

Tingle, Tim, Choctaw Storyteller. *Walking the Choctaw
Road.* Cinco Puntos Press, 2004

Updale, Eleanor. *Montmorency: Thief, Liar, Gentleman?*
Narrated by Stephen Fry. Listening Library, 2004, 3
cassettes, 5.25 hours

Van Draanen, Wendelin. *Flipped.* Narrated by Andy Paris
and Carine Montertrand, Recorded Books, 2004, 5
cassettes, 7.25 hours

1999–2005 (available on the website)

TEENS' TOP TEN (Where Teens Choose the Winners)

Members of YALSA's YA Galley Project, teen book groups
in five school and public libraries around the country—
Alabama, Indiana, Michigan, Texas, and Washington
state—selected the books nominated for this year's list.
(Nominating groups change every two years and are selected for their experience in discussing books.) The list is
voted on by teens all over the country during Teen Read
Week, which was October 17–23 in 2004. Readers 12–18
years old can vote online at any time during Teen Read
Week. The 44 books on the nomination list were all published in 2003 and 2004. Over 2,000 online votes were cast
by teens for their top three titles. Results were combined
with the vote cast by the nominating groups to create the
Teens' Top Ten list.

2004

1. *Harry Potter and the Order of the Phoenix* by J. K.
   Rowling (Scholastic, 2003) Fantasy.
2. *Eragon* by Christopher Paolini (Knopf, 2003) Fantasy.
3. *Pirates!* by Celia Rees (Bloomsbury, 2003) Historical
   Fiction.
4. *Trickster's Choice* by Tamora Pierce (Random House,
   2003) Fantasy.
5. *Inkheart* by Cornelia Funke (Chicken House/
   Scholastic, 2003) Fantasy.
6. *A Great and Terrible Beauty* by Libba Bray (Delacorte,
   2004) Supernatural.
7. *The Goose Girl* by Shannon Hale (Bloomsbury, 2003)
   Fantasy.
8. *Princess in Pink* by Meg Cabot (HarperCollins, 2004)
   Realistic.
9. *The Earth, My Butt, and Other Big Round Things* by
   Carolyn Mackler (Candlewick, 2003) Realistic.
10. *Curse of the Blue Tattoo* by L.A. Meyer (Harcourt,
    2004) Historical Fiction.

The complete list of nominations for the 2003 list is also
available on the website, along with the 2003 Teens' Top
Ten winners.

NATIONAL COUNCIL OF TEACHERS OF ENGLISH AWARDS

THE AWARD FOR EXCELLENCE IN POETRY FOR CHIL-
DREN WWW.NCTE.ORG/ABOUT/AWARDS/SECT/ELEM/
106857.HTM

The National Council of Teachers of English (NCTE)
wishes to recognize and foster excellence in children's
poetry by encouraging its publication and by exploring
ways to acquaint teachers and children with poetry through
such means as publications, programs, and displays. As one
means of accomplishing this goal, NCTE established its
Award for Excellence in Poetry for Children in 1977 to
honor a living American poet for his or her aggregate work
for children ages 3–13. The NCTE Poetry Selection Committee gave the award annually until 1982, at which time it
was decided that the award would be given every three
years. The next award will be given in 2006. A collection
of poetry books of all winners of the NCTE Award for Excellence in Poetry for Children, past and future, is sustained
and preserved at the University of Minnesota Children's
Literature Research Collections (CLRC) / Kerlan Collection
at the Andersen Library as well as the Boston Public
Library / Special Collections.

2003 Mary Ann Hoberman
2006 Date When Next Award Will Be Given

NCTE ORBIS PICTUS NONFICTION AWARD www.ncte.org/elem/awards/orbispictus

The world of children's literature contains a variety of
genres, all of which have appeal to the diverse interests of
children as well as potential for classroom teaching. In recent years, however, nonfiction or information books have
emerged as a very attractive, exciting, and popular genre.
NCTE, through the Committee on the Orbis Pictus Award
for Outstanding Nonfiction for Children, has established an
annual award for promoting and recognizing excellence in
the writing of nonfiction for children. The name *Orbis Pictus,* commemorates the work of Johannes Amos Comenius,
Orbis Pictus: The World in Pictures (1657), considered to
be the first book actually planned for children. The award is
presented each November by the Orbis Pictus Committee
Chair during the Books for Children Luncheon at the Annual NCTE Convention. Although only one title is singled
out for the award, up to five Honor Books are also recognized.

2001 Winner: Jerry Stanley. *Hurry Freedom: African Americans in Gold Rush California.* Crown

Honor Books:

Adler, David A. *America's Champion Swimmer: Gertrude Ederle.* Illustrated by Terry Widdener, Gulliver Books
Arnosky, Jim. *Wild & Swampy.* HarperCollins
Giblin, James Cross. *The Amazing Life of Benjamin Franklin.* Illustrated by Michael Dooling. Scholastic Press.
Govenar, Alan B. *Osceola: Memories of a Sharecropper's Daughter.* Illustrated by Shane W. Evans. Jump at the Sun
Stanley, Diane. *Michelangelo.* HarperCollins

2002 Winner: Susan Campbell Bartoletti. *Black Potatoes: The Story of the Great Irish Famine, 1845–1850.* Houghton Mifflin

Honor Books:

Kerley, Barbara. *The Dinosaurs of Waterhouse Hawkins: An Illuminating History of Mr. Waterhouse Hawkins, Artist and Lecturer : True Dinosaur Story in Three Ages. . . .* Illustrated by Brian Selznick. Scholastic Press
Kurlansky, Mark. *The Cod's Tale.* Illustrated by S. D. Schindler. Penguin Putnam Books
Rappaport, Doreen. *Martin's Big Words: The Life of Dr. Martin Luther King, Jr.* Illustrated by Bryan Collier. Hyperion Books for Children

2003 Winner: Pam Munoz Ryan. *When Marian Sang: The True Recital of Marian Anderson.* Illustrated by Brian Selznick. Scholastic Press

Honor Books:

Bial, Raymond. *Tenement: Immigrant Life on the Lower East Side.* Houghton Mifflin
Fleischman, John. *Phineas Gage: A Gruesome but True Story About Brain Science.* Houghton Mifflin
Freedman, Russell. *Confucius: The Golden Rule.* Arthur A. Levine Books
O'Connor, Jane. *Emperor's Silent Army: Terracotta Warriors of Ancient China.* Viking Children's Books
Old, Wendie. *To Fly: The Story Of The Wright Brothers.* Illustrated by Robert Andrew Parker. Clarion Books

2004 Winner: Jim Murphy. *An American Plague: The True and Terrifying Story of the Yellow Fever Epidemic of 1793.* Clarion Books

Honor Books:

Byrd, Robert. *Leonardo: Beautiful Dreamer.* Dutton Children's Books

Freedman, Russell. *In Defense of Liberty: The Story of America's Bill of Rights.* Holiday House
Hopkinson, Deborah. *Shutting Out The Sky: Life In The Tenements Of New York, 1880–1924.* Orchard Books
Lasky, Kathryn. *The Man Who Made Time Travel.* Farrar, Straus and Giroux
Mann, Elizabeth. *Empire State Building: When New York Reached for the Skies.* Mikaya Press

2005 Winner: Rhoda Blumberg. *York's Adventures with Lewis and Clark: An African-American's Part in the Great Expedition.* HarperCollins

Honor Books:

Burleigh, Robert. *Seurat and La Grande Jatte: Connecting the Dots.* Abrams Book for Young Readers
Freedman, Russell. *The Voice That Challenged A Nation: Marian Anderson and the Struggle for Equal Rights.* Clarion Books
Hoose, Phillip. *The Race to Save the Lord God Bird.* Farrar, Straus and Giroux
Jenkins, Steve. *Actual Size.* Houghton Mifflin

For Orbis Pictus Award winners 1990–2000, see page 831.

INTERNATIONAL READING ASSOCIATION AWARDS
www.reading.org

IRA Children's Book Awards

Children's Book Awards are given for an author's first or second published book written for children or young adults (ages birth to 17 years). Awards are given for fiction and nonfiction in each of three categories: primary, intermediate, and young adult. Books from any country and in any language published for the first time during the 2004 calendar year will be considered. Each award carries a monetary stipend.

2002

Intermediate Fiction: Yin. *Coolies.* Philomel, Penguin Putnam Books
Intermediate Nonfiction: Dorinda Makanaonalani Nicholson and Larry Nicholson. *Pearl Harbor Warriors.* Woodson House

Young Adult Fiction: An Na. *A Step from Heaven.* Front Street
Young Adult Nonfiction: Wilborn Hampton. *Meltdown: A Race against Nuclear Disaster at Three Mile Island.* Candlewick Press

2003

Intermediate Fiction: Marlene Carvell. *Who Will Tell My Brother?* Hyperion

Intermediate Nonfiction: David J. Smith. *If the World Were a Village: A Book About the World's People.* Kids Can Press

Young Adult Fiction: Chris Crowe. *Mississippi Trial, 1955.* Phyllis Fogelman Books

Young Adult Nonfiction: Duane Damon. *Headin' for Better Times: The Arts of the Great Depression.* Lerner

2004

Intermediate Fiction: Esme Raji Codell. *Sahara Special.* Hyperion Books

Intermediate Nonfiction: Penelope Niven. *Carl Sandburg: Adventures of a Poet.* Harcourt

Young Adult Fiction: Kathe Koja. *Buddha Boy.* Farrar Straus Giroux

Young Adult Nonfiction: Miriam Stone. *At the End of Words: A Daughter's Memoir.* Candlewick Press

2005

Intermediate Fiction: Maiya Williams. *The Golden Hour.* Amulet Books

Intermediate Nonfiction: Joan Marie Arbogast. *Buildings in Disguise.* Boyds Mill Press

Young Adult Fiction: Brenda Woods. *Emako Blue.* G.P. Putnam's Sons

Young Adult Nonfiction: Brent Runyon. *The Burn Journals.* Alfred A. Knopf

For IRA Award winners 1975–2001, see page 832 below.

Lee Bennett Hopkins Promising Poet Award
www.reading.org/association/awards/childrens_hopkins.html

The Lee Bennett Hopkins Promising Poet Award is a US$500 award given every three years to a promising new poet who writes for children and young adults, and who has published no more than two books of children's poetry. A book-length single poem may be submitted. ("Children's poetry" is defined as poetry, rather than light verse.) The award is for published works only. Poetry in any language may be submitted; non-English poetry must be accompanied by an English translation.

1995   Deborah Chandra. *Rich Lizard and Other Poems.* Farrar, Straus and Giroux
1998   Kristine O'Connell George. *The Great Frog Race and Other Poems.* Clarion

2001   Craig Crist-Evans. *Moon Over Tennessee: A Boy's Civil War Journal.* Houghton Mifflin
2004   Lindsay Lee Johnson. *Soul Moon Soup.* Front Street

INTERNATIONAL AWARDS

Carnegie Medal (The Library Association of UK)
www.carnegiegreenaway.org.uk/carnegie/carn.html

The Carnegie Medal is awarded in July each year to the writer of an outstanding book for children written in English and first published in the United Kingdom during the preceding year. It was established by The Library Association in 1936, in memory of the great Scottish-born philanthropist, Andrew Carnegie (1835–1919). Carnegie was a self-made industrialist who made his fortune in steel in the USA. His experience of using a library as a child led him to resolve that "if ever wealth came to me that it should be used to establish free libraries." Carnegie set up more than 2,800 libraries across the English speaking world and, by the time of his death, over half the library authorities in Great Britain had Carnegie libraries. It was first awarded to Arthur Ransome for *Pigeon Post.*

2001   Beverly Naidoo. *The Other Side of Truth.* Puffin
2002   Terry Pratchett. *The Amazing Maurice and His Educated Rodents.* Doubleday
2003   Sharon Creech. *Ruby Holler.* Bloomsbury Children's Books
2004   Jennifer Donnelly. *A Gathering Light.* Bloomsbury Children's Books (American Title: *A Northern Light.*)

For Carnegie Medal winners 1936–99, see page 834 below.

The Hans Christian Andersen Award (International Board on Books for Young People)
http://www.ibby.org/Seiten/04_andersen.htm

The Hans Christian Andersen Award, established in 1956, is given biennially to a living author and since 1966 an illustrator whose complete works have made a lasting contribution to children's literature. Often called the "Little Nobel Prize," the Hans Christian Andersen Award is the highest international recognition given to an author and an illustrator of children's books. Her Majesty Queen Margrethe II of Denmark is the Patron of the Andersen Awards. The nominations are made by the National Sections of International Board on Books for Young People (IBBY) and the recipients are selected by a distinguished international jury of children's literature specialists.

Hans Christian Andersen Award for Writing

2002   Aidan Chambers (UK)
2004   Martin Waddell (Ireland)

For Hans Christian Andersen Award winners
1956–2000, see page 834 below.

WHITBREAD BOOK AWARDS (for people who love reading) http://www.whitbread-bookawards.co.uk/index.cfm

Whitbread Book Awards are announced each year in five
categories: the Novel, First Novel, Biography, Poetry and
Children's Book Award. The Awards, which recognize the
most enjoyable books each year by writers based in the UK
and Ireland and were established by Whitbread, the UK's
leading hospitality business, in 1971. The first Whitbread
Children's Book Award was given in 1972. In 2004 the
awards attracted 450 entries—the second highest total
ever—and included a record number of entries (113) in the
Children's Book Award category. Winners in the five categories each receive £5,000 and are announced at the beginning of January. The overall winner of the Whitbread Book
of the Year, selected from the five category winners, receives £25,000 and is announced at the Whitbread Book
Awards ceremony in central London at the end of January.
The Whitbread Book Awards, in partnership with the National Reading Campaign, CILIP (Chartered Institute of Library and Information Professionals), amazon.co.uk and the
Booksellers Association, continue to explore new ways of
promoting the enjoyment of reading in the UK.

Whitbread Children's Book Award

1972   Rumer Godden. *The Diddakoi.*
1973   Alan Aldridge & William Plomer. *The Butterfly Ball & The Grasshopper's Feast.*
1974   Russell Hoban and Quentin Blake. *How Tom Beat Captain Najork & His Hired Sportsmen.* Tied with: Jill Paton Walsh. *The Emperor's Winding Sheet.*
1975   No Whitbread Children's Book Award
1976   Penelope Lively. *A Stitch in Time.*
1977   Shelagh Macdonald. *No End to Yesterday.*
1978   Philippa Pearce. *The Battle of Bubble & Squeak.*
1979   Peter Dickinson. *Tulku.*
1980   Leon Garfield. *John Diamond.*
1981   Jane Gardam. *The Hollow Land.*
1982   W J Corbett. *The Song of Pentecost.*
1983   Roald Dahl. *The Witches.*
1984   Barbara Willard. *The Queen of the Pharisees' Children.*
1985   Janni Howker. *The Nature of the Beast.*
1986   Andrew Taylor. *The Coal House.*
1987   Geraldine McCaughrean. *A Little Lower than the Angels.*
1988   Judy Allen. *Awaiting Developments.*
1989   Hugh Scott. *Why Weeps the Brogan?*

1990   Peter Dickinson. *AK.*
1991   Diana Hendry. *Harvey Angell.*
1992   Gillian Cross. *The Great Elephant Chase.*
1993   Anne Fine. *Flour Babies.*
1994   Geraldine McCaughrean. *Gold Dust.*
1995   Michael Morpurgo. *The Wreck of the Zanzibar.*
1996   Anne Fine. *The Tulip Touch.*
1997   Andrew Norriss. *Aquila.*
1998   David Almond. *Skellig.*
1999   J K Rowling, *Harry Potter and the Prisoner of Azkaban.*
2000   Jamila Gavin. *Coram Boy.*
2001   Philip Pullman. *The Amber Spyglass. His Dark Materials* Vol. III (Only Children's Book ever to win the Whitbread)
2002   Hilary McKay. *Saffy's Angel.*
2003   David Almond. *The Fire-Eaters.*
2004   Geraldine McCaughrean. *Not the End of the World.*

Children's Book Award Shortlist (Honor Books)

2000 Shortlist: *Heaven Eyes* by David Almond
                  The Seeing Stone by Kevin Crossley-Holland
                  Troy by Adele Geras

2001 Shortlist: *Artemis Fowl* by Eoin Colfer
                  Journey to the River Sea by Eva Ibbotson
                  The Lady and the Squire by Terry Jones

2002 Shortlist   *Exodus* by Julie Bertagna
                 Sorceress by Celia Rees
                 Mortal Engines by Philip Reeve

2003 Shortlist   *The Oracle* by Catherine Fisher
                 Private Peaceful by Michael Morpurgo
                 Naked Without a Hat by Jeanne Willis

2004 Shortlist   *Looking for JJ* by Anne Cassidy
                 how i live now by Meg Rosoff
                 No Shame, No Fear by Ann Turnbull

BOOKTRUST TEENAGE PRIZE SHORTLIST 2004 www.jubileebooks.co.uk/jubilee/newsn news_stories/2004/040611_01asp?

Booktrust, the independent educational charity that encourages people of all ages to read books, announced
eight shortlisted titles for the 2004 Booktrust Teenage
Prize. The Booktrust Teenage Prize was launched in 2003
with the aim of recognizing and celebrating contemporary
teenage fiction.

The inaugural prize was won by Mark Haddon for his
highly acclaimed book *The Curious Incident of the Dog in
the Night-Time,* which went on to win the Guardian Chil-

dren's Fiction Prize, the Whitbread Prize and the 2004 Commonwealth Writers Prize, as well as being longlisted for the Man Booker Prize.

A panel of five judges, who discussed every aspect of the books before reaching their decision, chose the eight shortlisted titles.

The eight shortlisted books are:

The Dark Beneath by Alan Gibbons (Orion)
Looking for JJ by Anne Cassidy (Scholastic)
Deep Secret by Berlie Doherty (Puffin)
Rani and Sukh by Bali Rai (Corgi)
Boy Kills Man by Matt Whyman (Hodder)
Fat Boy Swim by Catherine Forde (Egmont)
The Opposite of Chocolate by Julie Bertagna (Macmillan)
Unique by Alison Allen-Gray (Oxford University Press)

OTHER AWARDS

The *Boston Globe–Horn Book* Awards
http://www.hbook.com/awards/bghb/default.asp

Awarded annually since 1967 by the *Boston Globe* newspaper and the *Horn Book Magazine*, the *Boston Globe–Horn Book* Awards for Excellence in Children's Literature honor outstanding titles in three categories: Fiction and Poetry, Nonfiction, and Picture Book.

2001
Fiction and Poetry: *Carver: A Life in Poems* by Marilyn Nelson (Front Street)

Honors:

Everything on a Waffle by Polly Horvath (Farrar)
Troy by Adele Geras (Harcourt)

Nonfiction: *The Longitude Prize* by Joan Dash. Illustrated by Dusan Petricic (Foster/Farrar)

Honors:

Rocks in His Head by Carol Otis Hurst. Illustrated by James Stevenson (Greenwillow)
Uncommon Traveler: Mary Kingsley in Africa written and illustrated by Don Brown (Houghton)

2002
Fiction and Poetry: *Lord of the Deep* by Graham Salisbury (Delacorte)

Honors:

Saffy's Angel by Hilary McKay (McElderry)
Amber Was Brave, Essie Was Smart written and illustrated by Vera B. Williams (Greenwillow)

Nonfiction: *This Land Was Made for You and Me: The Life and Songs of Woody Guthrie* by Elizabeth Partridge (Viking)

Honors:

Handel, Who Knew What He Liked by M. T. Anderson. Illustrated by Kevin Hawkes (Candlewick)
Woody Guthrie: Poet of the People written and illustrated by Bonnie Christensen (Knopf)

2003
Fiction and Poetry: *The Jamie and Angus Stories* by Anne Fine. Illustrated by Penny Dale (Candlewick)

Honors:

Feed by M. T. Anderson (Candlewick)
Locomotion by Jacqueline Woodson (Putnam)

Nonfiction: *Fireboat: The Heroic Adventures of the John J. Harvey* by Maira Kalman (Putnam)

Honors:

To Fly: The Story Of The Wright Brothers by Wendie Old. Illustrated by Robert Andrew Parker (Clarion)
Revenge of the Whale: The True Story of the Whaleship Essex by Nathaniel Philbrick (Putnam)

2004
Fiction: *The Fire-Eaters* by David Almond (Delacorte)

Fiction Honors:

God Went to Beauty School by Cynthia Rylant (HarperTempest)
The Amulet of Samarkand: Bartimaeus Trilogy, Book One by Jonathan Stroud (Hyperion)

Nonfiction: *An American Plague: The True and Terrifying Story of the Yellow Fever Epidemic of 1793* by Jim Murphy (Clarion)

Nonfiction Honors:

Surprising Sharks by Surprising Sharks. Illustrated by James Croft (Candlewick)
The Man Who Went to the Far Side of the Moon: The Story of Apollo 11 Astronaut Michael Collins by Bea Uusma Schyffert (Chronicle)

For *Boston Globe–Horn Book* Award winners 1967–2000, see page 837 below.

THE LEE BENNETT HOPKINS POETRY AWARD http://www.pabook.libraries.psu.edu/hopkins/

The Lee Bennett Hopkins Award, established in 1993, is presented annually to an American poet or anthologist for the most outstanding new book of children's poetry published in the previous calendar year. Since its inception in 1993, the winning poet or anthologist has received a handsome plaque and a $500 honorarium made possible by Mr. Hopkins. Selected by a panel of nationally recognized teachers, librarians, and scholars, the Lee Bennett Hopkins Award for Children's Poetry is the first award of its kind in the United States. It is presented each year by The Children's Literature Council of Pennsylvania.

2002
Winner: *Pieces: A Year in Poems and Quilts* by Anna Grossnickle Hines (Greenwillow)

Honorees:

A Humble Life: Plain Poems by Linda Oatman High. Illustrated by Bill Farnsworth (Wm. B. Eerdmans Publishing Co)
A Poke in the I: A Collection of Concrete Poems by Paul Janeczko. Illustrated by Chris Raschka (Candlewick Press)
Short Takes: Fast Break Basketball Poetry by Smith, Charles R., Jr. (Dutton)

2003
Winner: *Splash! Poems of Our Watery World* by Constance Levy. Illustrated by David Soman (Orchard Books)

Honorees:

Girl Coming in for a Landing—A Novel in Poems by April Halprin Wayland. Illustrated by Elaine Clayton (Alfred A. Knopf)
Becoming Joe DiMaggio by Maria Testa. Illustrated by Scott Hunt (Candlewick Press)
The Song Shoots Out of My Mouth: A Celebration of Music by Jaime Adoff. Illustrated by Martin French (Dutton Children's Books)

2004
Winner: *The Wishing Bone and Other Poems* by Stephen Mitchell. Illustrated by Tom Pohrt (Candlewick)

Honorees:

Animal Sense by Diane Ackerman. Illustrated by Peter Sis (Knopf)

Blues Journey by Walter Dean Myers. Illustrated by Christopher Myers (Holiday House)
The Pond God and Other Stories by Samuel Jay Keyser. Illustrated by Robert Shetterly (Front Street)
The Way A Door Closes by Hope Anita Smith. Illustrated by Shane W. Evans (Henry Holt)

2005
Winner: *Here in Harlem* by Walter Dean Myers. (Holiday House)

Honorees:

Is This Forever, or What?: Poems and Paintings from Texas by Naomi Shihab Nye. (Greenwillow).
Creature Carnival by Marilyn Singer. Illustrated by Gris Grimly (Hyperion).

For Lee Bennett Hopkins Award winners 1993–2001, see page 840 below.

THE JOHN NEWBERY MEDAL AND HONOR BOOKS, 1922–2001

1922

The Story of Mankind by Hendrik Willem van Loon, Liveright

HONOR BOOKS: *The Great Quest* by Charles Hawes, Little, Brown; *Cedric the Forester* by Bernard Marshall, Appleton; *The Old Tobacco Shop* by William Bowen, Macmillan; *The Golden Fleece and the Heroes Who Lived Before Achilles* by Padraic Colum, Macmillan; *Windy Hill* by Cornelia Meigs, Macmillan

1923

The Voyages of Dr. Doolittle by Hugh Lofting, Harper

HONOR BOOKS: No Record

1924

The Dark Frigate by Charles Hawes, Little, Brown

HONOR BOOKS: No Record

1925

Tales from Silver Lands by Charles Finger, Doubleday

HONOR BOOKS: *Nicholas* by Anne Carroll Moore, Putnam; *Dream Coach* by Anne Parrish, Macmillan

1926

Shen of the Sea by Arthur Bowie Chrisman, Dutton

HONOR BOOK: *Voyagers* by Padraic Colum, Macmillan

1927

Smoky, The Cowhorse by Will James, Scribner's

HONOR BOOKS: No record

1928

Gayneck, The Story of a Pigeon by Dhan Gopat Mukeri, Dutton

HONOR BOOKS: *The Wonder Smith and His Son* by Ella Young, Longmans; *Downright Dencey* by Caroline Snedeker, Doubleday

1929

The Trumpeter of Krakow by Eric P. Kelly, Macmillan

HONOR BOOKS: *Pigtail of Ah Lee Ben Loo* by John Benett, Longmans; *Millions of Cats* by Wanda Gág, Coward-McCann; *The Boy Who Was* by Grace Hallock, Dutton; *Clearing Weather* by Cornelia Meigs, Little, Brown; *Runaway Papoose* by Grace Moon, Doubleday; *Tod of the Fens* by Elinor Whitney, Macmillan

1930

Hitty, Her First Hundred Years by Rachel Field, Macmillan

HONOR BOOKS: *Daughter of the Seine* by Jeanette Eaton, Harper; *Pran of Albania* by Elizabeth Miller, Doubleday; *Jumping-Off Place* by Marian Hurd McNeely, Longmans; *Tangle-Coated Horse and Other Tales* by Ella Young, Longmans; *Vaino* by Julia Davis Adams, Dutton; *Little Blacknose* by Hildegarde Swift, Harcourt

1931

The Cat Who Went to Heaven by Elizabeth Coatsworth, Macmillan

HONOR BOOKS: *Floating Island* by Anne Parrish, Harper; *The Dark Star of Itza* by Alida Malkus, Harcourt; *Queer Person* by Ralph Hubbard, Doubleday; *Mountains Are Free* by Julia Davis Adams, Dutton; *Spice and the Devil's Cave* by Agnes Hewes, Knopf; *Meggy Macintosh* by Elizabeth Janet Gray, Doubleday; *Garram the Hunter* by Herbert Best, Doubleday; *Ood-Le-Uk the Wanderer* by Alice Lide and Margaret Johansen, Little, Brown

1932

Waterless Mountain by Laura Adams Armer, Longmans

HONOR BOOKS: *The Fairy Circus* by Dorothy P. Lathrop, Macmillan; *Calico Bush* by Rachel Field, Macmillan; *Boy of the South Seas* by Eunice Tietjens, Coward-McCann; *Out of the Flame* by Eloise Lownsbery, Longmans; *Jane's Island* by Majorie Allee, Houghton; *Truce of the Wolf and Other Tales of Old Italy* by Mary Gould Davis, Harcourt

1933

Young Fu of the Upper Yangtze by Elizabeth Foreman Lewis, Winston

HONOR BOOKS: *Swift Rivers* by Cornelia Meigs, Little, Brown; *The Railroad to Freedom* by Hildegarde Swift, Harcourt; *Children of the Soil* by Nora Burglon, Doubleday

1934

Invincible Louisa by Cornelia Meigs, Little, Brown

HONOR BOOKS: *The Forgotten Daughter* by Caroline Snedeker, Doubleday; *Swords of Steel* by Elsie Singmaster, Houghton; *ABC Bunny* by Wanda Gág, Coward-McCann; *Winged Girl of Knossos* by Erik Berry, Appleton; *New Land* by Sarah Schmidt, McBride; *Big Tree of Buntahy* by Padraic Colum, Macmillan; *Glory of the Seas* by Agnes Hewes, Knopf; *Apprentice of Florence* by Ann Kyle, Houghton

1935

Dobry by Monica Shannon, Viking

HONOR BOOKS: *Pageant of Chinese History* by Elizabeth Seeger, Longmans; *Davy Crockett* by Constance Rourke, Harcourt; *A Day on Skates* by Hilda Van Stockum, Harper

1936

Caddie Woodlawn by Carol Ryrie Brink, Macmillan

HONOR BOOKS: *Honk, the Moose* by Phil Stong, Dodd, Mead; *The Good Master* by Kate Seredy, Viking; *Young Walter Scott* by Elizabeth Janet Gray, Viking; *All Sail Set* by Armstrong Sperry, Winston

1937

Roller Skates by Ruth Sawyer, Viking

HONOR BOOKS: *Phoebe Fairchild: Her Book* by Lois Lenski, Stokes; *Whistler's Van* by Idwal Jones, Viking; *Golden Basket* by Ludwig Bemelmans, Viking; *Winterbound* by Margery Bianco, Viking; *Audubon* by Constance Rourke, Harcourt; *The Codfish Musket* by Agnes Hewes, Doubleday

1938

The White Stag by Kate Scredy, Viking

HONOR BOOKS: *Pecos Bill* by James Cloyd Bowman, Little, Brown; *Bright Island* by Mabel Robinson, Random; *On the Banks of Plum Creek* by Laura Ingalls Wilder, Harper

1939

Thimble Summer by Elizabeth Enright, Rinehart

HONOR BOOKS: *Nino* by Valenti Angelo, Viking; *Mr. Popper's Penguins* by Richard and Florence Atwater, Little, Brown; *"Hello the Boat!"* by Phyllis Crawford, Holt; *Leader by Destiny: George Washington, Man and Patriot* by Jeanette Eaton, Harcourt; *Penn* by Elizabeth Janet Gray, Viking

1940

Daniel Boone by James Daugherty, Viking

HONOR BOOKS: *The Singing Tree* by Kate Seredy, Viking; *Runner of the Mountain Tops* by Mabel Robinson, Random; *By the Shores of Silver Lake* by Laura Ingalls Wilder, Harper; *Boy with a Pack* by Stephen W. Meader, Harcourt

1941

Call It Courage by Armstrong Sperry, Macmillan

HONOR BOOKS: *Blue Willow* by Doris Gates, Viking; *Young Mac of Fort Vancouver* by Mary Jane Carr, Harper; *The Long Winter* by Laura Ingalls Wilder, Harper; *Nansen* by Anna Gertrude Hall, Viking

1942

The Matchlock Gun by Walter D. Edmonds, Dodd, Mead

HONOR BOOKS: *Little Town on the Prairie* by Laura Ingalls Wilder, Harper; *George Washington's World* by Genevieve Foster, Scribner's; *Indian Captive: The Story of Mary Jemison* by Lois Lenski, Harper, *Down Ryton Water* by Eva Roe Gaggin, Viking

1943

Adam of the Road by Elizabeth Janet Gray, Viking

HONOR BOOKS: *The Middle Moffat* by Eleanor Estes, Harcourt; *Have You Seen Tom Thumb?* by Mabel Leigh Hunt, Harper

1944

Johnny Tremain by Esther Forbes, Houghton

HONOR BOOKS: *These Happy Golden Years* by Laura Ingalls Wilder, Harper; *Fog Magic* by Julia Sauer, Viking; *Rufus M.* by Eleanor Estes, Harcourt; *Mountain Born* by Elizabeth Yates, Coward-McCann

1945

Rabbit Hill by Robert Lawson, Viking

HONOR BOOKS: *The Hundred Dresses* by Eleanor Estes, Harcourt; *The Silver Pencil* by Alice Dalgliesh, Scribner's; *Abraham Lincoln's World* by Genevieve Foster, Scribner's; *Lone Journey: The Life of Roger Williams* by Jeanette Eaton, Harcourt

1946

Strawberry Girl by Lois Lenski, Harper

HONOR BOOKS: *Justin Morgan Had a Horse* by Marguerite Henry, Rand; *The Moved-Outers* by Florence Crannel Means, Houghton; *Bhimsa, the Dancing Bear* by Christine Weston, Scribner's; *New Found World* by Katherine Shippen, Viking

1947

Miss Hickory by Carolyn Sherwin Bailey, Viking

HONOR BOOKS: *Wonderful Year* by Nancy Barnes, Messner; *Big Tree* by Mary and Conrad Buff, Viking; *The Heavenly Tenants* by William Maxwell, Harper; *The Avion My Uncle Flew* by Cyrus Fisher, Appleton; *The Hidden Treasure of Glaston* by Eleanore Jewett, Viking

1948

The Twenty-One Balloons by William Pene du Bois, Viking

HONOR BOOKS: *Pancakes-Paris* by Claire Huchet Bishop, Viking; *Li Lun, Lad of Courage* by Carolyn Treffinger, Abingdon; *The Quaint and Curious Quest of Johnny Longfoot* by Catherine Besterman, Bobbs; *The Cow-Tail Switch, and Other West African Stories* by Harold Courlander, Holt; *Misty of Chincoteague* by Marguerite Henry, Rand

1949

King of the Wind by Marguerite Henry, Rand McNally

HONOR BOOKS: *Seabird* by Holling C. Holling, Houghton; *Daughter of the Mountains* by Louise Rankin, Viking; *My Father's Dragon* by Ruth S. Gannett, Random; *Story of the Negro* by Arna Bontemps, Knopf

1950

The Door in the Wall by Marguerite de Angeli, Doubleday

HONOR BOOKS: *Tree of Freedom* by Rebecca Caudill, Viking; *The Blue Cat of Castle Town* by Catherine Coblentz, Longmans; *Kildee House* by Rutherford Montgomery, Doubleday; *George Washington* by Genevieve Foster, Scribner's; *Song of the Pines* by Walter and Marion Havighurst, Winston

1951

Amos Fortune, Free Man by Elizabeth Yates, Aladdin

HONOR BOOKS: *Better Known as Johnny Appleseed* by Mabel Leigh Hunt, Harper; *Gandhi; Fighter Without a*

Sword by Jeanette Eaton, Morrow; *Abraham Lincoln, Friend of the People* by Clara Ingram Judson, Follett; *The Story of Appleby Capple* by Anne Parrish, Harper

1952

Ginger Pye by Eleanor Estes, Harcourt

HONOR BOOKS: *Americans Before Columbus* by Elizabeth Baity, Viking; *Minn of the Mississippi* by Holling C. Holling, Houghton; *The Defender* by Nicholas Kalashnikoff, Scribner's; *The Light at Tern Rock* by Julia Sauer, Viking; *The Apple and the Arrow* by Mary and Conrad Buff, Houghton

1953

Secret of the Andes by Ann Nolan Clark, Viking

HONOR BOOKS: *Charlotte's Web* by E. B. White, HarperCollins; *Moccasin Trail* by Eloise McGraw, Coward-McCann; *Red Sails to Capri* by Ann Weil, Viking; *The Bears on Hemlock Mountain* by Alice Dalgliesh, Scribner's; *Birthdays of Freedom,* Vol. 1, by Genevieve Foster, Scribner's

1954

. . . and now Miguel by Joseph Krumgold, HarperCollins

HONOR BOOKS: *All Alone* by Claire Huchet Bishop, Viking; *Shadrach* by Meindert DeJong, HarperCollins; *Hurry Home, Candy* by Meindert DeJong, HarperCollins; *Theodore Roosevelt, Fighting Patriot* by Clara Ingram Judson, Follett; *Magic Maize* by Mary and Conrad Buff, Houghton

1955

The Wheel on the School by Meindert DeJong, HarperCollins

HONOR BOOKS: *The Courage of Sarah Noble* by Alice Dalgliesh, Scribner's; *Banner in the Sky* by James Ullman, HarperCollins

1956

Carry on, Mr. Bowditch by Jean Lee Latham, Houghton Mifflin

HONOR BOOKS: *The Secret River* by Marjorie Kinnan Rawlings, Scribner's; *The Golden Name Day* by Jennie Linquist, HarperCollins; *Men, Microscopes, and Living Things* by Katherine Shippen, Viking

1957

Miracles on Maple Hill by Virginia Sorensen, Harcourt

HONOR BOOKS: *Old Yeller* by Fred Gipson, HarperCollins; *The House of Sixty Fathers* by Meindert DeJong, Harper-Collins; *Mr. Justice Holmes* by Clara Ingram Judson, Follett; *The Corn Grows Ripe* by Dorothy Rhoads, Viking; *Black Fox of Lorne* by Marguerite de Angeli, Doubleday

1958

Rifles for Watie by Harold Keith, Crowell

HONOR BOOKS: *The Horsecatcher* by Mari Sandoz, Westminster; *Gone-Away Lake* by Elizabeth Enright, Harcourt Brace; *The Great Wheel* by Robert Lawson, Viking; *Tom Paine, Freedom's Apostle* by Leo Gurko, HarperCollins

1959

The Witch of Blackbird Pond by Elizabeth George Speare, Houghton Mifflin

HONOR BOOKS: *The Family Under the Bridge* by Natalie Savage Carlson, HarperCollins; *Along Came a Dog* by Meindert DeJong, HarperCollins; *Chucaro: Wild Pony of the Pampa* by Francis Kalnay, Harcourt Brace; *The Perilous Road* by William O. Steele, Harcourt Brace

1960

Onion John by Joseph Krumgold, HarperCollins

HONOR BOOKS: *My Side of the Mountain* by Jean George, Dutton; *America Is Born* by Gerald W. Johnson, Morrow; *The Gammage Cup* by Carol Kendall, Harcourt Brace

1961

Island of the Blue Dolphins by Scott O'Dell, Houghton Mifflin

HONOR BOOKS: *America Moves Forward* by Gerald W. Johnson, Morrow; *Old Ramon* by Jack Schaefer, Houghton Mifflin; *The Cricket in Times Square* by George Selden, Farrar, Straus and Giroux

1962

The Bronze Bow by Elizabeth George Speare, Houghton Mifflin

HONOR BOOKS: *Frontier Living* by Edwin Tunis, World; *The Golden Goblet* by Eloise McGraw, Coward-McCann; *Belling the Tiger* by Mary Stolz, HarperCollins

1963

A Wrinkle in Time by Madeleine L'Engle, Farrar, Straus and Giroux

HONOR BOOKS: *Thistle and Thyme* by Sorche Nic Leodhas, Holt; *Men of Athens* by Olivia Coolidge, Houghton

1964

It's Like This, Cat by Emily Cheney Neville, Harper

HONOR BOOKS: *Rascal* by Sterling North Dutton; *The Loner* by Ester Wier, McKay

1965

Shadow of a Bull by Maia Wojciechowska, Atheneum

HONOR BOOK: *Across Five Aprils* by Irene Hunt, Follett

1966

I, Juan de Pareja by Elizabeth Borten de Treviño, Farrar, Straus and Giroux

HONOR BOOKS: *The Black Cauldron* by Lloyd Alexander, Holt; *The Animal Family* by Randall Jarrell, Pantheon; *The Noonday Friends* by Mary Stolz, Harper

1967

Up a Road Slowly by Irene Hunt, Follett

HONOR BOOKS: *The King's Fifth* by Scott O'Dell, Houghton; *Zlateh the Goat and Other Stories* by Isaac Bashevis Singer, Harper; *The Jazz Man* by Mary H. Weik, Atheneum

1968

From the Mixed-Up Files of Mrs. Basil E. Frankweiler by E. L. Konigsburg, Atheneum

HONOR BOOKS: *Jennifer, Hecate, Macbeth, William McKinley, and Me, Elizabeth* by E. L. Konigsburg, Atheneum; *The Black Pearl* by Scott O'Dell, Houghton; *The Fearsome Inn* by Isaac Bashevis Singer, Scribner's; *The Egypt Game* by Zilpha Keatley Snyder, Atheneum

1969

The High King by Lloyd Alexander, Holt

HONOR BOOKS: *To Be a Slave* by Julius Lester, Dial; *When Shlemiel Went to Warsaw and Other Stories* by Isaac Bashevis Singer, Farrar, Straus and Giroux

1970

Sounder by William H. Armstrong, Harper

HONOR BOOKS: *Our Eddie* by Sulamith Ish-Kishor, Pantheon; *The Many Ways of Seeing: An Introduction to the Pleasures of Art* by Janet Gaylord Moore, World; *Journey Outside* by Mary Q. Steele, Viking

1971

Summer of the Swans by Betsy Byars, Viking

HONOR BOOKS: *Kneeknock Rise* by Natalie Babbitt, Farrar, Straus and Giroux; *Enchantress from the Stars* by Sylvia Louise Engdahl, Atheneum; *Sing Down the Moon* by Scott O'Dell, Houghton

1972

Mrs. Frisby and the Rats of NIMH by Robert C. O'Brien, Atheneum

HONOR BOOKS: *Incident at Hawk's Hill* by Allan W. Eckert, Little, Brown; *The Planet of Junior Brown* by Virginia Hamilton, Macmillan; *The Tombs of Atuan* by Ursula K. Le Guin, Atheneum; *Annie and the Old One* by Miska Miles, Little, Atlantic; *The Headless Cupid* by Zilpha Keatley Snyder, Atheneum

1973

Julie of the Wolves by Jean Craighead George, Harper

HONOR BOOKS: *Frog and Toad Together* by Arnold Lobel, Harper; *The Upstairs Room* by Johanna Reiss, Harper; *The Witches of Worm* by Zilpha Keatley Snyder, Atheneum

1974

The Slave Dancer by Paula Fox, Bradbury

HONOR BOOKS: *The Dark Is Rising* by Susan Cooper, Atheneum, McElderry

1975

M. C. Higgins, the Great by Virginia Hamilton, Macmillan

HONOR BOOKS: *Figgs and Phantoms* by Ellen Raskin, Dutton; *My Brother Sam Is Dead* by James Lincoln and Christopher Collier, Four Winds; *The Perilous Guard* by Elizabeth Marie Pope, Houghton; *Philip Hall Likes Me. I Reckon Maybe* by Bette Greene, Dial

1976

The Grey King by Susan Cooper, Atheneum, McElderry

HONOR BOOKS: *The Hundred Penny Box* by Sharon Bell Mathis, Viking; *Dragonwings* by Laurence Yep, Harper

1977

Roll of Thunder, Hear My Cry by Mildred D. Taylor, Dial

HONOR BOOKS: *Abel's Island* by William Steig, Farrar, Straus and Giroux; *A String in the Harp* by Nancy Bond, McElderry

1978

Bridge to Terabithia by Katherine Paterson, Harper

HONOR BOOKS: *Ramona and Her Father* by Beverly Cleary, Morrow; *Anpao: An American Indian Odyssey* by Jamake Highwater, Harper

1979

The Westing Game by Ellen Raskin, Dutton

HONOR BOOKS: *The Great Gilly Hopkins* by Katherine Paterson, Harper

1980

A Gathering of Days: A New England Girl's Journal, 1830–32 by Joan Blos, Scribner's

HONOR BOOK: *The Road from Home: The Story of an Armenian Girl* by David Kherdian, Greenwillow

1981

Jacob Have I Loved by Katherine Paterson, Harper

HONOR BOOKS: *The Fledgling* by Jane Langton, Harper; *A Ring of Endless Light* by Madeleine L'Engle, Farrar, Straus and Giroux

1982

A Visit to William Blake's Inn: Poems for Innocent and Experienced Travelers by Nancy Willard, Harcourt

HONOR BOOKS: *Ramona Quimby, Age 8* by Beverly Cleary, Morrow; *Upon the Head of the Goat: A Childhood in Hungary, 1939–1944* by Aranka Siegel, Farrar, Straus and Giroux

1983

Dicey's Song by Cynthia Voigt, Atheneum

HONOR BOOKS: *The Blue Sword* by Robin McKinley, Greenwillow; *Dr. De Soto* by William Steig, Farrar, Straus and Giroux; *Graven Images* by Paul Fleischman, Harper; *Homesick: My Own Story* by Jean Fritz, Putnam; *Sweet Whispers, Brother Rush* by Virginia Hamilton, Philomel

1984

Dear Mr. Henshaw by Beverly Cleary, Morrow

HONOR BOOKS: *The Wish Giver: Three Tales of Coven Tree* by Bill Brittain, Harper; *A Solitary Blue* by Cynthia Voigt, Atheneum; *The Sign of the Beaver* by Elizabeth George Speare, Houghton; *Sugaring Time* by Kathryn Lasky, Macmillan

1985

The Hero and the Crown by Robin McKinley, Greenwillow

HONOR BOOKS: *The Moves Make the Man* by Bruce Brooks, Harper; *One-Eyed Cat* by Paula Fox, Bradbury; *Like Jake and Me* by Mavis Jukes, Knopf

1986

Sarah, Plain and Tall by Patricia MacLachlan, Harper

HONOR BOOKS: *Commodore Perry in the Land of Shogun* by Rhoda Blumberg, Lothrop: *Dogsong* by Gary Paulsen, Bradbury

1987

The Whipping Boy by Sid Fleischman, Greenwillow

HONOR BOOKS: *On My Honor* by Marion Dane Bauer, Clarion; *A Fine White Dust* by Cynthia Rylant, Bradbury; *Volcano* by Patricia Lauber, Bradbury

1988

Lincoln: A Photobiography by Russell Freedman, Clarion

HONOR BOOKS: *Hatchet* by Gary Paulsen, Bradbury; *After the Rain* by Norma Fox Mazer, Morrow

1989

Joyful Noise: Poems for Two Voices by Paul Fleischman, Harper

HONOR BOOKS: *In the Beginning: Creation Stories from Around the World* by Virginia Hamilton, Harcourt; *Scorpions* by Walter Dean Myers, Harper

1990

Number the Stars by Lois Lowry, Houghton

HONOR BOOKS: *Afternoon of the Elves* by Janet Taylor Lisle, Orchard; *Shabanu: Daughter of the Wind* by Suzanne Fisher Staples, Knopf; *The Winter Room* by Gary Paulsen, Orchard

1991

Maniac Magee by Jerry Spinelli, Little, Brown

HONOR BOOK: *The True Confessions of Charlotte Doyle* by Avi, Orchard

1992

Shiloh by Phyllis Reynolds Naylor, Atheneum

HONOR BOOKS: *Nothing but the Truth: A Documentary Novel* by Avi, Orchard, *The Wright Brothers: How They Invented the Airplane* by Russell Freedman, Holiday

1993

Missing May by Cynthia Rylant, Orchard

HONOR BOOKS: *What Hearts* by Bruce Brooks, Harper; *The Dark Thirty: Southern Tales of the Supernatural* by Patricia C. McKissack, Knopf; *Somewhere in the Darkness* by Walter Dean Myers, Sholastic

1994

The Giver by Lois Lowry, Houghton

HONOR BOOKS: *Crazy Lady!* by Jane Leslie Conley, Harper; *Dragon's Gate* by Laurence Yep, Harper; *Eleanor Roosevelt: A Life of Discovery* by Russell Freedman, Clarion

1995

Walk Two Moons by Sharon Creech, Harper

HONOR BOOKS: *Catherine, Called Birdy* by Karen Cushman, Clarion; *The Ear, the Eye and the Arm* by Nancy Farmer, Orchard

1996

The Midwife's Apprentice by Karen Cushman, Clarion

HONOR BOOKS: *The Great Fire* by Jim Murphy, Scholastic; *The Watsons Go to Birmingham—1963* by Christopher Paul Curtis, Delacorte; *What Jamie Saw* by Carolyn Coman, Front Street; *Yolanda's Genius* by Carol Fenner, McElderry

1997

The View from Saturday by E. L. Konigsburg, Karl/ Atheneum

HONOR BOOKS: *A Girl Named Disaster* by Nancy Farmer, Jackson/Orchard; *The Moorchild* by Eloise McGraw, McElderry; *The Thief* by Megan Whalen Turner, Greenwillow; *Belle Prater's Boy* by Ruth White, Farrar, Straus and Giroux

1998

Out of the Dust by Karen Hesse, Scholastic Press

HONOR BOOKS: *Lilly's Crossing* by Patricia Reilly Giff, Delacorte; *Ella Enchanted* by Gail C. Levine, HarperCollins; *Wringer* by Jerry Spinelli, HarperCollins

1999

Holes by Louis Sachar, Farrar, Straus and Giroux

HONOR BOOK: *A Long Way from Chicago* by Richard Peck, Dial

2000

Bud, Not Buddy by Christopher Paul Curtis, Delacorte

HONOR BOOKS: *Getting Near to Baby* by Audrey Couloumbis, Delacorte; *26 Fairmount Avenue* by Tomie dePaola, Putnam; *Our Only May Amelia* by Jennifer L. Holm, HarperCollins

2001

A Year down Yonder by Richard Peck, Penguin Putnam Dial, Phyllis Fogelman Books

HONOR BOOKS: *Hope Was Here* by Joan Bauer, Putnam; *The Wanderer* by Sharon Creech, HarperCollins/Joanna Cotler Books; *Because of Winn-Dixie* by Kate DiCamillo, Candlewick; *Joey Pigza Loses Control* by Jack Gantos, Farrar, Straus and Giroux

THE CORETTA SCOTT KING AWARD AND HONOR BOOKS

1970

AUTHOR AWARD: *Martin Luther King, Jr.: Man of Peace* by Lillie Patterson, Garrard

1971

AUTHOR AWARD: *Black Troubador: Langston Hughes* by Charlemae Rollins, Rand

1972

AUTHOR AWARD: *17 Black Artists* by Elton C. Fax, Dodd

1973

AUTHOR AWARD: *I Never Had It Made* by Jackie Robinson as told to Alfred Duckett, Putnam

1974

AUTHOR AWARD: *Ray Charles* by Sharon Bell Mathis, Crowell
ILLUSTRATOR AWARD: *Ray Charles,* illus. by George Ford, by Sharon Bell Mathis, Crowell

1975

AUTHOR AWARD: *The Legend of Africania* by Dorothy Robinson, Johnson Publishing
ILLUSTRATOR AWARD: No award given

1976

AUTHOR AWARD: *Duey's Tale* by Pearl Bailey, Harcourt
ILLUSTRATOR AWARD: No award given

1977

AUTHOR AWARD: *The Story of Stevie Wonder* by James Haskins, Lothrop
ILLUSTRATOR AWARD: No award given

1978

AUTHOR AWARD: *Africa Dream* by Eloise Greenfield, Crowell
AUTHOR HONOR BOOKS: *The Days When the Animals Talked: Black Folk Tales and How They Came to Be* by William J. Faulkner, Follett; *Marvin and Tige* by Frankcina Glass, St. Martin's; *Mary McCleod Bethune* by Eloise Greenfield, Crowell; *Barbara Jordan* by James Haskins, Dial; *Coretta Scott King* by Lillie Patterson, Garrard; *Portia: The Life of Portia Washington Pittman, the Daughter of Booker T. Washington* by Ruth Ann Stewart, Doubleday
ILLUSTRATOR AWARD: *Africa Dream,* illus. by Carole Bayard, by Eloise Greenfield, Crowell

1979

AUTHOR AWARD: *Escape to Freedom* by Ossie Davis, Viking
AUTHOR HONOR BOOKS: *Benjamin Banneker* by Lillie Patterson, Abingdon; *I Have a Sister, My Sister Is Deaf* by Jeanne W. Peterson, Harper; *Justice and Her Brothers* by Virginia Hamilton, Greenwillow; *Skates of Uncle Richard* by Carol Fenner, Random House
ILLUSTRATOR AWARD: *Something on My Mind,* illus. by Tom Feelings, by Nikki Grimes, Dial

1980

AUTHOR AWARD: *The Young Landlords* by Walter Dean Myers, Viking
AUTHOR HONOR BOOKS: *Movin' Up* by Berry Gordy, Harper; *Childtimes: A Three-Generation Memoir* by Eloise Greenfield and Lessie Jones Little, Harper; *Andrew Young: Young Man With a Mission* by James Haskins, Lothrop; *James Van Der Zee: The Picture Takin' Man* by James Haskins, Dodd; *Let the Lion Eat Straw* by Ellease Southerland, Scribner's
ILLUSTRATOR AWARD: *Cornrows,* illus. by Carole Bayard, by Camille Yarbrough, Coward

1981

AUTHOR AWARD: *This Life* by Sidney Poitier, Knopf
AUTHOR HONOR BOOK: *Don't Explain: A Song of Billie Holiday* by Alexis De Veaux, Harper
ILLUSTRATOR AWARD: *Beat the Story Drum, Pum-Pum* by Ashley Bryan, Atheneum
ILLUSTRATOR HONOR BOOKS: *Grandmama's Joy,* illus. by Carole Bayard, by Eloise Greenfield, Collins; *Count on Your Fingers African Style,* illus. by Jerry Pinkney, by Claudia Zaslavsky, Crowell

1982

AUTHOR AWARD: *Let the Circle Be Unbroken* by Mildred Taylor, Dial
AUTHOR HONOR BOOKS: *Rainbow Jordan* by Alice Childress, Coward-McCann; *Lou in the Limelight* by Kristin Hunter, Scribner; *Mary: An Autobiography* by Mary E. Mebane, Viking
ILLUSTRATOR AWARD: *Mother Crocodile* by John Steptoe, Delacorte
ILLUSTRATOR HONOR BOOK: *Daydreamers,* illus. by Tom Feelings, by Eloise Greenfield, Dial

1983

AUTHOR AWARD: *Sweet Whispers, Brother Rush* by Virginia Hamilton, Philomel
AUTHOR HONOR BOOK: *This Strange New Feeling* by Julius Lester, Dial
ILLUSTRATOR AWARD: *Black Child* by Peter Magubane, Knopf
ILLUSTRATOR HONOR BOOKS: *All the Colors of the Race,* illus. by John Steptoe, by Arnold Adoff, Lothrop; *I'm Going to Sing: Black American Spirituals,* illus. by Ashley Bryan, Atheneum; *Just Us Women,* illus. by Pat Cummings, by Jeanette Caines, Harper

1984

AUTHOR AWARD: *Everett Anderson's Goodbye* by Lucille Clifton, Holt
SPECIAL CITATION: *The Words of Martin Luther King, Jr.,* compiled by Coretta Scott King, Newmarket Press
AUTHOR HONOR BOOKS: *The Magical Adventures of Pretty Pearl* by Virginia Hamilton, Harper; *Lena Horne* by James Haskins, Coward-McCann; *Bright Shadow* by Joyce Carol Thomas, Avon; *Because We Are* by Mildred Pitts Walter
ILLUSTRATOR AWARD: *My Mama Needs Me,* illus. by Pat Cummings, by Mildred P. Walter, Lothrop

1985

AUTHOR AWARD: *Motown and Didi* by Walter Dean Myers, Viking
HONOR BOOKS: *Circle of Gold* by Candy Dawson Boyd, Apple, Scholastic; *A Little Love* by Virginia Hamilton, Philomel
ILLUSTRATOR AWARD: No award given

1986

AUTHOR AWARD: *The People Could Fly: American Black Folktales* by Virginia Hamilton, Knopf

AUTHOR HONOR BOOKS: *Junius Over Far* by Virginia Hamilton, Harper; *Trouble's Child* by Mildred Pitts Walter, Lothrop
ILLUSTRATOR AWARD: *The Patchwork Quilt,* illus. by Jerry Pinkney, by Valerie Flourney, Dial
ILLUSTRATOR HONOR BOOK: *The People Could Fly: American Black Folktales,* illus. by Leo and Diane Dillon, by Virginia Hamilton, Knopf

1987

AUTHOR AWARD: *Justin and the Best Biscuits in the World* by Mildred Pitts Walter, Lothrop
AUTHOR HONOR BOOKS: *Lion and the Ostrich Chicks and Other African Folk Tales* by Ashley Bryan, Atheneum; *Which Way Freedom* by Joyce Hansen, Walker
ILLUSTRATOR AWARD: *Half a Moon and One Whole Star,* illus. by Jerry Pinkney, by Crescent Dragonwagon, Macmillan
ILLUSTRATOR HONOR BOOKS: *Lion and the Ostrich Chicks and Other African Folk Tales* by Ashley Bryan, Atheneum; *C.L.O.U.D.S.* by Pat Cummings, Lothrop

1988

AUTHOR AWARD: *The Friendship* by Mildred Taylor, Dial
AUTHOR HONOR BOOKS: *An Enchanted Hair Tale* by Alexis De Veaux, Harper; *The Tales of Uncle Remus: The Adventures of Brer Rabbit* by Julius Lester, Dial
ILLUSTRATOR AWARD: *Mufaro's Beautiful Daughters: An African Tale* by John Steptoe, Lothrop
ILLUSTRATOR HONOR BOOKS: *What a Morning! The Christmas Story in Black Spirituals,* illus. by Ashley Bryan, selected by John Langstaff, Macmillan; *The Invisible Hunters: A Legend from the Miskito Indians of Nicaragua,* illus. by Joe Sam, compiled by Harriet Rohmer, et al., Children's Press

1989

AUTHOR AWARD: *Fallen Angels* by Walter Dean Myers, Scholastic
AUTHOR HONOR BOOKS: *A Thief in the Village and Other Stories* by James Berry, Orchard; *Anthony Burns: The Defeat and Triumph of a Fugitive Slave* by Virginia Hamilton, Knopf
ILLUSTRATOR AWARD: *Mirandy and Brother Wind,* illus. by Jerry Pinkney, by Patricia McKissack, Knopf
ILLUSTRATOR HONOR BOOKS: *Under the Sunday Tree,* illus. by Amos Ferguson, by Eloise Greenfield, Harper; *Storm in the Night,* illus. by Pat Cummings, by Mary Stolz, Harper

1990

AUTHOR AWARD: *A Long Hard Journey: The Story of the Pullman Porter* by Patricia and Frederick McKissack, Walker

AUTHOR HONOR BOOKS: *Nathaniel Talking* by Eloise Greenfield, illus. by Jan Spivey Gilchrist, Black Butterfly; *The Bells of Christmas* by Virginia Hamilton, Harcourt; *Martin Luther King, Jr., and the Freedom Movement* by Lillie Patterson, Facts on File
ILLUSTRATOR AWARD: *Nathaniel Talking,* illus. by Jan Gilchrist, by Eloise Greenfield, Black Butterfly Press
ILLUSTRATOR HONOR BOOK: *The Talking Eggs,* illus. by Jerry Pinkney, by Robert San Souci, Dial

1991

AUTHOR AWARD: *The Road to Memphis* by Mildred D. Taylor, Dial
AUTHOR HONOR BOOKS: *Black Dance in America* by James Haskins, Crowell; *When I Am Old with You* by Angela Johnson, Orchard
ILLUSTRATOR AWARD: *Aïda,* illus. by Leo and Diane Dillard, told by Leontyne Price, Harcourt

1992

AUTHOR AWARD: *Now Is Your Time! The African American Struggle for Freedom* by Walter Dean Myers, Harper
AUTHOR HONOR BOOK: *Night on Neighborhood Street* by Eloise Greenfield, illus. by Jan Spivey Gilchrist, Dial
ILLUSTRATOR AWARD: *Tar Beach* by Faith Ringgold, Crown
ILLUSTRATOR HONOR BOOKS: *All Night, All Day: A Child's First Book of African American Spirituals* by Ashley Bryan, Atheneum; *Night on Neighborhood Street,* illus. by Jan Spivey Gilchrist, by Eloise Greenfield, Dial

1993

AUTHOR AWARD: *The Dark Thirty: Southern Tales of the Supernatural* by Patricia C. McKissack, Knopf
AUTHOR HONOR BOOKS: *Mississippi Challenge* by Mildred Pitts Walter, Bradbury; *Sojourner Truth: Ain't I a Woman?* by Patricia C. and Frederick L. McKissack, Scholastic; *Somewhere in the Darkness* by Walter Dean Myers, Scholastic
ILLUSTRATOR AWARD: *The Origin of Life on Earth: An African Creation Myth,* illus. by Kathleen Atkins Wilson, retold by David Anderson, Sights Productions
ILLUSTRATOR HONOR BOOKS: *Little Eight John,* illus. by Wil Clay, by Jan Wahl, Lodestar; *Sukey and the Mermaid,* illus. by Brian Pinkney, text by Robert San Souci, Four Winds; *Working Cotton,* illus. by Carole Byard, by Sherley Anne Williams, Harcourt

1994

AUTHOR AWARD: *Toning the Sweep* by Angela Johnson, Orchard
AUTHOR HONOR BOOKS: *Brown Honey in Broom Wheat Tea*

by Joyce Carol Thomas, illus. by Floyd Cooper, HarperCollins; *Malcolm X: By Any Means Necessary* by Walter Dean Myers, Scholastic; *Soul Looks Back in Wonder,* ed. by Phyllis Fogelman, illus. by Tom Feelings, Dial Books for Young Readers

ILLUSTRATOR AWARD: *Soul Looks Back in Wonder* by Tom Feelings, Dial

ILLUSTRATOR HONOR BOOKS: *Brown Honey in Broom Wheat Tea,* illus. by Floyd Cooper, by Joyce Carol Thomas, HarperCollins; *Uncle Jed's Barbershop,* illus. by James Ransome, by Margaree King Mitchell, Simon and Schuster

1995

AUTHOR AWARD: *Christmas in the Big House, Christmas in the Quarters* by Patricia C. and Fredrick L. McKissack, Scholastic

AUTHOR HONOR BOOKS: *The Captive* by Joyce Hansen, Scholastic; *I Hadn't Meant to Tell You This* by Jacqueline Woodson, Delacorte; *Black Diamond: Story of the Negro Baseball League* by Patricia C. and Fredrick L. McKissack, Scholastic

ILLUSTRATOR AWARD: *The Creation* illus. by James E. Ransome, by James Weldon Johnson, Holiday

ILLUSTRATOR HONOR BOOKS: *The Singing Man,* illus. by Terea Shaffer, by Angela Shelf Medearis, Holiday House; *Meet Danitra Brown,* illus. by Floyd Cooper, by Nikki Grimes, Lothrop, Lee and Shepard

1996

AUTHOR AWARD: *Her Stories: African American Folktales, Fairy Tales, and True Tales* by Virginia Hamilton, illus. by Leo and Diane Dillon, Blue Sky/Scholastic

AUTHOR HONOR BOOKS: *The Watsons Go to Birmingham—1963* by Christopher Paul Curtis, Delacorte; *Like Sisters on the Homefront* by Rita Williams-Garcia, Delacorte; *From the Notebooks of Melanin Sun* by Jacqueline Woodson, Scholastic/Blue Sky Press

ILLUSTRATOR AWARD: *The Middle Passage: White Ships Black Cargo* by Tom Feelings, Dial

ILLUSTRATOR HONOR BOOKS: *Her Stories,* illus. by Leo and Diane Dillon, by Virginia Hamilton, Scholastic/Blue Sky Press; *The Faithful Friend,* illus. by Brian Pinkney, by Robert San Souci, Simon and Schuster Books for Young Readers

1997

AUTHOR AWARD: *Slam* by Walter Dean Myers, Scholastic

AUTHOR HONOR BOOKS: *Rebels Against Slavery: American Slave Revolts* by Patricia and Fredrick McKissack, Scholastic

ILLUSTRATOR AWARD: *Minty: A Story of Harriet Tubman* illus. by Jerry Pinkney, by Alan Schroeder, Dial

ILLUSTRATOR HONOR BOOKS: *The Palm of My Heart: Poetry*

by African American Children, illus. by Gregorie Christie, ed. by Davida Adedjourma, Lee and Low Books; *Running The Road to ABC,* illus. by Reynold Ruffins, by Denize Lauture, Simon and Schuster Books for Young Readers; *Neeny Coming, Neeny Going,* illus. by Synthia Saint James, by Karen English, BridgeWater Books

1998

AUTHOR AWARD: *Forged by Fire* by Sharon M. Draper, Atheneum

AUTHOR HONOR BOOKS: *Bayard Rustin: Behind the Scenes of the Civil Rights Movement* by James Haskins, Hyperion; *I Thought My Soul Would Rise and Fly: The Diary of Patsy, A Freed Girl* by Joyce Hansen, Scholastic

ILLUSTRATOR AWARD: *In Daddy's Arms I Am Tall: African Americans Celebrating Fathers,* illus. by Javaka Steptoe, by Alan Schroeder, Lee and Low

ILLUSTRATOR HONOR BOOKS: *Ashley Bryan's ABC of African American Poetry* by Ashley Bryan, Jean Karl/Atheneum; *Harlem,* illus. by Christopher Myers, by Walter Dean Myers, Scholastic; *The Hunterman and the Crocodile* by Baba Wagué Diakité, Scholastic

1999

AUTHOR AWARD: *Heaven* by Angela Johnson, Simon and Schuster

AUTHOR HONOR BOOKS: *Jazmin's Notebook* by Nikki Grimes, Dial Books; *Breaking Ground, Breaking Silence: The Story of New York's African Burial Ground* by Joyce Hansen and Gary McGowan, Henry Holt and Company; *The Other Side: Shorter Poems* by Angela Johnson, Orchard Books

ILLUSTRATOR AWARD: *I See the Rhythm,* illus. by Michele Wood, by Toyomi Igus, Children's Book Press

ILLUSTRATOR HONOR BOOKS: *I Have Heard of a Land,* illus. by Floyd Cooper, by Joyce Carol Thomas, Joanna Cotler Books/HarperCollins; *The Bat Boy and His Violin,* illus. by E. B. Lewis, by Gavin Curtis, Simon and Schuster; *Duke Ellington: The Piano Prince and His Orchestra,* illus. by Brian Pinkney, by Andrea David Pinkney, Hyperion Books for Children

2000

AUTHOR AWARD: *Bud, Not Buddy* by Christopher Paul Curtis, Delacorte

AUTHOR HONOR BOOKS: *Francie* by Karen English, Farrar, Straus and Giroux; *Black Hands, White Sails: The Story of African-American Whalers* by Patricia C. and Frederick L. McKissack, Scholastic Press; *Monster* by Walter Dean Myers, HarperCollins

ILLUSTRATOR AWARD: *In the Time of Drums,* illus. by Brian

Pinkney, by Kim L. Siegelson, Jump at the Sun/Hyperion Books for Children

ILLUSTRATOR HONOR BOOKS: *My Rows and Piles of Coins,* illus. by E. B. Lewis, by Tololwa M. Mollel, Clarion Books; *Black Cat* by Christopher Myers, Scholastic

2001

AUTHOR AWARD: *Miracle's Boys* by Jacqueline Woodson, Putnam

AUTHOR HONOR BOOKS: *Let It Shine! Stories of Black Women Freedom Fighters* by Andrea Davis Pinkney, illus. by Stephen Alcorn, Gulliver Books, Harcourt

ILLUSTRATOR AWARD: *Uptown* by Bryan Collier, Henry Holt

ILLUSTRATOR HONOR BOOKS: *Freedom River* by Bryan Collier, Jump at the Sun/Hyperion; *Only Passing Through: The Story of Sojourner Truth,* illus. by R. Gregory Christie, by Anne Rockwell, Random House; *Virgie Goes to School with Us Boys,* illus. by E. B. Lewis, by Elizabeth Fitzgerald Howard, Simon and Schuster

THE PURA BELPRÉ AWARD

1996

NARRATIVE WINNER: *An Island Like You: Stories of the Barrio* by Judith Ortiz Cofer, Melanie Kroupa/Orchard Books, 1995

HONOR BOOKS FOR NARRATIVE: *The Bossy Gallito / El Gallo de Bodas: A Traditional Cuban Folktale* by Lucía González, illus. by Lulu Delacre, Scholastic, 1994; *Baseball in April, and Other Stories,* by Gary Soto, Harcourt, 1994

ILLUSTRATION WINNER: *Chato's Kitchen* illus. by Susan Guevara, by Gary Soto, Putnam, 1995

HONOR BOOKS FOR ILLUSTRATION: *Pablo Remembers: The Fiesta of the Day of the Dead* by George Ancona, Lothrop, 1993 (Also available in a Spanish-language edition: *Pablo Recuerda: La Fiesta de Dia de los Muertos,* Lothrop, 1993); *The Bossy Gallito/El Gallo de Bodas: A Traditional Cuban Folktale* illus. by Lulu Delacre, retold by Lucia Gonzalez, Scholastic, 1994; *Family Pictures/Cuadros de Familia* by Carmen Lomas Garza, Spanish text by Rosalma Zubizarreta, Children's Book Press, 1990

1998

NARRATIVE WINNER: *Parrot in the Oven: mi vida* by Victor Martinez, Joanna Cotler/HarperCollins, 1996

HONOR BOOKS FOR NARRATIVE: *Laughing Tomatoes and Other Spring Poems/Jitomates Risuenos y Otros Poemas de Primavera* by Francisco Alarcón, illus. by Maya Christina Gonzalez, Children's Book Press, 1997; *Spirits of the High Mesa* by Floyd Marinez, Arte Publico Press, 1997

ILLUSTRATION WINNER: *Snapshots from the Wedding,* illus. by Stephanie Garcia, by Gary Soto, Putnam, 1997

HONOR BOOKS FOR ILLUSTRATION: *In My Family/En mi familia* by Carmen Lomas Garza, Children's Book Press, 1996; *The Golden Flower: A Taino Myth from Puerto Rico,* illus. by Enrique O. Sánchez, by Nina Jaffe, Simon and Schuster, 1996; *Gathering the Sun: An Alphabet in Spanish and English,* illus. by Simon Silva, by Alma Flor Ada, English tr. by Rosa Zubizarreta, Lothrop, 1997

2000

NARRATIVE WINNER: *Under the Royal Palms: A Childhood in Cuba* by Alma Flor Ada, Atheneum, 1998

HONOR BOOKS FOR NARRATIVE: *From the Bellybutton of the Moon and Other Summer Poems/Del Ombligo de la Luna y Otro Poemas de Verano* by Francisco X. Alarcón, illus. by Maya Christina Gonzalez, Children's Book Press, 1998; *Laughing Out Loud, I Fly: Poems in English and Spanish* by Juan Felipe Herrera, illus. by Karen Barbour, HarperCollins, 1998

ILLUSTRATION WINNER: *Magic Windows* by Carmen Lomas Garza, Children's Book Press, 1999

HONOR BOOKS FOR ILLUSTRATION: *Barrio: Jose's Neighborhood* by George Ancona, Harcourt, 1998; *The Secret Stars,* illus. by Felipe Dávalos, by Joseph Slate, Marshall Cavendish, 1998; *Mama and Papa Have a Store* by Amelia Lau Carling, Dial, 1998

THE ROBERT F. SIBERT AWARD

2001

Sir Walter Ralegh and the Quest for El Dorado by Marc Aronson, Clarion Books

HONOR BOOKS: *The Longitude Prize* by Joan Dash, illus. by Susan Petricic, Frances Foster Books/Farrar, Straus and Giroux; *Blizzard* by Jim Murphy, Scholastic; *My Season with Penguins: An Antarctic Journal* by Sophie Webb, Houghton; *Pedro and Me: Friendship, Loss, and What I Learned* by Judd Winick, Henry Holt

THE LAURA INGALLS WILDER MEDAL

1954	Laura Ingalls Wilder
1960	Clara Ingram Judson
1965	Ruth Sawyer
1970	E. B. White
1975	Beverly Cleary
1980	Theodor S. Geisel (Dr. Seuss)
1983	Maurice Sendak
1986	Jean Fritz
1989	Elizabeth George Speare

1992   Marcia Brown
1995   Virginia Hamilton
1998   Russell Freedman
2001   Milton Meltzer

THE MARGARET A. EDWARDS AWARD

1988   S. E. Hinton
1990   Richard Peck
1991   Robert Cormier
1992   Lois Duncan
1993   M. E. Kerr
1994   Walter Dean Myers
1995   Cynthia Voigt
1996   Judy Blume
1997   Gary Paulsen
1998   Madeleine L'Engle
1999   Anne McCaffrey
2000   Chris Crutcher
2001   Robert Lipsyte

THE MICHAEL L. PRINTZ AWARD

2000

Monster by Walter Dean Myers, HarperCollins

HONOR BOOKS: *Skellig* by David Almond, Delacorte Press; *Speak* by Laurie Halse Anderson, Farrar, Straus and Giroux; *Hard Love* by Ellen Wittlinger, Simon and Schuster

2001

Kit's Wilderness by David Almond, Delacorte Press

HONOR BOOKS: *Many Stones* by Carolyn Coman, Front Street Press; *The Body of Christopher Creed* by Carol Plum-Ucci, Harcourt; *Angus, Thongs, and Full-Frontal Snogging* by Louise Rennison, HarperCollins; *Stuck in Neutral* by Terry Trueman, HarperCollins

NATIONAL COUNCIL OF TEACHERS OF ENGLISH AWARDS

The Award for Excellence in Poetry for Children

The NCTE Award for Excellence in Poetry for Children, established in memory of Jonathan Cullinan (1969–1975) is given to a living American poet in recognition of an outstanding body of poetry for children. The award is administered by the National Council of Teachers of English and was given annually from 1977 to 1982; currently, the award is presented every three years. The poet receives a citation. A medallion designed by Karla Kuskin is available for use on dust jackets of all the poet's books. An archival collec-

tion of the poets' books is housed at the Children's Literature Research Center, Andersen Library, at the University of Minnesota. Another collection is housed at Boston Public Library in the David McCord Room.

1977   David McCord
1978   Aileen Fisher
1979   Karla Kuskin
1980   Myra Cohn Livingston
1981   Eve Merriam
1982   John Ciardi
1985   Lilian Moore
1988   Arnold Adoff
1991   Valerie Worth
1994   Barbara Esbensen
1997   Eloise Greenfield
2000   X. J. Kennedy
2003   Mary Ann Hoberman

THE ORBIS PICTUS AWARD AND HONOR BOOKS

The Orbis Pictus Award, established in 1990, is administered by the National Council of Teachers of English and honors the author of an outstanding nonfiction book.

1990

The Great Little Madison by Jean Fritz, Putnam

HONOR BOOKS: *The Great American Gold Rush* by Rhoda Blumberg, Bradbury Press; *The News About Dinosaurs* by Patricia Lauber, Bradbury Press

1991

Franklin Delano Roosevelt by Russell Freedman, Clarion Books

HONOR BOOKS: *Arctic Memories* by Normee Ekoomiak, Henry Holt; *Seeing Earth from Space* by Patricia Lauber, Orchard Books

1992

Flight: The Journey of Charles Lindbergh by Robert Burleigh and Mike Wimmer, Philomel Books

HONOR BOOKS: *Now Is Your Time! The African American Struggle for Freedom* by Walter Dean Myers, HarperCollins; *Prairie Vision: The Life and Times of Solomon Butcher* by Pam Conrad, HarperCollins

1993

Children of the Dust Bowl: The True Story of the School at Weedpatch Camp by Jerry Stanley, Crown

HONOR BOOKS: *Talking with Artists* by Pat Cummins, Bradbury Press; *Come Back, Salmon* by Molly Cone, Sierra Club Books

1994

Across America on an Emigrant Train by Jim Murphy, Clarion Books

HONOR BOOKS: *To the Top of the World: Adventures with Arctic Wolves* by Jim Brandenburg, Walker and Company; *Making Sense: Animal Perception and Communication* by Bruce Brooks, Farrar, Straus and Giroux

1995

Safari Beneath the Sea: The Wonder of the North Pacific Coast by Diane Swanson, Sierra Club Books

HONOR BOOKS: *Wildlife Rescue: The Work of Dr. Kathleen Ramsay* by Jennifer Owings Dewey, Boyds Mills Press; *Kids at Work: Lewis Hine and the Crusade Against Child Labor* by Russell Freedman, Clarion Books; *Christmas in the Big House, Christmas in the Quarters* by Patricia McKissack and Fredrick McKissack, Scholastic

1996

The Great Fire by Jim Murphy, Scholastic

HONOR BOOKS: *Dolphin Man: Exploring the World of Dolphins* by Laurence Pringle, photos by Randall S. Wells, Atheneum; *Rosie the Riveter: Women Working on the Home Front in World War II* by Penny Colman, Crown

1997

Leonardo da Vinci by Diane Stanley, Morrow Junior Books

HONOR BOOKS: *Full Steam Ahead: The Race to Build a Transcontinental Railroad* by Rhoda Blumberg, National Geographic Society; *The Life and Death of Crazy Horse* by Russell Freedman, Holiday House; *One World, Many Religions: The Way We Worship* by Mary Pope Osborne, Knopf

1998

An Extraordinary Life: The Story of a Monarch Butterfly by Laurence Pringle, illus. by Bob Marstall, Orchard Books

HONOR BOOKS: *A Drop of Water: A Book of Science and Wonder* by Walter Wick, Scholastic; *A Tree Is Growing* by Arthur Dorros, illus. by S. D. Schindler, Scholastic; *Charles A. Lindbergh: A Human Hero* by James Cross Giblin, Clarion; *Kennedy Assassinated! The World Mourns: A Reporter's Story* by Wilborn Hampton, Candlewick; *Digger: The Tragic Fate of the California Indians from the Missions to the Gold Rush* by Jerry Stanley, Crown

1999

Shipwreck at the Bottom of the World: The Extraordinary True Story of Schackleton and the Endurance by Jennifer Armstrong, Crown

HONOR BOOKS: *Black Whiteness: Admiral Byrd Alone in the Antarctic* by Robert Burleigh, illus. by Walter Lyon Krudop, Atheneum; *Fossil Feud: The Rivalry of the First American Dinosaur Hunters* by Thom Holmes, Messner; *Hottest, Coldest, Highest, Deepest* by Steve Jenkins, Houghton; *No Pretty Pictures: A Child of War* by Anita Lobel, Greenwillow

2000

Through My Eyes by Ruby Bridges, Margo Lundell, Scholastic

HONOR BOOKS: *At Her Majesty's Request: An African Princess in Victorian England* by Walter Dean Myers, Scholastic; *Clara Schumann: Piano Virtuoso* by Susanna Reich, Clarion; *Mapping the World* by Sylvia A. Johnson, Atheneum; *The Snake Scientist* by Sy Montgomery, illus. by Nic Bishop, Houghton; *The Top of the World: Climbing Mount Everest* by Steve Jenkins, Houghton

INTERNATIONAL READING ASSOCIATION AWARDS

The IRA Children's Book Award

1975

Transport 7–41 by T. Degens, Viking

1976

Dragonwings by Laurence Yep, Harper

1977

A String in the Harp by Nancy Bond, McElderry/Atheneum

1978

A Summer to Die by Lois Lowry, Houghton

1979

Reserved for Mark Anthony Crowder by Alison Smith, Dutton

1980

Words by Heart by Ouida Sebestyen, Atlantic/Little

1981

My Own Private Sky by Delores Beckman, Dutton

1982

Good Night, Mr. Tom by Michelle Magorian, Kestrel/Penguin, Great Britain, Harper, USA

1983

The Darkangel by Meredith Ann Pierce, Atlantic/Little

1984

Ratha's Creature by Clare Bell, Atheneum

1985

Badger on the Barge by Janni Howker, Greenwillow

1986

Prairie Songs by Pam Conrad, Harper

1987

PICTURE BOOK: *The Line Up Book* by Marisabina Russo, Greenwillow
NOVEL: *After the Dancing Days* by Margaret I. Rostkowski, Harper

1988

PICTURE BOOK: *Third Story Cat* by Leslie Baker, Little, Brown
NOVEL: *The Ruby in the Smoke* by Philip Pullman, Knopf

1989

PICTURE BOOK: *Rechenka's Eggs* by Patricia Polacco, Philomel
NOVEL: *Probably Still Nick Swansen* by Virginia Euwer Wolff, Holt

1990

PICTURE BOOK: *No Star Nights* by Anna Egan Smucker, Knopf
NOVEL: *Children of the River* by Linda Crew, Delacorte

1991

PICTURE BOOK: *Is This a House for Hermit Crab?* by Megan McDonald, Orchard
NOVEL: *Under the Hawthorn Tree* by Maria Conlon-McKenna, O'Brien Press

1992

PICTURE BOOK: *Ten Little Rabbits* by Virginia Grossman, Chronicle
NOVEL: *Rescue Josh McGuire* by Ben Mikaelsen, Hyperion

1993

PICTURE BOOK: *Old Turtle* by Douglas Wood, Pfeiffer-Hamilton
NOVEL: *Letters From Rifka* by Karen Hesse, Holt

1994

PICTURE BOOK: *Sweet Clara and the Freedom Quilt* by Deborah Hopkinson, illus. by James E. Ransome, Knopf
NOVEL: *Behind the Secret Window: A Memoir of a Hidden Childhood* by Nelly S. Toll, Dutton

1995

PICTURE BOOK: *The Ledgerbook of Thomas Blue Eagle* by Gay Matthaei and Jewel Grutman, illus. by Adam Cvijanovic, Thomasson-Grant
NOVEL: *Spite Fences* by Trudy Krisher, Bantam
INFORMATION BOOK: *Stranded at Plimoth Plantation 1626* by Gary Bowen, Harper

1996

PICTURE BOOK: *More Than Anything Else* by Marie Bradby and Chris K. Soentpiet, Orchard
NOVEL: *The King's Shadow* by Elizabeth Adler, Farrar, Straus and Giroux
INFORMATION BOOK: *The Case of the Mummified Pigs and Other Mysteries in Nature* by Susan E. Quinlan, Boyds Mills

1997

PICTURE BOOK: *The Fabulous Flying Fandinis* by Ingrid Slyder, Cobblehill/Dutton
NOVEL: *Don't You Dare Read This, Mrs. Dunphrey* by Margaret P. Haddix, Simon and Schuster
INFORMATION BOOK: *The Brooklyn Bridge* by Elizabeth Mann, Mikaya Press

1998

YOUNGER READER: *Nim and the War Effort* by Milly Lee and Yangsook Choi, Farrar, Straus and Giroux
OLDER READER: *Moving Mama to Town* by Ronder Thomas Young, Orchard
INFORMATIONAL READER: *Just What the Doctor Ordered: The History of American Medicine* by Brandon Marie Miller, Lerner

1999

YOUNGER READER: *My Freedom Trip: A Child's Escape from North Korea* by Frances and Ginger Park, Boyds Mills Press
OLDER READER: *Choosing Up Sides* by John H. Ritter, Philomel Books
INFORMATIONAL READER: *First in the Field: Baseball Hero Jackie Robinson* by Derek T. Dingle Hyperion Books

2000

YOUNGER READER: *The Snake Scientist* by Sy Montgomery, Houghton Mifflin
YOUNGER READER: *Molly Bannaky* by Alice McGill, Houghton Mifflin
OLDER READER: *Bud, Not Buddy* by Christopher Paul Curtis, Delacorte Press, Random House; *Eleanor's Story: An American Girl in Hitler's Germany* by Eleanor Ramrath Garner, Peachtree

2001

YOUNGER READER: *Stranger in the Woods* by Carl R. Sams II and Jean Stoick, Carl R. Sams II Photography
YOUNGER READER: *My Season with Penguins* by Sophie Webb, Houghton Mifflin
OLDER READER: *Jake's Orphan* by Peggy Brooke, Dorling-Kindersley; *Girls Think of Everything* by Catherine Thimmesh, Houghton Mifflin

THE LIBRARY ASSOCIATION CARNEGIE MEDALLISTS

1936 Arthur Ransome, *Pigeon Post*
1937 Eve Garnet, *The Family from One End Street*
1938 Noel Streatfield, *The Circus Is Coming*
1939 Eleanor Doorly, *The Radium Woman* (biography of Marie Curie)
1940 Kitty Barne, *Visitors from London*
1941 Mary Treadgold, *We Couldn't Leave Dinah*
1942 'B.B.' (D. J. Watkins-Pitchford), *The Little Grey Men*
1943 No award
1944 Eric Linklater, *The Wind on the Moon*
1945 No award
1946 Elizabeth Goudge, *The Little White Horse*
1947 Walter de la Mare, *Collected Stories for Children*
1948 Richard Armstrong, *Sea Change*
1949 Agnes Allen, *The Story of Your Home* (nonfiction)
1950 Elfrida Vipont, *The Lark on the Wing*
1951 Cynthia Harnett, *The Wool-Pack*
1952 Mary Norton, *The Borrowers*
1953 Edward Osmond, *A Valley Grows Up* (nonfiction)
1954 Ronald Welch, *Knight Crusaders*
1955 Eleanor Farjeon, *The Little Bookroom*
1956 C. S. Lewis, *The Last Battle*
1957 William Mayne, *A Grass Rope*
1958 Philippa Pearce, *Tom's Midnight Garden*
1959 Rosemary Sutcliff, *The Lantern Bearers*
1960 Ian W. Cornwall and Howard M. Maitland, *The Making of Man* (nonfiction)
1961 Lucy M. Boston, *A Stranger at Green Knowe*

1962 Pauline Clark, *The Twelve and the Genii*
1963 Hester Burton, *Time of Trial*
1964 Sheena Porter, *Nordy Bank*
1965 Philip Turner, *The Grange at High Force*
1966 No award
1967 Alan Garner, *The Owl Service*
1968 Rosemary Harris, *The Moon in the Cloud*
1969 K. M. Peyton, *The Edge of the Cloud*
1970 Edward Blishen and Leon Garfield, *The God Beneath the Sea*
1971 Ivan Southall, *Josh*
1972 Richard Adams, *Watership Down*
1973 Penelope Lively, *The Ghost of Thomas Kempe*
1974 Mollie Hunter, *The Stronghold*
1975 Robert Westall, *The Machine Gunners*
1976 Jan Mark, *Thunder and Lightnings*
1977 Gene Kemp, *The Turbulent Term of Tyke Tyler*
1978 David Rees, *The Exeter Blitz*
1979 Peter Dickinson, *Tulku*
1980 Peter Dickinson, *City of Gold*
1981 Robert Westall, *The Scarecrows*
1982 Margaret Mahy, *The Haunting*
1983 Jan Mark, *Handles*
1984 Margaret Mahy, *The Changeover*
1985 Kevin Crossley-Holland, *Storm*
1986 Berlie Doherty, *Granny Was a Buffer Girl*
1987 Susan Price, *The Ghost Drum*
1988 Geraldine McCaughrean, *A Pack of Lies*
1989 Anne Fine, *Goggle-Eyes*
1990 Gillian Cross, *Wolf*
1991 Berlie Doherty, *Dear Nobody*
1992 Anne Fine, *Flour Babies*
1993 Robert Swindells, *Stone Cold*
1994 Theresa Breslin, *Whispers in the Graveyard*
1995 Philip Pullman, *Northern Lights*
1996 Melvin Burgess, *Junk*
1997 Tim Bowler, *River Boy*
1998 David Almond, *Skellig*
1999 Aiden Chambers, *Postcards from No Man's Land*

THE HANS CHRISTIAN ANDERSEN AWARD

The Hans Christian Andersen Award, established in 1956, is given biennially and administered by the International Board on Books for Young People. It is given to one author and, since 1966, to one illustrator in recognition of his or her entire body of work. A medal is presented to the recipient.

1956

Eleanor Farjeon, Great Britain

1958

Astrid Lindgren, Sweden

1960

Erich Kästner, Germany

1962

Meindert DeJong, USA

1964

René Guillot, France

1966

AUTHOR: Tove Jansson, Finland
ILLUSTRATOR: Alois Carigiet, Switzerland

1968

AUTHORS: James Krüss, Germany, and José Maria Sanchez-Silva, Spain
ILLUSTRATOR: Jiri Trnka, Czechoslovakia

1970

AUTHOR: Gianni Rodari, Italy
ILLUSTRATOR: Maurice Sendak, USA

1972

AUTHOR: Scott O'Dell, USA
ILLUSTRATOR: Ib Spang Olsen, Denmark

1974

AUTHOR: Maria Gripe, Sweden
ILLUSTRATOR: Farshid Mesghali, Iran

1976

AUTHOR: Cecil Bodker, Denmark
ILLUSTRATOR: Tatjana Mawrina, USSR

1978

AUTHOR: Paula Fox, USA
ILLUSTRATOR: Otto S. Svend, Denmark

1980

AUTHOR: Bohumil Ríha, Czechoslovakia
ILLUSTRATOR: Suekichi Akaba, Japan

1982

AUTHOR: Lygia Bojunga Nunes, Brazil
ILLUSTRATOR: Zbigniew Rychlicki, Poland

1984

AUTHOR: Christine Nöstlinger, Austria
ILLUSTRATOR: Mitsumasa Anno, Japan

1986

AUTHOR: Patricia Wrightson, Australia
ILLUSTRATOR: Robert Ingpen, Australia

1988

AUTHOR: Annie M. G. Schmidt, Holland
ILLUSTRATOR: Dusan Kallay, Czechoslovakia

1990

AUTHOR: Tormod Haugen, Norway
ILLUSTRATOR: Lisbeth Zwerger, Austria

1992

AUTHOR: Virginia Hamilton, USA
ILLUSTRATOR: Kveta Pacovská, Czechoslovakia

1994

AUTHOR: Michio Mado, Japan
ILLUSTRATOR: Jörg Müller, Switzerland

1996

AUTHOR: Uri Orlev, Israel
ILLUSTRATOR: Klaus Ensikat, Germany

1998

AUTHOR: Katherine Paterson, USA
ILLUSTRATOR: Tomi Ungerer, France

2000

AUTHOR: Ana Maria Machado, Brazil
ILLUSTRATOR: Anthony Browne, United Kingdom

THE MILDRED L. BATCHELDER AWARD

1968

The Little Man by Erich Kastner, tr. by James Kirkup, illus. by Rick Schreiter, Knopf, Germany

1969

Don't Take Teddy by Babbis Friis-Baastad, tr. by Lise Somme McKinnon, Scribner's, Norway

1970

Wildcat Under Glass by Alki Zei, tr. by Edward Fenton, Holt, Greece

1971

In the Land of Ur by Hans Baumann, tr. by Stella Humphries, Pantheon, Germany

1972

Friedrich by Hans Peter Richter, tr. by Edite Kroll, Holt, Germany

1973

Pulga by S. R. Van Iterson, tr. by Alison and Alexander Gode, Morrow, Netherlands

1974

Petros' War by Aldi Zei, tr. by Edward Fenton, Dutton, Greece

1975

An Old Tale Carved Out of Stone by A. Linevsky, tr. by Maria Polushkin, Crown, Russia

1976

The Cat and Mouse Who Shared a House by Ruth Hurlimann, tr. by Anthea Bell, illus. by the author, Walck, Germany

1977

The Leopard by Cecil Bødker, tr. by Gunnar Poulsen, Atheneum, Denmark

1978

Konrad by Christine Nostlinger, illus. by Carol Nicklaus, Watts, Germany

1979

Rabbit Island by Jörg Steiner, tr. by Ann Conrad Lammers, illus. by Jörg Müller, Harcourt, Germany

1980

The Sound of the Dragons Feet by Alki Zei, tr. by Edward Fenton, Dutton, Greece

1981

The Winter When Time Was Frozen by Els Pelgrom, tr. by Maryka and Rafael Rudnik, Morrow, Netherlands

1982

The Battle Horse by Harry Kullman, tr. by George Blecherand Lone Thygesen-Blecher, Bradbury, Sweden

1983

Hiroshima No Pika by Toshi Maruki, Lothrop, Japan

1984

Ronia, the Robber's Daughter by Astrid Lindgren, tr. by Patricia Crampton, Viking, Sweden

1985

The Island on Bird Street by Uri Orlev, tr. by Hillel Halkin, Houghton, Israel

1986

Rose Blanche by Christophe Gallaz and Roberto Innocenti, tr. by Martha Coventry and Richard Graglia, Creative Education, Italy

1987

No Hero for the Kaiser by Rudolf Frank, tr. by Patricia Crampton, Lothrop, Germany

1988

If You Didn't Have Me by Ulf Nilsson, tr. by Lone Tygesen-Blecher and George Blecher, illus. by Eva Eriksson, McElderry, Sweden

1989

Crutches by Peter Hätling, tr. by Elizabeth D. Crawford, Lothrop, Germany

1990

Buster's World by Bjarne Reuter, tr. by Anthea Bell, Dutton, Denmark

1991

Two Long and One Short by Nina Ring Aamundsen, Houghton, Norway

1992

The Man from the Other Side by Uri Orlev, tr. by Hillel Halkin, Houghton, Israel

1993

No Award

1994

The Apprentice by Molina Llorente, tr. by Robin Longshaw, Farrar, Straus and Giroux, Spain

1995

The Boys from St. Petri by Bjarne Reuter, tr. by Anthea Bell, Dutton, Denmark

1996

The Lady with the Hat by Uri Orlev, tr. by Hillel Halkin, Houghton, Israel

1997

The Friends by Kazumi Yumoto, tr. by Cathy Hirano, Farrar, Straus and Giroux

1998

The Robber and Me by Josef Holub, edited by Mark Aronson and tr. by Elizabeth D. Crawford, Henry Holt, Germany

1999

Thanks to My Mother by Schoschana Rabinovici, tr. by James Skofield, Dial

2000

The Baboon King by Anton Quintana, tr. by John Nieuwenhuizen, Walker and Company, Holland

2001

Samir and Yonatan, tr. by Arthur A. Levine, Scholastic, Israel

THE *BOSTON GLOBE–HORN BOOK* AWARDS

1967

TEXT: *The Little Fishes* by Erik Christian Haugaard, Houghton
ILLUSTRATION: *London Bridge Is Falling Down!* illus. by Peter Spier, Doubleday

1968

TEXT: *The Spring Rider* by John Lawson, Harper
ILLUSTRATION: *Tikki Tikki Tembo* by Arlene Mosel, illus. by Blair Lent, Holt

1969

TEXT: *A Wizard of Earthsea* by Ursula K. Le Guin, Houghton, Parnassus
ILLUSTRATION: *The Adventures of Paddy Pork* by John S. Goodall, Harcourt

1970

TEXT: *The Intruder* by John Rowe Townsend, Harper
ILLUSTRATION: *Hi, Cat!* by Ezra Jack Keats, Macmillan

1971

TEXT: *A Room Made of Windows* by Eleanor Cameron, Little, Brown
ILLUSTRATION: *If I Built a Village* by Kazue Mizumura, Harper

1972

TEXT: *Tristan and Iseult* by Rosemary Sutcliff, Dutton
ILLUSTRATION: *Mr. Grumpy's Outing* by John Burningham, Holt

1973

TEXT: *The Dark Is Rising* by Susan Cooper, Atheneum, McElderry
ILLUSTRATION: *King Stork* by Trina Schart Hyman, Little, Brown

1974

TEXT: *M. C. Higgins, the Great* by Virginia Hamilton, Macmillan
ILLUSTRATION: *Jambo Means Hello* by Muriel Feelings, illus. by Tom Feelings, Dial

1975

TEXT: *Transport 7-41-R* by T. Degens, Viking
ILLUSTRATION: *Anno's Alphabet* by Mitsumasa Anno, Harper

1976

FICTION: *Unleaving* by Jill Paton Walsh, Farrar, Straus and Giroux
NONFICTION: *Voyaging to Cathay: Americans in the China Trade* by Alfred Tamarin and Shirley Glubok, Viking
ILLUSTRATION: *Thirteen* by Remy Charlip and Jerry Joyner, Four Winds

1977

FICTION: *Child of the Owl* by Laurence Yep, Harper
NONFICTION: *Chance, Luck and Destiny* by Peter Dickinson, Little, Brown

ILLUSTRATION: *Grandfa' Grig Had a Pig and Other Rhymes without Reason from Mother Goose* by Wallace Tripp, Little, Brown

1978

FICTION: *The Westing Game* by Ellen Raskin, Dutton
NONFICTION: *Mischling, Second Degree: My Childhood in Nazi Germany* by Ilse Koehn, Greenwillow
ILLUSTRATION: *Anno's Journey* by Mitsumasa Anno, Philomel

1979

FICTION: *Humbug Mountain* by Sid Fleischman, Little, Brown
NONFICTION: *The Road from Home: The Story of an Armenian Girl* by David Kherdian, Greenwillow
ILLUSTRATION: *The Snowman* by Raymond Briggs, Random

1980

FICTION: *Conrad's War* by Andrew Davies, Crown
NONFICTION: *Building: The Fight Against Gravity* by Mario Salvadori, McElderry
ILLUSTRATION: *The Garden of Abdul Gasazi* by Chris Van Allsburg, Houghton

1981

FICTION: *The Leaving* by Lynn Hall, Scribner's
NONFICTION: *The Weaver's Gift* by Kathryn Lasky, Warne
ILLUSTRATION: *Outside Over There* by Maurice Sendak, Harper

1982

FICTION: *Playing Beatie Bow* by Ruth Park, Atheneum
NONFICTION: *Upon the Head of the Goat: A Childhood in Hungary 1939–1944* by Aranka Siegal, Farrar, Straus and Giroux
ILLUSTRATION: *A Visit to William Blake's Inn: Poems for Innocent and Experienced Travelers* by Nancy Willard, illus. by Alice and Martin Provensen, Harcourt

1983

FICTION: *Sweet Whisper, Brother Rush* by Virginia Hamilton, Philomel
NONFICTION: *Behind Barbed Wire: The Imprisonment of Japanese Americans During World War II* by Daniel S. Davis, Dutton
ILLUSTRATION: *A Chair for My Mother* by Vera B. Williams, Greenwillow

1984

FICTION: *A Little Fear* by Patricia Wrightson, Atheneum, McElderry
NONFICTION: *The Double Life of Pocahontas* by Jean Fritz, Putnam
ILLUSTRATION: *Jonah and the Great Fish* by Warwick Hutton, McElderry

1985

FICTION: *The Moves Make the Man* by Bruce Books, Harper
NONFICTION: *Commodore Perry in the Land of the Shogun* by Rhoda Blumberg, Lothrop
ILLUSTRATION: *Mama Don't Allow* by Thacher Hurd, Harper
SPECIAL AWARD: *1, 2, 3* by Tana Hoban, Greenwillow

1986

FICTION: *In Summer Light* by Zibby Oneal, Viking
NONFICTION: *Auks, Rocks, and the Odd Dinosaur: Inside Stories from the Smithsonian's Museum of Natural History* by Peggy Thomsen, Harper
ILLUSTRATION: *The Paper Crane* by Molly Bang, Greenwillow

1987

FICTION: *Rabble Starkey* by Lois Lowry, Houghton
NONFICTION: *The Pilgrims of Plimoth* by Marcia Sewall, Atheneum
ILLUSTRATION: *Mufaro's Beautiful Daughters* by John Steptoe, Lothrop

1988

FICTION: *The Friendship* by Mildred Taylor, Dial
NONFICTION: *Anthony Burns: The Defeat and Triumph of a Fugitive Slave* by Virginia Hamilton, Knopf
PICTURE BOOK: *The Boy of the Three-Year Nap* by Diane Snyder, Houghton

1989

FICTION: *The Village by the Sea* by Paula Fox, Orchard
NONFICTION: *The Way Things Work* by David Macaulay, Houghton
PICTURE BOOK: *Shy Charles* by Rosemary Wells, Dial

1990

FICTION: *Maniac Magee* by Jerry Spinelli, Little, Brown
NONFICTION: *The Great Little Madison* by Jean Fritz, Putnam
PICTURE BOOK: *Lon Po Po: A Red-Riding Hood Story from China* by Ed Young, Philomel

SPECIAL AWARD: *Valentine and Orson* by Nancy Ekholm Burkert, Farrar, Straus and Giroux

1991

FICTION: *The True Confessions of Charlotte Doyle* by Avi, Orchard
NONFICTION: *Appalachia: The Voices of Sleeping Birds* by Cynthia Rylant, Harcourt
PICTURE BOOK: *The Tale of the Mandarin Ducks* by Katherine Paterson, illus. by Haru Wells, Lodestar

1992

FICTION: *Missing May* by Cynthia Rylant, Orchard
NONFICTION: *Talking with Artists* by Pat Cummings, Bradbury
PICTURE BOOK: *Seven Blind Mice* by Ed Young, Philomel

1993

FICTION: *Ajeemah and His Son* by James Berry, Harper
NONFICTION: *Sojourner Truth: Ain't I a Woman?* by Patricia C. and Fredrick L. McKissack, Scholastic
PICTURE BOOK: *The Fortune Tellers* by Lloyd Alexander, illus. by Trina Schart Hyman, Dutton

1994

FICTION: *Scooter* by Vera B. Williams, Greenwillow
NONFICTION: *Eleanor Roosevelt: A Life of Discovery* by Russell Freedman, Clarion
PICTURE BOOK: *Grandfather's Journey* by Allen Say, Houghton

1995

FICTION: *Some of the Kinder Planets* by Tim Wynne-Jones, Orchard
NONFICTION: *Abigail Adams, Witness to a Revolution* by Natalie S. Bober, Atheneum
PICTURE BOOK: *John Henry* by Julius Lester, illus. by Jerry Pinkney, Dial

1996

FICTION: *Poppy* by Avi, illus. by Brian Floca, Jackson/Orchard
NONFICTION: *Orphan Train Rider: One Boy's True Story* by Andrea Warren, Houghton
PICTURE BOOK: *In the Rain with Baby Duck* by Amy Hest, illus. by Jill Barton, Candlewick

1997

FICTION AND POETRY: *The Friends* by Kazumi Yumoto, tr. by Cathy Hirano, Farrar

FICTION AND POETRY HONORS: *Lily's Crossing* by Patricia Reilly Giff, Delacourt; *Harlem* by Walter Dean Myers, illus. by Christopher Myers, Scholastic
NONFICTION: *A Drop of Water: A Book of Science and Wonder* by Walter Wick, Scholastic
NONFICTION HONORS: *Lou Gehrig: The Luckiest Man* by David A. Adler, illus. by Terry Widener, Gulliver/Harcourt; *Leonardo da Vinci* by Diane Stanley, Morrow
PICTURE BOOK: *The Adventures of Sparrowboy* by Brian Pinkney, Simon
PICTURE BOOK HONORS: *Home on the Bayou: A Cowboy's Story* by G. Brian Karas, Simon; *Potato: A Tale from the Great Depression* by Kate Lied, illus. by Lisa Campbell Ernst, National Geographic

1998

FICTION AND POETRY: *The Circuit: Stories from the Life of a Migrant Child* by Francisco Jiménez, University of New Mexico Press
FICTION AND POETRY HONORS: *While No One Was Watching* by Jane Leslie Conly, Holt; *My Louisiana Sky* by Kimberly Willis Holt, Holt
NONFICTION: *Leon's Story* by Leon Walter Tillage, illus. by Susan L. Roth, Farrar
NONFICTION HONORS: *Martha Graham: A Dancer's Life* by Russell Freedman, Clarion; *Chuck Close Up Close* by Jan Greenberg and Sandra Jordan, DK Ink
PICTURE BOOK: *And If the Moon Could Talk* by Kate Banks, illus. by Georg Hallensleben, Foster/Farrar
PICTURE BOOK HONORS: *Seven Brave Women* by Betsy Hearne, illus. by Bethanne Andersen, Greenwillow; *Popcorn: Poems* by James Stevenson, Greenwillow

1999

FICTION: *Holes* by Louis Sachar, Foster/Farrar
FICTION HONORS: *The Trolls* by Polly Horvath, Farrar; *Monster* by Walter Dean Myers, illus. by Christopher Myers, HarperCollins
NONFICTION: *The Top of the World: Climbing Mount Everest* by Steve Jenkins, Houghton
NONFICTION HONORS: *Shipwreck at the Bottom of the World: The Extraordinary True Story of Shackleton and the Endurance* by Jennifer Armstrong, Crown; *William Shakespeare and the Globe* by Aliki, HarperCollins
PICTURE BOOK: *Red-Eyed Tree Frog* by Joy Cowley, illus. by Nic Bishop, Scholastic Press
PICTURE BOOK HONORS: *Dance* by Bill T. Jones and Susan Kuklin, illus. by Susan Kuklin, Hyperion; *The Owl and the Pussycat* by Edward Lear, illus. by James Marshall, di Capua/HarperCollins
SPECIAL CITATION: *Tibet: Through the Red Box* by Peter Sís, Foster/Farrar

2000

FICTION: *The Folk Keeper* by Franny Billingsley, Atheneum
FICTION HONORS: *King of Shadows* by Susan Cooper, Mc-Elderry; *145th Street: Short Stories* by Walter Dean Myers, Delacorte
NONFICTION: *Sir Walter Ralegh and the Quest for El Dorado* by Marc Aronson, Clarion
NONFICTION HONORS: *Osceola: Memories of a Sharecropper's Daughter* collected and edited by Alan Govenar; illus. by Shane W. Evans, Jump at the Sun/Hyperion; *Sitting Bull and His World* by Albert Marrin, Dutton
PICTURE BOOK: *Henry Hikes to Fitchburg* by D. B. Johnson, Houghton
PICTURE BOOK HONORS: *Buttons* by Brock Cole, Farrar; *A Day, A Dog* by Gabrielle Vincent, Front Street

THE LEE BENNETT HOPKINS POETRY AWARD

1993

Sing to the Sun by Ashley Bryan, McElderry

1994

Spirit Walker by Nancy Wood, Doubleday

1995

Beast Feast by Douglas Florian, Greenwillow

1996

Dance with Me by Barbara Juster Esbensen, Harper

1997

Voices from the Wild by David Bouchard, Chronicle

1998

The Great Frog Race by Kristine O'Connell George, Clarion

1999

The Other Side: Shorter Poems by Angela Johnson, Orchard

HONOR BOOK: *A Crack in the Clouds* by Constance Levy, McElderry

2000

What Have You Lost? ed. by Naomi Shihab Nye, Greenwillow

HONOR BOOKS: *An Old Shell* by Tony Johnston, Farrar, Straus and Giroux; *The Rainbow Hand* by Janet S. Wong, McElderry

2001

Light Gathering Poems ed. by Liz Rosenberg, Henry Holt

HONOR BOOK: *Stone Bench in an Empty Park* edited by Paul Janeczko, Orchard

BEST BOOKS FOR YOUNG ADULTS (BBYA) 2000–2004

Author	Title	Grade	Genre	Subjects	List Date
Abelove, Joan	*Saying It Out Loud*	8+	FIC	Death Dying Father	BBYA 00
Alexander, Caroline	*The Endurance: Shackleton's Legendary Antarctic Expedition*	Adult	NF	Exploration Antarctica	BBYA 00
Allison, Anthony	*Hear These Voices: Youth at the Edge of the Millennium*	7+	NF	Multicultural Essays	BBYA 00
Anderson, Laurie Halse	*Speak*	8+	FIC	Rape Art Mute High Schools	BBYA 00
Armstrong, Jennifer	*Ship Wreck at the Bottom of the World*	6+	NF	Exploration Antarctica	BBYA 00
Atkins, Catherine	*When Jeff Comes Home*	8+	FIC	Kidnapping Sexual Abuse	BBYA 00
Barrett, Tracy	*Anna of Byzantium*	6–10	HF	Byzantium Middle Ages	BBYA 00
Bat-Ami, Miriam	*Two Suns in the Sky*	8+	HF	New York 1940s Love Refugee Camp	BBYA 00
Calabro, Marian	*The Perilous Journey of the Donner Party*	6+	NF	Cannibalism West 19th Cent	BBYA 00
Calhoun, Dia	*Firegold*	6–9	FAN	Quest Family	BBYA 00

Author	Title	Grade	Genre	Subjects	List Date
Carbone, Elisa	*Stealing Freedom*	6–10	HF	Afro-Amer Canada Slavery Underground rr	BBYA 00
Card, Orson Scott	*Ender's Shadow*	Adult	SF	Aliens War Battle School	BBYA 00
Cart, Michael	*Tomorrowland*	6–10	SS	Future Antholog	BBYA 00
Chbosky, Stephen	*The Perks of Being a Wall-flower*	9 +	FIC	Coming of Age Friendship PA	BBYA 00
Cooper, Susan	*King of Shadows*	5–8	SF	Shakespeare Time Travel	BBYA 00
Curtis, Christopher Paul	*Bud, Not Buddy*	4–7	HF	Afro-Amer Orphan 1920s	BBYA 00
Dessen, Sarah	*Keeping the Moon*	7 +	FIC	Humor Aunt Weight Loss	BBYA 00
Dominick, Andie	*Needles*	Adult	BIO	Diabetes Sisters	BBYA 00
Ferris, Jean	*Bad*	9 +	FIC	Robbery Juvenile Deten	BBYA 00
Fleischman, Paul	*Mind's Eye*	8 +	FIC	Nursing Home Physical Handic	BBYA 00
Freedman, Russell	*Babe Didrikson Zaharias: The Making of a Champion*	5 +	BIO	Female Athletes Olympics	BBYA 00
Friesen, Gayle	*Janey's Girl*	6–9	FIC	Family Secrets	BBYA 00
Gaiman, Neil	*Stardust*	Adult	FAN	Faerie Witches	BBYA 00
Garner, Eleanor Ramrath	*Eleanor's Story: An American Girl in Hitler's Germany*	7 +	BIO	WW II Berlin Survival	BBYA 00
Gaskins, Pearl Fuyo	*What Are You? Voices of Mixed-Race Young People*	8 +	NF	Multicultural Essays	BBYA 00
Gilmore, Kate	*The Exchange Student*	6–10	SF	Endangered Species	BBYA 00
Gourley, Catherine	*Good Girl Work*	4–8	NF	Industrial Rev 19th Cen women	BBYA 00
Haddix, Margaret Peterson	*Just Ella*	7–9	FAN	Cinderella Fairytales	BBYA 00
Hewett, Lorri	*Dancer*	6–10	FIC	Afro-Amer Ballet Dance	BBYA 00
Hickam, Homer H., Jr.	*Rocket Boys: A Memoir*	Adult	BIO	Sputnik Rockets Coal Mines	BBYA 00
Hobbs, Will	*Jason's Gold*	5–8	HF	Gold Rush Alaska Brothers	BBYA 00
Holt, Kimberly Willis	*When Zachary Beaver Came to Town*	5–8	HF	1971 Sideshow TX Fattest Boy	BBYA 00
Holtwijk, Ineke	*Asphalt Angels*	8–10	FIC	Homeless Street Kids Rio de Jan	BBYA 00
Holubitsky, Katherine	*Alone at Ninety Foot*	7–9	FIC	Suicide Grief Mother Daughtr	BBYA 00
Hoobler, Dorothy and Thomas	*The Ghost in the Tokaido Inn*	6–8	HF MYS	Samurai 18th Cen Japan Judge	BBYA 00
Howe, Norma	*The Adventures of Blue Avenger*	7 +	FIC	Death Humor Superhero	BBYA 00
Jennings, Peter	*The Century for Young People*	4–9	NF	US 20th Century	BBYA 00
Johnson, Scott	*Safe at Second*	7 +	FIC	Baseball Friends Accident	BBYA 00
Jordan, Sherryl	*The Raging Quiet*	8 +	HF	Deaf Middle Ages Witches	BBYA 00
Kalergis, Mary Motley	*Seen and Heard: Teenagers Talk about Their Lives*	Adult	NF	Interviews Coming of Age	BBYA 00

Author	Title	Grade	Genre	Subjects	List Date
King, Stephen	*The Girl Who Loved Tom Gordon*	Adult	HOR	Appalachian Tr Lost Baseball	BBYA 00
Krizmanic, Judy	*Teen's Vegetarian Cookbook*	5 +	NF	Cookery	BBYA 00
Kuhn, Betsy	*Angels of Mercy: The Army Nurses of WW II*	6 +	NF	WW II Military Wars Nurses	BBYA 00
Lawrence, Iain	*The Smugglers*	5–9	HF	18th Century Pirates Ships	BBYA 00
Levine, Gail Carson	*Dave at Night*	5–9	HF	Orphan Hebrew Home Harlem R	BBYA 00
Lubar, David	*Hidden Talents*	6–8	SF	Supernatural	BBYA 00
Mah, Adeline Yen	*Chinese Cinderella: The True Story of an Unwanted Daughter*	6 +	BIO	Chinese Real-life Cinderella	BBYA 00
Marchetta, Melina	*Looking for Alibrandi*	8 +	FIC	Schools Family Australia	BBYA 00
Marrin, Albert	*Terror of the Spanish Main: Sir Henry Morgan and His Buccaneers*	6 +	NF	Adventure Buccaneers 17th Centur England	BBYA 00
Mattison, Chris	*Snake*	Adult	NF	Reptiles Photos	BBYA 00
McNamee, Graham	*Hate You*	8 +	FIC	Abuse Fathers Songwriting	BBYA 00
McNeal, Laura and Tom	*Crooked*	6–10	FIC	Death Grief Love Bullies	BBYA 00
Meyer, Carolyn	*Mary, Bloody Mary*	6 +	HF	Survival Englan Henry VIII	BBYA 00
Morris, Gerald	*The Squire, His Knight & His Lady*	5–9	HF FAN	King Arthur Sir Gawain Green Knight	BBYA 00
Myers, Walter Dean	*Monster*	7 +	FIC	Afro-Amer Trial Robbery Script	BBYA 00
Namioka, Lensey	*Ties That Bind, Ties That Break*	7–10	HF	China 1911 Foot Binding Family	BBYA 00
Nye, Naomi Shihab	*What Have You Lost?*	7 +	POE	Contemporary International	BBYA 00
Okutoro, Lydia Omolola	*Quiet Storm—Voices of Young Black Poets*	6 +	POE	Afro-Amer Anthology	BBYA 00
Opdyke, Irene Gut	*In My Hands: Memories of a Holocaust Rescuer*	6 +	BIO	Holocaust Jews Poland WW II	BBYA 00
Partridge, Elizabeth & Dorothea Lange	*Restless Spirit: The Life and Work of Dorothea Lange*	6 +	BIO	Photography Women Early 20th Century	BBYA 00
Porter, Connie	*Imani All Mine*	Adult	FIC	Afro-Amer Teen Mother Urban	BBYA 00
Powell, Randy	*Tribute to Another Dead Rock Star*	8 +	FIC	Death Grief Brothers Mental	BBYA 00
Qualey, Marsha	*Close to a Killer*	6–8	MYS	Murder Mothers	BBYA 00
Randle, Kristen D.	*Breaking Rank*	9 +	FIC	Friendship Love Gangs High Sch	BBYA 00
Reich, Susanna	*Clara Schumann: Piano Virtuoso*	5–8	BIO	Classical Music 19th Century	BBYA 00
Rottman, S. L.	*Head above Water*	9 +	FIC	Swimming Down Syndrome	BBYA 00

Author	Title	Grade	Genre	Subjects	List Date
Rowling, J. K.	*Harry Potter and the Chamber of Secrets*	4+	FAN	Wizards Magic School Friends	BBYA 00
Rowling, J. K.	*Harry Potter and the Prisoner of Azkaban*	4+	FAN	Wizards Magic School Friends	BBYA 00
Rubin, Susan Goldman	*Margaret Bourke-White: Her Pictures Were Her Life*	5+	BIO	Photography Women 20th C	BBYA 00
Savage, Deborah	*Summer Hawk*	6–10	FIC	Birds Friendship	BBYA 00
Schmidt, Thomas & Jeremy	*The Saga of Lewis and Clark into the Uncharted West*	Adult	NF	Exploration 19th Century	BBYA 00
Schwager, Tina & Michele Schuerger	*Gusty Girls: Young Women Who Dare*	7+	BIO	Essays Self-Help Sports Personal Achievements	BBYA 00
Shusterman, Neal	*Downsiders*	8+	FAN	Underground	BBYA 00
Skurzynski, Gloria	*Spider's Voice*	8+	HF	Middle Ages Mute Love	BBYA 00
Sones, Sonya	*Stop Pretending*	6–9	POE	Mental Problem Sisters	BBYA 00
Stanley, Diane	*A Time Apart*	5–8	FIC	Cancer Iron Age Archaeology Eng	BBYA 00
Thesman, Jean	*The Other Ones*	7–9	FIC	Wicca Friends	BBYA 00
Tomey, Ingrid	*Nobody Else Has to Know*	8–10	FIC	Accident Grandfathers	BBYA 00
Vande Velde, Vivian	*Never Trust a Dead Man*	6–9	HF MYS	Middle Ages Bats Witchcraft	BBYA 00
Voigt, Cynthia	*Elske*	9+	HF	Middle Ages Battles Royalty	BBYA 00
Whitmore, Arvella	*Trapped between the Lash and the Gun*	5–8	HF	Time Travel Slavery	BBYA 00
Wittlinger, Ellen	*Hard Love*	8+	FIC	Love 'Zines Gays Lesbians	BBYA 00
Young, Karen Romano	*The Beetle and Me—A Love Story*	6–10	FIC	Love Cars Volkswagen	BBYA 00
Almond, David	*Kit's Wilderness*	6–9	FIC	Ghosts Mines Grandfathers	BBYA 01
Anderson, Laurie Halse	*Fever 1793*	6–10	HF	Yellow Fever PA	BBYA 01
Appelt, Kathi	*Kissing Tennessee and Other Stories from the Stardust Dance*	6–9	SS	High Schools Dance	BBYA 01
Armstrong, Lance with Sally Jenkins	*It's Not about the Bike . . . My Journey Back to Life*	Adult	BIO	Cancer Cycling Sports Race	BBYA 01
Bachrach, Susan D.	*The Nazi Olympics: Berlin 1936*	7+	NF	Sports Germany Olympics	BBYA 01
Bagdasarian, Adam	*Forgotten Fire*	8+	FIC	Turkey Armenia Massacre	BBYA 01
Bartoletti, Susan Campbell	*Kids on Strike!*	5–8	NF	19th Century Children Strikes	BBYA 01
Bauer, Cat	*Harley, Like a Person*	7–10	FIC	Adoption Artist	BBYA 01
Bauer, Joan	*Hope Was Here*	8+	FIC	Politics Cancer	BBYA 01
Beckett, Wendy	*My Favorite Things: 75 Works of Art from around the World*	Adult	NF	Art Criticism Appreciation	BBYA 01
Blackwood, Gary	*Shakespeare's Scribe*	5–8	HF	Shakespeare Shorthand	BBYA 01
Brooks, Martha	*Being with Henry*	7+	FIC	Runaway Old Man Abuse	BBYA 01
Cabot, Meg	*The Princess Diaries*	7–9	FIC	Royalty Fathers	BBYA 01

Author	Title	Grade	Genre	Subjects	List Date
Calhoun, Dia	*Aria of the Sea*	6–9	FAN	Magic Dance	BBYA 01
Chevalier, Tracy	*Girl with the Pearl Earring*	Adult	HF	Artist Maid Love Vermeer	BBYA 01
Coman, Carolyn	*Many Stones*	8 +	FIC	Death Grief South Africa	BBYA 01
Creech, Sharon	*The Wanderer*	5–9	FIC	Sailing Family	BBYA 01
Crichton, Michael	*Timeline*	Adult	SF	Time Travel Middle Ages	BBYA 01
Cross, Gillian	*Tightrope*	7–10	MYS	Graffiti Bullies	BBYA 01
Dessen, Sarah	*Dreamland*	9 +	FIC	Abuse Boyfriend	BBYA 01
Deuker, Carl	*Night Hoops*	8–10	FIC	Basketball Sport	BBYA 01
Fienberg, Anna	*Borrowed Light*	9 +	FIC	Teen Pregnancy	BBYA 01
Fogelin, Adrian	*Crossing Jordan*	5–8	FIC	Friends Racism Afro-Amer Run	BBYA 01
Fradin, Dennis Brindell & Judith	*Ida B. Wells: Mother of the Civil Rights Movement*	5 +	BIO	Afro-Amer Civil Rights Women	BBYA 01
Franco, Betsy, ed.	*You Hear Me?: Poems and Writings by Teenage Boys*	7 +	NF	Anthology Essays	BBYA 01
Freedman, Russell	*Give Me Liberty!: The Story of the Declaration of Independence*	5–8	NF	Revolutionary War Colonial	BBYA 01
Giff, Patricia Reilly	*Nory Ryan's Song*	5–8	HF	Irish Famine Immigration	BBYA 01
Glenn, Mel	*Split Image*	8 +	POE	Suicide HS Chinese Amer	BBYA 01
Glover, Savion & Bruce Weber	*Savion: My Life in Tap*	5 +	BIO	Afro-Amer Tap Dancing	BBYA 01
Gottlieb, Lori	*Stick Figure: A Diary of My Former Self*	Adult	BIO	Anorexia Diaries Girl	BBYA 01
Gray, Dianne E.	*Holding Up the Earth*	5–8	HF	Farm Orphans	BBYA 01
Haruf, Kent	*Plainsong*	Adult	FIC	Teen Pregnancy	BBYA 01
Hyde, Catherine Ryan	*Pay It Forward*	Adult	FAN	Teacher Student Good Deeds	BBYA 01
Isaacs, Anne	*Torn Thread*	6–8	HF	Holocaust Jews	BBYA 01
Karr, Kathleen	*The Boxer*	7 +	HF	Boxing 19th Cent	BBYA 01
Katz, Jon	*Geeks: How Two Boys Rode the Internet out of Idaho*	Adult	NF	Internet Computers	BBYA 01
Kessler, Cristina	*No Condition Is Permanent*	7 +	FIC	Africa Female Circumcision	BBYA 01
Konigsburg, E. L.	*Silent to the Bone*	6–8	FIC	Mute Siblings Abuse Nanny	BBYA 01
Koss, Amy Goldman	*The Girls*	5–8	FIC	Cliques Peer Pressure MS	BBYA 01
Lalicki, Tom	*Spellbinder: The Life of Harry Houdini*	5–9	BIO	Magicians Escape Artist	BBYA 01
Lanier, Shannon & Jane Feldman	*Jefferson's Children: The Story of One American Family*	8 +	BIO	DNA Jefferson Descendents	BBYA 01
Lawrence, Iain	*Ghost Boy*	8–10	FIC	Albino Circus Runaway	BBYA 01
Lebert, Benjamin	*Crazy*	Adult	FIC	Boarding School	BBYA 01
Logue, Mary	*Dancing with an Alien*	8–10	SF	Love Aliens	BBYA 01
Lynch, Chris	*Gold Dust*	5–8	FIC	Baseball Racism	BBYA 01
Marillier, Juliet	*Daughter of the Forest*	Adult	FAN	Magic Swans	BBYA 01

844

Author	Title	Grade	Genre	Subjects	List Date
Marrin, Albert	*Sitting Bull and His World*	6+	BIO	Native Amer	BBYA 01
Morris, Gerald	*The Savage Damsel and the Dwarf*	6–9	FAN	King Arthur Knights	BBYA 01
Murphy, Rita	*Night Flying*	5–9	FIC	Flying Women	BBYA 01
Myers, Walter Dean	*145th Street: Short Stories*	6+	SS	Afro-Amer New York City	BBYA 01
Oughton, Jerrie	*Perfect Family*	8–10	FIC	Teenage Pregnancy	BBYA 01
Paulsen, Gary	*The Beet Fields*	9+	BIO	Runaway Farm Work Carnival	BBYA 01
Peck, Richard	*A Year Down Yonder*	5–8	HF	Humor Rural Grand-mothers	BBYA 01
Peters, Julie Anne	*Define "Normal"*	7–10	FIC	Humor Friends Peer Counselor	BBYA 01
Philbrick, Rodman	*The Last Book in the Universe*	6–9	SF	Dystopia Epilepsy	BBYA 01
Platt, Randall Beth	*The Likes of Me*	7–10	HF	Logging Camp Albino Seattle	BBYA 01
Plummer, Louise	*A Dance for Three*	9+	FIC	Teen Pregnancy	BBYA 01
Plum-Ucci, Carol	*The Body of Christopher Creed*	8+	MYS	Missing Student Harassment HS	BBYA 01
Rennison, Louise	*Angus, Thongs and Full-Frontal Snogging: Confessions of Georgia Nicolson*	7–9	FIC	Humor Diaries Cat Sisters England Friends	BBYA 01
Ryan, Pam Munoz	*Esperanza Rising*	6–9	FIC	Mexican Amer Labor Hispanic	BBYA 01
Schwartz, Virginia Frances	*Send One Angel Down*	5–8	HF	Afro-Americans Slavery	BBYA 01
Spinelli, Jerry	*Stargirl*	6–10	FIC	Peer Pressure Eccentric Love	BBYA 01
St. George, Judith	*In the Line of Fire: Presidents' Lives at Stake*	5+	NF	Assassination US History	BBYA 01
Trueman, Terry	*Stuck in Neutral*	5–9	FIC	Cerebral Palsy	BBYA 01
Turner, Ann	*Learning to Swim*	6+	POE	Sexual Abuse	BBYA 01
Ung, Loung	*First They Killed My Father: A Daughter of Cambodia Remembers*	Adult	BIO	Political Atrocities Asia 1970s Cambodia	BBYA 01
Wallace, Rich	*Playing without a Ball*	8+	FIC	Basketball Sport	BBYA 01
Wells, Ken	*Meely LaBauve*	Adult	FIC	Humor Bayou	BBYA 01
White, Ruth	*Memories of Summer*	7–10	FIC	Mental Illness Sisters 1955	BBYA 01
Williams, Lori Aurelia	*When Kambia Elaine Flew in from Nepture*	8+	FIC	Afro-Amer Abuse Friends	BBYA 01
Winick, Judd	*Pedro and Me: Friendship, Loss and What I Learned*	9+	NF	Aids Graphic Novel MTV	BBYA 01
Wittlinger, Ellen	*What's in a Name*	7+	FIC	Friendship Multiple Voices	BBYA 01
Woodson, Jacqueline	*Miracle's Boys*	6–10	FIC	Death Brothers Mother Grief	BBYA 01
Yolen, Jane and Robert J. Harris	*Queen's Own Fool*	7+	HF	Mary, Queen of Scots Jester	BBYA 01

845

Author	Title	Grade	Genre	Subjects	List Date
Bell, Hilari	*A Matter of Profit*	6–10	SF	Aliens Assassins Scholar Warrior	BBYA 02
Brashares, Ann	*The Sisterhood of the Traveling Pants*	9+	FIC	Friendship Jeans Sharing	BBYA 02
Brooks, Bruce	*All That Remains*	7+	SS	Death Grief Golf Ice Hockey	BBYA 02
Card, Orson Scott	*Shadow of the Hegemon*	Adult	SF	Bean Politics Peter Wiggin	BBYA 02
Cart, Michael, ed.	*Love and Sex: Ten Stories of Truth*	9+	SS	Relationships	BBYA 02
Clement-Davies, David	*Fire Bringer*	6+	FAN	Deer Scotland Animal Epic	BBYA 02
Colton, Larry	*Counting Coup: The True Story of Basketball and Honor on the Little Big Horn*	Adult	NF	Basketball Native Amer	BBYA 02
Cooper, Michael L.	*Fighting for Honor: Japanese Americans and World War II*	6+	NF	Japanese Amer WWII Relocate	BBYA 02
Cormier, Robert	*The Rag and Bone Shop*	7+	MYS	Murder Teen Interrogation	BBYA 02
Crutcher, Chris	*Whale Talk*	8+	FIC	Adoption Swim Mixed Race	BBYA 02
Ferris, Jean	*Eight Seconds*	9+	FIC	Homosexuals Rodeo Prejudice	BBYA 02
Ferris, Jean	*Of Sound Mind*	8+	FIC	Anger Deaf Sign Language	BBYA 02
Fisher, Antwone Quenton	*Finding Fish (with Mim Eichler Rivas)*	Adult	BIO	Afro-Amer Abuse Foster Child Homeless	BBYA 02
Fleischman, Paul	*Seek*	7+	FIC	Fathers Sons Radio Dialogue	BBYA 02
Flinn, Alex	*Breathing Underwater*	9+	FIC	Date Abuse Diaries Anger	BBYA 02
Fradin, Dennis Brindell	*Bound for the North Star: True Stories of Fugitive Slaves*	5+	NF	Afro-Amer Fugitive Slaves Underground rr	BBYA 02
Franco, Betsy, ed.	*Things I Have to Tell You: Poems and Writings by Teenage Girls*	8+	POE	Secrets Sexual Orientation Youth Writings	BBYA 02
Gallo, Don, ed.	*On the Fringe*	7+	SS	Peer Pressure Outsiders	BBYA 02
Greenberg, Jan & Sandra Jordan	*Vincent Van Gogh: Portrait of an Artist*	5+	BIO	Artists	BBYA 02
Greenberg, Jan, ed.	*Heart to Heart: New Poems Inspired by 20th Century Art*	5+	POE	Amer Poetry Art, Modern	BBYA 02
Griffin, Adele	*Amandine*	6–9	FAN	Emotional Problems School	BBYA 02
Heneghan, James	*The Grave*	7–10	FAN	Time Travel 1847 Ireland	BBYA 02
Holm, Jennifer	*Boston Jane: An Adventure*	6–10	HF	Chinook Indians Frontier Life	BBYA 02
Hoose, Phillip	*We Were There, Too!: Young People in U.S. History*	6+	NF	Children Youth	BBYA 02
Howe, James, ed.	*The Color of Absence: Twelve Stories about Love and Hope*	7–10	SS	Adolescence Grief	BBYA 02
Jenkins, A. M.	*Damage*	9+	FIC	Depression Mental Football	BBYA 02

Author	Title	Grade	Genre	Subjects	List Date
Jimenez, Francisco	*Breaking Through*	5–8	FIC	Mexican Americans	BBYA 02
Jordan, Sherryl	*Secret Sacrament*	7+	FAN	Magic Healer	BBYA 02
Kendall, Martha E.	*Failure Is Impossible: The History of American Women's Rights*	5–9	NF	Women's Rights Feminism US History	BBYA 02
Ketchum, Liza	*Into a New Country: Eight Remarkable Women of the West*	6+	BIO	Pioneers Women Frontier	BBYA 02
King, Daniel	*Chess: From First Moves to Checkmate*	4+	NF	Chess How-To-Guide Basics	BBYA 02
Klass, David	*You Don't Know Me*	7+	FIC	HS Child Abuse	BBYA 02
Koertge, Ron	*The Brimstone Journals*	9+	POE	School Violence	BBYA 02
Lawlor, Laurie	*Helen Keller: Rebellious Spirit*	5–7	BIO		BBYA 02
Lee, Bruce	*Bruce Lee: The Celebrated Life of the Golden Dragon*	Adult	BIO	Martial Arts Movie Actor	BBYA 02
Les Becquets, Diane	*The Stones of Mourning Creek*	7–10	HF	Race Relations Friendship	BBYA 02
Lynch, Chris	*Freewill*	9+	FIC	Death Suicide Emotional Prob	BBYA 02
Marrin, Albert	*George Washington and the Founding of a Nation*	6+	BIO	Amer Revolutn Generals	BBYA 02
McCormick, Patricia	*Cut*	7–10	FIC	Self-Mutilation Psych Hospital	BBYA 02
McDonald, Janet	*Spellbound*	7+	FIC	Teen Mothers Afro Americans	BBYA 02
McDonald, Joyce	*Shades of Simon Gray*	7+	MYS	Cheating Coma Astral projection	BBYA 02
Mikaelsen, Ben	*Touching Spirit Bear*	7+	FIC	Anger Bears Juv Delinquent Tlingit Abuse	BBYA 02
Moriarty, Jaclyn	*Feeling Sorry for Cecilia*	7+	FIC	Friends Austral Epistolary	BBYA 02
Murphy, Jim	*Blizzard!*	5–9	NF	NYC 1888 Blizzards	BBYA 02
Myers, Walter Dean	*Bad Boy: A Memoir*	7+	BIO	Afro-American Memoir Author	BBYA 02
Myers, Walter Dean	*The Greatest: Muhammad Ali*	7+	BIO	Afro-American Boxing Vietnam	BBYA 02
Na, An	*A Step From Heaven*	8+	FIC	Korean Amer Family Immigrt	BBYA 02
Naidoo, Beverly	*The Other Side of Truth*	5–8	FIC	Nigeria Immigrants	BBYA 02
Nam, Vickie	*Yell-OH Girls!: Emerging Voices Explore Culture, Identity and Growing-Up Asian American*	8+	SS POE	Asian American Stories Poetry Teen Authors Essays	BBYA 02
Nelson Marilyn	*Carver: A Life in Poems*	6+	POE	Afro-Amer Agriculturalist	BBYA 02
Nix, Garth	*Lirael: Daughter of the Clayr*	7+	FAN	Necromancy Librarian Magic	BBYA 02
Nolan, Han	*Born Blue*	8+	FIC	Singers Abandoned	BBYA 02
Orgill, Roxane	*Shout, Sister, Shout!: Ten Girl Singers Who Shaped a Century*	6–9	BIO	Singers Women	BBYA 02

Author	Title	Grade	Genre	Subjects	List Date
Owen David	*Hidden Evidence: Forty True Crimes and How Forensic Science Helped Solve Them*	Adult	NF	Forensic Science Crime Investigation	BBYA 02
Park, Linda Sue	*A Single Shard*	5–8	HF	Korea Pottery	BBYA 02
Peck, Richard	*Fair Weather*	5–8	HF	World's Fair Humor Family	BBYA 02
Pierce, Meredith Ann	*Treasure at the Heart of the Tanglewood*	8–10	FAN	Healer Boar Sorcerer Magic	BBYA 02
Pierce, Tamora	*Squire: Protector of the Small*	5–8	FAN	Knights and Knighthood	BBYA 02
Pratchett, Terry	*The Amazing Maurice and His Educated Rodents*	7+	FAN	Pied Piper Discworld	BBYA 02
Pullman, Philip	*The Amber Sypglass: His Dark Materials #3*	6+	FAN	Religion Adventure	BBYA 02
Rees, Celia	*Witch Child*	8+	HF	Witches Trials Persecution	BBYA 02
Rice, David	*Crazy Loco*	7+	SS	Mexican Americans	BBYA 02
Rochelle, Belinda, ed.	*Words with Wings: A Treasury of African-American Poetry and Art*	4–8	POE	Afro-Amer Artists Poets Collections BBYA 02	
Ryan, Sara	*Empress of the World*	9+	FIC	Lesbians Friend Summer Institut	BBYA 02
Salisbury, Graham	*The Lord of the Deep*	5–8	FIC	Hawaii Deep Sea Fishing	BBYA 02
Sanchez, Alex	*Rainbow Boys*	9+	FIC	Gay Teens Homosexuality	BBYA 02
Shinn, Sharon	*Summers at Castle Auburn*	Adult	FAN	Persecution	BBYA 02
Sones, Sonya	*What My Mother Doesn't Know*	9+	POE	Dating Love	BBYA 02
Stratton, Allan	*Leslie's Journal*	8+	FIC	Dating Violence Journals	BBYA 02
Tashjian, Janet	*The Gospel According to Larry*	8+	FIC	Web Sites Fame Identity Humor	BBYA 02
Taylor, Mildred	*The Land*	7–10	HF	Logan Family	BBYA 02
Tingle, Rebecca	*The Edge of the Sword*	6–10	HF	Ethelfled Viking Anglo Saxons	BBYA 02
Vance, Susanne	*Sights*	6–9	FAN	Precognition Child Abuse	BBYA 02
Vande Velde, Vivian	*Being Dead: Stories*	7+	SS	Supernatural Horror Stories	BBYA 02
Vijayaraghaven, Vineeta	*Motherland*	A/YA	FIC	India	BBYA 02
Weaver, Beth Nixon	*Rooster*	7–10	FIC	Farm Life FLA Mentally Handic	BBYA 02
Werlin, Nancy	*Black Mirror*	7+	MYS	Brother Murder Suicide School	BBYA 02
Williams, Garcia, Rita	*Every Time a Rainbow Dies*	9+	FIC	Caribbean-Amer Rape Love NYC	BBYA 02
Wittlinger, Ellen	*Razzle*	7–10	FIC	Photography Friendship	BBYA 02
Wolff, Virginia Euwer	*True Believer*	6+	FIC	Poverty Family Single Parent	BBYA 02
Zusak, Markus	*Fighting Ruben Wolfe*	7+	FIC	Boxing Brothers	BBYA 02
Alvarez, Julia	*Before We Were Free*	7–10	HF	Dominican Rep Trujillo 1960	BBYA 03
Anderson, Laurie Halse	*Catalyst*	10+	FIC	Death, HS, Fathers	BBYA 03

Author	Title	Grade	Genre	Subjects	List Date
Anderson, M. T.	*Feed*	8 +	SF	Computer Implants	BBYA 03
Armstrong, Jennifer, Editor	*Shattered: Stories of Children and War*	6 +	SS	Wars Young Adult Authors	BBYA 03
Auch, Mary Jane	*Ashes of Roses*	7 +	HF	Irish Americans Immigrants Fire	BBYA 03
Bardi, Abby	*The Book of Fred: A Novel*	A/YA	FIC	Foster Care Cult Fundamentalist	BBYA 03
Barker, Clive	*Abarat*	7 +	FAN	Islands, Journey	BBYA 03
Bartoletti, Susan Campbell	*Black Potatoes: The Story of the Great Irish Famine*	6 +	NF	Potato Famine Blight Ireland	BBYA 03
Bechard, Margaret	*Hanging on to Max*	8 +	FIC	Teenage Fathers Fathers & Sons	BBYA 03
Black, Holly	*Tithe: A Modern Faerie Tale*	9 +	FAN	Fairies Magic	BBYA 03
Blackwood, Gary	*The Year of the Hangman*	8–10	HF	Revolutionary War, Alt History	BBYA 03
Breslin, Theresa	*Remembrance*	7 +	HF	WWI Nursing	BBYA 03
Chambers, Aidan	*Postcards from No Man's Land*	9 +	HF	WWII; Assisted Suicide Holland	BBYA 03 Printz W
Clements, Andrew	*Things Not Seen*	7–10	SF	Invisibility; Blind, Friends	BBYA 03
Cohn, Rachel	*Gingerbread*	9 +	FIC	Family, NY	BBYA 03
Crowe, Chris	*Mississippi Trial, 1955*	7 +	HF	Civil Rights, Racism, Afro-Americans	BBYA 03
Datlow, Ellen & Terri Windling	*The Green Man: Tales from the Mythic Forest*	7 +	SS FAN	Fairytales, Urban Myths	BBYA 03
Dessen, Sarah	*This Lullaby*	9 +	FIC	Dating, Bands	BBYA 03
Ellis, Deborah	*Parvana's Journey*	7–10	FIC	Afghanistan, Disguise; War	BBYA 03
Etchemendy, Nancy	*Cat in Glass and Other Tales of the Unnatural*	9 +	SS/ HOR	Supernatural	BBYA 03
Fama, Elizabeth	*Overboard*	4–8	FIC	Sumatra, Ferry	BBYA 03
Farmer, Nancy	*The House of the Scorpion*	6–10	SF	Clones Drugs	BBYA 03
Ferris, Jean	*Once upon a Marigold*	5–9	FAN	Fairytales Humor Royalty	BBYA 03
Fleischman, John	*Phineas Gage: A Gruesome but True Story About Brain Science*	7–10	NF	Brain Injury Science	BBYA 03
Frank, E. R.	*America*	10 +	FIC	Racially Mixed, Foster Homes	BBYA 03
Frank, Hillary	*Better Than Running at Night*	10 +	FIC	Art School	BBYA 03
Freymann-Weyr, Garret	*My Heartbeat*	9 +	FIC	Homosexuality Bisexuality	BBYA 03
Froese, Deborah	*Out of the Fire*	8–11	FIC	Burns Bonfire	BBYA 03
Gaiman, Neil	*Coraline*	5–8	FAN	Alternate Univ; Button Eyes	BBYA 03
Gantos, Jack	*Hole in My Life*	8 +	BIO	Drugs Prison	BBYA 03
Giff, Patricia Reilly	*Pictures of Hollis Woods*	5–7	FIC	Orphans, Artists Foster Care	BBYA 03
Giles, Gail	*Shattering Glass*	9 +	FIC	Violence, HS, Popularity	BBYA 03
Grimes, Nikki	*Bronx Masquerade*	8 +	POE	Race, Multiple Voices	BBYA 03

Author	Title	Grade	Genre	Subjects	List Date
Halam, Ann	*Dr. Franklin's Island*	8+	SF	Clones, Genetic Engineering	BBYA 03
Hampton, Wilborn	*Meltdown: A Race against Nuclear Disaster at Three Mile Island*	7+	NF	Nuclear Power Plants, Accidents	BBYA 03
Hiaasen, Carl	*Hoot*	6–9	MYS	Owls, Humor, Endangered Species, FL	BBYA 03
Holeman, Linda	*Search of the Moon King's Daughter*	8–11	HF	Chimney Sweeps England	BBYA 03
Jordan, Sherryl	*The Hunting of the Last Dragon*	6–10	FAN	Middle Ages Dragons Britain	BBYA 03
Kidd, Sue Monk	*The Secret Life of Bees*	A/YA	HF	Bees Jailbreak Civil Right	BBYA 03
Koertge, Ron	*Stoner & Spaz: A Love Story*	9+	FIC	Cerebral Palsey Drugs HS Love	BBYA 03
Korman, Gordon	*Son of the Mob*	7+	FIC ROM	Mob, FBI, Humor, Love	BBYA 03
Lawrence, Iain	*The Lightkeeper's Daughter*	9+	FIC	Brothers Sisters Family problems	BBYA 03
Leavitt, Martine	*The Dollmage*	6+	FAN	Magic Jealousy	BBYA 03
McCaughrean, Geraldine	*The Kite Rider*	6–9	HF	China Mongols Kites Circus	BBYA 03
McPherson, James M.	*Fields of Fury: The American Civil War*	6–8	NF	Civil War Battles History	BBYA 03
Miller, Mary Beth	*Aimee*	9+	MYS	Suicide Murder Investigation	BBYA 03
Moore, Christopher	*Lamb: The Gospel According to Biff, Christ's Childhood Pal*	A/YA	FAN	Jesus Angels Messiah Friends	BBYA 03
Nelson, Peter	*Left For Dead: A Young Man's Search for Justice for the USS Indianapolis*	6+	NF	Trial USS Investigation Trial	BBYA 03
Nye, Naomi Shihab	*19 Varieties of Gazelle: Poems of the Middle East*	6+	POE	Peace Struggle Love Fear	BBYA 03
Oates, Joyce Carol	*Big Mouth & Ugly Girl*	8+	FIC	Friendship HS Violence Threat	BBYA 03
Park, Linda Sue	*When My Name Was Keoko: A Novel of Korea in World War II*	6–9	HF	WWII Korea Kamikaze	BBYA 03
Partridge, Elizabeth	*This Land Was Made for You and Me: The Life & Songs of Woody Guthrie*	6+	NF	Huntington's Disease Folk Singers	BBYA 03
Philbrick, Nathaniel	*Revenge of the Whale: The True Story of the Whaleship Essex*	6–10	NF	Shipwrecks Whaling	BBYA 03
Placide, Jaira	*Fresh Girl*	9+	FIC	Violence Rape Haiti Immigrant	BBYA 03
Plum-Ucci, Carol	*What Happened to Lani Garver?*	9+	FIC	Gay Bashing Alcoholism Leukemia	BBYA 03
Powell, Randy	*Three Clams and an Oyster*	7–10	FIC	Flag Football Humor Friends	BBYA 03

Author	Title	Grade	Genre	Subjects	List Date
Rall, Ted	*To Afghanistan and Back: A Graphic Travelogue*	A/YA	GN	Afghanistan Trip Politics	BBYA 03
Rottman, S. L.	*Stetson*	9+	FIC	Alcoholism Brothers Sisters	BBYA 03
Santana, Patricia	*Motorcycle Ride on the Sea of Tranquility*	Adult	HF	Mexican-Amer Vietnam 1969	BBYA 03
Savage, Deborah	*Kotuku*	10+	FIC	Grief Anorexia New Zealand	BBYA 03
Sebold, Alice	*The Lovely Bones: A Novel*	A/YA	MYS	Serial Killer Heaven Murder	BBYA 03
Sheppard, Mary C.	*Seven for a Secret*	10+	MYS	Summer Romance	BBYA 03
Smith, Kevin	*Green Arrow: Quiver*	10+	GN	Superheroes Archers	BBYA 03
Smith, Sherri L.	*Lucy the Giant*	7–10	FIC	Runaways Fishing Boats	BBYA 03
Steinberg, Jacques	*The Gatekeepers: Inside the Admissions Process of a Premier College*	A/YA	NF	Wesleyan Univ College Admissions	BBYA 03
Tolan, Stephanie S.	*Surviving the Applewhites*	6–9	FIC	Theater Juvenile Delinquent	BBYA 03
Toten, Teresa	*The Game*	7+	FIC	Suicide, Sisters, Psych Hospital	BBYA 03
Van Pelt, James	*Strangers and Beggars: Stories*	Adult	SF	Supernatural Horror	BBYA 03
Woodson, Jacqueline	*Hush*	6–9	MYS	Afro-American Witness Protect	BBYA 03
Yolen, Jane and Robert J. Harris	*Girl in a Cage*	6–10	HF	Robert the Bruce Scotland 1306	BBYA 03
Adichie, Chimamanda Ngozi	*Purple Hibiscus*	A/YA	FIC	Nigeria, Fathers Physical Abuse, Coming of Age	BBYA 04
Bell, Hilari	*The Goblin Wood*	6–10	FAN	Hedgewitch Knight Goblin	BBYA 04
Bird, Eugenie	*Fairie-ality: The Fashion Collection from the House of Ellwand*	6+	NF	Fairies Fashion	BBYA 04
Bray, Libba	*A Great and Terrible Beauty*	9+	FAN	Magic Boarding Schools India	BBYA 04
Brenna, Herbie	*Faerie Wars*	6–8	FAN	Faerie Animals	BBYA 04
Brooks, Kevin	*Lucas*	9+	FIC	Bullies England	BBYA 04
Brooks, Martha	*True Confessions of a Heartless Girl*	9+	FIC	Pregnancy Coming of Age	BBYA 04
Buckingham, Dorothea N.	*Staring Down the Dragon*	7+	FIC	Cancer; Hawaii; Death	BBYA 04
Burt, Guy	*Sophie*	Adult	FIC	Psychol Thriller Kidnapping	BBYA 04
Calhoun, Dia	*White Midnight*	9+	FAN	Social Classes Tolerance	BBYA 04
Capuzzo, Michael	*Close to Shore: The Terrifying Shark Attacks of 1916*	7+	NF	Shark Attack NJ Atlantic Coast	BBYA 04
Coburn, Jake	*Prep*	9+	FIC	Drugs Gangs Graffiti Artist	BBYA 04
Cofer, Judith Ortiz	*The Meaning of Consuelo*	Adult	HF	Schizophrenia Puerto Rico 1950	BBYA 04

851

Author	Title	Grade	Genre	Subjects	List Date
Crowe, Chris	*Getting Away With Murder: The True Story of the Emmett Till Case*	7+	NF	Civil Rights 1955 Miss Afro Amer	BBYA 04
Crutcher, Chris	*King of the Mild Frontier: An Ill-Advised Autobiography*	8+	BIO Autob	Humor Childhood	BBYA 04
Davis, Amanda	*Wonder When You'll Miss Me*	Adult	FIC	Suicide Attempt Race Circus	BBYA 04
Donnelly, Jennifer	*A Northern Light*	10+	MYS HF	Murder 1906 Adirondacks	BBYA 04
Fleming, Candace	*Ben Franklin's Alamanc: Being a True Account of the Good Gentleman's Life*	6–9	BIO	Statesmen Inventors	BBYA 04
Fradin, Dennis Brindell & Judith Bloom Fradin	*Fight On! Mary Church Terrell's Battle for Integration*	6–9	BIO	Civil Rights; Afro-Amer; Women	BBYA 04
Frank, E. R.	*Friction*	6–10	FIC	Sexual Abuse	BBYA 04
Freedman, Russell	*In Defense of Liberty: The Story of America's Bill of Rights*	5+	NF	Constitutional Amendments	BBYA 04
Freese, Barbara	*Coal: A Human History*	Adult	NF	Industrial Revol Pollution Minig	BBYA 04
Frost, Helen	*Keesha's House*	9+	POE	Foster Home	BBYA 04
Going, K. L.	*Fat Kid Rules the World*	8+	FIC	Obesity Band	BBYA 04
Goodman, Alison	*Singing the Dogstar Blues*	7+	SF	Time Travel	BBYA 04
Haddon, Mark	*The Curious Incident of the Dog in the Night-time: A Novel*	A/YA	MYS	Autism Dogs Math Investigate	BBYA 04
Hampton, Wilborn	*September 11, 2001: Attack on New York City*	7+	NF	World Trade Centr Terrorism	BBYA 04
Hautman, Pete	*Sweetblood*	9+	FIC	Vampires Goths Diabetes HS	BBYA 04
Hearn, Lian	*Across the Nightingale Floor: Tales of the Otori, Book One.*	A/YA	FAN	Feudal Japan-like Secrets Epic	BBYA 04
Henkes, Kevin	*Olive's Ocean*	5–8	FIC	Summer Beach Grandmothers	BBYA 04
Hoffman, Nina Kiriki	*A Stir of Bones*	Adult	FAN	Ghosts, Haunted House, Friends	BBYA 04
Holt, Kimberly	*Keeper of the Night*	6–10	FIC	Guam Suicide	BBYA 04
Horvath, Polly	*The Canning Season*	6–9	FIC	Twins Maine Summer Humor	BBYA 04
Jenkins, A. M.	*Out of Order*	8+	FIC	Baseball HS Relationship	BBYA 04
Johnson, Angela	*The First Part Last*	8+	FIC	Teen Fathers Afro-Americans	BBYA 04
Johnson, Kathleen Jeffrie	*Target*	10+	FIC	Rape Anorexia Homosexuality	BBYA 04
Juby, Susan	*Alice, I Think*	8+	FIC	Humor com age	BBYA 04
Koja, Kathe	*Buddha Boy*	7+	FIC	Bullies Abuse	BBYA 04

852

Author	Title	Grade	Genre	Subjects	List Date
Korman, Gordon	*Jake, Reinvented*	9 +	FIC	Peer Pressure, HS, Popularity	BBYA 04
Krisher, Trudy	*Uncommon Faith*	7–10	HF	Women's Rights Slavery Religion	BBYA 04
Levithan, David	*Boy Meets Boy*	9 +	FIC	Gay Lesbian HS Cross-Dressing	BBYA 04
Little, Jason	*Shutterbug Follies*	A/YA	GN MYS	Photo shop Murder	BBYA 04
Lowachee, Karin	*Burndive*	Adult	SF	Assassins	BBYA 04
Mack, Tracy	*Birdland*	7–10	FIC	Skateboarding Video NYC	BBYA 04
Mackler, Carolyn	*The Earth, My Butt, and Other Big Round Things*	7–10	FIC	Weight Control Humor HS	BBYA 04
Martinez, Manuel Luis	*Drift*	Adult	FIC	Chicano Texas Divorce Grandm	BBYA 04
Maynard, Joyce	*The Usual Rules*	Adult	FIC	9/11 Death	BBYA 04
McNamee, Graham	*Acceleration*	8 +	MYS	Toronto Diaries Transit Authority	BBYA 04
Meyer, L. A.	*Bloody Jack: Being an Account of the Curious Adventures of Mary "Jacky" Faber, Ship's Boy*	6–9	HF	Orphans Pirates Sex Role Girl Disguised Boy	BBYA 04
Murphy, Jim	*An American Plague: The True and Terrifying Story of the Yellow Fever Epidemic of 1793*	6 +	NF	Philadelphia Yellow Fever Plague 1793	BBYA 04
Murphy, Jim	*Inside the Alamo*	6 +	NF	Alamo 1836	BBYA 04
Murray, Jaye	*Bottled Up: A Novel*	7 +	FIC	Brothers Family Problems	BBYA 04
Myracle, Lauren	*Kissing Kate*	9 +	FIC	Girlfriends Kiss Lesbians	BBYA 04
Naidoo, Beverly	*Out of Bounds: Seven Stories of Conflict and Hope*	6–10	SS	Apartheid Race Relations	BBYA 04
Napoli, Donna Jo	*Breath*	8 +	FAN	Fairy Tales; Pied Piper	BBYA 04
November, Sharyn, ed.	*Firebirds: An Anthology of Original Fantasy and Science Fiction*	9 +	SS FAN	Fairytale Retellings	BBYA 04
Osa, Nancy	*Cuba 15*	6–10	FIC	Hispanic Amer	BBYA 04
Parker, Jeff	*The Interman*	YA	GN	Assassin; Adven	BBYA 04
Pattou, Edith	*East*	6 +	FAN	Fairytale Retelling	BBYA 04
Paulsen, Gary	*How Angel Peterson Got His Name and Other Outrageous Tales about Extreme Sports*	6–9	BIO	skis, bicycles, target kites, and skateboards	BBYA 04
Peck, Richard	*The River between Us*	7 +	HF	Civil War; Race Relations	BBYA 04
Pierce, Tamora	*Trickster's Choice*	7 +	FAN	Tortall Pirates Slaves Spies	BBYA 04
Pratchett, Terry	*The Wee Free Men: A Story of Discworld*	6–10	FAN	Discworld Fairies Witches	BBYA 04
Rapp, Adam	*33 Snowfish*	9 +	FIC	Runaways	BBYA 04
Rees, Celia	*Pirates!: The True and Remarkable Adventures of Min-*	6–9	HF	Female disguised as a male; pirates; 1722	BBYA 04

Author	Title	Grade	Genre	Subjects	List Date
	erva Sharpe and Nancy King-ton, Female Pirates				
Reeve, Philip	*Mortal Engines: A Novel*	7–10	SF	Mobile Cities Battles London	BBYA 04
Roach, Mary	*STIFF: The Curious Lives of Human Cadavers*	A/YA	NF	Corpses Forensic Science	BBYA 04
Rowling, J. K.	*Harry Potter and the Order of the Phoenix*	4+	FAN	Magic Boarding Schools Wizards	BBYA 04
Rylant, Cynthia	*God Went to Beauty School*	6+	POE	Humor Religion	BBYA 04
Satrapi, Marjane	*Persepolis: Story of a Child-hood*	Adult	GN	Iran Tehran war	BBYA 04
Sis, Peter	*The Tree of Life: A Book De-picting the Life of Charles Dar-win Naturalist, Geologist and Thinker*	4+	BIO	Naturalists 19th Century Beagle Diary Entries	BBYA 04
Slade, Arthur	*Dust*	6–9	FAN	Supernatural Drought	BBYA 04
Spinelli, Jerry	*Milkweed*	B 4–9	HF	Warsaw; Poland; Ghetto	BBYA 04
Stroud, Jonathan	*The Amulet of Samarkand: Bartimaeus Trilogy, Book One*	6+	FAN	Djin Magicians Apprentice London Murder	BBYA 04
Thompson, Craig	*Blankets: An Illustrated Novel*	A/YA	GN	Sibling Rivalry Wisconsin Love	BBYA 04
Trueman, Terry	*Inside Out*	9+	FIC	Schizophrenia Suicide, Hostage	BBYA 04
Vance, Susana	*Deep*	7–10	FIC	Modern Pirates	BBYA 04
Vande Velde, Vivian	*Heir Apparent*	6–9	SF	Virtual Reality; Games; Humor	BBYA 04
Wittlinger, Ellen	*Zigzag*	8+	FIC	Vacations; car travel; aunts	BBYA 04
Woodson, Jacqueline	*Locomotion*	4–6	POE	Fire Grief Loss of Parents	BBYA 04
Wrede, Patricia C. and Caroline Stevermer	*Sorcery and Cecelia, or, The Enchanted Chocolate Pot: being the Correspondence of Two Young Ladies of Quality Regarding Various Magical Scandals in London and the Country*	Adult	FAN	Cousins London Wizards Magic Regency Romance	BBYA 04
Yolen, Jane	*Sword Of The Rightful King: A Novel Of King Arthur*	6–9	FAN	Arthurian Knights	BBYA 04
Zahn, Timothy	*Dragon and Thief: A Dragon-back Adventure*	Adult	SF	Orphans Thieves Aliens	BBYA 04

BEST OF THE BEST YOUNG ADULTS BOOKS—BY PRECONFERENCE

Author	Title	Date	Grade	Genre	Still Alive	Best of Best	Nothin' But the Best	Here We Go	Awards
Adams, Richard	*Watership Down*	2001	9 +	FAN	*	*			
Adamson, Joy	*Born Free*	2000	8 +	NF	*				
Angelou, Maya	*Gather Together in My Name*	1997	Adult	Autobio	*				
Angelou, Maya	*I Know Why the Caged Bird Sings*	2002	Adult	Autobio	*	*	*	*	CSK Honor 1971
Anonymous	*Go Ask Alice*	1998	7 +	FIC	*	*		*	
Asimov, Isaac	*Fantastic Voyage*		7 +	SF	*				
Baldwin, James	*If Beale Street Could Talk*	2000	Adult	FIC	*	*		*	
Borland, Hal	*When the Legend Dies*				*				
Boston Women's Health Book Collective	*Our Bodies, Ourselves: A Book by and for Women*			NF	*	*		*	
Braithwaite, E. R.	*To Sir, with Love*			FIC	*				
Brautigan, Richard	*Trout Fishing in America*	1989	Adult	NF	*				
Brown, Claude	*Manchild in the Promised Land*	1999	8 +	Autobio	*				
Burnford, Sheila	*Incredible Journey*	1996		FIC	*				
Carson, Rachel	*Silent Spring*			NF	*				
Castaneda, Carlos	*Journey to Ixtlan: The Lessons of Don Juan*			NF	*				
Childress, Alice	*Hero Ain't Nothin but a Sandwich*			FIC	*	*	*		
Clarke, Arthur C.	*2001: A Space Odyssey*			SF	*				
Cleaver, Eldridge	*Soul on Ice*			NF	*				
Cormier, Robert	*Chocolate War: A Novel*			FIC	*	*	*		
Craven, Margaret	*I Heard the Owl Call My Name*			FIC	*				
Crichton, Michael	*Andromeda Strain*			SF	*				
Dunning, Stephen, ed.	*Reflections on a Gift of Watermelon Pickle*	1966	6 +	POE	*				
Elfman, Blossom	*Girls of Huntington House*			FIC	*	*			
Fast, Howard	*April Morning*			HF	*				
Frazier, Walt, and Ira Berkow	*Rockin' Steady: A Guide to Basketball and Cool*			NF	*				
Friedman, Myra	*Buried Alive: The Biography of Janis Joplin*			BIO	*				
Gaines, Ernest J.	*The Autobiography of Miss Jane Pittman*			HF	*			*	

Author	Title	Date	Grade	Genre	Still Alive	Best of Best	Nothin' But the Best	Here We Go	Awards
Gaines, William and Albert Feldstein, eds.	Ridiculously Expensive MAD			NF	*				
Graham, Robin Lee and Derek L. T. Gill	Dove			NF	*				
Green, Hannah	I Never Promised You a Rose Garden			FIC	*				
Griffin, John	Black Like Me			NF	*				
Guy, Rosa	The Friends			FIC	*	*	*	*	
Hall, Lynn	Sticks and Stones			FIC	*				
Harris, Marilyn	Hatter Fox			FIC	*	*			
Head, Ann	Mr. and Mrs. Bo Jo Jones			FIC	*		*		
Heinlein, Robert	Stranger in a Strange Land			SF	*				
Heller, Joseph	Catch-22			FIC	*				
Herbert, Frank	Dune			SF	*				
Herriot, James	All Creatures Great and Small			NF	*				
Herzog, Arthur	Swarm			HOR	*				
Hinton, S. E.	The Outsiders			FIC	*		*	*	MAE
Hinton, S. E.	That Was Then, This Is Now			FIC	*		*		MAE
Jackson, Shirley	We Have Always Lived in the Castle				*				
Kellogg, Marjorie	Tell Me That You Love Me, Junie Moon			FIC	*				
Kesey, Ken	One Flew Over the Cuckoo's Nest			FIC	*				
Keyes, Daniel	Flowers for Algernon			SF	*		*		
Knowles, John	Separate Peace			FIC	*				
Krentz, Harold	To Race the Wind: An Autobiography			Autobio	*				
Lee, Harper	To Kill a Mockingbird			HF	*				
Maas, Peter	Serpico			NF	*				
Meriwether, Louise	Daddy Was a Numbers Runner			HF	*			*	
Moody, Anne	Coming of Age in Mississippi: An Autobiography			Autobio	*				
Neufeld, John	Lisa Bright and Dark			FIC	*				
Peck, Robert Newton	Day No Pigs Would Die			HF	*				
Plath, Sylvia	The Bell Jar			Autobio	*	*	*	*	

Author	Title	Date	Grade	Genre	Still Alive	Best of Best	Nothin' But the Best	Here We Go	Awards
Potok, Chaim	*The Chosen*			FIC	*		*		
Read, Piers Paul	*Alive: The Story of the Andes Survivors*			NF	*				
Robertson, Dougal	*Survive the Savage Sea*			NF	*	*			
Samuels, Gertrude	*Run, Shelley, Run!*			FIC	*	*			
Schultz, Charles	*Peanuts Treasury*			GN	*				
Scoppettone, Sandra	*Trying Hard to Hear You*			FIC	*	*		*	
Sleator, William	*House of Stairs*			SF	*	*	*		
Solzhenitsyn, Alexander	*One Day in the Life of Ivan Denisovich*				*				
Swarthout, Glendon	*Bless the Beasts and Children*			FIC	*	*	*	*	
Thompson, Jean	*House of Tomorrow*			NF	*				
Vonnegut, Kurt, Jr.	*Slaughterhouse Five: or, The Children's Crusade*				*				
Westheimer, David	*My Sweet Charlie*				*				
Westheimer, David	*Von Ryan's Express*			HF	*				
White, Robb	*Deathwatch*			MYS	*	*	*	*	
Wigginton, Eliot	*Foxfire Book*				*				
X Malcolm and Alex Haley	*Autobiography of Malcolm X*			Autobio	*				
Zindel, Paul	*The Pigman*			FIC	*	*		*	MAE
Alexander, Lloyd	*Westmark*			FAN		*			
Ali, Muhammad and Richard Durham	*Greatest: My Own Story*			Autobio		*			
Arrick, Fran	*Tunnel Vision*			FIC		*			
Auel, Jean	*Clan of the Cave Bear*			HF		*			
Bell, Ruth	*Changing Bodies, Changing Lives: A Book for Teens on Sex and Relationships*			NF		*	*		
Bethancourt, T. Ernesto	*Tune in Yesterday*					*			
Bleier, Rocky and Terry O'Neill	*Fighting Back*			NF		*			
Blume, Judy	*Forever*			FIC		*	*	*	MAE
Brancato, Robin F.	*Winning*			FIC		*	*		
Bridgers, Sue Ellen	*Notes for Another Life*			FIC		*			
Brown, Dee	*Bury My Heart at Wounded Knee: An Indian History of the American West*			NF		*			

Author	Title	Date	Grade	Genre	Still Alive	Best of Best	Nothin' But the Best	Here We Go	Awards
Christopher, John	*Empty World*			FAN		*			
Conroy, Pat	*Great Santini*					*			
Cormier, Robert	*After the First Death*			FIC		*	*		
Cormier, Robert	*I Am the Cheese*			FIC		*			
Due, Linnea A.	*High and Outside*			FIC		*			
Duncan, Lois	*Killing Mr. Griffin*			MYS		*	*	*	
Duncan, Lois	*Stranger with My Face*			MYS		*			
Elder, Lauren and Shirley Streshinsky	*And I Alone Survived*			NF		*			
Garden, Nancy	*Annie on My Mind*			FIC		*	*	*	MAE
Glenn, Mel	*Class Dismissed! High School Poems*			POE		*			
Greenberg, Joanne	*In This Sign*			FIC		*	*		
Greene, Bette	*Summer of My German Soldier*			FIC		*			
Guest, Judith	*Ordinary People*			FIC		*	*	*	
Guy, Rosa	*Edith Jackson*			FIC		*			
Hamilton, Virginia	*Sweet Whispers, Brother Rush*			FIC		*			
Hayden, Torey L.	*One Child*			NF		*			
Hinton, S. E.	*Tex*			FIC		*	*		MAE
Hogan, William	*Quartzsite Trip*			FIC		*	*		
Holland, Isabelle	*Man without a Face*			FIC		*	*		
Holman, Felice	*Slake's Limbo*			FIC		*	*	*	
Johnston, Norma	*Keeping Days*					*			
Jordan, June	*His Own Where*			FIC		*			
Kerr, M. E.	*Dinky Hocker Shoots Smack*			FIC		*			
King, Stephen	*Carrie*			HOR		*		*	
Le Guin, Ursula	*Farthest Shore*			FAN		*			MAE
Le Guin, Ursula	*Tombs of Atuan*			FAN		*			MAE
Le Guin, Ursula K.	*Very Far Away from Anywhere Else*			FIC		*			MAE
Leitner, Isabella	*Fragments of Isabella: A Memoir of Auschwitz*			HF		*			
Levenkron, Steven	*Best Little Girl in the World*			FIC		*			
Lipsyte, Robert	*One Fat Summer*			FIC		*	*		
MacCracken, Mary	*Circle of Children*			NF		*			
MacDougall, Ruth	*Cheerleader*					*			
Mazer, Harry	*Last Mission*			HF		*	*		
Mazer, Norma Fox	*Up in Seth's Room*			FIC		*			
McCaffrey, Anne	*Dragonsong*			SF		*	*		MAE

Author	Title	Date	Grade	Genre	Still Alive	Best of Best	Nothin' But the Best	Here We Go	Awards
McCoy, Kathy and Charles Wibbelsman	The New Teenage Body Book			NF		*		*	
McIntyre, Vonda N.	Dreamsnake			SF		*	*		
McKinley, Robin	Beauty: A Retelling of the Story of Beauty and the Beast			FAN		*	*	*	
McKinley, Robin	Blue Sword			FAN		*			
Meltzer, Milton	Never to Forget: The Jews of the Holocaust			NF		*			
Niven, Larry	Ringworld			SF		*			
O'Brien, Robert C.	Z for Zachariah			SF		*		*	
Oneal, Zibby	Formal Feeling			FIC		*			
Oneal, Zibby	Language of Goldfish			FIC		*			
Peck, Richard	Are You in the House Alone?			FIC		*	*	*	MAE
Peck, Richard	Father Figure: A Novel			FIC		*			MAE
Peck, Richard	Ghosts I Have Been			FIC		*	*		MAE
Pierce, Meredith Ann	The Darkangel			FAN		*		*	
Platt, Kin	Headman			FIC		*			
Powers, John R.	Last Catholic in America: A Fictionalized Memoir					*			
Santoli, Al	Everything We Had: An Oral History of the Vietnam War As Told by Thirty-three American Soldiers Who Fought It			NF		*			
Schulke, Flip	Martin Luther King, Jr.: A Documentary . . . Montgomery to Memphis			NF		*			
Stewart, Mary	Crystal Cave			FAN		*			
Taylor, Mildred D.	Roll of Thunder, Hear My Cry			HF		*			
Wersba, Barbara	Run Softly, Go Fast			FIC		*	*	*	
Wilkinson, Brenda	Ludell and Willie			FIC		*			
Zindel, Paul	Effects of Gamma Rays on Man-in-the-Moon-Marigolds			PLAY		*	*		MAE
	Rolling Stone Illustrated History of Rock and Roll, 1950–1980			NF			*		

Author	Title	Date	Grade	Genre	Still Alive	Best of Best	Nothin' But the Best	Here We Go	Awards
Adams, Douglas	*The Hitchhiker's Guide to the Galaxy*			SF			*	*	
Bridgers, Sue Ellen	*All Together Now*			FIC	*				
Briggs, Raymond	*When the Wind Blows*			FIC			*		
Callahan, Steven	*Adrift: Seventy-Six Days Lost at Sea*			NF			*		
Card, Orson Scott	*Ender's Game*			SF			*	*	
Childress, Alice	*Rainbow Jordan*			FIC			*	*	
Clark, Mary Higgins	*Where Are the Children?*			MYS			*		
Crutcher, Chris	*Running Loose*			FIC			*		
Crutcher, Chris	*Stotan!*			FIC			*	*	
Edelman, Bernard	*Dear America: Letters Home from Vietnam*			NF			*		
Fox, Paula	*One-Eyed Cat*			FIC			*	*	
Gallo, Donald R., ed.	*Sixteen: Short Stories by Outstanding Writers for Young Adults*			SS			*	*	
Garfield, Brian	*Paladin*			HF			*		
Guy, Rosa	*Disappearance*			MYS			*		
Irwin, Hadley	*Abby, My Love*			FIC			*		
Kazimiroff, Theodore L.	*Last Algonquin*			NF			*		
Kerr, M. E.	*Gentlehands*			HF			*	*	
Kerr, M. E.	*Night Kites*			FIC			*		
King, Stephen	*Night Shift*			HOR			*		
Koehn, Ilse	*Mischling Second Degree: My Childhood in Nazi Germany*			NF			*		
MacKinnon, Bernie	*Meantime*			FIC			*		
Mason, Bobbie Ann	*In Country*			FIC			*		
Myers, Walter Dean	*Hoops*			FIC			*		
Naylor, Phyllis Reynolds	*Keeper*			FIC			*		
Newton, Suzanne	*I Will Call It Georgie's Blues*			FIC			*		
Richards, Arlene Kramer and Irene Willis	*Under Eighteen and Pregnant: What to Do If You or Someone You Know Is*			NF			*		

Author	Title	Date	Grade	Genre	Still Alive	Best of Best	Nothin' But the Best	Here We Go	Awards
Robeson, Susan	Whole World in His Hands: A Pictorial Biography of Paul Robeson			BIO			*		
Segal, Erich	Love Story			FIC			*		
Silverberg, Robert	Lord Valentine's Castle			SF			*		
Sleator, William	Interstellar Pig			SF			*	*	
Strasser, Todd	Friends till the End			FIC			*		
Van Devanter, Lynda and Christopher Morgan	Home Before Morning: The Story of an Army Nurse in Vietnam			NF			*		
Vinge, Joan D.	Psion			SF			*		
Voigt, Cynthia	Homecoming			FIC			*		
Voigt, Cynthia	Izzy, Willy-Nilly			FIC			*	*	
Voigt, Cynthia	Runner			FIC			*		
Voigt, Cynthia	Solitary Blue			FIC			*		
Walker, Alice	In Search of Our Mothers' Gardens: Womanist Prose			NF			*		
Webb, Sheyann and Rachel West Nelson	Selma, Lord, Selma: Girlhood Memories of the Civil-Rights Days			Autobio			*		
Anthony, Piers	On a Pale Horse			FAN				*	
Avi	Nothing But the Truth			FIC				*	
Barlow, Wayne Douglas and Ian Summers	Barlow's Guide to Extraterrestrials			SF				*	
Block, Francesca Lia	Weetzie Bat			FIC				*	MAE
Bridgers, Sue Ellen	Permanent Connections			FIC				*	
Brooks, Bruce	The Moves Make the Man			FIC				*	
Cannon, A. E.	Amazing Gracie			FIC				*	
Carter, Alden	Up Country			FIC				*	
Cole, Brock	The Goats			FIC				*	
Corman, Avery	Prized Possessions			FIC				*	
Cormier, Robert	We All Fall Down			FIC				*	
Crew, Linda	Children of the River			FIC				*	
Crutcher, Chris	Athletic Shorts: Six Short Stories			SS				*	
Dahl, Roald	Boy: Tales of Childhood			Autobio				*	
Davis, Jenny	Sex Education			FIC				*	
Davis, Terry	Vision Quest			FIC				*	
Deuker, Carl	On the Devil's Court			FIC				*	

Author	Title	Date	Grade	Genre	Still Alive	Best of Best	Nothin' But the Best	Here We Go	Awards
Dickinson, Peter	*Eva*			SF				*	
Gies, Miep and Alison Leslie Gold	*Anne Frank Remembered: The Story of Miep Gies, Who Helped to Hide the Frank Family*			NF				*	
Goldman, Peter and Tony Fuller	*Charlie Company: What Vietnam Did to Us*			NF				*	
Grant, Cynthia D.	*Phoenix Rising: or, How to Survive Your Life*			FIC				*	
Greenberg, Joanne	*Of Such Small Differences*			FIC				*	
Hayden, Torey L.	*Ghost Girl: The True Story of a Child Who Refused to Talk*			NF				*	
Hentoff, Nat	*American Heroes: In and Out of School*			NF				*	
Hobbs, Will	*Downriver*			FIC				*	
Hoover, H. M.	*Another Heaven, Another Earth*			SF				*	
Houston, James	*Ghost Fox*			HF				*	
Jaques, Brian	*Redwall*			FAN				*	
Jones, Diana Wynne	*Howl's Moving Castle*			FAN				*	
Klass, David	*Wrestling with Honor*			FIC				*	
Klause, Annette Curtis	*The Silver Kiss*			FAN				*	
Knudson, R. R. and May Swenson, Eds.	*American Sports Poems*			POE				*	
Koertge, Ron	*The Arizona Kid*			FIC				*	
Kotlowitz, Alex	*There Are No Children Here: The Story of Two Boys Growing Up in the Other America*			NF				*	
Lee, Gus	*China Boy*			BIO				*	
Levoy, Myron	*Alan and Naomi*			FIC				*	
Lipsyte, Robert	*The Contender*			FIC				*	
Lopes, Sal, ed.	*Wall: Images and Offerings from the Vietnam Veterans Memorial*			NF				*	
Madaras, Lynda and Area	*What's Happening to My Body? Book for Boys: A Growing Up Guide for Parents and Sons*			NF				*	

Author	Title	Date	Grade	Genre	Still Alive	Best of Best	Nothin' But the Best	Here We Go	Awards
Madaras, Lynda and Area	*What's Happening to My Body? Book for Girls: A Growing Up Guide for Parents and Daughters*			NF				*	
Mahy, Margaret	*The Changeover: A supernatural Romance*			FAN				*	
Mazer, Harry and Norma Fox	*Solid Gold Kid*			FIC				*	
Mazer, Norma Fox	*Silver*			FIC				*	
McCaffrey, Anne	*Dragonsinger*			SF				*	
Miller, Frances A.	*The Truth Trap*			FIC				*	
Murphy, Barbara Beasley and Judie Wolkoff	*Ace Hits the Big Time*			FIC				*	
Myers, Walter Dean	*Scorpions*			FIC				*	
Palmer, Laura	*Shrapnel in the Heart: Letters and Remembrances from the Vietnam Memorial*			NF				*	
Paterson, Katherine	*Jacob Have I Loved*			FIC				*	
Paulsen, Gary	*Hatchet*			FIC				*	
Pfeffer, Susan Beth	*The Year without Michael*			FIC				*	
Pullman, Philip	*The Ruby in the Smoke*			MYS				*	
Rinaldi, Ann	*Wolf by the Ears*			HF				*	
Rogasky, Barbara	*Smoke and Ashes: The Story of the Holocaust*			NF				*	
Salzman, Mark	*Iron and Silk*			FIC				*	
Shilts, Randy	*And the Band Played On: Politics, People, and the AIDS Epidemic*			NF				*	
Spiegelman, Art	*Maus: A Survivor's Tale*			GN				*	
Stoll, Cliff	*The Cuckoo's Egg: Tracking a Spy through the Maze of Computer Espionage*			NF				*	
Strieber, Whitley	*Wolf of Shadows*			SF				*	
Sullivan, Charles, ed.	*Children of Promise: African-American Literature and Art for Young People*			NF				*	
Tan, Amy	*The Joy Luck Club*			FIC				*	
Walker, Alice	*The Color Purple*			FIC				*	

Author	Title	Date	Grade	Genre	Still Alive	Best of Best	Nothin' But the Best	Here We Go	Awards
Westall, Robert	*Blitzcat*			HF				*	
Wolff, Virginia Euwer	*Probably Still Nick Swansen*			FIC				*	
Wrede, Patricia C.	*Dealing with Dragons*			FAN				*	
Wyss, Thelma Hatch	*Here at the Scenic-Vu Motel*			FIC				*	
Yolen, Jane and Martin H. Greenberg, eds.	*Vampires: A Collection of Original Stories*			SS				*	

Autobio	Autobiography
BIO	Biography
FAN	Fantasy
FIC	Fiction
GN	Graphic Novel
HF	Historical Fiction
HOR	Horror
NF	Non-Fiction
POE	Poetry
SF	Science Fiction
SS	Short Stories

YALSA BEST OF THE BEST LISTS:

STILL ALIVE (Selections from 1960 to 1974)

THE BEST OF THE BEST BOOKS (Selections from 1970 to 1983)

NOTHIN' BUT THE BEST (Selections from 1966 to 1986)

HERE WE GO AGAIN . . . 25 YEARS OF BEST BOOKS (Selections from 1967 to 1992)

Acknowledgments
& Contributors List of YA Encyclopedia

The three editors of this work want to thank all of the contributors who gave generously of their time, wealth of knowledge, and talent. Although each entry is signed, the contributors are also listed below. Our colleagues, students, family, and friends around the world have given generously of their time and talent to help us produce this first encyclopedia of young adult literature. They suggested names to be included, they wrote and edited entries, they proofread and helped us in every way.

Rachel Witmer was willing to work as many hours as needed to finish the task, even after she accepted a full-time position with a highly regarded publishing house. Her e-mail address includes "tiger lily," and when we were over our heads to meet deadlines we would say, "It is time for tiger lily." We will be eternally grateful to tiger lily. The publishing world is richer because she is devoting her life to it.

Sarah Katz and her brother Daniel Katz began working with us when the project germinated. They served successfully until college programs demanded that they return to campus.

Joie Gavigan Hinden, English literature teacher at Manhasset High School, used her literature curriculum to help us shape the list of authors whom readers ought to know.

Katelyn Wooten helped her mother identify important authors and books teens know. She wrote entries and urged her classmate Kyle Fox to share his poem with us.

Special thanks also go to Trisha Carley, a fifteen year old reader; Ernesta Gallo and Zoya Yupova who kept Bee looking presentable; Jack Martin, New York Public Library, Young Adult Librarian; Gabriella Page-Fort who kept track of all the segments; Suzanne Ponzini, Young Adult Librarian, Port Washington Public Library; Eduardo Zeiger for his computer help.

About the Contributors

Ira Aaron, Professor Emeritus, University of Georgia, Past President, International Reading Association • Richard Abrahamson, professor, University of Texas • Kate Adams, University of British Columbia, Canada • Trevor Agnew, Papanui, Christchurch, New Zealand • Denise E. Agosto, College of Information and Technology, Drexel University, Philadelphia, PA • Laurie M. Allen, Library Student, Emporia State University, Winfield, KS • Kirsten Andersen, Richmond Public Library, Richmond, BC V6Y IR9 Canada • Britt Anderson, Librarian and former middle-school teacher, Oakland, CA • Elizabeth Anderson, Doctoral student, University of Tennessee, Knoxville, TN • Mary Arnold, Librarian, Cuyahoga, Cleveland, OH • John C. Baken, Student of Library Science, University of Wisconsin, Madison, WI • Amy Ballmer, New York Public Library, New York, NY • Julie Bartel, Teen Librarian, Salt Lake City Public Library, Salt Lake City, UT • Terry Beck, Librarian, Bothell, WA • Claudia L. Bennett, MLS Student, University of Pennsylvania, Brownsville, PA • Laurie Berg, Student of Library Science, Roseville, MN • Joann Boboris, Student, New York University • Rita Bode, Trent University, Petersborough, Ontario • Christine E. S. Borne, Librarian, Cleveland Heights, OH • Erin Boyd, elementary-school librarian, Denton, TX • Dexter Braithwaite, graduate student, Yale University • Patricia Bricker, assistant professor, Western Carolina University • Nancy A. Buggé, graduate, Queens College, NY • Kristine Buller, MLTS candidate, San Jose State University, Cypress, CA • Michelle A. Carryl, student, New York University • Michael Cart, Former president of Young Adult Library Services Association, author, professor, UCLA • Betty Carter, retired, Texas Woman's University, Denton, TX • Sebsastien Chapleau, research student, Cardiff University, Cardiff, Wales, UK • Laura Charron, MLS • Barbara Chatton, Professor, University of Wyoming • Cathy Chauvette • Shu-Hsien L. Chen, assistant professor, GSLIS, Queens College, NY • Janet Ciarrocca, student, school-library media specialist • Jennifer Claiborne, high-school English teacher, Knoxville, TN • Amanda Cockrell • S. D. Collins, assistant professor, Tennessee Technological University • Sarah Cornish, young adult librarian, Warren Township, NJ • Hilary Crew, graduate coordinator EMS program, Keen University, NJ • Shannon Cuff, young adult librarian, Boston Public Library • Bernice E. Cullinan, professor emeritus, New York University, poetry editor, Wordsong • Cathy Delneo, adult-services librarian, Bridgewater, NJ • Cathy Denman, Titusville, FL • Karen Dennison, library-science student, San Jose State University • Kimberly DeStefano, student, Queens College, NY • Geri Diorio, MLS student, Southern Connecticut State University, Stratford, CT • Ken Donelson, professor • Sarah Spink Downing, assistant curator, Outer Banks History Center, Mateo, NC • Janet Duschack, Wisconsin Library Services, Madison, WI • Will Eisner, artist author of graphic novels, comics (died 2005) • Barbara Elleman, Founder, Book Links, Distinguished Scholar, Marquette University • Rhoda El-Said, Anderson Elementary School, Minneapolis, Minnesota • Kevin R. Ferst, teen librarian, Jacksonville, FL • Susan Fichteiberg, children's librarian and post president of Children's Services Section NJLA • Jana Fine, Librarian, Youth Services Manager, Clearwater Florida Public Library, former president of YALSA • Danny Fingeroth, writer, editor • Deborah Fink, MLS student, Syracuse University • Kathie Fitch, Fairfax, VA • Kristel Fleuren, MLS student, University of British Columbia • J. Flood, professor, San Diego State University • Michelle Crowell Fossum, librarian, Pittsburgh, PA • Kyle Fox, high school student, Knoxville, TN • James Gahagan, student and reference librarian, University of South Carolina • Carra Gamberdella, editor of young adult books, Scholastic, Inc. • Christine Gerloff, library tech–reference desk, Walnut, CA • Gretchen H. Gerzina, author of a scholarly work on F. H. Burnett • James Cross Giblin, author, editor • Colleen P. Gilrane, associate professor, literacy education, University of Tennessee • Kenneth Seeman Giniger, publisher of adult nonfiction • Catherine Given, student, Queens College, NY • Kerry Gleason, graduate student, Madison, WI • Cathy Goodwin, library technical assistant, Central Carolina University • Lanette Granger, SJSU SLIS student, CA • Sansanee S. Graves, MLS student, Pratt Institute, NY • Heidi Hauser Green, reviewer, Children's Literature Comprehensive Database • Edward Grinewich, student, Buffalo State College, NY • Rose F. Hagar, associate media specialist, Rowan University graduate student • Theresa Hahn • Kelly Milner Halls, freelance writer and reviewer, Spokane, WA • Judah Hamer, Ph.D. student, Rutgers University, NJ • Barbara J. Hampton, MLS, Southern Connecticut State University • Liz Hane, MLIS student, University of South Carolina • Terry Haugen, library specialist in an elementary school and on-call clerk Santa Cruz Public Library • Molly Ker Hawn, associate director, Children's Book Council • Sara Heaney • Joan Henry, director, Dunellen Public Library, NJ • Diana Tixier Herald, director, Center for Adolescent Reading, and an author–editor • Tina Hertel, Information Literary Specialist, Mary Wood University Library, Scranton, PA • Michele Hilton, faculty of science, Dalhousie University, Dartmouth, Canada • Ted Hipple, professor of English, University of Tennessee, Knoxville (died 2004) • Ruth Hitchcock, graduate student, University of Iowa, Ames • Nancy Spence Horton, assistant professor of reading, University of Texas, Tyler • Sara Catherine Howard, instructor, dept. of library science, Sam Houston State University, TX • Jennifer Hubert, Coordinator, Middle School Librarian, Little Red School House, Sunnyside, NY • Clara Hudson, library director, Mill Memorial Library, Nanticoke, PA • Peter Hunt, Professor, University of Wales, Cardiff • Andrew W. Hunter, Collection Development Librarian/Youth Materials Selector, Dallas Public Library, TX • Joann Janosko, Acquisitions/Serials Librarian, Indiana University of Pennsylvania, Indiana, PA • Susan Jones, MLIS graduate student, San Jose State University School of Library and Information Science, CA • Mia Kammerling, adjunct professor, Southern Connecticut State University • Katharine Kan, freelance book selector, Brodart • David Katz, student, Minneapolis • Sarah Katz, student, Allston, MA • Tricia Keane, student, Keen College, NJ • Carolyn Kim, graduate student, MA program for children's literature, University of British Columbia, Canada • Molly Kinney, assistant director, Peach Public Libraries, Fort Valley, GA • Sandra Kitain, student, Clarion University, Yardley, PA • Ilona N. Koti, MLS, Syracuse University • Karen Krizman, Littleton, CO • Christina Kruger, graduate student, University of Wisconsin • Bonnie L. Kunzel, former president of YALSA, Youth Services Consultant, New Jersey State Library • Diane Lapp, professor, San Diego State University • Rebecca Lasswell, MLIS student, San Jose State University • Dan Lawrence, San Jose State University

School of Library Information Science • Alice R. Leone, student, Queens College, NY • Teri S. Lesesne, editor *Book Talk, Voices from Middle,* professor, Dept. of Library Science, Sam Houston University • Andrea Lipinski, student/senior young adult librarian, Kingsbridge Regional Library, NY • Nancy Livingston, Professor, Brigham Young University • Sarah Lloyd, doctoral student, University of Tennessee, Knoxville • Laurene Madsen, graduate student (SJSU), Kodiak High School librarian, AK • Sara M. Marcus, student of library science, Queens College, NY • Mary Mariano, teacher, New York public schools • William Mariano, teacher, New York public schools • Susan Marinoff, teacher, New York Public Schools, graduate of New York University • Janelle Mathis, assistant professor of reading/children's literature, department of teacher education and administration, University of North Texas • Holly E. May, student, USC • Dawna McClendon, children's librarian, Monmouth County Library–Eastern Branch, NJ • Annette MacIntyre, SLIS student, Dalhousie University School, Dalhousie, Hfx., Canada • Rebecca Osa Mendell, graduate student, MLS Program, San Jose State University, CA • Mary Menzel, second-year MLIS student, UCLA • Kris Michell • Tammy Mielke, Ph.D. research student, University College, Worcester, UK • Suzy Moorhead, graduate student, San Jose State University • Hector L. Morey, library technician and ILS student, College Park, MD • Susan E. Morton, student MLIS Program, Dalhousie University, Hfx., Canada • Joy Morse, graduate student, University of North Carolina, Charlotte • Ginger Mullen, UBC, Vancouver, Canada • Myron Mykyta, former SJSU MLIS student • Bill Nagelkerke, children's and young adult services coordinator, Christchurch City Libraries, New Zealand • Kate Nagy, LMT, San Diego, CA • Sarah Nelsen, graduate SJSU MLIS program • Anastasia Niehof, library of science student, University of Iowa, Ames • Alleen Pace Nilsen, coauthor, *Literature for Today's Young Adults* • Jenna Obee, student, School of Library Information Management, Emporia (Kansas) State University • Deborah O'Keefe, author of *Good Girl Messages* and *Readers in Wonderland* • Mimi O'Malley, library education student, Clarion University, PA • Valerie Palazolo, elementary-school librarian, Bronx, NY • Roxanna Pandya, assistant managing librarian, Lynwood Library Sno-Isle Regional Libraries, WA • Kimberley L. Paone, Adult/Young Adult Services, Elizabeth Public Library, NJ • Patricia Payne, assistant to chairperson, UCLA Department of Information Studies, Los Angeles, CA • Joan Pearlman, teacher, Pingry School, New Jersey • Megan Pearlman, theater, editor, Scholastic Books, Inc. • Kristin Pehnke, student, Queens College, NY • Jennifer Burek Pierce, assistant professor, Indiana University • Jodi Pilgrim, contributor to *The Continuum Encyclopedia of Children's Literature,* Lindale, TX • Elizabeth Poe, editor, *Journal of Children's Literature, Signal Journal,* formerly West Virginia University; board member this volume • Karen Praeger, student, San Jose State SLIS program • Trevor Pross, graduate student and teacher, Hfx., Canada • Gabriella L. Radujko, SCILS student, Rutgers University, NJ • Cara Randall, library assistant, Sacramento Public Library • Sharon Rawlins, adult/young adult librarian, Piscataway, NJ • Sarah Loyd Raymer, educator, New York City • Connie Repplinger, senior youth librarian, Salem, OR • Allison Richardson Ogden, MLIS student, University of British Columbia, Canada • Susan Riley, director, Mount Kisco Public Library, Mount Kisco, NY • Hazel Rochman, YA editor Booklist, author *Against Borders,* coeditor *Bearing Witness: Stories of the Holocaust* • Aviva Roseman, MA student children's literature, UBC, Vancouver, Canada • Jennifer Roy, MA library and information science, Sunnyvale, CA • Jeanne Marie Ryan, director, Louis Bay Second Library and Community Center, NJ • Heidi L. Sacchitella, MLS graduate student, Southern Connecticut University • Heidi Sanchez, student, Queens College, NY • Karen Sands-O'Connor, associate professor of English, Buffalo State College, NY • Stephanie Schott, student, Rutgers/SCLIS, NJ • Ann Seefeldt, grant manager, Minnesota Dept. of Health • Emily Seitz, student, Rutgers/SCLIS, New Brunswick, NJ • Ken Setterington, Ph.D. student, University of Toronto • Julie Shen, publication assistant, Hannold/Mudd Library, Claremont Colleges, CA • Joel Shoemaker, Library Media Specialist, Iowa City, past president, YALSA • Heather Shumaker, high-school library science specialist, Newport, PA • Karlan Sick, YA Coordinator, New York Public Library, past chairperson ALEX Committee • Judy L. Silva, electronic access/serials librarian, Bailey Library, Slippery Rock University, PA • Caryn Sipos, Fort Vancouver Regional Library, La Center, WA • DeDe Small, assistant professor, Drake University, Des Moines, IA • Karen Patricia Smith, professor, Queens College Graduate School of Library and Information Studies, NY • Terri Snethen, library-media specialist, Blue Valley North High School, Overland Park, KS • Margaret Steffler • Jennifer Still, student–high-school librarian, George Washington High School, Astoria, NY • Dorothy Strickland, professor,

Rutgers University, past president, International Reading Association • Edward T. Sullivan, librarian, Knox County, TN, past board member YALSA • Lowell Swortzell, professor of music and theater, New York University (died 2005) • Nancy Swortzell, professor of music and theater, New York University • Laureen Tedesco, assistant professor English, East Carolina University, Greenville, SC • Mary McMillan Terry, Spanish teacher, Knoxville, TN • Carol Tilley, lecturer–coordinator of distance education, IN • Diane Tuccillo, librarian–young adult coordinator, City of Mesa Library, AZ • Ellie Tweedy, graduate student, LIS program, Pratt Institute, NY • Kathy Vanstrom • Rebecca B. Vargha, librarian School of Information and Library Science, University of North Carolina, Chapel Hill • Carlisle Kraft Webber, young adult and reference librarian, Kinnelon Public Library, NJ • Christine Maria Welter, student, librarian, freelance writer, Santa Clara County Library, CA • Amanda Werhane, graduate student, University of Wisconsin–Madison School of Library and Information Studies • Andrew Westover, student, Webb School, Knoxville, TN • Joyce Ann Wheatley, student MLIS Program, research assistant Center for Natural Language Processing, Syracuse University • Carol Wickstrom, assistant professor, University of North Texas, Denton • Kristine Wickson, student, San Jose University, CA • Trilby Wilde, student, New York University • Andrea L. Williams, curriculum-materials librarian, Midwestern State University, Moffett Library, TX • Valerie Williams, graduate student, Emporia State University, KS • Naomi Williamson, assistant professor of Library Services, James C. Kirkpatrick Library, MO • Nance Wilson, doctoral student, University of Illinois Chicago • Evie Wilson-Lingbloom, Sno-Isie Regional Library System, WA • Rachel Witmer, editor, John Wiley and Sons • Deborah A. Wooten, assistant professor of reading education, University of Tennessee, Knoxville • Katelyn Wooten, undergraduate student • Matthew Wooten, student Webb School, Knoxville, TN • Molly Rose Zeigler • Stephanie Zvirin, Books for Youth editor, *Booklist,* and board member this volume

Index

Drummond, Walter. *See* Silverberg, Robert
Dryden, John, 72
Dryden, Pamela. *See* Johnston, Norma
DuAime, Albert W. *See* Wharton, William
Duane, Diane, 760
Duder, Tessa, 204, 215–16
Dudley, A. T., 222, 367, 638, 791
DuJardin, Rosamund, 156, 639, 783, 785, 792
Dunbar, Paul Laurence, 4, 465
Duncan, Lois, 151, 216–17, 478, 518, 603, 645, 738
Dunning, Stephen, 217–18
Dunn, J. R., 710, 710
Dunsany, Lord, 204
Dunst, Kirsten, 504–5
Durban, Alan, 371
Durham, Victor G., 638
Durrell, Gerald, 218–19
Duvall, Robert, 334
Dwyer, Deanna. *See* Koontz, Dean
Dwyer, K. R. *See* Koontz, Dean
Dygard, Thomas, 665
Dylan, Bob, 208

E

Earhardt, Amelia, 223, 639, 791
Earls, Nick, 41
Early, Jack. *See* Scoppetone, Sandra
Easton, M. Coleman. *See* Bell, Clare Louise
Echlin, Kim, 524
Edelman, Bernard, 220
Ed, Eung Won, 555
Edghill, Rosemary, 415
Edwards, Margaret Alexander, 5–6, 224, 339, 477–78, 665, 782, 787, 788
Edwards, Nicholas. *See* White, Ellen Emerson
Edwards, Pamela Duncan, 599
Eichmann, Adolph, 366
Einstein, Albert, 487, 615
Eisner, Will, 220–22, 289, 290, 291
Elfman, Blossom, 222
Eliot, Dan. *See* Silverberg, Robert
Eliot, T. S., 58
Ellington, Duke, 326, 575
Elliott, Don. *See* Silverberg, Robert
Elliott, Duong Van Mai, 33
Ellis, Deborah, 127, 450
Ellison, Harlan, 121, 290
Ellison, Ralph, 19
Ellis, Sarah, 128
Eluard, Paul, 15
Emergence of Young Adult Literature in the Twentieth Century, 222–24
Emerson, Alice B., 638
Emerson, Ralph Waldo, 12

Emerson, Zack. *See* White, Ellen Emerson
Engdahl, Sylvia, 634
Engle, William, 223, 638, 791
Erdoes, Richard, 523
Erdrich, Lise, 449
Erdrich, Louise, 508
Ericson, Walter. *See* Fast, Howard Melvin
Eriksson, Inga-Karen, 450
Erwin, Carol, 725
Esquivel, Laura, 520
Ethical Decisions and the Young Adult Novel, 224–26
Evans, Linda, 710
Evers, Medgar, 46, 161
Exploring the World From Home, 226
Eyerley, Jeanette, 784

F

Fairbairn, Joyce, 159
Fairy Tale Retellings, 227–30
Fakih, Kimberly Olson, 647
Fallon, Martin. *See* Higgins, Jack
Falsen, Henry Gregor, 784
Family in Young Adult Literature, 230–32
Fantasy, 232–34
Fantasy Gaming in Young Adult Literature, 234–36
Farley, Randall and Cynthia, 32
Farmer, Harold, 236, 714
Farmer, Nancy, 231, 236–37, 633–34
Farquharson, Margaret, 367
Fast, Howard Melvin, 237–38
Faulkner, William, 73, 276
Feder, Harriet, 368
Feelings, Muriel, 239
Feelings, Tom (Thomas), 238–39
Feiffer, Jules, 289
Feiwel, Jean, 206
Feldman, Eva, 618
Feldstein, Al, 683
Felsen, Henry Gregor, 141, 783
Feminist Fairy Tales for Young Adults, 239–42
Ferguson, Dale, 276
Ferguson, Donald, 223, 638, 792
Ferris, Alfred G., 243
Ferris, Jean, 242–44, 445
Fest, Joachim, 365
Fforde, Jasper, 271
Fiedler, Lisa, 156
Field, Edward, 657
Fielding, Helen, 155
Field, Sally, 156, 245
Fields, W. C., 92
Fienberg, Anna, 244
Filipovic, Zlata, 74
Filo, David, 642
Fine, Anne, 244–45, 779

Finley, Margaret. *See* Farquharson, Margaret
Finney, Jack (Walter Braden), 245–46, 709, 710
Fiore, Candace, 87
Firbank Ronald, 19
Fischer, Klaus P., 365
Fisher, Antwone, 73
Fitch, John IV. *See* Cormier, Robert
Fitzgerald, Ella, 575
Fitzgerald, F. Scott, 132
Fitzhugh, Louise, 390–91, 635
Fitzhugh, Percy Keese, 638
Flake, Sharon G., 246
Fleischman, Paul, 27, 246–47, 444, 447
Fleischman, Sid, 246–47
Fleming, Ian, 778
Fletcher, Hilda Carter, 146, 229
Fletcher, Ralph, 247–48
Fletcher, Susan (Clemens), 67, 248–49, 445, 524, 761–62
Flinn, Alex, 249–50
Flinn, Gene, 250
Flower, Jessie Graham. *See* Chase, Josephine
Foote, Horton, 581
Ford, Hilary. *See* Christopher, John
Ford, Vince, 250
Foreman, James Douglas, 250–51
Forester, C. S., 196
Forest, Heather, 523
Foster, Alan Dean, 670, 671
Foster, Hal, 94
Fowke, Edith, 468
Fox, Kyle, 316–17
Fox, Paula, 251–52
Fox, Philip, 618
Fradin, Dennis Brindell, 252–53
Francis, Dick, 518
Franco, Betsy, 253–54
Frank, Anne(lies) Marie, 73, 83, 254, 348–49, 362
Frank, E. R., 77, 231, 254–55, 698, 786
Franklin, Benjamin, 253, 364–65, 494
Franklin, Kristine, 450
Frank, Otto, 253
Fraustino, Lisa Rowe, 255–57, 462
Frazier, James, 370
Freedman, Russell, 448, 480, 786
Freedman, Russell (Bruce), 74, 256–57, 277, 366
Freeman, Martin, 2
French, Albert, 257–58
French, Margaret, 404
Frenkel, Jim, 725
Freud, Sigmund, 188
Freymann-Weyr, Garret, 258, 788
Friedman, Myra, 258
Friesen, Gayle, 258–59
Friesner, Esther, 259
Fritz, Jean, 694

Mack, Louise, 40
Maclachlan, Patricia, 469–70, 580
Macy, Sue, 472–73
Madaras, Area, 473
Madaras, Lynda, 473
Madonna, 201, 504
Magazines and Periodicals, 473–75
Magorian, Michelle, 779
Maguire, Gregory, 228
Mah, Adeline Yen, 74
Mahotti, Lorenzo, 290
Mahy, Margaret, 335, 475–76, 789
Major, Kevin (Gerald), 127, 476–77
Malcolm, Dan. *See* Silverberg, Robert
Malcolm X, 46, 305
Malkovich, John, 2
Mallory, George, 650
Mallory, Thomas, 204
Malone, Jenna, 275
Malone, Paul B., 638
Mamet, David, 581
Mandela, Nelson, 509
Margaret A. Edwards Award (Alex
    Award), xviii, 5–6, 224, 339,
    477–78, 665, 782, 788
Marillier, Juliet, 228, 273, 479, 520
Marineau, Michele, 128
Marino, Jan, 479–80
Mark, J. *See* Highwater, Jamake
Mark, Jan, 779
Marks, Hershy, 348
Marks-Highwater, J. *See* Highwater, Ja-
    make
Marlowe, Hugh. *See* Higgins, Jack
Márquez, Gabriel García, 423, 657
Marrin, Albert, 73, 480–81
Marriott, Janice, 481, 790
Marsden, W. John, 40–41, 209, 733
Marston, John, 19
Martel, Suzanne, 127
Martel, Yann, 7–8, 714
Marti, José, 421
Martin, Ann Matthews, 162, 202, 209,
    224, 481–83, 640, 792
Martin, David, 41, 42
Martin, Edie, 481
Martinek, Frank V., 223, 639, 791
Martinez, Victor, 422
Martin, Henry, 481
Martin, Rafe, 524
Martin, Webber. *See* Silverberg, Robert
Maruki, Toshi, 32
Masefield, John, 210
Masereel, Frans, 289
Maslansky, Paul, 399
Mason, Bobbie Ann, 483–84
Mason, Lisa, 709, 710
Mason, Rosalie, 746
Mass, Wendy, 523
Matas, Carol, 349, 368, 484–85
Matcheck, Diane, 485–86

Mathabane, Mark, 507–8
Mathewson, Christy, 367
Mathis, Sharon Bell, 444, 486
Matthiesen, Peter, 494
Maurer, Richard, 73
Maxwell, Katie, 156
Maxwell, Robin, 487
May, Julian, 710
May, Karl, 487
Mayne, William, 233, 445
Mazer, Anne, 487–88
Mazer, Harry, 487, 488–89, 645
Mazer, Norma Fox, 231, 487, 489–90
Mead, Alice, 490–91, 733
Meader, Stephen, 141
Mead, Margaret, 410
Meaker, Marijane. *See* Kerr, M. E.
A Meditation on Writing Landscape,
    491–94
Meltzer, Milton, 349, 480, 494–96
Melville, Herman, 494, 674
Memmi, Albert, 296
Mercatante, Anthony S., 522
Merriman, Alex. *See* Silverberg, Robert
Merriwell, Frank, 554
Mertz, Barbara. *See* Michaels, Barbara
Merwin, W. S., 657
Metzger, George, 289
Metzger, Lois, 445
Metz, Melinda, 18, 640–41
Meyer, Carolyn, 9, 496–97
Mezieries, 290
Michael L. Printz Award, 212, 224, 591–
    92, 782
Michaels, Barbara, 497–98, 518
Michelangelo, 412
Mikaelsen, Ben, 498–99
Miklowitz, Gloria D., 499–500
Millay, Edna St. Vincent, 199
Miller, Arthur, 135
Miller, Frances A., 500
Miller, Frank, 290
Miller-Lachmann, Lyn, 584
Miller, Patricia, 83
Miller, William, 600
Mills, Sharon. *See* Draper, Sharon M.
Milne, A. A., 266
Misikiam, Jo Ellen, 417
Mitchell, Anne, 208
Mitchell, Clyde. *See* Silverberg, Robert
Mixon, Laura, 287
Mobieus, 290
Modine, Mathew, 201, 504
Moeri, Louise, 500–501
Moesta, Rebecca, 673
Mohr, Nicholasa, 501–2
Monfort, Simon de, 565
Monjo, Ferdinand, 158
Monjo, Justin, 759
Monroe, Lyle. *See* Heinlein, Robert
    A(nson)

Monseau, Virginia, 11
Montgomery, Lucy Maud, 126–27, 222–
    23, 265, 639, 791
Moore, Allen, 290
Moore, Anne Carroll, 442
Moore, Martha, 502
Moore, Peter, 446
Moore, Yvette, 162
Mora, Pat, 422
Morgan, Francis Xavier, 713
Morgan, Sally, 42
Moriarty, Jaclyn, 503
Mori, Kyoto, 502–3
Morpurgo, Michael, 503
Morris, Gerald Paul, 68, 503–4, 524
Morrison, Toni, xviii, 135, 151, 609, 754
Morse, Anne Christensen. *See* Head,
    Ann
Mosevitzsky, Adena, 585
Moss, Marissa, 599
Mother Jones, 169
Mouly, François, 660, 661
Mousdale, Chris, 183
Movies, 504–6
Mowat, Farley, 127
Mowry, Jess, 506–7
Mozart, Wolfgang Amadeus, 412
Mukherjee, Bharati, 32
Multicultural Literature, 507–11
Muñoz, Esperanza, 619
Munsch, Robert, 448
Munson, Amelia, 87, 88
Murphy, Jim, 366, 480, 511–12, 786
Murphy, Pat, 512, 707, 710
Murphy, Rita, 162, 512–13
Murphy, Shirley Rousseau, 228
Murray, Peter. *See* Hautman, Pete
Murrow, Edward R., 563
Musgrave, Susan, 128
Music in Teen Fiction, 513–15
Myers, Anna, 515–16
Myers, Bill, 367
Myers, Walter Dean, 8, 74, 149, 150,
    151, 174, 224, 478, 516–17, 553,
    572, 592, 601–2, 733, 782, 784,
    792
Mystery Novels, 517–18
Mythic Fiction, 519–21
Mythology and Legend, 521–25

N

Na, An, 526, 602, 788
Nabokov, Vladimir, 19
Naidoo, Beverly, 449, 527–28
Namioka, Lensey, 528–29
Napoli, Donna Jo, 191, 227, 228, 229,
    231, 240, 242, 523, 529–30
Nardo, Don, 523
Naylor, Phyllis R., 151, 191, 530–31
Neal, Patricia, 196
Nelson, Marilyn, 531–32